Laura Holmes

10/7/15

The Guidebook

The NRSV Student Bible

Study It

Connect It

Pray It

Live It

N R S V

New Revised Standard Version

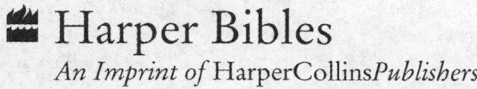

Harper Bibles

An Imprint of HarperCollinsPublishers

Acknowledgments

Project Editors

Marlene Baer Hekkert

Janna Jones

Jeremy Jones

Managing Editor

Terri Leonard

Production Editor

Suzanne Quist

Writers

Eduardo Arnouil

Lisa-Marie Calderone-Stewart

Carmen Maria Cervantes

Catherine Cory

Gary Dreier

Karen Emmerich

Carole Goodwin

Ron Kenney

Edward P. Kunzman

Judi Lanciotti

Joseph A. Morris, CM

Daniel Ponsetto

Rosa Sanchez

Larry Schatz, FSC

Vikki Shepp

Valerie Shields

Brian Singer-Towns

Tony Tamberino

Michael Theisen

Victor Valenzuela

Art Direction

Cover design by Claudine Mansour

Interior design by Mike Heath | Magnus Creative

Interior typesetting and additional design by Sally Dunn

Contents

The Old Testament

The New Testament

Alphabetical List of the Books of the Bible

Welcome!
This Bible is for YOU!

The Guidebook is focused on you—a young person seeking direction, advice, and answers to life's important questions. As the title suggests, think of this Bible as a guidebook as it helps you navigate and find the answers you seek while perhaps raising new questions along the way that will help you go deeper in your relationship with Jesus.

As you use this Bible, keep in mind two important points. First, the Bible is for everyone. Wherever you are in your relationship with God, the Bible can speak to you. The study notes in this Bible invite you to ask questions and to consider the meaning and relevance of God's message in the Bible, whether you've committed your life to Christ or are still looking for answers, or somewhere in between.

Second, all the special features are designed to help you understand the Bible's message, while encouraging you to go deeper in your reading of the Bible itself. They are also designed to help you see yourself in God's image and likeness—a vital part of God's saving work in a world full of diversity. The Bible's core message of God's love for human beings speaks to people of any culture. Many of the study note articles will help you learn what it means to be part of God's family as well as part of a global family that cares for the needs of others.

God desires a loving relationship with us. The special features of this Bible can help you understand God's message. But it is God's Word in the Bible, and the Holy Spirit at work in your heart, that can CHANGE YOUR LIFE!

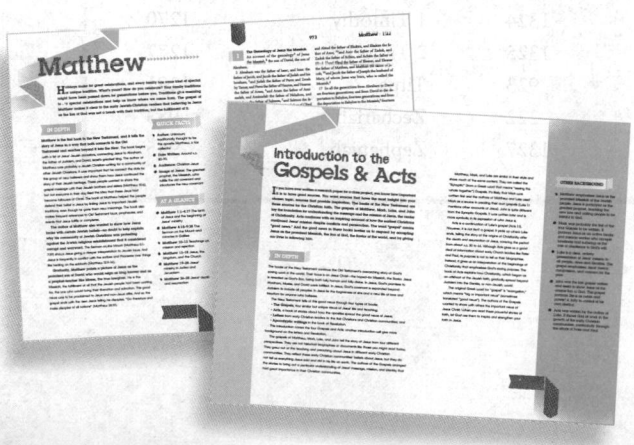

What's in This Bible

The Guidebook is loaded with special features to help make it easier for you to read and understand the Bible. Here is a list of some of those features and where to find them.

Section Introductions

Each major section of the Bible (the Pentateuch, the Historical Books, the Wisdom and Poetry Books, the Prophets, the Gospels and Acts, and the Letters and Revelation) begins with a brief introduction to the background, style, and themes of the books you'll find in that section.

Book Introductions

Introductions give insight into each book's central message and an overview of its contents.

Study Notes

Hundreds of relevant study note articles are woven throughout the Bible text. These articles—Study It!, Connect It!, Pray It!, Live It!—will encourage you to go deeper in your faith and knowledge of God's Word and inspire you to change your world.

Where Do I Find It?

Several indexes are located at the back of the Bible. The first index helps you locate Bible passages on events and the teachings of Jesus. The second index helps you find Bible passages related to life and faith issues. The third index lists the people or organizations profiled in the "Connect It!" articles. The fourth index lists the study note articles by topic to make it easy for you to find the content that relates to whatever you may be seeking guidance on in life.

Study Aids

A timeline of biblical history, a chart of biblical festivals, feasts, and fasts, a glossary of terms, a concordance for finding key verses, and maps are all found at the back of the Bible.

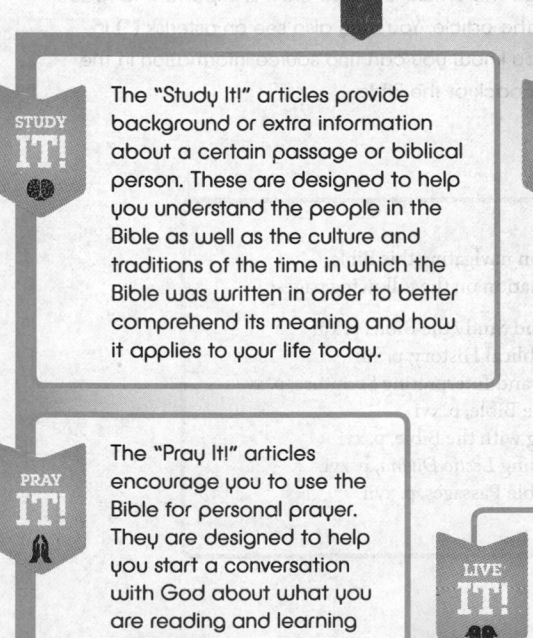

STUDY IT! The "Study It!" articles provide background or extra information about a certain passage or biblical person. These are designed to help you understand the people in the Bible as well as the culture and traditions of the time in which the Bible was written in order to better comprehend its meaning and how it applies to your life today.

CONNECT IT! The "Connect It!" articles profile historical and modern-day teens, adults, and organizations that are making a difference in our world. Each article will help you connect what you are reading to the world around you and to see living examples of what it means to follow God's Word.

PRAY IT! The "Pray It!" articles encourage you to use the Bible for personal prayer. They are designed to help you start a conversation with God about what you are reading and learning in God's Word.

LIVE IT! The "Live It!" articles are practical. They help you apply the Bible's messages to situations you may be facing now or will face in the future.

Getting Started
with your Bible!

If you haven't spent much time reading the Bible, it may seem overwhelming. It's a big book with some long words, funny names, and potentially confusing stories. But with a little instruction you'll find it is easy to navigate and fascinating to read.

Start with the contents on p. vii. This will give you a good overview of what is in the Bible and serve as a continuous reference point. You can read the Bible from front to back like a book, start with the life of Jesus (in the Gospels), or look for passages that relate to what you are dealing with in life (use the indexes at the back to find topics you are interested in).

For each study note article throughout the Bible, you'll see a scripture reference to the Bible passage the article is based on. It is important to read the passage before reading the article. You may also see an asterisk (*) in some study notes. This lets you know you can find source information in the "Works Cited" section at the back of the Bible.

For additional help on navigating this Bible,
check out the information on the following pages:

- How to Read and Study the Bible, p. xiii
- Overview of Biblical History, p. xiii
- Understanding and Interpreting Scripture, p. xv
- Praying with the Bible, p. xvi
- Tips for Praying with the Bible, p. xvi
- How to Pray Using *Lectio Divina*, p. xvi
- Memorizing Bible Passages, p. xvii

How to Read and Study the Bible

What is the Bible? The Bible tells the story of the loving relationship between God and humankind. Through the sacred writings, God reveals to humankind the truth about God and God's will for us. It is a library of books that is divided into two parts: the Old Testament (before Jesus) and the New Testament (Jesus' birth and after). The Old Testament books begin with a section called the Pentateuch, followed by the Historical Books, the Wisdom and Poetry Books, and the Prophets. The New Testament consists of two sections: the Gospels and the book of Acts, and the Letters and Revelation.

- The **Pentateuch** tells about God's chosen people, the Israelites. You'll read about their early stories, their history, and the laws God gave them.

- The **Historical Books** pick up Israelite history from 1250 to 400 B.C. You will find accounts of the Israelites' settling of the promised land, the rise and fall of their kings, their dispersion into exile, and their eventual return to the promised land.

- The **Wisdom and Poetry Books** are a collection of hymns, poems, proverbs, and stories. They use imaginative language to make their points.

- The **Prophets** are the books of those who speak God's word. In these books, you will find comfort and promise as well as be challenged to act with justice and mercy.

- The **Gospels** focus on the person and teachings of Jesus. **Acts** shows how the Church was formed and how the first Christians spread the good news. These books cover the time period from 5 B.C. to the early A.D. 60s.

- The **Letters** (written by Paul, his followers, and other disciples) are actual letters that describe the new Christian faith, give advice, and offer words of hope. **Revelation** is a collection of mystical visions written to encourage early Christians who were being persecuted.

Overview of Biblical History

Understanding some basics of history can go a long way in helping you see how the stories of the Bible fit together. They shed light on the specific stories of the Bible as well as God's story throughout history. The information below coupled with the Expanded Timeline of Biblical History, p. 1368, will give you a good overview.

Primeval History

The Bible starts with stories that tell how God made everything, along with the first humans, Adam and Eve. God's Creation was good, but evil crept into the world. After several generations, God decided to flood the world. But God saved Noah, his family, and specimens of land animals on an ark (boat) in order to give humans a chance to start over.

Patriarchs and Matriarchs (2000–1500 B.C.)

Abraham and Sarah arrived in Canaan, the land God had promised them. They were old, but God gave them a son, Isaac, who had two sons with his wife, Rebekah. The younger was Jacob, whom God named Israel. Israel had twelve sons, but his favorite was Joseph. Joseph's jealous brothers sold him as a slave in Egypt, but God helped him prosper. When Joseph's brothers visited Egypt, Joseph recognized them and told them to come live with him.

Egypt and the Exodus (1500–1250 B.C.)

Israel's descendants (sometimes called the Hebrews, the Israelites, the tribes of Israel, or the children of Israel) became a small nation. But a new Egyptian dynasty came to power and made the Hebrews slaves. Eventually, God told Moses to bring them out of Egypt. To convince Pharaoh to let his cheap labor go, God sent a series of plagues, including the killing of all firstborn sons. The Hebrews were saved by putting the blood of a lamb over their doors. After the Hebrews left, Pharaoh sent his army to bring them back, trapping them at the Red Sea. God made the waters separate, so the Hebrew people could cross over; then God made the waters fall back, drowning the pursuing army. The Passover meal celebrates this victory.

Settling the Promised Land (1250–1020 B.C.)

While the Hebrew people were on their way back to Canaan, God made a covenant (an agreement) with them at Mount Sinai. God gave them laws, including the Ten Commandments. God told them to build a tabernacle (worship tent) and the ark of the covenant (a box symbolizing God's presence). After a generation, the Hebrew people invaded Canaan under the leadership of Joshua. The land was divided into territories, roughly corresponding to the twelve tribes of Israel. For over two hundred years, the Hebrews fought for the land; there was no central power, so God would occasionally raise up local leaders called judges.

The Monarchy (1020–922 B.C.)

God allowed Samuel, the last of the judges, to make Saul the first king. Samuel poured oil on Saul's head, anointing him for leadership. The Hebrew word for an "anointed person" is *messiah* (the Greek word is *christos*, or Christ). The next king was David, the greatest human king the little nation of Israel would ever have. God promised that David's house would be established forever. Next was David's son Solomon, who was known for his wisdom and who built a great palace and the first temple in Jerusalem. But during Solomon's son's reign, the kingdom divided in two.

The Divided Kingdom (922–587 B.C.)

The northern kingdom was called Israel, and it went through several dynasties. The southern kingdom was Judah, and the Davidic dynasty stayed in power. Sadly, most of the kings were not faithful to God. So God would send prophets like Elijah to speak the word of God and call the people to faithfulness. When the northern kingdom fell to Assyria, it ceased to exist. Babylon in turn defeated Assyria and then later crushed Judah; Jerusalem and the temple were utterly destroyed. Many Jews (inhabitants of Judah) were sent into exile in Babylon.

The Exile and Return (587–5 B.C.)

Stories about heroes like Daniel kept the faith alive for Jews who were in exile. When Persia defeated Babylon (539 B.C.), the Jews were allowed to return home. By 515 B.C., the temple had been rebuilt. After Persian and then Greek rule, Israel was free for a short time until Rome conquered the region in 63 B.C. Weary from dark centuries of domination, the Jews began to hope for a new king, a Messiah (Christ), a son of David, who would restore glory to Israel. In time millions would recognize a baby lying in a manger as the Christ—a light shining in the darkness.

The Life of Jesus (5 B.C.– A.D. 30)

The angel Gabriel appeared to Mary, a young virgin, and told her she was going to have a baby—Jesus. The child would be conceived by the Holy Spirit and called the Son of God. Jesus was born in Bethlehem, with only a manger for a bed; we celebrate his birth on Christmas. Jesus grew up in Nazareth in Galilee. Meanwhile, John the Baptist was baptizing people in the Jordan River, when he recognized Jesus as the "Lamb of God." Jesus began teaching, often using stories called parables; he soon had a large following of disciples. Jesus preached the gospel—good news—with words that were both challenging and promising. He told us we are to love God and our neighbor—God's greatest commandment. Even though we sin, God loves us—unconditionally—and offers us forgiveness; this is God's promise. Jesus performed many miracles, which were signs of the coming of the kingdom of God. Some believed, and their faith was strengthened; others rejected Jesus.

The Death and Resurrection of Jesus, the Christ (A.D. 30)

Many of the Jewish leaders were upset because Jesus talked as though he was above Jewish law, claimed to be the Christ, and even claimed to be God. The authorities felt their power was threatened and planned to kill him. Shortly before he was arrested, Jesus rode into Jerusalem like a king, while crowds honored him with palm branches (Palm Sunday). Later that week, Jesus ate a Passover meal with his disciples, called the Last Supper, at which Jesus instituted the sharing of bread and wine in remembrance of him (Communion). The next day (Good Friday), Jesus was crucified on a cross under the authority of the Roman governor Pontius Pilate. Early Sunday morning (Easter), some women came to visit his tomb and were told that Jesus had come back to life; several times after his resurrection, Jesus appeared to his disciples. Forty days later (Ascension Day), Jesus was lifted up into heaven.

The Early Christian Church (A.D. 30–70)

Fifty days after Jesus' resurrection, on Pentecost, the Holy Spirit came to the disciples, and they started preaching in many languages. Thousands believed! Some refer to it as the birth of the Church. Stephen was the first martyr. Paul saw a vision of Jesus and became the first Christian missionary. Peter also had a startling vision—God told him salvation was for the Jews and the Gentiles (non-Jews). Days of persecution were ahead; Rome became increasingly intolerant and destroyed the temple in A.D. 70. But Christianity kept spreading and growing. Jesus' mission of spreading the good news of salvation continues through all who believe today.

Understanding and Interpreting Scripture

The Bible was written under the inspiration of the Holy Spirit to reveal the truths about God's saving plan for humanity and for all of creation. But like any work of ancient literature, written thousands of years ago in a culture very different from our own, the Bible must be interpreted to be properly understood. If we do not follow good principles of interpretation when reading the Bible, we can arrive at misleading and even erroneous conclusions about what God is trying to say to us. One way to describe this is to say that there are *lenses* through which we can look at the Bible's books and stories in order to understand what the human authors were trying to communicate to the people of their time. These lenses can also be called *contexts,* because they help us put a particular book or story in its proper context or perspective. These are the lenses or contexts:

Six Important Questions for Interpreting the Bible

Based on the six contexts used for interpreting the Bible, here are six summary questions you can ask when studying any book or story in the Bible.

1. What was the historical situation at the time this book was written and how did the human author(s) address this situation?

2. What is the literary genre of this book or passage and how does the genre impact my understanding or provide helpful context?

3. Is there a cultural practice or attitude reflected in this book or passage that we need to understand to appreciate the human author's intention?

4. How does this book or story fit into the overall story of salvation history?

5. Is the truth I understand from this book or story consistent with the rest of scripture?

6. When I look at everything I learned from these six contexts, what spiritual truth is God revealing?

Historical Context:
Conditions of the Time and Culture

The human authors of the Bible assumed the readers of their time knew basic facts about their world. Two thousand years later, those facts may not be as apparent to us! But the work of biblical scholars has helped us to be more aware of some of the history behind the Bible's books and stories. And the more you know about biblical history, the better you will understand the meaning of certain words and events.

Literary Context:
Literary Genres in Use at the Time

It is important to remember that the Bible is more like a library than a one-volume history book. The authors of the sixty-six books of the Bible used many different literary styles to communicate their ideas. Some books are short hero stories; some are religious history; some are collections of the sayings of prophets, collections of short wise sayings, or letters; and some are written in poetic or symbolic language. To properly understand a book, we must first understand what kind of literary style, or genre, the book uses. We do this automatically with writing styles we come across every day. In a news story, we expect facts based on real events; in a fairy tale, we expect to learn some truth, but we know the story itself didn't happen in real life. We must apply the same process to the Bible.

Cultural Context:
Practices and Traditions of the Time

Every culture has its own practices and traditions. The impact of culture affects almost every facet of life, such as the way we cut our hair; the way we dress; what we eat; the way we speak and even feel about certain things; how we relate to family, friends, and strangers; the way we do business; even whether we keep pets and, if we do, what kind. Without an understanding of another culture's traditions, many of that culture's practices may seem strange or even repulsive to us.

Unity of the Whole Scripture Context:
Salvation History

In order to understand what the human authors intended, we must consider the books of the Bible as independent documents. This is done to discover each author's purpose when the book was first written. But the Bible is more than just a collection of independent books that have no relationship to one another. When we put them all together, we can see God's bigger plan emerging—a plan the human authors could not fully see or comprehend until the New Testament was written. This overall plan for the salvation of God's people is often called salvation history. Our interpretation of the Bible does not end after we consider what the human author's intention was in writing a particular book or passage. Next we must ask, "How does this book or passage fit into salvation history?" Many books and resources are available to help us learn about salvation history; being familiar with it is important if we hope to interpret the Bible correctly.

Living Tradition Context

Not all God's revealed truths are contained within the Bible. An oral tradition preceded the writing of the Gospels. Not everything in the oral tradition was written down in the Gospels (see John 21:25) or even fully understood at the time the New Testament was written. But guided by the Holy Spirit, all that God revealed through the life and teaching of Christ has been kept alive. This revelation is passed on through the Bible and through the living tradition of the lives of believers.

Harmony Between Elements of Faith Context

This context, also called "the analogy of faith," means that ultimately there can be no contradiction between the truths God has revealed. The truths God reveals for our salvation are in harmony with one another. When, at times, there appear to be contradictions from the human authors' points of view, there are no contradictions in God's revealed truth.

Praying with the Bible

The Bible is one of the greatest sources of inspiration we can tap into. When we pray with the Bible, God can deeply touch and change our lives. The more we are willing to pray with the scriptures, the more we can enter into the profound mystery of God's relationship with all of humanity. God's word is the compass that leads us more deeply into the immense heart of God. This is why the Church proclaims the scriptures every time we worship together and why all are encouraged to use the Bible in private prayer.

The following sections teach specific techniques for praying with the Bible. Look these over and think about which suggestions might work for you.

Tips for Praying with the Bible

God has given us Jesus as a guide for our spiritual journey. He is a guide who knows the human experience from the inside out. Through his example during his life on earth, Jesus shows us the importance of prayer for our own journey. Through prayer Jesus understood the will of his Father. Through prayer Jesus gained and maintained his burning desire to do the will of God. We know from the Gospels that the Hebrew scriptures were an important part of Jesus' prayer life. Scripture was a compass that helped point Jesus to his Father, and God wants the Bible to be the same for us. Here are some tips for using the Bible in your times of prayer:

• **Be creative in making time for prayer.** Life is busy. But let your daily routine call you to prayer. Mark a favorite psalm in your Bible and pray it when you get up in the morning—maybe one like Psalm 118:24: "This is the day that the LORD has made; let us rejoice and be glad in it." Before going to bed, spend a few minutes using *lectio divina* (see below) to listen to God before going to sleep.

• **Engage your imagination.** When praying with the Bible, use your imagination to let the stories come alive. Put yourself in the Bible story, and ask, "What do I see?" "What do I smell?" "What do I hear?" Pretend you're one of the people in the story, and ask, "How do I feel about what's happening or what's being said?"

• **Listen.** Prayer is a dialogue with God, and scripture is one of the primary ways God speaks to us. So when you read the Bible, it's always a good idea to take a quiet moment to "listen." What might God be saying to you through these sacred words?

• **Live out your prayer.** God's story is our story, and God's life is intimately connected with our lives. The unfinished part of the story is our response to God's love for us. Each of us has a part in the great story of God's salvation of all humanity. Move through your day with an awareness of God's presence and work around you and an attitude of humility and thankfulness for being part of it.

How to Pray Using *Lectio Divina*

Lectio divina (Latin for "divine reading") is a very ancient method of praying with the Bible. It was practiced in the early Christian monasteries of the third and fourth centuries and even written into the *Rule of St. Benedict* as a requirement for the spiritual life of monks. But despite its ancient history, it is a great way for us to read the Bible today.

In traditional *lectio divina,* five movements lead you from hearing the word of God to applying God's word to your everyday life.

STEP 1: *Lectio* (LEX-ee-oh). This step is the reading of and listening to the word of God. In this step, read the scripture passage. Try reading it out loud. Try reading it several times. Let the words sink in deeply and open your mind and heart to the meaning of the words.

STEP 2: *Meditatio* (med-i-TOT-see-oh). This step is meditation on the scripture passage. Reflect on the scripture passage and allow the word of God to interact with your thoughts, hopes, memories, and desires. Ask yourself questions like the following, and take notes on the insights you gain through reflection:

- What does this passage say to me?
- Who am I in this passage? What character do I identify with?
- What do I see, hear, or think?
- What do I most need to learn from this?

STEP 3: *Oratio* (or-OT-see-oh). This step is responding to God with conscious prayer. Pray with the passage you are reflecting on. What does the word invite you to pray about? Let the following questions guide you as you express your inner thoughts to God in prayer:

- What do I want to communicate to God?
- What am I longing for in my relationship with God?
- What do I desire in my prayer life?
- What secrets of my heart are ready to be expressed? Is there joy, grief, fear, or gratitude?

STEP 4: *Contemplatio* (con-tem-PLOT-see-oh). This step is contemplation. Let go of distracting thoughts and simply let yourself rest in the presence of God.

STEP 5: *Actio* (AX-ee-oh; also known as *operatio*). In this step, answer these questions with total honesty:

- How is God challenging me?
- Is there a good thing God is calling me to do?
- Is there a harmful thing God wants me to stop doing?
- What is the next step I need to take?

Decide on a course of action (large or small). Commit to following through with your plan.

Memorizing Bible Passages

Saint Augustine provides us with an image for short, effective prayers that are based on scripture. He describes the prayers of monks in Egyptian monasteries of the third century A.D. The monks' prayers were short and to the point, and the monks continuously repeated them, as if trying to bombard God with prayer.

We too can pray this way by memorizing short passages of scripture and repeating them regularly. To do this, find short passages of scripture that you can memorize and pray when you face certain situations in your life. In other words, let your daily life trigger your prayer. Here are some examples of life situations and corresponding prayers:

- A prayer before a test: "Let the favor of the Lord our God be upon us, and prosper for us the work of our hands" (Psalm 90:17).
- A prayer when you feel fearful: "Do not let your hearts be troubled, and do not let them be afraid" (John 14:27).
- A prayer whenever you are outdoors in God's creation: "How great are your works, O LORD!" (Psalm 92:5).
- A morning prayer as you set out on a new day: "Create in me a clean heart, O God" (Psalm 51:10).

You can create your own daily scripture prayers. As you read and reflect on scripture, write down verses that speak to you. Then ask yourself, What things in my everyday life do these phrases connect with? Allow these experiences to trigger your memory to pray the scripture phrase. A rich source for such prayers is the book of Psalms.

To the Reader

This preface is addressed to you by the Committee of translators, who wish to explain, as briefly as possible, the origin and character of our work. The publication of our revision is yet another step in the long, continual process of making the Bible available in the form of the English language that is most widely current in our day. To summarize in a single sentence: the New Revised Standard Version of the Bible is an authorized revision of the Revised Standard Version, published in 1952, which was a revision of the American Standard Version, published in 1901, which, in turn, embodied earlier revisions of the King James Version, published in 1611.

In the course of time, the King James Version came to be regarded as "the Authorized Version." With good reason it has been termed "the noblest monument of English prose," and it has entered, as no other book has, into the making of the personal character and the public institutions of the English-speaking peoples. We owe to it an incalculable debt.

Yet the King James Version has serious defects. By the middle of the nineteenth century, the development of biblical studies and the discovery of many biblical manuscripts more ancient than those on which the King James Version was based made it apparent that these defects were so many as to call for revision. The task was begun, by authority of the Church of England, in 1870. The (British) Revised Version of the Bible was published in 1881–1885; and the American Standard Version, its variant embodying the preferences of the American scholars associated with the work, was published, as was mentioned above, in 1901. In 1928 the copyright of the latter was acquired by the International Council of Religious Education and thus passed into the ownership of the Churches of the United States and Canada that were associated in this Council through their boards of education and publication.

The Council appointed a committee of scholars to have charge of the text of the American Standard Version and to undertake inquiry concerning the need for further revision. After studying the questions whether or not revision should be undertaken, and if so, what its nature and extent should be, in 1937 the Council authorized a revision. The scholars who served as members of the Committee worked in two sections, one dealing with the Old Testament and one with the New Testament. In 1946 the Revised Standard Version of the New Testament was published. The publication of the Revised Standard Version of the Bible, containing the Old and New Testaments, took place on September 30, 1952. A translation of the *Apocryphal/Deuterocanonical Books of the Old Testament* followed in 1957. In 1977 this collection was issued in an expanded edition, containing three additional texts received by Eastern Orthodox communions (3 and 4 Maccabees and Psalm 151). Thereafter the Revised Standard Version gained the distinction of being officially authorized for use by all major Christian churches: Protestant, Anglican, Roman Catholic, and Eastern Orthodox.

The Revised Standard Version Bible Committee is a continuing body, comprising about thirty members, both men and women. Ecumenical in representation, it includes scholars affiliated with various Protestant denominations, as well as several Roman Catholic members, an Eastern Orthodox member, and a Jewish member who serves in the Old Testament section. For a period of time the Committee included several members from Canada and from England.

Because no translation of the Bible is perfect or is acceptable to all groups of readers, and because discoveries of older manuscripts and further investigation of linguistic features of the text continue to become available, renderings of the Bible have proliferated. During the years following the publication of the Revised Standard Version, twenty-six other English translations and revisions of the Bible were produced by committees and by individual scholars—not to mention twenty-five other translations and revisions of the New Testament alone. One of the latter was the second edition of the RSV New Testament, issued in 1971, twenty-five years after its initial publication.

Following the publication of the RSV Old Testament in 1952, significant advances were made in the discovery and interpretation of documents in Semitic languages related to Hebrew. In addition to the information that had become available in the late 1940s from the Dead Sea texts of Isaiah and Habakkuk, subsequent acquisitions from the same area brought to light many other early copies of all the books of the Hebrew Scriptures (except Esther), though most of these copies are fragmentary. During the same period early Greek manuscript copies of books of the New Testament also became available.

In order to take these discoveries into account, along with recent studies of documents in Semitic languages related to Hebrew, in 1974 the Policies Committee of the Revised Standard Version, which is a standing committee of the National Council of the Churches of Christ in the U.S.A., authorized the preparation of a revision of the entire RSV Bible.

For the Old Testament the Committee has made use of the *Biblia Hebraica Stuttgartensia* (1977; ed. sec. emendata, 1983). This is an edition of the Hebrew and Aramaic text as current early in the Christian era and fixed by Jewish scholars (the "Masoretes") of the sixth to the ninth centuries. The vowel signs, which were added by the Masoretes, are accepted in the main, but where a more probable and convincing reading can be obtained by assuming different vowels, this has been done. No notes are given in such cases, because the vowel points are less ancient and reliable than the consonants. When an alternative reading given by the Masoretes is translated in a footnote, this is identified by the words "Another reading is."

Departures from the consonantal text of the best manuscripts have been made only where it seems clear that errors in copying had been made before the text was standardized. Most of the corrections adopted are based on the ancient versions (translations into Greek, Aramaic, Syriac, and Latin), which were made prior to the time of the work of the Masoretes and which therefore may reflect earlier forms of the Hebrew text. In such instances a footnote specifies the version or versions from which the correction has been derived and also gives a translation of the Masoretic Text. Where it was deemed appropriate to do so, information is supplied in footnotes from subsidiary Jewish traditions concerning other textual readings (the *Tiqqune Sopherim*, "emendations of the scribes"). These are identified in the footnotes as "Ancient Heb tradition."

Occasionally it is evident that the text has suffered in transmission and that none of the versions provides a satisfactory restoration. Here we can only follow the best judgment of competent scholars as to the most probable reconstruction of the original text. Such reconstructions are indicated in footnotes by the abbreviation Cn ("Correction"), and a translation of the Masoretic Text is added.

For the New Testament the Committee has based its work on the most recent edition of *The Greek New Testament*, prepared by an interconfessional and international committee and published by the United Bible Societies (1966; 3rd ed. corrected, 1983; information concerning changes to be introduced into the critical apparatus of the forthcoming 4th edition was available to the Committee). As in that edition, double brackets are used to enclose a few passages that are generally regarded to be later additions to the text, but which we have retained because of their evident antiquity and their importance in the textual tradition. Only in very rare instances have we replaced the text or the punctuation of the Bible Societies' edition by an alternative that seemed to us to be superior. Here and there in the footnotes the phrase, "Other ancient authorities read," identifies alternative readings preserved by Greek manuscripts and early versions. In both Testaments, alternative renderings of the text are indicated by the word "Or."

As for the style of English adopted for the present revision, among the mandates given to the Committee in 1980 by the Division of Education and Ministry of the National Council of Churches of Christ (which now holds the copyright of the RSV Bible) was the directive to continue in the tradition of the King James Bible, but to introduce such changes as are warranted on the basis of accuracy, clarity, euphony, and current English usage. Within the constraints set by the original texts and by the mandates of the Division, the Committee has followed the maxim, "As literal as possible, as free as necessary." As a consequence, the New Revised Standard Version (NRSV) remains essentially a literal translation. Paraphrastic renderings have been adopted only sparingly, and then chiefly to compensate for a deficiency in the English language— the lack of a common gender third person singular pronoun.

During the almost half a century since the publication of the RSV, many in the churches have become sensitive to the danger of linguistic sexism arising from the inherent bias of the English language towards the masculine gender, a bias that in the case of the Bible has often restricted or obscured the meaning of the original text. The mandates from the Division specified that, in references to men and women, masculine-oriented language should be eliminated as far as this can be done without altering passages that reflect the historical situation of ancient patriarchal culture. As can be appreciated, more than once the Committee found that the several mandates stood in tension and even in conflict. The various concerns had to be balanced case by case in order to provide a faithful and acceptable rendering without using contrived English. Only very occasionally has the pronoun "he" or "him" been retained in passages where the reference may have been to a woman as well as to a man; for example, in several legal texts in Leviticus and Deuteronomy. In such instances of formal, legal language, the options of either putting the passage in the plural or of introducing additional nouns to avoid masculine pronouns in English seemed to the Committee to obscure the historic structure and literary character of the original. In the vast majority of cases, however, inclusiveness has been attained by simple rephrasing or by introducing plural forms when this does not distort the meaning of the passage. Of course, in narrative and in parable no attempt was made to generalize the sex of individual persons.

Another aspect of style will be detected by readers who compare the more stately English rendering of the Old Testament with the less formal rendering adopted for the New Testament. For example, the traditional distinction between *shall* and *will* in English has been retained in the Old Testament as appropriate in rendering a document that embodies what may be termed the classic form of Hebrew, while in the New Testament the abandonment of such distinctions in the usage of the future tense in English reflects the more colloquial nature of the koine Greek used by most New Testament authors except when they are quoting the Old Testament.

Careful readers will notice that here and there in the Old Testament the word LORD (or in certain cases GOD) is printed in capital letters. This represents the traditional manner in English versions of rendering the Divine Name: the "Tetragrammaton" (see the notes on Exodus 3.14, 15), following the precedent of the ancient Greek and Latin translators and the long established practice in the reading of the Hebrew Scriptures in the synagogue. While it is almost if not quite certain that the Name was originally pronounced "Yahweh," this pronunciation was not indicated when the Masoretes added vowel sounds to the consonantal Hebrew text. To the four consonants YHWH of the Name, which had come to be regarded as too sacred to be pronounced, they attached vowel signs indicating that in its place should be read the Hebrew word *Adonai* meaning "Lord" (or *Elohim* meaning "God"). Ancient Greek translators employed the word *Kyrios* ("Lord") for the Name. The Vulgate likewise used the Latin word *Dominus* ("Lord"). The form "Jehovah" is of late medieval origin; it is a combination of the consonants of the Divine Name and the vowels attached to it by the Masoretes but belonging to an entirely different word. Although the American Standard Version (1901) had used "Jehovah" to render the Tetragrammaton (the sound of Y being represented by J and the sound of W by V, as in Latin), for two reasons the Committees that produced the RSV and the NRSV returned to the more familiar usage of the King James Version. (1) The word "Jehovah" does not accurately represent any form of the Name ever used in Hebrew. (2) The use of any proper name for the one and only God, as though there were other gods from whom the true God had to be distinguished, began to be discontinued in Judaism before the Christian era and is inappropriate for the universal faith of the Christian Church.

It will be seen that in the Psalms and in other prayers addressed to God the archaic second person singular pronouns (*thee, thou, thine*) and verb forms (*art, hast, hadst*) are no longer used. Although some readers may regret this change, it should be pointed out that in the original languages neither the Old Testament nor the New makes any linguistic distinction between addressing a human being and addressing the Deity. Furthermore, in the tradition of the King James Version one will not expect to find the use of capital letters for pronouns that refer to the Deity—such capitalization is an unnecessary innovation that has only recently been introduced into a few English translations of the Bible. Finally, we have left to the discretion of the licensed publishers such matters as section headings, cross-references, and clues to the pronunciation of proper names.

This new version seeks to preserve all that is best in the English Bible as it has been known and used through the years. It is intended for use in public reading and congregational worship, as well as in private study, instruction, and meditation. We have resisted the temptation to introduce terms and phrases that merely reflect current moods, and have tried to put the message of the Scriptures in simple, enduring words and expressions that are worthy to stand in the great tradition of the King James Bible and its predecessors.

In traditional Judaism and Christianity, the Bible has been more than a historical document to be preserved or a classic of literature to be cherished and admired; it is recognized as the unique record of God's dealings with people over the ages. The Old Testament sets forth the call of a special people to enter into covenant relation with the God of justice and steadfast love and to bring God's law to the nations. The New Testament records the life and work of Jesus Christ, the one in whom "the Word became flesh," as well as describes the rise and spread of the early Christian Church. The Bible carries its full message, not to those who regard it simply as a noble literary heritage of the past or who wish to use it to enhance political purposes and advance otherwise desirable goals, but to all persons and communities who read it so that they may discern and understand what God is saying to them. That message must not be dis- guised in phrases that are no longer clear, or hidden under words that have changed or lost their mean- ing; it must be presented in language that is direct and plain and meaningful to people today. It is the hope and prayer of the translators that this version of the Bible may continue to hold a large place in congregational life and to speak to all readers, young and old alike, helping them to understand and believe and respond to its message.

For the Committee,
Bruce M. Metzger

THE OLD TESTAMENT

"God saw everything that he had made, and indeed, it was **very good.**"

—Genesis 1:31

Introduction to the
Pentateuch

Have you ever been late to a movie? Have you ever bugged your friends who got there on time by asking, "What's happening? Why'd he do that? What did she mean by that?" The opening scenes are crucial to understanding the rest of the movie.

The Pentateuch contains the Bible's opening scenes. These first five books set the stage for much of what happens in the rest of the Bible. If you're clueless about their epic stories, you might later find yourself in other books asking: "What's happening? Why is he doing that? Why did she say that?"

IN DEPTH

"Pentateuch" literally means "five-part writing." The Pentateuch is the first five books of the Old Testament: Genesis, Exodus, Leviticus, Numbers, and Deuteronomy. These books are special to Jewish and Christian believers because they tell of the origins of God's people and their unique relationship with God—sometimes called salvation history. They are the blueprint needed for properly understanding the rest of the Bible. The Pentateuch introduces the idea of a single God who is responsible for all creation. It also tells that this God is active in the world and in the lives of its people, and that the Israelites have been called into a special relationship with God.

One of the central elements of the special relationship between God and the Israelites described in the Pentateuch is the Sinai covenant. A covenant is a solemn promise between two parties who both agree to fulfill certain obligations. The Sinai covenant is the most famous one between God and Israel, and Moses is its mediator. You'll read about it in Exodus. In Genesis, you'll read about the covenants God makes with Noah, Abraham, and Jacob. Those lead up to the Sinai covenant.

Consider a time you've looked at a tapestry in a museum. Reading the Pentateuch is like appreciating a fine tapestry. When you view a tapestry from the front, all the threads combine to make a beautiful, coherent image. In the same way, an overall look at the covenants, stories, and laws in the Pentateuch combines them into a picture of the love relationship between God and the people of Israel. A close look at the back of a tapestry shows a more chaotic mix of colors and yarn. So too a closer look at the writings in the Pentateuch reveals not one story, but many.

Biblical scholars speak of four primary sources for the Pentateuch's stories and traditions. The sources reflect four different schools of thought about Israel's relationship with God. For convenience, each source is referred to as an individual author.

• The Yahwist used Yahweh as God's name. This writer focused on the southern kingdom, Judah, used lots of stories, emphasized God's closeness to humanity, and portrayed God acting as a human person.

• The Elohist referred to God as Elohim or Lord. The Elohist wrote about the northern kingdom, Israel, and was concerned about idolatry and morality. The writings of the Elohist present God's presence as mediated, such as through a burning bush.

• The Deuteronomist emphasized the law as the foundation of the kingdom of Judah. The Deuteronomist emerged toward the end of the monarchy (the time of the Israelite kings), when the covenant law seemed to have been forgotten.

• Finally, the priestly writer emphasized religious rituals and the role of the priesthood. This writer portrayed God as more distant and used a more formal style. This source was written after the Babylonian exile.

Knowing that these four sources contributed to the final form of the Pentateuch can help us understand that the Pentateuch books are not simply records of events as they occurred, but rather faith accounts about the Israelites' growing relationship with God, inspired by God and told from different perspectives.

The Pentateuch reveals how much God loves the human race collectively and how much God loves us personally. God wishes to be in a relationship with us today just as much as God did back then. The Pentateuch reminds us that we are all children of God.

OTHER BACKGROUND

● Some of the most famous stories and people of the Old Testament are found in Genesis and Exodus. Genesis includes the stories of Creation, Adam and Eve, Noah and the flood, Abraham and Sarah, and Joseph and his brothers. Exodus contains the stories of Moses and the burning bush, Pharaoh and the ten plagues, the parting of the Red Sea, and the Ten Commandments.

● Jewish people refer to the five books of the Pentateuch as the Torah, meaning "teaching" or "instruction."

● Ancient tradition named Moses as the author of the Pentateuch. This was no doubt due to Moses' importance in the Pentateuch itself. But evidence suggests that most of the Pentateuch was written hundreds of years after Moses' death.

● The two types of writing in the Pentateuch are stories and laws. Genesis is all stories, Leviticus and Deuteronomy are mostly laws, and Exodus and Numbers are approximately half and half.

The Names of God in the Old Testament

The theology of the Hebrew Bible flowered from its Semitic roots, where El was a generic term for any Canaanite deity. In early texts, El and its derivatives were used for the one true God of Israel, also known as Yahweh.

Name	Significance	References
El ("God")	A generic Semitic title for deity; the mighty, powerful Creator; God of the covenant; the protector	Gen. 1:1, 3, 4, 22; 17:7; 31:24; Isa. 44:24
Eloah; El Echad ("the one God")	A generic name for deity; the one God who is savior, redeemer, and deliverer; the source of living water	Gen. 45:5-6; Num. 23:22; Isa. 41:14; 43:3; 45:21; Jer. 2:13; Mal. 2:10
El Shaddai ("God Almighty")	A title of respect for the gods in the Canaanite pantheon; later a name for Yahweh of Israel	Gen. 17:1, 7; 28:3; 35:11; 49:25; Ruth 1:20-21; Ezra 1:2-4; 6:3; Ps. 91:1; Isa. 9:6
El Rachum ("God of compassion")	God, the compassionate one who suffers with the child in the "womb" ("rechem" in Hebrew means "womb")	Deut. 4:31; Neh. 9:17
El Elyon ("God Most High")	Pre-Davidic God of Jerusalem; the faithful God; the most high	Gen. 14:19-20; Num. 24:16; Deut. 7:9; Ps. 47:2-3
El Olam ("God everlasting")	Eternal God of the universe; God of refuge and truth; originally a name for the Canaanite god of Beer-sheba, but later a name for Yahweh	Gen. 21:33; Pss. 31:5-6; 90:1-3; 93:2; 106:48; Isa. 26:4
El Yisrael; Hai; Elohe ("God of Israel")	The living God; the Lord God of Israel; the Holy One	Gen. 33:20; Deut. 5:26; 1 Sam. 23:10; Ps. 68:36; Isa. 5:16
El Gibbor ("mighty God")	The God of war and strength; Lord; savior	Exod. 15:2-3; Isa. 9:6
El Berith ("God of the covenant")	Pre-Israelite title for the Canaanite god of Shechem, later a name for Yahweh	Josh. 23:16; Judg. 9:46
Elohim ("the single God")	Generic title for deity; signifies the singular, majestic God of Israel; plural form of El or Eloah—"sons of heaven"; can refer to Israel's God or to false gods	Gen. 1:1, 26; 6:2; 17:19; Exod. 3:6; 20:3
Yahweh ("life" "existence" "to be" "Lord")	Personal name for God; "I AM WHO I AM"; the Creator; ruler of history; the deliverer; the Hebrew word for God, YHWH (pronounced Yahweh), which was not spoken but was replaced with the word "Adonai"	Gen. 4:26; 49:24-25; Exod. 3:13-15; 2 Sam. 22:2; Prov. 9:10
Adonai ("my great Lord")	Used as a substitute for Yahweh; also commonly used as a title of respect for a significant male, a lower lord, a social superior, a king, husband, father, or slave master	Ps. 11:7; Jer. 31:32; Hos. 2:18; Mal. 1:6
Yahweh Sabaoth ("Lord of hosts")	Lord Almighty; conqueror and ruler of angels and deities; king of glory	Neh. 9:6; Pss. 24:10; 89:9-19; Isa. 1:24
Immanuel (Emmanuel); Yireh; El Roi ("God with us")	A child who is a sign of God's presence; the one who sees all, hears the cries of his people, knows the affliction of slavery, and saves	Gen. 16:13-14; 22:13-14; Deut. 11:12; 2 Chron. 16:9; 42:1; Job 34:21-22; Isa. 7:10-17

Genesis

A wesome cosmic powers, tender love stories, tearful family reunions, and tales of deceit, rape, murder, and worldwide destruction. Sound like the script for next summer's blockbuster movie? Wrong. It's the book of Genesis—the story of how a perfect world created for love and harmony goes astray. Through it all, God is at work, forming a people to restore the trust and perfection that were lost.

IN DEPTH

Genesis gathers together inspired stories and traditions that reveal God's nature and purpose and the beginning of the Israelites' special relationship with God. Genesis has two main sections. The first section, Genesis 1-11, contains some of the Bible's most memorable stories about creation and the fall. Genesis 1-2 tells two stories of creation that portray the beauty and wonder of the natural world and emphasize the goodness and unity that God intended in creation. Creation culminates in human beings, made in God's own image. Those human beings, symbolic of us all, live in a wonderful garden in harmony with God, creation, and each other. But in chapter 3, the perfect world God created is disrupted. As a result, Adam and Eve experience separation, suffering, and ultimately death.

Although Genesis itself does not specifically mention sin as the reason for the fall, the strong tradition of belief in the Church is based on Paul's later writings in the Bible as well as the writings of Church leaders like Augustine. Although sin is a key element in the stories of Genesis, the wider themes of alienation and broken trust are important as well.

And sin spreads, first to the family (Cain and Abel in Genesis 4), then to all of society (Noah and the flood in Genesis 6-9). Even after the flood and God's covenant with Noah, the story of the tower of Babel demonstrates that sin pits nation against nation. As you read these chapters, remember that they were written not as historical accounts or scientific explanations, but as symbolic stories for sharing faith experiences and teaching important religious truths.

The second section, Genesis 12-50, tells the story of the origins of the Israelite people. The story begins with Abraham and Sarah (originally called Abram and Sarai) and continues with Ishmael and Isaac, and with Isaac and Rebekah's children, Esau and Jacob. Genesis ends with Joseph, one of Jacob's twelve sons, cleverly saving Egypt and Israel from famine. These sections introduce the covenant God makes with Abraham and remind us that God's plans will overcome human sin and weakness.

QUICK FACTS

- **Dates Covered:** The stories in the first eleven chapters are primeval history (the earliest human history). The remainder of the book covers the period of the ancestors, or patriarchs and matriarchs, 2000-1500 B.C.

- **Author:** An unknown author who gathered oral traditions and stories from tribal peoples sometime between 1225 and 1000 B.C., though Genesis was often attributed to Moses

- **Themes:** The goodness of creation, human responsibility, the effects of sin, and God's covenant, power, creativity, desire for relationship, and ability to bring good out of evil

AT A GLANCE

- **Genesis 1-11** The creation of the world and human beings by God

- **Genesis 12-50** Stories of the ancestors (matriarchs and patriarchs) of Israel

1 Six Days of Creation and the Sabbath

In the beginning when God created[a] the heavens and the earth, [2]the earth was a formless void and darkness covered the face of the deep, while a wind from God[b] swept over the face of the waters. [3]Then God said, "Let there be light"; and there was light. [4]And God saw that the light was good; and God separated the light from the darkness. [5]God called the light Day, and the darkness he called Night. And there was evening and there was morning, the first day.

6 And God said, "Let there be a dome in the midst of the waters, and let it separate the waters from the waters." [7]So God made the dome and separated the waters that were under the dome from the waters that were above the dome. And it was so. [8]God called the dome Sky. And there was evening and there was morning, the second day.

9 And God said, "Let the waters under the sky be gathered together into one place, and let the dry land appear." And it was so. [10]God called the dry land Earth, and the waters that were gathered together he called Seas. And God saw that it was good. [11]Then God said, "Let the earth put forth vegetation: plants yielding seed, and fruit trees of every kind on earth that bear fruit with the seed in it." And it was so. [12]The earth brought forth vegetation: plants yielding seed of every kind, and trees of every

kind bearing fruit with the seed in it. And God saw that it was good. [13]And there was evening and there was morning, the third day.

14 And God said, "Let there be lights in the dome of the sky to separate the day from the night; and let them be for signs and for seasons and for days and years, [15]and let them be lights in the dome of the sky to give light upon the earth." And it was so. [16]God made the two great lights—the greater light to rule the day and the lesser light to rule the night—and the stars. [17]God set them in the dome of the sky to give light upon the earth, [18]to rule over the day and over the night, and to separate the light from the darkness. And God saw that it was good. [19]And there was evening and there was morning, the fourth day.

20 And God said, "Let the waters bring forth swarms of living creatures, and let birds fly above the earth across the dome of the sky." [21]So God

STUDY IT!

In the Beginning · Genesis 1:1–2:4

"In the beginning when God created the heavens and the earth . . ." (Genesis 1:1). It's a simple verse, but one of the foundational beliefs of Christianity. We're not a random collection of atoms. The world is not a lucky combination of cosmic circumstances. The universe didn't just accidentally happen.

The beginning of wisdom is acknowledging that a higher power is at work in our lives, that the universe has purpose, and that everything was created by God. The ancient writers and editors of Genesis expressed these ideas in the Creation stories. The Church affirms these beliefs. They are expressed in a prayer, the Apostles' Creed, which begins, "I believe in God the Father Almighty, Creator of heaven and earth."

Here's another foundational belief expressed in Genesis: God created everything good! Read the story in this passage and see how this belief is constantly repeated. And humankind is "very good," created in God's own image. This is God's message to you in the first chapter of the Bible: you carry God's image within you. You are very good! Don't let anyone ever try to convince you otherwise.

a Or *when God began to create* or *In the beginning God created* b Or *while the spirit of God* or *while a mighty wind*

created the great sea monsters and every living creature that moves, of every kind, with which the waters swarm, and every winged bird of every kind. And God saw that it was good. ²²God blessed them, saying, "Be fruitful and multiply and fill the waters in the seas, and let birds multiply on the earth." ²³And there was evening and there was morning, the fifth day.

24 And God said, "Let the earth bring forth living creatures of every kind: cattle and creeping things

STUDY IT!

How Do You Read It? · Genesis 1:1–2:4

Some Christians believe God actually created the world in seven twenty-four-hour days. That belief comes from a literal reading of the first chapter of Genesis, as though it were a scientific textbook. However, Genesis was written not as a science article, but as a series of symbolic stories, sometimes called mythic stories, that convey great moral and spiritual truths. We should not try to make any scientific conclusions about the creation of the world from reading these stories.

Mythic stories are one literary type, or genre. Just look at a newspaper to see examples of different literary genres: news stories, advice columns, editorials, and comics. Each genre has different rules for interpreting its meaning. The Bible also contains many types of literary genres including hero stories, poetry, laws, legends, fictional satire, debates, and letters. To properly understand the Bible, pay attention to the literary genre—otherwise, you might believe the Bible is saying something it doesn't intend.

LIVE IT!

Taking Care of Creation · Genesis 1–2

The opening chapters of Genesis give us the wonderful story of God's creation of the universe. With each new day, God creates the light and darkness, the earth and sea, the plants and animals, and ultimately humankind. On the seventh day, when God looked at the amazing creation, "God saw everything that he had made, and indeed, it was very good" (Genesis 1:31).

God created the man and woman, then commanded them to "fill the earth and subdue it" (Genesis 1:28). In other words, human beings are to cooperate with God in the care of creation. With God's grace, we participate in laying the foundation for God's reign on earth.

We are co-workers with God in caring for and sustaining the world. That gives us a responsibility to protect the dignity of both the human person and the planet. We have to ask hard questions about topics like cloning, stem-cell research, the genetic alteration of agricultural products, agricultural practices, and energy production. Will these practices sustain our world or ultimately destroy it? Do they focus on shortsighted plunder of resources or long-term renewal? Do these practices really revere and value human life and the created order?

God has given us amazing intellectual gifts, which can lead to wonderful advancements for our world. But we must always ask how we might help promote ethical approaches to research and resource management, so that future generations can continue to enjoy creation's beauty and thrive in the universe.

- As a co-worker with God, how do you sustain and care for God's creation?
- How might you use your gifts of knowledge and education to really improve the world and help bring about God's reign on earth?

CONNECT IT!

Anna Jayne Joyner: Seeking Renewal for the Earth
Genesis 1–2

Anna Jayne Joyner fell in love with God's creation during college. She grew up the daughter of a pastor and studied abroad in New Zealand. That educational experience started her quest to combine her faith with her environmental ethics. And as she searched, she found others who were seeking ways to care for God's creation. Together they explored ways to connect, inspire, and equip the growing movement of Christian students engaging in environmental issues as an expression of their faith. Joyner and company launched an organization called Renewal. A student-initiated, student-led network, Renewal seeks to follow Jesus' example of love, stewardship, and reconciliation. According to **renewingcreation.org**, that means these students are doing their best to take care of everything that God so lovingly created: the earth and everyone in it. Read the first two chapters of Genesis, which describe the creation of the world and of people. The amazing creation described here—the light and darkness, land and sea, trees and plants and animals—is what Anna is inspired to care for. Like her, we all have a role to play in protecting and caring for the world we live in, not only because it impacts us, but because it is the miraculous creation of God. What aspect of nature are you most inspired to care for?

LIVE IT!

Made in God's Image
Genesis 1:26–27

God doesn't make mistakes, but people do. People make snap judgments based on a glance at the outside of another person. We spend way too many hours and dollars trying to look like movie stars on magazine covers— even though those images have been airbrushed and created by an army of makeup artists. Some people try to deny their racial heritage. Some change their appearance to fit the latest fads and definitions of beauty. Remember that physical features are not accidents, but part of God's plan. Read **Genesis 1:26–27**. We're all made in God's image—physically and at much deeper levels. To authentically love ourselves, we must love our whole selves: tall or short, dark or light skin, straight or curly hair, thin or full lips, and every other physical variation possible. Whatever we look like, we're all blessed by God.

and wild animals of the earth of every kind." And it was so. ²⁵ God made the wild animals of the earth of every kind, and the cattle of every kind, and everything that creeps upon the ground of every kind. And God saw that it was good.

26 Then God said, "Let us make humankind*[a]* in our image, according to our likeness; and let them have dominion over the fish of the sea, and over the birds of the air, and over the cattle, and over all the wild animals of the earth,*[b]* and over every creeping thing that creeps upon the earth."

27 So God created humankind*[a]* in his image,
     in the image of God he created them;*[c]*
     male and female he created them.

²⁸ God blessed them, and God said to them, "Be fruitful and multiply, and fill the earth and subdue it; and have dominion over the fish of the sea and over the birds of the air and over every living thing that moves upon the earth." ²⁹ God said, "See, I have given you every plant yielding seed that is upon the face of all the earth, and every tree with seed in its fruit; you shall have them for food. ³⁰ And to every beast of the earth, and to every bird of the air, and to everything that creeps on the earth, everything that has the breath of life, I have given every green plant for food." And it was so. ³¹ God saw everything that he had made, and indeed, it was very good. And there was evening and there was morning, the sixth day.

a Heb *adam* *b* Syr: Heb *and over all the earth* *c* Heb *him*

2 Thus the heavens and the earth were finished, and all their multitude. ²And on the seventh day God finished the work that he had done, and he rested on the seventh day from all the work that he had done. ³So God blessed the seventh day and hallowed it, because on it God rested from all the work that he had done in creation.

4 These are the generations of the heavens and the earth when they were created.

Another Account of the Creation

In the day that the LORD*ᵃ* God made the earth and the heavens, ⁵when no plant of the field was yet in the earth and no herb of the field had yet sprung up—for the LORD God had not caused it to rain upon the earth, and there was no one to till the ground; ⁶but a stream would rise from the earth, and water the whole face of the ground— ⁷then the LORD God formed man from the dust of the ground,*ᵇ* and breathed into his nostrils the breath of life; and the man became a living being. ⁸And the LORD God planted a garden in Eden, in the east; and there he put the man whom he had formed. ⁹Out of the ground the LORD God made to grow every tree that is pleasant to the sight and good for food, the tree of life also in the midst of the garden, and the tree of the knowledge of good and evil.

10 A river flows out of Eden to water the garden, and from there it divides and becomes four branches. ¹¹The name of the first is Pishon; it is the one that flows around the whole land of Havilah, where there is gold; ¹²and the gold of that land is good; bdellium and onyx stone are there. ¹³The name of the second river is Gihon; it is the one that flows around the whole land of Cush. ¹⁴The name of the third river is Tigris, which flows east of Assyria. And the fourth river is the Euphrates.

15 The LORD God took the man and put him in the garden of Eden to till it and keep it. ¹⁶And the LORD God commanded the man, "You may freely

LIVE IT!

Your Creator Wants You · Genesis 1–2

According to these chapters, God created the universe and is the source of order in all creation. Creation is good, and its goodness is reflected in the harmony, peace, and love between the Creator and his creatures and among the creatures themselves. In theological traditions, this ideal relationship—symbolized by the way God and Adam and Eve relate in the Garden of Eden—is considered the foundation in which salvation history is rooted.

• How do your relationships with God, your friends and family, and nature reflect harmony, peace, and love?

• Think about how you can improve some of your strained relationships, and ask God for help.

Human beings are created in God's image and likeness. We share God's attributes: freedom, love, knowledge, and the ability to create. With these gifts comes the responsibility to care for all creation.

• What inspires you in creation? Praise God for it. Thank God for your own life and for the people around you.

• Think of how you, your family, and your community can take better care of all creation. Ask God to help you love fully, to know the truth, and to use your freedom wisely.

God offers us a covenant from the moment of our creation. We keep it by freely placing ourselves in God's hands and being responsive to God's invitation to live in communion with God and people.

• How do you respond to God's invitation?

• In what areas of life is it hardest to live in harmony and love? Ask for God's wisdom. Put yourself in God's hands, and let God help and direct you.

ɑ Heb *YHWH*, as in other places where "LORD" is spelled with capital letters (see also Ex 3.14-15 with notes)   **b** Or *formed a man* (Heb *adam*) *of dust from the ground* (Heb *adamah*)

PRAY IT!

Take a Break
Genesis 2:1–3

Even God took a rest. The writer of Genesis makes this point to remind us to set aside a day for rest and spiritual refreshment. In Jewish tradition, this day is called the sabbath. Honoring the sabbath is an act of trust in God. It means we believe that the world will not fall apart if we stop our normal activity. The world is in God's hands, and this truth echoes in Jesus' words:

Consider the lilies, how they grow: they neither toil nor spin; yet I tell you, even Solomon in all his glory was not clothed like one of these. But if God so clothes the grass of the field, which is alive today and tomorrow is thrown into the oven, how much more will he clothe you. (Luke 12:27–28)

Christians traditionally rest and worship together on Sunday because it's the day Jesus was resurrected. It seems many people are abandoning this practice in our culture today. There are benefits we could gain by recommitting ourselves to a day of rest, celebration, and prayer.

- What can you do to honor the concept of sabbath rest?
- What things could you take a sabbath break from for one day a week: cell phones, computers, TV, video games, sports or music practices?
- Pray and ask God to help you choose one way you can live out the concept of a sabbath rest.

God formed every animal of the field and every bird of the air, and brought them to the man to see what he would call them; and whatever the man called every living creature, that was its name. ²⁰The man gave names to all cattle, and to the birds of the air, and to every animal of the field; but for the man*ᵃ* there was not found a helper as his partner. ²¹So the LORD God caused a deep sleep to fall upon the man, and he slept; then he took one of his ribs and closed up its place with flesh. ²²And the rib that the LORD God had taken from the man he made into a woman and brought her to the man. ²³Then the man said,

"This at last is bone of my bones
and flesh of my flesh;
this one shall be called Woman,*ᵇ*
for out of Man*ᶜ* this one was taken."

²⁴Therefore a man leaves his father and his mother and clings to his wife, and they become one flesh. ²⁵And the man and his wife were both naked, and were not ashamed.

The First Sin and Its Punishment

3 Now the serpent was more crafty than any other wild animal that the LORD God had made. He said to the woman, "Did God say, 'You shall not eat from any tree in the garden'?" ²The woman said to the serpent, "We may eat of the fruit of the trees in the garden; ³but God said, 'You shall not eat of the fruit of the tree that is in the middle of the garden, nor shall you touch it, or you shall die.'" ⁴But the serpent said to the woman, "You will not die; ⁵for God knows that when you eat of it your eyes will be opened, and you will be like God,*ᵈ* knowing good and evil." ⁶So when the woman saw that the tree was good for food, and that it was a delight to the eyes, and that the tree was to be desired to make one wise, she took of its fruit and ate; and she also gave some to her husband, who was with her, and he ate. ⁷Then the eyes of both were opened, and they knew that they were naked; and they sewed fig leaves together and made loincloths for themselves.

8 They heard the sound of the LORD God walking in the garden at the time of the evening breeze, and the man and his wife hid themselves from the presence of the LORD God among the trees of the garden. ⁹But the LORD God called to the man, and said to him, "Where are you?" ¹⁰He said, "I heard the sound of you in the garden, and I was afraid, because I was naked; and I hid myself." ¹¹He said, "Who told you that you were naked? Have you eaten from the tree

eat of every tree of the garden; ¹⁷but of the tree of the knowledge of good and evil you shall not eat, for in the day that you eat of it you shall die."

18 Then the LORD God said, "It is not good that the man should be alone; I will make him a helper as his partner." ¹⁹So out of the ground the LORD

ᵃ Or for Adam ᵇ Heb ishshah ᶜ Heb ish ᵈ Or gods

of which I commanded you not to eat?" [12]The man said, "The woman whom you gave to be with me, she gave me fruit from the tree, and I ate." [13]Then the LORD God said to the woman, "What is this that you have done?" The woman said, "The serpent tricked me, and I ate." [14]The LORD God said to the serpent,

"Because you have done this,
    cursed are you among all animals
    and among all wild creatures;
upon your belly you shall go,
    and dust you shall eat
    all the days of your life.
[15] I will put enmity between you and the woman,
    and between your offspring and hers;
he will strike your head,
    and you will strike his heel."

[16] To the woman he said,

"I will greatly increase your pangs in
    childbearing;
in pain you shall bring forth children,
yet your desire shall be for your husband,
    and he shall rule over you."

[17]And to the man[a] he said,

"Because you have listened to the voice of your
    wife,
and have eaten of the tree
about which I commanded you,
    'You shall not eat of it,'
cursed is the ground because of you;
    in toil you shall eat of it all the days of
        your life;
[18] thorns and thistles it shall bring forth for
    you;
    and you shall eat the plants of the field.
[19] By the sweat of your face
    you shall eat bread
until you return to the ground,
    for out of it you were taken;
you are dust,
    and to dust you shall return."

20 The man named his wife Eve,[b] because she was the mother of all living. [21]And the LORD God made garments of skins for the man[c] and for his wife, and clothed them.

22 Then the LORD God said, "See, the man has become like one of us, knowing good and evil; and now, he might reach out his hand and take also from the tree of life, and eat, and live forever"— [23]therefore the LORD God sent him forth from the garden of Eden, to till the ground from which he was taken. [24]He drove out the man; and at the east of the garden of Eden he placed the cherubim, and

STUDY IT!

The Start of All Sin · Genesis 3

Before the fall, Adam and Eve had it all. God gave them freedom and enjoyed a close friendship with them. They lived in complete harmony with each other and all of creation without fear, suffering, or death. It was a perfect life. But Adam and Eve wanted more. They believed the serpent's lie and tried to make themselves equal to God. They distrusted God's goodness, directly disobeyed God, and abused the freedom God had given them. The results were tragic. The friendship Adam and Eve felt toward God turned into fear as they hid in the garden. After being expelled from the garden, tension and strife entered Adam and Eve's once harmonious relationship. The creation they once helped tend with God so easily became hazardous and difficult to manage. Ultimately, death became a reality for Adam and Eve.

We have come to know this as original sin, and its consequences have been handed down to every generation throughout all of history, with the exception of Jesus. Just because we're part of the human race, our nature makes us inclined to sin and subject to death. Fortunately, Jesus Christ came to earth in total obedience to God's will. As a result, the brokenness first experienced by Adam and Eve has been overcome by the life, death, and resurrection of Jesus. (Read Romans 5:12-21 to learn more about the relationship between Adam and Jesus.) By grace, through Jesus, we are freed from original sin and turned back toward God. And we look forward to the day when Jesus will come again, restore our fallen world, and make our relationship with God completely whole.

---

a Or *to Adam*　**b** In Heb *Eve* resembles the word for *living*　**c** Or *for Adam*

a sword flaming and turning to guard the way to the tree of life.

Cain Murders Abel

4 Now the man knew his wife Eve, and she conceived and bore Cain, saying, "I have produced[a] a man with the help of the LORD." [2]Next she bore his brother Abel. Now Abel was a keeper of sheep, and Cain a tiller of the ground. [3]In the course of time Cain brought to the LORD an offering of the fruit of the ground, [4]and Abel for his part brought of the firstlings of his flock, their fat portions. And the LORD had regard for Abel and his offering, [5]but for Cain and his offering he had no regard. So Cain was very angry, and his countenance fell. [6]The LORD said to Cain, "Why are you angry, and why has your countenance fallen? [7]If you do well, will you not be accepted? And if you do not do well, sin is lurking at the door; its desire is for you, but you must master it."

8 Cain said to his brother Abel, "Let us go out to the field."[b] And when they were in the field, Cain rose up against his brother Abel, and killed him. [9]Then the LORD said to Cain, "Where is your brother Abel?" He said, "I do not know; am I my brother's keeper?" [10]And the LORD said, "What have you done? Listen; your brother's blood is crying out to me from the ground! [11]And now you are cursed from the ground, which has opened its mouth to receive your brother's blood from your hand. [12]When you till the ground, it will no longer yield to you its strength; you will be a fugitive and a wanderer on the earth." [13]Cain said to the LORD, "My punishment is greater than I can bear! [14]Today you have driven me away from the soil, and I shall be hidden from your face; I shall be a fugitive and a wanderer on the earth, and anyone who meets me may kill me." [15]Then the LORD said to him,

"Not so!"[c] Whoever kills Cain will suffer a sevenfold vengeance." And the LORD put a mark on Cain, so that no one who came upon him would kill him. [16]Then Cain went away from the presence of the LORD, and settled in the land of Nod,[d] east of Eden.

Beginnings of Civilization

17 Cain knew his wife, and she conceived and bore Enoch; and he built a city, and named it Enoch after his son Enoch. [18]To Enoch was born Irad; and Irad was the father of Mehujael, and Mehujael the father of Methushael, and Methushael the father of Lamech. [19]Lamech took two wives; the name of the one was Adah, and the name of the other Zillah. [20]Adah bore Jabal; he was the ancestor of those who live in tents

LIVE IT!

Violence and More Violence
Genesis 4:15

Cain was a murderer. Some might say he deserved the death penalty. But in **Genesis 4:15,** God marks Cain so that he is protected from being killed. God seeks to stop the cycle of violence.

Think of a TV show or movie with violent scenes that you have seen recently. What attitude did it portray toward violence? Often, violence in revenge is showed as justified, even satisfying. How does violence on TV or in the movies affect your own attitude toward it? How can you respond to God's call to stop the cycle of violence?

LIVE IT!

Brothers and Sisters · Genesis 4:9

"Am I my brother's keeper?" (Genesis 4:9). With that famous question, Cain pretends he doesn't know where his brother is. God does not answer Cain's question directly, but each of us knows the response. We are—each and every one of us—responsible for one another: family, friends, and strangers. We are brothers and sisters, because God has created us that way. We cannot avoid our obligation to watch out for one another.

• Are there people in your life who need you to be a brother or sister to them?
• How can you reach out to them today?

---

a The verb in Heb resembles the word for *Cain*   **b** Sam Gk Syr Compare Vg: MT lacks *Let us go out to the field*   **c** Gk Syr Vg: Heb *Therefore*   **d** That is *Wandering*

and have livestock. [21]His brother's name was Jubal; he was the ancestor of all those who play the lyre and pipe. [22]Zillah bore Tubal-cain, who made all kinds of bronze and iron tools. The sister of Tubal-cain was Naamah.

23 Lamech said to his wives:

"Adah and Zillah, hear my voice;
    you wives of Lamech, listen to what I say:
I have killed a man for wounding me,
    a young man for striking me.
[24] If Cain is avenged sevenfold,
    truly Lamech seventy-sevenfold."

25 Adam knew his wife again, and she bore a son and named him Seth, for she said, "God has appointed[a] for me another child instead of Abel, because Cain killed him." [26]To Seth also a son was born, and he named him Enosh. At that time people began to invoke the name of the LORD.

5 Adam's Descendants to Noah and His Sons

This is the list of the descendants of Adam. When God created humankind,[b] he made them[c] in the likeness of God. [2]Male and female he created them, and he blessed them and named them "Humankind"[b] when they were created.

3 When Adam had lived one hundred thirty years, he became the father of a son in his likeness, according to his image, and named him Seth. [4]The days of Adam after he became the father of Seth were eight hundred years; and he had other sons and daughters. [5]Thus all the days that Adam lived were nine hundred thirty years; and he died.

6 When Seth had lived one hundred five years, he became the father of Enosh. [7]Seth lived after the birth of Enosh eight hundred seven years, and had other sons and daughters. [8]Thus all the days of Seth were nine hundred twelve years; and he died.

9 When Enosh had lived ninety years, he became the father of Kenan. [10]Enosh lived after the birth of Kenan eight hundred fifteen years, and had other sons and daughters. [11]Thus all the days of Enosh were nine hundred five years; and he died.

12 When Kenan had lived seventy years, he became the father of Mahalalel. [13]Kenan lived after the birth of Mahalalel eight hundred and forty years, and had other sons and daughters. [14]Thus all the days of Kenan were nine hundred and ten years; and he died.

15 When Mahalalel had lived sixty-five years, he became the father of Jared. [16]Mahalalel lived after the birth of Jared eight hundred thirty years, and had other sons and daughters. [17]Thus all the days of Mahalalel were eight hundred ninety-five years; and he died.

18 When Jared had lived one hundred sixty-two years he became the father of Enoch. [19]Jared lived after the birth of Enoch eight hundred years, and had other sons and daughters. [20]Thus all the days of Jared were nine hundred sixty-two years; and he died.

21 When Enoch had lived sixty-five years, he became the father of Methuselah. [22]Enoch walked with God after the birth of Methuselah three hundred years, and had other sons and daughters. [23]Thus all the days of Enoch were three hundred sixty-five years. [24]Enoch walked with God; then he was no more, because God took him.

25 When Methuselah had lived one hundred eighty-seven years, he became the father of Lamech. [26]Methuselah lived after the birth of Lamech seven hundred eighty-two years, and had other sons and daughters. [27]Thus all the days of Methuselah were nine hundred sixty-nine years; and he died.

28 When Lamech had lived one hundred eighty-two years, he became the father of a son; [29]he named him Noah, saying, "Out of the ground that the LORD has cursed this one shall bring us relief from our work and from the toil of our hands." [30]Lamech lived after the birth of Noah five hundred ninety-five years, and had other sons and daughters. [31]Thus all the days of Lamech were seven hundred seventy-seven years; and he died.

32 After Noah was five hundred years old, Noah became the father of Shem, Ham, and Japheth.

6 The Wickedness of Humankind

When people began to multiply on the face of the ground, and daughters were born to them, [2]the sons of God saw that they were fair; and they took wives for themselves of all that they chose. [3]Then the LORD said, "My spirit shall not abide[d] in mortals forever, for they are flesh; their days shall be one hundred twenty years." [4]The Nephilim were on the earth in those days—and also afterward—when the sons of God went in to the daughters of humans, who bore children to them. These were the heroes that were of old, warriors of renown.

5 The LORD saw that the wickedness of humankind was great in the earth, and that every inclination of the thoughts of their hearts was only evil continually. [6]And the LORD was sorry that he had made

---

a The verb in Heb resembles the word for *Seth* b Heb *adam* c Heb *him* d Meaning of Heb uncertain

CONNECT IT!

Kendall Ciesemier: Kids Caring 4 Kids
Genesis 6:5–8

You know Noah—the guy with a boat full of animals, right? The story of Noah's ark has become such a childhood favorite that sometimes we forget that God had Noah build the ark, because God was going to destroy the whole earth with a flood. Pretty harsh, huh? The sin of the world had become so great that God could not tolerate it any longer. It wasn't that people were just making a few bad choices. The world was permeated with wickedness.

When widespread sin becomes part of our social systems and our institutions, it is called social sin. Think of it as group sin. Social sin involves individual choices, but is bigger than any one person's choice. Examples of social sin include the unequal distribution of the world's wealth, slave labor, genocide, the exploitation of workers, and discrimination based on race or gender.

Kendall Ciesemier was only eleven years old when she first found out that children in Africa were being orphaned by the AIDS epidemic by the millions. The disease itself was not sinful. It was the lack of compassion and help on the part of those who could help that was part of the bigger problem. Kendall knew she wanted to help and immediately sponsored a child in Africa. Then, faced with her own medical challenges, she used her kidney-transplant surgeries as an opportunity to raise more money to help AIDS victims. Now Kendall is in high school and the organization she started, Kids Caring 4 Kids, inspires others. She believes that, with God's help, one regular kid can make a difference around the world. So KC4K works to raise money for AIDS victims and to inspire young people to have a global vision for helping others. You can find out more at **kidscaring4kids.org**.

humankind on the earth, and it grieved him to his heart. [7]So the LORD said, "I will blot out from the earth the human beings I have created—people together with animals and creeping things and birds of the air, for I am sorry that I have made them." [8]But Noah found favor in the sight of the LORD.

Noah Pleases God

9 These are the descendants of Noah. Noah was a righteous man, blameless in his generation; Noah walked with God. [10]And Noah had three sons, Shem, Ham, and Japheth.

11 Now the earth was corrupt in God's sight, and the earth was filled with violence. [12]And God saw that the earth was corrupt; for all flesh had corrupted its ways upon the earth. [13]And God said to Noah, "I have determined to make an end of all flesh, for the earth is filled with violence because of them; now I am going to destroy them along with the earth. [14]Make yourself an ark of cypress[a] wood; make rooms in the ark, and cover it inside and out with pitch. [15]This is how you are to make it: the length of the ark three hundred cubits, its width fifty cubits, and its height thirty cubits. [16]Make a roof[b] for the ark, and finish it to a cubit above; and put the door of the ark in its side; make it with lower, second, and third decks. [17]For my part, I am going to bring a flood of waters on the earth, to destroy from under heaven all flesh in which is the breath of life; everything that is on the earth shall die. [18]But I will establish my covenant with you; and you shall come into the ark, you, your sons, your wife, and your sons' wives with you. [19]And of every living thing, of all flesh, you shall bring two of every kind into the ark, to keep them alive with you; they shall be male and female. [20]Of the birds according to their kinds, and of the animals according to their kinds, of every creeping thing of the ground according to its kind, two of every kind shall come in to you, to keep them alive. [21]Also take with you every kind of food that is eaten, and store it up; and it shall serve as food for you and for them." [22]Noah did this; he did all that God commanded him.

The Great Flood

7 Then the LORD said to Noah, "Go into the ark, you and all your household, for I have seen that you alone are righteous before me in this generation. [2]Take with you seven pairs of all clean animals, the male and its mate; and a pair of the animals that are not clean, the male and its mate; [3]and

a Meaning of Heb uncertain   b Or window

STUDY IT!

The Flood · Genesis 6–9

Adam and Eve's choices in the garden start a disastrous chain reaction. Each generation adds to sin in the world, which leads to the corruption of the world and the destruction of human beings. The great flood illustrates the ancient belief that God washed the world clean of this sinfulness and gave another chance to those who were faithful to God.

Other ancient cultures had stories about great floods. But in those stories, vindictive gods caused the floods for petty reasons. These gods had no real love for humanity. The Bible's flood story is unique, because it insists that God acted out of justice and in response to great, widespread evil.

God takes great care to save Noah and his family, because they are faithful and obedient. After the flood, God makes a covenant with Noah, promising never to destroy the earth by flood again—another unique element not found in the stories of other cultures.

seven pairs of the birds of the air also, male and female, to keep their kind alive on the face of all the earth. [4]For in seven days I will send rain on the earth for forty days and forty nights; and every living thing that I have made I will blot out from the face of the ground." [5]And Noah did all that the LORD had commanded him.

6 Noah was six hundred years old when the flood of waters came on the earth. [7]And Noah with his sons and his wife and his sons' wives went into the ark to escape the waters of the flood. [8]Of clean animals, and of animals that are not clean, and of birds, and of everything that creeps on the ground, [9]two and two, male and female, went into the ark with Noah, as God had commanded Noah. [10]And after seven days the waters of the flood came on the earth.

11 In the six hundredth year of Noah's life, in the second month, on the seventeenth day of the month, on that day all the fountains of the great deep burst forth, and the windows of the heavens were opened. [12]The rain fell on the earth forty days and forty nights. [13]On the very same day Noah with his sons, Shem and Ham and Japheth, and Noah's wife and the three wives of his sons entered the ark, [14]they and every wild animal of every kind, and all domestic animals of every kind, and every creeping thing that creeps on the earth, and every bird of every kind—every bird, every winged creature. [15]They went into the ark with Noah, two and two of all flesh in which there was the breath of life. [16]And those that entered, male and female of all flesh, went in as God had commanded him; and the LORD shut him in.

17 The flood continued forty days on the earth;

STUDY IT!

Water Flows Through the Bible Genesis 7

For the ancient Hebrews, although water often represented a source of life, it also represented forces of destruction over which God triumphs. In the story of Creation, God is portrayed as mastering the waters that represent chaos (see Genesis 1:1-2)—God constructs the upper and lower firmaments to hold back the waters. At the time of the great flood, God releases the waters, and they destroy life on earth. At the time of the exodus, God will once again display divine mastery of the waters with the parting of the Red Sea. Jesus will later do the same when he calms the storm and walks on water (see Mark 6:45-52).

and the waters increased, and bore up the ark, and it rose high above the earth. [18]The waters swelled and increased greatly on the earth; and the ark floated on the face of the waters. [19]The waters swelled so mightily on the earth that all the high mountains under the whole heaven were covered; [20]the waters swelled above the mountains, covering them fifteen cubits deep. [21]And all flesh died that moved on the earth, birds, domestic animals, wild animals, all swarming creatures that swarm on the earth, and all human beings; [22]everything on dry land in whose nostrils was the breath of life died. [23]He blotted out every living thing that was on the face of the ground, human beings and animals and creeping things and birds of the air; they were blotted out from the earth. Only Noah was left, and those that were with him in the ark. [24]And the waters swelled on the earth for one hundred fifty days.

The Flood Subsides

8 But God remembered Noah and all the wild animals and all the domestic animals that were with him in the ark. And God made a wind blow over the earth, and the waters subsided; [2]the fountains of the deep and the windows of the heavens were closed, the rain from the heavens was restrained, [3]and the waters gradually receded from the earth. At the end of one hundred fifty days the waters had abated; [4]and in the seventh month, on the seventeenth day of the month, the ark came to rest on the mountains of Ararat. [5]The waters continued to abate until the tenth month; in the tenth month, on the first day of the month, the tops of the mountains appeared.

6 At the end of forty days Noah opened the window of the ark that he had made [7]and sent out the raven; and it went to and fro until the waters were dried up from the earth. [8]Then he sent out the dove from him, to see if the waters had subsided from the face of the ground; [9]but the dove found no place to set its foot, and it returned to him to the ark, for the waters were still on the face of the whole earth. So he put out his hand and took it and brought it into the ark with him. [10]He waited another seven days, and again he sent out the dove from the ark; [11]and the dove came back to him in the evening, and there in its beak was a freshly plucked olive leaf; so Noah knew that the waters had subsided from the earth. [12]Then he waited another seven days, and sent out the dove; and it did not return to him any more.

13 In the six hundred first year, in the first month, on the first day of the month, the waters were dried up from the earth; and Noah removed the covering of the ark, and looked, and saw that the face of the ground was drying. [14]In the second month, on the twenty-seventh day of the month, the earth was dry. [15]Then God said to Noah, [16]"Go out of the ark, you and your wife, and your sons and your sons' wives with you. [17]Bring out with you every living thing that is with you of all flesh—birds and animals and every creeping thing that creeps on the earth—so that they may abound on the earth, and be fruitful and multiply on the earth." [18]So Noah went out with his sons and his wife and his sons' wives. [19]And every animal, every creeping thing, and every bird, everything that moves on the earth, went out of the ark by families.

God's Promise to Noah

20 Then Noah built an altar to the Lord, and took of every clean animal and of every clean bird, and offered burnt offerings on the altar. [21]And when the Lord smelled the pleasing odor, the Lord said in his heart, "I will never again curse the ground because of humankind, for the inclination of the human heart is evil from youth; nor will I ever again destroy every living creature as I have done.

22 As long as the earth endures,
seedtime and harvest, cold and heat,
summer and winter, day and night,
shall not cease."

The Covenant with Noah

9 God blessed Noah and his sons, and said to them, "Be fruitful and multiply, and fill the earth. [2]The fear and dread of you shall rest on every animal of the earth, and on every bird of the air, on everything that creeps on the ground, and on all the fish of the sea; into your hand they are delivered. [3]Every moving thing that lives shall be food for you; and just as I gave you the green plants, I give you everything. [4]Only, you shall not eat flesh with its life, that is, its blood. [5]For your own lifeblood I will surely require a reckoning: from every animal I will require it and from human beings, each one for the blood of another, I will require a reckoning for human life.

6 Whoever sheds the blood of a human,
by a human shall that person's blood be shed;

God's Promise · Genesis 9:8–17

PRAY IT!

What do you see when you see a rainbow? Do you see a multicolored arc caused by the refraction of sunlight through droplets of water? Or do you see a wonder of nature that causes you to stop and stare in awe? Something as remarkable as a rainbow is more than just science. It's no wonder the writer of Genesis used it as a symbol of God's covenant promise. When God and the Israelites see the rainbow in the clouds, they will recall their covenant together.

• If not a rainbow, what in nature fills you with awe of God's promises, love, power, and creativity?

• Praise and thank God for those reminders today.

for in his own image
God made humankind.
⁷And you, be fruitful and multiply, abound on the earth and multiply in it."

8 Then God said to Noah and to his sons with him, ⁹"As for me, I am establishing my covenant with you and your descendants after you, ¹⁰and with every living creature that is with you, the birds, the domestic animals, and every animal of the earth with you, as many as came out of the ark.^a ¹¹I establish my covenant with you, that never again shall all flesh be cut off by the waters of a flood, and never again shall there be a flood to destroy the earth." ¹²God said, "This is the sign of the covenant that I make between me and you and every living creature that is with you, for all future generations: ¹³I have set my bow in the clouds, and it shall be a sign of the covenant between me and the earth. ¹⁴When I bring clouds over the earth and the bow is seen in the clouds, ¹⁵I will remember my covenant that is between me and you and every living creature of all flesh; and the waters shall never again become a flood to destroy all flesh. ¹⁶When the bow is in the clouds, I will see it and remember the everlasting covenant between God and every living creature of all flesh that is on the earth." ¹⁷God said to Noah, "This is the sign of the covenant that I have established between me and all flesh that is on the earth."

Noah and His Sons

18 The sons of Noah who went out of the ark were Shem, Ham, and Japheth. Ham was the father of Canaan. ¹⁹These three were the sons of Noah; and from these the whole earth was peopled.

20 Noah, a man of the soil, was the first to plant a vineyard. ²¹He drank some of the wine and became drunk, and he lay uncovered in his tent. ²²And Ham, the father of Canaan, saw the nakedness of his father, and told his two brothers outside. ²³Then Shem and Japheth took a garment, laid it on both their shoulders, and walked backward and covered the nakedness of their father; their faces were turned away, and they did not see their father's nakedness. ²⁴When Noah awoke from his wine and knew what his youngest son had done to him, ²⁵he said,

"Cursed be Canaan;
   lowest of slaves shall he be to his brothers."
²⁶He also said,

"Blessed by the Lord my God be Shem;
   and let Canaan be his slave.
²⁷ May God make space for^b Japheth,
   and let him live in the tents of Shem;
   and let Canaan be his slave."

28 After the flood Noah lived three hundred fifty years. ²⁹All the days of Noah were nine hundred fifty years; and he died.

Nations Descended from Noah

10 These are the descendants of Noah's sons, Shem, Ham, and Japheth; children were born to them after the flood.

2 The descendants of Japheth: Gomer, Magog, Madai, Javan, Tubal, Meshech, and Tiras. ³The descendants of Gomer: Ashkenaz, Riphath, and Togarmah. ⁴The descendants of Javan: Elishah, Tarshish, Kittim, and Rodanim.^c ⁵From these the coastland peoples spread. These are the descendants of Japheth^d in their lands, with their own language, by their families, in their nations.

6 The descendants of Ham: Cush, Egypt, Put, and

Canaan. ⁷The descendants of Cush: Seba, Havilah, Sabtah, Raamah, and Sabteca. The descendants of Raamah: Sheba and Dedan. ⁸Cush became the father of Nimrod; he was the first on earth to become a mighty warrior. ⁹He was a mighty hunter before the LORD; therefore it is said, "Like Nimrod a mighty hunter before the LORD." ¹⁰The beginning of his kingdom was Babel, Erech, and Accad, all of them in the land of Shinar. ¹¹From that land he went into Assyria, and built Nineveh, Rehoboth-ir, Calah, and ¹²Resen between Nineveh and Calah; that is the great city. ¹³Egypt became the father of Ludim, Anamim, Lehabim, Naphtuhim, ¹⁴Pathrusim, Casluhim, and Caphtorim, from which the Philistines come.ᵃ

15 Canaan became the father of Sidon his firstborn, and Heth, ¹⁶and the Jebusites, the Amorites, the Girgashites, ¹⁷the Hivites, the Arkites, the Sinites, ¹⁸the Arvadites, the Zemarites, and the Hamathites. Afterward the families of the Canaanites spread abroad. ¹⁹And the territory of the Canaanites extended from Sidon, in the direction of Gerar, as far as Gaza, and in the direction of Sodom, Gomorrah, Admah, and Zeboiim, as far as Lasha. ²⁰These are the descendants of Ham, by their families, their languages, their lands, and their nations.

21 To Shem also, the father of all the children of Eber, the elder brother of Japheth, children were born. ²²The descendants of Shem: Elam, Asshur, Arpachshad, Lud, and Aram. ²³The descendants of Aram: Uz, Hul, Gether, and Mash. ²⁴Arpachshad became the father of Shelah; and Shelah became the father of Eber. ²⁵To Eber were born two sons: the name of the one was Peleg,ᵇ for in his days the earth was divided, and his brother's name was Joktan. ²⁶Joktan became the father of Almodad, Sheleph, Hazarmaveth, Jerah, ²⁷Hadoram, Uzal, Diklah, ²⁸Obal, Abimael, Sheba, ²⁹Ophir, Havilah, and Jobab; all these were the descendants of Joktan. ³⁰The territory in which they lived extended from Mesha in the direction of Sephar, the hill country of the east. ³¹These are the descendants of Shem, by their families, their languages, their lands, and their nations.

32 These are the families of Noah's sons, according to their genealogies, in their nations; and from these the nations spread abroad on the earth after the flood.

The Tower of Babel

11 Now the whole earth had one language and the same words. ²And as they migrated from the east,ᶜ they came upon a plain in the land of Shinar and settled there. ³And they said to one another, "Come, let us make bricks, and burn them thoroughly." And they had brick for stone, and bitumen for mortar. ⁴Then they said, "Come, let us build ourselves a city, and a tower with its top in the heavens, and let us make a name for ourselves; otherwise we shall be scattered abroad upon the face of the whole earth." ⁵The LORD came down to see the city and the tower, which mortals had built. ⁶And the LORD said, "Look, they are one people, and they have all one language; and this is only the beginning of what they will do; nothing that they propose to do will now be impossible for them. ⁷Come, let us go down, and confuse their language there, so that they will not understand one another's speech." ⁸So the LORD scattered them abroad from there over the face of all the earth, and they left off building the city. ⁹Therefore

STUDY IT!

More Than Words
Genesis 11:1–9

We connect with other people through our words. You've probably also heard that love, music, and a smile are universal languages. Yet languages can also separate and confuse us. They can symbolize differences between cultures and nations that can cause wars and other atrocities to occur.

The story of the tower of Babel is an ancient explanation of why the separation between people, symbolized by different languages, occurs. The people ignore God's command to "fill the earth" (Genesis 1:28). Instead, they gather in one place to try to build a tower reaching to heaven, a sin of pride and arrogance. God confuses their language to foil their plan. But ultimately, it's not language that separates us; it's pride.

In **Acts 2**, language serves as a bridge. The Holy Spirit enables the people from many different lands to hear the apostles speaking in their own languages. The Spirit unifies us, no matter what earthly language we speak. The good news is universal and unites us!

ᵃ Cn: Heb *Casluhim, from which the Philistines come, and Caphtorim* ᵇ That is *Division* ᶜ Or *migrated eastward*

it was called Babel, because there the LORD confused[a] the language of all the earth; and from there the LORD scattered them abroad over the face of all the earth.

Descendants of Shem

10 These are the descendants of Shem. When Shem was one hundred years old, he became the father of Arpachshad two years after the flood; [11]and Shem lived after the birth of Arpachshad five hundred years, and had other sons and daughters.

12 When Arpachshad had lived thirty-five years, he became the father of Shelah; [13]and Arpachshad lived after the birth of Shelah four hundred three years, and had other sons and daughters.

14 When Shelah had lived thirty years, he became the father of Eber; [15]and Shelah lived after the birth of Eber four hundred three years, and had other sons and daughters.

16 When Eber had lived thirty-four years, he became the father of Peleg; [17]and Eber lived after the birth of Peleg four hundred thirty years, and had other sons and daughters.

18 When Peleg had lived thirty years, he became the father of Reu; [19]and Peleg lived after the birth of Reu two hundred nine years, and had other sons and daughters.

20 When Reu had lived thirty-two years, he became the father of Serug; [21]and Reu lived after the birth of Serug two hundred seven years, and had other sons and daughters.

22 When Serug had lived thirty years, he became the father of Nahor; [23]and Serug lived after the birth of Nahor two hundred years, and had other sons and daughters.

24 When Nahor had lived twenty-nine years, he became the father of Terah; [25]and Nahor lived after the birth of Terah one hundred nineteen years, and had other sons and daughters.

26 When Terah had lived seventy years, he became the father of Abram, Nahor, and Haran.

Descendants of Terah

27 Now these are the descendants of Terah. Terah was the father of Abram, Nahor, and Haran; and Haran was the father of Lot. [28]Haran died before his father Terah in the land of his birth, in Ur of the Chaldeans. [29]Abram and Nahor took wives; the name of Abram's wife was Sarai, and the name of Nahor's wife was Milcah. She was the daughter of Haran the father of Milcah and Iscah. [30]Now Sarai was barren; she had no child.

31 Terah took his son Abram and his grandson Lot son of Haran, and his daughter-in-law Sarai, his son Abram's wife, and they went out together from Ur of the Chaldeans to go into the land of Canaan; but when they came to Haran, they settled there. [32]The days of Terah were two hundred five years; and Terah died in Haran.

12 The Call of Abram

Now the LORD said to Abram, "Go from your country and your kindred and your father's house to the land that I will show you. [2]I will make of you a great nation, and I will bless you, and make your name great, so that you will be a blessing. [3]I will bless those who bless you, and the one who curses you I will curse; and in you all the families of the earth shall be blessed."[b]

4 So Abram went, as the LORD had told him; and Lot went with him. Abram was seventy-five years old when he departed from Haran. [5]Abram took his wife Sarai and his brother's son Lot, and all the possessions that they had gathered, and the persons whom they had acquired in Haran; and they set forth to go to the land of Canaan. When they had come to the land of Canaan, [6]Abram passed through the land to the place at Shechem, to the oak[c] of Moreh. At that time the Canaanites were in the land. [7]Then the LORD appeared to Abram, and said, "To your offspring[d] I will give this land." So he built there an altar to the LORD, who had appeared to him. [8]From there he moved on to the hill country on the east of Bethel, and pitched his tent, with Bethel on the west and Ai on the east; and there he built an altar to the LORD and invoked the name of the LORD. [9]And Abram journeyed on by stages toward the Negeb.

Abram and Sarai in Egypt

10 Now there was a famine in the land. So Abram went down to Egypt to reside there as an alien, for the famine was severe in the land. [11]When he was about to enter Egypt, he said to his wife Sarai, "I know well that you are a woman beautiful in appearance; [12]and when the Egyptians see you, they will say, 'This is his wife'; then they will kill me, but they will let you live. [13]Say you are my sister, so that it may go well with me because of you, and that my life may be spared on your account." [14]When Abram entered Egypt the Egyptians saw that the woman was very

---

a Heb *balal*, meaning *to confuse* b Or *by you all the families of the earth shall bless themselves* c Or *terebinth* d Heb *seed*

Introducing . . . Abraham and Sarah · Genesis 12:1–25:11

Abraham, whose name was originally Abram (Genesis 11:26), is an important figure for three major world religions: Judaism, Christianity, and Islam. Abraham is regarded as the great example of faith in God. For many years, Abram lives in Haran in northern Mesopotamia with his wife, Sarai. (See Map 1: "The World of the Patriarchs.") God calls Abram and Sarai to leave their home, seals a covenant with them, and changes their names to Abraham and Sarah. God's covenant promises that they will be the parents "of a multitude of nations" (Genesis 17:5) and that their descendants will be as numerous as the "stars of heaven" (Genesis 22:17).

As you will discover in their story, becoming the parents of many nations was a faith builder; it took longer than they could have imagined to even bear their first and only son, Isaac. Later, God requests that Abraham sacrifice Isaac as a burnt offering. God stops him from going through with it, but Abraham's willingness to cooperate with and completely trust God becomes the foundation for Israel's faith. Not surprisingly, in the Old Testament, when a prophet or teacher needed an example of someone with unwavering trust in God, Abraham was often cited. In the New Testament, Abraham is revered as the first patriarch to enter into a covenant with God (see Matthew 1:1; Luke 16:19-31) and the great pioneer of Israel's faith (Acts 7:2-50; Romans 4:1-25; Hebrews 7:1-10).

beautiful. [15]When the officials of Pharaoh saw her, they praised her to Pharaoh. And the woman was taken into Pharaoh's house. [16]And for her sake he dealt well with Abram; and he had sheep, oxen, male donkeys, male and female slaves, female donkeys, and camels.

17 But the LORD afflicted Pharaoh and his house with great plagues because of Sarai, Abram's wife. [18]So Pharaoh called Abram, and said, "What is this you have done to me? Why did you not tell me that she was your wife? [19]Why did you say, 'She is my sister,' so that I took her for my wife? Now then, here is your wife, take her, and be gone." [20]And Pharaoh gave his men orders concerning him; and they set him on the way, with his wife and all that he had.

Abram and Lot Separate

13 So Abram went up from Egypt, he and his wife, and all that he had, and Lot with him, into the Negeb.

2 Now Abram was very rich in livestock, in silver, and in gold. [3]He journeyed on by stages from the Negeb as far as Bethel, to the place where his tent had been at the beginning, between Bethel and Ai, [4]to the place where he had made an altar at the first; and there Abram called on the name of the LORD. [5]Now Lot, who went with Abram, also had flocks and herds and tents, [6]so that the land could not support both

of them living together; for their possessions were so great that they could not live together, [7]and there was strife between the herders of Abram's livestock and the herders of Lot's livestock. At that time the Canaanites and the Perizzites lived in the land.

8 Then Abram said to Lot, "Let there be no strife between you and me, and between your herders and my herders; for we are kindred. [9]Is not the whole land before you? Separate yourself from me. If you take the left hand, then I will go to the right; or if you take the right hand, then I will go to the left." [10]Lot looked about him, and saw that the plain of the Jordan was well watered everywhere like the garden of the LORD, like the land of Egypt, in the direction of Zoar; this was before the LORD had destroyed Sodom and Gomorrah. [11]So Lot chose for himself all the plain of the Jordan, and Lot journeyed eastward; thus they separated from each other. [12]Abram settled in the land of Canaan, while Lot settled among the cities of the Plain and moved his tent as far as Sodom. [13]Now the people of Sodom were wicked, great sinners against the LORD.

14 The LORD said to Abram, after Lot had separated from him, "Raise your eyes now, and look from the place where you are, northward and southward and eastward and westward; [15]for all the land that you see I will give to you and to your offspring[a] forever. [16]I will make your offspring like the dust of the

α Heb *seed*

earth; so that if one can count the dust of the earth, your offspring also can be counted. [17]Rise up, walk through the length and the breadth of the land, for I will give it to you." [18]So Abram moved his tent, and came and settled by the oaks[a] of Mamre, which are at Hebron; and there he built an altar to the LORD.

Lot's Captivity and Rescue

14 In the days of King Amraphel of Shinar, King Arioch of Ellasar, King Chedorlaomer of Elam, and King Tidal of Goiim, [2]these kings made war with King Bera of Sodom, King Birsha of Gomorrah, King Shinab of Admah, King Shemeber of Zeboiim, and the king of Bela (that is, Zoar). [3]All these joined forces in the Valley of Siddim (that is, the Dead Sea).[b] [4]Twelve years they had served Chedorlaomer, but in the thirteenth year they rebelled. [5]In the fourteenth year Chedorlaomer and the kings who were with him came and subdued the Rephaim in Ashteroth-karnaim, the Zuzim in Ham, the Emim in Shaveh-kiriathaim, [6]and the Horites in the hill country of Seir as far as El-paran on the edge of the wilderness; [7]then they turned back and came to En-mishpat (that is, Kadesh), and subdued all the country of the Amalekites, and also the Amorites who lived in Hazazon-tamar. [8]Then the king of Sodom, the king of Gomorrah, the king of Admah, the king of Zeboiim, and the king of Bela (that is, Zoar) went out, and they joined battle in the Valley of Siddim [9]with King Chedorlaomer of Elam, King Tidal of Goiim, King Amraphel of Shinar, and King Arioch of Ellasar, four kings against five. [10]Now the Valley of Siddim was full of bitumen pits; and as the kings of Sodom and Gomorrah fled, some fell into them, and the rest fled to the hill country. [11]So the enemy took all the goods of Sodom and Gomorrah, and all their provisions, and went their way; [12]they also took Lot, the son of Abram's brother, who lived in Sodom, and his goods, and departed.

13 Then one who had escaped came and told Abram the Hebrew, who was living by the oaks[a] of Mamre the Amorite, brother of Eshcol and of Aner; these were allies of Abram. [14]When Abram heard that his nephew had been taken captive, he led forth his trained men, born in his house, three hundred eighteen of them, and went in pursuit as far as Dan. [15]He divided his forces against them by night, he and his servants, and routed them and pursued them

STUDY IT!

Spiritual Symbols
Genesis 14:17–20

Sometimes words alone are not enough. Consider Abram's inexpressible joy and relief in **Genesis 14:17–20**. Abram's nephew Lot had been captured by foreign invaders, and Abram took his men to battle and rescued Lot safely. The king and priest Melchizedek meets Abram when he returns to rejoice in the great victory. As part of their celebration, Melchizedek uses not only words, but the everyday objects of bread and wine in a ritual to offer a blessing on Abram and to give praise to God.

We still use symbols today to express and deepen our relationship with God. We see this in celebrations of faith like baptism and Communion, or the Lord's Supper. The symbols used are normal, everyday things like water, bread, and wine, combined with the words and history given to us in the Bible. We see this most clearly when we celebrate Communion—we use the symbols of bread and wine (or juice) along with words and gestures that Jesus used when he celebrated the Passover with his disciples on the eve of his crucifixion.

These symbols and traditions make God's grace more real and tangible in our everyday lives. And when we see them around us at home, school, or work, those symbols can remind us that God's power and presence are with us and in us everywhere—not just at church on Sunday.

to Hobah, north of Damascus. [16]Then he brought back all the goods, and also brought back his nephew Lot with his goods, and the women and the people.

Abram Blessed by Melchizedek

17 After his return from the defeat of Chedorlaomer and the kings who were with him, the king of

---

a Or *terebinths*   **b** Heb *Salt Sea*

Sodom went out to meet him at the Valley of Shaveh (that is, the King's Valley). [18]And King Melchizedek of Salem brought out bread and wine; he was priest of God Most High.[a] [19]He blessed him and said,

"Blessed be Abram by God Most High,[a]
  maker of heaven and earth;
[20] and blessed be God Most High,[a]
    who has delivered your enemies into your hand!"

And Abram gave him one-tenth of everything. [21]Then the king of Sodom said to Abram, "Give me the persons, but take the goods for yourself." [22]But Abram said to the king of Sodom, "I have sworn to the LORD, God Most High,[a] maker of heaven and earth, [23]that I would not take a thread or a sandal-thong or anything that is yours, so that you might not say, 'I have made Abram rich.' [24]I will take nothing but what the young men have eaten, and the share of the men who went with me—Aner, Eshcol, and Mamre. Let them take their share."

God's Covenant with Abram

15 After these things the word of the LORD came to Abram in a vision, "Do not be afraid, Abram, I am your shield; your reward shall be very great." [2]But Abram said, "O Lord GOD, what will you give me, for I continue childless, and the heir of my house is Eliezer of Damascus?"[b] [3]And Abram said, "You have given me no offspring, and so a slave born in my house is to be my heir." [4]But the word of the LORD came to him, "This man shall not be your heir; no one but your very own issue shall be your heir." [5]He brought him outside and said, "Look toward heaven and count the stars, if you are able to count them." Then he said to him, "So shall your descendants be." [6]And he believed the LORD; and the LORD[c] reckoned it to him as righteousness.

7 Then he said to him, "I am the LORD who brought you from Ur of the Chaldeans, to give you this land to possess." [8]But he said, "O Lord GOD, how am I to know that I shall possess it?" [9]He said to him, "Bring me a heifer three years old, a female goat three years old, a ram three years old, a turtle-dove, and a young pigeon." [10]He brought him all these and cut them in two, laying each half over against the other; but he did not cut the birds in two. [11]And when birds of prey came down on the carcasses, Abram drove them away.

12 As the sun was going down, a deep sleep fell upon Abram, and a deep and terrifying darkness descended upon him. [13]Then the LORD[c] said to Abram, "Know this for certain, that your offspring shall be aliens in a land that is not theirs, and shall be slaves there, and they shall be oppressed for four hundred years; [14]but I will bring judgment on the nation that they serve, and afterward they shall come out with great possessions. [15]As for yourself, you shall go to your ancestors in peace; you shall be buried in a good old age. [16]And they shall come back here in the fourth generation; for the iniquity of the Amorites is not yet complete."

17 When the sun had gone down and it was dark, a smoking fire pot and a flaming torch passed between these pieces. [18]On that day the LORD made a covenant with Abram, saying, "To your descendants I give this land, from the river of Egypt to the great river, the river Euphrates, [19]the land of the Kenites, the Kenizzites, the Kadmonites, [20]the Hittites, the Perizzites, the Rephaim, [21]the Amorites, the Canaanites, the Girgashites, and the Jebusites."

The Birth of Ishmael

16 Now Sarai, Abram's wife, bore him no children. She had an Egyptian slave-girl whose name was Hagar, [2]and Sarai said to Abram, "You see that the LORD has prevented me from bearing children; go in to my slave-girl; it may be that I shall

STUDY IT!

On Fire
Genesis 15:17

Fire appears frequently throughout the Old Testament, symbolizing two aspects of God: presence and holiness. Fire symbolizes a special presence of God in the sealing of the covenant with Abraham (Genesis 15:17), in the burning bush seen by Moses (Exodus 3:2), and in the pillar of fire leading Israel through the desert (Exodus 13:21). Fire also symbolizes God's holiness appearing to purge and purify those who stray from God's ways, as in the destruction of Sodom and Gomorrah (Genesis 19:24) and in the seventh plague against Egypt (Exodus 9:23).

a Heb El Elyon   b Meaning of Heb uncertain   c Heb he

obtain children by her." And Abram listened to the voice of Sarai. ³So, after Abram had lived ten years in the land of Canaan, Sarai, Abram's wife, took Hagar the Egyptian, her slave-girl, and gave her to her husband Abram as a wife. ⁴He went in to Hagar, and she conceived; and when she saw that she had conceived, she looked with contempt on her mistress. ⁵Then Sarai said to Abram, "May the wrong done to me be on you! I gave my slave-girl to your embrace, and when she saw that she had conceived, she looked on me with contempt. May the LORD judge between you and me!" ⁶But Abram said to Sarai, "Your slave-girl is in your power; do to her as you please." Then Sarai dealt harshly with her, and she ran away from her.

7 The angel of the LORD found her by a spring of water in the wilderness, the spring on the way to Shur. ⁸And he said, "Hagar, slave-girl of Sarai, where have you come from and where are you going?" She said, "I am running away from my mistress Sarai." ⁹The angel of the LORD said to her, "Return to your mistress, and submit to her." ¹⁰The angel of the LORD also said to her, "I will so greatly multiply your offspring that they cannot be counted for multitude." ¹¹And the angel of the LORD said to her,

"Now you have conceived and shall bear a son;
     you shall call him Ishmael,ᵃ
     for the Lord has given heed to your
          affliction.
¹² He shall be a wild ass of a man,
     with his hand against everyone,
     and everyone's hand against him;
     and he shall live at odds with all his kin."

¹³So she named the LORD who spoke to her, "You are El-roi";ᵇ for she said, "Have I really seen God and remained alive after seeing him?"ᶜ ¹⁴Therefore the well was called Beer-lahai-roi;ᵈ it lies between Kadesh and Bered.

15 Hagar bore Abram a son; and Abram named his son, whom Hagar bore, Ishmael. ¹⁶Abram was eighty-six years old when Hagar bore himᵉ Ishmael.

The Sign of the Covenant

17 When Abram was ninety-nine years old, the LORD appeared to Abram, and said to him, "I am God Almighty;ᶠ walk before me, and be blameless. ²And I will make my covenant between me and you, and will make you exceedingly numerous." ³Then Abram fell on his face; and God said to him, ⁴"As for me, this is my covenant with you: You shall

LIVE IT!

A Message of Dignity
Genesis 16

A love triangle in the Bible? The relationship between Abram, Sarai, and Hagar is shocking by Christian moral standards, but it wasn't unusual in their time. Patriarchs like Abram often had children by several wives, slaves, and concubines (something like an official mistress who lived with the household). It's not surprising that such relationships would have fostered jealousy and tension. The conflict between Hagar and Sarai must have been fierce, for Hagar left the security of Abram's household—a big deal in an age when women had few or no rights of their own.

So why does God's angel seek out Hagar and ask her to return to a place where she is likely to be mistreated? To answer this, we have to remember that the writer of Genesis was concerned more with explaining the rise of nations than with teaching a moral lesson. Hagar must return to bear her son, Ishmael, so that the Ishmaelites (his descendants) have a clear connection to Abraham as their ancestor. God does not like injustice, but God does have the power to work in the midst of injustice to fulfill his greater plans. And Hagar's story isn't over yet. Check out **Genesis 21** for more!

Today, we encourage victims of abuse and harassment to speak out and take action. When we encounter people who have been abused or harassed, we also need to help them seek justice and set things right. Remember the larger message in Genesis—that every person is created in God's image and is to be treated with the utmost dignity and respect. Carrying out this message is our responsibility as one another's brothers and sisters.

ᵃ That is *God hears*   ᵇ Perhaps *God of seeing* or *God who sees*   ᶜ Meaning of Heb uncertain   ᵈ That is *the Well of the Living One who sees me*   ᵉ Heb *Abram*   ᶠ Traditional rendering of Heb *El Shaddai*

be the ancestor of a multitude of nations. [5]No longer shall your name be Abram,[a] but your name shall be Abraham;[b] for I have made you the ancestor of a multitude of nations. [6]I will make you exceedingly fruitful; and I will make nations of you, and kings shall come from you. [7]I will establish my covenant between me and you, and your offspring after you throughout their generations, for an everlasting covenant, to be God to you and to your offspring[c] after you. [8]And I will give to you, and to your offspring after you, the land where you are now an alien, all the land of Canaan, for a perpetual holding; and I will be their God."

9 God said to Abraham, "As for you, you shall keep my covenant, you and your offspring after you throughout their generations. [10]This is my covenant, which you shall keep, between me and you and your offspring after you: Every male among you shall be circumcised. [11]You shall circumcise the flesh of your foreskins, and it shall be a sign of the covenant between me and you. [12]Throughout your generations every male among you shall be circumcised when he is eight days old, including the slave born in your house and the one bought with your money from any foreigner who is not of your offspring. [13]Both the slave born in your house and the one bought with your money must be circumcised. So shall my covenant be in your flesh an everlasting covenant. [14]Any uncircumcised male who is not circumcised in the flesh of his foreskin shall be cut off from his people; he has broken my covenant."

15 God said to Abraham, "As for Sarai your wife, you shall not call her Sarai, but Sarah shall be her name. [16]I will bless her, and moreover I will give you a son by her. I will bless her, and she shall give rise to nations; kings of peoples shall come from her." [17]Then Abraham fell on his face and laughed, and said to himself, "Can a child be born to a man who is a hundred years old? Can Sarah, who is ninety years old, bear a child?" [18]And Abraham said to God, "O that Ishmael might live in your sight!" [19]God said, "No, but your wife Sarah shall bear you a son, and you shall name him Isaac.[d] I will establish my covenant with him as an everlasting covenant for his offspring after him. [20]As for Ishmael, I have heard you; I will bless him and make him fruitful and exceedingly numerous; he shall be the father of twelve princes, and I will make him a great nation. [21]But my covenant I will establish with Isaac,

LIVE IT!

The Power of Covenant
Genesis 17

"Covenant" is a powerful word in the Bible, with deep spiritual significance, because it expresses the intimate relationship between God and God's people. At its most basic level, a covenant is a promise made by two parties to do certain things. In the covenant God makes with Noah, God promises never to destroy the earth again, and Noah's family promises to fill the earth and tend it (Genesis 9:1-17). In the covenant with Abraham, God promises that Abraham's descendants will be numerous and become a great nation. As a sign of this covenant, all the males of Abraham's household and descendants must practice circumcision to mark that they belong to God. In the covenant made at Mount Sinai with Moses and the Hebrew people, God promises to give them the promised land. In return, they promise to follow the laws God gives them (Exodus 19:1-9).

These covenants are always initiated by God, who wants to lead the people to a better way of life. But the people must respond to God's offer as a sign of their faith in God. Each of us is part of these ancient promises. Like the many faithful people who have gone before us, we too are believers in the one God and members of God's family. But unlike the covenants of the Old Testament, we live under a new covenant offered through the sacrifice of Jesus. This new covenant is for all people. Anyone who believes in Jesus becomes an heir to an intimate relationship with the Holy One through the new covenant in Jesus (see Luke 22:14-23). How does this new covenant impact how you live your life and make your decisions?

---

a That is exalted ancestor   b Here taken to mean ancestor of a multitude   c Heb seed   d That is he laughs

STUDY IT!

The Symbol of Circumcision · Genesis 17:9–14

Circumcision, a symbolic mark for the male member and rite of passage, symbolized that a person belonged to God. It was required by the covenant that God made first with Abraham and then with Moses and all of Israel. In ancient Israel, circumcision was usually performed shortly after birth. Today most Jews and many Muslims continue circumcision as a religious tradition, and it is a common cultural practice in the United States. But the practice of circumcision is not as common in other cultures and religions around the world.

In the early Church, circumcision became the center of a controversy; the issue was whether Gentiles who wanted to become Christians had to first become Jews by being circumcised (see Acts 15; Philippians 3:2-9). But the Bible teaches that circumcision is no longer required under the new covenant in Jesus. Colossians 3:11 says, "In that renewal there is no longer Greek and Jew, circumcised and uncircumcised, barbarian, Scythian, slave and free; but Christ is all and in all!"

whom Sarah shall bear to you at this season next year." [22] And when he had finished talking with him, God went up from Abraham.

23 Then Abraham took his son Ishmael and all the slaves born in his house or bought with his money, every male among the men of Abraham's house, and he circumcised the flesh of their foreskins that very day, as God had said to him. [24] Abraham was ninety-nine years old when he was circumcised in the flesh of his foreskin. [25] And his son Ishmael was thirteen years old when he was circumcised in the flesh of his foreskin. [26] That very day Abraham and his son Ishmael were circumcised; [27] and all the men of his house, slaves born in the house and those bought with money from a foreigner, were circumcised with him.

A Son Promised to Abraham and Sarah

18

The Lord appeared to Abraham[a] by the oaks[b] of Mamre, as he sat at the entrance of his tent in the heat of the day. [2] He looked up and saw three men standing near him. When he saw them, he ran from the tent entrance to meet them, and bowed down to the ground. [3] He said, "My lord, if I find favor with you, do not pass by your servant. [4] Let a little water be brought, and wash your feet, and rest yourselves under the tree. [5] Let me bring a little bread, that you may refresh yourselves, and after that you may pass on—since you have come to your servant." So they said, "Do as you have said." [6] And Abraham hastened into the tent to Sarah, and said, "Make ready quickly three measures[c] of choice flour, knead it, and

make cakes." [7] Abraham ran to the herd, and took a calf, tender and good, and gave it to the servant, who hastened to prepare it. [8] Then he took curds and milk and the calf that he had prepared, and set it before them; and he stood by them under the tree while they ate.

9 They said to him, "Where is your wife Sarah?" And he said, "There, in the tent." [10] Then one said, "I will surely return to you in due season, and your wife Sarah shall have a son." And Sarah was listening at the tent entrance behind him. [11] Now Abraham and Sarah were old, advanced in age; it had ceased to be with Sarah after the manner of women. [12] So Sarah laughed to herself, saying, "After I have grown old, and my husband is old, shall I have pleasure?" [13] The Lord said to Abraham, "Why did Sarah laugh, and say, 'Shall I indeed bear a child, now that I am old?' [14] Is anything too wonderful for the Lord? At the set time I will return to you, in due season, and Sarah shall have a son." [15] But Sarah denied, saying, "I did not laugh"; for she was afraid. He said, "Oh yes, you did laugh."

Judgment Pronounced on Sodom

16 Then the men set out from there, and they looked toward Sodom; and Abraham went with them to set them on their way. [17] The Lord said, "Shall I hide from Abraham what I am about to do, [18] seeing that Abraham shall become a great and mighty nation, and all the nations of the earth shall be blessed in him?[d] [19] No, for I have chosen[e] him, that he may charge his children and his household after him to keep the way of the Lord by doing righteousness

a Heb *him*   b Or *terebinths*   c Heb *seahs*   d Or *and all the nations of the earth shall bless themselves by him*   e Heb *known*

What's So Funny? · Genesis 18:9–15

"Laughter" is not a word we always associate with the Bible, especially not with the Old Testament. Most of the stories are serious, filled with accounts of sacrifice, battles, and important covenants. In this passage, Sarah is an old woman and long past childbearing age. She overhears one of Abraham's mysterious guests tell him that in a year he and Sarah will have a son. And she can't help but laugh. The idea seems impossible to her. But sure enough, she and Abraham do have a son, called Isaac, whose Hebrew name, Yishaq, means "laughed." Sarah's cynical chuckles must have turned to joyful laughter at the birth of her beloved son—one she had waited her entire life for.

Laughter is a wonderful response to the gift of life and is a natural and often spontaneous response to God's presence within us and around us. We are all tempted to laugh and question the notion that miracles can happen to us, as Sarah did. But, remember, "Is anything too wonderful for the Lord?" (Genesis 18:14). As we grow in faith and open ourselves to God's goodness, our laughter can change from skepticism to joy.

and justice; so that the Lord may bring about for Abraham what he has promised him." 20Then the Lord said, "How great is the outcry against Sodom and Gomorrah and how very grave their sin! 21I must go down and see whether they have done altogether according to the outcry that has come to me; and if not, I will know."

22 So the men turned from there, and went toward Sodom, while Abraham remained standing before the Lord.ᵃ 23Then Abraham came near and said, "Will you indeed sweep away the righteous with the wicked? 24Suppose there are fifty righteous within the city; will you then sweep away the place and not forgive it for the fifty righteous who are in it? 25Far be it from you to do such a thing, to slay the righteous with the wicked, so that the righteous fare as the wicked! Far be that from you! Shall not the Judge of all the earth do what is just?" 26And the Lord said, "If I find at Sodom fifty righteous in the city, I will forgive the whole place for their sake." 27Abraham answered, "Let me take it upon myself to speak to the Lord, I who am but dust and ashes. 28Suppose five of the fifty righteous are lacking? Will you destroy the whole city for lack of five?" And he said, "I will not destroy it if I find forty-five there." 29Again he spoke to him, "Suppose forty are found there." He answered, "For the sake of forty I will not do it." 30Then he said, "Oh do not let the Lord be angry if I speak. Suppose thirty are found there." He answered, "I will not do it, if I find thirty there." 31He said, "Let me take it upon myself to speak to the Lord. Suppose twenty

Be Honest with God
Genesis 18:22–33

Our prayers reveal what we believe about God and what we value. Abraham's bargaining for the residents of Sodom and Gomorrah shows his faith, his care for others, and his closeness to God. Although he is humble, he deals with God as a friend he is not afraid to be honest with.

We too must be honest with God in our prayers. It can be tough to trust God enough to share our doubts, anger, grief, and frustrations. But God is big enough to handle it all. Find a way to share your innermost thoughts and feelings with God. Writing or journaling helps some people get things out; others yell and shout out loud at the Lord. Remember that being willing to share your deepest feelings can open the door to experiencing God's healing. Tell God what's on your mind right now.

are found there." He answered, "For the sake of twenty I will not destroy it." 32Then he said, "Oh do not let the Lord be angry if I speak just once more. Suppose

---

ᵃ Another ancient tradition reads *while the Lord remained standing before Abraham*

ten are found there." He answered, "For the sake of ten I will not destroy it." [33]And the LORD went his way, when he had finished speaking to Abraham; and Abraham returned to his place.

The Depravity of Sodom

19 The two angels came to Sodom in the evening, and Lot was sitting in the gateway of Sodom. When Lot saw them, he rose to meet them, and bowed down with his face to the ground. [2]He said, "Please, my lords, turn aside to your servant's house and spend the night, and wash your feet; then you can rise early and go on your way." They said, "No; we will spend the night in the square." [3]But he urged them strongly; so they turned aside to him and entered his house; and he made them a feast, and baked unleavened bread, and they ate. [4]But before they lay down, the men of the city, the men of Sodom, both young and old, all the people to the last man, surrounded the house; [5]and they called to Lot, "Where are the men who came to you tonight? Bring them out to us, so that we may know them." [6]Lot went out of the door to the men, shut the door after him, [7]and said, "I beg you, my brothers, do not act so wickedly. [8]Look, I have two daughters who have not known a man; let me bring them out to you, and do to them as you please; only do nothing to these men, for they have come under the shelter of my roof." [9]But they replied, "Stand back!" And they said, "This fellow came here as an alien, and he would play the judge! Now we will deal worse with you than with them." Then they pressed hard against the man Lot, and came near the door to break it down. [10]But the men inside reached out their hands and brought Lot into the house with them, and shut the door. [11]And they struck with blindness the men who were at the door

of the house, both small and great, so that they were unable to find the door.

Sodom and Gomorrah Destroyed

12 Then the men said to Lot, "Have you anyone else here? Sons-in-law, sons, daughters, or anyone you have in the city—bring them out of the place. [13]For we are about to destroy this place, because the outcry against its people has become great before the LORD, and the LORD has sent us to destroy it." [14]So Lot went out and said to his sons-in-law, who were to marry his daughters, "Up, get out of this place; for the LORD is about to destroy the city." But he seemed to his sons-in-law to be jesting.

15 When morning dawned, the angels urged Lot, saying, "Get up, take your wife and your two daughters who are here, or else you will be consumed in the punishment of the city." [16]But he lingered; so the men seized him and his wife and his two daughters by the hand, the LORD being merciful to him, and they brought him out and left him outside the city. [17]When they had brought them outside, they[a] said, "Flee for your life; do not look back or stop anywhere in the Plain; flee to the hills, or else you will be consumed." [18]And Lot said to them, "Oh, no, my lords; [19]your servant has found favor with you, and you have shown me great kindness in saving my life; but I cannot flee to the hills, for fear the disaster will overtake me and I die. [20]Look, that city is near enough to flee to, and it is a little one. Let me escape there—is it not a little one?—and my life will be saved!" [21]He said to him, "Very well, I grant you this favor too, and will not overthrow the city of which you have spoken. [22]Hurry, escape there, for I can do nothing

Be Kind to Strangers · Genesis 19

First impressions say a lot. What if our first gestures to outsiders showed respect, kindness, and gracious hospitality? How could that change our world? The story of Sodom and Gomorrah shows us the results of disrespect, inhospitality, and the attempted sexual abuse of strangers. Like Abraham, Lot is a wonderful host. But the people of Sodom want Lot's visitors for their own sexual pleasure or to humiliate them, which in this story amounts to homosexual rape. God had already spared Sodom from destruction (Genesis 18:22-33), but this horrendous crime is the last straw that calls for the most severe punishment.

As God's children, it is our responsibility to extend kindness to strangers and friends alike. So how are visitors or new students treated in your school? How do you treat new neighbors or guests?

a Gk Syr Vg: Heb *he*

until you arrive there." Therefore the city was called Zoar.[a] 23The sun had risen on the earth when Lot came to Zoar.

24 Then the LORD rained on Sodom and Gomorrah sulfur and fire from the LORD out of heaven; 25and he overthrew those cities, and all the Plain, and all the inhabitants of the cities, and what grew on the ground. 26But Lot's wife, behind him, looked back, and she became a pillar of salt.

27 Abraham went early in the morning to the place where he had stood before the LORD; 28and he looked down toward Sodom and Gomorrah and toward all the land of the Plain and saw the smoke of the land going up like the smoke of a furnace.

29 So it was that, when God destroyed the cities of the Plain, God remembered Abraham, and sent Lot out of the midst of the overthrow, when he overthrew the cities in which Lot had settled.

The Shameful Origin of Moab and Ammon

30 Now Lot went up out of Zoar and settled in the hills with his two daughters, for he was afraid to stay in Zoar; so he lived in a cave with his two daughters. 31And the firstborn said to the younger, "Our father is old, and there is not a man on earth to come in to us after the manner of all the world. 32Come, let us make our father drink wine, and we will lie with him, so that we may preserve offspring through our father." 33So they made their father drink wine that night; and the firstborn went in, and lay with her father; he did not know when she lay down or when she rose. 34On the next day, the firstborn said to the younger, "Look, I lay last night with my father; let us make him drink wine tonight also; then you go in and lie with him, so that we may preserve offspring through our father." 35So they made their father drink wine that night also; and the younger rose, and lay with him; and he did not know when she lay down or when she rose. 36Thus both the daughters of Lot became pregnant by their father. 37The firstborn bore a son, and named him Moab; he is the ancestor of the Moabites to this day. 38The younger also bore a son and named him Ben-ammi; he is the ancestor of the Ammonites to this day.

20 Abraham and Sarah at Gerar

From there Abraham journeyed toward the region of the Negeb, and settled between Kadesh and Shur. While residing in Gerar as an alien, 2Abraham said of his wife Sarah, "She is my sister."

And King Abimelech of Gerar sent and took Sarah. 3But God came to Abimelech in a dream by night, and said to him, "You are about to die because of the woman whom you have taken; for she is a married woman." 4Now Abimelech had not approached her; so he said, "Lord, will you destroy an innocent people? 5Did he not himself say to me, 'She is my sister'? And she herself said, 'He is my brother.' I did this in the integrity of my heart and the innocence of my hands." 6Then God said to him in the dream, "Yes, I know that you did this in the integrity of your heart; furthermore it was I who kept you from sinning against me. Therefore I did not let you touch her. 7Now then, return the man's wife; for he is a prophet, and he will pray for you and you shall live. But if you do not restore her, know that you shall surely die, you and all that are yours."

8 So Abimelech rose early in the morning, and called all his servants and told them all these things; and the men were very much afraid. 9Then Abimelech called Abraham, and said to him, "What have you done to us? How have I sinned against you, that you have brought such great guilt on me and my kingdom? You have done things to me that ought not to be done." 10And Abimelech said to Abraham, "What were you thinking of, that you did this thing?" 11Abraham said, "I did it because I thought, There is no fear of God at all in this place, and they will kill me because of my wife. 12Besides, she is indeed my sister, the daughter of my father but not the daughter of my mother; and she became my wife. 13And when God caused me to wander from my father's house, I said to her, 'This is the kindness you must do me: at every place to which we come, say of me, He is my brother.' " 14Then Abimelech took sheep and oxen, and male and female slaves, and gave them to Abraham, and restored his wife Sarah to him. 15Abimelech said, "My land is before you; settle where it pleases you." 16To Sarah he said, "Look, I have given your brother a thousand pieces of silver; it is your exoneration before all who are with you; you are completely vindicated." 17Then Abraham prayed to God; and God healed Abimelech, and also healed his wife and female slaves so that they bore children. 18For the LORD had closed fast all the wombs of the house of Abimelech because of Sarah, Abraham's wife.

21 The Birth of Isaac

The LORD dealt with Sarah as he had said, and the LORD did for Sarah as he had prom-

---

a That is *Little*

ised. [2]Sarah conceived and bore Abraham a son in his old age, at the time of which God had spoken to him. [3]Abraham gave the name Isaac to his son whom Sarah bore him. [4]And Abraham circumcised his son Isaac when he was eight days old, as God had commanded him. [5]Abraham was a hundred years old when his son Isaac was born to him. [6]Now Sarah said, "God has brought laughter for me; everyone who hears will laugh with me." [7]And she said, "Who would ever have said to Abraham that Sarah would nurse children? Yet I have borne him a son in his old age."

Hagar and Ishmael Sent Away

8 The child grew, and was weaned; and Abraham made a great feast on the day that Isaac was weaned. [9]But Sarah saw the son of Hagar the Egyptian, whom she had borne to Abraham, playing with her son Isaac.[a] [10]So she said to Abraham, "Cast out this slave woman with her son; for the son of this slave woman shall not inherit along with my son Isaac." [11]The matter was very distressing to Abraham on account of his son. [12]But God said to Abraham, "Do not be distressed because of the boy and because of your slave woman; whatever Sarah says to you, do as she tells you, for it is through Isaac that offspring shall be named for you. [13]As for the son of the slave woman, I will make a nation of him also, because he is your offspring." [14]So Abraham rose early in the morning, and took bread and a skin of water, and gave it to Hagar, putting it on her shoulder, along with the child, and sent her away. And she departed, and wandered about in the wilderness of Beer-sheba.

15 When the water in the skin was gone, she cast the child under one of the bushes. [16]Then she went and sat down opposite him a good way off, about the distance of a bowshot; for she said, "Do not let me look on the death of the child." And as she sat opposite him, she lifted up her voice and wept. [17]And God heard the voice of the boy; and the angel of God called to Hagar from heaven, and said to her, "What troubles you, Hagar? Do not be afraid; for God has heard the voice of the boy where he is. [18]Come, lift up the boy and hold him fast with your hand, for I will make a great nation of him." [19]Then God opened her eyes and she saw a well of water. She went, and filled the skin with water, and gave the boy a drink.

20 God was with the boy, and he grew up; he lived in the wilderness, and became an expert with the bow. [21]He lived in the wilderness of Paran; and his mother got a wife for him from the land of Egypt.

Abraham and Abimelech Make a Covenant

22 At that time Abimelech, with Phicol the commander of his army, said to Abraham, "God is with you in all that you do; [23]now therefore swear to me here by God that you will not deal falsely with me or with my offspring or with my posterity, but as I have dealt loyally with you, you will deal with me and with the land where you have resided as an alien." [24]And Abraham said, "I swear it."

25 When Abraham complained to Abimelech about a well of water that Abimelech's servants had seized, [26]Abimelech said, "I do not know who has done this; you did not tell me, and I have not heard

PRAY IT!

Hagar's Rescue · Genesis 21:8–21

This section of **Genesis 21** is part two of the Hagar and Ishmael story begun in **Genesis 16:1–16**. Once again, Hagar is the victim of Sarah's jealousy. But this time God does not send her back. Facing banishment and certain death, Hagar receives from God the ability to see the opportunity for life in front of her. This time the writer of Genesis makes the point that God rescues the abused and abandoned. Hagar and Ishmael survive, and a great people emerges from their descendants.

Hagar's story reminds us that God wants to rescue us from oppression, injustice, and abuse. Often we want to ask God to magically take these things away. But because God has given human beings free will, we can't always be spared from the mistreatment and injustice of others. If you are in an unjust or abusive situation, pray for God to rescue you. You can also ask God to give you the vision and ability to make healthy choices to improve your situation. Do that right now and take heart from Hagar's story. God can provide a way out.

a Gk Vg: Heb lacks *with her son Isaac*

of it until today." ²⁷So Abraham took sheep and oxen and gave them to Abimelech, and the two men made a covenant. ²⁸Abraham set apart seven ewe lambs of the flock. ²⁹And Abimelech said to Abraham, "What is the meaning of these seven ewe lambs that you have set apart?" ³⁰He said, "These seven ewe lambs you shall accept from my hand, in order that you may be a witness for me that I dug this well." ³¹Therefore that place was called Beer-sheba;ᵃ because there both of them swore an oath. ³²When they had made a covenant at Beer-sheba, Abimelech, with Phicol the commander of his army, left and returned to the land of the Philistines. ³³Abrahamᵇ planted a tamarisk tree in Beer-sheba, and called there on the name of the LORD, the Everlasting God.ᶜ ³⁴And Abraham resided as an alien many days in the land of the Philistines.

The Command to Sacrifice Isaac

22 After these things God tested Abraham. He said to him, "Abraham!" And he said, "Here I am." ²He said, "Take your son, your only son Isaac, whom you love, and go to the land of Moriah, and offer him there as a burnt offering on one of the mountains that I shall show you." ³So Abraham rose early in the morning, saddled his donkey, and took two of his young men with him, and his son Isaac; he cut the wood for the burnt offering, and set out and went to the place in the distance that God had shown him. ⁴On the third day Abraham looked up and saw the place far away. ⁵Then Abraham said to his young men, "Stay here with the donkey; the boy and I will go over there; we will worship, and then we will come back to you." ⁶Abraham took the wood of the burnt offering and laid it on his son Isaac, and he himself carried the fire and the knife. So the two of them walked on together. ⁷Isaac said to his father Abraham, "Father!" And he said, "Here I am, my son." He said, "The fire and the wood are here, but where is the lamb for a burnt offering?" ⁸Abraham said, "God himself will provide the lamb for a burnt offering, my son." So the two of them walked on together.

9 When they came to the place that God had shown him, Abraham built an altar there and laid the wood in order. He bound his son Isaac, and laid him on the altar, on top of the wood. ¹⁰Then Abraham reached out his hand and took the knife to killᵈ his son. ¹¹But the angel of the LORD called to him from heaven, and said, "Abraham, Abraham!" And he said, "Here I am." ¹²He said, "Do not lay your hand on the boy or do anything to him; for now I know that you fear God, since you have not withheld your son, your only son, from me." ¹³And Abraham looked up and saw a ram, caught in a thicket by its horns. Abraham went and took the ram and offered it up as a burnt offering instead of his son. ¹⁴So Abraham called that place "The LORD will provide";ᵉ as it is said to this day, "On the mount of the LORD it shall be provided."ᶠ

15 The angel of the LORD called to Abraham a

You Want Me to Sacrifice What?! · Genesis 22:1–19

It seems inconceivable to us that God would ask Abraham to sacrifice his son Isaac. But this story is meant to be a sign of Abraham's complete trust in God. Ultimately, God prevented the sacrifice, because God wanted not Isaac's death, but Abraham's faith. Because of his willingness to obey God's command, Abraham is recognized as the father of our faith. Our trust in God should be as total as Abraham's trust was.

We probably won't ever be faced with a test like Abraham's, but we might be faced with different, equally difficult tests of our own. The story of Abraham shows us the power of faith. Because of Abraham's trust in God's promise, Isaac lived and became the father of Jacob, whose twelve sons' descendants became the twelve tribes of Israel. During your prayer time, reflect or journal on the following questions:

- Have you ever had to give up someone or something that was precious to you because of your beliefs?
- How has your life been enriched as a result of trusting God in a difficult situation?
- Is there anything you sense God is asking you to give up?

ᵃ That is *Well of seven* or *Well of the oath*   ᵇ Heb *He*   ᶜ Or *the LORD, El Olam*   ᵈ Or *to slaughter*   ᵉ Or *will see;* Heb traditionally transliterated *Jehovah Jireh*   ᶠ Or *he shall be seen*

second time from heaven, [16]and said, "By myself I have sworn, says the LORD: Because you have done this, and have not withheld your son, your only son, [17]I will indeed bless you, and I will make your offspring as numerous as the stars of heaven and as the sand that is on the seashore. And your offspring shall possess the gate of their enemies, [18]and by your offspring shall all the nations of the earth gain blessing for themselves, because you have obeyed my voice." [19]So Abraham returned to his young men, and they arose and went together to Beer-sheba; and Abraham lived at Beer-sheba.

The Children of Nahor

20 Now after these things it was told Abraham, "Milcah also has borne children, to your brother Nahor: [21]Uz the firstborn, Buz his brother, Kemuel the father of Aram, [22]Chesed, Hazo, Pildash, Jidlaph, and Bethuel." [23]Bethuel became the father of Rebekah. These eight Milcah bore to Nahor, Abraham's brother. [24]Moreover, his concubine, whose name was Reumah, bore Tebah, Gaham, Tahash, and Maacah.

Sarah's Death and Burial

23 Sarah lived one hundred twenty-seven years; this was the length of Sarah's life. [2]And Sarah died at Kiriath-arba (that is, Hebron) in the land of Canaan; and Abraham went in to mourn for Sarah and to weep for her. [3]Abraham rose up from beside his dead, and said to the Hittites, [4]"I am a stranger and an alien residing among you; give me property among you for a burying place, so that I may bury my dead out of my sight." [5]The Hittites answered Abraham, [6]"Hear us, my lord; you are a mighty prince among us. Bury your dead in the choicest of our burial places; none of us will withhold from you any burial ground for burying your dead." [7]Abraham rose and bowed to the Hittites, the people of the land. [8]He said to them, "If you are willing that I should bury my dead out of my sight, hear me, and entreat for me Ephron son of Zohar, [9]so that he may give me the cave of Machpelah, which he owns; it is at the end of his field. For the full price let him give it to me in your presence as a possession for a burying place." [10]Now Ephron was sitting among the Hittites; and Ephron the Hittite answered Abraham in the hearing of the Hittites, of all who went in at the gate of his city, [11]"No, my lord, hear me; I give you the field, and I give you the cave that is in it; in the presence of my people I give it to you; bury your dead." [12]Then

Abraham bowed down before the people of the land. [13]He said to Ephron in the hearing of the people of the land, "If you only will listen to me! I will give the price of the field; accept it from me, so that I may bury my dead there." [14]Ephron answered Abraham, [15]"My lord, listen to me; a piece of land worth four hundred shekels of silver—what is that between you and me? Bury your dead." [16]Abraham agreed with Ephron; and Abraham weighed out for Ephron the silver that he had named in the hearing of the Hittites, four hundred shekels of silver, according to the weights current among the merchants.

17 So the field of Ephron in Machpelah, which was to the east of Mamre, the field with the cave that was in it and all the trees that were in the field, throughout its whole area, passed [18]to Abraham as a possession in the presence of the Hittites, in the presence of all who went in at the gate of his city. [19]After this, Abraham buried Sarah his wife in the cave of the field of Machpelah facing Mamre (that is, Hebron) in the land of Canaan. [20]The field and the cave that is in it passed from the Hittites into Abraham's possession as a burying place.

The Marriage of Isaac and Rebekah

24 Now Abraham was old, well advanced in years; and the LORD had blessed Abraham in all things. [2]Abraham said to his servant, the oldest of his house, who had charge of all that he had, "Put your hand under my thigh [3]and I will make you swear by the LORD, the God of heaven and earth, that you will not get a wife for my son from the daughters of the Canaanites, among whom I live, [4]but will go to my country and to my kindred and get a wife for my son Isaac." [5]The servant said to him, "Perhaps the woman may not be willing to follow me to this land; must I then take your son back to the land from which you came?" [6]Abraham said to him, "See to it that you do not take my son back there. [7]The LORD, the God of heaven, who took me from my father's house and from the land of my birth, and who spoke to me and swore to me, 'To your offspring I will give this land,' he will send his angel before you, and you shall take a wife for my son from there. [8]But if the woman is not willing to follow you, then you will be free from this oath of mine; only you must not take my son back there." [9]So the servant put his hand under the thigh of Abraham his master and swore to him concerning this matter.

10 Then the servant took ten of his master's cam-

els and departed, taking all kinds of choice gifts from his master; and he set out and went to Aram-naharaim, to the city of Nahor. ¹¹He made the camels kneel down outside the city by the well of water; it was toward evening, the time when women go out to draw water. ¹²And he said, "O LORD, God of my master Abraham, please grant me success today and show steadfast love to my master Abraham. ¹³I am standing here by the spring of water, and the daughters of the townspeople are coming out to draw water. ¹⁴Let the girl to whom I shall say, 'Please offer your jar that I may drink,' and who shall say, 'Drink, and I will water your camels'—let her be the one whom you have appointed for your servant Isaac. By this I shall know that you have shown steadfast love to my master."

15 Before he had finished speaking, there was Rebekah, who was born to Bethuel son of Milcah, the wife of Nahor, Abraham's brother, coming out with her water jar on her shoulder. ¹⁶The girl was very fair to look upon, a virgin, whom no man had known. She went down to the spring, filled her jar, and came up. ¹⁷Then the servant ran to meet her and said, "Please let me sip a little water from your jar." ¹⁸"Drink, my lord," she said, and quickly lowered her jar upon her hand and gave him a drink. ¹⁹When she had finished giving him a drink, she said, "I will draw for your camels also, until they have finished drinking." ²⁰So she quickly emptied her jar into the trough and ran again to the well to draw, and she drew for all his camels. ²¹The man gazed at her in silence to learn whether or not the LORD had made his journey successful.

22 When the camels had finished drinking, the man took a gold nose-ring weighing a half shekel, and two bracelets for her arms weighing ten gold shekels, ²³and said, "Tell me whose daughter you are. Is there room in your father's house for us to spend the night?" ²⁴She said to him, "I am the daughter of Bethuel son of Milcah, whom she bore to Nahor." ²⁵She added, "We have plenty of straw and fodder and a place to spend the night." ²⁶The man bowed his head and worshiped the LORD ²⁷and said, "Blessed be the LORD, the God of my master Abraham, who has not forsaken his steadfast love and his faithfulness toward my master. As for me, the LORD has led me on the way to the house of my master's kin."

28 Then the girl ran and told her mother's household about these things. ²⁹Rebekah had a brother whose name was Laban; and Laban ran out to the man, to the spring. ³⁰As soon as he had seen the nose-ring, and the bracelets on his sister's arms, and when he heard the words of his sister Rebekah, "Thus the man spoke to me," he went to the man; and there he was, standing by the camels at the spring. ³¹He said, "Come in, O blessed of the LORD. Why do you stand outside when I have prepared the house and a place for the camels?" ³²So the man came into the house; and Laban unloaded the camels, and gave him straw and fodder for the camels, and water to wash his feet and the feet of the men who were with him. ³³Then food was set before him to eat; but he said, "I will not eat until I have told my errand." He said, "Speak on."

34 So he said, "I am Abraham's servant. ³⁵The LORD has greatly blessed my master, and he has become wealthy; he has given him flocks and herds, silver and gold, male and female slaves, camels and donkeys. ³⁶And Sarah my master's wife bore a son to my master when she was old; and he has given him all that he has. ³⁷My master made me swear, saying, 'You shall not take a wife for my son from the daughters of the Canaanites, in whose land I live; ³⁸but you shall go to my father's house, to my kindred, and get a wife for my son.' ³⁹I said to my master, 'Perhaps the woman will not follow me.' ⁴⁰But he said to me, 'The LORD, before whom I walk, will send his angel with you and make your way successful. You shall get a wife for my son from my kindred, from my father's house. ⁴¹Then you will be free from my oath, when you come to my kindred; even if they will not give her to you, you will be free from my oath.'

42 "I came today to the spring, and said, 'O LORD, the God of my master Abraham, if now you will only make successful the way I am going! ⁴³I am standing here by the spring of water; let the young woman who comes out to draw, to whom I shall say, "Please

give me a little water from your jar to drink," [44]and who will say to me, "Drink, and I will draw for your camels also"—let her be the woman whom the LORD has appointed for my master's son.'

45 "Before I had finished speaking in my heart, there was Rebekah coming out with her water jar on her shoulder; and she went down to the spring, and drew. I said to her, 'Please let me drink.' [46]She quickly let down her jar from her shoulder, and said, 'Drink, and I will also water your camels.' So I drank, and she also watered the camels. [47]Then I asked her, 'Whose daughter are you?' She said, 'The daughter of Bethuel, Nahor's son, whom Milcah bore to him.' So I put the ring on her nose, and the bracelets on her arms. [48]Then I bowed my head and worshiped the LORD, and blessed the LORD, the God of my master Abraham, who had led me by the right way to obtain the daughter of my master's kinsman for his son. [49]Now then, if you will deal loyally and truly with my master, tell me; and if not, tell me, so that I may turn either to the right hand or to the left."

50 Then Laban and Bethuel answered, "The thing comes from the LORD; we cannot speak to you anything bad or good. [51]Look, Rebekah is before you, take her and go, and let her be the wife of your master's son, as the LORD has spoken."

52 When Abraham's servant heard their words, he bowed himself to the ground before the LORD. [53]And the servant brought out jewelry of silver and of gold, and garments, and gave them to Rebekah; he also gave to her brother and to her mother costly ornaments. [54]Then he and the men who were with him ate and drank, and they spent the night there. When they rose in the morning, he said, "Send me back to my master." [55]Her brother and her mother said, "Let the girl remain with us a while, at least ten days; after that she may go." [56]But he said to them, "Do not delay me, since the LORD has made my journey successful; let me go that I may go to my master." [57]They said, "We will call the girl, and ask her." [58]And they called Rebekah, and said to her, "Will you go with this man?" She said, "I will." [59]So they sent away their sister Rebekah and her nurse along with Abraham's servant and his men. [60]And they blessed Rebekah and said to her,

"May you, our sister, become
    thousands of myriads;
may your offspring gain possession
    of the gates of their foes."

[61]Then Rebekah and her maids rose up, mounted the camels, and followed the man; thus the servant took Rebekah, and went his way.

62 Now Isaac had come from[a] Beer-lahai-roi, and was settled in the Negeb. [63]Isaac went out in the evening to walk[b] in the field; and looking up, he saw camels coming. [64]And Rebekah looked up, and when she saw Isaac, she slipped quickly from the camel, [65]and said to the servant, "Who is the man over there, walking in the field to meet us?" The servant said, "It is my master." So she took her veil and covered herself. [66]And the servant told Isaac all the things that he had done. [67]Then Isaac brought her into his mother Sarah's tent. He took Rebekah, and she became his wife; and he loved her. So Isaac was comforted after his mother's death.

Abraham Marries Keturah

25 Abraham took another wife, whose name was Keturah. [2]She bore him Zimran, Jokshan, Medan, Midian, Ishbak, and Shuah. [3]Jokshan was the father of Sheba and Dedan. The sons of Dedan were Asshurim, Letushim, and Leummim. [4]The sons of Midian were Ephah, Epher, Hanoch, Abida, and Eldaah. All these were the children of Keturah. [5]Abraham gave all he had to Isaac. [6]But to the sons of his concubines Abraham gave gifts, while he was still living, and he sent them away from his son Isaac, eastward to the east country.

The Death of Abraham

7 This is the length of Abraham's life, one hundred seventy-five years. [8]Abraham breathed his last and died in a good old age, an old man and full of years, and was gathered to his people. [9]His sons Isaac and Ishmael buried him in the cave of Machpelah, in the field of Ephron son of Zohar the Hittite, east of Mamre, [10]the field that Abraham purchased from the Hittites. There Abraham was buried, with his wife Sarah. [11]After the death of Abraham God blessed his son Isaac. And Isaac settled at Beer-lahai-roi.

Ishmael's Descendants

12 These are the descendants of Ishmael, Abraham's son, whom Hagar the Egyptian, Sarah's slave-girl, bore to Abraham. [13]These are the names of the sons of Ishmael, named in the order of their birth: Nebaioth, the firstborn of Ishmael; and Kedar, Adbeel, Mibsam, [14]Mishma, Dumah, Massa, [15]Hadad, Tema, Jetur, Naphish, and Kedemah. [16]These are the sons of Ishmael and these are their names, by

---

a Syr Tg: Heb *from coming to*   b Meaning of Heb word is uncertain

STUDY IT!

Abraham's Towering Family Tree · Genesis 25:12–18

God promised Hagar that her son, Ishmael, would be made "a great nation" (Genesis 21:18). The Old Testament lists twelve princely tribes that descended from Abraham's older son, Ishmael (Genesis 25:13-16), tribes traditionally associated with the people of ancient Edom. A much later Islamic tradition identifies Muhammad and his descendants—the Muslims—as "children of Ishmael."

Abraham's younger son, Isaac, was the father of Jacob. The Jewish people trace their lineage to Jacob and his twelve sons. Because Jesus was a Jew, Christians ultimately trace their ancestry through Jacob to Abraham as well.

Thus, three major world religions—Judaism, Christianity, and Islam—all see Abraham as their father in faith.

their villages and by their encampments, twelve princes according to their tribes. ¹⁷(This is the length of the life of Ishmael, one hundred thirty-seven years; he breathed his last and died, and was gathered to his people.) ¹⁸They settled from Havilah to Shur, which is opposite Egypt in the direction of Assyria; he settled down*ᵃ* alongside of*ᵇ* all his people.

The Birth and Youth of Esau and Jacob

19 These are the descendants of Isaac, Abraham's son: Abraham was the father of Isaac, ²⁰and Isaac was forty years old when he married Rebekah, daughter of Bethuel the Aramean of Paddan-aram, sister of Laban the Aramean. ²¹Isaac prayed to the Lᴏʀᴅ for his wife, because she was barren; and the Lᴏʀᴅ granted his prayer, and his wife Rebekah conceived. ²²The children struggled together within her; and she said, "If it is to be this way, why do I live?"*ᶜ* So she went to inquire of the Lᴏʀᴅ. ²³And the Lᴏʀᴅ said to her,

"Two nations are in your womb,
　　and two peoples born of you shall be
　　　　divided;
the one shall be stronger than the other,
　　the elder shall serve the younger."
²⁴When her time to give birth was at hand, there were twins in her womb. ²⁵The first came out red, all his body like a hairy mantle; so they named him Esau. ²⁶Afterward his brother came out, with his hand gripping Esau's heel; so he was named Jacob.*ᵈ* Isaac was sixty years old when she bore them.

27 When the boys grew up, Esau was a skillful hunter, a man of the field, while Jacob was a quiet

STUDY IT!

Introducing . . . Jacob
Genesis 25:19–50:14

Abraham was the father of Isaac, and Isaac was the father of Jacob, and Jacob was the father of twelve sons who became the leaders of the twelve tribes of Israel. Jacob, like his ancestors, participated in the covenant with God that promised a great land and many descendants. He is portrayed as a very human character with a wide range of emotions and actions, both good and bad. Read **Genesis 25:29–34; 27:1–29.** Jacob is a repentant brother, a kind father, and a successful herder, but he is also a trickster who steals his brother Esau's birthright and his father's blessing. It's no wonder that Jacob's name in Hebrew means "supplanter" or "heel grabber."

God renews the covenant promises to Jacob in a dream (Genesis 28:10-17), and God changes Jacob's name to Israel (Genesis 32:22-32; 35:9-15). Jacob's descendants become known as the Israelites. His story reveals that God's blessing continues to work even through flawed human beings.

---

a Heb *he fell*　**b** Or *down in opposition to*　**c** Syr: Meaning of Heb uncertain　**d** That is *He takes by the heel* or *He supplants*

man, living in tents. [28]Isaac loved Esau, because he was fond of game; but Rebekah loved Jacob.

Esau Sells His Birthright

29 Once when Jacob was cooking a stew, Esau came in from the field, and he was famished. [30]Esau said to Jacob, "Let me eat some of that red stuff, for I am famished!" (Therefore he was called Edom.[a]) [31]Jacob said, "First sell me your birthright." [32]Esau said, "I am about to die; of what use is a birthright to me?" [33]Jacob said, "Swear to me first."[b] So he swore to him, and sold his birthright to Jacob. [34]Then Jacob gave Esau bread and lentil stew, and he ate and drank, and rose and went his way. Thus Esau despised his birthright.

Isaac and Abimelech

26 Now there was a famine in the land, besides the former famine that had occurred in the days of Abraham. And Isaac went to Gerar, to King Abimelech of the Philistines. [2]The LORD appeared to Isaac[c] and said, "Do not go down to Egypt; settle in the land that I shall show you. [3]Reside in this land as an alien, and I will be with you, and will bless you; for to you and to your descendants I will give all these lands, and I will fulfill the oath that I swore to your father Abraham. [4]I will make your offspring as numerous as the stars of heaven, and will give to your offspring all these lands; and all the nations of the earth shall gain blessing for themselves through your offspring, [5]because Abraham obeyed my voice and kept my charge, my commandments, my statutes, and my laws."

6 So Isaac settled in Gerar. [7]When the men of the place asked him about his wife, he said, "She is my sister"; for he was afraid to say, "My wife," thinking, "or else the men of the place might kill me for the sake of Rebekah, because she is attractive in appearance." [8]When Isaac had been there a long time, King Abimelech of the Philistines looked out of a window and saw him fondling his wife Rebekah. [9]So Abimelech called for Isaac, and said, "So she is your wife! Why then did you say, 'She is my sister'?" Isaac said to him, "Because I thought I might die because of her." [10]Abimelech said, "What is this you have done to us? One of the people might easily have lain with your wife, and you would have brought guilt upon us." [11]So Abimelech warned all the people, saying, "Whoever touches this man or his wife shall be put to death."

12 Isaac sowed seed in that land, and in the same year reaped a hundredfold. The LORD blessed him, [13]and the man became rich; he prospered more and more until he became very wealthy. [14]He had possessions of flocks and herds, and a great household, so that the Philistines envied him. [15](Now the Philistines had stopped up and filled with earth all the wells that his father's servants had dug in the days of his father Abraham.) [16]And Abimelech said to Isaac, "Go away from us; you have become too powerful for us."

17 So Isaac departed from there and camped in the valley of Gerar and settled there. [18]Isaac dug again the wells of water that had been dug in the days of his father Abraham; for the Philistines had stopped them up after the death of Abraham; and he gave them the names that his father had given them. [19]But when

PRAY IT!

Sibling Rivalry · Genesis 25:19–34

It's common for siblings to have conflict, but Jacob and Esau's rivalry gets extreme. Follow their story in **Genesis 27–28; 33.**

For another story of extreme sibling rivalry, see **Genesis 37:12–36.** Joseph's brothers (all sons of Jacob) are so jealous of him that they plot to kill him. Instead, they sell Joseph as a slave. (Of course, that backfires on the brothers, when it turns into a great career move for Joseph.)

Jesus gives us yet another example of sibling rivalry in the story of the prodigal son (Luke 15:11-32).

- Do you have any brothers or sisters? If so, how do you treat them? Do you ever pray for them? Do you ever tell them you care about them—even if they drive you crazy at times?
- If you don't have any brothers or sisters, how about cousins, neighbors, or friends? Who comes to mind? Pray for them today.

a That is *Red*   b Heb *today*   c Heb *him*

Isaac's servants dug in the valley and found there a well of spring water, [20]the herders of Gerar quarreled with Isaac's herders, saying, "The water is ours." So he called the well Esek,[a] because they contended with him. [21]Then they dug another well, and they quarreled over that one also; so he called it Sitnah.[b] [22]He moved from there and dug another well, and they did not quarrel over it; so he called it Rehoboth,[c] saying, "Now the LORD has made room for us, and we shall be fruitful in the land."

23 From there he went up to Beer-sheba. [24]And that very night the LORD appeared to him and said, "I am the God of your father Abraham; do not be afraid, for I am with you and will bless you and make your offspring numerous for my servant Abraham's sake." [25]So he built an altar there, called on the name of the LORD, and pitched his tent there. And there Isaac's servants dug a well.

26 Then Abimelech went to him from Gerar, with Ahuzzath his adviser and Phicol the commander of his army. [27]Isaac said to them, "Why have you come to me, seeing that you hate me and have sent me away from you?" [28]They said, "We see plainly that the LORD has been with you; so we say, let there be an oath between you and us, and let us make a covenant with you [29]so that you will do us no harm, just as we have not touched you and have done to you nothing but good and have sent you away in peace. You are now the blessed of the LORD." [30]So he made them a feast, and they ate and drank. [31]In the morning they rose early and exchanged oaths; and Isaac set them on their way, and they departed from him in peace. [32]That same day Isaac's servants came and told him about the well that they had dug, and said to him, "We have found water!" [33]He called it Shibah;[d] therefore the name of the city is Beer-sheba[e] to this day.

Esau's Hittite Wives

34 When Esau was forty years old, he married Judith daughter of Beeri the Hittite, and Basemath daughter of Elon the Hittite; [35]and they made life bitter for Isaac and Rebekah.

27 Isaac Blesses Jacob

When Isaac was old and his eyes were dim so that he could not see, he called his elder son Esau and said to him, "My son"; and he answered, "Here I am." [2]He said, "See, I am old; I do not know the day of my death. [3]Now then, take your weapons, your quiver and your bow, and go out to the field, and hunt game for me. [4]Then prepare for me savory food, such as I like, and bring it to me to eat, so that I may bless you before I die."

5 Now Rebekah was listening when Isaac spoke to his son Esau. So when Esau went to the field to hunt for game and bring it, [6]Rebekah said to her son Jacob, "I heard your father say to your brother Esau, [7]'Bring me game, and prepare for me savory food to eat, that I may bless you before the LORD before I die.' [8]Now therefore, my son, obey my word as I command you. [9]Go to the flock, and get me two choice kids, so that I may prepare from them savory food for your father, such as he likes; [10]and you shall take it to your father to eat, so that he may bless you before he dies." [11]But Jacob said to his mother Rebekah, "Look, my brother Esau is a hairy man, and I am a man of smooth skin. [12]Perhaps my father will feel me, and I shall seem to be mocking him, and bring a curse on myself and not a blessing." [13]His mother said to him, "Let your curse be on me, my son; only obey my word, and go, get them for me." [14]So he went and got them and brought them to his mother; and his mother prepared savory food, such as his father loved. [15]Then Rebekah took the best garments of her elder son Esau, which were with her in the house, and put them on her younger son Jacob; [16]and she put the skins of the kids on his hands and on the smooth part of his neck. [17]Then she handed the savory food, and the bread that she had prepared, to her son Jacob.

18 So he went in to his father, and said, "My father"; and he said, "Here I am; who are you, my son?" [19]Jacob said to his father, "I am Esau your firstborn. I have done as you told me; now sit up and eat of my game, so that you may bless me." [20]But Isaac said to his son, "How is it that you have found it so quickly, my son?" He answered, "Because the LORD your God granted me success." [21]Then Isaac said to Jacob, "Come near, that I may feel you, my son, to know whether you are really my son Esau or not." [22]So Jacob went up to his father Isaac, who felt him and said, "The voice is Jacob's voice, but the hands are the hands of Esau." [23]He did not recognize him, because his hands were hairy like his brother Esau's hands; so he blessed him. [24]He said, "Are you really my son Esau?" He answered, "I am." [25]Then he said, "Bring it to me, that I may eat of my son's game and bless you." So he brought it to him, and he ate; and he brought him wine, and he drank. [26]Then his father Isaac said to him, "Come near and kiss me, my son."

---

a That is *Contention* b That is *Enmity* c That is *Broad places* or *Room* d A word resembling the word for *oath* e That is *Well of the oath* or *Well of seven*

STUDY IT!

God's Surprising Choice · Genesis 27:1–40

In most ancient cultures, including Israel's, the oldest son of the family was expected to inherit his father's property (the birthright) and authority (the blessing). In the story of Esau and Jacob, Jacob tricks the older Esau out of his birthright (Genesis 25:29-34) and deceives his blind father into giving him the blessing (Genesis 27:1-29).

It's surprising that Genesis makes no comment on Jacob's actions. Ultimately, the story is about God's justice, not a commentary on Jacob's morality. God is not bound by cultural expectations. Again and again in the Old Testament, God defies human norms by choosing the "little ones" for big responsibilities: Jacob, Joseph, Ruth, David, and Esther, for example. Even the Israelites themselves were an unlikely choice on God's part. Why didn't God choose a nation of great wealth and power instead of a group that was enslaved?

The story of Jacob and Esau reminds us that God does not bow to human expectations or plans. God's ways are often surprising!

²⁷So he came near and kissed him; and he smelled the smell of his garments, and blessed him, and said,
"Ah, the smell of my son
  is like the smell of a field that the Lord has
   blessed.
²⁸ May God give you of the dew of heaven,
  and of the fatness of the earth,
  and plenty of grain and wine.
²⁹ Let peoples serve you,
  and nations bow down to you.
Be lord over your brothers,
  and may your mother's sons bow down
   to you.
Cursed be everyone who curses you,
  and blessed be everyone who blesses you!"

Esau's Lost Blessing

30 As soon as Isaac had finished blessing Jacob, when Jacob had scarcely gone out from the presence of his father Isaac, his brother Esau came in from his hunting. ³¹He also prepared savory food, and brought it to his father. And he said to his father, "Let my father sit up and eat of his son's game, so that you may bless me." ³²His father Isaac said to him, "Who are you?" He answered, "I am your firstborn son, Esau." ³³Then Isaac trembled violently, and said, "Who was it then that hunted game and brought it to me, and I ate it all[a] before you came, and I have blessed him?—yes, and blessed he shall be!" ³⁴When Esau heard his father's words, he cried out with an exceedingly great and bitter cry, and said to his father, "Bless me, me also, father!" ³⁵But he said, "Your brother came deceitfully, and he has taken away your blessing." ³⁶Esau said, "Is he not rightly named Jacob?[b] For he has supplanted me these two times. He took away my birthright; and look, now he has taken away my blessing." Then he said, "Have you not reserved a blessing for me?" ³⁷Isaac answered Esau, "I have already made him your lord, and I have given him all his brothers as servants, and with grain and wine I have sustained him. What then can I do for you, my son?" ³⁸Esau said to his father, "Have you only one blessing, father? Bless me, me also, father!" And Esau lifted up his voice and wept.
 39 Then his father Isaac answered him:
"See, away from[c] the fatness of the earth shall
  your home be,
  and away from[d] the dew of heaven on high.
40 By your sword you shall live,
  and you shall serve your brother;
but when you break loose,[e]
  you shall break his yoke from your neck."

Jacob Escapes Esau's Fury

41 Now Esau hated Jacob because of the blessing with which his father had blessed him, and Esau said to himself, "The days of mourning for my father are approaching; then I will kill my brother Jacob." ⁴²But the words of her elder son Esau were told to Rebekah; so she sent and called her younger son Jacob and said to him, "Your brother Esau is consoling himself by planning to kill you. ⁴³Now therefore, my son, obey my voice; flee at once to my brother Laban in Haran,

a Cn: Heb *of all* b That is *He supplants* or *He takes by the heel* c Or *See, of* d Or *and of* e Meaning of Heb uncertain

44 and stay with him a while, until your brother's fury turns away— 45 until your brother's anger against you turns away, and he forgets what you have done to him; then I will send, and bring you back from there. Why should I lose both of you in one day?"

46 Then Rebekah said to Isaac, "I am weary of my life because of the Hittite women. If Jacob marries one of the Hittite women such as these, one of the women of the land, what good will my life be to me?"

28 Then Isaac called Jacob and blessed him, and charged him, "You shall not marry one of the Canaanite women. 2 Go at once to Paddan-aram to the house of Bethuel, your mother's father; and take as wife from there one of the daughters of Laban, your mother's brother. 3 May God Almighty[a] bless you and make you fruitful and numerous, that you may become a company of peoples. 4 May he give to you the blessing of Abraham, to you and to your offspring with you, so that you may take possession of the land where you now live as an alien—land that God gave to Abraham." 5 Thus Isaac sent Jacob away; and he went to Paddan-aram, to Laban son of Bethuel the Aramean, the brother of Rebekah, Jacob's and Esau's mother.

Esau Marries Ishmael's Daughter

6 Now Esau saw that Isaac had blessed Jacob and sent him away to Paddan-aram to take a wife from there, and that as he blessed him he charged him, "You shall not marry one of the Canaanite women," 7 and that Jacob had obeyed his father and his mother and gone to Paddan-aram. 8 So when Esau saw that the Canaanite women did not please his father Isaac, 9 Esau went to Ishmael and took Mahalath daughter of Abraham's son Ishmael, and sister of Nebaioth, to be his wife in addition to the wives he had.

Jacob's Dream at Bethel

10 Jacob left Beer-sheba and went toward Haran. 11 He came to a certain place and stayed there for the night, because the sun had set. Taking one of the stones of the place, he put it under his head and lay down in that place. 12 And he dreamed that there was a ladder[b] set up on the earth, the top of it reaching to heaven; and the angels of God were ascending and descending on it. 13 And the LORD stood beside him[c]

PRAY IT!

Friends with God
Genesis 28:10–22

Just as Jacob is leaving his home and everything he knows, God establishes a personal relationship with him in a dream. In **Genesis 28:15,** God tells Jacob, "Know that I am with you and will keep you wherever you go." This reminder of God's presence will sustain Jacob through the tough times ahead. See **Genesis 32:22–32** for further developments in Jacob's relationship with God.

God, I want to know your presence. Use my dreams and my thoughts; use my family, friends, and neighbors; use your Word. Use them all to reach and guide me. And please let your presence sustain and help me with my biggest problems, just as you did for Jacob. Amen.

and said, "I am the LORD, the God of Abraham your father and the God of Isaac; the land on which you lie I will give to you and to your offspring; 14 and your offspring shall be like the dust of the earth, and you shall spread abroad to the west and to the east and to the north and to the south; and all the families of the earth shall be blessed[d] in you and in your offspring. 15 Know that I am with you and will keep you wherever you go, and will bring you back to this land; for I will not leave you until I have done what I have promised you." 16 Then Jacob woke from his sleep and said, "Surely the LORD is in this place—and I did not know it!" 17 And he was afraid, and said, "How awesome is this place! This is none other than the house of God, and this is the gate of heaven." 18 So Jacob rose early in the morning, and he took the stone that he had put under his head and set it up for a pillar and poured oil on the top of it. 19 He called that place Bethel;[e] but the name of the city was Luz at the first. 20 Then Jacob made a vow, saying, "If God

> "Know that I am with you and will keep you wherever you go."
> —Genesis 28:15

a Traditional rendering of Heb *El Shaddai*   b Or *stairway* or *ramp*   c Or *stood above it*   d Or *shall bless themselves*   e That is *House of God*

will be with me, and will keep me in this way that I go, and will give me bread to eat and clothing to wear, [21]so that I come again to my father's house in peace, then the LORD shall be my God, [22]and this stone, which I have set up for a pillar, shall be God's house; and of all that you give me I will surely give one-tenth to you."

Jacob Meets Rachel

29 Then Jacob went on his journey, and came to the land of the people of the east. [2]As he looked, he saw a well in the field and three flocks of sheep lying there beside it; for out of that well the flocks were watered. The stone on the well's mouth was large, [3]and when all the flocks were gathered there, the shepherds would roll the stone from the mouth of the well, and water the sheep, and put the stone back in its place on the mouth of the well.

4 Jacob said to them, "My brothers, where do you come from?" They said, "We are from Haran." [5]He said to them, "Do you know Laban son of Nahor?" They said, "We do." [6]He said to them, "Is it well with him?" "Yes," they replied, "and here is his daughter Rachel, coming with the sheep." [7]He said, "Look, it is still broad daylight; it is not time for the animals to be gathered together. Water the sheep, and go, pasture them." [8]But they said, "We cannot until all the flocks are gathered together, and the stone is rolled from the mouth of the well; then we water the sheep."

9 While he was still speaking with them, Rachel came with her father's sheep; for she kept them. [10]Now when Jacob saw Rachel, the daughter of his mother's brother Laban, and the sheep of his mother's brother Laban, Jacob went up and rolled the stone from the well's mouth, and watered the flock of his mother's brother Laban. [11]Then Jacob kissed Rachel, and wept aloud. [12]And Jacob told Rachel that he was her father's kinsman, and that he was Rebekah's son; and she ran and told her father.

13 When Laban heard the news about his sister's son Jacob, he ran to meet him; he embraced him and kissed him, and brought him to his house. Jacob[a] told Laban all these things, [14]and Laban said to him, "Surely you are my bone and my flesh!" And he stayed with him a month.

Jacob Marries Laban's Daughters

15 Then Laban said to Jacob, "Because you are my kinsman, should you therefore serve me for nothing? Tell me, what shall your wages be?" [16]Now Laban had two daughters; the name of the elder was Leah, and the name of the younger was Rachel. [17]Leah's eyes were lovely,[b] and Rachel was graceful and beautiful. [18]Jacob loved Rachel; so he said, "I will serve you seven years for your younger daughter Rachel." [19]Laban said, "It is better that I give her to you than that I should give her to any other man; stay with me." [20]So Jacob served seven years for Rachel, and they seemed to him but a few days because of the love he had for her.

21 Then Jacob said to Laban, "Give me my wife that I may go in to her, for my time is completed." [22]So Laban gathered together all the people of the place, and made a feast. [23]But in the evening he took his daughter Leah and brought her to Jacob; and he went in to her. [24](Laban gave his maid Zilpah to his daughter Leah to be her maid.) [25]When morning came, it was Leah! And Jacob said to Laban, "What is this you have done to me? Did I not serve with you for Rachel? Why then have you deceived me?" [26]Laban said, "This is not done in our country—giving the younger before the firstborn. [27]Complete the week of this one, and we will give you the other also in return for serving me another seven years."

When Lies Boomerang   Genesis 29:15–30

You can't blame Jacob for getting upset when he finds out he has been deceived by Laban (Genesis 29:25). But you could say the phrase "what goes around, comes around" applies here. The very reason Jacob is working for his uncle Laban is because he fled from his brother, Esau, whom he deceived several years ago (Genesis 27:1-40). Jacob's lies and deceit have boomeranged, so now he is the victim.

Our lies, gossip, and manipulation of others often come back to haunt us.

• When have you been the one to stir up gossip?

• Consider how you can respond in the future out of love and respect for others.

a Heb *He*   **b** Meaning of Heb uncertain

[28]Jacob did so, and completed her week; then Laban gave him his daughter Rachel as a wife. [29](Laban gave his maid Bilhah to his daughter Rachel to be her maid.) [30]So Jacob went in to Rachel also, and he loved Rachel more than Leah. He served Laban[a] for another seven years.

31 When the LORD saw that Leah was unloved, he opened her womb; but Rachel was barren. [32]Leah conceived and bore a son, and she named him Reuben;[b] for she said, "Because the LORD has looked on my affliction; surely now my husband will love me." [33]She conceived again and bore a son, and said, "Because the LORD has heard[c] that I am hated, he has given me this son also"; and she named him Simeon. [34]Again she conceived and bore a son, and said, "Now this time my husband will be joined[d] to me, because I have borne him three sons"; therefore he was named Levi. [35]She conceived again and bore a son, and said, "This time I will praise[e] the LORD"; therefore she named him Judah; then she ceased bearing.

30 When Rachel saw that she bore Jacob no children, she envied her sister; and she said to Jacob, "Give me children, or I shall die!" [2]Jacob became very angry with Rachel and said, "Am I in the place of God, who has withheld from you the fruit of the womb?" [3]Then she said, "Here is my maid Bilhah; go in to her, that she may bear upon my knees and that I too may have children through her." [4]So she gave him her maid Bilhah as a wife; and Jacob went in to her. [5]And Bilhah conceived and bore Jacob a son. [6]Then Rachel said, "God has judged me, and has also heard my voice and given me a son"; therefore she named him Dan.[f] [7]Rachel's maid Bilhah conceived again and bore Jacob a second son. [8]Then Rachel said, "With mighty wrestlings I have wrestled[g] with my sister, and have prevailed"; so she named him Naphtali.

9 When Leah saw that she had ceased bearing children, she took her maid Zilpah and gave her to Jacob as a wife. [10]Then Leah's maid Zilpah bore Jacob a son. [11]And Leah said, "Good fortune!" so she named him Gad.[h] [12]Leah's maid Zilpah bore Jacob a second son. [13]And Leah said, "Happy am I! For the women will call me happy"; so she named him Asher.[i]

14 In the days of wheat harvest Reuben went and found mandrakes in the field, and brought them to his mother Leah. Then Rachel said to Leah, "Please give me some of your son's mandrakes." [15]But she said to her, "Is it a small matter that you have taken away my husband? Would you take away my son's mandrakes also?" Rachel said, "Then he may lie with you tonight for your son's mandrakes." [16]When Jacob came from the field in the evening, Leah went out to meet him, and said, "You must come in to me; for I have hired you with my son's mandrakes." So he lay with her that night. [17]And God heeded Leah, and she conceived and bore Jacob a fifth son. [18]Leah said, "God has given me my hire[j] because I gave my maid to my husband"; so she named him Issachar. [19]And Leah conceived again, and she bore Jacob a sixth son. [20]Then Leah said, "God has endowed me with a good dowry; now my husband will honor[k] me, because I have borne him six sons"; so she named him Zebulun. [21]Afterwards she bore a daughter, and named her Dinah.

22 Then God remembered Rachel, and God heeded her and opened her womb. [23]She conceived and bore a son, and said, "God has taken away my reproach"; [24]and she named him Joseph,[l] saying, "May the LORD add to me another son!"

Jacob Prospers at Laban's Expense

25 When Rachel had borne Joseph, Jacob said to Laban, "Send me away, that I may go to my own home and country. [26]Give me my wives and my children for whom I have served you, and let me go; for you know very well the service I have given you." [27]But Laban said to him, "If you will allow me to say so, I have learned by divination that the LORD has blessed me because of you; [28]name your wages, and I will give it." [29]Jacob said to him, "You yourself know how I have served you, and how your cattle have fared with me. [30]For you had little before I came, and it has increased abundantly; and the LORD has blessed you wherever I turned. But now when shall I provide for my own household also?" [31]He said, "What shall I give you?" Jacob said, "You shall not give me anything; if you will do this for me, I will again feed your flock and keep it: [32]let me pass through all your flock today, removing from it every speckled and spotted sheep and every black lamb, and the spotted and speckled among the goats; and such shall be my wages. [33]So my honesty will answer for me later, when you come to look into my wages with you. Every one that is not speckled and spotted among the goats and black among the lambs, if found with me, shall be counted stolen." [34]Laban said, "Good! Let it be as you have said." [35]But that day Laban removed the male goats that were striped and

---

a Heb *him*   *b* That is *See, a son*   *c* Heb *shama*   *d* Heb *lawah*   *e* Heb *hodah*   *f* That is *He judged*   *g* Heb *niphtal*   *h* That is *Fortune*   *i* That is *Happy*   *j* Heb *sakar*   *k* Heb *zabal*   *l* That is *He adds*

spotted, and all the female goats that were speckled and spotted, every one that had white on it, and every lamb that was black, and put them in charge of his sons; [36]and he set a distance of three days' journey between himself and Jacob, while Jacob was pasturing the rest of Laban's flock.

37 Then Jacob took fresh rods of poplar and almond and plane, and peeled white streaks in them, exposing the white of the rods. [38]He set the rods that he had peeled in front of the flocks in the troughs, that is, the watering places, where the flocks came to drink. And since they bred when they came to drink, [39]the flocks bred in front of the rods, and so the flocks produced young that were striped, speckled, and spotted. [40]Jacob separated the lambs, and set the faces of the flocks toward the striped and the completely black animals in the flock of Laban; and he put his own droves apart, and did not put them with Laban's flock. [41]Whenever the stronger of the flock were breeding, Jacob laid the rods in the troughs before the eyes of the flock, that they might breed among the rods, [42]but for the feebler of the flock he did not lay them there; so the feebler were Laban's, and the stronger Jacob's. [43]Thus the man grew exceedingly rich, and had large flocks, and male and female slaves, and camels and donkeys.

31 Jacob Flees with Family and Flocks

Now Jacob heard that the sons of Laban were saying, "Jacob has taken all that was our father's; he has gained all this wealth from what belonged to our father." [2]And Jacob saw that Laban did not regard him as favorably as he did before. [3]Then the LORD said to Jacob, "Return to the land of your ancestors and to your kindred, and I will be with you." [4]So Jacob sent and called Rachel and Leah into the field where his flock was, [5]and said to them, "I see that your father does not regard me as favorably as he did before. But the God of my father has been with me. [6]You know that I have served your father with all my strength; [7]yet your father has cheated me and changed my wages ten times, but God did not permit him to harm me. [8]If he said, 'The speckled shall be your wages,' then all the flock bore speckled; and if he said, 'The striped shall be your wages,' then all the flock bore striped. [9]Thus God has taken away the livestock of your father, and given them to me. 10 "During the mating of the flock I once had a dream in which I looked up and saw that the male goats that leaped upon the flock were striped, speck-

led, and mottled. [11]Then the angel of God said to me in the dream, 'Jacob,' and I said, 'Here I am!' [12]And he said, 'Look up and see that all the goats that leap on the flock are striped, speckled, and mottled; for I have seen all that Laban is doing to you. [13]I am the God of Bethel,[a] where you anointed a pillar and made a vow to me. Now leave this land at once and return to the land of your birth.' " [14]Then Rachel and Leah answered him, "Is there any portion or inheritance left to us in our father's house? [15]Are we not regarded by him as foreigners? For he has sold us, and he has been using up the money given for us. [16]All the property that God has taken away from our father belongs to us and to our children; now then, do whatever God has said to you."

17 So Jacob arose, and set his children and his wives on camels; [18]and he drove away all his livestock, all the property that he had gained, the livestock in his possession that he had acquired in Paddan-aram, to go to his father Isaac in the land of Canaan.

19 Now Laban had gone to shear his sheep, and Rachel stole her father's household gods. [20]And Jacob deceived Laban the Aramean, in that he did not tell him that he intended to flee. [21]So he fled with all that he had; starting out he crossed the Euphrates,[b] and set his face toward the hill country of Gilead.

Laban Overtakes Jacob

22 On the third day Laban was told that Jacob had fled. [23]So he took his kinsfolk with him and pursued him for seven days until he caught up with him in the hill country of Gilead. [24]But God came to Laban the Aramean in a dream by night, and said to him, "Take heed that you say not a word to Jacob, either good or bad."

25 Laban overtook Jacob. Now Jacob had pitched his tent in the hill country, and Laban with his kinsfolk camped in the hill country of Gilead. [26]Laban said to Jacob, "What have you done? You have deceived me, and carried away my daughters like captives of the sword. [27]Why did you flee secretly and deceive me and not tell me? I would have sent you away with mirth and songs, with tambourine and lyre. [28]And why did you not permit me to kiss my sons and my daughters farewell? What you have done is foolish. [29]It is in my power to do you harm; but the God of your father spoke to me last night, saying, 'Take heed that you speak to Jacob neither good nor bad.' [30]Even though you had to go because you longed greatly for your father's house, why did you steal my

a Cn: Meaning of Heb uncertain   b Heb the river

gods?" [31]Jacob answered Laban, "Because I was afraid, for I thought that you would take your daughters from me by force. [32]But anyone with whom you find your gods shall not live. In the presence of our kinsfolk, point out what I have that is yours, and take it." Now Jacob did not know that Rachel had stolen the gods.[a]

33 So Laban went into Jacob's tent, and into Leah's tent, and into the tent of the two maids, but he did not find them. And he went out of Leah's tent, and entered Rachel's. [34]Now Rachel had taken the household gods and put them in the camel's saddle, and sat on them. Laban felt all about in the tent, but did not find them. [35]And she said to her father, "Let not my lord be angry that I cannot rise before you, for the way of women is upon me." So he searched, but did not find the household gods.

36 Then Jacob became angry, and upbraided Laban. Jacob said to Laban, "What is my offense? What is my sin, that you have hotly pursued me? [37]Although you have felt about through all my goods, what have you found of all your household goods? Set it here before my kinsfolk and your kinsfolk, so that they may decide between us two. [38]These twenty years I have been with you; your ewes and your female goats have not miscarried, and I have not eaten the rams of your flocks. [39]That which was torn by wild beasts I did not bring to you; I bore the loss of it myself; of my hand you required it, whether stolen by day or stolen by night. [40]It was like this with me: by day the heat consumed me, and the cold by night, and my sleep fled from my eyes. [41]These twenty years I have been in your house; I served you fourteen years for your two daughters, and six years for your flock, and you have changed my wages ten times. [42]If the God of my father, the God of Abraham and the Fear[b] of Isaac, had not been on my side, surely now you would have sent me away empty-handed. God saw my affliction and the labor of my hands, and rebuked you last night."

Laban and Jacob Make a Covenant

43 Then Laban answered and said to Jacob, "The daughters are my daughters, the children are my children, the flocks are my flocks, and all that you see is mine. But what can I do today about these daughters of mine, or about their children whom they have borne? [44]Come now, let us make a covenant, you and I; and let it be a witness between you and me." [45]So Jacob took a stone, and set it up

as a pillar. [46]And Jacob said to his kinsfolk, "Gather stones," and they took stones, and made a heap; and they ate there by the heap. [47]Laban called it Jegar-sahadutha:[c] but Jacob called it Galeed.[d] [48]Laban said, "This heap is a witness between you and me today." Therefore he called it Galeed, [49]and the pillar[e] Mizpah,[f] for he said, "The LORD watch between you and me, when we are absent one from the other. [50]If you ill-treat my daughters, or if you take wives in addition to my daughters, though no one else is with us, remember that God is witness between you and me."

51 Then Laban said to Jacob, "See this heap and see the pillar, which I have set between you and me. [52]This heap is a witness, and the pillar is a witness, that I will not pass beyond this heap to you, and you will not pass beyond this heap and this pillar to me, for harm. [53]May the God of Abraham and the God of Nahor"—the God of their father— "judge between us." So Jacob swore by the Fear[b] of his father Isaac, [54]and Jacob offered a sacrifice on the height and called his kinsfolk to eat bread; and they ate bread and tarried all night in the hill country.

55[g] Early in the morning Laban rose up, and kissed his grandchildren and his daughters and blessed them; then he departed and returned home.

32 Jacob went on his way and the angels of God met him; [2]and when Jacob saw them he said, "This is God's camp!" So he called that place Mahanaim.[h]

Jacob Sends Presents to Appease Esau

3 Jacob sent messengers before him to his brother Esau in the land of Seir, the country of Edom, [4]instructing them, "Thus you shall say to my lord Esau: Thus says your servant Jacob, 'I have lived with Laban as an alien, and stayed until now; [5]and I have oxen, donkeys, flocks, male and female slaves; and I have sent to tell my lord, in order that I may find favor in your sight.' "

6 The messengers returned to Jacob, saying, "We came to your brother Esau, and he is coming to meet you, and four hundred men are with him." [7]Then Jacob was greatly afraid and distressed; and he divided the people that were with him, and the flocks and herds and camels, into two companies, [8]thinking, "If Esau comes to the one company and destroys it, then the company that is left will escape." 9 And Jacob said, "O God of my father Abraham

---

a Heb *them*   **b** Meaning of Heb uncertain   **c** In Aramaic *The heap of witness*   **d** In Hebrew *The heap of witness*   **e** Compare Sam: MT lacks *the pillar*
f That is *Watchpost*   **g** Ch 32.1 in Heb   **h** Here taken to mean *Two camps*

and God of my father Isaac, O LORD who said to me, 'Return to your country and to your kindred, and I will do you good,' [10]I am not worthy of the least of all the steadfast love and all the faithfulness that you have shown to your servant, for with only my staff I crossed this Jordan; and now I have become two companies. [11]Deliver me, please, from the hand of my brother, from the hand of Esau, for I am afraid of him; he may come and kill us all, the mothers with the children. [12]Yet you have said, 'I will surely do you good, and make your offspring as the sand of the sea, which cannot be counted because of their number.' "

13 So he spent that night there, and from what he had with him he took a present for his brother Esau, [14]two hundred female goats and twenty male goats, two hundred ewes and twenty rams, [15]thirty milch camels and their colts, forty cows and ten bulls, twenty female donkeys and ten male donkeys. [16]These he delivered into the hand of his servants, every drove by itself, and said to his servants, "Pass on ahead of me, and put a space between drove and drove." [17]He instructed the foremost, "When Esau my brother meets you, and asks you, 'To whom do you belong? Where are you going? And whose are these ahead of you?' [18]then you shall say, 'They belong to your servant Jacob; they are a present sent to my lord Esau; and moreover he is behind us.' " [19]He likewise instructed the second and the third and all who followed the droves, "You shall say the same thing to Esau when you meet him, [20]and you shall say, 'Moreover your servant Jacob is behind us.' " For he thought, "I may appease him with the present that goes ahead of me, and afterwards I shall see his face; perhaps he will accept me." [21]So the present passed on ahead of him; and he himself spent that night in the camp.

Jacob Wrestles at Peniel

22 The same night he got up and took his two wives, his two maids, and his eleven children, and crossed the ford of the Jabbok. [23]He took them and sent them across the stream, and likewise everything that he had. [24]Jacob was left alone; and a man wrestled with him until daybreak. [25]When the man saw that he did not prevail against Jacob, he struck him on the hip socket; and Jacob's hip was put out of joint as he wrestled with him. [26]Then he said, "Let me go, for the day is breaking." But Jacob said, "I will not let you go, unless you bless me." [27]So he said to him, "What is your name?" And he said, "Jacob." [28]Then the man[a] said, "You shall no longer be called Jacob, but Israel,[b] for you have striven with God and with humans,[c] and have prevailed." [29]Then Jacob asked him, "Please tell me your name." But he said, "Why is it that you ask my name?" And there he blessed him. [30]So Jacob called the place Peniel,[d] saying, "For I have seen God face to face, and yet my life is preserved." [31]The sun rose upon him as he passed Penuel, limping because of his hip. [32]Therefore to this day the Israelites do not eat the thigh muscle that is on the hip socket, because he struck Jacob on the hip socket at the thigh muscle.

PRAY IT!

Wrestling with God · Genesis 32:22–32

Jacob is anxious about meeting Esau again, even after twenty years. This time Jacob uses his craftiness not to deceive Esau, but to gain Esau's good graces. Then on the way to meet Esau, Jacob has an amazing experience. Many scripture scholars believe the strange wrestling encounter is a symbol that Jacob has become a changed person. He finally realizes that in all his troubles, he was fighting against God.

Perhaps at times you have wrestled with yourself or with God. When you face challenges, especially big ones, the person you are now often wrestles with the person God is calling you to be.

Reflect or journal on the following questions during your prayer time:

• When does it seem as though you're trying to wrestle with God? What does it feel like?

• Is God challenging you about something in your life right now?

• What blessings can you gain from accepting God's challenge and calling in your life?

---

a Heb *he*   **b** That is *The one who strives with God* or *God strives*   **c** Or *with divine and human beings*   **d** That is *The face of God*

33 Jacob and Esau Meet

Now Jacob looked up and saw Esau coming, and four hundred men with him. So he divided the children among Leah and Rachel and the two maids. [2]He put the maids with their children in front, then Leah with her children, and Rachel and Joseph last of all. [3]He himself went on ahead of them, bowing himself to the ground seven times, until he came near his brother.

4 But Esau ran to meet him, and embraced him, and fell on his neck and kissed him, and they wept. [5]When Esau looked up and saw the women and children, he said, "Who are these with you?" Jacob said, "The children whom God has graciously given your servant." [6]Then the maids drew near, they and their children, and bowed down; [7]Leah likewise and her children drew near and bowed down; and finally Joseph and Rachel drew near, and they bowed down. [8]Esau said, "What do you mean by all this company that I met?" Jacob answered, "To find favor with my lord." [9]But Esau said, "I have enough, my brother; keep what you have for yourself." [10]Jacob said, "No, please; if I find favor with you, then accept my present from my hand; for truly to see your face is like seeing the face of God—since you have received me with such favor. [11]Please accept my gift that is brought to you, because God has dealt graciously with me, and because I have everything I want." So he urged him, and he took it.

12 Then Esau said, "Let us journey on our way, and I will go alongside you." [13]But Jacob said to him, "My lord knows that the children are frail and that the flocks and herds, which are nursing, are a care to me; and if they are overdriven for one day, all the flocks will die. [14]Let my lord pass on ahead of his servant, and I will lead on slowly, according to the pace of the cattle that are before me and according to the pace of the children, until I come to my lord in Seir."

15 So Esau said, "Let me leave with you some of the people who are with me." But he said, "Why should my lord be so kind to me?" [16]So Esau returned that day on his way to Seir. [17]But Jacob journeyed to Succoth,[a] and built himself a house, and made booths for his cattle; therefore the place is called Succoth.

Jacob Reaches Shechem

18 Jacob came safely to the city of Shechem, which is in the land of Canaan, on his way from Paddan-aram; and he camped before the city. [19]And from the sons of Hamor, Shechem's father, he bought for one hundred pieces of money[b] the plot of land on which he had pitched his tent. [20]There he erected an altar and called it El-Elohe-Israel.[c]

34 The Rape of Dinah

Now Dinah the daughter of Leah, whom she had borne to Jacob, went out to visit the women of the region. [2]When Shechem son of Hamor the Hivite, prince of the region, saw her, he seized her and lay with her by force. [3]And his soul was drawn to Dinah daughter of Jacob; he loved the girl, and spoke tenderly to her. [4]So Shechem spoke

LIVE IT!

Letting Go of the Past · Genesis 33:1–17

Jacob is understandably nervous as he approaches his long-estranged twin brother—and the four hundred men with him! But Esau, who was wronged by Jacob, runs to meet him and gives him a hug. All is forgiven, and the two are reconciled at last. This story is like the parable of the prodigal son (Luke 15:11-32).

All of us have wronged others, especially the people we care about most. All of us have also experienced forgiveness. Nothing is quite like the freedom that comes with genuine forgiveness and reconciliation. A burden is lifted. A heavy heart is made lighter. A vengeful anger is transformed into inner peace. This is the work of God's grace. Forgiveness and reconciliation are powerful signs of God's presence. We can almost feel the enormous sense of relief Jacob experiences as he realizes that his brother holds no grudge.

• What relationship in your life needs forgiveness and reconciliation?

• What step can you take to bring healing in this relationship?

---

a That is *Booths*   b Heb *one hundred qesitah*   c That is *God, the God of Israel*

to his father Hamor, saying, "Get me this girl to be my wife."

5 Now Jacob heard that Shechem[a] had defiled his daughter Dinah; but his sons were with his cattle in the field, so Jacob held his peace until they came. [6]And Hamor the father of Shechem went out to Jacob to speak with him, [7]just as the sons of Jacob came in from the field. When they heard of it, the men were indignant and very angry, because he had committed an outrage in Israel by lying with Jacob's daughter, for such a thing ought not to be done.

8 But Hamor spoke with them, saying, "The heart of my son Shechem longs for your daughter; please give her to him in marriage. [9]Make marriages with us; give your daughters to us, and take our daughters for yourselves. [10]You shall live with us; and the land shall be open to you; live and trade in it, and get property in it." [11]Shechem also said to her father and to her brothers, "Let me find favor with you, and whatever you say to me I will give. [12]Put the marriage present and gift as high as you like, and I will give whatever you ask me; only give me the girl to be my wife."

13 The sons of Jacob answered Shechem and his father Hamor deceitfully, because he had defiled their sister Dinah. [14]They said to them, "We cannot do this thing, to give our sister to one who is uncircumcised, for that would be a disgrace to us. [15]Only on this condition will we consent to you: that you will become as we are and every male among you be circumcised. [16]Then we will give our daughters to you, and we will take your daughters for ourselves, and we will live among you and become one people. [17]But if you will not listen to us and be circumcised, then we will take our daughter and be gone."

18 Their words pleased Hamor and Hamor's son Shechem. [19]And the young man did not delay to do the thing, because he was delighted with Jacob's daughter. Now he was the most honored of all his family. [20]So Hamor and his son Shechem came to the gate of their city and spoke to the men of their city, saying, [21]"These people are friendly with us; let them live in the land and trade in it, for the land is large enough for them; let us take their daughters in marriage, and let us give them our daughters. [22]Only on this condition will they agree to live among us, to become one people: that every male among us be circumcised as they are circumcised. [23]Will not their livestock, their property, and all their animals be ours? Only let us agree with them, and they will live among

us." [24]And all who went out of the city gate heeded Hamor and his son Shechem; and every male was circumcised, all who went out of the gate of his city.

Dinah's Brothers Avenge Their Sister

25 On the third day, when they were still in pain, two of the sons of Jacob, Simeon and Levi, Dinah's brothers, took their swords and came against the city unawares, and killed all the males. [26]They killed Hamor and his son Shechem with the sword, and

LIVE IT!

Rape: It's in the Bible Too
Genesis 34

Genesis doesn't beat around the bush, even when it comes to harsh topics like rape. The story in **Genesis 34** tells us of Shechem, a local prince who rapes Jacob's daughter, Dinah. Apparently Shechem figured he could do whatever he wanted to Dinah because of his power or social status. But in the end his life is taken when Dinah's brothers get revenge.

Rape is more about power and aggression than it is about sex. Perpetrators of this evil act violate the dignity of their victims and attempt to dominate them. Whenever individuals are raped, they are violated against their will, causing severe emotional damage.

We are called to respect one another. Position or power does not give us the right to commit sexual violence. Desire or spending money on a date does not make it okay to force any girl or guy into any kind of sexual activity. Rape and any other types of sexual abuse are an outrage to God.

- Have you been a victim of rape or sexual abuse?
- It's not your fault. God can bring healing, but you need to talk to a counselor and get help. Talk to a parent or trusted adult at school or church, or call a help line today.

took Dinah out of Shechem's house, and went away. [27] And the other sons of Jacob came upon the slain, and plundered the city, because their sister had been defiled. [28] They took their flocks and their herds, their donkeys, and whatever was in the city and in the field. [29] All their wealth, all their little ones and their wives, all that was in the houses, they captured and made their prey. [30] Then Jacob said to Simeon and Levi, "You have brought trouble on me by making me odious to the inhabitants of the land, the Canaanites and the Perizzites; my numbers are few, and if they gather themselves against me and attack me, I shall be destroyed, both I and my household." [31] But they said, "Should our sister be treated like a whore?"

Jacob Returns to Bethel

35 God said to Jacob, "Arise, go up to Bethel, and settle there. Make an altar there to the God who appeared to you when you fled from your brother Esau." [2] So Jacob said to his household and to all who were with him, "Put away the foreign gods that are among you, and purify yourselves, and change your clothes; [3] then come, let us go up to Bethel, that I may make an altar there to the God who answered me in the day of my distress and has been with me wherever I have gone." [4] So they gave to Jacob all the foreign gods that they had, and the rings that were in their ears; and Jacob hid them under the oak that was near Shechem.

5 As they journeyed, a terror from God fell upon the cities all around them, so that no one pursued them. [6] Jacob came to Luz (that is, Bethel), which is in the land of Canaan, he and all the people who were with him, [7] and there he built an altar and called the place El-bethel,[a] because it was there that God had revealed himself to him when he fled from his brother. [8] And Deborah, Rebekah's nurse, died, and she was buried under an oak below Bethel. So it was called Allon-bacuth.[b]

9 God appeared to Jacob again when he came from Paddan-aram, and he blessed him. [10] God said to him, "Your name is Jacob; no longer shall you be called Jacob, but Israel shall be your name." So he was called Israel. [11] God said to him, "I am God Almighty:[c] be fruitful and multiply; a nation and a company of nations shall come from you, and kings shall spring from you. [12] The land that I gave to Abraham and Isaac I will give to you, and I will give the land to your offspring after you." [13] Then God went up from him at the place where he had spoken with him. [14] Jacob set up a pillar in the place where he had spoken with him, a pillar of stone; and he poured out a drink offering on it, and poured oil on it. [15] So Jacob called the place where God had spoken with him Bethel.

The Birth of Benjamin and the Death of Rachel

16 Then they journeyed from Bethel; and when they were still some distance from Ephrath, Rachel was in childbirth, and she had hard labor. [17] When she was in her hard labor, the midwife said to her, "Do not be afraid; for now you will have another son." [18] As her soul was departing (for she died), she named him Ben-oni;[d] but his father called him Benjamin.[e] [19] So Rachel died, and she was buried on the way to Ephrath (that is, Bethlehem), [20] and Jacob set up a pillar at her grave; it is the pillar of Rachel's tomb, which is there to this day. [21] Israel journeyed on, and pitched his tent beyond the tower of Eder.

22 While Israel lived in that land, Reuben went and lay with Bilhah his father's concubine; and Israel heard of it.

Now the sons of Jacob were twelve. [23] The sons of Leah: Reuben (Jacob's firstborn), Simeon, Levi, Judah, Issachar, and Zebulun. [24] The sons of Rachel: Joseph and Benjamin. [25] The sons of Bilhah, Rachel's maid: Dan and Naphtali. [26] The sons of Zilpah, Leah's maid: Gad and Asher. These were the sons of Jacob who were born to him in Paddan-aram.

The Death of Isaac

27 Jacob came to his father Isaac at Mamre, or Kiriath-arba (that is, Hebron), where Abraham and Isaac had resided as aliens. [28] Now the days of Isaac were one hundred eighty years. [29] And Isaac breathed his last; he died and was gathered to his people, old and full of days; and his sons Esau and Jacob buried him.

Esau's Descendants

36 These are the descendants of Esau (that is, Edom). [2] Esau took his wives from the Canaanites: Adah daughter of Elon the Hittite, Oholibamah daughter of Anah son[f] of Zibeon the Hivite, [3] and Basemath, Ishmael's daughter, sister of Nebaioth. [4] Adah bore Eliphaz to Esau; Basemath bore Reuel; [5] and Oholibamah bore Jeush, Jalam, and Korah. These are the sons of Esau who were born to him in the land of Canaan.

6 Then Esau took his wives, his sons, his daughters,

---

a That is *God of Bethel* **b** That is *Oak of weeping* **c** Traditional rendering of Heb *El Shaddai* **d** That is *Son of my sorrow* **e** That is *Son of the right hand* or *Son of the South* **f** Sam Gk Syr: Heb *daughter*

and all the members of his household, his cattle, all his livestock, and all the property he had acquired in the land of Canaan; and he moved to a land some distance from his brother Jacob. [7]For their possessions were too great for them to live together; the land where they were staying could not support them because of their livestock. [8]So Esau settled in the hill country of Seir; Esau is Edom.

9 These are the descendants of Esau, ancestor of the Edomites, in the hill country of Seir. [10]These are the names of Esau's sons: Eliphaz son of Adah the wife of Esau; Reuel, the son of Esau's wife Basemath. [11]The sons of Eliphaz were Teman, Omar, Zepho, Gatam, and Kenaz. [12](Timna was a concubine of Eliphaz, Esau's son; she bore Amalek to Eliphaz.) These were the sons of Adah, Esau's wife. [13]These were the sons of Reuel: Nahath, Zerah, Shammah, and Mizzah. These were the sons of Esau's wife, Basemath. [14]These were the sons of Esau's wife Oholibamah, daughter of Anah son[a] of Zibeon: she bore to Esau Jeush, Jalam, and Korah.

Clans and Kings of Edom

15 These are the clans[b] of the sons of Esau. The sons of Eliphaz the firstborn of Esau: the clans[b] Teman, Omar, Zepho, Kenaz, [16]Korah, Gatam, and Amalek; these are the clans[b] of Eliphaz in the land of Edom; they are the sons of Adah. [17]These are the sons of Esau's son Reuel: the clans[b] Nahath, Zerah, Shammah, and Mizzah; these are the clans[b] of Reuel in the land of Edom; they are the sons of Esau's wife Basemath. [18]These are the sons of Esau's wife Oholibamah: the clans[b] Jeush, Jalam, and Korah; these are the clans[b] born of Esau's wife Oholibamah, the daughter of Anah. [19]These are the sons of Esau (that is, Edom), and these are their clans.[b]

20 These are the sons of Seir the Horite, the inhabitants of the land: Lotan, Shobal, Zibeon, Anah, [21]Dishon, Ezer, and Dishan; these are the clans[b] of the Horites, the sons of Seir in the land of Edom. [22]The sons of Lotan were Hori and Heman; and Lotan's sister was Timna. [23]These are the sons of Shobal: Alvan, Manahath, Ebal, Shepho, and Onam. [24]These are the sons of Zibeon: Aiah and Anah; he is the Anah who found the springs[c] in the wilderness, as he pastured the donkeys of his father Zibeon. [25]These are the children of Anah: Dishon and Oholibamah daughter of Anah. [26]These are the sons of Dishon: Hemdan, Eshban, Ithran, and Cheran. [27]These are the sons of Ezer: Bilhan, Zaavan, and Akan. [28]These are the sons of Dishan: Uz and Aran. [29]These are the clans[b] of the Horites: the clans[b] Lotan, Shobal, Zibeon, Anah, [30]Dishon, Ezer, and Dishan; these are the clans[b] of the Horites, clan by clan[d] in the land of Seir.

31 These are the kings who reigned in the land of Edom, before any king reigned over the Israelites. [32]Bela son of Beor reigned in Edom, the name of his city being Dinhabah. [33]Bela died, and Jobab son of Zerah of Bozrah succeeded him as king. [34]Jobab died, and Husham of the land of the Temanites succeeded him as king. [35]Husham died, and Hadad son of Bedad, who defeated Midian in the country of Moab, succeeded him as king, the name of his city being Avith. [36]Hadad died, and Samlah of Masrekah succeeded him as king. [37]Samlah died, and Shaul of Rehoboth on the Euphrates succeeded him as king. [38]Shaul died, and Baal-hanan son of Achbor succeeded him as king. [39]Baal-hanan son of Achbor died, and Hadar succeeded him as king, the name of his city being Pau; his wife's name was Mehetabel, the daughter of Matred, daughter of Me-zahab.

40 These are the names of the clans[b] of Esau, according to their families and their localities by their names: the clans[b] Timna, Alvah, Jetheth, [41]Oholibamah, Elah, Pinon, [42]Kenaz, Teman, Mibzar, [43]Magdiel, and Iram; these are the clans[b] of Edom (that is, Esau, the father of Edom), according to their settlements in the land that they held.

Joseph Dreams of Greatness

37 Jacob settled in the land where his father had lived as an alien, the land of Canaan. [2]This is the story of the family of Jacob.

Joseph, being seventeen years old, was shepherding the flock with his brothers; he was a helper to the sons of Bilhah and Zilpah, his father's wives; and Joseph brought a bad report of them to their father. [3]Now Israel loved Joseph more than any other of his children, because he was the son of his old age; and he had made him a long robe with sleeves.[e] [4]But when his brothers saw that their father loved him more than all his brothers, they hated him, and could not speak peaceably to him.

5 Once Joseph had a dream, and when he told it to his brothers, they hated him even more. [6]He said to them, "Listen to this dream that I dreamed. [7]There we were, binding sheaves in the field. Suddenly my sheaf rose and stood upright; then your sheaves gathered around it, and bowed down to my sheaf." [8]His

---

a Gk Syr: Heb *daughter*   b Or *chiefs*   c Meaning of Heb uncertain   d Or *chief by chief*   e Traditional rendering (compare Gk): *a coat of many colors*; meaning of Heb uncertain

brothers said to him, "Are you indeed to reign over us? Are you indeed to have dominion over us?" So they hated him even more because of his dreams and his words.

9 He had another dream, and told it to his brothers, saying, "Look, I have had another dream: the sun, the moon, and eleven stars were bowing down to me." ¹⁰But when he told it to his father and to his brothers, his father rebuked him, and said to him, "What kind of dream is this that you have had? Shall we indeed come, I and your mother and your brothers, and bow to the ground before you?" ¹¹So his brothers were jealous of him, but his father kept the matter in mind.

Joseph Is Sold by His Brothers

12 Now his brothers went to pasture their father's flock near Shechem. ¹³And Israel said to Joseph, "Are not your brothers pasturing the flock at Shechem? Come, I will send you to them." He answered, "Here I am." ¹⁴So he said to him, "Go now, see if it is well with your brothers and with the flock; and bring word back to me." So he sent him from the valley of Hebron.

He came to Shechem, ¹⁵and a man found him wandering in the fields; the man asked him, "What are you seeking?" ¹⁶"I am seeking my brothers," he said; "tell me, please, where they are pasturing the flock." ¹⁷The man said, "They have gone away, for I heard them say, 'Let us go to Dothan.'" So Joseph went after his brothers, and found them at Dothan. ¹⁸They saw him from a distance, and before he came near to them, they conspired to kill him. ¹⁹They said to one another, "Here comes this dreamer. ²⁰Come now, let us kill him and throw him into one of the pits; then we shall say that a wild animal has devoured him, and we shall see what will become of his dreams." ²¹But when Reuben heard it, he delivered him out of their hands, saying, "Let us not take his life." ²²Reuben said to them, "Shed no blood; throw him into this pit here in the wilderness, but lay no hand on him"—that he might rescue him out of their hand and restore him to his father. ²³So when Joseph came to his brothers, they stripped him of his robe, the long robe with sleeves[a] that he wore; ²⁴and they took him and threw him into a pit. The pit was empty; there was no water in it.

25 Then they sat down to eat; and looking up they saw a caravan of Ishmaelites coming from Gilead, with their camels carrying gum, balm, and resin, on their way to carry it down to Egypt. ²⁶Then Judah said to his brothers, "What profit is it if we kill our brother and conceal his blood? ²⁷Come, let us sell him to the Ishmaelites, and not lay our hands on him, for he is our brother, our own flesh." And his brothers agreed. ²⁸When some Midianite traders passed by, they drew Joseph up, lifting him out of the pit, and sold

STUDY IT!

Dreams and Visions · Genesis 37:1–11; 40:1–41:36

Belief in the reality and significance of dreams was widespread in the ancient world. People believed that dreams and visions revealed messages, prophecies, and healing from their gods. Israel shared this view of the importance of dreams. Joseph is described as an interpreter of dreams, and this skill earns him Pharaoh's respect (see Genesis 41:37-45) as well as his brothers' jealousy (see Genesis 37:5-11).

The Old Testament prophets are often referred to as seers, because the word of God often came to them through dreams and visions. The focus, however, is always on the word of God and its meaning, not on the dream itself. In fact, a character in the story usually interprets the dreams through inspiration from God, and that interpretation aims to lead the people to more faithful observance of the covenant. If the dream doesn't do this, it is to be considered a false dream (Deuteronomy 13:1-6). (See other references to dreams in Genesis 28:10-22; Jeremiah 27:9-10; 29:8-9; Joel 2:28; and Matthew 1:20; 2:13.)

---

a Traditional rendering (compare Gk): *a coat of many colors*; meaning of Heb uncertain

him to the Ishmaelites for twenty pieces of silver. And they took Joseph to Egypt.

29 When Reuben returned to the pit and saw that Joseph was not in the pit, he tore his clothes. [30]He returned to his brothers, and said, "The boy is gone; and I, where can I turn?" [31]Then they took Joseph's robe, slaughtered a goat, and dipped the robe in the blood. [32]They had the long robe with sleeves[a] taken to their father, and they said, "This we have found; see now whether it is your son's robe or not." [33]He recognized it, and said, "It is my son's robe! A wild animal has devoured him; Joseph is without doubt torn to pieces." [34]Then Jacob tore his garments, and put sackcloth on his loins, and mourned for his son many days. [35]All his sons and all his daughters sought to comfort him; but he refused to be comforted, and said, "No, I shall go down to Sheol to my son, mourning." Thus his father bewailed him. [36]Meanwhile the Midianites had sold him in Egypt to Potiphar, one of Pharaoh's officials, the captain of the guard.

38 Judah and Tamar

It happened at that time that Judah went down from his brothers and settled near a certain Adullamite whose name was Hirah. [2]There Judah saw the daughter of a certain Canaanite whose name was Shua; he married her and went in to her. [3]She conceived and bore a son; and he named him Er. [4]Again she conceived and bore a son whom she named Onan. [5]Yet again she bore a son, and she named him Shelah. She[b] was in Chezib when she bore him. [6]Judah took a wife for Er his firstborn; her name was Tamar. [7]But Er, Judah's firstborn, was wicked in the sight of the LORD, and the LORD put him to death. [8]Then Judah said to Onan, "Go in to your brother's wife and perform the duty of a brother-in-law to her; raise up offspring for your brother." [9]But since Onan knew that the offspring would not be his, he spilled his semen on the ground whenever he went in to his brother's wife, so that he would not give offspring to his brother. [10]What he did was displeasing in the sight of the LORD, and he put him to death also. [11]Then Judah said to his daughter-in-law Tamar, "Remain a widow in your father's house until my son Shelah grows up"—for he feared that he too would die, like his brothers. So Tamar went to live in her father's house.

12 In course of time the wife of Judah, Shua's daughter, died; when Judah's time of mourning was over,[c] he went up to Timnah to his sheepshearers, he and his friend Hirah the Adullamite. [13]When Tamar was told, "Your father-in-law is going up to Timnah to shear his sheep," [14]she put off her widow's garments, put on a veil, wrapped herself up, and sat down at the entrance to Enaim, which is on the road to Timnah. She saw that Shelah was grown up, yet she had not been given to him in marriage. [15]When

---

a Traditional rendering (compare Gk): *a coat of many colors*; meaning of Heb uncertain   b Gk: Heb *He*   c Heb *when Judah was comforted*

Judah saw her, he thought her to be a prostitute, for she had covered her face. ¹⁶He went over to her at the roadside, and said, "Come, let me come in to you," for he did not know that she was his daughter-in-law. She said, "What will you give me, that you may come in to me?" ¹⁷He answered, "I will send you a kid from the flock." And she said, "Only if you give me a pledge, until you send it." ¹⁸He said, "What pledge shall I give you?" She replied, "Your signet and your cord, and the staff that is in your hand." So he gave them to her, and went in to her, and she conceived by him. ¹⁹Then she got up and went away, and taking off her veil she put on the garments of her widowhood.

20 When Judah sent the kid by his friend the Adullamite, to recover the pledge from the woman, he could not find her. ²¹He asked the townspeople, "Where is the temple prostitute who was at Enaim by the wayside?" But they said, "No prostitute has been here." ²²So he returned to Judah, and said, "I have not found her; moreover the townspeople said, 'No prostitute has been here.' " ²³Judah replied, "Let her keep the things as her own, otherwise we will be laughed at; you see, I sent this kid, and you could not find her."

24 About three months later Judah was told, "Your daughter-in-law Tamar has played the whore; moreover she is pregnant as a result of whoredom." And Judah said, "Bring her out, and let her be burned." ²⁵As she was being brought out, she sent word to her father-in-law, "It was the owner of these who made me pregnant." And she said, "Take note, please, whose these are, the signet and the cord and the staff." ²⁶Then Judah acknowledged them and said, "She is more in the right than I, since I did not give her to my son Shelah." And he did not lie with her again.

27 When the time of her delivery came, there were twins in her womb. ²⁸While she was in labor, one put out a hand; and the midwife took and bound on his hand a crimson thread, saying, "This one came out first." ²⁹But just then he drew back his hand, and out came his brother; and she said, "What a breach you have made for yourself!" Therefore he was named Perez.ᵃ ³⁰Afterward his brother came out with the crimson thread on his hand; and he was named Zerah.ᵇ

Joseph and Potiphar's Wife

39 Now Joseph was taken down to Egypt, and Potiphar, an officer of Pharaoh, the captain

STUDY IT!

Taking Care of Relatives
Genesis 38:8–10

Why does Onan have to marry his dead brother's wife and have a son by her? One of the laws specified in **Deuteronomy 25:5–10** regulates what is called levirate marriage. "Levirate" means "brother-in-law." When a man's married brother died without a son, that man was obligated to marry the wife who was left. The firstborn son then became the heir of the man who had died (Deuteronomy 25:6). Onan's sin was refusing to take the responsibility for his brother's wife. This marriage practice seems to have developed in Israel for several reasons:

- A male child was needed to inherit a dead man's property, because women generally did not own property.
- The widow needed support and protection.
- A male heir ensured that the family property was kept within the immediate family.

of the guard, an Egyptian, bought him from the Ishmaelites who had brought him down there. ²The LORD was with Joseph, and he became a successful man; he was in the house of his Egyptian master. ³His master saw that the LORD was with him, and that the LORD caused all that he did to prosper in his hands. ⁴So Joseph found favor in his sight and attended him; he made him overseer of his house and put him in charge of all that he had. ⁵From the time that he made him overseer in his house and over all that he had, the LORD blessed the Egyptian's house for Joseph's sake; the blessing of the LORD was on all that he had, in house and field. ⁶So he left all that he had in Joseph's charge; and, with him there, he had no concern for anything but the food that he ate.

Now Joseph was handsome and good-looking. ⁷And after a time his master's wife cast her eyes on Joseph and said, "Lie with me." ⁸But he refused and said to his master's wife, "Look, with me here, my

ᵃ That is *A breach* ᵇ That is *Brightness*; perhaps alluding to the crimson thread master has no concern about anything in the house, and he has put everything that he has in my hand. ⁹He is not greater in this house than I am, nor has he kept back anything from me except yourself, because you are his wife. How then could I do this great wickedness, and sin against God?" ¹⁰And although she spoke to Joseph day after day, he would not consent to lie beside her or to be with her. ¹¹One day, however, when he went into the house to do his work, and while no one else was in the house, ¹²she caught hold of his garment, saying, "Lie with me!" But he left his garment in her hand, and fled and ran outside. ¹³When she saw that he had left his garment in her hand and had fled outside, ¹⁴she called out to the members of her household and said to them, "See, my husband*a* has brought among us a Hebrew to insult us! He came in to me to lie with me, and I cried out with a loud voice; ¹⁵and when he heard me raise my voice and cry out, he left his garment beside me, and fled outside." ¹⁶Then she kept his garment by her until his master came home, ¹⁷and she told him the same story, saying, "The Hebrew servant, whom you have brought among us, came in to me to insult me; ¹⁸but as soon as I raised my voice and cried out, he left his garment beside me, and fled outside."

19 When his master heard the words that his wife spoke to him, saying, "This is the way your servant treated me," he became enraged. ²⁰And Joseph's master took him and put him into the prison, the place where the king's prisoners were confined; he remained there in prison. ²¹But the LORD was with Joseph and showed him steadfast love; he gave him favor in the sight of the chief jailer. ²²The chief jailer committed to Joseph's care all the prisoners who were in the prison, and whatever was done there, he was the one who did it. ²³The chief jailer paid no heed to anything that was in Joseph's care, because the LORD was with him; and whatever he did, the LORD made it prosper.

The Dreams of Two Prisoners
Some time after this, the cupbearer of the king of Egypt and his baker offended their lord the king of Egypt. ²Pharaoh was angry with his two officers, the chief cupbearer and the chief baker, ³and he put them in custody in the house of the captain of the guard, in the prison where Joseph was confined. ⁴The captain of the guard charged Joseph with them, and he waited on them; and they continued for some time in custody. ⁵One night they both dreamed—the cupbearer and the baker of the king of Egypt, who were confined in the prison—each his own dream, and each dream with its own meaning. ⁶When Joseph came to them in the morning, he saw that they were troubled. ⁷So he asked Pharaoh's officers, who were with him in custody in his master's house, "Why are your faces downcast today?" ⁸They said to him, "We have had dreams, and there is no one to interpret them." And Joseph said to them, "Do not interpretations belong to God? Please tell them to me."

9 So the chief cupbearer told his dream to Joseph, and said to him, "In my dream there was a vine before me, ¹⁰and on the vine there were three branches. As soon as it budded, its blossoms came out and the clusters ripened into grapes. ¹¹Pharaoh's cup was in my hand; and I took the grapes and pressed them into Pharaoh's cup, and placed the cup in Pharaoh's hand." ¹²Then Joseph said to him, "This is its interpretation: the three branches are three days; ¹³within three days Pharaoh will lift up your head and restore you to your office; and you shall place Pharaoh's cup in his hand, just as you used to do when you were his cupbearer. ¹⁴But remember me when it is well with you; please do me the kindness to make mention of me to Pharaoh, and so get me out of this place. ¹⁵For in fact I was stolen out of the land of the Hebrews; and here also I have done nothing that they should have put me into the dungeon."

16 When the chief baker saw that the interpretation was favorable, he said to Joseph, "I also had a dream: there were three cake baskets on my head, ¹⁷and in the uppermost basket there were all sorts of baked food for Pharaoh, but the birds were eating it out of the basket on my head." ¹⁸And Joseph answered, "This is its interpretation: the three baskets are three days; ¹⁹within three days Pharaoh will lift up your head—from you!—and hang you on a pole; and the birds will eat the flesh from you."

20 On the third day, which was Pharaoh's birthday, he made a feast for all his servants, and lifted up the head of the chief cupbearer and the head of the chief baker among his servants. ²¹He restored the chief

a Heb *he*

cupbearer to his cupbearing, and he placed the cup in Pharaoh's hand; [22] but the chief baker he hanged, just as Joseph had interpreted to them. [23] Yet the chief cupbearer did not remember Joseph, but forgot him.

Joseph Interprets Pharaoh's Dream

41 After two whole years, Pharaoh dreamed that he was standing by the Nile, [2] and there came up out of the Nile seven sleek and fat cows, and they grazed in the reed grass. [3] Then seven other cows, ugly and thin, came up out of the Nile after them, and stood by the other cows on the bank of the Nile. [4] The ugly and thin cows ate up the seven sleek and fat cows. And Pharaoh awoke. [5] Then he fell asleep and dreamed a second time; seven ears of grain, plump and good, were growing on one stalk. [6] Then seven ears, thin and blighted by the east wind, sprouted after them. [7] The thin ears swallowed up the seven plump and full ears. Pharaoh awoke, and it was a dream. [8] In the morning his spirit was troubled; so he sent and called for all the magicians of Egypt and all its wise men. Pharaoh told them his dreams, but there was no one who could interpret them to Pharaoh.

9 Then the chief cupbearer said to Pharaoh, "I remember my faults today. [10] Once Pharaoh was angry with his servants, and put me and the chief baker in custody in the house of the captain of the guard. [11] We dreamed on the same night, he and I, each having a dream with its own meaning. [12] A young Hebrew was there with us, a servant of the captain of the guard. When we told him, he interpreted our dreams to us, giving an interpretation to each according to his dream. [13] As he interpreted to us, so it turned out; I was restored to my office, and the baker was hanged."

14 Then Pharaoh sent for Joseph, and he was hurriedly brought out of the dungeon. When he had shaved himself and changed his clothes, he came in before Pharaoh. [15] And Pharaoh said to Joseph, "I have had a dream, and there is no one who can interpret it. I have heard it said of you that when you hear a dream you can interpret it." [16] Joseph answered Pharaoh, "It is not I; God will give Pharaoh a favorable answer." [17] Then Pharaoh said to Joseph, "In my dream I was standing on the banks of the Nile; [18] and seven cows, fat and sleek, came up out of the Nile and fed in the reed grass. [19] Then seven other cows came up after them, poor, very ugly, and thin. Never had I seen such ugly ones in all the land of Egypt. [20] The thin and ugly cows ate up the first seven fat cows, [21] but when they had eaten them no one would have

known that they had done so, for they were still as ugly as before. Then I awoke. [22] I fell asleep a second time[a] and I saw in my dream seven ears of grain, full and good, growing on one stalk, [23] and seven ears, withered, thin, and blighted by the east wind, sprouting after them; [24] and the thin ears swallowed up the seven good ears. But when I told it to the magicians, there was no one who could explain it to me."

25 Then Joseph said to Pharaoh, "Pharaoh's dreams are one and the same; God has revealed to Pharaoh what he is about to do. [26] The seven good cows are seven years, and the seven good ears are seven years; the dreams are one. [27] The seven lean and ugly cows that came up after them are seven years, as are the seven empty ears blighted by the east wind. They are seven years of famine. [28] It is as I told Pharaoh; God has shown to Pharaoh what he is about to do. [29] There will come seven years of great plenty throughout all the land of Egypt. [30] After them there will arise seven years of famine, and all the plenty will be forgotten in the land of Egypt; the famine will consume the land. [31] The plenty will no longer be known in the land because of the famine that will follow, for it will be very grievous. [32] And the doubling of Pharaoh's dream means that the thing is fixed by God, and God will shortly bring it about. [33] Now therefore let Pharaoh select a man who is discerning and wise, and set him over the land of Egypt. [34] Let Pharaoh proceed to appoint overseers over the land, and take one-fifth of the produce of the land of Egypt during the seven plenteous years. [35] Let them gather all the food of these good years that are coming, and lay up grain under the authority of Pharaoh for food in the cities, and let them keep it. [36] That food shall be a reserve for the land against the seven years of famine that are to befall the land of Egypt, so that the land may not perish through the famine."

Joseph's Rise to Power

37 The proposal pleased Pharaoh and all his servants. [38] Pharaoh said to his servants, "Can we find anyone else like this—one in whom is the spirit of God?" [39] So Pharaoh said to Joseph, "Since God has shown you all this, there is no one so discerning and wise as you. [40] You shall be over my house, and all my people shall order themselves as you command; only with regard to the throne will I be greater than you." [41] And Pharaoh said to Joseph, "See, I have set you over all the land of Egypt." [42] Removing his signet ring from his hand, Pharaoh put it on Joseph's hand; he

---

a Gk Syr Vg: Heb lacks *I fell asleep a second time*

arrayed him in garments of fine linen, and put a gold chain around his neck. [43]He had him ride in the chariot of his second-in-command; and they cried out in front of him, "Bow the knee!"[a] Thus he set him over all the land of Egypt. [44]Moreover Pharaoh said to Joseph, "I am Pharaoh, and without your consent no one shall lift up hand or foot in all the land of Egypt." [45]Pharaoh gave Joseph the name Zaphenath-paneah; and he gave him Asenath daughter of Potiphera, priest of On, as his wife. Thus Joseph gained authority over the land of Egypt.

46 Joseph was thirty years old when he entered the service of Pharaoh king of Egypt. And Joseph went out from the presence of Pharaoh, and went through all the land of Egypt. [47]During the seven plenteous years the earth produced abundantly. [48]He gathered up all the food of the seven years when there was plenty[b] in the land of Egypt, and stored up food in the cities; he stored up in every city the food from the fields around it. [49]So Joseph stored up grain in such abundance—like the sand of the sea—that he stopped measuring it; it was beyond measure.

50 Before the years of famine came, Joseph had two sons, whom Asenath daughter of Potiphera, priest of On, bore to him. [51]Joseph named the first-born Manasseh,[c] "For," he said, "God has made me forget all my hardship and all my father's house." [52]The second he named Ephraim,[d] "For God has made me fruitful in the land of my misfortunes."

53 The seven years of plenty that prevailed in the land of Egypt came to an end; [54]and the seven years of famine began to come, just as Joseph had said. There was famine in every country, but throughout the land of Egypt there was bread. [55]When all the land of Egypt was famished, the people cried to Pharaoh for bread. Pharaoh said to all the Egyptians, "Go to Joseph; what he says to you, do." [56]And since the famine had spread over all the land, Joseph opened all the storehouses,[e] and sold to the Egyptians, for the famine was severe in the land of Egypt. [57]Moreover, all the world came to Joseph in Egypt to buy grain, because the famine became severe throughout the world.

Joseph's Brothers Go to Egypt

42 When Jacob learned that there was grain in Egypt, he said to his sons, "Why do you keep looking at one another? [2]I have heard," he said, "that there is grain in Egypt; go down and buy grain for us there, that we may live and not die." [3]So ten of Joseph's brothers went down to buy grain in Egypt. [4]But Jacob did not send Joseph's brother Benjamin with his brothers, for he feared that harm might come to him. [5]Thus the sons of Israel were among the other people who came to buy grain, for the famine had reached the land of Canaan.

6 Now Joseph was governor over the land; it was he who sold to all the people of the land. And Joseph's brothers came and bowed themselves before him with their faces to the ground. [7]When Joseph saw his brothers, he recognized them, but he treated them like strangers and spoke harshly to them. "Where do you come from?" he said. They said, "From the land of Canaan, to buy food." [8]Although Joseph had recognized his brothers, they did not recognize him. [9]Joseph also remembered the dreams that he had dreamed about them. He said to them, "You are spies; you have come to see the nakedness of the land!" [10]They said to him, "No, my lord; your servants have come to buy food. [11]We are all sons of one man; we are honest men; your servants have never been spies." [12]But he said to them, "No, you have come to see the nakedness of the land!" [13]They said, "We, your servants, are twelve brothers, the sons of a certain man in the land of Canaan; the youngest, however, is now with our father, and one is no more." [14]But Joseph said to them, "It is just as I have said to you; you are spies! [15]Here is how you shall be tested: as Pharaoh lives, you shall not leave this place unless your youngest brother comes here! [16]Let one of you go and bring your brother, while the rest of you remain in prison, in order that your words may be tested, whether there is truth in you; or else, as Pharaoh lives, surely you are spies." [17]And he put them all together in prison for three days.

18 On the third day Joseph said to them, "Do this and you will live, for I fear God: [19]if you are honest men, let one of your brothers stay here where you are imprisoned. The rest of you shall go and carry grain for the famine of your households, [20]and bring your youngest brother to me. Thus your words will be verified, and you shall not die." And they agreed to do so. [21]They said to one another, "Alas, we are paying the penalty for what we did to our brother; we saw his anguish when he pleaded with us, but we would not listen. That is why this anguish has come upon us." [22]Then Reuben answered them, "Did I not tell you not to wrong the boy? But you would not listen. So now there comes a reckoning for his blood." [23]They did not know that Joseph understood them,

---

a *Abrek,* apparently an Egyptian word similar in sound to the Hebrew word meaning *to kneel*　　**b** Sam Gk: MT *the seven years that were*　　**c** That is *Making to forget*　　**d** From a Hebrew word meaning *to be fruitful*　　**e** Gk Vg Compare Syr: Heb *opened all that was in* (or, *among*) *them*

since he spoke with them through an interpreter. [24]He turned away from them and wept; then he returned and spoke to them. And he picked out Simeon and had him bound before their eyes. [25]Joseph then gave orders to fill their bags with grain, to return every man's money to his sack, and to give them provisions for their journey. This was done for them.

Joseph's Brothers Return to Canaan

26 They loaded their donkeys with their grain, and departed. [27]When one of them opened his sack to give his donkey fodder at the lodging place, he saw his money at the top of the sack. [28]He said to his brothers, "My money has been put back; here it is in my sack!" At this they lost heart and turned trembling to one another, saying, "What is this that God has done to us?"

29 When they came to their father Jacob in the land of Canaan, they told him all that had happened to them, saying, [30]"The man, the lord of the land, spoke harshly to us, and charged us with spying on the land. [31]But we said to him, 'We are honest men, we are not spies. [32]We are twelve brothers, sons of our father; one is no more, and the youngest is now with our father in the land of Canaan.' [33]Then the man, the lord of the land, said to us, 'By this I shall know that you are honest men: leave one of your brothers with me, take grain for the famine of your households, and go your way. [34]Bring your youngest brother to me, and I shall know that you are not spies but honest men. Then I will release your brother to you, and you may trade in the land.'"

35 As they were emptying their sacks, there in each one's sack was his bag of money. When they and their father saw their bundles of money, they were dismayed. [36]And their father Jacob said to them, "I am the one you have bereaved of children: Joseph is no more, and Simeon is no more, and now you would take Benjamin. All this has happened to me!" [37]Then Reuben said to his father, "You may kill my two sons if I do not bring him back to you. Put him in my hands, and I will bring him back to you." [38]But he said, "My son shall not go down with you, for his brother is dead, and he alone is left. If harm should come to him on the journey that you are to make, you would bring down my gray hairs with sorrow to Sheol."

43 The Brothers Come Again, Bringing Benjamin

Now the famine was severe in the land.

[2]And when they had eaten up the grain that they had brought from Egypt, their father said to them, "Go again, buy us a little more food." [3]But Judah said to him, "The man solemnly warned us, saying, 'You shall not see my face unless your brother is with you.' [4]If you will send our brother with us, we will go down and buy you food; [5]but if you will not send him, we will not go down, for the man said to us, 'You shall not see my face, unless your brother is with you.'" [6]Israel said, "Why did you treat me so badly as to tell the man that you had another brother?" [7]They replied, "The man questioned us carefully about ourselves and our kindred, saying, 'Is your father still alive? Have you another brother?' What we told him was in answer to these questions. Could we in any way know that he would say, 'Bring your brother down'?" [8]Then Judah said to his father Israel, "Send the boy with me, and let us be on our way, so that we may live and not die—you and we and also our little ones. [9]I myself will be surety for him; you can hold me accountable for him. If I do not bring him back to you and set him before you, then let me bear the blame forever. [10]If we had not delayed, we would now have returned twice."

11 Then their father Israel said to them, "If it must be so, then do this: take some of the choice fruits of the land in your bags, and carry them down as a present to the man—a little balm and a little honey, gum, resin, pistachio nuts, and almonds. [12]Take double the money with you. Carry back with you the money that was returned in the top of your sacks; perhaps it was an oversight. [13]Take your brother also, and be on your way again to the man; [14]may God Almighty[a] grant you mercy before the man, so that he may send back your other brother and Benjamin. As for me, if I am bereaved of my children, I am bereaved." [15]So the men took the present, and they took double the money with them, as well as Benjamin. Then they went on their way down to Egypt, and stood before Joseph.

16 When Joseph saw Benjamin with them, he said to the steward of his house, "Bring the men into the house, and slaughter an animal and make ready, for the men are to dine with me at noon." [17]The man did as Joseph said, and brought the men to Joseph's house. [18]Now the men were afraid because they were brought to Joseph's house, and they said, "It is because of the money, replaced in our sacks the first time, that we have been brought in, so that he may have an opportunity to fall upon us, to make slaves

---

α Traditional rendering of Heb *El Shaddai*

of us and take our donkeys." [19]So they went up to the steward of Joseph's house and spoke with him at the entrance to the house. [20]They said, "Oh, my lord, we came down the first time to buy food; [21]and when we came to the lodging place we opened our sacks, and there was each one's money in the top of his sack, our money in full weight. So we have brought it back with us. [22]Moreover we have brought down with us additional money to buy food. We do not know who put our money in our sacks." [23]He replied, "Rest assured, do not be afraid; your God and the God of your father must have put treasure in your sacks for you; I received your money." Then he brought Simeon out to them. [24]When the steward[a] had brought the men into Joseph's house, and given them water, and they had washed their feet, and when he had given their donkeys fodder, [25]they made the present ready for Joseph's coming at noon, for they had heard that they would dine there.

26 When Joseph came home, they brought him the present that they had carried into the house, and bowed to the ground before him. [27]He inquired about their welfare, and said, "Is your father well, the old man of whom you spoke? Is he still alive?" [28]They said, "Your servant our father is well; he is still alive." And they bowed their heads and did obeisance. [29]Then he looked up and saw his brother Benjamin, his mother's son, and said, "Is this your youngest brother, of whom you spoke to me? God be gracious to you, my son!" [30]With that, Joseph hurried out, because he was overcome with affection for his brother, and he was about to weep. So he went into a private room and wept there. [31]Then he washed his face and came out; and controlling himself he said, "Serve the meal." [32]They served him by himself, and them by themselves, and the Egyptians who ate with him by themselves, because the Egyptians could not eat with the Hebrews, for that is an abomination to the Egyptians. [33]When they were seated before him, the firstborn according to his birthright and the youngest according to his youth, the men looked at one another in amazement. [34]Portions were taken to them from Joseph's table, but Benjamin's portion was five times as much as any of theirs. So they drank and were merry with him.

Joseph Detains Benjamin

44 Then he commanded the steward of his house, "Fill the men's sacks with food, as much as they can carry, and put each man's money in the top of his sack. [2]Put my cup, the silver cup, in the top of the sack of the youngest, with his money for the grain." And he did as Joseph told him. [3]As soon as the morning was light, the men were sent away with their donkeys. [4]When they had gone only a short distance from the city, Joseph said to his steward, "Go, follow after the men; and when you overtake them, say to them, 'Why have you returned evil for good? Why have you stolen my silver cup?[b] [5]Is it not from this that my lord drinks? Does he not indeed use it for divination? You have done wrong in doing this.'"

6 When he overtook them, he repeated these words to them. [7]They said to him, "Why does my lord speak such words as these? Far be it from your servants that they should do such a thing! [8]Look, the money that we found at the top of our sacks, we brought back to you from the land of Canaan; why then would we steal silver or gold from your lord's house? [9]Should it be found with any one of your servants, let him die; moreover the rest of us will become my lord's slaves." [10]He said, "Even so; in accordance with your words, let it be: he with whom it is found shall become my slave, but the rest of you shall go free." [11]Then each one quickly lowered his sack to the ground, and each opened his sack. [12]He searched, beginning with the eldest and ending with the youngest; and the cup was found in Benjamin's sack. [13]At this they tore their clothes. Then each one loaded his donkey, and they returned to the city.

14 Judah and his brothers came to Joseph's house while he was still there; and they fell to the ground before him. [15]Joseph said to them, "What deed is this that you have done? Do you not know that one such as I can practice divination?" [16]And Judah said, "What can we say to my lord? What can we speak? How can we clear ourselves? God has found out the guilt of your servants; here we are then, my lord's slaves, both we and also the one in whose possession the cup has been found." [17]But he said, "Far be it from me that I should do so! Only the one in whose possession the cup was found shall be my slave; but as for you, go up in peace to your father."

Judah Pleads for Benjamin's Release

18 Then Judah stepped up to him and said, "O my lord, let your servant please speak a word in my lord's ears, and do not be angry with your servant; for you are like Pharaoh himself. [19]My lord asked his ser-

---

a Heb *the man*   b Gk Compare Vg: Heb lacks *Why have you stolen my silver cup?*

vants, saying, 'Have you a father or a brother?' ²⁰And we said to my lord, 'We have a father, an old man, and a young brother, the child of his old age. His brother is dead; he alone is left of his mother's children, and his father loves him.' ²¹Then you said to your servants, 'Bring him down to me, so that I may set my eyes on him.' ²²We said to my lord, 'The boy cannot leave his father, for if he should leave his father, his father would die.' ²³Then you said to your servants, 'Unless your youngest brother comes down with you, you shall see my face no more.' ²⁴When we went back to your servant my father we told him the words of my lord. ²⁵And when our father said, 'Go again, buy us a little food,' ²⁶we said, 'We cannot go down. Only if our youngest brother goes with us, will we go down; for we cannot see the man's face unless our youngest brother is with us.' ²⁷Then your servant my father said to us, 'You know that my wife bore me two sons; ²⁸one left me, and I said, Surely he has been torn to pieces; and I have never seen him since. ²⁹If you take this one also from me, and harm comes to him, you will bring down my gray hairs in sorrow to Sheol.' ³⁰Now therefore, when I come to your servant my father and the boy is not with us, then, as his life is bound up in the boy's life, ³¹when he sees that the boy is not with us, he will die; and your servants will bring down the gray hairs of your servant our father with sorrow to Sheol. ³²For your servant became surety for the boy to my father, saying, 'If I do not bring him back to you, then I will bear the blame in the sight of my father all my life.' ³³Now therefore, please let your servant remain as a slave to my lord in place of the boy; and let the boy go back with his brothers. ³⁴For how can I go back to my father if the boy is not with me? I fear to see the suffering that would come upon my father."

45 Joseph Reveals Himself to His Brothers

Then Joseph could no longer control himself before all those who stood by him, and he cried out, "Send everyone away from me." So no one stayed with him when Joseph made himself known to his brothers. ²And he wept so loudly that the Egyptians heard it, and the household of Pharaoh heard it. ³Joseph said to his brothers, "I am Joseph. Is my father still alive?" But his brothers could not answer him, so dismayed were they at his presence.

4 Then Joseph said to his brothers, "Come closer to me." And they came closer. He said, "I am your brother, Joseph, whom you sold into Egypt. ⁵And now do not be distressed, or angry with yourselves, because you sold me here; for God sent me before you to preserve life. ⁶For the famine has been in the land these two years; and there are five more years in which there will be neither plowing nor harvest. ⁷God sent me before you to preserve for you a remnant on earth, and to keep alive for you many survivors. ⁸So it was not you who sent me here, but God; he has made me a father to Pharaoh, and lord of all his house and ruler over all the land of Egypt. ⁹Hurry and go up to my father and say to him, 'Thus says your son Joseph, God has made me lord of all Egypt; come down to me, do not delay. ¹⁰You shall settle in the land of Goshen, and you shall be near me, you and your children and your children's children, as well as your flocks, your herds, and all that you have. ¹¹I will provide for you there—since there are five more years of famine to come—so that you and your household, and all that you have, will not come to poverty.' ¹²And now your eyes and the eyes of my brother Benjamin see that it is my own mouth that speaks to you. ¹³You must tell my father how greatly I am honored in Egypt, and all that you have seen. Hurry and bring my father down here." ¹⁴Then he fell upon his brother Benjamin's neck and wept, while Benjamin wept upon his neck. ¹⁵And he kissed all his brothers and wept upon them; and after that his brothers talked with him.

16 When the report was heard in Pharaoh's house, "Joseph's brothers have come," Pharaoh and his servants were pleased. ¹⁷Pharaoh said to Joseph, "Say to your brothers, 'Do this: load your animals and go back to the land of Canaan. ¹⁸Take your father and your households and come to me, so that I may give you the best of the land of Egypt, and you may enjoy the fat of the land.' ¹⁹You are further charged to say, 'Do this: take wagons from the land of Egypt for your little ones and for your wives, and bring your father, and come. ²⁰Give no thought to your possessions, for the best of all the land of Egypt is yours.' "

21 The sons of Israel did so. Joseph gave them wagons according to the instruction of Pharaoh, and he gave them provisions for the journey. ²²To each one of them he gave a set of garments; but to Benjamin he gave three hundred pieces of silver and five sets of garments. ²³To his father he sent the following: ten donkeys loaded with the good things of Egypt, and ten female donkeys loaded with grain,

God's Master Plan · Genesis 45:4–8

After Joseph's emotional reconciliation with his brothers, he tells them about God's bigger picture. Because they sold him into slavery, Joseph was able to rise to power in Egypt and save them from famine. Now he can invite them to stay as guests of the pharaoh. Joseph realizes that good has come out of evil. He sees the events of his family's life as part of God's plan to preserve life and to make sure the covenant continues.

Joseph's insight doesn't justify what his brothers did, but it shows that good can even come out of tragedy. It's hard to see the purpose when we're in the middle of a hard situation, but time often helps give us perspective and insight. These are the rewards of trust and faith. Joseph remained faithful despite many difficulties. Do your best to do the same, confident that nothing can thwart God's saving plans.

- When have you experienced good things coming out of a bad situation? Have you ever felt as though God has messed up part of your life, but then realized God has worked out something good that you never expected?
- What problems are you facing now? Offer them to God by writing them down and, through a symbolic act of surrender, burn the paper in a fireplace.

bread, and provision for his father on the journey. [24] Then he sent his brothers on their way, and as they were leaving he said to them, "Do not quarrel[a] along the way."

25 So they went up out of Egypt and came to their father Jacob in the land of Canaan. [26] And they told him, "Joseph is still alive! He is even ruler over all the land of Egypt." He was stunned; he could not believe them. [27] But when they told him all the words of Joseph that he had said to them, and when he saw the wagons that Joseph had sent to carry him, the spirit of their father Jacob revived. [28] Israel said, "Enough! My son Joseph is still alive. I must go and see him before I die."

Jacob Brings His Whole Family to Egypt

46 When Israel set out on his journey with all that he had and came to Beer-sheba, he offered sacrifices to the God of his father Isaac. [2] God spoke to Israel in visions of the night, and said, "Jacob, Jacob." And he said, "Here I am." [3] Then he said, "I am God,[b] the God of your father; do not be afraid to go down to Egypt, for I will make of you a great nation there. [4] I myself will go down with you to Egypt, and I will also bring you up again; and Joseph's own hand shall close your eyes."

5 Then Jacob set out from Beer-sheba; and the sons of Israel carried their father Jacob, their little ones, and their wives, in the wagons that Pharaoh had sent to carry him. [6] They also took their livestock and the goods that they had acquired in the land of Canaan, and they came into Egypt, Jacob and all his offspring with him, [7] his sons, and his sons' sons with him, his daughters, and his sons' daughters; all his offspring he brought with him into Egypt.

8 Now these are the names of the Israelites, Jacob and his offspring, who came to Egypt. Reuben, Jacob's firstborn, [9] and the children of Reuben: Hanoch, Pallu, Hezron, and Carmi. [10] The children of Simeon: Jemuel, Jamin, Ohad, Jachin, Zohar, and Shaul,[c] the son of a Canaanite woman. [11] The children of Levi: Gershon, Kohath, and Merari. [12] The children of Judah: Er, Onan, Shelah, Perez, and Zerah (but Er and Onan died in the land of Canaan); and the children of Perez were Hezron and Hamul. [13] The children of Issachar: Tola, Puvah, Jashub,[d] and Shimron. [14] The children of Zebulun: Sered, Elon, and Jahleel [15] (these are the sons of Leah, whom she bore to Jacob in Paddan-aram, together with his daughter Dinah; in all his sons and his daughters numbered thirty-three). [16] The children of Gad: Ziphion, Haggi, Shuni, Ezbon, Eri, Arodi, and Areli. [17] The children of Asher: Imnah, Ishvah, Ishvi, Beriah, and their sister Serah. The children of Beriah: Heber and Malchiel [18] (these are the children of Zilpah, whom Laban gave to his

a Or *be agitated*   b Heb *the God*   c Or *Saul*   d Compare Sam Gk Num 26.24; 1 Chr 7.1: MT *Iob*

daughter Leah; and these she bore to Jacob—sixteen persons). [19]The children of Jacob's wife Rachel: Joseph and Benjamin. [20]To Joseph in the land of Egypt were born Manasseh and Ephraim, whom Asenath daughter of Potiphera, priest of On, bore to him. [21]The children of Benjamin: Bela, Becher, Ashbel, Gera, Naaman, Ehi, Rosh, Muppim, Huppim, and Ard [22](these are the children of Rachel, who were born to Jacob—fourteen persons in all). [23]The children of Dan: Hashum.[a] [24]The children of Naphtali: Jahzeel, Guni, Jezer, and Shillem [25](these are the children of Bilhah, whom Laban gave to his daughter Rachel, and these she bore to Jacob—seven persons in all). [26]All the persons belonging to Jacob who came into Egypt, who were his own offspring, not including the wives of his sons, were sixty-six persons in all. [27]The children of Joseph, who were born to him in Egypt, were two; all the persons of the house of Jacob who came into Egypt were seventy.

Jacob Settles in Goshen

28 Israel[b] sent Judah ahead to Joseph to lead the way before him into Goshen. When they came to the land of Goshen, [29]Joseph made ready his chariot and went up to meet his father Israel in Goshen. He presented himself to him, fell on his neck, and wept on his neck a good while. [30]Israel said to Joseph, "I can die now, having seen for myself that you are still alive." [31]Joseph said to his brothers and to his father's household, "I will go up and tell Pharaoh, and will say to him, 'My brothers and my father's household, who were in the land of Canaan, have come to me. [32]The men are shepherds, for they have been keepers of livestock; and they have brought their flocks, and their herds, and all that they have.' [33]When Pharaoh calls you, and says, 'What is your occupation?' [34]you shall say, 'Your servants have been keepers of livestock from our youth even until now, both we and our ancestors'—in order that you may settle in the land of Goshen, because all shepherds are abhorrent to the Egyptians."

47 So Joseph went and told Pharaoh, "My father and my brothers, with their flocks and herds and all that they possess, have come from the land of Canaan; they are now in the land of Goshen." [2]From among his brothers he took five men and presented them to Pharaoh. [3]Pharaoh said to his brothers, "What is your occupation?" And they said to Pharaoh, "Your servants are shepherds, as our ancestors were." [4]They said to Pharaoh, "We have come to reside as aliens in the land; for there is no pasture for your servants' flocks because the famine is severe in the land of Canaan. Now, we ask you, let your servants settle in the land of Goshen." [5]Then Pharaoh said to Joseph, "Your father and your brothers have come to you. [6]The land of Egypt is before you; settle your father and your brothers in the best part of the land; let them live in the land of Goshen; and if you know that there are capable men among them, put them in charge of my livestock."

7 Then Joseph brought in his father Jacob, and presented him before Pharaoh, and Jacob blessed Pharaoh. [8]Pharaoh said to Jacob, "How many are the years of your life?" [9]Jacob said to Pharaoh, "The years of my earthly sojourn are one hundred thirty; few and hard have been the years of my life. They do not compare with the years of the life of my ancestors during their long sojourn." [10]Then Jacob blessed Pharaoh, and went out from the presence of Pharaoh. [11]Joseph settled his father and his brothers, and granted them a holding in the land of Egypt, in the best part of the land, in the land of Rameses, as Pharaoh had instructed. [12]And Joseph provided his father, his brothers, and all his father's household with food, according to the number of their dependents.

The Famine in Egypt

13 Now there was no food in all the land, for the famine was very severe. The land of Egypt and the land of Canaan languished because of the famine. [14]Joseph collected all the money to be found in the land of Egypt and in the land of Canaan, in exchange for the grain that they bought; and Joseph brought the money into Pharaoh's house. [15]When the money from the land of Egypt and from the land of Canaan was spent, all the Egyptians came to Joseph, and said, "Give us food! Why should we die before your eyes? For our money is gone." [16]And Joseph answered, "Give me your livestock, and I will give you food in exchange for your livestock, if your money is gone." [17]So they brought their livestock to Joseph; and Joseph gave them food in exchange for the horses, the flocks, the herds, and the donkeys. That year he supplied them with food in exchange for all their livestock. [18]When that year was ended, they came to him the following year, and said to him, "We can not hide from my lord that our money is all spent; and the herds of cattle are my lord's. There is nothing left in the sight of my lord but our bodies and our lands. [19]Shall we die before your eyes, both we and our land?

Buy us and our land in exchange for food. We with our land will become slaves to Pharaoh; just give us seed, so that we may live and not die, and that the land may not become desolate."

20 So Joseph bought all the land of Egypt for Pharaoh. All the Egyptians sold their fields, because the famine was severe upon them; and the land became Pharaoh's. [21]As for the people, he made slaves of them[a] from one end of Egypt to the other. [22]Only the land of the priests he did not buy; for the priests had a fixed allowance from Pharaoh, and lived on the allowance that Pharaoh gave them; therefore they did not sell their land. [23]Then Joseph said to the people, "Now that I have this day bought you and your land for Pharaoh, here is seed for you; sow the land. [24]And at the harvests you shall give one-fifth to Pharaoh, and four-fifths shall be your own, as seed for the field and as food for yourselves and your households, and as food for your little ones." [25]They said, "You have saved our lives; may it please my lord, we will be slaves to Pharaoh." [26]So Joseph made it a statute concerning the land of Egypt, and it stands to this day, that Pharaoh should have the fifth. The land of the priests alone did not become Pharaoh's.

The Last Days of Jacob

27 Thus Israel settled in the land of Egypt, in the region of Goshen, and they gained possessions in it, and were fruitful and multiplied exceedingly. [28]Jacob lived in the land of Egypt seventeen years; so the days of Jacob, the years of his life, were one hundred forty-seven years.

29 When the time of Israel's death drew near, he called his son Joseph and said to him, "If I have found favor with you, put your hand under my thigh and promise to deal loyally and truly with me. Do not bury me in Egypt. [30]When I lie down with my ancestors, carry me out of Egypt and bury me in their burial place." He answered, "I will do as you have said." [31]And he said, "Swear to me"; and he swore to him. Then Israel bowed himself on the head of his bed.

48

Jacob Blesses Joseph's Sons

After this Joseph was told, "Your father is ill." So he took with him his two sons, Manasseh and Ephraim. [2]When Jacob was told, "Your son Joseph has come to you," he[b] summoned his strength and sat up in bed. [3]And Jacob said to Joseph, "God Almighty[c] appeared to me at Luz in the land of Canaan, and he blessed me, [4]and said to me, 'I am

going to make you fruitful and increase your numbers; I will make of you a company of peoples, and will give this land to your offspring after you for a perpetual holding.' [5]Therefore your two sons, who were born to you in the land of Egypt before I came to you in Egypt, are now mine; Ephraim and Manasseh shall be mine, just as Reuben and Simeon are. [6]As for the offspring born to you after them, they shall be yours. They shall be recorded under the names of their brothers with regard to their inheritance. [7]For when I came from Paddan, Rachel, alas, died in the land of Canaan on the way, while there was still some distance to go to Ephrath; and I buried her there on the way to Ephrath" (that is, Bethlehem).

8 When Israel saw Joseph's sons, he said, "Who are these?" [9]Joseph said to his father, "They are my sons, whom God has given me here." And he said, "Bring them to me, please, that I may bless them." [10]Now the eyes of Israel were dim with age, and he could not see well. So Joseph brought them near him; and he kissed them and embraced them. [11]Israel said to Joseph, "I did not expect to see your face; and here God has let me see your children also." [12]Then Joseph removed them from his father's knees,[d] and he bowed himself with his face to the earth. [13]Joseph took them both, Ephraim in his right hand toward Israel's left, and Manasseh in his left hand toward Israel's right, and brought them near him. [14]But Israel stretched out his right hand and laid it on the head of Ephraim, who was the younger, and his left hand on the head of Manasseh, crossing his hands, for Manasseh was the firstborn. [15]He blessed Joseph, and said,

"The God before whom my ancestors Abraham
and Isaac walked,
the God who has been my shepherd all my life
to this day,
16 the angel who has redeemed me from all harm,
bless the boys;
and in them let my name be perpetuated, and
the name of my ancestors Abraham
and Isaac;
and let them grow into a multitude on the
earth."

17 When Joseph saw that his father laid his right hand on the head of Ephraim, it displeased him; so he took his father's hand, to remove it from Ephraim's head to Manasseh's head. [18]Joseph said to his father, "Not so, my father! Since this one is the firstborn, put your right hand on his head." [19]But his father refused, and said, "I know, my son, I know; he also shall be-

---

a Sam Gk Compare Vg: MT *He removed them to the cities*   b Heb *Israel*   c Traditional rendering of Heb *El Shaddai*   d Heb *from his knees*

come a people, and he also shall be great. Nevertheless his younger brother shall be greater than he, and his offspring shall become a multitude of nations." [20]So he blessed them that day, saying,

"By you[a] Israel will invoke blessings, saying,

'God make you[a] like Ephraim and like
     Manasseh.' "

So he put Ephraim ahead of Manasseh. [21]Then Israel said to Joseph, "I am about to die, but God will be with you and will bring you again to the land of your

---

STUDY IT!

Israel's Ancestry · Genesis 49:1–28

Although the Israelites descended from many different relatives, the book of Genesis traces their origins back to a series of common ancestors. This connected family tree served to unite them as a people. Genesis tells the stories of those great ancestors, men and women called patriarchs and matriarchs, who were the founders of what later became the people of Israel. The twelve tribes of Israel are understood to be descendants of Jacob's twelve sons. Twelve becomes an important number that comes up again and again in the Bible. For example, the twelve apostles are Jesus' closest followers in the New Testament.

It can be confusing to remember who is related to whom, so here's a chart to keep everyone straight:

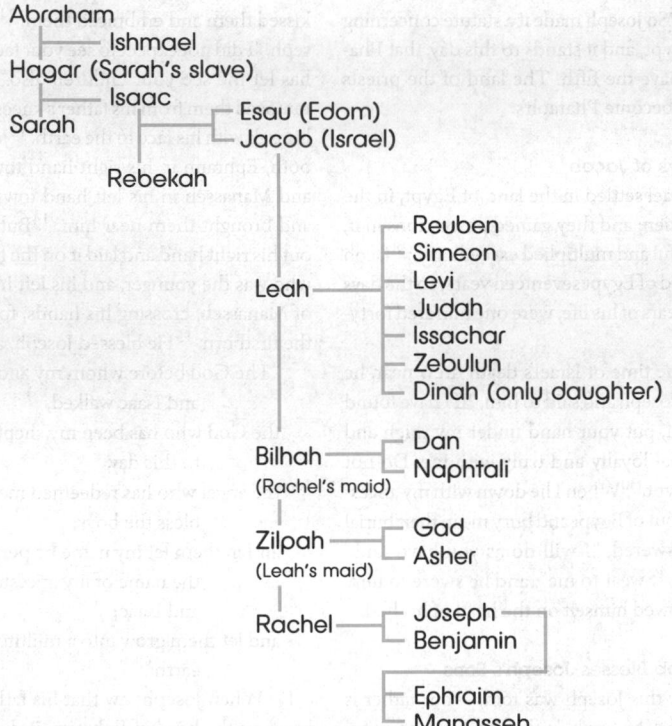

- Levi's tribe was set aside as priests and was not assigned land after the conquest of Canaan.
- Joseph is the father of two tribes, because Jacob adopted Joseph's sons, Ephraim and Manasseh.

---

a you here is singular in Heb

ancestors. [22]I now give to you one portion[a] more than to your brothers, the portion[a] that I took from the hand of the Amorites with my sword and with my bow."

49 Jacob's Last Words to His Sons

Then Jacob called his sons, and said: "Gather around, that I may tell you what will happen to you in days to come.

2 Assemble and hear, O sons of Jacob;
   listen to Israel your father.

3 Reuben, you are my firstborn,
   my might and the first fruits of my vigor,
   excelling in rank and excelling in power.

4 Unstable as water, you shall no longer excel
   because you went up onto your father's
      bed;
   then you defiled it—you[b] went up onto
      my couch!

5 Simeon and Levi are brothers;
   weapons of violence are their swords.

6 May I never come into their council;
   may I not be joined to their company—
   for in their anger they killed men,
   and at their whim they hamstrung oxen.

7 Cursed be their anger, for it is fierce,
   and their wrath, for it is cruel!
   I will divide them in Jacob,
   and scatter them in Israel.

8 Judah, your brothers shall praise you;
   your hand shall be on the neck of your
      enemies;
   your father's sons shall bow down
      before you.

9 Judah is a lion's whelp;
   from the prey, my son, you have gone up.
   He crouches down, he stretches out like a lion,
   like a lioness—who dares rouse him up?

10 The scepter shall not depart from Judah,
   nor the ruler's staff from between his feet,
   until tribute comes to him;[c]
   and the obedience of the peoples is his.

11 Binding his foal to the vine
   and his donkey's colt to the choice vine,
   he washes his garments in wine
   and his robe in the blood of grapes;

12 his eyes are darker than wine,
   and his teeth whiter than milk.

13 Zebulun shall settle at the shore of the sea;
   he shall be a haven for ships,
   and his border shall be at Sidon.

14 Issachar is a strong donkey,
   lying down between the sheepfolds;

15 he saw that a resting place was good,
   and that the land was pleasant;
   so he bowed his shoulder to the burden,
   and became a slave at forced labor.

16 Dan shall judge his people
   as one of the tribes of Israel.

17 Dan shall be a snake by the roadside,
   a viper along the path,
   that bites the horse's heels
   so that its rider falls backward.

18 I wait for your salvation, O Lord.

19 Gad shall be raided by raiders,
   but he shall raid at their heels.

20 Asher's[d] food shall be rich,
   and he shall provide royal delicacies.

21 Naphtali is a doe let loose
   that bears lovely fawns.[e]

22 Joseph is a fruitful bough,
   a fruitful bough by a spring;
   his branches run over the wall.[f]

23 The archers fiercely attacked him;
   they shot at him and pressed him hard.

24 Yet his bow remained taut,
   and his arms[g] were made agile
   by the hands of the Mighty One of Jacob,
   by the name of the Shepherd, the Rock of
      Israel,

25 by the God of your father, who will help
      you,
   by the Almighty[h] who will bless you
   with blessings of heaven above,
   blessings of the deep that lies beneath,
   blessings of the breasts and of the womb.

26 The blessings of your father
   are stronger than the blessings of the
      eternal mountains,
   the bounties[i] of the everlasting hills;
   may they be on the head of Joseph,

a Or *mountain slope* (Heb *shekem*, a play on the name of the town and district of Shechem)   b Gk Syr Tg: Heb *he*   c Or *until Shiloh comes* or *until he comes to Shiloh* or (with Syr) *until he comes to whom it belongs*   d Gk Vg Syr: Heb *From Asher*   e Or *that gives beautiful words*   f Meaning of Heb uncertain   g Heb *the arms of his hands*   h Traditional rendering of Heb *Shaddai*   i Cn Compare Gk: Heb *of my progenitors to the boundaries*

on the brow of him who was set apart from
  his brothers.
27 Benjamin is a ravenous wolf,
    in the morning devouring the prey,
    and at evening dividing the spoil."

28 All these are the twelve tribes of Israel, and this
is what their father said to them when he blessed them,
blessing each one of them with a suitable blessing.

Jacob's Death and Burial

29 Then he charged them, saying to them, "I am
about to be gathered to my people. Bury me with my
ancestors—in the cave in the field of Ephron the
Hittite, [30]in the cave in the field at Machpelah, near
Mamre, in the land of Canaan, in the field that Abraham bought from Ephron the Hittite as a burial site.
[31]There Abraham and his wife Sarah were buried;
there Isaac and his wife Rebekah were buried; and
there I buried Leah— [32]the field and the cave that is
in it were purchased from the Hittites." [33]When Jacob
ended his charge to his sons, he drew up his feet into
the bed, breathed his last, and was gathered to his
people.

50 Then Joseph threw himself on his father's
face and wept over him and kissed him.
[2]Joseph commanded the physicians in his
service to embalm his father. So the physicians embalmed Israel; [3]they spent forty days in doing this,
for that is the time required for embalming. And the
Egyptians wept for him seventy days.

4 When the days of weeping for him were past,
Joseph addressed the household of Pharaoh, "If now
I have found favor with you, please speak to Pharaoh
as follows: [5]My father made me swear an oath; he
said, 'I am about to die. In the tomb that I hewed out
for myself in the land of Canaan, there you shall bury
me.' Now therefore let me go up, so that I may bury
my father; then I will return." [6]Pharaoh answered,
"Go up, and bury your father, as he made you swear
to do."

7 So Joseph went up to bury his father. With him
went up all the servants of Pharaoh, the elders of his
household, and all the elders of the land of Egypt, [8]as
well as all the household of Joseph, his brothers, and
his father's household. Only their children, their
flocks, and their herds were left in the land of Goshen.
[9]Both chariots and charioteers went up with him. It
was a very great company. [10]When they came to the
threshing floor of Atad, which is beyond the Jordan,
they held there a very great and sorrowful lamentation; and he observed a time of mourning for his
father seven days. [11]When the Canaanite inhabitants
of the land saw the mourning on the threshing floor
of Atad, they said, "This is a grievous mourning on
the part of the Egyptians." Therefore the place was
named Abel-mizraim;[a] it is beyond the Jordan.
[12]Thus his sons did for him as he had instructed
them. [13]They carried him to the land of Canaan and
buried him in the cave of the field at Machpelah, the
field near Mamre, which Abraham bought as a burial
site from Ephron the Hittite. [14]After he had buried
his father, Joseph returned to Egypt with his brothers and all who had gone up with him to bury his
father.

Joseph Forgives His Brothers

15 Realizing that their father was dead, Joseph's
brothers said, "What if Joseph still bears a grudge
against us and pays us back in full for all the wrong
that we did to him?" [16]So they approached[b] Joseph,
saying, "Your father gave this instruction before he
died, [17]'Say to Joseph: I beg you, forgive the crime
of your brothers and the wrong they did in harming
you.' Now therefore please forgive the crime of the
servants of the God of your father." Joseph wept
when they spoke to him. [18]Then his brothers also
wept,[c] fell down before him, and said, "We are here
as your slaves." [19]But Joseph said to them, "Do not
be afraid! Am I in the place of God? [20]Even though
you intended to do harm to me, God intended it for
good, in order to preserve a numerous people, as he
is doing today. [21]So have no fear; I myself will provide for you and your little ones." In this way he
reassured them, speaking kindly to them.

Joseph's Last Days and Death

22 So Joseph remained in Egypt, he and his father's household; and Joseph lived one hundred ten
years. [23]Joseph saw Ephraim's children of the third
generation; the children of Machir son of Manasseh
were also born on Joseph's knees.

24 Then Joseph said to his brothers, "I am about
to die; but God will surely come to you, and bring
you up out of this land to the land that he swore to
Abraham, to Isaac, and to Jacob." [25]So Joseph made
the Israelites swear, saying, "When God comes to
you, you shall carry up my bones from here." [26]And
Joseph died, being one hundred ten years old; he
was embalmed and placed in a coffin in Egypt.

a That is *mourning* (or *meadow*) *of Egypt*   b Gk Syr: Heb *they commanded*   c Cn: Heb *also came*

Exodus

Clank! Chains snap tight around your ankles. Crack! The tip of a whip slices across your back. Bang! A door slams, leaving you in darkness. These are the sounds of slavery—along with the groans of an oppressed people—and they come as a surprise at the beginning of Exodus. What happened after the happy ending in Genesis? Like an action-packed drama, Exodus tells a story of deceit and broken promises and of how God's miraculous interventions delivered the Israelites from their slavery in Egypt.

IN DEPTH

Exodus is the story of Israel's liberation. "Exodus" literally means "departure," and this book's central story shows God liberating the people from slavery in Egypt (an event called the exodus). Its main character is Moses, who is chosen by God to become the voice and the instrument of God's power. Exodus was written hundreds of years after these events, using oral traditions that described the origin of many of the Israelites' beliefs and religious rituals.

Exodus is divided into two main sections. The first section, Exodus 1-18, begins with the Israelites enslaved in Egypt and prohibited from worshiping their God. Israel cries out to God, and God answers by sending Moses. When Pharaoh refuses to let the Israelites go, God sends ten devastating plagues, and Pharaoh finally gives in. Then Pharaoh changes his mind and chases the Israelites, only to have his army destroyed after the Israelites' escape through the Red Sea. This section ends with the people wandering through the wilderness, sustained by food and water miraculously provided by God.

Section two, Exodus 19-40, occurs at Mount Sinai. There God enters into a covenant with all the people. God's part of the Sinai covenant is to guarantee continued protection. The Israelites' part is to be faithful to God alone, a faithfulness marked by special laws (Exodus 20-23) and special worship (Exodus 24-31) that unite them as a people. Exodus ends with Israel still encamped at Mount Sinai, struggling to become a people of the covenant.

The stories and laws in Exodus are at the heart of both Jewish and Christian belief in a God who saves, a God of freedom. Knowing these stories brings a richer understanding to the meaning of Jesus' life, death, and resurrection.

QUICK FACTS

- **Dates Covered:** From 1500 to 1250 B.C.
- **Author:** An unknown author who gathered oral traditions and stories from various tribal peoples around 500 to 400 B.C.
- **Themes:** The liberation of God's people from slavery and oppression, their wandering in the wilderness, and God's covenant marked by laws and rituals, much of which foreshadows the liberation, freedom, and new covenant that is to come through Jesus

AT A GLANCE

- **Exodus 1–10** Pharaoh's oppression, the call of Moses, the plagues
- **Exodus 11:1–15:21** The Passover, deliverance at the Red Sea
- **Exodus 15:22–18:27** The journey through the wilderness
- **Exodus 19:1–35:3** The covenant at Mount Sinai, difficulty living the covenant
- **Exodus 35:4–40:38** Construction of the tabernacle

1 These are the names of the sons of Israel who came to Egypt with Jacob, each with his household: [2]Reuben, Simeon, Levi, and Judah, [3]Issachar, Zebulun, and Benjamin, [4]Dan and Naphtali, Gad and Asher. [5]The total number of people born to Jacob was seventy. Joseph was already in Egypt. [6]Then Joseph died, and all his brothers, and that whole generation. [7]But the Israelites were fruitful and prolific; they multiplied and grew exceedingly strong, so that the land was filled with them.

The Israelites Are Oppressed

8 Now a new king arose over Egypt, who did not know Joseph. [9]He said to his people, "Look, the Israelite people are more numerous and more powerful than we. [10]Come, let us deal shrewdly with them, or they will increase and, in the event of war, join our enemies and fight against us and escape from the land." [11]Therefore they set taskmasters over them to oppress them with forced labor. They built supply cities, Pithom and Rameses, for Pharaoh. [12]But the more they were oppressed, the more they multiplied and spread, so that the Egyptians came to dread the Israelites. [13]The Egyptians became ruthless in imposing tasks on the Israelites, [14]and made their lives bitter with hard service in mortar and brick and in every kind of field labor. They were ruthless in all the tasks that they imposed on them.

15 The king of Egypt said to the Hebrew midwives, one of whom was named Shiphrah and the other Puah, [16]"When you act as midwives to the Hebrew women, and see them on the birthstool, if it is a boy, kill him; but if it is a girl, she shall live." [17]But the midwives feared God; they did not do as the king of Egypt commanded them, but they let the boys live. [18]So the king of Egypt summoned the midwives and said to them, "Why have you done this, and allowed the boys to live?" [19]The midwives said to Pharaoh, "Because the Hebrew women are not like the Egyptian women; for they are vigorous and give birth before the midwife comes to them." [20]So God dealt well with the midwives; and the people multiplied and became very strong. [21]And because the midwives feared God, he gave them families. [22]Then Pharaoh commanded all his people, "Every boy that is born to the Hebrews[a] you shall throw into the Nile, but you shall let every girl live."

Birth and Youth of Moses

2 Now a man from the house of Levi went and married a Levite woman. [2]The woman conceived and bore a son; and when she saw that he was a fine baby, she hid him three months. [3]When she could hide him no longer she got a papyrus basket for him, and plastered it with bitumen and pitch; she put the child in it and placed it among the reeds on the bank of the river. [4]His sister stood at a distance, to see what would happen to him.

LIVE IT!

Lifesavers · Exodus 1:15–22

You don't hear much about the midwives in the story of Moses, but they are the unsung heroes of the Israelites in captivity. Pharaoh, feeling threatened by the increase in the number of Israelites, told the Hebrew midwives to kill every Hebrew baby boy immediately when he was born. Pharaoh was in charge. He had all the power and the ability to deal with people who didn't obey. But the midwives feared an even higher power than Pharaoh—God. They knew it was not right to kill the babies, and so they let them live and lied to Pharaoh about how it happened (Exodus 1:19). The midwives' disobedience to these unjust laws not only saved the lives of many Hebrew boys, including Moses, but gives us an example of how disobedience to unjust laws can be exactly what God wants from us.

• Do you face any unjust rules or expectations at school or in other activities you are involved in—not rules you just don't like or think are unfair, but rules that go against the core of what the Bible teaches?

• How can you make a stand against these rules or expectations and work to make a change?

a Sam Gk Tg: Heb lacks *to the Hebrews*

Introducing . . . Moses · Exodus 2

Moses is, without doubt, one of the most important characters in the Pentateuch, if not the entire Old Testament. Struggling to find language to describe his greatness, Deuteronomy says, "Never since has there arisen a prophet in Israel like Moses, whom the LORD knew face to face" (34:10). Born to a couple from the tribe of Levi and raised as an Egyptian by Pharaoh's daughter, Moses was perfectly suited to negotiate Israel's freedom from slavery in Egypt. In event after event, the author of Exodus shows us Moses' wonder-working power, his prophetic skill, and his intimacy with God.

Despite all of Moses' great accomplishments, he never loses his humanness. He lacks confidence in his ability to speak (Exodus 4:10); he is angry and frustrated with his people (Exodus 32:19), and he bargains with God out of love for his people (Exodus 32:11-14). Moses is noble, but also knows sadness. He is elegantly portrayed in **Deuteronomy 34** when he dies within sight of the promised land. These qualities paint a picture of someone whose perseverance and trust allow God to work through him.

A prophet is literally God's voice, and Moses was indeed God's voice shaping Israel into a people of the covenant. All other leaders and figures in the Old Testament are compared with Moses. And, in the New Testament, even Jesus is compared with him.

5 The daughter of Pharaoh came down to bathe at the river, while her attendants walked beside the river. She saw the basket among the reeds and sent her maid to bring it. [6] When she opened it, she saw the child. He was crying, and she took pity on him. "This must be one of the Hebrews' children," she said. [7] Then his sister said to Pharaoh's daughter, "Shall I go and get you a nurse from the Hebrew women to nurse the child for you?" [8] Pharaoh's daughter said to her, "Yes." So the girl went and called the child's mother. [9] Pharaoh's daughter said to her, "Take this child and nurse it for me, and I will give you your wages." So the woman took the child and nursed it. [10] When the child grew up, she brought him to Pharaoh's daughter, and she took him as her son. She named him Moses,[a] "because," she said, "I drew him out[b] of the water."

Moses Flees to Midian

11 One day, after Moses had grown up, he went out to his people and saw their forced labor. He saw an Egyptian beating a Hebrew, one of his kinsfolk. [12] He looked this way and that, and seeing no one he killed the Egyptian and hid him in the sand. [13] When he went out the next day, he saw two Hebrews fighting; and he said to the one who was in the wrong, "Why do you strike your fellow Hebrew?" [14] He answered, "Who made you a ruler and judge over us? Do you mean to kill me as you killed the Egyptian?" Then Moses was afraid and thought, "Surely the thing is known." [15] When Pharaoh heard of it, he sought to kill Moses.

But Moses fled from Pharaoh. He settled in the land of Midian, and sat down by a well. [16] The priest of Midian had seven daughters. They came to draw water, and filled the troughs to water their father's flock. [17] But some shepherds came and drove them away. Moses got up and came to their defense and watered their flock. [18] When they returned to their father Reuel, he said, "How is it that you have come back so soon today?" [19] They said, "An Egyptian helped us against the shepherds; he even drew water for us and watered the flock." [20] He said to his daughters, "Where is he? Why did you leave the man? Invite him to break bread." [21] Moses agreed to stay with the man, and he gave Moses his daughter Zipporah in marriage. [22] She bore a son, and he named him Gershom; for he said, "I have been an alien[c] residing in a foreign land."

23 After a long time the king of Egypt died. The Israelites groaned under their slavery, and cried out. Out of the slavery their cry for help rose up to God. [24] God heard their groaning, and God remembered his covenant with Abraham, Isaac, and Jacob. [25] God looked upon the Israelites, and God took notice of them.

a Heb *Mosheh*   b Heb *mashah*   c Heb *ger*

3 · Moses at the Burning Bush

Moses was keeping the flock of his father-in-law Jethro, the priest of Midian; he led his flock beyond the wilderness, and came to Horeb, the mountain of God. ²There the angel of the Lord appeared to him in a flame of fire out of a bush; he looked, and the bush was blazing, yet it was not consumed. ³Then Moses said, "I must turn aside and look at this great sight, and see why the bush is not burned up." ⁴When the Lord saw that he had turned aside to see, God called to him out of the bush, "Moses, Moses!" And he said, "Here I am." ⁵Then he said, "Come no closer! Remove the sandals from your feet, for the place on which you are standing is holy ground." ⁶He said further, "I am the God of your father, the God of Abraham, the God of Isaac, and the God of Jacob." And Moses hid his face, for he was afraid to look at God.

7 Then the Lord said, "I have observed the misery of my people who are in Egypt; I have heard their cry on account of their taskmasters. Indeed, I know their sufferings, ⁸and I have come down to deliver them from the Egyptians, and to bring them up out of that land to a good and broad land, a land flowing with milk and honey, to the country of the Canaanites, the Hittites, the Amorites, the Perizzites, the Hivites, and the Jebusites. ⁹The cry of the Israelites has now come to me; I have also seen how the Egyptians oppress them. ¹⁰So come, I will send you to Pharaoh to bring my people, the Israelites, out of Egypt." ¹¹But Moses said to God, "Who am I that I should go to Pharaoh, and bring the Israelites out of Egypt?" ¹²He said, "I will be with you; and this shall be the sign for you that it is I who sent you: when you have brought the people out of Egypt, you shall worship God on this mountain."

The Divine Name Revealed

13 But Moses said to God, "If I come to the Israelites and say to them, 'The God of your ancestors has sent me to you,' and they ask me, 'What is his name?' what shall I say to them?" ¹⁴God said to Moses, "I am who I am."ᵃ He said further, "Thus you shall say to the Israelites, 'I am has sent me to you.'" ¹⁵God also said to Moses, "Thus you shall say to the Israelites, 'The Lord,ᵇ the God of your ancestors, the God of Abraham, the God of Isaac, and the God of Jacob, has sent me to you':

This is my name forever,
and this my title for all generations.

¹⁶Go and assemble the elders of Israel, and say to them, 'The Lord, the God of your ancestors, the God of Abraham, of Isaac, and of Jacob, has appeared to me, saying: I have given heed to you and to what has been done to you in Egypt. ¹⁷I declare that I will bring you up out of the misery of Egypt, to the land of the Canaanites, the Hittites, the Amorites, the Perizzites, the Hivites, and the Jebusites, a

STUDY IT!

Holy Ground
Exodus 3:1–6

Removing one's shoes before entering a home is a common practice in Asian cultures and has spread to many others around the world. Maybe you remove your shoes before entering your own home. People of many religions also remove their shoes before entering a mosque, temple, or other place of worship as an act of respect and cleanliness. Read **Exodus 3:5**. Moses is commanded to remove his sandals. Why? Because he is standing on holy ground. What makes the ground holy? God is present. Moses is awestruck and humbled by his experience of God's presence.

We are rarely awed by anything in today's multimedia culture. Even the burning bush would be just another special effect. How can we regain our sense of awe at God's majesty? Some people experience it in nature by looking at a star-filled sky, climbing a high mountain, or watching ocean waves roll in. Others experience it in getting to know other people deeply. Still others find it in the amazing patterns that science reveals. The one element common to experiencing awe seems to be the ability to slow down, look closely, and appreciate what we discover—especially when it reveals the much bigger picture around us.

So slow down, find your own holy ground, take your shoes off, and let God fill you with awe!

ᵃ Or *I am what I am* or *I will be what I will be*   ᵇ The word "Lord" when spelled with capital letters stands for the divine name, *YHWH*, which is here connected with the verb *hayah*, "to be"

God's Mysterious Name · Exodus 3:13–15

Have you ever asked your parents what your name means or why they chose it for you? Most names have special significance or meaning. The same is true about God's own name, which was revealed to Moses from the burning bush.

God tells Moses that his name in Hebrew is Yahweh, which can be translated as "I AM WHO I AM." Some scholars suggest a better translation might be "he causes to be what exists." In any case, the four Hebrew letters YHWH (or Yahweh) are difficult to translate.

Over the centuries, the Jewish people stopped pronouncing the four letters out of reverence for God and replaced them with the word "Adonai," meaning "my Lord." Most English translations of the Bible respect this long-standing tradition, translating the original YHWH as "LORD." This mysterious name of God reminds us that no name or symbol can fully express who God is. Perhaps that's why the Old Testament uses many other descriptive names for God, such as "God Almighty" (Genesis 17:1), "the everlasting God" (Isaiah 40:28), and "the Most High" (Isaiah 14:14).

land flowing with milk and honey.' [18] They will listen to your voice; and you and the elders of Israel shall go to the king of Egypt and say to him, 'The LORD, the God of the Hebrews, has met with us; let us now go a three days' journey into the wilderness, so that we may sacrifice to the LORD our God.' [19] I know, however, that the king of Egypt will not let you go unless compelled by a mighty hand.[a] [20] So I will stretch out my hand and strike Egypt with all my wonders that I will perform in it; after that he will let you go. [21] I will bring this people into such favor with the Egyptians that, when you go, you will not go empty-handed; [22] each woman shall ask her neighbor and any woman living in the neighbor's house for jewelry of silver and of gold, and clothing, and you shall put them on your sons and on your daughters; and so you shall plunder the Egyptians."

Moses' Miraculous Power

4 Then Moses answered, "But suppose they do not believe me or listen to me, but say, 'The LORD did not appear to you.'" [2] The LORD said to him, "What is that in your hand?" He said, "A staff." [3] And he said, "Throw it on the ground." So he threw the staff on the ground, and it became a snake; and Moses drew back from it. [4] Then the LORD said to Moses, "Reach out your hand, and seize it by the tail"—so he reached out his hand and grasped it, and it became a staff in his hand— [5] "so that they may believe that the LORD, the God of their ancestors, the God of Abraham, the God of Isaac, and the God of Jacob, has appeared to you."

[6] Again, the LORD said to him, "Put your hand inside your cloak." He put his hand into his cloak; and when he took it out, his hand was leprous,[b] as white as snow. [7] Then God said, "Put your hand back into your cloak"—so he put his hand back into his cloak, and when he took it out, it was restored like the rest of his body— [8] "If they will not believe you or heed the first sign, they may believe the second sign. [9] If they will not believe even these two signs or heed you, you shall take some water from the Nile and pour it on the dry ground; and the water that you shall take from the Nile will become blood on the dry ground."

[10] But Moses said to the LORD, "O my Lord, I have never been eloquent, neither in the past nor even now that you have spoken to your servant; but I am slow of speech and slow of tongue." [11] Then the LORD said to him, "Who gives speech to mortals? Who makes them mute or deaf, seeing or blind? Is it not I, the LORD? [12] Now go, and I will be with your mouth and teach you what you are to speak." [13] But he said, "O my Lord, please send someone else." [14] Then the anger of the LORD was kindled against Moses and he said, "What of your brother Aaron the Levite? I know that he can speak fluently; even now he is coming out to meet you, and when he sees you his heart will be glad. [15] You shall speak to him and put the words in his mouth; and I will be with your mouth and with his mouth, and will teach you what you shall do. [16] He indeed shall speak for you to the people; he shall serve as a mouth for you, and you shall serve as God for him.

a Gk Vg: Heb *no, not by a mighty hand*   b A term for several skin diseases; precise meaning uncertain

LIVE IT!

Set Them Free! · Exodus 4:1–17

God responded to the cries of the Israelites by choosing Moses as a prophet to lead them to freedom. Moses was scared and questioned his ability, but he became an effective and powerful leader with God's help. God's mission of liberation was bigger than Moses' doubts.

In more modern times, great spiritual leaders have risen up to lead people to freedom: Martin Luther King Jr., Mohandas Gandhi, Nelson Mandela, William Wilberforce, Harriet Tubman, and even today's Gary Haugen of International Justice Mission are just a few. As with Moses, God inspired these leaders to see people experiencing injustice and to liberate them. These leaders most likely had their doubts, but they relied on God for strength and hope. We too need to speak out against injustice and with God's help work to free the victims of oppression.

- Are you aware of any group that's being oppressed today? How might God be calling you to help?
- Ask God for wisdom, strength, and help to fight injustice.

[17] Take in your hand this staff, with which you shall perform the signs."

Moses Returns to Egypt

18 Moses went back to his father-in-law Jethro and said to him, "Please let me go back to my kindred in Egypt and see whether they are still living." And Jethro said to Moses, "Go in peace." [19] The LORD said to Moses in Midian, "Go back to Egypt; for all those who were seeking your life are dead." [20] So Moses took his wife and his sons, put them on a donkey, and went back to the land of Egypt; and Moses carried the staff of God in his hand.

21 And the LORD said to Moses, "When you go back to Egypt, see that you perform before Pharaoh all the wonders that I have put in your power; but I will harden his heart, so that he will not let the people go. [22] Then you shall say to Pharaoh, 'Thus says the LORD: Israel is my firstborn son. [23] I said to you, "Let my son go that he may worship me." But you refused to let him go; now I will kill your firstborn son.' "

24 On the way, at a place where they spent the night, the LORD met him and tried to kill him. [25] But Zipporah took a flint and cut off her son's foreskin, and touched Moses'[a] feet with it, and said, "Truly you are a bridegroom of blood to me!" [26] So he let him alone. It was then she said, "A bridegroom of blood by circumcision."

27 The LORD said to Aaron, "Go into the wilderness to meet Moses." So he went; and he met him

at the mountain of God and kissed him. [28] Moses told Aaron all the words of the LORD with which he had sent him, and all the signs with which he had charged him. [29] Then Moses and Aaron went and assembled all the elders of the Israelites. [30] Aaron spoke all the words that the LORD had spoken to Moses, and performed the signs in the sight of the people. [31] The people believed; and when they heard that the LORD had given heed to the Israelites and that he had seen their misery, they bowed down and worshiped.

Bricks without Straw

5 Afterward Moses and Aaron went to Pharaoh and said, "Thus says the LORD, the God of Israel, 'Let my people go, so that they may celebrate a festival to me in the wilderness.' " [2] But Pharaoh said, "Who is the LORD, that I should heed him and let Israel go? I do not know the LORD, and I will not let Israel go." [3] Then they said, "The God of the Hebrews has revealed himself to us; let us go a three days' journey into the wilderness to sacrifice

---

α Heb his

to the Lord our God, or he will fall upon us with pestilence or sword." [4]But the king of Egypt said to them, "Moses and Aaron, why are you taking the people away from their work? Get to your labors!" [5]Pharaoh continued, "Now they are more numerous than the people of the land[a] and yet you want them to stop working!" [6]That same day Pharaoh commanded the taskmasters of the people, as well as their supervisors, [7]"You shall no longer give the people straw to make bricks, as before; let them go and gather straw for themselves. [8]But you shall require of them the same quantity of bricks as they have made previously; do not diminish it, for they are lazy; that is why they cry, 'Let us go and offer sacrifice to our God.' [9]Let heavier work be laid on them; then they will labor at it and pay no attention to deceptive words."

10 So the taskmasters and the supervisors of the people went out and said to the people, "Thus says Pharaoh, 'I will not give you straw. [11]Go and get straw yourselves, wherever you can find it; but your work will not be lessened in the least.' " [12]So the people scattered throughout the land of Egypt, to gather stubble for straw. [13]The taskmasters were urgent, saying, "Complete your work, the same daily assignment as when you were given straw." [14]And the supervisors of the Israelites, whom Pharaoh's taskmasters had set over them, were beaten, and were asked, "Why did you not finish the required quantity of bricks yesterday and today, as you did before?"

15 Then the Israelite supervisors came to Pharaoh and cried, "Why do you treat your servants like this? [16]No straw is given to your servants, yet they say to us, 'Make bricks!' Look how your servants are beaten! You are unjust to your own people."[b] [17]He said, "You are lazy, lazy; that is why you say, 'Let us go and sacrifice to the Lord.' [18]Go now, and work; for no straw shall be given you, but you shall still deliver the same number of bricks." [19]The Israelite supervisors saw that they were in trouble when they were told, "You shall not lessen your daily number of bricks." [20]As they left Pharaoh, they came upon Moses and Aaron who were waiting to meet them. [21]They said to them, "The Lord look upon you and judge! You have brought us into bad odor with

CONNECT IT!

William Wilberforce: Fighting Slave Labor · Exodus 5

Demanding bosses. Long hours. Poor working conditions. Unfortunately, the description of Pharaoh's unjust treatment of the Israelites almost thirty-five hundred years ago is remarkably similar to the work lives of many laborers throughout the world today. Read this chapter and note some of the practices that are still used by companies around the world today. Some companies—even companies we all know—require long hours for low wages in unsafe working conditions.

William Wilberforce was a British politician best known for his tireless work to abolish slavery throughout the British Empire. His faith in God would not let him stand by while people were treated unjustly and even cruelly. After dedicating his life to this cause, he died just three days after he was told that an act of Parliament to end slavery in the British Empire was a sure thing. Wilberforce's life and work brought freedom to many, but it didn't end slavery everywhere. It still exists in various forms, even in the United States today. Surprised? Public awareness has grown somewhat and pressured companies to follow ethical business practices. But you still might be wearing clothes right now that have been manufactured under unjust conditions—maybe even by slaves—without even knowing it!

And though you may feel called, like Wilberforce, to dedicate your life to the abolition of slavery, you may not. But either way, we all have a responsibility to act as we become more aware of the origins of the things we buy. Fair-trade products may cost a little more, but when we make small choices to buy products from companies with fair labor practices, we encourage justice. We make a stand for the fact that low wages, unfair labor practices, and dangerous working conditions are unjust and unacceptable in our world today.

---

a Sam: Heb *The people of the land are now many*   **b** Gk Compare Syr Vg: Heb *beaten, and the sin of your people*

Why Me?
Exodus 5:22–23

Can you imagine how Moses must have felt? He did what God told him to do, and things only got worse for the Israelites. But Moses still kept talking to God, even if only to say, "Why did you ever send me?" (Exodus 5:22).

Thomas Merton, a famous Trappist monk and spiritual writer, understood that Christians sometimes feel the way Moses did:

The Christian
must have the courage
to follow Christ.
The Christian
who is risen in Christ
must dare
to be like Christ:
he must dare
to follow conscience
even in unpopular causes.
He must, if necessary,
be able to disagree with the majority
and make decisions
that he knows
to be according to the Gospel
and teaching of Christ,
even when others
do not understand
why he is acting this way.*

The next time you are feeling a little like Moses and wondering, Why me? try this prayer:

Faithful God, help me to trust in you even when I feel disappointed and disillusioned. I want to believe you are working in ways I cannot see. Please help my disbelief. Amen.

Pharaoh and his officials, and have put a sword in their hand to kill us."

22 Then Moses turned again to the LORD and said, "O LORD, why have you mistreated this people? Why did you ever send me? 23 Since I first came to Pharaoh to speak in your name, he has mistreated this people, and you have done nothing at all to deliver your people."

Israel's Deliverance Assured

6 Then the LORD said to Moses, "Now you shall see what I will do to Pharaoh: Indeed, by a mighty hand he will let them go; by a mighty hand he will drive them out of his land."

2 God also spoke to Moses and said to him: "I am the LORD. 3 I appeared to Abraham, Isaac, and Jacob as God Almighty,[a] but by my name 'The LORD'[b] I did not make myself known to them. 4 I also established my covenant with them, to give them the land of Canaan, the land in which they resided as aliens. 5 I have also heard the groaning of the Israelites whom the Egyptians are holding as slaves, and I have remembered my covenant. 6 Say therefore to the Israelites, 'I am the LORD, and I will free you from the burdens of the Egyptians and deliver you from slavery to them. I will redeem you with an outstretched arm and with mighty acts of judgment. 7 I will take you as my people, and I will be your God. You shall know that I am the LORD your God, who has freed you from the burdens of the Egyptians. 8 I will bring you into the land that I swore to give to Abraham, Isaac, and Jacob; I will give it to you for a possession. I am the LORD.' " 9 Moses told this to the Israelites; but they would not listen to Moses, because of their broken spirit and their cruel slavery.

10 Then the LORD spoke to Moses, 11 "Go and tell Pharaoh king of Egypt to let the Israelites go out of his land." 12 But Moses spoke to the LORD, "The Israelites have not listened to me; how then shall Pharaoh listen to me, poor speaker that I am?"[c] 13 Thus the LORD spoke to Moses and Aaron, and gave them orders regarding the Israelites and Pharaoh king of Egypt, charging them to free the Israelites from the land of Egypt.

The Genealogy of Moses and Aaron

14 The following are the heads of their ancestral houses: the sons of Reuben, the firstborn of Israel: Hanoch, Pallu, Hezron, and Carmi; these are the families of Reuben. 15 The sons of Simeon: Jemuel, Jamin, Ohad, Jachin, Zohar, and Shaul,[d] the son of a Canaanite woman; these are the families of Simeon. 16 The following are the names of the sons

---

a Traditional rendering of Heb *El Shaddai* b Heb *YHWH*; see note at 3.15 c Heb *me? I am uncircumcised of lips* d Or *Saul*

God, You Promised · Exodus 6:1–9

The Israelites had been slaves for so long, they were discouraged and didn't believe Moses' liberating message in **Exodus 6:1–9**. Moses probably sounded crazy to them. The writer of Exodus reminds us that God is faithful to God's promises and that human weakness can't stop God's plans. We too might find it hard to believe in God's power in our lives when we feel burdened and oppressed, especially over a long time.

Think or journal about the following during your prayer time:

- When is it hard for you to believe in God's promises?
- Who do you know who has trouble accepting God's power in their lives?
- What barriers are keeping you and them from trusting God?
- Say or write your own prayer expressing your desire to believe in God's promises.

of Levi according to their genealogies: Gershon,[a] Kohath, and Merari, and the length of Levi's life was one hundred thirty-seven years. ¹⁷The sons of Gershon:[a] Libni and Shimei, by their families. ¹⁸The sons of Kohath: Amram, Izhar, Hebron, and Uzziel, and the length of Kohath's life was one hundred thirty-three years. ¹⁹The sons of Merari: Mahli and Mushi. These are the families of the Levites according to their genealogies. ²⁰Amram married Jochebed his father's sister and she bore him Aaron and Moses, and the length of Amram's life was one hundred thirty-seven years. ²¹The sons of Izhar: Korah, Nepheg, and Zichri. ²²The sons of Uzziel: Mishael, Elzaphan, and Sithri. ²³Aaron married Elisheba, daughter of Amminadab and sister of Nahshon, and she bore him Nadab, Abihu, Eleazar, and Ithamar. ²⁴The sons of Korah: Assir, Elkanah, and Abiasaph; these are the families of the Korahites. ²⁵Aaron's son Eleazar married one of the daughters of Putiel, and she bore him Phinehas. These are the heads of the ancestral houses of the Levites by their families.

26 It was this same Aaron and Moses to whom the LORD said, "Bring the Israelites out of the land of Egypt, company by company." ²⁷It was they who spoke to Pharaoh king of Egypt to bring the Israelites out of Egypt, the same Moses and Aaron.

Moses and Aaron Obey God's Commands

28 On the day when the LORD spoke to Moses in the land of Egypt, ²⁹he said to him, "I am the LORD; tell Pharaoh king of Egypt all that I am speaking to you." ³⁰But Moses said in the LORD's

presence, "Since I am a poor speaker,[b] why would Pharaoh listen to me?"

7 The LORD said to Moses, "See, I have made you like God to Pharaoh, and your brother Aaron shall be your prophet. ²You shall speak all that I command you, and your brother Aaron shall tell Pharaoh to let the Israelites go out of his land. ³But I will harden Pharaoh's heart, and I will multiply my signs and wonders in the land of Egypt. ⁴When Pharaoh does not listen to you, I will lay my hand upon Egypt and bring my people the Israelites, company by company, out of the land of Egypt by great acts of judgment. ⁵The Egyptians shall know that I am the LORD, when I stretch out my hand against Egypt and bring the Israelites out from among them." ⁶Moses and Aaron did so; they did just as the LORD commanded them. ⁷Moses was eighty years old and Aaron eighty-three when they spoke to Pharaoh.

Aaron's Miraculous Rod

8 The LORD said to Moses and Aaron, ⁹"When Pharaoh says to you, 'Perform a wonder,' then you

---

a Also spelled *Gershom*; see 2.22   **b** Heb *am uncircumcised of lips*; see 6.12

shall say to Aaron, 'Take your staff and throw it down before Pharaoh, and it will become a snake.' " ¹⁰So Moses and Aaron went to Pharaoh and did as the LORD had commanded; Aaron threw down his staff before Pharaoh and his officials, and it became a snake. ¹¹Then Pharaoh summoned the wise men and the sorcerers; and they also, the magicians of Egypt, did the same by their secret arts. ¹²Each one threw down his staff, and they became snakes; but Aaron's staff swallowed up theirs. ¹³Still Pharaoh's heart was hardened, and he would not listen to them, as the LORD had said.

The First Plague: Water Turned to Blood

14 Then the LORD said to Moses, "Pharaoh's heart is hardened; he refuses to let the people go. ¹⁵Go to Pharaoh in the morning, as he is going out to the water; stand by at the river bank to meet him, and take in your hand the staff that was turned into a snake. ¹⁶Say to him, 'The LORD, the God of the Hebrews, sent me to you to say, "Let my people go, so that they may worship me in the wilderness." But

until now you have not listened. ¹⁷Thus says the LORD, "By this you shall know that I am the LORD." See, with the staff that is in my hand I will strike the water that is in the Nile, and it shall be turned to blood. ¹⁸The fish in the river shall die, the river itself shall stink, and the Egyptians shall be unable to drink water from the Nile.' " ¹⁹The LORD said to Moses, "Say to Aaron, 'Take your staff and stretch out your hand over the waters of Egypt—over its rivers, its canals, and its ponds, and all its pools of water—so that they may become blood; and there shall be blood throughout the whole land of Egypt, even in vessels of wood and in vessels of stone.' "

20 Moses and Aaron did just as the LORD commanded. In the sight of Pharaoh and of his officials he lifted up the staff and struck the water in the river, and all the water in the river was turned into blood, ²¹and the fish in the river died. The river stank so that the Egyptians could not drink its water, and there was blood throughout the whole land of Egypt. ²²But the magicians of Egypt did the same by their secret arts; so Pharaoh's heart remained

STUDY IT!

The Miraculous Escape · Exodus 7–14

The writer of Exodus combines several versions of what happened in describing the ten plagues and the crossing of the Red Sea. The various story lines and types of writing are woven together to produce a complete and suspenseful story.

When Pharaoh refuses to let the Israelites go, God sends ten plagues to convince Pharaoh to cooperate. The first nine plagues are exaggerations of naturally occurring events. For example, Exodus says the first plague is the water of the Nile River turning to blood. Silt and microbes pollute and redden the Nile sometimes, making the water undrinkable. And frogs, bugs, and disease are also things that occur naturally. However, the timing and extent of these plagues set them apart from natural occurrences and show them to be miraculous.

Finally, God resorts to drastic measures. For the tenth plague, God sends an angel of death to kill the firstborn children of the Egyptians. Moses has the Israelites mark their doorposts with the blood of a lamb, so that the angel of death "passes over" their homes. Pharaoh is now eager to get rid of the Israelites and releases them from service. They gladly begin their journey to God's promised land.

It doesn't take long, though, for Pharaoh to regret his decision and send his army after the Israelites. The Israelites seem to be trapped at the marshlands by the Red Sea as the Egyptians close in (see Map 3: "Exodus and Conquest of Canaan"). Although the prose version of this situation (Exodus 14) and the poetic version (Exodus 15) differ in many details, both stress that the Israelites are able to pass through a section of land made dry by a strong wind. The chariots of the Egyptians get stuck, and the army drowns as the water returns. Again, the timing and method of God's help enable the miraculous escape. God hears the Israelite people and sets them free.

hardened, and he would not listen to them, as the LORD had said. ²³Pharaoh turned and went into his house, and he did not take even this to heart. ²⁴And all the Egyptians had to dig along the Nile for water to drink, for they could not drink the water of the river.

25 Seven days passed after the LORD had struck the Nile.

The Second Plague: Frogs

8 ᵃ Then the LORD said to Moses, "Go to Pharaoh and say to him, 'Thus says the LORD: Let my people go, so that they may worship me. ²If you refuse to let them go, I will plague your whole country with frogs. ³The river shall swarm with frogs; they shall come up into your palace, into your bedchamber and your bed, and into the houses of your officials and of your people,ᵇ and into your ovens and your kneading bowls. ⁴The frogs shall come up on you and on your people and on all your officials.' " ⁵ᶜ And the LORD said to Moses, "Say to Aaron, 'Stretch out your hand with your staff over the rivers, the canals, and the pools, and make frogs come up on the land of Egypt.' " ⁶So Aaron stretched out his hand over the waters of Egypt; and the frogs came up and covered the land of Egypt. ⁷But the magicians did the same by their secret arts, and brought frogs up on the land of Egypt.

8 Then Pharaoh called Moses and Aaron, and said, "Pray to the LORD to take away the frogs from me and my people, and I will let the people go to sacrifice to the LORD." ⁹Moses said to Pharaoh, "Kindly tell me when I am to pray for you and for your officials and for your people, that the frogs may be removed from you and your houses and be left only in the Nile." ¹⁰And he said, "Tomorrow." Moses said, "As you say! So that you may know that there is no one like the LORD our God, ¹¹the frogs shall leave you and your houses and your officials and your people; they shall be left only in the Nile." ¹²Then Moses and Aaron went out from Pharaoh; and Moses cried out to the LORD concerning the frogs that he had brought upon Pharaoh.ᵈ ¹³And the LORD did as Moses requested: the frogs died in the houses, the courtyards, and the fields. ¹⁴And they gathered them together in heaps, and the land stank. ¹⁵But when Pharaoh saw that there was a respite, he hardened his heart, and would not listen to them, just as the LORD had said.

The Third Plague: Gnats

16 Then the LORD said to Moses, "Say to Aaron, 'Stretch out your staff and strike the dust of the earth, so that it may become gnats throughout the whole land of Egypt.' " ¹⁷And they did so; Aaron stretched out his hand with his staff and struck the dust of the earth, and gnats came on humans and animals alike; all the dust of the earth turned into gnats throughout the whole land of Egypt. ¹⁸The magicians tried to produce gnats by their secret arts, but they could not. There were gnats on both humans and animals. ¹⁹And the magicians said to Pharaoh, "This is the finger of God!" But Pharaoh's heart was hardened, and he would not listen to them, just as the LORD had said.

The Fourth Plague: Flies

20 Then the LORD said to Moses, "Rise early in the morning and present yourself before Pharaoh, as he goes out to the water, and say to him, 'Thus says the LORD: Let my people go, so that they may worship me. ²¹For if you will not let my people go, I will send swarms of flies on you, your officials, and your people, and into your houses; and the houses of the Egyptians shall be filled with swarms of flies; so also the land where they live. ²²But on that day I will set apart the land of Goshen, where my people live, so that no swarms of flies shall be there, that you may know that I the LORD am in this land. ²³Thus I will make a distinctionᵉ between my people and your people. This sign shall appear tomorrow.' " ²⁴The LORD did so, and great swarms of flies came into the house of Pharaoh and into his officials' houses; in all of Egypt the land was ruined because of the flies.

25 Then Pharaoh summoned Moses and Aaron, and said, "Go, sacrifice to your God within the land." ²⁶But Moses said, "It would not be right to do so;

ᵃ Ch 7.26 in Heb　ᵇ Gk: Heb *upon your people*　ᶜ Ch 8.1 in Heb　ᵈ Or *frogs, as he had agreed with Pharaoh*　ᵉ Gk Vg: Heb *will set redemption* for the sacrifices that we offer to the LORD our God are offensive to the Egyptians. If we offer in the sight of the Egyptians sacrifices that are offensive to them, will they not stone us? [27] We must go a three days' journey into the wilderness and sacrifice to the LORD our God as he commands us." [28] So Pharaoh said, "I will let you go to sacrifice to the LORD your God in the wilderness, provided you do not go very far away. Pray for me." [29] Then Moses said, "As soon as I leave you, I will pray to the LORD that the swarms of flies may depart tomorrow from Pharaoh, from his officials, and from his people; only do not let Pharaoh again deal falsely by not letting the people go to sacrifice to the LORD."

30 So Moses went out from Pharaoh and prayed to the LORD. [31] And the LORD did as Moses asked: he removed the swarms of flies from Pharaoh, from his officials, and from his people; not one remained. [32] But Pharaoh hardened his heart this time also, and would not let the people go.

9 The Fifth Plague: Livestock Diseased

Then the LORD said to Moses, "Go to Pharaoh, and say to him, 'Thus says the LORD, the God of the Hebrews: Let my people go, so that they may worship me. [2] For if you refuse to let them go and still hold them, [3] the hand of the LORD will strike with a deadly pestilence your livestock in the field: the horses, the donkeys, the camels, the herds, and the flocks. [4] But the LORD will make a distinction between the livestock of Israel and the livestock of Egypt, so that nothing shall die of all that belongs to the Israelites.' " [5] The LORD set a time, saying, "Tomorrow the LORD will do this thing in the land." [6] And on the next day the LORD did so; all the livestock of the Egyptians died, but of the livestock of the Israelites not one died. [7] Pharaoh inquired and found that not one of the livestock of the Israelites was dead. But the heart of Pharaoh was hardened, and he would not let the people go.

The Sixth Plague: Boils

8 Then the LORD said to Moses and Aaron, "Take handfuls of soot from the kiln, and let Moses throw it in the air in the sight of Pharaoh. [9] It shall become fine dust all over the land of Egypt, and shall cause festering boils on humans and animals throughout the whole land of Egypt." [10] So they took soot from the kiln, and stood before Pharaoh, and Moses threw it in the air, and it caused festering boils on humans and animals. [11] The magicians could not stand before Moses because of the boils, for the boils afflicted the magicians as well as all the Egyptians. [12] But the LORD hardened the heart of Pharaoh, and he would not listen to them, just as the LORD had spoken to Moses.

The Seventh Plague: Thunder and Hail

13 Then the LORD said to Moses, "Rise up early in the morning and present yourself before Pharaoh, and say to him, 'Thus says the LORD, the God of the Hebrews: Let my people go, so that they may worship me. [14] For this time I will send all my plagues upon you yourself, and upon your officials, and upon your people, so that you may know that there is no one like me in all the earth. [15] For by now I could have stretched out my hand and struck you and your people with pestilence, and you would have been cut off from the earth. [16] But this is why I have let you live: to show you my power, and to make my name resound through all the earth. [17] You are still exalting yourself against my people, and will not let them go. [18] Tomorrow at this time I will cause the heaviest hail to fall that has ever fallen in Egypt from the day it was founded until now. [19] Send, therefore, and have your livestock and everything that you have in the open field brought to a secure place; every human or animal that is in the open field and is not brought under shelter will die when the hail comes down upon them.' " [20] Those officials of Pharaoh who feared the word of the LORD hurried their slaves and livestock off to a secure place. [21] Those who did not regard the word of the LORD left their slaves and livestock in the open field.

22 The LORD said to Moses, "Stretch out your hand toward heaven so that hail may fall on the whole land of Egypt, on humans and animals and all the plants of the field in the land of Egypt." [23] Then Moses stretched out his staff toward heaven, and the LORD sent thunder and hail, and fire came down on the earth. And the LORD rained hail on the land of Egypt; [24] there was hail with fire flashing continually in the midst of it, such heavy hail as had never fallen in all the land of Egypt since it became a nation. [25] The hail struck down everything that was in the open field throughout all the land of Egypt, both human and animal; the hail also struck down all the plants of the field, and shattered every tree in the field. [26] Only in the land of Goshen, where the Israelites were, there was no hail.

27 Then Pharaoh summoned Moses and Aaron, and said to them, "This time I have sinned; the LORD is in the right, and I and my people are in the wrong. [28]Pray to the LORD! Enough of God's thunder and hail! I will let you go; you need stay no longer." [29]Moses said to him, "As soon as I have gone out of the city, I will stretch out my hands to the LORD; the thunder will cease, and there will be no more hail, so that you may know that the earth is the LORD's. [30]But as for you and your officials, I know that you do not yet fear the LORD God." [31](Now the flax and the barley were ruined, for the barley was in the ear and the flax was in bud. [32]But the wheat and the spelt were not ruined, for they are late in coming up.) [33]So Moses left Pharaoh, went out of the city, and stretched out his hands to the LORD; then the thunder and the hail ceased, and the rain no longer poured down on the earth. [34]But when Pharaoh saw that the rain and the hail and the thunder had ceased, he sinned once more and hardened his heart, he and his officials. [35]So the heart of Pharaoh was hardened, and he would not let the Israelites go, just as the LORD had spoken through Moses.

The Eighth Plague: Locusts

10 Then the LORD said to Moses, "Go to Pharaoh; for I have hardened his heart and the heart of his officials, in order that I may show these signs of mine among them, [2]and that you may tell your children and grandchildren how I have made fools of the Egyptians and what signs I have done among them—so that you may know that I am the LORD."

3 So Moses and Aaron went to Pharaoh, and said to him, "Thus says the LORD, the God of the Hebrews, 'How long will you refuse to humble yourself before me? Let my people go, so that they may worship me. [4]For if you refuse to let my people go, tomorrow I will bring locusts into your country. [5]They shall cover the surface of the land, so that no one will be able to see the land. They shall devour the last remnant left you after the hail, and they shall devour every tree of yours that grows in the field. [6]They shall fill your houses, and the houses of all your officials and of all the Egyptians—something that neither your parents nor your grandparents have seen, from the day they came on earth to this day.' " Then he turned and went out from Pharaoh.

7 Pharaoh's officials said to him, "How long shall this fellow be a snare to us? Let the people go, so that they may worship the LORD their God; do you not yet understand that Egypt is ruined?" [8]So Moses and Aaron were brought back to Pharaoh, and he said to them, "Go, worship the LORD your God! But which ones are to go?" [9]Moses said, "We will go with our young and our old; we will go with our sons and daughters and with our flocks and herds, because we have the LORD's festival to celebrate." [10]He said to them, "The LORD indeed will be with you, if ever I let your little ones go with you! Plainly, you have some evil purpose in mind. [11]No, never! Your men may go and worship the LORD, for that is what you are asking." And they were driven out from Pharaoh's presence.

12 Then the LORD said to Moses, "Stretch out your hand over the land of Egypt, so that the locusts may come upon it and eat every plant in the land, all that the hail has left." [13]So Moses stretched out his staff over the land of Egypt, and the LORD brought an east wind upon the land all that day and all that night; when morning came, the east wind had brought the locusts. [14]The locusts came upon all the land of Egypt and settled on the whole country of Egypt, such a dense swarm of locusts as had never been before, nor ever shall be again. [15]They covered the surface of the whole land, so that the land was black; and they ate all the plants in the land and all the fruit of the trees that the hail had left; nothing green was left, no tree, no plant in the field, in all the land of Egypt. [16]Pharaoh hurriedly summoned Moses and Aaron and said, "I have sinned against the LORD your God, and against you. [17]Do forgive my sin just this once, and pray to the LORD your God that at the least he remove this deadly thing from me." [18]So he went out from Pharaoh and prayed to the LORD. [19]The LORD changed the wind into a very strong west wind, which lifted the locusts and drove them into the Red Sea;[a] not a single locust was left in all the country of Egypt. [20]But the LORD hardened Pharaoh's heart, and he would not let the Israelites go.

The Ninth Plague: Darkness

21 Then the LORD said to Moses, "Stretch out

[a] Or *Sea of Reeds*

your hand toward heaven so that there may be darkness over the land of Egypt, a darkness that can be felt." [22] So Moses stretched out his hand toward heaven, and there was dense darkness in all the land of Egypt for three days. [23] People could not see one another, and for three days they could not move from where they were; but all the Israelites had light where they lived. [24] Then Pharaoh summoned Moses, and said, "Go, worship the LORD. Only your flocks and your herds shall remain behind. Even your children may go with you." [25] But Moses said, "You must also let us have sacrifices and burnt offerings to sacrifice to the LORD our God. [26] Our livestock also must go with us; not a hoof shall be left behind, for we must choose some of them for the worship of the LORD our God, and we will not know what to use to worship the LORD until we arrive there." [27] But the LORD hardened Pharaoh's heart, and he was unwilling to let them go. [28] Then Pharaoh said to him, "Get away from me! Take care that you do not see my face again, for on the day you see my face you shall die." [29] Moses said, "Just as you say! I will never see your face again."

Warning of the Final Plague

11 The LORD said to Moses, "I will bring one more plague upon Pharaoh and upon Egypt; afterwards he will let you go from here; indeed, when he lets you go, he will drive you away. [2] Tell the people that every man is to ask his neighbor and every woman is to ask her neighbor for objects of silver and gold." [3] The LORD gave the people favor in the sight of the Egyptians. Moreover, Moses himself was a man of great importance in the land of Egypt, in the sight of Pharaoh's officials and in the sight of the people.

4 Moses said, "Thus says the LORD: About midnight I will go out through Egypt. [5] Every firstborn in the land of Egypt shall die, from the firstborn of Pharaoh who sits on his throne to the firstborn of the female slave who is behind the handmill, and all the firstborn of the livestock. [6] Then there will be a loud cry throughout the whole land of Egypt, such as has never been or will ever be again. [7] But not a dog shall growl at any of the Israelites—not at people, not at animals—so that you may know that the LORD makes a distinction between Egypt and Israel. [8] Then all these officials of yours shall come down to me, and bow low to me, saying, 'Leave us, you and all the people who follow you.'

After that I will leave." And in hot anger he left Pharaoh.

9 The LORD said to Moses, "Pharaoh will not listen to you, in order that my wonders may be multiplied in the land of Egypt." [10] Moses and Aaron performed all these wonders before Pharaoh; but the LORD hardened Pharaoh's heart, and he did not let the people of Israel go out of his land.

The First Passover Instituted

12 The LORD said to Moses and Aaron in the land of Egypt: [2] This month shall mark for you the beginning of months; it shall be the first month of the year for you. [3] Tell the whole congregation of Israel that on the tenth of this month they are to take a lamb for each family, a lamb for each household. [4] If a household is too small for a whole lamb, it shall join its closest neighbor in obtaining one; the lamb shall be divided in proportion to the number of people who eat of it. [5] Your lamb shall be without blemish, a year-old male; you may take it from the sheep or from the goats. [6] You shall keep it until the fourteenth day of this month; then the whole assembled congregation of Israel shall slaughter it at twilight. [7] They shall take some of the blood and put it on the two doorposts and the lintel of the houses in which they eat it. [8] They shall eat the lamb that same night; they shall eat it roasted over the fire with unleavened bread and bitter herbs. [9] Do not eat any of it raw or boiled in water, but roasted over the fire, with its head, legs, and inner organs. [10] You shall let none of it remain until the morning; anything that remains until the morning you shall burn. [11] This is how you shall eat it: your loins girded, your sandals on your feet, and your staff in your hand; and you shall eat it hurriedly. It is the passover of the LORD. [12] For I will pass through the land of Egypt that night, and I will strike down every firstborn in the land of Egypt, both human beings and animals; on all the gods of Egypt I will execute judgments: I am the LORD. [13] The blood shall be a sign for you on the houses where you live: when I see the blood, I will pass over you, and no plague shall destroy you when I strike the land of Egypt.

14 This day shall be a day of remembrance for you. You shall celebrate it as a festival to the LORD; throughout your generations you shall observe it as a perpetual ordinance. [15] Seven days you shall eat unleavened bread; on the first day you shall remove leaven from your houses, for whoever eats leavened

STUDY IT!

The Passover
Exodus 12:14–28

"Why is this night so different from all other nights?" This question is asked by the youngest member of the family as part of the Jewish celebration of the Passover, which Jewish people still celebrate today.

The Passover is celebrated around a meal that traditionally includes lamb and unleavened bread. The lamb recalls the Passover lamb, whose blood was placed on the doorpost to protect the firstborn from the angel of death. The unleavened bread recalls the haste of the people as they prepared to leave Egypt. Retelling the ancient story, generations of Jews have remembered that "night of nights" when the angel of death passed over the Israelites' houses and struck down the firstborn of the Egyptians. It was the night that the people of God were finally released from slavery. So Passover is a celebration of God's gift of freedom—a religious Independence Day, so to speak.

It was during the Passover celebration that Jesus and the disciples shared a farewell dinner (Luke 22:14-20), at which he explained to them that he was about to establish a new covenant. Christians see Jesus as the new Passover. It's his blood instead of the lamb's. It's through his death and resurrection that we're finally set free from all bondage, including sin and death.

perpetual ordinance. [18]In the first month, from the evening of the fourteenth day until the evening of the twenty-first day, you shall eat unleavened bread. [19]For seven days no leaven shall be found in your houses; for whoever eats what is leavened shall be cut off from the congregation of Israel, whether an alien or a native of the land. [20]You shall eat nothing leavened; in all your settlements you shall eat unleavened bread.

21 Then Moses called all the elders of Israel and said to them, "Go, select lambs for your families, and slaughter the passover lamb. [22]Take a bunch of hyssop, dip it in the blood that is in the basin, and touch the lintel and the two doorposts with the blood in the basin. None of you shall go outside the door of your house until morning. [23]For the LORD will pass through to strike down the Egyptians; when he sees the blood on the lintel and on the two doorposts, the LORD will pass over that door and will not allow the destroyer to enter your houses to strike you down. [24]You shall observe this rite as a perpetual ordinance for you and your children. [25]When you come to the land that the LORD will give you, as he has promised, you shall keep this observance. [26]And when your children ask you, 'What do you mean by this observance?' [27]you shall say, 'It is the passover sacrifice to the LORD, for he passed over the houses of the Israelites in Egypt, when he struck down the Egyptians but spared our houses.'" And the people bowed down and worshiped.

28 The Israelites went and did just as the LORD had commanded Moses and Aaron.

The Tenth Plague: Death of the Firstborn

29 At midnight the LORD struck down all the firstborn in the land of Egypt, from the firstborn of Pharaoh who sat on his throne to the firstborn of the prisoner who was in the dungeon, and all the firstborn of the livestock. [30]Pharaoh arose in the night, he and all his officials and all the Egyptians; and there was a loud cry in Egypt, for there was not a house without someone dead. [31]Then he summoned Moses and Aaron in the night, and said, "Rise up, go away from my people, both you and the Israelites! Go, worship the LORD, as you said. [32]Take your flocks and your herds, as you said, and be gone. And bring a blessing on me too!"

The Exodus: From Rameses to Succoth

33 The Egyptians urged the people to hasten their

bread from the first day until the seventh day shall be cut off from Israel. [16]On the first day you shall hold a solemn assembly, and on the seventh day a solemn assembly; no work shall be done on those days; only what everyone must eat, that alone may be prepared by you. [17]You shall observe the festival of unleavened bread, for on this very day I brought your companies out of the land of Egypt: you shall observe this day throughout your generations as a

departure from the land, for they said, "We shall all be dead." [34]So the people took their dough before it was leavened, with their kneading bowls wrapped up in their cloaks on their shoulders. [35]The Israelites had done as Moses told them; they had asked the Egyptians for jewelry of silver and gold, and for clothing, [36]and the LORD had given the people favor in the sight of the Egyptians, so that they let them have what they asked. And so they plundered the Egyptians.

37 The Israelites journeyed from Rameses to Succoth, about six hundred thousand men on foot, besides children. [38]A mixed crowd also went up with them, and livestock in great numbers, both flocks and herds. [39]They baked unleavened cakes of the dough that they had brought out of Egypt; it was not leavened, because they were driven out of Egypt and could not wait, nor had they prepared any provisions for themselves.

40 The time that the Israelites had lived in Egypt was four hundred thirty years. [41]At the end of four hundred thirty years, on that very day, all the companies of the LORD went out from the land of Egypt. [42]That was for the LORD a night of vigil, to bring them out of the land of Egypt. That same night is a vigil to be kept for the LORD by all the Israelites throughout their generations.

Directions for the Passover

43 The LORD said to Moses and Aaron: This is the ordinance for the passover: no foreigner shall eat of it, [44]but any slave who has been purchased may eat of it after he has been circumcised; [45]no bound or hired servant may eat of it. [46]It shall be eaten in one house; you shall not take any of the animal outside the house, and you shall not break any of its bones. [47]The whole congregation of Israel shall celebrate it. [48]If an alien who resides with you wants to celebrate the passover to the LORD, all his males shall be circumcised; then he may draw near to celebrate it; he shall be regarded as a native of the land. But no uncircumcised person shall eat of it; [49]there shall be one law for the native and for the alien who resides among you.

50 All the Israelites did just as the LORD had commanded Moses and Aaron. [51]That very day the LORD brought the Israelites out of the land of Egypt, company by company.

13 The LORD said to Moses: [2]Consecrate to me all the firstborn; whatever is the first to open the womb among the Israelites, of human beings and animals, is mine.

The Festival of Unleavened Bread

3 Moses said to the people, "Remember this day on which you came out of Egypt, out of the house of slavery, because the LORD brought you out from there by strength of hand; no leavened bread shall be eaten. [4]Today, in the month of Abib, you are going out. [5]When the LORD brings you into the land of the Canaanites, the Hittites, the Amorites, the Hivites, and the Jebusites, which he swore to your ancestors to give you, a land flowing with milk and honey, you shall keep this observance in this month. [6]Seven days you shall eat unleavened bread, and on the seventh day there shall be a festival to the LORD. [7]Unleavened bread shall be eaten for seven days; no leavened bread shall be seen in your possession, and no leaven shall be seen among you in all your territory. [8]You shall tell your child on that day, 'It is because of what the LORD did for me when I came out of Egypt.' [9]It shall serve for you as a sign on your hand and as a reminder on your forehead, so that the teaching of the LORD may be on your lips; for with a strong hand the LORD brought you out of Egypt. [10]You shall keep this ordinance at its proper time from year to year.

The Consecration of the Firstborn

11 "When the LORD has brought you into the land of the Canaanites, as he swore to you and your ancestors, and has given it to you, [12]you shall set apart to the LORD all that first opens the womb. All the firstborn of your livestock that are males shall be the LORD's. [13]But every firstborn donkey you shall redeem with a sheep; if you do not redeem it, you must break its neck. Every firstborn male among your children you shall redeem. [14]When in the future your child asks you, 'What does this mean?' you shall answer, 'By strength of hand the LORD brought us out of Egypt, from the house of slavery. [15]When Pharaoh stubbornly refused to let us go, the LORD killed all the firstborn in the land of Egypt, from human firstborn to the firstborn of animals. Therefore I sacrifice to the LORD every male that first opens the womb, but every firstborn of my sons I redeem.' [16]It shall serve as a sign on your hand and as an emblem[a] on your forehead that by strength of hand the LORD brought us out of Egypt."

a Or as a frontlet; meaning of Heb uncertain

The Pillars of Cloud and Fire

17 When Pharaoh let the people go, God did not lead them by way of the land of the Philistines, although that was nearer; for God thought, "If the people face war, they may change their minds and return to Egypt." [18]So God led the people by the roundabout way of the wilderness toward the Red Sea.[a] The Israelites went up out of the land of Egypt prepared for battle. [19]And Moses took with him the bones of Joseph who had required a solemn oath of the Israelites, saying, "God will surely take notice of you, and then you must carry my bones with you from here." [20]They set out from Succoth, and camped at Etham, on the edge of the wilderness. [21]The LORD went in front of them in a pillar of cloud by day, to lead them along the way, and in a pillar of fire by night, to give them light, so that they might travel by day and by night. [22]Neither the pil-

lar of cloud by day nor the pillar of fire by night left its place in front of the people.

14 Crossing the Red Sea

Then the LORD said to Moses: [2]Tell the Israelites to turn back and camp in front of Pi-hahiroth, between Migdol and the sea, in front of Baal-zephon; you shall camp opposite it, by the sea. [3]Pharaoh will say of the Israelites, "They are wandering aimlessly in the land; the wilderness has closed in on them." [4]I will harden Pharaoh's heart, and he will pursue them, so that I will gain glory for myself over Pharaoh and all his army; and the Egyptians shall know that I am the LORD. And they did so.

5 When the king of Egypt was told that the people had fled, the minds of Pharaoh and his officials were changed toward the people, and they said, "What have we done, letting Israel leave our ser-

Look Up · Exodus 14

Imagine the Israelites as they walked across the ground the Red Sea had covered. What if they had kept their eyes looking down at their feet as they walked, grumbling to one another? "Look at my feet," one might have said. "They're covered with mud. This is some mess Moses led us into." They would have crossed the sea without ever looking up. They would never have seen the sea parted on either side. As they wiped the mud from their feet and clothes, they would have completely missed the sea closing and the Egyptians being swallowed up at God's command!

It seems impossible to miss something so amazing as the parting of the Red Sea, but it's sometimes easy to focus so much on the negative that we miss the positive. Some people—especially those facing rejection, oppression, injustice, or struggles—keep looking down and miss seeing God's power and their own talents and gifts. Looking up is a tough challenge in the middle of hardship, but when we do, we have the chance to see God at work beyond the circumstances of our lives.

Jesus rose from the dead to give hope to you and me and people of every race and culture—so look up! Keep your eyes on the high calling of God in Christ Jesus. Remember the hopeful words in **Psalm 121:1–2**:

I lift up my eyes to the hills—
from where will my help come?
My help comes from the LORD,
who made heaven and earth.

- What do you do when self-doubt and negativity tempt you to keep looking down? What reminds you to look up?
- How can you encourage others when it seems their problems and injustices have beaten them down?

a Or *Sea of Reeds*

vice?" ⁶So he had his chariot made ready, and took his army with him; ⁷he took six hundred picked chariots and all the other chariots of Egypt with officers over all of them. ⁸The LORD hardened the heart of Pharaoh king of Egypt and he pursued the Israelites, who were going out boldly. ⁹The Egyptians pursued them, all Pharaoh's horses and chariots, his chariot drivers and his army; they overtook them camped by the sea, by Pi-hahiroth, in front of Baal-zephon.

10 As Pharaoh drew near, the Israelites looked back, and there were the Egyptians advancing on them. In great fear the Israelites cried out to the LORD. ¹¹They said to Moses, "Was it because there were no graves in Egypt that you have taken us away to die in the wilderness? What have you done to us, bringing us out of Egypt? ¹²Is this not the very thing we told you in Egypt, 'Let us alone and let us serve the Egyptians'? For it would have been better for us to serve the Egyptians than to die in the wilderness." ¹³But Moses said to the people, "Do not be afraid, stand firm, and see the deliverance that the LORD will accomplish for you today; for the Egyptians whom you see today you shall never see again.

¹⁴The LORD will fight for you, and you have only to keep still."

15 Then the LORD said to Moses, "Why do you cry out to me? Tell the Israelites to go forward. ¹⁶But you lift up your staff, and stretch out your hand over the sea and divide it, that the Israelites may go into the sea on dry ground. ¹⁷Then I will harden the hearts of the Egyptians so that they will go in after them; and so I will gain glory for myself over Pharaoh and all his army, his chariots, and his chariot drivers. ¹⁸And the Egyptians shall know that I am the LORD, when I have gained glory for myself over Pharaoh, his chariots, and his chariot drivers."

19 The angel of God who was going before the Israelite army moved and went behind them; and the pillar of cloud moved from in front of them and took its place behind them. ²⁰It came between the army of Egypt and the army of Israel. And so the cloud was there with the darkness, and it lit up the night; one did not come near the other all night.

21 Then Moses stretched out his hand over the sea. The LORD drove the sea back by a strong east wind all night, and turned the sea into dry land; and the waters were divided. ²²The Israelites went into

---

God Frees Us · Exodus 14

Many centuries before Christ, the Israelites migrated to Egypt from Canaan, seeking food because of an extreme drought in their land. The Egyptians took advantage of the Israelites' need for food and shelter; they enslaved the Israelites, ruled over them, and made their lives bitter with hard service.

- Do you know of any situations in which people are being oppressed or exploited because of their immigrant status, their educational level, or their need for food or shelter?
- Pray for God's liberating power. Ask God to give you strength to fight unjust situations and oppression.

The Israelite people groaned under their slavery and asked God for help. God responded to their plight and sent Moses to lead them to freedom. But they needed to overcome their fear of the unknown future and step out in trust. Their liberation was accomplished when they responded to God's initiative to free them from a life of bondage. To be free, we must first be willing to admit that we're enslaved to something.

- What pressures or oppression have taken away your freedom to live according to God's will? Do ever feel pressured to hide or go against your beliefs at school, to cheat on a test, or to treat someone else unkindly?
- How can your community help young people recognize when they're enslaved by social and peer pressures?
- Pray with **Psalm 54** to ask for God's help in your problems. Or pray with **Psalm 146** to praise and thank God for freedom that you've experienced.

the sea on dry ground, the waters forming a wall for them on their right and on their left. [23] The Egyptians pursued, and went into the sea after them, all of Pharaoh's horses, chariots, and chariot drivers. [24] At the morning watch the LORD in the pillar of fire and cloud looked down upon the Egyptian army, and threw the Egyptian army into panic. [25] He clogged[a] their chariot wheels so that they turned with difficulty. The Egyptians said, "Let us flee from the Israelites, for the LORD is fighting for them against Egypt."

The Pursuers Drowned

26 Then the LORD said to Moses, "Stretch out your hand over the sea, so that the water may come back upon the Egyptians, upon their chariots and chariot drivers." [27] So Moses stretched out his hand over the sea, and at dawn the sea returned to its normal depth. As the Egyptians fled before it, the LORD tossed the Egyptians into the sea. [28] The waters returned and covered the chariots and the chariot drivers, the entire army of Pharaoh that had followed them into the sea; not one of them remained. [29] But the Israelites walked on dry ground through the sea, the waters forming a wall for them on their right and on their left.

30 Thus the LORD saved Israel that day from the Egyptians; and Israel saw the Egyptians dead on the seashore. [31] Israel saw the great work that the LORD did against the Egyptians. So the people feared the LORD and believed in the LORD and in his servant Moses.

The Song of Moses

15 Then Moses and the Israelites sang this song to the LORD:

"I will sing to the Lord, for he has triumphed gloriously;
      horse and rider he has thrown into the sea.
[2] The Lord is my strength and my might,[b]
      and he has become my salvation;
   this is my God, and I will praise him,
      my father's God, and I will exalt him.
[3] The Lord is a warrior;
      the Lord is his name.

[4] "Pharaoh's chariots and his army he cast into
         the sea;
      his picked officers were sunk in the Red
         Sea.[c]

[5] The floods covered them;
      they went down into the depths like a
         stone.
[6] Your right hand, O Lord, glorious in power—
      your right hand, O Lord, shattered the
         enemy.
[7] In the greatness of your majesty you
         overthrew your adversaries;
      you sent out your fury, it consumed them
         like stubble.
[8] At the blast of your nostrils the waters
         piled up,
      the floods stood up in a heap;
      the deeps congealed in the heart of the sea.
[9] The enemy said, 'I will pursue, I will overtake,
      I will divide the spoil, my desire shall have
         its fill of them.
   I will draw my sword, my hand shall
         destroy them.'
[10] You blew with your wind, the sea covered
         them;
      they sank like lead in the mighty waters.

[11] "Who is like you, O Lord, among the gods?
      Who is like you, majestic in holiness,
      awesome in splendor, doing wonders?

STUDY IT!

Oldest Song in the Bible
Exodus 15:1–21

This song at the Red Sea is probably the oldest writing in the Bible. It's an example of how the Israelites turned stories of God's mighty deeds into song to be remembered and passed on from generation to generation.

Exodus 15:20–21 tell us that the prophetess Miriam held a key role in leading the people in praising God through music and dancing. Miriam was Moses' and Aaron's sister, and the three of them worked as a team to lead the Israelites. Many biblical scholars believe she may be the author of the song. This is one of the few biblical stories that clearly shows a woman serving as a leader of prayer and praise.

a Sam Gk Syr: MT *removed*   b Or *song*   c Or *Sea of Reeds*

12 You stretched out your right hand,
    the earth swallowed them.

13 "In your steadfast love you led the people
    whom you redeemed;
    you guided them by your strength to your
    holy abode.
14 The peoples heard, they trembled;
    pangs seized the inhabitants of Philistia.
15 Then the chiefs of Edom were dismayed;
    trembling seized the leaders of Moab;
    all the inhabitants of Canaan melted away.
16 Terror and dread fell upon them;
    by the might of your arm, they became still
    as a stone
until your people, O Lord, passed by,
    until the people whom you acquired
    passed by.
17 You brought them in and planted them on the
    mountain of your own possession,
    the place, O Lord, that you made your
    abode,
    the sanctuary, O Lord, that your hands
    have established.
18 The Lord will reign forever and ever."

19 When the horses of Pharaoh with his chariots and his chariot drivers went into the sea, the Lord brought back the waters of the sea upon them; but the Israelites walked through the sea on dry ground.

The Song of Miriam

20 Then the prophet Miriam, Aaron's sister, took a tambourine in her hand; and all the women went out after her with tambourines and with dancing. 21 And Miriam sang to them:

"Sing to the Lord, for he has triumphed
    gloriously;
horse and rider he has thrown into the sea."

Bitter Water Made Sweet

22 Then Moses ordered Israel to set out from the Red Sea,[a] and they went into the wilderness of Shur.

They went three days in the wilderness and found no water. 23 When they came to Marah, they could not drink the water of Marah because it was bitter. That is why it was called Marah.[b] 24 And the people complained against Moses, saying, "What shall we drink?" 25 He cried out to the Lord; and the Lord showed him a piece of wood;[c] he threw it into the water, and the water became sweet.

There the Lord[d] made for them a statute and an ordinance and there he put them to the test. 26 He said, "If you will listen carefully to the voice of the Lord your God, and do what is right in his sight, and give heed to his commandments and keep all his statutes, I will not bring upon you any of the diseases that I brought upon the Egyptians; for I am the Lord who heals you."

27 Then they came to Elim, where there were twelve springs of water and seventy palm trees; and they camped there by the water.

Bread from Heaven

16 The whole congregation of the Israelites set out from Elim; and Israel came to the wilderness of Sin, which is between Elim and Sinai, on the fifteenth day of the second month after they had departed from the land of Egypt. 2 The whole congregation of the Israelites complained against Moses and Aaron in the wilderness. 3 The Israelites said to them, "If only we had died by the hand of the Lord in the land of Egypt, when we sat by the fleshpots and ate our fill of bread; for you have brought us out into this wilderness to kill this whole assembly with hunger."

4 Then the Lord said to Moses, "I am going to rain bread from heaven for you, and each day the people shall go out and gather enough for that day. In that way I will test them, whether they will follow my instruction or not. 5 On the sixth day, when they prepare what they bring in, it will be twice as much as they gather on other days." 6 So Moses and Aaron said to all the Israelites, "In the evening you shall know that it was the Lord who brought you out of the land of Egypt, 7 and in the morning you shall see the glory of the Lord, because he has heard your complaining against the Lord. For what are we, that you complain against us?" 8 And Moses said, "When the Lord gives you meat to eat in the evening and your fill of bread in the morning, because the Lord has heard the complaining that you utter against him—what are we?

a Or *Sea of Reeds* b That is *Bitterness* c Or *a tree* d Heb *he*

LIVE IT!

Those Whiny Israelites • Exodus 16:1–3

It's so easy to complain, isn't it? We all do it. We start fussing and whining and grumbling as soon as things aren't quite the way we would like. We're no different from the Israelites, who started complaining after a few days in the wilderness—despite having just been miraculously delivered from slavery. "Why would God lead us through the Red Sea only to let us die of hunger?" they asked.

Perspective. Faith. That's what it takes. Once you've been through a crisis on your own or spent time with people in serious need—maybe in another country or place with truly poor and hungry people—you gain perspective on your own life and culture. You see your own tendency to want everything your own way, just the way you like it, as soon as possible. But even then, it's easy to forget. The next time you catch yourself complaining, stop, step back, and take a look at the bigger picture—perhaps the one that God sees. Then ask yourself, "Is this really worth complaining about?"

Your complaining is not against us but against the LORD."

9 Then Moses said to Aaron, "Say to the whole congregation of the Israelites, 'Draw near to the LORD, for he has heard your complaining.' " [10] And as Aaron spoke to the whole congregation of the Israelites, they looked toward the wilderness, and the glory of the LORD appeared in the cloud. [11] The LORD spoke to Moses and said, [12] "I have heard the complaining of the Israelites; say to them, 'At twilight you shall eat meat, and in the morning you shall have your fill of bread; then you shall know that I am the LORD your God.' "

13 In the evening quails came up and covered the camp; and in the morning there was a layer of dew around the camp. [14] When the layer of dew lifted, there on the surface of the wilderness was a fine flaky substance, as fine as frost on the ground. [15] When the Israelites saw it, they said to one another, "What is it?"[a] For they did not know what it was. Moses said to them, "It is the bread that the LORD has given you to eat. [16] This is what the LORD has commanded: 'Gather as much of it as each of you needs, an omer to a person according to the number of persons, all providing for those in their own tents.' " [17] The Israelites did so, some gathering more, some less. [18] But when they measured it with an omer, those who gathered much had nothing over, and those who gathered little had no shortage; they gathered as much as each of them needed. [19] And Moses said to them, "Let no one leave any of it over until morning." [20] But they did not listen to Moses; some left part of it until morning, and it bred worms

and became foul. And Moses was angry with them. [21] Morning by morning they gathered it, as much as each needed; but when the sun grew hot, it melted.

22 On the sixth day they gathered twice as much food, two omers apiece. When all the leaders of the congregation came and told Moses, [23] he said to them, "This is what the LORD has commanded: 'Tomorrow is a day of solemn rest, a holy sabbath to the LORD; bake what you want to bake and boil what you want to boil, and all that is left over put aside to be kept until morning.' " [24] So they put it aside until morning, as Moses commanded them; and it did not become foul, and there were no worms in it. [25] Moses said, "Eat it today, for today is a sabbath to the LORD; today you will not find it in the field. [26] Six days you shall gather it; but on the seventh day, which is a sabbath, there will be none."

27 On the seventh day some of the people went out to gather, and they found none. [28] The LORD said to Moses, "How long will you refuse to keep my commandments and instructions? [29] See! The LORD has given you the sabbath, therefore on the sixth day he gives you food for two days; each of you stay where you are; do not leave your place on the seventh day." [30] So the people rested on the seventh day.

31 The house of Israel called it manna; it was like coriander seed, white, and the taste of it was like wafers made with honey. [32] Moses said, "This is what the LORD has commanded: 'Let an omer of it be kept throughout your generations, in order that they may see the food with which I fed you in the wilderness, when I brought you out of the land of Egypt.' "

a Or "It is manna" (Heb man hu, see verse 31)

³³And Moses said to Aaron, "Take a jar, and put an omer of manna in it, and place it before the LORD, to be kept throughout your generations." ³⁴As the LORD commanded Moses, so Aaron placed it before the covenant,ᵃ for safekeeping. ³⁵The Israelites ate manna forty years, until they came to a habitable land; they ate manna, until they came to the border of the land of Canaan. ³⁶An omer is a tenth of an ephah.

17 Water from the Rock

From the wilderness of Sin the whole congregation of the Israelites journeyed by stages, as the LORD commanded. They camped at Rephidim, but there was no water for the people to drink. ²The people quarreled with Moses, and said, "Give us water to drink." Moses said to them, "Why do you quarrel with me? Why do you test the LORD?" ³But the people thirsted there for water; and the people complained against Moses and said, "Why did you bring us out of Egypt, to kill us and our children and livestock with thirst?" ⁴So Moses cried out to the LORD, "What shall I do with this people? They are almost ready to stone me." ⁵The LORD said to Moses, "Go on ahead of the people, and take some of the elders of Israel with you; take in your hand the staff with which you struck the Nile, and go. ⁶I will be standing there in front of you on the rock at Horeb. Strike the rock, and water will come out of it, so that the people may drink." Moses did so, in the sight of the elders of Israel. ⁷He called the place Massahᵇ and Meribah,ᶜ because the Israelites quarreled and tested the LORD, saying, "Is the LORD among us or not?"

Amalek Attacks Israel and Is Defeated

8 Then Amalek came and fought with Israel at Rephidim. ⁹Moses said to Joshua, "Choose some men for us and go out, fight with Amalek. Tomorrow I will stand on the top of the hill with the staff of God in my hand." ¹⁰So Joshua did as Moses told

PRAY IT!

No One Stands Alone
Exodus 17:8–16

Our modern army would never follow God's strange battle plans for the Israelites. When Moses held up his staff, the symbol of God's power, the Israelites were winning. When he couldn't keep his arms up, the Israelites began to lose. Moses needed help. Enter Aaron and Hur, two trusted friends who held up Moses' tired arms. They stood by Moses and supported him, literally. It took all three of them to accomplish their important task.

Moses' outstretched arms can also be understood as a prayer of support for the Israelites. Prayer makes a difference. Research has shown that prayer even helps our emotional and physical health and healing, though it cannot explain why. Prayer is a proven, powerful force.

When you pray, you don't always need words. To hold someone in prayer, just think of the person, and quietly take that person's pain or joy into your heart.

- Who in your life needs prayer? Take a minute to pray for those people.
- Who needs support? Whose hands can you hold up in a hard task or long process? List tangible ways you can help; then do them.

him, and fought with Amalek, while Moses, Aaron, and Hur went up to the top of the hill. ¹¹Whenever Moses held up his hand, Israel prevailed; and whenever he lowered his hand, Amalek prevailed. ¹²But Moses' hands grew weary; so they took a stone and put it under him, and he sat on it. Aaron and Hur held up his hands, one on one side, and the other on the other side; so his hands were steady until the sun set. ¹³And Joshua defeated Amalek and his people with the sword.

14 Then the LORD said to Moses, "Write this as

ᵃ Or *treaty* or *testimony*; Heb *eduth*   ᵇ That is *Test*   ᶜ That is *Quarrel* a reminder in a book and recite it in the hearing of Joshua: I will utterly blot out the remembrance of Amalek from under heaven." ¹⁵And Moses built an altar and called it, The LORD is my banner. ¹⁶He said, "A hand upon the banner of the LORD!^{*a*} The LORD will have war with Amalek from generation to generation."

Jethro's Advice

18 Jethro, the priest of Midian, Moses' father-in-law, heard of all that God had done for Moses and for his people Israel, how the LORD had brought Israel out of Egypt. ²After Moses had sent away his wife Zipporah, his father-in-law Jethro took her back, ³along with her two sons. The name of the one was Gershom (for he said, "I have been an alien^{*b*} in a foreign land"), ⁴and the name of the other, Eliezer^{*c*} (for he said, "The God of my father was my help, and delivered me from the sword of Pharaoh"). ⁵Jethro, Moses' father-in-law, came into the wilderness where Moses was encamped at the mountain of God, bringing Moses' sons and wife to him. ⁶He sent word to Moses, "I, your father-in-law Jethro, am coming to you, with your wife and her two sons." ⁷Moses went out to meet his father-in-law; he bowed down and kissed him; each asked after the other's welfare, and they went into the tent. ⁸Then Moses told his father-in-law all that the LORD had done to Pharaoh and to the Egyptians for Israel's sake, all the hardship that had beset them on the way, and how

the LORD had delivered them. ⁹Jethro rejoiced for all the good that the LORD had done to Israel, in delivering them from the Egyptians.

10 Jethro said, "Blessed be the LORD, who has delivered you from the Egyptians and from Pharaoh. ¹¹Now I know that the LORD is greater than all gods, because he delivered the people from the Egyptians,^{*d*} when they dealt arrogantly with them." ¹²And Jethro, Moses' father-in-law, brought a burnt offering and sacrifices to God; and Aaron came with all the elders of Israel to eat bread with Moses' father-in-law in the presence of God.

13 The next day Moses sat as judge for the people, while the people stood around him from morning until evening. ¹⁴When Moses' father-in-law saw all that he was doing for the people, he said, "What is this that you are doing for the people? Why do you sit alone, while all the people stand around you from morning until evening?" ¹⁵Moses said to his father-in-law, "Because the people come to me to inquire of God. ¹⁶When they have a dispute, they come to me and I decide between one person and another, and I make known to them the statutes and instructions of God." ¹⁷Moses' father-in-law said to him, "What you are doing is not good. ¹⁸You will surely wear yourself out, both you and these people with you. For the task is too heavy for you; you cannot do it alone. ¹⁹Now listen to me. I will give you counsel, and God be with you! You should represent the people before God, and you should bring their cases be-

---

LIVE IT!

Sometimes You've Got to Ask for Help · Exodus 18:13–26

Was Moses a workaholic? That's what his father-in-law calls him (Exodus 18:17–18). Maybe he just found himself suddenly overwhelmed by too many responsibilities. Fortunately for Moses, his wise father-in-law could see a solution Moses couldn't or maybe didn't want to see.

Which person in this story do you feel most like?

• Moses, surrounded by people clamoring for your attention

• Jethro, concerned about Moses and able to offer some advice

• One of the people hoping Moses has a few minutes to listen to your problem

• One of the trustworthy judges chosen by Moses to make sure the Israelites practice justice in all their day-to-day business

When leaders share responsibility, they are saying to other people, "I trust you, we're in this together, and you are needed." When you are in a leadership position, remember Jethro's advice to Moses, and don't be a lone ranger; ask others for help!

---

^{*a*} Cn: Meaning of Heb uncertain ^{*b*} Heb *ger* ^{*c*} Heb *Eli*, my God; *ezer*, help ^{*d*} The clause *because . . . Egyptians* has been transposed from verse 10

fore God; [20]teach them the statutes and instructions and make known to them the way they are to go and the things they are to do. [21]You should also look for able men among all the people, men who fear God, are trustworthy, and hate dishonest gain; set such men over them as officers over thousands, hundreds, fifties, and tens. [22]Let them sit as judges for the people at all times; let them bring every important case to you, but decide every minor case themselves. So it will be easier for you, and they will bear the burden with you. [23]If you do this, and God so commands you, then you will be able to endure, and all these people will go to their home in peace."

24 So Moses listened to his father-in-law and did all that he had said. [25]Moses chose able men from all Israel and appointed them as heads over the people, as officers over thousands, hundreds, fifties, and tens. [26]And they judged the people at all times; hard cases they brought to Moses, but any minor case they decided themselves. [27]Then Moses let his father-in-law depart, and he went off to his own country.

19 The Israelites Reach Mount Sinai

On the third new moon after the Israelites had gone out of the land of Egypt, on that very day, they came into the wilderness of Sinai. [2]They had journeyed from Rephidim, entered the wilderness of Sinai, and camped in the wilderness; Israel camped there in front of the mountain. [3]Then Moses went up to God; the LORD called to him from the mountain, saying, "Thus you shall say to the house of Jacob, and tell the Israelites: [4]You have seen what I did to the Egyptians, and how I bore you on eagles' wings and brought you to myself. [5]Now therefore, if you obey my voice and keep my covenant, you shall be my treasured possession out of all the peoples. Indeed, the whole earth is mine, [6]but you shall be for me a priestly kingdom and a holy nation. These are the words that you shall speak to the Israelites."

7 So Moses came, summoned the elders of the people, and set before them all these words that the LORD had commanded him. [8]The people all answered as one: "Everything that the LORD has spoken we will do." Moses reported the words of the people to the LORD. [9]Then the LORD said to Moses, "I am going to come to you in a dense cloud, in order that the people may hear when I speak with you and so trust you ever after."

The People Consecrated

When Moses had told the words of the people to the LORD, [10]the LORD said to Moses: "Go to the people and consecrate them today and tomorrow. Have them wash their clothes [11]and prepare for the third day, because on the third day the LORD will come down upon Mount Sinai in the sight of all the people. [12]You shall set limits for the people all around, saying, 'Be careful not to go up the mountain or to touch the edge of it. Any who touch the mountain shall be put to death. [13]No hand shall touch them, but they shall be stoned or shot with arrows;[a] whether animal or human being, they shall not live.' When the trumpet sounds a long blast, they may go up on the mountain." [14]So Moses went down from the mountain to the people. He consecrated the people, and they washed their clothes. [15]And he said to the people, "Prepare for the third day; do not go near a woman."

16 On the morning of the third day there was thunder and lightning, as well as a thick cloud on the mountain, and a blast of a trumpet so loud that all the people who were in the camp trembled. [17]Moses brought the people out of the camp to meet God. They took their stand at the foot of the mountain. [18]Now Mount Sinai was wrapped in smoke, because the LORD had descended upon it in fire; the smoke went up like the smoke of a kiln, while the whole mountain shook violently. [19]As the blast of the trumpet grew louder and louder, Moses would speak and God would answer him in thunder. [20]When the LORD descended upon Mount Sinai, to the top of the mountain, the LORD summoned Moses to the top of the mountain, and Moses went up. [21]Then the LORD said to Moses, "Go down and warn the people not to break through to the LORD to look; otherwise many of them will perish. [22]Even the priests who approach the LORD must consecrate themselves or the LORD will break out against them." [23]Moses said to the LORD, "The people are not permitted to come up to Mount Sinai; for you yourself warned us, saying, 'Set limits around the mountain and keep it holy.' " [24]The LORD said to him, "Go down, and come up bringing Aaron with you; but do not let either the priests or the people break through to come up to the LORD; otherwise he will break out against them." [25]So Moses went down to the people and told them.

a Heb lacks *with arrows*

The Ten Commandments

20 Then God spoke all these words:

2 I am the LORD your God, who brought you out of the land of Egypt, out of the house of slavery; ³you shall have no other gods before*ᵃ* me.

4 You shall not make for yourself an idol, whether in the form of anything that is in heaven above, or that is on the earth beneath, or that is in the water under the earth. ⁵You shall not bow down to them or worship them; for I the LORD your God am a jealous God, punishing children for the iniquity of parents, to the third and the fourth generation of those who reject me, ⁶but showing steadfast love to the thousandth generation*ᵇ* of those who love me and keep my commandments.

7 You shall not make wrongful use of the name of the LORD your God, for the LORD will not acquit anyone who misuses his name.

> "I am the LORD your God . . . you shall have no other gods before me."
> —Exodus 20:2–3

8 Remember the sabbath day, and keep it holy. ⁹Six days you shall labor and do all your work. ¹⁰But the seventh day is a sabbath to the LORD your God; you shall not do any work—you, your son or your daughter, your male or female slave, your livestock, or the alien resident in your towns. ¹¹For in six days the LORD made heaven and earth, the sea, and all that is in them, but rested the seventh day; therefore the LORD blessed the sabbath day and consecrated it.

STUDY IT!

Covenant Commandments   Exodus 20:1–17

The covenant God made with the Israelites is often called the Sinai covenant. The Ten Commandments are a handy summary of the Sinai covenant—literally handy, because they can be counted on one's fingers. They are also easy to memorize, because they're short (so short they are sometimes called the Ten Words) and most of them begin with a similar phrase ("you shall not").

1. I am the LORD your God; . . . you shall have no other gods before me.
2. You shall not make for yourself an idol.
3. You shall not make wrongful use of the name of the LORD your God.
4. Remember the sabbath day, and keep it holy.
5. Honor your father and your mother.
6. You shall not murder.
7. You shall not commit adultery.
8. You shall not steal.
9. You shall not bear false witness against your neighbor.
10. You shall not covet your neighbor's house; you shall not covet your neighbor's wife, . . . or anything that belongs to your neighbor.

The ancient Israelites believed that everyone had to know and observe these basic rules if God's people were to live together in peace and security. Today three major world religions—Judaism, Christianity, and Islam—continue to revere the Ten Commandments as basic building blocks of human community.

For the ancient Israelites, the Ten Commandments covered specific behaviors that made them different from the neighboring cultures. Through the centuries, Christians have applied the principles of the Ten Commandments to many other moral questions and issues. For Jesus' teaching on the Ten Commandments, see **Matthew 5:1–7:29; 22:34–40;** and **Mark 12:28–34.**

a Or *besides* *b* Or *to thousands*

LIVE IT!

Living Out the Commandments
Exodus 20:1–17

The Ten Commandments are probably the most famous part of the Old Testament. They are so basic and so familiar to us, mainly because they make so much sense. The actions they address happen all around us today, just as they did four thousand years ago. And we see the negative results and pain caused by disobeying authority, stealing, lying, killing, and committing adultery. The Ten Commandments lead us, instead, to behaviors that bring health, life, and peace. The Ten Commandments still make sense, because human nature hasn't really changed, and God knows that. So look them over carefully, memorize them, and ask God to help you with the ones that are the most challenging for you to understand and obey.

12 Honor your father and your mother, so that your days may be long in the land that the LORD your God is giving you.

13 You shall not murder.*a*

14 You shall not commit adultery.

15 You shall not steal.

16 You shall not bear false witness against your neighbor.

17 You shall not covet your neighbor's house; you shall not covet your neighbor's wife, or male or female slave, or ox, or donkey, or anything that belongs to your neighbor.

18 When all the people witnessed the thunder and lightning, the sound of the trumpet, and the mountain smoking, they were afraid*b* and trembled and stood at a distance, ¹⁹and said to Moses, "You speak to us, and we will listen; but do not let God speak to us, or we will die." ²⁰Moses said to the people, "Do not be afraid; for God has come only to test you and to put the fear of him upon you so that you do not sin." ²¹Then the people stood at a distance, while Moses drew near to the thick darkness where God was.

The Law concerning the Altar

22 The LORD said to Moses: Thus you shall say to the Israelites: "You have seen for yourselves that I spoke with you from heaven. ²³You shall not make gods of silver alongside me, nor shall you make for yourselves gods of gold. ²⁴You need make for me only an altar of earth and sacrifice on it your burnt offerings and your offerings of well-being, your sheep and your oxen; in every place where I cause my name to be remembered I will come to you and bless you. ²⁵But if you make for me an altar of stone, do not build it of hewn stones; for if you use a chisel upon it you profane it. ²⁶You shall not go up by steps to my altar, so that your nakedness may not be exposed on it."

The Law concerning Slaves

21 These are the ordinances that you shall set before them:

2 When you buy a male Hebrew slave, he shall serve six years, but in the seventh he shall go out a free person, without debt. ³If he comes in single, he shall go out single; if he comes in married, then his wife shall go out with him. ⁴If his master gives him a wife and she bears him sons or daughters, the wife and her children shall be her master's and he shall go out alone. ⁵But if the slave declares, "I love my master, my wife, and my children; I will not go out a free person," ⁶then his master shall bring him before God.*c* He shall be brought to the door or the doorpost; and his master shall pierce his ear with an awl; and he shall serve him for life.

7 When a man sells his daughter as a slave, she shall not go out as the male slaves do. ⁸If she does not please her master, who designated her for himself, then he shall let her be redeemed; he shall have no right to sell her to a foreign people, since he has dealt unfairly with her. ⁹If he designates her for his son, he shall deal with her as with a daughter. ¹⁰If he takes another wife to himself, he shall not diminish the food, clothing, or marital rights of the first wife.*d* ¹¹And if he does not do these three things for her, she shall go out without debt, without payment of money.

The Law concerning Violence

12 Whoever strikes a person mortally shall be put to death. ¹³If it was not premeditated, but came about by an act of God, then I will appoint for you a place to which the killer may flee. ¹⁴But if someone

a Or kill   *b* Sam Gk Syr Vg: MT *they saw*   *c* Or *to the judges*   *d* Heb *of her*

willfully attacks and kills another by treachery, you shall take the killer from my altar for execution.

15 Whoever strikes father or mother shall be put to death.

16 Whoever kidnaps a person, whether that person has been sold or is still held in possession, shall be put to death.

17 Whoever curses father or mother shall be put to death.

18 When individuals quarrel and one strikes the other with a stone or fist so that the injured party, though not dead, is confined to bed, 19but recovers and walks around outside with the help of a staff, then the assailant shall be free of liability, except to pay for the loss of time, and to arrange for full recovery.

20 When a slaveowner strikes a male or female slave with a rod and the slave dies immediately, the owner shall be punished. 21But if the slave survives a day or two, there is no punishment; for the slave is the owner's property.

22 When people who are fighting injure a pregnant woman so that there is a miscarriage, and yet no further harm follows, the one responsible shall be fined what the woman's husband demands, paying as much as the judges determine. 23If any harm follows, then you shall give life for life, 24eye for eye, tooth for tooth, hand for hand, foot for foot, 25burn for burn, wound for wound, stripe for stripe.

26 When a slaveowner strikes the eye of a male or female slave, destroying it, the owner shall let the slave go, a free person, to compensate for the eye. 27If the owner knocks out a tooth of a male or female slave, the slave shall be let go, a free person, to compensate for the tooth.

Laws concerning Property

28 When an ox gores a man or a woman to death, the ox shall be stoned, and its flesh shall not be eaten; but the owner of the ox shall not be liable. 29If the ox has been accustomed to gore in the past, and its owner has been warned but has not restrained it, and it kills a man or a woman, the ox shall be stoned, and its owner also shall be put to death. 30If a ransom is imposed on the owner, then the owner shall pay whatever is imposed for the redemption of the victim's life. 31If it gores a boy or a girl, the owner shall be dealt with according to this same rule. 32If the ox gores a male or female slave, the owner shall pay to the slaveowner thirty shekels of silver, and the ox shall be stoned.

33 If someone leaves a pit open, or digs a pit and does not cover it, and an ox or a donkey falls into it, 34the owner of the pit shall make restitution, giving money to its owner, but keeping the dead animal.

35 If someone's ox hurts the ox of another, so that it dies, then they shall sell the live ox and divide the price of it; and the dead animal they shall also divide. 36But if it was known that the ox was accustomed to gore in the past, and its owner has not restrained it, the owner shall restore ox for ox, but keep the dead animal.

22 Laws of Restitution

aWhen someone steals an ox or a sheep, and slaughters it or sells it, the thief shall pay five oxen for an ox, and four sheep for a sheep.b The thief shall make restitution, but if unable to do so, shall be sold for the theft. 4When the animal, whether ox or donkey or sheep, is found alive in the thief's possession, the thief shall pay double.

2c If a thief is found breaking in, and is beaten to death, no bloodguilt is incurred; 3but if it happens after sunrise, bloodguilt is incurred.

5 When someone causes a field or vineyard to be grazed over, or lets livestock loose to graze in someone else's field, restitution shall be made from the best in the owner's field or vineyard.

6 When fire breaks out and catches in thorns so that the stacked grain or the standing grain or the field is consumed, the one who started the fire shall make full restitution.

7 When someone delivers to a neighbor money or goods for safekeeping, and they are stolen from the neighbor's house, then the thief, if caught, shall pay double. 8If the thief is not caught, the owner of the house shall be brought before God,d to determine whether or not the owner had laid hands on the neighbor's goods.

9 In any case of disputed ownership involving ox, donkey, sheep, clothing, or any other loss, of which one party says, "This is mine," the case of both parties shall come before God;d the one whom God condemnse shall pay double to the other.

10 When someone delivers to another a donkey, ox, sheep, or any other animal for safekeeping, and it dies or is injured or is carried off, without anyone seeing it, 11an oath before the LORD shall decide between the two of them that the one has not laid

a Ch 21.37 in Heb   b Verses 2, 3, and 4 rearranged thus: 3b, 4, 2, 3a   c Ch 22.1 in Heb   d Or before the judges   e Or the judges condemn

hands on the property of the other; the owner shall accept the oath, and no restitution shall be made. [12] But if it was stolen, restitution shall be made to its owner. [13] If it was mangled by beasts, let it be brought as evidence; restitution shall not be made for the mangled remains.

14 When someone borrows an animal from another and it is injured or dies, the owner not being present, full restitution shall be made. [15] If the owner was present, there shall be no restitution; if it was hired, only the hiring fee is due.

Social and Religious Laws

16 When a man seduces a virgin who is not engaged to be married, and lies with her, he shall give the bride-price for her and make her his wife. [17] But if her father refuses to give her to him, he shall pay an amount equal to the bride-price for virgins.

18 You shall not permit a female sorcerer to live.

19 Whoever lies with an animal shall be put to death.

20 Whoever sacrifices to any god, other than the LORD alone, shall be devoted to destruction.

21 You shall not wrong or oppress a resident alien, for you were aliens in the land of Egypt. [22] You shall not abuse any widow or orphan. [23] If you do abuse them, when they cry out to me, I will surely heed their cry; [24] my wrath will burn, and I will kill you with the sword, and your wives shall become widows and your children orphans.

25 If you lend money to my people, to the poor among you, you shall not deal with them as a creditor; you shall not exact interest from them. [26] If you take your neighbor's cloak in pawn, you shall restore it before the sun goes down; [27] for it may be your neighbor's only clothing to use as cover; in what else shall that person sleep? And if your neighbor cries out to me, I will listen, for I am compassionate.

28 You shall not revile God, or curse a leader of your people.

29 You shall not delay to make offerings from the fullness of your harvest and from the outflow of your presses.[a]

CONNECT IT!

Neema Syovata: Teen Immigrant · Exodus 22:21–27

Moving to a new home is always hard—especially when it's in a new country. Fifteen-year-old Neema Syovata had positive hopes when her family moved from Kenya to the United States. According to her story online at PBS IN THE MIX,* she found out that many of the good things she'd heard about America were true, but she was in for some harsh surprises when she started her new school in Connecticut. Some kids cursed at her and told her to go back to Africa. Other people acted like racists, treating her like an outcast because of her black skin. Cruelty like that was certainly hard to deal with, but Neema did have some friends who stuck by her. Together they formed a diversity club to welcome people and embrace their unique differences. These students understood that people's unique abilities make the world a richer place. They thought it was cool that Neema knew how to speak Swahili—and was learning Spanish and Arabic! Thankfully, Neema was able to stay positive and enjoy friends who supported her through dealing with others' ignorance and prejudice.

Unfortunately, there are many other immigrants around us still struggling to find acceptance and kindness. Many young people who come to our country face insults and mockery, and so do their families. Immigration sometimes becomes a heated political topic, and as battle lines are drawn, the real people living among us become treated with suspicion and hostility.

Exodus 22:21–22 tells us, "You shall not wrong or oppress a resident alien. . . . You shall not abuse any widow or orphan." This section of the Sinai laws reminded the Israelites to take care of the poor and vulnerable around them and not to become abusive, as the Egyptians were to them. It applies to us today too. As individuals and as a society we are obliged to always be mindful of how our actions impact others and to treat them with God's love and compassion.

α Meaning of Heb uncertain

The firstborn of your sons you shall give to me. [30]You shall do the same with your oxen and with your sheep: seven days it shall remain with its mother; on the eighth day you shall give it to me.

31 You shall be people consecrated to me; therefore you shall not eat any meat that is mangled by beasts in the field; you shall throw it to the dogs.

23 Justice for All

You shall not spread a false report. You shall not join hands with the wicked to act as a malicious witness. [2]You shall not follow a majority in wrongdoing; when you bear witness in a lawsuit, you shall not side with the majority so as to pervert justice; [3]nor shall you be partial to the poor in a lawsuit.

4 When you come upon your enemy's ox or donkey going astray, you shall bring it back.

5 When you see the donkey of one who hates you lying under its burden and you would hold back from setting it free, you must help to set it free.[a]

6 You shall not pervert the justice due to your poor in their lawsuits. [7]Keep far from a false charge, and do not kill the innocent and those in the right, for I will not acquit the guilty. [8]You shall take no bribe, for a bribe blinds the officials, and subverts the cause of those who are in the right.

9 You shall not oppress a resident alien; you know the heart of an alien, for you were aliens in the land of Egypt.

Sabbatical Year and Sabbath

10 For six years you shall sow your land and gather in its yield; [11]but the seventh year you shall let it rest and lie fallow, so that the poor of your people may eat; and what they leave the wild animals may eat. You shall do the same with your vineyard, and with your olive orchard.

12 Six days you shall do your work, but on the seventh day you shall rest, so that your ox and your donkey may have relief, and your homeborn slave and the resident alien may be refreshed. [13]Be attentive to all that I have said to you. Do not invoke the names of other gods; do not let them be heard on your lips.

The Annual Festivals

14 Three times in the year you shall hold a festival for me. [15]You shall observe the festival of unleavened bread; as I commanded you, you shall eat unleavened bread for seven days at the appointed time in the month of Abib, for in it you came out of Egypt.

No one shall appear before me empty-handed.

16 You shall observe the festival of harvest, of the first fruits of your labor, of what you sow in the field. You shall observe the festival of ingathering at the end of the year, when you gather in from the field the fruit of your labor. [17]Three times in the year all your males shall appear before the Lord GOD.

18 You shall not offer the blood of my sacrifice with anything leavened, or let the fat of my festival remain until the morning.

19 The choicest of the first fruits of your ground you shall bring into the house of the LORD your God.

You shall not boil a kid in its mother's milk.

The Conquest of Canaan Promised

20 I am going to send an angel in front of you, to guard you on the way and to bring you to the place that I have prepared. [21]Be attentive to him and listen to his voice; do not rebel against him, for he will not pardon your transgression; for my name is in him.

22 But if you listen attentively to his voice and do all that I say, then I will be an enemy to your enemies and a foe to your foes.

23 When my angel goes in front of you, and brings you to the Amorites, the Hittites, the Perizzites, the Canaanites, the Hivites, and the Jebusites, and I blot them out, [24]you shall not bow down to their gods, or worship them, or follow their practices, but you shall utterly demolish them and break their pillars in pieces. [25]You shall worship the LORD your God, and I[b] will bless your bread and your water; and I will take sickness away from among you. [26]No one shall miscarry or be barren in your land; I will fulfill the number of your days. [27]I will send my terror in front of you, and will throw into confusion all the people against whom you shall come, and I will make all your enemies turn their backs to you. [28]And I will send the pestilence[c] in front of you, which shall drive out the Hivites, the Canaanites, and the Hittites from before you. [29]I will not drive them out from before you in one year, or the land would become desolate and the wild animals would multiply against you. [30]Little by little I will drive them out from before you, until you have increased and possess the land. [31]I will set your borders from the Red Sea[d] to the sea of the

---

a Meaning of Heb uncertain   b Gk Vg: Heb *he*   c Or *hornets:* Meaning of Heb uncertain   d Or *Sea of Reeds*

Philistines, and from the wilderness to the Euphrates; for I will hand over to you the inhabitants of the land, and you shall drive them out before you. ³²You shall make no covenant with them and their gods. ³³They shall not live in your land, or they will make you sin against me; for if you worship their gods, it will surely be a snare to you.

24 The Blood of the Covenant

Then he said to Moses, "Come up to the LORD, you and Aaron, Nadab, and Abihu, and seventy of the elders of Israel, and worship at a distance. ²Moses alone shall come near the LORD;

STUDY IT!

Sacrifice and Communion Exodus 24:1–8

Sacrifice is defined as an offering made to God that becomes holy by being set apart, blessed, burned, and consumed. The people of Israel brought animals to God and sacrificed them in the same way food and gifts were brought to a king as a form of tribute and worship. Their blood shed on the altar symbolized God's gift of life, and their meat was cooked and eaten as a form of worship that brought communion with God. In this passage when Israel is about to ratify the covenant with God, Moses smears the animal's blood on the altar to demonstrate the Israelites' union with God through the observance of the covenant.

In the New Testament, Jesus uses language at the Last Supper that reflects this sacrificial understanding. Jesus shares bread and wine and speaks of a new covenant that will be formed by the giving of his body and the shedding of his blood. Even today, we share the bread and wine of the Lord's Supper, celebrating the new covenant of love he established through his death and resurrection.

but the others shall not come near, and the people shall not come up with him."

3 Moses came and told the people all the words of the LORD and all the ordinances; and all the people answered with one voice, and said, "All the words that the LORD has spoken we will do." ⁴And Moses wrote down all the words of the LORD. He rose early in the morning, and built an altar at the foot of the mountain, and set up twelve pillars, corresponding to the twelve tribes of Israel. ⁵He sent young men of the people of Israel, who offered burnt offerings and sacrificed oxen as offerings of well-being to the LORD. ⁶Moses took half of the blood and put it in basins, and half of the blood he dashed against the altar. ⁷Then he took the book of the covenant, and read it in the hearing of the people; and they said, "All that the LORD has spoken we will do, and we will be obedient." ⁸Moses took the blood and dashed it on the people, and said, "See the blood of the covenant that the LORD has made with you in accordance with all these words."

On the Mountain with God

9 Then Moses and Aaron, Nadab, and Abihu, and seventy of the elders of Israel went up, ¹⁰and they saw the God of Israel. Under his feet there was something like a pavement of sapphire stone, like the very heaven for clearness. ¹¹God*ᵃ* did not lay his hand on the chief men of the people of Israel; also they beheld God, and they ate and drank.

12 The LORD said to Moses, "Come up to me on the mountain, and wait there; and I will give you the tablets of stone, with the law and the commandment, which I have written for their instruction." ¹³So Moses set out with his assistant Joshua, and Moses went up into the mountain of God. ¹⁴To the elders he had said, "Wait here for us, until we come to you again; for Aaron and Hur are with you; whoever has a dispute may go to them."

15 Then Moses went up on the mountain, and the cloud covered the mountain. ¹⁶The glory of the LORD settled on Mount Sinai, and the cloud covered it for six days; on the seventh day he called to Moses out of the cloud. ¹⁷Now the appearance of the glory of the LORD was like a devouring fire on the top of the mountain in the sight of the people of Israel. ¹⁸Moses entered the cloud, and went up on the mountain. Moses was on the mountain for forty days and forty nights.

ᵃ Heb *He*

Offerings for the Tabernacle

25 The LORD said to Moses: [2]Tell the Israelites to take for me an offering; from all
whose hearts prompt them to give you shall receive
the offering for me. [3]This is the offering that you
shall receive from them: gold, silver, and bronze,
[4]blue, purple, and crimson yarns and fine linen,
goats' hair, [5]tanned rams' skins, fine leather,[a] acacia
wood, [6]oil for the lamps, spices for the anointing
oil and for the fragrant incense, [7]onyx stones and
gems to be set in the ephod and for the breastpiece.
[8]And have them make me a sanctuary, so that I may
dwell among them. [9]In accordance with all that I
show you concerning the pattern of the tabernacle
and of all its furniture, so you shall make it.

The Ark of the Covenant

10 They shall make an ark of acacia wood; it shall
be two and a half cubits long, a cubit and a half
wide, and a cubit and a half high. [11]You shall overlay it with pure gold, inside and outside you shall
overlay it, and you shall make a molding of gold
upon it all around. [12]You shall cast four rings of
gold for it and put them on its four feet, two rings
on the one side of it, and two rings on the other
side. [13]You shall make poles of acacia wood, and
overlay them with gold. [14]And you shall put the
poles into the rings on the sides of the ark, by which
to carry the ark. [15]The poles shall remain in the
rings of the ark; they shall not be taken from it.
[16]You shall put into the ark the covenant[b] that I
shall give you.

17 Then you shall make a mercy seat[c] of pure
gold; two cubits and a half shall be its length, and
a cubit and a half its width. [18]You shall make two
cherubim of gold; you shall make them of hammered work, at the two ends of the mercy seat.[d]
[19]Make one cherub at the one end, and one cherub
at the other; of one piece with the mercy seat[d] you
shall make the cherubim at its two ends. [20]The
cherubim shall spread out their wings above, overshadowing the mercy seat[d] with their wings. They
shall face one to another; the faces of the cherubim
shall be turned toward the mercy seat.[d] [21]You shall
put the mercy seat[d] on the top of the ark; and in
the ark you shall put the covenant[b] that I shall give
you. [22]There I will meet with you, and from above
the mercy seat,[d] from between the two cherubim
that are on the ark of the covenant,[b] I will deliver
to you all my commands for the Israelites.

The Table for the Bread of the Presence

23 You shall make a table of acacia wood, two
cubits long, one cubit wide, and a cubit and a half
high. [24]You shall overlay it with pure gold, and make
a molding of gold around it. [25]You shall make around
it a rim a handbreadth wide, and a molding of gold
around the rim. [26]You shall make for it four rings of
gold, and fasten the rings to the four corners at its
four legs. [27]The rings that hold the poles used for
carrying the table shall be close to the rim. [28]You shall
make the poles of acacia wood, and overlay them with
gold, and the table shall be carried with these. [29]You
shall make its plates and dishes for incense, and its
flagons and bowls with which to pour drink offerings;
you shall make them of pure gold. [30]And you shall
set the bread of the Presence on the table before me
always.

The Lampstand

31 You shall make a lampstand of pure gold. The
base and the shaft of the lampstand shall be made of
hammered work; its cups, its calyxes, and its petals
shall be of one piece with it; [32]and there shall be six
branches going out of its sides, three branches of the
lampstand out of one side of it and three branches of
the lampstand out of the other side of it; [33]three cups
shaped like almond blossoms, each with calyx and
petals, on one branch, and three cups shaped like
almond blossoms, each with calyx and petals, on the
other branch—so for the six branches going out of
the lampstand. [34]On the lampstand itself there shall
be four cups shaped like almond blossoms, each with
its calyxes and petals. [35]There shall be a calyx of one
piece with it under the first pair of branches, a calyx
of one piece with it under the next pair of branches,
and a calyx of one piece with it under the last pair of
branches—so for the six branches that go out of the
lampstand. [36]Their calyxes and their branches shall
be of one piece with it, the whole of it one hammered
piece of pure gold. [37]You shall make the seven lamps
for it; and the lamps shall be set up so as to give light
on the space in front of it. [38]Its snuffers and trays shall
be of pure gold. [39]It, and all these utensils, shall be
made from a talent of pure gold. [40]And see that you
make them according to the pattern for them, which
is being shown you on the mountain.

The Tabernacle

26 Moreover you shall make the tabernacle
with ten curtains of fine twisted linen, and

---

a Meaning of Heb uncertain **b** Or *treaty,* or *testimony;* Heb *eduth* **c** Or *a cover* **d** Or *the cover*

blue, purple, and crimson yarns; you shall make them with cherubim skillfully worked into them. ²The length of each curtain shall be twenty-eight cubits, and the width of each curtain four cubits; all the curtains shall be of the same size. ³Five curtains shall be joined to one another; and the other five curtains shall be joined to one another. ⁴You shall make loops of blue on the edge of the outermost curtain in the first set; and likewise you shall make loops on the edge of the outermost curtain in the second set. ⁵You shall make fifty loops on the one curtain, and you shall make fifty loops on the edge of the curtain that is in the second set; the loops shall be opposite one another. ⁶You shall make fifty clasps of gold, and join the curtains to one another with the clasps, so that the tabernacle may be one whole.

7 You shall also make curtains of goats' hair for a tent over the tabernacle; you shall make eleven curtains. ⁸The length of each curtain shall be thirty cubits, and the width of each curtain four cubits; the eleven curtains shall be of the same size. ⁹You shall join five curtains by themselves, and six curtains by themselves, and the sixth curtain you shall double over at the front of the tent. ¹⁰You shall make fifty loops on the edge of the curtain that is outermost in one set, and fifty loops on the edge of the curtain that is outermost in the second set.

11 You shall make fifty clasps of bronze, and put the clasps into the loops, and join the tent together, so that it may be one whole. ¹²The part that remains of the curtains of the tent, the half curtain that remains, shall hang over the back of the tabernacle. ¹³The cubit on the one side, and the cubit on the other side, of what remains in the length of the curtains of the tent, shall hang over the sides of the tabernacle, on this side and that side, to cover it. ¹⁴You shall make for the tent a covering of tanned rams' skins and an outer covering of fine leather.ᵃ

The Framework

15 You shall make upright frames of acacia wood for the tabernacle. ¹⁶Ten cubits shall be the length of a frame, and a cubit and a half the width of each frame. ¹⁷There shall be two pegs in each frame to fit the frames together; you shall make these for all the frames of the tabernacle. ¹⁸You shall make the frames for the tabernacle: twenty frames for the south side; ¹⁹and you shall make forty bases of silver under the twenty frames, two bases under the first frame for its two pegs, and two bases under the next frame for its

two pegs; ²⁰and for the second side of the tabernacle, on the north side twenty frames, ²¹and their forty bases of silver, two bases under the first frame, and two bases under the next frame; ²²and for the rear of the tabernacle westward you shall make six frames. ²³You shall make two frames for corners of the tabernacle in the rear; ²⁴they shall be separate beneath, but joined at the top, at the first ring; it shall be the same with both of them; they shall form the two corners. ²⁵And so there shall be eight frames, with their bases of silver, sixteen bases; two bases under the first frame, and two bases under the next frame.

26 You shall make bars of acacia wood, five for the frames of the one side of the tabernacle, ²⁷and five bars for the frames of the other side of the tabernacle, and five bars for the frames of the side of the tabernacle at the rear westward. ²⁸The middle bar, halfway up the frames, shall pass through from end to end. ²⁹You shall overlay the frames with gold, and shall make their rings of gold to hold the bars; and you shall overlay the bars with gold. ³⁰Then you shall erect the tabernacle according to the plan for it that you were shown on the mountain.

The Curtain

31 You shall make a curtain of blue, purple, and crimson yarns, and of fine twisted linen; it shall be made with cherubim skillfully worked into it. ³²You shall hang it on four pillars of acacia overlaid with gold, which have hooks of gold and rest on four bases of silver. ³³You shall hang the curtain under the clasps, and bring the ark of the covenantᵇ in there, within the curtain; and the curtain shall separate for you the holy place from the most holy. ³⁴You shall put the mercy seatᶜ on the ark of the covenantᵇ in the most holy place. ³⁵You shall set the table outside the curtain, and the lampstand on the south side of the tabernacle opposite the table; and you shall put the table on the north side.

36 You shall make a screen for the entrance of the tent, of blue, purple, and crimson yarns, and of fine twisted linen, embroidered with needlework. ³⁷You shall make for the screen five pillars of acacia, and overlay them with gold; their hooks shall be of gold, and you shall cast five bases of bronze for them.

The Altar of Burnt Offering

27 You shall make the altar of acacia wood, five cubits long and five cubits wide; the altar shall be square, and it shall be three cubits high. ²You

---

ᵃ Meaning of Heb uncertain ᵇ Or *treaty*, or *testimony*; Heb *eduth* ᶜ Or *the cover*

shall make horns for it on its four corners; its horns shall be of one piece with it, and you shall overlay it with bronze. ³You shall make pots for it to receive its ashes, and shovels and basins and forks and firepans; you shall make all its utensils of bronze. ⁴You shall also make for it a grating, a network of bronze; and on the net you shall make four bronze rings at its four corners. ⁵You shall set it under the ledge of the altar so that the net shall extend halfway down the altar. ⁶You shall make poles for the altar, poles of acacia wood, and overlay them with bronze; ⁷the poles shall be put through the rings, so that the poles shall be on the two sides of the altar when it is carried. ⁸You shall make it hollow, with boards. They shall be made just as you were shown on the mountain.

The Court and Its Hangings

9 You shall make the court of the tabernacle. On the south side the court shall have hangings of fine twisted linen one hundred cubits long for that side; ¹⁰its twenty pillars and their twenty bases shall be of bronze, but the hooks of the pillars and their bands shall be of silver. ¹¹Likewise for its length on the north side there shall be hangings one hundred cubits long, their pillars twenty and their bases twenty, of bronze, but the hooks of the pillars and their bands shall be of silver. ¹²For the width of the court on the west side there shall be fifty cubits of hangings, with ten pillars and ten bases. ¹³The width of the court on the front to the east shall be fifty cubits. ¹⁴There shall be fifteen cubits of hangings on the one side, with three pillars and three bases. ¹⁵There shall be fifteen cubits of hangings on the other side, with three pillars and three bases. ¹⁶For the gate of the court there shall be a screen twenty cubits long, of blue, purple, and crimson yarns, and of fine twisted linen, embroidered with needlework; it shall have four pillars and with them four bases. ¹⁷All the pillars around the court shall be banded with silver; their hooks shall be of silver, and their bases of bronze. ¹⁸The length of the court shall be one hundred cubits, the width fifty, and the height five cubits, with hangings of fine twisted linen and bases of bronze. ¹⁹All the utensils of the tabernacle for every use, and all its pegs and all the pegs of the court, shall be of bronze.

The Oil for the Lamp

20 You shall further command the Israelites to bring you pure oil of beaten olives for the light, so that a lamp may be set up to burn regularly. ²¹In the

tent of meeting, outside the curtain that is before the covenant,ᵃ Aaron and his sons shall tend it from evening to morning before the LORD. It shall be a perpetual ordinance to be observed throughout their generations by the Israelites.

28   Vestments for the Priesthood

Then bring near to you your brother Aaron, and his sons with him, from among the Israelites, to serve me as priests—Aaron and Aaron's sons, Nadab and Abihu, Eleazar and Ithamar. ²You shall make sacred vestments for the glorious adornment of your brother Aaron. ³And you shall speak to all who have ability, whom I have endowed with skill, that they make Aaron's vestments to consecrate him for my priesthood. ⁴These are the vestments that they shall make: a breastpiece, an ephod, a robe, a checkered tunic, a turban, and a sash. When they make these sacred vestments for your brother Aaron and his sons to serve me as priests, ⁵they shall use gold, blue, purple, and crimson yarns, and fine linen.

The Ephod

6 They shall make the ephod of gold, of blue, purple, and crimson yarns, and of fine twisted linen, skillfully worked. ⁷It shall have two shoulder-pieces attached to its two edges, so that it may be joined together. ⁸The decorated band on it shall be of the same workmanship and materials, of gold, of blue, purple, and crimson yarns, and of fine twisted linen. ⁹You shall take two onyx stones, and engrave on them the names of the sons of Israel, ¹⁰six of their names on the one stone, and the names of the remaining six on the other stone, in the order of their birth. ¹¹As a gem-cutter engraves signets, so you shall engrave the two stones with the names of the sons of Israel; you shall mount them in settings of gold filigree. ¹²You shall set the two stones on the shoulder-pieces of the ephod, as stones of remembrance for the sons of Israel; and Aaron shall bear their names before the LORD on his two shoulders for remembrance.

ᵃ Or *treaty*, or *testimony*; Heb *eduth*

[13]You shall make settings of gold filigree, [14]and two chains of pure gold, twisted like cords; and you shall attach the corded chains to the settings.

The Breastplate

15 You shall make a breastpiece of judgment, in skilled work; you shall make it in the style of the ephod; of gold, of blue and purple and crimson yarns, and of fine twisted linen you shall make it. [16]It shall be square and doubled, a span in length and a span in width. [17]You shall set in it four rows of stones. A row of carnelian,[a] chrysolite, and emerald shall be the first row; [18]and the second row a turquoise, a sapphire,[b] and a moonstone; [19]and the third row a jacinth, an agate, and an amethyst; [20]and the fourth row a beryl, an onyx, and a jasper; they shall be set in gold filigree. [21]There shall be twelve stones with names corresponding to the names of the sons of Israel; they shall be like signets, each engraved with its name, for the twelve tribes. [22]You shall make for the breastpiece chains of pure gold, twisted like cords; [23]and you shall make for the breastpiece two rings of gold, and put the two rings on the two edges of the breastpiece. [24]You shall put the two cords of gold in the two rings at the edges of the breastpiece; [25]the two ends of the two cords you shall attach to the two settings, and so attach it in front to the shoulder-pieces of the ephod. [26]You shall make two rings of gold, and put them at the two ends of the breastpiece, on its inside edge next to the ephod. [27]You shall make two rings of gold, and attach them in front to the lower part of the two shoulder-pieces of the ephod, at its joining above the decorated band of the ephod. [28]The breastpiece shall be bound by its rings to the rings of the ephod with a blue cord, so that it may lie on the decorated band of the ephod, and so that the breastpiece shall not come loose from the ephod. [29]So Aaron shall bear the names of the sons of Israel in the breastpiece of judgment on his heart when he goes into the holy place, for a continual remembrance before the LORD. [30]In the breastpiece of judgment you shall put the Urim and the Thummim, and they shall be on Aaron's heart when he goes in before the LORD; thus Aaron shall bear the judgment of the Israelites on his heart before the LORD continually.

Other Priestly Vestments

31 You shall make the robe of the ephod all of blue. [32]It shall have an opening for the head in the middle of it, with a woven binding around the opening, like the opening in a coat of mail,[c] so that it may not be torn. [33]On its lower hem you shall make pomegranates of blue, purple, and crimson yarns, all around the lower hem, with bells of gold between them all around— [34]a golden bell and a pomegranate alternating all around the lower hem of the robe. [35]Aaron shall wear it when he ministers, and its sound shall be heard when he goes into the holy place before the LORD, and when he comes out, so that he may not die.

36 You shall make a rosette of pure gold, and engrave on it, like the engraving of a signet, "Holy to the LORD." [37]You shall fasten it on the turban with a blue cord; it shall be on the front of the turban. [38]It shall be on Aaron's forehead, and Aaron shall take on himself any guilt incurred in the holy offering that the Israelites consecrate as their sacred donations; it shall always be on his forehead, in order that they may find favor before the LORD.

39 You shall make the checkered tunic of fine linen, and you shall make a turban of fine linen, and you shall make a sash embroidered with needlework.

40 For Aaron's sons you shall make tunics and sashes and headdresses; you shall make them for their glorious adornment. [41]You shall put them on your brother Aaron, and on his sons with him, and shall anoint them and ordain them and consecrate them, so that they may serve me as priests. [42]You shall make for them linen undergarments to cover their naked flesh; they shall reach from the hips to the thighs; [43]Aaron and his sons shall wear them when they go into the tent of meeting, or when they come near the altar to minister in the holy place; or they will bring guilt on themselves and die. This shall be a perpetual ordinance for him and for his descendants after him.

The Ordination of the Priests

29 Now this is what you shall do to them to consecrate them, so that they may serve me as priests. Take one young bull and two rams without blemish, [2]and unleavened bread, unleavened cakes mixed with oil, and unleavened wafers spread with oil. You shall make them of choice wheat flour. [3]You shall put them in one basket and bring them in the basket, and bring the bull and the two rams. [4]You shall bring Aaron and his sons to the entrance of the tent of meeting, and wash them with water. [5]Then you shall take the vestments, and put

---

a The identity of several of these stones is uncertain　b Or *lapis lazuli*　c Meaning of Heb uncertain

on Aaron the tunic and the robe of the ephod, and the ephod, and the breastpiece, and gird him with the decorated band of the ephod; [6]and you shall set the turban on his head, and put the holy diadem on the turban. [7]You shall take the anointing oil, and pour it on his head and anoint him. [8]Then you shall bring his sons, and put tunics on them, [9]and you shall gird them with sashes[a] and tie headdresses on them; and the priesthood shall be theirs by a perpetual ordinance. You shall then ordain Aaron and his sons.

10 You shall bring the bull in front of the tent of meeting. Aaron and his sons shall lay their hands on the head of the bull, [11]and you shall slaughter the bull before the LORD, at the entrance of the tent of meeting, [12]and shall take some of the blood of the bull and put it on the horns of the altar with your finger, and all the rest of the blood you shall pour out at the base of the altar. [13]You shall take all the fat that covers the entrails, and the appendage of the liver, and the two kidneys with the fat that is on them, and turn them into smoke on the altar. [14]But the flesh of the bull, and its skin, and its dung, you shall burn with fire outside the camp; it is a sin offering.

15 Then you shall take one of the rams, and Aaron and his sons shall lay their hands on the head of the ram, [16]and you shall slaughter the ram, and shall take its blood and dash it against all sides of the altar. [17]Then you shall cut the ram into its parts, and wash its entrails and its legs, and put them with its parts and its head, [18]and turn the whole ram into smoke on the altar; it is a burnt offering to the LORD; it is a pleasing odor, an offering by fire to the LORD.

19 You shall take the other ram; and Aaron and his sons shall lay their hands on the head of the ram, [20]and you shall slaughter the ram, and take some of its blood and put it on the lobe of Aaron's right ear and on the lobes of the right ears of his sons, and on the thumbs of their right hands, and on the big toes of their right feet, and dash the rest of the blood against all sides of the altar. [21]Then you shall take some of the blood that is on the altar, and some of the anointing oil, and sprinkle it on Aaron and his vestments and on his sons and his sons' vestments with him; then he and his vestments shall be holy, as well as his sons and his sons' vestments.

22 You shall also take the fat of the ram, the fat tail, the fat that covers the entrails, the appendage of the liver, the two kidneys with the fat that is on them, and the right thigh (for it is a ram of ordination), [23]and one loaf of bread, one cake of bread made with oil, and one wafer, out of the basket of unleavened bread that is before the LORD; [24]and you shall place all these on the palms of Aaron and on the palms of his sons, and raise them as an elevation offering before the LORD. [25]Then you shall take them from their hands, and turn them into smoke on the altar on top of the burnt offering of pleasing odor before the LORD; it is an offering by fire to the LORD.

26 You shall take the breast of the ram of Aaron's ordination and raise it as an elevation offering before the LORD; and it shall be your portion. [27]You shall consecrate the breast that was raised as an elevation offering and the thigh that was raised as an elevation offering from the ram of ordination, from that which belonged to Aaron and his sons. [28]These things shall be a perpetual ordinance for Aaron and his sons from the Israelites, for this is an offering; and it shall be an offering by the Israelites from their sacrifice of offerings of well-being, their offering to the LORD.

29 The sacred vestments of Aaron shall be passed on to his sons after him; they shall be anointed in them and ordained in them. [30]The son who is priest in his place shall wear them seven days, when he comes into the tent of meeting to minister in the holy place.

31 You shall take the ram of ordination, and boil its flesh in a holy place; [32]and Aaron and his sons shall eat the flesh of the ram and the bread that is in the basket, at the entrance of the tent of meeting. [33]They themselves shall eat the food by which atonement is made, to ordain and consecrate them, but no one else shall eat of them, because they are holy. [34]If any of the flesh for the ordination, or of the bread, remains until the morning, then you shall burn the remainder with fire; it shall not be eaten, because it is holy.

35 Thus you shall do to Aaron and to his sons, just as I have commanded you; through seven days you shall ordain them. [36]Also every day you shall offer a bull as a sin offering for atonement. Also you shall offer a sin offering for the altar, when you make atonement for it, and shall anoint it, to consecrate it. [37]Seven days you shall make atonement for the altar, and consecrate it, and the altar shall be most holy; whatever touches the altar shall become holy.

a Gk: Heb *sashes, Aaron and his sons*

The Daily Offerings

38 Now this is what you shall offer on the altar: two lambs a year old regularly each day. [39]One lamb you shall offer in the morning, and the other lamb you shall offer in the evening; [40]and with the first lamb one-tenth of a measure of choice flour mixed with one-fourth of a hin of beaten oil, and one-fourth of a hin of wine for a drink offering. [41]And the other lamb you shall offer in the evening, and shall offer with it a grain offering and its drink offering, as in the morning, for a pleasing odor, an offering by fire to the LORD. [42]It shall be a regular burnt offering throughout your generations at the entrance of the tent of meeting before the LORD, where I will meet with you, to speak to you there. [43]I will meet with the Israelites there, and it shall be sanctified by my glory; [44]I will consecrate the tent of meeting and the altar; Aaron also and his sons I will consecrate, to serve me as priests. [45]I will dwell among the Israelites, and I will be their God. [46]And they shall know that I am the LORD their God, who brought them out of the land of Egypt that I might dwell among them; I am the LORD their God.

30 The Altar of Incense

You shall make an altar on which to offer incense; you shall make it of acacia wood. [2]It shall be one cubit long, and one cubit wide; it shall be square, and shall be two cubits high; its horns shall be of one piece with it. [3]You shall overlay it with pure gold, its top, and its sides all around and its horns; and you shall make for it a molding of gold all around. [4]And you shall make two golden rings for it; under its molding on two opposite sides of it you shall make them, and they shall hold the poles with which to carry it. [5]You shall make the poles of acacia wood, and overlay them with gold. [6]You shall place it in front of the curtain that is above the ark of the covenant,[a] in front of the mercy seat[b] that is over the covenant,[a] where I will meet with you. [7]Aaron shall offer fragrant incense on it; every morning when he dresses the lamps he shall offer it, [8]and when Aaron sets up the lamps in the evening, he shall offer it, a regular incense offering before the LORD throughout your generations. [9]You

shall not offer unholy incense on it, or a burnt offering, or a grain offering; and you shall not pour a drink offering on it. [10]Once a year Aaron shall perform the rite of atonement on its horns. Throughout your generations he shall perform the atonement for it once a year with the blood of the atoning sin offering. It is most holy to the LORD.

The Half Shekel for the Sanctuary

11 The LORD spoke to Moses: [12]When you take a census of the Israelites to register them, at registration all of them shall give a ransom for their lives to the LORD, so that no plague may come upon them for being registered. [13]This is what each one who is registered shall give: half a shekel according to the shekel of the sanctuary (the shekel is twenty gerahs), half a shekel as an offering to the LORD. [14]Each one who is registered, from twenty years old and upward, shall give the LORD's offering. [15]The rich shall not give more, and the poor shall not give less, than the half shekel, when you bring this offering to the LORD to make atonement for your lives. [16]You shall take the atonement money from the Israelites and shall designate it for the service of the tent of meeting; before the LORD it will be a reminder to the Israelites of the ransom given for your lives.

The Bronze Basin

17 The LORD spoke to Moses: [18]You shall make a bronze basin with a bronze stand for washing. You shall put it between the tent of meeting and the altar, and you shall put water in it; [19]with the water[c] Aaron and his sons shall wash their hands and their feet. [20]When they go into the tent of meeting, or when they come near the altar to minister, to make an offering by fire to the LORD, they shall wash with water, so that they may not die. [21]They shall wash their hands and their feet, so that they may not die: it shall be a perpetual ordinance for them, for him and for his descendants throughout their generations.

The Anointing Oil and Incense

22 The LORD spoke to Moses: [23]Take the finest spices: of liquid myrrh five hundred shekels, and of

---

a Or treaty, or testimony; Heb eduth   b Or the cover   c Heb it sweet-smelling cinnamon half as much, that is, two hundred fifty, and two hundred fifty of aromatic cane, [24]and five hundred of cassia—measured by the sanctuary shekel—and a hin of olive oil; [25]and you shall make of these a sacred anointing oil blended as by the perfumer; it shall be a holy anointing oil. [26]With it you shall anoint the tent of meeting and the ark of the covenant,[a] [27]and the table and all its utensils, and the lampstand and its utensils, and the altar of incense, [28]and the altar of burnt offering with all its utensils, and the basin with its stand; [29]you shall consecrate them, so that they may be most holy; whatever touches them will become holy. [30]You shall anoint Aaron and his sons, and consecrate them, in order that they may serve me as priests. [31]You shall say to the Israelites, "This shall be my holy anointing oil throughout your generations. [32]It shall not be used in any ordinary anointing of the body, and you shall make no other like it in composition; it is holy, and it shall be holy to you. [33]Whoever compounds any like it or whoever puts any of it on an unqualified person shall be cut off from the people."

34 The LORD said to Moses: Take sweet spices, stacte, and onycha, and galbanum, sweet spices with pure frankincense (an equal part of each), [35]and make an incense blended as by the perfumer, seasoned with salt, pure and holy; [36]and you shall beat some of it into powder, and put part of it before the covenant[a] in the tent of meeting where I shall meet with you; it shall be for you most holy. [37]When you make incense according to this composition, you shall not make it for yourselves; it shall be regarded by you as holy to the LORD. [38]Whoever makes any like it to use as perfume shall be cut off from the people.

Bezalel and Oholiab

31 The LORD spoke to Moses: [2]See, I have called by name Bezalel son of Uri son of Hur, of the tribe of Judah: [3]and I have filled him with divine spirit,[b] with ability, intelligence, and knowledge in every kind of craft, [4]to devise artistic designs, to work in gold, silver, and bronze, [5]in cutting stones for setting, and in carving wood, in every kind of craft. [6]Moreover, I have appointed with him Oholiab son of Ahisamach, of the tribe of Dan; and I have given skill to all the skillful, so that they may make all that I have commanded you: [7]the tent of meeting, and the ark of the covenant,[a] and the

mercy seat[c] that is on it, and all the furnishings of the tent, [8]the table and its utensils, and the pure lampstand with all its utensils, and the altar of incense, [9]and the altar of burnt offering with all its utensils, and the basin with its stand, [10]and the finely worked vestments, the holy vestments for the priest Aaron and the vestments of his sons, for their service as priests, [11]and the anointing oil and the fragrant incense for the holy place. They shall do just as I have commanded you.

The Sabbath Law

12 The LORD said to Moses: [13]You yourself are to speak to the Israelites: "You shall keep my sabbaths, for this is a sign between me and you throughout your generations, given in order that you may know that I, the LORD, sanctify you. [14]You shall keep the sabbath, because it is holy for you; everyone who profanes it shall be put to death; whoever does any work on it shall be cut off from among the people. [15]Six days shall work be done, but the seventh day is a sabbath of solemn rest, holy to the LORD; whoever does any work on the sabbath day shall be put to death. [16]Therefore the Israelites shall keep the sabbath, observing the sabbath throughout their generations, as a perpetual covenant. [17]It is a sign forever between me and the people of Israel that in six days the LORD made heaven and earth, and on the seventh day he rested, and was refreshed."

The Two Tablets of the Covenant

18 When God[d] finished speaking with Moses on Mount Sinai, he gave him the two tablets of the covenant,[a] tablets of stone, written with the finger of God.

The Golden Calf

32 When the people saw that Moses delayed to come down from the mountain, the people gathered around Aaron, and said to him, "Come, make gods for us, who shall go before us; as for this Moses, the man who brought us up out of the land of Egypt, we do not know what has become of him." [2]Aaron said to them, "Take off the gold rings that are on the ears of your wives, your sons, and your daughters, and bring them to me." [3]So all the people took off the gold rings from their ears, and brought them to Aaron. [4]He took the gold from them, formed it in a mold,[e] and cast an image of a calf; and they said, "These are your gods, O Is-

---

a Or treaty, or testimony; Heb eduth   b Or with the spirit of God   c Or the cover   d Heb he   e Or fashioned it with a graving tool; Meaning of Heb uncertain

Some People Never Learn · Exodus 32

Seriously? The Israelites have forgotten already? It has only been three weeks since they left Egypt—miraculously left Egypt. Remember the plagues, the angel of death, the parting of the Red Sea? Amazing stuff! Then came bread and meat every day from heaven (Exodus 16:13-15) and water pouring out of a rock (Exodus 17:6). God keeps doing miracles to care for the people, but they seem to forget God when Moses is gone for a few weeks. And they don't just forget—they try to replace God. The Israelites demand that Aaron make them new gods or idols, and for some reason he agrees. Next thing we know the Israelites are throwing a huge party to worship a golden cow. How dense can these people be?

The Israelites' actions are almost laughable as we read about them from the comfort of our present day. But the truth is we're just the same. We make the same kind of dumb decisions. We forget all the good God has done for us, even the miracles. We get bored and try to find excitement in ways God has told us not to. We grow impatient waiting for direction and strike out blindly in our own ways. And we form our own idols to worship. No, not golden statues, but we bow down and worship many other things. We devote all our energy, efforts, time, money, or attention to our own entertainment, achievement, comfort, or pleasure. We'd be much wiser to see ourselves in the failures of the Israelites and learn from their mistakes.

• What fills your thoughts and time? Have you placed it before God in your life? Talk with God about it, and ask for help to realign your priorities.

• What blessings from God have you been forgetting? Make a list and get thankful again.

rael, who brought you up out of the land of Egypt!" ⁵When Aaron saw this, he built an altar before it; and Aaron made proclamation and said, "Tomorrow shall be a festival to the LORD." ⁶They rose early the next day, and offered burnt offerings and brought sacrifices of well-being; and the people sat down to eat and drink, and rose up to revel.

7 The LORD said to Moses, "Go down at once! Your people, whom you brought up out of the land of Egypt, have acted perversely; ⁸they have been quick to turn aside from the way that I commanded them; they have cast for themselves an image of a calf, and have worshiped it and sacrificed to it, and said, 'These are your gods, O Israel, who brought you up out of the land of Egypt!' " ⁹The LORD said to Moses, "I have seen this people, how stiff-necked they are. ¹⁰Now let me alone, so that my wrath may burn hot against them and I may consume them; and of you I will make a great nation."

11 But Moses implored the LORD his God, and said, "O LORD, why does your wrath burn hot against your people, whom you brought out of the land of Egypt with great power and with a mighty hand? ¹²Why should the Egyptians say, 'It was with evil intent that he brought them out to kill them in the mountains, and to consume them from the face of the earth'? Turn from your fierce wrath; change your mind and do not bring disaster on your people. ¹³Remember Abraham, Isaac, and Israel, your servants, how you swore to them by your own self, saying to them, 'I will multiply your descendants like the stars of heaven, and all this land that I have promised I will give to your descendants, and they shall inherit it forever.' " ¹⁴And the LORD changed his mind about the disaster that he planned to bring on his people.

15 Then Moses turned and went down from the mountain, carrying the two tablets of the covenant*a* in his hands, tablets that were written on both sides, written on the front and on the back. ¹⁶The tablets were the work of God, and the writing was the writing of God, engraved upon the tablets. ¹⁷When Joshua heard the noise of the people as they shouted, he said to Moses, "There is a noise of war in the camp." ¹⁸But he said,

"It is not the sound made by victors,

a Or *treaty*, or *testimony*; Heb *eduth*

or the sound made by losers;
it is the sound of revelers that I hear."
[19]As soon as he came near the camp and saw the calf and the dancing, Moses' anger burned hot, and he threw the tablets from his hands and broke them at the foot of the mountain. [20]He took the calf that they had made, burned it with fire, ground it to powder, scattered it on the water, and made the Israelites drink it.

21 Moses said to Aaron, "What did this people do to you that you have brought so great a sin upon them?" [22]And Aaron said, "Do not let the anger of my lord burn hot; you know the people, that they are bent on evil. [23]They said to me, 'Make us gods, who shall go before us; as for this Moses, the man who brought us up out of the land of Egypt, we do not know what has become of him.' [24]So I said to them, 'Whoever has gold, take it off'; so they gave it to me, and I threw it into the fire, and out came this calf!"

25 When Moses saw that the people were running wild (for Aaron had let them run wild, to the derision of their enemies), [26]then Moses stood in the gate of the camp, and said, "Who is on the LORD's side? Come to me!" And all the sons of Levi gathered around him. [27]He said to them, "Thus says the LORD, the God of Israel, 'Put your sword on your side, each of you! Go back and forth from gate to gate throughout the camp, and each of you kill your brother, your friend, and your neighbor.' " [28]The sons of Levi did as Moses commanded, and about three thousand of the people fell on that day. [29]Moses said, "Today you have ordained yourselves[a] for the service of the LORD, each one at the cost of a son or a brother, and so have brought a blessing on yourselves this day."

30 On the next day Moses said to the people, "You have sinned a great sin. But now I will go up to the LORD; perhaps I can make atonement for your sin." [31]So Moses returned to the LORD and said, "Alas, this people has sinned a great sin; they have made for themselves gods of gold. [32]But now, if you will only forgive their sin—but if not, blot me out of the book that you have written." [33]But the LORD said to Moses, "Whoever has sinned against me I will blot out of my book. [34]But now go, lead the people to the place about which I have spoken to you; see, my angel shall go in front of you. Nevertheless, when the day comes for punishment, I will punish them for their sin."

35 Then the LORD sent a plague on the people, because they made the calf—the one that Aaron made.

The Command to Leave Sinai

33 The LORD said to Moses, "Go, leave this place, you and the people whom you have brought up out of the land of Egypt, and go to the land of which I swore to Abraham, Isaac, and Jacob, saying, 'To your descendants I will give it.' [2]I will send an angel before you, and I will drive out the Canaanites, the Amorites, the Hittites, the Perizzites, the Hivites, and the Jebusites. [3]Go up to a land flowing with milk and honey; but I will not go up among you, or I would consume you on the way, for you are a stiff-necked people."

4 When the people heard these harsh words, they mourned, and no one put on ornaments. [5]For the LORD had said to Moses, "Say to the Israelites, 'You are a stiff-necked people; if for a single moment I should go up among you, I would consume you. So now take off your ornaments, and I will decide what to do to you.' " [6]Therefore the Israelites stripped themselves of their ornaments, from Mount Horeb onward.

The Tent outside the Camp

7 Now Moses used to take the tent and pitch it outside the camp, far off from the camp; he called it the tent of meeting. And everyone who sought the LORD would go out to the tent of meeting, which was outside the camp. [8]Whenever Moses went out to the tent, all the people would rise and stand, each of them, at the entrance of their tents and watch Moses until he had gone into the tent. [9]When Moses entered the tent, the pillar of cloud would descend and stand at the entrance of the tent, and the LORD would speak with Moses. [10]When all the people saw the pillar of cloud standing at the entrance of the tent, all the people would rise and bow down, all of them, at the entrance of their tent. [11]Thus the LORD used to speak to Moses face to face, as one speaks to a friend. Then he would return to the camp; but his young assistant, Joshua son of Nun, would not leave the tent.

Moses' Intercession

12 Moses said to the LORD, "See, you have said to me, 'Bring up this people'; but you have not let me know whom you will send with me. Yet you have said, 'I know you by name, and you have also found favor

---

a Gk Vg Compare Tg: Heb *Today ordain yourselves*

in my sight.' [13]Now if I have found favor in your sight, show me your ways, so that I may know you and find favor in your sight. Consider too that this nation is your people." [14]He said, "My presence will go with you, and I will give you rest." [15]And he said to him, "If your presence will not go, do not carry us up from here. [16]For how shall it be known that I have found favor in your sight, I and your people, unless you go with us? In this way, we shall be distinct, I and your people, from every people on the face of the earth."

17 The LORD said to Moses, "I will do the very thing that you have asked; for you have found favor in my sight, and I know you by name." [18]Moses said, "Show me your glory, I pray." [19]And he said, "I will make all my goodness pass before you, and will proclaim before you the name, 'The LORD';[a] and I will be gracious to whom I will be gracious, and will show mercy on whom I will show mercy. [20]But," he said, "you cannot see my face; for no one shall see me and live." [21]And the LORD continued, "See, there is a place by me where you shall stand on the rock; [22]and while my glory passes by I will put you in a cleft of the rock, and I will cover you with my hand until I have passed by; [23]then I will take away my hand, and you shall see my back; but my face shall not be seen."

Moses Makes New Tablets

34 The LORD said to Moses, "Cut two tablets of stone like the former ones, and I will write on the tablets the words that were on the former tablets, which you broke. [2]Be ready in the morning, and come up in the morning to Mount Sinai and present yourself there to me, on the top of the mountain. [3]No one shall come up with you, and do not let anyone be seen throughout all the mountain; and do not let flocks or herds graze in front of that mountain." [4]So Moses cut two tablets of stone like the former ones; and he rose early in the morning and went up on Mount Sinai, as the LORD had commanded him, and took in his hand the two tablets of stone. [5]The LORD descended in the cloud and stood with him there, and proclaimed the name, "The LORD."[a] [6]The LORD passed before him, and proclaimed,

"The LORD, the LORD,
a God merciful and gracious,
  slow to anger,
and abounding in steadfast love and
    faithfulness,
[7] keeping steadfast love for the thousandth
    generation,[b]
forgiving iniquity and transgression and sin,
yet by no means clearing the guilty,
but visiting the iniquity of the parents
  upon the children
and the children's children,
to the third and the fourth generation."

[8]And Moses quickly bowed his head toward the

PRAY IT!

Getting Close to God   Exodus 33:17–23

How close can we get to God without actually seeing God's face? If anyone would know, it is Moses. His amazing encounter with God is recorded in this passage. Though most of us will never experience what Moses did, many believers and mystics have experienced a deep intimacy with God. The great thing is that we can too!

Moses' encounters with God often happened in or through nature. Creation is a reflection of God's glory, and a great place for us to connect and experience God's presence. Do you have a favorite outdoor spot? Maybe it's a favorite beach, a rock by a stream, a tree in your backyard, or even a park near your house. You may not actually see or feel the hand of God, but somehow when you spend time in nature, you have a chance to think, pray, and connect with God and catch a glimpse of God's glory. And sometimes, like Moses (see Exodus 34:29), you are transformed by the power of God's presence.

- What is it about nature that makes you feel close to God?
- Where do you most fully experience the presence of God?
- Spend some time in prayer there today.

---

a Heb *YHWH*; see note at 3.15   **b** Or *for thousands*

earth, and worshiped. [9]He said, "If now I have found favor in your sight, O Lord, I pray, let the Lord go with us. Although this is a stiff-necked people, pardon our iniquity and our sin, and take us for your inheritance."

The Covenant Renewed

10 He said. I hereby make a covenant. Before all your people I will perform marvels, such as have not been performed in all the earth or in any nation; and all the people among whom you live shall see the work of the Lord; for it is an awesome thing that I will do with you.

11 Observe what I command you today. See, I will drive out before you the Amorites, the Canaanites, the Hittites, the Perizzites, the Hivites, and the Jebusites. [12]Take care not to make a covenant with the inhabitants of the land to which you are going, or it will become a snare among you. [13]You shall tear down their altars, break their pillars, and cut down their sacred poles[a] [14](for you shall worship no other god, because the Lord, whose name is Jealous, is a jealous God). [15]You shall not make a covenant with the inhabitants of the land, for when they prostitute themselves to their gods and sacrifice to their gods, someone among them will invite you, and you will eat of the sacrifice. [16]And you will take wives from among their daughters for your sons, and their daughters who prostitute themselves to their gods will make your sons also prostitute themselves to their gods.

17 You shall not make cast idols.

18 You shall keep the festival of unleavened bread. Seven days you shall eat unleavened bread, as I commanded you, at the time appointed in the month of Abib; for in the month of Abib you came out from Egypt.

19 All that first opens the womb is mine, all your male[b] livestock, the firstborn of cow and sheep. [20]The firstborn of a donkey you shall redeem with a lamb, or if you will not redeem it you shall break its neck. All the firstborn of your sons you shall redeem.

No one shall appear before me empty-handed.

21 Six days you shall work, but on the seventh day you shall rest; even in plowing time and in harvest time you shall rest. [22]You shall observe the festival of weeks, the first fruits of wheat harvest, and the festival of ingathering at the turn of the

STUDY IT!

Israelite Parties
Exodus 34:18–26

Remember how Christmas Eve felt when you were a kid? The magic, the anticipation, the energy, the excitement! The three festivals described in **Exodus 34:18–26** (and in Exodus 23:14-17) brought the same kind of anticipation and excitement to the Israelites.

The Festival of Unleavened Bread probably originated as a pre-Passover agricultural holiday marking the beginning of the barley harvest. After the Passover, the festival was celebrated for one week starting on the day after the anniversary of the Passover. Unleavened bread came to be seen as a reminder of how quickly the Israelites left Egypt—baking bread without yeast, because they didn't have time for it to rise.

The Festival of Weeks, or Pentecost, began seven weeks after the barley harvest to celebrate the start of the wheat harvest. Because of the timing of the festival and the Israelites' arrival at Mount Sinai, it later took on added significance as a celebration of God's covenant with Israel and the Ten Commandments.

The third weeklong festival was called the Festival of Booths, or the Festival of Tabernacles. It was celebrated as the produce of the land was gathered in and was a lot like our own Thanksgiving Day, a time set aside to thank God for the bounty of the earth. It was the most popular of these festivals. Part of the instructions for this festival are that the people live in booths, or tents, to remind them of the time they spent wandering in the desert and living in tents (Leviticus 23:42-43). (See also "Study It: More Jewish Festivals," near Numbers 29:1-11.)

a Heb *Asherim* b Gk Theodotion Vg Tg: Meaning of Heb uncertain

year. [23] Three times in the year all your males shall appear before the LORD God, the God of Israel. [24] For I will cast out nations before you, and enlarge your borders; no one shall covet your land when you go up to appear before the LORD your God three times in the year.

25 You shall not offer the blood of my sacrifice with leaven, and the sacrifice of the festival of the passover shall not be left until the morning.

26 The best of the first fruits of your ground you shall bring to the house of the LORD your God.

You shall not boil a kid in its mother's milk.

27 The LORD said to Moses: Write these words; in accordance with these words I have made a covenant with you and with Israel. [28] He was there with the LORD forty days and forty nights; he neither ate bread nor drank water. And he wrote on the tablets the words of the covenant, the ten commandments. [a]

The Shining Face of Moses

29 Moses came down from Mount Sinai. As he came down from the mountain with the two tablets of the covenant [b] in his hand, Moses did not know that the skin of his face shone because he had been talking with God. [30] When Aaron and all the Israelites saw Moses, the skin of his face was shining, and they were afraid to come near him. [31] But Moses called to them; and Aaron and all the leaders of the congregation returned to him, and Moses spoke with them. [32] Afterward all the Israelites came near, and he gave them in commandment all that the LORD had spoken with him on Mount Sinai. [33] When Moses had finished speaking with them, he put a veil on his face; [34] but whenever Moses went in before the LORD to speak with him, he would take the veil off, until he came out; and when he came out, and told the Israelites what he had been commanded, [35] the Israelites would see the face of Moses, that the skin of his face was shining; and Moses would put the veil on his face again, until he went in to speak with him.

Sabbath Regulations

35 Moses assembled all the congregation of the Israelites and said to them: These are the things that the LORD has commanded you to do:

2 Six days shall work be done, but on the seventh day you shall have a holy sabbath of solemn rest to the LORD; whoever does any work on it shall be put to death. [3] You shall kindle no fire in all your dwellings on the sabbath day.

Preparations for Making the Tabernacle

4 Moses said to all the congregation of the Israelites: This is the thing that the LORD has commanded: [5] Take from among you an offering to the LORD; let whoever is of a generous heart bring the LORD's offering: gold, silver, and bronze; [6] blue, purple, and crimson yarns, and fine linen; goats' hair, [7] tanned rams' skins, and fine leather; [c] acacia wood, [8] oil for the light, spices for the anointing oil and for the fragrant incense, [9] and onyx stones and gems to be set in the ephod and the breastpiece.

10 All who are skillful among you shall come and make all that the LORD has commanded: the tabernacle, [11] its tent and its covering, its clasps and its frames, its bars, its pillars, and its bases; [12] the ark with its poles, the mercy seat, [d] and the curtain for the screen; [13] the table with its poles and all its utensils, and the bread of the Presence; [14] the lampstand also for the light, with its utensils and its lamps, and the oil for the light; [15] and the altar of incense, with its poles, and the anointing oil and the fragrant incense, and the screen for the entrance, the entrance of the tabernacle; [16] the altar of burnt offering, with its grating of bronze, its poles, and all its utensils, the basin with its stand; [17] the hangings of the court, its pillars and its bases, and the screen for the gate of the court; [18] the pegs of the tabernacle and the pegs of the court, and their cords; [19] the finely worked vestments for ministering in the holy place, the holy vestments for the priest Aaron, and the vestments of his sons, for their service as priests.

Offerings for the Tabernacle

20 Then all the congregation of the Israelites withdrew from the presence of Moses. [21] And they came, everyone whose heart was stirred, and everyone whose spirit was willing, and brought the LORD's offering to be used for the tent of meeting, and for all its service, and for the sacred vestments. [22] So they came, both men and women; all who were of a willing heart brought brooches and earrings and signet rings and pendants, all sorts of gold objects, everyone bringing an offering of gold to the LORD. [23] And everyone who possessed blue or purple or crimson yarn or fine linen or goats' hair or tanned

---

a Heb *words*   b Or *treaty*, or *testimony*; Heb *eduth*   c Meaning of Heb uncertain   d Or *the cover*

rams' skins or fine leather,[a] brought them. [24]Everyone who could make an offering of silver or bronze brought it as the LORD's offering; and everyone who possessed acacia wood of any use in the work, brought it. [25]All the skillful women spun with their hands, and brought what they had spun in blue and purple and crimson yarns and fine linen; [26]all the women whose hearts moved them to use their skill spun the goats' hair. [27]And the leaders brought onyx stones and gems to be set in the ephod and the breastpiece, [28]and spices and oil for the light, and for the anointing oil, and for the fragrant incense. [29]All the Israelite men and women whose hearts made them willing to bring anything for the work that the LORD had commanded by Moses to be done, brought it as a freewill offering to the LORD.

Bezalel and Oholiab

30 Then Moses said to the Israelites: See, the LORD has called by name Bezalel son of Uri son of Hur, of the tribe of Judah; [31]he has filled him with divine spirit,[b] with skill, intelligence, and knowledge in every kind of craft, [32]to devise artistic designs, to work in gold, silver, and bronze, [33]in cutting stones for setting, and in carving wood, in every kind of craft. [34]And he has inspired him to teach, both him and Oholiab son of Ahisamach, of the tribe of Dan. [35]He has filled them with skill to do every kind of work done by an artisan or by a designer or by an embroiderer in blue, purple, and crimson yarns, and in fine linen, or by a weaver—by any sort of artisan or skilled designer.

36 Bezalel and Oholiab and every skillful one to whom the LORD has given skill and understanding to know how to do any work in the construction of the sanctuary shall work in accordance with all that the LORD has commanded.

2 Moses then called Bezalel and Oholiab and every skillful one to whom the LORD had given skill, everyone whose heart was stirred to come to do the work; [3]and they received from Moses all the freewill offerings that the Israelites had brought for doing the work on the sanctuary. They still kept bringing him freewill offerings every morning, [4]so that all the artisans who were doing every sort of task on the sanctuary came, each from the task being performed, [5]and said to Moses, "The people are bringing much more than enough for doing the work that the LORD has commanded us to do." [6]So Moses gave

command, and word was proclaimed throughout the camp: "No man or woman is to make anything else as an offering for the sanctuary." So the people were restrained from bringing; [7]for what they had already brought was more than enough to do all the work.

Construction of the Tabernacle

8 All those with skill among the workers made the tabernacle with ten curtains; they were made of fine twisted linen, and blue, purple, and crimson yarns, with cherubim skillfully worked into them. [9]The length of each curtain was twenty-eight cubits, and the width of each curtain four cubits; all the curtains were of the same size.

10 He joined five curtains to one another, and the other five curtains he joined to one another. [11]He made loops of blue on the edge of the outermost curtain of the first set; likewise he made them on the edge of the outermost curtain of the second set; [12]he made fifty loops on the one curtain, and he made fifty loops on the edge of the curtain that was in the second set; the loops were opposite one another. [13]And he made fifty clasps of gold, and joined the curtains one to the other with clasps; so the tabernacle was one whole.

14 He also made curtains of goats' hair for a tent over the tabernacle; he made eleven curtains. [15]The length of each curtain was thirty cubits, and the width of each curtain four cubits; the eleven curtains were of the same size. [16]He joined five curtains by themselves, and six curtains by themselves. [17]He made fifty loops on the edge of the outermost curtain of the one set, and fifty loops on the edge of the other connecting curtain. [18]He made fifty clasps of bronze to join the tent together so that it might be one whole. [19]And he made for the tent a covering of tanned rams' skins and an outer covering of fine leather.[a]

20 Then he made the upright frames for the tabernacle of acacia wood. [21]Ten cubits was the length of a frame, and a cubit and a half the width of each frame. [22]Each frame had two pegs for fitting together; he did this for all the frames of the tabernacle. [23]The frames for the tabernacle he made in this way: twenty frames for the south side; [24]and he made forty bases of silver under the twenty frames, two bases under the first frame for its two pegs, and two bases under the next frame for its two pegs. [25]For the second side of the tabernacle, on the north

a Meaning of Heb uncertain b Or the spirit of God

side, he made twenty frames ²⁶ and their forty bases of silver, two bases under the first frame and two bases under the next frame. ²⁷ For the rear of the tabernacle westward he made six frames. ²⁸ He made two frames for corners of the tabernacle in the rear. ²⁹ They were separate beneath, but joined at the top, at the first ring; he made two of them in this way, for the two corners. ³⁰ There were eight frames with their bases of silver: sixteen bases, under every frame two bases.

31 He made bars of acacia wood, five for the frames of the one side of the tabernacle, ³² and five bars for the frames of the other side of the tabernacle, and five bars for the frames of the tabernacle at the rear westward. ³³ He made the middle bar to pass through from end to end halfway up the frames. ³⁴ And he overlaid the frames with gold, and made rings of gold for them to hold the bars, and overlaid the bars with gold.

35 He made the curtain of blue, purple, and crimson yarns, and fine twisted linen, with cherubim skillfully worked into it. ³⁶ For it he made four pillars of acacia, and overlaid them with gold; their hooks were of gold, and he cast for them four bases of silver. ³⁷ He also made a screen for the entrance to the tent, of blue, purple, and crimson yarns, and fine twisted linen, embroidered with needlework; ³⁸ and its five pillars with their hooks. He overlaid their capitals and their bases with gold, but their five bases were of bronze.

Making the Ark of the Covenant

37 Bezalel made the ark of acacia wood; it was two and a half cubits long, a cubit and a half wide, and a cubit and a half high. ² He overlaid it with pure gold inside and outside, and made a molding of gold around it. ³ He cast for it four rings of gold for its four feet, two rings on its one side and two rings on its other side. ⁴ He made poles of acacia wood, and overlaid them with gold, ⁵ and put the poles into the rings on the sides of the ark, to carry the ark. ⁶ He made a mercy seat[a] of pure gold; two cubits and a half was its length, and a cubit and a half its width. ⁷ He made two cherubim of hammered gold; at the two ends of the mercy seat[b] he made them, ⁸ one cherub at the one end, and one cherub at the other end; of one piece with the mercy seat[b] he made the cherubim at its two ends. ⁹ The cherubim spread out their wings above, overshadowing the mercy seat[b] with their wings. They faced one another; the faces of the cherubim were turned toward the mercy seat.[b]

Making the Table for the Bread of the Presence

10 He also made the table of acacia wood, two cubits long, one cubit wide, and a cubit and a half high. ¹¹ He overlaid it with pure gold, and made a molding of gold around it. ¹² He made around it a

a Or *a cover* b Or *the cover*

STUDY IT!

The Ark of the Covenant
Exodus 37:1–9

The ark of the covenant was a portable box in which the Israelites kept the tablets of the law (Deuteronomy 10:1-5; 1 Kings 8:9) and possibly other sacred items. The large box was made by Bezalel in fulfillment of God's command. It included gold-plated wood with four rings attached to its lower corners, so priests could insert gold-plated poles and carry the ark in processions. On top of the ark sat two golden angels facing each other, their wings touching over their heads.

The ark of the covenant was a symbol of God's saving presence among the Israelites. It accompanied them during their forty years in the desert (Numbers 10:33-36) and was solemnly carried through the Jordan River when they entered the promised land (Joshua 3:1-17). Later, the Israelite soldiers took the ark into battle, invoking God's strength against their enemies (1 Samuel 4:1-11). After the ark was lost in battle to the Philistines, David retrieved it and brought it to Jerusalem (2 Samuel 6:1-23), where his son Solomon eventually enthroned it in the Holy of Holies, it's own special room in the temple (1 Kings 8:1-11). The ark remained there until the destruction of Jerusalem in 587 B.C., when it was lost to history.

rim a handbreadth wide, and made a molding of gold around the rim. [13]He cast for it four rings of gold, and fastened the rings to the four corners at its four legs. [14]The rings that held the poles used for carrying the table were close to the rim. [15]He made the poles of acacia wood to carry the table, and overlaid them with gold. [16]And he made the vessels of pure gold that were to be on the table, its plates and dishes for incense, and its bowls and flagons with which to pour drink offerings.

Making the Lampstand

17 He also made the lampstand of pure gold. The base and the shaft of the lampstand were made of hammered work; its cups, its calyxes, and its petals were of one piece with it. [18]There were six branches going out of its sides, three branches of the lampstand out of one side of it and three branches of the lampstand out of the other side of it; [19]three cups shaped like almond blossoms, each with calyx and petals, on one branch, and three cups shaped like almond blossoms, each with calyx and petals, on the other branch—so for the six branches going out of the lampstand. [20]On the lampstand itself there were four cups shaped like almond blossoms, each with its calyxes and petals. [21]There was a calyx of one piece with it under the first pair of branches, a calyx of one piece with it under the next pair of branches, and a calyx of one piece with it under the last pair of branches. [22]Their calyxes and their branches were of one piece with it, the whole of it one hammered piece of pure gold. [23]He made its seven lamps and its snuffers and its trays of pure gold. [24]He made it and all its utensils of a talent of pure gold.

Making the Altar of Incense

25 He made the altar of incense of acacia wood, one cubit long, and one cubit wide; it was square, and was two cubits high; its horns were of one piece with it. [26]He overlaid it with pure gold, its top, and its sides all around, and its horns; and he made for it a molding of gold all around, [27]and made two golden rings for it under its molding, on two opposite sides of it, to hold the poles with which to carry it. [28]And he made the poles of acacia wood, and overlaid them with gold.

Making the Anointing Oil and the Incense

29 He made the holy anointing oil also, and the pure fragrant incense, blended as by the perfumer.

Making the Altar of Burnt Offering

38 He made the altar of burnt offering also of acacia wood; it was five cubits long, and five cubits wide; it was square, and three cubits high. [2]He made horns for it on its four corners; its horns were of one piece with it, and he overlaid it with bronze. [3]He made all the utensils of the altar, the pots, the shovels, the basins, the forks, and the firepans: all its utensils he made of bronze. [4]He made for the altar a grating, a network of bronze, under its ledge, extending halfway down. [5]He cast four rings on the four corners of the bronze grating to hold the poles; [6]he made the poles of acacia wood, and overlaid them with bronze. [7]And he put the poles through the rings on the sides of the altar, to carry it with them; he made it hollow, with boards.

8 He made the basin of bronze with its stand of bronze, from the mirrors of the women who served at the entrance to the tent of meeting.

Making the Court of the Tabernacle

9 He made the court; for the south side the hangings of the court were of fine twisted linen, one hundred cubits long; [10]its twenty pillars and their twenty bases were of bronze, but the hooks of the pillars and their bands were of silver. [11]For the north side there were hangings one hundred cubits long; its twenty pillars and their twenty bases were of bronze, but the hooks of the pillars and their bands were of silver. [12]For the west side there were hangings fifty cubits long, with ten pillars and ten bases; the hooks of the pillars and their bands were of silver. [13]And for the front to the east, fifty cubits. [14]The hangings for one side of the gate were fifteen cubits, with three pillars and three bases. [15]And so for the other side; on each side of the gate of the court were hangings of fifteen cubits, with three pillars and three bases. [16]All the hangings around the court were of fine twisted linen. [17]The bases for the pillars were of bronze, but the hooks of the pillars and their bands were of silver; the overlaying of their capitals was also of silver, and all the pillars of the court were banded with silver. [18]The screen for the entrance to the court was embroidered with needlework in blue, purple, and crimson yarns and fine twisted linen. It was twenty cubits long and, along the width of it, five cubits high, corresponding to the hangings of the court. [19]There were four pillars; their four bases were of bronze, their hooks of silver, and the overlaying of their capitals and their

bands of silver. [20] All the pegs for the tabernacle and for the court all around were of bronze.

Materials of the Tabernacle

21 These are the records of the tabernacle, the tabernacle of the covenant,[a] which were drawn up at the commandment of Moses, the work of the Levites being under the direction of Ithamar son of the priest Aaron. [22] Bezalel son of Uri son of Hur, of the tribe of Judah, made all that the LORD commanded Moses; [23] and with him was Oholiab son of Ahisamach, of the tribe of Dan, engraver, designer, and embroiderer in blue, purple, and crimson yarns, and in fine linen.

24 All the gold that was used for the work, in all the construction of the sanctuary, the gold from the offering, was twenty-nine talents and seven hundred thirty shekels, measured by the sanctuary shekel. [25] The silver from those of the congregation who were counted was one hundred talents and one thousand seven hundred seventy-five shekels, measured by the sanctuary shekel; [26] a beka a head (that is, half a shekel, measured by the sanctuary shekel), for everyone who was counted in the census, from twenty years old and upward, for six hundred three thousand, five hundred fifty men. [27] The hundred talents of silver were for casting the bases of the sanctuary, and the bases of the curtain; one hundred bases for the hundred talents, a talent for a base. [28] Of the thousand seven hundred seventy-five shekels he made hooks for the pillars, and overlaid their capitals and made bands for them. [29] The bronze that was contributed was seventy talents, and two thousand four hundred shekels; [30] with it he made the bases for the entrance of the tent of meeting, the bronze altar and the bronze grating for it and all the utensils of the altar, [31] the bases all around the court, and the bases of the gate of the court, all the pegs of the tabernacle, and all the pegs around the court.

39 Making the Vestments for the Priesthood

Of the blue, purple, and crimson yarns they made finely worked vestments, for ministering in the holy place; they made the sacred vestments for Aaron; as the LORD had commanded Moses.

2 He made the ephod of gold, of blue, purple, and crimson yarns, and of fine twisted linen. [3] Gold leaf was hammered out and cut into threads to work into the blue, purple, and crimson yarns and into the fine twisted linen, in skilled design. [4] They made for the ephod shoulder-pieces, joined to it at its two edges. [5] The decorated band on it was of the same materials and workmanship, of gold, of blue, purple, and crimson yarns, and of fine twisted linen; as the LORD had commanded Moses.

6 The onyx stones were prepared, enclosed in settings of gold filigree and engraved like the engravings of a signet, according to the names of the sons of Israel. [7] He set them on the shoulder-pieces of the ephod, to be stones of remembrance for the sons of Israel; as the LORD had commanded Moses.

8 He made the breastpiece, in skilled work, like the work of the ephod, of gold, of blue, purple, and crimson yarns, and of fine twisted linen. [9] It was square; the breastpiece was made double, a span in length and a span in width when doubled. [10] They set in it four rows of stones. A row of carnelian,[b] chrysolite, and emerald was the first row; [11] and the second row, a turquoise, a sapphire,[c] and a moonstone; [12] and the third row, a jacinth, an agate, and an amethyst; [13] and the fourth row, a beryl, an onyx, and a jasper; they were enclosed in settings of gold filigree. [14] There were twelve stones with names corresponding to the names of the sons of Israel; they were like signets, each engraved with its name, for the twelve tribes. [15] They made on the breastpiece chains of pure gold, twisted like cords; [16] and they made two settings of gold filigree and two gold rings, and put the two rings on the two edges of the breastpiece; [17] and they put the two cords of gold in the two rings at the edges of the breastpiece. [18] Two ends of the two cords they had attached to the two settings of filigree; in this way they attached it in front to the shoulder-pieces of the ephod. [19] Then they made two rings of gold, and put them at the two ends of the breastpiece, on its inside edge next to the ephod. [20] They made two rings of gold, and attached them in front to the lower part of the two shoulder-pieces of the ephod, at its joining above the decorated band of the ephod. [21] They bound the breastpiece by its rings to the rings of the ephod with a blue cord, so that it should lie on the decorated band of the ephod, and that the breastpiece should not come loose from the ephod; as the LORD had commanded Moses.

22 He also made the robe of the ephod woven all of blue yarn; [23] and the opening of the robe in the middle of it was like the opening in a coat of mail,[d] with a binding around the opening, so that it might

---

a Or *treaty*, or *testimony*; Heb *eduth*   b The identification of several of these stones is uncertain   c Or *lapis lazuli*   d Meaning of Heb uncertain

not be torn. [24]On the lower hem of the robe they made pomegranates of blue, purple, and crimson yarns, and of fine twisted linen. [25]They also made bells of pure gold, and put the bells between the pomegranates on the lower hem of the robe all around, between the pomegranates; [26]a bell and a pomegranate, a bell and a pomegranate all around on the lower hem of the robe for ministering; as the LORD had commanded Moses.

27 They also made the tunics, woven of fine linen, for Aaron and his sons, [28]and the turban of fine linen, and the headdresses of fine linen, and the linen undergarments of fine twisted linen, [29]and the sash of fine twisted linen, and of blue, purple, and crimson yarns, embroidered with needlework; as the LORD had commanded Moses.

30 They made the rosette of the holy diadem of pure gold, and wrote on it an inscription, like the engraving of a signet, "Holy to the LORD." [31]They tied to it a blue cord, to fasten it on the turban above; as the LORD had commanded Moses.

The Work Completed

32 In this way all the work of the tabernacle of the tent of meeting was finished; the Israelites had done everything just as the LORD had commanded Moses. [33]Then they brought the tabernacle to Moses, the tent and all its utensils, its hooks, its frames, its bars, its pillars, and its bases; [34]the covering of tanned rams' skins and the covering of fine leather,[a] and the curtain for the screen; [35]the ark of the covenant[b] with its poles and the mercy seat;[c] [36]the table with all its utensils, and the bread of the Presence; [37]the pure lampstand with its lamps set on it and all its utensils, and the oil for the light; [38]the golden altar, the anointing oil and the fragrant incense, and the screen for the entrance of the tent; [39]the bronze altar, and its grating of bronze, its poles, and all its utensils; the basin with its stand; [40]the hangings of the court, its pillars, and its bases, and the screen for the gate of the court, its cords, and its pegs; and all the utensils for the service of the tabernacle, for the tent of meeting; [41]the finely worked vestments for ministering in the holy place, the sacred vestments for the priest Aaron, and the vestments of his sons to serve as priests. [42]The Israelites had done all of the work just as the LORD had commanded Moses. [43]When Moses saw that they had done all the work just as the LORD had commanded, he blessed them.

40 The Tabernacle Erected and Its Equipment Installed

The LORD spoke to Moses: [2]On the first day of the first month you shall set up the tabernacle of the tent of meeting. [3]You shall put in it the ark of the covenant,[b] and you shall screen the ark with the curtain. [4]You shall bring in the table, and arrange its setting; and you shall bring in the lampstand, and set up its lamps. [5]You shall put the golden altar for incense before the ark of the covenant,[b] and set up the screen for the entrance of the tabernacle. [6]You shall set the altar of burnt offering before the entrance of the tabernacle of the tent of meeting, [7]and place the basin between the tent of meeting and the altar, and put water in it. [8]You shall set up the court all around, and hang up the screen for the gate of the court. [9]Then you shall take the anointing oil, and anoint the tabernacle and all that is in it, and consecrate it and all its furniture, so that it shall become holy. [10]You shall also anoint the altar of burnt offering and all its utensils, and consecrate the altar, so that the altar shall be most holy. [11]You shall also anoint the basin with its stand, and consecrate it. [12]Then you shall bring Aaron and his sons to the entrance of the tent of meeting, and shall wash them with water, [13]and put on Aaron the sacred vestments, and you shall anoint him and consecrate him, so that he may serve me as priest. [14]You shall bring his sons also and put tunics on them, [15]and anoint them, as you anointed their father, that they may serve me as priests: and their anointing shall admit them to a perpetual priesthood throughout all generations to come.

16 Moses did everything just as the LORD had commanded him. [17]In the first month in the second year, on the first day of the month, the tabernacle was set up. [18]Moses set up the tabernacle; he laid its bases, and set up its frames, and put in its poles, and raised up its pillars; [19]and he spread the tent over the tabernacle, and put the covering of the tent over it; as the LORD had commanded Moses. [20]He took the covenant[b] and put it into the ark, and put the poles on the ark, and set the mercy seat[c] above the ark; [21]and he brought the ark into the tabernacle, and set up the curtain for screening, and screened the ark of the covenant;[b] as the LORD had commanded Moses. [22]He put the table in the tent of meeting, on the north side of the tabernacle, outside the curtain, [23]and set the bread in order on it before the LORD; as the LORD had commanded

---

a Meaning of Heb uncertain   b Or *treaty*, or *testimony*; Heb *eduth*   c Or *the cover*

Moses. [24]He put the lampstand in the tent of meeting, opposite the table on the south side of the tabernacle, [25]and set up the lamps before the LORD; as the LORD had commanded Moses. [26]He put the golden altar in the tent of meeting before the curtain, [27]and offered fragrant incense on it; as the LORD had commanded Moses. [28]He also put in place the screen for the entrance of the tabernacle. [29]He set the altar of burnt offering at the entrance of the tabernacle of the tent of meeting, and offered on it the burnt offering and the grain offering as the LORD had commanded Moses. [30]He set the basin between the tent of meeting and the altar, and put water in it for washing, [31]with which Moses and Aaron and his sons washed their hands and their feet. [32]When they went into the tent of meeting, and when they approached the altar, they washed; as the LORD had

a Heb *it*

commanded Moses. [33]He set up the court around the tabernacle and the altar, and put up the screen at the gate of the court. So Moses finished the work.

The Cloud and the Glory

34 Then the cloud covered the tent of meeting, and the glory of the LORD filled the tabernacle. [35]Moses was not able to enter the tent of meeting because the cloud settled upon it, and the glory of the LORD filled the tabernacle. [36]Whenever the cloud was taken up from the tabernacle, the Israelites would set out on each stage of their journey; [37]but if the cloud was not taken up, then they did not set out until the day that it was taken up. [38]For the cloud of the LORD was on the tabernacle by day, and fire was in the cloud*a* by night, before the eyes of all the house of Israel at each stage of their journey.

Leviticus

Come to a complete stop before proceeding through a stop sign. No texting in class. The line forms here. No shoes, no shirt, no service.

Sometimes it seems that life is just made up of a bunch of rules and laws. But have you ever thought about what life would be like without them? Traffic would be chaos. Mobs would rule. And survival of the fittest would be the way things work. When we really think about it, we realize that rules and laws are designed to help society work smoothly and to make sure we respect one another's rights. Leviticus has a similar function. It is primarily a list of laws, rules, and instructions to ensure holiness and order in worship and the people's way of life.

IN DEPTH

Leviticus, the third book of the Pentateuch, is named after the tribe of Levi, whose male members were designated priests in Israel. It was their responsibility to conduct appropriate worship of God. For that reason, the book has often been referred to as the Torah (law) of the Priests.

Most scripture scholars believe that the laws and regulations in Leviticus developed over hundreds of years after the people entered the promised land. The book was compiled at a time when the priests were struggling to unify Israel as it lay in ruins after its conquest by the Babylonians. They wished to gather together the various traditions and regulations that governed Israel's way of life. The author of Leviticus, referred to as the priestly writer, writes as if these gathered traditions and regulations were given by God to Moses at Mount Sinai as part of the original law. The author wishes to show that these laws are an extension of the Sinai covenant.

If the goal of Israel's existence is to be holy, as their God is holy (Leviticus 11:45), then the book of Leviticus records how holiness becomes part of every aspect of Israel's existence. Leviticus 17–26 is described as the Holiness Code. The words on love of neighbor in Leviticus 19:18 are quoted several times in the New Testament. The purpose of Leviticus is to call Israel to follow the law, and thus become a holy people and make its land a suitable place for God to dwell.

The customs and rites in Jesus' time are observances of the laws in Leviticus. Jesus fulfilled the law with his resurrection, and many of those customs and rites were left behind as Christianity emerged as a distinct religion.

QUICK FACTS

- **Dates Covered:** After the exodus, during the Israelites' encampment at Mount Sinai, around 1300 B.C.

- **Author:** The priestly writer, writing after the Babylonian exile in the sixth century B.C.

- **Themes:** The way of holiness through observance of the law and religious ritual, and how impossible it is for anyone, including us, to be holy without the grace and salvation God provides

AT A GLANCE

- **Leviticus 1–7** Laws regulating various sacrifices

- **Leviticus 8–10** The ordination ceremony of Aaron and his sons

- **Leviticus 11–16** Purity laws and the celebration of Yom Kippur

- **Leviticus 17–26** Holiness laws

- **Leviticus 27–34** The rededication of holy things

The Burnt Offering

1 The LORD summoned Moses and spoke to him from the tent of meeting, saying: [2]Speak to the people of Israel and say to them: When any of you bring an offering of livestock to the LORD, you shall bring your offering from the herd or from the flock.

3 If the offering is a burnt offering from the herd, you shall offer a male without blemish; you shall bring it to the entrance of the tent of meeting, for acceptance in your behalf before the LORD. [4]You shall lay your hand on the head of the burnt offering, and it shall be acceptable in your behalf as atonement for you. [5]The bull shall be slaughtered before the LORD; and Aaron's sons the priests shall offer the blood, dashing the blood against all sides of the altar that is at the entrance of the tent of meeting. [6]The burnt offering shall be flayed and cut up into its parts. [7]The sons of the priest Aaron shall put fire on the altar and arrange wood on the fire. [8]Aaron's sons the priests shall arrange the parts, with the head and the suet, on the wood that is on the fire on the altar; [9]but its entrails and its legs shall be washed with water. Then the priest shall turn the whole into smoke on the altar as a burnt offering, an offering by fire of pleasing odor to the LORD.

10 If your gift for a burnt offering is from the flock, from the sheep or goats, your offering shall be a male without blemish. [11]It shall be slaughtered on the north side of the altar before the LORD, and Aaron's sons the priests shall dash its blood against all sides of the altar. [12]It shall be cut up into its parts, with its head and its suet, and the priest shall arrange them on the wood that is on the fire on the altar; [13]but the entrails and the legs shall be washed with water. Then the priest shall offer the whole and turn it into smoke on the altar; it is a burnt offering, an offering by fire of pleasing odor to the LORD.

14 If your offering to the LORD is a burnt offering of birds, you shall choose your offering from turtle-doves or pigeons. [15]The priest shall bring it to the altar and wring off its head, and turn it into smoke on the altar; and its blood shall be drained out against the side of the altar. [16]He shall remove its crop with its contents[a] and throw it at the east side of the altar, in the place for ashes. [17]He shall tear it open by its wings without severing it. Then the priest shall turn it into smoke on the altar, on the wood that is on the fire; it is a burnt offering, an offering by fire of pleasing odor to the LORD.

Grain Offerings

2 When anyone presents a grain offering to the LORD, the offering shall be of choice flour; the worshiper shall pour oil on it, and put frankincense on it, [2]and bring it to Aaron's sons the priests. After taking from it a handful of the choice flour and oil, with all its frankincense, the priest shall turn this token portion into smoke on the altar, an offering by fire of pleasing odor to the LORD. [3]And what is left of the grain offering shall be for Aaron and his sons, a most holy part of the offerings by fire to the LORD.

4 When you present a grain offering baked in the oven, it shall be of choice flour: unleavened cakes mixed with oil, or unleavened wafers spread with oil. [5]If your offering is grain prepared on a griddle, it shall be of choice flour mixed with oil, unleavened; [6]break it in pieces, and pour oil on it; it is a grain offering. [7]If your offering is grain prepared in a pan, it shall be made of choice flour in oil. [8]You shall bring to the LORD the grain offering that is prepared in any of these ways; and when it is presented to the priest, he shall take it to the altar. [9]The priest shall remove from the grain offering its token portion and turn this into smoke on the altar, an offering by fire of pleasing odor to the LORD. [10]And what is left of the grain offering shall be for Aaron and his sons; it is a most holy part of the offerings by fire to the LORD.

11 No grain offering that you bring to the LORD shall be made with leaven, for you must not turn any leaven or honey into smoke as an offering by fire to the LORD. [12]You may bring them to the LORD as an offering of choice products, but they shall not be offered on the altar for a pleasing odor. [13]You shall not omit from your grain offerings the salt of the covenant with your God; with all your offerings you shall offer salt.

14 If you bring a grain offering of first fruits to the LORD, you shall bring as the grain offering of

a Meaning of Heb uncertain

your first fruits coarse new grain from fresh ears, parched with fire. ¹⁵You shall add oil to it and lay frankincense on it; it is a grain offering. ¹⁶And the priest shall turn a token portion of it into smoke—some of the coarse grain and oil with all its frankincense; it is an offering by fire to the LORD.

Offerings of Well-Being

3 If the offering is a sacrifice of well-being, if you offer an animal of the herd, whether male or female, you shall offer one without blemish before the LORD. ²You shall lay your hand on the head of the offering and slaughter it at the entrance of the tent of meeting; and Aaron's sons the priests shall dash the blood against all sides of the altar. ³You shall offer from the sacrifice of well-being, as an offering by fire to the LORD, the fat that covers the entrails and all the fat that is around the entrails; ⁴the two kidneys with the fat that is on them at the loins, and the appendage of the liver, which he shall remove with the kidneys. ⁵Then Aaron's sons shall turn these into smoke on the altar, with the burnt offering that is on the wood on the fire, as an offering by fire of pleasing odor to the LORD.

6 If your offering for a sacrifice of well-being to the LORD is from the flock, male or female, you shall offer one without blemish. ⁷If you present a sheep as your offering, you shall bring it before the LORD ⁸and lay your hand on the head of the offering. It shall be slaughtered before the tent of meeting, and

Aaron's sons shall dash its blood against all sides of the altar. ⁹You shall present its fat from the sacrifice of well-being, as an offering by fire to the LORD: the whole broad tail, which shall be removed close to the backbone, the fat that covers the entrails, and all the fat that is around the entrails; ¹⁰the two kidneys with the fat that is on them at the loins, and the appendage of the liver, which you shall remove with the kidneys. ¹¹Then the priest shall turn these into smoke on the altar as a food offering by fire to the LORD.

12 If your offering is a goat, you shall bring it before the LORD ¹³and lay your hand on its head; it shall be slaughtered before the tent of meeting; and the sons of Aaron shall dash its blood against all sides of the altar. ¹⁴You shall present as your offering from it, as an offering by fire to the LORD, the fat that covers the entrails, and all the fat that is around the entrails; ¹⁵the two kidneys with the fat that is on them at the loins, and the appendage of the liver, which you shall remove with the kidneys. ¹⁶Then the priest shall turn these into smoke on the altar as a food offering by fire for a pleasing odor.

All fat is the LORD's. ¹⁷It shall be a perpetual statute throughout your generations, in all your settlements: you must not eat any fat or any blood.

Sin Offerings

4 The LORD spoke to Moses, saying, ²Speak to the people of Israel, saying: When anyone sins unintentionally in any of the Lord's commandments about things not to be done, and does any one of them:

3 If it is the anointed priest who sins, thus bringing guilt on the people, he shall offer for the sin that he has committed a bull of the herd without blemish as a sin offering to the Lord. [4]He shall bring the bull to the entrance of the tent of meeting before the Lord and lay his hand on the head of the bull; the bull shall be slaughtered before the Lord. [5]The anointed priest shall take some of the blood of the bull and bring it into the tent of meeting. [6]The priest shall dip his finger in the blood and sprinkle some of the blood seven times before the Lord in front of the curtain of the sanctuary. [7]The priest shall put some of the blood on the horns of the altar of fragrant incense that is in the tent of meeting before the Lord; and the rest of the blood of the bull he shall pour out at the base of the altar of burnt offering, which is at the entrance of the tent of meeting. [8]He shall remove all the fat from the bull of sin offering: the fat that covers the entrails and all the fat that is around the entrails; [9]the two kidneys with the fat that is on them at the loins; and the appendage of the liver, which he shall remove with the kidneys, [10]just as these are removed from the ox of the sacrifice of well-being. The priest shall turn them into smoke upon the altar of burnt offering. [11]But the skin of the bull and all its flesh, as well as its head, its legs,

its entrails, and its dung— [12]all the rest of the bull— he shall carry out to a clean place outside the camp, to the ash heap, and shall burn it on a wood fire; at the ash heap it shall be burned.

13 If the whole congregation of Israel errs unintentionally and the matter escapes the notice of the assembly, and they do any one of the things that by the Lord's commandments ought not to be done and incur guilt; [14]when the sin that they have committed becomes known, the assembly shall offer a bull of the herd for a sin offering and bring it before the tent of meeting. [15]The elders of the congregation shall lay their hands on the head of the bull before the Lord, and the bull shall be slaughtered before the Lord. [16]The anointed priest shall bring some of the blood of the bull into the tent of meeting, [17]and the priest shall dip his finger in the blood and sprinkle it seven times before the Lord, in front of the curtain. [18]He shall put some of the blood on the horns of the altar that is before the Lord in the tent of meeting; and the rest of the blood he shall pour out at the base of the altar of burnt offering that is at the entrance of the tent of meeting. [19]He shall remove all its fat and turn it into smoke on the altar. [20]He shall do with the bull just as is done with the bull of sin offering; he shall do the same with this. The priest shall make atonement for them, and they shall be forgiven. [21]He shall carry the bull outside the camp, and burn it as he burned the first bull; it is the sin offering for the assembly.

22 When a ruler sins, doing unintentionally any one of all the things that by commandments of the Lord his God ought not to be done and incurs guilt, [23]once the sin that he has committed is made known to him, he shall bring as his offering a male goat without blemish. [24]He shall lay his hand on the head of the goat; it shall be slaughtered at the spot where the burnt offering is slaughtered before the Lord; it is a sin offering. [25]The priest shall take some of the blood of the sin offering with his finger and put it on the horns of the altar of burnt offering, and pour out the rest of its blood at the base of the altar of burnt offering. [26]All its fat he shall turn into smoke on the altar, like the fat of the sacrifice of well-being. Thus the priest shall make atonement on his behalf for his sin, and he shall be forgiven.

27 If anyone of the ordinary people among you sins unintentionally in doing any one of the things that by the Lord's commandments ought not to be done and incurs guilt, [28]when the sin that you have

PRAY IT!

Settling Sin
Leviticus 4:1–6:7

The Israelites understood that sin affects not only the sinner, but everyone close to that person. They also understood sin as incurring a debt that had to be repaid, so they made guilt offerings to atone for sin. Christians believe that Jesus became the sin offering who took on the debt of the sins of the whole world, once and for all. We still have an obligation to confess and turn away from our sin, but the payment was made once for all in Jesus Christ. Take a minute to thank God for the great gift of Jesus and for the forgiveness of our sins.

committed is made known to you, you shall bring a female goat without blemish as your offering, for the sin that you have committed. [29]You shall lay your hand on the head of the sin offering; and the sin offering shall be slaughtered at the place of the burnt offering. [30]The priest shall take some of its blood with his finger and put it on the horns of the altar of burnt offering, and he shall pour out the rest of its blood at the base of the altar. [31]He shall remove all its fat, as the fat is removed from the offering of well-being, and the priest shall turn it into smoke on the altar for a pleasing odor to the LORD. Thus the priest shall make atonement on your behalf, and you shall be forgiven.

32 If the offering you bring as a sin offering is a sheep, you shall bring a female without blemish. [33]You shall lay your hand on the head of the sin offering; and it shall be slaughtered as a sin offering at the spot where the burnt offering is slaughtered. [34]The priest shall take some of the blood of the sin offering with his finger and put it on the horns of the altar of burnt offering, and pour out the rest of its blood at the base of the altar. [35]You shall remove all its fat, as the fat of the sheep is removed from the sacrifice of well-being, and the priest shall turn it into smoke on the altar, with the offerings by fire to the LORD. Thus the priest shall make atonement on your behalf for the sin that you have committed, and you shall be forgiven.

5 When any of you sin in that you have heard a public adjuration to testify and—though able to testify as one who has seen or learned of the matter—do not speak up, you are subject to punishment. [2]Or when any of you touch any unclean thing—whether the carcass of an unclean beast or the carcass of unclean livestock or the carcass of an unclean swarming thing—and are unaware of it, you have become unclean, and are guilty. [3]Or when you touch human uncleanness— any uncleanness by which one can become unclean—and are unaware of it, when you come to know it, you shall be guilty. [4]Or when any of you utter aloud a rash oath for a bad or a good purpose, whatever people utter in an oath, and are unaware of it, when you come to know it, you shall in any of these be guilty. [5]When you realize your guilt in any of these, you shall confess the sin that you have committed. [6]And you shall bring to the LORD, as your penalty for the sin that you have committed, a

female from the flock, a sheep or a goat, as a sin offering; and the priest shall make atonement on your behalf for your sin.

7 But if you cannot afford a sheep, you shall bring to the LORD, as your penalty for the sin that you have committed, two turtledoves or two pigeons, one for a sin offering and the other for a burnt offering. [8]You shall bring them to the priest, who shall offer first the one for the sin offering, wringing its head at the nape without severing it. [9]He shall sprinkle some of the blood of the sin offering on the side of the altar, while the rest of the blood shall be drained out at the base of the altar; it is a sin offering. [10]And the second he shall offer for a burnt offering according to the regulation. Thus the priest shall make atonement on your behalf for the sin that you have committed, and you shall be forgiven.

11 But if you cannot afford two turtledoves or two pigeons, you shall bring as your offering for the sin that you have committed one-tenth of an ephah of choice flour for a sin offering; you shall not put oil on it or lay frankincense on it, for it is a sin offering. [12]You shall bring it to the priest, and the priest shall scoop up a handful of it as its memorial portion, and turn this into smoke on the altar, with the offerings by fire to the LORD; it is a sin offering. [13]Thus the priest shall make atonement on your behalf for whichever of these sins you have committed, and you shall be forgiven. Like the grain offering, the rest shall be for the priest.

Offerings with Restitution

14 The LORD spoke to Moses, saying: [15]When any of you commit a trespass and sin unintentionally in any of the holy things of the LORD, you shall bring, as your guilt offering to the LORD, a ram without blemish from the flock, convertible into silver by the sanctuary shekel; it is a guilt offering. [16]And you shall make restitution for the holy thing in which you were remiss, and shall add one-fifth to it and give it to the priest. The priest shall make atonement on your behalf with the ram of the guilt offering, and you shall be forgiven.

17 If any of you sin without knowing it, doing any of the things that by the Lord's commandments ought not to be done, you have incurred guilt, and are subject to punishment. [18]You shall bring to the priest a ram without blemish from the flock, or the equivalent, as a guilt offering; and the priest shall make atonement on your behalf for the error that you committed unintentionally, and you shall be forgiven. [19]It is a guilt offering; you have incurred guilt before the Lord.

6 [a] The Lord spoke to Moses, saying: [2]When any of you sin and commit a trespass against the Lord by deceiving a neighbor in a matter of a deposit or a pledge, or by robbery, or if you have defrauded a neighbor, [3]or have found something lost and lied about it—if you swear falsely regarding any of the various things that one may do and sin thereby— [4]when you have sinned and realize your guilt, and would restore what you took by robbery or by fraud or the deposit that was committed to you, or the lost thing that you found, [5]or anything else about which you have sworn falsely, you shall repay the principal amount and shall add one-fifth to it. You shall pay it to its owner when you realize your guilt. [6]And you shall bring to the priest, as your guilt offering to the Lord, a ram without blemish from the flock, or its equivalent, for a guilt offering. [7]The priest shall make atonement on your behalf before the Lord, and you shall be forgiven for any of the things that one may do and incur guilt thereby.

Instructions concerning Sacrifices

8[b] The Lord spoke to Moses, saying: [9]Command Aaron and his sons, saying: This is the ritual of the burnt offering. The burnt offering itself shall remain on the hearth upon the altar all night until the morning, while the fire on the altar shall be kept burning. [10]The priest shall put on his linen vestments after putting on his linen undergarments next to his body; and he shall take up the ashes to which the fire has reduced the burnt offering on the altar, and place them beside the altar. [11]Then he shall take off his vestments and put on other garments, and carry the ashes out to a clean place outside the camp. [12]The fire on the altar shall be kept burning; it shall not go out. Every morning the priest shall add wood to it, lay out the burnt offering on it, and turn into smoke the fat pieces of the offerings of

well-being. [13]A perpetual fire shall be kept burning on the altar; it shall not go out.

14 This is the ritual of the grain offering: The sons of Aaron shall offer it before the Lord, in front of the altar. [15]They shall take from it a handful of the choice flour and oil of the grain offering, with all the frankincense that is on the offering, and they shall turn its memorial portion into smoke on the altar as a pleasing odor to the Lord. [16]Aaron and his sons shall eat what is left of it; it shall be eaten as unleavened cakes in a holy place; in the court of the tent of meeting they shall eat it. [17]It shall not be baked with leaven. I have given it as their portion of my offerings by fire; it is most holy, like the sin offering and the guilt offering. [18]Every male among the descendants of Aaron shall eat of it, as their perpetual due throughout your generations, from the Lord's offerings by fire; anything that touches them shall become holy.

19 The Lord spoke to Moses, saying: [20]This is the offering that Aaron and his sons shall offer to the Lord on the day when he is anointed: one-tenth of an ephah of choice flour as a regular offering, half of it in the morning and half in the evening. [21]It shall be made with oil on a griddle; you shall bring it well soaked, as a grain offering of baked[c] pieces, and you shall present it as a pleasing odor to the Lord. [22]And so the priest, anointed from among Aaron's descendants as a successor, shall prepare it; it is the Lord's—a perpetual due—to be turned entirely into smoke. [23]Every grain offering of a priest shall be wholly burned; it shall not be eaten.

24 The Lord spoke to Moses, saying: [25]Speak to Aaron and his sons, saying: This is the ritual of the sin offering. The sin offering shall be slaughtered before the Lord at the spot where the burnt offering is slaughtered; it is most holy. [26]The priest who offers it as a sin offering shall eat of it; it shall be eaten in a holy place, in the court of the tent of meeting. [27]Whatever touches its flesh shall become holy; and when any of its blood is spattered on a garment, you shall wash the bespattered part in a holy place. [28]An earthen vessel in which it was boiled shall be broken; but if it is boiled in a bronze vessel, that shall be scoured and rinsed in water. [29]Every male among the priests shall eat of it; it is most holy. [30]But no sin offering shall be eaten from which any blood is brought into the tent of meeting for atonement in the holy place; it shall be burned with fire.

---

a Ch 5.20 in Heb   b Ch 6.1 in Heb   c Meaning of Heb uncertain

7 This is the ritual of the guilt offering. It is most holy; [2] at the spot where the burnt offering is slaughtered, they shall slaughter the guilt offering, and its blood shall be dashed against all sides of the altar. [3] All its fat shall be offered: the broad tail, the fat that covers the entrails, [4] the two kidneys with the fat that is on them at the loins, and the appendage of the liver, which shall be removed with the kidneys. [5] The priest shall turn them into smoke on the altar as an offering by fire to the Lord; it is a guilt offering. [6] Every male among the priests shall eat of it; it shall be eaten in a holy place; it is most holy.

7 The guilt offering is like the sin offering, there is the same ritual for them; the priest who makes atonement with it shall have it. [8] So, too, the priest who offers anyone's burnt offering shall keep the skin of the burnt offering that he has offered. [9] And every grain offering baked in the oven, and all that is prepared in a pan or on a griddle, shall belong to the priest who offers it. [10] But every other grain offering, mixed with oil or dry, shall belong to all the sons of Aaron equally.

Further Instructions

11 This is the ritual of the sacrifice of the offering of well-being that one may offer to the Lord. [12] If you offer it for thanksgiving, you shall offer with the thank offering unleavened cakes mixed with oil, unleavened wafers spread with oil, and cakes of choice flour well soaked in oil. [13] With your thanksgiving sacrifice of well-being you shall bring your offering with cakes of leavened bread. [14] From this you shall offer one cake from each offering, as a gift to the Lord; it shall belong to the priest who dashes the blood of the offering of well-being. [15] And the flesh of your thanksgiving sacrifice of well-being shall be eaten on the day it is offered; you shall not leave any of it until morning. [16] But if the sacrifice you offer is a votive offering or a freewill offering, it shall be eaten on the day that you offer your sacrifice, and what is left of it shall be eaten the next day; [17] but what is left of the flesh of the sacrifice shall be burned up on the third day. [18] If any of the flesh of your sacrifice of well-being is eaten on the third day, it shall not be acceptable, nor shall it be credited to the one who offers it; it shall be an abomination, and the one who eats of it shall incur guilt.

19 Flesh that touches any unclean thing shall not be eaten; it shall be burned up. As for other flesh, all who are clean may eat such flesh. [20] But those who eat flesh from the Lord's sacrifice of well-being while in a state of uncleanness shall be cut off from their kin. [21] When any one of you touches any unclean thing—human uncleanness or an unclean animal or any unclean creature—and then eats flesh from the Lord's sacrifice of well-being, you shall be cut off from your kin.

22 The Lord spoke to Moses, saying: [23] Speak to the people of Israel, saying: You shall eat no fat of ox or sheep or goat. [24] The fat of an animal that died or was torn by wild animals may be put to any other use, but you must not eat it. [25] If any one of you eats the fat from an animal of which an offering by fire may be made to the Lord, you who eat it shall be cut off from your kin. [26] You must not eat any blood whatever, either of bird or of animal, in any of your settlements. [27] Any one of you who eats any blood shall be cut off from your kin.

28 The Lord spoke to Moses, saying: [29] Speak to the people of Israel, saying: Any one of you who would offer to the Lord your sacrifice of well-being must yourself bring to the Lord your offering from your sacrifice of well-being. [30] Your own hands shall bring the Lord's offering by fire; you shall bring the fat with the breast, so that the breast may be raised as an elevation offering before the Lord. [31] The priest shall turn the fat into smoke on the altar, but the breast shall belong to Aaron and his sons. [32] And the right thigh from your sacrifices of well-being you shall give to the priest as an offering; [33] the one among the sons of Aaron who offers the blood and fat of the offering of well-being shall have the right thigh for a portion. [34] For I have taken the breast of the elevation offering, and the thigh that is offered, from the people of Israel, from their sacrifices of well-being, and have given them to Aaron the priest and to his sons, as a perpetual due from the people of Israel. [35] This is the portion allotted to Aaron and to his sons from the offerings made by fire to the Lord, once they have been brought forward to serve the Lord as priests; [36] these the Lord commanded to be given them, when he anointed them, as a perpetual due from the people of Israel throughout their generations.

37 This is the ritual of the burnt offering, the grain offering, the sin offering, the guilt offering, the offering of ordination, and the sacrifice of well-being, [38] which the Lord commanded Moses on

Mount Sinai, when he commanded the people of Israel to bring their offerings to the Lord, in the wilderness of Sinai.

The Rites of Ordination

8 The Lord spoke to Moses, saying: ²Take Aaron and his sons with him, the vestments, the anointing oil, the bull of sin offering, the two rams, and the basket of unleavened bread; ³and assemble the whole congregation at the entrance of the tent of meeting. ⁴And Moses did as the Lord commanded him. When the congregation was assembled at the entrance of the tent of meeting, ⁵Moses said to the congregation, "This is what the Lord has commanded to be done."

6 Then Moses brought Aaron and his sons forward, and washed them with water. ⁷He put the tunic on him, fastened the sash around him, clothed him with the robe, and put the ephod on him. He then put the decorated band of the ephod around him, tying the ephod to him with it. ⁸He placed the breastpiece on him, and in the breastpiece he put the Urim and the Thummim. ⁹And he set the turban on his head, and on the turban, in front, he set the golden ornament, the holy crown, as the Lord commanded Moses.

10 Then Moses took the anointing oil and anointed the tabernacle and all that was in it, and consecrated them. ¹¹He sprinkled some of it on the altar seven times, and anointed the altar and all its utensils, and the basin and its base, to consecrate them. ¹²He poured some of the anointing oil on Aaron's head and anointed him, to consecrate him. ¹³And Moses brought forward Aaron's sons, and clothed them with tunics, and fastened sashes around them, and tied headdresses on them, as the Lord commanded Moses.

14 He led forward the bull of sin offering; and Aaron and his sons laid their hands upon the head of the bull of sin offering, ¹⁵and it was slaughtered. Moses took the blood and with his finger put some on each of the horns of the altar, purifying the altar; then he poured out the blood at the base of the altar. Thus he consecrated it, to make atonement for it. ¹⁶Moses took all the fat that was around the entrails, and the appendage of the liver, and the two kidneys with their fat, and turned them into smoke on the altar. ¹⁷But the bull itself, its skin and flesh and its dung, he burned with fire outside the camp, as the Lord commanded Moses.

18 Then he brought forward the ram of burnt offering. Aaron and his sons laid their hands on the head of the ram, ¹⁹and it was slaughtered. Moses dashed the blood against all sides of the altar. ²⁰The ram was cut into its parts, and Moses turned into smoke the head and the parts and the suet. ²¹And after the entrails and the legs were washed with water, Moses turned into smoke the whole ram on the altar; it was a burnt offering for a pleasing odor, an offering by fire to the Lord, as the Lord commanded Moses.

22 Then he brought forward the second ram, the ram of ordination. Aaron and his sons laid their hands on the head of the ram, ²³and it was slaughtered. Moses took some of its blood and put it on the lobe of Aaron's right ear and on the thumb of his right hand and on the big toe of his right foot. ²⁴After Aaron's sons were brought forward, Moses put some of the blood on the lobes of their right ears and on the thumbs of their right hands and on the big toes of their right feet; and Moses dashed the rest of the blood against all sides of the altar. ²⁵He took the fat—the broad tail, all the fat that was around the entrails, the appendage of the liver, and the two kidneys with their fat—and the right thigh. ²⁶From the basket of unleavened bread that was before the Lord, he took one cake of unleavened bread, one cake of bread with oil, and one wafer, and placed them on the fat and on the right thigh. ²⁷He placed all these on the palms of Aaron and on the palms of his sons, and raised them as an elevation offering before the Lord. ²⁸Then Moses took them from their hands and turned them into smoke on the altar with the burnt offering. This was an ordination offering for a pleasing odor, an offering by fire to the Lord. ²⁹Moses took the breast and raised it as an elevation offering before the Lord; it was Moses' portion of the ram of ordination, as the Lord commanded Moses.

30 Then Moses took some of the anointing oil and some of the blood that was on the altar and sprinkled them on Aaron and his vestments, and also on his sons and their vestments. Thus he consecrated Aaron and his vestments, and also his sons and their vestments.

31 And Moses said to Aaron and his sons, "Boil the flesh at the entrance of the tent of meeting, and eat it there with the bread that is in the basket of ordination offerings, as I was commanded, 'Aaron and his sons shall eat it'; ³²and what remains of the

flesh and the bread you shall burn with fire. ³³You shall not go outside the entrance of the tent of meeting for seven days, until the day when your period of ordination is completed. For it will take seven days to ordain you; ³⁴as has been done today, the LORD has commanded to be done to make atonement for you. ³⁵You shall remain at the entrance of the tent of meeting day and night for seven days, keeping the LORD's charge so that you do not die; for so I am commanded." ³⁶Aaron and his sons did all the things that the LORD commanded through Moses.

Aaron's Priesthood Inaugurated

9 On the eighth day Moses summoned Aaron and his sons and the elders of Israel. ²He said to Aaron, "Take a bull calf for a sin offering and a ram for a burnt offering, without blemish, and offer them before the LORD. ³And say to the people of Israel, 'Take a male goat for a sin offering; a calf and a lamb, yearlings without blemish, for a burnt offering; ⁴and an ox and a ram for an offering of well-being to sacrifice before the LORD; and a grain offering mixed with oil. For today the LORD will appear to you.' " ⁵They brought what Moses commanded to the front of the tent of meeting; and the whole congregation drew near and stood before the LORD. ⁶And Moses said, "This is the thing that the LORD commanded you to do, so that the glory of the LORD may appear to you." ⁷Then Moses said to Aaron, "Draw near to the altar and sacrifice your sin offering and your burnt offering, and make atonement for yourself and for the people; and sacrifice the offering of the people, and make atonement for them; as the LORD has commanded."

⁸ Aaron drew near to the altar,

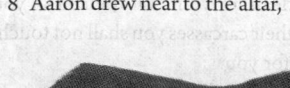

and slaughtered the calf of the sin offering, which was for himself. ⁹The sons of Aaron presented the blood to him, and he dipped his finger in the blood and put it on the horns of the altar; and the rest of the blood he poured out at the base of the altar. ¹⁰But the fat, the kidneys, and the appendage of the liver from the sin offering he turned into smoke on the altar, as the LORD commanded Moses; ¹¹and the flesh and the skin he burned with fire outside the camp.

12 Then he slaughtered the burnt offering. Aaron's sons brought him the blood, and he dashed it against all sides of the altar. ¹³And they brought him the burnt offering piece by piece, and the head, which he turned into smoke on the altar. ¹⁴He washed the entrails and the legs and, with the burnt offering, turned them into smoke on the altar.

15 Next he presented the people's offering. He took the goat of the sin offering that was for the people, and slaughtered it, and presented it as a sin offering like the first one. ¹⁶He presented the burnt offering, and sacrificed it according to regulation. ¹⁷He presented the grain offering, and, taking a handful of it, he turned it into smoke on the altar, in addition to the burnt offering of the morning.

18 He slaughtered the ox and the ram as a sacrifice of well-being for the people. Aaron's sons brought him the blood, which he dashed against all sides of the altar, ¹⁹and the fat of the ox and of the ram—the broad tail, the fat that covers the entrails, the two kidneys and the fat on them,^a and the appendage of the liver. ²⁰They first laid the fat on the breasts, and the fat was turned into smoke on the altar; ²¹and the breasts and the right thigh Aaron raised as an elevation offering before the LORD, as Moses had commanded.

22 Aaron lifted his hands toward the people and blessed them; and he came down after sacrificing the sin offering, the burnt offering, and the offering of well-being. ²³Moses and Aaron entered the tent of meeting, and then came out and blessed the people; and the glory of the LORD appeared to all the people. ²⁴Fire came out from the LORD and consumed the burnt offering and the fat on the altar; and when all the people saw it, they shouted and fell on their faces.

Nadab and Abihu

10 Now Aaron's sons, Nadab and Abihu, each took his censer, put fire in it, and laid in-

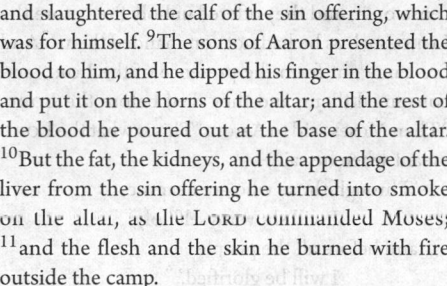

---

a Gk: Heb *the broad tail, and that which covers, and the kidneys*

cense on it; and they offered unholy fire before the LORD, such as he had not commanded them. [2]And fire came out from the presence of the LORD and consumed them, and they died before the LORD. [3]Then Moses said to Aaron, "This is what the LORD meant when he said,

'Through those who are near me
     I will show myself holy,
and before all the people
     I will be glorified.'"

And Aaron was silent.

4 Moses summoned Mishael and Elzaphan, sons of Uzziel the uncle of Aaron, and said to them, "Come forward, and carry your kinsmen away from the front of the sanctuary to a place outside the camp." [5]They came forward and carried them by their tunics out of the camp, as Moses had ordered. [6]And Moses said to Aaron and to his sons Eleazar and Ithamar, "Do not dishevel your hair, and do not tear your vestments, or you will die and wrath will strike all the congregation; but your kindred, the whole house of Israel, may mourn the burning that the LORD has sent. [7]You shall not go outside the entrance of the tent of meeting, or you will die; for the anointing oil of the LORD is on you." And they did as Moses had ordered.

8 And the LORD spoke to Aaron: [9]Drink no wine or strong drink, neither you nor your sons, when you enter the tent of meeting, that you may not die; it is a statute forever throughout your generations. [10]You are to distinguish between the holy and the common, and between the unclean and the clean; [11]and you are to teach the people of Israel all the statutes that the LORD has spoken to them through Moses.

12 Moses spoke to Aaron and to his remaining sons, Eleazar and Ithamar: Take the grain offering that is left from the LORD's offerings by fire, and eat it unleavened beside the altar, for it is most holy; [13]you shall eat it in a holy place, because it is your due and your sons' due, from the offerings by fire to the LORD; for so I am commanded. [14]But the breast that is elevated and the thigh that is raised, you and your sons and daughters as well may eat in any clean place; for they have been assigned to you and your children from the sacrifices of the offerings of well-being of the people of Israel. [15]The thigh that is raised and the breast that is elevated they shall bring, together with the offerings by fire of the fat, to raise for an elevation offering before the LORD;

they are to be your due and that of your children forever, as the LORD has commanded.

16 Then Moses made inquiry about the goat of the sin offering, and—it had already been burned! He was angry with Eleazar and Ithamar, Aaron's remaining sons, and said, [17]"Why did you not eat the sin offering in the sacred area? For it is most holy, and God[a] has given it to you that you may remove the guilt of the congregation, to make atonement on their behalf before the LORD. [18]Its blood was not brought into the inner part of the sanctuary. You should certainly have eaten it in the sanctuary, as I commanded." [19]And Aaron spoke to Moses, "See, today they offered their sin offering and their burnt offering before the LORD; and yet such things as these have befallen me! If I had eaten the sin offering today, would it have been agreeable to the LORD?" [20]And when Moses heard that, he agreed.

Clean and Unclean Foods

11 The LORD spoke to Moses and Aaron, saying to them: [2]Speak to the people of Israel, saying:

From among all the land animals, these are the creatures that you may eat. [3]Any animal that has divided hoofs and is cleft-footed and chews the cud—such you may eat. [4]But among those that chew the cud or have divided hoofs, you shall not eat the following: the camel, for even though it chews the cud, it does not have divided hoofs; it is unclean for you. [5]The rock badger, for even though it chews the cud, it does not have divided hoofs; it is unclean for you. [6]The hare, for even though it chews the cud, it does not have divided hoofs; it is unclean for you. [7]The pig, for even though it has divided hoofs and is cleft-footed, it does not chew the cud; it is unclean for you. [8]Of their flesh you shall not eat, and their carcasses you shall not touch; they are unclean for you.

9 These you may eat, of all that are in the waters. Everything in the waters that has fins and scales, whether in the seas or in the streams—such you may eat. [10]But anything in the seas or the streams that does not have fins and scales, of the swarming creatures in the waters and among all the other living creatures that are in the waters—they are detestable to you [11]and detestable they shall remain. Of their flesh you shall not eat, and their carcasses you shall regard as detestable. [12]Everything in the waters that does not have fins and scales is detestable to you.

a Heb *he*

13 These you shall regard as detestable among the birds. They shall not be eaten; they are an abomination: the eagle, the vulture, the osprey, [14]the buzzard, the kite of any kind; [15]every raven of any kind; [16]the ostrich, the nighthawk, the sea gull, the hawk of any kind; [17]the little owl, the cormorant, the great owl, [18]the water hen, the desert owl,[a] the carrion vulture, [19]the stork, the heron of any kind, the hoopoe, and the bat.[b]

20 All winged insects that walk upon all fours are detestable to you. [21]But among the winged insects that walk on all fours you may eat those that have jointed legs above their feet, with which to leap on the ground. [22]Of them you may eat: the locust according to its kind, the bald locust according to its kind, the cricket according to its kind, and the grasshopper according to its kind. [23]But all other winged insects that have four feet are detestable to you.

Unclean Animals

24 By these you shall become unclean; whoever touches the carcass of any of them shall be unclean until the evening, [25]and whoever carries any part of the carcass of any of them shall wash his clothes and be unclean until the evening. [26]Every animal that has divided hoofs but is not cleft-footed or does not chew the cud is unclean for you; everyone who touches one of them shall be unclean. [27]All that walk on their paws, among the animals that walk on all fours, are unclean for you; whoever touches the carcass of any of them shall be unclean until the evening, [28]and the one who carries the carcass shall wash his clothes and be unclean until the evening; they are unclean for you.

29 These are unclean for you among the creatures that swarm upon the earth: the weasel, the mouse, the great lizard according to its kind, [30]the gecko, the land crocodile, the lizard, the sand lizard, and the chameleon. [31]These are unclean for you among all that swarm; whoever touches one of them when they are dead shall be unclean until the evening. [32]And anything upon which any of them falls when they are dead shall be unclean, whether an article of wood or cloth or skin or sacking, any article that is used for any purpose; it shall be dipped into water, and it shall be unclean until the evening,

STUDY IT!

The Israelite Diet · Leviticus 11

The ancient Israelites ate mainly breads, cereals, fruits, vegetables, and dairy products. Meat was served only on special occasions, because it was expensive. A typical family meal was made up of barley or wheat bread, grapes, figs, olive oil, beans, cucumbers, onions, and cheese. Beef or lamb might grace the table on festive occasions.

The laws in **Leviticus 11** contain many restrictions about eating animals. The reasons for these restrictions aren't clear, but many scholars believe that one purpose was to keep Israelites from consuming animals used in pagan worship (for example, the pig offered in Babylonian services). Hygiene was likely another consideration.

The basic "meat laws" were as follows:

- Larger animals that chewed their cud and had split hooves could be eaten. So lamb was acceptable, but pork was not.
- Sea creatures to be eaten had to have both fins and scales. So catfish and eels were to be avoided.
- Eagles, vultures, buzzards, and many other birds were excluded from the table.
- Rodents, reptiles, and insects (except locusts and grasshoppers) were rejected from the diet as well.

The blood from all animals had to be drained completely before cooking, because blood was seen as the life force and therefore as belonging to God alone. It was also unlawful to touch or eat any animal found dead; contact with any dead body made one impure.

---

a Or *pelican*   *b* Identification of several of the birds in verses 13-19 is uncertain

and then it shall be clean. [33]And if any of them falls into any earthen vessel, all that is in it shall be unclean, and you shall break the vessel. [34]Any food that could be eaten shall be unclean if water from any such vessel comes upon it; and any liquid that could be drunk shall be unclean if it was in any such vessel. [35]Everything on which any part of the carcass falls shall be unclean; whether an oven or stove, it shall be broken in pieces; they are unclean, and shall remain unclean for you. [36]But a spring or a cistern holding water shall be clean, while whatever touches the carcass in it shall be unclean. [37]If any part of their carcass falls upon any seed set aside for sowing, it is clean; [38]but if water is put on the seed and any part of their carcass falls on it, it is unclean for you.

39 If an animal of which you may eat dies, anyone who touches its carcass shall be unclean until the evening. [40]Those who eat of its carcass shall wash their clothes and be unclean until the evening; and those who carry the carcass shall wash their clothes and be unclean until the evening.

41 All creatures that swarm upon the earth are detestable; they shall not be eaten. [42]Whatever moves on its belly, and whatever moves on all fours, or whatever has many feet, all the creatures that swarm upon the earth, you shall not eat; for they are detestable. [43]You shall not make yourselves detestable with any creature that swarms; you shall not defile yourselves with them, and so become unclean. [44]For I am the LORD your God; sanctify yourselves therefore, and be holy, for I am holy. You shall not defile yourselves with any swarming creature that moves on the earth. [45]For I am the LORD who brought you up from the land of Egypt, to be your God; you shall be holy, for I am holy.

46 This is the law pertaining to land animal and bird and every living creature that moves through the waters and every living creature that swarms upon the earth, [47]to make a distinction between the unclean and the clean, and between the living creature that may be eaten and the living creature that may not be eaten.

<table>
<tr><td>12</td><td></td></tr>
</table>

Purification of Women after Childbirth
The LORD spoke to Moses, saying: [2]Speak to the people of Israel, saying:

If a woman conceives and bears a male child, she shall be ceremonially unclean seven days; as at the time of her menstruation, she shall be unclean. [3]On the eighth day the flesh of his foreskin shall be cir-

cumcised. [4]Her time of blood purification shall be thirty-three days; she shall not touch any holy thing, or come into the sanctuary, until the days of her purification are completed. [5]If she bears a female child, she shall be unclean two weeks, as in her menstruation; her time of blood purification shall be sixty-six days.

6 When the days of her purification are completed, whether for a son or for a daughter, she shall bring to the priest at the entrance of the tent of meeting a lamb in its first year for a burnt offering, and a pigeon or a turtledove for a sin offering. [7]He shall offer it before the LORD, and make atonement on her behalf; then she shall be clean from her flow of blood. This is the law for her who bears a child, male or female. [8]If she cannot afford a sheep, she shall take two turtledoves or two pigeons, one for a burnt offering and the other for a sin offering; and the priest shall make atonement on her behalf, and she shall be clean.

Leprosy, Varieties and Symptoms

<table>
<tr><td>13</td><td></td></tr>
</table>

The LORD spoke to Moses and Aaron, saying:

2 When a person has on the skin of his body a swelling or an eruption or a spot, and it turns into a leprous[a] disease on the skin of his body, he shall be brought to Aaron the priest or to one of his sons the priests. [3]The priest shall examine the disease on the skin of his body, and if the hair in the diseased area has turned white and the disease appears to be deeper than the skin of his body, it is a leprous[a] disease; after the priest has examined him he shall pronounce him ceremonially unclean. [4]But if the spot is white in the skin of his body, and appears no deeper than the skin, and the hair in it has not turned white, the priest shall confine the diseased person for seven days. [5]The priest shall examine him on the seventh day, and if he sees that the disease is checked and the disease has not spread in the skin, then the priest shall confine him seven days more. [6]The priest shall examine him again on the seventh day, and if the disease has abated and the disease has not spread in the skin, the priest shall pronounce him clean; it is only an eruption; and he shall wash his clothes, and be clean. [7]But if the eruption spreads in the skin after he has shown himself to the priest for his cleansing, he shall appear again before the priest. [8]The priest shall make an examination, and if the eruption has spread in the skin, the priest shall pronounce him unclean; it is a leprous[a] disease.

---

a A term for several skin diseases; precise meaning uncertain

CONNECT IT!

A Mother's Prayer at Childbirth · Leviticus 12:1–8

The specifics of the purification ritual after the birth of a child seem foreign and strange to us today, but they show that childbirth was an important event in Israelite society. Customs and prayers associated with childbirth have changed over time, but are present in almost all cultures. In this mother's prayer of the Native American Omaha tribe, the four hills refer to the four parts of human life: childhood, youth, adulthood, and old age. What a wonderful reminder that life is a journey and that all creation is invited to celebrate new life!

Sun, moon, stars,
you that move in the heavens,
hear this mother!
A new life has come among you.
Make its path smooth that it may reach
the brow of the first hill.

Winds, clouds, rain, mist,
all that move in the air,
hear this mother!
A new life has come among you.
Make its path smooth that it may reach
the brow of the second hill.

Hills, valleys, rivers, lakes, trees, grasses,
all of the earth,
hear this mother!
A new life has come among you.

Make its path smooth that it may reach
the brow of the third hill.

Birds that fly in the air,
animals that dwell in the forest,
insects that creep in the grasses
and burrow in the ground,
hear this mother!
A new life has come among you.
Make its path smooth that it may reach
the brow of the fourth hill.

All the heavens, air and earth,
hear this mother!
A new life has come among you.
Make its path smooth—then shall it
travel beyond the four hills!*

9 When a person contracts a leprous[a] disease, he shall be brought to the priest. [10]The priest shall make an examination, and if there is a white swelling in the skin that has turned the hair white, and there is quick raw flesh in the swelling, [11]it is a chronic leprous[a] disease in the skin of his body. The priest shall pronounce him unclean; he shall not confine him, for he is unclean. [12]But if the disease breaks out in the skin, so that it covers all the skin of the diseased person from head to foot, so far as the priest can see, [13]then the priest shall make an examination, and if the disease has covered all his body, he shall pronounce him clean of the disease; since it has all turned white, he is clean. [14]But if raw flesh ever appears on him, he shall be unclean; [15]the priest shall examine the raw flesh and pronounce him unclean. Raw flesh is unclean, for it is a leprous[a] disease. [16]But if the raw flesh again turns white, he shall come to the priest; [17]the priest shall examine him, and if the disease has turned white, the priest shall pronounce the diseased person clean. He is clean.

18 When there is on the skin of one's body a boil that has healed, [19]and in the place of the boil there appears a white swelling or a reddish-white spot, it shall be shown to the priest. [20]The priest shall make an examination, and if it appears deeper than the skin and its hair has turned white, the priest shall pronounce him unclean; this is a leprous[a] disease, broken out in the boil. [21]But if the priest examines it and the hair on it is not white, nor is it deeper than the skin but has abated, the priest shall confine him seven days. [22]If it spreads in the skin, the priest shall pronounce him unclean; it is diseased. [23]But if the

a A term for several skin diseases; precise meaning uncertain

spot remains in one place and does not spread, it is the scar of the boil; the priest shall pronounce him clean.

24 Or, when the body has a burn on the skin and the raw flesh of the burn becomes a spot, reddish-white or white, [25]the priest shall examine it. If the hair in the spot has turned white and it appears deeper than the skin, it is a leprous[a] disease; it has broken out in the burn, and the priest shall pronounce him unclean. This is a leprous[a] disease. [26]But if the priest examines it and the hair in the spot is not white, and it is no deeper than the skin but has abated, the priest shall confine him seven days. [27]The priest shall examine him the seventh day; if it is spreading in the skin, the priest shall pronounce him unclean. This is a leprous[a] disease. [28]But if the spot remains in one place and does not spread in the skin but has abated, it is a swelling from the burn, and the priest shall pronounce him clean; for it is the scar of the burn.

29 When a man or woman has a disease on the head or in the beard, [30]the priest shall examine the disease. If it appears deeper than the skin and the hair in it is yellow and thin, the priest shall pronounce him unclean; it is an itch, a leprous[a] disease of the head or the beard. [31]If the priest examines the itching disease, and it appears no deeper than the skin and there is no black hair in it, the priest shall confine the person with the itching disease for seven days. [32]On the seventh day the priest shall examine the itch; if the itch has not spread, and there is no yellow hair in it, and the itch appears to be no deeper than the skin, [33]he shall shave, but the itch he shall not shave. The priest shall confine the person with the itch for seven days more. [34]On the seventh day the priest shall examine the itch; if the itch has not spread in the skin and it appears to be no deeper than the skin, the priest shall pronounce him clean. He shall wash his clothes and be clean. [35]But if the itch spreads in the skin after he was pronounced clean, [36]the priest shall examine him. If the itch has spread in the skin, the priest need not seek for the yellow hair; he is unclean. [37]But if in his eyes the itch is checked, and black hair has grown in it, the itch is healed, he is clean; and the priest shall pronounce him clean.

38 When a man or a woman has spots on the skin of the body, white spots, [39]the priest shall make an examination, and if the spots on the skin of the body are of a dull white, it is a rash that has broken out on the skin; he is clean.

40 If anyone loses the hair from his head, he is bald but he is clean. [41]If he loses the hair from his forehead and temples, he has baldness of the forehead but he is clean. [42]But if there is on the bald head or the bald forehead a reddish-white diseased spot, it is a leprous[a] disease breaking out on his bald head or his bald forehead. [43]The priest shall examine him; if the diseased swelling is reddish-white on his bald head or on his bald forehead, which resembles a leprous[a] disease in the skin of the body, [44]he is leprous,[a] he is unclean. The priest shall pronounce him unclean; the disease is on his head.

45 The person who has the leprous[a] disease shall wear torn clothes and let the hair of his head be disheveled; and he shall cover his upper lip and cry out, "Unclean, unclean." [46]He shall remain unclean as long as he has the disease; he is unclean. He shall live alone; his dwelling shall be outside the camp.

47 Concerning clothing: when a leprous[a] disease appears in it, in woolen or linen cloth, [48]in warp or woof of linen or wool, or in a skin or in anything made of skin, [49]if the disease shows greenish or reddish in the garment, whether in warp or woof or in skin or in anything made of skin, it is a leprous[a] disease and shall be shown to the priest. [50]The priest shall examine the disease, and put the diseased article aside for seven days. [51]He shall examine the disease on the seventh day. If the disease has spread in the cloth, in warp or woof, or in the skin, whatever be the use of the skin, this is a spreading leprous[a] disease; it is unclean. [52]He shall burn the clothing, whether diseased in warp or woof, woolen or linen, or anything of skin, for it is a spreading leprous[a] disease; it shall be burned in fire.

53 If the priest makes an examination, and the disease has not spread in the clothing, in warp or woof or in anything of skin, [54]the priest shall command them to wash the article in which the disease appears, and he shall put it aside seven days more. [55]The priest shall examine the diseased article after it has been washed. If the diseased spot has not changed color, though the disease has not spread, it is unclean; you shall burn it in fire, whether the leprous[a] spot is on the inside or on the outside.

56 If the priest makes an examination, and the disease has abated after it is washed, he shall tear the spot out of the cloth, in warp or woof, or out of skin. [57]If it appears again in the garment, in warp

---

[a] A term for several skin diseases; precise meaning uncertain

or woof, or in anything of skin, it is spreading; you shall burn with fire that in which the disease appears. [58]But the cloth, warp or woof, or anything of skin from which the disease disappears when you have washed it, shall then be washed a second time, and it shall be clean.

59 This is the ritual for a leprous[a] disease in a cloth of wool or linen, either in warp or woof, or in anything of skin, to decide whether it is clean or unclean.

14 Purification of Lepers and Leprous Houses

The LORD spoke to Moses, saying: [2]This shall be the ritual for the leprous[a] person at the time of his cleansing:

He shall be brought to the priest; [3]the priest shall go out of the camp, and the priest shall make an examination. If the disease is healed in the leprous[a] person, [4]the priest shall command that two living clean birds and cedarwood and crimson yarn and hyssop be brought for the one who is to be cleansed. [5]The priest shall command that one of the birds be slaughtered over fresh water in an earthen vessel. [6]He shall take the living bird with the cedarwood and the crimson yarn and the hyssop, and dip them and the living bird in the blood of the bird that was slaughtered over the fresh water. [7]He shall sprinkle it seven times upon the one who is to be cleansed of the leprous[a] disease; then he shall pronounce him clean, and he shall let the living bird go into the open field. [8]The one who is to be cleansed shall wash his clothes, and shave off all his hair, and bathe himself in water, and he shall be clean. After that he shall come into the camp, but shall live outside his tent seven days. [9]On the seventh day he shall shave all his hair: of head, beard, eyebrows; he shall shave all his hair. Then he shall wash his clothes, and bathe his body in water, and he shall be clean.

10 On the eighth day he shall take two male lambs without blemish, and one ewe lamb in its first year without blemish, and a grain offering of three-tenths of an ephah of choice flour mixed with oil, and one log[b] of oil. [11]The priest who cleanses shall set the person to be cleansed, along with these things, before the LORD, at the entrance of the tent of meeting. [12]The priest shall take one of the lambs, and offer it as a guilt offering, along with the log[b] of oil, and raise them as an elevation offering before the LORD. [13]He shall slaughter the lamb in the place where the sin offering and the burnt offering are slaughtered in the holy place; for the guilt offering, like the sin offering, belongs to the priest: it is most holy. [14]The priest shall take some of the blood of the guilt offering and put it on the lobe of the right ear of the one to be cleansed, and on the thumb of the right hand, and on the big toe of the right foot. [15]The priest shall take some of the log[b] of oil and pour it into the palm of his own left hand, [16]and dip his right finger in the oil that is in his left hand and sprinkle some oil with his finger seven times before the LORD. [17]Some of the oil that remains in his hand the priest shall put on the lobe of the right ear of the one to be cleansed, and on the thumb of the right hand, and on the big toe of the right foot, on top of the blood of the guilt offering. [18]The rest of the oil that is in the priest's hand he shall put on the head of the one to be cleansed. Then the priest shall make atonement on his behalf before the LORD: [19]the priest shall offer the sin offering, to make atonement for the one to be cleansed from his uncleanness. Afterward he shall slaughter the burnt offering; [20]and the priest shall offer the burnt offering and the grain offering on the altar. Thus the priest shall make atonement on his behalf and he shall be clean.

21 But if he is poor and cannot afford so much, he shall take one male lamb for a guilt offering to be elevated, to make atonement on his behalf, and one-tenth of an ephah of choice flour mixed with oil for a grain offering and a log[b] of oil; [22]also two turtledoves or two pigeons, such as he can afford, one for a sin offering and the other for a burnt offering. [23]On the eighth day he shall bring them for his cleansing to the priest, to the entrance of the tent of meeting, before the LORD; [24]and the priest shall take the lamb of the guilt offering and the log[a] of oil, and the priest shall raise them as an elevation offering before the LORD. [25]The priest shall slaughter the lamb of the guilt offering and shall take some of the blood of the guilt offering, and put it on the lobe of the right ear of the one to be cleansed, and on the thumb of the right hand, and on the big toe of the right foot. [26]The priest shall pour some of the oil into the palm of his own left hand, [27]and shall sprinkle with his right finger some of the oil that is in his left hand seven times before the LORD. [28]The priest shall put some of the oil that is in his hand on the lobe of the right ear of the one to be cleansed, and on the thumb of

---

a A term for several skin diseases; precise meaning uncertain   b A liquid measure

the right hand, and the big toe of the right foot, where the blood of the guilt offering was placed. ^{29}The rest of the oil that is in the priest's hand he shall put on the head of the one to be cleansed, to make atonement on his behalf before the LORD. ^{30}And he shall offer, of the turtledoves or pigeons such as he can afford, ^{31}one^a for a sin offering and the other for a burnt offering, along with a grain offering; and the priest shall make atonement before the LORD on behalf of the one being cleansed. ^{32}This is the ritual for the one who has a leprous^b disease, who cannot afford the offerings for his cleansing.

33 The LORD spoke to Moses and Aaron, saying:

34 When you come into the land of Canaan, which I give you for a possession, and I put a leprous^b disease in a house in the land of your possession, ^{35}the owner of the house shall come and tell the priest, saying, "There seems to me to be some sort of disease in my house." ^{36}The priest shall command that they empty the house before the priest goes to examine the disease, or all that is in the house will become unclean; and afterward the priest shall go in to inspect the house. ^{37}He shall examine the disease; if the disease is in the walls of the house with greenish or reddish spots, and if it appears to be deeper than the surface, ^{38}the priest shall go outside to the door of the house and shut up the house seven days. ^{39}The priest shall come again on the seventh day and make an inspection; if the disease has spread in the walls of the house, ^{40}the priest shall command that the stones in which the disease appears be taken out and thrown into an unclean place outside the city. ^{41}He shall have the inside of the house scraped thoroughly, and the plaster that is scraped off shall be dumped in an unclean place outside the city. ^{42}They shall take other stones and put them in the place of those stones, and take other plaster and plaster the house.

43 If the disease breaks out again in the house, after he has taken out the stones and scraped the house and plastered it, ^{44}the priest shall go and make inspection; if the disease has spread in the house, it is a spreading leprous^b disease in the house; it is unclean. ^{45}He shall have the house torn down, its stones and timber and all the plaster of the house, and taken outside the city to an unclean place. ^{46}All who enter the house while it is shut up shall be unclean until the evening; ^{47}and all who

sleep in the house shall wash their clothes; and all who eat in the house shall wash their clothes.

48 If the priest comes and makes an inspection, and the disease has not spread in the house after the house was plastered, the priest shall pronounce the house clean; the disease is healed. ^{49}For the cleansing of the house he shall take two birds, with cedarwood and crimson yarn and hyssop, ^{50}and shall slaughter one of the birds over fresh water in an earthen vessel, ^{51}and shall take the cedarwood and the hyssop and the crimson yarn, along with the living bird, and dip them in the blood of the slaughtered bird and the fresh water, and sprinkle the house seven times. ^{52}Thus he shall cleanse the house with the blood of the bird, and with the fresh water, and with the living bird, and with the cedarwood and hyssop and crimson yarn; ^{53}and he shall let the living bird go out of the city into the open field; so he shall make atonement for the house, and it shall be clean.

54 This is the ritual for any leprous^b disease: for an itch, ^{55}for leprous^b diseases in clothing and houses, ^{56}and for a swelling or an eruption or a spot, ^{57}to determine when it is unclean and when it is clean. This is the ritual for leprous^b diseases.

Concerning Bodily Discharges

15 The LORD spoke to Moses and Aaron, saying: ^{2}Speak to the people of Israel and say to them:

When any man has a discharge from his member,^{c} his discharge makes him ceremonially unclean. ^{3}The uncleanness of his discharge is this: whether his member^b flows with his discharge, or his member^c is stopped from discharging, it is uncleanness for him. ^{4}Every bed on which the one with the discharge lies shall be unclean; and everything on which he sits shall be unclean. ^{5}Anyone who touches his bed shall wash his clothes, and bathe in water, and be unclean until the evening. ^{6}All who sit on anything on which the one with the discharge has sat shall wash their clothes, and bathe in water, and be unclean until the evening. ^{7}All who touch the body of the one with the discharge shall wash their clothes, and bathe in water, and be unclean until the evening. ^{8}If the one with the discharge spits on persons who are clean, then they shall wash their clothes, and bathe in water, and be unclean until the evening. ^{9}Any saddle on which the one with the discharge rides shall be unclean. ^{10}All who touch

---

a Gk Syr: Heb *afford*, ^{31}*such as he can afford, one* b A term for several skin diseases; precise meaning uncertain c Heb *flesh*

anything that was under him shall be unclean until the evening, and all who carry such a thing shall wash their clothes, and bathe in water, and be unclean until the evening. [11]All those whom the one with the discharge touches without his having rinsed his hands in water shall wash their clothes, and bathe in water, and be unclean until the evening. [12]Any earthen vessel that the one with the discharge touches shall be broken; and every vessel of wood shall be rinsed in water.

13 When the one with a discharge is cleansed of his discharge, he shall count seven days for his cleansing; he shall wash his clothes and bathe his body in fresh water, and he shall be clean. [14]On the eighth day he shall take two turtledoves or two pigeons and come before the Lord to the entrance of the tent of meeting and give them to the priest. [15]The priest shall offer them, one for a sin offering and the other for a burnt offering; and the priest shall make atonement on his behalf before the Lord for his discharge.

16 If a man has an emission of semen, he shall bathe his whole body in water, and be unclean until the evening. [17]Everything made of cloth or of skin on which the semen falls shall be washed with water, and be unclean until the evening. [18]If a man lies with a woman and has an emission of semen, both of them shall bathe in water, and be unclean until the evening.

19 When a woman has a discharge of blood that is her regular discharge from her body, she shall be in her impurity for seven days, and whoever touches her shall be unclean until the evening. [20]Everything upon which she lies during her impurity shall be unclean; everything also upon which she sits shall be unclean. [21]Whoever touches her bed shall wash his clothes, and bathe in water, and be unclean until the evening. [22]Whoever touches anything upon which she sits shall wash his clothes, and bathe in water, and be unclean until the evening; [23]whether it is the bed or anything upon which she sits, when he touches it he shall be unclean until the evening. [24]If any man lies with her, and her impurity falls on him, he shall be unclean seven days; and every bed on which he lies shall be unclean.

25 If a woman has a discharge of blood for many days, not at the time of her impurity, or if she has a discharge beyond the time of her impurity, all the days of the discharge she shall continue in uncleanness; as in the days of her impurity, she shall be unclean. [26]Every bed on which she lies during all the days of her discharge shall be treated as the bed of her impurity; and everything on which she sits shall be unclean, as in the uncleanness of her impurity. [27]Whoever touches these things shall be unclean, and shall wash his clothes, and bathe in water, and be unclean until the evening. [28]If she is cleansed of her discharge, she shall count seven days, and after that she shall be clean. [29]On the eighth day she shall take two turtledoves or two pigeons and bring them to the priest at the entrance of the tent of meeting. [30]The priest shall offer one for a sin offering and the other for a burnt offering; and the priest shall make atonement on her behalf before the Lord for her unclean discharge.

31 Thus you shall keep the people of Israel separate from their uncleanness, so that they do not die in their uncleanness by defiling my tabernacle that is in their midst.

32 This is the ritual for those who have a discharge: for him who has an emission of semen, be-

STUDY IT!

Monthly Periods
Leviticus 15:19–33

Imagine the situation of women in Old Testament days. Everyday life wasn't easy, and menstrual periods brought even bigger challenges: No sanitary supplies, just strips of old cloth. Not much privacy. Not much sympathy from men. Very limited understanding of human biology. Just the monthly flow of blood and the trouble and discomfort of dealing with it.

And on top of all that, women were considered unclean during their menstrual period (Leviticus 15:19). It seems unfair and insensitive to us who live in a culture that has grown in our understanding of biology and human dignity. How did this concept of uncleanness develop anyway? We don't know all the history, but blood was a powerful sign of life to the ancient Israelites, so the loss of blood may have symbolized illness and death.

coming unclean thereby, ³³for her who is in the infirmity of her period, for anyone, male or female, who has a discharge, and for the man who lies with a woman who is unclean.

16 The Day of Atonement

The LORD spoke to Moses after the death of the two sons of Aaron, when they drew near before the LORD and died. ²The LORD said to Moses:

Tell your brother Aaron not to come just at any time into the sanctuary inside the curtain before the mercy seat^a that is upon the ark, or he will die; for I appear in the cloud upon the mercy seat.^{a 3}Thus shall Aaron come into the holy place: with a young bull for a sin offering and a ram for a burnt offering. ⁴He shall put on the holy linen tunic, and shall have the linen undergarments next to his body, fasten the linen sash, and wear the linen turban; these are the holy vestments. He shall bathe his body in water, and then put them on. ⁵He shall take from the congregation of the people of Israel two male goats for a sin offering, and one ram for a burnt offering.

6 Aaron shall offer the bull as a sin offering for himself, and shall make atonement for himself and for his house. ⁷He shall take the two goats and set them before the LORD at the entrance of the tent of meeting; ⁸and Aaron shall cast lots on the two goats, one lot for the LORD and the other lot for Azazel.^b ⁹Aaron shall present the goat on which the lot fell for the LORD, and offer it as a sin offering; ¹⁰but the goat on which the lot fell for Azazel^b shall be presented alive before the LORD to make atonement over it, that it may be sent away into the wilderness to Azazel.^b

11 Aaron shall present the bull as a sin offering for himself, and shall make atonement for himself and for his house; he shall slaughter the bull as a sin offering for himself. ¹²He shall take a censer full of coals of fire from the altar before the LORD, and two handfuls of crushed sweet incense, and he shall bring it inside the curtain ¹³and put the incense on the fire before the LORD, that the cloud of the incense may cover the mercy seat^a that is upon the covenant,^c or he will die. ¹⁴He shall take some of the blood of the bull, and sprinkle it with his finger on the front of the mercy seat,^a and before the mercy seat^a he shall sprinkle the blood with his finger seven times.

15 He shall slaughter the goat of the sin offering that is for the people and bring its blood inside the curtain, and do with its blood as he did with the blood of the bull, sprinkling it upon the mercy seat^a and before the mercy seat.^a ¹⁶Thus he shall make atonement for the sanctuary, because of the uncleannesses of the people of Israel, and because of their

LIVE IT!

The Scapegoat · Leviticus 16:20–21

So that's where the word "scapegoat" came from! In this interesting Israelite ritual the leader symbolically transfers all the people's sins onto a goat and drives it away. It's a liberating act that allows a fresh start.

But today, the idea of a scapegoat conveys oppression rather than freedom. A person becomes the scapegoat when other people blame that person for their problems. Here's an example.

Suppose you are on a soccer team that expects this week's game to be easy, so no one works hard at practice. On game day, the score is tied near the end of the game. While your team is preoccupied with thoughts of going home, the other team scores a goal and wins the game. Everyone gets mad at the goalie for not preventing the goal, but the defense stood still while the opponent dribbled around them to the wide-open goal. The goalie is the scapegoat, but you all should share in the fault for the loss, because none of you practiced well or played your best.

- Have you ever been the scapegoat for someone else's problems? If so, how did that feel? What did you do?
- Have you ever scapegoated someone else when you were partly to blame for some situation? What happened?
- How will you prevent scapegoating in the future?

---

a Or *the cover* **b** Traditionally rendered *a scapegoat* **c** Or *treaty*, or *testament*; Heb *eduth*

transgressions, all their sins; and so he shall do for the tent of meeting, which remains with them in the midst of their uncleannesses. [17]No one shall be in the tent of meeting from the time he enters to make atonement in the sanctuary until he comes out and has made atonement for himself and for his house and for all the assembly of Israel. [18]Then he shall go out to the altar that is before the LORD and make atonement on its behalf, and shall take some of the blood of the bull and of the blood of the goat, and put it on each of the horns of the altar. [19]He shall sprinkle some of the blood on it with his finger seven times, and cleanse it and hallow it from the uncleannesses of the people of Israel.

20 When he has finished atoning for the holy place and the tent of meeting and the altar, he shall present the live goat. [21]Then Aaron shall lay both his hands on the head of the live goat, and confess over it all the iniquities of the people of Israel, and all their transgressions, all their sins, putting them on the head of the goat, and sending it away into the wilderness by means of someone designated for the task.[a] [22]The goat shall bear on itself all their iniquities to a barren region; and the goat shall be set free in the wilderness.

23 Then Aaron shall enter the tent of meeting, and shall take off the linen vestments that he put on when he went into the holy place, and shall leave them there. [24]He shall bathe his body in water in a holy place, and put on his vestments; then he shall come out and offer his burnt offering and the burnt offering of the people, making atonement for himself and for the people. [25]The fat of the sin offering he shall turn into smoke on the altar. [26]The one who sets the goat free for Azazel[b] shall wash his clothes and bathe his body in water, and afterward may come into the camp. [27]The bull of the sin offering and the goat of the sin offering, whose blood was brought in to make atonement in the holy place, shall be taken outside the camp; their skin and their flesh and their dung shall be consumed in fire. [28]The one who burns them shall wash his clothes and bathe his body in water, and afterward may come into the camp.

29 This shall be a statute to you forever: In the seventh month, on the tenth day of the month, you shall deny yourselves,[c] and shall do no work, neither the citizen nor the alien who resides among you. [30]For on this day atonement shall be made for you, to cleanse you; from all your sins you shall be clean before the LORD. [31]It is a sabbath of complete rest to you, and you shall deny yourselves;[c] it is a statute forever. [32]The priest who is anointed and consecrated as priest in his father's place shall make atonement, wearing the linen vestments, the holy vestments. [33]He shall make atonement for the sanctuary, and he shall make atonement for the tent of meeting and for the altar, and he shall make atonement for the priests and for all the people of the assembly. [34]This shall be an everlasting statute for you, to make atonement for the people of Israel once in the year for all their sins. And Moses did as the LORD had commanded him.

17 The Slaughtering of Animals

The LORD spoke to Moses:

2 Speak to Aaron and his sons and to all the people of Israel and say to them: This is what the LORD has commanded. [3]If anyone of the house of Israel slaughters an ox or a lamb or a goat in the camp, or slaughters it outside the camp, [4]and does not bring it to the entrance of the tent of meeting, to present it as an offering to the LORD before the tabernacle of the LORD, he shall be held guilty of bloodshed; he has shed blood, and he shall be cut off from the people. [5]This is in order that the people of Israel may bring their sacrifices that they offer in the open field, that they may bring them to the LORD, to the priest at the entrance of the tent of meeting, and offer them as sacrifices of well-being to the LORD. [6]The priest shall dash the blood against the altar of the LORD at the entrance of the tent of meeting, and turn the fat into smoke as a pleasing odor to the LORD, [7]so that they may no longer offer their sacrifices for goat-demons, to whom they prostitute themselves. This shall be a statute forever to them throughout their generations.

8 And say to them further: Anyone of the house of Israel or of the aliens who reside among them who offers a burnt offering or sacrifice, [9]and does not bring it to the entrance of the tent of meeting, to sacrifice it to the LORD, shall be cut off from the people.

Eating Blood Prohibited

10 If anyone of the house of Israel or of the aliens who reside among them eats any blood, I will set my face against that person who eats blood, and will cut that person off from the people. [11]For the life of the flesh is in the blood; and I have given it to you for making atonement for your lives on the altar; for, as life, it is the blood that makes atonement. [12]Therefore

---

a Meaning of Heb uncertain   b Traditionally rendered a *scapegoat*   c Or *shall fast*

I have said to the people of Israel: No person among you shall eat blood, nor shall any alien who resides among you eat blood. [13]And anyone of the people of Israel, or of the aliens who reside among them, who hunts down an animal or bird that may be eaten shall pour out its blood and cover it with earth.

14 For the life of every creature—its blood is its life; therefore I have said to the people of Israel: You shall not eat the blood of any creature, for the life of every creature is its blood; whoever eats it shall be cut off. [15]All persons, citizens or aliens, who eat what dies of itself or what has been torn by wild animals, shall wash their clothes, and bathe themselves in water, and be unclean until the evening; then they shall be clean. [16]But if they do not wash themselves or bathe their body, they shall bear their guilt.

18 Sexual Relations

The LORD spoke to Moses, saying: 2 Speak to the people of Israel and say to them: I am the LORD your God. [3]You shall not do as they do in the land of Egypt, where you lived, and you shall not do as they do in the land of Canaan, to which I am bringing you. You shall not follow their statutes. [4]My ordinances you shall observe and my statutes you shall keep, following them: I am the LORD your God. [5]You shall keep my statutes and my ordinances; by doing so one shall live: I am the LORD.

6 None of you shall approach anyone near of kin to uncover nakedness: I am the LORD. [7]You shall not uncover the nakedness of your father, which is the nakedness of your mother; she is your mother, you shall not uncover her nakedness. [8]You shall not uncover the nakedness of your father's wife; it is the nakedness of your father. [9]You shall not uncover the nakedness of your sister, your father's daughter or your mother's daughter, whether born at home or born abroad. [10]You shall not uncover the nakedness of your son's daughter or of your daughter's daughter, for their nakedness is your own nakedness. [11]You shall not uncover the nakedness of your father's wife's daughter, begotten by your father, since she is your sister. [12]You shall not uncover the nakedness of your father's sister; she is your father's flesh. [13]You shall not uncover the nakedness of your mother's sister, for she is your mother's flesh. [14]You shall not uncover the nakedness of your father's brother, that is, you shall not approach his wife; she is your aunt. [15]You shall not uncover the nakedness of your daughter-in-law: she is your son's wife; you shall not uncover her nakedness. [16]You shall not uncover the nakedness of your brother's wife; it is your brother's nakedness.

Keeping Sex Special · Leviticus 18

Holiness extended to all aspects of life for the Israelites, even sex. This chapter spells out laws about sexual relations. The people had experienced the sexual promiscuity of other cultures (Genesis 19). To become a great nation, the children of God, they had to abandon unhealthy and unholy sexual practices and follow God's way.

Young people today also receive many confusing cultural messages about when it's okay to have sex. Our movies, TV, and music show and describe sex happening all the time between unmarried people, usually with no consequences. But the Church, parents, and youth leaders say to wait until marriage. What's a person to believe?

Sex is a wonderful gift from God, meant for that day when you say "I do" to someone you are committed to in marriage. Only in marriage can sex fully unite a couple as God intended. Practicing it before or outside the commitment of marriage can bring emotional scars and physical disease— pain not intended as part of God's good plans for sex. Just as some of Leviticus' sexual laws were meant to protect people from harm and disease, so will following God's parameters for sex protect us. That's why the Bible tells us to wait until we are married to have sex. In **1 Corinthians 7:2–3** the Bible talks about the importance of the marriage commitment between a man and a woman. And **Hebrews 13:4** makes it clear that sex is for marriage alone. Why the restrictions? So this gift will be as special as it is meant to be and so we can enjoy it in emotional and spiritual freedom.

[17]You shall not uncover the nakedness of a woman and her daughter, and you shall not take[a] her son's daughter or her daughter's daughter to uncover her nakedness; they are your[b] flesh; it is depravity. [18]And you shall not take[a] a woman as a rival to her sister, uncovering her nakedness while her sister is still alive.

19 You shall not approach a woman to uncover her nakedness while she is in her menstrual uncleanness. [20]You shall not have sexual relations with your kinsman's wife, and defile yourself with her. [21]You shall not give any of your offspring to sacrifice them[c] to Molech, and so profane the name of your God: I am the LORD. [22]You shall not lie with a male as with a woman; it is an abomination. [23]You shall not have sexual relations with any animal and defile yourself with it, nor shall any woman give herself to an animal to have sexual relations with it: it is perversion.

24 Do not defile yourselves in any of these ways, for by all these practices the nations I am casting out before you have defiled themselves. [25]Thus the land became defiled; and I punished it for its iniquity, and the land vomited out its inhabitants. [26]But you shall keep my statutes and my ordinances and commit none of these abominations, either the citizen or the alien who resides among you [27](for the inhabitants of the land, who were before you, committed all of these abominations, and the land became defiled); [28]otherwise the land will vomit you out for defiling it, as it vomited out the nation that was before you. [29]For whoever commits any of these abominations shall be cut off from their people. [30]So keep my charge not to commit any of these abominations that were done before you, and not to defile yourselves by them: I am the LORD your God.

Ritual and Moral Holiness

19 The LORD spoke to Moses, saying: 2 Speak to all the congregation of the people of Israel and say to them: You shall be holy, for I the LORD your God am holy. [3]You shall each revere your mother and father, and you shall keep my sabbaths: I am the LORD your God. [4]Do not turn to idols or make cast images for yourselves: I am the LORD your God.

5 When you offer a sacrifice of well-being to the LORD, offer it in such a way that it is acceptable in your behalf. [6]It shall be eaten on the same day you offer it, or on the next day; and anything left over until the third day shall be consumed in fire. [7]If it is eaten at all on the third day, it is an abomination; it will not be acceptable. [8]All who eat it shall be subject to punishment, because they have profaned what is holy to the LORD; and any such person shall be cut off from the people.

9 When you reap the harvest of your land, you shall not reap to the very edges of your field, or gather the gleanings of your harvest. [10]You shall not strip your vineyard bare, or gather the fallen grapes of your vineyard; you shall leave them for the poor and the alien: I am the LORD your God.

11 You shall not steal; you shall not deal falsely; and you shall not lie to one another. [12]And you shall not swear falsely by my name, profaning the name of your God: I am the LORD.

13 You shall not defraud your neighbor; you shall not steal; and you shall not keep for yourself the wages of a laborer until morning. [14]You shall not revile the deaf or put a stumbling block before the blind; you shall fear your God: I am the LORD.

15 You shall not render an unjust judgment; you shall not be partial to the poor or defer to the great: with justice you shall judge your neighbor. [16]You shall not go around as a slanderer[d] among your people, and you shall not profit by the blood[e] of your neighbor: I am the LORD.

17 You shall not hate in your heart anyone of your kin; you shall reprove your neighbor, or you will incur guilt yourself. [18]You shall not take vengeance or bear a grudge against any of your people, but you shall love your neighbor as yourself: I am the LORD.

19 You shall keep my statutes. You shall not let your animals breed with a different kind; you shall not sow your field with two kinds of seed; nor shall you put on a garment made of two different materials.

20 If a man has sexual relations with a woman who is a slave, designated for another man but not ransomed or given her freedom, an inquiry shall be held. They shall not be put to death, since she has not been freed; [21]but he shall bring a guilt offering

> "Do not turn to idols or make cast images for yourselves: I am the LORD your God." —Leviticus 19:4

---

a Or *marry*   b Gk: Heb lacks *your*   c Heb *to pass them over*   d Meaning of Heb uncertain   e Heb *stand against the blood*

Be Holy
Leviticus 19–20

As the Israelites' image of God developed, so did their sense of how they needed to live as God's people. They were God's chosen people and were called to behave according to God's plan for them by keeping themselves pure as individuals and as a community. The laws in the book of Leviticus are examples of how they lived out the call to be holy. Holiness for them was not just for the sabbath or the temple, but for every day and everything.

Think about the choices you make in your own life. How do your choices help you to be holy in today's world? Think about these questions:

- How do you treat your friends?
- How do you spend your money?
- How much time do you spend alone with God?

Being holy has a lot to do with how we live out the moments of our day and how often we remember that we are in God's presence.

for himself to the LORD, at the entrance of the tent of meeting, a ram as guilt offering. ²²And the priest shall make atonement for him with the ram of guilt offering before the LORD for his sin that he committed; and the sin he committed shall be forgiven him.

23 When you come into the land and plant all kinds of trees for food, then you shall regard their fruit as forbidden;ᵃ three years it shall be forbiddenᵇ to you, it must not be eaten. ²⁴In the fourth year all their fruit shall be set apart for rejoicing in the LORD. ²⁵But in the fifth year you may eat of their fruit, that their yield may be increased for you: I am the LORD your God.

26 You shall not eat anything with its blood. You shall not practice augury or witchcraft. ²⁷You shall not round off the hair on your temples or mar the edges of your beard. ²⁸You shall not make any gashes in your flesh for the dead or tattoo any marks upon you: I am the LORD.

29 Do not profane your daughter by making her a prostitute, that the land not become prostituted and full of depravity. ³⁰You shall keep my sabbaths and reverence my sanctuary: I am the LORD.

31 Do not turn to mediums or wizards; do not seek them out, to be defiled by them: I am the LORD your God.

32 You shall rise before the aged, and defer to the old; and you shall fear your God: I am the LORD.

33 When an alien resides with you in your land, you shall not oppress the alien. ³⁴The alien who resides with you shall be to you as the citizen among you; you shall love the alien as yourself, for you were aliens in the land of Egypt: I am the LORD your God.

35 You shall not cheat in measuring length, weight, or quantity. ³⁶You shall have honest balances, honest weights, an honest ephah, and an honest hin: I am the LORD your God, who brought you out of the land of Egypt. ³⁷You shall keep all my statutes and all my ordinances, and observe them: I am the LORD.

Penalties for Violations of Holiness

20 The LORD spoke to Moses, saying: ²Say further to the people of Israel:

Any of the people of Israel, or of the aliens who reside in Israel, who give any of their offspring to Molech shall be put to death; the people of the land shall stone them to death. ³I myself will set my face against them, and will cut them off from the people, because they have given of their offspring to Molech, defiling my sanctuary and profaning my holy name. ⁴And if the people of the land should ever close their eyes to them, when they give of their offspring to Molech, and do not put them to death, ⁵I myself will set my face against them and against their family, and will cut them off from among their people, them and all who follow them in prostituting themselves to Molech.

6 If any turn to mediums and wizards, prostituting themselves to them, I will set my face against them, and will cut them off from the people. ⁷Consecrate yourselves therefore, and be holy; for I am the LORD your God. ⁸Keep my statutes, and observe them; I am the LORD; I sanctify you. ⁹All who curse father or mother shall be put to death; having cursed father or mother, their blood is upon them.

a Heb *as their uncircumcision*   b Heb *uncircumcision*

10 If a man commits adultery with the wife of[a] his neighbor, both the adulterer and the adulteress shall be put to death. [11]The man who lies with his father's wife has uncovered his father's nakedness; both of them shall be put to death; their blood is upon them. [12]If a man lies with his daughter-in-law, both of them shall be put to death; they have committed perversion, their blood is upon them. [13]If a man lies with a male as with a woman, both of them have committed an abomination; they shall be put to death; their blood is upon them. [14]If a man takes a wife and her mother also, it is depravity; they shall be burned to death, both he and they, that there may be no depravity among you. [15]If a man has sexual relations with an animal, he shall be put to death; and you shall kill the animal. [16]If a woman approaches any animal and has sexual relations with it, you shall kill the woman and the animal; they shall be put to death, their blood is upon them.

17 If a man takes his sister, a daughter of his father or a daughter of his mother, and sees her nakedness, and she sees his nakedness, it is a disgrace, and they shall be cut off in the sight of their people; he has uncovered his sister's nakedness, he shall be subject to punishment. [18]If a man lies with a woman having her sickness and uncovers her nakedness, he has laid bare her flow and she has laid bare her flow of blood; both of them shall be cut off from their people. [19]You shall not uncover the nakedness of your mother's sister or of your father's sister, for that is to lay bare one's own flesh; they shall be subject to punishment. [20]If a man lies with his uncle's wife, he has uncovered his uncle's nakedness; they shall be subject to punishment; they shall die childless. [21]If a man takes his brother's wife, it is impurity; he has uncovered his brother's nakedness; they shall be childless.

22 You shall keep all my statutes and all my ordinances, and observe them, so that the land to which I bring you to settle in may not vomit you out. [23]You shall not follow the practices of the nation that I am driving out before you. Because they did all these things, I abhorred them. [24]But I have said to you: You shall inherit their land, and I will give it to you to possess, a land flowing with milk and honey. I am the LORD your God; I have separated you from the peoples. [25]You shall therefore make a distinction between the clean animal and the unclean, and between the unclean bird and the clean; you shall not bring abomination on your-

selves by animal or by bird or by anything with which the ground teems, which I have set apart for you to hold unclean. [26]You shall be holy to me; for I the LORD am holy, and I have separated you from the other peoples to be mine.

27 A man or a woman who is a medium or a wizard shall be put to death; they shall be stoned to death, their blood is upon them.

The Holiness of Priests

21 The LORD said to Moses: Speak to the priests, the sons of Aaron, and say to them: No one shall defile himself for a dead person among his relatives, [2]except for his nearest kin: his mother, his father, his son, his daughter, his brother; [3]likewise, for a virgin sister, close to him because she has had no husband, he may defile himself for her. [4]But he shall not defile himself as a husband among his people and so profane himself. [5]They shall not make bald spots upon their heads, or shave off the edges of their beards, or make any gashes in their flesh. [6]They shall be holy to their God, and not profane the name of their God; for they offer the LORD's offerings by fire, the food of their God; therefore they shall be holy. [7]They shall not marry a prostitute or a woman who has been defiled; neither shall they marry a woman divorced from her husband. For they are holy to their God, [8]and you shall treat them as holy, since they offer the food of your God; they shall be holy to you, for I the LORD, I who sanctify you, am holy. [9]When the daughter of a priest profanes herself through prostitution, she profanes her father; she shall be burned to death.

10 The priest who is exalted above his fellows, on whose head the anointing oil has been poured and who has been consecrated to wear the vestments, shall not dishevel his hair, nor tear his vestments. [11]He shall not go where there is a dead body; he shall not defile himself even for his father or mother. [12]He shall not go outside the sanctuary and thus profane the sanctuary of his God; for the consecration of the anointing oil of his God is upon him: I am the LORD. [13]He shall marry only a woman who is a virgin. [14]A widow, or a divorced woman, or a woman who has been defiled, a prostitute, these he shall not marry. He shall marry a virgin of his own kin, [15]that he may not profane his offspring among his kin; for I am the LORD; I sanctify him.

16 The LORD spoke to Moses, saying: [17]Speak

---

a Heb repeats *if a man commits adultery with the wife of*

to Aaron and say: No one of your offspring throughout their generations who has a blemish may approach to offer the food of his God. [18]For no one who has a blemish shall draw near, one who is blind or lame, or one who has a mutilated face or a limb too long, [19]or one who has a broken foot or a broken hand, [20]or a hunchback, or a dwarf, or a man with a blemish in his eyes or an itching disease or scabs or crushed testicles. [21]No descendant of Aaron the priest who has a blemish shall come near to offer the LORD's offerings by fire; since he has a blemish, he shall not come near to offer the food of his God. [22]He may eat the food of his God, of the most holy as well as of the holy. [23]But he shall not come near the curtain or approach the altar, because he has a blemish, that he may not profane my sanctuaries; for I am the LORD; I sanctify them. [24]Thus Moses spoke to Aaron and to his sons and to all the people of Israel.

The Use of Holy Offerings

22 The LORD spoke to Moses, saying: [2]Direct Aaron and his sons to deal carefully with the sacred donations of the people of Israel, which they dedicate to me, so that they may not profane my holy name; I am the LORD. [3]Say to them: If anyone among all your offspring throughout your generations comes near the sacred donations, which the people of Israel dedicate to the LORD, while he is in a state of uncleanness, that person shall be cut off from my presence: I am the LORD. [4]No one of Aaron's offspring who has a leprous[a] disease or suffers a discharge may eat of the sacred donations until he is clean. Whoever touches anything made unclean by a corpse or a man who has had an emission of semen, [5]and whoever touches any swarming thing by which he may be made unclean or any human being by whom he may be made unclean—whatever his uncleanness may be— [6]the person who touches any such shall be unclean until evening and shall not eat of the sacred donations unless he has washed his body in water. [7]When the sun sets he shall be clean; and afterward he may eat of the sacred donations, for they are his food. [8]That which died or was torn by wild animals he shall not eat, becoming unclean by it: I am the LORD. [9]They shall keep my charge, so that they may not incur guilt and die in the sanctuary[b] for having profaned it: I am the LORD; I sanctify them.

10 No lay person shall eat of the sacred donations.

No bound or hired servant of the priest shall eat of the sacred donations; [11]but if a priest acquires anyone by purchase, the person may eat of them; and those that are born in his house may eat of his food. [12]If a priest's daughter marries a layman, she shall not eat of the offering of the sacred donations; [13]but if a priest's daughter is widowed or divorced, without offspring, and returns to her father's house, as in her youth, she may eat of her father's food. No lay person shall eat of it. [14]If a man eats of the sacred donation unintentionally, he shall add one-fifth of its value to it, and give the sacred donation to the priest. [15]No one shall profane the sacred donations of the people of Israel, which they offer to the LORD, [16]causing them to bear guilt requiring a guilt offering, by eating their sacred donations: for I am the LORD; I sanctify them.

Acceptable Offerings

17 The LORD spoke to Moses, saying: [18]Speak to Aaron and his sons and all the people of Israel and say to them: When anyone of the house of Israel or of the aliens residing in Israel presents an offering, whether in payment of a vow or as a freewill offering that is offered to the LORD as a burnt offering, [19]to be acceptable in your behalf it shall be a male without blemish, of the cattle or the sheep or the goats. [20]You shall not offer anything that has a blemish, for it will not be acceptable in your behalf.

21 When anyone offers a sacrifice of well-being to the LORD, in fulfillment of a vow or as a freewill offering, from the herd or from the flock, to be acceptable it must be perfect; there shall be no blemish in it. [22]Anything blind, or injured, or maimed, or having a discharge or an itch or scabs—these you shall not offer to the LORD or put any of them on the altar as offerings by fire to the LORD. [23]An ox or a lamb that has a limb too long or too short you may present for a freewill offering; but it will not be accepted for a vow. [24]Any animal that has its testicles bruised or crushed or torn or cut, you shall not offer to the LORD; such you shall not do within your land, [25]nor shall you accept any such animals from a foreigner to offer as food to your God; since they are mutilated, with a blemish in them, they shall not be accepted in your behalf.

26 The LORD spoke to Moses, saying: [27]When an ox or a sheep or a goat is born, it shall remain seven days with its mother, and from the eighth day on it shall be acceptable as the LORD's offering by

---

a A term for several skin diseases; precise meaning uncertain b Vg: Heb *incur guilt for it and die in it*

fire. [28]But you shall not slaughter, from the herd or the flock, an animal with its young on the same day. [29]When you sacrifice a thanksgiving offering to the LORD, you shall sacrifice it so that it may be acceptable in your behalf. [30]It shall be eaten on the same day; you shall not leave any of it until morning: I am the LORD.

31 Thus you shall keep my commandments and observe them: I am the LORD. [32]You shall not profane my holy name, that I may be sanctified among the people of Israel: I am the LORD; I sanctify you, [33]I who brought you out of the land of Egypt to be your God: I am the LORD.

Appointed Festivals

23 The LORD spoke to Moses, saying: [2]Speak to the people of Israel and say to them: These are the appointed festivals of the LORD that you shall proclaim as holy convocations, my appointed festivals.

The Sabbath, Passover, and Unleavened Bread

3 Six days shall work be done; but the seventh day is a sabbath of complete rest, a holy convocation; you shall do no work: it is a sabbath to the LORD throughout your settlements.

4 These are the appointed festivals of the LORD, the holy convocations, which you shall celebrate at the time appointed for them. [5]In the first month, on the fourteenth day of the month, at twilight,[a] there shall be a passover offering to the LORD, [6]and on the fifteenth day of the same month is the festival of unleavened bread to the LORD; seven days you shall eat unleavened bread. [7]On the first day you shall have a holy convocation; you shall not work at your occupations. [8]For seven days you shall present the LORD's offerings by fire; on the seventh day there shall be a holy convocation: you shall not work at your occupations.

The Offering of First Fruits

9 The LORD spoke to Moses: [10]Speak to the people of Israel and say to them: When you enter the land that I am giving you and you reap its harvest, you shall bring the sheaf of the first fruits of your harvest to the priest. [11]He shall raise the sheaf before the LORD, that you may find acceptance; on the day after the sabbath the priest shall raise it. [12]On the day when you raise the sheaf, you shall

offer a lamb a year old, without blemish, as a burnt offering to the LORD. [13]And the grain offering with it shall be two-tenths of an ephah of choice flour mixed with oil, an offering by fire of pleasing odor to the LORD; and the drink offering with it shall be of wine, one-fourth of a hin. [14]You shall eat no bread or parched grain or fresh ears until that very day, until you have brought the offering of your God: it is a statute forever throughout your generations in all your settlements.

The Festival of Weeks

15 And from the day after the sabbath, from the day on which you bring the sheaf of the elevation offering, you shall count off seven weeks; they shall be complete. [16]You shall count until the day after the seventh sabbath, fifty days; then you shall present an offering of new grain to the LORD. [17]You shall bring from your settlements two loaves of bread as an elevation offering, each made of two-tenths of an ephah; they shall be of choice flour, baked with leaven, as first fruits to the LORD. [18]You shall present with the bread seven lambs a year old without blemish, one young bull, and two rams; they shall be a burnt offering to the LORD, along with their grain offering and their drink offerings, an offering by fire of pleasing odor to the LORD. [19]You shall also offer one male goat for a sin offering, and two male lambs a year old as a sacrifice of well-being. [20]The priest shall raise them with the bread of the first fruits as an elevation offering before the LORD, together with the two lambs; they shall be holy to the LORD for the priest. [21]On that same day you shall make proclamation; you shall hold a holy convocation; you shall not work at your occupations. This is a statute forever in all your settlements throughout your generations.

22 When you reap the harvest of your land, you shall not reap to the very edges of your field, or gather the gleanings of your harvest; you shall leave them for the poor and for the alien: I am the LORD your God.

The Festival of Trumpets

23 The LORD spoke to Moses, saying: [24]Speak to the people of Israel, saying: In the seventh month, on the first day of the month, you shall observe a day of complete rest, a holy convocation commemorated with trumpet blasts. [25]You shall not work at your occupations; and you shall present the LORD's offering by fire.

---

a Heb *between the two evenings*

The Day of Atonement

26 The LORD spoke to Moses, saying: [27]Now, the tenth day of this seventh month is the day of atonement; it shall be a holy convocation for you: you shall deny yourselves[a] and present the LORD's offering by fire; [28]and you shall do no work during that entire day; for it is a day of atonement, to make atonement on your behalf before the LORD your God. [29]For anyone who does not practice self-denial[b] during that entire day shall be cut off from the people. [30]And anyone who does any work during that entire day, such a one I will destroy from the midst of the people. [31]You shall do no work: it is a statute forever throughout your generations in all your settlements. [32]It shall be to you a sabbath of complete rest, and you shall deny yourselves;[a] on the ninth day of the month at evening, from evening to evening you shall keep your sabbath.

The Festival of Booths

33 The LORD spoke to Moses, saying: [34]Speak to the people of Israel, saying: On the fifteenth day of this seventh month, and lasting seven days, there shall be the festival of booths[c] to the LORD. [35]The first day shall be a holy convocation; you shall not work at your occupations. [36]Seven days you shall present the LORD's offerings by fire; on the eighth day you shall observe a holy convocation and present the LORD's offerings by fire; it is a solemn assembly; you shall not work at your occupations.

37 These are the appointed festivals of the LORD, which you shall celebrate as times of holy convocation, for presenting to the LORD offerings by fire— burnt offerings and grain offerings, sacrifices and drink offerings, each on its proper day— [38]apart from the sabbaths of the LORD, and apart from your gifts, and apart from all your votive offerings, and apart from all your freewill offerings, which you give to the LORD.

39 Now, the fifteenth day of the seventh month, when you have gathered in the produce of the land, you shall keep the festival of the LORD, lasting seven days; a complete rest on the first day, and a complete rest on the eighth day. [40]On the first day you shall take the fruit of majestic[d] trees, branches of palm trees, boughs of leafy trees, and willows of the brook; and you shall rejoice before the LORD your God for seven days. [41]You shall keep it as a festival to the LORD seven days in the year; you shall keep it in the seventh month as a statute forever through-

out your generations. [42]You shall live in booths for seven days; all that are citizens in Israel shall live in booths, [43]so that your generations may know that I made the people of Israel live in booths when I brought them out of the land of Egypt: I am the LORD your God.

44 Thus Moses declared to the people of Israel the appointed festivals of the LORD.

The Lamp

24 The LORD spoke to Moses, saying: [2]Command the people of Israel to bring you pure oil of beaten olives for the lamp, that a light may be kept burning regularly. [3]Aaron shall set it up in the tent of meeting, outside the curtain of the covenant,[e] to burn from evening to morning before the LORD regularly; it shall be a statute forever throughout your generations. [4]He shall set up the lamps on the lampstand of pure gold[f] before the LORD regularly.

The Bread for the Tabernacle

5 You shall take choice flour, and bake twelve loaves of it; two-tenths of an ephah shall be in each loaf. [6]You shall place them in two rows, six in a row, on the table of pure gold.[g] [7]You shall put pure frankincense with each row, to be a token offering for the bread, as an offering by fire to the LORD. [8]Every sabbath day Aaron shall set them in order before the LORD regularly as a commitment of the people of Israel, as a covenant forever. [9]They shall be for Aaron and his descendants, who shall eat them in a holy place, for they are most holy portions for him from the offerings by fire to the LORD, a perpetual due.

Blasphemy and Its Punishment

10 A man whose mother was an Israelite and whose father was an Egyptian came out among the

---

a Or *shall fast*   *b* Or *does not fast*   *c* Or *tabernacles*: Heb *succoth*   *d* Meaning of Heb uncertain   *e* Or *treaty, or testament*; Heb *eduth*   *f* Heb *pure lampstand*   *g* Heb *pure table*

people of Israel; and the Israelite woman's son and a certain Israelite began fighting in the camp. [11] The Israelite woman's son blasphemed the Name in a curse. And they brought him to Moses—now his mother's name was Shelomith, daughter of Dibri, of the tribe of Dan— [12] and they put him in custody, until the decision of the LORD should be made clear to them.

13 The LORD said to Moses, saying: [14] Take the blasphemer outside the camp; and let all who were within hearing lay their hands on his head, and let the whole congregation stone him. [15] And speak to the people of Israel, saying: Anyone who curses God shall bear the sin. [16] One who blasphemes the name of the LORD shall be put to death; the whole congregation shall stone the blasphemer. Aliens as well as citizens, when they blaspheme the Name, shall be put to death. [17] Anyone who kills a human being shall be put to death. [18] Anyone who kills an animal shall make restitution for it, life for life. [19] Anyone who maims another shall suffer the same injury in return: [20] fracture for fracture, eye for eye, tooth for tooth; the injury inflicted is the injury to be suffered. [21] One who kills an animal shall make restitution for it; but one who kills a human being shall be put to death. [22] You shall have one law for the alien and for the citizen: for I am the LORD your God. [23] Moses spoke thus to the people of Israel; and they took the blasphemer outside the camp, and stoned him to death. The people of Israel did as the LORD had commanded Moses.

The Sabbatical Year

25 The LORD spoke to Moses on Mount Sinai, saying: [2] Speak to the people of Israel and say to them: When you enter the land that I am giving you, the land shall observe a sabbath for the LORD. [3] Six years you shall sow your field, and six years you shall prune your vineyard, and gather in their yield; [4] but in the seventh year there shall be a sabbath of complete rest for the land, a sabbath for the LORD: you shall not sow your field or prune your vineyard. [5] You shall not reap the aftergrowth of your harvest or gather the grapes of your unpruned vine: it shall be a year of complete rest for the land. [6] You may eat what the land yields during its sabbath—you, your male and female slaves, your hired and your bound laborers who live with you; [7] for your livestock also, and for the wild animals in your land all its yield shall be for food.

The Year of Jubilee

8 You shall count off seven weeks[a] of years, seven times seven years, so that the period of seven weeks of years gives forty-nine years. [9] Then you shall have the trumpet sounded loud; on the tenth day of the seventh month—on the day of atonement—you shall have the trumpet sounded throughout all your land. [10] And you shall hallow the fiftieth year and you shall proclaim liberty throughout the land to all its inhabitants. It shall be a jubilee for you: you shall return, every one of you, to your property and every one of you to your family. [11] That fiftieth year shall be a jubilee for you: you shall not sow, or reap the aftergrowth, or harvest the unpruned vines. [12] For it is a jubilee; it shall be holy to you: you shall eat only what the field itself produces.

13 In this year of jubilee you shall return, every one of you, to your property. [14] When you make a sale to your neighbor or buy from your neighbor, you shall not cheat one another. [15] When you buy from your neighbor, you shall pay only for the number of years since the jubilee; the seller shall charge you only for the remaining crop years. [16] If the years are more, you shall increase the price, and if the years are fewer, you shall diminish the price; for it is a certain number of harvests that are being sold to you. [17] You shall not cheat one another, but you shall fear your God; for I am the LORD your God.

18 You shall observe my statutes and faithfully keep my ordinances, so that you may live on the land securely. [19] The land will yield its fruit, and you will eat your fill and live on it securely. [20] Should you ask, "What shall we eat in the seventh year, if we may not sow or gather in our crop?" [21] I will order my blessing for you in the sixth year, so that it will yield a crop for three years. [22] When you sow in the eighth year, you will be eating from the old crop; until the ninth year, when its produce comes in, you shall eat the old. [23] The land shall not be sold in perpetuity, for the land is mine; with me you are but aliens and tenants. [24] Throughout the land that you hold, you shall provide for the redemption of the land.

25 If anyone of your kin falls into difficulty and sells a piece of property, then the next of kin shall come and redeem what the relative has sold. [26] If the person has no one to redeem it, but then prospers and finds sufficient means to do so, [27] the years since its sale shall be computed and the difference shall be refunded to the person to whom it was sold, and the property shall be returned. [28] But if there are not

α Or *sabbaths*

7 x 7 + 1 = Jubilee! · Leviticus 25

Seven is a special number in the Bible. Just as the seventh day of the week was set aside as a day of rest in ancient Israel, so the seventh year was set aside as a year of rest for the land. Fields were to remain uncultivated during the seventh year; whatever fruits or grains grew on their own were to be left for the poor. The sabbatical year was to give the land a rest and to remind the people that the land actually belonged to God, not to them. As our own scientific understanding has grown, we now recognize the wisdom in allowing soils to replenish and rejuvenate, making them healthier and more fruitful in the long run.

Seven may be a special number, but seven times seven plus one is very special. The fiftieth year was declared the jubilee year, and God's law demanded some very special things. The people were to take a year of vacation from their normal routine. This meant no planting for a farmer, no lending for a banker, and no big sales for a merchant. Why this break? Because God wanted the jubilee year to be a time when everyone started over with a clean slate. During the jubilee, all land was to be returned to its original owners, and all Israelite slaves were to be set free. Debts were to be forgiven and justly settled. The year of jubilee was like the reset button on a computer, stopping everything and returning it to its original settings. It was a check against the unjust distribution of property and wealth.

Today our society does not observe the jubilee, but we can still personally apply the principles in our individual lives. We can consider things like those we need to forgive, what we need to return to others, and what work we could rest from in order to spend more time with God. We can also share our time and resources with those less fortunate in order to fight against injustice.

sufficient means to recover it, what was sold shall remain with the purchaser until the year of jubilee; in the jubilee it shall be released, and the property shall be returned.

29 If anyone sells a dwelling house in a walled city, it may be redeemed until a year has elapsed since its sale; the right of redemption shall be one year. [30] If it is not redeemed before a full year has elapsed, a house that is in a walled city shall pass in perpetuity to the purchaser, throughout the generations; it shall not be released in the jubilee. [31] But houses in villages that have no walls around them shall be classed as open country; they may be redeemed, and they shall be released in the jubilee. [32] As for the cities of the Levites, the Levites shall forever have the right of redemption of the houses in the cities belonging to them. [33] Such property as may be redeemed from the Levites— houses sold in a city belonging to them—shall be released in the jubilee; because the houses in the cities of the Levites are their possession among the people of Israel. [34] But the open land around their

cities may not be sold; for that is their possession for all time.

35 If any of your kin fall into difficulty and become dependent on you,[a] you shall support them; they shall live with you as though resident aliens. [36] Do not take interest in advance or otherwise make a profit from them, but fear your God; let them live with you. [37] You shall not lend them your money at interest taken in advance, or provide them food at a profit. [38] I am the Lord your God, who brought you out of the land of Egypt, to give you the land of Canaan, to be your God.

39 If any who are dependent on you become so impoverished that they sell themselves to you, you shall not make them serve as slaves. [40] They shall remain with you as hired or bound laborers. They shall serve with you until the year of the jubilee. [41] Then they and their children with them shall be free from your authority; they shall go back to their own family and return to their ancestral property. [42] For they are my servants, whom I brought out of the land of Egypt; they shall not be sold as slaves

a Meaning of Heb uncertain

are sold. [43]You shall not rule over them with harshness, but shall fear your God. [44]As for the male and female slaves whom you may have, it is from the nations around you that you may acquire male and female slaves. [45]You may also acquire them from among the aliens residing with you, and from their families that are with you, who have been born in your land; and they may be your property. [46]You may keep them as a possession for your children after you, for them to inherit as property. These you may treat as slaves, but as for your fellow Israelites, no one shall rule over the other with harshness.

47 If resident aliens among you prosper, and if any of your kin fall into difficulty with one of them and sell themselves to an alien, or to a branch of the alien's family, [48]after they have sold themselves they shall have the right of redemption; one of their brothers may redeem them, [49]or their uncle or their uncle's son may redeem them, or anyone of their family who is of their own flesh may redeem them; or if they prosper they may redeem themselves. [50]They shall compute with the purchaser the total from the year when they sold themselves to the alien until the jubilee year; the price of the sale shall be applied to the number of years: the time they were with the owner shall be rated as the time of a hired laborer. [51]If many years remain, they shall pay for their redemption in proportion to the purchase price; [52]and if few years remain until the jubilee year, they shall compute thus: according to the years involved they shall make payment for their redemption. [53]As a laborer hired by the year they shall be under the alien's authority, who shall not, however, rule with harshness over them in your sight. [54]And if they have not been redeemed in any of these ways, they and their children with them shall go free in the jubilee year. [55]For to me the people of Israel are servants; they are my servants whom I brought out from the land of Egypt: I am the LORD your God.

Rewards for Obedience

26 You shall make for yourselves no idols and erect no carved images or pillars, and you shall not place figured stones in your land, to worship at them; for I am the LORD your God. [2]You shall keep my sabbaths and reverence my sanctuary: I am the LORD.

3 If you follow my statutes and keep my commandments and observe them faithfully, [4]I will give you your rains in their season, and the land shall yield its produce, and the trees of the field shall yield their fruit. [5]Your threshing shall overtake the vintage, and the vintage shall overtake the sowing; you shall eat your bread to the full, and live securely in your land. [6]And I will grant peace in the land, and you shall lie down, and no one shall make you afraid; I will remove dangerous animals from the land, and no sword shall go through your land. [7]You shall give chase to your enemies, and they shall fall before you by the sword. [8]Five of you shall give chase to a hundred, and a hundred of you shall give chase to ten thousand; your enemies shall fall before you by the sword. [9]I will look with favor upon you and make you fruitful and multiply you; and I will maintain my covenant with you. [10]You shall eat old grain long stored, and you shall have to clear out the old to make way for the new. [11]I will place my dwelling in your midst, and I shall not abhor you. [12]And I will walk among you, and will be your God, and you shall be my people. [13]I am the LORD your God who brought you out of the land of Egypt, to be their slaves no more; I have broken the bars of your yoke and made you walk erect.

Penalties for Disobedience

14 But if you will not obey me, and do not observe all these commandments, [15]if you spurn my statutes, and abhor my ordinances, so that you will not observe all my commandments, and you break my covenant, [16]I in turn will do this to you: I will bring terror on you; consumption and fever that waste the eyes and cause life to pine away. You shall sow your seed in vain, for your enemies shall eat it. [17]I will set my face against you, and you shall be struck down by your enemies; your foes shall rule over you, and you shall flee though no one pursues you. [18]And if in spite of this you will not obey me, I will continue to punish you sevenfold for your sins. [19]I will break your proud glory, and I will make your sky like iron and your earth like copper. [20]Your strength shall be spent to no purpose: your land shall not yield its produce, and the trees of the land shall not yield their fruit.

21 If you continue hostile to me, and will not obey me, I will continue to plague you sevenfold for your sins. [22]I will let loose wild animals against you, and they shall bereave you of your children and destroy your livestock; they shall make you few in number, and your roads shall be deserted.

23 If in spite of these punishments you have not

turned back to me, but continue hostile to me, [24]then I too will continue hostile to you: I myself will strike you sevenfold for your sins. [25]I will bring the sword against you, executing vengeance for the covenant; and if you withdraw within your cities, I will send pestilence among you, and you shall be delivered into enemy hands. [26]When I break your staff of bread, ten women shall bake your bread in a single oven, and they shall dole out your bread by weight; and though you eat, you shall not be satisfied.

27 But if, despite this, you disobey me, and continue hostile to me, [28]I will continue hostile to you in fury; I in turn will punish you myself sevenfold for your sins. [29]You shall eat the flesh of your sons, and you shall eat the flesh of your daughters. [30]I will destroy your high places and cut down your incense altars; I will heap your carcasses on the carcasses of your idols. I will abhor you. [31]I will lay your cities waste, will make your sanctuaries desolate, and I will not smell your pleasing odors. [32]I will devastate the land, so that your enemies who come to settle in it shall be appalled at it. [33]And you I will scatter among the nations, and I will unsheathe the sword against you; your land shall be a desolation, and your cities a waste.

34 Then the land shall enjoy[a] its sabbath years as long as it lies desolate, while you are in the land of your enemies; then the land shall rest, and enjoy[a] its sabbath years. [35]As long as it lies desolate, it shall have the rest it did not have on your sabbaths when you were living on it. [36]And as for those of you who survive, I will send faintness into their hearts in the lands of their enemies; the sound of a driven leaf shall put them to flight, and they shall flee as one flees from the sword, and they shall fall though no one pursues. [37]They shall stumble over one another, as if to escape a sword, though no one pursues; and you shall have no power to stand against your enemies. [38]You shall perish among the nations, and the land of your enemies shall devour you. [39]And those of you who survive shall languish in the land of your enemies because of their iniquities; also they shall languish because of the iniquities of their ancestors.

40 But if they confess their iniquity and the iniquity of their ancestors, in that they committed treachery against me and, moreover, that they continued hostile to me— [41]so that I, in turn, continued hostile to them and brought them into the land of their enemies; if then their uncircumcised heart is humbled and they make amends for their iniquity, [42]then will I remember my covenant with Jacob; I will remember also my covenant with Isaac and also my covenant with Abraham, and I will remember the land. [43]For the land shall be deserted by them, and enjoy[a] its sabbath years by lying desolate without them, while they shall make amends for their iniquity, because they dared to spurn my ordinances, and they abhorred my statutes. [44]Yet for all that, when they are in the land of their enemies, I will not spurn them, or abhor them so as to destroy them utterly and break my covenant with them; for I am the LORD their God; [45]but I will remember in their favor the covenant with their ancestors whom I brought out of the land of Egypt in the sight of the nations, to be their God: I am the LORD.

46 These are the statutes and ordinances and laws that the LORD established between himself and the people of Israel on Mount Sinai through Moses.

Votive Offerings

27 The LORD spoke to Moses, saying: [2]Speak to the people of Israel and say to them: When a person makes an explicit vow to the LORD concerning the equivalent for a human being, [3]the equivalent for a male shall be: from twenty to sixty years of age the equivalent shall be fifty shekels of silver by the sanctuary shekel. [4]If the person is a female, the equivalent is thirty shekels. [5]If the age is from five to twenty years of age, the equivalent is twenty shekels for a male and ten shekels for a female. [6]If the age is from one month to five years, the equivalent for a male is five shekels of silver, and for a female the equivalent is three shekels of silver. [7]And if the person is sixty years old or over, then the equivalent for a male is fifteen shekels, and for a female ten shekels. [8]If any cannot afford the equivalent, they shall be brought before the priest and the priest shall assess them; the priest shall assess them according to what each one making a vow can afford.

9 If it concerns an animal that may be brought as an offering to the LORD, any such that may be given to the LORD shall be holy. [10]Another shall not be exchanged or substituted for it, either good for bad or bad for good; and if one animal is substituted for another, both that one and its substitute shall be holy. [11]If it concerns any unclean animal that may not be brought as an offering to the LORD, the animal shall be presented before the priest. [12]The priest shall assess it: whether good or bad, according to the assessment of the priest, so it shall be. [13]But if

it is to be redeemed, one-fifth must be added to the assessment.

14 If a person consecrates a house to the Lord, the priest shall assess it: whether good or bad, as the priest assesses it, so it shall stand. [15]And if the one who consecrates the house wishes to redeem it, one-fifth shall be added to its assessed value, and it shall revert to the original owner.

16 If a person consecrates to the Lord any inherited landholding, its assessment shall be in accordance with its seed requirements: fifty shekels of silver to a homer of barley seed. [17]If the person consecrates the field as of the year of jubilee, that assessment shall stand; [18]but if the field is consecrated after the jubilee, the priest shall compute the price for it according to the years that remain until the year of jubilee, and the assessment shall be reduced. [19]And if the one who consecrates the field wishes to redeem it, then one-fifth shall be added to its assessed value, and it shall revert to the original owner; [20]but if the field is not redeemed, or if it has been sold to someone else, it shall no longer be redeemable. [21]But when the field is released in the jubilee, it shall be holy to the Lord as a devoted field; it becomes the priest's holding. [22]If someone consecrates to the Lord a field that has been purchased, which is not a part of the inherited landholding, [23]the priest shall compute for it the proportionate assessment up to the year of jubilee, and the assessment shall be paid as of that day, a sacred donation to the Lord. [24]In the year of jubilee the field shall return to the one from whom it was bought, whose holding the land is. [25]All assessments shall be by the sanctuary shekel: twenty gerahs shall make a shekel.

26 A firstling of animals, however, which as a firstling belongs to the Lord, cannot be consecrated by anyone; whether ox or sheep, it is the Lord's. [27]If it is an unclean animal, it shall be ransomed at its assessment, with one-fifth added; if it is not redeemed, it shall be sold at its assessment.

28 Nothing that a person owns that has been devoted to destruction for the Lord, be it human or animal, or inherited landholding, may be sold or redeemed; every devoted thing is most holy to the Lord. [29]No human beings who have been devoted to destruction can be ransomed; they shall be put to death.

30 All tithes from the land, whether the seed from the ground or the fruit from the tree, are the Lord's; they are holy to the Lord. [31]If persons wish to redeem any of their tithes, they must add one-fifth to them. [32]All tithes of herd and flock, every tenth one that passes under the shepherd's staff, shall be holy to the Lord. [33]Let no one inquire whether it is good or bad, or make substitution for it; if one makes substitution for it, then both it and the substitute shall be holy and cannot be redeemed.

34 These are the commandments that the Lord gave to Moses for the people of Israel on Mount Sinai.

Numbers ▶▶▶▶▶▶▶▶▶▶▶▶▶▶

Sound the trumpet. Beat the drum. We're going to war! The call to arms brings out the best and the worst in people—courage and cowardice, love and hate, hope and fear. Numbers records the varied experiences of the Israelites as they prepare for the armed conquest of the promised land and endure the delays they bring upon themselves. Most important, Numbers tells of God's insistence that they maintain their purity and holiness to be worthy recipients of God's promises.

IN DEPTH

Although the book of Numbers is named for the two censuses mentioned in it (Numbers 1; 26), the book's original Hebrew name describes it better: "bemidbar" means "in the desert." Numbers picks up the story of the Israelites where Exodus leaves off. The first section, about the first ten chapters of the book, opens with a census at Mount Sinai to determine who is eligible for military service. As the people prepare to enter the promised land, their leaders review the laws and regulations with them.

The Israelites begin their journey to the promised land in the second section, approximately chapters 10–25. Unfortunately, they haven't learned to put their faith in God, and their journey is marked by grumbling, rebellion, and even idolatry. When the first army refuses to enter the promised land because of reports that it is inhabited by a race of giants (Numbers 13:32-33), God decrees that none of the older generation who left Egypt shall enter the promised land. So the Israelites begin their desert wandering, which lasts thirty-eight years. (See Map 3: "Exodus and Conquest of Canaan.")

The third section of Numbers, beginning at chapter 26, paints a more hopeful picture. The people of the new generation are faithful and obedient as they prepare to enter the promised land. They experience victory against the Midianites (Numbers 31) and conquer the land east of the Jordan River (Numbers 32). The God who liberated their ancestors from Egypt and sustained and led them through the wilderness with Moses is the same God who now is ready to fulfill the promise of the land to Israel.

Numbers was compiled and edited by priestly scribes hundreds of years after these events, after the people had lost the promised land to the Babylonians. They fully appreciated the gift of the land only after they had lost it. For the Israelites in the Babylonian exile, Numbers portrayed the hopeful, grateful, and faithful hearts required to receive God's blessing.

QUICK FACTS

- **Dates Covered:** The thirty-eight years of wandering in the desert after the exodus, sometime between 1400 and 1200 B.C.

- **Authors:** Priestly scribes writing during the Babylonian exile (587-538 B.C.)

- **Themes:** The history of the Israelites during their time in the wilderness as they learned that faithfulness and gratefulness to God were necessary for obtaining the promised land; the importance of remembering who we are, where we have come from, and who God is in our own life journeys

AT A GLANCE

- **Numbers 1:1–10:10** Preparation at Mount Sinai for conquest of the promised land

- **Numbers 10:11–25:18** The desert journey and death of the older generation

- **Numbers 26–36** The birth of a new generation and instructions for entering the promised land

The First Census of Israel

1 The LORD spoke to Moses in the wilderness of Sinai, in the tent of meeting, on the first day of the second month, in the second year after they had come out of the land of Egypt, saying: ²Take a census of the whole congregation of Israelites, in their clans, by ancestral houses, according to the number of names, every male individually; ³from twenty years old and upward, everyone in Israel able to go to war. You and Aaron shall enroll them, company by company. ⁴A man from each tribe shall be with you, each man the head of his ancestral house. ⁵These are the names of the men who shall assist you:

From Reuben, Elizur son of Shedeur.
⁶ From Simeon, Shelumiel son of Zurishaddai.
⁷ From Judah, Nahshon son of Amminadab.
⁸ From Issachar, Nethanel son of Zuar.
⁹ From Zebulun, Eliab son of Helon.
¹⁰ From the sons of Joseph:
from Ephraim, Elishama son of Ammihud;
from Manasseh, Gamaliel son of Pedahzur.
¹¹ From Benjamin, Abidan son of Gideoni.
¹² From Dan, Ahiezer son of Ammishaddai.
¹³ From Asher, Pagiel son of Ochran.
¹⁴ From Gad, Eliasaph son of Deuel.
¹⁵ From Naphtali, Ahira son of Enan.

¹⁶These were the ones chosen from the congregation, the leaders of their ancestral tribes, the heads of the divisions of Israel.

17 Moses and Aaron took these men who had been designated by name, ¹⁸and on the first day of the second month they assembled the whole congregation together. They registered themselves in their clans, by their ancestral houses, according to the number of names from twenty years old and upward, individually, ¹⁹as the LORD commanded Moses. So he enrolled them in the wilderness of Sinai.

20 The descendants of Reuben, Israel's firstborn, their lineage, in their clans, by their ancestral houses, according to the number of names, individually, every male from twenty years old and upward, everyone able to go to war: ²¹those enrolled of the tribe of Reuben were forty-six thousand five hundred.

22 The descendants of Simeon, their lineage, in their clans, by their ancestral houses, those of them that were numbered, according to the number of names, individually, every male from twenty years old and upward, everyone able to go to war: ²³those enrolled of the tribe of Simeon were fifty-nine thousand three hundred.

24 The descendants of Gad, their lineage, in their

STUDY IT!

Holy War
Numbers 1:3

The book of Numbers begins with a census of "everyone in Israel able to go to war" (Numbers 1:3) in preparation for taking the promised land. This is no ordinary war, but a holy war—one the Israelites believe is divinely inspired, even a war God commands. Later Moses says to the Israelites, "Arm some of your number . . . to execute the LORD's vengeance on Midian" (Numbers 31:2). The Israelites go on to kill every Midianite except for the young girls who are virgins.

How should we understand this? Does God really order the killing of innocent people? To answer this, let's first remember that the writers of the Bible were influenced by their own cultural background and understanding of God. Three main things were probably on the minds of the writers of Numbers. First, the early Israelites viewed God as a warrior god fighting for them. Second, they believed the Canaanites were a wicked and idolatrous people who deserved punishment. And finally, they believed the Midianites deserved special punishment, because they had led the Israelites into idolatry and sin at Shittim (Numbers 25:1-5).

Holy wars are dangerous. Throughout history, people have committed atrocities in the name of God. Christians must interpret the Old Testament in the light of Jesus' teachings in the New Testament. Jesus clearly taught about a God of mercy and love, not a God of war and vengeance. This is one area where New Testament teaching replaces an earlier Old Testament understanding. Holy wars have no place in the lives of Christians.

clans, by their ancestral houses, according to the number of the names, from twenty years old and upward, everyone able to go to war: [25]those enrolled of the tribe of Gad were forty-five thousand six hundred fifty.

26 The descendants of Judah, their lineage, in their clans, by their ancestral houses, according to the number of the names, from twenty years old and upward, everyone able to go to war: [27]those enrolled of the tribe of Judah were seventy-four thousand six hundred.

28 The descendants of Issachar, their lineage, in their clans, by their ancestral houses, according to the number of the names, from twenty years old and upward, everyone able to go to war: [29]those enrolled of the tribe of Issachar were fifty-four thousand four hundred.

30 The descendants of Zebulun, their lineage, in their clans, by their ancestral houses, according to the number of names, from twenty years old and upward, everyone able to go to war: [31]those enrolled of the tribe of Zebulun were fifty-seven thousand four hundred.

32 The descendants of Joseph, namely, the descendants of Ephraim, their lineage, in their clans, by their ancestral houses, according to the number of names, from twenty years old and upward, everyone able to go to war: [33]those enrolled of the tribe of Ephraim were forty thousand five hundred.

34 The descendants of Manasseh, their lineage, in their clans, by their ancestral houses, according to the number of names, from twenty years old and upward, everyone able to go to war: [35]those enrolled of the tribe of Manasseh were thirty-two thousand two hundred.

36 The descendants of Benjamin, their lineage, in their clans, by their ancestral houses, according to the number of names, from twenty years old and upward, everyone able to go to war: [37]those enrolled of the tribe of Benjamin were thirty-five thousand four hundred.

38 The descendants of Dan, their lineage, in their clans, by their ancestral houses, according to the number of names, from twenty years old and upward, everyone able to go to war: [39]those enrolled of the tribe of Dan were sixty-two thousand seven hundred.

40 The descendants of Asher, their lineage, in their clans, by their ancestral houses, according to the number of names, from twenty years old and upward, everyone able to go to war: [41]those enrolled of the tribe of Asher were forty-one thousand five hundred.

42 The descendants of Naphtali, their lineage, in their clans, by their ancestral houses, according to the number of names, from twenty years old and upward, everyone able to go to war: [43]those enrolled of the tribe of Naphtali were fifty-three thousand four hundred.

44 These are those who were enrolled, whom Moses and Aaron enrolled with the help of the leaders of Israel, twelve men, each representing his ancestral house. [45]So the whole number of the Israelites, by their ancestral houses, from twenty years old and upward, everyone able to go to war in Israel— [46]their whole number was six hundred three thousand five hundred fifty. [47]The Levites, however, were not numbered by their ancestral tribe along with them.

48 The LORD had said to Moses: [49]Only the tribe of Levi you shall not enroll, and you shall not take a census of them with the other Israelites. [50]Rather you shall appoint the Levites over the tabernacle of the covenant,[a] and over all its equipment, and over all that belongs to it; they are to carry the tabernacle and all its equipment, and they shall tend it, and shall camp around the tabernacle. [51]When the tabernacle is to set out, the Levites shall take it down; and when the tabernacle is to be pitched, the Levites shall set it up. And any outsider who comes near shall be put to death. [52]The other Israelites shall camp in their respective regimental camps, by companies; [53]but the Levites shall camp around the tabernacle of the covenant,[a] that there may be no wrath on the congregation of the Israelites; and the Levites shall perform the guard duty of the tabernacle of the covenant.[a] [54]The Israelites did so; they did just as the LORD commanded Moses.

The Order of Encampment and Marching

2 The LORD spoke to Moses and Aaron, saying: [2]The Israelites shall camp each in their respective regiments, under ensigns by their ancestral houses; they shall camp facing the tent of meeting on every side. [3]Those to camp on the east side toward the sunrise shall be of the regimental encampment of Judah by companies. The leader of the people of Judah shall be Nahshon son of Amminadab, [4]with a company as enrolled of seventy-

---

a Or treaty, or testimony; Heb eduth

four thousand six hundred. [5]Those to camp next to him shall be the tribe of Issachar. The leader of the Issacharites shall be Nethanel son of Zuar, [6]with a company as enrolled of fifty-four thousand four hundred. [7]Then the tribe of Zebulun: The leader of the Zebulunites shall be Eliab son of Helon, [8]with a company as enrolled of fifty-seven thousand four hundred. [9]The total enrollment of the camp of Judah, by companies, is one hundred eighty-six thousand four hundred. They shall set out first on the march.

10 On the south side shall be the regimental encampment of Reuben by companies. The leader of the Reubenites shall be Elizur son of Shedeur, [11]with a company as enrolled of forty-six thousand five hundred. [12]And those to camp next to him shall be the tribe of Simeon. The leader of the Simeonites shall be Shelumiel son of Zurishaddai, [13]with a company as enrolled of fifty-nine thousand three hundred. [14]Then the tribe of Gad: The leader of the Gadites shall be Eliasaph son of Reuel, [15]with a company as enrolled of forty-five thousand six hundred fifty. [16]The total enrollment of the camp of Reuben, by companies, is one hundred fifty-one thousand four hundred fifty. They shall set out second.

17 The tent of meeting, with the camp of the Levites, shall set out in the center of the camps; they shall set out just as they camp, each in position, by their regiments.

18 On the west side shall be the regimental encampment of Ephraim by companies. The leader of the people of Ephraim shall be Elishama son of Ammihud, [19]with a company as enrolled of forty thousand five hundred. [20]Next to him shall be the tribe of Manasseh. The leader of the people of Manasseh shall be Gamaliel son of Pedahzur, [21]with a company as enrolled of thirty-two thousand two hundred. [22]Then the tribe of Benjamin: The leader of the Benjaminites shall be Abidan son of Gideoni, [23]with a company as enrolled of thirty-five thousand four hundred. [24]The total enrollment of the camp of Ephraim, by companies, is one hundred eight thousand one hundred. They shall set out third on the march.

25 On the north side shall be the regimental encampment of Dan by companies. The leader of the Danites shall be Ahiezer son of Ammishaddai, [26]with a company as enrolled of sixty-two thousand seven hundred. [27]Those to camp next to him shall

be the tribe of Asher. The leader of the Asherites shall be Pagiel son of Ochran, [28]with a company as enrolled of forty-one thousand five hundred. [29]Then the tribe of Naphtali: The leader of the Naphtalites shall be Ahira son of Enan, [30]with a company as enrolled of fifty-three thousand four hundred. [31]The total enrollment of the camp of Dan is one hundred fifty-seven thousand six hundred. They shall set out last, by companies.[a]

32 This was the enrollment of the Israelites by their ancestral houses; the total enrollment in the camps by their companies was six hundred three thousand five hundred fifty. [33]Just as the LORD had commanded Moses, the Levites were not enrolled among the other Israelites.

34 The Israelites did just as the LORD had commanded Moses: They camped by regiments, and they set out the same way, everyone by clans, according to ancestral houses.

The Sons of Aaron

3 This is the lineage of Aaron and Moses at the time when the LORD spoke with Moses on Mount Sinai. [2]These are the names of the sons of Aaron: Nadab the firstborn, and Abihu, Eleazar, and Ithamar; [3]these are the names of the sons of Aaron, the anointed priests, whom he ordained to minister as priests. [4]Nadab and Abihu died before the LORD when they offered unholy fire before the LORD in the wilderness of Sinai, and they had no children. Eleazar and Ithamar served as priests in the lifetime of their father Aaron.

The Duties of the Levites

5 Then the LORD spoke to Moses, saying: [6]Bring the tribe of Levi near, and set them before Aaron the priest, so that they may assist him. [7]They shall perform duties for him and for the whole congregation in front of the tent of meeting, doing service at the tabernacle; [8]they shall be in charge of all the furnishings of the tent of meeting, and attend to the duties for the Israelites as they do service at the tabernacle. [9]You shall give the Levites to Aaron and his descendants; they are unreservedly given to him from among the Israelites. [10]But you shall make a register of Aaron and his descendants; it is they who shall attend to the priesthood, and any outsider who comes near shall be put to death.

11 Then the LORD spoke to Moses, saying: [12]I hereby accept the Levites from among the Israelites

a Compare verses 9, 16, 24: Heb by their regiments

as substitutes for all the firstborn that open the womb among the Israelites. The Levites shall be mine, [13]for all the firstborn are mine; when I killed all the firstborn in the land of Egypt, I consecrated for my own all the firstborn in Israel, both human and animal; they shall be mine. I am the LORD.

A Census of the Levites

14 Then the LORD spoke to Moses in the wilderness of Sinai, saying: [15]Enroll the Levites by ancestral houses and by clans. You shall enroll every male from a month old and upward. [16]So Moses enrolled them according to the word of the LORD, as he was commanded. [17]The following were the sons of Levi, by their names: Gershon, Kohath, and Merari. [18]These are the names of the sons of Gershon by their clans: Libni and Shimei. [19]The sons of Kohath by their clans: Amram, Izhar, Hebron, and Uzziel. [20]The sons of Merari by their clans: Mahli and Mushi. These are the clans of the Levites, by their ancestral houses.

21 To Gershon belonged the clan of the Libnites and the clan of the Shimeites; these were the clans of the Gershonites. [22]Their enrollment, counting all the males from a month old and upward, was seven thousand five hundred. [23]The clans of the Gershonites were to camp behind the tabernacle on the west, [24]with Eliasaph son of Lael as head of the ancestral house of the Gershonites. [25]The responsibility of the sons of Gershon in the tent of meeting was to be the tabernacle, the tent with its covering, the screen for the entrance of the tent of meeting, [26]the hangings of the court, the screen for the entrance of the court that is around the tabernacle and the altar, and its cords—all the service pertaining to these.

27 To Kohath belonged the clan of the Amramites, the clan of the Izharites, the clan of the Hebronites, and the clan of the Uzzielites; these are the clans of the Kohathites. [28]Counting all the males, from a month old and upward, there were eight thousand six hundred, attending to the duties of the sanctuary. [29]The clans of the Kohathites were to camp on the south side of the tabernacle, [30]with Elizaphan son of Uzziel as head of the ancestral house of the clans of the Kohathites. [31]Their responsibility was to be the ark, the table, the lampstand, the altars, the vessels of the sanctuary with which the priests minister, and the screen—all the service pertaining to these. [32]Eleazar son of Aaron the priest was to be chief over the leaders of the Levites, and to have oversight of those who had charge of the sanctuary.

33 To Merari belonged the clan of the Mahlites and the clan of the Mushites: these are the clans of Merari. [34]Their enrollment, counting all the males from a month old and upward, was six thousand two hundred. [35]The head of the ancestral house of the clans of Merari was Zuriel son of Abihail; they were to camp on the north side of the tabernacle. [36]The responsibility assigned to the sons of Merari was to be the frames of the tabernacle, the bars, the pillars, the bases, and all their accessories—all the service pertaining to these; [37]also the pillars of the court all around, with their bases and pegs and cords.

38 Those who were to camp in front of the tabernacle on the east—in front of the tent of meeting toward the east—were Moses and Aaron and Aaron's sons, having charge of the rites within the sanctuary, whatever had to be done for the Israelites; and any outsider who came near was to be put to death. [39]The total enrollment of the Levites whom Moses and Aaron enrolled at the commandment of the LORD, by their clans, all the males from a month old and upward, was twenty-two thousand.

The Redemption of the Firstborn

40 Then the LORD said to Moses: Enroll all the firstborn males of the Israelites, from a month old and upward, and count their names. [41]But you shall accept the Levites for me—I am the LORD—as substitutes for all the firstborn among the Israelites, and the livestock of the Levites as substitutes for all the firstborn among the livestock of the Israelites. [42]So Moses enrolled all the firstborn among the Israelites, as the LORD commanded him. [43]The total enrollment, all the firstborn males from a month old and upward, counting the number of names, was twenty-two thousand two hundred seventy-three.

44 Then the LORD spoke to Moses, saying: [45]Accept the Levites as substitutes for all the firstborn among the Israelites, and the livestock of the Levites as substitutes for their livestock; and the Levites shall be mine. I am the LORD. [46]As the price of redemption of the two hundred seventy-three of the firstborn of the Israelites, over and above the number of the Levites, [47]you shall accept five shekels apiece, reckoning by the shekel of the sanctuary, a shekel of twenty gerahs. [48]Give to Aaron and his

sons the money by which the excess number of them is redeemed. [49]So Moses took the redemption money from those who were over and above those redeemed by the Levites; [50]from the firstborn of the Israelites he took the money, one thousand three hundred sixty-five shekels, reckoned by the shekel of the sanctuary; [51]and Moses gave the redemption money to Aaron and his sons, according to the word of the LORD, as the LORD had commanded Moses.

The Kohathites

4 The LORD spoke to Moses and Aaron, saying: [2]Take a census of the Kohathites separate from the other Levites, by their clans and their ancestral houses, [3]from thirty years old up to fifty years old, all who qualify to do work relating to the tent of meeting. [4]The service of the Kohathites relating to the tent of meeting concerns the most holy things.

5 When the camp is to set out, Aaron and his sons shall go in and take down the screening curtain, and cover the ark of the covenant[a] with it; [6]then they shall put on it a covering of fine leather,[b] and spread over that a cloth all of blue, and shall put its poles in place. [7]Over the table of the bread of the Presence they shall spread a blue cloth, and put on it the plates, the dishes for incense, the bowls, and the flagons for the drink offering; the regular bread also shall be on it; [8]then they shall spread over them a crimson cloth, and cover it with a covering of fine leather,[b] and shall put its poles in place. [9]They shall take a blue cloth, and cover the lampstand for the light, with its lamps, its snuffers, its trays, and all the vessels for oil with which it is supplied; [10]and they shall put it with all its utensils in a covering of fine leather,[b] and put it on the carrying frame. [11]Over the golden altar they shall spread a blue cloth, and cover it with a covering of fine leather,[b] and shall put its poles in place; [12]and they shall take all the utensils of the service that are used in the sanctuary, and put them in a blue cloth, and cover them with a covering of fine leather,[b] and put them on the carrying frame. [13]They shall take away the ashes from the altar, and spread a purple cloth over it; [14]and they shall put on it all the utensils of the altar, which are used for the service there, the firepans, the forks, the shovels, and the basins, all the utensils of the altar; and they shall spread on it a covering of fine leather,[b] and

shall put its poles in place. [15]When Aaron and his sons have finished covering the sanctuary and all the furnishings of the sanctuary, as the camp sets out, after that the Kohathites shall come to carry these, but they must not touch the holy things, or they will die. These are the things of the tent of meeting that the Kohathites are to carry.

16 Eleazar son of Aaron the priest shall have charge of the oil for the light, the fragrant incense, the regular grain offering, and the anointing oil, the oversight of all the tabernacle and all that is in it, in the sanctuary and in its utensils.

17 Then the LORD spoke to Moses and Aaron, saying: [18]You must not let the tribe of the clans of the Kohathites be destroyed from among the Levites. [19]This is how you must deal with them in order that they may live and not die when they come near to the most holy things: Aaron and his sons shall go in and assign each to a particular task or burden. [20]But the Kohathites[c] must not go in to look on the holy things even for a moment; otherwise they will die.

The Gershonites and Merarites

21 Then the LORD spoke to Moses, saying: [22]Take a census of the Gershonites also, by their ancestral houses and by their clans; [23]from thirty years old up to fifty years old you shall enroll them, all who qualify to do work in the tent of meeting. [24]This is the service of the clans of the Gershonites, in serving and bearing burdens: [25]They shall carry the curtains of the tabernacle, and the tent of meeting with its covering, and the outer covering of fine leather[b] that is on top of it, and the screen for the entrance of the tent of meeting, [26]and the hangings of the court, and the screen for the entrance of the gate of the court that is around the tabernacle and the altar, and their cords, and all the equipment for their service; and they shall do all that needs to be done with regard to them. [27]All the service of the Gershonites shall be at the command of Aaron and his sons, in all that they are to carry, and in all that they have to do; and you shall assign to their charge all that they are to carry. [28]This is the service of the clans of the Gershonites relating to the tent of meeting, and their responsibilities are to be under the oversight of Ithamar son of Aaron the priest.

29 As for the Merarites, you shall enroll them by their clans and their ancestral houses; [30]from thirty years old up to fifty years old you shall enroll them, everyone who qualifies to do the work of the tent

a Or *treaty,* or *testimony;* Heb *eduth*   b Meaning of Heb uncertain   c Heb *they*

of meeting. [31] This is what they are charged to carry, as the whole of their service in the tent of meeting: the frames of the tabernacle, with its bars, pillars, and bases, [32] and the pillars of the court all around with their bases, pegs, and cords, with all their equipment and all their related service; and you shall assign by name the objects that they are required to carry. [33] This is the service of the clans of the Merarites, the whole of their service relating to the tent of meeting, under the hand of Ithamar son of Aaron the priest.

Census of the Levites

34 So Moses and Aaron and the leaders of the congregation enrolled the Kohathites, by their clans and their ancestral houses, [35] from thirty years old up to fifty years old, everyone who qualified for work relating to the tent of meeting; [36] and their enrollment by clans was two thousand seven hundred fifty. [37] This was the enrollment of the clans of the Kohathites, all who served at the tent of meeting, whom Moses and Aaron enrolled according to the commandment of the LORD by Moses.

38 The enrollment of the Gershonites, by their clans and their ancestral houses, [39] from thirty years old up to fifty years old, everyone who qualified for work relating to the tent of meeting— [40] their enrollment by their clans and their ancestral houses was two thousand six hundred thirty. [41] This was the enrollment of the clans of the Gershonites, all who served at the tent of meeting, whom Moses and Aaron enrolled according to the commandment of the LORD.

42 The enrollment of the clans of the Merarites, by their clans and their ancestral houses, [43] from thirty years old up to fifty years old, everyone who qualified for work relating to the tent of meeting— [44] their enrollment by their clans was three thousand two hundred. [45] This is the enrollment of the clans of the Merarites, whom Moses and Aaron enrolled according to the commandment of the LORD by Moses.

46 All those who were enrolled of the Levites, whom Moses and Aaron and the leaders of Israel enrolled, by their clans and their ancestral houses, [47] from thirty years old up to fifty years old, everyone who qualified to do the work of service and the work of bearing burdens relating to the tent of meeting, [48] their enrollment was eight thousand five hundred eighty. [49] According to the commandment of the LORD through Moses they were appointed to their several tasks of serving or carrying; thus they were enrolled by him, as the LORD commanded Moses.

5 Unclean Persons

The LORD spoke to Moses, saying: [2] Command the Israelites to put out of the camp everyone who is leprous,[a] or has a discharge, and everyone who is unclean through contact with a corpse; [3] you shall put out both male and female, putting them outside the camp; they must not defile their camp, where I dwell among them. [4] The Israelites did so, putting them outside the camp; as the LORD had spoken to Moses, so the Israelites did.

Confession and Restitution

5 The LORD spoke to Moses, saying: [6] Speak to the Israelites: When a man or a woman wrongs another, breaking faith with the LORD, that person incurs guilt [7] and shall confess the sin that has been committed. The person shall make full restitution for the wrong, adding one-fifth to it, and giving it to the one who was wronged. [8] If the injured party has no next of kin to whom restitution may be made for the wrong, the restitution for wrong shall go to the LORD for the priest, in addition to the ram of atonement with which atonement is made for the guilty party. [9] Among all the sacred donations of the Israelites, every gift that they bring to the priest shall be his. [10] The sacred donations of all are their own; whatever anyone gives to the priest shall be his.

Concerning an Unfaithful Wife

11 The LORD spoke to Moses, saying: [12] Speak to the Israelites and say to them: If any man's wife goes astray and is unfaithful to him, [13] if a man has had intercourse with her but it is hidden from her husband, so that she is undetected though she has defiled herself, and there is no witness against her since she was not caught in the act; [14] if a spirit of jealousy comes on him, and he is jealous of his wife who has defiled herself; or if a spirit of jealousy comes on him, and he is jealous of his wife, though she has not defiled herself; [15] then the man shall bring his wife to the priest. And he shall bring the offering required for her, one-tenth of an ephah of barley flour. He shall pour no oil on it and put no frankincense on it, for it is a grain offering of jealousy, a grain offering of remembrance, bringing iniquity to remembrance.

a A term for several skin diseases; precise meaning uncertain

16 Then the priest shall bring her near, and set her before the LORD; [17]the priest shall take holy water in an earthen vessel, and take some of the dust that is on the floor of the tabernacle and put it into the water. [18]The priest shall set the woman before the LORD, dishevel the woman's hair, and place in her hands the grain offering of remembrance, which is the grain offering of jealousy. In his own hand the priest shall have the water of bitterness that brings the curse. [19]Then the priest shall make her take an oath, saying, "If no man has lain with you, if you have not turned aside to uncleanness while under your husband's authority, be immune to this water of bitterness that brings the curse. [20]But if you have gone astray while under your husband's authority, if you have defiled yourself and some man other than your husband has had intercourse with you," [21]—let the priest make the woman take the oath of the curse and say to the woman—"the LORD make you an execration and an oath among your people, when the LORD makes your uterus drop, your womb discharge; [22]now may this water that brings the curse enter your bowels and make your womb discharge, your uterus drop!" And the woman shall say, "Amen. Amen."

23 Then the priest shall put these curses in writing, and wash them off into the water of bitterness. [24]He shall make the woman drink the water of bitterness that brings the curse, and the water that brings the curse shall enter her and cause bitter pain. [25]The priest shall take the grain offering of jealousy out of the woman's hand, and shall elevate the grain offering before the LORD and bring it to the altar; [26]and the priest shall take a handful of the grain offering, as its memorial portion, and turn it into smoke on the altar, and afterward shall make the woman drink the water. [27]When he has made her drink the water, then, if she has defiled herself and has been unfaithful to her husband, the water that brings the curse shall enter into her and cause bitter pain, and her womb shall discharge, her uterus drop, and the woman shall become an execration among her people. [28]But if the woman has not defiled herself and is clean, then she shall be immune and be able to conceive children.

29 This is the law in cases of jealousy, when a wife, while under her husband's authority, goes astray and defiles herself, [30]or when a spirit of jealousy comes on a man and he is jealous of his wife; then he shall set the woman before the LORD, and the priest shall apply this entire law to her. [31]The man shall be free from iniquity, but the woman shall bear her iniquity.

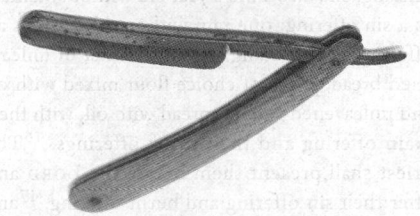

6 The Nazirites

The LORD spoke to Moses, saying: [2]Speak to the Israelites and say to them: When either men or women make a special vow, the vow of a nazirite,[a] to separate themselves to the LORD, [3]they shall separate themselves from wine and strong drink; they shall drink no wine vinegar or other vinegar, and shall not drink any grape juice or eat grapes, fresh or dried. [4]All their days as nazirites[b] they shall eat nothing that is produced by the grapevine, not even the seeds or the skins.

5 All the days of their nazirite vow no razor shall come upon the head; until the time is completed for which they separate themselves to the LORD, they shall be holy; they shall let the locks of the head grow long.

6 All the days that they separate themselves to the LORD they shall not go near a corpse. [7]Even if their father or mother, brother or sister, should die, they may not defile themselves; because their consecration to God is upon the head. [8]All their days as nazirites[b] they are holy to the LORD.

9 If someone dies very suddenly nearby, defiling the consecrated head, then they shall shave the head on the day of their cleansing; on the seventh day they shall shave it. [10]On the eighth day they shall bring two turtledoves or two young pigeons to the priest at the entrance of the tent of meeting, [11]and the priest shall offer one as a sin offering and the other as a burnt offering, and make atonement for them, because they incurred guilt by reason of the corpse. They shall sanctify the head that same day, [12]and separate themselves to the LORD for their days as nazirites,[b] and bring a male lamb a year old as a guilt offering. The former time shall be void, because the consecrated head was defiled.

a That is *one separated* or *one consecrated*   b That is *those separated* or *those consecrated*

13 This is the law for the nazirites[a] when the time of their consecration has been completed: they shall be brought to the entrance of the tent of meeting, [14]and they shall offer their gift to the LORD, one male lamb a year old without blemish as a burnt offering, one ewe lamb a year old without blemish as a sin offering, one ram without blemish as an offering of well-being, [15]and a basket of unleavened bread, cakes of choice flour mixed with oil and unleavened wafers spread with oil, with their grain offering and their drink offerings. [16]The priest shall present them before the LORD and offer their sin offering and burnt offering, [17]and shall offer the ram as a sacrifice of well-being to the LORD, with the basket of unleavened bread; the priest also shall make the accompanying grain offering and drink offering. [18]Then the nazirites[a] shall shave the consecrated head at the entrance of the tent of meeting, and shall take the hair from the consecrated head and put it on the fire under the sacrifice of well-being. [19]The priest shall take the shoulder of the ram, when it is boiled, and one unleavened cake out of the basket, and one unleavened wafer, and shall put them in the palms of the nazirites,[a] after they have shaved the consecrated head. [20]Then the priest shall elevate them as an elevation offering before the LORD; they are a holy portion for the priest, together with the breast that is elevated and the thigh that is offered. After that the nazirites[a] may drink wine.

21 This is the law for the nazirites[a] who take a vow. Their offering to the LORD must be in accordance with the nazirite[b] vow, apart from what else they can afford. In accordance with whatever vow they take, so they shall do, following the law for their consecration.

The Priestly Benediction

22 The LORD spoke to Moses, saying: [23]Speak to Aaron and his sons, saying, Thus you shall bless the Israelites: You shall say to them,

[24] The Lord bless you and keep you;

[25] the Lord make his face to shine upon you, and
　be gracious to you;

[26] the Lord lift up his countenance upon you,
　and give you peace.

27 So they shall put my name on the Israelites, and I will bless them.

Offerings of the Leaders

7 On the day when Moses had finished setting up the tabernacle, and had anointed and consecrated it with all its furnishings, and had anointed and consecrated the altar with all its utensils, [2]the leaders of Israel, heads of their ancestral houses, the leaders of the tribes, who were over those who were enrolled, made offerings. [3]They brought their offerings before the LORD, six covered wagons and twelve oxen, a wagon for every two of the leaders, and for each one an ox; they presented them before the tabernacle. [4]Then the LORD said to Moses: [5]Accept these from them, that they may be used in doing the service of the tent of meeting, and give them to the Levites, to each according to

PRAY IT!

God Bless You · Numbers 6:22–27

This Jewish blessing (some of which is repeated in Psalms 4:6 and 67:1) was not originally a Christian blessing, but it has become a favorite in churches today, often used to end church services. However, the concept behind the blessing is much bigger than words said at the end of church. There is power in our words, power to build up or tear down others. We all can extend life and hope through what we say to others, or we can hurl death and pain. Blessing was an important practice for God's people. And the value of a blessing was enough to pit brother against brother and divide a family. (Read the story of Jacob and Esau seeking Isaac's blessing in Genesis 25-28.) Those who believe in God today are also called to bless others—even our enemies. We should not repay evil with evil, but with blessings (see 1 Peter 3:9).

• Ask God who you can bless today.
• Look for ways to build others up with your words.

---

a That is *those separated* or *those consecrated*　**b** That is *one separated* or *one consecrated*

his service. [6]So Moses took the wagons and the oxen, and gave them to the Levites. [7]Two wagons and four oxen he gave to the Gershonites, according to their service; [8]and four wagons and eight oxen he gave to the Merarites, according to their service, under the direction of Ithamar son of Aaron the priest. [9]But to the Kohathites he gave none, because they were charged with the care of the holy things that had to be carried on the shoulders.

10 The leaders also presented offerings for the dedication of the altar at the time when it was anointed; the leaders presented their offering before the altar. [11]The LORD said to Moses: They shall present their offerings, one leader each day, for the dedication of the altar.

12 The one who presented his offering the first day was Nahshon son of Amminadab, of the tribe of Judah; [13]his offering was one silver plate weighing one hundred thirty shekels, one silver basin weighing seventy shekels, according to the shekel of the sanctuary, both of them full of choice flour mixed with oil for a grain offering; [14]one golden dish weighing ten shekels, full of incense; [15]one young bull, one ram, one male lamb a year old, for a burnt offering; [16]one male goat for a sin offering; [17]and for the sacrifice of well-being, two oxen, five rams, five male goats, and five male lambs a year old. This was the offering of Nahshon son of Amminadab.

18 On the second day Nethanel son of Zuar, the leader of Issachar, presented an offering; [19]he presented for his offering one silver plate weighing one hundred thirty shekels, one silver basin weighing seventy shekels, according to the shekel of the sanctuary, both of them full of choice flour mixed with oil for a grain offering; [20]one golden dish weighing ten shekels, full of incense; [21]one young bull, one ram, one male lamb a year old, as a burnt offering; [22]one male goat as a sin offering; [23]and for the sacrifice of well-being, two oxen, five rams, five male goats, and five male lambs a year old. This was the offering of Nethanel son of Zuar.

24 On the third day Eliab son of Helon, the leader of the Zebulunites: [25]his offering was one silver plate weighing one hundred thirty shekels, one silver basin weighing seventy shekels, according to the shekel of the sanctuary, both of them full of choice flour mixed with oil for a grain offering; [26]one golden dish weighing ten shekels, full of incense; [27]one young bull, one ram, one male lamb a year old, for a burnt offering; [28]one male goat for a sin

offering; [29]and for the sacrifice of well-being, two oxen, five rams, five male goats, and five male lambs a year old. This was the offering of Eliab son of Helon.

30 On the fourth day Elizur son of Shedeur, the leader of the Reubenites: [31]his offering was one silver plate weighing one hundred thirty shekels, one silver basin weighing seventy shekels, according to the shekel of the sanctuary, both of them full of choice flour mixed with oil for a grain offering; [32]one golden dish weighing ten shekels, full of incense; [33]one young bull, one ram, one male lamb a year old, for a burnt offering; [34]one male goat for a sin offering; [35]and for the sacrifice of well-being, two oxen, five rams, five male goats, and five male lambs a year old. This was the offering of Elizur son of Shedeur.

36 On the fifth day Shelumiel son of Zurishaddai, the leader of the Simeonites: [37]his offering was one silver plate weighing one hundred thirty shekels, one silver basin weighing seventy shekels, according to the shekel of the sanctuary, both of them full of choice flour mixed with oil for a grain offering; [38]one golden dish weighing ten shekels, full of incense; [39]one young bull, one ram, one male lamb a year old, for a burnt offering; [40]one male goat for a sin offering; [41]and for the sacrifice of well-being, two oxen, five rams, five male goats, and five male lambs a year old. This was the offering of Shelumiel son of Zurishaddai.

42 On the sixth day Eliasaph son of Deuel, the leader of the Gadites: [43]his offering was one silver plate weighing one hundred thirty shekels, one silver basin weighing seventy shekels, according to the shekel of the sanctuary, both of them full of choice flour mixed with oil for a grain offering; [44]one golden dish weighing ten shekels, full of incense; [45]one young bull, one ram, one male lamb a year old, for a burnt offering; [46]one male goat for a sin offering; [47]and for the sacrifice of well-being, two oxen, five rams, five male goats, and five male lambs a year old. This was the offering of Eliasaph son of Deuel.

48 On the seventh day Elishama son of Ammihud, the leader of the Ephraimites: [49]his offering was one silver plate weighing one hundred thirty shekels, one silver basin weighing seventy shekels, according to the shekel of the sanctuary, both of them full of choice flour mixed with oil for a grain offering; [50]one golden dish weighing ten shekels, full of in-

cense; [51]one young bull, one ram, one male lamb a year old, for a burnt offering; [52]one male goat for a sin offering; [53]and for the sacrifice of well-being, two oxen, five rams, five male goats, and five male lambs a year old. This was the offering of Elishama son of Ammihud.

54 On the eighth day Gamaliel son of Pedahzur, the leader of the Manassites: [55]his offering was one silver plate weighing one hundred thirty shekels, one silver basin weighing seventy shekels, according to the shekel of the sanctuary, both of them full of choice flour mixed with oil for a grain offering; [56]one golden dish weighing ten shekels, full of incense; [57]one young bull, one ram, one male lamb a year old, for a burnt offering; [58]one male goat for a sin offering; [59]and for the sacrifice of well-being, two oxen, five rams, five male goats, and five male lambs a year old. This was the offering of Gamaliel son of Pedahzur.

60 On the ninth day Abidan son of Gideoni, the leader of the Benjaminites: [61]his offering was one silver plate weighing one hundred thirty shekels, one silver basin weighing seventy shekels, according to the shekel of the sanctuary, both of them full of choice flour mixed with oil for a grain offering; [62]one golden dish weighing ten shekels, full of incense; [63]one young bull, one ram, one male lamb a year old, for a burnt offering; [64]one male goat for a sin offering; [65]and for the sacrifice of well-being, two oxen, five rams, five male goats, and five male lambs a year old. This was the offering of Abidan son of Gideoni.

66 On the tenth day Ahiezer son of Ammishaddai, the leader of the Danites: [67]his offering was one silver plate weighing one hundred thirty shekels, one silver basin weighing seventy shekels, according to the shekel of the sanctuary, both of them full of choice flour mixed with oil for a grain offering; [68]one golden dish weighing ten shekels, full of incense; [69]one young bull, one ram, one male lamb a year old, for a burnt offering; [70]one male goat for a sin offering; [71]and for the sacrifice of well-being, two oxen, five rams, five male goats, and five male lambs a year old. This was the offering of Ahiezer son of Ammishaddai.

72 On the eleventh day Pagiel son of Ochran, the leader of the Asherites: [73]his offering was one silver plate weighing one hundred thirty shekels, one silver basin weighing seventy shekels, according to the shekel of the sanctuary, both of them full of choice flour mixed with oil for a grain offering; [74]one golden dish weighing ten shekels, full of incense; [75]one young bull, one ram, one male lamb a year old, for a burnt offering; [76]one male goat for a sin offering; [77]and for the sacrifice of well-being, two oxen, five rams, five male goats, and five male lambs a year old. This was the offering of Pagiel son of Ochran.

78 On the twelfth day Ahira son of Enan, the leader of the Naphtalites: [79]his offering was one silver plate weighing one hundred thirty shekels, one silver basin weighing seventy shekels, according to the shekel of the sanctuary, both of them full of choice flour mixed with oil for a grain offering; [80]one golden dish weighing ten shekels, full of incense; [81]one young bull, one ram, one male lamb a year old, for a burnt offering; [82]one male goat for a sin offering; [83]and for the sacrifice of well-being, two oxen, five rams, five male goats, and five male lambs a year old. This was the offering of Ahira son of Enan.

84 This was the dedication offering for the altar, at the time when it was anointed, from the leaders of Israel: twelve silver plates, twelve silver basins, twelve golden dishes, [85]each silver plate weighing one hundred thirty shekels and each basin seventy, all the silver of the vessels two thousand four hundred shekels according to the shekel of the sanctuary, [86]the twelve golden dishes, full of incense, weighing ten shekels apiece according to the shekel of the sanctuary, all the gold of the dishes being one hundred twenty shekels; [87]all the livestock for the burnt offering twelve bulls, twelve rams, twelve male lambs a year old, with their grain offering; and twelve male goats for a sin offering; [88]and all the livestock for the sacrifice of well-being twenty-four bulls, the rams sixty, the male goats sixty, the male lambs a year old sixty. This was the dedication offering for the altar, after it was anointed.

89 When Moses went into the tent of meeting to speak with the LORD,[a] he would hear the voice speaking to him from above the mercy seat[b] that was on the ark of the covenant[c] from between the two cherubim; thus it spoke to him.

The Seven Lamps

8 The LORD spoke to Moses, saying: [2]Speak to Aaron and say to him: When you set up the lamps, the seven lamps shall give light in front of the lampstand. [3]Aaron did so; he set up its lamps

a Heb *him* b Or *the cover* c Or *treaty*, or *testimony*; Heb *eduth*

to give light in front of the lampstand, as the LORD had commanded Moses. [4]Now this was how the lampstand was made, out of hammered work of gold. From its base to its flowers, it was hammered work; according to the pattern that the LORD had shown Moses, so he made the lampstand.

Consecration and Service of the Levites

5 The LORD spoke to Moses, saying: [6]Take the Levites from among the Israelites and cleanse them. [7]Thus you shall do to them, to cleanse them: sprinkle the water of purification on them, have them shave their whole body with a razor and wash their clothes, and so cleanse themselves. [8]Then let them take a young bull and its grain offering of choice flour mixed with oil, and you shall take another young bull for a sin offering. [9]You shall bring the Levites before the tent of meeting, and assemble the whole congregation of the Israelites. [10]When you bring the Levites before the LORD, the Israelites shall lay their hands on the Levites, [11]and Aaron shall present the Levites before the LORD as an elevation offering from the Israelites, that they may do the service of the LORD. [12]The Levites shall lay their hands on the heads of the bulls, and he shall offer the one for a sin offering and the other for a burnt offering to the LORD, to make atonement for the Levites. [13]Then you shall have the Levites stand before Aaron and his sons, and you shall present them as an elevation offering to the LORD.

14 Thus you shall separate the Levites from among the other Israelites, and the Levites shall be mine. [15]Thereafter the Levites may go in to do service at the tent of meeting, once you have cleansed them and presented them as an elevation offering. [16]For they are unreservedly given to me from among the Israelites; I have taken them for myself, in place of all that open the womb, the firstborn of all the Israelites. [17]For all the firstborn among the Israelites are mine, both human and animal. On the day that I struck down all the firstborn in the land of Egypt I consecrated them for myself, [18]but I have taken the Levites in place of all the firstborn among the Israelites. [19]Moreover, I have given the Levites as a gift to Aaron and his sons from among the Israelites, to do the service for the Israelites at the tent of meeting, and to make atonement for the Israelites, in order that there may be no plague among the Israelites for coming too close to the sanctuary.

20 Moses and Aaron and the whole congregation of the Israelites did with the Levites accordingly; the Israelites did with the Levites just as the LORD had commanded Moses concerning them. [21]The Levites purified themselves from sin and washed their clothes; then Aaron presented them as an elevation offering before the LORD, and Aaron made atonement for them to cleanse them. [22]Thereafter the Levites went in to do their service in the tent of meeting in attendance on Aaron and his sons. As the LORD had commanded Moses concerning the Levites, so they did with them.

23 The LORD spoke to Moses, saying: [24]This applies to the Levites: from twenty-five years old and upward they shall begin to do duty in the service of the tent of meeting; [25]and from the age of fifty years they shall retire from the duty of the service and serve no more. [26]They may assist their brothers in the tent of meeting in carrying out their duties, but they shall perform no service. Thus you shall do with the Levites in assigning their duties.

9 The Passover at Sinai

The LORD spoke to Moses in the wilderness of Sinai, in the first month of the second year after they had come out of the land of Egypt, saying: [2]Let the Israelites keep the passover at its appointed time. [3]On the fourteenth day of this month, at twilight,[a] you shall keep it at its appointed time; according to all its statutes and all its regulations you shall keep it. [4]So Moses told the Israelites that they should keep the passover. [5]They kept the passover in the first month, on the fourteenth day of the month, at twilight,[a] in the wilderness of Sinai. Just as the LORD had commanded Moses, so the Israelites did. [6]Now there were certain people who were unclean through touching a corpse, so that they could not keep the passover on that day. They came before Moses and Aaron on that day, [7]and said to him, "Although we are unclean through touching a corpse, why must we be kept from presenting the LORD's offering at its appointed time among the Israelites?" [8]Moses spoke to them, "Wait, so that I may hear what the LORD will command concerning you."

9 The LORD spoke to Moses, saying: [10]Speak to the Israelites, saying: Anyone of you or your descendants who is unclean through touching a corpse, or is away on a journey, shall still keep the passover to the LORD. [11]In the second month on

α Heb *between the two evenings*

the fourteenth day, at twilight,[a] they shall keep it; they shall eat it with unleavened bread and bitter herbs. [12]They shall leave none of it until morning, nor break a bone of it; according to all the statute for the passover they shall keep it. [13]But anyone who is clean and is not on a journey, and yet refrains from keeping the passover, shall be cut off from the people for not presenting the LORD's offering at its appointed time; such a one shall bear the consequences for the sin. [14]Any alien residing among you who wishes to keep the passover to the LORD shall do so according to the statute of the passover and according to its regulation; you shall have one statute for both the resident alien and the native.

The Cloud and the Fire

15 On the day the tabernacle was set up, the cloud covered the tabernacle, the tent of the covenant;[b] and from evening until morning it was over the tabernacle, having the appearance of fire. [16]It was always so: the cloud covered it by day[c] and the appearance of fire by night. [17]Whenever the cloud lifted from over the tent, then the Israelites would set out; and in the place where the cloud settled down, there the Israelites would camp. [18]At the command of the LORD the Israelites would set out, and at the command of the LORD they would camp. As long as the cloud rested over the tabernacle, they would remain in camp. [19]Even when the cloud continued over the tabernacle many days, the Israelites would keep the charge of the LORD, and would not set out. [20]Sometimes the cloud would remain a few days over the tabernacle, and according to the command of the LORD they would remain in camp; then according to the command of the LORD they would set out.

[21]Sometimes the cloud would remain from evening until morning; and when the cloud lifted in the morning, they would set out, or if it continued for a day and a night, when the cloud lifted they would set out. [22]Whether it was two days, or a month, or a longer time, that the cloud continued over the tabernacle, resting upon it, the Israelites would remain in camp and would not set out; but when it lifted they would set out. [23]At the command of the LORD they would camp, and at the command of the LORD they would set out. They kept the charge of the LORD, at the command of the LORD by Moses.

The Silver Trumpets

10 The LORD spoke to Moses, saying: [2]Make two silver trumpets; you shall make them of hammered work; and you shall use them for summoning the congregation, and for breaking camp. [3]When both are blown, the whole congregation shall assemble before you at the entrance of the tent of meeting. [4]But if only one is blown, then the leaders, the heads of the tribes of Israel, shall assemble before you. [5]When you blow an alarm, the camps on the east side shall set out; [6]when you blow a second alarm, the camps on the south side shall set out. An alarm is to be blown whenever they are to set out. [7]But when the assembly is to be gathered, you shall blow, but you shall not sound an alarm. [8]The sons of Aaron, the priests, shall blow the trumpets; this shall be a perpetual institution for you throughout your generations. [9]When you go to war in your land against the adversary who oppresses you, you shall sound an alarm with the trumpets, so that you may be remembered before the LORD your God and be saved from your enemies. [10]Also on your days of rejoicing, at your appointed festivals, and at the beginnings of your months, you shall blow the trumpets over your burnt offerings and over your sacrifices of well-being; they shall serve as a reminder on your behalf before the LORD your God: I am the LORD your God.

Departure from Sinai

11 In the second year, in the second month, on the twentieth day of the month, the cloud lifted from over the tabernacle of the covenant.[b] [12]Then the Israelites set out by stages from the wilderness of Sinai, and the cloud settled down in the wilderness of Paran. [13]They set out for the first time at the command of the LORD by Moses. [14]The standard

a Heb *between the two evenings* b Or *treaty,* or *testimony;* Heb *eduth* c Gk Syr Vg: Heb lacks *by day*

of the camp of Judah set out first, company by company, and over the whole company was Nahshon of Amminadab. [15]Over the company of the tribe of Issachar was Nethanel son of Zuar; [16]and over the company of the tribe of Zebulun was Eliab son of Helon.

17 Then the tabernacle was taken down, and the Gershonites and the Merarites, who carried the tabernacle, set out. [18]Next the standard of the camp of Reuben set out, company by company; and over the whole company was Elizur son of Shedeur. [19]Over the company of the tribe of Simeon was Shelumiel son of Zurishaddai, [20]and over the company of the tribe of Gad was Eliasaph son of Deuel.

21 Then the Kohathites, who carried the holy things, set out; and the tabernacle was set up before their arrival. [22]Next the standard of the Ephraimite camp set out, company by company, and over the whole company was Elishama son of Ammihud. [23]Over the company of the tribe of Manasseh was Gamaliel son of Pedahzur, [24]and over the company of the tribe of Benjamin was Abidan son of Gideoni.

25 Then the standard of the camp of Dan, acting as the rear guard of all the camps, set out, company by company, and over the whole company was Ahiezer son of Ammishaddai. [26]Over the company of the tribe of Asher was Pagiel son of Ochran, [27]and over the company of the tribe of Naphtali was Ahira son of Enan. [28]This was the order of march of the Israelites, company by company, when they set out.

29 Moses said to Hobab son of Reuel the Midianite, Moses' father-in-law, "We are setting out for the place of which the Lord said, 'I will give it to you'; come with us, and we will treat you well; for the Lord has promised good to Israel." [30]But he said to him, "I will not go, but I will go back to my own land and to my kindred." [31]He said, "Do not leave us, for you know where we should camp in the wilderness, and you will serve as eyes for us. [32]Moreover, if you go with us, whatever good the Lord does for us, the same we will do for you."

33 So they set out from the mount of the Lord three days' journey with the ark of the covenant of the Lord going before them three days' journey, to seek out a resting place for them, [34]the cloud of the Lord being over them by day when they set out from the camp.

35 Whenever the ark set out, Moses would say,
"Arise, O Lord, let your enemies be scattered,
    and your foes flee before you."

[36]And whenever it came to rest, he would say,
"Return, O Lord of the ten thousand
    thousands of Israel."[a]

Complaining in the Desert

11 Now when the people complained in the hearing of the Lord about their misfortunes, the Lord heard it and his anger was kindled. Then the fire of the Lord burned against them, and consumed some outlying parts of the camp. [2]But the people cried out to Moses; and Moses prayed to the Lord, and the fire abated. [3]So that place was called Taberah,[b] because the fire of the Lord burned against them.

4 The rabble among them had a strong craving; and the Israelites also wept again, and said, "If only we had meat to eat! [5]We remember the fish we used to eat in Egypt for nothing, the cucumbers, the melons, the leeks, the onions, and the garlic; [6]but now our strength is dried up, and there is nothing at all but this manna to look at."

7 Now the manna was like coriander seed, and its color was like the color of gum resin. [8]The people went around and gathered it, ground it in mills or beat it in mortars, then boiled it in pots and made cakes of it; and the taste of it was like the taste of cakes baked with oil. [9]When the dew fell on the camp in the night, the manna would fall with it.

10 Moses heard the people weeping throughout their families, all at the entrances of their tents. Then the Lord became very angry, and Moses was displeased. [11]So Moses said to the Lord, "Why have you treated your servant so badly? Why have I not found favor in your sight, that you lay the burden of all this people on me? [12]Did I conceive all this people? Did I give birth to them, that you should say to me, 'Carry them in your bosom, as a nurse carries a sucking child, to the land that you promised on oath to their ancestors'? [13]Where am I to get meat to give to all this people? For they come weeping to me and say, 'Give us meat to eat!' [14]I am not able to carry all this people alone, for they are too heavy for me. [15]If this is the way you are going to treat me, put me to death at once—if I have found favor in your sight—and do not let me see my misery."

The Seventy Elders

16 So the Lord said to Moses, "Gather for me seventy of the elders of Israel, whom you know to

a Meaning of Heb uncertain   b That is *Burning*

be the elders of the people and officers over them; bring them to the tent of meeting, and have them take their place there with you. [17] I will come down and talk with you there; and I will take some of the spirit that is on you and put it on them; and they shall bear the burden of the people along with you so that you will not bear it all by yourself. [18] And say to the people: Consecrate yourselves for tomorrow, and you shall eat meat; for you have wailed in the hearing of the LORD, saying, 'If only we had meat to eat! Surely it was better for us in Egypt.' Therefore the LORD will give you meat, and you shall eat. [19] You shall eat not only one day, or two days, or five days, or ten days, or twenty days, [20] but for a whole month—until it comes out of your nostrils and becomes loathsome to you—because you have rejected the LORD who is among you, and have wailed before him, saying, 'Why did we ever leave Egypt?' " [21] But Moses said, "The people I am with number six hundred thousand on foot; and you say, 'I will give them meat, that they may eat for a whole month'! [22] Are there enough flocks and herds to slaughter for them? Are there enough fish in the sea to catch for them?" [23] The LORD said to Moses, "Is the LORD's power limited?[a] Now you shall see whether my word will come true for you or not."

24 So Moses went out and told the people the words of the LORD; and he gathered seventy elders of the people, and placed them all around the tent. [25] Then the LORD came down in the cloud and spoke to him, and took some of the spirit that was on him and put it on the seventy elders; and when the spirit rested upon them, they prophesied. But they did not do so again.

26 Two men remained in the camp, one named Eldad, and the other named Medad, and the spirit rested on them; they were among those registered, but they had not gone out to the tent, and so they prophesied in the camp. [27] And a young man ran and told Moses, "Eldad and Medad are prophesying in the camp." [28] And Joshua son of Nun, the assistant of Moses, one of his chosen men,[b] said, "My lord Moses, stop them!" [29] But Moses said to him, "Are you jealous for my sake? Would that all the LORD's people were prophets, and that the LORD would put his spirit on them!" [30] And Moses and the elders of Israel returned to the camp.

The Quails

31 Then a wind went out from the LORD, and it brought quails from the sea and let them fall beside the camp, about a day's journey on this side and a day's journey on the other side, all around the camp, about two cubits deep on the ground. [32] So the people worked all that day and night and all the

Overcoming Jealousy · Numbers 12

Brothers and sisters inevitably have their squabbles. Even Moses, Aaron, and Miriam are no exception. Miriam and Aaron are jealous of Moses. Miriam might have said something like, "Moses really gets to me sometimes! How can he think God only speaks through him?" Aaron may have thought, "I know he has a special connection with God, but does he always have to set himself apart, acting like he's better than the rest of us?"

Miriam and Aaron knew Moses was called by God, but still they let jealousy creep in. And they were later punished for challenging Moses' authority (check out what happens to Miriam in Numbers 12:10-16). Jealousy is like a dangerous cancer, growing until it affects your whole outlook on life.

• What happens inside of you when you feel jealous?
• How does feeling jealous affect your attitude toward other people?

a Heb LORD's hand too short? **b** Or of Moses from his youth

next day, gathering the quails; the least anyone gathered was ten homers; and they spread them out for themselves all around the camp. [33]But while the meat was still between their teeth, before it was consumed, the anger of the LORD was kindled against the people, and the LORD struck the people with a very great plague. [34]So that place was called Kibroth-hattaavah,[a] because there they buried the people who had the craving. [35]From Kibroth-hattaavah the people journeyed to Hazeroth.

Aaron and Miriam Jealous of Moses

12 While they were at Hazeroth, Miriam and Aaron spoke against Moses because of the Cushite woman whom he had married (for he had indeed married a Cushite woman); [2]and they said, "Has the LORD spoken only through Moses? Has he not spoken through us also?" And the LORD heard it. [3]Now the man Moses was very humble,[b] more so than anyone else on the face of the earth. [4]Suddenly the LORD said to Moses, Aaron, and Miriam, "Come out, you three, to the tent of meeting." So the three of them came out. [5]Then the LORD came down in a pillar of cloud, and stood at the entrance of the tent, and called Aaron and Miriam; and they both came forward. [6]And he said, "Hear my words:

When there are prophets among you,
    I the LORD make myself known to them in
        visions;
    I speak to them in dreams.
[7] Not so with my servant Moses;
    he is entrusted with all my house.
[8] With him I speak face to face— clearly, not in
        riddles;
    and he beholds the form of the LORD.

Why then were you not afraid to speak against my servant Moses?" [9]And the anger of the LORD was kindled against them, and he departed.

[10] When the cloud went away from over the tent, Miriam had become leprous,[c] as white as snow. And Aaron turned towards Miriam and saw that she was leprous. [11]Then Aaron said to Moses, "Oh, my lord, do not punish us[d] for a sin that we have so foolishly committed. [12]Do not let her be like one stillborn, whose flesh is half consumed when it comes out of its mother's womb." [13]And Moses cried to the LORD, "O God, please heal her." [14]But the LORD said to Moses, "If her father had but spit in her face, would she not bear her shame for seven days? Let her be

shut out of the camp for seven days, and after that she may be brought in again." [15]So Miriam was shut out of the camp for seven days; and the people did not set out on the march until Miriam had been brought in again. [16]After that the people set out from Hazeroth, and camped in the wilderness of Paran.

Spies Sent into Canaan

13 The LORD said to Moses, [2]"Send men to spy out the land of Canaan, which I am giving to the Israelites; from each of their ancestral tribes you shall send a man, every one a leader among them." [3]So Moses sent them from the wilderness of Paran, according to the command of the LORD, all of them leading men among the Israelites. [4]These were their names: From the tribe of Reuben, Shammua son of Zaccur; [5]from the tribe of Simeon, Shaphat son of Hori; [6]from the tribe of Judah, Caleb son of Jephunneh; [7]from the tribe of Issachar, Igal son of Joseph; [8]from the tribe of Ephraim, Hoshea son of Nun; [9]from the tribe of Benjamin, Palti son of Raphu; [10]from the tribe of Zebulun, Gaddiel son of Sodi; [11]from the tribe of Joseph (that is, from the tribe of Manasseh), Gaddi son of Susi; [12]from the tribe of Dan, Ammiel son of Gemalli; [13]from the tribe of Asher, Sethur son of Michael; [14]from the tribe of Naphtali, Nahbi son of Vophsi; [15]from the tribe of Gad, Geuel son of Machi. [16]These were the names of the men whom Moses sent to spy out the land. And Moses changed the name of Hoshea son of Nun to Joshua.

[17] Moses sent them to spy out the land of Canaan, and said to them, "Go up there into the Negeb, and go up into the hill country, [18]and see what the land is like, and whether the people who live in it are strong or weak, whether they are few or many, [19]and whether the land they live in is good or bad, and whether the towns that they live in are unwalled or fortified, [20]and whether the land is rich or poor, and whether there are trees in it or not. Be bold, and bring some of the fruit of the land." Now it was the season of the first ripe grapes.

[21] So they went up and spied out the land from the wilderness of Zin to Rehob, near Lebo-hamath. [22]They went up into the Negeb, and came to Hebron; and Ahiman, Sheshai, and Talmai, the Anakites, were there. (Hebron was built seven years before Zoan in Egypt.) [23]And they came to the Wadi Eshcol, and cut down from there a branch with a single cluster of grapes, and they carried it on a pole

---

a That is *Graves of craving*   b Or *devout*   c A term for several skin diseases; precise meaning uncertain   d Heb *do not lay sin upon us*

between two of them. They also brought some pomegranates and figs. ²⁴That place was called the Wadi Eshcol,ᵃ because of the cluster that the Israelites cut down from there.

The Report of the Spies

25 At the end of forty days they returned from spying out the land. ²⁶And they came to Moses and Aaron and to all the congregation of the Israelites in the wilderness of Paran, at Kadesh; they brought back word to them and to all the congregation, and showed them the fruit of the land. ²⁷And they told him, "We came to the land to which you sent us; it flows with milk and honey, and this is its fruit. ²⁸Yet the people who live in the land are strong, and the towns are fortified and very large; and besides, we saw the descendants of Anak there. ²⁹The Amalekites live in the land of the Negeb; the Hittites, the Jebusites, and the Amorites live in the hill country; and the Canaanites live by the sea, and along the Jordan."

30 But Caleb quieted the people before Moses, and said, "Let us go up at once and occupy it, for we are well able to overcome it." ³¹Then the men who had

PRAY IT!

Bugs vs. Giants
Numbers 13:25–33

The Israelites were scared and intimidated when they heard the amazing things their spies reported about the promised land. In comparison to the "giants" reported there, they saw themselves as tiny bugs, or "grasshoppers," forgetting the overpowering value of their identity as the chosen children of God. Joshua and Caleb understood that their task was more about God than the people's own abilities (Numbers 14:6-9), and that faith gave them courage.

• Pray about the areas or situations in your life where you feel small or weak.

• Ask for God's help and trust God's power instead of your own. God will build his identity in you and give you boldness.

gone up with him said, "We are not able to go up against this people, for they are stronger than we." ³²So they brought to the Israelites an unfavorable report of the land that they had spied out, saying, "The land that we have gone through as spies is a land that devours its inhabitants; and all the people that we saw in it are of great size. ³³There we saw the Nephilim (the Anakites come from the Nephilim); and to ourselves we seemed like grasshoppers, and so we seemed to them."

The People Rebel

14 Then all the congregation raised a loud cry, and the people wept that night. ²And all the Israelites complained against Moses and Aaron; the whole congregation said to them, "Would that we had died in the land of Egypt! Or would that we had died in this wilderness! ³Why is the LORD bringing us into this land to fall by the sword? Our wives and our little ones will become booty; would it not be better for us to go back to Egypt?" ⁴So they said to one another, "Let us choose a captain, and go back to Egypt."

5 Then Moses and Aaron fell on their faces before all the assembly of the congregation of the Israelites. ⁶And Joshua son of Nun and Caleb son of Jephunneh, who were among those who had spied out the land, tore their clothes ⁷and said to all the congregation of the Israelites, "The land that we went through as spies is an exceedingly good land. ⁸If the LORD is pleased with us, he will bring us into this land and give it to us, a land that flows with milk and honey. ⁹Only, do not rebel against the LORD; and do not fear the people of the land, for they are no more than bread for us; their protection is removed from them, and the LORD is with us; do not fear them." ¹⁰But the whole congregation threatened to stone them.

Then the glory of the LORD appeared at the tent of meeting to all the Israelites. ¹¹And the LORD said to Moses, "How long will this people despise me? And how long will they refuse to believe in me, in spite of all the signs that I have done among them? ¹²I will strike them with pestilence and disinherit them, and I will make of you a nation greater and mightier than they."

Moses Intercedes for the People

13 But Moses said to the LORD, "Then the Egyptians will hear of it, for in your might you brought up this people from among them, ¹⁴and they will

ᵃ That is *Cluster*

Krochet Kids: From Spokane to Uganda · Numbers 13–14

Every day a group of women in northern Uganda gather in a simple brick hut and begin to work. Their tools are small, just a hook and some yarn, but their results are huge. Their products are style accessories and much, much more. The crocheted hats these women make have a far-reaching impact. They provide immediate stability for their families and communicate the realities of poverty around the world. And each sale promotes the development of their community, according to **krochetkids.org**.

These ten women in Uganda have hope because three friends from Spokane, Washington, didn't let the depth of pain or the breadth of poverty stop them. Instead, these three friends used what they knew to make a difference. Cofounders Kohl Crecellus, Travis Nartanov, and Stewart Ramsey learned to crochet in high school. They thought it was only a hobby. But when they came face-to-face with the world's poverty during college, they thought they'd do something about it with crochet. Crazy, right? Tackle the poverty of Africa with crochet?

It can be tempting to look at the issues of the world and come to conclusions like that of the ten spies in **Numbers 13:27–29**. They reported that the land of Canaan was filled with challenges they couldn't face, forgetting that it was by God's power that they would be able to overcome. Only Caleb and Joshua gave a report based on God's ability (Numbers 14:6-9) and were the only two spies to enter the promised land (Numbers 14:36-38). Like Caleb and Joshua, the founders of Krochet Kids saw the huge challenges of Uganda, but were not scared away. Instead, they saw them as an opportunity for God to work powerfully.

Today Krochet Kids is a nonprofit organization that trains Ugandan women to crochet and sells their products. The small skill of three friends is creating a sustainable source of empowerment and change for an African community.

tell the inhabitants of this land. They have heard that you, O LORD, are in the midst of this people; for you, O LORD, are seen face to face, and your cloud stands over them and you go in front of them, in a pillar of cloud by day and in a pillar of fire by night. [15]Now if you kill this people all at one time, then the nations who have heard about you will say, [16]'It is because the LORD was not able to bring this people into the land he swore to give them that he has slaughtered them in the wilderness.' [17]And now, therefore, let the power of the LORD be great in the way that you promised when you spoke, saying,

[18] 'The LORD is slow to anger,
   and abounding in steadfast love,
   forgiving iniquity and transgression,
   but by no means clearing the guilty,
   visiting the iniquity of the parents
     upon the children
   to the third and the fourth generation.'
[19]Forgive the iniquity of this people according to the greatness of your steadfast love, just as you have pardoned this people, from Egypt even until now."

20 Then the LORD said, "I do forgive, just as you have asked; [21]nevertheless—as I live, and as all the earth shall be filled with the glory of the LORD— [22]none of the people who have seen my glory and the signs that I did in Egypt and in the wilderness, and yet have tested me these ten times and have not obeyed my voice, [23]shall see the land that I swore to give to their ancestors; none of those who despised me shall see it. [24]But my servant Caleb, because he has a different spirit and has followed me wholeheartedly, I will bring into the land into which he went, and his descendants shall possess it. [25]Now, since the Amalekites and the Canaanites live in the valleys, turn tomorrow and set out for the wilderness by the way to the Red Sea."[a]

An Attempted Invasion is Repulsed

26 And the LORD spoke to Moses and to Aaron, saying: [27]How long shall this wicked congregation complain against me? I have heard the complaints

of the Israelites, which they complain against me. [28] Say to them, "As I live," says the LORD, "I will do to you the very things I heard you say: [29] your dead bodies shall fall in this very wilderness; and of all your number, included in the census, from twenty years old and upward, who have complained against me, [30] not one of you shall come into the land in which I swore to settle you, except Caleb son of Jephunneh and Joshua son of Nun. [31] But your little ones, who you said would become booty, I will bring in, and they shall know the land that you have despised. [32] But as for you, your dead bodies shall fall in this wilderness. [33] And your children shall be shepherds in the wilderness for forty years, and shall suffer for your faithlessness, until the last of your dead bodies lies in the wilderness. [34] According to the number of the days in which you spied out the land, forty days, for every day a year, you shall bear your iniquity, forty years, and you shall know my displeasure." [35] I the LORD have spoken; surely I will do thus to all this wicked congregation gathered together against me: in this wilderness they shall come to a full end, and there they shall die.

36 And the men whom Moses sent to spy out the land, who returned and made all the congregation complain against him by bringing a bad report about the land— [37] the men who brought an unfavorable report about the land died by a plague before the LORD. [38] But Joshua son of Nun and Caleb son of Jephunneh alone remained alive, of those men who went to spy out the land.

39 When Moses told these words to all the Israelites, the people mourned greatly. [40] They rose early in the morning and went up to the heights of the hill country, saying, "Here we are. We will go up to the place that the LORD has promised, for we have sinned." [41] But Moses said, "Why do you continue to transgress the command of the LORD? That will not succeed. [42] Do not go up, for the LORD is not with you; do not let yourselves be struck down before your enemies. [43] For the Amalekites and the Canaanites will confront you there, and you shall fall by the sword; because you have turned back from following the LORD, the LORD will not be with you." [44] But they presumed to go up to the heights of the hill country, even though the ark of the covenant of the LORD, and Moses, had not left the camp. [45] Then the Amalekites and the Canaanites who lived in that hill country came down and defeated them, pursuing them as far as Hormah.

Various Offerings

15 The LORD spoke to Moses, saying: [2] Speak to the Israelites and say to them: When you come into the land you are to inhabit, which I am giving you, [3] and you make an offering by fire to the LORD from the herd or from the flock—whether a burnt offering or a sacrifice, to fulfill a vow or as a freewill offering or at your appointed festivals—to make a pleasing odor for the LORD, [4] then whoever presents such an offering to the LORD shall present also a grain offering, one-tenth of an ephah of choice flour, mixed with one-fourth of a hin of oil. [5] Moreover, you shall offer one-fourth of a hin of wine as a drink offering with the burnt offering or the sacrifice, for each lamb. [6] For a ram, you shall offer a grain offering, two-tenths of an ephah of choice flour mixed with one-third of a hin of oil; [7] and as a drink offering you shall offer one-third of a hin of wine, a pleasing odor to the LORD. [8] When you offer a bull as a burnt offering or a sacrifice, to fulfill a vow or as an offering of well-being to the LORD, [9] then you shall present with the bull a grain offering, three-tenths of an ephah of choice flour, mixed with half a hin of oil, [10] and you shall present as a drink offering half a hin of wine, as an offering by fire, a pleasing odor to the LORD.

11 Thus it shall be done for each ox or ram, or for each of the male lambs or the kids. [12] According to the number that you offer, so you shall do with each and every one. [13] Every native Israelite shall do these things in this way, in presenting an offering by fire, a pleasing odor to the LORD. [14] An alien who lives with you, or who takes up permanent residence among you, and wishes to offer an offering by fire, a pleasing odor to the LORD, shall do as you do. [15] As for the assembly, there shall be for both you and the resident alien a single statute, a perpetual statute throughout your generations; you and the alien shall be alike before the LORD. [16] You and the alien who resides with you shall have the same law and the same ordinance.

17 The LORD spoke to Moses, saying: [18] Speak to the Israelites and say to them: After you come into the land to which I am bringing you, [19] whenever you eat of the bread of the land, you shall present a donation to the LORD. [20] From your first batch of dough you shall present a loaf as a donation; you shall present it just as you present a donation from the threshing floor. [21] Throughout your generations you shall give to the LORD a donation from the first of your batch of dough.

22 But if you unintentionally fail to observe all these commandments that the LORD has spoken to Moses— ²³everything that the LORD has commanded you by Moses, from the day the LORD gave commandment and thereafter, throughout your generations— ²⁴then if it was done unintentionally without the knowledge of the congregation, the whole congregation shall offer one young bull for a burnt offering, a pleasing odor to the LORD, together with its grain offering and its drink offering, according to the ordinance, and one male goat for a sin offering. ²⁵The priest shall make atonement for all the congregation of the Israelites, and they shall be forgiven; it was unintentional, and they have brought their offering, an offering by fire to the LORD, and their sin offering before the LORD, for their error. ²⁶All the congregation of the Israelites shall be forgiven, as well as the aliens residing among them, because the whole people was involved in the error.

27 An individual who sins unintentionally shall present a female goat a year old for a sin offering. ²⁸And the priest shall make atonement before the LORD for the one who commits an error, when it is unintentional, to make atonement for the person, who then shall be forgiven. ²⁹For both the native among the Israelites and the alien residing among them—you shall have the same law for anyone who acts in error. ³⁰But whoever acts high-handedly, whether a native or an alien, affronts the LORD, and shall be cut off from among the people. ³¹Because of having despised the word of the LORD and broken his commandment, such a person shall be utterly cut off and bear the guilt.

Penalty for Violating the Sabbath

32 When the Israelites were in the wilderness, they found a man gathering sticks on the sabbath day. ³³Those who found him gathering sticks brought him to Moses, Aaron, and to the whole congregation. ³⁴They put him in custody, because it was not clear what should be done to him. ³⁵Then the LORD said to Moses, "The man shall be put to death; all the congregation shall stone him outside the camp." ³⁶The whole congregation brought him outside the camp and stoned him to death, just as the LORD had commanded Moses.

Fringes on Garments

37 The LORD said to Moses: ³⁸Speak to the Israelites, and tell them to make fringes on the corners of their garments throughout their generations and to put a blue cord on the fringe at each corner. ³⁹You have the fringe so that, when you see it, you will remember all the commandments of the LORD and do them, and not follow the lust of your own heart and your own eyes. ⁴⁰So you shall remember and do all my commandments, and you shall be holy to your God. ⁴¹I am the LORD your God, who brought you out of the land of Egypt, to be your God: I am the LORD your God.

Revolt of Korah, Dathan, and Abiram

16 Now Korah son of Izhar son of Kohath son of Levi, along with Dathan and Abiram sons of Eliab, and On son of Peleth—descendants of Reuben—took ²two hundred fifty Israelite men, leaders of the congregation, chosen from the assembly, well-known men,ᵃ and they confronted Moses. ³They assembled against Moses and against Aaron, and said to them, "You have gone too far! All the congregation are holy, every one of them, and the LORD is among them. So why then do you exalt yourselves above the assembly of the LORD?" ⁴When Moses heard it, he fell on his face. ⁵Then he said to Korah and all his company, "In the morning the LORD will make known who is his, and who is holy, and who will be allowed to approach him; the one whom he will choose he will allow to approach him. ⁶Do this: take censers, Korah and all yourᵇ company, ⁷and tomorrow put fire in them, and lay incense on them before the LORD; and the man whom the LORD chooses shall be the holy one. You Levites have gone too far!" ⁸Then Moses said to Korah, "Hear now, you Levites! ⁹Is it too little for you that the God of Israel has separated you from the congregation of Israel, to allow you to approach him in order to perform the duties of the LORD's tabernacle, and to stand before the congregation and serve them? ¹⁰He has allowed you to approach him, and all your brother Levites with you; yet you seek the priesthood as well! ¹¹Therefore you and all your company have gathered together against the LORD. What is Aaron that you rail against him?"

12 Moses sent for Dathan and Abiram sons of Eliab; but they said, "We will not come! ¹³Is it too little that you have brought us up out of a land flowing with milk and honey to kill us in the wilderness, that you must also lord it over us? ¹⁴It is clear you have not brought us into a land flowing with milk and honey, or given us an inheritance of fields and

---

ᵃ Cn: Heb *and they confronted Moses, and two hundred fifty men . . . well-known men*   ᵇ Heb *his*

vineyards. Would you put out the eyes of these men? We will not come!"

15 Moses was very angry and said to the LORD, "Pay no attention to their offering. I have not taken one donkey from them, and I have not harmed any one of them." [16]And Moses said to Korah, "As for you and all your company, be present tomorrow before the LORD, you and they and Aaron; [17]and let each one of you take his censer, and put incense on it, and each one of you present his censer before the LORD, two hundred fifty censers; you also, and Aaron, each his censer." [18]So each man took his censer, and they put fire in the censers and laid incense on them, and they stood at the entrance of the tent of meeting with Moses and Aaron. [19]Then Korah assembled the whole congregation against them at the entrance of the tent of meeting. And the glory of the LORD appeared to the whole congregation.

20 Then the LORD spoke to Moses and to Aaron, saying: [21]Separate yourselves from this congregation, so that I may consume them in a moment. [22]They fell on their faces, and said, "O God, the God of the spirits of all flesh, shall one person sin and you become angry with the whole congregation?"

23 And the LORD spoke to Moses, saying: [24]Say to the congregation: Get away from the dwellings of Korah, Dathan, and Abiram. [25]So Moses got up and went to Dathan and Abiram; the elders of Israel followed him. [26]He said to the congregation, "Turn away from the tents of these wicked men, and touch nothing of theirs, or you will be swept away for all their sins." [27]So they got away from the dwellings of Korah, Dathan, and Abiram; and Dathan and Abiram came out and stood at the entrance of their tents, together with their wives, their children, and their little ones. [28]And Moses said, "This is how you shall know that the LORD has sent me to do all these works; it has not been of my own accord: [29]If these people die a natural death, or if a natural fate comes on them, then the LORD has not sent me. [30]But if the LORD creates something new, and the ground opens its mouth and swallows them up, with all that belongs to them, and they go down alive into Sheol, then you shall know that these men have despised the LORD."

31 As soon as he finished speaking all these words, the ground under them was split apart. [32]The earth opened its mouth and swallowed them up, along with their households—everyone who belonged to Korah and all their goods. [33]So they with all that

belonged to them went down alive into Sheol; the earth closed over them, and they perished from the midst of the assembly. [34]All Israel around them fled at their outcry, for they said, "The earth will swallow us too!" [35]And fire came out from the LORD and consumed the two hundred fifty men offering the incense.

36[a] Then the LORD spoke to Moses, saying: [37]Tell Eleazar son of Aaron the priest to take the censers out of the blaze; then scatter the fire far and wide. [38]For the censers of these sinners have become holy at the cost of their lives. Make them into hammered plates as a covering for the altar, for they presented them before the LORD and they became holy. Thus they shall be a sign to the Israelites. [39]So Eleazar the priest took the bronze censers that had been presented by those who were burned; and they were hammered out as a covering for the altar— [40]a reminder to the Israelites that no outsider, who is not of the descendants of Aaron, shall approach to offer incense before the LORD, so as not to become like Korah and his company—just as the LORD had said to him through Moses.

41 On the next day, however, the whole congregation of the Israelites rebelled against Moses and against Aaron, saying, "You have killed the people of the LORD." [42]And when the congregation had assembled against them, Moses and Aaron turned toward the tent of meeting; the cloud had covered it and the glory of the LORD appeared. [43]Then Moses and Aaron came to the front of the tent of meeting, [44]and the LORD spoke to Moses, saying, [45]"Get away from this congregation, so that I may consume them in a moment." And they fell on their faces. [46]Moses said to Aaron, "Take your censer, put fire on it from the altar and lay incense on it, and carry it quickly to the congregation and make atonement for them. For wrath has gone out from the LORD; the plague has begun." [47]So Aaron took it as Moses had ordered, and ran into the middle of the assembly, where the plague had already begun among the people. He put on the incense, and made atonement for the people. [48]He stood between the dead and the living; and the plague was stopped. [49]Those who died by the plague were fourteen thousand seven hundred, besides those who died in the affair of Korah. [50]When the plague was stopped, Aaron returned to Moses at the entrance of the tent of meeting.

a Ch 17.1 in Heb

The Budding of Aaron's Rod

17 [a] The LORD spoke to Moses, saying: [2]Speak to the Israelites, and get twelve staffs from them, one for each ancestral house, from all the leaders of their ancestral houses. Write each man's name on his staff, [3]and write Aaron's name on the staff of Levi. For there shall be one staff for the head of each ancestral house. [4]Place them in the tent of meeting before the covenant,[b] where I meet with you. [5]And the staff of the man whom I choose shall sprout; thus I will put a stop to the complaints of the Israelites that they continually make against you. [6]Moses spoke to the Israelites; and all their leaders gave him staffs, one for each leader, according to their ancestral houses, twelve staffs; and the staff of Aaron was among theirs. [7]So Moses placed the staffs before the LORD in the tent of the covenant.[b]

8 When Moses went into the tent of the covenant[b] on the next day, the staff of Aaron for the house of Levi had sprouted. It put forth buds, produced blossoms, and bore ripe almonds. [9]Then Moses brought out all the staffs from before the LORD to all the Israelites; and they looked, and each man took his staff. [10]And the LORD said to Moses, "Put back the staff of Aaron before the covenant,[b] to be kept as a warning to rebels, so that you may make an end of their complaints against me, or else they will die." [11]Moses did so; just as the LORD commanded him, so he did.

12 The Israelites said to Moses, "We are perishing; we are lost, all of us are lost! [13]Everyone who approaches the tabernacle of the LORD will die. Are we all to perish?"

Responsibility of Priests and Levites

18 The LORD said to Aaron: You and your sons and your ancestral house with you shall bear responsibility for offenses connected with the sanctuary, while you and your sons alone shall bear responsibility for offenses connected with the priesthood. [2]So bring with you also your brothers of the tribe of Levi, your ancestral tribe, in order that they may be joined to you, and serve you while you and your sons with you are in front of the tent of the covenant.[b] [3]They shall perform duties for you and for the whole tent. But they must not approach either the utensils of the sanctuary or the altar, otherwise both they and you will die. [4]They are attached to you in order to perform the duties of the tent of meeting, for all the service of the tent; no outsider shall approach you.

[5]You yourselves shall perform the duties of the sanctuary and the duties of the altar, so that wrath may never again come upon the Israelites. [6]It is I who now take your brother Levites from among the Israelites; they are now yours as a gift, dedicated to the LORD, to perform the service of the tent of meeting. [7]But you and your sons with you shall diligently perform your priestly duties in all that concerns the altar and the area behind the curtain. I give your priesthood as a gift;[c] any outsider who approaches shall be put to death.

The Priests' Portion

8 The LORD spoke to Aaron: I have given you charge of the offerings made to me, all the holy gifts of the Israelites; I have given them to you and your sons as a priestly portion due you in perpetuity. [9]This shall be yours from the most holy things, reserved from the fire: every offering of theirs that they render to me as a most holy thing, whether grain offering, sin offering, or guilt offering, shall belong to you and your sons. [10]As a most holy thing you shall eat it; every male may eat it; it shall be holy to you. [11]This also is yours: I have given to you, together with your sons and daughters, as a perpetual due, whatever is set aside from the gifts of all the elevation offerings of the Israelites; everyone who is clean in your house may eat them. [12]All the best of the oil and all the best of the wine and of the grain, the choice produce that they give to the LORD, I have given to you. [13]The first fruits of all that is in their land, which they bring to the LORD, shall be yours; everyone who is clean in your house may eat of it. [14]Every devoted thing in Israel shall be yours. [15]The first issue of the womb of all creatures, human and animal, which is offered to the LORD, shall be yours; but the firstborn of human beings you shall redeem, and the firstborn of unclean animals you shall redeem. [16]Their redemption price, reckoned from one month of age, you shall fix at five shekels of silver, according to the shekel of the sanctuary (that is, twenty gerahs). [17]But the firstborn of a cow, or the firstborn of a sheep, or the firstborn of a goat, you shall not redeem; they are holy. You shall dash their blood on the altar, and shall turn their fat into smoke as an offering by fire for a pleasing odor to the LORD; [18]but their flesh shall be yours, just as the breast that is elevated and as the right thigh are yours. [19]All the holy offerings that the Israelites present to the LORD I have given to you, together with your sons and daughters, as a perpetual due; it is a

---

a Ch 17.16 in Heb   **b** Or *treaty,* or *testimony;* Heb *eduth*   **c** Heb *as a service of gift*

covenant of salt forever before the LORD for you and your descendants as well. ²⁰ Then the LORD said to Aaron: You shall have no allotment in their land, nor shall you have any share among them; I am your share and your possession among the Israelites.

21 To the Levites I have given every tithe in Israel for a possession in return for the service that they perform, the service in the tent of meeting. ²² From now on the Israelites shall no longer approach the tent of meeting, or else they will incur guilt and die. ²³ But the Levites shall perform the service of the tent of meeting, and they shall bear responsibility for their own offenses; it shall be a perpetual statute throughout your generations. But among the Israelites they shall have no allotment, ²⁴ because I have given to the Levites as their portion the tithe of the Israelites, which they set apart as an offering to the LORD. Therefore I have said of them that they shall have no allotment among the Israelites.

25 Then the LORD spoke to Moses, saying: ²⁶ You shall speak to the Levites, saying: When you receive from the Israelites the tithe that I have given you from them for your portion, you shall set apart an offering from it to the LORD, a tithe of the tithe. ²⁷ It shall be reckoned to you as your gift, the same as the grain of the threshing floor and the fullness of the wine press. ²⁸ Thus you also shall set apart an offering to the LORD from all the tithes that you receive from the Israelites; and from them you shall give the LORD's offering to the priest Aaron. ²⁹ Out of all the gifts to you, you shall set apart every offering due to the LORD; the best of all of them is the part to be consecrated. ³⁰ Say also to them: When you have set apart the best of it, then the rest shall be reckoned to the Levites as produce of the threshing floor, and as produce of the wine press. ³¹ You may eat it in any place, you and your households; for it is your payment for your service in the tent of meeting. ³² You shall incur no guilt by reason of it, when you have offered the best of it. But you shall not profane the holy gifts of the Israelites, on pain of death.

> "You shall set apart every offering due to the LORD; the best of all of them is the part to be consecrated."
> —Numbers 18:29

19 Ceremony of the Red Heifer

The LORD spoke to Moses and Aaron, saying: ² This is a statute of the law that the LORD has commanded: Tell the Israelites to bring you a red heifer without defect, in which there is no blemish and on which no yoke has been laid. ³ You shall give it to the priest Eleazar, and it shall be taken outside the camp and slaughtered in his presence. ⁴ The priest Eleazar shall take some of its blood with his finger and sprinkle it seven times towards the front of the tent of meeting. ⁵ Then the heifer shall be burned in his sight; its skin, its flesh, and its blood, with its dung, shall be burned. ⁶ The priest shall take cedarwood, hyssop, and crimson material, and throw them into the fire in which the heifer is burning. ⁷ Then the priest shall wash his clothes and bathe his body in water, and afterwards he may come into the camp; but the priest shall remain unclean until evening. ⁸ The one who burns the heifer[a] shall wash his clothes in water and bathe his body in water; he shall remain unclean until evening. ⁹ Then someone who is clean shall gather up the ashes of the heifer, and deposit them outside the camp in a clean place; and they shall be kept for the congregation of the Israelites for the water for cleansing. It is a purification offering. ¹⁰ The one who gathers the ashes of the heifer shall wash his clothes and be unclean until evening.

This shall be a perpetual statute for the Israelites and for the alien residing among them. ¹¹ Those who touch the dead body of any human being shall be unclean seven days. ¹² They shall purify themselves with the water on the third day and on the seventh day, and so be clean; but if they do not purify themselves on the third day and on the seventh day, they will not become clean. ¹³ All who touch a corpse, the body of a human being who has died, and do not purify themselves, defile the tabernacle of the LORD; such persons shall be cut off from Israel. Since water for cleansing was not dashed on them, they remain unclean; their uncleanness is still on them.

14 This is the law when someone dies in a tent: everyone who comes into the tent, and everyone

a Heb *it*

who is in the tent, shall be unclean seven days. ¹⁵And every open vessel with no cover fastened on it is unclean. ¹⁶Whoever in the open field touches one who has been killed by a sword, or who has died naturally,ᵃ or a human bone, or a grave, shall be unclean seven days. ¹⁷For the unclean they shall take some ashes of the burnt purification offering, and running water shall be added in a vessel; ¹⁸then a clean person shall take hyssop, dip it in the water, and sprinkle it on the tent, on all the furnishings, on the persons who were there, and on whoever touched the bone, the slain, the corpse, or the grave. ¹⁹The clean person shall sprinkle the unclean ones on the third day and on the seventh day, thus purifying them on the seventh day. Then they shall wash their clothes and bathe themselves in water, and at evening they shall be clean. ²⁰Any who are unclean but do not purify themselves, those persons shall be cut off from the assembly, for they have defiled the sanctuary of the LORD. Since the water for cleansing has not been dashed on them, they are unclean.

21 It shall be a perpetual statute for them. The one who sprinkles the water for cleansing shall wash his clothes, and whoever touches the water for cleansing shall be unclean until evening. ²²Whatever the unclean person touches shall be unclean, and anyone who touches it shall be unclean until evening.

20 ## The Waters of Meribah

The Israelites, the whole congregation, came into the wilderness of Zin in the first month, and the people stayed in Kadesh. Miriam died there, and was buried there.

2 Now there was no water for the congregation; so they gathered together against Moses and against Aaron. ³The people quarreled with Moses and said, "Would that we had died when our kindred died before the LORD! ⁴Why have you brought the assembly of the LORD into this wilderness for us and our livestock to die here? ⁵Why have you brought us up out of Egypt, to bring us to this wretched place? It is no place for grain, or figs, or vines, or pomegranates; and there is no water to drink." ⁶Then Moses and Aaron went away from the assembly to the entrance of the tent of meeting; they fell on their faces, and the glory of the LORD appeared to them. ⁷The LORD spoke to Moses, saying: ⁸Take the staff, and assemble the congregation, you and your brother Aaron, and command the rock

before their eyes to yield its water. Thus you shall bring water out of the rock for them; thus you shall provide drink for the congregation and their livestock.

9 So Moses took the staff from before the LORD, as he had commanded him. ¹⁰Moses and Aaron gathered the assembly together before the rock, and he said to them, "Listen, you rebels, shall we bring water for you out of this rock?" ¹¹Then Moses lifted up his hand and struck the rock twice with his staff; water came out abundantly, and the congregation and their livestock drank. ¹²But the LORD said to Moses and Aaron, "Because you did not trust in me, to show my holiness before the eyes of the Israelites, therefore you shall not bring this assembly into the land that I have given them." ¹³These are the waters of Meribah,ᵇ where the people of Israel quarreled with the LORD, and by which he showed his holiness.

Passage through Edom Refused

14 Moses sent messengers from Kadesh to the king of Edom, "Thus says your brother Israel: You know all the adversity that has befallen us: ¹⁵how our ancestors went down to Egypt, and we lived in Egypt a long time; and the Egyptians oppressed us and our ancestors; ¹⁶and when we cried to the LORD, he heard our voice, and sent an angel and brought us out of Egypt; and here we are in Kadesh, a town on the edge of your territory. ¹⁷Now let us pass through your land. We will not pass through field or vineyard, or drink water from any well; we will go along the King's Highway, not turning aside to the right hand or to the left until we have passed through your territory."

18 But Edom said to him, "You shall not pass through, or we will come out with the sword against you." ¹⁹The Israelites said to him, "We will stay on the highway; and if we drink of your water, we and our livestock, then we will pay for it. It is only a small matter; just let us pass through on foot." ²⁰But he said, "You shall not pass through." And Edom came out against them with a large force, heavily armed. ²¹Thus Edom refused to give Israel passage through their territory; so Israel turned away from them.

The Death of Aaron

22 They set out from Kadesh, and the Israelites, the whole congregation, came to Mount Hor. ²³Then the LORD said to Moses and Aaron at Mount

ᵃ Heb lacks *naturally*   ᵇ That is *Quarrel*

Hor, on the border of the land of Edom, [24]"Let Aaron be gathered to his people. For he shall not enter the land that I have given to the Israelites, because you rebelled against my command at the waters of Meribah. [25]Take Aaron and his son Eleazar, and bring them up Mount Hor; [26]strip Aaron of his vestments, and put them on his son Eleazar. But Aaron shall be gathered to his people,[a] and shall die there." [27]Moses did as the LORD had commanded; they went up Mount Hor in the sight of the whole congregation. [28]Moses stripped Aaron of his vestments, and put them on his son Eleazar; and Aaron died there on the top of the mountain. Moses and Eleazar came down from the mountain. [29]When all the congregation saw that Aaron had died, all the house of Israel mourned for Aaron thirty days.

The Bronze Serpent

21 When the Canaanite, the king of Arad, who lived in the Negeb, heard that Israel was coming by the way of Atharim, he fought against Israel and took some of them captive. [2]Then Israel made a vow to the LORD and said, "If you will indeed give this people into our hands, then we will utterly destroy their towns." [3]The LORD listened to the voice of Israel, and handed over the Canaanites; and they utterly destroyed them and their towns; so the place was called Hormah.[b]

4 From Mount Hor they set out by the way to the Red Sea,[c] to go around the land of Edom; but the people became impatient on the way. [5]The people spoke against God and against Moses, "Why have you brought us up out of Egypt to die in the wilderness? For there is no food and no water, and we detest this miserable food." [6]Then the LORD sent poisonous[d] serpents among the people, and they bit the people, so that many Israelites died. [7]The people came to Moses and said, "We have sinned by speaking against the LORD and against you; pray to the LORD to take away the serpents from us." So Moses prayed for the people. [8]And the LORD said to Moses, "Make a poisonous[e] serpent, and set it on a pole; and everyone who is bitten shall look at it and live." [9]So Moses made a serpent of bronze, and put it upon a pole; and whenever a serpent bit someone, that person would look at the serpent of bronze and live.

The Journey to Moab

10 The Israelites set out, and camped in Oboth. [11]They set out from Oboth, and camped at Iye-

STUDY IT!

Snake on a Stick
Numbers 21:6–9

It's an odd image and an even stranger concept—a bronze serpent on a pole that people can look at and be healed. It makes no sense in light of our modern-day understanding of medicine, but it was a gift given by God to heal the Israelites. And the symbolism has meaning for us today. The serpent raised up on a pole foreshadows the cross of Christ (see John 3:14). When people saw Jesus on the cross, they lost hope. It appeared that Satan had won. But as we look to the empty cross, knowing the truth of Christ's resurrection, we are healed from our sin when we believe in Jesus' sacrifice.

abarim, in the wilderness bordering Moab toward the sunrise. [12]From there they set out, and camped in the Wadi Zered. [13]From there they set out, and camped on the other side of the Arnon, in[f] the wilderness that extends from the boundary of the Amorites; for the Arnon is the boundary of Moab, between Moab and the Amorites. [14]Wherefore it is said in the Book of the Wars of the LORD,

"Waheb in Suphah and the wadis.

The Arnon [15]and the slopes of the wadis
   that extend to the seat of Ar,
   and lie along the border of Moab."[g]

16 From there they continued to Beer;[h] that is the well of which the LORD said to Moses, "Gather the people together, and I will give them water." [17]Then Israel sang this song:

"Spring up, O well!—Sing to it!—
[18] the well that the leaders sank,
   that the nobles of the people dug,
   with the scepter, with the staff."

From the wilderness to Mattanah, [19]from Mattanah to Nahaliel, from Nahaliel to Bamoth, [20]and from Bamoth to the valley lying in the region of Moab by the top of Pisgah that overlooks the wasteland.[i]

King Sihon Defeated

21 Then Israel sent messengers to King Sihon of

---

a Heb lacks *to his people*   b Heb *Destruction*   c Or *Sea of Reeds*   d Or *fiery;* Heb *seraphim*   e Or *fiery;* Heb *seraph*   f Gk: Heb *which is in*   g Meaning of Heb uncertain   h That is *Well*   i Or *Jeshimon*

the Amorites, saying, [22]"Let me pass through your land; we will not turn aside into field or vineyard; we will not drink the water of any well; we will go by the King's Highway until we have passed through your territory." [23]But Sihon would not allow Israel to pass through his territory. Sihon gathered all his people together, and went out against Israel to the wilderness; he came to Jahaz, and fought against Israel. [24]Israel put him to the sword, and took possession of his land from the Arnon to the Jabbok, as far as to the Ammonites; for the boundary of the Ammonites was strong. [25]Israel took all these towns, and Israel settled in all the towns of the Amorites, in Heshbon, and in all its villages. [26]For Heshbon was the city of King Sihon of the Amorites, who had fought against the former king of Moab and captured all his land as far as the Arnon. [27]Therefore the ballad singers say,

"Come to Heshbon, let it be built;
        let the city of Sihon be established.
[28] For fire came out from Heshbon,
        flame from the city of Sihon.
    It devoured Ar of Moab,
        and swallowed up[a] the heights of the Arnon.
[29] Woe to you, O Moab!
        You are undone, O people of Chemosh!
    He has made his sons fugitives,
        and his daughters captives,
        to an Amorite king, Sihon.
[30] So their posterity perished
        from Heshbon[b] to Dibon,
        and we laid waste until fire spread to
        Medeba."[c]

[31] Thus Israel settled in the land of the Amorites. [32]Moses sent to spy out Jazer; and they captured its villages, and dispossessed the Amorites who were there.

King Og Defeated

[33] Then they turned and went up the road to Bashan; and King Og of Bashan came out against them, he and all his people, to battle at Edrei. [34]But the LORD said to Moses, "Do not be afraid of him; for I have given him into your hand, with all his people, and all his land. You shall do to him as you did to King Sihon of the Amorites, who ruled in Heshbon." [35]So they killed him, his sons, and all his people, until there was no survivor left; and they took possession of his land.

22

Balak Summons Balaam to Curse Israel

The Israelites set out, and camped in the plains of Moab across the Jordan from Jericho. [2]Now Balak son of Zippor saw all that Israel had done to the Amorites. [3]Moab was in great dread of the people, because they were so numerous; Moab was overcome with fear of the people of Israel. [4]And Moab said to the elders of Midian, "This horde will now lick up all that is around us, as an ox licks up the grass of the field." Now Balak son of Zippor was king of Moab at that time. [5]He sent messengers to Balaam son of Beor at Pethor, which is on the Euphrates, in the land of Amaw,[d] to summon him, saying, "A people has come out of Egypt; they have spread over the face of the earth, and they have settled next to me. [6]Come now, curse this people for me, since they are stronger than I; perhaps I shall be able to defeat them and drive them from the land; for I know that whomever you bless is blessed, and whomever you curse is cursed."

7 So the elders of Moab and the elders of Midian departed with the fees for divination in their hand; and they came to Balaam, and gave him Balak's message. [8]He said to them, "Stay here tonight, and I will bring back word to you, just as the LORD speaks to me"; so the officials of Moab stayed with Balaam. [9]God came to Balaam and said, "Who are these men with you?" [10]Balaam said to God, "King Balak son of Zippor of Moab, has sent me this message: [11]'A people has come out of Egypt and has spread over the face of the earth; now come, curse them for me; perhaps I shall be able to fight against them and drive them out.'" [12]God said to Balaam, "You shall not go with them; you shall not curse the people, for they are blessed." [13]So Balaam rose in the morning, and said to the officials of Balak, "Go to your own land, for the LORD has refused to let me go with you." [14]So the officials of Moab rose and went to Balak, and said, "Balaam refuses to come with us."

15 Once again Balak sent officials, more numerous and more distinguished than these. [16]They came to Balaam and said to him, "Thus says Balak son of Zippor: 'Do not let anything hinder you from coming to me; [17]for I will surely do you great honor, and whatever you say to me I will do; come, curse this people for me.'" [18]But Balaam replied to the servants of Balak, "Although Balak were to give me his house full of silver and gold, I could not go be-

---

a Gk: Heb *and the lords of*   b Gk: Heb *we have shot at them; Heshbon has perished*   c Compare Sam Gk: Meaning of MT uncertain   d Or *land of his kinsfolk*

yond the command of the Lord my God, to do less or more. [19]You remain here, as the others did, so that I may learn what more the Lord may say to me." [20]That night God came to Balaam and said to him, "If the men have come to summon you, get up and go with them; but do only what I tell you to do." [21]So Balaam got up in the morning, saddled his donkey, and went with the officials of Moab.

Balaam, the Donkey, and the Angel

22 God's anger was kindled because he was going, and the angel of the Lord took his stand in the road as his adversary. Now he was riding on the donkey, and his two servants were with him. [23]The donkey saw the angel of the Lord standing in the road, with a drawn sword in his hand; so the donkey turned off the road, and went into the field; and Balaam struck the donkey, to turn it back onto the road. [24]Then the angel of the Lord stood in a narrow path between the vineyards, with a wall on either side. [25]When the donkey saw the angel of the Lord, it scraped against the wall, and scraped Balaam's foot against the wall; so he struck it again. [26]Then the angel of the Lord went ahead, and stood in a narrow place, where there was no way to turn either to the right or to the left. [27]When the donkey saw the angel of the Lord, it lay down under Balaam; and Balaam's anger was kindled, and he struck the donkey with his staff. [28]Then the Lord opened the mouth of the donkey, and it said to Balaam, "What have I done to you, that you have struck me these three times?" [29]Balaam said to the donkey, "Because you have made a fool of me! I wish I had a sword in my hand! I would kill you right now!" [30]But the donkey said to Balaam, "Am I not your donkey, which you have ridden all your life to this day? Have I been in the habit of treating you this way?" And he said, "No."

31 Then the Lord opened the eyes of Balaam, and he saw the angel of the Lord standing in the road, with his drawn sword in his hand; and he bowed down, falling on his face. [32]The angel of the Lord said to him, "Why have you struck your donkey these three times? I have come out as an adversary, because your way is perverse[a] before me. [33]The donkey saw me, and turned away from me these three times. If it had not turned away from me, surely just now I would have killed you and let it live." [34]Then Balaam said to the angel of the Lord, "I have sinned, for I did not know that you were standing in the road to oppose me. Now therefore, if it is displeasing to you, I will return home." [35]The angel of the Lord said to Balaam, "Go with the men; but speak only what I tell you to speak."

PRAY IT!

The Talking Donkey · Numbers 22:22–35

Balaam, who was not an Israelite, seems to be a sort of prophet for hire in this story. Balak, the king of Moab, hires him to prophesy against Israel. But God speaks to Balaam through his donkey, so instead of cursing the Israelites, Balaam blesses them four times. Even though the Israelites were unfaithful, God continues to be with them and bless them.

This story gives us two insights into prayer. First, if God can use a donkey to talk to Balaam, God can use anything to talk to us. God speaks to us in many ways—through the scriptures, our experiences, poetry and music, nature, other people, and more. Are we paying attention? Second, God wants us to hear the voices of those who often go unheard—particularly those who are poor and oppressed. Do you hear God's voice expressed through them? Practice paying attention to God—you might just hear from God in an unlikely way.

α Meaning of Heb uncertain

So Balaam went on with the officials of Balak.

36 When Balak heard that Balaam had come, he went out to meet him at Ir-moab, on the boundary formed by the Arnon, at the farthest point of the boundary. [37]Balak said to Balaam, "Did I not send to summon you? Why did you not come to me? Am I not able to honor you?" [38]Balaam said to Balak, "I have come to you now, but do I have power to say just anything? The word God puts in my mouth, that is what I must say." [39]Then Balaam went with Balak, and they came to Kiriath-huzoth. [40]Balak sacrificed oxen and sheep, and sent them to Balaam and to the officials who were with him.

Balaam's First Oracle

41 On the next day Balak took Balaam and brought him up to Bamoth-baal; and from there he could see part of the people of Israel.[a] [1]Then Balaam said to Balak, "Build me seven altars here, and prepare seven bulls and seven rams for me." [2]Balak did as Balaam had said; and Balak and Balaam offered a bull and a ram on each altar. [3]Then Balaam said to Balak, "Stay here beside your burnt offerings while I go aside. Perhaps the LORD will come to meet me. Whatever he shows me I will tell you." And he went to a bare height.

4 Then God met Balaam; and Balaam said to him, "I have arranged the seven altars, and have offered a bull and a ram on each altar. [5]The LORD put a word in Balaam's mouth, and said, "Return to Balak, and this is what you must say." [6]So he returned to Balak,[b] who was standing beside his burnt offerings with all the officials of Moab. [7]Then Balaam[c] uttered his oracle, saying:

"Balak has brought me from Aram,
　　the king of Moab from the eastern
　　　　mountains:
'Come, curse Jacob for me;
　Come, denounce Israel!'
[8] How can I curse whom God has not cursed?
　　How can I denounce those whom the LORD
　　　　has not denounced?
[9] For from the top of the crags I see him,
　　from the hills I behold him.
Here is a people living alone,
　　and not reckoning itself among the nations!
[10] Who can count the dust of Jacob,
　　or number the dust-cloud[d] of Israel?
Let me die the death of the upright,
　　and let my end be like his!"

11 Then Balak said to Balaam, "What have you done to me? I brought you to curse my enemies, but now you have done nothing but bless them." [12]He answered, "Must I not take care to say what the LORD puts into my mouth?"

Balaam's Second Oracle

13 So Balak said to him, "Come with me to another place from which you may see them; you shall see only part of them, and shall not see them all; then curse them for me from there." [14]So he took him to the field of Zophim, to the top of Pisgah. He built seven altars, and offered a bull and a ram on each altar. [15]Balaam said to Balak, "Stand here beside your burnt offerings, while I meet the LORD over there." [16]The LORD met Balaam, put a word into his mouth, and said, "Return to Balak, and this is what you shall say." [17]When he came to him, he was standing beside his burnt offerings with the officials of Moab. Balak said to him, "What has the LORD said?" [18]Then Balaam uttered his oracle, saying:

"Rise, Balak, and hear;
　　listen to me, O son of Zippor:
[19] God is not a human being, that he should lie,
　　or a mortal, that he should change his mind.
Has he promised, and will he not do it?
　　Has he spoken, and will he not fulfill it?
[20] See, I received a command to bless;
　　he has blessed, and I cannot revoke it.
[21] He has not beheld misfortune in Jacob;
　　nor has he seen trouble in Israel.
The LORD their God is with them,
　　acclaimed as a king among them.
[22] God, who brings them out of Egypt,
　　is like the horns of a wild ox for them.
[23] Surely there is no enchantment against Jacob,
　　no divination against Israel;
now it shall be said of Jacob and Israel,
　　'See what God has done!'
[24] Look, a people rising up like a lioness,
　　and rousing itself like a lion!
It does not lie down until it has eaten the prey
　　and drunk the blood of the slain."

25 Then Balak said to Balaam, "Do not curse them at all, and do not bless them at all." [26]But Balaam answered Balak, "Did I not tell you, 'Whatever the LORD says, that is what I must do'?"

27 So Balak said to Balaam, "Come now, I will take you to another place; perhaps it will please God

---

a Heb lacks *of Israel*　b Heb *him*　c Heb *he*　d Or *fourth part* that you may curse them for me from there." ²⁸ So Balak took Balaam to the top of Peor, which overlooks the wasteland.^a ²⁹ Balaam said to Balak, "Build me seven altars here, and prepare seven bulls and seven rams for me." ³⁰ So Balak did as Balaam had said, and offered a bull and a ram on each altar.

Balaam's Third Oracle

24 Now Balaam saw that it pleased the LORD to bless Israel, so he did not go, as at other times, to look for omens, but set his face toward the wilderness. ² Balaam looked up and saw Israel camping tribe by tribe. Then the spirit of God came upon him, ³ and he uttered his oracle, saying:

"The oracle of Balaam son of Beor,
    the oracle of the man whose eye is clear,^b
⁴ the oracle of one who hears the words of God,
    who sees the vision of the Almighty,^c
    who falls down, but with eyes uncovered:
⁵ how fair are your tents, O Jacob,
    your encampments, O Israel!
⁶ Like palm groves that stretch far away,
    like gardens beside a river,
    like aloes that the LORD has planted,
    like cedar trees beside the waters.
⁷ Water shall flow from his buckets,
    and his seed shall have abundant water,
    his king shall be higher than Agag,
    and his kingdom shall be exalted.
⁸ God who brings him out of Egypt,
    is like the horns of a wild ox for him;
    he shall devour the nations that are his foes
    and break their bones.
    He shall strike with his arrows.^d
⁹ He crouched, he lay down like a lion,
    and like a lioness; who will rouse him up?
    Blessed is everyone who blesses you,
    and cursed is everyone who curses you."

¹⁰ Then Balak's anger was kindled against Balaam, and he struck his hands together. Balak said to Balaam, "I summoned you to curse my enemies, but instead you have blessed them these three times. ¹¹ Now be off with you! Go home! I said, 'I will reward you richly,' but the LORD has denied you any reward." ¹² And Balaam said to Balak, "Did I not tell your messengers whom you sent to me, ¹³ 'If Balak should give me his house full of silver and gold, I would not be able to go beyond the word of the LORD, to do either good or bad of my own will; what the LORD says, that is what I will say'? ¹⁴ So now, I am going to my people; let me advise you what this people will do to your people in days to come."

Balaam's Fourth Oracle

¹⁵ So he uttered his oracle, saying:

"The oracle of Balaam son of Beor,
    the oracle of the man whose eye is clear,^b
¹⁶ the oracle of one who hears the words of God,
    and knows the knowledge of the Most High,^e
    who sees the vision of the Almighty,^c
    who falls down, but with his eyes uncovered:
¹⁷ I see him, but not now;
    I behold him, but not near—
    a star shall come out of Jacob,
    and a scepter shall rise out of Israel;
    it shall crush the borderlands^f of Moab,
    and the territory^g of all the Shethites.
¹⁸ Edom will become a possession,
    Seir a possession of its enemies,^h
    while Israel does valiantly.
¹⁹ One out of Jacob shall rule,
    and destroy the survivors of Ir."

²⁰ Then he looked on Amalek, and uttered his oracle, saying:

"First among the nations was Amalek,
    but its end is to perish forever."

²¹ Then he looked on the Kenite, and uttered his oracle, saying:

"Enduring is your dwelling place,
    and your nest is set in the rock;
²² yet Kain is destined for burning.
    How long shall Asshur take you away captive?"

²³ Again he uttered his oracle, saying:
"Alas, who shall live when God does this?
²⁴   But ships shall come from Kittim
    and shall afflict Asshur and Eber;
    and he also shall perish forever."

²⁵ Then Balaam got up and went back to his place, and Balak also went his way.

Worship of Baal of Peor

25 While Israel was staying at Shittim, the people began to have sexual relations with the women of Moab. ² These invited the people to the sacrifices of their gods, and the people ate and bowed down to their gods. ³ Thus Israel yoked itself to the Baal of Peor, and the LORD's anger was kindled against Israel. ⁴ The LORD said to Moses, "Take all the chiefs of the people, and impale them in the sun

---

^a Or *overlooks Jeshimon* ^b Or *closed* or *open* ^c Traditional rendering of Heb *Shaddai* ^d Meaning of Heb uncertain ^e Or *of Elyon* ^f Or *forehead* ^g Some Mss read *skull* ^h Heb *Seir, its enemies, a possession*

before the LORD, in order that the fierce anger of the LORD may turn away from Israel." [5]And Moses said to the judges of Israel, "Each of you shall kill any of your people who have yoked themselves to the Baal of Peor."

6 Just then one of the Israelites came and brought a Midianite woman into his family, in the sight of Moses and in the sight of the whole congregation of the Israelites, while they were weeping at the entrance of the tent of meeting. [7]When Phinehas son of Eleazar, son of Aaron the priest, saw it, he got up and left the congregation. Taking a spear in his hand, [8]he went after the Israelite man into the tent, and pierced the two of them, the Israelite and the woman, through the belly. So the plague was stopped among the people of Israel. [9]Nevertheless those that died by the plague were twenty-four thousand.

10 The LORD spoke to Moses, saying: [11]"Phinehas son of Eleazar, son of Aaron the priest, has turned back my wrath from the Israelites by manifesting such zeal among them on my behalf that in my jealousy I did not consume the Israelites. [12]Therefore say, 'I hereby grant him my covenant of peace. [13]It shall be for him and for his descendants after him a covenant of perpetual priesthood, because he was zealous for his God, and made atonement for the Israelites.'"

14 The name of the slain Israelite man, who was killed with the Midianite woman, was Zimri son of Salu, head of an ancestral house belonging to the Simeonites. [15]The name of the Midianite woman who was killed was Cozbi daughter of Zur, who was the head of a clan, an ancestral house in Midian. 16 The LORD said to Moses, [17]"Harass the Midianites, and defeat them; [18]for they have harassed you by the trickery with which they deceived you in the affair of Peor, and in the affair of Cozbi, the daughter of a leader of Midian, their sister; she was killed on the day of the plague that resulted from Peor."

26 A Census of the New Generation

After the plague the LORD said to Moses and to Eleazar son of Aaron the priest, [2]"Take a census of the whole congregation of the Israelites, from twenty years old and upward, by their ancestral houses, everyone in Israel able to go to war." [3]Moses and Eleazar the priest spoke with them in the plains of Moab by the Jordan opposite Jericho, saying, [4]"Take a census of the people,[a] from

twenty years old and upward," as the LORD commanded Moses.

The Israelites, who came out of the land of Egypt, were:

5 Reuben, the firstborn of Israel. The descendants of Reuben: of Hanoch, the clan of the Hanochites; of Pallu, the clan of the Palluites; [6]of Hezron, the clan of the Hezronites; of Carmi, the clan of the Carmites. [7]These are the clans of the Reubenites; the number of those enrolled was forty-three thousand seven hundred thirty. [8]And the descendants of Pallu: Eliab. [9]The descendants of Eliab: Nemuel, Dathan, and Abiram. These are the same Dathan and Abiram, chosen from the congregation, who rebelled against Moses and Aaron in the company of Korah, when they rebelled against the LORD, [10]and the earth opened its mouth and swallowed them up along with Korah, when that company died, when the fire devoured two hundred fifty men; and they became a warning. [11]Notwithstanding, the sons of Korah did not die.

12 The descendants of Simeon by their clans: of Nemuel, the clan of the Nemuelites; of Jamin, the clan of the Jaminites; of Jachin, the clan of the Jachinites; [13]of Zerah, the clan of the Zerahites; of Shaul, the clan of the Shaulites.[b] [14]These are the clans of the Simeonites, twenty-two thousand two hundred.

15 The children of Gad by their clans: of Zephon, the clan of the Zephonites; of Haggi, the clan of the Haggites; of Shuni, the clan of the Shunites; [16]of Ozni, the clan of the Oznites; of Eri, the clan of the Erites; [17]of Arod, the clan of the Arodites; of Areli, the clan of the Arelites. [18]These are the clans of the Gadites: the number of those enrolled was forty thousand five hundred.

19 The sons of Judah: Er and Onan; Er and Onan died in the land of Canaan. [20]The descendants of Judah by their clans were: of Shelah, the clan of the Shelanites; of Perez, the clan of the Perezites; of Zerah, the clan of the Zerahites. [21]The descendants of Perez were: of Hezron, the clan of the Hezronites; of Hamul, the clan of the Hamulites. [22]These are the clans of Judah: the number of those enrolled was seventy-six thousand five hundred.

23 The descendants of Issachar by their clans: of Tola, the clan of the Tolaites; of Puvah, the clan of the Punites; [24]of Jashub, the clan of the Jashubites; of Shimron, the clan of the Shimronites. [25]These are the clans of Issachar: sixty-four thousand three hundred enrolled.

a Heb lacks *take a census of the people*: Compare verse 2   b Or *Saul . . . Saulites*

26 The descendants of Zebulun by their clans: of Sered, the clan of the Seredites; of Elon, the clan of the Elonites; of Jahleel, the clan of the Jahleelites. [27] These are the clans of the Zebulunites; the number of those enrolled was sixty thousand five hundred.

28 The sons of Joseph by their clans: Manasseh and Ephraim. [29] The descendants of Manasseh: of Machir, the clan of the Machirites; and Machir was the father of Gilead; of Gilead, the clan of the Gileadites. [30] These are the descendants of Gilead: of Iezer, the clan of the Iezerites; of Helek, the clan of the Helekites; [31] and of Asriel, the clan of the Asrielites; and of Shechem, the clan of the Shechemites; [32] and of Shemida, the clan of the Shemidaites; and of Hepher, the clan of the Hepherites. [33] Now Zelophehad son of Hepher had no sons, but daughters: and the names of the daughters of Zelophehad were Mahlah, Noah, Hoglah, Milcah, and Tirzah. [34] These are the clans of Manasseh; the number of those enrolled was fifty-two thousand seven hundred.

35 These are the descendants of Ephraim according to their clans: of Shuthelah, the clan of the Shuthelahites; of Becher, the clan of the Becherites; of Tahan, the clan of the Tahanites. [36] And these are the descendants of Shuthelah: of Eran, the clan of the Eranites. [37] These are the clans of the Ephraimites: the number of those enrolled was thirty-two thousand five hundred. These are the descendants of Joseph by their clans.

38 The descendants of Benjamin by their clans: of Bela, the clan of the Belaites; of Ashbel, the clan of the Ashbelites; of Ahiram, the clan of the Ahiramites; [39] of Shephupham, the clan of the Shuphamites; of Hupham, the clan of the Huphamites. [40] And the sons of Bela were Ard and Naaman: of Ard, the clan of the Ardites; of Naaman, the clan of the Naamites. [41] These are the descendants of Benjamin by their clans; the number of those enrolled was forty-five thousand six hundred.

42 These are the descendants of Dan by their clans: of Shuham, the clan of the Shuhamites. These are the clans of Dan by their clans. [43] All the clans of the Shuhamites: sixty-four thousand four hundred enrolled.

44 The descendants of Asher by their families: of Imnah, the clan of the Imnites; of Ishvi, the clan of the Ishvites; of Beriah, the clan of the Beriites. [45] Of the descendants of Beriah: of Heber, the clan of the Heberites; of Malchiel, the clan of the Mal-

chielites. [46] And the name of the daughter of Asher was Serah. [47] These are the clans of the Asherites: the number of those enrolled was fifty-three thousand four hundred.

48 The descendants of Naphtali by their clans: of Jahzeel, the clan of the Jahzeelites; of Guni, the clan of the Gunites; [49] of Jezer, the clan of the Jezerites; of Shillem, the clan of the Shillemites. [50] These are the Naphtalites[a] by their clans: the number of those enrolled was forty-five thousand four hundred.

51 This was the number of the Israelites enrolled: six hundred and one thousand seven hundred thirty.

52 The LORD spoke to Moses, saying: [53] To these the land shall be apportioned for inheritance according to the number of names. [54] To a large tribe you shall give a large inheritance, and to a small tribe you shall give a small inheritance; every tribe shall be given its inheritance according to its enrollment. [55] But the land shall be apportioned by lot; according to the names of their ancestral tribes they shall inherit. [56] Their inheritance shall be apportioned according to lot between the larger and the smaller.

57 This is the enrollment of the Levites by their clans: of Gershon, the clan of the Gershonites; of Kohath, the clan of the Kohathites; of Merari, the clan of the Merarites. [58] These are the clans of Levi: the clan of the Libnites, the clan of the Hebronites, the clan of the Mahlites, the clan of the Mushites, the clan of the Korahites. Now Kohath was the father of Amram. [59] The name of Amram's wife was Jochebed daughter of Levi, who was born to Levi in Egypt; and she bore to Amram: Aaron, Moses, and their sister Miriam. [60] To Aaron were born Nadab, Abihu, Eleazar, and Ithamar. [61] But Nadab and Abihu died when they offered unholy fire before the LORD. [62] The number of those enrolled was twenty-three thousand, every male one month old and upward; for they were not enrolled among the Israelites because there was no allotment given to them among the Israelites.

63 These were those enrolled by Moses and Eleazar the priest, who enrolled the Israelites in the plains of Moab by the Jordan opposite Jericho. [64] Among these there was not one of those enrolled by Moses and Aaron the priest, who had enrolled the Israelites in the wilderness of Sinai. [65] For the LORD had said of them, "They shall die in the wilderness." Not one of them was left, except Caleb son of Jephunneh and Joshua son of Nun.

a Heb *clans of Naphtali*

The Daughters of Zelophehad

27 Then the daughters of Zelophehad came forward. Zelophehad was son of Hepher son of Gilead son of Machir son of Manasseh son of Joseph, a member of the Manassite clans. The names of his daughters were: Mahlah, Noah, Hoglah, Milcah, and Tirzah. ²They stood before Moses, Eleazar the priest, the leaders, and all the congregation, at the entrance of the tent of meeting, and they said, ³"Our father died in the wilderness; he was not among the company of those who gathered themselves together against the LORD in the company of Korah, but died for his own sin; and he had no sons. ⁴Why should the name of our father be taken away from his clan because he had no son? Give to us a possession among our father's brothers."

5 Moses brought their case before the LORD. ⁶And the LORD spoke to Moses, saying: ⁷The daughters of Zelophehad are right in what they are saying; you shall indeed let them possess an inheritance among their father's brothers and pass the inheritance of their father on to them. ⁸You shall also say to the Israelites, "If a man dies, and has no son, then you shall pass his inheritance on to his daughter. ⁹If he has no daughter, then you shall give his inheritance to his brothers. ¹⁰If he has no brothers, then you shall give his inheritance to his father's brothers. ¹¹And if his father has no brothers, then you shall give his inheritance to the nearest kinsman of his clan, and he shall possess it. It shall be for the Israelites a statute and ordinance, as the LORD commanded Moses."

Joshua Appointed Moses' Successor

12 The LORD said to Moses, "Go up this mountain of the Abarim range, and see the land that I have given to the Israelites. ¹³When you have seen it, you also shall be gathered to your people, as your brother Aaron was, ¹⁴because you rebelled against my word in the wilderness of Zin when the congregation quarreled with me.[a] You did not show my holiness before their eyes at the waters." (These are the waters of Meribath-kadesh in the wilderness of Zin.) ¹⁵Moses spoke to the LORD, saying, ¹⁶"Let the LORD, the God of the spirits of all flesh, appoint someone over the congregation ¹⁷who shall go out before them and come in before them, who shall lead them out and bring them in, so that the congregation of the LORD may not be like sheep without a shepherd." ¹⁸So the LORD said to Moses, "Take Joshua son of Nun, a man in whom is the spirit, and lay your hand

upon him; ¹⁹have him stand before Eleazar the priest and all the congregation, and commission him in their sight. ²⁰You shall give him some of your authority, so that all the congregation of the Israelites may obey. ²¹But he shall stand before Eleazar the priest, who shall inquire for him by the decision of the Urim before the LORD; at his word they shall go out, and at his word they shall come in, both he and all the Israelites with him, the whole congregation." ²²So Moses did as the LORD commanded him. He took Joshua and had him stand before Eleazar the priest and the whole congregation; ²³he laid his hands on him and commissioned him—as the LORD had directed through Moses.

Daily Offerings

28 The LORD spoke to Moses, saying: ²Command the Israelites, and say to them: My offering, the food for my offerings by fire, my pleasing odor, you shall take care to offer to me at its appointed time. ³And you shall say to them, This is the offering by fire that you shall offer to the LORD: two male lambs a year old without blemish, daily, as a regular offering. ⁴One lamb you shall offer in the morning, and the other lamb you shall offer at twilight;[b] ⁵also one-tenth of an ephah of choice flour for a grain offering, mixed with one-fourth of a hin of beaten oil. ⁶It is a regular burnt offering, ordained at Mount Sinai for a pleasing odor, an offering by fire to the LORD. ⁷Its drink offering shall be one-fourth of a hin for each lamb; in the sanctuary you shall pour out a drink offering of strong drink to the LORD. ⁸The other lamb you shall offer at twilight[b] with a grain offering and a drink offering like the one in the morning; you shall offer it as an offering by fire, a pleasing odor to the LORD.

Sabbath Offerings

9 On the sabbath day: two male lambs a year old without blemish, and two-tenths of an ephah of choice flour for a grain offering, mixed with oil, and its drink offering— ¹⁰this is the burnt offering for every sabbath, in addition to the regular burnt offering and its drink offering.

Monthly Offerings

11 At the beginnings of your months you shall offer a burnt offering to the LORD: two young bulls, one ram, seven male lambs a year old without blemish; ¹²also three-tenths of an ephah of choice flour

---

a Heb lacks *with me*   b Heb *between the two evenings*

for a grain offering, mixed with oil, for each bull; and two-tenths of choice flour for a grain offering, mixed with oil, for the one ram; [13]and one-tenth of choice flour mixed with oil as a grain offering for every lamb—a burnt offering of pleasing odor, an offering by fire to the LORD. [14]Their drink offerings shall be half a hin of wine for a bull, one-third of a hin for a ram, and one-fourth of a hin for a lamb. This is the burnt offering of every month throughout the months of the year. [15]And there shall be one male goat for a sin offering to the LORD; it shall be offered in addition to the regular burnt offering and its drink offering.

Offerings at Passover

16 On the fourteenth day of the first month there shall be a passover offering to the LORD. [17]And on the fifteenth day of this month is a festival; seven days shall unleavened bread be eaten. [18]On the first day there shall be a holy convocation. You shall not work at your occupations. [19]You shall offer an offering by fire, a burnt offering to the LORD: two young bulls, one ram, and seven male lambs a year old; see that they are without blemish. [20]Their grain offering shall be of choice flour mixed with oil: three-tenths of an ephah shall you offer for a bull, and two-tenths for a ram; [21]one-tenth shall you offer for each of the seven lambs; [22]also one male goat for a sin offering, to make atonement for you. [23]You shall offer these in addition to the burnt offering of the morning, which belongs to the regular burnt offering. [24]In the same way you shall offer daily, for seven days, the food of an offering by fire, a pleasing odor to the LORD; it shall be offered in addition to the regular burnt offering and its drink offering. [25]And on the seventh day you shall have a holy convocation; you shall not work at your occupations.

Offerings at the Festival of Weeks

26 On the day of the first fruits, when you offer a grain offering of new grain to the LORD at your festival of weeks, you shall have a holy convocation; you shall not work at your occupations. [27]You shall offer a burnt offering, a pleasing odor to the LORD: two young bulls, one ram, seven male lambs a year old. [28]Their grain offering shall be of choice flour mixed with oil, three-tenths of an ephah for each bull, two-tenths for one ram, [29]one-tenth for each of the seven lambs; [30]with one male goat, to make

atonement for you. [31]In addition to the regular burnt offering with its grain offering, you shall offer them and their drink offering. They shall be without blemish.

29 ### Offerings at the Festival of Trumpets
On the first day of the seventh month you shall have a holy convocation; you shall not work at your occupations. It is a day for you to blow the trumpets, [2]and you shall offer a burnt offering, a pleasing odor to the LORD: one young bull, one ram, seven male lambs a year old without blemish. [3]Their grain offering shall be of choice flour mixed with oil, three-tenths of one ephah for the bull, two-tenths for the ram, [4]and one-tenth for each of the seven lambs; [5]with one male goat for a sin offering, to make atonement for you. [6]These are in addition to the burnt offering of the new moon and its grain offering, and the regular burnt offering and its grain offering, and their drink offerings, according to the ordinance for them, a pleasing odor, an offering by fire to the LORD.

STUDY IT!

More Jewish Festivals
Numbers 29:1–11

Here we find the instructions for two more Jewish festivals. (For other Jewish festivals, see "Study It: Israelite Parties," near Exodus 34:18–26.) The Festival of Trumpets is a fall celebration calling for a day of rest marked by trumpet blasts and sacrifices. It came to be called Rosh Hashanah, the Jewish New Year.

On the tenth day of the seventh month, Israelites celebrated the Day of Atonement (Yom Kippur). On this solemn day of penance and fasting, the high priest laid the sins of the people on a so-called scapegoat (Leviticus 16:20-21), then ran the beast into the wilderness, thus symbolically purifying the nation and bringing the people freedom from their sin.

Offerings on the Day of Atonement

7 On the tenth day of this seventh month you shall have a holy convocation, and deny yourselves;[a] you shall do no work. [8]You shall offer a burnt offering to the LORD, a pleasing odor: one young bull, one ram, seven male lambs a year old. They shall be without blemish. [9]Their grain offering shall be of choice flour mixed with oil, three-tenths of an ephah for the bull, two-tenths for the one ram, [10]one-tenth for each of the seven lambs; [11]with one male goat for a sin offering, in addition to the sin offering of atonement, and the regular burnt offering and its grain offering, and their drink offerings.

Offerings at the Festival of Booths

12 On the fifteenth day of the seventh month you shall have a holy convocation; you shall not work at your occupations. You shall celebrate a festival to the LORD seven days. [13]You shall offer a burnt offering, an offering by fire, a pleasing odor to the LORD: thirteen young bulls, two rams, fourteen male lambs a year old. They shall be without blemish. [14]Their grain offering shall be of choice flour mixed with oil, three-tenths of an ephah for each of the thirteen bulls, two-tenths for each of the two rams, [15]and one-tenth for each of the fourteen lambs; [16]also one male goat for a sin offering, in addition to the regular burnt offering, its grain offering and its drink offering.

17 On the second day: twelve young bulls, two rams, fourteen male lambs a year old without blemish, [18]with the grain offering and the drink offerings for the bulls, for the rams, and for the lambs, as prescribed in accordance with their number; [19]also one male goat for a sin offering, in addition to the regular burnt offering and its grain offering, and their drink offerings.

20 On the third day: eleven bulls, two rams, fourteen male lambs a year old without blemish, [21]with the grain offering and the drink offerings for the bulls, for the rams, and for the lambs, as prescribed in accordance with their number; [22]also one male goat for a sin offering, in addition to the regular burnt offering and its grain offering and its drink offering.

23 On the fourth day: ten bulls, two rams, fourteen male lambs a year old without blemish, [24]with the grain offering and the drink offerings for the bulls, for the rams, and for the lambs, as prescribed in accordance with their number; [25]also one male goat for a sin offering, in addition to the regular burnt offering, its grain offering and its drink offering.

26 On the fifth day: nine bulls, two rams, fourteen male lambs a year old without blemish, [27]with the grain offering and the drink offerings for the bulls, for the rams, and for the lambs, as prescribed in accordance with their number; [28]also one male goat for a sin offering, in addition to the regular burnt offering and its grain offering and its drink offering.

29 On the sixth day: eight bulls, two rams, fourteen male lambs a year old without blemish, [30]with the grain offering and the drink offerings for the bulls, for the rams, and for the lambs, as prescribed in accordance with their number; [31]also one male goat for a sin offering, in addition to the regular burnt offering, its grain offering, and its drink offerings.

32 On the seventh day: seven bulls, two rams, fourteen male lambs a year old without blemish, [33]with the grain offering and the drink offerings for the bulls, for the rams, and for the lambs, as prescribed in accordance with their number; [34]also one male goat for a sin offering, besides the regular burnt offering, its grain offering, and its drink offering.

35 On the eighth day you shall have a solemn assembly; you shall not work at your occupations. [36]You shall offer a burnt offering, an offering by fire, a pleasing odor to the LORD: one bull, one ram, seven male lambs a year old without blemish, [37]and the grain offering and the drink offerings for the bull, for the ram, and for the lambs, as prescribed in accordance with their number; [38]also one male goat for a sin offering, in addition to the regular burnt offering and its grain offering and its drink offering.

39 These you shall offer to the LORD at your appointed festivals, in addition to your votive offerings and your freewill offerings, as your burnt offerings, your grain offerings, your drink offerings, and your offerings of well-being.

40[b] So Moses told the Israelites everything just as the LORD had commanded Moses.

Vows Made by Women

30 Then Moses said to the heads of the tribes of the Israelites: This is what the LORD has commanded. [2]When a man makes a vow to the LORD, or swears an oath to bind himself by a pledge, he shall not break his word; he shall do according to all that proceeds out of his mouth.

3 When a woman makes a vow to the LORD, or binds herself by a pledge, while within her father's

a Or *and fast*   b Ch 30.1 in Heb

STUDY IT!

Making a Vow · Numbers 30:2–5

"Vow." Such a simple word. Three letters. One syllable. But its significance is huge.

We rarely even use the word "vow," except for the most important promises we make—like those made at a wedding. Vows were very important to the Israelites too, as we can see from the laws in **Numbers 30**. We can also see the patriarchal nature of the ancient culture, in which women had few rights. For example, a father or a husband could veto a woman's vows. Such laws were acceptable in the Israelites' patriarchal society, but not in ours today. Still, the laws do show us that the Israelites understood the importance of vows and took them seriously.

From a faith perspective, a person making a vow is making a deep, binding promise before God. A vow cannot fully be captured on paper. It must be internalized. A vow must be lived out. It's the foundation for a life choice—one we keep choosing to follow every day.

house, in her youth, [4] and her father hears of her vow or her pledge by which she has bound herself, and says nothing to her; then all her vows shall stand, and any pledge by which she has bound herself shall stand. [5] But if her father expresses disapproval to her at the time that he hears of it, no vow of hers, and no pledge by which she has bound herself, shall stand; and the LORD will forgive her, because her father had expressed to her his disapproval.

[6] If she marries, while obligated by her vows or any thoughtless utterance of her lips by which she has bound herself, [7] and her husband hears of it and says nothing to her at the time that he hears, then her vows shall stand, and her pledges by which she has bound herself shall stand. [8] But if, at the time that her husband hears of it, he expresses disapproval to her, then he shall nullify the vow by which she was obligated, or the thoughtless utterance of her lips, by which she bound herself; and the LORD will forgive her. [9] (But every vow of a widow or of a divorced woman, by which she has bound herself, shall be binding upon her.) [10] And if she made a vow in her husband's house, or bound herself by a pledge with an oath, [11] and her husband heard it and said nothing to her, and did not express disapproval to her, then all her vows shall stand, and any pledge by which she bound herself shall stand. [12] But if her husband nullifies them at the time that he hears them, then whatever proceeds out of her lips concerning her vows, or concerning her pledge of herself, shall not stand. Her husband has nullified them, and the LORD will forgive her. [13] Any vow or any

binding oath to deny herself,[a] her husband may allow to stand, or her husband may nullify. [14] But if her husband says nothing to her from day to day,[b] then he validates all her vows, or all her pledges, by which she is obligated; he has validated them, because he said nothing to her at the time that he heard of them. [15] But if he nullifies them some time after he has heard of them, then he shall bear her guilt.

[16] These are the statutes that the LORD commanded Moses concerning a husband and his wife, and a father and his daughter while she is still young and in her father's house.

War against Midian

31 The LORD spoke to Moses, saying, [2] "Avenge the Israelites on the Midianites; afterward you shall be gathered to your people." [3] So Moses said to the people, "Arm some of your number for the war, so that they may go against Midian, to execute the LORD's vengeance on Midian. [4] You shall send a thousand from each of the tribes of Israel to the war." [5] So out of the thousands of Israel, a thousand from each tribe were conscripted, twelve thousand armed for battle. [6] Moses sent them to the war, a thousand from each tribe, along with Phinehas son of Eleazar the priest,[c] with the vessels of the sanctuary and the trumpets for sounding the alarm in his hand. [7] They did battle against Midian, as the LORD had commanded Moses, and killed every male. [8] They killed the kings of Midian: Evi, Rekem, Zur, Hur, and Reba, the five kings of Midian, in addition to others who were slain by them;

a Or *to fast*   b Or *from that day to the next*   c Gk: Heb adds *to the war* and they also killed Balaam son of Beor with the sword. [9] The Israelites took the women of Midian and their little ones captive; and they took all their cattle, their flocks, and all their goods as booty. [10] All their towns where they had settled, and all their encampments, they burned, [11] but they took all the spoil and all the booty, both people and animals. [12] Then they brought the captives and the booty and the spoil to Moses, to Eleazar the priest, and to the congregation of the Israelites, at the camp on the plains of Moab by the Jordan at Jericho.

Return from the War

13 Moses, Eleazar the priest, and all the leaders of the congregation went to meet them outside the camp. [14] Moses became angry with the officers of the army, the commanders of thousands and the commanders of hundreds, who had come from service in the war. [15] Moses said to them, "Have you allowed all the women to live? [16] These women here, on Balaam's advice, made the Israelites act treacherously against the LORD in the affair of Peor, so that the plague came among the congregation of the LORD. [17] Now therefore, kill every male among the little ones, and kill every woman who has known a man by sleeping with him. [18] But all the young girls who have not known a man by sleeping with him, keep alive for yourselves. [19] Camp outside the camp seven days; whoever of you has killed any person or touched a corpse, purify yourselves and your captives on the third and on the seventh day. [20] You shall purify every garment, every article of skin, everything made of goats' hair, and every article of wood."

21 Eleazar the priest said to the troops who had gone to battle: "This is the statute of the law that the LORD has commanded Moses: [22] gold, silver, bronze, iron, tin, and lead— [23] everything that can withstand fire, shall be passed through fire, and it shall be clean. Nevertheless it shall also be purified with the water for purification; and whatever cannot withstand fire, shall be passed through the water. [24] You must wash your clothes on the seventh day, and you shall be clean; afterward you may come into the camp."

Disposition of Captives and Booty

25 The LORD spoke to Moses, saying, [26] "You and Eleazar the priest and the heads of the ancestral houses of the congregation make an inventory of the booty captured, both human and animal. [27] Divide the booty into two parts, between the warriors who went out to battle and all the congregation. [28] From the share of the warriors who went out to battle, set aside as tribute for the LORD, one item out of every five hundred, whether persons, oxen, donkeys, sheep, or goats. [29] Take it from their half and give it to Eleazar the priest as an offering to the LORD. [30] But from the Israelites' half you shall take one out of every fifty, whether persons, oxen, donkeys, sheep, or goats—all the animals—and give them to the Levites who have charge of the tabernacle of the LORD."

31 Then Moses and Eleazar the priest did as the LORD had commanded Moses:

32 The booty remaining from the spoil that the troops had taken totaled six hundred seventy-five thousand sheep, [33] seventy-two thousand oxen, [34] sixty-one thousand donkeys, [35] and thirty-two thousand persons in all, women who had not known a man by sleeping with him.

36 The half-share, the portion of those who had gone out to war, was in number three hundred thirty-seven thousand five hundred sheep and goats, [37] and the LORD's tribute of sheep and goats was six hundred seventy-five. [38] The oxen were thirty-six thousand, of which the LORD's tribute was seventy two. [39] The donkeys were thirty thousand five hundred, of which the LORD's tribute was sixty-one. [40] The persons were sixteen thousand, of which the LORD's tribute was thirty-two persons. [41] Moses gave the tribute, the offering for the LORD, to Eleazar the priest, as the LORD had commanded Moses.

42 As for the Israelites' half, which Moses separated from that of the troops, [43] the congregation's half was three hundred thirty-seven thousand five hundred sheep and goats, [44] thirty-six thousand oxen, [45] thirty thousand five hundred donkeys, [46] and sixteen thousand persons. [47] From the Israelites' half Moses took one of every fifty, both of persons and of animals, and gave them to the Levites who had charge of the tabernacle of the LORD; as the LORD had commanded Moses.

48 Then the officers who were over the thousands of the army, the commanders of thousands and the commanders of hundreds, approached Moses, [49] and said to Moses, "Your servants have counted the warriors who are under our command, and not one of us is missing. [50] And we have brought the LORD's

offering, what each of us found, articles of gold, armlets and bracelets, signet rings, earrings, and pendants, to make atonement for ourselves before the Lord." ⁵¹Moses and Eleazar the priest received the gold from them, all in the form of crafted articles. ⁵²And all the gold of the offering that they offered to the Lord, from the commanders of thousands and the commanders of hundreds, was sixteen thousand seven hundred fifty shekels. ⁵³(The troops had all taken plunder for themselves.) ⁵⁴So Moses and Eleazar the priest received the gold from the commanders of thousands and of hundreds, and brought it into the tent of meeting as a memorial for the Israelites before the Lord.

Conquest and Division of Transjordan

32 Now the Reubenites and the Gadites owned a very great number of cattle. When they saw that the land of Jazer and the land of Gilead was a good place for cattle, ²the Gadites and the Reubenites came and spoke to Moses, to Eleazar the priest, and to the leaders of the congregation, saying, ³"Ataroth, Dibon, Jazer, Nimrah, Heshbon, Elealeh, Sebam, Nebo, and Beon— ⁴the land that the Lord subdued before the congregation of Israel—is a land for cattle; and your servants have cattle." ⁵They continued, "If we have found favor in your sight, let this land be given to your servants for a possession; do not make us cross the Jordan."

6 But Moses said to the Gadites and to the Reubenites, "Shall your brothers go to war while you sit here? ⁷Why will you discourage the hearts of the Israelites from going over into the land that the Lord has given them? ⁸Your fathers did this, when I sent them from Kadesh-barnea to see the land. ⁹When they went up to the Wadi Eshcol and saw the land, they discouraged the hearts of the Israelites from going into the land that the Lord had given them. ¹⁰The Lord's anger was kindled on that day and he swore, saying, ¹¹'Surely none of the people who came up out of Egypt, from twenty years old and upward, shall see the land that I swore to give to Abraham, to Isaac, and to Jacob, because they have not unreservedly followed me— ¹²none except Caleb son of Jephunneh the Kenizzite and Joshua son of Nun, for they have unreservedly followed the Lord.' ¹³And the Lord's anger was kindled against Israel, and he made them wander in the wilderness for forty years, until all the generation that had done evil in the sight of the Lord

had disappeared. ¹⁴And now you, a brood of sinners, have risen in place of your fathers, to increase the Lord's fierce anger against Israel! ¹⁵If you turn away from following him, he will again abandon them in the wilderness; and you will destroy all this people."

16 Then they came up to him and said, "We will build sheepfolds here for our flocks, and towns for our little ones, ¹⁷but we will take up arms as a vanguard[a] before the Israelites, until we have brought them to their place. Meanwhile our little ones will stay in the fortified towns because of the inhabitants of the land. ¹⁸We will not return to our homes until all the Israelites have obtained their inheritance. ¹⁹We will not inherit with them on the other side of the Jordan and beyond, because our inheritance has come to us on this side of the Jordan to the east."

20 So Moses said to them, "If you do this—if you take up arms to go before the Lord for the war, ²¹and all those of you who bear arms cross the Jordan before the Lord, until he has driven out his enemies from before him ²²and the land is subdued before the Lord—then after that you may return and be free of obligation to the Lord and to Israel, and this land shall be your possession before the Lord. ²³But if you do not do this, you have sinned against the Lord; and be sure your sin will find you out. ²⁴Build towns for your little ones, and folds for your flocks; but do what you have promised."

25 Then the Gadites and the Reubenites said to Moses, "Your servants will do as my lord commands. ²⁶Our little ones, our wives, our flocks, and all our livestock shall remain there in the towns of Gilead; ²⁷but your servants will cross over, everyone armed for war, to do battle for the Lord, just as my lord orders."

28 So Moses gave command concerning them to Eleazar the priest, to Joshua son of Nun, and to the heads of the ancestral houses of the Israelite tribes. ²⁹And Moses said to them, "If the Gadites and the Reubenites, everyone armed for battle before the Lord, will cross over the Jordan with you and the land shall be subdued before you, then you shall give them the land of Gilead for a possession; ³⁰but if they will not cross over with you armed, they shall have possessions among you in the land of Canaan." ³¹The Gadites and the Reubenites answered, "As the Lord has spoken to your servants, so we will do. ³²We will cross over armed

a Cn: Heb *hurrying*

before the LORD into the land of Canaan, but the possession of our inheritance shall remain with us on this side of[a] the Jordan."

33 Moses gave to them—to the Gadites and to the Reubenites and to the half-tribe of Manasseh son of Joseph—the kingdom of King Sihon of the Amorites and the kingdom of King Og of Bashan, the land and its towns, with the territories of the surrounding towns. [34]And the Gadites rebuilt Dibon, Ataroth, Aroer, [35]Atroth-shophan, Jazer, Jogbehah, [36]Beth-nimrah, and Beth-haran, fortified cities, and folds for sheep. [37]And the Reubenites rebuilt Heshbon, Elealeh, Kiriathaim, [38]Nebo, and Baal-meon (some names being changed), and Sibmah; and they gave names to the towns that they rebuilt. [39]The descendants of Machir son of Manasseh went to Gilead, captured it, and dispossessed the Amorites who were there; [40]so Moses gave Gilead to Machir son of Manasseh, and he settled there. [41]Jair son of Manasseh went and captured their villages, and renamed them Havvoth-jair.[b] [42]And Nobah went and captured Kenath and its villages, and renamed it Nobah after himself.

33 The Stages of Israel's Journey from Egypt

These are the stages by which the Israelites went out of the land of Egypt in military formation under the leadership of Moses and Aaron. [2]Moses wrote down their starting points, stage by stage, by command of the LORD; and these are their stages according to their starting places. [3]They set out from Rameses in the first month, on the fifteenth day of the first month; on the day after the passover the Israelites went out boldly in the sight of all the Egyptians, [4]while the Egyptians were burying all their firstborn, whom the LORD had struck down among them. The LORD executed judgments even against their gods.

5 So the Israelites set out from Rameses, and camped at Succoth. [6]They set out from Succoth, and camped at Etham, which is on the edge of the wilderness. [7]They set out from Etham, and turned back to Pi-hahiroth, which faces Baal-zephon; and they camped before Migdol. [8]They set out from Pi-hahiroth, passed through the sea into the wilderness, went a three days' journey in the wilderness of Etham, and camped at Marah. [9]They set out from Marah and came to Elim; at Elim there were twelve springs of water and seventy palm trees, and they camped there.

[10]They set out from Elim and camped by the Red Sea.[c] [11]They set out from the Red Sea[c] and camped in the wilderness of Sin. [12]They set out from the wilderness of Sin and camped at Dophkah. [13]They set out from Dophkah and camped at Alush. [14]They set out from Alush and camped at Rephidim, where there was no water for the people to drink. [15]They set out from Rephidim and camped in the wilderness of Sinai. [16]They set out from the wilderness of Sinai and camped at Kibroth-hattaavah. [17]They set out from Kibroth-hattaavah and camped at Hazeroth. [18]They set out from Hazeroth and camped at Rithmah. [19]They set out from Rithmah and camped at Rimmon-perez. [20]They set out from Rimmon-perez and camped at Libnah. [21]They set out from Libnah and camped at Rissah. [22]They set out from Rissah and camped at Kehelathah. [23]They set out from Kehelathah and camped at Mount Shepher. [24]They set out from Mount Shepher and camped at Haradah. [25]They set out from Haradah and camped at Makheloth. [26]They set out from Makheloth and camped at Tahath. [27]They set out from Tahath and camped at Terah. [28]They set out from Terah and camped at Mithkah. [29]They set out from Mithkah and camped at Hashmonah. [30]They set out from Hashmonah and camped at Moseroth. [31]They set out from Moseroth and camped at Bene-jaakan. [32]They set out from Bene-jaakan and camped at Hor-haggidgad. [33]They set out from Hor-haggidgad and camped at Jotbathah. [34]They set out from Jotbathah and camped at Abronah. [35]They set out from Abronah and camped at Ezion-geber. [36]They set out from Ezion-geber and camped in the wilderness of Zin (that is, Kadesh). [37]They set out from Kadesh and camped at Mount Hor, on the edge of the land of Edom.

38 Aaron the priest went up Mount Hor at the command of the LORD and died there in the fortieth year after the Israelites had come out of the land of Egypt, on the first day of the fifth month. [39]Aaron was one hundred twenty-three years old when he died on Mount Hor.

40 The Canaanite, the king of Arad, who lived in the Negeb in the land of Canaan, heard of the coming of the Israelites.

41 They set out from Mount Hor and camped at Zalmonah. [42]They set out from Zalmonah and camped at Punon. [43]They set out from Punon and camped at Oboth. [44]They set out from Oboth and camped at Iye-abarim, in the territory of

---

a Heb *beyond*   b That is *the villages of Jair*   c Or *Sea of Reeds*

Moab. [45]They set out from Iyim and camped at Dibon-gad. [46]They set out from Dibon-gad and camped at Almon-diblathaim. [47]They set out from Almon-diblathaim and camped in the mountains of Abarim, before Nebo. [48]They set out from the mountains of Abarim and camped in the plains of Moab by the Jordan at Jericho; [49]they camped by the Jordan from Beth-jeshimoth as far as Abel-shittim in the plains of Moab.

Directions for the Conquest of Canaan

50 In the plains of Moab by the Jordan at Jericho, the LORD spoke to Moses, saying: [51]Speak to the Israelites, and say to them: When you cross over the Jordan into the land of Canaan, [52]you shall drive out all the inhabitants of the land from before you, destroy all their figured stones, destroy all their cast images, and demolish all their high places. [53]You shall take possession of the land and settle in it, for I have given you the land to possess. [54]You shall apportion the land by lot according to your clans; to a large one you shall give a large inheritance, and to a small one you shall give a small inheritance; the inheritance shall belong to the person on whom the lot falls; according to your ancestral tribes you shall inherit. [55]But if you do not drive out the inhabitants of the land from before you, then those whom you let remain shall be as barbs in your eyes and thorns in your sides; they shall trouble you in the land where you are settling. [56]And I will do to you as I thought to do to them.

The Boundaries of the Land

34 The LORD spoke to Moses, saying: [2]Command the Israelites, and say to them: When you enter the land of Canaan (this is the land that shall fall to you for an inheritance, the land of Canaan, defined by its boundaries), [3]your south sector shall extend from the wilderness of Zin along the side of Edom. Your southern boundary shall begin from the end of the Dead Sea[a] on the east; [4]your boundary shall turn south of the ascent of Akrabbim, and cross to Zin, and its outer limit shall be south of Kadesh-barnea; then it shall go on to Hazar-addar, and cross to Azmon; [5]the boundary shall turn from Azmon to the Wadi of Egypt, and its termination shall be at the Sea.

6 For the western boundary, you shall have the Great Sea and its[b] coast; this shall be your western boundary.

7 This shall be your northern boundary: from the

Great Sea you shall mark out your line to Mount Hor; [8]from Mount Hor you shall mark it out to Lebo-hamath, and the outer limit of the boundary shall be at Zedad; [9]then the boundary shall extend to Ziphron, and its end shall be at Hazar-enan; this shall be your northern boundary.

10 You shall mark out your eastern boundary from Hazar-enan to Shepham; [11]and the boundary shall continue down from Shepham to Riblah on the east side of Ain; and the boundary shall go down, and reach the eastern slope of the sea of Chinnereth; [12]and the boundary shall go down to the Jordan, and its end shall be at the Dead Sea.[a] This shall be your land with its boundaries all around.

13 Moses commanded the Israelites, saying: This is the land that you shall inherit by lot, which the LORD has commanded to give to the nine tribes and to the half-tribe; [14]for the tribe of the Reubenites by their ancestral houses and the tribe of the Gadites by their ancestral houses have taken their inheritance, and also the half-tribe of Manasseh; [15]the two tribes and the half-tribe have

a Heb *Salt Sea* b Syr: Heb lacks *its*

taken their inheritance beyond the Jordan at Jericho eastward, toward the sunrise.

Tribal Leaders

16 The LORD spoke to Moses, saying: [17]These are the names of the men who shall apportion the land to you for inheritance: the priest Eleazar and Joshua son of Nun. [18]You shall take one leader of every tribe to apportion the land for inheritance. [19]These are the names of the men: Of the tribe of Judah, Caleb son of Jephunneh. [20]Of the tribe of the Simeonites, Shemuel son of Ammihud. [21]Of the tribe of Benjamin, Elidad son of Chislon. [22]Of the tribe of the Danites a leader, Bukki son of Jogli. [23]Of the Josephites: of the tribe of the Manassites a leader, Hanniel son of Ephod, [24]and of the tribe of the Ephraimites a leader, Kemuel son of Shiphtan. [25]Of the tribe of the Zebulunites a leader, Eli-zaphan son of Parnach. [26]Of the tribe of the Issacharites a leader, Paltiel son of Azzan. [27]And of the tribe of the Asherites a leader, Ahihud son of Shelomi. [28]Of the tribe of the Naphtalites a leader, Pedahel son of Ammihud. [29]These were the ones whom the LORD commanded to apportion the inheritance for the Israelites in the land of Canaan.

35 Cities for the Levites

In the plains of Moab by the Jordan at Jericho, the LORD spoke to Moses, saying: [2]Command the Israelites to give, from the inheritance that they possess, towns for the Levites to live in; you shall also give to the Levites pasture lands surrounding the towns. [3]The towns shall be theirs to live in, and their pasture lands shall be for their cattle, for their livestock, and for all their animals. [4]The pasture lands of the towns, which you shall give to the Levites, shall reach from the wall of the town outward a thousand cubits all around. [5]You shall measure, outside the town, for the east side two thousand cubits, for the south side two thousand cubits, for the west side two thousand cubits, and for the north side two thousand cubits, with the town in the middle; this shall belong to them as pasture land for their towns.

6 The towns that you give to the Levites shall include the six cities of refuge, where you shall permit a slayer to flee, and in addition to them you shall give forty-two towns. [7]The towns that you give to the Levites shall total forty-eight, with their pasture lands. [8]And as for the towns that you shall

[a] Heb *without seeing*

give from the possession of the Israelites, from the larger tribes you shall take many, and from the smaller tribes you shall take few; each, in proportion to the inheritance that it obtains, shall give of its towns to the Levites.

Cities of Refuge

9 The LORD spoke to Moses, saying: [10]Speak to the Israelites, and say to them: When you cross the Jordan into the land of Canaan, [11]then you shall select cities to be cities of refuge for you, so that a slayer who kills a person without intent may flee there. [12]The cities shall be for you a refuge from the avenger, so that the slayer may not die until there is a trial before the congregation.

13 The cities that you designate shall be six cities of refuge for you: [14]you shall designate three cities beyond the Jordan, and three cities in the land of Canaan, to be cities of refuge. [15]These six cities shall serve as refuge for the Israelites, for the resident or transient alien among them, so that anyone who kills a person without intent may flee there.

Concerning Murder and Blood Revenge

16 But anyone who strikes another with an iron object, and death ensues, is a murderer; the murderer shall be put to death. [17]Or anyone who strikes another with a stone in hand that could cause death, and death ensues, is a murderer; the murderer shall be put to death. [18]Or anyone who strikes another with a weapon of wood in hand that could cause death, and death ensues, is a murderer; the murderer shall be put to death. [19]The avenger of blood is the one who shall put the murderer to death; when they meet, the avenger of blood shall execute the sentence. [20]Likewise, if someone pushes another from hatred, or hurls something at another, lying in wait, and death ensues, [21]or in enmity strikes another with the hand, and death ensues, then the one who struck the blow shall be put to death; that person is a murderer; the avenger of blood shall put the murderer to death, when they meet.

22 But if someone pushes another suddenly without enmity, or hurls any object without lying in wait, [23]or, while handling any stone that could cause death, unintentionally[a] drops it on another and death ensues, though they were not enemies, and no harm was intended, [24]then the congregation shall judge between the slayer and the avenger of blood, in accordance with these ordinances; [25]and

the congregation shall rescue the slayer from the avenger of blood. Then the congregation shall send the slayer back to the original city of refuge. The slayer shall live in it until the death of the high priest who was anointed with the holy oil. [26]But if the slayer shall at any time go outside the bounds of the original city of refuge, [27]and is found by the avenger of blood outside the bounds of the city of refuge, and is killed by the avenger, no bloodguilt shall be incurred. [28]For the slayer must remain in the city of refuge until the death of the high priest; but after the death of the high priest the slayer may return home.

29 These things shall be a statute and ordinance for you throughout your generations wherever you live.

30 If anyone kills another, the murderer shall be put to death on the evidence of witnesses; but no one shall be put to death on the testimony of a single witness. [31]Moreover you shall accept no ransom for the life of a murderer who is subject to the death penalty; a murderer must be put to death. [32]Nor shall you accept ransom for one who has fled to a city of refuge, enabling the fugitive to return to live in the land before the death of the high priest. [33]You shall not pollute the land in which you live; for blood pollutes the land, and no expiation can be made for the land, for the blood that is shed in it, except by the blood of the one who shed it. [34]You shall not defile the land in which you live, in which I also dwell; for I the LORD dwell among the Israelites.

Marriage of Female Heirs

36 The heads of the ancestral houses of the clans of the descendants of Gilead son of Machir son of Manasseh, of the Josephite clans, came forward and spoke in the presence of Moses and the leaders, the heads of the ancestral houses of the Israelites; [2]they said, "The LORD commanded my lord to give the land for inheritance by lot to the Israelites; and my lord was commanded by the LORD to give the inheritance of our brother Zelophehad to his daughters. [3]But if they are married into another Israelite tribe, then their inheritance will be taken from the inheritance of our ancestors and added to the inheritance of the tribe into which they marry; so it will be taken away from the allotted portion of our inheritance. [4]And when the jubilee of the Israelites comes, then their inheritance will be added to the inheritance of the tribe into which they have married; and their inheritance will be taken from the inheritance of our ancestral tribe."

5 Then Moses commanded the Israelites according to the word of the LORD, saying, "The descendants of the tribe of Joseph are right in what they are saying. [6]This is what the LORD commands concerning the daughters of Zelophehad, 'Let them marry whom they think best; only it must be into a clan of their father's tribe that they are married, [7]so that no inheritance of the Israelites shall be transferred from one tribe to another; for all Israelites shall retain the inheritance of their ancestral tribes. [8]Every daughter who possesses an inheritance in any tribe of the Israelites shall marry one from the clan of her father's tribe, so that all Israelites may continue to possess their ancestral inheritance. [9]No inheritance shall be transferred from one tribe to another; for each of the tribes of the Israelites shall retain its own inheritance.' "

10 The daughters of Zelophehad did as the LORD had commanded Moses. [11]Mahlah, Tirzah, Hoglah, Milcah, and Noah, the daughters of Zelophehad, married sons of their father's brothers. [12]They were married into the clans of the descendants of Manasseh son of Joseph, and their inheritance remained in the tribe of their father's clan.

13 These are the commandments and the ordinances that the LORD commanded through Moses to the Israelites in the plains of Moab by the Jordan at Jericho.

Deuteronomy

▶▶▶▶▶▶▶▶▶▶▶▶▶▶▶▶▶

If you haven't done so lately, take some time to really listen to a grandparent or older friend. Their stories can be more entertaining than you'd expect. And they're usually filled with wisdom and insight that only comes from years of experience. Deuteronomy is filled with the stories of Moses, the wise leader of Israel who has led the Israelites through the wilderness and now, like an aging grandparent, shares instruction and encourages them not to forget their covenant with God.

IN DEPTH

The word "Deuteronomy" means "second law" in Greek. The first law was given by God on Mount Sinai to guide Israel in its wilderness journey. Deuteronomy is a second law, or a second giving of the law, as Moses presents and applies the law to the Israelites on the verge of entering the promised land. Because Moses will not go with them into the promised land, this collection of his teachings serves as a reminder to the people to live by the covenant.

Deuteronomy also includes some difficult teachings and laws that are no longer relevant in our culture today. For example, we do not stone people caught in adultery (Deuteronomy 22:22-24), or (luckily for you) rebellious children (Deuteronomy 21:18-21). We do not offer burnt sacrifices (Deuteronomy 12:13), make tassels on the four corners of our cloaks (Deuteronomy 22:12), or concern ourselves with shaving our forelocks (Deuteronomy 14:1). But that doesn't mean this book has no meaning for us. The law showed people their need for God. It's clear that none of the Israelites were able to perfectly follow all of God's laws—just as none of us today can live a perfect life. We deserve judgment just as the Israelites did. Jesus is the only one able to perfectly keep God's law. Jesus completely fulfilled the old law through his death and resurrection (Matthew 5:17-20) and established a new covenant with his followers (Luke 22:20). That new covenant takes away the need to live up to all these rules and regulations and, instead, gives us the assurance through grace that we are accepted by God. God makes us holy and worthy through Jesus, so that we may experience new, abundant life.

More than anything else, Deuteronomy stresses Israel as one people, with one God, one sanctuary, and now one land. These elements not only make Israel a unique people, but also bind them together in unity. The promised land now becomes a symbol of God's blessing and favor, the fulfillment of God's promises in the covenant.

QUICK FACTS

- **Dates Covered:** Just before the Israelites enter the promised land, sometime between 1400 and 1200 B.C.

- **Authors:** Scribes from the eighth century B.C. who adapted the earlier covenant law to Israel's changing situation

- **Themes:** Covenant laws and requirements, and on a deeper level God's faithfulness in sustaining the people; a good reminder to us that we are to obey and respect God as well as trust God's provision and faithfulness

AT A GLANCE

- **Deuteronomy 1:1–4:43** Moses reviews Israel's history.

- **Deuteronomy 4:44–11:32** Moses proclaims obedience to the Torah.

- **Deuteronomy 12–26** Moses adapts the covenant for settlement in the land.

- **Deuteronomy 27–34** Moses gives a farewell address and dies.

Events at Horeb Recalled

1 These are the words that Moses spoke to all Israel beyond the Jordan—in the wilderness, on the plain opposite Suph, between Paran and Tophel, Laban, Hazeroth, and Di-zahab. [2](By the way of Mount Seir it takes eleven days to reach Kadesh-barnea from Horeb.) [3]In the fortieth year, on the first day of the eleventh month, Moses spoke to the Israelites just as the Lord had commanded him to speak to them. [4]This was after he had defeated King Sihon of the Amorites, who reigned in Heshbon, and King Og of Bashan, who reigned in Ashtaroth and[a] in Edrei. [5]Beyond the Jordan in the land of Moab, Moses undertook to expound this law as follows:

6 The Lord our God spoke to us at Horeb, saying, "You have stayed long enough at this mountain. [7]Resume your journey, and go into the hill country of the Amorites as well as into the neighboring regions—the Arabah, the hill country, the Shephelah, the Negeb, and the seacoast—the land of the Canaanites and the Lebanon, as far as the great river, the river Euphrates. [8]See, I have set the land before you; go in and take possession of the land that I[b] swore to your ancestors, to Abraham, to Isaac, and to Jacob, to give to them and to their descendants after them."

Appointment of Tribal Leaders

9 At that time I said to you, "I am unable by myself to bear you. [10]The Lord your God has multiplied you, so that today you are as numerous as the stars of heaven. [11]May the Lord, the God of your ancestors, increase you a thousand times more and bless you, as he has promised you! [12]But how can I bear the heavy burden of your disputes all by myself? [13]Choose for each of your tribes individuals who are wise, discerning, and reputable to be your leaders." [14]You answered me, "The plan you have proposed is a good one." [15]So I took the leaders of your tribes, wise and reputable individuals, and installed them as leaders over you, commanders of thousands, commanders of hundreds, commanders of fifties, commanders of tens, and officials, throughout your tribes. [16]I charged your judges at that time: "Give the members of your community a fair hearing, and judge rightly between one person and another, whether citizen or resident alien. [17]You must not be partial in judging: hear out the small and the great alike; you shall not be intimidated by anyone, for the judgment is God's. Any case that is too hard for you, bring to me, and I will hear it." [18]So I charged you at that time with all the things that you should do.

Israel's Refusal to Enter the Land

19 Then, just as the Lord our God had ordered us, we set out from Horeb and went through all that great and terrible wilderness that you saw, on the way to the hill country of the Amorites, until we reached Kadesh-barnea. [20]I said to you, "You have reached the hill country of the Amorites, which the Lord our God is giving us. [21]See, the Lord your God has given the land to you; go up, take possession, as the Lord, the God of your ancestors, has promised you; do not fear or be dismayed."

22 All of you came to me and said, "Let us send men ahead of us to explore the land for us and bring back a report to us regarding the route by which we should go up and the cities we will come to." [23]The plan seemed good to me, and I selected twelve of you, one from each tribe. [24]They set out and went up into the hill country, and when they reached the Valley of Eshcol they spied it out [25]and gathered some of the land's produce, which they brought down to us. They brought back a report to us, and said, "It is a good land that the Lord our God is giving us."

26 But you were unwilling to go up. You rebelled against the command of the Lord your God; [27]you grumbled in your tents and said, "It is because the Lord hates us that he has brought us out of the land of Egypt, to hand us over to the Amorites to destroy us. [28]Where are we headed? Our kindred have made our hearts melt by reporting, 'The people are stronger and taller than we; the cities are large and fortified up to heaven! We actually saw there the offspring of the Anakim!' " [29]I said to you, "Have no dread or fear of them. [30]The Lord your God, who goes before you, is the one who will fight for you, just as he did for you in Egypt before your very eyes, [31]and in the wilderness, where you saw how the Lord your God carried you, just as one carries a child, all the way that you traveled until you reached this place. [32]But in spite of this, you have no trust in the Lord your God, [33]who goes before you on the way to seek out a place for you to camp, in fire by night, and in the cloud by day, to show you the route you should take."

The Penalty for Israel's Rebellion

34 When the Lord heard your words, he was

a Gk Syr Vg Compare Josh 12.4: Heb lacks and   b Sam Gk: MT *the* Lord wrathful and swore: [35]"Not one of these—not one of this evil generation—shall see the good land that I swore to give to your ancestors, [36]except Caleb son of Jephunneh. He shall see it, and to him and to his descendants I will give the land on which he set foot, because of his complete fidelity to the LORD." [37]Even with me the LORD was angry on your account, saying, "You also shall not enter there. [38]Joshua son of Nun, your assistant, shall enter there; encourage him, for he is the one who will secure Israel's possession of it. [39]And as for your little ones, who you thought would become booty, your children, who today do not yet know right from wrong, they shall enter there; to them I will give it, and they shall take possession of it. [40]But as for you, journey back into the wilderness, in the direction of the Red Sea."[a]

41 You answered me, "We have sinned against the LORD! We are ready to go up and fight, just as the LORD our God commanded us." So all of you strapped on your battle gear, and thought it easy to go up into the hill country. [42]The LORD said to me, "Say to them, 'Do not go up and do not fight, for I am not in the midst of you; otherwise you will be defeated by your enemies.'" [43]Although I told you, you would not listen. You rebelled against the command of the LORD and presumptuously went up into the hill country. [44]The Amorites who lived in that hill country then came out against you and chased you as bees do. They beat you down in Seir as far as Hormah. [45]When you returned and wept before the LORD, the LORD would neither heed your voice nor pay you any attention.

The Desert Years

46 After you had stayed at Kadesh as many days

2 as you did, [1]we journeyed back into the wilderness, in the direction of the Red Sea,[a] as the LORD had told me and skirted Mount Seir for many days. [2]Then the LORD said to me: [3]"You have been skirting this hill country long enough. Head north, [4]and charge the people as follows: You are about to pass through the territory of your kindred, the descendants of Esau, who live in Seir. They will be afraid of you, so, be very careful [5]not to engage in battle with them, for I will not give you even so much as a foot's length of their land, since I have given Mount Seir to Esau as a possession. [6]You shall purchase food from them for money, so that you may eat; and you shall also buy water

from them for money, so that you may drink. [7]Surely the LORD your God has blessed you in all your undertakings; he knows your going through this great wilderness. These forty years the LORD your God has been with you; you have lacked nothing." [8]So we passed by our kin, the descendants of Esau who live in Seir, leaving behind the route of the Arabah, and leaving behind Elath and Ezion-geber.

When we had headed out along the route of the wilderness of Moab, [9]the LORD said to me: "Do not harass Moab or engage them in battle, for I will not give you any of its land as a possession, since I have given Ar as a possession to the descendants of Lot." [10](The Emim—a large and numerous people, as tall as the Anakim—had formerly inhabited it. [11]Like the Anakim, they are usually reckoned as Rephaim, though the Moabites call them Emim. [12]Moreover, the Horim had formerly inhabited Seir, but the descendants of Esau dispossessed them, destroying them and settling in their place, as Israel has done in the land that the LORD gave them as a possession.)

STUDY IT!

Waiting
Deuteronomy 1–3

History shapes us. Whether you groan about your history class in school or you can't get enough of the History Channel, history influences our present and our future. As the Israelites stood on the verge of entering the promised land, Moses didn't want them to forget their history. The first few chapters of Deuteronomy retell all that the Israelites had gone through since Mount Sinai. And it's a retelling of God's faithfulness, including God's final go-ahead ("Go in and take possession of the land," 1:8). Imagine how excited the people were— they'd waited decades for this day of entering the promised land—the fulfillment of promises from long ago. Have you ever had to wait for a promise to be fulfilled? It's tough. But reading about God's faithfulness can help us wait patiently for God's promises to be fulfilled in our lives.

---

a Or *Sea of Reeds*

[13]"Now then, proceed to cross over the Wadi Zered."

So we crossed over the Wadi Zered. [14]And the length of time we had traveled from Kadesh-barnea until we crossed the Wadi Zered was thirty-eight years, until the entire generation of warriors had perished from the camp, as the LORD had sworn concerning them. [15]Indeed, the LORD's own hand was against them, to root them out from the camp, until all had perished.

16 Just as soon as all the warriors had died off from among the people, [17]the LORD spoke to me, saying, [18]"Today you are going to cross the boundary of Moab at Ar. [19]When you approach the frontier of the Ammonites, do not harass them or engage them in battle, for I will not give the land of the Ammonites to you as a possession, because I have given it to the descendants of Lot." [20](It also is usually reckoned as a land of Rephaim. Rephaim formerly inhabited it, though the Ammonites call them Zamzummim, [21]a strong and numerous people, as tall as the Anakim. But the LORD destroyed them from before the Ammonites so that they could dispossess them and settle in their place. [22]He did the same for the descendants of Esau, who live in Seir, by destroying the Horim before them so that they could dispossess them and settle in their place even to this day. [23]As for the Avvim, who had lived in settlements in the vicinity of Gaza, the Caphtorim, who came from Caphtor, destroyed them and settled in their place.) [24]"Proceed on your journey and cross the Wadi Arnon. See, I have handed over to you King Sihon the Amorite of Heshbon, and his land. Begin to take possession by engaging him in battle. [25]This day I will begin to put the dread and fear of you upon the peoples everywhere under heaven; when they hear report of you, they will tremble and be in anguish because of you."

Defeat of King Sihon

26 So I sent messengers from the wilderness of Kedemoth to King Sihon of Heshbon with the following terms of peace: [27]"If you let me pass through your land, I will travel only along the road; I will turn aside neither to the right nor to the left. [28]You shall sell me food for money, so that I may eat, and supply me water for money, so that I may drink. Only allow me to pass through on foot— [29]just as the descendants of Esau who live in Seir have done for me and likewise the Moabites who live in Ar—until I cross the Jordan into the land that the LORD our God is giving us." [30]But King Sihon of Heshbon was not willing to let us pass through, for the LORD your God had hardened his spirit and made his heart defiant in order to hand him over to you, as he has now done.

31 The LORD said to me, "See, I have begun to give Sihon and his land over to you. Begin now to take possession of his land." [32]So when Sihon came out against us, he and all his people for battle at Jahaz, [33]the LORD our God gave him over to us; and we struck him down, along with his offspring and all his people. [34]At that time we captured all his towns, and in each town we utterly destroyed men, women, and children. We left not a single survivor. [35]Only the livestock we kept as spoil for ourselves, as well as the plunder of the towns that we had captured. [36]From Aroer on the edge of the Wadi Arnon (including the town that is in the wadi itself) as far as Gilead, there was no citadel too high for us. The LORD our God gave everything to us. [37]You did not encroach, however, on the land of the Ammonites, avoiding the whole upper region of the Wadi Jabbok as well as the towns of the hill country, just as[a] the LORD our God had charged.

Defeat of King Og

3 When we headed up the road to Bashan, King Og of Bashan came out against us, he and all his people, for battle at Edrei. [2]The LORD said to me, "Do not fear him, for I have handed him over to you, along with his people and his land. Do to him as you did to King Sihon of the Amorites, who reigned in Heshbon." [3]So the LORD our God also handed over to us King Og of Bashan and all his people. We struck him down until not a single survivor was left. [4]At that time we captured all his towns; there was no citadel that we did not take from them—sixty towns, the whole region of Argob, the kingdom of Og in Bashan. [5]All these were fortress towns with high walls, double gates, and bars, besides a great many villages. [6]And we utterly destroyed them, as we had done to King Sihon of Heshbon, in each city utterly destroying men, women, and children. [7]But all the livestock and the plunder of the towns we kept as spoil for ourselves.

8 So at that time we took from the two kings of the Amorites the land beyond the Jordan, from the Wadi Arnon to Mount Hermon [9](the Sidonians call Hermon Sirion, while the Amorites call it Senir), [10]all the towns of the tableland, the whole of Gilead, and all of Bashan, as far as Salecah and Edrei, towns

_a_ Gk Tg: Heb _and all_

of Og's kingdom in Bashan. [11](Now only King Og of Bashan was left of the remnant of the Rephaim. In fact his bed, an iron bed, can still be seen in Rabbah of the Ammonites. By the common cubit it is nine cubits long and four cubits wide.) [12]As for the land that we took possession of at that time, I gave to the Reubenites and Gadites the territory north of Aroer,[a] that is on the edge of the Wadi Arnon, as well as half the hill country of Gilead with its towns, [13]and I gave to the half-tribe of Manasseh the rest of Gilead and all of Bashan, Og's kingdom. (The whole region of Argob: all that portion of Bashan used to be called a land of Rephaim; [14]Jair the Manassite acquired the whole region of Argob as far as the border of the Geshurites and the Maacathites, and he named them—that is, Bashan—after himself, Havvoth-jair,[b] as it is to this day.) [15]To Machir I gave Gilead. [16]And to the Reubenites and the Gadites I gave the territory from Gilead as far as the Wadi Arnon, with the middle of the wadi as a boundary, and up to the Jabbok, the wadi being boundary of the Ammonites; [17]the Arabah also, with the Jordan and its banks, from Chinnereth down to the sea of the Arabah, the Dead Sea,[c] with the lower slopes of Pisgah on the east.

18 At that time, I charged you as follows: "Although the LORD your God has given you this land to occupy, all your troops shall cross over armed as the vanguard of your Israelite kin. [19]Only your wives, your children, and your livestock—I know that you have much livestock—shall stay behind in the towns that I have given to you. [20]When the LORD gives rest to your kindred, as to you, and they too have occupied the land that the LORD your God is giving them beyond the Jordan, then each of you may return to the property that I have given to you." [21]And I charged Joshua as well at that time, saying: "Your own eyes have seen everything that the LORD your God has done to these two kings; so the LORD will do to all the kingdoms into which you are about to cross. [22]Do not fear them, for it is the LORD your God who fights for you."

Moses Views Canaan from Pisgah

23 At that time, too, I entreated the LORD, saying: [24]"O Lord GOD, you have only begun to show your servant your greatness and your might; what god in heaven or on earth can perform deeds and mighty acts like yours! [25]Let me cross over to see the good land beyond the Jordan, that good hill country and

the Lebanon." [26]But the LORD was angry with me on your account and would not heed me. The LORD said to me, "Enough from you! Never speak to me of this matter again! [27]Go up to the top of Pisgah and look around you to the west, to the north, to the south, and to the east. Look well, for you shall not cross over this Jordan. [28]But charge Joshua, and encourage and strengthen him, because it is he who shall cross over at the head of this people and who shall secure their possession of the land that you will see." [29]So we remained in the valley opposite Beth-peor.

Moses Commands Obedience

4 So now, Israel, give heed to the statutes and ordinances that I am teaching you to observe, so that you may live to enter and occupy the land that the LORD, the God of your ancestors, is giving you. [2]You must neither add anything to what I command you nor take away anything from it, but keep the commandments of the LORD your God with which I am charging you. [3]You have seen for yourselves what the LORD did with regard to the Baal of Peor—how the LORD your God destroyed from among you everyone who followed the Baal of Peor, [4]while those of you who held fast to the LORD your God are all alive today.

5 See, just as the LORD my God has charged me, I now teach you statutes and ordinances for you to observe in the land that you are about to enter and occupy. [6]You must observe them diligently, for this will show your wisdom and discernment to the peoples, who, when they hear all these statutes, will say, "Surely this great nation is a wise and discerning people!" [7]For what other great nation has a god so near to it as the LORD our God is whenever we call to him? [8]And what other great nation has statutes and ordinances as just as this entire law that I am setting before you today?

9 But take care and watch yourselves closely, so as neither to forget the things that your eyes have seen nor to let them slip from your mind all the days of your life; make them known to your children and your children's children— [10]how you once stood before the LORD your God at Horeb, when the LORD said to me, "Assemble the people for me, and I will let them hear my words, so that they may learn to fear me as long as they live on the earth, and may teach their children so"; [11]you approached and stood at the foot of the mountain while the mountain was

---

a Heb *territory from Aroer* **b** That is *Settlement of Jair* **c** Heb *Salt Sea*

blazing up to the very heavens, shrouded in dark clouds. [12]Then the LORD spoke to you out of the fire. You heard the sound of words but saw no form; there was only a voice. [13]He declared to you his covenant, which he charged you to observe, that is, the ten commandments;[a] and he wrote them on two stone tablets. [14]And the LORD charged me at that time to teach you statutes and ordinances for you to observe in the land that you are about to cross into and occupy.

15 Since you saw no form when the LORD spoke to you at Horeb out of the fire, take care and watch yourselves closely, [16]so that you do not act corruptly by making an idol for yourselves, in the form of any figure—the likeness of male or female, [17]the likeness of any animal that is on the earth, the likeness of any winged bird that flies in the air, [18]the likeness of anything that creeps on the ground, the likeness of any fish that is in the water under the earth. [19]And when you look up to the heavens and see the sun, the moon, and the stars, all the host of heaven, do not be led astray and bow down to them and serve them, things that the LORD your God has allotted to all the peoples everywhere under heaven. [20]But the LORD has taken you and brought you out of the iron-smelter, out of Egypt, to become a people of his very own possession, as you are now.

21 The LORD was angry with me because of you, and he vowed that I should not cross the Jordan and that I should not enter the good land that the LORD your God is giving for your possession. [22]For I am going to die in this land without crossing over the Jordan, but you are going to cross over to take possession of that good land. [23]So be careful not to forget the covenant that the LORD your God made with you, and not to make for yourselves an idol in the form of anything that the LORD your God has forbidden you. [24]For the LORD your God is a devouring fire, a jealous God.

25 When you have had children and children's children, and become complacent in the land, if you act corruptly by making an idol in the form of anything, thus doing what is evil in the sight of the LORD your God, and provoking him to anger, [26]I call heaven and earth to witness against you today that you will soon utterly perish from the land that you are crossing the Jordan to occupy; you will not live long on it, but will be utterly destroyed. [27]The LORD will scatter you among the peoples; only a

few of you will be left among the nations where the LORD will lead you. [28]There you will serve other gods made by human hands, objects of wood and stone that neither see, nor hear, nor eat, nor smell. [29]From there you will seek the LORD your God, and you will find him if you search after him with all your heart and soul. [30]In your distress, when all these things have happened to you in time to come, you will return to the LORD your God and heed him. [31]Because the LORD your God is a merciful God, he will neither abandon you nor destroy you; he will not forget the covenant with your ancestors that he swore to them.

32 For ask now about former ages, long before your own, ever since the day that God created human beings on the earth; ask from one end of heaven to the other: has anything so great as this ever happened or has its like ever been heard of? [33]Has any people ever heard the voice of a god speaking out of a fire, as you have heard, and lived? [34]Or has any god ever attempted to go and take a nation for himself from the midst of another nation, by trials, by signs and wonders, by war, by a mighty hand and an outstretched arm, and by terrifying displays of power, as the LORD your God did for you in Egypt before your very eyes? [35]To you it was shown so that you would acknowledge that the LORD is God; there is no other besides him. [36]From heaven he made you hear his voice to discipline you. On earth he showed you his great fire, while you heard his words coming out of the fire. [37]And because he loved your ancestors, he chose their descendants after them. He brought you out of Egypt with his own presence, by his great power, [38]driving out before you nations greater and mightier than yourselves, to bring you in, giving you their land for a possession, as it is still today. [39]So acknowledge today and take to heart that the LORD is God in heaven above and on the earth beneath; there is no other. [40]Keep his statutes and his commandments, which I am commanding you today for your own well-being and that of your descendants after you, so that you may long remain in the land that the LORD your God is giving you for all time.

Cities of Refuge East of the Jordan

41 Then Moses set apart on the east side of the Jordan three cities [42]to which a homicide could flee, someone who unintentionally kills another

a Heb *the ten words*

person, the two not having been at enmity before; the homicide could flee to one of these cities and live: [43]Bezer in the wilderness on the tableland belonging to the Reubenites, Ramoth in Gilead belonging to the Gadites, and Golan in Bashan belonging to the Manassites.

Transition to the Second Address

44 This is the law that Moses set before the Israelites. [45]These are the decrees and the statutes and ordinances that Moses spoke to the Israelites when they had come out of Egypt, [46]beyond the Jordan in the valley opposite Beth-peor, in the land of King Sihon of the Amorites, who reigned at Heshbon, whom Moses and the Israelites defeated when they came out of Egypt. [47]They occupied his land and the land of King Og of Bashan, the two kings of the Amorites on the eastern side of the Jordan: [48]from Aroer, which is on the edge of the Wadi Arnon, as far as Mount Sirion[a] (that is, Hermon), [49]together with all the Arabah on the east side of the Jordan as far as the Sea of the Arabah, under the slopes of Pisgah.

The Ten Commandments

5 Moses convened all Israel, and said to them:

Hear, O Israel, the statutes and ordinances that I am addressing to you today; you shall learn them and observe them diligently. [2]The LORD our God made a covenant with us at Horeb. [3]Not with our ancestors did the LORD make this covenant, but with us, who are all of us here alive today. [4]The LORD spoke with you face to face at the mountain, out of the fire. [5](At that time I was standing between the LORD and you to declare to you the words[b] of the LORD; for you were afraid because of the fire and did not go up the mountain.) And he said:

6 I am the LORD your God, who brought you out of the land of Egypt, out of the house of slavery; [7]you shall have no other gods before[c] me.

8 You shall not make for yourself an idol, whether in the form of anything that is in heaven above, or that is on the earth beneath, or that is in the water under the earth. [9]You shall not bow down to them or worship them; for I the LORD your God am a jealous God, punishing children for the iniquity of

The Lakota Code · Deuteronomy 5:1–21

These guidelines are taken from a Native American tribal code. Check out their similarity to the Ten Commandments (Deuteronomy 5:6–21), not to mention many of our civil laws, school policies, and even family rules.

• Love one another.

• Pity orphan children. Be kind to them because they are poor; feed them and clothe them.

• Do not kill one another.

• Do not steal anything from anyone, especially from your own people.

• Do not tell lies to anyone, or lie about anyone.

• Respect your brothers and sisters. Do not marry in your own family.

• The ability to make good speech is a great gift from the maker, owner of all things, to the people. This is why you should not talk badly about anyone. Bad talk can hurt one's family or everyday life.

• Never quarrel among one another. Be good to others and always be friendly to whomever you meet, wherever you meet them.

• Do not brag about yourself or try to hurt another's feelings. The generous person is the one who is respected.*

What can we learn from these guidelines?

How does their similarity to the Ten Commandments show that God's truth is not relative, but true for everyone?

a Syr: Heb *Sion*   b Q Mss Sam Gk Syr Vg Tg: MT *word*   c Or *besides*

parents, to the third and fourth generation of those who reject me, [10]but showing steadfast love to the thousandth generation[a] of those who love me and keep my commandments.

11 You shall not make wrongful use of the name of the LORD your God, for the LORD will not acquit anyone who misuses his name.

12 Observe the sabbath day and keep it holy, as the LORD your God commanded you. [13]Six days you shall labor and do all your work. [14]But the seventh day is a sabbath to the LORD your God; you shall not do any work—you, or your son or your daughter, or your male or female slave, or your ox or your donkey, or any of your livestock, or the resident alien in your towns, so that your male and female slave may rest as well as you. [15]Remember that you were a slave in the land of Egypt, and the LORD your God brought you out from there with a mighty hand and an outstretched arm; therefore the LORD your God commanded you to keep the sabbath day.

16 Honor your father and your mother, as the LORD your God commanded you, so that your days may be long and that it may go well with you in the land that the LORD your God is giving you.

17 You shall not murder.[b]

18 Neither shall you commit adultery.

19 Neither shall you steal.

20 Neither shall you bear false witness against your neighbor.

21 Neither shall you covet your neighbor's wife.

Neither shall you desire your neighbor's house, or field, or male or female slave, or ox, or donkey, or anything that belongs to your neighbor.

Moses the Mediator of God's Will

22 These words the LORD spoke with a loud voice to your whole assembly at the mountain, out of the fire, the cloud, and the thick darkness, and he added no more. He wrote them on two stone tablets, and gave them to me. [23]When you heard the voice out of the darkness, while the mountain was burning with fire, you approached me, all the heads of your tribes and your elders; [24]and you said, "Look, the LORD our God has shown us his glory and greatness, and we have heard his voice out of the fire. Today we have seen that God may speak to someone and the person may still live. [25]So now why should we die? For this great fire will consume us; if we hear the voice of the LORD our God any longer, we shall die. [26]For who is there of all flesh that has heard the voice

of the living God speaking out of fire, as we have, and remained alive? [27]Go near, you yourself, and hear all that the LORD our God will say. Then tell us everything that the LORD our God tells you, and we will listen and do it."

28 The LORD heard your words when you spoke to me, and the LORD said to me: "I have heard the words of this people, which they have spoken to you; they are right in all that they have spoken. [29]If only they had such a mind as this, to fear me and to keep all my commandments always, so that it might go well with them and with their children forever! [30]Go say to them, 'Return to your tents.' [31]But you, stand here by me, and I will tell you all the commandments, the statutes and the ordinances, that you shall teach them, so that they may do them in the land that I am giving them to possess." [32]You must therefore be careful to do as the LORD your God has commanded you; you shall not turn to the right or to the left. [33]You must follow exactly the path that the LORD your God has commanded you, so that you may live, and that it may go well with you, and that you may live long in the land that you are to possess.

6
The Great Commandment

Now this is the commandment—the statutes and the ordinances—that the LORD your God charged me to teach you to observe in the land that you are about to cross into and occupy, [2]so that you and your children and your children's children may fear the LORD your God all the days of your life, and keep all his decrees and his commandments that I am commanding you, so that your days may be long. [3]Hear therefore, O Israel, and observe them diligently, so that it may go well with you, and so that you may multiply greatly in a land flowing with milk and honey, as the LORD, the God of your ancestors, has promised you.

4 Hear, O Israel: The LORD is our God, the LORD alone.[c] [5]You shall love the LORD your God with all your heart, and with all your soul, and with all your might. [6]Keep these words that I am commanding you today in your heart. [7]Recite them to your children and talk about them when you are at home and when you are away, when you lie down and when you rise. [8]Bind them as a sign on your hand, fix them as an emblem[d] on your forehead, [9]and write them on the doorposts of your house and on your gates.

---

a Or to thousands b Or kill c Or The LORD our God is one LORD, or The LORD our God, the LORD is one, or The LORD is our God, the LORD is one d Or as a frontlet

Caution against Disobedience

10 When the LORD your God has brought you into the land that he swore to your ancestors, to Abraham, to Isaac, and to Jacob, to give you—a land with fine, large cities that you did not build, [11]houses filled with all sorts of goods that you did not fill, hewn cisterns that you did not hew, vineyards and olive groves that you did not plant—and when you have eaten your fill, [12]take care that you do not forget the LORD, who brought you out of the land of Egypt, out of the house of slavery. [13]The LORD your God you shall fear; him you shall serve, and by his name alone you shall swear. [14]Do not follow other gods, any of the gods of the peoples who are all around you, [15]because the LORD your God, who is present with you, is a jealous God. The anger of the LORD your God would be kindled against you and he would destroy you from the face of the earth.

16 Do not put the LORD your God to the test, as you tested him at Massah. [17]You must diligently keep the commandments of the LORD your God, and his decrees, and his statutes that he has commanded you. [18]Do what is right and good in the sight of the LORD, so that it may go well with you, and so that you may go in and occupy the good land that the LORD swore to your ancestors to give you,

"Hear O Israel:
The LORD is our God,
the LORD alone.
You shall love
the LORD your God
with all your heart,
and with all
your soul,
and with all
your might."
—Deuteronomy 6:4–5

[19]thrusting out all your enemies from before you, as the LORD has promised.

20 When your children ask you in time to come, "What is the meaning of the decrees and the statutes and the ordinances that the LORD our God has commanded you?" [21]then you shall say to your children, "We were Pharaoh's slaves in Egypt, but the LORD brought us out of Egypt with a mighty hand. [22]The LORD displayed before our eyes great and awesome signs and wonders against Egypt, against Pharaoh and all his household. [23]He brought us out from there in order to bring us in, to give us the land that he promised on oath to our ancestors. [24]Then the LORD commanded us to observe all these statutes, to fear the LORD our God, for our lasting good, so as to keep us alive, as is now the case. [25]If we diligently observe this entire commandment before the LORD our God, as he has commanded us, we will be in the right."

A Chosen People

7 When the LORD your God brings you into the land that you are about to enter and occupy, and he clears away many nations before you—the Hittites, the Girgashites, the Amorites, the Canaanites, the Perizzites, the Hivites, and the

PRAY IT!

Chosen · Deuteronomy 7:7–11

God did not love Israel because it was such a great nation—numerous, strong, or especially holy. In fact, they were the smallest group of all people (Deuteronomy 7:7). Israel's special position and close relationship with God in the Old Testament was because God chose to love the Israelites and make them a great nation. Sounds familiar, doesn't it? God does not choose us because of our own greatness. He chooses us out of love and grace (see Ephesians 2:8-10). Our response should be humility, obedience, and thankfulness. Say a prayer of thankfulness for God's love and grace, which saves you.

Jebusites, seven nations mightier and more numerous than you— [2]and when the LORD your God gives them over to you and you defeat them, then you must utterly destroy them. Make no covenant with them and show them no mercy. [3]Do not intermarry with them, giving your daughters to their sons or taking their daughters for your sons, [4]for that would turn away your children from following me, to serve other gods. Then the anger of the LORD would be kindled against you, and he would destroy you quickly. [5]But this is how you must deal with them: break down their altars, smash their pillars, hew down their sacred poles,[a] and burn their idols with fire. [6]For you are a people holy to the LORD your God; the LORD your God has chosen you out of all the peoples on earth to be his people, his treasured possession.

7 It was not because you were more numerous than any other people that the LORD set his heart on you and chose you—for you were the fewest of all peoples. [8]It was because the LORD loved you and kept the oath that he swore to your ancestors, that the LORD has brought you out with a mighty hand, and redeemed you from the house of slavery, from the hand of Pharaoh king of Egypt. [9]Know therefore that the LORD your God is God, the faithful God who maintains covenant loyalty with those who love him and keep his commandments, to a thousand generations, [10]and who repays in their own person those who reject him. He does not delay but repays in their own person those who reject him. [11]Therefore, observe diligently the commandment—the statutes and the ordinances—that I am commanding you today.

Blessings for Obedience

12 If you heed these ordinances, by diligently observing them, the LORD your God will maintain with you the covenant loyalty that he swore to your ancestors; [13]he will love you, bless you, and multiply you; he will bless the fruit of your womb and the fruit of your ground, your grain and your wine and your oil, the increase of your cattle and the issue of your flock, in the land that he swore to your ancestors to give you. [14]You shall be the most blessed of peoples, with neither sterility nor barrenness among you or your livestock. [15]The LORD will turn away from you every illness; all the dread diseases of Egypt that you experienced, he will not inflict on you, but he will lay them on all who hate you. [16]You shall devour

all the peoples that the LORD your God is giving over to you, showing them no pity; you shall not serve their gods, for that would be a snare to you.

17 If you say to yourself, "These nations are more numerous than I; how can I dispossess them?" [18]do not be afraid of them. Just remember what the LORD your God did to Pharaoh and to all Egypt, [19]the great trials that your eyes saw, the signs and wonders, the mighty hand and the outstretched arm by which the LORD your God brought you out. The LORD your God will do the same to all the peoples of whom you are afraid. [20]Moreover, the LORD your God will send the pestilence[b] against them, until even the survivors and the fugitives are destroyed. [21]Have no dread of them, for the LORD your God, who is present with you, is a great and awesome God. [22]The LORD your God will clear away these nations before you little by little; you will not be able to make a quick end of them, otherwise the wild animals would become too numerous for you. [23]But the LORD your God will give them over to you, and throw them into great panic, until they are destroyed. [24]He will hand their kings over to you and you shall blot out their name from under heaven; no one will be able to stand against you, until you have destroyed them. [25]The images of their gods you shall burn with fire. Do not covet the silver or the gold that is on them and take it for yourself, because you could be ensnared by it; for it is abhorrent to the LORD your God. [26]Do not bring an abhorrent thing into your house, or you will be set apart for destruction like it. You must utterly detest and abhor it, for it is set apart for destruction.

8

A Warning Not to Forget God in Prosperity

This entire commandment that I command you today you must diligently observe, so that you may live and increase, and go in and occupy the land that the LORD promised on oath to your ancestors. [2]Remember the long way that the LORD your God has led you these forty years in the wilderness, in order to humble you, testing you to know what was in your heart, whether or not you would keep his commandments. [3]He humbled you by letting you hunger, then by feeding you with manna, with which neither you nor your ancestors were acquainted, in order to make you understand that one does not live by bread alone, but by every word that comes from the mouth of the LORD.[c] [4]The clothes on your back did not wear out and your feet did not swell these

---

a Heb *Asherim* b Or *hornets*: Meaning of Heb uncertain c Or *by anything that the* LORD *decrees*

Josh Schack: 30 Hour Famine · Deuteronomy 8:3

Josh Schack was hungry. Really hungry. He hadn't eaten in over twenty-four hours. But this student from Washington wasn't being forced to avoid food. He was doing it by choice. Why? Josh took part in World Vision's 30 Hour Famine, a program that is simply about students around the world loving God and fighting hunger. By going without food for thirty hours, students experience hunger. They also do something about the injustice of hunger in the world by raising money. When Josh took part in a famine with friends from his church youth group, he experienced his need for God in a new way and found that God was his help and sustainer as he relied on God's strength. **Deuteronomy 8:3** tells us that we can't live by bread alone, but by every word that comes from the mouth of God. A 30 Hour Famine can bring a new appreciation for hunger, a deeper compassion for those who face it every day, and inspiration to do something to help. At the same time, it can also bring home the truth that rich or poor, well fed or hungry, God is our true provider and sustainer. You can learn more at **30hourfamine.org**.

forty years. [5]Know then in your heart that as a parent disciplines a child so the Lord your God disciplines you. [6]Therefore keep the commandments of the Lord your God, by walking in his ways and by fearing him. [7]For the Lord your God is bringing you into a good land, a land with flowing streams, with springs and underground waters welling up in valleys and hills, [8]a land of wheat and barley, of vines and fig trees and pomegranates, a land of olive trees and honey, [9]a land where you may eat bread without scarcity, where you will lack nothing, a land whose stones are iron and from whose hills you may mine copper. [10]You shall eat your fill and bless the Lord your God for the good land that he has given you.

11 Take care that you do not forget the Lord your God, by failing to keep his commandments, his ordinances, and his statutes, which I am commanding you today. [12]When you have eaten your fill and have built fine houses and live in them, [13]and when your herds and flocks have multiplied, and your silver and gold is multiplied, and all that you have is multiplied, [14]then do not exalt yourself, forgetting the Lord your God, who brought you out of the land of Egypt, out of the house of slavery, [15]who led you through the great and terrible wilderness, an arid wasteland with poisonous[a] snakes and scorpions. He made water flow for you from flint rock, [16]and fed you in the wilderness with manna that your ancestors did not know, to humble you and to test you, and in the end to do you good. [17]Do not say to yourself, "My power and the might of my own hand have gotten

me this wealth." [18]But remember the Lord your God, for it is he who gives you power to get wealth, so that he may confirm his covenant that he swore to your ancestors, as he is doing today. [19]If you do forget the Lord your God and follow other gods to serve and worship them, I solemnly warn you today that you shall surely perish. [20]Like the nations that the Lord is destroying before you, so shall you perish, because you would not obey the voice of the Lord your God.

The Consequences of Rebelling against God

9

Hear, O Israel! You are about to cross the Jordan today, to go in and dispossess nations larger and mightier than you, great cities, fortified to the heavens, [2]a strong and tall people, the offspring of the Anakim, whom you know. You have heard it said of them, "Who can stand up to the Anakim?" [3]Know then today that the Lord your God is the one who crosses over before you as a devouring fire; he will defeat them and subdue them before you, so that you may dispossess and destroy them quickly, as the Lord has promised you.

4 When the Lord your God thrusts them out before you, do not say to yourself, "It is because of my righteousness that the Lord has brought me in to occupy this land"; it is rather because of the wickedness of these nations that the Lord is dispossessing them before you. [5]It is not because of your righteousness or the uprightness of your heart that you

a Or *fiery*; Heb *seraph*

are going in to occupy their land; but because of the wickedness of these nations the LORD your God is dispossessing them before you, in order to fulfill the promise that the LORD made on oath to your ancestors, to Abraham, to Isaac, and to Jacob.

6 Know, then, that the LORD your God is not giving you this good land to occupy because of your righteousness; for you are a stubborn people. [7]Remember and do not forget how you provoked the LORD your God to wrath in the wilderness; you have been rebellious against the LORD from the day you came out of the land of Egypt until you came to this place.

8 Even at Horeb you provoked the LORD to wrath, and the LORD was so angry with you that he was ready to destroy you. [9]When I went up the mountain to receive the stone tablets, the tablets of the covenant that the LORD made with you, I remained on the mountain forty days and forty nights; I neither ate bread nor drank water. [10]And the LORD gave me the two stone tablets written with the finger of God; on them were all the words that the LORD had spoken to you at the mountain out of the fire on the day of the assembly. [11]At the end of forty days and forty nights the LORD gave me the two stone tablets, the tablets of the covenant. [12]Then the LORD said to me, "Get up, go down quickly from here, for your people whom you have brought from Egypt have acted corruptly. They have been quick to turn from the way that I commanded them; they have cast an image for themselves." [13]Furthermore the LORD said to me, "I have seen that this people is indeed a stubborn people. [14]Let me alone that I may destroy them and blot out their name from under heaven; and I will make of you a nation mightier and more numerous than they."

15 So I turned and went down from the mountain, while the mountain was ablaze; the two tablets of the covenant were in my two hands. [16]Then I saw that you had indeed sinned against the LORD your God, by casting for yourselves an image of a calf; you had been quick to turn from the way that the LORD had commanded you. [17]So I took hold of the two tablets and flung them from my two hands, smashing them before your eyes. [18]Then I lay prostrate before the LORD as before, forty days and forty nights; I neither ate bread nor drank water, because of all the sin you had committed, provoking the LORD by doing what was evil in his sight. [19]For I was afraid that the anger that the LORD bore against you was

so fierce that he would destroy you. But the LORD listened to me that time also. [20]The LORD was so angry with Aaron that he was ready to destroy him, but I interceded also on behalf of Aaron at that same time. [21]Then I took the sinful thing you had made, the calf, and burned it with fire and crushed it, grinding it thoroughly, until it was reduced to dust; and I threw the dust of it into the stream that runs down the mountain.

22 At Taberah also, and at Massah, and at Kibroth-hattaavah, you provoked the LORD to wrath. [23]And when the LORD sent you from Kadesh-barnea, saying, "Go up and occupy the land that I have given you," you rebelled against the command of the LORD your God, neither trusting him nor obeying him. [24]You have been rebellious against the LORD as long as he has[a] known you.

25 Throughout the forty days and forty nights that I lay prostrate before the LORD when the LORD intended to destroy you, [26]I prayed to the LORD and said, "Lord GOD, do not destroy the people who are your very own possession, whom you redeemed in your greatness, whom you brought out of Egypt with a mighty hand. [27]Remember your servants, Abraham, Isaac, and Jacob; pay no attention to the stubbornness of this people, their wickedness and their sin, [28]otherwise the land from which you have brought us might say, 'Because the LORD was not able to bring them into the land that he promised them, and because he hated them, he has brought them out to let them die in the wilderness.' [29]For they are the people of your very own possession, whom you brought out by your great power and by your outstretched arm."

The Second Pair of Tablets

10 At that time the LORD said to me, "Carve out two tablets of stone like the former ones, and come up to me on the mountain, and make an ark of wood. [2]I will write on the tablets the words that were on the former tablets, which you smashed, and you shall put them in the ark." [3]So I made an ark of acacia wood, cut two tablets of stone like the former ones, and went up the mountain with the two tablets in my hand. [4]Then he wrote on the tablets the same words as before, the ten commandments[b] that the LORD had spoken to you on the mountain out of the fire on the day of the assembly; and the LORD gave them to me. [5]So I turned and came down from the mountain, and put the tablets in the ark that

a Sam Gk: MT *I have*   b Heb *the ten words*

I had made; and there they are, as the LORD commanded me.

6 (The Israelites journeyed from Beeroth-bene-jaakan[a] to Moserah. There Aaron died, and there he was buried; his son Eleazar succeeded him as priest. [7]From there they journeyed to Gudgodah, and from Gudgodah to Jotbathah, a land with flowing streams. [8]At that time the LORD set apart the tribe of Levi to carry the ark of the covenant of the LORD, to stand before the LORD to minister to him, and to bless in his name, to this day. [9]Therefore Levi has no allotment or inheritance with his kindred; the LORD is his inheritance, as the LORD your God promised him.)

10 I stayed on the mountain forty days and forty nights, as I had done the first time. And once again the LORD listened to me. The LORD was unwilling to destroy you. [11]The LORD said to me, "Get up, go on your journey at the head of the people, that they may go in and occupy the land that I swore to their ancestors to give them."

The Essence of the Law

12 So now, O Israel, what does the LORD your God require of you? Only to fear the LORD your God, to walk in all his ways, to love him, to serve the LORD your God with all your heart and with all your soul, [13]and to keep the commandments of the LORD your God[b] and his decrees that I am commanding you today, for your own well-being. [14]Although heaven and the heaven of heavens belong to the LORD your God, the earth with all that is in it, [15]yet the LORD set his heart in love on your ancestors alone and chose you, their descendants after them, out of all the peoples, as it is today. [16]Circumcise, then, the foreskin of your heart, and do not be stubborn any longer. [17]For the LORD your God is God of gods and Lord of lords, the great God, mighty and awesome, who is not partial and takes no bribe, [18]who executes justice for the orphan and the widow, and who loves the strangers, providing them food and clothing. [19]You shall also love the stranger, for you were strangers in the land of Egypt. [20]You shall fear the LORD your God; him alone you shall worship; to him you shall hold fast, and by his name you shall swear. [21]He is your praise; he is your God, who has done for you these great and awesome things that your own eyes have seen. [22]Your ancestors went down to Egypt seventy persons; and now the LORD your God has made you as numerous as the stars in heaven.

Rewards for Obedience

11 You shall love the LORD your God, therefore, and keep his charge, his decrees, his ordinances, and his commandments always. [2]Remember today that it was not your children (who have not known or seen the discipline of the LORD your God), but it is you who must acknowledge his greatness, his mighty hand and his outstretched arm, [3]his signs and his deeds that he did in Egypt to Pharaoh, the king of Egypt, and to all his land; [4]what he did to the Egyptian army, to their horses and chariots, how he made the water of the Red Sea[c] flow over them as they pursued you, so that the LORD has destroyed them to this day; [5]what he did to you in the wilderness, until you came to this place; [6]and what he did to Dathan and Abiram, sons of Eliab son of Reuben, how in the midst of all Israel the earth opened its mouth and swallowed them up, along with their households, their tents, and every living being in their company; [7]for it is your own eyes that have seen every great deed that the LORD did.

8 Keep, then, this entire commandment that I am commanding you today, so that you may have strength to go in and occupy the land that you are crossing over to occupy, [9]and so that you may live long in the land that the LORD swore to your ancestors to give them and to their descendants, a land flowing with milk and honey. [10]For the land that you are about to enter to occupy is not like the land of Egypt, from which you have come, where you sow your seed and irrigate by foot like a vegetable garden. [11]But the land that you are crossing over to occupy is a land of hills and valleys, watered by rain from the sky, [12]a land that the LORD your God looks after. The eyes of the LORD your God are always on it, from the beginning of the year to the end of the year.

13 If you will only heed his every commandment[d] that I am commanding you today—loving the LORD your God, and serving him with all your heart and with all your soul— [14]then he[e] will give the rain for your land in its season, the early rain and the later rain, and you will gather in your grain, your wine, and your oil; [15]and he[e] will give grass in your fields for your livestock, and you will eat your fill. [16]Take care, or you will be seduced into turning away, serving other gods and worshiping them, [17]for then the anger of the LORD will be kindled against you and he will shut up the heavens, so that there will be no rain and the land will yield no fruit; then you will perish quickly off the good land that the LORD is giving you.

18 You shall put these words of mine in your heart and soul, and you shall bind them as a sign on your hand, and fix them as an emblem[a] on your forehead. [19]Teach them to your children, talking about them when you are at home and when you are away, when you lie down and when you rise. [20]Write them on the doorposts of your house and on your gates, [21]so that your days and the days of your children may be multiplied in the land that the LORD swore to your ancestors to give them, as long as the heavens are above the earth.

22 If you will diligently observe this entire commandment that I am commanding you, loving the LORD your God, walking in all his ways, and holding fast to him, [23]then the LORD will drive out all these nations before you, and you will dispossess nations larger and mightier than yourselves. [24]Every place on which you set foot shall be yours; your territory shall extend from the wilderness to the Lebanon and from the River, the river Euphrates, to the Western Sea. [25]No one will be able to stand against you; the LORD your God will put the fear and dread of you on all the land on which you set foot, as he promised you.

26 See, I am setting before you today a blessing and a curse: [27]the blessing, if you obey the commandments of the LORD your God that I am commanding you today; [28]and the curse, if you do not obey the commandments of the LORD your God, but turn from the way that I am commanding you today, to follow other gods that you have not known.

29 When the LORD your God has brought you into the land that you are entering to occupy, you shall set the blessing on Mount Gerizim and the curse on Mount Ebal. [30]As you know, they are beyond the Jordan, some distance to the west, in the land of the Canaanites who live in the Arabah, opposite Gilgal, beside the oak[b] of Moreh.

31 When you cross the Jordan to go in to occupy the land that the LORD your God is giving you, and when you occupy it and live in it, [32]you must diligently observe all the statutes and ordinances that I am setting before you today.

12
Pagan Shrines to Be Destroyed
These are the statutes and ordinances that you must diligently observe in the land that the LORD, the God of your ancestors, has given you to occupy all the days that you live on the earth.
2 You must demolish completely all the places

where the nations whom you are about to dispossess served their gods, on the mountain heights, on the hills, and under every leafy tree. [3]Break down their altars, smash their pillars, burn their sacred poles[c] with fire, and hew down the idols of their gods, and thus blot out their name from their places. [4]You shall not worship the LORD your God in such ways. [5]But you shall seek the place that the LORD your God will choose out of all your tribes as his habitation to put his name there. You shall go there, [6]bringing there your burnt offerings and your sacrifices, your tithes and your donations, your votive gifts, your freewill offerings, and the firstlings of your herds and flocks. [7]And you shall eat there in the presence of the LORD your God, you and your households together, rejoicing in all the undertakings in which the LORD your God has blessed you.

8 You shall not act as we are acting here today, all of us according to our own desires, [9]for you have not yet come into the rest and the possession that the LORD your God is giving you. [10]When you cross over the Jordan and live in the land that the LORD your God is allotting to you, and when he gives you rest from your enemies all around so that you live in safety, [11]then you shall bring everything that I command you to the place that the LORD your God will choose as a dwelling for his name: your burnt offerings and your sacrifices, your tithes and your donations, and all your choice votive gifts that you vow to the LORD. [12]And you shall rejoice before the LORD your God, you together with your sons and your daughters, your male and female slaves, and the Levites who reside in your towns (since they have no allotment or inheritance with you).

A Prescribed Place of Worship

13 Take care that you do not offer your burnt offerings at any place you happen to see. [14]But only at the place that the LORD will choose in one of your tribes—there you shall offer your burnt

---

a Or *as a frontlet*   *b* Gk Syr: Compare Gen 12.6; Heb *oaks* or *terebinths*   *c* Heb *Asherim*

offerings and there you shall do everything I command you.

15 Yet whenever you desire you may slaughter and eat meat within any of your towns, according to the blessing that the LORD your God has given you; the unclean and the clean may eat of it, as they would of gazelle or deer. [16]The blood, however, you must not eat; you shall pour it out on the ground like water. [17]Nor may you eat within your towns the tithe of your grain, your wine, and your oil, the firstlings of your herds and your flocks, any of your votive gifts that you vow, your freewill offerings, or your donations; [18]these you shall eat in the presence of the LORD your God at the place that the LORD your God will choose, you together with your son and your daughter, your male and female slaves, and the Levites resident in your towns, rejoicing in the presence of the LORD your God in all your undertakings. [19]Take care that you do not neglect the Levite as long as you live in your land.

20 When the LORD your God enlarges your territory, as he has promised you, and you say, "I am going to eat some meat," because you wish to eat meat, you may eat meat whenever you have the desire. [21]If the place where the LORD your God will choose to put his name is too far from you, and you slaughter as I have commanded you any of your herd or flock that the LORD has given you, then you may eat within your towns whenever you desire. [22]Indeed, just as gazelle or deer is eaten, so you may eat it; the unclean and the clean alike may eat it. [23]Only be sure that you do not eat the blood; for the blood is the life, and you shall not eat the life with the meat. [24]Do not eat it; you shall pour it out on the ground like water. [25]Do not eat it, so that all may go well with you and your children after you, because you do what is right in the sight of the LORD. [26]But the sacred donations that are due from you, and your votive gifts, you shall bring to the place that the LORD will choose. [27]You shall present your burnt offerings, both the meat and the blood, on the altar of the LORD your God; the blood of your other sacrifices shall be poured out beside[a] the altar of the LORD your God, but the meat you may eat.

28 Be careful to obey all these words that I command you today,[b] so that it may go well with you and with your children after you forever, because you will be doing what is good and right in the sight of the LORD your God.

Warning against Idolatry

29 When the LORD your God has cut off before you the nations whom you are about to enter to dispossess them, when you have dispossessed them and live in their land, [30]take care that you are not snared into imitating them, after they have been destroyed before you: do not inquire concerning their gods, saying, "How did these nations worship their gods? I also want to do the same." [31]You must not do the same for the LORD your God, because every abhorrent thing that the LORD hates they have done for their gods. They would even burn their sons and their daughters in the fire to their gods. [32][c] You must diligently observe everything that I command you; do not add to it or take anything from it.

13 [d] If prophets or those who divine by dreams appear among you and promise you omens or portents, [2]and the omens or the portents declared by them take place, and they say, "Let us follow other gods" (whom you have not known) "and let us serve them," [3]you must not heed the words of those prophets or those who divine by dreams; for the LORD your God is testing you, to know whether you indeed love the LORD your God with all your heart and soul. [4]The LORD your God you shall follow, him alone you shall fear, his commandments you shall keep, his voice you shall obey, him you shall serve, and to him you shall hold fast. [5]But those prophets or those who divine by dreams shall be put to death for having spoken treason against the LORD your God—who brought you out of the land of Egypt and redeemed you from the house of slavery—to turn you from the way in which the LORD your God commanded you to walk. So you shall purge the evil from your midst.

6 If anyone secretly entices you—even if it is your brother, your father's son or[e] your mother's son, or your own son or daughter, or the wife you embrace, or your most intimate friend—saying, "Let us go worship other gods," whom neither you nor your ancestors have known, [7]any of the gods of the peoples that are around you, whether near you or far away from you, from one end of the earth to the other, [8]you must not yield to or heed any such persons. Show them no pity or compassion and do not shield them. [9]But you shall surely kill them; your own hand shall be first against them to execute them, and afterwards the hand of all the people. [10]Stone them to death for trying to turn you away from the

---

a Or *on*   b Gk Sam Syr: MT lacks *today*   c Ch 13.1 in Heb   d Ch 13.2 in Heb   e Sam Gk Compare Tg: MT lacks *your father's son or*

LORD your God, who brought you out of the land of Egypt, out of the house of slavery. [11]Then all Israel shall hear and be afraid, and never again do any such wickedness.

12 If you hear it said about one of the towns that the LORD your God is giving you to live in, [13]that scoundrels from among you have gone out and led the inhabitants of the town astray, saying, "Let us go and worship other gods," whom you have not known, [14]then you shall inquire and make a thorough investigation. If the charge is established that such an abhorrent thing has been done among you, [15]you shall put the inhabitants of that town to the sword, utterly destroying it and everything in it—even putting its livestock to the sword. [16]All of its spoil you shall gather into its public square; then burn the town and all its spoil with fire, as a whole burnt offering to the LORD your God. It shall remain a perpetual ruin, never to be rebuilt. [17]Do not let anything devoted to destruction stick to your hand, so that the LORD may turn from his fierce anger and show you compassion, and in his compassion multiply you, as he swore to your ancestors, [18]if you obey the voice of the LORD your God by keeping all his commandments that I am commanding you today, doing what is right in the sight of the LORD your God.

Pagan Practices Forbidden

14 You are children of the LORD your God. You must not lacerate yourselves or shave your forelocks for the dead. [2]For you are a people holy to the LORD your God; it is you the LORD has chosen out of all the peoples on earth to be his people, his treasured possession.

Clean and Unclean Foods

3 You shall not eat any abhorrent thing. [4]These are the animals you may eat: the ox, the sheep, the goat, [5]the deer, the gazelle, the roebuck, the wild goat, the ibex, the antelope, and the mountain-sheep. [6]Any animal that divides the hoof and has the hoof cleft in two, and chews the cud, among the animals, you may eat. [7]Yet of those that chew the cud or have the hoof cleft you shall not eat these: the camel, the hare, and the rock badger, because they chew the cud but do not divide the hoof; they are unclean for you. [8]And the pig, because it divides the hoof but does not chew the cud, is unclean for you. You shall not eat their meat, and you shall not touch their carcasses.

9 Of all that live in water you may eat these: whatever has fins and scales you may eat. [10]And whatever does not have fins and scales you shall not eat; it is unclean for you.

11 You may eat any clean birds. [12]But these are the ones that you shall not eat: the eagle, the vulture, the osprey, [13]the buzzard, the kite of any kind; [14]every raven of any kind; [15]the ostrich, the nighthawk, the sea gull, the hawk of any kind; [16]the little owl and the great owl, the water hen [17]and the desert owl,[a] the carrion vulture and the cormorant, [18]the stork, the heron of any kind; the hoopoe and the bat.[b] [19]And all winged insects are unclean for you; they shall not be eaten. [20]You may eat any clean winged creature.

21 You shall not eat anything that dies of itself; you may give it to aliens residing in your towns for them to eat, or you may sell it to a foreigner. For you are a people holy to the LORD your God.

You shall not boil a kid in its mother's milk.

Regulations concerning Tithes

22 Set apart a tithe of all the yield of your seed that is brought in yearly from the field. [23]In the presence of the LORD your God, in the place that he will choose as a dwelling for his name, you shall eat the tithe of your grain, your wine, and your oil, as well as the firstlings of your herd and flock, so that you may learn to fear the LORD your God always. [24]But if, when the LORD your God has blessed you, the distance is so great that you are unable to transport it, because the place where the LORD your God will choose to set his name is too far away from you, [25]then you may turn it into money. With the money secure in hand, go to the place that the LORD your God will choose; [26]spend the money for whatever you wish—oxen, sheep, wine, strong drink, or whatever you desire. And you shall eat there in the presence of the LORD your God, you and your household rejoicing together. [27]As for the Levites resident in your towns, do not neglect them, because they have no allotment or inheritance with you.

28 Every third year you shall bring out the full tithe of your produce for that year, and store it within your towns; [29]the Levites, because they have no allotment or inheritance with you, as well as the resident aliens, the orphans, and the widows in your towns, may come and eat their fill so that the LORD your God may bless you in all the work that you undertake.

---

a Or *pelican* b Identification of several of the birds in verses 12-18 is uncertain

15

Laws concerning the Sabbatical Year

Every seventh year you shall grant a remission of debts. [2] And this is the manner of the remission: every creditor shall remit the claim that is held against a neighbor, not exacting it of a neighbor who is a member of the community, because the Lord's remission has been proclaimed. [3] Of a foreigner you may exact it, but you must remit your claim on whatever any member of your community owes you. [4] There will, however, be no one in need among you, because the Lord is sure to bless you in the land that the Lord your God is giving you as a possession to occupy, [5] if only you will obey the Lord your God by diligently observing this entire commandment that I command you today. [6] When the Lord your God has blessed you, as he promised you, you will lend to many nations, but you will not borrow; you will rule over many nations, but they will not rule over you.

7 If there is among you anyone in need, a member of your community in any of your towns within the land that the Lord your God is giving you, do not be hard-hearted or tight-fisted toward your needy neighbor. [8] You should rather open your hand, willingly lending enough to meet the need, whatever it may be. [9] Be careful that you do not entertain a mean thought, thinking, "The seventh year, the year of remission, is near," and therefore view your needy neighbor with hostility and give nothing; your neighbor might cry to the Lord against you, and you would incur guilt. [10] Give liberally and be ungrudging when you do so, for on this account the Lord your God will bless you in all your work and in all that you undertake. [11] Since there will never cease to be some in need on the earth, I therefore command you, "Open your hand to the poor and needy neighbor in your land."

12 If a member of your community, whether a Hebrew man or a Hebrew woman, is sold[a] to you and works for you six years, in the seventh year you shall set that person free. [13] And when you send a male slave[b] out from you a free person, you shall not send him out empty-handed. [14] Provide liberally out of your flock, your threshing floor, and your wine press, thus giving to him some of the bounty with which the Lord your God has blessed you. [15] Remember that you were a slave in the land of Egypt, and the Lord your God redeemed you; for this reason I lay this command upon you today. [16] But if he says to you, "I will not go out from you,"

because he loves you and your household, since he is well off with you, [17] then you shall take an awl and thrust it through his earlobe into the door, and he shall be your slave[c] forever.

You shall do the same with regard to your female slave.[d]

18 Do not consider it a hardship when you send them out from you free persons, because for six years they have given you services worth the wages of hired laborers; and the Lord your God will bless you in all that you do.

The Firstborn of Livestock

19 Every firstling male born of your herd and flock you shall consecrate to the Lord your God; you shall not do work with your firstling ox nor shear the firstling of your flock. [20] You shall eat it, you together with your household, in the presence of the Lord your God year by year at the place that the Lord will choose. [21] But if it has any defect—any serious defect, such as lameness or blindness—you shall not sacrifice it to the Lord your God; [22] within your towns may eat it, the unclean and the clean alike, as you would a gazelle or deer. [23] Its blood, however, you must not eat; you shall pour it out on the ground like water.

16

The Passover Reviewed

Observe the month[e] of Abib by keeping the passover to the Lord your God, for in the month of Abib the Lord your God brought you out of Egypt by night. [2] You shall offer the passover sacrifice to the Lord your God, from the flock and the herd, at the place that the Lord will choose as a dwelling for his name. [3] You must not eat with it anything leavened. For seven days you shall eat unleavened bread with it—the bread of affliction—because you came out of the land of Egypt in great haste, so that all the days of your life you may remember the day of your departure from the land of Egypt. [4] No leaven shall be seen with you in all your territory for seven days; and none of the meat of what you slaughter on the evening of the first day shall remain until morning. [5] You are not permitted to offer the passover sacrifice within any of your towns that the Lord your God is giving you. [6] But at the place that the Lord your God will choose as a dwelling for his name, only there shall you offer the passover sacrifice, in the evening at sunset, the time of day when you de-

---

a Or *sells himself or herself* b Heb *him* c Or *bondman* d Or *bondwoman* e Or *new moon* parted from Egypt. [7]You shall cook it and eat it at the place that the LORD your God will choose; the next morning you may go back to your tents. [8]For six days you shall continue to eat unleavened bread, and on the seventh day there shall be a solemn assembly for the LORD your God, when you shall do no work.

The Festival of Weeks Reviewed

9 You shall count seven weeks; begin to count the seven weeks from the time the sickle is first put to the standing grain. [10]Then you shall keep the festival of weeks to the LORD your God, contributing a freewill offering in proportion to the blessing that you have received from the LORD your God. [11]Rejoice before the LORD your God—you and your sons and your daughters, your male and female slaves, the Levites resident in your towns, as well as the strangers, the orphans, and the widows who are among you—at the place that the LORD your God will choose as a dwelling for his name. [12]Remember that you were a slave in Egypt, and diligently observe these statutes.

The Festival of Booths Reviewed

13 You shall keep the festival of booths[a] for seven days, when you have gathered in the produce from your threshing floor and your wine press. [14]Rejoice during your festival, you and your sons and your daughters, your male and female slaves, as well as the Levites, the strangers, the orphans, and the widows resident in your towns. [15]Seven days you shall keep the festival to the LORD your God at the place that the LORD will choose; for the LORD your God will bless you in all your produce and in all your undertakings, and you shall surely celebrate.

16 Three times a year all your males shall appear before the LORD your God at the place that he will choose: at the festival of unleavened bread, at the festival of weeks, and at the festival of booths.[a] They shall not appear before the LORD empty-handed; [17]all shall give as they are able, according to the blessing of the LORD your God that he has given you.

Municipal Judges and Officers

18 You shall appoint judges and officials throughout your tribes, in all your towns that the LORD your God is giving you, and they shall render just decisions for the people. [19]You must not distort justice; you must not show partiality; and you must not accept bribes, for a bribe blinds the eyes of the wise and subverts the cause of those who are in the right. [20]Justice, and only justice, you shall pursue, so that you may live and occupy the land that the LORD your God is giving you.

Forbidden Forms of Worship

21 You shall not plant any tree as a sacred pole[b] beside the altar that you make for the LORD your God; [22]nor shall you set up a stone pillar—things that the LORD your God hates.

17 You must not sacrifice to the LORD your God an ox or a sheep that has a defect, anything seriously wrong; for that is abhorrent to the LORD your God.

2 If there is found among you, in one of your towns that the LORD your God is giving you, a man or woman who does what is evil in the sight of the LORD your God, and transgresses his covenant [3]by going to serve other gods and worshiping them—whether the sun or the moon or any of the host of heaven, which I have forbidden— [4]and if it is reported to you or you hear of it, and you make a thorough inquiry, and the charge is proved true that such an abhorrent thing has occurred in Israel, [5]then you shall bring out to your gates that man or that woman who has committed this crime and you shall stone the man or woman to death. [6]On the evidence of two or three witnesses the death sentence shall be executed; a person must not be put to death on the evidence of only one witness. [7]The hands of the witnesses shall be the first raised against the person to execute the death penalty, and afterward the hands of all the people. So you shall purge the evil from your midst.

Legal Decisions by Priests and Judges

8 If a judicial decision is too difficult for you to make between one kind of bloodshed and another, one kind of legal right and another, or one kind of assault and another—any such matters of dispute in your towns—then you shall immediately go up to the place that the LORD your God will choose, [9]where you shall consult with the levitical priests and the judge who is in office in those days; they shall announce to you the decision in the case. [10]Carry out exactly the decision that they announce to you from the place that the LORD will choose,

a Or tabernacles; Heb succoth   b Heb Asherah

STUDY IT!

The Torah · Deuteronomy 17:8–11

The Hebrew word "torah" means "instruction" or "teaching." Only over time has it come to refer to the law. Torah refers most fundamentally to the law that was recorded as given by God to Moses on Mount Sinai. As the Israelites lived the Torah, it became equated with their very life and existence. It was the key for their organization as a people and gave consistency to their struggle to live their covenant with God.

Jewish people refer to the first five books of the Bible (the Pentateuch) as the Torah, because those books contain the law and instructions on how to live it. The other books of the Old Testament are also strongly connected to the Torah. The historical books record how the people and their kings kept the Torah or disobeyed it. The prophets in the prophetic books call the people to faithfulness to the law. They condemn idolatry and injustice and call the people to live the spirit of the Torah.

What laws are Christians called to live by today? Read the New Testament books of Galatians and James to find out or check out the Sermon on the Mount (Matthew 5:1-7:28).

diligently observing everything they instruct you. [11] You must carry out fully the law that they interpret for you or the ruling that they announce to you; do not turn aside from the decision that they announce to you, either to the right or to the left. [12] As for anyone who presumes to disobey the priest appointed to minister there to the LORD your God, or the judge, that person shall die. So you shall purge the evil from Israel. [13] All the people will hear and be afraid, and will not act presumptuously again.

Limitations of Royal Authority

14 When you have come into the land that the LORD your God is giving you, and have taken possession of it and settled in it, and you say, "I will set a king over me, like all the nations that are around me," [15] you may indeed set over you a king whom the LORD your God will choose. One of your own community you may set as king over you; you are not permitted to put a foreigner over you, who is not of your own community. [16] Even so, he must not acquire many horses for himself, or return the people to Egypt in order to acquire more horses, since the LORD has said to you, "You must never return that way again." [17] And he must not acquire many wives for himself, or else his heart will turn away; also silver and gold he must not acquire in great quantity for himself. [18] When he has taken the throne of his kingdom, he shall have a copy of this law written for him in the presence of the levitical priests. [19] It shall remain with him and he shall read

in it all the days of his life, so that he may learn to fear the LORD his God, diligently observing all the words of this law and these statutes, [20] neither exalting himself above other members of the community nor turning aside from the commandment, either to the right or to the left, so that he and his descendants may reign long over his kingdom in Israel.

Privileges of Priests and Levites

18 The levitical priests, the whole tribe of Levi, shall have no allotment or inheritance within Israel. They may eat the sacrifices that are the LORD's portion[a] [2] but they shall have no inheritance among the other members of the community; the LORD is their inheritance, as he promised them.

3 This shall be the priests' due from the people, from those offering a sacrifice, whether an ox or a sheep: they shall give to the priest the shoulder, the two jowls, and the stomach. [4] The first fruits of your grain, your wine, and your oil, as well as the first of the fleece of your sheep, you shall give him. [5] For the LORD your God has chosen Levi[b] out of all your tribes, to stand and minister in the name of the LORD, him and his sons for all time.

6 If a Levite leaves any of your towns, from wherever he has been residing in Israel, and comes to the place that the LORD will choose (and he may come whenever he wishes), [7] then he may minister in the name of the LORD his God, like all his fellow-Levites who stand to minister there before the LORD. [8] They shall have equal portions to eat, even

a Meaning of Heb uncertain   b Heb *him*

though they have income from the sale of family possessions.[a]

Child-Sacrifice, Divination, and Magic Prohibited

9 When you come into the land that the LORD your God is giving you, you must not learn to imitate the abhorrent practices of those nations. [10]No one shall be found among you who makes a son or daughter pass through fire, or who practices divination, or is a soothsayer, or an augur, or a sorcerer, [11]or one who casts spells, or who consults ghosts or spirits, or who seeks oracles from the dead. [12]For whoever does these things is abhorrent to the LORD; it is because of such abhorrent practices that the LORD your God is driving them out before you. [13]You must remain completely loyal to the LORD your God. [14]Although these nations that you are about to dispossess do give heed to soothsayers and diviners, as for you, the LORD your God does not permit you to do so.

A New Prophet Like Moses

15 The LORD your God will raise up for you a prophet[b] like me from among your own people; you shall heed such a prophet.[c] [16]This is what you requested of the LORD your God at Horeb on the day of the assembly when you said: "If I hear the voice of the LORD my God any more, or ever again see this great fire, I will die." [17]Then the LORD replied to me: "They are right in what they have said. [18]I will raise up for them a prophet[b] like you from among their own people; I will put my words in the mouth of the prophet,[d] who shall speak to them everything that I command. [19]Anyone who does not heed the words that the prophet[e] shall speak in my name, I myself will hold accountable. [20]But any prophet who speaks in the name of other gods, or who presumes to speak in my name a word that I have not commanded the prophet to speak—that prophet shall die." [21]You may say to yourself, "How can we recognize a word that the LORD has not spoken?" [22]If a prophet speaks in the name of the LORD but the thing does not take place or prove true, it is a word that the LORD has not spoken. The prophet has spoken it presumptuously; do not be frightened by it.

19 Laws concerning the Cities of Refuge

When the LORD your God has cut off the nations whose land the LORD your God is giving you, and you have dispossessed them and settled in their towns and in their houses, [2]you shall set apart three cities in the land that the LORD your God is giving you to possess. [3]You shall calculate the distances[f] and divide into three regions the land that the LORD your God gives you as a possession, so that any homicide can flee to one of them.

4 Now this is the case of a homicide who might flee there and live, that is, someone who has killed another person unintentionally when the two had not been at enmity before: [5]Suppose someone goes into the forest with another to cut wood, and when one of them swings the ax to cut down a tree, the head slips from the handle and strikes the other person who then dies; the killer may flee to one of these cities and live. [6]But if the distance is too great, the avenger of blood in hot anger might pursue and overtake and put the killer to death, although a death sentence was not deserved, since the two had not been at enmity before. [7]Therefore I command you: You shall set apart three cities.

8 If the LORD your God enlarges your territory, as he swore to your ancestors—and he will give you all the land that he promised your ancestors to give you, [9]provided you diligently observe this entire commandment that I command you today, by loving the LORD your God and walking always in his ways— then you shall add three more cities to these three, [10]so that the blood of an innocent person may not be shed in the land that the LORD your God is giving you as an inheritance, thereby bringing bloodguilt upon you.

11 But if someone at enmity with another lies in wait and attacks and takes the life of that person, and flees into one of these cities, [12]then the elders of the killer's city shall send to have the culprit taken from there and handed over to the avenger of blood to be put to death. [13]Show no pity; you shall purge the guilt of innocent blood from Israel, so that it may go well with you.

Property Boundaries

14 You must not move your neighbor's boundary marker, set up by former generations, on the property that will be allotted to you in the land that the LORD your God is giving you to possess.

Law concerning Witnesses

15 A single witness shall not suffice to convict a person of any crime or wrongdoing in connection

with any offense that may be committed. Only on the evidence of two or three witnesses shall a charge be sustained. [16]If a malicious witness comes forward to accuse someone of wrongdoing, [17]then both parties to the dispute shall appear before the LORD, before the priests and the judges who are in office in those days, [18]and the judges shall make a thorough inquiry. If the witness is a false witness, having testified falsely against another, [19]then you shall do to the false witness just as the false witness had meant to do to the other. So you shall purge the evil from your midst. [20]The rest shall hear and be afraid, and a crime such as this shall never again be committed among you. [21]Show no pity: life for life, eye for eye, tooth for tooth, hand for hand, foot for foot.

Rules of Warfare

20 When you go out to war against your enemies, and see horses and chariots, an army larger than your own, you shall not be afraid of them; for the LORD your God is with you, who brought you up from the land of Egypt. [2]Before you engage in battle, the priest shall come forward and speak to the troops, [3]and shall say to them: "Hear, O Israel! Today you are drawing near to do battle against your enemies. Do not lose heart, or be afraid, or panic, or be in dread of them; [4]for it is the LORD your God who goes with you, to fight for you against your enemies, to give you victory." [5]Then the officials shall address the troops, saying, "Has anyone built a new house but not dedicated it? He should go back to his house, or he might die in the battle and another dedicate it. [6]Has anyone planted a vineyard but not yet enjoyed its fruit? He should go back to his house, or he might die in the battle and another be first to enjoy its fruit. [7]Has anyone become engaged to a woman but not yet married her? He should go back to his house, or he might die in the battle and another marry her." [8]The officials shall continue to address the troops, saying, "Is anyone afraid or disheartened? He should go back to his house, or he might cause the heart of his comrades to melt like his own." [9]When the officials have finished addressing the troops, then the commanders shall take charge of them.

10 When you draw near to a town to fight against it, offer it terms of peace. [11]If it accepts your terms of peace and surrenders to you, then all the people in it shall serve you at forced labor. [12]If it does not submit to you peacefully, but makes war against you,

Facing Life's Battles
Deuteronomy 20:1

What are the wars in your life? Where do you experience problems, conflict, and lack of peace? We all hope we won't face war in armed conflict. But in a sense, war is around us in the struggles of everyday life.

We have fights with family and friends. We battle the pressures of society and our peers. We're at odds with the future. But this verse tells us we are not to fear times of war because our God is with us and will be our strength.

Our faith will be tested when we face conflict, but we must hold strong and be true to what God tells us. If we let our hearts be filled with God, the wars we face will become opportunities for God's love to triumph.

- What conflicts do you encounter daily?
- Do you sense that God is with you in these conflicts? If so, how?
- Pray for peace-filled ways to resolve conflict.

then you shall besiege it; [13]and when the LORD your God gives it into your hand, you shall put all its males to the sword. [14]You may, however, take as your booty the women, the children, livestock, and everything else in the town, all its spoil. You may enjoy the spoil of your enemies, which the LORD your God has given you. [15]Thus you shall treat all the towns that are very far from you, which are not towns of the nations here. [16]But as for the towns of these peoples that the LORD your God is giving you as an inheritance, you must not let anything that breathes remain alive. [17]You shall annihilate them—the Hittites and the Amorites, the Canaanites and the Perizzites, the Hivites and the Jebusites—just as the LORD your God has commanded, [18]so that they may not teach you to do all the abhorrent things that they do for their gods, and you thus sin against the LORD your God.

19 If you besiege a town for a long time, making

war against it in order to take it, you must not destroy its trees by wielding an ax against them. Although you may take food from them, you must not cut them down. Are trees in the field human beings that they should come under siege from you? [20]You may destroy only the trees that you know do not produce food; you may cut them down for use in building siegeworks against the town that makes war with you, until it falls.

21 Law concerning Murder by Persons Unknown

If, in the land that the LORD your God is giving you to possess, a body is found lying in open country, and it is not known who struck the person down, [2]then your elders and your judges shall come out to measure the distances to the towns that are near the body. [3]The elders of the town nearest the body shall take a heifer that has never been worked, one that has not pulled in the yoke; [4]the elders of that town shall bring the heifer down to a wadi with running water, which is neither plowed nor sown, and shall break the heifer's neck there in the wadi. [5]Then the priests, the sons of Levi, shall come forward, for the LORD your God has chosen them to minister to him and to pronounce blessings in the name of the LORD, and by their decision all cases of dispute and assault shall be settled. [6]All the elders of that town nearest the body shall wash their hands over the heifer whose neck was broken in the wadi, [7]and they shall declare: "Our hands did not shed this blood, nor were we witnesses to it. [8]Absolve, O LORD, your people Israel, whom you redeemed; do not let the guilt of innocent blood remain in the midst of your people Israel." Then they will be absolved of bloodguilt. [9]So you shall purge the guilt of innocent blood from your midst, because you must do what is right in the sight of the LORD.

Female Captives

10 When you go out to war against your enemies, and the LORD your God hands them over to you and you take them captive, [11]suppose you see among the captives a beautiful woman whom you desire and want to marry, [12]and so you bring her home to your house: she shall shave her head, pare her nails, [13]discard her captive's garb, and shall remain in your house a full month, mourning for her father and mother; after that you may go in to her and be her husband, and she shall be your wife. [14]But if you are not satisfied with her, you shall let her go free and not sell her for money. You must not treat her as a slave, since you have dishonored her.

The Right of the Firstborn

15 If a man has two wives, one of them loved and the other disliked, and if both the loved and the disliked have borne him sons, the firstborn being the son of the one who is disliked, [16]then on the day when he wills his possessions to his sons, he is not permitted to treat the son of the loved as the firstborn in preference to the son of the disliked, who is the firstborn. [17]He must acknowledge as firstborn the son of the one who is disliked, giving him a double portion[a] of all that he has; since he is the first issue of his virility, the right of the firstborn is his.

Rebellious Children

18 If someone has a stubborn and rebellious son who will not obey his father and mother, who does not heed them when they discipline him, [19]then his father and his mother shall take hold of him and bring him out to the elders of his town at the gate of that place. [20]They shall say to the elders of his town, "This son of ours is stubborn and rebellious. He will not obey us. He is a glutton and a drunkard." [21]Then all the men of the town shall stone him to death. So you shall purge the evil from your midst; and all Israel will hear, and be afraid.

Miscellaneous Laws

22 When someone is convicted of a crime punishable by death and is executed, and you hang him on a tree, [23]his corpse must not remain all night upon the tree; you shall bury him that same day, for anyone hung on a tree is under God's curse. You must not defile the land that the LORD your God is giving you for possession.

22

You shall not watch your neighbor's ox or sheep straying away and ignore them; you shall take them back to their owner. [2]If the owner does not reside near you or you do not know who the owner is, you shall bring it to your own house, and it shall remain with you until the owner claims it; then you shall return it. [3]You shall do the same with a neighbor's donkey; you shall do the same with a neighbor's garment; and you shall do the same with anything else that your neighbor loses and you find. You may not withhold your help.

4 You shall not see your neighbor's donkey or ox

a Heb *two-thirds*

fallen on the road and ignore it; you shall help to lift it up.

5 A woman shall not wear a man's apparel, nor shall a man put on a woman's garment; for whoever does such things is abhorrent to the LORD your God.

6 If you come on a bird's nest, in any tree or on the ground, with fledglings or eggs, with the mother sitting on the fledglings or on the eggs, you shall not take the mother with the young. [7]Let the mother go, taking only the young for yourself, in order that it may go well with you and you may live long.

8 When you build a new house, you shall make a parapet for your roof; otherwise you might have bloodguilt on your house, if anyone should fall from it.

9 You shall not sow your vineyard with a second kind of seed, or the whole yield will have to be forfeited, both the crop that you have sown and the yield of the vineyard itself.

10 You shall not plow with an ox and a donkey yoked together.

11 You shall not wear clothes made of wool and linen woven together.

12 You shall make tassels on the four corners of the cloak with which you cover yourself.

Laws concerning Sexual Relations

13 Suppose a man marries a woman, but after going in to her, he dislikes her [14]and makes up charges against her, slandering her by saying, "I married this woman; but when I lay with her, I did not find evidence of her virginity." [15]The father of the young woman and her mother shall then submit the evidence of the young woman's virginity to the elders of the city at the gate. [16]The father of the young woman shall say to the elders: "I gave my daughter in marriage to this man but he dislikes her; [17]now he has made up charges against her, saying, 'I did not find evidence of your daughter's virginity.' But here is the evidence of my daughter's virginity." Then they shall spread out the cloth before the elders of the town. [18]The elders of that town shall take the man and punish him; [19]they shall fine him one hundred shekels of silver (which they shall give to the young woman's father) because he has slandered a virgin of Israel. She shall remain his wife; he shall not be permitted to divorce her as long as he lives.

20 If, however, this charge is true, that evidence of the young woman's virginity was not found, [21]then they shall bring the young woman out to the entrance of her father's house and the men of her town shall stone her to death, because she committed a disgraceful act in Israel by prostituting herself in her father's house. So you shall purge the evil from your midst.

22 If a man is caught lying with the wife of another man, both of them shall die, the man who lay with the woman as well as the woman. So you shall purge the evil from Israel.

23 If there is a young woman, a virgin already engaged to be married, and a man meets her in the town and lies with her, [24]you shall bring both of them to the gate of that town and stone them to death, the young woman because she did not cry for help in the town and the man because he violated his neighbor's wife. So you shall purge the evil from your midst.

25 But if the man meets the engaged woman in the open country, and the man seizes her and lies with her, then only the man who lay with her shall die. [26]You shall do nothing to the young woman; the young woman has not committed an offense punishable by death, because this case is like that of someone who attacks and murders a neighbor. [27]Since he found her in the open country, the engaged woman may have cried for help, but there was no one to rescue her.

28 If a man meets a virgin who is not engaged, and seizes her and lies with her, and they are caught in the act, [29]the man who lay with her shall give fifty shekels of silver to the young woman's father, and she shall become his wife. Because he violated her he shall not be permitted to divorce her as long as he lives.

30[a] A man shall not marry his father's wife, thereby violating his father's rights.[b]

23 Those Excluded from the Assembly

No one whose testicles are crushed or whose penis is cut off shall be admitted to the assembly of the LORD.

2 Those born of an illicit union shall not be admitted to the assembly of the LORD. Even to the tenth generation, none of their descendants shall be admitted to the assembly of the LORD.

3 No Ammonite or Moabite shall be admitted to the assembly of the LORD. Even to the tenth generation, none of their descendants shall be admitted to the assembly of the LORD, [4]because they did not meet you with food and water on your journey out of Egypt, and because they hired against you Balaam

---

a Ch 23.1 in Heb   b Heb *uncovering his father's skirt*

son of Beor, from Pethor of Mesopotamia, to curse you. [5](Yet the LORD your God refused to heed Balaam; the LORD your God turned the curse into a blessing for you, because the LORD your God loved you.) [6]You shall never promote their welfare or their prosperity as long as you live.

7 You shall not abhor any of the Edomites, for they are your kin. You shall not abhor any of the Egyptians, because you were an alien residing in their land. [8]The children of the third generation that are born to them may be admitted to the assembly of the LORD.

Sanitary, Ritual, and Humanitarian Precepts

9 When you are encamped against your enemies you shall guard against any impropriety.

10 If one of you becomes unclean because of a nocturnal emission, then he shall go outside the camp; he must not come within the camp. [11]When evening comes, he shall wash himself with water, and when the sun has set, he may come back into the camp.

12 You shall have a designated area outside the camp to which you shall go. [13]With your utensils you shall have a trowel; when you relieve yourself outside, you shall dig a hole with it and then cover up your excrement. [14]Because the LORD your God travels along with your camp, to save you and to hand over your enemies to you, therefore your camp must be holy, so that he may not see anything indecent among you and turn away from you.

15 Slaves who have escaped to you from their owners shall not be given back to them. [16]They shall reside with you, in your midst, in any place they choose in any one of your towns, wherever they please; you shall not oppress them.

17 None of the daughters of Israel shall be a temple prostitute; none of the sons of Israel shall be a temple prostitute. [18]You shall not bring the fee of a prostitute or the wages of a male prostitute[a] into the house of the LORD your God in payment for any vow, for both of these are abhorrent to the LORD your God.

19 You shall not charge interest on loans to another Israelite, interest on money, interest on provisions, interest on anything that is lent. [20]On loans to a foreigner you may charge interest, but on loans to another Israelite you may not charge interest, so that the LORD your God may bless you in all your under-

takings in the land that you are about to enter and possess.

21 If you make a vow to the LORD your God, do not postpone fulfilling it; for the LORD your God will surely require it of you, and you would incur guilt. [22]But if you refrain from vowing, you will not incur guilt. [23]Whatever your lips utter you must diligently perform, just as you have freely vowed to the LORD your God with your own mouth.

24 If you go into your neighbor's vineyard, you may eat your fill of grapes, as many as you wish, but you shall not put any in a container.

25 If you go into your neighbor's standing grain, you may pluck the ears with your hand, but you shall not put a sickle to your neighbor's standing grain.

24 Laws concerning Marriage and Divorce

Suppose a man enters into marriage with a woman, but she does not please him because he finds something objectionable about her, and so he writes her a certificate of divorce, puts it in her hand, and sends her out of his house; she then leaves his house [2]and goes off to become another man's wife. [3]Then suppose the second man dislikes her, writes her a bill of divorce, puts it in her hand, and sends her out of his house (or the second man who married her dies); [4]her first husband, who sent her away, is not permitted to take her again to be his wife after she has been defiled; for that would be abhorrent to the LORD, and you shall not bring guilt on the land that the LORD your God is giving you as a possession.

Miscellaneous Laws

5 When a man is newly married, he shall not go out with the army or be charged with any related duty. He shall be free at home one year, to be happy with the wife whom he has married.

α Heb *a dog*

The Outsiders • Deuteronomy 24:10–21

One remarkable aspect of Israel's covenant was the command to care for the poor, aliens or strangers, widows, and orphans. These four groups were the outsiders in ancient Israel because they fell outside Israel's socioeconomic system. The poor often had no means to sustain themselves. Strangers, or aliens, were not part of Israel's tribal organization. Widows depended on the charity of others. Orphans were destitute because they had no family to help them survive.

God reminds the Israelites that they were once enslaved in Egypt—poor, oppressed, orphans in a foreign land. God responded to their cry for help and wants them in turn to care for the poor, oppressed, forgotten, and marginalized in their midst.

In a world that is more connected than ever, we are surrounded by those in need of care—in our backyard and around the world. God's command to care for them is repeated in the New Testament (James 1:27; Mark 10:17-31), and it's as true for us today as it was for the Israelites.

6 No one shall take a mill or an upper millstone in pledge, for that would be taking a life in pledge.

7 If someone is caught kidnaping another Israelite, enslaving or selling the Israelite, then that kidnaper shall die. So you shall purge the evil from your midst.

8 Guard against an outbreak of a leprous[a] skin disease by being very careful; you shall carefully observe whatever the levitical priests instruct you, just as I have commanded them. [9]Remember what the LORD your God did to Miriam on your journey out of Egypt.

10 When you make your neighbor a loan of any kind, you shall not go into the house to take the pledge. [11]You shall wait outside, while the person to whom you are making the loan brings the pledge out to you. [12]If the person is poor, you shall not sleep in the garment given you as[b] the pledge. [13]You shall give the pledge back by sunset, so that your neighbor may sleep in the cloak and bless you; and it will be to your credit before the LORD your God.

14 You shall not withhold the wages of poor and needy laborers, whether other Israelites or aliens who reside in your land in one of your towns. [15]You shall pay them their wages daily before sunset, because they are poor and their livelihood depends on them; otherwise they might cry to the LORD against you, and you would incur guilt.

16 Parents shall not be put to death for their children, nor shall children be put to death for their parents; only for their own crimes may persons be put to death.

17 You shall not deprive a resident alien or an orphan of justice; you shall not take a widow's garment in pledge. [18]Remember that you were a slave in Egypt and the LORD your God redeemed you from there; therefore I command you to do this.

19 When you reap your harvest in your field and forget a sheaf in the field, you shall not go back to get it; it shall be left for the alien, the orphan, and the widow, so that the LORD your God may bless you in all your undertakings. [20]When you beat your olive trees, do not strip what is left; it shall be for the alien, the orphan, and the widow.

21 When you gather the grapes of your vineyard, do not glean what is left; it shall be for the alien, the orphan, and the widow. [22]Remember that you were a slave in the land of Egypt; therefore I am commanding you to do this.

25 Suppose two persons have a dispute and enter into litigation, and the judges decide between them, declaring one to be in the right and the other to be in the wrong. [2]If the one in the wrong deserves to be flogged, the judge shall make that person lie down and be beaten in his presence with the number of lashes proportionate to the offense. [3]Forty lashes may be given but not more; if more lashes than these are given, your neighbor will be degraded in your sight.

4 You shall not muzzle an ox while it is treading out the grain.

Levirate Marriage

5 When brothers reside together, and one of them

---

a A term for several skin diseases; precise meaning uncertain **b** Heb lacks *the garment given you as*

dies and has no son, the wife of the deceased shall not be married outside the family to a stranger. Her husband's brother shall go in to her, taking her in marriage, and performing the duty of a husband's brother to her, [6]and the firstborn whom she bears shall succeed to the name of the deceased brother, so that his name may not be blotted out of Israel. [7]But if the man has no desire to marry his brother's widow, then his brother's widow shall go up to the elders at the gate and say, "My husband's brother refuses to perpetuate his brother's name in Israel; he will not perform the duty of a husband's brother to me." [8]Then the elders of his town shall summon him and speak to him. If he persists, saying, "I have no desire to marry her," [9]then his brother's wife shall go up to him in the presence of the elders, pull his sandal off his foot, spit in his face, and declare, "This is what is done to the man who does not build up his brother's house." [10]Throughout Israel his family shall be known as "the house of him whose sandal was pulled off."

Various Commands

11 If men get into a fight with one another, and the wife of one intervenes to rescue her husband from the grip of his opponent by reaching out and seizing his genitals, [12]you shall cut off her hand; show no pity.

13 You shall not have in your bag two kinds of weights, large and small. [14]You shall not have in your house two kinds of measures, large and small. [15]You shall have only a full and honest weight; you shall have only a full and honest measure, so that your days may be long in the land that the LORD your God is giving you. [16]For all who do such things, all who act dishonestly, are abhorrent to the LORD your God.

17 Remember what Amalek did to you on your journey out of Egypt, [18]how he attacked you on the way, when you were faint and weary, and struck down all who lagged behind you; he did not fear God. [19]Therefore when the LORD your God has given you rest from all your enemies on every hand, in the land that the LORD your God is giving you as an inheritance to possess, you shall blot out the remembrance of Amalek from under heaven; do not forget.

First Fruits and Tithes

26 When you have come into the land that the LORD your God is giving you as an inheritance to possess, and you possess it, and settle in it, [2]you shall take some of the first of all the fruit of the ground, which you harvest from the land that the LORD your God is giving you, and you shall put it in a basket and go to the place that the LORD your God will choose as a dwelling for his name. [3]You shall go to the priest who is in office at that time, and say to him, "Today I declare to the LORD your God that I have come into the land that the LORD swore to our ancestors to give us." [4]When the priest takes the basket from your hand and sets it down before the altar of the LORD your God, [5]you shall make this response before the LORD your God: "A wandering Aramean was my ancestor; he went down into Egypt and lived there as an alien, few in number, and there he became a great nation, mighty and populous. [6]When the Egyptians treated us harshly and afflicted us, by imposing hard labor on us, [7]we cried to the LORD, the God of our ancestors; the LORD heard our voice and saw our affliction, our toil, and our oppression. [8]The LORD brought us out of Egypt with a mighty hand and an outstretched arm, with a terrifying display of power, and with signs and wonders; [9]and he brought us into this place and gave us this land, a land flowing with milk and honey. [10]So now I bring the first of the fruit of the ground that you, O LORD, have given me." You shall set it down before the LORD your God and bow down before the LORD your God. [11]Then you, together with the Levites and the aliens who reside among you, shall celebrate with all the bounty that the LORD your God has given to you and to your house.

12 When you have finished paying all the tithe of your produce in the third year (which is the year of the tithe), giving it to the Levites, the aliens, the orphans, and the widows, so that they may eat their fill within your towns, [13]then you shall say before the LORD your God: "I have removed the sacred portion from the house, and I have given it to the Levites, the resident aliens, the orphans, and the widows, in accordance with your entire commandment that you commanded me; I have neither transgressed nor forgotten any of your commandments: [14]I have not eaten of it while in mourning; I have not removed any of it while I was unclean; and I have not offered any of it to the dead. I have obeyed the LORD my God, doing just as you commanded me. [15]Look down from your holy habitation, from heaven, and bless your people Israel and

the ground that you have given us, as you swore to our ancestors—a land flowing with milk and honey."

Concluding Exhortation

16 This very day the LORD your God is commanding you to observe these statutes and ordinances; so observe them diligently with all your heart and with all your soul. [17]Today you have obtained the LORD's agreement: to be your God; and for you to walk in his ways, to keep his statutes, his commandments, and his ordinances, and to obey him. [18]Today the LORD has obtained your agreement: to be his treasured people, as he promised you, and to keep his commandments; [19]for him to set you high above all nations that he has made, in praise and in fame and in honor; and for you to be a people holy to the LORD your God, as he promised.

27 ### The Inscribed Stones and Altar on Mount Ebal

Then Moses and the elders of Israel charged all the people as follows: Keep the entire commandment that I am commanding you today. [2]On the day that you cross over the Jordan into the land that the LORD your God is giving you, you shall set up large stones and cover them with plaster. [3]You shall write on them all the words of this law when you have crossed over, to enter the land that the LORD your God is giving you, a land flowing with milk and honey, as the LORD, the God of your ancestors, promised you. [4]So when you have crossed over the Jordan, you shall set up these stones, about which I am commanding you today, on Mount Ebal, and you shall cover them with plaster. [5]And you shall build an altar there to the LORD your God, an altar of stones on which you have not used an iron tool. [6]You must build the altar of the LORD your God of unhewn[a] stones. Then offer up burnt offerings on it to the LORD your God, [7]make sacrifices of well-being, and eat them there, rejoicing before the LORD your God. [8]You shall write on the stones all the words of this law very clearly.

9 Then Moses and the levitical priests spoke to all Israel, saying: Keep silence and hear, O Israel! This very day you have become the people of the LORD your God. [10]Therefore obey the LORD your God, observing his commandments and his statutes that I am commanding you today.

Twelve Curses

11 The same day Moses charged the people as follows: [12]When you have crossed over the Jordan, these shall stand on Mount Gerizim for the blessing of the people: Simeon, Levi, Judah, Issachar, Joseph, and Benjamin. [13]And these shall stand on Mount Ebal for the curse: Reuben, Gad, Asher, Zebulun, Dan, and Naphtali. [14]Then the Levites shall declare in a loud voice to all the Israelites:

15 "Cursed be anyone who makes an idol or casts an image, anything abhorrent to the LORD, the work of an artisan, and sets it up in secret." All the people shall respond, saying, "Amen!"

16 "Cursed be anyone who dishonors father or mother." All the people shall say, "Amen!"

17 "Cursed be anyone who moves a neighbor's boundary marker." All the people shall say, "Amen!"

18 "Cursed be anyone who misleads a blind person on the road." All the people shall say, "Amen!"

19 "Cursed be anyone who deprives the alien, the orphan, and the widow of justice." All the people shall say, "Amen!"

20 "Cursed be anyone who lies with his father's wife, because he has violated his father's rights."[b] All the people shall say, "Amen!"

21 "Cursed be anyone who lies with any animal." All the people shall say, "Amen!"

22 "Cursed be anyone who lies with his sister, whether the daughter of his father or the daughter of his mother." All the people shall say, "Amen!"

23 "Cursed be anyone who lies with his mother-in-law." All the people shall say, "Amen!"

24 "Cursed be anyone who strikes down a neighbor in secret." All the people shall say, "Amen!"

25 "Cursed be anyone who takes a bribe to shed innocent blood." All the people shall say, "Amen!"

26 "Cursed be anyone who does not uphold the words of this law by observing them." All the people shall say, "Amen!"

28 ### Blessings for Obedience

If you will only obey the LORD your God, by diligently observing all his commandments that I am commanding you today, the LORD your God will set you high above all the nations of the earth; [2]all these blessings shall come upon you and overtake you, if you obey the LORD your God:

3 Blessed shall you be in the city, and blessed shall you be in the field.

4 Blessed shall be the fruit of your womb, the fruit

---

a Heb *whole*   b Heb *uncovered his father's skirt*

of your ground, and the fruit of your livestock, both the increase of your cattle and the issue of your flock.

5 Blessed shall be your basket and your kneading bowl.

6 Blessed shall you be when you come in, and blessed shall you be when you go out.

7 The LORD will cause your enemies who rise against you to be defeated before you; they shall come out against you one way, and flee before you seven ways. [8]The LORD will command the blessing upon you in your barns, and in all that you undertake; he will bless you in the land that the LORD your God is giving you. [9]The LORD will establish you as his holy people, as he has sworn to you, if you keep the commandments of the LORD your God and walk in his ways. [10]All the peoples of the earth shall see that you are called by the name of the LORD, and they shall be afraid of you. [11]The LORD will make you abound in prosperity, in the fruit of your womb, in the fruit of your livestock, and in the fruit of your ground in the land that the LORD swore to your ancestors to give you. [12]The LORD will open for you his rich storehouse, the heavens, to give the rain of your land in its season and to bless all your undertakings. You will lend to many nations, but you will not borrow. [13]The LORD will make you the head, and not the tail; you shall be only at the top, and not at the bottom—if you obey the commandments of the LORD your God, which I am commanding you today, by diligently observing them, [14]and if you do not turn aside from any of the words that I am commanding you today, either to the right or to the left, following other gods to serve them.

Warnings against Disobedience

15 But if you will not obey the LORD your God by diligently observing all his commandments and decrees, which I am commanding you today, then all these curses shall come upon you and overtake you:

16 Cursed shall you be in the city, and cursed shall you be in the field.

17 Cursed shall be your basket and your kneading bowl.

18 Cursed shall be the fruit of your womb, the fruit of your ground, the increase of your cattle and the issue of your flock.

19 Cursed shall you be when you come in, and cursed shall you be when you go out.

20 The LORD will send upon you disaster, panic, and frustration in everything you attempt to do, until you are destroyed and perish quickly, on account of the evil of your deeds, because you have forsaken me. [21]The LORD will make the pestilence cling to you until it has consumed you off the land that you are entering to possess. [22]The LORD will afflict you with consumption, fever, inflammation, with fiery heat and drought, and with blight and mildew; they shall pursue you until you perish. [23]The sky over your head shall be bronze, and the earth under you iron. [24]The LORD will change the rain of your land into powder, and only dust shall come down upon you from the sky until you are destroyed.

25 The LORD will cause you to be defeated before your enemies; you shall go out against them one way and flee before them seven ways. You shall become an object of horror to all the kingdoms of the earth. [26]Your corpses shall be food for every bird of the air and animal of the earth, and there shall be no one to frighten them away. [27]The LORD will afflict you with the boils of Egypt, with ulcers, scurvy, and itch, of which you cannot be healed. [28]The LORD will afflict you with madness, blindness, and confusion of mind; [29]you shall grope about at noon as blind people grope in darkness, but you shall be unable to find your way; and you shall be continually abused and robbed, without anyone to help. [30]You shall become engaged to a woman, but another man shall lie with her. You shall build a house, but not live in it. You shall plant a vineyard, but not enjoy its fruit. [31]Your ox shall be butchered before your eyes, but you shall not eat of it. Your donkey shall be stolen in front of you, and shall not be restored to you. Your sheep shall be given to your enemies, without anyone to help you. [32]Your sons and daughters shall be given to another people, while you look on; you will strain your eyes looking for them all day but be powerless to do anything. [33]A people whom you do not know shall eat up the fruit of your ground and of all your labors; you shall be continually abused and crushed, [34]and driven mad by the sight that your eyes shall see. [35]The LORD will strike you on the knees and on the legs with grievous boils of which you cannot be healed, from the sole of your foot to the crown of your head. [36]The LORD will bring you, and the king whom you set over you, to a nation that neither you nor your ancestors have known, where you shall serve other gods, of wood and stone. [37]You shall become an object of horror, a proverb, and a byword among

all the peoples where the LORD will lead you.
38 You shall carry much seed into the field but shall gather little in, for the locust shall consume it. [39]You shall plant vineyards and dress them, but you shall neither drink the wine nor gather the grapes, for the worm shall eat them. [40]You shall have olive trees throughout all your territory, but you shall not anoint yourself with the oil, for your olives shall drop off. [41]You shall have sons and daughters, but they shall not remain yours, for they shall go into captivity. [42]All your trees and the fruit of your ground the cicada shall take over. [43]Aliens residing among you shall ascend above you higher and higher, while you shall descend lower and lower. [44]They shall lend to you but you shall not lend to them; they shall be the head and you shall be the tail.

45 All these curses shall come upon you, pursuing and overtaking you until you are destroyed, because you did not obey the LORD your God, by observing the commandments and the decrees that he commanded you. [46]They shall be among you and your descendants as a sign and a portent forever.

47 Because you did not serve the LORD your God joyfully and with gladness of heart for the abundance of everything, [48]therefore you shall serve your enemies whom the LORD will send against you, in hunger and thirst, in nakedness and lack of everything. He will put an iron yoke on your neck until he has destroyed you. [49]The LORD will bring a nation from far away, from the end of the earth, to swoop down on you like an eagle, a nation whose language you do not understand, [50]a grim-faced nation showing no respect to the old or favor to the young. [51]It shall consume the fruit of your livestock and the fruit of your ground until you are destroyed, leaving you neither grain, wine, and oil, nor the increase of your cattle and the issue of your flock, until it has made you perish. [52]It shall besiege you in all your towns until your high and fortified walls, in which you trusted, come down throughout your land; it shall besiege you in all your towns throughout the land that the LORD your God has given you. [53]In the desperate straits to which the enemy siege reduces you, you will eat the fruit of your womb, the flesh of your own sons and daughters whom the LORD your God has given you. [54]Even the most refined and gentle of men among you will begrudge food to his own brother, to the wife whom he embraces, and to the last of his remaining children, [55]giving to none of them any of the flesh of his children whom he is eating, because nothing else remains to him, in the desperate straits to which the enemy siege will reduce you in all your towns. [56]She who is the most refined and gentle among you, so gentle and refined that she does not venture to set the sole of her foot on the ground, will begrudge food to the husband whom she embraces, to her own son, and to her own daughter, [57]begrudging even the afterbirth that comes out from between her thighs, and the children that she bears, because she is eating them in secret for lack of anything else, in the desperate straits to which the enemy siege will reduce you in your towns.

58 If you do not diligently observe all the words of this law that are written in this book, fearing this glorious and awesome name, the LORD your God, [59]then the LORD will overwhelm both you and your offspring with severe and lasting afflictions and grievous and lasting maladies. [60]He will bring back upon you all the diseases of Egypt, of which you were in dread, and they shall cling to you. [61]Every other malady and affliction, even though not recorded in the book of this law, the LORD will inflict on you until you are destroyed. [62]Although once you were as numerous as the stars in heaven, you shall be left few in number, because you did not obey the LORD your God. [63]And just as the LORD took delight in making you prosperous and numerous, so the LORD will take delight in bringing you to ruin and destruction; you shall be plucked off the land that you are entering to possess. [64]The LORD will scatter you among all peoples, from one end of the earth to the other; and there you shall serve other gods, of wood and stone, which neither you nor your ancestors have known. [65]Among those nations you shall find no ease, no resting place for the sole of your foot. There the LORD will give you a trembling heart, failing eyes, and a languishing spirit. [66]Your life shall hang in doubt before you; night and day you shall be in dread, with no assurance of your life. [67]In the morning you shall say, "If only it were evening!" and at evening you shall say, "If only it were morning!"— because of the dread that your heart shall feel and the sights that your eyes shall see. [68]The LORD will bring you back in ships to Egypt, by a route that I promised you would never see again; and there you shall offer yourselves for sale to your enemies as male and female slaves, but there will be no buyer.

29 [a] These are the words of the covenant that the LORD commanded Moses to make with the Israelites in the land of Moab, in addition to the covenant that he had made with them at Horeb.

The Covenant Renewed in Moab

2[a] Moses summoned all Israel and said to them: You have seen all that the LORD did before your eyes in the land of Egypt, to Pharaoh and to all his servants and to all his land, [3]the great trials that your eyes saw, the signs, and those great wonders. [4]But to this day the LORD has not given you a mind to understand, or eyes to see, or ears to hear. [5]I have led you forty years in the wilderness. The clothes on your back have not worn out, and the sandals on your feet have not worn out; [6]you have not eaten bread, and you have not drunk wine or strong drink—so that you may know that I am the LORD your God. [7]When you came to this place, King Sihon of Heshbon and King Og of Bashan came out against us for battle, but we defeated them. [8]We took their land and gave it as an inheritance to the Reubenites, the Gadites, and the half-tribe of Manasseh. [9]Therefore diligently observe the words of this covenant, in order that you may succeed[b] in everything that you do.

10 You stand assembled today, all of you, before the LORD your God—the leaders of your tribes,[c] your elders, and your officials, all the men of Israel, [11]your children, your women, and the aliens who are in your camp, both those who cut your wood and those who draw your water— [12]to enter into the covenant of the LORD your God, sworn by an oath, which the LORD your God is making with you today; [13]in order that he may establish you today as his people, and that he may be your God, as he promised you and as he swore to your ancestors, to Abraham, to Isaac, and to Jacob. [14]I am making this covenant, sworn by an oath, not only with you who stand here with us today before the LORD our God, [15]but also with those who are not here with us today. [16]You know how we lived in the land of Egypt, and how we came through the midst of the nations through which you passed. [17]You have seen their detestable things, the filthy idols of wood and stone, of silver and gold, that were among them. [18]It may be that there is among you a man or woman, or a family or tribe, whose heart is already turning away from the LORD our God to serve the gods of those nations. It may be that there is among you a root sprouting poisonous and bitter growth. [19]All who hear the words of this oath and bless themselves, thinking in their hearts, "We are safe even though we go our own stubborn ways" (thus bringing disaster on moist and dry alike)[d]— [20]the LORD will be unwilling to pardon them, for the LORD's anger and passion will smoke against them. All the curses written in this book will descend on them, and the LORD will blot out their names from under heaven. [21]The LORD will single them out from all the tribes of Israel for calamity, in accordance with all the curses of the covenant written in this book of the law. [22]The next generation, your children who rise up after you, as well as the foreigner who comes from a distant country, will see the devastation of that land and the afflictions with which the LORD has afflicted it— [23]all its soil burned out by sulfur and salt, nothing planted, nothing sprouting, unable to support any vegetation, like the destruction of Sodom and Gomorrah, Admah and Zeboiim, which the LORD destroyed in his fierce anger— [24]they and indeed all the nations will wonder, "Why has the LORD done thus to this land? What caused this great display of anger?" [25]They will conclude, "It is because they abandoned the covenant of the LORD, the God of their ancestors, which he made with them when he brought them out of the land of Egypt. [26]They turned and served other gods, worshiping them, gods whom they had not known and whom he had not allotted to them; [27]so the anger of the LORD was kindled against that land, bringing on it every curse written in this book. [28]The LORD uprooted them from their land in anger, fury, and great wrath, and cast them into another land, as is now the case." [29]The secret things belong to the LORD our God, but the revealed things belong to us and to our children forever, to observe all the words of this law.

God's Fidelity Assured

30 When all these things have happened to you, the blessings and the curses that I have set before you, if you call them to mind among all the nations where the LORD your God has driven you, [2]and return to the LORD your God, and you and your children obey him with all your heart and with all your soul, just as I am commanding you today, [3]then the LORD your God will restore your fortunes and have compassion on you, gathering you again from all the peoples among whom the LORD your God has scattered you. [4]Even if you are exiled to the ends of the world,[e] from there the LORD your God will gather you, and from there he will bring you back. [5]The LORD your God will bring you into the land that your

---

a Ch 29.1 in Heb   b Or deal wisely   c Gk Syr: Heb your leaders, your tribes   d Meaning of Heb uncertain   e Heb of heaven

LIVE IT!

Choose Life · Deuteronomy 30:19–20

We live in a culture that is constantly filled with images of violence and death, especially in the media. Many people seem to choose options that lead to death rather than life. Temptations to do so are everywhere.

These verses are a powerful call to choose life through obedience to God. What options lead us to life rather than death? What choices give life to others?

We are called to a full life, lived out in God's presence and in service to others. Think about the choices you make each day. Something as simple as the choice to smile at someone and start a conversation can make a big difference. That is a life-giving choice and can even make a lifesaving difference.

- How can you love, obey, and hold fast to God today?
- What choices can you make now to serve others—friends, family, or people in need in your community and around the world?
- Think of someone you know who is facing some tough choices. How can you encourage that person to choose the things that bring fullness of life?

ancestors possessed, and you will possess it; he will make you more prosperous and numerous than your ancestors.

6 Moreover, the LORD your God will circumcise your heart and the heart of your descendants, so that you will love the LORD your God with all your heart and with all your soul, in order that you may live. [7]The LORD your God will put all these curses on your enemies and on the adversaries who took advantage of you. [8]Then you shall again obey the LORD, observing all his commandments that I am commanding you today, [9]and the LORD your God will make you abundantly prosperous in all your undertakings, in the fruit of your body, in the fruit of your livestock, and in the fruit of your soil. For the LORD will again take delight in prospering you, just as he delighted in prospering your ancestors, [10]when you obey the LORD your God by observing his commandments and decrees that are written in this book of the law, because you turn to the LORD your God with all your heart and with all your soul.

Exhortation to Choose Life

11 Surely, this commandment that I am commanding you today is not too hard for you, nor is it too far away. [12]It is not in heaven, that you should say, "Who will go up to heaven for us, and get it for us so that we may hear it and observe it?" [13]Neither is it beyond the sea, that you should say, "Who will cross to the other side of the sea for us, and get it for us so that we may hear it and observe it?" [14]No, the word is very near to you; it is in your mouth and in your heart for you to observe.

15 See, I have set before you today life and prosperity, death and adversity. [16]If you obey the commandments of the LORD your God[a] that I am commanding you today, by loving the LORD your God, walking in his ways, and observing his commandments, decrees, and ordinances, then you shall live and become numerous, and the LORD your God will bless you in the land that you are entering to possess. [17]But if your heart turns away and you do not hear, but are led astray to bow down to other gods and serve them, [18]I declare to you today that you shall perish; you shall not live long in the land that you are crossing the Jordan to enter and possess. [19]I call heaven and earth to witness against you today that I have set before you life and death, blessings and curses. Choose life so that you and your descendants may live, [20]loving the LORD your God, obeying him, and holding fast to him; for that means life to you and length of days, so that you may live in the land that the LORD swore to give to your ancestors, to Abraham, to Isaac, and to Jacob.

Joshua Becomes Moses' Successor

When Moses had finished speaking all[b] these words to all Israel, [2]he said to them:

a Gk: Heb lacks *If you obey the commandments of the LORD your God*   b Q Ms Gk: MT *Moses went and spoke*

"I am now one hundred twenty years old. I am no longer able to get about, and the Lord has told me, 'You shall not cross over this Jordan.' ³The Lord your God himself will cross over before you. He will destroy these nations before you, and you shall dispossess them. Joshua also will cross over before you, as the Lord promised.

⁴The Lord will do to them as he did to Sihon and Og, the kings of the Amorites, and to their land, when he destroyed them. ⁵The Lord will give them over to you and you shall deal with them in full accord with the command that I have given to you. ⁶Be strong and bold; have no fear or dread of them, because it is the Lord your God who goes with you; he will not fail you or forsake you."

7 Then Moses summoned Joshua and said to him in the sight of all Israel: "Be strong and bold, for you are the one who will go with this people into the land that the Lord has sworn to their ancestors to give them; and you will put them in possession of it. ⁸It is the Lord who goes before you. He will be with you; he will not fail you or forsake you. Do not fear or be dismayed."

The Law to Be Read Every Seventh Year

9 Then Moses wrote down this law, and gave it to the priests, the sons of Levi, who carried the ark of the covenant of the Lord, and to all the elders of Israel. ¹⁰Moses commanded them: "Every seventh year, in the scheduled year of remission, during the festival of booths,ᵃ ¹¹when all Israel comes to appear before the Lord your God at the place that he will choose, you shall read this law before all Israel in their hearing. ¹²Assemble the people—men, women, and children, as well as the aliens residing in your towns—so that they may hear and learn to fear the Lord your God and to observe diligently all the words of this law, ¹³and so that their children, who have not known it, may hear and learn to fear the Lord your God, as long as you live in the land that you are crossing over the Jordan to possess."

Moses and Joshua Receive God's Charge

14 The Lord said to Moses, "Your time to die is near; call Joshua and present yourselves in the tent of meeting, so that I may commission him." So Mo-

ses and Joshua went and presented themselves in the tent of meeting, ¹⁵and the Lord appeared at the tent in a pillar of cloud; the pillar of cloud stood at the entrance to the tent.

16 The Lord said to Moses, "Soon you will lie down with your ancestors. Then this people will begin to prostitute themselves to the foreign gods in their midst, the gods of the land into which they are going; they will forsake me, breaking my covenant that I have made with them. ¹⁷My anger will be kindled against them in that day. I will forsake them and hide my face from them; they will become easy prey, and many terrible troubles will come upon them. In that day they will say, 'Have not these troubles come upon us because our God is not in our midst?' ¹⁸On that day I will surely hide my face on account of all the evil they have done by turning to other gods. ¹⁹Now therefore write this song, and teach it to the Israelites; put it in their mouths, in order that this song may be a witness for me against the Israelites. ²⁰For when I have brought them into the land flowing with milk and honey, which I promised on oath to their ancestors, and they have eaten their fill and grown fat, they will turn to other gods and serve them, despising me and breaking my covenant. ²¹And when many terrible troubles come upon them, this song will confront them as a witness, because it will not be lost from the mouths of their descendants. For I know what they are inclined to do even now, before I have brought them into the land that I promised them on oath." ²²That very day Moses wrote this song and taught it to the Israelites.

23 Then the Lord commissioned Joshua son of Nun and said, "Be strong and bold, for you shall bring the Israelites into the land that I promised them; I will be with you."

24 When Moses had finished writing down in a book the words of this law to the very end, ²⁵Moses commanded the Levites who carried the ark of the covenant of the Lord, saying, ²⁶"Take this book of the law and put it beside the ark of the covenant of the Lord your God; let it remain there as a witness against you. ²⁷For I know well how rebellious and stubborn you are. If you already have

"It is the Lord who goes before you . . . he will not fail you."
—Deuteronomy 31:8

ᵃ Or *tabernacles*; Heb *succoth*

been so rebellious toward the LORD while I am still alive among you, how much more after my death! ²⁸Assemble to me all the elders of your tribes and your officials, so that I may recite these words in their hearing and call heaven and earth to witness against them. ²⁹For I know that after my death you will surely act corruptly, turning aside from the way that I have commanded you. In time to come trouble will befall you, because you will do what is evil in the sight of the LORD, provoking him to anger through the work of your hands."

The Song of Moses

30 Then Moses recited the words of this song, to the very end, in the hearing of the whole assembly of Israel:

32 Give ear, O heavens, and I will speak;
    let the earth hear the words of my
        mouth.
² May my teaching drop like the rain,
    my speech condense like the dew;
like gentle rain on grass,
    like showers on new growth.

³ For I will proclaim the name of the LORD;
    ascribe greatness to our God!

⁴ The Rock, his work is perfect,
    and all his ways are just.
A faithful God, without deceit,

just and upright is he;
⁵ yet his degenerate children have dealt falsely
    with him,^a
    a perverse and crooked generation.

⁶ Do you thus repay the LORD,
    O foolish and senseless people?
Is not he your father, who created you,
    who made you and established you?

⁷ Remember the days of old,
    consider the years long past;
ask your father, and he will inform you;
    your elders, and they will tell you.

⁸ When the Most High^b apportioned the
        nations,
    when he divided humankind,
he fixed the boundaries of the peoples
    according to the number of the gods;^c
⁹ the LORD's own portion was his people,
    Jacob his allotted share.

¹⁰ He sustained^d him in a desert land,
    in a howling wilderness waste;
he shielded him, cared for him,
    guarded him as the apple of his eye.
¹¹ As an eagle stirs up its nest,
    and hovers over its young;
as it spreads its wings, takes them up,
    and bears them aloft on its pinions,
¹² the LORD alone guided him;
    no foreign god was with him.
¹³ He set him atop the heights of the land,
    and fed him with^e produce of the field;
he nursed him with honey from the crags,
    with oil from flinty rock;
¹⁴ curds from the herd, and milk from the flock,
    with fat of lambs and rams;
Bashan bulls and goats,
    together with the choicest wheat—
    you drank fine wine from the blood of
        grapes.
¹⁵ Jacob ate his fill;^f
    Jeshurun grew fat, and kicked.
    You grew fat, bloated, and gorged!
He abandoned God who made him,
    and scoffed at the Rock of his salvation.
¹⁶ They made him jealous with strange gods,
    with abhorrent things they provoked him.
¹⁷ They sacrificed to demons, not God,
    to deities they had never known,
to new ones recently arrived,

PRAY IT!

**Life Song
Deuteronomy
31:30–32:47**

Before the Israelites enter the promised land, Moses recites a song for the people, gives a final blessing, and dies. It is history and teaching and praise all in one.

- Write your own life song. Take some time to write down the highlights, challenges, and lessons of your life to this point. Write about your own experiences and about God's faithfulness.
- Then find a favorite place and read it as a time of prayer to God.

---

a Meaning of Heb uncertain   **b** Traditional rendering of Heb *Elyon*   **c** Q Ms Compare Gk Tg: MT *the Israelites*   **d** Sam Gk Compare Tg: MT *found*
e Sam Gk Syr Tg: MT *he ate*   **f** Q Mss Sam Gk: MT lacks *Jacob ate his fill*

whom your ancestors had not feared.

18 You were unmindful of the Rock that bore
   you;[a]
   you forgot the God who gave you birth.

19 The LORD saw it, and was jealous;[b]
   he spurned[c] his sons and daughters.
20 He said: I will hide my face from
      them,
   I will see what their end will be;
   for they are a perverse generation,
      children in whom there is no faithfulness.
21 They made me jealous with what is no god,
      provoked me with their idols.
   So I will make them jealous with what is no
         people,
      provoke them with a foolish nation.
22 For a fire is kindled by my anger,
      and burns to the depths of Sheol;
   it devours the earth and its increase,
      and sets on fire the foundations of the
         mountains.
23 I will heap disasters upon them,
      spend my arrows against them:
24 wasting hunger,
      burning consumption,
      bitter pestilence.
   The teeth of beasts I will send against them,
      with venom of things crawling in the dust.
25 In the street the sword shall bereave,
      and in the chambers terror,
   for young man and woman alike,
      nursing child and old gray head.
26 I thought to scatter them[d]
      and blot out the memory of them from
         humankind;
27 but I feared provocation by the enemy,
      for their adversaries might misunderstand
   and say, "Our hand is triumphant;
      it was not the LORD who did all this."

28 They are a nation void of sense;
      there is no understanding in them.
29 If they were wise, they would understand
         this;
      they would discern what the end
         would be.
30 How could one have routed a thousand,
      and two put a myriad to flight,
   unless their Rock had sold them,

the LORD had given them up?
31 Indeed their rock is not like our Rock;
      our enemies are fools.[d]
32 Their vine comes from the vinestock of
         Sodom,
      from the vineyards of Gomorrah;
   their grapes are grapes of poison,
      their clusters are bitter;
33 their wine is the poison of serpents,
      the cruel venom of asps.

34 Is not this laid up in store with me,
      sealed up in my treasuries?
35 Vengeance is mine, and recompense,
      for the time when their foot shall slip;
   because the day of their calamity is at hand,
      their doom comes swiftly.

36 Indeed the LORD will vindicate his people,
      have compassion on his servants,
   when he sees that their power is gone,
      neither bond nor free remaining.
37 Then he will say: Where are their gods,
      the rock in which they took refuge,
38 who ate the fat of their sacrifices,
      and drank the wine of their libations?
   Let them rise up and help you,
      let them be your protection!

39 See now that I, even I, am he;
      there is no god besides me.
   I kill and I make alive;
      I wound and I heal;
      and no one can deliver from my hand.
40 For I lift up my hand to heaven,
      and swear: As I live forever,
41 when I whet my flashing sword,
      and my hand takes hold on judgment;
   I will take vengeance on my adversaries,
      and will repay those who hate me.
42 I will make my arrows drunk with blood,
      and my sword shall devour flesh—
   with the blood of the slain and the captives,
      from the long-haired enemy.

43 Praise, O heavens,[e] his people,
      worship him, all you gods![f]
   For he will avenge the blood of his children,[g]
      and take vengeance on his adversaries;
   he will repay those who hate him,[f]

---

a Or *that begot you*   b Q Mss Gk: MT lacks *was jealous*   c Cn: Heb *he spurned because of provocation*   d Gk: Meaning of Heb uncertain   e Q Ms Gk:
MT *nations*   f Q Ms Gk: MT lacks this line   g Q Ms Gk: MT *his servants*

and cleanse the land for his people.[a]

44 Moses came and recited all the words of this song in the hearing of the people, he and Joshua[b] son of Nun. [45]When Moses had finished reciting all these words to all Israel, [46]he said to them: "Take to heart all the words that I am giving in witness against you today; give them as a command to your children, so that they may diligently observe all the words of this law. [47]This is no trifling matter for you, but rather your very life; through it you may live long in the land that you are crossing over the Jordan to possess."

Moses' Death Foretold

48 On that very day the LORD addressed Moses as follows: [49]"Ascend this mountain of the Abarim, Mount Nebo, which is in the land of Moab, across from Jericho, and view the land of Canaan, which I am giving to the Israelites for a possession; [50]you shall die there on the mountain that you ascend and shall be gathered to your kin, as your brother Aaron died on Mount Hor and was gathered to his kin; [51]because both of you broke faith with me among the Israelites at the waters of Meribath-kadesh in the wilderness of Zin, by failing to maintain my holiness among the Israelites. [52]Although you may view the land from a distance, you shall not enter it—the land that I am giving to the Israelites."

33 Moses' Final Blessing on Israel

This is the blessing with which Moses, the man of God, blessed the Israelites before his death. [2]He said:

The LORD came from Sinai,
   and dawned from Seir upon us;[c]
he shone forth from Mount Paran.
With him were myriads of holy ones;[d]
   at his right, a host of his own.[e]
[3] Indeed, O favorite among[f] peoples,
   all his holy ones were in your charge;
they marched at your heels,
   accepted direction from you.
[4] Moses charged us with the law,
   as a possession for the assembly of Jacob.
[5] There arose a king in Jeshurun,
   when the leaders of the people assembled—
   the united tribes of Israel.

[6] May Reuben live, and not die out,
   even though his numbers are few.

[7]And this he said of Judah:
   O LORD, give heed to Judah,
      and bring him to his people;
   strengthen his hands for him,[g]
      and be a help against his adversaries.

[8]And of Levi he said:
   Give to Levi[h] your Thummim,
      and your Urim to your loyal one,
   whom you tested at Massah,
      with whom you contended at the waters of
         Meribah;
[9] who said of his father and mother,
      "I regard them not";
   he ignored his kin,
      and did not acknowledge his children.
   For they observed your word,
      and kept your covenant.
[10] They teach Jacob your ordinances,
      and Israel your law;
   they place incense before you,
      and whole burnt offerings on your altar.
[11] Bless, O LORD, his substance,
      and accept the work of his hands;
   crush the loins of his adversaries,
      of those that hate him, so that they do not
         rise again.

[12]Of Benjamin he said:
   The beloved of the LORD rests in safety—
      the High God[i] surrounds him all day long—
      the beloved[j] rests between his shoulders.

[13]And of Joseph he said:
   Blessed by the LORD be his land,
      with the choice gifts of heaven above,
      and of the deep that lies beneath;
[14] with the choice fruits of the sun,
      and the rich yield of the months;
[15] with the finest produce of the ancient
         mountains,
      and the abundance of the everlasting hills;
[16] with the choice gifts of the earth and its fullness,
      and the favor of the one who dwells on
         Sinai.[k]
   Let these come on the head of Joseph,
      on the brow of the prince among his
         brothers.
[17] A firstborn[l] bull—majesty is his!
      His horns are the horns of a wild ox;

---

a Q Ms Sam Gk Vg: MT *his land his people* **b** Sam Gk Syr Vg: MT *Hoshea* **c** Gk Syr Vg Compare Tg: Heb *upon them* **d** Cn Compare Gk Sam Syr Vg: MT *He came from Ribeboth-kodesh,* **e** Cn Compare Gk: meaning of Heb uncertain **f** Or *O lover of the* **g** Cn: Heb *with his hands he contended* **h** Q Ms Gk: MT lacks *Give to Levi* **i** Heb *above him* **j** Heb *he* **k** Cn: Heb *in the bush* **l** Q Ms Gk Syr Vg: MT *His firstborn*

with them he gores the peoples,
  driving them to[a] the ends of the earth;
such are the myriads of Ephraim,
  such the thousands of Manasseh.

18 And of Zebulun he said:
  Rejoice, Zebulun, in your going out;
    and Issachar, in your tents.
19   They call peoples to the mountain;
    there they offer the right sacrifices;
  for they suck the affluence of the seas
    and the hidden treasures of the sand.

20 And of Gad he said:
  Blessed be the enlargement of Gad!
    Gad lives like a lion;
  he tears at arm and scalp.
21   He chose the best for himself,
    for there a commander's allotment was
      reserved;
  he came at the head of the people,
    he executed the justice of the LORD,
    and his ordinances for Israel.

22 And of Dan he said:
  Dan is a lion's whelp
    that leaps forth from Bashan.

23 And of Naphtali he said:

O Naphtali, sated with favor,
  full of the blessing of the LORD,
  possess the west and the south.

24 And of Asher he said:
  Most blessed of sons be Asher;
  may he be the favorite of his brothers,
  and may he dip his foot in oil.
25   Your bars are iron and bronze;
  and as your days, so is your strength.
26   There is none like God, O Jeshurun,
  who rides through the heavens to your
    help,
  majestic through the skies.
27   He subdues the ancient gods,[b]
  shatters[c] the forces of old;[d]
  he drove out the enemy before you,
  and said, "Destroy!"
28   So Israel lives in safety,
  untroubled is Jacob's abode[e]
  in a land of grain and wine,
  where the heavens drop down dew.
29   Happy are you, O Israel! Who is like you,
  a people saved by the LORD,
  the shield of your help,
  and the sword of your triumph!
  Your enemies shall come fawning to you,
  and you shall tread on their backs.

Moses' Death · Deuteronomy 34

He came tantalizingly close! Why did Moses die on the brink of entering the promised land? This question has disturbed many generations of believers. The one who received God's call to lead the Israelites out of slavery, who amazed Pharaoh with wonders and called down plagues on Egypt, who opened the Red Sea and received the tablets of the law on Mount Sinai—this great leader did not get to enjoy the success of his work, because he disobeyed God earlier (Numbers 20:12)! **Deuteronomy 34:1–6** simply tells us that Moses died on Mount Nebo and that his burial place was forgotten.

We also experience times when we don't get to enjoy the success of our work or are waiting for a promise to be fulfilled. For example, you may volunteer for some project and never really see the results of your time and effort. But that's not the point, is it? We don't volunteer so that we can take credit for the result. Rather, we do it because God has called us to serve and to love our neighbor. So it was with Moses. He had done what he was called to do—no more, no less. And as the Israelites stood on the verge of entering the promised land, we too stand on the verge of our final destination—eternity with God in heaven.

a Cn: Heb *the peoples, together*   b Or *The eternal God is a dwelling place*   c Cn: Heb *from underneath*   d Or *the everlasting arms*   e Or *fountain*

Martin Luther King Jr.: Unseen Freedom
Deuteronomy 34:4–5

Martin Luther King Jr. had a lot in common with Moses. Like Moses, Dr. King led his people out of a wilderness—a postslavery no-man's-land of abuse and second-class citizenship. Moses constantly reminded his people to faithfully follow God's law; Dr. King continually called people to follow Jesus' way of loving their enemies, even when those enemies treated them violently. Both leaders relied on God's strength to answer their calling and spent the bulk of their lives working on their difficult tasks. Unfortunately, both Moses and Dr. King died before seeing their work complete and their people reach freedom.

Dr. King referenced Moses in his last speech when he said, "I've been to the mountaintop . . . and I've seen the promised land. I may not get there with you, but I want you to know that we as a people will get to the promised land." His words were an incredible foreshadowing, as Dr. King was assassinated the next day, but those words rang out as a final call to the people to stay true to God and their mission. Dr. King knew he might not live to see his people completely freed from prejudice and discrimination. But he spent and ultimately sacrificed his life working with others toward that goal.

34 Moses Dies and Is Buried in the Land of Moab

Then Moses went up from the plains of Moab to Mount Nebo, to the top of Pisgah, which is opposite Jericho, and the LORD showed him the whole land: Gilead as far as Dan, [2]all Naphtali, the land of Ephraim and Manasseh, all the land of Judah as far as the Western Sea, [3]the Negeb, and the Plain—that is, the valley of Jericho, the city of palm trees—as far as Zoar. [4]The LORD said to him, "This is the land of which I swore to Abraham, to Isaac, and to Jacob, saying, 'I will give it to your descendants'; I have let you see it with your eyes, but you shall not cross over there." [5]Then Moses, the servant of the LORD, died there in the land of Moab, at the LORD's command. [6]He was buried in a valley in the land of Moab, opposite Beth-peor, but no one knows his burial place to this day. [7]Moses was one hundred twenty years old when he died; his sight was unimpaired and his vigor had not abated. [8]The Israelites wept for Moses in the plains of Moab thirty days; then the period of mourning for Moses was ended.

9 Joshua son of Nun was full of the spirit of wisdom, because Moses had laid his hands on him; and the Israelites obeyed him, doing as the LORD had commanded Moses.

10 Never since has there arisen a prophet in Israel like Moses, whom the LORD knew face to face. [11]He was unequaled for all the signs and wonders that the LORD sent him to perform in the land of Egypt, against Pharaoh and all his servants and his entire land, [12]and for all the mighty deeds and all the terrifying displays of power that Moses performed in the sight of all Israel.

Introduction to the
Historical Books

When's the last time you looked through old family photos? Give it a try if it's been a while. Open an old album or scroll through the digital pics, and you'll most likely find yourself reliving some great moments and telling old stories. If you really want to hear some family classics, look through the pictures with a parent or grandparent. The twelve historical books of the Old Testament are like the photo album of ancient Israel. They didn't have cameras back then, but they had stories. And these books are like the voices of respected elders walking us through the tales of God at work. We can see more clearly how God works in today's world by reading these stories of the past.

IN DEPTH

The historical books recount the period of Israelite history from 1250 to 400 B.C. In these books, we read about:

- The Israelites' settlement in the promised land and their struggle to protect themselves from their enemies (Joshua and Judges)
- King David's ancestry (Ruth)
- The rise of a united kingdom under David (1 and 2 Samuel, 1 Kings)
- The division of Israel into northern and southern kingdoms and the various kings and prophets of each until the fall of Jerusalem in 587 B.C. (1 and 2 Kings, 1 and 2 Chronicles)
- The return from exile and the rebuilding of the nation (Ezra and Nehemiah)
- A threat to a group of Jews living outside their homeland and the heroine who trusts God and saves them (Esther)

The historical books of the Old Testament are not like the history books we read in school. Those who write history books today generally try to report the facts with little interpretation. "Let the events speak for themselves," they say. However, those who wrote the historical books of the Old Testament had a different purpose; they are saying, "Let us tell you what the events mean in the light of our faith in God." So the history contained in these books is often called sacred history, because it reveals God's message and God's purpose in history.

Scripture scholars find evidence of two general groups shaping the final form of the historical books. The first group wrote from the same point of view as the book of Deuteronomy (and are often called the Deuteronomists). This group wrote Joshua, Judges, 1 and 2 Samuel, and 1 and 2 Kings and was convinced that God rewarded the good and punished the wicked in this world. So you will find in these books a repeated pattern of (1) God's offer of love, (2) the people's faithlessness and sin, (3) God's just punishment, (4) the people's repentance and cry for help, (5) God's forgiveness and mercy, and (6) the people's repeated sin.

The second group (or person), sometimes called the Chronicler, was responsible for 1 and 2 Chronicles and probably Ezra and Nehemiah. The Chronicler also emphasized that God rewards the faithful and punishes the unfaithful, but the definition of faithfulness had changed. Instead of emphasizing faithfulness to the Sinai covenant (the Ten Commandments), the Chronicler emphasized faithfulness to proper worship, particularly worship at the temple in Jerusalem. Some scholars believe that the Chronicler wrote during the time when the Jewish people were rebuilding the temple.

Some of the religious truths you will learn from reading these historical books are:

- God is not removed from the affairs of this world, but cares deeply about what's happening in human history.
- People are happier when they follow the law of God than when they turn away from the law.
- All human beings, from the beginning of history, are joined in a common struggle to find sense and meaning in the ups and downs of life.

As you read these books, remember that the authors' understanding of God is not the same as Jesus' understanding. Christians can learn many truths about God taught by these books, but we also have a larger context for understanding God's unconditional love and unlimited mercy: Jesus' teaching in the New Testament.

OTHER BACKGROUND

- Ruth wasn't originally one of the historical books. It was written later than the books it is now sandwiched between.

- The books of 1 and 2 Chronicles review the same historical period as 1 and 2 Samuel and 1 and 2 Kings.

- Esther is inspired folklore that uses history only as a backdrop. Its purpose is to encourage faithfulness to God's law in hard times.

Joshua ▶▶▶▶▶▶▶▶▶▶▶▶▶▶▶▶▶▶▶▶▶▶▶▶▶

Remember when you were young and you asked to hear your favorite story over and over again? We often like familiar stories where good triumphs over evil. There's something reassuring in knowing that the "good guys" win and evil is punished in the end. That theme never gets old, and it's the basic message of the book of Joshua. In the conquest of the promised land, the author reminds us that those who follow God are rewarded and those who do not are punished—pure and simple.

IN DEPTH

The book of Joshua is named after the Israelite hero who succeeds Moses and leads the people in their takeover and settlement of the promised land. At the beginning, Joshua promises the Israelites they will conquer the land of Canaan and make it their own if they are faithful to the covenant of Moses. They respond with enthusiasm: "Just as we obeyed Moses in all things, so we will obey you" (Joshua 1:17). The author describes how the various Israelite tribes remain true to God's commandments, take over the land, and settle in it with their families and livestock—all under Joshua's leadership. (See Map 3: "Exodus and Conquest of Canaan.")

Today biblical scholars doubt that the conquest of the promised land by the twelve tribes of Israel was as complete and easy as it is portrayed in Joshua. Archaeologists have found evidence that Canaanites continued to live in the area after the time of the conquest. The historical memories preserved in the book were reshaped by subsequent storytellers who lived later, after the Holy Land had been lost. They wanted to emphasize an important faith lesson: God would preserve the Israelites on their land as long as they obeyed the commandments.

The belief in the triumph of good and the punishment of evil is at the heart of the book of Joshua. Joshua is written from the same point of view as Deuteronomy, which insists that God rewards the just and punishes the wicked in this world (Deuteronomy 30:15-20). And you'll find the same perspective in Judges, 1 and 2 Samuel, and 1 and 2 Kings too. Joshua challenges us to remember that God is our surest hope in all the ups and downs of history and of our lives.

QUICK FACTS

- **Dates Covered:** After the desert wandering, from about 1250 to 1200 B.C.
- **Author:** An unknown author writing in the same style as Deuteronomy in the seventh or sixth century B.C.
- **Themes:** The triumph of good and the punishment of evil in Israel's conquest of the promised land; the importance of following God's ways in our own lives; and a reminder of the consequences of our good and bad actions
- **Noteworthy:** The name Jesus is the Greek form of Joshua, which means "God saves."

AT A GLANCE

- **Joshua 1–12** The conquest of the land of Canaan
- **Joshua 13–22** The division of the land among the twelve tribes
- **Joshua 23–24** Joshua's last words and death

God's Commission to Joshua

1 After the death of Moses the servant of the LORD, the LORD spoke to Joshua son of Nun, Moses' assistant, saying, [2]"My servant Moses is dead. Now proceed to cross the Jordan, you and all this people, into the land that I am giving to them, to the Israelites. [3]Every place that the sole of your foot will tread upon I have given to you, as I promised to Moses. [4]From the wilderness and the Lebanon as far as the great river, the river Euphrates, all the land of the Hittites, to the Great Sea in the west shall be your territory. [5]No one shall be able to stand against you all the days of your life. As I was with Moses, so I will be with you; I will not fail you or forsake you. [6]Be strong and courageous; for you shall put this people in possession of the land that I swore to their ancestors to give them. [7]Only be strong and very courageous, being careful to act in accordance with all the law that my servant Moses commanded you; do not turn from it to the right hand or to the left, so that you may be successful wherever you go. [8]This book of the law shall not depart out of your mouth; you shall meditate on it day and night, so that you may be careful to act in accordance with all that is written in it. For then you shall make your way prosperous, and then you shall be successful. [9]I hereby command you: Be strong and courageous; do not be frightened or dismayed, for the LORD your God is with you wherever you go."

Preparations for the Invasion

10 Then Joshua commanded the officers of the people, [11]"Pass through the camp, and command the people: 'Prepare your provisions; for in three days you are to cross over the Jordan, to go in to take possession of the land that the LORD your God gives you to possess.'"

12 To the Reubenites, the Gadites, and the half-tribe of Manasseh Joshua said, [13]"Remember the word that Moses the servant of the LORD commanded you, saying, 'The LORD your God is providing you a place of rest, and will give you this land.' [14]Your wives, your little ones, and your livestock shall remain in the land that Moses gave you beyond the Jordan. But all the warriors among you shall cross over armed before your kindred and shall help them, [15]until the LORD gives rest to your kindred as well as to you, and they too take possession of the land that the LORD your God is giving them. Then you shall return to your own land and take possession of

---

CONNECT IT!

Florence Nightingale, Corrie ten Boom, Jim Elliot: No Fear
Joshua 1:5–9

"Be strong and courageous; do not be frightened or dismayed, for the LORD your God is with you wherever you go" (Joshua 1:9). Here are some people who are living proof that you can live out this scripture.

Florence Nightingale, born to a wealthy English family in Italy, left her home and position to serve God by tending to the sick and wounded in wars around the world. She overcame the stigma of the job, the limitations of being a woman in the late nineteenth century, and the horrendous nature of war to bring peace and healing to many soldiers and change to the way soldiers were medically treated during war.

Corrie ten Boom defied the Nazi invaders of Holland by hiding and protecting Jews during World War II. She was eventually betrayed and imprisoned in concentration camps, but survived the war and continued to speak about God's faithfulness.

Jim Elliot was a missionary to the Waodani tribe in Ecuador. He and four others were killed by the tribe they were trying to reach, but family members continued their mission to bring Christ's love to the people. Their widows and children even lived among the tribe for a time. Elliot and his friends' story of obedience and personal tragedy became famous as an example of faith and dedication to God's story, which is much bigger than any individual.

These people, along with many others, have taken to heart God's words to Joshua. If you are not familiar with their stories, take time to learn more about these heroes of the Christian faith.

it, the land that Moses the servant of the LORD gave you beyond the Jordan to the east."

16 They answered Joshua: "All that you have commanded us we will do, and wherever you send us we will go. ¹⁷Just as we obeyed Moses in all things, so we will obey you. Only may the LORD your God be with you, as he was with Moses! ¹⁸Whoever rebels against your orders and disobeys your words, whatever you command, shall be put to death. Only be strong and courageous."

Spies Sent to Jericho

2 Then Joshua son of Nun sent two men secretly from Shittim as spies, saying, "Go, view the land, especially Jericho." So they went, and entered the house of a prostitute whose name was Rahab, and spent the night there. ²The king of Jericho was told, "Some Israelites have come here tonight to search out the land." ³Then the king of Jericho sent orders to Rahab, "Bring out the men who have come to you, who entered your house, for they have come only to search out the whole land." ⁴But the woman took the two men and hid them. Then she said, "True, the men came to me, but I did not know where they came from. ⁵And when it was time to close the gate at dark, the men went out. Where the men went I do not know. Pursue them quickly, for you can overtake them." ⁶She had, however, brought them up to the roof and hidden them with the stalks of flax that she had laid out on the roof. ⁷So the men pursued them on the way to the Jordan as far as the fords. As soon as the pursuers had gone out, the gate was shut.

8 Before they went to sleep, she came up to them on the roof ⁹and said to the men: "I know that the LORD has given you the land, and that dread of you has fallen on us, and that all the inhabitants of the land melt in fear before you. ¹⁰For we have heard how the LORD dried up the water of the Red Sea^a before you when you came out of Egypt, and what you did to the two kings of the Amorites that were beyond the Jordan, to Sihon and Og, whom you utterly destroyed. ¹¹As soon as we heard it, our hearts melted, and there was no courage left in any of us because of you. The LORD your God is indeed God in heaven above and on earth below. ¹²Now then, since I have dealt kindly with you, swear to me by the LORD that you in turn will deal kindly with my family. Give me a sign of good faith ¹³that you will spare my father and mother, my brothers and sisters, and all who belong to them, and deliver our lives from death." ¹⁴The men said to her, "Our life for yours! If you do not tell this business of ours, then we will deal kindly and faithfully with you when the LORD gives us the land."

15 Then she let them down by a rope through the window, for her house was on the outer side of the city wall and she resided within the wall itself. ¹⁶She said to them, "Go toward the hill country, so that the pursuers may not come upon you. Hide yourselves there three days, until the pursuers have returned; then afterward you may go your way." ¹⁷The men

PRAY IT!

Pray Against Prejudice · Joshua 2

The Israelite spies needed help to check out Jericho to see what kind of enemies the Israelites were up against—especially when the king of Jericho got wind of their mission. That help came from an unlikely source, a prostitute who lived in the city. Rahab lied to the king's messengers and risked her life to hide these foreign spies. But she showed great faith in God by doing so. Her actions showed that she was committed to putting God before any differences in nationality or race.

Dear God, you made many different and diverse people—all in your image. Please help me to be open to making friends with people who are different from me—just as the Israelites did with Rahab when she was outside their group.

Please give me your eyes to see past skin color and clothing styles and nationalities and clique labels. Forgive me and my friends for every time we've looked down on someone different. Forgive us for talking about people as if we're better than they are. Forgive us for ignoring and not associating with them. And help us forgive people who have looked down on us. Amen.

---

^a Or *Sea of Reeds*

said to her, "We will be released from this oath that you have made us swear to you [18]if we invade the land and you do not tie this crimson cord in the window through which you let us down, and you do not gather into your house your father and mother, your brothers, and all your family. [19]If any of you go out of the doors of your house into the street, they shall be responsible for their own death, and we shall be innocent; but if a hand is laid upon any who are with you in the house, we shall bear the responsibility for their death. [20]But if you tell this business of ours, then we shall be released from this oath that you made us swear to you." [21]She said, "According to your words, so be it." She sent them away and they departed. Then she tied the crimson cord in the window.

22 They departed and went into the hill country and stayed there three days, until the pursuers returned. The pursuers had searched all along the way and found nothing. [23]Then the two men came down again from the hill country. They crossed over, came to Joshua son of Nun, and told him all that had happened to them. [24]They said to Joshua, "Truly the LORD has given all the land into our hands; moreover all the inhabitants of the land melt in fear before us."

Israel Crosses the Jordan

3 Early in the morning Joshua rose and set out from Shittim with all the Israelites, and they came to the Jordan. They camped there before crossing over. [2]At the end of three days the officers went through the camp [3]and commanded the people, "When you see the ark of the covenant of the LORD your God being carried by the levitical priests, then you shall set out from your place. Follow it, [4]so that you may know the way you should go, for you have not passed this way before. Yet there shall be a space between you and it, a distance of about two thousand cubits; do not come any nearer to it." [5]Then Joshua said to the people, "Sanctify yourselves; for tomorrow the LORD will do wonders among you." [6]To the priests Joshua said, "Take up the ark of the covenant, and pass on in front of the people." So they took up the ark of the covenant and went in front of the people.

7 The LORD said to Joshua, "This day I will begin to exalt you in the sight of all Israel, so that they may know that I will be with you as I was with Moses. [8]You are the one who shall command the priests who bear the ark of the covenant, 'When you come

to the edge of the waters of the Jordan, you shall stand still in the Jordan.' " [9]Joshua then said to the Israelites, "Draw near and hear the words of the LORD your God." [10]Joshua said, "By this you shall know that among you is the living God who without fail will drive out from before you the Canaanites, Hittites, Hivites, Perizzites, Girgashites, Amorites, and Jebusites: [11]the ark of the covenant of the Lord of all the earth is going to pass before you into the Jordan. [12]So now select twelve men from the tribes of Israel, one from each tribe. [13]When the soles of the feet of the priests who bear the ark of the LORD, the Lord of all the earth, rest in the waters of the Jordan, the waters of the Jordan flowing from above shall be cut off; they shall stand in a single heap."

14 When the people set out from their tents to cross over the Jordan, the priests bearing the ark of the covenant were in front of the people. [15]Now the Jordan overflows all its banks throughout the time of harvest. So when those who bore the ark had come to the Jordan, and the feet of the priests bearing the ark were dipped in the edge of the water, [16]the waters flowing from above stood still, rising up in a single heap far off at Adam, the city that is beside Zarethan, while those flowing toward the sea of the Arabah, the Dead Sea,[a] were wholly cut off. Then the people crossed over opposite Jericho. [17]While all Israel were crossing over on dry ground, the priests who bore the ark of the covenant of the LORD stood on dry ground in the middle of the Jordan, until the entire nation finished crossing over the Jordan.

Twelve Stones Set Up at Gilgal

4 When the entire nation had finished crossing over the Jordan, the LORD said to Joshua: [2]"Select twelve men from the people, one from each tribe, [3]and command them, 'Take twelve stones from here out of the middle of the Jordan, from the place where the priests' feet stood, carry them over with you, and lay them down in the place where you camp tonight.' " [4]Then Joshua summoned the twelve men from the Israelites, whom he had appointed, one from each tribe. [5]Joshua said to them, "Pass on before the ark of the LORD your God into the middle of the Jordan, and each of you take up a stone on his shoulder, one for each of the tribes of the Israelites, [6]so that this may be a sign among you. When your children ask in time to come, 'What do those stones mean to you?' [7]then you shall tell them that the waters of the Jordan were cut off in front of

a Heb *Salt Sea*

the ark of the covenant of the LORD. When it crossed over the Jordan, the waters of the Jordan were cut off. So these stones shall be to the Israelites a memorial forever."

8 The Israelites did as Joshua commanded. They took up twelve stones out of the middle of the Jordan, according to the number of the tribes of the Israelites, as the LORD told Joshua, carried them over with them to the place where they camped, and laid them down there. ⁹(Joshua set up twelve stones in the middle of the Jordan, in the place where the feet of the priests bearing the ark of the covenant had stood; and they are there to this day.)

10 The priests who bore the ark remained standing in the middle of the Jordan, until everything was finished that the LORD commanded Joshua to tell the people, according to all that Moses had commanded Joshua. The people crossed over in haste. ¹¹As soon as all the people had finished crossing over, the ark of the LORD, and the priests, crossed over in front of the people. ¹²The Reubenites, the Gadites, and the half-tribe of Manasseh crossed over armed before the Israelites, as Moses had ordered them. ¹³About forty thousand armed for war crossed over before the LORD to the plains of Jericho for battle.

14 On that day the LORD exalted Joshua in the sight of all Israel; and they stood in awe of him, as they had stood in awe of Moses, all the days of his life.

15 The LORD said to Joshua, ¹⁶"Command the priests who bear the ark of the covenant,ᵃ to come up out of the Jordan." ¹⁷Joshua therefore commanded the priests, "Come up out of the Jordan." ¹⁸When the priests bearing the ark of the covenant of the LORD came up from the middle of the Jordan, and the soles of the priests' feet touched dry ground, the waters of the Jordan returned to their place and overflowed all its banks, as before.

19 The people came up out of the Jordan on the tenth day of the first month, and they camped in Gilgal on the east border of Jericho. ²⁰Those twelve stones, which they had taken out of the Jordan, Joshua set up in Gilgal, ²¹saying to the Israelites, "When your children ask their parents in time to come, 'What do these stones mean?' ²²then you shall let your children know, 'Israel crossed over the Jordan here on dry ground.' ²³For the LORD your God dried up the waters of the Jordan for you until you crossed over, as the LORD your God did to the Red Sea,ᵇ which he dried up for us until we crossed over, ²⁴so that all the peoples of the earth may know that the hand of the LORD is mighty, and so that you may fear the LORD your God forever."

The New Generation Circumcised

5 When all the kings of the Amorites beyond the Jordan to the west, and all the kings of the Canaanites by the sea, heard that the LORD had dried up the waters of the Jordan for the Israelites until they had crossed over, their hearts melted, and there was no longer any spirit in them, because of the Israelites.

2 At that time the LORD said to Joshua, "Make flint knives and circumcise the Israelites a second time." ³So Joshua made flint knives, and circumcised the Israelites at Gibeath-haaraloth.ᶜ ⁴This is the reason why Joshua circumcised them: all the males of the people who came out of Egypt, all the warriors, had died during the journey through the wilderness after they had come out of Egypt. ⁵Although all the people who came out had been circumcised, yet all the people born on the journey through the wilderness after they had come out of Egypt had not been circumcised. ⁶For the Israelites traveled forty years in the wilderness, until all the nation, the warriors who came out of Egypt, perished, not having listened to the voice of the LORD. To them the LORD swore that he would not let them see the land that he had sworn to their ancestors to give us, a land flowing with milk and honey. ⁷So it was their children, whom he raised up in their place, that Joshua circumcised; for they were uncircumcised, because they had not been circumcised on the way.

8 When the circumcising of all the nation was done, they remained in their places in the camp until they were healed. ⁹The LORD said to Joshua, "Today I have rolled away from you the disgrace of Egypt." And so that place is called Gilgalᵈ to this day.

The Passover at Gilgal

10 While the Israelites were camped in Gilgal they kept the passover in the evening on the fourteenth day of the month in the plains of Jericho. ¹¹On the day after the passover, on that very day, they ate the produce of the land, unleavened cakes and parched grain. ¹²The manna ceased on the day they ate the produce of the land, and the Israelites no longer had manna; they ate the crops of the land of Canaan that year.

ᵃ Or *treaty*, or *testimony*; Heb *eduth*   ᵇ Or *Sea of Reeds*   ᶜ That is *the Hill of the Foreskins*   ᵈ Related to Heb *galal* to roll

Joshua's Vision

13 Once when Joshua was by Jericho, he looked up and saw a man standing before him with a drawn sword in his hand. Joshua went to him and said to him, "Are you one of us, or one of our adversaries?" [14]He replied, "Neither; but as commander of the army of the LORD I have now come." And Joshua fell on his face to the earth and worshiped, and he said to him, "What do you command your servant, my lord?" [15]The commander of the army of the LORD said to Joshua, "Remove the sandals from your feet, for the place where you stand is holy." And Joshua did so.

Jericho Taken and Destroyed

6 Now Jericho was shut up inside and out because of the Israelites; no one came out and no one went in. [2]The LORD said to Joshua, "See, I have handed Jericho over to you, along with its king and soldiers. [3]You shall march around the city, all the warriors circling the city once. Thus you shall do for six days, [4]with seven priests bearing seven trumpets of rams' horns before the ark. On the seventh day you shall march around the city seven times, the priests blowing the trumpets. [5]When they make a long blast with the ram's horn, as soon as you hear the sound of the trumpet, then all the people shall shout with a great shout; and the wall of the city will fall down flat, and all the people shall charge straight ahead." [6]So Joshua son of Nun summoned the priests and said to them, "Take up the ark of the covenant, and have seven priests carry seven trumpets of rams' horns in front of the ark of the LORD." [7]To the people he said, "Go forward and march around the city; have the armed men pass on before the ark of the LORD."

8 As Joshua had commanded the people, the seven priests carrying the seven trumpets of rams' horns before the LORD went forward, blowing the trumpets, with the ark of the covenant of the LORD following them. [9]And the armed men went before the priests who blew the trumpets; the rear guard came after the ark, while the trumpets blew continually. [10]To the people Joshua gave this command: "You shall not shout or let your voice be heard, nor shall you utter a word, until the day I tell you to shout. Then you shall shout." [11]So the ark of the LORD went around the city, circling it once; and they came into the camp, and spent the night in the camp.

12 Then Joshua rose early in the morning, and the priests took up the ark of the LORD. [13]The seven priests carrying the seven trumpets of rams' horns before the ark of the LORD passed on, blowing the trumpets continually. The armed men went before them, and the rear guard came after the ark of the LORD, while the trumpets blew continually. [14]On the second day they marched around the city once and then returned to the camp. They did this for six days.

15 On the seventh day they rose early, at dawn, and marched around the city in the same manner seven times. It was only on that day that they marched around the city seven times. [16]And at the seventh time, when the priests had blown the trumpets, Joshua said to the people, "Shout! For the LORD has given you the city. [17]The city and all that is in it shall be devoted to the LORD for destruction. Only Rahab the prostitute and all who are with her in her house shall live because she hid the messengers we sent. [18]As for you, keep away from the things devoted to destruction, so as not to covet[a] and take any of the devoted things and make the camp of Israel an object for destruction, bringing trouble upon it. [19]But all silver and gold, and vessels of bronze and iron, are sacred to the LORD; they shall go into the treasury of the LORD." [20]So the people shouted, and the trumpets were blown. As soon as the people heard the sound of the trumpets, they raised a great shout, and the wall fell down flat; so the people charged straight ahead into the city and captured it. [21]Then they devoted to destruction by the edge of the sword all in the city, both men and women, young and old, oxen, sheep, and donkeys.

22 Joshua said to the two men who had spied out the land, "Go into the prostitute's house, and bring the woman out of it and all who belong to her, as you swore to her." [23]So the young men who had been spies went in and brought Rahab out, along with her father, her mother, her brothers, and all who belonged to her—they brought all her kindred out—and set them outside the camp of Israel. [24]They burned down the city, and everything in it; only the silver and gold, and the vessels of bronze and iron,

a Gk: Heb *devote to destruction* Compare 7.21

they put into the treasury of the house of the LORD. [25]But Rahab the prostitute, with her family and all who belonged to her, Joshua spared. Her family[a] has lived in Israel ever since. For she hid the messengers whom Joshua sent to spy out Jericho.

26 Joshua then pronounced this oath, saying,

"Cursed before the LORD be anyone who tries
    to build this city—this Jericho!
At the cost of his firstborn he shall lay its
    foundation,
    and at the cost of his youngest he shall set up
    its gates!"

27 So the LORD was with Joshua; and his fame was in all the land.

7   The Sin of Achan and Its Punishment

But the Israelites broke faith in regard to the devoted things: Achan son of Carmi son of Zabdi son of Zerah, of the tribe of Judah, took some of the devoted things; and the anger of the LORD burned against the Israelites.

2 Joshua sent men from Jericho to Ai, which is near Beth-aven, east of Bethel, and said to them, "Go up and spy out the land." And the men went up and spied out Ai. [3]Then they returned to Joshua and said to him, "Not all the people need go up; about two or three thousand men should go up and attack Ai. Since they are so few, do not make the whole people toil up there." [4]So about three thousand of the people went up there; and they fled before the men of Ai. [5]The men of Ai killed about thirty-six of them, chasing them from outside the gate as far as Shebarim and killing them on the slope. The hearts of the people melted and turned to water.

6 Then Joshua tore his clothes, and fell to the ground on his face before the ark of the LORD until the evening, he and the elders of Israel; and they put dust on their heads. [7]Joshua said, "Ah, Lord GOD! Why have you brought this people across the Jordan at all, to hand us over to the Amorites so as to destroy us? Would that we had been content to settle beyond the Jordan! [8]O Lord, what can I say, now that Israel has turned their backs to their enemies! [9]The Canaanites and all the inhabitants of the land will hear of it, and surround us, and cut off our name from the earth. Then what will you do for your great name?"

10 The LORD said to Joshua, "Stand up! Why have you fallen upon your face? [11]Israel has sinned; they have transgressed my covenant that I imposed on them. They have taken some of the devoted things; they have stolen, they have acted deceitfully, and they have put them among their own belongings. [12]Therefore the Israelites are unable to stand before their enemies; they turn their backs to their enemies, because they have become a thing devoted for destruction themselves. I will be with you no more, unless you destroy the devoted things from among you. [13]Proceed to sanctify the people, and say, 'Sanctify yourselves for tomorrow; for thus says the LORD, the God of Israel, "There are devoted things among you, O Israel; you will be unable to stand before your enemies until you take away the devoted things from among you." [14]In the morning therefore you shall come forward tribe by tribe. The tribe that the LORD takes shall come near by clans, the clan that the LORD takes shall come near by households, and the household that the LORD takes shall come near one by one. [15]And the one who is taken as having the devoted things shall be burned with fire, together with all that he has, for having transgressed the covenant of the LORD, and for having done an outrageous thing in Israel.' "

16 So Joshua rose early in the morning, and brought Israel near tribe by tribe, and the tribe of Judah was taken. [17]He brought near the clans of Judah, and the clan of the Zerahites was taken; and he brought near the clan of the Zerahites, family by family,[b] and Zabdi was taken. [18]And he brought near his household one by one, and Achan son of Carmi son of Zabdi son of Zerah, of the tribe of Judah, was taken. [19]Then Joshua said to Achan, "My son, give glory to the LORD God of Israel and make confession to him. Tell me now what you have done; do not hide it from me." [20]And Achan answered Joshua, "It is true; I am the one who sinned against the LORD God of Israel. This is what I did: [21]when I saw among the spoil a beautiful mantle from Shinar, and two hundred shekels of silver, and a bar of gold weighing fifty shekels, then I coveted them and took them. They now lie hidden in the ground inside my tent, with the silver underneath."

22 So Joshua sent messengers, and they ran to the tent; and there it was, hidden in his tent with the silver underneath. [23]They took them out of the tent and brought them to Joshua and all the Israelites; and they spread them out before the LORD. [24]Then Joshua and all Israel with him took Achan son of Zerah, with the silver, the mantle, and the bar of gold, with his sons and daughters, with his oxen, donkeys, and sheep, and his tent and all that he had; and they

---

a Heb *She*   b Mss Syr: MT *man by man*

brought them up to the Valley of Achor. [25]Joshua said, "Why did you bring trouble on us? The LORD is bringing trouble on you today." And all Israel stoned him to death; they burned them with fire, cast stones on them, [26]and raised over him a great heap of stones that remains to this day. Then the LORD turned from his burning anger. Therefore that place to this day is called the Valley of Achor.[a]

8

Ai Captured by a Stratagem and Destroyed

Then the LORD said to Joshua, "Do not fear or be dismayed; take all the fighting men with you, and go up now to Ai. See, I have handed over to you the king of Ai with his people, his city, and his land. [2]You shall do to Ai and its king as you did to Jericho and its king; only its spoil and its livestock you may take as booty for yourselves. Set an ambush against the city, behind it."

3 So Joshua and all the fighting men set out to go up against Ai. Joshua chose thirty thousand warriors and sent them out by night [4]with the command, "You shall lie in ambush against the city, behind it; do not go very far from the city, but all of you stay alert. [5]I and all the people who are with me will approach the city. When they come out against us, as before, we shall flee from them. [6]They will come out after us until we have drawn them away from the city; for they will say, 'They are fleeing from us, as before.' While we flee from them, [7]you shall rise up from the ambush and seize the city; for the LORD your God will give it into your hand. [8]And when you have taken the city, you shall set the city on fire, doing as the LORD has ordered; see, I have commanded you." [9]So Joshua sent them out; and they went to the place of ambush, and lay between Bethel and Ai, to the west of Ai; but Joshua spent that night in the camp.[b]

10 In the morning Joshua rose early and mustered the people, and went up, with the elders of Israel, before the people to Ai. [11]All the fighting men who were with him went up, and drew near before the city, and camped on the north side of Ai, with a ravine between them and Ai. [12]Taking about five thousand men, he set them in ambush between Bethel and Ai, to the west of the city. [13]So they stationed the forces, the main encampment that was north of the city and its rear guard west of the city. But Joshua spent that night in the valley. [14]When the king of Ai saw this, he and all his people, the inhabitants of the city, hurried out early in the morning to the meeting place facing the Arabah to meet Israel in battle; but he did not know that there was an ambush against him behind the city. [15]And Joshua and all Israel made a pretense of being beaten before them, and fled in the direction of the wilderness. [16]So all the people who were in the city were called together to pursue them, and as they pursued Joshua they were drawn away from the city. [17]There was not a man left in Ai or Bethel who did not go out after Israel; they left the city open, and pursued Israel.

18 Then the LORD said to Joshua, "Stretch out the sword that is in your hand toward Ai; for I will give it into your hand." And Joshua stretched out the sword that was in his hand toward the city. [19]As soon as he stretched out his hand, the troops in ambush rose quickly out of their place and rushed forward. They entered the city, took it, and at once set the city on fire. [20]So when the men of Ai looked back, the smoke of the city was rising to the sky. They had no power to flee this way or that, for the people who fled to the wilderness turned back against the pursuers. [21]When Joshua and all Israel saw that the ambush had taken the city and that the smoke of the city was rising, then they turned back and struck down the men of Ai. [22]And the others came out from the city against them; so they were surrounded by Israelites, some on one side, and some on the other; and Israel struck them down until no one was left who survived or escaped. [23]But the king of Ai was taken alive and brought to Joshua.

24 When Israel had finished slaughtering all the inhabitants of Ai in the open wilderness where they pursued them, and when all of them to the very last had fallen by the edge of the sword, all Israel returned to Ai, and attacked it with the edge of the sword. [25]The total of those who fell that day, both men and women, was twelve thousand—all the people of Ai. [26]For Joshua did not draw back his hand, with which he stretched out the sword, until he had utterly destroyed all the inhabitants of Ai. [27]Only the livestock and the spoil of that city Israel took as their booty, according to the word of the LORD that he had issued to Joshua. [28]So Joshua burned Ai, and made it forever a heap of ruins, as it is to this day. [29]And he hanged the king of Ai on a tree until evening; and at sunset Joshua commanded, and they took his body down from the tree, threw it down at the entrance of the gate of the city, and raised over it a great heap of stones, which stands there to this day.

a That is Trouble   b Heb among the people

Joshua Renews the Covenant

30 Then Joshua built on Mount Ebal an altar to the LORD, the God of Israel, [31]just as Moses the servant of the LORD had commanded the Israelites, as it is written in the book of the law of Moses, "an altar of unhewn[a] stones, on which no iron tool has been used"; and they offered on it burnt offerings to the LORD, and sacrificed offerings of well-being. [32]And there, in the presence of the Israelites, Joshua[b] wrote on the stones a copy of the law of Moses, which he had written. [33]All Israel, alien as well as citizen, with their elders and officers and their judges, stood on opposite sides of the ark in front of the levitical priests who carried the ark of the covenant of the LORD, half of them in front of Mount Gerizim and half of them in front of Mount Ebal, as Moses the servant of the LORD had commanded at the first, that they should bless the people of Israel. [34]And afterward he read all the words of the law, blessings and curses, according to all that is written in the book of the law. [35]There was not a word of all that Moses commanded that Joshua did not read before all the assembly of Israel, and the women, and the little ones, and the aliens who resided among them.

9 ### The Gibeonites Save Themselves by Trickery

Now when all the kings who were beyond the Jordan in the hill country and in the lowland all along the coast of the Great Sea toward Lebanon—the Hittites, the Amorites, the Canaanites, the Perizzites, the Hivites, and the Jebusites—heard of this, [2]they gathered together with one accord to fight Joshua and Israel.

3 But when the inhabitants of Gibeon heard what Joshua had done to Jericho and to Ai, [4]they on their part acted with cunning: they went and prepared provisions,[c] and took worn-out sacks for their donkeys, and wineskins, worn-out and torn and mended, [5]with worn-out, patched sandals on their feet, and worn-out clothes; and all their provisions were dry and moldy. [6]They went to Joshua in the camp at Gilgal, and said to him and to the Israelites, "We have come from a far country; so now make a treaty with us." [7]But the Israelites said to the Hivites, "Perhaps you live among us; then how can we make a treaty with you?" [8]They said to Joshua, "We are your servants." And Joshua said to them, "Who are you? And where do you come from?" [9]They said to him, "Your servants have come from a very far country, because

LIVE IT!

Remember and Renew
Joshua 8:30–35

Not long after entering the promised land, the Israelites followed Moses' command to renew their covenant with God. They prepared the altar, gathered everyone together, brought out the ark of the covenant, read from the law of Moses, and agreed to renew the covenant. Through these acts, the Israelites thanked God and reaffirmed their relationship with God.

The Israelites gathered at the altar to remember God's presence with them and their need for rededication and renewal as God's people. We gather in the same way when we celebrate communion, which is a symbol of Christ's presence in our lives. Any gathering to celebrate Jesus' resurrection and our new covenant with God helps us remember the story of our faith, renews our commitment to Christ, and joins us together as a community of believers.

of the name of the LORD your God; for we have heard a report of him, of all that he did in Egypt, [10]and of all that he did to the two kings of the Amorites who were beyond the Jordan, King Sihon of Heshbon, and King Og of Bashan who lived in Ashtaroth. [11]So our elders and all the inhabitants of our country said to us, 'Take provisions in your hand for the journey; go to meet them, and say to them, "We are your servants; come now, make a treaty with us." ' [12]Here is our bread; it was still warm when we took it from our houses as our food for the journey, on the day we set out to come to you, but now, see, it is dry and moldy; [13]these wineskins were new when we filled them, and see, they are burst; and these garments and sandals of ours are worn out from the very long journey." [14]So the leaders[d] partook of their provisions, and did not ask direction from the LORD. [15]And Joshua made peace with them, guaranteeing their lives by a treaty; and the leaders of the congregation swore an oath to them.

a Heb *whole* b Heb *he* c Cn: Meaning of Heb uncertain d Gk: Heb *men*

16 But when three days had passed after they had made a treaty with them, they heard that they were their neighbors and were living among them. [17]So the Israelites set out and reached their cities on the third day. Now their cities were Gibeon, Chephirah, Beeroth, and Kiriath-jearim. [18]But the Israelites did not attack them, because the leaders of the congregation had sworn to them by the LORD, the God of Israel. Then all the congregation murmured against the leaders. [19]But all the leaders said to all the congregation, "We have sworn to them by the LORD, the God of Israel, and now we must not touch them. [20]This is what we will do to them: We will let them live, so that wrath may not come upon us, because of the oath that we swore to them." [21]The leaders said to them, "Let them live." So they became hewers of wood and drawers of water for all the congregation, as the leaders had decided concerning them.

22 Joshua summoned them, and said to them, "Why did you deceive us, saying, 'We are very far from you,' while in fact you are living among us? [23]Now therefore you are cursed, and some of you shall always be slaves, hewers of wood and drawers of water for the house of my God." [24]They answered Joshua, "Because it was told to your servants for a certainty that the LORD your God had commanded his servant Moses to give you all the land, and to destroy all the inhabitants of the land before you; so we were in great fear for our lives because of you, and did this thing. [25]And now we are in your hand: do as it seems good and right in your sight to do to us." [26]This is what he did for them: he saved them from the Israelites; and they did not kill them. [27]But on that day Joshua made them hewers of wood and drawers of water for the congregation and for the altar of the LORD, to continue to this day, in the place that he should choose.

The Sun Stands Still

10 When King Adoni-zedek of Jerusalem heard how Joshua had taken Ai, and had utterly destroyed it, doing to Ai and its king as he had done to Jericho and its king, and how the inhabitants of Gibeon had made peace with Israel and were among them, [2]he[a] became greatly frightened, because Gibeon was a large city, like one of the royal cities, and was larger than Ai, and all its men were warriors. [3]So King Adoni-zedek of Jerusalem sent a message to King Hoham of Hebron, to King Piram of Jarmuth, to King Japhia of Lachish, and to King Debir of Eglon, saying, [4]"Come up and help me, and let us attack Gibeon; for it has made peace with Joshua and with the Israelites." [5]Then the five kings of the Amorites—the king of Jerusalem, the king of Hebron, the king of Jarmuth, the king of Lachish, and the king of Eglon—gathered their forces, and went up with all their armies and camped against Gibeon, and made war against it.

6 And the Gibeonites sent to Joshua at the camp in Gilgal, saying, "Do not abandon your servants; come up to us quickly, and save us, and help us; for all the kings of the Amorites who live in the hill country are gathered against us." [7]So Joshua went up from Gilgal, he and all the fighting force with him, all the mighty warriors. [8]The LORD said to Joshua, "Do not fear them, for I have handed them over to you; not one of them shall stand before you." [9]So Joshua came upon them suddenly, having marched up all night from Gilgal. [10]And the LORD threw them into a panic before Israel, who inflicted a great slaughter on them at Gibeon, chased them by the way of the ascent of Beth-horon, and struck them down as far as Azekah and Makkedah. [11]As they fled before Israel, while they were going down the slope of Beth-horon, the LORD threw down huge stones from heaven on them as far as Azekah, and they died; there were more who died because of the hailstones than the Israelites killed with the sword.

12 On the day when the LORD gave the Amorites over to the Israelites, Joshua spoke to the LORD; and he said in the sight of Israel,

"Sun, stand still at Gibeon,
    and Moon, in the valley of Aijalon."
[13] And the sun stood still, and the moon stopped,
    until the nation took vengeance on their
        enemies.

Is this not written in the Book of Jashar? The sun stopped in midheaven, and did not hurry to set for about a whole day. [14]There has been no day like it before or since, when the LORD heeded a human voice; for the LORD fought for Israel.

15 Then Joshua returned, and all Israel with him, to the camp at Gilgal.

Five Kings Defeated

16 Meanwhile, these five kings fled and hid themselves in the cave at Makkedah. [17]And it was told Joshua, "The five kings have been found, hidden in the cave at Makkedah." [18]Joshua said, "Roll

---

a Heb *they*

large stones against the mouth of the cave, and set men by it to guard them; [19]but do not stay there yourselves; pursue your enemies, and attack them from the rear. Do not let them enter their towns, for the LORD your God has given them into your hand." [20]When Joshua and the Israelites had finished inflicting a very great slaughter on them, until they were wiped out, and when the survivors had entered into the fortified towns, [21]all the people returned safe to Joshua in the camp at Makkedah; no one dared to speak[a] against any of the Israelites.

22 Then Joshua said, "Open the mouth of the cave, and bring those five kings out to me from the cave." [23]They did so, and brought the five kings out to him from the cave, the king of Jerusalem, the king of Hebron, the king of Jarmuth, the king of Lachish, and the king of Eglon. [24]When they brought the kings out to Joshua, Joshua summoned all the Israelites, and said to the chiefs of the warriors who had gone with him, "Come near, put your feet on the necks of these kings." Then they came near and put their feet on their necks. [25]And Joshua said to them, "Do not be afraid or dismayed; be strong and courageous; for thus the LORD will do to all the enemies against whom you fight." [26]Afterward Joshua struck them down and put them to death, and he hung them on five trees. And they hung on the trees until evening. [27]At sunset Joshua commanded, and they took them down from the trees and threw them into the cave where they had hidden themselves; they set large stones against the mouth of the cave, which remain to this very day.

28 Joshua took Makkedah on that day, and struck it and its king with the edge of the sword; he utterly destroyed every person in it; he left no one remaining. And he did to the king of Makkedah as he had done to the king of Jericho.

29 Then Joshua passed on from Makkedah, and all Israel with him, to Libnah, and fought against Libnah. [30]The LORD gave it also and its king into the hand of Israel; and he struck it with the edge of the sword, and every person in it; he left no one remaining in it; and he did to its king as he had done to the king of Jericho.

31 Next Joshua passed on from Libnah, and all Israel with him, to Lachish, and laid siege to it, and assaulted it. [32]The LORD gave Lachish into the hand of Israel, and he took it on the second day, and struck it with the edge of the sword, and every person in it, as he had done to Libnah.

33 Then King Horam of Gezer came up to help Lachish; and Joshua struck him and his people, leaving him no survivors.

34 From Lachish Joshua passed on with all Israel to Eglon; and they laid siege to it, and assaulted it; [35]and they took it that day, and struck it with the edge of the sword; and every person in it he utterly destroyed that day, as he had done to Lachish.

36 Then Joshua went up with all Israel from Eglon to Hebron; they assaulted it, [37]and took it, and struck it with the edge of the sword, and its king and its towns, and every person in it; he left no one remaining, just as he had done to Eglon, and utterly destroyed it with every person in it.

38 Then Joshua, with all Israel, turned back to Debir and assaulted it, [39]and he took it with its king and all its towns; they struck them with the edge of the sword, and utterly destroyed every person in it; he left no one remaining; just as he had done to Hebron, and, as he had done to Libnah and its king, so he did to Debir and its king.

40 So Joshua defeated the whole land, the hill country and the Negeb and the lowland and the slopes, and all their kings; he left no one remaining, but utterly destroyed all that breathed, as the LORD God of Israel commanded. [41]And Joshua defeated them from Kadesh-barnea to Gaza, and all the country of Goshen, as far as Gibeon. [42]Joshua took all these kings and their land at one time, because the LORD God of Israel fought for Israel. [43]Then Joshua returned, and all Israel with him, to the camp at Gilgal.

The United Kings of Northern Canaan Defeated

11 When King Jabin of Hazor heard of this, he sent to King Jobab of Madon, to the king of Shimron, to the king of Achshaph, [2]and to the kings who were in the northern hill country, and in the Arabah south of Chinneroth, and in the lowland, and in Naphoth-dor on the west, [3]to the Canaanites in the east and the west, the Amorites, the Hittites, the Perizzites, and the Jebusites in the hill country, and the Hivites under Hermon in the land of Mizpah. [4]They came out, with all their troops, a great army, in number like the sand on the seashore, with very many horses and chariots. [5]All these kings joined their forces, and came and camped together at the waters of Merom, to fight with Israel.

6 And the LORD said to Joshua, "Do not be afraid

---

a Heb *moved his tongue*

of them, for tomorrow at this time I will hand over all of them, slain, to Israel; you shall hamstring their horses, and burn their chariots with fire." [7] So Joshua came suddenly upon them with all his fighting force, by the waters of Merom, and fell upon them. [8] And the LORD handed them over to Israel, who attacked them and chased them as far as Great Sidon and Misrephoth-maim, and eastward as far as the valley of Mizpeh. They struck them down, until they had left no one remaining. [9] And Joshua did to them as the LORD commanded him; he hamstrung their horses, and burned their chariots with fire.

10 Joshua turned back at that time, and took Hazor, and struck its king down with the sword. Before that time Hazor was the head of all those kingdoms. [11] And they put to the sword all who were in it, utterly destroying them; there was no one left who breathed, and he burned Hazor with fire. [12] And all the towns of those kings, and all their kings, Joshua took, and struck them with the edge of the sword, utterly destroying them, as Moses the servant of the LORD had commanded. [13] But Israel burned none of the towns that stood on mounds except Hazor, which Joshua did burn. [14] All the spoil of these towns, and the livestock, the Israelites took for their booty; but all the people they struck down with the edge of the sword, until they had destroyed them, and they did not leave any who breathed. [15] As the LORD had commanded his servant Moses, so Moses commanded Joshua, and so Joshua did; he left nothing undone of all that the LORD had commanded Moses.

Summary of Joshua's Conquests

16 So Joshua took all that land: the hill country and all the Negeb and all the land of Goshen and the lowland and the Arabah and the hill country of Israel and its lowland, [17] from Mount Halak, which rises toward Seir, as far as Baal-gad in the valley of Lebanon below Mount Hermon. He took all their kings, struck them down, and put them to death. [18] Joshua made war a long time with all those kings. [19] There was not a town that made peace with the Israelites, except the Hivites, the inhabitants of Gibeon; all were taken in battle. [20] For it was the LORD's doing to harden their hearts so that they would come against Israel in battle, in order that they might be utterly destroyed, and might receive no mercy, but be exterminated, just as the LORD had commanded Moses.

21 At that time Joshua came and wiped out the Anakim from the hill country, from Hebron, from Debir, from Anab, and from all the hill country of Judah, and from all the hill country of Israel; Joshua utterly destroyed them with their towns. [22] None of the Anakim was left in the land of the Israelites; some remained only in Gaza, in Gath, and in Ashdod. [23] So Joshua took the whole land, according to all that the LORD had spoken to Moses; and Joshua gave it for an inheritance to Israel according to their tribal allotments. And the land had rest from war.

The Kings Conquered by Moses

12 Now these are the kings of the land, whom the Israelites defeated, whose land they occupied beyond the Jordan toward the east, from the Wadi Arnon to Mount Hermon, with all the Arabah eastward: [2] King Sihon of the Amorites who lived at Heshbon, and ruled from Aroer, which is on the edge of the Wadi Arnon, and from the middle of the valley as far as the river Jabbok, the boundary of the Ammonites, that is, half of Gilead, [3] and the Arabah to the Sea of Chinneroth eastward, and in the direction of Beth-jeshimoth, to the sea of the Arabah, the Dead Sea,[a] southward to the foot of the slopes of Pisgah; [4] and King Og[b] of Bashan, one of the last of the Rephaim, who lived at Ashtaroth and at Edrei [5] and ruled over Mount Hermon and Salecah and all Bashan to the boundary of the Geshurites and the Maacathites, and over half of Gilead to the boundary of King Sihon of Heshbon. [6] Moses, the servant of the LORD, and the Israelites defeated them; and Moses the servant of the LORD gave their land for a possession to the Reubenites and the Gadites and the half-tribe of Manasseh.

The Kings Conquered by Joshua

7 The following are the kings of the land whom Joshua and the Israelites defeated on the west side of the Jordan, from Baal-gad in the valley of Lebanon to Mount Halak, that rises toward Seir (and Joshua gave their land to the tribes of Israel as a possession according to their allotments, [8] in the hill country, in the lowland, in the Arabah, in the slopes, in the wilderness, and in the Negeb, the land of the Hittites, Amorites, Canaanites, Perizzites, Hivites, and Jebusites):

9   the king of Jericho   one
    the king of Ai, which is next to Bethel   one

---

a Heb *Salt Sea* b Gk: Heb *the boundary of King Og*

STUDY IT!

The Conquest of Canaan · Joshua 12

The beginning of the story of Joshua makes several strong parallels with the events of the exodus from Egypt. The crossing of the Jordan River looks similar to the crossing of the Red Sea. God's direction and protection of the Israelites, symbolized by the ark, is much like God's protection and provision in the desert. And the renewal of the covenant at Mount Ebal reflects the Israelites' original commitment to the covenant. These parallels reinforce how the conquest of Canaan was part of God's continued liberation of the Israelites and a key time in their history.

As the Israelites moved into the promised land, the Canaanites were one of several groups of people the Israelites had to deal with. They were primarily an agricultural society and believed that their gods, called "baals," controlled the rain, the seasons, and the fertility of the soil. For the Israelites, there was only one God over all creation and history.

The conquest of the Canaanites through violence might make you wonder what the Israelites believed about God. They believed that the Canaanite baals were an offense against God. Because the Canaanites wouldn't change, the Israelites felt justified in killing them and taking their land. Later Christians would not be able to justify such actions, because of Jesus' teaching that we are all loved by God and that we must love even our enemies. But God's plan for humanity had not yet been fully revealed at the time Joshua was written.

10 the king of Jerusalem	one
the king of Hebron	one
11 the king of Jarmuth	one
the king of Lachish	one
12 the king of Eglon	one
the king of Gezer	one
13 the king of Debir	one
the king of Geder	one
14 the king of Hormah	one
the king of Arad	one
15 the king of Libnah	one
the king of Adullam	one
16 the king of Makkedah	one
the king of Bethel	one
17 the king of Tappuah	one
the king of Hepher	one
18 the king of Aphek	one
the king of Lasharon	one
19 the king of Madon	one
the king of Hazor	one
20 the king of Shimron-meron	one
the king of Achshaph	one
21 the king of Taanach	one
the king of Megiddo	one
22 the king of Kedesh	one
the king of Jokneam in Carmel	one
23 the king of Dor in Naphath-dor	one

the king of Goiim in Galilee,[a]	one
24 the king of Tirzah	one
thirty-one kings in all.	

13 The Parts of Canaan Still Unconquered

Now Joshua was old and advanced in years; and the LORD said to him, "You are old and advanced in years, and very much of the land still remains to be possessed. ²This is the land that still remains: all the regions of the Philistines, and all those of the Geshurites ³(from the Shihor, which is east of Egypt, northward to the boundary of Ekron, it is reckoned as Canaanite; there are five rulers of the Philistines, those of Gaza, Ashdod, Ashkelon, Gath, and Ekron), and those of the Avvim ⁴in the south; all the land of the Canaanites, and Mearah that belongs to the Sidonians, to Aphek, to the boundary of the Amorites, ⁵and the land of the Gebalites, and all Lebanon, toward the east, from Baal-gad below Mount Hermon to Lebo-hamath, ⁶all the inhabitants of the hill country from Lebanon to Misrephoth-maim, even all the Sidonians. I will myself drive them out from before the Israelites; only allot the land to Israel for an inheritance, as I have commanded you. ⁷Now therefore divide this land for an inheritance to the nine tribes and the half-tribe of Manasseh."

a Gk: Heb *Gilgal*

The Territory East of the Jordan

8 With the other half-tribe of Manasseh[a] the Reubenites and the Gadites received their inheritance, which Moses gave them, beyond the Jordan eastward, as Moses the servant of the LORD gave them: [9]from Aroer, which is on the edge of the Wadi Arnon, and the town that is in the middle of the valley, and all the tableland from[b] Medeba as far as Dibon; [10]and all the cities of King Sihon of the Amorites, who reigned in Heshbon, as far as the boundary of the Ammonites; [11]and Gilead, and the region of the Geshurites and Maacathites, and all Mount Hermon, and all Bashan to Salecah; [12]all the kingdom of Og in Bashan, who reigned in Ashtaroth and in Edrei (he alone was left of the survivors of the Rephaim); these Moses had defeated and driven out. [13]Yet the Israelites did not drive out the Geshurites or the Maacathites; but Geshur and Maacath live within Israel to this day.

14 To the tribe of Levi alone Moses gave no inheritance; the offerings by fire to the LORD God of Israel are their inheritance, as he said to them.

The Territory of Reuben

15 Moses gave an inheritance to the tribe of the Reubenites according to their clans. [16]Their territory was from Aroer, which is on the edge of the Wadi Arnon, and the town that is in the middle of the valley, and all the tableland by Medeba; [17]with Heshbon, and all its towns that are in the tableland; Dibon, and Bamoth-baal, and Beth-baal-meon, [18]and Jahaz, and Kedemoth, and Mephaath, [19]and Kiriathaim, and Sibmah, and Zereth-shahar on the hill of the valley, [20]and Beth-peor, and the slopes of Pisgah, and Beth-jeshimoth, [21]that is, all the towns of the tableland, and all the kingdom of King Sihon of the Amorites, who reigned in Heshbon, whom Moses defeated with the leaders of Midian, Evi and Rekem and Zur and Hur and Reba, as princes of Sihon, who lived in the land. [22]Along with the rest of those they put to death, the Israelites also put to the sword Balaam son of Beor, who practiced divination. [23]And the border of the Reubenites was the Jordan and its banks. This was the inheritance of the Reubenites according to their families with their towns and villages.

The Territory of Gad

24 Moses gave an inheritance also to the tribe of the Gadites, according to their families. [25]Their territory was Jazer, and all the towns of Gilead, and half the land of the Ammonites, to Aroer, which is east of

Rabbah, [26]and from Heshbon to Ramath-mizpeh and Betonim, and from Mahanaim to the territory of Debir,[c] [27]and in the valley Beth-haram, Beth-nimrah, Succoth, and Zaphon, the rest of the kingdom of King Sihon of Heshbon, the Jordan and its banks, as far as the lower end of the Sea of Chinnereth, eastward beyond the Jordan. [28]This is the inheritance of the Gadites according to their clans, with their towns and villages.

The Territory of the Half-Tribe of Manasseh (East)

29 Moses gave an inheritance to the half-tribe of Manasseh; it was allotted to the half-tribe of the Manassites according to their families. [30]Their territory extended from Mahanaim, through all Bashan, the whole kingdom of King Og of Bashan, and all the settlements of Jair, which are in Bashan, sixty towns, [31]and half of Gilead, and Ashtaroth, and Edrei, the towns of the kingdom of Og in Bashan; these were allotted to the people of Machir son of Manasseh according to their clans—for half the Machirites.

32 These are the inheritances that Moses distributed in the plains of Moab, beyond the Jordan east of Jericho. [33]But to the tribe of Levi Moses gave no inheritance; the LORD God of Israel is their inheritance, as he said to them.

The Distribution of Territory West of the Jordan

14 These are the inheritances that the Israelites received in the land of Canaan, which the priest Eleazar, and Joshua son of Nun, and the heads of the families of the tribes of the Israelites distributed to them. [2]Their inheritance was by lot, as the LORD had commanded Moses for the nine and one-half tribes. [3]For Moses had given an inheritance to the two and one-half tribes beyond the Jordan; but to the Levites he gave no inheritance among them. [4]For the people of Joseph were two tribes, Manasseh and Ephraim; and no portion was given to the Levites in the land, but only towns to live in, with their pasture lands for their flocks and herds. [5]The Israelites did as the LORD commanded Moses; they allotted the land.

Hebron Allotted to Caleb

6 Then the people of Judah came to Joshua at Gilgal; and Caleb son of Jephunneh the Kenizzite said to him, "You know what the LORD said to Moses the man of God in Kadesh-barnea concerning you and me. [7]I was forty years old when Moses the

servant of the LORD sent me from Kadesh-barnea to spy out the land; and I brought him an honest report. [8]But my companions who went up with me made the heart of the people melt; yet I wholeheartedly followed the LORD my God. [9]And Moses swore on that day, saying, 'Surely the land on which your foot has trodden shall be an inheritance for you and your children forever, because you have wholeheartedly followed the LORD my God.' [10]And now, as you see, the LORD has kept me alive, as he said, these forty-five years since the time that the LORD spoke this word to Moses, while Israel was journeying through the wilderness; and here I am today, eighty-five years old. [11]I am still as strong today as I was on the day that Moses sent me; my strength now is as my strength was then, for war, and for going and coming. [12]So now give me this hill country of which the LORD spoke on that day; for you heard on that day how the Anakim were there, with great fortified cities; it may be that the LORD will be with me, and I shall drive them out, as the LORD said."

13 Then Joshua blessed him, and gave Hebron to Caleb son of Jephunneh for an inheritance. [14]So Hebron became the inheritance of Caleb son of Jephunneh the Kenizzite to this day, because he wholeheartedly followed the LORD, the God of Israel. [15]Now the name of Hebron formerly was Kiriath-arba;[a] this Arba was[b] the greatest man among the Anakim. And the land had rest from war.

The Territory of Judah

15 The lot for the tribe of the people of Judah according to their families reached southward to the boundary of Edom, to the wilderness of Zin at the farthest south. [2]And their south boundary ran from the end of the Dead Sea,[c] from the bay that faces southward; [3]it goes out southward of the ascent of Akrabbim, passes along to Zin, and goes up south of Kadesh-barnea, along by Hezron, up to Addar, makes a turn to Karka, [4]passes along to Azmon, goes out by the Wadi of Egypt, and comes to its end at the sea. This shall be your south boundary. [5]And the east boundary is the Dead Sea,[c] to the mouth of the Jordan. And the boundary on the north side runs from the bay of the sea at the mouth of the Jordan; [6]and the boundary goes up to Beth-hoglah, and passes along north of Beth-arabah; and the boundary goes up to

the Stone of Bohan, Reuben's son; [7]and the boundary goes up to Debir from the Valley of Achor, and so northward, turning toward Gilgal, which is opposite the ascent of Adummim, which is on the south side of the valley; and the boundary passes along to the waters of En-shemesh, and ends at En-rogel; [8]then the boundary goes up by the valley of the son of Hinnom at the southern slope of the Jebusites (that is, Jerusalem); and the boundary goes up to the top of the mountain that lies over against the valley of Hinnom, on the west, at the northern end of the valley of Rephaim; [9]then the boundary extends from the top of the mountain to the spring of the Waters of Nephtoah, and from there to the towns of Mount Ephron; then the boundary bends around to Baalah (that is, Kiriath-jearim); [10]and the boundary circles west of Baalah to Mount Seir, passes along to the northern slope of Mount Jearim (that is, Chesalon), and goes down to Beth-shemesh, and passes along by Timnah; [11]the boundary goes out to the slope of the hill north of Ekron, then the boundary bends around to Shikkeron, and passes along to Mount Baalah, and goes out to Jabneel; then the boundary comes to an end at the sea. [12]And the west boundary was the Mediterranean with its coast. This is the boundary surrounding the people of Judah according to their families.

Caleb Occupies His Portion

13 According to the commandment of the LORD to Joshua, he gave to Caleb son of Jephunneh a portion among the people of Judah, Kiriath-arba,[a] that is, Hebron (Arba was the father of Anak). [14]And Caleb drove out from there the three sons of Anak: Sheshai, Ahiman, and Talmai, the descendants of Anak. [15]From there he went up against the inhabitants of Debir; now the name of Debir formerly was Kiriath-sepher. [16]And Caleb said, "Whoever attacks Kiriath-sepher and takes it, to him I will give my daughter Achsah as wife." [17]Othniel son of Kenaz, the brother of Caleb, took it; and he gave him his daughter Achsah as wife. [18]When she came to him, she urged him to ask her father for a field. As she dismounted from her donkey, Caleb said to her, "What do you wish?" [19]She said to him, "Give me a present; since you have set me in the land of the Negeb, give me springs of water as well." So Caleb gave her the upper springs and the lower springs.

---

a That is the city of Arba　b Heb lacks this Arba was　c Heb Salt Sea

The Towns of Judah

20 This is the inheritance of the tribe of the people of Judah according to their families. [21] The towns belonging to the tribe of the people of Judah in the extreme south, toward the boundary of Edom, were Kabzeel, Eder, Jagur, [22] Kinah, Dimonah, Adadah, [23] Kedesh, Hazor, Ithnan, [24] Ziph, Telem, Bealoth, [25] Hazor-hadattah, Kerioth-hezron (that is, Hazor), [26] Amam, Shema, Moladah, [27] Hazar-gaddah, Heshmon, Beth-pelet, [28] Hazar-shual, Beer-sheba, Biziothiah, [29] Baalah, Iim, Ezem, [30] El-tolad, Chesil, Hormah, [31] Ziklag, Madmannah, Sansannah, [32] Lebaoth, Shilhim, Ain, and Rimmon: in all, twenty-nine towns, with their villages.

33 And in the lowland, Eshtaol, Zorah, Ashnah, [34] Zanoah, En-gannim, Tappuah, Enam, [35] Jarmuth, Adullam, Socoh, Azekah, [36] Shaaraim, Adithaim, Gederah, Gederothaim: fourteen towns with their villages.

37 Zenan, Hadashah, Migdal-gad, [38] Dilan, Mizpeh, Jokthe-el, [39] Lachish, Bozkath, Eglon, [40] Cabbon, Lahmam, Chitlish, [41] Gederoth, Beth-dagon, Naamah, and Makkedah: sixteen towns with their villages.

42 Libnah, Ether, Ashan, [43] Iphtah, Ashnah, Nezib, [44] Keilah, Achzib, and Mareshah: nine towns with their villages.

45 Ekron, with its dependencies and its villages; [46] from Ekron to the sea, all that were near Ashdod, with their villages.

47 Ashdod, its towns and its villages; Gaza, its towns and its villages; to the Wadi of Egypt, and the Great Sea with its coast.

48 And in the hill country, Shamir, Jattir, Socoh, [49] Dannah, Kiriath-sannah (that is, Debir), [50] Anab, Eshtemoh, Anim, [51] Goshen, Holon, and Giloh: eleven towns with their villages.

52 Arab, Dumah, Eshan, [53] Janim, Beth-tappuah, Aphekah, [54] Humtah, Kiriath-arba (that is, Hebron), and Zior: nine towns with their villages.

55 Maon, Carmel, Ziph, Juttah, [56] Jezreel, Jokdeam, Zanoah, [57] Kain, Gibeah, and Timnah: ten towns with their villages.

58 Halhul, Beth-zur, Gedor, [59] Maarath, Beth-anoth, and Eltekon: six towns with their villages.

60 Kiriath-baal (that is, Kiriath-jearim) and Rabbah: two towns with their villages.

61 In the wilderness, Beth-arabah, Middin, Secacah, [62] Nibshan, the City of Salt, and En-gedi: six towns with their villages.

63 But the people of Judah could not drive out the Jebusites, the inhabitants of Jerusalem; so the Jebusites live with the people of Judah in Jerusalem to this day.

16 The Territory of Ephraim

The allotment of the Josephites went from the Jordan by Jericho, east of the waters of Jericho, into the wilderness, going up from Jericho into the hill country to Bethel; [2] then going from Bethel to Luz, it passes along to Ataroth, the territory of the Archites; [3] then it goes down westward to the territory of the Japhletites, as far as the territory of Lower Beth-horon, then to Gezer, and it ends at the sea.

4 The Josephites—Manasseh and Ephraim—received their inheritance.

5 The territory of the Ephraimites by their families was as follows: the boundary of their inheritance on the east was Ataroth-addar as far as Upper Beth-horon, [6] and the boundary goes from there to the sea; on the north is Michmethath; then on the east the boundary makes a turn toward Taanath-shiloh, and passes along beyond it on the east to Janoah, [7] then it goes down from Janoah to Ataroth and to Naarah, and touches Jericho, ending at the Jordan. [8] From Tappuah the boundary goes westward to the Wadi Kanah, and ends at the sea. Such is the inheritance of the tribe of the Ephraimites by their families, [9] together with the towns that were set apart for the Ephraimites within the inheritance of the Manassites, all those towns with their villages. [10] They did not, however, drive out the Canaanites who lived in Gezer: so the Canaanites have lived within Ephraim to this day but have been made to do forced labor.

17 The Other Half-Tribe of Manasseh (West)

Then allotment was made to the tribe of Manasseh, for he was the firstborn of Joseph. To Machir the firstborn of Manasseh, the father of Gilead, were allotted Gilead and Bashan, because he was a warrior. [2] And allotments were made to the rest of the tribe of Manasseh, by their families, Abiezer, Helek, Asriel, Shechem, Hepher, and Shemida; these were the male descendants of Manasseh son of Joseph, by their families.

3 Now Zelophehad son of Hepher son of Gilead son of Machir son of Manasseh had no sons, but only daughters; and these are the names of his daughters:

Mahlah, Noah, Hoglah, Milcah, and Tirzah. [4]They came before the priest Eleazar and Joshua son of Nun and the leaders, and said, "The LORD commanded Moses to give us an inheritance along with our male kin." So according to the commandment of the LORD he gave them an inheritance among the kinsmen of their father. [5]Thus there fell to Manasseh ten portions, besides the land of Gilead and Bashan, which is on the other side of the Jordan, [6]because the daughters of Manasseh received an inheritance along with his sons. The land of Gilead was allotted to the rest of the Manassites.

[7] The territory of Manasseh reached from Asher to Michmethath, which is east of Shechem; then the boundary goes along southward to the inhabitants of En-tappuah. [8]The land of Tappuah belonged to Manasseh, but the town of Tappuah on the boundary of Manasseh belonged to the Ephraimites. [9]Then the boundary went down to the Wadi Kanah. The towns here, to the south of the wadi, among the towns of Manasseh, belong to Ephraim. Then the boundary of Manasseh goes along the north side of the wadi and ends at the sea. [10]The land to the south is Ephraim's and that to the north is Manasseh's, with the sea forming its boundary; on the north Asher is reached, and on the east Issachar. [11]Within Issachar and Asher, Manasseh had Beth-shean and its villages, Ibleam and its villages, the inhabitants of Dor and its villages, the inhabitants of En-dor and its villages, the inhabitants of Taanach and its villages, and the inhabitants of Megiddo and its villages (the third is Naphath).[a] [12]Yet the Manassites could not take possession of those towns; but the Canaanites continued to live in that land. [13]But when the Israelites grew strong, they put the Canaanites to forced labor, but did not utterly drive them out.

The Tribe of Joseph Protests

[14] The tribe of Joseph spoke to Joshua, saying, "Why have you given me but one lot and one portion as an inheritance, since we are a numerous people, whom all along the LORD has blessed?" [15]And Joshua said to them, "If you are a numerous people, go up to the forest, and clear ground there for yourselves in the land of the Perizzites and the Rephaim, since the hill country of Ephraim is too narrow for you." [16]The tribe of Joseph said, "The hill country is not enough for us; yet all the Canaanites who live in the plain have chariots of iron, both those in Beth-shean and its villages and those in the Valley of Jezreel."

[17]Then Joshua said to the house of Joseph, to Ephraim and Manasseh, "You are indeed a numerous people, and have great power; you shall not have one lot only, [18]but the hill country shall be yours, for though it is a forest, you shall clear it and possess it to its farthest borders; for you shall drive out the Canaanites, though they have chariots of iron, and though they are strong."

The Territories of the Remaining Tribes

18 Then the whole congregation of the Israelites assembled at Shiloh, and set up the tent of meeting there. The land lay subdued before them.

[2] There remained among the Israelites seven tribes whose inheritance had not yet been apportioned. [3]So Joshua said to the Israelites, "How long will you be slack about going in and taking possession of the land that the LORD, the God of your ancestors, has given you? [4]Provide three men from each tribe, and I will send them out that they may begin to go throughout the land, writing a description of it with a view to their inheritances. Then come back to me. [5]They shall divide it into seven portions, Judah continuing in its territory on the south, and the house of Joseph in their territory on the north. [6]You shall describe the land in seven divisions and bring the description here to me; and I will cast lots for you here before the LORD our God. [7]The Levites have no portion among you, for the priesthood of the LORD is their heritage; and Gad and Reuben and the half-tribe of Manasseh have received their inheritance beyond the Jordan eastward, which Moses the servant of the LORD gave them."

[8] So the men started on their way; and Joshua charged those who went to write the description of the land, saying, "Go throughout the land and write a description of it, and come back to me; and I will cast lots for you here before the LORD in Shiloh." [9]So the men went and traversed the land and set down in a book a description of it by towns in seven divisions; then they came back to Joshua in the camp at Shiloh, [10]and Joshua cast lots for them in Shiloh before the LORD; and there Joshua apportioned the land to the Israelites, to each a portion.

The Territory of Benjamin

[11] The lot of the tribe of Benjamin according to its families came up, and the territory allotted to it fell between the tribe of Judah and the tribe of Jo-

---

[a] Meaning of Heb uncertain

seph. [12]On the north side their boundary began at the Jordan; then the boundary goes up to the slope of Jericho on the north, then up through the hill country westward; and it ends at the wilderness of Beth-aven. [13]From there the boundary passes along southward in the direction of Luz, to the slope of Luz (that is, Bethel), then the boundary goes down to Ataroth-addar, on the mountain that lies south of Lower Beth-horon. [14]Then the boundary goes in another direction, turning on the western side southward from the mountain that lies to the south, opposite Beth-horon, and it ends at Kiriath-baal (that is, Kiriath-jearim), a town belonging to the tribe of Judah. This forms the western side. [15]The southern side begins at the outskirts of Kiriath-jearim; and the boundary goes from there to Ephron,[a] to the spring of the Waters of Nephtoah; [16]then the boundary goes down to the border of the mountain that overlooks the valley of the son of Hinnom, which is at the north end of the valley of Rephaim; and it then goes down the valley of Hinnom, south of the slope of the Jebusites, and downward to En-rogel; [17]then it bends in a northerly direction going on to En-shemesh, and from there goes to Geliloth, which is opposite the ascent of Adummim; then it goes down to the Stone of Bohan, Reuben's son; [18]and passing on to the north of the slope of Beth-arabah[b] it goes down to the Arabah; [19]then the boundary passes on to the north of the slope of Beth-hoglah; and the boundary ends at the northern bay of the Dead Sea,[c] at the south end of the Jordan: this is the southern border. [20]The Jordan forms its boundary on the eastern side. This is the inheritance of the tribe of Benjamin, according to its families, boundary by boundary all around.

21 Now the towns of the tribe of Benjamin according to their families were Jericho, Beth-hoglah, Emek-keziz, [22]Beth-arabah, Zemaraim, Bethel, [23]Avvim, Parah, Ophrah, [24]Chephar-ammoni, Ophni, and Geba—twelve towns with their villages: [25]Gibeon, Ramah, Beeroth, [26]Mizpeh, Chephirah, Mozah, [27]Rekem, Irpeel, Taralah, [28]Zela, Haeleph, Jebus[d] (that is, Jerusalem), Gibeah[e] and Kiriath-jearim[f]—fourteen towns with their villages. This is the inheritance of the tribe of Benjamin according to its families.

The Territory of Simeon

19 The second lot came out for Simeon, for the tribe of Simeon, according to its fami-

lies; its inheritance lay within the inheritance of the tribe of Judah. [2]It had for its inheritance Beer-sheba, Sheba, Moladah, [3]Hazar-shual, Balah, Ezem, [4]Eltolad, Bethul, Hormah, [5]Ziklag, Beth-marcaboth, Hazar-susah, [6]Beth-lebaoth, and Sharuhen—thirteen towns with their villages; [7]Ain, Rimmon, Ether, and Ashan—four towns with their villages; [8]together with all the villages all around these towns as far as Baalath-beer, Ramah of the Negeb. This was the inheritance of the tribe of Simeon according to its families. [9]The inheritance of the tribe of Simeon formed part of the territory of Judah; because the portion of the tribe of Judah was too large for them, the tribe of Simeon obtained an inheritance within their inheritance.

The Territory of Zebulun

10 The third lot came up for the tribe of Zebulun, according to its families. The boundary of its inheritance reached as far as Sarid; [11]then its boundary goes up westward, and on to Maralah, and touches Dabbesheth, then the wadi that is east of Jokneam; [12]from Sarid it goes in the other direction eastward toward the sunrise to the boundary of Chisloth-tabor; from there it goes to Daberath, then up to Japhia; [13]from there it passes along on the east toward the sunrise to Gath-hepher, to Eth-kazin, and going on to Rimmon it bends toward Neah; [14]then on the north the boundary makes a turn to Hannathon, and it ends at the valley of Iphtah-el; [15]and Kattath, Nahalal, Shimron, Idalah, and Bethlehem—twelve towns with their villages. [16]This is the inheritance of the tribe of Zebulun, according to its families—these towns with their villages.

The Territory of Issachar

17 The fourth lot came out for Issachar, for the tribe of Issachar, according to its families. [18]Its territory included Jezreel, Chesulloth, Shunem, [19]Hapharaim, Shion, Anaharath, [20]Rabbith, Kishion, Ebez, [21]Remeth, En-gannim, En-haddah, Beth-pazzez; [22]the boundary also touches Tabor, Shahazumah, and Beth-shemesh, and its boundary ends at the Jordan—sixteen towns with their villages. [23]This is the inheritance of the tribe of Issachar, according to its families—the towns with their villages.

The Territory of Asher

24 The fifth lot came out for the tribe of Asher according to its families. [25]Its boundary included

---

a Cn See 15.9. Heb *westward* b Gk: Heb *to the slope over against the Arabah* c Heb *Salt Sea* d Gk Syr Vg: Heb *the Jebusite* e Heb *Gibeath* f Gk: Heb *Kiriath*

Helkath, Hali, Beten, Achshaph, [26]Allammelech, Amad, and Mishal; on the west it touches Carmel and Shihor-libnath, [27]then it turns eastward, goes to Beth-dagon, and touches Zebulun and the valley of Iphtah-el northward to Beth-emek and Neiel; then it continues in the north to Cabul, [28]Ebron, Rehob, Hammon, Kanah, as far as Great Sidon; [29]then the boundary turns to Ramah, reaching to the fortified city of Tyre; then the boundary turns to Hosah, and it ends at the sea; Mahalab,[a] Achzib, [30]Ummah, Aphek, and Rehob—twenty-two towns with their villages. [31]This is the inheritance of the tribe of Asher according to its families—these towns with their villages.

The Territory of Naphtali

32 The sixth lot came out for the tribe of Naphtali, for the tribe of Naphtali, according to its families. [33]And its boundary ran from Heleph, from the oak in Zaanannim, and Adami-nekeb, and Jabneel, as far as Lakkum; and it ended at the Jordan; [34]then the boundary turns westward to Aznoth-tabor, and goes from there to Hukkok, touching Zebulun at the south, and Asher on the west, and Judah on the east at the Jordan. [35]The fortified towns are Ziddim, Zer, Hammath, Rakkath, Chinnereth, [36]Adamah, Ramah, Hazor, [37]Kedesh, Edrei, En-hazor, [38]Iron, Migdal-el, Horem, Beth-anath, and Beth-shemesh—nineteen towns with their villages. [39]This is the inheritance of the tribe of Naphtali according to its families—the towns with their villages.

The Territory of Dan

40 The seventh lot came out for the tribe of Dan, according to its families. [41]The territory of its inheritance included Zorah, Eshtaol, Ir-shemesh, [42]Shaalabbin, Aijalon, Ithlah, [43]Elon, Timnah, Ekron, [44]Eltekeh, Gibbethon, Baalath, [45]Jehud, Bene-berak, Gath-rimmon, [46]Me-jarkon, and Rakkon at the border opposite Joppa. [47]When the territory of the Danites was lost to them, the Danites went up and fought against Leshem, and after capturing it and putting it to the sword, they took possession of it and settled in it, calling Leshem, Dan, after their ancestor Dan. [48]This is the inheritance of the tribe of Dan, according to their families—these towns with their villages.

Joshua's Inheritance

49 When they had finished distributing the several territories of the land as inheritances, the Israelites gave an inheritance among them to Joshua son of Nun. [50]By command of the LORD they gave him the town that he asked for, Timnath-serah in the hill country of Ephraim; he rebuilt the town, and settled in it.

51 These are the inheritances that the priest Eleazar and Joshua son of Nun and the heads of the families of the tribes of the Israelites distributed by lot at Shiloh before the LORD, at the entrance of the tent of meeting. So they finished dividing the land.

The Cities of Refuge

20 Then the LORD spoke to Joshua, saying, [2]"Say to the Israelites, 'Appoint the cities of refuge, of which I spoke to you through Moses, [3]so that anyone who kills a person without intent or by mistake may flee there; they shall be for you a refuge from the avenger of blood. [4]The slayer shall flee to one of these cities and shall stand at the entrance of the gate of the city, and explain the case to the elders of that city; then the fugitive shall be taken into the city, and given a place, and shall remain with them. [5]And if the avenger of blood is in pursuit, they shall not give up the slayer, because the neighbor was killed by mistake, there having been no enmity between them before. [6]The slayer shall remain in that city until there is a trial before the congregation, until the death of the one who is high priest at the time: then the slayer may return home, to the town in which the deed was done.'"

7 So they set apart Kedesh in Galilee in the hill country of Naphtali, and Shechem in the hill country of Ephraim, and Kiriath-arba (that is, Hebron) in the hill country of Judah. [8]And beyond the Jordan east of Jericho, they appointed Bezer in the wilderness on the tableland, from the tribe of Reuben, and Ramoth in Gilead, from the tribe of Gad, and Golan in Bashan, from the tribe of Manasseh. [9]These were the cities designated for all the Israelites, and for the aliens residing among them, that anyone who killed a person without intent could flee there, so as not to die by the hand of the avenger of blood, until there was a trial before the congregation.

Cities Allotted to the Levites

21 Then the heads of the families of the Levites came to the priest Eleazar and to Joshua son of Nun and to the heads of the families of the tribes of the Israelites; [2]they said to them at Shiloh in the land of Canaan, "The LORD com-

---

a Cn Compare Gk: Heb *Mehebel*

manded through Moses that we be given towns to live in, along with their pasture lands for our livestock." [3]So by command of the LORD the Israelites gave to the Levites the following towns and pasture lands out of their inheritance.

4 The lot came out for the families of the Kohathites. So those Levites who were descendants of Aaron the priest received by lot thirteen towns from the tribes of Judah, Simeon, and Benjamin.

5 The rest of the Kohathites received by lot ten towns from the families of the tribe of Ephraim, from the tribe of Dan, and the half-tribe of Manasseh.

6 The Gershonites received by lot thirteen towns from the families of the tribe of Issachar, from the tribe of Asher, from the tribe of Naphtali, and from the half-tribe of Manasseh in Bashan.

7 The Merarites according to their families received twelve towns from the tribe of Reuben, the tribe of Gad, and the tribe of Zebulun.

8 These towns and their pasture lands the Israelites gave by lot to the Levites, as the LORD had commanded through Moses.

9 Out of the tribe of Judah and the tribe of Simeon they gave the following towns mentioned by name, [10]which went to the descendants of Aaron, one of the families of the Kohathites who belonged to the Levites, since the lot fell to them first. [11]They gave them Kiriath-arba (Arba being the father of Anak), that is Hebron, in the hill country of Judah, along with the pasture lands around it. [12]But the fields of the town and its villages had been given to Caleb son of Jephunneh as his holding.

13 To the descendants of Aaron the priest they gave Hebron, the city of refuge for the slayer, with its pasture lands, Libnah with its pasture lands, [14]Jattir with its pasture lands, Eshtemoa with its pasture lands, [15]Holon with its pasture lands, Debir with its pasture lands, [16]Ain with its pasture lands, Juttah with its pasture lands, and Beth-shemesh with its pasture lands—nine towns out of these two tribes. [17]Out of the tribe of Benjamin: Gibeon with its pasture lands, Geba with its pasture lands, [18]Anathoth with its pasture lands, and Almon with its pasture lands—four towns. [19]The towns of the descendants of Aaron—the priests—were thirteen in all, with their pasture lands.

20 As to the rest of the Kohathites belonging to the Kohathite families of the Levites, the towns allotted to them were out of the tribe of Ephraim. [21]To them were given Shechem, the city of refuge for the slayer, with its pasture lands in the hill country of Ephraim, Gezer with its pasture lands, [22]Kibzaim with its pasture lands, and Beth-horon with its pasture lands—four towns. [23]Out of the tribe of Dan: Elteke with its pasture lands, Gibbethon with its pasture lands, [24]Aijalon with its pasture lands, Gath-rimmon with its pasture lands—four towns. [25]Out of the half-tribe of Manasseh: Taanach with its pasture lands, and Gath-rimmon with its pasture lands—two towns. [26]The towns of the families of the rest of the Kohathites were ten in all, with their pasture lands.

27 To the Gershonites, one of the families of the Levites, were given out of the half-tribe of Manasseh, Golan in Bashan with its pasture lands, the city of refuge for the slayer, and Beeshterah with its pasture lands—two towns. [28]Out of the tribe of Issachar: Kishion with its pasture lands, Daberath with its pasture lands, [29]Jarmuth with its pasture lands, Engannim with its pasture lands—four towns. [30]Out of the tribe of Asher: Mishal with its pasture lands, Abdon with its pasture lands, [31]Helkath with its pasture lands, and Rehob with its pasture lands—four towns. [32]Out of the tribe of Naphtali: Kedesh in Galilee with its pasture lands, the city of refuge for the slayer, Hammoth-dor with its pasture lands, and Kartan with its pasture lands—three towns. [33]The towns of the several families of the Gershonites were in all thirteen, with their pasture lands.

34 To the rest of the Levites—the Merarite families—were given out of the tribe of Zebulun: Jokneam with its pasture lands, Kartah with its pasture lands, [35]Dimnah with its pasture lands, Nahalal with its pasture lands—four towns. [36]Out of the tribe of Reuben: Bezer with its pasture lands, Jahzah with its pasture lands, [37]Kedemoth with its pasture lands, and Mephaath with its pasture lands—four towns. [38]Out of the tribe of Gad: Ramoth in Gilead with its pasture lands, the city of refuge for the slayer, Mahanaim with its pasture lands, [39]Heshbon with its pasture lands, Jazer with its pasture lands—four towns in all. [40]As for the towns of the several Merarite families, that is, the remainder of the families of the Levites, those allotted to them were twelve in all.

41 The towns of the Levites within the holdings of the Israelites were in all forty-eight towns with their pasture lands. [42]Each of these towns had its pasture lands around it; so it was with all these towns.

43 Thus the LORD gave to Israel all the land that he swore to their ancestors that he would give them; and having taken possession of it, they settled there.

[44] And the LORD gave them rest on every side just as he had sworn to their ancestors; not one of all their enemies had withstood them, for the LORD had given all their enemies into their hands. [45] Not one of all the good promises that the LORD had made to the house of Israel had failed; all came to pass.

22 The Eastern Tribes Return to Their Territory

Then Joshua summoned the Reubenites, the Gadites, and the half-tribe of Manasseh, [2] and said to them, "You have observed all that Moses the servant of the LORD commanded you, and have obeyed me in all that I have commanded you; [3] you have not forsaken your kindred these many days, down to this day, but have been careful to keep the charge of the LORD your God. [4] And now the LORD your God has given rest to your kindred, as he promised them; therefore turn and go to your tents in the land where your possession lies, which Moses the servant of the LORD gave you on the other side of the Jordan. [5] Take good care to observe the commandment and instruction that Moses the servant of the LORD commanded you, to love the LORD your God, to walk in all his ways, to keep his commandments, and to hold fast to him, and to serve him with all your heart and with all your soul." [6] So Joshua blessed them and sent them away, and they went to their tents.

[7] Now to the one half of the tribe of Manasseh Moses had given a possession in Bashan; but to the other half Joshua had given a possession beside their fellow Israelites in the land west of the Jordan. And when Joshua sent them away to their tents and blessed them, [8] he said to them, "Go back to your tents with much wealth, and with very much livestock, with silver, gold, bronze, and iron, and with a great quantity of clothing; divide the spoil of your enemies with your kindred." [9] So the Reubenites and the Gadites and the half-tribe of Manasseh returned home, parting from the Israelites at Shiloh, which is in the land of Canaan, to go to the land of Gilead, their own land

of which they had taken possession by command of the LORD through Moses.

A Memorial Altar East of the Jordan

[10] When they came to the region[a] near the Jordan that lies in the land of Canaan, the Reubenites and the Gadites and the half-tribe of Manasseh built there an altar by the Jordan, an altar of great size. [11] The Israelites heard that the Reubenites and the Gadites and the half-tribe of Manasseh had built an altar at the frontier of the land of Canaan, in the region[b] near the Jordan, on the side that belongs to the Israelites. [12] And when the people of Israel heard of it, the whole assembly of the Israelites gathered at Shiloh, to make war against them.

[13] Then the Israelites sent the priest Phinehas son of Eleazar to the Reubenites and the Gadites and the half-tribe of Manasseh, in the land of Gilead, [14] and with him ten chiefs, one from each of the tribal families of Israel, every one of them the head of a family among the clans of Israel. [15] They came to the Reubenites, the Gadites, and the half-tribe of Manasseh, in the land of Gilead, and they said to them, [16] "Thus says the whole congregation of the LORD, 'What is this treachery that you have committed against the God of Israel in turning away today from following the LORD, by building yourselves an altar today in rebellion against the LORD? [17] Have we not had enough of the sin at Peor from which even yet we have not cleansed ourselves, and for which a plague came upon the congregation of the LORD, [18] that you must turn away today from following the LORD! If you rebel against the LORD today, he will be angry with the whole congregation of Israel tomorrow. [19] But now, if your land is unclean, cross over into the LORD's land where the LORD's tabernacle now stands, and take for yourselves a possession among us; only do not rebel against the LORD, or rebel against us[c] by building yourselves an altar other than the altar of the LORD our God. [20] Did not Achan son of Zerah break faith in the matter of the devoted things, and wrath fell upon all the congrega-

> "Take good care to observe the commandment … to love the LORD your God, to walk in all his ways … and to serve him with all your heart and with all your soul."
> —Joshua 22:5

a Or *to Geliloth*   b Or *at Geliloth*   c Or *make rebels of us*

A Prayer for Understanding · Joshua 22:10–34

The Israelite tribes who settled west of the Jordan River become concerned when the Israelite tribes on the east side of the Jordan built a large altar to worship God. They thought that by building more altars, the tribes to the east were compromising their belief in one God. Some were ready to go to war over this issue. But maintaining unity among the tribes was also important. So the western tribes wisely sent Phinehas and others to insist on the importance of one place of worship. When Phinehas listened to the eastern tribes, he understood their good intentions, and war was avoided.

Think about times when you have jumped to conclusions about other people's actions. Then say the following prayer:

Dear God, you are God of love, wisdom, and mercy. A misunderstanding almost led to war among your people, the Israelites. Help me to avoid jumping to conclusions about the actions of others. Help me to listen and understand their intentions, as Phinehas did. And let me be gracious in recognizing when I'm wrong. Amen.

tion of Israel? And he did not perish alone for his iniquity!' "

21 Then the Reubenites, the Gadites, and the half-tribe of Manasseh said in answer to the heads of the families of Israel, [22]"The Lord, God of gods! The Lord, God of gods! He knows; and let Israel itself know! If it was in rebellion or in breach of faith toward the Lord, do not spare us today [23]for building an altar to turn away from following the Lord; or if we did so to offer burnt offerings or grain offerings or offerings of well-being on it, may the Lord himself take vengeance. [24]No! We did it from fear that in time to come your children might say to our children, 'What have you to do with the Lord, the God of Israel? [25]For the Lord has made the Jordan a boundary between us and you, you Reubenites and Gadites; you have no portion in the Lord.' So your children might make our children cease to worship the Lord. [26]Therefore we said, 'Let us now build an altar, not for burnt offering, nor for sacrifice, [27]but to be a witness between us and you, and between the generations after us, that we do perform the service of the Lord in his presence with our burnt offerings and sacrifices and offerings of well-being; so that your children may never say to our children in time to come, "You have no portion in the Lord." ' [28]And we thought, If this should be said to us or to our descendants in time to come, we could say, 'Look at this copy of the altar of the Lord, which our ancestors made, not for burnt offerings, nor for sacrifice, but to be a witness between us and you.' [29]Far be it from us

that we should rebel against the Lord, and turn away this day from following the Lord by building an altar for burnt offering, grain offering, or sacrifice, other than the altar of the Lord our God that stands before his tabernacle!"

30 When the priest Phinehas and the chiefs of the congregation, the heads of the families of Israel who were with him, heard the words that the Reubenites and the Gadites and the Manassites spoke, they were satisfied. [31]The priest Phinehas son of Eleazar said to the Reubenites and the Gadites and the Manassites, "Today we know that the Lord is among us, because you have not committed this treachery against the Lord; now you have saved the Israelites from the hand of the Lord."

32 Then the priest Phinehas son of Eleazar and the chiefs returned from the Reubenites and the Gadites in the land of Gilead to the land of Canaan, to the Israelites, and brought back word to them. [33]The report pleased the Israelites; and the Israelites blessed God and spoke no more of making war against them, to destroy the land where the Reubenites and the Gadites were settled. [34]The Reubenites and the Gadites called the altar Witness;[a] "For," said they, "it is a witness between us that the Lord is God."

Joshua Exhorts the People

23 A long time afterward, when the Lord had given rest to Israel from all their enemies all around, and Joshua was old and well advanced in years, [2]Joshua summoned all Israel, their elders and

a Cn Compare Syr: Heb lacks *Witness*

heads, their judges and officers, and said to them, "I am now old and well advanced in years; ³and you have seen all that the LORD your God has done to all these nations for your sake, for it is the LORD your God who has fought for you. ⁴I have allotted to you as an inheritance for your tribes those nations that remain, along with all the nations that I have already cut off, from the Jordan to the Great Sea in the west. ⁵The LORD your God will push them back before you, and drive them out of your sight; and you shall possess their land, as the LORD your God promised you. ⁶Therefore be very steadfast to observe and do all that is written in the book of the law of Moses, turning aside from it neither to the right nor to the left, ⁷so that you may not be mixed with these nations left here among you, or make mention of the names of their gods, or swear by them, or serve them, or bow yourselves down to them, ⁸but hold fast to the LORD your God, as you have done to this day. ⁹For the LORD has driven out before you great and strong nations; and as for you, no one has been able to withstand you to this day. ¹⁰One of you puts to flight a thousand, since it is the LORD your God who fights for you, as he promised you. ¹¹Be very careful, therefore, to love the LORD your God. ¹²For if you turn back, and join the survivors of these nations left here among you, and intermarry with them, so that you marry their women and they yours, ¹³know assuredly that the LORD your God will not continue to drive out these nations before you; but they shall be a snare and a trap for you, a scourge on your sides, and thorns in your eyes, until you perish from this good land that the LORD your God has given you.

14 "And now I am about to go the way of all the earth, and you know in your hearts and souls, all of you, that not one thing has failed of all the good things that the LORD your God promised concerning you; all have come to pass for you, not one of them has failed. ¹⁵But just as all the good things that the LORD your God promised concerning you have been fulfilled for you, so the LORD will bring upon you all the bad things, until he has destroyed you from this good land that the LORD your God has given you. ¹⁶If you transgress the covenant of the LORD your God, which he enjoined on you, and go and serve other gods and bow down to them, then the anger of the LORD will be kindled against you, and you shall perish quickly from the good land that he has given to you."

The Tribes Renew the Covenant

24 Then Joshua gathered all the tribes of Israel to Shechem, and summoned the elders, the heads, the judges, and the officers of Israel; and they presented themselves before God. ²And Joshua said to all the people, "Thus says the LORD, the God of Israel: Long ago your ancestors—Terah and his sons Abraham and Nahor—lived beyond the Euphrates and served other gods. ³Then I took your father Abraham from beyond the River and led him through all the land of Canaan and made his offspring many. I gave him Isaac; ⁴and to Isaac I gave Jacob and Esau. I gave Esau the hill country of Seir to possess, but Jacob and his children went down to Egypt. ⁵Then I sent Moses and Aaron, and I plagued Egypt with what I did in its midst; and afterwards I brought you out. ⁶When I brought your ancestors out of Egypt, you came to the sea; and the Egyptians pursued your ancestors with chariots and horsemen to the Red Sea.ᵃ ⁷When they cried out to the LORD, he put darkness between you and the Egyptians, and made the sea come upon them and cover them; and your eyes saw what I did to Egypt. Afterwards you lived in the wilderness a long time. ⁸Then I brought you to the land of the Amorites, who lived on the other side of the Jordan; they fought with you, and I handed them over to you, and you took possession of their land, and I destroyed them before you. ⁹Then King Balak son of Zippor of Moab, set out to fight against Israel. He sent and invited Balaam son of Beor to curse you, ¹⁰but I would not listen to Balaam; therefore he blessed you; so I rescued you out of his hand. ¹¹When you went over the Jordan and came to Jericho, the citizens of Jericho fought against you, and also the Amorites, the Perizzites, the Canaanites, the Hittites, the Girgashites, the Hivites, and the Jebusites; and I handed them over to you. ¹²I sent the hornetᵇ ahead of you, which drove out before you the two kings of the Amorites; it was not by your sword or by your bow. ¹³I gave you a land on which you had not labored, and towns that you had not

---

a Or *Sea of Reeds*　**b** Meaning of Heb uncertain

God's Church—Unified · Joshua 24:1–28

Some people think the Israelites always got along and never had any differences, but nothing could be farther from the truth. In this passage, Joshua summoned the leaders of the twelve tribes to present themselves before God, embrace their common faith, and renew the covenant of Sinai, setting aside their differences and political struggles.

Imagine if all Christian churches could come together and embrace a common identity before God as the tribes did in Joshua's time. Imagine if all the clubs, cliques, and gangs in our schools and neighborhoods could work toward the good of all. What strength we would have to help each other face life's challenges!

- What can you do to foster this type of unity in your local schools, churches, and neighborhoods?
- Who can help you work toward this goal?

built, and you live in them; you eat the fruit of vineyards and oliveyards that you did not plant.

14 "Now therefore revere the LORD, and serve him in sincerity and in faithfulness; put away the gods that your ancestors served beyond the River and in Egypt, and serve the LORD. ¹⁵Now if you are unwilling to serve the LORD, choose this day whom you will serve, whether the gods your ancestors served in the region beyond the River or the gods of the Amorites in whose land you are living; but as for me and my household, we will serve the LORD."

16 Then the people answered, "Far be it from us that we should forsake the LORD to serve other gods; ¹⁷for it is the LORD our God who brought us and our ancestors up from the land of Egypt, out of the house of slavery, and who did those great signs in our sight. He protected us along all the way that we went, and among all the peoples through whom we passed; ¹⁸and the LORD drove out before us all the peoples, the Amorites who lived in the land. Therefore we also will serve the LORD, for he is our God."

19 But Joshua said to the people, "You cannot serve the LORD, for he is a holy God. He is a jealous God; he will not forgive your transgressions or your sins. ²⁰If you forsake the LORD and serve foreign gods, then he will turn and do you harm, and consume you, after having done you good." ²¹And the people said to Joshua, "No, we will serve the LORD!" ²²Then Joshua said to the people, "You are witnesses against yourselves that you have chosen the LORD, to serve him." And they said, "We are witnesses." ²³He said, "Then put away the foreign gods that are among you,

and incline your hearts to the LORD, the God of Israel." ²⁴The people said to Joshua, "The LORD our God we will serve, and him we will obey." ²⁵So Joshua made a covenant with the people that day, and made statutes and ordinances for them at Shechem. ²⁶Joshua wrote these words in the book of the law of God; and he took a large stone, and set it up there under the oak in the sanctuary of the LORD. ²⁷Joshua said to all the people, "See, this stone shall be a witness against us; for it has heard all the words of the LORD that he spoke to us; therefore it shall be a witness against you, if you deal falsely with your God." ²⁸So Joshua sent the people away to their inheritances.

Death of Joshua and Eleazar

29 After these things Joshua son of Nun, the servant of the LORD, died, being one hundred ten years old. ³⁰They buried him in his own inheritance at Timnath-serah, which is in the hill country of Ephraim, north of Mount Gaash.

31 Israel served the LORD all the days of Joshua, and all the days of the elders who outlived Joshua and had known all the work that the LORD did for Israel.

32 The bones of Joseph, which the Israelites had brought up from Egypt, were buried at Shechem, in the portion of ground that Jacob had bought from the children of Hamor, the father of Shechem, for one hundred pieces of money;ᵃ it became an inheritance of the descendants of Joseph.

33 Eleazar son of Aaron died; and they buried him at Gibeah, the town of his son Phinehas, which had been given him in the hill country of Ephraim.

ᵃ Heb *one hundred qesitah*

Judges ▶▶▶▶▶▶▶▶▶▶▶▶▶▶▶▶▶▶▶▶▶▶▶▶▶

Do you ever feel caught in the middle between being treated like a child and being expected to act like an adult? For example, you feel more independent and may even have your driver's license, but you still have to obey curfew. You need a job, but employers want someone with experience—which you can't get without a job. You can die in a war for your country, but you can't buy alcohol. This time of your life is full of paradox and transitions that hold many challenges. The book of Judges in some ways is about Israel's teenage years. It tells about the difficulties faced by God's people during an in-between time: the two hundred years between the conquest of Canaan under Joshua and the establishment of the kingdom of Israel under Saul.

IN DEPTH

The twelve tribes of Israel face two especially difficult challenges in Judges: how to live peacefully together and how to withstand the attacks of foreign armies. God answers the Israelites' prayers for help by raising up extraordinary men and women to lead the tribes. These famous leaders—Gideon, Deborah, Samson, and nine others—are called judges, but they aren't judges in courtrooms wearing black robes. They are local elders and military heroes chosen by God's Spirit to lead the Israelites in times of crisis.

The same pattern we observe in the book of Joshua also appears in Judges: When the people obey God's laws, they thrive; when they are disobedient, they suffer and need to be rescued by a God-given leader. The stories in Judges probably began as regional tales about local heroes. As they were collected and edited by the author of Judges, they became national stories influenced by this message of Deuteronomy: faithfulness to God is the only road to security.

Judges reminds us that life's challenges, especially during the in-between times, are best handled through prayer and reliance on God. We can trust God to lead us through all our difficulties, the big and the small.

QUICK FACTS

- **Dates Covered:** From 1220 to 1000 B.C.
- **Author:** An unknown author writing in the same style as Deuteronomy around the end of the Babylonian exile (538 B.C.)
- **Themes:** God's raising up of mighty heroes, even flawed ones, to protect the people; a reminder of how God uses us in mighty ways too, even though we're not perfect

AT A GLANCE

- **Judges 1:1–3:6** Historical introduction
- **Judges 3:7–16:31** The stories of individual judges
- **Judges 17–21** Two appendices, including stories of moral disorder

1 Israel's Failure to Complete the Conquest of Canaan

After the death of Joshua, the Israelites inquired of the LORD, "Who shall go up first for us against the Canaanites, to fight against them?" [2]The LORD said, "Judah shall go up. I hereby give the land into his hand." [3]Judah said to his brother Simeon, "Come up with me into the territory allotted to me, that we may fight against the Canaanites; then I too will go with you into the territory allotted to you." So Simeon went with him. [4]Then Judah went up and the LORD gave the Canaanites and the Perizzites into their hand; and they defeated ten thousand of them at Bezek. [5]They came upon Adoni-bezek at Bezek, and fought against him, and defeated the Canaanites and the Perizzites. [6]Adoni-bezek fled; but they pursued him, and caught him, and cut off his thumbs and big toes. [7]Adoni-bezek said, "Seventy kings with their thumbs and big toes cut off used to pick up scraps under my table; as I have done, so God has paid me back." They brought him to Jerusalem, and he died there.

8 Then the people of Judah fought against Jerusalem and took it. They put it to the sword and set the city on fire. [9]Afterward the people of Judah went down to fight against the Canaanites who lived in the hill country, in the Negeb, and in the lowland. [10]Judah went against the Canaanites who lived in Hebron (the name of Hebron was formerly Kiriath-arba); and they defeated Sheshai and Ahiman and Talmai.

11 From there they went against the inhabitants of Debir (the name of Debir was formerly Kiriath-sepher). [12]Then Caleb said, "Whoever attacks Kiriath-sepher and takes it, I will give him my daughter Achsah as wife." [13]And Othniel son of Kenaz, Caleb's younger brother, took it; and he gave him his daughter Achsah as wife. [14]When she came to him, she urged him to ask her father for a field. As she dismounted from her donkey, Caleb said to her, "What do you wish?" [15]She said to him, "Give me a present; since you have set me in the land of the Negeb, give me also Gulloth-mayim."[a] So Caleb gave her Upper Gulloth and Lower Gulloth.

16 The descendants of Hobab[b] the Kenite, Moses' father-in-law, went up with the people of Judah from the city of palms into the wilderness of Judah, which lies in the Negeb near Arad. Then they went and settled with the Amalekites.[c] [17]Judah went with his brother Simeon, and they defeated the Canaanites who inhabited Zephath, and devoted it to destruction. So the city was called Hormah. [18]Judah took Gaza with its territory, Ashkelon with its territory, and Ekron with its territory. [19]The LORD was with Judah, and he took possession of the hill country, but could not drive out the inhabitants of the plain, because they had chariots of iron. [20]Hebron was given to Caleb, as Moses had said; and he drove out from it the three sons of

a That is Basins of Water   b Gk: Heb lacks Hobab   c See 1 Sam 15.6: Heb people

Anak. [21] But the Benjaminites did not drive out the Jebusites who lived in Jerusalem; so the Jebusites have lived in Jerusalem among the Benjaminites to this day.

22 The house of Joseph also went up against Bethel; and the LORD was with them. [23] The house of Joseph sent out spies to Bethel (the name of the city was formerly Luz). [24] When the spies saw a man coming out of the city, they said to him, "Show us the way into the city, and we will deal kindly with you." [25] So he showed them the way into the city; and they put the city to the sword, but they let the man and all his family go. [26] So the man went to the land of the Hittites and built a city, and named it Luz; that is its name to this day.

27 Manasseh did not drive out the inhabitants of Beth-shean and its villages, or Taanach and its villages, or the inhabitants of Dor and its villages, or the inhabitants of Ibleam and its villages, or the inhabitants of Megiddo and its villages; but the Canaanites continued to live in that land. [28] When Israel grew strong, they put the Canaanites to forced labor, but did not in fact drive them out.

29 And Ephraim did not drive out the Canaanites who lived in Gezer; but the Canaanites lived among them in Gezer.

30 Zebulun did not drive out the inhabitants of Kitron, or the inhabitants of Nahalol; but the Canaanites lived among them, and became subject to forced labor.

31 Asher did not drive out the inhabitants of Acco, or the inhabitants of Sidon, or of Ahlab, or of Achzib, or of Helbah, or of Aphik, or of Rehob; [32] but the Asherites lived among the Canaanites, the inhabitants of the land; for they did not drive them out.

33 Naphtali did not drive out the inhabitants of Beth-shemesh, or the inhabitants of Beth-anath, but lived among the Canaanites, the inhabitants of the land; nevertheless the inhabitants of Beth-shemesh and of Beth-anath became subject to forced labor for them.

34 The Amorites pressed the Danites back into the hill country; they did not allow them to come down to the plain. [35] The Amorites continued to live in Har-heres, in Aijalon, and in Shaalbim, but the hand of the house of Joseph rested heavily on them, and they became subject to forced labor. [36] The border of the Amorites ran from the ascent of Akrabbim, from Sela and upward.

Israel's Disobedience

2 Now the angel of the LORD went up from Gilgal to Bochim, and said, "I brought you up from Egypt, and brought you into the land that I had promised to your ancestors. I said, 'I will never break my covenant with you. [2] For your part, do not make a covenant with the inhabitants of this land; tear down their altars.' But you have not obeyed my command. See what you have done! [3] So now I say, I will not drive them out before you; but they shall become adversaries[a] to you, and their gods shall be a snare to you." [4] When the angel of the LORD spoke these words to all the Israelites, the people lifted up their voices and wept. [5] So they named that place Bochim,[b] and there they sacrificed to the LORD.

Death of Joshua

6 When Joshua dismissed the people, the Israelites all went to their own inheritances to take possession of the land. [7] The people worshiped the LORD all the days of Joshua, and all the days of the elders who outlived Joshua, who had seen all the great work that the LORD had done for Israel. [8] Joshua son of Nun, the servant of the LORD, died at the age of one hundred ten years. [9] So they buried him within the bounds of his inheritance in Timnath-heres, in the hill country of Ephraim, north of Mount Gaash. [10] Moreover, that whole generation was gathered to their ancestors, and another generation grew up after them, who did not know the LORD or the work that he had done for Israel.

Israel's Unfaithfulness

11 Then the Israelites did what was evil in the sight of the LORD and worshiped the Baals; [12] and they abandoned the LORD, the God of their ancestors, who had brought them out of the land of Egypt; they followed other gods, from among the gods of the peoples who were all around them, and bowed down to them; and they provoked the LORD to anger. [13] They abandoned the LORD, and worshiped Baal and the Astartes. [14] So the anger of the LORD was kindled against Israel, and he gave them over to plunderers who plundered them, and he sold them into the power of their enemies all around, so that they could no longer withstand their enemies. [15] Whenever they marched out, the hand of the LORD was against them to bring misfortune, as the LORD had warned them and sworn to them; and they were in great distress.

a OL Vg Compare Gk: Heb *sides*   b That is *Weepers*

Don't Forget
Judges 2:10–15

It's easy to look at the Israelites from our perspective of history and wonder how they could be so dense and thickheaded. After all God has done for them, how could they forget so easily and turn away to worship a statue (representing one of the gods of the people around them)? Then again, don't we do the same thing? It's actually all too easy to get caught up in our current challenges, follow after the "gods" in our world, like fashion, popularity, or the latest celebrity icon, and forget the amazing things God has done in our lives. Then we wonder why we feel distant from God, when we're the ones who have turned away and disobeyed. The key to avoiding this? Remembering. Write down the times in your life when you know God was with you, helped you, saved you, blessed you. Then review your list and add to it often, so that you do not turn away from God's faithfulness out of forgetfulness.

16 Then the Lord raised up judges, who delivered them out of the power of those who plundered them. [17] Yet they did not listen even to their judges; for they lusted after other gods and bowed down to them. They soon turned aside from the way in which their ancestors had walked, who had obeyed the commandments of the Lord; they did not follow their example. [18] Whenever the Lord raised up judges for them, the Lord was with the judge, and he delivered them from the hand of their enemies all the days of the judge; for the Lord would be moved to pity by their groaning because of those who persecuted and oppressed them. [19] But whenever the judge died, they would relapse and behave worse than their ancestors, following other gods, worshiping them and bowing down to them. They would not drop any of their practices or their stubborn ways. [20] So the anger of the Lord was kindled against Israel; and he said, "Because this people

have transgressed my covenant that I commanded their ancestors, and have not obeyed my voice, [21] I will no longer drive out before them any of the nations that Joshua left when he died." [22] In order to test Israel, whether or not they would take care to walk in the way of the Lord as their ancestors did, [23] the Lord had left those nations, not driving them out at once, and had not handed them over to Joshua.

3 **Nations Remaining in the Land**

Now these are the nations that the Lord left to test all those in Israel who had no experience of any war in Canaan [2] (it was only that successive generations of Israelites might know war, to teach those who had no experience of it before): [3] the five lords of the Philistines, and all the Canaanites, and the Sidonians, and the Hivites who lived on Mount Lebanon, from Mount Baal-hermon as far as Lebo-hamath. [4] They were for the testing of Israel, to know whether Israel would obey the commandments of the Lord, which he commanded their ancestors by Moses. [5] So the Israelites lived among the Canaanites, the Hittites, the Amorites, the Perizzites, the Hivites, and the Jebusites; [6] and they took their daughters as wives for themselves, and their own daughters they gave to their sons; and they worshiped their gods.

Othniel

7 The Israelites did what was evil in the sight of the Lord, forgetting the Lord their God, and worshiping the Baals and the Asherahs. [8] Therefore the anger of the Lord was kindled against Israel, and he sold them into the hand of King Cushan-rishathaim of Aram-naharaim; and the Israelites served Cushan-rishathaim eight years. [9] But when the Israelites cried out to the Lord, the Lord raised up a deliverer for the Israelites, who delivered them, Othniel son of Kenaz, Caleb's younger brother. [10] The spirit of the Lord came upon him, and he judged Israel; he went out to war, and the Lord gave King Cushan-rishathaim of Aram into his hand; and his hand prevailed over Cushan-rishathaim. [11] So the land had rest forty years. Then Othniel son of Kenaz died.

Ehud

12 The Israelites again did what was evil in the sight of the Lord; and the Lord strengthened King

Eglon of Moab against Israel, because they had done what was evil in the sight of the LORD. [13]In alliance with the Ammonites and the Amalekites, he went and defeated Israel; and they took possession of the city of palms. [14]So the Israelites served King Eglon of Moab eighteen years.

15 But when the Israelites cried out to the LORD, the LORD raised up for them a deliverer, Ehud son of Gera, the Benjaminite, a left-handed man. The Israelites sent tribute by him to King Eglon of Moab. [16]Ehud made for himself a sword with two edges, a cubit in length; and he fastened it on his right thigh under his clothes. [17]Then he presented the tribute to King Eglon of Moab. Now Eglon was a very fat man. [18]When Ehud had finished presenting the tribute, he sent the people who carried the tribute on their way. [19]But he himself turned back at the sculptured stones near Gilgal, and said, "I have a secret message for you, O king." So the king said,[a] "Silence!" and all his attendants went out from his presence. [20]Ehud came to him, while he was sitting alone in his cool roof chamber, and said, "I have a message from God for you." So he rose from his seat. [21]Then Ehud reached with his left hand, took the sword from his right thigh, and thrust it into Eglon's[b] belly; [22]the hilt also went in after the blade, and the fat closed over the blade, for he did not draw the sword out of his belly; and the dirt came out.[c] [23]Then Ehud went out into the vestibule,[d] and closed the doors of the roof chamber on him, and locked them.

24 After he had gone, the servants came. When they saw that the doors of the roof chamber were locked, they thought, "He must be relieving himself[e] in the cool chamber." [25]So they waited until they were embarrassed. When he still did not open the doors of the roof chamber, they took the key and opened them. There was their lord lying dead on the floor.

26 Ehud escaped while they delayed, and passed beyond the sculptured stones, and escaped to Seirah. [27]When he arrived, he sounded the trumpet in the hill country of Ephraim; and the Israelites went down with him from the hill country, having him at their head. [28]He said to them, "Follow after me; for the LORD has given your enemies the Moabites into your hand." So they went down after him, and seized the fords of the Jordan against the Moabites, and allowed no one to cross over. [29]At that time they killed about ten thousand of the Moabites, all strong, able-bodied men; no one escaped. [30]So Moab was subdued that day under the hand of Israel. And the land had rest eighty years.

Shamgar

31 After him came Shamgar son of Anath, who killed six hundred of the Philistines with an oxgoad. He too delivered Israel.

Deborah and Barak

4 The Israelites again did what was evil in the sight of the LORD, after Ehud died. [2]So the LORD sold them into the hand of King Jabin of Canaan, who reigned in Hazor; the commander of his army was Sisera, who lived in Harosheth-ha-goiim. [3]Then the Israelites cried out to the LORD for help; for he had nine hundred chariots of iron, and had oppressed the Israelites cruelly twenty years.

4 At that time Deborah, a prophetess, wife of Lappidoth, was judging Israel. [5]She used to sit under the palm of Deborah between Ramah and Bethel in the hill country of Ephraim; and the Israelites came up to her for judgment. [6]She sent and summoned Barak son of Abinoam from Kedesh in Naphtali, and said to him, "The LORD, the God of Israel, commands you, 'Go, take position at Mount Tabor, bringing ten thousand from the tribe of Naphtali and the tribe of Zebulun. [7]I will draw out Sisera, the general of Jabin's army, to meet you by the Wadi Kishon with his chariots and his troops; and I will give him into your hand.' " [8]Barak said to her, "If you will go with me, I will go; but if you will not go with me, I will not go." [9]And she said, "I will surely go with you; nevertheless, the road on which you are going will not lead to your glory, for the LORD will sell Sisera into the hand of a woman." Then Deborah got up and went with Barak to Kedesh. [10]Barak summoned Zebulun and Naphtali to Kedesh; and ten thousand warriors went up behind him; and Deborah went up with him.

11 Now Heber the Kenite had separated from the other Kenites,[f] that is, the descendants of Hobab the father-in-law of Moses, and had encamped as far away as Elon-bezaanannim, which is near Kedesh.

12 When Sisera was told that Barak son of Abinoam had gone up to Mount Tabor, [13]Sisera called out all his chariots, nine hundred chariots of iron, and all the troops who were with him, from

---

a Heb *he said*　b Heb *his*　c With Tg Vg: Meaning of Heb uncertain　d Meaning of Heb uncertain　e Heb *covering his feet*　f Heb *from the Kain*

Harosheth-ha-goiim to the Wadi Kishon. ¹⁴Then Deborah said to Barak, "Up! For this is the day on which the LORD has given Sisera into your hand. The LORD is indeed going out before you." So Barak went down from Mount Tabor with ten thousand warriors following him. ¹⁵And the LORD threw Sisera and all his chariots and all his army into a panic*a* before Barak; Sisera got down from his chariot and fled away on foot, ¹⁶while Barak pursued the chariots and the army to Harosheth-ha-goiim. All the army of Sisera fell by the sword; no one was left.

17 Now Sisera had fled away on foot to the tent of Jael wife of Heber the Kenite; for there was peace between King Jabin of Hazor and the clan of Heber the Kenite. ¹⁸Jael came out to meet Sisera, and said to him, "Turn aside, my lord, turn aside to me; have no fear." So he turned aside to her into the tent, and she covered him with a rug. ¹⁹Then he said to her, "Please give me a little water to drink; for I am thirsty." So she opened a skin of milk and gave him a drink and covered him. ²⁰He said to her, "Stand at the entrance of the tent, and if anybody comes and asks you, 'Is anyone here?' say, 'No.' " ²¹But Jael wife of Heber took a tent peg, and took a hammer in her hand, and went softly to him and drove the peg into his temple, until it went down into the ground—he was lying fast asleep from weariness—and he died. ²²Then, as Barak came in pursuit of

Sisera, Jael went out to meet him, and said to him, "Come, and I will show you the man whom you are seeking." So he went into her tent; and there was Sisera lying dead, with the tent peg in his temple.

23 So on that day God subdued King Jabin of Canaan before the Israelites. ²⁴Then the hand of the Israelites bore harder and harder on King Jabin of Canaan, until they destroyed King Jabin of Canaan.

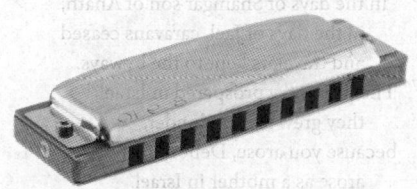

The Song of Deborah

5 Then Deborah and Barak son of Abinoam sang on that day, saying:

2 "When locks are long in Israel,
    when the people offer themselves willingly—
    bless*b* the LORD!

3 "Hear, O kings; give ear, O princes;
       to the LORD I will sing,
    I will make melody to the LORD, the God of Israel.

STUDY IT!

Introducing . . . Deborah · Judges 4–5

Deborah was a judge, prophet, and spiritual leader in Israel. During her day, the Israelites had again begun worshiping other gods and were being punished for their idolatry. When they cried out to God, God used Deborah to bring them back to obedience and devotion. Deborah directed the Israelites' military commander and led them to an unusual victory—unusual because it was victory at the hands of a woman and because she drove a tent peg into the enemy commander's head (Judges 4:21). When it was all over, Deborah sang a song of thankfulness for winning the battle (Judges 5). Even more important, it was a song of thankfulness for turning the hearts of the people back to true worship of God.

Deborah is an example of consistency and commitment in a nation that constantly waivered in its devotion. And in a society dominated by men, she took on the highest role of leadership, allowing God to use her passion and devotion to direct the entire nation. Deborah must have faced criticism, doubt, and complaints due to her unusual role. We will often face the same when we're obeying God. When we do, we should stay true to God's calling and God's word, just as Deborah did, and trust that God is in control.

---

a Heb adds *to the sword*; compare verse 16   **b** Or *You who offer yourselves willingly among the people, bless*

4 "Lord, when you went out from Seir,
    when you marched from the region of Edom,
the earth trembled,
    and the heavens poured,
    the clouds indeed poured water.
5 The mountains quaked before the Lord, the
        One of Sinai,
    before the Lord, the God of Israel.

6 "In the days of Shamgar son of Anath,
    in the days of Jael, caravans ceased
    and travelers kept to the byways.
7 The peasantry prospered in Israel,
    they grew fat on plunder,
because you arose, Deborah,
    arose as a mother in Israel.
8 When new gods were chosen,
    then war was in the gates.
Was shield or spear to be seen
    among forty thousand in Israel?
9 My heart goes out to the commanders of Israel
    who offered themselves willingly among the
        people.
    Bless the Lord.

10 "Tell of it, you who ride on white donkeys,
    you who sit on rich carpets[a]
    and you who walk by the way.
11 To the sound of musicians[a] at the watering
        places,
    there they repeat the triumphs of the Lord,
    the triumphs of his peasantry in Israel.

"Then down to the gates marched the people of
        the Lord.

12 "Awake, awake, Deborah!
    Awake, awake, utter a song!
Arise, Barak, lead away your captives,
    O son of Abinoam.
13 Then down marched the remnant of the noble;
    the people of the Lord marched down for
        him[b] against the mighty.
14 From Ephraim they set out[c] into the valley,[d]
    following you, Benjamin, with your kin;
from Machir marched down the commanders,
    and from Zebulun those who bear the
        marshal's staff;
15 the chiefs of Issachar came with Deborah,
    and Issachar faithful to Barak;

PRAY IT!

Wartime Women
Judges 4–5

Deborah, a judge and prophet, rallies Barak and the Israelites to war in **Judges 4**. Jael, another woman (a non-Israelite), delivers the final blow to the enemy's commander, Sisera. In **Judges 5**, Deborah leads the victory celebration with an elaborate prayer-song that is probably one of the oldest texts in the Bible. (See also the Song of Moses and the Song of Miriam in Exodus 15:1-21.)

In this case, a woman is credited with the victory, and it stands out as inspiring because it is so unusual. Throughout biblical history and modern times, women are often innocent victims of war. They usually don't do the fighting, but are raped, killed, or widowed. Many groups and organizations helping in war-torn countries recognize that one of the main keys to preventing future wars is to work to rehabilitate and educate women. By doing this, women are given purpose and hope that they pass on to their children and the rest of their community. It's hard to imagine the horror and pain women around the world have faced in war, but we can still pray for healing and peace.

God of love, please bring peace where there is fighting, and healing where there is pain. Be close to those who suffer, especially women who have survived or are still facing the horrors of war. Give them hope, and help us to know what part we can play in making them and their communities whole again. Amen.

into the valley they rushed out at his heels.
Among the clans of Reuben
    there were great searchings of heart.
16 Why did you tarry among the sheepfolds,
    to hear the piping for the flocks?
Among the clans of Reuben

---

a Meaning of Heb uncertain   b Gk: Heb me   c Cn: Heb From Ephraim their root   d Gk: Heb in Amalek

there were great searchings of heart.

17 Gilead stayed beyond the Jordan;
    and Dan, why did he abide with the ships?
  Asher sat still at the coast of the sea,
    settling down by his landings.

18 Zebulun is a people that scorned death;
    Naphtali too, on the heights of the field.

19 "The kings came, they fought;
    then fought the kings of Canaan,
  at Taanach, by the waters of Megiddo;
    they got no spoils of silver.

20 The stars fought from heaven,
    from their courses they fought against Sisera.

21 The torrent Kishon swept them away,
    the onrushing torrent, the torrent Kishon.
  March on, my soul, with might!

22 "Then loud beat the horses' hoofs
    with the galloping, galloping of his steeds.

23 "Curse Meroz, says the angel of the LORD,
    curse bitterly its inhabitants,
  because they did not come to the help of the
      LORD,
    to the help of the LORD against the mighty.

24 "Most blessed of women be Jael,
    the wife of Heber the Kenite,
  of tent-dwelling women most blessed.

25 He asked water and she gave him milk,
    she brought him curds in a lordly bowl.

26 She put her hand to the tent peg
    and her right hand to the workmen's mallet;
  she struck Sisera a blow,
    she crushed his head,
    she shattered and pierced his temple.

27 He sank, he fell,
    he lay still at her feet;
  at her feet he sank, he fell;
    where he sank, there he fell dead.

28 "Out of the window she peered,
    the mother of Sisera gazed*a* through the
        lattice:
  'Why is his chariot so long in coming?
    Why tarry the hoofbeats of his chariots?'

29 Her wisest ladies make answer,
    indeed, she answers the question herself:

30 'Are they not finding and dividing the spoil?—

A girl or two for every man;
  spoil of dyed stuffs for Sisera,
    spoil of dyed stuffs embroidered,
  two pieces of dyed work embroidered for my
      neck as spoil?'

31 "So perish all your enemies, O LORD!
    But may your friends be like the sun as it rises
        in its might."

And the land had rest forty years.

The Midianite Oppression

6 The Israelites did what was evil in the sight of the LORD, and the LORD gave them into the hand of Midian seven years. 2 The hand of Midian prevailed over Israel; and because of Midian the Israelites provided for themselves hiding places in the mountains, caves and strongholds. 3 For whenever the Israelites put in seed, the Midianites and the Amalekites and the people of the east would come up against them. 4 They would encamp against them and destroy the produce of the land, as far as the neighborhood of Gaza, and leave no sustenance in Israel, and no sheep or ox or donkey. 5 For they and their livestock would come up, and they would even bring their tents, as thick as locusts; neither they nor their camels could be counted; so they wasted the land as they came in. 6 Thus Israel was greatly impoverished because of Midian; and the Israelites cried out to the LORD for help.

7 When the Israelites cried to the LORD on account of the Midianites, 8 the LORD sent a prophet to the Israelites; and he said to them, "Thus says the LORD, the God of Israel: I led you up from Egypt, and brought you out of the house of slavery; 9 and I delivered you from the hand of the Egyptians, and from the hand of all who oppressed you, and drove them out before you, and gave you their land; 10 and I said to you, 'I am the LORD your God; you shall not pay reverence to the gods of the Amorites, in whose land you live.' But you have not given heed to my voice."

The Call of Gideon

11 Now the angel of the LORD came and sat under the oak at Ophrah, which belonged to Joash the Abiezrite, as his son Gideon was beating out wheat in the wine press, to hide it from the Midianites. 12 The angel of the LORD appeared to him and said

a Gk Compare Tg: Heb *exclaimed*

to him, "The LORD is with you, you mighty warrior." [13] Gideon answered him, "But sir, if the LORD is with us, why then has all this happened to us? And where are all his wonderful deeds that our ancestors recounted to us, saying, 'Did not the LORD bring us up from Egypt?' But now the LORD has cast us off, and given us into the hand of Midian." [14] Then the LORD turned to him and said, "Go in this might of yours and deliver Israel from the hand of Midian; I hereby commission you." [15] He responded, "But sir, how can I deliver Israel? My clan is the weakest in Manasseh, and I am the least in my family." [16] The LORD said to him, "But I will be with you, and you shall strike down the Midianites, every one of them." [17] Then he said to him, "If now I have found favor with you, then show me a sign that it is you who speak with me. [18] Do not depart from here until I come to you, and bring out my present, and set it before you." And he said, "I will stay until you return."

19 So Gideon went into his house and prepared a kid, and unleavened cakes from an ephah of flour; the meat he put in a basket, and the broth he put in a pot, and brought them to him under the oak and presented them. [20] The angel of God said to him, "Take the meat and the unleavened cakes, and put them on this rock, and pour out the broth." And he did so. [21] Then the angel of the LORD reached out the tip of the staff that was in his hand, and touched the meat and the unleavened cakes; and fire sprang up from the rock and consumed the meat and the unleavened cakes; and the angel

of the LORD vanished from his sight. [22] Then Gideon perceived that it was the angel of the LORD; and Gideon said, "Help me, Lord GOD! For I have seen the angel of the LORD face to face." [23] But the LORD said to him, "Peace be to you; do not fear, you shall not die." [24] Then Gideon built an altar there to the LORD, and called it, The LORD is peace. To this day it still stands at Ophrah, which belongs to the Abiezrites.

25 That night the LORD said to him, "Take your father's bull, the second bull seven years old, and pull down the altar of Baal that belongs to your father, and cut down the sacred pole[a] that is beside it; [26] and build an altar to the LORD your God on the top of the stronghold here, in proper order; then take the second bull, and offer it as a burnt offering with the wood of the sacred pole[a] that you shall cut down." [27] So Gideon took ten of his servants, and did as the LORD had told him; but because he was too afraid of his family and the townspeople to do it by day, he did it by night.

Gideon Destroys the Altar of Baal

28 When the townspeople rose early in the morning, the altar of Baal was broken down, and the sacred pole[a] beside it was cut down, and the second bull was offered on the altar that had been built. [29] So they said to one another, "Who has done this?" After searching and inquiring, they were told, "Gideon son of Joash did it." [30] Then the townspeople said to Joash, "Bring out your son, so that he may die, for he has pulled down the altar

Trusting or Testing God · Judges 6:36–40

The true test of faith is to obey without testing. In this passage Gideon keeps testing God; he can't bring himself to believe God's promises. **Judges 6–8** gives a full picture of this hero, who never quite understands what loving God is all about. Even after his victory and his words of devotion to God, he makes a golden idol (Judges 8:22-28).

Most of us are tempted to test God in some way: "God, I'll know you are there for me, if I make this team or band," or "If you really want me to break up with him, make him call me right now." God is big enough to face our testing, but God won't be manipulated by our doubt. So don't expect God to answer every request—at least not exactly the way you would like.

How do you test God? Is your prayer more trusting than Gideon's prayer? The next time you feel anxious or afraid, read one of these scripture passages and make it your prayer: **Psalm 25; Psalm 27; John 14; 1 John 4:7–21.** Challenge yourself to trust God without testing.

a Heb *Asherah*

of Baal and cut down the sacred pole[a] beside it." [31]But Joash said to all who were arrayed against him, "Will you contend for Baal? Or will you defend his cause? Whoever contends for him shall be put to death by morning. If he is a god, let him contend for himself, because his altar has been pulled down." [32]Therefore on that day Gideon[a] was called Jerubbaal, that is to say, "Let Baal contend against him," because he pulled down his altar.

33 Then all the Midianites and the Amalekites and the people of the east came together, and crossing the Jordan they encamped in the Valley of Jezreel. [34]But the spirit of the Lord took possession of Gideon; and he sounded the trumpet, and the Abiezrites were called out to follow him. [35]He sent messengers throughout all Manasseh, and they too were called out to follow him. He also sent messengers to Asher, Zebulun, and Naphtali, and they went up to meet them.

The Sign of the Fleece

36 Then Gideon said to God, "In order to see whether you will deliver Israel by my hand, as you have said, [37]I am going to lay a fleece of wool on the threshing floor; if there is dew on the fleece alone, and it is dry on all the ground, then I shall know that you will deliver Israel by my hand, as you have said." [38]And it was so. When he rose early next morning and squeezed the fleece, he wrung enough dew from the fleece to fill a bowl with water. [39]Then Gideon said to God, "Do not let your anger burn against me, let me speak one more time; let me, please, make trial with the fleece just once more; let it be dry only on the fleece, and on all the ground let there be dew." [40]And God did so that night. It was dry on the fleece only, and on all the ground there was dew.

Gideon Surprises and Routs the Midianites

7   Then Jerubbaal (that is, Gideon) and all the troops that were with him rose early and encamped beside the spring of Harod; and the camp of Midian was north of them, below[b] the hill of Moreh, in the valley.

2 The Lord said to Gideon, "The troops with you are too many for me to give the Midianites into their hand. Israel would only take the credit away from me, saying, 'My own hand has delivered me.' [3]Now therefore proclaim this in the hearing of the

troops, 'Whoever is fearful and trembling, let him return home.' " Thus Gideon sifted them out;[c] twenty-two thousand returned, and ten thousand remained.

4 Then the Lord said to Gideon, "The troops are still too many; take them down to the water and I will sift them out for you there. When I say, 'This one shall go with you,' he shall go with you; and when I say, 'This one shall not go with you,' he shall not go." [5]So he brought the troops down to the water; and the Lord said to Gideon, "All those who lap the water with their tongues, as a dog laps, you shall put to one side; all those who kneel down to drink, putting their hands to their mouths,[d] you shall put to the other side." [6]The number of those that lapped was three hundred; but all the rest of the troops knelt down to drink water. [7]Then the Lord said to Gideon, "With the three hundred that lapped I will deliver you, and give the Midianites into your hand. Let all the others go to their homes." [8]So he took the jars of the troops from their hands,[e] and their trumpets; and he sent all the rest of Israel back to their own tents, but retained the three hundred. The camp of Midian was below him in the valley.

9 That same night the Lord said to him, "Get up, attack the camp; for I have given it into your hand. [10]But if you fear to attack, go down to the camp with your servant Purah; [11]and you shall hear what they say, and afterward your hands shall be strengthened to attack the camp." Then he went down with his servant Purah to the outposts of the armed men that were in the camp. [12]The Midianites and the Amalekites and all the people of the east lay along the valley as thick as locusts; and their camels were without number, countless as the sand on the seashore. [13]When Gideon arrived, there was a man telling a dream to his comrade; and he said, "I had a dream, and in it a cake of barley bread tumbled into the camp of Midian, and came to the tent, and struck it so that it fell; it turned upside down, and the tent collapsed." [14]And his comrade answered, "This is no other than the sword of Gideon son of Joash, a man of Israel; into his hand God has given Midian and all the army."

15 When Gideon heard the telling of the dream and its interpretation, he worshiped; and he returned to the camp of Israel, and said, "Get up; for the Lord has given the army of Midian into your hand." [16]After he divided the three hundred men

---

a Heb *he*   b Heb *from*   c Cn: Heb *home, and depart from Mount Gilead' "*   d Heb places the words *putting their hands to their mouths* after the word *lapped* in verse 6   e Cn: Heb *So the people took provisions in their hands*

into three companies, and put trumpets into the hands of all of them, and empty jars, with torches inside the jars, [17] he said to them, "Look at me, and do the same; when I come to the outskirts of the camp, do as I do. [18] When I blow the trumpet, I and all who are with me, then you also blow the trumpets around the whole camp, and shout, 'For the LORD and for Gideon!' "

19 So Gideon and the hundred who were with him came to the outskirts of the camp at the beginning of the middle watch, when they had just set the watch; and they blew the trumpets and smashed the jars that were in their hands. [20] So the three companies blew the trumpets and broke the jars, holding in their left hands the torches, and in their right hands the trumpets to blow; and they cried, "A sword for the LORD and for Gideon!" [21] Every man stood in his place all around the camp, and all the men in camp ran; they cried out and fled. [22] When they blew the three hundred trumpets, the LORD set every man's sword against his fellow and against all the army; and the army fled as far as Beth-shittah toward Zererah,[a] as far as the border of Abel-meholah, by Tabbath. [23] And the men of Israel were called out from Naphtali and from Asher and from all Manasseh, and they pursued after the Midianites.

24 Then Gideon sent messengers throughout all the hill country of Ephraim, saying, "Come down against the Midianites and seize the waters against them, as far as Beth-barah, and also the Jordan." So all the men of Ephraim were called out, and they seized the waters as far as Beth-barah, and also the Jordan. [25] They captured the two captains of Midian, Oreb and Zeeb; they killed Oreb at the rock of Oreb, and Zeeb they killed at the wine press of Zeeb, as they pursued the Midianites. They brought the heads of Oreb and Zeeb to Gideon beyond the Jordan.

8 Gideon's Triumph and Vengeance

Then the Ephraimites said to him, "What have you done to us, not to call us when you went to fight against the Midianites?" And they upbraided him violently. [2] So he said to them, "What have I done now in comparison with you? Is not the gleaning of the grapes of Ephraim better than the vintage of Abiezer? [3] God has given into your hands the captains of Midian, Oreb and Zeeb; what have I been able to do in comparison with

you?" When he said this, their anger against him subsided.

4 Then Gideon came to the Jordan and crossed over, he and the three hundred who were with him, exhausted and famished.[b] [5] So he said to the people of Succoth, "Please give some loaves of bread to my followers, for they are exhausted, and I am pursuing Zebah and Zalmunna, the kings of Midian." [6] But the officials of Succoth said, "Do you already have in your possession the hands of Zebah and Zalmunna, that we should give bread to your army?" [7] Gideon replied, "Well then, when the LORD has given Zebah and Zalmunna into my hand, I will trample your flesh on the thorns of the wilderness and on briers." [8] From there he went up to Penuel, and made the same request of them; and the people of Penuel answered him as the people of Succoth had answered. [9] So he said to the people of Penuel, "When I come back victorious, I will break down this tower."

10 Now Zebah and Zalmunna were in Karkor with their army, about fifteen thousand men, all who were left of all the army of the people of the east; for one hundred twenty thousand men bearing arms had fallen. [11] So Gideon went up by the caravan route east of Nobah and Jogbehah, and attacked the army; for the army was off its guard. [12] Zebah and Zalmunna fled; and he pursued them and took the two kings of Midian, Zebah and Zalmunna, and threw all the army into a panic.

13 When Gideon son of Joash returned from the battle by the ascent of Heres, [14] he caught a young man, one of the people of Succoth, and questioned him; and he listed for him the officials and elders of Succoth, seventy-seven people. [15] Then he came to the people of Succoth, and said, "Here are Zebah and Zalmunna, about whom you taunted me, saying, 'Do you already have in your possession the hands of Zebah and Zalmunna, that we should give bread to your troops who are exhausted?' " [16] So he took the elders of the city and he took thorns of the wilderness and briers and with them he trampled[c] the people of Succoth. [17] He also broke down the tower of Penuel, and killed the men of the city.

18 Then he said to Zebah and Zalmunna, "What about the men whom you killed at Tabor?" They answered, "As you are, so were they, every one of them; they resembled the sons of a king." [19] And he replied, "They were my brothers, the sons of my mother; as the LORD lives, if you had saved them

---

a Another reading is *Zeredah*   b Gk: Heb *pursuing*   c With verse 7, Compare Gk: Heb *he taught*

alive, I would not kill you." ²⁰So he said to Jether his firstborn, "Go kill them!" But the boy did not draw his sword, for he was afraid, because he was still a boy. ²¹Then Zebah and Zalmunna said, "You come and kill us; for as the man is, so is his strength." So Gideon proceeded to kill Zebah and Zalmunna; and he took the crescents that were on the necks of their camels.

Gideon's Idolatry

22 Then the Israelites said to Gideon, "Rule over us, you and your son and your grandson also; for you have delivered us out of the hand of Midian." ²³Gideon said to them, "I will not rule over you, and my son will not rule over you; the LORD will rule over you." ²⁴Then Gideon said to them, "Let me make a request of you; each of you give me an earring he has taken as booty." (For the enemy*a* had golden earrings, because they were Ishmaelites.) ²⁵"We will willingly give them," they answered. So they spread a garment, and each threw into it an earring he had taken as booty. ²⁶The weight of the golden earrings that he requested was one thousand seven hundred shekels of gold (apart from the crescents and the pendants and the purple garments worn by the kings of Midian, and the collars that were on the necks of their camels). ²⁷Gideon made an ephod of it and put it in his town, in Ophrah; and all Israel prostituted themselves to it there, and it became a snare to Gideon and to his family. ²⁸So Midian was subdued before the Israelites, and they lifted up their heads no more. So the land had rest forty years in the days of Gideon.

Death of Gideon

29 Jerubbaal son of Joash went to live in his own house. ³⁰Now Gideon had seventy sons, his own offspring, for he had many wives. ³¹His concubine who was in Shechem also bore him a son, and he named him Abimelech. ³²Then Gideon son of Joash died at a good old age, and was buried in the tomb of his father Joash at Ophrah of the Abiezrites. 33 As soon as Gideon died, the Israelites relapsed and prostituted themselves with the Baals, making Baal-berith their god. ³⁴The Israelites did not remember the LORD their God, who had rescued them from the hand of all their enemies on every side; ³⁵and they did not exhibit loyalty to the house of Jerubbaal (that is, Gideon) in return for all the good that he had done to Israel.

9 Abimelech Attempts to Establish a Monarchy

Now Abimelech son of Jerubbaal went to Shechem to his mother's kinsfolk and said to them and to the whole clan of his mother's family, ²"Say in the hearing of all the lords of Shechem, 'Which is better for you, that all seventy of the sons of Jerubbaal rule over you, or that one rule over you?' Remember also that I am your bone and your flesh." ³So his mother's kinsfolk spoke all these words on his behalf in the hearing of all the lords of Shechem; and their hearts inclined to follow Abimelech, for they said, "He is our brother." ⁴They gave him seventy pieces of silver out of the temple of Baal-berith with which Abimelech hired worthless and reckless fellows, who followed him. ⁵He went to his father's house at Ophrah, and killed his brothers the sons of Jerubbaal, seventy men, on one stone; but Jotham, the youngest son of Jerubbaal, survived, for he hid himself. ⁶Then all the lords of Shechem and all Beth-millo came together, and they went and made Abimelech king, by the oak of the pillar*b* at Shechem.

The Parable of the Trees

7 When it was told to Jotham, he went and stood on the top of Mount Gerizim, and cried aloud and said to them, "Listen to me, you lords of Shechem, so that God may listen to you.

8 The trees once went out
         to anoint a king over themselves.
    So they said to the olive tree,
         'Reign over us.'
9 The olive tree answered them,
         'Shall I stop producing my rich oil
    by which gods and mortals are honored,
         and go to sway over the trees?'
10 Then the trees said to the fig tree,
         'You come and reign over us.'

a Heb *they*   *b* Cn: Meaning of Heb uncertain

11   But the fig tree answered them,
      'Shall I stop producing my sweetness
         and my delicious fruit,
         and go to sway over the trees?'
12   Then the trees said to the vine,
      'You come and reign over us.'
13   But the vine said to them,
      'Shall I stop producing my wine
         that cheers gods and mortals,
         and go to sway over the trees?'
14   So all the trees said to the bramble,
      'You come and reign over us.'
15   And the bramble said to the trees,
      'If in good faith you are anointing me king
         over you,
         then come and take refuge in my shade;
      but if not, let fire come out of the bramble
         and devour the cedars of Lebanon.'

16   "Now therefore, if you acted in good faith and honor when you made Abimelech king, and if you have dealt well with Jerubbaal and his house, and have done to him as his actions deserved— 17 for my father fought for you, and risked his life, and rescued you from the hand of Midian; 18 but you have risen up against my father's house this day, and have killed his sons, seventy men on one stone, and have made Abimelech, the son of his slave woman, king over the lords of Shechem, because he is your kinsman— 19 if, I say, you have acted in good faith and honor with Jerubbaal and with his house this day, then rejoice in Abimelech, and let him also rejoice in you; 20 but if not, let fire come out from Abimelech, and devour the lords of Shechem, and Beth-millo; and let fire come out from the lords of Shechem, and from Beth-millo, and devour Abimelech." 21 Then Jotham ran away and fled, going to Beer, where he remained for fear of his brother Abimelech.

The Downfall of Abimelech

22   Abimelech ruled over Israel three years. 23 But God sent an evil spirit between Abimelech and the lords of Shechem; and the lords of Shechem dealt treacherously with Abimelech. 24 This happened so that the violence done to the seventy sons of Jerubbaal might be avenged[a] and their blood be laid on their brother Abimelech, who killed them, and on the lords of Shechem, who strengthened his hands to kill his brothers. 25 So, out of hostility to him, the lords of Shechem set ambushes on the mountain tops. They robbed all who passed by them along that way; and it was reported to Abimelech.

26   When Gaal son of Ebed moved into Shechem with his kinsfolk, the lords of Shechem put confidence in him. 27 They went out into the field and gathered the grapes from their vineyards, trod them, and celebrated. Then they went into the temple of their god, ate and drank, and ridiculed Abimelech. 28 Gaal son of Ebed said, "Who is Abimelech, and who are we of Shechem, that we should serve him? Did not the son of Jerubbaal and Zebul his officer serve the men of Hamor father of Shechem? Why then should we serve him? 29 If only this people were under my command! Then I would remove Abimelech; I would say[b] to him, 'Increase your army, and come out.'"

30   When Zebul the ruler of the city heard the words of Gaal son of Ebed, his anger was kindled. 31 He sent messengers to Abimelech at Arumah,[c] saying, "Look, Gaal son of Ebed and his kinsfolk have come to Shechem, and they are stirring up[d] the city against you. 32 Now therefore, go by night, you and the troops that are with you, and lie in wait in the fields. 33 Then early in the morning, as soon as the sun rises, get up and rush on the city; and when he and the troops that are with him come out against you, you may deal with them as best you can."

34   So Abimelech and all the troops with him got up by night and lay in wait against Shechem in four companies. 35 When Gaal son of Ebed went out and stood in the entrance of the gate of the city, Abimelech and the troops with him rose from the ambush. 36 And when Gaal saw them, he said to Zebul, "Look, people are coming down from the mountain tops!" And Zebul said to him, "The shadows on the mountains look like people to you." 37 Gaal spoke again and said, "Look, people are coming down from Tabbur erez, and one company is coming from the direction of Elon-meonenim."[e] 38 Then Zebul said to him, "Where is your boast[f] now, you who said, 'Who is Abimelech, that we should serve him?' Are not these the troops you made light of? Go out now and fight with them." 39 So Gaal went out at the head of the lords of Shechem, and fought with Abimelech. 40 Abimelech chased him, and he fled before him. Many fell wounded, up to the entrance of the gate. 41 So Abimelech resided at Arumah; and Zebul drove out Gaal and his kinsfolk, so that they could not live on at Shechem.

a Heb might come   b Gk: Heb and he said   c Cn See 9.41. Heb Tormah   d Cn: Heb are besieging   e That is Diviners' Oak   f Heb mouth

42 On the following day the people went out into the fields. When Abimelech was told, 43he took his troops and divided them into three companies, and lay in wait in the fields. When he looked and saw the people coming out of the city, he rose against them and killed them. 44Abimelech and the company that was*a* with him rushed forward and stood at the entrance of the gate of the city, while the two companies rushed on all who were in the fields and killed them. 45Abimelech fought against the city all that day; he took the city, and killed the people that were in it; and he razed the city and sowed it with salt.

46 When all the lords of the Tower of Shechem heard of it, they entered the stronghold of the temple of El-berith. 47Abimelech was told that all the lords of the Tower of Shechem were gathered together. 48So Abimelech went up to Mount Zalmon, he and all the troops that were with him. Abimelech took an ax in his hand, cut down a bundle of brushwood, and took it up and laid it on his shoulder. Then he said to the troops with him, "What you have seen me do, do quickly, as I have done." 49So every one of the troops cut down a bundle and following Abimelech put it against the stronghold, and they set the stronghold on fire over them, so that all the people of the Tower of Shechem also died, about a thousand men and women.

50 Then Abimelech went to Thebez, and encamped against Thebez, and took it. 51But there was a strong tower within the city, and all the men and women and all the lords of the city fled to it and shut themselves in; and they went to the roof of the tower.

52Abimelech came to the tower, and fought against it, and came near to the entrance of the tower to burn it with fire. 53But a certain woman threw an upper millstone on Abimelech's head, and crushed his skull. 54Immediately he called to the young man who carried his armor and said to him, "Draw your sword and kill me, so people will not say about me, 'A woman killed him.' " So the young man thrust him through, and he died. 55When the Israelites saw that Abimelech was dead, they all went home. 56Thus God repaid Abimelech for the crime he committed against his father in killing his seventy brothers; 57and God also made all the wickedness of the people of Shechem fall back on their heads, and on them came the curse of Jotham son of Jerubbaal.

Tola and Jair

10 After Abimelech, Tola son of Puah son of Dodo, a man of Issachar, who lived at Shamir in the hill country of Ephraim, rose to deliver Israel. 2He judged Israel twenty-three years. Then he died, and was buried at Shamir.

3 After him came Jair the Gileadite, who judged Israel twenty-two years. 4He had thirty sons who rode on thirty donkeys; and they had thirty towns, which are in the land of Gilead, and are called Havvoth-jair to this day. 5Jair died, and was buried in Kamon.

Oppression by the Ammonites

6 The Israelites again did what was evil in the sight of the Lord, worshiping the Baals and the Astartes,

PRAY IT!

The Effects of Sin · Judges 10:6–16

The Israelites must have liked hitting the "repeat" button and learning things the hard way. Once again they lapsed into sin and worshiped other gods, and their sin brought consequences (Judges 10:6). The Israelites were oppressed by their enemies for eighteen years (Judges 10:7-8). That's a long time! Their sin not only had personal consequences, but it affected the whole nation before they reached the point of turning and crying out to God to save them (Judges 10:10).

When you look at your life, do you see ways that you are suffering the consequences of a choice you made to turn from God? Have your poor choices impacted others? The amazing news is that God hears us when we return and cry out for help.

Lord, you know all things. You've seen everything I've done. Please turn your love to me and forgive my sins. Give me strength to turn away from the lure of sin. Help me to be more generous in serving you and people around me. Help me to be a true follower of your Son, Jesus. Amen.

a   Vg and some Gk Mss: Heb *companies that were*

the gods of Aram, the gods of Sidon, the gods of Moab, the gods of the Ammonites, and the gods of the Philistines. Thus they abandoned the LORD, and did not worship him. [7]So the anger of the LORD was kindled against Israel, and he sold them into the hand of the Philistines and into the hand of the Ammonites, [8]and they crushed and oppressed the Israelites that year. For eighteen years they oppressed all the Israelites that were beyond the Jordan in the land of the Amorites, which is in Gilead. [9]The Ammonites also crossed the Jordan to fight against Judah and against Benjamin and against the house of Ephraim; so that Israel was greatly distressed.

10 So the Israelites cried to the LORD, saying, "We have sinned against you, because we have abandoned our God and have worshiped the Baals." [11]And the LORD said to the Israelites, "Did I not deliver you[a] from the Egyptians and from the Amorites, from the Ammonites and from the Philistines? [12]The Sidonians also, and the Amalekites, and the Maonites, oppressed you; and you cried to me, and I delivered you out of their hand. [13]Yet you have abandoned me and worshiped other gods; therefore I will deliver you no more. [14]Go and cry to the gods whom you have chosen; let them deliver you in the time of your distress." [15]And the Israelites said to the LORD, "We have sinned; do to us whatever seems good to you; but deliver us this day!" [16]So they put away the foreign gods from among them and worshiped the LORD; and he could no longer bear to see Israel suffer.

17 Then the Ammonites were called to arms, and they encamped in Gilead; and the Israelites came together, and they encamped at Mizpah. [18]The commanders of the people of Gilead said to one another, "Who will begin the fight against the Ammonites? He shall be head over all the inhabitants of Gilead."

Jephthah

11 Now Jephthah the Gileadite, the son of a prostitute, was a mighty warrior. Gilead was the father of Jephthah. [2]Gilead's wife also bore him sons; and when his wife's sons grew up, they drove Jephthah away, saying to him, "You shall not inherit anything in our father's house; for you are the son of another woman." [3]Then Jephthah fled from his brothers and lived in the land of Tob. Outlaws collected around Jephthah and went raiding with him.

4 After a time the Ammonites made war against Israel. [5]And when the Ammonites made war against Israel, the elders of Gilead went to bring Jephthah from the land of Tob. [6]They said to Jephthah, "Come and be our commander, so that we may fight with the Ammonites." [7]But Jephthah said to the elders of Gilead, "Are you not the very ones who rejected me and drove me out of my father's house? So why do you come to me now when you are in trouble?" [8]The elders of Gilead said to Jephthah, "Nevertheless, we have now turned back to you, so that you may go with us and fight with the Ammonites, and become head over us, over all the inhabitants of Gilead." [9]Jephthah said to the elders of Gilead, "If you bring me home again to fight with the Ammonites, and the LORD gives them over to me, I will be your head." [10]And the elders of Gilead said to Jephthah, "The LORD will be witness between us; we will surely do as you say." [11]So Jephthah went with the elders of Gilead, and the people made him head and commander over them; and Jephthah spoke all his words before the LORD at Mizpah.

12 Then Jephthah sent messengers to the king of the Ammonites and said, "What is there between you and me, that you have come to me to fight against my land?" [13]The king of the Ammonites answered the messengers of Jephthah, "Because Israel, on coming from Egypt, took away my land from the Arnon to the Jabbok and to the Jordan; now therefore restore it peaceably." [14]Once again Jephthah sent messengers to the king of the Ammonites [15]and said to him: "Thus says Jephthah: Israel did not take away the land of Moab or the land of the Ammonites, [16]but when they came up from Egypt, Israel went through the wilderness to the Red Sea[b] and came to Kadesh. [17]Israel then sent messengers to the king of Edom, saying, 'Let us pass through your land'; but the king of Edom would not listen. They also sent to the king of Moab, but he would not consent. So Israel remained at Kadesh. [18]Then they journeyed through the wilderness, went around the land of Edom and the land of Moab, arrived on the east side of the land of Moab, and camped on the other side of the Arnon. They did not enter the territory of Moab, for the Arnon was the boundary of Moab. [19]Israel then sent messengers to King Sihon of the Amorites, king of Heshbon; and Israel said to him, 'Let us pass through your land to our country.' [20]But Sihon did not trust Israel to pass through his territory; so Sihon gathered all his people together, and encamped at Jahaz, and fought with Israel. [21]Then the LORD, the God of Israel, gave Sihon and all his people into the hand

a Heb lacks *Did I not deliver you* **b** Or *Sea of Reeds* of Israel, and they defeated them; so Israel occupied all the land of the Amorites, who inhabited that country. ²²They occupied all the territory of the Amorites from the Arnon to the Jabbok and from the wilderness to the Jordan. ²³So now the LORD, the God of Israel, has conquered the Amorites for the benefit of his people Israel. Do you intend to take their place? ²⁴Should you not possess what your god Chemosh gives you to possess? And should we not be the ones to possess everything that the LORD our God has conquered for our benefit? ²⁵Now are you any better than King Balak son of Zippor of Moab? Did he ever enter into conflict with Israel, or did he ever go to war with them? ²⁶While Israel lived in Heshbon and its villages, and in Aroer and its villages, and in all the towns that are along the Arnon, three hundred years, why did you not recover them within that time? ²⁷It is not I who have sinned against you, but you are the one who does me wrong by making war on me. Let the LORD, who is judge, decide today for the Israelites or for the Ammonites." ²⁸But the king of the Ammonites did not heed the message that Jephthah sent him.

Jephthah's Vow

29 Then the spirit of the LORD came upon Jephthah, and he passed through Gilead and Manasseh. He passed on to Mizpah of Gilead, and from Mizpah of Gilead he passed on to the Ammonites. ³⁰And Jephthah made a vow to the LORD, and said, "If you will give the Ammonites into my hand, ³¹then whoever comes out of the doors of my house to meet me, when I return victorious from the Ammonites, shall be the LORD's, to be offered up by me as a burnt offering." ³²So Jephthah crossed over to the Ammonites to fight against them; and the LORD gave them into his hand. ³³He inflicted a massive defeat on them from Aroer to the neighborhood of Minnith, twenty towns, and as far as Abel-keramim. So the Ammonites were subdued before the people of Israel.

Jephthah's Daughter

34 Then Jephthah came to his home at Mizpah; and there was his daughter coming out to meet him with timbrels and with dancing. She was his only child; he had no son or daughter except her. ³⁵When he saw her, he tore his clothes, and said, "Alas, my daughter! You have brought me very low;

you have become the cause of great trouble to me. For I have opened my mouth to the LORD, and I cannot take back my vow." ³⁶She said to him, "My father, if you have opened your mouth to the LORD, do to me according to what has gone out of your mouth, now that the LORD has given you vengeance against your enemies, the Ammonites." ³⁷And she said to her father, "Let this thing be done for me: Grant me two months, so that I may go and wander^a on the mountains, and bewail my virginity, my companions and I." ³⁸"Go," he said and sent her away for two months. So she departed, she and her companions, and bewailed her virginity on the mountains. ³⁹At the end of two months, she returned to her father, who did with her according to the vow he had made. She had never slept with a man. So there arose an Israelite custom that ⁴⁰for four days every year the daughters of Israel would go out to lament the daughter of Jephthah the Gileadite.

Intertribal Dissension

12 The men of Ephraim were called to arms, and they crossed to Zaphon and said to Jephthah, "Why did you cross over to fight against the Ammonites, and did not call us to go with you? We will burn your house down over you!" ²Jephthah said to them, "My people and I were engaged in conflict with the Ammonites who oppressed us^b severely. But when I called you, you did not deliver me from their hand. ³When I saw that you would not deliver me, I took my life in my hand, and crossed over against the Ammonites, and the LORD gave them into my hand. Why then have you come up to me this day, to fight against me?" ⁴Then Jephthah gathered all the men of Gilead and fought with Ephraim; and the men of Gilead defeated Ephraim, because they said, "You are fugitives from Ephraim, you Gileadites—in the heart of Ephraim and Manasseh."^c ⁵Then the Gileadites took the fords of the Jordan against the Ephraimites. Whenever one of the fugitives of Ephraim said, "Let me go over," the men of Gilead would say to him, "Are you an Ephraimite?" When he said, "No," ⁶they said to him, "Then say Shibboleth," and he said, "Sibboleth," for he could not pronounce it right. Then they seized him and killed him at the fords of the Jordan. Forty-two thousand of the Ephraimites fell at that time.

7 Jephthah judged Israel six years. Then

---

a Cn: Heb *go down*   **b** Gk OL, Syr H: Heb lacks *who oppressed us*   **c** Meaning of Heb uncertain: Gk omits *because . . . Manasseh*

Jephthah the Gileadite died, and was buried in his town in Gilead.[a]

Ibzan, Elon, and Abdon

8 After him Ibzan of Bethlehem judged Israel. [9]He had thirty sons. He gave his thirty daughters in marriage outside his clan and brought in thirty young women from outside for his sons. He judged Israel seven years. [10]Then Ibzan died, and was buried at Bethlehem.

11 After him Elon the Zebulunite judged Israel; and he judged Israel ten years. [12]Then Elon the Zebulunite died, and was buried at Aijalon in the land of Zebulun.

13 After him Abdon son of Hillel the Pirathonite judged Israel. [14]He had forty sons and thirty grandsons, who rode on seventy donkeys; he judged Israel eight years. [15]Then Abdon son of Hillel the Pirathonite died, and was buried at Pirathon in the land of Ephraim, in the hill country of the Amalekites.

13 The Birth of Samson

The Israelites again did what was evil in the sight of the LORD, and the LORD gave them into the hand of the Philistines forty years.

2 There was a certain man of Zorah, of the tribe of the Danites, whose name was Manoah. His wife was barren, having borne no children. [3]And the angel of the LORD appeared to the woman and said to her, "Although you are barren, having borne no children, you shall conceive and bear a son. [4]Now be careful not to drink wine or strong drink, or to eat anything unclean, [5]for you shall conceive and bear a son. No razor is to come on his head, for the boy shall be a nazirite[b] to God from birth. It is he who shall begin to deliver Israel from the hand of the Philistines." [6]Then the woman came and told her husband, "A man of God came to me, and his appearance was like that of an angel[c] of God, most awe-inspiring; I did not ask him where he came from, and he did not tell me his name; [7]but he said to me, 'You shall conceive and bear a son. So then drink no wine or strong drink, and eat nothing unclean, for the boy shall be a nazirite[c] to God from birth to the day of his death.'"

8 Then Manoah entreated the LORD, and said, "O LORD, I pray, let the man of God whom you sent come to us again and teach us what we are to do concerning the boy who will be born." [9]God listened to Manoah, and the angel of God came again to the

STUDY IT!

Introducing . . . Samson
Judges 13–16

Samson is one of the Bible's most famous judges, and his story is one of the most well known. When you think of Samson, you may remember him for his long hair and great feats of strength, such as killing a lion bare-handed and slaying a thousand men with the jawbone of a donkey. But did you also know that Samson's birth was announced by an angel and that the "spirit of the LORD rushed on him" more often for Samson than for any other judge (Judges 14:6, 19; 15:14)? Samson was a Nazirite as well as a judge. Nazirites took vows to abstain from alcohol, avoid contact with dead bodies, and refrain from cutting their hair—all as signs of their devotion to God.

Samson was a flawed hero, like many of the other judges. He broke all his Nazirite vows, was controlled by lust, and used his great strength for personal revenge. But God chose to use Samson despite these flaws. Samson paid for his sins, but his tragic death ultimately brought victory over the Philistines. Once again God's purposes were accomplished, even through a flawed and sinful human being.

woman as she sat in the field; but her husband Manoah was not with her. [10]So the woman ran quickly and told her husband, "The man who came to me the other day has appeared to me." [11]Manoah got up and followed his wife, and came to the man and said to him, "Are you the man who spoke to this woman?" And he said, "I am." [12]Then Manoah said, "Now when your words come true, what is to be the boy's rule of life; what is he to do?" [13]The angel of the LORD said to Manoah, "Let the woman give heed to all that I said to her. [14]She may not eat of anything that comes from the vine. She is not to drink wine or strong drink, or eat any unclean thing. She is to observe everything that I commanded her."

---

a Gk: Heb *in the towns of Gilead*   **b** That is *one separated* or *one consecrated*   **c** Or *the angel*

15 Manoah said to the angel of the LORD, "Allow us to detain you, and prepare a kid for you." [16]The angel of the LORD said to Manoah, "If you detain me, I will not eat your food; but if you want to prepare a burnt offering, then offer it to the LORD." (For Manoah did not know that he was the angel of the LORD.) [17]Then Manoah said to the angel of the LORD, "What is your name, so that we may honor you when your words come true?" [18]But the angel of the LORD said to him, "Why do you ask my name? It is too wonderful."

19 So Manoah took the kid with the grain offering, and offered it on the rock to the LORD, to him who works[a] wonders.[b] [20]When the flame went up toward heaven from the altar, the angel of the LORD ascended in the flame of the altar while Manoah and his wife looked on; and they fell on their faces to the ground. [21]The angel of the LORD did not appear again to Manoah and his wife. Then Manoah realized that it was the angel of the LORD. [22]And Manoah said to his wife, "We shall surely die, for we have seen God." [23]But his wife said to him, "If the LORD had meant to kill us, he would not have accepted a burnt offering and a grain offering at our hands, or shown us all these things, or now announced to us such things as these."

24 The woman bore a son, and named him Samson. The boy grew, and the LORD blessed him. [25]The spirit of the LORD began to stir him in Mahaneh-dan, between Zorah and Eshtaol.

Samson's Marriage

14 Once Samson went down to Timnah, and at Timnah he saw a Philistine woman. [2]Then he came up, and told his father and mother, "I saw a Philistine woman at Timnah; now get her for me as my wife." [3]But his father and mother said to him, "Is there not a woman among your kin, or among all our[c] people, that you must go to take a wife from the uncircumcised Philistines?" But Samson said to his father, "Get her for me, because she pleases me." [4]His father and mother did not know that this was from the LORD; for he was seeking a pretext to act against the Philistines. At that time the Philistines had dominion over Israel.

5 Then Samson went down with his father and mother to Timnah. When he came to the vineyards of Timnah, suddenly a young lion roared at him. [6]The spirit of the LORD rushed on him, and he tore the lion apart barehanded as one might tear apart a kid. But he did not tell his father or his mother what he had done. [7]Then he went down and talked with the woman, and she pleased Samson. [8]After a while he returned to marry her, and he turned aside to see the carcass of the lion, and there was a swarm of bees in the body of the lion, and honey. [9]He scraped it out into his hands, and went on, eating as he went. When he came to his father and mother, he gave some to them, and they ate it. But he did not tell them that he had taken the honey from the carcass of the lion.

10 His father went down to the woman, and Samson made a feast there as the young men were accustomed to do. [11]When the people saw him, they brought thirty companions to be with him. [12]Samson said to them, "Let me now put a riddle to you. If you can explain it to me within the seven days of the feast, and find it out, then I will give you thirty linen garments and thirty festal garments. [13]But if you cannot explain it to me, then you shall give me thirty linen garments and thirty festal garments." So they said to him, "Ask your riddle; let us hear it." [14]He said to them,

"Out of the eater came something to eat.
Out of the strong came something sweet."

But for three days they could not explain the riddle.

15 On the fourth[d] day they said to Samson's wife, "Coax your husband to explain the riddle to us, or we will burn you and your father's house with fire. Have you invited us here to impoverish us?" [16]So Samson's wife wept before him, saying, "You hate me; you do not really love me. You have asked a riddle of my people, but you have not explained it to me." He said to her, "Look, I have not told my father or my mother. Why should I tell you?" [17]She wept before him the seven days that their feast lasted; and because she nagged him, on the seventh day he told her. Then she explained the riddle to her people. [18]The men of the town said to him on the seventh day before the sun went down,

"What is sweeter than honey?
What is stronger than a lion?"

And he said to them,

"If you had not plowed with my heifer,
you would not have found out my riddle."

[19]Then the spirit of the LORD rushed on him, and he went down to Ashkelon. He killed thirty men of the town, took their spoil, and gave the festal garments to those who had explained the riddle. In hot anger he went back to his father's house. [20]And

a Gk Vg: Heb *and working*   b Heb *wonders, while Manoah and his wife looked on*   c Cn: Heb *my*   d Gk Syr: Heb *seventh*

Samson's wife was given to his companion, who had been his best man.

Samson Defeats the Philistines

15 After a while, at the time of the wheat harvest, Samson went to visit his wife, bringing along a kid. He said, "I want to go into my wife's room." But her father would not allow him to go in. [2] Her father said, "I was sure that you had rejected her; so I gave her to your companion. Is not her younger sister prettier than she? Why not take her instead?" [3] Samson said to them, "This time, when I do mischief to the Philistines, I will be without blame." [4] So Samson went and caught three hundred foxes, and took some torches; and he turned the foxes[a] tail to tail, and put a torch between each pair of tails. [5] When he had set fire to the torches, he let the foxes go into the standing grain of the Philistines, and burned up the shocks and the standing grain, as well as the vineyards and[b] olive groves. [6] Then the Philistines asked, "Who has done this?" And they said, "Samson, the son-in-law of the Timnite, because he has taken Samson's wife and given her to his companion." So the Philistines came up, and burned her and her father. [7] Samson said to them, "If this is what you do, I swear I will not stop until I have taken revenge on you." [8] He struck them down hip and thigh with great slaughter; and he went down and stayed in the cleft of the rock of Etam.

9 Then the Philistines came up and encamped in Judah, and made a raid on Lehi. [10] The men of Judah said, "Why have you come up against us?" They said, "We have come up to bind Samson, to do to him as he did to us." [11] Then three thousand men of Judah went down to the cleft of the rock of Etam, and they said to Samson, "Do you not know that the Philistines are rulers over us? What then have you done to us?" He replied, "As they did to me, so I have done to them." [12] They said to him, "We have come down to bind you, so that we may give you into the hands of the Philistines." Samson answered them, "Swear to me that you yourselves will not attack me." [13] They said to him, "No, we will only bind you and give you into their hands; we will not kill you." So they bound him with two new ropes, and brought him up from the rock.

14 When he came to Lehi, the Philistines came shouting to meet him; and the spirit of the Lord rushed on him, and the ropes that were on his arms became like flax that has caught fire, and his bonds melted off his hands. [15] Then he found a fresh jawbone of a donkey, reached down and took it, and with it he killed a thousand men. [16] And Samson said,

"With the jawbone of a donkey,
    heaps upon heaps,
with the jawbone of a donkey
    I have slain a thousand men."

[17] When he had finished speaking, he threw away the jawbone; and that place was called Ramath-lehi.[c]

18 By then he was very thirsty, and he called on the Lord, saying, "You have granted this great victory by the hand of your servant. Am I now to die of thirst, and fall into the hands of the uncircumcised?" [19] So God split open the hollow place that is at Lehi, and water came from it. When he drank, his spirit returned, and he revived. Therefore it was named En-hakkore,[d] which is at Lehi to this day. [20] And he judged Israel in the days of the Philistines twenty years.

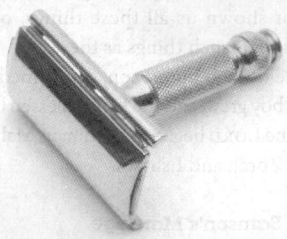

Samson and Delilah

16 Once Samson went to Gaza, where he saw a prostitute and went in to her. [2] The Gazites were told,[e] "Samson has come here." So they circled around and lay in wait for him all night at the city gate. They kept quiet all night, thinking, "Let us wait until the light of the morning; then we will kill him." [3] But Samson lay only until midnight. Then at midnight he rose up, took hold of the doors of the city gate and the two posts, pulled them up, bar and all, put them on his shoulders, and carried them to the top of the hill that is in front of Hebron.

4 After this he fell in love with a woman in the valley of Sorek, whose name was Delilah. [5] The lords of the Philistines came to her and said to her, "Coax him, and find out what makes his strength so great, and how we may overpower him, so that

---

a Heb *them*   b Gk Tg Vg: Heb lacks *and*   c That is *The Hill of the Jawbone*   d That is *The Spring of the One who Called*   e Gk: Heb lacks *were told*

we may bind him in order to subdue him; and we will each give you eleven hundred pieces of silver." [6]So Delilah said to Samson, "Please tell me what makes your strength so great, and how you could be bound, so that one could subdue you." [7]Samson said to her, "If they bind me with seven fresh bowstrings that are not dried out, then I shall become weak, and be like anyone else." [8]Then the lords of the Philistines brought her seven fresh bowstrings that had not dried out, and she bound him with them. [9]While men were lying in wait in an inner chamber, she said to him, "The Philistines are upon you, Samson!" But he snapped the bowstrings, as a strand of fiber snaps when it touches the fire. So the secret of his strength was not known.

10 Then Delilah said to Samson, "You have mocked me and told me lies; please tell me how you could be bound." [11]He said to her, "If they bind me with new ropes that have not been used, then I shall become weak, and be like anyone else." [12]So Delilah took new ropes and bound him with them, and said to him, "The Philistines are upon you, Samson!" (The men lying in wait were in an inner chamber.) But he snapped the ropes off his arms like a thread.

13 Then Delilah said to Samson, "Until now you have mocked me and told me lies; tell me how you could be bound." He said to her, "If you weave the seven locks of my head with the web and make it tight with the pin, then I shall become weak, and be like anyone else." [14]So while he slept, Delilah took the seven locks of his head and wove them into the web,[a] and made them tight with the pin. Then she said to him, "The Philistines are upon you, Samson!" But he awoke from his sleep, and pulled away the pin, the loom, and the web.

15 Then she said to him, "How can you say, 'I love you,' when your heart is not with me? You have mocked me three times now and have not told me what makes your strength so great." [16]Finally, after she had nagged him with her words day after day, and pestered him, he was tired to death. [17]So he told her his whole secret, and said to her, "A razor has never come upon my head; for I have been a nazirite[b] to God from my mother's womb. If my head were shaved, then my strength would leave me; I would become weak, and be like anyone else."

18 When Delilah realized that he had told her his whole secret, she sent and called the lords of the Philistines, saying, "This time come up, for he has told his whole secret to me." Then the lords of the Philistines came up to her, and brought the money in their hands. [19]She let him fall asleep on her lap; and she called a man, and had him shave

LIVE IT!

Manipulation and Betrayal · Judges 16:4–22

Delilah is the master manipulator in trying to coax from Samson the secret of his strength. By the third attempt, it seems rather obvious that she wants to betray him to the Philistines. You'd think Samson would catch on! But Samson still stays with her and is finally pestered into revealing his secret. Of course, Delilah immediately uses the information to betray him.

Have you ever been betrayed by a friend? Have you ever trusted someone with a secret only to discover later that your secret is out? That makes it hard to trust again, to be open, and to share yourself with another person. And the betrayal is even more painful when the person who betrays your confidence is someone you love.

It may be easy to remember times we were betrayed, but we don't often like to think about the times we have betrayed others. Ask yourself: Am I the kind of person who can be trusted with someone's secret? Have I ever betrayed a confidence?

It's easier than we think to be like Delilah—abusing the trust built up in a relationship and manipulating another person, even someone we care deeply about. We need to resolve to be people of integrity who would never betray our friends or use them for personal gain. If you have betrayed a friend or if a friend has betrayed you, take the tough road and seek forgiveness and ways to restore that relationship.

a Compare Gk: in verses 13–14, Heb lacks *and make it tight . . . into the web*   b That is *one separated* or *one consecrated* off the seven locks of his head. He began to weaken,[a] and his strength left him. [20]Then she said, "The Philistines are upon you, Samson!" When he awoke from his sleep, he thought, "I will go out as at other times, and shake myself free." But he did not know that the LORD had left him. [21]So the Philistines seized him and gouged out his eyes. They brought him down to Gaza and bound him with bronze shackles; and he ground at the mill in the prison. [22]But the hair of his head began to grow again after it had been shaved.

Samson's Death

23 Now the lords of the Philistines gathered to offer a great sacrifice to their god Dagon, and to rejoice; for they said, "Our god has given Samson our enemy into our hand." [24]When the people saw him, they praised their god; for they said, "Our god has given our enemy into our hand, the ravager of our country, who has killed many of us." [25]And when their hearts were merry, they said, "Call Samson, and let him entertain us." So they called Samson out of the prison, and he performed for them. They made him stand between the pillars; [26]and Samson said to the attendant who held him by the hand, "Let me feel the pillars on which the house rests, so that I may lean against them." [27]Now the house was full of men and women; all the lords of the Philistines were there, and on the roof there were about three thousand men and women, who looked on while Samson performed.

28 Then Samson called to the LORD and said, "Lord GOD, remember me and strengthen me only this once, O God, so that with this one act of revenge I may pay back the Philistines for my two eyes."[b] [29]And Samson grasped the two middle pillars on which the house rested, and he leaned his weight against them, his right hand on the one and his left hand on the other. [30]Then Samson said, "Let me die with the Philistines." He strained with all his might; and the house fell on the lords and all the people who were in it. So those he killed at his death were more than those he had killed during

his life. [31]Then his brothers and all his family came down and took him and brought him up and buried him between Zorah and Eshtaol in the tomb of his father Manoah. He had judged Israel twenty years.

17 ### Micah and the Levite

There was a man in the hill country of Ephraim whose name was Micah. [2]He said to his mother, "The eleven hundred pieces of silver that were taken from you, about which you uttered a curse, and even spoke it in my hearing,—that silver is in my possession; I took it; but now I will return it to you."[c] And his mother said, "May my son be blessed by the LORD!" [3]Then he returned the eleven hundred pieces of silver to his mother; and his mother said, "I consecrate the silver to the LORD from my hand for my son, to make an idol of cast metal." [4]So when he returned the money to his mother, his mother took two hundred pieces of silver, and gave it to the silversmith, who made it into an idol of cast metal; and it was in the house of Micah. [5]This man Micah had a shrine, and he made an ephod and teraphim, and installed one of his sons, who became his priest. [6]In those days there was no king in Israel; all the people did what was right in their own eyes.

7 Now there was a young man of Bethlehem in Judah, of the clan of Judah. He was a Levite residing there. [8]This man left the town of Bethlehem in Judah, to live wherever he could find a place. He came to the house of Micah in the hill country of Ephraim to carry on his work.[d] [9]Micah said to him, "From where do you come?" He replied, "I am a Levite of Bethlehem in Judah, and I am going to live wherever I can find a place." [10]Then Micah said to him, "Stay with me, and be to me a father and a priest, and I will give you ten pieces of silver a year, a set of clothes, and your living."[e] [11]The Levite agreed to stay with the man; and the young man became to him like one of his sons. [12]So Micah installed the Levite, and the young man became his priest, and was in the house of Micah. [13]Then Micah said, "Now I know that the LORD

> "In those days there was no king in Israel; all the people did what was right in their own eyes."
> —Judges 17:6

---

a Gk: Heb *She began to torment him*   b Or *so that I may be avenged upon the Philistines for one of my two eyes*   c The words *but now I will return it to you* are transposed from the end of verse 3 in Heb   d Or *Ephraim, continuing his journey*   e Heb *living, and the Levite went*

will prosper me, because the Levite has become my priest."

The Migration of Dan

18 In those days there was no king in Israel. And in those days the tribe of the Danites was seeking for itself a territory to live in; for until then no territory among the tribes of Israel had been allotted to them. [2]So the Danites sent five valiant men from the whole number of their clan, from Zorah and from Eshtaol, to spy out the land and to explore it; and they said to them, "Go, explore the land." When they came to the hill country of Ephraim, to the house of Micah, they stayed there. [3]While they were at Micah's house, they recognized the voice of the young Levite; so they went over and asked him, "Who brought you here? What are you doing in this place? What is your business here?" [4]He said to them, "Micah did such and such for me, and he hired me, and I have become his priest." [5]Then they said to him, "Inquire of God that we may know whether the mission we are undertaking will succeed." [6]The priest replied, "Go in peace. The mission you are on is under the eye of the LORD."

7 The five men went on, and when they came to Laish, they observed the people who were there living securely, after the manner of the Sidonians, quiet and unsuspecting, lacking[a] nothing on earth, and possessing wealth.[b] Furthermore, they were far from the Sidonians and had no dealings with Aram.[c] [8]When they came to their kinsfolk at Zorah and Eshtaol, they said to them, "What do you report?" [9]They said, "Come, let us go up against them; for we have seen the land, and it is very good. Will you do nothing? Do not be slow to go, but enter in and possess the land. [10]When you go, you will come to an unsuspecting people. The land is broad—God has indeed given it into your hands—a place where there is no lack of anything on earth."

11 Six hundred men of the Danite clan, armed with weapons of war, set out from Zorah and Eshtaol, [12]and went up and encamped at Kiriath-jearim in Judah. On this account that place is called Mahaneh-dan[d] to this day; it is west of Kiriath-jearim. [13]From there they passed on to the hill country of Ephraim, and came to the house of Micah.

14 Then the five men who had gone to spy out the land (that is, Laish) said to their comrades, "Do you know that in these buildings there are an ephod,

teraphim, and an idol of cast metal? Now therefore consider what you will do." [15]So they turned in that direction and came to the house of the young Levite, at the home of Micah, and greeted him. [16]While the six hundred men of the Danites, armed with their weapons of war, stood by the entrance of the gate, [17]the five men who had gone to spy out the land proceeded to enter and take the idol of cast metal, the ephod, and the teraphim.[e] The priest was standing by the entrance of the gate with the six hundred men armed with weapons of war. [18]When the men went into Micah's house and took the idol of cast metal, the ephod, and the teraphim, the priest said to them, "What are you doing?" [19]They said to him, "Keep quiet! Put your hand over your mouth, and come with us, and be to us a father and a priest. Is it better for you to be priest to the house of one person, or to be priest to a tribe and clan in Israel?" [20]Then the priest accepted the offer. He took the ephod, the teraphim, and the idol, and went along with the people.

21 So they resumed their journey, putting the little ones, the livestock, and the goods in front of them. [22]When they were some distance from the home of Micah, the men who were in the houses near Micah's house were called out, and they overtook the Danites. [23]They shouted to the Danites, who turned around and said to Micah, "What is the matter that you come with such a company?" [24]He replied, "You take my gods that I made, and the priest, and go away, and what have I left? How then can you ask me, 'What is the matter?'" [25]And the Danites said to him, "You had better not let your voice be heard among us or else hot-tempered fellows will attack you, and you will lose your life and the lives of your household." [26]Then the Danites went their way. When Micah saw that they were too strong for him, he turned and went back to his home.

The Danites Settle in Laish

27 The Danites, having taken what Micah had made, and the priest who belonged to him, came to Laish, to a people quiet and unsuspecting, put them to the sword, and burned down the city. [28]There was no deliverer, because it was far from Sidon and they had no dealings with Aram.[f] It was in the valley that belongs to Beth-rehob. They rebuilt the city, and lived in it. [29]They named the city Dan, after their ancestor Dan, who was born to Israel; but the name of the city was formerly Laish. [30]Then the

---

a Cn Compare 18.10: Meaning of Heb uncertain   b Meaning of Heb uncertain   c Symmachus: Heb *with anyone*   d That is *Camp of Dan*   e Compare 17.4, 5; 18.14: Heb *teraphim and the cast metal*   f Cn Compare verse 7: Heb *with anyone*

Danites set up the idol for themselves. Jonathan son of Gershom, son of Moses,[a] and his sons were priests to the tribe of the Danites until the time the land went into captivity. ³¹ So they maintained as their own Micah's idol that he had made, as long as the house of God was at Shiloh.

19 The Levite's Concubine

In those days, when there was no king in Israel, a certain Levite, residing in the remote parts of the hill country of Ephraim, took to himself a concubine from Bethlehem in Judah. ² But his concubine became angry with[b] him, and she went away from him to her father's house at Bethlehem in Judah, and was there some four months. ³ Then her husband set out after her, to speak tenderly to her and bring her back. He had with him his servant and a couple of donkeys. When he reached[c] her father's house, the girl's father saw him and came with joy to meet him. ⁴ His father-in-law, the girl's father, made him stay, and he remained with him three days; so they ate and drank, and he[d] stayed there. ⁵ On the fourth day they got up early in the morning, and he prepared to go; but the girl's father said to his son-in-law, "Fortify yourself with a bit of food, and after that you may go." ⁶ So the two men sat and ate and drank together; and the girl's father said to the man, "Why not spend the night and enjoy yourself?" ⁷ When the man got up to go, his father-in-law kept urging him until he spent the night there again. ⁸ On the fifth day he got up early in the morning to leave; and the girl's father said, "Fortify yourself." So they lingered[e] until the day declined, and the two of them ate and drank.[f] ⁹ When the man with his concubine and his servant got up to leave, his father-in-law, the girl's father, said to him, "Look, the day has worn on until it is almost evening. Spend the night. See, the day has drawn to a close. Spend the night here and enjoy yourself. Tomorrow you can get up early in the morning for your journey, and go home."

10 But the man would not spend the night; he got up and departed, and arrived opposite Jebus (that is, Jerusalem). He had with him a couple of saddled donkeys, and his concubine was with him. ¹¹ When they were near Jebus, the day was far spent, and the servant said to his master, "Come now, let us turn aside to this city of the Jebusites, and spend the night in it." ¹² But his master said to him, "We will not turn aside into a city of foreigners, who do not belong to the people of Israel; but we will continue on to Gibeah." ¹³ Then he said to his servant, "Come, let us try to reach one of these places, and spend the night at Gibeah or at Ramah." ¹⁴ So they passed on and went their way; and the sun went down on them near Gibeah, which belongs to Benjamin. ¹⁵ They turned aside there, to go in and spend the night at Gibeah. He went in and sat down in the open square of the city, but no one took them in to spend the night.

16 Then at evening there was an old man coming from his work in the field. The man was from the hill country of Ephraim, and he was residing in Gibeah. (The people of the place were Benjaminites.) ¹⁷ When the old man looked up and saw the wayfarer in the open square of the city, he said, "Where are you going and where do you come from?" ¹⁸ He answered him, "We are passing from Bethlehem in Judah to the remote parts of the hill country of Ephraim, from which I come. I went to Bethlehem in Judah; and I am going to my home.[g] Nobody has offered to take me in. ¹⁹ We your servants have straw and fodder for our donkeys, with bread and wine for me and the woman and the young man along with us. We need nothing more." ²⁰ The old man said, "Peace be to you. I will care for all your wants; only do not spend the night in the square." ²¹ So he brought him into his house, and fed the donkeys; they washed their feet, and ate and drank.

Gibeah's Crime

22 While they were enjoying themselves, the men of the city, a perverse lot, surrounded the house, and started pounding on the door. They said to the old man, the master of the house, "Bring out the man who came into your house, so that we may have intercourse with him." ²³ And the man, the master of the house, went out to them and said to them, "No, my brothers, do not act so wickedly. Since this man is my guest, do not do this vile thing. ²⁴ Here are my virgin daughter and his concubine; let me bring them out now. Ravish them and do whatever you want to them; but against this man do not do such a vile thing." ²⁵ But the men would not listen to him. So the man seized his concubine, and put her out to them. They wantonly raped her, and abused her all through the night until the morning. And as the dawn began

a Another reading is *son of Manasseh*   b Gk OL: Heb *prostituted herself against*   c Gk: Heb *she brought him to*   d Compare verse 7 and Gk: Heb *they*
e Cn: Heb *Linger*   f Gk: Heb lacks *and drank*   g Gk Compare 19.29. Heb *to the house of the LORD*

to break, they let her go. ²⁶As morning appeared, the woman came and fell down at the door of the man's house where her master was, until it was light.

27 In the morning her master got up, opened the doors of the house, and when he went out to go on his way, there was his concubine lying at the door of the house, with her hands on the threshold. ²⁸"Get up," he said to her, "we are going." But there was no answer. Then he put her on the donkey; and the man set out for his home. ²⁹When he had entered his house, he took a knife, and grasping his concubine he cut her into twelve pieces, limb by limb, and sent her throughout all the territory of Israel. ³⁰Then he commanded the men whom he sent, saying, "Thus shall you say to all the Israelites, 'Has such a thing ever happened[a] since the day that the Israelites came up from the land of Egypt until this day? Consider it, take counsel, and speak out.' "

The Other Tribes Attack Benjamin

20 Then all the Israelites came out, from Dan to Beer-sheba, including the land of Gilead, and the congregation assembled in one body before the LORD at Mizpah. ²The chiefs of all the people, of all the tribes of Israel, presented themselves in the assembly of the people of God, four hundred thousand foot-soldiers bearing arms. ³(Now the Benjaminites heard that the people of Israel had gone up to Mizpah.) And the Israelites said, "Tell us, how did this criminal act come about?" ⁴The Levite, the husband of the woman who was murdered, answered, "I came to Gibeah that belongs to Benjamin, I and my concubine, to spend the night. ⁵The lords of Gibeah rose up against me, and surrounded the house at night. They intended to kill me, and they raped my concubine until she died. ⁶Then I took my concubine and cut her into pieces, and sent her throughout the whole extent of Israel's territory; for they have committed a vile outrage in Israel. ⁷So now, you Israelites, all of you, give your advice and counsel here."

8 All the people got up as one, saying, "We will not any of us go to our tents, nor will any of us return to our houses. ⁹But now this is what we will do to Gibeah: we will go up[b] against it by lot. ¹⁰We will take ten men of a hundred throughout all the tribes of Israel, and a hundred of a thousand, and a thousand of ten thousand, to bring provisions for the troops, who are going to repay[c] Gibeah of Benjamin for all the disgrace that they have done in Israel." ¹¹So all the men of Israel gathered against the city, united as one.

12 The tribes of Israel sent men through all the tribe of Benjamin, saying, "What crime is this that has been committed among you? ¹³Now then, hand over those scoundrels in Gibeah, so that we may put them to death, and purge the evil from Israel." But the Benjaminites would not listen to their kinsfolk, the Israelites. ¹⁴The Benjaminites came together out of the towns to Gibeah, to go out to battle against the Israelites. ¹⁵On that day the Benjaminites mustered twenty-six thousand armed men from their towns, besides the inhabitants of Gibeah. ¹⁶Of all this force, there were seven hundred picked men who were left-handed; every one could sling a stone at a hair, and not miss. ¹⁷And the Israelites, apart from Benjamin, mustered four hundred thousand armed men, all of them warriors.

18 The Israelites proceeded to go up to Bethel, where they inquired of God, "Which of us shall go up first to battle against the Benjaminites?" And the LORD answered, "Judah shall go up first."

19 Then the Israelites got up in the morning, and encamped against Gibeah. ²⁰The Israelites went out to battle against Benjamin; and the Israelites drew up the battle line against them at Gibeah. ²¹The Benjaminites came out of Gibeah, and struck down on that day twenty-two thousand of the Israelites. ²³[d] The Israelites went up and wept before the LORD until the evening; and they inquired of the LORD, "Shall we again draw near to battle against our kinsfolk the Benjaminites?" And the LORD said, "Go up against them." ²²The Israelites took courage, and again formed the battle line in the same place where they had formed it on the first day.

24 So the Israelites advanced against the Benjaminites the second day. ²⁵Benjamin moved out against them from Gibeah the second day, and struck down eighteen thousand of the Israelites, all of them armed men. ²⁶Then all the Israelites, the whole army, went back to Bethel and wept, sitting there before the LORD; they fasted that day until evening. Then they offered burnt offerings and sacrifices of well-being before the LORD. ²⁷And the Israelites inquired of the LORD (for the ark of the covenant of God was there in those days, ²⁸and Phinehas son of Eleazar, son of Aaron, ministered before it in those days), saying, "Shall we go out once

---

a Compare Gk: Heb ³⁰*And all who saw it said, "Such a thing has not happened or been seen* **b** Gk: Heb lacks *we will go up* **c** Compare Gk: Meaning of Heb uncertain **d** Verses 22 and 23 are transposed

more to battle against our kinsfolk the Benjaminites, or shall we desist?" The LORD answered, "Go up, for tomorrow I will give them into your hand."

29 So Israel stationed men in ambush around Gibeah. [30]Then the Israelites went up against the Benjaminites on the third day, and set themselves in array against Gibeah, as before. [31]When the Benjaminites went out against the army, they were drawn away from the city. As before they began to inflict casualties on the troops, along the main roads, one of which goes up to Bethel and the other to Gibeah, as well as in the open country, killing about thirty men of Israel. [32]The Benjaminites thought, "They are being routed before us, as previously." But the Israelites said, "Let us retreat and draw them away from the city toward the roads." [33]The main body of the Israelites drew back its battle line to Baal-tamar, while those Israelites who were in ambush rushed out of their place west[a] of Geba. [34]There came against Gibeah ten thousand picked men out of all Israel, and the battle was fierce. But the Benjaminites did not realize that disaster was close upon them.

35 The LORD defeated Benjamin before Israel; and the Israelites destroyed twenty-five thousand one hundred men of Benjamin that day, all of them armed.

36 Then the Benjaminites saw that they were defeated.[b]

The Israelites gave ground to Benjamin, because they trusted to the troops in ambush that they had stationed against Gibeah. [37]The troops in ambush rushed quickly upon Gibeah. Then they put the whole city to the sword. [38]Now the agreement between the main body of Israel and the men in ambush was that when they sent up a cloud of smoke out of the city [39]the main body of Israel should turn in battle. But Benjamin had begun to inflict casualties on the Israelites, killing about thirty of them; so they thought, "Surely they are defeated before us, as in the first battle." [40]But when the cloud, a column of smoke, began to rise out of the city, the Benjaminites looked behind them—and there was the whole city going up in smoke toward the sky! [41]Then the main body of Israel turned, and the Benjaminites were dismayed, for they saw that disaster was close upon them. [42]Therefore they turned away from the Israelites in the direction of the wilderness; but the battle overtook them, and those who came out of the city[c] were slaughtering them

in between.[d] [43]Cutting down[e] the Benjaminites, they pursued them from Nohah[f] and trod them down as far as a place east of Gibeah. [44]Eighteen thousand Benjaminites fell, all of them courageous fighters. [45]When they turned and fled toward the wilderness to the rock of Rimmon, five thousand of them were cut down on the main roads, and they were pursued as far as Gidom, and two thousand of them were slain. [46]So all who fell that day of Benjamin were twenty-five thousand arms-bearing men, all of them courageous fighters. [47]But six hundred turned and fled toward the wilderness to the rock of Rimmon, and remained at the rock of Rimmon for four months. [48]Meanwhile, the Israelites turned back against the Benjaminites, and put them to the sword—the city, the people, the animals, and all that remained. Also the remaining towns they set on fire.

21 The Benjaminites Saved from Extinction

Now the Israelites had sworn at Mizpah, "No one of us shall give his daughter in marriage to Benjamin." [2]And the people came to Bethel, and sat there until evening before God, and they lifted up their voices and wept bitterly. [3]They said, "O LORD, the God of Israel, why has it come to pass that today there should be one tribe lacking in Israel?" [4]On the next day, the people got up early, and built an altar there, and offered burnt offerings and sacrifices of well-being. [5]Then the Israelites said, "Which of all the tribes of Israel did not come up in the assembly to the LORD?" For a solemn oath had been taken concerning whoever did not come up to the LORD to Mizpah, saying, "That one shall be put to death." [6]But the Israelites had compassion for Benjamin their kin, and said, "One tribe is cut off from Israel this day. [7]What shall we do for wives for those who are left, since we have sworn by the LORD that we will not give them any of our daughters as wives?"

8 Then they said, "Is there anyone from the tribes of Israel who did not come up to the LORD to Mizpah?" It turned out that no one from Jabesh-gilead had come to the camp, to the assembly. [9]For when the roll was called among the people, not one of the inhabitants of Jabesh-gilead was there. [10]So the congregation sent twelve thousand soldiers there and commanded them, "Go, put the inhabitants of Jabesh-gilead to the sword, including the women and the little ones. [11]This is what you

---

a Gk Vg: Heb *in the plain*   b This sentence is continued by verse 45.   c Compare Vg and some Gk Mss: Heb *cities*   d Compare Syr: Meaning of Heb uncertain   e Gk: Heb *Surrounding*   f Gk: Heb *pursued them at their resting place*

shall do; every male and every woman that has lain with a male you shall devote to destruction." [12]And they found among the inhabitants of Jabesh-gilead four hundred young virgins who had never slept with a man and brought them to the camp at Shiloh, which is in the land of Canaan.

13 Then the whole congregation sent word to the Benjaminites who were at the rock of Rimmon, and proclaimed peace to them. [14]Benjamin returned at that time; and they gave them the women whom they had saved alive of the women of Jabesh-gilead; but they did not suffice for them.

15 The people had compassion on Benjamin because the LORD had made a breach in the tribes of Israel. [16]So the elders of the congregation said, "What shall we do for wives for those who are left, since there are no women left in Benjamin?" [17]And they said, "There must be heirs for the survivors of Benjamin, in order that a tribe may not be blotted out from Israel. [18]Yet we cannot give any of our daughters to them as wives." For the Israelites had sworn, "Cursed be anyone who gives a wife to Benjamin." [19]So they said, "Look, the yearly festival of the LORD is taking place at Shiloh, which is north of Bethel, on the east of the highway that goes up from Bethel to Shechem, and south of Lebonah." [20]And they instructed the Benjaminites, saying, "Go and lie in wait in the vineyards, [21]and watch; when the young women of Shiloh come out to dance in the dances, then come out of the vineyards and each of you carry off a wife for himself from the young women of Shiloh, and go to the land of Benjamin. [22]Then if their fathers or their brothers come to complain to us, we will say to them, 'Be generous and allow us to have them; because we did not capture in battle a wife for each man. But neither did you incur guilt by giving your daughters to them.' " [23]The Benjaminites did so; they took wives for each of them from the dancers whom they abducted. Then they went and returned to their territory, and rebuilt the towns, and lived in them. [24]So the Israelites departed from there at that time by tribes and families, and they went out from there to their own territories.

25 In those days there was no king in Israel; all the people did what was right in their own eyes.

Ruth ▶▶▶▶▶▶▶▶▶▶▶▶▶▶▶▶▶▶▶▶▶▶▶▶▶▶▶▶▶▶▶▶▶▶▶

Have you ever had to move to a new city, home, or school? How about a totally different country? Nobody likes to be an outsider or a "new kid." It can be confusing and lonely to find your way around in a new place or a new culture. No one likes to feel alone, and it can be overwhelming when it seems as though everything is different.

But if you've gone through an experience like that, you've probably learned about the importance of family loyalty and support—and the power of one person to reach out with kindness. Ruth found herself in this situation. Her story is a beautiful message of God's love and loyalty and the power of friendship and faithfulness.

IN DEPTH

The book of Ruth offers a surprising revelation about the family tree of King David: Ruth, King David's great-grandmother, was a foreigner, born and reared in the land of Moab. The book of Ruth took its final form long after the death of her famous great-grandson, but it seems to preserve an accurate memory: King David was of mixed ancestry. Many Israelites were probably shocked that God worked through a member of an enemy tribe to advance God's divine plan.

The book of Ruth is sandwiched between the books of Judges and 1 Samuel, because its events take place during the time of the judges. It teaches some extremely important lessons:

• Ruth was faithful to Naomi, her mother-in-law, even though she was of a different ethnic group and different faith. Ruth's character challenged the perception of the ancient Israelites, who tended to view foreigners with suspicion and to see nothing good in their enemies.

• If God's plan included a foreign Moabite woman among David's ancestors, then God's love and favor must extend beyond the boundaries of Israel. After the exile, when Jewish marriages to foreigners were outlawed, the little book of Ruth presented a huge challenge!

• God works through the faithfulness of ordinary people living ordinary lives. No kings, wars, or dramatic miracles appear in the book of Ruth.

Ruth is action packed and full of dialogue. We gain a deeper understanding of ourselves and our faith by reading this story of King David's great-grandmother.

QUICK FACTS

● **Dates Covered:** Sometime between 1200 and 1000 B.C.

◢ **Author:** An unknown author probably writing during the sixth century B.C.

● **Themes:** The inclusion of non-Israelites and ordinary people in God's plan; a reminder that God still invites everyone into a relationship and wants to work in the ordinary details and events of our lives and friendships

AT A GLANCE

● **Ruth 1** Ruth's decision to go with her mother-in-law to Bethlehem

◢ **Ruth 2–3** Ruth's encounter with Boaz

● **Ruth 4** The marriage of Ruth and Boaz; Ruth's descendants

Elimelech's Family Goes to Moab

1 In the days when the judges ruled, there was a famine in the land, and a certain man of Bethlehem in Judah went to live in the country of Moab, he and his wife and two sons. ²The name of the man was Elimelech and the name of his wife Naomi, and the names of his two sons were Mahlon and Chilion; they were Ephrathites from Bethlehem in Judah. They went into the country of Moab and remained there. ³But Elimelech, the husband of Naomi, died, and she was left with her two sons. ⁴These took Moabite wives; the name of the one was Orpah and the name of the other Ruth. When they had lived there about ten years, ⁵both Mahlon and Chilion also died, so that the woman was left without her two sons and her husband.

Naomi and Her Moabite Daughters-in-Law

6 Then she started to return with her daughters-in-law from the country of Moab, for she had heard in the country of Moab that the LORD had considered his people and given them food. ⁷So she set out from the place where she had been living, she and her two daughters-in-law, and they went on their way to go back to the land of Judah. ⁸But Naomi said to her two daughters-in-law, "Go back each of you to your mother's house. May the LORD deal kindly with you, as you have dealt with the dead and with me. ⁹The LORD grant that you may find security, each of you in the house of your husband." Then she kissed them, and they wept aloud. ¹⁰They said to her, "No, we will return with you to your people." ¹¹But Naomi said, "Turn back, my daughters, why will you go with me? Do I still have sons in my womb that they may become your husbands? ¹²Turn back, my daughters, go your way, for I am too old to have a husband. Even if I thought there was hope for me, even if I should have a husband tonight and bear sons, ¹³would you then wait until they were grown? Would you then refrain from marrying? No, my daughters, it has been far more bitter for me than for you, because the hand of the LORD has turned against me." ¹⁴Then they wept aloud again. Orpah kissed her mother-in-law, but Ruth clung to her.

15 So she said, "See, your sister-in-law has gone back to her people and to her gods; return after your sister-in-law." ¹⁶But Ruth said,

"Do not press me to leave you
    or to turn back from following you!
Where you go, I will go;
    where you lodge, I will lodge;
your people shall be my people,
    and your God my God.
¹⁷ Where you die, I will die—
    there will I be buried.
May the LORD do thus and so to me,
    and more as well,
if even death parts me from you!"

¹⁸When Naomi saw that she was determined to go with her, she said no more to her.

19 So the two of them went on until they came to Bethlehem. When they came to Bethlehem, the whole town was stirred because of them; and the women said, "Is this Naomi?" ²⁰She said to them, "Call me no longer Naomi,ᵃ
    call me Mara,ᵇ
for the Almightyᶜ has dealt bitterly with me.
²¹ I went away full,
    but the LORD has brought me back empty;
why call me Naomi
    when the LORD has dealt harshly withᵈ me,
    and the Almightyᶜ has brought calamity upon me?"

PRAY IT!

Wherever You Go
Ruth 1:16

Ruth is under no obligation to leave her homeland and go to Israel with her mother-in-law. It would most likely mean facing a life of poverty. But Ruth's loyalty is rewarded, and she finds new life among God's people.

After reading Ruth's story, reflect on these questions:

- What do you find inspiring in Ruth's story?
- What would have to be present in a relationship for you to have the kind of loyalty Ruth showed to Naomi?
- Consider making Ruth's words to Naomi your prayer of loyalty to God: Where you lead, I will follow; where you direct me, I will live; your people will be my family (Ruth 1:16, adapted).

---

a That is *Pleasant*   **b** That is *Bitter*   **c** Traditional rendering of Heb *Shaddai*   **d** Or *has testified against*

Stand by Me · Ruth 1:1–18

The word "loyalty" might sound old-fashioned. We're more likely to hear someone say, "I've got your back," but that's the same timeless concept in different words. The story of Naomi and Ruth gives us an inspiring example of loyalty.

After Ruth's husband dies, her mother-in-law, Naomi, decides to return home to Bethlehem and tells her two widowed daughters-in-law that they should return to their homes and marry again. That was their best route to security and safety in their culture. But Ruth decides to stay with Naomi, which means leaving her own land of Moab and settling in Judea, a foreign land. Ruth's words to Naomi are a powerful statement of what it means to be loyal: "Where you go, I will go; where you lodge, I will lodge; your people shall be my people, and your God my God" (Ruth 1:16). In other words, "No matter what, I will stand by you."

We are also called to be loyal—especially to our families and friends. We are to stand by the people we are close to, especially when they are experiencing hard times. We should stay faithful even when it's tough to do so. Loyalty creates trust and deepens relationships.

• Who or what are you loyal to?
• When have you experienced disloyalty, especially in a friend?
• How have you proven your loyalty to others? To God?

22 So Naomi returned together with Ruth the Moabite, her daughter-in-law, who came back with her from the country of Moab. They came to Bethlehem at the beginning of the barley harvest.

Ruth Meets Boaz

2 Now Naomi had a kinsman on her husband's side, a prominent rich man, of the family of Elimelech, whose name was Boaz. ²And Ruth the Moabite said to Naomi, "Let me go to the field and glean among the ears of grain, behind someone in whose sight I may find favor." She said to her, "Go, my daughter." ³So she went. She came and gleaned in the field behind the reapers. As it happened, she came to the part of the field belonging to Boaz, who was of the family of Elimelech. ⁴Just then Boaz came from Bethlehem. He said to the reapers, "The LORD be with you." They answered, "The LORD bless you." ⁵Then Boaz said to his servant who was in charge of the reapers, "To whom does this young woman belong?" ⁶The servant who was in charge of the reapers answered, "She is the Moabite who came back with Naomi from the country of Moab. ⁷She said, 'Please, let me glean and gather among the sheaves behind the reapers.' So she came, and she has been on her feet from early this morning until now, without resting even for a moment."ᵃ

8 Then Boaz said to Ruth, "Now listen, my daughter, do not go to glean in another field or leave this one, but keep close to my young women. ⁹Keep your eyes on the field that is being reaped, and follow behind them. I have ordered the young men not to bother you. If you get thirsty, go to the vessels and drink from what the young men have drawn." ¹⁰Then she fell prostrate, with her face to the ground, and said to him, "Why have I found favor in your sight, that you should take notice of me, when I am a foreigner?" ¹¹But Boaz answered her, "All that you have done for your mother-in-law since the death of your husband has been fully told me, and how you left your father and mother and your native land and came to a people that you did not know before. ¹²May the LORD reward you for your deeds, and may you have a full reward from the LORD, the God of Israel, under whose wings you have come for refuge!" ¹³Then she said, "May I continue to find favor in your sight, my lord, for you have comforted me and spoken kindly to your servant, even though I am not one of your servants."

14 At mealtime Boaz said to her, "Come here, and eat some of this bread, and dip your morsel in the sour wine." So she sat beside the reapers, and he heaped up for her some parched grain. She ate until she was satisfied, and she had some left over. ¹⁵When she got up to glean, Boaz instructed his young men, "Let her glean even among the standing sheaves, and

ᵃ Compare Gk Vg: Meaning of Heb uncertain

do not reproach her. [16]You must also pull out some handfuls for her from the bundles, and leave them for her to glean, and do not rebuke her."

17 So she gleaned in the field until evening. Then she beat out what she had gleaned, and it was about an ephah of barley. [18]She picked it up and came into the town, and her mother-in-law saw how much she had gleaned. Then she took out and gave her what was left over after she herself had been satisfied. [19]Her mother-in-law said to her, "Where did you glean today? And where have you worked? Blessed be the man who took notice of you." So she told her mother-in-law with whom she had worked, and said, "The name of the man with whom I worked today is Boaz." [20]Then Naomi said to her daughter-in-law, "Blessed be he by the LORD, whose kindness has not forsaken the living or the dead!" Naomi also said to her, "The man is a relative of ours, one of our nearest kin."[a] [21]Then Ruth the Moabite said, "He even said to me, 'Stay close by my servants, until they have finished all my harvest.'" [22]Naomi said to Ruth, her daughter-in-law, "It is better, my daughter, that you go out with his young women, otherwise you might be bothered in another field." [23]So she stayed close to the young women of Boaz, gleaning until the end of the barley and wheat harvests; and she lived with her mother-in-law.

Ruth and Boaz at the Threshing Floor

3 Naomi her mother-in-law said to her, "My daughter, I need to seek some security for you, so that it may be well with you. [2]Now here is our kinsman Boaz, with whose young women you have been working. See, he is winnowing barley tonight at the threshing floor. [3]Now wash and anoint yourself, and put on your best clothes and go down to the threshing floor; but do not make yourself known to the man until he has finished eating and drinking. [4]When he lies down, observe the place where he lies; then, go and uncover his feet and lie down; and he will tell you what to do." [5]She said to her, "All that you tell me I will do."

6 So she went down to the threshing floor and did just as her mother-in-law had instructed her. [7]When Boaz had eaten and drunk, and he was in a contented mood, he went to lie down at the end of the heap of grain. Then she came stealthily and uncovered his feet, and lay down. [8]At midnight the man was startled, and turned over, and there, lying at his feet, was a woman! [9]He said, "Who are you?"

And she answered, "I am Ruth, your servant; spread your cloak over your servant, for you are next-of-kin."[a] [10]He said, "May you be blessed by the LORD, my daughter; this last instance of your loyalty is better than the first; you have not gone after young men, whether poor or rich. [11]And now, my daughter, do not be afraid, I will do for you all that you ask, for all the assembly of my people know that you are a worthy woman. [12]But now, though it is true that I am a near kinsman, there is another kinsman more closely related than I. [13]Remain this night, and in the morning, if he will act as next-of-kin[a] for you, good; let him do it. If he is not willing to act as next-of-kin[a] for you, then, as the LORD lives, I will act as next-of-kin[a] for you. Lie down until the morning."

14 So she lay at his feet until morning, but got up before one person could recognize another; for he said, "It must not be known that the woman came to the threshing floor." [15]Then he said, "Bring the cloak you are wearing and hold it out." So she held it, and he measured out six measures of barley, and put it on her back; then he went into the city. [16]She came to her mother-in-law, who said, "How did things go with you,[b] my daughter?" Then she told her all that the man had done for her, [17]saying, "He gave me these six measures of barley, for he said, 'Do not go back to your mother-in-law empty-handed.'" [18]She replied, "Wait, my daughter, until you learn how the matter turns out, for the man will not rest, but will settle the matter today."

The Marriage of Boaz and Ruth

4 No sooner had Boaz gone up to the gate and sat down there than the next-of-kin,[a] of whom Boaz had spoken, came passing by. So Boaz said, "Come over, friend; sit down here." And he went over and sat down. [2]Then Boaz took ten men of the elders of the city, and said, "Sit down here"; so they sat down. [3]He then said to the next-of-kin,[a] "Naomi, who has come back from the country of Moab, is selling the parcel of land that belonged to

---

a Or one with the right to redeem   **b** Or "Who are you,

our kinsman Elimelech. [4]So I thought I would tell you of it, and say: Buy it in the presence of those sitting here, and in the presence of the elders of my people. If you will redeem it, redeem it; but if you will not, tell me, so that I may know; for there is no one prior to you to redeem it, and I come after you." So he said, "I will redeem it." [5]Then Boaz said, "The day you acquire the field from the hand of Naomi, you are also acquiring Ruth[a] the Moabite, the widow of the dead man, to maintain the dead man's name on his inheritance." [6]At this, the next-of-kin[b] said, "I cannot redeem it for myself without damaging my own inheritance. Take my right of redemption yourself, for I cannot redeem it."

7 Now this was the custom in former times in Israel concerning redeeming and exchanging: to confirm a transaction, the one took off a sandal and gave it to the other; this was the manner of attesting in Israel. [8]So when the next-of-kin[b] said to Boaz, "Acquire it for yourself," he took off his sandal. [9]Then Boaz said to the elders and all the people, "Today you are witnesses that I have acquired from the hand of Naomi all that belonged to Elimelech and all that belonged to Chilion and Mahlon. [10]I have also acquired Ruth the Moabite, the wife of Mahlon, to be my wife, to maintain the dead man's name on his inheritance, in order that the name of the dead may not be cut off from his kindred and from the gate of his native place; today you are witnesses." [11]Then all the people who were at the gate, along with the elders, said, "We are witnesses. May the LORD make the woman who is coming into your house like Rachel and Leah, who together built up the house of Israel. May you produce children in Ephrathah and bestow a name in Bethlehem; [12]and, through the children that the LORD will give you by this young woman, may your house be like the house of Perez, whom Tamar bore to Judah."

The Genealogy of David

13 So Boaz took Ruth and she became his wife. When they came together, the LORD made her conceive, and she bore a son. [14]Then the women said to Naomi, "Blessed be the LORD, who has not left you this day without next-of-kin;[b] and may his name be renowned in Israel! [15]He shall be to you a restorer of life and a nourisher of your old age; for your daughter-in-law who loves you, who is more to you than seven sons, has borne him." [16]Then Naomi took the child and laid him in her bosom, and became his nurse. [17]The women of the neighborhood gave him a name, saying, "A son has been born to Naomi." They named him Obed; he became the father of Jesse, the father of David.

18 Now these are the descendants of Perez: Perez became the father of Hezron, [19]Hezron of Ram, Ram of Amminadab, [20]Amminadab of Nahshon, Nahshon of Salmon, [21]Salmon of Boaz, Boaz of Obed, [22]Obed of Jesse, and Jesse of David.

LIVE IT!

Caring for Foreigners and the Poor · Ruth 4:14–17

The story of Ruth was a challenge to the Israelites' tendency to distrust foreigners. It's also an example of how service to the poor was an integral part of Israel's society. In the story, Boaz, a wealthy and respected man, both provides for the poor and looks beyond ethnic differences to marry Ruth. Boaz's goal is to do God's will. His marriage to Ruth ensures that Naomi's land is redeemed and that she will have descendants to claim the land. Ruth's faithfulness and Boaz's integrity serve to gradually restore Naomi's hope in God's care.

In the New Testament, it becomes even clearer that God makes no distinctions between people of different races and cultures (Romans 10:11-13). And Jesus teaches that caring for the poor is one of the requirements of God's people (Matthew 19:16-23).

- How do you treat people of different races?
- Are you serving poor people? How can you?
- Pray for the courage to follow Ruth and Boaz's example and to be an instrument of faith, hope, and justice for people in need.

a OL Vg: Heb *from the hand of Naomi and from Ruth* b Or *one with the right to redeem*

1 Samuel

The role of government is one of the basic ongoing tensions in many countries. Some believe the government interferes too much in their lives; others feel the government should do more. Some leaders are corrupt; others are good-hearted. Issues like health care and the environment often become the focus of argument and tension. The book of 1 Samuel reflects a similar tension in Israel as the days of the judges come to an end and the first kings make their appearance. This period of Israelite history is filled with mighty struggles and colorful personalities, including a king who gradually loses his sanity and a shining hero who replaces him.

IN DEPTH

This book is named after Samuel, the last of the judges and a reluctant kingmaker. Samuel was a prophet anointed to speak God's words to the nation. God worked through the prophet's words to remind the people of Israel to be faithful to the terms of the covenant. In 1 Samuel, the rule of the judges gradually gives way to the rule of the kings, with obvious gains and obvious losses for the people.

When kings began to rule Israel in place of judges and prophets, the people gained a more structured way of life and developed a greater national identity. These changes also made them stronger in facing threats from other nations. At the same time, the people lost a great deal of personal freedom and independence. They were taxed and even forced into labor to support the king's government and building plans. Echoes of the debate between the charismatic style of judges and the structured rule of kings can be found throughout 1 Samuel. (See "Study It: Different Opinions," near 1 Samuel 8–11.)

Yet the people wanted a king, so Samuel anointed Saul to be the first king to rule the whole nation. Israel's kings were understood as being chosen by God and as being responsible for God's interests. First Samuel clearly emphasizes that the success of kings depends on their obedience to God's law and reminds us that final authority in human affairs rests in God alone. Human systems are never perfect; they must constantly be reviewed and renewed.

QUICK FACTS

- **Dates Covered:** From approximately 1080 to 1040 B.C.
- **Author:** An unknown author writing around 600 to 500 B.C., probably using ancient court records and hero stories
- **Themes:** Israel's tension between the need for a king and the people's reliance on God; the benefits of following God's ways in our lives as well as the consequences of rejecting them
- **Noteworthy:** Samuel was originally one book, but was made into 1 Samuel and 2 Samuel when translated from Hebrew into Greek.

AT A GLANCE

- **1 Samuel 1–7** Stories of Eli and Samuel
- **1 Samuel 8–15** The beginning of Saul's kingship
- **1 Samuel 16–31** Stories of King Saul and the young David

Samuel's Birth and Dedication

1 There was a certain man of Ramathaim, a Zuphite[a] from the hill country of Ephraim, whose name was Elkanah son of Jeroham son of Elihu son of Tohu son of Zuph, an Ephraimite. [2]He had two wives; the name of the one was Hannah, and the name of the other Peninnah. Peninnah had children, but Hannah had no children.

3 Now this man used to go up year by year from his town to worship and to sacrifice to the LORD of hosts at Shiloh, where the two sons of Eli, Hophni and Phinehas, were priests of the LORD. [4]On the day when Elkanah sacrificed, he would give portions to his wife Peninnah and to all her sons and daughters; [5]but to Hannah he gave a double portion,[b] because he loved her, though the LORD had closed her womb. [6]Her rival used to provoke her severely, to irritate her, because the LORD had closed her womb. [7]So it went on year by year; as often as she went up to the house of the LORD, she used to provoke her. Therefore Hannah wept and would not eat. [8]Her husband Elkanah said to her, "Hannah, why do you weep? Why do you not eat? Why is your heart sad? Am I not more to you than ten sons?"

9 After they had eaten and drunk at Shiloh, Hannah rose and presented herself before the LORD.[c] Now Eli the priest was sitting on the seat beside the doorpost of the temple of the LORD. [10]She was deeply distressed and prayed to the LORD, and wept bitterly. [11]She made this vow: "O LORD of hosts, if only you will look on the misery of your servant, and remember me, and not forget your servant, but will give to your servant a male child, then I will set him before you as a nazirite[d] until the day of his death. He shall drink neither wine nor intoxicants,[e] and no razor shall touch his head."

12 As she continued praying before the LORD, Eli observed her mouth. [13]Hannah was praying silently; only her lips moved, but her voice was not heard; therefore Eli thought she was drunk. [14]So Eli said to her, "How long will you make a drunken spectacle of yourself? Put away your wine." [15]But Hannah answered, "No, my lord, I am a woman deeply troubled; I have drunk neither wine nor strong drink, but I have been pouring out my soul before the LORD. [16]Do not regard your servant as a worthless woman, for I have been speaking out of my great anxiety and vexation all this time." [17]Then Eli answered, "Go in peace; the God of Israel grant the petition you have made to him." [18]And she said, "Let your servant find favor in your sight." Then the woman went to her quarters,[f] ate and drank with her husband,[g] and her countenance was sad no longer.[h]

19 They rose early in the morning and worshiped before the LORD; then they went back to their house at Ramah. Elkanah knew his wife Hannah, and the LORD remembered her. [20]In due time Hannah conceived and bore a son. She named him Samuel, for she said, "I have asked him of the LORD."

21 The man Elkanah and all his household went up to offer to the LORD the yearly sacrifice, and to pay his vow. [22]But Hannah did not go up, for she said to her husband, "As soon as the child is weaned, I will bring him, that he may appear in the presence of the LORD, and remain there forever; I will offer him as a nazirite[d] for all time."[i] [23]Her husband Elkanah said to her, "Do what seems best to you, wait until you have weaned him; only—may the LORD establish his word."[j] So the woman remained and nursed her son, until she weaned him. [24]When she had weaned him, she took him up with her, along with a three-year-old bull,[k] an ephah of flour, and a skin of wine. She brought him to the house of the LORD at Shiloh; and the child was young. [25]Then they slaughtered the bull, and they brought the child to Eli. [26]And she said, "Oh, my lord! As you live, my lord, I am the woman who was standing here in your presence, praying to the LORD. [27]For this child I prayed; and the LORD has granted me the petition that I made to him. [28]Therefore I have lent him to the LORD; as long as he lives, he is given to the LORD."

She left him there for[l] the LORD.

Hannah's Prayer

2 Hannah prayed and said,
"My heart exults in the LORD;
    my strength is exalted in my God.[m]
My mouth derides my enemies,
    because I rejoice in my[n] victory.

2 "There is no Holy One like the LORD,
    no one besides you;
    there is no Rock like our God.
3 Talk no more so very proudly,
    let not arrogance come from your mouth;
for the LORD is a God of knowledge,
    and by him actions are weighed.
4 The bows of the mighty are broken,

---

a Compare Gk and 1 Chr 6.35-36: Heb *Ramathaim-zophim*   **b** Syr: Meaning of Heb uncertain   **c** Gk: Heb lacks *and presented herself before the LORD*   **d** That is *one separated* or *one consecrated*   **e** Cn Compare Gk Q Ms 1.22: MT *then I will give him to the LORD all the days of his life*   **f** Gk: Heb *went her way*   **g** Gk: Heb lacks *and drank with her husband*   **h** Gk: Meaning of Heb uncertain   **i** Cn Compare Q Ms: MT lacks *I will offer him as a nazirite for all time*   **j** MT: Q Ms Gk Compare Syr *that which goes out of your mouth*   **k** Q Ms Gk Syr: MT *three bulls*   **l** Gk (Compare Q Ms) and Gk at 2.11: MT *And he* (that is, Elkanah) *worshiped there before*   **m** Gk: Heb *the LORD*   **n** Q Ms: MT *your*

Strong Women Pray · 1 Samuel 2:1–10

Compare Hannah's prayer to Mary's prayer in **Luke 1:46–55**. Notice the joy, the confident faith in God's way, and the understanding that God will raise up those who are hungry, poor, and in need. Notice also how God will deal with the proud, the powerful, and the rich, especially in Mary's prayer. These women saw life from a larger perspective and recognized God's plans at work in the world.

- What strong and holy women in your life keep you in their prayers?
- Take some time now to pray for each of them.

but the feeble gird on strength.

5 Those who were full have hired themselves out
 for bread,
 but those who were hungry are fat with spoil.
 The barren has borne seven,
 but she who has many children is forlorn.

6 The LORD kills and brings to life;
 he brings down to Sheol and raises up.

7 The LORD makes poor and makes rich;
 he brings low, he also exalts.

8 He raises up the poor from the dust;
 he lifts the needy from the ash heap,
 to make them sit with princes
 and inherit a seat of honor.*a*
 For the pillars of the earth are the LORD's,
 and on them he has set the world.

9 "He will guard the feet of his faithful ones,
 but the wicked shall be cut off in darkness;
 for not by might does one prevail.

10 The LORD! His adversaries shall be shattered;
 the Most High*b* will thunder in heaven.
 The LORD will judge the ends of the earth;
 he will give strength to his king,
 and exalt the power of his anointed."

Eli's Wicked Sons

11 Then Elkanah went home to Ramah, while the boy remained to minister to the LORD, in the presence of the priest Eli.

12 Now the sons of Eli were scoundrels; they had no regard for the LORD 13 or for the duties of the priests to the people. When anyone offered sacrifice, the priest's servant would come, while the meat was boiling, with a three-pronged fork in his hand, 14 and he would thrust it into the pan, or kettle, or caldron, or pot; all that the fork brought up the priest would take for himself.*c* This is what they did at Shiloh to

all the Israelites who came there. 15 Moreover, before the fat was burned, the priest's servant would come and say to the one who was sacrificing, "Give meat for the priest to roast; for he will not accept boiled meat from you, but only raw." 16 And if the man said to him, "Let them burn the fat first, and then take whatever you wish," he would say, "No, you must give it now; if not, I will take it by force." 17 Thus the sin of the young men was very great in the sight of the LORD; for they treated the offerings of the LORD with contempt.

The Child Samuel at Shiloh

18 Samuel was ministering before the LORD, a boy wearing a linen ephod. 19 His mother used to make for him a little robe and take it to him each year, when she went up with her husband to offer the yearly sacrifice. 20 Then Eli would bless Elkanah and his wife, and say, "May the LORD repay*d* you with children by this woman for the gift that she made to*e* the LORD"; and then they would return to their home.

21 And*f* the LORD took note of Hannah; she conceived and bore three sons and two daughters. And the boy Samuel grew up in the presence of the LORD.

Prophecy against Eli's Household

22 Now Eli was very old. He heard all that his sons were doing to all Israel, and how they lay with the women who served at the entrance to the tent of meeting. 23 He said to them, "Why do you do such things? For I hear of your evil dealings from all these people. 24 No, my sons; it is not a good report that I hear the people of the LORD spreading abroad. 25 If one person sins against another, someone can intercede for the sinner with the LORD;*g* but if someone sins against the LORD, who can make intercession?"

a Gk (Compare Q Ms) adds *He grants the vow of the one who vows, and blesses the years of the just* *b* Cn Heb *against him he* *c* Gk Syr Vg: Heb *with it* *d* Q Ms Gk: MT *give* *e* Q Ms Gk: MT *for the petition that she asked of* *f* Q Ms Gk: MT *When* *g* Gk Compare Q Ms: MT *another, God will mediate for him*

But they would not listen to the voice of their father; for it was the will of the LORD to kill them.

26 Now the boy Samuel continued to grow both in stature and in favor with the LORD and with the people.

27 A man of God came to Eli and said to him, "Thus the LORD has said, 'I revealed[a] myself to the family of your ancestor in Egypt when they were slaves[b] to the house of Pharaoh. [28]I chose him out of all the tribes of Israel to be my priest, to go up to my altar, to offer incense, to wear an ephod before me; and I gave to the family of your ancestor all my offerings by fire from the people of Israel. [29]Why then look with greedy eye[c] at my sacrifices and my offerings that I commanded, and honor your sons more than me by fattening yourselves on the choicest parts of every offering of my people Israel?' [30]Therefore the LORD the God of Israel declares: 'I promised that your family and the family of your ancestor should go in and out before me forever'; but now the LORD declares: 'Far be it from me; for those who honor me I will honor, and those who despise me shall be treated with contempt. [31]See, a time is coming when I will cut off your strength and the strength of your ancestor's family, so that no one in your family will live to old age. [32]Then in distress you will look with greedy eye[d] on all the prosperity that shall be bestowed upon Israel; and no one in your family shall ever live to old age. [33]The only one of you whom I shall not cut off from my altar shall be spared to weep out his[e] eyes and grieve his[f] heart; all the members of your household shall die by the sword.[g] [34]The fate of your two sons, Hophni and Phinehas, shall be the sign to you—both of them shall die on the same day. [35]I will raise up for myself a faithful priest, who shall do according to what is in my heart and in my mind. I will build him a sure house, and he shall go in and out before my anointed one forever. [36]Everyone who is left in your family shall come to implore him for a piece of silver or a loaf of bread, and shall say, Please put me in one of the priest's places, that I may eat a morsel of bread.' "

3 Samuel's Calling and Prophetic Activity

Now the boy Samuel was ministering to the LORD under Eli. The word of the LORD was rare in those days; visions were not widespread.

2 At that time Eli, whose eyesight had begun to grow dim so that he could not see, was lying down in his room; [3]the lamp of God had not yet gone out, and Samuel was lying down in the temple of the LORD, where the ark of God was. [4]Then the LORD called, "Samuel! Samuel!"[h] and he said, "Here I am!" [5]and ran to Eli, and said, "Here I am, for you called me." But he said, "I did not call; lie down again." So he went and lay down. [6]The LORD called again, "Samuel!" Samuel got up and went to Eli, and said, "Here I am, for you called me." But he said, "I did not call, my son; lie down again." [7]Now Samuel did not yet know the LORD, and the word of the LORD had not yet been revealed to him. [8]The LORD called Samuel again, a third time. And he got up and went to Eli, and said, "Here I am, for you called me." Then Eli perceived that the LORD was calling the boy. [9]Therefore Eli said to Samuel, "Go, lie down; and if he calls you, you shall say, 'Speak, LORD, for your servant is listening.' " So Samuel went and lay down in his place.

10 Now the LORD came and stood there, calling as before, "Samuel! Samuel!" And Samuel said,

PRAY IT!

Learning How to Pray
1 Samuel 3:1–19

Eli taught Samuel to listen to God's voice with a simple sentence: "Speak, LORD, for your servant is listening" (1 Samuel 3:9). What would it look like if we made that our prayer?

"Speak, LORD . . ." This is an invitation. It shows openness and readiness. It shows your recognition of God: "You are the Almighty, and I am ready to hear what you have to say."

". . . for your servant . . ." This shows humility. It's a recognition of your place as God's servant: "It's my desire to do what you want. My life's purpose is to serve you."

". . . is listening." This demonstrates your response: "I am not going to ignore you. I am not going to daydream or just pretend to pay attention. I will let your message become part of me."

---

a Gk Tg Syr: Heb *Did I reveal*   b Q Ms Gk: MT lacks *slaves*   c Q Ms Gk: MT *then kick*   d Q Ms Gk: MT *will kick*   e Q Ms Gk: MT *your*   f Q Ms Gk: Heb *your*   g Q Ms See Gk: MT *die like mortals*   h Q Ms Gk See 3.10: MT *the LORD called Samuel*

"Speak, for your servant is listening." [11]Then the LORD said to Samuel, "See, I am about to do something in Israel that will make both ears of anyone who hears of it tingle. [12]On that day I will fulfill against Eli all that I have spoken concerning his house, from beginning to end. [13]For I have told him that I am about to punish his house forever, for the iniquity that he knew, because his sons were blaspheming God,[a] and he did not restrain them. [14]Therefore I swear to the house of Eli that the iniquity of Eli's house shall not be expiated by sacrifice or offering forever."

15 Samuel lay there until morning; then he opened the doors of the house of the LORD. Samuel was afraid to tell the vision to Eli. [16]But Eli called Samuel and said, "Samuel, my son." He said, "Here I am." [17]Eli said, "What was it that he told you? Do not hide it from me. May God do so to you and more also, if you hide anything from me of all that he told you." [18]So Samuel told him everything and hid nothing from him. Then he said, "It is the LORD; let him do what seems good to him."

19 As Samuel grew up, the LORD was with him and let none of his words fall to the ground. [20]And all Israel from Dan to Beer-sheba knew that Samuel was a trustworthy prophet of the LORD. [21]The LORD continued to appear at Shiloh, for the LORD revealed himself to Samuel at Shiloh by the word of the LORD.

 **4** [1]And the word of Samuel came to all Israel.

The Ark of God Captured

In those days the Philistines mustered for war against Israel,[b] and Israel went out to battle against them;[c] they encamped at Ebenezer, and the Philistines encamped at Aphek. [2]The Philistines drew up in line against Israel, and when the battle was joined,[d] Israel was defeated by the Philistines, who killed about four thousand men on the field of battle. [3]When the troops came to the camp, the elders of Israel said, "Why has the LORD put us to rout today before the Philistines? Let us bring the ark of the covenant of the LORD here from Shiloh, so that he may come among us and save us from the power of our enemies." [4]So the people sent to Shiloh, and brought from there the ark of the covenant of the LORD of hosts, who is enthroned on the cherubim. The two sons of Eli, Hophni and Phinehas, were there with the ark of the covenant of God.

5 When the ark of the covenant of the LORD came into the camp, all Israel gave a mighty shout, so that the earth resounded. [6]When the Philistines heard the noise of the shouting, they said, "What does this great shouting in the camp of the Hebrews mean?" When they learned that the ark of the LORD had come to the camp, [7]the Philistines were afraid; for they said, "Gods have[e] come into the camp." They also said, "Woe to us! For nothing like this has happened before. [8]Woe to us! Who can deliver us from the power of these mighty gods? These are the gods who struck the Egyptians with every sort of plague in the wilderness. [9]Take courage, and be men, O Philistines, in order not to become slaves to the Hebrews as they have been to you; be men and fight."

10 So the Philistines fought; Israel was defeated, and they fled, everyone to his home. There was a very great slaughter, for there fell of Israel thirty thousand foot soldiers. [11]The ark of God was captured; and the two sons of Eli, Hophni and Phinehas, died.

Death of Eli

12 A man of Benjamin ran from the battle line, and came to Shiloh the same day, with his clothes torn and with earth upon his head. [13]When he arrived, Eli was sitting upon his seat by the road watching, for his heart trembled for the ark of God. When the man came into the city and told the news, all the city cried out. [14]When Eli heard the sound of the outcry, he said, "What is this uproar?" Then the man came quickly and told Eli. [15]Now Eli was ninety-eight years old and his eyes were set, so that he could not see. [16]The man said to Eli, "I have just come from the battle; I fled from the battle today." He said, "How did it go, my son?" [17]The messenger replied, "Israel has fled before the Philistines, and there has also been a great slaughter among the troops; your two sons also, Hophni and Phinehas, are dead, and the ark of God has been captured." [18]When he mentioned the ark of God, Eli[f] fell over backward from his seat by the side of the gate; and his neck was broken and he died, for he was an old man, and heavy. He had judged Israel forty years.

19 Now his daughter-in-law, the wife of Phinehas, was pregnant, about to give birth. When she heard the news that the ark of God was captured, and that her father-in-law and her husband were dead, she bowed and gave birth; for her labor pains overwhelmed her. [20]As she was about to die, the women attending her said to her, "Do not be afraid, for you

---

a Another reading is *for themselves* **b** Gk: Heb lacks *In those days the Philistines mustered for war against Israel* **c** Gk: Heb *against the Philistines*
d Meaning of Heb uncertain **e** Or *A god has* **f** Heb *he*

have borne a son." But she did not answer or give heed. [21] She named the child Ichabod, meaning, "The glory has departed from Israel," because the ark of God had been captured and because of her father-in-law and her husband. [22] She said, "The glory has departed from Israel, for the ark of God has been captured."

The Philistines and the Ark

5 When the Philistines captured the ark of God, they brought it from Ebenezer to Ashdod; [2] then the Philistines took the ark of God and brought it into the house of Dagon and placed it beside Dagon. [3] When the people of Ashdod rose early the next day, there was Dagon, fallen on his face to the ground before the ark of the LORD. So they took Dagon and put him back in his place. [4] But when they rose early on the next morning, Dagon had fallen on his face to the ground before the ark of the LORD, and the head of Dagon and both his hands were lying cut off upon the threshold; only the trunk of[a] Dagon was left to him. [5] This is why the priests of Dagon and all who enter the house of Dagon do not step on the threshold of Dagon in Ashdod to this day.

6 The hand of the LORD was heavy upon the people of Ashdod, and he terrified and struck them with tumors, both in Ashdod and in its territory. [7] And when the inhabitants of Ashdod saw how things were, they said, "The ark of the God of Israel must not remain with us; for his hand is heavy on us and on our god Dagon." [8] So they sent and gathered together all the lords of the Philistines, and said, "What shall we do with the ark of the God of Israel?" The inhabitants of Gath replied, "Let the ark of God be moved on to us."[b] So they moved the ark of the God of Israel to Gath.[c] [9] But after they had brought it to Gath,[d] the hand of the LORD was against the city, causing a very great panic; he struck the inhabitants of the city, both young and old, so that tumors broke out on them. [10] So they sent the ark of the God of Israel[e] to Ekron. But when the ark of God came to Ekron, the people of Ekron cried out, "Why[f] have they brought around to us[g] the ark of the God of Israel to kill us[g] and our[h] people?" [11] They sent therefore and gathered together all the lords of the Philistines, and said, "Send away the ark of the God of Israel, and let it return to its own place, that it may not kill us and our people." For there was a deathly panic[i] throughout the whole city. The

hand of God was very heavy there; [12] those who did not die were stricken with tumors, and the cry of the city went up to heaven.

The Ark Returned to Israel

6 The ark of the LORD was in the country of the Philistines seven months. [2] Then the Philistines called for the priests and the diviners and said, "What shall we do with the ark of the LORD? Tell us what we should send with it to its place." [3] They said, "If you send away the ark of the God of Israel, do not send it empty, but by all means return him a guilt offering. Then you will be healed and will be ransomed;[j] will not his hand then turn from you?" [4] And they said, "What is the guilt offering that we shall return to him?" They answered, "Five gold tumors and five gold mice, according to the number of the lords of the Philistines; for the same plague was upon all of you and upon your lords. [5] So you must make images of your tumors and images of your mice that ravage the land, and give glory to the God of Israel; perhaps he will lighten his hand on you and your gods and your land. [6] Why should you harden your hearts as the Egyptians and Pharaoh hardened their hearts? After he had made fools of them, did they not let the people go, and they departed? [7] Now then, get ready a new cart and two milch cows that have never borne a yoke, and yoke the cows to the cart, but take their calves home, away from them. [8] Take the ark of the LORD and place it on the cart, and put in a box at its side the figures of gold, which you are returning to him as a guilt offering. Then send it off, and let it go its way. [9] And watch; if it goes up on the way to its own land, to Beth-shemesh, then it is he who has done us this great harm; but if not, then we shall know that it is not his hand that struck us; it happened to us by chance."

10 The men did so; they took two milch cows and yoked them to the cart, and shut up their calves at home. [11] They put the ark of the LORD on the cart, and the box with the gold mice and the images of their tumors. [12] The cows went straight in the direction of Beth-shemesh along one highway, lowing as they went; they turned neither to the right nor to the left, and the lords of the Philistines went after them as far as the border of Beth-shemesh.

13 Now the people of Beth-shemesh were reaping their wheat harvest in the valley. When they looked up and saw the ark, they went with rejoicing to meet

---

a Heb lacks *the trunk of*   **b** Gk Compare Q Ms: MT *They answered, "Let the ark of the God of Israel be brought around to Gath."*   **c** Gk: Heb lacks *to Gath*
d Q Ms: MT lacks *to Gath*   **e** Q Ms Gk: MT lacks *of Israel*   **f** Q Ms Gk: MT lacks *Why*   **g** Heb *me*   **h** Heb *my*   **i** Q Ms reads *a panic from the LORD*
j Q Ms Gk: MT *and it will be known to you*

it.*a* [14]The cart came into the field of Joshua of Beth-shemesh, and stopped there. A large stone was there; so they split up the wood of the cart and offered the cows as a burnt offering to the LORD. [15]The Levites took down the ark of the LORD and the box that was beside it, in which were the gold objects, and set them upon the large stone. Then the people of Beth-shemesh offered burnt offerings and presented sacrifices on that day to the LORD. [16]When the five lords of the Philistines saw it, they returned that day to Ekron.

17 These are the gold tumors, which the Philistines returned as a guilt offering to the LORD: one for Ashdod, one for Gaza, one for Ashkelon, one for Gath, one for Ekron; [18]also the gold mice, according to the number of all the cities of the Philistines belonging to the five lords, both fortified cities and unwalled villages. The great stone, beside which they set down the ark of the LORD, is a witness to this day in the field of Joshua of Beth-shemesh.

The Ark at Kiriath-jearim

19 The descendants of Jeconiah did not rejoice with the people of Beth-shemesh when they greeted*b* the ark of the LORD; and he killed seventy men of them.*c* The people mourned because the LORD had made a great slaughter among the people. [20]Then the people of Beth-shemesh said, "Who is able to stand before the LORD, this holy God? To whom shall he go so that we may be rid of him?" [21]So they sent messengers to the inhabitants of Kiriath-jearim, saying, "The Philistines have returned the ark of the LORD. Come down and take it up to you." [1]And the people of Kiriath-jearim came and took up the ark of the LORD, and brought it to the house of Abinadab on the hill. They consecrated his son, Eleazar, to have charge of the ark of the LORD.

7

2 From the day that the ark was lodged at Kiriath-jearim, a long time passed, some twenty years, and all the house of Israel lamented*d* after the LORD.

Samuel as Judge

3 Then Samuel said to all the house of Israel, "If you are returning to the LORD with all your heart, then put away the foreign gods and the Astartes from among you. Direct your heart to the LORD, and serve him only, and he will deliver you out of the hand of the Philistines." [4]So Israel put away the Baals and the Astartes, and they served the LORD only.

5 Then Samuel said, "Gather all Israel at Mizpah, and I will pray to the LORD for you." [6]So they gathered at Mizpah, and drew water and poured it out before the LORD. They fasted that day, and said, "We have sinned against the LORD." And Samuel judged the people of Israel at Mizpah.

7 When the Philistines heard that the people of Israel had gathered at Mizpah, the lords of the Philistines went up against Israel. And when the people of Israel heard of it they were afraid of the Philistines. [8]The people of Israel said to Samuel, "Do not cease to cry out to the LORD our God for us, and pray that he may save us from the hand of the Philistines." [9]So Samuel took a sucking lamb and offered it as a whole burnt offering to the LORD; Samuel cried out to the LORD for Israel, and the LORD answered him. [10]As Samuel was offering up the burnt offering, the Philistines drew near to attack Israel; but the LORD thundered with a mighty voice that day against the Philistines and threw them into confusion; and they were routed before Israel. [11]And the men of Israel went out of Mizpah and pursued the Philistines, and struck them down as far as beyond Beth-car.

12 Then Samuel took a stone and set it up between Mizpah and Jeshanah,*e* and named it Ebenezer;*f* for he said, "Thus far the LORD has helped us." [13]So the Philistines were subdued and did not again enter the territory of Israel; the hand of the LORD was against the Philistines all the days of Samuel. [14]The towns that the Philistines had taken from Israel were restored to Israel, from Ekron to Gath; and Israel recovered their territory from the hand of the Philistines. There was peace also between Israel and the Amorites.

15 Samuel judged Israel all the days of his life. [16]He went on a circuit year by year to Bethel, Gilgal, and Mizpah; and he judged Israel in all these places. [17]Then he would come back to Ramah, for his home was there; he administered justice there to Israel, and built there an altar to the LORD.

Israel Demands a King

8

When Samuel became old, he made his sons judges over Israel. [2]The name of his firstborn son was Joel, and the name of his second, Abijah; they were judges in Beer-sheba. [3]Yet his

---

a Gk: Heb *rejoiced to see it*   *b* Gk: Heb *And he killed some of the people of Beth-shemesh, because they looked into*   *c* Heb *killed seventy men, fifty thousand men*   *d* Meaning of Heb uncertain   *e* Gk Syr: Heb *Shen*   *f* That is *Stone of Help*

sons did not follow in his ways, but turned aside after gain; they took bribes and perverted justice.

4 Then all the elders of Israel gathered together and came to Samuel at Ramah, [5]and said to him, "You are old and your sons do not follow in your ways; appoint for us, then, a king to govern us, like other nations." [6]But the thing displeased Samuel when they said, "Give us a king to govern us." Samuel prayed to the LORD, [7]and the LORD said to Samuel, "Listen to the voice of the people in all that they say to you; for they have not rejected you, but they have rejected me from being king over them. [8]Just as they have done to me,[a] from the day I brought them up out of Egypt to this day, forsaking me and serving other gods, so also they are doing to you. [9]Now then, listen to their voice; only—you shall solemnly warn them, and show them the ways of the king who shall reign over them."

10 So Samuel reported all the words of the LORD to the people who were asking him for a king. [11]He said, "These will be the ways of the king who will reign over you: he will take your sons and appoint them to his chariots and to be his horsemen, and to run before his chariots; [12]and he will appoint for himself commanders of thousands and commanders of fifties, and some to plow his ground and to reap his harvest, and to make his implements of war and the equipment of his chariots. [13]He will take your daughters to be perfumers and cooks and bakers. [14]He will take the best of your fields and vineyards and olive orchards and give them to his courtiers. [15]He will take one-tenth of your grain and of your vineyards and give it to his officers and his courtiers. [16]He will take your male and female slaves, and the best of your cattle[b] and donkeys, and put them to his work. [17]He will take one-tenth of your flocks, and you shall be his slaves. [18]And in that day you will cry out because of your king, whom you have chosen for yourselves; but the LORD will not answer you in that day."

Israel's Request for a King Granted

19 But the people refused to listen to the voice of Samuel; they said, "No! but we are determined to have a king over us, [20]so that we also may be like other nations, and that our king may govern us and go out before us and fight our battles." [21]When Samuel had heard all the words of the people, he repeated them in the ears of the LORD. [22]The LORD said to Samuel, "Listen to their voice and set a king over them." Samuel then said to the people of Israel, "Each of you return home."

9

Saul Chosen to Be King

There was a man of Benjamin whose name was Kish son of Abiel son of Zeror son of Becorath son of Aphiah, a Benjaminite, a man of wealth. [2]He had a son whose name was Saul, a handsome young man. There was not a man among the people of Israel more handsome than he; he stood head and shoulders above everyone else.

3 Now the donkeys of Kish, Saul's father, had strayed. So Kish said to his son Saul, "Take one of the boys with you; go and look for the donkeys." [4]He passed through the hill country of Ephraim and passed through the land of Shalishah, but they did not find them. And they passed through the land of Shaalim, but they were not there. Then he passed through the land of Benjamin, but they did not find them.

5 When they came to the land of Zuph, Saul said to the boy who was with him, "Let us turn back, or my father will stop worrying about the donkeys and worry about us." [6]But he said to him, "There is a man of God in this town; he is a man held in honor. Whatever he says always comes true. Let us go there now; perhaps he will tell us about the journey on which we have set out." [7]Then Saul replied to the boy, "But if we go, what can we bring the man? For the bread in our sacks is gone, and there is no present to bring to the man of God. What have we?" [8]The boy answered Saul again, "Here, I have with me a quarter shekel of silver; I will give it to the man of God, to tell us our way." [9](Formerly in Israel, anyone who went to inquire of God would say, "Come, let us go to the seer"; for the one who is now called a prophet was formerly called a seer.) [10]Saul said to the boy, "Good; come, let us go." So they went to the town where the man of God was.

11 As they went up the hill to the town, they met some girls coming out to draw water, and said to them, "Is the seer here?" [12]They answered, "Yes, there he is just ahead of you. Hurry; he has come just now to the town, because the people have a sacrifice today at the shrine. [13]As soon as you enter the town, you will find him, before he goes up to the shrine to eat. For the people will not eat until he comes, since he must bless the sacrifice; afterward those eat who are invited. Now go up, for you will meet him immediately." [14]So they went up to

a Gk: Heb lacks *to me*   b Gk: Heb *young men*

the town. As they were entering the town, they saw Samuel coming out toward them on his way up to the shrine.

15 Now the day before Saul came, the LORD had revealed to Samuel: ¹⁶"Tomorrow about this time I will send to you a man from the land of Benjamin, and you shall anoint him to be ruler over my people Israel. He shall save my people from the hand of the Philistines; for I have seen the suffering of[a] my people, because their outcry has come to me." ¹⁷When Samuel saw Saul, the LORD told him, "Here is the man of whom I spoke to you. He it is who shall rule over my people." ¹⁸Then Saul approached Samuel inside the gate, and said, "Tell me, please, where is the house of the seer?" ¹⁹Samuel answered Saul, "I am the seer; go up before me to the shrine, for today you shall eat with me, and in the morning I will let you go and will tell you all that is on your mind. ²⁰As for your donkeys that were lost three days ago, give no further thought to them, for they have been found. And on whom is all Israel's desire fixed, if not on you and on all your ancestral house?" ²¹Saul answered, "I am only a Benjaminite, from the least of the tribes of Israel, and my family is the humblest of all the families of the tribe of Benjamin. Why then have you spoken to me in this way?"

22 Then Samuel took Saul and his servant-boy and brought them into the hall, and gave them a place at the head of those who had been invited, of whom there were about thirty. ²³And Samuel said to the cook, "Bring the portion I gave you, the one I asked you to put aside." ²⁴The cook took up the thigh and what went with it[b] and set them before Saul. Samuel said, "See, what was kept is set before you. Eat; for it is set[c] before you at the appointed time, so that you might eat with the guests."[d]

So Saul ate with Samuel that day. ²⁵When they came down from the shrine into the town, a bed was spread for Saul[e] on the roof, and he lay down to sleep.[f] ²⁶Then at the break of dawn[g] Samuel called to Saul upon the roof, "Get up, so that I may send you on your way." Saul got up, and both he and Samuel went out into the street.

Samuel Anoints Saul

27 As they were going down to the outskirts of the town, Samuel said to Saul, "Tell the boy to go on before us, and when he has passed on, stop here yourself for a while, that I may make known to you

STUDY IT!

Different Opinions 1 Samuel 8–11

The Bible often records more than one version of a story. Genesis has two stories of the Creation (Genesis 1:1–2:4a; 2:4b–25). And 1 Samuel has two different attitudes toward the request to have a king in Israel. Compare the anti-king passages of **1 Samuel 8:10–22; 10:17–19** with the pro-king passages of **1 Samuel 9:15–16; 11**. The difference of opinion most likely came from different parts of Israel. The Bible sometimes uses two versions of a story, called doublets, to allow consideration of both sides of an issue.

10 the word of God." ¹Samuel took a vial of oil and poured it on his head, and kissed him; he said, "The LORD has anointed you ruler over his people Israel. You shall reign over the people of the LORD and you will save them from the hand of their enemies all around. Now this shall be the sign to you that the LORD has anointed you ruler[h] over his heritage: ²When you depart from me today you will meet two men by Rachel's tomb in the territory of Benjamin at Zelzah; they will say to you, 'The donkeys that you went to seek are found, and now your father has stopped worrying about them and is worrying about you, saying: What shall I do about my son?' ³Then you shall go on from there further and come to the oak of Tabor; three men going up to God at Bethel will meet you there, one carrying three kids, another carrying three loaves of bread, and another carrying a skin of wine. ⁴They will greet you and give you two loaves of bread, which you shall accept from them. ⁵After that you shall come to Gibeath-elohim,[i] at the place where the Philistine garrison is; there, as you come to the town, you will meet a band of prophets coming down from the shrine with harp, tambourine, flute, and lyre playing in front of them; they will be in a prophetic frenzy. ⁶Then the spirit of the LORD will possess you, and you will be in a prophetic frenzy along with them and be turned into a different person. ⁷Now when

a Gk: Heb lacks the suffering of   b Meaning of Heb uncertain   c Q Ms Gk: MT it was kept   d Cn: Heb it was kept for you, saying, I have invited the people
e Gk: Heb and he spoke with Saul   f Gk: Heb lacks and he lay down to sleep   g Gk: Heb and they arose early and at break of dawn   h Gk: Heb lacks over his
people Israel. You shall . . . anointed you ruler   i Or the Hill of God

these signs meet you, do whatever you see fit to do, for God is with you. [8] And you shall go down to Gilgal ahead of me; then I will come down to you to present burnt offerings and offer sacrifices of well-being. Seven days you shall wait, until I come to you and show you what you shall do."

Saul Prophesies

9 As he turned away to leave Samuel, God gave him another heart; and all these signs were fulfilled that day. [10] When they were going from there[a] to Gibeah,[b] a band of prophets met him; and the spirit of God possessed him, and he fell into a prophetic frenzy along with them. [11] When all who knew him before saw how he prophesied with the prophets, the people said to one another, "What has come over the son of Kish? Is Saul also among the prophets?" [12] A man of the place answered, "And who is their father?" Therefore it became a proverb, "Is Saul also among the prophets?" [13] When his prophetic frenzy had ended, he went home.[c]

14 Saul's uncle said to him and to the boy, "Where did you go?" And he replied, "To seek the donkeys; and when we saw they were not to be found, we went to Samuel." [15] Saul's uncle said, "Tell me what Samuel said to you." [16] Saul said to his uncle, "He told us that the donkeys had been found." But about the matter of the kingship, of which Samuel had spoken, he did not tell him anything.

Saul Proclaimed King

17 Samuel summoned the people to the LORD at Mizpah [18] and said to them,[d] "Thus says the LORD, the God of Israel, 'I brought up Israel out of Egypt, and I rescued you from the hand of the Egyptians and from the hand of all the kingdoms that were oppressing you.' [19] But today you have rejected your God, who saves you from all your calamities and your distresses; and you have said, 'No! but set a king over us.' Now therefore present yourselves before the LORD by your tribes and by your clans."

20 Then Samuel brought all the tribes of Israel near, and the tribe of Benjamin was taken by lot. [21] He brought the tribe of Benjamin near by its families, and the family of the Matrites was taken by lot. Finally he brought the family of the Matrites near man by man,[e] and Saul the son of Kish was taken by lot. But when they sought him, he could not be found. [22] So they inquired again of the LORD, "Did the man come here?"[f] and the LORD said, "See, he has hidden

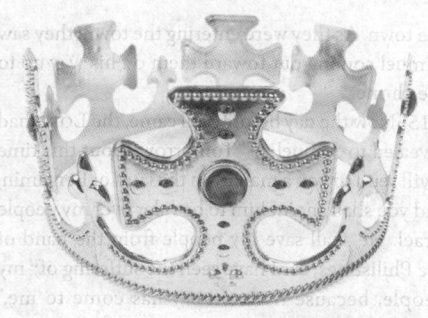

himself among the baggage." [23] Then they ran and brought him from there. When he took his stand among the people, he was head and shoulders taller than any of them. [24] Samuel said to all the people, "Do you see the one whom the LORD has chosen? There is no one like him among all the people." And all the people shouted, "Long live the king!"

25 Samuel told the people the rights and duties of the kingship; and he wrote them in a book and laid it up before the LORD. Then Samuel sent all the people back to their homes. [26] Saul also went to his home at Gibeah, and with him went warriors whose hearts God had touched. [27] But some worthless fellows said, "How can this man save us?" They despised him and brought him no present. But he held his peace.

Now Nahash, king of the Ammonites, had been grievously oppressing the Gadites and the Reubenites. He would gouge out the right eye of each of them and would not grant Israel a deliverer. No one was left of the Israelites across the Jordan whose right eye Nahash, king of the Ammonites, had not gouged out. But there were seven thousand men who had escaped from the Ammonites and had entered Jabesh-gilead.[g]

Saul Defeats the Ammonites

11 About a month later,[h] Nahash the Ammonite went up and besieged Jabesh-gilead; and all the men of Jabesh said to Nahash, "Make a treaty with us, and we will serve you." [2] But Nahash the Ammonite said to them, "On this condition I will make a treaty with you, namely that I gouge out everyone's right eye, and thus put disgrace upon all Israel." [3] The elders of Jabesh said to him, "Give us seven days' respite that we may send messengers through all the territory of Israel. Then, if there is no one to save us, we will give ourselves up to you." [4] When the messengers came to Gibeah of Saul, they

---

a Gk: Heb *they came there* b Or *the hill* c Cn: Heb *he came to the shrine* d Heb *to the people of Israel* e Gk: Heb lacks *Finally ... man by man*
f Gk: Heb *Is there yet a man to come here?* g Q Ms Compare Josephus, *Antiquities* VI.v.1 (68-71): MT lacks *Now Nahash ... entered Jabesh-gilead.* h Q Ms
Gk: MT lacks *About a month later*

reported the matter in the hearing of the people; and all the people wept aloud.

5 Now Saul was coming from the field behind the oxen; and Saul said, "What is the matter with the people, that they are weeping?" So they told him the message from the inhabitants of Jabesh. 6And the spirit of God came upon Saul in power when he heard these words, and his anger was greatly kindled. 7He took a yoke of oxen, and cut them in pieces and sent them throughout all the territory of Israel by messengers, saying, "Whoever does not come out after Saul and Samuel, so shall it be done to his oxen!" Then the dread of the LORD fell upon the people, and they came out as one. 8When he mustered them at Bezek, those from Israel were three hundred thousand, and those from Judah seventy*a* thousand. 9They said to the messengers who had come, "Thus shall you say to the inhabitants of Jabesh-gilead: 'Tomorrow, by the time the sun is hot, you shall have deliverance.' " When the messengers came and told the inhabitants of Jabesh, they rejoiced. 10So the inhabitants of Jabesh said, "Tomorrow we will give ourselves up to you, and you may do to us whatever seems good to you." 11The next day Saul put the people in three companies. At the morning watch they came into the camp and cut down the Ammonites until the heat of the day; and those who survived were scattered, so that no two of them were left together.

12 The people said to Samuel, "Who is it that said, 'Shall Saul reign over us?' Give them to us so that we may put them to death." 13But Saul said, "No one shall be put to death this day, for today the LORD has brought deliverance to Israel."

14 Samuel said to the people, "Come, let us go to Gilgal and there renew the kingship." 15So all the people went to Gilgal, and there they made Saul king before the LORD in Gilgal. There they sacrificed offerings of well-being before the LORD, and there Saul and all the Israelites rejoiced greatly.

12 Samuel's Farewell Address

Samuel said to all Israel, "I have listened to you in all that you have said to me, and have set a king over you. 2See, it is the king who leads you now; I am old and gray, but my sons are with you. I have led you from my youth until this day. 3Here I am; testify against me before the LORD and before his anointed. Whose ox have I taken? Or whose donkey have I taken? Or whom have I defrauded? Whom have I oppressed? Or from whose hand have I taken a bribe to blind my eyes with it? Testify against me*b* and I will restore it to you." 4They said, "You have not defrauded us or oppressed us or taken anything from the hand of anyone." 5He said to them, "The LORD is witness against you, and his anointed is witness this day, that you have not found anything in my hand." And they said, "He is witness."

6 Samuel said to the people, "The LORD is witness, who*c* appointed Moses and Aaron and brought your ancestors up out of the land of Egypt. 7Now therefore take your stand, so that I may enter into judgment with you before the LORD, and I will declare to you*d* all the saving deeds of the LORD that he performed for you and for your ancestors. 8When Jacob went into Egypt and the Egyptians oppressed them,*e* then your ancestors cried to the LORD and the LORD sent Moses and Aaron, who brought forth your ancestors out of Egypt, and settled them in this place. 9But they forgot the LORD their God; and he sold them into the hand of Sisera, commander of the army of King Jabin of*f* Hazor, and into the hand of the Philistines, and into the hand of the king of Moab; and they fought against them. 10Then they cried to the LORD, and said, 'We have sinned, because we have forsaken the LORD, and have served the Baals and the Astartes; but now rescue us out of the hand of our enemies, and we will serve you.' 11And the LORD sent Jerubbaal and Barak,*g* and Jephthah, and Samson,*h* and rescued you out of the hand of your enemies on every side; and you lived in safety. 12But when you saw that King Nahash of the Ammonites came against you, you said to me, 'No, but a king shall reign over us,' though the LORD your God was your king. 13See, here is the king whom you have chosen, for whom you have asked; see, the LORD has set a king over you. 14If you will fear the LORD and serve him and heed his voice and not rebel against the commandment of the LORD, and if both you and the king who reigns over you will follow the LORD your God, it will be well; 15but if you will not heed the voice of the LORD, but rebel against the commandment of the LORD, then the hand of the LORD will be against you and your king.*i* 16Now therefore take your stand and see this great thing that the LORD will do before your eyes. 17Is it not the wheat harvest today? I will call upon the LORD, that he may send thunder and rain; and you shall know and see that the wickedness that you have done in the sight of the LORD is great in demanding a king for yourselves."

---

a Q Ms Gk: MT *thirty*   b Gk: Heb lacks *Testify against me*   c Gk: Heb lacks *is witness, who*   d Gk: Heb lacks *and I will declare to you*   e Gk: Heb lacks *and the Egyptians oppressed them*   f Gk: Heb lacks *King Jabin of*   g Gk Syr: Heb *Bedan*   h Gk: Heb *Samuel*   i Gk: Heb *and your ancestors*

[18]So Samuel called upon the LORD, and the LORD sent thunder and rain that day; and all the people greatly feared the LORD and Samuel.

19 All the people said to Samuel, "Pray to the LORD your God for your servants, so that we may not die; for we have added to all our sins the evil of demanding a king for ourselves." [20]And Samuel said to the people, "Do not be afraid; you have done all this evil, yet do not turn aside from following the LORD, but serve the LORD with all your heart; [21]and do not turn aside after useless things that cannot profit or save, for they are useless. [22]For the LORD will not cast away his people, for his great name's sake, because it has pleased the LORD to make you a people for himself. [23]Moreover as for me, far be it from me that I should sin against the LORD by ceasing to pray for you; and I will instruct you in the good and the right way. [24]Only fear the LORD, and serve him faithfully with all your heart; for consider what great things he has done for you. [25]But if you still do wickedly, you shall be swept away, both you and your king."

Saul's Unlawful Sacrifice

13 Saul was . . .[a] years old when he began to reign; and he reigned . . . and two[b] years over Israel.

2 Saul chose three thousand out of Israel; two thousand were with Saul in Michmash and the hill country of Bethel, and a thousand were with Jonathan in Gibeah of Benjamin; the rest of the people he sent home to their tents. [3]Jonathan defeated the garrison of the Philistines that was at Geba; and the Philistines heard of it. And Saul blew the trumpet throughout all the land, saying, "Let the Hebrews hear!" [4]When all Israel heard that Saul had defeated the garrison of the Philistines, and also that Israel had become odious to the Philistines, the people were called out to join Saul at Gilgal.

5 The Philistines mustered to fight with Israel, thirty thousand chariots, and six thousand horsemen, and troops like the sand on the seashore in multitude; they came up and encamped at Michmash, to the east of Beth-aven. [6]When the Israelites saw that they were in distress (for the troops were hard pressed), the people hid themselves in caves and in holes and in rocks and in tombs and in cisterns. [7]Some Hebrews crossed the Jordan to the land of Gad and Gilead. Saul was still at Gilgal, and all the people followed him trembling.

8 He waited seven days, the time appointed by Samuel; but Samuel did not come to Gilgal, and the people began to slip away from Saul.[c] [9]So Saul said, "Bring the burnt offering here to me, and the offerings of well-being." And he offered the burnt offering. [10]As soon as he had finished offering the burnt offering, Samuel arrived; and Saul went out to meet him and salute him. [11]Samuel said, "What have you done?" Saul replied, "When I saw that the people were slipping away from me, and that you did not come within the days appointed, and that the Philistines were mustering at Michmash, [12]I said, 'Now the Philistines will come down upon me at Gilgal, and I have not entreated the favor of the LORD'; so I forced myself, and offered the burnt offering." [13]Samuel said to Saul, "You have done foolishly; you have not kept the commandment of the LORD your God, which he commanded you. The LORD would have established your kingdom over Israel forever, [14]but now your kingdom will not continue; the LORD has sought out a man after his own heart; and the LORD has appointed him to be ruler over his people, because you have not kept what the LORD commanded you." [15]And Samuel left and went on his way from Gilgal.[d] The rest of the people followed Saul to join the army; they went up from Gilgal toward Gibeah of Benjamin.[e]

Preparations for Battle

Saul counted the people who were present with him, about six hundred men. [16]Saul, his son Jonathan, and the people who were present with them stayed in Geba of Benjamin; but the Philistines encamped at Michmash. [17]And raiders came out of the camp of the Philistines in three companies; one company turned toward Ophrah, to the land of Shual, [18]another company turned toward Beth-horon, and another company turned toward the mountain[f] that looks down upon the valley of Zeboim toward the wilderness.

19 Now there was no smith to be found throughout all the land of Israel; for the Philistines said, "The Hebrews must not make swords or spears for themselves"; [20]so all the Israelites went down to the Philistines to sharpen their plowshares, mattocks, axes, or sickles;[g] [21]The charge was two-thirds of a shekel[h] for the plowshares and for the mattocks, and one-third of a shekel for sharpening the axes and for setting the goads.[i] [22]So on the day

---

a The number is lacking in the Heb text (the verse is lacking in the Septuagint). **b** *Two is not the entire number; something has dropped out.* **c** Heb *him* **d** Gk: Heb *went up from Gilgal to Gibeah of Benjamin* **e** Gk: Heb lacks *The rest . . . of Benjamin* **f** Cn Compare Gk: Heb *toward the border* **g** Gk: Heb *plowshare* **h** Heb *was a pim* **i** Cn: Meaning of Heb uncertain

of the battle neither sword nor spear was to be found in the possession of any of the people with Saul and Jonathan; but Saul and his son Jonathan had them.

Jonathan Surprises and Routs the Philistines

23 Now a garrison of the Philistines had gone out to the pass of Michmash. [1]One day Jonathan son of Saul said to the young man who carried his armor, "Come, let us go over to the Philistine garrison on the other side." But he did not tell his father. [2]Saul was staying in the outskirts of Gibeah under the pomegranate tree that is at Migron; the troops that were with him were about six hundred men, [3]along with Ahijah son of Ahitub, Ichabod's brother, son of Phinehas son of Eli, the priest of the LORD in Shiloh, carrying an ephod. Now the people did not know that Jonathan had gone. [4]In the pass,[a] by which Jonathan tried to go over to the Philistine garrison, there was a rocky crag on one side and a rocky crag on the other; the name of the one was Bozez, and the name of the other Seneh. [5]One crag rose on the north in front of Michmash, and the other on the south in front of Geba.

6 Jonathan said to the young man who carried his armor, "Come, let us go over to the garrison of these uncircumcised; it may be that the LORD will act for us; for nothing can hinder the LORD from saving by many or by few." [7]His armor-bearer said to him, "Do all that your mind inclines to.[b] I am with you; as your mind is, so is mine."[c] [8]Then Jonathan said, "Now we will cross over to those men and will show ourselves to them. [9]If they say to us, 'Wait until we come to you,' then we will stand still in our place, and we will not go up to them. [10]But if they say, 'Come up to us,' then we will go up; for the LORD has given them into our hand. That will be the sign for us." [11]So both of them showed themselves to the garrison of the Philistines; and the Philistines said, "Look, Hebrews are coming out of the holes where they have hidden themselves." [12]The men of the garrison hailed Jonathan and his armor-bearer, saying, "Come up to us, and we will show you something." Jonathan said to his armor-bearer, "Come up after me; for the LORD has given them into the hand of Israel." [13]Then Jonathan climbed up on his hands and feet, with his armor-bearer following after him. The Philistines[d] fell before Jonathan, and his armor-bearer, coming after him, killed them. [14]In that first slaughter Jonathan and his armor-bearer killed about

twenty men within an area about half a furrow long in an acre[e] of land. [15]There was a panic in the camp, in the field, and among all the people; the garrison and even the raiders trembled; the earth quaked; and it became a very great panic.

16 Saul's lookouts in Gibeah of Benjamin were watching as the multitude was surging back and forth.[f] [17]Then Saul said to the troops that were with him, "Call the roll and see who has gone from us." When they had called the roll, Jonathan and his armor-bearer were not there. [18]Saul said to Ahijah, "Bring the ark[g] of God here." For at that time the ark[g] of God went with the Israelites. [19]While Saul was talking to the priest, the tumult in the camp of the Philistines increased more and more; and Saul said to the priest, "Withdraw your hand." [20]Then Saul and all the people who were with him rallied and went into the battle; and every sword was against the other, so that there was very great confusion. [21]Now the Hebrews who previously had been with the Philistines and had gone up with them into the camp turned and joined the Israelites who were with Saul and Jonathan. [22]Likewise, when all the Israelites who had gone into hiding in the hill country of Ephraim heard that the Philistines were fleeing, they too followed closely after them in the battle. [23]So the LORD gave Israel the victory that day.

The battle passed beyond Beth-aven, and the troops with Saul numbered altogether about ten thousand men. The battle spread out over the hill country of Ephraim.

Saul's Rash Oath

24 Now Saul committed a very rash act on that day.[h] He had laid an oath on the troops, saying, "Cursed be anyone who eats food before it is evening and I have been avenged on my enemies." So none of the troops tasted food. [25]All the troops[i] came upon a honeycomb; and there was honey on the ground. [26]When the troops came upon the honeycomb, the honey was dripping out; but they did not put their hands to their mouths, for they feared the oath. [27]But Jonathan had not heard his father charge the troops with the oath; so he extended the staff that was in his hand, and dipped the tip of it in the honeycomb, and put his hand to his mouth; and his eyes brightened. [28]Then one of the soldiers said, "Your father strictly charged the troops with an oath, saying, 'Cursed be anyone who eats food this day.'

---

a Heb *Between the passes* b Gk: Heb *Do all that is in your mind. Turn* c Gk: Heb lacks *so is mine* d Heb *They* e Heb *yoke* f Gk: Heb *they went and there* g Gk *the ephod* h Gk: Heb *The Israelites were distressed that day* i Heb *land*

And so the troops are faint." [29] Then Jonathan said, "My father has troubled the land; see how my eyes have brightened because I tasted a little of this honey. [30] How much better if today the troops had eaten freely of the spoil taken from their enemies; for now the slaughter among the Philistines has not been great."

31 After they had struck down the Philistines that day from Michmash to Aijalon, the troops were very faint; [32] so the troops flew upon the spoil, and took sheep and oxen and calves, and slaughtered them on the ground; and the troops ate them with the blood. [33] Then it was reported to Saul, "Look, the troops are sinning against the LORD by eating with the blood." And he said, "You have dealt treacherously; roll a large stone before me here."[a] [34] Saul said, "Disperse yourselves among the troops, and say to them, 'Let all bring their oxen or their sheep, and slaughter them here, and eat; and do not sin against the LORD by eating with the blood.'" So all of the troops brought their oxen with them that night, and slaughtered them there. [35] And Saul built an altar to the LORD; it was the first altar that he built to the LORD.

Jonathan in Danger of Death

36 Then Saul said, "Let us go down after the Philistines by night and despoil them until the morning light; let us not leave one of them." They said, "Do whatever seems good to you." But the priest said, "Let us draw near to God here." [37] So Saul inquired of God, "Shall I go down after the Philistines? Will you give them into the hand of Israel?" But he did not answer him that day. [38] Saul said, "Come here, all you leaders of the people; and let us find out how this sin has arisen today. [39] For as the LORD lives who saves Israel, even if it is in my son Jonathan, he shall surely die!" But there was no one among all the people who answered him. [40] He said to all Israel, "You shall be on one side, and I and my son Jonathan will be on the other side." The people said to Saul, "Do what seems good to you." [41] Then Saul said, "O LORD God of Israel, why have you not answered your servant today? If this guilt is in me or in my son Jonathan, O LORD God of Israel, give Urim; but if this guilt is in your people Israel,[b] give Thummim." And Jonathan and Saul were indicated by the lot, but the people were cleared. [42] Then Saul said, "Cast the lot between me and my son Jonathan." And Jonathan was taken.

43 Then Saul said to Jonathan, "Tell me what you have done." Jonathan told him, "I tasted a little honey with the tip of the staff that was in my hand; here I am, I will die." [44] Saul said, "God do so to me and more also; you shall surely die, Jonathan!" [45] Then the people said to Saul, "Shall Jonathan die, who has accomplished this great victory in Israel? Far from it! As the LORD lives, not one hair of his head shall fall to the ground; for he has worked with God today." So the people ransomed Jonathan, and he did not die. [46] Then Saul withdrew from pursuing the Philistines; and the Philistines went to their own place.

Saul's Continuing Wars

47 When Saul had taken the kingship over Israel, he fought against all his enemies on every side—against Moab, against the Ammonites, against Edom, against the kings of Zobah, and against the Philistines; wherever he turned he routed them. [48] He did valiantly, and struck down the Amalekites, and rescued Israel out of the hands of those who plundered them.

49 Now the sons of Saul were Jonathan, Ishvi, and Malchishua; and the names of his two daughters were these: the name of the firstborn was Merab, and the name of the younger, Michal. [50] The name of Saul's wife was Ahinoam daughter of Ahimaaz. And the name of the commander of his army was Abner son of Ner, Saul's uncle; [51] Kish was the father of Saul, and Ner the father of Abner was the son of Abiel.

52 There was hard fighting against the Philistines all the days of Saul; and when Saul saw any strong or valiant warrior, he took him into his service.

15 Saul Defeats the Amalekites but Spares Their King

Samuel said to Saul, "The LORD sent me to anoint you king over his people Israel; now therefore listen to the words of the LORD. [2] Thus says the LORD of hosts, 'I will punish the Amalekites for what they did in opposing the Israelites when they came up out of Egypt. [3] Now go and attack Amalek, utterly destroy all that they have; do not spare them, but kill both man and woman, child and infant, ox and sheep, camel and donkey.'"

4 So Saul summoned the people, and numbered them in Telaim, two hundred thousand foot soldiers, and ten thousand soldiers of Judah. [5] Saul came to the city of the Amalekites and lay in wait in the valley. [6] Saul said to the Kenites, "Go! Leave! Withdraw from among the Amalekites, or I will destroy you with

---

a Gk: Heb *me this day*   b Vg Compare Gk: Heb *"Saul said to the LORD, the God of Israel*

them; for you showed kindness to all the people of Israel when they came up out of Egypt." So the Kenites withdrew from the Amalekites. ⁷Saul defeated the Amalekites, from Havilah as far as Shur, which is east of Egypt. ⁸He took King Agag of the Amalekites alive, but utterly destroyed all the people with the edge of the sword. ⁹Saul and the people spared Agag, and the best of the sheep and of the cattle and of the fatlings, and the lambs, and all that was valuable, and would not utterly destroy them; all that was despised and worthless they utterly destroyed.

Saul Rejected as King

10 The word of the LORD came to Samuel: ¹¹"I regret that I made Saul king, for he has turned back from following me, and has not carried out my commands." Samuel was angry; and he cried out to the LORD all night. ¹²Samuel rose early in the morning to meet Saul, and Samuel was told, "Saul went to Carmel, where he set up a monument for himself, and on returning he passed on down to Gilgal." ¹³When Samuel came to Saul, Saul said to him, "May you be blessed by the LORD; I have carried out the command of the LORD." ¹⁴But Samuel said, "What then is this bleating of sheep in my ears, and the lowing of cattle that I hear?" ¹⁵Saul said, "They have brought them from the Amalekites; for the people spared the best of the sheep and the cattle, to sacrifice to the LORD your God; but the rest we have utterly destroyed." ¹⁶Then Samuel said to Saul, "Stop! I will tell you what the LORD said to me last night." He replied, "Speak."

17 Samuel said, "Though you are little in your own eyes, are you not the head of the tribes of Israel? The LORD anointed you king over Israel. ¹⁸And the LORD sent you on a mission, and said, 'Go, utterly destroy the sinners, the Amalekites, and fight against them until they are consumed.' ¹⁹Why then did you not obey the voice of the LORD? Why did you swoop down on the spoil, and do what was evil in the sight of the LORD?" ²⁰Saul said to Samuel, "I have obeyed the voice of the LORD, I have gone on the mission on which the LORD sent me, I have brought Agag the king of Amalek, and I have utterly destroyed the Amalekites. ²¹But from the spoil the people took sheep and cattle, the best of the things devoted to destruction, to sacrifice to the LORD your God in Gilgal." ²²And Samuel said,

"Has the LORD as great delight in burnt offerings
    and sacrifices,

LIVE IT!

Power and Corruption
1 Samuel 15:22–23

Power corrupts. We see headlines almost daily about its effect on athletes, celebrities, politicians, and even religious leaders. This passage gives us a vivid example as well. King Saul once again decides to take matters into his own hands and goes against the word of the Lord. He seems to assume that his role as king exempts him from obeying God. But Samuel reminds Saul that he assumes way too much. No king, no president, no prime minister is above the law, especially when that law comes from God.

• In what ways have you served in a leadership role?

• Were you ever tempted to abuse your privileges? How?

as in obedience to the voice of the LORD?
Surely, to obey is better than sacrifice,
    and to heed than the fat of rams.
²³ For rebellion is no less a sin than divination,
    and stubbornness is like iniquity and idolatry.
Because you have rejected the word of the LORD,
    he has also rejected you from being king."

24 Saul said to Samuel, "I have sinned; for I have transgressed the commandment of the LORD and your words, because I feared the people and obeyed their voice. ²⁵Now therefore, I pray, pardon my sin, and return with me, so that I may worship the LORD." ²⁶Samuel said to Saul, "I will not return with you; for you have rejected the word of the LORD, and the LORD has rejected you from being king over Israel." ²⁷As Samuel turned to go away, Saul caught hold of the hem of his robe, and it tore. ²⁸And Samuel said to him, "The LORD has torn the kingdom of Israel from you this very day, and has given it to a neighbor of yours, who is better than you. ²⁹Moreover the Glory of Israel will not recant[a] or change his mind; for he is not a mortal, that he should change his mind." ³⁰Then Saul[b] said, "I have sinned; yet honor me now before the elders of my people and before Israel, and return with me, so that I may worship the

a Q Ms Gk: MT *deceive*   b Heb *he*

LORD your God." [31] So Samuel turned back after Saul; and Saul worshiped the LORD.

32 Then Samuel said, "Bring Agag king of the Amalekites here to me." And Agag came to him haltingly.[a] Agag said, "Surely this is the bitterness of death."[b] [33] But Samuel said,

"As your sword has made women childless,
    so your mother shall be childless among women."

And Samuel hewed Agag in pieces before the LORD in Gilgal.

34 Then Samuel went to Ramah; and Saul went up to his house in Gibeah of Saul. [35] Samuel did not see Saul again until the day of his death, but Samuel grieved over Saul. And the LORD was sorry that he had made Saul king over Israel.

David Anointed as King

16 The LORD said to Samuel, "How long will you grieve over Saul? I have rejected him from being king over Israel. Fill your horn with oil and set out; I will send you to Jesse the Bethlehemite, for I have provided for myself a king among his sons." [2] Samuel said, "How can I go? If Saul hears of it, he will kill me." And the LORD said, "Take a heifer with you, and say, 'I have come to sacrifice to the LORD.' [3] Invite Jesse to the sacrifice, and I will show you what you shall do; and you shall anoint for me the one whom I name to you." [4] Samuel did what the LORD commanded, and came to Bethlehem. The elders of the city came to meet him trembling, and said, "Do you come peaceably?" [5] He said, "Peaceably; I have come to sacrifice to the LORD; sanctify yourselves and come with me to the sacrifice." And he sanctified Jesse and his sons and invited them to the sacrifice.

6 When they came, he looked on Eliab and thought, "Surely the LORD's anointed is now before the LORD."[c] [7] But the LORD said to Samuel, "Do not look on his appearance or on the height of his stature, because I have rejected him; for the LORD does not see as mortals see; they look on the outward appearance, but the LORD looks on the heart."

[8] Then Jesse called Abinadab, and made him pass before Samuel. He said, "Neither has the LORD chosen this one." [9] Then Jesse made Shammah pass by. And he said, "Neither has the LORD chosen this one." [10] Jesse made seven of his sons pass before Samuel, and Samuel said to Jesse, "The LORD has not chosen any of these." [11] Samuel said to Jesse, "Are all your sons here?" And he said, "There remains yet the youngest, but he is keeping the sheep." And Samuel said to Jesse, "Send and bring him; for we will not sit down until he comes here." [12] He sent and brought him in. Now he was ruddy, and had beautiful eyes, and was handsome. The LORD said, "Rise and anoint him; for this is the one." [13] Then Samuel took the horn of oil, and anointed him in the presence of his brothers; and the spirit of the LORD came mightily upon David from that day forward. Samuel then set out and went to Ramah.

David Plays the Lyre for Saul

14 Now the spirit of the LORD departed from Saul, and an evil spirit from the LORD tormented him. [15] And Saul's servants said to him, "See now, an evil spirit from God is tormenting you. [16] Let our lord now command the servants who attend you to look for someone who is skillful in playing the lyre; and when the evil spirit from God is upon you, he will play it, and you will feel better." [17] So Saul said to his servants, "Provide for me someone who can play well, and bring him to me." [18] One of the young men answered, "I have seen a son of Jesse the Bethlehemite who is skillful in playing, a man of valor, a warrior, prudent in speech, and a man of good presence; and the LORD is with him." [19] So Saul sent messengers to Jesse, and said, "Send me your son David who is with the sheep." [20] Jesse took a donkey loaded with bread, a skin of wine, and a kid, and sent them by his son David to Saul. [21] And David came to Saul, and entered his service. Saul loved him greatly, and he became his armor-bearer. [22] Saul sent to Jesse, saying, "Let David remain in my service, for he has found favor in my sight." [23] And whenever the evil spirit from God came upon Saul, David took the

> "The LORD does not see as mortals see; they look on the outward appearance, but the LORD looks on the heart."
> —1 Samuel 16:7

---

a Cn Compare Gk: Meaning of Heb uncertain b Q Ms Gk: MT *Surely the bitterness of death is past* c Heb *him*

lyre and played it with his hand, and Saul would be relieved and feel better, and the evil spirit would depart from him.

David and Goliath

17 Now the Philistines gathered their armies for battle; they were gathered at Socoh, which belongs to Judah, and encamped between Socoh and Azekah, in Ephes-dammim. ²Saul and the Israelites gathered and encamped in the valley of Elah, and formed ranks against the Philistines. ³The Philistines stood on the mountain on the one side, and Israel stood on the mountain on the other side, with a valley between them. ⁴And there came out from the camp of the Philistines a champion named Goliath, of Gath, whose height was six*ᵃ* cubits and a span. ⁵He had a helmet of bronze on his head, and he was armed with a coat of mail; the weight of the coat was five thousand shekels of bronze. ⁶He had greaves of bronze on his legs and a javelin of bronze slung between his shoulders. ⁷The shaft of his spear was like a weaver's beam, and his spear's head weighed six hundred shekels of iron; and his shield-bearer went before him. ⁸He stood and shouted to the ranks of Israel, "Why have you come out to draw up for battle? Am I not a Philistine, and are you not servants of Saul? Choose a man for yourselves, and let him come down to me. ⁹If he is able to fight with me and kill me, then we will be your servants; but if I prevail against him and kill him, then you shall be our servants and serve us." ¹⁰And the Philistine said, "Today I defy the ranks of Israel! Give me a man, that we may fight together." ¹¹When Saul and all Israel heard these words of the Philistine, they were dismayed and greatly afraid.

12 Now David was the son of an Ephrathite of Bethlehem in Judah, named Jesse, who had eight sons. In the days of Saul the man was already old and advanced in years.*ᵇ* ¹³The three eldest sons of Jesse had followed Saul to the battle; the names of his three sons who went to the battle were Eliab the firstborn, and next to him Abinadab, and the third Shammah. ¹⁴David was the youngest; the three eldest followed Saul, ¹⁵but David went back and forth from Saul to feed his father's sheep at Bethlehem. ¹⁶For forty days the Philistine came forward and took his stand, morning and evening.

17 Jesse said to his son David, "Take for your brothers an ephah of this parched grain and these ten loaves, and carry them quickly to the camp to

LIVE IT!

Taking On Goliath
1 Samuel 17

David makes it look so easy. A slingshot, a stone, skillful aim, and it's game over. Goliath is dead, and the Israelites win the day. It's a story that challenges each of us to see ourselves and the giants in our own lives from God's perspective rather than the perspective of the world.

There are plenty of modern-day Goliaths out there ready to defeat us. Our personal Goliaths might include peer pressure, addiction, an abusive situation, or self-doubt. There are also widespread Goliaths like poverty, hunger, disease, and war that threaten the well-being of entire nations. We may feel overpowered by these Goliaths, sure that they are too big for us to handle. But they're not! We can believe in God as David did and remember that we're not alone. True, we're not strong enough to defeat them on our own, but God is. And God works through us to do just that.

- Identify a Goliath in your life or in the world right now, and journal about it.
- What stepping-stone can you take in defeating it with God's help and guidance?

your brothers; ¹⁸also take these ten cheeses to the commander of their thousand. See how your brothers fare, and bring some token from them."

19 Now Saul, and they, and all the men of Israel, were in the valley of Elah, fighting with the Philistines. ²⁰David rose early in the morning, left the sheep with a keeper, took the provisions, and went as Jesse had commanded him. He came to the encampment as the army was going forth to the battle line, shouting the war cry. ²¹Israel and the Philistines drew up for battle, army against army. ²²David left the things in charge of the keeper of the baggage, ran to the ranks, and went and greeted his brothers. ²³As he talked with them, the champion, the Philistine of Gath, Goliath by name, came up out of the ranks of

---

ᵃ MT: Q Ms Gk *four*   *ᵇ* Gk Syr: Heb *among men*

the Philistines, and spoke the same words as before. And David heard him.

24 All the Israelites, when they saw the man, fled from him and were very much afraid. [25]The Israelites said, "Have you seen this man who has come up? Surely he has come up to defy Israel. The king will greatly enrich the man who kills him, and will give him his daughter and make his family free in Israel." [26]David said to the men who stood by him, "What shall be done for the man who kills this Philistine, and takes away the reproach from Israel? For who is this uncircumcised Philistine that he should defy the armies of the living God?" [27]The people answered him in the same way, "So shall it be done for the man who kills him."

28 His eldest brother Eliab heard him talking to the men; and Eliab's anger was kindled against David. He said, "Why have you come down? With whom have you left those few sheep in the wilderness? I know your presumption and the evil of your heart; for you have come down just to see the battle." [29]David said, "What have I done now? It was only a question." [30]He turned away from him toward another and spoke in the same way; and the people answered him again as before.

31 When the words that David spoke were heard, they repeated them before Saul; and he sent for him. [32]David said to Saul, "Let no one's heart fail because of him; your servant will go and fight with this Philistine." [33]Saul said to David, "You are not able to go against this Philistine to fight with him; for you are just a boy, and he has been a warrior from his youth." [34]But David said to Saul, "Your servant used to keep sheep for his father; and whenever a lion or a bear came, and took a lamb from the flock, [35]I went after it and struck it down, rescuing the lamb from its mouth; and if it turned against me, I would catch it by the jaw, strike it down, and kill it. [36]Your servant has killed both lions and bears; and this uncircumcised Philistine shall be like one of them, since he has defied the armies of the living God." [37]David said, "The LORD, who saved me from the paw of the lion and from the paw of the bear, will save me from the hand of this Philistine." So Saul said to David, "Go, and may the LORD be with you!"

38 Saul clothed David with his armor; he put a bronze helmet on his head and clothed him with a coat of mail. [39]David strapped Saul's sword over the armor, and he tried in vain to walk, for he was not

used to them. Then David said to Saul, "I cannot walk with these; for I am not used to them." So David removed them. [40]Then he took his staff in his hand, and chose five smooth stones from the wadi, and put them in his shepherd's bag, in the pouch; his sling was in his hand, and he drew near to the Philistine.

41 The Philistine came on and drew near to David, with his shield-bearer in front of him. [42]When the Philistine looked and saw David, he disdained him, for he was only a youth, ruddy and handsome in appearance. [43]The Philistine said to David, "Am I a dog, that you come to me with sticks?" And the Philistine cursed David by his gods. [44]The Philistine said to David, "Come to me, and I will give your flesh to the birds of the air and to the wild animals of the field." [45]But David said to the Philistine, "You come to me with sword and spear and javelin; but I come to you in the name of the LORD of hosts, the God of the armies of Israel, whom you have defied. [46]This very day the LORD will deliver you into my hand, and I will strike you down and cut off your head; and I will give the dead bodies of the Philistine army this very day to the birds of the air and to the wild animals of the earth, so that all the earth may know that there is a God in Israel, [47]and that all this assembly may know that the LORD does not save by sword and spear; for the battle is the LORD's and he will give you into our hand."

48 When the Philistine drew nearer to meet David, David ran quickly toward the battle line to meet the Philistine. [49]David put his hand in his bag, took out a stone, slung it, and struck the Philistine on his forehead; the stone sank into his forehead, and he fell face down on the ground.

50 So David prevailed over the Philistine with a sling and a stone, striking down the Philistine and killing him; there was no sword in David's hand.

⁵¹Then David ran and stood over the Philistine; he grasped his sword, drew it out of its sheath, and killed him; then he cut off his head with it.

When the Philistines saw that their champion was dead, they fled. ⁵²The troops of Israel and Judah rose up with a shout and pursued the Philistines as far as Gath*ᵃ* and the gates of Ekron, so that the wounded Philistines fell on the way from Shaaraim as far as Gath and Ekron. ⁵³The Israelites came back from chasing the Philistines, and they plundered their camp. ⁵⁴David took the head of the Philistine and brought it to Jerusalem; but he put his armor in his tent.

55 When Saul saw David go out against the Philistine, he said to Abner, the commander of the army, "Abner, whose son is this young man?" Abner said, "As your soul lives, O king, I do not know." ⁵⁶The king said, "Inquire whose son the stripling is." ⁵⁷On David's return from killing the Philistine, Abner took him and brought him before Saul, with the head of the Philistine in his hand. ⁵⁸Saul said to him, "Whose son are you, young man?" And David answered, "I am the son of your servant Jesse the Bethlehemite."

Jonathan's Covenant with David

18 When David*ᵇ* had finished speaking to Saul, the soul of Jonathan was bound to the soul of David, and Jonathan loved him as his own soul. ²Saul took him that day and would not let him return to his father's house. ³Then Jonathan made a covenant with David, because he loved him as his own soul. ⁴Jonathan stripped himself of the robe that he was wearing, and gave it to David, and his armor, and even his sword and his bow and his belt. ⁵David went out and was successful wherever Saul sent him; as a result, Saul set him over the army. And all the people, even the servants of Saul, approved.

6 As they were coming home, when David returned from killing the Philistine, the women came out of all the towns of Israel, singing and dancing, to meet King Saul, with tambourines, with songs of joy, and with musical instruments.*ᶜ* ⁷And the women sang to one another as they made merry,

"Saul has killed his thousands,
    and David his ten thousands."

⁸Saul was very angry, for this saying displeased him. He said, "They have ascribed to David ten thousands, and to me they have ascribed thousands; what more can he have but the kingdom?" ⁹So Saul eyed David from that day on.

Saul Tries to Kill David

10 The next day an evil spirit from God rushed upon Saul, and he raved within his house, while David was playing the lyre, as he did day by day. Saul had his spear in his hand; ¹¹and Saul threw the spear, for he thought, "I will pin David to the wall." But David eluded him twice.

12 Saul was afraid of David, because the LORD was with him but had departed from Saul. ¹³So Saul removed him from his presence, and made him a commander of a thousand; and David marched out and came in, leading the army. ¹⁴David had success in all his undertakings; for the LORD was with him. ¹⁵When Saul saw that he had great success, he stood in awe of him. ¹⁶But all Israel and Judah loved David; for it was he who marched out and came in leading them.

David Marries Michal

17 Then Saul said to David, "Here is my elder daughter Merab; I will give her to you as a wife; only be valiant for me and fight the LORD's battles." For Saul thought, "I will not raise a hand against him; let the Philistines deal with him." ¹⁸David said to Saul, "Who am I and who are my kinsfolk, my father's family in Israel, that I should be son-in-law to the king?" ¹⁹But at the time when Saul's daughter Merab should have been given to David, she was given to Adriel the Meholathite as a wife.

20 Now Saul's daughter Michal loved David. Saul was told, and the thing pleased him. ²¹Saul thought, "Let me give her to him that she may be a snare for him and that the hand of the Philistines may be against him." Therefore Saul said to David a second time,*ᵈ* "You shall now be my son-in-law." ²²Saul commanded his servants, "Speak to David in private and say, 'See, the king is delighted with you, and all his servants love you; now then, become the king's son-in-law.'" ²³So Saul's servants reported these words to David in private. And David said, "Does it seem to you a little thing to become the king's son-in-law, seeing that I am a poor man and of no repute?" ²⁴The servants of Saul told him, "This is what David said." ²⁵Then Saul said, "Thus shall you say to David, 'The king desires no marriage present except a hundred foreskins of the Philistines, that he may be avenged on the king's enemies.'" Now Saul planned to make David fall by the hand of the Philistines. ²⁶When his servants told David these words, David was well pleased to be the king's son-in-law. Before

---

ᵃ Gk Syr: Heb *Gai* *ᵇ* Heb *he* *ᶜ* Or *triangles, or three-stringed instruments* *ᵈ* Heb *by two*

the time had expired, [27]David rose and went, along with his men, and killed one hundred[a] of the Philistines; and David brought their foreskins, which were given in full number to the king, that he might become the king's son-in-law. Saul gave him his daughter Michal as a wife. [28]But when Saul realized that the LORD was with David, and that Saul's daughter Michal loved him, [29]Saul was still more afraid of David. So Saul was David's enemy from that time forward.

30 Then the commanders of the Philistines came out to battle; and as often as they came out, David had more success than all the servants of Saul, so that his fame became very great.

Jonathan Intercedes for David

19 Saul spoke with his son Jonathan and with all his servants about killing David. But Saul's son Jonathan took great delight in David. [2]Jonathan told David, "My father Saul is trying to kill you; therefore be on guard tomorrow morning; stay in a secret place and hide yourself. [3]I will go out and stand beside my father in the field where you are, and I will speak to my father about you; if I learn anything I will tell you." [4]Jonathan spoke well of David to his father Saul, saying to him, "The king should not sin against his servant David, because he has not sinned against you, and because his deeds have been of good service to you; [5]for he took his life in his hand when he attacked the Philistine, and the LORD brought about a great victory for all Israel. You saw it, and rejoiced; why then will you sin against an innocent person by killing David without cause?" [6]Saul heeded the voice of Jonathan; Saul swore, "As the LORD lives, he shall not be put to death." [7]So Jonathan called David and related all these things to him. Jonathan then brought David to Saul, and he was in his presence as before.

Michal Helps David Escape from Saul

8 Again there was war, and David went out to fight the Philistines. He launched a heavy attack on them, so that they fled before him. [9]Then an evil spirit from the LORD came upon Saul, as he sat in his house with his spear in his hand, while David was playing music. [10]Saul sought to pin David to the wall with the spear; but he eluded Saul, so that he struck the spear into the wall. David fled and escaped that night.

11 Saul sent messengers to David's house to keep watch over him, planning to kill him in the morning. David's wife Michal told him, "If you do not save your life tonight, tomorrow you will be killed." [12]So Michal let David down through the window; he fled away and escaped. [13]Michal took an idol[b] and laid it on the bed; she put a net[c] of goats' hair on its head, and covered it with the clothes. [14]When Saul sent messengers to take David, she said, "He is sick." [15]Then Saul sent the messengers to see David for themselves. He said, "Bring him up to me in the bed, that I may kill him." [16]When the messengers came in, the idol[d] was in the bed, with the covering[c] of goats' hair on its head. [17]Saul said to Michal, "Why have you deceived me like this, and let my enemy go, so that he has escaped?" Michal answered Saul, "He said to me, 'Let me go; why should I kill you?' "

David Joins Samuel in Ramah

18 Now David fled and escaped; he came to Samuel at Ramah, and told him all that Saul had done to him. He and Samuel went and settled at Naioth. [19]Saul was told, "David is at Naioth in Ramah." [20]Then Saul sent messengers to take David. When they saw the company of the prophets in a frenzy, with Samuel standing in charge of[e] them, the spirit of God came upon the messengers of Saul, and they also fell into a prophetic frenzy. [21]When Saul was told, he sent other messengers, and they also fell into a frenzy. Saul sent messengers again the third time, and they also fell into a frenzy. [22]Then he himself went to Ramah. He came to the great well that is in Secu;[g] he asked, "Where are Samuel and David?" And someone said, "They are at Naioth in Ramah." [23]He went there, toward Naioth in Ramah; and the spirit of God came upon him. As he was going, he fell into a prophetic frenzy, until he came to Naioth in Ramah. [24]He too stripped off his clothes, and he too fell into a frenzy before Samuel. He lay naked all that day and all that night. Therefore it is said, "Is Saul also among the prophets?"

The Friendship of David and Jonathan

20 David fled from Naioth in Ramah. He came before Jonathan and said, "What have I done? What is my guilt? And what is my sin against your father that he is trying to take my life?" [2]He said to him, "Far from it! You shall not die. My father does nothing either great or small without disclosing it to me; and why should my father hide this from me?

---

a Gk Compare 2 Sam 3.14: Heb *two hundred*   b Heb *took the teraphim*   c Meaning of Heb uncertain   d Heb *the teraphim*   e Gk reads *to the well of the threshing floor on the bare height*

Never!" ³But David also swore, "Your father knows well that you like me; and he thinks, 'Do not let Jonathan know this, or he will be grieved.' But truly, as the LORD lives and as you yourself live, there is but a step between me and death." ⁴Then Jonathan said to David, "Whatever you say, I will do for you." ⁵David said to Jonathan, "Tomorrow is the new moon, and I should not fail to sit with the king at the meal; but let me go, so that I may hide in the field until the third evening. ⁶If your father misses me at all, then say, 'David earnestly asked leave of me to run to Bethlehem his city; for there is a yearly sacrifice there for all the family.' ⁷If he says, 'Good!' it will be well with your servant; but if he is angry, then know that evil has been determined by him. ⁸Therefore deal kindly with your servant, for you have brought your servant into a sacred covenant^a with you. But if there is guilt in me, kill me yourself; why should you bring me to your father?" ⁹Jonathan said, "Far be it from you! If I knew that it was decided by my father that evil should come upon you, would I not tell you?" ¹⁰Then David said to Jonathan, "Who will tell me if your father answers you harshly?" ¹¹Jonathan replied to David, "Come, let us go out into the field." So they both went out into the field.

12 Jonathan said to David, "By the LORD, the God of Israel! When I have sounded out my father, about this time tomorrow, or on the third day, if he is well disposed toward David, shall I not then send and disclose it to you? ¹³But if my father intends to do you harm, the LORD do so to Jonathan, and more also, if I do not disclose it to you, and send you away, so that you may go in safety. May the LORD be with you, as he has been with my father. ¹⁴If I am still alive, show me the faithful love of the LORD; but if I die,^b ¹⁵never cut off your faithful love from my house, even if the LORD were to cut off every one of the enemies of David from the face of the earth." ¹⁶Thus Jonathan made a covenant with the house of David, saying, "May the LORD seek out the enemies of David." ¹⁷Jonathan made David swear again by his love for him; for he loved him as he loved his own life.

18 Jonathan said to him, "Tomorrow is the new moon; you will be missed, because your place will be empty. ¹⁹On the day after tomorrow, you shall go a long way down; go to the place where you hid yourself earlier, and remain beside the stone there.^b ²⁰I will shoot three arrows to the side of it, as though I shot at a mark. ²¹Then I will send the boy, saying, 'Go, find the arrows.' If I say to the boy, 'Look, the arrows are on this side of you, collect them,' then you are to come, for, as the LORD lives, it is safe for you and there is no danger. ²²But if I say to the young man, 'Look, the arrows are beyond you,' then go; for the LORD has sent you away. ²³As for the matter

STUDY IT!

Biblical BFF · 1 Samuel 20

David and Jonathan's friendship is an amazing picture of commitment and faithfulness. In 1 Samuel 18:1–4, Jonathan makes a special covenant with David. In this chapter their deep love leads them to risk their lives for each other. Saul, the king and Jonathan's father, is acting like a madman. He is insanely jealous of David and wants him dead.

But Jonathan and David's friendship is strong—and made stronger because God is part of it. This gives them the wisdom to see what is right and the courage to do it. When they have to part (1 Samuel 20:41-42), they cry and embrace and remind each other of their vows.

Fortunately, your father isn't likely to take Saul's strategy to hunt down and try to kill a friend of yours. But it's not unusual to feel some tension with parents over your choice of friends. Parents may not understand why you like a person they dislike. And parents often have great wisdom in this area. But if you know God is at the center of your friendship and that your friend is helping you follow God better, your response should be like David and Jonathan's.

Keep God part of all your relationships and act out of commitment and love. Trust God to lead you to good decisions and to keep the bond between you and your friends strong, even when you're faced with challenges or time apart from each other.

a Heb *a covenant of the LORD*   b Meaning of Heb uncertain

STUDY IT!

Introducing . . . David
1 Samuel 16–30

David, the shepherd turned king, is one of the great tragic heroes of the Old Testament. David, whose name means "beloved," was the second king (1000–961 B.C.) of the new nation formed from the twelve tribes of Israel. David was the youngest son of Jesse of the tribe of Judah and a member of King Saul's court as a young man. Later, when Saul disappointed God, Samuel the prophet anointed David as Saul's successor. After Saul was killed, David established the neutral city of Jerusalem as his capital. (See Map 5: "Kingdom of David and Solomon.") He moved the ark of the covenant there, making this city the new religious center of Israel. Jerusalem is also known as the City of David.

David was a successful warrior, a capable king, and a gifted poet, having written some of the psalms himself. He was also capable of great sin. His affair with Bathsheba led to acts of violence and betrayal that affected his whole family (see 2 Samuel 11). One of his sons, Absalom, even incited a revolt against David. But through it all, David was passionately in love with God. God recognized this and promised David that someone from his line would sit upon the throne in Israel.

When Israel was destroyed and its kings taken prisoners, the people developed a hope that another anointed one, a messiah from the house of David, would rise up and lead Israel in God's ways once again. It's this hope for the Davidic Messiah that is fulfilled by Jesus in the New Testament.

about which you and I have spoken, the LORD is witness[a] between you and me forever."

24 So David hid himself in the field. When the new moon came, the king sat at the feast to eat. 25 The king sat upon his seat, as at other times, upon the seat by the wall. Jonathan stood, while Abner sat by Saul's side; but David's place was empty.

26 Saul did not say anything that day; for he thought, "Something has befallen him; he is not clean, surely he is not clean." 27 But on the second day, the day after the new moon, David's place was empty. And Saul said to his son Jonathan, "Why has the son of Jesse not come to the feast, either yesterday or today?" 28 Jonathan answered Saul, "David earnestly asked leave of me to go to Bethlehem; 29 he said, 'Let me go; for our family is holding a sacrifice in the city, and my brother has commanded me to be there. So now, if I have found favor in your sight, let me get away, and see my brothers.' For this reason he has not come to the king's table."

30 Then Saul's anger was kindled against Jonathan. He said to him, "You son of a perverse, rebellious woman! Do I not know that you have chosen the son of Jesse to your own shame, and to the shame of your mother's nakedness? 31 For as long as the son of Jesse lives upon the earth, neither you nor your kingdom shall be established. Now send and bring him to me, for he shall surely die." 32 Then Jonathan answered his father Saul, "Why should he be put to death? What has he done?" 33 But Saul threw his spear at him to strike him; so Jonathan knew that it was the decision of his father to put David to death. 34 Jonathan rose from the table in fierce anger and ate no food on the second day of the month, for he was grieved for David, and because his father had disgraced him.

35 In the morning Jonathan went out into the field to the appointment with David, and with him was a little boy. 36 He said to the boy, "Run and find the arrows that I shoot." As the boy ran, he shot an arrow beyond him. 37 When the boy came to the place where Jonathan's arrow had fallen, Jonathan called after the boy and said, "Is the arrow not beyond you?" 38 Jonathan called after the boy, "Hurry, be quick, do not linger." So Jonathan's boy gathered up the arrows and came to his master. 39 But the boy knew nothing; only Jonathan and David knew the arrangement. 40 Jonathan gave his weapons to the boy and said to him, "Go and carry them to the city." 41 As soon as the boy had gone, David rose from beside the stone heap[b] and prostrated himself with his face to the ground. He bowed three times, and they kissed each other, and wept with each other; David wept the more.[c] 42 Then Jonathan said to David, "Go in peace,

a Gk: Heb lacks witness   b Gk: Heb from beside the south   c Vg: Meaning of Heb uncertain

since both of us have sworn in the name of the LORD, saying, 'The LORD shall be between me and you, and between my descendants and your descendants, forever.' " He got up and left; and Jonathan went into the city.[a]

David and the Holy Bread

21 [b] David came to Nob to the priest Ahimelech. Ahimelech came trembling to meet David, and said to him, "Why are you alone, and no one with you?" [2] David said to the priest Ahimelech, "The king has charged me with a matter, and said to me, 'No one must know anything of the matter about which I send you, and with which I have charged you.' I have made an appointment[c] with the young men for such and such a place. [3] Now then, what have you at hand? Give me five loaves of bread, or whatever is here." [4] The priest answered David, "I have no ordinary bread at hand, only holy bread—provided that the young men have kept themselves from women." [5] David answered the priest, "Indeed women have been kept from us as always when I go on an expedition; the vessels of the young men are holy even when it is a common journey; how much more today will their vessels be holy?" [6] So the priest gave him the holy bread; for there was no bread there except the bread of the Presence, which is removed from before the LORD, to be replaced by hot bread on the day it is taken away.

7 Now a certain man of the servants of Saul was there that day, detained before the LORD; his name was Doeg the Edomite, the chief of Saul's shepherds.

8 David said to Ahimelech, "Is there no spear or sword here with you? I did not bring my sword or my weapons with me, because the king's business required haste." [9] The priest said, "The sword of Goliath the Philistine, whom you killed in the valley of Elah, is here wrapped in a cloth behind the ephod; if you will take that, take it, for there is none here except that one." David said, "There is none like it; give it to me."

David Flees to Gath

10 David rose and fled that day from Saul; he went to King Achish of Gath. [11] The servants of Achish said to him, "Is this not David the king of the land? Did they not sing to one another of him in dances,

'Saul has killed his thousands,
and David his ten thousands'?"

[12] David took these words to heart and was very much afraid of King Achish of Gath. [13] So he changed his behavior before them; he pretended to be mad when in their presence.[d] He scratched marks on the doors of the gate, and let his spittle run down his beard. [14] Achish said to his servants, "Look, you see the man is mad; why then have you brought him to me? [15] Do I lack madmen, that you have brought this fellow to play the madman in my presence? Shall this fellow come into my house?"

David and His Followers at Adullam

22 David left there and escaped to the cave of Adullam; when his brothers and all his father's house heard of it, they went down there to him. [2] Everyone who was in distress, and everyone who was in debt, and everyone who was discontented gathered to him; and he became captain over them. Those who were with him numbered about four hundred.

3 David went from there to Mizpeh of Moab. He said to the king of Moab, "Please let my father and mother come[e] to you, until I know what God will do for me." [4] He left them with the king of Moab, and they stayed with him all the time that David was in the stronghold. [5] Then the prophet Gad said to David, "Do not remain in the stronghold; leave, and go into the land of Judah." So David left, and went into the forest of Hereth.

Saul Slaughters the Priests at Nob

6 Saul heard that David and those who were with him had been located. Saul was sitting at Gibeah, under the tamarisk tree on the height, with his spear in his hand, and all his servants were standing around him. [7] Saul said to his servants who stood around him, "Hear now, you Benjaminites; will the son of Jesse give every one of you fields and vineyards, will he make you all commanders of thousands and commanders of hundreds? [8] Is that why all of you have conspired against me? No one discloses to me when my son makes a league with the son of Jesse, none of you is sorry for me or discloses to me that my son has stirred up my servant against me, to lie in wait, as he is doing today." [9] Doeg the Edomite, who was in charge of Saul's servants, answered, "I saw the son of Jesse coming to Nob, to Ahimelech son of Ahitub; [10] he inquired of the LORD for him, gave him provisions, and gave him the sword of Goliath the Philistine."

11 The king sent for the priest Ahimelech son of

α This sentence is 21.1 in Heb   b Ch 21.2 in Heb   c Q Ms Vg Compare Gk: Meaning of MT uncertain   d Heb *in their hands*   e Syr Vg: Heb *come out*

Ahitub and for all his father's house, the priests who were at Nob; and all of them came to the king. ¹²Saul said, "Listen now, son of Ahitub." He answered, "Here I am, my lord." ¹³Saul said to him, "Why have you conspired against me, you and the son of Jesse, by giving him bread and a sword, and by inquiring of God for him, so that he has risen against me, to lie in wait, as he is doing today?"

14 Then Ahimelech answered the king, "Who among all your servants is so faithful as David? He is the king's son-in-law, and is quick*a* to do your bidding, and is honored in your house. ¹⁵Is today the first time that I have inquired of God for him? By no means! Do not let the king impute anything to his servant or to any member of my father's house; for your servant has known nothing of all this, much or little." ¹⁶The king said, "You shall surely die, Ahimelech, you and all your father's house." ¹⁷The king said to the guard who stood around him, "Turn and kill the priests of the LORD, because their hand also is with David; they knew that he fled, and did not disclose it to me." But the servants of the king would not raise their hand to attack the priests of the LORD. ¹⁸Then the king said to Doeg, "You, Doeg, turn and attack the priests." Doeg the Edomite turned and attacked the priests; on that day he killed eighty-five who wore the linen ephod. ¹⁹Nob, the city of the priests, he put to the sword; men and women, children and infants, oxen, donkeys, and sheep, he put to the sword.

20 But one of the sons of Ahimelech son of Ahitub, named Abiathar, escaped and fled after David. ²¹Abiathar told David that Saul had killed the priests of the LORD. ²²David said to Abiathar, "I knew on that day, when Doeg the Edomite was there, that he would surely tell Saul. I am responsible*b* for the lives of all your father's house. ²³Stay with me, and do not be afraid; for the one who seeks my life seeks your life; you will be safe with me."

David Saves the City of Keilah

23 Now they told David, "The Philistines are fighting against Keilah, and are robbing the threshing floors." ²David inquired of the LORD, "Shall I go and attack these Philistines?" The LORD said to David, "Go and attack the Philistines and save Keilah." ³But David's men said to him, "Look, we are afraid here in Judah; how much more then if we go to Keilah against the armies of the Philistines?" ⁴Then David inquired of the LORD again. The LORD answered him, "Yes, go down to Keilah; for I will give the Philistines into your hand." ⁵So David and his men went to Keilah, fought with the Philistines, brought away their livestock, and dealt them a heavy defeat. Thus David rescued the inhabitants of Keilah.

6 When Abiathar son of Ahimelech fled to David at Keilah, he came down with an ephod in his hand. ⁷Now it was told Saul that David had come to Keilah. And Saul said, "God has given*c* him into my hand; for he has shut himself in by entering a town that has gates and bars." ⁸Saul summoned all the people to war, to go down to Keilah, to besiege David and his men. ⁹When David learned that Saul was plotting evil against him, he said to the priest Abiathar, "Bring the ephod here." ¹⁰David said, "O LORD, the God of Israel, your servant has heard that Saul seeks to come to Keilah, to destroy the city on my account. ¹¹And now, will*d* Saul come down as your servant has heard? O LORD, the God of Israel, I beseech you, tell your servant." The LORD said, "He will come down." ¹²Then David said, "Will the men of Keilah surrender me and my men into the hand of Saul?" The LORD said, "They will surrender you." ¹³Then David and his men, who were about six hundred, set out and left Keilah; they wandered wherever they could go. When Saul was told that David had escaped from Keilah, he gave up the expedition. ¹⁴David remained in the strongholds in the wilderness, in the hill country of the Wilderness of Ziph. Saul sought him every day, but the LORD*e* did not give him into his hand.

David Eludes Saul in the Wilderness

15 David was in the Wilderness of Ziph at Horesh when he learned that*f* Saul had come out to seek his life. ¹⁶Saul's son Jonathan set out and came to David at Horesh; there he strengthened his hand through the LORD.*g* ¹⁷He said to him, "Do not be afraid; for the hand of my father Saul shall not find you; you shall be king over Israel, and I shall be second to you; my father Saul also knows that this is so." ¹⁸Then the two of them made a covenant before the LORD; David remained at Horesh, and Jonathan went home.

19 Then some Ziphites went up to Saul at Gibeah and said, "David is hiding among us in the strongholds of Horesh, on the hill of Hachilah, which is south of Jeshimon. ²⁰Now, O king, whenever you wish to come down, do so; and our part will be to surrender him into the king's hand." ²¹Saul said, "May you be blessed by the LORD for showing me compassion! ²²Go and make sure once more; find out ex-

---

a Heb *and turns aside*   *b* Gk Vg: Meaning of Heb uncertain   *c* Gk Tg: Heb *made a stranger of*   *d* Q Ms Compare Gk: MT *Will the men of Keilah surrender me into his hand? Will*   *e* Q Ms Gk: MT *God*   *f* Or *saw that*   *g* Compare Q Ms Gk: MT *God*

actly where he is, and who has seen him there; for I am told that he is very cunning. ²³Look around and learn all the hiding places where he lurks, and come back to me with sure information. Then I will go with you; and if he is in the land, I will search him out among all the thousands of Judah." ²⁴So they set out and went to Ziph ahead of Saul.

David and his men were in the wilderness of Maon, in the Arabah to the south of Jeshimon. ²⁵Saul and his men went to search for him. When David was told, he went down to the rock and stayed in the wilderness of Maon. When Saul heard that, he pursued David into the wilderness of Maon. ²⁶Saul went on one side of the mountain, and David and his men on the other side of the mountain. David was hurrying to get away from Saul, while Saul and his men were closing in on David and his men to capture them. ²⁷Then a messenger came to Saul, saying, "Hurry and come; for the Philistines have made a raid on the land." ²⁸So Saul stopped pursuing David, and went against the Philistines; therefore that place was called the Rock of Escape.ᵃ ²⁹ᵇ David then went up from there, and lived in the strongholds of En-gedi.

David Spares Saul's Life

24 When Saul returned from following the Philistines, he was told, "David is in the wilderness of En-gedi." ²Then Saul took three thousand chosen men out of all Israel, and went to look for David and his men in the direction of the Rocks of the Wild Goats. ³He came to the sheepfolds beside the road, where there was a cave; and Saul went in to relieve himself.ᶜ Now David and his men were sitting in the innermost parts of the cave. ⁴The men of David said to him, "Here is the day of which the LORD said to you, 'I will give your enemy into your hand, and you shall do to him as it seems good to you.'" Then David went and stealthily cut off a corner of Saul's cloak. ⁵Afterward David was stricken to the heart because he had cut off a corner of Saul's cloak. ⁶He said to his men, "The LORD forbid that I should do this thing to my lord, the LORD's anointed, to raise my hand against him; for he is the LORD's anointed." ⁷So David scolded his men severely and did not permit them to attack Saul. Then Saul got up and left the cave, and went on his way.

8 Afterwards David also rose up and went out of the cave and called after Saul, "My lord the king!"

STUDY IT!

Anointed
1 Samuel 24

Oil has been used throughout human history as medicine, perfume, and a symbol of blessing. The Israelite kings and prophets were anointed with oil to symbolize the powerful spirit of God with them as they fulfilled their important roles. Often it was olive oil mixed with a small amount of perfume. Throughout the Bible, oil signifies a setting apart of something as holy and chosen by God.

The Hebrew word "mashiah," translated as "anointed (one)" (1 Samuel 24:6), is the root of the English word "messiah." Often applied to kings in the Old Testament, this title was attached in the second century B.C. to the one "like David" who was expected to come (see Daniel 9:25). "Mashiah" in Greek is "christos," which became the title given to Jesus by his followers: Jesus, the Christ. Jesus, the anointed one. Jesus, the Messiah.

When Saul looked behind him, David bowed with his face to the ground, and did obeisance. ⁹David said to Saul, "Why do you listen to the words of those who say, 'David seeks to do you harm'? ¹⁰This very day your eyes have seen how the LORD gave you into my hand in the cave; and some urged me to kill you, but I sparedᵈ you. I said, 'I will not raise my hand against my lord; for he is the LORD's anointed.' ¹¹See, my father, see the corner of your cloak in my hand; for by the fact that I cut off the corner of your cloak, and did not kill you, you may know for certain that there is no wrong or treason in my hands. I have not sinned against you, though you are hunting me to take my life. ¹²May the LORD judge between me and you! May the LORD avenge me on you; but my hand shall not be against you. ¹³As the ancient proverb says, 'Out of the wicked comes forth wickedness'; but my hand shall not be against you. ¹⁴Against whom has the king of Israel come out? Whom do you pursue? A dead dog? A single flea? ¹⁵May the LORD therefore be judge, and give sentence between me and you. May he see to

ɑ Or Rock of Division; meaning of Heb uncertain   b Ch 24.1 in Heb   c Heb to cover his feet   d Gk Syr Tg Vg: Heb it (my eye) spared

it, and plead my cause, and vindicate me against you."

16 When David had finished speaking these words to Saul, Saul said, "Is this your voice, my son David?" Saul lifted up his voice and wept. [17]He said to David, "You are more righteous than I; for you have repaid me good, whereas I have repaid you evil. [18]Today you have explained how you have dealt well with me, in that you did not kill me when the LORD put me into your hands. [19]For who has ever found an enemy, and sent the enemy safely away? So may the LORD reward you with good for what you have done to me this day. [20]Now I know that you shall surely be king, and that the kingdom of Israel shall be established in your hand. [21]Swear to me therefore by the LORD that you will not cut off my descendants after me, and that you will not wipe out my name from my father's house." [22]So David swore this to Saul. Then Saul went home; but David and his men went up to the stronghold.

Death of Samuel

25 Now Samuel died; and all Israel assembled and mourned for him. They buried him at his home in Ramah.

Then David got up and went down to the wilderness of Paran.

David and the Wife of Nabal

2 There was a man in Maon, whose property was in Carmel. The man was very rich; he had three thousand sheep and a thousand goats. He was shearing his sheep in Carmel. [3]Now the name of the man was Nabal, and the name of his wife Abigail. The woman was clever and beautiful, but the man was surly and mean; he was a Calebite. [4]David heard in the wilderness that Nabal was shearing his sheep. [5]So David sent ten young men; and David said to the young men, "Go up to Carmel, and go to Nabal, and greet him in my name. [6]Thus you shall salute him: 'Peace be to you, and peace be to your house, and peace be to all that you have. [7]I hear that you have shearers; now your shepherds have been with us, and we did them no harm, and they missed nothing, all the time they were in Carmel. [8]Ask your young men, and they will tell you. Therefore let my young men find favor in your sight; for we have come on a feast day. Please give whatever you have at hand to your servants and to your son David.' "

9 When David's young men came, they said all this to Nabal in the name of David; and then they waited. [10]But Nabal answered David's servants, "Who is David? Who is the son of Jesse? There are many servants today who are breaking away from their masters. [11]Shall I take my bread and my water and the meat that I have butchered for my shearers, and give it to men who come from I do not know where?" [12]So David's young men turned away, and came back and told him all this. [13]David said to his men, "Every man strap on his sword!" And every one of them strapped on his sword; David also strapped on his sword; and about four hundred men went up after David, while two hundred remained with the baggage.

14 But one of the young men told Abigail, Nabal's wife, "David sent messengers out of the wilderness to salute our master; and he shouted insults at them. [15]Yet the men were very good to us, and we suffered no harm, and we never missed anything when we were in the fields, as long as we were with them; [16]they were a wall to us both by night and by day, all the while we were with them keeping the sheep. [17]Now therefore know this and consider what you should do; for evil has been decided against our master and against all his house; he is so ill-natured that no one can speak to him."

18 Then Abigail hurried and took two hundred loaves, two skins of wine, five sheep ready dressed, five measures of parched grain, one hundred clusters of raisins, and two hundred cakes of figs. She loaded them on donkeys [19]and said to her young men, "Go on ahead of me; I am coming after you." But she did not tell her husband Nabal. [20]As she rode on the donkey and came down under cover of the mountain, David and his men came down toward her; and she met them. [21]Now David had said, "Surely it was in vain that I protected all that this fellow has in the wilderness, so that nothing was missed of all that belonged to him; but he has returned me evil for good. [22]God do so to David[a] and more also, if by morning I leave so much as one male of all who belong to him."

23 When Abigail saw David, she hurried and alighted from the donkey, and fell before David on her face, bowing to the ground. [24]She fell at his feet and said, "Upon me alone, my lord, be the guilt; please let your servant speak in your ears, and hear the words of your servant. [25]My lord, do not take seriously this ill-natured fellow, Nabal; for as his

---

α Gk Compare Syr: Heb *the enemies of David*

name is, so is he; Nabal[a] is his name, and folly is with him; but I, your servant, did not see the young men of my lord, whom you sent.

26 "Now then, my lord, as the LORD lives, and as you yourself live, since the LORD has restrained you from bloodguilt and from taking vengeance with your own hand, now let your enemies and those who seek to do evil to my lord be like Nabal. [27]And now let this present that your servant has brought to my lord be given to the young men who follow my lord. [28]Please forgive the trespass of your servant; for the LORD will certainly make my lord a sure house, because my lord is fighting the battles of the LORD; and evil shall not be found in you so long as you live. [29]If anyone should rise up to pursue you and to seek your life, the life of my lord shall be bound in the bundle of the living under the care of the LORD your God; but the lives of your enemies he shall sling out as from the hollow of a sling. [30]When the LORD has done to my lord according to all the good that he has spoken concerning you, and has appointed you prince over Israel, [31]my lord shall have no cause of grief, or pangs of conscience, for having shed blood without cause or for having saved himself. And when the LORD has dealt well with my lord, then remember your servant."

32 David said to Abigail, "Blessed be the LORD, the God of Israel, who sent you to meet me today! [33]Blessed be your good sense, and blessed be you, who have kept me today from bloodguilt and from avenging myself by my own hand! [34]For as surely as the LORD the God of Israel lives, who has restrained me from hurting you, unless you had hurried and come to meet me, truly by morning there would not have been left to Nabal so much as one male." [35]Then David received from her hand what she had brought him; he said to her, "Go up to your house in peace; see, I have heeded your voice, and I have granted your petition."

36 Abigail came to Nabal; he was holding a feast in his house, like the feast of a king. Nabal's heart was merry within him, for he was very drunk; so she told him nothing at all until the morning light. [37]In the morning, when the wine had gone out of Nabal, his wife told him these things, and his heart died within him; he became like a stone. [38]About ten days later the LORD struck Nabal, and he died.

39 When David heard that Nabal was dead, he said, "Blessed be the LORD who has judged the case of Nabal's insult to me, and has kept back his servant from evil; the LORD has returned the evildoing of Nabal upon his own head." Then David sent and wooed Abigail, to make her his wife. [40]When David's servants came to Abigail at Carmel, they said to her, "David has sent us to you to take you to him as his wife." [41]She rose and bowed down, with her face to the ground, and said, "Your servant is a slave to wash the feet of the servants of my lord." [42]Abigail got up hurriedly and rode away on a donkey; her five maids attended her. She went after the messengers of David and became his wife.

43 David also married Ahinoam of Jezreel; both of them became his wives. [44]Saul had given his daughter Michal, David's wife, to Palti son of Laish, who was from Gallim.

David Spares Saul's Life a Second Time

26 Then the Ziphites came to Saul at Gibeah, saying, "David is in hiding on the hill of Hachilah, which is opposite Jeshimon."[b] [2]So Saul rose and went down to the Wilderness of Ziph, with three thousand chosen men of Israel, to seek David in the Wilderness of Ziph. [3]Saul encamped on the hill of Hachilah, which is opposite Jeshimon[b] beside the road. But David remained in the wilderness. When he learned that Saul had come after him into the wilderness, [4]David sent out spies, and learned that Saul had indeed arrived. [5]Then David set out and came to the place where Saul had encamped; and David saw the place where Saul lay, with Abner son of Ner, the commander of his army. Saul was lying within the encampment, while the army was encamped around him.

6 Then David said to Ahimelech the Hittite, and to Joab's brother Abishai son of Zeruiah, "Who will go down with me into the camp to Saul?" Abishai said, "I will go down with you." [7]So David and Abishai went to the army by night; there Saul lay sleeping within the encampment, with his spear stuck in the ground at his head; and Abner and the army lay around him. [8]Abishai said to David, "God has given your enemy into your hand today; now therefore let me pin him to the ground with one stroke of the spear; I will not strike him twice." [9]But David said to Abishai, "Do not destroy him; for who can raise his hand against the LORD's anointed, and be guiltless?" [10]David said, "As the LORD lives, the LORD will strike him down; or his day will come to die; or he will go down into battle and perish. [11]The

LORD forbid that I should raise my hand against the LORD's anointed; but now take the spear that is at his head, and the water jar, and let us go." [12]So David took the spear that was at Saul's head and the water jar, and they went away. No one saw it, or knew it, nor did anyone awake; for they were all asleep, because a deep sleep from the LORD had fallen upon them.

13 Then David went over to the other side, and stood on top of a hill far away, with a great distance between them. [14]David called to the army and to Abner son of Ner, saying, "Abner! Will you not answer?" Then Abner replied, "Who are you that calls to the king?" [15]David said to Abner, "Are you not a man? Who is like you in Israel? Why then have you not kept watch over your lord the king? For one of the people came in to destroy your lord the king. [16]This thing that you have done is not good. As the LORD lives, you deserve to die, because you have not kept watch over your lord, the LORD's anointed. See now, where is the king's spear, or the water jar that was at his head?"

17 Saul recognized David's voice, and said, "Is this your voice, my son David?" David said, "It is my voice, my lord, O king." [18]And he added, "Why does my lord pursue his servant? For what have I done? What guilt is on my hands? [19]Now therefore let my lord the king hear the words of his servant. If it is the LORD who has stirred you up against me, may he accept an offering; but if it is mortals, may they be cursed before the LORD, for they have driven me out today from my share in the heritage of the LORD, saying, 'Go, serve other gods.' [20]Now therefore, do not let my blood fall to the ground, away from the presence of the LORD; for the king of Israel has come out to seek a single flea, like one who hunts a partridge in the mountains."

21 Then Saul said, "I have done wrong; come back, my son David, for I will never harm you again, because my life was precious in your sight today; I have been a fool, and have made a great mistake." [22]David replied, "Here is the spear, O king! Let one of the young men come over and get it. [23]The LORD rewards everyone for his righteousness and his faithfulness; for the LORD gave you into my hand today, but I would not raise my hand against the LORD's anointed. [24]As your life was precious today in my sight, so may my life be precious in the sight of the LORD, and may he rescue me from all tribulation." [25]Then Saul said to David, "Blessed be you,

my son David! You will do many things and will succeed in them." So David went his way, and Saul returned to his place.

David Serves King Achish of Gath

27 David said in his heart, "I shall now perish one day by the hand of Saul; there is nothing better for me than to escape to the land of the Philistines; then Saul will despair of seeking me any longer within the borders of Israel, and I shall escape out of his hand." [2]So David set out and went over, he and the six hundred men who were with him, to King Achish son of Maoch of Gath. [3]David stayed with Achish at Gath, he and his troops, every man with his household, and David with his two wives, Ahinoam of Jezreel, and Abigail of Carmel, Nabal's widow. [4]When Saul was told that David had fled to Gath, he no longer sought for him.

5 Then David said to Achish, "If I have found favor in your sight, let a place be given me in one of the country towns, so that I may live there; for why should your servant live in the royal city with you?" [6]So that day Achish gave him Ziklag; therefore Ziklag has belonged to the kings of Judah to this day. [7]The length of time that David lived in the country of the Philistines was one year and four months.

8 Now David and his men went up and made raids on the Geshurites, the Girzites, and the Amalekites; for these were the landed settlements from Telam[a] on the way to Shur and on to the land of Egypt. [9]David struck the land, leaving neither man nor woman alive, but took away the sheep, the oxen, the donkeys, the camels, and the clothing, and came back to Achish. [10]When Achish asked, "Against whom[b] have you made a raid today?" David would say, "Against the Negeb of Judah," or "Against the Negeb of the Jerahmeelites," or, "Against the Negeb of the Kenites." [11]David left neither man nor woman alive to be brought back to Gath, thinking, "They might tell about us, and say, 'David has done so and so.'" Such was his practice all the time he lived in the country of the Philistines. [12]Achish trusted David, thinking, "He has made himself utterly abhorrent to his people Israel; therefore he shall always be my servant."

28 In those days the Philistines gathered their forces for war, to fight against Israel. Achish said to David, "You know, of course, that you and your men are to go out with me in the army." [2]David said to Achish, "Very well, then you shall

---

a Compare Gk 15.4: Heb *from of old*   **b** Q Ms Gk Vg: MT lacks *whom*

know what your servant can do." Achish said to David, "Very well, I will make you my bodyguard for life."

Saul Consults a Medium

3 Now Samuel had died, and all Israel had mourned for him and buried him in Ramah, his own city. Saul had expelled the mediums and the wizards from the land. [4]The Philistines assembled, and came and encamped at Shunem. Saul gathered all Israel, and they encamped at Gilboa. [5]When Saul saw the army of the Philistines, he was afraid, and his heart trembled greatly. [6]When Saul inquired of the LORD, the LORD did not answer him, not by dreams, or by Urim, or by prophets. [7]Then Saul said to his servants, "Seek out for me a woman who is a medium, so that I may go to her and inquire of her." His servants said to him, "There is a medium at Endor."

8 So Saul disguised himself and put on other clothes and went there, he and two men with him. They came to the woman by night. And he said, "Consult a spirit for me, and bring up for me the one whom I name to you." [9]The woman said to him, "Surely you know what Saul has done, how he has cut off the mediums and the wizards from the land. Why then are you laying a snare for my life to bring about my death?" [10]But Saul swore to her by the LORD, "As the LORD lives, no punishment shall come upon you for this thing." [11]Then the woman said, "Whom shall I bring up for you?" He answered, "Bring up Samuel for me." [12]When the woman saw Samuel, she cried out with a loud voice; and the woman said to Saul, "Why have you deceived me? You are Saul!" [13]The king said to her, "Have no fear; what do you see?" The woman said to Saul, "I see a divine being[a] coming up out of the ground." [14]He said to her, "What is his appearance?" She said, "An old man is coming up; he is wrapped in a robe." So Saul knew that it was Samuel, and he bowed with his face to the ground, and did obeisance.

15 Then Samuel said to Saul, "Why have you disturbed me by bringing me up?" Saul answered, "I am in great distress, for the Philistines are warring against me, and God has turned away from me and answers me no more, either by prophets or by dreams; so I have summoned you to tell me what I should do." [16]Samuel said, "Why then do you ask me, since the LORD has turned from me and become your enemy? [17]The LORD has done to you just as he spoke by me; for the LORD has torn the kingdom out

of your hand, and given it to your neighbor, David. [18]Because you did not obey the voice of the LORD, and did not carry out his fierce wrath against Amalek, therefore the LORD has done this thing to you today. [19]Moreover the LORD will give Israel along with you into the hands of the Philistines; and tomorrow you and your sons shall be with me; the LORD will also give the army of Israel into the hands of the Philistines."

20 Immediately Saul fell full length on the ground, filled with fear because of the words of Samuel; and there was no strength in him, for he had eaten nothing all day and all night. [21]The woman came to Saul, and when she saw that he was terrified, she said to him, "Your servant has listened to you; I have taken my life in my hand, and have listened to what you have said to me. [22]Now therefore, you also listen to your servant; let me set a morsel of bread before you. Eat, that you may have strength when you go on your way." [23]He refused, and said, "I will not eat." But his servants, together with the woman, urged him; and he listened to their words. So he got up from the ground and sat on the bed. [24]Now the woman had a fatted calf in the house. She quickly slaughtered it, and she took flour, kneaded it, and baked unleavened cakes. [25]She put them before Saul and his servants, and they ate. Then they rose and went away that night.

29 The Philistines Reject David

Now the Philistines gathered all their forces at Aphek, while the Israelites were encamped by the fountain that is in Jezreel. [2]As the lords of the Philistines were passing on by hundreds and by thousands, and David and his men were passing on in the rear with Achish, [3]the commanders of the Philistines said, "What are these Hebrews doing here?" Achish said to the commanders of the Philistines, "Is this not David, the servant of King Saul of Israel, who has been with me now for days and years? Since he deserted to me I have found no fault in him to this day." [4]But the commanders of the Philistines were angry with him; and the commanders of the Philistines said to him, "Send the man back, so that he may return to the place that you have assigned to him; he shall not go down with us to battle, or else he may become an adversary to us in the battle. For how could this fellow reconcile himself to his lord? Would it not be with the heads of the men here? [5]Is this not David, of whom they sing to one another in dances,

a Or *a god*; or *gods*

'Saul has killed his thousands,
    and David his ten thousands'?"

6 Then Achish called David and said to him, "As the LORD lives, you have been honest, and to me it seems right that you should march out and in with me in the campaign; for I have found nothing wrong in you from the day of your coming to me until today. Nevertheless the lords do not approve of you. ⁷So go back now; and go peaceably; do nothing to displease the lords of the Philistines." ⁸David said to Achish, "But what have I done? What have you found in your servant from the day I entered your service until now, that I should not go and fight against the enemies of my lord the king?" ⁹Achish replied to David, "I know that you are as blameless in my sight as an angel of God; nevertheless, the commanders of the Philistines have said, 'He shall not go up with us to the battle.' ¹⁰Now then rise early in the morning, you and the servants of your lord who came with you, and go to the place that I appointed for you. As for the evil report, do not take it to heart, for you have done well before me.ᵃ Start early in the morning, and leave as soon as you have light." ¹¹So David set out with his men early in the morning, to return to the land of the Philistines. But the Philistines went up to Jezreel.

30 David Avenges the Destruction of Ziklag

Now when David and his men came to Ziklag on the third day, the Amalekites had made a raid on the Negeb and on Ziklag. They had attacked Ziklag, burned it down, ²and taken captive the women and allᵇ who were in it, both small and great; they killed none of them, but carried them off, and went their way. ³When David and his men came to the city, they found it burned down, and their wives and sons and daughters taken captive. ⁴Then David and the people who were with him raised their voices and wept, until they had no more strength to weep. ⁵David's two wives also had been taken captive, Ahinoam of Jezreel, and Abigail the widow of Nabal of Carmel. ⁶David was in great danger; for the people spoke of stoning him, because all the people were bitter in spirit for their sons and daughters. But David strengthened himself in the LORD his God.

7 David said to the priest Abiathar son of Ahimelech, "Bring me the ephod." So Abiathar brought the ephod to David. ⁸David inquired of the LORD, "Shall I pursue this band? Shall I overtake them?" He an-

swered him, "Pursue; for you shall surely overtake and shall surely rescue." ⁹So David set out, he and the six hundred men who were with him. They came to the Wadi Besor, where those stayed who were left behind. ¹⁰But David went on with the pursuit, he and four hundred men; two hundred stayed behind, too exhausted to cross the Wadi Besor.

11 In the open country they found an Egyptian, and brought him to David. They gave him bread and he ate; they gave him water to drink; ¹²they also gave him a piece of fig cake and two clusters of raisins. When he had eaten, his spirit revived; for he had not eaten bread or drunk water for three days and three nights. ¹³Then David said to him, "To whom do you belong? Where are you from?" He said, "I am a young man of Egypt, servant to an Amalekite. My master left me behind because I fell sick three days ago. ¹⁴We had made a raid on the Negeb of the Cherethites and on that which belongs to Judah and on the Negeb of

LIVE IT!

Suicide Is Not the Answer
1 Samuel 31:1–6

In this troubling account, Saul commits suicide out of fear of what his enemies would do to him. His death leaves a gap for the Israelites, and David, Saul's enemy, deeply mourns his death (2 Samuel 1:1-27).

For some, pain, fear, and hopelessness can feel so overwhelming that death seems the only escape. But God's love and grace provide a way out that leads to life, not death.

No life is worthless! No pain is invincible! No matter how overwhelming your struggles and challenges seem, there are people who can help you, and people who could not bear to lose you. Seek God for help. Seek others for help. Even if you can't bring yourself to talk to people around you, there are many national suicide hotlines and websites you can contact. Suicide is NEVER a solution!

(For more on suicide, see "Live It: Second Chances," near Matthew 27:3-10.)

ᵃ Gk: Heb lacks *and go to the place . . . done well before me*   ᵇ Gk: Heb lacks *and all*

Caleb; and we burned Ziklag down." [15]David said to him, "Will you take me down to this raiding party?" He said, "Swear to me by God that you will not kill me, or hand me over to my master, and I will take you down to them."

16 When he had taken him down, they were spread out all over the ground, eating and drinking and dancing, because of the great amount of spoil they had taken from the land of the Philistines and from the land of Judah. [17]David attacked them from twilight until the evening of the next day. Not one of them escaped, except four hundred young men, who mounted camels and fled. [18]David recovered all that the Amalekites had taken; and David rescued his two wives. [19]Nothing was missing, whether small or great, sons or daughters, spoil or anything that had been taken; David brought back everything. [20]David also captured all the flocks and herds, which were driven ahead of the other cattle; people said, "This is David's spoil."

21 Then David came to the two hundred men who had been too exhausted to follow David, and who had been left at the Wadi Besor. They went out to meet David and to meet the people who were with him. When David drew near to the people he saluted them. [22]Then all the corrupt and worthless fellows among the men who had gone with David said, "Because they did not go with us, we will not give them any of the spoil that we have recovered, except that each man may take his wife and children, and leave." [23]But David said, "You shall not do so, my brothers, with what the LORD has given us; he has preserved us and handed over to us the raiding party that attacked us. [24]Who would listen to you in this matter? For the share of the one who goes down into the battle shall be the same as the share of the one who stays by the baggage; they shall share alike." [25]From that day forward he made it a statute and an ordinance for Israel; it continues to the present day.

26 When David came to Ziklag, he sent part of the spoil to his friends, the elders of Judah, saying, "Here is a present for you from the spoil of the enemies of the LORD"; [27]it was for those in Bethel, in Ramoth of the Negeb, in Jattir, [28]in Aroer, in Siphmoth, in Eshtemoa, [29]in Racal, in the towns of the Jerahmeelites, in the towns of the Kenites, [30]in Hormah, in Bor-ashan, in Athach, [31]in Hebron, all the places where David and his men had roamed.

The Death of Saul and His Sons

31 Now the Philistines fought against Israel; and the men of Israel fled before the Philistines, and many fell[a] on Mount Gilboa. [2]The Philistines overtook Saul and his sons; and the Philistines killed Jonathan and Abinadab and Malchishua, the sons of Saul. [3]The battle pressed hard upon Saul; the archers found him, and he was badly wounded by them. [4]Then Saul said to his armor-bearer, "Draw your sword and thrust me through with it, so that these uncircumcised may not come and thrust me through, and make sport of me." But his armor-bearer was unwilling; for he was terrified. So Saul took his own sword and fell upon it. [5]When his armor-bearer saw that Saul was dead, he also fell upon his sword and died with him. [6]So Saul and his three sons and his armor-bearer and all his men died together on the same day. [7]When the men of Israel who were on the other side of the valley and those beyond the Jordan saw that the men of Israel had fled and that Saul and his sons were dead, they forsook their towns and fled; and the Philistines came and occupied them.

8 The next day, when the Philistines came to strip the dead, they found Saul and his three sons fallen on Mount Gilboa. [9]They cut off his head, stripped off his armor, and sent messengers throughout the land of the Philistines to carry the good news to the houses of their idols and to the people. [10]They put his armor in the temple of Astarte;[b] and they fastened his body to the wall of Beth-shan. [11]But when the inhabitants of Jabesh-gilead heard what the Philistines had done to Saul, [12]all the valiant men set out, traveled all night long, and took the body of Saul and the bodies of his sons from the wall of Beth-shan. They came to Jabesh and burned them there. [13]Then they took their bones and buried them under the tamarisk tree in Jabesh, and fasted seven days.

a Heb *and they fell slain*   b Heb plural

2 Samuel ▶▶▶▶▶▶▶▶▶▶▶▶▶▶

"**P**olitician Guilty of Taking Bribes!" "Military Officer Charged with Sexual Misconduct!" "Pro Athlete Convicted of Using Drugs!" It seems as if the news is filled with one scandal after another. What's happening in the world today? we might be tempted to ask. Where are the honest, decent people? Are there any left? After reading 2 Samuel, you'll realize that scandals involving the rich and powerful are nothing new. But more important, God's will rises above human sin and weakness to accomplish good.

IN DEPTH

King David, whom we already met in 1 Samuel, is the main character in 2 Samuel. The youngest of Jesse's sons, David is secretly anointed to succeed King Saul. He kills Goliath, plays music in Saul's court, and becomes best friends with the king's son Jonathan. David takes the throne at the beginning of 2 Samuel and quickly extends Israel's boundaries in every direction. Everything looks hopeful for the nation.

As 2 Samuel continues, however, we discover that this hero is far from perfect. He sleeps with Bathsheba, the wife of one of his soldiers, and then tries to deceive the man when Bathsheba reports that she is pregnant. Later, he has the soldier killed and takes Bathsheba as his own. Soon, several tragedies hit his family, and more bad decisions hurt his reign, leaving us with a mixed picture of Israel's second king. Was David a great saint or a great sinner?

It was during David's reign that the people's understanding of their covenant relationship with God began to center less on the exodus experience and more on their desire for a king and kingdom (2 Samuel 7:1–17). This fact is underlined in a memorable way when David, after completing his own magnificent palace, declares that he will build a house for God. But God does not want a temple; God wants a relationship. God wants to maintain a covenant relationship with the people of Israel through all history (2 Samuel 7:16).

King David was a talented military leader and a powerful ruler, but he shared our broken human nature. The author of 2 Samuel reminds us that even the great and the mighty stand in need of God's help and mercy. Even they must keep God's covenant. David became a symbol of the ideal king and of the future messiah because of his reliance on God. This is where true greatness is born.

QUICK FACTS

- **Dates Covered:** From 1000 to 961 B.C.
- **Author:** An unknown author writing around 600 to 500 B.C., probably using ancient court records and hero stories
- **Themes:** David's rise to power and descent into sin; the importance of obeying God and the ways God works in our lives
- **Noteworthy:** The prophet Samuel doesn't appear in this book, even though it carries his name.

AT A GLANCE

- **2 Samuel 1** David's mourning for Saul and Jonathan
- **2 Samuel 2–20** The reign of David
- **2 Samuel 21–24** Miscellaneous texts, including David's last words

1 David Mourns for Saul and Jonathan

After the death of Saul, when David had returned from defeating the Amalekites, David remained two days in Ziklag. ²On the third day, a man came from Saul's camp, with his clothes torn and dirt on his head. When he came to David, he fell to the ground and did obeisance. ³David said to him, "Where have you come from?" He said to him, "I have escaped from the camp of Israel." ⁴David said to him, "How did things go? Tell me!" He answered, "The army fled from the battle, but also many of the army fell and died; and Saul and his son Jonathan also died." ⁵Then David asked the young man who was reporting to him, "How do you know that Saul and his son Jonathan died?" ⁶The young man reporting to him said, "I happened to be on Mount Gilboa; and there was Saul leaning on his spear, while the chariots and the horsemen drew close to him. ⁷When he looked behind him, he saw me, and called to me. I answered, 'Here sir.' ⁸And he said to me, 'Who are you?' I answered him, 'I am an Amalekite.' ⁹He said to me, 'Come, stand over me and kill me; for convulsions have seized me, and yet my life still lingers.' ¹⁰So I stood over him, and killed him, for I knew that he could not live after he had fallen. I took the crown that was on his head and the armlet that was on his arm, and I have brought them here to my lord."

11 Then David took hold of his clothes and tore them; and all the men who were with him did the same. ¹²They mourned and wept, and fasted until evening for Saul and for his son Jonathan, and for the army of the LORD and for the house of Israel, because they had fallen by the sword. ¹³David said to the young man who had reported to him, "Where do you come from?" He answered, "I am the son of a resident alien, an Amalekite." ¹⁴David said to him, "Were you not afraid to lift your hand to destroy the LORD's anointed?" ¹⁵Then David called one of the young men and said, "Come here and strike him down." So he struck him down and he died. ¹⁶David said to him, "Your blood be on your head; for your own mouth has testified against you, saying, 'I have killed the LORD's anointed.'"

17 David intoned this lamentation over Saul and his son Jonathan. ¹⁸(He ordered that The Song of the Bow*a* be taught to the people of Judah; it is written in the Book of Jashar.) He said:

¹⁹ Your glory, O Israel, lies slain upon your high
            places!
        How the mighty have fallen!
²⁰ Tell it not in Gath,
        proclaim it not in the streets of Ashkelon;
    or the daughters of the Philistines will rejoice,
        the daughters of the uncircumcised will
            exult.

²¹ You mountains of Gilboa,
        let there be no dew or rain upon you,
        nor bounteous fields!*b*

a Heb *that The Bow*   *b* Meaning of Heb uncertain

For there the shield of the mighty was defiled,
　　the shield of Saul, anointed with oil no
　　　more.

22 From the blood of the slain,
　　from the fat of the mighty,
　the bow of Jonathan did not turn
　　　back,
　　nor the sword of Saul return empty.

23 Saul and Jonathan, beloved and
　　　lovely!
　　In life and in death they were not divided;
　they were swifter than eagles,
　　they were stronger than lions.

24 O daughters of Israel, weep over Saul,
　　who clothed you with crimson, in luxury,
　　who put ornaments of gold on your
　　　apparel.

25 How the mighty have fallen
　　in the midst of the battle!

Jonathan lies slain upon your high places.
26 　I am distressed for you, my brother
　　　Jonathan;
　greatly beloved were you to me;
　　your love to me was wonderful,
　　passing the love of women.

27 How the mighty have fallen,
　　and the weapons of war perished!

David Anointed King of Judah

2 After this David inquired of the Lord, "Shall I go up into any of the cities of Judah?" The Lord said to him, "Go up." David said, "To which shall I go up?" He said, "To Hebron." [2]So David went up there, along with his two wives, Ahinoam of Jezreel, and Abigail the widow of Nabal of Carmel. [3]David brought up the men who were with him, every one with his household; and they settled in the towns of Hebron. [4]Then the people of Judah came, and there they anointed David king over the house of Judah.

When they told David, "It was the people of Jabesh-gilead who buried Saul," [5]David sent messengers to the people of Jabesh-gilead, and said to them, "May you be blessed by the Lord, because you showed this loyalty to Saul your lord, and buried him! [6]Now may the Lord show steadfast love and faithfulness to you! And I too will reward you because you have done this thing. [7]Therefore let your hands be strong, and be valiant; for Saul your lord is dead, and the house of Judah has anointed me king over them."

Ishbaal King of Israel

8 But Abner son of Ner, commander of Saul's army, had taken Ishbaal[a] son of Saul, and brought him over to Mahanaim. [9]He made him king over Gilead, the Ashurites, Jezreel, Ephraim, Benjamin, and over all Israel. [10]Ishbaal,[a] Saul's son, was forty years old when he began to reign over Israel, and he reigned two years. But the house of Judah followed David. [11]The time that David was king in Hebron over the house of Judah was seven years and six months.

The Battle of Gibeon

12 Abner son of Ner, and the servants of Ishbaal[a] son of Saul, went out from Mahanaim to Gibeon. [13]Joab son of Zeruiah, and the servants of David, went out and met them at the pool of Gibeon. One group sat on one side of the pool, while the other sat on the other side of the pool. [14]Abner said to Joab, "Let the young men come forward and have a contest before us." Joab said, "Let them come forward." [15]So they came forward and were counted as they passed by, twelve for Benjamin and Ishbaal[a] son of Saul, and twelve of the servants of David. [16]Each grasped his opponent by the head, and thrust his sword in his opponent's side; so they fell down together. Therefore that place was called Helkath-hazzurim,[b] which is at Gibeon. [17]The battle was very fierce that day; and Abner and the men of Israel were beaten by the servants of David.

18 The three sons of Zeruiah were there, Joab, Abishai, and Asahel. Now Asahel was as swift of foot as a wild gazelle. [19]Asahel pursued Abner, turning neither to the right nor to the left as he followed him. [20]Then Abner looked back and said, "Is it you, Asahel?" He answered, "Yes, it is." [21]Abner said to him, "Turn to your right or to your left, and seize one of the young men, and take his spoil." But Asahel would not turn away from following him. [22]Abner said again to Asahel, "Turn away from following me; why should I strike you to the ground? How then could I show my face to your brother Joab?" [23]But he refused to turn away. So Abner struck him in the stomach with

---

a Gk Compare 1 Chr 8.33; 9.39: Heb *Ish-bosheth*, "man of shame"　b That is *Field of Sword-edges*

the butt of his spear, so that the spear came out at his back. He fell there, and died where he lay. And all those who came to the place where Asahel had fallen and died, stood still.

24 But Joab and Abishai pursued Abner. As the sun was going down they came to the hill of Ammah, which lies before Giah on the way to the wilderness of Gibeon. [25]The Benjaminites rallied around Abner and formed a single band; they took their stand on the top of a hill. [26]Then Abner called to Joab, "Is the sword to keep devouring forever? Do you not know that the end will be bitter? How long will it be before you order your people to turn from the pursuit of their kinsmen?" [27]Joab said, "As God lives, if you had not spoken, the people would have continued to pursue their kinsmen, not stopping until morning." [28]Joab sounded the trumpet and all the people stopped; they no longer pursued Israel or engaged in battle any further.

29 Abner and his men traveled all that night through the Arabah; they crossed the Jordan, and, marching the whole forenoon,[a] they came to Mahanaim. [30]Joab returned from the pursuit of Abner; and when he had gathered all the people together, there were missing of David's servants nineteen men besides Asahel. [31]But the servants of David had killed of Benjamin three hundred sixty of Abner's men. [32]They took up Asahel and buried him in the tomb of his father, which was at Bethlehem. Joab and his men marched all night, and the day broke upon them at Hebron.

Abner Defects to David

3 There was a long war between the house of Saul and the house of David; David grew stronger and stronger, while the house of Saul became weaker and weaker.

2 Sons were born to David at Hebron: his firstborn was Amnon, of Ahinoam of Jezreel; [3]his second, Chileab, of Abigail the widow of Nabal of Carmel; the third, Absalom son of Maacah, daughter of King Talmai of Geshur; [4]the fourth, Adonijah son of Haggith; the fifth, Shephatiah son of Abital; [5]and the sixth, Ithream, of David's wife Eglah. These were born to David in Hebron.

6 While there was war between the house of Saul and the house of David, Abner was making himself strong in the house of Saul. [7]Now Saul had a concubine whose name was Rizpah daughter of Aiah. And Ishbaal[b] said to Abner, "Why have you gone in to my father's concubine?" [8]The words of Ishbaal[c] made Abner very angry; he said, "Am I a dog's head for Judah? Today I keep showing loyalty to the house of your father Saul, to his brothers, and to his friends, and have not given you into the hand of David; and yet you charge me now with a crime concerning this woman. [9]So may God do to Abner and so may he add to it! For just what the LORD has sworn to David, that will I accomplish for him, [10]to transfer the kingdom from the house of Saul, and set up the throne of David over Israel and over Judah, from Dan to Beer-sheba." [11]And Ishbaal[b] could not answer Abner another word, because he feared him.

12 Abner sent messengers to David at Hebron,[d] saying, "To whom does the land belong? Make your covenant with me, and I will give you my support to bring all Israel over to you." [13]He said, "Good; I will make a covenant with you. But one thing I require of you: you shall never appear in my presence unless you bring Saul's daughter Michal when you come to see me." [14]Then David sent messengers to Saul's son Ishbaal,[e] saying, "Give me my wife Michal, to whom I became engaged at the price of one hundred foreskins of the Philistines." [15]Ishbaal[e] sent and took her from her husband Paltiel the son of Laish. [16]But her husband went with her, weeping as he walked behind her all the way to Bahurim. Then Abner said to him, "Go back home!" So he went back.

17 Abner sent word to the elders of Israel, saying, "For some time past you have been seeking David as king over you. [18]Now then bring it about; for the LORD has promised David: Through my servant David I will save my people Israel from the hand of the Philistines, and from all their enemies." [19]Abner also spoke directly to the Benjaminites; then Abner went to tell David at Hebron all that Israel and the whole house of Benjamin were ready to do.

20 When Abner came with twenty men to David at Hebron, David made a feast for Abner and the men who were with him. [21]Abner said to David, "Let me go and rally all Israel to my lord the king, in order that they may make a covenant with you, and that you may reign over all that your heart desires." So David dismissed Abner, and he went away in peace.

Abner Is Killed by Joab

22 Just then the servants of David arrived with Joab from a raid, bringing much spoil with them.

---

a Meaning of Heb uncertain   b Heb *And he*   c Gk Compare 1 Chr 8.33; 9.39: Heb *Ish-bosheth*, "man of shame"   d Gk: Heb *where he was*   e Heb *Ish-bosheth*

But Abner was not with David at Hebron, for David[a] had dismissed him, and he had gone away in peace. 23When Joab and all the army that was with him came, it was told Joab, "Abner son of Ner came to the king, and he has dismissed him, and he has gone away in peace." 24Then Joab went to the king and said, "What have you done? Abner came to you; why did you dismiss him, so that he got away? 25You know that Abner son of Ner came to deceive you, and to learn your comings and goings and to learn all that you are doing."

26 When Joab came out from David's presence, he sent messengers after Abner, and they brought him back from the cistern of Sirah; but David did not know about it. 27When Abner returned to Hebron, Joab took him aside in the gateway to speak with him privately, and there he stabbed him in the stomach. So he died for shedding[b] the blood of Asahel, Joab's[c] brother. 28Afterward, when David heard of it, he said, "I and my kingdom are forever guiltless before the LORD for the blood of Abner son of Ner. 29May the guilt[d] fall on the head of Joab, and on all his father's house; and may the house of Joab never be without one who has a discharge, or who is leprous,[e] or who holds a spindle, or who falls by the sword, or who lacks food!" 30So Joab and his brother Abishai murdered Abner because he had killed their brother Asahel in the battle at Gibeon.

31 Then David said to Joab and to all the people who were with him, "Tear your clothes, and put on sackcloth, and mourn over Abner." And King David followed the bier. 32They buried Abner at Hebron. The king lifted up his voice and wept at the grave of Abner, and all the people wept. 33The king lamented for Abner, saying,

"Should Abner die as a fool dies?
34 Your hands were not bound,
        your feet were not fettered;
    as one falls before the wicked
        you have fallen."

And all the people wept over him again. 35Then all the people came to persuade David to eat something while it was still day; but David swore, saying, "So may God do to me, and more, if I taste bread or anything else before the sun goes down!" 36All the people took notice of it, and it pleased them; just as everything the king did pleased all the people. 37So all the people and all Israel understood that day that the king had no part in the killing of Abner son of Ner. 38And the king said to his servants, "Do you not know that a prince and a great man has fallen this day in Israel? 39Today I am powerless, even though anointed king; these men, the sons of Zeruiah, are too violent for me. The LORD pay back the one who does wickedly in accordance with his wickedness!"

Ishbaal Assassinated

4 When Saul's son Ishbaal[f] heard that Abner had died at Hebron, his courage failed, and all Israel was dismayed. 2Saul's son had two captains of raiding bands; the name of the one was Baanah, and the name of the other Rechab. They were sons of Rimmon a Benjaminite from Beeroth—for Beeroth is considered to belong to Benjamin. 3(Now the people of Beeroth had fled to Gittaim and are there as resident aliens to this day).

4 Saul's son Jonathan had a son who was crippled in his feet. He was five years old when the news about Saul and Jonathan came from Jezreel. His nurse picked him up and fled; and, in her haste to flee, it happened that he fell and became lame. His name was Mephibosheth.[g]

5 Now the sons of Rimmon the Beerothite, Rechab and Baanah, set out, and about the heat of the day they came to the house of Ishbaal,[h] while he was taking his noonday rest. 6They came inside the house as though to take wheat, and they struck him in the stomach; then Rechab and his brother Baanah escaped.[i] 7Now they had come into the house while he was lying on his couch in his bedchamber; they attacked him, killed him, and beheaded him. Then they took his head and traveled by way of the Arabah all night long. 8They brought the head of Ishbaal[h] to David at Hebron and said to the king, "Here is the head of Ishbaal,[h] son of Saul, your enemy, who sought your life; the LORD has avenged my lord the king this day on Saul and on his offspring."

9 David answered Rechab and his brother Baanah, the sons of Rimmon the Beerothite, "As the LORD lives, who has redeemed my life out of every adversity, 10when the one who told me, 'See, Saul is dead,' thought he was bringing good news, I seized him and killed him at Ziklag—this was the reward I gave him for his news. 11How much more then, when wicked men have killed a righteous man on his bed in his own house! And now shall I not require his blood at your hand, and destroy you from the earth?" 12So David commanded the young men, and they killed them; they cut off their hands and

---

a Heb *he*   b Heb lacks *shedding*   c Heb *his*   d Heb *May it*   e A term for several skin diseases; precise meaning uncertain   f Heb lacks *Ishbaal*
g In 1 Chr 8.34 and 9.40, *Merib-baal*   h Heb *Ish-bosheth*   i Meaning of Heb of verse 6 uncertain

feet, and hung their bodies beside the pool at Hebron. But the head of Ishbaal[a] they took and buried in the tomb of Abner at Hebron.

5 David Anointed King of All Israel

Then all the tribes of Israel came to David at Hebron, and said, "Look, we are your bone and flesh. [2]For some time, while Saul was king over us, it was you who led out Israel and brought it in. The LORD said to you: It is you who shall be shepherd of my people Israel, you who shall be ruler over Israel." [3]So all the elders of Israel came to the king at Hebron; and King David made a covenant with them at Hebron before the LORD, and they anointed David king over Israel. [4]David was thirty years old when he began to reign, and he reigned forty years. [5]At Hebron he reigned over Judah seven years and six months; and at Jerusalem he reigned over all Israel and Judah thirty-three years.

Jerusalem Made Capital of the United Kingdom

6 The king and his men marched to Jerusalem against the Jebusites, the inhabitants of the land, who said to David, "You will not come in here, even the blind and the lame will turn you back"—thinking, "David cannot come in here." [7]Nevertheless David took the stronghold of Zion, which is now the city of David. [8]David had said on that day, "Whoever would strike down the Jebusites, let him get up the water shaft to attack the lame and the blind, those whom David hates."[b] Therefore it is said, "The blind and the lame shall not come into the house." [9]David occupied the stronghold, and named it the city of David. David built the city all around from the Millo inward. [10]And David became greater and greater, for the LORD, the God of hosts, was with him.

11 King Hiram of Tyre sent messengers to David, along with cedar trees, and carpenters and masons who built David a house. [12]David then perceived

that the LORD had established him king over Israel, and that he had exalted his kingdom for the sake of his people Israel.

13 In Jerusalem, after he came from Hebron, David took more concubines and wives; and more sons and daughters were born to David. [14]These are the names of those who were born to him in Jerusalem: Shammua, Shobab, Nathan, Solomon, [15]Ibhar, Elishua, Nepheg, Japhia, [16]Elishama, Eliada, and Eliphelet.

Philistine Attack Repulsed

17 When the Philistines heard that David had been anointed king over Israel, all the Philistines went up in search of David; but David heard about it and went down to the stronghold. [18]Now the Philistines had come and spread out in the valley of Rephaim. [19]David inquired of the LORD, "Shall I go up against the Philistines? Will you give them into my hand?" The LORD said to David, "Go up; for I will certainly give the Philistines into your hand." [20]So David came to Baal-perazim, and David defeated them there. He said, "The LORD has burst forth against[c] my enemies before me, like a bursting flood." Therefore that place is called Baal-perazim.[d] [21]The Philistines abandoned their idols there, and David and his men carried them away.

22 Once again the Philistines came up, and were spread out in the valley of Rephaim. [23]When David inquired of the LORD, he said, "You shall not go up; go around to their rear, and come upon them opposite the balsam trees. [24]When you hear the sound of marching in the tops of the balsam trees, then be on the alert; for then the LORD has gone out before you to strike down the army of the Philistines." [25]David did just as the LORD had commanded him; and he struck down the Philistines from Geba all the way to Gezer.

6 David Brings the Ark to Jerusalem

David again gathered all the chosen men of Israel, thirty thousand. [2]David and all the people with him set out and went from Baale-judah, to bring up from there the ark of God, which is called by the name of the LORD of hosts who is enthroned on the cherubim. [3]They carried the ark of God on a new cart, and brought it out of the house of Abinadab, which was on the hill. Uzzah and Ahio,[e] the sons of Abinadab, were driving the new cart [4]with the ark of God;[f] and Ahio[e] went in front of

---

a Heb *Ish-bosheth*   b Another reading is *those who hate David*   c Heb *paraz*   d That is *Lord of Bursting Forth*   e Or *and his brother*   f Compare Gk: Heb *and brought it out of the house of Abinadab, which was on the hill with the ark of God*

the ark. [5]David and all the house of Israel were dancing before the LORD with all their might, with songs[a] and lyres and harps and tambourines and castanets and cymbals.

6 When they came to the threshing floor of Nacon, Uzzah reached out his hand to the ark of God and took hold of it, for the oxen shook it. [7]The anger of the LORD was kindled against Uzzah; and God struck him there because he reached out his hand to the ark;[b] and he died there beside the ark of God. [8]David was angry because the LORD had burst forth with an outburst upon Uzzah; so that place is called Perez-uzzah,[c] to this day. [9]David was afraid of the LORD that day; he said, "How can the ark of the LORD come into my care?" [10]So David was unwilling to take the ark of the LORD into his care in the city of David; instead David took it to the house of Obed-edom the Gittite. [11]The ark of the LORD remained in the house of Obed-edom the Gittite three months; and the LORD blessed Obed-edom and all his household.

12 It was told King David, "The LORD has blessed the household of Obed-edom and all that belongs to him, because of the ark of God." So David went and brought up the ark of God from the house of Obed-edom to the city of David with rejoicing; [13]and when those who bore the ark of the LORD had gone six paces, he sacrificed an ox and a fatling. [14]David danced before the LORD with all his might; David was girded with a linen ephod. [15]So David and all the house of Israel brought up the ark of the LORD with shouting, and with the sound of the trumpet.

16 As the ark of the LORD came into the city of David, Michal daughter of Saul looked out of the window, and saw King David leaping and dancing before the LORD; and she despised him in her heart.

17 They brought in the ark of the LORD, and set it in its place, inside the tent that David had pitched for it; and David offered burnt offerings and offerings of well-being before the LORD. [18]When David had finished offering the burnt offerings and the offerings of well-being, he blessed the people in the name of the LORD of hosts, [19]and distributed food among all the people, the whole multitude of Israel, both men and women, to each a cake of bread, a portion of meat,[d] and a cake of raisins. Then all the people went back to their homes.

20 David returned to bless his household. But Michal the daughter of Saul came out to meet David, and said, "How the king of Israel honored himself today, uncovering himself today before the eyes of his servants' maids, as any vulgar fellow might shamelessly uncover himself!" [21]David said to Michal, "It was before the LORD, who chose me in place of your father and all his household, to appoint me as prince over Israel, the people of the LORD, that I have danced before the LORD. [22]I will make myself yet more contemptible than this, and I will be abased in my own eyes; but by the maids of whom you have spoken, by them I shall be held in honor." [23]And Michal the daughter of Saul had no child to the day of her death.

God's Covenant with David

7 Now when the king was settled in his house, and the LORD had given him rest

LIVE IT!

Holding Nothing Back · 2 Samuel 6:11–19

It's a party! How else could we describe the festivities surrounding the triumphant bringing of the ark of the Lord into Jerusalem? And King David is leading the way, dancing before the Lord "with all his might" (2 Samuel 6:14). What a scene that must have been! King David was wonderfully uninhibited when it came to expressing his great joy at escorting the ark into the city he had made his own.

We often attend church or Christian events as critical and uninvolved observers, much like Michal, David's wife. David shows us the true way to celebrate—with singing and dancing and eating. We need to celebrate together God's presence in our lives! Here David is our role model. Let's sing the song in our heart and dance to the music God has planted within us.

• Are you an observer or a participant in the dance of life?

• How can you better celebrate the Lord in your life?

---

a Q Ms Gk 1 Chr 13.8: Heb *fir trees*   **b** 1 Chr 13.10 Compare Q Ms: Meaning of Heb uncertain   **c** That is *Bursting Out Against Uzzah*   **d** Vg: Meaning of Heb uncertain

Take Time for Praise · 2 Samuel 7:18–29

"Then King David went in and sat before the LORD, and said, 'Who am I, O Lord GOD, and what is my house, that you have brought me thus far?'" (2 Samuel 7:18). When was the last time you brought yourself before God, like King David, just to offer praise for all God has done for you?

It's easy to feel too busy to take time for God, and then complain and get frustrated because God feels distant when you suddenly want direction. It's important and necessary to humbly place yourself before God and to praise God for the good you experience.

Find a quiet place. Take fifteen minutes. No iPod, no TV, no laptop or book. Think of all the positive and happy things in your life and, in your own words, say a prayer of thanks to God for caring for you and the people you love.

from all his enemies around him, [2] the king said to the prophet Nathan, "See now, I am living in a house of cedar, but the ark of God stays in a tent." [3] Nathan said to the king, "Go, do all that you have in mind; for the LORD is with you."

4 But that same night the word of the LORD came to Nathan: [5] Go and tell my servant David: Thus says the LORD: Are you the one to build me a house to live in? [6] I have not lived in a house since the day I brought up the people of Israel from Egypt to this day, but I have been moving about in a tent and a tabernacle. [7] Wherever I have moved about among all the people of Israel, did I ever speak a word with any of the tribal leaders[a] of Israel, whom I commanded to shepherd my people Israel, saying, "Why have you not built me a house of cedar?" [8] Now therefore thus you shall say to my servant David: Thus says the LORD of hosts: I took you from the pasture, from following the sheep to be prince over my people Israel; [9] and I have been with you wherever you went, and have cut off all your enemies from before you; and I will make for you a great name, like the name of the great ones of the earth. [10] And I will appoint a place for my people Israel and will plant them, so that they may live in their own place, and be disturbed no more; and evildoers shall afflict them no more, as formerly, [11] from the time that I appointed judges over my people Israel; and I will give you rest from all your enemies. Moreover the LORD declares to you that the LORD will make you a house. [12] When your days are fulfilled and you lie down with your ancestors, I will raise up your offspring after you, who shall come forth from your body, and I will establish his kingdom. [13] He shall

build a house for my name, and I will establish the throne of his kingdom forever. [14] I will be a father to him, and he shall be a son to me. When he commits iniquity, I will punish him with a rod such as mortals use, with blows inflicted by human beings. [15] But I will not take[b] my steadfast love from him, as I took it from Saul, whom I put away from before you. [16] Your house and your kingdom shall be made sure forever before me;[c] your throne shall be established forever. [17] In accordance with all these words and with all this vision, Nathan spoke to David.

David's Prayer

18 Then King David went in and sat before the LORD, and said, "Who am I, O Lord GOD, and what is my house, that you have brought me thus far? [19] And yet this was a small thing in your eyes, O Lord GOD; you have spoken also of your servant's house for a great while to come. May this be instruction for the people,[d] O Lord GOD! [20] And what more can David say to you? For you know your servant, O Lord GOD! [21] Because of your promise, and according to your own heart, you have wrought all this greatness, so that your servant may know it. [22] Therefore you are great, O LORD God; for there is no one like you, and there is no God besides you, according to all that we have heard with our ears. [23] Who is like your people, like Israel? Is there another[e] nation on earth whose God went to redeem it as a people, and to make a name for himself, doing great and awesome things for them,[f] by driving out[g] before his people nations and their gods?[h] [24] And you established your people Israel for yourself to be your people forever; and you, O LORD, became their

God. [25]And now, O LORD God, as for the word that you have spoken concerning your servant and concerning his house, confirm it forever; do as you have promised. [26]Thus your name will be magnified forever in the saying, 'The LORD of hosts is God over Israel'; and the house of your servant David will be established before you. [27]For you, O LORD of hosts, the God of Israel, have made this revelation to your servant, saying, 'I will build you a house'; therefore your servant has found courage to pray this prayer to you. [28]And now, O Lord GOD, you are God, and your words are true, and you have promised this good thing to your servant; [29]now therefore may it please you to bless the house of your servant, so that it may continue forever before you; for you, O Lord GOD, have spoken, and with your blessing shall the house of your servant be blessed forever."

David's Wars

8 Some time afterward, David attacked the Philistines and subdued them; David took Metheg-ammah out of the hand of the Philistines. 2 He also defeated the Moabites and, making them lie down on the ground, measured them off with a cord; he measured two lengths of cord for those who were to be put to death, and one length[a] for those who were to be spared. And the Moabites became servants to David and brought tribute.

3 David also struck down King Hadadezer son of Rehob of Zobah, as he went to restore his monument[b] at the river Euphrates. [4]David took from him one thousand seven hundred horsemen, and twenty thousand foot soldiers. David hamstrung all the chariot horses, but left enough for a hundred chariots. [5]When the Arameans of Damascus came to help King Hadadezer of Zobah, David killed twenty-two thousand men of the Arameans. [6]Then David put garrisons among the Arameans of Damascus; and the Arameans became servants to David and brought tribute. The LORD gave victory to David wherever he went. [7]David took the gold shields that were carried by the servants of Hadadezer, and brought them to Jerusalem. [8]From Betah and from Berothai, towns of Hadadezer, King David took a great amount of bronze.

9 When King Toi of Hamath heard that David had defeated the whole army of Hadadezer, [10]Toi sent his son Joram to King David, to greet him and to congratulate him because he had fought against Hadadezer and defeated him. Now Hadadezer had often been at war with Toi. Joram brought with him articles of silver, gold, and bronze; [11]these also King David dedicated to the LORD, together with the silver and gold that he dedicated from all the nations he subdued, [12]from Edom, Moab, the Ammonites, the Philistines, Amalek, and from the spoil of King Hadadezer son of Rehob of Zobah.

13 David won a name for himself. When he returned, he killed eighteen thousand Edomites[c] in the Valley of Salt. [14]He put garrisons in Edom; throughout all Edom he put garrisons, and all the Edomites became David's servants. And the LORD gave victory to David wherever he went.

David's Officers

15 So David reigned over all Israel; and David administered justice and equity to all his people. [16]Joab son of Zeruiah was over the army; Jehoshaphat son of Ahilud was recorder; [17]Zadok son of Ahitub and Ahimelech son of Abiathar were priests; Seraiah was secretary; [18]Benaiah son of Jehoiada was over[d] the Cherethites and the Pelethites; and David's sons were priests.

David's Kindness to Mephibosheth

9 David asked, "Is there still anyone left of the house of Saul to whom I may show kindness for Jonathan's sake?" [2]Now there was a servant of the house of Saul whose name was Ziba, and he was summoned to David. The king said to him, "Are you Ziba?" And he said, "At your service!" [3]The king said, "Is there anyone remaining of the house of Saul to whom I may show the kindness of God?" Ziba said to the king, "There remains a son of Jonathan; he is crippled in his feet." [4]The king said to him, "Where is he?" Ziba said to the king, "He is in the house of Machir son of Ammiel, at Lo-debar." [5]Then King David sent and brought him from the house of Machir son of Ammiel, at Lo-debar. [6]Mephibosheth[e] son of Jonathan son of Saul came to David, and fell on his face and did obeisance. David said, "Mephibosheth!"[e] He answered, "I am your servant." [7]David said to him, "Do not be afraid, for I will show you kindness for the sake of your father Jonathan; I will restore to you all the land of your grandfather Saul, and you yourself shall eat at my table always." [8]He did obeisance and said, "What is your servant, that you should look upon a dead dog such as I?"

---

a Heb *one full length*   b Compare 1 Sam 15.12 and 2 Sam 18.18   c Gk: Heb *returned from striking down eighteen thousand Arameans*   d Syr Tg Vg 20.23; 1 Chr 18.17: Heb lacks *was over*   e Or *Merib-baal*: See 4.4 note

9 Then the king summoned Saul's servant Ziba, and said to him, "All that belonged to Saul and to all his house I have given to your master's grandson. [10]You and your sons and your servants shall till the land for him, and shall bring in the produce, so that your master's grandson may have food to eat; but your master's grandson Mephibosheth[a] shall always eat at my table." Now Ziba had fifteen sons and twenty servants. [11]Then Ziba said to the king, "According to all that my lord the king commands his servant, so your servant will do." Mephibosheth[a] ate at David's[b] table, like one of the king's sons. [12]Mephibosheth[a] had a young son whose name was Mica. And all who lived in Ziba's house became Mephibosheth's[c] servants. [13]Mephibosheth[a] lived in Jerusalem, for he always ate at the king's table. Now he was lame in both his feet.

10

The Ammonites and Arameans Are Defeated

Some time afterward, the king of the Ammonites died, and his son Hanun succeeded him. [2]David said, "I will deal loyally with Hanun son of Nahash, just as his father dealt loyally with me." So David sent envoys to console him concerning his father. When David's envoys came into the land of the Ammonites, [3]the princes of the Ammonites said to their lord Hanun, "Do you really think that David is honoring your father just because he has sent messengers with condolences to you? Has not David sent his envoys to you to search the city, to spy it out, and to overthrow it?" [4]So Hanun seized David's envoys, shaved off half the beard of each, cut off their garments in the middle at their hips, and sent them away. [5]When David was told, he sent to meet them, for the men were greatly ashamed. The king said, "Remain at Jericho until your beards have grown, and then return."

6 When the Ammonites saw that they had become odious to David, the Ammonites sent and hired the Arameans of Beth-rehob and the Arameans of Zobah, twenty thousand foot soldiers, as well as the king of Maacah, one thousand men, and the men of Tob, twelve thousand men. [7]When David heard of it, he sent Joab and all the army with the warriors. [8]The Ammonites came out and drew up in battle array at the entrance of the gate; but the Arameans of Zobah and of Rehob, and the men of Tob and Maacah, were by themselves in the open country.

9 When Joab saw that the battle was set against

him both in front and in the rear, he chose some of the picked men of Israel, and arrayed them against the Arameans; [10]the rest of his men he put in the charge of his brother Abishai, and he arrayed them against the Ammonites. [11]He said, "If the Arameans are too strong for me, then you shall help me; but if the Ammonites are too strong for you, then I will come and help you. [12]Be strong, and let us be courageous for the sake of our people, and for the cities of our God; and may the LORD do what seems good to him." [13]So Joab and the people who were with him moved forward into battle against the Arameans; and they fled before him. [14]When the Ammonites saw that the Arameans fled, they likewise fled before Abishai, and entered the city. Then Joab returned from fighting against the Ammonites, and came to Jerusalem.

15 But when the Arameans saw that they had been defeated by Israel, they gathered themselves together. [16]Hadadezer sent and brought out the Arameans who were beyond the Euphrates; and they came to Helam, with Shobach the commander of the army of Hadadezer at their head. [17]When it was told David, he gathered all Israel together, and crossed the Jordan, and came to Helam. The Arameans arrayed themselves against David and fought with him. [18]The Arameans fled before Israel; and David killed of the Arameans seven hundred chariot teams, and forty thousand horsemen,[d] and wounded Shobach the commander of their army, so that he died there. [19]When all the kings who were servants of Hadadezer saw that they had been defeated by Israel, they made peace with Israel, and became subject to them. So the Arameans were afraid to help the Ammonites any more.

11

David Commits Adultery with Bathsheba

In the spring of the year, the time when kings go out to battle, David sent Joab with his officers and all Israel with him; they ravaged the Ammonites, and besieged Rabbah. But David remained at Jerusalem.

2 It happened, late one afternoon, when David rose from his couch and was walking about on the roof of the king's house, that he saw from the roof a woman bathing; the woman was very beautiful. [3]David sent someone to inquire about the woman. It was reported, "This is Bathsheba daughter of Eliam, the wife of Uriah the Hittite." [4]So David sent messengers to

---

a Or *Merib-baal*: See 4.4 note   b Gk: Heb *my*   c Or *Merib-baal's*: See 4.4 note   d 1 Chr 19.18 and some Gk Mss read *foot soldiers*

LIVE IT!

Lust Destroys · 2 Samuel 11:1–5

What the king wants, the king gets. That seems to be the message of this passage. We are spared many of the details about the encounter between David and Bathsheba, but we do know this: Bathsheba is married to Uriah, so David has coveted another man's wife and committed adultery. When Bathsheba becomes pregnant, David attempts a cover-up. He brings Uriah home from the battlefield to have sex with Bathsheba, so that Uriah will think the baby is his. But Uriah refuses to do so, because he and his men are in the middle of a war. Finally, David arranges for Uriah to be murdered in battle.

In one brief episode, David has broken four commandments—murder, adultery, theft, and coveting (see Exodus 20:1–17). He has given in to lust, and it has led him into unexpected pain that will affect his family, his kingship, and the whole nation of Israel. It's so easy to give in to temptation, especially lust, because it's so alluring and tricks us into not thinking beyond the moment.

We find a clue to defeating lust in David's story. For reasons we're not sure of, David was slacking in his kingly duties. Instead of leading his men, he was kicking back in his palace—inviting temptation. Lust and temptation often blindside us when we're slacking in our own responsibilities. The best way for us to beat temptation is to avoid it altogether.

• Where are you getting snagged by sin?

• What steps can you take to avoid temptation?

---

get her, and she came to him, and he lay with her. (Now she was purifying herself after her period.) Then she returned to her house. [5]The woman conceived; and she sent and told David, "I am pregnant."

6 So David sent word to Joab, "Send me Uriah the Hittite." And Joab sent Uriah to David. [7]When Uriah came to him, David asked how Joab and the people fared, and how the war was going. [8]Then David said to Uriah, "Go down to your house, and wash your feet." Uriah went out of the king's house, and there followed him a present from the king. [9]But Uriah slept at the entrance of the king's house with all the servants of his lord, and did not go down to his house. [10]When they told David, "Uriah did not go down to his house," David said to Uriah, "You have just come from a journey. Why did you not go down to your house?" [11]Uriah said to David, "The ark and Israel and Judah remain in booths;[a] and my lord Joab and the servants of my lord are camping in the open field; shall I then go to my house, to eat and to drink, and to lie with my wife? As you live, and as your soul lives, I will not do such a thing." [12]Then David said to Uriah, "Remain here today also, and tomorrow I will send you back." So Uriah remained in Jerusalem that day. On the next day, [13]David invited him to eat

and drink in his presence and made him drunk; and in the evening he went out to lie on his couch with the servants of his lord, but he did not go down to his house.

David Has Uriah Killed

14 In the morning David wrote a letter to Joab, and sent it by the hand of Uriah. [15]In the letter he wrote, "Set Uriah in the forefront of the hardest fighting, and then draw back from him, so that he may be struck down and die." [16]As Joab was besieging the city, he assigned Uriah to the place where he knew there were valiant warriors. [17]The men of the city came out and fought with Joab; and some of the servants of David among the people fell. Uriah the Hittite was killed as well. [18]Then Joab sent and told David all the news about the fighting; [19]and he instructed the messenger, "When you have finished telling the king all the news about the fighting, [20]then, if the king's anger rises, and if he says to you, 'Why did you go so near the city to fight? Did you not know that they would shoot from the wall? [21]Who killed Abimelech son of Jerubbaal?[b] Did not a woman throw an upper millstone on him from the wall, so that he died at Thebez? Why did you go so

---

a Or at Succoth   b Gk Syr Judg 7.1: Heb Jerubbesheth

near the wall?' then you shall say, 'Your servant Uriah the Hittite is dead too.' "

22 So the messenger went, and came and told David all that Joab had sent him to tell. ²³The messenger said to David, "The men gained an advantage over us, and came out against us in the field; but we drove them back to the entrance of the gate. ²⁴Then the archers shot at your servants from the wall; some of the king's servants are dead; and your servant Uriah the Hittite is dead also." ²⁵David said to the messenger, "Thus you shall say to Joab, 'Do not let this matter trouble you, for the sword devours now one and now another; press your attack on the city, and overthrow it.' And encourage him."

26 When the wife of Uriah heard that her husband was dead, she made lamentation for him. ²⁷When the mourning was over, David sent and brought her to his house, and she became his wife, and bore him a son.

Nathan Condemns David

But the thing that David had done displeased the LORD, ¹and the LORD sent Nathan to David. He came to him, and said to him, "There were two men in a certain city, the one rich and the other poor. ²The rich man had very many flocks and herds; ³but the poor man had nothing but one little ewe lamb, which he had bought. He brought it up, and it grew up with him and with his children; it used to eat of his meager fare, and drink from his cup, and lie in his bosom, and it was like a daughter to him. ⁴Now there came a traveler to the rich man, and he was loath to take one of his own flock or herd to prepare for the wayfarer who had come to him, but he took the poor man's lamb, and prepared that for the guest who had come to him." ⁵Then David's anger was greatly kindled against the man. He said to Nathan, "As the LORD lives, the man who has done this deserves to die; ⁶he shall restore the lamb fourfold, because he did this thing, and because he had no pity."

7 Nathan said to David, "You are the man! Thus says the LORD, the God of Israel: I anointed you king over Israel, and I rescued you from the hand of Saul; ⁸I gave you your master's house, and your master's wives into your bosom, and gave you the house of Israel and of Judah; and if that had been too little, I would have added as much more. ⁹Why have you despised the word of the LORD, to do what is evil in his sight? You have struck down Uriah the Hittite

with the sword, and have taken his wife to be your wife, and have killed him with the sword of the Ammonites. ¹⁰Now therefore the sword shall never depart from your house, for you have despised me, and have taken the wife of Uriah the Hittite to be your wife. ¹¹Thus says the LORD: I will raise up trouble against you from within your own house; and I will take your wives before your eyes, and give them to your neighbor, and he shall lie with your wives in the sight of this very sun. ¹²For you did it secretly; but I will do this thing before all Israel, and before the sun." ¹³David said to Nathan, "I have sinned against the LORD." Nathan said to David, "Now the LORD has put away your sin; you shall not die. ¹⁴Nevertheless, because by this deed you have utterly scorned the LORD,ᵃ the child that is born to you shall die." ¹⁵Then Nathan went to his house.

Bathsheba's Child Dies

The LORD struck the child that Uriah's wife bore

STUDY IT!

The Power of Story
2 Samuel 12:1–14

Stories can be powerful. Jesus knew the power of stories, so he often responded to questions by telling a parable or story (see Matthew 13). The prophet Nathan also knew the power of stories. His challenge was to force David to come to grips with what he had done with Bathsheba and Uriah. Nathan cleverly brings a story to David in his familiar role as judge. David hears the case and is furious at the actions of the rich man. David declares that the rich man should die for what he's done. Then, with four words, Nathan turns David's world upside down: "You are the man!" (2 Samuel 12:7).

What can David say? He just condemned himself, and he knows it. Nathan has cleverly forced him into a moment of truth. You may want to read **Psalm 51**, which poetically records David's confession. Yes, a story can be a powerful thing. Just ask Nathan. Or David. Or Jesus.

ᵃ Ancient scribal tradition: Compare 1 Sam 25.22 note: Heb *scorned the enemies of the LORD*

CONNECT IT!

C. S. Lewis: Master Storyteller · 2 Samuel 12:1–14

All it takes is a mention of Aslan, and you probably know the story. THE LION, THE WITCH AND THE WARDROBE and the other books of The Chronicles of Narnia have been read and loved by millions of children and adults for decades. (Some have also been turned into movies.) That's because C. S. Lewis was a master storyteller. Few writers have been able to match his ability to create such a simple yet imaginative story filled with such deep spiritual truth.

Clive Staples Lewis was an Irish scholar and professor of literature at Oxford and Cambridge universities from 1925 to 1963, but he shared a skill with the ancient prophet Nathan. When Nathan confronted King David about his sin, he told a story that moved David and opened his eyes with a powerful spiritual punch (2 Samuel 12:7). Lewis' tales of Narnia also reveal fresh and meaningful spiritual insights for those willing to look at them.

Lewis' writing both entertains and challenges us to open fresh eyes toward God. We can also be inspired to use whatever creative gifts we have to point others toward God as well.

---

to David, and it became very ill. [16]David therefore pleaded with God for the child; David fasted, and went in and lay all night on the ground. [17]The elders of his house stood beside him, urging him to rise from the ground; but he would not, nor did he eat food with them. [18]On the seventh day the child died. And the servants of David were afraid to tell him that the child was dead; for they said, "While the child was still alive, we spoke to him, and he did not listen to us; how then can we tell him the child is dead? He may do himself some harm." [19]But when David saw that his servants were whispering together, he perceived that the child was dead; and David said to his servants, "Is the child dead?" They said, "He is dead."

20 Then David rose from the ground, washed, anointed himself, and changed his clothes. He went into the house of the LORD, and worshiped; he then went to his own house; and when he asked, they set food before him and he ate. [21]Then his servants said to him, "What is this thing that you have done? You fasted and wept for the child while it was alive; but when the child died, you rose and ate food." [22]He said, "While the child was still alive, I fasted and wept; for I said, 'Who knows? The LORD may be gracious to me, and the child may live.' [23]But now he is dead; why should I fast? Can I bring him back again? I shall go to him, but he will not return to me."

Solomon Is Born

24 Then David consoled his wife Bathsheba, and went to her, and lay with her; and she bore a son, and he named him Solomon. The LORD loved him, [25]and sent a message by the prophet Nathan; so he named him Jedidiah,[a] because of the LORD.

The Ammonites Crushed

26 Now Joab fought against Rabbah of the Ammonites, and took the royal city. [27]Joab sent messengers to David, and said, "I have fought against Rabbah; moreover, I have taken the water city. [28]Now, then, gather the rest of the people together, and encamp against the city, and take it; or I myself will take the city, and it will be called by my name." [29]So David gathered all the people together and went to Rabbah, and fought against it and took it. [30]He took the crown of Milcom[b] from his head; the weight of it was a talent of gold, and in it was a precious stone; and it was placed on David's head. He also brought forth the spoil of the city, a very great amount. [31]He brought out the people who were in it, and set them to work with saws and iron picks and iron axes, or sent them to the brickworks. Thus he did to all the cities of the Ammonites. Then David and all the people returned to Jerusalem.

13

Amnon and Tamar

Some time passed. David's son Absalom had a beautiful sister whose name was Tamar; and David's son Amnon fell in love with her. [2]Amnon was so tormented that he made himself ill because of his sister Tamar, for she was a virgin and it seemed impossible to Amnon to do anything to

---

a That is *Beloved of the LORD*   **b** Gk See 1 Kings 11.5, 33: Heb *their kings*

her. ³But Amnon had a friend whose name was Jonadab, the son of David's brother Shimeah; and Jonadab was a very crafty man. ⁴He said to him, "O son of the king, why are you so haggard morning after morning? Will you not tell me?" Amnon said to him, "I love Tamar, my brother Absalom's sister." ⁵Jonadab said to him, "Lie down on your bed, and pretend to be ill; and when your father comes to see you, say to him, 'Let my sister Tamar come and give me something to eat, and prepare the food in my sight, so that I may see it and eat it from her hand.' " ⁶So Amnon lay down, and pretended to be ill; and when the king came to see him, Amnon said to the king, "Please let my sister Tamar come and make a couple of cakes in my sight, so that I may eat from her hand."

7 Then David sent home to Tamar, saying, "Go to your brother Amnon's house, and prepare food for him." ⁸So Tamar went to her brother Amnon's house, where he was lying down. She took dough, kneaded it, made cakes in his sight, and baked the cakes. ⁹Then she took the pan and set them*ᵃ* out before him, but he refused to eat. Amnon said, "Send out everyone from me." So everyone went out from him. ¹⁰Then Amnon said to Tamar, "Bring the food into the chamber, so that I may eat from your hand." So Tamar took the cakes she had made, and brought them into the chamber to Amnon her brother. ¹¹But when she brought them near him to eat, he took hold of her, and said to her, "Come, lie with me, my sister." ¹²She answered him, "No, my brother, do not force me; for such a thing is not done in Israel; do not do anything so vile! ¹³As for me, where could I carry my shame? And as for you, you would be as one of the scoundrels in Israel. Now therefore, I beg you, speak to the king; for he will not withhold me from you." ¹⁴But he would not listen to her; and being stronger than she, he forced her and lay with her.

15 Then Amnon was seized with a very great loathing for her; indeed, his loathing was even greater than the lust he had felt for her. Amnon said to her, "Get out!" ¹⁶But she said to him, "No, my brother;*ᵇ* for this wrong in sending me away is greater than the other that you did to me." But he would not listen to her. ¹⁷He called the young man who served him and said, "Put this woman out of my presence, and bolt the door after her." ¹⁸(Now she was wearing a long robe with sleeves; for this is how the virgin daughters of the king were clothed

Family Dysfunction · 2 Samuel 13:1–29

This story is straight out of a soap opera or a bestselling novel. It's filled with lust, cruelty, deceit, and revenge. It might come as a surprise to find it in the Bible. Tamar is raped by her half brother, Amnon, so another brother, Absalom, murders Amnon to avenge his sister's disgrace. What's going on here?

We have to remind ourselves that these are all David's children, and they are living out the consequences of the sin of their father. After Nathan confronts David about his affair with Bathsheba and his arrangement of Uriah's death, he tells David, "The sword shall never depart from your house" (2 Samuel 12:10).

This brutal chain of events unfolds within one family. The actions of one impact all the others, and the cycle escalates. You may know a family that doesn't get along or lives in a cycle of bad habits, addiction, or violence. We see this most clearly in families caught up in domestic violence, which can pass from one generation to the next. So how do we stop the "sword of violence" within families?

Each of us needs to make sure we're doing what we can to build bridges in our own families rather than putting up walls. And we need to seek help for individuals who are affected by domestic violence. Look around. Pay attention. Be willing to listen. There are many resources available for people suffering from abuse and violence.

• What can you do to help someone affected by family violence?
• Where can you go for help?

ᵃ Heb *and poured*   ᵇ Cn Compare Gk Vg: Meaning of Heb uncertain

in earlier times.*a*) So his servant put her out, and bolted the door after her. ¹⁹But Tamar put ashes on her head, and tore the long robe that she was wearing; she put her hand on her head, and went away, crying aloud as she went.

20 Her brother Absalom said to her, "Has Amnon your brother been with you? Be quiet for now, my sister; he is your brother; do not take this to heart." So Tamar remained, a desolate woman, in her brother Absalom's house. ²¹When King David heard of all these things, he became very angry, but he would not punish his son Amnon, because he loved him, for he was his firstborn.*b* ²²But Absalom spoke to Amnon neither good nor bad; for Absalom hated Amnon, because he had raped his sister Tamar.

Absalom Avenges the Violation of His Sister

23 After two full years Absalom had sheepshearers at Baal-hazor, which is near Ephraim, and Absalom invited all the king's sons. ²⁴Absalom came to the king, and said, "Your servant has sheepshearers; will the king and his servants please go with your servant?" ²⁵But the king said to Absalom, "No, my son, let us not all go, or else we will be burdensome to you." He pressed him, but he would not go but gave him his blessing. ²⁶Then Absalom said, "If not, please let my brother Amnon go with us." The king said to him, "Why should he go with you?" ²⁷But Absalom pressed him until he let Amnon and all the king's sons go with him. Absalom made a feast like a king's feast.*c* ²⁸Then Absalom commanded his servants, "Watch when Amnon's heart is merry with wine, and when I say to you, 'Strike Amnon,' then kill him. Do not be afraid; have I not myself commanded you? Be courageous and valiant." ²⁹So the servants of Absalom did to Amnon as Absalom had commanded. Then all the king's sons rose, and each mounted his mule and fled.

30 While they were on the way, the report came to David that Absalom had killed all the king's sons, and not one of them was left. ³¹The king rose, tore his garments, and lay on the ground; and all his servants who were standing by tore their garments. ³²But Jonadab, the son of David's brother Shimeah, said, "Let not my lord suppose that they have killed all the young men the king's sons; Amnon alone is dead. This has been determined by Absalom from the day Amnon*d* raped his sister Tamar. ³³Now therefore, do not let my lord the king take it to

heart, as if all the king's sons were dead; for Amnon alone is dead."

34 But Absalom fled. When the young man who kept watch looked up, he saw many people coming from the Horonaim road*e* by the side of the mountain. ³⁵Jonadab said to the king, "See, the king's sons have come; as your servant said, so it has come about." ³⁶As soon as he had finished speaking, the king's sons arrived, and raised their voices and wept; and the king and all his servants also wept very bitterly.

37 But Absalom fled, and went to Talmai son of Ammihud, king of Geshur. David mourned for his son day after day. ³⁸Absalom, having fled to Geshur, stayed there three years. ³⁹And the heart of*f* the king went out, yearning for Absalom; for he was now consoled over the death of Amnon.

Absalom Returns to Jerusalem

14 Now Joab son of Zeruiah perceived that the king's mind was on Absalom. ²Joab sent to Tekoa and brought from there a wise woman. He said to her, "Pretend to be a mourner; put on mourning garments, do not anoint yourself with oil, but behave like a woman who has been mourning many days for the dead. ³Go to the king and speak to him as follows." And Joab put the words into her mouth.

4 When the woman of Tekoa came to the king, she fell on her face to the ground and did obeisance, and said, "Help, O king!" ⁵The king asked her, "What is your trouble?" She answered, "Alas, I am a widow; my husband is dead. ⁶Your servant had two sons, and they fought with one another in the field; there was no one to part them, and one struck the other and killed him. ⁷Now the whole family has risen against your servant. They say, 'Give up the man who struck his brother, so that we may kill him for the life of his brother whom he murdered, even if we destroy the heir as well.' Thus they would quench my one remaining ember, and leave to my husband neither name nor remnant on the face of the earth."

8 Then the king said to the woman, "Go to your house, and I will give orders concerning you." ⁹The woman of Tekoa said to the king, "On me be the guilt, my lord the king, and on my father's house; let the king and his throne be guiltless." ¹⁰The king said, "If anyone says anything to you, bring him to me, and he shall never touch you again." ¹¹Then she said, "Please, may the king keep the LORD your God

---

a Cn: Heb *were clothed in robes*   **b** Q Ms Gk: MT lacks *but he would not punish . . . firstborn*   **c** Gk Compare Q Ms: MT lacks *Absalom made a feast like a king's feast*   **d** Heb *he*   **e** Cn Compare Gk: Heb *the road behind him*   **f** Q Ms Gk: MT *And David*

in mind, so that the avenger of blood may kill no more, and my son not be destroyed." He said, "As the LORD lives, not one hair of your son shall fall to the ground."

12 Then the woman said, "Please let your servant speak a word to my lord the king." He said, "Speak." [13]The woman said, "Why then have you planned such a thing against the people of God? For in giving this decision the king convicts himself, inasmuch as the king does not bring his banished one home again. [14]We must all die; we are like water spilled on the ground, which cannot be gathered up. But God will not take away a life; he will devise plans so as not to keep an outcast banished forever from his presence.[a] [15]Now I have come to say this to my lord the king because the people have made me afraid; your servant thought, 'I will speak to the king; it may be that the king will perform the request of his servant. [16]For the king will hear, and deliver his servant from the hand of the man who would cut both me and my son off from the heritage of God.' [17]Your servant thought, 'The word of my lord the king will set me at rest'; for my lord the king is like the angel of God, discerning good and evil. The LORD your God be with you!"

18 Then the king answered the woman, "Do not withhold from me anything I ask you." The woman said, "Let my lord the king speak." [19]The king said, "Is the hand of Joab with you in all this?" The woman answered and said, "As surely as you live, my lord the king, one cannot turn right or left from anything that my lord the king has said. For it was your servant Joab who commanded me; it was he who put all these words into the mouth of your servant. [20]In order to change the course of affairs your servant Joab did this. But my lord has wisdom like the wisdom of the angel of God to know all things that are on the earth."

21 Then the king said to Joab, "Very well, I grant this; go, bring back the young man Absalom." [22]Joab prostrated himself with his face to the ground and did obeisance, and blessed the king; and Joab said, "Today your servant knows that I have found favor in your sight, my lord the king, in that the king has granted the request of his servant." [23]So Joab set off, went to Geshur, and brought Absalom to Jerusalem. [24]The king said, "Let him go to his own house; he is not to come into my presence." So Absalom went to his own house, and did not come into the king's presence.

David Forgives Absalom

25 Now in all Israel there was no one to be praised so much for his beauty as Absalom; from the sole of his foot to the crown of his head there was no blemish in him. [26]When he cut the hair of his head (for at the end of every year he used to cut it; when it was heavy on him, he cut it), he weighed the hair of his head, two hundred shekels by the king's weight. [27]There were born to Absalom three sons, and one daughter whose name was Tamar; she was a beautiful woman.

28 So Absalom lived two full years in Jerusalem, without coming into the king's presence. [29]Then Absalom sent for Joab to send him to the king; but Joab would not come to him. He sent a second time, but Joab would not come. [30]Then he said to his servants, "Look, Joab's field is next to mine, and he has barley there; go and set it on fire." So Absalom's servants set the field on fire. [31]Then Joab rose and went to Absalom at his house, and said to him, "Why have your servants set my field on fire?" [32]Absalom answered Joab, "Look, I sent word to you: Come here, that I may send you to the king with the question, 'Why have I come from Geshur? It would be better for me to be there still.' Now let me go into the king's presence; if there is guilt in me, let him kill me!" [33]Then Joab went to the king and told him; and he summoned Absalom. So he came to the king and prostrated himself with his face to the ground before the king; and the king kissed Absalom.

15 Absalom Usurps the Throne

After this Absalom got himself a chariot and horses, and fifty men to run ahead of him. [2]Absalom used to rise early and stand beside the road into the gate; and when anyone brought a suit before the king for judgment, Absalom would call out and say, "From what city are you?" When the person said, "Your servant is of such and such a tribe in Israel," [3]Absalom would say, "See, your claims are good and right; but there is no one deputed by the king to hear you." [4]Absalom said moreover, "If only I were judge in the land! Then all who had a suit or cause might come to me, and I would give them justice." [5]Whenever people came near to do obeisance to him, he would put out his hand and take hold of them, and kiss them. [6]Thus Absalom did to every Israelite who came to the king for judgment; so Absalom stole the hearts of the people of Israel.

---

a Meaning of Heb uncertain

7 At the end of four*a* years Absalom said to the king, "Please let me go to Hebron and pay the vow that I have made to the LORD. ⁸For your servant made a vow while I lived at Geshur in Aram: If the LORD will indeed bring me back to Jerusalem, then I will worship the LORD in Hebron."*b* ⁹The king said to him, "Go in peace." So he got up, and went to Hebron. ¹⁰But Absalom sent secret messengers throughout all the tribes of Israel, saying, "As soon as you hear the sound of the trumpet, then shout: Absalom has become king at Hebron!" ¹¹Two hundred men from Jerusalem went with Absalom; they were invited guests, and they went in their innocence, knowing nothing of the matter. ¹²While Absalom was offering the sacrifices, he sent for*c* Ahithophel the Gilonite, David's counselor, from his city Giloh. The conspiracy grew in strength, and the people with Absalom kept increasing.

David Flees from Jerusalem

13 A messenger came to David, saying, "The hearts of the Israelites have gone after Absalom." ¹⁴Then David said to all his officials who were with him at Jerusalem, "Get up! Let us flee, or there will be no escape for us from Absalom. Hurry, or he will soon overtake us, and bring disaster down upon us, and attack the city with the edge of the sword." ¹⁵The king's officials said to the king, "Your servants are ready to do whatever our lord the king decides." ¹⁶So the king left, followed by all his household, except ten concubines whom he left behind to look after the house. ¹⁷The king left, followed by all the people; and they stopped at the last house. ¹⁸All his officials passed by him; and all the Cherethites, and all the Pelethites, and all the six hundred Gittites who had followed him from Gath, passed on before the king.

19 Then the king said to Ittai the Gittite, "Why are you also coming with us? Go back, and stay with the king; for you are a foreigner, and also an exile from your home. ²⁰You came only yesterday, and shall I today make you wander about with us, while I go wherever I can? Go back, and take your kinsfolk with you; and may the LORD show*d* steadfast love and faithfulness to you." ²¹But Ittai answered the king, "As the LORD lives, and as my lord the king lives, wherever my lord the king may be, whether for death or for life, there also your servant will be." ²²David said to Ittai, "Go then, march on." So Ittai the Gittite marched on, with all his men and all the little ones who were with him. ²³The whole country wept aloud as all the people passed by; the king crossed the Wadi Kidron, and all the people moved on toward the wilderness.

24 Abiathar came up, and Zadok also, with all the Levites, carrying the ark of the covenant of God. They set down the ark of God, until the people had all passed out of the city. ²⁵Then the king said to Zadok, "Carry the ark of God back into the city. If I find favor in the eyes of the LORD, he will bring me back and let me see both it and the place where it stays. ²⁶But if he says, 'I take no pleasure in you,' here I am, let him do to me what seems good to him." ²⁷The king also said to the priest Zadok, "Look,*e* go back to the city in peace, you and Abiathar,*f* with your two sons, Ahimaaz your son, and Jonathan son of Abiathar. ²⁸See, I will wait at the fords of the wilderness until word comes from you to inform me." ²⁹So Zadok and Abiathar carried the ark of God back to Jerusalem, and they remained there.

30 But David went up the ascent of the Mount of Olives, weeping as he went, with his head covered and walking barefoot; and all the people who were with him covered their heads and went up, weeping as they went. ³¹David was told that Ahithophel was among the conspirators with Absalom. And David said, "O LORD, I pray you, turn the counsel of Ahithophel into foolishness."

Hushai Becomes David's Spy

32 When David came to the summit, where God was worshiped, Hushai the Archite came to meet him with his coat torn and earth on his head. ³³David said to him, "If you go on with me, you will be a burden to me. ³⁴But if you return to the city and say to Absalom, 'I will be your servant, O king; as I have been your father's servant in time past, so now I will be your servant,' then you will defeat for me the counsel of Ahithophel. ³⁵The priests Zadok and Abiathar will be with you there. So whatever you hear from the king's house, tell it to the priests Zadok and Abiathar. ³⁶Their two sons are with them there, Zadok's son Ahimaaz and Abiathar's son Jonathan; and by them you shall report to me everything you hear." ³⁷So Hushai, David's friend, came into the city, just as Absalom was entering Jerusalem.

David's Adversaries

16 When David had passed a little beyond the summit, Ziba the servant of Me-

---

a Gk Syr: Heb *forty* *b* Gk Mss: Heb lacks *in Hebron* *c* Or *he sent* *d* Gk Compare 2.6: Heb lacks *may the LORD show* *e* Gk: Heb *Are you a seer* or *Do you see?* *f* Cn: Heb lacks *and Abiathar*

phibosheth[a] met him, with a couple of donkeys saddled, carrying two hundred loaves of bread, one hundred bunches of raisins, one hundred of summer fruits, and one skin of wine. [2]The king said to Ziba, "Why have you brought these?" Ziba answered, "The donkeys are for the king's household to ride, the bread and summer fruit for the young men to eat, and the wine is for those to drink who faint in the wilderness." [3]The king said, "And where is your master's son?" Ziba said to the king, "He remains in Jerusalem; for he said, 'Today the house of Israel will give me back my grandfather's kingdom.' " [4]Then the king said to Ziba, "All that belonged to Mephibosheth[a] is now yours." Ziba said, "I do obeisance; let me find favor in your sight, my lord the king."

Shimei Curses David

5 When King David came to Bahurim, a man of the family of the house of Saul came out whose name was Shimei son of Gera; he came out cursing. [6]He threw stones at David and at all the servants of King David; now all the people and all the warriors were on his right and on his left. [7]Shimei shouted while he cursed, "Out! Out! Murderer! Scoundrel! [8]The LORD has avenged on all of you the blood of the house of Saul, in whose place you have reigned; and the LORD has given the kingdom into the hand of your son Absalom. See, disaster has overtaken you; for you are a man of blood."

9 Then Abishai son of Zeruiah said to the king, "Why should this dead dog curse my lord the king? Let me go over and take off his head." [10]But the king said, "What have I to do with you, you sons of Zeruiah? If he is cursing because the LORD has said to him, 'Curse David,' who then shall say, 'Why have you done so?' " [11]David said to Abishai and to all his servants, "My own son seeks my life; how much more now may this Benjaminite! Let him alone, and let him curse; for the LORD has bidden him. [12]It may be that the LORD will look on my distress,[b] and the LORD will repay me with good for this cursing of me today." [13]So David and his men went on the road, while Shimei went along on the hillside opposite him and cursed as he went, throwing stones and flinging dust at him. [14]The king and all the people who were with him arrived weary at the Jordan;[c] and there he refreshed himself.

The Counsel of Ahithophel

15 Now Absalom and all the Israelites[d] came to Jerusalem; Ahithophel was with him. [16]When Hushai the Archite, David's friend, came to Absalom, Hushai said to Absalom, "Long live the king! Long live the king!" [17]Absalom said to Hushai, "Is this your loyalty to your friend? Why did you not go with your friend?" [18]Hushai said to Absalom, "No; but the one whom the LORD and this people and all the Israelites have chosen, his I will be, and with him I will remain. [19]Moreover, whom should I serve? Should it not be his son? Just as I have served your father, so I will serve you."

20 Then Absalom said to Ahithophel, "Give us your counsel; what shall we do?" [21]Ahithophel said to Absalom, "Go in to your father's concubines, the ones he has left to look after the house; and all Israel will hear that you have made yourself odious to your father, and the hands of all who are with you will be strengthened." [22]So they pitched a tent for Absalom upon the roof; and Absalom went in to his father's concubines in the sight of all Israel. [23]Now in those days the counsel that Ahithophel gave was as if one consulted the oracle[e] of God; so all the counsel of Ahithophel was esteemed, both by David and by Absalom.

17 Moreover Ahithophel said to Absalom, "Let me choose twelve thousand men, and I will set out and pursue David tonight. [2]I will come upon him while he is weary and discouraged, and throw him into a panic; and all the people who are with him will flee. I will strike down only the king, [3]and I will bring all the people back to you as a bride comes home to her husband. You seek the life of only one man,[f] and all the people will be at peace." [4]The advice pleased Absalom and all the elders of Israel.

The Counsel of Hushai

5 Then Absalom said, "Call Hushai the Archite also, and let us hear too what he has to say." [6]When Hushai came to Absalom, Absalom said to him, "This is what Ahithophel has said; shall we do as he advises? If not, you tell us." [7]Then Hushai said to Absalom, "This time the counsel that Ahithophel has given is not good." [8]Hushai continued, "You know that your father and his men are warriors, and that they are enraged, like a bear robbed of her cubs in the field. Besides, your father is expert in war; he will not spend the night with the troops. [9]Even now he has hidden himself in one of the pits, or in some other place. And when some of our

---

a Or *Merib-baal*: See 4.4 note b Gk Vg: Heb *iniquity* c Gk: Heb lacks *at the Jordan* d Gk: Heb *all the people, the men of Israel* e Heb *word*
f Gk: Heb *like the return of the whole (is) the man whom you seek*

troops[a] fall at the first attack, whoever hears it will say, 'There has been a slaughter among the troops who follow Absalom.' [10]Then even the valiant warrior, whose heart is like the heart of a lion, will utterly melt with fear; for all Israel knows that your father is a warrior, and that those who are with him are valiant warriors. [11]But my counsel is that all Israel be gathered to you, from Dan to Beer-sheba, like the sand by the sea for multitude, and that you go to battle in person. [12]So we shall come upon him in whatever place he may be found, and we shall light on him as the dew falls on the ground; and he will not survive, nor will any of those with him. [13]If he withdraws into a city, then all Israel will bring ropes to that city, and we shall drag it into the valley, until not even a pebble is to be found there." [14]Absalom and all the men of Israel said, "The counsel of Hushai the Archite is better than the counsel of Ahithophel." For the LORD had ordained to defeat the good counsel of Ahithophel, so that the LORD might bring ruin on Absalom.

Hushai Warns David to Escape

[15] Then Hushai said to the priests Zadok and Abiathar, "Thus and so did Ahithophel counsel Absalom and the elders of Israel; and thus and so I have counseled. [16]Therefore send quickly and tell David, 'Do not lodge tonight at the fords of the wilderness, but by all means cross over; otherwise the king and all the people who are with him will be swallowed up.' " [17]Jonathan and Ahimaaz were waiting at En-rogel; a servant-girl used to go and tell them, and they would go and tell King David; for they could not risk being seen entering the city. [18]But a boy saw them, and told Absalom; so both of them went away quickly, and came to the house of a man at Bahurim, who had a well in his courtyard; and they went down into it. [19]The man's wife took a covering, stretched it over the well's mouth, and spread out grain on it; and nothing was known of it. [20]When Absalom's servants came to the woman at the house, they said, "Where are Ahimaaz and Jonathan?" The woman said to them, "They have crossed over the brook[b] of water." And when they had searched and could not find them, they returned to Jerusalem.

[21] After they had gone, the men came up out of the well, and went and told King David. They said to David, "Go and cross the water quickly; for thus and so has Ahithophel counseled against you." [22]So

David and all the people who were with him set out and crossed the Jordan; by daybreak not one was left who had not crossed the Jordan.

[23] When Ahithophel saw that his counsel was not followed, he saddled his donkey and went off home to his own city. He set his house in order, and hanged himself; he died and was buried in the tomb of his father.

[24] Then David came to Mahanaim, while Absalom crossed the Jordan with all the men of Israel. [25]Now Absalom had set Amasa over the army in the place of Joab. Amasa was the son of a man named Ithra the Ishmaelite,[c] who had married Abigal daughter of Nahash, sister of Zeruiah, Joab's mother. [26]The Israelites and Absalom encamped in the land of Gilead.

[27] When David came to Mahanaim, Shobi son of Nahash from Rabbah of the Ammonites, and Machir son of Ammiel from Lo-debar, and Barzillai the Gileadite from Rogelim, [28]brought beds, basins, and earthen vessels, wheat, barley, meal, parched grain, beans and lentils,[d] [29]honey and curds, sheep, and cheese from the herd, for David and the people with him to eat; for they said, "The troops are hungry and weary and thirsty in the wilderness."

The Defeat and Death of Absalom

18 Then David mustered the men who were with him, and set over them commanders of thousands and commanders of hundreds. [2]And David divided the army into three groups:[e] one third under the command of Joab, one third under the command of Abishai son of Zeruiah, Joab's brother, and one third under the command of Ittai the Gittite. The king said to the men, "I myself will also go out with you." [3]But the men said, "You shall not go out. For if we flee, they will not care about us. If half of us die, they will not care about us. But you are worth ten thousand of us;[f] therefore it is better that you send us help from the city." [4]The king said to them, "Whatever seems best to you I will do." So the king stood at the side of the gate, while all the army marched out by hundreds and by thousands. [5]The king ordered Joab and Abishai and Ittai, saying, "Deal gently for my sake with the young man Absalom." And all the people heard when the king gave orders to all the commanders concerning Absalom.

[6] So the army went out into the field against Israel; and the battle was fought in the forest of Ephraim. [7]The men of Israel were defeated there by

---

a Gk Mss: Heb *some of them* b Meaning of Heb uncertain c 1 Chr 2.17: Heb *Israelite* d Heb *and lentils and parched grain* e Gk: Heb *sent forth the army* f Gk Vg Symmachus: Heb *for now there are ten thousand such as we*

the servants of David, and the slaughter there was great on that day, twenty thousand men. [8]The battle spread over the face of all the country; and the forest claimed more victims that day than the sword.

9 Absalom happened to meet the servants of David. Absalom was riding on his mule, and the mule went under the thick branches of a great oak. His head caught fast in the oak, and he was left hanging[a] between heaven and earth, while the mule that was under him went on. [10]A man saw it, and told Joab, "I saw Absalom hanging in an oak." [11]Joab said to the man who told him, "What, you saw him! Why then did you not strike him there to the ground? I would have been glad to give you ten pieces of silver and a belt." [12]But the man said to Joab, "Even if I felt in my hand the weight of a thousand pieces of silver, I would not raise my hand against the king's son; for in our hearing the king commanded you and Abishai and Ittai, saying: For my sake protect the young man Absalom! [13]On the other hand, if I had dealt treacherously against his life[b] (and there is nothing hidden from the king), then you yourself would have stood aloof." [14]Joab said, "I will not waste time like this with you." He took three spears in his hand, and thrust them into the heart of Absalom, while he was still alive in the oak. [15]And ten young men, Joab's armor-bearers, surrounded Absalom and struck him, and killed him.

16 Then Joab sounded the trumpet, and the troops came back from pursuing Israel, for Joab restrained the troops. [17]They took Absalom, threw him into a great pit in the forest, and raised over him a very great heap of stones. Meanwhile all the Israelites fled to their homes. [18]Now Absalom in his lifetime had taken and set up for himself a pillar that is in the King's Valley, for he said, "I have no son to keep my name in remembrance"; he called the pillar by his own name. It is called Absalom's Monument to this day.

David Hears of Absalom's Death

19 Then Ahimaaz son of Zadok said, "Let me run, and carry tidings to the king that the LORD has delivered him from the power of his enemies." [20]Joab said to him, "You are not to carry tidings today; you may carry tidings another day, but today you shall not do so, because the king's son is dead." [21]Then Joab said to a Cushite, "Go, tell the king what you have seen." The Cushite bowed before Joab, and ran. [22]Then Ahimaaz son of Zadok said again to Joab,

"Come what may, let me also run after the Cushite." And Joab said, "Why will you run, my son, seeing that you have no reward[c] for the tidings?" [23]"Come what may," he said, "I will run." So he said to him, "Run." Then Ahimaaz ran by the way of the Plain, and outran the Cushite.

24 Now David was sitting between the two gates. The sentinel went up to the roof of the gate by the wall, and when he looked up, he saw a man running alone. [25]The sentinel shouted and told the king. The king said, "If he is alone, there are tidings in his mouth." He kept coming, and drew near. [26]Then the sentinel saw another man running; and the sentinel called to the gatekeeper and said, "See, another man running alone!" The king said, "He also is bringing tidings." [27]The sentinel said, "I think the running of the first one is like the running of Ahimaaz son of Zadok." The king said, "He is a good man, and comes with good tidings."

28 Then Ahimaaz cried out to the king, "All is well!" He prostrated himself before the king with his face to the ground, and said, "Blessed be the LORD your God, who has delivered up the men who raised their hand against my lord the king." [29]The king said, "Is it well with the young man Absalom?" Ahimaaz answered, "When Joab sent your servant,[d] I saw a great tumult, but I do not know what it was." [30]The king said, "Turn aside, and stand here." So he turned aside, and stood still.

31 Then the Cushite came; and the Cushite said, "Good tidings for my lord the king! For the LORD has vindicated you this day, delivering you from the power of all who rose up against you." [32]The king said to the Cushite, "Is it well with the young man Absalom?" The Cushite answered, "May the enemies of my lord the king, and all who rise up to do you harm, be like that young man."

---

a Gk Syr Tg: Heb *was put*   b Another reading is *at the risk of my life*   c Meaning of Heb uncertain   d Heb *the king's servant, your servant*

LIVE IT!

Surviving Grief
2 Samuel
18:33–19:8

There is no greater loss for parents than the death of a child. King David is devastated by the death of his son Absalom, despite Absalom's betrayal (2 Samuel 18:33). There is no easy answer or explanation when someone we love dies. How could God allow this? It's too hard to understand. What helps is to allow ourselves to mourn like David and to place ourselves in God's healing hands.

Life continues—in the Bible and for us today. Joab challenges David not to forget the people who have served him faithfully and count on his leadership (2 Samuel 19:6-8). In our grief, we must not forget the family and friends who grieve with us. We need them, and they need us to heal the pain of loss.

David Mourns for Absalom

33[a] The king was deeply moved, and went up to the chamber over the gate, and wept; and as he went, he said, "O my son Absalom, my son, my son Absalom! Would I had died instead of you, O Absalom, my son, my son!"

19 It was told Joab, "The king is weeping and mourning for Absalom." [2] So the victory that day was turned into mourning for all the troops; for the troops heard that day, "The king is grieving for his son." [3] The troops stole into the city that day as soldiers steal in who are ashamed when they flee in battle. [4] The king covered his face, and the king cried with a loud voice, "O my son Absalom, O Absalom, my son, my son!" [5] Then Joab came into the house to the king, and said, "Today you have covered with shame the faces of all your officers who have saved your life today, and the lives of your sons and your daughters, and the lives of your wives and your concubines, [6] for love of those who hate you and for hatred of those who love you. You have made it clear today that commanders and officers are nothing to you; for I perceive that if Absalom were alive and all of us were dead today, then you would be pleased. [7] So go out at once and speak kindly to your servants; for I swear by the LORD, if you do not go, not a man will stay with you this night; and this will be worse for you than any disaster that has come upon you from your youth until now." [8] Then the king got up and took his seat in the gate. The troops were all told, "See, the king is sitting in the gate"; and all the troops came before the king.

David Recalled to Jerusalem

Meanwhile, all the Israelites had fled to their homes. [9] All the people were disputing throughout all the tribes of Israel, saying, "The king delivered us from the hand of our enemies, and saved us from the hand of the Philistines; and now he has fled out of the land because of Absalom. [10] But Absalom, whom we anointed over us, is dead in battle. Now therefore why do you say nothing about bringing the king back?"

11 King David sent this message to the priests Zadok and Abiathar, "Say to the elders of Judah, 'Why should you be the last to bring the king back to his house? The talk of all Israel has come to the king.[b] [12] You are my kin, you are my bone and my flesh; why then should you be the last to bring back the king?' [13] And say to Amasa, 'Are you not my bone and my flesh? So may God do to me, and more, if you are not the commander of my army from now on, in place of Joab.'" [14] Amasa[c] swayed the hearts of all the people of Judah as one, and they sent word to the king, "Return, both you and all your servants." [15] So the king came back to the Jordan; and Judah came to Gilgal to meet the king and to bring him over the Jordan.

16 Shimei son of Gera, the Benjaminite, from Bahurim, hurried to come down with the people of Judah to meet King David; [17] with him were a thousand people from Benjamin. And Ziba, the servant of the house of Saul, with his fifteen sons and his twenty servants, rushed down to the Jordan ahead of the king, [18] while the crossing was taking place,[d] to bring over the king's household, and to do his pleasure.

David's Mercy to Shimei

Shimei son of Gera fell down before the king, as he was about to cross the Jordan, [19] and said to the king, "May my lord not hold me guilty or remember how your servant did wrong on the day my lord the

a Ch 19.1 in Heb   b Gk: Heb *to the king, to his house*   c Heb *He*   d Cn: Heb *the ford crossed* king left Jerusalem; may the king not bear it in mind. ²⁰For your servant knows that I have sinned; therefore, see, I have come this day, the first of all the house of Joseph to come down to meet my lord the king." ²¹Abishai son of Zeruiah answered, "Shall not Shimei be put to death for this, because he cursed the LORD's anointed?" ²²But David said, "What have I to do with you, you sons of Zeruiah, that you should today become an adversary to me? Shall anyone be put to death in Israel this day? For do I not know that I am this day king over Israel?" ²³The king said to Shimei, "You shall not die." And the king gave him his oath.

David and Mephibosheth Meet

24 Mephibosheth[a] grandson of Saul came down to meet the king; he had not taken care of his feet, or trimmed his beard, or washed his clothes, from the day the king left until the day he came back in safety. ²⁵When he came from Jerusalem to meet the king, the king said to him, "Why did you not go with me, Mephibosheth?"[a] ²⁶He answered, "My lord, O king, my servant deceived me; for your servant said to him, 'Saddle a donkey for me,[b] so that I may ride on it and go with the king.' For your servant is lame. ²⁷He has slandered your servant to my lord the king. But my lord the king is like the angel of God; do therefore what seems good to you. ²⁸For all my father's house were doomed to death before my lord the king; but you set your servant among those who eat at your table. What further right have I, then, to appeal to the king?" ²⁹The king said to him, "Why speak any more of your affairs? I have decided: you and Ziba shall divide the land." ³⁰Mephibosheth[a] said to the king, "Let him take it all, since my lord the king has arrived home safely."

David's Kindness to Barzillai

31 Now Barzillai the Gileadite had come down from Rogelim; he went on with the king to the Jordan, to escort him over the Jordan. ³²Barzillai was a very aged man, eighty years old. He had provided the king with food while he stayed at Mahanaim, for he was a very wealthy man. ³³The king said to Barzillai, "Come over with me, and I will provide for you in Jerusalem at my side." ³⁴But Barzillai said to the king, "How many years have I still to live, that I should go up with the king to Jerusalem? ³⁵Today I am eighty years old; can I discern what is pleasant and what is not? Can your servant taste what he eats or what he drinks? Can I still listen to the voice of singing men and singing women? Why then should your servant be an added burden to my lord the king? ³⁶Your servant will go a little way over the Jordan with the king. Why should the king recompense me with such a reward? ³⁷Please let your servant return, so that I may die in my own town, near the graves of my father and my mother. But here is your servant Chimham; let him go over with my lord the king; and do for him whatever seems good to you." ³⁸The king answered, "Chimham shall go over with me, and I will do for him whatever seems good to you; and all that you desire of me I will do for you." ³⁹Then all the people crossed over the Jordan, and the king crossed over; the king kissed Barzillai and blessed him, and he returned to his own home. ⁴⁰The king went on to Gilgal, and Chimham went on with him; all the people of Judah, and also half the people of Israel, brought the king on his way.

41 Then all the people of Israel came to the king, and said to him, "Why have our kindred the people of Judah stolen you away, and brought the king and his household over the Jordan, and all David's men with him?" ⁴²All the people of Judah answered the people of Israel, "Because the king is near of kin to us. Why then are you angry over this matter? Have we eaten at all at the king's expense? Or has he given us any gift?" ⁴³But the people of Israel answered the people of Judah, "We have ten shares in the king, and in David also we have more than you. Why then did you despise us? Were we not the first to speak of bringing back our king?" But the words of the people of Judah were fiercer than the words of the people of Israel.

The Rebellion of Sheba

20 Now a scoundrel named Sheba son of Bichri, a Benjaminite, happened to be there. He sounded the trumpet and cried out,

"We have no portion in David,
no share in the son of Jesse!
Everyone to your tents, O Israel!"

²So all the people of Israel withdrew from David and followed Sheba son of Bichri; but the people of Judah followed their king steadfastly from the Jordan to Jerusalem.

3 David came to his house at Jerusalem; and the king took the ten concubines whom he had left to look after the house, and put them in a house under

---

a Or *Merib-baal*: See 4.4 note   **b** Gk Syr Vg: Heb *said, 'I will saddle a donkey for myself*

guard, and provided for them, but did not go in to them. So they were shut up until the day of their death, living as if in widowhood.

4 Then the king said to Amasa, "Call the men of Judah together to me within three days, and be here yourself." [5]So Amasa went to summon Judah; but he delayed beyond the set time that had been appointed him. [6]David said to Abishai, "Now Sheba son of Bichri will do us more harm than Absalom; take your lord's servants and pursue him, or he will find fortified cities for himself, and escape from us." [7]Joab's men went out after him, along with the Cherethites, the Pelethites, and all the warriors; they went out from Jerusalem to pursue Sheba son of Bichri. [8]When they were at the large stone that is in Gibeon, Amasa came to meet them. Now Joab was wearing a soldier's garment and over it was a belt with a sword in its sheath fastened at his waist; as he went forward it fell out. [9]Joab said to Amasa, "Is it well with you, my brother?" And Joab took Amasa by the beard with his right hand to kiss him. [10]But Amasa did not notice the sword in Joab's hand; Joab struck him in the belly so that his entrails poured out on the ground, and he died. He did not strike a second blow.

Then Joab and his brother Abishai pursued Sheba son of Bichri. [11]And one of Joab's men took his stand by Amasa, and said, "Whoever favors Joab, and whoever is for David, let him follow Joab." [12]Amasa lay wallowing in his blood on the highway, and the man saw that all the people were stopping. Since he saw that all who came by him were stopping, he carried Amasa from the highway into a field, and threw a garment over him. [13]Once he was removed from the highway, all the people went on after Joab to pursue Sheba son of Bichri.

14 Sheba[a] passed through all the tribes of Israel to Abel of Beth-maacah;[b] and all the Bichrites[c] assembled, and followed him inside. [15]Joab's forces[d] came and besieged him in Abel of Beth-maacah; they threw up a siege ramp against the city, and it stood against the rampart. Joab's forces were battering the wall to break it down. [16]Then a wise woman called from the city, "Listen! Listen! Tell Joab, 'Come here, I want to speak to you.' " [17]He came near her; and the woman said, "Are you Joab?" He answered, "I am." Then she said to him, "Listen to the words of your servant." He answered, "I am listening." [18]Then she said, "They used to say in the old days, 'Let them inquire at Abel'; and so they

would settle a matter. [19]I am one of those who are peaceable and faithful in Israel; you seek to destroy a city that is a mother in Israel; why will you swallow up the heritage of the LORD?" [20]Joab answered, "Far be it from me, far be it, that I should swallow up or destroy! [21]That is not the case! But a man of the hill country of Ephraim, called Sheba son of Bichri, has lifted up his hand against King David; give him up alone, and I will withdraw from the city." The woman said to Joab, "His head shall be thrown over the wall to you." [22]Then the woman went to all the people with her wise plan. And they cut off the head of Sheba son of Bichri, and threw it out to Joab. So he blew the trumpet, and they dispersed from the city, and all went to their homes, while Joab returned to Jerusalem to the king.

23 Now Joab was in command of all the army of Israel;[e] Benaiah son of Jehoiada was in command of the Cherethites and the Pelethites; [24]Adoram was in charge of the forced labor; Jehoshaphat son of Ahilud was the recorder; [25]Sheva was secretary; Zadok and Abiathar were priests; [26]and Ira the Jairite was also David's priest.

David Avenges the Gibeonites

21 Now there was a famine in the days of David for three years, year after year; and David inquired of the LORD. The LORD said, "There is bloodguilt on Saul and on his house, because he put the Gibeonites to death." [2]So the king called the Gibeonites and spoke to them. (Now the Gibeonites were not of the people of Israel, but of the remnant of the Amorites; although the people of Israel had sworn to spare them, Saul had tried to wipe them out in his zeal for the people of Israel and Judah.) [3]David said to the Gibeonites, "What shall I do for you? How shall I make expiation, that you may bless the heritage of the LORD?" [4]The Gibeonites said to him, "It is not a matter of silver or gold between us and Saul or his house; neither is it for us to put anyone to death in Israel." He said, "What do you say that I should do for you?" [5]They said to the king, "The man who consumed us and planned to destroy us, so that we should have no place in all the territory of Israel— [6]let seven of his sons be handed over to us, and we will impale them before the LORD at Gibeon on the mountain of the LORD."[f] The king said, "I will hand them over."

7 But the king spared Mephibosheth,[g] the son of Saul's son Jonathan, because of the oath of the LORD

---

a Heb *He* **b** Compare 20.15: Heb *and Beth-maacah* **c** Compare Gk Vg: Heb *Berites* **d** Heb *They* **e** Cn: Heb *Joab to all the army, Israel*
f Cn Compare Gk and 21.9: Heb *at Gibeah of Saul, the chosen of the LORD* **g** Or *Merib-baal*: See 4.4 note

that was between them, between David and Jonathan son of Saul. [8]The king took the two sons of Rizpah daughter of Aiah, whom she bore to Saul, Armoni and Mephibosheth;[a] and the five sons of Merab[b] daughter of Saul, whom she bore to Adriel son of Barzillai the Meholathite; [9]he gave them into the hands of the Gibeonites, and they impaled them on the mountain before the LORD. The seven of them perished together. They were put to death in the first days of harvest, at the beginning of barley harvest.

10 Then Rizpah the daughter of Aiah took sackcloth, and spread it on a rock for herself, from the beginning of harvest until rain fell on them from the heavens; she did not allow the birds of the air to come on the bodies[c] by day, or the wild animals by night. [11]When David was told what Rizpah daughter of Aiah, the concubine of Saul, had done, [12]David went and took the bones of Saul and the bones of his son Jonathan from the people of Jabesh-gilead, who had stolen them from the public square of Beth-shan, where the Philistines had hung them up, on the day the Philistines killed Saul on Gilboa. [13]He brought up from there the bones of Saul and the bones of his son Jonathan; and they gathered the bones of those who had been impaled. [14]They buried the bones of Saul and of his son Jonathan in the land of Benjamin in Zela, in the tomb of his father Kish; they did all that the king commanded. After that, God heeded supplications for the land.

Exploits of David's Men

15 The Philistines went to war again with Israel, and David went down together with his servants. They fought against the Philistines, and David grew weary. [16]Ishbi-benob, one of the descendants of the giants, whose spear weighed three hundred shekels of bronze, and who was fitted out with new weapons,[d] said he would kill David. [17]But Abishai son of Zeruiah came to his aid, and attacked the Philistine and killed him. Then David's men swore to him, "You shall not go out with us to battle any longer, so that you do not quench the lamp of Israel."

18 After this a battle took place with the Philistines, at Gob; then Sibbecai the Hushathite killed Saph, who was one of the descendants of the giants. [19]Then there was another battle with the Philistines at Gob; and Elhanan son of Jaare-oregim, the Bethlehemite, killed Goliath the Gittite, the shaft of whose spear was like a weaver's beam. [20]There was again war at Gath, where there was a man of great size, who had six fingers on each hand, and six toes on each foot, twenty-four in number; he too was descended from the giants. [21]When he taunted Israel, Jonathan son of David's brother Shimei, killed him. [22]These four were descended from the giants in Gath; they fell by the hands of David and his servants.

David's Song of Thanksgiving

David spoke to the LORD the words of this song on the day when the LORD delivered

The Lord Is My Rock · 2 Samuel 22:1–4

Have you ever watched a house being built? One of the first things a contractor does is level the ground and put in a foundation. It's the base that everything stands on. From there, the structure begins to grow. A solid foundation will enable that house to stand for decades.

We need a solid foundation in our lives too, both personally and communally. What is the foundation—the rock—that your life is built on? King David says to the Lord, "(You are) my rock, my fortress, and my deliverer" (2 Samuel 22:2). David built his life on the rock and foundation of the Lord. And he found refuge in times of fear as a result. It was this rock that saved David and the people of Israel from the hands of their enemies. Because of David's reliance on God, his kingdom is seen by later generations of Jews as the ideal kingdom for Israel.

You too can find this same refuge and saving grace. Starting today, build your life with the Lord as your foundation (see Matthew 7:24-27). The next time you face a battle—whether drugs, envy, grief, or lust—stand on the rock!

---

a Or *Merib-baal*: See 4.4 note b Two Heb Mss Syr Compare Gk: MT *Michal* c Heb *them* d Heb *was belted anew*

him from the hand of all his enemies, and from the hand of Saul. ²He said:

The LORD is my rock, my fortress, and my
    deliverer,
3   my God, my rock, in whom I take refuge,
my shield and the horn of my salvation,
    my stronghold and my refuge,
    my savior; you save me from violence.
4 I call upon the LORD, who is worthy to be
    praised,
    and I am saved from my enemies.

5 For the waves of death
        encompassed me,
    the torrents of perdition assailed me;
6 the cords of Sheol entangled me,
    the snares of death confronted me.

7 In my distress I called upon the LORD;
    to my God I called.
From his temple he heard my voice,
    and my cry came to his ears.

8 Then the earth reeled and rocked;
    the foundations of the heavens trembled
    and quaked, because he was angry.
9 Smoke went up from his nostrils,
    and devouring fire from his mouth;
    glowing coals flamed forth from him.
10 He bowed the heavens, and came down;
    thick darkness was under his feet.
11 He rode on a cherub, and flew;
    he was seen upon the wings of the wind.
12 He made darkness around him a canopy,
    thick clouds, a gathering of water.
13 Out of the brightness before him
    coals of fire flamed forth.
14 The LORD thundered from heaven;
    the Most High uttered his voice.
15 He sent out arrows, and scattered them
        —lightning, and routed them.
16 Then the channels of the sea were seen,
    the foundations of the world were laid bare
at the rebuke of the LORD,
    at the blast of the breath of his nostrils.

17 He reached from on high, he took me,
    he drew me out of mighty waters.
18 He delivered me from my strong enemy,
    from those who hated me;

for they were too mighty for me.
19 They came upon me in the day of my
    calamity,
    but the LORD was my stay.
20 He brought me out into a broad place;
    he delivered me, because he delighted
    in me.

21 The LORD rewarded me according to my
    righteousness;
    according to the cleanness of my hands he
    recompensed me.
22 For I have kept the ways of the LORD,
    and have not wickedly departed from
    my God.
23 For all his ordinances were before me,
    and from his statutes I did not turn aside.
24 I was blameless before him,
    and I kept myself from guilt.
25 Therefore the LORD has recompensed me
    according to my righteousness,
    according to my cleanness in his sight.

26 With the loyal you show yourself loyal;
    with the blameless you show yourself
    blameless;
27 with the pure you show yourself pure,
    and with the crooked you show yourself
    perverse.
28 You deliver a humble people,
    but your eyes are upon the haughty to
    bring them down.
29 Indeed, you are my lamp, O LORD,
    the LORD lightens my darkness.
30 By you I can crush a troop,
    and by my God I can leap over a wall.
31 This God—his way is perfect;
    the promise of the LORD proves true;

> "This God—his way is perfect; the promise of the LORD proves true; he is a shield for all who take refuge in him."
> —2 Samuel 22:31

he is a shield for all who take refuge
   in him.

32 For who is God, but the Lord?
   And who is a rock, except our God?
33 The God who has girded me with strength[a]
   has opened wide my path.[b]
34 He made my[c] feet like the feet of deer,
   and set me secure on the heights.
35 He trains my hands for war,
   so that my arms can bend a bow of
      bronze.
36 You have given me the shield of your
      salvation,
   and your help[d] has made me great.
37 You have made me stride freely,
   and my feet do not slip;
38 I pursued my enemies and destroyed them,
   and did not turn back until they were
      consumed.
39 I consumed them; I struck them down, so
      that they did not rise;
   they fell under my feet.
40 For you girded me with strength for the
      battle;
   you made my assailants sink
      under me.
41 You made my enemies turn their backs to me,
   those who hated me, and I destroyed
      them.
42 They looked, but there was no one to save
      them;
   they cried to the Lord, but he did not
      answer them.
43 I beat them fine like the dust of the earth,
   I crushed them and stamped them down
      like the mire of the streets.

44 You delivered me from strife with the
      peoples;[e]
   you kept me as the head of the nations;
   people whom I had not known served me.
45 Foreigners came cringing to me;
   as soon as they heard of me, they
      obeyed me.
46 Foreigners lost heart,
   and came trembling out of their
      strongholds.

47 The Lord lives! Blessed be my rock,

and exalted be my God, the rock of my
      salvation,
48 the God who gave me vengeance
   and brought down peoples under me,
49 who brought me out from my enemies;
   you exalted me above my adversaries,
   you delivered me from the violent.

50 For this I will extol you, O Lord, among the
      nations,
   and sing praises to your name.
51 He is a tower of salvation for his king,
   and shows steadfast love to his anointed,
   to David and his descendants forever.

23 The Last Words of David

Now these are the last words of David:
   The oracle of David, son of Jesse,
   the oracle of the man whom God exalted,[f]
the anointed of the God of Jacob,
   the favorite of the Strong One of Israel:

2 The spirit of the Lord speaks through me,
   his word is upon my tongue.
3 The God of Israel has spoken,
   the Rock of Israel has said to me:
One who rules over people justly,
   ruling in the fear of God,
4 is like the light of morning,
   like the sun rising on a cloudless morning,
   gleaming from the rain on the grassy land.

5 Is not my house like this with God?
   For he has made with me an everlasting
      covenant,
   ordered in all things and secure.
Will he not cause to prosper
   all my help and my desire?
6 But the godless are[g] all like thorns that are
      thrown away;
   for they cannot be picked up with the
      hand;
7 to touch them one uses an iron bar
   or the shaft of a spear.
   And they are entirely consumed in fire on
      the spot.[h]

David's Mighty Men

8 These are the names of the warriors whom
David had: Josheb-basshebeth a Tahchemonite; he

a Q Ms Gk Syr Vg Compare Ps 18.32: MT *God is my strong refuge* b Meaning of Heb uncertain c Another reading is *his* d Q Ms: MT *your answering* e Gk: Heb *from strife with my people* f Q Ms: MT *who was raised on high* g Heb *But worthlessness* h Heb *in sitting*

was chief of the Three;[a] he wielded his spear[b] against eight hundred whom he killed at one time.

9 Next to him among the three warriors was Eleazar son of Dodo son of Ahohi. He was with David when they defied the Philistines who were gathered there for battle. The Israelites withdrew, [10]but he stood his ground. He struck down the Philistines until his arm grew weary, though his hand clung to the sword. The LORD brought about a great victory that day. Then the people came back to him—but only to strip the dead.

11 Next to him was Shammah son of Agee, the Hararite. The Philistines gathered together at Lehi, where there was a plot of ground full of lentils; and the army fled from the Philistines. [12]But he took his stand in the middle of the plot, defended it, and killed the Philistines; and the LORD brought about a great victory.

13 Towards the beginning of harvest three of the thirty[c] chiefs went down to join David at the cave of Adullam, while a band of Philistines was encamped in the valley of Rephaim. [14]David was then in the stronghold; and the garrison of the Philistines was then at Bethlehem. [15]David said longingly, "O that someone would give me water to drink from the well of Bethlehem that is by the gate!" [16]Then the three warriors broke through the camp of the Philistines, drew water from the well of Bethlehem that was by the gate, and brought it to David. But he would not drink of it; he poured it out to the LORD, [17]for he said, "The LORD forbid that I should do this. Can I drink the blood of the men who went at the risk of their lives?" Therefore he would not drink it. The three warriors did these things.

18 Now Abishai son of Zeruiah, the brother of Joab, was chief of the Thirty.[d] With his spear he fought against three hundred men and killed them, and won a name beside the Three. [19]He was the most renowned of the Thirty,[e] and became their commander; but he did not attain to the Three.

20 Benaiah son of Jehoiada was a valiant warrior[f] from Kabzeel, a doer of great deeds; he struck down two sons of Ariel[g] of Moab. He also went down and killed a lion in a pit on a day when snow had fallen. [21]And he killed an Egyptian, a handsome man. The Egyptian had a spear in his hand; but Benaiah went against him with a staff, snatched the spear out of the Egyptian's hand, and killed him with his own spear. [22]Such were the things Benaiah son of Jehoiada did, and won a name beside the three warriors. [23]He was renowned among the Thirty, but did not attain to the Three. And David put him in charge of his bodyguard.

24 Among the Thirty were Asahel brother of Joab; Elhanan son of Dodo of Bethlehem; [25]Shammah of Harod; Elika of Harod; [26]Helez the Paltite; Ira son of Ikkesh of Tekoa; [27]Abiezer of Anathoth; Mebunnai the Hushathite; [28]Zalmon the Ahohite; Maharai of Netophah; [29]Heleb son of Baanah of Netophah; Ittai son of Ribai of Gibeah of the Benjaminites; [30]Benaiah of Pirathon; Hiddai of the torrents of Gaash; [31]Abi-albon the Arbathite; Azmaveth of Bahurim; [32]Eliahba of Shaalbon; the sons of Jashen: Jonathan [33]son of[h] Shammah the Hararite; Ahiam son of Sharar the Hararite; [34]Eliphelet son of Ahasbai of Maacah; Eliam son of Ahithophel the Gilonite; [35]Hezro[i] of Carmel; Paarai the Arbite; [36]Igal son of Nathan of Zobah; Bani the Gadite; [37]Zelek the Ammonite; Naharai of Beeroth, the armor-bearer of Joab son of Zeruiah; [38]Ira the Ithrite; Gareb the Ithrite; [39]Uriah the Hittite— thirty-seven in all.

24 David's Census of Israel and Judah

Again the anger of the LORD was kindled against Israel, and he incited David against them, saying, "Go, count the people of Israel and Judah." [2]So the king said to Joab and the commanders of the army,[j] who were with him, "Go through all the tribes of Israel, from Dan to Beer-sheba, and take a census of the people, so that I may know how many there are." [3]But Joab said to the king, "May the LORD your God increase the number of the people a hundredfold, while the eyes of my lord the king can still see it! But why does my lord the king want to do this?" [4]But the king's word prevailed against Joab and the commanders of the army. So Joab and the commanders of the army went out from the presence of the king to take a census of the people of Israel. [5]They crossed the Jordan, and began from[k] Aroer and from the city that is in the middle of the valley, toward Gad and on to Jazer. [6]Then they came to Gilead, and to Kadesh in the land of the Hittites;[l] and they came to Dan, and from Dan[m] they went around to Sidon, [7]and came to the fortress of Tyre and to all the cities of the Hivites and Canaanites; and they went out to the Negeb of Judah at Beer-sheba. [8]So when they had gone through all the land, they came back to Jerusalem at the end of nine months and twenty days. [9]Joab

---

a Gk Vg Compare 1 Chr 11.11: Meaning of Heb uncertain   b 1 Chr 11.11: Meaning of Heb uncertain   c Heb adds head   d Two Heb Mss Syr: MT *Three*   e Syr Compare 1 Chr 11.25: Heb *Was he the most renowned of the Three?*   f Another reading is *the son of Ish-hai*   g Gk: Heb lacks *sons of* h Gk: Heb lacks *son of*   i Another reading is *Hezrai*   j 1 Chr 21.2 Gk: Heb *to Joab the commander of the army*   k Gk Mss: Heb *encamped in Aroer south of* l Gk: Heb *to the land of Tahtim-hodshi*   m Cn Compare Gk: Heb *they came to Dan-jaan and*

reported to the king the number of those who had been recorded: in Israel there were eight hundred thousand soldiers able to draw the sword, and those of Judah were five hundred thousand.

Judgment on David's Sin

10 But afterward, David was stricken to the heart because he had numbered the people. David said to the LORD, "I have sinned greatly in what I have done. But now, O LORD, I pray you, take away the guilt of your servant; for I have done very foolishly." [11] When David rose in the morning, the word of the LORD came to the prophet Gad, David's seer, saying, [12] "Go and say to David: Thus says the LORD: Three things I offer[a] you; choose one of them, and I will do it to you." [13] So Gad came to David and told him; he asked him, "Shall three[b] years of famine come to you on your land? Or will you flee three months before your foes while they pursue you? Or shall there be three days' pestilence in your land? Now consider, and decide what answer I shall return to the one who sent me." [14] Then David said to Gad, "I am in great distress; let us fall into the hand of the LORD, for his mercy is great; but let me not fall into human hands."

15 So the LORD sent a pestilence on Israel from that morning until the appointed time; and seventy thousand of the people died, from Dan to Beersheba. [16] But when the angel stretched out his hand toward Jerusalem to destroy it, the LORD relented concerning the evil, and said to the angel who was bringing destruction among the people, "It is enough; now stay your hand." The angel of the LORD was then by the threshing floor of Araunah the Jebusite. [17] When David saw the angel who was destroying the people, he said to the LORD, "I alone have sinned, and I alone have done wickedly; but these sheep, what have they done? Let your hand, I pray, be against me and against my father's house."

David's Altar on the Threshing Floor

18 That day Gad came to David and said to him, "Go up and erect an altar to the LORD on the threshing floor of Araunah the Jebusite." [19] Following Gad's instructions, David went up, as the LORD had commanded. [20] When Araunah looked down, he saw the king and his servants coming toward him; and Araunah went out and prostrated himself before the king with his face to the ground. [21] Araunah said, "Why has my lord the king come to his servant?" David said, "To buy the threshing floor from you in order to build an altar to the LORD, so that the plague may be averted from the people." [22] Then Araunah said to David, "Let my lord the king take and offer up what seems good to him; here are the oxen for the burnt offering, and the threshing sledges and the yokes of the oxen for the wood. [23] All this, O king, Araunah gives to the king." And Araunah said to the king, "May the LORD your God respond favorably to you."

24 But the king said to Araunah, "No, but I will buy them from you for a price; I will not offer burnt offerings to the LORD my God that cost me nothing." So David bought the threshing floor and the oxen for fifty shekels of silver. [25] David built there an altar to the LORD, and offered burnt offerings and offerings of well-being. So the LORD answered his supplication for the land, and the plague was averted from Israel.

a Or *hold over*   b 1 Chr 21.12 Gk: Heb *seven*

1 Kings ▶▶▶▶▶▶▶▶▶▶▶▶▶▶▶▶▶▶▶▶▶▶▶▶▶

The ancient Egyptians had an advanced civilization, yet today the remains of their handiwork lie buried under centuries of sand. The great Roman Empire spanned and ruled the Western world at the time of Jesus, yet today only scattered ruins testify to its existence. The same is true of the glorious but short-lived Israelite kingdom. The books of 1 and 2 Kings trace its tragic collapse from the glories of Solomon's temple to the Babylonian exile.

IN DEPTH

If the kingships of Saul and David could be described as the spring and summer of the Israelite kingdom, the books of 1 and 2 Kings describe its fall and winter. The beginning of 1 Kings covers the glorious late summer under King Solomon, during which he accumulated great riches, constructed a beautiful temple, and built Jerusalem into a city rivaling any other center of power. But summer was over quickly when the kingdom split in two at Solomon's death. (See Map 5: "Kingdom of David and Solomon.") The northern kingdom was called Israel, and the southern kingdom was called Judah. They were ruled by a succession of kings, most of whom proved to be weak and sinful leaders. Their incompetence had disastrous consequences: the two kingdoms fell to foreign powers. Israel fell to the Assyrians in 722 B.C., and Judah to the Babylonians in 587 B.C.

The sorrow we hear in 1 and 2 Kings is accompanied by a clear explanation: The people have fallen because of their wickedness and the wickedness of their leaders. Not surprisingly, the author of 1 and 2 Kings fashions the history of God's people into a kind of morality tale, emphasizing the importance of faithfulness to the covenant and the law.

Of special interest in these books is the appearance of the classical prophet. Unlike the prophets of other lands, who were mere tools in the ruler's hand, the great prophets of Israel and Judah, such as Elijah and Elisha, often directly opposed royal decisions and actions. Their job was not to pamper the ruler's pride, but to speak God's word clearly and boldly.

As we read about the terrible crises that the kingdoms of Judah and Israel faced, we see that there is no hope apart from God. And we can reflect on one of the basic truths of human history: only God's promise remains true as history passes.

QUICK FACTS

- **Dates Covered:** From 961 to 587 B.C.
- **Author:** An unknown author writing in the same style as Deuteronomy after the fall of Jerusalem in 587 B.C.
- **Themes:** The history of the kings of Israel and Judah from Solomon until the fall of Jerusalem; the people's and rulers' faithfulness or lack of faithfulness to God; God's faithfulness, then and now
- **Noteworthy:** 1 and 2 Kings were originally one book.

AT A GLANCE

- **1 Kings 1–11** The reign of King Solomon
- **1 Kings 12–2 Kings 17** The various kings of Israel and Judah
- **2 Kings 18–25** The kings of Judah until its fall in 587 B.C.

The Struggle for the Succession

1 King David was old and advanced in years; and although they covered him with clothes, he could not get warm. ²So his servants said to him, "Let a young virgin be sought for my lord the king, and let her wait on the king, and be his attendant; let her lie in your bosom, so that my lord the king may be warm." ³So they searched for a beautiful girl throughout all the territory of Israel, and found Abishag the Shunammite, and brought her to the king. ⁴The girl was very beautiful. She became the king's attendant and served him, but the king did not know her sexually.

5 Now Adonijah son of Haggith exalted himself, saying, "I will be king"; he prepared for himself chariots and horsemen, and fifty men to run before him. ⁶His father had never at any time displeased him by asking, "Why have you done thus and so?" He was also a very handsome man, and he was born next after Absalom. ⁷He conferred with Joab son of Zeruiah and with the priest Abiathar, and they supported Adonijah. ⁸But the priest Zadok, and Benaiah son of Jehoiada, and the prophet Nathan, and Shimei, and Rei, and David's own warriors did not side with Adonijah.

9 Adonijah sacrificed sheep, oxen, and fatted cattle by the stone Zoheleth, which is beside En-rogel, and he invited all his brothers, the king's sons, and all the royal officials of Judah, ¹⁰but he did not invite the prophet Nathan or Benaiah or the warriors or his brother Solomon.

11 Then Nathan said to Bathsheba, Solomon's mother, "Have you not heard that Adonijah son of Haggith has become king and our lord David does not know it? ¹²Now therefore come, let me give you advice, so that you may save your own life and the life of your son Solomon. ¹³Go in at once to King David, and say to him, 'Did you not, my lord the king, swear to your servant, saying: Your son Solomon shall succeed me as king, and he shall sit on my throne? Why then is Adonijah king?' ¹⁴Then while you are still there speaking with the king, I will come in after you and confirm your words."

15 So Bathsheba went to the king in his room. The king was very old; Abishag the Shunammite was attending the king. ¹⁶Bathsheba bowed and did obeisance to the king, and the king said, "What do you wish?" ¹⁷She said to him, "My lord, you swore to your servant by the LORD your God, saying: Your son Solomon shall succeed me as king, and he shall sit on my throne. ¹⁸But now suddenly Adonijah has become king, though you, my lord the king, do not know it. ¹⁹He has sacrificed oxen, fatted cattle, and sheep in abundance, and has invited all the children of the king, the priest Abiathar, and Joab the commander of the army; but your servant Solomon he has not invited. ²⁰But you, my lord the king—the eyes of all Israel are on you to tell them who shall sit on the throne of my lord the king after him. ²¹Otherwise it will come to pass, when my lord the king sleeps with his ancestors, that my son Solomon and I will be counted offenders."

STUDY IT!

Introducing . . . Solomon · 1 Kings 1–11

Solomon was one of the sons of David and Bathsheba. He ruled for forty years after King David died, and he was the third and last king to rule over the united kingdom of Israel.

There's an old saying that often our personal strengths are our greatest weaknesses. This was true of Solomon. He was a tremendous organizer, an able ruler, a clever politician, and a great builder—it was during his reign that the first temple was built in Jerusalem. Solomon accomplished these things, however, by taxing his people heavily, marrying foreign women to seal political alliances with other nations, and using forced labor to complete his building projects. These things offended God and made Solomon unpopular with the people of Israel.

When Solomon died, ten of the original twelve tribes left and set up their own kingdom in the northern part of Israel. Israel never again existed as a united kingdom ruled by an Israelite king. The author of Kings attributes this more to Solomon's acceptance of other gods near the end of his life than to his political mistakes.

22 While she was still speaking with the king, the prophet Nathan came in. [23]The king was told, "Here is the prophet Nathan." When he came in before the king, he did obeisance to the king, with his face to the ground. [24]Nathan said, "My lord the king, have you said, 'Adonijah shall succeed me as king, and he shall sit on my throne'? [25]For today he has gone down and has sacrificed oxen, fatted cattle, and sheep in abundance, and has invited all the king's children, Joab the commander[a] of the army, and the priest Abiathar, who are now eating and drinking before him, and saying, 'Long live King Adonijah!' [26]But he did not invite me, your servant, and the priest Zadok, and Benaiah son of Jehoiada, and your servant Solomon. [27]Has this thing been brought about by my lord the king and you have not let your servants know who should sit on the throne of my lord the king after him?"

The Accession of Solomon

28 King David answered, "Summon Bathsheba to me." So she came into the king's presence, and stood before the king. [29]The king swore, saying, "As the LORD lives, who has saved my life from every adversity, [30]as I swore to you by the LORD, the God of Israel, 'Your son Solomon shall succeed me as king, and he shall sit on my throne in my place,' so will I do this day." [31]Then Bathsheba bowed with her face to the ground, and did obeisance to the king, and said, "May my lord King David live forever!"

32 King David said, "Summon to me the priest Zadok, the prophet Nathan, and Benaiah son of Jehoiada." When they came before the king, [33]the king said to them, "Take with you the servants of your lord, and have my son Solomon ride on my own mule, and bring him down to Gihon. [34]There let the priest Zadok and the prophet Nathan anoint him king over Israel; then blow the trumpet, and say, 'Long live King Solomon!' [35]You shall go up following him. Let him enter and sit on my throne; he shall be king in my place; for I have appointed him to be ruler over Israel and over Judah." [36]Benaiah son of Jehoiada answered the king, "Amen! May the LORD, the God of my lord the king, so ordain. [37]As the LORD has been with my lord the king, so may he be with Solomon, and make his throne greater than the throne of my lord King David."

38 So the priest Zadok, the prophet Nathan, and Benaiah son of Jehoiada, and the Cherethites and the Pelethites, went down and had Solomon ride on

King David's mule, and led him to Gihon. [39]There the priest Zadok took the horn of oil from the tent and anointed Solomon. Then they blew the trumpet, and all the people said, "Long live King Solomon!" [40]And all the people went up following him, playing on pipes and rejoicing with great joy, so that the earth quaked at their noise.

41 Adonijah and all the guests who were with him heard it as they finished feasting. When Joab heard the sound of the trumpet, he said, "Why is the city in an uproar?" [42]While he was still speaking, Jonathan son of the priest Abiathar arrived. Adonijah said, "Come in, for you are a worthy man and surely you bring good news." [43]Jonathan answered Adonijah, "No, for our lord King David has made Solomon king; [44]the king has sent with him the priest Zadok, the prophet Nathan, and Benaiah son of Jehoiada, and the Cherethites and the Pelethites; and they had him ride on the king's mule; [45]the priest Zadok and the prophet Nathan have anointed him king at Gihon; and they have gone up from there rejoicing, so that the city is in an uproar. This is the noise that you heard. [46]Solomon now sits on the royal throne. [47]Moreover the king's servants came to congratulate our lord King David, saying, 'May God make the name of Solomon more famous than yours, and make his throne greater than your throne.' The king bowed in worship on the bed [48]and went on to pray thus, 'Blessed be the LORD, the God of Israel, who today has granted one of my offspring[b] to sit on my throne and permitted me to witness it.' "

49 Then all the guests of Adonijah got up trembling and went their own ways. [50]Adonijah, fearing Solomon, got up and went to grasp the horns of the altar. [51]Solomon was informed, "Adonijah is afraid of King Solomon; see, he has laid hold of the horns of the altar, saying, 'Let King Solomon swear to me first that he will not kill his servant with the sword.' " [52]So Solomon responded, "If he proves to be a worthy man, not one of his hairs shall fall to the ground; but if wickedness is found in him, he shall die." [53]Then King Solomon sent to have him brought down from the altar. He came to do obeisance to King Solomon; and Solomon said to him, "Go home."

David's Instruction to Solomon

2 When David's time to die drew near, he charged his son Solomon, saying: [2]"I am about to go the way of all the earth. Be strong, be

---

a Gk: Heb *the commanders*   b Gk: Heb *one*

courageous, [3]and keep the charge of the LORD your God, walking in his ways and keeping his statutes, his commandments, his ordinances, and his testimonies, as it is written in the law of Moses, so that you may prosper in all that you do and wherever you turn. [4]Then the LORD will establish his word that he spoke concerning me: 'If your heirs take heed to their way, to walk before me in faithfulness with all their heart and with all their soul, there shall not fail you a successor on the throne of Israel.'

5 "Moreover you know also what Joab son of Zeruiah did to me, how he dealt with the two commanders of the armies of Israel, Abner son of Ner, and Amasa son of Jether, whom he murdered, retaliating in time of peace for blood that had been shed in war, and putting the blood of war on the belt around his waist, and on the sandals on his feet. [6]Act therefore according to your wisdom, but do not let his gray head go down to Sheol in peace. [7]Deal loyally, however, with the sons of Barzillai the Gileadite, and let them be among those who eat at your table; for with such loyalty they met me when I fled from your brother Absalom. [8]There is also with you Shimei son of Gera, the Benjaminite from Bahurim, who cursed me with a terrible curse on the day when I went to Mahanaim; but when he came down to meet me at the Jordan, I swore to him by the LORD, 'I will not put you to death with the sword.' [9]Therefore do not hold him guiltless, for you are a wise man; you will know what you ought to do to him, and you must bring his gray head down with blood to Sheol."

Death of David

10 Then David slept with his ancestors, and was buried in the city of David. [11]The time that David reigned over Israel was forty years; he reigned seven years in Hebron, and thirty-three years in Jerusalem. [12]So Solomon sat on the throne of his father David; and his kingdom was firmly established.

Solomon Consolidates His Reign

13 Then Adonijah son of Haggith came to Bath-sheba, Solomon's mother. She asked, "Do you come peaceably?" He said, "Peaceably." [14]Then he said, "May I have a word with you?" She said, "Go on."

[15]He said, "You know that the kingdom was mine, and that all Israel expected me to reign; however, the kingdom has turned about and become my brother's, for it was his from the LORD. [16]And now I have one request to make of you; do not refuse me." She said to him, "Go on." [17]He said, "Please ask King Solomon—he will not refuse you—to give me Abishag the Shunammite as my wife." [18]Bath-sheba said, "Very well; I will speak to the king on your behalf."

19 So Bathsheba went to King Solomon, to speak to him on behalf of Adonijah. The king rose to meet her, and bowed down to her; then he sat on his throne, and had a throne brought for the king's mother, and she sat on his right. [20]Then she said, "I have one small request to make of you; do not refuse me." And the king said to her, "Make your request, my mother; for I will not refuse you." [21]She said, "Let Abishag the Shunammite be given to your brother Adonijah as his wife." [22]King Solomon answered his mother, "And why do you ask Abishag the Shunammite for Adonijah? Ask for him the kingdom as well! For he is my elder brother; ask not only for him but also for the priest Abiathar and for Joab son of Zeruiah!" [23]Then King Solomon swore by the LORD, "So may God do to me, and more also, for Adonijah has devised this scheme at the risk of his life! [24]Now therefore as the LORD lives, who has established me and placed me on the throne of my father David, and who has made me a house as he promised, today Adonijah shall be put to death." [25]So King Solomon sent Benaiah son of Jehoiada; he struck him down, and he died.

26 The king said to the priest Abiathar, "Go to Anathoth, to your estate; for you deserve death. But I will not at this time put you to death, because you carried the ark of the Lord GOD before my father David, and because you shared in all the hardships my father endured." [27]So Solomon banished Abiathar from being priest to the LORD, thus fulfilling the

> "Be strong, be courageous, and keep the charge of the LORD your God, walking in his ways ... so that you may prosper in all that you do."
> —1 Kings 2:2–3

word of the LORD that he had spoken concerning the house of Eli in Shiloh.

28 When the news came to Joab—for Joab had supported Adonijah though he had not supported Absalom—Joab fled to the tent of the LORD and grasped the horns of the altar. [29]When it was told King Solomon, "Joab has fled to the tent of the LORD and now is beside the altar," Solomon sent Benaiah son of Jehoiada, saying, "Go, strike him down." [30]So Benaiah came to the tent of the LORD and said to him, "The king commands, 'Come out.' " But he said, "No, I will die here." Then Benaiah brought the king word again, saying, "Thus said Joab, and thus he answered me." [31]The king replied to him, "Do as he has said, strike him down and bury him; and thus take away from me and from my father's house the guilt for the blood that Joab shed without cause. [32]The LORD will bring back his bloody deeds on his own head, because, without the knowledge of my father David, he attacked and killed with the sword two men more righteous and better than himself, Abner son of Ner, commander of the army of Israel, and Amasa son of Jether, commander of the army of Judah. [33]So shall their blood come back on the head of Joab and on the head of his descendants forever; but to David, and to his descendants, and to his house, and to his throne, there shall be peace from the LORD forevermore." [34]Then Benaiah son of Jehoiada went up and struck him down and killed him; and he was buried at his own house near the wilderness. [35]The king put Benaiah son of Jehoiada over the army in his place, and the king put the priest Zadok in the place of Abiathar.

36 Then the king sent and summoned Shimei, and said to him, "Build yourself a house in Jerusalem, and live there, and do not go out from there to any place whatever. [37]For on the day you go out, and cross the Wadi Kidron, know for certain that you shall die; your blood shall be on your own head." [38]And Shimei said to the king, "The sentence is fair; as my lord the king has said, so will your servant do." So Shimei lived in Jerusalem many days.

39 But it happened at the end of three years that two of Shimei's slaves ran away to King Achish son of Maacah of Gath. When it was told Shimei, "Your slaves are in Gath," [40]Shimei arose and saddled a donkey, and went to Achish in Gath, to search for his slaves; Shimei went and brought his slaves from Gath. [41]When Solomon was told that Shimei had gone from Jerusalem to Gath and returned, [42]the king sent and summoned Shimei, and said to him, "Did I not make you swear by the LORD, and solemnly adjure you, saying, 'Know for certain that on the day you go out and go to any place whatever, you shall die'? And you said to me, 'The sentence is fair; I accept.' [43]Why then have you not kept your oath to the LORD and the commandment with which I charged you?" [44]The king also said to Shimei, "You know in your own heart all the evil that you did to my father David; so the LORD will bring back your evil on your own head. [45]But King Solomon shall be blessed, and the throne of David shall be established before the LORD forever." [46]Then the king commanded Benaiah son of Jehoiada; and he went out and struck him down, and he died.

So the kingdom was established in the hand of Solomon.

Solomon's Prayer for Wisdom

3 Solomon made a marriage alliance with Pharaoh king of Egypt; he took Pharaoh's daughter and brought her into the city of David, until he had finished building his own house and the house of the LORD and the wall around Jerusalem. [2]The people were sacrificing at the high places, however, because no house had yet been built for the name of the LORD.

3 Solomon loved the LORD, walking in the statutes of his father David; only, he sacrificed and offered incense at the high places. [4]The king went to Gibeon to sacrifice there, for that was the principal high place; Solomon used to offer a thousand burnt offerings on that altar. [5]At Gibeon the LORD appeared to Solomon in a dream by night; and God said, "Ask what I should give you." [6]And Solomon said, "You have shown great and steadfast love to your servant my father David, because he walked before you in faithfulness, in righteousness, and in uprightness of heart toward you; and you have kept for him this great and steadfast love, and have given him a son to sit on his throne today. [7]And now, O LORD my God, you have made your servant king in place of my father David, although I am only a little child; I do not know how to go out or come in. [8]And your servant is in the midst of the people whom you have chosen, a great people, so numerous they cannot be numbered or counted. [9]Give your servant therefore an understanding mind to govern your people, able to discern between good and evil; for who can govern this your great people?"

10 It pleased the Lord that Solomon had asked this.

CONNECT IT!

Saint Francis of Assisi: Dream Big, Seek Wisdom
1 Kings 3:9

Saint Francis remains one of the most famous Catholic saints, even though he's been dead since 1226. The founder of the Franciscan order of monks is best known for his extreme generosity, for treating all of nature as part of his family in Christ, and for choosing to live in poverty so that he'd be completely dependent on God. But in his younger years, Francis lacked nothing growing up the son of a wealthy Italian merchant. His transformation from rich party boy to absolute follower of Jesus began with a dream from God, and he devoted the rest of his life to living out Jesus' teachings as literally as possible.

Francis' prayer, often called the Peace Prayer, contains the line, "Lord, grant that I may not so much seek to be . . . understood, as to understand." Like Solomon in his youth when he asked God for wisdom and understanding (1 Kings 3:9), Saint Francis understood that a wise heart is much more valuable than worldly riches. We would be wise to follow their example.

PRAY IT!

God, Give Me Wisdom!
1 Kings 3:4–15

Solomon could have asked God for anything in the world, and he chose . . . wisdom. Actually, he asked for an understanding mind (1 Kings 3:9). And it's a wonderful thing to ask God for. Solomon was noted for his wisdom, far and wide. In fact, he's still famous for it.

We usually associate wisdom with old age, because we tend to grow wiser as we go through life and gain experience. But we have a choice as we grow older. We can choose to grow bitter and self-focused or we can choose to grow wiser from life's experiences. Whether we're young or old, we have to trust God to use the events of our life to teach us wisdom and discernment.

Why not make Solomon's prayer for an understanding heart your own? "'Give your servant therefore an understanding mind . . . able to discern between good and evil'" (1 Kings 3:9).

[11] God said to him, "Because you have asked this, and have not asked for yourself long life or riches, or for the life of your enemies, but have asked for yourself understanding to discern what is right, [12] I now do according to your word. Indeed I give you a wise and discerning mind; no one like you has been before you and no one like you shall arise after you. [13] I give you also what you have not asked, both riches and honor all your life; no other king shall compare with you. [14] If you will walk in my ways, keeping my statutes and my commandments, as your father David walked, then I will lengthen your life."

15 Then Solomon awoke; it had been a dream. He came to Jerusalem where he stood before the ark of the covenant of the LORD. He offered up burnt offerings and offerings of well-being, and provided a feast for all his servants.

Solomon's Wisdom in Judgment

16 Later, two women who were prostitutes came to the king and stood before him. [17] The one woman said, "Please, my lord, this woman and I live in the same house; and I gave birth while she was in the house. [18] Then on the third day after I gave birth, this woman also gave birth. We were together; there was no one else with us in the house, only the two of us were in the house. [19] Then this woman's son died in the night, because she lay on him. [20] She got up in the middle of the night and took my son from beside me while your servant slept. She laid him at her breast, and laid her dead son at my breast. [21] When I rose in

the morning to nurse my son, I saw that he was dead; but when I looked at him closely in the morning, clearly it was not the son I had borne." [22]But the other woman said, "No, the living son is mine, and the dead son is yours." The first said, "No, the dead son is yours, and the living son is mine." So they argued before the king.

23 Then the king said, "The one says, 'This is my son that is alive, and your son is dead'; while the other says, 'Not so! Your son is dead, and my son is the living one.' " [24]So the king said, "Bring me a sword," and they brought a sword before the king. [25]The king said, "Divide the living boy in two; then give half to the one, and half to the other." [26]But the woman whose son was alive said to the king—because compassion for her son burned within her—"Please, my lord, give her the living boy; certainly do not kill him!" The other said, "It shall be neither mine nor yours; divide it." [27]Then the king responded: "Give the first woman the living boy; do not kill him. She is his mother." [28]All Israel heard of the judgment that the king had rendered; and they stood in awe of the king, because they perceived that the wisdom of God was in him, to execute justice.

Solomon's Administrative Officers

4 King Solomon was king over all Israel, [2]and these were his high officials: Azariah son of Zadok was the priest; [3]Elihoreph and Ahijah sons of Shisha were secretaries; Jehoshaphat son of Ahilud was recorder; [4]Benaiah son of Jehoiada was in command of the army; Zadok and Abiathar were priests; [5]Azariah son of Nathan was over the officials; Zabud son of Nathan was priest and king's friend; [6]Ahishar was in charge of the palace; and Adoniram son of Abda was in charge of the forced labor.

7 Solomon had twelve officials over all Israel, who provided food for the king and his household; each one had to make provision for one month in the year. [8]These were their names: Ben-hur, in the hill country of Ephraim; [9]Ben-deker, in Makaz, Shaalbim, Beth-shemesh, and Elon-beth-hanan; [10]Ben-hesed, in Arubboth (to him belonged Socoh and all the land of Hepher); [11]Ben-abinadab, in all Naphath-dor (he had Taphath, Solomon's daughter, as his wife); [12]Baana son of Ahilud, in Taanach, Megiddo, and all Beth-shean, which is beside Zarethan below Jezreel, and from Beth-shean to Abel-meholah, as far as the other side of Jokmeam; [13]Ben-geber, in Ramoth-gilead (he had the villages of Jair son of Manasseh,

which are in Gilead, and he had the region of Argob, which is in Bashan, sixty great cities with walls and bronze bars); [14]Ahinadab son of Iddo, in Mahanaim; [15]Ahimaaz, in Naphtali (he had taken Basemath, Solomon's daughter, as his wife); [16]Baana son of Hushai, in Asher and Bealoth; [17]Jehoshaphat son of Paruah, in Issachar; [18]Shimei son of Ela, in Benjamin; [19]Geber son of Uri, in the land of Gilead, the country of King Sihon of the Amorites and of King Og of Bashan. And there was one official in the land of Judah.

Magnificence of Solomon's Rule

20 Judah and Israel were as numerous as the sand by the sea; they ate and drank and were happy. [21][a] Solomon was sovereign over all the kingdoms from the Euphrates to the land of the Philistines, even to the border of Egypt; they brought tribute and served Solomon all the days of his life.

22 Solomon's provision for one day was thirty cors of choice flour, and sixty cors of meal, [23]ten fat oxen, and twenty pasture-fed cattle, one hundred sheep, besides deer, gazelles, roebucks, and fatted fowl. [24]For he had dominion over all the region west of the Euphrates from Tiphsah to Gaza, over all the kings west of the Euphrates; and he had peace on all sides. [25]During Solomon's lifetime Judah and Israel lived in safety, from Dan even to Beer-sheba, all of them under their vines and fig trees. [26]Solomon also had forty thousand stalls of horses for his chariots, and twelve thousand horsemen. [27]Those officials supplied provisions for King Solomon and for all who came to King Solomon's table, each one in his month; they let nothing be lacking. [28]They also brought to the required place barley and straw for the horses and swift steeds, each according to his charge.

Fame of Solomon's Wisdom

29 God gave Solomon very great wisdom, discernment, and breadth of understanding as vast as the sand on the seashore, [30]so that Solomon's wisdom surpassed the wisdom of all the people of the east, and all the wisdom of Egypt. [31]He was wiser than anyone else, wiser than Ethan the Ezrahite, and Heman, Calcol, and Darda, children of Mahol; his fame spread throughout all the surrounding nations. [32]He composed three thousand proverbs, and his songs numbered a thousand and five. [33]He would speak of trees, from the cedar that is in the Lebanon to the hyssop that grows in the wall; he would speak

α Ch 5.1 in Heb

of animals, and birds, and reptiles, and fish. [34]People came from all the nations to hear the wisdom of Solomon; they came from all the kings of the earth who had heard of his wisdom.

Preparations and Materials for the Temple

5 [a] Now King Hiram of Tyre sent his servants to Solomon, when he heard that they had anointed him king in place of his father; for Hiram had always been a friend to David. [2]Solomon sent word to Hiram, saying, [3]"You know that my father David could not build a house for the name of the LORD his God because of the warfare with which his enemies surrounded him, until the LORD put them under the soles of his feet.[b] [4]But now the LORD my God has given me rest on every side; there is neither adversary nor misfortune. [5]So I intend to build a house for the name of the LORD my God, as the LORD said to my father David, 'Your son, whom I will set on your throne in your place, shall build the house for my name.' [6]Therefore command that cedars from the Lebanon be cut for me. My servants will join your servants, and I will give you whatever wages you set for your servants; for you know that there is no one among us who knows how to cut timber like the Sidonians."

[7] When Hiram heard the words of Solomon, he rejoiced greatly, and said, "Blessed be the LORD today, who has given to David a wise son to be over this great people." [8]Hiram sent word to Solomon, "I have heard the message that you have sent to me; I will fulfill all your needs in the matter of cedar and cypress timber. [9]My servants shall bring it down to the sea from the Lebanon; I will make it into rafts to go by sea to the place you indicate. I will have them broken up there for you to take away. And you shall meet my needs by providing food for my household." [10]So Hiram supplied Solomon's every need for timber of cedar and cypress. [11]Solomon in turn gave Hiram twenty thousand cors of wheat as food for his household, and twenty cors of fine oil. Solomon gave this to Hiram year by year. [12]So the LORD gave Solomon wisdom, as he promised him. There was peace between Hiram and Solomon; and the two of them made a treaty.

[13] King Solomon conscripted forced labor out of all Israel; the levy numbered thirty thousand men. [14]He sent them to the Lebanon, ten thousand a month in shifts; they would be a month in the Lebanon and two months at home; Adoniram was in charge of the forced labor. [15]Solomon also had seventy thousand laborers and eighty thousand stonecutters in the hill country, [16]besides Solomon's three thousand three hundred supervisors who were over the work, having charge of the people who did the work. [17]At the king's command, they quarried out great, costly stones in order to lay the foundation of the house with dressed stones. [18]So Solomon's builders and Hiram's builders and the Gebalites did the stonecutting and prepared the timber and the stone to build the house.

Solomon Builds the Temple

6 In the four hundred eightieth year after the Israelites came out of the land of Egypt, in the fourth year of Solomon's reign over Israel, in the month of Ziv, which is the second month, he began to build the house of the LORD. [2]The house that King Solomon built for the LORD was sixty cubits long, twenty cubits wide, and thirty cubits high. [3]The vestibule in front of the nave of the house was twenty cubits wide, across the width of the house. Its depth was ten cubits in front of the house. [4]For the house he made windows with recessed frames.[c] [5]He also built a structure against the wall of the house, running around the walls of the house, both the nave and the inner sanctuary; and he made side chambers all around. [6]The lowest story[d] was five cubits wide, the middle one was six cubits wide, and the third was seven cubits wide; for around the outside of the house he made offsets on the wall in order that the supporting beams should not be inserted into the walls of the house.

[7] The house was built with stone finished at the quarry, so that neither hammer nor ax nor any tool of iron was heard in the temple while it was being built.

---

a Ch 5.15 in Heb   b Gk Tg Vg: Heb *my feet* or *his feet*   c Gk: Meaning of Heb uncertain   d Gk: Heb *structure*

8 The entrance for the middle story was on the south side of the house: one went up by winding stairs to the middle story, and from the middle story to the third. ⁹So he built the house, and finished it; he roofed the house with beams and planks of cedar. ¹⁰He built the structure against the whole house, each story*ᵃ* five cubits high, and it was joined to the house with timbers of cedar.

11 Now the word of the LORD came to Solomon, ¹²"Concerning this house that you are building, if you will walk in my statutes, obey my ordinances, and keep all my commandments by walking in them, then I will establish my promise with you, which I made to your father David. ¹³I will dwell among the children of Israel, and will not forsake my people Israel."

14 So Solomon built the house, and finished it. ¹⁵He lined the walls of the house on the inside with boards of cedar; from the floor of the house to the rafters of the ceiling, he covered them on the inside with wood; and he covered the floor of the house with boards of cypress. ¹⁶He built twenty cubits of the rear of the house with boards of cedar from the floor to the rafters, and he built this within as an inner sanctuary, as the most holy place. ¹⁷The house, that is, the nave in front of the inner sanctuary, was forty cubits long. ¹⁸The cedar within the house had carvings of gourds and open flowers; all was cedar, no stone was seen. ¹⁹The inner sanctuary he prepared in the innermost part of the house, to set there the ark of the covenant of the LORD. ²⁰The interior of the inner sanctuary was twenty cubits long, twenty cubits wide, and twenty cubits high; he overlaid it with pure gold. He also overlaid the altar with cedar.*ᵇ* ²¹Solomon overlaid the inside of the house with pure gold, then he drew chains of gold across, in front of the inner sanctuary, and overlaid it with gold. ²²Next he overlaid the whole house with gold, in order that the whole house might be perfect; even the whole altar that belonged to the inner sanctuary he overlaid with gold.

The Furnishings of the Temple

23 In the inner sanctuary he made two cherubim of olivewood, each ten cubits high. ²⁴Five cubits was the length of one wing of the cherub, and five cubits the length of the other wing of the cherub; it was ten cubits from the tip of one wing to the tip of the other. ²⁵The other cherub also measured ten cubits; both cherubim had the same measure and the same form. ²⁶The height of one cherub was ten cubits, and so

was that of the other cherub. ²⁷He put the cherubim in the innermost part of the house; the wings of the cherubim were spread out so that a wing of one was touching the one wall, and a wing of the other cherub was touching the other wall; their other wings toward the center of the house were touching wing to wing. ²⁸He also overlaid the cherubim with gold.

29 He carved the walls of the house all around about with carved engravings of cherubim, palm trees, and open flowers, in the inner and outer rooms. ³⁰The floor of the house he overlaid with gold, in the inner and outer rooms.

31 For the entrance to the inner sanctuary he made doors of olivewood; the lintel and the doorposts were five-sided.*ᵇ* ³²He covered the two doors of olivewood with carvings of cherubim, palm trees, and open flowers; he overlaid them with gold, and spread gold on the cherubim and on the palm trees.

33 So also he made for the entrance to the nave doorposts of olivewood, four-sided each, ³⁴and two doors of cypress wood; the two leaves of the one door were folding, and the two leaves of the other door were folding. ³⁵He carved cherubim, palm trees, and open flowers, overlaying them with gold evenly applied upon the carved work. ³⁶He built the inner court with three courses of dressed stone to one course of cedar beams.

37 In the fourth year the foundation of the house of the LORD was laid, in the month of Ziv. ³⁸In the eleventh year, in the month of Bul, which is the eighth month, the house was finished in all its parts, and according to all its specifications. He was seven years in building it.

Solomon's Palace and Other Buildings

7 Solomon was building his own house thirteen years, and he finished his entire house.

2 He built the House of the Forest of the Lebanon one hundred cubits long, fifty cubits wide, and thirty cubits high, built on four rows of cedar pillars, with cedar beams on the pillars. ³It was roofed with cedar on the forty-five rafters, fifteen in each row, which were on the pillars. ⁴There were window frames in the three rows, facing each other in the three rows. ⁵All the doorways and doorposts had four-sided frames, opposite, facing each other in the three rows.

6 He made the Hall of Pillars fifty cubits long and thirty cubits wide. There was a porch in front with pillars, and a canopy in front of them.

7 He made the Hall of the Throne where he was

---

a Heb lacks *each story*   *b* Meaning of Heb uncertain

to pronounce judgment, the Hall of Justice, covered with cedar from floor to floor.

8 His own house where he would reside, in the other court back of the hall, was of the same construction. Solomon also made a house like this hall for Pharaoh's daughter, whom he had taken in marriage.

9 All these were made of costly stones, cut according to measure, sawed with saws, back and front, from the foundation to the coping, and from outside to the great court. [10]The foundation was of costly stones, huge stones, stones of eight and ten cubits. [11]There were costly stones above, cut to measure, and cedarwood. [12]The great court had three courses of dressed stone to one layer of cedar beams all around; so had the inner court of the house of the LORD, and the vestibule of the house.

Products of Hiram the Bronzeworker

13 Now King Solomon invited and received Hiram from Tyre. [14]He was the son of a widow of the tribe of Naphtali, whose father, a man of Tyre, had been an artisan in bronze; he was full of skill, intelligence, and knowledge in working bronze. He came to King Solomon, and did all his work.

15 He cast two pillars of bronze. Eighteen cubits was the height of the one, and a cord of twelve cubits would encircle it; the second pillar was the same.[a] [16]He also made two capitals of molten bronze, to set on the tops of the pillars; the height of the one capital was five cubits, and the height of the other capital was five cubits. [17]There were nets of checker work with wreaths of chain work for the capitals on the tops of the pillars; seven[b] for the one capital, and seven[c] for the other capital. [18]He made the columns with two rows around each latticework to cover the capitals that were above the pomegranates; he did the same with the other capital. [19]Now the capitals that were on the tops of the pillars in the vestibule were of lily-work, four cubits high. [20]The capitals were on the two pillars and also above the rounded projection that was beside the latticework; there were two hundred pomegranates in rows all around; and so with the other capital. [21]He set up the pillars at the vestibule of the temple; he set up the pillar on the south and called it Jachin; and he set up the pillar on the north and called it Boaz. [22]On the tops of the pillars was lily-work. Thus the work of the pillars was finished.

23 Then he made the molten sea; it was round, ten cubits from brim to brim, and five cubits high. A line

of thirty cubits would encircle it completely. [24]Under its brim were panels all around it, each of ten cubits, surrounding the sea; there were two rows of panels, cast when it was cast. [25]It stood on twelve oxen, three facing north, three facing west, three facing south, and three facing east; the sea was set on them. The hindquarters of each were toward the inside. [26]Its thickness was a handbreadth; its brim was made like the brim of a cup, like the flower of a lily; it held two thousand baths.[c]

27 He also made the ten stands of bronze; each stand was four cubits long, four cubits wide, and three cubits high. [28]This was the construction of the stands: they had borders; the borders were within the frames; [29]on the borders that were set in the frames were lions, oxen, and cherubim. On the frames, both above and below the lions and oxen, there were wreaths of beveled work. [30]Each stand had four bronze wheels and axles of bronze; at the four corners were supports for a basin. The supports were cast with wreaths at the side of each. [31]Its opening was within the crown whose height was one cubit; its opening was round, as a pedestal is made; it was a cubit and a half wide. At its opening there were carvings; its borders were four-sided, not round. [32]The four wheels were underneath the borders; the axles of the wheels were in the stands; and the height of a wheel was a cubit and a half. [33]The wheels were made like a chariot wheel, their axles, their rims, their spokes, and their hubs were all cast. [34]There were four supports at the four corners of each stand; the supports were of one piece with the stands. [35]On the top of the stand there was a round band half a cubit high; on the top of the stand, its stays and its borders were of one piece with it. [36]On the surfaces of its stays and on its borders he carved cherubim, lions, and palm trees, where each had space, with wreaths all around. [37]In this way he made the ten stands; all of them were cast alike, with the same size and the same form.

38 He made ten basins of bronze; each basin held forty baths,[c] each basin measured four cubits; there was a basin for each of the ten stands. [39]He set five of the stands on the south side of the house, and five on the north side of the house; he set the sea on the southeast corner of the house.

40 Hiram also made the pots, the shovels, and the basins. So Hiram finished all the work that he did for King Solomon on the house of the LORD: [41]the two pillars, the two bowls of the capitals that were on the tops of the pillars, the two latticeworks to

---

a Cn: Heb *and a cord of twelve cubits encircled the second pillar*; Compare Jer 52.21   b Heb: Gk *a net*   c A Heb measure of volume

cover the two bowls of the capitals that were on the tops of the pillars; [42]the four hundred pomegranates for the two latticeworks, two rows of pomegranates for each latticework, to cover the two bowls of the capitals that were on the pillars; [43]the ten stands, the ten basins on the stands; [44]the one sea, and the twelve oxen underneath the sea.

45 The pots, the shovels, and the basins, all these vessels that Hiram made for King Solomon for the house of the LORD were of burnished bronze. [46]In the plain of the Jordan the king cast them, in the clay ground between Succoth and Zarethan. [47]Solomon left all the vessels unweighed, because there were so many of them; the weight of the bronze was not determined.

48 So Solomon made all the vessels that were in the house of the LORD: the golden altar, the golden table for the bread of the Presence, [49]the lampstands of pure gold, five on the south side and five on the north, in front of the inner sanctuary; the flowers, the lamps, and the tongs, of gold; [50]the cups, snuffers, basins, dishes for incense, and firepans, of pure gold; the sockets for the doors of the innermost part of the house, the most holy place, and for the doors of the nave of the temple, of gold.

51 Thus all the work that King Solomon did on the house of the LORD was finished. Solomon brought in the things that his father David had dedicated, the silver, the gold, and the vessels, and stored them in the treasuries of the house of the LORD.

Dedication of the Temple

8 Then Solomon assembled the elders of Israel and all the heads of the tribes, the leaders of the ancestral houses of the Israelites, before King Solomon in Jerusalem, to bring up the ark of the covenant of the LORD out of the city of David, which is Zion. [2]All the people of Israel assembled to King Solomon at the festival in the month Ethanim, which is the seventh month. [3]And all the elders of Israel came, and the priests carried the ark. [4]So they brought up the ark of the LORD, the tent of meeting, and all the holy vessels that were in the tent; the priests and the Levites brought them up. [5]King Solomon and all the congregation of Israel, who had assembled before him, were with him before the ark, sacrificing so many sheep and oxen that they could not be counted or numbered. [6]Then the priests brought the ark of the covenant of the LORD

to its place, in the inner sanctuary of the house, in the most holy place, underneath the wings of the cherubim. [7]For the cherubim spread out their wings over the place of the ark, so that the cherubim made a covering above the ark and its poles. [8]The poles were so long that the ends of the poles were seen from the holy place in front of the inner sanctuary; but they could not be seen from outside; they are there to this day. [9]There was nothing in the ark except the two tablets of stone that Moses had placed there at Horeb, where the LORD made a covenant with the Israelites, when they came out of the land of Egypt. [10]And when the priests came out of the holy place, a cloud filled the house of the LORD, [11]so that the priests could not stand to minister because of the cloud; for the glory of the LORD filled the house of the LORD.

12 Then Solomon said,

"The LORD has said that he would dwell in
    thick darkness.
[13] I have built you an exalted house,
    a place for you to dwell in forever."

Solomon's Speech

14 Then the king turned around and blessed all the assembly of Israel, while all the assembly of Israel stood. [15]He said, "Blessed be the LORD, the God of Israel, who with his hand has fulfilled what he promised with his mouth to my father David, saying, [16]'Since the day that I brought my people Israel out of Egypt, I have not chosen a city from any of the tribes of Israel in which to build a house, that my name might be there; but I chose David to be over my people Israel.' [17]My father David had it in mind to build a house for the name of the LORD, the God of Israel. [18]But the LORD said to my father David, 'You did well to consider building a house for my name; [19]nevertheless you shall not build the house, but your son who shall be born to you shall build the house for my name.' [20]Now the LORD has upheld the promise that he made; for I have risen in the place of my father David; I sit on the throne of Israel, as the LORD promised, and have built the house for the name of the LORD, the God of Israel. [21]There I have provided a place for the ark, in which is the covenant of the LORD that he made with our ancestors when he brought them out of the land of Egypt."

Solomon's Prayer of Dedication

22 Then Solomon stood before the altar of the

LORD in the presence of all the assembly of Israel, and spread out his hands to heaven. ²³He said, "O LORD, God of Israel, there is no God like you in heaven above or on earth beneath, keeping covenant and steadfast love for your servants who walk before you with all their heart, ²⁴the covenant that you kept for your servant my father David as you declared to him; you promised with your mouth and have this day fulfilled with your hand. ²⁵Therefore, O LORD, God of Israel, keep for your servant my father David that which you promised him, saying, 'There shall never fail you a successor before me to sit on the throne of Israel, if only your children look to their way, to walk before me as you have walked before me.' ²⁶Therefore, O God of Israel, let your word be confirmed, which you promised to your servant my father David.

27 "But will God indeed dwell on the earth? Even heaven and the highest heaven cannot contain you, much less this house that I have built! ²⁸Regard your servant's prayer and his plea, O LORD my God, heeding the cry and the prayer that your servant prays to

PRAY IT!

Holy Places
1 Kings 8:27–30

Solomon knew that the temple would not hold God. But he asked God to choose to hear the prayers of the people offered in that place. Holy places are not cages to keep God contained, but physical reminders of God's presence. People need holy places more than God does. We gather together in church or other public holy places to experience God's presence as a community. But we can also meet God one-on-one in places special to us alone.

Try creating a holy space of your own. Use a corner of your bedroom, a favorite tree or rock near your house, or any other place you go frequently to connect with God. Ask God to be present there with you, just as Solomon and the Israelites did. Then trust that the God who listened to them will also hear and answer your prayers.

you today; ²⁹that your eyes may be open night and day toward this house, the place of which you said, 'My name shall be there,' that you may heed the prayer that your servant prays toward this place. ³⁰Hear the plea of your servant and of your people Israel when they pray toward this place; O hear in heaven your dwelling place; heed and forgive.

31 "If someone sins against a neighbor and is given an oath to swear, and comes and swears before your altar in this house, ³²then hear in heaven, and act, and judge your servants, condemning the guilty by bringing their conduct on their own head, and vindicating the righteous by rewarding them according to their righteousness.

33 "When your people Israel, having sinned against you, are defeated before an enemy but turn again to you, confess your name, pray and plead with you in this house, ³⁴then hear in heaven, forgive the sin of your people Israel, and bring them again to the land that you gave to their ancestors.

35 "When heaven is shut up and there is no rain because they have sinned against you, and then they pray toward this place, confess your name, and turn from their sin, because you punishᵃ them, ³⁶then hear in heaven, and forgive the sin of your servants, your people Israel, when you teach them the good way in which they should walk; and grant rain on your land, which you have given to your people as an inheritance.

37 "If there is famine in the land, if there is plague, blight, mildew, locust, or caterpillar; if their enemy besieges them in anyᵇ of their cities; whatever plague, whatever sickness there is; ³⁸whatever prayer, whatever plea there is from any individual or from all your people Israel, all knowing the afflictions of their own hearts so that they stretch out their hands toward this house; ³⁹then hear in heaven your dwelling place, forgive, act, and render to all whose hearts you know—according to all their ways, for only you know what is in every human heart— ⁴⁰so that they may fear you all the days that they live in the land that you gave to our ancestors.

41 "Likewise when a foreigner, who is not of your people Israel, comes from a distant land because of your name ⁴²—for they shall hear of your great name, your mighty hand, and your outstretched arm—when a foreigner comes and prays toward this house, ⁴³then hear in heaven your dwelling place, and do according to all that the foreigner calls to you, so that all the peoples of the earth may know

ᵃ Or when you answer ᵇ Gk Syr: Heb in the land

your name and fear you, as do your people Israel, and so that they may know that your name has been invoked on this house that I have built.

44 "If your people go out to battle against their enemy, by whatever way you shall send them, and they pray to the Lord toward the city that you have chosen and the house that I have built for your name, [45] then hear in heaven their prayer and their plea, and maintain their cause.

46 "If they sin against you—for there is no one who does not sin—and you are angry with them and give them to an enemy, so that they are carried away captive to the land of the enemy, far off or near; [47] yet if they come to their senses in the land to which they have been taken captive, and repent, and plead with you in the land of their captors, saying, 'We have sinned, and have done wrong; we have acted wickedly'; [48] if they repent with all their heart and soul in the land of their enemies, who took them captive, and pray to you toward their land, which you gave to their ancestors, the city that you have chosen, and the house that I have built for your name; [49] then hear in heaven your dwelling place their prayer and their plea, maintain their cause [50] and forgive your people who have sinned against you, and all their transgressions that they have committed against you; and grant them compassion in the sight of their captors, so that they may have compassion on them [51] (for they are your people and heritage, which you brought out of Egypt, from the midst of the iron-smelter). [52] Let your eyes be open to the plea of your servant, and to the plea of your people Israel, listening to them whenever they call to you. [53] For you have separated them from among all the peoples of the earth, to be your heritage, just as you promised through Moses, your servant, when you brought our ancestors out of Egypt, O Lord God."

Solomon Blesses the Assembly

54 Now when Solomon finished offering all this prayer and this plea to the Lord, he arose from facing the altar of the Lord, where he had knelt with hands outstretched toward heaven; [55] he stood and blessed all the assembly of Israel with a loud voice: 56 "Blessed be the Lord, who has given rest to his people Israel according to all that he promised; not one word has failed of all his good promise, which he spoke through his servant Moses. [57] The Lord our God be with us, as he was with our ances-

tors; may he not leave us or abandon us, [58] but incline our hearts to him, to walk in all his ways, and to keep his commandments, his statutes, and his ordinances, which he commanded our ancestors. [59] Let these words of mine, with which I pleaded before the Lord, be near to the Lord our God day and night, and may he maintain the cause of his servant and the cause of his people Israel, as each day requires; [60] so that all the peoples of the earth may know that the Lord is God; there is no other. [61] Therefore devote yourselves completely to the Lord our God, walking in his statutes and keeping his commandments, as at this day."

Solomon Offers Sacrifices

62 Then the king, and all Israel with him, offered sacrifice before the Lord. [63] Solomon offered as sacrifices of well-being to the Lord twenty-two thousand oxen and one hundred twenty thousand sheep. So the king and all the people of Israel dedicated the house of the Lord. [64] The same day the king consecrated the middle of the court that was in front of the house of the Lord; for there he offered the burnt offerings and the grain offerings and the fat pieces of the sacrifices of well-being, because the bronze altar that was before the Lord was too small to receive the burnt offerings and the grain offerings and the fat pieces of the sacrifices of well-being.

65 So Solomon held the festival at that time, and all Israel with him—a great assembly, people from Lebo-hamath to the Wadi of Egypt—before the Lord our God, seven days.[a] [66] On the eighth day he sent the people away; and they blessed the king, and went to their tents, joyful and in good spirits because of all the goodness that the Lord had shown to his servant David and to his people Israel.

God Appears Again to Solomon

9 When Solomon had finished building the house of the Lord and the king's house and all that Solomon desired to build, [2] the Lord appeared to Solomon a second time, as he had appeared to him at Gibeon. [3] The Lord said to him, "I have heard your prayer and your plea, which you made before me; I have consecrated this house that you have built, and put my name there forever; my eyes and my heart will be there for all time. [4] As for you, if you will walk before me, as David your father walked, with integrity of heart and uprightness,

---

a Compare Gk: Heb *seven days and seven days, fourteen days*

doing according to all that I have commanded you, and keeping my statutes and my ordinances, [5]then I will establish your royal throne over Israel forever, as I promised your father David, saying, 'There shall not fail you a successor on the throne of Israel.'

6 "If you turn aside from following me, you or your children, and do not keep my commandments and my statutes that I have set before you, but go and serve other gods and worship them, [7]then I will cut Israel off from the land that I have given them; and the house that I have consecrated for my name I will cast out of my sight; and Israel will become a proverb and a taunt among all peoples. [8]This house will become a heap of ruins;[a] everyone passing by it will be astonished, and will hiss; and they will say, 'Why has the LORD done such a thing to this land and to this house?' [9]Then they will say, 'Because they have forsaken the LORD their God, who brought their ancestors out of the land of Egypt, and embraced other gods, worshiping them and serving them; therefore the LORD has brought this disaster upon them.' "

10 At the end of twenty years, in which Solomon had built the two houses, the house of the LORD and the king's house, [11]King Hiram of Tyre having supplied Solomon with cedar and cypress timber and gold, as much as he desired, King Solomon gave to Hiram twenty cities in the land of Galilee. [12]But when Hiram came from Tyre to see the cities that Solomon had given him, they did not please him. [13]Therefore he said, "What kind of cities are these that you have given me, my brother?" So they are called the land of Cabul[b] to this day. [14]But Hiram had sent to the king one hundred twenty talents of gold.

Other Acts of Solomon

15 This is the account of the forced labor that King Solomon conscripted to build the house of the LORD and his own house, the Millo and the wall of Jerusalem, Hazor, Megiddo, Gezer [16](Pharaoh king of Egypt had gone up and captured Gezer and burned it down, had killed the Canaanites who lived in the city, and had given it as dowry to his daughter, Solomon's wife; [17]so Solomon rebuilt Gezer), Lower Beth-horon, [18]Baalath, Tamar in the wilderness, within the land, [19]as well as all of Solomon's storage cities, the cities for his chariots, the cities for his cavalry, and whatever Solomon desired to build, in Jerusalem, in Lebanon, and in all the land of his dominion. [20]All the people who were left of the Amorites, the Hittites, the Perizzites, the Hivites, and the Jebusites, who were not of the people of Israel— [21]their descendants who were still left in the land, whom the Israelites were unable to destroy completely—these Solomon conscripted for slave labor, and so they are to this day. [22]But of the Israelites Solomon made no slaves; they were the soldiers, they were his officials, his commanders, his captains, and the commanders of his chariotry and cavalry.

23 These were the chief officers who were over Solomon's work: five hundred fifty, who had charge of the people who carried on the work.

24 But Pharaoh's daughter went up from the city of David to her own house that Solomon had built for her; then he built the Millo.

25 Three times a year Solomon used to offer up burnt offerings and sacrifices of well-being on the altar that he built for the LORD, offering incense[c] before the LORD. So he completed the house.

Solomon's Commercial Activity

26 King Solomon built a fleet of ships at Eziongeber, which is near Eloth on the shore of the Red Sea,[d] in the land of Edom. [27]Hiram sent his servants with the fleet, sailors who were familiar with the sea, together with the servants of Solomon. [28]They went to Ophir, and imported from there four hundred twenty talents of gold, which they delivered to King Solomon.

Visit of the Queen of Sheba

10 When the queen of Sheba heard of the fame of Solomon (fame due to[e] the name of the LORD), she came to test him with hard questions. [2]She came to Jerusalem with a very great retinue, with camels bearing spices, and very much gold, and precious stones; and when she came to Solomon, she told him all that was on her mind. [3]Solomon answered all her questions; there was nothing hidden from the king that he could not explain to her. [4]When the queen of Sheba had observed all the wisdom of Solomon, the house that he had built, [5]the food of his table, the seating of his officials, and the attendance of his servants, their clothing, his valets, and his burnt offerings that he offered at the house of the LORD, there was no more spirit in her.

6 So she said to the king, "The report was true

---

a Syr Old Latin: Heb *will become high*   b Perhaps meaning *a land good for nothing*   c Gk: Heb *offering incense with it that was*   d Or *Sea of Reeds*
e Meaning of Heb uncertain

that I heard in my own land of your accomplishments and of your wisdom, [7]but I did not believe the reports until I came and my own eyes had seen it. Not even half had been told me; your wisdom and prosperity far surpass the report that I had heard. [8]Happy are your wives![a] Happy are these your servants, who continually attend you and hear your wisdom! [9]Blessed be the LORD your God, who has delighted in you and set you on the throne of Israel! Because the LORD loved Israel forever, he has made you king to execute justice and righteousness." [10]Then she gave the king one hundred twenty talents of gold, a great quantity of spices, and precious stones; never again did spices come in such quantity as that which the queen of Sheba gave to King Solomon.

11 Moreover, the fleet of Hiram, which carried gold from Ophir, brought from Ophir a great quantity of almug wood and precious stones. [12]From the almug wood the king made supports for the house of the LORD, and for the king's house, lyres also and harps for the singers; no such almug wood has come or been seen to this day.

13 Meanwhile King Solomon gave to the queen of Sheba every desire that she expressed, as well as what he gave her out of Solomon's royal bounty. Then she returned to her own land, with her servants.

14 The weight of gold that came to Solomon in one year was six hundred sixty-six talents of gold, [15]besides that which came from the traders and from the business of the merchants, and from all the kings of Arabia and the governors of the land. [16]King Solomon made two hundred large shields of beaten gold; six hundred shekels of gold went into each large shield. [17]He made three hundred shields of beaten gold; three minas of gold went into each shield; and the king put them in the House of the Forest of Lebanon. [18]The king also made a great ivory throne, and overlaid it with the finest gold. [19]The throne had six steps. The top of the throne was rounded in the back, and on each side of the seat were arm rests and two lions standing beside the arm rests, [20]while twelve lions were standing, one on each end of a step on the six steps. Nothing like it was ever made in any kingdom. [21]All King Solomon's drinking vessels were of gold, and all the vessels of the House of the Forest of Lebanon were of pure gold; none were of silver—it was not considered as anything in the days of Solomon. [22]For the king had a fleet of ships of Tarshish at sea with the fleet of Hiram. Once every three years the fleet of ships of Tarshish used to come bringing gold, silver, ivory, apes, and peacocks.[b]

23 Thus King Solomon excelled all the kings of the earth in riches and in wisdom. [24]The whole earth sought the presence of Solomon to hear his wisdom, which God had put into his mind. [25]Every one of them brought a present, objects of silver and gold, garments, weaponry, spices, horses, and mules, so much year by year.

26 Solomon gathered together chariots and horses; he had fourteen hundred chariots and twelve thousand horses, which he stationed in the chariot cities and with the king in Jerusalem. [27]The king made silver as common in Jerusalem as stones, and he made cedars as numerous as the sycamores of the Shephelah. [28]Solomon's import of horses was from Egypt and Kue, and the king's traders received them from Kue at a price. [29]A chariot could be imported from Egypt for six hundred shekels of silver, and a horse for one hundred fifty; so through the king's traders they were exported to all the kings of the Hittites and the kings of Aram.

Solomon's Errors

11 King Solomon loved many foreign women along with the daughter of Pharaoh: Moabite, Ammonite, Edomite, Sidonian, and Hittite women, [2]from the nations concerning which the LORD had said to the Israelites, "You shall not enter into marriage with them, neither shall they with you; for they will surely incline your heart to follow their gods"; Solomon clung to these in love. [3]Among his wives were seven hundred princesses and three hundred concubines; and his wives turned away his heart. [4]For when Solomon was old, his wives turned away his heart after other gods; and his heart was not true to the LORD his God, as was the heart of his father David. [5]For Solomon followed Astarte the goddess of the Sidonians, and Milcom the abomination of the Ammonites. [6]So Solomon did what was evil in the sight of the LORD, and did not completely follow the LORD, as his father David had done. [7]Then Solomon built a high place for Chemosh the abomination of Moab, and for Molech the abomination of the Ammonites, on the mountain east of Jerusalem. [8]He did the same for all his foreign wives, who offered incense and sacrificed to their gods.

9 Then the LORD was angry with Solomon, be-

---

a Gk Syr: Heb *men*   b Or *baboons*

PRAY IT!

Solomon's Sin · 1 Kings 11:1–8

Sometimes when we think we are strongest, we are actually weakest. Solomon replaces his poverty of spirit (see 1 Kings 3:4-14) with pride. He seems to believe that he is strong enough to go against God's command not to take foreign wives and that he can withstand the influence of their foreign gods. But Solomon falls into the sin of idolatry (worshiping other gods) and breaks the covenant.

Have you ever considered doing something you knew was wrong? Did you tell yourself that it wouldn't hurt to do it just this once? Or that the benefits were worth the risk of the consequences? Maybe that's what Solomon said when he took his first foreign wife.

During your prayer time, reflect or journal on the following questions:

- Think of a time when you deliberately gave in to temptation. What excuses did you use?
- What takes your attention away from God?
- Have you ever tried asking God to give you strength to avoid doing something wrong?
- Pray **Psalm 86:11** to end your prayer.

cause his heart had turned away from the Lord, the God of Israel, who had appeared to him twice, [10]and had commanded him concerning this matter, that he should not follow other gods; but he did not observe what the Lord commanded. [11]Therefore the Lord said to Solomon, "Since this has been your mind and you have not kept my covenant and my statutes that I have commanded you, I will surely tear the kingdom from you and give it to your servant. [12]Yet for the sake of your father David I will not do it in your lifetime; I will tear it out of the hand of your son. [13]I will not, however, tear away the entire kingdom; I will give one tribe to your son, for the sake of my servant David and for the sake of Jerusalem, which I have chosen."

Adversaries of Solomon

14 Then the Lord raised up an adversary against Solomon, Hadad the Edomite; he was of the royal house in Edom. [15]For when David was in Edom, and Joab the commander of the army went up to bury the dead, he killed every male in Edom [16](for Joab and all Israel remained there six months, until he had eliminated every male in Edom); [17]but Hadad fled to Egypt with some Edomites who were servants of his father. He was a young boy at that time. [18]They set out from Midian and came to Paran; they took people with them from Paran and came to Egypt, to Pharaoh king of Egypt, who gave him a house, assigned him an allowance of food, and gave him land. [19]Hadad found great favor in the

sight of Pharaoh, so that he gave him his sister-in-law for a wife, the sister of Queen Tahpenes. [20]The sister of Tahpenes gave birth by him to his son Genubath, whom Tahpenes weaned in Pharaoh's house; Genubath was in Pharaoh's house among the children of Pharaoh. [21]When Hadad heard in Egypt that David slept with his ancestors and that Joab the commander of the army was dead, Hadad said to Pharaoh, "Let me depart, that I may go to my own country." [22]But Pharaoh said to him, "What do you lack with me that you now seek to go to your own country?" And he said, "No, do let me go."

23 God raised up another adversary against Solomon,[a] Rezon son of Eliada, who had fled from his master, King Hadadezer of Zobah. [24]He gathered followers around him and became leader of a marauding band, after the slaughter by David; they

a Heb *him*

went to Damascus, settled there, and made him king in Damascus. [25]He was an adversary of Israel all the days of Solomon, making trouble as Hadad did; he despised Israel and reigned over Aram.

Jeroboam's Rebellion

26 Jeroboam son of Nebat, an Ephraimite of Zeredah, a servant of Solomon, whose mother's name was Zeruah, a widow, rebelled against the king. [27]The following was the reason he rebelled against the king. Solomon built the Millo, and closed up the gap in the wall[a] of the city of his father David. [28]The man Jeroboam was very able, and when Solomon saw that the young man was industrious he gave him charge over all the forced labor of the house of Joseph. [29]About that time, when Jeroboam was leaving Jerusalem, the prophet Ahijah the Shilonite found him on the road. Ahijah had clothed himself with a new garment. The two of them were alone in the open country [30]when Ahijah laid hold of the new garment he was wearing and tore it into twelve pieces. [31]He then said to Jeroboam: Take for yourself ten pieces; for thus says the Lord, the God of Israel, "See, I am about to tear the kingdom from the hand of Solomon, and will give you ten tribes. [32]One tribe will remain his, for the sake of my servant David and for the sake of Jerusalem, the city that I have chosen out of all the tribes of Israel. [33]This is because he has[b] forsaken me, worshiped Astarte the goddess of the Sidonians, Chemosh the god of Moab, and Milcom the god of the Ammonites, and has[b] not walked in my ways, doing what is right in my sight and keeping my statutes and my ordinances, as his father David did. [34]Nevertheless I will not take the whole kingdom away from him but will make him ruler all the days of his life, for the sake of my servant David whom I chose and who did keep my commandments and my statutes; [35]but I will take the kingdom away from his son and give it to you—that is, the ten tribes. [36]Yet to his son I will give one tribe, so that my servant David may always have a lamp before me in Jerusalem, the city where I have chosen to put my name. [37]I will take you, and you shall reign over all that your soul desires; you shall be king over Israel. [38]If you will listen to all that I command you, walk in my ways, and do what is right in my sight by keeping my statutes and my commandments, as David my servant did, I will be with you, and will build you an enduring house, as I built for David, and I will give Israel to you. [39]For this reason I will punish the descendants of David, but not forever." [40]Solomon sought therefore to kill Jeroboam; but Jeroboam promptly fled to Egypt, to King Shishak of Egypt, and remained in Egypt until the death of Solomon.

Death of Solomon

41 Now the rest of the acts of Solomon, all that he did as well as his wisdom, are they not written in the Book of the Acts of Solomon? [42]The time that Solomon reigned in Jerusalem over all Israel was forty years. [43]Solomon slept with his ancestors and was buried in the city of his father David; and his son Rehoboam succeeded him.

The Northern Tribes Secede

12 Rehoboam went to Shechem, for all Israel had come to Shechem to make him king. [2]When Jeroboam son of Nebat heard of it (for he was still in Egypt, where he had fled from King Solomon), then Jeroboam returned from[c] Egypt. [3]And they sent and called him; and Jeroboam and all the assembly of Israel came and said to Rehoboam, [4]"Your father made our yoke heavy. Now therefore lighten the hard service of your father and his heavy yoke that he placed on us, and we will serve you." [5]He said to them, "Go away for three days, then come again to me." So the people went away.

6 Then King Rehoboam took counsel with the older men who had attended his father Solomon while he was still alive, saying, "How do you advise me to answer this people?" [7]They answered him, "If you will be a servant to this people today and serve them, and speak good words to them when you answer them, then they will be your servants forever." [8]But he disregarded the advice that the older men gave him, and consulted with the young men who had grown up with him and now attended him. [9]He said to them, "What do you advise that we answer this people who have said to me, 'Lighten the yoke that your father put on us'?" [10]The young men who had grown up with him said to him, "Thus you should say to this people who spoke to you, 'Your father made our yoke heavy, but you must lighten it for us'; thus you should say to them, 'My little finger is thicker than my father's loins. [11]Now, whereas my father laid on you a heavy yoke, I will add to your yoke. My father disciplined you with whips, but I will discipline you with scorpions.' "

12 So Jeroboam and all the people came to Rehoboam the third day, as the king had said, "Come

---

a Heb lacks *in the wall* b Gk Syr Vg: Heb *they have* c Gk Vg Compare 2 Chr 10.2: Heb *lived in*

STUDY IT!

The Kingdom Splits
1 Kings 12:1-19

When the people of Israel first settled in Canaan, they organized into twelve tribes, ruled by chieftains, that supported and protected one another. As Israel grew, though, it became necessary to have one central ruler who would unite the tribes into one nation. Saul was the first king of this united Israel. David followed Saul and expanded the kingdom's territory. David's son Solomon continued ruling over the expanded kingdom and engaged in expensive building projects.

At Solomon's death, many Israelites wanted a less demanding king. They had suffered under the burden of heavy taxes and forced labor. When Solomon's son Rehoboam refused to make any changes (1 Kings 12:11), ten of the northern tribes pulled away and placed their own king, Jeroboam, on the throne. The northern kingdom was called Israel. The southern kingdom, composed of two tribes, was called Judah. (See Map 6: "Kingdoms of Israel and Judah.") The kingdom was now split in two, and it was never again reunited.

Saul (1020 B.C.)

David (1000 B.C.)

Solomon (961 B.C.)

Kingdom splits (931 B.C.)

JUDAH (SOUTH)	ISRAEL (NORTH)
Capital: Jerusalem	Capital: Samaria
Twenty kings	Twenty kings
Falls to Babylonians (587 B.C.)	Falls to Assyrians (722 B.C.)
Exile to Babylon	Exile to Assyria

to me again the third day." [13] The king answered the people harshly. He disregarded the advice that the older men had given him [14] and spoke to them according to the advice of the young men, "My father made your yoke heavy, but I will add to your yoke; my father disciplined you with whips, but I will discipline you with scorpions." [15] So the king did not listen to the people, because it was a turn of affairs brought about by the LORD that he might fulfill his word, which the LORD had spoken by Ahijah the Shilonite to Jeroboam son of Nebat.

16 When all Israel saw that the king would not listen to them, the people answered the king,

"What share do we have in David?
    We have no inheritance in the son of Jesse.
To your tents, O Israel!
    Look now to your own house, O David."

So Israel went away to their tents. [17] But Rehoboam reigned over the Israelites who were living in the towns of Judah. [18] When King Rehoboam sent Adoram, who was taskmaster over the forced labor, all Israel stoned him to death. King Rehoboam then hurriedly mounted his chariot to flee to Jerusalem. [19] So Israel has been in rebellion against the house of David to this day.

First Dynasty: Jeroboam Reigns over Israel

20 When all Israel heard that Jeroboam had returned, they sent and called him to the assembly and made him king over all Israel. There was no one who followed the house of David, except the tribe of Judah alone.

21 When Rehoboam came to Jerusalem, he assembled all the house of Judah and the tribe of Benjamin, one hundred eighty thousand chosen troops to fight against the house of Israel, to restore the kingdom to Rehoboam son of Solomon. [22] But the word of God came to Shemaiah the man of God: [23] Say to King Rehoboam of Judah, son of Solomon, and to all the house of Judah and Benjamin, and to the rest of the people, [24] "Thus says the LORD, You shall not go up or fight against your kindred the people of Israel. Let everyone go home, for this thing is from me." So they heeded the word of the LORD and went home again, according to the word of the LORD.

Jeroboam's Golden Calves

25 Then Jeroboam built Shechem in the hill country of Ephraim, and resided there; he went out from

there and built Penuel. ²⁶Then Jeroboam said to himself, "Now the kingdom may well revert to the house of David. ²⁷If this people continues to go up to offer sacrifices in the house of the LORD at Jerusalem, the heart of this people will turn again to their master, King Rehoboam of Judah; they will kill me and return to King Rehoboam of Judah." ²⁸So the king took counsel, and made two calves of gold. He said to the people,ᵃ "You have gone up to Jerusalem long enough. Here are your gods, O Israel, who brought you up out of the land of Egypt." ²⁹He set one in Bethel, and the other he put in Dan. ³⁰And this thing became a sin, for the people went to worship before the one at Bethel and before the other as far as Dan.ᵇ ³¹He also made housesᶜ on high places, and appointed priests from among all the people, who were not Levites. ³²Jeroboam appointed a festival on the fifteenth day of the eighth month like the festival that was in Judah, and he offered sacrifices on the altar; so he did in Bethel, sacrificing to the calves that he had made. And he placed in Bethel the priests of the high places that he had made. ³³He went up to the altar that he had made in Bethel on the fifteenth day in the eighth month, in the month that he alone had devised; he appointed a festival for the people of Israel, and he went up to the altar to offer incense.

A Man of God from Judah

13 While Jeroboam was standing by the altar to offer incense, a man of God came out of Judah by the word of the LORD to Bethel ²and proclaimed against the altar by the word of the LORD, and said, "O altar, altar, thus says the LORD: 'A son shall be born to the house of David, Josiah by name; and he shall sacrifice on you the priests of the high places who offer incense on you, and human bones shall be burned on you.' " ³He gave a sign the same day, saying, "This is the sign that the LORD has spoken: 'The altar shall be torn down, and the ashes that are on it shall be poured out.' " ⁴When the king heard what the man of God cried out against the altar at Bethel, Jeroboam stretched out his hand from the altar, saying, "Seize him!" But the hand that he stretched out against him withered so that he could not draw it back to himself. ⁵The altar also was torn down, and the ashes poured out from the altar, according to the sign that the man of God had given by the word of the LORD. ⁶The king said to the man of God, "Entreat now the favor of the LORD your

God, and pray for me, so that my hand may be restored to me." So the man of God entreated the LORD; and the king's hand was restored to him, and became as it was before. ⁷Then the king said to the man of God, "Come home with me and dine, and I will give you a gift." ⁸But the man of God said to the king, "If you give me half your kingdom, I will not go in with you; nor will I eat food or drink water in this place. ⁹For thus I was commanded by the word of the LORD: You shall not eat food, or drink water, or return by the way that you came." ¹⁰So he went another way, and did not return by the way that he had come to Bethel.

11 Now there lived an old prophet in Bethel. One of his sons came and told him all that the man of God had done that day in Bethel; the words also that he had spoken to the king, they told to their father. ¹²Their father said to them, "Which way did he go?" And his sons showed him the way that the man of God who came from Judah had gone. ¹³Then he said to his sons, "Saddle a donkey for me." So they saddled a donkey for him, and he mounted it. ¹⁴He went after the man of God, and found him sitting under an oak tree. He said to him, "Are you the man of God who came from Judah?" He answered, "I am." ¹⁵Then he said to him, "Come home with me and eat some food." ¹⁶But he said, "I cannot return with you, or go in with you; nor will I eat food or drink water with you in this place; ¹⁷for it was said to me by the word of the LORD: You shall not eat food or drink water there, or return by the way that you came." ¹⁸Then the otherᵈ said to him, "I also am a prophet as you are, and an angel spoke to me by the word of the LORD: Bring him back with you into your house so that he may eat food and drink water." But he was deceiving him. ¹⁹Then the man of Godᵈ went back with him, and ate food and drank water in his house.

20 As they were sitting at the table, the word of the LORD came to the prophet who had brought him back; ²¹and he proclaimed to the man of God who came from Judah, "Thus says the LORD: Because you have disobeyed the word of the LORD, and have not kept the commandment that the LORD your God commanded you, ²²but have come back and have eaten food and drunk water in the place of which he said to you, 'Eat no food, and drink no water,' your body shall not come to your ancestral tomb." ²³After the man of Godᵈ had eaten food and had drunk, they saddled for him a donkey belonging to the prophet who had brought him back. ²⁴Then as he went away,

---

ᵃ Gk: Heb *to them*   ᵇ Compare Gk: Heb *went to the one as far as Dan*   ᶜ Gk Vg Compare 13.32: Heb *a house*   ᵈ Heb *he*

a lion met him on the road and killed him. His body was thrown in the road, and the donkey stood beside it; the lion also stood beside the body. ²⁵People passed by and saw the body thrown in the road, with the lion standing by the body. And they came and told it in the town where the old prophet lived.

26 When the prophet who had brought him back from the way heard of it, he said, "It is the man of God who disobeyed the word of the LORD; therefore the LORD has given him to the lion, which has torn him and killed him according to the word that the LORD spoke to him." ²⁷Then he said to his sons, "Saddle a donkey for me." So they saddled one, ²⁸and he went and found the body thrown in the road, with the donkey and the lion standing beside the body. The lion had not eaten the body or attacked the donkey. ²⁹The prophet took up the body of the man of God, laid it on the donkey, and brought it back to the city,ᵃ to mourn and to bury him. ³⁰He laid the body in his own grave; and they mourned over him, saying, "Alas, my brother!" ³¹After he had buried him, he said to his sons, "When I die, bury me in the grave in which the man of God is buried; lay my bones beside his bones. ³²For the saying that he proclaimed by the word of the LORD against the altar in Bethel, and against all the houses of the high places that are in the cities of Samaria, shall surely come to pass."

33 Even after this event Jeroboam did not turn from his evil way, but made priests for the high places again from among all the people; any who wanted to be priests he consecrated for the high places. ³⁴This matter became sin to the house of Jeroboam, so as to cut it off and to destroy it from the face of the earth.

Judgment on the House of Jeroboam

14 At that time Abijah son of Jeroboam fell sick. ²Jeroboam said to his wife, "Go, disguise yourself, so that it will not be known that you are the wife of Jeroboam, and go to Shiloh; for the prophet Ahijah is there, who said of me that I should be king over this people. ³Take with you ten loaves, some cakes, and a jar of honey, and go to him; he will tell you what shall happen to the child."

4 Jeroboam's wife did so; she set out and went to Shiloh, and came to the house of Ahijah. Now Ahijah could not see, for his eyes were dim because of his age. ⁵But the LORD said to Ahijah, "The wife of Jeroboam is coming to inquire of you concerning

her son; for he is sick. Thus and thus you shall say to her."

When she came, she pretended to be another woman. ⁶But when Ahijah heard the sound of her feet, as she came in at the door, he said, "Come in, wife of Jeroboam; why do you pretend to be another? For I am charged with heavy tidings for you. ⁷Go, tell Jeroboam, 'Thus says the LORD, the God of Israel: Because I exalted you from among the people, made you leader over my people Israel, ⁸and tore the kingdom away from the house of David to give it to you; yet you have not been like my servant David, who kept my commandments and followed me with all his heart, doing only that which was right in my sight, ⁹but you have done evil above all those who were before you and have gone and made for yourself other gods, and cast images, provoking me to anger, and have thrust me behind your back; ¹⁰therefore, I will bring evil upon the house of Jeroboam. I will cut off from Jeroboam every male, both bond and free in Israel, and will consume the house of Jeroboam, just as one burns up dung until it is all gone. ¹¹Anyone belonging to Jeroboam who dies in the city, the dogs shall eat; and anyone who dies in the open country, the birds of the air shall eat; for the LORD has spoken.' ¹²Therefore set out, go to your house. When your feet enter the city, the child shall die. ¹³All Israel shall mourn for him and bury him; for he alone of Jeroboam's family shall come to the grave, because in him there is found something pleasing to the LORD, the God of Israel, in the house of Jeroboam. ¹⁴Moreover the LORD will raise up for himself a king over Israel, who shall cut off the house of Jeroboam today, even right now!ᵇ

15 "The LORD will strike Israel, as a reed is shaken in the water; he will root up Israel out of this good land that he gave to their ancestors, and scatter them beyond the Euphrates, because they have made their sacred poles,ᶜ provoking the LORD to anger. ¹⁶He will give Israel up because of the sins of Jeroboam, which he sinned and which he caused Israel to commit."

17 Then Jeroboam's wife got up and went away, and she came to Tirzah. As she came to the threshold of the house, the child died. ¹⁸All Israel buried him and mourned for him, according to the word of the LORD, which he spoke by his servant the prophet Ahijah.

ᵃ Gk: Heb *he came to the town of the old prophet*   ᵇ Meaning of Heb uncertain   ᶜ Heb *Asherim*

Death of Jeroboam

19 Now the rest of the acts of Jeroboam, how he warred and how he reigned, are written in the Book of the Annals of the Kings of Israel. ²⁰The time that Jeroboam reigned was twenty-two years; then he slept with his ancestors, and his son Nadab succeeded him.

Rehoboam Reigns over Judah

21 Now Rehoboam son of Solomon reigned in Judah. Rehoboam was forty-one years old when he began to reign, and he reigned seventeen years in Jerusalem, the city that the LORD had chosen out of all the tribes of Israel, to put his name there. His mother's name was Naamah the Ammonite. ²²Judah did what was evil in the sight of the LORD; they provoked him to jealousy with their sins that they committed, more than all that their ancestors had done. ²³For they also built for themselves high places, pillars, and sacred poles*ᵃ* on every high hill and under every green tree; ²⁴there were also male temple prostitutes in the land. They committed all the abominations of the nations that the LORD drove out before the people of Israel.

25 In the fifth year of King Rehoboam, King Shishak of Egypt came up against Jerusalem; ²⁶he took away the treasures of the house of the LORD and the treasures of the king's house; he took everything. He also took away all the shields of gold that Solomon had made; ²⁷so King Rehoboam made shields of bronze instead, and committed them to the hands of the officers of the guard, who kept the door of the king's house. ²⁸As often as the king went into the house of the LORD, the guard carried them and brought them back to the guardroom.

29 Now the rest of the acts of Rehoboam, and all that he did, are they not written in the Book of the Annals of the Kings of Judah? ³⁰There was war between Rehoboam and Jeroboam continually. ³¹Rehoboam slept with his ancestors and was buried with his ancestors in the city of David. His mother's name was Naamah the Ammonite. His son Abijam succeeded him.

Abijam Reigns over Judah: Idolatry and War

15 Now in the eighteenth year of King Jeroboam son of Nebat, Abijam began to reign over Judah. ²He reigned for three years in Jerusalem. His mother's name was Maacah daughter of Abishalom.

ᵃ Heb *Asherim*

³He committed all the sins that his father did before him; his heart was not true to the LORD his God, like the heart of his father David. ⁴Nevertheless for David's sake the LORD his God gave him a lamp in Jerusalem, setting up his son after him, and establishing Jerusalem; ⁵because David did what was right in the sight of the LORD, and did not turn aside from anything that he commanded him all the days of his life, except in the matter of Uriah the Hittite. ⁶The war begun between Rehoboam and Jeroboam continued all the days of his life. ⁷The rest of the acts of Abijam, and all that he did, are they not written in the Book of the Annals of the Kings of Judah? There was war between Abijam and Jeroboam. ⁸Abijam slept with his ancestors, and they buried him in the city of David. Then his son Asa succeeded him.

Asa Reigns over Judah

9 In the twentieth year of King Jeroboam of Israel, Asa began to reign over Judah; ¹⁰he reigned forty-one years in Jerusalem. His mother's name was Maacah daughter of Abishalom. ¹¹Asa did what was right in the sight of the LORD, as his father David had done. ¹²He put away the male temple prostitutes out of the land, and removed all the idols that his ancestors had made. ¹³He also removed his mother Maacah from being queen mother, because she had made an abominable image for Asherah; Asa cut down her image and burned it at the Wadi Kidron. ¹⁴But the high places were not taken away. Nevertheless the heart of Asa was true to the LORD all his days. ¹⁵He brought into the house of the LORD the votive gifts of his father and his own votive gifts—silver, gold, and utensils.

Alliance with Aram against Israel

16 There was war between Asa and King Baasha of Israel all their days. ¹⁷King Baasha of Israel went up against Judah, and built Ramah, to prevent anyone from going out or coming in to King Asa of Judah. ¹⁸Then Asa took all the silver and the gold that were left in the treasures of the house of the LORD and the treasures of the king's house, and gave them into the hands of his servants. King Asa sent them to King Ben-hadad son of Tabrimmon son of Hezion of Aram, who resided in Damascus, saying, ¹⁹"Let there be an alliance between me and you, like that between my father and your father: I am sending you a present of silver and gold; go, break your alliance with King Baasha of Israel, so that he may withdraw from me."

^{20}Ben-hadad listened to King Asa, and sent the commanders of his armies against the cities of Israel. He conquered Ijon, Dan, Abel-beth-maacah, and all Chinneroth, with all the land of Naphtali. ^{21}When Baasha heard of it, he stopped building Ramah and lived in Tirzah. ^{22}Then King Asa made a proclamation to all Judah, none was exempt: they carried away the stones of Ramah and its timber, with which Baasha had been building; with them King Asa built Geba of Benjamin and Mizpah. ^{23}Now the rest of all the acts of Asa, all his power, all that he did, and the cities that he built, are they not written in the Book of the Annals of the Kings of Judah? But in his old age he was diseased in his feet. ^{24}Then Asa slept with his ancestors, and was buried with his ancestors in the city of his father David; his son Jehoshaphat succeeded him.

Nadab Reigns over Israel

25 Nadab son of Jeroboam began to reign over Israel in the second year of King Asa of Judah; he reigned over Israel two years. ^{26}He did what was evil in the sight of the LORD, walking in the way of his ancestor and in the sin that he caused Israel to commit.

27 Baasha son of Ahijah, of the house of Issachar, conspired against him; and Baasha struck him down at Gibbethon, which belonged to the Philistines; for Nadab and all Israel were laying siege to Gibbethon. ^{28}So Baasha killed Nadab^a in the third year of King Asa of Judah, and succeeded him. ^{29}As soon as he was king, he killed all the house of Jeroboam; he left to the house of Jeroboam not one that breathed, until he had destroyed it, according to the word of the LORD that he spoke by his servant Ahijah the Shilonite— ^{30}because of the sins of Jeroboam that he committed and that he caused Israel to commit, and because of the anger to which he provoked the LORD, the God of Israel.

31 Now the rest of the acts of Nadab, and all that he did, are they not written in the Book of the Annals of the Kings of Israel? ^{32}There was war between Asa and King Baasha of Israel all their days.

Second Dynasty: Baasha Reigns over Israel

33 In the third year of King Asa of Judah, Baasha son of Ahijah began to reign over all Israel at Tirzah; he reigned twenty-four years. ^{34}He did what was evil in the sight of the LORD, walking in

the way of Jeroboam and in the sin that he caused Israel to commit.

16 The word of the LORD came to Jehu son of Hanani against Baasha, saying, ^{2}"Since I exalted you out of the dust and made you leader over my people Israel, and you have walked in the way of Jeroboam, and have caused my people Israel to sin, provoking me to anger with their sins, ^{3}therefore, I will consume Baasha and his house, and I will make your house like the house of Jeroboam son of Nebat. ^{4}Anyone belonging to Baasha who dies in the city the dogs shall eat; and anyone of his who dies in the field the birds of the air shall eat."

5 Now the rest of the acts of Baasha, what he did, and his power, are they not written in the Book of the Annals of the Kings of Israel? ^{6}Baasha slept with his ancestors, and was buried at Tirzah; and his son Elah succeeded him. ^{7}Moreover the word of the LORD came by the prophet Jehu son of Hanani against Baasha and his house, both because of all the evil that he did in the sight of the LORD, provoking him to anger with the work of his hands, in being like the house of Jeroboam, and also because he destroyed it.

Elah Reigns over Israel

8 In the twenty-sixth year of King Asa of Judah, Elah son of Baasha began to reign over Israel in Tirzah; he reigned two years. ^{9}But his servant Zimri, commander of half his chariots, conspired against him. When he was at Tirzah, drinking himself drunk in the house of Arza, who was in charge of the palace at Tirzah, ^{10}Zimri came in and struck him down and killed him, in the twenty-seventh year of King Asa of Judah, and succeeded him.

11 When he began to reign, as soon as he had seated himself on his throne, he killed all the house of Baasha; he did not leave him a single male of his kindred or his friends. ^{12}Thus Zimri destroyed all the house of Baasha, according to the word of the LORD, which he spoke against Baasha by the prophet Jehu— ^{13}because of all the sins of Baasha and the sins of his son Elah that they committed, and that they caused Israel to commit, provoking the LORD God of Israel to anger with their idols. ^{14}Now the rest of the acts of Elah, and all that he did, are they not written in the Book of the Annals of the Kings of Israel?

a Heb him

Third Dynasty: Zimri Reigns over Israel

15 In the twenty-seventh year of King Asa of Judah, Zimri reigned seven days in Tirzah. Now the troops were encamped against Gibbethon, which belonged to the Philistines, [16]and the troops who were encamped heard it said, "Zimri has conspired, and he has killed the king"; therefore all Israel made Omri, the commander of the army, king over Israel that day in the camp. [17]So Omri went up from Gibbethon, and all Israel with him, and they besieged Tirzah. [18]When Zimri saw that the city was taken, he went into the citadel of the king's house; he burned down the king's house over himself with fire, and died— [19]because of the sins that he committed, doing evil in the sight of the LORD, walking in the way of Jeroboam, and for the sin that he committed, causing Israel to sin. [20]Now the rest of the acts of Zimri, and the conspiracy that he made, are they not written in the Book of the Annals of the Kings of Israel?

Fourth Dynasty: Omri Reigns over Israel

21 Then the people of Israel were divided into two parts; half of the people followed Tibni son of Ginath, to make him king, and half followed Omri. [22]But the people who followed Omri overcame the people who followed Tibni son of Ginath; so Tibni died, and Omri became king. [23]In the thirty-first year of King Asa of Judah, Omri began to reign over Israel; he reigned for twelve years, six of them in Tirzah.

Samaria the New Capital

24 He bought the hill of Samaria from Shemer for two talents of silver; he fortified the hill, and called the city that he built, Samaria, after the name of Shemer, the owner of the hill.

25 Omri did what was evil in the sight of the LORD; he did more evil than all who were before him. [26]For he walked in all the way of Jeroboam son of Nebat, and in the sins that he caused Israel to commit, provoking the LORD, the God of Israel, to anger by their idols. [27]Now the rest of the acts of Omri that he did, and the power that he showed, are they not written in the Book of the Annals of the Kings of Israel? [28]Omri slept with his ancestors, and was buried in Samaria; his son Ahab succeeded him.

Ahab Reigns over Israel

29 In the thirty-eighth year of King Asa of Judah,

Ahab son of Omri began to reign over Israel; Ahab son of Omri reigned over Israel in Samaria twenty-two years. [30]Ahab son of Omri did evil in the sight of the LORD more than all who were before him.

Ahab Marries Jezebel and Worships Baal

31 And as if it had been a light thing for him to walk in the sins of Jeroboam son of Nebat, he took as his wife Jezebel daughter of King Ethbaal of the Sidonians, and went and served Baal, and worshiped him. [32]He erected an altar for Baal in the house of Baal, which he built in Samaria. [33]Ahab also made a sacred pole.[a] Ahab did more to provoke the anger of the LORD, the God of Israel, than had all the kings of Israel who were before him. [34]In his days Hiel of Bethel built Jericho; he laid its foundation at the cost of Abiram his firstborn, and set up its gates at the cost of his youngest son Segub, according to the word of the LORD, which he spoke by Joshua son of Nun.

Elijah Predicts a Drought

17 Now Elijah the Tishbite, of Tishbe[b] in Gilead, said to Ahab, "As the LORD the God of Israel lives, before whom I stand, there shall be neither dew nor rain these years, except by my word." [2]The word of the LORD came to him, saying, [3]"Go from here and turn eastward, and hide yourself by the Wadi Cherith, which is east of the Jordan. [4]You shall drink from the wadi, and I have commanded the ravens to feed you there." [5]So he went and did according to the word of the LORD; he went and lived by the Wadi Cherith, which is east of the Jordan. [6]The ravens brought him bread and meat in the morning, and bread and meat in the evening; and he drank from the wadi. [7]But after a while the wadi dried up, because there was no rain in the land.

The Widow of Zarephath

8 Then the word of the LORD came to him, saying, [9]"Go now to Zarephath, which belongs to Sidon, and live there; for I have commanded a widow there to feed you." [10]So he set out and went to Zarephath. When he came to the gate of the town, a widow was there gathering sticks; he called to her and said, "Bring me a little water in a vessel, so that I may drink." [11]As she was going to bring it, he called to her and said, "Bring me a morsel of bread in your hand." [12]But she said, "As the LORD your God lives, I have nothing baked, only a handful of meal in a jar,

---

a Heb Asherah   b Gk: Heb of the settlers

and a little oil in a jug; I am now gathering a couple of sticks, so that I may go home and prepare it for myself and my son, that we may eat it, and die." [13]Elijah said to her, "Do not be afraid; go and do as you have said; but first make me a little cake of it and bring it to me, and afterwards make something for yourself and your son. [14]For thus says the LORD the God of Israel: The jar of meal will not be emptied and the jug of oil will not fail until the day that the LORD sends rain on the earth." [15]She went and did as Elijah said, so that she as well as he and her household ate for many days. [16]The jar of meal was not emptied, neither did the jug of oil fail, according to the word of the LORD that he spoke by Elijah.

Elijah Revives the Widow's Son

17 After this the son of the woman, the mistress of the house, became ill; his illness was so severe that there was no breath left in him. [18]She then said to Elijah, "What have you against me, O man of God? You have come to me to bring my sin to remembrance, and to cause the death of my son!" [19]But he said to her, "Give me your son." He took him from her bosom, carried him up into the upper chamber where he was lodging, and laid him on his own bed. [20]He cried out to the LORD, "O LORD my God, have you brought calamity even upon the widow with whom I am staying, by killing her son?" [21]Then he stretched himself upon the child three times, and cried out to the LORD, "O LORD my God, let this child's life come into him again." [22]The LORD listened to the voice of Elijah; the life of the child came into him again, and he revived. [23]Elijah took the child, brought him down from the upper chamber into the house, and gave him to his mother; then Elijah said, "See, your son is alive." [24]So the woman said to Elijah, "Now I know that you are a man of God, and that the word of the LORD in your mouth is truth."

Elijah's Message to Ahab

18 After many days the word of the LORD came to Elijah, in the third year of the drought,[a] saying, "Go, present yourself to Ahab; I will send rain on the earth." [2]So Elijah went to present himself to Ahab. The famine was severe in Samaria. [3]Ahab summoned Obadiah, who was in charge of the palace. (Now Obadiah revered the LORD greatly; [4]when Jezebel was killing off the prophets of the LORD, Obadiah took a hundred

---

Introducing . . . Elijah and Elisha · 1 Kings 17–19

You don't want to mess with Elijah and Elisha. They are the take-no-prisoners kind of prophets. According to 1 Kings, Elijah has 450 prophets of Baal killed after publicly humiliating them (1 Kings 18:40). And in 2 Kings when a bunch of boys call Elisha "baldhead," he curses them and they are attacked by bears (2 Kings 2:23-24).

Elijah, whose name means "Yahweh is my God," shows up in the second half of 1 Kings, reminding the Israelites that God is their only God and that keeping God's covenant means not worshiping the Canaanite baals (gods). In a dramatic story, he shows the idol-worshiping King Ahab and Queen Jezebel that God is superior to their false gods (1 Kings 18:21-40).

Elijah was recorded as being carried to heaven in a fiery chariot (2 Kings 2:11) as a sign of his greatness, and he was expected to reappear before the "day of the LORD" arrived (Malachi 4:5). By New Testament times, Elijah had come to represent the prophets as Moses had come to represent the law. Referring to Moses and Elijah was a way of summarizing everything God had revealed before Christ.

Elisha was Elijah's disciple and successor. He plays an important role in the first half of 2 Kings. Elisha's name means "God is salvation." He was a man of wisdom and a miracle worker.

These tough guys also had tender hearts. Both miraculously multiplied food for widows (1 Kings 17:16; 2 Kings 4:5), and both brought a dead child back to life (1 Kings 17:22; 2 Kings 4:34). Elijah and Elisha are revered for both their uncompromising faith and their compassion for children.

---

a Heb lacks *of the drought*

prophets, hid them fifty to a cave, and provided them with bread and water.) [5]Then Ahab said to Obadiah, "Go through the land to all the springs of water and to all the wadis; perhaps we may find grass to keep the horses and mules alive, and not lose some of the animals." [6]So they divided the land between them to pass through it; Ahab went in one direction by himself, and Obadiah went in another direction by himself.

7 As Obadiah was on the way, Elijah met him; Obadiah recognized him, fell on his face, and said, "Is it you, my lord Elijah?" [8]He answered him, "It is I. Go, tell your lord that Elijah is here." [9]And he said, "How have I sinned, that you would hand your servant over to Ahab, to kill me? [10]As the Lord your God lives, there is no nation or kingdom to which my lord has not sent to seek you; and when they would say, 'He is not here,' he would require an oath of the kingdom or nation, that they had not found you. [11]But now you say, 'Go, tell your lord that Elijah is here.' [12]As soon as I have gone from you, the spirit of the Lord will carry you I know not where; so, when I come and tell Ahab and he cannot find you, he will kill me, although I your servant have revered the Lord from my youth. [13]Has it not been told my lord what I did when Jezebel killed the prophets of the Lord, how I hid a hundred of the Lord's prophets fifty to a cave, and provided them with bread and water? [14]Yet now you say, 'Go, tell your lord that Elijah is here'; he will surely kill me." [15]Elijah said, "As the Lord of hosts lives, before whom I stand, I will surely show myself to him today." [16]So Obadiah went to meet Ahab, and told him; and Ahab went to meet Elijah.

17 When Ahab saw Elijah, Ahab said to him, "Is it you, you troubler of Israel?" [18]He answered, "I have not troubled Israel; but you have, and your father's house, because you have forsaken the commandments of the Lord and followed the Baals. [19]Now therefore have all Israel assemble for me at Mount Carmel, with the four hundred fifty prophets of Baal and the four hundred prophets of Asherah, who eat at Jezebel's table."

Elijah's Triumph over the Priests of Baal

20 So Ahab sent to all the Israelites, and assembled the prophets at Mount Carmel. [21]Elijah then came near to all the people, and said, "How long will you go limping with two different opinions? If the Lord is God, follow him; but if Baal, then follow

him." The people did not answer him a word. [22]Then Elijah said to the people, "I, even I only, am left a prophet of the Lord; but Baal's prophets number four hundred fifty. [23]Let two bulls be given to us; let them choose one bull for themselves, cut it in pieces, and lay it on the wood, but put no fire to it; I will prepare the other bull and lay it on the wood, but put no fire to it. [24]Then you call on the name of your god and I will call on the name of the Lord; the god who answers by fire is indeed God." All the people answered, "Well spoken!" [25]Then Elijah said to the prophets of Baal, "Choose for yourselves one bull and prepare it first, for you are many; then call on the name of your god, but put no fire to it." [26]So they took the bull that was given them, prepared it, and called on the name of Baal from morning until noon, crying, "O Baal, answer us!" But there was no voice, and no answer. They limped about the altar that they had made. [27]At noon Elijah mocked them, saying, "Cry aloud! Surely he is a god; either he is meditating, or he has wandered away, or he is on a journey, or perhaps he is asleep and must be awakened." [28]Then they cried aloud and, as was their custom, they cut themselves with swords and lances until the blood gushed out over them. [29]As midday passed, they raved on until the time of the offering of the oblation, but there was no voice, no answer, and no response.

30 Then Elijah said to all the people, "Come closer to me"; and all the people came closer to him. First he repaired the altar of the Lord that had been thrown down; [31]Elijah took twelve stones, according to the number of the tribes of the sons of Jacob, to whom the word of the Lord came, saying, "Israel shall be your name"; [32]with the stones he built an altar in the name of the Lord. Then he made a trench around the altar, large enough to contain two measures of seed. [33]Next he put the wood in order, cut the bull in pieces, and laid it on the wood. He said, "Fill four jars with water and pour it on the burnt offering and on the wood." [34]Then he said, "Do it a second time"; and they did it a second time. Again he said, "Do it a third time"; and they did it a third time, [35]so that the water ran all around the altar, and filled the trench also with water.

36 At the time of the offering of the oblation, the prophet Elijah came near and said, "O Lord, God of Abraham, Isaac, and Israel, let it be known this day that you are God in Israel, that I am your servant, and that I have done all these things at your bidding. [37]Answer me, O Lord, answer me, so that this peo-

ple may know that you, O LORD, are God, and that you have turned their hearts back." [38]Then the fire of the LORD fell and consumed the burnt offering, the wood, the stones, and the dust, and even licked up the water that was in the trench. [39]When all the people saw it, they fell on their faces and said, "The LORD indeed is God; the LORD indeed is God." [40]Elijah said to them, "Seize the prophets of Baal; do not let one of them escape." Then they seized them; and Elijah brought them down to the Wadi Kishon, and killed them there.

The Drought Ends

41 Elijah said to Ahab, "Go up, eat and drink; for there is a sound of rushing rain." [42]So Ahab went up to eat and to drink. Elijah went up to the top of Carmel; there he bowed himself down upon the earth and put his face between his knees. [43]He said to his servant, "Go up now, look toward the sea." He went up and looked, and said, "There is nothing." Then he said, "Go again seven times." [44]At the seventh time he said, "Look, a little cloud no bigger than a person's hand is rising out of the sea." Then he said, "Go say to Ahab, 'Harness your chariot and go down before the rain stops you.' " [45]In a little while the heavens grew black with clouds and wind; there was a heavy rain. Ahab rode off and went to Jezreel. [46]But the hand of the LORD was on Elijah; he girded up his loins and ran in front of Ahab to the entrance of Jezreel.

19 Elijah Flees from Jezebel

Ahab told Jezebel all that Elijah had done, and how he had killed all the prophets with the sword. [2]Then Jezebel sent a messenger to Elijah, saying, "So may the gods do to me, and more also, if I do not make your life like the life of one of them by this time tomorrow." [3]Then he was afraid; he got up and fled for his life, and came to Beersheba, which belongs to Judah; he left his servant there.

4 But he himself went a day's journey into the wilderness, and came and sat down under a solitary broom tree. He asked that he might die: "It is enough; now, O LORD, take away my life, for I am no better than my ancestors." [5]Then he lay down under the broom tree and fell asleep. Suddenly an angel touched him and said to him, "Get up and eat." [6]He looked, and there at his head was a cake baked on hot stones, and a jar of water. He ate and drank, and lay down again. [7]The angel of the LORD came a second time, touched him, and said, "Get up and eat, otherwise the journey will be too much for you." [8]He got up, and ate and drank; then he went in the strength of that food forty days and forty nights to Horeb the mount of God. [9]At that place he came to a cave, and spent the night there.

Then the word of the LORD came to him, saying, "What are you doing here, Elijah?" [10]He answered, "I have been very zealous for the LORD, the God of hosts; for the Israelites have forsaken your covenant, thrown down your altars, and killed your prophets with the sword. I alone am left, and they are seeking my life, to take it away."

Elijah Meets God at Horeb

11 He said, "Go out and stand on the mountain before the LORD, for the LORD is about to pass by." Now there was a great wind, so strong that it was splitting mountains and breaking rocks in pieces before the LORD, but the LORD was not in the wind; and after the wind an earthquake, but the LORD was not in the earthquake; [12]and after the earthquake a fire, but the LORD was not in the fire; and after the fire a sound of sheer silence. [13]When Elijah heard it, he wrapped his face in his mantle and went out and stood at the entrance of the cave. Then there came a voice to him that said, "What are you doing here, Elijah?" [14]He answered, "I have been very zealous for the LORD, the God of hosts; for the Israelites have forsaken your covenant, thrown down your altars, and killed your prophets with the sword. I alone am left, and they are seeking my life, to take it away." [15]Then the LORD said to him, "Go, return on your way to the wilderness of Damascus; when you arrive, you shall anoint Hazael as king over Aram. [16]Also you shall anoint Jehu son of Nimshi as king over Israel; and you shall anoint Elisha son of Shaphat of Abel-meholah as prophet in your place. [17]Whoever escapes from the sword of Hazael, Jehu shall kill; and whoever escapes from the sword of Jehu, Elisha shall kill. [18]Yet I will leave seven thousand in Israel, all the knees that have not bowed to Baal, and every mouth that has not kissed him."

Elisha Becomes Elijah's Disciple

19 So he set out from there, and found Elisha son of Shaphat, who was plowing. There were twelve yoke of oxen ahead of him, and he was with the twelfth. Elijah passed by him and threw his mantle

PRAY IT!

Listening for God
1 Kings 19:9–13

Elijah was told to meet God on the mountain.

A great wind, an earthquake, and fire all passed by, but God's presence was in none of these. God was in the "sound of sheer silence," sometimes translated as "a gentle whisper" (1 Kings 19:12).

Let's face it. Our lives tend to be pretty noisy and cluttered. How will we ever hear that tiny whispering sound? In order to hear God's voice, we need to take time away from the noise and clutter to be quiet in God's presence. We also know that God often "whispers" to us through our friends, family, teachers, and youth leaders. Like Elijah, we have to be open to hearing God's voice speaking through other people and the events of our lives—even those times and places we least expect it.

God is always with us, in the quiet depths of our heart and in the people and situations God has placed in our lives. We need to be like Elijah—tuning out things that are not God and tuning in to God's presence. Take time today to find a quiet place, without distractions, where you can pray and listen for God's voice.

over him. ²⁰He left the oxen, ran after Elijah, and said, "Let me kiss my father and my mother, and then I will follow you." Then Elijah[a] said to him, "Go back again; for what have I done to you?" ²¹He returned from following him, took the yoke of oxen, and slaughtered them; using the equipment from the oxen, he boiled their flesh, and gave it to the people, and they ate. Then he set out and followed Elijah, and became his servant.

20 ### Ahab's Wars with the Arameans

King Ben-hadad of Aram gathered all his army together; thirty-two kings were with him, along with horses and chariots. He marched against Samaria, laid siege to it, and attacked it.

²Then he sent messengers into the city to King Ahab of Israel, and said to him: "Thus says Ben-hadad: ³Your silver and gold are mine; your fairest wives and children also are mine." ⁴The king of Israel answered, "As you say, my lord, O king, I am yours, and all that I have." ⁵The messengers came again and said: "Thus says Ben-hadad: I sent to you, saying, 'Deliver to me your silver and gold, your wives and children'; ⁶nevertheless I will send my servants to you tomorrow about this time, and they shall search your house and the houses of your servants, and lay hands on whatever pleases them,[b] and take it away."

7 Then the king of Israel called all the elders of the land, and said, "Look now! See how this man is seeking trouble; for he sent to me for my wives, my children, my silver, and my gold; and I did not refuse him." ⁸Then all the elders and all the people said to him, "Do not listen or consent." ⁹So he said to the messengers of Ben-hadad, "Tell my lord the king: All that you first demanded of your servant I will do; but this thing I cannot do." The messengers left and brought him word again. ¹⁰Ben-hadad sent to him and said, "The gods do so to me, and more also, if the dust of Samaria will provide a handful for each of the people who follow me." ¹¹The king of Israel answered, "Tell him: One who puts on armor should not brag like one who takes it off." ¹²When Ben-hadad heard this message—now he had been drinking with the kings in the booths—he said to his men, "Take your positions!" And they took their positions against the city.

Prophetic Opposition to Ahab

13 Then a certain prophet came up to King Ahab of Israel and said, "Thus says the LORD, Have you seen all this great multitude? Look, I will give it into your hand today; and you shall know that I am the LORD." ¹⁴Ahab said, "By whom?" He said, "Thus says the LORD, By the young men who serve the district governors." Then he said, "Who shall begin the battle?" He answered, "You." ¹⁵Then he mustered the young men who served the district governors, two hundred thirty-two; after them he mustered all the people of Israel, seven thousand.

16 They went out at noon, while Ben-hadad was drinking himself drunk in the booths, he and the thirty-two kings allied with him. ¹⁷The young men who served the district governors went out first. Ben-hadad had sent out scouts,[c] and they reported to him, "Men have come out from Samaria." ¹⁸He

a Heb *he*　b Gk Syr Vg: Heb *you*　c Heb lacks *scouts*

said, "If they have come out for peace, take them alive; if they have come out for war, take them alive."

19 But these had already come out of the city: the young men who served the district governors, and the army that followed them. [20]Each killed his man; the Arameans fled and Israel pursued them, but King Ben-hadad of Aram escaped on a horse with the cavalry. [21]The king of Israel went out, attacked the horses and chariots, and defeated the Arameans with a great slaughter.

22 Then the prophet approached the king of Israel and said to him, "Come, strengthen yourself, and consider well what you have to do; for in the spring the king of Aram will come up against you."

The Arameans Are Defeated

23 The servants of the king of Aram said to him, "Their gods are gods of the hills, and so they were stronger than we; but let us fight against them in the plain, and surely we shall be stronger than they. [24]Also do this: remove the kings, each from his post, and put commanders in place of them; [25]and muster an army like the army that you have lost, horse for horse, and chariot for chariot; then we will fight against them in the plain, and surely we shall be stronger than they." He heeded their voice, and did so.

26 In the spring Ben-hadad mustered the Arameans and went up to Aphek to fight against Israel. [27]After the Israelites had been mustered and provisioned, they went out to engage them; the people of Israel encamped opposite them like two little flocks of goats, while the Arameans filled the country. [28]A man of God approached and said to the king of Israel, "Thus says the LORD: Because the Arameans have said, 'The LORD is a god of the hills but he is not a god of the valleys,' therefore I will give all this great multitude into your hand, and you shall know that I am the LORD." [29]They encamped opposite one another seven days. Then on the seventh day the battle began; the Israelites killed one hundred thousand Aramean foot soldiers in one day. [30]The rest fled into the city of Aphek; and the wall fell on twenty-seven thousand men that were left.

Ben-hadad also fled, and entered the city to hide. [31]His servants said to him, "Look, we have heard that the kings of the house of Israel are merciful kings; let us put sackcloth around our waists and ropes on our heads, and go out to the king of Israel; perhaps he will spare your life." [32]So they tied sack-

cloth around their waists, put ropes on their heads, went to the king of Israel, and said, "Your servant Ben-hadad says, 'Please let me live.' " And he said, "Is he still alive? He is my brother." [33]Now the men were watching for an omen; they quickly took it up from him and said, "Yes, Ben-hadad is your brother." Then he said, "Go and bring him." So Ben-hadad came out to him; and he had him come up into the chariot. [34]Ben-hadad[a] said to him, "I will restore the towns that my father took from your father; and you may establish bazaars for yourself in Damascus, as my father did in Samaria." The king of Israel responded,[b] "I will let you go on those terms." So he made a treaty with him and let him go.

A Prophet Condemns Ahab

35 At the command of the LORD a certain member of a company of prophets[c] said to another, "Strike me!" But the man refused to strike him. [36]Then he said to him, "Because you have not obeyed the voice of the LORD, as soon as you have left me, a lion will kill you." And when he had left him, a lion met him and killed him. [37]Then he found another man and said, "Strike me!" So the man hit him, striking and wounding him. [38]Then the prophet departed, and waited for the king along the road, disguising himself with a bandage over his eyes. [39]As the king passed by, he cried to the king and said, "Your servant went out into the thick of the battle; then a soldier turned and brought a man to me, and said, 'Guard this man; if he is missing, your life shall be given for his life, or else you shall pay a talent of silver.' [40]While your servant was busy here and there, he was gone." The king of Israel said to him, "So shall your judgment be; you yourself have decided it." [41]Then he quickly took the bandage away from his eyes. The king of Israel recognized him as one of the prophets. [42]Then he said to him, "Thus says the LORD, 'Because you have let the man go whom I had devoted to destruction, therefore your life shall be for his life, and your people for his people.' " [43]The king of Israel set out toward home, resentful and sullen, and came to Samaria.

Naboth's Vineyard

21 Later the following events took place: Naboth the Jezreelite had a vineyard in Jezreel, beside the palace of King Ahab of Samaria. [2]And Ahab said to Naboth, "Give me your vineyard, so that I may have it for a vegetable garden, because

---

a Heb He   b Heb lacks The king of Israel responded   c Heb of the sons of the prophets

it is near my house; I will give you a better vineyard for it; or, if it seems good to you, I will give you its value in money." ³But Naboth said to Ahab, "The LORD forbid that I should give you my ancestral inheritance." ⁴Ahab went home resentful and sullen because of what Naboth the Jezreelite had said to him; for he had said, "I will not give you my ancestral inheritance." He lay down on his bed, turned away his face, and would not eat.

5 His wife Jezebel came to him and said, "Why are you so depressed that you will not eat?" ⁶He said to her, "Because I spoke to Naboth the Jezreelite and said to him, 'Give me your vineyard for money; or else, if you prefer, I will give you another vineyard for it'; but he answered, 'I will not give you my vineyard.' " ⁷His wife Jezebel said to him, "Do you now govern Israel? Get up, eat some food, and be cheerful; I will give you the vineyard of Naboth the Jezreelite."

8 So she wrote letters in Ahab's name and sealed them with his seal; she sent the letters to the elders and the nobles who lived with Naboth in his city. ⁹She wrote in the letters, "Proclaim a fast, and seat Naboth at the head of the assembly; ¹⁰seat two scoundrels opposite him, and have them bring a charge against him, saying, 'You have cursed God and the king.' Then take him out, and stone him to death." ¹¹The men of his city, the elders and the nobles who lived in his city, did as Jezebel had sent word to them. Just as it was written in the letters that she had sent to them, ¹²they proclaimed a fast and seated Naboth at the head of the assembly. ¹³The two scoundrels came in and sat opposite him; and the scoundrels brought a charge against Naboth, in the presence of the people, saying, "Naboth cursed God and the king." So they took him outside the city, and stoned him to death. ¹⁴Then they sent to Jezebel, saying, "Naboth has been stoned; he is dead."

15 As soon as Jezebel heard that Naboth had been stoned and was dead, Jezebel said to Ahab, "Go, take

possession of the vineyard of Naboth the Jezreelite, which he refused to give you for money; for Naboth is not alive, but dead." ¹⁶As soon as Ahab heard that Naboth was dead, Ahab set out to go down to the vineyard of Naboth the Jezreelite, to take possession of it.

Elijah Pronounces God's Sentence

17 Then the word of the LORD came to Elijah the Tishbite, saying: ¹⁸Go down to meet King Ahab of Israel, who rules*a* in Samaria; he is now in the vineyard of Naboth, where he has gone to take possession. ¹⁹You shall say to him, "Thus says the LORD: Have you killed, and also taken possession?" You shall say to him, "Thus says the LORD: In the place where dogs licked up the blood of Naboth, dogs will also lick up your blood."

20 Ahab said to Elijah, "Have you found me, O my enemy?" He answered, "I have found you. Because you have sold yourself to do what is evil in the sight of the LORD, ²¹I will bring disaster on you; I will consume you, and will cut off from Ahab every male, bond or free, in Israel; ²²and I will make your house like the house of Jeroboam son of Nebat, and like the house of Baasha son of Ahijah, because you have provoked me to anger and have caused Israel to sin. ²³Also concerning Jezebel the LORD said, 'The dogs shall eat Jezebel within the bounds of Jezreel.' ²⁴Anyone belonging to Ahab who dies in the city the dogs shall eat; and anyone of his who dies in the open country the birds of the air shall eat."

25 (Indeed, there was no one like Ahab, who sold himself to do what was evil in the sight of the LORD, urged on by his wife Jezebel. ²⁶He acted most abominably in going after idols, as the Amorites had done, whom the LORD drove out before the Israelites.)

27 When Ahab heard those words, he tore his clothes and put sackcloth over his bare flesh; he fasted, lay in the sackcloth, and went about dejectedly. ²⁸Then the word of the LORD came to Elijah the Tishbite: ²⁹"Have you seen how Ahab has humbled himself before me? Because he has humbled himself before me, I will not bring the disaster in his days; but in his son's days I will bring the disaster on his house."

22 Joint Campaign with Judah against Aram

For three years Aram and Israel continued without war. ²But in the third year King Jehoshaphat

a Heb *who is*

of Judah came down to the king of Israel. [3]The king of Israel said to his servants, "Do you know that Ramoth-gilead belongs to us, yet we are doing nothing to take it out of the hand of the king of Aram?" [4]He said to Jehoshaphat, "Will you go with me to battle at Ramoth-gilead?" Jehoshaphat replied to the king of Israel, "I am as you are; my people are your people, my horses are your horses."

5 But Jehoshaphat also said to the king of Israel, "Inquire first for the word of the LORD." [6]Then the king of Israel gathered the prophets together, about four hundred of them, and said to them, "Shall I go to battle against Ramoth-gilead, or shall I refrain?" They said, "Go up; for the LORD will give it into the hand of the king." [7]But Jehoshaphat said, "Is there no other prophet of the LORD here of whom we may inquire?" [8]The king of Israel said to Jehoshaphat, "There is still one other by whom we may inquire of the LORD, Micaiah son of Imlah; but I hate him, for he never prophesies anything favorable about me, but only disaster." Jehoshaphat said, "Let the king not say such a thing." [9]Then the king of Israel summoned an officer and said, "Bring quickly Micaiah son of Imlah." [10]Now the king of Israel and King Jehoshaphat of Judah were sitting on their thrones, arrayed in their robes, at the threshing floor at the entrance of the gate of Samaria; and all the prophets were prophesying before them. [11]Zedekiah son of Chenaanah made for himself horns of iron, and he said, "Thus says the LORD: With these you shall gore the Arameans until they are destroyed." [12]All the prophets were prophesying the same and saying, "Go up to Ramoth-gilead and triumph; the LORD will give it into the hand of the king."

Micaiah Predicts Failure

13 The messenger who had gone to summon Micaiah said to him, "Look, the words of the prophets with one accord are favorable to the king; let your word be like the word of one of them, and speak favorably." [14]But Micaiah said, "As the LORD lives, whatever the LORD says to me, that I will speak."

15 When he had come to the king, the king said to him, "Micaiah, shall we go to Ramoth-gilead to battle, or shall we refrain?" He answered him, "Go up and triumph; the LORD will give it into the hand of the king." [16]But the king said to him, "How many times must I make you swear to tell me nothing but the truth in the name of the LORD?" [17]Then Mi-

caiah[a] said, "I saw all Israel scattered on the mountains, like sheep that have no shepherd; and the LORD said, 'These have no master; let each one go home in peace.'" [18]The king of Israel said to Jehoshaphat, "Did I not tell you that he would not prophesy anything favorable about me, but only disaster?"

19 Then Micaiah[a] said, "Therefore hear the word of the LORD: I saw the LORD sitting on his throne, with all the host of heaven standing beside him to the right and to the left of him. [20]And the LORD said, 'Who will entice Ahab, so that he may go up and fall at Ramoth-gilead?' Then one said one thing, and another said another, [21]until a spirit came forward and stood before the LORD, saying, 'I will entice him.' [22]'How?' the LORD asked him. He replied, 'I will go out and be a lying spirit in the mouth of all his prophets.' Then the LORD[a] said, 'You are to entice him, and you shall succeed; go out and do it.' [23]So you see, the LORD has put a lying spirit in the mouth of all these your prophets; the LORD has decreed disaster for you."

24 Then Zedekiah son of Chenaanah came up to Micaiah, slapped him on the cheek, and said, "Which way did the spirit of the LORD pass from me to speak to you?" [25]Micaiah replied, "You will find out on that day when you go in to hide in an inner chamber." [26]The king of Israel then ordered, "Take Micaiah, and return him to Amon the governor of the city and to Joash the king's son, [27]and say, 'Thus says the king: Put this fellow in prison, and feed him on reduced rations of bread and water until I come in peace.'" [28]Micaiah said, "If you return in peace, the LORD has not spoken by me." And he said, "Hear, you peoples, all of you!"

Defeat and Death of Ahab

29 So the king of Israel and King Jehoshaphat of Judah went up to Ramoth-gilead. [30]The king of Israel said to Jehoshaphat, "I will disguise myself and go into battle, but you wear your robes." So the king of Israel disguised himself and went into battle. [31]Now the king of Aram had commanded the thirty-two captains of his chariots, "Fight with no one small or great, but only with the king of Israel." [32]When the captains of the chariots saw Jehoshaphat, they said, "It is surely the king of Israel." So they turned to fight against him; and Jehoshaphat cried out. [33]When the captains of the chariots saw that it was not the king of Israel, they turned back from pursu-

a Heb *he*

ing him. ³⁴But a certain man drew his bow and unknowingly struck the king of Israel between the scale armor and the breastplate; so he said to the driver of his chariot, "Turn around, and carry me out of the battle, for I am wounded." ³⁵The battle grew hot that day, and the king was propped up in his chariot facing the Arameans, until at evening he died; the blood from the wound had flowed into the bottom of the chariot. ³⁶Then about sunset a shout went through the army, "Every man to his city, and every man to his country!"

37 So the king died, and was brought to Samaria; they buried the king in Samaria. ³⁸They washed the chariot by the pool of Samaria; the dogs licked up his blood, and the prostitutes washed themselves in it,ᵃ according to the word of the LORD that he had spoken. ³⁹Now the rest of the acts of Ahab, and all that he did, and the ivory house that he built, and all the cities that he built, are they not written in the Book of the Annals of the Kings of Israel? ⁴⁰So Ahab slept with his ancestors; and his son Ahaziah succeeded him.

Jehoshaphat Reigns over Judah

41 Jehoshaphat son of Asa began to reign over Judah in the fourth year of King Ahab of Israel. ⁴²Jehoshaphat was thirty-five years old when he began to reign, and he reigned twenty-five years in Jerusalem. His mother's name was Azubah daughter of Shilhi. ⁴³He walked in all the way of his father Asa; he did not turn aside from it, doing what was

ᵃ Heb lacks in it

right in the sight of the LORD; yet the high places were not taken away, and the people still sacrificed and offered incense on the high places. ⁴⁴Jehoshaphat also made peace with the king of Israel.

45 Now the rest of the acts of Jehoshaphat, and his power that he showed, and how he waged war, are they not written in the Book of the Annals of the Kings of Judah? ⁴⁶The remnant of the male temple prostitutes who were still in the land in the days of his father Asa, he exterminated.

47 There was no king in Edom; a deputy was king. ⁴⁸Jehoshaphat made ships of the Tarshish type to go to Ophir for gold; but they did not go, for the ships were wrecked at Ezion-geber. ⁴⁹Then Ahaziah son of Ahab said to Jehoshaphat, "Let my servants go with your servants in the ships," but Jehoshaphat was not willing. ⁵⁰Jehoshaphat slept with his ancestors and was buried with his ancestors in the city of his father David; his son Jehoram succeeded him.

Ahaziah Reigns over Israel

51 Ahaziah son of Ahab began to reign over Israel in Samaria in the seventeenth year of King Jehoshaphat of Judah; he reigned two years over Israel. ⁵²He did what was evil in the sight of the LORD, and walked in the way of his father and mother, and in the way of Jeroboam son of Nebat, who caused Israel to sin. ⁵³He served Baal and worshiped him; he provoked the LORD, the God of Israel, to anger, just as his father had done.

▶▶▶▶▶▶▶▶▶▶▶▶▶▶▶▶▶▶▶▶▶▶▶

2 Kings

For background on this book, see the introduction to 1 and 2 Kings at the beginning of 1 Kings.

Elijah Denounces Ahaziah

1 After the death of Ahab, Moab rebelled against Israel.

2 Ahaziah had fallen through the lattice in his upper chamber in Samaria, and lay injured; so he sent messengers, telling them, "Go, inquire of Baal-zebub, the god of Ekron, whether I shall recover from this injury." ³But the angel of the LORD said to Elijah the Tishbite, "Get up, go to meet the messengers of the king of Samaria, and say to them, 'Is it because there is no God in Israel that you are going to inquire of Baal-zebub, the god of Ekron?' ⁴Now therefore thus says the LORD, 'You shall not leave the bed to which you have gone, but you shall surely die.'" So Elijah went.

5 The messengers returned to the king, who said to them, "Why have you returned?" ⁶They answered him, "There came a man to meet us, who said to us, 'Go back to the king who sent you, and say to him: Thus says the LORD: Is it because there is no God in Israel that you are sending to inquire of Baal-zebub, the god of Ekron? Therefore you shall not leave the bed to which you have gone, but shall surely die.'" ⁷He said to them, "What sort of man was he who came to meet you and told you these things?" ⁸They answered him, "A hairy man, with a leather belt around his waist." He said, "It is Elijah the Tishbite."

9 Then the king sent to him a captain of fifty with his fifty men. He went up to Elijah, who was sitting on the top of a hill, and said to him, "O man of God, the king says, 'Come down.'" ¹⁰But Elijah answered the captain of fifty, "If I am a man of God, let fire come down from heaven and consume you and your fifty." Then fire came down from heaven, and consumed him and his fifty.

11 Again the king sent to him another captain of fifty with his fifty. He went up*ᵃ* and said to him, "O man of God, this is the king's order: Come down quickly!" ¹²But Elijah answered them, "If I am a man of God, let fire come down from heaven and con-

sume you and your fifty." Then the fire of God came down from heaven and consumed him and his fifty.

13 Again the king sent the captain of a third fifty with his fifty. So the third captain of fifty went up, and came and fell on his knees before Elijah, and entreated him, "O man of God, please let my life, and the life of these fifty servants of yours, be precious in your sight. ¹⁴Look, fire came down from heaven and consumed the two former captains of fifty men with their fifties; but now let my life be precious in your sight." ¹⁵Then the angel of the LORD said to Elijah, "Go down with him; do not be afraid of him." So he set out and went down with him to the king, ¹⁶and said to him, "Thus says the LORD: Because you have sent messengers to inquire of Baal-zebub, the god of Ekron,—is it because there is no God in Israel to inquire of his word?—therefore you shall not leave the bed to which you have gone, but you shall surely die."

Death of Ahaziah

17 So he died according to the word of the LORD that Elijah had spoken. His brother,*ᵇ* Jehoram succeeded him as king in the second year of King Jehoram son of Jehoshaphat of Judah, because Ahaziah had no son. ¹⁸Now the rest of the acts of Ahaziah that he did, are they not written in the Book of the Annals of the Kings of Israel?

---

a Gk Compare verses 9, 13: Heb *He answered*   b Gk Syr: Heb lacks *His brother*

Elijah Ascends to Heaven

2 Now when the LORD was about to take Elijah up to heaven by a whirlwind, Elijah and Elisha were on their way from Gilgal. ²Elijah said to Elisha, "Stay here; for the LORD has sent me as far as Bethel." But Elisha said, "As the LORD lives, and as you yourself live, I will not leave you." So they went down to Bethel. ³The company of prophets*a* who were in Bethel came out to Elisha, and said to him, "Do you know that today the LORD will take your master away from you?" And he said, "Yes, I know; keep silent."

4 Elijah said to him, "Elisha, stay here; for the LORD has sent me to Jericho." But he said, "As the LORD lives, and as you yourself live, I will not leave you." So they came to Jericho. ⁵The company of prophets*a* who were at Jericho drew near to Elisha, and said to him, "Do you know that today the LORD will take your master away from you?" And he answered, "Yes, I know; be silent."

6 Then Elijah said to him, "Stay here; for the LORD has sent me to the Jordan." But he said, "As the LORD lives, and as you yourself live, I will not leave you." So the two of them went on. ⁷Fifty men of the company of prophets*a* also went, and stood at some distance from them, as they both were standing by the Jordan. ⁸Then Elijah took his mantle and rolled it up, and struck the water; the water was parted to the one side and to the other, until the two of them crossed on dry ground.

9 When they had crossed, Elijah said to Elisha, "Tell me what I may do for you, before I am taken from you." Elisha said, "Please let me inherit a double share of your spirit." ¹⁰He responded, "You have asked a hard thing; yet, if you see me as I am being taken from you, it will be granted you; if not, it will not." ¹¹As they continued walking and talking, a chariot of fire and horses of fire separated the two of them, and Elijah ascended in a whirlwind into heaven. ¹²Elisha kept watching and crying out, "Father, father! The chariots of Israel and its horsemen!" But when he could no longer see him, he grasped his own clothes and tore them in two pieces.

Elisha Succeeds Elijah

13 He picked up the mantle of Elijah that had fallen from him, and went back and stood on the bank of the Jordan. ¹⁴He took the mantle of Elijah that had fallen from him, and struck the water, saying, "Where is the LORD, the God of Elijah?" When he had struck the water, the water was parted to the one side and to the other, and Elisha went over.

15 When the company of prophets*a* who were at Jericho saw him at a distance, they declared, "The spirit of Elijah rests on Elisha." They came to meet him and bowed to the ground before him. ¹⁶They said to him, "See now, we have fifty strong men among your servants; please let them go and seek your master; it may be that the spirit of the LORD has caught him up and thrown him down on some

LIVE IT!

Looking Out for the Little Guy · 2 Kings 2:11

Elijah was a passionate prophet who understood the history of Israel's kings from God's perspective. He saw division in the people of Israel. On the one hand were the kings, the noblemen, and the leaders of the army. On the other hand were the peasants, the widows, and the persecuted prophets. The covenant had been broken. Elijah denounced the unfaithfulness of Queen Jezebel and Kings Ahab and Ahaziah. They had introduced idolatry in the form of the false god Baal, who favored the powerful and allowed injustices.

Elijah's faithfulness to the covenant and his defense of the poor led him to speak against kings and queens, to fight false prophets, and to intervene in national affairs. The powerful rulers wanted to kill him and silence his voice. After his dramatic departure from earth (2 Kings 2:11), the people never forgot him. They always expected his return.

- Who is like Elijah in our world today?
- In what ways and situations are you called to act like a prophet, standing for what's right and fighting injustice?

a Heb *sons of the prophets*

mountain or into some valley." He responded, "No, do not send them." [17]But when they urged him until he was ashamed, he said, "Send them." So they sent fifty men who searched for three days but did not find him. [18]When they came back to him (he had remained at Jericho), he said to them, "Did I not say to you, Do not go?"

Elisha Performs Miracles

19 Now the people of the city said to Elisha, "The location of this city is good, as my lord sees; but the water is bad, and the land is unfruitful." [20]He said, "Bring me a new bowl, and put salt in it." So they brought it to him. [21]Then he went to the spring of water and threw the salt into it, and said, "Thus says the LORD, I have made this water wholesome; from now on neither death nor miscarriage shall come from it." [22]So the water has been wholesome to this day, according to the word that Elisha spoke.

23 He went up from there to Bethel; and while he was going up on the way, some small boys came out of the city and jeered at him, saying, "Go away, baldhead! Go away, baldhead!" [24]When he turned around and saw them, he cursed them in the name of the LORD. Then two she-bears came out of the woods and mauled forty-two of the boys. [25]From there he went on to Mount Carmel, and then returned to Samaria.

Jehoram Reigns over Israel

3 In the eighteenth year of King Jehoshaphat of Judah, Jehoram son of Ahab became king over Israel in Samaria; he reigned twelve years. [2]He did what was evil in the sight of the LORD, though not like his father and mother, for he removed the pillar of Baal that his father had made. [3]Nevertheless he clung to the sin of Jeroboam son of Nebat, which he caused Israel to commit; he did not depart from it.

War with Moab

4 Now King Mesha of Moab was a sheep breeder, who used to deliver to the king of Israel one hundred thousand lambs, and the wool of one hundred thousand rams. [5]But when Ahab died, the king of Moab rebelled against the king of Israel. [6]So King Jehoram marched out of Samaria at that time and mustered all Israel. [7]As he went he sent word to King Jehoshaphat of Judah, "The king of Moab has rebelled against me; will you go with me to battle against

Moab?" He answered, "I will; I am with you, my people are your people, my horses are your horses." [8]Then he asked, "By which way shall we march?" Jehoram answered, "By the way of the wilderness of Edom."

9 So the king of Israel, the king of Judah, and the king of Edom set out; and when they had made a roundabout march of seven days, there was no water for the army or for the animals that were with them. [10]Then the king of Israel said, "Alas! The LORD has summoned us, three kings, only to be handed over to Moab." [11]But Jehoshaphat said, "Is there no prophet of the LORD here, through whom we may inquire of the LORD?" Then one of the servants of the king of Israel answered, "Elisha son of Shaphat, who used to pour water on the hands of Elijah, is here." [12]Jehoshaphat said, "The word of the LORD is with him." So the king of Israel and Jehoshaphat and the king of Edom went down to him.

13 Elisha said to the king of Israel, "What have I to do with you? Go to your father's prophets or to your mother's." But the king of Israel said to him, "No; it is the LORD who has summoned us, three kings, only to be handed over to Moab." [14]Elisha said, "As the LORD of hosts lives, whom I serve, were it not that I have regard for King Jehoshaphat of Judah, I would give you neither a look nor a glance. [15]But get me a musician." And then, while the musician was playing, the power of the LORD came on him. [16]And he said, "Thus says the LORD, 'I will make this wadi full of pools.' [17]For thus says the LORD, 'You shall see neither wind nor rain, but the wadi shall be filled with water, so that you shall drink, you, your cattle, and your animals.' [18]This is only a trifle in the sight of the LORD, for he will also hand Moab over to you. [19]You shall conquer every fortified city and every choice city; every good tree you shall fell, all springs of water you shall stop up, and every good piece of land you shall ruin with stones." [20]The next day, about the time of the morning offering, suddenly water began to flow from the direction of Edom, until the country was filled with water.

21 When all the Moabites heard that the kings had come up to fight against them, all who were able to put on armor, from the youngest to the oldest, were called out and were drawn up at the frontier. [22]When they rose early in the morning, and the sun shone upon the water, the Moabites saw the water opposite them as red as blood. [23]They said, "This is blood; the kings must have fought together, and killed one

another. Now then, Moab, to the spoil!" [24]But when they came to the camp of Israel, the Israelites rose up and attacked the Moabites, who fled before them; as they entered Moab they continued the attack.[a] [25]The cities they overturned, and on every good piece of land everyone threw a stone, until it was covered; every spring of water they stopped up, and every good tree they felled. Only at Kir-hareseth did the stone walls remain, until the slingers surrounded and attacked it. [26]When the king of Moab saw that the battle was going against him, he took with him seven hundred swordsmen to break through, opposite the king of Edom; but they could not. [27]Then he took his firstborn son who was to succeed him, and offered him as a burnt offering on the wall. And great wrath came upon Israel, so they withdrew from him and returned to their own land.

Elisha and the Widow's Oil

4 Now the wife of a member of the company of prophets[b] cried to Elisha, "Your servant my husband is dead; and you know that your servant feared the LORD, but a creditor has come to take my two children as slaves." [2]Elisha said to her, "What shall I do for you? Tell me, what do you have in the house?" She answered, "Your servant has nothing in the house, except a jar of oil." [3]He said, "Go outside, borrow vessels from all your neighbors, empty vessels and not just a few. [4]Then go in, and shut the door behind you and your children, and start pouring into all these vessels; when each is full, set it aside." [5]So she left him and shut the door behind her and her children; they kept bringing vessels to her, and she kept pouring. [6]When the vessels were full, she said to her son, "Bring me another vessel." But he said to her, "There are no more." Then the oil stopped flowing. [7]She came and told the man of God, and he said, "Go sell the oil and pay your debts, and you and your children can live on the rest."

Elisha Raises the Shunammite's Son

8 One day Elisha was passing through Shunem, where a wealthy woman lived, who urged him to have a meal. So whenever he passed that way, he would stop there for a meal. [9]She said to her husband, "Look, I am sure that this man who regularly passes our way is a holy man of God. [10]Let us make a small roof chamber with walls, and put there for him a bed, a table, a chair, and a lamp, so that he can stay there whenever he comes to us."

11 One day when he came there, he went up to the chamber and lay down there. [12]He said to his servant Gehazi, "Call the Shunammite woman." When he had called her, she stood before him. [13]He said to him, "Say to her, Since you have taken all this trouble for us, what may be done for you? Would you have a word spoken on your behalf to the king or to the commander of the army?" She answered, "I live among my own people." [14]He said, "What then may be done for her?" Gehazi answered, "Well, she has no son, and her husband is old." [15]He said, "Call her." When he had called her, she stood at the door. [16]He said, "At this season, in due time, you shall embrace a son." She replied, "No, my lord, O man of God; do not deceive your servant."

17 The woman conceived and bore a son at that season, in due time, as Elisha had declared to her.

18 When the child was older, he went out one day to his father among the reapers. [19]He complained to his father, "Oh, my head, my head!" The father said to his servant, "Carry him to his mother." [20]He carried him and brought him to his mother; the child sat on her lap until noon, and he died. [21]She went up and laid him on the bed of the man of God, closed the door on him, and left. [22]Then she called to her husband, and said, "Send me one of the servants and one of the donkeys, so that I may quickly go to the man of God and come back again." [23]He said, "Why go to him today? It is neither new moon nor sabbath." She said, "It will be all right." [24]Then she saddled the donkey and said to her servant, "Urge the animal on; do not hold back for me unless I tell you." [25]So she set out, and came to the man of God at Mount Carmel.

When the man of God saw her coming, he said to Gehazi his servant, "Look, there is the Shunammite woman; [26]run at once to meet her, and say to her, Are you all right? Is your husband all right? Is the child all right?" She answered, "It is all right." [27]When she came to the man of God at the mountain, she caught hold of his feet. Gehazi approached to push her away. But the man of God said, "Let her alone, for she is in bitter distress; the LORD has hidden it from me and has not told me." [28]Then she said, "Did I ask my lord for a son? Did I not say, Do not mislead me?" [29]He said to Gehazi, "Gird up your loins, and take my staff in your hand, and go. If you meet anyone, give no greeting, and if anyone greets you, do not answer; and lay my staff on the face of the child." [30]Then the mother of the child said, "As the LORD

a Compare Gk Syr: Meaning of Heb uncertain   b Heb *the sons of the prophets*

Feed Your Soul · 2 Kings 4:42–44

Elisha's miracle fed the body, but it's just as important to feed the appetite of the soul—the need for hope, peace, and love. There is more than enough food in restaurants and grocery stores to satisfy your physical appetite, but where do you go when it comes to feeding your soul?

God gives us plenty of opportunities to feed our soul and grow in faith. We just need to take advantage of them. Go to church. Be part of your youth group. Start a Bible study. Go on a retreat, conference, or mission trip. Talk to friends about your faith and theirs. Take a walk and pray. You'll find that feeding your soul can be fun and fulfilling, and it often costs less than a value meal at your favorite fast-food restaurant.

Sounds Familiar
2 Kings 4:42–44

Several events in the Old Testament have close parallels in the New Testament. This story of Elisha feeding a crowd with the small amount of food offered by one man reminds us of a famous story about Jesus. In all four gospels, Jesus feeds a crowd of five thousand (Matthew 14:13-21; Mark 6:34-44; Luke 9:10-17; John 6:1-14) and a crowd of four thousand in two gospels (Matthew 15:32-39; Mark 8:1-9). In light of Jesus' life and ministry, these Old Testament parallels have even richer meaning.

lives, and as you yourself live, I will not leave without you." So he rose up and followed her. ³¹Gehazi went on ahead and laid the staff on the face of the child, but there was no sound or sign of life. He came back to meet him and told him, "The child has not awakened."

32 When Elisha came into the house, he saw the child lying dead on his bed. ³³So he went in and closed the door on the two of them, and prayed to the LORD. ³⁴Then he got up on the bed*a* and lay upon the child, putting his mouth upon his mouth, his eyes upon his eyes, and his hands upon his hands; and while he lay bent over him, the flesh of the child became warm. ³⁵He got down, walked once to and fro in the room, then got up again and bent over him;

the child sneezed seven times, and the child opened his eyes. ³⁶Elisha*b* summoned Gehazi and said, "Call the Shunammite woman." So he called her. When she came to him, he said, "Take your son." ³⁷She came and fell at his feet, bowing to the ground; then she took her son and left.

Elisha Purifies the Pot of Stew

38 When Elisha returned to Gilgal, there was a famine in the land. As the company of prophets was*c* sitting before him, he said to his servant, "Put the large pot on, and make some stew for the company of prophets."*d* ³⁹One of them went out into the field to gather herbs; he found a wild vine and gathered from it a lapful of wild gourds, and came and cut them up into the pot of stew, not knowing what they were. ⁴⁰They served some for the men to eat. But while they were eating the stew, they cried out, "O man of God, there is death in the pot!" They could not eat it. ⁴¹He said, "Then bring some flour." He threw it into the pot, and said, "Serve the people and let them eat." And there was nothing harmful in the pot.

Elisha Feeds One Hundred Men

42 A man came from Baal-shalishah, bringing food from the first fruits to the man of God: twenty loaves of barley and fresh ears of grain in his sack. Elisha said, "Give it to the people and let them eat." ⁴³But his servant said, "How can I set this before a hundred people?" So he repeated, "Give it to the people and let them eat, for thus says the LORD, 'They shall eat and have some left.' " ⁴⁴He set it before them, they ate, and had some left, according to the word of the LORD.

a Heb lacks *on the bed* b Heb *he* c Heb *sons of the prophets were* d Heb *sons of the prophets*

5

The Healing of Naaman

Naaman, commander of the army of the king of Aram, was a great man and in high favor with his master, because by him the LORD had given victory to Aram. The man, though a mighty warrior, suffered from leprosy.[a] 2 Now the Arameans on one of their raids had taken a young girl captive from the land of Israel, and she served Naaman's wife. 3 She said to her mistress, "If only my lord were with the prophet who is in Samaria! He would cure him of his leprosy."[a] 4 So Naaman[b] went in and told his lord just what the girl from the land of Israel had said. 5 And the king of Aram said, "Go then, and I will send along a letter to the king of Israel."

He went, taking with him ten talents of silver, six thousand shekels of gold, and ten sets of garments. 6 He brought the letter to the king of Israel, which read, "When this letter reaches you, know that I have sent to you my servant Naaman, that you may cure him of his leprosy."[a] 7 When the king of Israel read the letter, he tore his clothes and said, "Am I God, to give death or life, that this man sends word to me to cure a man of his leprosy?[a] Just look and see how he is trying to pick a quarrel with me."

8 But when Elisha the man of God heard that the king of Israel had torn his clothes, he sent a message to the king, "Why have you torn your clothes? Let him come to me, that he may learn that there is a prophet in Israel." 9 So Naaman came with his horses and chariots, and halted at the entrance of Elisha's house. 10 Elisha sent a messenger to him, saying, "Go, wash in the Jordan seven times, and your flesh shall be restored and you shall be clean." 11 But Naaman became angry and went away, saying, "I thought that for me he would surely come out, and stand and call on the name of the LORD his God, and would wave his hand over the spot, and cure the leprosy![a] 12 Are not Abana[c] and Pharpar, the rivers of Damascus, better than all the waters of Israel? Could I not wash in them, and be clean?" He turned and went away in a rage. 13 But his servants approached and said to him, "Father, if the prophet had commanded you to do something difficult, would you not have done it? How much more, when all he said to you was, 'Wash, and be clean'?" 14 So he went down and immersed himself seven times in the Jordan, according to the word of the man of God; his flesh was restored like the flesh of a young boy, and he was clean.

15 Then he returned to the man of God, he and all his company; he came and stood before him and said, "Now I know that there is no God in all the earth except in Israel; please accept a present from your servant." 16 But he said, "As the LORD lives, whom I serve, I will accept nothing!" He urged him to accept, but he refused. 17 Then Naaman said, "If not, please let two mule-loads of earth be given to your servant; for your servant will no longer offer burnt offering or sacrifice to any god except the LORD. 18 But may the LORD pardon your servant on one count: when my master goes into the house of Rimmon to worship there, leaning on my arm, and I bow down in the house of Rimmon, when I do bow down in the house of Rimmon, may the LORD pardon your servant on this one count." 19 He said to him, "Go in peace."

Gehazi's Greed

But when Naaman had gone from him a short distance, 20 Gehazi, the servant of Elisha the man of God, thought, "My master has let that Aramean Naaman off too lightly by not accepting from him what he offered. As the LORD lives, I will run after him and get something out of him." 21 So Gehazi went after Naaman. When Naaman saw someone running after him, he jumped down from the chariot to meet him and said, "Is everything all right?" 22 He replied, "Yes, but my master has sent me to say, 'Two members of a company of prophets[d] have just come to me from the hill country of Ephraim; please give them a talent of silver and two changes of clothing.' " 23 Naaman said, "Please accept two talents." He urged him, and tied up two talents of silver in two bags, with two changes of clothing, and gave them to two of his servants, who carried them in front of Gehazi.[e] 24 When he came to the citadel, he took the bags[f] from them, and stored them inside; he dismissed the men, and they left.

25 He went in and stood before his master; and Elisha said to him, "Where have you been, Gehazi?" He answered, "Your servant has not gone anywhere at all." 26 But he said to him, "Did I not go with you in spirit when someone left his chariot to meet you? Is this a time to accept money and to accept clothing, olive orchards and vineyards, sheep and oxen, and male and female slaves? 27 Therefore the leprosy[a] of Naaman shall cling to you, and to your descendants forever." So he left his presence leprous,[a] as white as snow.

---

[a] A term for several skin diseases; precise meaning uncertain   [b] Heb *he*   [c] Another reading is *Amana*   [d] Heb *sons of the prophets*   [e] Heb *him*
[f] Heb lacks *the bags*

The Miracle of the Ax Head

6 Now the company of prophets[a] said to Elisha, "As you see, the place where we live under your charge is too small for us. [2]Let us go to the Jordan, and let us collect logs there, one for each of us, and build a place there for us to live." He answered, "Do so." [3]Then one of them said, "Please come with your servants." And he answered, "I will." [4]So he went with them. When they came to the Jordan, they cut down trees. [5]But as one was felling a log, his ax head fell into the water; he cried out, "Alas, master! It was borrowed." [6]Then the man of God said, "Where did it fall?" When he showed him the place, he cut off a stick, and threw it in there, and made the iron float. [7]He said, "Pick it up." So he reached out his hand and took it.

The Aramean Attack Is Thwarted

8 Once when the king of Aram was at war with Israel, he took counsel with his officers. He said, "At such and such a place shall be my camp." [9]But the man of God sent word to the king of Israel, "Take care not to pass this place, because the Arameans are going down there." [10]The king of Israel sent word to the place of which the man of God spoke. More than once or twice he warned such a place[b] so that it was on the alert.

11 The mind of the king of Aram was greatly perturbed because of this; he called his officers and said to them, "Now tell me who among us sides with the king of Israel?" [12]Then one of his officers said, "No one, my lord king. It is Elisha, the prophet in Israel, who tells the king of Israel the words that you speak in your bedchamber." [13]He said, "Go and find where he is; I will send and seize him." He was told, "He is in Dothan." [14]So he sent horses and chariots there and a great army; they came by night, and surrounded the city.

15 When an attendant of the man of God rose early in the morning and went out, an army with horses and chariots was all around the city. His servant said, "Alas, master! What shall we do?" [16]He replied, "Do not be afraid, for there are more with us than there are with them." [17]Then Elisha prayed: "O LORD, please open his eyes that he may see." So the LORD opened the eyes of the servant, and he saw; the mountain was full of horses and chariots of fire all around Elisha. [18]When the Arameans[c] came down against him, Elisha prayed to the LORD, and said, "Strike this people, please, with blindness." So he struck them with blindness as Elisha had asked. [19]Elisha said to them, "This is not the way, and this is not the city; follow me, and I will bring you to the man whom you seek." And he led them to Samaria.

20 As soon as they entered Samaria, Elisha said, "O LORD, open the eyes of these men so that they may see." The LORD opened their eyes, and they saw that they were inside Samaria. [21]When the king of Israel saw them he said to Elisha, "Father, shall I kill them? Shall I kill them?" [22]He answered, "No! Did you capture with your sword and your bow those whom you want to kill? Set food and water before them so that they may eat and drink; and let them go to their master." [23]So he prepared for them a great feast; after they ate and drank, he sent them on their way, and they went to their master. And the Arameans no longer came raiding into the land of Israel.

Ben-hadad's Siege of Samaria

24 Some time later King Ben-hadad of Aram mustered his entire army; he marched against Samaria and laid siege to it. [25]As the siege continued, famine in Samaria became so great that a donkey's head was sold for eighty shekels of silver, and one-fourth of a kab of dove's dung for five shekels of silver. [26]Now as the king of Israel was walking on the city wall, a woman cried out to him, "Help, my lord king!" [27]He said, "No! Let the LORD help you. How can I help you? From the threshing floor or from the wine press?" [28]But then the king asked her, "What is your complaint?" She answered, "This woman said to me, 'Give up your son; we will eat him today, and we will eat my son tomorrow.' [29]So we cooked my son and ate him. The next day I said to her, 'Give up your son and we will eat him.' But she has hidden her son." [30]When the king heard the words of the woman he tore his clothes—now since he was walking on the city wall, the people could see that he had sackcloth on his body underneath— [31]and he said, "So may God do to me, and more, if

---

a Heb *sons of the prophets*   b Heb *warned it*   c Heb *they*

the head of Elisha son of Shaphat stays on his shoulders today." [32] So he dispatched a man from his presence.

Now Elisha was sitting in his house, and the elders were sitting with him. Before the messenger arrived, Elisha said to the elders, "Are you aware that this murderer has sent someone to take off my head? When the messenger comes, see that you shut the door and hold it closed against him. Is not the sound of his master's feet behind him?" [33]While he was still speaking with them, the king[a] came down to him and said, "This trouble is from the LORD! Why should I hope in the LORD any longer?"

7 [1]But Elisha said, "Hear the word of the LORD: thus says the LORD, Tomorrow about this time a measure of choice meal shall be sold for a shekel, and two measures of barley for a shekel, at the gate of Samaria." [2]Then the captain on whose hand the king leaned said to the man of God, "Even if the LORD were to make windows in the sky, could such a thing happen?" But he said, "You shall see it with your own eyes, but you shall not eat from it."

The Arameans Flee

3 Now there were four leprous[b] men outside the city gate, who said to one another, "Why should we sit here until we die? [4]If we say, 'Let us enter the city,' the famine is in the city, and we shall die there; but if we sit here, we shall also die. Therefore, let us desert to the Aramean camp; if they spare our lives, we shall live; and if they kill us, we shall but die." [5]So they arose at twilight to go to the Aramean camp; but when they came to the edge of the Aramean camp, there was no one there at all. [6]For the Lord had caused the Aramean army to hear the sound of chariots, and of horses, the sound of a great army, so that they said to one another, "The king of Israel has hired the kings of the Hittites and the kings of Egypt to fight against us." [7]So they fled away in the twilight and abandoned their tents, their horses, and their donkeys leaving the camp just as it was, and fled for their lives. [8]When these leprous[b] men had come to the edge of the camp, they went into a tent, ate and drank, carried off silver, gold, and clothing, and went and hid them. Then they came back, entered another tent, carried off things from it, and went and hid them.

9 Then they said to one another, "What we are doing is wrong. This is a day of good news; if we are silent and wait until the morning light, we will be found guilty; therefore let us go and tell the king's household." [10]So they came and called to the gatekeepers of the city, and told them, "We went to the Aramean camp, but there was no one to be seen or heard there, nothing but the horses tied, the donkeys tied, and the tents as they were." [11]Then the gatekeepers called out and proclaimed it to the king's household. [12]The king got up in the night, and said to his servants, "I will tell you what the Arameans have prepared against us. They know that we are starving; so they have left the camp to hide themselves in the open country, thinking, 'When they come out of the city, we shall take them alive and get into the city.' " [13]One of his servants said, "Let some men take five of the remaining horses, since those left here will suffer the fate of the whole multitude of Israel that have perished already;[c] let us send and find out." [14]So they took two mounted men, and the king sent them after the Aramean army, saying, "Go and find out." [15]So they went after them as far as the Jordan; the whole way was littered with garments and equipment that the Arameans had thrown away in their haste. So the messengers returned, and told the king.

16 Then the people went out, and plundered the camp of the Arameans. So a measure of choice meal was sold for a shekel, and two measures of barley for a shekel, according to the word of the LORD. [17]Now the king had appointed the captain on whose hand he leaned to have charge of the gate; the people trampled him to death in the gate, just as the man of God had said when the king came down to him. [18]For when the man of God had said to the king, "Two measures of barley shall be sold for a shekel, and a measure of choice meal for a shekel, about this time tomorrow in the gate of Samaria," [19]the captain had answered the man of God, "Even if the LORD were to make windows in the sky, could such a thing happen?" And he had answered, "You shall see it with your own eyes, but you shall not eat from it." [20]It did indeed happen to him; the people trampled him to death in the gate.

8 **The Shunammite Woman's Land Restored**

Now Elisha had said to the woman whose son he had restored to life, "Get up and go with your household, and settle wherever you can; for the

---

a See 7.2: Heb *messenger*   b A term for several skin diseases; precise meaning uncertain   c Compare Gk Syr Vg: Meaning of Heb uncertain

LORD has called for a famine, and it will come on the land for seven years." ²So the woman got up and did according to the word of the man of God; she went with her household and settled in the land of the Philistines seven years. ³At the end of the seven years, when the woman returned from the land of the Philistines, she set out to appeal to the king for her house and her land. ⁴Now the king was talking with Gehazi the servant of the man of God, saying, "Tell me all the great things that Elisha has done." ⁵While he was telling the king how Elisha had restored a dead person to life, the woman whose son he had restored to life appealed to the king for her house and her land. Gehazi said, "My lord king, here is the woman, and here is her son whom Elisha restored to life." ⁶When the king questioned the woman, she told him. So the king appointed an official for her, saying, "Restore all that was hers, together with all the revenue of the fields from the day that she left the land until now."

Death of Ben-hadad

7 Elisha went to Damascus while King Ben-hadad of Aram was ill. When it was told him, "The man of God has come here," ⁸the king said to Hazael, "Take a present with you and go to meet the man of God. Inquire of the LORD through him, whether I shall recover from this illness." ⁹So Hazael went to meet him, taking a present with him, all kinds of goods of Damascus, forty camel loads. When he entered and stood before him, he said, "Your son King Ben-hadad of Aram has sent me to you, saying, 'Shall I recover from this illness?' " ¹⁰Elisha said to him, "Go, say to him, 'You shall certainly recover'; but the LORD has shown me that he shall certainly die." ¹¹He fixed his gaze and stared at him, until he was ashamed. Then the man of God wept. ¹²Hazael asked, "Why does my lord weep?" He answered, "Because I know the

evil that you will do to the people of Israel; you will set their fortresses on fire, you will kill their young men with the sword, dash in pieces their little ones, and rip up their pregnant women." ¹³Hazael said, "What is your servant, who is a mere dog, that he should do this great thing?" Elisha answered, "The LORD has shown me that you are to be king over Aram." ¹⁴Then he left Elisha, and went to his master Ben-hadad,ᵃ who said to him, "What did Elisha say to you?" And he answered, "He told me that you would certainly recover." ¹⁵But the next day he took the bed-cover and dipped it in water and spread it over the king's face, until he died. And Hazael succeeded him.

Jehoram Reigns over Judah

16 In the fifth year of King Joram son of Ahab of Israel,ᵇ Jehoram son of King Jehoshaphat of Judah began to reign. ¹⁷He was thirty-two years old when he became king, and he reigned eight years in Jerusalem. ¹⁸He walked in the way of the kings of Israel, as the house of Ahab had done, for the daughter of Ahab was his wife. He did what was evil in the sight of the LORD. ¹⁹Yet the LORD would not destroy Judah, for the sake of his servant David, since he had promised to give a lamp to him and to his descendants forever.

20 In his days Edom revolted against the rule of Judah, and set up a king of their own. ²¹Then Joram crossed over to Zair with all his chariots. He set out by night and attacked the Edomites and their chariot commanders who had surrounded him;ᶜ but his army fled home. ²²So Edom has been in revolt against the rule of Judah to this day. Libnah also revolted at the same time. ²³Now the rest of the acts of Joram, and all that he did, are they not written in the Book of the Annals of the Kings of Judah? ²⁴So Joram slept with his ancestors, and was buried with

Grading Kings · 2 Kings 8–25

As you read the remaining chapters of 2 Kings, notice that the author gives a kind of report card for each of the rulers of Israel and Judah. Jehoram, for example, receives an F: "He did what was evil in the sight of the LORD" (2 Kings 8:18). Josiah receives an A: "He did what was right in the sight of the LORD" (2 Kings 22:2). The author, who wrote after the fall of both kingdoms, provides a theological reason for the failure of Israel and Judah: the spiritual failure of their leaders. Because most of the rulers continually violated God's law, they were largely responsible for the fall of the kingdoms.

---

a Heb lacks *Ben-hadad*   **b** Gk Syr: Heb adds *Jehoshaphat being king of Judah,*   **c** Meaning of Heb uncertain

them in the city of David; his son Ahaziah succeeded him.

Ahaziah Reigns over Judah

25 In the twelfth year of King Joram son of Ahab of Israel, Ahaziah son of King Jehoram of Judah began to reign. 26 Ahaziah was twenty-two years old when he began to reign; he reigned one year in Jerusalem. His mother's name was Athaliah, a granddaughter of King Omri of Israel. 27 He also walked in the way of the house of Ahab, doing what was evil in the sight of the LORD, as the house of Ahab had done, for he was son-in-law to the house of Ahab.

28 He went with Joram son of Ahab to wage war against King Hazael of Aram at Ramoth-gilead, where the Arameans wounded Joram. 29 King Joram returned to be healed in Jezreel of the wounds that the Arameans had inflicted on him at Ramah, when he fought against King Hazael of Aram. King Ahaziah son of Jehoram of Judah went down to see Joram son of Ahab in Jezreel, because he was wounded.

9 ## Anointing of Jehu

Then the prophet Elisha called a member of the company of prophets[a] and said to him, "Gird up your loins; take this flask of oil in your hand, and go to Ramoth-gilead. 2 When you arrive, look there for Jehu son of Jehoshaphat, son of Nimshi; go in and get him to leave his companions, and take him into an inner chamber. 3 Then take the flask of oil, pour it on his head, and say, 'Thus says the LORD: I anoint you king over Israel.' Then open the door and flee; do not linger."

4 So the young man, the young prophet, went to Ramoth-gilead. 5 He arrived while the commanders of the army were in council, and he announced, "I have a message for you, commander." "For which one of us?" asked Jehu. "For you, commander." 6 So Jehu[b] got up and went inside; the young man poured the oil on his head, saying to him, "Thus says the LORD the God of Israel: I anoint you king over the people of the LORD, over Israel. 7 You shall strike down the house of your master Ahab, so that I may avenge on Jezebel the blood of my servants the prophets, and the blood of all the servants of the LORD. 8 For the whole house of Ahab shall perish; I will cut off from Ahab every male, bond or free, in Israel. 9 I will make the house of Ahab like the house of Jeroboam son of Nebat, and like the house of Baasha son of Ahijah. 10 The dogs shall eat Jezebel in the territory of Jezreel,

and no one shall bury her." Then he opened the door and fled.

11 When Jehu came back to his master's officers, they said to him, "Is everything all right? Why did that madman come to you?" He answered them, "You know the sort and how they babble." 12 They said, "Liar! Come on, tell us!" So he said, "This is just what he said to me: 'Thus says the LORD, I anoint you king over Israel.' " 13 Then hurriedly they all took their cloaks and spread them for him on the bare[c] steps; and they blew the trumpet, and proclaimed, "Jehu is king."

Joram of Israel Killed

14 Thus Jehu son of Jehoshaphat son of Nimshi conspired against Joram. Joram with all Israel had been on guard at Ramoth-gilead against King Hazael of Aram; 15 but King Joram had returned to be healed in Jezreel of the wounds that the Arameans had inflicted on him, when he fought against King Hazael of Aram. So Jehu said, "If this is your wish, then let no one slip out of the city to go and tell the news in Jezreel." 16 Then Jehu mounted his chariot and went to Jezreel, where Joram was lying ill. King Ahaziah of Judah had come down to visit Joram.

17 In Jezreel, the sentinel standing on the tower spied the company of Jehu arriving, and said, "I see a company." Joram said, "Take a horseman; send him to meet them, and let him say, 'Is it peace?' " 18 So the horseman went to meet him; he said, "Thus says the king, 'Is it peace?' " Jehu responded, "What have you to do with peace? Fall in behind me." The sentinel reported, saying, "The messenger reached them, but he is not coming back." 19 Then he sent out a second horseman, who came to them and said, "Thus says the king, 'Is it peace?' " Jehu answered, "What have you to do with peace? Fall in behind me." 20 Again the sentinel reported, "He reached them, but he is not coming back. It looks like the driving of Jehu son of Nimshi; for he drives like a maniac."

21 Joram said, "Get ready." And they got his chariot ready. Then King Joram of Israel and King Ahaziah of Judah set out, each in his chariot, and went to meet Jehu; they met him at the property of Naboth the Jezreelite. 22 When Joram saw Jehu, he said, "Is it peace, Jehu?" He answered, "What peace can there be, so long as the many whoredoms and sorceries of your mother Jezebel continue?" 23 Then Joram reined about and fled, saying to Ahaziah, "Treason, Ahaziah!" 24 Jehu drew his bow with all his strength, and

---

a Heb *sons of the prophets*   **b** Heb *he*   **c** Meaning of Heb uncertain

shot Joram between the shoulders, so that the arrow pierced his heart; and he sank in his chariot. ^{25}Jehu said to his aide Bidkar, "Lift him out, and throw him on the plot of ground belonging to Naboth the Jezreelite; for remember, when you and I rode side by side behind his father Ahab how the LORD uttered this oracle against him: ^{26}'For the blood of Naboth and for the blood of his children that I saw yesterday, says the LORD, I swear I will repay you on this very plot of ground.' Now therefore lift him out and throw him on the plot of ground, in accordance with the word of the LORD."

Ahaziah of Judah Killed

27 When King Ahaziah of Judah saw this, he fled in the direction of Beth-haggan. Jehu pursued him, saying, "Shoot him also!" And they shot him^a in the chariot at the ascent to Gur, which is by Ibleam. Then he fled to Megiddo, and died there. ^{28}His officers carried him in a chariot to Jerusalem, and buried him in his tomb with his ancestors in the city of David.

29 In the eleventh year of Joram son of Ahab, Ahaziah began to reign over Judah.

Jezebel's Violent Death

30 When Jehu came to Jezreel, Jezebel heard of it; she painted her eyes, and adorned her head, and looked out of the window. ^{31}As Jehu entered the gate, she said, "Is it peace, Zimri, murderer of your master?" ^{32}He looked up to the window and said, "Who is on my side? Who?" Two or three eunuchs looked out at him. ^{33}He said, "Throw her down." So they threw her down; some of her blood spattered on the wall and on the horses, which trampled on her. ^{34}Then he went in and ate and drank; he said, "See to that cursed woman and bury her; for she is a king's daughter." ^{35}But when they went to bury her, they found no more of her than the skull and the feet and the palms of her hands. ^{36}When they came back and told him, he said, "This is the word of the LORD, which he spoke by his servant Elijah the Tishbite, 'In the territory of Jezreel the dogs shall eat the flesh of Jezebel; ^{37}the corpse of Jezebel shall be like dung on the field in the territory of Jezreel, so that no one can say, This is Jezebel.' "

Massacre of Ahab's Descendants

10 Now Ahab had seventy sons in Samaria. So Jehu wrote letters and sent them to Samaria, to the rulers of Jezreel,^{b} to the elders, and to the guardians of the sons of^c Ahab, saying, ^{2}"Since your master's sons are with you and you have at your disposal chariots and horses, a fortified city, and weapons, ^{3}select the son of your master who is the best qualified, set him on his father's throne, and fight for your master's house." ^{4}But they were utterly terrified and said, "Look, two kings could not withstand him; how then can we stand?" ^{5}So the steward of the palace, and the governor of the city, along with the elders and the guardians, sent word to Jehu: "We are your servants; we will do anything you say. We will not make anyone king; do whatever you think right." ^{6}Then he wrote them a second letter, saying, "If you are on my side, and if you are ready to obey me, take the heads of your master's sons and come to me at Jezreel tomorrow at this time." Now the king's sons, seventy persons, were with the leaders of the city, who were charged with their upbringing. ^{7}When the letter reached them, they took the king's sons and killed them, seventy persons; they put their heads in baskets and sent them to him at Jezreel. ^{8}When the messenger came and told him, "They have brought the heads of the king's sons," he said, "Lay them in two heaps at the entrance of the gate until the morning." ^{9}Then in the morning when he went out, he stood and said to all the people, "You are innocent. It was I who conspired against my master and killed him; but who struck down all these? ^{10}Know then that there shall fall to the earth nothing of the word of the LORD, which the LORD spoke concerning the house of Ahab; for the LORD has done what he said through his servant Elijah." ^{11}So Jehu killed all who were left of the house of Ahab in Jezreel, all his leaders, close friends, and priests, until he left him no survivor.

12 Then he set out and went to Samaria. On the way, when he was at Beth-eked of the Shepherds, ^{13}Jehu met relatives of King Ahaziah of Judah and said, "Who are you?" They answered, "We are kin of Ahaziah; we have come down to visit the royal princes and the sons of the queen mother." ^{14}He said, "Take them alive." They took them alive, and slaughtered them at the pit of Beth-eked, forty-two in all; he spared none of them.

15 When he left there, he met Jehonadab son of Rechab coming to meet him; he greeted him, and said to him, "Is your heart as true to mine as mine is to yours?"^{d} Jehonadab answered, "It is." Jehu said,^{e} "If it is, give me your hand." So he gave him his hand. Jehu took him up with him into the chariot. ^{16}He

---

a Syr Vg Compare Gk: Heb lacks *and they shot him* b Or *of the city*; Vg Compare Gk c Gk: Heb lacks *of the sons of* d Gk: Heb *Is it right with your heart, as my heart is with your heart?* e Gk: Heb lacks *Jehu said*

said, "Come with me, and see my zeal for the LORD."
So he*a* had him ride in his chariot. [17]When he came
to Samaria, he killed all who were left to Ahab in
Samaria, until he had wiped them out, according to
the word of the LORD that he spoke to Elijah.

Slaughter of Worshipers of Baal

18 Then Jehu assembled all the people and said
to them, "Ahab offered Baal small service; but Jehu
will offer much more. [19]Now therefore summon to
me all the prophets of Baal, all his worshipers, and
all his priests; let none be missing, for I have a great
sacrifice to offer to Baal; whoever is missing shall not
live." But Jehu was acting with cunning in order to
destroy the worshipers of Baal. [20]Jehu decreed,
"Sanctify a solemn assembly for Baal." So they proclaimed it. [21]Jehu sent word throughout all Israel; all
the worshipers of Baal came, so that there was no
one left who did not come. They entered the temple
of Baal, until the temple of Baal was filled from wall
to wall. [22]He said to the keeper of the wardrobe,
"Bring out the vestments for all the worshipers of
Baal." So he brought out the vestments for them.
[23]Then Jehu entered the temple of Baal with Jehonadab son of Rechab; he said to the worshipers
of Baal, "Search and see that there is no worshiper of
the LORD here among you, but only worshipers of
Baal." [24]Then they proceeded to offer sacrifices and
burnt offerings.

Now Jehu had stationed eighty men outside, saying, "Whoever allows any of those to escape whom
I deliver into your hands shall forfeit his life." [25]As
soon as he had finished presenting the burnt offering,
Jehu said to the guards and to the officers, "Come in
and kill them; let no one escape." So they put them
to the sword. The guards and the officers threw them
out, and then went into the citadel of the temple of
Baal. [26]They brought out the pillar*b* that was in the
temple of Baal, and burned it. [27]Then they demolished the pillar of Baal, and destroyed the temple of
Baal, and made it a latrine to this day.

28 Thus Jehu wiped out Baal from Israel. [29]But
Jehu did not turn aside from the sins of Jeroboam
son of Nebat, which he caused Israel to commit—the
golden calves that were in Bethel and in Dan. [30]The
LORD said to Jehu, "Because you have done well in
carrying out what I consider right, and in accordance
with all that was in my heart have dealt with the
house of Ahab, your sons of the fourth generation
shall sit on the throne of Israel." [31]But Jehu was not

careful to follow the law of the LORD the God of
Israel with all his heart; he did not turn from the sins
of Jeroboam, which he caused Israel to commit.

Death of Jehu

32 In those days the LORD began to trim off parts
of Israel. Hazael defeated them throughout the territory of Israel: [33]from the Jordan eastward, all the
land of Gilead, the Gadites, the Reubenites, and the
Manassites, from Aroer, which is by the Wadi Arnon,
that is, Gilead and Bashan. [34]Now the rest of the acts
of Jehu, all that he did, and all his power, are they not
written in the Book of the Annals of the Kings of
Israel? [35]So Jehu slept with his ancestors, and they
buried him in Samaria. His son Jehoahaz succeeded
him. [36]The time that Jehu reigned over Israel in
Samaria was twenty-eight years.

Athaliah Reigns over Judah

11 Now when Athaliah, Ahaziah's mother, saw
that her son was dead, she set about to
destroy all the royal family. [2]But Jehosheba, King
Joram's daughter, Ahaziah's sister, took Joash son of
Ahaziah, and stole him away from among the king's
children who were about to be killed; she put*c* him
and his nurse in a bedroom. Thus she*d* hid him from
Athaliah, so that he was not killed; [3]he remained
with her six years, hidden in the house of the LORD,
while Athaliah reigned over the land.

Jehoiada Anoints the Child Joash

4 But in the seventh year Jehoiada summoned the
captains of the Carites and of the guards and had
them come to him in the house of the LORD. He
made a covenant with them and put them under oath
in the house of the LORD; then he showed them the
king's son. [5]He commanded them, "This is what you
are to do: one-third of you, those who go off duty
on the sabbath and guard the king's house [6](another
third being at the gate Sur and a third at the gate
behind the guards), shall guard the palace; [7]and your
two divisions that come on duty in force on the sabbath and guard the house of the LORD*e* [8]shall surround the king, each with weapons in hand; and
whoever approaches the ranks is to be killed. Be with
the king in his comings and goings."

9 The captains did according to all that the priest
Jehoiada commanded; each brought his men who
were to go off duty on the sabbath, with those who
were to come on duty on the sabbath, and came to

---

a Gk Syr Tg: Heb *they*   *b* Gk Vg Syr Tg: Heb *pillars*   *c* With 2 Chr 22.11: Heb lacks *she put*   *d* Gk Syr Vg Compare 2 Chr 22.11: Heb *they*   *e* Heb *the*
LORD *to the king*

the priest Jehoiada. ¹⁰The priest delivered to the captains the spears and shields that had been King David's, which were in the house of the LORD; ¹¹the guards stood, every man with his weapons in his hand, from the south side of the house to the north side of the house, around the altar and the house, to guard the king on every side. ¹²Then he brought out the king's son, put the crown on him, and gave him the covenant;ᵃ they proclaimed him king, and anointed him; they clapped their hands and shouted, "Long live the king!"

Death of Athaliah

13 When Athaliah heard the noise of the guard and of the people, she went into the house of the LORD to the people; ¹⁴when she looked, there was the king standing by the pillar, according to custom, with the captains and the trumpeters beside the king, and all the people of the land rejoicing and blowing trumpets. Athaliah tore her clothes and cried, "Treason! Treason!" ¹⁵Then the priest Jehoiada commanded the captains who were set over the army, "Bring her out between the ranks, and kill with the sword anyone who follows her." For the priest said, "Let her not be killed in the house of the LORD." ¹⁶So they laid hands on her; she went through the horses' entrance to the king's house, and there she was put to death.

17 Jehoiada made a covenant between the LORD and the king and people, that they should be the LORD's people; also between the king and the people. ¹⁸Then all the people of the land went to the house of Baal, and tore it down; his altars and his images they broke in pieces, and they killed Mattan, the priest of Baal, before the altars. The priest posted guards over the house of the LORD. ¹⁹He took the captains, the Carites, the guards, and all the people of the land; then they brought the king down from the house of the LORD, marching through the gate of the guards to the king's house. He took his seat on the throne of the kings. ²⁰So all the people of the land rejoiced; and the city was quiet after Athaliah had been killed with the sword at the king's house. 21ᵇ Jehoashᶜ was seven years old when he began to reign.

The Temple Repaired

12 In the seventh year of Jehu, Jehoash began to reign; he reigned forty years in Jerusalem. His mother's name was Zibiah of Beer-sheba.

²Jehoash did what was right in the sight of the LORD all his days, because the priest Jehoiada instructed him. ³Nevertheless the high places were not taken away; the people continued to sacrifice and make offerings on the high places.

4 Jehoash said to the priests, "All the money offered as sacred donations that is brought into the house of the LORD, the money for which each person is assessed—the money from the assessment of persons—and the money from the voluntary offerings brought into the house of the LORD, ⁵let the priests receive from each of the donors; and let them repair the house wherever any need of repairs is discovered." ⁶But by the twenty-third year of King Jehoash the priests had made no repairs on the house. ⁷Therefore King Jehoash summoned the priest Jehoiada with the other priests and said to them, "Why are you not repairing the house? Now therefore do not accept any more money from your donors but hand it over for the repair of the house." ⁸So the priests agreed that they would neither accept more money from the people nor repair the house.

9 Then the priest Jehoiada took a chest, made a hole in its lid, and set it beside the altar on the right side as one entered the house of the LORD; the priests who guarded the threshold put in it all the money that was brought into the house of the LORD. ¹⁰Whenever they saw that there was a great deal of money in the chest, the king's secretary and the high priest went up, counted the money that was found in the house of the LORD, and tied it up in bags. ¹¹They would give the money that was weighed out into the hands of the workers who had the oversight of the house of the LORD; then they paid it out to the carpenters and the builders who worked on the house of the LORD, ¹²to the masons and the stonecutters, as well as to buy timber and quarried stone for making repairs on the house of the LORD, as well as for any outlay for repairs of the house. ¹³But for the house of the LORD no basins of silver, snuffers, bowls, trumpets, or any vessels of gold, or of silver, were made from the money that was brought into the house of the LORD, ¹⁴for that was given to the workers who were repairing the house of the LORD with it. ¹⁵They did not ask an accounting from those into whose hand they delivered the money to pay out to the workers, for they dealt honestly. ¹⁶The money from the guilt offerings and the money from the sin offerings was not brought into the house of the LORD; it belonged to the priests.

---

a Or *treaty* or *testimony*; Heb *eduth*　b Ch 12.1 in Heb　c Another spelling is *Joash*; see verse 19

Hazael Threatens Jerusalem

17 At that time King Hazael of Aram went up, fought against Gath, and took it. But when Hazael set his face to go up against Jerusalem, [18] King Jehoash of Judah took all the votive gifts that Jehoshaphat, Jehoram, and Ahaziah, his ancestors, the kings of Judah, had dedicated, as well as his own votive gifts, all the gold that was found in the treasuries of the house of the LORD and of the king's house, and sent these to King Hazael of Aram. Then Hazael withdrew from Jerusalem.

Death of Joash

19 Now the rest of the acts of Joash, and all that he did, are they not written in the Book of the Annals of the Kings of Judah? [20] His servants arose, devised a conspiracy, and killed Joash in the house of Millo, on the way that goes down to Silla. [21] It was Jozacar son of Shimeath and Jehozabad son of Shomer, his servants, who struck him down, so that he died. He was buried with his ancestors in the city of David; then his son Amaziah succeeded him.

Jehoahaz Reigns over Israel

13 In the twenty-third year of King Joash son of Ahaziah of Judah, Jehoahaz son of Jehu began to reign over Israel in Samaria; he reigned seventeen years. [2] He did what was evil in the sight of the LORD, and followed the sins of Jeroboam son of Nebat, which he caused Israel to sin; he did not depart from them. [3] The anger of the LORD was kindled against Israel, so that he gave them repeatedly into the hand of King Hazael of Aram, then into the hand of Ben-hadad son of Hazael. [4] But Jehoahaz entreated the LORD, and the LORD heeded him; for he saw the oppression of Israel, how the king of Aram oppressed them. [5] Therefore the LORD gave Israel a savior, so that they escaped from the hand of the Arameans; and the people of Israel lived in their homes as formerly. [6] Nevertheless they did not depart from the sins of the house of Jeroboam, which he caused Israel to sin, but walked[a] in them; the sacred pole[b] also remained in Samaria. [7] So Jehoahaz was left with an army of not more than fifty horsemen, ten chariots and ten thousand footmen; for the king of Aram had destroyed them and made them like the dust at threshing. [8] Now the rest of the acts of Jehoahaz and all that he did, including his might, are they not written in the Book of the Annals of the Kings of Israel? [9] So Jehoahaz slept with his ancestors, and

they buried him in Samaria; then his son Joash succeeded him.

Jehoash Reigns over Israel

10 In the thirty-seventh year of King Joash of Judah, Jehoash son of Jehoahaz began to reign over Israel in Samaria; he reigned sixteen years. [11] He also did what was evil in the sight of the LORD; he did not depart from all the sins of Jeroboam son of Nebat, which he caused Israel to sin, but he walked in them. [12] Now the rest of the acts of Joash, and all that he did, as well as the might with which he fought against King Amaziah of Judah, are they not written in the Book of the Annals of the Kings of Israel? [13] So Joash slept with his ancestors, and Jeroboam sat upon his throne; Joash was buried in Samaria with the kings of Israel.

Death of Elisha

14 Now when Elisha had fallen sick with the illness of which he was to die, King Joash of Israel went down to him, and wept before him, crying, "My father, my father! The chariots of Israel and its horsemen!" [15] Elisha said to him, "Take a bow and arrows"; so he took a bow and arrows. [16] Then he said to the king of Israel, "Draw the bow"; and he drew it. Elisha laid his hands on the king's hands. [17] Then he said, "Open the window eastward"; and he opened it. Elisha said, "Shoot"; and he shot. Then he said, "The LORD's arrow of victory, the arrow of victory over Aram! For you shall fight the Arameans in Aphek until you have made an end of them." [18] He continued, "Take the arrows"; and he took them. He said to the king of Israel, "Strike the ground with them"; he struck three times, and stopped. [19] Then the man of God was angry with him, and said, "You should have struck five or six times; then you would have struck down Aram until you had made an end of it, but now you will strike down Aram only three times."

20 So Elisha died, and they buried him. Now bands of Moabites used to invade the land in the spring of the year. [21] As a man was being buried, a marauding band was seen and the man was thrown into the grave of Elisha; as soon as the man touched

a Gk Syr Tg Vg: Heb *he walked*   *b* Heb *Asherah*

the bones of Elisha, he came to life and stood on his feet.

Israel Recaptures Cities from Aram

22 Now King Hazael of Aram oppressed Israel all the days of Jehoahaz. ²³But the LORD was gracious to them and had compassion on them; he turned toward them, because of his covenant with Abraham, Isaac, and Jacob, and would not destroy them; nor has he banished them from his presence until now.

24 When King Hazael of Aram died, his son Benhadad succeeded him. ²⁵Then Jehoash son of Jehoahaz took again from Ben-hadad son of Hazael the towns that he had taken from his father Jehoahaz in war. Three times Joash defeated him and recovered the towns of Israel.

Amaziah Reigns over Judah

14 In the second year of King Joash son of Joahaz of Israel, King Amaziah son of Joash of Judah, began to reign. ²He was twenty-five years old when he began to reign, and he reigned twenty-nine years in Jerusalem. His mother's name was Jehoaddin of Jerusalem. ³He did what was right in the sight of the LORD, yet not like his ancestor David; in all things he did as his father Joash had done. ⁴But the high places were not removed; the people still sacrificed and made offerings on the high places. ⁵As soon as the royal power was firmly in his hand he killed his servants who had murdered his father the king. ⁶But he did not put to death the children of the murderers; according to what is written in the book of the law of Moses, where the LORD commanded, "The parents shall not be put to death for the children, or the children be put to death for the parents; but all shall be put to death for their own sins."

7 He killed ten thousand Edomites in the Valley of Salt and took Sela by storm; he called it Joktheel, which is its name to this day.

8 Then Amaziah sent messengers to King Jehoash son of Jehoahaz, son of Jehu, of Israel, saying, "Come, let us look one another in the face." ⁹King Jehoash of Israel sent word to King Amaziah of Judah, "A thornbush on Lebanon sent to a cedar on Lebanon, saying, 'Give your daughter to my son for a wife'; but a wild animal of Lebanon passed by and trampled down the thornbush. ¹⁰You have indeed defeated Edom, and your heart has lifted you up. Be

content with your glory, and stay at home; for why should you provoke trouble so that you fall, you and Judah with you?"

11 But Amaziah would not listen. So King Jehoash of Israel went up; he and King Amaziah of Judah faced one another in battle at Beth-shemesh, which belongs to Judah. ¹²Judah was defeated by Israel; everyone fled home. ¹³King Jehoash of Israel captured King Amaziah of Judah son of Jehoash, son of Ahaziah, at Beth-shemesh; he came to Jerusalem, and broke down the wall of Jerusalem from the Ephraim Gate to the Corner Gate, a distance of four hundred cubits. ¹⁴He seized all the gold and silver, and all the vessels that were found in the house of the LORD and in the treasuries of the king's house, as well as hostages; then he returned to Samaria.

15 Now the rest of the acts that Jehoash did, his might, and how he fought with King Amaziah of Judah, are they not written in the Book of the Annals of the Kings of Israel? ¹⁶Jehoash slept with his ancestors, and was buried in Samaria with the kings of Israel; then his son Jeroboam succeeded him.

17 King Amaziah son of Joash of Judah lived fifteen years after the death of King Jehoash son of Jehoahaz of Israel. ¹⁸Now the rest of the deeds of Amaziah, are they not written in the Book of the Annals of the Kings of Judah? ¹⁹They made a conspiracy against him in Jerusalem, and he fled to Lachish. But they sent after him to Lachish, and killed him there. ²⁰They brought him on horses; he was buried in Jerusalem with his ancestors in the city of David. ²¹All the people of Judah took Azariah, who was sixteen years old, and made him king to succeed his father Amaziah. ²²He rebuilt Elath and restored it to Judah, after King Amaziah*ᵃ* slept with his ancestors.

Jeroboam II Reigns over Israel

23 In the fifteenth year of King Amaziah son of Joash of Judah, King Jeroboam son of Joash of Israel began to reign in Samaria; he reigned forty-one years. ²⁴He did what was evil in the sight of the LORD; he did not depart from all the sins of Jeroboam son of Nebat, which he caused Israel to sin. ²⁵He restored the border of Israel from Lebo-hamath as far as the Sea of the Arabah, according to the word of the LORD, the God of Israel, which he spoke by his servant Jonah son of Amittai, the prophet, who was from Gath-hepher. ²⁶For the LORD saw that the distress of Israel was very bitter; there was no one

ᵃ Heb *the king*

left, bond or free, and no one to help Israel. ²⁷But the LORD had not said that he would blot out the name of Israel from under heaven, so he saved them by the hand of Jeroboam son of Joash.

28 Now the rest of the acts of Jeroboam, and all that he did, and his might, how he fought, and how he recovered for Israel Damascus and Hamath, which had belonged to Judah, are they not written in the Book of the Annals of the Kings of Israel? ²⁹Jeroboam slept with his ancestors, the kings of Israel; his son Zechariah succeeded him.

Azariah Reigns over Judah

15 In the twenty-seventh year of King Jeroboam of Israel King Azariah son of Amaziah of Judah began to reign. ²He was sixteen years old when he began to reign, and he reigned fifty-two years in Jerusalem. His mother's name was Jecoliah of Jerusalem. ³He did what was right in the sight of the LORD, just as his father Amaziah had done. ⁴Nevertheless the high places were not taken away; the people still sacrificed and made offerings on the high places. ⁵The LORD struck the king, so that he was leprous^a to the day of his death, and lived in a separate house. Jotham the king's son was in charge of the palace, governing the people of the land. ⁶Now the rest of the acts of Azariah, and all that he did, are they not written in the Book of the Annals of the Kings of Judah? ⁷Azariah slept with his ancestors; they buried him with his ancestors in the city of David; his son Jotham succeeded him.

Zechariah Reigns over Israel

8 In the thirty-eighth year of King Azariah of Judah, Zechariah son of Jeroboam reigned over Israel in Samaria six months. ⁹He did what was evil in the sight of the LORD, as his ancestors had done. He did not depart from the sins of Jeroboam son of Nebat, which he caused Israel to sin. ¹⁰Shallum son of Jabesh conspired against him, and struck him down in public and killed him, and reigned in place of him. ¹¹Now the rest of the deeds of Zechariah are written in the Book of the Annals of the Kings of Israel. ¹²This was the promise of the LORD that he gave to Jehu, "Your sons shall sit on the throne of Israel to the fourth generation." And so it happened.

Shallum Reigns over Israel

13 Shallum son of Jabesh began to reign in the thirty-ninth year of King Uzziah of Judah; he reigned one month in Samaria. ¹⁴Then Menahem son of Gadi came up from Tirzah and came to Samaria; he struck down Shallum son of Jabesh in Samaria and killed him; he reigned in place of him. ¹⁵Now the rest of the deeds of Shallum, including the conspiracy that he made, are written in the Book of the Annals of the Kings of Israel. ¹⁶At that time Menahem sacked Tiphsah, all who were in it and its territory from Tirzah on; because they did not open it to him, he sacked it. He ripped open all the pregnant women in it.

Menahem Reigns over Israel

17 In the thirty-ninth year of King Azariah of Judah, Menahem son of Gadi began to reign over Israel; he reigned ten years in Samaria. ¹⁸He did what was evil in the sight of the LORD; he did not depart all his days from any of the sins of Jeroboam son of Nebat, which he caused Israel to sin. ¹⁹King Pul of Assyria came against the land; Menahem gave Pul a thousand talents of silver, so that he might help him confirm his hold on the royal power. ²⁰Menahem exacted the money from Israel, that is, from all the wealthy, fifty shekels of silver from each one, to give to the king of Assyria. So the king of Assyria turned back, and did not stay there in the land. ²¹Now the rest of the deeds of Menahem, and all that he did, are they not written in the Book of the Annals of the Kings of Israel? ²²Menahem slept with his ancestors, and his son Pekahiah succeeded him.

Pekahiah Reigns over Israel

23 In the fiftieth year of King Azariah of Judah, Pekahiah son of Menahem began to reign over Israel in Samaria; he reigned two years. ²⁴He did what was evil in the sight of the LORD; he did not turn away from the sins of Jeroboam son of Nebat, which he caused Israel to sin. ²⁵Pekah son of Remaliah, his captain, conspired against him with fifty of the Gileadites, and attacked him in Samaria, in the citadel of the palace along with Argob and Arieh; he killed him, and reigned in place of him. ²⁶Now the rest of the deeds of Pekahiah, and all that he did, are written in the Book of the Annals of the Kings of Israel.

Pekah Reigns over Israel

27 In the fifty-second year of King Azariah of Judah, Pekah son of Remaliah began to reign over Israel in Samaria; he reigned twenty years. ²⁸He did what was evil in the sight of the LORD; he did not

^a A term for several skin diseases; precise meaning uncertain

depart from the sins of Jeroboam son of Nebat, which he caused Israel to sin.

29 In the days of King Pekah of Israel, King Tiglath-pileser of Assyria came and captured Ijon, Abel-beth-maacah, Janoah, Kedesh, Hazor, Gilead, and Galilee, all the land of Naphtali; and he carried the people captive to Assyria. [30]Then Hoshea son of Elah made a conspiracy against Pekah son of Remaliah, attacked him, and killed him; he reigned in place of him, in the twentieth year of Jotham son of Uzziah. [31]Now the rest of the acts of Pekah, and all that he did, are written in the Book of the Annals of the Kings of Israel.

Jotham Reigns over Judah

32 In the second year of King Pekah son of Remaliah of Israel, King Jotham son of Uzziah of Judah began to reign. [33]He was twenty-five years old when he began to reign and reigned sixteen years in Jerusalem. His mother's name was Jerusha daughter of Zadok. [34]He did what was right in the sight of the LORD, just as his father Uzziah had done. [35]Nevertheless the high places were not removed; the people still sacrificed and made offerings on the high places. He built the upper gate of the house of the LORD. [36]Now the rest of the acts of Jotham, and all that he did, are they not written in the Book of the Annals of the Kings of Judah? [37]In those days the LORD began to send King Rezin of Aram and Pekah son of Remaliah against Judah. [38]Jotham slept with his ancestors, and was buried with his ancestors in the city of David, his ancestor; his son Ahaz succeeded him.

Ahaz Reigns over Judah

16 In the seventeenth year of Pekah son of Remaliah, King Ahaz son of Jotham of Judah began to reign. [2]Ahaz was twenty years old when he began to reign; he reigned sixteen years in Jerusalem. He did not do what was right in the sight of the LORD his God, as his ancestor David had done, [3]but he walked in the way of the kings of Israel. He even made his son pass through fire, according to the abominable practices of the nations whom the LORD drove out before the people of Israel. [4]He sacrificed and made offerings on the high places, on the hills, and under every green tree.

5 Then King Rezin of Aram and King Pekah son of Remaliah of Israel came up to wage war on Jerusalem; they besieged Ahaz but could not conquer

him. [6]At that time the king of Edom[a] recovered Elath for Edom,[b] and drove the Judeans from Elath; and the Edomites came to Elath, where they live to this day. [7]Ahaz sent messengers to King Tiglath-pileser of Assyria, saying, "I am your servant and your son. Come up, and rescue me from the hand of the king of Aram and from the hand of the king of Israel, who are attacking me." [8]Ahaz also took the silver and gold found in the house of the LORD and in the treasures of the king's house, and sent a present to the king of Assyria. [9]The king of Assyria listened to him; the king of Assyria marched up against Damascus, and took it, carrying its people captive to Kir; then he killed Rezin.

10 When King Ahaz went to Damascus to meet King Tiglath-pileser of Assyria, he saw the altar that was at Damascus. King Ahaz sent to the priest Uriah a model of the altar, and its pattern, exact in all its details. [11]The priest Uriah built the altar; in accordance with all that King Ahaz had sent from Damascus, just so did the priest Uriah build it, before King Ahaz arrived from Damascus. [12]When the king came from Damascus, the king viewed the altar. Then the king drew near to the altar, went up on it, [13]and offered his burnt offering and his grain offering, poured his drink offering, and dashed the blood of his offerings of well-being against the altar. [14]The bronze altar that was before the LORD he removed from the front of the house, from the place between his altar and the house of the LORD, and put it on the north side of his altar. [15]King Ahaz commanded the priest Uriah, saying, "Upon the great altar offer the morning burnt offering, and the evening grain offering, and the king's burnt offering, and his grain offering, with the burnt offering of all the people of the land, their grain offering, and their drink offering; then dash against it all the blood of the burnt offering, and all the blood of the sacrifice; but the bronze altar shall be for me to inquire by." [16]The priest Uriah did everything that King Ahaz commanded.

17 Then King Ahaz cut off the frames of the stands, and removed the laver from them; he removed the sea from the bronze oxen that were under it, and put it on a pediment of stone. [18]The covered portal for use on the sabbath that had been built inside the palace, and the outer entrance for the king he removed from[c] the house of the LORD. He did this because of the king of Assyria. [19]Now the rest of the acts of Ahaz that he did, are they not written in the Book of the Annals of the Kings of Judah?

a Cn: Heb *King Rezin of Aram*   **b** Cn: Heb *Aram*   **c** Cn: Heb lacks *from*

²⁰Ahaz slept with his ancestors, and was buried with his ancestors in the city of David; his son Hezekiah succeeded him.

Hoshea Reigns over Israel

17 In the twelfth year of King Ahaz of Judah, Hoshea son of Elah began to reign in Samaria over Israel; he reigned nine years. ²He did what was evil in the sight of the LORD, yet not like the kings of Israel who were before him. ³King Shalmaneser of Assyria came up against him; Hoshea became his vassal, and paid him tribute. ⁴But the king of Assyria found treachery in Hoshea; for he had sent messengers to King So of Egypt, and offered no tribute to the king of Assyria, as he had done year by year; therefore the king of Assyria confined him and imprisoned him.

Israel Carried Captive to Assyria

5 Then the king of Assyria invaded all the land and came to Samaria; for three years he besieged it. ⁶In the ninth year of Hoshea the king of Assyria captured Samaria; he carried the Israelites away to Assyria. He placed them in Halah, on the Habor, the river of Gozan, and in the cities of the Medes.

7 This occurred because the people of Israel had sinned against the LORD their God, who had brought them up out of the land of Egypt from under the hand of Pharaoh king of Egypt. They had worshiped other gods ⁸and walked in the customs of the nations whom the LORD drove out before the people of Israel, and in the customs that the kings of Israel had introduced.ᵃ ⁹The people of Israel secretly did things

that were not right against the LORD their God. They built for themselves high places at all their towns, from watchtower to fortified city; ¹⁰they set up for themselves pillars and sacred polesᵇ on every high hill and under every green tree; ¹¹there they made offerings on all the high places, as the nations did whom the LORD carried away before them. They did wicked things, provoking the LORD to anger; ¹²they served idols, of which the LORD had said to them, "You shall not do this." ¹³Yet the LORD warned Israel and Judah by every prophet and every seer, saying, "Turn from your evil ways and keep my commandments and my statutes, in accordance with all the law that I commanded your ancestors and that I sent to you by my servants the prophets." ¹⁴They would not listen but were stubborn, as their ancestors had been, who did not believe in the LORD their God. ¹⁵They despised his statutes, and his covenant that he made with their ancestors, and the warnings that he gave them. They went after false idols and became false; they followed the nations that were around them, concerning whom the LORD had commanded them that they should not do as they did. ¹⁶They rejected all the commandments of the LORD their God and made for themselves cast images of two calves; they made a sacred pole,ᶜ worshiped all the host of heaven, and served Baal. ¹⁷They made their sons and their daughters pass through fire; they used divination and augury; and they sold themselves to do evil in the sight of the LORD, provoking him to anger. ¹⁸Therefore the LORD was very angry with Israel and removed them out of his sight; none was left but the tribe of Judah alone.

STUDY IT!

The First Exile · 2 Kings 17:5–18

Two exiles are described in 2 Kings. The first one is the Assyrian conquest of the northern kingdom, Israel, which occurred in 722 B.C. (See Map 8a: "Assyrian Empire.") According to the author of 2 Kings, Israel fell first because its kings and people were even less faithful to God than the kings and people of Judah, the southern kingdom (2 Kings 17:18).

Notice that the Assyrian conquest is described in the briefest detail (2 Kings 17:5–6), but the reasons for it are described in great detail (2 Kings 17:7–18). That's a good reminder to us of what God's higher priority is. We can learn from the Israelites' mistakes. The people of Israel worshiped idols, lived for other gods, and acted like their ungodly neighbors instead of God's people. Even when God reminded and warned them through the prophets, they stayed stubborn and ignored God's messages. The people of Israel essentially chose to learn the hard way.

---

a Meaning of Heb uncertain   b Heb *Asherim*   c Heb *Asherah*

19 Judah also did not keep the commandments of the Lord their God but walked in the customs that Israel had introduced. [20]The Lord rejected all the descendants of Israel; he punished them and gave them into the hand of plunderers, until he had banished them from his presence.

21 When he had torn Israel from the house of David, they made Jeroboam son of Nebat king. Jeroboam drove Israel from following the Lord and made them commit great sin. [22]The people of Israel continued in all the sins that Jeroboam committed; they did not depart from them [23]until the Lord removed Israel out of his sight, as he had foretold through all his servants the prophets. So Israel was exiled from their own land to Assyria until this day.

Assyria Resettles Samaria

24 The king of Assyria brought people from Babylon, Cuthah, Avva, Hamath, and Sepharvaim, and placed them in the cities of Samaria in place of the people of Israel; they took possession of Samaria, and settled in its cities. [25]When they first settled there, they did not worship the Lord; therefore the Lord sent lions among them, which killed some of them. [26]So the king of Assyria was told, "The nations that you have carried away and placed in the cities of Samaria do not know the law of the god of the land; therefore he has sent lions among them; they are killing them, because they do not know the law of the god of the land." [27]Then the king of Assyria commanded, "Send there one of the priests whom you carried away from there; let him[a] go and live there, and teach them the law of the god of the land." [28]So one of the priests whom they had carried away from Samaria came and lived in Bethel; he taught them how they should worship the Lord.

29 But every nation still made gods of its own and put them in the shrines of the high places that the people of Samaria had made, every nation in the cities in which they lived; [30]the people of Babylon made Succoth-benoth, the people of Cuth made Nergal, the people of Hamath made Ashima; [31]the Avvites made Nibhaz and Tartak; the Sepharvites burned their children in the fire to Adrammelech and Anammelech, the gods of Sepharvaim. [32]They also worshiped the Lord and appointed from among themselves all sorts of people as priests of the high places, who sacrificed for them in the shrines of the high places. [33]So they worshiped the Lord but also served their own gods, after the manner of the nations from among whom they had been carried away. [34]To this day they continue to practice their former customs.

They do not worship the Lord and they do not follow the statutes or the ordinances or the law or the commandment that the Lord commanded the children of Jacob, whom he named Israel. [35]The Lord had made a covenant with them and commanded them, "You shall not worship other gods or bow yourselves to them or serve them or sacrifice to them, [36]but you shall worship the Lord, who brought you out of the land of Egypt with great power and with an outstretched arm; you shall bow yourselves to him, and to him you shall sacrifice. [37]The statutes and the ordinances and the law and the commandment that he wrote for you, you shall always be careful to observe. You shall not worship other gods; [38]you shall not forget the covenant that I have made with you. You shall not worship other gods, [39]but you shall worship the Lord your God; he will deliver you out of the hand of all your enemies." [40]They would not listen, however, but they continued to practice their former custom.

41 So these nations worshiped the Lord, but also served their carved images; to this day their children and their children's children continue to do as their ancestors did.

Hezekiah's Reign over Judah

18 In the third year of King Hoshea son of Elah of Israel, Hezekiah son of King Ahaz of Judah began to reign. [2]He was twenty-five years old when he began to reign; he reigned twenty-nine years in Jerusalem. His mother's name was Abi daughter of Zechariah. [3]He did what was right in the sight of the Lord just as his ancestor David had done. [4]He removed the high places, broke down the pillars, and cut down the sacred pole.[b] He broke in pieces the bronze serpent that Moses had made, for until those days the people of Israel had made offerings to it; it was called Nehushtan. [5]He trusted in the Lord the God of Israel; so that there was no one like him among all the kings of Judah after him, or among those who were before him. [6]For he held fast to the Lord; he did not depart from following him but kept the commandments that the Lord commanded Moses. [7]The Lord was with him; wherever he went, he prospered. He rebelled against the king of Assyria and

a Syr Vg: Heb *them*   b Heb *Asherah*

would not serve him. ⁸He attacked the Philistines as far as Gaza and its territory, from watchtower to fortified city.

9 In the fourth year of King Hezekiah, which was the seventh year of King Hoshea son of Elah of Israel, King Shalmaneser of Assyria came up against Samaria, besieged it, ¹⁰and at the end of three years, took it. In the sixth year of Hezekiah, which was the ninth year of King Hoshea of Israel, Samaria was taken. ¹¹The king of Assyria carried the Israelites away to Assyria, settled them in Halah, on the Habor, the river of Gozan, and in the cities of the Medes, ¹²because they did not obey the voice of the LORD their God but transgressed his covenant—all that Moses the servant of the LORD had commanded; they neither listened nor obeyed.

Sennacherib Invades Judah

13 In the fourteenth year of King Hezekiah, King Sennacherib of Assyria came up against all the fortified cities of Judah and captured them. ¹⁴King Hezekiah of Judah sent to the king of Assyria at Lachish, saying, "I have done wrong; withdraw from me; whatever you impose on me I will bear." The king of Assyria demanded of King Hezekiah of Judah three hundred talents of silver and thirty talents of gold. ¹⁵Hezekiah gave him all the silver that was found in the house of the LORD and in the treasuries of the king's house. ¹⁶At that time Hezekiah stripped the gold from the doors of the temple of the LORD, and from the doorposts that King Hezekiah of Judah had overlaid and gave it to the king of Assyria. ¹⁷The king of Assyria sent the Tartan, the Rabsaris, and the Rabshakeh with a great army from Lachish to King Hezekiah at Jerusalem. They went up and came to Jerusalem. When they arrived, they came and stood by the conduit of the upper pool, which is on the highway to the Fuller's Field. ¹⁸When they called for the king, there came out to them Eliakim son of Hilkiah, who was in charge of the palace, and Shebnah the secretary, and Joah son of Asaph, the recorder.

19 The Rabshakeh said to them, "Say to Hezekiah: Thus says the great king, the king of Assyria: On what do you base this confidence of yours? ²⁰Do you think that mere words are strategy and power for war? On whom do you now rely, that you have rebelled against me? ²¹See, you are relying now on Egypt, that broken reed of a staff, which will pierce the hand of anyone who leans on it. Such is Pharaoh

king of Egypt to all who rely on him. ²²But if you say to me, 'We rely on the LORD our God,' is it not he whose high places and altars Hezekiah has removed, saying to Judah and to Jerusalem, 'You shall worship before this altar in Jerusalem'? ²³Come now, make a wager with my master the king of Assyria: I will give you two thousand horses, if you are able on your part to set riders on them. ²⁴How then can you repulse a single captain among the least of my master's servants, when you rely on Egypt for chariots and for horsemen? ²⁵Moreover, is it without the LORD that I have come up against this place to destroy it? The LORD said to me, Go up against this land, and destroy it."

26 Then Eliakim son of Hilkiah, and Shebnah, and Joah said to the Rabshakeh, "Please speak to your servants in the Aramaic language, for we understand it; do not speak to us in the language of Judah within the hearing of the people who are on the wall." ²⁷But the Rabshakeh said to them, "Has my master sent me to speak these words to your master and to you, and not to the people sitting on the wall, who are doomed with you to eat their own dung and to drink their own urine?"

28 Then the Rabshakeh stood and called out in a loud voice in the language of Judah, "Hear the word of the great king, the king of Assyria! ²⁹Thus says the king: 'Do not let Hezekiah deceive you, for he will not be able to deliver you out of my hand. ³⁰Do not let Hezekiah make you rely on the LORD by saying, The LORD will surely deliver us, and this city will not be given into the hand of the king of Assyria.' ³¹Do not listen to Hezekiah; for thus says the king of Assyria: 'Make your peace with me and come out to me; then every one of you will eat from your own vine and your own fig tree, and drink water from your own cistern, ³²until I come and take you away to a land like your own land, a land of grain and wine, a land of bread and vineyards, a land of olive oil and honey, that you may live and not die. Do not listen to Hezekiah when he misleads you by saying, The LORD will deliver us. ³³Has any of the gods of the nations ever delivered its land out of the hand of the king of Assyria? ³⁴Where are the gods of Hamath and Arpad? Where are the gods of Sepharvaim, Hena, and Ivvah? Have they delivered Samaria out of my hand? ³⁵Who among all the gods of the countries have delivered their countries out of my hand, that the LORD should deliver Jerusalem out of my hand?'"

36 But the people were silent and answered him not a word, for the king's command was, "Do not answer him." [37] Then Eliakim son of Hilkiah, who was in charge of the palace, and Shebna the secretary, and Joah son of Asaph, the recorder, came to Hezekiah with their clothes torn and told him the words of the Rabshakeh.

Hezekiah Consults Isaiah

19 When King Hezekiah heard it, he tore his clothes, covered himself with sackcloth, and went into the house of the LORD. [2] And he sent Eliakim, who was in charge of the palace, and Shebna the secretary, and the senior priests, covered with sackcloth, to the prophet Isaiah son of Amoz. [3] They said to him, "Thus says Hezekiah, This day is a day of distress, of rebuke, and of disgrace; children have come to the birth, and there is no strength to bring them forth. [4] It may be that the LORD your God heard all the words of the Rabshakeh, whom his master the king of Assyria has sent to mock the living God, and will rebuke the words that the LORD your God has heard; therefore lift up your prayer for the remnant that is left." [5] When the servants of King Hezekiah came to Isaiah, [6] Isaiah said to them, "Say to your master, 'Thus says the LORD: Do not be afraid because of the words that you have heard, with which the servants of the king of Assyria have reviled me. [7] I myself will put a spirit in him, so that he shall hear a rumor and return to his own land; I will cause him to fall by the sword in his own land.' "

Sennacherib's Threat

8 The Rabshakeh returned, and found the king of Assyria fighting against Libnah; for he had heard that the king had left Lachish. [9] When the king[a] heard concerning King Tirhakah of Ethiopia,[b] "See, he has set out to fight against you," he sent messengers again to Hezekiah, saying, [10] "Thus shall you speak to King Hezekiah of Judah: Do not let your God on whom you rely deceive you by promising that Jerusalem will not be given into the hand of the king of Assyria. [11] See, you have heard what the kings of Assyria have done to all lands, destroying them utterly. Shall you be delivered? [12] Have the gods of the nations delivered them, the nations that my predecessors destroyed, Gozan, Haran, Rezeph, and the people of Eden who were in Telassar? [13] Where is the king of Hamath, the king of Arpad, the king of the city of Sepharvaim, the king of Hena, or the king of Ivvah?"

Hezekiah's Prayer

14 Hezekiah received the letter from the hand of the messengers and read it; then Hezekiah went up to the house of the LORD and spread it before the LORD. [15] And Hezekiah prayed before the LORD, and said: "O LORD the God of Israel, who are enthroned above the cherubim, you are God, you alone, of all the kingdoms of the earth; you have made heaven and earth. [16] Incline your ear, O LORD, and hear; open your eyes, O LORD, and see; hear the words of Sennacherib, which he has sent to mock the living God. [17] Truly, O LORD, the kings of Assyria have laid waste the nations and their lands, [18] and have hurled their gods into the fire, though they were no gods but the work of human hands—wood and stone— and so they were destroyed. [19] So now, O LORD our God, save us, I pray you, from his hand, so that all the kingdoms of the earth may know that you, O LORD, are God alone."

20 Then Isaiah son of Amoz sent to Hezekiah, saying, "Thus says the LORD, the God of Israel: I have heard your prayer to me about King Sennacherib of Assyria. [21] This is the word that the LORD has spoken concerning him:

She despises you, she scorns you—
     virgin daughter Zion;
she tosses her head—behind your back,
     daughter Jerusalem.

22 "Whom have you mocked and reviled?
     Against whom have you raised your voice
and haughtily lifted your eyes?
     Against the Holy One of Israel!
23 By your messengers you have mocked the
     Lord,
     and you have said, 'With my many chariots
I have gone up the heights of the mountains,
     to the far recesses of Lebanon;
I felled its tallest cedars,
     its choicest cypresses;
I entered its farthest retreat,
     its densest forest.
24 I dug wells
     and drank foreign waters,
I dried up with the sole of my foot
     all the streams of Egypt.'
25 "Have you not heard
     that I determined it long ago?
I planned from days of old

a Heb *he* b Or *Nubia*; Heb *Cush*

what now I bring to pass,
  that you should make fortified cities
    crash into heaps of ruins,
26 while their inhabitants, shorn of strength,
    are dismayed and confounded;
  they have become like plants of the field
    and like tender grass,
  like grass on the housetops,
    blighted before it is grown.

27 "But I know your rising[a] and your sitting,
    your going out and coming in,
    and your raging against me.
28 Because you have raged against me
    and your arrogance has come to my ears,
  I will put my hook in your nose
    and my bit in your mouth;
  I will turn you back on the way
    by which you came.

29 "And this shall be the sign for you: This year you shall eat what grows of itself, and in the second year what springs from that; then in the third year sow, reap, plant vineyards, and eat their fruit. 30 The surviving remnant of the house of Judah shall again take root downward, and bear fruit upward; 31 for from Jerusalem a remnant shall go out, and from Mount Zion a band of survivors. The zeal of the LORD of hosts will do this.

32 "Therefore thus says the LORD concerning the king of Assyria: He shall not come into this city, shoot an arrow there, come before it with a shield, or cast up a siege ramp against it. 33 By the way that he came, by the same he shall return; he shall not come into this city, says the LORD. 34 For I will defend this city to save it, for my own sake and for the sake of my servant David."

Sennacherib's Defeat and Death

35 That very night the angel of the LORD set out and struck down one hundred eighty-five thousand in the camp of the Assyrians; when morning dawned, they were all dead bodies. 36 Then King Sennacherib of Assyria left, went home, and lived at Nineveh. 37 As he was worshiping in the house of his god Nisroch,

his sons Adrammelech and Sharezer killed him with the sword, and they escaped into the land of Ararat. His son Esar-haddon succeeded him.

20 Hezekiah's Illness

In those days Hezekiah became sick and was at the point of death. The prophet Isaiah son of Amoz came to him, and said to him, "Thus says the LORD: Set your house in order, for you shall die; you shall not recover." 2 Then Hezekiah turned his face to the wall and prayed to the LORD: 3 "Remember now, O LORD, I implore you, how I have walked before you in faithfulness with a whole heart, and have done what is good in your sight." Hezekiah wept bitterly. 4 Before Isaiah had gone out of the middle court, the word of the LORD came to him: 5 "Turn back, and say to Hezekiah prince of my people, Thus says the LORD, the God of your ancestor David: I have heard your prayer, I have seen your tears; indeed, I will heal you; on the third day you shall go up to the house of the LORD. 6 I will add fifteen years to your life. I will deliver you and this city out of the hand of the king of Assyria; I will defend this city for my own sake and for my servant David's sake." 7 Then Isaiah said, "Bring a lump of figs. Let them take it and apply it to the boil, so that he may recover."

8 Hezekiah said to Isaiah, "What shall be the sign that the LORD will heal me, and that I shall go up to the house of the LORD on the third day?" 9 Isaiah said, "This is the sign to you from the LORD, that the LORD will do the thing that he has promised: the shadow has now advanced ten intervals; shall it retreat ten intervals?" 10 Hezekiah answered, "It is normal for the shadow to lengthen ten intervals; rather let the shadow retreat ten intervals." 11 The prophet Isaiah cried to the LORD; and he brought the shadow back the ten intervals, by which the sun[b] had declined on the dial of Ahaz.

Envoys from Babylon

12 At that time King Merodach-baladan son of Baladan of Babylon sent envoys with letters and a present to Hezekiah, for he had heard that Hezekiah

> "Thus says the LORD ...
> I have heard your
> prayer, I have seen
> your tears; indeed,
> I will heal you."
> —2 Kings 20:5

---

a Gk Compare Isa 37.27 Q Ms: MT lacks rising   b Syr See Isa 38.8 and Tg: Heb it had been sick. [13]Hezekiah welcomed them;[a] he showed them all his treasure house, the silver, the gold, the spices, the precious oil, his armory, all that was found in his storehouses; there was nothing in his house or in all his realm that Hezekiah did not show them. [14]Then the prophet Isaiah came to King Hezekiah, and said to him, "What did these men say? From where did they come to you?" Hezekiah answered, "They have come from a far country, from Babylon." [15]He said, "What have they seen in your house?" Hezekiah answered, "They have seen all that is in my house; there is nothing in my storehouses that I did not show them."

16 Then Isaiah said to Hezekiah, "Hear the word of the LORD: [17]Days are coming when all that is in your house, and that which your ancestors have stored up until this day, shall be carried to Babylon; nothing shall be left, says the LORD. [18]Some of your own sons who are born to you shall be taken away; they shall be eunuchs in the palace of the king of Babylon." [19]Then Hezekiah said to Isaiah, "The word of the LORD that you have spoken is good." For he thought, "Why not, if there will be peace and security in my days?"

Death of Hezekiah

20 The rest of the deeds of Hezekiah, all his power, how he made the pool and the conduit and brought water into the city, are they not written in the Book of the Annals of the Kings of Judah? [21]Hezekiah slept with his ancestors; and his son Manasseh succeeded him.

21 Manasseh Reigns over Judah

Manasseh was twelve years old when he began to reign; he reigned fifty-five years in Jerusalem. His mother's name was Hephzibah. [2]He did what was evil in the sight of the LORD, following the abominable practices of the nations that the LORD drove out before the people of Israel. [3]For he rebuilt the high places that his father Hezekiah had destroyed; he erected altars for Baal, made a sacred pole,[b] as King Ahab of Israel had done, worshiped all the host of heaven, and served them. [4]He built altars in the house of the LORD, of which the LORD had said, "In Jerusalem I will put my name." [5]He built altars for all the host of heaven in the two courts of the house of the LORD. [6]He made his son pass through fire; he practiced soothsaying and augury, and dealt with mediums and with wizards. He

did much evil in the sight of the LORD, provoking him to anger. [7]The carved image of Asherah that he had made he set in the house of which the LORD said to David and to his son Solomon, "In this house, and in Jerusalem, which I have chosen out of all the tribes of Israel, I will put my name forever; [8]I will not cause the feet of Israel to wander any more out of the land that I gave to their ancestors, if only they will be careful to do according to all that I have commanded them, and according to all the law that my servant Moses commanded them." [9]But they did not listen; Manasseh misled them to do more evil than the nations had done that the LORD destroyed before the people of Israel.

10 The LORD said by his servants the prophets, [11]"Because King Manasseh of Judah has committed these abominations, has done things more wicked than all that the Amorites did, who were before him, and has caused Judah also to sin with his idols; [12]therefore thus says the LORD, the God of Israel, I am bringing upon Jerusalem and Judah such evil that the ears of everyone who hears of it will tingle. [13]I will stretch over Jerusalem the measuring line for Samaria, and the plummet for the house of Ahab; I will wipe Jerusalem as one wipes a dish, wiping it and turning it upside down. [14]I will cast off the remnant of my heritage, and give them into the hand of their enemies; they shall become a prey and a spoil to all their enemies, [15]because they have done what is evil in my sight and have provoked me to anger, since the day their ancestors came out of Egypt, even to this day."

16 Moreover Manasseh shed very much innocent blood, until he had filled Jerusalem from one end to another, besides the sin that he caused Judah to sin so that they did what was evil in the sight of the LORD.

17 Now the rest of the acts of Manasseh, all that he did, and the sin that he committed, are they not written in the Book of the Annals of the Kings of Judah? [18]Manasseh slept with his ancestors, and was buried in the garden of his house, in the garden of Uzza. His son Amon succeeded him.

Amon Reigns over Judah

19 Amon was twenty-two years old when he began to reign; he reigned two years in Jerusalem. His mother's name was Meshullemeth daughter of Haruz of Jotbah. [20]He did what was evil in the sight of the LORD, as his father Manasseh had done.

---

a Gk Vg Syr: Heb *When Hezekiah heard about them*   b Heb *Asherah*

21He walked in all the way in which his father walked, served the idols that his father served, and worshiped them; 22he abandoned the LORD, the God of his ancestors, and did not walk in the way of the LORD. 23The servants of Amon conspired against him, and killed the king in his house. 24But the people of the land killed all those who had conspired against King Amon, and the people of the land made his son Josiah king in place of him. 25Now the rest of the acts of Amon that he did, are they not written in the Book of the Annals of the Kings of Judah? 26He was buried in his tomb in the garden of Uzza; then his son Josiah succeeded him.

Josiah Reigns over Judah

22 Josiah was eight years old when he began to reign; he reigned thirty-one years in Jerusalem. His mother's name was Jedidah daughter of Adaiah of Bozkath. 2He did what was right in the sight of the LORD, and walked in all the way of his father David; he did not turn aside to the right or to the left.

Hilkiah Finds the Book of the Law

3 In the eighteenth year of King Josiah, the king sent Shaphan son of Azaliah, son of Meshullam, the secretary, to the house of the LORD, saying, 4"Go up to the high priest Hilkiah, and have him count the entire sum of the money that has been brought into the house of the LORD, which the keepers of the threshold have collected from the people; 5let it be given into the hand of the workers who have the oversight of the house of the LORD; let them give it to the workers who are at the house of the LORD, repairing the house, 6that is, to the carpenters, to the builders, to the masons; and let them use it to buy timber and quarried stone to repair the house. 7But no accounting shall be asked from them for the money that is delivered into their hand, for they deal honestly."

8 The high priest Hilkiah said to Shaphan the secretary, "I have found the book of the law in the house of the LORD." When Hilkiah gave the book to Shaphan, he read it. 9Then Shaphan the secretary came to the king, and reported to the king, "Your servants have emptied out the money that was found in the house, and have delivered it into the hand of the workers who have oversight of the house of the LORD." 10Shaphan the secretary informed the king, "The priest Hilkiah has given me a book." Shaphan then read it aloud to the king.

11 When the king heard the words of the book of the law, he tore his clothes. 12Then the king commanded the priest Hilkiah, Ahikam son of Shaphan, Achbor son of Micaiah, Shaphan the secretary, and the king's servant Asaiah, saying, 13"Go,

LIVE IT!

Reading and Remembering · 2 Kings 22–23

What happened to the covenant? What happened to the Israelites' true traditions and prayer rituals? After worshiping false gods for so long, it seems as if people forgot about the covenant! Then Hilkiah discovers an old book in the temple (2 Kings 22:8), King Josiah reads it, and a religious renewal is started. Josiah's reform is an effort to know and obey God's law and to restore worship of the one true God. The holy days and holy ways of God are back—at least for a while. (See also 2 Chronicles 34–35.)

Reading can be powerful. Christians have a tremendous tradition of spiritual writings that inspire and renew faith. Spiritual autobiographies like THE CONFESSIONS OF SAINT AUGUSTINE, THE STORY OF A SOUL by Saint Thérèse of Lisieux, and THE SEVEN STOREY MOUNTAIN by Thomas Merton are classics. You might try starting with entertaining fictional books that have strong spiritual messages, like the seven volumes of The Chronicles of Narnia by C. S. Lewis. For other suggestions of spiritual writings you might enjoy, ask a friend, parent, youth leader, teacher, or pastor. Reading can open our eyes to see new things, and wise authors like these can serve as mentors and teachers for us. Reading can point us to new understanding of God's truths and help change our lives, just like Josiah's.

inquire of the LORD for me, for the people, and for all Judah, concerning the words of this book that has been found; for great is the wrath of the LORD that is kindled against us, because our ancestors did not obey the words of this book, to do according to all that is written concerning us."

14 So the priest Hilkiah, Ahikam, Achbor, Shaphan, and Asaiah went to the prophetess Huldah the wife of Shallum son of Tikvah, son of Harhas, keeper of the wardrobe; she resided in Jerusalem in the Second Quarter, where they consulted her. [15]She declared to them, "Thus says the LORD, the God of Israel: Tell the man who sent you to me, [16]Thus says the LORD, I will indeed bring disaster on this place and on its inhabitants—all the words of the book that the king of Judah has read. [17]Because they have abandoned me and have made offerings to other gods, so that they have provoked me to anger with all the work of their hands, therefore my wrath will be kindled against this place, and it will not be quenched. [18]But as to the king of Judah, who sent you to inquire of the LORD, thus shall you say to him, Thus says the LORD, the God of Israel: Regarding the words that you have heard, [19]because your heart was penitent, and you humbled yourself before the LORD, when you heard how I spoke against this place, and against its inhabitants, that they should become a desolation and a curse, and because you have torn your clothes and wept before me, I also have heard you, says the LORD. [20]Therefore, I will gather you to your ancestors, and you shall be gathered to your grave in peace; your eyes shall not see all the disaster that I will bring on this place." They took the message back to the king.

Josiah's Reformation

23 Then the king directed that all the elders of Judah and Jerusalem should be gathered to him. [2]The king went up to the house of the LORD, and with him went all the people of Judah, all the inhabitants of Jerusalem, the priests, the prophets, and all the people, both small and great; he read in their hearing all the words of the book of the covenant that had been found in the house of the LORD. [3]The king stood by the pillar and made a covenant before the LORD, to follow the LORD, keeping his commandments, his decrees, and his statutes, with all his heart and all his soul, to perform the words of this covenant that were written in this book. All the people joined in the covenant.

4 The king commanded the high priest Hilkiah,

the priests of the second order, and the guardians of the threshold, to bring out of the temple of the LORD all the vessels made for Baal, for Asherah, and for all the host of heaven; he burned them outside Jerusalem in the fields of the Kidron, and carried their ashes to Bethel. [5]He deposed the idolatrous priests whom the kings of Judah had ordained to make offerings in the high places at the cities of Judah and around Jerusalem; those also who made offerings to Baal, to the sun, the moon, the constellations, and all the host of the heavens. [6]He brought out the image of[a] Asherah from the house of the LORD, outside Jerusalem, to the Wadi Kidron, burned it at the Wadi Kidron, beat it to dust and threw the dust of it upon the graves of the common people. [7]He broke down the houses of the male temple prostitutes that were in the house of the LORD, where the women did weaving for Asherah. [8]He brought all the priests out of the towns of Judah, and defiled the high places where the priests had made offerings, from Geba to Beer-sheba; he broke down the high places of the gates that were at the entrance of the gate of Joshua the governor of the city, which were on the left at the gate of the city. [9]The priests of the high places, however, did not come up to the altar of the LORD in Jerusalem, but ate unleavened bread among their kindred. [10]He defiled Topheth, which is in the valley of Ben-hinnom, so that no one would make a son or a daughter pass through fire as an offering to Molech. [11]He removed the horses that the kings of Judah had dedicated to the sun, at the entrance to the house of the LORD, by the chamber of the eunuch Nathan-melech, which was in the precincts;[b] then he burned the chariots of the sun with fire. [12]The altars on the roof of the upper chamber of Ahaz, which the kings of Judah had made, and the altars that Manasseh had made in the two courts of the house of the LORD, he pulled down from there and broke in pieces, and threw the rubble into the Wadi Kidron. [13]The king defiled the high places that were east of Jerusalem, to the south of the Mount of Destruction, which King Solomon of Israel had built for Astarte the abomination of the Sidonians, for Chemosh the abomination of Moab, and for Milcom the abomination of the Ammonites. [14]He broke the pillars in pieces, cut down the sacred poles,[c] and covered the sites with human bones.

15 Moreover, the altar at Bethel, the high place erected by Jeroboam son of Nebat, who caused Israel to sin—he pulled down that altar along with the high

a Heb lacks *image of*   b Meaning of Heb uncertain   c Heb *Asherim*

place. He burned the high place, crushing it to dust; he also burned the sacred pole.*ᵃ* ¹⁶As Josiah turned, he saw the tombs there on the mount; and he sent and took the bones out of the tombs, and burned them on the altar, and defiled it, according to the word of the LORD that the man of God proclaimed,*ᵇ* when Jeroboam stood by the altar at the festival; he turned and looked up at the tomb of the man of God who had predicted these things. ¹⁷Then he said, "What is that monument that I see?" The people of the city told him, "It is the tomb of the man of God who came from Judah and predicted these things that you have done against the altar at Bethel." ¹⁸He said, "Let him rest; let no one move his bones." So they let his bones alone, with the bones of the prophet who came out of Samaria. ¹⁹Moreover, Josiah removed all the shrines of the high places that were in the towns of Samaria, which kings of Israel had made, provoking the LORD to anger; he did to them just as he had done at Bethel. ²⁰He slaughtered on the altars all the priests of the high places who were there, and burned human bones on them. Then he returned to Jerusalem.

The Passover Celebrated

21 The king commanded all the people, "Keep the passover to the LORD your God as prescribed in this book of the covenant." ²²No such passover had been kept since the days of the judges who judged Israel, even during all the days of the kings of Israel and of the kings of Judah; ²³but in the eighteenth year of King Josiah this passover was kept to the LORD in Jerusalem.

24 Moreover Josiah put away the mediums, wizards, teraphim,*ᶜ* idols, and all the abominations that were seen in the land of Judah and in Jerusalem, so that he established the words of the law that were written in the book that the priest Hilkiah had found in the house of the LORD. ²⁵Before him there was no king like him, who turned to the LORD with all his heart, with all his soul, and with all his might, according to all the law of Moses; nor did any like him arise after him.

26 Still the LORD did not turn from the fierceness of his great wrath, by which his anger was kindled against Judah, because of all the provocations with which Manasseh had provoked him. ²⁷The LORD said, "I will remove Judah also out of my sight, as I have removed Israel; and I will reject this city that I have chosen, Jerusalem, and the house of which I said, My name shall be there."

Josiah Dies in Battle

28 Now the rest of the acts of Josiah, and all that he did, are they not written in the Book of the Annals of the Kings of Judah? ²⁹In his days Pharaoh Neco king of Egypt went up to the king of Assyria to the river Euphrates. King Josiah went to meet him; but when Pharaoh Neco met him at Megiddo, he killed him. ³⁰His servants carried him dead in a chariot from Megiddo, brought him to Jerusalem, and buried him in his own tomb. The people of the land took Jehoahaz son of Josiah, anointed him, and made him king in place of his father.

Reign and Captivity of Jehoahaz

31 Jehoahaz was twenty-three years old when he began to reign; he reigned three months in Jerusalem. His mother's name was Hamutal daughter of Jeremiah of Libnah. ³²He did what was evil in the sight of the LORD, just as his ancestors had done. ³³Pharaoh Neco confined him at Riblah in the land of Hamath, so that he might not reign in Jerusalem, and imposed tribute on the land of one hundred talents of silver and a talent of gold. ³⁴Pharaoh Neco made Eliakim son of Josiah king in place of his father Josiah, and changed his name to Jehoiakim. But he took Jehoahaz away; he came to Egypt, and died there. ³⁵Jehoiakim gave the silver and the gold to Pharaoh, but he taxed the land in order to meet Pharaoh's demand for money. He exacted the silver and the gold from the people of the land, from all according to their assessment, to give it to Pharaoh Neco.

Jehoiakim Reigns over Judah

36 Jehoiakim was twenty-five years old when he began to reign; he reigned eleven years in Jerusalem. His mother's name was Zebidah daughter of Pedaiah of Rumah. ³⁷He did what was evil in the sight of the LORD, just as all his ancestors had done.

Judah Overrun by Enemies

24 In his days King Nebuchadnezzar of Babylon came up; Jehoiakim became his servant for three years; then he turned and rebelled against him. ²The LORD sent against him bands of the Chaldeans, bands of the Arameans, bands of the Moabites, and bands of the Ammonites; he sent them against Judah to destroy it, according to the word of

a Heb *Asherah*   *b* Gk: Heb *proclaimed, who had predicted these things*   *c* Or *household gods*

the LORD that he spoke by his servants the prophets. ³Surely this came upon Judah at the command of the LORD, to remove them out of his sight, for the sins of Manasseh, for all that he had committed, ⁴and also for the innocent blood that he had shed; for he filled Jerusalem with innocent blood, and the LORD was not willing to pardon. ⁵Now the rest of the deeds of Jehoiakim, and all that he did, are they not written in the Book of the Annals of the Kings of Judah? ⁶So Jehoiakim slept with his ancestors; then his son Jehoiachin succeeded him. ⁷The king of Egypt did not come again out of his land, for the king of Babylon had taken over all that belonged to the king of Egypt from the Wadi of Egypt to the River Euphrates.

Reign and Captivity of Jehoiachin

8 Jehoiachin was eighteen years old when he began to reign; he reigned three months in Jerusalem. His mother's name was Nehushta daughter of Elnathan of Jerusalem. ⁹He did what was evil in the sight of the LORD, just as his father had done.

10 At that time the servants of King Nebuchadnezzar of Babylon came up to Jerusalem, and the city was besieged. ¹¹King Nebuchadnezzar of Babylon came to the city, while his servants were besieging it; ¹²King Jehoiachin of Judah gave himself up to the king of Babylon, himself, his mother, his servants, his officers, and his palace officials. The king of Babylon took him prisoner in the eighth year of his reign.

Capture of Jerusalem

13 He carried off all the treasures of the house of the LORD, and the treasures of the king's house; he cut in pieces all the vessels of gold in the temple of the LORD, which King Solomon of Israel had made, all this as the LORD had foretold. ¹⁴He carried away all Jerusalem, all the officials, all the warriors, ten thousand captives, all the artisans and the smiths; no one remained, except the poorest people of the land. ¹⁵He carried away Jehoiachin to Babylon; the king's mother, the king's wives, his officials, and the elite of the land, he took into captivity from Jerusalem to Babylon. ¹⁶The king of Babylon brought captive to Babylon all the men of valor, seven thousand, the artisans and the smiths, one thousand, all of them strong and fit for war. ¹⁷The king of Babylon made Mattaniah, Jehoiachin's uncle, king in his place, and changed his name to Zedekiah.

Zedekiah Reigns over Judah

18 Zedekiah was twenty-one years old when he began to reign; he reigned eleven years in Jerusalem. His mother's name was Hamutal daughter of Jeremiah of Libnah. ¹⁹He did what was evil in the sight of the LORD, just as Jehoiakim had done. ²⁰Indeed, Jerusalem and Judah so angered the LORD that he expelled them from his presence.

The Fall and Captivity of Judah

Zedekiah rebelled against the king of Babylon. ¹And in the ninth year of his reign, in the tenth month, on the tenth day of the month, King Nebuchadnezzar of Babylon came with all his army against Jerusalem, and laid siege to it; they built siegeworks against it all around. ²So the city was besieged until the eleventh year of King Zedekiah. ³On the ninth day of the fourth month the famine became so severe in the city that there was no food for the people of the land. ⁴Then a breach was made in the city

STUDY IT!

The Fall of Jerusalem
2 Kings 25:1–21

The second conquest and exile described in 2 Kings involves Judah, the southern kingdom. (See "Study It: The First Exile," near 2 Kings 17:5-18, for the first conquest.) Judah was conquered by the Babylonians in 587 B.C., which is why the exile that occurred after it is often referred to as the Babylonian exile. (See Map 8b: "Babylonian Empire.") The author of 1 and 2 Kings implies that the kingdom of Judah lasted longer than the kingdom of Israel, because it had faithful reformer kings like Hezekiah and Josiah. The fall of Judah was particularly devastating, because both Jerusalem (David's city) and the temple (the central place of worship) were destroyed. The whole book of Lamentations is an expression of the sorrow and grief the people experienced as a result.

wall;[a] the king with all the soldiers fled[b] by night by the way of the gate between the two walls, by the king's garden, though the Chaldeans were all around the city. They went in the direction of the Arabah. [5]But the army of the Chaldeans pursued the king, and overtook him in the plains of Jericho; all his army was scattered, deserting him. [6]Then they captured the king and brought him up to the king of Babylon at Riblah, who passed sentence on him. [7]They slaughtered the sons of Zedekiah before his eyes, then put out the eyes of Zedekiah; they bound him in fetters and took him to Babylon.

[8] In the fifth month, on the seventh day of the month—which was the nineteenth year of King Nebuchadnezzar, king of Babylon—Nebuzaradan, the captain of the bodyguard, a servant of the king of Babylon, came to Jerusalem. [9]He burned the house of the LORD, the king's house, and all the houses of Jerusalem; every great house he burned down. [10]All the army of the Chaldeans who were with the captain of the guard broke down the walls around Jerusalem. [11]Nebuzaradan the captain of the guard carried into exile the rest of the people who were left in the city and the deserters who had defected to the king of Babylon—all the rest of the population. [12]But the captain of the guard left some of the poorest people of the land to be vinedressers and tillers of the soil.

[13] The bronze pillars that were in the house of the LORD, as well as the stands and the bronze sea that were in the house of the LORD, the Chaldeans broke in pieces, and carried the bronze to Babylon. [14]They took away the pots, the shovels, the snuffers, the dishes for incense, and all the bronze vessels used in the temple service, [15]as well as the firepans and the basins. What was made of gold the captain of the guard took away for the gold, and what was made of silver, for the silver. [16]As for the two pillars, the one sea, and the stands, which Solomon had made for the house of the LORD, the bronze of all these vessels was beyond weighing. [17]The height of the one pillar was eighteen cubits, and on it was a bronze capital; the height of the capital was three cubits; latticework and pomegranates, all of bronze, were on the capital all around. The second pillar had the same, with the latticework.

[18] The captain of the guard took the chief priest Seraiah, the second priest Zephaniah, and the three

guardians of the threshold; [19]from the city he took an officer who had been in command of the soldiers, and five men of the king's council who were found in the city; the secretary who was the commander of the army who mustered the people of the land; and sixty men of the people of the land who were found in the city. [20]Nebuzaradan the captain of the guard took them, and brought them to the king of Babylon at Riblah. [21]The king of Babylon struck them down and put them to death at Riblah in the land of Hamath. So Judah went into exile out of its land.

Gedaliah Made Governor of Judah

[22] He appointed Gedaliah son of Ahikam son of Shaphan as governor over the people who remained in the land of Judah, whom King Nebuchadnezzar of Babylon had left. [23]Now when all the captains of the forces and their men heard that the king of Babylon had appointed Gedaliah as governor, they came with their men to Gedaliah at Mizpah, namely, Ishmael son of Nethaniah, Johanan son of Kareah, Seraiah son of Tanhumeth the Netophathite, and Jaazaniah son of the Maacathite. [24]Gedaliah swore to them and their men, saying, "Do not be afraid because of the Chaldean officials; live in the land, serve the king of Babylon, and it shall be well with you." [25]But in the seventh month, Ishmael son of Nethaniah son of Elishama, of the royal family, came with ten men; they struck down Gedaliah so that he died, along with the Judeans and Chaldeans who were with him at Mizpah. [26]Then all the people, high and low,[c] and the captains of the forces set out and went to Egypt; for they were afraid of the Chaldeans.

Jehoiachin Released from Prison

[27] In the thirty-seventh year of the exile of King Jehoiachin of Judah, in the twelfth month, on the twenty-seventh day of the month, King Evilmerodach of Babylon, in the year that he began to reign, released King Jehoiachin of Judah from prison; [28]he spoke kindly to him, and gave him a seat above the other seats of the kings who were with him in Babylon. [29]So Jehoiachin put aside his prison clothes. Every day of his life he dined regularly in the king's presence. [30]For his allowance, a regular allowance was given him by the king, a portion every day, as long as he lived.

---

a Heb lacks *wall*   b Gk Compare Jer 39.4; 52.7: Heb lacks *the king* and lacks *fled*   c Or *young and old*

1 Chronicles

"Wait! That's not the way I saw it!" There is always more than one version of a story. Any two people can witness the exact same thing and have different interpretations. The books of 1 and 2 Chronicles (originally one book) present the history of the Israelites from a different perspective than the history told in the books of Joshua through 2 Kings. Chronicles was written at a later date, and the lessons this generation draws from the past are different than those drawn by the generations before them. In contrast to the previous account, Chronicles tends to downplay the covenant. Instead, it emphasizes the importance of worship in the spiritual formation of God's people.

IN DEPTH

The Chronicler is the name given to the unknown author (or authors) of 1 and 2 Chronicles. The Chronicler has a unique perspective, writing after the Israelites' return from the exile in Babylon, and almost never mentions the Sinai covenant (the Ten Commandments) or Moses (central themes throughout other parts of the Old Testament). The Israelites still hope to have their own king, and the Chronicler makes it clear that they must stay faithful in worship in order for God's promises regarding land and kingship to be fulfilled.

The Chronicler uses two types of material: genealogies and legends edited to emphasize the Chronicler's point. Both summarize Israel's history from the Creation to around 538 B.C., but focus primarily on the kings David and Solomon. Those kings are praised extensively because of their role in centralizing worship in Jerusalem and building the temple. Many of the negative stories about David from 2 Samuel—such as his affair with Bathsheba—are not even mentioned. The Chronicler wants nothing to tarnish the people's memory of an ideal kingdom that might one day be restored.

Second Chronicles also focuses on the southern kingdom, Judah, and ignores the northern kingdom, Israel, after Solomon's death. This may well be due to a bias of the priestly class in Jerusalem against the religious practice of the northern tribes. This bias lasted into Jesus' time.

The goal of 1 and 2 Chronicles was to give the Israelites hope for the future after returning from exile in Babylon. The Chronicler reminds them that if they maintain their religious practices and worship of God, they will continue to be God's people.

From Adam to Abraham

1 Adam, Seth, Enosh; [2]Kenan, Mahalalel, Jared; [3]Enoch, Methuselah, Lamech; [4]Noah, Shem, Ham, and Japheth.

5 The descendants of Japheth: Gomer, Magog, Madai, Javan, Tubal, Meshech, and Tiras. [6]The descendants of Gomer: Ashkenaz, Diphath,[a] and Togarmah. [7]The descendants of Javan: Elishah, Tarshish, Kittim, and Rodanim.[b]

8 The descendants of Ham: Cush, Egypt, Put, and Canaan. [9]The descendants of Cush: Seba, Havilah, Sabta, Raama, and Sabteca. The descendants of Raamah: Sheba and Dedan. [10]Cush became the father of Nimrod; he was the first to be a mighty one on the earth.

11 Egypt became the father of Ludim, Anamim, Lehabim, Naphtuhim, [12]Pathrusim, Casluhim, and Caphtorim, from whom the Philistines come.[c]

13 Canaan became the father of Sidon his firstborn, and Heth, [14]and the Jebusites, the Amorites, the Girgashites, [15]the Hivites, the Arkites, the Sinites, [16]the Arvadites, the Zemarites, and the Hamathites.

17 The descendants of Shem: Elam, Asshur, Arpachshad, Lud, Aram, Uz, Hul, Gether, and Meshech.[d] [18]Arpachshad became the father of Shelah; and Shelah became the father of Eber. [19]To Eber were born two sons: the name of the one was Peleg (for in his days the earth was divided), and the name of his brother Joktan. [20]Joktan became the father of Almodad, Sheleph, Hazarmaveth, Jerah, [21]Hadoram, Uzal, Diklah, [22]Ebal, Abimael, Sheba, [23]Ophir, Havilah, and Jobab; all these were the descendants of Joktan.

24 Shem, Arpachshad, Shelah; [25]Eber, Peleg, Reu; [26]Serug, Nahor, Terah; [27]Abram, that is, Abraham.

From Abraham to Jacob

28 The sons of Abraham: Isaac and Ishmael. [29]These are their genealogies: the firstborn of Ishmael, Nebaioth; and Kedar, Adbeel, Mibsam, [30]Mishma, Dumah, Massa, Hadad, Tema, [31]Jetur, Naphish, and Kedemah. These are the sons of Ishmael. [32]The sons of Keturah, Abraham's concubine: she bore Zimran, Jokshan, Medan, Midian, Ishbak, and Shuah. The sons of Jokshan: Sheba and Dedan. [33]The sons of Midian: Ephah, Epher, Hanoch, Abida, and Eldaah. All these were the descendants of Keturah.

34 Abraham became the father of Isaac. The sons of Isaac: Esau and Israel. [35]The sons of Esau: Eliphaz, Reuel, Jeush, Jalam, and Korah. [36]The sons of Eliphaz: Teman, Omar, Zephi, Gatam, Kenaz, Timna, and Amalek. [37]The sons of Reuel: Nahath, Zerah, Shammah, and Mizzah.

38 The sons of Seir: Lotan, Shobal, Zibeon, Anah, Dishon, Ezer, and Dishan. [39]The sons of Lotan: Hori and Homam; and Lotan's sister was Timna. [40]The sons of Shobal: Alian, Manahath, Ebal, Shephi, and Onam. The sons of Zibeon: Aiah and Anah. [41]The sons of Anah: Dishon. The sons of Dishon: Hamran, Eshban, Ithran, and Cheran. [42]The sons of Ezer: Bilhan, Zaavan, and Jaakan.[e] The sons of Dishan:[f] Uz and Aran.

43 These are the kings who reigned in the land of Edom before any king reigned over the Israelites: Bela son of Beor, whose city was called Dinhabah. [44]When Bela died, Jobab son of Zerah of Bozrah succeeded him. [45]When Jobab died, Husham of the land of the Temanites succeeded him. [46]When Husham died, Hadad son of Bedad, who defeated Midian in the country of Moab, succeeded him; and the name of his city was Avith. [47]When Hadad died, Samlah of Masrekah succeeded him. [48]When Samlah died, Shaul[g] of Rehoboth on the Euphrates succeeded him. [49]When Shaul[g] died, Baal-hanan son of Achbor succeeded him. [50]When Baal-hanan died, Hadad succeeded him; the name of his city was Pai, and his wife's name Mehetabel daughter of Matred, daughter of Me-zahab. [51]And Hadad died.

The clans[h] of Edom were: clans[h] Timna, Aliah,[i] Jetheth, [52]Oholibamah, Elah, Pinon, [53]Kenaz, Teman, Mibzar, [54]Magdiel, and Iram; these are the clans[h] of Edom.

2 The Sons of Israel and the Descendants of Judah

These are the sons of Israel: Reuben, Simeon, Levi, Judah, Issachar, Zebulun, [2]Dan, Joseph, Benjamin, Naphtali, Gad, and Asher. [3]The sons of Judah: Er, Onan, and Shelah; these three the Canaanite woman Bath-shua bore to him. Now Er, Judah's firstborn, was wicked in the sight of the LORD, and he put him to death. [4]His daughter-in-law Tamar also bore him Perez and Zerah. Judah had five sons in all.

5 The sons of Perez: Hezron and Hamul. [6]The sons of Zerah: Zimri, Ethan, Heman, Calcol, and Dara,[j] five in all. [7]The sons of Carmi: Achar, the troubler of Israel, who transgressed in the matter of the devoted thing; [8]and Ethan's son was Azariah.

---

a Gen 10.3 *Ripath;* See Gk Vg b Gen 10.4 *Dodanim;* See Syr Vg c Heb *Casluhim, from which the Philistines come, Caphtorim;* See Am 9.7, Jer 47.4
d *Mash* in Gen 10.23 e Or *and Akan;* See Gen 36.27 f See 1.38: Heb *Dishon* g Or *Saul* h Or *chiefs* i Or *Alvah;* See Gen 36.40 j Or *Darda;*
Compare Syr Tg some Gk Mss; See 1 Kings 4.31

9 The sons of Hezron, who were born to him: Jerahmeel, Ram, and Chelubai. [10]Ram became the father of Amminadab, and Amminadab became the father of Nahshon, prince of the sons of Judah. [11]Nahshon became the father of Salma, Salma of Boaz, [12]Boaz of Obed, Obed of Jesse. [13]Jesse became the father of Eliab his firstborn, Abinadab the second, Shimea the third, [14]Nethanel the fourth, Raddai the fifth, [15]Ozem the sixth, David the seventh; [16]and their sisters were Zeruiah and Abigail. The sons of Zeruiah: Abishai, Joab, and Asahel, three. [17]Abigail bore Amasa, and the father of Amasa was Jether the Ishmaelite.

18 Caleb son of Hezron had children by his wife Azubah, and by Jerioth; these were her sons: Jesher, Shobab, and Ardon. [19]When Azubah died, Caleb married Ephrath, who bore him Hur. [20]Hur became the father of Uri, and Uri became the father of Bezalel.

21 Afterward Hezron went in to the daughter of Machir father of Gilead, whom he married when he was sixty years old; and she bore him Segub; [22]and Segub became the father of Jair, who had twenty-three towns in the land of Gilead. [23]But Geshur and Aram took from them Havvoth-jair, Kenath and its villages, sixty towns. All these were descendants of Machir, father of Gilead. [24]After the death of Hezron, in Caleb-ephrathah, Abijah wife of Hezron bore him Ashhur, father of Tekoa.

25 The sons of Jerahmeel, the firstborn of Hezron: Ram his firstborn, Bunah, Oren, Ozem, and Ahijah. [26]Jerahmeel also had another wife, whose name was Atarah; she was the mother of Onam. [27]The sons of Ram, the firstborn of Jerahmeel: Maaz, Jamin, and Eker. [28]The sons of Onam: Shammai and Jada. The sons of Shammai: Nadab and Abishur. [29]The name of Abishur's wife was Abihail, and she bore him Ahban and Molid. [30]The sons of Nadab: Seled and Appaim; and Seled died childless. [31]The son[a] of Appaim: Ishi. The son[a] of Ishi: Sheshan. The son[a] of Sheshan: Ahlai. [32]The sons of Jada, Shammai's brother: Jether and Jonathan; and Jether died childless. [33]The sons of Jonathan: Peleth and Zaza. These were the descendants of Jerahmeel. [34]Now Sheshan had no sons, only daughters; but Sheshan had an Egyptian slave, whose name was Jarha. [35]So Sheshan gave his daughter in marriage to his slave Jarha; and she bore him Attai. [36]Attai became the father of Nathan, and Nathan of Zabad. [37]Zabad became the father of Ephlal, and Ephlal of Obed. [38]Obed became

the father of Jehu, and Jehu of Azariah. [39]Azariah became the father of Helez, and Helez of Eleasah. [40]Eleasah became the father of Sismai, and Sismai of Shallum. [41]Shallum became the father of Jekamiah, and Jekamiah of Elishama.

42 The sons of Caleb brother of Jerahmeel: Mesha[b] his firstborn, who was father of Ziph. The sons of Mareshah father of Hebron. [43]The sons of Hebron: Korah, Tappuah, Rekem, and Shema. [44]Shema became father of Raham, father of Jorkeam; and Rekem became the father of Shammai. [45]The son of Shammai: Maon; and Maon was the father of Beth-zur. [46]Ephah also, Caleb's concubine, bore Haran, Moza, and Gazez; and Haran became the father of Gazez. [47]The sons of Jahdai: Regem, Jotham, Geshan, Pelet, Ephah, and Shaaph. [48]Maacah, Caleb's concubine, bore Sheber and Tirhanah. [49]She also bore Shaaph father of Madmannah, Sheva father of Machbenah and father of Gibea; and the daughter of Caleb was Achsah. [50]These were the descendants of Caleb.

The sons[c] of Hur the firstborn of Ephrathah: Shobal father of Kiriath-jearim, [51]Salma father of Bethlehem, and Hareph father of Beth-gader. [52]Shobal father of Kiriath-jearim had other sons: Haroeh, half of the Menuhoth. [53]And the families of Kiriath-jearim: the Ithrites, the Puthites, the Shumathites, and the Mishraites; from these came the Zorathites and the Eshtaolites. [54]The sons of Salma: Bethlehem, the Netophathites, Atroth-beth-joab, and half of the Manahathites, the Zorites. [55]The families also of the scribes that lived at Jabez: the Tirathites, the Shimeathites, and the Sucathites. These are the Kenites who came from Hammath, father of the house of Rechab.

Descendants of David and Solomon

3 These are the sons of David who were born to him in Hebron: the firstborn Amnon, by Ahinoam the Jezreelite; the second Daniel, by Abigail the Carmelite; [2]the third Absalom, son of Maacah, daughter of King Talmai of Geshur; the fourth Adonijah, son of Haggith; [3]the fifth Shephatiah, by Abital; the sixth Ithream, by his wife Eglah; [4]six were born to him in Hebron, where he reigned for seven years and six months. And he reigned thirty-three years in Jerusalem. [5]These were born to him in Jerusalem: Shimea, Shobab, Nathan, and Solomon, four by Bath-shua, daughter of Ammiel; [6]then Ibhar, Elishama, Eliphelet, [7]Nogah, Nepheg, Japhia,

---

a Heb *sons*   **b** Gk reads *Mareshah*   **c** Gk Vg: Heb *son*

[8]Elishama, Eliada, and Eliphelet, nine. [9]All these were David's sons, besides the sons of the concubines; and Tamar was their sister.

10 The descendants of Solomon: Rehoboam, Abijah his son, Asa his son, Jehoshaphat his son, [11]Joram his son, Ahaziah his son, Joash his son, [12]Amaziah his son, Azariah his son, Jotham his son, [13]Ahaz his son, Hezekiah his son, Manasseh his son, [14]Amon his son, Josiah his son. [15]The sons of Josiah: Johanan the firstborn, the second Jehoiakim, the third Zedekiah, the fourth Shallum. [16]The descendants of Jehoiakim: Jeconiah his son, Zedekiah his son; [17]and the sons of Jeconiah, the captive: Shealtiel his son, [18]Malchiram, Pedaiah, Shenazzar, Jekamiah, Hoshama, and Nedabiah; [19]The sons of Pedaiah: Zerubbabel and Shimei; and the sons of Zerubbabel: Meshullam and Hananiah, and Shelomith was their sister; [20]and Hashubah, Ohel, Berechiah, Hasadiah, and Jushab-hesed, five. [21]The sons of Hananiah: Pelatiah and Jeshaiah, his son[a] Rephaiah, his son[a] Arnan, his son[a] Obadiah, his son[a] Shecaniah. [22]The son[b] of Shecaniah: Shemaiah. And the sons of Shemaiah: Hattush, Igal, Bariah, Neariah, and Shaphat, six. [23]The sons of Neariah: Elioenai, Hizkiah, and Azrikam, three. [24]The sons of Elioenai: Hodaviah, Eliashib, Pelaiah, Akkub, Johanan, Delaiah, and Anani, seven.

Descendants of Judah

4 The sons of Judah: Perez, Hezron, Carmi, Hur, and Shobal. [2]Reaiah son of Shobal became the father of Jahath, and Jahath became the father of Ahumai and Lahad. These were the families of the Zorathites. [3]These were the sons[c] of Etam: Jezreel, Ishma, and Idbash; and the name of their sister was Hazzelelponi, [4]and Penuel was the father of Gedor, and Ezer the father of Hushah. These were the sons of Hur, the firstborn of Ephrathah, the father of Bethlehem. [5]Ashhur father of Tekoa had two wives, Helah and Naarah; [6]Naarah bore him Ahuzzam, Hepher, Temeni, and Haahashtari.[d] These were the sons of Naarah. [7]The sons of Helah: Zereth, Izhar,[e] and Ethnan. [8]Koz became the father of Anub, Zobebah, and the families of Aharhel son of Harum. [9]Jabez was honored more than his brothers; and his mother named him Jabez, saying, "Because I bore him in pain." [10]Jabez called on the God of Israel, saying, "Oh that you would bless me and enlarge my border, and that your hand might be with me, and that you would keep me from hurt and harm!" And God granted what he asked. [11]Chelub the brother of Shuhah became the father of Mehir, who was the father of Eshton. [12]Eshton became the father of Beth-rapha, Paseah, and Tehinnah the father of Ir-nahash. These are the men of Recah. [13]The sons of Kenaz: Othniel and Seraiah; and the sons of Othniel: Hathath and Meonothai.[f] [14]Meonothai became the father of Ophrah; and Seraiah became the father of Joab father of Ge-harashim,[g] so-called because they were artisans. [15]The sons of Caleb son of Jephunneh: Iru, Elah, and Naam; and the son[b] of Elah: Kenaz. [16]The sons of Jehallelel: Ziph, Ziphah, Tiria, and Asarel. [17]The sons of Ezrah: Jether, Mered, Epher, and Jalon. These are the sons of Bithiah, daughter of Pharaoh, whom Mered married;[h] and she conceived and bore[i] Miriam, Shammai, and Ishbah father of Eshtemoa. [18]And his Judean wife bore Jered father of Gedor, Heber father of Soco, and Jekuthiel father of Zanoah. [19]The sons of the wife of Hodiah, the sister of Naham, were the fathers of Keilah the Garmite and Eshtemoa the Maacathite. [20]The sons of Shimon: Amnon, Rinnah, Ben-hanan, and Tilon. The sons of Ishi: Zoheth and Ben-zoheth. [21]The sons of Shelah son of Judah: Er father of Lecah, Laadah father of Mareshah, and the families of the guild of linen workers at Beth-ashbea; [22]and Jokim, and the men of Cozeba, and Joash, and Saraph, who married into Moab but returned to Lehem[j] (now the records[k] are ancient). [23]These were the potters and inhabitants of Netaim and Gederah; they lived there with the king in his service.

Descendants of Simeon

24 The sons of Simeon: Nemuel, Jamin, Jarib, Zerah, Shaul;[l] [25]Shallum was his son, Mibsam his son, Mishma his son. [26]The sons of Mishma: Hammuel his son, Zaccur his son, Shimei his son. [27]Shimei had sixteen sons and six daughters; but his brothers did not have many children, nor did all their family multiply like the Judeans. [28]They lived in Beer-sheba, Moladah, Hazar-shual, [29]Bilhah, Ezem, Tolad, [30]Bethuel, Hormah, Ziklag, [31]Beth-marcaboth, Hazar-susim, Beth-biri, and Shaaraim. These were their towns until David became king. [32]And their villages were Etam, Ain, Rimmon, Tochen, and Ashan, five towns, [33]along with all their villages that were around these towns as far as Baal. These were their settlements. And they kept a genealogical record.

---

a Gk Compare Syr Vg: Heb *sons of* b Heb *sons* c Gk Compare Vg: Heb *the father* d Or *Ahashtari* e Another reading is *Zohar* f Gk Vg: Heb lacks *and Meonothai* g That is *Valley of artisans* h The clause: *These are ... married* is transposed from verse 18 i Heb lacks *and bore* j Vg Compare Gk: Heb *and Jashubi-lehem* k Or *matters* l Or *Saul*

STUDY IT!

Genealogies · 1 Chronicles 1–9

Look at all these names! The first nine chapters of 1 Chronicles consist entirely of family trees, or genealogies, tracing the history of Israel from Adam to Saul. It was essential to be able to trace one's tribal roots in a culture where not only money and identity, but also the offices of priest and king, passed from one generation to another.

The many genealogies of the Old Testament answer important questions. How were the various tribes related to one another? Who were a particular tribe's ancestors? What right did a certain group or person have to the office of priest or king? The Chronicler lists the genealogies of King David and the priest Levi in considerable detail. The kingship and the priesthood were clearly of special interest to him. To trace the genealogy of Jesus, read **Matthew 1:1–17.**

34 Meshobab, Jamlech, Joshah son of Amaziah, [35]Joel, Jehu son of Joshibiah son of Seraiah son of Asiel, [36]Elioenai, Jaakobah, Jeshohaiah, Asaiah, Adiel, Jesimiel, Benaiah, [37]Ziza son of Shiphi son of Allon son of Jedaiah son of Shimri son of Shemaiah— [38]these mentioned by name were leaders in their families, and their clans increased greatly. [39]They journeyed to the entrance of Gedor, to the east side of the valley, to seek pasture for their flocks, [40]where they found rich, good pasture, and the land was very broad, quiet, and peaceful; for the former inhabitants there belonged to Ham. [41]These, registered by name, came in the days of King Hezekiah of Judah, and attacked their tents and the Meunim who were found there, and exterminated them to this day, and settled in their place, because there was pasture there for their flocks. [42]And some of them, five hundred men of the Simeonites, went to Mount Seir, having as their leaders Pelatiah, Neariah, Rephaiah, and Uzziel, sons of Ishi; [43]they destroyed the remnant of the Amalekites that had escaped, and they have lived there to this day.

Descendants of Reuben

5 The sons of Reuben the firstborn of Israel. (He was the firstborn, but because he defiled his father's bed his birthright was given to the sons of Joseph son of Israel, so that he is not enrolled in the genealogy according to the birthright; [2]though Judah became prominent among his brothers and a ruler came from him, yet the birthright belonged to Joseph.) [3]The sons of Reuben, the firstborn of Israel: Hanoch, Pallu, Hezron, and Carmi. [4]The sons of Joel: Shemaiah his son, Gog his son, Shimei his son,

[5]Micah his son, Reaiah his son, Baal his son, [6]Beerah his son, whom King Tilgath-pilneser of Assyria carried away into exile; he was a chieftain of the Reubenites. [7]And his kindred by their families, when the genealogy of their generations was reckoned: the chief, Jeiel, and Zechariah, [8]and Bela son of Azaz, son of Shema, son of Joel, who lived in Aroer, as far as Nebo and Baal-meon. [9]He also lived to the east as far as the beginning of the desert this side of the Euphrates, because their cattle had multiplied in the land of Gilead. [10]And in the days of Saul they made war on the Hagrites, who fell by their hand; and they lived in their tents throughout all the region east of Gilead.

Descendants of Gad

11 The sons of Gad lived beside them in the land of Bashan as far as Salecah: [12]Joel the chief, Shapham the second, Janai, and Shaphat in Bashan. [13]And their kindred according to their clans: Michael, Meshullam, Sheba, Jorai, Jacan, Zia, and Eber, seven. [14]These were the sons of Abihail son of Huri, son of Jaroah, son of Gilead, son of Michael, son of Jeshishai, son of Jahdo, son of Buz; [15]Ahi son of Abdiel, son of Guni, was chief in their clan; [16]and they lived in Gilead, in Bashan and in its towns, and in all the pasture lands of Sharon to their limits. [17]All of these were enrolled by genealogies in the days of King Jotham of Judah, and in the days of King Jeroboam of Israel.

18 The Reubenites, the Gadites, and the half-tribe of Manasseh had valiant warriors, who carried shield and sword, and drew the bow, expert in war, forty-four thousand seven hundred sixty, ready for service.

[19]They made war on the Hagrites, Jetur, Naphish, and Nodab; [20]and when they received help against them, the Hagrites and all who were with them were given into their hands, for they cried to God in the battle, and he granted their entreaty because they trusted in him. [21]They captured their livestock: fifty thousand of their camels, two hundred fifty thousand sheep, two thousand donkeys, and one hundred thousand captives. [22]Many fell slain, because the war was of God. And they lived in their territory until the exile.

The Half-Tribe of Manasseh

23 The members of the half-tribe of Manasseh lived in the land; they were very numerous from Bashan to Baal-hermon, Senir, and Mount Hermon. [24]These were the heads of their clans: Epher,[a] Ishi, Eliel, Azriel, Jeremiah, Hodaviah, and Jahdiel, mighty warriors, famous men, heads of their clans. [25]But they transgressed against the God of their ancestors, and prostituted themselves to the gods of the peoples of the land, whom God had destroyed before them. [26]So the God of Israel stirred up the spirit of King Pul of Assyria, the spirit of King Tilgath-pilneser of Assyria, and he carried them away, namely, the Reubenites, the Gadites, and the half-tribe of Manasseh, and brought them to Halah, Habor, Hara, and the river Gozan, to this day.

Descendants of Levi

6 [b]The sons of Levi: Gershom,[c] Kohath, and Merari. [2]The sons of Kohath: Amram, Izhar, Hebron, and Uzziel. [3]The children of Amram: Aaron, Moses, and Miriam. The sons of Aaron: Nadab, Abihu, Eleazar, and Ithamar. [4]Eleazar became the father of Phinehas, Phinehas of Abishua, [5]Abishua of Bukki, Bukki of Uzzi, [6]Uzzi of Zerahiah, Zerahiah of Meraioth, [7]Meraioth of Amariah, Amariah of Ahitub, [8]Ahitub of Zadok, Zadok of Ahimaaz, [9]Ahimaaz of Azariah, Azariah of Johanan, [10]and Johanan of Azariah (it was he who served as priest in the house that Solomon built in Jerusalem). [11]Azariah became the father of Amariah, Amariah of Ahitub, [12]Ahitub of Zadok, Zadok of Shallum, [13]Shallum of Hilkiah, Hilkiah of Azariah, [14]Azariah of Seraiah, Seraiah of Jehozadak; [15]and Jehozadak went into exile when the LORD sent Judah and Jerusalem into exile by the hand of Nebuchadnezzar.

[16][d]The sons of Levi: Gershom, Kohath, and Merari. [17]These are the names of the sons of Gershom: Libni and Shimei. [18]The sons of Kohath: Amram, Izhar, Hebron, and Uzziel. [19]The sons of Merari: Mahli and Mushi. These are the clans of the Levites according to their ancestry. [20]Of Gershom: Libni his son, Jahath his son, Zimmah his son, [21]Joah his son, Iddo his son, Zerah his son, Jeatherai his son. [22]The sons of Kohath: Amminadab his son, Korah his son, Assir his son, [23]Elkanah his son, Ebiasaph his son, Assir his son, [24]Tahath his son, Uriel his son, Uzziah his son, and Shaul his son. [25]The sons of Elkanah: Amasai and Ahimoth, [26]Elkanah his son, Zophai his son, Nahath his son, [27]Eliab his son, Jeroham his son, Elkanah his son. [28]The sons of Samuel: Joel[e] his firstborn, the second Abijah.[f] [29]The sons of Merari: Mahli, Libni his son, Shimei his son, Uzzah his son, [30]Shimea his son, Haggiah his son, and Asaiah his son.

Musicians Appointed by David

31 These are the men whom David put in charge of the service of song in the house of the LORD, after the ark came to rest there. [32]They ministered with song before the tabernacle of the tent of meeting, until Solomon had built the house of the LORD in Jerusalem; and they performed their service in due order. [33]These are the men who served; and their sons were: Of the Kohathites: Heman, the singer, son of Joel, son of Samuel, [34]son of Elkanah, son of Jeroham, son of Eliel, son of Toah, [35]son of Zuph, son of Elkanah, son of Mahath, son of Amasai, [36]of Elkanah, son of Joel, son of Azariah, son of Zephaniah, [37]son of Tahath, son of Assir, son of Ebiasaph, son of Korah, [38]son of Izhar, son of Kohath, son of Levi, son of Israel; [39]and his brother Asaph, who stood on his right, namely, Asaph son of Berechiah, son of Shimea, [40]son of Michael, son of Baaseiah, son of Malchijah, [41]son of Ethni, son of Zerah, son of Adaiah, [42]son of Ethan, son of Zimmah, son of Shimei, [43]son of Jahath, son of Gershom, son of Levi. [44]On the left were their kindred the sons of Merari: Ethan son of Kishi, son of Abdi, son of Malluch,

---

a Gk Vg: Heb and Epher b Ch 5.27 in Heb c Heb Gershon, variant of Gershom; See 6.16 d Ch 6.1 in Heb e Gk Syr Compare verse 33 and 1 Sam 8.2: Heb lacks Joel f Heb reads Vashni, and Abijah for the second Abijah, taking the second as a proper name

[45]son of Hashabiah, son of Amaziah, son of Hilkiah, [46]son of Amzi, son of Bani, son of Shemer, [47]son of Mahli, son of Mushi, son of Merari, son of Levi; [48]and their kindred the Levites were appointed for all the service of the tabernacle of the house of God.

49 But Aaron and his sons made offerings on the altar of burnt offering and on the altar of incense, doing all the work of the most holy place, to make atonement for Israel, according to all that Moses the servant of God had commanded. [50]These are the sons of Aaron: Eleazar his son, Phinehas his son, Abishua his son, [51]Bukki his son, Uzzi his son, Zerahiah his son, [52]Meraioth his son, Amariah his son, Ahitub his son, [53]Zadok his son, Ahimaaz his son.

Settlements of the Levites

54 These are their dwelling places according to their settlements within their borders: to the sons of Aaron of the families of Kohathites—for the lot fell to them first— [55]to them they gave Hebron in the land of Judah and its surrounding pasture lands, [56]but the fields of the city and its villages they gave to Caleb son of Jephunneh. [57]To the sons of Aaron they gave the cities of refuge: Hebron, Libnah with its pasture lands, Jattir, Eshtemoa with its pasture lands, [58]Hilen[a] with its pasture lands, Debir with its pasture lands, [59]Ashan with its pasture lands, and Beth-shemesh with its pasture lands. [60]From the tribe of Benjamin, Geba with its pasture lands, Alemeth with its pasture lands, and Anathoth with its pasture lands. All their towns throughout their families were thirteen.

61 To the rest of the Kohathites were given by lot out of the family of the tribe, out of the half-tribe, the half of Manasseh, ten towns. [62]To the Gershomites according to their families were allotted thirteen towns out of the tribes of Issachar, Asher, Naphtali, and Manasseh in Bashan. [63]To the Merarites according to their families were allotted twelve towns out of the tribes of Reuben, Gad, and Zebulun. [64]So the people of Israel gave the Levites the towns with their pasture lands. [65]They also gave them by lot out of the tribes of Judah, Simeon, and Benjamin these towns that are mentioned by name.

66 And some of the families of the sons of Kohath had towns of their territory out of the tribe of Ephraim. [67]They were given the cities of refuge: Shechem with its pasture lands in the hill country of Ephraim, Gezer with its pasture lands, [68]Jokmeam with its pasture lands, Beth-horon with its pasture lands, [69]Aijalon with its pasture lands, Gath-rimmon with its pasture lands; [70]and out of the half-tribe of Manasseh, Aner with its pasture lands, and Bileam with its pasture lands, for the rest of the families of the Kohathites.

71 To the Gershomites: out of the half-tribe of Manasseh: Golan in Bashan with its pasture lands and Ashtaroth with its pasture lands; [72]and out of the tribe of Issachar: Kedesh with its pasture lands, Daberath[b] with its pasture lands, [73]Ramoth with its pasture lands, and Anem with its pasture lands; [74]out of the tribe of Asher: Mashal with its pasture lands, Abdon with its pasture lands, [75]Hukok with its pasture lands, and Rehob with its pasture lands; [76]and out of the tribe of Naphtali: Kedesh in Galilee with its pasture lands, Hammon with its pasture lands, and Kiriathaim with its pasture lands. [77]To the rest of the Merarites out of the tribe of Zebulun: Rimmono with its pasture lands, Tabor with its pasture lands, [78]and across the Jordan from Jericho, on the east side of the Jordan, out of the tribe of Reuben: Bezer in the steppe with its pasture lands, Jahzah with its pasture lands, [79]Kedemoth with its pasture lands, and Mephaath with its pasture lands; [80]and out of the tribe of Gad: Ramoth in Gilead with its pasture lands, Mahanaim with its pasture lands, [81]Heshbon with its pasture lands, and Jazer with its pasture lands.

Descendants of Issachar

7 The sons[c] of Issachar: Tola, Puah, Jashub, and Shimron, four. [2]The sons of Tola: Uzzi, Rephaiah, Jeriel, Jahmai, Ibsam, and Shemuel, heads of their ancestral houses, namely of Tola, mighty warriors of their generations, their number in the days of David being twenty-two thousand six hundred. [3]The son[d] of Uzzi: Izrahiah. And the sons of Izrahiah: Michael, Obadiah, Joel, and Isshiah, five, all of them chiefs; [4]and along with them, by their generations, according to their ancestral houses, were units of the fighting force, thirty-six thousand, for they had many wives and sons. [5]Their kindred belonging to all the families of Issachar were in all eighty-seven thousand mighty warriors, enrolled by genealogy.

Descendants of Benjamin

6 The sons of Benjamin: Bela, Becher, and Jediael, three. [7]The sons of Bela: Ezbon, Uzzi, Uzziel, Jerimoth, and Iri, five, heads of ancestral houses, mighty warriors; and their enrollment by genealogies was

---

a Other readings *Hilez, Holon;* See Josh 21.15   b Or *Dobrath*   c Syr Compare Vg: Heb *And to the sons*   d Heb *sons*

twenty-two thousand thirty-four. [8]The sons of Becher: Zemirah, Joash, Eliezer, Elioenai, Omri, Jeremoth, Abijah, Anathoth, and Alemeth. All these were the sons of Becher; [9]and their enrollment by genealogies, according to their generations, as heads of their ancestral houses, mighty warriors, was twenty thousand two hundred. [10]The sons of Jediael: Bilhan. And the sons of Bilhan: Jeush, Benjamin, Ehud, Chenaanah, Zethan, Tarshish, and Ahishahar. [11]All these were the sons of Jediael according to the heads of their ancestral houses, mighty warriors, seventeen thousand two hundred, ready for service in war. [12]And Shuppim and Huppim were the sons of Ir, Hushim the son[a] of Aher.

Descendants of Naphtali

13 The descendants of Naphtali: Jahziel, Guni, Jezer, and Shallum, the descendants of Bilhah.

Descendants of Manasseh

14 The sons of Manasseh: Asriel, whom his Aramean concubine bore; she bore Machir the father of Gilead. [15]And Machir took a wife for Huppim and for Shuppim. The name of his sister was Maacah. And the name of the second was Zelophehad; and Zelophehad had daughters. [16]Maacah the wife of Machir bore a son, and she named him Peresh; the name of his brother was Sheresh; and his sons were Ulam and Rekem. [17]The son[a] of Ulam: Bedan. These were the sons of Gilead son of Machir, son of Manasseh. [18]And his sister Hammolecheth bore Ishhod, Abiezer, and Mahlah. [19]The sons of Shemida were Ahian, Shechem, Likhi, and Aniam.

Descendants of Ephraim

20 The sons of Ephraim: Shuthelah, and Bered his son, Tahath his son, Eleadah his son, Tahath his son, [21]Zabad his son, Shuthelah his son, and Ezer and Elead. Now the people of Gath, who were born in the land, killed them, because they came down to raid their cattle. [22]And their father Ephraim mourned many days, and his brothers came to comfort him. [23]Ephraim[b] went in to his wife, and she conceived and bore a son; and he named him Beriah, because disaster[c] had befallen his house. [24]His daughter was Sheerah, who built both Lower and Upper Beth-horon, and Uzzen-sheerah. [25]Rephah was his son, Resheph his son, Telah his son, Tahan his son, [26]Ladan his son, Ammihud his son, Elishama his son, [27]Nun[d] his son, Joshua his son. [28]Their posses-

sions and settlements were Bethel and its towns, and eastward Naaran, and westward Gezer and its towns, Shechem and its towns, as far as Ayyah and its towns; [29]also along the borders of the Manassites, Beth-shean and its towns, Taanach and its towns, Megiddo and its towns, Dor and its towns. In these lived the sons of Joseph son of Israel.

Descendants of Asher

30 The sons of Asher: Imnah, Ishvah, Ishvi, Beriah, and their sister Serah. [31]The sons of Beriah: Heber and Malchiel, who was the father of Birzaith. [32]Heber became the father of Japhlet, Shomer, Hotham, and their sister Shua. [33]The sons of Japhlet: Pasach, Bimhal, and Ashvath. These are the sons of Japhlet. [34]The sons of Shemer: Ahi, Rohgah, Hubbah, and Aram. [35]The sons of Helem[e] his brother: Zophah, Imna, Shelesh, and Amal. [36]The sons of Zophah: Suah, Harnepher, Shual, Beri, Imrah, [37]Bezer, Hod, Shamma, Shilshah, Ithran, and Beera. [38]The sons of Jether: Jephunneh, Pispa, and Ara. [39]The sons of Ulla: Arah, Hanniel, and Rizia. [40]All of these were men of Asher, heads of ancestral houses, select mighty warriors, chief of the princes. Their number enrolled by genealogies, for service in war, was twenty-six thousand men.

Descendants of Benjamin

8 Benjamin became the father of Bela his firstborn, Ashbel the second, Aharah the third, [2]Nohah the fourth, and Rapha the fifth. [3]And Bela had sons: Addar, Gera, Abihud,[f] [4]Abishua, Naaman, Ahoah, [5]Gera, Shephuphan, and Huram. [6]These are the sons of Ehud (they were heads of ancestral houses of the inhabitants of Geba, and they were carried into exile to Manahath): [7]Naaman,[g] Ahijah, and Gera, that is, Heglam,[h] who became the father of Uzza and Ahihud. [8]And Shaharaim had sons in the country of Moab after he had sent away his wives Hushim and Baara. [9]He had sons by his wife Hodesh: Jobab, Zibia, Mesha, Malcam, [10]Jeuz, Sachia, and Mirmah. These were his sons, heads of ancestral houses. [11]He also had sons by Hushim: Abitub and Elpaal. [12]The sons of Elpaal: Eber, Misham, and Shemed, who built Ono and Lod with its towns, [13]and Beriah and Shema (they were heads of ancestral houses of the inhabitants of Aijalon, who put to flight the inhabitants of Gath); [14]and Ahio, Shashak, and Jeremoth. [15]Zebadiah, Arad, Eder, [16]Michael, Ishpah, and Joha were sons of Beriah.

---

a Heb sons b Heb He c Heb beraah d Here spelled Non; see Ex 33.11 e Or Hotham; see 7.32 f Or father of Ehud; see 8.6 g Heb and Naaman
h Or he carried them into exile

[17] Zebadiah, Meshullam, Hizki, Heber, [18] Ishmerai, Izliah, and Jobab were the sons of Elpaal. [19] Jakim, Zichri, Zabdi, [20] Elienai, Zillethai, Eliel, [21] Adaiah, Beraiah, and Shimrath were the sons of Shimei. [22] Ishpan, Eber, Eliel, [23] Abdon, Zichri, Hanan, [24] Hananiah, Elam, Anthothijah, [25] Iphdeiah, and Penuel were the sons of Shashak. [26] Shamsherai, Shchariah, Athaliah, [27] Jaareshiah, Elijah, and Zichri were the sons of Jeroham. [28] These were the heads of ancestral houses, according to their generations, chiefs. These lived in Jerusalem.

[29] Jeiel[a] the father of Gibeon lived in Gibeon, and the name of his wife was Maacah. [30] His firstborn son: Abdon, then Zur, Kish, Baal,[b] Nadab, [31] Gedor, Ahio, Zecher, [32] and Mikloth, who became the father of Shimeah. Now these also lived opposite their kindred in Jerusalem, with their kindred. [33] Ner became the father of Kish, Kish of Saul,[c] Saul[c] of Jonathan, Malchishua, Abinadab, and Esh-baal; [34] and the son of Jonathan was Merib-baal; and Merib-baal became the father of Micah. [35] The sons of Micah: Pithon, Melech, Tarea, and Ahaz. [36] Ahaz became the father of Jehoaddah; and Jehoaddah became the father of Alemeth, Azmaveth, and Zimri; Zimri became the father of Moza. [37] Moza became the father of Binea; Raphah was his son, Eleasah his son, Azel his son. [38] Azel had six sons, and these are their names: Azrikam, Bocheru, Ishmael, Sheariah, Obadiah, and Hanan; all these were the sons of Azel. [39] The sons of his brother Eshek: Ulam his firstborn, Jeush the second, and Eliphelet the third. [40] The sons of Ulam were mighty warriors, archers, having many children and grandchildren, one hundred fifty. All these were Benjaminites.

9 So all Israel was enrolled by genealogies; and these are written in the Book of the Kings of Israel. And Judah was taken into exile in Babylon because of their unfaithfulness. [2] Now the first to live again in their possessions in their towns were Israelites, priests, Levites, and temple servants.

Inhabitants of Jerusalem after the Exile

[3] And some of the people of Judah, Benjamin, Ephraim, and Manasseh lived in Jerusalem: [4] Uthai son of Ammihud, son of Omri, son of Imri, son of Bani, from the sons of Perez son of Judah. [5] And of the Shilonites: Asaiah the firstborn, and his sons. [6] Of the sons of Zerah: Jeuel and their kin, six hundred ninety. [7] Of the Benjaminites: Sallu son of Meshullam, son of Hodaviah, son of Hassenuah, [8] Ibneiah son of Jeroham, Elah son of Uzzi, son of Michri, and Meshullam son of Shephatiah, son of Reuel, son of Ibnijah; [9] and their kindred according to their generations, nine hundred fifty-six. All these were heads of families according to their ancestral houses.

Priestly Families

[10] Of the priests: Jedaiah, Jehoiarib, Jachin, [11] and Azariah son of Hilkiah, son of Meshullam, son of Zadok, son of Meraioth, son of Ahitub, the chief officer of the house of God; [12] and Adaiah son of Jeroham, son of Pashhur, son of Malchijah, and Maasai son of Adiel, son of Jahzerah, son of Meshullam, son of Meshillemith, son of Immer; [13] besides their kindred, heads of their ancestral houses, one thousand seven hundred sixty, qualified for the work of the service of the house of God.

Levitical Families

[14] Of the Levites: Shemaiah son of Hasshub, son of Azrikam, son of Hashabiah, of the sons of Merari; [15] and Bakbakkar, Heresh, Galal, and Mattaniah son of Mica, son of Zichri, son of Asaph; [16] and Obadiah son of Shemaiah, son of Galal, son of Jeduthun, and Berechiah son of Asa, son of Elkanah, who lived in the villages of the Netophathites.

[17] The gatekeepers were: Shallum, Akkub, Talmon, Ahiman; and their kindred Shallum was the chief, [18] stationed previously in the king's gate on the east side. These were the gatekeepers of the camp of the Levites. [19] Shallum son of Kore, son of Ebiasaph, son of Korah, and his kindred of his ancestral house, the Korahites, were in charge of the work of the service, guardians of the thresholds of the tent, as their ancestors had been in charge of the camp of the LORD, guardians of the entrance. [20] And Phinehas son of Eleazar was chief over them in former times; the LORD was with him. [21] Zechariah son of Meshelemiah was gatekeeper at the entrance of the tent of meeting. [22] All these, who were chosen as gatekeepers at the thresholds, were two hundred twelve. They were enrolled by genealogies in their villages. David and the seer Samuel established them in their office of trust. [23] So they and their descendants were in charge of the gates of the house of the LORD, that is, the house of the tent, as guards. [24] The gatekeepers were on the four sides, east, west, north, and south; [25] and their kindred who were in their villages

---

a Compare 9.35: Heb lacks *Jeiel*　**b** Gk Ms adds *Ner*; Compare 8.33 and 9.36　**c** Or *Shaul*

were obliged to come in every seven days, in turn, to be with them; [26]for the four chief gatekeepers, who were Levites, were in charge of the chambers and the treasures of the house of God. [27]And they would spend the night near the house of God; for on them lay the duty of watching, and they had charge of opening it every morning.

28 Some of them had charge of the utensils of service, for they were required to count them when they were brought in and taken out. [29]Others of them were appointed over the furniture, and over all the holy utensils, also over the choice flour, the wine, the oil, the incense, and the spices. [30]Others, of the sons of the priests, prepared the mixing of the spices, [31]and Mattithiah, one of the Levites, the firstborn of Shallum the Korahite, was in charge of making the flat cakes. [32]Also some of their kindred of the Kohathites had charge of the rows of bread, to prepare them for each sabbath.

33 Now these are the singers, the heads of ancestral houses of the Levites, living in the chambers of the temple free from other service, for they were on duty day and night. [34]These were heads of ancestral houses of the Levites, according to their generations; these leaders lived in Jerusalem.

The Family of King Saul

35 In Gibeon lived the father of Gibeon, Jeiel, and the name of his wife was Maacah. [36]His firstborn son was Abdon, then Zur, Kish, Baal, Ner, Nadab, [37]Gedor, Ahio, Zechariah, and Mikloth; [38]and Mikloth became the father of Shimeam; and these also lived opposite their kindred in Jerusalem, with their kindred. [39]Ner became the father of Kish, Kish of Saul, Saul of Jonathan, Malchishua, Abinadab, and Eshbaal; [40]and the son of Jonathan was Merib-baal; and Merib-baal became the father of Micah. [41]The sons of Micah: Pithon, Melech, Tahrea, and Ahaz;[a] [42]and Ahaz became the father of Jarah, and Jarah of Alemeth, Azmaveth, and Zimri; and Zimri became the father of Moza. [43]Moza became the father of Binea; and Rephaiah was his son, Eleasah his son, Azel his son. [44]Azel had six sons, and these are their names: Azrikam, Bocheru, Ishmael, Sheariah, Obadiah, and Hanan; these were the sons of Azel.

Death of Saul and His Sons

10 Now the Philistines fought against Israel; and the men of Israel fled before the Philistines, and fell slain on Mount Gilboa. [2]The Philis-

tines overtook Saul and his sons; and the Philistines killed Jonathan and Abinadab and Malchishua, sons of Saul. [3]The battle pressed hard on Saul; and the archers found him, and he was wounded by the archers. [4]Then Saul said to his armor-bearer, "Draw your sword, and thrust me through with it, so that these uncircumcised may not come and make sport of me." But his armor-bearer was unwilling, for he was terrified. So Saul took his own sword and fell on it. [5]When his armor-bearer saw that Saul was dead, he also fell on his sword and died. [6]Thus Saul died; he and his three sons and all his house died together. [7]When all the men of Israel who were in the valley saw that the army[b] had fled and that Saul and his sons were dead, they abandoned their towns and fled; and the Philistines came and occupied them.

8 The next day when the Philistines came to strip the dead, they found Saul and his sons fallen on Mount Gilboa. [9]They stripped him and took his head and his armor, and sent messengers throughout the land of the Philistines to carry the good news to their idols and to the people. [10]They put his armor in the temple of their gods, and fastened his head in the temple of Dagon. [11]But when all Jabesh-gilead heard everything that the Philistines had done to Saul, [12]all the valiant warriors got up and took away the body of Saul and the bodies of his sons, and brought them to Jabesh. Then they buried their bones under the oak in Jabesh, and fasted seven days.

13 So Saul died for his unfaithfulness; he was unfaithful to the LORD in that he did not keep the command of the LORD; moreover, he had consulted a medium, seeking guidance, [14]and did not seek guidance from the LORD. Therefore the LORD[c] put him to death and turned the kingdom over to David son of Jesse.

David Anointed King of All Israel

11 Then all Israel gathered together to David at Hebron and said, "See, we are your bone and flesh. [2]For some time now, even while Saul was king, it was you who commanded the army of Israel. The LORD your God said to you: It is you who shall be shepherd of my people Israel, you who shall be ruler over my people Israel." [3]So all the elders of Israel came to the king at Hebron, and David made a covenant with them at Hebron before the LORD. And they anointed David king over Israel, according to the word of the LORD by Samuel.

a Compare 8.35: Heb lacks and Ahaz   b Heb they   c Heb he

Jerusalem Captured

4 David and all Israel marched to Jerusalem, that is Jebus, where the Jebusites were, the inhabitants of the land. [5]The inhabitants of Jebus said to David, "You will not come in here." Nevertheless David took the stronghold of Zion, now the city of David. [6]David had said, "Whoever attacks the Jebusites first shall be chief and commander." And Joab son of Zeruiah went up first, so he became chief. [7]David resided in the stronghold; therefore it was called the city of David. [8]He built the city all around, from the Millo in complete circuit; and Joab repaired the rest of the city. [9]And David became greater and greater, for the LORD of hosts was with him.

David's Mighty Men and Their Exploits

10 Now these are the chiefs of David's warriors, who gave him strong support in his kingdom, together with all Israel, to make him king, according to the word of the LORD concerning Israel. [11]This is an account of David's mighty warriors: Jashobeam, son of Hachmoni,[a] was chief of the Three;[b] he wielded his spear against three hundred whom he killed at one time.

12 And next to him among the three warriors was Eleazar son of Dodo, the Ahohite. [13]He was with David at Pas-dammim when the Philistines were gathered there for battle. There was a plot of ground full of barley. Now the people had fled from the Philistines, [14]but he and David took their stand in the middle of the plot, defended it, and killed the Philistines; and the LORD saved them by a great victory.

15 Three of the thirty chiefs went down to the rock to David at the cave of Adullam, while the army of Philistines was encamped in the valley of Rephaim. [16]David was then in the stronghold; and the garrison of the Philistines was then at Bethlehem. [17]David said longingly, "O that someone would give me water to drink from the well of Bethlehem that is by the gate!" [18]Then the Three broke through the camp of the Philistines, and drew water from the well of Bethlehem that was by the gate, and they brought it to David. But David would not drink of it; he poured it out to the LORD, [19]and said, "My God forbid that I should do this. Can I drink the blood of these men? For at the risk of their lives they brought it." Therefore he would not drink it. The three warriors did these things.

20 Now Abishai,[c] the brother of Joab, was chief of the Thirty.[d] With his spear he fought against three hundred and killed them, and won a name beside the Three. [21]He was the most renowned[e] of the Thirty,[d] and became their commander; but he did not attain to the Three.

22 Benaiah son of Jehoiada was a valiant man[f] of Kabzeel, a doer of great deeds; he struck down two sons of[g] Ariel of Moab. He also went down and killed a lion in a pit on a day when snow had fallen. [23]And he killed an Egyptian, a man of great stature, five cubits tall. The Egyptian had in his hand a spear like a weaver's beam; but Benaiah went against him with a staff, snatched the spear out of the Egyptian's hand, and killed him with his own spear. [24]Such were the things Benaiah son of Jehoiada did, and he won a name beside the three warriors. [25]He was renowned among the Thirty, but he did not attain to the Three. And David put him in charge of his bodyguard.

26 The warriors of the armies were Asahel brother of Joab, Elhanan son of Dodo of Bethlehem, [27]Shammoth of Harod,[h] Helez the Pelonite, [28]Ira son of Ikkesh of Tekoa, Abiezer of Anathoth, [29]Sibbecai the Hushathite, Ilai the Ahohite, [30]Maharai of Netophah, Heled son of Baanah of Netophah, [31]Ithai son of Ribai of Gibeah of the Benjaminites, Benaiah of Pir-athon, [32]Hurai of the wadis of Gaash, Abiel the Arbathite, [33]Azmaveth of Baharum, Eliahba of Shaalbon, [34]Hashem[i] the Gizonite, Jonathan son of Shagee the Hararite, [35]Ahiam son of Sachar the Hararite, Eliphal son of Ur, [36]Hepher the Mecherathite, Ahijah the Pelonite, [37]Hezro of Carmel, Naarai son of Ezbai, [38]Joel the brother of Nathan, Mibhar son of Hagri, [39]Zelek the Ammonite, Naharai of Beeroth, the armor-bearer of Joab son of Zeruiah, [40]Ira the Ithrite, Gareb the Ithrite, [41]Uriah the Hittite, Zabad son of Ahlai, [42]Adina son of Shiza the Reubenite, a leader of the Reubenites, and thirty with him, [43]Hanan son of Maacah, and Joshaphat the Mithnite, [44]Uzzia the Ashterathite, Shama and Jeiel sons of Hotham the Aroerite, [45]Jediael son of Shimri, and his brother Joha the Tizite, [46]Eliel the Mahavite, and Jeribai and Joshaviah sons of Elnaam, and Ithmah the Moabite, [47]Eliel, and Obed, and Jaasiel the Mezobaite.

David's Followers in the Wilderness

12 The following are those who came to David at Ziklag, while he could not move about freely because of Saul son of Kish; they were among the mighty warriors who helped him in war. [2]They were archers, and could shoot arrows and sling stones

a Or *a Hachmonite*   **b** Compare 2 Sam 23.8: Heb *Thirty* or *captains*   **c** Gk Vg Tg Compare 2 Sam 23.18: Heb *Abshai*   **d** Syr: Heb *Three*   **e** Compare 2 Sam 23.19: Heb *more renowned among the two*   **f** Syr: Heb *the son of a valiant man*   **g** See 2 Sam 23.20: Heb lacks *sons of*   **h** Compare 2 Sam 23.25: Heb *the Harorite*   **i** Compare Gk and 2 Sam 23.32: Heb *the sons of Hashem* with either the right hand or the left; they were Benjaminites, Saul's kindred. ³The chief was Ahiezer, then Joash, both sons of Shemaah of Gibeah; also Jeziel and Pelet sons of Azmaveth; Beracah, Jehu of Anathoth, ⁴Ishmaiah of Gibeon, a warrior among the Thirty and a leader over the Thirty; Jeremiah,ᵃ Jahaziel, Johanan, Jozabad of Gederah, ⁵Eluzai,ᵇ Jerimoth, Bealiah, Shemariah, Shephatiah the Haruphite; ⁶Elkanah, Isshiah, Azarel, Joezer, and Jashobeam, the Korahites; ⁷and Joelah and Zebadiah, sons of Jeroham of Gedor.

8 From the Gadites there went over to David at the stronghold in the wilderness mighty and experienced warriors, expert with shield and spear, whose faces were like the faces of lions, and who were swift as gazelles on the mountains: ⁹Ezer the chief, Obadiah second, Eliab third, ¹⁰Mishmannah fourth, Jeremiah fifth, ¹¹Attai sixth, Eliel seventh, ¹²Johanan eighth, Elzabad ninth, ¹³Jeremiah tenth, Machbannai eleventh. ¹⁴These Gadites were officers of the army, the least equal to a hundred and the greatest to a thousand. ¹⁵These are the men who crossed the Jordan in the first month, when it was overflowing all its banks, and put to flight all those in the valleys, to the east and to the west.

16 Some Benjaminites and Judahites came to the stronghold to David. ¹⁷David went out to meet them and said to them, "If you have come to me in friendship, to help me, then my heart will be knit to you; but if you have come to betray me to my adversaries, though my hands have done no wrong, then may the God of our ancestors see and give judgment." ¹⁸Then the spirit came upon Amasai, chief of the Thirty, and he said,

"We are yours, O David;
　and with you, O son of Jesse!
Peace, peace to you,
　and peace to the one who helps you!
For your God is the one who
　helps you."

Then David received them, and made them officers of his troops.

19 Some of the Manassites deserted to David when he came with the Philistines for the battle against Saul. (Yet he did not help them, for the rulers of the Philistines took counsel and sent him away, saying, "He will desert to his master Saul at the cost of our heads.") ²⁰As he went to Ziklag these Manassites deserted to him: Adnah, Jozabad, Jediael, Michael, Jozabad, Elihu, and Zillethai, chiefs of the thousands in Manasseh. ²¹They helped David against the band of raiders,ᶜ for they were all warriors and commanders in the army. ²²Indeed from day to day people kept coming to David to help him, until there was a great army, like an army of God.

David's Army at Hebron

23 These are the numbers of the divisions of the armed troops who came to David in Hebron to turn the kingdom of Saul over to him, according to the word of the LORD. ²⁴The people of Judah bearing shield and spear numbered six thousand eight hundred armed troops. ²⁵Of the Simeonites, mighty warriors, seven thousand one hundred. ²⁶Of the Levites four thousand six hundred. ²⁷Jehoiada, leader of the house of Aaron, and with him three thousand seven hundred. ²⁸Zadok, a young warrior, and twenty-two commanders from his own ancestral house. ²⁹Of the Benjaminites, the kindred of Saul, three thousand, of whom the majority had continued to keep their allegiance to the house of Saul. ³⁰Of the Ephraimites, twenty thousand eight hundred, mighty warriors, notables in their ancestral houses. ³¹Of the half-tribe of Manasseh, eighteen thousand, who were expressly named to come and make David king. ³²Of Issachar, those who had understanding of the times, to know what Israel ought to do, two hundred chiefs, and all their kindred under their command. ³³Of Zebulun, fifty thousand seasoned troops, equipped for battle with all the weapons of war, to help Davidᵈ with singleness of purpose. ³⁴Of Naphtali, a thousand commanders, with whom there were thirty-seven thousand armed with shield and spear. ³⁵Of the Danites, twenty-eight thousand six hundred equipped for battle. ³⁶Of Asher, forty thousand seasoned troops ready for battle. ³⁷Of the Reubenites and Gadites and the half-tribe of Manasseh from beyond the Jordan, one hundred twenty thousand armed with all the weapons of war.

"Your God is the
one who helps you."
—1 Chronicles 12:18

ᵃ Heb verse 5　ᵇ Heb verse 6　ᶜ Or *as officers of his troops*　ᵈ Gk: Heb lacks *David*

38 All these, warriors arrayed in battle order, came to Hebron with full intent to make David king over all Israel; likewise all the rest of Israel were of a single mind to make David king. ³⁹They were there with David for three days, eating and drinking, for their kindred had provided for them. ⁴⁰And also their neighbors, from as far away as Issachar and Zebulun and Naphtali, came bringing food on donkeys, camels, mules, and oxen—abundant provisions of meal, cakes of figs, clusters of raisins, wine, oil, oxen, and sheep, for there was joy in Israel.

The Ark Brought from Kiriath-jearim

13 David consulted with the commanders of the thousands and of the hundreds, with every leader. ²David said to the whole assembly of Israel, "If it seems good to you, and if it is the will of the LORD our God, let us send abroad to our kindred who remain in all the land of Israel, including the priests and Levites in the cities that have pasture lands, that they may come together to us. ³Then let us bring again the ark of our God to us; for we did not turn to it in the days of Saul." ⁴The whole assembly agreed to do so, for the thing pleased all the people.

5 So David assembled all Israel from the Shihor of Egypt to Lebo-hamath, to bring the ark of God from Kiriath-jearim. ⁶And David and all Israel went up to Baalah, that is, to Kiriath-jearim, which belongs to Judah, to bring up from there the ark of God, the LORD, who is enthroned on the cherubim, which is called by his*a* name. ⁷They carried the ark of God on a new cart, from the house of Abinadab, and Uzzah and Ahio*b* were driving the cart. ⁸David and all Israel were dancing before God with all their might, with song and lyres and harps and tambourines and cymbals and trumpets.

9 When they came to the threshing floor of Chidon, Uzzah put out his hand to hold the ark, for the oxen shook it. ¹⁰The anger of the LORD was kindled against Uzzah; he struck him down because he put out his hand to the ark; and he died there before God. ¹¹David was angry because the LORD had burst out against Uzzah; so that place is called Perez-uzzah*c* to this day. ¹²David was afraid of God that day; he said, "How can I bring the ark of God into my care?" ¹³So David did not take the ark into his care into the city of David; he took it instead to the house of Obed-edom the Gittite. ¹⁴The ark of God remained with the household of Obed-edom in his house three

months, and the LORD blessed the household of Obed-edom and all that he had.

David Established at Jerusalem

14 King Hiram of Tyre sent messengers to David, along with cedar logs, and masons and carpenters to build a house for him. ²David then perceived that the LORD had established him as king over Israel, and that his kingdom was highly exalted for the sake of his people Israel.

3 David took more wives in Jerusalem, and David became the father of more sons and daughters. ⁴These are the names of the children whom he had in Jerusalem: Shammua, Shobab, and Nathan; Solomon, ⁵Ibhar, Elishua, and Elpelet; ⁶Nogah, Nepheg, and Japhia; ⁷Elishama, Beeliada, and Eliphelet.

Defeat of the Philistines

8 When the Philistines heard that David had been anointed king over all Israel, all the Philistines went up in search of David; and David heard of it and went out against them. ⁹Now the Philistines had come and made a raid in the valley of Rephaim. ¹⁰David inquired of God, "Shall I go up against the Philistines? Will you give them into my hand?" The LORD said to him, "Go up, and I will give them into your hand." ¹¹So he went up to Baal-perazim, and David defeated them there. David said, "God has burst out*d* against my enemies by my hand, like a bursting flood." Therefore that place is called Baal-perazim.*e* ¹²They abandoned their gods there, and at David's command they were burned.

13 Once again the Philistines made a raid in the valley. ¹⁴When David again inquired of God, God said to him, "You shall not go up after them; go around and come on them opposite the balsam trees. ¹⁵When you hear the sound of marching in the tops of the balsam trees, then go out to battle; for God has gone out before you to strike down the army of the Philistines." ¹⁶David did as God had commanded him, and they struck down the Philistine army from Gibeon to Gezer. ¹⁷The fame of David went out into all lands, and the LORD brought the fear of him on all nations.

The Ark Brought to Jerusalem

15 David*f* built houses for himself in the city of David, and he prepared a place for the ark of God and pitched a tent for it. ²Then David commanded that no one but the Levites were to carry

---

a Heb lacks *his*   **b** Or *and his brother*   **c** That is *Bursting Out Against Uzzah*   **d** Heb *paraz*   **e** That is *Lord of Bursting Out*   **f** Heb *He*

the ark of God, for the Lord had chosen them to carry the ark of the Lord and to minister to him forever. [3]David assembled all Israel in Jerusalem to bring up the ark of the Lord to its place, which he had prepared for it. [4]Then David gathered together the descendants of Aaron and the Levites: [5]of the sons of Kohath, Uriel the chief, with one hundred twenty of his kindred; [6]of the sons of Merari, Asaiah the chief, with two hundred twenty of his kindred; [7]of the sons of Gershom, Joel the chief, with one hundred thirty of his kindred; [8]of the sons of Elizaphan, Shemaiah the chief, with two hundred of his kindred; [9]of the sons of Hebron, Eliel the chief, with eighty of his kindred; [10]of the sons of Uzziel, Amminadab the chief, with one hundred twelve of his kindred.

11 David summoned the priests Zadok and Abiathar, and the Levites Uriel, Asaiah, Joel, Shemaiah, Eliel, and Amminadab. [12]He said to them, "You are the heads of families of the Levites; sanctify yourselves, you and your kindred, so that you may bring up the ark of the Lord, the God of Israel, to the place that I have prepared for it. [13]Because you did not carry it the first time,[a] the Lord our God burst out against us, because we did not give it proper care." [14]So the priests and the Levites sanctified themselves to bring up the ark of the Lord, the God of Israel. [15]And the Levites carried the ark of God on their shoulders with the poles, as Moses had commanded according to the word of the Lord.

16 David also commanded the chiefs of the Levites to appoint their kindred as the singers to play on musical instruments, on harps and lyres and cymbals, to raise loud sounds of joy. [17]So the Levites appointed Heman son of Joel; and of his kindred Asaph son of Berechiah; and of the sons of Merari, their kindred, Ethan son of Kushaiah; [18]and with them their kindred of the second order, Zechariah, Jaaziel, Shemiramoth, Jehiel, Unni, Eliab, Benaiah, Maaseiah, Mattithiah, Eliphelehu, and Mikneiah, and the gatekeepers Obed-edom and Jeiel. [19]The singers Heman, Asaph, and Ethan were to sound bronze cymbals; [20]Zechariah, Aziel, Shemiramoth, Jehiel, Unni, Eliab, Maaseiah, and Benaiah were to play harps according to Alamoth; [21]but Mattithiah, Eliphelehu, Mikneiah, Obed-edom, Jeiel, and Azaziah were to lead with lyres according to the Sheminith. [22]Chenaniah, leader of the Levites in music, was to direct the music, for he understood it. [23]Berechiah and Elkanah were to be gatekeepers for the ark. [24]Shebaniah,

Joshaphat, Nethanel, Amasai, Zechariah, Benaiah, and Eliezer, the priests, were to blow the trumpets before the ark of God. Obed-edom and Jehiah also were to be gatekeepers for the ark.

25 So David and the elders of Israel, and the commanders of the thousands, went to bring up the ark of the covenant of the Lord from the house of Obed-edom with rejoicing. [26]And because God helped the Levites who were carrying the ark of the covenant of the Lord, they sacrificed seven bulls and seven rams. [27]David was clothed with a robe of fine linen, as also were all the Levites who were carrying the ark, and the singers, and Chenaniah the leader of the music of the singers; and David wore a linen ephod. [28]So all Israel brought up the ark of the covenant of the Lord with shouting, to the sound of the horn, trumpets, and cymbals, and made loud music on harps and lyres.

29 As the ark of the covenant of the Lord came to the city of David, Michal daughter of Saul looked out of the window, and saw King David leaping and dancing; and she despised him in her heart.

The Ark Placed in the Tent

16 They brought in the ark of God, and set it inside the tent that David had pitched for it; and they offered burnt offerings and offerings of well-being before God. [2]When David had finished offering the burnt offerings and the offerings of well-being, he blessed the people in the name of the Lord; [3]and he distributed to every person in Israel—man and woman alike—to each a loaf of bread, a portion of meat,[b] and a cake of raisins.

4 He appointed certain of the Levites as ministers before the ark of the Lord, to invoke, to thank, and to praise the Lord, the God of Israel. [5]Asaph was the chief, and second to him Zechariah, Jeiel, Shemiramoth, Jehiel, Mattithiah, Eliab, Benaiah, Obed-edom, and Jeiel, with harps and lyres; Asaph was to sound the cymbals, [6]and the priests Benaiah and Jahaziel were to blow trumpets regularly, before the ark of the covenant of God.

David's Psalm of Thanksgiving

7 Then on that day David first appointed the singing of praises to the Lord by Asaph and his kindred.

8 O give thanks to the Lord, call on his name,
     make known his deeds among the peoples.

---

a Meaning of Heb uncertain b Compare Gk Syr Vg: Meaning of Heb uncertain

CONNECT IT!

Pete Greig: Praying 24–7 · 1 Chronicles 16:1–37

They started praying in 1999 and haven't stopped yet. Pete Greig was a young pastor in England who scheduled a prayer gathering and hoped his church could manage to keep someone praying continuously for one month. They did—and kept right on going, growing into the 24-7 Prayer movement, which spread by word of mouth to more than one hundred nations. In prayer rooms around the world, someone has been praying every minute of every hour of every day for more than a decade.

Sound boring? This movement is much more than mumbling empty phrases into the sky. It's all about action—action that begins with seeking God and putting Jesus' two greatest commandments into real practice: to love God with all your heart and to love your neighbor as yourself (see Mark 12:30). Participants pray for spiritual, social, and environmental reconciliation, and many go on to serve and act to bring about those changes they pray for. The movement has formed many communities and churches and launched other initiatives to serve the poor and spread prayer groups to every college campus in the United States (Campus America).

"One thing I've learned is that prayer is not a big switch in the sky that makes revival happen," says Greig. "Don't get me wrong; we've seen plenty of remarkable answers to prayer, but it's just not like a Coke machine. You don't put in your prayer and get out a miracle. You sow something and you harvest it later, and it's often quite different from what you sowed."*

Greig and the 24-7 Prayer movement reflect David's passion for prayer (1 Chronicles 16:7-10) and remind us that those who spend time with God in prayer naturally seek God's heart in their actions as well. To learn more, visit the website: **24-7prayer.com**.

---

9 Sing to him, sing praises to him,
   tell of all his wonderful works.
10 Glory in his holy name;
   let the hearts of those who seek the LORD
      rejoice.
11 Seek the LORD and his strength,
   seek his presence continually.
12 Remember the wonderful works he has done,
   his miracles, and the judgments he uttered,
13 O offspring of his servant Israel,[a]
   children of Jacob, his chosen ones.

14 He is the LORD our God;
   his judgments are in all the earth.
15 Remember his covenant forever,
   the word that he commanded, for a
      thousand generations,
16 the covenant that he made with Abraham,
   his sworn promise to Isaac,
17 which he confirmed to Jacob as a statute,
   to Israel as an everlasting covenant,
18 saying, "To you I will give the land of Canaan
   as your portion for an inheritance."

19 When they were few in number,
   of little account, and strangers in the land,[b]
20 wandering from nation to nation,
   from one kingdom to another people,
21 he allowed no one to oppress them;
   he rebuked kings on their account,
22 saying, "Do not touch my anointed ones;
   do my prophets no harm."

23 Sing to the LORD, all the earth.
   Tell of his salvation from day to day.
24 Declare his glory among the nations,
   his marvelous works among all the peoples.
25 For great is the LORD, and greatly to be praised;
   he is to be revered above all gods.
26 For all the gods of the peoples are
      idols,
   but the LORD made the heavens.
27 Honor and majesty are before him;
   strength and joy are in his place.

28 Ascribe to the LORD, O families of the peoples,
   ascribe to the LORD glory and strength.

---

a Another reading is *Abraham* (compare Ps 105.6) b Heb *in it*

29 Ascribe to the LORD the glory due his name;
  bring an offering, and come before him.
Worship the LORD in holy splendor;
30   tremble before him, all the earth.
  The world is firmly established; it shall
    never be moved.
31 Let the heavens be glad, and let the earth
    rejoice,
  and let them say among the nations, "The
    LORD is king!"
32 Let the sea roar, and all that fills it;
  let the field exult, and everything
    in it.
33 Then shall the trees of the forest sing for joy
  before the LORD, for he comes to judge the
    earth.
34 O give thanks to the LORD, for he is good;
  for his steadfast love endures forever.

35 Say also:
"Save us, O God of our salvation,
  and gather and rescue us from among the
    nations,
that we may give thanks to your holy name,
  and glory in your praise.
36 Blessed be the LORD, the God of Israel,
  from everlasting to everlasting."
Then all the people said "Amen!" and praised the
LORD.

Regular Worship Maintained

37 David left Asaph and his kinsfolk there before
the ark of the covenant of the LORD to minister
regularly before the ark as each day required, 38 and
also Obed-edom and his^a sixty-eight kinsfolk; while
Obed-edom son of Jeduthun and Hosah were to be
gatekeepers. 39 And he left the priest Zadok and his

Ways to Pray · 1 Chronicles 16:37–42

Think of all the time you spend texting, chatting, or talking on the phone with your friends. What would happen to a friendship if one of you never responded? The relationship probably wouldn't last long. Our relationship with God also relies on good communication. In this passage, King David wanted to help the Israelites stay close to God, so he established regular times and forms of prayer to remind the Israelites of God's presence and their identity as God's people.

Our need to be close to God through prayer is just as important today as it was for King David. Prayer opens our heart and lets us keep a conversation going with God. You can use the events of your day as a guide to help you open those lines of communication. Here are some suggestions.

- Had a good day? Offer "prayers of blessing and adoration" in response to all the ways you've been blessed by God's goodness.
- Need something? Offer a "prayer of petition" by simply asking God for whatever you need and acknowledging your dependency on and trust in God.
- Got a friend in need? Offer a "prayer of intercession" asking God to help your friend.
- Feeling thankful? Offer a "prayer of thanksgiving" for God's mercy and love. Join in the ultimate prayer of thanksgiving by participating in the Lord's Supper at church.
- In awe of God? Offer a "prayer of praise" not for what God has done for you, but for simply being God.

There are different ways we can express any form of prayer. We can put the desires of our heart into words spoken aloud or silently in "vocal prayer." We can concentrate on the scriptures or other spiritual writings and listen to what God is saying to us through them in "meditative prayer." Or we can pray deep in our hearts by focusing on Jesus in "contemplative prayer," which enables us to simply be present with Christ in love.

No matter where you are in your relationship with Christ, set aside a regular time for prayer each day. It will help your relationship grow and remind you that God is with you.

a Gk Syr Vg: Heb their

God Won't Stay in a Box · 1 Chronicles 17:1–15

Our world loves boxes and containers and compartments. We have complete stores filled with nothing else! There's a sense of comfort that comes when everything is in its place. But don't we often try to put God away in a special place too? It's just more convenient to think of God as residing "up there" in heaven or in the church sanctuary than to try to wrap our brains around the complexity of God's presence with and in us. Maybe that's why God seems less than enthusiastic about David's desire to build a temple (1 Chronicles 17:4–6). The danger is clear. If you identify God with a building, however grand and beautiful, people will begin to think God stays there.

When we enter a chapel or a church, we become reverent, sensing that we are in the presence of God. Indeed, we are. But we need to remember that we don't leave God behind when we step out of that building. Simply put, God cannot and will not be confined, despite our best efforts.

Our God walks with us. God's place is everywhere. How can you practice living in the constant presence of God?

kindred the priests before the tabernacle of the LORD in the high place that was at Gibeon, [40]to offer burnt offerings to the LORD on the altar of burnt offering regularly, morning and evening, according to all that is written in the law of the LORD that he commanded Israel. [41]With them were Heman and Jeduthun, and the rest of those chosen and expressly named to render thanks to the LORD, for his steadfast love endures forever. [42]Heman and Jeduthun had with them trumpets and cymbals for the music, and instruments for sacred song. The sons of Jeduthun were appointed to the gate.

43 Then all the people departed to their homes, and David went home to bless his household.

God's Covenant with David

17 Now when David settled in his house, David said to the prophet Nathan, "I am living in a house of cedar, but the ark of the covenant of the LORD is under a tent." [2]Nathan said to David, "Do all that you have in mind, for God is with you."

3 But that same night the word of the LORD came to Nathan, saying: [4]Go and tell my servant David: Thus says the LORD: You shall not build me a house to live in. [5]For I have not lived in a house since the day I brought out Israel to this very day, but I have lived in a tent and a tabernacle.[a] [6]Wherever I have moved about among all Israel, did I ever speak a word with any of the judges of Israel, whom I commanded to shepherd my people, saying, Why have you not built me a house of cedar? [7]Now therefore thus you

shall say to my servant David: Thus says the LORD of hosts: I took you from the pasture, from following the sheep, to be ruler over my people Israel; [8]and I have been with you wherever you went, and have cut off all your enemies before you; and I will make for you a name, like the name of the great ones of the earth. [9]I will appoint a place for my people Israel, and will plant them, so that they may live in their own place, and be disturbed no more; and evildoers shall wear them down no more, as they did formerly, [10]from the time that I appointed judges over my people Israel; and I will subdue all your enemies.

Moreover I declare to you that the LORD will build you a house. [11]When your days are fulfilled to go to be with your ancestors, I will raise up your offspring after you, one of your own sons, and I will establish his kingdom. [12]He shall build a house for me, and I will establish his throne forever. [13]I will be a father to him, and he shall be a son to me. I will not take my steadfast love from him, as I took it from him who was before you, [14]but I will confirm him in my house and in my kingdom forever, and his throne shall be established forever. [15]In accordance with all these words and all this vision, Nathan spoke to David.

David's Prayer

16 Then King David went in and sat before the LORD, and said, "Who am I, O LORD God, and what is my house, that you have brought me thus far? [17]And even this was a small thing in your sight,

a Gk 2 Sam 7.6: Heb *but I have been from tent to tent and from tabernacle*

O God; you have also spoken of your servant's house for a great while to come. You regard me as someone of high rank,[a] O LORD God! [18]And what more can David say to you for honoring your servant? You know your servant. [19]For your servant's sake, O LORD, and according to your own heart, you have done all these great deeds, making known all these great things. [20]There is no one like you, O LORD, and there is no God besides you, according to all that we have heard with our ears. [21]Who is like your people Israel, one nation on the earth whom God went to redeem to be his people, making for yourself a name for great and terrible things, in driving out nations before your people whom you redeemed from Egypt? [22]And you made your people Israel to be your people forever; and you, O LORD, became their God.

23 "And now, O LORD, as for the word that you have spoken concerning your servant and concerning his house, let it be established forever, and do as you have promised. [24]Thus your name will be established and magnified forever in the saying, 'The LORD of hosts, the God of Israel, is Israel's God'; and the house of your servant David will be established in your presence. [25]For you, my God, have revealed to your servant that you will build a house for him; therefore your servant has found it possible to pray before you. [26]And now, O LORD, you are God, and you have promised this good thing to your servant; [27]therefore may it please you to bless the house of your servant, that it may continue forever before you. For you, O LORD, have blessed and are blessed[b] forever."

18 David's Kingdom Established and Extended

Some time afterward, David attacked the Philistines and subdued them; he took Gath and its villages from the Philistines.

2 He defeated Moab, and the Moabites became subject to David and brought tribute.

3 David also struck down King Hadadezer of Zobah, toward Hamath,[a] as he went to set up a monument at the river Euphrates. [4]David took from him one thousand chariots, seven thousand cavalry, and twenty thousand foot soldiers. David hamstrung all the chariot horses, but left one hundred of them. [5]When the Arameans of Damascus came to help King Hadadezer of Zobah, David killed twenty-two thousand Arameans. [6]Then David put garrisons[c] in Aram of Damascus; and the Arameans became sub-

ject to David, and brought tribute. The LORD gave victory to David wherever he went. [7]David took the gold shields that were carried by the servants of Hadadezer, and brought them to Jerusalem. [8]From Tibhath and from Cun, cities of Hadadezer, David took a vast quantity of bronze; with it Solomon made the bronze sea and the pillars and the vessels of bronze.

9 When King Tou of Hamath heard that David had defeated the whole army of King Hadadezer of Zobah, [10]he sent his son Hadoram to King David, to greet him and to congratulate him, because he had fought against Hadadezer and defeated him. Now Hadadezer had often been at war with Tou. He sent all sorts of articles of gold, of silver, and of bronze; [11]these also King David dedicated to the LORD, together with the silver and gold that he had carried off from all the nations, from Edom, Moab, the Ammonites, the Philistines, and Amalek.

12 Abishai son of Zeruiah killed eighteen thousand Edomites in the Valley of Salt. [13]He put garrisons in Edom; and all the Edomites became subject to David. And the LORD gave victory to David wherever he went.

David's Administration

14 So David reigned over all Israel; and he administered justice and equity to all his people. [15]Joab son of Zeruiah was over the army; Jehoshaphat son of Ahilud was recorder; [16]Zadok son of Ahitub and Ahimelech son of Abiathar were priests; Shavsha was secretary; [17]Benaiah son of Jehoiada was over the Cherethites and the Pelethites; and David's sons were the chief officials in the service of the king.

19 Defeat of the Ammonites and Arameans

Some time afterward, King Nahash of the Ammonites died, and his son succeeded him. [2]David said, "I will deal loyally with Hanun son of Nahash, for his father dealt loyally with me." So David sent messengers to console him concerning his father. When David's servants came to Hanun in the land of the Ammonites, to console him, [3]the officials of the Ammonites said to Hanun, "Do you think, because David has sent consolers to you, that he is honoring your father? Have not his servants come to you to search and to overthrow and to spy out the land?" [4]So Hanun seized David's servants, shaved them, cut off their garments in the middle at their

a Meaning of Heb uncertain b Or and it is blessed c Gk Vg 2 Sam 8.6 Compare Syr: Heb lacks garrisons

hips, and sent them away; [5]and they departed. When David was told about the men, he sent messengers to them, for they felt greatly humiliated. The king said, "Remain at Jericho until your beards have grown, and then return."

6 When the Ammonites saw that they had made themselves odious to David, Hanun and the Ammonites sent a thousand talents of silver to hire chariots and cavalry from Mesopotamia, from Aram-maacah and from Zobah. [7]They hired thirty-two thousand chariots and the king of Maacah with his army, who came and camped before Medeba. And the Ammonites were mustered from their cities and came to battle. [8]When David heard of it, he sent Joab and all the army of the warriors. [9]The Ammonites came out and drew up in battle array at the entrance of the city, and the kings who had come were by themselves in the open country.

10 When Joab saw that the line of battle was set against him both in front and in the rear, he chose some of the picked men of Israel and arrayed them against the Arameans; [11]the rest of his troops he put in the charge of his brother Abishai, and they were arrayed against the Ammonites. [12]He said, "If the Arameans are too strong for me, then you shall help me; but if the Ammonites are too strong for you, then I will help you. [13]Be strong, and let us be courageous for our people and for the cities of our God; and may the LORD do what seems good to him." [14]So Joab and the troops who were with him advanced toward the Arameans for battle; and they fled before him. [15]When the Ammonites saw that the Arameans fled, they likewise fled before Abishai, Joab's brother, and entered the city. Then Joab came to Jerusalem.

16 But when the Arameans saw that they had been defeated by Israel, they sent messengers and brought out the Arameans who were beyond the Euphrates, with Shophach the commander of the army of Hadadezer at their head. [17]When David was informed, he gathered all Israel together, crossed the Jordan, came to them, and drew up his forces against them. When David set the battle in array against the Arameans, they fought with him. [18]The Arameans fled before Israel; and David killed seven thousand Aramean charioteers and forty thousand foot soldiers, and also killed Shophach the commander of their army. [19]When the servants of Hadadezer saw that they had been defeated by Israel, they made peace with David, and became subject to him. So the Arameans were not willing to help the Ammonites any more.

Siege and Capture of Rabbah

20 In the spring of the year, the time when kings go out to battle, Joab led out the army, ravaged the country of the Ammonites, and came and besieged Rabbah. But David remained at Jerusalem. Joab attacked Rabbah, and overthrew it. [2]David took the crown of Milcom[a] from his head; he found that it weighed a talent of gold, and in it was a precious stone; and it was placed on David's head. He also brought out the booty of the city, a very great amount. [3]He brought out the people who were in it, and set them to work[b] with saws and iron picks and axes.[c] Thus David did to all the cities of the Ammonites. Then David and all the people returned to Jerusalem.

Exploits against the Philistines

4 After this, war broke out with the Philistines at Gezer; then Sibbecai the Hushathite killed Sippai, who was one of the descendants of the giants; and the Philistines were subdued. [5]Again there was war with the Philistines; and Elhanan son of Jair killed Lahmi the brother of Goliath the Gittite, the shaft of whose spear was like a weaver's beam. [6]Again there was war at Gath, where there was a man of great size, who had six fingers on each hand, and six toes on each foot, twenty-four in number; he also was descended from the giants. [7]When he taunted Israel, Jonathan son of Shimea, David's brother, killed him. [8]These were descended from the giants in Gath; they fell by the hand of David and his servants.

The Census and Plague

21 Satan stood up against Israel, and incited David to count the people of Israel. [2]So David said to Joab and the commanders of the army, "Go, number Israel, from Beer-sheba to Dan, and bring me a report, so that I may know their number." [3]But Joab said, "May the LORD increase the number of his people a hundredfold! Are they not, my lord the king, all of them my lord's servants? Why then should my lord require this? Why should he bring guilt on Israel?" [4]But the king's word prevailed against Joab. So Joab departed and went throughout all Israel, and came back to Jerusalem. [5]Joab gave the total count of the people to David. In all Israel

a Gk Vg See 1 Kings 11.5, 33: MT *of their king*   **b** Compare 2 Sam 12.31: Heb *and he sawed*   **c** Compare 2 Sam 12.31: Heb *saws*

LIVE IT!

True Repentance
1 Chronicles 21:1–17

Think of a time when you said "I'm sorry" just because you felt you had to. Now think of a time when you truly were sorry for hurting another person. There's a big difference between going through the motions of repentance and being truly sorry. David learned the difference when he sinned by ordering a census to count his people (1 Chronicles 21:2). He accepted a consequence that he hoped would be the easiest (1 Chronicles 21:13). But when he saw the harm he had caused, he became truly repentant and asked God's mercy upon the Israelites (1 Chronicles 21:17).

Repentance requires true sorrow and asking God to change our heart. It leads to reconciliation—making things right with God and others.

- Is there anything in your life that needs repentance or anyone you need to reconcile with?
- Go make things right.

there were one million one hundred thousand men who drew the sword, and in Judah four hundred seventy thousand who drew the sword. [6]But he did not include Levi and Benjamin in the numbering, for the king's command was abhorrent to Joab.

7 But God was displeased with this thing, and he struck Israel. [8]David said to God, "I have sinned greatly in that I have done this thing. But now, I pray you, take away the guilt of your servant; for I have done very foolishly." [9]The LORD spoke to Gad, David's seer, saying, [10]"Go and say to David, 'Thus says the LORD: Three things I offer you; choose one of them, so that I may do it to you.'" [11]So Gad came to David and said to him, "Thus says the LORD, 'Take your choice: [12]either three years of famine; or three months of devastation by your foes, while the sword of your enemies overtakes you; or three days of the sword of the LORD,

pestilence on the land, and the angel of the LORD destroying throughout all the territory of Israel.' Now decide what answer I shall return to the one who sent me." [13]Then David said to Gad, "I am in great distress; let me fall into the hand of the LORD, for his mercy is very great; but let me not fall into human hands."

14 So the LORD sent a pestilence on Israel; and seventy thousand persons fell in Israel. [15]And God sent an angel to Jerusalem to destroy it; but when he was about to destroy it, the LORD took note and relented concerning the calamity; he said to the destroying angel, "Enough! Stay your hand." The angel of the LORD was then standing by the threshing floor of Ornan the Jebusite. [16]David looked up and saw the angel of the LORD standing between earth and heaven, and in his hand a drawn sword stretched out over Jerusalem. Then David and the elders, clothed in sackcloth, fell on their faces. [17]And David said to God, "Was it not I who gave the command to count the people? It is I who have sinned and done very wickedly. But these sheep, what have they done? Let your hand, I pray, O LORD my God, be against me and against my father's house; but do not let your people be plagued!"

David's Altar and Sacrifice

18 Then the angel of the LORD commanded Gad to tell David that he should go up and erect an altar to the LORD on the threshing floor of Ornan the Jebusite. [19]So David went up following Gad's instructions, which he had spoken in the name of the LORD. [20]Ornan turned and saw the angel; and while his four sons who were with him hid themselves, Ornan continued to thresh wheat. [21]As David came to Ornan, Ornan looked and saw David; he went out from the threshing floor, and did obeisance to David with his face to the ground. [22]David said to Ornan, "Give me the site of the threshing floor that I may build on it an altar to the LORD—give it to me at its full price—so that the plague may be averted from the people." [23]Then Ornan said to David, "Take it; and let my lord the king do what seems good to him; see, I present the oxen for burnt offerings, and the threshing sledges for the wood, and the wheat for a grain offering. I give it all." [24]But King David said to Ornan, "No; I will buy them for the full price. I will not take for the LORD what is yours, nor offer burnt offerings

that cost me nothing." ²⁵So David paid Ornan six hundred shekels of gold by weight for the site. ²⁶David built there an altar to the LORD and presented burnt offerings and offerings of well-being. He called upon the LORD, and he answered him with fire from heaven on the altar of burnt offering. ²⁷Then the LORD commanded the angel, and he put his sword back into its sheath.

The Place Chosen for the Temple

28 At that time, when David saw that the LORD had answered him at the threshing floor of Ornan the Jebusite, he made his sacrifices there. ²⁹For the tabernacle of the LORD, which Moses had made in the wilderness, and the altar of burnt offering were at that time in the high place at Gibeon; ³⁰but David could not go before it to inquire of God, for he was afraid of the sword of the angel of the LORD. ¹Then David said, "Here shall be the house of the LORD God and here the altar of burnt offering for Israel."

22

David Prepares to Build the Temple

2 David gave orders to gather together the aliens who were residing in the land of Israel, and he set stonecutters to prepare dressed stones for building the house of God. ³David also provided great stores of iron for nails for the doors of the gates and for clamps, as well as bronze in quantities beyond weighing, ⁴and cedar logs without number—for the Sidonians and Tyrians brought great quantities of cedar to David. ⁵For David said, "My son Solomon is young and inexperienced, and the house that is to be built for the LORD must be exceedingly magnificent, famous and glorified throughout all lands; I will therefore make prepa-

ration for it." So David provided materials in great quantity before his death.

David's Charge to Solomon and the Leaders

6 Then he called for his son Solomon and charged him to build a house for the LORD, the God of Israel. ⁷David said to Solomon, "My son, I had planned to build a house to the name of the LORD my God. ⁸But the word of the LORD came to me, saying, 'You have shed much blood and have waged great wars; you shall not build a house to my name, because you have shed so much blood in my sight on the earth. ⁹See, a son shall be born to you; he shall be a man of peace. I will give him peace from all his enemies on every side; for his name shall be Solomon,^a and I will give peace^b and quiet to Israel in his days. ¹⁰He shall build a house for my name. He shall be a son to me, and I will be a father to him, and I will establish his royal throne in Israel forever.' ¹¹Now, my son, the LORD be with you, so that you may succeed in building the house of the LORD your God, as he has spoken concerning you. ¹²Only, may the LORD grant you discretion and understanding, so that when he gives you charge over Israel you may keep the law of the LORD your God. ¹³Then you will prosper if you are careful to observe the statutes and the ordinances that the LORD commanded Moses for Israel. Be strong and of good courage. Do not be afraid or dismayed. ¹⁴With great pains I have provided for the house of the LORD one hundred thousand talents of gold, one million talents of silver, and bronze and iron beyond weighing, for there is so much of it; timber and stone too I have provided. To these you must add more. ¹⁵You have an abundance of workers: stonecutters, masons, carpenters, and all kinds of artisans without number, skilled in working ¹⁶gold, silver, bronze, and iron. Now begin the work, and the LORD be with you."

17 David also commanded all the leaders of Israel to help his son Solomon, saying, ¹⁸"Is not the LORD your God with you? Has he not given you peace on every side? For he has delivered the inhabitants of the land into my hand; and the land is subdued before the LORD and his people. ¹⁹Now set your mind and heart to seek the LORD your God. Go and build the sanctuary of the LORD God so that the ark of the covenant of the LORD and the holy vessels of God may be brought into a house built for the name of the LORD."

a Heb *Shelomoh* *b* Heb *shalom*

23 Families of the Levites and Their Functions

When David was old and full of days, he made his son Solomon king over Israel.

2 David assembled all the leaders of Israel and the priests and the Levites. [3]The Levites, thirty years old and upward, were counted, and the total was thirty-eight thousand. [4]"Twenty-four thousand of these," David said, "shall have charge of the work in the house of the LORD, six thousand shall be officers and judges, [5]four thousand gatekeepers, and four thousand shall offer praises to the LORD with the instruments that I have made for praise." [6]And David organized them in divisions corresponding to the sons of Levi: Gershon,[a] Kohath, and Merari.

7 The sons of Gershon[b] were Ladan and Shimei. [8]The sons of Ladan: Jehiel the chief, Zetham, and Joel, three. [9]The sons of Shimei: Shelomoth, Haziel, and Haran, three. These were the heads of families of Ladan. [10]And the sons of Shimei: Jahath, Zina, Jeush, and Beriah. These four were the sons of Shimei. [11]Jahath was the chief, and Zizah the second; but Jeush and Beriah did not have many sons, so they were enrolled as a single family.

12 The sons of Kohath: Amram, Izhar, Hebron, and Uzziel, four. [13]The sons of Amram: Aaron and Moses. Aaron was set apart to consecrate the most holy things, so that he and his sons forever should make offerings before the LORD, and minister to him and pronounce blessings in his name forever; [14]but as for Moses the man of God, his sons were to be reckoned among the tribe of Levi. [15]The sons of Moses: Gershom and Eliezer. [16]The sons of Gershom: Shebuel the chief. [17]The sons of Eliezer: Rehabiah the chief; Eliezer had no other sons, but the sons of Rehabiah were very numerous. [18]The sons of Izhar: Shelomith the chief. [19]The sons of Hebron: Jeriah the chief, Amariah the second, Jahaziel the third, and Jekameam the fourth. [20]The sons of Uzziel: Micah the chief and Isshiah the second.

21 The sons of Merari: Mahli and Mushi. The sons of Mahli: Eleazar and Kish. [22]Eleazar died having no sons, but only daughters; their kindred, the sons of Kish, married them. [23]The sons of Mushi: Mahli, Eder, and Jeremoth, three.

24 These were the sons of Levi by their ancestral houses, the heads of families as they were enrolled according to the number of the names of the individuals from twenty years old and upward who were to do the work for the service of the house of the LORD. [25]For David said, "The LORD, the God of Israel, has given rest to his people; and he resides in Jerusalem forever. [26]And so the Levites no longer need to carry the tabernacle or any of the things for its service"— [27]for according to the last words of David these were the number of the Levites from twenty years old and upward— [28]"but their duty shall be to assist the descendants of Aaron for the service of the house of the LORD, having the care of the courts and the chambers, the cleansing of all that is holy, and any work for the service of the house of God; [29]to assist also with the rows of bread, the choice flour for the grain offering, the wafers of unleavened bread, the baked offering, the offering mixed with oil, and all measures of quantity or size. [30]And they shall stand every morning, thanking and praising the LORD, and likewise at evening, [31]and whenever burnt offerings are offered to the LORD on sabbaths, new moons, and appointed festivals, according to the number required of them, regularly before the LORD. [32]Thus they shall keep charge of the tent of meeting and the sanctuary, and shall attend the descendants of Aaron, their kindred, for the service of the house of the LORD."

24 Divisions of the Priests

The divisions of the descendants of Aaron were these. The sons of Aaron: Nadab, Abihu, Eleazar, and Ithamar. [2]But Nadab and Abihu died before their father, and had no sons; so Eleazar and Ithamar became the priests. [3]Along with Zadok of the sons of Eleazar, and Ahimelech of the sons of Ithamar, David organized them according to the appointed duties in their service. [4]Since more chief men were found among the sons of Eleazar than among the sons of Ithamar, they organized them under sixteen heads of ancestral houses of the sons of Eleazar, and eight of the sons of Ithamar. [5]They organized them by lot, all alike, for there were officers of the sanctuary and officers of God among both the sons of Eleazar and the sons of Ithamar. [6]The scribe Shemaiah son of Nethanel, a Levite, recorded them in the presence of the king, and the officers, and Zadok the priest, and Ahimelech son of Abiathar, and the heads of ancestral houses of the priests and of the Levites; one ancestral house being chosen for Eleazar and one chosen for Ithamar.

7 The first lot fell to Jehoiarib, the second to Jedaiah, [8]the third to Harim, the fourth to Seorim, [9]the fifth to Malchijah, the sixth to Mijamin, [10]the seventh

---

a Or *Gershom*; See 1 Chr 6.1, note, and 23.15   **b** Vg Compare Gk Syr: Heb *to the Gershonite*

to Hakkoz, the eighth to Abijah, [11] the ninth to Jeshua, the tenth to Shecaniah, [12] the eleventh to Eliashib, the twelfth to Jakim, [13] the thirteenth to Huppah, the fourteenth to Jeshebeab, [14] the fifteenth to Bilgah, the sixteenth to Immer, [15] the seventeenth to Hezir, the eighteenth to Happizzez, [16] the nineteenth to Pethahiah, the twentieth to Jehezkel, [17] the twenty-first to Jachin, the twenty-second to Gamul, [18] the twenty-third to Delaiah, the twenty-fourth to Maaziah. [19] These had as their appointed duty in their service to enter the house of the LORD according to the procedure established for them by their ancestor Aaron, as the LORD God of Israel had commanded him.

Other Levites

20 And of the rest of the sons of Levi: of the sons of Amram, Shubael; of the sons of Shubael, Jehdeiah. [21] Of Rehabiah: of the sons of Rehabiah, Isshiah the chief. [22] Of the Izharites, Shelomoth; of the sons of Shelomoth, Jahath. [23] The sons of Hebron:[a] Jeriah the chief,[b] Amariah the second, Jahaziel the third, Jekameam the fourth. [24] The sons of Uzziel, Micah; of the sons of Micah, Shamir. [25] The brother of Micah, Isshiah; of the sons of Isshiah, Zechariah. [26] The sons of Merari: Mahli and Mushi. The sons of Jaaziah: Beno.[c] [27] The sons of Merari: of Jaaziah, Beno,[c] Shoham, Zaccur, and Ibri. [28] Of Mahli: Eleazar, who had no sons. [29] Of Kish, the sons of Kish: Jerahmeel. [30] The sons of Mushi: Mahli, Eder, and Jerimoth. These were the sons of the Levites according to their ancestral houses. [31] These also cast lots corresponding to their kindred, the descendants of Aaron, in the presence of King David, Zadok, Ahimelech, and the heads of ancestral houses of the priests and of the Levites, the chief as well as the youngest brother.

The Temple Musicians

25 David and the officers of the army also set apart for the service the sons of Asaph, and of Heman, and of Jeduthun, who should prophesy with lyres, harps, and cymbals. The list of those who did the work and of their duties was: [2] Of the sons of Asaph: Zaccur, Joseph, Nethaniah, and Asarelah, sons of Asaph, under the direction of Asaph, who prophesied under the direction of the king. [3] Of Jeduthun, the sons of Jeduthun: Gedaliah, Zeri, Jeshaiah, Shimei,[d] Hashabiah, and Mattithiah, six, under the direction of their father Jeduthun, who prophesied

with the lyre in thanksgiving and praise to the LORD. [4] Of Heman, the sons of Heman: Bukkiah, Mattaniah, Uzziel, Shebuel, and Jerimoth, Hananiah, Hanani, Eliathah, Giddalti, and Romamti-ezer, Joshbekashah, Mallothi, Hothir, Mahazioth. [5] All these were the sons of Heman the king's seer, according to the promise of God to exalt him; for God had given Heman fourteen sons and three daughters. [6] They were all under the direction of their father for the music in the house of the LORD with cymbals, harps, and lyres for the service of the house of God. Asaph, Jeduthun, and Heman were under the order of the king. [7] They and their kindred, who were trained in singing to the LORD, all of whom were skillful, numbered two hundred eighty-eight. [8] And they cast lots for their duties, small and great, teacher and pupil alike.

9 The first lot fell for Asaph to Joseph; the second to Gedaliah, to him and his brothers and his sons, twelve; [10] the third to Zaccur, his sons and his brothers, twelve; [11] the fourth to Izri, his sons and his brothers, twelve; [12] the fifth to Nethaniah, his sons and his brothers, twelve; [13] the sixth to Bukkiah, his sons and his brothers, twelve; [14] the seventh to Jesarelah,[e] his sons and his brothers, twelve; [15] the eighth to Jeshaiah, his sons and his brothers, twelve; [16] the ninth to Mattaniah, his sons and his brothers, twelve; [17] the tenth to Shimei, his sons and his brothers, twelve; [18] the eleventh to Azarel, his sons and his brothers, twelve; [19] the twelfth to Hashabiah, his sons and his brothers, twelve; [20] to the thirteenth, Shubael, his sons and his brothers, twelve; [21] to the fourteenth, Mattithiah, his sons and his brothers, twelve; [22] to the fifteenth, to Jeremoth, his sons and his brothers, twelve; [23] to the sixteenth, to Hananiah, his sons and his brothers, twelve; [24] to the seventeenth, to Joshbekashah, his sons and his brothers, twelve; [25] to the eighteenth, to Hanani, his sons and his brothers, twelve; [26] to the nineteenth, to Mallothi, his sons and his brothers, twelve; [27] to the twentieth, to Eliathah, his sons and his brothers, twelve; [28] to the twenty-first, to Hothir, his sons and his brothers, twelve; [29] to the twenty-second, to Giddalti, his sons and his brothers, twelve; [30] to the twenty-third, to Mahazioth, his sons and his brothers, twelve; [31] to the twenty-fourth, to Romamti-ezer, his sons and his brothers, twelve.

The Gatekeepers

26 As for the divisions of the gatekeepers: of the Korahites, Meshelemiah son of Kore, of the sons of Asaph. [2] Meshelemiah had sons: Zech-

---

a See 23.19: Heb lacks *Hebron*   b See 23.19: Heb lacks *the chief*   c Or *his son*: Meaning of Heb uncertain   d One Ms: Gk: MT lacks *Shimei*
e Or *Asarelah*; see 25.2

ariah the firstborn, Jediael the second, Zebadiah the third, Jathniel the fourth, [3]Elam the fifth, Jehohanan the sixth, Eliehoenai the seventh. [4]Obed-edom had sons: Shemaiah the firstborn, Jehozabad the second, Joah the third, Sachar the fourth, Nethanel the fifth, [5]Ammiel the sixth, Issachar the seventh, Peullethai the eighth; for God blessed him. [6]Also to his son Shemaiah sons were born who exercised authority in their ancestral houses, for they were men of great ability. [7]The sons of Shemaiah: Othni, Rephael, Obed, and Elzabad, whose brothers were able men, Elihu and Semachiah. [8]All these, sons of Obed-edom with their sons and brothers, were able men qualified for the service; sixty-two of Obed-edom. [9]Meshelemiah had sons and brothers, able men, eighteen. [10]Hosah, of the sons of Merari, had sons: Shimri the chief (for though he was not the firstborn, his father made him chief), [11]Hilkiah the second, Tebaliah the third, Zechariah the fourth: all the sons and brothers of Hosah totaled thirteen.

12 These divisions of the gatekeepers, corresponding to their leaders, had duties, just as their kindred did, ministering in the house of the LORD; [13]and they cast lots by ancestral houses, small and great alike, for their gates. [14]The lot for the east fell to Shelemiah. They cast lots also for his son Zechariah, a prudent counselor, and his lot came out for the north. [15]Obed-edom's came out for the south, and to his sons was allotted the storehouse. [16]For Shuppim and Hosah it came out for the west, at the gate of Shallecheth on the ascending road. Guard corresponded to guard. [17]On the east there were six Levites each day,[a] on the north four each day, on the south four each day, as well as two and two at the storehouse; [18]and for the colonnade[b] on the west there were four at the road and two at the colonnade.[b] [19]These were the divisions of the gatekeepers among the Korahites and the sons of Merari.

The Treasurers, Officers, and Judges

20 And of the Levites, Ahijah had charge of the treasuries of the house of God and the treasuries of the dedicated gifts. [21]The sons of Ladan, the sons of the Gershonites belonging to Ladan, the heads of families belonging to Ladan the Gershonite: Jehieli.[c]

22 The sons of Jehieli, Zetham and his brother Joel, were in charge of the treasuries of the house of the LORD. [23]Of the Amramites, the Izharites, the Hebronites, and the Uzzielites: [24]Shebuel son of

Gershom, son of Moses, was chief officer in charge of the treasuries. [25]His brothers: from Eliezer were his son Rehabiah, his son Jeshaiah, his son Joram, his son Zichri, and his son Shelomoth. [26]This Shelomoth and his brothers were in charge of all the treasuries of the dedicated gifts that King David, and the heads of families, and the officers of the thousands and the hundreds, and the commanders of the army, had dedicated. [27]From booty won in battles they dedicated gifts for the maintenance of the house of the LORD. [28]Also all that Samuel the seer, and Saul son of Kish, and Abner son of Ner, and Joab son of Zeruiah had dedicated—all dedicated gifts were in the care of Shelomoth[d] and his brothers.

29 Of the Izharites, Chenaniah and his sons were appointed to outside duties for Israel, as officers and judges. [30]Of the Hebronites, Hashabiah and his brothers, one thousand seven hundred men of ability, had the oversight of Israel west of the Jordan for all the work of the LORD and for the service of the king. [31]Of the Hebronites, Jerijah was chief of the Hebronites. (In the fortieth year of David's reign search was made, of whatever genealogy or family, and men of great ability among them were found at Jazer in Gilead.) [32]King David appointed him and his brothers, two thousand seven hundred men of ability, heads of families, to have the oversight of the Reubenites, the Gadites, and the half-tribe of the Manassites for everything pertaining to God and for the affairs of the king.

The Military Divisions

27 This is the list of the people of Israel, the heads of families, the commanders of the thousands and the hundreds, and their officers who served the king in all matters concerning the divisions that came and went, month after month throughout the year, each division numbering twenty-four thousand:

2 Jashobeam son of Zabdiel was in charge of the first division in the first month; in his division were twenty-four thousand. [3]He was a descendant of Perez, and was chief of all the commanders of the army for the first month. [4]Dodai the Ahohite was in charge of the division of the second month; Mikloth was the chief officer of his division. In his division were twenty-four thousand. [5]The third commander, for the third month, was Benaiah son of the priest Jehoiada, as chief; in his division were twenty-four thousand. [6]This is the Benaiah who was a mighty

man of the Thirty and in command of the Thirty; his son Ammizabad was in charge of his division.[a] [7]Asahel brother of Joab was fourth, for the fourth month, and his son Zebadiah after him; in his division were twenty-four thousand. [8]The fifth commander, for the fifth month, was Shamhuth, the Izrahite; in his division were twenty-four thousand. [9]Sixth, for the sixth month, was Ira son of Ikkesh the Tekoite; in his division were twenty-four thousand. [10]Seventh, for the seventh month, was Helez the Pelonite, of the Ephraimites; in his division were twenty-four thousand. [11]Eighth, for the eighth month, was Sibbecai the Hushathite, of the Zerahites; in his division were twenty-four thousand. [12]Ninth, for the ninth month, was Abiezer of Anathoth, a Benjaminite; in his division were twenty-four thousand. [13]Tenth, for the tenth month, was Maharai of Netophah, of the Zerahites; in his division were twenty-four thousand. [14]Eleventh, for the eleventh month, was Benaiah of Pirathon, of the Ephraimites; in his division were twenty-four thousand. [15]Twelfth, for the twelfth month, was Heldai the Netophathite, of Othniel; in his division were twenty-four thousand.

Leaders of Tribes

16 Over the tribes of Israel, for the Reubenites, Eliezer son of Zichri was chief officer; for the Simeonites, Shephatiah son of Maacah; [17]for Levi, Hashabiah son of Kemuel; for Aaron, Zadok; [18]for Judah, Elihu, one of David's brothers; for Issachar, Omri son of Michael; [19]for Zebulun, Ishmaiah son of Obadiah; for Naphtali, Jerimoth son of Azriel; [20]for the Ephraimites, Hoshea son of Azaziah; for the half-tribe of Manasseh, Joel son of Pedaiah; [21]for the half-tribe of Manasseh in Gilead, Iddo son of Zechariah; for Benjamin, Jaasiel son of Abner; [22]for Dan, Azarel son of Jeroham. These were the leaders of the tribes of Israel. [23]David did not count those below twenty years of age, for the LORD had promised to make Israel as numerous as the stars of heaven. [24]Joab son of Zeruiah began to count them, but did not finish; yet wrath came upon Israel for this, and the number was not entered into the account of the Annals of King David.

Other Civic Officials

25 Over the king's treasuries was Azmaveth son of Adiel. Over the treasuries in the country, in the cities, in the villages and in the towers, was Jonathan son of Uzziah. [26]Over those who did the work of the field,

tilling the soil, was Ezri son of Chelub. [27]Over the vineyards was Shimei the Ramathite. Over the produce of the vineyards for the wine cellars was Zabdi the Shiphmite. [28]Over the olive and sycamore trees in the Shephelah was Baal-hanan the Gederite. Over the stores of oil was Joash. [29]Over the herds that pastured in Sharon was Shitrai the Sharonite. Over the herds in the valleys was Shaphat son of Adlai. [30]Over the camels was Obil the Ishmaelite. Over the donkeys was Jehdeiah the Meronothite. Over the flocks was Jaziz the Hagrite. [31]All these were stewards of King David's property.

32 Jonathan, David's uncle, was a counselor, being a man of understanding and a scribe; Jehiel son of Hachmoni attended the king's sons. [33]Ahithophel was the king's counselor, and Hushai the Archite was the king's friend. [34]After Ahithophel came Jehoiada son of Benaiah, and Abiathar. Joab was commander of the king's army.

28

Solomon Instructed to Build the Temple

David assembled at Jerusalem all the officials of Israel, the officials of the tribes, the officers of the divisions that served the king, the commanders of the thousands, the commanders of the hundreds, the stewards of all the property and cattle of the king and his sons, together with the palace officials, the mighty warriors, and all the warriors. [2]Then King David rose to his feet and said: "Hear me, my brothers and my people. I had planned to build a house of rest for the ark of the covenant of the LORD, for the footstool of our God; and I made preparations for building. [3]But God said to me, 'You shall not build a house for my name, for you are a warrior and have shed blood.' [4]Yet the LORD God of Israel chose me from all my ancestral house to be king over Israel forever; for he chose Judah as leader, and in the house of Judah my father's house, and among my father's sons he took delight in making me king over all Israel. [5]And of all my sons, for the LORD has given me many, he has chosen my son Solomon to sit upon the throne of the kingdom of the LORD over Israel. [6]He said to me, 'It is your son Solomon who shall build my house and my courts, for I have chosen him to be a son to me, and I will be a father to him. [7]I will establish his kingdom forever if he continues resolute in keeping my commandments and my ordinances, as he is today.' [8]Now therefore in the sight of all Israel, the assembly of

---

[a] Gk Vg: Heb *Ammizabad was his division*

the Lord, and in the hearing of our God, observe and search out all the commandments of the Lord your God; that you may possess this good land, and leave it for an inheritance to your children after you forever.

9 "And you, my son Solomon, know the God of your father, and serve him with single mind and willing heart; for the Lord searches every mind, and understands every plan and thought. If you seek him, he will be found by you; but if you forsake him, he will abandon you forever. ¹⁰Take heed now, for the Lord has chosen you to build a house as the sanctuary; be strong, and act."

11 Then David gave his son Solomon the plan of the vestibule of the temple, and of its houses, its treasuries, its upper rooms, and its inner chambers, and of the room for the mercy seat; [a] ¹²and the plan of all that he had in mind: for the courts of the house of the Lord, all the surrounding chambers, the treasuries of the house of God, and the treasuries for dedicated gifts; ¹³for the divisions of the priests and of the Levites, and all the work of the service in the house of the Lord; for all the vessels for the service in the house of the Lord, ¹⁴the weight of gold for all golden vessels for each service, the weight of silver vessels for each service, ¹⁵the weight of the golden lampstands and their lamps, the weight of gold for each lampstand and its lamps, the weight of silver for a lampstand and its lamps, according to the use of each in the service, ¹⁶the weight of gold for each table for the rows of bread, the silver for the silver tables, ¹⁷and pure gold for the forks, the basins, and the cups; for the golden bowls and the weight of each; for the silver bowls and the weight of each; ¹⁸for the altar of incense made of refined gold, and its weight; also his plan for the golden chariot of the cherubim that spread their wings and covered the ark of the covenant of the Lord.

19 "All this, in writing at the Lord's direction, he made clear to me—the plan of all the works."

20 David said further to his son Solomon, "Be strong and of good courage, and act. Do not be afraid or dismayed; for the Lord God, my God, is with you. He will not fail you or forsake you, until all the work for the service of the house of the Lord is finished. ²¹Here are the divisions of the priests and the Levites for all the service of the house of God; and with you in all the work will be every volunteer who has skill for any kind of service; also the officers and all the people will be wholly at your command."

a Or the cover   b Heb fortress

29 Offerings for Building the Temple

King David said to the whole assembly, "My son Solomon, whom alone God has chosen, is young and inexperienced, and the work is great; for the temple[b] will not be for mortals but for the Lord God. ²So I have provided for the house of my God, so far as I was able, the gold for the things of gold, the silver for the things of silver, and the bronze for the things of bronze, the iron for the things of iron, and wood for the things of wood, besides great quantities of onyx and stones for setting, antimony, colored stones, all sorts of precious stones, and marble in abundance. ³Moreover, in addition to all that I have provided for the holy house, I have a treasure of my own of gold and silver, and because of my devotion to the house of my God I give it to the house of my God: ⁴three thousand talents of gold, of the gold of Ophir, and seven thousand talents of refined silver, for overlaying the walls of the house, ⁵and for all the work to be done by artisans, gold for the things of gold and silver for the things of silver. Who then will offer willingly, consecrating themselves today to the Lord?"

6 Then the leaders of ancestral houses made their freewill offerings, as did also the leaders of the tribes, the commanders of the thousands and of the hundreds, and the officers over the king's work. ⁷They gave for the service of the house of God five thousand talents and ten thousand darics of gold, ten thousand talents of silver, eighteen thousand talents of bronze, and one hundred thousand talents of iron. ⁸Whoever had precious stones gave them to the treasury of the house of the Lord, into the care of Jehiel the Gershonite. ⁹Then the people rejoiced because these had given willingly, for with single mind they had offered freely to the Lord; King David also rejoiced greatly.

David's Praise to God

10 Then David blessed the Lord in the presence of all the assembly; David said: "Blessed are you, O Lord, the God of our ancestor Israel, forever and ever. ¹¹Yours, O Lord, are the greatness, the power, the glory, the victory, and the majesty; for all that is in the heavens and on the earth is yours; yours is the kingdom, O Lord, and you are exalted as head above all. ¹²Riches and honor come from you, and you rule over all. In your hand are power and might; and it is in your hand to make great and

CONNECT IT!

The Karen People: The Sacred Name of God
1 Chronicles 29:10–22

As David neared the end of his life and reign, he blessed God's name in the midst of the people. The Israelites believed in one God, but were surrounded by people of other cultures who believed in many different gods. The name of God was sacred and precious to the Israelites. When David publicly praised God's name, he affirmed God's power, glory, majesty, and victory over all creation (1 Chronicles 29:11).

Other cultures around the world have their own names for God. The Karen people of Burma (also known today as Myanmar) called their supreme god Y'wa. Even though they were surrounded by Buddhist cultures, they had clung to their beliefs—and their prophecy that one day a white brother would bring them God's book, which their ancestors had lost, to reveal God's ways. In the early 1800s, the Karen were overjoyed when American missionaries arrived with the Bible, and they readily accepted Jesus. By remaining true to their belief in Y'wa, one God with power over all creation, these people were prepared for God's revelation and news of Jesus.

own. ¹⁷I know, my God, that you search the heart, and take pleasure in uprightness; in the uprightness of my heart I have freely offered all these things, and now I have seen your people, who are present here, offering freely and joyously to you. ¹⁸O Lᴏʀᴅ, the God of Abraham, Isaac, and Israel, our ancestors, keep forever such purposes and thoughts in the hearts of your people, and direct their hearts toward you. ¹⁹Grant to my son Solomon that with single mind he may keep your commandments, your decrees, and your statutes, performing all of them, and that he may build the temple*a* for which I have made provision."

20 Then David said to the whole assembly, "Bless the Lᴏʀᴅ your God." And all the assembly blessed the Lᴏʀᴅ, the God of their ancestors, and bowed their heads and prostrated themselves before the Lᴏʀᴅ and the king. ²¹On the next day they offered sacrifices and burnt offerings to the Lᴏʀᴅ, a thousand bulls, a thousand rams, and a thousand lambs, with their libations, and sacrifices in abundance for all Israel; ²²and they ate and drank before the Lᴏʀᴅ on that day with great joy.

Solomon Anointed King

They made David's son Solomon king a second time; they anointed him as the Lᴏʀᴅ's prince, and Zadok as priest. ²³Then Solomon sat on the throne of the Lᴏʀᴅ, succeeding his father David as king; he prospered, and all Israel obeyed him. ²⁴All the leaders and the mighty warriors, and also all the sons of King David, pledged their allegiance to King Solomon. ²⁵The Lᴏʀᴅ highly exalted Solomon in the sight of all Israel, and bestowed upon him such royal majesty as had not been on any king before him in Israel.

Summary of David's Reign

26 Thus David son of Jesse reigned over all Israel. ²⁷The period that he reigned over Israel was forty years; he reigned seven years in Hebron, and thirty-three years in Jerusalem. ²⁸He died in a good old age, full of days, riches, and honor; and his son Solomon succeeded him. ²⁹Now the acts of King David, from first to last, are written in the records of the seer Samuel, and in the records of the prophet Nathan, and in the records of the seer Gad, ³⁰with accounts of all his rule and his might and of the events that befell him and Israel and all the kingdoms of the earth.

to give strength to all. ¹³And now, our God, we give thanks to you and praise your glorious name. 14 "But who am I, and what is my people, that we should be able to make this freewill offering? For all things come from you, and of your own have we given you. ¹⁵For we are aliens and transients before you, as were all our ancestors; our days on the earth are like a shadow, and there is no hope. ¹⁶O Lᴏʀᴅ our God, all this abundance that we have provided for building you a house for your holy name comes from your hand and is all your

a Heb *fortress*

2 Chronicles ►►►

For background on this book, see the introduction to 1 and 2 Chronicles at the beginning of 1 Chronicles.

Solomon Requests Wisdom

1 Solomon son of David established himself in his kingdom; the Lord his God was with him and made him exceedingly great.

2 Solomon summoned all Israel, the commanders of the thousands and of the hundreds, the judges, and all the leaders of all Israel, the heads of families. ³Then Solomon, and the whole assembly with him, went to the high place that was at Gibeon; for God's tent of meeting, which Moses the servant of the Lord had made in the wilderness, was there. ⁴(But David had brought the ark of God up from Kiriath-jearim to the place that David had prepared for it; for he had pitched a tent for it in Jerusalem.) ⁵Moreover the bronze altar that Bezalel son of Uri, son of Hur, had made, was there in front of the tabernacle of the Lord. And Solomon and the assembly inquired at it. ⁶Solomon went up there to the bronze altar before the Lord, which was at the tent of meeting, and offered a thousand burnt offerings on it.

7 That night God appeared to Solomon, and said to him, "Ask what I should give you." ⁸Solomon said to God, "You have shown great and steadfast love to my father David, and have made me succeed him as king. ⁹O Lord God, let your promise to my father David now be fulfilled, for you have made me king over a people as numerous as the dust of the earth. ¹⁰Give me now wisdom and knowledge to go out and come in before this people, for who can rule this great people of yours?" ¹¹God answered Solomon, "Because this was in your heart, and you have not asked for possessions, wealth, honor, or the life of those who hate you, and have not even asked for long life, but have asked for wisdom and knowledge for yourself that you may rule my people over whom I have made you king, ¹²wisdom and knowledge are granted to you. I will also give you riches, possessions, and honor, such as none of the kings had who were before you, and none after you shall have the like." ¹³So Solomon came from*ᵃ* the high place at Gibeon, from the tent of meeting, to Jerusalem. And he reigned over Israel.

Solomon's Military and Commercial Activity

14 Solomon gathered together chariots and horses; he had fourteen hundred chariots and twelve thousand horses, which he stationed in the

---

STUDY IT!

What Is Wisdom? • 2 Chronicles 1:7–12

What a deal for Solomon: ask for anything, and you'll get it (2 Chronicles 1:7). It's like our genie-in-a-bottle fantasy come true. So what does Solomon ask for? Wealth? Power? Fame? Nope. Wisdom. This pleases God, because it shows Solomon's desire to rule according to God's will.

But what is wisdom? For the Chronicler, wisdom was more than just knowing what was right. It meant living according to God's instruction, or the Torah (see Deuteronomy 17:8–11). A wise person worships God correctly and lives a moral life in keeping with the law. A wise leader or king governs justly. To learn more about the Israelites' view of wisdom, take a look at the wisdom books in the next section of the Old Testament (such as the book of Proverbs). For a New Testament perspective, see **Luke 2:41–52** and **1 Corinthians 1:18–31.**

ᵃ Gk Vg: Heb *to*

chariot cities and with the king in Jerusalem. [15] The king made silver and gold as common in Jerusalem as stone, and he made cedar as plentiful as the sycamore of the Shephelah. [16] Solomon's horses were imported from Egypt and Kue; the king's traders received them from Kue at the prevailing price. [17] They imported from Egypt, and then exported, a chariot for six hundred shekels of silver, and a horse for one hundred fifty; so through them these were exported to all the kings of the Hittites and the kings of Aram.

Preparations for Building the Temple

[a] Solomon decided to build a temple for the name of the LORD, and a royal palace for himself. [2] [b] Solomon conscripted seventy thousand laborers and eighty thousand stonecutters in the hill country, with three thousand six hundred to oversee them.

Alliance with Huram of Tyre

3 Solomon sent word to King Huram of Tyre: "Once you dealt with my father David and sent him cedar to build himself a house to live in. [4] I am now about to build a house for the name of the LORD my God and dedicate it to him for offering fragrant incense before him, and for the regular offering of the rows of bread, and for burnt offerings morning and evening, on the sabbaths and the new moons and the appointed festivals of the LORD our God, as ordained forever for Israel. [5] The house that I am about to build will be great, for our God is greater than other gods. [6] But who is able to build him a house, since heaven, even highest heaven, cannot contain him? Who am I to build a house for him, except as a place to make offerings before him? [7] So now send me an artisan skilled to work in gold, silver, bronze, and iron, and in purple, crimson, and blue fabrics, trained also in engraving, to join the skilled workers who are with me in Judah and Jerusalem, whom my father David provided. [8] Send me also cedar, cypress, and algum timber from Lebanon, for I know that your servants are skilled in cutting Lebanon timber. My servants will work with your servants [9] to prepare timber for me in abundance, for the house I am about to build will be great and wonderful. [10] I will provide for your servants, those who cut the timber, twenty thousand cors of crushed wheat, twenty thousand

cors of barley, twenty thousand baths[c] of wine, and twenty thousand baths of oil."

11 Then King Huram of Tyre answered in a letter that he sent to Solomon, "Because the LORD loves his people he has made you king over them." [12] Huram also said, "Blessed be the LORD God of Israel, who made heaven and earth, who has given King David a wise son, endowed with discretion and understanding, who will build a temple for the LORD, and a royal palace for himself.

13 "I have dispatched Huram-abi, a skilled artisan, endowed with understanding, [14] the son of one of the Danite women, his father a Tyrian. He is trained to work in gold, silver, bronze, iron, stone, and wood, and in purple, blue, and crimson fabrics and fine linen, and to do all sorts of engraving and execute any design that may be assigned him, with your artisans, the artisans of my lord, your father David. [15] Now, as for the wheat, barley, oil, and wine, of which my lord has spoken, let him send them to his servants. [16] We will cut whatever timber you need from Lebanon, and bring it to you as rafts by sea to Joppa; you will take it up to Jerusalem."

17 Then Solomon took a census of all the aliens who were residing in the land of Israel, after the census that his father David had taken; and there were found to be one hundred fifty-three thousand six hundred. [18] Seventy thousand of them he assigned as laborers, eighty thousand as stonecutters in the hill country, and three thousand six hundred as overseers to make the people work.

Solomon Builds the Temple

Solomon began to build the house of the LORD in Jerusalem on Mount Moriah, where the LORD had appeared to his father David, at the place that David had designated, on the threshing floor of Ornan the Jebusite. [2] He began to build on the second day of the second month of the fourth year of his reign. [3] These are Solomon's measurements[d] for building the house of God: the length, in cubits of the old standard, was sixty cubits, and the width twenty cubits. [4] The vestibule in front of the nave of the house was twenty cubits long, across the width of the house;[e] and its height was one hundred twenty cubits. He overlaid it on the inside with pure gold. [5] The nave he lined with cypress, covered it with fine gold, and made palms and chains on it. [6] He adorned the house with settings of precious stones. The gold was gold from Parvaim.

a Ch 1.18 in Heb   b Ch 2.1 in Heb   c A Hebrew measure of volume   d Syr: Heb *foundations*   e Compare 1 Kings 6.3: Meaning of Heb uncertain

7 So he lined the house with gold—its beams, its thresholds, its walls, and its doors; and he carved cherubim on the walls.

8 He made the most holy place; its length, corresponding to the width of the house, was twenty cubits, and its width was twenty cubits; he overlaid it with six hundred talents of fine gold. 9 The weight of the nails was fifty shekels of gold. He overlaid the upper chambers with gold.

10 In the most holy place he made two carved cherubim and overlaid[a] them with gold. 11 The wings of the cherubim together extended twenty cubits: one wing of the one, five cubits long, touched the wall of the house, and its other wing, five cubits long, touched the wing of the other cherub; 12 and of this cherub, one wing, five cubits long, touched the wall of the house, and the other wing, also five cubits long, was joined to the wing of the first cherub. 13 The wings of these cherubim extended twenty cubits; the cherubim[b] stood on their feet, facing the nave. 14 And Solomon[c] made the curtain of blue and purple and crimson fabrics and fine linen, and worked cherubim into it.

15 In front of the house he made two pillars thirty-five cubits high, with a capital of five cubits on the top of each. 16 He made encircling[d] chains and put them on the tops of the pillars; and he made one hundred pomegranates, and put them on the chains. 17 He set up the pillars in front of the temple, one on the right, the other on the left; the one on the right he called Jachin, and the one on the left, Boaz.

Furnishings of the Temple

4 He made an altar of bronze, twenty cubits long, twenty cubits wide, and ten cubits high. 2 Then he made the molten sea; it was round, ten cubits from rim to rim, and five cubits high. A line of thirty cubits would encircle it completely. 3 Under it were panels all around, each of ten cubits, surrounding the sea; there were two rows of panels, cast when it was cast. 4 It stood on twelve oxen, three facing north, three facing west, three facing south, and three facing east; the sea was set on them. The hindquarters of each were toward the inside. 5 Its thickness was a handbreadth; its rim was made like the rim of a cup, like the flower of a lily; it held three thousand baths.[e] 6 He also made ten basins in which to wash, and set five on the right side, and five on the left. In these they were to rinse what was used

for the burnt offering. The sea was for the priests to wash in.

7 He made ten golden lampstands as prescribed, and set them in the temple, five on the south side and five on the north. 8 He also made ten tables and placed them in the temple, five on the right side and five on the left. And he made one hundred basins of gold. 9 He made the court of the priests, and the great court, and doors for the court; he overlaid their doors with bronze. 10 He set the sea at the southeast corner of the house.

11 And Huram made the pots, the shovels, and the basins. Thus Huram finished the work that he did for King Solomon on the house of God: 12 the two pillars, the bowls, and the two capitals on the top of the pillars; and the two latticeworks to cover the two bowls of the capitals that were on the top of the pillars; 13 the four hundred pomegranates for the two latticeworks, two rows of pomegranates for each latticework, to cover the two bowls of the capitals that were on the pillars. 14 He made the stands, the basins on the stands, 15 the one sea, and the twelve oxen underneath it. 16 The pots, the shovels, the forks, and all the equipment for these Huram-abi made of burnished bronze for King Solomon for the house of the LORD. 17 In the plain of the Jordan the king cast them, in the clay ground between Succoth and Zeredah. 18 Solomon made all these things in great quantities, so that the weight of the bronze was not determined.

19 So Solomon made all the things that were in the house of God: the golden altar, the tables for the bread of the Presence, 20 the lampstands and their lamps of pure gold to burn before the inner sanctuary, as prescribed; 21 the flowers, the lamps, and the tongs, of purest gold; 22 the snuffers, basins, ladles, and firepans, of pure gold. As for the entrance to the temple: the inner doors to the most holy place and the doors of the nave of the temple were of gold.

5 Thus all the work that Solomon did for the house of the LORD was finished. Solomon brought in the things that his father David had dedicated, and stored the silver, the gold, and all the vessels in the treasuries of the house of God.

The Ark Brought into the Temple

2 Then Solomon assembled the elders of Israel and all the heads of the tribes, the leaders of the ancestral houses of the people of Israel, in Jerusalem, to bring up the ark of the covenant of the LORD out

---

a Heb *they overlaid* b Heb *they* c Heb *he* d Cn: Heb *in the inner sanctuary* e A Hebrew measure of volume

of the city of David, which is Zion. ³And all the Israelites assembled before the king at the festival that is in the seventh month. ⁴And all the elders of Israel came, and the Levites carried the ark. ⁵So they brought up the ark, the tent of meeting, and all the holy vessels that were in the tent; the priests and the Levites brought them up. ⁶King Solomon and all the congregation of Israel, who had assembled before him, were before the ark, sacrificing so many sheep and oxen that they could not be numbered or counted. ⁷Then the priests brought the ark of the covenant of the Lord to its place, in the inner sanctuary of the house, in the most holy place, underneath the wings of the cherubim. ⁸For the cherubim spread out their wings over the place of the ark, so that the cherubim made a covering above the ark and its poles. ⁹The poles were so long that the ends of the poles were seen from the holy place in front of the inner sanctuary; but they could not be seen from outside; they are there to this day. ¹⁰There was nothing in the ark except the two tablets that Moses put there at Horeb, where the Lord made a covenant*ᵃ* with the people of Israel after they came out of Egypt.

11 Now when the priests came out of the holy place (for all the priests who were present had sanctified themselves, without regard to their divisions), ¹²all the levitical singers, Asaph, Heman, and Jeduthun, their sons and kindred, arrayed in fine linen, with cymbals, harps, and lyres, stood east of the altar with one hundred twenty priests who were trumpeters. ¹³It was the duty of the trumpeters and singers to make themselves heard in unison in praise and thanksgiving to the Lord, and when the song was raised, with trumpets and cymbals and other musical instruments, in praise to the Lord,

"For he is good,
        for his steadfast love endures forever,"

the house, the house of the Lord, was filled with a cloud, ¹⁴so that the priests could not stand to minister because of the cloud; for the glory of the Lord filled the house of God.

Dedication of the Temple

6 Then Solomon said, "The Lord has said that he would reside in thick darkness. ²I have built you an exalted house, a place for you to reside in forever."

3 Then the king turned around and blessed all the assembly of Israel, while all the assembly of Israel

stood. ⁴And he said, "Blessed be the Lord, the God of Israel, who with his hand has fulfilled what he promised with his mouth to my father David, saying, ⁵'Since the day that I brought my people out of the land of Egypt, I have not chosen a city from any of the tribes of Israel in which to build a house, so that my name might be there, and I chose no one as ruler over my people Israel; ⁶but I have chosen Jerusalem in order that my name may be there, and I have chosen David to be over my people Israel.' ⁷My father David had it in mind to build a house for the name of the Lord, the God of Israel. ⁸But the Lord said to my father David, 'You did well to consider building a house for my name; ⁹nevertheless you shall not build the house, but your son who shall be born to you shall build the house for my name.' ¹⁰Now the Lord has fulfilled his promise that he made; for I have succeeded my father David, and sit on the throne of Israel, as the Lord promised, and have built the house for the name of the Lord, the God of Israel. ¹¹There I have set the ark, in which is the covenant of the Lord that he made with the people of Israel."

Solomon's Prayer of Dedication

12 Then Solomon*ᵇ* stood before the altar of the Lord in the presence of the whole assembly of Israel, and spread out his hands. ¹³Solomon had made a bronze platform five cubits long, five cubits wide, and three cubits high, and had set it in the court; and he stood on it. Then he knelt on his knees in the presence of the whole assembly of Israel, and spread out his hands toward heaven. ¹⁴He said, "O Lord, God of Israel, there is no God like you, in heaven or on earth, keeping covenant in steadfast love with your servants who walk before you with all their heart— ¹⁵you who have kept for your servant, my father David, what you promised to him. Indeed, you promised with your mouth and this day have fulfilled with your hand. ¹⁶Therefore, O Lord, God of Israel, keep for your servant, my father David, that which you promised him, saying, 'There shall never fail you a successor before me to sit on the throne of Israel, if only your children keep to their way, to walk in my law as you have walked before me.' ¹⁷Therefore, O Lord, God of Israel, let your word be confirmed, which you promised to your servant David.

18 "But will God indeed reside with mortals on earth? Even heaven and the highest heaven cannot

ᵃ Heb lacks *a covenant* ᵇ Heb *he*

contain you, how much less this house that I have built! [19]Regard your servant's prayer and his plea, O LORD my God, heeding the cry and the prayer that your servant prays to you. [20]May your eyes be open day and night toward this house, the place where you promised to set your name, and may you heed the prayer that your servant prays toward this place. [21]And hear the plea of your servant and of your people Israel, when they pray toward this place; may you hear from heaven your dwelling place; hear and forgive.

[22] "If someone sins against another and is required to take an oath and comes and swears before your altar in this house, [23]may you hear from heaven, and act, and judge your servants, repaying the guilty by bringing their conduct on their own head, and vindicating those who are in the right by rewarding them in accordance with their righteousness.

[24] "When your people Israel, having sinned against you, are defeated before an enemy but turn again to you, confess your name, pray and plead with you in this house, [25]may you hear from heaven, and forgive the sin of your people Israel, and bring them again to the land that you gave to them and to their ancestors.

[26] "When heaven is shut up and there is no rain because they have sinned against you, and then they pray toward this place, confess your name, and turn from their sin, because you punish them, [27]may you hear in heaven, forgive the sin of your servants, your people Israel, when you teach them the good way in which they should walk; and send down rain upon your land, which you have given to your people as an inheritance.

[28] "If there is famine in the land, if there is plague, blight, mildew, locust, or caterpillar; if their enemies besiege them in any of the settlements of the lands; whatever suffering, whatever sickness there is; [29]whatever prayer, whatever plea from any individual or from all your people Israel, all knowing their own suffering and their own sorrows so that they stretch out their hands toward this house; [30]may you hear from heaven, your dwelling place, forgive, and render to all whose heart you know, according to all their ways, for only you know the human heart. [31]Thus may they fear you and walk in your ways all the days that they live in the land that you gave to our ancestors.

[32] "Likewise when foreigners, who are not of your people Israel, come from a distant land because of your great name, and your mighty hand, and your outstretched arm, when they come and pray toward this house, [33]may you hear from heaven your dwelling place, and do whatever the foreigners ask of you, in order that all the peoples of the earth may know your name and fear you, as do your people Israel, and that they may know that your name has been invoked on this house that I have built.

[34] "If your people go out to battle against their enemies, by whatever way you shall send them, and they pray to you toward this city that you have chosen and the house that I have built for your name, [35]then hear from heaven their prayer and their plea, and maintain their cause.

[36] "If they sin against you—for there is no one who does not sin—and you are angry with them and give them to an enemy, so that they are carried away captive to a land far or near; [37]then if they come to their senses in the land to which they have been taken captive, and repent, and plead with you in the land of their captivity, saying, 'We have sinned, and have done wrong; we have acted wickedly'; [38]if they repent with all their heart and soul in the land of their captivity, to which they were taken captive, and pray toward their land, which you gave to their ancestors, the city that you have chosen, and the house that I have built for your name, [39]then hear from heaven your dwelling place their prayer and their pleas, maintain their cause and forgive your people who have sinned against you. [40]Now, O my God, let your eyes be open and your ears attentive to prayer from this place.

[41] "Now rise up, O LORD God, and go to your
  resting place,
  you and the ark of your might.
Let your priests, O LORD God, be clothed
  with salvation,
  and let your faithful rejoice in your
  goodness.
[42] O LORD God, do not reject your
  anointed one.
Remember your steadfast love for your
  servant David."

Solomon Dedicates the Temple

7 When Solomon had ended his prayer, fire came down from heaven and consumed the burnt offering and the sacrifices; and the glory of the LORD filled the temple. [2]The priests could not enter the house of the LORD, because the glory of the LORD filled the LORD's house. [3]When all the people of Israel saw the fire come down and the glory of the LORD on the temple, they bowed down on the pavement with their faces to the ground, and worshiped and gave thanks to the LORD, saying,

"For he is good,

for his steadfast love endures forever."

[4] Then the king and all the people offered sacrifice before the LORD. [5]King Solomon offered as a sacrifice twenty-two thousand oxen and one hundred twenty thousand sheep. So the king and all the people dedicated the house of God. [6]The priests stood at their posts; the Levites also, with the instruments for music to the LORD that King David had made for giving thanks to the LORD—for his steadfast love endures forever—whenever David offered praises by their ministry. Opposite them the priests sounded trumpets; and all Israel stood.

[7] Solomon consecrated the middle of the court that was in front of the house of the LORD; for there he offered the burnt offerings and the fat of the offerings of well-being because the bronze altar Solomon had made could not hold the burnt offering and the grain offering and the fat parts.

[8] At that time Solomon held the festival for seven days, and all Israel with him, a very great congregation, from Lebo-hamath to the Wadi of Egypt. [9]On the eighth day they held a solemn assembly; for they had observed the dedication of the altar seven days and the festival seven days. [10]On the twenty-third day of the seventh month he sent the people away to their homes, joyful and in good spirits because of the goodness that the LORD had shown to David and to Solomon and to his people Israel.

[11] Thus Solomon finished the house of the LORD and the king's house; all that Solomon had planned to do in the house of the LORD and in his own house he successfully accomplished.

God's Second Appearance to Solomon

[12] Then the LORD appeared to Solomon in the night and said to him: "I have heard your prayer, and have chosen this place for myself as a house of sacrifice. [13]When I shut up the heavens so that there is no rain, or command the locust to devour the land, or send pestilence among my people, [14]if my people who are called by my name humble themselves, pray, seek my face, and turn from their wicked ways, then I will hear from heaven, and will forgive their sin and heal their land. [15]Now my eyes will be open and my ears attentive to the prayer that is made in this place. [16]For now I have chosen and consecrated this house so that my name may be there forever; my eyes and my heart will be there for all time. [17]As for you, if you walk before me, as your father David walked, doing according to all that I have commanded you and keeping my statutes and my ordinances, [18]then I will establish your royal throne, as I made covenant with your father David saying, 'You shall never lack a successor to rule over Israel.'

[19] "But if you[a] turn aside and forsake my statutes and my commandments that I have set before you, and go and serve other gods and worship them, [20]then I will pluck you[b] up from the land that I have given you;[b] and this house, which I have consecrated for my name, I will cast out of my sight, and will make it a proverb and a byword among all peoples. [21]And regarding this house, now exalted, everyone passing by will be astonished, and say, 'Why has the LORD done such a thing to this land and to this house?' [22]Then they will say, 'Because they abandoned the LORD the God of their ancestors who brought them out of the land of Egypt, and they adopted other gods, and worshiped them and served them; therefore he has brought all this calamity upon them.' "

Various Activities of Solomon

8 At the end of twenty years, during which Solomon had built the house of the LORD and his own house, [2]Solomon rebuilt the cities that

---

a The word *you* in this verse is plural   *b* Heb *them*

> "If my people who are called by my name humble themselves, pray, seek my face, and turn from their wicked ways, then I will hear from heaven, and will forgive their sin and heal their land."
> —2 Chronicles 7:14

Huram had given to him, and settled the people of Israel in them.

3 Solomon went to Hamath-zobah, and captured it. ⁴He built Tadmor in the wilderness and all the storage towns that he built in Hamath. ⁵He also built Upper Beth-horon and Lower Beth-horon, fortified cities, with walls, gates, and bars, ⁶and Baalath, as well as all Solomon's storage towns, and all the towns for his chariots, the towns for his cavalry, and whatever Solomon desired to build, in Jerusalem, in Lebanon, and in all the land of his dominion. ⁷All the people who were left of the Hittites, the Amorites, the Perizzites, the Hivites, and the Jebusites, who were not of Israel, ⁸from their descendants who were still left in the land, whom the people of Israel had not destroyed—these Solomon conscripted for forced labor, as is still the case today. ⁹But of the people of Israel Solomon made no slaves for his work; they were soldiers, and his officers, the commanders of his chariotry and cavalry. ¹⁰These were the chief officers of King Solomon, two hundred fifty of them, who exercised authority over the people.

11 Solomon brought Pharaoh's daughter from the city of David to the house that he had built for her, for he said, "My wife shall not live in the house of King David of Israel, for the places to which the ark of the LORD has come are holy."

12 Then Solomon offered up burnt offerings to the LORD on the altar of the LORD that he had built in front of the vestibule, ¹³as the duty of each day required, offering according to the commandment of Moses for the sabbaths, the new moons, and the three annual festivals—the festival of unleavened bread, the festival of weeks, and the festival of booths. ¹⁴According to the ordinance of his father David, he appointed the divisions of the priests for their service, and the Levites for their offices of praise and ministry alongside the priests as the duty of each day required, and the gatekeepers in their divisions for the several gates; for so David the man of God had commanded. ¹⁵They did not turn away from what the king had commanded the priests and Levites regarding anything at all, or regarding the treasuries.

16 Thus all the work of Solomon was accomplished from^a the day the foundation of the house of the LORD was laid until the house of the LORD was finished completely.

17 Then Solomon went to Ezion-geber and Eloth on the shore of the sea, in the land of Edom. ¹⁸Huram sent him, in the care of his servants, ships and servants familiar with the sea. They went to Ophir, together with the servants of Solomon, and imported from there four hundred fifty talents of gold and brought it to King Solomon.

Visit of the Queen of Sheba

9 When the queen of Sheba heard of the fame of Solomon, she came to Jerusalem to test him with hard questions, having a very great retinue and camels bearing spices and very much gold and precious stones. When she came to Solomon, she discussed with him all that was on her mind. ²Solomon answered all her questions; there was nothing hidden from Solomon that he could not explain to her. ³When the queen of Sheba had observed the wisdom of Solomon, the house that he had built, ⁴the food of his table, the seating of his officials, and the attendance of his servants, and their clothing, his valets, and their clothing, and his burnt offerings^b that he offered at the house of the LORD, there was no more spirit left in her.

5 So she said to the king, "The report was true that I heard in my own land of your accomplishments and of your wisdom, ⁶but I did not believe the^c reports until I came and my own eyes saw it. Not even half of the greatness of your wisdom had been told to me; you far surpass the report that I had heard. ⁷Happy are your people! Happy are these your servants, who continually attend you and hear your wisdom! ⁸Blessed be the LORD your God, who has delighted in you and set you on his throne as king for the LORD your God. Because your God loved Israel and would establish them forever, he has made you king over them, that you may execute justice and righteousness." ⁹Then she gave the king one hundred twenty talents of gold, a very great quantity of spices, and precious stones: there were no spices such as those that the queen of Sheba gave to King Solomon.

10 Moreover the servants of Huram and the servants of Solomon who brought gold from Ophir brought algum wood and precious stones. ¹¹From the algum wood, the king made steps^d for the house of the LORD and for the king's house, lyres also and harps for the singers; there never was seen the like of them before in the land of Judah.

12 Meanwhile King Solomon granted the queen of Sheba every desire that she expressed, well be-

---

a Gk Syr Vg: Heb *to*   b Gk Syr Vg 1 Kings 10.5: Heb *ascent*   c Heb *their*   d Gk Vg: Meaning of Heb uncertain

yond what she had brought to the king. Then she returned to her own land, with her servants.

Solomon's Great Wealth

13 The weight of gold that came to Solomon in one year was six hundred sixty-six talents of gold, [14]besides that which the traders and merchants brought; and all the kings of Arabia and the governors of the land brought gold and silver to Solomon. [15]King Solomon made two hundred large shields of beaten gold; six hundred shekels of beaten gold went into each large shield. [16]He made three hundred shields of beaten gold; three hundred shekels of gold went into each shield; and the king put them in the House of the Forest of Lebanon. [17]The king also made a great ivory throne, and overlaid it with pure gold. [18]The throne had six steps and a footstool of gold, which were attached to the throne, and on each side of the seat were arm rests and two lions standing beside the arm rests, [19]while twelve lions were standing, one on each end of a step on the six steps. The like of it was never made in any kingdom. [20]All King Solomon's drinking vessels were of gold, and all the vessels of the House of the Forest of Lebanon were of pure gold; silver was not considered as anything in the days of Solomon. [21]For the king's ships went to Tarshish with the servants of Huram; once every three years the ships of Tarshish used to come bringing gold, silver, ivory, apes, and peacocks.[a]

22 Thus King Solomon excelled all the kings of the earth in riches and in wisdom. [23]All the kings of the earth sought the presence of Solomon to hear his wisdom, which God had put into his mind. [24]Every one of them brought a present, objects of silver and gold, garments, weaponry, spices, horses, and mules, so much year by year. [25]Solomon had four thousand stalls for horses and chariots, and twelve thousand horses, which he stationed in the chariot cities and with the king in Jerusalem. [26]He ruled over all the kings from the Euphrates to the land of the Philistines, and to the border of Egypt. [27]The king made silver as common in Jerusalem as stone, and cedar as plentiful as the sycamore of the Shephelah. [28]Horses were imported for Solomon from Egypt and from all lands.

Death of Solomon

29 Now the rest of the acts of Solomon, from first to last, are they not written in the history of the prophet Nathan, and in the prophecy of Ahijah the Shilonite, and in the visions of the seer Iddo concerning Jeroboam son of Nebat? [30]Solomon

Money Talks · 2 Chronicles 9:13–28

King Solomon, with all his wealth, would be right at home in our world, which seems so obsessed with the rich and famous. Even though Solomon saw his riches as a blessing from God, he still became distracted by his power and wealth and turned from God (see 1 Kings 11:1-13).

Solomon's life teaches us important lessons about the devotion of our hearts. Even the wisest of all men got caught up in wealth, power, and wrong relationships. This great king forgot God's ways and put his own comfort and power ahead of caring for the poor under his rule.

"Live simply, so others may simply live" is a common saying of those promoting sustainable living, and it's a powerful call to us who live in a society consumed with shopping and buying and always having the latest and the greatest. This is a helpful reminder, since it's easy for us to forget that much of the world around us doesn't even have the basic necessities of life.

- Think about the clothes in your closet. Do you wear them all?
- What do you spend your money on? Are you generous or tightfisted? What does your spending say about what you care about?
- Is there a way that you can use your money to improve the lives of others?
- What's one thing you can do today to live more simply?

a Or baboons

reigned in Jerusalem over all Israel forty years. [31]Solomon slept with his ancestors and was buried in the city of his father David; and his son Rehoboam succeeded him.

The Revolt against Rehoboam

10 Rehoboam went to Shechem, for all Israel had come to Shechem to make him king. [2]When Jeroboam son of Nebat heard of it (for he was in Egypt, where he had fled from King Solomon), then Jeroboam returned from Egypt. [3]They sent and called him; and Jeroboam and all Israel came and said to Rehoboam, [4]"Your father made our yoke heavy. Now therefore lighten the hard service of your father and his heavy yoke that he placed on us, and we will serve you." [5]He said to them, "Come to me again in three days." So the people went away. 6 Then King Rehoboam took counsel with the older men who had attended his father Solomon while he was still alive, saying, "How do you advise me to answer this people?" [7]They answered him, "If you will be kind to this people and please them, and speak good words to them, then they will be your servants forever." [8]But he rejected the advice that the older men gave him, and consulted the young men who had grown up with him and now attended him. [9]He said to them, "What do you advise that we answer this people who have said to me, 'Lighten the yoke that your father put on us'?" [10]The young men who had grown up with him said to him, "Thus should you speak to the people who said to you, 'Your father made our yoke heavy, but you must lighten it for us'; tell them, 'My little finger is thicker than my father's loins. [11]Now, whereas my father laid on you a heavy yoke, I will add to your yoke. My father disciplined you with whips, but I will discipline you with scorpions.'"

12 So Jeroboam and all the people came to Rehoboam the third day, as the king had said, "Come to me again the third day." [13]The king answered them harshly. King Rehoboam rejected the advice of the older men; [14]he spoke to them in accordance with the advice of the young men, "My father made your yoke heavy, but I will add to it; my father disciplined you with whips, but I will discipline you with scorpions." [15]So the king did not listen to the people, because it was a turn of affairs brought about by God so that the LORD might fulfill his word, which he had spoken by Ahijah the Shilonite to Jeroboam son of Nebat.

16 When all Israel saw that the king would not listen to them, the people answered the king,

"What share do we have in David?
    We have no inheritance in the son of Jesse.
Each of you to your tents, O Israel!
    Look now to your own house, O David."

So all Israel departed to their tents. [17]But Rehoboam reigned over the people of Israel who were living in the cities of Judah. [18]When King Rehoboam sent Hadoram, who was taskmaster over the forced labor, the people of Israel stoned him to death. King Rehoboam hurriedly mounted his chariot to flee to Jerusalem. [19]So Israel has been in rebellion against the house of David to this day.

Judah and Benjamin Fortified

11 When Rehoboam came to Jerusalem, he assembled one hundred eighty thousand chosen troops of the house of Judah and Benjamin to fight against Israel, to restore the kingdom to Rehoboam. [2]But the word of the LORD came to Shemaiah the man of God: [3]Say to King Rehoboam of Judah, son of Solomon, and to all Israel in Judah and Benjamin, [4]"Thus says the LORD: You shall not go up or fight against your kindred. Let everyone return home, for this thing is from me." So they heeded the word of the LORD and turned back from the expedition against Jeroboam.

5 Rehoboam resided in Jerusalem, and he built cities for defense in Judah. [6]He built up Bethlehem, Etam, Tekoa, [7]Beth-zur, Soco, Adullam, [8]Gath, Mareshah, Ziph, [9]Adoraim, Lachish, Azekah, [10]Zorah, Aijalon, and Hebron, fortified cities that are in Judah and in Benjamin. [11]He made the fortresses strong, and put commanders in them, and stores of food, oil, and wine. [12]He also put large shields and spears in all the cities, and made them very strong. So he held Judah and Benjamin.

Priests and Levites Support Rehoboam

13 The priests and the Levites who were in all

Israel presented themselves to him from all their territories. [14]The Levites had left their common lands and their holdings and had come to Judah and Jerusalem, because Jeroboam and his sons had prevented them from serving as priests of the LORD, [15]and had appointed his own priests for the high places, and for the goat-demons, and for the calves that he had made. [16]Those who had set their hearts to seek the LORD God of Israel came after them from all the tribes of Israel to Jerusalem to sacrifice to the LORD, the God of their ancestors. [17]They strengthened the kingdom of Judah, and for three years they made Rehoboam son of Solomon secure, for they walked for three years in the way of David and Solomon.

Rehoboam's Marriages

18 Rehoboam took as his wife Mahalath daughter of Jerimoth son of David, and of Abihail daughter of Eliab son of Jesse. [19]She bore him sons: Jeush, Shemariah, and Zaham. [20]After her he took Maacah daughter of Absalom, who bore him Abijah, Attai, Ziza, and Shelomith. [21]Rehoboam loved Maacah daughter of Absalom more than all his other wives and concubines (he took eighteen wives and sixty concubines, and became the father of twenty-eight sons and sixty daughters). [22]Rehoboam appointed Abijah son of Maacah as chief prince among his brothers, for he intended to make him king. [23]He dealt wisely, and distributed some of his sons through all the districts of Judah and Benjamin, in all the fortified cities; he gave them abundant provisions, and found many wives for them.

Egypt Attacks Judah

12 When the rule of Rehoboam was established and he grew strong, he abandoned the law of the LORD, he and all Israel with him. [2]In the fifth year of King Rehoboam, because they had been unfaithful to the LORD, King Shishak of Egypt came up against Jerusalem [3]with twelve hundred chariots and sixty thousand cavalry. A countless army came with him from Egypt—Libyans, Sukkiim, and Ethiopians.[a] [4]He took the fortified cities of Judah and came as far as Jerusalem. [5]Then the prophet Shemaiah came to Rehoboam and to the officers of Judah, who had gathered at Jerusalem because of Shishak, and said to them, "Thus says the LORD: You abandoned me, so I have abandoned you to the hand of Shishak." [6]Then the officers of

Israel and the king humbled themselves and said, "The LORD is in the right." [7]When the LORD saw that they humbled themselves, the word of the LORD came to Shemaiah, saying: "They have humbled themselves; I will not destroy them, but I will grant them some deliverance, and my wrath shall not be poured out on Jerusalem by the hand of Shishak. [8]Nevertheless they shall be his servants, so that they may know the difference between serving me and serving the kingdoms of other lands."

9 So King Shishak of Egypt came up against Jerusalem; he took away the treasures of the house of the LORD and the treasures of the king's house; he took everything. He also took away the shields of gold that Solomon had made; [10]but King Rehoboam made in place of them shields of bronze, and committed them to the hands of the officers of the guard, who kept the door of the king's house. [11]Whenever the king went into the house of the LORD, the guard would come along bearing them, and would then bring them back to the guardroom. [12]Because he humbled himself the wrath of the LORD turned from him, so as not to destroy them completely; moreover, conditions were good in Judah.

Death of Rehoboam

13 So King Rehoboam established himself in Jerusalem and reigned. Rehoboam was forty-one years old when he began to reign; he reigned seventeen years in Jerusalem, the city that the LORD had chosen out of all the tribes of Israel to put his name there. His mother's name was Naamah the Ammonite. [14]He did evil, for he did not set his heart to seek the LORD.

15 Now the acts of Rehoboam, from first to last, are they not written in the records of the prophet Shemaiah and of the seer Iddo, recorded by genealogy? There were continual wars between Rehoboam and Jeroboam. [16]Rehoboam slept with his ancestors and was buried in the city of David; and his son Abijah succeeded him.

Abijah Reigns over Judah

13 In the eighteenth year of King Jeroboam, Abijah began to reign over Judah. [2]He reigned for three years in Jerusalem. His mother's name was Micaiah daughter of Uriel of Gibeah.

Now there was war between Abijah and Jeroboam. [3]Abijah engaged in battle, having an army of valiant warriors, four hundred thousand picked men; and

a Or *Nubians*; Heb *Cushites*

Jeroboam drew up his line of battle against him with eight hundred thousand picked mighty warriors. [4]Then Abijah stood on the slope of Mount Zemaraim that is in the hill country of Ephraim, and said, "Listen to me, Jeroboam and all Israel! [5]Do you not know that the LORD God of Israel gave the kingship over Israel forever to David and his sons by a covenant of salt? [6]Yet Jeroboam son of Nebat, a servant of Solomon son of David, rose up and rebelled against his lord; [7]and certain worthless scoundrels gathered around him and defied Rehoboam son of Solomon, when Rehoboam was young and irresolute and could not withstand them.

[8] "And now you think that you can withstand the kingdom of the LORD in the hand of the sons of David, because you are a great multitude and have with you the golden calves that Jeroboam made as gods for you. [9]Have you not driven out the priests of the LORD, the descendants of Aaron, and the Levites, and made priests for yourselves like the peoples of other lands? Whoever comes to be consecrated with a young bull or seven rams becomes a priest of what are no gods. [10]But as for us, the LORD is our God, and we have not abandoned him. We have priests ministering to the LORD who are descendants of Aaron, and Levites for their service. [11]They offer to the LORD every morning and every evening burnt offerings and fragrant incense, set out the rows of bread on the table of pure gold, and care for the golden lampstand so that its lamps may burn every evening; for we keep the charge of the LORD our God, but you have abandoned him. [12]See, God is with us at our head, and his priests have their battle trumpets to sound the call to battle against you. O Israelites, do not fight against the LORD, the God of your ancestors; for you cannot succeed."

[13] Jeroboam had sent an ambush around to come on them from behind; thus his troops[a] were in front of Judah, and the ambush was behind them. [14]When Judah turned, the battle was in front of them and behind them. They cried out to the LORD, and the priests blew the trumpets. [15]Then the people of Judah raised the battle shout. And when the people of Judah shouted, God defeated Jeroboam and all Israel before Abijah and Judah. [16]The Israelites fled before Judah, and God gave them into their hands. [17]Abijah and his army defeated them with great slaughter; five hundred thousand picked men of Israel fell slain. [18]Thus the Israelites were subdued at that time, and the people of Judah prevailed,

because they relied on the LORD, the God of their ancestors. [19]Abijah pursued Jeroboam, and took cities from him: Bethel with its villages and Jeshanah with its villages and Ephron[b] with its villages. [20]Jeroboam did not recover his power in the days of Abijah; the LORD struck him down, and he died. [21]But Abijah grew strong. He took fourteen wives, and became the father of twenty-two sons and sixteen daughters. [22]The rest of the acts of Abijah, his behavior and his deeds, are written in the story of the prophet Iddo.

Asa Reigns

14 [c]So Abijah slept with his ancestors, and they buried him in the city of David. His son Asa succeeded him. In his days the land had rest for ten years. [2][d] Asa did what was good and right in the sight of the LORD his God. [3]He took away the foreign altars and the high places, broke down the pillars, hewed down the sacred poles,[e] [4]and commanded Judah to seek the LORD, the God of their ancestors, and to keep the law and the commandment. [5]He also removed from all the cities of Judah the high places and the incense altars. And the kingdom had rest under him. [6]He built fortified cities in Judah while the land had rest. He had no war in those years, for the LORD gave him peace. [7]He said to Judah, "Let us build these cities, and surround them with walls and towers, gates and bars; the land is still ours because we have sought the LORD our God; we have sought him, and he has given us peace on every side." So they built and prospered. [8]Asa had an army of three hundred thousand from Judah, armed with large shields and spears, and two hundred eighty thousand troops from Benjamin who carried shields and drew bows; all these were mighty warriors.

Ethiopian Invasion Repulsed

[9] Zerah the Ethiopian[f] came out against them with an army of a million men and three hundred chariots, and came as far as Mareshah. [10]Asa went out to meet him, and they drew up their lines of battle in the valley of Zephathah at Mareshah. [11]Asa cried to the LORD his God, "O LORD, there is no difference for you between helping the mighty and the weak. Help us, O LORD our God, for we rely on you, and in your name we have come against this multitude. O LORD, you are our God; let no mortal prevail against you." [12]So the LORD defeated the

---

a Heb *they*   b Another reading is *Ephrain*   c Ch 13.23 in Heb   d Ch 14.1 in Heb   e Heb *Asherim*   f Or *Nubian*; Heb *Cushite*

Ethiopians[a] before Asa and before Judah, and the Ethiopians[a] fled. [13]Asa and the army with him pursued them as far as Gerar, and the Ethiopians[a] fell until no one remained alive; for they were broken before the LORD and his army. The people of Judah[b] carried away a great quantity of booty. [14]They defeated all the cities around Gerar, for the fear of the LORD was on them. They plundered all the cities; for there was much plunder in them. [15]They also attacked the tents of those who had livestock,[c] and carried away sheep and goats in abundance, and camels. Then they returned to Jerusalem.

15 The spirit of God came upon Azariah son of Oded. [2]He went out to meet Asa and said to him, "Hear me, Asa, and all Judah and Benjamin: The LORD is with you, while you are with him. If you seek him, he will be found by you, but if you abandon him, he will abandon you. [3]For a long time Israel was without the true God, and without a teaching priest, and without law; [4]but when in their distress they turned to the LORD, the God of Israel, and sought him, he was found by them. [5]In those times it was not safe for anyone to go or come, for great disturbances afflicted all the inhabitants of the lands. [6]They were broken in pieces, nation against nation and city against city, for God troubled them with every sort of distress. [7]But you, take courage! Do not let your hands be weak, for your work shall be rewarded."

8 When Asa heard these words, the prophecy of Azariah son of Oded,[d] he took courage, and put away the abominable idols from all the land of Judah and Benjamin and from the towns that he had taken in the hill country of Ephraim. He repaired the altar of the LORD that was in front of the vestibule of the house of the LORD.[e] [9]He gathered all Judah and Benjamin, and those from Ephraim, Manasseh, and Simeon who were residing as aliens with them, for great numbers had deserted to him from Israel when they saw that the LORD his God was with him. [10]They were gathered at Jerusalem in the third month of the fifteenth year of the reign of Asa. [11]They sacrificed to the LORD on that day, from the booty that they had brought, seven hundred oxen and seven thousand sheep. [12]They entered into a covenant to seek the LORD, the God of their ancestors, with all their heart and with all their soul. [13]Whoever would not seek the LORD, the God of Israel, should be put to death, whether young or old, man or woman. [14]They took an oath to the LORD

PRAY IT!

**Turning Back to God
2 Chronicles 15:8–15**

"Conversion" is probably a word you've come across in church before. Its Latin root means "to turn around." We turn from sin and toward God when we choose to follow God with our lives. In this passage, King Asa and his people heard the words of the prophet Azariah and then turned away from idols and back to God.

Conversion is not a onetime event. It's a process all of us go through again and again as our faith and understanding grow. The Israelites are a great example of this—again and again, they were called to turn back to God. If we are committed to following Jesus, conversion is a lifelong process of deepening our faith.

• Where in your life do you need to turn back to God?

• Pray for the strength and wisdom to turn toward God today.

with a loud voice, and with shouting, and with trumpets, and with horns. [15]All Judah rejoiced over the oath; for they had sworn with all their heart, and had sought him with their whole desire, and he was found by them, and the LORD gave them rest all around.

16 King Asa even removed his mother Maacah from being queen mother because she had made an abominable image for Asherah. Asa cut down her image, crushed it, and burned it at the Wadi Kidron. [17]But the high places were not taken out of Israel. Nevertheless the heart of Asa was true all his days. [18]He brought into the house of God the votive gifts of his father and his own votive gifts—silver, gold, and utensils. [19]And there was no more war until the thirty-fifth year of the reign of Asa.

Alliance with Aram Condemned

16 In the thirty-sixth year of the reign of Asa, King Baasha of Israel went up against Judah, and built Ramah, to prevent anyone from going

a Or *Nubians*; Heb *Cushites* b Heb *They* c Meaning of Heb uncertain d Compare Syr Vg: Heb *the prophecy, the prophet Obed* e Heb *the vestibule of the LORD*

out or coming into the territory of^a King Asa of Judah. ²Then Asa took silver and gold from the treasures of the house of the LORD and the king's house, and sent them to King Ben-hadad of Aram, who resided in Damascus, saying, ³"Let there be an alliance between me and you, like that between my father and your father; I am sending to you silver and gold; go, break your alliance with King Baasha of Israel, so that he may withdraw from me." ⁴Ben-hadad listened to King Asa, and sent the commanders of his armies against the cities of Israel. They conquered Ijon, Dan, Abel-maim, and all the store-cities of Naphtali. ⁵When Baasha heard of it, he stopped building Ramah, and let his work cease. ⁶Then King Asa brought all Judah, and they carried away the stones of Ramah and its timber, with which Baasha had been building, and with them he built up Geba and Mizpah.

7 At that time the seer Hanani came to King Asa of Judah, and said to him, "Because you relied on the king of Aram, and did not rely on the LORD your God, the army of the king of Aram has escaped you. ⁸Were not the Ethiopians^b and the Libyans a huge army with exceedingly many chariots and cavalry? Yet because you relied on the LORD, he gave them into your hand. ⁹For the eyes of the LORD range throughout the entire earth, to strengthen those whose heart is true to him. You have done foolishly in this; for from now on you will have wars." ¹⁰Then Asa was angry with the seer, and put him in the stocks, in prison, for he was in a rage with him because of this. And Asa inflicted cruelties on some of the people at the same time.

Asa's Disease and Death

11 The acts of Asa, from first to last, are written in the Book of the Kings of Judah and Israel. ¹²In the thirty-ninth year of his reign Asa was diseased in his feet, and his disease became severe; yet even in his disease he did not seek the LORD, but sought help from physicians. ¹³Then Asa slept with his ancestors, dying in the forty-first year of his reign. ¹⁴They buried him in the tomb that he had hewn out for himself in the city of David. They laid him on a bier that had been filled with various kinds of spices prepared by the perfumer's art; and they made a very great fire in his honor.

17 Jehoshaphat's Reign

His son Jehoshaphat succeeded him, and strengthened himself against Israel. ²He placed forces in all the fortified cities of Judah, and set garrisons in the land of Judah, and in the cities of Ephraim that his father Asa had taken. ³The LORD was with Jehoshaphat, because he walked in the earlier ways of his father;^c he did not seek the Baals, ⁴but sought the God of his father and walked in his commandments, and not according to the ways of Israel. ⁵Therefore the LORD established the kingdom in his hand. All Judah brought tribute to Jehoshaphat, and he had great riches and honor. ⁶His heart was courageous in the ways of the LORD; and furthermore he removed the high places and the sacred poles^d from Judah.

7 In the third year of his reign he sent his officials, Ben-hail, Obadiah, Zechariah, Nethanel, and Micaiah, to teach in the cities of Judah. ⁸With them were the Levites, Shemaiah, Nethaniah, Zebadiah, Asahel, Shemiramoth, Jehonathan, Adonijah, Tobijah, and Tob-adonijah; and with these Levites, the priests Elishama and Jehoram. ⁹They taught in Judah, having the book of the law of the LORD with them; they went around through all the cities of Judah and taught among the people.

10 The fear of the LORD fell on all the kingdoms of the lands around Judah, and they did not make war against Jehoshaphat. ¹¹Some of the Philistines brought Jehoshaphat presents, and silver for tribute; and the Arabs also brought him seven thousand seven hundred rams and seven thousand seven hundred male goats. ¹²Jehoshaphat grew steadily greater. He built fortresses and storage cities in Judah. ¹³He carried out great works in the cities of Judah. He had soldiers, mighty warriors, in Jerusalem. ¹⁴This was the muster of them by ancestral houses: Of Judah, the commanders of the thousands: Adnah the commander, with three hundred thousand mighty warriors, ¹⁵and next to him Jehohanan the commander, with two hundred eighty thousand, ¹⁶and next to him Amasiah son of Zichri, a volunteer for the service of the LORD, with two hundred thousand mighty warriors. ¹⁷Of Benjamin: Eliada, a mighty warrior, with two hundred thousand armed with bow and shield, ¹⁸and next to him Jehozabad with one hundred eighty thousand armed for war. ¹⁹These were in the service of the king, besides those whom the king had placed in the fortified cities throughout all Judah.

18 Micaiah Predicts Failure

Now Jehoshaphat had great riches and honor; and he made a marriage alliance

---

a Heb lacks *the territory of* **b** Or *Nubians;* Heb *Cushites* **c** Another reading is *his father David* **d** Heb *Asherim*

with Ahab. [2]After some years he went down to Ahab in Samaria. Ahab slaughtered an abundance of sheep and oxen for him and for the people who were with him, and induced him to go up against Ramoth-gilead. [3]King Ahab of Israel said to King Jehoshaphat of Judah, "Will you go with me to Ramoth-gilead?" He answered him, "I am with you, my people are your people. We will be with you in the war."

4 But Jehoshaphat also said to the king of Israel, "Inquire first for the word of the LORD." [5]Then the king of Israel gathered the prophets together, four hundred of them, and said to them, "Shall we go to battle against Ramoth-gilead, or shall I refrain?" They said, "Go up; for God will give it into the hand of the king." [6]But Jehoshaphat said, "Is there no other prophet of the LORD here of whom we may inquire?" [7]The king of Israel said to Jehoshaphat, "There is still one other by whom we may inquire of the LORD, Micaiah son of Imlah; but I hate him, for he never prophesies anything favorable about me, but only disaster." Jehoshaphat said, "Let the king not say such a thing." [8]Then the king of Israel summoned an officer and said, "Bring quickly Micaiah son of Imlah." [9]Now the king of Israel and King Jehoshaphat of Judah were sitting on their thrones, arrayed in their robes; and they were sitting at the threshing floor at the entrance of the gate of Samaria; and all the prophets were prophesying before them. [10]Zedekiah son of Chenaanah made for himself horns of iron, and he said, "Thus says the LORD: With these you shall gore the Arameans until they are destroyed." [11]All the prophets were prophesying the same and saying, "Go up to Ramoth-gilead and triumph; the LORD will give it into the hand of the king."

12 The messenger who had gone to summon Micaiah said to him, "Look, the words of the prophets with one accord are favorable to the king; let your word be like the word of one of them, and speak favorably." [13]But Micaiah said, "As the LORD lives, whatever my God says, that I will speak."

14 When he had come to the king, the king said to him, "Micaiah, shall we go to Ramoth-gilead to battle, or shall I refrain?" He answered, "Go up and triumph; they will be given into your hand." [15]But the king said to him, "How many times must I make you swear to tell me nothing but the truth in the name of the LORD?" [16]Then Micaiah[a] said, "I saw all Israel scattered on the mountains, like sheep

without a shepherd; and the LORD said, 'These have no master; let each one go home in peace.' " [17]The king of Israel said to Jehoshaphat, "Did I not tell you that he would not prophesy anything favorable about me, but only disaster?"

18 Then Micaiah[a] said, "Therefore hear the word of the LORD: I saw the LORD sitting on his throne, with all the host of heaven standing to the right and to the left of him. [19]And the LORD said, 'Who will entice King Ahab of Israel, so that he may go up and fall at Ramoth-gilead?' Then one said one thing, and another said another, [20]until a spirit came forward and stood before the LORD, saying, 'I will entice him.' The LORD asked him, 'How?' [21]He replied, 'I will go out and be a lying spirit in the mouth of all his prophets.' Then the LORD[a] said, 'You are to entice him, and you shall succeed; go out and do it.' [22]So you see, the LORD has put a lying spirit in the mouth of these your prophets; the LORD has decreed disaster for you."

23 Then Zedekiah son of Chenaanah came up to Micaiah, slapped him on the cheek, and said, "Which way did the spirit of the LORD pass from me to speak to you?" [24]Micaiah replied, "You will find out on that day when you go in to hide in an inner chamber." [25]The king of Israel then ordered, "Take Micaiah, and return him to Amon the governor of the city and to Joash the king's son; [26]and say, 'Thus says the king: Put this fellow in prison, and feed him on reduced rations of bread and water until I return in peace.' " [27]Micaiah said, "If you return in peace, the LORD has not spoken by me." And he said, "Hear, you peoples, all of you!"

Defeat and Death of Ahab

28 So the king of Israel and King Jehoshaphat of Judah went up to Ramoth-gilead. [29]The king of Israel said to Jehoshaphat, "I will disguise myself and go into battle, but you wear your robes." So the king of Israel disguised himself, and they went into battle. [30]Now the king of Aram had commanded the captains of his chariots, "Fight with no one small or great, but only with the king of Israel." [31]When the captains of the chariots saw Jehoshaphat, they said, "It is the king of Israel." So they turned to fight against him; and Jehoshaphat cried out, and the LORD helped him. God drew them away from him, [32]for when the captains of the chariots saw that it was not the king of Israel, they turned back from pursuing him. [33]But a certain

α Heb he

man drew his bow and unknowingly struck the king of Israel between the scale armor and the breastplate; so he said to the driver of his chariot, "Turn around, and carry me out of the battle, for I am wounded." [34]The battle grew hot that day, and the king of Israel propped himself up in his chariot facing the Arameans until evening; then at sunset he died.

19 King Jehoshaphat of Judah returned in safety to his house in Jerusalem. [2]Jehu son of Hanani the seer went out to meet him and said to King Jehoshaphat, "Should you help the wicked and love those who hate the LORD? Because of this, wrath has gone out against you from the LORD. [3]Nevertheless, some good is found in you, for you destroyed the sacred poles[a] out of the land, and have set your heart to seek God."

The Reforms of Jehoshaphat

4 Jehoshaphat resided at Jerusalem; then he went out again among the people, from Beer-sheba to the hill country of Ephraim, and brought them back to the LORD, the God of their ancestors. [5]He appointed judges in the land in all the fortified cities of Judah, city by city, [6]and said to the judges, "Consider what you are doing, for you judge not on behalf of human beings but on the LORD's behalf; he is with you in giving judgment. [7]Now, let the fear of the LORD be upon you; take care what you do, for there is no perversion of justice with the LORD our God, or partiality, or taking of bribes."

8 Moreover in Jerusalem Jehoshaphat appointed certain Levites and priests and heads of families of Israel, to give judgment for the LORD and to decide disputed cases. They had their seat at Jerusalem. [9]He charged them: "This is how you shall act: in the fear of the LORD, in faithfulness, and with your whole heart; [10]whenever a case comes to you from your kindred who live in their cities, concerning bloodshed, law or commandment, statutes or ordinances, then you shall instruct them, so that they may not incur guilt before the LORD and wrath may not come on you and your kindred. Do so, and you will not incur guilt. [11]See, Amariah the chief priest is over you in all matters of the LORD; and Zebadiah son of Ishmael, the governor of the house of Judah, in all the king's matters; and the Levites will serve you as officers. Deal courageously, and may the LORD be with the good!"

Invasion from the East

20 After this the Moabites and Ammonites, and with them some of the Meunites,[b] came against Jehoshaphat for battle. [2]Messengers[c] came and told Jehoshaphat, "A great multitude is coming against you from Edom,[d] from beyond the sea; already they are at Hazazon-tamar" (that is, En-gedi). [3]Jehoshaphat was afraid; he set himself to seek the LORD, and proclaimed a fast throughout all Judah. [4]Judah assembled to seek help from the LORD; from all the towns of Judah they came to seek the LORD.

Jehoshaphat's Prayer and Victory

5 Jehoshaphat stood in the assembly of Judah and Jerusalem, in the house of the LORD, before the new court, [6]and said, "O LORD, God of our ancestors, are you not God in heaven? Do you not rule over all the kingdoms of the nations? In your hand are power and might, so that no one is able to withstand you. [7]Did you not, O our God, drive out the inhabitants of this land before your people Israel, and give it forever to the descendants of your friend Abraham? [8]They have lived in it, and in it have built you a sanctuary for your name, saying, [9]'If disaster comes upon us, the sword, judgment,[e] or pestilence, or famine, we will stand before this house, and before you, for your name is in this house, and cry to you in our distress, and you will hear and save.' [10]See now, the people of Ammon, Moab, and Mount Seir, whom you would not let Israel invade when they came from the land of Egypt, and whom they avoided and did not destroy— [11]they reward us by coming to drive us out of your possession that you have given us to inherit. [12]O our God, will you not execute judgment upon them? For we are powerless against this great multitude that is coming against us. We do not know what to do, but our eyes are on you."

13 Meanwhile all Judah stood before the LORD, with their little ones, their wives, and their children. [14]Then the spirit of the LORD came upon Jahaziel son of Zechariah, son of Benaiah, son of Jeiel, son of Mattaniah, a Levite of the sons of Asaph, in the middle of the assembly. [15]He said, "Listen, all Judah and inhabitants of Jerusalem, and King Jehoshaphat: Thus says the LORD to you: 'Do not fear or be dismayed at this great multitude; for the battle is not yours but God's. [16]Tomorrow go down against them; they will come up by the as-

---

a Heb Asheroth   b Compare 26.7: Heb Ammonites   c Heb They   d One Ms: MT Aram   e Or the sword of judgment

cent of Ziz; you will find them at the end of the valley, before the wilderness of Jeruel. [17] This battle is not for you to fight; take your position, stand still, and see the victory of the Lord on your behalf, O Judah and Jerusalem.' Do not fear or be dismayed; tomorrow go out against them, and the Lord will be with you."

18 Then Jehoshaphat bowed down with his face to the ground, and all Judah and the inhabitants of Jerusalem fell down before the Lord, worshiping the Lord. [19] And the Levites, of the Kohathites and the Korahites, stood up to praise the Lord, the God of Israel, with a very loud voice.

20 They rose early in the morning and went out into the wilderness of Tekoa; and as they went out, Jehoshaphat stood and said, "Listen to me, O Judah and inhabitants of Jerusalem! Believe in the Lord your God and you will be established; believe his prophets." [21] When he had taken counsel with the people, he appointed those who were to sing to the Lord and praise him in holy splendor, as they went before the army, saying,

"Give thanks to the Lord,
    for his steadfast love endures forever."

[22] As they began to sing and praise, the Lord set an ambush against the Ammonites, Moab, and Mount Seir, who had come against Judah, so that they were routed. [23] For the Ammonites and Moab attacked the inhabitants of Mount Seir, destroying them utterly; and when they had made an end of the inhabitants of Seir, they all helped to destroy one another.

24 When Judah came to the watchtower of the wilderness, they looked toward the multitude; they were corpses lying on the ground; no one had escaped. [25] When Jehoshaphat and his people came to take the booty from them, they found livestock[a] in great numbers, goods, clothing, and precious things, which they took for themselves until they could carry no more. They spent three days taking the booty, because of its abundance. [26] On the fourth day they assembled in the Valley of Beracah, for there they blessed the Lord; therefore that place has been called the Valley of Beracah[b] to this day. [27] Then all the people of Judah and Jerusalem, with Jehoshaphat at their head, returned to Jerusalem with joy, for the Lord had enabled them to rejoice over their enemies. [28] They came to Jerusalem, with harps and lyres and trumpets, to the house of the Lord. [29] The fear of God came on all

the kingdoms of the countries when they heard that the Lord had fought against the enemies of Israel. [30] And the realm of Jehoshaphat was quiet, for his God gave him rest all around.

The End of Jehoshaphat's Reign

31 So Jehoshaphat reigned over Judah. He was thirty-five years old when he began to reign; he reigned twenty-five years in Jerusalem. His mother's name was Azubah daughter of Shilhi. [32] He walked in the way of his father Asa and did not turn aside from it, doing what was right in the sight of the Lord. [33] Yet the high places were not removed; the people had not yet set their hearts upon the God of their ancestors.

34 Now the rest of the acts of Jehoshaphat, from first to last, are written in the Annals of Jehu son of Hanani, which are recorded in the Book of the Kings of Israel.

35 After this King Jehoshaphat of Judah joined with King Ahaziah of Israel, who did wickedly. [36] He joined him in building ships to go to Tarshish; they built the ships in Ezion-geber. [37] Then Eliezer son of Dodavahu of Mareshah prophesied against Jehoshaphat, saying, "Because you have joined with Ahaziah, the Lord will destroy what you have made." And the ships were wrecked and were not able to go to Tarshish.

Jehoram's Reign

21 Jehoshaphat slept with his ancestors and was buried with his ancestors in the city of David; his son Jehoram succeeded him. [2] He had brothers, the sons of Jehoshaphat: Azariah, Jehiel, Zechariah, Azariah, Michael, and Shephatiah; all these were the sons of King Jehoshaphat of Judah.[c] [3] Their father gave them many gifts, of silver, gold, and valuable possessions, together with fortified cities in Judah; but he gave the kingdom to Jehoram, because he was the firstborn. [4] When Jehoram had ascended the throne of his father and was established, he put all his brothers to the sword, and also some of the officials of Israel. [5] Jehoram was thirty-two years old when he began to reign; he reigned eight years in Jerusalem. [6] He walked in the way of the kings of Israel, as the house of Ahab had done; for the daughter of Ahab was his wife. He did what was evil in the sight of the Lord. [7] Yet the Lord would not destroy the house of David because of the covenant that he had made with David, and since

a Gk: Heb *among them*   b That is *Blessing*   c Gk Syr: Heb *Israel* he had promised to give a lamp to him and to his descendants forever.

Revolt of Edom

8 In his days Edom revolted against the rule of Judah and set up a king of their own. ⁹Then Jehoram crossed over with his commanders and all his chariots. He set out by night and attacked the Edomites, who had surrounded him and his chariot commanders. ¹⁰So Edom has been in revolt against the rule of Judah to this day. At that time Libnah also revolted against his rule, because he had forsaken the LORD, the God of his ancestors.

Elijah's Letter

11 Moreover he made high places in the hill country of Judah, and led the inhabitants of Jerusalem into unfaithfulness, and made Judah go astray. ¹²A letter came to him from the prophet Elijah, saying: "Thus says the LORD, the God of your father David: Because you have not walked in the ways of your father Jehoshaphat or in the ways of King Asa of Judah, ¹³but have walked in the way of the kings of Israel, and have led Judah and the inhabitants of Jerusalem into unfaithfulness, as the house of Ahab led Israel into unfaithfulness, and because you also have killed your brothers, members of your father's house, who were better than yourself, ¹⁴see, the LORD will bring a great plague on your people, your children, your wives, and all your possessions, ¹⁵and you yourself will have a severe sickness with a disease of your bowels, until your bowels come out, day after day, because of the disease."

16 The LORD aroused against Jehoram the anger of the Philistines and of the Arabs who are near the Ethiopians.ᵃ ¹⁷They came up against Judah, invaded it, and carried away all the possessions they found that belonged to the king's house, along with his sons and his wives, so that no son was left to him except Jehoahaz, his youngest son.

Disease and Death of Jehoram

18 After all this the LORD struck him in his bowels with an incurable disease. ¹⁹In course of time, at the end of two years, his bowels came out because of the disease, and he died in great agony. His people made no fire in his honor, like the fires made for his ancestors. ²⁰He was thirty-two years old when he began to reign; he reigned eight years in Jerusalem. He departed with no one's regret. They buried him in the city of David, but not in the tombs of the kings.

Ahaziah's Reign

22 The inhabitants of Jerusalem made his youngest son Ahaziah king as his successor; for the troops who came with the Arabs to the camp had killed all the older sons. So Ahaziah son of Jehoram reigned as king of Judah. ²Ahaziah was forty-two years old when he began to reign; he reigned one year in Jerusalem. His mother's name was Athaliah, a granddaughter of Omri. ³He also walked in the ways of the house of Ahab, for his mother was his counselor in doing wickedly. ⁴He did what was evil in the sight of the LORD, as the house of Ahab had done; for after the death of his father they were his counselors, to his ruin. ⁵He even followed their advice, and went with Jehoram son of King Ahab of Israel to make war against King Hazael of Aram at Ramoth-gilead. The Arameans wounded Joram, ⁶and he returned to be healed in Jezreel of the wounds that he had received at Ramah, when he fought King Hazael of Aram. And

A Prophet's Job · 2 Chronicles 21:12–15

The letter from Elijah to King Jehoram underscores the principal role of the Hebrew prophet: to be God's voice, the one who speaks for God. Although many early figures are called prophets, including Moses and Deborah, the classical prophet—"nabi'" in Hebrew—appeared later in Israelite history. The primary function of the prophet was not to foretell the future, but to announce God's judgment, to confront those who violated God's law, and to console those who suffered. In short, prophets were the conscience of the Israelite nation.

ᵃ Or Nubians; Heb Cushites

Ahaziah son of King Jehoram of Judah went down to see Joram son of Ahab in Jezreel, because he was sick. 7 But it was ordained by God that the downfall of Ahaziah should come about through his going to visit Joram. For when he came there he went out with Jehoram to meet Jehu son of Nimshi, whom the LORD had anointed to destroy the house of Ahab. [8]When Jehu was executing judgment on the house of Ahab, he met the officials of Judah and the sons of Ahaziah's brothers, who attended Ahaziah, and he killed them. [9]He searched for Ahaziah, who was captured while hiding in Samaria and was brought to Jehu, and put to death. They buried him, for they said, "He is the grandson of Jehoshaphat, who sought the LORD with all his heart." And the house of Ahaziah had no one able to rule the kingdom.

Athaliah Seizes the Throne

10 Now when Athaliah, Ahaziah's mother, saw that her son was dead, she set about to destroy all the royal family of the house of Judah. [11]But Jehoshabeath, the king's daughter, took Joash son of Ahaziah, and stole him away from among the king's children who were about to be killed; she put him and his nurse in a bedroom. Thus Jehoshabeath, daughter of King Jehoram and wife of the priest Jehoiada—because she was a sister of Ahaziah—hid him from Athaliah, so that she did not kill him; [12]he remained with them six years, hidden in the house of God, while Athaliah reigned over the land.

23 But in the seventh year Jehoiada took courage, and entered into a compact with the commanders of the hundreds, Azariah son of Jeroham, Ishmael son of Jehohanan, Azariah son of Obed, Maaseiah son of Adaiah, and Elishaphat son of Zichri. [2]They went around through Judah and gathered the Levites from all the towns of Judah, and the heads of families of Israel, and they came to Jerusalem. [3]Then the whole assembly made a covenant with the king in the house of God. Jehoiada[a] said to them, "Here is the king's son! Let him reign, as the LORD promised concerning the sons of David. [4]This is what you are to do: one-third of you, priests and Levites, who come on duty on the sabbath, shall be gatekeepers, [5]one-third shall be at the king's house, and one-third at the Gate of the Foundation; and all the people shall be in the courts of the house of

the LORD. [6]Do not let anyone enter the house of the LORD except the priests and ministering Levites; they may enter, for they are holy, but all the other[b] people shall observe the instructions of the LORD. [7]The Levites shall surround the king, each with his weapons in his hand; and whoever enters the house shall be killed. Stay with the king in his comings and goings."

Joash Crowned King

8 The Levites and all Judah did according to all that the priest Jehoiada commanded; each brought his men, who were to come on duty on the sabbath, with those who were to go off duty on the sabbath; for the priest Jehoiada did not dismiss the divisions. [9]The priest Jehoiada delivered to the captains the spears and the large and small shields that had been King David's, which were in the house of God; [10]and he set all the people as a guard for the king, everyone with weapon in hand, from the south side of the house to the north side of the house, around the altar and the house. [11]Then he brought out the king's son, put the crown on him, and gave him the covenant;[c] they proclaimed him king, and Jehoiada and his sons anointed him; and they shouted, "Long live the king!"

Athaliah Murdered

12 When Athaliah heard the noise of the people running and praising the king, she went into the house of the LORD to the people; [13]and when she looked, there was the king standing by his pillar at the entrance, and the captains and the trumpeters beside the king, and all the people of the land rejoicing and blowing trumpets, and the singers with their musical instruments leading in the celebration. Athaliah tore her clothes, and cried, "Treason! Treason!" [14]Then the priest Jehoiada brought out the captains who were set over the army, saying to them, "Bring her out between the ranks; anyone who follows her is to be put to the sword." For the priest said, "Do not put her to death in the house of the LORD." [15]So they laid hands on her; she went into the entrance of the Horse Gate of the king's house, and there they put her to death.

16 Jehoiada made a covenant between himself and all the people and the king that they should be the LORD's people. [17]Then all the people went to the house of Baal, and tore it down; his altars and his images they broke in pieces, and they killed

a Heb He b Heb lacks other c Or treaty, or testimony; Heb eduth

Mattan, the priest of Baal, in front of the altars. [18]Jehoiada assigned the care of the house of the LORD to the levitical priests whom David had organized to be in charge of the house of the LORD, to offer burnt offerings to the LORD, as it is written in the law of Moses, with rejoicing and with singing, according to the order of David. [19]He stationed the gatekeepers at the gates of the house of the LORD so that no one should enter who was in any way unclean. [20]And he took the captains, the nobles, the governors of the people, and all the people of the land, and they brought the king down from the house of the LORD, marching through the upper gate to the king's house. They set the king on the royal throne. [21]So all the people of the land rejoiced, and the city was quiet after Athaliah had been killed with the sword.

24

Joash Repairs the Temple

Joash was seven years old when he began to reign; he reigned forty years in Jerusalem; his mother's name was Zibiah of Beer-sheba. [2]Joash did what was right in the sight of the LORD all the days of the priest Jehoiada. [3]Jehoiada got two wives for him, and he became the father of sons and daughters.

4 Some time afterward Joash decided to restore the house of the LORD. [5]He assembled the priests and the Levites and said to them, "Go out to the cities of Judah and gather money from all Israel to repair the house of your God, year by year; and see that you act quickly." But the Levites did not act quickly. [6]So the king summoned Jehoiada the chief, and said to him, "Why have you not required the Levites to bring in from Judah and Jerusalem the tax levied by Moses, the servant of the LORD, on[a] the congregation of Israel for the tent of the covenant?"[b] [7]For the children of Athaliah, that wicked woman, had broken into the house of God, and had even used all the dedicated things of the house of the LORD for the Baals.

8 So the king gave command, and they made a chest, and set it outside the gate of the house of the LORD. [9]A proclamation was made throughout Judah and Jerusalem to bring in for the LORD the tax that Moses the servant of God laid on Israel in the wilderness. [10]All the leaders and all the people rejoiced and brought their tax and dropped it into the chest until it was full. [11]Whenever the chest was brought to the king's officers by the Levites,

when they saw that there was a large amount of money in it, the king's secretary and the officer of the chief priest would come and empty the chest and take it and return it to its place. So they did day after day, and collected money in abundance. [12]The king and Jehoiada gave it to those who had charge of the work of the house of the LORD, and they hired masons and carpenters to restore the house of the LORD, and also workers in iron and bronze to repair the house of the LORD. [13]So those who were engaged in the work labored, and the repairing went forward at their hands, and they restored the house of God to its proper condition and strengthened it. [14]When they had finished, they brought the rest of the money to the king and Jehoiada, and with it were made utensils for the house of the LORD, utensils for the service and for the burnt offerings, and ladles, and vessels of gold and silver. They offered burnt offerings in the house of the LORD regularly all the days of Jehoiada.

Apostasy of Joash

15 But Jehoiada grew old and full of days, and died; he was one hundred thirty years old at his death. [16]And they buried him in the city of David among the kings, because he had done good in Israel, and for God and his house.

17 Now after the death of Jehoiada the officials of Judah came and did obeisance to the king; then the king listened to them. [18]They abandoned the house of the LORD, the God of their ancestors, and served the sacred poles[c] and the idols. And wrath came upon Judah and Jerusalem for this guilt of theirs. [19]Yet he sent prophets among them to bring them back to the LORD; they testified against them, but they would not listen.

20 Then the spirit of God took possession of[d]

---

a Compare Vg: Heb *and*   b Or *treaty, or testimony*; Heb *eduth*   c Heb *Asherim*   d Heb *clothed itself with*

Zechariah son of the priest Jehoiada; he stood above the people and said to them, "Thus says God: Why do you transgress the commandments of the LORD, so that you cannot prosper? Because you have forsaken the LORD, he has also forsaken you." [21] But they conspired against him, and by command of the king they stoned him to death in the court of the house of the LORD. [22] King Joash did not remember the kindness that Jehoiada, Zechariah's father, had shown him, but killed his son. As he was dying, he said, "May the LORD see and avenge!"

Death of Joash

23 At the end of the year the army of Aram came up against Joash. They came to Judah and Jerusalem, and destroyed all the officials of the people from among them, and sent all the booty they took to the king of Damascus. [24] Although the army of Aram had come with few men, the LORD delivered into their hand a very great army, because they had abandoned the LORD, the God of their ancestors. Thus they executed judgment on Joash.

25 When they had withdrawn, leaving him severely wounded, his servants conspired against him because of the blood of the son[a] of the priest Jehoiada, and they killed him on his bed. So he died; and they buried him in the city of David, but they did not bury him in the tombs of the kings. [26] Those who conspired against him were Zabad son of Shimeath the Ammonite, and Jehozabad son of Shimrith the Moabite. [27] Accounts of his sons, and of the many oracles against him, and of the rebuilding[b] of the house of God are written in the Commentary on the Book of the Kings. And his son Amaziah succeeded him.

25 Reign of Amaziah

Amaziah was twenty-five years old when he began to reign, and he reigned twenty-nine years in Jerusalem. His mother's name was Jehoaddan of Jerusalem. [2] He did what was right in the sight of the LORD, yet not with a true heart. [3] As soon as the royal power was firmly in his hand he killed his servants who had murdered his father the king. [4] But he did not put their children to death, according to what is written in the law, in the book of Moses, where the LORD commanded, "The parents shall not be put to death for the children, or the children be put to death for the parents; but all shall be put to death for their own sins."

Slaughter of the Edomites

5 Amaziah assembled the people of Judah, and set them by ancestral houses under commanders of the thousands and of the hundreds for all Judah and Benjamin. He mustered those twenty years old and upward, and found that they were three hundred thousand picked troops fit for war, able to handle spear and shield. [6] He also hired one hundred thousand mighty warriors from Israel for one hundred talents of silver. [7] But a man of God came to him and said, "O king, do not let the army of Israel go with you, for the LORD is not with Israel—all these Ephraimites. [8] Rather, go by yourself and act; be strong in battle, or God will fling you down before the enemy; for God has power to help or to overthrow." [9] Amaziah said to the man of God, "But what shall we do about the hundred talents that I have given to the army of Israel?" The man of God answered, "The LORD is able to give you much more than this." [10] Then Amaziah discharged the army that had come to him from Ephraim, letting them go home again. But they became very angry with Judah, and returned home in fierce anger.

11 Amaziah took courage, and led out his people; he went to the Valley of Salt, and struck down ten thousand men of Seir. [12] The people of Judah captured another ten thousand alive, took them to the top of Sela, and threw them down from the top of Sela, so that all of them were dashed to pieces. [13] But the men of the army whom Amaziah sent back, not letting them go with him to battle, fell on the cities of Judah from Samaria to Beth-horon; they killed three thousand people in them, and took much booty.

14 Now after Amaziah came from the slaughter of the Edomites, he brought the gods of the people of Seir, set them up as his gods, and worshiped them, making offerings to them. [15] The LORD was angry with Amaziah and sent to him a prophet, who said to him, "Why have you resorted to a people's gods who could not deliver their own people from your hand?" [16] But as he was speaking the king[c] said to him, "Have we made you a royal counselor? Stop! Why should you be put to death?" So the prophet stopped, but said, "I know that God has determined to destroy you, because you have done this and have not listened to my advice."

Israel Defeats Judah

17 Then King Amaziah of Judah took counsel and

a Gk Vg: Heb sons   b Heb founding   c Heb he

sent to King Joash son of Jehoahaz son of Jehu of Israel, saying, "Come, let us look one another in the face." [18]King Joash of Israel sent word to King Amaziah of Judah, "A thornbush on Lebanon sent to a cedar on Lebanon, saying, 'Give your daughter to my son for a wife'; but a wild animal of Lebanon passed by and trampled down the thornbush. [19]You say, 'See, I have defeated Edom,' and your heart has lifted you up in boastfulness. Now stay at home; why should you provoke trouble so that you fall, you and Judah with you?"

20 But Amaziah would not listen—it was God's doing, in order to hand them over, because they had sought the gods of Edom. [21]So King Joash of Israel went up; he and King Amaziah of Judah faced one another in battle at Beth-shemesh, which belongs to Judah. [22]Judah was defeated by Israel; everyone fled home. [23]King Joash of Israel captured King Amaziah of Judah, son of Joash, son of Ahaziah, at Beth-shemesh; he brought him to Jerusalem, and broke down the wall of Jerusalem from the Ephraim Gate to the Corner Gate, a distance of four hundred cubits. [24]He seized all the gold and silver, and all the vessels that were found in the house of God, and Obed-edom with them; he seized also the treasuries of the king's house, also hostages; then he returned to Samaria.

Death of Amaziah

25 King Amaziah son of Joash of Judah, lived fifteen years after the death of King Joash son of Jehoahaz of Israel. [26]Now the rest of the deeds of Amaziah, from first to last, are they not written in the Book of the Kings of Judah and Israel? [27]From the time that Amaziah turned away from the LORD they made a conspiracy against him in Jerusalem, and he fled to Lachish. But they sent after him to Lachish, and killed him there. [28]They brought him back on horses; he was buried with his ancestors in the city of David.

Reign of Uzziah

26 Then all the people of Judah took Uzziah, who was sixteen years old, and made him king to succeed his father Amaziah. [2]He rebuilt Eloth and restored it to Judah, after the king slept with his ancestors. [3]Uzziah was sixteen years old when he began to reign, and he reigned fifty-two years in Jerusalem. His mother's name was Jecoliah of Jerusalem. [4]He did what was right in the sight of the LORD, just as his father Amaziah had done. [5]He set himself to seek God in the days of Zechariah, who instructed him in the fear of God; and as long as he sought the LORD, God made him prosper.

6 He went out and made war against the Philistines, and broke down the wall of Gath and the wall of Jabneh and the wall of Ashdod; he built cities in the territory of Ashdod and elsewhere among the Philistines. [7]God helped him against the Philistines, against the Arabs who lived in Gur-baal, and against the Meunites. [8]The Ammonites paid tribute to Uzziah, and his fame spread even to the border of Egypt, for he became very strong. [9]Moreover Uzziah built towers in Jerusalem at the Corner Gate, at the Valley Gate, and at the Angle, and fortified them. [10]He built towers in the wilderness and hewed out many cisterns, for he had large herds, both in the Shephelah and in the plain, and he had farmers and vinedressers in the hills and in the fertile lands, for he loved the soil. [11]Moreover Uzziah had an army of soldiers, fit for war, in divisions according to the numbers in the muster made by the secretary Jeiel and the officer Maaseiah, under the direction of Hananiah, one of the king's commanders. [12]The whole number of the heads of ancestral houses of mighty warriors was two thousand six hundred. [13]Under their command was an army of three hundred seven thousand five hundred, who could make war with mighty power, to help the king against the enemy. [14]Uzziah provided for all the army the shields, spears, helmets, coats of mail, bows, and stones for slinging. [15]In Jerusalem he set up machines, invented by skilled workers, on the towers and the corners for shooting arrows and large stones. And his fame spread far, for he was marvelously helped until he became strong.

Pride and Apostasy

16 But when he had become strong he grew proud, to his destruction. For he was false to the LORD his God, and entered the temple of the LORD to make offering on the altar of incense. [17]But the priest Azariah went in after him, with eighty priests of the LORD who were men of valor; [18]they withstood King Uzziah, and said to him, "It is not for you, Uzziah, to make offering to the LORD, but for the priests the descendants of Aaron, who are consecrated to make offering. Go out of the sanctuary; for you have done wrong, and it will bring you no honor from the LORD God." [19]Then Uzziah was

angry. Now he had a censer in his hand to make offering, and when he became angry with the priests a leprous[a] disease broke out on his forehead, in the presence of the priests in the house of the LORD, by the altar of incense. [20]When the chief priest Azariah, and all the priests, looked at him, he was leprous[a] in his forehead. They hurried him out, and he himself hurried to get out, because the LORD had struck him. [21]King Uzziah was leprous[a] to the day of his death, and being leprous[a] lived in a separate house, for he was excluded from the house of the LORD. His son Jotham was in charge of the palace of the king, governing the people of the land.

22 Now the rest of the acts of Uzziah, from first to last, the prophet Isaiah son of Amoz wrote. [23]Uzziah slept with his ancestors; they buried him near his ancestors in the burial field that belonged to the kings, for they said, "He is leprous."[a] His son Jotham succeeded him.

Reign of Jotham

27 Jotham was twenty-five years old when he began to reign; he reigned sixteen years in Jerusalem. His mother's name was Jerushah daughter of Zadok. [2]He did what was right in the sight of the LORD just as his father Uzziah had done—only he did not invade the temple of the LORD. But the people still followed corrupt practices. [3]He built the upper gate of the house of the LORD, and did extensive building on the wall of Ophel. [4]Moreover he built cities in the hill country of Judah, and forts and towers on the wooded hills. [5]He fought with the king of the Ammonites and prevailed against them. The Ammonites gave him that year one hundred talents of silver, ten thousand cors of wheat and ten thousand of barley. The Ammonites paid him the same amount in the second and the third years. [6]So Jotham became strong because he ordered his ways before the LORD his God. [7]Now the rest of the acts of Jotham, and all his wars and his ways, are written in the Book of the Kings of Israel and Judah. [8]He was twenty-five years old when he began to reign; he reigned sixteen years in Jerusalem. [9]Jotham slept with his ancestors, and they buried him in the city of David; and his son Ahaz succeeded him.

Reign of Ahaz

28 Ahaz was twenty years old when he began to reign; he reigned sixteen years in Jeru-

salem. He did not do what was right in the sight of the LORD, as his ancestor David had done, [2]but he walked in the ways of the kings of Israel. He even made cast images for the Baals; [3]and he made offerings in the valley of the son of Hinnom, and made his sons pass through fire, according to the abominable practices of the nations whom the LORD drove out before the people of Israel. [4]He sacrificed and made offerings on the high places, on the hills, and under every green tree.

Aram and Israel Defeat Judah

5 Therefore the LORD his God gave him into the hand of the king of Aram, who defeated him and took captive a great number of his people and brought them to Damascus. He was also given into the hand of the king of Israel, who defeated him with great slaughter. [6]Pekah son of Remaliah killed one hundred twenty thousand in Judah in one day, all of them valiant warriors, because they had abandoned the LORD, the God of their ancestors. [7]And Zichri, a mighty warrior of Ephraim, killed the king's son Maaseiah, Azrikam the commander of the palace, and Elkanah the next in authority to the king.

Intervention of Oded

8 The people of Israel took captive two hundred thousand of their kin, women, sons, and daughters; they also took much booty from them and brought the booty to Samaria. [9]But a prophet of the LORD was there, whose name was Oded; he went out to meet the army that came to Samaria, and said to them, "Because the LORD, the God of your ancestors, was angry with Judah, he gave them into your hand, but you have killed them in a rage that has reached up to heaven. [10]Now you intend to subjugate the people of Judah and Jerusalem, male and female, as your slaves. But what have you except sins against the LORD your God? [11]Now hear me, and send back the captives whom you have taken from your kindred, for the fierce wrath of the LORD is upon you." [12]Moreover, certain chiefs of the Ephraimites, Azariah son of Johanan, Berechiah son of Meshillemoth, Jehizkiah son of Shallum, and Amasa son of Hadlai, stood up against those who were coming from the war, [13]and said to them, "You shall not bring the captives in here, for you propose to bring on us guilt against the LORD in addition to our present sins and guilt. For our guilt is already

---

a A term for several skin diseases; precise meaning uncertain

great, and there is fierce wrath against Israel." [14]So the warriors left the captives and the booty before the officials and all the assembly. [15]Then those who were mentioned by name got up and took the captives, and with the booty they clothed all that were naked among them; they clothed them, gave them sandals, provided them with food and drink, and anointed them; and carrying all the feeble among them on donkeys, they brought them to their kindred at Jericho, the city of palm trees. Then they returned to Samaria.

Assyria Refuses to Help Judah

16 At that time King Ahaz sent to the king[a] of Assyria for help. [17]For the Edomites had again invaded and defeated Judah, and carried away captives. [18]And the Philistines had made raids on the cities in the Shephelah and the Negeb of Judah, and had taken Beth-shemesh, Aijalon, Gederoth, Soco with its villages, Timnah with its villages, and Gimzo with its villages; and they settled there. [19]For the LORD brought Judah low because of King Ahaz of Israel, for he had behaved without restraint in Judah and had been faithless to the LORD. [20]So King Tilgath-pilneser of Assyria came against him, and oppressed him instead of strengthening him. [21]For Ahaz plundered the house of the LORD and the houses of the king and of the officials, and gave tribute to the king of Assyria; but it did not help him.

Apostasy and Death of Ahaz

22 In the time of his distress he became yet more faithless to the LORD—this same King Ahaz. [23]For he sacrificed to the gods of Damascus, which had defeated him, and said, "Because the gods of the kings of Aram helped them, I will sacrifice to them so that they may help me." But they were the ruin of him, and of all Israel. [24]Ahaz gathered together the utensils of the house of God, and cut in pieces the utensils of the house of God. He shut up the doors of the house of the LORD and made himself altars in every corner of Jerusalem. [25]In every city of Judah he made high places to make offerings to other gods, provoking to anger the LORD, the God of his ancestors. [26]Now the rest of his acts and all his ways, from first to last, are written in the Book of the Kings of Judah and Israel. [27]Ahaz slept with his ancestors, and they buried him in the city, in Jerusalem; but they did not bring him into the tombs of the kings of Israel. His son Hezekiah succeeded him.

Reign of Hezekiah

29 Hezekiah began to reign when he was twenty-five years old; he reigned twenty-nine years in Jerusalem. His mother's name was Abijah daughter of Zechariah. [2]He did what was right in the sight of the LORD, just as his ancestor David had done.

The Temple Cleansed

3 In the first year of his reign, in the first month, he opened the doors of the house of the LORD and repaired them. [4]He brought in the priests and the Levites and assembled them in the square on the east. [5]He said to them, "Listen to me, Levites! Sanctify yourselves, and sanctify the house of the LORD, the God of your ancestors, and carry out the filth from the holy place. [6]For our ancestors have been unfaithful and have done what was evil in the sight of the LORD our God; they have forsaken him, and have turned away their faces from the dwelling of the LORD, and turned their backs. [7]They also shut the doors of the vestibule and put out the lamps, and have not offered incense or made burnt offerings in the holy place to the God of Israel. [8]Therefore the wrath of the LORD came upon Judah and Jerusalem, and he has made them an object of horror, of astonishment, and of hissing, as you see with your own eyes. [9]Our fathers have fallen by the sword and our sons and our daughters and our wives are in captivity for this. [10]Now it is in my heart to make a covenant with the LORD, the God of Israel, so that his fierce anger may turn away from us. [11]My sons, not now be negligent, for the LORD has chosen you to stand in his presence to minister to him, and to be his ministers and make offerings to him."

12 Then the Levites arose, Mahath son of Amasai, and Joel son of Azariah, of the sons of the Ko-

a Gk Syr Vg Compare 2 Kings 16.7: Heb kings

hathites; and of the sons of Merari, Kish son of Abdi, and Azariah son of Jehallelel; and of the Gershonites, Joah son of Zimmah, and Eden son of Joah; [13]and of the sons of Elizaphan, Shimri and Jeuel; and of the sons of Asaph, Zechariah and Mattaniah; [14]and of the sons of Heman, Jehuel and Shimei; and of the sons of Jeduthun, Shemaiah and Uzziel. [15]They gathered their brothers, sanctified themselves, and went in as the king had commanded, by the words of the LORD, to cleanse the house of the LORD. [16]The priests went into the inner part of the house of the LORD to cleanse it, and they brought out all the unclean things that they found in the temple of the LORD into the court of the house of the LORD; and the Levites took them and carried them out to the Wadi Kidron. [17]They began to sanctify on the first day of the first month, and on the eighth day of the month they came to the vestibule of the LORD; then for eight days they sanctified the house of the LORD, and on the sixteenth day of the first month they finished. [18]Then they went inside to King Hezekiah and said, "We have cleansed all the house of the LORD, the altar of burnt offering and all its utensils, and the table for the rows of bread and all its utensils. [19]All the utensils that King Ahaz repudiated during his reign when he was faithless, we have made ready and sanctified; see, they are in front of the altar of the LORD."

Temple Worship Restored

20 Then King Hezekiah rose early, assembled the officials of the city, and went up to the house of the LORD. [21]They brought seven bulls, seven rams, seven lambs, and seven male goats for a sin offering for the kingdom and for the sanctuary and for Judah. He commanded the priests the descendants of Aaron to offer them on the altar of the LORD. [22]So they slaughtered the bulls, and the priests received the blood and dashed it against the altar; they slaughtered the rams and their blood was dashed against the altar; they also slaughtered the lambs and their blood was dashed against the altar. [23]Then the male goats for the sin offering were brought to the king and the assembly; they laid their hands on them, [24]and the priests slaughtered them and made a sin offering with their blood at the altar, to make atonement for all Israel. For the king commanded that the burnt offering and the sin offering should be made for all Israel.

25 He stationed the Levites in the house of the LORD with cymbals, harps, and lyres, according to the commandment of David and of Gad the king's seer and of the prophet Nathan, for the commandment was from the LORD through his prophets. [26]The Levites stood with the instruments of David, and the priests with the trumpets. [27]Then Hezekiah commanded that the burnt offering be offered on the altar. When the burnt offering began, the song to the LORD began also, and the trumpets, accompanied by the instruments of King David of Israel. [28]The whole assembly worshiped, the singers sang, and the trumpeters sounded; all this continued until the burnt offering was finished. [29]When the offering was finished, the king and all who were present with him bowed down and worshiped. [30]King Hezekiah and the officials commanded the Levites to sing praises to the LORD with the words of David and of the seer Asaph. They sang praises with gladness, and they bowed down and worshiped.

31 Then Hezekiah said, "You have now consecrated yourselves to the LORD; come near, bring sacrifices and thank offerings to the house of the LORD." The assembly brought sacrifices and thank offerings; and all who were of a willing heart brought burnt offerings. [32]The number of the burnt offerings that the assembly brought was seventy bulls, one hundred rams, and two hundred lambs; all these were for a burnt offering to the LORD. [33]The consecrated offerings were six hundred bulls and three thousand sheep. [34]But the priests were too few and could not skin all the burnt offerings, so, until other priests had sanctified themselves, their kindred, the Levites, helped them until the work was finished— for the Levites were more conscientious[a] than the priests in sanctifying themselves. [35]Besides the great number of burnt offerings there was the fat of the offerings of well-being, and there were the drink offerings for the burnt offerings. Thus the service of the house of the LORD was restored. [36]And Hezekiah and all the people rejoiced because of what God had done for the people; for the thing had come about suddenly.

The Great Passover

30 Hezekiah sent word to all Israel and Judah, and wrote letters also to Ephraim and Manasseh, that they should come to the house of the LORD at Jerusalem, to keep the passover to the LORD the God of Israel. [2]For the king and his officials and all the assembly in Jerusalem had taken

---

a Heb upright in heart

counsel to keep the passover in the second month [3](for they could not keep it at its proper time because the priests had not sanctified themselves in sufficient number, nor had the people assembled in Jerusalem). [4]The plan seemed right to the king and all the assembly. [5]So they decreed to make a proclamation throughout all Israel, from Beer-sheba to Dan, that the people should come and keep the passover to the LORD the God of Israel, at Jerusalem; for they had not kept it in great numbers as prescribed. [6]So couriers went throughout all Israel and Judah with letters from the king and his officials, as the king had commanded, saying, "O people of Israel, return to the LORD, the God of Abraham, Isaac, and Israel, so that he may turn again to the remnant of you who have escaped from the hand of the kings of Assyria. [7]Do not be like your ancestors and your kindred, who were faithless to the LORD God of their ancestors, so that he made them a desolation, as you see. [8]Do not now be stiff-necked as your ancestors were, but yield yourselves to the LORD and come to his sanctuary, which he has sanctified forever, and serve the LORD your God, so that his fierce anger may turn away from you. [9]For as you return to the LORD, your kindred and your children will find compassion with their captors, and return to this land. For the LORD your God is gracious and merciful, and will not turn away his face from you, if you return to him."

10 So the couriers went from city to city through the country of Ephraim and Manasseh, and as far as Zebulun; but they laughed them to scorn, and mocked them. [11]Only a few from Asher, Manasseh, and Zebulun humbled themselves and came to Jerusalem. [12]The hand of God was also on Judah to give them one heart to do what the king and the officials commanded by the word of the LORD.

13 Many people came together in Jerusalem to keep the festival of unleavened bread in the second month, a very large assembly. [14]They set to work and removed the altars that were in Jerusalem, and all the altars for offering incense they took away and threw into the Wadi Kidron. [15]They slaughtered the passover lamb on the fourteenth day of the second month. The priests and the Levites were ashamed, and they sanctified themselves and brought burnt offerings into the house of the LORD. [16]They took their accustomed posts according to the law of Moses the man of God; the priests dashed the blood that they received[a] from the hands of the Levites. [17]For there were many in the assembly who had not

sanctified themselves; therefore the Levites had to slaughter the passover lamb for everyone who was not clean, to make it holy to the LORD. [18]For a multitude of the people, many of them from Ephraim, Manasseh, Issachar, and Zebulun, had not cleansed themselves, yet they ate the passover otherwise than as prescribed. But Hezekiah prayed for them, saying, "The good LORD pardon all [19]who set their hearts to seek God, the LORD the God of their ancestors, even though not in accordance with the sanctuary's rules of cleanness." [20]The LORD heard Hezekiah, and healed the people. [21]The people of Israel who were present at Jerusalem kept the festival of unleavened bread seven days with great gladness; and the Levites and the priests praised the LORD day by day, accompanied by loud instruments for the LORD. [22]Hezekiah spoke encouragingly to all the Levites who showed good skill in the service of the LORD. So the people ate the food of the festival for seven days, sacrificing offerings of well-being and giving thanks to the LORD the God of their ancestors.

23 Then the whole assembly agreed together to keep the festival for another seven days; so they kept it for another seven days with gladness. [24]For King Hezekiah of Judah gave the assembly a thousand bulls and seven thousand sheep for offerings, and the officials gave the assembly a thousand bulls and ten thousand sheep. The priests sanctified themselves in great numbers. [25]The whole assembly of Judah, the priests and the Levites, and the whole assembly that came out of Israel, and the resident aliens who came out of the land of Israel, and the resident aliens who lived in Judah, rejoiced. [26]There was great joy in Jerusalem, for since the time of Solomon son of King David of Israel there had been nothing like this in Jerusalem. [27]Then the priests and the Levites stood up and blessed the people, and their voice was heard; their prayer came to his holy dwelling in heaven.

Pagan Shrines Destroyed

31 Now when all this was finished, all Israel who were present went out to the cities of Judah and broke down the pillars, hewed down the sacred poles,[b] and pulled down the high places and the altars throughout all Judah and Benjamin, and in Ephraim and Manasseh, until they had destroyed them all. Then all the people of Israel returned to their cities, all to their individual properties.

2 Hezekiah appointed the divisions of the priests

---

a Heb lacks *that they received* b Heb *Asherim*

Giving the Best of the Best • 2 Chronicles 31:2–10

When King Hezekiah called upon the people to support the priests and the restoration of temple worship, they "gave in abundance the first fruits of grain, wine, oil, honey, and of all the produce of the field; and they brought in abundantly the tithe of everything" (2 Chronicles 31:5). They gave the best of the best in gratitude for the gifts from God. That's what being generous is all about. True generosity springs from the heart and motivates us to give the best of what we have, not just what we don't want or need anymore.

The word "tithe" appears in this verse. For the Israelites, to tithe meant to give 10 percent of one's earnings as a tax for the upkeep of the temple. Many Christians continue the spirit of tithing by giving 10 percent of all they earn to their church and other charities. When we tithe, it's important to remember to offer God our best, the first fruits of our time, talents, and treasure (see Luke 21:1-4; Acts 4:32-37).

We all need to search our hearts and continue this tradition of offering our best back to God—not because it makes us look good and gives us extra points with God, but because it comes from our gratitude for the gifts we have received and reminds us that everything we have is God's.

and of the Levites, division by division, everyone according to his service, the priests and the Levites, for burnt offerings and offerings of well-being, to minister in the gates of the camp of the LORD and to give thanks and praise. ³The contribution of the king from his own possessions was for the burnt offerings: the burnt offerings of morning and evening, and the burnt offerings for the sabbaths, the new moons, and the appointed festivals, as it is written in the law of the LORD. ⁴He commanded the people who lived in Jerusalem to give the portion due to the priests and the Levites, so that they might devote themselves to the law of the LORD. ⁵As soon as the word spread, the people of Israel gave in abundance the first fruits of grain, wine, oil, honey, and of all the produce of the field; and they brought in abundantly the tithe of everything. ⁶The people of Israel and Judah who lived in the cities of Judah also brought in the tithe of cattle and sheep, and the tithe of the dedicated things that had been consecrated to the LORD their God, and laid them in heaps. ⁷In the third month they began to pile up the heaps, and finished them in the seventh month. ⁸When Hezekiah and the officials came and saw the heaps, they blessed the LORD and his people Israel. ⁹Hezekiah questioned the priests and the Levites about the heaps. ¹⁰The chief priest Azariah, who was of the house of Zadok, answered him, "Since

they began to bring the contributions into the house of the LORD, we have had enough to eat and have plenty to spare; for the LORD has blessed his people, so that we have this great supply left over."

Reorganization of Priests and Levites

11 Then Hezekiah commanded them to prepare store-chambers in the house of the LORD; and they prepared them. ¹²Faithfully they brought in the contributions, the tithes and the dedicated things. The chief officer in charge of them was Conaniah the Levite, with his brother Shimei as second; ¹³while Jehiel, Azaziah, Nahath, Asahel, Jerimoth, Jozabad, Eliel, Ismachiah, Mahath, and Benaiah were overseers assisting Conaniah and his brother Shimei, by the appointment of King Hezekiah and of Azariah the chief officer of the house of God. ¹⁴Kore son of Imnah the Levite, keeper of the east gate, was in charge of the freewill offerings to God, to apportion the contribution reserved for the LORD and the most holy offerings. ¹⁵Eden, Miniamin, Jeshua, Shemaiah, Amariah, and Shecaniah were faithfully assisting him in the cities of the priests, to distribute the portions to their kindred, old and young alike, by divisions, ¹⁶except those enrolled by genealogy, males from three years old and upwards, all who entered the house of the LORD as the duty of each day required, for their service according to their

offices, by their divisions. [17] The enrollment of the priests was according to their ancestral houses; that of the Levites from twenty years old and upwards was according to their offices, by their divisions. [18] The priests were enrolled with all their little children, their wives, their sons, and their daughters, the whole multitude; for they were faithful in keeping themselves holy. [19] And for the descendants of Aaron, the priests, who were in the fields of common land belonging to their towns, town by town, the people designated by name were to distribute portions to every male among the priests and to everyone among the Levites who was enrolled.

20 Hezekiah did this throughout all Judah; he did what was good and right and faithful before the LORD his God. [21] And every work that he undertook in the service of the house of God, and in accordance with the law and the commandments, to seek his God, he did with all his heart; and he prospered.

Sennacherib's Invasion

32 After these things and these acts of faithfulness, King Sennacherib of Assyria came and invaded Judah and encamped against the fortified cities, thinking to win them for himself. [2] When Hezekiah saw that Sennacherib had come and intended to fight against Jerusalem, [3] he planned with his officers and his warriors to stop the flow of the springs that were outside the city; and they helped him. [4] A great many people were gathered, and they stopped all the springs and the wadi that flowed through the land, saying, "Why should the Assyrian kings come and find water in abundance?" [5] Hezekiah[a] set to work resolutely and built up the entire wall that was broken down, and raised towers on it,[b] and outside it he built another wall; he also strengthened the Millo in the city of David, and made weapons and shields in abundance. [6] He appointed combat commanders over the people, and gathered them together to him in the square at the gate of the city and spoke encouragingly to them, saying, [7] "Be strong and of good courage. Do not be afraid or dismayed before the king of Assyria and all the horde that is with him; for there is one greater with us than with him. [8] With him is an arm of flesh; but with us is the LORD our God, to help us and to fight our battles." The people were encouraged by the words of King Hezekiah of Judah.

9 After this, while King Sennacherib of Assyria was at Lachish with all his forces, he sent his servants to Jerusalem to King Hezekiah of Judah and to all the people of Judah that were in Jerusalem, saying, [10] "Thus says King Sennacherib of Assyria: On what are you relying, that you undergo the siege of Jerusalem? [11] Is not Hezekiah misleading you, handing you over to die by famine and by thirst, when he tells you, 'The LORD our God will save us from the hand of the king of Assyria'? [12] Was it not this same Hezekiah who took away his high places and his altars and commanded Judah and Jerusalem, saying, 'Before one altar you shall worship, and upon it you shall make your offerings'? [13] Do you not know what I and my ancestors have done to all the peoples of other lands? Were the gods of the nations of those lands at all able to save their lands out of my hand? [14] Who among all the gods of those nations that my ancestors utterly destroyed was able to save his people from my hand, that your God should be able to save you from my hand? [15] Now therefore do not let Hezekiah deceive you or mislead you in this fashion, and do not believe him, for no god of any nation or kingdom has been able to save his people from my hand or from the hand of my ancestors. How much less will your God save you out of my hand!"

16 His servants said still more against the Lord GOD and against his servant Hezekiah. [17] He also wrote letters to throw contempt on the LORD the God of Israel and to speak against him, saying, "Just as the gods of the nations in other lands did not rescue their people from my hands, so the God of Hezekiah will not rescue his people from my hand." [18] They shouted it with a loud voice in the language of Judah to the people of Jerusalem who were on the wall, to frighten and terrify them, in order that they might take the city. [19] They spoke of the God of Jerusalem as if he were like the gods of the peoples of the earth, which are the work of human hands.

Sennacherib's Defeat and Death

20 Then King Hezekiah and the prophet Isaiah son of Amoz prayed because of this and cried to heaven. [21] And the LORD sent an angel who cut off all the mighty warriors and commanders and officers in the camp of the king of Assyria. So he returned in disgrace to his own land. When he came into the house of his god, some of his own sons struck him down there with the sword. [22] So the LORD saved Hezekiah and the inhabitants of Jerusalem from the hand of King Sennacherib of Assyria and from the hand of all his enemies; he gave them rest[c] on every

---

a Heb He   b Vg: Heb and raised on the towers   c Gk Vg: Heb guided them side. [23]Many brought gifts to the LORD in Jerusalem and precious things to King Hezekiah of Judah, so that he was exalted in the sight of all nations from that time onward.

Hezekiah's Sickness

24 In those days Hezekiah became sick and was at the point of death. He prayed to the LORD, and he answered him and gave him a sign. [25]But Hezekiah

LIVE IT!

Perseverance
2 Chronicles 32:27–33

Who or what motivates you to persevere when you're faced with an obstacle or difficult situation? King Hezekiah persevered and prospered while providing for the people in his kingdom. One great example of Hezekiah's perseverance was a tunnel he dug under the City of David (2 Chronicles 32:3-4, 30). The tunnel allowed the springs of Gihon to flow into the city, so that the people had easier access to water in the event of a siege.

That tunnel, more than 1,700 feet long, was carved through stone. It wouldn't take much to complete such a task today with explosives and modern machinery. But in Hezekiah's time, it was done by hand, little by little, with simple tools.

Perseverance is a valuable skill that everyone can benefit from, especially when great obstacles stand in the way. People can get discouraged and lose heart when faced with difficult tasks. Those who refuse to be discouraged or to give up can serve as a source of encouragement and vision for others.

- When have you gotten discouraged and given up (for example, at school, in a relationship)? Why?
- What are you tempted to give up on today? Recommit yourself to making it through.

did not respond according to the benefit done to him, for his heart was proud. Therefore wrath came upon him and upon Judah and Jerusalem. [26]Then Hezekiah humbled himself for the pride of his heart, both he and the inhabitants of Jerusalem, so that the wrath of the LORD did not come upon them in the days of Hezekiah.

Hezekiah's Prosperity and Achievements

27 Hezekiah had very great riches and honor; and he made for himself treasuries for silver, for gold, for precious stones, for spices, for shields, and for all kinds of costly objects; [28]storehouses also for the yield of grain, wine, and oil; and stalls for all kinds of cattle, and sheepfolds.[a] [29]He likewise provided cities for himself, and flocks and herds in abundance; for God had given him very great possessions. [30]This same Hezekiah closed the upper outlet of the waters of Gihon and directed them down to the west side of the city of David. Hezekiah prospered in all his works. [31]So also in the matter of the envoys of the officials of Babylon, who had been sent to him to inquire about the sign that had been done in the land, God left him to himself, in order to test him and to know all that was in his heart.

32 Now the rest of the acts of Hezekiah, and his good deeds, are written in the vision of the prophet Isaiah son of Amoz in the Book of the Kings of Judah and Israel. [33]Hezekiah slept with his ancestors, and they buried him on the ascent to the tombs of the descendants of David; and all Judah and the inhabitants of Jerusalem did him honor at his death. His son Manasseh succeeded him.

33 Reign of Manasseh

Manasseh was twelve years old when he began to reign; he reigned fifty-five years in Jerusalem. [2]He did what was evil in the sight of the LORD, according to the abominable practices of the nations whom the LORD drove out before the people of Israel. [3]For he rebuilt the high places that his father Hezekiah had pulled down, and erected altars to the Baals, made sacred poles,[b] worshiped all the host of heaven, and served them. [4]He built altars in the house of the LORD, of which the LORD had said, "In Jerusalem shall my name be forever." [5]He built altars for all the host of heaven in the two courts of the house of the LORD. [6]He made his son pass through fire in the valley of the son of Hinnom, practiced soothsaying and augury and sorcery, and

---

a Gk Vg: Heb *flocks for folds*   b Heb *Asheroth*

dealt with mediums and with wizards. He did much evil in the sight of the LORD, provoking him to anger. [7]The carved image of the idol that he had made he set in the house of God, of which God said to David and to his son Solomon, "In this house, and in Jerusalem, which I have chosen out of all the tribes of Israel, I will put my name forever; [8]I will never again remove the feet of Israel from the land that I appointed for your ancestors, if only they will be careful to do all that I have commanded them, all the law, the statutes, and the ordinances given through Moses." [9]Manasseh misled Judah and the inhabitants of Jerusalem, so that they did more evil than the nations whom the LORD had destroyed before the people of Israel.

Manasseh Restored after Repentance

10 The LORD spoke to Manasseh and to his people, but they gave no heed. [11]Therefore the LORD brought against them the commanders of the army of the king of Assyria, who took Manasseh captive in manacles, bound him with fetters, and brought him to Babylon. [12]While he was in distress he entreated the favor of the LORD his God and humbled himself greatly before the God of his ancestors. [13]He prayed to him, and God received his entreaty, heard his plea, and restored him again to Jerusalem and to his kingdom. Then Manasseh knew that the LORD indeed was God.

14 Afterward he built an outer wall for the city of David west of Gihon, in the valley, reaching the entrance at the Fish Gate; he carried it around Ophel, and raised it to a very great height. He also put commanders of the army in all the fortified cities in Judah. [15]He took away the foreign gods and the idol from the house of the LORD, and all the altars that he had built on the mountain of the house of the LORD and in Jerusalem, and he threw them out of the city. [16]He also restored the altar of the LORD and offered on it sacrifices of well-being and of thanksgiving; and he commanded Judah to serve the LORD the God of Israel. [17]The people, however, still sacrificed at the high places, but only to the LORD their God.

Death of Manasseh

18 Now the rest of the acts of Manasseh, his prayer to his God, and the words of the seers who spoke to him in the name of the LORD God of Israel, these are in the Annals of the Kings of Israel. [19]His prayer, and how God received his entreaty, all his sin and his faithlessness, the sites on which he built high places and set up the sacred poles[a] and the images, before he humbled himself, these are written in the records of the seers.[b] [20]So Manasseh slept with his ancestors, and they buried him in his house. His son Amon succeeded him.

Amon's Reign and Death

21 Amon was twenty-two years old when he began to reign; he reigned two years in Jerusalem. [22]He did what was evil in the sight of the LORD, as his father Manasseh had done. Amon sacrificed to all the images that his father Manasseh had made, and served them. [23]He did not humble himself before the LORD, as his father Manasseh had humbled himself, but this Amon incurred more and more guilt. [24]His servants conspired against him and killed him in his house. [25]But the people of the land killed all those who had conspired against King Amon; and the people of the land made his son Josiah king to succeed him.

34 Reign of Josiah

Josiah was eight years old when he began to reign; he reigned thirty-one years in Jerusalem. [2]He did what was right in the sight of the LORD, and walked in the ways of his ancestor David; he did not turn aside to the right or to the left. [3]For in the eighth year of his reign, while he was still a boy, he began to seek the God of his ancestor David, and in the twelfth year he began to purge Judah and Jerusalem of the high places, the sacred poles,[a] and the carved and the cast images. [4]In his presence they pulled down the altars of the Baals; he demolished the incense altars that stood above them. He broke down the sacred poles[a] and the carved and the cast images; he made dust of them and scattered it over the graves of those who had sacrificed to them. [5]He also burned the bones of the priests on their altars, and purged Judah and Jerusalem. [6]In the towns of Manasseh, Ephraim, and Simeon, and as far as Naphtali, in their ruins[c] all around, [7]he broke down the altars, beat the sacred poles[a] and the images into powder, and demolished all the incense altars throughout all the land of Israel. Then he returned to Jerusalem.

Discovery of the Book of the Law

8 In the eighteenth year of his reign, when he had purged the land and the house, he sent Shaphan son of Azaliah, Maaseiah the governor of the city,

---

a Heb *Asherim*   b One Ms Gk: MT *of Hozai*   c Meaning of Heb uncertain

and Joah son of Joahaz, the recorder, to repair the house of the LORD his God. [9]They came to the high priest Hilkiah and delivered the money that had been brought into the house of God, which the Levites, the keepers of the threshold, had collected from Manasseh and Ephraim and from all the remnant of Israel and from all Judah and Benjamin and from the inhabitants of Jerusalem. [10]They delivered it to the workers who had the oversight of the house of the LORD, and the workers who were working in the house of the LORD gave it for repairing and restoring the house. [11]They gave it to the carpenters and the builders to buy quarried stone, and timber for binders, and beams for the buildings that the kings of Judah had let go to ruin. [12]The people did the work faithfully. Over them were appointed the Levites Jahath and Obadiah, of the sons of Merari, along with Zechariah and Meshullam, of the sons of the Kohathites, to have oversight. Other Levites, all skillful with instruments of music, [13]were over the burden bearers and directed all who did work in every kind of service; and some of the Levites were scribes, and officials, and gatekeepers.

14 While they were bringing out the money that had been brought into the house of the LORD, the priest Hilkiah found the book of the law of the LORD given through Moses. [15]Hilkiah said to the secretary Shaphan, "I have found the book of the law in the house of the LORD"; and Hilkiah gave the book to Shaphan. [16]Shaphan brought the book to the king, and further reported to the king, "All that was committed to your servants they are doing. [17]They have emptied out the money that was found in the house of the LORD and have delivered it into the hand of the overseers and the workers." [18]The secretary Shaphan informed the king, "The priest Hilkiah has given me a book." Shaphan then read it aloud to the king.

19 When the king heard the words of the law he tore his clothes. [20]Then the king commanded Hilkiah, Ahikam son of Shaphan, Abdon son of Micah, the secretary Shaphan, and the king's servant Asaiah: [21]"Go, inquire of the LORD for me and for those who are left in Israel and in Judah, concerning the words of the book that has been found; for the wrath of the LORD that is poured out on us is great, because our ancestors did not keep the word of the LORD, to act in accordance with all that is written in this book."

The Prophet Huldah Consulted

22 So Hilkiah and those whom the king had sent went to the prophet Huldah, the wife of Shallum son of Tokhath son of Hasrah, keeper of the wardrobe (who lived in Jerusalem in the Second Quarter) and spoke to her to that effect. [23]She declared to them, "Thus says the LORD, the God of Israel: Tell the man who sent you to me, [24]Thus says the LORD: I will indeed bring disaster upon this place and upon its inhabitants, all the curses that are written in the book that was read before the king of Judah. [25]Because they have forsaken me and have made offerings to other gods, so that they have provoked me to anger with all the works of their hands, my wrath will be poured out on this place and will not be quenched. [26]But as to the king of Judah, who sent you to inquire of the LORD, thus shall you say to him: Thus says the LORD, the God of Israel: Regarding the words that you have heard, [27]because your heart was penitent and you humbled yourself before God when you heard his words against this place and its inhabitants, and you have humbled yourself before me, and have torn your clothes and wept before me, I also have heard you, says the LORD. [28]I will gather you to your ancestors and you shall be gathered to your grave in peace; your eyes shall not see all the disaster that I will bring on this place and its inhabitants." They took the message back to the king.

The Covenant Renewed

29 Then the king sent word and gathered together all the elders of Judah and Jerusalem. [30]The king went up to the house of the LORD, with all the people of Judah, the inhabitants of Jerusalem, the priests and the Levites, all the people both great and small; he read in their hearing all the words of the book of the covenant that had been found in the house of the LORD. [31]The king stood in his place and made a covenant before the LORD, to follow the LORD, keeping his commandments, his decrees, and his statutes, with all his heart and all his soul, to perform the words of the covenant that were written in this book. [32]Then he made all who were present in Jerusalem and in Benjamin pledge themselves to it. And the inhabitants of Jerusalem acted according to the covenant of God, the God of their ancestors. [33]Josiah took away all the abominations from all the territory that belonged to the people of Israel, and made all who were in Israel

worship the LORD their God. All his days they did not turn away from following the LORD the God of their ancestors.

Celebration of the Passover

35 Josiah kept a passover to the LORD in Jerusalem; they slaughtered the passover lamb on the fourteenth day of the first month. [2]He appointed the priests to their offices and encouraged them in the service of the house of the LORD. [3]He said to the Levites who taught all Israel and who were holy to the LORD, "Put the holy ark in the house that Solomon son of David, king of Israel, built; you need no longer carry it on your shoulders. Now serve the LORD your God and his people Israel. [4]Make preparations by your ancestral houses by your divisions, following the written directions of King David of Israel and the written directions of his son Solomon. [5]Take position in the holy place according to the groupings of the ancestral houses of your kindred the people, and let there be Levites for each division of an ancestral house.[a] [6]Slaughter the passover lamb, sanctify yourselves, and on behalf of your kindred make preparations, acting according to the word of the LORD by Moses."

7 Then Josiah contributed to the people, as passover offerings for all that were present, lambs and kids from the flock to the number of thirty thousand, and three thousand bulls; these were from the king's possessions. [8]His officials contributed willingly to the people, to the priests, and to the Levites. Hilkiah, Zechariah, and Jehiel, the chief officers of the house of God, gave to the priests for the passover offerings two thousand six hundred lambs and kids and three hundred bulls. [9]Conaniah also, and his brothers Shemaiah and Nethanel, and Hashabiah and Jeiel and Jozabad, the chiefs of the Levites, gave to the Levites for the passover offerings five thousand lambs and kids and five hundred bulls.

10 When the service had been prepared for, the priests stood in their place, and the Levites in their divisions according to the king's command. [11]They slaughtered the passover lamb, and the priests dashed the blood that they received[b] from them, while the Levites did the skinning. [12]They set aside the burnt offerings so that they might distribute them according to the groupings of the ancestral houses of the people, to offer to the LORD, as it is written in the book of Moses. And they did the same with the bulls. [13]They roasted the passover lamb with fire according to the ordinance; and they boiled the holy offerings in pots, in caldrons, and in pans, and carried them quickly to all the people. [14]Afterward they made preparations for themselves and for the priests, because the priests the descendants of Aaron were occupied in offering the burnt offerings and the fat parts until night; so the Levites made preparations for themselves and for the priests, the descendants of Aaron. [15]The singers, the descendants of Asaph, were in their place according to the command of David, and Asaph, and Heman, and the king's seer Jeduthun. The gatekeepers were at each gate; they did not need to interrupt their service, for their kindred the Levites made preparations for them.

16 So all the service of the LORD was prepared that day, to keep the passover and to offer burnt offerings on the altar of the LORD, according to the command of King Josiah. [17]The people of Israel who were present kept the passover at that time, and the festival of unleavened bread seven days. [18]No passover like it had been kept in Israel since the days of the prophet Samuel; none of the kings of Israel had kept such a passover as was kept by Josiah, by the priests and the Levites, by all Judah and Israel who were present, and by the inhabitants of Jerusalem. [19]In the eighteenth year of the reign of Josiah this passover was kept.

Defeat by Pharaoh Neco and Death of Josiah

20 After all this, when Josiah had set the temple in order, King Neco of Egypt went up to fight at Carchemish on the Euphrates, and Josiah went out against him. [21]But Neco[c] sent envoys to him, saying, "What have I to do with you, king of Judah? I am not coming against you today, but against the house with which I am at war; and God has commanded me to hurry. Cease opposing God, who is with me, so that he will not destroy you." [22]But Josiah would not turn away from him, but disguised himself in order to fight with him. He did not listen to the words of Neco from the mouth of God, but joined battle in the plain of Megiddo. [23]The archers shot King Josiah; and the king said to his servants, "Take me away, for I am badly wounded." [24]So his servants took him out of the chariot and carried him in his second chariot[d] and brought him to Jerusalem. There he died, and was buried in the tombs of his ancestors. All Judah and Jerusalem mourned for

---

a Meaning of Heb uncertain   b Heb lacks *that they received*   c Heb *he*   d Or *the chariot of his deputy*

Schools for Schools: Providing Education Instead of Weapons · 2 Chronicles 35:22

King Josiah didn't listen to God's words, but instead, he rushed into war and it cost him his life. Even when God did command the Israelites to fight against people who were committed to doing evil, it was brutal.

War is a destroyer—of life and of opportunity for its survivors. And today, brutal civil wars have torn apart much of Africa, including Uganda. Young people there have seen their families killed and their homes, towns, and schools destroyed. Even young children have had to run for their lives. Those who are captured have been brainwashed and forced to become soldiers—killing machines who prey on innocent civilians.

Many American students are doing something about it through Schools for Schools (S4S), a program run by Invisible Children that helps American schools partner with and rebuild Ugandan secondary schools. At schools such as Bridgeport High School in Bridgeport, West Virginia, American students are using car washes, dog washes, raffles, loose change collections, and whatever creative ideas they can come up with to raise money. "It's just great to be able to realize that you're making a difference in someone's education. Sometimes we take that for granted," says cofounder Thomas Collins.*

It's even greater for African students—education means a chance that new life can replace the horror and death of war. Learn more about S4S at **s4s.invisiblechildren.com**.

Josiah. [25]Jeremiah also uttered a lament for Josiah, and all the singing men and singing women have spoken of Josiah in their laments to this day. They made these a custom in Israel; they are recorded in the Laments. [26]Now the rest of the acts of Josiah and his faithful deeds in accordance with what is written in the law of the LORD, [27]and his acts, first and last, are written in the Book of the Kings of Israel and Judah.

Reign of Jehoahaz

36 The people of the land took Jehoahaz son of Josiah and made him king to succeed his father in Jerusalem. [2]Jehoahaz was twenty-three years old when he began to reign; he reigned three months in Jerusalem. [3]Then the king of Egypt deposed him in Jerusalem and laid on the land a tribute of one hundred talents of silver and one talent of gold. [4]The king of Egypt made his brother Eliakim king over Judah and Jerusalem, and changed his name to Jehoiakim; but Neco took his brother Jehoahaz and carried him to Egypt.

Reign and Captivity of Jehoiakim

5 Jehoiakim was twenty-five years old when he began to reign; he reigned eleven years in Jerusalem. He did what was evil in the sight of the LORD his God. [6]Against him King Nebuchadnezzar of Babylon came up, and bound him with fetters to take him to Babylon. [7]Nebuchadnezzar also carried some of the vessels of the house of the LORD to Babylon and put them in his palace in Babylon. [8]Now the rest of the acts of Jehoiakim, and the abominations that he did, and what was found against him, are written in the Book of the Kings of Israel and Judah; and his son Jehoiachin succeeded him.

Reign and Captivity of Jehoiachin

9 Jehoiachin was eight years old when he began to reign; he reigned three months and ten days in Jerusalem. He did what was evil in the sight of the LORD. [10]In the spring of the year King Nebuchadnezzar sent and brought him to Babylon, along with the precious vessels of the house of the LORD, and made his brother Zedekiah king over Judah and Jerusalem.

Reign of Zedekiah

11 Zedekiah was twenty-one years old when he began to reign; he reigned eleven years in Jerusalem.

Stiff Neck · 2 Chronicles 36:11–14

"Whiplash!" It can happen so quickly. You're waiting at a stoplight when the car behind you slams into your car and snaps your neck back. It hurts, but it doesn't seem very serious at first. The adrenaline and shock of the moment make you much more upset about the damage done to your car. But by the next morning, you're in agony—your neck is stiff and sore and you can barely move it from side to side. By the end of the day you have a brace and medication from the doctor.

No wonder the Bible so often uses the metaphor of stiff-necked people for those who rebel against God (2 Chronicles 36:13). Unable or unwilling to turn their heads, they lose their ability to look toward God. They keep looking straight ahead stubbornly, as if it were impossible to look in any other direction.

- How often have you refused to turn toward God or to gain a new perspective on life?
- How can you keep from becoming spiritually stiff-necked?

---

¹²He did what was evil in the sight of the LORD his God. He did not humble himself before the prophet Jeremiah who spoke from the mouth of the LORD. ¹³He also rebelled against King Nebuchadnezzar, who had made him swear by God; he stiffened his neck and hardened his heart against turning to the LORD, the God of Israel. ¹⁴All the leading priests and the people also were exceedingly unfaithful, following all the abominations of the nations; and they polluted the house of the LORD that he had consecrated in Jerusalem.

The Fall of Jerusalem

15 The LORD, the God of their ancestors, sent persistently to them by his messengers, because he had compassion on his people and on his dwelling place; ¹⁶but they kept mocking the messengers of God, despising his words, and scoffing at his prophets, until the wrath of the LORD against his people became so great that there was no remedy.

17 Therefore he brought up against them the king of the Chaldeans, who killed their youths with the sword in the house of their sanctuary, and had no compassion on young man or young woman, the aged or the feeble; he gave them all into his hand. ¹⁸All the vessels of the house of God, large and small, and the treasures of the house of the LORD, and the treasures of the king and of his officials, all these he brought to Babylon. ¹⁹They burned the house of God, broke down the wall of Jerusalem, burned all its palaces with fire, and destroyed all its precious vessels. ²⁰He took into exile in Babylon those who had escaped from the sword, and they became servants to him and to his sons until the establishment of the kingdom of Persia, ²¹to fulfill the word of the LORD by the mouth of Jeremiah, until the land had made up for its sabbaths. All the days that it lay desolate it kept sabbath, to fulfill seventy years.

Cyrus Proclaims Liberty for the Exiles

22 In the first year of King Cyrus of Persia, in fulfillment of the word of the LORD spoken by Jeremiah, the LORD stirred up the spirit of King Cyrus of Persia so that he sent a herald throughout all his kingdom and also declared in a written edict: ²³"Thus says King Cyrus of Persia: The LORD, the God of heaven, has given me all the kingdoms of the earth, and he has charged me to build him a house at Jerusalem, which is in Judah. Whoever is among you of all his people, may the LORD his God be with him! Let him go up."

Ezra

I magine the worst vacation ever. The car breaks down twice. Your whole family is sick the whole time, and your beach resort is hit by a hurricane. You can't wait to get home, but when you walk in the front door, your house is trashed. That's how the Israelites felt—but even worse. They didn't just have a bad vacation; they spent fifty years as captives in a foreign land. When they finally returned home, they faced the overwhelming task of rebuilding a destroyed Jerusalem and starting life anew. Fortunately, they had Ezra and Nehemiah to lead and encourage them.

IN DEPTH

In 587 B.C., the land of Judah and the city of Jerusalem were conquered by the Babylonians, and many Israelites were taken away as prisoners to Babylon. The books of Ezra and Nehemiah pick up the story with the return of some Israelites from Babylon to Judah about fifty years later, in 538 B.C. The two books were originally a single work, perhaps written in their final form by the same person (or persons) who wrote 1 and 2 Chronicles.

Ezra, a descendant of Israelite priests, was born in Babylonian captivity and became a priest. Because priests couldn't exercise their religious functions during the exile, they dedicated themselves to studying the scriptures. Eventually, Ezra was sent to Judah by the Persian emperor Artaxerxes to restore Israel's faithfulness to God. Ezra appointed scribes and judges to establish civil and moral order in the new community returned from exile.

Nehemiah was a Jewish cupbearer for Emperor Artaxerxes (a cupbearer tastes whatever the emperor drinks to make sure it isn't poisoned). When Nehemiah heard reports of Jerusalem's poverty and ruin, he persuaded the emperor to appoint him governor of Judah to help rebuild the city. Nehemiah turned out to be a gifted governor. Under Nehemiah's direction, Jerusalem's walls were rebuilt, and economic and social reforms helped restore order and hope to the community.

The leadership of Ezra and Nehemiah was extremely important to Israel as the people returned and began the difficult task of rebuilding Jerusalem. The need to save the faith and customs of the Israelites led to a strict observance of the law and the beginnings of modern Judaism.

QUICK FACTS

- **Dates Covered:** From the exiles' return to Jerusalem through Nehemiah's tenure as governor of Judah, from 538 to about 400 B.C.

- **Author:** A scribe (perhaps the Chronicler) drawing on Ezra's and Nehemiah's memoirs and other sources, completed around 400 B.C.

- **Themes:** The Israelites' return from exile and the rebuilding of Jerusalem and the temple, showing the power of people working together for God's purposes

AT A GLANCE

- **Ezra 1–6** The return of the exiled Israelites to Judah

- **Ezra 7–10** The story of Ezra and his works

- **Nehemiah 1:1–7:72** Nehemiah's appointment as governor

- **Nehemiah 7:73–9:38** Ezra's proclaiming of the Torah

- **Nehemiah 10–13** The various reforms of Nehemiah

End of the Babylonian Captivity

1 In the first year of King Cyrus of Persia, in order that the word of the LORD by the mouth of Jeremiah might be accomplished, the LORD stirred up the spirit of King Cyrus of Persia so that he sent a herald throughout all his kingdom, and also in a written edict declared:

2 "Thus says King Cyrus of Persia: The LORD, the God of heaven, has given me all the kingdoms of the earth, and he has charged me to build him a house at Jerusalem in Judah. ³Any of those among you who are of his people—may their God be with them!—are now permitted to go up to Jerusalem in Judah, and rebuild the house of the LORD, the God of Israel—he is the God who is in Jerusalem; ⁴and let all survivors, in whatever place they reside, be assisted by the people of their place with silver and gold, with goods and with animals, besides freewill offerings for the house of God in Jerusalem."

5 The heads of the families of Judah and Benjamin, and the priests and the Levites—everyone whose spirit God had stirred—got ready to go up and rebuild the house of the LORD in Jerusalem. ⁶All their neighbors aided them with silver vessels, with gold, with goods, with animals, and with valuable gifts, besides all that was freely offered. ⁷King Cyrus himself brought out the vessels of the house of the LORD that Nebuchadnezzar had carried away from Jerusalem and placed in the house of his gods. ⁸King Cyrus of Persia had them released into the charge of Mithredath the treasurer, who counted them out to Sheshbazzar the prince of Judah. ⁹And this was the inventory: gold basins, thirty; silver basins, one thousand; knives,ᵃ twenty-nine; ¹⁰gold bowls, thirty; other silver bowls, four hundred ten; other vessels, one thousand; ¹¹the total of the gold and silver vessels was five thousand four hundred. All these Sheshbazzar brought up, when the exiles were brought up from Babylonia to Jerusalem.

List of the Returned Exiles

2 Now these were the people of the province who came from those captive exiles whom King Nebuchadnezzar of Babylon had carried captive to Babylonia; they returned to Jerusalem and Judah, all to their own towns. ²They came with Zerubbabel, Jeshua, Nehemiah, Seraiah, Reelaiah, Mordecai, Bilshan, Mispar, Bigvai, Rehum, and Baanah.

The number of the Israelite people: ³the descendants of Parosh, two thousand one hundred seventy-two. ⁴Of Shephatiah, three hundred seventy-two. ⁵Of Arah, seven hundred seventy-five. ⁶Of Pahath-moab, namely the descendants of Jeshua and Joab, two thousand eight hundred twelve. ⁷Of Elam, one thousand two hundred fifty-four. ⁸Of Zattu, nine hundred forty-five. ⁹Of Zaccai, seven hundred sixty. ¹⁰Of Bani, six hundred forty-two. ¹¹Of Bebai, six hundred twenty-three. ¹²Of Azgad, one thousand two hundred twenty-two. ¹³Of Adonikam, six hundred sixty-six. ¹⁴Of Bigvai, two thousand fifty-six. ¹⁵Of Adin, four hundred fifty-four. ¹⁶Of Ater, namely of Hezekiah, ninety-eight. ¹⁷Of Bezai, three hundred twenty-three. ¹⁸Of Jorah, one hundred twelve. ¹⁹Of Hashum, two hundred twenty-three. ²⁰Of Gibbar, ninety-five. ²¹Of Bethlehem, one hundred twenty-three. ²²The people of Netophah, fifty-six. ²³Of Anathoth, one hundred twenty-eight. ²⁴The descendants of Azmaveth, forty-two. ²⁵Of Kiriatharim, Chephirah, and Beeroth, seven hundred forty-three. ²⁶Of Ramah and Geba, six hundred twenty-one. ²⁷The people of Michmas, one hundred twenty-two. ²⁸Of Bethel and Ai, two hundred twenty-three. ²⁹The descendants of Nebo, fifty-two. ³⁰Of Magbish, one hundred fifty-six. ³¹Of the other Elam, one thousand two hundred fifty-four. ³²Of Harim, three hundred twenty. ³³Of Lod, Hadid, and Ono, seven hundred twenty-five. ³⁴Of Jericho, three hundred forty-five. ³⁵Of Senaah, three thousand six hundred thirty.

36 The priests: the descendants of Jedaiah, of the house of Jeshua, nine hundred seventy-three. ³⁷Of Immer, one thousand fifty-two. ³⁸Of Pashhur, one thousand two hundred forty-seven. ³⁹Of Harim, one thousand seventeen.

40 The Levites: the descendants of Jeshua and Kadmiel, of the descendants of Hodaviah, seventy-four. ⁴¹The singers: the descendants of Asaph, one hundred twenty-eight. ⁴²The descendants of the gatekeepers: of Shallum, of Ater, of Talmon, of Akkub, of Hatita, and of Shobai, in all one hundred thirty-nine.

43 The temple servants: the descendants of Ziha, Hasupha, Tabbaoth, ⁴⁴Keros, Siaha, Padon, ⁴⁵Lebanah, Hagabah, Akkub, ⁴⁶Hagab, Shamlai, Hanan, ⁴⁷Giddel, Gahar, Reaiah, ⁴⁸Rezin, Nekoda, Gazzam, ⁴⁹Uzza, Paseah, Besai, ⁵⁰Asnah, Meunim, Nephisim, ⁵¹Bakbuk, Hakupha, Harhur, ⁵²Bazluth, Mehida, Harsha, ⁵³Barkos, Sisera, Temah, ⁵⁴Neziah, and Hatipha.

ᵃ Vg: Meaning of Heb uncertain

LIVE IT!

The Spirit of Giving · Ezra 1:6–11

9/11. Whenever we hear it, we're reminded of a horrible day in the history of the United States. On September 11, 2001, suicidal terrorists hijacked four commercial airplanes. Two were crashed into the Twin Towers of the World Trade Center in New York City. One was crashed into the Pentagon in Washington, D.C., and the other missed its target in Washington, D.C., and crashed in Pennsylvania when the passengers fought to regain control of the flight. The towers in New York City collapsed and killed more than three thousand people.

That event impacted all Americans, especially those living in New York City. In the midst of such great tragedy, many stories of heroism emerged. New Yorkers and the entire nation came together to grieve and then to rebuild. Countless people volunteered untold hours to help with rescue efforts and clean-up. Countless more donated money to the families of those directly affected by the tragedy. Despite the horror of the attack, the aftermath of 9/11 brought millions of people together to help rebuild a broken city. It was perhaps one of our finest hours as a nation.

For the Jews returning to Jerusalem, the task of rebuilding their ruined city must have seemed even more overwhelming. (Their whole city was destroyed.) The Persian king Cyrus understood this and asked family, friends, and neighbors to help by giving whatever they could to the rebuilding effort.

• Who has been there to help you when you have felt completely overwhelmed or defeated?
• How can you offer help to others in their times of tragedy and crisis?

---

55 The descendants of Solomon's servants: Sotai, Hassophereth, Peruda, ⁵⁶Jaalah, Darkon, Giddel, ⁵⁷Shephatiah, Hattil, Pochereth-hazzebaim, and Ami.

58 All the temple servants and the descendants of Solomon's servants were three hundred ninety-two.

59 The following were those who came up from Tel-melah, Tel-harsha, Cherub, Addan, and Immer, though they could not prove their families or their descent, whether they belonged to Israel: ⁶⁰the descendants of Delaiah, Tobiah, and Nekoda, six hundred fifty-two. ⁶¹Also, of the descendants of the priests: the descendants of Habaiah, Hakkoz, and Barzillai (who had married one of the daughters of Barzillai the Gileadite, and was called by their name). ⁶²These looked for their entries in the genealogical records, but they were not found there, and so they were excluded from the priesthood as unclean; ⁶³the governor told them that they were not to partake of the most holy food, until there should be a priest to consult Urim and Thummim.

64 The whole assembly together was forty-two thousand three hundred sixty, ⁶⁵besides their male and female servants, of whom there were seven thousand three hundred thirty-seven; and they had two hundred male and female singers. ⁶⁶They had seven hundred thirty-six horses, two hundred forty-five mules, ⁶⁷four hundred thirty-five camels, and six thousand seven hundred twenty donkeys.

68 As soon as they came to the house of the LORD in Jerusalem, some of the heads of families made freewill offerings for the house of God, to erect it on its site. ⁶⁹According to their resources they gave to the building fund sixty-one thousand darics of gold, five thousand minas of silver, and one hundred priestly robes.

70 The priests, the Levites, and some of the people lived in Jerusalem and its vicinity;ᵃ and the singers, the gatekeepers, and the temple servants lived in their towns, and all Israel in their towns.

Worship Restored at Jerusalem

3 When the seventh month came, and the Israelites were in the towns, the people gathered together in Jerusalem. ²Then Jeshua son of Jozadak, with his fellow priests, and Zerubbabel son of Shealtiel with his kin set out to build the altar

ᵃ 1 Esdras 5.46: Heb lacks *lived in Jerusalem and its vicinity*

of the God of Israel, to offer burnt offerings on it, as prescribed in the law of Moses the man of God. [3]They set up the altar on its foundation, because they were in dread of the neighboring peoples, and they offered burnt offerings upon it to the LORD, morning and evening. [4]And they kept the festival of booths,[a] as prescribed, and offered the daily burnt offerings by number according to the ordinance, as required for each day, [5]and after that the regular burnt offerings, the offerings at the new moon and at all the sacred festivals of the LORD, and the offerings of everyone who made a freewill offering to the LORD. [6]From the first day of the seventh month they began to offer burnt offerings to the LORD. But the foundation of the temple of the LORD was not yet laid. [7]So they gave money to the masons and the carpenters, and food, drink, and oil to the Sidonians and the Tyrians to bring cedar trees from Lebanon to the sea, to Joppa, according to the grant that they had from King Cyrus of Persia.

Foundation Laid for the Temple

8　In the second year after their arrival at the house of God at Jerusalem, in the second month, Zerubbabel son of Shealtiel and Jeshua son of Jozadak made a beginning, together with the rest of their people, the priests and the Levites and all who had come to Jerusalem from the captivity. They appointed the Levites, from twenty years old and upward, to have the oversight of the work on the house of the LORD. [9]And Jeshua with his sons and his kin, and Kadmiel and his sons, Binnui and Hodaviah[b] along with the sons of Henadad, the Levites, their sons and kin, together took charge of the workers in the house of God.

10　When the builders laid the foundation of the temple of the LORD, the priests in their vestments were stationed to praise the LORD with trumpets, and the Levites, the sons of Asaph, with cymbals, according to the directions of King David of Israel; [11]and they sang responsively, praising and giving thanks to the LORD,

"For he is good,
　for his steadfast love endures forever toward
　　Israel."

And all the people responded with a great shout when they praised the LORD, because the foundation of the house of the LORD was laid. [12]But many of the priests and Levites and heads of families, old people who had seen the first house on its foundations, wept with a loud voice when they saw this house, though many shouted aloud for joy, [13]so that the people could not distinguish the sound of the joyful shout from the sound of the people's weeping, for the people shouted so loudly that the sound was heard far away.

PRAY IT!

Holy Tears
Ezra 3:10–13

Many of the older Israelites who remembered the first temple wept at the grand celebration that marked its rebirth (Ezra 3:12). Were they shedding tears of joy that the temple was being built again? Or were they shedding tears of sorrow over what they had lost and never regained? Most likely, they were doing both.

Weeping can be a holy and healing part of life. Unfortunately, some people believe that strong men and women never cry. But tears are appropriate on many occasions: the loss of a dear friend or family member, reconciliation with someone after a long separation, and the moment we recognize we have sinned and hurt someone deeply, to name a few. Recall that moving scene in Luke's gospel in which the sinful woman washes Jesus' feet with her tears (Luke 7:36–50). We should bring our tears to God in prayer, knowing that God hears the cries of our hearts (see Romans 8:26–27).

Resistance to Rebuilding the Temple

4 When the adversaries of Judah and Benjamin heard that the returned exiles were building a temple to the LORD, the God of Israel, [2]they approached Zerubbabel and the heads of families and said to them, "Let us build with you, for we worship your God as you do, and we have been sacrificing to him ever since the days of King Esar-haddon of Assyria who brought us here." [3]But Zerubbabel, Jeshua, and the rest of the heads of families in Israel said to them, "You shall have no

---

a Or *tabernacles*; Heb *succoth*　b Compare 2.40; Neh 7.43; 1 Esdras 5.58: Heb *sons of Judah*

part with us in building a house to our God; but we alone will build to the LORD, the God of Israel, as King Cyrus of Persia has commanded us."

4 Then the people of the land discouraged the people of Judah, and made them afraid to build, ⁵and they bribed officials to frustrate their plan throughout the reign of King Cyrus of Persia and until the reign of King Darius of Persia.

Rebuilding of Jerusalem Opposed

6 In the reign of Ahasuerus, in his accession year, they wrote an accusation against the inhabitants of Judah and Jerusalem.

7 And in the days of Artaxerxes, Bishlam and Mithredath and Tabeel and the rest of their associates wrote to King Artaxerxes of Persia; the letter was written in Aramaic and translated.[a] [8]Rehum the royal deputy and Shimshai the scribe wrote a letter against Jerusalem to King Artaxerxes as follows [9](then Rehum the royal deputy, Shimshai the scribe, and the rest of their associates, the judges, the envoys, the officials, the Persians, the people of Erech, the Babylonians, the people of Susa, that is, the Elamites, [10]and the rest of the nations whom the great and noble Osnappar deported and settled in the cities of Samaria and in the rest of the province Beyond the River wrote—and now [11]this is a copy of the letter that they sent):

"To King Artaxerxes: Your servants, the people of the province Beyond the River, send greeting. And now [12]may it be known to the king that the Jews who came up from you to us have gone to Jerusalem. They are rebuilding that rebellious and wicked city; they are finishing the walls and repairing the foundations. [13]Now may it be known to the king that, if this city is rebuilt and the walls finished, they will not pay tribute, custom, or toll, and the royal revenue will be reduced. [14]Now because we share the salt of the palace and it is not fitting for us to witness the king's dishonor, therefore we send and inform the king, [15]so that a search may be made in the annals of your ancestors. You will discover in the annals that this is a rebellious city, hurtful to kings and provinces, and that sedition was stirred up in it from long ago. On that account this city was laid waste. [16]We make known to the king that, if this city is rebuilt and its walls finished, you will then have no possession in the province Beyond the River."

17 The king sent an answer: "To Rehum the royal deputy and Shimshai the scribe and the rest of their associates who live in Samaria and in the rest of the province Beyond the River, greeting. And now [18]the letter that you sent to us has been read in translation before me. [19]So I made a decree, and someone searched and discovered that this city has risen against kings from long ago, and that rebellion and sedition have been made in it. [20]Jerusalem has had mighty kings who ruled over the whole province Beyond the River, to whom tribute, custom, and toll were paid. [21]Therefore issue an order that these people be made to cease, and that this city not be rebuilt, until I make a decree. [22]Moreover, take care not to be slack in this matter; why should damage grow to the hurt of the king?"

23 Then when the copy of King Artaxerxes' letter was read before Rehum and the scribe Shimshai and their associates, they hurried to the Jews in Jerusalem and by force and power made them cease. [24]At that time the work on the house of God in Jerusalem stopped and was discontinued until the second year of the reign of King Darius of Persia.

Restoration of the Temple Resumed

5 Now the prophets, Haggai[b] and Zechariah son of Iddo, prophesied to the Jews who were in Judah and Jerusalem, in the name of the God of Israel who was over them. [2]Then Zerubbabel son of Shealtiel and Jeshua son of Jozadak set out to rebuild the house of God in Jerusalem; and with them were the prophets of God, helping them.

3 At the same time Tattenai the governor of the province Beyond the River and Shethar-bozenai and their associates came to them and spoke to them thus, "Who gave you a decree to build this house and to finish this structure?" [4]They[c] also asked them this, "What are the names of the men who are building this building?" [5]But the eye of their God was upon the elders of the Jews, and they did not stop them until a report reached Darius and then answer was returned by letter in reply to it.

a Heb adds in Aramaic, indicating that 4.8–6.18 is in Aramaic. Another interpretation is The letter was written in the Aramaic script and set forth in the Aramaic language   b Aram adds the prophet   c Gk Syr: Aram We

The Second Temple · Ezra 5–6

The first temple was built during Solomon's reign and destroyed in 587 B.C. when the southern kingdom, Judah, was conquered by the Babylonians. The Persian king Cyrus II conquered Babylon in 539 B.C. and a year later freed the Jewish exiles in Babylon. He also decreed that the temple in Jerusalem be rebuilt (Ezra 6:3). Between the years 520 and 515 B.C., the second temple was rebuilt in Jerusalem. The second temple was essential to the Israelites rebuilding their life, culture, and religion after the Babylonian exile. This temple became the central focus of Jewish identity instead of a king.

6 The copy of the letter that Tattenai the governor of the province Beyond the River and Shethar-bozenai and his associates the envoys who were in the province Beyond the River sent to King Darius; [7]they sent him a report, in which was written as follows: "To Darius the king, all peace! [8]May it be known to the king that we went to the province of Judah, to the house of the great God. It is being built of hewn stone, and timber is laid in the walls; this work is being done diligently and prospers in their hands. [9]Then we spoke to those elders and asked them, 'Who gave you a decree to build this house and to finish this structure?' [10]We also asked them their names, for your information, so that we might write down the names of the men at their head. [11]This was their reply to us: 'We are the servants of the God of heaven and earth, and we are rebuilding the house that was built many years ago, which a great king of Israel built and finished. [12]But because our ancestors had angered the God of heaven, he gave them into the hand of King Nebuchadnezzar of Babylon, the Chaldean, who destroyed this house and carried away the people to Babylonia. [13]However, King Cyrus of Babylon, in the first year of his reign, made a decree that this house of God should be rebuilt. [14]Moreover, the gold and silver vessels of the house of God, which Nebuchadnezzar had taken out of the temple in Jerusalem and had brought into the temple of Babylon, these King Cyrus took out of the temple of Babylon, and they were delivered to a man named Sheshbazzar, whom he had made governor. [15]He said to him, "Take these vessels; go and put them in the temple in Jerusalem, and let the house of God be rebuilt on its site." [16]Then this Sheshbazzar came and laid the foundations of the house of God in Jerusalem; and from that time until now it has been under construction, and it is not yet finished.' [17]And now, if it seems good to the king, have a search made in the royal archives there in Babylon, to see whether a decree was issued by King Cyrus for the rebuilding of this house of God in Jerusalem. Let the king send us his pleasure in this matter."

The Decree of Darius

6 Then King Darius made a decree, and they searched the archives where the documents were stored in Babylon. [2]But it was in Ecbatana, the capital in the province of Media, that a scroll was found on which this was written: "A record. [3]In the first year of his reign, King Cyrus issued a decree: Concerning the house of God at Jerusalem, let the house be rebuilt, the place where sacrifices are offered and burnt offerings are brought;[a] its height shall be sixty cubits and its width sixty cubits, [4]with three courses of hewn stones and one course of timber; let the cost be paid from the royal treasury. [5]Moreover, let the gold and silver vessels of the house of God, which Nebuchadnezzar took out of the temple in Jerusalem and brought to Babylon, be restored and brought back to the temple in Jerusalem, each to its place; you shall put them in the house of God."

6 "Now you, Tattenai, governor of the province Beyond the River, Shethar-bozenai, and you, their associates, the envoys in the province Beyond the River, keep away; [7]let the work on this house of God alone; let the governor of the Jews and the elders of the Jews rebuild this house of God on its site. [8]Moreover I make a decree regarding what you shall do for these elders of the Jews for the rebuilding of this house of God: the cost is to be paid to these people, in full and without delay, from the royal revenue, the tribute of the province Beyond the River. [9]Whatever is needed—young bulls, rams, or sheep for burnt offerings to the God of heaven, wheat, salt,

---

a Meaning of Aram uncertain

wine, or oil, as the priests in Jerusalem require—let that be given to them day by day without fail, [10]so that they may offer pleasing sacrifices to the God of heaven, and pray for the life of the king and his children. [11]Furthermore I decree that if anyone alters this edict, a beam shall be pulled out of the house of the perpetrator, who then shall be impaled on it. The house shall be made a dunghill. [12]May the God who has established his name there overthrow any king or people that shall put forth a hand to alter this, or to destroy this house of God in Jerusalem. I, Darius, make a decree; let it be done with all diligence."

Completion and Dedication of the Temple

13 Then, according to the word sent by King Darius, Tattenai, the governor of the province Beyond the River, Shethar-bozenai, and their associates did with all diligence what King Darius had ordered. [14]So the elders of the Jews built and prospered, through the prophesying of the prophet Haggai and Zechariah son of Iddo. They finished their building by command of the God of Israel and by decree of Cyrus, Darius, and King Artaxerxes of Persia; [15]and this house was finished on the third day of the month of Adar, in the sixth year of the reign of King Darius.

16 The people of Israel, the priests and the Levites, and the rest of the returned exiles, celebrated the dedication of this house of God with joy. [17]They offered at the dedication of this house of God one hundred bulls, two hundred rams, four hundred lambs, and as a sin offering for all Israel, twelve male goats, according to the number of the tribes of Israel. [18]Then they set the priests in their divisions and the Levites in their courses for the service of God at Jerusalem, as it is written in the book of Moses.

The Passover Celebrated

19 On the fourteenth day of the first month the returned exiles kept the passover. [20]For both the priests and the Levites had purified themselves; all of them were clean. So they killed the passover lamb for all the returned exiles, for their fellow priests, and for themselves. [21]It was eaten by the people of Israel who had returned from exile, and also by all who had joined them and separated themselves from the pollutions of the nations of the land to worship the LORD, the God of Israel. [22]With joy they celebrated the festival of unleavened bread seven days;

for the LORD had made them joyful, and had turned the heart of the king of Assyria to them, so that he aided them in the work on the house of God, the God of Israel.

The Coming and Work of Ezra

7 After this, in the reign of King Artaxerxes of Persia, Ezra son of Seraiah, son of Azariah, son of Hilkiah, [2]son of Shallum, son of Zadok, son of Ahitub, [3]son of Amariah, son of Azariah, son of Meraioth, [4]son of Zerahiah, son of Uzzi, son of Bukki, [5]son of Abishua, son of Phinehas, son of Eleazar, son of the chief priest Aaron— [6]this Ezra went up from Babylonia. He was a scribe skilled in the law of Moses that the LORD the God of Israel had given; and the king granted him all that he asked, for the hand of the LORD his God was upon him.

7 Some of the people of Israel, and some of the priests and Levites, the singers and gatekeepers, and the temple servants also went up to Jerusalem, in the seventh year of King Artaxerxes. [8]They came to Jerusalem in the fifth month, which was in the seventh year of the king. [9]On the first day of the first month the journey up from Babylon was begun, and on the first day of the fifth month he came to Jerusalem, for the gracious hand of his God was upon him. [10]For Ezra had set his heart to study the law of the LORD, and to do it, and to teach the statutes and ordinances in Israel.

The Letter of Artaxerxes to Ezra

11 This is a copy of the letter that King Artaxerxes gave to the priest Ezra, the scribe, a scholar of the text of the commandments of the LORD and his statutes for Israel: [12]"Artaxerxes, king of kings, to the priest Ezra, the scribe of the law of the God of heaven: Peace.[a] And now [13]I decree that any of the people of Israel or their priests or Levites in my kingdom who freely offers to go to Jerusalem may go with you. [14]For you are sent by the king and his seven counselors to make inquiries about Judah and Jerusalem according to the law of your God, which is in your hand, [15]and also to convey the silver and gold that the king and his counselors have freely offered to the God of Israel, whose dwelling is in Jerusalem, [16]with all the silver and gold that you shall find in the whole province of Babylonia, and with the freewill offerings of the people and the priests, given willingly for the house of their God in Jerusalem. [17]With this money, then, you shall with

a Syr Vg 1 Esdras 8.9: Aram *Perfect*

all diligence buy bulls, rams, and lambs, and their grain offerings and their drink offerings, and you shall offer them on the altar of the house of your God in Jerusalem. [18]Whatever seems good to you and your colleagues to do with the rest of the silver and gold, you may do, according to the will of your God. [19]The vessels that have been given you for the service of the house of your God, you shall deliver before the God of Jerusalem. [20]And whatever else is required for the house of your God, which you are responsible for providing, you may provide out of the king's treasury.

[21] "I, King Artaxerxes, decree to all the treasurers in the province Beyond the River: Whatever the priest Ezra, the scribe of the law of the God of heaven, requires of you, let it be done with all diligence, [22]up to one hundred talents of silver, one hundred cors of wheat, one hundred baths[a] of wine, one hundred baths[a] of oil, and unlimited salt. [23]Whatever is commanded by the God of heaven, let it be done with zeal for the house of the God of heaven, or wrath will come upon the realm of the king and his heirs. [24]We also notify you that it shall not be lawful to impose tribute, custom, or toll on any of the priests, the Levites, the singers, the doorkeepers, the temple servants, or other servants of this house of God.

[25] "And you, Ezra, according to the God-given wisdom you possess, appoint magistrates and judges who may judge all the people in the province Beyond the River who know the laws of your God; and you shall teach those who do not know them. [26]All who will not obey the law of your God and the law of the king, let judgment be strictly executed on them, whether for death or for banishment or for confiscation of their goods or for imprisonment."

[27] Blessed be the LORD, the God of our ancestors, who put such a thing as this into the heart of the king to glorify the house of the LORD in Jerusalem, [28]and who extended to me steadfast love before the king and his counselors, and before all the king's mighty officers. I took courage, for the hand of the LORD my God was upon me, and I gathered leaders from Israel to go up with me.

8

Heads of Families Who Returned with Ezra

These are their family heads, and this is the genealogy of those who went up with me from Babylonia, in the reign of King Artaxerxes: [2]Of the descendants of Phinehas, Gershom. Of Ithamar, Daniel. Of David, Hattush, [3]of the descendants of Shecaniah. Of Parosh, Zechariah, with whom were registered one hundred fifty males. [4]Of the descendants of Pahath-moab, Eliehoenai son of Zerahiah, and with him two hundred males. [5]Of the descendants of Zattu,[b] Shecaniah son of Jahaziel, and with him three hundred males. [6]Of the descendants of Adin, Ebed son of Jonathan, and with him fifty males. [7]Of the descendants of Elam, Jeshaiah son of Athaliah, and with him seventy males. [8]Of the descendants of Shephatiah, Zebadiah son of Michael, and with him eighty males. [9]Of the descendants of Joab, Obadiah son of Jehiel, and with him two hundred eighteen males. [10]Of the descendants of Bani,[c] Shelomith son of Josiphiah, and with him one hundred sixty males. [11]Of the descendants of Bebai, Zechariah son of Bebai, and with him twenty-eight males. [12]Of the descendants of Azgad, Johanan son of Hakkatan, and with him one hundred ten males. [13]Of the descendants of Adonikam, those who came later, their names being Eliphelet, Jeuel, and Shemaiah, and with them sixty males. [14]Of the descendants of Bigvai, Uthai and Zaccur, and with them seventy males.

Servants for the Temple

[15] I gathered them by the river that runs to Ahava, and there we camped three days. As I reviewed the people and the priests, I found there none of the descendants of Levi. [16]Then I sent for Eliezer, Ariel, Shemaiah, Elnathan, Jarib, Elnathan, Nathan, Zechariah, and Meshullam, who were leaders, and for Joiarib and Elnathan, who were wise, [17]and sent them to Iddo, the leader at the place called Casiphia, telling them what to say to Iddo and his colleagues the temple servants at Casiphia, namely, to send us ministers for the house of our God. [18]Since the gracious hand of our God was upon us, they brought us a man of discretion, of the descendants of Mahli son of Levi son of Israel, namely Sherebiah, with his sons and kin, eighteen; [19]also Hashabiah and with him Jeshaiah of the descendants of Merari, with his kin and their sons, twenty; [20]besides two hundred twenty of the temple servants, whom David and his officials had set apart to attend the Levites. These were all mentioned by name.

Fasting and Prayer for Protection

[21] Then I proclaimed a fast there, at the river

---

a A Heb measure of volume   b Gk 1 Esdras 8.32: Heb lacks *of Zattu*   c Gk 1 Esdras 8.36: Heb lacks *Bani*

Ahava, that we might deny ourselves[a] before our God, to seek from him a safe journey for ourselves, our children, and all our possessions. [22]For I was ashamed to ask the king for a band of soldiers and cavalry to protect us against the enemy on our way, since we had told the king that the hand of our God is gracious to all who seek him, but his power and his wrath are against all who forsake him. [23]So we fasted and petitioned our God for this, and he listened to our entreaty.

Gifts for the Temple

24 Then I set apart twelve of the leading priests: Sherebiah, Hashabiah, and ten of their kin with them. [25]And I weighed out to them the silver and the gold and the vessels, the offering for the house of our God that the king, his counselors, his lords, and all Israel there present had offered; [26]I weighed out into their hand six hundred fifty talents of silver, and one hundred silver vessels worth . . . talents,[b] and one hundred talents of gold, [27]twenty gold bowls worth a thousand darics, and two vessels of fine polished bronze as precious as gold. [28]And I said to them, "You are holy to the LORD, and the vessels are holy; and the silver and the gold are a freewill offering to the LORD, the God of your ancestors. [29]Guard them and keep them until you weigh them before the chief priests and the Levites and the heads of families in Israel at Jerusalem, within the chambers of the house of the LORD." [30]So the priests and the Levites took over the silver, the gold, and the vessels as they were weighed out, to bring them to Jerusalem, to the house of our God.

The Return to Jerusalem

31 Then we left the river Ahava on the twelfth day of the first month, to go to Jerusalem; the hand of our God was upon us, and he delivered us from the hand of the enemy and from ambushes along the way. [32]We came to Jerusalem and remained there three days. [33]On the fourth day, within the house of our God, the silver, the gold, and the vessels were weighed into the hands of the priest Meremoth son of Uriah, and with him was Eleazar son of Phinehas, and with them were the Levites, Jozabad son of Jeshua and Noadiah son of Binnui. [34]The total was counted and weighed, and the weight of everything was recorded.

35 At that time those who had come from captivity, the returned exiles, offered burnt offerings to the God of Israel, twelve bulls for all Israel, ninety-six rams, seventy-seven lambs, and as a sin offering twelve male goats; all this was a burnt offering to the LORD. [36]They also delivered the king's commissions to the king's satraps and to the governors of the province Beyond the River; and they supported the people and the house of God.

Denunciation of Mixed Marriages

9 After these things had been done, the officials approached me and said, "The people of Israel, the priests, and the Levites have not separated themselves from the peoples of the lands with their abominations, from the Canaanites, the Hittites, the Perizzites, the Jebusites, the Ammonites, the Moabites, the Egyptians, and the Amorites. [2]For they have taken some of their daughters as wives for themselves and for their sons. Thus the holy seed has mixed itself with the peoples of the lands, and in this faithlessness the officials and leaders have led the way." [3]When I heard this, I tore my garment and my mantle, and pulled hair from my head and beard, and sat appalled. [4]Then all who trembled at the words of the God of Israel, because of the faithlessness of the returned exiles, gathered around me while I sat appalled until the evening sacrifice.

Ezra's Prayer

5 At the evening sacrifice I got up from my fasting, with my garments and my mantle torn, and fell on my knees, spread out my hands to the LORD my God, [6]and said,

"O my God, I am too ashamed and embarrassed to lift my face to you, my God, for our iniquities have risen higher than our heads, and our guilt has mounted up to the heavens. [7]From the days of our ancestors to this day we have been deep in guilt, and for our iniquities we, our kings, and our priests have been handed over to the kings of the lands, to the sword, to captivity, to plundering, and to utter shame, as is now the case. [8]But now for a brief moment favor has been shown by the LORD our God, who has left us a remnant, and given us a stake in his holy place, in order that he[c] may brighten our eyes and grant us a little sustenance in our slavery. [9]For we are slaves; yet our God has not forsaken us in our slavery, but has extended to us his steadfast love before the kings of Persia, to give us new life to set up the house of our God, to repair its ruins, and to give us a wall in Judea and Jerusalem.

10 "And now, our God, what shall we say after this? For we have forsaken your commandments, [11]which you commanded by your servants the prophets, saying, 'The land that you are entering to possess is a land unclean with the pollutions of the peoples of the lands, with their abominations. They have filled it from end to end with their uncleanness. [12]Therefore do not give your daughters to their sons, neither take their daughters for your sons, and never seek their peace or prosperity, so that you may be strong and eat the good of the land and leave it for an inheritance to your children forever.' [13]After all that has come upon us for our evil deeds and for our great guilt, seeing that you, our God, have punished us less than our iniquities deserved and have given us such a remnant as this, [14]shall we break your commandments again and intermarry with the peoples who practice these abominations? Would you not be angry with us until you destroy us without remnant or survivor? [15]O LORD, God of Israel, you are just, but we have escaped as a remnant, as is now the case. Here we are before you in our guilt, though no one can face you because of this."

The People's Response

10 While Ezra prayed and made confession, weeping and throwing himself down before the house of God, a very great assembly of men, women, and children gathered to him out of Israel; the people also wept bitterly. [2]Shecaniah son of Jehiel, of the descendants of Elam, addressed Ezra, saying, "We have broken faith with our God and have married foreign women from the peoples of the land, but even now there is hope for Israel in spite of this. [3]So now let us make a covenant with our God to send away all these wives and their children, according to the counsel of my lord and of those who tremble at the commandment of our God; and let it be done according to the law. [4]Take action, for it is your duty, and we are with you; be strong, and do it." [5]Then Ezra stood up and made the leading priests, the Levites, and all Israel swear that they would do as had been said. So they swore.

Foreign Wives and Their Children Rejected

6 Then Ezra withdrew from before the house of God, and went to the chamber of Jehohanan son of Eliashib, where he spent the night.[a] He did not eat bread or drink water, for he was mourning over the faithlessness of the exiles. [7]They made a proclamation throughout Judah and Jerusalem to all the returned exiles that they should assemble at Jerusalem, [8]and that if any did not come within three days, by order of the officials and the elders all their property should be forfeited, and they themselves banned from the congregation of the exiles.

9 Then all the people of Judah and Benjamin assembled at Jerusalem within the three days; it was the ninth month, on the twentieth day of the month. All the people sat in the open square before the house of God, trembling because of this matter and because of the heavy rain. [10]Then Ezra the priest stood up and said to them, "You have trespassed and married foreign women, and so increased the guilt of Israel. [11]Now make confession to the LORD the God of your ancestors, and do his will; separate yourselves from the peoples of the land and from the foreign wives." [12]Then all the assembly answered with a loud voice, "It is so; we must do as you have said. [13]But the people are many, and it is a time of heavy rain; we cannot stand in the open. Nor is this a task for one day or for two, for many of us have transgressed in this matter. [14]Let our officials represent the whole assembly, and let all in our towns who have taken foreign wives come at appointed times, and with them the elders and judges of every town, until the fierce wrath of our God on this account is averted from us." [15]Only Jonathan son of Asahel and Jahzeiah son of Tikvah opposed this, and Meshullam and Shabbethai the Levites supported them.

16 Then the returned exiles did so. Ezra the priest selected men,[b] heads of families, according to their families, each of them designated by name. On the first day of the tenth month they sat down to exam-

> "Our God has not forsaken us in our slavery, but has extended to us his steadfast love."
> —Ezra 9:9

---

a 1 Esdras 9.2: Heb *where he went*   b 1 Esdras 9.16: Syr: Heb *And there were selected Ezra,*

Who Belongs and Who Doesn't? · Ezra 9–10

Ezra tells the people to reject their foreign wives and children. Nehemiah does the same (Nehemiah 13:23-27). This probably strikes us as harsh, but we can try to understand the Israelites' situation. Only a remnant of the Israelites was left to reestablish Israel's identity. History had taught the Israelites that intermarriage led to a watering down of their faith and of the people's loyalty to their religious practices. In that time period, separation from outsiders preserved the identity of a group of people or a nation.

This separation led to an even greater animosity between the Jews from Judah and their cousins in faith, the Samaritans. We see some of this prejudice in the gospels (see John 4:1-42; and "Live It: The Good Samaritan," near Luke 10:25-37). Christians have also discriminated against others at times throughout our history, which causes separation and mistrust. But now that our world is more and more connected through technology and travel, our challenge becomes remaining faithful to our beliefs, but open and loving toward others who believe differently. Together we can discover what we have in common and learn to accept our differences in peace.

- Why is it often so hard for people to be open to those from other faith traditions or cultures?
- Do you know individuals of another faith? How does knowing them personally help you learn to love others despite your differences?

ine the matter. [17]By the first day of the first month they had come to the end of all the men who had married foreign women.

18 There were found of the descendants of the priests who had married foreign women, of the descendants of Jeshua son of Jozadak and his brothers: Maaseiah, Eliezer, Jarib, and Gedaliah. [19]They pledged themselves to send away their wives, and their guilt offering was a ram of the flock for their guilt. [20]Of the descendants of Immer: Hanani and Zebadiah. [21]Of the descendants of Harim: Maaseiah, Elijah, Shemaiah, Jehiel, and Uzziah. [22]Of the descendants of Pashhur: Elioenai, Maaseiah, Ishmael, Nethanel, Jozabad, and Elasah.

23 Of the Levites: Jozabad, Shimei, Kelaiah (that is, Kelita), Pethahiah, Judah, and Eliezer. [24]Of the singers: Eliashib. Of the gatekeepers: Shallum, Telem, and Uri.

25 And of Israel: of the descendants of Parosh: Ramiah, Izziah, Malchijah, Mijamin, Eleazar, Hashabiah,[a] and Benaiah. [26]Of the descendants of Elam: Mattaniah, Zechariah, Jehiel, Abdi, Jeremoth, and

Elijah. [27]Of the descendants of Zattu: Elioenai, Eliashib, Mattaniah, Jeremoth, Zabad, and Aziza. [28]Of the descendants of Bebai: Jehohanan, Hananiah, Zabbai, and Athlai. [29]Of the descendants of Bani: Meshullam, Malluch, Adaiah, Jashub, Sheal, and Jeremoth. [30]Of the descendants of Pahath-moab: Adna, Chelal, Benaiah, Maaseiah, Mattaniah, Bezalel, Binnui, and Manasseh. [31]Of the descendants of Harim: Eliezer, Isshijah, Malchijah, Shemaiah, Shimeon, [32]Benjamin, Malluch, and Shemariah. [33]Of the descendants of Hashum: Mattenai, Mattattah, Zabad, Eliphelet, Jeremai, Manasseh, and Shimei. [34]Of the descendants of Bani: Maadai, Amram, Uel, [35]Benaiah, Bedeiah, Cheluhi, [36]Vaniah, Meremoth, Eliashib, [37]Mattaniah, Mattenai, and Jaasu. [38]Of the descendants of Binnui:[b] Shimei, [39]Shelemiah, Nathan, Adaiah, [40]Machnadebai, Shashai, Sharai, [41]Azarel, Shelemiah, Shemariah, [42]Shallum, Amariah, and Joseph. [43]Of the descendants of Nebo: Jeiel, Mattithiah, Zabad, Zebina, Jaddai, Joel, and Benaiah. [44]All these had married foreign women, and they sent them away with their children.[c]

a 1 Esdras 9.26 Gk: Heb Malchijah   b Gk: Heb Bani, Binnui   c 1 Esdras 9.36; meaning of Heb uncertain

Nehemiah ▶▶▶▶▶▶▶▶

For background on this book, see the introduction to Ezra and Nehemiah at the beginning of Ezra.

1

Nehemiah Prays for His People

The words of Nehemiah son of Hacaliah.

In the month of Chislev, in the twentieth year, while I was in Susa the capital, ²one of my brothers, Hanani, came with certain men from Judah; and I asked them about the Jews that survived, those who had escaped the captivity, and about Jerusalem. ³They replied, "The survivors there in the province who escaped captivity are in great trouble and shame; the wall of Jerusalem is broken down, and its gates have been destroyed by fire."

4 When I heard these words I sat down and wept, and mourned for days, fasting and praying before the God of heaven. ⁵I said, "O LORD God of heaven, the great and awesome God who keeps covenant and steadfast love with those who love him and keep his commandments; ⁶let your ear be attentive and your eyes open to hear the prayer of your servant that I now pray before you day and night for your servants, the people of Israel, confessing the sins of the people of Israel, which we have sinned against you. Both I and my family have sinned. ⁷We have offended you deeply, failing to keep the commandments, the statutes, and the ordinances that you commanded your servant Moses. ⁸Remember the word that you commanded your servant Moses, 'If you are unfaithful, I will scatter you among the peoples; ⁹but if you return to me and keep my commandments and do them, though your outcasts are under the farthest skies, I will gather them from there and bring them to the place at which I have chosen to establish my name.' ¹⁰They are your servants and your people, whom you redeemed by your great power and your strong hand. ¹¹O Lord, let your ear be attentive to the prayer of your servant, and to the prayer of your servants who delight in revering your name. Give success to your servant today, and grant him mercy in the sight of this man!"

At the time, I was cupbearer to the king.

PRAY IT!

Ready for Action · Nehemiah 1

Do you ever watch the news and think, "Why bother trying to make the world a better place?" Poverty, racism, violence, materialism, and indifference—these problems often seem too big for any individual to do much about. It's easy to be overwhelmed and give up.

But Christians are called to social action—action for justice, action to make the world a better place. Nehemiah is a great example for us today. When Nehemiah heard of the Israelites' collective sin and their captivity, he could have said, "I give up." Instead, he turned to God in fasting and prayer, repenting of sin and asking God to help him make a difference (Nehemiah 1:4-11). During your prayer time, reflect on or journal about the following questions:

• What social issue are you most concerned about?
• What can you do to learn more about this issue?
• How can you get more involved in acting on this issue?
• What do you need to bring to God in prayer about this issue?

Nehemiah Sent to Judah

2 In the month of Nisan, in the twentieth year of King Artaxerxes, when wine was served him, I carried the wine and gave it to the king. Now, I had never been sad in his presence before. [2]So the king said to me, "Why is your face sad, since you are not sick? This can only be sadness of the heart." Then I was very much afraid. [3]I said to the king, "May the king live forever! Why should my face not be sad, when the city, the place of my ancestors' graves, lies waste, and its gates have been destroyed by fire?" [4]Then the king said to me, "What do you request?" So I prayed to the God of heaven. [5]Then I said to the king, "If it pleases the king, and if your servant has found favor with you, I ask that you send me to Judah, to the city of my ancestors' graves, so that I may rebuild it." [6]The king said to me (the queen also was sitting beside him), "How long will you be gone, and when will you return?" So it pleased the king to send me, and I set him a date. [7]Then I said to the king, "If it pleases the king, let letters be given me to the governors of the province Beyond the River, that they may grant me passage until I arrive in Judah; [8]and a letter to Asaph, the keeper of the king's forest, directing him to give me timber to make beams for the gates of the temple fortress, and for the wall of the city, and for the house that I shall occupy." And the king granted me what I asked, for the gracious hand of my God was upon me.

[9] Then I came to the governors of the province Beyond the River, and gave them the king's letters. Now the king had sent officers of the army and cavalry with me. [10]When Sanballat the Horonite and Tobiah the Ammonite official heard this, it displeased them greatly that someone had come to seek the welfare of the people of Israel.

Nehemiah's Inspection of the Walls

[11] So I came to Jerusalem and was there for three days. [12]Then I got up during the night, I and a few men with me; I told no one what my God had put into my heart to do for Jerusalem. The only animal I took was the animal I rode. [13]I went out by night by the Valley Gate past the Dragon's Spring and to the Dung Gate, and I inspected the walls of Jerusalem that had been broken down and its gates that had been destroyed by fire. [14]Then I went on to the Fountain Gate and to the King's Pool; but there was no place for the animal I was riding to continue. [15]So

I went up by way of the valley by night and inspected the wall. Then I turned back and entered by the Valley Gate, and so returned. [16]The officials did not know where I had gone or what I was doing; I had not yet told the Jews, the priests, the nobles, the officials, and the rest that were to do the work.

Decision to Restore the Walls

[17] Then I said to them, "You see the trouble we are in, how Jerusalem lies in ruins with its gates burned. Come, let us rebuild the wall of Jerusalem, so that we may no longer suffer disgrace." [18]I told them that the hand of my God had been gracious upon me, and also the words that the king had spoken to me. Then they said, "Let us start building!" So they committed themselves to the common good. [19]But when Sanballat the Horonite and Tobiah the Ammonite official, and Geshem the Arab heard of it, they mocked and ridiculed us, saying, "What is this that you are doing? Are you rebelling against the king?" [20]Then I replied to them, "The God of heaven is the one who will give us success, and we his servants are going to start building; but you have no share or claim or historic right in Jerusalem."

Organization of the Work

3 Then the high priest Eliashib set to work with his fellow priests and rebuilt the Sheep Gate. They consecrated it and set up its doors; they consecrated it as far as the Tower of the Hundred and as far as the Tower of Hananel. [2]And the men of Jericho built next to him. And next to them[a] Zaccur son of Imri built.

[3] The sons of Hassenaah built the Fish Gate; they laid its beams and set up its doors, its bolts, and its bars. [4]Next to them Meremoth son of Uriah son of Hakkoz made repairs. Next to them Meshullam son of Berechiah son of Meshezabel made repairs. Next to them Zadok son of Baana made repairs. [5]Next to them the Tekoites made repairs; but their nobles would not put their shoulders to the work of their Lord.[b]

[6] Joiada son of Paseah and Meshullam son of Besodeiah repaired the Old Gate; they laid its beams and set up its doors, its bolts, and its bars. [7]Next to them repairs were made by Melatiah the Gibeonite and Jadon the Meronothite—the men of Gibeon and of Mizpah—who were under the jurisdiction of[c] the governor of the province Beyond the River.

a Heb *him*   b Or *lords*   c Meaning of Heb uncertain

CONNECT IT!

Habitat for Humanity: Rebuilding Lives · Nehemiah 3

The rebuilding of the walls of Jerusalem was a huge job. But Nehemiah tackled it by creating a vision and recruiting the people of Jerusalem to work together. The list of people and their contributions in this chapter is easy to skip over. (Who can even say half those names?) But a closer look shows that the list includes all types of people—businessmen, priests, community leaders, people from neighboring cities, artists, common people, and entire families, including daughters. They all did their part to rebuild their city.

Today Habitat for Humanity is playing a role similar to that of Nehemiah. It doesn't rebuild city walls, but it does help to build and rebuild a central aspect of community—the home. Habitat's purpose is to eliminate poverty housing and homelessness from the world. To accomplish this they invite people of all backgrounds, races, and religions to build houses together with families in need. From local projects in low-income neighborhoods to major relief programs in countries devastated by natural disasters, Habitat has built 50,000 houses around the world, providing safe, affordable shelter for more than 1.75 million people in 3,000 communities.

And Habitat believes in the power of youth. The organization has many opportunities for young people, including leadership conferences, student-led Habitat groups, short-term local and international building trips, and fund-raising projects. If you're looking for a way to rebuild like Nehemiah, learn more at **habitat.org**.

⁸Next to them Uzziel son of Harhaiah, one of the goldsmiths, made repairs. Next to him Hananiah, one of the perfumers, made repairs; and they restored Jerusalem as far as the Broad Wall. ⁹Next to them Rephaiah son of Hur, ruler of half the district of*ᵃ* Jerusalem, made repairs. ¹⁰Next to them Jedaiah son of Harumaph made repairs opposite his house; and next to him Hattush son of Hashabneiah made repairs. ¹¹Malchijah son of Harim and Hasshub son of Pahath-moab repaired another section and the Tower of the Ovens. ¹²Next to him Shallum son of Hallohesh, ruler of half the district of*ᵃ* Jerusalem, made repairs, he and his daughters.

13 Hanun and the inhabitants of Zanoah repaired the Valley Gate; they rebuilt it and set up its doors, its bolts, and its bars, and repaired a thousand cubits of the wall, as far as the Dung Gate.

14 Malchijah son of Rechab, ruler of the district of*ᵇ* Beth-haccherem, repaired the Dung Gate; he rebuilt it and set up its doors, its bolts, and its bars.

15 And Shallum son of Col-hozeh, ruler of the district of*ᵇ* Mizpah, repaired the Fountain Gate; he rebuilt it and covered it and set up its doors, its bolts, and its bars; and he built the wall of the Pool of Shelah of the king's garden, as far as the stairs that go down from the City of David. ¹⁶After him Nehe-

miah son of Azbuk, ruler of half the district of*ᵃ* Beth-zur, repaired from a point opposite the graves of David, as far as the artificial pool and the house of the warriors. ¹⁷After him the Levites made repairs: Rehum son of Bani; next to him Hashabiah, ruler of half the district of*ᵃ* Keilah, made repairs for his district. ¹⁸After him their kin made repairs: Binnui,*ᶜ* son of Henadad, ruler of half the district of*ᵃ* Keilah; ¹⁹next to him Ezer son of Jeshua, ruler*ᵈ* of Mizpah, repaired another section opposite the ascent to the armory at the Angle. ²⁰After him Baruch son of Zabbai repaired another section from the Angle to the door of the house of the high priest Eliashib. ²¹After him Meremoth son of Uriah son of Hakkoz repaired another section from the door of the house of Eliashib to the end of the house of Eliashib. ²²After him the priests, the men of the surrounding area, made repairs. ²³After them Benjamin and Hasshub made repairs opposite their house. After them Azariah son of Maaseiah son of Ananiah made repairs beside his own house. ²⁴After him Binnui son of Henadad repaired another section, from the house of Azariah to the Angle and to the corner. ²⁵Palal son of Uzai repaired opposite the Angle and the tower projecting from the upper house of the king at the court of the guard. After him Pedaiah son of Parosh

[26] and the temple servants living[a] on Ophel made repairs up to a point opposite the Water Gate on the east and the projecting tower. [27] After him the Tekoites repaired another section opposite the great projecting tower as far as the wall of Ophel.

28 Above the Horse Gate the priests made repairs, each one opposite his own house. [29] After them Zadok son of Immer made repairs opposite his own house. After him Shemaiah son of Shecaniah, the keeper of the East Gate, made repairs. [30] After him Hananiah son of Shelemiah and Hanun sixth son of Zalaph repaired another section. After him Meshullam son of Berechiah made repairs opposite his living quarters. [31] After him Malchijah, one of the goldsmiths, made repairs as far as the house of the temple servants and of the merchants, opposite the Muster Gate,[b] and to the upper room of the corner. [32] And between the upper room of the corner and the Sheep Gate the goldsmiths and the merchants made repairs.

Hostile Plots Thwarted

4 [c] Now when Sanballat heard that we were building the wall, he was angry and greatly enraged, and he mocked the Jews. [2] He said in the presence of his associates and of the army of Samaria, "What are these feeble Jews doing? Will they restore things? Will they sacrifice? Will they finish it in a day? Will they revive the stones out of the heaps of rubbish—and burned ones at that?" [3] Tobiah the Ammonite was beside him, and he said, "That stone wall they are building—any fox going up on it would break it down!" [4] Hear, O our God, for we are despised; turn their taunt back on their own heads, and give them over as plunder in a land of captivity. [5] Do not cover their guilt, and do not let their sin be blotted out from your sight; for they have hurled insults in the face of the builders.

6 So we rebuilt the wall, and all the wall was joined together to half its height; for the people had a mind to work.

7[d] But when Sanballat and Tobiah and the Arabs and the Ammonites and the Ashdodites heard that the repairing of the walls of Jerusalem was going forward and the gaps were beginning to be closed, they were very angry, [8] and all plotted together to come and fight against Jerusalem and to cause confusion in it. [9] So we prayed to our God, and set a guard as a protection against them day and night.

10 But Judah said, "The strength of the burden bearers is failing, and there is too much rubbish so that we are unable to work on the wall." [11] And our enemies said, "They will not know or see anything before we come upon them and kill them and stop the work." [12] When the Jews who lived near them came, they said to us ten times, "From all the places where they live[e] they will come up against us."[f] [13] So in the lowest parts of the space behind the wall, in open places, I stationed the people according to their families,[g] with their swords, their spears, and their bows. [14] After I looked these things over, I stood up and said to the nobles and the officials and the rest of the people, "Do not be afraid of them. Remember the LORD, who is great and awesome, and fight for your kin, your sons, your daughters, your wives, and your homes."

15 When our enemies heard that their plot was

Rising Above · Nehemiah 4

Parents' divorce. Domestic and community violence. The death of a loved one. Prejudice. Poverty. These are common experiences of young people. Some come through them as victims, unable to take any control in their lives. Others become cynical, violent, or antisocial. But some rise above their hurt to live happy and healthy lives. What makes the difference in people's reactions?

Perhaps Nehemiah provides a clue. He was confronted by cynical people (Nehemiah 4:2-3) and violent people (Nehemiah 4:7-9). But he trusted in something bigger than himself. "The God of heaven is the one who will give us success," he proclaimed to those with negative attitudes (Nehemiah 2:20).

Prayer and faith in God gave Nehemiah strength to take action in difficult times. You can do the same, trusting God for the strength to meet your problems with action.

a Cn: Heb *were living* b Or *Hammiphkad Gate* c Ch 3.33 in Heb d Ch 4.1 in Heb e Cn: Heb *you return* f Compare Gk Syr: Meaning of Heb uncertain g Meaning of Heb uncertain

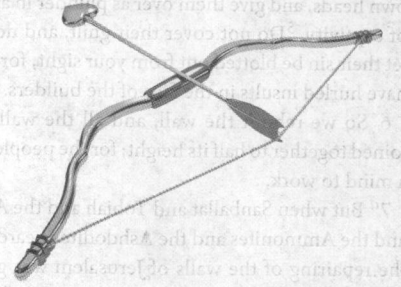

known to us, and that God had frustrated it, we all returned to the wall, each to his work. [16] From that day on, half of my servants worked on construction, and half held the spears, shields, bows, and body-armor; and the leaders posted themselves behind the whole house of Judah, [17] who were building the wall. The burden bearers carried their loads in such a way that each labored on the work with one hand and with the other held a weapon. [18] And each of the builders had his sword strapped at his side while he built. The man who sounded the trumpet was beside me. [19] And I said to the nobles, the officials, and the rest of the people, "The work is great and widely spread out, and we are separated far from one another on the wall. [20] Rally to us wherever you hear the sound of the trumpet. Our God will fight for us."

[21] So we labored at the work, and half of them held the spears from break of dawn until the stars came out. [22] I also said to the people at that time, "Let every man and his servant pass the night inside Jerusalem, so that they may be a guard for us by night and may labor by day." [23] So neither I nor my brothers nor my servants nor the men of the guard who followed me ever took off our clothes; each kept his weapon in his right hand.[a]

Nehemiah Deals with Oppression

5 Now there was a great outcry of the people and of their wives against their Jewish kin. [2] For there were those who said, "With our sons and our daughters, we are many; we must get grain, so that we may eat and stay alive." [3] There were also those who said, "We are having to pledge our fields, our vineyards, and our houses in order to get grain during the famine." [4] And there were those who said, "We are having to borrow money on our fields and vineyards to pay the king's tax. [5] Now our flesh is the same as that of our kindred; our children are the same as their children; and yet we are forcing our sons and daughters to be slaves, and some of our daughters have been ravished; we are powerless, and our fields and vineyards now belong to others."

[6] I was very angry when I heard their outcry and these complaints. [7] After thinking it over, I brought

Hunger Pains · Nehemiah 5:7–11

"I'm starving. Let's go get something to eat."

It's so easy. If we're hungry, we eat. If we're thirsty, we grab something to drink. If we're not feeling well, we get medicine to make us feel better. We forget sometimes that our way of doing things is the exception in the world, not the rule. Right now, people around the world and even in your city are truly starving and have no idea where their next meal is coming from.

When Nehemiah's people were hungry, he saw the problem right away. The problem wasn't a lack of food. It was that some people were using their wealth and influence to control who got the food (Nehemiah 5:7-8). Nehemiah took the radical step of demanding that the wealthy restore the money and property they had taken from others by charging unjust interest (Nehemiah 5:10-11).

Experts tell us that similar injustices still happen today. People are starving not because food is scarce, but because political and economic conditions prevent them from getting the food. We may not have Nehemiah's power to demand that the powerful and wealthy reform, but we can make a difference. We can educate ourselves and speak out through letters and phone calls to elected officials. And while we're calling for society to change, let's volunteer at a neighborhood pantry or soup kitchen to help feed the hungry in our own backyard.

a Cn: Heb *each his weapon the water*

charges against the nobles and the officials; I said to them, "You are all taking interest from your own people." And I called a great assembly to deal with them, [8]and said to them, "As far as we were able, we have bought back our Jewish kindred who had been sold to other nations; but now you are selling your own kin, who must then be bought back by us!" They were silent, and could not find a word to say. [9]So I said, "The thing that you are doing is not good. Should you not walk in the fear of our God, to prevent the taunts of the nations our enemies? [10]Moreover I and my brothers and my servants are lending them money and grain. Let us stop this taking of interest. [11]Restore to them, this very day, their fields, their vineyards, their olive orchards, and their houses, and the interest on money, grain, wine, and oil that you have been exacting from them." [12]Then they said, "We will restore everything and demand nothing more from them. We will do as you say." And I called the priests, and made them take an oath to do as they had promised. [13]I also shook out the fold of my garment and said, "So may God shake out everyone from house and from property who does not perform this promise. Thus may they be shaken out and emptied." And all the assembly said, "Amen," and praised the LORD. And the people did as they had promised.

The Generosity of Nehemiah

14 Moreover from the time that I was appointed to be their governor in the land of Judah, from the twentieth year to the thirty-second year of King Artaxerxes, twelve years, neither I nor my brothers ate the food allowance of the governor. [15]The former governors who were before me laid heavy burdens on the people, and took food and wine from them, besides forty shekels of silver. Even their servants lorded it over the people. But I did not do so, because of the fear of God. [16]Indeed, I devoted myself to the work on this wall, and acquired no land; and all my servants were gathered there for the work. [17]Moreover there were at my table one hundred fifty people, Jews and officials, besides those who came to us from the nations around us. [18]Now that which was prepared for one day was one ox and six choice sheep; also fowls were prepared for me, and every ten days skins of wine in abundance; yet with all this I did not demand the food allowance of the governor, because

of the heavy burden of labor on the people. [19]Remember for my good, O my God, all that I have done for this people.

Intrigues of Enemies Foiled

6 Now when it was reported to Sanballat and Tobiah and to Geshem the Arab and to the rest of our enemies that I had built the wall and that there was no gap left in it (though up to that time I had not set up the doors in the gates), [2]Sanballat and Geshem sent to me, saying, "Come and let us meet together in one of the villages in the plain of Ono." But they intended to do me harm. [3]So I sent messengers to them, saying, "I am doing a great work and I cannot come down. Why should the work stop while I leave it to come down to you?" [4]They sent to me four times in this way, and I answered them in the same manner. [5]In the same way Sanballat for the fifth time sent his servant to me with an open letter in his hand. [6]In it was written, "It is reported among the nations—and Geshem[a] also says it—that you and the Jews intend to rebel; that is why you are building the wall; and according to this report you wish to become their king. [7]You have also set up prophets to proclaim in Jerusalem concerning you, 'There is a king in Judah!' And now it will be reported to the king according to these words. So come, therefore, and let us confer together." [8]Then I sent to him, saying, "No such things as you say have been done; you are inventing them out of your own mind" [9]—for they all wanted to frighten us, thinking, "Their hands will drop from the work, and it will not be done." But now, O God, strengthen my hands.

10 One day when I went into the house of Shemaiah son of Delaiah son of Mehetabel, who was confined to his house, he said, "Let us meet together in the house of God, within the temple, and let us close the doors of the temple, for they are coming to kill you; indeed, tonight they are coming to kill you." [11]But I said, "Should a man like me run away? Would a man like me go into the temple to save his life? I will not go in!" [12]Then I perceived and saw that God had not sent him at all, but he had pronounced the prophecy against me because Tobiah and Sanballat had hired him. [13]He was hired for this purpose, to intimidate me and make me sin by acting in this way, and so they could give me a bad name, in order to taunt me. [14]Remember Tobiah and Sanballat, O my God, according to these things

a Heb *Gashmu*

that they did, and also the prophetess Noadiah and the rest of the prophets who wanted to make me afraid.

The Wall Completed

15 So the wall was finished on the twenty-fifth day of the month Elul, in fifty-two days. [16]And when all our enemies heard of it, all the nations around us were afraid[a] and fell greatly in their own esteem; for they perceived that this work had been accomplished with the help of our God. [17]Moreover in those days the nobles of Judah sent many letters to Tobiah, and Tobiah's letters came to them. [18]For many in Judah were bound by oath to him, because he was the son-in-law of Shecaniah son of Arah: and his son Jehohanan had married the daughter of Meshullam son of Berechiah. [19]Also they spoke of his good deeds in my presence, and reported my words to him. And Tobiah sent letters to intimidate me.

7 Now when the wall had been built and I had set up the doors, and the gatekeepers, the singers, and the Levites had been appointed, [2]I gave my brother Hanani charge over Jerusalem, along with Hananiah the commander of the citadel—for he was a faithful man and feared God more than many. [3]And I said to them, "The gates of Jerusalem are not to be opened until the sun is hot; while the gatekeepers[b] are still standing guard, let them shut and bar the doors. Appoint guards from among the inhabitants of Jerusalem, some at their watch posts, and others before their own houses." [4]The city was wide and large, but the people within it were few and no houses had been built.

Lists of the Returned Exiles

5 Then my God put it into my mind to assemble the nobles and the officials and the people to be enrolled by genealogy. And I found the book of the genealogy of those who were the first to come back, and I found the following written in it:

6 These are the people of the province who came up out of the captivity of those exiles whom King Nebuchadnezzar of Babylon had carried into exile; they returned to Jerusalem and Judah, each to his town. [7]They came with Zerubbabel, Jeshua, Nehemiah, Azariah, Raamiah, Nahamani, Mordecai, Bilshan, Mispereth, Bigvai, Nehum, Baanah.

The number of the Israelite people: [8]the descendants of Parosh, two thousand one hundred seventy-two. [9]Of Shephatiah, three hundred seventy-two. [10]Of Arah, six hundred fifty-two. [11]Of Pahath-moab, namely the descendants of Jeshua and Joab, two thousand eight hundred eighteen. [12]Of Elam, one thousand two hundred fifty-four. [13]Of Zattu, eight hundred forty-five. [14]Of Zaccai, seven hundred sixty. [15]Of Binnui, six hundred forty-eight. [16]Of Bebai, six hundred twenty-eight. [17]Of Azgad, two thousand three hundred twenty-two. [18]Of Adonikam, six hundred sixty-seven. [19]Of Bigvai, two thousand sixty-seven. [20]Of Adin, six hundred fifty-five. [21]Of Ater, namely of Hezekiah, ninety-eight. [22]Of Hashum, three hundred twenty-eight. [23]Of Bezai, three hundred twenty-four. [24]Of Hariph, one hundred twelve. [25]Of Gibeon, ninety-five. [26]The people of Bethlehem and Netophah, one hundred eighty-eight. [27]Of Anathoth, one hundred twenty-eight. [28]Of Beth-azmaveth, forty-two. [29]Of Kiriath-jearim, Chephirah, and Beeroth, seven hundred forty-three. [30]Of Ramah and Geba, six hundred twenty-one. [31]Of Michmas, one hundred twenty-two. [32]Of Bethel and Ai, one hundred twenty-three. [33]Of the other Nebo, fifty-two. [34]The descendants of the other Elam, one thousand two hundred fifty-four. [35]Of Harim, three hundred twenty. [36]Of Jericho, three hundred forty-five. [37]Of Lod, Hadid, and Ono, seven hundred twenty-one. [38]Of Senaah, three thousand nine hundred thirty.

39 The priests: the descendants of Jedaiah, namely the house of Jeshua, nine hundred seventy-three. [40]Of Immer, one thousand fifty-two. [41]Of Pashhur, one thousand two hundred forty-seven. [42]Of Harim, one thousand seventeen.

43 The Levites: the descendants of Jeshua, namely of Kadmiel of the descendants of Hodevah, seventy-four. [44]The singers: the descendants of Asaph, one hundred forty-eight. [45]The gatekeepers: the descendants of Shallum, of Ater, of Talmon, of Akkub, of Hatita, of Shobai, one hundred thirty-eight.

46 The temple servants: the descendants of Ziha, of Hasupha, of Tabbaoth, [47]of Keros, of Sia, of Padon, [48]of Lebana, of Hagaba, of Shalmai, [49]of Hanan, of Giddel, of Gahar, [50]of Reaiah, of Rezin, of Nekoda, [51]of Gazzam, of Uzza, of Paseah, [52]of Besai, of Meunim, of Nephushesim, [53]of Bakbuk, of Hakupha, of Harhur, [54]of Bazlith, of Mehida, of Harsha, [55]of Barkos, of Sisera, of Temah, [56]of Neziah, of Hatipha.

---

a Another reading is *saw* b Heb *while they*

57 The descendants of Solomon's servants: of Sotai, of Sophereth, of Perida, 58 of Jaala, of Darkon, of Giddel, 59 of Shephatiah, of Hattil, of Pochereth-hazzebaim, of Amon.

60 All the temple servants and the descendants of Solomon's servants were three hundred ninety-two.

61 The following were those who came up from Tel-melah, Tel-harsha, Cherub, Addon, and Immer, but they could not prove their ancestral houses or their descent, whether they belonged to Israel: 62 the descendants of Delaiah, of Tobiah, of Nekoda, six hundred forty-two. 63 Also, of the priests: the descendants of Hobaiah, of Hakkoz, of Barzillai (who had married one of the daughters of Barzillai the Gileadite and was called by their name). 64 These sought their registration among those enrolled in the genealogies, but it was not found there, so they were excluded from the priesthood as unclean; 65 the governor told them that they were not to partake of the most holy food, until a priest with Urim and Thummim should come.

66 The whole assembly together was forty-two thousand three hundred sixty, 67 besides their male and female slaves, of whom there were seven thousand three hundred thirty-seven; and they had two hundred forty-five singers, male and female. 68 They had seven hundred thirty-six horses, two hundred forty-five mules,ᵃ 69 four hundred thirty-five camels, and six thousand seven hundred twenty donkeys.

70 Now some of the heads of ancestral houses contributed to the work. The governor gave to the treasury one thousand darics of gold, fifty basins, and five hundred thirty priestly robes. 71 And some of the heads of ancestral houses gave into the building fund twenty thousand darics of gold and two thousand two hundred minas of silver. 72 And what the rest of the people gave was twenty thousand darics of gold, two thousand minas of silver, and sixty-seven priestly robes.

73 So the priests, the Levites, the gatekeepers, the singers, some of the people, the temple servants, and all Israel settled in their towns.

Ezra Summons the People to Obey the Law

When the seventh month came—the people of Israel being settled in their towns— 1 all the people gathered together into the square before the Water Gate. They told the scribe Ezra to bring the book of the law of Moses, which the LORD had given to Israel. 2 Accordingly, the priest Ezra brought the law before the assembly, both men and women and all who could hear with understanding. This was on the first day of the seventh month. 3 He read from it facing the square before the Water Gate from early morning until midday, in the presence of the men and the women and those who could understand; and the ears of all the people were attentive to the book of the law. 4 The scribe Ezra stood on a wooden platform that had been made for the purpose; and beside him stood Mattithiah, Shema, Anaiah, Uriah, Hilkiah, and Maaseiah on his right hand; and Pedaiah, Mishael, Malchijah, Hashum, Hash-baddanah, Zechariah, and Meshullam on his left hand. 5 And Ezra opened the book in the sight of all the people, for he was standing above all the people; and when he opened it, all the people stood up. 6 Then Ezra blessed the LORD, the great God, and all the people answered, "Amen, Amen," lifting up their hands. Then they bowed their heads and worshiped the LORD with their faces to the ground. 7 Also Jeshua, Bani, Sherebiah, Jamin, Akkub, Shabbethai, Hodiah, Maaseiah, Kelita, Azariah, Jozabad, Hanan, Pelaiah, the Levites,ᵇ helped the people to understand the law, while the people remained in their places. 8 So they read from the book, from the law of God, with interpretation. They gave the sense, so that the people understood the reading.

9 And Nehemiah, who was the governor, and Ezra the priest and scribe, and the Levites who taught the people said to all the people, "This day is holy to the LORD your God; do not mourn or weep." For all the people wept when they heard the words of the law. 10 Then he said to them, "Go your way, eat the fat and drink sweet wine and send portions of them to those for whom nothing is prepared, for this day is holy to our LORD; and do not be grieved, for the joy of the LORD is your strength." 11 So the Levites stilled all the people, saying, "Be quiet, for this day is holy; do not be grieved." 12 And all the people went their way to eat and drink and to send portions and to make great rejoicing, because they had understood the words that were declared to them.

The Festival of Booths Celebrated

13 On the second day the heads of ancestral houses of all the people, with the priests and the

---

ᵃ Ezra 2.66 and the margins of some Hebrew Mss: MT lacks *They had . . . forty-five mules*   ᵇ 1 Esdras 9.48 Vg: Heb *and the Levites*

Levites, came together to the scribe Ezra in order to study the words of the law. [14]And they found it written in the law, which the LORD had commanded by Moses, that the people of Israel should live in booths[a] during the festival of the seventh month, [15]and that they should publish and proclaim in all their towns and in Jerusalem as follows, "Go out to the hills and bring branches of olive, wild olive, myrtle, palm, and other leafy trees to make booths,[a] as it is written." [16]So the people went out and brought them, and made booths[a] for themselves, each on the roofs of their houses, and in their courts and in the courts of the house of God, and in the square at the Water Gate and in the square at the Gate of Ephraim. [17]And all the assembly of those who had returned from the captivity made booths[a] and lived in them; for from the days of Jeshua son of Nun to that day the people of Israel had not done so. And there was very great rejoicing. [18]And day by day, from the first day to the last day, he read from the book of the law of God. They kept the festival seven days; and on the eighth day there was a solemn assembly, according to the ordinance.

National Confession

9 Now on the twenty-fourth day of this month the people of Israel were assembled with fasting and in sackcloth, and with earth on their heads.[b] [2]Then those of Israelite descent separated themselves from all foreigners, and stood and confessed their sins and the iniquities of their ancestors. [3]They stood up in their place and read from the book of the law of the LORD their God for a fourth part of the day, and for another fourth they made confession and worshiped the LORD their God. [4]Then Jeshua, Bani, Kadmiel, Shebaniah, Bunni, Sherebiah, Bani, and Chenani stood on the stairs of the Levites and cried out with a loud voice to the LORD their God. [5]Then the Levites, Jeshua, Kadmiel, Bani, Hashabneiah, Sherebiah, Hodiah, Shebaniah, and Pethahiah, said, "Stand up and bless the LORD your God from everlasting to everlasting. Blessed be your glorious name, which is exalted above all blessing and praise."

[6] And Ezra said:[c] "You are the LORD, you alone; you have made heaven, the heaven of heavens, with all their host, the earth and all that is on it, the seas and all that is in them. To all of them you give life, and the host of heaven worships you. [7]You are the LORD, the God who chose Abram and brought him out of Ur of the Chaldeans and gave him the name Abraham; [8]and you found his heart faithful before you, and made with him a covenant to give to his descendants the land of the Canaanite, the Hittite, the Amorite, the Perizzite, the Jebusite, and the Girgashite; and you have fulfilled your promise, for you are righteous.

[9] "And you saw the distress of our ancestors in Egypt and heard their cry at the Red Sea.[d] [10]You performed signs and wonders against Pharaoh and all his servants and all the people of his land, for you knew that they acted insolently against our ancestors. You made a name for yourself, which remains to this day. [11]And you divided the sea before them, so that they passed through the sea on dry land, but you threw their pursuers into the depths, like a stone into mighty waters. [12]Moreover, you led them by day with a pillar of cloud, and by night with a pillar of fire, to give them light on the way in which they should go. [13]You came down also upon Mount Sinai, and spoke with them from heaven, and gave them right ordinances and true laws, good statutes and commandments, [14]and you made known your holy sabbath to them and gave them commandments and statutes and a law through your servant Moses. [15]For their hunger you gave them bread from heaven, and for their thirst you brought water for them out of the rock, and you told them to go in to possess the land that you swore to give them.

16 "But they and our ancestors acted presumptuously and stiffened their necks and did not obey your commandments; [17]they refused to obey, and were not mindful of the wonders that you performed among them; but they stiffened their necks and determined to return to their slavery in Egypt. But you are a God ready to forgive, gracious and merciful, slow to anger and abounding in steadfast love, and you did not forsake them. [18]Even when they had cast an image of a calf

> "Stand up and bless
> the LORD your God
> from everlasting
> to everlasting."
> —Nehemiah 9:5

---

a Or *tabernacles;* Heb *succoth*   b Heb *on them*   c Gk: Heb lacks *And Ezra said*   d Or *Sea of Reeds*

for themselves and said, 'This is your God who brought you up out of Egypt,' and had committed great blasphemies, [19]you in your great mercies did not forsake them in the wilderness; the pillar of cloud that led them in the way did not leave them by day, nor the pillar of fire by night that gave them light on the way by which they should go. [20]You gave your good spirit to instruct them, and did not withhold your manna from their mouths, and gave them water for their thirst. [21]Forty years you sustained them in the wilderness so that they lacked nothing; their clothes did not wear out and their feet did not swell. [22]And you gave them kingdoms and peoples, and allotted to them every corner,[a] so they took possession of the land of King Sihon of Heshbon and the land of King Og of Bashan. [23]You multiplied their descendants like the stars of heaven, and brought them into the land that you had told their ancestors to enter and possess. [24]So the descendants went in and possessed the land, and you subdued before them the inhabitants of the land, the Canaanites, and gave them into their hands, with their kings and the peoples of the land, to do with them as they pleased. [25]And they captured fortress cities and a rich land, and took possession of houses filled with all sorts of goods, hewn cisterns, vineyards, olive orchards, and fruit trees in abundance; so they ate, and were filled and became fat, and delighted themselves in your great goodness.

26 "Nevertheless they were disobedient and rebelled against you and cast your law behind their backs and killed your prophets, who had warned them in order to turn them back to you, and they committed great blasphemies. [27]Therefore you gave them into the hands of their enemies, who made them suffer. Then in the time of their suffering they cried out to you and you heard them from heaven, and according to your great mercies you gave them saviors who saved them from the hands of their enemies. [28]But after they had rest, they again did evil before you, and you abandoned them to the hands of their enemies, so that they had dominion over them; yet when they turned and cried to you, you heard from heaven, and many times you rescued them according to your mercies. [29]And you warned them in order to turn them back to your law. Yet they acted presumptuously and did not obey your commandments, but sinned against your ordinances, by the observance of which a person shall live. They turned a stubborn shoulder and stiffened

their neck and would not obey. [30]Many years you were patient with them, and warned them by your spirit through your prophets; yet they would not listen. Therefore you handed them over to the peoples of the lands. [31]Nevertheless, in your great mercies you did not make an end of them or forsake them, for you are a gracious and merciful God.

32 "Now therefore, our God—the great and mighty and awesome God, keeping covenant and steadfast love—do not treat lightly all the hardship that has come upon us, upon our kings, our officials, our priests, our prophets, our ancestors, and all your people, since the time of the kings of Assyria until today. [33]You have been just in all that has come upon us, for you have dealt faithfully and we have acted wickedly; [34]our kings, our officials, our priests, and our ancestors have not kept your law or heeded the commandments and the warnings that you gave them. [35]Even in their own kingdom, and in the great goodness you bestowed on them, and in the large and rich land that you set before them, they did not serve you and did not turn from their wicked works. [36]Here we are, slaves to this day—slaves in the land that you gave to our ancestors to enjoy its fruit and its good gifts. [37]Its rich yield goes to the kings whom you have set over us because of our sins; they have power also over our bodies and over our livestock at their pleasure, and we are in great distress."

Those Who Signed the Covenant

38[b] Because of all this we make a firm agreement in writing, and on that sealed document are inscribed the names of our officials, our Levites, and our priests.

10 [c] Upon the sealed document are the names of Nehemiah the governor, son of Hacaliah, and Zedekiah; [2]Seraiah, Azariah, Jeremiah, [3]Pashhur, Amariah, Malchijah, [4]Hattush, Shebaniah, Malluch, [5]Harim, Meremoth, Obadiah, [6]Daniel, Ginnethon, Baruch, [7]Meshullam, Abijah, Mijamin, [8]Maaziah, Bilgai, Shemaiah; these are the priests. [9]And the Levites: Jeshua son of Azaniah, Binnui of the sons of Henadad, Kadmiel; [10]and their associates, Shebaniah, Hodiah, Kelita, Pelaiah, Hanan, [11]Mica, Rehob, Hashabiah, [12]Zaccur, Sherebiah, Shebaniah, [13]Hodiah, Bani, Beninu. [14]The leaders of the people: Parosh, Pahath-moab, Elam, Zattu, Bani, [15]Bunni, Azgad, Bebai, [16]Adonijah, Bigvai, Adin, [17]Ater, Hezekiah, Azzur, [18]Hodiah,

a Meaning of Heb uncertain   b Ch 10.1 in Heb   c Ch 10.2 in Heb

Hashum, Bezai, [19]Hariph, Anathoth, Nebai, [20]Magpiash, Meshullam, Hezir, [21]Meshezabel, Zadok, Jaddua, [22]Pelatiah, Hanan, Anaiah, [23]Hoshea, Hananiah, Hasshub, [24]Hallohesh, Pilha, Shobek, [25]Rehum, Hashabnah, Maaseiah, [26]Ahiah, Hanan, Anan, [27]Malluch, Harim, and Baanah.

Summary of the Covenant

28 The rest of the people, the priests, the Levites, the gatekeepers, the singers, the temple servants, and all who have separated themselves from the peoples of the lands to adhere to the law of God, their wives, their sons, their daughters, all who have knowledge and understanding, [29]join with their kin, their nobles, and enter into a curse and an oath to walk in God's law, which was given by Moses the servant of God, and to observe and do all the commandments of the LORD our Lord and his ordinances and his statutes. [30]We will not give our daughters to the peoples of the land or take their daughters for our sons; [31]and if the peoples of the land bring in merchandise or any grain on the sabbath day to sell, we will not buy it from them on the sabbath or on a holy day; and we will forego the crops of the seventh year and the exaction of every debt.

32 We also lay on ourselves the obligation to charge ourselves yearly one-third of a shekel for the service of the house of our God: [33]for the rows of bread, the regular grain offering, the regular burnt offering, the sabbaths, the new moons, the appointed festivals, the sacred donations, and the sin offerings to make atonement for Israel, and for all the work of the house of our God. [34]We have also cast lots among the priests, the Levites, and the people, for the wood offering, to bring it into the house of our God, by ancestral houses, at appointed times, year by year, to burn on the altar of the LORD our God, as it is written in the law. [35]We obligate ourselves to bring the first fruits of our soil and the first fruits of all fruit of every tree, year by year, to the house of the LORD; [36]also to bring to the house of our God, to the priests who minister in the house of our God, the firstborn of our sons and of our livestock, as it is written in the law, and the firstlings of our herds and of our flocks; [37]and to bring the first of our dough, and our contributions, the fruit of every tree, the wine and the oil, to the priests, to the chambers of the house of our God; and to bring to the Levites the tithes from our soil, for it is the Levites who collect the tithes in all our rural towns. [38]And the priest, the descendant of Aaron, shall be with the Levites when the Levites receive the tithes; and the Levites shall bring up a tithe of the tithes to the house of our God, to the chambers of the storehouse. [39]For the people of Israel and the sons of Levi shall bring the contribution of grain, wine, and oil to the storerooms where the vessels of the sanctuary are, and where the priests that minister, and the gatekeepers and the singers are. We will not neglect the house of our God.

Population of the City Increased

11 Now the leaders of the people lived in Jerusalem; and the rest of the people cast lots to bring one out of ten to live in the holy city Jerusalem, while nine-tenths remained in the other towns. [2]And the people blessed all those who willingly offered to live in Jerusalem.

3 These are the leaders of the province who lived in Jerusalem; but in the towns of Judah all lived on their property in their towns: Israel, the priests, the Levites, the temple servants, and the descendants of Solomon's servants. [4]And in Jerusalem lived some of the Judahites and of the Benjaminites. Of the Judahites: Athaiah son of Uzziah son of Zechariah son of Amariah son of Shephatiah son of Mahalalel, of the descendants of Perez; [5]and Maaseiah son of Baruch son of Col-hozeh son of Hazaiah son of Adaiah son of Joiarib son of Zechariah son of the Shilonite. [6]All the descendants of Perez who lived in Jerusalem were four hundred sixty-eight valiant warriors.

7 And these are the Benjaminites: Sallu son of Meshullam son of Joed son of Pedaiah son of Kolaiah son of Maaseiah son of Ithiel son of Jeshaiah. [8]And his brothers[a] Gabbai, Sallai: nine hundred twenty-eight. [9]Joel son of Zichri was their overseer; and Judah son of Hassenuah was second in charge of the city.

10 Of the priests: Jedaiah son of Joiarib, Jachin, [11]Seraiah son of Hilkiah son of Meshullam son of Zadok son of Meraioth son of Ahitub, officer of the house of God, [12]and their associates who did the work of the house, eight hundred twenty-two; and Adaiah son of Jeroham son of Pelaliah son of Amzi son of Zechariah son of Pashhur son of Malchijah, [13]and his associates, heads of ancestral houses, two hundred forty-two; and Amashsai son of Azarel son of Ahzai son of Meshillemoth son of Immer, [14]and

---

a Gk Mss: Heb *And after him*

their associates, valiant warriors, one hundred twenty-eight; their overseer was Zabdiel son of Haggedolim.

15 And of the Levites: Shemaiah son of Hasshub son of Azrikam son of Hashabiah son of Bunni; [16]and Shabbethai and Jozabad, of the leaders of the Levites, who were over the outside work of the house of God; [17]and Mattaniah son of Mica son of Zabdi son of Asaph, who was the leader to begin the thanksgiving in prayer, and Bakbukiah, the second among his associates; and Abda son of Shammua son of Galal son of Jeduthun. [18]All the Levites in the holy city were two hundred eighty-four.

19 The gatekeepers, Akkub, Talmon and their associates, who kept watch at the gates, were one hundred seventy-two. [20]And the rest of Israel, and of the priests and the Levites, were in all the towns of Judah, all of them in their inheritance. [21]But the temple servants lived on Ophel; and Ziha and Gishpa were over the temple servants.

22 The overseer of the Levites in Jerusalem was Uzzi son of Bani son of Hashabiah son of Mattaniah son of Mica, of the descendants of Asaph, the singers, in charge of the work of the house of God. [23]For there was a command from the king concerning them, and a settled provision for the singers, as was required every day. [24]And Pethahiah son of Meshezabel, of the descendants of Zerah son of Judah, was at the king's hand in all matters concerning the people.

Villages outside Jerusalem

25 And as for the villages, with their fields, some of the people of Judah lived in Kiriath-arba and its villages, and in Dibon and its villages, and in Jekabzeel and its villages, [26]and in Jeshua and in Moladah and Beth-pelet, [27]in Hazar-shual, in Beer-sheba and its villages, [28]in Ziklag, in Meconah and its villages, [29]in En-rimmon, in Zorah, in Jarmuth, [30]Zanoah, Adullam, and their villages, Lachish and its fields, and

Azekah and its villages. So they camped from Beer-sheba to the valley of Hinnom. [31]The people of Benjamin also lived from Geba onward, at Michmash, Aija, Bethel and its villages, [32]Anathoth, Nob, Ananiah, [33]Hazor, Ramah, Gittaim, [34]Hadid, Zeboim, Neballat, [35]Lod, and Ono, the valley of artisans. [36]And certain divisions of the Levites in Judah were joined to Benjamin.

A List of Priests and Levites

12 These are the priests and the Levites who came up with Zerubbabel son of Shealtiel, and Jeshua: Seraiah, Jeremiah, Ezra, [2]Amariah, Malluch, Hattush, [3]Shecaniah, Rehum, Meremoth, [4]Iddo, Ginnethoi, Abijah, [5]Mijamin, Maadiah, Bilgah, [6]Shemaiah, Joiarib, Jedaiah, [7]Sallu, Amok, Hilkiah, Jedaiah. These were the leaders of the priests and of their associates in the days of Jeshua.

8 And the Levites: Jeshua, Binnui, Kadmiel, Sherebiah, Judah, and Mattaniah, who with his associates was in charge of the songs of thanksgiving. [9]And Bakbukiah and Unno their associates stood opposite them in the service. [10]Jeshua was the father of Joiakim, Joiakim the father of Eliashib, Eliashib the father of Joiada, [11]Joiada the father of Jonathan, and Jonathan the father of Jaddua.

12 In the days of Joiakim the priests, heads of ancestral houses, were: of Seraiah, Meraiah; of Jeremiah, Hananiah; [13]of Ezra, Meshullam; of Amariah, Jehohanan; [14]of Malluchi, Jonathan; of Shebaniah, Joseph; [15]of Harim, Adna; of Meraioth, Helkai; [16]of Iddo, Zechariah; of Ginnethon, Meshullam; [17]of Abijah, Zichri; of Miniamin, of Moadiah, Piltai; [18]of Bilgah, Shammua; of Shemaiah, Jehonathan; [19]of Joiarib, Mattenai; of Jedaiah, Uzzi; [20]of Sallai, Kallai; of Amok, Eber; [21]of Hilkiah, Hashabiah; of Jedaiah, Nethanel.

22 As for the Levites, in the days of Eliashib, Joiada, Johanan, and Jaddua, there were recorded the heads of ancestral houses; also the priests until the reign of Darius the Persian. [23]The Levites, heads of ancestral houses, were recorded in the Book of the Annals until the days of Johanan son of Eliashib. [24]And the leaders of the Levites: Hashabiah, Sherebiah, and Jeshua son of Kadmiel, with their associates over against them, to praise and to give thanks, according to the commandment of David the man of God, section opposite to section. [25]Mattaniah, Bakbukiah, Obadiah, Meshullam, Talmon, and Akkub were gatekeepers standing guard at the store-

houses of the gates. [26]These were in the days of Joiakim son of Jeshua son of Jozadak, and in the days of the governor Nehemiah and of the priest Ezra, the scribe.

Dedication of the City Wall

27 Now at the dedication of the wall of Jerusalem they sought out the Levites in all their places, to bring them to Jerusalem to celebrate the dedication with rejoicing, with thanksgivings and with singing, with cymbals, harps, and lyres. [28]The companies of the singers gathered together from the circuit around Jerusalem and from the villages of the Netophathites; [29]also from Beth-gilgal and from the region of Geba and Azmaveth; for the singers had built for themselves villages around Jerusalem. [30]And the priests and the Levites purified themselves; and they purified the people and the gates and the wall.

31 Then I brought the leaders of Judah up onto the wall, and appointed two great companies that gave thanks and went in procession. One went to the right on the wall to the Dung Gate; [32]and after them went Hoshaiah and half the officials of Judah, [33]and Azariah, Ezra, Meshullam, [34]Judah, Benjamin, Shemaiah, and Jeremiah, [35]and some of the young priests with trumpets: Zechariah son of Jonathan son of Shemaiah son of Mattaniah son of Micaiah son of Zaccur son of Asaph; [36]and his kindred, Shemaiah, Azarel, Milalai, Gilalai, Maai, Nethanel, Judah, and Hanani, with the musical instruments of David the man of God; and the scribe Ezra went in front of them. [37]At the Fountain Gate, in front of them, they went straight up by the stairs of the city of David, at the ascent of the wall, above the house of David, to the Water Gate on the east.

38 The other company of those who gave thanks went to the left,[a] and I followed them with half of the people on the wall, above the Tower of the Ovens, to the Broad Wall, [39]and above the Gate of Ephraim, and by the Old Gate, and by the Fish Gate and the Tower of Hananel and the Tower of the Hundred, to the Sheep Gate; and they came to a halt at the Gate of the Guard. [40]So both companies of those who gave thanks stood in the house of God, and I and half of the officials with me; [41]and the priests Eliakim, Maaseiah, Miniamin, Micaiah, Elioenai, Zechariah, and Hananiah, with trumpets; [42]and Maaseiah, Shemaiah, Eleazar, Uzzi, Jehohanan, Malchijah, Elam, and Ezer. And the singers sang with Jezrahiah as their leader. [43]They offered great sacrifices that day and rejoiced, for God had made them rejoice with great joy; the women and children also rejoiced. The joy of Jerusalem was heard far away.

Temple Responsibilities

44 On that day men were appointed over the chambers for the stores, the contributions, the first fruits, and the tithes, to gather into them the portions required by the law for the priests and for the Levites from the fields belonging to the towns; for Judah rejoiced over the priests and the Levites who ministered. [45]They performed the service of their God and the service of purification, as did the singers and the gatekeepers, according to the command of David and his son Solomon. [46]For in the days of David and Asaph long ago there was a leader of the singers, and there were songs of praise and thanksgiving to God. [47]In the days of Zerubbabel and in the days of Nehemiah all Israel gave the daily portions for the singers and the gatekeepers. They set apart that which was for the Levites; and the Levites set apart that which was for the descendants of Aaron.

Foreigners Separated from Israel

13 On that day they read from the book of Moses in the hearing of the people; and in it was found written that no Ammonite or Moabite should ever enter the assembly of God, [2]because they did not meet the Israelites with bread and water, but hired Balaam against them to curse them—yet our God turned the curse into a blessing. [3]When the people heard the law, they separated from Israel all those of foreign descent.

The Reforms of Nehemiah

4 Now before this, the priest Eliashib, who was appointed over the chambers of the house of our God, and who was related to Tobiah, [5]prepared for Tobiah a large room where they had previously put the grain offering, the frankincense, the vessels, and the tithes of grain, wine, and oil, which were given by commandment to the Levites, singers, and gatekeepers, and the contributions for the priests. [6]While this was taking place I was not in Jerusalem, for in the thirty-second year of King Artaxerxes of Babylon I went to the king. After some time I asked leave of the king [7]and returned to Jerusalem. I then

---

α Cn: Heb opposite

discovered the wrong that Eliashib had done on behalf of Tobiah, preparing a room for him in the courts of the house of God. [8]And I was very angry, and I threw all the household furniture of Tobiah out of the room. [9]Then I gave orders and they cleansed the chambers, and I brought back the vessels of the house of God, with the grain offering and the frankincense.

10 I also found out that the portions of the Levites had not been given to them; so that the Levites and the singers, who had conducted the service, had gone back to their fields. [11]So I remonstrated with the officials and said, "Why is the house of God forsaken?" And I gathered them together and set them in their stations. [12]Then all Judah brought the tithe of the grain, wine, and oil into the storehouses. [13]And I appointed as treasurers over the storehouses the priest Shelemiah, the scribe Zadok, and Pedaiah of the Levites, and as their assistant Hanan son of Zaccur son of Mattaniah, for they were considered faithful; and their duty was to distribute to their associates. [14]Remember me, O my God, concerning this, and do not wipe out my good deeds that I have done for the house of my God and for his service.

Sabbath Reforms Begun

15 In those days I saw in Judah people treading wine presses on the sabbath, and bringing in heaps of grain and loading them on donkeys; and also wine, grapes, figs, and all kinds of burdens, which they brought into Jerusalem on the sabbath day; and I warned them at that time against selling food. [16]Tyrians also, who lived in the city, brought in fish and all kinds of merchandise and sold them on the sabbath to the people of Judah, and in Jerusalem. [17]Then I remonstrated with the nobles of Judah and said to them, "What is this evil thing that you are doing, profaning the sabbath day? [18]Did not your ancestors act in this way, and did not our God bring all this disaster on us and on this city? Yet you bring more wrath on Israel by profaning the sabbath."

19 When it began to be dark at the gates of Jerusalem before the sabbath, I commanded that the doors should be shut and gave orders that they should not be opened until after the sabbath. And I set some of my servants over the gates, to prevent any burden from being brought in on the sabbath day. [20]Then the merchants and sellers of all kinds of merchandise spent the night outside Jerusalem once or twice. [21]But I warned them and said to them, "Why do you spend the night in front of the wall? If you do so again, I will lay hands on you." From that time on they did not come on the sabbath. [22]And I commanded the Levites that they should purify themselves and come and guard the gates, to keep the sabbath day holy. Remember this also in my favor, O my God, and spare me according to the greatness of your steadfast love.

Mixed Marriages Condemned

23 In those days also I saw Jews who had married women of Ashdod, Ammon, and Moab; [24]and half of their children spoke the language of Ashdod, and they could not speak the language of Judah, but spoke the language of various peoples. [25]And I contended with them and cursed them and beat some of them and pulled out their hair; and I made them take an oath in the name of God, saying, "You shall not give your daughters to their sons, or take their daughters for your sons or for yourselves. [26]Did not King Solomon of Israel sin on account of such women? Among the many nations there was no king like him, and he was beloved by his God, and God made him king over all Israel; nevertheless, foreign women made even him to sin. [27]Shall we then listen to you and do all this great evil and act treacherously against our God by marrying foreign women?"

28 And one of the sons of Jehoiada, son of the high priest Eliashib, was the son-in-law of Sanballat the Horonite; I chased him away from me. [29]Remember them, O my God, because they have defiled the priesthood, the covenant of the priests and the Levites.

30 Thus I cleansed them from everything foreign, and I established the duties of the priests and Levites, each in his work; [31]and I provided for the wood offering, at appointed times, and for the first fruits. Remember me, O my God, for good.

Esther

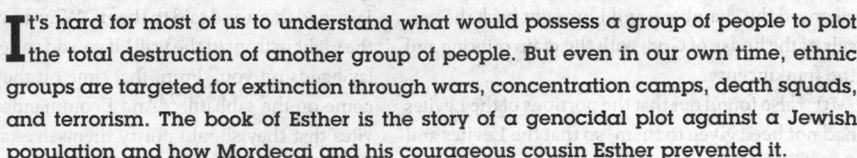

It's hard for most of us to understand what would possess a group of people to plot the total destruction of another group of people. But even in our own time, ethnic groups are targeted for extinction through wars, concentration camps, death squads, and terrorism. The book of Esther is the story of a genocidal plot against a Jewish population and how Mordecai and his courageous cousin Esther prevented it.

IN DEPTH

During the five centuries before Jesus, many of the Jewish people were uprooted from their homeland and had settled in foreign lands. The stories in Daniel and Esther reflect the challenges these emigrant Jews had to face, especially the concern for their safety. Esther rose to a position of power in a foreign government much as Joseph did in Egypt. When a plot was hatched to destroy the Jews, she used her influence with the king of Persia to save her people. Each year, Esther's victory is celebrated in the Jewish festival of Purim (Esther 9:18-32)—the festival celebrating the triumph of ordinary people over larger forces.

Esther is a unique book of the Bible. It's the only account of the Jewish people scattered in ancient Persia after the destruction of Jerusalem and the Babylonian exile. And it's the only book that does not specifically mention God. No one speaks to or about God, and God doesn't speak to anyone. Some scholars interpret God's absence as a sign of divine judgment for Israel's disobedience. Others view God's veiled presence as a signal for readers to look for God's work in between the lines of the story—and in our own lives.

All of us have or will face times in our lives when we ask, "Where is God?" The book of Esther gives us the reassurance that our questions are okay. It challenges us to trust God even when we don't have all the answers. And it reminds us that spiritual growth is about seeking God with and in our questions rather than demanding simple or easy answers.

QUICK FACTS

- **Setting:** Persia
- **Dates Covered:** After the Babylonian exile, which ended in 538 B.C.
- **Authors:** Unknown authors probably writing in the late fourth century B.C.
- **Themes:** God's protection of the Israelites; lessons about God's timing and purpose for our lives

AT A GLANCE

- **Esther 1–2** The choice of Esther as queen
- **Esther 3–5** The plot against the Jews
- **Esther 6–10** Haman's downfall and the rescue of the Jews

King Ahasuerus Deposes Queen Vashti

This happened in the days of Ahasuerus, the same Ahasuerus who ruled over one hundred twenty-seven provinces from India to Ethiopia.[a] 2In those days when King Ahasuerus sat on his royal throne in the citadel of Susa, 3in the third year of his reign, he gave a banquet for all his officials and ministers. The army of Persia and Media and the nobles and governors of the provinces were present, 4while he displayed the great wealth of his kingdom and the splendor and pomp of his majesty for many days, one hundred eighty days in all.

5 When these days were completed, the king gave for all the people present in the citadel of Susa, both great and small, a banquet lasting for seven days, in the court of the garden of the king's palace. 6There were white cotton curtains and blue hangings tied with cords of fine linen and purple to silver rings[b] and marble pillars. There were couches of gold and silver on a mosaic pavement of porphyry, marble, mother-of-pearl, and colored stones. 7Drinks were served in golden goblets, goblets of different kinds, and the royal wine was lavished according to the bounty of the king. 8Drinking was by flagons, without restraint; for the king had given orders to all the officials of his palace to do as each one desired. 9Furthermore, Queen Vashti gave a banquet for the women in the palace of King Ahasuerus.

10 On the seventh day, when the king was merry with wine, he commanded Mehuman, Biztha, Harbona, Bigtha and Abagtha, Zethar and Carkas, the seven eunuchs who attended him, 11to bring Queen Vashti before the king, wearing the royal crown, in order to show the peoples and the officials her beauty; for she was fair to behold. 12But Queen Vashti refused to come at the king's command conveyed by the eunuchs. At this the king was enraged, and his anger burned within him.

13 Then the king consulted the sages who knew the laws[c] (for this was the king's procedure toward all who were versed in law and custom, 14and those next to him were Carshena, Shethar, Admatha, Tarshish, Meres, Marsena, and Memucan, the seven officials of Persia and Media, who had access to the king, and sat first in the kingdom): 15"According to the law, what is to be done to Queen Vashti because she has not performed the command of King Ahasuerus conveyed by

STUDY IT!

The Case of the Missing Books · Esther

The book of Esther is one of the Old Testament books whose content has been disputed throughout history. Some versions include additional text that isn't printed here. So what's the story? A look at history holds the explanation.

Sometime in the second or third century B.C., Jewish scholars translated the scriptures from Hebrew and Aramaic into Greek. Many Jews living throughout the Mediterranean world spoke Greek, which had become a common language at that time. Because most of the early Christians spoke Greek, including Jews such as Paul, this Greek translation, called the Septuagint, was adopted by the Church as its Bible (Old Testament).

After the destruction of the Jerusalem temple by the Romans in A.D. 70, rabbis tried to reorganize Jewish worship, which could no longer center on the temple in Jerusalem. They reviewed the existing editions of the Bible and developed an official list of thirty-nine holy books. They rejected certain books contained in the Septuagint for which there were no existing original Hebrew or Aramaic texts, such as Tobit, Judith, 1 and 2 Maccabees, Wisdom, Sirach, Baruch, and additions to the books of Esther and Daniel.

Many centuries later, the Christian Reformer Martin Luther used the Jewish set, or canon, of the Old Testament as his translation of the Bible. He placed the additional books in a separate section called the Apocrypha (Greek for "hidden"). Most Protestant Bibles do not include these books. The Catholic and Orthodox churches continue to use the Greek canon, including the Apocrypha. But they prefer the term "deuterocanonical" (Greek for "second canon") for the disputed books.

a Or Nubia; Heb Cush   b Or rods   c Cn: Heb times

the eunuchs?" ¹⁶Then Memucan said in the presence of the king and the officials, "Not only has Queen Vashti done wrong to the king, but also to all the officials and all the peoples who are in all the provinces of King Ahasuerus. ¹⁷For this deed of the queen will be made known to all women, causing them to look with contempt on their husbands, since they will say, 'King Ahasuerus commanded Queen Vashti to be brought before him, and she did not come.' ¹⁸This very day the noble ladies of Persia and Media who have heard of the queen's behavior will rebel against^a the king's officials, and there will be no end of contempt and wrath! ¹⁹If it pleases the king, let a royal order go out from him, and let it be written among the laws of the Persians and the Medes so that it may not be altered, that Vashti is never again to come before King Ahasuerus; and let the king give her royal position to another who is better than she. ²⁰So when the decree made by the king is proclaimed throughout all his kingdom, vast as it is, all women will give honor to their husbands, high and low alike."

21 This advice pleased the king and the officials, and the king did as Memucan proposed; ²²he sent letters to all the royal provinces, to every province in its own script and to every people in its own language, declaring that every man should be master in his own house.^b

Esther Becomes Queen

2 After these things, when the anger of King Ahasuerus had abated, he remembered Vashti and what she had done and what had been decreed against her. ²Then the king's servants who attended him said, "Let beautiful young virgins be sought out for the king. ³And let the king appoint commissioners in all the provinces of his kingdom to gather all the beautiful young virgins to the harem in the citadel of Susa under custody of Hegai, the king's eunuch, who is in charge of the women; let their cosmetic treatments be given them. ⁴And let the girl who pleases the king be queen instead of Vashti." This pleased the king, and he did so.

5 Now there was a Jew in the citadel of Susa whose name was Mordecai son of Jair son of Shimei son of Kish, a Benjaminite. ⁶Kish^c had been carried away from Jerusalem among the captives carried away with King Jeconiah of Judah, whom King Nebuchadnezzar of Babylon had carried away. ⁷Mordecai^d had brought up Hadassah, that is Esther, his cousin, for she had neither father nor

STUDY IT!

Scattered People
Esther 2

The story of Esther implies that Mordecai and Esther were members of the Diaspora. The Greek word "diaspora" means "scattered abroad." It refers to the Jews who lived outside of Palestine. When the Babylonians destroyed Jerusalem (587 B.C.), many of the Jews who were forced to leave the land of Israel settled in various Greco-Roman cities. They maintained their Jewish identity by adapting the language and customs of their new home to their Jewish traditions. The Diaspora Jews were responsible for the translation of the Hebrew Bible into Greek, a translation called the Septuagint.

mother; the girl was fair and beautiful, and when her father and her mother died, Mordecai adopted her as his own daughter. ⁸So when the king's order and his edict were proclaimed, and when many young women were gathered in the citadel of Susa in custody of Hegai, Esther also was taken into the king's palace and put in custody of Hegai, who had charge of the women. ⁹The girl pleased him and won his favor, and he quickly provided her with her cosmetic treatments and her portion of food, and with seven chosen maids from the king's palace, and advanced her and her maids to the best place in the harem. ¹⁰Esther did not reveal her people or kindred, for Mordecai had charged her not to tell. ¹¹Every day Mordecai would walk around in front of the court of the harem, to learn how Esther was and how she fared.

12 The turn came for each girl to go in to King Ahasuerus, after being twelve months under the regulations for the women, since this was the regular period of their cosmetic treatment, six months with oil of myrrh and six months with perfumes and cosmetics for women. ¹³When the girl went in to the king she was given whatever she asked for to take with her from the harem to the king's palace. ¹⁴In the evening she went in; then in the morning she came back to the second harem in custody of

---

a Cn: Heb *will tell*   b Heb adds *and speak according to the language of his people*   c Heb *a Benjaminite* ⁶*who*   d Heb *He*

Shaashgaz, the king's eunuch, who was in charge of the concubines; she did not go in to the king again, unless the king delighted in her and she was summoned by name.

15 When the turn came for Esther daughter of Abihail the uncle of Mordecai, who had adopted her as his own daughter, to go in to the king, she asked for nothing except what Hegai the king's eunuch, who had charge of the women, advised. Now Esther was admired by all who saw her. ¹⁶When Esther was taken to King Ahasuerus in his royal palace in the tenth month, which is the month of Tebeth, in the seventh year of his reign, ¹⁷the king loved Esther more than all the other women; of all the virgins she won his favor and devotion, so that he set the royal crown on her head and made her queen instead of Vashti. ¹⁸Then the king gave a great banquet to all his officials and ministers—"Esther's banquet." He also granted a holiday*a* to the provinces, and gave gifts with royal liberality.

Mordecai Discovers a Plot

19 When the virgins were being gathered together,*b* Mordecai was sitting at the king's gate. ²⁰Now Esther had not revealed her kindred or her people, as Mordecai had charged her; for Esther obeyed Mordecai just as when she was brought up by him. ²¹In those days, while Mordecai was sitting

at the king's gate, Bigthan and Teresh, two of the king's eunuchs, who guarded the threshold, became angry and conspired to assassinate*c* King Ahasuerus. ²²But the matter came to the knowledge of Mordecai, and he told it to Queen Esther, and Esther told the king in the name of Mordecai. ²³When the affair was investigated and found to be so, both the men were hanged on the gallows. It was recorded in the book of the annals in the presence of the king.

Haman Undertakes to Destroy the Jews

3 After these things King Ahasuerus promoted Haman son of Hammedatha the Agagite, and advanced him and set his seat above all the officials who were with him. ²And all the king's servants who were at the king's gate bowed down and did obeisance to Haman; for the king had so commanded concerning him. But Mordecai did not bow down or do obeisance. ³Then the king's servants who were at the king's gate said to Mordecai, "Why do you disobey the king's command?" ⁴When they spoke to him day after day and he would not listen to them, they told Haman, in order to see whether Mordecai's words would avail; for he had told them that he was a Jew. ⁵When Haman saw that Mordecai did not bow down or do obeisance to him, Haman was infuriated. ⁶But he thought it beneath him to lay hands

Body Count · Esther 3:1–7

"Genocide" is a scary word. It's the complete annihilation of a people. This is what King Ahasuerus plots in the book of Esther: to destroy all the Jews in his kingdom. Fortunately, he doesn't succeed.

In our time, we know too well that the past two centuries have been marked by many attempts to exterminate whole groups of people. The most systematic and ambitious of these attempts was that of Adolf Hitler and the Third Reich. Six million Jews were put to death in Nazi concentration camps, along with four million other "undesirables." Every decade seems to bring new stories of genocide and ethnic cleansing even in our lifetime. In the 1990s, genocide happened in Rwanda and Bosnia. In the early 2000s, it was Darfur, Sudan.

As Christians we are called to love and see others as God does—humans in need of forgiveness and grace, regardless of culture, ethnicity, or language. We must strive to promote unity and work for justice, which will lead to a lasting peace. We must always think globally, for we are part of a very large family!

• What can you do to promote unity in your school, community, or church?
• Where is genocide or violence happening in the world today? What steps can you take to help stop it or to create awareness about it?

---

a Or *an amnesty* *b* Heb adds *a second time* *c* Heb *to lay hands on* on Mordecai alone. So, having been told who Mordecai's people were, Haman plotted to destroy all the Jews, the people of Mordecai, throughout the whole kingdom of Ahasuerus.

7 In the first month, which is the month of Nisan, in the twelfth year of King Ahasuerus, they cast Pur—which means "the lot"—before Haman for the day and for the month, and the lot fell on the thirteenth day[a] of the twelfth month, which is the month of Adar. [8]Then Haman said to King Ahasuerus, "There is a certain people scattered and separated among the peoples in all the provinces of your kingdom; their laws are different from those of every other people, and they do not keep the king's laws, so that it is not appropriate for the king to tolerate them. [9]If it pleases the king, let a decree be issued for their destruction, and I will pay ten thousand talents of silver into the hands of those who have charge of the king's business, so that they may put it into the king's treasuries." [10]So the king took his signet ring from his hand and gave it to Haman son of Hammedatha the Agagite, the enemy of the Jews. [11]The king said to Haman, "The money is given to you, and the people as well, to do with them as it seems good to you."

12 Then the king's secretaries were summoned on the thirteenth day of the first month, and an edict, according to all that Haman commanded, was written to the king's satraps and to the governors over all the provinces and to the officials of all the peoples, to every province in its own script and every people in its own language; it was written in the name of King Ahasuerus and sealed with the king's ring. [13]Letters were sent by couriers to all the king's provinces, giving orders to destroy, to kill, and to annihilate all Jews, young and old, women and children, in one day, the thirteenth day of the twelfth month, which is the month of Adar, and to plunder their goods. [14]A copy of the document was to be issued as a decree in every province by proclamation, calling on all the peoples to be ready for that day. [15]The couriers went quickly by order of the king, and the decree was issued in the citadel of Susa. The king and Haman sat down to drink; but the city of Susa was thrown into confusion.

Esther Agrees to Help the Jews

4 When Mordecai learned all that had been done, Mordecai tore his clothes and put on sackcloth and ashes, and went through the city,

wailing with a loud and bitter cry; [2]he went up to the entrance of the king's gate, for no one might enter the king's gate clothed with sackcloth. [3]In every province, wherever the king's command and his decree came, there was great mourning among the Jews, with fasting and weeping and lamenting, and most of them lay in sackcloth and ashes.

4 When Esther's maids and her eunuchs came and told her, the queen was deeply distressed; she sent garments to clothe Mordecai, so that he might take off his sackcloth; but he would not accept them. [5]Then Esther called for Hathach, one of the king's eunuchs, who had been appointed to attend her, and ordered him to go to Mordecai to learn what was happening and why. [6]Hathach went out to Mordecai in the open square of the city in front of the king's gate, [7]and Mordecai told him all that had happened

CONNECT IT!

Sojourner Truth: Speaking Out
Esther 4:9–16

Sojourner Truth was an American hero who refused to keep quiet despite being mistreated and devalued. Like Esther, she spoke up within an unjust system to bring about freedom and justice for her people. Born into slavery in 1797, Truth lived a tragic life of hard work, abuse, and injustice. But after her escape to freedom in 1826 and her emancipation one year later under New York law, she dedicated herself to speaking out against slavery.

In her famous speech "Ain't I a Woman?" Truth said, "That man over there says that women need to be helped into carriages, and lifted over ditches, and to have the best place everywhere. Nobody ever helps me into carriages, or over mud puddles, or gives me any best place! And ain't I a woman?"*

Truth was an abolitionist and a women's rights activist. Her womanhood was slighted and her personhood was trampled, yet she traveled America telling all who would listen about the evils of slavery.

---

a Cn Compare Gk and verse 13 below: Heb *the twelfth month*

LIVE IT!

For Such a Time as This
Esther 4:14

Esther is faced with a tough choice. Speaking out to save the Jews could mean losing her own life. But Mordecai reminds her that, although the ultimate fate of the Jewish people will not change no matter what she does, this is her responsibility and she will face the consequences if she disobeys. God has placed her in the right place at the right time to save her people. **Esther 4:14** is a good reminder that sometimes God engineers our circumstances for a particular purpose. It's our job to prepare and grow stronger by seeking God daily. Then when "such a time" arrives, we can be ready and willing to obey God and seize the opportunity given to us.

- What position have you been given?
- What opportunities are you facing?
- What is God asking you to do?
- How will you respond?

to him, and the exact sum of money that Haman had promised to pay into the king's treasuries for the destruction of the Jews. [8]Mordecai also gave him a copy of the written decree issued in Susa for their destruction, that he might show it to Esther, explain it to her, and charge her to go to the king to make supplication to him and entreat him for her people.

9 Hathach went and told Esther what Mordecai had said. [10]Then Esther spoke to Hathach and gave him a message for Mordecai, saying, [11]"All the king's servants and the people of the king's provinces know that if any man or woman goes to the king inside the inner court without being called, there is but one law—all alike are to be put to death. Only if the king holds out the golden scepter to someone, may that person live. I myself have not been called to come in to the king for thirty days." [12]When they told Mordecai what Esther had said, [13]Mordecai told them to reply to Esther, "Do not think that in the king's palace you will escape any more than all the other Jews. [14]For if you keep silence at such a time as this, relief and deliverance will rise for the Jews from another quarter, but you and your father's family will perish. Who knows? Perhaps you have come to royal dignity for just such a time as this." [15]Then Esther said in reply to Mordecai, [16]"Go, gather all the Jews to be found in Susa, and hold a fast on my behalf, and neither eat nor drink for three

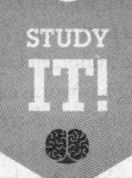

STUDY IT!

Women of the Bible · Esther 4:17

What a surprise to hear of a man in the ancient world taking orders from a woman! As a fictional character, Esther has an exceptional role in the Old Testament. However, many women who appear in stories that have a historical core are not even named, Jephthah's daughter and Samson's mother, for instance. Even the Hebrew women whose names have become famous—Sarah, Rebekah, Rachel, Miriam, Bathsheba—played second fiddle to their more famous husbands or brothers.

In the biblical world, a woman was defined by her relationships with men. Before marriage she belonged to her father's household and had no status outside of it. Once married, a woman left her father's family and joined the family of her husband. If her husband died, she remained in the new family, rearing children for her deceased spouse or, if childless, marrying a brother-in-law. Although many women undoubtedly lived happily under this system, many others just as surely suffered abuse or felt oppressed. The stories of Lot's daughters (see Genesis 19:8) and the woman of Gibeah (see Judges 19:24-30) testify to this horrifying truth.

More and more biblical scholars are seeking to give voice to the many silent and forgotten women of the Bible—searching for quiet messages that have long been overlooked. All of us can benefit from this effort to listen to the voices of these women!

days, night or day. I and my maids will also fast as you do. After that I will go to the king, though it is against the law; and if I perish, I perish." [17]Mordecai then went away and did everything as Esther had ordered him.

5 Esther's Banquet

On the third day Esther put on her royal robes and stood in the inner court of the king's palace, opposite the king's hall. The king was sitting on his royal throne inside the palace opposite the entrance to the palace. [2]As soon as the king saw Queen Esther standing in the court, she won his favor and he held out to her the golden scepter that was in his hand. Then Esther approached and touched the top of the scepter. [3]The king said to her, "What is it, Queen Esther? What is your request? It shall be given you, even to the half of my kingdom." [4]Then Esther said, "If it pleases the king, let the king and Haman come today to a banquet that I have prepared for the king." [5]Then the king said, "Bring Haman quickly, so that we may do as Esther desires." So the king and Haman came to the banquet that Esther had prepared. [6]While they were drinking wine, the king said to Esther, "What is your petition? It shall be granted you. And what is your request? Even to the half of my kingdom, it shall be fulfilled." [7]Then Esther said, "This is my petition and request: [8]If I have won the king's favor, and if it pleases the king to grant my petition and fulfill my request, let the king and Haman come tomorrow to the banquet that I will prepare for them, and then I will do as the king has said."

Haman Plans to Have Mordecai Hanged

[9] Haman went out that day happy and in good spirits. But when Haman saw Mordecai in the king's gate, and observed that he neither rose nor trembled before him, he was infuriated with Mordecai; [10]nevertheless Haman restrained himself and went home. Then he sent and called for his friends and his wife Zeresh, [11]and Haman recounted to them the splendor of his riches, the number of his sons, all the promotions with which the king had honored him, and how he had advanced him above the officials and the ministers of the king. [12]Haman added, "Even Queen Esther let no one but myself come with the king to the banquet that she prepared. Tomorrow also I am invited by her, together with the king. [13]Yet all this does me no good so long as I see the Jew Mordecai sitting at the king's gate." [14]Then his wife Zeresh and all his friends said to him, "Let a gallows fifty cubits high be made, and in the morning tell the king to have Mordecai hanged on it; then go with the king to the banquet in good spirits." This advice pleased Haman, and he had the gallows made.

6 The King Honors Mordecai

On that night the king could not sleep, and he gave orders to bring the book of records, the annals, and they were read to the king. [2]It was found written how Mordecai had told about Bigthana and Teresh, two of the king's eunuchs, who guarded the threshold, and who had conspired to assassinate[a] King Ahasuerus. [3]Then the king said, "What honor or distinction has been bestowed on Mordecai for this?" The king's servants who attended him said, "Nothing has been done for him." [4]The king said, "Who is in the court?" Now Haman had just entered the outer court of the king's palace to speak to the king about having Mordecai hanged on the gallows that he had prepared for him. [5]So the king's servants told him, "Haman is there, standing in the court." The king said, "Let him come in." [6]So Haman came in, and the king said to him, "What shall be done for the man whom the king wishes to honor?" Haman said to himself, "Whom would the king wish to honor more than me?" [7]So Haman said to the king, "For the man whom the king wishes to honor, [8]let royal robes be brought, which the king has worn, and a horse that the king has ridden, with a royal crown on its head. [9]Let the robes and the horse be handed over to one of the king's most noble officials; let him[b] robe the man whom the king wishes to honor, and let him[b] conduct the man on horseback through the open square of the city, proclaiming before him: 'Thus shall it be done for the man whom the king wishes to honor.' " [10]Then the king said to Haman, "Quickly, take the robes and the horse, as you have said, and do so to the Jew Mordecai who sits at the king's gate. Leave out nothing that you have mentioned." [11]So Haman took the robes and the horse and robed Mordecai and led him riding through the open square of the city, proclaiming, "Thus shall it be done for the man whom the king wishes to honor."

[12] Then Mordecai returned to the king's gate,

---

a Heb *to lay hands on*   **b** Heb *them*

but Haman hurried to his house, mourning and with his head covered. [13]When Haman told his wife Zeresh and all his friends everything that had happened to him, his advisers and his wife Zeresh said to him, "If Mordecai, before whom your downfall has begun, is of the Jewish people, you will not prevail against him, but will surely fall before him."

Haman's Downfall and Mordecai's Advancement

14 While they were still talking with him, the king's eunuchs arrived and hurried Haman off to the banquet that Esther had prepared. [1]So the king and Haman went in to feast with Queen Esther. [2]On the second day, as they were drinking wine, the king again said to Esther, "What is your petition, Queen Esther? It shall be granted you. And what is your request? Even to the half of my kingdom, it shall be fulfilled." [3]Then Queen Esther answered, "If I have won your favor, O king, and if it pleases the king, let my life be given me—that is my petition—and the lives of my people—that is my request. [4]For we have been sold, I and my people, to be destroyed, to be killed, and to be annihilated. If we had been sold merely as slaves, men and women, I would have held my peace; but no enemy can compensate for this damage to the king."[a] [5]Then King Ahasuerus said to Queen Esther, "Who is he, and where is he, who has presumed to do this?" [6]Esther said, "A foe and enemy, this wicked Haman!" Then Haman was terrified before the king and the queen. [7]The king rose from the feast in wrath and went into the palace garden, but Haman stayed to beg his life from Queen Esther, for he saw that the king had determined to destroy him. [8]When the king returned from the palace garden to the banquet hall, Haman had thrown himself on the couch where Esther was reclining; and the king said, "Will he even assault the queen in my presence, in my own house?" As the words left the mouth of the king, they covered Haman's face. [9]Then Harbona, one of the eunuchs in attendance on the king, said, "Look, the very gallows that Haman has prepared for Mordecai, whose word saved the king, stands at Haman's house, fifty cubits high." And the king said, "Hang him on that." [10]So they hanged Haman on the gallows that he had prepared for Mordecai. Then the anger of the king abated.

Esther Saves the Jews

On that day King Ahasuerus gave to Queen Esther the house of Haman, the enemy of the Jews; and Mordecai came before the king, for Esther had told what he was to her. [2]Then the king took off his signet ring, which he had taken from Haman, and gave it to Mordecai. So Esther set Mordecai over the house of Haman.

3 Then Esther spoke again to the king; she fell at his feet, weeping and pleading with him to avert the evil design of Haman the Agagite and the plot that he had devised against the Jews. [4]The king held out the golden scepter to Esther, [5]and Esther rose and stood before the king. She said, "If it pleases the king, and if I have won his favor, and if the thing seems right before the king, and I have his approval, let an order be written to revoke the letters devised by Haman son of Hammedatha the Agagite, which he wrote giving orders to destroy the Jews who are in all the provinces of the king. [6]For how can I bear to see the calamity that is coming on my people? Or how can I bear to see the destruction of my kindred?" [7]Then King Ahasuerus said to Queen Esther and to the Jew Mordecai, "See, I have given Esther the house of Haman, and they have hanged him on the gallows, because he plotted to lay hands on the Jews. [8]You may write as you please with regard to the Jews, in the name of the king, and seal it with the king's ring; for an edict written in the name of the king and sealed with the king's ring cannot be revoked."

9 The king's secretaries were summoned at that time, in the third month, which is the month of Sivan, on the twenty-third day; and an edict was written, according to all that Mordecai commanded, to the Jews and to the satraps and the governors and the officials of the provinces from India to Ethiopia,[b] one hundred twenty-seven provinces, to every province in its own script and to every people in its own language, and also to the Jews in their script and their language. [10]He wrote letters in the name of

a Meaning of Heb uncertain   b Or Nubia; Heb Cush

King Ahasuerus, sealed them with the king's ring, and sent them by mounted couriers riding on fast steeds bred from the royal herd.[a] 11 By these letters the king allowed the Jews who were in every city to assemble and defend their lives, to destroy, to kill, and to annihilate any armed force of any people or province that might attack them, with their children and women, and to plunder their goods 12 on a single day throughout all the provinces of King Ahasuerus, on the thirteenth day of the twelfth month, which is the month of Adar. 13 A copy of the writ was to be issued as a decree in every province and published to all peoples, and the Jews were to be ready on that day to take revenge on their enemies. 14 So the couriers, mounted on their swift royal steeds, hurried out, urged by the king's command. The decree was issued in the citadel of Susa.

15 Then Mordecai went out from the presence of the king, wearing royal robes of blue and white, with a great golden crown and a mantle of fine linen and purple, while the city of Susa shouted and rejoiced. 16 For the Jews there was light and gladness, joy and honor. 17 In every province and in every city, wherever the king's command and his edict came, there was gladness and joy among the Jews, a festival and a holiday. Furthermore, many of the peoples of the country professed to be Jews, because the fear of the Jews had fallen upon them.

9 **Destruction of the Enemies of the Jews**

Now in the twelfth month, which is the month of Adar, on the thirteenth day, when the king's command and edict were about to be executed, on the very day when the enemies of the Jews hoped to gain power over them, but which had been changed to a day when the Jews would gain power over their foes, 2 the Jews gathered in their cities throughout all the provinces of King Ahasuerus to lay hands on those who had sought their ruin; and no one could withstand them, because the fear of them had fallen upon all peoples. 3 All the officials of the provinces, the satraps and the governors, and the royal officials were supporting the Jews, because the fear of Mordecai had fallen upon them. 4 For Mordecai was powerful in the king's house, and his fame spread throughout all the provinces as the man Mordecai grew more and more powerful. 5 So the Jews struck down all their enemies with the sword, slaughtering, and destroying them, and did as they pleased to those who hated them. 6 In the citadel of Susa the Jews killed and destroyed five hundred people. 7 They killed Parshandatha, Dalphon, Aspatha, 8 Poratha, Adalia, Aridatha, 9 Parmashta, Arisai, Aridai, Vaizatha, 10 the ten sons of Haman son of Hammedatha, the enemy of the Jews; but they did not touch the plunder.

11 That very day the number of those killed in the citadel of Susa was reported to the king. 12 The king said to Queen Esther, "In the citadel of Susa the Jews have killed five hundred people and also the ten sons of Haman. What have they done in the rest of the king's provinces? Now what is your petition? It shall be granted you. And what further is your request? It shall be fulfilled." 13 Esther said, "If it pleases the king, let the Jews who are in Susa be allowed tomorrow also to do according to this day's edict, and let the ten sons of Haman be hanged on the gallows." 14 So the king commanded this to be done; a decree was issued in Susa, and the ten sons of Haman were hanged. 15 The Jews who were in Susa gathered also on the fourteenth day of the month of Adar and they killed three hundred persons in Susa; but they did not touch the plunder.

16 Now the other Jews who were in the king's provinces also gathered to defend their lives, and gained relief from their enemies, and killed seventy-five thousand of those who hated them; but they laid no hands on the plunder. 17 This was on the thirteenth day of the month of Adar, and on the fourteenth day they rested and made that a day of feasting and gladness.

The Feast of Purim Inaugurated

18 But the Jews who were in Susa gathered on the thirteenth day and on the fourteenth, and rested on the fifteenth day, making that a day of feasting and gladness. 19 Therefore the Jews of the villages, who live in the open towns, hold the fourteenth day of the month of Adar as a day for gladness and feasting, a holiday on which they send gifts of food to one another.

20 Mordecai recorded these things, and sent letters to all the Jews who were in all the provinces of King Ahasuerus, both near and far, 21 enjoining them that they should keep the fourteenth day of

---

a Meaning of Heb uncertain

STUDY IT!

Purim
Esther 9:20–32

Purim ("lots" in Hebrew) is a minor festival in the Jewish calendar celebrated in late winter and marked by the retelling and acting out of the legendary victory of Queen Esther and Mordecai. It's a celebration of a deliverance that almost didn't happen. The celebration includes the exchange of gifts, the sharing of meals, and giving to the poor.

the month Adar and also the fifteenth day of the same month, year by year, [22] as the days on which the Jews gained relief from their enemies, and as the month that had been turned for them from sorrow into gladness and from mourning into a holiday; that they should make them days of feasting and gladness, days for sending gifts of food to one another and presents to the poor. [23] So the Jews adopted as a custom what they had begun to do, as Mordecai had written to them.

[24] Haman son of Hammedatha the Agagite, the enemy of all the Jews, had plotted against the Jews to destroy them, and had cast Pur—that is "the lot"—to crush and destroy them; [25] but when Esther came before the king, he gave orders in writing that the wicked plot that he had devised against the Jews should come upon his own head, and that he and his sons should be hanged on the gallows. [26] Therefore these days are called Purim, from the word Pur.

Thus because of all that was written in this letter, and of what they had faced in this matter, and of what had happened to them, [27] the Jews established and accepted as a custom for themselves and their descendants and all who joined them, that without fail they would continue to observe these two days every year, as it was written and at the time appointed. [28] These days should be remembered and kept throughout every generation, in every family, province, and city; and these days of Purim should never fall into disuse among the Jews, nor should the commemoration of these days cease among their descendants.

[29] Queen Esther daughter of Abihail, along with the Jew Mordecai, gave full written authority, confirming this second letter about Purim. [30] Letters were sent wishing peace and security to all the Jews, to the one hundred twenty-seven provinces of the kingdom of Ahasuerus, [31] and giving orders that these days of Purim should be observed at their appointed seasons, as the Jew Mordecai and Queen Esther enjoined on the Jews, just as they had laid down for themselves and for their descendants regulations concerning their fasts and their lamentations. [32] The command of Queen Esther fixed these practices of Purim, and it was recorded in writing.

10 King Ahasuerus laid tribute on the land and on the islands of the sea. [2] All the acts of his power and might, and the full account of the high honor of Mordecai, to which the king advanced him, are they not written in the annals of the kings of Media and Persia? [3] For Mordecai the Jew was next in rank to King Ahasuerus, and he was powerful among the Jews and popular with his many kindred, for he sought the good of his people and interceded for the welfare of all his descendants.

Introduction to the
Wisdom &
Poetry Books

"The Lord is my shepherd, I shall not want" (Psalm 23:1). "A soft answer turns away wrath, but a harsh word stirs up anger" (Proverbs 15:1). "For everything there is a season, and a time for every matter under heaven" (Ecclesiastes 3:1). These words are taken from the wisdom and poetry books of the Old Testament. They are among the most quoted books of the Bible. Their distilled wisdom and beautiful language have universal appeal. Across cultures and time, these books touch thoughtful minds and inquiring hearts.

IN DEPTH

This section of the Bible contains a variety of books written in different literary styles. The book of Job is a debate about why innocent people suffer. Psalms consists of songs and hymns, many written for use in Jewish worship. Advice on moral and virtuous living is found in Proverbs. Ecclesiastes is a sort of journal on the purpose of human life. And the Song of Solomon is a love poem.

The most obvious common element in these books is the use of poetic language to convey their messages. These aren't the only books of the Old Testament that use poetry, but they use so much of it that a little background on the nature of Hebrew poetry is helpful for reading them.

The most important feature of Hebrew poetry is parallelism, which involves the repetition of words or ideas in successive lines of a verse. Sometimes the second line contrasts with the first:

The Lord watches over the way of the righteous,
but the way of the wicked will perish. (Psalm 1:6)

Other times, the second line completes the thought of the first:

The Lord looks down from heaven on humankind
to see if there are any who are wise, who seek after God. (Psalm 14:2)

Still other times, the second line seems to restate the first line more forcefully:

For I know my transgressions,
and my sin is ever before me. (Psalm 51:3)

Parallelism isn't a rhythmic or rhyming pattern; it's the organizing principle of Hebrew poetry. Hebrew poetry also uses symbolic language just as poetry does in any language. This includes metaphors such as, "My God, my rock in whom I take refuge" (Psalm 18:2). It also includes similes like, "As a deer longs for flowing streams, so my soul longs for you, O God" (Psalm 42:1). To appreciate the beauty of Old Testament poetry and to feel its impact, readers must be willing to wrestle with symbolic ways of interpreting words and phrases.

The other books of the Old Testament emphasize ancient Israel's distinctive religious values, but the wisdom and poetry books focus on Israel's unique view of wisdom. Other ancient cultures surrounding Israel produced wisdom literature too. The Egyptians, Sumerians, and Babylonians all had literature that offered practical, time-tested advice for people seeking trustworthy guidance. For the Israelites, however, true wisdom was more than mere common sense—it was a gift from God given to those who sought it.

In general, the wisdom writings have these characteristics:

- Few references to the law or the covenant
- A minimal interest in Israel's history
- A search for harmony and the meaning of life
- A willingness to explore the difficult mysteries of life, such as suffering and death
- A commitment to discovering the moral lessons of everyday experiences
- A fundamental belief that good and wise living is rewarded, but evil and foolish ways lead to ruin

The poetry and wisdom books of the Old Testament had an enormous influence on the writers of the New Testament and continue to be popular today. Their poetic structure, which often makes them hard to comprehend, also gives them a richness and depth that centuries of reading and rereading have not exhausted. Each time you read from these books, you will discover new treasures to enrich your life.

OTHER BACKGROUND

- The book of Psalms is quoted more often in the New Testament than any other Old Testament book.

- Job and Ecclesiastes posed serious challenges to the traditional understanding of Israelite faith. For help in understanding why, see the introductions to these books.

- Solomon's reputation for wisdom was so great that he was indicated as the author of three books actually written by others: Proverbs, Ecclesiastes, and the Song of Solomon.

Job

▶▶▶

Suffering is a harsh but unavoidable reality in our world. You've seen the images—a mother holding her starving child in a country ravaged by drought; the glazed faces of innocent victims of war and violence; the devastation from natural disasters like hurricanes and earthquakes. You also might have watched someone close to you suffer from a horrible illness or felt the grief of losing a loved one. You can't help but ask the questions: Why do innocent people suffer? How can God allow this to happen? These are the basic questions the book of Job wrestles with.

IN DEPTH

Most Israelites living at the time Job was written believed God would bless and protect them if they obeyed God's commandments. The Israelites also believed that if people were poor or suffering, God was punishing them for some sin they or their parents had committed, even if they didn't know what that sin was. The Israelites' thinking was extremely logical—they thought that because God was all-powerful and completely just, God would not allow people to suffer unless they somehow deserved it because of their sin.

The book of Job challenges that way of thinking. Job is a good man who has received great wealth and a wonderful family from God. The book begins with God's allowing Job's health and wealth and children to be taken from him. Three friends come to mourn with Job, and in a series of lengthy debates they point out that his misfortunes must be the result of some wrong he has committed. Job maintains his innocence. In fact, Job's final defense in Job 31 is one of the finest summaries of the Old Testament version of a righteous person. Job demands another explanation from God in his search for an answer. Finally, God appears and overwhelms Job with questions about the nature of the universe. Job realizes that God is beyond human knowledge and that some mysteries—including suffering—can never be completely understood; they can only be accepted.

The book of Job doesn't give the final answer about why bad things happen to good people. But it does make it clear that good people do suffer and that their suffering is not a punishment sent by God. Job is a reminder to the Israelites and to us that God's purposes are far beyond our human understanding.

QUICK FACTS

● **Date Written:** Between 600 and 400 B.C.

◢ **Author:** Unknown

◗ **Theme:** The question of why good people suffer—both in biblical times and in ours

● **Noteworthy:** Job is a story within a story: Job 1-2 and 42:7-17 tell the main story; Job 3:1-42:6 is a poetic debate about the causes of suffering set within the story.

AT A GLANCE

● **Job 1-2** God and Satan's agreement to test Job

◢ **Job 3-37** Job and his friends' debate on the cause of his suffering

◗ **Job 38:1-42:6** God's response to Job

◗ **Job 42:7-17** God's blessing of Job

Job and His Family

1 There was once a man in the land of Uz whose name was Job. That man was blameless and upright, one who feared God and turned away from evil. [2] There were born to him seven sons and three daughters. [3] He had seven thousand sheep, three thousand camels, five hundred yoke of oxen, five hundred donkeys, and very many servants; so that this man was the greatest of all the people of the east. [4] His sons used to go and hold feasts in one another's houses in turn; and they would send and invite their three sisters to eat and drink with them. [5] And when the feast days had run their course, Job would send and sanctify them, and he would rise early in the morning and offer burnt offerings according to the number of them all; for Job said, "It may be that my children have sinned, and cursed God in their hearts." This is what Job always did.

Attack on Job's Character

[6] One day the heavenly beings[a] came to present themselves before the LORD, and Satan[b] also came among them. [7] The LORD said to Satan,[b] "Where have you come from?" Satan[b] answered the LORD, "From going to and fro on the earth, and from walking up and down on it." [8] The LORD said to Satan,[b] "Have you considered my servant Job? There is no one like him on the earth, a blameless and upright man who fears God and turns away from evil." [9] Then Satan[b] answered the LORD, "Does Job fear God for nothing? [10] Have you not put a fence around him and his house and all that he has, on every side? You have blessed the work of his hands, and his possessions have increased in the land. [11] But stretch out your hand now, and touch all that he has, and he will curse you to your face." [12] The LORD said to Satan,[b] "Very well, all that he has is in your power; only do not stretch out your hand against him!" So Satan[b] went out from the presence of the LORD.

Job Loses Property and Children

[13] One day when his sons and daughters were eating and drinking wine in the eldest brother's house, [14] a messenger came to Job and said, "The oxen were plowing and the donkeys were feeding beside them, [15] and the Sabeans fell on them and carried them off, and killed the servants with the edge of the sword; I alone have escaped to tell you." [16] While he was still speaking, another came and said, "The fire of God fell from heaven and burned up the sheep and the servants, and consumed them; I alone have escaped to tell you." [17] While

STUDY IT!

Introducing . . . Job · Job 1:13–21

Have you ever felt loss so deep or anger so intense that you cursed and swore at God? Have you ever felt like just giving up on God? In **Job 1:13–19**, a man named Job experiences an unimaginable loss. His children, his home, and his property are all destroyed at the same time. Job responds with great anger and pain, but instead of cursing or blaming God, he blesses and praises God (Job 1:21).

Job never loses his faith in God, even when he loses so much else. Through most of the rest of this book, he struggles to understand why this has happened to him.

We can learn a lot from Job. When faced with great suffering, Job is real with God about his struggles, but does not lose his belief in the goodness of God. We too can face the reality of pain without losing sight of God's goodness. Job's friends try to force him into false confessions of sin, but Job refuses, firmly maintaining his claim to innocence and right living. When we know we have not sinned, we need to stand firm against the feelings of guilt that come so easily. And we need to be slow to judge others who face struggles of their own. Bad things are not necessarily punishment from God.

Although the question of suffering may haunt us, we cannot explain it. Instead, like Job, we must reach out to God, the good and compassionate healer who offers us comfort and grace in our times of distress.

---

a Heb *sons of God*   b Or *the Accuser*; Heb *ha-satan*

he was still speaking, another came and said, "The Chaldeans formed three columns, made a raid on the camels and carried them off, and killed the servants with the edge of the sword; I alone have escaped to tell you." ¹⁸While he was still speaking, another came and said, "Your sons and daughters were eating and drinking wine in their eldest brother's house, ¹⁹and suddenly a great wind came across the desert, struck the four corners of the house, and it fell on the young people, and they are dead; I alone have escaped to tell you."

20 Then Job arose, tore his robe, shaved his head, and fell on the ground and worshiped. ²¹He said, "Naked I came from my mother's womb, and naked shall I return there; the LORD gave, and the LORD has taken away; blessed be the name of the LORD."

22 In all this Job did not sin or charge God with wrongdoing.

Attack on Job's Health

2 One day the heavenly beings*ᵃ* came to present themselves before the LORD, and Satan*ᵇ* also came among them to present himself before the LORD. ²The LORD said to Satan,*ᵇ* "Where have you come from?" Satan*ᵇ* answered the LORD, "From going to and fro on the earth, and from walking up and down on it." ³The LORD said to Satan,*ᵃ* "Have you considered my servant Job? There is no one like him on the earth, a blameless and upright man who fears God and turns away from evil. He still persists in his integrity, although

CONNECT IT!

Darrell Scott: A Chain Reaction Starts with You
Job 1:20–22

Darrell Scott's life changed forever on April 20, 1999. His daughter, Rachel Scott, was the first of twelve students and one teacher killed in the terrible school shooting at Columbine High School in Littleton, Colorado. In many ways, Scott experienced the pain of Job that day with the sudden loss of his daughter. But like Job, who worshiped in the midst of his loss by saying, "The LORD gave, and the LORD has taken away; blessed be the name of the LORD" (Job 1:21), Scott chose hope in the midst of grief. With the help of others, Rachel's dad formed an organization called Rachel's Challenge, which he speaks about to more than a million students each year. Based on an essay Rachel wrote before her death, the organization challenges people to create a chain reaction of kindness and compassion in their own school or community. Rachel's essay said, "I have this theory that if one person can go out of their way to show compassion, then it will start a chain reaction of the same. People will never know how far a little kindness can go."*

STUDY IT!

Satan: The Accuser · Job 1:6–2:10

Does the name Satan conjure up an image of a demon with horns and a tail, torturing people in the fires of hell? Or perhaps an evil presence wandering the world looking for souls to corrupt? The Hebrew word "satan" is more of a job description than a name; it means "adversary." Satan is depicted in the Old Testament as a member of God's court who has the responsibility to accuse or test humans before God.

It's only much later that Satan is seen as the enemy of God and the leader of the forces of evil. The notion of Satan as an evildoer seems to have been borrowed from a similar figure in Persian religion and developed in Israel as time passed. By the New Testament period, Satan is identified as a powerful agent of evil fighting against God (1 Thessalonians 2:18), is instrumental in Jesus' death (Luke 22:3), tempts people to sin (1 Corinthians 7:5), and is called the devil (Revelation 12:9). The good news is that through the death and resurrection of Jesus, God overcomes the evil associated with Satan both now and forever.

---

a Heb *sons of God*   *b* Or *the Accuser*; Heb *ha-satan*

you incited me against him, to destroy him for no reason." [4]Then Satan[a] answered the LORD, "Skin for skin! All that people have they will give to save their lives.[b] [5]But stretch out your hand now and touch his bone and his flesh, and he will curse you to your face." [6]The LORD said to Satan,[a] "Very well, he is in your power; only spare his life."

7 So Satan[a] went out from the presence of the LORD, and inflicted loathsome sores on Job from the sole of his foot to the crown of his head. [8]Job[c] took a potsherd with which to scrape himself, and sat among the ashes.

9 Then his wife said to him, "Do you still persist in your integrity? Curse[d] God, and die." [10]But he said to her, "You speak as any foolish woman would speak. Shall we receive the good at the hand of God, and not receive the bad?" In all this Job did not sin with his lips.

Job's Three Friends

11 Now when Job's three friends heard of all these troubles that had come upon him, each of them set out from his home—Eliphaz the Temanite, Bildad the Shuhite, and Zophar the Naamathite. They met together to go and console and comfort him. [12]When they saw him from a distance, they did not recognize him, and they raised their voices and wept aloud; they tore their robes and threw dust in the air upon their heads. [13]They sat with him on the ground seven days and seven nights, and no one spoke a word to him, for they saw that his suffering was very great.

Being There
Job 2:11–13

Most of us steer clear of hospitals and funerals as much as possible. They're all about realities we don't like to face. We often feel awkward and don't know what to do or say. Even when our intentions are good, it's tough to know how to respond to someone else's suffering.

After his loss, Job was visited by three friends. They didn't recognize him at first because of his great suffering. Then they cried. And then something remarkable happened: "They sat with him on the ground seven days and seven nights, and no one spoke a word to him, for they saw that his suffering was very great" (Job 2:13).

Although Job's friends get a bad reputation for their assumptions and words later in the story, they deserve credit for their initial actions. They were there, spent time with Job, and let him know they cared. That's all we have to do for a friend who is hurting—offer a hug and a simple "I'm sorry," and then just be there to listen. It sounds easy, but it can be very hard. We can feel so helpless or awkward. But what matters most is that we're there for a friend. That's what he or she will remember.

If you know people are hurting or grieving, don't avoid them. Go to them, let them know how you feel, and just be there for them. That's all. And that's a lot.

3

Job Curses the Day He Was Born

After this Job opened his mouth and cursed the day of his birth. [2]Job said:

3 "Let the day perish in which I was born,
    and the night that said,
    'A man-child is conceived.'
4 Let that day be darkness!
    May God above not seek it,
    or light shine on it.
5 Let gloom and deep darkness claim it.
    Let clouds settle upon it;
    let the blackness of the day terrify it.
6 That night—let thick darkness seize it!
    let it not rejoice among the days of the
        year;
    let it not come into the number of the
        months.
7 Yes, let that night be barren;
    let no joyful cry be heard[e] in it.
8 Let those curse it who curse the Sea,[f]
    those who are skilled to rouse up
        Leviathan.
9 Let the stars of its dawn be dark;
    let it hope for light, but have none;
    may it not see the eyelids of the
        morning—

---

a Or the Accuser; Heb ha-satan   b Or All that the man has he will give for his life   c Heb He   d Heb Bless   e Heb come   f Cn: Heb day

10 because it did not shut the doors of my
        mother's womb,
    and hide trouble from my eyes.

11 "Why did I not die at birth,
    come forth from the womb and expire?
12 Why were there knees to receive me,
    or breasts for me to suck?
13 Now I would be lying down and quiet;
    I would be asleep; then I would be at rest
14 with kings and counselors of the earth
    who rebuild ruins for themselves,
15 or with princes who have gold,
    who fill their houses with silver.
16 Or why was I not buried like a stillborn
        child,
    like an infant that never sees the light?
17 There the wicked cease from troubling,
    and there the weary are at rest.
18 There the prisoners are at ease together;
    they do not hear the voice of the
        taskmaster.
19 The small and the great are there,
    and the slaves are free from their masters.

20 "Why is light given to one in misery,
    and life to the bitter in soul,
21 who long for death, but it does not come,
    and dig for it more than for hidden
        treasures;
22 who rejoice exceedingly,
    and are glad when they find the grave?
23 Why is light given to one who cannot see
        the way,
    whom God has fenced in?
24 For my sighing comes like[a] my bread,
    and my groanings are poured out like
        water.
25 Truly the thing that I fear comes upon me,
    and what I dread befalls me.
26 I am not at ease, nor am I quiet;
    I have no rest; but trouble comes."

Eliphaz Speaks: Job Has Sinned

4 Then Eliphaz the Temanite answered:
2 "If one ventures a word with you, will
        you be offended?
    But who can keep from speaking?
3 See, you have instructed many;
    you have strengthened the weak hands.

4 Your words have supported those who were
        stumbling,
    and you have made firm the feeble knees.
5 But now it has come to you, and you are
        impatient;
    it touches you, and you are
        dismayed.
6 Is not your fear of God your confidence,
    and the integrity of your ways your hope?

7 "Think now, who that was innocent ever
        perished?
    Or where were the upright cut off?
8 As I have seen, those who plow iniquity
    and sow trouble reap the same.
9 By the breath of God they perish,
    and by the blast of his anger they are
        consumed.
10 The roar of the lion, the voice of the fierce
        lion,
    and the teeth of the young lions are
        broken.
11 The strong lion perishes for lack of prey,
    and the whelps of the lioness are scattered.

12 "Now a word came stealing to me,
    my ear received the whisper of it.
13 Amid thoughts from visions of the night,
    when deep sleep falls on mortals,
14 dread came upon me, and trembling,
    which made all my bones shake.
15 A spirit glided past my face;
    the hair of my flesh bristled.
16 It stood still,
    but I could not discern its appearance.
    A form was before my eyes;
    there was silence, then I heard a voice:
17 'Can mortals be righteous before[b] God?
    Can human beings be pure before[b] their
        Maker?
18 Even in his servants he puts no trust,
    and his angels he charges with error;
19 how much more those who live in houses of
        clay,
    whose foundation is in the dust,
    who are crushed like a moth.
20 Between morning and evening they are
        destroyed;
    they perish forever without any
        regarding it.

a Heb *before* b Or *more than*

²¹ Their tent-cord is plucked up within them,
  and they die devoid of wisdom.'

Job Is Corrected by God

5 "Call now; is there anyone who will
  answer you?
To which of the holy ones will you turn?
² Surely vexation kills the fool,
  and jealousy slays the simple.
³ I have seen fools taking root,
  but suddenly I cursed their dwelling.
⁴ Their children are far from safety,
  they are crushed in the gate,
  and there is no one to deliver them.
⁵ The hungry eat their harvest,
  and they take it even out of the thorns;^a
  and the thirsty^b pant after their wealth.
⁶ For misery does not come from the earth,
  nor does trouble sprout from the ground;
⁷ but human beings are born to trouble
  just as sparks^c fly upward.

⁸ "As for me, I would seek God,
  and to God I would commit my cause.
⁹ He does great things and unsearchable,
  marvelous things without number.
¹⁰ He gives rain on the earth
  and sends waters on the fields;
¹¹ he sets on high those who are lowly,
  and those who mourn are lifted to safety.
¹² He frustrates the devices of the crafty,
  so that their hands achieve no success.
¹³ He takes the wise in their own craftiness;
  and the schemes of the wily are brought
    to a quick end.
¹⁴ They meet with darkness in the daytime,
  and grope at noonday as in the night.
¹⁵ But he saves the needy from the sword of
    their mouth,

from the hand of the mighty.
¹⁶ So the poor have hope,
  and injustice shuts its mouth.

¹⁷ "How happy is the one whom God reproves;
  therefore do not despise the discipline of
    the Almighty.^d
¹⁸ For he wounds, but he binds up;
  he strikes, but his hands heal.
¹⁹ He will deliver you from six troubles;
  in seven no harm shall touch you.
²⁰ In famine he will redeem you from death,
  and in war from the power of the sword.
²¹ You shall be hidden from the scourge of the
    tongue,
  and shall not fear destruction when it
    comes.
²² At destruction and famine you shall laugh,
  and shall not fear the wild animals of the
    earth.
²³ For you shall be in league with the stones of
    the field,
  and the wild animals shall be at peace
    with you.
²⁴ You shall know that your tent is safe,
  you shall inspect your fold and miss
    nothing.
²⁵ You shall know that your descendants will be
    many,
  and your offspring like the grass of the
    earth.
²⁶ You shall come to your grave in ripe old age,
  as a shock of grain comes up to the
    threshing floor in its season.
²⁷ See, we have searched this out; it is true.
  Hear, and know it for yourself."

Job Replies: My Complaint Is Just

6 Then Job answered:
² "O that my vexation were weighed,
  and all my calamity laid in the balances!
³ For then it would be heavier than the sand of
    the sea;
  therefore my words have been rash.
⁴ For the arrows of the Almighty^d are
    in me;
  my spirit drinks their poison;
  the terrors of God are arrayed against me.
⁵ Does the wild ass bray over its grass,
  or the ox low over its fodder?

---

a Meaning of Heb uncertain   *b* Aquila Symmachus Syr Vg: Heb *snare*   *c* Or *birds*; Heb *sons of Resheph*   *d* Traditional rendering of Heb *Shaddai*

6 Can that which is tasteless be eaten without
salt,
or is there any flavor in the juice of
mallows?*a*

7 My appetite refuses to touch them;
they are like food that is loathsome
to me.*a*

8 "O that I might have my request,
and that God would grant my desire;

9 that it would please God to crush me,
that he would let loose his hand and cut
me off!

10 This would be my consolation;
I would even exult*a* in unrelenting pain;
for I have not denied the words of the
Holy One.

11 What is my strength, that I should wait?
And what is my end, that I should be
patient?

12 Is my strength the strength of stones,
or is my flesh bronze?

13 In truth I have no help in me,
and any resource is driven from me.

14 "Those who withhold*b* kindness from a friend
forsake the fear of the Almighty.*c*

15 My companions are treacherous like a
torrent-bed,
like freshets that pass away,

16 that run dark with ice,
turbid with melting snow.

17 In time of heat they disappear;
when it is hot, they vanish from their
place.

18 The caravans turn aside from their course;
they go up into the waste, and perish.

19 The caravans of Tema look,
the travelers of Sheba hope.

20 They are disappointed because they were
confident;
they come there and are confounded.

21 Such you have now become to me;*d*
you see my calamity, and are afraid.

22 Have I said, 'Make me a gift'?
Or, 'From your wealth offer a bribe
for me'?

23 Or, 'Save me from an opponent's hand'?
Or, 'Ransom me from the hand of
oppressors'?

24 "Teach me, and I will be silent;
make me understand how I have gone
wrong.

25 How forceful are honest words!
But your reproof, what does it reprove?

26 Do you think that you can reprove words,
as if the speech of the desperate were
wind?

27 You would even cast lots over the orphan,
and bargain over your friend.

28 "But now, be pleased to look at me;
for I will not lie to your face.

29 Turn, I pray, let no wrong be done.
Turn now, my vindication is at stake.

30 Is there any wrong on my tongue?
Cannot my taste discern calamity?

Job: My Suffering Is without End

7 "Do not human beings have a hard
service on earth,
and are not their days like the days of a
laborer?

2 Like a slave who longs for the shadow,
and like laborers who look for their
wages,

3 so I am allotted months of emptiness,
and nights of misery are apportioned
to me.

4 When I lie down I say, 'When shall I rise?'
But the night is long,
and I am full of tossing until dawn.

5 My flesh is clothed with worms and dirt;
my skin hardens, then breaks out again.

6 My days are swifter than a weaver's shuttle,
and come to their end without hope.*e*

7 "Remember that my life is a breath;
my eye will never again see good.

8 The eye that beholds me will see me no
more;
while your eyes are upon me, I shall be
gone.

9 As the cloud fades and vanishes,
so those who go down to Sheol do not
come up;

10 they return no more to their houses,
nor do their places know them any more.

11 "Therefore I will not restrain my mouth;

---

a Meaning of Heb uncertain　*b* Syr Vg Compare Tg: Meaning of Heb uncertain　*c* Traditional rendering of Heb *Shaddai*　*d* Cn Compare Gk Syr:
Meaning of Heb uncertain　*e* Or *as the thread runs out*

Be Honest · Job 7:1–21

Job's words in **Job 7** are almost a prayer describing his suffering and asking, "Why me?" Job isn't worried about being polite; he says it like it is. What can you learn from Job about prayer during suffering?

First, you need to be honest with God and yourself. If you are hurt or in pain, don't play games with God. Tell God what you're feeling in your own words. Write it down in a journal if that helps. And be honest. If you aren't honest with God, you probably aren't being honest with yourself.

Second, let all your feelings out, just as Job did—including your anger. God is big enough to handle it. When you suppress your negative feelings, they may come out in unhealthy ways. Let God help you deal with them instead.

Third, let your prayer lead you to some action. Job debated with his friends. You might need to talk with others, such as a friend, youth pastor, counselor, or parent, to help you process your pain.

Finally, allow the depth of your pain to push you deeper into God's grace. Job worshiped God in the midst of accusations and pain (Job 19:25). Cling tightly to God's promises and character, even as you face questions and doubt.

God, I trust that you know what's on my mind anyway, so here goes. . . . I don't understand. Why did it have to happen? Why does it hurt so bad and seem so unfair? Why didn't you stop it? Please help me to understand and trust you, and please help me to feel your love and peace even more strongly than my pain.

I will speak in the anguish of my spirit;
    I will complain in the bitterness of my
        soul.
12 Am I the Sea, or the Dragon,
    that you set a guard over me?
13 When I say, 'My bed will comfort me,
    my couch will ease my complaint,'
14 then you scare me with dreams
    and terrify me with visions,
15 so that I would choose strangling
    and death rather than this body.
16 I loathe my life; I would not live forever.
    Let me alone, for my days are a breath.
17 What are human beings, that you make so
        much of them,
    that you set your mind on them,
18 visit them every morning,
    test them every moment?
19 Will you not look away from me for a while,
    let me alone until I swallow my spittle?
20 If I sin, what do I do to you, you watcher of
        humanity?
    Why have you made me your target?
    Why have I become a burden to you?

21 Why do you not pardon my transgression
    and take away my iniquity?
    For now I shall lie in the earth;
    you will seek me, but I shall not be."

8   Bildad Speaks: Job Should Repent

Then Bildad the Shuhite answered:
2 "How long will you say these things,
    and the words of your mouth be a great
        wind?
3 Does God pervert justice?
    Or does the Almighty[a] pervert the right?
4 If your children sinned against him,
    he delivered them into the power of their
        transgression.
5 If you will seek God
    and make supplication to the Almighty,[a]
6 if you are pure and upright,
    surely then he will rouse himself for you
    and restore to you your rightful place.
7 Though your beginning was small,
    your latter days will be very great.

8 "For inquire now of bygone generations,

---

a Traditional rendering of Heb *Shaddai*

and consider what their ancestors have
found;

9 for we are but of yesterday, and we know
nothing,
for our days on earth are but a shadow.

10 Will they not teach you and tell you
and utter words out of their
understanding?

11 "Can papyrus grow where there is no marsh?
Can reeds flourish where there is no water?

12 While yet in flower and not cut down,
they wither before any other plant.

13 Such are the paths of all who forget God;
the hope of the godless shall perish.

14 Their confidence is gossamer,
a spider's house their trust.

15 If one leans against its house, it will not stand;
if one lays hold of it, it will not endure.

16 The wicked thrive*a* before the sun,
and their shoots spread over the garden.

17 Their roots twine around the stoneheap;
they live among the rocks.*b*

18 If they are destroyed from their place,
then it will deny them, saying, 'I have never
seen you.'

19 See, these are their happy ways,*c*
and out of the earth still others will spring.

20 "See, God will not reject a blameless person,
nor take the hand of evildoers.

21 He will yet fill your mouth with laughter,
and your lips with shouts of joy.

22 Those who hate you will be clothed with
shame,
and the tent of the wicked will be no
more."

Job Replies: There Is No Mediator

9 Then Job answered:
2 "Indeed I know that this is so;
but how can a mortal be just before God?

3 If one wished to contend with him,
one could not answer him once in a
thousand.

4 He is wise in heart, and mighty in strength
—who has resisted him, and succeeded?—

5 he who removes mountains, and they do not
know it,
when he overturns them in his anger;

6 who shakes the earth out of its place,
and its pillars tremble;

7 who commands the sun, and it does not rise;
who seals up the stars;

8 who alone stretched out the heavens
and trampled the waves of the Sea;*d*

9 who made the Bear and Orion,
the Pleiades and the chambers of the
south;

10 who does great things beyond understanding,
and marvelous things without number.

11 Look, he passes by me, and I do not see him;
he moves on, but I do not perceive him.

12 He snatches away; who can stop him?
Who will say to him, 'What are you
doing?'

13 "God will not turn back his anger;
the helpers of Rahab bowed beneath him.

14 How then can I answer him,
choosing my words with him?

15 Though I am innocent, I cannot answer him;
I must appeal for mercy to my accuser.*e*

16 If I summoned him and he answered me,
I do not believe that he would listen to my
voice.

17 For he crushes me with a tempest,
and multiplies my wounds without cause;

18 he will not let me get my breath,
but fills me with bitterness.

19 If it is a contest of strength, he is the
strong one!
If it is a matter of justice, who can summon
him?*f*

20 Though I am innocent, my own mouth would
condemn me;
though I am blameless, he would prove me
perverse.

21 I am blameless; I do not know myself;
I loathe my life.

22 It is all one; therefore I say,
he destroys both the blameless and the
wicked.

23 When disaster brings sudden death,
he mocks at the calamity*c* of the innocent.

24 The earth is given into the hand of the wicked;
he covers the eyes of its judges—
if it is not he, who then is it?

25 "My days are swifter than a runner;

---

a Heb *He thrives*   b Gk Vg: Meaning of Heb uncertain   c Meaning of Heb uncertain   d Or *trampled the back of the sea dragon*   e Or *for my right*
f Compare Gk: Heb *me*

they flee away, they see no good.
26 They go by like skiffs of reed,
    like an eagle swooping on the prey.
27 If I say, 'I will forget my complaint;
    I will put off my sad countenance and be of
        good cheer,'
28 I become afraid of all my suffering,
    for I know you will not hold me innocent.
29 I shall be condemned;
    why then do I labor in vain?
30 If I wash myself with soap
    and cleanse my hands with lye,
31 yet you will plunge me into filth,
    and my own clothes will abhor me.
32 For he is not a mortal, as I am, that I might
        answer him,
    that we should come to trial together.
33 There is no umpire^a between us,
    who might lay his hand on us both.
34 If he would take his rod away from me,
    and not let dread of him terrify me,
35 then I would speak without fear of him,
    for I know I am not what I am thought
        to be.^{b}

10 Job: I Loathe My Life

"I loathe my life;
    I will give free utterance to my
        complaint;
    I will speak in the bitterness of my soul.
2 I will say to God, Do not condemn me;
    let me know why you contend against me.
3 Does it seem good to you to oppress,
    to despise the work of your hands
    and favor the schemes of the wicked?
4 Do you have eyes of flesh?
    Do you see as humans see?
5 Are your days like the days of mortals,
    or your years like human years,
6 that you seek out my iniquity
    and search for my sin,
7 although you know that I am not guilty,
    and there is no one to deliver out of your
        hand?
8 Your hands fashioned and made me;
    and now you turn and destroy me.^{c}
9 Remember that you fashioned me like clay;
    and will you turn me to dust again?
10 Did you not pour me out like milk
    and curdle me like cheese?

> "You have granted me
> life and steadfast love,
> and your care has
> preserved my spirit."
> —Job 10:12

11 You clothed me with skin and flesh,
    and knit me together with bones and
        sinews.
12 You have granted me life and steadfast love,
    and your care has preserved my spirit.
13 Yet these things you hid in your heart;
    I know that this was your purpose.
14 If I sin, you watch me,
    and do not acquit me of my iniquity.
15 If I am wicked, woe to me!
    If I am righteous, I cannot lift up my head,
for I am filled with disgrace
    and look upon my affliction.
16 Bold as a lion you hunt me;
    you repeat your exploits against me.
17 You renew your witnesses against me,
    and increase your vexation toward me;
    you bring fresh troops against me.^{d}

18 "Why did you bring me forth from the womb?
    Would that I had died before any eye had
        seen me,
19 and were as though I had not been,
    carried from the womb to the grave.
20 Are not the days of my life few?^{e}
    Let me alone, that I may find a little
        comfort^f
21 before I go, never to return,
    to the land of gloom and deep darkness,
22 the land of gloom^g and chaos,
    where light is like darkness."

11 Zophar Speaks: Job's Guilt Deserves Punishment

Then Zophar the Naamathite answered:
2 "Should a multitude of words go unanswered,
    and should one full of talk be vindicated?
3 Should your babble put others to silence,
    and when you mock, shall no one
        shame you?
4 For you say, 'My conduct^h is pure,

a Another reading is *Would that there were an umpire*   b Cn: Heb *for I am not so in myself*   c Cn Compare Gk Syr: Heb *made me together all around, and you destroy me*   d Cn Compare Gk: Heb *toward me; changes and a troop are with me*   e Cn Compare Gk Syr: Heb *Are not my days few? Let him cease!*
f Heb *that I may brighten up a little*   g Heb *gloom as darkness, deep darkness*   h Gk: Heb *teaching*

and I am clean in God's[a] sight.'
5 But O that God would speak,
and open his lips to you,
6 and that he would tell you the secrets of
wisdom!
For wisdom is many-sided.[b]
Know then that God exacts of you less than
your guilt deserves.

7 "Can you find out the deep things of God?
Can you find out the limit of the
Almighty?[c]
8 It is higher than heaven[d]—what can you do?
Deeper than Sheol—what can you know?
9 Its measure is longer than the earth,
and broader than the sea.
10 If he passes through, and imprisons,
and assembles for judgment, who can
hinder him?
11 For he knows those who are worthless;
when he sees iniquity, will he not
consider it?
12 But a stupid person will get understanding,
when a wild ass is born human.[b]

13 "If you direct your heart rightly,
you will stretch out your hands
toward him.
14 If iniquity is in your hand, put it far away,
and do not let wickedness reside in your
tents.
15 Surely then you will lift up your face without
blemish;
you will be secure, and will not fear.
16 You will forget your misery;
you will remember it as waters that have
passed away.
17 And your life will be brighter than the
noonday;
its darkness will be like the morning.
18 And you will have confidence, because there is
hope;
you will be protected[e] and take your rest in
safety.
19 You will lie down, and no one will make you
afraid;
many will entreat your favor.
20 But the eyes of the wicked will fail;
all way of escape will be lost to them,
and their hope is to breathe their last."

Job Replies: I Am a Laughingstock

12 Then Job answered:
2 "No doubt you are the people,
and wisdom will die with you.
3 But I have understanding as well as you;
I am not inferior to you.
Who does not know such things as these?
4 I am a laughingstock to my friends;
I, who called upon God and he
answered me,
a just and blameless man, I am a
laughingstock.
5 Those at ease have contempt for misfortune,[b]
but it is ready for those whose feet are
unstable.
6 The tents of robbers are at peace,
and those who provoke God are secure,
who bring their god in their hands.[f]

7 "But ask the animals, and they will teach you;
the birds of the air, and they will tell you;
8 ask the plants of the earth,[g] and they will
teach you;
and the fish of the sea will declare to you.
9 Who among all these does not know
that the hand of the LORD has done this?
10 In his hand is the life of every living thing
and the breath of every human being.
11 Does not the ear test words
as the palate tastes food?
12 Is wisdom with the aged,
and understanding in length of days?

13 "With God[h] are wisdom and strength;
he has counsel and understanding.
14 If he tears down, no one can rebuild;
if he shuts someone in, no one can
open up.
15 If he withholds the waters, they dry up;
if he sends them out, they overwhelm the
land.
16 With him are strength and wisdom;
the deceived and the deceiver are his.
17 He leads counselors away stripped,
and makes fools of judges.
18 He looses the sash of kings,
and binds a waistcloth on their
loins.
19 He leads priests away stripped,
and overthrows the mighty.

---

a Heb *your* b Meaning of Heb uncertain c Traditional rendering of Heb *Shaddai* d Heb *The heights of heaven* e Or *you will look around* f Or *whom God brought forth by his hand*; Meaning of Heb uncertain g Or *speak to the earth* h Heb *him*

20 He deprives of speech those who are trusted,
　　and takes away the discernment of the
　　　elders.
21 He pours contempt on princes,
　　and looses the belt of the strong.
22 He uncovers the deeps out of darkness,
　　and brings deep darkness to light.
23 He makes nations great, then destroys them;
　　he enlarges nations, then leads them away.
24 He strips understanding from the leaders[a] of
　　　the earth,
　　and makes them wander in a pathless
　　　waste.
25 They grope in the dark without light;
　　he makes them stagger like a drunkard.

13 "Look, my eye has seen all this,
　　my ear has heard and
　　　understood it.
2 What you know, I also know;
　　I am not inferior to you.
3 But I would speak to the Almighty,[b]
　　and I desire to argue my case with God.
4 As for you, you whitewash with lies;
　　all of you are worthless physicians.
5 If you would only keep silent,
　　that would be your wisdom!
6 Hear now my reasoning,
　　and listen to the pleadings of my lips.
7 Will you speak falsely for God,
　　and speak deceitfully for him?
8 Will you show partiality toward him,
　　will you plead the case for God?
9 Will it be well with you when he searches
　　　you out?
　　Or can you deceive him, as one person
　　　deceives another?
10 He will surely rebuke you
　　if in secret you show partiality.
11 Will not his majesty terrify you,
　　and the dread of him fall upon you?
12 Your maxims are proverbs of ashes,
　　your defenses are defenses of clay.
13 "Let me have silence, and I will speak,
　　and let come on me what may.
14 I will take my flesh in my teeth,
　　and put my life in my hand.[c]
15 See, he will kill me; I have no hope;[d]
　　but I will defend my ways to his face.

16 This will be my salvation,
　　that the godless shall not come
　　　before him.
17 Listen carefully to my words,
　　and let my declaration be in your ears.
18 I have indeed prepared my case;
　　I know that I shall be vindicated.
19 Who is there that will contend with me?
　　For then I would be silent and die.

Job's Despondent Prayer

20 Only grant two things to me,
　　then I will not hide myself from your face:
21 withdraw your hand far from me,
　　and do not let dread of you terrify me.
22 Then call, and I will answer;
　　or let me speak, and you reply to me.
23 How many are my iniquities and my sins?
　　Make me know my transgression and
　　　my sin.
24 Why do you hide your face,
　　and count me as your enemy?
25 Will you frighten a windblown leaf
　　and pursue dry chaff?
26 For you write bitter things against me,
　　and make me reap[e] the iniquities of my
　　　youth.
27 You put my feet in the stocks,
　　and watch all my paths;
　　you set a bound to the soles of my feet.
28 One wastes away like a rotten thing,
　　like a garment that is moth-eaten.

14 "A mortal, born of woman, few of days
　　　and full of trouble,
　　2comes up like a flower and withers,
　　flees like a shadow and does not last.
3 Do you fix your eyes on such a one?
　　Do you bring me into judgment with you?
4 Who can bring a clean thing out of an
　　　unclean?
　　No one can.
5 Since their days are determined,
　　and the number of their months is known
　　　to you,
　　and you have appointed the bounds that
　　　they cannot pass,
6 look away from them, and desist,[f]
　　that they may enjoy, like laborers, their
　　　days.

---

a Heb adds *of the people* b Traditional rendering of Heb *Shaddai* c Gk: Heb *Why should I take . . . in my hand?* d Or *Though he kill me, yet I will trust in him* e Heb *inherit* f Cn: Heb *that they may desist*

7 "For there is hope for a tree,
   if it is cut down, that it will sprout again,
   and that its shoots will not cease.
8 Though its root grows old in the earth,
   and its stump dies in the ground,
9 yet at the scent of water it will bud
   and put forth branches like a young plant.
10 But mortals die, and are laid low;
    humans expire, and where are they?
11 As waters fail from a lake,
    and a river wastes away and dries up,
12 so mortals lie down and do not rise again;
    until the heavens are no more, they will
       not awake
    or be roused out of their sleep.
13 O that you would hide me in Sheol,
    that you would conceal me until your
       wrath is past,
    that you would appoint me a set time, and
       remember me!
14 If mortals die, will they live again?
    All the days of my service I would wait
    until my release should come.
15 You would call, and I would answer you;
    you would long for the work of your hands.
16 For then you would not[a] number my steps,
    you would not keep watch over my sin;
17 my transgression would be sealed up in a bag,
    and you would cover over my iniquity.

18 "But the mountain falls and crumbles away,
    and the rock is removed from its place;
19 the waters wear away the stones;
    the torrents wash away the soil of the
       earth;
    so you destroy the hope of mortals.
20 You prevail forever against them, and they pass
       away;
    you change their countenance, and send
       them away.
21 Their children come to honor, and they do not
       know it;
    they are brought low, and it goes
       unnoticed.
22 They feel only the pain of their own bodies,
    and mourn only for themselves."

15 **Eliphaz Speaks: Job Undermines Religion**
    Then Eliphaz the Temanite answered:

2 "Should the wise answer with windy
       knowledge,
    and fill themselves with the east wind?
3 Should they argue in unprofitable talk,
    or in words with which they can do no
       good?
4 But you are doing away with the fear of God,
    and hindering meditation before God.
5 For your iniquity teaches your mouth,
    and you choose the tongue of the crafty.
6 Your own mouth condemns you, and not I;
    your own lips testify against you.

7 "Are you the firstborn of the human race?
    Were you brought forth before the hills?
8 Have you listened in the council of God?
    And do you limit wisdom to yourself?
9 What do you know that we do not know?
    What do you understand that is not clear
       to us?
10 The gray-haired and the aged are on our side,
    those older than your father.
11 Are the consolations of God too small for you,
    or the word that deals gently with you?
12 Why does your heart carry you away,
    and why do your eyes flash,[b]
13 so that you turn your spirit against God,
    and let such words go out of your mouth?
14 What are mortals, that they can be clean?
    Or those born of woman, that they can be
       righteous?
15 God puts no trust even in his holy ones,
    and the heavens are not clean in his sight;
16 how much less one who is abominable and
       corrupt,
    one who drinks iniquity like water!

17 "I will show you; listen to me;
    what I have seen I will declare—
18 what sages have told,
    and their ancestors have not hidden,
19 to whom alone the land was given,
    and no stranger passed among them.
20 The wicked writhe in pain all their days,
    through all the years that are laid up for the
       ruthless.
21 Terrifying sounds are in their ears;
    in prosperity the destroyer will come upon
       them.
22 They despair of returning from darkness,

a Syr: Heb lacks *not*   b Meaning of Heb uncertain

and they are destined for the sword.

23 They wander abroad for bread, saying, 'Where
      is it?'
   They know that a day of darkness is ready
      at hand;

24 distress and anguish terrify them;
   they prevail against them, like a king
      prepared for battle.

25 Because they stretched out their hands
      against God,
   and bid defiance to the Almighty,*a*

26 running stubbornly against him
   with a thick-bossed shield;

27 because they have covered their faces with
      their fat,
   and gathered fat upon their loins,

28 they will live in desolate cities,
   in houses that no one should inhabit,
   houses destined to become heaps of ruins;

29 they will not be rich, and their wealth will not
      endure,
   nor will they strike root in the earth;*b*

30 they will not escape from darkness;
   the flame will dry up their shoots,
   and their blossom*c* will be swept away*d* by
      the wind.

31 Let them not trust in emptiness, deceiving
      themselves;
   for emptiness will be their recompense.

32 It will be paid in full before their time,
   and their branch will not be green.

33 They will shake off their unripe grape, like the
      vine,
   and cast off their blossoms, like the olive
      tree.

34 For the company of the godless is barren,
   and fire consumes the tents of bribery.

35 They conceive mischief and bring forth evil
   and their heart prepares deceit."

Job Reaffirms His Innocence

16 Then Job answered:
   2 "I have heard many such things;
   miserable comforters are you all.

3 Have windy words no limit?
   Or what provokes you that you keep on
      talking?

4 I also could talk as you do,
   if you were in my place;
   I could join words together against you,

and shake my head at you.

5 I could encourage you with my mouth,
   and the solace of my lips would assuage
      your pain.

6 "If I speak, my pain is not assuaged,
   and if I forbear, how much of it leaves me?

7 Surely now God has worn me out;
   he has*e* made desolate all my company.

8 And he has*e* shriveled me up,
   which is a witness against me;
   my leanness has risen up against me,
   and it testifies to my face.

9 He has torn me in his wrath, and hated me;
   he has gnashed his teeth at me;
   my adversary sharpens his eyes
      against me.

10 They have gaped at me with their mouths;
   they have struck me insolently on the
      cheek;
   they mass themselves together against me.

11 God gives me up to the ungodly,
   and casts me into the hands of the
      wicked.

12 I was at ease, and he broke me in two;
   he seized me by the neck and dashed me
      to pieces;
   he set me up as his target;

13   his archers surround me.
   He slashes open my kidneys, and shows no
      mercy;
   he pours out my gall on the ground.

14 He bursts upon me again and again;
   he rushes at me like a warrior.

15 I have sewed sackcloth upon my skin,
   and have laid my strength in the dust.

16 My face is red with weeping,
   and deep darkness is on my eyelids,

17 though there is no violence in my hands,
   and my prayer is pure.

18 "O earth, do not cover my blood;
   let my outcry find no resting place.

19 Even now, in fact, my witness is in heaven,
   and he that vouches for me is on high.

20 My friends scorn me;
   my eye pours out tears to God,

21 that he would maintain the right of a mortal
      with God,
   as*f* one does for a neighbor.

---

a Traditional rendering of Heb *Shaddai* *b* Vg: Meaning of Heb uncertain *c* Gk: Heb *mouth* *d* Cn: Heb *will depart* *e* Heb *you have* *f* Syr Vg Tg: Heb *and*

22 For when a few years have come,
   I shall go the way from which I shall not
     return.

17 Job Prays for Relief

My spirit is broken, my days are extinct,
   the grave is ready for me.
2 Surely there are mockers around me,
   and my eye dwells on their provocation.

3 "Lay down a pledge for me with yourself;
   who is there that will give surety for me?
4 Since you have closed their minds to
     understanding,
   therefore you will not let them triumph.
5 Those who denounce friends for reward—
   the eyes of their children will fail.

6 "He has made me a byword of the peoples,
   and I am one before whom people spit.
7 My eye has grown dim from grief,
   and all my members are like a shadow.
8 The upright are appalled at this,
   and the innocent stir themselves up against
     the godless.
9 Yet the righteous hold to their way,
   and they that have clean hands grow
     stronger and stronger.
10 But you, come back now, all of you,
   and I shall not find a sensible person
     among you.
11 My days are past, my plans are broken off,
   the desires of my heart.
12 They make night into day;
   'The light,' they say, 'is near to the
     darkness.'*a*
13 If I look for Sheol as my house,
   if I spread my couch in darkness,
14 if I say to the Pit, 'You are my father,'
   and to the worm, 'My mother,' or 'My
     sister,'
15 where then is my hope?
   Who will see my hope?
16 Will it go down to the bars of Sheol?
   Shall we descend together into the dust?"

18 Bildad Speaks: God Punishes the Wicked

Then Bildad the Shuhite answered:
2 "How long will you hunt for words?

   Consider, and then we shall speak.
3 Why are we counted as cattle?
   Why are we stupid in your sight?
4 You who tear yourself in your anger—
   shall the earth be forsaken because of you,
   or the rock be removed out of its place?

5 "Surely the light of the wicked is put out,
   and the flame of their fire does not shine.
6 The light is dark in their tent,
   and the lamp above them is put out.
7 Their strong steps are shortened,
   and their own schemes throw them down.
8 For they are thrust into a net by their own feet,
   and they walk into a pitfall.
9 A trap seizes them by the heel;
   a snare lays hold of them.
10 A rope is hid for them in the ground,
   a trap for them in the path.
11 Terrors frighten them on every side,
   and chase them at their heels.
12 Their strength is consumed by hunger,*b*
   and calamity is ready for their stumbling.
13 By disease their skin is consumed,*c*
   the firstborn of Death consumes their
     limbs.
14 They are torn from the tent in which they
     trusted,
   and are brought to the king of terrors.
15 In their tents nothing remains;
   sulfur is scattered upon their habitations.
16 Their roots dry up beneath,
   and their branches wither above.
17 Their memory perishes from the earth,
   and they have no name in the street.
18 They are thrust from light into darkness,
   and driven out of the world.
19 They have no offspring or descendant among
     their people,
   and no survivor where they used to live.
20 They of the west are appalled at their fate,
   and horror seizes those of the east.
21 Surely such are the dwellings of the ungodly,
   such is the place of those who do not know
     God."

19 Job Replies: I Know That My Redeemer Lives

Then Job answered:
2 "How long will you torment me,

---

a Meaning of Heb uncertain   b Or *Disaster is hungry for them*   c Cn: Heb *It consumes the limbs of his skin* and break me in pieces with words?

3 These ten times you have cast reproach
upon me;
are you not ashamed to wrong me?

4 And even if it is true that I have erred,
my error remains with me.

5 If indeed you magnify yourselves against me,
and make my humiliation an argument
against me,

6 know then that God has put me in the wrong,
and closed his net around me.

7 Even when I cry out, 'Violence!' I am not
answered;
I call aloud, but there is no justice.

8 He has walled up my way so that I cannot pass,
and he has set darkness upon my paths.

9 He has stripped my glory from me,
and taken the crown from my head.

10 He breaks me down on every side, and I am
gone,
he has uprooted my hope like a tree.

11 He has kindled his wrath against me,
and counts me as his adversary.

12 His troops come on together;
they have thrown up siegeworks^a
against me,
and encamp around my tent.

13 "He has put my family far from me,
and my acquaintances are wholly estranged
from me.

14 My relatives and my close friends have
failed me;

15   the guests in my house have forgotten me;
my serving girls count me as a stranger;
I have become an alien in their eyes.

16 I call to my servant, but he gives me no
answer;
I must myself plead with him.

17 My breath is repulsive to my wife;
I am loathsome to my own family.

18 Even young children despise me;
when I rise, they talk against me.

19 All my intimate friends abhor me,
and those whom I loved have turned
against me.

20 My bones cling to my skin and to my flesh,
and I have escaped by the skin of my teeth.

21 Have pity on me, have pity on me, O you my
friends,

for the hand of God has touched me!

22 Why do you, like God, pursue me,
never satisfied with my flesh?

23 "O that my words were written down!
O that they were inscribed in a book!

24 O that with an iron pen and with lead
they were engraved on a rock forever!

25 For I know that my Redeemer^b lives,
and that at the last he^c will stand upon the
earth;^{d}

26 and after my skin has been thus destroyed,
then in^e my flesh I shall see God,^{f}

27 whom I shall see on my side,^{g}
and my eyes shall behold, and not another.
My heart faints within me!

28 If you say, 'How we will persecute him!'
and, 'The root of the matter is found in
him';

29 be afraid of the sword,
for wrath brings the punishment of the
sword,
so that you may know there is a judgment."

20 Zophar Speaks: Wickedness
Receives Just Retribution

Then Zophar the Naamathite answered:

2 "Pay attention! My thoughts urge me to answer,
because of the agitation within me.

3 I hear censure that insults me,
and a spirit beyond my understanding
answers me.

4 Do you not know this from of old,
ever since mortals were placed on earth,

5 that the exulting of the wicked is short,
and the joy of the godless is but for a
moment?

6 Even though they mount up high as the
heavens,
and their head reaches to the clouds,

7 they will perish forever like their own dung;
those who have seen them will say, 'Where
are they?'

8 They will fly away like a dream, and not be
found;
they will be chased away like a vision of the
night.

9 The eye that saw them will see them no more,
nor will their place behold them any
longer.

---

a Cn: Heb *their way*   b Or *Vindicator*   c Or *that he the Last*   d Heb *dust*   e Or *without*   f Meaning of Heb of this verse uncertain   g Or *for myself*

10 Their children will seek the favor of the poor,
　　and their hands will give back their wealth.
11 Their bodies, once full of youth,
　　will lie down in the dust with them.

12 "Though wickedness is sweet in their mouth,
　　though they hide it under their tongues,
13 though they are loath to let it go,
　　and hold it in their mouths,
14 yet their food is turned in their stomachs;
　　it is the venom of asps within them.
15 They swallow down riches and vomit them up
　　　again;
　　God casts them out of their bellies.
16 They will suck the poison of asps;
　　the tongue of a viper will kill them.
17 They will not look on the rivers,
　　the streams flowing with honey and curds.
18 They will give back the fruit of their toil,
　　and will not swallow it down;
　　from the profit of their trading
　　they will get no enjoyment.
19 For they have crushed and abandoned the
　　　poor,
　　they have seized a house that they did not
　　　build.

20 "They knew no quiet in their bellies;
　　in their greed they let nothing escape.
21 There was nothing left after they had eaten;
　　therefore their prosperity will not endure.
22 In full sufficiency they will be in distress;

all the force of misery will come upon
　　them.
23 To fill their belly to the full
　　God*a* will send his fierce anger into them,
　　and rain it upon them as their food.*b*
24 They will flee from an iron weapon;
　　a bronze arrow will strike them through.
25 It is drawn forth and comes out of their body,
　　and the glittering point comes out of their
　　　gall;
　　terrors come upon them.
26 Utter darkness is laid up for their treasures;
　　a fire fanned by no one will devour them;
　　what is left in their tent will be consumed.
27 The heavens will reveal their iniquity,
　　and the earth will rise up against them.
28 The possessions of their house will be carried
　　　away,
　　dragged off in the day of God's*c* wrath.
29 This is the portion of the wicked from God,
　　the heritage decreed for them by God."

21 Job Replies: The Wicked Often Go Unpunished

Then Job answered:
2 "Listen carefully to my words,
　　and let this be your consolation.
3 Bear with me, and I will speak;
　　then after I have spoken, mock on.
4 As for me, is my complaint addressed to
　　　mortals?
　　Why should I not be impatient?

STUDY IT!

Good vs. Evil: The Debate · Job 20–24

Why are Job's friends so insistent that sin and suffering are connected? Why do they go on, chapter after chapter, telling Job that his suffering is a punishment for his sins? The author of Job uses the debate of Job and his friends to contrast two positions. The position of Job's friends is that God rewards people who are good and punishes those who are wicked. If Job is suffering terribly, then Job must have sinned terribly. Job's repeated denial of sin reveals the second position, which is that sometimes innocent people suffer. This second position is harder to argue, because it leaves a huge question: Why?

Job doesn't get an answer, but God does appear to Job in an awesome show of power (Job 38-41) and reminds Job that human intelligence is too limited to comprehend the deeper mysteries of creation. God alone knows why innocent people suffer; Job must trust God's plan.

Read **Job 20–24**. This long debate about human suffering reflects the Israelites' long history of wrestling with this complex question.

a Heb *he*　b Cn: Meaning of Heb uncertain　c Heb *his*

5 Look at me, and be appalled,
   and lay your hand upon your mouth.
6 When I think of it I am dismayed,
   and shuddering seizes my flesh.
7 Why do the wicked live on,
   reach old age, and grow mighty in power?
8 Their children are established in their presence,
   and their offspring before their eyes.
9 Their houses are safe from fear,
   and no rod of God is upon them.
10 Their bull breeds without fail;
   their cow calves and never miscarries.
11 They send out their little ones like a flock,
   and their children dance around.
12 They sing to the tambourine and the lyre,
   and rejoice to the sound of the pipe.
13 They spend their days in prosperity,
   and in peace they go down to Sheol.
14 They say to God, 'Leave us alone!
   We do not desire to know your ways.
15 What is the Almighty,[a] that we should
       serve him?
   And what profit do we get if we pray
       to him?'
16 Is not their prosperity indeed their own
       achievement?[b]
   The plans of the wicked are repugnant
       to me.
17 "How often is the lamp of the wicked put out?
   How often does calamity come upon them?
   How often does God[c] distribute pains in
       his anger?
18 How often are they like straw before the wind,
   and like chaff that the storm carries away?
19 You say, 'God stores up their iniquity for their
       children.'
   Let it be paid back to them, so that they
       may know it.
20 Let their own eyes see their destruction,
   and let them drink of the wrath of the
       Almighty.[a]
21 For what do they care for their household after
       them,
   when the number of their months is
       cut off?
22 Will any teach God knowledge,
   seeing that he judges those that are on
       high?
23 One dies in full prosperity,

being wholly at ease and secure,
24 his loins full of milk
   and the marrow of his bones moist.
25 Another dies in bitterness of soul,
   never having tasted of good.
26 They lie down alike in the dust,
   and the worms cover them.

27 "Oh, I know your thoughts,
   and your schemes to wrong me.
28 For you say, 'Where is the house of the prince?
   Where is the tent in which the wicked
       lived?'
29 Have you not asked those who travel the roads,
   and do you not accept their testimony,
30 that the wicked are spared in the day of
       calamity,
   and are rescued in the day of wrath?
31 Who declares their way to their face,
   and who repays them for what they have
       done?
32 When they are carried to the grave,
   a watch is kept over their tomb.
33 The clods of the valley are sweet to them;
   everyone will follow after,
   and those who went before are
       innumerable.
34 How then will you comfort me with empty
       nothings?
   There is nothing left of your answers but
       falsehood."

22 Eliphaz Speaks: Job's Wickedness Is Great

Then Eliphaz the Temanite answered:
2 "Can a mortal be of use to God?
   Can even the wisest be of service to him?
3 Is it any pleasure to the Almighty[a] if you are
       righteous,
   or is it gain to him if you make your ways
       blameless?
4 Is it for your piety that he reproves you,

a Traditional rendering of Heb *Shaddai* b Heb *in their hand* c Heb *he*

and enters into judgment with you?

5 Is not your wickedness great?
 There is no end to your iniquities.
6 For you have exacted pledges from your family
  for no reason,
 and stripped the naked of their clothing.
7 You have given no water to the weary to drink,
 and you have withheld bread from the
  hungry.
8 The powerful possess the land,
 and the favored live in it.
9 You have sent widows away empty-handed,
 and the arms of the orphans you have
  crushed.[a]
10 Therefore snares are around you,
 and sudden terror overwhelms you,
11 or darkness so that you cannot see;
 a flood of water covers you.

12 "Is not God high in the heavens?
 See the highest stars, how lofty they are!
13 Therefore you say, 'What does God know?
 Can he judge through the deep darkness?
14 Thick clouds enwrap him, so that he does
  not see,
 and he walks on the dome of heaven.'
15 Will you keep to the old way
 that the wicked have trod?
16 They were snatched away before their time;
 their foundation was washed away by a
  flood.
17 They said to God, 'Leave us alone,'
 and 'What can the Almighty[b] do to us?'[c]
18 Yet he filled their houses with good things—
 but the plans of the wicked are repugnant
  to me.
19 The righteous see it and are glad;
 the innocent laugh them to scorn,
20 saying, 'Surely our adversaries are cut off,
 and what they left, the fire has consumed.'

21 "Agree with God,[d] and be at peace;
 in this way good will come to you.
22 Receive instruction from his mouth,
 and lay up his words in your heart.
23 If you return to the Almighty,[b] you will be
  restored,
  if you remove unrighteousness from your
   tents,
24 if you treat gold like dust,

and gold of Ophir like the stones of the
  torrent-bed,
25 and if the Almighty[b] is your gold
 and your precious silver,
26 then you will delight yourself in the
  Almighty,[b]
 and lift up your face to God.
27 You will pray to him, and he will hear you,
 and you will pay your vows.
28 You will decide on a matter, and it will be
  established for you,
 and light will shine on your ways.
29 When others are humiliated, you say it is
  pride;
 for he saves the humble.
30 He will deliver even those who are guilty;
 they will escape because of the cleanness
  of your hands."[e]

23 Job Replies: My Complaint Is Bitter

Then Job answered:
2 "Today also my complaint is bitter;[f]
 his[g] hand is heavy despite my groaning.
3 Oh, that I knew where I might find him,
 that I might come even to his dwelling!
4 I would lay my case before him,
 and fill my mouth with arguments.
5 I would learn what he would answer me,
 and understand what he would say to me.
6 Would he contend with me in the greatness of
  his power?
 No; but he would give heed to me.
7 There an upright person could reason with him,
 and I should be acquitted forever by my
  judge.

8 "If I go forward, he is not there;
 or backward, I cannot perceive him;
9 on the left he hides, and I cannot behold him;
 I turn[h] to the right, but I cannot see him.
10 But he knows the way that I take;
 when he has tested me, I shall come out like
  gold.
11 My foot has held fast to his steps;
 I have kept his way and have not turned
  aside.
12 I have not departed from the commandment of
  his lips;
 I have treasured in[i] my bosom the words of
  his mouth.

---

a Gk Syr Tg Vg: Heb *were crushed*   b Traditional rendering of Heb *Shaddai*   c Gk Syr: Heb *them*   d Heb *him*   e Meaning of Heb uncertain   f Syr Vg Tg: Heb *rebellious*   g Gk Syr: Heb *my*   h Syr Vg: Heb *he turns*   i Gk Vg: Heb *from*

13 But he stands alone and who can
      dissuade him?
    What he desires, that he does.
14 For he will complete what he appoints for me;
    and many such things are in his mind.
15 Therefore I am terrified at his presence;
    when I consider, I am in dread of him.
16 God has made my heart faint;
    the Almighty[a] has terrified me;
17 If only I could vanish in darkness,
    and thick darkness would cover my face![b]

24 Job Complains of Violence on the Earth

    "Why are times not kept by the
      Almighty,[a]
    and why do those who know him never see
      his days?
2 The wicked[c] remove landmarks;
    they seize flocks and pasture them.
3 They drive away the donkey of the orphan;
    they take the widow's ox for a pledge.
4 They thrust the needy off the road;
    the poor of the earth all hide themselves.
5 Like wild asses in the desert
    they go out to their toil,
  scavenging in the wasteland
    food for their young.
6 They reap in a field not their own
    and they glean in the vineyard of the
      wicked.
7 They lie all night naked, without clothing,
    and have no covering in the cold.
8 They are wet with the rain of the mountains,
    and cling to the rock for want of shelter.

9 "There are those who snatch the orphan child
      from the breast,
    and take as a pledge the infant of the poor.
10 They go about naked, without clothing;
    though hungry, they carry the sheaves;
11 between their terraces[d] they press out oil;
    they tread the wine presses, but suffer
      thirst.
12 From the city the dying groan,
    and the throat of the wounded cries for
      help;
    yet God pays no attention to their prayer.

13 "There are those who rebel against the light,

    who are not acquainted with its ways,
    and do not stay in its paths.
14 The murderer rises at dusk
    to kill the poor and needy,
    and in the night is like a thief.
15 The eye of the adulterer also waits for the
      twilight,
    saying, 'No eye will see me';
    and he disguises his face.
16 In the dark they dig through houses;
    by day they shut themselves up;
    they do not know the light.
17 For deep darkness is morning to all of them;
    for they are friends with the terrors of
      deep darkness.

18 "Swift are they on the face of the waters;
    their portion in the land is cursed;
    no treader turns toward their vineyards.
19 Drought and heat snatch away the snow
      waters;
    so does Sheol those who have sinned.
20 The womb forgets them;
    the worm finds them sweet;
  they are no longer remembered;
    so wickedness is broken like a tree.

21 "They harm[e] the childless woman,
    and do no good to the widow.
22 Yet God[f] prolongs the life of the mighty by
      his power;
    they rise up when they despair of life.
23 He gives them security, and they are
      supported;
    his eyes are upon their ways.
24 They are exalted a little while, and then are
      gone;
    they wither and fade like the mallow;[g]
    they are cut off like the heads of grain.
25 If it is not so, who will prove me a liar,
    and show that there is nothing in what I
      say?"

25 Bildad Speaks: How Can a Mortal Be Righteous Before God?

    Then Bildad the Shuhite answered:
2 "Dominion and fear are with God;[h]
    he makes peace in his high heaven.
3 Is there any number to his armies?
    Upon whom does his light not arise?

---

a Traditional rendering of Heb *Shaddai* b Or *But I am not destroyed by the darkness; he has concealed the thick darkness from me* c Gk: Heb *they*
d Meaning of Heb uncertain e Gk Tg: Heb *feed on* or *associate with* f Heb *he* g Gk: Heb *like all others* h Heb *him*

4 How then can a mortal be righteous
        before God?
    How can one born of woman be pure?
5 If even the moon is not bright
    and the stars are not pure in his sight,
6 how much less a mortal, who is a maggot,
    and a human being, who is a worm!"

26 Job Replies: God's Majesty Is Unsearchable

Then Job answered:
2 "How you have helped one who has no power!
    How you have assisted the arm that has no
        strength!
3 How you have counseled one who has no
        wisdom,
    and given much good advice!
4 With whose help have you uttered words,
    and whose spirit has come forth from you?
5 The shades below tremble,
    the waters and their inhabitants.
6 Sheol is naked before God,
    and Abaddon has no covering.
7 He stretches out Zaphon[a] over the void,
    and hangs the earth upon nothing.
8 He binds up the waters in his thick clouds,
    and the cloud is not torn open by them.
9 He covers the face of the full moon,
    and spreads over it his cloud.
10 He has described a circle on the face of the
        waters,
    at the boundary between light and
        darkness.
11 The pillars of heaven tremble,
    and are astounded at his rebuke.
12 By his power he stilled the Sea;
    by his understanding he struck down
        Rahab.
13 By his wind the heavens were made
        fair;
    his hand pierced the fleeing serpent.
14 These are indeed but the outskirts of his ways;
    and how small a whisper do we hear
        of him!
    But the thunder of his power who can
        understand?"

27 Job Maintains His Integrity

Job again took up his discourse and
said:

2 "As God lives, who has taken away my right,
    and the Almighty,[b] who has made my soul
        bitter,
3 as long as my breath is in me
    and the spirit of God is in my nostrils,
4 my lips will not speak falsehood,
    and my tongue will not utter deceit.
5 Far be it from me to say that you are right;
    until I die I will not put away my integrity
        from me.
6 I hold fast my righteousness, and will not let
        it go;
    my heart does not reproach me for any of
        my days.

7 "May my enemy be like the wicked,
    and may my opponent be like the
        unrighteous.
8 For what is the hope of the godless when God
        cuts them off,
    when God takes away their lives?
9 Will God hear their cry
    when trouble comes upon them?
10 Will they take delight in the Almighty?[b]
    Will they call upon God at all times?
11 I will teach you concerning the hand of God;
    that which is with the Almighty[b] I will not
        conceal.
12 All of you have seen it yourselves;
    why then have you become altogether
        vain?

13 "This is the portion of the wicked with God,
    and the heritage that oppressors receive
        from the Almighty:[b]
14 If their children are multiplied, it is for the
        sword;
    and their offspring have not enough to eat.
15 Those who survive them the pestilence buries,
    and their widows make no lamentation.
16 Though they heap up silver like dust,
    and pile up clothing like clay—
17 they may pile it up, but the just will wear it,
    and the innocent will divide the silver.
18 They build their houses like nests,
    like booths made by sentinels of the
        vineyard.
19 They go to bed with wealth, but will do so no
        more;
    they open their eyes, and it is gone.

---

a Or *the North*   b Traditional rendering of Heb *Shaddai*

²⁰ Terrors overtake them like a flood;
     in the night a whirlwind carries them off.
²¹ The east wind lifts them up and they are gone;
     it sweeps them out of their place.
²² It*a* hurls at them without pity;
     they flee from its*b* power in headlong
        flight.
²³ It*a* claps its*b* hands at them,
     and hisses at them from its*b* place.

28 Interlude: Where Wisdom Is Found

"Surely there is a mine for silver,
     and a place for gold to be refined.
² Iron is taken out of the earth,
     and copper is smelted from ore.
³ Miners put*c* an end to darkness,
     and search out to the farthest bound
     the ore in gloom and deep darkness.
⁴ They open shafts in a valley away from human
        habitation;
     they are forgotten by travelers,
     they sway suspended, remote from people.
⁵ As for the earth, out of it comes bread;
     but underneath it is turned up as by fire.
⁶ Its stones are the place of sapphires,*d*
     and its dust contains gold.

⁷ "That path no bird of prey knows,
     and the falcon's eye has not seen it.
⁸ The proud wild animals have not trodden it;
     the lion has not passed over it.

⁹ "They put their hand to the flinty rock,
     and overturn mountains by the roots.
¹⁰ They cut out channels in the rocks,
     and their eyes see every precious thing.
¹¹ The sources of the rivers they probe;*e*
     hidden things they bring to light.

¹² "But where shall wisdom be found?
     And where is the place of understanding?
¹³ Mortals do not know the way to it,*f*
     and it is not found in the land of the
        living.
¹⁴ The deep says, 'It is not in me,'
     and the sea says, 'It is not with me.'
¹⁵ It cannot be gotten for gold,
     and silver cannot be weighed out as its
        price.
¹⁶ It cannot be valued in the gold of Ophir,

in precious onyx or sapphire.*d*
¹⁷ Gold and glass cannot equal it,
     nor can it be exchanged for jewels of fine
        gold.
¹⁸ No mention shall be made of coral or of
        crystal;
     the price of wisdom is above pearls.
¹⁹ The chrysolite of Ethiopia*g* cannot compare
        with it,
     nor can it be valued in pure gold.

²⁰ "Where then does wisdom come from?
     And where is the place of understanding?
²¹ It is hidden from the eyes of all living,
     and concealed from the birds of the air.
²² Abaddon and Death say,
     'We have heard a rumor of it with our ears.'

²³ "God understands the way to it,
     and he knows its place.
²⁴ For he looks to the ends of the earth,
     and sees everything under the heavens.
²⁵ When he gave to the wind its weight,
     and apportioned out the waters by
        measure;
²⁶ when he made a decree for the rain,
     and a way for the thunderbolt;
²⁷ then he saw it and declared it;
     he established it, and searched it out.
²⁸ And he said to humankind,
     'Truly, the fear of the Lord, that is wisdom;
     and to depart from evil is understanding.' "

29 Job Finishes His Defense

Job again took up his discourse and said:
²"O that I were as in the months of old,
     as in the days when God watched over me;
³ when his lamp shone over my head,
     and by his light I walked through
        darkness;
⁴ when I was in my prime,
     when the friendship of God was upon my
        tent;
⁵ when the Almighty*h* was still with me,
     when my children were around me;
⁶ when my steps were washed with milk,
     and the rock poured out for me streams
        of oil!
⁷ When I went out to the gate of the city,
     when I took my seat in the square,

a Or *He* (that is God) b Or *his* c Heb *He puts* d Or *lapis lazuli* e Gk Vg: Heb *bind* f Gk: Heb *its price* g Or *Nubia*; Heb *Cush* h Traditional
rendering of Heb *Shaddai*

8 the young men saw me and withdrew,
 and the aged rose up and stood;
9 the nobles refrained from talking,
 and laid their hands on their
  mouths;
10 the voices of princes were hushed,
 and their tongues stuck to the roof of their
  mouths.
11 When the ear heard, it commended me,
 and when the eye saw, it approved;
12 because I delivered the poor who cried,
 and the orphan who had no helper.
13 The blessing of the wretched came upon me,
 and I caused the widow's heart to sing
  for joy.
14 I put on righteousness, and it clothed me;
 my justice was like a robe and a
  turban.
15 I was eyes to the blind,
 and feet to the lame.
16 I was a father to the needy,
 and I championed the cause of the
  stranger.
17 I broke the fangs of the unrighteous,
 and made them drop their prey from their
  teeth.
18 Then I thought, 'I shall die in my nest,
 and I shall multiply my days like the
  phoenix;[a]
19 my roots spread out to the waters,
 with the dew all night on my
  branches;
20 my glory was fresh with me,
 and my bow ever new in my hand.'
21 "They listened to me, and waited,
 and kept silence for my counsel.
22 After I spoke they did not speak again,
 and my word dropped upon them like
  dew.[b]
23 They waited for me as for the rain;
 they opened their mouths as for the spring
  rain.
24 I smiled on them when they had no
  confidence;
 and the light of my countenance they did
  not extinguish.[c]
25 I chose their way, and sat as chief,
 and I lived like a king among his troops,
 like one who comforts mourners.

30 "But now they make sport of me,
 those who are younger than I,
 whose fathers I would have disdained
 to set with the dogs of my flock.
2 What could I gain from the strength of their
  hands?
 All their vigor is gone.
3 Through want and hard hunger
 they gnaw the dry and desolate ground,
4 they pick mallow and the leaves of bushes,
 and to warm themselves the roots of
  broom.
5 They are driven out from society;
 people shout after them as after a thief.
6 In the gullies of wadis they must live,
 in holes in the ground, and in the rocks.
7 Among the bushes they bray;
 under the nettles they huddle together.
8 A senseless, disreputable brood,
 they have been whipped out of the land.
9 "And now they mock me in song;
 I am a byword to them.
10 They abhor me, they keep aloof from me;
 they do not hesitate to spit at the sight
  of me.
11 Because God has loosed my bowstring and
  humbled me,
 they have cast off restraint in my presence.
12 On my right hand the rabble rise up;
 they send me sprawling,
 and build roads for my ruin.
13 They break up my path,
 they promote my calamity;
 no one restrains[d] them.
14 As through a wide breach they come;
 amid the crash they roll on.
15 Terrors are turned upon me;
 my honor is pursued as by the wind,
 and my prosperity has passed away like a
  cloud.
16 "And now my soul is poured out within me;
 days of affliction have taken hold of me.
17 The night racks my bones,
 and the pain that gnaws me takes no rest.
18 With violence he seizes my garment;[e]
 he grasps me by[f] the collar of my tunic.
19 He has cast me into the mire,
 and I have become like dust and ashes.

a *Or* like sand b *Heb lacks* like dew c *Meaning of Heb uncertain* d *Cn: Heb* helps e *Gk: Heb* my garment is disfigured f *Heb* like

20 I cry to you and you do not answer me;
   I stand, and you merely look at me.
21 You have turned cruel to me;
   with the might of your hand you
       persecute me.
22 You lift me up on the wind, you make me ride
       on it,
   and you toss me about in the roar of the
       storm.
23 I know that you will bring me to death,
   and to the house appointed for all living.

24 "Surely one does not turn against the needy,[a]
   when in disaster they cry for help.[b]
25 Did I not weep for those whose day was hard?
   Was not my soul grieved for the poor?

LIVE IT!

Hey, God! Did You Hear Me?
Job 30:20

How do we know God hears and answers our prayers? The books of Job and Psalms describe many cries for help and God's responses to those cries. Answers to prayer throughout the Old Testament came in dramatic, miraculous forms—a burning bush or an angel with a message. Other times, as in **Job 30:20**, the answer was silence. So what do we do when faced with the silence of God?

- Keep praying. Silence is not a sign of God's absence or lack of caring.
- Read the Bible. It's the Word of God and, although it won't always give you specific answers, it will draw you closer to God's heart and teach you how to live according to God's will.
- Pay attention to the common, ordinary experiences and relationships of your everyday life—the experiences and relationships in which God is abundantly present, helping you to understand more about yourself and your place in this world.

26 But when I looked for good, evil came;
   and when I waited for light, darkness came.
27 My inward parts are in turmoil, and are never
       still;
   days of affliction come to meet me.
28 I go about in sunless gloom;
   I stand up in the assembly and cry for help.
29 I am a brother of jackals,
   and a companion of ostriches.
30 My skin turns black and falls from me,
   and my bones burn with heat.
31 My lyre is turned to mourning,
   and my pipe to the voice of those who weep.

31 "I have made a covenant with my eyes;
   how then could I look upon a virgin?
2 What would be my portion from God
       above,
   and my heritage from the Almighty[c] on
       high?
3 Does not calamity befall the unrighteous,
   and disaster the workers of iniquity?
4 Does he not see my ways,
   and number all my steps?

5 "If I have walked with falsehood,
   and my foot has hurried to deceit—
6 let me be weighed in a just balance,
   and let God know my integrity!—
7 if my step has turned aside from the way,
   and my heart has followed my eyes,
   and if any spot has clung to my hands;
8 then let me sow, and another eat;
   and let what grows for me be rooted out.

9 "If my heart has been enticed by a woman,
   and I have lain in wait at my neighbor's
       door;
10 then let my wife grind for another,
   and let other men kneel over her.
11 For that would be a heinous crime;
   that would be a criminal offense;
12 for that would be a fire consuming down to
       Abaddon,
   and it would burn to the root all my harvest.

13 "If I have rejected the cause of my male or
       female slaves,
   when they brought a complaint
       against me;

14 what then shall I do when God rises up?
     When he makes inquiry, what shall I
          answer him?
15 Did not he who made me in the womb make
          them?
     And did not one fashion us in the womb?

16 "If I have withheld anything that the poor
          desired,
     or have caused the eyes of the widow to fail,
17 or have eaten my morsel alone,
     and the orphan has not eaten from it—
18 for from my youth I reared the orphan*a* like a
          father,
     and from my mother's womb I guided the
          widow*b*—
19 if I have seen anyone perish for lack of clothing,
     or a poor person without covering,
20 whose loins have not blessed me,
     and who was not warmed with the fleece of
          my sheep;
21 if I have raised my hand against the orphan,
     because I saw I had supporters at the gate;
22 then let my shoulder blade fall from my
          shoulder,
     and let my arm be broken from its socket.
23 For I was in terror of calamity from God,
     and I could not have faced his majesty.

24 "If I have made gold my trust,
     or called fine gold my confidence;
25 if I have rejoiced because my wealth was
          great,
     or because my hand had gotten much;
26 if I have looked at the sun*c* when it shone,
     or the moon moving in splendor,
27 and my heart has been secretly enticed,
     and my mouth has kissed my hand;
28 this also would be an iniquity to be punished
          by the judges,
     for I should have been false to God above.

29 "If I have rejoiced at the ruin of those who
          hated me,
     or exulted when evil overtook them—
30 I have not let my mouth sin
     by asking for their lives with a curse—
31 if those of my tent ever said,
     'O that we might be sated with his
          flesh!'*d*—

32 the stranger has not lodged in the street;
     I have opened my doors to the traveler—
33 if I have concealed my transgressions as
          others do,*e*
     by hiding my iniquity in my bosom,
34 because I stood in great fear of the multitude,
     and the contempt of families terrified me,
     so that I kept silence, and did not go out
          of doors—
35 O that I had one to hear me!
     (Here is my signature! Let the Almighty*f*
          answer me!)
     O that I had the indictment written by my
          adversary!
36 Surely I would carry it on my shoulder;
     I would bind it on me like a crown;
37 I would give him an account of all my steps;
     like a prince I would approach him.

38 "If my land has cried out against me,
     and its furrows have wept together;
39 if I have eaten its yield without payment,
     and caused the death of its owners;
40 let thorns grow instead of wheat,
     and foul weeds instead of barley."

The words of Job are ended.

Elihu Rebukes Job's Friends

32 So these three men ceased to answer Job, because he was righteous in his own eyes. ²Then Elihu son of Barachel the Buzite, of the family of Ram, became angry. He was angry at Job because he justified himself rather than God; ³he was angry also at Job's three friends because they had found no answer, though they had declared Job to be in the wrong.*g* ⁴Now Elihu had waited to speak to Job, because they were older than he. ⁵But when Elihu saw that there was no answer in the mouths of these three men, he became angry.

6 Elihu son of Barachel the Buzite answered:
"I am young in years,
     and you are aged;
therefore I was timid and afraid
     to declare my opinion to you.
7 I said, 'Let days speak,
     and many years teach wisdom.'
8 But truly it is the spirit in a mortal,
     the breath of the Almighty,*f* that makes for
          understanding.

---

a Heb *him* b Heb *her* c Heb *the light* d Meaning of Heb uncertain e Or *as Adam did* f Traditional rendering of Heb *Shaddai* g Another ancient tradition reads *answer, and had put God in the wrong*

9 It is not the old[a] that are wise,
    nor the aged that understand what is right.
10 Therefore I say, 'Listen to me;
    let me also declare my opinion.'

11 "See, I waited for your words,
    I listened for your wise sayings,
    while you searched out what to say.
12 I gave you my attention,
    but there was in fact no one that
      confuted Job,
    no one among you that answered his
      words.
13 Yet do not say, 'We have found wisdom;
    God may vanquish him, not a human.'
14 He has not directed his words against me,
    and I will not answer him with your
      speeches.

15 "They are dismayed, they answer no more;
    they have not a word to say.
16 And am I to wait, because they do not speak,
    because they stand there, and answer no
      more?
17 I also will give my answer;
    I also will declare my opinion.
18 For I am full of words;
    the spirit within me constrains me.
19 My heart is indeed like wine that has no vent;
    like new wineskins, it is ready to burst.
20 I must speak, so that I may find relief;
    I must open my lips and answer.
21 I will not show partiality to any person
    or use flattery toward anyone.
22 For I do not know how to flatter—
    or my Maker would soon put an end
      to me!

Elihu Rebukes Job

33 "But now, hear my speech, O Job,
    and listen to all my words.
2 See, I open my mouth;
    the tongue in my mouth speaks.
3 My words declare the uprightness of my
      heart,
    and what my lips know they speak
      sincerely.
4 The spirit of God has made me,
    and the breath of the Almighty[b] gives me
      life.

5 Answer me, if you can;
    set your words in order before me; take
      your stand.
6 See, before God I am as you are;
    I too was formed from a piece of clay.
7 No fear of me need terrify you;
    my pressure will not be heavy on you.

8 "Surely, you have spoken in my hearing,
    and I have heard the sound of your words.
9 You say, 'I am clean, without transgression;
    I am pure, and there is no iniquity
      in me.
10 Look, he finds occasions against me,
    he counts me as his enemy;
11 he puts my feet in the stocks,
    and watches all my paths.'

12 "But in this you are not right. I will
      answer you:
    God is greater than any mortal.
13 Why do you contend against him,
    saying, 'He will answer none of my[c]
      words'?
14 For God speaks in one way,
    and in two, though people do not
      perceive it.
15 In a dream, in a vision of the night,
    when deep sleep falls on mortals,
    while they slumber on their beds,
16 then he opens their ears,
    and terrifies them with warnings,
17 that he may turn them aside from their deeds,
    and keep them from pride,
18 to spare their souls from the Pit,
    their lives from traversing the River.
19 They are also chastened with pain upon their
      beds,
    and with continual strife in their bones,
20 so that their lives loathe bread,
    and their appetites dainty food.
21 Their flesh is so wasted away that it cannot be
      seen;
    and their bones, once invisible, now
      stick out.
22 Their souls draw near the Pit,
    and their lives to those who bring death.
23 Then, if there should be for one of them an
      angel,
    a mediator, one of a thousand,

a Gk Syr Vg: Heb *many*   b Traditional rendering of Heb *Shaddai*   c Compare Gk: Heb *his*

one who declares a person upright,

24 and he is gracious to that person, and says,
   'Deliver him from going down into the Pit;
   I have found a ransom;

25 let his flesh become fresh with youth;
   let him return to the days of his youthful
      vigor';

26 then he prays to God, and is accepted by him,
   he comes into his presence with joy,
   and God*a* repays him for his righteousness.

27   That person sings to others and says,
   'I sinned, and perverted what was right,
      and it was not paid back to me.

28 He has redeemed my soul from going down to
      the Pit,
   and my life shall see the light.'

29 "God indeed does all these things,
   twice, three times, with mortals,

30 to bring back their souls from the Pit,
   so that they may see the light of life.*b*

31 Pay heed, Job, listen to me;
   be silent, and I will speak.

32 If you have anything to say, answer me;
   speak, for I desire to justify you.

33 If not, listen to me;
   be silent, and I will teach you wisdom."

Elihu Proclaims God's Justice

34 Then Elihu continued and said:
   ² "Hear my words, you wise men,
   and give ear to me, you who know;

3 for the ear tests words
   as the palate tastes food.

4 Let us choose what is right;
   let us determine among ourselves what is
      good.

5 For Job has said, 'I am innocent,
   and God has taken away my right;

6 in spite of being right I am counted a liar;
   my wound is incurable, though I am
      without transgression.'

7 Who is there like Job,
   who drinks up scoffing like water,

8 who goes in company with evildoers
   and walks with the wicked?

9 For he has said, 'It profits one nothing
   to take delight in God.'

10 "Therefore, hear me, you who have sense,

far be it from God that he should do
      wickedness,
   and from the Almighty*c* that he should do
      wrong.

11 For according to their deeds he will repay
      them,
   and according to their ways he will make it
      befall them.

12 Of a truth, God will not do wickedly,
   and the Almighty*c* will not pervert justice.

13 Who gave him charge over the earth
   and who laid on him*d* the whole world?

14 If he should take back his spirit*e* to himself,
   and gather to himself his breath,

15 all flesh would perish together,
   and all mortals return to dust.

16 "If you have understanding, hear this;
   listen to what I say.

17 Shall one who hates justice govern?
   Will you condemn one who is righteous
      and mighty,

18 who says to a king, 'You scoundrel!'
   and to princes, 'You wicked men!';

19 who shows no partiality to nobles,
   nor regards the rich more than the poor,
   for they are all the work of his hands?

20 In a moment they die;
   at midnight the people are shaken and pass
      away,
   and the mighty are taken away by no
      human hand.

21 "For his eyes are upon the ways of mortals,
   and he sees all their steps.

22 There is no gloom or deep darkness
   where evildoers may hide themselves.

23 For he has not appointed a time*f* for anyone
   to go before God in judgment.

24 He shatters the mighty without investigation,
   and sets others in their place.

25 Thus, knowing their works,
   he overturns them in the night, and they
      are crushed.

26 He strikes them for their wickedness
   while others look on,

27 because they turned aside from following him,
   and had no regard for any of his ways,

28 so that they caused the cry of the poor to
      come to him,

---

a Heb *he*   *b* Syr: Heb *to be lighted with the light of life*   *c* Traditional rendering of Heb *Shaddai*   *d* Heb lacks *on him*   *e* Heb *his heart his spirit*
f Cn: Heb *yet*

and he heard the cry of the
afflicted—

29 When he is quiet, who can condemn?
When he hides his face, who can
behold him,
whether it be a nation or an individual?—

30 so that the godless should not reign,
or those who ensnare the people.

31 "For has anyone said to God,
'I have endured punishment; I will not
offend any more;

32 teach me what I do not see;
if I have done iniquity, I will do it no
more'?

33 Will he then pay back to suit you,
because you reject it?
For you must choose, and not I;
therefore declare what you know.[a]

34 Those who have sense will say to me,
and the wise who hear me will say,

35 'Job speaks without knowledge,
his words are without insight.'

36 Would that Job were tried to the limit,
because his answers are those of the
wicked.

37 For he adds rebellion to his sin;
he claps his hands among us,
and multiplies his words against God."

Elihu Condemns Self-Righteousness

35 Elihu continued and said:
2 "Do you think this to be just?
You say, 'I am in the right before God.'

3 If you ask, 'What advantage have I?
How am I better off than if I had sinned?'

4 I will answer you
and your friends with you.

5 Look at the heavens and see;
observe the clouds, which are higher
than you.

6 If you have sinned, what do you accomplish
against him?
And if your transgressions are multiplied,
what do you do to him?

7 If you are righteous, what do you give to him;
or what does he receive from your hand?

8 Your wickedness affects others like you,
and your righteousness, other human
beings.

9 "Because of the multitude of oppressions
people cry out;
they call for help because of the arm of the
mighty.

10 But no one says, 'Where is God my Maker,
who gives strength in the night,

11 who teaches us more than the animals of the
earth,
and makes us wiser than the birds of the
air?'

12 There they cry out, but he does not answer,
because of the pride of evildoers.

13 Surely God does not hear an empty cry,
nor does the Almighty[b] regard it.

14 How much less when you say that you do not
see him,
that the case is before him, and you are
waiting for him!

15 And now, because his anger does not punish,
and he does not greatly heed
transgression,[c]

16 Job opens his mouth in empty talk,
he multiplies words without knowledge."

Elihu Exalts God's Goodness

36 Elihu continued and said:
2 "Bear with me a little, and I will
show you,
for I have yet something to say on God's
behalf.

3 I will bring my knowledge from far away,
and ascribe righteousness to my Maker.

4 For truly my words are not false;
one who is perfect in knowledge is
with you.

5 "Surely God is mighty and does not
despise any;
he is mighty in strength of understanding.

6 He does not keep the wicked alive,
but gives the afflicted their right.

7 He does not withdraw his eyes from the
righteous,
but with kings on the throne
he sets them forever, and they are exalted.

8 And if they are bound in fetters
and caught in the cords of affliction,

9 then he declares to them their work
and their transgressions, that they are
behaving arrogantly.

---

a Meaning of Heb of verses 29–33 uncertain   b Traditional rendering of Heb *Shaddai*   c Theodotion Symmachus Compare Vg: Meaning of Heb
uncertain

10 He opens their ears to instruction,
   and commands that they return from
      iniquity.
11 If they listen, and serve him,
   they complete their days in prosperity,
   and their years in pleasantness.
12 But if they do not listen, they shall perish by
      the sword,
   and die without knowledge.

13 "The godless in heart cherish anger;
   they do not cry for help when he binds
      them.
14 They die in their youth,
   and their life ends in shame.*a*
15 He delivers the afflicted by their affliction,
   and opens their ear by adversity.
16 He also allured you out of distress
   into a broad place where there was no
      constraint,
   and what was set on your table was full of
      fatness.

17 "But you are obsessed with the case of the
      wicked;
   judgment and justice seize you.
18 Beware that wrath does not entice you into
      scoffing,
   and do not let the greatness of the ransom
      turn you aside.
19 Will your cry avail to keep you from distress,
   or will all the force of your strength?
20 Do not long for the night,
   when peoples are cut off in their place.
21 Beware! Do not turn to iniquity;
   because of that you have been tried by
      affliction.
22 See, God is exalted in his power;
   who is a teacher like him?
23 Who has prescribed for him his way,
   or who can say, 'You have done wrong'?

Elihu Proclaims God's Majesty
24 "Remember to extol his work,
   of which mortals have sung.
25 All people have looked on it;
   everyone watches it from far away.
26 Surely God is great, and we do not know him;
   the number of his years is unsearchable.
27 For he draws up the drops of water;

   he distills*b* his mist in rain,
28 which the skies pour down
   and drop upon mortals abundantly.
29 Can anyone understand the spreading of the
      clouds,
   the thunderings of his pavilion?
30 See, he scatters his lightning around him
   and covers the roots of the sea.
31 For by these he governs peoples;
   he gives food in abundance.
32 He covers his hands with the lightning,
   and commands it to strike the mark.
33 Its crashing*c* tells about him;
   he is jealous*c* with anger against iniquity.

37 "At this also my heart trembles,
   and leaps out of its place.
2 Listen, listen to the thunder of his
      voice
   and the rumbling that comes from his
      mouth.
3 Under the whole heaven he lets it loose,
   and his lightning to the corners of the
      earth.
4 After it his voice roars;
   he thunders with his majestic voice
   and he does not restrain the lightnings*d*
      when his voice is heard.
5 God thunders wondrously with his voice;
   he does great things that we cannot
      comprehend.
6 For to the snow he says, 'Fall on the earth';
   and the shower of rain, his heavy shower
      of rain,
7 serves as a sign on everyone's hand,
   so that all whom he has made may
      know it.*e*
8 Then the animals go into their lairs
   and remain in their dens.
9 From its chamber comes the whirlwind,
   and cold from the scattering winds.
10 By the breath of God ice is given,
   and the broad waters are frozen fast.
11 He loads the thick cloud with moisture;
   the clouds scatter his lightning.
12 They turn round and round by his guidance,
   to accomplish all that he commands them
   on the face of the habitable world.
13 Whether for correction, or for his land,
   or for love, he causes it to happen.

---

a Heb *ends among the temple prostitutes*   *b* Cn: Heb *they distill*   *c* Meaning of Heb uncertain   *d* Heb *them*   *e* Meaning of Heb of verse 7 uncertain

14 "Hear this, O Job;
    stop and consider the wondrous works
      of God.
15 Do you know how God lays his command
      upon them,
    and causes the lightning of his cloud to
      shine?
16 Do you know the balancings of the clouds,
    the wondrous works of the one whose
      knowledge is perfect,
17 you whose garments are hot
    when the earth is still because of the
      south wind?
18 Can you, like him, spread out the skies,
    hard as a molten mirror?
19 Teach us what we shall say to him;
    we cannot draw up our case because of
      darkness.
20 Should he be told that I want to speak?
    Did anyone ever wish to be
      swallowed up?
21 Now, no one can look on the light
    when it is bright in the skies,
    when the wind has passed and cleared
      them.
22 Out of the north comes golden splendor;
    around God is awesome majesty.
23 The Almighty[a]—we cannot find him;
    he is great in power and justice,
    and abundant righteousness he will not
      violate.
24 Therefore mortals fear him;
    he does not regard any who are wise in
      their own conceit."

The LORD Answers Job

38 Then the LORD answered Job out of the
whirlwind:
2 "Who is this that darkens counsel by words
      without knowledge?
3 Gird up your loins like a man,
    I will question you, and you shall declare
      to me.

4 "Where were you when I laid the foundation
      of the earth?
    Tell me, if you have understanding.
5 Who determined its measurements—surely
      you know!
    Or who stretched the line upon it?

STUDY IT!

Heaven and Earth
Job 38:4–38

The questions God asks Job about the formation of the cosmos give us a clue about how the ancient Israelites thought the universe was put together. They believed God had created it in three levels. The heavens were contained in a giant vault above the earth. The earth was a disk that rested on the waters of the abyss, and the abyss was the underworld. Over time the heavens and the earth developed symbolic meanings. The heavens became known as the place where God dwells, and the earth as the place where humans live. Even later, the abyss became known as the place of the dead.

6 On what were its bases sunk,
    or who laid its cornerstone
7 when the morning stars sang
      together
    and all the heavenly beings[b] shouted
      for joy?

8 "Or who shut in the sea with doors
    when it burst out from the womb?—
9 when I made the clouds its garment,
    and thick darkness its swaddling band,
10 and prescribed bounds for it,
    and set bars and doors,
11 and said, 'Thus far shall you come, and no
      farther,
    and here shall your proud waves be
      stopped'?

12 "Have you commanded the morning since
      your days began,
    and caused the dawn to know its place,
13 so that it might take hold of the skirts of the
      earth,
    and the wicked be shaken out
      of it?
14 It is changed like clay under the seal,
    and it is dyed[c] like a garment.

a Traditional rendering of Heb *Shaddai* b Heb *sons of God* c Cn: Heb *and they stand forth*

Why? · Job 38:1–42:6

So, that's it? God just shows up, overwhelms Job with a bunch of questions he can't answer, and then gives Job back double of everything he lost? God doesn't even answer Job's question about why he had to suffer!

Maybe you've asked God some of the following questions. Why do innocent children die? Why was someone I love taken from me? Why do people die from hunger in a world that has so much? Why did that plane crash?

Why was Job satisfied with God's response? Perhaps Job's mind and heart struggled with God's answer, and his heart won. Maybe his heart told him to trust in God's love even when his mind couldn't understand the mystery of his suffering.

With Job the Israelite people began to see the suffering of innocent people as mystery and not as punishment. In the New Testament, this suffering would continue to be seen as mystery, but also as something more. The death of Jesus—the ultimate innocent suffering person—and his resurrection led to the understanding that God ultimately brings good out of the suffering of faithful people (see John 12:24-25 and the introduction to 1 Peter).

Thankfully, the story of our faith doesn't end with Jesus' suffering on the cross, but with the glory of Jesus' resurrection. For Christians death, sin, and suffering hold no power if we believe in the truth of the resurrection. We may not be able to explain why bad things happen, but we are empowered by a faith that shows us that suffering and evil never have the final word.

15 Light is withheld from the wicked,
  and their uplifted arm is broken.

16 "Have you entered into the springs of
    the sea,
  or walked in the recesses of the deep?
17 Have the gates of death been revealed
    to you,
  or have you seen the gates of deep
    darkness?
18 Have you comprehended the expanse of the
    earth?
  Declare, if you know all this.

19 "Where is the way to the dwelling of light,
  and where is the place of darkness,
20 that you may take it to its territory
  and that you may discern the paths to its
    home?
21 Surely you know, for you were born then,
  and the number of your days is great!

22 "Have you entered the storehouses of the
    snow,
  or have you seen the storehouses of the
    hail,

23 which I have reserved for the time of trouble,
  for the day of battle and war?
24 What is the way to the place where the light is
    distributed,
  or where the east wind is scattered upon
    the earth?

25 "Who has cut a channel for the torrents of
    rain,
  and a way for the thunderbolt,
26 to bring rain on a land where no one lives,
  on the desert, which is empty of human
    life,
27 to satisfy the waste and desolate land,
  and to make the ground put forth grass?

28 "Has the rain a father,
  or who has begotten the drops of dew?
29 From whose womb did the ice come forth,
  and who has given birth to the hoarfrost of
    heaven?
30 The waters become hard like stone,
  and the face of the deep is frozen.

31 "Can you bind the chains of the Pleiades,
  or loose the cords of Orion?

³² Can you lead forth the Mazzaroth in their
    season,
      or can you guide the Bear with its
      children?

³³ Do you know the ordinances of the heavens?
    Can you establish their rule on the earth?

³⁴ "Can you lift up your voice to the clouds,
    so that a flood of waters may cover you?

³⁵ Can you send forth lightnings, so that they
    may go
    and say to you, 'Here we are'?

³⁶ Who has put wisdom in the inward parts,^{*a*}
    or given understanding to the mind?^{*a*}

³⁷ Who has the wisdom to number the clouds?
    Or who can tilt the waterskins of the
    heavens,

³⁸ when the dust runs into a mass
    and the clods cling together?

³⁹ "Can you hunt the prey for the lion,
    or satisfy the appetite of the young
    lions,

⁴⁰ when they crouch in their dens,
    or lie in wait in their covert?

⁴¹ Who provides for the raven its prey,
    when its young ones cry to God,
    and wander about for lack of food?

39 "Do you know when the mountain goats
    give birth?
    Do you observe the calving of the deer?

² Can you number the months that they fulfill,
    and do you know the time when they give
    birth,

³ when they crouch to give birth to their
    offspring,
    and are delivered of their young?

⁴ Their young ones become strong, they grow
    up in the open;
    they go forth, and do not return to them.

⁵ "Who has let the wild ass go free?
    Who has loosed the bonds of the swift ass,

⁶ to which I have given the steppe for its home,
    the salt land for its dwelling place?

⁷ It scorns the tumult of the city;
    it does not hear the shouts of the driver.

⁸ It ranges the mountains as its pasture,
    and it searches after every green thing.

⁹ "Is the wild ox willing to serve you?
    Will it spend the night at your crib?

¹⁰ Can you tie it in the furrow with ropes,
    or will it harrow the valleys after you?

¹¹ Will you depend on it because its strength is
    great,
    and will you hand over your labor
    to it?

¹² Do you have faith in it that it will return,
    and bring your grain to your threshing
    floor?^{*b*}

¹³ "The ostrich's wings flap wildly,
    though its pinions lack plumage.^{*a*}

¹⁴ For it leaves its eggs to the earth,
    and lets them be warmed on the ground,

¹⁵ forgetting that a foot may crush them,
    and that a wild animal may trample them.

PRAY IT!

Too Big to Understand
Job 38–41

When God asks Job a series of questions about creation and good and evil, he's trying to make one simple point: "You can never understand me. I am too big. You are too small."

The author of Job seems to be saying to readers, "If you think you've got God all figured out—as Job's friends thought they had, or as even Job wanted to—you're wrong." The author is reminding readers that God is a mystery, powerful and awesome beyond our imagination and control.

During your prayer time, reflect or journal on the following questions:

- In what ways has God been too big for you to understand?
- Do you expect God to provide you with happiness? Peace? Friends?
- What happens if God doesn't meet your expectations in the ways you want?
- Can you let go of your expectations and trust in God's love? Why or why not?

---

a Meaning of Heb uncertain *b* Heb *your grain and your threshing floor*

16 It deals cruelly with its young, as if they were
  not its own;
    though its labor should be in vain, yet it
    has no fear;
17 because God has made it forget wisdom,
    and given it no share in understanding.
18 When it spreads its plumes aloft,[a]
    it laughs at the horse and its rider.

19 "Do you give the horse its might?
    Do you clothe its neck with mane?
20 Do you make it leap like the locust?
    Its majestic snorting is terrible.
21 It paws[b] violently, exults mightily;
    it goes out to meet the weapons.
22 It laughs at fear, and is not dismayed;
    it does not turn back from the sword.
23 Upon it rattle the quiver,
    the flashing spear, and the javelin.
24 With fierceness and rage it swallows the
    ground;
    it cannot stand still at the sound of the
    trumpet.
25 When the trumpet sounds, it says 'Aha!'
    From a distance it smells the battle,
    the thunder of the captains, and the
    shouting.

26 "Is it by your wisdom that the hawk soars,
    and spreads its wings toward the south?
27 Is it at your command that the eagle
    mounts up
    and makes its nest on high?
28 It lives on the rock and makes its home
    in the fastness of the rocky crag.
29 From there it spies the prey;
    its eyes see it from far away.
30 Its young ones suck up blood;
    and where the slain are, there it is."

40 And the LORD said to Job:
2 "Shall a faultfinder contend with the
    Almighty?[c]
    Anyone who argues with God must
    respond."

Job's Response to God

3 Then Job answered the LORD:
4 "See, I am of small account; what shall I
    answer you?
    I lay my hand on my mouth.
5 I have spoken once, and I will not answer;
    twice, but will proceed no further."

God's Challenge to Job

6 Then the LORD answered Job out of the whirlwind:
7 "Gird up your loins like a man;
    I will question you, and you declare to me.
8 Will you even put me in the wrong?
    Will you condemn me that you may be
    justified?
9 Have you an arm like God,
    and can you thunder with a voice like his?

10 "Deck yourself with majesty and dignity;
    clothe yourself with glory and splendor.
11 Pour out the overflowings of your anger,
    and look on all who are proud, and abase
    them.
12 Look on all who are proud, and bring
    them low;
    tread down the wicked where they stand.
13 Hide them all in the dust together;
    bind their faces in the world below.[d]
14 Then I will also acknowledge to you
    that your own right hand can give you
    victory.

15 "Look at Behemoth,
    which I made just as I made you;
    it eats grass like an ox.
16 Its strength is in its loins,
    and its power in the muscles of its belly.
17 It makes its tail stiff like a cedar;
    the sinews of its thighs are knit together.
18 Its bones are tubes of bronze,
    its limbs like bars of iron.

19 "It is the first of the great acts of God—

a Meaning of Heb uncertain b Gk Syr Vg: Heb they dig c Traditional rendering of Heb Shaddai d Heb the hidden place

only its Maker can approach it with the
sword.

20 For the mountains yield food for it
where all the wild animals play.

21 Under the lotus plants it lies,
in the covert of the reeds and in the marsh.

22 The lotus trees cover it for shade;
the willows of the wadi surround it.

23 Even if the river is turbulent, it is not
frightened;
it is confident though Jordan rushes against
its mouth.

24 Can one take it with hooks[a]
or pierce its nose with a snare?

41

[b] "Can you draw out Leviathan[c] with a
fishhook,
or press down its tongue with a cord?

2 Can you put a rope in its nose,
or pierce its jaw with a hook?

3 Will it make many supplications to you?
Will it speak soft words to you?

4 Will it make a covenant with you
to be taken as your servant forever?

5 Will you play with it as with a bird,
or will you put it on leash for your girls?

6 Will traders bargain over it?
Will they divide it up among the
merchants?

7 Can you fill its skin with harpoons,
or its head with fishing spears?

8 Lay hands on it;
think of the battle; you will not do it again!

9[d] Any hope of capturing it[e] will be disappointed;
were not even the gods[f] overwhelmed at
the sight of it?

10 No one is so fierce as to dare to stir
it up.
Who can stand before it?[g]

11 Who can confront it[g] and be safe?[h]
—under the whole heaven, who?[i]

12 "I will not keep silence concerning its limbs,
or its mighty strength, or its splendid
frame.

13 Who can strip off its outer garment?
Who can penetrate its double coat of mail?[j]

14 Who can open the doors of its face?
There is terror all around its teeth.

15 Its back[k] is made of shields in rows,

shut up closely as with a seal.

16 One is so near to another
that no air can come between them.

17 They are joined one to another;
they clasp each other and cannot be
separated.

18 Its sneezes flash forth light,
and its eyes are like the eyelids of the dawn.

19 From its mouth go flaming torches;
sparks of fire leap out.

20 Out of its nostrils comes smoke,
as from a boiling pot and burning rushes.

21 Its breath kindles coals,
and a flame comes out of its mouth.

22 In its neck abides strength,
and terror dances before it.

23 The folds of its flesh cling together;
it is firmly cast and immovable.

24 Its heart is as hard as stone,
as hard as the lower millstone.

25 When it raises itself up the gods are afraid;
at the crashing they are beside themselves.

26 Though the sword reaches it, it does not avail,
nor does the spear, the dart, or the javelin.

27 It counts iron as straw,
and bronze as rotten wood.

28 The arrow cannot make it flee;
slingstones, for it, are turned to chaff.

29 Clubs are counted as chaff;
it laughs at the rattle of javelins.

30 Its underparts are like sharp potsherds;
it spreads itself like a threshing sledge on
the mire.

31 It makes the deep boil like a pot;
it makes the sea like a pot of ointment.

32 It leaves a shining wake behind it;
one would think the deep to be
white-haired.

33 On earth it has no equal,
a creature without fear.

34 It surveys everything that is lofty;
it is king over all that are proud."

42

Job Is Humbled and Satisfied

Then Job answered the LORD:

2 "I know that you can do all things,
and that no purpose of yours can be
thwarted.

3 'Who is this that hides counsel without
knowledge?'

---

a Cn: Heb *in his eyes* b Ch 40.25 in Heb c Or *the crocodile* d Ch 41.1 in Heb e Heb *of it* f Cn Compare Symmachus Syr: Heb *one is* g Heb *me*
h Gk: Heb *that I shall repay* i Heb *to me* j Gk: Heb *bridle* k Cn Compare Gk Vg: Heb *pride*

Therefore I have uttered what I did not
    understand,
  things too wonderful for me, which I did
    not know.
4 'Hear, and I will speak;
  I will question you, and you declare to me.'
5 I had heard of you by the hearing of the ear,
  but now my eye sees you;
6 therefore I despise myself,
  and repent in dust and ashes."

Job's Friends Are Humiliated

7 After the LORD had spoken these words to Job,
the LORD said to Eliphaz the Temanite: "My wrath is
kindled against you and against your two friends; for
you have not spoken of me what is right, as my servant
Job has. 8 Now therefore take seven bulls and seven
rams, and go to my servant Job, and offer up for
yourselves a burnt offering; and my servant Job shall
pray for you, for I will accept his prayer not to deal
with you according to your folly; for you have not
spoken of me what is right, as my servant Job has
done." 9 So Eliphaz the Temanite and Bildad the
Shuhite and Zophar the Naamathite went and did

<hr/>

α Heb a *qesitah*

what the LORD had told them; and the LORD accepted Job's prayer.

Job's Fortunes Are Restored Twofold

10 And the LORD restored the fortunes of Job when
he had prayed for his friends; and the LORD gave Job
twice as much as he had before. 11 Then there came
to him all his brothers and sisters and all who had
known him before, and they ate bread with him in
his house; they showed him sympathy and comforted
him for all the evil that the LORD had brought upon
him; and each of them gave him a piece of money[a]
and a gold ring. 12 The LORD blessed the latter days
of Job more than his beginning; and he had fourteen
thousand sheep, six thousand camels, a thousand
yoke of oxen, and a thousand donkeys. 13 He also had
seven sons and three daughters. 14 He named the first
Jemimah, the second Keziah, and the third Keren-
happuch. 15 In all the land there were no women so
beautiful as Job's daughters; and their father gave them
an inheritance along with their brothers. 16 After this
Job lived one hundred and forty years, and saw his
children, and his children's children, four generations.
17 And Job died, old and full of days.

Psalms

Rock. Pop. Indie. R&B. Hip-hop. Singer-songwriter. Alternative. Country. Jazz. Latin. World. What's your favorite style of music? Music resonates deep inside us and often is able to express our attitudes and philosophy toward life—so much so that we often refer to it as "our" music, even though it was written by someone else. In the same way, the psalms were written by various authors, but together they are Israel's music. They are the hymns or songs that Israel used in its temple worship. They give voice to the souls of the Israelites and express the ups and downs of the Israelites' relationship with God.

The Hebrew version of Psalms is titled "Tehillim," or "Praises," because its hymns praise God. The Greek translation calls them "Psalmoi," or "Psalms," which means "religious songs performed to music." The 150 psalms can be grouped into one or more of five general categories:

- The **hymns of praise and thanksgiving** sing of God's majesty, power, and wisdom (for example, Psalms 8; 24; 47; 93; 95-99; 113-118; 136; 150).
- The **hymns of lament or petition** include both individual and communal cries to God for help in some need (for example, Psalms 38; 51; 55; 58; 59; 74; 78; 105; 106).
- The **hymns of wisdom sing** of Israel's insights into how to live according to God's law and what brings true happiness (for example, Psalms 1; 34; 37; 49; 73; 112; 128).
- The **liturgical or worship psalms** are used as entrance hymns in liturgies or during worship services at the temple (for example, Psalms 15; 24; 134).
- The **historical psalms** sing of the great wonders God has worked throughout the history of Israel (for example, Psalms 78; 105; 106; 135; 136).

Because of King David's reputation for writing and performing music, he is named as the author of many of the psalms despite the fact that some of them were written long after his death. It's more accurate to understand Psalms as a collection of songs that reflect different times and experiences throughout Israel's existence. Psalms tells us about Israel and its wondrous relationship with God and encourages each of us to pursue our own relationship with the God of the universe.

- **Date Written:** It is impossible to determine when any individual psalm was composed. The collection spans Israel's history.
- **Authors:** Unknown, although many psalms are attributed to David
- **Themes:** The full range of human emotions expressed to God including love, anger, joy, and hope (see "Study It: The Themes of Psalms," near the end of Psalms, for an index of the many different themes)
- **Noteworthy:** The psalms are often used as worship songs. They invite us to look at our lives our own and relationship with God.

Psalms is divided into five books without any particular organizing theme:

- Psalms 1–41 Book I
- Psalms 42–72 Book II
- Psalms 73–89 Book III
- Psalms 90–106 Book IV
- Psalms 107–150 Book V

BOOK I
(Psalms 1–41)

1 **The Two Ways**
Happy are those
  who do not follow the advice of the
    wicked,
or take the path that sinners tread,
  or sit in the seat of scoffers;
2 but their delight is in the law of the LORD,
  and on his law they meditate day and
    night.
3 They are like trees
  planted by streams of water,
which yield their fruit in its season,
  and their leaves do not wither.
In all that they do, they prosper.

4 The wicked are not so,
  but are like chaff that the wind drives away.
5 Therefore the wicked will not stand in the
    judgment,

The Ways of God
Psalm 1

Psalms begins with a clear distinction between the ways of God and the ways of the wicked. The actions mentioned at the beginning of the first psalm—follow, take, sit, delight, meditate (Psalm 1:1-2)—are not onetime actions, but habits. They invite us to look at what we give our time and attention to. From beginning to end, in a variety of ways, Psalms asks us to take a good look at whether or not we're following God's ways in our lives here on earth. Through prayers of individuals, small groups, or even the entire Jewish nation, Psalms shows us that every human experience can also be a faith experience—one in which we can choose the ways of God.

• Who or what do you choose to follow?
• How does your life show it day to day?

nor sinners in the congregation of the
    righteous;
6 for the LORD watches over the way of the
    righteous,
  but the way of the wicked will perish.

2 **God's Promise to His Anointed**
Why do the nations conspire,
  and the peoples plot in vain?
2 The kings of the earth set themselves,
  and the rulers take counsel
    together,
  against the LORD and his anointed,
    saying,
3 "Let us burst their bonds asunder,
  and cast their cords from us."

4 He who sits in the heavens laughs;
  the LORD has them in derision.
5 Then he will speak to them in his
    wrath,
  and terrify them in his fury, saying,
6 "I have set my king on Zion, my holy hill."

7 I will tell of the decree of the LORD:
He said to me, "You are my son;
  today I have begotten you.
8 Ask of me, and I will make the nations your
    heritage,
  and the ends of the earth your possession.
9 You shall break them with a rod of
    iron,
  and dash them in pieces like a potter's
    vessel."

10 Now therefore, O kings, be wise;
  be warned, O rulers of the earth.
11 Serve the LORD with fear,
  with trembling 12kiss his feet,*a*
or he will be angry, and you will perish in
    the way;
  for his wrath is quickly kindled.

Happy are all who take refuge in him.

3 **Trust in God under Adversity**
*A Psalm of David, when he fled from his
son Absalom.*

O LORD, how many are my foes!
  Many are rising against me;

---

a Cn: Meaning of Heb of verses 11b and 12a is uncertain

Songs and Prayers · Psalms 1–150

Psalms is Israel's book of religious poetry and song. It expresses the people's very real and concrete experiences of God. Psalms is filled with the same wide range of feelings and moods that we experience in our lives today. The people who wrote the psalms poured out their hearts to God in words of joy and sorrow, regret and celebration, earnest pleading and praise. These are the prayers of people who struggled to live righteous lives.

There are many different kinds of psalms. There are psalms of lament, which express the anguish and sorrow experienced in illness, death, and personal loss. There are psalms of thanksgiving and rejoicing, which recognize God's hand when the people are rescued from evil or wickedness. There are psalms of praise to a majestic God, witnessed in all of creation.

Psalms serves as a common book of prayer for Jews and Christians. Because the psalms address feelings and experiences common to everyone, the words speak to us today just as strongly as they did to the people who first used them thousands of years ago.

Read the psalms slowly, savoring the words as if God is saying them to you or you are expressing those thoughts to God for the first time. You'll gain deeper insights if you take your time with the psalms. Look for their rhythm and repetition. Just as modern music and poetry use rhythm and repetition to emphasize certain things, so the psalmists used rhythm and repetition to emphasize keen insights into our relationship with God. (See "Study It: The Themes of Psalms," near the end of Psalms, for an index of themes.)

---

2   many are saying to me,
     "There is no help for you*a* in God."
                                    Selah

3   But you, O LORD, are a shield around me,
       my glory, and the one who lifts up my head.
4   I cry aloud to the LORD,
       and he answers me from his holy hill.
                                    Selah

5   I lie down and sleep;
       I wake again, for the LORD sustains me.
6   I am not afraid of ten thousands of people
       who have set themselves against me all
          around.

7   Rise up, O LORD!
       Deliver me, O my God!
   For you strike all my enemies on the cheek;
       you break the teeth of the wicked.

8   Deliverance belongs to the LORD;
       may your blessing be on your
          people!   *Selah*

 4

**Confident Plea for Deliverance
from Enemies**

*To the leader: with stringed instruments.
A Psalm of David.*

Answer me when I call, O God of my right!
   You gave me room when I was in distress.
   Be gracious to me, and hear my prayer.

2   How long, you people, shall my honor suffer
          shame?
       How long will you love vain words, and seek
          after lies?   *Selah*
3   But know that the LORD has set apart the
          faithful for himself;
       the LORD hears when I call to him.

4   When you are disturbed,*b* do not sin;
       ponder it on your beds, and be silent.
                                    Selah
5   Offer right sacrifices,
       and put your trust in the LORD.

6   There are many who say, "O that we might
          see some good!

---

a Syr: Heb *him*   **b** Or *are angry*

Let the light of your face shine on us,
　　O Lᴏʀᴅ!"
7 You have put gladness in my heart
　　more than when their grain and wine
　　abound.

8 I will both lie down and sleep in peace;
　　for you alone, O Lᴏʀᴅ, make me lie down
　　in safety.

5 Trust in God for Deliverance from Enemies

To the leader: for the flutes. A Psalm of David.

Give ear to my words, O Lᴏʀᴅ;
　　give heed to my sighing.
2 Listen to the sound of my cry,
　　my King and my God,
　　for to you I pray.
3 O Lᴏʀᴅ, in the morning you hear my voice;
　　in the morning I plead my case to you,
　　and watch.

4 For you are not a God who delights in
　　wickedness;
　　evil will not sojourn with you.
5 The boastful will not stand before your eyes;
　　you hate all evildoers.
6 You destroy those who speak lies;
　　the Lᴏʀᴅ abhors the bloodthirsty and
　　deceitful.

7 But I, through the abundance of your
　　steadfast love,
　　will enter your house,
I will bow down toward your holy temple
　　in awe of you.
8 Lead me, O Lᴏʀᴅ, in your righteousness
　　because of my enemies;
　　make your way straight before me.

9 For there is no truth in their mouths;
　　their hearts are destruction;
their throats are open graves;
　　they flatter with their tongues.
10 Make them bear their guilt, O God;
　　let them fall by their own counsels;
because of their many transgressions cast
　　them out,
　　for they have rebelled against you.

11 But let all who take refuge in you rejoice;
　　let them ever sing for joy.
Spread your protection over them,
　　so that those who love your name may
　　exult in you.
12 For you bless the righteous, O Lᴏʀᴅ;
　　you cover them with favor as with a
　　shield.

6 Prayer for Recovery from Grave Illness

To the leader: with stringed instruments; according to The Sheminith. A Psalm of David.

O Lᴏʀᴅ, do not rebuke me in your anger,
　　or discipline me in your wrath.
2 Be gracious to me, O Lᴏʀᴅ, for I am
　　languishing;
　　O Lᴏʀᴅ, heal me, for my bones are
　　shaking with terror.
3 My soul also is struck with terror,
　　while you, O Lᴏʀᴅ—how long?

PRAY IT!

Hope in the Hearing
Psalm 6

The psalmist is praying in **Psalm 6** for healing from physical and mental suffering. It's a prayer that calls on the compassion and steadfast love of God—a love that is even stronger than pain, grief, or anger. Hope comes when the writer realizes God has heard his prayers. Even when our circumstances don't change, we can continue to pray and trust that God does hear our prayers and will transform our suffering by using it for good in our life and the lives of others. (See Romans 8:28.)

- When have you prayed for healing from illness or suffering? How have your prayers been answered?
- Like the psalmist, write a song or poem to pour out your heart to God.

4 Turn, O Lord, save my life;
   deliver me for the sake of your steadfast
      love.
5 For in death there is no remembrance of you;
   in Sheol who can give you praise?

6 I am weary with my moaning;
   every night I flood my bed with
      tears;
   I drench my couch with my
      weeping.
7 My eyes waste away because of grief;
   they grow weak because of all my foes.

8 Depart from me, all you workers of
      evil,
   for the Lord has heard the sound of my
      weeping.
9 The Lord has heard my supplication;
   the Lord accepts my prayer.
10 All my enemies shall be ashamed and struck
      with terror;
   they shall turn back, and in a moment be
      put to shame.

7   **Plea for Help against Persecutors**
*A Shiggaion of David, which he sang to
the Lord concerning Cush, a Benjaminite.*

O Lord my God, in you I take refuge;
   save me from all my pursuers, and
      deliver me,
2 or like a lion they will tear me apart;
   they will drag me away, with no one to
      rescue.

3 O Lord my God, if I have done this,
   if there is wrong in my hands,
4 if I have repaid my ally with harm
   or plundered my foe without
      cause,
5 then let the enemy pursue and
      overtake me,
   trample my life to the ground,
   and lay my soul in the dust.   *Selah*

6 Rise up, O Lord, in your anger;
   lift yourself up against the fury of my
      enemies;
   awake, O my God;[a] you have appointed a
      judgment.

7 Let the assembly of the peoples be gathered
      around you,
   and over it take your seat[b] on high.
8 The Lord judges the peoples;
   judge me, O Lord, according to my
      righteousness
   and according to the integrity that is in me.

9 O let the evil of the wicked come to an end,
   but establish the righteous,
 you who test the minds and hearts,
   O righteous God.
10 God is my shield,
   who saves the upright in heart.
11 God is a righteous judge,
   and a God who has indignation every day.

12 If one does not repent, God[c] will whet his
      sword;
   he has bent and strung his bow;
13 he has prepared his deadly weapons,
   making his arrows fiery shafts.
14 See how they conceive evil,
   and are pregnant with mischief,
   and bring forth lies.
15 They make a pit, digging it out,
   and fall into the hole that they have made.
16 Their mischief returns upon their own heads,
   and on their own heads their violence
      descends.

17 I will give to the Lord the thanks due to his
      righteousness,
   and sing praise to the name of the Lord,
      the Most High.

8   **Divine Majesty and Human Dignity**
*To the leader: according to The Gittith. A
Psalm of David.*

O Lord, our Sovereign,
   how majestic is your name in all the earth!

You have set your glory above the heavens.
2   Out of the mouths of babes and infants
 you have founded a bulwark because of your
      foes,
   to silence the enemy and the avenger.

3 When I look at your heavens, the work of
      your fingers,

a Or *awake for me*   b Cn: Heb *return*   c Heb *he*

the moon and the stars that you have
established;
4 what are human beings that you are mindful
of them,
mortals*a* that you care for them?

5 Yet you have made them a little lower than
God,*b*
and crowned them with glory and honor.
6 You have given them dominion over the
works of your hands;
you have put all things under their feet,
7 all sheep and oxen,
and also the beasts of the field,
8 the birds of the air, and the fish of the sea,
whatever passes along the paths of the
seas.

9 O Lord, our Sovereign,
how majestic is your name in all the earth!

9 God's Power and Justice

*To the leader: according to Muth-labben.
A Psalm of David.*

I will give thanks to the Lord with my whole
heart;
I will tell of all your wonderful deeds.
2 I will be glad and exult in you;
I will sing praise to your name, O Most
High.

3 When my enemies turned back,
they stumbled and perished before you.
4 For you have maintained my just cause;
you have sat on the throne giving
righteous judgment.

5 You have rebuked the nations, you have
destroyed the wicked;

you have blotted out their name forever
and ever.
6 The enemies have vanished in everlasting
ruins;
their cities you have rooted out;
the very memory of them has perished.

7 But the Lord sits enthroned forever,
he has established his throne for
judgment.
8 He judges the world with righteousness;
he judges the peoples with equity.

9 The Lord is a stronghold for the oppressed,
a stronghold in times of trouble.
10 And those who know your name put their
trust in you,
for you, O Lord, have not forsaken those
who seek you.

11 Sing praises to the Lord, who dwells in
Zion.
Declare his deeds among the peoples.
12 For he who avenges blood is mindful of them;
he does not forget the cry of the afflicted.

13 Be gracious to me, O Lord.
See what I suffer from those who hate me;
you are the one who lifts me up from the
gates of death,
14 so that I may recount all your praises,
and, in the gates of daughter Zion,
rejoice in your deliverance.

15 The nations have sunk in the pit that they
made;
in the net that they hid has their own foot
been caught.
16 The Lord has made himself known, he has
executed judgment;
the wicked are snared in the work of their
own hands.   *Higgaion. Selah*

17 The wicked shall depart to Sheol,
all the nations that forget God.

18 For the needy shall not always be forgotten,
nor the hope of the poor perish forever.

19 Rise up, O Lord! Do not let mortals prevail;

a Heb *ben adam*, lit. *son of man*   *b* Or *than the divine beings* or *angels*: Heb *elohim*

let the nations be judged before you.
20 Put them in fear, O Lord;
    let the nations know that they are only
        human.   *Selah*

Prayer for Deliverance from Enemies

10 Why, O Lord, do you stand far off?
    Why do you hide yourself in times of
        trouble?
2 In arrogance the wicked persecute the poor—
    let them be caught in the schemes they
        have devised.

3 For the wicked boast of the desires of their
        heart,
    those greedy for gain curse and renounce
        the Lord.
4 In the pride of their countenance the wicked
        say, "God will not seek it out";
    all their thoughts are, "There is no God."

5 Their ways prosper at all times;
    your judgments are on high, out of their
        sight;
    as for their foes, they scoff at them.
6 They think in their heart, "We shall not be
        moved;
    throughout all generations we shall not
        meet adversity."

7 Their mouths are filled with cursing and
        deceit and oppression;
    under their tongues are mischief and
        iniquity.
8 They sit in ambush in the villages;
    in hiding places they murder the
        innocent.

Their eyes stealthily watch for the helpless;
9   they lurk in secret like a lion in its
        covert;
    they lurk that they may seize the poor;
    they seize the poor and drag them off in
        their net.

10 They stoop, they crouch,
    and the helpless fall by their might.
11 They think in their heart, "God has forgotten,
    he has hidden his face, he will never
        see it."

12 Rise up, O Lord; O God, lift up your hand;
    do not forget the oppressed.
13 Why do the wicked renounce God,
    and say in their hearts, "You will not call us
        to account"?

14 But you do see! Indeed you note trouble and
        grief,
    that you may take it into your hands;
    the helpless commit themselves to you;
    you have been the helper of the orphan.

15 Break the arm of the wicked and evildoers;
    seek out their wickedness until you find
        none.
16 The Lord is king forever and ever;
    the nations shall perish from his land.

17 O Lord, you will hear the desire of the meek;
    you will strengthen their heart, you will
        incline your ear
18 to do justice for the orphan and the oppressed,
    so that those from earth may strike terror
        no more.[a]

Song of Trust in God

11 *To the leader. Of David.*

In the Lord I take refuge; how can you say to
        me,
    "Flee like a bird to the mountains;[b]
2 for look, the wicked bend the bow,
    they have fitted their arrow to the string,
    to shoot in the dark at the upright in heart.
3 If the foundations are destroyed,
    what can the righteous do?"

4 The Lord is in his holy temple;
    the Lord's throne is in heaven.
    His eyes behold, his gaze examines
        humankind.
5 The Lord tests the righteous and the wicked,
    and his soul hates the lover of violence.
6 On the wicked he will rain coals of fire and
        sulfur;
    a scorching wind shall be the portion of
        their cup.
7 For the Lord is righteous;
    he loves righteous deeds;
    the upright shall behold his face.

a Meaning of Heb uncertain   b Gk Syr Jerome Tg: Heb *flee to your mountain, O bird*

12 Plea for Help in Evil Times

To the leader: according to The Sheminith.
A Psalm of David.

Help, O LORD, for there is no longer anyone
      who is godly;
   the faithful have disappeared from
      humankind.
2 They utter lies to each other;
   with flattering lips and a double heart they
      speak.

3 May the LORD cut off all flattering lips,
   the tongue that makes great boasts,
4 those who say, "With our tongues we will
      prevail;
   our lips are our own—who is our master?"

5 "Because the poor are despoiled, because the
      needy groan,
   I will now rise up," says the LORD;
   "I will place them in the safety for which
      they long."
6 The promises of the LORD are promises that
      are pure,
   silver refined in a furnace on the ground,
   purified seven times.

7 You, O LORD, will protect us;
   you will guard us from this generation
      forever.
8 On every side the wicked prowl,
   as vileness is exalted among humankind.

13 Prayer for Deliverance from Enemies

To the leader. A Psalm of David.

How long, O LORD? Will you forget me forever?
   How long will you hide your face
      from me?
2 How long must I bear pain[a] in my soul,
   and have sorrow in my heart all day long?
   How long shall my enemy be exalted over me?

3 Consider and answer me, O LORD my God!
   Give light to my eyes, or I will sleep the sleep
      of death,
4 and my enemy will say, "I have prevailed";
   my foes will rejoice because I am shaken.

5 But I trusted in your steadfast love;

a Syr: Heb *hold counsels*

my heart shall rejoice in your salvation.
6 I will sing to the LORD,
   because he has dealt bountifully
      with me.

14 Denunciation of Godlessness

To the leader. Of David.

Fools say in their hearts, "There is no God."
   They are corrupt, they do abominable
      deeds;
   there is no one who does good.

2 The LORD looks down from heaven on
      humankind
   to see if there are any who are wise,
   who seek after God.

3 They have all gone astray, they are all alike
      perverse;
   there is no one who does good,
   no, not one.

LIVE IT!

Believing Psalm 14

Although it was written
thousands of years
ago, **Psalm 14** could
have been written about our world today.
It's quite common to hear people say
there is no God. Our faith may tell us that
such beliefs are foolish, but everyone has
the freedom to believe as they choose.
You can't force someone to believe in God.

How do we talk about faith with
people who refuse to believe in God?
Maybe the most powerful way we can
show others that God exists is through our
own actions. God's presence in our world
is most clearly revealed when we love
each other. We must also trust that God is
already at work in the lives of those who
don't believe, and hope and pray that one
day their eyes will be opened to the
presence of God in their lives.

4 Have they no knowledge, all the evildoers
   who eat up my people as they eat bread,
   and do not call upon the LORD?

5 There they shall be in great terror,
   for God is with the company of the
      righteous.
6 You would confound the plans of the poor,
   but the LORD is their refuge.

7 O that deliverance for Israel would come from
      Zion!
   When the LORD restores the fortunes of
      his people,
   Jacob will rejoice; Israel will be glad.

15 Who Shall Abide in God's Sanctuary?
A Psalm of David.

O Lord, who may abide in your tent?
   Who may dwell on your holy hill?
2 Those who walk blamelessly, and do what is
      right,
   and speak the truth from their heart;
3 who do not slander with their tongue,
   and do no evil to their friends,
   nor take up a reproach against their
      neighbors;
4 in whose eyes the wicked are despised,
   but who honor those who fear the
      LORD;
   who stand by their oath even to their hurt;
5 who do not lend money at interest,
   and do not take a bribe against the
      innocent.

Those who do these things shall never be
   moved.

16 Song of Trust and Security in God
A Miktam of David.

Protect me, O God, for in you I take refuge.
2 I say to the LORD, "You are my Lord;
   I have no good apart from you."[a]

3 As for the holy ones in the land, they are the
      noble,
   in whom is all my delight.

4 Those who choose another god multiply their
      sorrows;[b]
   their drink offerings of blood I will not
      pour out
   or take their names upon my lips.

5 The LORD is my chosen portion and
      my cup;
   you hold my lot.
6 The boundary lines have fallen for me in
      pleasant places;
   I have a goodly heritage.

7 I bless the LORD who gives me counsel;
   in the night also my heart instructs me.
8 I keep the LORD always before me;
   because he is at my right hand, I shall not
      be moved.

9 Therefore my heart is glad, and my soul
      rejoices;
   my body also rests secure.
10 For you do not give me up to Sheol,
   or let your faithful one see the Pit.

11 You show me the path of life.
   In your presence there is fullness of joy;
   in your right hand are pleasures
      forevermore.

17 Prayer for Deliverance from Persecutors
A Prayer of David.

Hear a just cause, O LORD; attend to
      my cry;
   give ear to my prayer from lips free of
      deceit.

> "You show me the
> path of life. In your
> presence there is
> fullness of joy;
> in your right hand
> are pleasures
> forevermore."
> —Psalm 16:11

a Jerome Tg: Meaning of Heb uncertain   b Cn: Meaning of Heb uncertain

2 From you let my vindication come;
    let your eyes see the right.

3 If you try my heart, if you visit me by night,
    if you test me, you will find no wickedness
        in me;
    my mouth does not transgress.
4 As for what others do, by the word of
        your lips
    I have avoided the ways of the violent.
5 My steps have held fast to your paths;
    my feet have not slipped.

6 I call upon you, for you will answer me,
        O God;
    incline your ear to me, hear my words.
7 Wondrously show your steadfast love,
    O savior of those who seek refuge
    from their adversaries at your right
        hand.

8 Guard me as the apple of the eye;
    hide me in the shadow of your wings,
9 from the wicked who despoil me,
    my deadly enemies who surround me.
10 They close their hearts to pity;
    with their mouths they speak arrogantly.
11 They track me down;[a] now they surround me;
    they set their eyes to cast me to the
        ground.
12 They are like a lion eager to tear,
    like a young lion lurking in ambush.

13 Rise up, O Lord, confront them, overthrow
        them!
    By your sword deliver my life from the
        wicked,
14 from mortals—by your hand, O Lord—
    from mortals whose portion in life is in
        this world.
    May their bellies be filled with what you have
        stored up for them;
    may their children have more than enough;
    may they leave something over to their
        little ones.

15 As for me, I shall behold your face in
        righteousness;
    when I awake I shall be satisfied, beholding
        your likeness.

18

Royal Thanksgiving for Victory

To the leader. A Psalm of David the servant of the Lord, who addressed the words of this song to the Lord on the day when the Lord delivered him from the hand of all his enemies, and from the hand of Saul. He said:

I love you, O Lord, my strength.
2 The Lord is my rock, my fortress, and my
        deliverer,
    my God, my rock in whom I take refuge,
    my shield, and the horn of my salvation, my
        stronghold.
3 I call upon the Lord, who is worthy to be
        praised,
    so I shall be saved from my enemies.

4 The cords of death encompassed me;
    the torrents of perdition assailed me;
5 the cords of Sheol entangled me;
    the snares of death confronted me.

6 In my distress I called upon the Lord;
    to my God I cried for help.
    From his temple he heard my voice,
    and my cry to him reached his ears.

7 Then the earth reeled and rocked;
    the foundations also of the mountains
        trembled
    and quaked, because he was angry.
8 Smoke went up from his nostrils,
    and devouring fire from his mouth;
    glowing coals flamed forth from him.
9 He bowed the heavens, and came down;
    thick darkness was under his feet.
10 He rode on a cherub, and flew;
    he came swiftly upon the wings of the
        wind.
11 He made darkness his covering around him,
    his canopy thick clouds dark with water.
12 Out of the brightness before him
    there broke through his clouds
    hailstones and coals of fire.
13 The Lord also thundered in the heavens,
    and the Most High uttered his voice.[b]
14 And he sent out his arrows, and scattered them;
    he flashed forth lightnings, and routed
        them.
15 Then the channels of the sea were seen,

---

a One Ms Compare Syr: MT *Our steps*   b Gk See 2 Sam 22.14: Heb adds *hailstones and coals of fire*

and the foundations of the world were
    laid bare
at your rebuke, O Lord,
    at the blast of the breath of your nostrils.

16 He reached down from on high, he took me;
    he drew me out of mighty waters.
17 He delivered me from my strong enemy,
    and from those who hated me;
    for they were too mighty for me.
18 They confronted me in the day of my calamity;
    but the Lord was my support.
19 He brought me out into a broad place;
    he delivered me, because he delighted
      in me.

20 The Lord rewarded me according to my
    righteousness;
    according to the cleanness of my hands he
      recompensed me.
21 For I have kept the ways of the Lord,
    and have not wickedly departed from
      my God.
22 For all his ordinances were before me,
    and his statutes I did not put away
      from me.
23 I was blameless before him,
    and I kept myself from guilt.
24 Therefore the Lord has recompensed me
    according to my righteousness,
    according to the cleanness of my hands in
      his sight.

25 With the loyal you show yourself loyal;
    with the blameless you show yourself
      blameless;
26 with the pure you show yourself pure;
    and with the crooked you show yourself
      perverse.
27 For you deliver a humble people,
    but the haughty eyes you bring down.
28 It is you who light my lamp;
    the Lord, my God, lights up my darkness.
29 By you I can crush a troop,
    and by my God I can leap over a wall.
30 This God—his way is perfect;
    the promise of the Lord proves true;
    he is a shield for all who take refuge in him.

31 For who is God except the Lord?

    And who is a rock besides our God?—
32 the God who girded me with strength,
    and made my way safe.
33 He made my feet like the feet of a deer,
    and set me secure on the heights.
34 He trains my hands for war,
    so that my arms can bend a bow of bronze.
35 You have given me the shield of your salvation,
    and your right hand has
      supported me;
    your help*a* has made me great.
36 You gave me a wide place for my steps
    under me,
    and my feet did not slip.
37 I pursued my enemies and overtook them;
    and did not turn back until they were
      consumed.
38 I struck them down, so that they were not able
    to rise;
    they fell under my feet.
39 For you girded me with strength for the battle;
    you made my assailants sink
      under me.
40 You made my enemies turn their backs to me,
    and those who hated me I
      destroyed.
41 They cried for help, but there was no one to
    save them;
    they cried to the Lord, but he did not
      answer them.
42 I beat them fine, like dust before the wind;
    I cast them out like the mire of the streets.

43 You delivered me from strife with the peoples;*b*
    you made me head of the nations;
    people whom I had not known served me.
44 As soon as they heard of me they obeyed me;
    foreigners came cringing to me.
45 Foreigners lost heart,
    and came trembling out of their
      strongholds.

46 The Lord lives! Blessed be my rock,
    and exalted be the God of my salvation,
47 the God who gave me vengeance
    and subdued peoples under me;
48 who delivered me from my enemies;
    indeed, you exalted me above my
      adversaries;
    you delivered me from the violent.

a Or *gentleness* *b* Gk Tg: Heb *people*

49 For this I will extol you, O LORD, among the
        nations,
      and sing praises to your name.
50 Great triumphs he gives to his king,
      and shows steadfast love to his anointed,
      to David and his descendants forever.

19 God's Glory in Creation and the Law
To the leader. A Psalm of David.

The heavens are telling the glory of God;
    and the firmament[a] proclaims his
        handiwork.
2 Day to day pours forth speech,
    and night to night declares knowledge.
3 There is no speech, nor are there words;
    their voice is not heard;
4 yet their voice[b] goes out through all the
        earth,
    and their words to the end of the world.

In the heavens[c] he has set a tent for the sun,
5 which comes out like a bridegroom from his
        wedding canopy,

PRAY IT!

What the Heavens Say
Psalm 19

Have you ever watched the awesome show of
a thunder and lightning storm? Lost yourself
looking up into a star-filled night sky? Felt
breathless watching a magnificent sunrise
or sunset? Creation doesn't use words, but
it can speak deeply to our hearts when we
take the time to listen.

But as amazing as creation is, it only hints
at the astounding glory of God! In the second
half of **Psalm 19**, the psalmist reminds us
that God's law is equally wonderful and is to
be desired above all things. Read this psalm
as your own prayer of praise to God for the
many ways God communicates to you.
Better yet, go outside into nature and read it
as your prayer.

and like a strong man runs its course
        with joy.
6 Its rising is from the end of the heavens,
    and its circuit to the end of them;
    and nothing is hid from its heat.

7 The law of the LORD is perfect,
    reviving the soul;
  the decrees of the LORD are sure,
    making wise the simple;
8 the precepts of the LORD are right,
    rejoicing the heart;
  the commandment of the LORD is clear,
    enlightening the eyes;
9 the fear of the LORD is pure,
    enduring forever;
  the ordinances of the LORD are true
    and righteous altogether.
10 More to be desired are they than gold,
    even much fine gold;
  sweeter also than honey,
    and drippings of the honeycomb.

11 Moreover by them is your servant
        warned;
    in keeping them there is great reward.
12 But who can detect their errors?
    Clear me from hidden faults.
13 Keep back your servant also from the
        insolent;[d]
    do not let them have dominion
        over me.
  Then I shall be blameless,
    and innocent of great transgression.

14 Let the words of my mouth and the
        meditation of my heart
    be acceptable to you,
    O LORD, my rock and my redeemer.

20 Prayer for Victory
To the leader. A Psalm of David.

The LORD answer you in the day of trouble!
    The name of the God of Jacob protect you!
2 May he send you help from the sanctuary,
    and give you support from Zion.
3 May he remember all your offerings,
    and regard with favor your burnt
        sacrifices.   *Selah*

a Or *dome* b Gk Jerome Compare Syr: Heb *line* c Heb *In them* d Or *from proud thoughts*

4 May he grant you your heart's desire,
　and fulfill all your plans.
5 May we shout for joy over your victory,
　and in the name of our God set up our
　　banners.
May the LORD fulfill all your petitions.

6 Now I know that the LORD will help his
　　anointed;
　he will answer him from his holy heaven
　with mighty victories by his right hand.
7 Some take pride in chariots, and some in
　　horses,
　but our pride is in the name of the LORD
　　our God.
8 They will collapse and fall,
　but we shall rise and stand upright.

9 Give victory to the king, O LORD;
　answer us when we call. *a*

Thanksgiving for Victory

21 *To the leader. A Psalm of David.*

In your strength the king rejoices, O LORD,
　and in your help how greatly he exults!
2 You have given him his heart's desire,
　and have not withheld the request of his
　　lips.　　　　　　　　　　　*Selah*
3 For you meet him with rich blessings;
　you set a crown of fine gold on his head.
4 He asked you for life; you gave it to him—
　length of days forever and ever.
5 His glory is great through your help;
　splendor and majesty you bestow on him.
6 You bestow on him blessings forever;
　you make him glad with the joy of your
　　presence.
7 For the king trusts in the LORD,
　and through the steadfast love of the Most
　　High he shall not be moved.

8 Your hand will find out all your enemies;
　your right hand will find out those who
　　hate you.
9 You will make them like a fiery furnace
　when you appear.
The LORD will swallow them up in his
　　wrath,
　and fire will consume them.

10 You will destroy their offspring from the
　　earth,
　and their children from among
　　humankind.
11 If they plan evil against you,
　if they devise mischief, they will not
　　succeed.
12 For you will put them to flight;
　you will aim at their faces with your
　　bows.

13 Be exalted, O LORD, in your strength!
　We will sing and praise your power.

Plea for Deliverance from Suffering and Hostility

22 *To the leader: according to The Deer of the Dawn. A Psalm of David.*

My God, my God, why have you forsaken me?
　Why are you so far from helping me, from
　　the words of my groaning?
2 O my God, I cry by day, but you do not
　　answer;
　and by night, but find no rest.

3 Yet you are holy,
　enthroned on the praises of Israel.
4 In you our ancestors trusted;
　they trusted, and you delivered them.
5 To you they cried, and were saved;
　in you they trusted, and were not put to
　　shame.

6 But I am a worm, and not human;
　scorned by others, and despised by the
　　people.
7 All who see me mock at me;
　they make mouths at me, they shake their
　　heads;
8 "Commit your cause to the LORD; let him
　　deliver—
　let him rescue the one in whom he
　　delights!"

9 Yet it was you who took me from
　　the womb;
　you kept me safe on my mother's breast.
10 On you I was cast from my birth,
　and since my mother bore me you have
　　been my God.

a Gk: Heb *give victory, O LORD; let the King answer us when we call*

11 Do not be far from me,
      for trouble is near
      and there is no one to help.

12 Many bulls encircle me,
      strong bulls of Bashan surround me;
13 they open wide their mouths at me,
      like a ravening and roaring lion.

14 I am poured out like water,
      and all my bones are out of joint;
   my heart is like wax;
      it is melted within my breast;
15 my mouth[a] is dried up like a potsherd,
      and my tongue sticks to my jaws;
      you lay me in the dust of death.

16 For dogs are all around me;
      a company of evildoers encircles me.
   My hands and feet have shriveled;[b]
17 I can count all my bones.
   They stare and gloat over me;
18 they divide my clothes among themselves,
      and for my clothing they cast lots.

19 But you, O LORD, do not be far away!
      O my help, come quickly to my aid!
20 Deliver my soul from the sword,
      my life[c] from the power of the dog!
21   Save me from the mouth of the lion!

   From the horns of the wild oxen you have
      rescued[d] me.
22 I will tell of your name to my brothers and
      sisters;[e]
      in the midst of the congregation I will
      praise you:
23 You who fear the LORD, praise him!
      All you offspring of Jacob, glorify him;
      stand in awe of him, all you offspring of
      Israel!
24 For he did not despise or abhor
      the affliction of the afflicted;
   he did not hide his face from me,[f]
      but heard when I[g] cried to him.

25 From you comes my praise in the great
      congregation;
      my vows I will pay before those who
      fear him.

26 The poor[h] shall eat and be satisfied;
      those who seek him shall praise the
      LORD.
      May your hearts live forever!

27 All the ends of the earth shall remember
      and turn to the LORD;
   and all the families of the nations
      shall worship before him.[i]
28 For dominion belongs to the LORD,
      and he rules over the nations.

29 To him,[j] indeed, shall all who sleep in[k] the
      earth bow down;
      before him shall bow all who go down to
      the dust,
      and I shall live for him.[l]
30 Posterity will serve him;
      future generations will be told about the
      Lord,
31 and[m] proclaim his deliverance to a people
      yet unborn,
      saying that he has done it.

The Divine Shepherd

23 *A Psalm of David.*

   The LORD is my shepherd, I shall not want.
2   He makes me lie down in green pastures;
   he leads me beside still waters;[n]
3   he restores my soul.[o]
   He leads me in right paths[p]
      for his name's sake.

4 Even though I walk through the darkest
      valley,[q]
      I fear no evil;
   for you are with me;
      your rod and your staff—
      they comfort me.

5 You prepare a table before me
      in the presence of my enemies;
   you anoint my head with oil;
      my cup overflows.
6 Surely[r] goodness and mercy[s] shall follow
      me
      all the days of my life,
   and I shall dwell in the house of the LORD
      my whole life long.[t]

a Cn: Heb *strength* b Meaning of Heb uncertain c Heb *my only one* d Heb *answered* e Or *kindred* f Heb *him* g Heb *he* h Or *afflicted*
i Gk Syr Jerome: Heb *you* j Cn: Heb *They have eaten and* k Cn: Heb *all the fat ones* l Compare Gk Syr Vg: Heb *and he who cannot keep himself alive*
m Compare Gk: Heb *it will be told about the Lord to the generation,* 31*they will come and* n Heb *waters of rest* o Or *life* p Or *paths of righteousness*
q Or *the valley of the shadow of death* r Or *Only* s Or *kindness* t Heb *for length of days*

PRAY IT!

The LORD Is My Shepherd
Psalm 23

The famous **Psalm 23** offers two images of God: the Good Shepherd and a generous host. Both images speak of God's closeness and gentle care for us. They speak not of a God who cares for us out of obligation, but one who delights in protecting and providing generously. In the New Testament, Jesus appears as the Good Shepherd who gives his life for his sheep (John 10:1-29). He also appears several times as a host, particularly in the stories about the multiplication of the loaves and the Last Supper.

- Read the psalm slowly as a prayer, letting God fill you with peace and security.
- Pray the psalm again, this time thinking of friends or people throughout the world who might be feeling like sheep without a shepherd. How can you lead them to Jesus? How can you care more for them?
- The role of a shepherd was well known and understood when this was written, but those of us who live in urban settings may find it hard to identify with this image of God. Think of an image that feels relevant to you and apply **Psalm 23**. Start with "The Lord is my _____ ."

24 Entrance into the Temple
Of David. A Psalm.

The earth is the LORD's and all that is in it,
    the world, and those who live in it;
2 for he has founded it on the seas,
    and established it on the rivers.

3 Who shall ascend the hill of the LORD?
    And who shall stand in his holy place?
4 Those who have clean hands and pure hearts,

who do not lift up their souls to what is false,
    and do not swear deceitfully.
5 They will receive blessing from the LORD,
    and vindication from the God of their salvation.
6 Such is the company of those who seek him,
    who seek the face of the God of Jacob.[a]
                Selah

7 Lift up your heads, O gates!
    and be lifted up, O ancient doors!
    that the King of glory may come in.
8 Who is the King of glory?
    The LORD, strong and mighty,
    the LORD, mighty in battle.
9 Lift up your heads, O gates!
    and be lifted up, O ancient doors!
    that the King of glory may come in.
10 Who is this King of glory?
    The LORD of hosts,
    he is the King of glory.   *Selah*

25 Prayer for Guidance and for Deliverance
Of David.

To you, O LORD, I lift up my soul.
2 O my God, in you I trust;
    do not let me be put to shame;
    do not let my enemies exult over me.
3 Do not let those who wait for you be put to shame;
    let them be ashamed who are wantonly treacherous.

4 Make me to know your ways, O LORD;

> "Make me to know your ways, O LORD; teach me your paths. Lead me in your truth, and teach me, for you are the God of my salvation; for you I wait all day long."
> —Psalm 25:4–5

---

a Gk Syr: Heb *your face, O Jacob*

Temple Worship · Psalm 24

When Israel was ruled by kings (1000–587 B.C.), worship in the temple at Jerusalem was an important part of the people's religious life. Many of the psalms, including **Psalm 24**, refer to going up to the temple (the "holy place" in Psalm 24:3). Although the first temple was destroyed in 587 B.C., it was later rebuilt. Temple worship started again and continued into Jesus' time. This is what the priests did during some of the temple ceremonies:

Daily temple worship:

- Presented a burnt offering (a year-old male lamb), grain, drink, and an incense offering every morning
- Presented a second burnt offering and a cereal offering every evening

Sabbath (weekly) temple worship:

- Gave two additional burnt offerings
- Replaced the twelve loaves of bread, called the bread of the Presence (1 Kings 7:48; Matthew 12:4; Hebrews 9:2), recalling the manna God fed the Israelites in the desert
- Made an incense offering

Monthly and festival temple worship:

- Blew the trumpet
- Presented additional burnt offerings and a sin offering (a male goat)
- On the Day of Atonement, laid their hands on a living goat while confessing the people's sins and then sent the goat away into the wilderness

teach me your paths.
⁵ Lead me in your truth, and teach me,
     for you are the God of my salvation;
     for you I wait all day long.

⁶ Be mindful of your mercy, O LORD, and of
          your steadfast love,
     for they have been from of old.
⁷ Do not remember the sins of my youth or my
          transgressions;
     according to your steadfast love
     remember me,
     for your goodness' sake, O LORD!

⁸ Good and upright is the LORD;
     therefore he instructs sinners in the way.
⁹ He leads the humble in what is
          right,
     and teaches the humble his way.
¹⁰ All the paths of the LORD are steadfast love
          and faithfulness,
     for those who keep his covenant and his
          decrees.

¹¹ For your name's sake, O LORD,
     pardon my guilt, for it is great.
¹² Who are they that fear the LORD?
     He will teach them the way that they
          should choose.
¹³ They will abide in prosperity,
     and their children shall possess the land.
¹⁴ The friendship of the LORD is for those who
          fear him,
     and he makes his covenant known to them.
¹⁵ My eyes are ever toward the LORD,
     for he will pluck my feet out of the net.

¹⁶ Turn to me and be gracious to me,
     for I am lonely and afflicted.
¹⁷ Relieve the troubles of my heart,
     and bring me*ᵃ* out of my distress.
¹⁸ Consider my affliction and my
          trouble,
     and forgive all my sins.
¹⁹ Consider how many are my foes,

ᵃ Or *The troubles of my heart are enlarged; bring me*

and with what violent hatred they hate me.
20 O guard my life, and deliver me;
    do not let me be put to shame, for I take
        refuge in you.
21 May integrity and uprightness
        preserve me,
    for I wait for you.

22 Redeem Israel, O God,
    out of all its troubles.

26 Plea for Justice and Declaration of Righteousness

Of David.

Vindicate me, O LORD,
    for I have walked in my integrity,
    and I have trusted in the LORD without
        wavering.
2 Prove me, O LORD, and try me;
    test my heart and mind.
3 For your steadfast love is before my eyes,
    and I walk in faithfulness to you.*a*

4 I do not sit with the worthless,
    nor do I consort with hypocrites;
5 I hate the company of evildoers,
    and will not sit with the wicked.

6 I wash my hands in innocence,
    and go around your altar, O LORD,
7 singing aloud a song of thanksgiving,
    and telling all your wondrous deeds.

8 O LORD, I love the house in which you
        dwell,
    and the place where your glory abides.
9 Do not sweep me away with sinners,
    nor my life with the bloodthirsty,
10 those in whose hands are evil devices,
    and whose right hands are full of
        bribes.

11 But as for me, I walk in my integrity;
    redeem me, and be gracious to me.
12 My foot stands on level ground;
    in the great congregation I will bless the
        LORD.

27 Triumphant Song of Confidence

Of David.

The LORD is my light and my salvation;
    whom shall I fear?
The LORD is the stronghold*b* of my life;
    of whom shall I be afraid?

2 When evildoers assail me
    to devour my flesh—
my adversaries and foes—
    they shall stumble and fall.

3 Though an army encamp against me,
    my heart shall not fear;
though war rise up against me,
    yet I will be confident.

PRAY IT!

Integrity and Values · Psalm 26

What values are you committed to? Compassion, honesty, determination, generosity, love? Can you think of times when your actions didn't reflect your values or beliefs? People with integrity have a set of core values that guide them—values instilled in them by parents, teachers, mentors, and role models. People with integrity act consistently and make sure all their decisions accurately reflect these principles. There is no disconnect between what they say they believe and what they actually do.

It's impossible for us to have integrity if we follow one set of values in one situation and another set of values in a different situation. The integrity of the writer of this psalm comes from following God in everything (Psalm 26:1). The psalmist even wants to be tested by God (Psalm 26:2) to be sure of complete faithfulness! To have the kind of integrity that the psalmist writes about, we have to let God be the only ruler of our lives. That takes a lifetime of growth and change. Pray that God will give you strength to do what is right, even when it's most difficult.

---

a Or *in your faithfulness* **b** Or *refuge*

4 One thing I asked of the LORD,
    that will I seek after:
  to live in the house of the LORD
    all the days of my life,
  to behold the beauty of the LORD,
    and to inquire in his temple.

5 For he will hide me in his shelter
    in the day of trouble;
  he will conceal me under the cover of his tent;
    he will set me high on a rock.

6 Now my head is lifted up
    above my enemies all around me,
  and I will offer in his tent
    sacrifices with shouts of joy;
  I will sing and make melody to the LORD.

7 Hear, O LORD, when I cry aloud,
    be gracious to me and answer me!
8 "Come," my heart says, "seek his face!"
    Your face, LORD, do I seek.
9   Do not hide your face from me.

  Do not turn your servant away in anger,
    you who have been my help.
  Do not cast me off, do not forsake me,
    O God of my salvation!
10 If my father and mother forsake me,
    the LORD will take me up.

11 Teach me your way, O LORD,
    and lead me on a level path
    because of my enemies.
12 Do not give me up to the will of my
      adversaries,
    for false witnesses have risen against me,
    and they are breathing out violence.

13 I believe that I shall see the goodness of
      the LORD
    in the land of the living.
14 Wait for the LORD;
    be strong, and let your heart take courage;
    wait for the LORD!

28 **Prayer for Help and Thanksgiving for It**
Of David.
  To you, O LORD, I call;

  my rock, do not refuse to hear me,
  for if you are silent to me,
    I shall be like those who go down to the Pit.
2 Hear the voice of my supplication,
    as I cry to you for help,
  as I lift up my hands
    toward your most holy sanctuary.*a*

3 Do not drag me away with the wicked,
    with those who are workers of evil,
  who speak peace with their neighbors,
    while mischief is in their hearts.
4 Repay them according to their work,
    and according to the evil of their deeds;
  repay them according to the work of their
      hands;
    render them their due reward.
5 Because they do not regard the works of the
      LORD,
    or the work of his hands,
  he will break them down and build them up no
      more.

6 Blessed be the LORD,
    for he has heard the sound of my pleadings.
7 The LORD is my strength and my shield;
    in him my heart trusts;
  so I am helped, and my heart exults,
    and with my song I give thanks to him.

8 The LORD is the strength of his people;
    he is the saving refuge of his anointed.
9 O save your people, and bless your heritage;
    be their shepherd, and carry them forever.

29 **The Voice of God in a Great Storm**
A Psalm of David.

  Ascribe to the LORD, O heavenly beings,*b*
    ascribe to the LORD glory and strength.
2 Ascribe to the LORD the glory of his name;
    worship the LORD in holy splendor.

3 The voice of the LORD is over the waters;
    the God of glory thunders,
    the LORD, over mighty waters.
4 The voice of the LORD is powerful;
    the voice of the LORD is full of majesty.
5 The voice of the LORD breaks the cedars;

---

a Heb *your innermost sanctuary*   *b* Heb *sons of gods*

LIVE IT!

The Great Storm
Psalm 29

You may have left your fear of thunder back in childhood, but if you've ever stood on top of a mountain and watched a thunderstorm roll in, or felt the electricity of nearby lightning, or experienced the sheer force of wind as a storm ripped across the plains, you know that thunderstorms can still be frightening. They often come up quickly and without warning, causing destruction and demanding respect.

Psalm 29 uses images of nature to express the majesty and power of God. Statements like "The God of glory thunders" (Psalm 29:3), "The voice of the LORD breaks the cedars" (Psalm 29:5), and "The voice of the LORD flashes forth flames of fire" (Psalm 29:7) evoke a divine splendor that we don't often hear about. The psalmist speaks with admiration about the power and majesty of God.

- When have you experienced the awesome power of God?
- What places or surroundings remind you most of God?

the LORD breaks the cedars of Lebanon.
6 He makes Lebanon skip like a calf,
and Sirion like a young wild ox.

7 The voice of the LORD flashes forth flames of fire.
8 The voice of the LORD shakes the wilderness;
the LORD shakes the wilderness of Kadesh.

9 The voice of the LORD causes the oaks to whirl,[a]
and strips the forest bare;
and in his temple all say, "Glory!"

10 The LORD sits enthroned over the flood;

the LORD sits enthroned as king forever.
11 May the LORD give strength to his people!
May the LORD bless his people with peace!

30 **Thanksgiving for Recovery from Grave Illness**
A Psalm. A Song at the dedication of the temple. Of David.

I will extol you, O LORD, for you have drawn me up,
and did not let my foes rejoice over me.
2 O LORD my God, I cried to you for help,
and you have healed me.
3 O LORD, you brought up my soul from Sheol,
restored me to life from among those gone down to the Pit.[b]

4 Sing praises to the LORD, O you his faithful ones,
and give thanks to his holy name.
5 For his anger is but for a moment;
his favor is for a lifetime.
Weeping may linger for the night,
but joy comes with the morning.

6 As for me, I said in my prosperity,
"I shall never be moved."
7 By your favor, O LORD,
you had established me as a strong mountain;
you hid your face;
I was dismayed.

8 To you, O LORD, I cried,
and to the LORD I made supplication:
9 "What profit is there in my death,
if I go down to the Pit?
Will the dust praise you?
Will it tell of your faithfulness?
10 Hear, O LORD, and be gracious to me!
O LORD, be my helper!"

11 You have turned my mourning into dancing;
you have taken off my sackcloth
and clothed me with joy,
12 so that my soul[c] may praise you and not be silent.
O LORD my God, I will give thanks to you forever.

a *Or causes the deer to calve* b *Or that I should not go down to the Pit* c *Heb that glory*

31 Prayer and Praise for Deliverance from Enemies

To the leader. A Psalm of David.

In you, O LORD, I seek refuge;
do not let me ever be put to shame;
in your righteousness deliver me.
2 Incline your ear to me;
rescue me speedily.
Be a rock of refuge for me,
a strong fortress to save me.

3 You are indeed my rock and my fortress;
for your name's sake lead me and guide me,
4 take me out of the net that is hidden for me,
for you are my refuge.
5 Into your hand I commit my spirit;
you have redeemed me, O LORD,
faithful God.

6 You hate[a] those who pay regard to worthless
idols,
but I trust in the LORD.
7 I will exult and rejoice in your steadfast love,
because you have seen my affliction;
you have taken heed of my adversities,
8 and have not delivered me into the hand of the
enemy;
you have set my feet in a broad place.

9 Be gracious to me, O LORD, for I am in
distress;
my eye wastes away from grief,
my soul and body also.
10 For my life is spent with sorrow,
and my years with sighing;
my strength fails because of my misery,[b]
and my bones waste away.

11 I am the scorn of all my adversaries,
a horror[c] to my neighbors,
an object of dread to my acquaintances;
those who see me in the street flee
from me.
12 I have passed out of mind like one who is
dead;
I have become like a broken vessel.
13 For I hear the whispering of many—
terror all around!—
as they scheme together against me,
as they plot to take my life.

14 But I trust in you, O LORD;
I say, "You are my God."
15 My times are in your hand;
deliver me from the hand of my enemies
and persecutors.
16 Let your face shine upon your servant;

The Masai: Fierce Courage · Psalm 31

CONNECT IT!

The Masai are known for their fierce courage. Located mostly in Kenya and Tanzania, these African tribespeople have a rich history of traditions that have made them famous for courage. Although many of their rituals are changing today, traditionally their culture requires young men to hunt and kill a lion with only a spear and shield, undergo a circumcision ceremony (without anesthetic!), and protect their herds of cattle from wild animals. No doubt these young Masai warriors have demonstrated great courage.

But the courage spoken of in **Psalm 31** is a different kind of courage. It's the courage to take shelter in a strong fortress, trust in the faithfulness of God, and wait on the Lord. The psalm ends: "Be strong, and let your heart take courage, all you who wait for the LORD" (Psalm 31:24). Sometimes waiting on God doesn't feel courageous, but God's strength is where we can find true courage to face the challenges of life. It takes courage to make unpopular decisions and to go against peer pressure. It takes courage to do the right thing when the wrong thing seems easier or more enjoyable. It takes courage to protect others and care for their needs. Because these kinds of actions take courage, trusting God's strength and putting it into practice will earn you honor. What is the most courageous thing you have done for the sake of someone else?

a One Heb Ms Gk Syr Jerome: MT *I hate* b Gk Syr: Heb *my iniquity* c Cn: Heb *exceedingly*

save me in your steadfast love.
17 Do not let me be put to shame, O Lord,
    for I call on you;
let the wicked be put to shame;
    let them go dumbfounded to Sheol.
18 Let the lying lips be stilled
    that speak insolently against the righteous
    with pride and contempt.

19 O how abundant is your goodness
    that you have laid up for those who fear you,
and accomplished for those who take refuge
        in you,
    in the sight of everyone!
20 In the shelter of your presence you hide them
    from human plots;
you hold them safe under your shelter
    from contentious tongues.

21 Blessed be the Lord,
    for he has wondrously shown his steadfast
        love to me
    when I was beset as a city under siege.
22 I had said in my alarm,
    "I am driven far[a] from your sight."
But you heard my supplications
    when I cried out to you for help.

23 Love the Lord, all you his saints.
    The Lord preserves the faithful,
    but abundantly repays the one who acts
        haughtily.
24 Be strong, and let your heart take courage,
    all you who wait for the Lord.

The Joy of Forgiveness

32 *Of David. A Maskil.*

Happy are those whose transgression is forgiven,
    whose sin is covered.
2 Happy are those to whom the Lord imputes
        no iniquity,
    and in whose spirit there is no deceit.

3 While I kept silence, my body wasted away
    through my groaning all day long.
4 For day and night your hand was heavy
        upon me;
    my strength was dried up[b] as by the heat of
        summer.   *Selah*

5 Then I acknowledged my sin to you,
    and I did not hide my iniquity;
I said, "I will confess my transgressions to the
        Lord,"
    and you forgave the guilt of my sin.
                                         Selah

6 Therefore let all who are faithful
    offer prayer to you;
at a time of distress,[c] the rush of mighty waters
    shall not reach them.
7 You are a hiding place for me;
    you preserve me from trouble;
    you surround me with glad cries of
        deliverance.   *Selah*

8 I will instruct you and teach you the way you
        should go;
    I will counsel you with my eye upon you.
9 Do not be like a horse or a mule, without
        understanding,
    whose temper must be curbed with bit
        and bridle,
    else it will not stay near you.

10 Many are the torments of the
        wicked,
    but steadfast love surrounds those who
        trust in the Lord.
11 Be glad in the Lord and rejoice, O righteous,
    and shout for joy, all you upright in heart.

The Greatness and Goodness of God

33 Rejoice in the Lord, O you righteous.
    Praise befits the upright.
2 Praise the Lord with the lyre;
    make melody to him with the harp of ten
        strings.
3 Sing to him a new song;
    play skillfully on the strings, with loud
        shouts.

---

a Another reading is *cut off*   b Meaning of Heb uncertain   c Cn: Heb *at a time of finding only*

4 For the word of the LORD is upright,
   and all his work is done in faithfulness.
5 He loves righteousness and justice;
   the earth is full of the steadfast love of the
      LORD.

6 By the word of the LORD the heavens were
      made,
   and all their host by the breath of his
      mouth.
7 He gathered the waters of the sea as in a
      bottle;
   he put the deeps in storehouses.

8 Let all the earth fear the LORD;
   let all the inhabitants of the world stand
      in awe of him.
9 For he spoke, and it came to be;
   he commanded, and it stood firm.

10 The LORD brings the counsel of the nations
      to nothing;
   he frustrates the plans of the
      peoples.
11 The counsel of the LORD stands
      forever,
   the thoughts of his heart to all
      generations.
12 Happy is the nation whose God is the LORD,
   the people whom he has chosen as his
      heritage.

13 The LORD looks down from heaven;
   he sees all humankind.
14 From where he sits enthroned he watches
   all the inhabitants of the earth—
15 he who fashions the hearts of them all,
   and observes all their deeds.
16 A king is not saved by his great
      army;
   a warrior is not delivered by his great
      strength.
17 The war horse is a vain hope for
      victory,
   and by its great might it cannot
      save.

18 Truly the eye of the LORD is on those who
      fear him,
   on those who hope in his steadfast love,

19 to deliver their soul from death,
   and to keep them alive in famine.

20 Our soul waits for the LORD;
   he is our help and shield.
21 Our heart is glad in him,
   because we trust in his holy name.
22 Let your steadfast love, O LORD, be
      upon us,
   even as we hope in you.

34 Praise for Deliverance from Trouble

*Of David, when he feigned madness before
Abimelech, so that he drove him out, and
he went away.*

I will bless the LORD at all times;
   his praise shall continually be in my
      mouth.
2 My soul makes its boast in the LORD;
   let the humble hear and be glad.
3 O magnify the LORD with me,
   and let us exalt his name together.

4 I sought the LORD, and he answered me,
   and delivered me from all my fears.
5 Look to him, and be radiant;
   so your[a] faces shall never be ashamed.
6 This poor soul cried, and was heard by the
      LORD,
   and was saved from every trouble.
7 The angel of the LORD encamps
   around those who fear him, and delivers
      them.
8 O taste and see that the LORD is good;
   happy are those who take refuge in him.
9 O fear the LORD, you his holy ones,
   for those who fear him have no
      want.
10 The young lions suffer want and hunger,
   but those who seek the LORD lack no good
      thing.

11 Come, O children, listen to me;
   I will teach you the fear of the LORD.
12 Which of you desires life,
   and covets many days to enjoy good?
13 Keep your tongue from evil,
   and your lips from speaking deceit.
14 Depart from evil, and do good;
   seek peace, and pursue it.

a Gk Syr Jerome: Heb *their*

¹⁵ The eyes of the LORD are on the righteous,
  and his ears are open to their cry.
¹⁶ The face of the LORD is against evildoers,
  to cut off the remembrance of them from
  the earth.
¹⁷ When the righteous cry for help, the LORD
  hears,
  and rescues them from all their troubles.
¹⁸ The LORD is near to the brokenhearted,
  and saves the crushed in spirit.

¹⁹ Many are the afflictions of the righteous,
  but the LORD rescues them from them all.
²⁰ He keeps all their bones;
  not one of them will be broken.
²¹ Evil brings death to the wicked,
  and those who hate the righteous will be
  condemned.
²² The LORD redeems the life of his servants;
  none of those who take refuge in him will
  be condemned.

---

35   Prayer for Deliverance from Enemies
Of David.

Contend, O LORD, with those who contend
  with me;
  fight against those who fight
  against me!
² Take hold of shield and buckler,
  and rise up to help me!
³ Draw the spear and javelin
  against my pursuers;
  say to my soul,
  "I am your salvation."

⁴ Let them be put to shame and dishonor
  who seek after my life.
Let them be turned back and confounded
  who devise evil against me.
⁵ Let them be like chaff before the wind,
  with the angel of the LORD driving
  them on.
⁶ Let their way be dark and slippery,
  with the angel of the LORD pursuing
  them.

⁷ For without cause they hid their net*ᵃ* for me;
  without cause they dug a pit*ᵇ* for my life.
⁸ Let ruin come on them unawares.

And let the net that they hid ensnare them;
  let them fall in it—to their ruin.

⁹ Then my soul shall rejoice in the LORD,
  exulting in his deliverance.
¹⁰ All my bones shall say,
  "O LORD, who is like you?
You deliver the weak
  from those too strong for them,
  the weak and needy from those who despoil
  them."

¹¹ Malicious witnesses rise up;
  they ask me about things I do not know.
¹² They repay me evil for good;
  my soul is forlorn.
¹³ But as for me, when they were sick,
  I wore sackcloth;
  I afflicted myself with fasting.
I prayed with head bowed*ᶜ* on my bosom,
¹⁴   as though I grieved for a friend or a brother;
I went about as one who laments for a mother,
  bowed down and in mourning.

¹⁵ But at my stumbling they gathered in glee,
  they gathered together against me;
ruffians whom I did not know
  tore at me without ceasing;
¹⁶ they impiously mocked more and more,*ᵈ*
  gnashing at me with their teeth.

¹⁷ How long, O LORD, will you look on?
  Rescue me from their ravages,
  my life from the lions!
¹⁸ Then I will thank you in the great congregation;
  in the mighty throng I will praise you.

¹⁹ Do not let my treacherous enemies rejoice
  over me,
  or those who hate me without cause wink
  the eye.
²⁰ For they do not speak peace,
  but they conceive deceitful words
  against those who are quiet in the land.
²¹ They open wide their mouths against me;
  they say, "Aha, Aha,
  our eyes have seen it."

²² You have seen, O LORD; do not be silent!
  O Lord, do not be far from me!

ᵃ Heb a pit, their net ᵇ The word pit is transposed from the preceding line ᶜ Or My prayer turned back ᵈ Cn Compare Gk: Heb like the profanest of mockers of a cake

23 Wake up! Bestir yourself for my defense,
    for my cause, my God and my Lord!
24 Vindicate me, O LORD, my God,
    according to your righteousness,
    and do not let them rejoice over me.
25 Do not let them say to themselves,
    "Aha, we have our heart's desire."
    Do not let them say, "We have swallowed
      you*a* up."

26 Let all those who rejoice at my calamity
    be put to shame and confusion;
  let those who exalt themselves
    against me
    be clothed with shame and dishonor.

27 Let those who desire my vindication
    shout for joy and be glad,
    and say evermore,
  "Great is the LORD,
    who delights in the welfare of his servant."
28 Then my tongue shall tell of your
    righteousness
    and of your praise all day long.

36 Human Wickedness and Divine Goodness

*To the leader. Of David, the servant of the
LORD.*

Transgression speaks to the
    wicked
    deep in their hearts;
  there is no fear of God
    before their eyes.
2 For they flatter themselves in their own eyes
    that their iniquity cannot be found out and
      hated.
3 The words of their mouths are mischief and
      deceit;
    they have ceased to act wisely and do
      good.
4 They plot mischief while on their beds;
    they are set on a way that is not good;
    they do not reject evil.

5 Your steadfast love, O LORD, extends to the
      heavens,
    your faithfulness to the clouds.
6 Your righteousness is like the mighty
      mountains,

your judgments are like the great deep;
    you save humans and animals alike,
      O LORD.

7 How precious is your steadfast love, O God!
    All people may take refuge in the shadow
      of your wings.
8 They feast on the abundance of your house,
    and you give them drink from the river of
      your delights.
9 For with you is the fountain of life;
    in your light we see light.

10 O continue your steadfast love to those who
      know you,
    and your salvation to the upright of heart!
11 Do not let the foot of the arrogant tread
      on me,
    or the hand of the wicked drive me away.
12 There the evildoers lie prostrate;
    they are thrust down, unable to rise.

37 Exhortation to Patience and Trust

Of David.

Do not fret because of the wicked;
    do not be envious of wrongdoers,
2 for they will soon fade like the grass,
    and wither like the green herb.

3 Trust in the LORD, and do good;
    so you will live in the land, and enjoy
      security.
4 Take delight in the LORD,
    and he will give you the desires of your
      heart.

5 Commit your way to the LORD;

> "Take delight in the
> LORD, and he will
> give you the desires
> of your heart.
> Commit your way to
> the LORD; trust in him,
> and he will act."
> —Psalm 37:4–5

a Heb *him*

trust in him, and he will act.

6 He will make your vindication shine like the
   light,
   and the justice of your cause like the
   noonday.

7 Be still before the LORD, and wait patiently
   for him;
   do not fret over those who prosper in
   their way,
   over those who carry out evil
   devices.

8 Refrain from anger, and forsake wrath.
   Do not fret—it leads only to evil.
9 For the wicked shall be cut off,
   but those who wait for the LORD shall
   inherit the land.

10 Yet a little while, and the wicked will be no
   more;
   though you look diligently for their place,
   they will not be there.
11 But the meek shall inherit the land,
   and delight themselves in abundant
   prosperity.

12 The wicked plot against the righteous,
   and gnash their teeth at them;
13 but the LORD laughs at the wicked,
   for he sees that their day is coming.

14 The wicked draw the sword and bend
   their bows
   to bring down the poor and needy,
   to kill those who walk uprightly;
15 their sword shall enter their own heart,
   and their bows shall be broken.

16 Better is a little that the righteous person has
   than the abundance of many
   wicked.
17 For the arms of the wicked shall be broken,
   but the LORD upholds the righteous.

18 The LORD knows the days of the blameless,
   and their heritage will abide forever;
19 they are not put to shame in evil
   times,
   in the days of famine they have abundance.

20 But the wicked perish,
   and the enemies of the LORD are like the
   glory of the pastures;
   they vanish—like smoke they vanish away.

21 The wicked borrow, and do not pay back,
   but the righteous are generous and keep
   giving;
22 for those blessed by the LORD shall inherit the
   land,
   but those cursed by him shall be cut off.

23 Our steps*a* are made firm by the LORD,
   when he delights in our*b* way;
24 though we stumble,*c* we*d* shall not fall
   headlong,
   for the LORD holds us*e* by the hand.

25 I have been young, and now am old,
   yet I have not seen the righteous forsaken
   or their children begging bread.
26 They are ever giving liberally and lending,
   and their children become a blessing.

27 Depart from evil, and do good;
   so you shall abide forever.
28 For the LORD loves justice;
   he will not forsake his faithful ones.

   The righteous shall be kept safe
   forever,
   but the children of the wicked shall be
   cut off.
29 The righteous shall inherit the land,
   and live in it forever.

30 The mouths of the righteous utter wisdom,
   and their tongues speak justice.
31 The law of their God is in their hearts;
   their steps do not slip.

32 The wicked watch for the righteous,
   and seek to kill them.
33 The LORD will not abandon them to their
   power,
   or let them be condemned when they are
   brought to trial.

34 Wait for the LORD, and keep to his way,
   and he will exalt you to inherit the land;

a Heb *A man's steps*　b Heb *his*　c Heb *he stumbles*　d Heb *he*　e Heb *him*

you will look on the destruction of the
wicked.

35 I have seen the wicked oppressing,
and towering like a cedar of Lebanon. *a*
36 Again I *b* passed by, and they were no more;
though I sought them, they could not be
found.

37 Mark the blameless, and behold the upright,
for there is posterity for the peaceable.
38 But transgressors shall be altogether
destroyed;
the posterity of the wicked shall be cut off.

39 The salvation of the righteous is from the
Lord;
he is their refuge in the time of trouble.
40 The Lord helps them and rescues them;
he rescues them from the wicked, and
saves them,
because they take refuge in him.

A Penitent Sufferer's Plea for Healing

38
*A Psalm of David, for the memorial
offering.*

O Lord, do not rebuke me in your anger,
or discipline me in your wrath.
2 For your arrows have sunk into me,
and your hand has come down
on me.

3 There is no soundness in my flesh
because of your indignation;
there is no health in my bones
because of my sin.
4 For my iniquities have gone over my head;
they weigh like a burden too heavy for me.

5 My wounds grow foul and fester
because of my foolishness;
6 I am utterly bowed down and prostrate;
all day long I go around mourning.
7 For my loins are filled with burning,
and there is no soundness in my flesh.
8 I am utterly spent and crushed;
I groan because of the tumult of my heart.

9 O Lord, all my longing is known to you;
my sighing is not hidden from you.

10 My heart throbs, my strength fails me;
as for the light of my eyes—it also has
gone from me.
11 My friends and companions stand aloof from
my affliction,
and my neighbors stand far off.

12 Those who seek my life lay their snares;
those who seek to hurt me speak of ruin,
and meditate treachery all day long.

13 But I am like the deaf, I do not hear;
like the mute, who cannot speak.
14 Truly, I am like one who does not hear,
and in whose mouth is no retort.

15 But it is for you, O Lord, that I wait;
it is you, O Lord my God, who will
answer.
16 For I pray, "Only do not let them rejoice
over me,
those who boast against me when my foot
slips."

17 For I am ready to fall,
and my pain is ever with me.
18 I confess my iniquity;
I am sorry for my sin.
19 Those who are my foes without cause *c* are
mighty,
and many are those who hate me
wrongfully.
20 Those who render me evil for good
are my adversaries because I follow after
good.

21 Do not forsake me, O Lord;
O my God, do not be far from me;
22 make haste to help me,
O Lord, my salvation.

Prayer for Wisdom and Forgiveness

39
*To the leader: to Jeduthun. A Psalm
of David.*

I said, "I will guard my ways
that I may not sin with my tongue;
I will keep a muzzle on my mouth
as long as the wicked are in my presence."
2 I was silent and still;
I held my peace to no avail;

---

a Gk: Meaning of Heb uncertain   *b* Gk Syr Jerome: Heb *he*   *c* Q Ms: MT *my living foes*

my distress grew worse,
   3   my heart became hot within me.
While I mused, the fire burned;
   then I spoke with my tongue:

4 "LORD, let me know my end,
   and what is the measure of my days;
   let me know how fleeting my life is.
5 You have made my days a few handbreadths,
   and my lifetime is as nothing in your sight.
Surely everyone stands as a mere breath.
                           Selah
   6   Surely everyone goes about like a shadow.
Surely for nothing they are in turmoil;
   they heap up, and do not know who will
      gather.

7 "And now, O Lord, what do I wait for?
   My hope is in you.
8 Deliver me from all my transgressions.
   Do not make me the scorn of the fool.
9 I am silent; I do not open my mouth,
   for it is you who have done it.
10 Remove your stroke from me;
   I am worn down by the blows*a* of your
      hand.

11 "You chastise mortals
   in punishment for sin,
consuming like a moth what is dear to them;
   surely everyone is a mere breath.   *Selah*

12 "Hear my prayer, O LORD,
   and give ear to my cry;
   do not hold your peace at my tears.
For I am your passing guest,
   an alien, like all my forebears.
13 Turn your gaze away from me, that I may
      smile again,
   before I depart and am no more."

40 **Thanksgiving for Deliverance
and Prayer for Help**
To the leader. Of David. A Psalm.

I waited patiently for the LORD;
   he inclined to me and heard my cry.
2 He drew me up from the desolate pit,*b*
   out of the miry bog,
and set my feet upon a rock,

making my steps secure.
3 He put a new song in my mouth,
   a song of praise to our God.
Many will see and fear,
   and put their trust in the LORD.

4 Happy are those who make
   the LORD their trust,
who do not turn to the proud,
   to those who go astray after false gods.
5 You have multiplied, O LORD my God,
   your wondrous deeds and your thoughts
      toward us;
   none can compare with you.
Were I to proclaim and tell of them,
   they would be more than can be
      counted.

6 Sacrifice and offering you do not desire,
   but you have given me an open ear.*c*
Burnt offering and sin offering
   you have not required.
7 Then I said, "Here I am;
   in the scroll of the book it is written
      of me.*d*
8 I delight to do your will, O my God;
   your law is within my heart."

9 I have told the glad news of deliverance
   in the great congregation;
see, I have not restrained my lips,
   as you know, O LORD.
10 I have not hidden your saving help within my
      heart,
   I have spoken of your faithfulness and
      your salvation;
I have not concealed your steadfast love and
      your faithfulness
   from the great congregation.

11 Do not, O LORD, withhold
   your mercy from me;
let your steadfast love and your faithfulness
   keep me safe forever.
12 For evils have encompassed me
   without number;
my iniquities have overtaken me,
   until I cannot see;
they are more than the hairs of my head,
   and my heart fails me.

---

a Heb *hostility* b Cn: Heb *pit of tumult* c Heb *ears you have dug for me* d Meaning of Heb uncertain

13 Be pleased, O Lᴏʀᴅ, to deliver me;
    O Lᴏʀᴅ, make haste to help me.
14 Let all those be put to shame and confusion
    who seek to snatch away my life;
  let those be turned back and brought to
    dishonor
    who desire my hurt.
15 Let those be appalled because of their shame
    who say to me, "Aha, Aha!"

16 But may all who seek you
    rejoice and be glad in you;
  may those who love your salvation
    say continually, "Great is the Lᴏʀᴅ!"
17 As for me, I am poor and needy,
    but the Lord takes thought for me.
  You are my help and my deliverer;
    do not delay, O my God.

41   Assurance of God's Help and a Plea for Healing
To the leader. A Psalm of David.

Happy are those who consider the poor;*ᵃ*
    the Lᴏʀᴅ delivers them in the day of
    trouble.
2 The Lᴏʀᴅ protects them and keeps them
    alive;
  they are called happy in the land.
  You do not give them up to the will of
    their enemies.
3 The Lᴏʀᴅ sustains them on their sickbed;
  in their illness you heal all their
    infirmities.*ᵇ*

4 As for me, I said, "O Lᴏʀᴅ, be gracious
    to me;
  heal me, for I have sinned against you."
5 My enemies wonder in malice
    when I will die, and my name
      perish.
6 And when they come to see me, they utter
      empty words,
  while their hearts gather mischief;
  when they go out, they tell it abroad.
7 All who hate me whisper together about me;
  they imagine the worst for me.

8 They think that a deadly thing has fastened
    on me,

    that I will not rise again from where
    I lie.
9 Even my bosom friend in whom I trusted,
    who ate of my bread, has lifted the heel
    against me.
10 But you, O Lᴏʀᴅ, be gracious to me,
    and raise me up, that I may repay them.

11 By this I know that you are pleased
    with me;
  because my enemy has not triumphed
    over me.
12 But you have upheld me because of my
    integrity,
  and set me in your presence forever.

13 Blessed be the Lᴏʀᴅ, the God of Israel,
    from everlasting to everlasting.
      Amen and Amen.

BOOK II
(Psalms 42–72)

42   Longing for God and His Help in Distress
To the leader. A Maskil of the Korahites.

As a deer longs for flowing streams,
    so my soul longs for you, O God.
2 My soul thirsts for God,
    for the living God.
  When shall I come and behold
    the face of God?
3 My tears have been my food
    day and night,
  while people say to me continually,
    "Where is your God?"

4 These things I remember,
    as I pour out my soul:
  how I went with the throng,*ᶜ*
    and led them in procession to the house
      of God,
  with glad shouts and songs of thanksgiving,
    a multitude keeping festival.
5 Why are you cast down, O my soul,
    and why are you disquieted
      within me?
  Hope in God; for I shall again praise him,
    my help ⁶and my God.

---

a Or *weak* b Heb *you change all his bed* c Meaning of Heb uncertain

Longing
Psalm 42

Pain makes us search for God's comfort. Tears make us long for the flowing streams of God's love. Think of times when you have felt the most in need of God—times of rejection, depression, or loneliness. The writer of **Psalm 42** knows what it feels like to call out to God from a dark place in life. When you're in those hard times, what do you do? Sleep? Listen to music? Play video games? Shop? Run? Where do you place your hope? This psalm shows us where to turn: "Hope in God; for I shall again praise him, my help and my God" (Psalm 42:11).

My soul is cast down within me;
    therefore I remember you
from the land of Jordan and of
      Hermon,
    from Mount Mizar.
7 Deep calls to deep
    at the thunder of your cataracts;
all your waves and your billows
    have gone over me.
8 By day the Lord commands his steadfast
    love,
    and at night his song is with me,
    a prayer to the God of my life.

9 I say to God, my rock,
    "Why have you forgotten me?
Why must I walk about mournfully
    because the enemy oppresses me?"
10 As with a deadly wound in my body,
    my adversaries taunt me,
while they say to me continually,
    "Where is your God?"

11 Why are you cast down, O my soul,
    and why are you disquieted
      within me?
Hope in God; for I shall again praise him,
    my help and my God.

a Gk Syr: Heb *You are my King, O God; command*

43 Prayer to God in Time of Trouble

Vindicate me, O God, and defend my
    cause
    against an ungodly people;
from those who are deceitful and unjust
    deliver me!
2 For you are the God in whom I take refuge;
    why have you cast me off?
Why must I walk about mournfully
    because of the oppression of the enemy?

3 O send out your light and your truth;
    let them lead me;
let them bring me to your holy hill
    and to your dwelling.
4 Then I will go to the altar of God,
    to God my exceeding joy;
and I will praise you with the harp,
    O God, my God.

5 Why are you cast down, O my soul,
    and why are you disquieted within me?
Hope in God; for I shall again praise him,
    my help and my God.

44 National Lament and Prayer for Help

To the leader. Of the Korahites. A Maskil.

We have heard with our ears, O God,
    our ancestors have told us,
what deeds you performed in their days,
    in the days of old:
2 you with your own hand drove out the nations,
    but them you planted;
you afflicted the peoples,
    but them you set free;
3 for not by their own sword did they win the
      land,
    nor did their own arm give them victory;
but your right hand, and your arm,
    and the light of your countenance,
    for you delighted in them.

4 You are my King and my God;
    you command[a] victories for Jacob.
5 Through you we push down our foes;
    through your name we tread down our
      assailants.
6 For not in my bow do I trust,
    nor can my sword save me.

⁷ But you have saved us from our foes,
　　and have put to confusion those who
　　　hate us.
⁸ In God we have boasted continually,
　　and we will give thanks to your name
　　　forever.   *Selah*

⁹ Yet you have rejected us and abased us,
　　and have not gone out with our armies.
¹⁰ You made us turn back from the foe,
　　and our enemies have gotten spoil.
¹¹ You have made us like sheep for slaughter,
　　and have scattered us among the nations.
¹² You have sold your people for a trifle,
　　demanding no high price for them.

¹³ You have made us the taunt of our neighbors,
　　the derision and scorn of those around us.
¹⁴ You have made us a byword among the
　　　nations,
　　a laughingstock*ᵃ* among the peoples.
¹⁵ All day long my disgrace is before me,
　　and shame has covered my face
¹⁶ at the words of the taunters and revilers,
　　at the sight of the enemy and the avenger.

¹⁷ All this has come upon us,
　　yet we have not forgotten you,
　　or been false to your covenant.
¹⁸ Our heart has not turned back,
　　nor have our steps departed from your way,
¹⁹ yet you have broken us in the haunt of jackals,
　　and covered us with deep darkness.

²⁰ If we had forgotten the name of our God,
　　or spread out our hands to a strange god,
²¹ would not God discover this?
　　For he knows the secrets of the heart.
²² Because of you we are being killed all day
　　　long,
　　and accounted as sheep for the slaughter.

²³ Rouse yourself! Why do you sleep, O Lord?
　　Awake, do not cast us off forever!
²⁴ Why do you hide your face?
　　Why do you forget our affliction and
　　　oppression?
²⁵ For we sink down to the dust;
　　our bodies cling to the ground.
²⁶ Rise up, come to our help.

Redeem us for the sake of your steadfast
　　love.

45 Ode for a Royal Wedding
*To the leader: according to Lilies. Of the
Korahites. A Maskil. A love song.*

My heart overflows with a goodly theme;
　　I address my verses to the king;
　　my tongue is like the pen of a ready scribe.

² You are the most handsome of men;
　　grace is poured upon your lips;
　　therefore God has blessed you forever.
³ Gird your sword on your thigh, O mighty one,
　　in your glory and majesty.

⁴ In your majesty ride on victoriously
　　for the cause of truth and to defend*ᵇ* the
　　　right;
　　let your right hand teach you dread deeds.
⁵ Your arrows are sharp
　　in the heart of the king's enemies;
　　the peoples fall under you.

⁶ Your throne, O God,*ᶜ* endures forever and
　　　ever.
　　Your royal scepter is a scepter of equity;
⁷ you love righteousness and hate
　　　wickedness.
Therefore God, your God, has anointed you
　　with the oil of gladness beyond your
　　　companions;
⁸ your robes are all fragrant with myrrh and
　　　aloes and cassia.
From ivory palaces stringed instruments make
　　you glad;
⁹ daughters of kings are among your ladies of
　　　honor;
　　at your right hand stands the queen in gold
　　　of Ophir.

¹⁰ Hear, O daughter, consider and incline
　　　your ear;
　　forget your people and your father's house,
¹¹ and the king will desire your beauty.
Since he is your lord, bow to him;
¹² the people*ᵈ* of Tyre will seek your favor
　　　with gifts,
　　the richest of the people ¹³with all kinds of
　　　wealth.

ᵃ Heb *a shaking of the head*   *ᵇ* Cn: Heb *and the meekness of*   *ᶜ* Or *Your throne is a throne of God, it*   *ᵈ* Heb *daughter*

The princess is decked in her chamber with
    gold-woven robes;[a]
14 in many-colored robes she is led to the
    king;
    behind her the virgins, her companions,
    follow.
15 With joy and gladness they are led along
    as they enter the palace of the king.

16 In the place of ancestors you, O king,[b] shall
    have sons;
    you will make them princes in all the earth.
17 I will cause your name to be celebrated in all
    generations;
    therefore the peoples will praise you
    forever and ever.

God's Defense of His City and People

46 *To the leader. Of the Korahites. According
to Alamoth. A Song.*

God is our refuge and strength,
    a very present[c] help in trouble.
2 Therefore we will not fear, though the earth
    should change,
    though the mountains shake in the heart of
    the sea;
3 though its waters roar and foam,
    though the mountains tremble with its
    tumult.   *Selah*

4 There is a river whose streams make glad the
    city of God,
    the holy habitation of the Most High.
5 God is in the midst of the city;[d] it shall not be
    moved;
    God will help it when the morning dawns.
6 The nations are in an uproar, the kingdoms
    totter;
    he utters his voice, the earth melts.
7 The LORD of hosts is with us;
    the God of Jacob is our refuge.[e]   *Selah*

8 Come, behold the works of the LORD;
    see what desolations he has brought on the
    earth.
9 He makes wars cease to the end of the earth;
    he breaks the bow, and shatters the spear;
    he burns the shields with fire.
10 "Be still, and know that I am God!
    I am exalted among the nations,

I am exalted in the earth."
11 The LORD of hosts is with us;
    the God of Jacob is our refuge.[e]   *Selah*

God's Rule over the Nations

47 *To the leader. Of the Korahites. A Psalm.*

Clap your hands, all you peoples;
    shout to God with loud songs of joy.
2 For the LORD, the Most High, is awesome,
    a great king over all the earth.
3 He subdued peoples under us,
    and nations under our feet.
4 He chose our heritage for us,
    the pride of Jacob whom he loves.   *Selah*

5 God has gone up with a shout,
    the LORD with the sound of a trumpet.
6 Sing praises to God, sing praises;
    sing praises to our King, sing praises.
7 For God is the king of all the earth;
    sing praises with a psalm.[f]

8 God is king over the nations;
    God sits on his holy throne.
9 The princes of the peoples gather
    as the people of the God of Abraham.
For the shields of the earth belong to God;
    he is highly exalted.

The Glory and Strength of Zion

48 *A Song. A Psalm of the Korahites.*

Great is the LORD and greatly to be praised
    in the city of our God.
His holy mountain, 2beautiful in elevation,
    is the joy of all the earth,
Mount Zion, in the far north,
    the city of the great King.
3 Within its citadels God
    has shown himself a sure defense.

---

a *Or people.* [13]*All glorious is the princess within, gold embroidery is her clothing* **b** *Heb lacks O king* **c** *Or well proved* **d** *Heb of it* **e** *Or fortress*
f *Heb Maskil*

⁴ Then the kings assembled,
  they came on together.
⁵ As soon as they saw it, they were astounded;
  they were in panic, they took to flight;
⁶ trembling took hold of them there,
  pains as of a woman in labor,
⁷ as when an east wind shatters
  the ships of Tarshish.
⁸ As we have heard, so have we seen
  in the city of the LORD of hosts,
in the city of our God,
  which God establishes forever.   *Selah*

⁹ We ponder your steadfast love, O God,
  in the midst of your temple.
¹⁰ Your name, O God, like your praise,
  reaches to the ends of the earth.
Your right hand is filled with victory.
¹¹   Let Mount Zion be glad,
let the towns*ᵃ* of Judah rejoice
because of your judgments.

¹² Walk about Zion, go all around it,
  count its towers,
¹³ consider well its ramparts;
  go through its citadels,
that you may tell the next generation
¹⁴   that this is God,
our God forever and ever.
  He will be our guide forever.

49 The Folly of Trust in Riches
To the leader. Of the Korahites. A Psalm.

Hear this, all you peoples;
  give ear, all inhabitants of the world,
² both low and high,
  rich and poor together.
³ My mouth shall speak wisdom;
  the meditation of my heart shall be
    understanding.
⁴ I will incline my ear to a proverb;
  I will solve my riddle to the music of the
    harp.

⁵ Why should I fear in times of trouble,
  when the iniquity of my persecutors
    surrounds me,
⁶ those who trust in their wealth
  and boast of the abundance of their riches?

⁷ Truly, no ransom avails for one's life,*ᵇ*
  there is no price one can give to God
    for it.
⁸ For the ransom of life is costly,
  and can never suffice,
⁹ that one should live on forever
  and never see the grave.*ᶜ*

¹⁰ When we look at the wise, they die;
  fool and dolt perish together
  and leave their wealth to others.
¹¹ Their graves*ᵈ* are their homes forever,
  their dwelling places to all generations,
  though they named lands their own.
¹² Mortals cannot abide in their pomp;
  they are like the animals that perish.

¹³ Such is the fate of the foolhardy,
  the end of those*ᵉ* who are pleased with
    their lot.   *Selah*
¹⁴ Like sheep they are appointed for Sheol;
  Death shall be their shepherd;
straight to the grave they descend,*ᶠ*
  and their form shall waste away;
  Sheol shall be their home.*ᵍ*
¹⁵ But God will ransom my soul from the power
    of Sheol,
  for he will receive me.   *Selah*

¹⁶ Do not be afraid when some become rich,
  when the wealth of their houses increases.
¹⁷ For when they die they will carry nothing
    away;
  their wealth will not go down after them.
¹⁸ Though in their lifetime they count
    themselves happy
  —for you are praised when you do well
    for yourself—
¹⁹ they*ʰ* will go to the company of their
    ancestors,
  who will never again see the light.
²⁰ Mortals cannot abide in their pomp;
  they are like the animals that perish.

50 The Acceptable Sacrifice
A Psalm of Asaph.

The mighty one, God the LORD,
  speaks and summons the earth
  from the rising of the sun to its setting.

ᵃ Heb *daughters*   *ᵇ* Another reading is *no one can ransom a brother*   *ᶜ* Heb *the pit*   *ᵈ* Gk Syr Compare Tg: Heb *their inward* (thought)   *ᵉ* Tg: Heb *after them*   *ᶠ* Cn: Heb *the upright shall have dominion over them in the morning*   *ᵍ* Meaning of Heb uncertain   *ʰ* Cn: Heb *you*

2 Out of Zion, the perfection of beauty,
  God shines forth.

3 Our God comes and does not keep silence,
  before him is a devouring fire,
  and a mighty tempest all around him.
4 He calls to the heavens above
  and to the earth, that he may judge his
  people:
5 "Gather to me my faithful ones,
  who made a covenant with me by
  sacrifice!"
6 The heavens declare his righteousness,
  for God himself is judge.
  Selah

7 "Hear, O my people, and I will speak,
  O Israel, I will testify against you.
  I am God, your God.
8 Not for your sacrifices do I rebuke you;
  your burnt offerings are continually
  before me.
9 I will not accept a bull from your house,
  or goats from your folds.
10 For every wild animal of the forest is mine,
   the cattle on a thousand hills.
11 I know all the birds of the air,*a*
   and all that moves in the field is mine.

12 "If I were hungry, I would not tell you,
   for the world and all that is in it is
   mine.
13 Do I eat the flesh of bulls,
   or drink the blood of goats?
14 Offer to God a sacrifice of thanksgiving,*b*
   and pay your vows to the Most High.
15 Call on me in the day of trouble;
   I will deliver you, and you shall
   glorify me."

16 But to the wicked God says:
   "What right have you to recite my
   statutes,
   or take my covenant on your lips?
17 For you hate discipline,
   and you cast my words behind you.
18 You make friends with a thief when you
   see one,
   and you keep company with
   adulterers.

19 "You give your mouth free rein for evil,
   and your tongue frames deceit.
20 You sit and speak against your kin;
   you slander your own mother's child.
21 These things you have done and I have been
   silent;
   you thought that I was one just like
   yourself.
   But now I rebuke you, and lay the charge
   before you.

22 "Mark this, then, you who forget God,
   or I will tear you apart, and there will be
   no one to deliver.
23 Those who bring thanksgiving as their
   sacrifice honor me;
   to those who go the right way*c*
   I will show the salvation of God."

Prayer for Cleansing and Pardon

51 *To the leader. A Psalm of David,
when the prophet Nathan came to him,
after he had gone in to Bathsheba.*

Have mercy on me, O God,
  according to your steadfast love;
according to your abundant mercy
  blot out my transgressions.
2 Wash me thoroughly from my iniquity,
  and cleanse me from my sin.

3 For I know my transgressions,
  and my sin is ever before me.
4 Against you, you alone, have I sinned,
  and done what is evil in your sight,
so that you are justified in your sentence
  and blameless when you pass judgment.
5 Indeed, I was born guilty,
  a sinner when my mother
  conceived me.

6 You desire truth in the inward being;*d*
  therefore teach me wisdom in my secret
  heart.
7 Purge me with hyssop, and I shall be clean;
  wash me, and I shall be whiter than snow.
8 Let me hear joy and gladness;
  let the bones that you have crushed
  rejoice.
9 Hide your face from my sins,
  and blot out all my iniquities.

a Gk Syr Tg: Heb *mountains* b Or *make thanksgiving your sacrifice to God* c Heb *who set a way* d Meaning of Heb uncertain

PRAY IT!

A Fresh Start
Psalm 51

This is a beautiful prayer of sorrow and remorse. It is attributed to King David, who would have written it seeking forgiveness and a fresh start after committing adultery with Bathsheba. Take a few minutes to read this psalm prayerfully and reflect on the marvelous way it asks for God's help in starting over.

Today, people can also fall into a sinful pattern of having sex outside of marriage. Many people experience deep regret and sadness in losing their virginity. Their struggle with guilt and the loss of their sexual innocence often causes negative patterns in future relationships. But the promise of this psalm is that they can start fresh at any point in this cycle! Some people call this new beginning a secondary virginity. It's not, of course, a physical virginity, but a restored purity of the heart and soul. It means a commitment not to have sex again, except within marriage.

So whenever you're feeling the weight of sin, whether it's sexual or some other kind, say this psalm as your prayer. Let it mark your commitment to start fresh with God's help. Ask God to show you what situations to avoid and who you need to ask to support you. Remember, God is always ready to forgive you, and all of heaven rejoices when you make a fresh start!

10 Create in me a clean heart, O God,
　　and put a new and right[a] spirit
　　　　within me.
11 Do not cast me away from your presence,
　　and do not take your holy spirit
　　　　from me.
12 Restore to me the joy of your salvation,
　　and sustain in me a willing[b] spirit.

13 Then I will teach transgressors your ways,
　　and sinners will return to you.
14 Deliver me from bloodshed, O God,
　　O God of my salvation,
　　and my tongue will sing aloud of your
　　　　deliverance.

15 O Lord, open my lips,
　　and my mouth will declare your praise.
16 For you have no delight in sacrifice;
　　if I were to give a burnt offering, you would
　　　　not be pleased.
17 The sacrifice acceptable to God[c] is a broken
　　　　spirit;
　　a broken and contrite heart, O God, you will
　　　　not despise.

18 Do good to Zion in your good
　　　　pleasure;
　　rebuild the walls of Jerusalem,
19 then you will delight in right sacrifices,
　　in burnt offerings and whole burnt offerings;
　　then bulls will be offered on your altar.

52 **Judgment on the Deceitful**

To the leader. A Maskil of David, when Doeg the Edomite came to Saul and said to him, "David has come to the house of Ahimelech."

Why do you boast, O mighty one,
　　of mischief done against the godly?[d]
　　All day long ²you are plotting destruction.
Your tongue is like a sharp razor,
　　you worker of treachery.
3 You love evil more than good,
　　and lying more than speaking the truth.
　　　　　　　　　　　　　　　　Selah
4 You love all words that devour,
　　O deceitful tongue.

5 But God will break you down forever;
　　he will snatch and tear you from your tent;
　　he will uproot you from the land of the
　　　　living.　　　　　　　　　*Selah*
6 The righteous will see, and fear,
　　and will laugh at the evildoer,[e] saying,
7 "See the one who would not take
　　refuge in God,
　　but trusted in abundant riches,
　　and sought refuge in wealth!"[f]

---

a Or *steadfast*　b Or *generous*　c Or *My sacrifice, O God,*　d Cn Compare Syr: Heb *the kindness of God*　e Heb *him*　f Syr Tg: Heb *in his destruction*

8 But I am like a green olive tree
    in the house of God.
I trust in the steadfast love of God
    forever and ever.
9 I will thank you forever,
    because of what you have done.
In the presence of the faithful
    I will proclaim[a] your name, for it is good.

53 Denunciation of Godlessness

*To the leader: according to Mahalath.
A Maskil of David.*

Fools say in their hearts, "There is no God."
    They are corrupt, they commit abominable
        acts;
    there is no one who does good.

2 God looks down from heaven on humankind
    to see if there are any who are wise,
    who seek after God.

3 They have all fallen away, they are all alike
        perverse;
    there is no one who does good,
    no, not one.

4 Have they no knowledge, those evildoers,
    who eat up my people as they eat bread,
    and do not call upon God?

5 There they shall be in great terror,
    in terror such as has not been.
For God will scatter the bones of the
        ungodly;[b]
    they will be put to shame,[c] for God has
        rejected them.

6 O that deliverance for Israel would come from
        Zion!
    When God restores the fortunes of his
        people,
    Jacob will rejoice; Israel will be glad.

54 Prayer for Vindication

*To the leader: with stringed instruments.
A Maskil of David, when the Ziphites
went and told Saul, "David is in hiding
among us."*

Save me, O God, by your name,
    and vindicate me by your might.

2 Hear my prayer, O God;
    give ear to the words of my mouth.

3 For the insolent have risen against me,
    the ruthless seek my life;
    they do not set God before them.   *Selah*

4 But surely, God is my helper;
    the Lord is the upholder of[d] my life.
5 He will repay my enemies for their evil.
    In your faithfulness, put an end to them.

6 With a freewill offering I will sacrifice to you;
    I will give thanks to your name, O LORD, for
        it is good.
7 For he has delivered me from every trouble,
    and my eye has looked in triumph on my
        enemies.

55 Complaint about a Friend's Treachery

*To the leader: with stringed instruments.
A Maskil of David.*

Give ear to my prayer, O God;
    do not hide yourself from my
        supplication.
2 Attend to me, and answer me;
    I am troubled in my complaint.
I am distraught 3by the noise of the enemy,
    because of the clamor of the wicked.
For they bring[e] trouble upon me,
    and in anger they cherish enmity
        against me.

4 My heart is in anguish within me,
    the terrors of death have fallen
        upon me.
5 Fear and trembling come upon me,
    and horror overwhelms me.
6 And I say, "O that I had wings like a dove!
    I would fly away and be at rest;
7 truly, I would flee far away;
    I would lodge in the wilderness;   *Selah*
8 I would hurry to find a shelter for myself
    from the raging wind and tempest."

9 Confuse, O Lord, confound their speech;
    for I see violence and strife in the city.
10 Day and night they go around it
    on its walls,
    and iniquity and trouble are within it;

a Cn: Heb *wait for*   b Cn Compare Gk Syr: Heb *him who encamps against you*   c Gk: Heb *you have put (them) to shame*   d Gk Syr Jerome: Heb *is of those who uphold* or *is with those who uphold*   e Cn Compare Gk: Heb *they cause to totter*

Betrayed!
Psalm 55

Maybe you don't have enemies quite as bad as the ones described in **Psalm 55,** but you may be able to identify with these words: "My companion laid hands on a friend and violated a covenant with me" (Psalm 55:20). This psalmist feels betrayed. You can probably relate—maybe your friend didn't keep a promise or a parent seemed to treat you unfairly. Whatever the reason, call on God, and say a prayer like this:

I trust you, God. I want to believe you are with me. When others abandon or betray me, help me to know you are here and that I'm never alone. Help me to always stay true to you. Amen.

11 ruin is in its midst;
oppression and fraud
    do not depart from its marketplace.

12 It is not enemies who taunt me—
    I could bear that;
it is not adversaries who deal insolently
        with me—
    I could hide from them.
13 But it is you, my equal,
    my companion, my familiar friend,
14 with whom I kept pleasant company;
    we walked in the house of God with the
        throng.
15 Let death come upon them;
    let them go down alive to Sheol;
    for evil is in their homes and in their
        hearts.

16 But I call upon God,
    and the LORD will save me.
17 Evening and morning and at noon
    I utter my complaint and moan,
    and he will hear my voice.
18 He will redeem me unharmed
    from the battle that I wage,
    for many are arrayed against me.

19 God, who is enthroned from of old,   *Selah*
    will hear, and will humble them—
because they do not change,
    and do not fear God.

20 My companion laid hands on a friend
    and violated a covenant with me[a]
21 with speech smoother than butter,
    but with a heart set on war;
with words that were softer than oil,
    but in fact were drawn swords.

22 Cast your burden[b] on the LORD,
    and he will sustain you;
he will never permit
    the righteous to be moved.

23 But you, O God, will cast them down
    into the lowest pit;
the bloodthirsty and treacherous
    shall not live out half their days.
But I will trust in you.

56 Trust in God under Persecution

To the leader: according to The Dove on Far-off Terebinths. Of David. A Miktam, when the Philistines seized him in Gath.

Be gracious to me, O God, for people trample
        on me;
    all day long foes oppress me;
2 my enemies trample on me all day
        long,
    for many fight against me.
O Most High, 3 when I am afraid,
    I put my trust in you.
4 In God, whose word I praise,
    in God I trust; I am not afraid;
    what can flesh do to me?

5 All day long they seek to injure my cause;
    all their thoughts are against me for evil.
6 They stir up strife, they lurk,
    they watch my steps.
As they hoped to have my life,
7   so repay[c] them for their crime;
    in wrath cast down the peoples, O God!

8 You have kept count of my tossings;
    put my tears in your bottle.
    Are they not in your record?

---

a Heb lacks *with me*   b Or *Cast what he has given you*   c Cn: Heb *rescue*

9 Then my enemies will retreat
    in the day when I call.
    This I know, that[a] God is for me.
10 In God, whose word I praise,
    in the LORD, whose word I praise,
11 in God I trust; I am not afraid.
    What can a mere mortal do to me?

12 My vows to you I must perform, O God;
    I will render thank offerings to you.
13 For you have delivered my soul from
       death,
    and my feet from falling,
    so that I may walk before God
    in the light of life.

57 Praise and Assurance under Persecution

*To the leader: Do Not Destroy. Of David.
A Miktam, when he fled from Saul, in the
cave.*

Be merciful to me, O God, be merciful
      to me,
    for in you my soul takes refuge;
in the shadow of your wings I will take
    refuge,
    until the destroying storms pass by.
2 I cry to God Most High,
    to God who fulfills his purpose
      for me.
3 He will send from heaven and save me,
    he will put to shame those who trample
      on me.   *Selah*
God will send forth his steadfast love and his
    faithfulness.

4 I lie down among lions
    that greedily devour[b] human prey;

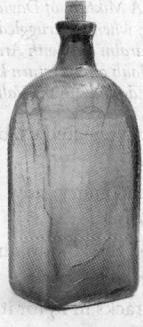

their teeth are spears and arrows,
    their tongues sharp swords.

5 Be exalted, O God, above the
      heavens.
    Let your glory be over all the earth.

6 They set a net for my steps;
    my soul was bowed down.
They dug a pit in my path,
    but they have fallen into it themselves.
                             Selah
7 My heart is steadfast, O God,
    my heart is steadfast.
I will sing and make melody.
8   Awake, my soul!
Awake, O harp and lyre!
    I will awake the dawn.
9 I will give thanks to you, O Lord, among the
      peoples;
    I will sing praises to you among the
      nations.
10 For your steadfast love is as high as the
      heavens;
    your faithfulness extends to the clouds.

11 Be exalted, O God, above the heavens.
    Let your glory be over all the earth.

58 Prayer for Vengeance

*To the leader: Do Not Destroy. Of David.
A Miktam.*

Do you indeed decree what is right, you
    gods?[c]
    Do you judge people fairly?
2 No, in your hearts you devise wrongs;
    your hands deal out violence on earth.

3 The wicked go astray from the womb;
    they err from their birth, speaking lies.
4 They have venom like the venom of a
      serpent,
    like the deaf adder that stops its ear,
5 so that it does not hear the voice of charmers
    or of the cunning enchanter.

6 O God, break the teeth in their mouths;
    tear out the fangs of the young lions,
      O LORD!
7 Let them vanish like water that runs away;

a Or *because* b Cn: Heb *are aflame for* c Or *mighty lords*

like grass let them be trodden down[a] and
    wither.
8 Let them be like the snail that dissolves into
        slime;
    like the untimely birth that never sees
        the sun.
9 Sooner than your pots can feel the heat of
        thorns,
    whether green or ablaze, may he sweep
        them away!

10 The righteous will rejoice when they see
        vengeance done;
    they will bathe their feet in the blood of
        the wicked.
11 People will say, "Surely there is a reward for
        the righteous;
    surely there is a God who judges on
        earth."

59 Prayer for Deliverance from Enemies

*To the leader: Do Not Destroy. Of David.
A Miktam, when Saul ordered his house to
be watched in order to kill him.*

Deliver me from my enemies, O my God;
    protect me from those who rise up
        against me.
2 Deliver me from those who work evil;
    from the bloodthirsty save me.

3 Even now they lie in wait for my life;
    the mighty stir up strife against me.
For no transgression or sin of mine, O LORD,
4   for no fault of mine, they run and make
        ready.

Rouse yourself, come to my help and see!
5   You, LORD God of hosts, are God of Israel.
Awake to punish all the nations;
    spare none of those who treacherously plot
        evil.   *Selah*

6 Each evening they come back,
    howling like dogs
    and prowling about the city.
7 There they are, bellowing with their mouths,
    with sharp words[b] on their lips—
    for "Who," they think,[c] "will hear us?"

8 But you laugh at them, O LORD;

you hold all the nations in derision.
9 O my strength, I will watch for you;
    for you, O God, are my fortress.
10 My God in his steadfast love will
        meet me;
    my God will let me look in triumph on my
        enemies.

11 Do not kill them, or my people may forget;
    make them totter by your power, and bring
        them down,
    O Lord, our shield.
12 For the sin of their mouths, the words of their
        lips,
    let them be trapped in their pride.
For the cursing and lies that they utter,
13   consume them in wrath;
    consume them until they are no more.
Then it will be known to the ends of the earth
    that God rules over Jacob.   *Selah*

14 Each evening they come back,
    howling like dogs
    and prowling about the city.
15 They roam about for food,
    and growl if they do not get their fill.

16 But I will sing of your might;
    I will sing aloud of your steadfast love in
        the morning.
For you have been a fortress for me
    and a refuge in the day of my distress.
17 O my strength, I will sing praises to you,
    for you, O God, are my fortress,
    the God who shows me steadfast love.

60 Prayer for National Victory after Defeat

*To the leader: according to the Lily of the
Covenant. A Miktam of David; for
instruction; when he struggled with
Aram-naharaim and with Aram-zobah,
and when Joab on his return killed twelve
thousand Edomites in the Valley of Salt.*

O God, you have rejected us, broken our
        defenses;
    you have been angry; now
        restore us!
2 You have caused the land to quake; you have
        torn it open;
    repair the cracks in it, for it is tottering.

a Cn: Meaning of Heb uncertain b Heb *with swords* c Heb lacks *they think*

The Agony of Defeat
Psalm 60:1–5

There's no such thing as a person who has never lost something or someone important. Just as all athletes eventually know the agony of defeat, every one of us experiences loss at some point.

The psalmist who sang **Psalm 60** knew how it felt to lose. Although the psalm was written after defeat in battle, its spirit has been echoed through the ages by others who have been defeated in other ways.

- The next time you experience loss, read this passage and think about how the psalmist calls on God as a helper.
- What have you learned from defeat or loss with the help of God's strength and inspiration?

3 You have made your people suffer hard things;
  you have given us wine to drink that made
    us reel.

4 You have set up a banner for those who
      fear you,
  to rally to it out of bowshot.[a]   Selah

5 Give victory with your right hand, and
      answer us,[b]
  so that those whom you love may be
      rescued.

6 God has promised in his sanctuary:[c]
  "With exultation I will divide up Shechem,
    and portion out the Vale of Succoth.

7 Gilead is mine, and Manasseh is mine;
  Ephraim is my helmet;
  Judah is my scepter.

8 Moab is my washbasin;
  on Edom I hurl my shoe;
  over Philistia I shout in triumph."

9 Who will bring me to the fortified
      city?

Who will lead me to Edom?

10 Have you not rejected us, O God?
  You do not go out, O God, with our
      armies.

11 O grant us help against the foe,
  for human help is worthless.

12 With God we shall do valiantly;
  it is he who will tread down our foes.

61   Assurance of God's Protection
*To the leader: with stringed instruments.
Of David.*

Hear my cry, O God;
  listen to my prayer.

2 From the end of the earth I call to you,
  when my heart is faint.

Lead me to the rock
  that is higher than I;

3 for you are my refuge,
  a strong tower against the enemy.

4 Let me abide in your tent forever,
  find refuge under the shelter of your
      wings.   *Selah*

5 For you, O God, have heard my vows;
  you have given me the heritage of those
      who fear your name.

6 Prolong the life of the king;
  may his years endure to all generations!

7 May he be enthroned forever before God;
  appoint steadfast love and faithfulness to
      watch over him!

8 So I will always sing praises to your name,
  as I pay my vows day after day.

62   Song of Trust in God Alone
*To the leader: according to Jeduthun. A
Psalm of David.*

For God alone my soul waits in silence;
  from him comes my salvation.

2 He alone is my rock and my salvation,
  my fortress; I shall never be shaken.

3 How long will you assail a person,
  will you batter your victim, all of you,
  as you would a leaning wall, a tottering
      fence?

a Gk Syr Jerome: Heb *because of the truth*   b Another reading is *me*   c Or *by his holiness*

LIVE IT!

Choose! · Psalm 62

Who do you trust? Where do you find your satisfaction? In popular people? The newest clothes? Money? The right car or the perfect job? Or can you trust God to be your rock and your salvation (Psalm 62:2)?

To place your trust in someone you know and can see is one thing, but to trust in someone who is unseen can feel really risky. But this is what Jesus calls his followers to do—place their lives and futures in the invisible hands of God, just as he did. Doing so builds strong faith in us and pulls us into God's refuge. But that's not all. By experiencing God's peace and the reassurance that God is in control of everything around us, we build courage to live boldly. We get strength to live out our faith in the world. We feel hope and certainty that, no matter what comes, God will always be our rock and refuge.

Choose to take refuge in God, and journal your thoughts and reflections on these questions:

• Why is it sometimes so hard to let your soul wait for God in silence (Psalm 62:1)?
• Will you let God be your refuge in hard times (Psalm 61:4; 62:7)?

---

4 Their only plan is to bring down a person of
     prominence.
  They take pleasure in falsehood;
they bless with their mouths,
  but inwardly they curse.   *Selah*

5 For God alone my soul waits in silence,
  for my hope is from him.
6 He alone is my rock and my salvation,
  my fortress; I shall not be shaken.
7 On God rests my deliverance and my
     honor;
  my mighty rock, my refuge is in God.

8 Trust in him at all times, O people;
  pour out your heart before him;
  God is a refuge for us.   *Selah*

9 Those of low estate are but a breath,
  those of high estate are a delusion;
in the balances they go up;
  they are together lighter than a breath.
10 Put no confidence in extortion,
  and set no vain hopes on robbery;
  if riches increase, do not set your heart on
     them.

11 Once God has spoken;
  twice have I heard this:
that power belongs to God,
12   and steadfast love belongs to you, O Lord.

For you repay to all
  according to their work.

63 · Comfort and Assurance in God's Presence

A Psalm of David, when he was in the Wilderness of Judah.

O God, you are my God, I seek you,
  my soul thirsts for you;
my flesh faints for you,
  as in a dry and weary land where there is
     no water.
2 So I have looked upon you in the sanctuary,
  beholding your power and glory.
3 Because your steadfast love is better than
     life,
  my lips will praise you.
4 So I will bless you as long as I live;
  I will lift up my hands and call on your
     name.

5 My soul is satisfied as with a rich feast,[a]
  and my mouth praises you with joyful lips
6 when I think of you on my bed,
  and meditate on you in the watches of the
     night;
7 for you have been my help,
  and in the shadow of your wings I sing
     for joy.
8 My soul clings to you;
  your right hand upholds me.

---

a Heb *with fat and fatness*

⁹ But those who seek to destroy my life
   shall go down into the depths of the earth;
¹⁰ they shall be given over to the power of the
      sword,
   they shall be prey for jackals.
¹¹ But the king shall rejoice in God;
   all who swear by him shall exult,
   for the mouths of liars will be stopped.

64 Prayer for Protection from Enemies
To the leader. A Psalm of David.

Hear my voice, O God, in my complaint;
   preserve my life from the dread enemy.
² Hide me from the secret plots of the wicked,
   from the scheming of evildoers,
³ who whet their tongues like swords,
   who aim bitter words like arrows,
⁴ shooting from ambush at the blameless;
   they shoot suddenly and without fear.
⁵ They hold fast to their evil purpose;
   they talk of laying snares secretly,
thinking, "Who can see us?"[a]
⁶   Who can search out our crimes?[b]
We have thought out a cunningly conceived
      plot."
   For the human heart and mind are deep.

⁷ But God will shoot his arrow at them;
   they will be wounded suddenly.
⁸ Because of their tongue he will bring them to
      ruin;[c]
   all who see them will shake with horror.
⁹ Then everyone will fear;
   they will tell what God has brought about,
   and ponder what he has done.

¹⁰ Let the righteous rejoice in the LORD
   and take refuge in him.
Let all the upright in heart glory.

65 Thanksgiving for Earth's Bounty
To the leader. A Psalm of David. A Song.

Praise is due to you,
   O God, in Zion;
and to you shall vows be performed,
²   O you who answer prayer!
To you all flesh shall come.
³ When deeds of iniquity overwhelm us,

you forgive our transgressions.
⁴ Happy are those whom you choose and bring
      near
   to live in your courts.
We shall be satisfied with the goodness of your
      house,
   your holy temple.

⁵ By awesome deeds you answer us with
      deliverance,
   O God of our salvation;
you are the hope of all the ends of the earth
   and of the farthest seas.
⁶ By your[d] strength you established the
      mountains;
   you are girded with might.
⁷ You silence the roaring of the seas,
   the roaring of their waves,
   the tumult of the peoples.
⁸ Those who live at earth's farthest bounds are
      awed by your signs;
you make the gateways of the morning and the
   evening shout for joy.

⁹ You visit the earth and water it,
   you greatly enrich it;
the river of God is full of water;
   you provide the people with grain,
   for so you have prepared it.
¹⁰ You water its furrows abundantly,
   settling its ridges,
softening it with showers,
   and blessing its growth.
¹¹ You crown the year with your bounty;
   your wagon tracks overflow with richness.
¹² The pastures of the wilderness overflow,
   the hills gird themselves with joy,
¹³ the meadows clothe themselves with flocks,
   the valleys deck themselves with grain,
   they shout and sing together for joy.

66 Praise for God's Goodness to Israel
To the leader. A Song. A Psalm.

Make a joyful noise to God, all the earth;
²   sing the glory of his name;
   give to him glorious praise.
³ Say to God, "How awesome are your deeds!
   Because of your great power, your enemies
      cringe before you.

---

a Syr: Heb *them*   b Cn: Heb *They search out crimes*   c Cn: Heb *They will bring him to ruin, their tongue being against them*   d Gk Jerome: Heb *his*

4 All the earth worships you;
      they sing praises to you,
      sing praises to your name."   *Selah*

5 Come and see what God has done:
      he is awesome in his deeds among mortals.
6 He turned the sea into dry land;
      they passed through the river on foot.
   There we rejoiced in him,
7   who rules by his might forever,
   whose eyes keep watch on the nations—
      let the rebellious not exalt themselves.   *Selah*

8 Bless our God, O peoples,
      let the sound of his praise be heard,
9 who has kept us among the living,
      and has not let our feet slip.
10 For you, O God, have tested us;
      you have tried us as silver is tried.
11 You brought us into the net;
      you laid burdens on our backs;
12 you let people ride over our heads;
      we went through fire and through water;
   yet you have brought us out to a spacious
         place.*a*

13 I will come into your house with burnt
         offerings;
   I will pay you my vows,
14 those that my lips uttered
      and my mouth promised when I was in
         trouble.
15 I will offer to you burnt offerings of fatlings,
      with the smoke of the sacrifice of rams;
   I will make an offering of bulls and goats.   *Selah*

16 Come and hear, all you who fear God,
      and I will tell what he has done
         for me.
17 I cried aloud to him,
      and he was extolled with my tongue.
18 If I had cherished iniquity in my heart,
      the Lord would not have listened.
19 But truly God has listened;
      he has given heed to the words of my prayer.

20 Blessed be God,
      because he has not rejected my prayer

      or removed his steadfast love
         from me.

67 The Nations Called to Praise God

To the leader: with stringed instruments.
A Psalm. A Song.

May God be gracious to us and bless us
   and make his face to shine upon us,   *Selah*
2 that your way may be known upon earth,
      your saving power among all nations.
3 Let the peoples praise you, O God;
      let all the peoples praise you.

4 Let the nations be glad and sing for joy,
      for you judge the peoples with equity
      and guide the nations upon earth.   *Selah*
5 Let the peoples praise you, O God;
      let all the peoples praise you.

6 The earth has yielded its increase;
      God, our God, has blessed us.
7 May God continue to bless us;
      let all the ends of the earth revere him.

68 Praise and Thanksgiving

To the leader. Of David. A Psalm. A Song.

Let God rise up, let his enemies be scattered;
      let those who hate him flee before him.
2 As smoke is driven away, so drive them away;
      as wax melts before the fire,
      let the wicked perish before God.
3 But let the righteous be joyful;
      let them exult before God;
      let them be jubilant with joy.

4 Sing to God, sing praises to his name;
      lift up a song to him who rides upon the
         clouds*b*—
   his name is the LORD—
      be exultant before him.

5 Father of orphans and protector of widows
      is God in his holy habitation.
6 God gives the desolate a home to
         live in;
      he leads out the prisoners to prosperity,
      but the rebellious live in a parched land.

α Cn Compare Gk Syr Jerome Tg: Heb *to a saturation*   b Or *cast up a highway for him who rides through the deserts*

STUDY IT!

Hey, You—Praise the Lord
Psalm 68

Psalm 68 commands us to sing praises to the Lord. We're told to praise the Lord, because God, the "Father of orphans and protector of widows" (Psalm 68:5), "gives the desolate a home to live in" and "leads out the prisoners to prosperity" (Psalm 68:6), "daily bears us up" (Psalm 68:19), and "will shatter the heads of his enemies" (Psalm 68:21).

Who should sing praises for these reasons? Everyone! All of us! No matter what your gender, race, family history, or social status is, you are invited to praise God. This psalm calls to men, women, and people of various tribes and nations. It's not a call to praise based on who we are, but on who God is. "Sing to God, O kingdoms of the earth; sing praises to the Lord" (Psalm 68:32).

7 O God, when you went out before your people,
 when you marched through the wilderness, *Selah*
8 the earth quaked, the heavens poured
  down rain
 at the presence of God, the God of Sinai,
 at the presence of God, the God of Israel.
9 Rain in abundance, O God, you showered
  abroad;
 you restored your heritage when it
  languished;
10 your flock found a dwelling in it;
 in your goodness, O God, you provided for
  the needy.

11 The Lord gives the command;
 great is the company of those[a] who bore the
  tidings:
12 "The kings of the armies, they flee, they
  flee!"
 The women at home divide the spoil,
13 though they stay among the sheepfolds—
 the wings of a dove covered with silver,

its pinions with green gold.
14 When the Almighty[b] scattered kings there,
 snow fell on Zalmon.

15 O mighty mountain, mountain of Bashan;
 O many-peaked mountain, mountain of
  Bashan!
16 Why do you look with envy,
 O many-peaked mountain,
 at the mount that God desired for his abode,
 where the Lord will reside forever?

17 With mighty chariotry, twice ten thousand,
 thousands upon thousands,
 the Lord came from Sinai into the holy
  place.[c]
18 You ascended the high mount,
 leading captives in your train
 and receiving gifts from people,
 even from those who rebel against the Lord
  God's abiding there.
19 Blessed be the Lord,
 who daily bears us up;
 God is our salvation. *Selah*
20 Our God is a God of salvation,
 and to God, the Lord, belongs escape from
  death.

21 But God will shatter the heads of his enemies,
 the hairy crown of those who walk in their
  guilty ways.
22 The Lord said,
 "I will bring them back from Bashan,
 I will bring them back from the depths of
  the sea,
23 so that you may bathe[d] your feet in blood,
 so that the tongues of your dogs may have
  their share from the foe."

24 Your solemn processions are seen,[e] O God,
 the processions of my God, my King, into
  the sanctuary—
25 the singers in front, the musicians last,
 between them girls playing tambourines:
26 "Bless God in the great congregation,
 the Lord, O you who are of Israel's
  fountain!"
27 There is Benjamin, the least of them, in the
  lead,
 the princes of Judah in a body,

a Or *company of the women* b Traditional rendering of Heb *Shaddai* c Cn: Heb *The Lord among them Sinai in the holy* (place) d Gk Syr Tg: Heb *shatter* e Or *have been seen*

the princes of Zebulun, the princes of
    Naphtali.

28 Summon your might, O God;
    show your strength, O God, as you have
      done for us before.
29 Because of your temple at Jerusalem
    kings bear gifts to you.
30 Rebuke the wild animals that live among the
      reeds,
    the herd of bulls with the calves of the
      peoples.
    Trample *a* under foot those who lust after
      tribute;
    scatter the peoples who delight in war.*b*
31 Let bronze be brought from Egypt;
    let Ethiopia*c* hasten to stretch out its
      hands to God.

32 Sing to God, O kingdoms of the earth;
    sing praises to the Lord,   Selah
33 O rider in the heavens, the ancient heavens;
    listen, he sends out his voice, his mighty
      voice.
34 Ascribe power to God,
    whose majesty is over Israel;
    and whose power is in the skies.
35 Awesome is God in his*d* sanctuary,
    the God of Israel;
    he gives power and strength to his people.

Blessed be God!

69 Prayer for Deliverance from Persecution

*To the leader: according to Lilies. Of
David.*

Save me, O God,
    for the waters have come up to my neck.
2 I sink in deep mire,
    where there is no foothold;
    I have come into deep waters,
    and the flood sweeps over me.
3 I am weary with my crying;
    my throat is parched.
    My eyes grow dim
    with waiting for my God.

4 More in number than the hairs of my head
    are those who hate me without cause;

many are those who would destroy me,
    my enemies who accuse me falsely.
    What I did not steal
    must I now restore?
5 O God, you know my folly;
    the wrongs I have done are not hidden
      from you.

6 Do not let those who hope in you be put to
      shame because of me,
    O Lord GOD of hosts;
    do not let those who seek you be dishonored
      because of me,
    O God of Israel.
7 It is for your sake that I have borne
      reproach,
    that shame has covered my face.
8 I have become a stranger to my kindred,
    an alien to my mother's children.
9 It is zeal for your house that has
      consumed me;
    the insults of those who insult you have
      fallen on me.
10 When I humbled my soul with fasting,*e*
    they insulted me for doing so.
11 When I made sackcloth my clothing,
    I became a byword to them.
12 I am the subject of gossip for those who sit in
      the gate,
    and the drunkards make songs
      about me.

13 But as for me, my prayer is to you, O LORD.
    At an acceptable time, O God,
    in the abundance of your steadfast love,
      answer me.
    With your faithful help 14rescue me
      from sinking in the mire;
    let me be delivered from my enemies
      and from the deep waters.
15 Do not let the flood sweep over me,
    or the deep swallow me up,
    or the Pit close its mouth over me.

16 Answer me, O LORD, for your steadfast love is
      good;
    according to your abundant mercy, turn
      to me.
17 Do not hide your face from your servant,

---

a Cn: Heb *Trampling* *b* Meaning of Heb of verse 30 is uncertain *c* Or *Nubia*; Heb *Cush* *d* Gk: Heb *from your* *e* Gk Syr: Heb *I wept, with fasting my
soul,* or *I made my soul mourn with fasting*

for I am in distress—make haste to
      answer me.
18 Draw near to me, redeem me,
      set me free because of my enemies.

19 You know the insults I receive,
      and my shame and dishonor;
      my foes are all known to you.
20 Insults have broken my heart,
      so that I am in despair.
   I looked for pity, but there was none;
      and for comforters, but I found none.
21 They gave me poison for food,
      and for my thirst they gave me vinegar to
      drink.

22 Let their table be a trap for them,
      a snare for their allies.
23 Let their eyes be darkened so that they
      cannot see,
      and make their loins tremble continually.
24 Pour out your indignation upon them,
      and let your burning anger overtake them.
25 May their camp be a desolation;
      let no one live in their tents.
26 For they persecute those whom you have
      struck down,
      and those whom you have wounded, they
      attack still more.[a]
27 Add guilt to their guilt;
      may they have no acquittal from you.
28 Let them be blotted out of the book of the
      living;
      let them not be enrolled among the
      righteous.
29 But I am lowly and in pain;
      let your salvation, O God, protect me.

30 I will praise the name of God with a song;
      I will magnify him with thanksgiving.
31 This will please the LORD more than
      an ox
      or a bull with horns and hoofs.
32 Let the oppressed see it and be glad;
      you who seek God, let your hearts revive.
33 For the LORD hears the needy,
      and does not despise his own that are in
      bonds.

34 Let heaven and earth praise him,

the seas and everything that moves in
      them.
35 For God will save Zion
      and rebuild the cities of Judah;
   and his servants shall live[b] there and
      possess it;
36 the children of his servants shall inherit it,
      and those who love his name shall live
      in it.

70 Prayer for Deliverance from Enemies

*To the leader. Of David, for the memorial
offering.*

Be pleased, O God, to deliver me.
      O LORD, make haste to help me!
2 Let those be put to shame and confusion
      who seek my life.
   Let those be turned back and brought to
      dishonor
      who desire to hurt me.
3 Let those who say, "Aha, Aha!"
      turn back because of their shame.

4 Let all who seek you
      rejoice and be glad in you.
   Let those who love your salvation
      say evermore, "God is great!"
5 But I am poor and needy;
      hasten to me, O God!
   You are my help and my deliverer;
      O LORD, do not delay!

71 Prayer for Lifelong Protection and Help

In you, O LORD, I take refuge;
      let me never be put to shame.
2 In your righteousness deliver me and
      rescue me;
      incline your ear to me and save me.
3 Be to me a rock of refuge,
      a strong fortress,[c] to save me,
      for you are my rock and my fortress.

4 Rescue me, O my God, from the hand of the
      wicked,
      from the grasp of the unjust and cruel.
5 For you, O Lord, are my hope,
      my trust, O LORD, from my youth.
6 Upon you I have leaned from my
      birth;

a Gk Syr: Heb *recount the pain of*   b Syr: Heb *and they shall live*   c Gk Compare 31.3: Heb *to come continually you have commanded*

it was you who took me from my mother's
      womb.
   My praise is continually of you.

7 I have been like a portent to many,
      but you are my strong refuge.
8 My mouth is filled with your praise,
      and with your glory all day long.
9 Do not cast me off in the time of old age;
      do not forsake me when my strength is
         spent.
10 For my enemies speak concerning me,
      and those who watch for my life consult
         together.
11 They say, "Pursue and seize that person
      whom God has forsaken,
      for there is no one to deliver."

12 O God, do not be far from me;
      O my God, make haste to help me!
13 Let my accusers be put to shame and
         consumed;
      let those who seek to hurt me
      be covered with scorn and disgrace.
14 But I will hope continually,
      and will praise you yet more and more.
15 My mouth will tell of your righteous acts,
      of your deeds of salvation all day long,
      though their number is past my knowledge.
16 I will come praising the mighty deeds of the
         Lord GOD,
      I will praise your righteousness, yours
         alone.

17 O God, from my youth you have taught me,
      and I still proclaim your wondrous deeds.
18 So even to old age and gray hairs,
      O God, do not forsake me,
   until I proclaim your might
      to all the generations to come.[a]
   Your power [19]and your righteousness, O God,
      reach the high heavens.

   You who have done great things,
      O God, who is like you?
20 You who have made me see many troubles
         and calamities
      will revive me again;
   from the depths of the earth
      you will bring me up again.

21 You will increase my honor,
      and comfort me once again.

22 I will also praise you with the harp
      for your faithfulness, O my God;
   I will sing praises to you with the lyre,
      O Holy One of Israel.
23 My lips will shout for joy
      when I sing praises to you;
      my soul also, which you have rescued.
24 All day long my tongue will talk of your
         righteous help,
   for those who tried to do me harm
      have been put to shame, and
         disgraced.

72 Prayer for Guidance and Support for the King
Of Solomon.

   Give the king your justice, O God,
      and your righteousness to a king's son.
2 May he judge your people with
         righteousness,
      and your poor with justice.
3 May the mountains yield prosperity for the
         people,
      and the hills, in righteousness.
4 May he defend the cause of the poor of the
         people,
      give deliverance to the needy,
      and crush the oppressor.

5 May he live[b] while the sun endures,
      and as long as the moon, throughout all
         generations.
6 May he be like rain that falls on the mown grass,
      like showers that water the earth.
7 In his days may righteousness flourish
      and peace abound, until the moon is no
         more.

8 May he have dominion from sea to sea,
      and from the River to the ends of the earth.
9 May his foes[c] bow down before him,
      and his enemies lick the dust.
10 May the kings of Tarshish and of the isles
      render him tribute,
   may the kings of Sheba and Seba
      bring gifts.

a Gk Compare Syr: Heb *to a generation, to all that come*   b Gk: Heb *may they fear you*   c Cn: Heb *those who live in the wilderness*

11 May all kings fall down before him,
  all nations give him service.

12 For he delivers the needy when they call,
  the poor and those who have no helper.
13 He has pity on the weak and the needy,
  and saves the lives of the needy.
14 From oppression and violence he redeems
    their life;
  and precious is their blood in his sight.

15 Long may he live!
  May gold of Sheba be given to him.
  May prayer be made for him continually,
  and blessings invoked for him all day long.
16 May there be abundance of grain in the land;
  may it wave on the tops of the mountains;
  may its fruit be like Lebanon;
  and may people blossom in the cities
  like the grass of the field.
17 May his name endure forever,
  his fame continue as long as the sun.
  May all nations be blessed in him;[a]
  may they pronounce him happy.

18 Blessed be the LORD, the God of Israel,
  who alone does wondrous things.
19 Blessed be his glorious name forever;
  may his glory fill the whole earth.
    Amen and Amen.

20 The prayers of David son of Jesse are ended.

BOOK III
(Psalms 73–89)

Plea for Relief from Oppressors
73 *A Psalm of Asaph.*

Truly God is good to the upright,[b]
  to those who are pure in heart.
2 But as for me, my feet had almost stumbled;
  my steps had nearly slipped.
3 For I was envious of the arrogant;
  I saw the prosperity of the wicked.

4 For they have no pain;
  their bodies are sound and sleek.
5 They are not in trouble as others are;
  they are not plagued like other people.
6 Therefore pride is their necklace;
  violence covers them like a garment.
7 Their eyes swell out with fatness;
  their hearts overflow with follies.
8 They scoff and speak with malice;
  loftily they threaten oppression.
9 They set their mouths against heaven,
  and their tongues range over the earth.
10 Therefore the people turn and praise them,[c]
  and find no fault in them.[d]
11 And they say, "How can God know?
  Is there knowledge in the Most High?"
12 Such are the wicked;
  always at ease, they increase in riches.

STUDY IT!

Why Do the Bad Guys Win? · Psalm 73

Life would have a happy ending if it were a movie or book. The bad guys would always get what they deserve. The good people would prosper and live in peace and happiness. But look around the world today—it's like a story gone bad. **Psalm 73** addresses the age-old question, Why do bad people prosper?

Isn't it supposed to be the other way around? How can God allow the wicked to become rich and powerful and successful—often at the expense of others? The psalmist asks all these questions and realizes that the answer lies at least partly in wisdom.

Wisdom is the ability to see clearly and not be taken in by illusions or outer appearances. A wise person knows that what's on the inside is more important than what can be seen on the outside, and that what is eternal is more important than what is temporary. Seeing the world through the eyes of wisdom shows us that God is in control and that the wicked will eventually get what they deserve. In the meantime, we are to stay near to God and live in the refuge of God's strength.

a Or *bless themselves by him* b Or *good to Israel* c Cn: Heb *his people return here* d Cn: Heb *abundant waters are drained by them*

13 All in vain I have kept my heart clean
   and washed my hands in innocence.
14 For all day long I have been plagued,
   and am punished every morning.

15 If I had said, "I will talk on in this way,"
   I would have been untrue to the circle of
      your children.
16 But when I thought how to understand this,
   it seemed to me a wearisome task,
17 until I went into the sanctuary of God;
   then I perceived their end.
18 Truly you set them in slippery places;
   you make them fall to ruin.
19 How they are destroyed in a moment,
   swept away utterly by terrors!
20 They are*a* like a dream when one awakes;
   on awaking you despise their phantoms.

21 When my soul was embittered,
   when I was pricked in heart,
22 I was stupid and ignorant;
   I was like a brute beast toward you.
23 Nevertheless I am continually with you;
   you hold my right hand.
24 You guide me with your counsel,
   and afterward you will receive me with
      honor.*b*
25 Whom have I in heaven but you?
   And there is nothing on earth that I desire
      other than you.
26 My flesh and my heart may fail,
   but God is the strength*c* of my heart and my
      portion forever.

27 Indeed, those who are far from you will perish;

> "Nevertheless I am
> continually with you;
> you hold my right
> hand. You guide me
> with your counsel,
> and afterward
> you will receive
> me with honor."
> —Psalm 73:23–24

   you put an end to those who are false
      to you.
28 But for me it is good to be near God;
   I have made the Lord GOD my refuge,
   to tell of all your works.

74 Plea for Help in Time of National Humiliation

A Maskil of Asaph.

O God, why do you cast us off forever?
   Why does your anger smoke against the
      sheep of your pasture?
2 Remember your congregation, which you
      acquired long ago,
   which you redeemed to be the tribe of
      your heritage.
   Remember Mount Zion, where you came
      to dwell.
3 Direct your steps to the perpetual ruins;
   the enemy has destroyed everything in the
      sanctuary.

4 Your foes have roared within your holy place;
   they set up their emblems there.
5 At the upper entrance they hacked
   the wooden trellis with axes.*d*
6 And then, with hatchets and hammers,
   they smashed all its carved work.
7 They set your sanctuary on fire;
   they desecrated the dwelling place of your
      name,
   bringing it to the ground.
8 They said to themselves, "We will utterly
      subdue them";
   they burned all the meeting places of God
      in the land.

9 We do not see our emblems;
   there is no longer any prophet,
   and there is no one among us who knows
      how long.
10 How long, O God, is the foe to scoff?
   Is the enemy to revile your name forever?
11 Why do you hold back your hand;
   why do you keep your hand in*e* your
      bosom?

12 Yet God my King is from of old,
   working salvation in the earth.

a Cn: Heb *Lord*   *b* Or *to glory*   *c* Heb *rock*   *d* Cn Compare Gk Syr: Meaning of Heb uncertain   *e* Cn: Heb *do you consume your right hand from*

13 You divided the sea by your might;
    you broke the heads of the dragons in the
        waters.
14 You crushed the heads of Leviathan;
    you gave him as food[a] for the creatures of
        the wilderness.
15 You cut openings for springs and torrents;
    you dried up ever-flowing streams.
16 Yours is the day, yours also the night;
    you established the luminaries[b] and
        the sun.
17 You have fixed all the bounds of the earth;
    you made summer and winter.

18 Remember this, O LORD, how the enemy
        scoffs,
    and an impious people reviles your name.
19 Do not deliver the soul of your dove to the wild
        animals;
    do not forget the life of your poor forever.

20 Have regard for your[c] covenant,
    for the dark places of the land are full of the
        haunts of violence.
21 Do not let the downtrodden be put to shame;
    let the poor and needy praise your name.
22 Rise up, O God, plead your cause;
    remember how the impious scoff at you all
        day long.
23 Do not forget the clamor of your foes,
    the uproar of your adversaries that goes up
        continually.

75 Thanksgiving for God's Wondrous Deeds

*To the leader: Do Not Destroy. A Psalm of
Asaph. A Song.*

We give thanks to you, O God;
    we give thanks; your name is near.
People tell of your wondrous deeds.

2 At the set time that I appoint
    I will judge with equity.
3 When the earth totters, with all its inhabitants,
    it is I who keep its pillars steady.   *Selah*
4 I say to the boastful, "Do not boast,"
    and to the wicked, "Do not lift up your
        horn;
5 do not lift up your horn on high,
    or speak with insolent neck."

6 For not from the east or from the west
    and not from the wilderness comes
        lifting up;
7 but it is God who executes judgment,
    putting down one and lifting up another.
8 For in the hand of the LORD there is a cup
    with foaming wine, well mixed;
he will pour a draught from it,
    and all the wicked of the earth
    shall drain it down to the dregs.
9 But I will rejoice[d] forever;
    I will sing praises to the God of Jacob.

10 All the horns of the wicked I will cut off,
    but the horns of the righteous shall be
        exalted.

76 Israel's God—Judge of All the Earth

*To the leader: with stringed instruments.
A Psalm of Asaph. A Song.*

In Judah God is known,
    his name is great in Israel.
2 His abode has been established in Salem,
    his dwelling place in Zion.
3 There he broke the flashing arrows,
    the shield, the sword, and the weapons
        of war.   *Selah*

4 Glorious are you, more majestic
    than the everlasting mountains.[e]
5 The stouthearted were stripped of their
        spoil;
    they sank into sleep;
none of the troops
    was able to lift a hand.
6 At your rebuke, O God of Jacob,
    both rider and horse lay stunned.

7 But you indeed are awesome!
    Who can stand before you
    when once your anger is roused?
8 From the heavens you uttered judgment;
    the earth feared and was still
9 when God rose up to establish judgment,
    to save all the oppressed of the earth.   *Selah*

10 Human wrath serves only to praise you,
    when you bind the last bit of your[f] wrath
        around you.

a Heb *food for the people* b Or *moon; Heb light* c Gk Syr: Heb *the* d Gk: Heb *declare* e Gk: Heb *the mountains of prey* f Heb lacks *your*

11 Make vows to the LORD your God, and
  perform them;
  let all who are around him bring gifts
  to the one who is awesome,
12 who cuts off the spirit of princes,
  who inspires fear in the kings of the earth.

God's Mighty Deeds Recalled

77 *To the leader: according to Jeduthun. Of Asaph. A Psalm.*

I cry aloud to God,
  aloud to God, that he may hear me.
2 In the day of my trouble I seek the Lord;
  in the night my hand is stretched out
   without wearying;
  my soul refuses to be comforted.
3 I think of God, and I moan;
  I meditate, and my spirit faints. *Selah*

4 You keep my eyelids from closing;
  I am so troubled that I cannot speak.
5 I consider the days of old,
  and remember the years of long ago.
6 I commune*a* with my heart in the night;
  I meditate and search my spirit:*b*
7 "Will the Lord spurn forever,
  and never again be favorable?
8 Has his steadfast love ceased forever?
  Are his promises at an end for all time?
9 Has God forgotten to be gracious?

Has he in anger shut up his compassion?"
         Selah
10 And I say, "It is my grief
  that the right hand of the Most High has
   changed."

11 I will call to mind the deeds of the LORD;
  I will remember your wonders of old.
12 I will meditate on all your work,
  and muse on your mighty deeds.
13 Your way, O God, is holy.
  What god is so great as our God?
14 You are the God who works wonders;
  you have displayed your might among the
   peoples.
15 With your strong arm you redeemed your
   people,
  the descendants of Jacob and Joseph.
         Selah

16 When the waters saw you, O God,
  when the waters saw you, they were afraid;
  the very deep trembled.
17 The clouds poured out water;
  the skies thundered;
  your arrows flashed on every side.
18 The crash of your thunder was in the
   whirlwind;
  your lightnings lit up the world;
  the earth trembled and shook.

The Big Picture · Psalm 77

It's easy for us to get caught up in the moment, overwhelmed by the stress of school assignments, extracurricular activities, and time with family and friends. It's hard to do, but we need to step back for a few minutes to try to grasp the big picture. We need to get some perspective.

When we look back at our lives and see where we have come from, the path often makes sense. We can see that the twists and turns that were so frustrating and confusing were just temporary diversions on our journey. Everything we experienced—the good and the bad—contains lessons for us. The question is: How good are we at learning?

The key to wisdom is reflection. **Psalm 77** recalls God's mighty deeds among the Israelites and calls us to reflect in different ways: "I meditate" (Psalm 77:3, 6, 12), "I consider" (Psalm 77:5), and "I will call to mind" (Psalm 77:11). If you don't already spend some time reflecting on the events of each day, start now. Keep a journal about how you felt or what you learned. Take the time to remember where you've been and to meditate on where you hope to go. Over time you'll see the big picture emerge and gain an even greater sense of God's presence in your life.

---

a Gk Syr: Heb *My music* *b* Syr Jerome: Heb *my spirit searches*

19 Your way was through the sea,
    your path, through the mighty waters;
    yet your footprints were unseen.
20 You led your people like a flock
    by the hand of Moses and Aaron.

78 God's Goodness and Israel's Ingratitude
A Maskil of Asaph.

Give ear, O my people, to my teaching;
    incline your ears to the words of my mouth.
2 I will open my mouth in a parable;
    I will utter dark sayings from of old,
3 things that we have heard and known,
    that our ancestors have told us.
4 We will not hide them from their children;
    we will tell to the coming generation
the glorious deeds of the Lord, and his might,
    and the wonders that he has done.

5 He established a decree in Jacob,
    and appointed a law in Israel,
which he commanded our ancestors
    to teach to their children;
6 that the next generation might know them,
    the children yet unborn,
and rise up and tell them to their children,
7   so that they should set their hope in God,
and not forget the works of God,
    but keep his commandments;
8 and that they should not be like their
        ancestors,
    a stubborn and rebellious generation,
a generation whose heart was not steadfast,
    whose spirit was not faithful to God.

9 The Ephraimites, armed with*a* the bow,
    turned back on the day of battle.
10 They did not keep God's covenant,
    but refused to walk according to his law.
11 They forgot what he had done,
    and the miracles that he had shown them.
12 In the sight of their ancestors he worked
        marvels
    in the land of Egypt, in the fields of Zoan.
13 He divided the sea and let them pass
        through it,
    and made the waters stand like a heap.
14 In the daytime he led them with a cloud,

and all night long with a fiery light.
15 He split rocks open in the wilderness,
    and gave them drink abundantly as from
        the deep.
16 He made streams come out of the rock,
    and caused waters to flow down like rivers.
17 Yet they sinned still more against him,
    rebelling against the Most High in the
        desert.
18 They tested God in their heart
    by demanding the food they craved.
19 They spoke against God, saying,
    "Can God spread a table in the wilderness?
20 Even though he struck the rock so that water
        gushed out
    and torrents overflowed,
can he also give bread,
    or provide meat for his people?"

21 Therefore, when the Lord heard, he was full
        of rage;
    a fire was kindled against Jacob,
    his anger mounted against Israel,
22 because they had no faith in God,
    and did not trust his saving power.
23 Yet he commanded the skies above,
    and opened the doors of heaven;
24 he rained down on them manna to eat,
    and gave them the grain of heaven.
25 Mortals ate of the bread of angels;
    he sent them food in abundance.
26 He caused the east wind to blow in the
        heavens,
    and by his power he led out the south
        wind;
27 he rained flesh upon them like dust,
    winged birds like the sand of the seas;
28 he let them fall within their camp,
    all around their dwellings.
29 And they ate and were well filled,
    for he gave them what they craved.
30 But before they had satisfied their craving,
    while the food was still in their mouths,
31 the anger of God rose against them
    and he killed the strongest of them,
    and laid low the flower of Israel.

32 In spite of all this they still sinned;
    they did not believe in his wonders.

a Heb *armed with shooting*

33 So he made their days vanish like a breath,
and their years in terror.

34 When he killed them, they sought for him;
they repented and sought God earnestly.

35 They remembered that God was their rock,
the Most High God their redeemer.

36 But they flattered him with their mouths;
they lied to him with their tongues.

37 Their heart was not steadfast toward him;
they were not true to his covenant.

38 Yet he, being compassionate,
forgave their iniquity,
and did not destroy them;
often he restrained his anger,
and did not stir up all his wrath.

39 He remembered that they were but flesh,
a wind that passes and does not come
again.

40 How often they rebelled against him in the
wilderness
and grieved him in the desert!

41 They tested God again and again,
and provoked the Holy One of Israel.

42 They did not keep in mind his power,
or the day when he redeemed them from
the foe;

43 when he displayed his signs in Egypt,
and his miracles in the fields of Zoan.

44 He turned their rivers to blood,
so that they could not drink of their
streams.

45 He sent among them swarms of flies, which
devoured them,
and frogs, which destroyed them.

46 He gave their crops to the caterpillar,
and the fruit of their labor to the locust.

47 He destroyed their vines with hail,
and their sycamores with frost.

48 He gave over their cattle to the hail,
and their flocks to thunderbolts.

49 He let loose on them his fierce anger,
wrath, indignation, and distress,
a company of destroying angels.

50 He made a path for his anger;
he did not spare them from death,
but gave their lives over to the plague.

51 He struck all the firstborn in Egypt,
the first issue of their strength in the tents
of Ham.

52 Then he led out his people like sheep,
and guided them in the wilderness like a
flock.

53 He led them in safety, so that they were not
afraid;
but the sea overwhelmed their enemies.

54 And he brought them to his holy hill,
to the mountain that his right hand
had won.

55 He drove out nations before them;
he apportioned them for a possession
and settled the tribes of Israel in their tents.

56 Yet they tested the Most High God,
and rebelled against him.
They did not observe his decrees,

57 but turned away and were faithless like their
ancestors;
they twisted like a treacherous bow.

58 For they provoked him to anger with their
high places;
they moved him to jealousy with their
idols.

59 When God heard, he was full of wrath,
and he utterly rejected Israel.

60 He abandoned his dwelling at Shiloh,
the tent where he dwelt among mortals,

61 and delivered his power to captivity,
his glory to the hand of the foe.

62 He gave his people to the sword,
and vented his wrath on his
heritage.

63 Fire devoured their young men,
and their girls had no marriage
song.

64 Their priests fell by the sword,
and their widows made no lamentation.

65 Then the Lord awoke as from sleep,
like a warrior shouting because of wine.

66 He put his adversaries to rout;
he put them to everlasting disgrace.

67 He rejected the tent of Joseph,
he did not choose the tribe of Ephraim;

68 but he chose the tribe of Judah,
Mount Zion, which he loves.

69 He built his sanctuary like the high heavens,
like the earth, which he has founded
forever.

70 He chose his servant David,
and took him from the sheepfolds;

71 from tending the nursing ewes he brought him
    to be the shepherd of his people Jacob,
    of Israel, his inheritance.
72 With upright heart he tended them,
    and guided them with skillful hand.

79 Plea for Mercy for Jerusalem
A Psalm of Asaph.

O God, the nations have come into your
    inheritance;
  they have defiled your holy temple;
  they have laid Jerusalem in ruins.
2 They have given the bodies of your servants
    to the birds of the air for food,
  the flesh of your faithful to the wild
    animals of the earth.
3 They have poured out their blood like water
    all around Jerusalem,
  and there was no one to bury them.
4 We have become a taunt to our neighbors,
    mocked and derided by those
    around us.

5 How long, O LORD? Will you be angry
    forever?
  Will your jealous wrath burn like
    fire?
6 Pour out your anger on the nations
    that do not know you,
  and on the kingdoms
    that do not call on your name.
7 For they have devoured Jacob
    and laid waste his habitation.

8 Do not remember against us the iniquities of
    our ancestors;
  let your compassion come speedily to
    meet us,
  for we are brought very low.
9 Help us, O God of our salvation,
    for the glory of your name;
  deliver us, and forgive our sins,
    for your name's sake.
10 Why should the nations say,
    "Where is their God?"
  Let the avenging of the outpoured blood of
    your servants
  be known among the nations before our
    eyes.

11 Let the groans of the prisoners come
    before you;
  according to your great power preserve
    those doomed to die.
12 Return sevenfold into the bosom of our
    neighbors
  the taunts with which they taunted you,
    O Lord!
13 Then we your people, the flock of your
    pasture,
  will give thanks to you forever;
  from generation to generation we will
    recount your praise.

80 Prayer for Israel's Restoration
To the leader: on Lilies, a Covenant. Of Asaph. A Psalm.

Give ear, O Shepherd of Israel,
  you who lead Joseph like a flock!
You who are enthroned upon the cherubim,
    shine forth
2   before Ephraim and Benjamin and
    Manasseh.
Stir up your might,
  and come to save us!

3 Restore us, O God;
  let your face shine, that we may be saved.

4 O LORD God of hosts,
  how long will you be angry with your
    people's prayers?
5 You have fed them with the bread of tears,
  and given them tears to drink in full
    measure.
6 You make us the scorn[a] of our neighbors;
  our enemies laugh among themselves.

7 Restore us, O God of hosts;
  let your face shine, that we may be saved.

8 You brought a vine out of Egypt;
  you drove out the nations and planted it.
9 You cleared the ground for it;
  it took deep root and filled the land.
10 The mountains were covered with its shade,
  the mighty cedars with its branches;
11 it sent out its branches to the sea,
  and its shoots to the River.
12 Why then have you broken down its walls,

a Syr: Heb *strife*

so that all who pass along the way pluck its
 fruit?

13 The boar from the forest ravages it,
 and all that move in the field feed
 on it.

14 Turn again, O God of hosts;
 look down from heaven, and see;
have regard for this vine,
15 the stock that your right hand planted.*a*
16 They have burned it with fire, they have cut it
 down;*b*
 may they perish at the rebuke of your
 countenance.
17 But let your hand be upon the one at your
 right hand,
 the one whom you made strong for
 yourself.
18 Then we will never turn back from you;
 give us life, and we will call on your name.

19 Restore us, O LORD God of hosts;
 let your face shine, that we may be saved.

God's Appeal to Stubborn Israel

*To the leader: according to The Gittith. Of
Asaph.*

Sing aloud to God our strength;
 shout for joy to the God of Jacob.
2 Raise a song, sound the tambourine,
 the sweet lyre with the harp.
3 Blow the trumpet at the new moon,
 at the full moon, on our festal day.
4 For it is a statute for Israel,
 an ordinance of the God of Jacob.
5 He made it a decree in Joseph,
 when he went out over*c* the land of Egypt.

I hear a voice I had not known:
6 "I relieved your*d* shoulder of the burden;
 your*d* hands were freed from the basket.
7 In distress you called, and I rescued you;
 I answered you in the secret place of
 thunder;
 I tested you at the waters of Meribah.
 Selah
8 Hear, O my people, while I admonish you;
 O Israel, if you would but listen
 to me!
9 There shall be no strange god among you;

you shall not bow down to a foreign god.
10 I am the LORD your God,
 who brought you up out of the land of
 Egypt.
 Open your mouth wide and I will
 fill it.

11 "But my people did not listen to my voice;
 Israel would not submit to me.
12 So I gave them over to their stubborn hearts,
 to follow their own counsels.
13 O that my people would listen to me,
 that Israel would walk in my ways!
14 Then I would quickly subdue their enemies,
 and turn my hand against their
 foes.
15 Those who hate the LORD would cringe
 before him,
 and their doom would last forever.
16 I would feed you*e* with the finest of the wheat,
 and with honey from the rock I would
 satisfy you."

A Plea for Justice

A Psalm of Asaph.

God has taken his place in the divine council;
 in the midst of the gods he holds
 judgment:
2 "How long will you judge unjustly
 and show partiality to the wicked?
 Selah
3 Give justice to the weak and the orphan;
 maintain the right of the lowly and the
 destitute.
4 Rescue the weak and the needy;
 deliver them from the hand of the wicked."

5 They have neither knowledge nor
 understanding,
 they walk around in darkness;
 all the foundations of the earth are shaken.

6 I say, "You are gods,
 children of the Most High, all of you;
7 nevertheless, you shall die like mortals,
 and fall like any prince."*f*

8 Rise up, O God, judge the earth;
 for all the nations belong to you!

---

a Heb adds from verse 17 *and upon the one whom you made strong for yourself*   *b* Cn: Heb *it is cut down*   *c* Or *against*   *d* Heb *his*   *e* Cn Compare verse
16b: Heb *he would feed him*   *f* Or *fall as one man, O princes*

LIVE IT!

AIDS and Compassion · Psalm 82

After a local man died of complications due to AIDS, a newspaper carried an article about his life. "His worst fears were not realized," the article said. "His church did not reject him in the end. It surrounded him with love." What an awesome example of love and justice! His church did not blame and condemn him; the people around him showed compassion for him.

God calls us to show compassion toward those who suffer, but it's easy for us to blame those who are suffering for the situation they are in and to excuse ourselves from any need to help. It's tempting to say that poor people are too lazy to work, that those who are homeless should get a job, or that people dying of AIDS deserve it because of their choices. These attitudes portray a cold justice without mercy. They are not from the mind of God. For God, mercy and justice go hand in hand.

Psalm 82 is a plea for God's justice—a cry to "maintain the right of the lowly" (Psalm 82:3). Every person's life has a God-given sense of dignity that must always be upheld. This is especially true for the weak, needy, orphaned, and destitute. We should never condemn or judge those in hard situations, even if they have made seemingly poor life decisions. Instead, we should direct our words and actions toward lifting up the lowly, surrounding them with great love in their time of need, as the AIDS victim's local church did.

- Who around you is hurting?
- What is one way you can act with compassion and help?

---

83. Prayer for Judgment on Israel's Foes

A Song. A Psalm of Asaph.

O God, do not keep silence;
  do not hold your peace or be still, O God!
2 Even now your enemies are in tumult;
  those who hate you have raised their heads.
3 They lay crafty plans against your people;
  they consult together against those you protect.
4 They say, "Come, let us wipe them out as a nation;
  let the name of Israel be remembered no more."
5 They conspire with one accord;
  against you they make a covenant—
6 the tents of Edom and the Ishmaelites,
  Moab and the Hagrites,
7 Gebal and Ammon and Amalek,
  Philistia with the inhabitants of Tyre;
8 Assyria also has joined them;
  they are the strong arm of the children of Lot.   *Selah*

9 Do to them as you did to Midian,
  as to Sisera and Jabin at the Wadi Kishon,
10 who were destroyed at En-dor,
  who became dung for the ground.
11 Make their nobles like Oreb and Zeeb,
  all their princes like Zebah and Zalmunna,
12 who said, "Let us take the pastures of God
  for our own possession."

13 O my God, make them like whirling dust,*a*
  like chaff before the wind.
14 As fire consumes the forest,
  as the flame sets the mountains ablaze,
15 so pursue them with your tempest
  and terrify them with your hurricane.
16 Fill their faces with shame,
  so that they may seek your name,
    O Lord.
17 Let them be put to shame and dismayed forever;
  let them perish in disgrace.
18 Let them know that you alone,
  whose name is the Lord,
  are the Most High over all the earth.

a Or *a tumbleweed*

CONNECT IT!

Matt Redman: Modern-Day Psalmist
Psalm 84:10

Worshipers have been singing since ancient days. Music has a way of engaging our emotions and connecting our head and heart to our spirit. Many of the psalms were sung for worship in the temple, and our worship songs serve a similar purpose today. Many of our songs are styled after the psalms or even directly quote psalms.

Matt Redman is considered by many to be a modern-day psalmist. Matt started out as a teenage worship leader when the Soul Survivor festival began in the early 1990s in England. Since then he has become a respected songwriter and has been leading worship around the world. You've probably sung his songs in worship at some time. "The Heart of Worship" and "Blessed Be Your Name" are among his most popular worship songs. Another of his famous songs, "Better Is One Day," draws its words directly from **Psalm 84:10**.

One of Matt's recent albums, WE SHALL NOT BE SHAKEN, celebrates the unchanging faithfulness of God in a world where everything seems to constantly shift and change. Sound familiar? The theme and the style are modeled after psalms. The songs are intentionally psalmlike, using simple poetic lyrics to express unbreakable truth in an age of utter brokenness. "Look at the psalms," Matt says on his website. "So many of them are very focused on a particular situation . . . so much of what people put their trust in is not ultimately dependable."* But God is. So Matt continues to write songs, not for fame or fortune, but, like the psalmists of old, for the church to benefit from and use in its worship of God.

---

84 The Joy of Worship in the Temple
To the leader: according to The Gittith. Of the Korahites. A Psalm.

How lovely is your dwelling place,
   O LORD of hosts!
2 My soul longs, indeed it faints
      for the courts of the LORD;
   my heart and my flesh sing for joy
      to the living God.

3 Even the sparrow finds a home,
      and the swallow a nest for herself,
         where she may lay her young,
   at your altars, O LORD of hosts,
      my King and my God.
4 Happy are those who live in your house,
      ever singing your praise.   *Selah*

5 Happy are those whose strength is in you,
      in whose heart are the highways to Zion.*a*
6 As they go through the valley of Baca
      they make it a place of springs;
      the early rain also covers it with pools.
7 They go from strength to strength;
      the God of gods will be seen in Zion.

8 O LORD God of hosts, hear my prayer;
      give ear, O God of Jacob!   *Selah*
9 Behold our shield, O God;
      look on the face of your anointed.

10 For a day in your courts is better
      than a thousand elsewhere.
   I would rather be a doorkeeper in the house of
         my God
      than live in the tents of wickedness.
11 For the LORD God is a sun and shield;
      he bestows favor and honor.
   No good thing does the LORD withhold
      from those who walk uprightly.
12 O LORD of hosts,
      happy is everyone who trusts in you.

---

a Heb lacks *to Zion*

85 Prayer for the Restoration of God's Favor
To the leader. Of the Korahites. A Psalm.

LORD, you were favorable to your land;
  you restored the fortunes of Jacob.
2 You forgave the iniquity of your people;
  you pardoned all their sin.   *Selah*
3 You withdrew all your wrath;
  you turned from your hot anger.

4 Restore us again, O God of our salvation,
  and put away your indignation toward us.
5 Will you be angry with us forever?
  Will you prolong your anger to all
    generations?
6 Will you not revive us again,
  so that your people may rejoice in you?
7 Show us your steadfast love, O LORD,
  and grant us your salvation.

8 Let me hear what God the LORD will speak,
  for he will speak peace to his people,
  to his faithful, to those who turn to him in
    their hearts.[a]
9 Surely his salvation is at hand for those who
    fear him,
  that his glory may dwell in our land.

10 Steadfast love and faithfulness will meet;
  righteousness and peace will kiss each
    other.
11 Faithfulness will spring up from the ground,
  and righteousness will look down from
    the sky.
12 The LORD will give what is good,
  and our land will yield its increase.
13 Righteousness will go before him,
  and will make a path for his steps.

86 Supplication for Help against Enemies
A Prayer of David.

Incline your ear, O LORD, and answer me,
  for I am poor and needy.
2 Preserve my life, for I am devoted to you;
  save your servant who trusts in you.
  You are my God; 3be gracious to me, O Lord,
  for to you do I cry all day long.

> "Give ear, O LORD,
> to my prayer; listen to
> my cry of supplication.
> In the day of
> my trouble I call
> on you, for you will
> answer me."
> —Psalm 86:6–7

4 Gladden the soul of your servant,
  for to you, O Lord, I lift up my soul.
5 For you, O Lord, are good and forgiving,
  abounding in steadfast love to all who call
    on you.
6 Give ear, O LORD, to my prayer;
  listen to my cry of supplication.
7 In the day of my trouble I call on you,
  for you will answer me.

8 There is none like you among the gods,
    O Lord,
  nor are there any works like yours.
9 All the nations you have made shall come
  and bow down before you, O Lord,
  and shall glorify your name.
10 For you are great and do wondrous things;
  you alone are God.
11 Teach me your way, O LORD,
  that I may walk in your truth;
  give me an undivided heart to revere your
    name.
12 I give thanks to you, O Lord my God, with my
    whole heart,
  and I will glorify your name forever.
13 For great is your steadfast love
    toward me;
  you have delivered my soul from the
    depths of Sheol.

14 O God, the insolent rise up against me;
  a band of ruffians seeks my life,
  and they do not set you before them.
15 But you, O Lord, are a God merciful and
    gracious,
  slow to anger and abounding in steadfast
    love and faithfulness.

a Gk: Heb *but let them not turn back to folly*

16 Turn to me and be gracious to me;
        give your strength to your servant;
        save the child of your serving girl.
17 Show me a sign of your favor,
        so that those who hate me may see it and
            be put to shame,
        because you, LORD, have helped me and
            comforted me.

87 The Joy of Living in Zion
Of the Korahites. A Psalm. A Song.

   On the holy mount stands the city he
        founded;
2   the LORD loves the gates of Zion
        more than all the dwellings of Jacob.
3 Glorious things are spoken of you,
        O city of God.   *Selah*

4 Among those who know me I mention Rahab
        and Babylon;
        Philistia too, and Tyre, with Ethiopia*a*—
        "This one was born there," they say.

5 And of Zion it shall be said,
        "This one and that one were born in it";
        for the Most High himself will establish it.
6 The LORD records, as he registers the
            peoples,
        "This one was born there."   *Selah*

7 Singers and dancers alike say,
        "All my springs are in you."

88 Prayer for Help in Despondency
*A Song. A Psalm of the Korahites. To the
leader: according to Mahalath Leannoth.
A Maskil of Heman the Ezrahite.*

   O LORD, God of my salvation,
        when, at night, I cry out in your presence,
2 let my prayer come before you;
        incline your ear to my cry.

3 For my soul is full of troubles,
        and my life draws near to Sheol.
4 I am counted among those who go down to
            the Pit;
        I am like those who have no help,
5 like those forsaken among the dead,
        like the slain that lie in the grave,

like those whom you remember no more,
        for they are cut off from your hand.
6 You have put me in the depths of the Pit,
        in the regions dark and deep.
7 Your wrath lies heavy upon me,
        and you overwhelm me with all your
            waves.   *Selah*

8 You have caused my companions to shun me;
        you have made me a thing of horror to
            them.
   I am shut in so that I cannot escape;
9   my eye grows dim through sorrow.
   Every day I call on you, O LORD;
        I spread out my hands to you.
10 Do you work wonders for the dead?
        Do the shades rise up to praise you?
                                          Selah
11 Is your steadfast love declared in the grave,
        or your faithfulness in Abaddon?
12 Are your wonders known in the darkness,
        or your saving help in the land of
            forgetfulness?

13 But I, O LORD, cry out to you;
        in the morning my prayer comes
            before you.
14 O LORD, why do you cast me off?
        Why do you hide your face from me?
15 Wretched and close to death from my
            youth up,
        I suffer your terrors; I am desperate.*b*
16 Your wrath has swept over me;
        your dread assaults destroy me.
17 They surround me like a flood all day long;
        from all sides they close in on me.
18 You have caused friend and neighbor to
            shun me;
        my companions are in darkness.

89 God's Covenant with David
A Maskil of Ethan the Ezrahite.

   I will sing of your steadfast love, O LORD,*c*
        forever;
        with my mouth I will proclaim your
            faithfulness to all generations.
2 I declare that your steadfast love is established
            forever;
        your faithfulness is as firm as the heavens.

---

a Or *Nubia*; Heb *Cush*   *b* Meaning of Heb uncertain   *c* Gk: Heb *the steadfast love of the* LORD

3 You said, "I have made a covenant with my
     chosen one,
   I have sworn to my servant David:
4 'I will establish your descendants forever,
     and build your throne for all generations.' "
                                         Selah

5 Let the heavens praise your wonders, O LORD,
     your faithfulness in the assembly of the
     holy ones.
6 For who in the skies can be compared to the
     LORD?
   Who among the heavenly beings is like the
     LORD,
7 a God feared in the council of the holy ones,
     great and awesome*a* above all that are
     around him?
8 O LORD God of hosts,
     who is as mighty as you, O LORD?
   Your faithfulness surrounds you.
9 You rule the raging of the sea;
     when its waves rise, you still them.
10 You crushed Rahab like a carcass;
     you scattered your enemies with your
     mighty arm.
11 The heavens are yours, the earth also is yours;
     the world and all that is in it—you have
     founded them.
12 The north and the south*b*—you created them;
     Tabor and Hermon joyously praise your
     name.
13 You have a mighty arm;
     strong is your hand, high your right hand.
14 Righteousness and justice are the foundation
     of your throne;
   steadfast love and faithfulness go
     before you.
15 Happy are the people who know the festal
     shout,
   who walk, O LORD, in the light of your
     countenance;
16 they exult in your name all day long,
     and extol*c* your righteousness.
17 For you are the glory of their strength;
     by your favor our horn is exalted.
18 For our shield belongs to the LORD,
     our king to the Holy One of Israel.

19 Then you spoke in a vision to your faithful
     one, and said:

"I have set the crown*d* on one who is
     mighty,
   I have exalted one chosen from the people.
20 I have found my servant David;
     with my holy oil I have anointed him;
21 my hand shall always remain with him;
     my arm also shall strengthen him.
22 The enemy shall not outwit him,
     the wicked shall not humble him.
23 I will crush his foes before him
     and strike down those who hate him.
24 My faithfulness and steadfast love shall be
     with him;
   and in my name his horn shall be exalted.
25 I will set his hand on the sea
     and his right hand on the rivers.
26 He shall cry to me, 'You are my Father,
     my God, and the Rock of my salvation!'
27 I will make him the firstborn,
     the highest of the kings of the earth.
28 Forever I will keep my steadfast love for him,
     and my covenant with him will stand
     firm.
29 I will establish his line forever,
     and his throne as long as the heavens
     endure.
30 If his children forsake my law
     and do not walk according to my
     ordinances,
31 if they violate my statutes
     and do not keep my commandments,
32 then I will punish their transgression with
     the rod
   and their iniquity with scourges;
33 but I will not remove from him my steadfast
     love,
   or be false to my faithfulness.
34 I will not violate my covenant,
     or alter the word that went forth from my
     lips.
35 Once and for all I have sworn by my holiness;
     I will not lie to David.
36 His line shall continue forever,
     and his throne endure before me like
     the sun.
37 It shall be established forever like the moon,
     an enduring witness in the skies."   *Selah*

38 But now you have spurned and rejected him;
     you are full of wrath against your anointed.

a Gk Syr: Heb *greatly awesome* b Or *Zaphon and Yamin* c Cn: Heb *are exalted in* d Cn: Heb *help*

39 You have renounced the covenant with your
      servant;
   you have defiled his crown in the dust.
40 You have broken through all his walls;
   you have laid his strongholds in
      ruins.
41 All who pass by plunder him;
   he has become the scorn of his neighbors.
42 You have exalted the right hand of his foes;
   you have made all his enemies rejoice.
43 Moreover, you have turned back the edge of his
      sword,
   and you have not supported him in battle.
44 You have removed the scepter from his hand,[a]
   and hurled his throne to the ground.
45 You have cut short the days of his youth;
   you have covered him with shame.
                                        Selah

46 How long, O Lord? Will you hide yourself
      forever?
   How long will your wrath burn like fire?
47 Remember how short my time is—[b]
   for what vanity you have created all mortals!
48 Who can live and never see death?
   Who can escape the power of Sheol?
                                        Selah

49 Lord, where is your steadfast love of old,
   which by your faithfulness you swore to
      David?
50 Remember, O Lord, how your servant is
      taunted;
   how I bear in my bosom the insults of the
      peoples,[c]
51 with which your enemies taunt, O Lord,
   with which they taunted the footsteps of
      your anointed.

52 Blessed be the Lord forever.
      Amen and Amen.

BOOK IV
(Psalms 90–106)

90 God's Eternity and Human Frailty
A Prayer of Moses, the man of God.

Lord, you have been our dwelling place[d]
   in all generations.

2 Before the mountains were brought forth,
   or ever you had formed the earth and the
      world,
   from everlasting to everlasting you
      are God.

3 You turn us[e] back to dust,
   and say, "Turn back, you mortals."
4 For a thousand years in your sight
   are like yesterday when it is past,
   or like a watch in the night.

5 You sweep them away; they are like a dream,
   like grass that is renewed in the morning;
6 in the morning it flourishes and is renewed;
   in the evening it fades and withers.

7 For we are consumed by your anger;
   by your wrath we are overwhelmed.
8 You have set our iniquities before you,
   our secret sins in the light of your
      countenance.

9 For all our days pass away under your wrath;
   our years come to an end[f] like a sigh.
10 The days of our life are seventy years,
   or perhaps eighty, if we are strong;
   even then their span[g] is only toil and
      trouble;
   they are soon gone, and we fly away.

11 Who considers the power of your anger?
   Your wrath is as great as the fear that is
      due you.
12 So teach us to count our days
   that we may gain a wise heart.

13 Turn, O Lord! How long?
   Have compassion on your servants!
14 Satisfy us in the morning with your steadfast
      love,
   so that we may rejoice and be glad all our
      days.
15 Make us glad as many days as you have
      afflicted us,
   and as many years as we have seen evil.
16 Let your work be manifest to your servants,
   and your glorious power to their children.
17 Let the favor of the Lord our God be
      upon us,

---

a Cn: Heb *removed his cleanness*   b Meaning of Heb uncertain   c Cn: Heb *bosom all of many peoples*   d Another reading is *our refuge*   e Heb *humankind*
f Syr: Heb *we bring our years to an end*   g Cn Compare Gk Syr Jerome Tg: Heb *pride*

Write Your Own Psalm

There are many types of psalms (see the introduction to Psalms), and more than one author of the book of Psalms. Even today there are psalmists, people who write songs or poems similar in tone and style to the psalms in the Bible. Try writing your own psalm:

- Choose the type of psalm you want to write based on what's in your heart.
- Use poetic language and symbolism.
- Illustrate your psalm.
- Set it to music (like the original ones) even if you can only hum.
- Or choose an existing psalm and rewrite it to reflect a current issue you're facing.

and prosper for us the work of our
    hands—
O prosper the work of our hands!

Assurance of God's Protection

91 You who live in the shelter of the Most
    High,
who abide in the shadow of the
    Almighty,[a]
2 will say to the LORD, "My refuge and my
    fortress;
my God, in whom I trust."
3 For he will deliver you from the snare of the
    fowler
and from the deadly pestilence;
4 he will cover you with his pinions,
and under his wings you will find
    refuge;
his faithfulness is a shield and buckler.
5 You will not fear the terror of the night,
or the arrow that flies by day,
6 or the pestilence that stalks in darkness,
or the destruction that wastes at noonday.

7 A thousand may fall at your side,
ten thousand at your right hand,
but it will not come near you.
8 You will only look with your eyes
and see the punishment of the wicked.

9 Because you have made the LORD your
    refuge,[b]
the Most High your dwelling place,
10 no evil shall befall you,
no scourge come near your tent.

11 For he will command his angels
    concerning you
to guard you in all your ways.
12 On their hands they will bear you up,
so that you will not dash your foot against
    a stone.
13 You will tread on the lion and the adder,
the young lion and the serpent you will
    trample under foot.

14 Those who love me, I will deliver;
I will protect those who know my name.
15 When they call to me, I will answer them;
I will be with them in trouble,
I will rescue them and honor them.
16 With long life I will satisfy them,
and show them my salvation.

Thanksgiving for Vindication

92 A Psalm. A Song for the Sabbath Day.

It is good to give thanks to the LORD,
to sing praises to your name,
    O Most High;
2 to declare your steadfast love in the morning,
and your faithfulness by night,
3 to the music of the lute and the harp,
to the melody of the lyre.
4 For you, O LORD, have made me glad by your
    work;
at the works of your hands I sing for joy.

5 How great are your works, O LORD!
Your thoughts are very deep!
6 The dullard cannot know,

the stupid cannot understand this:

7 though the wicked sprout like grass
and all evildoers flourish,
they are doomed to destruction forever,
8   but you, O LORD, are on high forever.
9 For your enemies, O LORD,
for your enemies shall perish;
all evildoers shall be scattered.

10 But you have exalted my horn like that of the
wild ox;
you have poured over me[a] fresh oil.
11 My eyes have seen the downfall of my
enemies;
my ears have heard the doom of my evil
assailants.

12 The righteous flourish like the palm
tree,
and grow like a cedar in Lebanon.
13 They are planted in the house of the
LORD;
they flourish in the courts of our God.
14 In old age they still produce fruit;
they are always green and full of sap,
15 showing that the LORD is upright;
he is my rock, and there is no
unrighteousness in him.

93 The Majesty of God's Rule

The LORD is king, he is robed in
majesty;
the LORD is robed, he is girded with
strength.
He has established the world; it shall never be
moved;
2   your throne is established from of old;
you are from everlasting.

3 The floods have lifted up, O LORD,
the floods have lifted up their voice;
the floods lift up their roaring.
4 More majestic than the thunders of mighty
waters,
more majestic than the waves[b] of the sea,
majestic on high is the LORD!

5 Your decrees are very sure;
holiness befits your house,
O LORD, forevermore.

94 God the Avenger of the Righteous

O LORD, you God of vengeance,
you God of vengeance, shine forth!
2 Rise up, O judge of the earth;
give to the proud what they deserve!
3 O LORD, how long shall the wicked,
how long shall the wicked exult?

4 They pour out their arrogant words;
all the evildoers boast.
5 They crush your people, O LORD,
and afflict your heritage.
6 They kill the widow and the stranger,
they murder the orphan,
7 and they say, "The LORD does not see;
the God of Jacob does not perceive."

8 Understand, O dullest of the people;
fools, when will you be wise?
9 He who planted the ear, does he not hear?
He who formed the eye, does he not see?
10 He who disciplines the nations,
he who teaches knowledge to humankind,
does he not chastise?
11 The LORD knows our thoughts,[c]
that they are but an empty breath.

12 Happy are those whom you discipline,
O LORD,
and whom you teach out of your law,
13 giving them respite from days of trouble,
until a pit is dug for the wicked.
14 For the LORD will not forsake his people;
he will not abandon his heritage;
15 for justice will return to the righteous,
and all the upright in heart will
follow it.

16 Who rises up for me against the wicked?
Who stands up for me against evildoers?
17 If the LORD had not been my help,
my soul would soon have lived in the land
of silence.
18 When I thought, "My foot is slipping,"
your steadfast love, O LORD, held
me up.
19 When the cares of my heart are many,
your consolations cheer my soul.
20 Can wicked rulers be allied with you,
those who contrive mischief by statute?

a Syr: Meaning of Heb uncertain   b Cn: Heb majestic are the waves   c Heb the thoughts of humankind

21 They band together against the life of the
    righteous,
    and condemn the innocent to death.
22 But the LORD has become my stronghold,
    and my God the rock of my refuge.
23 He will repay them for their iniquity
    and wipe them out for their wickedness;
    the LORD our God will wipe them out.

95   A Call to Worship and Obedience

O come, let us sing to the LORD;
    let us make a joyful noise to the rock of
    our salvation!
2 Let us come into his presence with
    thanksgiving;
    let us make a joyful noise to him with
    songs of praise!
3 For the LORD is a great God,
    and a great King above all gods.
4 In his hand are the depths of the earth;
    the heights of the mountains are his also.
5 The sea is his, for he made it,
    and the dry land, which his hands have
    formed.

6 O come, let us worship and bow down,
    let us kneel before the LORD, our Maker!
7 For he is our God,
    and we are the people of his pasture,
    and the sheep of his hand.

O that today you would listen to his voice!
8   Do not harden your hearts, as at Meribah,
    as on the day at Massah in the wilderness,
9 when your ancestors tested me,
    and put me to the proof, though they had
    seen my work.
10 For forty years I loathed that generation
    and said, "They are a people whose hearts
    go astray,
    and they do not regard my ways."
11 Therefore in my anger I swore,
    "They shall not enter my rest."

96   Praise to God Who Comes in Judgment

O sing to the LORD a new song;
    sing to the LORD, all the earth.
2 Sing to the LORD, bless his name;
    tell of his salvation from day to day.

> "O sing to the LORD
> a new song; sing to
> the LORD, all the earth.
> Sing to the LORD,
> bless his name;
> tell of his salvation
> from day to day."
> —Psalm 96:1–2

3 Declare his glory among the nations,
    his marvelous works among all the
    peoples.
4 For great is the LORD, and greatly to be
    praised;
    he is to be revered above all gods.
5 For all the gods of the peoples are idols,
    but the LORD made the heavens.
6 Honor and majesty are before him;
    strength and beauty are in his sanctuary.

7 Ascribe to the LORD, O families of the
    peoples,
    ascribe to the LORD glory and strength.
8 Ascribe to the LORD the glory due his name;
    bring an offering, and come into his courts.
9 Worship the LORD in holy splendor;
    tremble before him, all the earth.

10 Say among the nations, "The LORD is king!
    The world is firmly established; it shall
    never be moved.
    He will judge the peoples with equity."
11 Let the heavens be glad, and let the earth
    rejoice;
    let the sea roar, and all that fills it;
12   let the field exult, and everything in it.
    Then shall all the trees of the forest sing
    for joy
13   before the LORD; for he is coming,
    for he is coming to judge the earth.
    He will judge the world with righteousness,
    and the peoples with his truth.

97   The Glory of God's Reign

The LORD is king! Let the earth rejoice;
    let the many coastlands be glad!

2 Clouds and thick darkness are all around him;
    righteousness and justice are the
        foundation of his throne.
3 Fire goes before him,
    and consumes his adversaries on every side.
4 His lightnings light up the world;
    the earth sees and trembles.
5 The mountains melt like wax before the
        LORD,
    before the Lord of all the earth.

6 The heavens proclaim his righteousness;
    and all the peoples behold his glory.
7 All worshipers of images are put to shame,
    those who make their boast in worthless
        idols;
    all gods bow down before him.
8 Zion hears and is glad,
    and the towns[a] of Judah rejoice,
    because of your judgments, O God.
9 For you, O LORD, are most high over all the
        earth;
    you are exalted far above all gods.

10 The LORD loves those who hate[b] evil;
    he guards the lives of his faithful;
    he rescues them from the hand of the
        wicked.
11 Light dawns[c] for the righteous,
    and joy for the upright in heart.
12 Rejoice in the LORD, O you righteous,
    and give thanks to his holy name!

98 Praise the Judge of the World
A Psalm.

O sing to the LORD a new song,
    for he has done marvelous things.
His right hand and his holy arm
    have gotten him victory.
2 The LORD has made known his victory;
    he has revealed his vindication in the
        sight of the nations.
3 He has remembered his steadfast love and
        faithfulness
    to the house of Israel.
All the ends of the earth have seen
    the victory of our God.
4 Make a joyful noise to the LORD, all the earth;

break forth into joyous song and sing
    praises.
5 Sing praises to the LORD with the lyre,
    with the lyre and the sound of melody.
6 With trumpets and the sound of the horn
    make a joyful noise before the King, the
        LORD.

7 Let the sea roar, and all that fills it;
    the world and those who live in it.
8 Let the floods clap their hands;
    let the hills sing together for joy
9 at the presence of the LORD, for he is coming
    to judge the earth.
He will judge the world with righteousness,
    and the peoples with equity.

99 Praise to God for His Holiness
The LORD is king; let the peoples
        tremble!
He sits enthroned upon the cherubim; let
    the earth quake!
2 The LORD is great in Zion;
    he is exalted over all the peoples.
3 Let them praise your great and awesome
        name.
    Holy is he!
4 Mighty King,[d] lover of justice,
    you have established equity;
you have executed justice
    and righteousness in Jacob.
5 Extol the LORD our God;
    worship at his footstool.
    Holy is he!

6 Moses and Aaron were among his priests,
    Samuel also was among those who called
        on his name.
    They cried to the LORD, and he answered
        them.
7 He spoke to them in the pillar of cloud;
    they kept his decrees,
    and the statutes that he gave them.

8 O LORD our God, you answered them;
    you were a forgiving God to them,
    but an avenger of their wrongdoings.
9 Extol the LORD our God,
    and worship at his holy mountain;
    for the LORD our God is holy.

---

a Heb *daughters*   b Cn: Heb *You who love the LORD hate*   c Gk Syr Jerome: Heb *is sown*   d Cn: Heb *And a king's strength*

100 All Lands Summoned to Praise God
A Psalm of thanksgiving.

Make a joyful noise to the LORD, all the earth.
2 Worship the LORD with gladness;
   come into his presence with singing.
3 Know that the LORD is God.
   It is he that made us, and we are his;*a*
   we are his people, and the sheep of his
      pasture.

4 Enter his gates with thanksgiving,
   and his courts with praise.
   Give thanks to him, bless his name.

5 For the LORD is good;
   his steadfast love endures forever,
   and his faithfulness to all generations.

101 A Sovereign's Pledge of Integrity and Justice
Of David. A Psalm.

I will sing of loyalty and of justice;
   to you, O LORD, I will sing.
2 I will study the way that is blameless.
   When shall I attain it?

I will walk with integrity of heart
   within my house;
3 I will not set before my eyes
   anything that is base.

I hate the work of those who fall away;
   it shall not cling to me.
4 Perverseness of heart shall be far
      from me;
   I will know nothing of evil.

5 One who secretly slanders a neighbor
   I will destroy.
A haughty look and an arrogant heart
   I will not tolerate.

6 I will look with favor on the faithful in the
      land,
   so that they may live with me;
whoever walks in the way that is blameless
   shall minister to me.

7 No one who practices deceit
   shall remain in my house;
no one who utters lies
   shall continue in my presence.

8 Morning by morning I will destroy
   all the wicked in the land,
cutting off all evildoers
   from the city of the LORD.

102 Prayer to the Eternal King for Help
A prayer of one afflicted, when faint and pleading before the LORD.

Hear my prayer, O LORD;
   let my cry come to you.
2 Do not hide your face from me
   in the day of my distress.
Incline your ear to me;
   answer me speedily in the day when
      I call.

3 For my days pass away like smoke,
   and my bones burn like a furnace.
4 My heart is stricken and withered like grass;
   I am too wasted to eat my bread.
5 Because of my loud groaning
   my bones cling to my skin.
6 I am like an owl of the wilderness,
   like a little owl of the waste places.
7 I lie awake;
   I am like a lonely bird on the housetop.
8 All day long my enemies taunt me;
   those who deride me use my name for a
      curse.
9 For I eat ashes like bread,
   and mingle tears with my drink,
10 because of your indignation and anger;
   for you have lifted me up and thrown me
      aside.
11 My days are like an evening shadow;
   I wither away like grass.

12 But you, O LORD, are enthroned forever;
   your name endures to all generations.
13 You will rise up and have compassion on
      Zion,
   for it is time to favor it;
   the appointed time has come.
14 For your servants hold its stones dear,
   and have pity on its dust.

a Another reading is *and not we ourselves*

15 The nations will fear the name of the LORD,
　　and all the kings of the earth your glory.
16 For the LORD will build up Zion;
　　he will appear in his glory.
17 He will regard the prayer of the destitute,
　　and will not despise their prayer.

18 Let this be recorded for a generation to come,
　　so that a people yet unborn may praise the
　　　LORD:
19 that he looked down from his holy height,
　　from heaven the LORD looked at the earth,
20 to hear the groans of the prisoners,
　　to set free those who were doomed to die;
21 so that the name of the LORD may be declared
　　in Zion,
　　and his praise in Jerusalem,
22 when peoples gather together,
　　and kingdoms, to worship the LORD.

23 He has broken my strength in midcourse;
　　he has shortened my days.
24 "O my God," I say, "do not take me away
　　at the midpoint of my life,
　　you whose years endure
　　throughout all generations."

25 Long ago you laid the foundation of the earth,
　　and the heavens are the work of your
　　　hands.

26 They will perish, but you endure;
　　they will all wear out like a garment.
　　You change them like clothing, and they pass
　　　away;
27 but you are the same, and your years have
　　no end.
28 The children of your servants shall live secure;
　　their offspring shall be established in your
　　　presence.

103 Thanksgiving for God's Goodness
Of David.

Bless the LORD, O my soul,
　　and all that is within me,
　　bless his holy name.
2 Bless the LORD, O my soul,
　　and do not forget all his benefits—
3 who forgives all your iniquity,
　　who heals all your diseases,
4 who redeems your life from the Pit,
　　who crowns you with steadfast love and
　　　mercy,
5 who satisfies you with good as long as you
　　live[a]
　　so that your youth is renewed like the
　　　eagle's.

6 The LORD works vindication
　　and justice for all who are oppressed.

Letting Go of Anger · Psalm 103

This psalm is a beautiful prayer praising God's love and compassion. **Psalm 103:9** reminds us that God will not stay angry forever. What a great lesson for us to learn from God. Anger is a natural human emotion—but, in imitation of God, we shouldn't hold on to it. When we let go of our anger, we free ourselves from being consumed by bitterness. We also build better relationships, because hidden anger puts other people on the defensive and destroys trust.

How do you let go of anger? Here are some suggestions:

• Express your feelings in a letter or a journal.
• Tell the person you are angry with how you feel and that you would like to reconcile.
• Go for a walk or run or use another form of exercise to vent your anger and cool down.
• Relax with some quiet, worshipful music.
• Try to identify why you feel angry. Often anger is a symptom of another feeling, such as hurt, disappointment, or even tiredness.
• Express your anger in prayer to God, and ask for help in forgiveness.

a Meaning of Heb uncertain

7 He made known his ways to Moses,
     his acts to the people of Israel.
8 The Lord is merciful and gracious,
     slow to anger and abounding in steadfast
        love.
9 He will not always accuse,
     nor will he keep his anger forever.
10 He does not deal with us according to our sins,
     nor repay us according to our iniquities.
11 For as the heavens are high above the earth,
     so great is his steadfast love toward those
        who fear him;
12 as far as the east is from the west,
     so far he removes our transgressions
        from us.
13 As a father has compassion for his children,
     so the Lord has compassion for those who
        fear him.
14 For he knows how we were made;
     he remembers that we are dust.

15 As for mortals, their days are like grass;
     they flourish like a flower of the field;
16 for the wind passes over it, and it is gone,
     and its place knows it no more.
17 But the steadfast love of the Lord is from
        everlasting to everlasting
     on those who fear him,
     and his righteousness to children's
        children,
18 to those who keep his covenant
     and remember to do his commandments.

19 The Lord has established his throne in the
        heavens,
     and his kingdom rules over all.
20 Bless the Lord, O you his angels,
     you mighty ones who do his
        bidding,
     obedient to his spoken word.
21 Bless the Lord, all his hosts,
     his ministers that do his will.
22 Bless the Lord, all his works,
     in all places of his dominion.
     Bless the Lord, O my soul.

104   God the Creator and Provider

Bless the Lord, O my soul.
     O Lord my God, you are very great.
You are clothed with honor and majesty,

2 wrapped in light as with a garment.
You stretch out the heavens like a tent,
3   you set the beams of your^a chambers on
        the waters,
you make the clouds your^a chariot,
     you ride on the wings of the wind,
4 you make the winds your^a messengers,
     fire and flame your^a ministers.

5 You set the earth on its foundations,
     so that it shall never be shaken.
6 You cover it with the deep as with a garment;
     the waters stood above the mountains.
7 At your rebuke they flee;
     at the sound of your thunder they take to
        flight.
8 They rose up to the mountains, ran down to
        the valleys
     to the place that you appointed for them.
9 You set a boundary that they may not pass,
     so that they might not again cover the
        earth.

10 You make springs gush forth in the valleys;
     they flow between the hills,
11 giving drink to every wild animal;
     the wild asses quench their thirst.
12 By the streams^b the birds of the air have their
        habitation;
     they sing among the branches.
13 From your lofty abode you water the
        mountains;
     the earth is satisfied with the fruit of your
        work.

14 You cause the grass to grow for the cattle,
     and plants for people to use,^{c}
to bring forth food from the earth,
15 and wine to gladden the human heart,

a Heb his   b Heb By them   c Or to cultivate

Care for Our Planet · Psalm 104

The writer of this psalm describes the intimate and dependent relationship all living things have with their creator. There is beauty in creation, and God is actively involved in the unfolding of the natural world. We are called to revere God's creation and to care for it in a way that reflects God's boundless and ongoing care.

An important part of that call is to recognize that what we do with creation impacts people—and the negative effects seem to fall most often on the vulnerable of our world. We must recognize the interdependence of all creation and remember that any action we take must consider the common good. The destruction of a rain forest in one part of the world or the disproportionate use of resources in another part impacts the entire planet. Usually poorer countries and people have the least amount of power to affect political policies, and they suffer the most. Things will only get worse if steps are not taken to reverse this trend.

Caring for creation must be directed by God's plan and not by our own self-interests. When we contribute to the destruction of our environment, we dishonor God and all creation. Think about how your individual actions impact the global community, and pray for the wisdom to understand your role in restoring order to the natural world—our planet and survival depend on it. Consider these questions:

- How does your use of energy affect the environment and other people? What can you do to reduce your energy use?
- How dependent are you on material things? What are some ways you can live more simply so others can simply live?

oil to make the face shine,
and bread to strengthen the human heart.
16 The trees of the LORD are watered abundantly,
the cedars of Lebanon that he planted.
17 In them the birds build their nests;
the stork has its home in the fir trees.
18 The high mountains are for the wild goats;
the rocks are a refuge for the coneys.
19 You have made the moon to mark the seasons;
the sun knows its time for setting.
20 You make darkness, and it is night,
when all the animals of the forest come
creeping out.
21 The young lions roar for their prey,
seeking their food from God.
22 When the sun rises, they withdraw
and lie down in their dens.
23 People go out to their work
and to their labor until the evening.
24 O LORD, how manifold are your works!
In wisdom you have made them all;

the earth is full of your creatures.
25 Yonder is the sea, great and wide,
creeping things innumerable are there,
living things both small and great.
26 There go the ships,
and Leviathan that you formed to sport
in it.
27 These all look to you
to give them their food in due season;
28 when you give to them, they gather
it up;
when you open your hand, they are filled
with good things.
29 When you hide your face, they are dismayed;
when you take away their breath, they die
and return to their dust.
30 When you send forth your spirit,*a* they are
created;
and you renew the face of the ground.
31 May the glory of the LORD endure forever;

a Or your breath

may the LORD rejoice in his works—
³² who looks on the earth and it trembles,
     who touches the mountains and they
        smoke.
³³ I will sing to the LORD as long as I live;
     I will sing praise to my God while I have
        being.
³⁴ May my meditation be pleasing to him,
     for I rejoice in the LORD.
³⁵ Let sinners be consumed from the earth,
     and let the wicked be no more.
     Bless the LORD, O my soul.
     Praise the LORD!

God's Faithfulness to Israel

105 O give thanks to the LORD, call on his
        name,
     make known his deeds among the
        peoples.
² Sing to him, sing praises to him;
     tell of all his wonderful works.
³ Glory in his holy name;
     let the hearts of those who seek the LORD
        rejoice.
⁴ Seek the LORD and his strength;
     seek his presence continually.
⁵ Remember the wonderful works he has done,
     his miracles, and the judgments he has
        uttered,
⁶ O offspring of his servant Abraham,[a]
     children of Jacob, his chosen ones.

⁷ He is the LORD our God;
     his judgments are in all the earth.
⁸ He is mindful of his covenant forever,
     of the word that he commanded, for a
        thousand generations,
⁹ the covenant that he made with Abraham,
     his sworn promise to Isaac,
¹⁰ which he confirmed to Jacob as a statute,
     to Israel as an everlasting covenant,
¹¹ saying, "To you I will give the land of Canaan
     as your portion for an inheritance."

¹² When they were few in number,
     of little account, and strangers in it,
¹³ wandering from nation to nation,
     from one kingdom to another people,
¹⁴ he allowed no one to oppress them;
     he rebuked kings on their account,

¹⁵ saying, "Do not touch my anointed ones;
     do my prophets no harm."

¹⁶ When he summoned famine against the land,
     and broke every staff of bread,
¹⁷ he had sent a man ahead of them,
     Joseph, who was sold as a slave.
¹⁸ His feet were hurt with fetters,
     his neck was put in a collar of iron;
¹⁹ until what he had said came to pass,
     the word of the LORD kept testing him.
²⁰ The king sent and released him;
     the ruler of the peoples set him free.
²¹ He made him lord of his house,
     and ruler of all his possessions,
²² to instruct[b] his officials at his pleasure,
     and to teach his elders wisdom.

²³ Then Israel came to Egypt;
     Jacob lived as an alien in the land of Ham.
²⁴ And the LORD made his people very fruitful,
     and made them stronger than their foes,
²⁵ whose hearts he then turned to hate his
        people,
     to deal craftily with his servants.

²⁶ He sent his servant Moses,
     and Aaron whom he had chosen.
²⁷ They performed his signs among
        them,
     and miracles in the land of Ham.
²⁸ He sent darkness, and made the land dark;
     they rebelled[c] against his words.
²⁹ He turned their waters into blood,
     and caused their fish to die.
³⁰ Their land swarmed with frogs,
     even in the chambers of their kings.
³¹ He spoke, and there came swarms of flies,
     and gnats throughout their country.
³² He gave them hail for rain,
     and lightning that flashed through their
        land.
³³ He struck their vines and fig trees,
     and shattered the trees of their country.
³⁴ He spoke, and the locusts came,
     and young locusts without number;
³⁵ they devoured all the vegetation in their land,
     and ate up the fruit of their ground.
³⁶ He struck down all the firstborn in their land,
     the first issue of all their strength.

a Another reading is *Israel* (compare 1 Chr 16.13)   **b** Gk Syr Jerome: Heb *to bind*   **c** Cn Compare Gk Syr: Heb *they did not rebel*

37 Then he brought Israel[a] out with silver and
gold,
and there was no one among their tribes
who stumbled.
38 Egypt was glad when they departed,
for dread of them had fallen upon it.
39 He spread a cloud for a covering,
and fire to give light by night.
40 They asked, and he brought quails,
and gave them food from heaven in
abundance.
41 He opened the rock, and water gushed out;
it flowed through the desert like a river.
42 For he remembered his holy promise,
and Abraham, his servant.

43 So he brought his people out with joy,
his chosen ones with singing.
44 He gave them the lands of the nations,
and they took possession of the wealth of
the peoples,
45 that they might keep his statutes
and observe his laws.
Praise the Lord!

A Confession of Israel's Sins

106 Praise the Lord!
O give thanks to the Lord, for he is
good;
for his steadfast love endures forever.
2 Who can utter the mighty doings of the
Lord,
or declare all his praise?
3 Happy are those who observe justice,
who do righteousness at all times.

4 Remember me, O Lord, when you show
favor to your people;
help me when you deliver them;
5 that I may see the prosperity of your chosen
ones,
that I may rejoice in the gladness of your
nation,
that I may glory in your heritage.

6 Both we and our ancestors have sinned;
we have committed iniquity, have done
wickedly.
7 Our ancestors, when they were in Egypt,
did not consider your wonderful works;

they did not remember the abundance of your
steadfast love,
but rebelled against the Most High[b] at the
Red Sea.[c]
8 Yet he saved them for his name's sake,
so that he might make known his mighty
power.
9 He rebuked the Red Sea,[c] and it became dry;
he led them through the deep as through a
desert.
10 So he saved them from the hand of the foe,
and delivered them from the hand of the
enemy.
11 The waters covered their adversaries;
not one of them was left.
12 Then they believed his words;
they sang his praise.

13 But they soon forgot his works;
they did not wait for his counsel.
14 But they had a wanton craving in the
wilderness,
and put God to the test in the desert;
15 he gave them what they asked,
but sent a wasting disease among them.

16 They were jealous of Moses in the camp,
and of Aaron, the holy one of the Lord.
17 The earth opened and swallowed up Dathan,
and covered the faction of Abiram.
18 Fire also broke out in their company;
the flame burned up the wicked.

19 They made a calf at Horeb
and worshiped a cast image.
20 They exchanged the glory of God[d]
for the image of an ox that eats grass.
21 They forgot God, their Savior,
who had done great things in Egypt,
22 wondrous works in the land of Ham,
and awesome deeds by the Red Sea.[c]
23 Therefore he said he would destroy them—
had not Moses, his chosen one,
stood in the breach before him,
to turn away his wrath from destroying
them.

24 Then they despised the pleasant land,
having no faith in his promise.
25 They grumbled in their tents,

---

a Heb *them* b Cn Compare 78.17, 56: Heb *rebelled at the sea* c Or *Sea of Reeds* d Compare Gk Mss: Heb *exchanged their glory*

and did not obey the voice of the LORD.
26 Therefore he raised his hand and swore
      to them
      that he would make them fall in the
          wilderness,
27 and would disperse^a their descendants among
      the nations,
      scattering them over the lands.

28 Then they attached themselves to the Baal of
      Peor,
      and ate sacrifices offered to the
          dead;
29 they provoked the LORD to anger with their
      deeds,
      and a plague broke out among them.
30 Then Phinehas stood up and interceded,
      and the plague was stopped.
31 And that has been reckoned to him as
      righteousness
      from generation to generation forever.

32 They angered the LORD^b at the waters of
      Meribah,
      and it went ill with Moses on their
          account;
33 for they made his spirit bitter,
      and he spoke words that were rash.

34 They did not destroy the peoples,
      as the LORD commanded them,
35 but they mingled with the nations
      and learned to do as they did.
36 They served their idols,
      which became a snare to them.
37 They sacrificed their sons
      and their daughters to the demons;
38 they poured out innocent blood,
      the blood of their sons and daughters,
      whom they sacrificed to the idols of Canaan;
      and the land was polluted with blood.
39 Thus they became unclean by their acts,
      and prostituted themselves in their doings.

40 Then the anger of the LORD was kindled
          against his people,
      and he abhorred his heritage;
41 he gave them into the hand of the nations,
      so that those who hated them ruled over
          them.

42 Their enemies oppressed them,
      and they were brought into subjection
          under their power.
43 Many times he delivered them,
      but they were rebellious in their purposes,
      and were brought low through their
          iniquity.
44 Nevertheless he regarded their distress
      when he heard their cry.
45 For their sake he remembered his covenant,
      and showed compassion according to the
          abundance of his steadfast love.
46 He caused them to be pitied
      by all who held them captive.

47 Save us, O LORD our God,
      and gather us from among the nations,
      that we may give thanks to your holy name
      and glory in your praise.

48 Blessed be the LORD, the God of Israel,
      from everlasting to everlasting.
      And let all the people say, "Amen."
      Praise the LORD!

BOOK V
(Psalms 107–150)

107

Thanksgiving for Deliverance
from Many Troubles

O give thanks to the LORD, for he is
      good;
      for his steadfast love endures forever.
2 Let the redeemed of the LORD say so,
      those he redeemed from trouble
3 and gathered in from the lands,
      from the east and from the west,
      from the north and from the south.^c

4 Some wandered in desert wastes,
      finding no way to an inhabited town;
5 hungry and thirsty,
      their soul fainted within them.
6 Then they cried to the LORD in their trouble,
      and he delivered them from their distress;
7 he led them by a straight way,
      until they reached an inhabited town.
8 Let them thank the LORD for his steadfast
      love,
      for his wonderful works to humankind.

---

a Syr Compare Ezek 20.23: Heb *cause to fall*   b Heb *him*   c Cn: Heb *sea*

PRAY IT!

Thankfulness
Psalm 107

It's good and natural to express gratitude for our blessings. **Psalm 107** is an extended thanksgiving for God's love and saving power. It also shows us the importance of taking time to remember the specific things God has done for us. These memories will remind us of God's faithfulness and inspire our own thankfulness.

- Think back over your life and take time to remember specific times God has helped you.
- Do those memories inspire thankfulness? Express that thankfulness to God in prayer.

9 For he satisfies the thirsty,
and the hungry he fills with good things.

10 Some sat in darkness and in gloom,
prisoners in misery and in irons,
11 for they had rebelled against the words
of God,
and spurned the counsel of the Most High.
12 Their hearts were bowed down with hard
labor;
they fell down, with no one to help.
13 Then they cried to the LORD in their trouble,
and he saved them from their distress;
14 he brought them out of darkness and gloom,
and broke their bonds asunder.
15 Let them thank the LORD for his steadfast
love,
for his wonderful works to humankind.
16 For he shatters the doors of bronze,
and cuts in two the bars of iron.

17 Some were sick[a] through their sinful ways,
and because of their iniquities endured
affliction;
18 they loathed any kind of food,
and they drew near to the gates of death.
19 Then they cried to the LORD in their trouble,

and he saved them from their distress;
20 he sent out his word and healed them,
and delivered them from destruction.
21 Let them thank the LORD for his steadfast
love,
for his wonderful works to humankind.
22 And let them offer thanksgiving sacrifices,
and tell of his deeds with songs of joy.

23 Some went down to the sea in ships,
doing business on the mighty waters;
24 they saw the deeds of the LORD,
his wondrous works in the deep.
25 For he commanded and raised the stormy
wind,
which lifted up the waves of the sea.
26 They mounted up to heaven, they went down
to the depths;
their courage melted away in their
calamity;
27 they reeled and staggered like drunkards,
and were at their wits' end.
28 Then they cried to the LORD in their
trouble,
and he brought them out from their
distress;
29 he made the storm be still,
and the waves of the sea were hushed.
30 Then they were glad because they had quiet,
and he brought them to their desired
haven.
31 Let them thank the LORD for his steadfast
love,
for his wonderful works to humankind.
32 Let them extol him in the congregation of the
people,
and praise him in the assembly of the
elders.

33 He turns rivers into a desert,
springs of water into thirsty ground,
34 a fruitful land into a salty waste,
because of the wickedness of its
inhabitants.
35 He turns a desert into pools of water,
a parched land into springs of water.
36 And there he lets the hungry live,
and they establish a town to live in;
37 they sow fields, and plant vineyards,
and get a fruitful yield.

a Cn: Heb *fools*

38 By his blessing they multiply greatly,
   and he does not let their cattle decrease.

39 When they are diminished and brought low
   through oppression, trouble, and sorrow,
40 he pours contempt on princes
   and makes them wander in trackless
   wastes;
41 but he raises up the needy out of distress,
   and makes their families like flocks.
42 The upright see it and are glad;
   and all wickedness stops its mouth.
43 Let those who are wise give heed to these
   things,
   and consider the steadfast love of the
   LORD.

108 Praise and Prayer for Victory
A Song. A Psalm of David.

My heart is steadfast, O God, my heart is
   steadfast;[a]
   I will sing and make melody.
   Awake, my soul![b]
2 Awake, O harp and lyre!
   I will awake the dawn.
3 I will give thanks to you, O LORD, among the
   peoples,
   and I will sing praises to you among the
   nations.
4 For your steadfast love is higher than the
   heavens,
   and your faithfulness reaches to the clouds.

5 Be exalted, O God, above the heavens,
   and let your glory be over all the earth.
6 Give victory with your right hand, and
   answer me,
   so that those whom you love may be
   rescued.

7 God has promised in his sanctuary:[c]
   "With exultation I will divide up Shechem,
   and portion out the Vale of Succoth.
8 Gilead is mine; Manasseh is mine;
   Ephraim is my helmet;
   Judah is my scepter.
9 Moab is my washbasin;
   on Edom I hurl my shoe;
   over Philistia I shout in triumph."

10 Who will bring me to the fortified city?
   Who will lead me to Edom?
11 Have you not rejected us, O God?
   You do not go out, O God, with our armies.
12 O grant us help against the foe,
   for human help is worthless.
13 With God we shall do valiantly;
   it is he who will tread down our foes.

109 Prayer for Vindication and Vengeance
To the leader. Of David. A Psalm.

Do not be silent, O God of my praise.
2 For wicked and deceitful mouths are opened
   against me,
   speaking against me with lying tongues.
3 They beset me with words of hate,
   and attack me without cause.
4 In return for my love they accuse me,
   even while I make prayer for them.[d]
5 So they reward me evil for good,
   and hatred for my love.

6 They say,[e] "Appoint a wicked man
   against him;
   let an accuser stand on his right.
7 When he is tried, let him be found guilty;
   let his prayer be counted as sin.
8 May his days be few;
   may another seize his position.
9 May his children be orphans,
   and his wife a widow.
10 May his children wander about and beg;
   may they be driven out of[f] the ruins they
   inhabit.
11 May the creditor seize all that he has;
   may strangers plunder the fruits of his toil.
12 May there be no one to do him a kindness,
   nor anyone to pity his orphaned children.
13 May his posterity be cut off;
   may his name be blotted out in the second
   generation.
14 May the iniquity of his father[g] be remembered
   before the LORD,
   and do not let the sin of his mother be
   blotted out.
15 Let them be before the LORD continually,
   and may his[h] memory be cut off from the
   earth.

a Heb Mss Gk Syr: MT lacks *my heart is steadfast*   b Compare 57.8: Heb *also my soul*   c Or *by his holiness*   d Syr: Heb *I prayer*   e Heb lacks *They say*
f Gk: Heb *and seek*   g Cn: Heb *fathers*   h Gk: Heb *their*

16 For he did not remember to show kindness,
      but pursued the poor and needy
      and the brokenhearted to their death.
17 He loved to curse; let curses come on him.
      He did not like blessing; may it be far
         from him.
18 He clothed himself with cursing as his coat,
      may it soak into his body like water,
      like oil into his bones.
19 May it be like a garment that he wraps around
         himself,
      like a belt that he wears every day."

20 May that be the reward of my accusers from
      the Lord,
      of those who speak evil against my life.
21 But you, O Lord my Lord,
      act on my behalf for your name's sake;
      because your steadfast love is good,
         deliver me.
22 For I am poor and needy,
      and my heart is pierced within me.
23 I am gone like a shadow at evening;
      I am shaken off like a locust.
24 My knees are weak through fasting;
      my body has become gaunt.
25 I am an object of scorn to my accusers;
      when they see me, they shake their heads.

26 Help me, O Lord my God!
      Save me according to your steadfast love.
27 Let them know that this is your hand;
      you, O Lord, have done it.
28 Let them curse, but you will bless.
      Let my assailants be put to shame; *a* may
         your servant be glad.
29 May my accusers be clothed with dishonor;
      may they be wrapped in their own shame
         as in a mantle.
30 With my mouth I will give great thanks to the
      Lord;
      I will praise him in the midst of the throng.
31 For he stands at the right hand of the needy,
      to save them from those who would
         condemn them to death.

110 Assurance of Victory for God's Priest-King
Of David. A Psalm.

The Lord says to my lord,

"Sit at my right hand
until I make your enemies your
      footstool."
2 The Lord sends out from Zion
      your mighty scepter.
      Rule in the midst of your foes.
3 Your people will offer themselves willingly
      on the day you lead your forces
      on the holy mountains. *b*
From the womb of the morning,
      like dew, your youth*c* will come to you.
4 The Lord has sworn and will not change his
      mind,
      "You are a priest forever according to the
         order of Melchizedek."*d*

5 The Lord is at your right hand;
      he will shatter kings on the day of his
         wrath.
6 He will execute judgment among the nations,
      filling them with corpses;
he will shatter heads
      over the wide earth.
7 He will drink from the stream by the path;
      therefore he will lift up his head.

111 Praise for God's Wonderful Works
Praise the Lord!
      I will give thanks to the Lord with my
         whole heart,
      in the company of the upright, in the
         congregation.
2 Great are the works of the Lord,
      studied by all who delight in them.
3 Full of honor and majesty is his work,
      and his righteousness endures forever.
4 He has gained renown by his wonderful deeds;
      the Lord is gracious and merciful.
5 He provides food for those who fear him;
      he is ever mindful of his covenant.
6 He has shown his people the power of his
      works,
      in giving them the heritage of the nations.
7 The works of his hands are faithful and just;
      all his precepts are trustworthy.
8 They are established forever and ever,
      to be performed with faithfulness and
         uprightness.
9 He sent redemption to his people;
      he has commanded his covenant forever.

a Gk: Heb *They have risen up and have been put to shame* *b* Another reading is *in holy splendor* *c* Cn: Heb *the dew of your youth* *d* Or *forever, a rightful king by my edict*

Holy and awesome is his name.

10 The fear of the LORD is the beginning of
wisdom;
all those who practice it*ᵃ* have a good
understanding.
His praise endures forever.

112 Blessings of the Righteous

Praise the LORD!
Happy are those who fear the LORD,
who greatly delight in his commandments.

2 Their descendants will be mighty in the land;
the generation of the upright will be
blessed.

3 Wealth and riches are in their houses,
and their righteousness endures forever.

4 They rise in the darkness as a light for the
upright;
they are gracious, merciful, and righteous.

5 It is well with those who deal generously and
lend,
who conduct their affairs with justice.

6 For the righteous will never be moved;
they will be remembered forever.

7 They are not afraid of evil tidings;
their hearts are firm, secure in the LORD.

8 Their hearts are steady, they will not be afraid;
in the end they will look in triumph on
their foes.

9 They have distributed freely, they have given
to the poor;
their righteousness endures forever;
their horn is exalted in honor.

10 The wicked see it and are angry;
they gnash their teeth and melt away;
the desire of the wicked comes to nothing.

113 God the Helper of the Needy

Praise the LORD!
Praise, O servants of the LORD;
praise the name of the LORD.

2 Blessed be the name of the LORD
from this time on and forevermore.

3 From the rising of the sun to its setting
the name of the LORD is to be praised.

4 The LORD is high above all nations,
and his glory above the heavens.

5 Who is like the LORD our God,

LIVE IT!

**A Life of Generosity
Psalm 112**

A new iPod. A new car. The latest clothes and tech gadgets. Our culture assigns value to material possessions—so we focus a lot on getting them. But although it is human nature to want more, some cultures put a much higher value on generosity. This is why people are often surprised when they travel to other countries and are treated to a feast in the home of a family on the verge of starvation. Generosity is a matter of honor for those people. Security and honor can be found in giving generously. Here are a few ideas:

- Start close to home by sharing what you have with your family, friends, and neighbors.
- Go through your closet each season and give clothes you don't need to a homeless shelter or other ministry.
- Give of your time to help tutor a student who is struggling or teach English to an immigrant family.
- Save money for a month by choosing to give up a luxury (movies, coffee, music, etc.). Loan that money to someone in need through a microfinance organization such as Kiva (**kiva.org**). As the money is repaid, you can continue impacting the lives of people around the world by loaning it to others.

Now come up with some ideas of your own. Choose one, and take action. Let it be said of us, "They have distributed freely, they have given to the poor; their righteousness endures forever; their horn is exalted in honor" (Psalm 112:9).

---

who is seated on high,

6 who looks far down
on the heavens and the earth?

7 He raises the poor from the dust,

ᵃ Gk Syr: Heb *them*

and lifts the needy from the ash heap,
8 to make them sit with princes,
  with the princes of his people.
9 He gives the barren woman a home,
  making her the joyous mother of children.
Praise the LORD!

114 God's Wonders at the Exodus

When Israel went out from Egypt,
  the house of Jacob from a people of
  strange language,
2 Judah became God's[a] sanctuary,
  Israel his dominion.

3 The sea looked and fled;
  Jordan turned back.
4 The mountains skipped like rams,
  the hills like lambs.

5 Why is it, O sea, that you flee?
  O Jordan, that you turn back?
6 O mountains, that you skip like rams?
  O hills, like lambs?

7 Tremble, O earth, at the presence of the
  LORD,
  at the presence of the God of Jacob,
8 who turns the rock into a pool of water,
  the flint into a spring of water.

115 The Impotence of Idols and the Greatness of God

Not to us, O LORD, not to us, but to
  your name give glory,
for the sake of your steadfast love and your
  faithfulness.
2 Why should the nations say,
  "Where is their God?"

3 Our God is in the heavens;
  he does whatever he pleases.
4 Their idols are silver and gold,
  the work of human hands.
5 They have mouths, but do not speak;
  eyes, but do not see.
6 They have ears, but do not hear;
  noses, but do not smell.
7 They have hands, but do not feel;
  feet, but do not walk;
  they make no sound in their throats.

8 Those who make them are like them;
  so are all who trust in them.

9 O Israel, trust in the LORD!
  He is their help and their shield.
10 O house of Aaron, trust in the LORD!
  He is their help and their shield.
11 You who fear the LORD, trust in the LORD!
  He is their help and their shield.

12 The LORD has been mindful of us; he will
  bless us;
  he will bless the house of Israel;
  he will bless the house of Aaron;
13 he will bless those who fear the LORD,
  both small and great.

14 May the LORD give you increase,
  both you and your children.
15 May you be blessed by the LORD,
  who made heaven and earth.

LIVE IT!

What Lasts?
Psalm 115

A car won't last forever. Neither will a computer, cell phone, or your favorite sports team. Does anything other than God truly have no end? No matter how hard you look, you won't find such a thing. So why do we spend so much of our time with what won't last, rather than what WILL last?

Psalm 115 proclaims the greatness of God and the foolishness of idols. It's easy to think of idols as small statues that ancient people worshiped, but idols are anything we make more important than God. In the end, what matters most won't be how many awards you were given, how much money you made, or how many possessions you had, but rather how you loved God and others.

Find a mission trip, outreach, or a way in which you can serve others. Make a lasting impact!

---

a Heb his

16 The heavens are the LORD's heavens,
   but the earth he has given to human
      beings.
17 The dead do not praise the LORD,
   nor do any that go down into silence.
18 But we will bless the LORD
   from this time on and forevermore.
   Praise the LORD!

116 Thanksgiving for Recovery
from Illness

   I love the LORD, because he has heard
   my voice and my supplications.
2 Because he inclined his ear to me,
   therefore I will call on him as long as I
      live.
3 The snares of death encompassed me;
   the pangs of Sheol laid hold on me;
   I suffered distress and anguish.
4 Then I called on the name of the LORD:
   "O LORD, I pray, save my life!"

5 Gracious is the LORD, and righteous;
   our God is merciful.
6 The LORD protects the simple;
   when I was brought low, he
      saved me.
7 Return, O my soul, to your rest,
   for the LORD has dealt bountifully
      with you.

8 For you have delivered my soul from
      death,
   my eyes from tears,
   my feet from stumbling.
9 I walk before the LORD
   in the land of the living.

10 I kept my faith, even when I said,
   "I am greatly afflicted";
11 I said in my consternation,
   "Everyone is a liar."

12 What shall I return to the LORD
   for all his bounty to me?
13 I will lift up the cup of salvation
   and call on the name of the LORD,
14 I will pay my vows to the LORD
   in the presence of all his people.
15 Precious in the sight of the LORD
   is the death of his faithful ones.
16 O LORD, I am your servant;
   I am your servant, the child of your serving
      girl.
   You have loosed my bonds.
17 I will offer to you a thanksgiving sacrifice
   and call on the name of the LORD.
18 I will pay my vows to the LORD
   in the presence of all his people,
19 in the courts of the house of the LORD,
   in your midst, O Jerusalem.
   Praise the LORD!

117 Universal Call to Worship

   Praise the LORD, all you nations!
   Extol him, all you peoples!
2 For great is his steadfast love toward us,
   and the faithfulness of the LORD endures
      forever.
   Praise the LORD!

118 A Song of Victory

   O give thanks to the LORD, for he is
      good;
   his steadfast love endures forever!

LIVE IT!

Gratitude · Psalm 116

"Thank God!" Have you ever uttered these words in response to something finally going your way? Or maybe in response to a personal situation that turned out just as you hoped it would? Psalm 116 is all about this feeling—a feeling of true gratitude toward God for making life better.

It's easy to get caught up in our prayers asking God for help and treating God like a vending machine—so much so that we forget to give thanks for the ways God has already blessed our lives. This psalm reminds us to be grateful at all times, thanking and praising God for the many gifts we have received, especially those we have asked for so diligently. What are you thankful for today?

> "O give thanks to the Lord, for he is good; his steadfast love endures forever!"
> —Psalm 118:1

2 Let Israel say,
    "His steadfast love endures forever."
3 Let the house of Aaron say,
    "His steadfast love endures forever."
4 Let those who fear the Lord say,
    "His steadfast love endures forever."

5 Out of my distress I called on the Lord;
    the Lord answered me and set me in a
        broad place.
6 With the Lord on my side I do not fear.
    What can mortals do to me?
7 The Lord is on my side to help me;
    I shall look in triumph on those who
        hate me.
8 It is better to take refuge in the Lord
    than to put confidence in mortals.
9 It is better to take refuge in the Lord
    than to put confidence in princes.

10 All nations surrounded me;
    in the name of the Lord I cut them off!
11 They surrounded me, surrounded me on every
        side;
    in the name of the Lord I cut them off!
12 They surrounded me like bees;
    they blazed[a] like a fire of thorns;
    in the name of the Lord I cut them off!
13 I was pushed hard,[b] so that I was falling,
    but the Lord helped me.
14 The Lord is my strength and my might;
    he has become my salvation.

15 There are glad songs of victory in the tents of
        the righteous:
    "The right hand of the Lord does valiantly;
16   the right hand of the Lord is exalted;
    the right hand of the Lord does valiantly."
17 I shall not die, but I shall live,
    and recount the deeds of the Lord.

18 The Lord has punished me severely,
    but he did not give me over to death.

19 Open to me the gates of righteousness,
    that I may enter through them
    and give thanks to the Lord.

20 This is the gate of the Lord;
    the righteous shall enter through it.
21 I thank you that you have answered me
    and have become my salvation.
22 The stone that the builders rejected
    has become the chief cornerstone.
23 This is the Lord's doing;
    it is marvelous in our eyes.
24 This is the day that the Lord has made;
    let us rejoice and be glad in it.[c]
25 Save us, we beseech you, O Lord!
    O Lord, we beseech you, give us success!

26 Blessed is the one who comes in the name
        of the Lord.[d]
    We bless you from the house of the
        Lord.
27 The Lord is God,
    and he has given us light.
    Bind the festal procession with branches,
    up to the horns of the altar.[e]

28 You are my God, and I will give thanks to you;
    you are my God, I will extol you.

29 O give thanks to the Lord, for he is good,
    for his steadfast love endures forever.

119   The Glories of God's Law

Happy are those whose way is
    blameless,
    who walk in the law of the Lord.
2 Happy are those who keep his decrees,
    who seek him with their whole heart,
3 who also do no wrong,
    but walk in his ways.
4 You have commanded your precepts
    to be kept diligently.
5 O that my ways may be steadfast
    in keeping your statutes!
6 Then I shall not be put to shame,

---

a Gk: Heb *were extinguished*   b Gk Syr Jerome: Heb *You pushed me hard*   c Or *in him*   d Or *Blessed in the name of the Lord is the one who comes*
e Meaning of Heb uncertain

**The Longest Psalm
Psalm 119**

Psalm 119 is the longest psalm in the Bible. It has 176 verses and an interesting structure that cannot be appreciated in the English language. It consists of twenty-two sections, and all the lines of a particular section begin with the same letter of the Hebrew alphabet. All the lines of the first section begin with "aleph," the Hebrew equivalent of "A." All the lines of the second section begin with "beth," the Hebrew equivalent of "B." And so on through the whole Hebrew alphabet!

This type of structure is called an acrostic. An acrostic is a poem in which the beginning letters of each line form a word, a phrase, or a logical sequence. You may have written a poem like this in school using a simple word.

• Write your own acrostic prayer, beginning the lines of the prayer with the letters of your name or the name of someone or something you would like to pray for.

having my eyes fixed on all your
  commandments.
7 I will praise you with an upright heart,
  when I learn your righteous ordinances.
8 I will observe your statutes;
  do not utterly forsake me.

9 How can young people keep their way pure?
  By guarding it according to your word.
10 With my whole heart I seek you;
  do not let me stray from your
  commandments.
11 I treasure your word in my heart,
  so that I may not sin against you.
12 Blessed are you, O Lord;
  teach me your statutes.
13 With my lips I declare
  all the ordinances of your mouth.
14 I delight in the way of your decrees
  as much as in all riches.

15 I will meditate on your precepts,
  and fix my eyes on your ways.
16 I will delight in your statutes;
  I will not forget your word.

17 Deal bountifully with your servant,
  so that I may live and observe your word.
18 Open my eyes, so that I may behold
  wondrous things out of your law.
19 I live as an alien in the land;
  do not hide your commandments from me.
20 My soul is consumed with longing
  for your ordinances at all times.
21 You rebuke the insolent, accursed ones,
  who wander from your commandments;
22 take away from me their scorn and contempt,
  for I have kept your decrees.
23 Even though princes sit plotting against me,
  your servant will meditate on your statutes.
24 Your decrees are my delight,
  they are my counselors.

25 My soul clings to the dust;
  revive me according to your word.
26 When I told of my ways, you answered me;
  teach me your statutes.
27 Make me understand the way of your precepts,
  and I will meditate on your wondrous
  works.
28 My soul melts away for sorrow;
  strengthen me according to your word.
29 Put false ways far from me;
  and graciously teach me your law.
30 I have chosen the way of faithfulness;
  I set your ordinances before me.
31 I cling to your decrees, O Lord;
  let me not be put to shame.
32 I run the way of your commandments,
  for you enlarge my understanding.

33 Teach me, O Lord, the way of your statutes,
  and I will observe it to the end.
34 Give me understanding, that I may keep
  your law
  and observe it with my whole heart.
35 Lead me in the path of your commandments,
  for I delight in it.
36 Turn my heart to your decrees,
  and not to selfish gain.
37 Turn my eyes from looking at vanities;
  give me life in your ways.

38 Confirm to your servant your promise,
    which is for those who fear you.
39 Turn away the disgrace that I dread,
    for your ordinances are good.
40 See, I have longed for your precepts;
    in your righteousness give me life.

41 Let your steadfast love come to me, O LORD,
    your salvation according to your promise.
42 Then I shall have an answer for those who
        taunt me,
    for I trust in your word.
43 Do not take the word of truth utterly out of
        my mouth,
    for my hope is in your ordinances.
44 I will keep your law continually,
    forever and ever.
45 I shall walk at liberty,
    for I have sought your precepts.
46 I will also speak of your decrees before kings,
    and shall not be put to shame;
47 I find my delight in your commandments,
    because I love them.
48 I revere your commandments, which I love,
    and I will meditate on your statutes.

49 Remember your word to your servant,
    in which you have made me hope.
50 This is my comfort in my distress,
    that your promise gives me life.
51 The arrogant utterly deride me,
    but I do not turn away from your law.
52 When I think of your ordinances from of old,
    I take comfort, O LORD.
53 Hot indignation seizes me because of the
        wicked,
    those who forsake your law.
54 Your statutes have been my songs
    wherever I make my home.
55 I remember your name in the night, O LORD,
    and keep your law.
56 This blessing has fallen to me,
    for I have kept your precepts.

57 The LORD is my portion;
    I promise to keep your words.
58 I implore your favor with all my heart;
    be gracious to me according to your
        promise.
59 When I think of your ways,
    I turn my feet to your decrees;
60 I hurry and do not delay
    to keep your commandments.
61 Though the cords of the wicked ensnare me,
    I do not forget your law.
62 At midnight I rise to praise you,
    because of your righteous ordinances.
63 I am a companion of all who fear you,
    of those who keep your precepts.
64 The earth, O LORD, is full of your steadfast
        love;
    teach me your statutes.

65 You have dealt well with your servant,
    O LORD, according to your word.
66 Teach me good judgment and knowledge,
    for I believe in your commandments.
67 Before I was humbled I went astray,
    but now I keep your word.
68 You are good and do good;
    teach me your statutes.
69 The arrogant smear me with lies,
    but with my whole heart I keep your
        precepts.
70 Their hearts are fat and gross,
    but I delight in your law.
71 It is good for me that I was humbled,
    so that I might learn your statutes.
72 The law of your mouth is better to me
    than thousands of gold and silver pieces.

73 Your hands have made and fashioned me;
    give me understanding that I may learn
        your commandments.
74 Those who fear you shall see me and rejoice,
    because I have hoped in your word.
75 I know, O LORD, that your judgments are
        right,
    and that in faithfulness you have
        humbled me.
76 Let your steadfast love become my comfort
    according to your promise to your servant.
77 Let your mercy come to me, that I may live;
    for your law is my delight.
78 Let the arrogant be put to shame,
    because they have subverted me with
        guile;
    as for me, I will meditate on your precepts.
79 Let those who fear you turn to me,
    so that they may know your decrees.

80 May my heart be blameless in your statutes,
    so that I may not be put to shame.

81 My soul languishes for your salvation;
    I hope in your word.

82 My eyes fail with watching for your promise;
    I ask, "When will you comfort me?"

83 For I have become like a wineskin in the
       smoke,
    yet I have not forgotten your statutes.

84 How long must your servant endure?
    When will you judge those who
       persecute me?

85 The arrogant have dug pitfalls for me;
    they flout your law.

86 All your commandments are enduring;
    I am persecuted without cause;
       help me!

87 They have almost made an end of me on
       earth;
    but I have not forsaken your precepts.

88 In your steadfast love spare my life,
    so that I may keep the decrees of your
       mouth.

89 The LORD exists forever;
    your word is firmly fixed in heaven.

90 Your faithfulness endures to all generations;
    you have established the earth, and it
       stands fast.

91 By your appointment they stand today,
    for all things are your servants.

92 If your law had not been my delight,
    I would have perished in my misery.

93 I will never forget your precepts,
    for by them you have given me life.

94 I am yours; save me,
    for I have sought your precepts.

95 The wicked lie in wait to destroy me,
    but I consider your decrees.

96 I have seen a limit to all perfection,
    but your commandment is exceedingly
       broad.

97 Oh, how I love your law!
    It is my meditation all day long.

98 Your commandment makes me wiser than my
       enemies,
    for it is always with me.

99 I have more understanding than all my
       teachers,
    for your decrees are my meditation.

100 I understand more than the aged,
    for I keep your precepts.

101 I hold back my feet from every evil way,
    in order to keep your word.

Light the Way · Psalm 119:105

Light is available at the flip of a switch. But for the writer of this psalm, light was much harder to come by. A lamp for his feet would have meant the difference between life and death. A light for his path would have meant he was able to complete his journey without falling off a cliff, straying from the way, or making a wrong turn.

But **Psalm 119:105** still applies to many areas of our lives today. God's Word illuminates our surroundings and gives us direction. Where is your world the darkest? Where are you most likely to take a wrong step without the guidance of God's light? One possible place is the Internet. Although it is an amazing tool that provides us with information and communication, it's also an easy place to go the wrong way. Pornography, violence, bullying, and simple distractions that consume our time are only a click away. We need the light of God's Word, guiding our "steps" to help us make right choices as we navigate the wonders of technology.

102 I do not turn away from your ordinances,
    for you have taught me.
103 How sweet are your words to my taste,
    sweeter than honey to my mouth!
104 Through your precepts I get understanding;
    therefore I hate every false way.
105 Your word is a lamp to my feet
    and a light to my path.
106 I have sworn an oath and confirmed it,
    to observe your righteous ordinances.
107 I am severely afflicted;
    give me life, O LORD, according to your
     word.
108 Accept my offerings of praise, O LORD,
    and teach me your ordinances.
109 I hold my life in my hand continually,
    but I do not forget your law.
110 The wicked have laid a snare for me,
    but I do not stray from your precepts.
111 Your decrees are my heritage forever;
    they are the joy of my heart.
112 I incline my heart to perform your statutes
    forever, to the end.
113 I hate the double-minded,
    but I love your law.
114 You are my hiding place and my shield;
    I hope in your word.
115 Go away from me, you evildoers,
    that I may keep the commandments of
     my God.
116 Uphold me according to your promise, that I
    may live,
    and let me not be put to shame in my
     hope.
117 Hold me up, that I may be safe
    and have regard for your statutes
     continually.
118 You spurn all who go astray from your
    statutes;
    for their cunning is in vain.
119 All the wicked of the earth you count as
    dross;
    therefore I love your decrees.
120 My flesh trembles for fear of you,
    and I am afraid of your judgments.
121 I have done what is just and right;
    do not leave me to my oppressors.
122 Guarantee your servant's well-being;
    do not let the godless oppress me.
123 My eyes fail from watching for your salvation,

    and for the fulfillment of your righteous
     promise.
124 Deal with your servant according to your
    steadfast love,
    and teach me your statutes.
125 I am your servant; give me understanding,
    so that I may know your decrees.
126 It is time for the LORD to act,
    for your law has been broken.
127 Truly I love your commandments
    more than gold, more than fine
     gold.
128 Truly I direct my steps by all your precepts; [a]
    I hate every false way.
129 Your decrees are wonderful;
    therefore my soul keeps them.
130 The unfolding of your words gives light;
    it imparts understanding to the simple.
131 With open mouth I pant,
    because I long for your commandments.
132 Turn to me and be gracious to me,
    as is your custom toward those who love
     your name.
133 Keep my steps steady according to your
    promise,
    and never let iniquity have dominion
     over me.
134 Redeem me from human oppression,
    that I may keep your precepts.
135 Make your face shine upon your servant,
    and teach me your statutes.
136 My eyes shed streams of tears
    because your law is not kept.
137 You are righteous, O LORD,
    and your judgments are right.
138 You have appointed your decrees in
    righteousness
    and in all faithfulness.
139 My zeal consumes me
    because my foes forget your words.
140 Your promise is well tried,
    and your servant loves it.
141 I am small and despised,
    yet I do not forget your precepts.
142 Your righteousness is an everlasting
    righteousness,
    and your law is the truth.
143 Trouble and anguish have come
     upon me,
    but your commandments are my delight.

a Gk Jerome: Meaning of Heb uncertain

144 Your decrees are righteous forever;
    give me understanding that I may live.
145 With my whole heart I cry; answer me,
        O Lord.
    I will keep your statutes.
146 I cry to you; save me,
    that I may observe your decrees.
147 I rise before dawn and cry for help;
    I put my hope in your words.
148 My eyes are awake before each watch of the
        night,
    that I may meditate on your promise.
149 In your steadfast love hear my voice;
    O Lord, in your justice preserve my life.
150 Those who persecute me with evil purpose
        draw near;
    they are far from your law.
151 Yet you are near, O Lord,
    and all your commandments are true.
152 Long ago I learned from your decrees
    that you have established them forever.
153 Look on my misery and rescue me,
    for I do not forget your law.
154 Plead my cause and redeem me;
    give me life according to your promise.
155 Salvation is far from the wicked,
    for they do not seek your statutes.
156 Great is your mercy, O Lord;
    give me life according to your justice.
157 Many are my persecutors and my
        adversaries,
    yet I do not swerve from your decrees.
158 I look at the faithless with disgust,
    because they do not keep your
        commands.
159 Consider how I love your precepts;
    preserve my life according to your
        steadfast love.
160 The sum of your word is truth;
    and every one of your righteous
        ordinances endures forever.
161 Princes persecute me without cause,
    but my heart stands in awe of your words.
162 I rejoice at your word
    like one who finds great spoil.
163 I hate and abhor falsehood,
    but I love your law.
164 Seven times a day I praise you
    for your righteous ordinances.
165 Great peace have those who love your law;

nothing can make them stumble.
166 I hope for your salvation, O Lord,
    and I fulfill your commandments.
167 My soul keeps your decrees;
    I love them exceedingly.
168 I keep your precepts and decrees,
    for all my ways are before you.
169 Let my cry come before you, O Lord;
    give me understanding according to your
        word.
170 Let my supplication come before you;
    deliver me according to your promise.
171 My lips will pour forth praise,
    because you teach me your statutes.
172 My tongue will sing of your promise,
    for all your commandments are right.
173 Let your hand be ready to help me,
    for I have chosen your precepts.
174 I long for your salvation, O Lord,
    and your law is my delight.
175 Let me live that I may praise you,
    and let your ordinances help me.
176 I have gone astray like a lost sheep; seek out
        your servant,
    for I do not forget your commandments.

120 Prayer for Deliverance from Slanderers

A Song of Ascents.

In my distress I cry to the Lord,
    that he may answer me:
2 "Deliver me, O Lord,
    from lying lips,
    from a deceitful tongue."

3 What shall be given to you?
    And what more shall be done to you,
    you deceitful tongue?
4 A warrior's sharp arrows,
    with glowing coals of the broom tree!

5 Woe is me, that I am an alien in Meshech,
    that I must live among the tents
        of Kedar.
6 Too long have I had my dwelling
    among those who hate peace.
7 I am for peace;
    but when I speak,
    they are for war.

121 Assurance of God's Protection
A Song of Ascents.

I lift up my eyes to the hills—
  from where will my help come?
2 My help comes from the LORD,
  who made heaven and earth.

3 He will not let your foot be moved;
  he who keeps you will not slumber.
4 He who keeps Israel
  will neither slumber nor sleep.

5 The LORD is your keeper;
  the LORD is your shade at your right hand.
6 The sun shall not strike you by day,
  nor the moon by night.

7 The LORD will keep you from all evil;
  he will keep your life.
8 The LORD will keep
  your going out and your coming in
  from this time on and forevermore.

122 Song of Praise and Prayer for Jerusalem
A Song of Ascents. Of David.

I was glad when they said to me,
  "Let us go to the house of the LORD!"
2 Our feet are standing
  within your gates, O Jerusalem.

3 Jerusalem—built as a city
  that is bound firmly together.
4 To it the tribes go up,
    the tribes of the LORD,
  as was decreed for Israel,
    to give thanks to the name of the
    LORD.
5 For there the thrones for judgment were
    set up,
  the thrones of the house of David.

6 Pray for the peace of Jerusalem:
  "May they prosper who love you.
7 Peace be within your walls,
  and security within your towers."
8 For the sake of my relatives and friends
  I will say, "Peace be within you."

9 For the sake of the house of the LORD
  our God,
  I will seek your good.

123 Supplication for Mercy
A Song of Ascents.

To you I lift up my eyes,
  O you who are enthroned in the
    heavens!
2 As the eyes of servants
  look to the hand of their master,
as the eyes of a maid
  to the hand of her mistress,
so our eyes look to the LORD our God,
  until he has mercy upon us.

3 Have mercy upon us, O LORD, have mercy
    upon us,
  for we have had more than enough of
    contempt.
4 Our soul has had more than its fill
  of the scorn of those who are at
    ease,
  of the contempt of the proud.

124 Thanksgiving for Israel's Deliverance
A Song of Ascents. Of David.

If it had not been the LORD who was on
    our side
  —let Israel now say—
2 if it had not been the LORD who was on our
    side,
  when our enemies attacked us,
3 then they would have swallowed us up alive,
  when their anger was kindled against us;
4 then the flood would have swept us away,
  the torrent would have gone over us;
5 then over us would have gone
  the raging waters.

6 Blessed be the LORD,
  who has not given us
  as prey to their teeth.
7 We have escaped like a bird
  from the snare of the fowlers;
the snare is broken,
  and we have escaped.

LIVE IT!

God on Our Side
Psalm 124

The writer of **Psalm 124** knows the Israelites would never have made it through their challenges without God's presence and help. How do you recognize God's help in your life? It's God who carries us when we are down, who rescues us when we're in trouble, and who comforts us when we are hurt or afraid. When we reach out to God and take steps to grow in that relationship, God promises to be with us.

If you have ever been afraid or felt lost, read this psalm and be assured that others have felt the same way. Whether you're unsure about school, a relationship, a job, or your future, just remember, "Our help is in the name of the LORD, who made heaven and earth" (Psalm 124:8).

8 Our help is in the name of the LORD,
    who made heaven and earth.

125 The Security of God's People

A Song of Ascents.

Those who trust in the LORD are like Mount
        Zion,
    which cannot be moved, but abides forever.
2 As the mountains surround Jerusalem,
    so the LORD surrounds his people,
    from this time on and forevermore.
3 For the scepter of wickedness shall not rest
    on the land allotted to the righteous,
    so that the righteous might not stretch out
    their hands to do wrong.
4 Do good, O LORD, to those who are good,
    and to those who are upright in their
        hearts.
5 But those who turn aside to their own
        crooked ways
    the LORD will lead away with evildoers.
Peace be upon Israel!

126 A Harvest of Joy

A Song of Ascents.

When the LORD restored the fortunes of Zion,[a]
    we were like those who dream.
2 Then our mouth was filled with laughter,
    and our tongue with shouts of joy;
then it was said among the nations,
    "The LORD has done great things for them."
3 The LORD has done great things for us,
    and we rejoiced.

4 Restore our fortunes, O LORD,
    like the watercourses in the Negeb.
5 May those who sow in tears
    reap with shouts of joy.
6 Those who go out weeping,
    bearing the seed for sowing,
shall come home with shouts of joy,
    carrying their sheaves.

127 God's Blessings in the Home

A Song of Ascents. Of Solomon.

Unless the LORD builds the house,
    those who build it labor in vain.
Unless the LORD guards the city,
    the guard keeps watch in vain.
2 It is in vain that you rise up early
    and go late to rest,
eating the bread of anxious toil;
    for he gives sleep to his beloved.[b]

3 Sons are indeed a heritage from the LORD,
    the fruit of the womb a reward.
4 Like arrows in the hand of a warrior
    are the sons of one's youth.
5 Happy is the man who has
    his quiver full of them.
He shall not be put to shame
    when he speaks with his enemies in the
        gate.

128 The Happy Home of the Faithful

A Song of Ascents.

Happy is everyone who fears the LORD,
    who walks in his ways.
2 You shall eat the fruit of the labor of your
        hands;

---

a Or *brought back those who returned to Zion*   **b** Or *for he provides for his beloved during sleep*

you shall be happy, and it shall go well
with you.

3 Your wife will be like a fruitful vine
within your house;
your children will be like olive shoots
around your table.
4 Thus shall the man be blessed
who fears the Lord.

5 The Lord bless you from Zion.
May you see the prosperity of Jerusalem
all the days of your life.
6 May you see your children's children.
Peace be upon Israel!

129 Prayer for the Downfall of Israel's Enemies
A Song of Ascents.

"Often have they attacked me from my youth"
—let Israel now say—

2 "often have they attacked me from my youth,
yet they have not prevailed against me.
3 The plowers plowed on my back;
they made their furrows long."
4 The Lord is righteous;
he has cut the cords of the wicked.
5 May all who hate Zion
be put to shame and turned backward.
6 Let them be like the grass on the housetops
that withers before it grows up,
7 with which reapers do not fill their hands
or binders of sheaves their arms,
8 while those who pass by do not say,
"The blessing of the Lord be upon you!
We bless you in the name of the Lord!"

130 Waiting for Divine Redemption
A Song of Ascents.

Out of the depths I cry to you,
O Lord.
2 Lord, hear my voice!

STUDY IT!

Real Prayer for Real Life · Psalm 130:1–8

At some point, we all hit the bottom—sad and overwhelmed by our circumstances or our sin. That's the time to cry out to God! That's just what the psalmist did when faced with the weight of personal sins and the sins of the Israelites. This passage gives us insight into the nature of prayer.

Prayer is a turning away from sin and responding to God's endless offer of love and friendship. It's focusing our heart and mind on God and entering into dialogue with God. Prayer allows a loving and personal relationship with God to grow—just as communication and time together cause our human relationships to grow.

Just like the disciples, we need to ask Jesus to teach us how to pray. We need to call on the Holy Spirit and make prayer a daily practice. (See "Study It: The Lord's Prayer," near Luke 11:1-4, for more on how Jesus teaches us to pray.)

One way to pray is with the Bible, opening our heart to hear and respond to the living Word of God. (See "How to Pray Using 'Lectio Divina,'" p. xvi.) Another way is through worship or community prayers of the Church. We can also use our own words and emotions to pour out our hearts to God, and we can recognize God's presence in each moment of our day. (See "Pray It: Ways to Pray," near 1 Chronicles 16:37-42; and "Study It: Songs and Prayers," near Psalm 4.)

Praying isn't always easy. We get distracted by life and forget to focus on God. Yet that's when we need to take our distractions to God and let God purify our hearts. Other times, we may feel as though God isn't there or isn't answering. Keep trusting in God's faithfulness even in those times. Remember that God is always present and that God is working for the best for us even when we can't see it.

Let your ears be attentive
　　to the voice of my supplications!

3 If you, O LORD, should mark iniquities,
　　Lord, who could stand?
4 But there is forgiveness with you,
　　so that you may be revered.

5 I wait for the LORD, my soul waits,
　　and in his word I hope;
6 my soul waits for the Lord
　　more than those who watch for the
　　　　morning,
　　more than those who watch for the
　　　　morning.

7 O Israel, hope in the LORD!
　　For with the LORD there is steadfast love,
　　and with him is great power to redeem.
8 It is he who will redeem Israel
　　from all its iniquities.

131 **Song of Quiet Trust**
A Song of Ascents. Of David.

O LORD, my heart is not lifted up,
　　my eyes are not raised too high;
I do not occupy myself with things
　　too great and too marvelous for me.
2 But I have calmed and quieted my soul,
　　like a weaned child with its mother;
　　my soul is like the weaned child that is
　　　　with me.[a]

3 O Israel, hope in the LORD
　　from this time on and forevermore.

132 **The Eternal Dwelling of God**
in Zion
A Song of Ascents.

O LORD, remember in David's favor
　　all the hardships he endured;
2 how he swore to the LORD
　　and vowed to the Mighty One of Jacob,
3 "I will not enter my house
　　or get into my bed;
4 I will not give sleep to my eyes
　　or slumber to my eyelids,
5 until I find a place for the LORD,

a Or *my soul within me is like a weaned child*

PRAY IT!

God's Loving Arms
Psalm 131

Psalm 131 is a humble prayer of childlike trust. It gives the wonderful image of God holding us like a child in a mother's lap. God hugs us close, as a mother would, and keeps us safe and protected. In God's arms we don't need to solve problems or be concerned about our performance. We are loved just because we are. God created us; God loves us and cradles us.

Do you remember sitting quietly in your mother's or father's lap when you were a small child? Do you recall your parent telling you stories or singing you lullabies? How is God's love like that?

- During your prayer time, imagine being held by God as a child is held by a mother. You might be surprised how safe and secure you feel!
- Then pray: God, I put my trust in you. I'm like a baby who needs you for everything. Help me to trust and rest in your powerful arms. Thank you for taking care of all my needs.

　　a dwelling place for the Mighty One of
　　　　Jacob."

6 We heard of it in Ephrathah;
　　we found it in the fields of Jaar.
7 "Let us go to his dwelling place;
　　let us worship at his footstool."

8 Rise up, O LORD, and go to your resting
　　　　place,
　　you and the ark of your might.
9 Let your priests be clothed with
　　　　righteousness,
　　and let your faithful shout for joy.
10 For your servant David's sake
　　do not turn away the face of your
　　　　anointed one.

STUDY IT!

Jerusalem, Zion, City of David · Psalm 132

Jerusalem, Zion, City of David—you've probably noticed that these three names keep popping up throughout Psalms. They all refer to the heart of Israel, the city of Jerusalem. When David became king of Israel, he needed a place that was neutral to both the northern and the southern tribes. He conquered Jerusalem and elevated it as the political and religious center—thus, Jerusalem was known as the City of David. Mount Zion, located within Jerusalem, was the site of the temple—God's sacred dwelling place. So Zion became another way to refer to Jerusalem.

The Israelites at the time felt that Jerusalem was invincible, because it was God's dwelling place. But eventually Jerusalem and the temple were destroyed. Later, hope arose that one day a messiah from David's line would renew Jerusalem and the true worship of God on Zion. The New Testament portrays Jesus as the fulfillment of this hope.

11 The LORD swore to David a sure oath
    from which he will not turn back:
"One of the sons of your body
    I will set on your throne.
12 If your sons keep my covenant
    and my decrees that I shall teach them,
their sons also, forevermore,
    shall sit on your throne."

13 For the LORD has chosen Zion;
    he has desired it for his habitation:
14 "This is my resting place forever;
    here I will reside, for I have
        desired it.
15 I will abundantly bless its provisions;
    I will satisfy its poor with bread.
16 Its priests I will clothe with salvation,
    and its faithful will shout for joy.
17 There I will cause a horn to sprout up for David;
    I have prepared a lamp for my
        anointed one.
18 His enemies I will clothe with disgrace,
    but on him, his crown will gleam."

The Blessedness of Unity

133 *A Song of Ascents.*

How very good and pleasant it is
    when kindred live together in unity!
2 It is like the precious oil on the head,
    running down upon the beard,
on the beard of Aaron,
    running down over the collar of his robes.

3 It is like the dew of Hermon,
    which falls on the mountains of
        Zion.
For there the LORD ordained his blessing,
    life forevermore.

Praise in the Night

134 *A Song of Ascents.*

Come, bless the LORD, all you servants of the
    LORD,
    who stand by night in the house of the
        LORD!
2 Lift up your hands to the holy place,
    and bless the LORD.

3 May the LORD, maker of heaven and earth,
    bless you from Zion.

Praise for God's Goodness and Might

135
    Praise the LORD!
Praise the name of the LORD;
    give praise, O servants of the LORD,
2 you that stand in the house of the LORD,
    in the courts of the house of our God.
3 Praise the LORD, for the LORD is good;
    sing to his name, for he is gracious.
4 For the LORD has chosen Jacob for himself,
    Israel as his own possession.

5 For I know that the LORD is great;
    our Lord is above all gods.

6 Whatever the LORD pleases he does,
    in heaven and on earth,
    in the seas and all deeps.
7 He it is who makes the clouds rise at the end
        of the earth;
    he makes lightnings for the rain
    and brings out the wind from his
        storehouses.

8 He it was who struck down the firstborn of
        Egypt,
    both human beings and animals;
9 he sent signs and wonders
    into your midst, O Egypt,
    against Pharaoh and all his servants.
10 He struck down many nations
    and killed mighty kings—
11 Sihon, king of the Amorites,
    and Og, king of Bashan,
    and all the kingdoms of Canaan—
12 and gave their land as a heritage,
    a heritage to his people Israel.

13 Your name, O LORD, endures forever,
    your renown, O LORD, throughout all ages.
14 For the LORD will vindicate his people,
    and have compassion on his servants.

15 The idols of the nations are silver and gold,
    the work of human hands.
16 They have mouths, but they do not speak;
    they have eyes, but they do not see;
17 they have ears, but they do not hear,
    and there is no breath in their mouths.
18 Those who make them
    and all who trust them
    shall become like them.

19 O house of Israel, bless the LORD!
    O house of Aaron, bless the LORD!
20 O house of Levi, bless the LORD!
    You that fear the LORD, bless the LORD!
21 Blessed be the LORD from Zion,
    he who resides in Jerusalem.
    Praise the LORD!

136 God's Work in Creation and in History

O give thanks to the LORD, for he is
    good,
    for his steadfast love endures forever.

2 O give thanks to the God of gods,
    for his steadfast love endures forever.
3 O give thanks to the Lord of lords,
    for his steadfast love endures forever;

4 who alone does great wonders,
    for his steadfast love endures forever;
5 who by understanding made the heavens,
    for his steadfast love endures forever;
6 who spread out the earth on the waters,
    for his steadfast love endures forever;
7 who made the great lights,
    for his steadfast love endures forever;
8 the sun to rule over the day,
    for his steadfast love endures forever;
9 the moon and stars to rule over the night,
    for his steadfast love endures forever;

10 who struck Egypt through their firstborn,
    for his steadfast love endures forever;
11 and brought Israel out from among them,
    for his steadfast love endures forever;
12 with a strong hand and an outstretched arm,
    for his steadfast love endures forever;
13 who divided the Red Sea*a* in two,
    for his steadfast love endures forever;
14 and made Israel pass through the midst
        of it,
    for his steadfast love endures forever;
15 but overthrew Pharaoh and his army in the
        Red Sea,*a*
    for his steadfast love endures forever;
16 who led his people through the wilderness,
    for his steadfast love endures forever;
17 who struck down great kings,
    for his steadfast love endures forever;
18 and killed famous kings,
    for his steadfast love endures forever;
19 Sihon, king of the Amorites,
    for his steadfast love endures forever;
20 and Og, king of Bashan,
    for his steadfast love endures forever;
21 and gave their land as a heritage,
    for his steadfast love endures forever;
22 a heritage to his servant Israel,
    for his steadfast love endures forever;

23 It is he who remembered us in our low
        estate,
    for his steadfast love endures forever;

a Or *Sea of Reeds*

24 and rescued us from our foes,
  for his steadfast love endures forever;
25 who gives food to all flesh,
  for his steadfast love endures forever.

26 O give thanks to the God of heaven,
  for his steadfast love endures forever.

137 Lament over the Destruction of Jerusalem

By the rivers of Babylon—
  there we sat down and there we wept
  when we remembered Zion.
2 On the willows[a] there
  we hung up our harps.
3 For there our captors
  asked us for songs,
and our tormentors asked for mirth,
      saying,
  "Sing us one of the songs of Zion!"

4 How could we sing the LORD's song
  in a foreign land?
5 If I forget you, O Jerusalem,
  let my right hand wither!
6 Let my tongue cling to the roof of my mouth,
  if I do not remember you,
if I do not set Jerusalem
  above my highest joy.

7 Remember, O LORD, against the Edomites
  the day of Jerusalem's fall,
how they said, "Tear it down! Tear it down!
  Down to its foundations!"
8 O daughter Babylon, you devastator![b]
  Happy shall they be who pay you back
  what you have done to us!
9 Happy shall they be who take your
      little ones
  and dash them against the rock!

138 Thanksgiving and Praise
Of David.

I give you thanks, O LORD, with my whole
      heart;
  before the gods I sing your praise;
2 I bow down toward your holy temple
  and give thanks to your name for your
      steadfast love and your faithfulness;
  for you have exalted your name and
      your word
  above everything.[c]
3 On the day I called, you answered me,
  you increased my strength of soul.[d]

4 All the kings of the earth shall praise you,
      O LORD,
  for they have heard the words of your
      mouth.
5 They shall sing of the ways of the
      LORD,
  for great is the glory of the LORD.
6 For though the LORD is high, he regards the
      lowly;
  but the haughty he perceives from far away.

7 Though I walk in the midst of trouble,
  you preserve me against the wrath of my
      enemies;
you stretch out your hand,
  and your right hand delivers me.
8 The LORD will fulfill his purpose for me;
  your steadfast love, O LORD, endures
      forever.
  Do not forsake the work of your hands.

139 The Inescapable God
To the leader. Of David. A Psalm.

O LORD, you have searched me and
      known me.
2 You know when I sit down and when I
      rise up;
  you discern my thoughts from far away.
3 You search out my path and my lying down,
  and are acquainted with all my ways.
4 Even before a word is on my tongue,
  O LORD, you know it completely.
5 You hem me in, behind and before,
  and lay your hand upon me.

---

a Or *poplars* b Or *you who are devastated* c Cn: Heb *you have exalted your word above all your name* d Syr Compare Gk Tg: Heb *you made me arrogant in my soul with strength*

6 Such knowledge is too wonderful
     for me;
       it is so high that I cannot attain it.

7 Where can I go from your spirit?
     Or where can I flee from your presence?
8 If I ascend to heaven, you are there;
     if I make my bed in Sheol, you are there.
9 If I take the wings of the morning
     and settle at the farthest limits of the sea,
10 even there your hand shall lead me,
     and your right hand shall hold me fast.
11 If I say, "Surely the darkness shall cover me,
     and the light around me become night,"
12 even the darkness is not dark to you;
     the night is as bright as the day,
     for darkness is as light to you.

13 For it was you who formed my inward parts;
     you knit me together in my mother's
       womb.
14 I praise you, for I am fearfully and
     wonderfully made.

Wonderful are your works;
that I know very well.
15 My frame was not hidden from you,
when I was being made in secret,
     intricately woven in the depths of the
       earth.
16 Your eyes beheld my unformed substance.
In your book were written
     all the days that were formed for me,
     when none of them as yet existed.
17 How weighty to me are your thoughts,
     O God!
     How vast is the sum of them!
18 I try to count them—they are more than the
       sand;
     I come to the end[a]—I am still with you.

19 O that you would kill the wicked, O God,
     and that the bloodthirsty would depart
       from me—
20 those who speak of you maliciously,
     and lift themselves up against you for evil![b]
21 Do I not hate those who hate you, O LORD?
     And do I not loathe those who rise up
       against you?
22 I hate them with perfect hatred;
     I count them my enemies.
23 Search me, O God, and know my heart;
     test me and know my thoughts.
24 See if there is any wicked[c] way in me,
     and lead me in the way
       everlasting.[d]

STUDY IT!

Life Is Sacred
Psalm 139

"For it was you who formed my inward parts; you knit me together in my mother's womb" (Psalm 139:13). God cared intimately for each of us long before we were even created. It's perhaps the most powerful argument for the sacredness of life in the entire Bible. It speaks of a God who knew us, formed us, and gave us life long before we actually saw the light of day.

It's easy to get caught up in arguments about individual rights and scientific terminology. But this psalm is not about science or government or even when life begins. It's about poetry and love and the faith that God has created us as special and unique. We have been lovingly made in God's image—and because of that, every life has dignity.

140 Prayer for Deliverance from Enemies

To the leader. A Psalm of David.

Deliver me, O LORD, from evildoers;
     protect me from those who are violent,
2 who plan evil things in their minds
     and stir up wars continually.
3 They make their tongue sharp as a snake's,
     and under their lips is the venom of
       vipers.   *Selah*

4 Guard me, O LORD, from the hands of the
       wicked;
     protect me from the violent
     who have planned my downfall.
5 The arrogant have hidden a trap for me,

a Or *I awake* b Cn: Meaning of Heb uncertain c Heb *hurtful* d Or *the ancient way.* Compare Jer 6.16

LIVE IT!

God Cares for the Persecuted · Psalm 140

We like to think that persecution doesn't happen much today. Unfortunately, it does. People are persecuted every day in our world, because of their color, ethnic origin, or political or spiritual beliefs. Harassment can be as subtle as a rude comment or an attitude of being better than someone else; it can also be as aggressive as beating or killing. You may see persecution and bullying in your school. Young people experience it because of race, social prejudice, the way they look or talk, what they believe, or for no apparent reason.

Psalm 140 is one of several psalms that are prayers for God's help in times of persecution (see also Psalms 35; 86). These psalms typically have two parts. The first part asks for God's protection against persecutors, and the second part praises God's love, justice, and mercy. The combination shows the continual tension for all believers: feeling the need and calling for God's action while at the same time being certain that God still cares in the midst of persecution.

Jesus is the perfect model of the persecuted person. He was persecuted without reason (Luke 23:4), and he felt God's absence (Mark 15:34), but he still put his entire trust in God's will (Matthew 26:39). Following Jesus' example, Christians throughout history have bravely endured persecution, and even death, for their faith.

- Are you being persecuted? Ask for God's strength and talk to parents, teachers, counselors, or other authorities for help.
- Have you ever persecuted someone else, even with mean words? Pray for forgiveness, and do all you can to make amends.
- Where do you see persecution? Speak up for the defenseless and seek help on their behalf.

---

and with cords they have spread a
    net,[a]
along the road they have set snares
    for me.   *Selah*

6 I say to the LORD, "You are my God;
    give ear, O LORD, to the voice of my
        supplications."
7 O LORD, my Lord, my strong deliverer,
    you have covered my head in the day
        of battle.
8 Do not grant, O LORD, the desires of the
        wicked;
    do not further their evil plot.[b] *Selah*

9 Those who surround me lift up their
        heads;[c]
    let the mischief of their lips overwhelm
        them!
10 Let burning coals fall on them!
    Let them be flung into pits, no more to
        rise!

11 Do not let the slanderer be established in the
        land;
    let evil speedily hunt down the violent!

12 I know that the LORD maintains the cause of
        the needy,
    and executes justice for the poor.
13 Surely the righteous shall give thanks to your
        name;
    the upright shall live in your presence.

141 Prayer for Preservation from Evil
A Psalm of David.

I call upon you, O LORD; come quickly to me;
    give ear to my voice when I call to you.
2 Let my prayer be counted as incense
        before you,
    and the lifting up of my hands as an evening
        sacrifice.

3 Set a guard over my mouth, O LORD;

---

a *Or they have spread cords as a net* b *Heb adds they are exalted* c *Cn Compare Gk: Heb those who surround me are uplifted in head; Heb divides verses 8 and 9 differently*

keep watch over the door of my lips.
⁴ Do not turn my heart to any evil,
   to busy myself with wicked deeds
in company with those who work iniquity;
   do not let me eat of their delicacies.

⁵ Let the righteous strike me;
   let the faithful correct me.
Never let the oil of the wicked anoint my
      head,ᵃ
   for my prayer is continuallyᵇ against their
      wicked deeds.
⁶ When they are given over to those who shall
      condemn them,
   then they shall learn that my words were
      pleasant.
⁷ Like a rock that one breaks apart and shatters
      on the land,
   so shall their bones be strewn at the mouth
      of Sheol. ᶜ

⁸ But my eyes are turned toward you, O GOD,
      my Lord;
   in you I seek refuge; do not leave me
      defenseless.
⁹ Keep me from the trap that they have laid
      for me,
   and from the snares of evildoers.
¹⁰ Let the wicked fall into their own nets,
   while I alone escape.

142 Prayer for Deliverance from Persecutors

*A Maskil of David. When he was in the
cave. A Prayer.*

With my voice I cry to the LORD;
   with my voice I make supplication to the
      LORD.
² I pour out my complaint before him;
   I tell my trouble before him.
³ When my spirit is faint,
   you know my way.

In the path where I walk
   they have hidden a trap for me.
⁴ Look on my right hand and see—
   there is no one who takes notice of me;
no refuge remains to me;
   no one cares for me.

⁵ I cry to you, O LORD;
   I say, "You are my refuge,
   my portion in the land of the living."
⁶ Give heed to my cry,
   for I am brought very low.

Save me from my persecutors,
   for they are too strong for me.
⁷ Bring me out of prison,
   so that I may give thanks to your name.
The righteous will surround me,
   for you will deal bountifully with me.

143 Prayer for Deliverance from Enemies

A Psalm of David.

Hear my prayer, O LORD;
   give ear to my supplications in your
      faithfulness;
   answer me in your righteousness.
² Do not enter into judgment with your
      servant,
   for no one living is righteous
      before you.

³ For the enemy has pursued me,
   crushing my life to the ground,
   making me sit in darkness like those long
      dead.
⁴ Therefore my spirit faints within me;
   my heart within me is appalled.

⁵ I remember the days of old,
   I think about all your deeds,
   I meditate on the works of your hands.
⁶ I stretch out my hands to you;
   my soul thirsts for you like a parched
      land.   *Selah*

⁷ Answer me quickly, O LORD;
   my spirit fails.
Do not hide your face from me,
   or I shall be like those who go down to
      the Pit.
⁸ Let me hear of your steadfast love in the
      morning,
   for in you I put my trust.
Teach me the way I should go,
   for to you I lift up my soul.

ᵃ Gk: Meaning of Heb uncertain ᵇ Cn: Heb *for continually and my prayer* ᶜ Meaning of Heb of verses 5-7 is uncertain

9 Save me, O LORD, from my enemies;
   I have fled to you for refuge.[a]
10 Teach me to do your will,
   for you are my God.
   Let your good spirit lead me
      on a level path.

11 For your name's sake, O LORD, preserve my life.
   In your righteousness bring me out of
      trouble.
12 In your steadfast love cut off my enemies,
   and destroy all my adversaries,
   for I am your servant.

144 **Prayer for National Deliverance and Security**
Of David.

Blessed be the LORD, my rock,
   who trains my hands for war, and my fingers
      for battle;
2 my rock[b] and my fortress,
   my stronghold and my deliverer,
   my shield, in whom I take refuge,
   who subdues the peoples[c] under me.

3 O LORD, what are human beings that you
      regard them,
   or mortals that you think of them?
4 They are like a breath;
   their days are like a passing
      shadow.

5 Bow your heavens, O LORD, and come down;
   touch the mountains so that they smoke.
6 Make the lightning flash and scatter them;
   send out your arrows and rout
      them.
7 Stretch out your hand from on high;
   set me free and rescue me from the mighty
      waters,
   from the hand of aliens,
8 whose mouths speak lies,
   and whose right hands are false.

9 I will sing a new song to you,
      O God;
   upon a ten-stringed harp I will play to you,
10 the one who gives victory to kings,
   who rescues his servant David.

11 Rescue me from the cruel sword,
   and deliver me from the hand of aliens,
whose mouths speak lies,
   and whose right hands are false.

12 May our sons in their youth
      be like plants full grown,
our daughters like corner pillars,
   cut for the building of a palace.
13 May our barns be filled,
   with produce of every kind;
may our sheep increase by thousands,
   by tens of thousands in our fields,
14
      and may our cattle be heavy with young.
May there be no breach in the walls,[d] no
      exile,
   and no cry of distress in our streets.

15 Happy are the people to whom such blessings
      fall;
   happy are the people whose God is the
      LORD.

145 **The Greatness and the Goodness of God**
Praise. Of David.

I will extol you, my God and King,
   and bless your name forever and ever.
2 Every day I will bless you,
   and praise your name forever and ever.
3 Great is the LORD, and greatly to be praised;
   his greatness is unsearchable.

4 One generation shall laud your works to
      another,
   and shall declare your mighty acts.
5 On the glorious splendor of your majesty,
   and on your wondrous works, I will
      meditate.
6 The might of your awesome deeds shall be
      proclaimed,
   and I will declare your greatness.
7 They shall celebrate the fame of your
      abundant goodness,
   and shall sing aloud of your righteousness.

8 The LORD is gracious and merciful,
   slow to anger and abounding in steadfast
      love.

a One Heb Ms Gk: MT *to you I have hidden*   b With 18.2 and 2 Sam 22.2: Heb *my steadfast love*   c Heb Mss Syr Aquila Jerome: MT *my people*
d Heb lacks *in the walls*

> "The LORD is near
> to all who call on
> him, to all who call
> on him in truth."
> —Psalm 145:18

9 The LORD is good to all,
    and his compassion is over all that he has
        made.
10 All your works shall give thanks to you,
        O LORD,
    and all your faithful shall bless you.
11 They shall speak of the glory of your kingdom,
    and tell of your power,
12 to make known to all people your[a] mighty
        deeds,
    and the glorious splendor of your[b]
        kingdom.
13 Your kingdom is an everlasting kingdom,
    and your dominion endures throughout all
        generations.

The LORD is faithful in all his words,
    and gracious in all his deeds.[c]
14 The LORD upholds all who are falling,
    and raises up all who are bowed down.
15 The eyes of all look to you,
    and you give them their food in due season.
16 You open your hand,
    satisfying the desire of every living thing.
17 The LORD is just in all his ways,
    and kind in all his doings.
18 The LORD is near to all who call on him,
    to all who call on him in truth.
19 He fulfills the desire of all who fear him;
    he also hears their cry, and saves them.
20 The LORD watches over all who love him,
    but all the wicked he will destroy.

21 My mouth will speak the praise of the LORD,
    and all flesh will bless his holy name forever
        and ever.

Praise for God's Help

146 Praise the LORD!
    Praise the LORD, O my soul!

2 I will praise the LORD as long as I live;
    I will sing praises to my God all my life long.

3 Do not put your trust in princes,
    in mortals, in whom there is no
        help.
4 When their breath departs, they return to the
        earth;
    on that very day their plans perish.

5 Happy are those whose help is the God of
        Jacob,
    whose hope is in the LORD their God,
6 who made heaven and earth,
    the sea, and all that is in them;
who keeps faith forever;
7   who executes justice for the oppressed;
    who gives food to the hungry.

The LORD sets the prisoners free;
8   the LORD opens the eyes of the blind.
The LORD lifts up those who are bowed
        down;
    the LORD loves the righteous.
9 The LORD watches over the strangers;
    he upholds the orphan and the widow,
    but the way of the wicked he brings to ruin.

10 The LORD will reign forever,
    your God, O Zion, for all generations.
Praise the LORD!

Praise for God's Care for Jerusalem

147 Praise the LORD!
    How good it is to sing praises to
        our God;
    for he is gracious, and a song of praise is
        fitting.
2 The LORD builds up Jerusalem;
    he gathers the outcasts of Israel.
3 He heals the brokenhearted,
    and binds up their wounds.
4 He determines the number of the
        stars;
    he gives to all of them their names.
5 Great is our Lord, and abundant in power;
    his understanding is beyond
        measure.
6 The LORD lifts up the downtrodden;
    he casts the wicked to the ground.

a Gk Jerome Syr: Heb *his*   b Heb *his*   c These two lines supplied by Q Ms Gk Syr

7 Sing to the LORD with thanksgiving;
   make melody to our God on the
     lyre.
8 He covers the heavens with clouds,
   prepares rain for the earth,
   makes grass grow on the hills.
9 He gives to the animals their food,
   and to the young ravens when they cry.
10 His delight is not in the strength of the horse,
   nor his pleasure in the speed of a runner;[a]
11 but the LORD takes pleasure in those who
     fear him,
   in those who hope in his steadfast love.

12 Praise the LORD, O Jerusalem!
   Praise your God, O Zion!
13 For he strengthens the bars of your gates;
   he blesses your children within you.
14 He grants peace[b] within your borders;
   he fills you with the finest of wheat.
15 He sends out his command to the earth;
   his word runs swiftly.
16 He gives snow like wool;
   he scatters frost like ashes.
17 He hurls down hail like crumbs—
   who can stand before his cold?
18 He sends out his word, and melts them;
   he makes his wind blow, and the waters
     flow.
19 He declares his word to Jacob,
   his statutes and ordinances to Israel.
20 He has not dealt thus with any other nation;
   they do not know his ordinances.
   Praise the LORD!

148   Praise for God's Universal Glory

Praise the LORD!
Praise the LORD from the heavens;
   praise him in the heights!
2 Praise him, all his angels;
   praise him, all his host!

3 Praise him, sun and moon;
   praise him, all you shining stars!
4 Praise him, you highest heavens,
   and you waters above the heavens!

5 Let them praise the name of the LORD,
   for he commanded and they were
     created.

LIVE IT!

Care for God's Creation
Psalm 148

Psalm 148 calls on all of creation to praise God. By caring for God's creation, we can respond to God and the needs of others. We can work to keep water clean for safe drinking and for the protection of sea life. We can educate ourselves and others about the effects of pollution on animal habitats and nesting sites. We can protect endangered species and reduce our energy use and carbon emissions. All are ways we can fulfill our call to care for God's creation.

    Psalm 148 asks us to complete a cycle—God creates, and we "co-create," acting as caretakers for the good of the earth. That is often called stewardship. Stewardship is taking care of something that's been entrusted to us. Our time on earth is short, so we have a moral responsibility to take care of it for future generations. Indeed, God demands that we be good stewards of all that God has blessed us with, so that all people can share in the overwhelming goodness of God's creation.

- How can you be a better steward of God's creation?
- What are three small steps you can take to care for the resources around you? (For ideas, visit **BlessedEarth.org**.)

6 He established them forever and ever;
   he fixed their bounds, which cannot be
     passed.[c]

7 Praise the LORD from the earth,
   you sea monsters and all deeps,
8 fire and hail, snow and frost,
   stormy wind fulfilling his command!

9 Mountains and all hills,

---

a Heb *legs of a person* b Or *prosperity* c Or *he set a law that cannot pass away*

fruit trees and all cedars!
10 Wild animals and all cattle,
   creeping things and flying birds!

11 Kings of the earth and all peoples,
   princes and all rulers of the earth!
12 Young men and women alike,
   old and young together!

13 Let them praise the name of the LORD,
   for his name alone is exalted;
   his glory is above earth and heaven.
14 He has raised up a horn for his
         people,
   praise for all his faithful,
   for the people of Israel who are close to
         him.
   Praise the LORD!

149   **Praise for God's Goodness to Israel**
   Praise the LORD!
   Sing to the LORD a new song,
   his praise in the assembly of the faithful.
2 Let Israel be glad in its Maker;
   let the children of Zion rejoice in their
         King.
3 Let them praise his name with dancing,
   making melody to him with tambourine
         and lyre.
4 For the LORD takes pleasure in his people;

α Or *dome*

he adorns the humble with victory.
5 Let the faithful exult in glory;
   let them sing for joy on their couches.
6 Let the high praises of God be in their throats
   and two-edged swords in their hands,
7 to execute vengeance on the nations
   and punishment on the peoples,
8 to bind their kings with fetters
   and their nobles with chains of iron,
9 to execute on them the judgment decreed.
   This is glory for all his faithful ones.
   Praise the LORD!

150   **Praise for God's Surpassing
         Greatness**
   Praise the LORD!
   Praise God in his sanctuary;
   praise him in his mighty firmament!α
2 Praise him for his mighty deeds;
   praise him according to his surpassing
         greatness!

3 Praise him with trumpet sound;
   praise him with lute and harp!
4 Praise him with tambourine and dance;
   praise him with strings and pipe!
5 Praise him with clanging cymbals;
   praise him with loud clashing cymbals!
6 Let everything that breathes praise the LORD!
   Praise the LORD!

STUDY IT!

The Themes of Psalms · Psalms 1–150

Psalms is a wonderful place to turn when you are seeking ways to express your feelings in prayer. Use this index to read and pray the psalms in all of life's situations or to draw nearer to God.

- Ambiguity: Psalm 97:7-12
- Anger: Psalm 9:1-6; 25:19-22; 35:1-10; 37:8-17
- Anxiety: Psalm 69:1-8; 88:1-7; 94:16-23; 102:3-11
- Betrayal: Psalm 41:4-13; 55:12-23; 109:1-5
- Bullying: Psalm 70
- Compassion: Psalm 102:12-17; 113; 145:13-21; 146:5-10
- Confession: Psalm 38:12-22; 51:3-6; 119:65-72; 143:1-6
- Death: Psalm 6:1-10; 18:1-6; 39:1-6; 49:10-20; 88:13-18; 102:23-28; 116:1-19; 118:10-17
- Despair: Psalm 6:1-5; 22:1-21; 38:1-11; 40:11-17; 55:1-11; 119:25-32; 130:1-4
- Direction: Psalm 43:3-4; 119:105
- Envy: Psalm 73:1-3
- Face of God: Psalm 76:7-12
- Faith: Psalm 25:1-5; 116:1-10; 146:1-7
- Fear of God: Psalm 76:7-12
- Forgiveness: Psalm 25:1-18; 32:1-5; 51:7-9; 85:1-3; 103:6-13
- Generosity: Psalm 112:6-10
- Gossip: Psalm 7:6-17; 50:16-23; 141:1-4
- Guilt: Psalm 4:1-3; 25:11-18; 51:1-2; 79:8-10
- Holiness: Psalm 77:11-15; 93; 99:1-9
- Hope: Psalm 9:13-20; 33:14-22; 39:7-8; 43:1-5; 62:1-8; 65:1-8; 71:3-14; 91:1-12; 119:41-45; 146:1-7
- Hypocrisy: Psalm 36:1-6
- Joy: Psalm 16:1-22; 35:27-28; 43:1-5; 67:1-7; 71:20-24; 98:1-9; 126:1-6; 149:1-5
- Judgment: Psalm 50:1-6; 73:1-20; 111:6-10
- Justice: Psalm 9:7-10; 18:31-42; 33:1-5; 37:18-28; 101
- Law: Psalm 19:7-10; 37:28-34; 119:89-96
- Love: Psalm 17:6-9; 18:1-3; 25:6-10; 26:1-3; 36:5-10; 63:1-4; 98:1-6; 108:1-6; 136:1-26
- Love of God: Psalm 17:1-7; 86:14-17; 103:14-22; 117; 136:23-26
- Poverty: Psalm 9:11-20; 22:21-26; 34:1-10; 72:12-14; 107:39-43; 146:5-10; 147:1-6
- Pride: Psalm 20:6-9; 52; 94:1-11; 119:97-104; 119:161-168
- Resurrection: Psalm 16:9-11; 27:13-14; 88:8-12
- Righteousness: Psalm 5:8-12; 7:6-17; 11:1-5; 15; 31:1-8; 85:10-13; 119:137-144
- Self-Pity: Psalm 69:22-29; 119:25-32
- Sickness: Psalm 6:6-10; 38:1-11; 39:7-10; 107:17-22
- Sin: Psalm 32:1-5; 38:12-22; 51:1-6; 85:1-3; 130:1-8
- Success: Psalm 18:43-50
- Thanksgiving: Psalm 30:4-12; 75:1-3; 92:1-9; 100:1-5; 107:1-9; 118:19-29; 147:1-11
- Truth: Psalm 43; 86:8-13
- Waiting: Psalm 13; 37:28-34; 39:7-10; 119:122-128; 130:5-8
- Wisdom of God: Psalm 51:6; 104:24

Proverbs

▶▶▶▶▶▶▶▶▶▶▶▶▶▶▶▶▶▶

Advice columns. You can find them in newspapers, magazines, and all over the Internet, dealing with a wide variety of topics such as relationships, money, beauty, fitness, sex, and time management. Some offer sound advice, while others are questionable at best. The book of Proverbs deals with all these topics and more. But Proverbs is more than advice—it's a book of encouragement, offering stability and comfort in its words of godly wisdom.

IN DEPTH

Proverbs teaches that the wise person listens to the voices of history, which communicate experience, intelligence, and common sense. The ancient Israelites had a long tradition of reflecting on the challenges of life. Over the centuries, a whole body of writings developed to record their reflections. These writings gave advice on common problems, answered questions, and provided directions for wise living.

Proverbs is the best-known example of this type of literature in the Old Testament. It contains two basic kinds of writings: longer instructions addressed to young people and short sayings addressed to all. With advice on matters ranging from laziness (Proverbs 6:6-11), cheating (Proverbs 11:1), and pride (Proverbs 16:18) to training children (Proverbs 22:6) and being a good wife (Proverbs 31:10-31), Proverbs is a treasure chest of advice from the ancient world. Although some of the sayings may seem outdated or funny to us today, the overall lesson is something Jesus insists on in the Gospels: faith is not just a matter of right believing; it's also a matter of right living. And right living begins by growing closer to God, whose ways are far better than ours.

The poetic devices used in Proverbs—found in most wisdom literature—reveal another basic belief of our ancestors in faith: How something is said is as important as what is said. The proverbs are easy to read and easy to remember. So read them often and open your heart to God's wisdom.

QUICK FACTS

- **Date Written:** Between the reign of King Solomon (961-931 B.C.) and sometime after the Babylonian exile (587-538 B.C.)
- **Author:** Unknown, although the book is attributed to King Solomon, probably because of his legendary wisdom
- **Theme:** How to please God through wise living
- **Noteworthy:** The book is made up of several collections of proverbs.

AT A GLANCE

- **Proverbs 1–9** Introduction and instructions for young people
- **Proverbs 10:1–31:9** Assorted collections of proverbs and wise advice
- **Proverbs 31:10–31** A reflection on being a good wife

1

The proverbs of Solomon son of David, king of Israel:

Prologue

2 For learning about wisdom and instruction,
   for understanding words of insight,
3 for gaining instruction in wise dealing,
   righteousness, justice, and equity;
4 to teach shrewdness to the simple,
   knowledge and prudence to the young—
5 let the wise also hear and gain in learning,
   and the discerning acquire skill,
6 to understand a proverb and a figure,
   the words of the wise and their riddles.

7 The fear of the LORD is the beginning of
      knowledge;
   fools despise wisdom and
      instruction.

Warnings against Evil Companions

8 Hear, my child, your father's instruction,
   and do not reject your mother's teaching;
9 for they are a fair garland for your head,
   and pendants for your neck.
10 My child, if sinners entice you,
    do not consent.
11 If they say, "Come with us, let us lie in wait for
       blood;
    let us wantonly ambush the innocent;
12 like Sheol let us swallow them alive
    and whole, like those who go down to
       the Pit.
13 We shall find all kinds of costly things;
    we shall fill our houses with booty.
14 Throw in your lot among us;
    we will all have one purse"—
15 my child, do not walk in their way,
    keep your foot from their paths;
16 for their feet run to evil,
    and they hurry to shed blood.
17 For in vain is the net baited
    while the bird is looking on;
18 yet they lie in wait—to kill themselves!
    and set an ambush—for their own
       lives!
19 Such is the end^a of all who are greedy for
       gain;
    it takes away the life of its
       possessors.

a Gk: Heb *are the ways*

Media Madness
Proverbs 1:10

Every day we are bombarded with messages from the media. Our lives are so media saturated that we absorb much of it without even noticing.

Some of what we learn and experience through the media is incredibly valuable, but there are many negative messages as well. Our self-concept is skewed by the perfect bodies we see all around us. Our materialism is fueled by the attraction of the newest and best things. Our minds and emotions become numb to the constant parade of violent and sexual images.

So what do we do? Isolate ourselves from all media? Impossible. But we can educate ourselves to be aware of the messages we are receiving. Proverbs says that learning to be wise requires instruction, knowledge, and discernment. When we grow in wisdom, we can take the good and reject the bad. In this proverb we read, "My child, if sinners entice you, do not consent" (Proverbs 1:10). Take time to really think about a message in the media before you choose to follow it. And build your life on a foundation of wisdom instead of market-driven hype that will fade when the next fad comes along.

The Call of Wisdom

20 Wisdom cries out in the street;
    in the squares she raises her voice.
21 At the busiest corner she cries out;
    at the entrance of the city gates she speaks:
22 "How long, O simple ones, will you love being
       simple?
    How long will scoffers delight in their scoffing
       and fools hate knowledge?
23 Give heed to my reproof;
    I will pour out my thoughts to you;
    I will make my words known to you.
24 Because I have called and you refused,

have stretched out my hand and no one
　　heeded,
25 and because you have ignored all my counsel
　　and would have none of my reproof,
26 I also will laugh at your calamity;
　　I will mock when panic strikes you,
27 when panic strikes you like a storm,
　　and your calamity comes like a whirlwind,
　　when distress and anguish come upon you.
28 Then they will call upon me, but I will not
　　answer;
　　they will seek me diligently, but will not
　　find me.
29 Because they hated knowledge
　　and did not choose the fear of the LORD,
30 would have none of my counsel,
　　and despised all my reproof,
31 therefore they shall eat the fruit of their way
　　and be sated with their own devices.
32 For waywardness kills the simple,

and the complacency of fools destroys
　　them;
33 but those who listen to me will be secure
　　and will live at ease, without dread of
　　disaster."

The Value of Wisdom

2 My child, if you accept my words
　　and treasure up my commandments
　　within you,
2 making your ear attentive to wisdom
　　and inclining your heart to
　　understanding;
3 if you indeed cry out for insight,
　　and raise your voice for understanding;
4 if you seek it like silver,
　　and search for it as for hidden treasures—
5 then you will understand the fear of
　　the LORD
　　and find the knowledge of God.

STUDY IT!

Finding Truth · Proverbs 2

Many people say that morality is relative, that it's up to each individual to determine what's right and wrong. But scripture teaches that there is a moral law with moral truths that never change, and we must seek to know them. This isn't always easy. Proverbs speaks of the need to seek wisdom, understanding, and insight (Proverbs 2:2-5). We must be attentive and treat this knowledge as a highly treasured prize.

So where do we find this moral law we're supposed to seek? There are three expressions or sources. Together they provide the understanding and insight we need to obey God and work toward the common good.

- **Natural law** is the God-given ability to use reason to tell right from wrong. This ability can be found in all people throughout history, regardless of their religion. It leads us to do good and avoid evil. Sounds simple, but sometimes we forget that we each must use reason when confronted with a moral dilemma.

- The **old law** is the law given to Moses and summed up in the Ten Commandments (Exodus 20:2-17). This law provides us with moral truths regarding ways we are to love God and other people. Knowing and applying the Ten Commandments is essential to making a moral decision.

- The **new law** or **law of the gospel** was given to us by Jesus. The new law and the old law are both essential parts of the moral law that God has revealed to the world. The new law fulfills and gives us a deeper understanding of the old law. It not only shows us how to love God and others, but also gives us the grace and strength necessary to follow the law through the power of the Holy Spirit.

Through prayer and study, we all can seek moral truth as Proverbs calls us to do. Listen to God calling you to grow in wisdom and understanding as you seek to live out moral truth.

6 For the LORD gives wisdom;
   from his mouth come knowledge and
     understanding;
7 he stores up sound wisdom for the upright;
   he is a shield to those who walk
     blamelessly,
8 guarding the paths of justice
   and preserving the way of his faithful ones.
9 Then you will understand righteousness and
     justice
   and equity, every good path;
10 for wisdom will come into your heart,
   and knowledge will be pleasant to your
     soul;
11 prudence will watch over you;
   and understanding will guard you.
12 It will save you from the way of evil,
   from those who speak perversely,
13 who forsake the paths of uprightness
   to walk in the ways of darkness,
14 who rejoice in doing evil
   and delight in the perverseness of evil;
15 those whose paths are crooked,
   and who are devious in their ways.

16 You will be saved from the loose[a] woman,
   from the adulteress with her smooth words,
17 who forsakes the partner of her youth
   and forgets her sacred covenant;
18 for her way[b] leads down to death,
   and her paths to the shades;
19 those who go to her never come back,
   nor do they regain the paths of life.

20 Therefore walk in the way of the good,
   and keep to the paths of the just.
21 For the upright will abide in the land,

and the innocent will remain in it;
22 but the wicked will be cut off from the land,
   and the treacherous will be rooted out
     of it.

Admonition to Trust and Honor God

3 My child, do not forget my teaching,
   but let your heart keep my
     commandments;
2 for length of days and years of life
   and abundant welfare they will give you.

3 Do not let loyalty and faithfulness forsake you;
   bind them around your neck,
   write them on the tablet of your heart.
4 So you will find favor and good repute
   in the sight of God and of people.

5 Trust in the LORD with all your heart,
   and do not rely on your own insight.
6 In all your ways acknowledge him,
   and he will make straight your paths.

PRAY IT!

Your Future
Proverbs 3:5–8
Read **Proverbs 3:5–8** and think about your plans for the future. How does God play a part in them? Do they include prayerfully listening to (discerning) God's plans for you? Here are some clues for discerning where God is calling you:

- Pray about your future, and ask for God's direction.
- Look at your talents and interests. These are gifts from God to be used for the good of others as well as yourself.
- Imagine yourself doing whatever you're considering. What feelings surface? Do you feel peaceful or full of anxiety and fear?
- Talk with a trusted adult about your options. If this person is wise, she or he will help you sort out where God is leading, not give you a definitive answer.

> "Trust in the LORD with all your heart, and do not rely on your own insight. In all your ways acknowledge him, and he will make straight your paths."
> —Proverbs 3:5–6

a Heb *strange*   b Cn: Heb *house*

7 Do not be wise in your own eyes;
   fear the LORD, and turn away from evil.
8 It will be a healing for your flesh
   and a refreshment for your body.

9 Honor the LORD with your substance
   and with the first fruits of all your
      produce;
10 then your barns will be filled with plenty,
   and your vats will be bursting with wine.

11 My child, do not despise the LORD's discipline
   or be weary of his reproof,
12 for the LORD reproves the one he loves,
   as a father the son in whom he delights.

The True Wealth

13 Happy are those who find wisdom,
   and those who get understanding,
14 for her income is better than silver,
   and her revenue better than gold.
15 She is more precious than jewels,
   and nothing you desire can compare
      with her.
16 Long life is in her right hand;
   in her left hand are riches and honor.
17 Her ways are ways of pleasantness,
   and all her paths are peace.
18 She is a tree of life to those who lay hold
      of her;
   those who hold her fast are called happy.

God's Wisdom in Creation

19 The LORD by wisdom founded the earth;
   by understanding he established the
      heavens;
20 by his knowledge the deeps broke open,
   and the clouds drop down the dew.

The True Security

21 My child, do not let these escape from your
      sight:
   keep sound wisdom and prudence,
22 and they will be life for your soul
   and adornment for your neck.
23 Then you will walk on your way securely
   and your foot will not stumble.
24 If you sit down,*a* you will not be afraid;
   when you lie down, your sleep will be
      sweet.
25 Do not be afraid of sudden panic,
   or of the storm that strikes the wicked;
26 for the LORD will be your confidence
   and will keep your foot from being
      caught.

27 Do not withhold good from those to whom it
      is due,*b*
   when it is in your power to do it.
28 Do not say to your neighbor, "Go, and come
      again,
   tomorrow I will give it"—when you have
      it with you.
29 Do not plan harm against your neighbor
   who lives trustingly beside you.
30 Do not quarrel with anyone without cause,
   when no harm has been done to you.
31 Do not envy the violent
   and do not choose any of their ways;
32 for the perverse are an abomination to the
      LORD,
   but the upright are in his confidence.
33 The LORD's curse is on the house of the
      wicked,
   but he blesses the abode of the righteous.
34 Toward the scorners he is scornful,
   but to the humble he shows favor.

STUDY IT!

True Security · Proverbs 3:21–26

What do you think of when you hear the word "security"? An alarm system? An antiviral software program? A big bank account? A safe location? The problem is that all of those isolate and can easily fail when under attack. Proverbs tells us that wisdom provides a much better way to gain true security. When we embrace wisdom and let it guide the ways we treat others, we have true security. "Then you will walk on your way securely and your foot will not stumble" (Proverbs 3:23). For more on security, read **Job 19:25; Psalm 37:3;** and **Jeremiah 33:6.**

a Gk: Heb *lie down* *b* Heb *from its owners*

35 The wise will inherit honor,
   but stubborn fools, disgrace.

4

Parental Advice

Listen, children, to a father's instruction,
   and be attentive, that you may gain[a]
      insight;
2 for I give you good precepts:
   do not forsake my teaching.
3 When I was a son with my father,
   tender, and my mother's favorite,
4 he taught me, and said to me,
   "Let your heart hold fast my words;
   keep my commandments, and live.
5 Get wisdom; get insight: do not forget, nor
      turn away
   from the words of my mouth.
6 Do not forsake her, and she will keep you;
   love her, and she will guard you.
7 The beginning of wisdom is this: Get wisdom,
   and whatever else you get, get insight.
8 Prize her highly, and she will exalt you;
   she will honor you if you embrace her.
9 She will place on your head a fair garland;
   she will bestow on you a beautiful crown."

Admonition to Keep to the Right Path

10 Hear, my child, and accept my words,
   that the years of your life may be many.
11 I have taught you the way of wisdom;
   I have led you in the paths of uprightness.
12 When you walk, your step will not be
      hampered;
   and if you run, you will not stumble.
13 Keep hold of instruction; do not let go;
   guard her, for she is your life.
14 Do not enter the path of the wicked,
   and do not walk in the way of evildoers.
15 Avoid it; do not go on it;
   turn away from it and pass on.
16 For they cannot sleep unless they have done
      wrong;
   they are robbed of sleep unless they have
      made someone stumble.
17 For they eat the bread of wickedness
   and drink the wine of violence.
18 But the path of the righteous is like the light of
      dawn,
   which shines brighter and brighter until
      full day.

19 The way of the wicked is like deep darkness;
   they do not know what they stumble over.
20 My child, be attentive to my words;
   incline your ear to my sayings.
21 Do not let them escape from your sight;
   keep them within your heart.
22 For they are life to those who find them,
   and healing to all their flesh.
23 Keep your heart with all vigilance,
   for from it flow the springs of life.
24 Put away from you crooked speech,
   and put devious talk far from you.
25 Let your eyes look directly forward,
   and your gaze be straight before you.
26 Keep straight the path of your feet,
   and all your ways will be sure.
27 Do not swerve to the right or to the left;
   turn your foot away from evil.

5

Warning against Impurity and Infidelity

My child, be attentive to my wisdom;
   incline your ear to my understanding,
2 so that you may hold on to prudence,
   and your lips may guard knowledge.
3 For the lips of a loose[b] woman drip honey,
   and her speech is smoother than oil;
4 but in the end she is bitter as wormwood,
   sharp as a two-edged sword.
5 Her feet go down to death;
   her steps follow the path to Sheol.
6 She does not keep straight to the path of life;
   her ways wander, and she does not know it.
7 And now, my child,[c] listen to me,
   and do not depart from the words of my
      mouth.
8 Keep your way far from her,
   and do not go near the door of her house;
9 or you will give your honor to others,
   and your years to the merciless,
10 and strangers will take their fill of your wealth,
   and your labors will go to the house of an
      alien;
11 and at the end of your life you will groan,
   when your flesh and body are consumed,
12 and you say, "Oh, how I hated discipline,
   and my heart despised reproof!
13 I did not listen to the voice of my teachers
   or incline my ear to my instructors.

---

a Heb *know*   b Heb *strange*   c Gk Vg: Heb *children*

14 Now I am at the point of utter ruin
     in the public assembly.'"

15 Drink water from your own cistern,
     flowing water from your own well.
16 Should your springs be scattered abroad,
     streams of water in the streets?
17 Let them be for yourself alone,
     and not for sharing with strangers.
18 Let your fountain be blessed,
     and rejoice in the wife of your youth,
19   a lovely deer, a graceful doe.
May her breasts satisfy you at all times;
     may you be intoxicated always by her love.
20 Why should you be intoxicated, my son, by
              another woman
     and embrace the bosom of an adulteress?
21 For human ways are under the eyes of the
              Lord,

and he examines all their paths.
22 The iniquities of the wicked ensnare them,
     and they are caught in the toils of their sin.
23 They die for lack of discipline,
     and because of their great folly they are
         lost.

6   Practical Admonitions

My child, if you have given your pledge
     to your neighbor,
if you have bound yourself to another,[a]
2 you are snared by the utterance of your lips,[b]
     caught by the words of your mouth.
3 So do this, my child, and save yourself,
     for you have come into your neighbor's
         power:
     go, hurry,[c] and plead with your neighbor.
4 Give your eyes no sleep
     and your eyelids no slumber;
5 save yourself like a gazelle from the hunter,[d]
     like a bird from the hand of the fowler.

6 Go to the ant, you lazybones;
     consider its ways, and be wise.
7 Without having any chief
     or officer or ruler,
8 it prepares its food in summer,
     and gathers its sustenance in harvest.
9 How long will you lie there, O lazybones?
     When will you rise from your sleep?
10 A little sleep, a little slumber,
     a little folding of the hands to rest,
11 and poverty will come upon you like a robber,
     and want, like an armed warrior.

12 A scoundrel and a villain
     goes around with crooked speech,
13 winking the eyes, shuffling the feet,
     pointing the fingers,
14 with perverted mind devising evil,
     continually sowing discord;
15 on such a one calamity will descend suddenly;
     in a moment, damage beyond repair.

16 There are six things that the Lord hates,
     seven that are an abomination to him:
17 haughty eyes, a lying tongue,
     and hands that shed innocent blood,
18 a heart that devises wicked plans,
     feet that hurry to run to evil,

LIVE IT!

Intoxicating Love
Proverbs 5:15–23

We live in a society where promiscuity is accepted, even valued in some circles. The message of our culture is to follow our hearts in love—but to feel free to change course or relationships when our feelings change. The writer of Proverbs paints a different picture of love. It's one of commitment in marriage, even against the strongest temptations of adultery and lust. Think this kind of commitment sounds boring and confining? Think again! **Proverbs 5:18–19** speaks of the satisfaction and intoxicating love that can be found within marriage.

These verses are addressed to men, but they challenge and benefit men and women, married or unmarried. We're all called to live out sexual self-control in our relationships. This means we must never abuse the gift of sexuality by using it for self-serving purposes or immediate gratification, remembering that our "human ways are under the eyes of the Lord" (Proverbs 5:21).

a Or *a stranger*   **b** Cn Compare Gk Syr: Heb *the words of your mouth*   **c** Or *humble yourself*   **d** Cn: Heb *from the hand*

LIVE IT!

Leaders with Character
Proverbs 6:16–19

Look at the list of the things the Lord hates in **Proverbs 6:17–19**. It looks like a popular description of a corrupt politician or businessperson! Now turn those negative traits into positive ones: humble eyes, a truthful tongue, hands that protect the innocent, a heart that plans good, feet that hurry to help, a truthful witness, and someone who brings harmony to families. That's the kind of leader everyone wants! Maybe you know a leader in your school, family, church, or local community who exhibits many of these positive qualities. These sorts of leaders have a unique ability to inspire others to follow, providing great insight and direction when one is faced with difficult situations or decisions.

The author of Proverbs is constantly reminding us to be of good character. When you're given the chance to lead, keep the advice of Proverbs in mind. Be a leader of character and integrity by doing the things the Lord loves, not the things the Lord hates.

19 a lying witness who testifies falsely,
and one who sows discord in a family.

20 My child, keep your father's commandment,
and do not forsake your mother's teaching.
21 Bind them upon your heart always;
tie them around your neck.
22 When you walk, they[a] will lead you;
when you lie down, they[a] will watch
over you;
and when you awake, they[a] will talk
with you.
23 For the commandment is a lamp and the
teaching a light,
and the reproofs of discipline are the way
of life,

24 to preserve you from the wife of another,[b]
from the smooth tongue of the adulteress.
25 Do not desire her beauty in your heart,
and do not let her capture you with her
eyelashes;
26 for a prostitute's fee is only a loaf of bread,[c]
but the wife of another stalks a man's very
life.
27 Can fire be carried in the bosom
without burning one's clothes?
28 Or can one walk on hot coals
without scorching the feet?
29 So is he who sleeps with his neighbor's wife;
no one who touches her will go
unpunished.
30 Thieves are not despised who steal only
to satisfy their appetite when they are
hungry.
31 Yet if they are caught, they will pay sevenfold;
they will forfeit all the goods of their
house.
32 But he who commits adultery has no sense;
he who does it destroys himself.
33 He will get wounds and dishonor,
and his disgrace will not be wiped away.
34 For jealousy arouses a husband's fury,
and he shows no restraint when he takes
revenge.
35 He will accept no compensation,
and refuses a bribe no matter how great.

7 The False Attractions of Adultery

My child, keep my words
and store up my commandments
with you;
2 keep my commandments and live,
keep my teachings as the apple of your eye;
3 bind them on your fingers,
write them on the tablet of your heart.
4 Say to wisdom, "You are my sister,"
and call insight your intimate friend,
5 that they may keep you from the loose[d]
woman,
from the adulteress with her smooth
words.

6 For at the window of my house
I looked out through my lattice,
7 and I saw among the simple ones,
I observed among the youths,

a Heb *it* b Gk: MT *the evil woman* c Cn Compare Gk Syr Vg Tg: Heb *for because of a harlot to a piece of bread* d Heb *strange*

a young man without sense,
8 passing along the street near her corner,
　　taking the road to her house
9 in the twilight, in the evening,
　　at the time of night and darkness.

10 Then a woman comes toward him,
　　decked out like a prostitute, wily of heart.[a]
11 She is loud and wayward;
　　her feet do not stay at home;
12 now in the street, now in the squares,
　　and at every corner she lies in wait.
13 She seizes him and kisses him,
　　and with impudent face she says to him:
14 "I had to offer sacrifices,
　　and today I have paid my vows;
15 so now I have come out to meet you,
　　to seek you eagerly, and I have found you!
16 I have decked my couch with coverings,
　　colored spreads of Egyptian linen;
17 I have perfumed my bed with myrrh,
　　aloes, and cinnamon.
18 Come, let us take our fill of love until
　　morning;
　　let us delight ourselves with love.
19 For my husband is not at home;
　　he has gone on a long journey.
20 He took a bag of money with him;
　　he will not come home until full moon."

21 With much seductive speech she
　　persuades him;
　　with her smooth talk she compels him.
22 Right away he follows her,
　　and goes like an ox to the slaughter,
　or bounds like a stag toward the trap[b]

23 until an arrow pierces its entrails.
He is like a bird rushing into a snare,
　　not knowing that it will cost him his life.

24 And now, my children, listen to me,
　　and be attentive to the words of my mouth.
25 Do not let your hearts turn aside to her ways;
　　do not stray into her paths.
26 For many are those she has laid low,
　　and numerous are her victims.
27 Her house is the way to Sheol,
　　going down to the chambers of death.

8 The Gifts of Wisdom

Does not wisdom call,
　　and does not understanding raise her
　　　voice?
2 On the heights, beside the way,
　　at the crossroads she takes her stand;
3 beside the gates in front of the town,
　　at the entrance of the portals she cries out:
4 "To you, O people, I call,
　　and my cry is to all that live.
5 O simple ones, learn prudence;
　　acquire intelligence, you who lack it.
6 Hear, for I will speak noble things,
　　and from my lips will come what is right;
7 for my mouth will utter truth;
　　wickedness is an abomination to my lips.
8 All the words of my mouth are righteous;
　　there is nothing twisted or crooked in
　　　them.
9 They are all straight to one who understands
　　and right to those who find knowledge.
10 Take my instruction instead of silver,
　　and knowledge rather than choice gold;

STUDY IT!

Woman Wisdom · Proverbs 8:1–9:6

The description of wisdom in **Proverbs 8:1–9:6** might give you the impression
that you're reading about a goddess. Nope. The wisdom writers borrowed
the idea of describing wisdom as a beautiful and eternal aspect of God from
neighboring cultures. They exquisitely embodied the idea of wisdom in the
figure of Woman Wisdom. Woman Wisdom comes from God, she was present at the creation
of the world, and she has a special understanding of the world and its workings (see Proverbs 3:19;
8:22-31). For the wisdom writers, Woman Wisdom was an aspect of God that wise people would
want to pursue, because she reveals the right ways to live and behave.

a Meaning of Heb uncertain　b Cn Compare Gk: Meaning of Heb uncertain

The Gifts of Wisdom
Proverbs 8:1–21

What do you desire? Whatever it is, no matter how great, **Proverbs 8** says the gifts of wisdom are better. Wisdom's gifts include diligence, intelligence, knowledge, insight, strength, honor, and justice. They are better than silver, gold, or jewels. So how can you gain these gifts? By diligently seeking wisdom (Proverbs 8:17). This includes reading God's Word, listening to wise teachers, and making choices each day to follow the leading of the Holy Spirit. Spend some time asking God for the strength and courage to seek out these gifts.

> Dear God, please help me to pursue wisdom. When I'm distracted by meaningless pursuits, please remind me of wisdom's rewards and guide my decisions by your Spirit.

11 for wisdom is better than jewels,
    and all that you may desire cannot
        compare with her.
12 I, wisdom, live with prudence,[a]
    and I attain knowledge and discretion.
13 The fear of the LORD is hatred of evil.
    Pride and arrogance and the way of evil
        and perverted speech I hate.
14 I have good advice and sound wisdom;
    I have insight, I have strength.
15 By me kings reign,
    and rulers decree what is just;
16 by me rulers rule,
    and nobles, all who govern rightly.
17 I love those who love me,
    and those who seek me diligently find me.
18 Riches and honor are with me,
    enduring wealth and prosperity.
19 My fruit is better than gold, even fine gold,
    and my yield than choice silver.
20 I walk in the way of righteousness,
    along the paths of justice,
21 endowing with wealth those who love me,
    and filling their treasuries.

Wisdom's Part in Creation

22 The LORD created me at the beginning[b] of
    his work,[c]
    the first of his acts of long ago.
23 Ages ago I was set up,
    at the first, before the beginning of the
        earth.
24 When there were no depths I was brought
        forth,
    when there were no springs abounding
        with water.
25 Before the mountains had been shaped,
    before the hills, I was brought forth—
26 when he had not yet made earth and fields,[a]
    or the world's first bits of soil.
27 When he established the heavens, I was
        there,
    when he drew a circle on the face of the
        deep,
28 when he made firm the skies above,
    when he established the fountains of the
        deep,
29 when he assigned to the sea its limit,
    so that the waters might not transgress his
        command,
    when he marked out the foundations of the
        earth,
30   then I was beside him, like a master
        worker;[d]
    and I was daily his[e] delight,
    rejoicing before him always,
31 rejoicing in his inhabited world
    and delighting in the human race.

32 "And now, my children, listen to me:
    happy are those who keep my ways.
33 Hear instruction and be wise,
    and do not neglect it.
34 Happy is the one who listens to me,
    watching daily at my gates,
    waiting beside my doors.
35 For whoever finds me finds life
    and obtains favor from the LORD;
36 but those who miss me injure
        themselves;
    all who hate me love death."

a Meaning of Heb uncertain   b Or *me as the beginning*   c Heb *way*   d Another reading is *little child*   e Gk: Heb lacks *his*

9

Wisdom's Feast

Wisdom has built her house,
    she has hewn her seven pillars.

[2] She has slaughtered her animals, she has mixed
    her wine,
    she has also set her table.

[3] She has sent out her servant-girls, she calls
    from the highest places in the town,

[4] "You that are simple, turn in here!"
    To those without sense she says,

[5] "Come, eat of my bread
    and drink of the wine I have mixed.

[6] Lay aside immaturity,[a] and live,
    and walk in the way of insight."

General Maxims

[7] Whoever corrects a scoffer wins abuse;
    whoever rebukes the wicked gets hurt.

[8] A scoffer who is rebuked will only hate you;
    the wise, when rebuked, will love you.

[9] Give instruction[b] to the wise, and they will
    become wiser still;
    teach the righteous and they will gain in
    learning.

[10] The fear of the LORD is the beginning of
    wisdom,
    and the knowledge of the Holy One is
    insight.

[11] For by me your days will be multiplied,
    and years will be added to your life.

[12] If you are wise, you are wise for yourself;
    if you scoff, you alone will bear it.

Folly's Invitation and Promise

[13] The foolish woman is loud;
    she is ignorant and knows nothing.

[14] She sits at the door of her house,
    on a seat at the high places of the town,

[15] calling to those who pass by,
    who are going straight on their way,

[16] "You who are simple, turn in here!"
    And to those without sense she says,

[17] "Stolen water is sweet,
    and bread eaten in secret is pleasant."

[18] But they do not know that the dead[c] are there,
    that her guests are in the depths of Sheol.

10

Wise Sayings of Solomon

The proverbs of Solomon.

A wise child makes a glad father,
    but a foolish child is a mother's grief.

[2] Treasures gained by wickedness do not profit,
    but righteousness delivers from death.

[3] The LORD does not let the righteous go
    hungry,
    but he thwarts the craving of the wicked.

[4] A slack hand causes poverty,
    but the hand of the diligent makes rich.

[5] A child who gathers in summer is prudent,
    but a child who sleeps in harvest brings
    shame.

[6] Blessings are on the head of the righteous,
    but the mouth of the wicked conceals
    violence.

[7] The memory of the righteous is a blessing,
    but the name of the wicked will rot.

[8] The wise of heart will heed commandments,
    but a babbling fool will come to ruin.

[9] Whoever walks in integrity walks securely,
    but whoever follows perverse ways will be
    found out.

STUDY IT!

That's Righteous • Proverbs 10

This chapter is the beginning of a section of Proverbs (Proverbs 10-22) that uses parallelism—a style used in poetry to say something in a positive way first and then repeat in a negative way. The parallelism here contrasts the lifestyle and blessings of righteousness with those of wickedness.

Later, righteousness is directly linked to justice. **Proverbs 29:7** says, "The righteous know the rights of the poor." Throughout the New Testament, Jesus tells his followers that his way is the just way. The parables of the good Samaritan (Luke 10:29-37) and the unforgiving servant (Matthew 18:21-35) are reminders of this. Living as a just person may not be easy, but it's what Christ asks of his followers.

a Or *simpleness* b Heb lacks *instruction* c Heb *shades*

10 Whoever winks the eye causes trouble,
   but the one who rebukes boldly makes
      peace.[a]
11 The mouth of the righteous is a fountain of
      life,
   but the mouth of the wicked conceals
      violence.
12 Hatred stirs up strife,
   but love covers all offenses.
13 On the lips of one who has understanding
      wisdom is found,
   but a rod is for the back of one who lacks
      sense.
14 The wise lay up knowledge,
   but the babbling of a fool brings ruin near.
15 The wealth of the rich is their fortress;
   the poverty of the poor is their ruin.
16 The wage of the righteous leads to life,
   the gain of the wicked to sin.
17 Whoever heeds instruction is on the path to
      life,
   but one who rejects a rebuke goes astray.
18 Lying lips conceal hatred,
   and whoever utters slander is a fool.
19 When words are many, transgression is not
      lacking,
   but the prudent are restrained in speech.
20 The tongue of the righteous is choice silver;
   the mind of the wicked is of little worth.
21 The lips of the righteous feed many,
   but fools die for lack of sense.
22 The blessing of the LORD makes rich,
   and he adds no sorrow with it.[b]
23 Doing wrong is like sport to a fool,
   but wise conduct is pleasure to a person of
      understanding.

24 What the wicked dread will come upon them,
   but the desire of the righteous will be
      granted.
25 When the tempest passes, the wicked are no
      more,
   but the righteous are established forever.
26 Like vinegar to the teeth, and smoke to the
      eyes,
   so are the lazy to their employers.
27 The fear of the LORD prolongs life,
   but the years of the wicked will be short.
28 The hope of the righteous ends in gladness,
   but the expectation of the wicked comes to
      nothing.
29 The way of the LORD is a stronghold for the
      upright,
   but destruction for evildoers.
30 The righteous will never be removed,
   but the wicked will not remain in the land.
31 The mouth of the righteous brings forth
      wisdom,
   but the perverse tongue will be cut off.
32 The lips of the righteous know what is
      acceptable,
   but the mouth of the wicked what is
      perverse.

11 A false balance is an abomination to the
      LORD,
   but an accurate weight is his delight.
2 When pride comes, then comes disgrace;
   but wisdom is with the humble.
3 The integrity of the upright guides them,
   but the crookedness of the treacherous
      destroys them.
4 Riches do not profit in the day of wrath,
   but righteousness delivers from death.

Nothing but the Truth · Proverbs 10:18–21

"Do you swear to tell the truth, the whole truth, and nothing but the truth, so help you God?" These are the words asked of every witness about to testify in a U.S. courtroom. Requiring a witness to place a hand on the Bible and answer this question is an attempt to ensure that the witness will be honest. But despite this oath, some witnesses lie.

Proverbs 10:18 tells us, "Lying lips conceal hatred." Just as dishonesty is an act of hatred, so honesty is an act of love. Ultimately, our lies end up hurting others and damaging our integrity. Whether in the courtroom or in everyday life, we must always strive to tell "the truth, the whole truth, and nothing but the truth." And we can only really do that with God's help.

a Gk: Heb *but a babbling fool will come to ruin*   b Or *and toil adds nothing to it*

5 The righteousness of the blameless keeps their
     ways straight,
     but the wicked fall by their own
     wickedness.
6 The righteousness of the upright saves them,
     but the treacherous are taken captive by
     their schemes.
7 When the wicked die, their hope perishes,
     and the expectation of the godless comes
     to nothing.
8 The righteous are delivered from trouble,
     and the wicked get into it instead.
9 With their mouths the godless would destroy
     their neighbors,
     but by knowledge the righteous are
     delivered.
10 When it goes well with the righteous, the city
     rejoices;
     and when the wicked perish, there is
     jubilation.
11 By the blessing of the upright a city is exalted,
     but it is overthrown by the mouth of the
     wicked.
12 Whoever belittles another lacks sense,
     but an intelligent person remains
     silent.
13 A gossip goes about telling secrets,
     but one who is trustworthy in spirit keeps
     a confidence.
14 Where there is no guidance, a nation[a] falls,
     but in an abundance of counselors there is
     safety.
15 To guarantee loans for a stranger brings
     trouble,
     but there is safety in refusing to
     do so.
16 A gracious woman gets honor,
     but she who hates virtue is covered with
     shame.[b]
     The timid become destitute,[c]
     but the aggressive gain riches.
17 Those who are kind reward themselves,
     but the cruel do themselves harm.
18 The wicked earn no real gain,
     but those who sow righteousness get a true
     reward.
19 Whoever is steadfast in righteousness will live,
     but whoever pursues evil will die.
20 Crooked minds are an abomination to the
     LORD,
     but those of blameless ways are his delight.
21 Be assured, the wicked will not go
     unpunished,
     but those who are righteous will escape.
22 Like a gold ring in a pig's snout
     is a beautiful woman without good sense.
23 The desire of the righteous ends only in good;
     the expectation of the wicked in wrath.
24 Some give freely, yet grow all the richer;
     others withhold what is due, and only
     suffer want.
25 A generous person will be enriched,
     and one who gives water will get water.
26 The people curse those who hold back grain,
     but a blessing is on the head of those who
     sell it.
27 Whoever diligently seeks good seeks favor,
     but evil comes to the one who searches
     for it.
28 Those who trust in their riches will wither,[d]
     but the righteous will flourish like green
     leaves.
29 Those who trouble their households will
     inherit wind,
     and the fool will be servant to the wise.

PRAY IT!

Get Over Gossip
Proverbs 11:13
We're all guilty of belittling others with our words or telling secrets. Gossip can seem like fun, but it hurts people. When you find yourself going against the wisdom of **Proverbs 11:13**, say this prayer:
Oh, God, forgive me! I gossiped about someone today. I don't even know if what I said was true, but it made me feel important to tell it to my friends.
Help me keep my mouth shut! When someone tells me a secret, seal it into my heart, and keep it away from my lips!
I can't stop thinking about how the target of my gossip would feel if he or she knew what I said. God, teach me to be trustworthy!

a Or an army b Compare Gk Syr: Heb lacks but she . . . shame c Gk: Heb lacks The timid . . . destitute d Cn: Heb fall

CONNECT IT!

Living Water International: Water Is Life · Proverbs 11:25

There's nothing more refreshing than a cold drink or a dip in a cool swimming pool on a hot summer day. Water is health, growth, refreshment . . . . life. **Proverbs 11:25** says, "One who gives water will get water," and in Israel, then and now, water means life. Sharing the refreshment of water was sharing life. It still is. None of us can live without it. But a billion people in our world today lack clean water. The global water crisis is killing more people than war or natural disasters.

Can you imagine not being able to go to school or work because so much of your time is spent collecting and carrying water miles to your home? That's life for millions, mostly women and children. Even worse, the water they collect is usually filled with pollution and disease that makes them sick and often kills them. It's a silent crisis that doesn't often make the evening news. But organizations like Living Water International (LWI) are fighting hard to end it (visit **water.cc**).

LWI was formed after a group from Houston, Texas, visited Kenya and saw the desperate need for clean water. LWI's mission statement is: "To demonstrate the love of God by helping communities acquire desperately needed clean water, and to experience 'living water'—the gospel of Jesus Christ—which alone satisfies the deepest thirst." LWI does that by teaching and helping people to implement solutions in their own countries. By training and equipping local people to provide their own communities with clean water, LWI works to be sure the water solutions they provide are sustainable for the long term. In addition, they also take hundreds of volunteers on mission trips each year, allowing people to connect with their global neighbors and to provide life through clean water.

When we take part in providing water for people around our world through LWI or other organizations, we are acting out the wisdom of this verse.

30 The fruit of the righteous is a tree of life,
    but violence[a] takes lives away.
31 If the righteous are repaid on earth,
    how much more the wicked and the
        sinner!

12 Whoever loves discipline loves
        knowledge,
    but those who hate to be rebuked are
        stupid.
2 The good obtain favor from the LORD,
    but those who devise evil he condemns.
3 No one finds security by wickedness,
    but the root of the righteous will never be
        moved.
4 A good wife is the crown of her husband,
    but she who brings shame is like
        rottenness in his bones.
5 The thoughts of the righteous are just;
    the advice of the wicked is treacherous.
6 The words of the wicked are a deadly ambush,
    but the speech of the upright delivers
        them.

7 The wicked are overthrown and are no more,
    but the house of the righteous will stand.
8 One is commended for good sense,
    but a perverse mind is despised.
9 Better to be despised and have a servant,
    than to be self-important and lack food.
10 The righteous know the needs of their
        animals,
    but the mercy of the wicked is cruel.
11 Those who till their land will have plenty of
        food,
    but those who follow worthless pursuits
        have no sense.
12 The wicked covet the proceeds of
        wickedness,[b]
    but the root of the righteous bears fruit.
13 The evil are ensnared by the transgression of
        their lips,
    but the righteous escape from trouble.
14 From the fruit of the mouth one is filled with
        good things,
    and manual labor has its reward.

_a_ Cn Compare Gk Syr: Heb _a wise man_   _b_ Or _covet the catch of the wicked_

15 Fools think their own way is right,
  but the wise listen to advice.
16 Fools show their anger at once,
  but the prudent ignore an insult.
17 Whoever speaks the truth gives honest
    evidence,
  but a false witness speaks deceitfully.
18 Rash words are like sword thrusts,
  but the tongue of the wise brings healing.
19 Truthful lips endure forever,
  but a lying tongue lasts only a moment.
20 Deceit is in the mind of those who plan evil,
  but those who counsel peace have joy.
21 No harm happens to the righteous,
  but the wicked are filled with trouble.
22 Lying lips are an abomination to the LORD,
  but those who act faithfully are his delight.
23 One who is clever conceals knowledge,
  but the mind of a fool*a* broadcasts folly.
24 The hand of the diligent will rule,
  while the lazy will be put to forced labor.
25 Anxiety weighs down the human heart,
  but a good word cheers it up.
26 The righteous gives good advice to friends,*b*
  but the way of the wicked leads astray.
27 The lazy do not roast*c* their game,
  but the diligent obtain precious wealth.*c*
28 In the path of righteousness there is life,
    in walking its path there is no death.

13 A wise child loves discipline,*d*
  but a scoffer does not listen to rebuke.
2 From the fruit of their words good
    persons eat good things,
  but the desire of the treacherous is for
    wrongdoing.
3 Those who guard their mouths preserve their
    lives;
  those who open wide their lips come to
    ruin.
4 The appetite of the lazy craves, and gets
    nothing,
  while the appetite of the diligent is richly
    supplied.
5 The righteous hate falsehood,
  but the wicked act shamefully and
    disgracefully.
6 Righteousness guards one whose way is
    upright,
  but sin overthrows the wicked.
7 Some pretend to be rich, yet have nothing;

others pretend to be poor, yet have great
    wealth.
8 Wealth is a ransom for a person's life,
  but the poor get no threats.
9 The light of the righteous rejoices,
  but the lamp of the wicked goes out.
10 By insolence the heedless make strife,
  but wisdom is with those who take advice.
11 Wealth hastily gotten*e* will dwindle,
  but those who gather little by little will
    increase it.
12 Hope deferred makes the heart sick,
  but a desire fulfilled is a tree of life.
13 Those who despise the word bring destruction
    on themselves,
  but those who respect the commandment
    will be rewarded.
14 The teaching of the wise is a fountain of life,
  so that one may avoid the snares of death.
15 Good sense wins favor,
  but the way of the faithless is their ruin.*f*
16 The clever do all things intelligently,
  but the fool displays folly.
17 A bad messenger brings trouble,
  but a faithful envoy, healing.
18 Poverty and disgrace are for the one who
    ignores instruction,
  but one who heeds reproof is honored.
19 A desire realized is sweet to the soul,
  but to turn away from evil is an
    abomination to fools.
20 Whoever walks with the wise becomes wise,
  but the companion of fools suffers harm.
21 Misfortune pursues sinners,
  but prosperity rewards the righteous.
22 The good leave an inheritance to their
    children's children,
  but the sinner's wealth is laid up for the
    righteous.
23 The field of the poor may yield much food,
  but it is swept away through injustice.
24 Those who spare the rod hate their children,
  but those who love them are diligent to
    discipline them.
25 The righteous have enough to satisfy their
    appetite,
  but the belly of the wicked is empty.

14 The wise woman*g* builds her house,
  but the foolish tears it down with her
    own hands.

---

a Heb *the heart of fools* b Syr: Meaning of Heb uncertain c Meaning of Heb uncertain d Cn: Heb *A wise child the discipline of his father* e Gk Vg:
Heb *from vanity* f Cn Compare Gk Syr Vg Tg: Heb *is enduring* g Heb *Wisdom of women*

2 Those who walk uprightly fear the LORD,
    but one who is devious in conduct
        despises him.
3 The talk of fools is a rod for their backs,*a*
    but the lips of the wise preserve them.
4 Where there are no oxen, there is no grain;
    abundant crops come by the strength of
        the ox.
5 A faithful witness does not lie,
    but a false witness breathes out lies.
6 A scoffer seeks wisdom in vain,
    but knowledge is easy for one who
        understands.
7 Leave the presence of a fool,
    for there you do not find words of
        knowledge.
8 It is the wisdom of the clever to understand
    where they go,
    but the folly of fools misleads.
9 Fools mock at the guilt offering,*b*
    but the upright enjoy God's favor.
10 The heart knows its own bitterness,
    and no stranger shares its joy.
11 The house of the wicked is destroyed,
    but the tent of the upright flourishes.
12 There is a way that seems right to a person,
    but its end is the way to death.*c*
13 Even in laughter the heart is sad,
    and the end of joy is grief.
14 The perverse get what their ways deserve,
    and the good, what their deeds deserve.*d*
15 The simple believe everything,
    but the clever consider their steps.
16 The wise are cautious and turn away from evil,
    but the fool throws off restraint and is
        careless.
17 One who is quick-tempered acts foolishly,
    and the schemer is hated.
18 The simple are adorned with*e* folly,
    but the clever are crowned with knowledge.
19 The evil bow down before the good,
    the wicked at the gates of the righteous.
20 The poor are disliked even by their neighbors,
    but the rich have many friends.
21 Those who despise their neighbors are sinners,
    but happy are those who are kind to the
        poor.
22 Do they not err that plan evil?
    Those who plan good find loyalty and
        faithfulness.

23 In all toil there is profit,
    but mere talk leads only to poverty.
24 The crown of the wise is their wisdom,*f*
    but folly is the garland*g* of fools.
25 A truthful witness saves lives,
    but one who utters lies is a betrayer.
26 In the fear of the LORD one has strong
    confidence,
    and one's children will have a refuge.
27 The fear of the LORD is a fountain of life,
    so that one may avoid the snares of death.
28 The glory of a king is a multitude of people;
    without people a prince is ruined.
29 Whoever is slow to anger has great
    understanding,
    but one who has a hasty temper exalts folly.
30 A tranquil mind gives life to the flesh,
    but passion makes the bones rot.
31 Those who oppress the poor insult their Maker,
    but those who are kind to the needy
        honor him.
32 The wicked are overthrown by their evildoing,
    but the righteous find a refuge in their
        integrity.*h*
33 Wisdom is at home in the mind of one who has
    understanding,
    but it is not*i* known in the heart of fools.
34 Righteousness exalts a nation,
    but sin is a reproach to any people.
35 A servant who deals wisely has the king's favor,
    but his wrath falls on one who acts
        shamefully.

15 A soft answer turns away wrath,
    but a harsh word stirs up anger.
2 The tongue of the wise dispenses
    knowledge,*j*
    but the mouths of fools pour out folly.
3 The eyes of the LORD are in every place,
    keeping watch on the evil and the good.
4 A gentle tongue is a tree of life,
    but perverseness in it breaks the spirit.
5 A fool despises a parent's instruction,
    but the one who heeds admonition is
        prudent.
6 In the house of the righteous there is much
    treasure,
    but trouble befalls the income of the
        wicked.
7 The lips of the wise spread knowledge;
    not so the minds of fools.

---

a Cn: Heb *a rod of pride* *b* Meaning of Heb uncertain *c* Heb *ways of death* *d* Cn: Heb *from upon him* *e* Or *inherit* *f* Cn Compare Gk: Heb *riches*
g Cn: Heb *is the folly* *h* Gk Syr: Heb *in their death* *i* Gk Syr: Heb lacks *not* *j* Cn: Heb *makes knowledge good*

8 The sacrifice of the wicked is an abomination to
the LORD,
but the prayer of the upright is his delight.

9 The way of the wicked is an abomination to the
LORD,
but he loves the one who pursues
righteousness.

10 There is severe discipline for one who forsakes
the way,
but one who hates a rebuke will die.

11 Sheol and Abaddon lie open before the LORD,
how much more human hearts!

12 Scoffers do not like to be rebuked;
they will not go to the wise.

13 A glad heart makes a cheerful countenance,
but by sorrow of heart the spirit is broken.

14 The mind of one who has understanding seeks
knowledge,
but the mouths of fools feed on folly.

15 All the days of the poor are hard,
but a cheerful heart has a continual feast.

16 Better is a little with the fear of the LORD
than great treasure and trouble
with it.

17 Better is a dinner of vegetables where love is
than a fatted ox and hatred with it.

18 Those who are hot-tempered stir up strife,
but those who are slow to anger calm
contention.

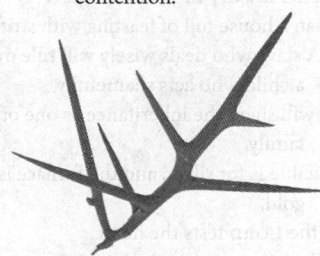

19 The way of the lazy is overgrown with thorns,
but the path of the upright is a level
highway.

20 A wise child makes a glad father,
but the foolish despise their mothers.

21 Folly is a joy to one who has no sense,
but a person of understanding walks straight
ahead.

22 Without counsel, plans go wrong,
but with many advisers they succeed.

23 To make an apt answer is a joy to anyone,
and a word in season, how good it is!

24 For the wise the path of life leads upward,
in order to avoid Sheol below.

25 The LORD tears down the house of the proud,
but maintains the widow's boundaries.

26 Evil plans are an abomination to the LORD,
but gracious words are pure.

27 Those who are greedy for unjust gain make
trouble for their households,
but those who hate bribes will live.

28 The mind of the righteous ponders how to
answer,
but the mouth of the wicked pours out evil.

29 The LORD is far from the wicked,
but he hears the prayer of the righteous.

30 The light of the eyes rejoices the heart,
and good news refreshes the body.

31 The ear that heeds wholesome admonition
will lodge among the wise.

32 Those who ignore instruction despise
themselves,
but those who heed admonition gain
understanding.

33 The fear of the LORD is instruction in wisdom,
and humility goes before honor.

16   The plans of the mind belong to mortals,
but the answer of the tongue is from the
LORD.

2 All one's ways may be pure in one's own eyes,
but the LORD weighs the spirit.

3 Commit your work to the LORD,
and your plans will be established.

4 The LORD has made everything for its
purpose,
even the wicked for the day of trouble.

PRAY IT!

Give Your Day to God
Proverbs 16:3

Follow the advice in this
verse and commit your
day to the Lord by starting each morning with
a prayer like this one:

Dear Lord, today I offer you all my
thoughts, deeds, and words. Let everything
I do reflect your love and goodness. Amen.

5 All those who are arrogant are an abomination
    to the LORD;
    be assured, they will not go unpunished.
6 By loyalty and faithfulness iniquity is
    atoned for,
    and by the fear of the LORD one avoids
    evil.
7 When the ways of people please the LORD,
    he causes even their enemies to be at peace
    with them.
8 Better is a little with righteousness
    than large income with injustice.
9 The human mind plans the way,
    but the LORD directs the steps.
10 Inspired decisions are on the lips of a king;
    his mouth does not sin in judgment.
11 Honest balances and scales are the LORD's;
    all the weights in the bag are his work.
12 It is an abomination to kings to do evil,
    for the throne is established by
    righteousness.
13 Righteous lips are the delight of a king,
    and he loves those who speak what is right.
14 A king's wrath is a messenger of death,
    and whoever is wise will appease it.
15 In the light of a king's face there is life,
    and his favor is like the clouds that bring
    the spring rain.
16 How much better to get wisdom than gold!
    To get understanding is to be chosen
    rather than silver.
17 The highway of the upright avoids evil;
    those who guard their way preserve their
    lives.
18 Pride goes before destruction,
    and a haughty spirit before a fall.
19 It is better to be of a lowly spirit among
    the poor
    than to divide the spoil with the proud.
20 Those who are attentive to a matter will
    prosper,
    and happy are those who trust in the
    LORD.
21 The wise of heart is called perceptive,
    and pleasant speech increases
    persuasiveness.
22 Wisdom is a fountain of life to one who has it,
    but folly is the punishment of fools.
23 The mind of the wise makes their speech
    judicious,
    and adds persuasiveness to their lips.
24 Pleasant words are like a honeycomb,
    sweetness to the soul and health to the
    body.
25 Sometimes there is a way that seems to be
    right,
    but in the end it is the way to death.
26 The appetite of workers works for
    them;
    their hunger urges them on.
27 Scoundrels concoct evil,
    and their speech is like a scorching fire.
28 A perverse person spreads strife,
    and a whisperer separates close friends.
29 The violent entice their neighbors,
    and lead them in a way that is not good.
30 One who winks the eyes plans[a] perverse
    things;
    one who compresses the lips brings evil to
    pass.
31 Gray hair is a crown of glory;
    it is gained in a righteous life.
32 One who is slow to anger is better than the
    mighty,
    and one whose temper is controlled than
    one who captures a city.
33 The lot is cast into the lap,
    but the decision is the LORD's alone.

17 Better is a dry morsel with quiet
    than a house full of feasting with strife.
2 A slave who deals wisely will rule over
    a child who acts shamefully,
    and will share the inheritance as one of the
    family.
3 The crucible is for silver, and the furnace is for
    gold,
    but the LORD tests the heart.
4 An evildoer listens to wicked lips;
    and a liar gives heed to a mischievous
    tongue.
5 Those who mock the poor insult their Maker;
    those who are glad at calamity will not go
    unpunished.
6 Grandchildren are the crown of the aged,
    and the glory of children is their parents.
7 Fine speech is not becoming to a fool;
    still less is false speech to a ruler.[b]
8 A bribe is like a magic stone in the eyes of
    those who give it;
    wherever they turn they prosper.

a Gk Syr Vg Tg: Heb to plan   b Or a noble person

9 One who forgives an affront fosters friendship,
   but one who dwells on disputes will
      alienate a friend.
10 A rebuke strikes deeper into a discerning
      person
   than a hundred blows into a fool.
11 Evil people seek only rebellion,
   but a cruel messenger will be sent against
      them.
12 Better to meet a she-bear robbed of its cubs
   than to confront a fool immersed in folly.
13 Evil will not depart from the house
   of one who returns evil for good.
14 The beginning of strife is like letting out
      water;
   so stop before the quarrel breaks out.
15 One who justifies the wicked and one who
      condemns the righteous
   are both alike an abomination to the LORD.
16 Why should fools have a price in hand
   to buy wisdom, when they have no mind
      to learn?
17 A friend loves at all times,
   and kinsfolk are born to share adversity.
18 It is senseless to give a pledge,
   to become surety for a neighbor.
19 One who loves transgression loves strife;
   one who builds a high threshold invites
      broken bones.
20 The crooked of mind do not prosper,
   and the perverse of tongue fall into
      calamity.

21 The one who begets a fool gets trouble;
   the parent of a fool has no joy.
22 A cheerful heart is a good medicine,
   but a downcast spirit dries up the bones.
23 The wicked accept a concealed bribe
   to pervert the ways of justice.
24 The discerning person looks to wisdom,
   but the eyes of a fool to the ends of the
      earth.
25 Foolish children are a grief to their father
   and bitterness to her who bore them.
26 To impose a fine on the innocent is not right,
   or to flog the noble for their integrity.
27 One who spares words is knowledgeable;
   one who is cool in spirit has
      understanding.
28 Even fools who keep silent are considered
      wise;
   when they close their lips, they are deemed
      intelligent.

18 The one who lives alone is
      self-indulgent,
   showing contempt for all who have
      sound judgment.[a]
2 A fool takes no pleasure in understanding,
   but only in expressing personal opinion.
3 When wickedness comes, contempt comes
      also;
   and with dishonor comes disgrace.
4 The words of the mouth are deep waters;
   the fountain of wisdom is a gushing
      stream.

a Meaning of Heb uncertain

5 It is not right to be partial to the guilty,
  or to subvert the innocent in judgment.
6 A fool's lips bring strife,
  and a fool's mouth invites a flogging.
7 The mouths of fools are their ruin,
  and their lips a snare to themselves.
8 The words of a whisperer are like delicious
    morsels;
    they go down into the inner parts of the
    body.
9 One who is slack in work
  is close kin to a vandal.
10 The name of the LORD is a strong tower;
  the righteous run into it and are safe.
11 The wealth of the rich is their strong city;
  in their imagination it is like a high wall.
12 Before destruction one's heart is haughty,
  but humility goes before honor.
13 If one gives answer before hearing,
  it is folly and shame.
14 The human spirit will endure sickness;
  but a broken spirit—who can bear?
15 An intelligent mind acquires knowledge,
  and the ear of the wise seeks knowledge.
16 A gift opens doors;
  it gives access to the great.
17 The one who first states a case seems right,
  until the other comes and
    cross-examines.
18 Casting the lot puts an end to disputes
  and decides between powerful
    contenders.
19 An ally offended is stronger than a city;[a]
  such quarreling is like the bars of a castle.
20 From the fruit of the mouth one's stomach is
    satisfied;
  the yield of the lips brings satisfaction.
21 Death and life are in the power of the tongue,
  and those who love it will eat its fruits.
22 He who finds a wife finds a good thing,
  and obtains favor from the LORD.
23 The poor use entreaties,
  but the rich answer roughly.
24 Some[b] friends play at friendship[c]
  but a true friend sticks closer than one's
    nearest kin.

19 Better the poor walking in integrity
  than one perverse of speech who is a
    fool.
2 Desire without knowledge is not good,

and one who moves too hurriedly misses
    the way.
3 One's own folly leads to ruin,
  yet the heart rages against the LORD.
4 Wealth brings many friends,
  but the poor are left friendless.
5 A false witness will not go unpunished,
  and a liar will not escape.
6 Many seek the favor of the generous,
  and everyone is a friend to a giver of gifts.
7 If the poor are hated even by their kin,
  how much more are they shunned by their
    friends!
  When they call after them, they are not
    there.[d]
8 To get wisdom is to love oneself;
  to keep understanding is to prosper.
9 A false witness will not go unpunished,
  and the liar will perish.
10 It is not fitting for a fool to live in luxury,
  much less for a slave to rule over princes.
11 Those with good sense are slow to anger,
  and it is their glory to overlook an offense.
12 A king's anger is like the growling of a lion,
  but his favor is like dew on the grass.
13 A stupid child is ruin to a father,
  and a wife's quarreling is a continual
    dripping of rain.
14 House and wealth are inherited from parents,
  but a prudent wife is from the LORD.
15 Laziness brings on deep sleep;
  an idle person will suffer hunger.
16 Those who keep the commandment will live;
  those who are heedless of their ways
    will die.
17 Whoever is kind to the poor lends to the
    LORD,
  and will be repaid in full.
18 Discipline your children while there is hope;
  do not set your heart on their destruction.
19 A violent tempered person will pay the
    penalty;
  if you effect a rescue, you will only have to
    do it again.[d]
20 Listen to advice and accept instruction,
  that you may gain wisdom for the future.
21 The human mind may devise many plans,
  but it is the purpose of the LORD that will
    be established.
22 What is desirable in a person is loyalty,

a Gk Syr Vg Tg: Meaning of Heb uncertain   b Syr Tg: Heb A man of   c Cn Compare Syr Vg Tg: Meaning of Heb uncertain   d Meaning of Heb
uncertain

LIVE IT!

Fear of the Lord · Proverbs 19:23

The phrase "fear of the LORD" is used fourteen times in Proverbs (for example, see Proverbs 19:23). You might ask why the author of Proverbs keeps telling us to be afraid of God. But in the Bible, fear of the Lord has less to do with terror and fright than with awe, reverence, and respect. It's a reminder that God is far from ordinary. To fear the Lord is to take God very seriously. Take some time to think or journal about these questions:

• What does fear of the Lord mean to you?

• Describe a time when you were awed by something about God, and explain how you showed God respect.

and it is better to be poor than a
    liar.
23 The fear of the LORD is life indeed;
    filled with it one rests secure
    and suffers no harm.
24 The lazy person buries a hand in the dish,
    and will not even bring it back to the
    mouth.
25 Strike a scoffer, and the simple will learn
    prudence;
    reprove the intelligent, and they will gain
    knowledge.
26 Those who do violence to their father and
    chase away their mother
    are children who cause shame and bring
    reproach.
27 Cease straying, my child, from the words of
    knowledge,
    in order that you may hear instruction.
28 A worthless witness mocks at justice,
    and the mouth of the wicked devours
    iniquity.
29 Condemnation is ready for scoffers,
    and flogging for the backs of fools.

20 Wine is a mocker, strong drink a
    brawler,
    and whoever is led astray by it is not
    wise.
2 The dread anger of a king is like the growling
    of a lion;
    anyone who provokes him to anger forfeits
    life itself.
3 It is honorable to refrain from strife,
    but every fool is quick to quarrel.
4 The lazy person does not plow in season;

harvest comes, and there is nothing to be
    found.
5 The purposes in the human mind are like
    deep water,
    but the intelligent will draw them out.
6 Many proclaim themselves loyal,
    but who can find one worthy of trust?
7 The righteous walk in integrity—
    happy are the children who follow them!
8 A king who sits on the throne of judgment
    winnows all evil with his eyes.
9 Who can say, "I have made my heart clean;
    I am pure from my sin"?
10 Diverse weights and diverse measures
    are both alike an abomination to the
    LORD.
11 Even children make themselves known by
    their acts,
    by whether what they do is pure and right.
12 The hearing ear and the seeing eye—
    the LORD has made them both.
13 Do not love sleep, or else you will come to
    poverty;
    open your eyes, and you will have plenty
    of bread.
14 "Bad, bad," says the buyer,
    then goes away and boasts.
15 There is gold, and abundance of costly stones;
    but the lips informed by knowledge are a
    precious jewel.
16 Take the garment of one who has given surety
    for a stranger;
    seize the pledge given as surety for
    foreigners.
17 Bread gained by deceit is sweet,

but afterward the mouth will be full of
  gravel.
18 Plans are established by taking advice;
  wage war by following wise guidance.
19 A gossip reveals secrets;
  therefore do not associate with a babbler.
20 If you curse father or mother,
  your lamp will go out in utter darkness.
21 An estate quickly acquired in the beginning
  will not be blessed in the end.
22 Do not say, "I will repay evil";
  wait for the LORD, and he will help you.
23 Differing weights are an abomination to the
  LORD,
  and false scales are not good.
24 All our steps are ordered by the LORD;
  how then can we understand our own
  ways?
25 It is a snare for one to say rashly, "It is holy,"
  and begin to reflect only after making
  a vow.
26 A wise king winnows the wicked,
  and drives the wheel over them.
27 The human spirit is the lamp of the LORD,
  searching every inmost part.
28 Loyalty and faithfulness preserve the king,
  and his throne is upheld by righteousness.[a]
29 The glory of youths is their strength,
  but the beauty of the aged is their gray hair.
30 Blows that wound cleanse away evil;
  beatings make clean the innermost parts.

21   The king's heart is a stream of water in
  the hand of the LORD;
  he turns it wherever he will.
2 All deeds are right in the sight of the doer,
  but the LORD weighs the heart.
3 To do righteousness and justice
  is more acceptable to the LORD than
  sacrifice.
4 Haughty eyes and a proud heart—
  the lamp of the wicked—are sin.
5 The plans of the diligent lead surely to
  abundance,
  but everyone who is hasty comes only to
  want.
6 The getting of treasures by a lying tongue
  is a fleeting vapor and a snare[b] of death.
7 The violence of the wicked will sweep them
  away,
  because they refuse to do what is just.

8 The way of the guilty is crooked,
  but the conduct of the pure is right.
9 It is better to live in a corner of the housetop
  than in a house shared with a contentious
  wife.
10 The souls of the wicked desire evil;
  their neighbors find no mercy in their eyes.
11 When a scoffer is punished, the simple
  become wiser;
  when the wise are instructed, they increase
  in knowledge.
12 The Righteous One observes the house of the
  wicked;
  he casts the wicked down to ruin.
13 If you close your ear to the cry of the poor,
  you will cry out and not be heard.
14 A gift in secret averts anger;
  and a concealed bribe in the bosom, strong
  wrath.
15 When justice is done, it is a joy to the
  righteous,
  but dismay to evildoers.
16 Whoever wanders from the way of
  understanding
  will rest in the assembly of the
  dead.
17 Whoever loves pleasure will suffer
  want;
  whoever loves wine and oil will not be
  rich.
18 The wicked is a ransom for the righteous,
  and the faithless for the upright.
19 It is better to live in a desert land
  than with a contentious and fretful wife.
20 Precious treasure remains[c] in the house of the
  wise,
  but the fool devours it.
21 Whoever pursues righteousness and kindness
  will find life[d] and honor.
22 One wise person went up against a city of
  warriors
  and brought down the stronghold in which
  they trusted.
23 To watch over mouth and tongue
  is to keep out of trouble.
24 The proud, haughty person, named "Scoffer,"
  acts with arrogant pride.
25 The craving of the lazy person is fatal,
  for lazy hands refuse to labor.
26 All day long the wicked covet,[e]

---

a Gk: Heb *loyalty* **b** Gk: Heb *seekers* **c** Gk: Heb *and oil* **d** Gk: Heb *life and righteousness* **e** Gk: Heb *all day long one covets covetously*

but the righteous give and do not hold
back.

27 The sacrifice of the wicked is an abomination;
how much more when brought with evil
intent.

28 A false witness will perish,
but a good listener will testify successfully.

29 The wicked put on a bold face,
but the upright give thought to[a] their
ways.

30 No wisdom, no understanding, no counsel,
can avail against the Lord.

31 The horse is made ready for the day of battle,
but the victory belongs to the Lord.

22   A good name is to be chosen rather than
great riches,
and favor is better than silver or gold.

2 The rich and the poor have this in common:
the Lord is the maker of them all.

3 The clever see danger and hide;
but the simple go on, and suffer for it.

4 The reward for humility and fear of the Lord
is riches and honor and life.

5 Thorns and snares are in the way of the
perverse;
the cautious will keep far from them.

6 Train children in the right way,
and when old, they will not stray.

7 The rich rule over the poor,
and the borrower is the slave of the lender.

8 Whoever sows injustice will reap calamity,
and the rod of anger will fail.

9 Those who are generous are blessed,
for they share their bread with the poor.

10 Drive out a scoffer, and strife goes out;
quarreling and abuse will cease.

11 Those who love a pure heart and are gracious
in speech
will have the king as a friend.

12 The eyes of the Lord keep watch over
knowledge,
but he overthrows the words of the
faithless.

13 The lazy person says, "There is a lion outside!
I shall be killed in the streets!"

14 The mouth of a loose[b] woman is a deep pit;
he with whom the Lord is angry falls
into it.

15 Folly is bound up in the heart of a boy,
but the rod of discipline drives it far away.

16 Oppressing the poor in order to enrich
oneself,
and giving to the rich, will lead only to
loss.

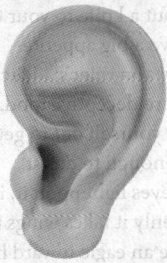

Sayings of the Wise

17   The words of the wise:

Incline your ear and hear my words,[c]
and apply your mind to my teaching;

18 for it will be pleasant if you keep them
within you,
if all of them are ready on your lips.

19 So that your trust may be in the Lord,
I have made them known to you today—
yes, to you.

20 Have I not written for you thirty sayings
of admonition and knowledge,

21 to show you what is right and true,
so that you may give a true answer to those
who sent you?

22 Do not rob the poor because they are poor,
or crush the afflicted at the gate;

23 for the Lord pleads their cause
and despoils of life those who despoil
them.

24 Make no friends with those given to anger,
and do not associate with hotheads,

25 or you may learn their ways
and entangle yourself in a snare.

26 Do not be one of those who give pledges,
who become surety for debts.

27 If you have nothing with which to pay,
why should your bed be taken from
under you?

28 Do not remove the ancient landmark
that your ancestors set up.

29 Do you see those who are skillful in their
work?

---

a Another reading is *establish*   b Heb *strange*   c Cn Compare Gk: Heb *Incline your ear, and hear the words of the wise*

They will serve kings;
they will not serve common people.

23 When you sit down to eat with a ruler,
observe carefully what*ª* is before you,
2 and put a knife to your throat
if you have a big appetite.
3 Do not desire the ruler's*ᵇ* delicacies,
for they are deceptive food.
4 Do not wear yourself out to get rich;
be wise enough to desist.
5 When your eyes light upon it, it is gone;
for suddenly it takes wings to itself,
flying like an eagle toward heaven.
6 Do not eat the bread of the stingy;
do not desire their delicacies;
7 for like a hair in the throat, so are they.*ᶜ*
"Eat and drink!" they say to you;
but they do not mean it.
8 You will vomit up the little you have eaten,
and you will waste your pleasant words.
9 Do not speak in the hearing of a fool,
who will only despise the wisdom of your
words.
10 Do not remove an ancient landmark
or encroach on the fields of orphans,
11 for their redeemer is strong;
he will plead their cause against you.
12 Apply your mind to instruction
and your ear to words of knowledge.
13 Do not withhold discipline from your
children;
if you beat them with a rod, they will
not die.
14 If you beat them with the rod,
you will save their lives from Sheol.
15 My child, if your heart is wise,
my heart too will be glad.
16 My soul will rejoice
when your lips speak what is right.
17 Do not let your heart envy sinners,
but always continue in the fear of the
Lord.
18 Surely there is a future,
and your hope will not be cut off.

19 Hear, my child, and be wise,
and direct your mind in the way.
20 Do not be among winebibbers,
or among gluttonous eaters of meat;

21 for the drunkard and the glutton will come to
poverty,
and drowsiness will clothe them with rags.
22 Listen to your father who begot you,
and do not despise your mother when she
is old.
23 Buy truth, and do not sell it;
buy wisdom, instruction, and
understanding.
24 The father of the righteous will greatly rejoice;
he who begets a wise son will be glad
in him.
25 Let your father and mother be glad;
let her who bore you rejoice.

26 My child, give me your heart,
and let your eyes observe*ᵈ* my ways.
27 For a prostitute is a deep pit;
an adulteress*ᵉ* is a narrow well.
28 She lies in wait like a robber
and increases the number of the faithless.

29 Who has woe? Who has sorrow?
Who has strife? Who has complaining?
Who has wounds without cause?
Who has redness of eyes?
30 Those who linger late over wine,
those who keep trying mixed wines.
31 Do not look at wine when it is red,
when it sparkles in the cup
and goes down smoothly.
32 At the last it bites like a serpent,
and stings like an adder.
33 Your eyes will see strange things,
and your mind utter perverse things.
34 You will be like one who lies down in the
midst of the sea,
like one who lies on the top of a mast.*ᶜ*
35 "They struck me," you will say,*ᶠ* "but I was not
hurt;
they beat me, but I did not feel it.
When shall I awake?
I will seek another drink."

24 Do not envy the wicked,
nor desire to be with them;
2 for their minds devise violence,
and their lips talk of mischief.

3 By wisdom a house is built,

---

a Or *who*   *b* Heb *his*   *c* Meaning of Heb uncertain   *d* Another reading is *delight in*   *e* Heb *an alien woman*   *f* Gk Syr Vg Tg: Heb lacks *you will say*

and by understanding it is established;

4 by knowledge the rooms are filled
　　with all precious and pleasant riches.
5 Wise warriors are mightier than strong ones,[a]
　　and those who have knowledge than those
　　　who have strength;
6 for by wise guidance you can wage your war,
　　and in abundance of counselors there is
　　　victory.
7 Wisdom is too high for fools;
　　in the gate they do not open their mouths.

8 Whoever plans to do evil
　　will be called a mischief-maker.
9 The devising of folly is sin,
　　and the scoffer is an abomination to all.

10 If you faint in the day of adversity,
　　your strength being small;
11 if you hold back from rescuing those taken
　　　away to death,
　　those who go staggering to the slaughter;
12 if you say, "Look, we did not know this"—
　　does not he who weighs the heart
　　　perceive it?
　　Does not he who keeps watch over your soul
　　　know it?
　　And will he not repay all according to their
　　　deeds?

13 My child, eat honey, for it is good,
　　and the drippings of the honeycomb are
　　　sweet to your taste.
14 Know that wisdom is such to your soul;
　　if you find it, you will find a future,
　　and your hope will not be cut off.

15 Do not lie in wait like an outlaw against the
　　　home of the righteous;
　　do no violence to the place where the
　　　righteous live;
16 for though they fall seven times, they will rise
　　　again;
　　but the wicked are overthrown by calamity.

17 Do not rejoice when your enemies fall,
　　and do not let your heart be glad when
　　　they stumble,
18 or else the LORD will see it and be displeased,
　　and turn away his anger from them.

19 Do not fret because of evildoers.
　　Do not envy the wicked;
20 for the evil have no future;
　　the lamp of the wicked will go out.

21 My child, fear the LORD and the king,
　　and do not disobey either of them;[b]
22 for disaster comes from them
　　　suddenly,
　　and who knows the ruin that both can
　　　bring?

Further Sayings of the Wise

23 　　These also are sayings of the wise:

Partiality in judging is not good.
24 Whoever says to the wicked, "You are
　　　innocent,"
　　will be cursed by peoples, abhorred by
　　　nations;
25 but those who rebuke the wicked will have
　　　delight,
　　and a good blessing will come upon them.
26 One who gives an honest answer
　　gives a kiss on the lips.

27 Prepare your work outside,
　　get everything ready for you in the field;
　　and after that build your house.

28 Do not be a witness against your neighbor
　　　without cause,
　　and do not deceive with your lips.
29 Do not say, "I will do to others as they have
　　　done to me;
　　I will pay them back for what they have
　　　done."

30 I passed by the field of one who was lazy,
　　by the vineyard of a stupid person;
31 and see, it was all overgrown with thorns;
　　the ground was covered with nettles,
　　and its stone wall was broken down.
32 Then I saw and considered it;
　　I looked and received instruction.
33 A little sleep, a little slumber,
　　a little folding of the hands to rest,
34 and poverty will come upon you like a
　　　robber,
　　and want, like an armed warrior.

a Gk Compare Syr Tg: Heb *A wise man is strength* 　b Gk: Heb *do not associate with those who change*

25 **Further Wise Sayings of Solomon**
These are other proverbs of Solomon that the officials of King Hezekiah of Judah copied.

2 It is the glory of God to conceal things,
  but the glory of kings is to search
    things out.
3 Like the heavens for height, like the earth for
      depth,
  so the mind of kings is unsearchable.
4 Take away the dross from the silver,
  and the smith has material for a vessel;
5 take away the wicked from the presence of
    the king,
  and his throne will be established in
    righteousness.
6 Do not put yourself forward in the king's
    presence
  or stand in the place of the great;
7 for it is better to be told, "Come up here,"
  than to be put lower in the presence of a
    noble.

What your eyes have seen
8   do not hastily bring into court;
for[a] what will you do in the end,
    when your neighbor puts you to shame?
9 Argue your case with your neighbor directly,
  and do not disclose another's secret;
10 or else someone who hears you will bring
    shame upon you,
  and your ill repute will have no end.

11 A word fitly spoken
  is like apples of gold in a setting of silver.
12 Like a gold ring or an ornament of gold
  is a wise rebuke to a listening ear.
13 Like the cold of snow in the time of harvest
  are faithful messengers to those who send
    them;
  they refresh the spirit of their masters.
14 Like clouds and wind without rain
  is one who boasts of a gift never given.
15 With patience a ruler may be persuaded,
  and a soft tongue can break bones.
16 If you have found honey, eat only enough
    for you,
  or else, having too much, you will
    vomit it.

17 Let your foot be seldom in your neighbor's
    house,
  otherwise the neighbor will become weary
    of you and hate you.
18 Like a war club, a sword, or a sharp arrow
  is one who bears false witness against a
    neighbor.
19 Like a bad tooth or a lame foot
  is trust in a faithless person in time of
    trouble.
20 Like vinegar on a wound[b]
  is one who sings songs to a heavy heart.
Like a moth in clothing or a worm in wood,
  sorrow gnaws at the human heart.[c]
21 If your enemies are hungry, give them bread
    to eat;
  and if they are thirsty, give them water to
    drink;
22 for you will heap coals of fire on their heads,
  and the LORD will reward you.
23 The north wind produces rain,
  and a backbiting tongue, angry looks.
24 It is better to live in a corner of the housetop
  than in a house shared with a contentious
    wife.
25 Like cold water to a thirsty soul,
  so is good news from a far country.
26 Like a muddied spring or a polluted fountain
  are the righteous who give way before the
    wicked.
27 It is not good to eat much honey,
  or to seek honor on top of honor.
28 Like a city breached, without walls,
  is one who lacks self-control.

26 Like snow in summer or rain in harvest,
  so honor is not fitting for a fool.
2 Like a sparrow in its flitting, like a
    swallow in its flying,
  an undeserved curse goes nowhere.
3 A whip for the horse, a bridle for the donkey,
  and a rod for the back of fools.
4 Do not answer fools according to their folly,
  or you will be a fool yourself.
5 Answer fools according to their folly,
  or they will be wise in their own eyes.
6 It is like cutting off one's foot and drinking
    down violence,
  to send a message by a fool.
7 The legs of a disabled person hang limp;
  so does a proverb in the mouth of a fool.

a Cn: Heb *or else* *b* Gk: Heb *Like one who takes off a garment on a cold day, like vinegar on lye* *c* Gk Syr Tg: Heb lacks *Like a moth ... human heart*

8 It is like binding a stone in a sling
   to give honor to a fool.
9 Like a thornbush brandished by the hand of a
      drunkard
   is a proverb in the mouth of a fool.
10 Like an archer who wounds everybody
   is one who hires a passing fool or
      drunkard.[a]
11 Like a dog that returns to its vomit
   is a fool who reverts to his folly.
12 Do you see persons wise in their own eyes?
   There is more hope for fools than for
      them.
13 The lazy person says, "There is a lion in the
      road!
   There is a lion in the streets!"
14 As a door turns on its hinges,
   so does a lazy person in bed.
15 The lazy person buries a hand in the dish,
   and is too tired to bring it back to the
      mouth.
16 The lazy person is wiser in self-esteem
   than seven who can answer discreetly.
17 Like somebody who takes a passing dog by
      the ears
   is one who meddles in the quarrel of
      another.
18 Like a maniac who shoots deadly firebrands
      and arrows,
19 so is one who deceives a neighbor
   and says, "I am only joking!"
20 For lack of wood the fire goes out,
   and where there is no whisperer, quarreling
      ceases.
21 As charcoal is to hot embers and wood to fire,
   so is a quarrelsome person for kindling
      strife.
22 The words of a whisperer are like delicious
      morsels;
   they go down into the inner parts of the
      body.
23 Like the glaze[b] covering an earthen vessel
   are smooth[c] lips with an evil heart.
24 An enemy dissembles in speaking
   while harboring deceit within;
25 when an enemy speaks graciously, do not
      believe it,
   for there are seven abominations concealed
      within;
26 though hatred is covered with guile,

the enemy's wickedness will be exposed in
   the assembly.
27 Whoever digs a pit will fall into it,
   and a stone will come back on the one who
      starts it rolling.
28 A lying tongue hates its victims,
   and a flattering mouth works ruin.
   Do not boast about tomorrow,
   for you do not know what a day may
      bring.

27

2 Let another praise you, and not your own
      mouth—
   a stranger, and not your own lips.
3 A stone is heavy, and sand is weighty,
   but a fool's provocation is heavier than
      both.
4 Wrath is cruel, anger is overwhelming,
   but who is able to stand before jealousy?
5 Better is open rebuke
   than hidden love.
6 Well meant are the wounds a friend inflicts,
   but profuse are the kisses of an enemy.
7 The sated appetite spurns honey,
   but to a ravenous appetite even the bitter is
      sweet.
8 Like a bird that strays from its nest
   is one who strays from home.
9 Perfume and incense make the heart glad,
   but the soul is torn by trouble.[d]
10 Do not forsake your friend or the friend of
      your parent;
   do not go to the house of your kindred in
      the day of your calamity.
   Better is a neighbor who is nearby
   than kindred who are far away.
11 Be wise, my child, and make my heart glad,
   so that I may answer whoever
      reproaches me.
12 The clever see danger and hide;
   but the simple go on, and suffer for it.
13 Take the garment of one who has given surety
      for a stranger;
   seize the pledge given as surety for
      foreigners.[e]
14 Whoever blesses a neighbor with a loud voice,
   rising early in the morning,
   will be counted as cursing.
15 A continual dripping on a rainy day
   and a contentious wife are alike;
16 to restrain her is to restrain the wind

---

a Meaning of Heb uncertain b Cn: Heb *silver of dross* c Gk: Heb *burning* d Gk: Heb *the sweetness of a friend is better than one's own counsel* e Vg and
20.16: Heb *for a foreign woman*

or to grasp oil in the right hand.[a]

17 Iron sharpens iron,
  and one person sharpens the wits[b] of
   another.
18 Anyone who tends a fig tree will eat its fruit,
  and anyone who takes care of a master will
   be honored.
19 Just as water reflects the face,
  so one human heart reflects another.
20 Sheol and Abaddon are never satisfied,
  and human eyes are never satisfied.
21 The crucible is for silver, and the furnace is for
   gold,
  so a person is tested[c] by being praised.
22 Crush a fool in a mortar with a pestle
  along with crushed grain,
  but the folly will not be driven out.

23 Know well the condition of your flocks,
  and give attention to your herds;
24 for riches do not last forever,
  nor a crown for all generations.
25 When the grass is gone, and new growth
   appears,
  and the herbage of the mountains is
   gathered,
26 the lambs will provide your clothing,
  and the goats the price of a field;
27 there will be enough goats' milk for your food,
  for the food of your household
  and nourishment for your servant-girls.

28 The wicked flee when no one pursues,
  but the righteous are as bold as a lion.
2 When a land rebels
 it has many rulers;
but with an intelligent ruler
 there is lasting order.[a]
3 A ruler[d] who oppresses the poor

is a beating rain that leaves no food.
4 Those who forsake the law praise the wicked,
  but those who keep the law struggle
   against them.
5 The evil do not understand justice,
  but those who seek the Lord understand
   it completely.
6 Better to be poor and walk in integrity
  than to be crooked in one's ways even
   though rich.
7 Those who keep the law are wise children,
  but companions of gluttons shame their
   parents.
8 One who augments wealth by exorbitant
   interest
  gathers it for another who is kind to the
   poor.
9 When one will not listen to the law,
  even one's prayers are an abomination.
10 Those who mislead the upright into evil ways
  will fall into pits of their own making,
  but the blameless will have a goodly
   inheritance.
11 The rich is wise in self-esteem,
  but an intelligent poor person sees through
   the pose.
12 When the righteous triumph, there is great
   glory,
  but when the wicked prevail, people go
   into hiding.
13 No one who conceals transgressions will
   prosper,
  but one who confesses and forsakes them
   will obtain mercy.
14 Happy is the one who is never without fear,
  but one who is hard-hearted will fall into
   calamity.
15 Like a roaring lion or a charging bear

Integrity · Proverbs 28:6

A person with integrity won't lie, steal, cheat, gossip, betray, or insult—not even when everyone else seems to be doing it. A person with integrity is trustworthy, dependable, and reliable. Such a person admits making mistakes and apologizes. Such a person forgives freely and doesn't hold grudges. Living with integrity isn't easy, but **Proverbs 28:6** says it's better to be poor with integrity than rich without it. Lord, I'm far from perfect. But with every word I speak, every action I take, every choice I make, teach me to choose integrity and grow closer to you.

a Meaning of Heb uncertain   b Heb *face*   c Heb lacks *is tested*   d Cn: Heb *A poor person* is a wicked ruler over a poor people.

16 A ruler who lacks understanding is a cruel
      oppressor;
    but one who hates unjust gain will enjoy a
      long life.

17 If someone is burdened with the blood of
      another,
    let that killer be a fugitive until
      death;
    let no one offer assistance.

18 One who walks in integrity will be safe,
    but whoever follows crooked ways will fall
      into the Pit.[a]

19 Anyone who tills the land will have plenty of
      bread,
    but one who follows worthless pursuits
      will have plenty of poverty.

20 The faithful will abound with blessings,
    but one who is in a hurry to be rich will
      not go unpunished.

21 To show partiality is not good—
    yet for a piece of bread a person may do
      wrong.

22 The miser is in a hurry to get rich
    and does not know that loss is sure to
      come.

23 Whoever rebukes a person will afterward find
      more favor
    than one who flatters with the tongue.

24 Anyone who robs father or mother
    and says, "That is no crime,"
    is partner to a thug.

25 The greedy person stirs up strife,
    but whoever trusts in the LORD will be
      enriched.

26 Those who trust in their own wits are fools;
    but those who walk in wisdom come
      through safely.

27 Whoever gives to the poor will lack nothing,
    but one who turns a blind eye will get
      many a curse.

28 When the wicked prevail, people go into
      hiding;
    but when they perish, the righteous
      increase.

29 One who is often reproved, yet remains
      stubborn,
    will suddenly be broken beyond healing.

2 When the righteous are in authority, the
      people rejoice;

but when the wicked rule, the people
      groan.

3 A child who loves wisdom makes a parent
      glad,
    but to keep company with prostitutes is to
      squander one's substance.

4 By justice a king gives stability to the land,
    but one who makes heavy exactions
      ruins it.

5 Whoever flatters a neighbor
    is spreading a net for the neighbor's feet.

6 In the transgression of the evil there is a
      snare,
    but the righteous sing and rejoice.

7 The righteous know the rights of the poor;
    the wicked have no such understanding.

8 Scoffers set a city aflame,
    but the wise turn away wrath.

9 If the wise go to law with fools,
    there is ranting and ridicule without relief.

10 The bloodthirsty hate the blameless,
    and they seek the life of the upright.

11 A fool gives full vent to anger,
    but the wise quietly holds it back.

12 If a ruler listens to falsehood,
    all his officials will be wicked.

13 The poor and the oppressor have this in
      common:
    the LORD gives light to the eyes of both.

14 If a king judges the poor with equity,
    his throne will be established forever.

15 The rod and reproof give wisdom,
    but a mother is disgraced by a neglected
      child.

16 When the wicked are in authority,
      transgression increases,
    but the righteous will look upon their
      downfall.

17 Discipline your children, and they will give
      you rest;
    they will give delight to your heart.

18 Where there is no prophecy, the people cast
      off restraint,
    but happy are those who keep the law.

19 By mere words servants are not disciplined,
    for though they understand, they will not
      give heed.

20 Do you see someone who is hasty in speech?
    There is more hope for a fool than for
      anyone like that.

a Syr: Heb *fall all at once*

21 A slave pampered from childhood
will come to a bad end.[a]
22 One given to anger stirs up strife,
and the hothead causes much
transgression.
23 A person's pride will bring humiliation,
but one who is lowly in spirit will obtain
honor.
24 To be a partner of a thief is to hate one's own
life;
one hears the victim's curse, but discloses
nothing.[b]
25 The fear of others[c] lays a snare,
but one who trusts in the LORD is secure.
26 Many seek the favor of a ruler,
but it is from the LORD that one gets
justice.
27 The unjust are an abomination to the
righteous,
but the upright are an abomination to the
wicked.

Sayings of Agur

30 The words of Agur son of Jakeh. An oracle.

Thus says the man: I am weary, O God,
I am weary, O God. How can I prevail?[d]
2 Surely I am too stupid to be human;
I do not have human understanding.
3 I have not learned wisdom,
nor have I knowledge of the holy ones.[e]
4 Who has ascended to heaven and come
down?
Who has gathered the wind in the hollow
of the hand?
Who has wrapped up the waters in a garment?
Who has established all the ends of the
earth?
What is the person's name?
And what is the name of the person's child?
Surely you know!

> "Every word of God
> proves true; he is a
> shield to those who
> take refuge in him."
> ----Proverbs 30:5

5 Every word of God proves true;
he is a shield to those who take refuge
in him.
6 Do not add to his words,
or else he will rebuke you, and you will be
found a liar.
7 Two things I ask of you;
do not deny them to me before I die:
8 Remove far from me falsehood and lying;
give me neither poverty nor riches;
feed me with the food that I need,
9 or I shall be full, and deny you,
and say, "Who is the LORD?"
or I shall be poor, and steal,
and profane the name of my God.
10 Do not slander a servant to a master,
or the servant will curse you, and you will
be held guilty.
11 There are those who curse their fathers
and do not bless their mothers.
12 There are those who are pure in their
own eyes
yet are not cleansed of their filthiness.
13 There are those—how lofty are their eyes,
how high their eyelids lift!—
14 there are those whose teeth are swords,
whose teeth are knives,
to devour the poor from off the earth,
the needy from among mortals.
15 The leech[b] has two daughters;
"Give, give," they cry.
Three things are never satisfied;
four never say, "Enough":
16 Sheol, the barren womb,
the earth ever thirsty for water,
and the fire that never says, "Enough."[b]
17 The eye that mocks a father
and scorns to obey a mother
will be pecked out by the ravens of the valley
and eaten by the vultures.
18 Three things are too wonderful for me;
four I do not understand:
19 the way of an eagle in the sky,
the way of a snake on a rock,

---

a Vg: Meaning of Heb uncertain **b** Meaning of Heb uncertain **c** Or *human fear* **d** Or *I am spent.* Meaning of Heb uncertain **e** Or *Holy One*

Birds of Prey · Proverbs 30:17

If this passage were literal, most of us would already be missing eyes or be eaten by vultures. Who hasn't at some point mocked their parents—if not to their faces, at least to their friends? And is there anyone who has not disobeyed a parent?

The vast majority of us are loved by our parents. Even if the parents you live with are stepparents, grandparents, or foster parents, they are most likely trying hard to do what is best for you. It doesn't always seem that way, but if we can accept this, it might be easier to forgive them their faults and overlook some of the things they do that irritate us.

Let's keep the vultures far away!

• What can you do to let your parents know you love them?

• What can you do today to show them more respect?

• If the situation with your parents is truly abusive or destructive, talk to a trusted pastor or teacher or call a help line. Although we are called to respect our parents, we are never called to live in abuse.

the way of a ship on the high seas,
  and the way of a man with a girl.

20 This is the way of an adulteress:
  she eats, and wipes her mouth,
  and says, "I have done no wrong."

21 Under three things the earth
    trembles;
  under four it cannot bear up:
22 a slave when he becomes king,
  and a fool when glutted with food;
23 an unloved woman when she gets a husband,
  and a maid when she succeeds her
    mistress.

24 Four things on earth are small,
  yet they are exceedingly wise:
25 the ants are a people without
    strength,
  yet they provide their food in the
    summer;
26 the badgers are a people without power,
  yet they make their homes in the rocks;
27 the locusts have no king,
  yet all of them march in rank;
28 the lizard*a* can be grasped in the hand,
  yet it is found in kings' palaces.

29 Three things are stately in their stride;
  four are stately in their gait:
30 the lion, which is mightiest among wild
    animals
  and does not turn back before any;
31 the strutting rooster,*b* the he-goat,
  and a king striding before*c* his people.

32 If you have been foolish, exalting yourself,
  or if you have been devising evil,
  put your hand on your mouth.
33 For as pressing milk produces curds,
  and pressing the nose produces blood,
  so pressing anger produces strife.

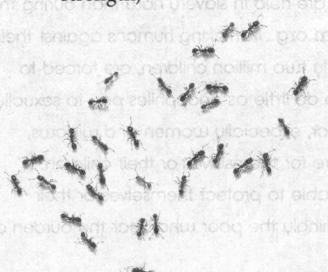

The Teaching of King Lemuel's Mother

31 The words of King Lemuel. An oracle that his mother taught him:

2 No, my son! No, son of my womb!

---

a Or *spider* *b* Gk Syr Tg Compare Vg: Meaning of Heb uncertain *c* Meaning of Heb uncertain

No, son of my vows!

3 Do not give your strength to women,
  your ways to those who destroy kings.

4 It is not for kings, O Lemuel,
  it is not for kings to drink wine,
  or for rulers to desire*a* strong drink;

5 or else they will drink and forget what has
    been decreed,
  and will pervert the rights of all the
    afflicted.

6 Give strong drink to one who is perishing,
  and wine to those in bitter distress;

7 let them drink and forget their poverty,
  and remember their misery no more.

8 Speak out for those who cannot speak,
  for the rights of all the destitute.*b*

9 Speak out, judge righteously,
  defend the rights of the poor and needy.

Ode to a Capable Wife

10 A capable wife who can find?

   She is far more precious than jewels.

11 The heart of her husband trusts in her,
   and he will have no lack of gain.

12 She does him good, and not harm,
   all the days of her life.

13 She seeks wool and flax,
   and works with willing hands.

14 She is like the ships of the merchant,
   she brings her food from far away.

15 She rises while it is still night
   and provides food for her household
   and tasks for her servant-girls.

16 She considers a field and buys it;
   with the fruit of her hands she plants a
     vineyard.

17 She girds herself with strength,
   and makes her arms strong.

18 She perceives that her merchandise is
     profitable.
   Her lamp does not go out at night.

19 She puts her hands to the distaff,

CONNECT IT!

Gary Haugen: International Justice Mission
Proverbs 31:8–9

Gary Haugen was a young attorney with degrees from Harvard and the University of Chicago who was sent by the U.S. Department of Justice to investigate the Rwandan genocide. He came face-to-face with unimaginable evil as he searched mass graves for evidence and heard the stories of victims. He was never the same after that.

Used to working with the law, Haugen saw the impact of lawlessness on people who had no power to speak out against it. **Proverbs 31:8–9** says, "Speak out for those who cannot speak, for the rights of the destitute. Speak out, judge righteously, defend the rights of the poor and needy." When Haugen returned to the United States, he began to do just that, forming International Justice Mission (IJM). IJM is committed to Christian beliefs and works as a human rights agency to secure justice for victims of slavery, sexual exploitation, and other forms of violent oppression. It works through local justice systems around the world to uphold laws that prosecute perpetrators and defend victims.

And the needs are great. More people, including children, are held in slavery now than during the entire transatlantic slave trade, according to IJM's website, **ijm.org**. Trafficking humans against their will is a $12 billion a year industry. Many slaves, including nearly two million children, are forced to work in the commercial sex industry. In many countries, police do little as pedophiles pay to sexually violate children. IJM also works to secure fair rights for the poor, especially women and widows, whose land rights are violated and who are left unable to care for themselves or their children.

"Often lacking access to their own justice systems and unable to protect themselves or their families from those more powerful," IJM says, "it is overwhelmingly the poor who bear the burden of these abuses." International Justice Mission fights for them.*

a Cn: Heb *where*   *b* Heb *all children of passing away*

STUDY IT!

A Woman's Place · Proverbs 31:10–31

You've probably noticed that women had a much different role in biblical times than they do now. Their place was usually in the home, raising a family, and doing household chores. At first glance the description of a capable wife in **Proverbs 31:10–31** can seem outdated and irrelevant to our modern times. After all, how many women do you know who "seek wool and flax" (Proverbs 31:13)? But a closer look shows a picture of a happy marriage and a strong family. The virtues of the husband and the wife are dependent on each other. They both work hard and are respected by others. And the values the wife displays are ones we appreciate today—she is strong, compassionate, successful, happy, and active. And above all, she fears the Lord.

and her hands hold the spindle.
20 She opens her hand to the poor,
and reaches out her hands to the needy.
21 She is not afraid for her household when it
snows,
for all her household are clothed in
crimson.
22 She makes herself coverings;
her clothing is fine linen and purple.
23 Her husband is known in the city gates,
taking his seat among the elders of the
land.
24 She makes linen garments and sells them;
she supplies the merchant with sashes.
25 Strength and dignity are her clothing,
and she laughs at the time to come.

26 She opens her mouth with wisdom,
and the teaching of kindness is on her
tongue.
27 She looks well to the ways of her household,
and does not eat the bread of idleness.
28 Her children rise up and call her
happy;
her husband too, and he praises her:
29 "Many women have done excellently,
but you surpass them all."
30 Charm is deceitful, and beauty is vain,
but a woman who fears the LORD is to be
praised.
31 Give her a share in the fruit of her hands,
and let her works praise her in the city
gates.

Ecclesiastes ▶▶▶▶▶▶

S ome of the phrases in the book of Ecclesiastes may make you think you're reading the handbook for Pessimists Anonymous:

There is nothing new under the sun. (Ecclesiastes 1:9)

For in much wisdom is much vexation, and those who increase knowledge increase sorrow. (Ecclesiastes 1:18)

For no one can anticipate the time of disaster. (Ecclesiastes 9:12)

Yet this book is hardly a defense of pessimism. The Teacher (identified as "Qoheleth" in Ecclesiastes 1:1) was pointing out to the Israelites the need for a new understanding of God and life.

IN DEPTH

The author of Ecclesiastes lived a long life of careful observation and was disturbed by many things: that wise people perished just like fools (Ecclesiastes 2:12-17); that those who worked hard for a living had to leave their possessions behind in death (Ecclesiastes 5:13-17); that bad people sometimes lived longer than good people (Ecclesiastes 7:15); and that the most deserving didn't always get what they had earned (Ecclesiastes 9:11-12).

Observing these puzzling things, the writer asked the obvious question: "Why should we work so hard to be wise and good?" For centuries, believers had struggled to be honest, law-abiding people in the hope of being rewarded by God. And what had they gotten? Sickness, suffering, and death—like everyone else! "Something's wrong!" the Teacher insisted. "Something's terribly wrong!"

The author of Ecclesiastes raised the question, but didn't provide an answer—there's not a convincing one to be found in other Old Testament writings either. However, later generations of Jews began to see things in a different light as they pondered the possibility of life after death, a concept that developed late in Jewish religion. Does God possibly reward the faithful in a life beyond the grave? For Christians, the New Testament answers that question with a resounding "yes."

The book of Ecclesiastes warns us against placing our trust in anything "under the sun"—it's all meaningless and leaves us unfulfilled. Instead, we must fear God and keep his commandments. In light of the New Testament, we can read Ecclesiastes knowing that Jesus came to a meaningless world in order to free us from it and bring meaning to life.

QUICK FACTS

- **Date Written:** Between 400 and 200 B.C.
- **Author:** An unknown scholar, although the book is attributed to King Solomon
- **Themes:** The lack of easy answers and the unfairness of life

AT A GLANCE

- **Ecclesiastes 1:1–6:9** Thoughts on life's difficulties, along with the Teacher's advice
- **Ecclesiastes 6:10–12:8** Thoughts on the future
- **Ecclesiastes 12:9–14** An editor's addition, affirming the Teacher's insights

Reflections of a Royal Philosopher

1 The words of the Teacher,[a] the son of David, king in Jerusalem.

2 Vanity of vanities, says the Teacher,[a]
   vanity of vanities! All is vanity.
3 What do people gain from all the toil
   at which they toil under the sun?
4 A generation goes, and a generation comes,
   but the earth remains forever.
5 The sun rises and the sun goes down,
   and hurries to the place where it rises.
6 The wind blows to the south,
   and goes around to the north;
round and round goes the wind,
   and on its circuits the wind returns.
7 All streams run to the sea,
   but the sea is not full;
to the place where the streams flow,
   there they continue to flow.
8 All things[b] are wearisome;
   more than one can express;
the eye is not satisfied with seeing,
   or the ear filled with hearing.
9 What has been is what will be,
   and what has been done is what will be done;
   there is nothing new under the sun.
10 Is there a thing of which it is said,
   "See, this is new"?
It has already been,
   in the ages before us.
11 The people of long ago are not remembered,
nor will there be any remembrance
   of people yet to come
by those who come after them.

The Futility of Seeking Wisdom

12 I, the Teacher,[a] when king over Israel in Jerusalem, 13 applied my mind to seek and to search out by wisdom all that is done under heaven; it is an unhappy business that God has given to human beings to be busy with. 14 I saw all the deeds that are done under the sun; and see, all is vanity and a chasing after wind.[c]

15 What is crooked cannot be made straight,
   and what is lacking cannot be counted.

16 I said to myself, "I have acquired great wisdom, surpassing all who were over Jerusalem before me; and my mind has had great experience of wisdom and knowledge." 17 And I applied my mind to know wisdom and to know madness and folly. I perceived that this also is but a chasing after wind.[c]

18 For in much wisdom is much vexation,
   and those who increase knowledge increase sorrow.

The Futility of Self-Indulgence

2 I said to myself, "Come now, I will make a test of pleasure; enjoy yourself." But again, this also was vanity. 2 I said of laughter, "It is mad," and of pleasure, "What use is it?" 3 I searched with my mind how to cheer my body with wine—my mind still guiding me with wisdom—and how to lay hold on folly, until I might see what was good

STUDY IT!

New and Improved! · Ecclesiastes 1:1–11

We like to think we are constantly improving our world. New and improved inventions, technologies, and ways of thinking and living are all making this a better world, right? The writer of Ecclesiastes disagrees. The writer looks back on history and forward to the future and sees the same problems continuing to exist. The same cycles of life and death and good and evil keep circling around. Ecclesiastes 1:9 says, "There is nothing new under the sun."

Sounds pretty hopeless, doesn't it? If everything is meaningless, why go on? But Ecclesiastes isn't meant to inspire hopelessness. In fact, we need to have a little bit of the attitude of the Teacher if we want to find the true source of contentment. Throughout Ecclesiastes, the writer invites us to enjoy what we have now, while keeping our focus on what will really last beyond this life. It's only in facing the reality that the things of this world are temporary that we can see the great value in pursuing things that are eternal.

---

a Heb Qoheleth, traditionally rendered Preacher   b Or words   c Or a feeding on wind. See Hos 12.1

for mortals to do under heaven during the few days of their life. [4]I made great works; I built houses and planted vineyards for myself; [5]I made myself gardens and parks, and planted in them all kinds of fruit trees. [6]I made myself pools from which to water the forest of growing trees. [7]I bought male and female slaves, and had slaves who were born in my house; I also had great possessions of herds and flocks, more than any who had been before me in Jerusalem. [8]I also gathered for myself silver and gold and the treasure of kings and of the provinces; I got singers, both men and women, and delights of the flesh, and many concubines.[a]

9 So I became great and surpassed all who were before me in Jerusalem; also my wisdom remained with me. [10]Whatever my eyes desired I did not keep from them; I kept my heart from no pleasure, for my heart found pleasure in all my toil, and this was my reward for all my toil. [11]Then I considered all that my hands had done and the toil I had spent in doing it, and again, all was vanity and a chasing after wind,[b] and there was nothing to be gained under the sun.

Wisdom and Joy Given to One Who Pleases God

12 So I turned to consider wisdom and madness and folly; for what can the one do who comes after the king? Only what has already been done. [13]Then I saw that wisdom excels folly as light excels darkness.
[14]   The wise have eyes in their head,
        but fools walk in darkness.

Yet I perceived that the same fate befalls all of them. [15]Then I said to myself, "What happens to the fool will happen to me also; why then have I been so very wise?" And I said to myself that this also is vanity. [16]For there is no enduring remembrance of the wise or of fools, seeing that in the days to come all will have been long forgotten. How can the wise die just like fools? [17]So I hated life, because what is done under the sun was grievous to me; for all is vanity and a chasing after wind.[b]

18 I hated all my toil in which I had toiled under the sun, seeing that I must leave it to those who come after me [19]—and who knows whether they will be wise or foolish? Yet they will be master of all for which I toiled and used my wisdom under the sun. This also is vanity. [20]So I turned and gave my heart up to despair concerning all the toil of my labors under the sun, [21]because sometimes one who has toiled with wisdom and knowledge and skill must leave all to be enjoyed by another who did not toil for it. This also is vanity and a great evil. [22]What do mortals get from all the toil and strain with which they toil under the sun? [23]For all their days are full of pain, and their work is a

PRAY IT!

The Balance of Life · Ecclesiastes 3:1–8

This passage, probably the most famous part of Ecclesiastes, reminds us that there is a time for everything. Some times are easier to handle than others, but God is faithful through everything. Pray this prayer as a reminder:

God of all seasons,
Help me to remember the sun when rain is falling.
Help me to remember the rain when the sun is shining.
When I win on the field, let me remember the times I lost.
When I lose on the field, let me remember the times I won.
Guide me to appreciate studying when I'm taking a hard test.
Guide me to appreciate hard tests when I'm studying.
During times with friends, remind me of times alone.
During times alone, remind me of times with friends.
Help me to live all moments and remember there is a balance to life.
Amen.

---

a Meaning of Heb uncertain   b Or *a feeding on wind.* See Hos 12.1

Dr. Robi Sonderegger: A Time to Heal · Ecclesiastes 3:1–8

Ecclesiastes 3 tells us there is a time for everything. Unfortunately, the horrors of war can last long past the fighting—especially when it's children who are being kidnapped, tortured, brainwashed, and forced to fight and kill as genocidal soldiers. That's what has been happening in certain areas of the world, including Uganda and Sudan. Psychologist Dr. Robi Sonderegger is doing something about it.

Based in Australia, Sonderegger and his partners go into war zones and walk refugees and trauma victims through steps of healing. Their efforts have helped thousands restore a time for hope and joy in childhood. "The world has been silent for far too long," Sonderegger says on his website, thefrontline.org. "It's about time we made some noise and became a voice for the children whose cries go unheard."* We can help make sure there's a time for healing for those who have experienced times of violence.

vexation; even at night their minds do not rest. This also is vanity.

24 There is nothing better for mortals than to eat and drink, and find enjoyment in their toil. This also, I saw, is from the hand of God; ^{25}for apart from him^a who can eat or who can have enjoyment? ^{26}For to the one who pleases him God gives wisdom and knowledge and joy; but to the sinner he gives the work of gathering and heaping, only to give to one who pleases God. This also is vanity and a chasing after wind.^{b}

Everything Has Its Time

3 For everything there is a season, and a time for every matter under heaven:

2 a time to be born, and a time to die;
  a time to plant, and a time to pluck up what is planted;
3 a time to kill, and a time to heal;
  a time to break down, and a time to build up;
4 a time to weep, and a time to laugh;
  a time to mourn, and a time to dance;
5 a time to throw away stones, and a time to gather stones together;
  a time to embrace, and a time to refrain from embracing;
6 a time to seek, and a time to lose;
  a time to keep, and a time to throw away;
7 a time to tear, and a time to sew;
  a time to keep silence, and a time to speak;
8 a time to love, and a time to hate;
  a time for war, and a time for peace.

The God-Given Task

9 What gain have the workers from their toil? ^{10}I have seen the business that God has given to everyone to be busy with. ^{11}He has made everything suitable for its time; moreover he has put a sense of past and future into their minds, yet they cannot find out what God has done from the beginning to the end. ^{12}I know that there is nothing better for them than to be happy and enjoy themselves as long as they live; ^{13}moreover, it is God's gift that all should eat and drink and take pleasure in all their toil. ^{14}I know that whatever God does endures forever; nothing can be added to it, nor anything taken from it; God has done this, so that all should stand in awe before him. ^{15}That which is, already has been; that which is to be, already is; and God seeks out what has gone by.^{c}

Judgment and the Future Belong to God

16 Moreover I saw under the sun that in the place of justice, wickedness was there, and in the place of righteousness, wickedness was there as well. ^{17}I said in my heart, God will judge the righteous and the wicked, for he has appointed a time for every matter, and for every work. ^{18}I said in my heart with regard to human beings that God is testing them to show that they are but animals. ^{19}For the fate of humans and the fate of animals is the same; as one dies, so dies the other. They all have the same breath, and humans have no advantage over the animals; for all is vanity. ^{20}All go to one place; all are from the dust, and all turn to dust again. ^{21}Who knows whether the human spirit goes upward and the spirit of ani-

a Gk Syr: Heb apart from me b Or a feeding on wind. See Hos 12.1 c Heb what is pursued mals goes downward to the earth? [22]So I saw that there is nothing better than that all should enjoy their work, for that is their lot; who can bring them to see what will be after them?

4 Again I saw all the oppressions that are practiced under the sun. Look, the tears of the oppressed—with no one to comfort them! On the side of their oppressors there was power—with no one to comfort them. [2]And I thought the dead, who have already died, more fortunate than the living, who are still alive; [3]but better than both is the one who has not yet been, and has not seen the evil deeds that are done under the sun.

4 Then I saw that all toil and all skill in work come from one person's envy of another. This also is vanity and a chasing after wind.[a]

5 Fools fold their hands
 and consume their own flesh.

6 Better is a handful with quiet
 than two handfuls with toil,
 and a chasing after wind.[a]

7 Again, I saw vanity under the sun: [8]the case of solitary individuals, without sons or brothers; yet there is no end to all their toil, and their eyes are never satisfied with riches. "For whom am I toiling," they ask, "and depriving myself of pleasure?" This also is vanity and an unhappy business.

The Value of a Friend

9 Two are better than one, because they have a good reward for their toil. [10]For if they fall, one will lift up the other; but woe to one who is alone and falls and does not have another to help. [11]Again, if two lie together, they keep warm; but how can one keep warm alone? [12]And though one might prevail against another, two will withstand one. A threefold cord is not quickly broken.

13 Better is a poor but wise youth than an old but foolish king, who will no longer take advice. [14]One can indeed come out of prison to reign, even though born poor in the kingdom. [15]I saw all the living who, moving about under the sun, follow that[b] youth who replaced the king;[c] [16]there was no end to all those people whom he led. Yet those who come later will not rejoice in him. Surely this also is vanity and a chasing after wind.[a]

5 **Reverence, Humility, and Contentment**

[d] Guard your steps when you go to the house of God; to draw near to listen is better than the sacrifice offered by fools; for they do not know how to keep from doing evil.[e] [2f]Never be rash with your mouth, nor let your heart be quick to utter a word before God, for God is in heaven, and you upon earth; therefore let your words be few.

3 For dreams come with many cares, and a fool's voice with many words.

4 When you make a vow to God, do not delay fulfilling it; for he has no pleasure in fools. Fulfill what you vow. [5]It is better that you should not vow than that you should vow and not fulfill it. [6]Do not let your mouth lead you into sin, and do not say before the messenger that it was a mistake; why should God be angry at your words, and destroy the work of your hands?

7 With many dreams come vanities and a multitude of words;[g] but fear God.

8 If you see in a province the oppression of the poor and the violation of justice and right, do not be amazed at the matter; for the high official is watched by a higher, and there are yet higher ones over them. [9]But all things considered, this is an advantage for a land: a king for a plowed field.[g]

10 The lover of money will not be satisfied with money; nor the lover of wealth, with gain. This also is vanity.

11 When goods increase, those who eat them increase; and what gain has their owner but to see them with his eyes?

12 Sweet is the sleep of laborers, whether they eat little or much; but the surfeit of the rich will not let them sleep.

13 There is a grievous ill that I have seen under the sun: riches were kept by their owners to their hurt, [14]and those riches were lost in a bad venture; though they are parents of children, they have nothing in their hands. [15]As they came from their mother's womb, so

> "Two are better than one, because they have a good reward for their toil. For if they fall, one will lift up the other."
> —Ecclesiastes 4:9–10

---

a Or *a feeding on wind*. See Hos 12.1 b Heb *the second* c Heb *him* d Ch 4.17 in Heb e Cn: Heb *they do not know how to do evil* f Ch 5.1 in Heb
g Meaning of Heb uncertain

LIVE IT!

How Much Is Enough?
Ecclesiastes 5:10

How much wealth does one person need? Most young people reply in surveys that they want just enough money to be happy. It's an interesting answer—they are implying they don't want to be greedy, but that it takes money to be happy!

According to the Teacher in **Ecclesiastes 5:10**, those who love money will always want more. What is God trying to tell us here? Maybe that real happiness is not found in material wealth. The more we want, the less satisfied we are. Money can be an evil when it's all we want and think about.

- For a week, try to do things with your family and friends that don't cost anything. Play board games. Go for walks or hikes. Even volunteer some time at a community organization.
- Think about what makes these times together great, even when no money is required.
- Consider taking the money you save and donating it to a charity.

---

they shall go again, naked as they came; they shall take nothing for their toil, which they may carry away with their hands. [16]This also is a grievous ill: just as they came, so shall they go; and what gain do they have from toiling for the wind? [17]Besides, all their days they eat in darkness, in much vexation and sickness and resentment.

18 This is what I have seen to be good: it is fitting to eat and drink and find enjoyment in all the toil with which one toils under the sun the few days of the life God gives us; for this is our lot. [19]Likewise all to whom God gives wealth and possessions and whom he enables to enjoy them, and to accept their lot and find enjoyment in their toil—this is the gift of God. [20]For they will scarcely brood over the days of their lives, because God keeps them occupied with the joy of their hearts.

6

The Frustration of Desires

There is an evil that I have seen under the sun, and it lies heavy upon humankind: [2]those to whom God gives wealth, possessions, and honor, so that they lack nothing of all that they desire, yet God does not enable them to enjoy these things, but a stranger enjoys them. This is vanity; it is a grievous ill. [3]A man may beget a hundred children, and live many years; but however many are the days of his years, if he does not enjoy life's good things, or has no burial, I say that a stillborn child is better off than he. [4]For it comes into vanity and goes into darkness, and in darkness its name is covered; [5]moreover it has not seen the sun or known anything; yet it finds rest rather than he. [6]Even though he should live a thousand years twice over, yet enjoy no good—do not all go to one place?

7 All human toil is for the mouth, yet the appetite is not satisfied. [8]For what advantage have the wise over fools? And what do the poor have who know how to conduct themselves before the living? [9]Better is the sight of the eyes than the wandering of desire; this also is vanity and a chasing after wind.[a]

10 Whatever has come to be has already been named, and it is known what human beings are, and that they are not able to dispute with those who are stronger. [11]The more words, the more vanity, so how is one the better? [12]For who knows what is good for mortals while they live the few days of their vain life, which they pass like a shadow? For who can tell them what will be after them under the sun?

7

A Disillusioned View of Life

A good name is better than precious
        ointment,
   and the day of death, than the day of birth.
2   It is better to go to the house of mourning
        than to go to the house of feasting;
   for this is the end of everyone,
        and the living will lay it to heart.
3   Sorrow is better than laughter,
        for by sadness of countenance the heart is
        made glad.
4   The heart of the wise is in the house of
        mourning;
        but the heart of fools is in the house of
        mirth.
5   It is better to hear the rebuke of the wise
        than to hear the song of fools.
6   For like the crackling of thorns under a pot,

a Or *a feeding on wind*. See Hos 12.1

so is the laughter of fools;
    this also is vanity.

7 Surely oppression makes the wise foolish,
    and a bribe corrupts the heart.
8 Better is the end of a thing than its beginning;
    the patient in spirit are better than the
        proud in spirit.
9 Do not be quick to anger,
    for anger lodges in the bosom of fools.
10 Do not say, "Why were the former days better
        than these?"
    For it is not from wisdom that you ask this.
11 Wisdom is as good as an inheritance,
    an advantage to those who see the sun.
12 For the protection of wisdom is like the
        protection of money,
    and the advantage of knowledge is that
        wisdom gives life to the one who
        possesses it.
13 Consider the work of God;
    who can make straight what he has made
        crooked?

14 In the day of prosperity be joyful, and in the day of adversity consider; God has made the one as well as the other, so that mortals may not find out anything that will come after them.

The Riddles of Life

15 In my vain life I have seen everything; there are righteous people who perish in their righteousness, and there are wicked people who prolong their life in their evildoing. [16]Do not be too righteous, and do not act too wise; why should you destroy yourself? [17]Do not be too wicked, and do not be a fool; why should you die before your time? [18]It is good that you should take hold of the one, without letting go of the other; for the one who fears God shall succeed with both.

19 Wisdom gives strength to the wise more than ten rulers that are in a city.

20 Surely there is no one on earth so righteous as to do good without ever sinning.

21 Do not give heed to everything that people say, or you may hear your servant cursing you; [22]your heart knows that many times you have yourself cursed others.

23 All this I have tested by wisdom; I said, "I will be wise," but it was far from me. [24]That which is, is far off, and deep, very deep; who can find it out? [25]I turned my mind to know and to search out and to seek wisdom and the sum of things, and to know that wickedness is folly and that foolishness is madness. [26]I found more bitter than death the woman who is a trap, whose heart is snares and nets, whose hands are fetters; one who pleases God escapes her, but the sinner is taken by her. [27]See, this is what I found, says the Teacher,[a] adding one thing to another to find the sum, [28]which my mind has sought repeatedly, but I have not found. One man among a thousand I found, but a woman among all these I have not found. [29]See, this alone I found, that God made human beings straightforward, but they have devised many schemes.

Obey the King and Enjoy Yourself

8 Who is like the wise man?
    And who knows the interpretation of a
        thing?
Wisdom makes one's face shine,
    and the hardness of one's countenance is
        changed.

2 Keep[b] the king's command because of your sacred oath. [3]Do not be terrified; go from his presence, do not delay when the matter is unpleasant, for he does whatever he pleases. [4]For the word of the king is powerful, and who can say to him, "What are you doing?" [5]Whoever obeys a command will meet no harm, and the wise mind will know the time and way. [6]For every matter has its time and way, although the troubles of mortals lie heavy upon them. [7]Indeed, they do not know what is to be, for who can tell them how it will be? [8]No one has power over the wind[c] to restrain the wind,[c] or power over the day of death; there is no discharge from the battle, nor does wickedness deliver those who practice it. [9]All this I observed, applying my mind to all that is done under the sun, while one person exercises authority over another to the other's hurt.

God's Ways Are Inscrutable

10 Then I saw the wicked buried; they used to go in and out of the holy place, and were praised in the city where they had done such things.[d] This also is vanity. [11]Because sentence against an evil deed is not executed speedily, the human heart is fully set to do evil. [12]Though sinners do evil a hundred times and prolong their lives, yet I know that it will be well with those who fear God, because they stand in fear before him, [13]but it will not be

---

a Qoheleth, traditionally rendered Preacher   b Heb I keep   c Or breath   d Meaning of Heb uncertain

well with the wicked, neither will they prolong their days like a shadow, because they do not stand in fear before God.

14 There is a vanity that takes place on earth, that there are righteous people who are treated according to the conduct of the wicked, and there are wicked people who are treated according to the conduct of the righteous. I said that this also is vanity. ¹⁵So I commend enjoyment, for there is nothing better for people under the sun than to eat, and drink, and enjoy themselves, for this will go with them in their toil through the days of life that God gives them under the sun.

16 When I applied my mind to know wisdom, and to see the business that is done on earth, how one's eyes see sleep neither day nor night, ¹⁷then I saw all the work of God, that no one can find out what is happening under the sun. However much they may toil in seeking, they will not find it out; even though those who are wise claim to know, they cannot find it out.

STUDY IT!

Imagine There's No Heaven
Ecclesiastes 9:5

Some people assume that the ancient Israelites believed in an afterlife as we do today. However, Ecclesiastes speaks of the end of earthly life without any hint of eternal life: "The dead know nothing; they have no more reward, and even the memory of them is lost" (Ecclesiastes 9:5). The book reflects the author's belief that all life ends with death. It was not until the last two centuries before Jesus that the idea of life after death began to take root among the Jewish people.

9   Take Life as It Comes

All this I laid to heart, examining it all, how the righteous and the wise and their deeds are in the hand of God; whether it is love or hate one does not know. Everything that confronts them ²is vanity,^a since the same fate comes to all, to the righteous and the wicked, to the good and the evil,^b to the clean and the unclean, to those who sacrifice and those who do not sacrifice. As are the good, so are the sinners; those who swear are like those who shun an oath. ³This is an evil in all that happens under the sun, that the same fate comes to everyone. Moreover, the hearts of all are full of evil; madness is in their hearts while they live, and after that they go to the dead. ⁴But whoever is joined with all the living has hope, for a living dog is better than a dead lion. ⁵The living know that they will die, but the dead know nothing; they have no more reward, and even the memory of them is lost. ⁶Their love and their hate and their envy have already perished; never again will they have any share in all that happens under the sun.

7 Go, eat your bread with enjoyment, and drink your wine with a merry heart; for God has long ago approved what you do. ⁸Let your garments always be white; do not let oil be lacking on your head. ⁹Enjoy life with the wife whom you love, all the days of your vain life that are given you under the sun, because that is your portion in life and in your toil at which you toil under the sun. ¹⁰Whatever your hand finds to do, do with your might; for there is no work or thought or knowledge or wisdom in Sheol, to which you are going.

11 Again I saw that under the sun the race is not to the swift, nor the battle to the strong, nor bread to the wise, nor riches to the intelligent, nor favor to the skillful; but time and chance happen to them all. ¹²For no one can anticipate the time of disaster. Like fish taken in a cruel net, and like birds caught in a snare, so mortals are snared at a time of calamity, when it suddenly falls upon them.

Wisdom Superior to Folly

13 I have also seen this example of wisdom under the sun, and it seemed great to me. ¹⁴There was a little city with few people in it. A great king came against it and besieged it, building great siegeworks against it. ¹⁵Now there was found in it a poor wise man, and he by his wisdom delivered the city. Yet no one remembered that poor man. ¹⁶So I said, "Wisdom is better than might; yet the poor man's wisdom is despised, and his words are not heeded."

17   The quiet words of the wise are more to be heeded
        than the shouting of a ruler among fools.
18   Wisdom is better than weapons of war,
        but one bungler destroys much good.

---

a Syr Compare Gk: Heb *Everything that confronts them* ²*is everything*   b Gk Syr Vg: Heb lacks *and the evil*

10 Miscellaneous Observations

Dead flies make the perfumer's ointment
give off a foul odor;
so a little folly outweighs wisdom and
honor.

2 The heart of the wise inclines to the right,
but the heart of a fool to the left.

3 Even when fools walk on the road, they lack
sense,
and show to everyone that they are fools.

4 If the anger of the ruler rises against you, do
not leave your post,
for calmness will undo great offenses.

5 There is an evil that I have seen under the sun,
as great an error as if it proceeded from the ruler:
6 folly is set in many high places, and the rich sit in
a low place. 7 I have seen slaves on horseback, and
princes walking on foot like slaves.

8 Whoever digs a pit will fall into it;
and whoever breaks through a wall will be
bitten by a snake.

9 Whoever quarries stones will be hurt by them;
and whoever splits logs will be endangered
by them.

10 If the iron is blunt, and one does not whet the
edge,
then more strength must be
exerted;
but wisdom helps one to succeed.

11 If the snake bites before it is charmed,
there is no advantage in a charmer.

12 Words spoken by the wise bring them favor,
but the lips of fools consume them.

13 The words of their mouths begin in
foolishness,
and their talk ends in wicked madness;

14 yet fools talk on and on.
No one knows what is to happen,
and who can tell anyone what the future
holds?

15 The toil of fools wears them out,
for they do not even know the way to
town.

16 Alas for you, O land, when your king is a
servant,[a]
and your princes feast in the morning!

17 Happy are you, O land, when your king is a
nobleman,

and your princes feast at the proper time—
for strength, and not for drunkenness!

18 Through sloth the roof sinks in,
and through indolence the house leaks.

19 Feasts are made for laughter;
wine gladdens life,
and money meets every need.

20 Do not curse the king, even in your thoughts,
or curse the rich, even in your bedroom;
for a bird of the air may carry your voice,
or some winged creature tell the matter.

11 The Value of Diligence

Send out your bread upon the waters,
for after many days you will get it
back.

2 Divide your means seven ways, or even eight,
for you do not know what disaster may
happen on earth.

3 When clouds are full,
they empty rain on the earth;
whether a tree falls to the south or to the
north,
in the place where the tree falls, there it
will lie.

4 Whoever observes the wind will not sow;
and whoever regards the clouds will not
reap.

5 Just as you do not know how the breath comes
to the bones in the mother's womb, so you do not
know the work of God, who makes everything.

6 In the morning sow your seed, and at evening
do not let your hands be idle; for you do not know
which will prosper, this or that, or whether both
alike will be good.

Youth and Old Age

7 Light is sweet, and it is pleasant for the eyes to
see the sun.

8 Even those who live many years should rejoice

a Or a child

"Carpe Diem"—Seize the Day! · Ecclesiastes 11:7–10

"Youth is wasted on the young." You might have heard that statement uttered by someone struggling with growing older. But there is some truth in it. It's easy to take for granted life as we know it. Many young people don't reflect on life or pause to appreciate being young.

Ecclesiastes says some beautiful and profound things about youthfulness. Its advice to young people is: "Follow the inclination of your heart" (Ecclesiastes 11:9) and "Banish anxiety from your mind" (Ecclesiastes 11:10). Today the advice might be: "Follow your heart, and don't spend so much time worrying." These verses also remind young people that God will hold them accountable for what they do, but still it encourages the enjoyment of youth. It's a blessing to be young, to have so much energy and so many dreams. There are many pressures and stresses on young people today, but don't let them dominate your life. Enjoy this special time of growth and discovery.

It's good to be young. Seize the day!

---

in them all; yet let them remember that the days of darkness will be many. All that comes is vanity.

9 Rejoice, young man, while you are young, and let your heart cheer you in the days of your youth. Follow the inclination of your heart and the desire of your eyes, but know that for all these things God will bring you into judgment.

10 Banish anxiety from your mind, and put away pain from your body; for youth and the dawn of life are vanity.

12 Remember your creator in the days of your youth, before the days of trouble come, and the years draw near when you will say, "I have no pleasure in them"; ²before the sun and the light and the moon and the stars are darkened and the clouds return with*ᵃ* the rain; ³in the day when the guards of the house tremble, and the strong men are bent, and the women who grind cease working because they are few, and those who look through the windows see dimly; ⁴when the doors on the street are shut, and the sound of the grinding is low, and one rises up at the sound of a bird, and all the daughters of song are brought low; ⁵when one is afraid of heights, and terrors are in the road; the almond tree blossoms, the grasshopper drags itself along*ᵇ* and desire fails; because all must go to their eternal home, and the mourners will go about the streets; ⁶before the silver cord is snapped,*ᶜ* and the golden bowl is broken, and the pitcher is broken at the fountain, and the wheel broken at the cistern, ⁷and the dust returns to the earth as it was, and the breath*ᵈ* returns to God who

Remember the Elderly
Ecclesiastes 12:1–8

To understand this bittersweet poem about the difficulties of the aging process, you need to be aware of the metaphors used:

- Guards of the house = arms and hands
- Strong men = legs
- Women who grind = teeth
- Windows = eyes
- Doors = ears or lips
- Silver cord, golden bowl = life itself

Aging is a natural part of life, but it can be a struggle. No one enjoys its accompanying loss of mobility, loss of strength, and problems with seeing and hearing. The struggle is even greater if one is alone.

If you have aging grandparents, family friends, or neighbors, keep in mind how much they need to be noticed by you. Stay in touch with them, so you can learn from their wisdom and so they can be strengthened by your youth!

---

a Or *after*; Heb *'ahar* **b** Or *is a burden* **c** Syr Vg Compare Gk: Heb *is removed* **d** Or *the spirit* gave it. [8]Vanity of vanities, says the Teacher;[a] all is vanity.

Epilogue

9 Besides being wise, the Teacher[a] also taught the people knowledge, weighing and studying and arranging many proverbs. [10]The Teacher[a] sought to find pleasing words, and he wrote words of truth plainly.

11 The sayings of the wise are like goads, and like nails firmly fixed are the collected sayings that are given by one shepherd.[b] [12]Of anything beyond these, my child, beware. Of making many books there is no end, and much study is a weariness of the flesh.

13 The end of the matter; all has been heard. Fear God, and keep his commandments; for that is the whole duty of everyone. [14]For God will bring every deed into judgment, including[c] every secret thing, whether good or evil.

a *Qoheleth,* traditionally rendered *Preacher* b Meaning of Heb uncertain c Or *into the judgment on*

Song of Solomon

Sex sells. When we see an ad with a beautiful woman slipping out of a sports car or a sculpted guy grabbing an ice-cold soda, we sit up and take notice. Advertisers love to take advantage of our fascination with sex. Once they have our attention, they can sell us something we might not even be interested in! The Song of Solomon—a collection of ancient love poems—reminds us that this powerful force is ultimately a gift from God.

IN DEPTH

The Song of Solomon is a well-kept secret. Are you aware of its explicit sexual images? Consider these verses:

Let him kiss me with the kisses of his mouth! (Song of Solomon 1:2)

Your lips distill nectar, my bride; honey and milk are under your tongue. (Song of Solomon 4:11)

May your breasts be like clusters of the vine, and the scent of your breath like apples. (Song of Solomon 7:8)

Some people find these images so surprising that they wonder why the Song of Solomon is found in the Bible at all.

Scholars believe that the naming of King Solomon in the first verse is the main reason this book was preserved and eventually included with the Jewish scriptures. Although written long after Solomon's death, this book—like Proverbs and Ecclesiastes—was attributed to him to give it authority.

Some people through the centuries have not been able to accept the Song of Solomon as simply love poetry and have hunted for a deeper meaning. Many people believe that the lover and the beloved in this book stand for Israel and God or for Jesus and the Church. Modern-day scholars, however, begin their interpretation of the Song of Solomon at the literal level—a collection of love poems. The book's inclusion among the other holy books is an affirmation of the goodness of human sexuality; human love is holy because it is a gift from God. The passion and beauty of human sexual attraction is a reflection of the passion and beauty of God's love for us!

QUICK FACTS

- **Date Written:** Probably after the Jews' return from the Babylonian exile in 538 B.C.
- **Author:** Unknown, but the book is often attributed to King Solomon because of his renowned marriages (see 1 Kings 11:3)
- **Theme:** The goodness and passion of human love
- **Noteworthy:** In other translations, it is called the Song of Songs or the Canticle of Canticles (the title in Hebrew means "the greatest song").

AT A GLANCE

- **Song of Solomon 1:1–2:7** Opening dialogue between the two lovers
- **Song of Solomon 2:8–8:4** Various reflections on human love and other dialogues
- **Song of Solomon 8:5–14** Final thoughts

The Song of Songs, which is Solomon's.

Colloquy of Bride and Friends

2 Let him kiss me with the kisses of his mouth!
  For your love is better than wine,
3   your anointing oils are fragrant,
  your name is perfume poured out;
    therefore the maidens love you.
4 Draw me after you, let us make haste.
    The king has brought me into his chambers.
  We will exult and rejoice in you;
    we will extol your love more than wine;
    rightly do they love you.

5 I am black and beautiful,
    O daughters of Jerusalem,
  like the tents of Kedar,
    like the curtains of Solomon.
6 Do not gaze at me because I am dark,
    because the sun has gazed on me.
  My mother's sons were angry with me;
    they made me keeper of the vineyards,
    but my own vineyard I have not kept!
7 Tell me, you whom my soul loves,
    where you pasture your flock,
    where you make it lie down at noon;
  for why should I be like one who is veiled
    beside the flocks of your companions?

8 If you do not know,
    O fairest among women,
  follow the tracks of the flock,
    and pasture your kids
    beside the shepherds' tents.

Colloquy of Bridegroom, Friends, and Bride

9 I compare you, my love,
    to a mare among Pharaoh's chariots.

10 Your cheeks are comely with ornaments,
    your neck with strings of jewels.
11 We will make you ornaments of gold,
    studded with silver.

12 While the king was on his couch,
    my nard gave forth its fragrance.
13 My beloved is to me a bag of myrrh
    that lies between my breasts.
14 My beloved is to me a cluster of henna
    blossoms
    in the vineyards of En-gedi.
15 Ah, you are beautiful, my love;
    ah, you are beautiful;
    your eyes are doves.
16 Ah, you are beautiful, my beloved,
    truly lovely.
  Our couch is green;
17   the beams of our house are cedar,
    our rafters[a] are pine.

    I am a rose[b] of Sharon,
    a lily of the valleys.
2 As a lily among brambles,
    so is my love among maidens.
3 As an apple tree among the trees of the wood,
    so is my beloved among young men.
  With great delight I sat in his shadow,
    and his fruit was sweet to my taste.
4 He brought me to the banqueting house,
    and his intention toward me was love.
5 Sustain me with raisins,
    refresh me with apples;
    for I am faint with love.
6 O that his left hand were under my head,
    and that his right hand embraced me!

STUDY IT!

Romantic Love · Song of Solomon 1

The book opens with the words of two lovers expressing their passion (the bride in Song of Solomon 1:2-8 and the groom in Song of Solomon 1:9-17). Their exchange is a picture of the good gifts God has given us in both spiritual and physical intimacy. Romantic, playful love was created by God for us to enjoy. The way we express such love can bring joy and delight; it also can devastate and destroy if it is disrespected and abused. Be careful with love. God gave us our sexuality as a gift, not as a weapon.

---

a Meaning of Heb uncertain b Heb crocus

The Illusion of Pornography · Song of Solomon 2

Pornography is all around us, on websites, in magazines, videos, and phone apps. Unfortunately, there's a good chance you've seen porn even if you didn't want to. It's natural to be both curious and excited by sex. The pornography industry knows this. Pornography strips away love and human intimacy from sex. It twists and exploits God's sacred gift by objectifying and degrading people. And it preys on people, especially males who are sexually excited visually, but also anyone who is lonely and searching for love, acceptance, or excitement.

The Song of Solomon is about passion and sexual longing between a bride and a bridegroom. Their love is committed: "My beloved is mine and I am his" (Song of Solomon 2:16). Their love is at once both urgent and patient: "Draw me after you, let us make haste" (Song of Solomon 1:4); "Do not stir up or awaken love until it is ready" (Song of Solomon 2:7). This is not the kind of love offered in pornography, which has nothing at all to do with real love.

If you find yourself snared by pornography, take these steps:

- Break free of its shame and secrecy by talking to a trusted Christian adult who is the same gender as you. Confess your sin and possible addiction, and ask for accountability and help.
- Get rid of any porn you own, and use software or other digital tools to beat temptation by avoiding and blocking it.
- Memorize scripture to combat temptation and replace pornographic images in your head.
- Pray and ask for help. God created sex and wants to help you be free to enjoy it fully in marriage.

---

7 I adjure you, O daughters of Jerusalem,
　　by the gazelles or the wild does:
do not stir up or awaken love
　　until it is ready!

Springtime Rhapsody

8 The voice of my beloved!
　　Look, he comes,
leaping upon the mountains,
　　bounding over the hills.
9 My beloved is like a gazelle
　　or a young stag.
Look, there he stands
　　behind our wall,
gazing in at the windows,
　　looking through the lattice.
10 My beloved speaks and says to me:
"Arise, my love, my fair one,
　　and come away;
11 for now the winter is past,
　　the rain is over and gone.
12 The flowers appear on the earth;
　　the time of singing has come,

and the voice of the turtledove
　　is heard in our land.
13 The fig tree puts forth its figs,
　　and the vines are in blossom;
　　they give forth fragrance.
Arise, my love, my fair one,
　　and come away.
14 O my dove, in the clefts of the rock,
　　in the covert of the cliff,
let me see your face,
　　let me hear your voice;
for your voice is sweet,
　　and your face is lovely.
15 Catch us the foxes,
　　the little foxes,
that ruin the vineyards—
　　for our vineyards are in blossom."
16 My beloved is mine and I am his;
　　he pastures his flock among the
　　　　lilies.
17 Until the day breathes
　　and the shadows flee,

turn, my beloved, be like a gazelle
    or a young stag on the cleft mountains.*a*

3 Love's Dream

Upon my bed at night
    I sought him whom my soul loves;
I sought him, but found him not;
    I called him, but he gave no
        answer.*b*
2 "I will rise now and go about the city,
    in the streets and in the squares;
I will seek him whom my soul loves."
    I sought him, but found him not.
3 The sentinels found me,
    as they went about in the city.
"Have you seen him whom my soul loves?"
4 Scarcely had I passed them,
    when I found him whom my soul loves.
I held him, and would not let him go
    until I brought him into my mother's
        house,
    and into the chamber of her that
        conceived me.
5 I adjure you, O daughters of Jerusalem,
    by the gazelles or the wild does:
do not stir up or awaken love
    until it is ready!

The Groom and His Party Approach

6 What is that coming up from the wilderness,
    like a column of smoke,
perfumed with myrrh and frankincense,
    with all the fragrant powders of the
        merchant?
7 Look, it is the litter of Solomon!
Around it are sixty mighty men
    of the mighty men of Israel,
8 all equipped with swords
    and expert in war,
each with his sword at his thigh
    because of alarms by night.
9 King Solomon made himself a palanquin
    from the wood of Lebanon.
10 He made its posts of silver,
    its back of gold, its seat of purple;
its interior was inlaid with love.*c*
    Daughters of Jerusalem,
11 come out.
Look, O daughters of Zion,
    at King Solomon,

at the crown with which his mother
      crowned him
on the day of his wedding,
    on the day of the gladness of his heart.

4 The Bride's Beauty Extolled

How beautiful you are, my love,
    how very beautiful!
Your eyes are doves
    behind your veil.
Your hair is like a flock of goats,
    moving down the slopes of Gilead.

CONNECT IT!

Eric and Leslie Ludy: Love Writers
Song of Solomon 3:5

Got questions about relationships, love, and sex? Has the Song of Solomon gotten you wondering what else the Bible has to say about these topics? Struggling with ways to talk to your boyfriend or girlfriend about physical issues? Where do you turn for answers? Advice columns and love stories fill magazines, TV shows, and websites, but many of their answers leave you asking more questions and searching for deeper answers. That's where Eric and Leslie Ludy come in.

The couple are bestselling authors and speakers, and their books answer tough questions and give biblical guidance to those seeking godly relationships. (Their most widely known book is WHEN GOD WRITES YOUR LOVE STORY.) Through their books and ministry, the Ludys challenge and encourage young adults to pursue holiness in every aspect of their lives. Through that pursuit comes a relationship with God that impacts every other relationship you have. That relationship with God allows you to be patient and "not stir up or awaken love until it is ready" (Song of Solomon 3:5), because instead of trying to make love happen, you are trusting God's timing.

---

a Or *on the mountains of Bether*; meaning of Heb uncertain   **b** Gk: Heb lacks this line   **c** Meaning of Heb uncertain

2 Your teeth are like a flock of shorn ewes
    that have come up from the washing,
all of which bear twins,
    and not one among them is bereaved.
3 Your lips are like a crimson thread,
    and your mouth is lovely.
Your cheeks are like halves of a pomegranate
    behind your veil.
4 Your neck is like the tower of David,
    built in courses;
on it hang a thousand bucklers,
    all of them shields of warriors.
5 Your two breasts are like two fawns,
    twins of a gazelle,
    that feed among the lilies.
6 Until the day breathes
    and the shadows flee,
I will hasten to the mountain of myrrh
    and the hill of frankincense.
7 You are altogether beautiful, my love;
    there is no flaw in you.
8 Come with me from Lebanon, my bride;
    come with me from Lebanon.
Depart*a* from the peak of Amana,
    from the peak of Senir and Hermon,
from the dens of lions,
    from the mountains of leopards.

9 You have ravished my heart, my sister, my
      bride,
    you have ravished my heart with a glance
      of your eyes,
    with one jewel of your necklace.
10 How sweet is your love, my sister, my bride!
    how much better is your love than wine,
    and the fragrance of your oils than any
      spice!
11 Your lips distill nectar, my bride;
    honey and milk are under your tongue;
    the scent of your garments is like the scent
      of Lebanon.
12 A garden locked is my sister, my bride,
    a garden locked, a fountain sealed.
13 Your channel*b* is an orchard of pomegranates
    with all choicest fruits,
    henna with nard,
14 nard and saffron, calamus and cinnamon,
    with all trees of frankincense,
myrrh and aloes,
    with all chief spices—

15 a garden fountain, a well of living water,
    and flowing streams from Lebanon.
16 Awake, O north wind,
    and come, O south wind!
Blow upon my garden
    that its fragrance may be wafted abroad.
Let my beloved come to his garden,
    and eat its choicest fruits.

5

    I come to my garden, my sister, my
      bride;
    I gather my myrrh with my spice,
I eat my honeycomb with my honey,
I drink my wine with my milk.

Eat, friends, drink,
    and be drunk with love.

Another Dream

2 I slept, but my heart was awake.
Listen! my beloved is knocking.
"Open to me, my sister, my love,
    my dove, my perfect one;
for my head is wet with dew,
    my locks with the drops of the night."
3 I had put off my garment;
    how could I put it on again?
I had bathed my feet;
    how could I soil them?
4 My beloved thrust his hand into the opening,
    and my inmost being yearned for him.
5 I arose to open to my beloved,
    and my hands dripped with myrrh,
my fingers with liquid myrrh,
    upon the handles of the bolt.
6 I opened to my beloved,
    but my beloved had turned and was gone.
My soul failed me when he spoke.

a Or *Look* *b* Meaning of Heb uncertain

Sexuality and Communication · Song of Solomon 2–7

Some of the love songs included in the Song of Solomon are addressed to the bridegroom and others to the beloved. It's as if a romantic dialogue has been recorded of lovers pouring out the depths of their feeling and desire for each other.

Communication is an essential part of any relationship. Open and honest dialogue maintains and deepens the bonds of respect, friendship, and love.

Are you in a dating relationship? Ask yourself this: Is it possible for the two of you to speak honestly with each other about anything—especially problems and difficulties? Are you willing and able to discuss all dimensions of your love—including sexual feelings, desires, boundaries, and standards?

Young couples often avoid such sensitive or embarrassing conversations and move through physical affection into sexual activity without considering the impact or consequences. Many important things are often left unsaid. Such failure to communicate can result in regret, hurt feelings, misunderstandings, and even behaviors that can lead to manipulation, selfishness, and sin.

Don't be afraid to discuss sexual issues. Always be ready to examine the nature of your relationships in the light of God's Word, especially when the power and passion of sexuality are present. True sexual love is rooted in dialogue, honest communication, and commitment. And its fullest expression is found only in the context of marriage.

I sought him, but did not find him;
    I called him, but he gave no answer.
7 Making their rounds in the city
    the sentinels found me;
they beat me, they wounded me,
    they took away my mantle,
    those sentinels of the walls.
8 I adjure you, O daughters of Jerusalem,
    if you find my beloved,
tell him this:
    I am faint with love.

Colloquy of Friends and Bride

9 What is your beloved more than another
      beloved,
    O fairest among women?
What is your beloved more than another
      beloved,
    that you thus adjure us?

10 My beloved is all radiant and ruddy,
    distinguished among ten thousand.
11 His head is the finest gold;
    his locks are wavy,
    black as a raven.

12 His eyes are like doves
    beside springs of water,
bathed in milk,
    fitly set.[a]
13 His cheeks are like beds of spices,
    yielding fragrance.
His lips are lilies,
    distilling liquid myrrh.
14 His arms are rounded gold,
    set with jewels.
His body is ivory work,[a]
    encrusted with sapphires.[b]
15 His legs are alabaster columns,
    set upon bases of gold.
His appearance is like Lebanon,
    choice as the cedars.
16 His speech is most sweet,
    and he is altogether desirable.
This is my beloved and this is my friend,
    O daughters of Jerusalem.

6   Where has your beloved gone,
      O fairest among women?
      Which way has your beloved turned,
    that we may seek him with you?

a Meaning of Heb uncertain   b Heb *lapis lazuli*

2 My beloved has gone down to his garden,
    to the beds of spices,
to pasture his flock in the gardens,
    and to gather lilies.
3 I am my beloved's and my beloved is mine;
    he pastures his flock among the lilies.

The Bride's Matchless Beauty

4 You are beautiful as Tirzah, my love,
    comely as Jerusalem,
    terrible as an army with banners.
5 Turn away your eyes from me,
    for they overwhelm me!
Your hair is like a flock of goats,
    moving down the slopes of Gilead.
6 Your teeth are like a flock of ewes,
    that have come up from the
        washing;
all of them bear twins,
    and not one among them is bereaved.
7 Your cheeks are like halves of a pomegranate
    behind your veil.
8 There are sixty queens and eighty
        concubines,
    and maidens without number.
9 My dove, my perfect one, is the only one,
    the darling of her mother,

flawless to her that bore her.
The maidens saw her and called her happy;
    the queens and concubines also, and they
        praised her.
10 "Who is this that looks forth like the dawn,
    fair as the moon, bright as the sun,
    terrible as an army with banners?"

11 I went down to the nut orchard,
    to look at the blossoms of the valley,
to see whether the vines had budded,
    whether the pomegranates were in bloom.
12 Before I was aware, my fancy set me
    in a chariot beside my prince.*a*

13*b* Return, return, O Shulammite!
    Return, return, that we may look
        upon you.

Why should you look upon the Shulammite,
    as upon a dance before two armies?*c*

7   Expressions of Praise

How graceful are your feet in sandals,
    O queenly maiden!
Your rounded thighs are like jewels,
    the work of a master hand.

STUDY IT!

Sex in the Old Testament · Song of Solomon 7:1–9

Through its descriptive sexual content (as seen in these verses), the Song of Solomon has surprised many generations of readers. It reminds us that one of the richest images in the Old Testament is a sexual one: God as the faithful lover of Israel. We hear of God's jealous love for God's people (Exodus 20:5). By the time of the early prophets, the image of God as lover was fully developed: "On that day, says the LORD, you will call me, 'My husband'" (Hosea 2:16).

Because of ancient Israel's conviction that human love reflects divine love—and vice versa—there was a high regard for human sexuality. This regard was reflected in Israel's sexual morality. Free-for-all sex stood in clear contradiction to the holiness of God, whose faithful love was the model for all human love. The Ten Commandments prohibit not only having sex with someone else's spouse, but also desiring someone else's spouse (see Exodus 20:14, 17).

Despite these high standards, some Bible stories do not comment on the morality of behavior that would be unacceptable today. They make no comment on the many patriarchs and kings who had more than one wife and take for granted the inferior status of women in marriage. Because moral insights developed over the centuries, we must remember to read biblical passages in light of the whole Bible and the Christian tradition. We can be inspired by the descriptions of God's love in the Old Testament while holding true to the moral requirements of the New Testament.

a Cn: Meaning of Heb uncertain   *b* Ch 7.1 in Heb   *c* Or *dance of Mahanaim*

2 Your navel is a rounded bowl
   that never lacks mixed wine.
Your belly is a heap of wheat,
   encircled with lilies.
3 Your two breasts are like two fawns,
   twins of a gazelle.
4 Your neck is like an ivory tower.
Your eyes are pools in Heshbon,
   by the gate of Bath-rabbim.
Your nose is like a tower of Lebanon,
   overlooking Damascus.
5 Your head crowns you like Carmel,
   and your flowing locks are like purple;
   a king is held captive in the tresses.*a*

6 How fair and pleasant you are,
   O loved one, delectable maiden!*b*
7 You are stately*c* as a palm tree,
   and your breasts are like its clusters.
8 I say I will climb the palm tree
   and lay hold of its branches.
O may your breasts be like clusters of the vine,
   and the scent of your breath like apples,
9 and your kisses*d* like the best wine
   that goes down*e* smoothly,
   gliding over lips and teeth.*f*

10 I am my beloved's,
   and his desire is for me.
11 Come, my beloved,
   let us go forth into the fields,
   and lodge in the villages;
12 let us go out early to the vineyards,
   and see whether the vines have budded,
whether the grape blossoms have opened
   and the pomegranates are in bloom.
There I will give you my love.
13 The mandrakes give forth fragrance,
   and over our doors are all choice fruits,
new as well as old,
   which I have laid up for you, O my
      beloved.

8

   O that you were like a brother to me,
      who nursed at my mother's breast!
      If I met you outside, I would kiss you,
   and no one would despise me.
2 I would lead you and bring you
   into the house of my mother,
   and into the chamber of the one who
      bore me.*g*

I would give you spiced wine to drink,
   the juice of my pomegranates.
3 O that his left hand were under my head,
   and that his right hand embraced me!
4 I adjure you, O daughters of Jerusalem,
   do not stir up or awaken love
   until it is ready!

Homecoming
5 Who is that coming up from the wilderness,
   leaning upon her beloved?

Under the apple tree I awakened you.
There your mother was in labor with you;
   there she who bore you was in
      labor.

PRAY IT!

Divine Love
Song of Solomon 8:6–7

God loves us passionately and seeks us with the enthusiasm of a lover who memorizes every detail and cherishes every moment. If you look at human love as a reflection of divine love, then parts of this love poem could be understood as prayer. Try reading parts of it as your words to God and other parts as God's words to you. Look at these sections:

• **Song of Solomon 2:2–6:** A prayer describing your passion for God
• **Song of Solomon 5:6–8:** A prayer to God when God seems absent
• **Song of Solomon 8:6–7:** God's words of love to you

The words may seem strange in this context, but if we're passionate about pursuing a human relationship, why can't we be passionate about pursuing our relationship with God? Some of the greatest saints expressed their love of God as a passionate, romantic love. You can do the same in your prayer with God!

---

a Meaning of Heb uncertain *b* Syr: Heb *in delights* *c* Heb *This your stature is* *d* Heb *palate* *e* Heb *down for my lover* *f* Gk Syr Vg: Heb *lips of sleepers* *g* Gk Syr: Heb *my mother; she (or you) will teach me*

6 Set me as a seal upon your heart,
   as a seal upon your arm;
   for love is strong as death,
   passion fierce as the grave.
   Its flashes are flashes of fire,
   a raging flame.
7 Many waters cannot quench love,
   neither can floods drown it.
   If one offered for love
   all the wealth of one's house,
   it would be utterly scorned.

8 We have a little sister,
   and she has no breasts.
   What shall we do for our sister,
   on the day when she is spoken for?
9 If she is a wall,
   we will build upon her a battlement of
   silver;
   but if she is a door,
   we will enclose her with boards of cedar.

10 I was a wall,
   and my breasts were like towers;
   then I was in his eyes
   as one who brings*a* peace.
11 Solomon had a vineyard at Baal-hamon;
   he entrusted the vineyard to keepers;
   each one was to bring for its fruit a
   thousand pieces of silver.
12 My vineyard, my very own, is for myself;
   you, O Solomon, may have the thousand,
   and the keepers of the fruit two hundred!

13 O you who dwell in the gardens,
   my companions are listening for your
   voice;
   let me hear it.

14 Make haste, my beloved,
   and be like a gazelle
   or a young stag
   upon the mountains of spices!

a Or *finds*

Introduction to the
Prophets

Who inspires you? Who challenges you to make changes in your life and gives you hope for the future? We all need someone who is not afraid to speak God's truth and challenge our choices. Is there someone like that in your life? Then you've encountered a modern-day prophet—a person who speaks the word of God into your life. In this section of the Old Testament, you will meet the prophets of the Bible—unique and courageous people who did this for ancient Israel.

IN DEPTH

What is a prophet? A prophet is a person—or sometimes a group—who speaks for God. The prophet's words spoken in God's name—usually called prophecies or oracles—are God's words. Some people think prophets can predict the future, but this is not their role in the Bible. The biblical prophets were called by God during times of crisis to offer God's people challenge or comfort, depending on their circumstances. To really understand biblical prophecies, we've got to understand the historical situation God was addressing through the prophets.

Through the prophets' inspired messages, God reminded the Israelites of the covenant God had made with them (see "Introduction to the Pentateuch," p. 2). If the people or their leaders were not keeping their part of the covenant, the prophets challenged them to do so. If the people were in despair that God was not keeping God's part of the covenant, the prophets promised that God would. Here are some common covenant themes the prophets emphasized:

• **Warnings against idolatry.** The Israelites were constantly tempted to worship the gods of other nations and cultures. The prophets had to keep reminding the kings and people of the first law of the Ten Commandments: "I am the Lord your God, who brought you out of the land of Egypt, out of the house of slavery; you shall have no other gods before me" (Exodus 20:2-3).

• **Warnings to act justly and to treat the poor fairly.** In their greed and struggle for power, the wealthy and the ruling class often cheated and oppressed other people. Operating as Israel's conscience, the prophets were unanimous in challenging Israel to act justly and to care for the poor and marginalized. This did not always make the prophets popular with the kings and the ruling class—they were often ridiculed and even threatened with violence.

• **Attempts to deepen the understanding of God's love and mercy.** Some Israelites felt God would not forgive them after Israel (the northern kingdom) and Judah (the southern kingdom) were conquered by foreign nations. The prophets assured them they would receive God's forgiveness if they turned to God and kept the covenant. In addition, some of the prophets began to teach that God cared for and was Lord over all nations, not just Israel.

• **Promises of hope for the future.** During these troubled and often violent times, it must have seemed to many Israelites that their world was coming to an end. The prophets responded to the people's despair with hope-filled promises that ultimately God's love and justice would prevail. These hopeful prophecies took different forms: the coming of the ideal ruler or king, the restoration of Jerusalem and the temple, a time of judgment when good is rewarded and evil punished, and so on.

The stories of the earliest prophets—Samuel, Nathan, Elijah, and Elisha—are in the Bible's historical books of 1 and 2 Samuel and 1 and 2 Kings. God's revelation through the later prophets is recorded in the books of this section of the Bible. The introduction to each book in this section gives background about the historical situation the prophet faced. The Expanded Timeline of Biblical History, p. 1368, identifies the time period for each prophet, and the chart "Prophets and Kings (1050-571 B.C.)," p. 680, shows the prophets and reigning kings before the fall of Jerusalem (587 B.C.).

As you read these books, keep this in mind: the role of prophets has not disappeared, only changed. In every age, there are people who challenge us to be faithful to God and remind us about God's faithful love for us. In fact, Christians believe that through their baptism God calls them to be priest, prophet, and king. You can fulfill your prophetic calling by challenging others to live justly and reminding them of God's love. It's exciting and humbling to be called into such a tradition.

OTHER BACKGROUND

- Isaiah, Jeremiah, and Ezekiel are sometimes called the major prophets, because their books are long.

- Hosea, Amos, Jeremiah, First Isaiah, Obadiah, Micah, Nahum, Habakkuk, and Zephaniah prophesied before the Babylonian exile.

- Ezekiel, Second Isaiah, and Lamentations are set during the exile.

- Joel, Haggai, Zechariah, Malachi, and Third Isaiah prophesied after the exile.

- Seven of the prophets talk about the "day of the LORD"—a final time of God's judgment when evil will be punished.

Prophets and Kings (1050–571 B.C.)

The Hebrew prophets proclaimed the will of God as the highest authority for honor and morality. The kings were anointed to lead the people according to the covenant values of justice and worship of the one true God. Some kings were great sages, brave warriors, and brilliant statesmen. Others were idolatrous despots who abandoned their call in favor of power and lust. The scripture writers of the ancient world hailed or condemned their kings based on how they heeded the word of God offered by the prophets. (All dates are approximate.)

Prophets	Kings of the United Monarchy	
Samuel (1050-1030): Last judge, first prophet (1 Sam. 3:20; 10:1; 16:13)	**Saul (1020-1000):** Warrior of the tribe of Benjamin who contained the Philistines, but disobeyed the Lord's command (1 Sam. 9:1–2, 15–16; 13:10–14)	
Gad (995): Counselor to David (1 Sam. 22:5; 2 Sam. 24:11–19)	**David (1000-961):** Greatest king of Israel; hero, warrior, man of repentance and faith; husband of Bathsheba, father of Solomon (1 Sam. 16:1–1 Kings 2:11)	
Nathan (975): Seer of David and Solomon; revealed the temple and the dynasty of David (2 Sam. 7:12–13, 17; 12:1–15; 1 Chron. 29:29; 2 Chron. 9:29)	**Solomon (961-931):** Son of David and Bathsheba renowned for his great wisdom, wealth, and power, but also idolatry; built the temple, but also imposed heavy taxes and forced labor (1 Kings 1:1–11:43)	

	Kings of Judah	Kings of Israel
Ahijah (924): Seer of Shiloh who, upon meeting Jeroboam, tore his cloak into twelve pieces to symbolize the civil war and the reign of Jeroboam as king of Israel (1 Kings 11:29–35)	**Rehoboam (922-915):** Idolatrous son of Solomon; increased taxation, which caused the northern tribes to secede, forming the two kingdoms of Israel and Judah (1 Kings 12:1–25)	**Jeroboam (922-901):** Israelite king who worshiped the golden calves of Samaria (1 Kings 12:26–28; 14:20)
	Abijam (915-913): Idolatrous son of Rehoboam who continued his father's war against Jeroboam (1 Kings 14:31–15:8)	**Nadab (901-900):** Idolatrous son of Jeroboam (1 Kings 15:25–31)
	Asa (913-873): Loyal son of Abijam; faithful to God (1 Kings 15:8–24)	**Baasha (900-877):** Built citadels and honored idols in Tirzah (1 Kings 15:33–34)
Jehu (902-884): Israelite prophet, son of Hanani, who condemned Baasha's idolatry and murder of Nadab (1 Kings 16:7)	**Jehoshaphat (873-849):** Diplomatic son of Asa who worked for peace with Israel (1 Kings 22:41–51)	**Elah (877-876):** Son of Baasha, murdered by his servant Zimri (1 Kings 16:8–14)
	Jehoram (Joram; 849-842): Serial murderer; son of Jehoshaphat; married Athaliah (842–837), daughter of Ahab and Jezebel (2 Kings 8:16–24)	**Zimri (876):** Charioteer who murdered Elah, his family, and himself (1 Kings 16:9–20)
		Omri (876-869): Commander and first king of the Omride dynasty (1 Kings 16:15–28)
Elijah (865-842): Israelite wonder worker (1 Kings 17:7–24); defeated the prophets of Baal and Asherah and reinstated worship of Yahweh (1 Kings 18:36–40); defeated the sons of Ahab and Jezebel (1 Kings 17:1); made Elisha his successor; taken to heaven in a fiery chariot (2 Kings 2:11–15)	**Ahaziah (842):** Son of Jehoram and Athaliah (842–837); killed by Jehu (2 Kings 8:25; 9:29; 11:1–20)	**Ahab (869-850):** King who, along with Jezebel, served Baal, offered human sacrifice, and killed the prophets of God (1 Kings 16:28–22:40)
	Athaliah (842-837): Daughter of Jezebel and Ahab and wife of Jehoram; made herself queen after death of Ahaziah (2 Kings 11:1–20)	**Ahaziah (850-849):** Son of Ahab and Jezebel (1 Kings 22:52–53); a devotee of Baalzebub, god of Ekron; death prophesied by Elijah (2 Kings 1:2–18)
	Joash (Jehoash; 837-800): Son of Ahaziah who survived the murderous reign of Athaliah, protected by his aunt Jehosheba; murdered by his servants (2 Kings 11:1–12:21)	**Jehoram (Joram; 849-842):** Son of Ahab, brother-in-law of Jehoram of Judah, who succeeded Ahaziah on the throne (2 Kings 3:1); the last of the Omride dynasty (2 Kings 1:1–18)

Prophets	Kings of Judah	Kings of Israel
Elisha (850-800): Israelite prophet and miracle worker who served Elijah and followed as his successor (1 Kings 19:19–21; 2 Kings 2:9–22); miraculously provided the poor with oil and bread, cured the leper, astounded the proud, raised the dead, offered hope, and anointed kings (2 Kings 4:1–5:27)	**Amaziah (800-783):** Son of Joash who took the throne after his father's murder (2 Kings 14:1–20)	**Jehu (842-815):** Defeated the house of Ahab and removed Baal of Tyre from Israel; worshiped the golden calves of Samaria (2 Kings 9:1–10:36)
		Jehoahaz (815-801): Warring king who mixed worship of Yahweh with worship of false gods (2 Kings 13:1–9)
Amos (760-740): Farm laborer from Judah who prophesied in the northern kingdom, Israel (Amos 7:14–15), condemning treatment of workers (Amos 5:7–17)	**Uzziah (Azariah; 783-742):** Faithful son of Amaziah who came to rule at age sixteen; reign was stable and victorious (2 Kings 14:21; 15:1–7)	**Jehoash (Joash; 801-786):** Son of Jehoahaz who persisted in the sins begun by Jeroboam; an adversary of Amaziah, king of Judah (2 Kings 13:10–13)
		Jeroboam II (786-746): A prosperous and unjust king; worshiped the golden calves of Samaria (2 Kings 14:23–29)
	Jotham (742-735): Regent for eight years, then king; left the high places intact (2 Kings 15:32–38)	**Zechariah (746-745):** The last in the line of Jehu whose six-month rule was marked by injustice (2 Kings 15:8–12)
Hosea (750-732): A northern kingdom prophet whose marriage to the adulterous Gomer became an allegory for the love of God for the unfaithful Israel (Hos. 3:1)		**Shallum (745):** Murdered Zechariah and was assassinated within one month (2 Kings 15:10–15)
Isaiah of Jerusalem (742-700): Mystic who lived with a prophetess wife; served in the temple of Jerusalem as Assyria pillaged Israel (Isa. 6:1–13; 8:3); revealed the birth of a child, Immanuel, who would save Israel (Isa. 7:14; 8:6–10)	**Ahaz (735-715):** Idolatrous king who sacrificed his own son to Molech; practiced Canaanite rites on the high places; refused to join the anti-Assyrian alliance and became an Assyrian vassal (2 Kings 16:1–20)	**Menahem (745-738):** Much-hated puppet ruler of the Assyrians who killed Shallum (2 Kings 15:14–22)
		Pekahiah (738-737): Pro-Assyrian son of Menahem who escalated the war (2 Kings 15:22–26)
		Pekah (737-732): Became king after killing Pekahiah; joined Damascus, Tyre, and Philistia against Assyria (2 Kings 15:25–31)

Prophet of the Assyrian Destruction

Micah (720-701): Judahite who prophesied the Assyrian conquest of the northern kingdom and taught that sin hides the truth and leads to economic collapse and war (Mic. 1:1; 2:1–10); envisioned a new Israel and foretold of the royal shepherd of Bethlehem who would bring peace to the earth (Mic. 4:1–7; 5:1–4)

Hoshea (732-724): Son of Elah, vassal to Shalmaneser of Assyria, but refused to pay the annual tribute; imprisoned and exiled with the Samarian people (2 Kings 17:1–6); last king of Israel

Prophets of Judah

Kings of Judah after the Assyrian Destruction of Israel

Zephaniah (640-609): Served in Jerusalem during the reign of Josiah (Zeph. 1:1–18; 3:14–20)

Hezekiah (715-687): Son of Ahaz; faithful ruler who healed ancient wounds; dug the tunnel of Siloam to protect the city's water supply from the Assyrians (2 Kings 18:1–20:21)

Nahum (612): Prophesied the destruction of Nineveh (Nah. 1:1–6)

Manasseh (687-642): Sacrificed his son to Baal and was taken captive by Assyria (2 Chron. 33:1–25; 2 Kings 21:1–18)

Amon (642-640): Evil adulterer who was murdered (2 Kings 21:19–26)

Jeremiah (626-582): Called to be a prophet as a child; advised the king and identified the Babylonian destruction and exile as sin (Jer. 1:1–10; 26:1–16)

Josiah (640-609): Great reformer who renewed the covenant and restored the temple (2 Kings 21:26–23:30)

Jehoahaz (609): Idolatrous son of Josiah who reigned three months, then was taken prisoner by Pharaoh Neco; died in Egypt (2 Kings 23:30–33)

Habakkuk (609-598): Revealed God's lament over Judah's sin (Heb. 2:1–20)

Jehoiakim (609-598): Son of Josiah named Eliakim; at age twenty-five renamed Jehoiakim by Pharaoh Neco and made king of Judah and vassal to Egypt (2 Kings 23:33–37)

Jehoiachin (597): Son of Jehoiakim; exiled to Babylon (2 Kings 24:6–16; 25:27–30)

Ezekiel (593-571): Israelite prophet in exile in Babylon whose strange visions warn of Jerusalem's fall (Ezek. 4:1–24:27)

Zedekiah (Mattaniah; 597-587): Jehoiachin's uncle; his family murdered and his eyes gouged out by Nebuchadnezzar; led to Babylon in chains and died in the shame of exile (2 Kings 24:17–25:11; Jer. 52:1–11); the last preexilic king of Judah

Isaiah ▸▸▸▸▸▸▸▸▸▸▸▸▸▸▸▸▸▸▸▸▸▸▸▸▸▸▸▸▸▸▸▸▸

Remember when Christmas morning seemed as though it would never come? The magic of the season was alive and well in your youthful imagination. That gift under the tree was calling you to rip off the paper. The good smells from the kitchen made your stomach rumble. You were wired with excited anticipation. Now imagine that you'd been waiting for this day for thousands of years. The words of Isaiah tell the Israelites of the coming of Jesus, the Messiah, God's ultimate gift given on Christmas Day.

IN DEPTH

The book of Isaiah was written by prophets from three different periods in Israel's history. Chapters 1-39 reflect the prophecies of the original Isaiah, called First Isaiah. His career began with his call in the temple during the reign of Uzziah around 742 B.C. (See the chart "Prophets and Kings (1050-571 B.C.)," p. 680.) First Isaiah advised the kings of Judah about the dangers of alliances with foreign nations and cautioned them to trust only in God. He cried out against the social injustices of the rich ruling class against the poor and taught that God had a plan for rich and poor, powerful and oppressed. First Isaiah is responsible for the messianic prophecies, which tell of the coming of a perfect king.

Years later, when Israel was exiled in Babylon (587–538 B.C.), another prophet, Second Isaiah, reworked First Isaiah's prophecies to address his own people (Isaiah 40–55). Second Isaiah's people were struggling to understand why God allowed them to be captives in a strange land. The prophet comforted them with a hopeful message. They had been taken captive so that they would turn away from their sinful practices. Now that they had learned their lesson, God would let them return to rebuild Israel. Contained in this prophet's writings are the famous servant songs (see "Study It: The Servant Leader," near Isaiah 42:1-7).

After the Israelites returned from exile and resettled in Judah (538–500 B.C.), they once again fell into patterns of social injustice and religious apathy. Third Isaiah responded by demanding that they practice justice toward one another, and even toward the Gentiles (non-Jews; Isaiah 56-66). Realizing that Israel would never be a perfect community, he spoke of "new heavens and a new earth" (Isaiah 65:17), where people would live according to God's plan.

QUICK FACTS

- **Dates Covered:** First Isaiah, before the Babylonian exile (742-700 B.C.); Second Isaiah, during the exile (587-538 B.C.); Third Isaiah, after the exile (538-500 B.C.)
- **Authors:** The three prophets known as Isaiah or their followers
- **Themes:** The importance of faithfulness to God; justice for the poor; hope for the future and messianic prophecies; and God as Lord over all nations

AT A GLANCE

- **Isaiah 1–39** First Isaiah; covering events during the kingdom of Judah
- **Isaiah 40–55** Second Isaiah; covering events during the Babylonian exile
- **Isaiah 56–66** Third Isaiah; covering events during the restoration of Judah

1 The vision of Isaiah son of Amoz, which he saw concerning Judah and Jerusalem in the days of Uzziah, Jotham, Ahaz, and Hezekiah, kings of Judah.

The Wickedness of Judah

2 Hear, O heavens, and listen, O earth;
  for the LORD has spoken:
I reared children and brought them up,
  but they have rebelled against me.
3 The ox knows its owner,
  and the donkey its master's crib;
but Israel does not know,
  my people do not understand.

4 Ah, sinful nation,
  people laden with iniquity,
offspring who do evil,
  children who deal corruptly,
who have forsaken the LORD,
  who have despised the Holy One of Israel,
  who are utterly estranged!

5 Why do you seek further beatings?
  Why do you continue to rebel?
The whole head is sick,
  and the whole heart faint.
6 From the sole of the foot even to the head,
  there is no soundness in it,

but bruises and sores
  and bleeding wounds;
they have not been drained, or bound up,
  or softened with oil.

7 Your country lies desolate,
  your cities are burned with fire;
in your very presence
  aliens devour your land;
  it is desolate, as overthrown by foreigners.
8 And daughter Zion is left
  like a booth in a vineyard,
like a shelter in a cucumber field,
  like a besieged city.
9 If the LORD of hosts
  had not left us a few survivors,
we would have been like Sodom,
  and become like Gomorrah.

10 Hear the word of the LORD,
  you rulers of Sodom!
Listen to the teaching of our God,
  you people of Gomorrah!
11 What to me is the multitude of your sacrifices?
  says the LORD;
I have had enough of burnt offerings of rams
  and the fat of fed beasts;
I do not delight in the blood of bulls,
  or of lambs, or of goats.

LIVE IT!

Empty Worship · Isaiah 1:10–20

It's easy to get caught up in the activities of worship, such as going to church, youth group, Bible study, or singing along to the songs without really thinking about them. The Israelites did. They were busy making sacrifices and going through the motions of ritual worship. But Isaiah says religious practices that are not grounded in justice, sincerity, and good deeds are meaningless and empty. God wants genuine change, not just ritual worship. Speaking for God, Isaiah calls the people to do good, seek justice, rescue the oppressed, and defend the orphans and the widows (Isaiah 1:17).

How can we do this today? By befriending the outcast at school; volunteering our time to serve those in need; speaking out against those who persecute, demean, or ridicule; educating ourselves about the plight of those who suffer; and praying for the poor, oppressed, orphaned, and widowed in our world.

• How do you actively seek justice and take care of people in need?
• Make a plan to do one thing in the next week that shows sincere worship as described in these verses. Choose an action from the list above and dedicate it to God with a silent prayer before or after you do it.

12 When you come to appear before me,^a
  who asked this from your hand?
  Trample my courts no more;
13 bringing offerings is futile;
  incense is an abomination to me.
  New moon and sabbath and calling of
    convocation—
  I cannot endure solemn assemblies with
    iniquity.
14 Your new moons and your appointed
    festivals
  my soul hates;
  they have become a burden to me,
  I am weary of bearing them.
15 When you stretch out your hands,
  I will hide my eyes from you;
  even though you make many prayers,
  I will not listen;
  your hands are full of blood.
16 Wash yourselves; make yourselves clean;
  remove the evil of your doings
    from before my eyes;
  cease to do evil,
17   learn to do good;
  seek justice,
  rescue the oppressed,
  defend the orphan,
  plead for the widow.

18 Come now, let us argue it out,
  says the LORD:
  though your sins are like scarlet,
  they shall be like snow;
  though they are red like crimson,
  they shall become like wool.
19 If you are willing and obedient,
  you shall eat the good of the land;
20 but if you refuse and rebel,
  you shall be devoured by the sword;
  for the mouth of the LORD has
    spoken.

The Degenerate City
21 How the faithful city
  has become a whore!
  She that was full of justice,
  righteousness lodged in her—
  but now murderers!
22 Your silver has become dross,
  your wine is mixed with water.

23 Your princes are rebels
  and companions of thieves.
  Everyone loves a bribe
  and runs after gifts.
  They do not defend the orphan,
  and the widow's cause does not come
    before them.

24 Therefore says the Sovereign, the LORD of
    hosts, the Mighty One of Israel:
  Ah, I will pour out my wrath on my enemies,
  and avenge myself on my foes!
25 I will turn my hand against you;
  I will smelt away your dross as with lye
  and remove all your alloy.
26 And I will restore your judges as at the first,
  and your counselors as at the beginning.
  Afterward you shall be called the city of
    righteousness,
  the faithful city.

27 Zion shall be redeemed by justice,
  and those in her who repent, by
    righteousness.
28 But rebels and sinners shall be destroyed
    together,
  and those who forsake the LORD shall be
    consumed.
29 For you shall be ashamed of the oaks
  in which you delighted;
  and you shall blush for the gardens
  that you have chosen.
30 For you shall be like an oak
  whose leaf withers,
  and like a garden without water.
31 The strong shall become like tinder,
  and their work^b like a spark;
  they and their work shall burn together,
  with no one to quench them.

The Future House of God

2 The word that Isaiah son of Amoz saw
  concerning Judah and Jerusalem.

2 In days to come
  the mountain of the LORD's house
  shall be established as the highest of the
    mountains,
  and shall be raised above the hills;
  all the nations shall stream to it.

a Or *see my face* b Or *its makers*

LIVE IT!

From Violence to Love · Isaiah 2:1–5

What exactly is a plowshare? A plowshare is a tool that farmers use to prepare fields for planting. And the picture of beating swords into plowshares is one of peace. Instead of tools of violence (swords), a world of peace needs only tools to feed and nourish its people (plowshares).

Our society often glorifies violence, weapons, battle, and war. Take a few minutes to reflect and journal on the following questions:

- Why does our society glorify violence?
- How do your actions support violence or nonviolence?
- What violent images do you frequently see in media? How can you limit those in your life?
- What nonviolent actions can you take when you find yourself in conflict situations? (Some examples might be walking away from the situation, remaining calm, and asking for help to work out the problem.)

3 Many peoples shall come and say,
"Come, let us go up to the mountain of the
    Lord,
    to the house of the God of Jacob;
that he may teach us his ways
    and that we may walk in his paths."
For out of Zion shall go forth instruction,
    and the word of the Lord from Jerusalem.
4 He shall judge between the nations,
    and shall arbitrate for many peoples;
they shall beat their swords into plowshares,
    and their spears into pruning hooks;
nation shall not lift up sword against nation,
    neither shall they learn war any more.

Judgment Pronounced on Arrogance
5 O house of Jacob,
    come, let us walk
    in the light of the Lord!
6 For you have forsaken the ways of[a] your
        people,
    O house of Jacob.
Indeed they are full of diviners[b] from the east
    and of soothsayers like the Philistines,
    and they clasp hands with foreigners.
7 Their land is filled with silver and gold,
    and there is no end to their treasures;
their land is filled with horses,
    and there is no end to their chariots.
8 Their land is filled with idols;
    they bow down to the work of their hands,
    to what their own fingers have made.

9 And so people are humbled,
    and everyone is brought low—
    do not forgive them!
10 Enter into the rock,
    and hide in the dust
    from the terror of the Lord,
    and from the glory of his majesty.
11 The haughty eyes of people shall be
            brought low,
    and the pride of everyone shall be
            humbled;
and the Lord alone will be exalted on
        that day.
12 For the Lord of hosts has a day
        against all that is proud and lofty,
        against all that is lifted up and high;[c]
13 against all the cedars of Lebanon,
        lofty and lifted up;
    and against all the oaks of Bashan;
14 against all the high mountains,
        and against all the lofty hills;
15 against every high tower,
        and against every fortified wall;
16 against all the ships of Tarshish,
        and against all the beautiful craft.[d]
17 The haughtiness of people shall be humbled,
        and the pride of everyone shall be
            brought low;
        and the Lord alone will be exalted on
            that day.
18 The idols shall utterly pass away.
19 Enter the caves of the rocks

a Heb lacks *the ways of*   b Cn: Heb lacks *of diviners*   c Cn Compare Gk: Heb *low*   d Compare Gk: Meaning of Heb uncertain

and the holes of the ground,
  from the terror of the LORD,
    and from the glory of his majesty,
      when he rises to terrify the earth.
20 On that day people will throw away
    to the moles and to the bats
  their idols of silver and their idols of gold,
    which they made for themselves to
      worship,
21 to enter the caverns of the rocks
    and the clefts in the crags,
  from the terror of the LORD,
    and from the glory of his majesty,
      when he rises to terrify the earth.
22 Turn away from mortals,
    who have only breath in their nostrils,
    for of what account are they?

3 For now the Sovereign, the LORD of
      hosts,
    is taking away from Jerusalem and from
      Judah
  support and staff—
    all support of bread,
    and all support of water—
2   warrior and soldier,
      judge and prophet,
      diviner and elder,
3   captain of fifty
      and dignitary,
    counselor and skillful magician
      and expert enchanter.
4 And I will make boys their princes,
    and babes shall rule over them.
5 The people will be oppressed,
    everyone by another
    and everyone by a neighbor;
  the youth will be insolent to the elder,
    and the base to the honorable.

6 Someone will even seize a relative,
    a member of the clan, saying,
  "You have a cloak;
    you shall be our leader,
  and this heap of ruins
    shall be under your rule."
7 But the other will cry out on that day, saying,
  "I will not be a healer;
    in my house there is neither bread nor
      cloak;
  you shall not make me

leader of the people."
8 For Jerusalem has stumbled
    and Judah has fallen,
  because their speech and their deeds are
      against the LORD,
    defying his glorious presence.
9 The look on their faces bears witness against
      them;
    they proclaim their sin like Sodom,
    they do not hide it.
  Woe to them!
    For they have brought evil on themselves.
10 Tell the innocent how fortunate they are,
    for they shall eat the fruit of their labors.
11 Woe to the guilty! How unfortunate they are,
    for what their hands have done shall be
      done to them.
12 My people—children are their oppressors,
    and women rule over them.
  O my people, your leaders mislead you,
    and confuse the course of your paths.

13 The LORD rises to argue his case;
    he stands to judge the peoples.
14 The LORD enters into judgment
    with the elders and princes of his people:
  It is you who have devoured the vineyard;
    the spoil of the poor is in your houses.
15 What do you mean by crushing my people,
    by grinding the face of the poor? says the
      Lord GOD of hosts.

16 The LORD said:
  Because the daughters of Zion are haughty
    and walk with outstretched necks,
    glancing wantonly with their eyes,
  mincing along as they go,
    tinkling with their feet;
17 the Lord will afflict with scabs
    the heads of the daughters of Zion,
    and the LORD will lay bare their secret
      parts.

18 In that day the Lord will take away the finery
of the anklets, the headbands, and the crescents;
19 the pendants, the bracelets, and the scarfs; 20 the
headdresses, the armlets, the sashes, the perfume
boxes, and the amulets; 21 the signet rings and nose
rings; 22 the festal robes, the mantles, the cloaks, and

the handbags; ²³the garments of gauze, the linen garments, the turbans, and the veils.
²⁴ Instead of perfume there will be a stench;
    and instead of a sash, a rope;
and instead of well-set hair, baldness;
    and instead of a rich robe, a binding of
        sackcloth;
    instead of beauty, shame.*
²⁵ Your men shall fall by the sword
    and your warriors in battle.
²⁶ And her gates shall lament and mourn;
    ravaged, she shall sit upon the ground.

4 Seven women shall take hold of one man
        in that day, saying,
    "We will eat our own bread and wear
        our own clothes;
    just let us be called by your name;
        take away our disgrace."

The Future Glory of the Survivors in Zion

2 On that day the branch of the Lord shall be beautiful and glorious, and the fruit of the land shall be the pride and glory of the survivors of Israel. ³Whoever is left in Zion and remains in Jerusalem will be called holy, everyone who has been recorded for life in Jerusalem, ⁴once the Lord has washed away the filth of the daughters of Zion and cleansed the bloodstains of Jerusalem from its midst by a spirit of judgment and by a spirit of burning. ⁵Then the Lord will create over the whole site of Mount Zion and over its places of assembly a cloud by day and smoke and the shining of a flaming fire by night. Indeed over all the glory there will be a canopy. ⁶It will serve as a pavilion, a shade by day from the heat, and a refuge and a shelter from the storm and rain.

The Song of the Unfruitful Vineyard

5 Let me sing for my beloved
    my love-song concerning his vineyard:
My beloved had a vineyard

α Q Ms: MT lacks shame

on a very fertile hill.
² He dug it and cleared it of stones,
    and planted it with choice vines;
he built a watchtower in the midst
        of it,
    and hewed out a wine vat in it;
he expected it to yield grapes,
    but it yielded wild grapes.

³ And now, inhabitants of Jerusalem
    and people of Judah,
judge between me
    and my vineyard.
⁴ What more was there to do for my vineyard
    that I have not done in it?
When I expected it to yield grapes,
    why did it yield wild grapes?

⁵ And now I will tell you
    what I will do to my vineyard.
I will remove its hedge,
    and it shall be devoured;
I will break down its wall,
    and it shall be trampled down.
⁶ I will make it a waste;
    it shall not be pruned or hoed,
    and it shall be overgrown with briers and
        thorns;
I will also command the clouds
    that they rain no rain upon it.

⁷ For the vineyard of the Lord of hosts
    is the house of Israel,
and the people of Judah
    are his pleasant planting;
he expected justice,
    but saw bloodshed;
righteousness,
    but heard a cry!

Social Injustice Denounced
⁸ Ah, you who join house to house,
    who add field to field,
until there is room for no one but you,
    and you are left to live alone
    in the midst of the land!
⁹ The Lord of hosts has sworn in my hearing:
    Surely many houses shall be desolate,
    large and beautiful houses, without
        inhabitant.

10 For ten acres of vineyard shall yield but one
        bath,
    and a homer of seed shall yield a mere
        ephah.*a*

11 Ah, you who rise early in the morning
        in pursuit of strong drink,
    who linger in the evening
        to be inflamed by wine,
12 whose feasts consist of lyre and harp,
        tambourine and flute and wine,
    but who do not regard the deeds of the
        LORD,
    or see the work of his hands!
13 Therefore my people go into exile without
        knowledge;
    their nobles are dying of hunger,
    and their multitude is parched with thirst.

14 Therefore Sheol has enlarged its appetite
        and opened its mouth beyond measure;
    the nobility of Jerusalem*b* and her multitude
        go down,
    her throng and all who exult in her.
15 People are bowed down, everyone is
        brought low,
    and the eyes of the haughty are humbled.
16 But the LORD of hosts is exalted by justice,
    and the Holy God shows himself holy by
        righteousness.
17 Then the lambs shall graze as in their pasture,
    fatlings and kids*c* shall feed among the
        ruins.

18 Ah, you who drag iniquity along with cords
        of falsehood,
    who drag sin along as with cart ropes,
19 who say, "Let him make haste,
        let him speed his work
        that we may see it;
    let the plan of the Holy One of Israel hasten
        to fulfillment,
        that we may know it!"
20 Ah, you who call evil good
        and good evil,
    who put darkness for light
        and light for darkness,
    who put bitter for sweet
        and sweet for bitter!
21 Ah, you who are wise in your own eyes,

    and shrewd in your own sight!
22 Ah, you who are heroes in drinking wine
        and valiant at mixing drink,
23 who acquit the guilty for a bribe,
        and deprive the innocent of their
            rights!

Foreign Invasion Predicted

24 Therefore, as the tongue of fire devours the
        stubble,
    and as dry grass sinks down in the flame,
    so their root will become rotten,
        and their blossom go up like dust;
    for they have rejected the instruction of the
        LORD of hosts,
    and have despised the word of the Holy
        One of Israel.

25 Therefore the anger of the LORD was kindled
        against his people,
    and he stretched out his hand against
        them and struck them;
    the mountains quaked,
    and their corpses were like refuse
        in the streets.
    For all this his anger has not turned away,
        and his hand is stretched out still.

26 He will raise a signal for a nation far away,
        and whistle for a people at the ends of the
            earth;
    Here they come, swiftly, speedily!
27 None of them is weary, none
        stumbles,
        none slumbers or sleeps,
    not a loincloth is loose,
        not a sandal-thong broken;
28 their arrows are sharp,
        all their bows bent,
    their horses' hoofs seem like flint,
        and their wheels like the whirlwind.
29 Their roaring is like a lion,
        like young lions they roar;
    they growl and seize their prey,
        they carry it off, and no one can rescue.
30 They will roar over it on that day,
        like the roaring of the sea.
    And if one look to the land—
        only darkness and distress;
    and the light grows dark with clouds.

a The Heb *bath, homer,* and *ephah* are measures of quantity   *b* Heb *her nobility*   *c* Cn Compare Gk: Heb *aliens*

A Vision of God in the Temple

6 In the year that King Uzziah died, I saw the Lord sitting on a throne, high and lofty; and the hem of his robe filled the temple. ²Seraphs were in attendance above him; each had six wings: with two they covered their faces, and with two they covered their feet, and with two they flew. ³And one called to another and said:

"Holy, holy, holy is the LORD of hosts;
the whole earth is full of his glory."

⁴The pivots*a* on the thresholds shook at the voices of those who called, and the house filled with smoke. ⁵And I said: "Woe is me! I am lost, for I am a man of unclean lips, and I live among a people of unclean lips; yet my eyes have seen the King, the LORD of hosts!"

6 Then one of the seraphs flew to me, holding a live coal that had been taken from the altar with a pair of tongs. ⁷The seraph*b* touched my mouth with it and said: "Now that this has touched your lips, your guilt has departed and your sin is blotted out." ⁸Then I heard the voice of the Lord saying, "Whom shall I send, and who will go for us?" And I said, "Here am I; send me!" ⁹And he said, "Go and say to this people:

'Keep listening, but do not comprehend;
keep looking, but do not understand.'

¹⁰ Make the mind of this people dull,

and stop their ears,
and shut their eyes,
so that they may not look with their eyes,
and listen with their ears,
and comprehend with their minds,
and turn and be healed."

¹¹ Then I said, "How long, O Lord?" And he said:

"Until cities lie waste
without inhabitant,
and houses without people,
and the land is utterly desolate;
¹² until the LORD sends everyone far away,
and vast is the emptiness in the midst of
the land.
¹³ Even if a tenth part remain in it,
it will be burned again,
like a terebinth or an oak
whose stump remains standing
when it is felled."*a*
The holy seed is its stump.

Isaiah Reassures King Ahaz

7 In the days of Ahaz son of Jotham son of Uzziah, king of Judah, King Rezin of Aram and King Pekah son of Remaliah of Israel went up to attack Jerusalem, but could not mount an attack against it. ²When the house of David heard that

Here I Am, Lord! · Isaiah 6

Wow! Isaiah has quite a vision in which he receives God's call. Isaiah's call follows a biblical pattern:

• **The person has an experience of God.** Isaiah has a dramatic vision of God in the temple.
• **God gives the person a mission.** God sends Isaiah to speak to the people.
• **The person denies being worthy.** Isaiah knows he has unclean (or sinful) lips.
• **God addresses the denial and reassures the person.** God purifies Isaiah with fire from the altar and words of forgiveness.

You can see the same pattern for Moses' call in **Exodus 3:1–12**, Samuel's call in **1 Samuel 3:1–14**, Jeremiah's call in **Jeremiah 1:4–10**, and Mary's call in **Luke 1:26–38**.

Christians are called by God to participate in Jesus' saving mission. And even if most experiences are less dramatic or direct than Isaiah's, we all need to discover the way God wants us to live out that call. At times that may mean trusting God to lead us into a specific situation, or it may mean living faithfully in the everyday moments of life.

• Do you believe God has a purpose for your life?
• How can you use your talents to create a more loving and just world?

a Meaning of Heb uncertain   *b* Heb *He*

Aram had allied itself with Ephraim, the heart of Ahaz*a* and the heart of his people shook as the trees of the forest shake before the wind.

3 Then the Lord said to Isaiah, Go out to meet Ahaz, you and your son Shear-jashub,*b* at the end of the conduit of the upper pool on the highway to the Fuller's Field, ⁴and say to him, Take heed, be quiet, do not fear, and do not let your heart be faint because of these two smoldering stumps of fire-brands, because of the fierce anger of Rezin and Aram and the son of Remaliah. ⁵Because Aram—with Ephraim and the son of Remaliah—has plotted evil against you, saying, ⁶Let us go up against Judah and cut off Jerusalem*c* and conquer it for ourselves and make the son of Tabeel king in it; ⁷therefore thus says the Lord God:

It shall not stand,
    and it shall not come to pass.
⁸ For the head of Aram is Damascus,
    and the head of Damascus is Rezin.
(Within sixty-five years Ephraim will be shattered, no longer a people.)
⁹ The head of Ephraim is Samaria,
    and the head of Samaria is the son of
        Remaliah.
If you do not stand firm in faith,
    you shall not stand at all.

Isaiah Gives Ahaz the Sign of Immanuel

10 Again the Lord spoke to Ahaz, saying, ¹¹Ask a sign of the Lord your God; let it be deep as Sheol or high as heaven. ¹²But Ahaz said, I will not ask, and I will not put the Lord to the test. ¹³Then Isaiah*d* said: "Hear then, O house of David! Is it too little for you to weary mortals, that you weary my God also? ¹⁴Therefore the Lord himself will give you a sign. Look, the young woman*e* is with child and shall bear a son, and shall name him Immanuel.*f* ¹⁵He shall eat curds and honey by the time he knows how to refuse the evil and choose the good. ¹⁶For before the child knows how to refuse the evil and choose the good, the land before whose two kings you are in dread will be deserted. ¹⁷The Lord will bring on you and on your people and on your ancestral house such days as have not come since the day that Ephraim departed from Judah—the king of Assyria."

18 On that day the Lord will whistle for the fly that is at the sources of the streams of Egypt, and for the bee that is in the land of Assyria. ¹⁹And they will all come and settle in the steep ravines, and in the

STUDY IT!

Introducing . . . Mary
Isaiah 7:14

Have you ever wondered what Mary, the mother of Jesus, was like as a young girl? Or, if Mary had heard this passage recited and what she thought of it? Imagine what it would be like to discover that you are destined to play such an important role in the salvation of the world! We know little of Mary's childhood, but the gospel writers give us insight into how Mary, through faith and the Holy Spirit, helped fulfill Isaiah's prophecy by becoming the mother of Jesus.

Mary was still a young virgin when the angel Gabriel told her she would give birth to God's only son, Jesus (Luke 1:26-38). Mary willingly responded "yes" to the angel. Mary had to have faith that God's Spirit was at work in Jesus' life as he grew from a child into a man (Luke 2:41-52). It was Mary's faith in God's plan that prompted her to encourage Jesus to begin his public ministry at the wedding at Cana (John 2:1-12), and it is what sustained her as she stood at the foot of the cross during her own son's crucifixion (John 19:17-30). After Jesus' resurrection, it was faith in Christ's promises that motivated Mary to stay with the disciples and pray for the coming of the Holy Spirit, who would guide them and give them the courage to spread the gospel message (Acts 1:12-14).

clefts of the rocks, and on all the thornbushes, and on all the pastures.

20 On that day the Lord will shave with a razor hired beyond the River—with the king of Assyria—the head and the hair of the feet, and it will take off the beard as well.

21 On that day one will keep alive a young cow and two sheep, ²²and will eat curds because of the abundance of milk that they give; for everyone that is left in the land shall eat curds and honey.

---

a Heb *his heart*   *b* That is *A remnant shall return*   *c* Heb *cut it off*   *d* Heb *he*   *e* Gk *the virgin*   *f* That is *God is with us*

23 On that day every place where there used to be a thousand vines, worth a thousand shekels of silver, will become briers and thorns. [24]With bow and arrows one will go there, for all the land will be briers and thorns; [25]and as for all the hills that used to be hoed with a hoe, you will not go there for fear of briers and thorns; but they will become a place where cattle are let loose and where sheep tread.

8   Isaiah's Son a Sign of the Assyrian Invasion

Then the LORD said to me, Take a large tablet and write on it in common characters, "Belonging to Maher-shalal-hash-baz,"[a] [2]and have it attested[b] for me by reliable witnesses, the priest Uriah and Zechariah son of Jeberechiah. [3]And I went to the prophetess, and she conceived and bore a son. Then the LORD said to me, Name him Maher-shalal-hash-baz; [4]for before the child knows how to call "My father" or "My mother," the wealth of Damascus and the spoil of Samaria will be carried away by the king of Assyria.

5 The LORD spoke to me again: [6]Because this people has refused the waters of Shiloah that flow gently, and melt in fear before[c] Rezin and the son of Remaliah; [7]therefore, the Lord is bringing up against it the mighty flood waters of the River, the king of Assyria and all his glory; it will rise above all its channels and overflow all its banks; [8]it will sweep on into Judah as a flood, and, pouring over, it will reach up to the neck; and its outspread wings will fill the breadth of your land, O Immanuel.

9   Band together, you peoples, and be dismayed;
    listen, all you far countries;
  gird yourselves and be dismayed;
  gird yourselves and be dismayed!
[10] Take counsel together, but it shall be brought to naught;
  speak a word, but it will not stand,
  for God is with us.[d]

11 For the LORD spoke thus to me while his hand was strong upon me, and warned me not to walk in the way of this people, saying: [12]Do not call conspiracy all that this people calls conspiracy, and do not fear what it fears, or be in dread. [13]But the LORD of hosts, him you shall regard as holy; let him be your fear, and let him be your dread. [14]He will become a sanctuary, a stone one strikes against; for both houses of Israel he will become a rock one stumbles over—a trap and a snare for the inhab-itants of Jerusalem. [15]And many among them shall stumble; they shall fall and be broken; they shall be snared and taken.

Disciples of Isaiah

16 Bind up the testimony, seal the teaching among my disciples. [17]I will wait for the LORD, who is hiding his face from the house of Jacob, and I will hope in him. [18]See, I and the children whom the LORD has given me are signs and portents in Israel from the LORD of hosts, who dwells on Mount Zion. [19]Now if people say to you, "Consult the ghosts and the familiar spirits that chirp and mutter; should not a people consult their gods, the dead on behalf of the living, [20]for teaching and for instruction?" surely, those who speak like this will have no dawn! [21]They will pass through the land,[e] greatly distressed and hungry; when they are hungry, they will be enraged and will curse[f] their king and their gods. They will turn their faces upward, [22]or they will look to the earth, but will see only distress and darkness, the gloom of anguish; and they will be thrust into thick darkness.[g]

STUDY IT!

God with Us · Isaiah 7–12

In these chapters, often referred to as the Book of Immanuel, Isaiah announces that Israel's salvation will come from a child from the family of Jesse, the father of King David. This child will be named Immanuel (also spelled Emmanuel), which means "God with us."

Biblical scholars agree that the first fulfillment of this prophecy is through the son of King Ahaz—the future king Hezekiah. But the gospel writers later see in this passage a prophecy of an even greater king—Jesus (Matthew 1:23), the Son of God, who is truly Immanuel, "God with us." Therefore, these chapters are most often read as the Christmas season approaches, in anticipation of the birth of Immanuel.

---

a That is *The spoil speeds, the prey hastens* b Q Ms Gk Syr: MT *and I caused to be attested* c Cn: Meaning of Heb uncertain d Heb *immanu el*
e Heb *it* f Or *curse by* g Meaning of Heb uncertain

9 The Righteous Reign of the Coming King

a But there will be no gloom for those who were in anguish. In the former time he brought into contempt the land of Zebulun and the land of Naphtali, but in the latter time he will make glorious the way of the sea, the land beyond the Jordan, Galilee of the nations.

2*b* The people who walked in darkness
　　have seen a great light;
　those who lived in a land of deep darkness—
　　on them light has shined.
3　You have multiplied the nation,
　　you have increased its joy;
　they rejoice before you
　　as with joy at the harvest,
　　as people exult when dividing plunder.
4　For the yoke of their burden,
　　and the bar across their shoulders,
　　the rod of their oppressor,
　　you have broken as on the day of Midian.
5　For all the boots of the tramping warriors
　　and all the garments rolled in blood

shall be burned as fuel for the fire.
6　For a child has been born for us,
　　a son given to us;
　authority rests upon his shoulders;
　　and he is named
　Wonderful Counselor, Mighty God,
　　Everlasting Father, Prince of Peace.
7　His authority shall grow continually,
　　and there shall be endless peace
　for the throne of David and his kingdom.
　　He will establish and uphold it
　with justice and with righteousness
　　from this time onward and forevermore.
　The zeal of the LORD of hosts will do this.

Judgment on Arrogance and Oppression

8　The Lord sent a word against Jacob,
　　and it fell on Israel;
9　and all the people knew it—
　　Ephraim and the inhabitants of Samaria—
　　but in pride and arrogance of heart they
　　　said:
10　"The bricks have fallen,
　　but we will build with dressed stones;
　the sycamores have been cut down,
　　but we will put cedars in their
　　　place."
11　So the LORD raised adversaries*c* against them,
　　and stirred up their enemies,
12　the Arameans on the east and the Philistines on
　　　the west,
　　and they devoured Israel with open mouth.
　For all this his anger has not turned away;
　　his hand is stretched out still.

13　The people did not turn to him who struck
　　　them,
　　or seek the LORD of hosts.
14　So the LORD cut off from Israel head and tail,
　　palm branch and reed in one day—
15　elders and dignitaries are the head,
　　and prophets who teach lies are the tail;
16　for those who led this people led them astray,
　　and those who were led by them were left in
　　　confusion.
17　That is why the Lord did not have pity on*d*
　　　their young people,
　　or compassion on their orphans and
　　　widows;
　for everyone was godless and an evildoer,

STUDY IT!

Prophecy About the Messiah
Isaiah 9:2–7

Isaiah 9:2–7 describes Immanuel as a wise, brave, courageous, virtuous, and righteous king. Isaiah may be referring here to King Hezekiah, the reformer king of Judah (see 2 Chronicles 29–33). However, after Hezekiah's death, the passage came to be understood as predicting the coming of a future savior or messiah. That's why the passage is called a messianic prophecy.

　Christians throughout the ages have seen in these words a perfect description of Jesus. These words are often read at Christmas to celebrate Jesus' presence in the world as a light dispelling the darkness of sin. For the fulfillment of other messianic prophecies, read **Micah 5:2** with **Matthew 2:1**, and **Isaiah 61:1** with **Luke 4:14–21**.

---

a Ch 8.23 in Heb　*b* Ch 9.1 in Heb　*c* Cn: Heb *the adversaries of Rezin*　*d* Q Ms: MT *rejoice over*

and every mouth spoke folly.
For all this his anger has not turned away;
  his hand is stretched out still.

18 For wickedness burned like a fire,
  consuming briers and thorns;
it kindled the thickets of the forest,
  and they swirled upward in a column of
    smoke.
19 Through the wrath of the Lord of hosts
  the land was burned,
and the people became like fuel for the fire;
  no one spared another.
20 They gorged on the right, but still were hungry,
  and they devoured on the left, but were not
    satisfied;
they devoured the flesh of their own kindred;[a]
21 Manasseh devoured Ephraim, and Ephraim
    Manasseh,
  and together they were against Judah.
For all this his anger has not turned away;
  his hand is stretched out still.

10   Ah, you who make iniquitous decrees,
  who write oppressive statutes,
  2 to turn aside the needy from justice
and to rob the poor of my people of their
    right,
that widows may be your spoil,
  and that you may make the orphans your
    prey!
3 What will you do on the day of punishment,
  in the calamity that will come from far
    away?
To whom will you flee for help,
  and where will you leave your wealth,
4 so as not to crouch among the prisoners
  or fall among the slain?
For all this his anger has not turned away;
  his hand is stretched out still.

Arrogant Assyria Also Judged

5 Ah, Assyria, the rod of my anger—
  the club in their hands is my fury!
6 Against a godless nation I send him,
  and against the people of my wrath I
    command him,
to take spoil and seize plunder,
  and to tread them down like the mire of the
    streets.

7 But this is not what he intends,
  nor does he have this in mind;
but it is in his heart to destroy,
  and to cut off nations not a few.
8 For he says:
  "Are not my commanders all kings?
9 Is not Calno like Carchemish?
  Is not Hamath like Arpad?
  Is not Samaria like Damascus?
10 As my hand has reached to the kingdoms of the
    idols
  whose images were greater than those of
    Jerusalem and Samaria,
11 shall I not do to Jerusalem and her idols
  what I have done to Samaria and her
    images?"

12 When the Lord has finished all his work on Mount Zion and on Jerusalem, he[b] will punish the arrogant boasting of the king of Assyria and his haughty pride. 13For he says:
  "By the strength of my hand I have done it,
  and by my wisdom, for I have
    understanding;
I have removed the boundaries of peoples,
  and have plundered their treasures;
like a bull I have brought down those who
    sat on thrones.
14 My hand has found, like a nest,
  the wealth of the peoples;
and as one gathers eggs that have been
    forsaken,
  so I have gathered all the earth;
and there was none that moved a wing,
  or opened its mouth, or chirped."

15 Shall the ax vaunt itself over the one who
    wields it,
  or the saw magnify itself against the one
    who handles it?

a Or arm   b Heb I

As if a rod should raise the one who lifts
    it up,
  or as if a staff should lift the one who is
    not wood!
16 Therefore the Sovereign, the Lord of hosts,
    will send wasting sickness among his
    stout warriors,
  and under his glory a burning will be kindled,
    like the burning of fire.
17 The light of Israel will become a fire,
    and his Holy One a flame;
  and it will burn and devour
    his thorns and briers in one day.
18 The glory of his forest and his fruitful land
    the Lord will destroy, both soul and
    body,
  and it will be as when an invalid wastes
    away.
19 The remnant of the trees of his forest will be
    so few
  that a child can write them down.

The Repentant Remnant of Israel

20 On that day the remnant of Israel and the survivors of the house of Jacob will no more lean on the one who struck them, but will lean on the Lord, the Holy One of Israel, in truth. 21 A remnant will return, the remnant of Jacob, to the mighty God. 22 For though your people Israel were like the sand of the sea, only a remnant of them will return. Destruction is decreed, overflowing with righteousness. 23 For the Lord God of hosts will make a full end, as decreed, in all the earth.[a]

24 Therefore thus says the Lord God of hosts: O my people, who live in Zion, do not be afraid of the Assyrians when they beat you with a rod and lift up their staff against you as the Egyptians did. 25 For in a very little while my indignation will come to an end, and my anger will be directed to their destruction. 26 The Lord of hosts will wield a whip against them, as when he struck Midian at the rock of Oreb; his staff will be over the sea, and he will lift it as he did in Egypt. 27 On that day his burden will be removed from your shoulder, and his yoke will be destroyed from your neck.

  He has gone up from Rimmon,[b]
28   he has come to Aiath;
  he has passed through Migron,
    at Michmash he stores his baggage;

29 they have crossed over the pass,
    at Geba they lodge for the night;
Ramah trembles,
    Gibeah of Saul has fled.
30 Cry aloud, O daughter Gallim!
    Listen, O Laishah!
    Answer her, O Anathoth!
31 Madmenah is in flight,
    the inhabitants of Gebim flee for safety.
32 This very day he will halt at Nob,
    he will shake his fist
    at the mount of daughter Zion,
    the hill of Jerusalem.

33 Look, the Sovereign, the Lord of hosts,
    will lop the boughs with terrifying power;
  the tallest trees will be cut down,
    and the lofty will be brought low.
34 He will hack down the thickets of the forest
    with an ax,
  and Lebanon with its majestic trees[a] will
    fall.

The Peaceful Kingdom

11 A shoot shall come out from the stump
    of Jesse,
  and a branch shall grow out of his roots.
2 The spirit of the Lord shall rest on him,
    the spirit of wisdom and understanding,
    the spirit of counsel and might,
    the spirit of knowledge and the fear of the
    Lord.
3 His delight shall be in the fear of the Lord.

  He shall not judge by what his eyes see,
    or decide by what his ears hear;
4 but with righteousness he shall judge the
    poor,
  and decide with equity for the meek of
    the earth;
  he shall strike the earth with the rod of his
    mouth,
  and with the breath of his lips he shall kill
    the wicked.
5 Righteousness shall be the belt around his
    waist,
  and faithfulness the belt around his loins.

6 The wolf shall live with the lamb,
    the leopard shall lie down with the kid,

---

a Or land   b Cn: Heb *and his yoke from your neck, and a yoke will be destroyed because of fatness*

PRAY IT!

The Character of the King · Isaiah 11:1–2

Have you ever wanted to make the world a better place, but didn't know where to begin? Isaiah's description of Jesus is a good place to start. Isaiah prophesied about a world marked by justice and peace and led by the ideal king. This ideal king would be full of wisdom, understanding, counsel, might, knowledge, and the fear of the Lord.

Nearly eight hundred years later, Isaiah's ideal king arrived—Jesus of Nazareth, the Son of God. Jesus' life, death, and resurrection reveal that Jesus truly is the ideal king, yet Jesus' perfect kingdom has not come to completion on earth. But we can be part of restoring the world by allowing the Holy Spirit to shape our hearts and grow the character of Christ in us.

Here are some suggestions for putting the character of Jesus into practice in your everyday life:

- Pray for **wisdom** when life gets complicated and you have lost sight of the big picture.
- Pray for **understanding** when you have a problem and need to figure out what is at the heart of it.
- Pray for **counsel (right judgment)** when a friend asks you for advice.
- Pray for **might (courage and strength)** when you know the right thing to do, but are afraid to do it.
- Pray for **knowledge** when you need to separate the truth from lies.
- Pray for **fear of the Lord (awe in God's presence)** every day, so that you may know in your heart the greatness of God.

---

the calf and the lion and the fatling
    together,
    and a little child shall lead them.
7 The cow and the bear shall graze,
    their young shall lie down together;
    and the lion shall eat straw like
        the ox.
8 The nursing child shall play over the hole of
        the asp,
    and the weaned child shall put its hand on
        the adder's den.
9 They will not hurt or destroy
    on all my holy mountain;
    for the earth will be full of the knowledge of
        the LORD
    as the waters cover the sea.

Return of the Remnant of Israel and Judah

10 On that day the root of Jesse shall stand as a signal to the peoples; the nations shall inquire of him, and his dwelling shall be glorious.

11 On that day the Lord will extend his hand yet a second time to recover the remnant that is left of his people, from Assyria, from Egypt, from Pathros, from Ethiopia,ª from Elam, from Shinar, from Hamath, and from the coastlands of the sea.

12 He will raise a signal for the nations,
    and will assemble the outcasts of Israel,
    and gather the dispersed of Judah
        from the four corners of the earth.
13 The jealousy of Ephraim shall depart,
    the hostility of Judah shall be cut off;
    Ephraim shall not be jealous of Judah,
    and Judah shall not be hostile towards
        Ephraim.
14 But they shall swoop down on the backs of
        the Philistines in the west,
    together they shall plunder the people of
        the east.
    They shall put forth their hand against Edom
        and Moab,
    and the Ammonites shall obey them.
15 And the LORD will utterly destroy
    the tongue of the sea of Egypt;
    and will wave his hand over the River
    with his scorching wind;
    and will split it into seven channels,
    and make a way to cross on foot;

ª Cn Compare Gk Vg: Heb *with a majestic one*

LIVE IT!

Lions and Lambs · Isaiah 11:6–9

Every week we hear new reports of violence and ethnic clashes somewhere in our world. War, poverty, ethnic cleansing, and discrimination all point to how easy it is to forget that we are all members of the human family.

It is the harsh realities of our world that make the peaceful descriptions in this passage so appealing. Imagine predators such as wolves and lions living together in harmony with lambs and calves. Harmony. Peace. Gentleness.

This is God's ultimate intent. And although its ultimate fulfillment will only come with Christ's return, it is a vision we can work toward.

- How can you live at peace with those around you, especially with your parents, brothers, and sisters?
- What organizations can you partner with to give help to areas of our world in desperate need of peace?

---

16 so there shall be a highway from Assyria
    for the remnant that is left of his people,
as there was for Israel
    when they came up from the land of
      Egypt.

Thanksgiving and Praise

12 You will say in that day:
I will give thanks to you, O Lord,
    for though you were angry with me,
your anger turned away,
    and you comforted me.

2 Surely God is my salvation;
    I will trust, and will not be afraid,
for the Lord God*b* is my strength and my
      might;
    he has become my salvation.

3 With joy you will draw water from the wells of salvation. ⁴And you will say in that day:
Give thanks to the Lord,
    call on his name;
make known his deeds among the nations;
    proclaim that his name is exalted.

5 Sing praises to the Lord, for he has done
      gloriously;
    let this be known*c* in all the earth.
6 Shout aloud and sing for joy, O royal*d* Zion,
    for great in your midst is the Holy One of
      Israel.

Proclamation against Babylon

13 The oracle concerning Babylon that Isaiah son of Amoz saw.

2 On a bare hill raise a signal,
    cry aloud to them;
wave the hand for them to enter
    the gates of the nobles.
3 I myself have commanded my consecrated
      ones,
    have summoned my warriors, my proudly
      exulting ones,
    to execute my anger.

4 Listen, a tumult on the mountains
    as of a great multitude!
Listen, an uproar of kingdoms,
    of nations gathering together!
The Lord of hosts is mustering
    an army for battle.
5 They come from a distant land,
    from the end of the heavens,
the Lord and the weapons of his indignation,
    to destroy the whole earth.

6 Wail, for the day of the Lord is near;
    it will come like destruction from the
      Almighty!*e*
7 Therefore all hands will be feeble,
    and every human heart will melt,
8   and they will be dismayed.
Pangs and agony will seize them;

---

a Or *Nubia;* Heb *Cush*　**b** Heb *for Yah, the* Lord　**c** Or *this is made known*　**d** Or *O inhabitant of*　**e** Traditional rendering of Heb *Shaddai*

they will be in anguish like a woman in labor.
They will look aghast at one another;
their faces will be aflame.

9 See, the day of the LORD comes,
cruel, with wrath and fierce anger,
to make the earth a desolation,
and to destroy its sinners from it.

10 For the stars of the heavens and their
constellations
will not give their light;
the sun will be dark at its rising,
and the moon will not shed its light.

11 I will punish the world for its evil,
and the wicked for their iniquity;
I will put an end to the pride of the arrogant,

and lay low the insolence of tyrants.

12 I will make mortals more rare than fine gold,
and humans than the gold of Ophir.

13 Therefore I will make the heavens tremble,
and the earth will be shaken out of its
place,
at the wrath of the LORD of hosts
in the day of his fierce anger.

14 Like a hunted gazelle,
or like sheep with no one to gather them,
all will turn to their own people,
and all will flee to their own lands.

15 Whoever is found will be thrust through,
and whoever is caught will fall by the
sword.

16 Their infants will be dashed to pieces
before their eyes;
their houses will be plundered,
and their wives ravished.

17 See, I am stirring up the Medes against them,
who have no regard for silver
and do not delight in gold.

18 Their bows will slaughter the young men;
they will have no mercy on the fruit of the
womb;
their eyes will not pity children.

19 And Babylon, the glory of kingdoms,
the splendor and pride of the Chaldeans,
will be like Sodom and Gomorrah
when God overthrew them.

20 It will never be inhabited
or lived in for all generations;
Arabs will not pitch their tents there,
shepherds will not make their flocks lie
down there.

21 But wild animals will lie down there,
and its houses will be full of howling
creatures;
there ostriches will live,
and there goat-demons will dance.

22 Hyenas will cry in its towers,
and jackals in the pleasant palaces;
its time is close at hand,
and its days will not be prolonged.

LIVE IT!

In God We Trust
Isaiah 12

"In God We Trust." Have you ever noticed that every piece of U.S. currency bears this statement? **Isaiah 12:2** proclaims the same message: "Surely God is my salvation; I will trust, and will not be afraid, for the LORD GOD is my strength and my might; he has become my salvation."

Fear is the enemy of trust. And there is plenty of fear to keep us paralyzed: fear of the unknown, fear of strangers, fear of failure, fear of rejection, and the list goes on. How often does fear keep you from being who God has called you to be and doing what you're called to do? Reach out to God and others in your life, and trust that God is with you. Jesus' life and death showed the depth of trust he had in his Father—a trust that overcame even the fear of death. That ability to conquer fear is yours when you trust in Jesus. You can celebrate as Israel did in **Isaiah 12:3–6**.

- How can you better live out the words, "In God We Trust"?
- What do you fear? How can you begin to replace that fear with trust?

Restoration of Judah

14 But the LORD will have compassion on Jacob and will again choose Israel, and will set them in their own land; and aliens will join them and attach themselves to the house of Jacob. 2 And the nations will take them and bring them to their place, and the house of Israel will possess the nations[a] as male and female slaves in the LORD's land; they will take captive those who were their captors, and rule over those who oppressed them.

Downfall of the King of Babylon

3 When the LORD has given you rest from your pain and turmoil and the hard service with which you were made to serve, [4] you will take up this taunt against the king of Babylon:

How the oppressor has ceased!
　　How his insolence[b] has ceased!
5 The LORD has broken the staff of the
　　　　wicked,
　　the scepter of rulers,
6 that struck down the peoples in wrath
　　with unceasing blows,
　that ruled the nations in anger
　　with unrelenting persecution.
7 The whole earth is at rest and quiet;
　　they break forth into singing.
8 The cypresses exult over you,
　　the cedars of Lebanon, saying,
"Since you were laid low,
　　no one comes to cut us down."
9 Sheol beneath is stirred up
　　to meet you when you come;
it rouses the shades to greet you,
　　all who were leaders of the earth;
it raises from their thrones
　　all who were kings of the nations.
10 All of them will speak
　　and say to you:
"You too have become as weak as we!
　　You have become like us!"
11 Your pomp is brought down to Sheol,
　　and the sound of your harps;

maggots are the bed beneath you,
　　and worms are your covering.
12 How you are fallen from heaven,
　　O Day Star, son of Dawn!
How you are cut down to the ground,
　　you who laid the nations low!
13 You said in your heart,
　　"I will ascend to heaven;
I will raise my throne
　　above the stars of God;
I will sit on the mount of assembly
　　on the heights of Zaphon;[c]
14 I will ascend to the tops of the clouds,
　　I will make myself like the Most High."
15 But you are brought down to Sheol,
　　to the depths of the Pit.
16 Those who see you will stare at you,
　　and ponder over you:
"Is this the man who made the earth tremble,
　　who shook kingdoms,
17 who made the world like a desert
　　and overthrew its cities,
　who would not let his prisoners go
　　　　home?"
18 All the kings of the nations lie in glory,
　　each in his own tomb;
19 but you are cast out, away from your grave,
　　like loathsome carrion,[d]
clothed with the dead, those pierced by the
　　　　sword,
　who go down to the stones of the Pit,
　　like a corpse trampled underfoot.
20 You will not be joined with them in burial,
　　because you have destroyed your land,
　　you have killed your people.

May the descendants of evildoers

Oracles · Isaiah 13–23

In the ancient world, an oracle was understood as a communication from the gods. By means of oracles, Isaiah presents God's judgment on Israel's enemies, including Egypt, Babylon, Assyria, Philistia, Moab, and Edom (Isaiah 13-23).

When we read these oracles today, we can understand their angry and vengeful spirit if we recall the terrible suffering that these nations inflicted on Israel. Still, we should also keep in mind the New Testament commandment to avoid revenge in all its forms (Matthew 5:38-48). Jesus calls us to be peacemakers in spite of our suffering.

a Heb *them*　b Q Ms Compare Gk Syr Vg: Meaning of MT uncertain　c Or *assembly in the far north*　d Cn Compare Gk: Heb *like a loathed branch*

nevermore be named!

²¹ Prepare slaughter for his sons
    because of the guilt of their father.ᵃ
Let them never rise to possess the earth
    or cover the face of the world with cities.

22 I will rise up against them, says the LORD of hosts, and will cut off from Babylon name and remnant, offspring and posterity, says the LORD. ²³And I will make it a possession of the hedgehog, and pools of water, and I will sweep it with the broom of destruction, says the LORD of hosts.

An Oracle concerning Assyria

²⁴ The LORD of hosts has sworn:
As I have designed,
    so shall it be;
and as I have planned,
    so shall it come to pass:
²⁵ I will break the Assyrian in my land,
    and on my mountains trample him under
        foot;
his yoke shall be removed from them,
    and his burden from their shoulders.
²⁶ This is the plan that is planned
    concerning the whole earth;
and this is the hand that is stretched out
    over all the nations.
²⁷ For the LORD of hosts has planned,
    and who will annul it?
His hand is stretched out,
    and who will turn it back?

An Oracle concerning Philistia

²⁸In the year that King Ahaz died this oracle came:

²⁹ Do not rejoice, all you Philistines,
    that the rod that struck you is broken,
for from the root of the snake will come
        forth an adder,
    and its fruit will be a flying fiery
        serpent.
³⁰ The firstborn of the poor will graze,
    and the needy lie down in safety;
but I will make your root die of famine,
    and your remnant Iᵇ will kill.
³¹ Wail, O gate; cry, O city;
    melt in fear, O Philistia, all of you!
For smoke comes out of the north,
    and there is no straggler in its ranks.

³² What will one answer the messengers of the
    nation?
"The LORD has founded Zion,
    and the needy among his people
    will find refuge in her."

15 An Oracle concerning Moab

An oracle concerning Moab.

Because Ar is laid waste in a night,
    Moab is undone;
because Kir is laid waste in a night,
    Moab is undone.
² Dibonᶜ has gone up to the temple,
    to the high places to weep;
over Nebo and over Medeba
    Moab wails.
On every head is baldness,
    every beard is shorn;
³ in the streets they bind on sackcloth;
    on the housetops and in the squares
    everyone wails and melts in tears.
⁴ Heshbon and Elealeh cry out,
    their voices are heard as far as
        Jahaz;
therefore the loins of Moab quiver;ᵈ
    his soul trembles.
⁵ My heart cries out for Moab;
    his fugitives flee to Zoar,
    to Eglath-shelishiyah.
For at the ascent of Luhith
    they go up weeping;
on the road to Horonaim
    they raise a cry of destruction;
⁶ the waters of Nimrim
    are a desolation;
the grass is withered, the new growth fails,
    the verdure is no more.
⁷ Therefore the abundance they have gained
    and what they have laid up
they carry away
    over the Wadi of the Willows.
⁸ For a cry has gone
    around the land of Moab;
the wailing reaches to Eglaim,
    the wailing reaches to Beer-elim.
⁹ For the waters of Dibonᵉ are full of blood;
    yet I will bring upon Dibonᵉ even more—
a lion for those of Moab who escape,
    for the remnant of the land.

16 Send lambs
to the ruler of the land,
from Sela, by way of the desert,
to the mount of daughter Zion.
2 Like fluttering birds,
like scattered nestlings,
so are the daughters of Moab
at the fords of the Arnon.
3 "Give counsel,
grant justice;
make your shade like night
at the height of noon;
hide the outcasts,
do not betray the fugitive;
4 let the outcasts of Moab
settle among you;
be a refuge to them
from the destroyer."

When the oppressor is no more,
and destruction has ceased,
and marauders have vanished from the land,
5 then a throne shall be established in
steadfast love
in the tent of David,
and on it shall sit in faithfulness
a ruler who seeks justice
and is swift to do what is right.

6 We have heard of the pride of Moab
—how proud he is!—
of his arrogance, his pride, and his insolence;
his boasts are false.
7 Therefore let Moab wail,
let everyone wail for Moab.
Mourn, utterly stricken,
for the raisin cakes of Kir-hareseth.

8 For the fields of Heshbon languish,
and the vines of Sibmah,
whose clusters once made drunk
the lords of the nations,
reached to Jazer
and strayed to the desert;
their shoots once spread abroad
and crossed over the sea.
9 Therefore I weep with the weeping of Jazer
for the vines of Sibmah;
I drench you with my tears,
O Heshbon and Elealeh;

for the shout over your fruit harvest
and your grain harvest has ceased.
10 Joy and gladness are taken away
from the fruitful field;
and in the vineyards no songs are sung,
no shouts are raised;
no treader treads out wine in the presses;
the vintage-shout is hushed.*a*
11 Therefore my heart throbs like a harp for Moab,
and my very soul for Kir-heres.
12 When Moab presents himself, when he wearies himself upon the high place, when he comes to his sanctuary to pray, he will not prevail.
13 This was the word that the Lord spoke concerning Moab in the past. 14But now the Lord says, In three years, like the years of a hired worker, the glory of Moab will be brought into contempt, in spite of all its great multitude; and those who survive will be very few and feeble.

An Oracle concerning Damascus

17 An oracle concerning Damascus.

See, Damascus will cease to be a city,
and will become a heap of ruins.
2 Her towns will be deserted forever;*b*
they will be places for flocks,
which will lie down, and no one will make
them afraid.
3 The fortress will disappear from Ephraim,
and the kingdom from Damascus;
and the remnant of Aram will be
like the glory of the children of Israel,
says the Lord of hosts.

4 On that day
the glory of Jacob will be brought low,
and the fat of his flesh will grow lean.
5 And it shall be as when reapers gather standing
grain
and their arms harvest the ears,
and as when one gleans the ears of grain
in the Valley of Rephaim.
6 Gleanings will be left in it,
as when an olive tree is beaten—
two or three berries
in the top of the highest bough,
four or five
on the branches of a fruit tree,
says the Lord God of Israel.

---

a Gk: Heb *I have hushed*   *b* Cn Compare Gk: Heb *the cities of Aroer are deserted*

7 On that day people will regard their Maker, and their eyes will look to the Holy One of Israel; ⁸they will not have regard for the altars, the work of their hands, and they will not look to what their own fingers have made, either the sacred poles^a or the altars of incense.

9 On that day their strong cities will be like the deserted places of the Hivites and the Amorites,^b which they deserted because of the children of Israel, and there will be desolation.

¹⁰ For you have forgotten the God of your
    salvation,
    and have not remembered the Rock of
      your refuge;
therefore, though you plant pleasant plants
    and set out slips of an alien god,
¹¹ though you make them grow on the day that
      you plant them,
    and make them blossom in the morning
      that you sow;
yet the harvest will flee away
    in a day of grief and incurable pain.

¹² Ah, the thunder of many peoples,
    they thunder like the thundering of
      the sea!
Ah, the roar of nations,
    they roar like the roaring of mighty
      waters!
¹³ The nations roar like the roaring of many
      waters,
    but he will rebuke them, and they will flee
      far away,
chased like chaff on the mountains before the
      wind
    and whirling dust before the storm.
¹⁴ At evening time, lo, terror!
    Before morning, they are no more.
This is the fate of those who despoil us,
    and the lot of those who plunder us.

18 An Oracle concerning Ethiopia

Ah, land of whirring wings
    beyond the rivers of Ethiopia,^c
² sending ambassadors by the Nile
    in vessels of papyrus on the waters!
Go, you swift messengers,
    to a nation tall and smooth,
    to a people feared near and far,

a nation mighty and conquering,
    whose land the rivers divide.

³ All you inhabitants of the world,
    you who live on the earth,
when a signal is raised on the mountains,
      look!
    When a trumpet is blown, listen!
⁴ For thus the LORD said to me:
I will quietly look from my dwelling
    like clear heat in sunshine,
    like a cloud of dew in the heat of harvest.
⁵ For before the harvest, when the blossom
      is over
    and the flower becomes a ripening grape,
he will cut off the shoots with pruning hooks,
    and the spreading branches he will hew
      away.
⁶ They shall all be left
    to the birds of prey of the mountains
    and to the animals of the earth.
And the birds of prey will summer on them,
    and all the animals of the earth will winter
      on them.

7 At that time gifts will be brought to the LORD of hosts from^d a people tall and smooth, from a people feared near and far, a nation mighty and conquering, whose land the rivers divide, to Mount Zion, the place of the name of the LORD of hosts.

19 An Oracle concerning Egypt

An oracle concerning Egypt.

See, the LORD is riding on a swift cloud
    and comes to Egypt;
the idols of Egypt will tremble at his presence,
    and the heart of the Egyptians will melt
      within them.
² I will stir up Egyptians against Egyptians,
    and they will fight, one against the other,
    neighbor against neighbor,
    city against city, kingdom against kingdom;
³ the spirit of the Egyptians within them will be
      emptied out,
    and I will confound their plans;
they will consult the idols and the spirits of
      the dead
    and the ghosts and the familiar spirits;
⁴ I will deliver the Egyptians

---

^a Heb *Asherim* ^b Cn Compare Gk: Heb *places of the wood and the highest bough* ^c Or *Nubia*; Heb *Cush* ^d Q Ms Gk Vg: MT *of*

into the hand of a hard master;
a fierce king will rule over them,
   says the Sovereign, the LORD of hosts.

5 The waters of the Nile will be dried up,
   and the river will be parched and dry;
6 its canals will become foul,
   and the branches of Egypt's Nile will
      diminish and dry up,
   reeds and rushes will rot away.
7 There will be bare places by the Nile,
   on the brink of the Nile;
and all that is sown by the Nile will
      dry up,
   be driven away, and be no more.
8 Those who fish will mourn;
   all who cast hooks in the Nile will lament,
   and those who spread nets on the water
      will languish.
9 The workers in flax will be in despair,
   and the carders and those at the loom will
      grow pale.
10 Its weavers will be dismayed,
   and all who work for wages will be grieved.

11 The princes of Zoan are utterly foolish;
   the wise counselors of Pharaoh give stupid
      counsel.
How can you say to Pharaoh,
   "I am one of the sages,
   a descendant of ancient kings"?
12 Where now are your sages?
   Let them tell you and make known
   what the LORD of hosts has planned
      against Egypt.
13 The princes of Zoan have become fools,
   and the princes of Memphis are deluded;
those who are the cornerstones of its tribes
   have led Egypt astray.
14 The LORD has poured into them[a]
   a spirit of confusion;
and they have made Egypt stagger in all its
      doings
   as a drunkard staggers around in vomit.
15 Neither head nor tail, palm branch or reed,
   will be able to do anything for Egypt.

16 On that day the Egyptians will be like women, and tremble with fear before the hand that the LORD of hosts raises against them. 17 And the land of Judah will become a terror to the Egyptians; everyone to whom it is mentioned will fear because of the plan that the LORD of hosts is planning against them.

Egypt, Assyria, and Israel Blessed

18 On that day there will be five cities in the land of Egypt that speak the language of Canaan and swear allegiance to the LORD of hosts. One of these will be called the City of the Sun.

19 On that day there will be an altar to the LORD in the center of the land of Egypt, and a pillar to the LORD at its border. 20 It will be a sign and a witness to the LORD of hosts in the land of Egypt; when they cry to the LORD because of oppressors, he will send them a savior, and will defend and deliver them. 21 The LORD will make himself known to the Egyptians; and the Egyptians will know the LORD on that day, and will worship with sacrifice and burnt offering, and they will make vows to the LORD and perform them. 22 The LORD will strike Egypt, striking and healing; they will return to the LORD, and he will listen to their supplications and heal them.

23 On that day there will be a highway from Egypt to Assyria, and the Assyrian will come into Egypt, and the Egyptian into Assyria, and the Egyptians will worship with the Assyrians. 24 On that day Israel will be the third with Egypt and Assyria, a blessing in the midst of the earth, 25 whom the LORD of hosts has blessed, saying, "Blessed be Egypt my people, and Assyria the work of my hands, and Israel my heritage."

20 Isaiah Dramatizes the Conquest of Egypt and Ethiopia

In the year that the commander-in-chief, who was sent by King Sargon of Assyria, came to Ashdod and fought against it and took it— 2 at that time the LORD had spoken to Isaiah son of Amoz, saying, "Go, and loose the sackcloth from your loins and take your sandals off your feet," and he had done so, walking naked and barefoot. 3 Then the LORD said, "Just as my servant Isaiah has walked naked and barefoot for three years as a sign and a portent against Egypt and Ethiopia,[b] 4 so shall the king of Assyria lead away the Egyptians as captives and the Ethiopians[c] as exiles, both the young and the old, naked and barefoot, with buttocks uncovered, to the shame of Egypt. 5 And they shall be dismayed and confounded because of Ethiopia[b] their hope and of Egypt their boast. 6 In that day the inhabitants of this coastland will say, 'See, this

---

a Gk Compare Tg: Heb it   b Or Nubia; Heb Cush   c Or Nubians; Heb Cushites

is what has happened to those in whom we hoped and to whom we fled for help and deliverance from the king of Assyria! And we, how shall we escape?' "

21   Oracles concerning Babylon, Edom, and Arabia

The oracle concerning the wilderness of
   the sea.

As whirlwinds in the Negeb sweep on,
   it comes from the desert,
   from a terrible land.
2 A stern vision is told to me;
   the betrayer betrays,
   and the destroyer destroys.
Go up, O Elam,
   lay siege, O Media;
all the sighing she has caused
   I bring to an end.
3 Therefore my loins are filled with anguish;
   pangs have seized me,
   like the pangs of a woman in labor;
I am bowed down so that I cannot hear,
   I am dismayed so that I cannot see.
4 My mind reels, horror has appalled me;
   the twilight I longed for
   has been turned for me into trembling.
5 They prepare the table,
   they spread the rugs,
   they eat, they drink.
Rise up, commanders,
   oil the shield!
6 For thus the Lord said to me:
"Go, post a lookout,
   let him announce what he sees.
7 When he sees riders, horsemen in pairs,
   riders on donkeys, riders on camels,
let him listen diligently,
   very diligently."
8 Then the watcher[b] called out:
"Upon a watchtower I stand, O Lord,
   continually by day,
and at my post I am stationed
   throughout the night.
9 Look, there they come, riders,
   horsemen in pairs!"
Then he responded,
   "Fallen, fallen is Babylon;
and all the images of her gods
   lie shattered on the ground."

10 O my threshed and winnowed one,
   what I have heard from the Lord of hosts,
   the God of Israel, I announce to you.

11 The oracle concerning Dumah.

One is calling to me from Seir,
   "Sentinel, what of the night?
   Sentinel, what of the night?"
12 The sentinel says:
"Morning comes, and also the night.
   If you will inquire, inquire;
   come back again."

13 The oracle concerning the desert plain.

In the scrub of the desert plain you will lodge,
   O caravans of Dedanites.
14 Bring water to the thirsty,
   meet the fugitive with bread,
   O inhabitants of the land of Tema.
15 For they have fled from the swords,
   from the drawn sword,
   from the bent bow,
   and from the stress of battle.

16 For thus the Lord said to me: Within a year, according to the years of a hired worker, all the glory of Kedar will come to an end; [17]and the remaining bows of Kedar's warriors will be few; for the Lord, the God of Israel, has spoken.

22   A Warning of Destruction of Jerusalem

The oracle concerning the valley of vision.

What do you mean that you have
      gone up,
   all of you, to the housetops,
2 you that are full of shoutings,
   tumultuous city, exultant town?
Your slain are not slain by the sword,
   nor are they dead in battle.
3 Your rulers have all fled together;
   they were captured without the use of a
      bow.[c]
All of you who were found were captured,
   though they had fled far away.[d]
4 Therefore I said:
Look away from me,
   let me weep bitter tears;

---

a Or Nubia; Heb Cush   b Q Ms: MT a lion   c Or without their bows   d Gk Syr Vg: Heb fled from far away

do not try to comfort me
    for the destruction of my beloved people.

5 For the Lord GOD of hosts has a day
    of tumult and trampling and confusion
    in the valley of vision,
  a battering down of walls
    and a cry for help to the mountains.
6 Elam bore the quiver
    with chariots and cavalry,*a*
  and Kir uncovered the shield.
7 Your choicest valleys were full of chariots,
    and the cavalry took their stand at the
      gates.
8 He has taken away the covering of Judah.

On that day you looked to the weapons of the House of the Forest, 9and you saw that there were many breaches in the city of David, and you collected the waters of the lower pool. 10You counted the houses of Jerusalem, and you broke down the houses to fortify the wall. 11You made a reservoir between the two walls for the water of the old pool. But you did not look to him who did it, or have regard for him who planned it long ago.

12 In that day the Lord GOD of hosts
    called to weeping and mourning,
    to baldness and putting on sackcloth;
13 but instead there was joy and festivity,
    killing oxen and slaughtering sheep,
    eating meat and drinking wine.
  "Let us eat and drink,
    for tomorrow we die."
14 The LORD of hosts has revealed himself in my
      ears:
  Surely this iniquity will not be forgiven you
    until you die,
  says the Lord GOD of hosts.

Denunciation of Self-Seeking Officials

15 Thus says the Lord GOD of hosts: Come, go to this steward, to Shebna, who is master of the household, and say to him: 16What right do you have here? Who are your relatives here, that you have cut out a tomb here for yourself, cutting a tomb on the height, and carving a habitation for yourself in the rock? 17The LORD is about to hurl you away violently, my fellow. He will seize firm hold on you, 18whirl you round and round, and throw you like a ball into a wide land; there you shall die, and there your splendid chariots shall lie, O you disgrace to your master's house! 19I will thrust you from your office, and you will be pulled down from your post.

20 On that day I will call my servant Eliakim son of Hilkiah, 21and will clothe him with your robe and

LIVE IT!

The Look of a Leader · Isaiah 22:15–25

Think about the groups you belong to: sports teams, bands, clubs, community service groups. What do they all have in common? A leader. And although we may not always get the privilege of choosing our leaders, we have a right to expect integrity from our leaders as well as a responsibility to practice it ourselves.

In **Isaiah 22:15–25**, the prophet denounces the steward Shebna for his self-seeking ways. Evidently, Shebna is using his position of leadership to prepare an expensive tomb for himself (Isaiah 22:16) and to acquire ornate chariots (Isaiah 22:18). Isaiah wants Eliakim to take over his position.

When we do have a part in choosing our school, community, and government leaders, we must seek out people who are committed to protecting basic human rights and enhancing the dignity of the human person. They must be people of integrity—people whose actions and decisions accurately reflect their core values and beliefs. Good leaders are also willing to speak up for the voiceless and advocate for those who are suffering, ensuring that every human being has the opportunity to live life abundantly.

• What qualities do you look for in a leader?

• How can you build those qualities into your own life?

a Meaning of Heb uncertain

bind your sash on him. I will commit your authority to his hand, and he shall be a father to the inhabitants of Jerusalem and to the house of Judah. ²²I will place on his shoulder the key of the house of David; he shall open, and no one shall shut; he shall shut, and no one shall open. ²³I will fasten him like a peg in a secure place, and he will become a throne of honor to his ancestral house. ²⁴And they will hang on him the whole weight of his ancestral house, the off-spring and issue, every small vessel, from the cups to all the flagons. ²⁵On that day, says the LORD of hosts, the peg that was fastened in a secure place will give way; it will be cut down and fall, and the load that was on it will perish, for the LORD has spoken.

23   An Oracle concerning Tyre

The oracle concerning Tyre.

Wail, O ships of Tarshish,
   for your fortress is destroyed.ᵃ
When they came in from Cyprus
   they learned of it.
2 Be still, O inhabitants of the coast,
   O merchants of Sidon,
your messengers crossed over the seaᵇ
3   and were on the mighty waters;
your revenue was the grain of Shihor,
   the harvest of the Nile;
   you were the merchant of the nations.
4 Be ashamed, O Sidon, for the sea has spoken,
   the fortress of the sea, saying:
"I have neither labored nor given birth,
   I have neither reared young men
   nor brought up young women."
5 When the report comes to Egypt,
   they will be in anguish over the report
     about Tyre.
6 Cross over to Tarshish—
   wail, O inhabitants of the coast!
7 Is this your exultant city
   whose origin is from days of old,
whose feet carried her
   to settle far away?
8 Who has planned this
   against Tyre, the bestower of crowns,
whose merchants were princes,
   whose traders were the honored of the
     earth?
9 The LORD of hosts has planned it—
   to defile the pride of all glory,

   to shame all the honored of the earth.
10 Cross over to your own land,
   O ships ofᶜ Tarshish;
   this is a harborᵈ no more.
11 He has stretched out his hand over the sea,
   he has shaken the kingdoms;
the LORD has given command concerning
     Canaan
   to destroy its fortresses.
12 He said:
You will exult no longer,
   O oppressed virgin daughter Sidon;
rise, cross over to Cyprus—
   even there you will have no rest.

13 Look at the land of the Chaldeans! This is the people; it was not Assyria. They destined Tyre for wild animals. They erected their siege towers, they tore down her palaces, they made her a ruin.ᵉ 14 Wail, O ships of Tarshish,
   for your fortress is destroyed.

15 From that day Tyre will be forgotten for seventy years, the lifetime of one king. At the end of seventy years, it will happen to Tyre as in the song about the prostitute:
16 Take a harp,
   go about the city,
   you forgotten prostitute!
Make sweet melody,
   sing many songs,
   that you may be remembered.

17 At the end of seventy years, the LORD will visit Tyre, and she will return to her trade, and will pros-titute herself with all the kingdoms of the world on the face of the earth. 18 Her merchandise and her wages will be dedicated to the LORD; her profitsᶠ will not be stored or hoarded, but her merchandise will supply abundant food and fine clothing for those who live in the presence of the LORD.

24   Impending Judgment on the Earth

Now the LORD is about to lay waste the
   earth and make it desolate,
and he will twist its surface and scatter its
     inhabitants.
2 And it shall be, as with the people, so with the
     priest;
as with the slave, so with his master;
as with the maid, so with her mistress;
as with the buyer, so with the seller;

ᵃ Cn Compare verse 14: Heb *for it is destroyed, without houses* ᵇ Q Ms: MT *crossing over the sea, they replenished you* ᶜ Cn Compare Gk: Heb *like the Nile, daughter* ᵈ Cn: Heb *restraint* ᵉ Meaning of Heb uncertain ᶠ Heb *it*

as with the lender, so with the borrower;
as with the creditor, so with the debtor.
3 The earth shall be utterly laid waste and
        utterly despoiled;
    for the LORD has spoken this word.

4 The earth dries up and withers,
        the world languishes and withers;
    the heavens languish together with the
        earth.
5 The earth lies polluted
        under its inhabitants;
    for they have transgressed laws,
        violated the statutes,
        broken the everlasting covenant.
6 Therefore a curse devours the earth,
        and its inhabitants suffer for their guilt;
    therefore the inhabitants of the earth
        dwindled,
        and few people are left.
7 The wine dries up,
        the vine languishes,
    all the merry-hearted sigh.
8 The mirth of the timbrels is stilled,
        the noise of the jubilant has ceased,
        the mirth of the lyre is stilled.
9 No longer do they drink wine with singing;
        strong drink is bitter to those who
        drink it.
10 The city of chaos is broken down,
        every house is shut up so that no one can
        enter.
11 There is an outcry in the streets for lack of
        wine;
    all joy has reached its eventide;
        the gladness of the earth is banished.
12 Desolation is left in the city,
        the gates are battered into ruins.
13 For thus it shall be on the earth
        and among the nations,
    as when an olive tree is beaten,
        as at the gleaning when the grape harvest
        is ended.

14 They lift up their voices, they sing for joy;
        they shout from the west over the majesty
        of the LORD.
15 Therefore in the east give glory to the LORD;
        in the coastlands of the sea glorify the
        name of the LORD, the God of Israel.

16 From the ends of the earth we hear songs of
        praise,
        of glory to the Righteous One.
    But I say, I pine away,
        I pine away. Woe is me!
    For the treacherous deal treacherously,
        the treacherous deal very treacherously.

17 Terror, and the pit, and the snare
        are upon you, O inhabitant of the earth!
18 Whoever flees at the sound of the terror
        shall fall into the pit;
    and whoever climbs out of the pit
        shall be caught in the snare.
    For the windows of heaven are opened,
        and the foundations of the earth tremble.
19 The earth is utterly broken,
        the earth is torn asunder,
        the earth is violently shaken.
20 The earth staggers like a drunkard,
        it sways like a hut;
    its transgression lies heavy upon it,
        and it falls, and will not rise again.

21 On that day the LORD will punish
        the host of heaven in heaven,
        and on earth the kings of the earth.
22 They will be gathered together
        like prisoners in a pit;
    they will be shut up in a prison,
        and after many days they will be
        punished.
23 Then the moon will be abashed,
        and the sun ashamed;
    for the LORD of hosts will reign
        on Mount Zion and in Jerusalem,
    and before his elders he will manifest his
        glory.

25 Praise for Deliverance
        from Oppression
    O LORD, you are my God;
        I will exalt you, I will praise your name;
    for you have done wonderful things,
        plans formed of old, faithful and sure.
2 For you have made the city a heap,
        the fortified city a ruin;
    the palace of aliens is a city no more,
        it will never be rebuilt.
3 Therefore strong peoples will glorify you;

cities of ruthless nations will fear you.
4 For you have been a refuge to the poor,
a refuge to the needy in their distress,
a shelter from the rainstorm and a shade
from the heat.
When the blast of the ruthless was like a
winter rainstorm,
5 the noise of aliens like heat in a dry place,
you subdued the heat with the shade of
clouds;
the song of the ruthless was stilled.

6 On this mountain the LORD of hosts will
make for all peoples
a feast of rich food, a feast of well-aged
wines,
of rich food filled with marrow, of
well-aged wines strained clear.

7 And he will destroy on this mountain
the shroud that is cast over all peoples,
the sheet that is spread over all nations;
8 he will swallow up death forever.
Then the Lord GOD will wipe away the tears
from all faces,
and the disgrace of his people he will take
away from all the earth,
for the LORD has spoken.
9 It will be said on that day,
Lo, this is our God; we have waited for
him, so that he might save us.
This is the LORD for whom we have
waited;
let us be glad and rejoice in his salvation.
10 For the hand of the LORD will rest on this
mountain.

"O LORD, you are my
God; I will exalt you, I
will praise your name;
for you have done
wonderful things,
plans formed of old,
faithful and sure."
—Isaiah 25:1

CONNECT IT!

Jacob Amaya: Nickels for Nails
Isaiah 25:4

Jacob Amaya was in fifth grade when he found out the true value of a nickel. That was the first year he helped to lead a campaign at his school to raise money for the safe, affordable housing being built by Habitat for Humanity in the Los Angeles area. The campaign, Nickels for Nails, asks young people to collect change and other donations in order to buy the nails and supplies needed to build a house. And though a nickel may not seem like much, the final result is life-changing for someone in need of shelter. For those who join in taking action, like Jacob, the words of **Isaiah 25:4** are true—they have been a refuge to the poor, a shelter from the rain, a shade from the heat.

The Moabites shall be trodden down in their
place
as straw is trodden down in a dung-pit.
11 Though they spread out their hands in the
midst of it,
as swimmers spread out their hands to
swim,
their pride will be laid low despite the
struggle[a] of their hands.
12 The high fortifications of his walls will be
brought down,
laid low, cast to the ground, even to the
dust.

Judah's Song of Victory

26 On that day this song will be sung in the
land of Judah:
We have a strong city;
he sets up victory
like walls and bulwarks.
2 Open the gates,
so that the righteous nation that keeps
faith

STUDY IT!

First Isaiah's Ideal King · Isaiah 25:6–10

The name Isaiah means "God is salvation" in Hebrew. The themes of salvation and God's holiness and the portrayal of God as the ideal king run throughout the first chapters of the book.

First Isaiah, the author of chapters 1-39 of the book of Isaiah, was probably a member of an aristocratic family and had ready access to Judah's kings. The style of his writing shows his education and is some of the loftiest and most beautiful poetry in the Old Testament. His devotion to the royal tradition of kings from the line of David is clear. Much of his writing celebrates three aspects of this tradition: God as the great king of heaven and earth, Jerusalem (Zion) as God's dwelling place, and the kings from the line of David as God's anointed earthly rulers. (See "Prophets and Kings (1050-571 B.C.)," p. 680, for a complete chart of when the prophets and kings of Israel lived.)

With this as the backdrop, much of First Isaiah's writing speaks of the future rule of God, the ideal king. **Isaiah 25:6–10** paints a picture of a beautiful day on which all who have waited on God will rejoice in salvation and celebrate on Mount Zion, the site of God's royal rule.

---

    may enter in.

3 Those of steadfast mind you keep in peace—
    in peace because they trust in you.
4 Trust in the LORD forever,
    for in the LORD GOD[b]
    you have an everlasting rock.
5 For he has brought low
    the inhabitants of the height;
    the lofty city he lays low.
He lays it low to the ground,
    casts it to the dust.
6 The foot tramples it,
    the feet of the poor,
    the steps of the needy.

7 The way of the righteous is level;
    O Just One, you make smooth the path of
      the righteous.
8 In the path of your judgments,
    O LORD, we wait for you;
your name and your renown
    are the soul's desire.
9 My soul yearns for you in the night,
    my spirit within me earnestly seeks you.
For when your judgments are in the earth,
    the inhabitants of the world learn
      righteousness.
10 If favor is shown to the wicked,
    they do not learn righteousness;
in the land of uprightness they deal perversely

    and do not see the majesty of the LORD.
11 O LORD, your hand is lifted up,
    but they do not see it.
Let them see your zeal for your people, and be
      ashamed.
    Let the fire for your adversaries consume
      them.
12 O LORD, you will ordain peace for us,
    for indeed, all that we have done, you have
      done for us.
13 O LORD our God,
    other lords besides you have ruled over us,
    but we acknowledge your name alone.
14 The dead do not live;
    shades do not rise—
because you have punished and destroyed
      them,
    and wiped out all memory of them.
15 But you have increased the nation, O LORD,
    you have increased the nation; you are
      glorified;
    you have enlarged all the borders of the
      land.

16 O LORD, in distress they sought you,
    they poured out a prayer[a]
    when your chastening was on them.
17 Like a woman with child,
    who writhes and cries out in her pangs
    when she is near her time,

---

a Meaning of Heb uncertain **b** Heb *in Yah, the* LORD

so were we because of you, O Lord;
18 we were with child, we writhed,
    but we gave birth only to wind.
We have won no victories on earth,
    and no one is born to inhabit the world.
19 Your dead shall live, their corpses*a* shall rise.
    O dwellers in the dust, awake and sing
        for joy!
For your dew is a radiant dew,
    and the earth will give birth to those long
        dead.*b*

20 Come, my people, enter your chambers,
    and shut your doors behind you;
hide yourselves for a little while
    until the wrath is past.
21 For the Lord comes out from his place
    to punish the inhabitants of the earth for
        their iniquity;
the earth will disclose the blood shed on it,
    and will no longer cover its slain.

Israel's Redemption

27 On that day the Lord with his cruel and
great and strong sword will punish
Leviathan the fleeing serpent, Leviathan the twisting serpent, and he will kill the dragon that is in
the sea.

2 On that day:
A pleasant vineyard, sing about it!
3 I, the Lord, am its keeper;
    every moment I water it.
I guard it night and day
    so that no one can harm it;
4 I have no wrath.
If it gives me thorns and briers,
    I will march to battle against it.
    I will burn it up.
5 Or else let it cling to me for
        protection,
    let it make peace with me,
    let it make peace with me.

6 In days to come*c* Jacob shall take root,
    Israel shall blossom and put forth shoots,
    and fill the whole world with fruit.

7 Has he struck them down as he struck down
    those who struck them?

Or have they been killed as their killers
    were killed?
8 By expulsion,*d* by exile you struggled against
        them;
    with his fierce blast he removed them in
        the day of the east wind.
9 Therefore by this the guilt of Jacob will be
        expiated,
    and this will be the full fruit of the
        removal of his sin:
when he makes all the stones of the altars
    like chalkstones crushed to pieces,
    no sacred poles*e* or incense altars will
        remain standing.
10 For the fortified city is solitary,
    a habitation deserted and forsaken, like
        the wilderness;
the calves graze there,
    there they lie down, and strip its
        branches.
11 When its boughs are dry, they are broken;
    women come and make a fire of them.
For this is a people without understanding;
    therefore he that made them will not have
        compassion on them,
    he that formed them will show them no
        favor.

12 On that day the Lord will thresh from the
channel of the Euphrates to the Wadi of Egypt, and
you will be gathered one by one, O people of Israel.
13 And on that day a great trumpet will be blown,
and those who were lost in the land of Assyria and
those who were driven out to the land of Egypt
will come and worship the Lord on the holy
mountain at Jerusalem.

Judgment on Corrupt Rulers, Priests, and Prophets

28 Ah, the proud garland of the drunkards
        of Ephraim,
    and the fading flower of its glorious
        beauty,
    which is on the head of those bloated
        with rich food, of those overcome
        with wine!
2 See, the Lord has one who is mighty and
        strong;
    like a storm of hail, a destroying tempest,
    like a storm of mighty, overflowing waters;

---

a Cn Compare Syr Tg: Heb *my corpse* *b* Heb *to the shades* *c* Heb *Those to come* *d* Meaning of Heb uncertain *e* Heb *Asherim*

with his hand he will hurl them down to
the earth.
3 Trampled under foot will be
the proud garland of the drunkards of
Ephraim.
4 And the fading flower of its glorious beauty,
which is on the head of those bloated
with rich food,
will be like a first-ripe fig before the summer;
whoever sees it, eats it up
as soon as it comes to hand.

5 In that day the LORD of hosts will be a
garland of glory,
and a diadem of beauty, to the remnant of
his people;
6 and a spirit of justice to the one who sits in
judgment,
and strength to those who turn back the
battle at the gate.

7 These also reel with wine
and stagger with strong drink;
the priest and the prophet reel with strong
drink,
they are confused with wine,
they stagger with strong drink;
they err in vision,
they stumble in giving judgment.
8 All tables are covered with filthy vomit;
no place is clean.

9 "Whom will he teach knowledge,
and to whom will he explain the
message?
Those who are weaned from milk,
those taken from the breast?
10 For it is precept upon precept, precept upon
precept,
line upon line, line upon line,
here a little, there a little."[a]

11 Truly, with stammering lip
and with alien tongue
he will speak to this people,
12 to whom he has said,
"This is rest;
give rest to the weary;
and this is repose";
yet they would not hear.

13 Therefore the word of the LORD will be to
them,
"Precept upon precept, precept upon
precept,
line upon line, line upon line,
here a little, there a little;"[a]
in order that they may go, and fall backward,
and be broken, and snared, and taken.

14 Therefore hear the word of the LORD, you
scoffers
who rule this people in Jerusalem.
15 Because you have said, "We have made a
covenant with death,
and with Sheol we have an agreement;
when the overwhelming scourge passes
through
it will not come to us;
for we have made lies our refuge,
and in falsehood we have taken shelter";
16 therefore thus says the Lord GOD,
See, I am laying in Zion a foundation stone,
a tested stone,
a precious cornerstone, a sure foundation:
"One who trusts will not panic."
17 And I will make justice the line,
and righteousness the plummet;
hail will sweep away the refuge of lies,
and waters will overwhelm the shelter.
18 Then your covenant with death will be
annulled,
and your agreement with Sheol will not
stand;
when the overwhelming scourge passes
through
you will be beaten down by it.
19 As often as it passes through, it will take you;
for morning by morning it will pass
through,
by day and by night;
and it will be sheer terror to understand the
message.
20 For the bed is too short to stretch oneself
on it,
and the covering too narrow to wrap
oneself in it.
21 For the LORD will rise up as on Mount
Perazim,
he will rage as in the valley of Gibeon
to do his deed—strange is his deed!—

a Meaning of Heb of this verse uncertain

and to work his work—alien is his work!

22 Now therefore do not scoff,
  or your bonds will be made stronger;
for I have heard a decree of destruction
  from the Lord GOD of hosts upon the
    whole land.

23 Listen, and hear my voice;
  Pay attention, and hear my speech.
24 Do those who plow for sowing plow
    continually?
  Do they continually open and harrow
    their ground?
25 When they have leveled its surface,
    do they not scatter dill, sow cummin,
  and plant wheat in rows
    and barley in its proper place,
    and spelt as the border?
26 For they are well instructed;
  their God teaches them.

27 Dill is not threshed with a threshing
    sledge,
  nor is a cart wheel rolled over cummin;
but dill is beaten out with a stick,
  and cummin with a rod.
28 Grain is crushed for bread,
  but one does not thresh it forever;
one drives the cart wheel and horses over it,
  but does not pulverize it.
29 This also comes from the LORD of hosts;
  he is wonderful in counsel,
  and excellent in wisdom.

The Siege of Jerusalem

29 Ah, Ariel, Ariel,
  the city where David encamped!
Add year to year;
  let the festivals run their round.
2 Yet I will distress Ariel,
  and there shall be moaning and
    lamentation,
  and Jerusalem*a* shall be to me like an
    Ariel.*b*
3 And like David*c* I will encamp against you;
  I will besiege you with towers
  and raise siegeworks against you.
4 Then deep from the earth you shall speak,
  from low in the dust your words shall
    come;

your voice shall come from the ground like the
    voice of a ghost,
  and your speech shall whisper out of the
    dust.

5 But the multitude of your foes*d* shall be like
    small dust,
  and the multitude of tyrants like flying
    chaff.
And in an instant, suddenly,
6   you will be visited by the LORD of hosts
with thunder and earthquake and great noise,
  with whirlwind and tempest, and the flame
    of a devouring fire.
7 And the multitude of all the nations that fight
    against Ariel,
  all that fight against her and her
    stronghold, and who distress her,
  shall be like a dream, a vision of the night.
8 Just as when a hungry person dreams of
    eating
  and wakes up still hungry,
or a thirsty person dreams of drinking
  and wakes up faint, still thirsty,
so shall the multitude of all the
    nations be
  that fight against Mount Zion.

9 Stupefy yourselves and be in a stupor,
  blind yourselves and be blind!
Be drunk, but not from wine;
  stagger, but not from strong drink!
10 For the LORD has poured out upon you
    a spirit of deep sleep;
he has closed your eyes, you prophets,
  and covered your heads, you seers.

11 The vision of all this has become for you like
the words of a sealed document. If it is given to
those who can read, with the command, "Read this,"
they say, "We cannot, for it is sealed." 12 And if it is
given to those who cannot read, saying, "Read this,"
they say, "We cannot read."

13 The Lord said:
Because these people draw near with their
    mouths
  and honor me with their lips,
    while their hearts are far from me,
  and their worship of me is a human
    commandment learned by rote;

---

a Heb *she* *b* Probable meaning, *altar hearth*; compare Ezek 43.15 *c* Gk: Meaning of Heb uncertain *d* Cn: Heb *strangers*

14 so I will again do
    amazing things with this people,
    shocking and amazing.
The wisdom of their wise shall perish,
    and the discernment of the discerning
      shall be hidden.

15 Ha! You who hide a plan too deep for the
      Lord,
    whose deeds are in the dark,
    and who say, "Who sees us? Who
      knows us?"
16 You turn things upside down!
    Shall the potter be regarded as the clay?
Shall the thing made say of its maker,
    "He did not make me";
or the thing formed say of the one who
      formed it,
    "He has no understanding"?

Hope for the Future

17 Shall not Lebanon in a very little while
    become a fruitful field,
    and the fruitful field be regarded as a
      forest?
18 On that day the deaf shall hear
    the words of a scroll,
and out of their gloom and darkness
    the eyes of the blind shall see.
19 The meek shall obtain fresh joy in the Lord,
    and the neediest people shall exult in the
      Holy One of Israel.
20 For the tyrant shall be no more,
    and the scoffer shall cease to be;
    all those alert to do evil shall be cut off—
21 those who cause a person to lose a lawsuit,
    who set a trap for the arbiter in the gate,
    and without grounds deny justice to the
      one in the right.

22 Therefore thus says the Lord, who redeemed
Abraham, concerning the house of Jacob:
    No longer shall Jacob be ashamed,
      no longer shall his face grow pale.
23 For when he sees his children,
      the work of my hands, in his midst,
      they will sanctify my name;
    they will sanctify the Holy One of Jacob,
      and will stand in awe of the God of Israel.

PRAY IT!

Hope for the Poor · Isaiah 29:17–21

Imagine a world where the deaf will hear, the blind will see, the meek will know joy, and the neediest of people will rejoice. Isaiah's words in **Isaiah 29:17–21** are reflected in Jesus' words in the Beatitudes (Luke 6:20-26). Both Jesus and Isaiah say that in God's reign the rights and needs of the lowliest and the weakest come first (see Isaiah 58 and 61).

There is hope for those living in poverty. And hope makes all the difference. Poverty is often seen simply as a lack of material possessions or wealth. But at a deeper level, it is a lack of hope that things can ever change.

So how can we be part of bringing this hope to the poor and helpless in our own country and around the world? How can we make our own communities ones where the most vulnerable people are treated with dignity and love?

- Write your own prayer describing God's vision for those who are poor. Use Isaiah's words and the Beatitudes for ideas.
- Share your prayer with your family or youth group.

24 And those who err in spirit will come to
       understanding,
    and those who grumble will accept
       instruction.

The Futility of Reliance on Egypt

30 Oh, rebellious children, says the LORD,
    who carry out a plan, but not mine;
who make an alliance, but against my will,
    adding sin to sin;
2 who set out to go down to Egypt
    without asking for my counsel,
to take refuge in the protection of Pharaoh,
    and to seek shelter in the shadow of Egypt;
3 Therefore the protection of Pharaoh shall
       become your shame,
    and the shelter in the shadow of Egypt your
       humiliation.
4 For though his officials are at Zoan
    and his envoys reach Hanes,
5 everyone comes to shame
    through a people that cannot profit them,
that brings neither help nor profit,
    but shame and disgrace.

6 An oracle concerning the animals of the Negeb.
 Through a land of trouble and distress,
    of lioness and roaring*a* lion,
    of viper and flying serpent,
they carry their riches on the backs of donkeys,
    and their treasures on the humps of camels,
    to a people that cannot profit them.
7 For Egypt's help is worthless and empty,
    therefore I have called her,
    "Rahab who sits still."*b*

A Rebellious People

8 Go now, write it before them on a tablet,
    and inscribe it in a book,
so that it may be for the time to come
    as a witness forever.
9 For they are a rebellious people,
    faithless children,
children who will not hear
    the instruction of the LORD;
10 who say to the seers, "Do not see";
    and to the prophets, "Do not prophesy to us
       what is right;
speak to us smooth things,
    prophesy illusions,

11 leave the way, turn aside from the path,
    let us hear no more about the Holy One of
       Israel."
12 Therefore thus says the Holy One of Israel:
 Because you reject this word,
    and put your trust in oppression and
       deceit,
    and rely on them;
13 therefore this iniquity shall become for you
    like a break in a high wall, bulging out, and
       about to collapse,
    whose crash comes suddenly, in an instant;
14 its breaking is like that of a potter's vessel
    that is smashed so ruthlessly
that among its fragments not a sherd is found
    for taking fire from the hearth,
    or dipping water out of the cistern.

15 For thus said the Lord GOD, the Holy One of
       Israel:
 In returning and rest you shall be saved;
    in quietness and in trust shall be your
       strength.
But you refused 16and said,
    "No! We will flee upon horses"—
    therefore you shall flee!
and, "We will ride upon swift steeds"—
    therefore your pursuers shall be swift!
17 A thousand shall flee at the threat of one,
    at the threat of five you shall flee,
until you are left
    like a flagstaff on the top of a mountain,
    like a signal on a hill.

God's Promise to Zion

18 Therefore the LORD waits to be gracious
       to you;
    therefore he will rise up to show mercy
       to you.
 For the LORD is a God of justice;
    blessed are all those who wait for him.
  19 Truly, O people in Zion, inhabitants of Jerusalem, you shall weep no more. He will surely be
gracious to you at the sound of your cry; when he
hears it, he will answer you. 20Though the Lord may
give you the bread of adversity and the water of affliction, yet your Teacher will not hide himself any
more, but your eyes shall see your Teacher. 21And
when you turn to the right or when you turn to the
left, your ears shall hear a word behind you, saying,

a Cn: Heb *from them*   *b* Meaning of Heb uncertain

> "When you turn to the right or when you turn to the left, your ears shall hear a word behind you, saying, 'This is the way; walk in it.'"
> —Isaiah 30:21

"This is the way; walk in it." [22] Then you will defile your silver-covered idols and your gold-plated images. You will scatter them like filthy rags; you will say to them, "Away with you!"

23 He will give rain for the seed with which you sow the ground, and grain, the produce of the ground, which will be rich and plenteous. On that day your cattle will graze in broad pastures; [24] and the oxen and donkeys that till the ground will eat silage, which has been winnowed with shovel and fork. [25] On every lofty mountain and every high hill there will be brooks running with water—on a day of the great slaughter, when the towers fall. [26] Moreover the light of the moon will be like the light of the sun, and the light of the sun will be sevenfold, like the light of seven days, on the day when the LORD binds up the injuries of his people, and heals the wounds inflicted by his blow.

Judgment on Assyria

27 See, the name of the LORD comes from far
  away,
    burning with his anger, and in thick rising
    smoke;[a]
  his lips are full of indignation,
    and his tongue is like a devouring fire;
28 his breath is like an overflowing stream
    that reaches up to the neck—
  to sift the nations with the sieve of
    destruction,
    and to place on the jaws of the peoples a
    bridle that leads them astray.

29 You shall have a song as in the night when a holy festival is kept; and gladness of heart, as when one sets out to the sound of the flute to go to the mountain of the LORD, to the Rock of Israel. [30] And

the LORD will cause his majestic voice to be heard and the descending blow of his arm to be seen, in furious anger and a flame of devouring fire, with a cloudburst and tempest and hailstones. [31] The Assyrian will be terror-stricken at the voice of the LORD, when he strikes with his rod. [32] And every stroke of the staff of punishment that the LORD lays upon him will be to the sound of timbrels and lyres; battling with brandished arm he will fight with him. [33] For his burning place[b] has long been prepared; truly it is made ready for the king,[c] its pyre made deep and wide, with fire and wood in abundance; the breath of the LORD, like a stream of sulfur, kindles it.

Alliance with Egypt Is Futile

31 Alas for those who go down to Egypt
      for help
    and who rely on horses,
  who trust in chariots because they are many
    and in horsemen because they are very
      strong,
  but do not look to the Holy One of Israel
    or consult the LORD!
2 Yet he too is wise and brings disaster;
    he does not call back his words,
  but will rise against the house of the evildoers,
    and against the helpers of those who work
      iniquity.
3 The Egyptians are human, and not God;
    their horses are flesh, and not spirit.
  When the LORD stretches out his hand,
    the helper will stumble, and the one helped
      will fall,
    and they will all perish together.

4 For thus the LORD said to me,
  As a lion or a young lion growls over its prey,
    and—when a band of shepherds is called
      out against it—
  is not terrified by their shouting
    or daunted at their noise,
  so the LORD of hosts will come down
    to fight upon Mount Zion and upon its
      hill.
5 Like birds hovering overhead, so the LORD of
      hosts
    will protect Jerusalem;
  he will protect and deliver it,
    he will spare and rescue it.

a Meaning of Heb uncertain   b Or Topheth   c Or Molech

6 Turn back to him whom you[a] have deeply betrayed, O people of Israel. 7 For on that day all of you shall throw away your idols of silver and idols of gold, which your hands have sinfully made for you.

8 "Then the Assyrian shall fall by a sword, not
        of mortals;
    and a sword, not of humans, shall
        devour him;
he shall flee from the sword,
    and his young men shall be put to forced
        labor.
9 His rock shall pass away in terror,
    and his officers desert the standard in
        panic,"
says the LORD, whose fire is in Zion,
    and whose furnace is in Jerusalem.

Government with Justice Predicted

32 See, a king will reign in righteousness,
    and princes will rule with justice.
2 Each will be like a hiding place from the
        wind,
    a covert from the tempest,
like streams of water in a dry place,
    like the shade of a great rock in a weary
        land.
3 Then the eyes of those who have sight will
        not be closed,
    and the ears of those who have hearing
        will listen.
4 The minds of the rash will have good
        judgment,
    and the tongues of stammerers will speak
        readily and distinctly.
5 A fool will no longer be called noble,
    nor a villain said to be honorable.
6 For fools speak folly,
    and their minds plot iniquity:
to practice ungodliness,
    to utter error concerning the LORD,
to leave the craving of the hungry unsatisfied,
    and to deprive the thirsty of drink.
7 The villainies of villains are evil;
    they devise wicked devices
to ruin the poor with lying words,
    even when the plea of the needy is
        right.
8 But those who are noble plan noble things,
    and by noble things they stand.

Complacent Women Warned of Disaster

9 Rise up, you women who are at ease, hear my
        voice;
    you complacent daughters, listen to my
        speech.
10 In little more than a year
    you will shudder, you complacent ones;
for the vintage will fail,
    the fruit harvest will not come.
11 Tremble, you women who are at ease,
    shudder, you complacent ones;
strip, and make yourselves bare,
    and put sackcloth on your loins.
12 Beat your breasts for the pleasant fields,
    for the fruitful vine,
13 for the soil of my people
    growing up in thorns and briers;
yes, for all the joyous houses
    in the jubilant city.
14 For the palace will be forsaken,
    the populous city deserted;
the hill and the watchtower
    will become dens forever,
the joy of wild asses,
    a pasture for flocks;
15 until a spirit from on high is poured out on us,
    and the wilderness becomes a fruitful
        field,
    and the fruitful field is deemed a forest.

The Peace of God's Reign

16 Then justice will dwell in the wilderness,
    and righteousness abide in the fruitful
        field.
17 The effect of righteousness will be peace,
    and the result of righteousness, quietness
        and trust forever.
18 My people will abide in a peaceful habitation,
    in secure dwellings, and in quiet resting
        places.
19 The forest will disappear completely,[a]
    and the city will be utterly laid low.
20 Happy will you be who sow beside every
        stream,
    who let the ox and the donkey range freely.

A Prophecy of Deliverance from Foes

33 Ah, you destroyer,
    who yourself have not been destroyed;
you treacherous one,

---

a Heb *they*

LIVE IT!

Shalom
Isaiah 32:16–20

In Israel, people greet one another by saying, "Shalom." In the Bible, the Hebrew word "shalom" means "peace." **Isaiah 32:16–20** describes peace in its fullest sense. Peace is not just the absence of war and violence, but also the presence of justice, righteousness, happiness, and fullness of life. What better way to greet your neighbors or friends than to wish them "shalom"?

In your own life, seek peace. Begin each day by praying for peace of mind and heart, and for God's help to live out peace by acting with justice in all that you do. The very prayer you speak will become the way you live.

with whom no one has dealt treacherously!
    When you have ceased to destroy,
        you will be destroyed;
    and when you have stopped dealing
        treacherously,
        you will be dealt with treacherously.

2 O LORD, be gracious to us; we wait for you.
    Be our arm every morning,
        our salvation in the time of trouble.
3 At the sound of tumult, peoples fled;
    before your majesty, nations scattered.
4 Spoil was gathered as the caterpillar gathers;
    as locusts leap, they leaped[b] upon it.
5 The LORD is exalted, he dwells on high;
    he filled Zion with justice and
        righteousness;
6 he will be the stability of your times,
    abundance of salvation, wisdom, and
        knowledge;
    the fear of the LORD is Zion's treasure.[c]

7 Listen! the valiant[b] cry in the streets;
    the envoys of peace weep bitterly.
8 The highways are deserted,
    travelers have quit the road.

The treaty is broken,
    its oaths[d] are despised,
    its obligation[e] is disregarded.
9 The land mourns and languishes;
    Lebanon is confounded and withers away;
Sharon is like a desert;
    and Bashan and Carmel shake off their
        leaves.

10 "Now I will arise," says the LORD,
    "now I will lift myself up;
    now I will be exalted.
11 You conceive chaff, you bring forth stubble;
    your breath is a fire that will consume you.
12 And the peoples will be as if burned to lime,
    like thorns cut down, that are burned in
        the fire."

13 Hear, you who are far away, what I have done;
    and you who are near, acknowledge my
        might.
14 The sinners in Zion are afraid;
    trembling has seized the godless:
"Who among us can live with the devouring
        fire?
    Who among us can live with everlasting
        flames?"
15 Those who walk righteously and speak
        uprightly,
    who despise the gain of oppression,
who wave away a bribe instead of accepting it,
    who stop their ears from hearing of
        bloodshed
    and shut their eyes from looking on evil,
16 they will live on the heights;
    their refuge will be the fortresses of rocks;
    their food will be supplied, their water
        assured.

The Land of the Majestic King
17 Your eyes will see the king in his beauty;
    they will behold a land that stretches far
        away.
18 Your mind will muse on the terror:
    "Where is the one who counted?
    Where is the one who weighed the
        tribute?
    Where is the one who counted the
        towers?"
19 No longer will you see the insolent people,

a Cn: Heb *And it will hail when the forest comes down*   b Meaning of Heb uncertain   c Heb *his treasure*; meaning of Heb uncertain   d Q Ms: MT *cities*
e Or *everyone*

the people of an obscure speech that you
    cannot comprehend,
    stammering in a language that you cannot
    understand.
20 Look on Zion, the city of our appointed
    festivals!
    Your eyes will see Jerusalem,
    a quiet habitation, an immovable tent,
whose stakes will never be pulled up,
    and none of whose ropes will be broken.
21 But there the LORD in majesty will be
        for us
    a place of broad rivers and streams,
where no galley with oars can go,
    nor stately ship can pass.
22 For the LORD is our judge, the LORD is our
        ruler,
    the LORD is our king; he will save us.

23 Your rigging hangs loose;
    it cannot hold the mast firm in its place,
    or keep the sail spread out.

Then prey and spoil in abundance will be
        divided;
    even the lame will fall to plundering.
24 And no inhabitant will say, "I am sick";
    the people who live there will be forgiven
        their iniquity.

34 Judgment on the Nations

Draw near, O nations, to hear;
    O peoples, give heed!
Let the earth hear, and all that fills it;
    the world, and all that comes from it.
2 For the LORD is enraged against all the nations,
    and furious against all their hordes;
    he has doomed them, has given them over
        for slaughter.
3 Their slain shall be cast out,
    and the stench of their corpses shall rise;
    the mountains shall flow with their blood.
4 All the host of heaven shall rot away,
    and the skies roll up like a scroll.
All their host shall wither
    like a leaf withering on a vine,
    or fruit withering on a fig tree.

5 When my sword has drunk its fill in the
        heavens,

lo, it will descend upon Edom,
    upon the people I have doomed to
        judgment.
6 The LORD has a sword; it is sated with blood,
    it is gorged with fat,
    with the blood of lambs and goats,
    with the fat of the kidneys of rams.
For the LORD has a sacrifice in Bozrah,
    a great slaughter in the land of Edom.
7 Wild oxen shall fall with them,
    and young steers with the mighty bulls.
Their land shall be soaked with blood,
    and their soil made rich with fat.

8 For the LORD has a day of vengeance,
    a year of vindication by Zion's cause.[a]
9 And the streams of Edom[b] shall be turned
        into pitch,
    and her soil into sulfur;
    her land shall become burning pitch.
10 Night and day it shall not be quenched;
    its smoke shall go up forever.
From generation to generation it shall lie
        waste;
    no one shall pass through it forever and
        ever.
11 But the hawk[c] and the hedgehog[c] shall
        possess it;
    the owl[c] and the raven shall live in it.
He shall stretch the line of confusion over it,
    and the plummet of chaos over[d] its
        nobles.
12 They shall name it No Kingdom There,
    and all its princes shall be nothing.
13 Thorns shall grow over its strongholds,
    nettles and thistles in its fortresses.
It shall be the haunt of jackals,
    an abode for ostriches.
14 Wildcats shall meet with hyenas,
    goat-demons shall call to each other;
there too Lilith shall repose,
    and find a place to rest.
15 There shall the owl nest
    and lay and hatch and brood in its
        shadow;
there too the buzzards shall gather,
    each one with its mate.
16 Seek and read from the book of the LORD:
    Not one of these shall be missing;
    none shall be without its mate.

a Or of recompense by Zion's defender b Heb her streams c Identification uncertain d Heb lacks over

For the mouth of the LORD has commanded,
    and his spirit has gathered them.
17 He has cast the lot for them,
    his hand has portioned it out to them
        with the line;
they shall possess it forever,
    from generation to generation they shall
        live in it.

35 The Return of the Redeemed to Zion

The wilderness and the dry land shall
    be glad,
the desert shall rejoice and blossom;
like the crocus ²it shall blossom abundantly,
    and rejoice with joy and singing.
The glory of Lebanon shall be given
    to it,
    the majesty of Carmel and Sharon.
They shall see the glory of the LORD,
    the majesty of our God.

3 Strengthen the weak hands,
    and make firm the feeble knees.
4 Say to those who are of a fearful heart,
    "Be strong, do not fear!
Here is your God.
    He will come with vengeance,
with terrible recompense.
    He will come and save you."

5 Then the eyes of the blind shall be opened,
    and the ears of the deaf unstopped;
6 then the lame shall leap like a deer,
    and the tongue of the speechless sing
        for joy.

For waters shall break forth in the wilderness,
    and streams in the desert;
7 the burning sand shall become a pool,
    and the thirsty ground springs of water;
the haunt of jackals shall become a swamp,ᵃ
    the grass shall become reeds and rushes.

8 A highway shall be there,
    and it shall be called the Holy Way;
the unclean shall not travel on it,ᵇ
    but it shall be for God's people;ᶜ
    no traveler, not even fools, shall go
        astray.
9 No lion shall be there,
    nor shall any ravenous beast come up
        on it;
they shall not be found there,
    but the redeemed shall walk there.
10 And the ransomed of the LORD shall return,
    and come to Zion with singing;
everlasting joy shall be upon their heads;
    they shall obtain joy and gladness,
    and sorrow and sighing shall flee away.

36 Sennacherib Threatens Jerusalem

In the fourteenth year of King Hezekiah, King Sennacherib of Assyria came up against all the fortified cities of Judah and captured them. ²The king of Assyria sent the Rabshakeh from Lachish to King Hezekiah at Jerusalem, with a great army. He stood by the conduit of the upper pool on the highway to the Fuller's Field. ³And there came out to him Eliakim son of Hilkiah, who was in charge of the palace, and Shebna the secretary, and Joah son of Asaph, the recorder.

Salvation Is Coming · Isaiah 35

Imagine the desperation of wandering through the desert hoping for water but never finding any. Then imagine the relief you'd feel when someone arrives and gives you word that not only is there water ahead, but the burning sand you are standing on will become a pool of clear, refreshing water. This is the poetic picture of hope that Isaiah offers in **Isaiah 35**. To followers of God who feel tired, weak, and fearful, Isaiah promises that God will save them and make their wilderness into an abundant land. This theme is repeated many times in Isaiah, giving hope to people in need.

And the hope of God's salvation is true for us today. Whether you feel as though you're wandering in a physical, mental, or emotional desert, God's power to meet you there with hope, salvation, and restoration is real.

ᵃ Cn: Heb *in the haunt of jackals is her resting place*   ᵇ Or *pass it by*   ᶜ Cn: Heb *for them*

4 The Rabshakeh said to them, "Say to Hezekiah: Thus says the great king, the king of Assyria: On what do you base this confidence of yours? [5]Do you think that mere words are strategy and power for war? On whom do you now rely, that you have rebelled against me? [6]See, you are relying on Egypt, that broken reed of a staff, which will pierce the hand of anyone who leans on it. Such is Pharaoh king of Egypt to all who rely on him. [7]But if you say to me, 'We rely on the LORD our God,' is it not he whose high places and altars Hezekiah has removed, saying to Judah and to Jerusalem, 'You shall worship before this altar'? [8]Come now, make a wager with my master the king of Assyria: I will give you two thousand horses, if you are able on your part to set riders on them. [9]How then can you repulse a single captain among the least of my master's servants, when you rely on Egypt for chariots and for horsemen? [10]Moreover, is it without the LORD that I have come up against this land to destroy it? The LORD said to me, Go up against this land, and destroy it."

11 Then Eliakim, Shebna, and Joah said to the Rabshakeh, "Please speak to your servants in Aramaic, for we understand it; do not speak to us in the language of Judah within the hearing of the people who are on the wall." [12]But the Rabshakeh said, "Has my master sent me to speak these words to your master and to you, and not to the people sitting on the wall, who are doomed with you to eat their own dung and drink their own urine?"

13 Then the Rabshakeh stood and called out in a loud voice in the language of Judah, "Hear the words of the great king, the king of Assyria! [14]Thus says the king: 'Do not let Hezekiah deceive you, for he will not be able to deliver you. [15]Do not let Hezekiah make you rely on the LORD by saying, The LORD will surely deliver us; this city will not be given into the hand of the king of Assyria.' [16]Do not listen to Hezekiah; for thus says the king of Assyria: 'Make your peace with me and come out to me; then every one of you will eat from your own vine and your own fig tree and drink water from your own cistern, [17]until I come and take you away to a land like your own land, a land of grain and wine, a land of bread and vineyards. [18]Do not let Hezekiah mislead you by saying, The LORD will save us. Has any of the gods of the nations saved their land out of the hand of the king of Assyria? [19]Where are the gods of Hamath and Arpad? Where are the gods of Sepharvaim? Have they delivered Samaria out of my hand? [20]Who among all the gods of these countries have saved their countries out of my hand, that the LORD should save Jerusalem out of my hand?' "

21 But they were silent and answered him not a word, for the king's command was, "Do not answer him." [22]Then Eliakim son of Hilkiah, who was in charge of the palace, and Shebna the secretary, and Joah son of Asaph, the recorder, came to Hezekiah with their clothes torn, and told him the words of the Rabshakeh.

Hezekiah Consults Isaiah

37 When King Hezekiah heard it, he tore his clothes, covered himself with sackcloth, and went into the house of the LORD. [2]And he sent Eliakim, who was in charge of the palace, and Shebna the secretary, and the senior priests, covered with sackcloth, to the prophet Isaiah son of Amoz. [3]They said to him, "Thus says Hezekiah, This day is a day of distress, of rebuke, and of disgrace; children have come to the birth, and there is no strength to bring them forth. [4]It may be that the LORD your God heard the words of the Rabshakeh, whom his master the king of Assyria has sent to mock the living God, and will rebuke the words that the LORD your God has heard; therefore lift up your prayer for the remnant that is left."

5 When the servants of King Hezekiah came to Isaiah, [6]Isaiah said to them, "Say to your master, 'Thus says the LORD: Do not be afraid because of the words that you have heard, with which the servants of the king of Assyria have reviled me. [7]I myself will put a spirit in him, so that he shall hear a rumor, and return to his own land; I will cause him to fall by the sword in his own land.' "

8 The Rabshakeh returned, and found the king of Assyria fighting against Libnah; for he had heard that the king had left Lachish. [9]Now the king[a] heard concerning King Tirhakah of Ethiopia,[b] "He has set out to fight against you." When he heard it, he sent messengers to Hezekiah, saying, [10]"Thus shall you speak to King Hezekiah of Judah: Do not let your God on whom you rely deceive you by promising that Jerusalem will not be given into the hand of the king of Assyria. [11]See, you have heard what the kings of Assyria have done to all lands, destroying them utterly. Shall you be delivered? [12]Have the gods of the nations delivered them, the nations that my predecessors destroyed, Gozan, Haran, Rezeph, and the people of Eden who were in Telassar?

a Heb *he* b Or *Nubia*; Heb *Cush*

¹³Where is the king of Hamath, the king of Arpad, the king of the city of Sepharvaim, the king of Hena, or the king of Ivvah?"

Hezekiah's Prayer

14 Hezekiah received the letter from the hand of the messengers and read it; then Hezekiah went up to the house of the LORD and spread it before the LORD. ¹⁵And Hezekiah prayed to the LORD, saying: ¹⁶"O LORD of hosts, God of Israel, who are enthroned above the cherubim, you are God, you alone, of all the kingdoms of the earth; you have made heaven and earth. ¹⁷Incline your ear, O LORD, and hear; open your eyes, O LORD, and see; hear all the words of Sennacherib, which he has sent to mock the living God. ¹⁸Truly, O LORD, the kings of Assyria have laid waste all the nations and their lands, ¹⁹and have hurled their gods into the fire, though they were no gods, but the work of human hands—wood and stone—and so they were destroyed. ²⁰So now, O LORD our God, save us from his hand, so that all the kingdoms of the earth may know that you alone are the LORD."

21 Then Isaiah son of Amoz sent to Hezekiah, saying: "Thus says the LORD, the God of Israel: Because you have prayed to me concerning King Sennacherib of Assyria, ²²this is the word that the LORD has spoken concerning him:

She despises you, she scorns you—
    virgin daughter Zion;
she tosses her head—behind your back,
    daughter Jerusalem.

²³ "Whom have you mocked and reviled?
    Against whom have you raised your voice
and haughtily lifted your eyes?
    Against the Holy One of Israel!
²⁴ By your servants you have mocked the Lord,
    and you have said, 'With my many
      chariots
I have gone up the heights of the mountains,
    to the far recesses of Lebanon;
I felled its tallest cedars,
    its choicest cypresses;
I came to its remotest height,
    its densest forest.
²⁵ I dug wells
    and drank waters,
I dried up with the sole of my foot
    all the streams of Egypt.'

²⁶ "Have you not heard
    that I determined it long ago?
I planned from days of old
    what now I bring to pass,
that you should make fortified cities
    crash into heaps of ruins,
²⁷ while their inhabitants, shorn of strength,
    are dismayed and confounded;
they have become like plants of the field
    and like tender grass,
like grass on the housetops,
    blighted^a before it is grown.

²⁸ "I know your rising up^b and your sitting
    down,
    your going out and coming in,
    and your raging against me.
²⁹ Because you have raged against me
    and your arrogance has come to my ears,
I will put my hook in your nose
    and my bit in your mouth;
I will turn you back on the way
    by which you came.

30 "And this shall be the sign for you: This year eat what grows of itself, and in the second year what springs from that; then in the third year sow, reap, plant vineyards, and eat their fruit. ³¹The surviving remnant of the house of Judah shall again take root downward, and bear fruit upward; ³²for from Jerusalem a remnant shall go out, and from Mount Zion a band of survivors. The zeal of the LORD of hosts will do this.

33 "Therefore thus says the LORD concerning the king of Assyria: He shall not come into this city, shoot an arrow there, come before it with a shield, or cast up a siege ramp against it. ³⁴By the way that he came, by the same he shall return; he shall not come into this city, says the LORD. ³⁵For I will defend this city to save it, for my own sake and for the sake of my servant David."

Sennacherib's Defeat and Death

36 Then the angel of the LORD set out and struck down one hundred eighty-five thousand in the camp of the Assyrians; when morning dawned, they were all dead bodies. ³⁷Then King Sennacherib of Assyria left, went home, and lived at Nineveh. ³⁸As he was worshiping in the house of his god Nisroch, his sons Adrammelech and Sharezer killed him with

a With 2 Kings 19.26: Heb *field*   *b* Q Ms Gk: MT lacks *your rising up*

the sword, and they escaped into the land of Ararat. His son Esar-haddon succeeded him.

Hezekiah's Illness

38 In those days Hezekiah became sick and was at the point of death. The prophet Isaiah son of Amoz came to him, and said to him, "Thus says the LORD: Set your house in order, for you shall die; you shall not recover." [2] Then Hezekiah turned his face to the wall, and prayed to the LORD: [3] "Remember now, O LORD, I implore you, how I have walked before you in faithfulness with a whole heart, and have done what is good in your sight." And Hezekiah wept bitterly.

4 Then the word of the LORD came to Isaiah: [5] "Go and say to Hezekiah, Thus says the LORD, the God of your ancestor David: I have heard your prayer, I have seen your tears; I will add fifteen years to your life. [6] I will deliver you and this city out of the hand of the king of Assyria, and defend this city.

7 "This is the sign to you from the LORD, that the LORD will do this thing that he has promised: [8] See, I will make the shadow cast by the declining sun on the dial of Ahaz turn back ten steps." So the sun turned back on the dial the ten steps by which it had declined.[a]

9 A writing of King Hezekiah of Judah, after he had been sick and had recovered from his sickness:
[10] I said: In the noontide of my days
    I must depart;
I am consigned to the gates of Sheol
    for the rest of my years.
[11] I said, I shall not see the LORD
    in the land of the living;
I shall look upon mortals no more
    among the inhabitants of the world.
[12] My dwelling is plucked up and removed
        from me
    like a shepherd's tent;
like a weaver I have rolled up my life;
    he cuts me off from the loom;
from day to night you bring me to an end;[a]
[13]   I cry for help[b] until morning;
like a lion he breaks all my bones;
    from day to night you bring me to an end.[a]

[14] Like a swallow or a crane[a] I clamor,
    I moan like a dove.
My eyes are weary with looking upward.

O Lord, I am oppressed; be my security!
[15] But what can I say? For he has spoken to me,
    and he himself has done it.
All my sleep has fled[c]
    because of the bitterness of my soul.

[16] O Lord, by these things people live,
    and in all these is the life of my spirit.[a]
    Oh, restore me to health and make me live!
[17] Surely it was for my welfare
    that I had great bitterness;
but you have held back[d] my life
    from the pit of destruction,
for you have cast all my sins
    behind your back.
[18] For Sheol cannot thank you,
    death cannot praise you;
those who go down to the Pit cannot hope
    for your faithfulness.
[19] The living, the living, they thank you,
    as I do this day;
fathers make known to children
    your faithfulness.

[20] The LORD will save me,
    and we will sing to stringed instruments[e]
all the days of our lives,
    at the house of the LORD.

21 Now Isaiah had said, "Let them take a lump of figs, and apply it to the boil, so that he may recover." [22] Hezekiah also had said, "What is the sign that I shall go up to the house of the LORD?"

Envoys from Babylon Welcomed

39 At that time King Merodach-baladan son of Baladan of Babylon sent envoys with letters and a present to Hezekiah, for he heard that he had been sick and had recovered. [2] Hezekiah welcomed them; he showed them his treasure house, the silver, the gold, the spices, the precious oil, his whole armory, all that was found in his storehouses. There was nothing in his house or in all his realm that Hezekiah did not show them. [3] Then the prophet Isaiah came to King Hezekiah and said to him, "What did these men say? From where did they come to you?" Hezekiah answered, "They have come to me from a far country, from Babylon." [4] He said, "What have they seen in your house?" Hezekiah answered, "They have seen all that is in my

---

a Meaning of Heb uncertain   b Cn: Meaning of Heb uncertain   c Cn Compare Syr: Heb *I will walk slowly all my years*   d Cn Compare Gk Vg: Heb *loved*   e Heb *my stringed instruments*

house; there is nothing in my storehouses that I did not show them."

5 Then Isaiah said to Hezekiah, "Hear the word of the LORD of hosts: ⁶Days are coming when all that is in your house, and that which your ancestors have stored up until this day, shall be carried to Babylon; nothing shall be left, says the LORD. ⁷Some of your own sons who are born to you shall be taken away; they shall be eunuchs in the palace of the king of Babylon." ⁸Then Hezekiah said to Isaiah, "The word of the LORD that you have spoken is good." For he thought, "There will be peace and security in my days."

God's People Are Comforted

40 Comfort, O comfort my people,
  says your God.
2 Speak tenderly to Jerusalem,
    and cry to her
that she has served her term,
    that her penalty is paid,
that she has received from the LORD's hand
    double for all her sins.

3 A voice cries out:
"In the wilderness prepare the way of the
    LORD,
    make straight in the desert a highway for
    our God.
4 Every valley shall be lifted up,

and every mountain and hill be made low;
  the uneven ground shall become level,
    and the rough places a plain.
5 Then the glory of the LORD shall be revealed,
    and all people shall see it together,
  for the mouth of the LORD has spoken."

6 A voice says, "Cry out!"
    And I said, "What shall I cry?"
All people are grass,
    their constancy is like the flower of the
    field.
7 The grass withers, the flower fades,
    when the breath of the LORD blows
      upon it;
    surely the people are grass.
8 The grass withers, the flower fades;
  but the word of our God will stand forever.
9 Get you up to a high mountain,
    O Zion, herald of good tidings;ᵃ
lift up your voice with strength,
    O Jerusalem, herald of good tidings,ᵇ
lift it up, do not fear;
say to the cities of Judah,
    "Here is your God!"
10 See, the Lord GOD comes with might,
    and his arm rules for him;
his reward is with him,
    and his recompense before him.
11 He will feed his flock like a shepherd;

PRAY IT!

The Hope of Second Isaiah · Isaiah 40:1–5

Second Isaiah, the author of chapters 40–55, prophesies to the Israelites living in exile in Babylon with words full of love and hope: "Comfort, O comfort my people, says your God" (Isaiah 40:1). Isaiah promises these Israelites a new liberation and the eventual restoration of Jerusalem and the temple (Isaiah 44:26–28).

The author of the gospel of Luke uses part of this passage (Isaiah 40:3–5) to describe the ministry of John the Baptist in announcing Jesus' arrival (Luke 3:4–6). This writer wants to make it clear that Isaiah's promises are answered by the coming of Jesus.

Say a prayer of thanks for the fulfillment of hope in Jesus. Then pray about or journal on the following questions:
• Is there hope for our world today?
• What are some things that you are hopeful for?
• Imagine God is speaking words of hope to you. What is God saying?
• Has the hope Jesus brought changed your life? How?

ᵃ Or *O herald of good tidings to Zion*   ᵇ Or *O herald of good tidings to Jerusalem*

he will gather the lambs in his arms,
and carry them in his bosom,
and gently lead the mother sheep.

12 Who has measured the waters in the hollow of
his hand
and marked off the heavens with a span,
enclosed the dust of the earth in a measure,
and weighed the mountains in scales
and the hills in a balance?
13 Who has directed the spirit of the LORD,
or as his counselor has instructed him?
14 Whom did he consult for his enlightenment,
and who taught him the path of justice?
Who taught him knowledge,
and showed him the way of understanding?

15 Even the nations are like a drop from a bucket,
and are accounted as dust on the scales;
see, he takes up the isles like fine dust.
16 Lebanon would not provide fuel enough,
nor are its animals enough for a burnt
offering.
17 All the nations are as nothing before him;
they are accounted by him as less than
nothing and emptiness.

18 To whom then will you liken God,
or what likeness compare with him?
19 An idol?—A workman casts it,
and a goldsmith overlays it with gold,
and casts for it silver chains.
20 As a gift one chooses mulberry wood*a*
—wood that will not rot—
then seeks out a skilled artisan
to set up an image that will not topple.

21 Have you not known? Have you not heard?
Has it not been told you from the
beginning?
Have you not understood from the
foundations of the earth?

22 It is he who sits above the circle of the earth,
and its inhabitants are like grasshoppers;
who stretches out the heavens like a curtain,
and spreads them like a tent to
live in;
23 who brings princes to naught,
and makes the rulers of the earth as
nothing.

24 Scarcely are they planted, scarcely sown,
scarcely has their stem taken root in the
earth,
when he blows upon them, and they wither,
and the tempest carries them off like
stubble.

25 To whom then will you compare me,
or who is my equal? says the Holy One.
26 Lift up your eyes on high and see:
Who created these?
He who brings out their host and numbers
them,
calling them all by name;
because he is great in strength,
mighty in power,
not one is missing.

27 Why do you say, O Jacob,
and speak, O Israel,
"My way is hidden from the LORD,
and my right is disregarded by my God"?
28 Have you not known? Have you not heard?
The LORD is the everlasting God,
the Creator of the ends of the earth.
He does not faint or grow weary;
his understanding is unsearchable.
29 He gives power to the faint,
and strengthens the powerless.
30 Even youths will faint and be weary,
and the young will fall exhausted;
31 but those who wait for the LORD shall renew
their strength,
they shall mount up with wings like
eagles,
they shall run and not be weary,
they shall walk and not faint.

Israel Assured of God's Help

41 Listen to me in silence, O coastlands;
let the peoples renew their strength;

a Meaning of Heb uncertain

let them approach, then let them speak;
 let us together draw near for judgment.

2 Who has roused a victor from the east,
 summoned him to his service?
He delivers up nations to him,
 and tramples kings under foot;
he makes them like dust with his sword,
 like driven stubble with his bow.
3 He pursues them and passes on safely,
 scarcely touching the path with his feet.
4 Who has performed and done this,
 calling the generations from the
 beginning?
I, the LORD, am first,
 and will be with the last.
5 The coastlands have seen and are afraid,
 the ends of the earth tremble;
 they have drawn near and come.
6 Each one helps the other,
 saying to one another, "Take courage!"
7 The artisan encourages the goldsmith,
 and the one who smooths with the
 hammer encourages the one who
 strikes the anvil,
saying of the soldering, "It is good";
 and they fasten it with nails so that it
 cannot be moved.
8 But you, Israel, my servant,
 Jacob, whom I have chosen,
 the offspring of Abraham, my friend;
9 you whom I took from the ends of the earth,
 and called from its farthest corners,
saying to you, "You are my servant,
 I have chosen you and not cast you off";
10 do not fear, for I am with you,
 do not be afraid, for I am your God;
I will strengthen you, I will help you,
 I will uphold you with my victorious right
 hand.

11 Yes, all who are incensed against you
 shall be ashamed and disgraced;
those who strive against you
 shall be as nothing and shall perish.
12 You shall seek those who contend with you,
 but you shall not find them;
those who war against you
 shall be as nothing at all.
13 For I, the LORD your God,

> "Do not fear,
> for I am with you, do
> not be afraid, for I
> am your God; I will
> strengthen you,
> I will help you, I will
> uphold you with my
> victorious right hand."
> —Isaiah 41:10

hold your right hand;
it is I who say to you, "Do not fear,
 I will help you."

14 Do not fear, you worm Jacob,
 you insect[a] Israel!
I will help you, says the LORD;
 your Redeemer is the Holy One of Israel.
15 Now, I will make of you a threshing sledge,
 sharp, new, and having teeth;
you shall thresh the mountains and crush
 them,
 and you shall make the hills like chaff.
16 You shall winnow them and the wind shall
 carry them away,
 and the tempest shall scatter them.
Then you shall rejoice in the LORD;
 in the Holy One of Israel you shall glory.

17 When the poor and needy seek water,
 and there is none,
 and their tongue is parched with thirst,
I the LORD will answer them,
 I the God of Israel will not forsake them.
18 I will open rivers on the bare heights,[b]
 and fountains in the midst of the valleys;
I will make the wilderness a pool of water,
 and the dry land springs of water.
19 I will put in the wilderness the cedar,
 the acacia, the myrtle, and the olive;
I will set in the desert the cypress,
 the plane and the pine together,
20 so that all may see and know,
 all may consider and understand,
that the hand of the LORD has done this,
 the Holy One of Israel has created it.

a Syr: Heb *men of* b Or *trails*

The Futility of Idols

21 Set forth your case, says the LORD;
     bring your proofs, says the King of Jacob.
22 Let them bring them, and tell us
     what is to happen.
   Tell us the former things, what they are,
     so that we may consider them,
   and that we may know their outcome;
     or declare to us the things to come.
23 Tell us what is to come hereafter,
     that we may know that you are gods;
   do good, or do harm,
     that we may be afraid and terrified.
24 You, indeed, are nothing
     and your work is nothing at all;
     whoever chooses you is an abomination.

25 I stirred up one from the north, and he has
     come,
   from the rising of the sun he was
     summoned by name.[a]
   He shall trample[b] on rulers as on mortar,
     as the potter treads clay.
26 Who declared it from the beginning, so that
     we might know,
   and beforehand, so that we might say, "He
     is right"?
   There was no one who declared it, none who
     proclaimed,
     none who heard your words.
27 I first have declared it to Zion,[c]
     and I give to Jerusalem a herald of good
     tidings.
28 But when I look there is no one;
     among these there is no counselor
   who, when I ask, gives an answer.

29 No, they are all a delusion;
     their works are nothing;
     their images are empty wind.

The Servant, a Light to the Nations

42 Here is my servant, whom I uphold,
     my chosen, in whom my soul delights;
   I have put my spirit upon him;
     he will bring forth justice to the nations.
2 He will not cry or lift up his voice,
     or make it heard in the street;
3 a bruised reed he will not break,
     and a dimly burning wick he will not
       quench;
   he will faithfully bring forth justice.
4 He will not grow faint or be crushed
     until he has established justice in the earth;
     and the coastlands wait for his teaching.

5 Thus says God, the LORD,
     who created the heavens and stretched
       them out,
   who spread out the earth and what comes
       from it,
   who gives breath to the people upon it
     and spirit to those who walk in it:
6 I am the LORD, I have called you in
       righteousness,
     I have taken you by the hand and kept you;
   I have given you as a covenant to the people,[d]
     a light to the nations,
7   to open the eyes that are blind,
   to bring out the prisoners from the dungeon,
     from the prison those who sit in darkness.
8 I am the LORD, that is my name;
     my glory I give to no other,

STUDY IT!

The Servant Leader · Isaiah 42:1–7

Isaiah's four songs of the servant (Isaiah 42:1-7; 49:1-6; 50:4-9; 52:13-53:12) have had an important place in Christian theology and worship. They portray the qualities of the ideal servant leader. Through these songs, the prophet speaks of hope: the faithful Israelites, though in exile, are still God's servants (Isaiah 42:1), chosen from the womb (Isaiah 49:1). Through their courageous suffering (Isaiah 50:7-8), Israel will be restored to bring salvation to all nations (Isaiah 53:5).

It is not surprising that the early Christians saw in the servant songs a remarkable similarity to Jesus' words and actions. The fourth song in particular—which talks of a suffering servant—helped the followers of Jesus understand his suffering and humiliating death on the cross.

a Cn Compare Q Ms Gk: MT *and he shall call on my name*   **b** Cn: Heb *come*   **c** Cn: Heb *First to Zion—Behold, behold them*   **d** Meaning of Heb uncertain

LIVE IT!

The Servant's Mission
Isaiah 42:1–7

Read the first song of the servant in **Isaiah 42:1–7.**

These are God's words of calling and direction to the servant, and they apply to the people of Isaiah's time, Jesus' time, and our time as well.

- What is the servant's mission from God?
- How does Jesus fulfill this mission (compare Isaiah 42:6-7 with Luke 4:18-19)?
- How can you participate in this mission?

nor my praise to idols.

⁹ See, the former things have come to pass,
  and new things I now declare;
before they spring forth,
  I tell you of them.

A Hymn of Praise

¹⁰ Sing to the LORD a new song,
  his praise from the end of the earth!
Let the sea roar*ᵃ* and all that fills it,
  the coastlands and their inhabitants.

¹¹ Let the desert and its towns lift up their voice,
  the villages that Kedar inhabits;
let the inhabitants of Sela sing for joy,
  let them shout from the tops of the
    mountains.

¹² Let them give glory to the LORD,
  and declare his praise in the coastlands.

¹³ The LORD goes forth like a soldier,
  like a warrior he stirs up his fury;
he cries out, he shouts aloud,
  he shows himself mighty against his foes.

¹⁴ For a long time I have held my peace,
  I have kept still and restrained myself;
now I will cry out like a woman in labor,
  I will gasp and pant.

¹⁵ I will lay waste mountains and hills,
  and dry up all their herbage;
I will turn the rivers into islands,
  and dry up the pools.

¹⁶ I will lead the blind
  by a road they do not know,
by paths they have not known
  I will guide them.
I will turn the darkness before them into light,
  the rough places into level ground.
These are the things I will do,
  and I will not forsake them.

¹⁷ They shall be turned back and utterly put to
    shame—
  those who trust in carved images,
who say to cast images,
  "You are our gods."

¹⁸ Listen, you that are deaf;
  and you that are blind, look up and see!

¹⁹ Who is blind but my servant,
  or deaf like my messenger whom I send?
Who is blind like my dedicated one,
  or blind like the servant of the LORD?

²⁰ He sees many things, but does*ᵇ* not observe
    them;
  his ears are open, but he does not hear.

Israel's Disobedience

²¹ The LORD was pleased, for the sake of his
    righteousness,
  to magnify his teaching and make it
    glorious.

²² But this is a people robbed and plundered,
  all of them are trapped in holes
  and hidden in prisons;
they have become a prey with no one to
    rescue,
  a spoil with no one to say, "Restore!"

²³ Who among you will give heed to this,
  who will attend and listen for the time to
    come?

²⁴ Who gave up Jacob to the spoiler,
  and Israel to the robbers?
Was it not the LORD, against whom we have
    sinned,
  in whose ways they would not walk,
  and whose law they would not obey?

²⁵ So he poured upon him the heat of his anger
  and the fury of war;
it set him on fire all around, but he did not
    understand;
  it burned him, but he did not take it to
    heart.

ᵃ Cn Compare Ps 96.11; 98.7: Heb *Those who go down to the sea* *ᵇ* Heb *You see many things but do*

43 Restoration and Protection Promised

But now thus says the LORD,
he who created you, O Jacob,
he who formed you, O Israel:
Do not fear, for I have redeemed you;
I have called you by name, you are mine.
2 When you pass through the waters, I will be
with you;
and through the rivers, they shall not
overwhelm you;
when you walk through fire you shall not be
burned,
and the flame shall not consume you.
3 For I am the LORD your God,
the Holy One of Israel, your Savior.
I give Egypt as your ransom,
Ethiopia[a] and Seba in exchange for you.
4 Because you are precious in my sight,
and honored, and I love you,
I give people in return for you,
nations in exchange for your life.
5 Do not fear, for I am with you;
I will bring your offspring from the east,
and from the west I will gather you;
6 I will say to the north, "Give them up,"
and to the south, "Do not withhold;
bring my sons from far away
and my daughters from the end of the
earth—
7 everyone who is called by my name,
whom I created for my glory,
whom I formed and made."

8 Bring forth the people who are blind, yet have
eyes,
who are deaf, yet have ears!
9 Let all the nations gather together,
and let the peoples assemble.
Who among them declared this,

and foretold to us the former things?
Let them bring their witnesses to justify them,
and let them hear and say, "It is true."
10 You are my witnesses, says the LORD,
and my servant whom I have chosen,
so that you may know and believe me
and understand that I am he.
Before me no god was formed,
nor shall there be any after me.
11 I, I am the LORD,
and besides me there is no savior.
12 I declared and saved and proclaimed,
when there was no strange god
among you;
and you are my witnesses, says the LORD.
13 I am God, and also henceforth I am He;
there is no one who can deliver from my
hand;
I work and who can hinder it?

14 Thus says the LORD,
your Redeemer, the Holy One of Israel:
For your sake I will send to Babylon
and break down all the bars,
and the shouting of the Chaldeans will be
turned to lamentation.[b]
15 I am the LORD, your Holy One,
the Creator of Israel, your King.
16 Thus says the LORD,
who makes a way in the sea,
a path in the mighty waters,
17 who brings out chariot and horse,
army and warrior;
they lie down, they cannot rise,
they are extinguished, quenched like a
wick:
18 Do not remember the former things,
or consider the things of old.
19 I am about to do a new thing;

STUDY IT!

No Fear! · Isaiah 43:1–5

The words of Isaiah 43:1–5 are a great comfort for all of us who struggle with fear. Originally addressed to the people of Israel, this section of Isaiah begins with the assurance that God has created and redeemed you, and that God knows you by name. It then goes on to tell the amazing ways God will be with you and protect you. Jesus echoes the assurance that we do not need to fear anything in this world when he says, "Do not let your hearts be troubled, and do not let them be afraid" (John 14:27).

a Or Nubia; Heb Cush   b Meaning of Heb uncertain

now it springs forth, do you not
　　perceive it?
I will make a way in the wilderness
　　and rivers in the desert.
20 The wild animals will honor me,
　　the jackals and the ostriches;
for I give water in the wilderness,
　　rivers in the desert,
to give drink to my chosen people,
21　　the people whom I formed for myself
so that they might declare my praise.

22 Yet you did not call upon me, O Jacob;
　　but you have been weary of me, O Israel!
23 You have not brought me your sheep for burnt
　　offerings,
　　or honored me with your sacrifices.
I have not burdened you with offerings,
　　or wearied you with frankincense.
24 You have not bought me sweet cane with
　　money,
　　or satisfied me with the fat of your sacrifices.
But you have burdened me with your sins;
　　you have wearied me with your iniquities.

25 I, I am He
　　who blots out your transgressions for my
　　　own sake,
　　and I will not remember your sins.
26 Accuse me, let us go to trial;
　　set forth your case, so that you may be
　　　proved right.
27 Your first ancestor sinned,
　　and your interpreters transgressed
　　　against me.
28 Therefore I profaned the princes of the
　　sanctuary,
　　I delivered Jacob to utter destruction,
　　and Israel to reviling.

44 God's Blessing on Israel

But now hear, O Jacob my servant,
　　Israel whom I have chosen!
2 Thus says the LORD who made you,
　　who formed you in the womb and will
　　　help you:
Do not fear, O Jacob my servant,
　　Jeshurun whom I have chosen.
3 For I will pour water on the thirsty land,
　　and streams on the dry ground;

I will pour my spirit upon your descendants,
　　and my blessing on your offspring.
4 They shall spring up like a green tamarisk,
　　like willows by flowing streams.
5 This one will say, "I am the LORD's,"
　　another will be called by the name of
　　　Jacob,
yet another will write on the hand, "The
　　LORD's,"
　　and adopt the name of Israel.

6 Thus says the LORD, the King of Israel,
　　and his Redeemer, the LORD of hosts:
I am the first and I am the last;
　　besides me there is no god.
7 Who is like me? Let them proclaim it,
　　let them declare and set it forth before me.
Who has announced from of old the things to
　　come?[a]
　　Let them tell us[b] what is yet to be.
8 Do not fear, or be afraid;
　　have I not told you from of old and
　　　declared it?
　　You are my witnesses!
Is there any god besides me?
　　There is no other rock; I know not one.

The Absurdity of Idol Worship

9 All who make idols are nothing, and the things
they delight in do not profit; their witnesses neither
see nor know. And so they will be put to shame.
10 Who would fashion a god or cast an image that
can do no good? 11 Look, all its devotees shall be
put to shame; the artisans too are merely human.
Let them all assemble, let them stand up; they shall
be terrified, they shall all be put to shame.

12 The ironsmith fashions it[c] and works it over
the coals, shaping it with hammers, and forging it
with his strong arm; he becomes hungry and his
strength fails, he drinks no water and is faint. 13 The
carpenter stretches a line, marks it out with a stylus,
fashions it with planes, and marks it with a compass;

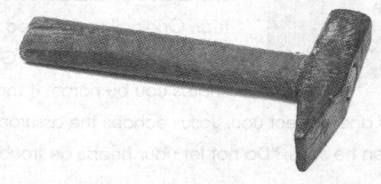

---

a Cn: Heb *from my placing an eternal people and things to come*　b Tg: Heb *them*　c Cn: Heb *an ax*

he makes it in human form, with human beauty, to be set up in a shrine. [14]He cuts down cedars or chooses a holm tree or an oak and lets it grow strong among the trees of the forest. He plants a cedar and the rain nourishes it. [15]Then it can be used as fuel. Part of it he takes and warms himself; he kindles a fire and bakes bread. Then he makes a god and worships it, makes it a carved image and bows down before it. [16]Half of it he burns in the fire; over this half he roasts meat, eats it and is satisfied. He also warms himself and says, "Ah, I am warm, I can feel the fire!" [17]The rest of it he makes into a god, his idol, bows down to it and worships it; he prays to it and says, "Save me, for you are my god!"

18 They do not know, nor do they comprehend; for their eyes are shut, so that they cannot see, and their minds as well, so that they cannot understand. [19]No one considers, nor is there knowledge or discernment to say, "Half of it I burned in the fire; I also baked bread on its coals, I roasted meat and have eaten. Now shall I make the rest of it an abomination? Shall I fall down before a block of wood?" [20]He feeds on ashes; a deluded mind has led him astray, and he cannot save himself or say, "Is not this thing in my right hand a fraud?"

Israel Is Not Forgotten

21 Remember these things, O Jacob,
    and Israel, for you are my servant;
I formed you, you are my servant;
    O Israel, you will not be forgotten
      by me.
22 I have swept away your transgressions like a
      cloud,
    and your sins like mist;
return to me, for I have redeemed you.

23 Sing, O heavens, for the LORD has done it;
    shout, O depths of the earth;
break forth into singing, O mountains,
    O forest, and every tree in it!
For the LORD has redeemed Jacob,
    and will be glorified in Israel.

24 Thus says the LORD, your Redeemer,
    who formed you in the womb:
I am the LORD, who made all things,
    who alone stretched out the heavens,
    who by myself spread out the earth;
25 who frustrates the omens of liars,

and makes fools of diviners;
who turns back the wise,
    and makes their knowledge foolish;
26 who confirms the word of his servant,
    and fulfills the prediction of his
      messengers;
who says of Jerusalem, "It shall be inhabited,"
    and of the cities of Judah, "They shall be
      rebuilt,
    and I will raise up their ruins";
27 who says to the deep, "Be dry—
    I will dry up your rivers";
28 who says of Cyrus, "He is my shepherd,
    and he shall carry out all my purpose";
and who says of Jerusalem, "It shall be
      rebuilt,"
    and of the temple, "Your foundation shall
      be laid."

Cyrus, God's Instrument

45 Thus says the LORD to his anointed, to
    Cyrus,
    whose right hand I have grasped
to subdue nations before him
    and strip kings of their robes,
to open doors before him—
    and the gates shall not be closed:
2 I will go before you
    and level the mountains,[a]
I will break in pieces the doors of bronze
    and cut through the bars of iron,
3 I will give you the treasures of darkness
    and riches hidden in secret places,
so that you may know that it is I, the LORD,
    the God of Israel, who call you by your
      name.
4 For the sake of my servant Jacob,
    and Israel my chosen,
I call you by your name,
    I surname you, though you do not
      know me.
5 I am the LORD, and there is no other;
    besides me there is no god.
    I arm you, though you do not
      know me,
6 so that they may know, from the rising of
      the sun
    and from the west, that there is no one
      besides me;
    I am the LORD, and there is no other.

a Q Ms Gk: MT *the swellings*

7 I form light and create darkness,
    I make weal and create woe;
    I the LORD do all these things.

8 Shower, O heavens, from above,
    and let the skies rain down righteousness;
let the earth open, that salvation may
      spring up,*a*
    and let it cause righteousness to sprout up
      also;
    I the LORD have created it.

9 Woe to you who strive with your
      Maker,
    earthen vessels with the potter!*b*
Does the clay say to the one who fashions it,
    "What are you making"?
    or "Your work has no handles"?
10 Woe to anyone who says to a father, "What are
      you begetting?"
    or to a woman, "With what are you in
      labor?"
11 Thus says the LORD,
    the Holy One of Israel, and its Maker:
Will you question me*c* about my children,
    or command me concerning the work of
      my hands?
12 I made the earth,
    and created humankind upon it;
it was my hands that stretched out the
      heavens,
    and I commanded all their host.
13 I have aroused Cyrus*d* in righteousness,
    and I will make all his paths straight;
he shall build my city
    and set my exiles free,
not for price or reward,
    says the LORD of hosts.
14 Thus says the LORD:
The wealth of Egypt and the merchandise of
      Ethiopia,*e*
    and the Sabeans, tall of stature,
shall come over to you and be yours,
    they shall follow you;
    they shall come over in chains and bow
      down to you.
They will make supplication to you, saying,
    "God is with you alone, and there is no
      other;
    there is no god besides him."

15 Truly, you are a God who hides himself,
    O God of Israel, the Savior.
16 All of them are put to shame and confounded,
    the makers of idols go in confusion
      together.
17 But Israel is saved by the LORD
    with everlasting salvation;
you shall not be put to shame or confounded
    to all eternity.

18 For thus says the LORD,
who created the heavens
    (he is God!),
who formed the earth and made it
    (he established it;
he did not create it a chaos,
    he formed it to be inhabited!):
I am the LORD, and there is no other.
19 I did not speak in secret,
    in a land of darkness;
I did not say to the offspring of Jacob,
    "Seek me in chaos."
I the LORD speak the truth,
    I declare what is right.

Idols Cannot Save Babylon

20 Assemble yourselves and come together,
    draw near, you survivors of the nations!
They have no knowledge—
    those who carry about their wooden idols,
and keep on praying to a god
    that cannot save.
21 Declare and present your case;
    let them take counsel together!
Who told this long ago?
    Who declared it of old?
Was it not I, the LORD?
    There is no other god besides me,
a righteous God and a Savior;
    there is no one besides me.

22 Turn to me and be saved,
    all the ends of the earth!
For I am God, and there is no other.
23 By myself I have sworn,
    from my mouth has gone forth in
      righteousness
    a word that shall not return:
"To me every knee shall bow,
    every tongue shall swear."

a Q Ms: MT *that they may bring forth salvation* b Cn: Heb *with the potsherds, or with the potters* c Cn: Heb *Ask me of things to come* d Heb *him*
e Or *Nubia*; Heb *Cush*

24 Only in the LORD, it shall be said of me,
    are righteousness and strength;
all who were incensed against him
    shall come to him and be ashamed.
25 In the LORD all the offspring of Israel
    shall triumph and glory.

46 Bel bows down, Nebo stoops,
    their idols are on beasts and cattle;
these things you carry are loaded
    as burdens on weary animals.
2 They stoop, they bow down together;
    they cannot save the burden,
but themselves go into captivity.

3 Listen to me, O house of Jacob,
    all the remnant of the house of Israel,
who have been borne by me from your birth,
    carried from the womb;
4 even to your old age I am he,
    even when you turn gray I will carry you.
I have made, and I will bear;
    I will carry and will save.

5 To whom will you liken me and make me
    equal,
and compare me, as though we were
    alike?
6 Those who lavish gold from the purse,
    and weigh out silver in the scales—
they hire a goldsmith, who makes it into a god;
    then they fall down and worship!
7 They lift it to their shoulders, they
    carry it,
they set it in its place, and it stands there;
    it cannot move from its place.
If one cries out to it, it does not answer
    or save anyone from trouble.

8 Remember this and consider,[a]
    recall it to mind, you transgressors,
9   remember the former things of old;
for I am God, and there is no other;
    I am God, and there is no one
    like me,
10 declaring the end from the beginning
    and from ancient times things not yet
    done,
saying, "My purpose shall stand,
    and I will fulfill my intention,"

11 calling a bird of prey from the east,
    the man for my purpose from a far country.
I have spoken, and I will bring it to pass;
    I have planned, and I will do it.

12 Listen to me, you stubborn of heart,
    you who are far from deliverance:
13 I bring near my deliverance, it is not far off,
    and my salvation will not tarry;
I will put salvation in Zion,
    for Israel my glory.

47 ### The Humiliation of Babylon
Come down and sit in the dust,
    virgin daughter Babylon!
Sit on the ground without a throne,
    daughter Chaldea!
For you shall no more be called
    tender and delicate.
2 Take the millstones and grind meal,
    remove your veil,
strip off your robe, uncover your legs,
    pass through the rivers.
3 Your nakedness shall be uncovered,
    and your shame shall be seen.
I will take vengeance,
    and I will spare no one.
4 Our Redeemer—the LORD of hosts is his
    name—
    is the Holy One of Israel.

5 Sit in silence, and go into darkness,
    daughter Chaldea!
For you shall no more be called
    the mistress of kingdoms.
6 I was angry with my people,
    I profaned my heritage;
I gave them into your hand,
    you showed them no mercy;
on the aged you made your yoke
    exceedingly heavy.
7 You said, "I shall be mistress forever,"
    so that you did not lay these things to heart
    or remember their end.

8 Now therefore hear this, you lover of
    pleasures,
who sit securely,
who say in your heart,
    "I am, and there is no one besides me;

a Meaning of Heb uncertain

I shall not sit as a widow
    or know the loss of children"—
9 both these things shall come upon you
    in a moment, in one day:
the loss of children and widowhood
    shall come upon you in full measure,
in spite of your many sorceries
    and the great power of your
        enchantments.

10 You felt secure in your wickedness;
    you said, "No one sees me."
Your wisdom and your knowledge
    led you astray,
and you said in your heart,
    "I am, and there is no one besides me."
11 But evil shall come upon you,
    which you cannot charm away;
disaster shall fall upon you,
    which you will not be able to ward off;
and ruin shall come on you suddenly,
    of which you know nothing.

12 Stand fast in your enchantments
    and your many sorceries,
    with which you have labored from your
        youth;
perhaps you may be able to succeed,
    perhaps you may inspire terror.
13 You are wearied with your many
        consultations;
    let those who study[a] the heavens
stand up and save you,
    those who gaze at the stars,
and at each new moon predict
    what[b] shall befall you.

14 See, they are like stubble,
    the fire consumes them;
they cannot deliver themselves
    from the power of the flame.
No coal for warming oneself is this,
    no fire to sit before!
15 Such to you are those with whom you
        have labored,
    who have trafficked with you from
        your youth;
they all wander about in their own
        paths;
    there is no one to save you.

God the Creator and Redeemer

48 Hear this, O house of Jacob,
    who are called by the name of Israel,
    and who came forth from the loins[c] of
        Judah;
who swear by the name of the LORD,
    and invoke the God of Israel,
    but not in truth or right.
2 For they call themselves after the holy city,
    and lean on the God of Israel;
    the LORD of hosts is his name.

3 The former things I declared long ago,
    they went out from my mouth and I made
        them known;
    then suddenly I did them and they came to
        pass.
4 Because I know that you are obstinate,
    and your neck is an iron sinew
    and your forehead brass,
5 I declared them to you from long ago,
    before they came to pass I announced
        them to you,
so that you would not say, "My idol did them,
    my carved image and my cast image
        commanded them."

6 You have heard; now see all this;
    and will you not declare it?
From this time forward I make you hear new
        things,
    hidden things that you have not known.
7 They are created now, not long ago;
    before today you have never heard of
        them,
    so that you could not say, "I already knew
        them."
8 You have never heard, you have never known,
    from of old your ear has not been opened.
For I knew that you would deal very
        treacherously,
    and that from birth you were called a rebel.

9 For my name's sake I defer my anger,
    for the sake of my praise I restrain it
        for you,
    so that I may not cut you off.
10 See, I have refined you, but not like[d] silver;
    I have tested you in the furnace of
        adversity.

---

a Meaning of Heb uncertain   b Gk Syr Compare Vg: Heb *from what*   c Cn: Heb *waters*   d Cn: Heb *with*

11 For my own sake, for my own sake, I do it,
     for why should my name[a] be profaned?
     My glory I will not give to another.

12 Listen to me, O Jacob,
     and Israel, whom I called:
     I am He; I am the first,
     and I am the last.
13 My hand laid the foundation of the earth,
     and my right hand spread out the heavens;
     when I summon them,
     they stand at attention.

14 Assemble, all of you, and hear!
     Who among them has declared these
     things?
     The LORD loves him;
     he shall perform his purpose on Babylon,
     and his arm shall be against the
     Chaldeans.
15 I, even I, have spoken and called him,
     I have brought him, and he will prosper in
     his way.
16 Draw near to me, hear this!
     From the beginning I have not spoken in
     secret,
     from the time it came to be I have been
     there.
     And now the Lord GOD has sent me and his
     spirit.

17 Thus says the LORD,
     your Redeemer, the Holy One of Israel:
     I am the LORD your God,
     who teaches you for your own good,
     who leads you in the way you
     should go.
18 O that you had paid attention to my
     commandments!
     Then your prosperity would have been like
     a river,
     and your success like the waves of the sea;
19 your offspring would have been like the sand,
     and your descendants like its grains;
     their name would never be cut off
     or destroyed from before me.

20 Go out from Babylon, flee from Chaldea,
     declare this with a shout of joy, proclaim it,
     send it forth to the end of the earth;

     say, "The LORD has redeemed his servant
     Jacob!"
21 They did not thirst when he led them through
     the deserts;
     he made water flow for them from the
     rock;
     he split open the rock and the water
     gushed out.

22 "There is no peace," says the LORD, "for the
     wicked."

The Servant's Mission

49 Listen to me, O coastlands,
     pay attention, you peoples from far away!
     The LORD called me before I was born,
     while I was in my mother's womb he
     named me.
2 He made my mouth like a sharp sword,
     in the shadow of his hand he hid me;
     he made me a polished arrow,
     in his quiver he hid me away.
3 And he said to me, "You are my servant,
     Israel, in whom I will be glorified."
4 But I said, "I have labored in vain,
     I have spent my strength for nothing and
     vanity;
     yet surely my cause is with the LORD,
     and my reward with my God."

PRAY IT!

Fear of Failure
Isaiah 49:1–6

Isaiah 49:1–6 is the second of the four servant songs (see "Study It: The Servant Leader," near Isaiah 42:1–7). In this passage, the servant expresses a feeling of failure (Isaiah 49:4). But God responds that the servant will be a success—a "light to the nations" (Isaiah 49:6).

- During your prayer time, reflect or journal on a time when you felt you failed, but something good happened anyway.
- How do you now see that God was at work in the situation?

a Gk Old Latin: Heb *for why should it*

5 And now the LORD says,
    who formed me in the womb to be his
       servant,
  to bring Jacob back to him,
    and that Israel might be gathered
       to him,
for I am honored in the sight of the LORD,
    and my God has become my strength—
6 he says,
  "It is too light a thing that you should be my
      servant
    to raise up the tribes of Jacob
    and to restore the survivors of Israel;
I will give you as a light to the nations,
    that my salvation may reach to the end of
      the earth."

7 Thus says the LORD,
    the Redeemer of Israel and his
      Holy One,
to one deeply despised, abhorred by the
      nations,
    the slave of rulers,
"Kings shall see and stand up,
    princes, and they shall prostrate
      themselves,
because of the LORD, who is faithful,
    the Holy One of Israel, who has chosen
      you."

Zion's Children to Be Brought Home
8 Thus says the LORD:

In a time of favor I have answered you,
    on a day of salvation I have helped you;
I have kept you and given you
    as a covenant to the people,[a]
to establish the land,
    to apportion the desolate heritages;
9 saying to the prisoners, "Come out,"
    to those who are in darkness, "Show
      yourselves."
They shall feed along the ways,
    on all the bare heights[b] shall be their
      pasture;
10 they shall not hunger or thirst,
    neither scorching wind nor sun shall strike
      them down,
for he who has pity on them will lead them,
    and by springs of water will guide them.
11 And I will turn all my mountains into a road,
    and my highways shall be raised up.
12 Lo, these shall come from far away,
    and lo, these from the north and from the
      west,
    and these from the land of Syene.[c]

13 Sing for joy, O heavens, and exult, O earth;
    break forth, O mountains, into singing!
For the LORD has comforted his people,
    and will have compassion on his suffering
      ones.

14 But Zion said, "The LORD has
      forsaken me,

The Love of a Mother · Isaiah 49:13–16

In **Isaiah 49** the love and commitment of God are compared to those of a mother for her child. Although we often use masculine words to describe God, it's easy to imagine God as a loving mother—forgiving us when we make mistakes, embracing us when we need comfort, nurturing us through difficult times, and acting gently toward us at all times. The Hebrew root of the word "compassion" actually means "womb." Thus, a God of compassion and love, a God who will never forget our suffering, is by definition a God of the womb—a God of motherly tenderness.

- Who has been a mother figure in your life—perhaps your birth mother, grandmother, adoptive mother, stepmother, godmother, or mentor?
- How do you see God's love reflected in her love?
- Have you experienced the even greater love of God?
- How can you share the caring, compassionate love of God with others?

---

a Meaning of Heb uncertain   b Or *the trails*   c Q Ms: MT *Sinim*

my Lord has forgotten me."

15 Can a woman forget her nursing child,
  or show no compassion for the child of her
    womb?
Even these may forget,
  yet I will not forget you.
16 See, I have inscribed you on the palms of my
    hands;
  your walls are continually
    before me.
17 Your builders outdo your destroyers,[a]
  and those who laid you waste go away
    from you.
18 Lift up your eyes all around and see;
  they all gather, they come to you.
As I live, says the LORD,
  you shall put all of them on like an
    ornament,
  and like a bride you shall bind
    them on.

19 Surely your waste and your desolate places
  and your devastated land—
surely now you will be too crowded for your
    inhabitants,
  and those who swallowed you up will be
    far away.
20 The children born in the time of your
    bereavement
  will yet say in your hearing:
"The place is too crowded for me;
  make room for me to settle."
21 Then you will say in your heart,
  "Who has borne me these?
I was bereaved and barren,
  exiled and put away—
so who has reared these?
I was left all alone—
  where then have these come from?"

22 Thus says the Lord GOD:
I will soon lift up my hand to the nations,
  and raise my signal to the peoples;
and they shall bring your sons in their bosom,
  and your daughters shall be carried on
    their shoulders.
23 Kings shall be your foster fathers,
  and their queens your nursing mothers.
With their faces to the ground they shall bow
    down to you,
  and lick the dust of your feet.
Then you will know that I am the LORD;
  those who wait for me shall not be put to
    shame.

24 Can the prey be taken from the mighty,
  or the captives of a tyrant[b] be rescued?
25 But thus says the LORD:
Even the captives of the mighty shall be taken,
  and the prey of the tyrant be rescued;
for I will contend with those who contend
    with you,
  and I will save your children.
26 I will make your oppressors eat their own
    flesh,
  and they shall be drunk with their own
    blood as with wine.
Then all flesh shall know
  that I am the LORD your Savior,
  and your Redeemer, the Mighty One of
    Jacob.

50 Thus says the LORD:
  Where is your mother's bill of divorce
    with which I put her away?
Or which of my creditors is it
  to whom I have sold you?
No, because of your sins you were sold,
  and for your transgressions your mother
    was put away.
2 Why was no one there when I came?
  Why did no one answer when I called?
Is my hand shortened, that it cannot redeem?
  Or have I no power to deliver?
By my rebuke I dry up the sea,
  I make the rivers a desert;
their fish stink for lack of water,
  and die of thirst.[c]
3 I clothe the heavens with blackness,
  and make sackcloth their covering.

The Servant's Humiliation and Vindication
4 The Lord GOD has given me
  the tongue of a teacher,[d]
that I may know how to sustain
  the weary with a word.
Morning by morning he wakens—
  wakens my ear
to listen as those who are taught.
5 The Lord GOD has opened my ear,

---

a Or *Your children come swiftly; your destroyers*   b Q Ms Syr Vg: MT *of a righteous person*   c Or *die on the thirsty ground*   d Cn: Heb *of those who are taught*

The Servant's Strength · Isaiah 50:4–9

This is the third of the four servant songs (see "Study It: The Servant Leader," near Isaiah 42:1-7). Read the song twice. The first time, think about how it reflects Jesus' relationship with his heavenly Father. The second time, focus on the verses that inspire you and give you strength. Pray that God will give you the strength to stand up and speak out for what is right among other young people.

and I was not rebellious,
    I did not turn backward.
6 I gave my back to those who struck me,
    and my cheeks to those who pulled out the
        beard;
I did not hide my face
    from insult and spitting.

7 The Lord GOD helps me;
    therefore I have not been disgraced;
therefore I have set my face like flint,
    and I know that I shall not be put to shame;
8   he who vindicates me is near.
Who will contend with me?
    Let us stand up together.
Who are my adversaries?
    Let them confront me.
9 It is the Lord GOD who helps me;
    who will declare me guilty?
All of them will wear out like a garment;
    the moth will eat them up.

10 Who among you fears the LORD
    and obeys the voice of his servant,
who walks in darkness
    and has no light,
yet trusts in the name of the LORD
    and relies upon his God?
11 But all of you are kindlers of fire,
    lighters of firebrands.*a*
Walk in the flame of your fire,
    and among the brands that you have
        kindled!
This is what you shall have from my hand:
    you shall lie down in torment.

Blessings in Store for God's People

51 Listen to me, you that pursue
    righteousness,

you that seek the LORD.
Look to the rock from which you were hewn,
    and to the quarry from which you
        were dug.
2 Look to Abraham your father
    and to Sarah who bore you;
for he was but one when I called him,
    but I blessed him and made him many.
3 For the LORD will comfort Zion;
    he will comfort all her waste places,
and will make her wilderness like Eden,
    her desert like the garden of the LORD;
joy and gladness will be found in her,
    thanksgiving and the voice of song.

4 Listen to me, my people,
    and give heed to me, my nation;
for a teaching will go out from me,
    and my justice for a light to the peoples.
5 I will bring near my deliverance swiftly,
    my salvation has gone out
    and my arms will rule the peoples;
the coastlands wait for me,
    and for my arm they hope.
6 Lift up your eyes to the heavens,
    and look at the earth beneath;
for the heavens will vanish like smoke,
    the earth will wear out like a garment,
    and those who live on it will die like
        gnats;*b*
but my salvation will be forever,
    and my deliverance will never be ended.

7 Listen to me, you who know righteousness,
    you people who have my teaching in your
        hearts;
do not fear the reproach of others,
    and do not be dismayed when they
        revile you.

a Syr: Heb *you gird yourselves with firebrands* *b* Or *in like manner*

8 For the moth will eat them up like a garment,
    and the worm will eat them like wool;
but my deliverance will be forever,
    and my salvation to all generations.

9 Awake, awake, put on strength,
    O arm of the LORD!
Awake, as in days of old,
    the generations of long ago!
Was it not you who cut Rahab in pieces,
    who pierced the dragon?
10 Was it not you who dried up the sea,
    the waters of the great deep;
who made the depths of the sea a way
    for the redeemed to cross over?
11 So the ransomed of the LORD shall return,
    and come to Zion with singing;
everlasting joy shall be upon their heads;
    they shall obtain joy and gladness,
    and sorrow and sighing shall flee away.

12 I, I am he who comforts you;
    why then are you afraid of a mere mortal
        who must die,
    a human being who fades like grass?
13 You have forgotten the LORD, your Maker,
    who stretched out the heavens
    and laid the foundations of the earth.
You fear continually all day long
    because of the fury of the oppressor,
who is bent on destruction.
    But where is the fury of the oppressor?
14 The oppressed shall speedily be released;
    they shall not die and go down to the Pit,
    nor shall they lack bread.
15 For I am the LORD your God,
    who stirs up the sea so that its waves roar—
    the LORD of hosts is his name.
16 I have put my words in your mouth,
    and hidden you in the shadow of my hand,
stretching out[a] the heavens
    and laying the foundations of the earth,
    and saying to Zion, "You are my people."

17 Rouse yourself, rouse yourself!
    Stand up, O Jerusalem,
you who have drunk at the hand of the LORD
    the cup of his wrath,
who have drunk to the dregs
    the bowl of staggering.

18 There is no one to guide her
    among all the children she has borne;
there is no one to take her by the hand
    among all the children she has brought up.
19 These two things have befallen you
    —who will grieve with you?—
devastation and destruction, famine and
        sword
    who will comfort you?[b]
20 Your children have fainted,
    they lie at the head of every street
    like an antelope in a net;
they are full of the wrath of the LORD,
    the rebuke of your God.

21 Therefore hear this, you who are wounded,[c]
    who are drunk, but not with wine:
22 Thus says your Sovereign, the LORD,
    your God who pleads the cause of his
        people:
See, I have taken from your hand the cup of
        staggering;
you shall drink no more
    from the bowl of my wrath.
23 And I will put it into the hand of your
        tormentors,
    who have said to you,
    "Bow down, that we may walk on you";
and you have made your back like the ground
    and like the street for them to walk on.

52 **Let Zion Rejoice**
Awake, awake,
    put on your strength, O Zion!
Put on your beautiful garments,
    O Jerusalem, the holy city;
for the uncircumcised and the unclean
    shall enter you no more.
2 Shake yourself from the dust, rise up,
    O captive[d] Jerusalem;
loose the bonds from your neck,
    O captive daughter Zion!

3 For thus says the LORD: You were sold for nothing, and you shall be redeemed without money. 4For
thus says the Lord GOD: Long ago, my people went
down into Egypt to reside there as aliens; the Assyrian, too, has oppressed them without cause. 5Now
therefore what am I doing here, says the LORD, seeing that my people are taken away without cause?

a Syr: Heb *planting*   b Q Ms Gk Syr Vg: MT *how may I comfort you?*   c Or *humbled*   d Cn: Heb *rise up, sit*

Their rulers howl, says the LORD, and continually, all day long, my name is despised. [6]Therefore my people shall know my name; therefore in that day they shall know that it is I who speak; here am I.

[7] How beautiful upon the mountains
　　　are the feet of the messenger who announces peace,
　　who brings good news,
　　　who announces salvation,
　　　who says to Zion, "Your God reigns."
[8] Listen! Your sentinels lift up their voices,
　　　together they sing for joy;
　　for in plain sight they see
　　　the return of the LORD to Zion.
[9] Break forth together into singing,
　　　you ruins of Jerusalem;
　　for the LORD has comforted his people,
　　　he has redeemed Jerusalem.
[10] The LORD has bared his holy arm
　　　before the eyes of all the nations;
　　and all the ends of the earth shall see
　　　the salvation of our God.

[11] Depart, depart, go out from there!
　　　Touch no unclean thing;
　　go out from the midst of it, purify yourselves,
　　　you who carry the vessels of the LORD.
[12] For you shall not go out in haste,
　　　and you shall not go in flight;
　　for the LORD will go before you,
　　　and the God of Israel will be your rear guard.

The Suffering Servant
[13] See, my servant shall prosper;
　　　he shall be exalted and lifted up,
　　　and shall be very high.
[14] Just as there were many who were astonished at him[a]
　　　—so marred was his appearance, beyond human semblance,
　　　and his form beyond that of mortals—
[15] so he shall startle[b] many nations;
　　　kings shall shut their mouths because of him;
　　for that which had not been told them they shall see,
　　　and that which they had not heard they shall contemplate.

PRAY IT!

The Suffering Servant
Isaiah 52:13–53:12

In the fourth servant song (see "Study It: The Servant Leader," near Isaiah 42:1-7), the servant suffers for the salvation of others. Can you see how this description fits Jesus? Compare these verses to **Matthew 27:57–60** and **Luke 22:37**. Take a moment to say your own prayer of thanksgiving to Jesus for enduring the suffering it took to save us from sin and death.

53 Who has believed what we have heard?
　　And to whom has the arm of the LORD been revealed?
[2] For he grew up before him like a young plant,
　　　and like a root out of dry ground;
　　he had no form or majesty that we should look at him,
　　　nothing in his appearance that we should desire him.
[3] He was despised and rejected by others;
　　　a man of suffering[c] and acquainted with infirmity;
　　and as one from whom others hide their faces[d]
　　　he was despised, and we held him of no account.

[4] Surely he has borne our infirmities
　　　and carried our diseases;
　　yet we accounted him stricken,
　　　struck down by God, and afflicted.
[5] But he was wounded for our transgressions,
　　　crushed for our iniquities;
　　upon him was the punishment that made us whole,
　　　and by his bruises we are healed.
[6] All we like sheep have gone astray;
　　　we have all turned to our own way,
　　and the LORD has laid on him
　　　the iniquity of us all.

[7] He was oppressed, and he was afflicted,

---

a Syr Tg: Heb *you*　**b** Meaning of Heb uncertain　**c** Or *a man of sorrows*　**d** Or *as one who hides his face from us*

yet he did not open his mouth;
like a lamb that is led to the slaughter,
  and like a sheep that before its shearers is
    silent,
so he did not open his mouth.

8 By a perversion of justice he was taken away.
  Who could have imagined his future?
For he was cut off from the land of the living,
  stricken for the transgression of my people.

9 They made his grave with the wicked
    and his tomb[a] with the rich,[b]
although he had done no violence,
    and there was no deceit in his mouth.

10 Yet it was the will of the LORD to crush him
    with pain.[c]
When you make his life an offering for sin,[d]
    he shall see his offspring, and shall prolong
      his days;
through him the will of the LORD shall prosper.

11   Out of his anguish he shall see light;[e]
he shall find satisfaction through his
    knowledge.
  The righteous one,[f] my servant, shall make
    many righteous,
  and he shall bear their iniquities.

12 Therefore I will allot him a portion with the
    great,
  and he shall divide the spoil with the
    strong;
because he poured out himself to death,
  and was numbered with the transgressors;
yet he bore the sin of many,
  and made intercession for the transgressors.

The Eternal Covenant of Peace

54 Sing, O barren one who did not bear;
  burst into song and shout,
you who have not been in labor!
For the children of the desolate woman will
    be more
  than the children of her that is married, says
    the LORD.

2 Enlarge the site of your tent,
  and let the curtains of your habitations be
    stretched out;
do not hold back; lengthen your cords
  and strengthen your stakes.

3 For you will spread out to the right and to the
    left,

and your descendants will possess the
    nations
  and will settle the desolate towns.

4 Do not fear, for you will not be ashamed;
  do not be discouraged, for you will not
    suffer disgrace;
for you will forget the shame of your youth,
  and the disgrace of your widowhood you
    will remember no more.

5 For your Maker is your husband,
  the LORD of hosts is his name;
the Holy One of Israel is your Redeemer,
  the God of the whole earth he is called.

6 For the LORD has called you
  like a wife forsaken and grieved in spirit,
like the wife of a man's youth when she is
    cast off,
  says your God.

7 For a brief moment I abandoned you,
  but with great compassion I will
    gather you.

8 In overflowing wrath for a moment
  I hid my face from you,
but with everlasting love I will have
    compassion on you,
  says the LORD, your Redeemer.

9 This is like the days of Noah to me:
  Just as I swore that the waters of Noah
    would never again go over the earth,
so I have sworn that I will not be angry
    with you
  and will not rebuke you.

10 For the mountains may depart
    and the hills be removed,
but my steadfast love shall not depart
    from you,
  and my covenant of peace shall not be
    removed,
says the LORD, who has compassion
    on you.

11 O afflicted one, storm-tossed, and not
    comforted,
  I am about to set your stones in antimony,
    and lay your foundations with sapphires.[g]

12 I will make your pinnacles of rubies,
  your gates of jewels,
    and all your wall of precious stones.

---

a Q Ms: MT *and in his death* b Cn: Heb *with a rich person* c Or *by disease*; meaning of Heb uncertain d Meaning of Heb uncertain e Q Mss: MT
lacks *light* f Or *and he shall find satisfaction. Through his knowledge, the righteous one* g Or *lapis lazuli*

13 All your children shall be taught by the
    Lord,
      and great shall be the prosperity of your
        children.
14 In righteousness you shall be established;
      you shall be far from oppression, for you
        shall not fear;
      and from terror, for it shall not come
        near you.
15 If anyone stirs up strife,
      it is not from me;
    whoever stirs up strife with you
      shall fall because of you.
16 See it is I who have created the smith
      who blows the fire of coals,
      and produces a weapon fit for its purpose;
    I have also created the ravager to destroy.
17   No weapon that is fashioned against you
      shall prosper,
    and you shall confute every tongue that
      rises against you in judgment.
    This is the heritage of the servants of
      the Lord
    and their vindication from me, says
      the Lord.

An Invitation to Abundant Life

55 Ho, everyone who thirsts,
    come to the waters;
and you that have no money,
    come, buy and eat!
Come, buy wine and milk
    without money and without price.
2 Why do you spend your money for that which
      is not bread,
    and your labor for that which does not
      satisfy?
Listen carefully to me, and eat what is
    good,
    and delight yourselves in rich food.
3 Incline your ear, and come to me;
    listen, so that you may live.
I will make with you an everlasting covenant,
    my steadfast, sure love for David.
4 See, I made him a witness to the peoples,
    a leader and commander for the peoples.
5 See, you shall call nations that you do not
    know,
    and nations that do not know you shall run
      to you,

because of the Lord your God, the Holy One
    of Israel,
    for he has glorified you.

6 Seek the Lord while he may be found,
    call upon him while he is near;
7 let the wicked forsake their way,
    and the unrighteous their thoughts;
let them return to the Lord, that he may have
    mercy on them,
    and to our God, for he will abundantly
      pardon.
8 For my thoughts are not your thoughts,
    nor are your ways my ways, says the
      Lord.
9 For as the heavens are higher than the earth,
    so are my ways higher than your ways
    and my thoughts than your thoughts.

10 For as the rain and the snow come down
      from heaven,
    and do not return there until they have
      watered the earth,
making it bring forth and sprout,
    giving seed to the sower and bread to the
      eater,

11 so shall my word be that goes out from my
      mouth;
    it shall not return to me empty,
but it shall accomplish that which I purpose,
    and succeed in the thing for which I
      sent it.

12 For you shall go out in joy,
    and be led back in peace;
the mountains and the hills before you
    shall burst into song,
    and all the trees of the field shall clap
      their hands.
13 Instead of the thorn shall come up the
    cypress;

instead of the brier shall come up the
  myrtle;
and it shall be to the LORD for a memorial,
  for an everlasting sign that shall not be
  cut off.

56 The Covenant Extended to All Who Obey

Thus says the LORD:
Maintain justice, and do what is right,
for soon my salvation will come,
  and my deliverance be revealed.

2 Happy is the mortal who does this,
  the one who holds it fast,
who keeps the sabbath, not profaning it,
  and refrains from doing any evil.

3 Do not let the foreigner joined to the
  LORD say,
  "The LORD will surely separate me from
  his people";
and do not let the eunuch say,
  "I am just a dry tree."
4 For thus says the LORD:
To the eunuchs who keep my sabbaths,
  who choose the things that please me
  and hold fast my covenant,
5 I will give, in my house and within my walls,
  a monument and a name
  better than sons and daughters;
I will give them an everlasting name
  that shall not be cut off.

6 And the foreigners who join themselves to
  the LORD,
  to minister to him, to love the name of
  the LORD,
  and to be his servants,
all who keep the sabbath, and do not
  profane it,
  and hold fast my covenant—
7 these I will bring to my holy mountain,
  and make them joyful in my house of
  prayer;
their burnt offerings and their sacrifices
  will be accepted on my altar;
for my house shall be called a house of prayer
  for all peoples.
8 Thus says the Lord GOD,

who gathers the outcasts of Israel,
I will gather others to them
  besides those already gathered.*a*

The Corruption of Israel's Rulers

9 All you wild animals,
  all you wild animals in the forest, come to
  devour!
10 Israel's*b* sentinels are blind,
  they are all without knowledge;
they are all silent dogs
  that cannot bark;
dreaming, lying down,
  loving to slumber.
11 The dogs have a mighty appetite;
  they never have enough.
The shepherds also have no understanding;
  they have all turned to their own way,
  to their own gain, one and all.

LIVE IT!

The Optimism of Third Isaiah
Isaiah 56–66

The last eleven chapters
of Isaiah contain the
messages of several prophets known
collectively as Third Isaiah. The common
element of their prophecies is optimism.
They proclaim the hopeful message that
God's covenant will be extended to all
nations and that Jerusalem will become
God's holy city, the throne of the eternal King.

Third Isaiah, in contrast to many of the
other biblical prophets, proclaims joy as a
sign of God's presence. Joy is absent in the
lives of many people today, as it was in the
time of Isaiah. Taking time to remember all
the wonderful things God has done for us
can help bring joy to our lives.

- When have you experienced true joy in
  your life?
- Where have you seen the presence of
  God in your life? In your world?
- How can you help others to experience
  joy?

a Heb *besides his gathered ones* b Heb *His*

12 "Come," they say, "let us[a] get wine;
    let us fill ourselves with strong drink.
And tomorrow will be like today,
    great beyond measure."

57 Israel's Futile Idolatry

The righteous perish,
    and no one takes it to heart;
the devout are taken away,
    while no one understands.
For the righteous are taken away from
    calamity,
2   and they enter into peace;
those who walk uprightly
    will rest on their couches.
3 But as for you, come here,
    you children of a sorceress,
    you offspring of an adulterer and a whore.[b]
4 Whom are you mocking?
    Against whom do you open your
        mouth wide
    and stick out your tongue?
Are you not children of transgression,
    the offspring of deceit—
5 you that burn with lust among the oaks,
    under every green tree;
you that slaughter your children in the
        valleys,
    under the clefts of the rocks?
6 Among the smooth stones of the valley is
        your portion;
    they, they, are your lot;
to them you have poured out a drink offering,
    you have brought a grain offering.
    Shall I be appeased for these things?
7 Upon a high and lofty mountain
    you have set your bed,
    and there you went up to offer sacrifice.
8 Behind the door and the doorpost
    you have set up your symbol;
for, in deserting me,[c] you have uncovered
        your bed,
    you have gone up to it,
    you have made it wide;
and you have made a bargain for yourself
        with them,
    you have loved their bed,
    you have gazed on their nakedness.[d]
9 You journeyed to Molech[e] with oil,
    and multiplied your perfumes;

you sent your envoys far away,
    and sent down even to Sheol.
10 You grew weary from your many wanderings,
    but you did not say, "It is useless."
You found your desire rekindled,
    and so you did not weaken.
11 Whom did you dread and fear
    so that you lied,
and did not remember me
    or give me a thought?
Have I not kept silent and closed my eyes,[f]
    and so you do not fear me?
12 I will concede your righteousness and your
        works,
    but they will not help you.
13 When you cry out, let your collection of idols
        deliver you!
    The wind will carry them off,
    a breath will take them away.
But whoever takes refuge in me shall possess
        the land
    and inherit my holy mountain.

A Promise of Help and Healing

14 It shall be said,
    "Build up, build up, prepare the way,
        remove every obstruction from my
        people's way."
15 For thus says the high and lofty one
    who inhabits eternity, whose name is
        Holy:
I dwell in the high and holy place,
    and also with those who are contrite and
        humble in spirit,
to revive the spirit of the humble,
    and to revive the heart of the contrite.
16 For I will not continually accuse,
    nor will I always be angry;
for then the spirits would grow faint
        before me,
    even the souls that I have made.
17 Because of their wicked covetousness I was
        angry;
    I struck them, I hid and was angry;
    but they kept turning back to their own
        ways.
18 I have seen their ways, but I will heal them;
    I will lead them and repay them with
        comfort,

---

a Q Ms Syr Vg Tg: MT me   b Heb an adulterer and she plays the whore   c Meaning of Heb uncertain   d Or their phallus; Heb the hand   e Or the king
f Gk Vg: Heb silent even for a long time

creating for their mourners the fruit of the
lips.*

19 Peace, peace, to the far and the near, says the
Lord;
and I will heal them.

20 But the wicked are like the tossing sea
that cannot keep still;
its waters toss up mire and mud.

21 There is no peace, says my God, for the
wicked.

58 False and True Worship

Shout out, do not hold back!
Lift up your voice like a trumpet!
Announce to my people their rebellion,
to the house of Jacob their sins.

2 Yet day after day they seek me
and delight to know my ways,
as if they were a nation that practiced
righteousness
and did not forsake the ordinance of
their God;
they ask of me righteous judgments,
they delight to draw near to God.

3 "Why do we fast, but you do not see?
Why humble ourselves, but you do not
notice?"
Look, you serve your own interest on your
fast day,
and oppress all your workers.

4 Look, you fast only to quarrel and to fight
and to strike with a wicked fist.
Such fasting as you do today
will not make your voice heard on high.

5 Is such the fast that I choose,
a day to humble oneself?
Is it to bow down the head like a bulrush,
and to lie in sackcloth and ashes?
Will you call this a fast,
a day acceptable to the Lord?

6 Is not this the fast that I choose:
to loose the bonds of injustice,
to undo the thongs of the yoke,
to let the oppressed go free,
and to break every yoke?

7 Is it not to share your bread with the hungry,
and bring the homeless poor into your
house;
when you see the naked, to cover them,

LIVE IT!

True Worship
Isaiah 58:1–7

Have you ever done something just to get others to notice you? The Israelites were apparently performing pious acts like fasting or humbling themselves to get God's attention and complaining when God didn't notice. In response, God points out that when they fast, they do it for self-serving reasons and commit numerous sins in the process. God then explains what true fasting, or worship, looks like. True worship involves not serving yourself, but serving others.

Isaiah mentions many ways of serving others, all founded on God's call for justice and self-sacrifice and Jesus' command to love our neighbors (Luke 10:27). They include meeting physical and spiritual needs such as fighting injustice, freeing the oppressed, feeding the hungry, clothing the naked, and giving shelter to the homeless. Through all of these acts, we honor God by showing respect for every human being God created.

and not to hide yourself from your
own kin?

8 Then your light shall break forth like the dawn,
and your healing shall spring up quickly;
your vindicator* shall go before you,
the glory of the Lord shall be your rear
guard.

9 Then you shall call, and the Lord will answer;
you shall cry for help, and he will say, Here
I am.

If you remove the yoke from among you,
the pointing of the finger, the speaking of
evil,

10 if you offer your food to the hungry
and satisfy the needs of the afflicted,
then your light shall rise in the
darkness
and your gloom be like the noonday.

11 The Lord will guide you continually,

a Meaning of Heb uncertain b Or *vindication*

LIVE IT!

Make a Difference
Isaiah 58:8–14

Think of all the time you spend wondering what God wants you to do with your life. Think of the many times you've heard other people talk about the darkness of the world we live in and the need for change. Think of the times you've wished you could make a difference, but wondered how. **Isaiah 58:8–14** holds at least part of the answer to those ponderings of life. It says that when we feed the hungry and provide for the needs of the suffering, our light rises in the darkness. God wants you to worship by serving others, and when you do, you also will be satisfied, made strong, and continually filled by God.

- Read this passage and make a list of the things it says to do.
- Now go back and make specific notes about how you can begin to do those things.
- Need some inspiration? Read the "Connect It" sections for profiles of people who are putting that call into action.

and satisfy your needs in parched places,
and make your bones strong;
and you shall be like a watered garden,
like a spring of water,
whose waters never fail.
12 Your ancient ruins shall be rebuilt;
you shall raise up the foundations of many
generations;
you shall be called the repairer of the breach,
the restorer of streets to live in.

13 If you refrain from trampling the sabbath,
from pursuing your own interests on my
holy day;
if you call the sabbath a delight
and the holy day of the LORD honorable;
if you honor it, not going your own ways,
serving your own interests, or pursuing
your own affairs;[a]
14 then you shall take delight in the LORD,
and I will make you ride upon the heights
of the earth;
I will feed you with the heritage of your
ancestor Jacob,
for the mouth of the LORD has spoken.

59 Injustice and Oppression to Be Punished

See, the LORD's hand is not too short to
save,
nor his ear too dull to hear.
2 Rather, your iniquities have been barriers
between you and your God,

CONNECT IT!

Dan Haseltine: Music and Justice for All
Isaiah 58:6–14

You may know Dan Haseltine as the lead vocalist for the band Jars of Clay. And though music is central to his identity and his songs have pointed many people to God, his life shows a more complete understanding of worship. Freeing the oppressed, feeding the hungry, giving shelter to the homeless, and clothing the naked—all acts of worship described in **Isaiah 58:6–14**—can be seen in the way Haseltine lives his life. He often writes and sings about social justice issues, sharing stories of the needs of friends in Africa. He is also the founder of Blood:Water Mission, an organization that works with communities to prevent and treat HIV/AIDS and to provide clean water (**bloodwatermission .com**). The words of the prophets, like Isaiah, echo through Haseltine's life and music in the ongoing pursuit of bringing hope and justice to our world.

a Heb *or speaking words*

and your sins have hidden his face from you
    so that he does not hear.
3 For your hands are defiled with blood,
    and your fingers with iniquity;
your lips have spoken lies,
    your tongue mutters wickedness.
4 No one brings suit justly,
    no one goes to law honestly;
they rely on empty pleas, they speak lies,
    conceiving mischief and begetting iniquity.
5 They hatch adders' eggs,
    and weave the spider's web;
whoever eats their eggs dies,
    and the crushed egg hatches out a viper.
6 Their webs cannot serve as clothing;
    they cannot cover themselves with what
        they make.
Their works are works of iniquity,
    and deeds of violence are in their hands.
7 Their feet run to evil,
    and they rush to shed innocent blood;
their thoughts are thoughts of iniquity,
    desolation and destruction are in their
        highways.
8 The way of peace they do not know,
    and there is no justice in their paths.
Their roads they have made crooked;
    no one who walks in them knows peace.

9 Therefore justice is far from us,
    and righteousness does not reach us;
we wait for light, and lo! there is darkness;
    and for brightness, but we walk in gloom.
10 We grope like the blind along a wall,
    groping like those who have no
        eyes;
we stumble at noon as in the twilight,
    among the vigorous[a] as though we were
        dead.
11 We all growl like bears;
    like doves we moan mournfully.
We wait for justice, but there is none;
    for salvation, but it is far from us.
12 For our transgressions before you are many,
    and our sins testify against us.
Our transgressions indeed are with us,
    and we know our iniquities:
13 transgressing, and denying the Lord,
    and turning away from following our God,
    talking oppression and revolt,

conceiving lying words and uttering them
    from the heart.
14 Justice is turned back,
    and righteousness stands at a distance;
for truth stumbles in the public square,
    and uprightness cannot enter.
15 Truth is lacking,
    and whoever turns from evil is despoiled.

The Lord saw it, and it displeased him
    that there was no justice.
16 He saw that there was no one,
    and was appalled that there was no one to
        intervene;
so his own arm brought him victory,
    and his righteousness upheld him.
17 He put on righteousness like a breastplate,
    and a helmet of salvation on his head;
he put on garments of vengeance for clothing,
    and wrapped himself in fury as in a
        mantle.
18 According to their deeds, so will he repay;
    wrath to his adversaries, requital to his
        enemies;
to the coastlands he will render requital.
19 So those in the west shall fear the name of the
    Lord,
and those in the east, his glory;
for he will come like a pent-up stream
    that the wind of the Lord drives on.

20 And he will come to Zion as Redeemer,
    to those in Jacob who turn from
        transgression, says the Lord.
21 And as for me, this is my covenant with them,
says the Lord: my spirit that is upon you, and my
words that I have put in your mouth, shall not depart out of your mouth, or out of the mouths of
your children, or out of the mouths of your children's children, says the Lord, from now on and
forever.

60 The Ingathering of the Dispersed

Arise, shine; for your light has come,
    and the glory of the Lord has risen
        upon you.
2 For darkness shall cover the earth,
    and thick darkness the peoples;
but the Lord will arise upon you,
    and his glory will appear over you.

a Meaning of Heb uncertain

3 Nations shall come to your light,
      and kings to the brightness of your dawn.

4 Lift up your eyes and look around;
      they all gather together, they come to you;
   your sons shall come from far away,
      and your daughters shall be carried on
         their nurses' arms.
5 Then you shall see and be radiant;
      your heart shall thrill and rejoice,[a]
   because the abundance of the sea shall be
         brought to you,
      the wealth of the nations shall come
         to you.
6 A multitude of camels shall cover you,
      the young camels of Midian and Ephah;
   all those from Sheba shall come.
   They shall bring gold and frankincense,
      and shall proclaim the praise of the LORD.
7 All the flocks of Kedar shall be gathered
         to you,
      the rams of Nebaioth shall minister
         to you;
   they shall be acceptable on my altar,
      and I will glorify my glorious house.

8 Who are these that fly like a cloud,
      and like doves to their windows?
9 For the coastlands shall wait for me,
      the ships of Tarshish first,
   to bring your children from far away,
      their silver and gold with them,
   for the name of the LORD your God,
      and for the Holy One of Israel,
         because he has glorified you.
10 Foreigners shall build up your walls,
      and their kings shall minister to you;
   for in my wrath I struck you down,
      but in my favor I have had mercy on you.
11 Your gates shall always be open;
      day and night they shall not be shut,
   so that nations shall bring you their wealth,
      with their kings led in procession.
12 For the nation and kingdom
      that will not serve you shall perish;
      those nations shall be utterly laid waste.
13 The glory of Lebanon shall come to you,
      the cypress, the plane, and the pine,
   to beautify the place of my sanctuary;
      and I will glorify where my feet rest.

14 The descendants of those who oppressed you
      shall come bending low to you,
   and all who despised you
      shall bow down at your feet;
   they shall call you the City of the LORD,
      the Zion of the Holy One of Israel.
15 Whereas you have been forsaken and hated,
      with no one passing through,
   I will make you majestic forever,
      a joy from age to age.
16 You shall suck the milk of nations,
      you shall suck the breasts of kings;
   and you shall know that I, the LORD, am your
         Savior
      and your Redeemer, the Mighty One of
         Jacob.

17 Instead of bronze I will bring gold,
      instead of iron I will bring silver;
   instead of wood, bronze,
      instead of stones, iron.
   I will appoint Peace as your overseer
      and Righteousness as your taskmaster.
18 Violence shall no more be heard in your land,
      devastation or destruction within your
         borders;
   you shall call your walls Salvation,
      and your gates Praise.

God the Glory of Zion
19 The sun shall no longer be
      your light by day,
   nor for brightness shall the moon
      give light to you by night;[b]
   but the LORD will be your everlasting light,
      and your God will be your glory.
20 Your sun shall no more go down,
      or your moon withdraw itself;
   for the LORD will be your everlasting light,
      and your days of mourning shall be
         ended.
21 Your people shall all be righteous;
      they shall possess the land forever.
   They are the shoot that I planted, the work of
         my hands,
      so that I might be glorified.
22 The least of them shall become a clan,
      and the smallest one a mighty nation;
   I am the LORD;
      in its time I will accomplish it quickly.

a Heb *be enlarged*   b Q Ms Gk Old Latin Tg: MT lacks *by night*

61 The Good News of Deliverance

The spirit of the Lord GOD is
      upon me,
because the LORD has anointed me;
he has sent me to bring good news to the
      oppressed,
to bind up the brokenhearted,
to proclaim liberty to the captives,
      and release to the prisoners;
2 to proclaim the year of the LORD's favor,
      and the day of vengeance of our God;
      to comfort all who mourn;
3 to provide for those who mourn in Zion—
      to give them a garland instead of ashes,
the oil of gladness instead of mourning,
      the mantle of praise instead of a faint spirit.
They will be called oaks of righteousness,
      the planting of the LORD, to display his
      glory.
4 They shall build up the ancient ruins,
      they shall raise up the former devastations;
they shall repair the ruined cities,
      the devastations of many generations.

5 Strangers shall stand and feed your flocks,
      foreigners shall till your land and dress your
      vines;
6 but you shall be called priests of the LORD,
      you shall be named ministers of our God;
you shall enjoy the wealth of the nations,
      and in their riches you shall glory.
7 Because their[a] shame was double,
      and dishonor was proclaimed as their lot,

therefore they shall possess a double portion;
      everlasting joy shall be theirs.

8 For I the LORD love justice,
      I hate robbery and wrongdoing;[b]
I will faithfully give them their recompense,
      and I will make an everlasting covenant
      with them.
9 Their descendants shall be known among the
      nations,
      and their offspring among the peoples;
all who see them shall acknowledge
      that they are a people whom the LORD has
      blessed.
10 I will greatly rejoice in the LORD,
      my whole being shall exult in my God;
for he has clothed me with the garments of
      salvation,
      he has covered me with the robe of
      righteousness,
as a bridegroom decks himself with a garland,
      and as a bride adorns herself with her
      jewels.
11 For as the earth brings forth its shoots,
      and as a garden causes what is sown in it to
      spring up,
so the Lord GOD will cause righteousness and
      praise
to spring up before all the nations.

62 The Vindication and Salvation of Zion

For Zion's sake I will not keep silent,

Like a Bride and Groom · Isaiah 61:10

The scene is a familiar one: A bride dressed in the most beautiful white wedding gown walks down the aisle to meet her waiting groom. Their happiness and love cannot be hidden as they prepare to join their lives together in marriage.

In ancient Israel, the bride and bridegroom gradually became a metaphor, or symbol, for the relationship between Israel and God (Isaiah 61:10; 62:5). Israel is the bride, and God is the faithful groom who loves her, lavishes her with blessings, and continues to be faithful to her. When Israel strays from the covenant or goes after foreign gods, she is compared to an unfaithful lover, even a prostitute who pursues other partners (for a graphic example, see Ezekiel 16:1-43). The prophet Hosea even marries a prostitute as a living example of God's faithfulness to an unfaithful people (Hosea 1:2)! The wonder of God's love is that through all of Israel's infidelity (and ours), God always remains willing to take her (and us) back with open, loving arms.

a Heb *your*   b Or *robbery with a burnt offering*

and for Jerusalem's sake I will not rest,
until her vindication shines out like the
   dawn,
and her salvation like a burning torch.
2 The nations shall see your vindication,
   and all the kings your glory;
and you shall be called by a new name
   that the mouth of the LORD will give.
3 You shall be a crown of beauty in the hand of
   the LORD,
   and a royal diadem in the hand of
     your God.
4 You shall no more be termed Forsaken,*a*
   and your land shall no more be termed
     Desolate;*b*
but you shall be called My Delight Is in Her,*c*
   and your land Married;*d*
for the LORD delights in you,
   and your land shall be married.
5 For as a young man marries a young woman,
   so shall your builder*e* marry you,
and as the bridegroom rejoices over the bride,
   so shall your God rejoice over you.
6 Upon your walls, O Jerusalem,
   I have posted sentinels;
all day and all night
   they shall never be silent.
You who remind the LORD,
   take no rest,
7 and give him no rest
   until he establishes Jerusalem
   and makes it renowned throughout the
     earth.
8 The LORD has sworn by his right hand
   and by his mighty arm:
I will not again give your grain
   to be food for your enemies,
and foreigners shall not drink the wine
   for which you have labored;
9 but those who garner it shall eat it
   and praise the LORD,
and those who gather it shall drink it
   in my holy courts.

10 Go through, go through the gates,
   prepare the way for the people;
build up, build up the highway,
   clear it of stones,
   lift up an ensign over the peoples.
11 The LORD has proclaimed

to the end of the earth:
Say to daughter Zion,
   "See, your salvation comes;
his reward is with him,
   and his recompense before him."
12 They shall be called, "The Holy People,
   The Redeemed of the LORD";
and you shall be called, "Sought Out,
   A City Not Forsaken."

Vengeance on Edom

63 "Who is this that comes from Edom,
   from Bozrah in garments stained
     crimson?
Who is this so splendidly robed,
   marching in his great might?"

"It is I, announcing vindication,
   mighty to save."

2 "Why are your robes red,
   and your garments like theirs who tread
     the wine press?"

3 "I have trodden the wine press alone,
   and from the peoples no one was with me;
I trod them in my anger
   and trampled them in my wrath;
their juice spattered on my garments,
   and stained all my robes.
4 For the day of vengeance was in my heart,
   and the year for my redeeming work had
     come.
5 I looked, but there was no helper;
   I stared, but there was no one to
     sustain me;
so my own arm brought me victory,
   and my wrath sustained me.
6 I trampled down peoples in my anger,
   I crushed them in my wrath,
   and I poured out their lifeblood on the
     earth."

God's Mercy Remembered

7 I will recount the gracious deeds of the
   LORD,
   the praiseworthy acts of the LORD,
because of all that the LORD has done
   for us,
   and the great favor to the house of Israel

---

a Heb *Azubah*   b Heb *Shemamah*   c Heb *Hephzibah*   d Heb *Beulah*   e Cn: Heb *your sons*

that he has shown them according to his
    mercy,
    according to the abundance of his
      steadfast love.
8 For he said, "Surely they are my people,
    children who will not deal falsely";
and he became their savior
9   in all their distress.
    It was no messenger*a* or angel
      but his presence that saved them;*b*
in his love and in his pity he redeemed them;
    he lifted them up and carried them all the
      days of old.

10 But they rebelled
    and grieved his holy spirit;
therefore he became their enemy;
    he himself fought against them.
11 Then they*c* remembered the days of old,
    of Moses his servant.*d*
Where is the one who brought them up out
    of the sea
    with the shepherds of his flock?
Where is the one who put within them
    his holy spirit,
12 who caused his glorious arm
    to march at the right hand of Moses,
who divided the waters before them
    to make for himself an everlasting
      name,
13   who led them through the depths?
Like a horse in the desert,
    they did not stumble.
14 Like cattle that go down into the valley,
    the spirit of the LORD gave them rest.
Thus you led your people,
    to make for yourself a glorious name.

A Prayer of Penitence

15 Look down from heaven and see,
    from your holy and glorious habitation.
Where are your zeal and your might?
    The yearning of your heart and your
      compassion?
    They are withheld from me.
16 For you are our father,
    though Abraham does not know us
    and Israel does not acknowledge us;
you, O LORD, are our father;
    our Redeemer from of old is your name.

17 Why, O LORD, do you make us stray from
    your ways
    and harden our heart, so that we do not
      fear you?
Turn back for the sake of your servants,
    for the sake of the tribes that are your
      heritage.
18 Your holy people took possession for a little
    while;
    but now our adversaries have trampled
      down your sanctuary.
19 We have long been like those whom you do
    not rule,
    like those not called by your name.

64 O that you would tear open the heavens
    and come down,
    so that the mountains would quake at
      your presence—
2*e* as when fire kindles brushwood
    and the fire causes water to boil—
to make your name known to your adversaries,
    so that the nations might tremble at your
      presence!
3 When you did awesome deeds that we did not
    expect,
    you came down, the mountains quaked at
      your presence.
4 From ages past no one has heard,
    no ear has perceived,
no eye has seen any God besides you,
    who works for those who wait for him.
5 You meet those who gladly do right,
    those who remember you in your ways.
But you were angry, and we sinned;
    because you hid yourself we transgressed.*f*
6 We have all become like one who is unclean,
    and all our righteous deeds are like a filthy
      cloth.
We all fade like a leaf,
    and our iniquities, like the wind, take us
      away.
7 There is no one who calls on your name,
    or attempts to take hold of you;
for you have hidden your face from us,
    and have delivered*g* us into the hand of our
      iniquity.
8 Yet, O LORD, you are our Father;
    we are the clay, and you are our potter;
    we are all the work of your hand.

a Gk: Heb *anguish* *b* Or *savior.* *⁹In all their distress he was distressed; the angel of his presence saved them;* *c* Heb *he* *d* Cn: Heb *his people*
e Ch 64.1 in Heb *f* Meaning of Heb uncertain *g* Gk Syr Old Latin Tg: Heb *melted*

PRAY IT!

In the Potter's Hands
Isaiah 64:8

Have you ever seen a potter at work? Maybe you've even worked at a potter's wheel yourself. Pot making is still practiced today much as it was at the time of Isaiah. The potter takes a lump of moist clay and begins to shape it by hand, with an image in mind of what the finished product will look like. The artisan then puts the piece of clay on a potter's wheel and spins the wheel, continuing to form the pot with his or her hands. Because it is designed by hand rather than mass-produced by machine, each work of the potter is original; there is no other just like it.

The image of God as a potter and each of us as a clay pot is also seen in the second Creation story in **Genesis 2:7**, where God scoops up clay from the earth, forms the first human being, and breathes life into him. It is also reflected in the description in **Psalm 139:13–16** of being knit together in our mother's womb.

The idea of God's hands shaping us like clay is intimate and comforting. No one but the potter knows how much time and love goes into the making of each pot, giving each one a special design and markings. The potter also knows its flaws. **Isaiah 64:8** gives us a vivid and beautiful image of God's relationship with each of us (see also Jeremiah 18:1-6).

During your prayer time, reflect or journal on the following questions:

- How has God molded you as a unique person?
- What are your special features and markings (gifts), and what are your flaws (weaknesses)?
- How is God still molding you?

9 Do not be exceedingly angry, O Lord,
　and do not remember iniquity forever.
　Now consider, we are all your people.
10 Your holy cities have become a wilderness,
　Zion has become a wilderness,
　Jerusalem a desolation.
11 Our holy and beautiful house,
　where our ancestors praised you,
has been burned by fire,
　and all our pleasant places have become
　　ruins.
12 After all this, will you restrain yourself, O Lord?
　Will you keep silent, and punish us so
　　severely?

65   The Righteousness of God's Judgment

I was ready to be sought out by those who
　did not ask,
　to be found by those who did not seek me.
I said, "Here I am, here I am,"
　to a nation that did not call on my name.
2 I held out my hands all day long
　to a rebellious people,
who walk in a way that is not good,
　following their own devices;
3 a people who provoke me
　to my face continually,
sacrificing in gardens
　and offering incense on bricks;
4 who sit inside tombs,
　and spend the night in secret places;
who eat swine's flesh,
　with broth of abominable things in their
　　vessels;
5 who say, "Keep to yourself,
　do not come near me, for I am too holy for
　　you."
These are a smoke in my nostrils,
　a fire that burns all day long.
6 See, it is written before me:
　I will not keep silent, but I will repay;
I will indeed repay into their laps
7 　their[a] iniquities and their[a] ancestors'
　　iniquities together,
　　　　　　　　　　　　says the Lord;
because they offered incense on the mountains
　and reviled me on the hills,
I will measure into their laps
　full payment for their actions.
8 Thus says the Lord:

As the wine is found in the cluster,
   and they say, "Do not destroy it,
   for there is a blessing in it,"
so I will do for my servants' sake,
   and not destroy them all.
9 I will bring forth descendants[a] from Jacob,
   and from Judah inheritors[b] of my
      mountains;
my chosen shall inherit it,
   and my servants shall settle there.
10 Sharon shall become a pasture for flocks,
   and the Valley of Achor a place for herds to
      lie down,
   for my people who have sought me.
11 But you who forsake the LORD,
   who forget my holy mountain,
who set a table for Fortune
   and fill cups of mixed wine for Destiny;
12 I will destine you to the sword,
   and all of you shall bow down to the
      slaughter;
because, when I called, you did not answer,
   when I spoke, you did not listen,
but you did what was evil in my sight,
   and chose what I did not delight in.
13 Therefore thus says the Lord GOD:
My servants shall eat,
   but you shall be hungry;
my servants shall drink,
   but you shall be thirsty;
my servants shall rejoice,
   but you shall be put to shame;
14 my servants shall sing for gladness of heart,
   but you shall cry out for pain of heart,
   and shall wail for anguish of spirit.
15 You shall leave your name to my chosen to use
      as a curse,
   and the Lord GOD will put you to death;
   but to his servants he will give a different
      name.
16 Then whoever invokes a blessing in the land
   shall bless by the God of faithfulness,
and whoever takes an oath in the land
   shall swear by the God of faithfulness;
because the former troubles are forgotten
   and are hidden from my sight.

The Glorious New Creation

17 For I am about to create new heavens
   and a new earth;

the former things shall not be remembered
   or come to mind.
18 But be glad and rejoice forever
   in what I am creating;
for I am about to create Jerusalem as a joy,
   and its people as a delight.
19 I will rejoice in Jerusalem,
   and delight in my people;
no more shall the sound of weeping be heard
      in it,
   or the cry of distress.
20 No more shall there be in it
   an infant that lives but a few days,
   or an old person who does not live out a
      lifetime;
for one who dies at a hundred years will be
      considered a youth,
   and one who falls short of a hundred will be
      considered accursed.
21 They shall build houses and inhabit them;
   they shall plant vineyards and eat their fruit.
22 They shall not build and another inhabit;
   they shall not plant and another eat;
for like the days of a tree shall the days of my
      people be,
   and my chosen shall long enjoy the work of
      their hands.
23 They shall not labor in vain,
   or bear children for calamity;[c]
for they shall be offspring blessed by the
      LORD—
   and their descendants as well.
24 Before they call I will answer,
   while they are yet speaking I will hear.
25 The wolf and the lamb shall feed together,
   the lion shall eat straw like the ox;
   but the serpent—its food shall be dust!
They shall not hurt or destroy
   on all my holy mountain,
                              says the LORD.

The Worship God Demands

66 Thus says the LORD:
Heaven is my throne
   and the earth is my footstool;
what is the house that you would build for me,
   and what is my resting place?
2 All these things my hand has made,
   and so all these things are mine,[d]
                              says the LORD.

a Or *a descendant*   b Or *an inheritor*   c Or *sudden terror*   d Gk Syr: Heb *these things came to be*

But this is the one to whom I will look,
   to the humble and contrite in spirit,
   who trembles at my word.

3 Whoever slaughters an ox is like one who kills
     a human being;
   whoever sacrifices a lamb, like one who
     breaks a dog's neck;
whoever presents a grain offering, like one
     who offers swine's blood;[a]
   whoever makes a memorial offering of
     frankincense, like one who blesses an
     idol.
These have chosen their own ways,
   and in their abominations they take
     delight;
4 I also will choose to mock[b] them,
   and bring upon them what they fear;
because, when I called, no one answered,
   when I spoke, they did not listen;
but they did what was evil in my sight,
   and chose what did not please me.

The LORD Vindicates Zion

5 Hear the word of the LORD,
   you who tremble at his word:
Your own people who hate you
   and reject you for my name's sake
have said, "Let the LORD be glorified,
   so that we may see your joy";
   but it is they who shall be put to
     shame.

6 Listen, an uproar from the city!
   A voice from the temple!
The voice of the LORD,
   dealing retribution to his enemies!

7 Before she was in labor
   she gave birth;
before her pain came upon her
   she delivered a son.
8 Who has heard of such a thing?
   Who has seen such things?
Shall a land be born in one day?
   Shall a nation be delivered in one moment?
Yet as soon as Zion was in labor
   she delivered her children.
9 Shall I open the womb and not deliver?
   says the LORD;

shall I, the one who delivers, shut the womb?
   says your God.

10 Rejoice with Jerusalem, and be glad for her,
   all you who love her;
rejoice with her in joy,
   all you who mourn over her—
11 that you may nurse and be satisfied
   from her consoling breast;
that you may drink deeply with delight
   from her glorious bosom.

12 For thus says the LORD:
I will extend prosperity to her like a river,
   and the wealth of the nations like an
     overflowing stream;
and you shall nurse and be carried on
     her arm,
   and dandled on her knees.
13 As a mother comforts her child,
   so I will comfort you;
   you shall be comforted in Jerusalem.

The Reign and Indignation of God

14 You shall see, and your heart shall rejoice;
   your bodies[c] shall flourish like the grass;
and it shall be known that the hand of the
     LORD is with his servants,
   and his indignation is against his enemies.
15 For the LORD will come in fire,
   and his chariots like the whirlwind,
to pay back his anger in fury,
   and his rebuke in flames of fire.
16 For by fire will the LORD execute judgment,
   and by his sword, on all flesh;
   and those slain by the LORD shall be many.

17 Those who sanctify and purify themselves to
go into the gardens, following the one in the center,
eating the flesh of pigs, vermin, and rodents, shall
come to an end together, says the LORD.

18 For I know[d] their works and their thoughts,
and I am[e] coming to gather all nations and tongues;
and they shall come and shall see my glory, 19and I
will set a sign among them. From them I will send
survivors to the nations, to Tarshish, Put,[f] and
Lud—which draw the bow—to Tubal and Javan, to
the coastlands far away that have not heard of my
fame or seen my glory; and they shall declare my

---

a Meaning of Heb uncertain   b Or *to punish*   c Heb *bones*   d Gk Syr: Heb lacks *know*   e Gk Syr Vg Tg: Heb *it is*   f Gk: Heb *Pul*

glory among the nations. ²⁰They shall bring all your kindred from all the nations as an offering to the LORD, on horses, and in chariots, and in litters, and on mules, and on dromedaries, to my holy mountain Jerusalem, says the LORD, just as the Israelites bring a grain offering in a clean vessel to the house of the LORD. ²¹And I will also take some of them as priests and as Levites, says the LORD.

²² For as the new heavens and the new earth,
  which I will make,
 shall remain before me, says the LORD;

so shall your descendants and your name
  remain.
²³ From new moon to new moon,
  and from sabbath to sabbath,
 all flesh shall come to worship before me,
  says the LORD.

24 And they shall go out and look at the dead bodies of the people who have rebelled against me; for their worm shall not die, their fire shall not be quenched, and they shall be an abhorrence to all flesh.

Jeremiah ▶▶▶▶▶▶▶▶▶▶▶▶▶▶

Imagine you're watching a movie. One of the lead characters imposes severe hardships on others and then goes off to dine in luxury. Immediately, you know the character is a villain. Another leading character calls for others to endure sacrifice and lives under the same conditions as they do. You know this one is a hero, because heroes practice what they preach. Jeremiah the prophet was such a hero; he not only preached a hard message, but accepted the trials that came with it.

IN DEPTH

At the beginning of Jeremiah's prophetic ministry, King Josiah ruled the southern kingdom, Judah (2 Chronicles 34–35). He was a good king who expanded Judah's territory and started a religious reform. Jeremiah approved of Josiah and Josiah's reforms, but he was afraid they were too little, too late. Chapters 2-5 contain his prophecies during Josiah's rule. In them, he speaks out against Israel's sin and corruption, but hopes things will improve if the people turn to God (Jeremiah 4:1-2). Unfortunately, King Josiah was suddenly killed in battle, and things went from bad to worse.

Kings Jehoiakim and Zedekiah were the main rulers who followed, and they were the complete opposite of Josiah (2 Chronicles 36:5–14). Both were ruthless, power hungry, and corrupt. During Jehoiakim's reign, Jeremiah had to go into hiding out of fear for his life. Jeremiah 7-20 contain his prophecies during this time, when his preaching against the sins of Israel became stronger. Jeremiah 21-29 and 34-45 record his life and preaching during Zedekiah's reign—the last few years before the Babylonian exile. While Zedekiah ruled, Jeremiah was imprisoned, beaten, and thrown into a well to die.

Jeremiah survived his experience in the well to see Jerusalem and the temple destroyed by the Babylonians. To give the people hope that God was still on their side, he prophesied the destruction of all Israel's enemies, especially Babylon (see Jeremiah 46-51).

Ultimately, Jeremiah realized that even a new king like David would not be enough to correct what was wrong. The people were unable to fulfill God's commandments, because they had hearts of stone. Jeremiah 30-33 is known as the Book of Consolation. In it, Jeremiah said the Lord would make a new covenant with Israel in the future, and this time the law would be written on the people's hearts (Jeremiah 31:31-34).

QUICK FACTS

- **Dates Covered:** Between 626 and 582 B.C.
- **Authors:** Jeremiah and his disciples, including Baruch
- **Theme:** The call to the ancient Israelites and to us to turn back to God and find hope for the future

AT A GLANCE

- **Jeremiah 1** Jeremiah's call to be a prophet to the nations
- **Jeremiah 2–25** Prophecies against Judah and Jerusalem
- **Jeremiah 26–45** Stories about Jeremiah and a discussion of the restoration of Israel
- **Jeremiah 46–52** Prophecies against other nations

1

The words of Jeremiah son of Hilkiah, of the priests who were in Anathoth in the land of Benjamin, [2]to whom the word of the LORD came in the days of King Josiah son of Amon of Judah, in the thirteenth year of his reign. [3]It came also in the days of King Jehoiakim son of Josiah of Judah, and until the end of the eleventh year of King Zedekiah son of Josiah of Judah, until the captivity of Jerusalem in the fifth month.

Jeremiah's Call and Commission

4 Now the word of the LORD came to me saying,
5   "Before I formed you in the womb I knew you,
    and before you were born I consecrated you;
    I appointed you a prophet to the nations."
[6]Then I said, "Ah, Lord GOD! Truly I do not know how to speak, for I am only a boy." [7]But the LORD said to me,
    "Do not say, 'I am only a boy';
    for you shall go to all to whom I send you,
    and you shall speak whatever I command you.
8   Do not be afraid of them,
    for I am with you to deliver you,
                        says the LORD."
[9]Then the LORD put out his hand and touched my mouth; and the LORD said to me,
    "Now I have put my words in your mouth.
10 See, today I appoint you over nations and over kingdoms,
    to pluck up and to pull down,
    to destroy and to overthrow,
    to build and to plant."

11 The word of the LORD came to me, saying, "Jeremiah, what do you see?" And I said, "I see a branch of an almond tree."[a] [12]Then the LORD said to me, "You have seen well, for I am watching[b] over

my word to perform it." [13]The word of the LORD came to me a second time, saying, "What do you see?" And I said, "I see a boiling pot, tilted away from the north."

14 Then the LORD said to me: Out of the north disaster shall break out on all the inhabitants of the land. [15]For now I am calling all the tribes of the kingdoms of the north, says the LORD; and they shall come and all of them shall set their thrones at the entrance of the gates of Jerusalem, against all its surrounding walls and against all the cities of Judah. [16]And I will utter my judgments against them, for all their wickedness in forsaking me; they have made offerings to other gods, and worshiped the works of their own hands. [17]But you, gird up your loins; stand up and tell them everything that I command you. Do not break down before them, or I will break you before them. [18]And I for my part have made you today a fortified city, an iron pillar, and a bronze wall, against the whole land—against the kings of Judah, its princes, its priests, and the people of the land. [19]They will fight against you; but they shall not prevail against you, for I am with you, says the LORD, to deliver you.

2

God Pleads with Israel to Repent

The word of the LORD came to me, saying: [2]Go and proclaim in the hearing of Jerusalem, Thus says the LORD:
    I remember the devotion of your youth,
        your love as a bride,
    how you followed me in the wilderness,
        in a land not sown.
3   Israel was holy to the LORD,
        the first fruits of his harvest.
    All who ate of it were held guilty;

You Are Not Too Young! • Jeremiah 1:4–10

Jeremiah was a young man when God tapped him on the shoulder. In response to God, Jeremiah said, "Truly I do not know how to speak, for I am only a boy" (Jeremiah 1:6). But God gave Jeremiah the words and the ability to do what God asked.

When you need to do something difficult for the good of others, remember God's response to Jeremiah: "Do not say, 'I am only a boy'" (Jeremiah 1:7). When we look at Jeremiah (and many others in the Bible), it becomes clear that God likes to call those who are too young, old, weak, timid, or immoral by worldly standards to do God's work. But it is not about you—it is about God working through you. God knows what you are able to do and say and be. Listen to God.

---

a Heb shaqed   b Heb shoqed

disaster came upon them,
    says the LORD.

4 Hear the word of the LORD, O house of Jacob,
and all the families of the house of Israel. ⁵Thus says
the LORD:
    What wrong did your ancestors find in me
        that they went far from me,
    and went after worthless things, and became
        worthless themselves?
6 They did not say, "Where is the LORD
        who brought us up from the land of Egypt,
    who led us in the wilderness,
        in a land of deserts and pits,
    in a land of drought and deep darkness,
        in a land that no one passes through,
        where no one lives?"
7 I brought you into a plentiful land
        to eat its fruits and its good things.
    But when you entered you defiled my land,
        and made my heritage an abomination.
8 The priests did not say, "Where is the LORD?"
        Those who handle the law did not
            know me;
    the rulers*a* transgressed against me;
        the prophets prophesied by Baal,
        and went after things that do not profit.

9 Therefore once more I accuse you,
    says the LORD,
        and I accuse your children's children.
10 Cross to the coasts of Cyprus and look,
        send to Kedar and examine with care;
    see if there has ever been such a thing.
11 Has a nation changed its gods,
        even though they are no gods?
    But my people have changed their glory
        for something that does not profit.
12 Be appalled, O heavens, at this,
        be shocked, be utterly desolate,
    says the LORD,
13 for my people have committed two evils:
        they have forsaken me,
    the fountain of living water,
        and dug out cisterns for themselves,
    cracked cisterns
        that can hold no water.

14 Is Israel a slave? Is he a homeborn servant?
    Why then has he become plunder?

15 The lions have roared against him,
        they have roared loudly.
    They have made his land a waste;
        his cities are in ruins, without inhabitant.
16 Moreover, the people of Memphis and
            Tahpanhes
        have broken the crown of your head.
17 Have you not brought this upon yourself
        by forsaking the LORD your God,
        while he led you in the way?
18 What then do you gain by going to Egypt,
        to drink the waters of the Nile?
    Or what do you gain by going to Assyria,
        to drink the waters of the Euphrates?
19 Your wickedness will punish you,
        and your apostasies will convict you.
    Know and see that it is evil and bitter
        for you to forsake the LORD your God;
        the fear of me is not in you,
    says the Lord GOD of hosts.

20 For long ago you broke your yoke
        and burst your bonds,
        and you said, "I will not serve!"
    On every high hill
        and under every green tree
        you sprawled and played the whore.
21 Yet I planted you as a choice vine,
        from the purest stock.
    How then did you turn degenerate
        and become a wild vine?
22 Though you wash yourself with lye
        and use much soap,
    the stain of your guilt is still before me,
        says the Lord GOD.
23 How can you say, "I am not defiled,
        I have not gone after the Baals"?
    Look at your way in the valley;
        know what you have done—
    a restive young camel interlacing her tracks,
24   a wild ass at home in the wilderness,
    in her heat sniffing the wind!
        Who can restrain her lust?
    None who seek her need weary themselves;
        in her month they will find her.
25 Keep your feet from going unshod
        and your throat from thirst.
    But you said, "It is hopeless,
        for I have loved strangers,
        and after them I will go."

a Heb *shepherds*

26 As a thief is shamed when caught,
      so the house of Israel shall be
          shamed—
   they, their kings, their officials,
      their priests, and their prophets,
27 who say to a tree, "You are my father,"
      and to a stone, "You gave me birth."
   For they have turned their backs to me,
      and not their faces.
   But in the time of their trouble they say,
      "Come and save us!"
28 But where are your gods
      that you made for yourself?
   Let them come, if they can save you,
      in your time of trouble;
   for you have as many gods
      as you have towns, O Judah.

29 Why do you complain against me?
      You have all rebelled against me,
                              says the LORD.
30 In vain I have struck down your children;
      they accepted no correction.
   Your own sword devoured your prophets
      like a ravening lion.
31 And you, O generation, behold the word of
          the LORD!*a*
   Have I been a wilderness to Israel,
      or a land of thick darkness?
   Why then do my people say, "We are free,
      we will come to you no more"?
32 Can a girl forget her ornaments,
      or a bride her attire?
   Yet my people have forgotten me,
      days without number.

33 How well you direct your course
      to seek lovers!
   So that even to wicked women
      you have taught your ways.
34 Also on your skirts is found
      the lifeblood of the innocent poor,
   though you did not catch them
          breaking in.
   Yet in spite of all these things*a*
35 you say, "I am innocent;
      surely his anger has turned from me."
   Now I am bringing you to judgment
      for saying, "I have not sinned."
36 How lightly you gad about,
   changing your ways!
   You shall be put to shame by Egypt
      as you were put to shame by Assyria.
37 From there also you will come away
      with your hands on your head;
   for the LORD has rejected those in whom you
          trust,
   and you will not prosper through them.

Unfaithful Israel

3 If*b* a man divorces his wife
      and she goes from him
   and becomes another man's wife,
      will he return to her?
   Would not such a land be greatly polluted?
   You have played the whore with many lovers;
      and would you return to me?
                              says the LORD.
2 Look up to the bare heights,*c* and see!
      Where have you not been lain with?
   By the waysides you have sat waiting for
          lovers,
      like a nomad in the wilderness.
   You have polluted the land
      with your whoring and wickedness.
3 Therefore the showers have been withheld,
      and the spring rain has not come;
   yet you have the forehead of a whore,
      you refuse to be ashamed.
4 Have you not just now called to me,
      "My Father, you are the friend of my
          youth—
5   will he be angry forever,
      will he be indignant to the end?"
   This is how you have spoken,
      but you have done all the evil that you
          could.

A Call to Repentance

6 The LORD said to me in the days of King Josiah:
Have you seen what she did, that faithless one, Israel,
how she went up on every high hill and under every
green tree, and played the whore there? 7 And I
thought, "After she has done all this she will return
to me"; but she did not return, and her false sister
Judah saw it. 8 She*d* saw that for all the adulteries of
that faithless one, Israel, I had sent her away with a
decree of divorce; yet her false sister Judah did not
fear, but she too went and played the whore. 9 Because she took her whoredom so lightly, she polluted

---

a Meaning of Heb uncertain   *b* Q Ms Gk Syr: MT *Saying, If*   *c* Or *the trails*   *d* Q Ms Gk Mss Syr: MT *I* the land, committing adultery with stone and tree. [10]Yet for all this her false sister Judah did not return to me with her whole heart, but only in pretense, says the LORD.

11 Then the LORD said to me: Faithless Israel has shown herself less guilty than false Judah. [12]Go, and proclaim these words toward the north, and say:

Return, faithless Israel,
                                        says the LORD.
I will not look on you in anger,
    for I am merciful,
                                        says the LORD;
I will not be angry forever.
[13] Only acknowledge your guilt,
    that you have rebelled against the LORD
        your God,
and scattered your favors among strangers
        under every green tree,
and have not obeyed my voice,
                                        says the LORD.
[14] Return, O faithless children,
                                        says the LORD,
    for I am your master;
I will take you, one from a city and two from a
        family,
and I will bring you to Zion.

15 I will give you shepherds after my own heart, who will feed you with knowledge and understanding. [16]And when you have multiplied and increased in the land, in those days, says the LORD, they shall no longer say, "The ark of the covenant of the LORD." It shall not come to mind, or be remembered, or missed; nor shall another one be made. [17]At that time Jerusalem shall be called the throne of the LORD, and all nations shall gather to it, to the presence of the LORD in Jerusalem, and they shall no longer stubbornly follow their own evil will. [18]In those days the house of Judah shall join the house of Israel, and together they shall come from the land of the north to the land that I gave your ancestors for a heritage.

[19] I thought
        how I would set you among my children,
    and give you a pleasant land,
        the most beautiful heritage of all the
            nations.
    And I thought you would call me, My Father,
and would not turn from following me.
20 Instead, as a faithless wife leaves her
        husband,
    so you have been faithless to me, O house
        of Israel,
                                        says the LORD.

[21] A voice on the bare heights[a] is heard,
        the plaintive weeping of Israel's children,
because they have perverted their way,
        they have forgotten the LORD their God:
[22] Return, O faithless children,
        I will heal your faithlessness.

"Here we come to you;
        for you are the LORD our God.
[23] Truly the hills are[b] a delusion,
        the orgies on the mountains.
Truly in the LORD our God
        is the salvation of Israel.
24 "But from our youth the shameful thing has devoured all for which our ancestors had labored, their flocks and their herds, their sons and their daughters. [25]Let us lie down in our shame, and let our dishonor cover us; for we have sinned against the LORD our God, we and our ancestors, from our youth even to this day; and we have not obeyed the voice of the LORD our God."

4   If you return, O Israel,
                                        says the LORD,
        if you return to me,
    if you remove your abominations from my
            presence,
        and do not waver,
2   and if you swear, "As the LORD lives!"
        in truth, in justice, and in uprightness,
    then nations shall be blessed[c] by him,
        and by him they shall boast.

3 For thus says the LORD to the people of Judah and to the inhabitants of Jerusalem:
    Break up your fallow ground,
        and do not sow among thorns.
[4] Circumcise yourselves to the LORD,
    remove the foreskin of your hearts,
        O people of Judah and inhabitants of
            Jerusalem,
    or else my wrath will go forth like fire,
        and burn with no one to quench it,
    because of the evil of your doings.

a Or *the trails* b Gk Syr Vg: Heb *Truly from the hills is* c Or *shall bless themselves*

Invasion and Desolation of Judah Threatened

5 Declare in Judah, and proclaim in Jerusalem,
and say:

Blow the trumpet through the land;
   shout aloud[a] and say,
"Gather together, and let us go
   into the fortified cities!"
6 Raise a standard toward Zion,
   flee for safety, do not delay,
for I am bringing evil from the north,
   and a great destruction.
7 A lion has gone up from its thicket,
   a destroyer of nations has set out;
he has gone out from his place
to make your land a waste;
   your cities will be ruins
   without inhabitant.
8 Because of this put on sackcloth,
   lament and wail:
"The fierce anger of the LORD
   has not turned away from us."

9 On that day, says the LORD, courage shall fail the
king and the officials; the priests shall be appalled
and the prophets astounded. 10 Then I said, "Ah,
Lord GOD, how utterly you have deceived this
people and Jerusalem, saying, 'It shall be well with
you,' even while the sword is at the throat!"

11 At that time it will be said to this people and
to Jerusalem: A hot wind comes from me out of the
bare heights[b] in the desert toward my poor people,
not to winnow or cleanse— 12 a wind too strong for
that. Now it is I who speak in judgment against them.
13   Look! He comes up like clouds,
   his chariots like the whirlwind;
his horses are swifter than eagles—
   woe to us, for we are ruined!
14 O Jerusalem, wash your heart clean of
   wickedness
   so that you may be saved.
How long shall your evil schemes
   lodge within you?
15 For a voice declares from Dan
   and proclaims disaster from Mount
    Ephraim.
16 Tell the nations, "Here they are!"
   Proclaim against Jerusalem,
"Besiegers come from a distant land;

   they shout against the cities of Judah.
17 They have closed in around her like watchers
   of a field,
   because she has rebelled against me,
       says the LORD.
18 Your ways and your doings
   have brought this upon you.
This is your doom; how bitter it is!
   It has reached your very heart."

Sorrow for a Doomed Nation

19 My anguish, my anguish! I writhe in pain!
   Oh, the walls of my heart!
My heart is beating wildly;
   I cannot keep silent;
for I[c] hear the sound of the trumpet,
   the alarm of war.

20 Disaster overtakes disaster,
   the whole land is laid waste.
Suddenly my tents are destroyed,
   my curtains in a moment.
21 How long must I see the standard,
   and hear the sound of the trumpet?
22 "For my people are foolish,
   they do not know me;
they are stupid children,
   they have no understanding.
They are skilled in doing evil,
   but do not know how to do good."

23 I looked on the earth, and lo, it was waste and
    void;
   and to the heavens, and they had no light.
24 I looked on the mountains, and lo, they were
    quaking,
   and all the hills moved to and fro.
25 I looked, and lo, there was no one
    at all,
   and all the birds of the air had fled.
26 I looked, and lo, the fruitful land was a desert,
   and all its cities were laid in ruins
   before the LORD, before his fierce anger.

---

a Or *shout, take your weapons*: Heb *shout, fill (your hand)*   b Or *the trails*   c Another reading is *for you, O my soul,*

27 For thus says the Lord: The whole land shall be a desolation; yet I will not make a full end.
28 Because of this the earth shall mourn,
and the heavens above grow black;
for I have spoken, I have purposed;
I have not relented nor will I turn back.

29 At the noise of horseman and archer
every town takes to flight;
they enter thickets; they climb among rocks;
all the towns are forsaken,
and no one lives in them.
30 And you, O desolate one,
what do you mean that you dress in crimson,
that you deck yourself with ornaments of
gold,
that you enlarge your eyes with paint?
In vain you beautify yourself.
Your lovers despise you;
they seek your life.
31 For I heard a cry as of a woman in labor,
anguish as of one bringing forth her first
child,
the cry of daughter Zion gasping for breath,
stretching out her hands,
"Woe is me! I am fainting before killers!"

The Utter Corruption of God's People

5 Run to and fro through the streets of
Jerusalem,
look around and take note!
Search its squares and see
if you can find one person
who acts justly
and seeks truth—
so that I may pardon Jerusalem.^{a}
2 Although they say, "As the Lord lives,"
yet they swear falsely.
3 O Lord, do your eyes not look for truth?
You have struck them,
but they felt no anguish;
you have consumed them,
but they refused to take correction.
They have made their faces harder than rock;
they have refused to turn back.

4 Then I said, "These are only the poor,
they have no sense;
for they do not know the way of the Lord,
the law of their God.

5 Let me go to the rich^b
and speak to them;
surely they know the way of the Lord,
the law of their God."
But they all alike had broken the yoke,
they had burst the bonds.

6 Therefore a lion from the forest shall kill them,
a wolf from the desert shall destroy them.
A leopard is watching against their cities;
everyone who goes out of them shall be
torn in pieces—
because their transgressions are many,
their apostasies are great.

7 How can I pardon you?
Your children have forsaken me,
and have sworn by those who are no gods.
When I fed them to the full,
they committed adultery
and trooped to the houses of prostitutes.
8 They were well-fed lusty stallions,
each neighing for his neighbor's wife.
9 Shall I not punish them for these things?
says the Lord;
and shall I not bring retribution
on a nation such as this?

10 Go up through her vine-rows and destroy,
but do not make a full end;
strip away her branches,
for they are not the Lord's.
11 For the house of Israel and the house of Judah
have been utterly faithless to me,
says the Lord.
12 They have spoken falsely of the Lord,
and have said, "He will do nothing.
No evil will come upon us,
and we shall not see sword or famine."
13 The prophets are nothing but wind,
for the word is not in them.
Thus shall it be done to them!

14 Therefore thus says the Lord, the God of
hosts:
Because they^c have spoken this word,
I am now making my words in your mouth a
fire,
and this people wood, and the fire shall
devour them.

a Heb it b Or the great c Heb you

15 I am going to bring upon you
     a nation from far away, O house of Israel,
                              says the LORD.
   It is an enduring nation,
     it is an ancient nation,
   a nation whose language you do not know,
     nor can you understand what they say.
16 Their quiver is like an open tomb;
     all of them are mighty warriors.
17 They shall eat up your harvest and your food;
     they shall eat up your sons and your
          daughters;
   they shall eat up your flocks and your herds;
     they shall eat up your vines and your fig
          trees;
   they shall destroy with the sword
     your fortified cities in which you trust.

18 But even in those days, says the LORD, I will
not make a full end of you. 19And when your people
say, "Why has the LORD our God done all these
things to us?" you shall say to them, "As you have
forsaken me and served foreign gods in your land,
so you shall serve strangers in a land that is not
yours."

20 Declare this in the house of Jacob,
     proclaim it in Judah:
21 Hear this, O foolish and senseless people,
     who have eyes, but do not see,
     who have ears, but do not hear.

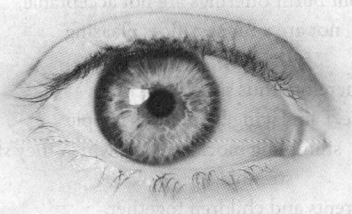

22 Do you not fear me? says the LORD;
     Do you not tremble before me?
   I placed the sand as a boundary for the sea,
     a perpetual barrier that it cannot pass;
   though the waves toss, they cannot prevail,
     though they roar, they cannot pass over it.
23 But this people has a stubborn and rebellious
          heart;
     they have turned aside and gone away.

24 They do not say in their hearts,
     "Let us fear the LORD our God,
   who gives the rain in its season,
     the autumn rain and the spring rain,
   and keeps for us
     the weeks appointed for the harvest."
25 Your iniquities have turned these away,
     and your sins have deprived you of good.
26 For scoundrels are found among my people;
     they take over the goods of others.
   Like fowlers they set a trap;[a]
     they catch human beings.
27 Like a cage full of birds,
     their houses are full of treachery;
   therefore they have become great and rich,
28   they have grown fat and sleek.
   They know no limits in deeds of wickedness;
     they do not judge with justice
   the cause of the orphan, to make it prosper,
     and they do not defend the rights of the
          needy.
29 Shall I not punish them for these things?
                              says the LORD,
     and shall I not bring retribution
     on a nation such as this?

30 An appalling and horrible thing
     has happened in the land:
31 the prophets prophesy falsely,
     and the priests rule as the prophets direct;[b]
   my people love to have it so,
     but what will you do when the end comes?

6 **The Imminence and Horror
of the Invasion**
     Flee for safety, O children of Benjamin,
       from the midst of Jerusalem!
   Blow the trumpet in Tekoa,
     and raise a signal on Beth-haccherem;
   for evil looms out of the north,
     and great destruction.
2 I have likened daughter Zion
     to the loveliest pasture.[c]
3 Shepherds with their flocks shall come
          against her.
     They shall pitch their tents around her;
     they shall pasture, all in their places.
4 "Prepare war against her;
     up, and let us attack at noon!"
   "Woe to us, for the day declines,

a Meaning of Heb uncertain   b Or rule by their own authority   c Or I will destroy daughter Zion, the loveliest pasture

the shadows of evening lengthen!"
5 "Up, and let us attack by night,
and destroy her palaces!"
6 For thus says the LORD of hosts:
Cut down her trees;
cast up a siege ramp against Jerusalem.
This is the city that must be punished;[a]
there is nothing but oppression within her.
7 As a well keeps its water fresh,
so she keeps fresh her wickedness;
violence and destruction are heard within her;
sickness and wounds are ever
before me.
8 Take warning, O Jerusalem,
or I shall turn from you in disgust,
and make you a desolation,
an uninhabited land.

9 Thus says the LORD of hosts:
Glean[b] thoroughly as a vine
the remnant of Israel;
like a grape-gatherer, pass your hand again
over its branches.

10 To whom shall I speak and give warning,
that they may hear?
See, their ears are closed,[c]
they cannot listen.
The word of the LORD is to them an object of
scorn;
they take no pleasure in it.
11 But I am full of the wrath of the LORD;
I am weary of holding it in.

Pour it out on the children in the street,
and on the gatherings of young men as well;
both husband and wife shall be taken,
the old folk and the very aged.
12 Their houses shall be turned over to others,
their fields and wives together;
for I will stretch out my hand
against the inhabitants of the land,
says the LORD.

13 For from the least to the greatest of them,
everyone is greedy for unjust gain;
and from prophet to priest,
everyone deals falsely.
14 They have treated the wound of my people
carelessly,

saying, "Peace, peace,"
when there is no peace.
15 They acted shamefully, they committed
abomination;
yet they were not ashamed,
they did not know how to blush.
Therefore they shall fall among those who fall;
at the time that I punish them, they shall
be overthrown,
says the LORD.
16 Thus says the LORD:
Stand at the crossroads, and look,
and ask for the ancient paths,
where the good way lies; and walk in it,
and find rest for your souls.
But they said, "We will not walk in it."
17 Also I raised up sentinels for you:
"Give heed to the sound of the trumpet!"
But they said, "We will not give heed."
18 Therefore hear, O nations,
and know, O congregation, what will
happen to them.
19 Hear, O earth; I am going to bring disaster on
this people,
the fruit of their schemes,
because they have not given heed to my
words;
and as for my teaching, they have
rejected it.
20 Of what use to me is frankincense that comes
from Sheba,
or sweet cane from a distant land?
Your burnt offerings are not acceptable,
nor are your sacrifices pleasing
to me.
21 Therefore thus says the LORD:
See, I am laying before this people
stumbling blocks against which they shall
stumble;
parents and children together,
neighbor and friend shall perish.

22 Thus says the LORD:
See, a people is coming from the land of the
north,
a great nation is stirring from the farthest
parts of the earth.
23 They grasp the bow and the javelin,
they are cruel and have no mercy,
their sound is like the roaring sea;

a Or the city of license   b Cn: Heb They shall glean   c Heb are uncircumcised

like dung upon the open field,
like sheaves behind the reaper,
and no one shall gather them."

23 Thus says the LORD: Do not let the wise boast in their wisdom, do not let the mighty boast in their might, do not let the wealthy boast in their wealth; [24]but let those who boast boast in this, that they understand and know me, that I am the LORD; I act with steadfast love, justice, and righteousness in the earth, for in these things I delight, says the LORD.

25 The days are surely coming, says the LORD, when I will attend to all those who are circumcised only in the foreskin: [26]Egypt, Judah, Edom, the Ammonites, Moab, and all those with shaven temples who live in the desert. For all these nations are uncircumcised, and all the house of Israel is uncircumcised in heart.

Idolatry Has Brought Ruin on Israel

10 Hear the word that the LORD speaks to you, O house of Israel. [2]Thus says the LORD:

Do not learn the way of the nations,
or be dismayed at the signs of the heavens;
for the nations are dismayed at
them.
[3] For the customs of the peoples are false:
a tree from the forest is cut down,
and worked with an ax by the hands of an
artisan;
[4] people deck it with silver and gold;
they fasten it with hammer and nails
so that it cannot move.
[5] Their idols[a] are like scarecrows in a cucumber
field,
and they cannot speak;
they have to be carried,
for they cannot walk.
Do not be afraid of them,
for they cannot do evil,
nor is it in them to do good.

[6] There is none like you, O LORD;
you are great, and your name is great in
might.
[7] Who would not fear you, O King of the
nations?
For that is your due;
among all the wise ones of the nations

> **"The LORD is the true God; he is the living God and the everlasting King."**
> **—Jeremiah 10:10**

and in all their kingdoms
there is no one like you.
[8] They are both stupid and foolish;
the instruction given by idols
is no better than wood![b]
[9] Beaten silver is brought from Tarshish,
and gold from Uphaz.
They are the work of the artisan and of the
hands of the goldsmith;
their clothing is blue and purple;
they are all the product of skilled
workers.
[10] But the LORD is the true God;
he is the living God and the everlasting
King.
At his wrath the earth quakes,
and the nations cannot endure his
indignation.

11 Thus shall you say to them: The gods who did not make the heavens and the earth shall perish from the earth and from under the heavens.[c]

[12] It is he who made the earth by his power,
who established the world by his wisdom,
and by his understanding stretched out
the heavens.
[13] When he utters his voice, there is a tumult of
waters in the heavens,
and he makes the mist rise from the ends
of the earth.
He makes lightnings for the rain,
and he brings out the wind from his
storehouses.
[14] Everyone is stupid and without knowledge;
goldsmiths are all put to shame by their
idols;
for their images are false,
and there is no breath in them.
[15] They are worthless, a work of
delusion;

---

a Heb *They*   b Meaning of Heb uncertain   c This verse is in Aramaic

at the time of their punishment they shall
perish.
16 Not like these is the Lord,^a the portion of
Jacob,
for he is the one who formed all things,
and Israel is the tribe of his
inheritance;
the Lord of hosts is his name.

The Coming Exile

17 Gather up your bundle from the ground,
O you who live under siege!
18 For thus says the Lord:
I am going to sling out the inhabitants of
the land
at this time,
and I will bring distress on them,
so that they shall feel it.

19 Woe is me because of my hurt!
My wound is severe.
But I said, "Truly this is my punishment,
and I must bear it."
20 My tent is destroyed,
and all my cords are broken;
my children have gone from me,
and they are no more;
there is no one to spread my tent again,
and to set up my curtains.
21 For the shepherds are stupid,
and do not inquire of the Lord;
therefore they have not prospered,
and all their flock is scattered.

22 Hear, a noise! Listen, it is coming—
a great commotion from the land of the
north
to make the cities of Judah a desolation,
a lair of jackals.

23 I know, O Lord, that the way of human beings
is not in their control,
that mortals as they walk cannot direct
their steps.
24 Correct me, O Lord, but in just measure;
not in your anger, or you will bring me to
nothing.

25 Pour out your wrath on the nations that do
not know you,

and on the peoples that do not call on your
name;
for they have devoured Jacob;
they have devoured him and consumed
him,
and have laid waste his habitation.

Israel and Judah Have Broken the Covenant

11 The word that came to Jeremiah from the
Lord: ²Hear the words of this covenant, and speak
to the people of Judah and the inhabitants of Jerusalem. ³You shall say to them, Thus says the Lord,
the God of Israel: Cursed be anyone who does not
heed the words of this covenant, ⁴which I commanded your ancestors when I brought them out
of the land of Egypt, from the iron-smelter, saying,
Listen to my voice, and do all that I command you.
So shall you be my people, and I will be your God,
⁵that I may perform the oath that I swore to your
ancestors, to give them a land flowing with milk and
honey, as at this day. Then I answered, "So be it,
Lord."

6 And the Lord said to me: Proclaim all these
words in the cities of Judah, and in the streets of Jerusalem: Hear the words of this covenant and do
them. ⁷For I solemnly warned your ancestors when
I brought them up out of the land of Egypt, warning
them persistently, even to this day, saying, Obey my
voice. ⁸Yet they did not obey or incline their ear, but
everyone walked in the stubbornness of an evil will.
So I brought upon them all the words of this covenant, which I commanded them to do, but they
did not.

9 And the Lord said to me: Conspiracy exists
among the people of Judah and the inhabitants of
Jerusalem. ¹⁰They have turned back to the iniquities
of their ancestors of old, who refused to heed my
words; they have gone after other gods to serve
them; the house of Israel and the house of Judah
have broken the covenant that I made with their
ancestors. ¹¹Therefore, thus says the Lord, assuredly I am going to bring disaster upon them that
they cannot escape; though they cry out to me, I
will not listen to them. ¹²Then the cities of Judah
and the inhabitants of Jerusalem will go and cry out
to the gods to whom they make offerings, but they
will never save them in the time of their trouble.
¹³For your gods have become as many as your
towns, O Judah; and as many as the streets of Jeru-

---

a Heb lacks *the* Lord

salem are the altars to shame you have set up, altars to make offerings to Baal.

14 As for you, do not pray for this people, or lift up a cry or prayer on their behalf, for I will not listen when they call to me in the time of their trouble. ¹⁵What right has my beloved in my house, when she has done vile deeds? Can vows^a and sacrificial flesh avert your doom? Can you then exult? ¹⁶The LORD once called you, "A green olive tree, fair with goodly fruit"; but with the roar of a great tempest he will set fire to it, and its branches will be consumed. ¹⁷The LORD of hosts, who planted you, has pronounced evil against you, because of the evil that the house of Israel and the house of Judah have done, provoking me to anger by making offerings to Baal.

Jeremiah's Life Threatened

¹⁸ It was the LORD who made it known to me,
        and I knew;
    then you showed me their evil deeds.
¹⁹ But I was like a gentle lamb
        led to the slaughter.
    And I did not know it was against me
        that they devised schemes, saying,
    "Let us destroy the tree with its fruit,
        let us cut him off from the land of the
            living,

so that his name will no longer be
        remembered!"
²⁰ But you, O LORD of hosts, who judge
        righteously,
    who try the heart and the mind,
    let me see your retribution upon them,
        for to you I have committed my cause.

21 Therefore thus says the LORD concerning the people of Anathoth, who seek your life, and say, "You shall not prophesy in the name of the LORD, or you will die by our hand"— ²²therefore thus says the LORD of hosts: I am going to punish them; the young men shall die by the sword; their sons and their daughters shall die by famine; ²³and not even a remnant shall be left of them. For I will bring disaster upon the people of Anathoth, the year of their punishment.

Jeremiah Complains to God

12 You will be in the right, O LORD,
        when I lay charges against you;
    but let me put my case to you.
    Why does the way of the guilty prosper?
        Why do all who are treacherous thrive?
² You plant them, and they take root;
        they grow and bring forth fruit;
    you are near in their mouths
        yet far from their hearts.

True Confessions · Jeremiah 12:1–6

What if your private journals ended up in print? Now imagine they were included in the Bible! Some scholars believe that several passages in Jeremiah were exactly that—a private journal kept by Jeremiah that he never intended to be made public.

Jeremiah 12:1–6 is the first of five passages that are sometimes called the confessions of Jeremiah (Jeremiah 12:1-6; 15:10-21; 17:14-18; 18:18-23; 20:7-18). In the confessions, Jeremiah speaks to God in a very personal, very direct way. He complains to God about the people's stubbornness, he complains about his treatment, and he accuses God of deceiving him.

In **Jeremiah 12:1–4**, Jeremiah asks God why God lets evil people prosper. Why doesn't God just slaughter them like sheep? God's reply in **Jeremiah 12:5–6** is that things are going to get worse before they get better and that even Jeremiah's own family will turn against him. God never answers Jeremiah directly in any of the confessions—although in **Jeremiah 15:19–21**, God does promise to support him.

If this famous prophet shared his anger, doubts, and fears with God honestly, so can we. Jeremiah's confessions are a good reminder that God wants to share everything with us—and God is strong enough to handle the hardest things our hearts and minds can bring to God.

---

a Gk: Heb *Can many*

³ But you, O LORD, know me;
>   You see me and test me—my heart is
>   with you.
> Pull them out like sheep for the slaughter,
>   and set them apart for the day of slaughter.

⁴ How long will the land mourn,
>   and the grass of every field wither?
> For the wickedness of those who live in it
>   the animals and the birds are swept away,
>   and because people said, "He is blind to
>   our ways."ᵃ

God Replies to Jeremiah

⁵ If you have raced with foot-runners and they
>   have wearied you,
>   how will you compete with horses?
> And if in a safe land you fall down,
>   how will you fare in the thickets of the
>   Jordan?

⁶ For even your kinsfolk and your own family,
>   even they have dealt treacherously
>   with you;
> they are in full cry after you;
> do not believe them,
>   though they speak friendly words to you.

⁷ I have forsaken my house,
>   I have abandoned my heritage;
> I have given the beloved of my heart
>   into the hands of her enemies.

⁸ My heritage has become to me
>   like a lion in the forest;
> she has lifted up her voice against me—
>   therefore I hate her.

⁹ Is the hyena greedyᵇ for my heritage at my
>   command?
>   Are the birds of prey all around her?
> Go, assemble all the wild animals;
>   bring them to devour her.

¹⁰ Many shepherds have destroyed my
>   vineyard,
>   they have trampled down my portion,
> they have made my pleasant portion
>   a desolate wilderness.

¹¹ They have made it a desolation;
>   desolate, it mourns to me.
> The whole land is made desolate,
>   but no one lays it to heart.

¹² Upon all the bare heightsᶜ in the desert
>   spoilers have come;

for the sword of the LORD devours
>   from one end of the land to the other;
>   no one shall be safe.

¹³ They have sown wheat and have reaped
>   thorns,
>   they have tired themselves out but profit
>   nothing.
> They shall be ashamed of theirᵈ harvests
>   because of the fierce anger of the LORD.

¹⁴ Thus says the LORD concerning all my evil neighbors who touch the heritage that I have given my people Israel to inherit: I am about to pluck them up from their land, and I will pluck up the house of Judah from among them. ¹⁵And after I have plucked them up, I will again have compassion on them, and I will bring them again to their heritage and to their land, every one of them. ¹⁶And then, if they will diligently learn the ways of my people, to swear by my name, "As the LORD lives," as they taught my people to swear by Baal, then they shall be built up in the midst of my people. ¹⁷But if any nation will not listen, then I will completely uproot it and destroy it, says the LORD.

The Linen Loincloth

13 Thus said the LORD to me, "Go and buy yourself a linen loincloth, and put it on your loins, but do not dip it in water." ²So I bought a loincloth according to the word of the LORD, and put it on my loins. ³And the word of the LORD came to me a second time, saying, ⁴"Take the loincloth that you bought and are wearing, and go now to the Euphrates,ᵉ and hide it there in a cleft of the rock." ⁵So I went, and hid it by the Euphrates,ᶠ as the LORD commanded me. ⁶And after many days the LORD said to me, "Go now to the Euphrates,ᵉ and take from there the loincloth that I commanded you to hide there." ⁷Then I went to the Euphrates,ᵉ and dug, and I took the loincloth from the place where I had hidden it. But now the loincloth was ruined; it was good for nothing.

⁸ Then the word of the LORD came to me: ⁹Thus says the LORD: Just so I will ruin the pride of Judah and the great pride of Jerusalem. ¹⁰This evil people, who refuse to hear my words, who stubbornly follow their own will and have gone after other gods to serve them and worship them, shall be like this loincloth, which is good for nothing. ¹¹For as the loincloth clings to one's loins, so I made the whole

---

ᵃ Gk: Heb *to our future*   ᵇ Cn: Heb *Is the hyena, the bird of prey*   ᶜ Or *the trails*   ᵈ Heb *your*   ᵉ Or *to Parah*; Heb *perath*   ᶠ Or *by Parah*; Heb *perath*

house of Israel and the whole house of Judah cling to me, says the LORD, in order that they might be for me a people, a name, a praise, and a glory. But they would not listen.

Symbol of the Wine-Jars

12 You shall speak to them this word: Thus says the LORD, the God of Israel: Every wine-jar should be filled with wine. And they will say to you, "Do you think we do not know that every wine-jar should be filled with wine?" [13] Then you shall say to them: Thus says the LORD: I am about to fill all the inhabitants of this land—the kings who sit on David's throne, the priests, the prophets, and all the inhabitants of Jerusalem—with drunkenness. [14] And I will dash them one against another, parents and children together, says the LORD. I will not pity or spare or have compassion when I destroy them.

Exile Threatened

15 Hear and give ear; do not be haughty,
　　for the LORD has spoken.
16 Give glory to the LORD your God
　　before he brings darkness,
and before your feet stumble
　　on the mountains at twilight;
while you look for light,
　　he turns it into gloom
and makes it deep darkness.
17 But if you will not listen,
　　my soul will weep in secret for your pride;
my eyes will weep bitterly and run down with
　　　　tears,
　　because the LORD's flock has been taken
　　　　captive.
18 Say to the king and the queen
　　　　mother:
　　"Take a lowly seat,
for your beautiful crown
　　has come down from your head."[a]
19 The towns of the Negeb are shut up
　　with no one to open them;
all Judah is taken into exile,
　　wholly taken into exile.
20 Lift up your eyes and see
　　those who come from the north.
Where is the flock that was given you,
　　your beautiful flock?

21 What will you say when they set as head
　　　　over you
　　those whom you have trained
　　to be your allies?
Will not pangs take hold of you,
　　like those of a woman in labor?
22 And if you say in your heart,
　　"Why have these things come
　　　　upon me?"
it is for the greatness of your iniquity
　　that your skirts are lifted up,
　　and you are violated.
23 Can Ethiopians[b] change their skin
　　or leopards their spots?
Then also you can do good
　　who are accustomed to do evil.
24 I will scatter you[c] like chaff
　　driven by the wind from the desert.
25 This is your lot,
　　the portion I have measured out to you,
　　　　says the LORD,
because you have forgotten me
　　and trusted in lies.
26 I myself will lift up your skirts over your face,
　　and your shame will be seen.
27 I have seen your abominations,
　　your adulteries and neighings, your
　　　　shameless prostitutions
　　on the hills of the countryside.
Woe to you, O Jerusalem!
　　How long will it be
　　before you are made clean?

The Great Drought

14 The word of the LORD that came to Jeremiah concerning the drought:

2 Judah mourns
　　and her gates languish;
they lie in gloom on the ground,
　　and the cry of Jerusalem goes up.
3 Her nobles send their servants for water;
　　they come to the cisterns,
they find no water,
　　they return with their vessels empty.
They are ashamed and dismayed
　　and cover their heads,
4 because the ground is cracked.
Because there has been no rain on the land
　　the farmers are dismayed;
　　they cover their heads.

---

a Gk Syr Vg: Meaning of Heb uncertain　*b* Or *Nubians*; Heb *Cushites*　*c* Heb *them*

5 Even the doe in the field forsakes her
　　　newborn fawn
　　because there is no grass.
6 The wild asses stand on the bare heights,[a]
　　they pant for air like jackals;
　their eyes fail
　　because there is no herbage.

7 Although our iniquities testify against us,
　　act, O LORD, for your name's sake;
　our apostasies indeed are many,
　　and we have sinned against you.
8 O hope of Israel,
　　its savior in time of trouble,
　why should you be like a stranger in the land,
　　like a traveler turning aside for the night?
9 Why should you be like someone confused,
　　like a mighty warrior who cannot give
　　　help?
　Yet you, O LORD, are in the midst of us,
　　and we are called by your name;
　　do not forsake us!

10 Thus says the LORD concerning this people:
　Truly they have loved to wander,
　　they have not restrained their feet;
　therefore the LORD does not accept them,
　　now he will remember their iniquity
　　and punish their sins.

11 The LORD said to me: Do not pray for the
welfare of this people. 12Although they fast, I do not
hear their cry, and although they offer burnt offering
and grain offering, I do not accept them; but by the
sword, by famine, and by pestilence I consume them.

Denunciation of Lying Prophets

13 Then I said: "Ah, Lord GOD! Here are the
prophets saying to them, 'You shall not see the
sword, nor shall you have famine, but I will give you
true peace in this place.'" 14And the LORD said to
me: The prophets are prophesying lies in my name;
I did not send them, nor did I command them or
speak to them. They are prophesying to you a lying
vision, worthless divination, and the deceit of their
own minds. 15Therefore thus says the LORD concerning the prophets who prophesy in my name
though I did not send them, and who say, "Sword
and famine shall not come on this land": By sword
and famine those prophets shall be consumed.

16And the people to whom they prophesy shall be
thrown out into the streets of Jerusalem, victims of
famine and sword. There shall be no one to bury
them—themselves, their wives, their sons, and their
daughters. For I will pour out their wickedness upon
them.

17 You shall say to them this word:
　Let my eyes run down with tears night
　　　and day,
　　and let them not cease,
　for the virgin daughter—my people—is struck
　　　down with a crushing blow,
　　with a very grievous wound.
18 If I go out into the field,
　　look—those killed by the sword!
　And if I enter the city,
　　look—those sick with[b] famine!
　For both prophet and priest ply their trade
　　　throughout the land,
　　and have no knowledge.

The People Plead for Mercy

19 Have you completely rejected Judah?
　　Does your heart loathe Zion?
　Why have you struck us down
　　so that there is no healing for us?
　We look for peace, but find no good;
　　for a time of healing, but there is terror
　　　instead.
20 We acknowledge our wickedness, O LORD,
　　the iniquity of our ancestors,
　　for we have sinned against you.
21 Do not spurn us, for your name's sake;
　　do not dishonor your glorious throne;
　　remember and do not break your covenant
　　　with us.
22 Can any idols of the nations bring rain?
　　Or can the heavens give showers?
　Is it not you, O LORD our God?
　　We set our hope on you,
　　for it is you who do all this.

Punishment Is Inevitable

15 Then the LORD said to me: Though Moses
and Samuel stood before me, yet my heart
would not turn toward this people. Send them out
of my sight, and let them go! 2And when they say
to you, "Where shall we go?" you shall say to them:
Thus says the LORD:

---

a Or the trails　b Heb look—the sicknesses of

Those destined for pestilence, to pestilence,
 and those destined for the sword, to the
 sword;
those destined for famine, to famine,
 and those destined for captivity, to
 captivity.
3 And I will appoint over them four kinds of destroyers, says the LORD: the sword to kill, the dogs to drag away, and the birds of the air and the wild animals of the earth to devour and destroy. 4 I will make them a horror to all the kingdoms of the earth because of what King Manasseh son of Hezekiah of Judah did in Jerusalem.

5 Who will have pity on you, O Jerusalem,
 or who will bemoan you?
Who will turn aside
 to ask about your welfare?
6 You have rejected me, says the LORD,
 you are going backward;
so I have stretched out my hand against you
 and destroyed you—
 I am weary of relenting.
7 I have winnowed them with a winnowing fork
 in the gates of the land;
I have bereaved them, I have destroyed my
 people;
 they did not turn from their ways.
8 Their widows became more numerous

than the sand of the seas;
I have brought against the mothers of youths
 a destroyer at noonday;
I have made anguish and terror
 fall upon her suddenly.
9 She who bore seven has languished;
 she has swooned away;
her sun went down while it was yet day;
 she has been shamed and disgraced.
And the rest of them I will give to the sword
 before their enemies,
 says the LORD.

Jeremiah Complains Again and Is Reassured

10 Woe is me, my mother, that you ever bore me, a man of strife and contention to the whole land! I have not lent, nor have I borrowed, yet all of them curse me. 11 The LORD said: Surely I have intervened in your life[a] for good, surely I have imposed enemies on you in a time of trouble and in a time of distress.[b] 12 Can iron and bronze break iron from the north?

13 Your wealth and your treasures I will give as plunder, without price, for all your sins, throughout all your territory. 14 I will make you serve your enemies in a land that you do not know, for in my anger a fire is kindled that shall burn forever.
15 O LORD, you know;

Ben Schumaker: The Memory Project · Jeremiah 15:15

Ben Schumaker's life was changed by a man he met in a Guatemalan orphanage. In 2003, Schumaker was visiting Guatemala and was dismayed by the great physical needs of the children he met. But a man who had grown up in a similar orphanage told him about a much deeper need—the children's need to have and preserve their identities. He told Schumaker that he himself had no photos or keepsakes from his childhood and no parents to tell him the stories. So Schumaker left Guatemala with an idea that has become The Memory Project. Art students in the United States, the United Kingdom, and Canada create portraits of children and teens around the world who have been orphaned, abandoned, or neglected. The portraits provide the children with a special memory of their youth and help build a positive identity and self-image. For the artists, the project provides a chance to learn about and open their hearts to children in need and to actively give kindness through their art. Since Schumaker's trip to Guatemala, tens of thousands of children have been given the gift of a portrait. As Jeremiah asked in **Jeremiah 15:15**, "O LORD, . . . remember me, and visit me," so these children cry out to be remembered. Their cry is being met through The Memory Project **(thememoryproject.org)**.

a Heb *intervened with you*   b Meaning of Heb uncertain

remember me and visit me,
and bring down retribution for me on my
persecutors.
In your forbearance do not take me away;
know that on your account I suffer insult.

16 Your words were found, and I ate
them,
and your words became to me a joy
and the delight of my heart;
for I am called by your name,
O LORD, God of hosts.

17 I did not sit in the company of merrymakers,
nor did I rejoice;
under the weight of your hand I sat alone,
for you had filled me with indignation.

18 Why is my pain unceasing,
my wound incurable,
refusing to be healed?
Truly, you are to me like a deceitful brook,
like waters that fail.

19 Therefore thus says the LORD:
If you turn back, I will take you back,
and you shall stand before me.
If you utter what is precious, and not what is
worthless,
you shall serve as my mouth.
It is they who will turn to you,
not you who will turn to them.

20 And I will make you to this people
a fortified wall of bronze;
they will fight against you,
but they shall not prevail over you,
for I am with you
to save you and deliver you,
says the LORD.

21 I will deliver you out of the hand of the
wicked,
and redeem you from the grasp of the
ruthless.

16

Jeremiah's Celibacy and Message

The word of the LORD came to me: [2]You
shall not take a wife, nor shall you have
sons or daughters in this place. [3]For thus says the
LORD concerning the sons and daughters who are
born in this place, and concerning the mothers who
bear them and the fathers who beget them in this
land: [4]They shall die of deadly diseases. They shall
not be lamented, nor shall they be buried; they shall

become like dung on the surface of the ground. They
shall perish by the sword and by famine, and their
dead bodies shall become food for the birds of the
air and for the wild animals of the earth.

5 For thus says the LORD: Do not enter the house
of mourning, or go to lament, or bemoan them; for I
have taken away my peace from this people, says the
LORD, my steadfast love and mercy. [6]Both great and
small shall die in this land; they shall not be buried,
and no one shall lament for them; there shall be no
gashing, no shaving of the head for them. [7]No one
shall break bread[a] for the mourner, to offer comfort
for the dead; nor shall anyone give them the cup of
consolation to drink for their fathers or their mothers.
[8]You shall not go into the house of feasting to sit with
them, to eat and drink. [9]For thus says the LORD of
hosts, the God of Israel: I am going to banish from
this place, in your days and before your eyes, the voice
of mirth and the voice of gladness, the voice of the
bridegroom and the voice of the bride.

10 And when you tell this people all these words,
and they say to you, "Why has the LORD pronounced
all this great evil against us? What is our iniquity?
What is the sin that we have committed against the
LORD our God?" [11]then you shall say to them: It is
because your ancestors have forsaken me, says the
LORD, and have gone after other gods and have
served and worshiped them, and have forsaken me
and have not kept my law; [12]and because you have
behaved worse than your ancestors, for here you are,
every one of you, following your stubborn evil will,
refusing to listen to me. [13]Therefore I will hurl you
out of this land into a land that neither you nor your
ancestors have known, and there you shall serve
other gods day and night, for I will show you no favor.

God Will Restore Israel

14 Therefore, the days are surely coming, says the
LORD, when it shall no longer be said, "As the LORD
lives who brought the people of Israel up out of the
land of Egypt," [15]but "As the LORD lives who
brought the people of Israel up out of the land of
the north and out of all the lands where he had
driven them." For I will bring them back to their
own land that I gave to their ancestors.

16 I am now sending for many fishermen, says the
LORD, and they shall catch them; and afterward I
will send for many hunters, and they shall hunt them
from every mountain and every hill, and out of the
clefts of the rocks. [17]For my eyes are on all their

a Two Mss Gk: MT *break for them*

ways; they are not hidden from my presence, nor is their iniquity concealed from my sight. [18]And[a] I will doubly repay their iniquity and their sin, because they have polluted my land with the carcasses of their detestable idols, and have filled my inheritance with their abominations.

19 O LORD, my strength and my stronghold,
  my refuge in the day of trouble,
to you shall the nations come
  from the ends of the earth and say:
Our ancestors have inherited nothing but lies,
  worthless things in which there is no
    profit.
20 Can mortals make for themselves gods?
  Such are no gods!

21 "Therefore I am surely going to teach them, this time I am going to teach them my power and my might, and they shall know that my name is the LORD."

Judah's Sin and Punishment

17 The sin of Judah is written with an iron pen; with a diamond point it is engraved on the tablet of their hearts, and on the horns of their altars, [2]while their children remember their altars and their sacred poles,[b] beside every green tree, and on the high hills, [3]on the mountains in the open country. Your wealth and all your treasures I will give for spoil as the price of your sin[c] throughout all your territory. [4]By your own act you shall lose the heritage that I gave you, and I will make you serve your enemies in a land that you do not know, for in my anger a fire is kindled[d] that shall burn forever.

5 Thus says the LORD:
Cursed are those who trust in mere mortals
  and make mere flesh their strength,
  whose hearts turn away from the LORD.
6 They shall be like a shrub in the desert,
  and shall not see when relief comes.
They shall live in the parched places of the
    wilderness,
  in an uninhabited salt land.

7 Blessed are those who trust in the LORD,
  whose trust is the LORD.
8 They shall be like a tree planted by water,

sending out its roots by the stream.
It shall not fear when heat comes,
  and its leaves shall stay green;
in the year of drought it is not anxious,
  and it does not cease to bear fruit.

9 The heart is devious above all else;
  it is perverse—
  who can understand it?
10 I the LORD test the mind
  and search the heart,
to give to all according to their ways,
  according to the fruit of their doings.

11 Like the partridge hatching what it did not lay,
  so are all who amass wealth unjustly;
in mid-life it will leave them,
  and at their end they will prove to be
    fools.

12 O glorious throne, exalted from the
    beginning,
  shrine of our sanctuary!
13 O hope of Israel! O LORD!
  All who forsake you shall be put to shame;
  those who turn away from you[e] shall be
    recorded in the underworld,[f]
  for they have forsaken the fountain of
    living water, the LORD.

Jeremiah Prays for Vindication

14 Heal me, O LORD, and I shall be healed;
  save me, and I shall be saved;
  for you are my praise.
15 See how they say to me,
  "Where is the word of the LORD?
  Let it come!"
16 But I have not run away from being a
    shepherd[g] in your service,
  nor have I desired the fatal day.
You know what came from my lips;
  it was before your face.
17 Do not become a terror to me;
  you are my refuge in the day of disaster;
18 Let my persecutors be shamed,
  but do not let me be shamed;
let them be dismayed,
  but do not let me be dismayed;
bring on them the day of disaster;
  destroy them with double destruction!

a Gk: Heb *And first* b Heb *Asherim* c Cn: Heb *spoil your high places for sin* d Two Mss Theodotion: *you kindled* e Heb *me* f Or *in the earth*
g Meaning of Heb uncertain

Hallow the Sabbath Day

19 Thus said the LORD to me: Go and stand in the People's Gate, by which the kings of Judah enter and by which they go out, and in all the gates of Jerusalem, [20]and say to them: Hear the word of the LORD, you kings of Judah, and all Judah, and all the inhabitants of Jerusalem, who enter by these gates. [21]Thus says the LORD: For the sake of your lives, take care that you do not bear a burden on the sabbath day or bring it in by the gates of Jerusalem. [22]And do not carry a burden out of your houses on the sabbath or do any work, but keep the sabbath day holy, as I commanded your ancestors. [23]Yet they did not listen or incline their ear; they stiffened their necks and would not hear or receive instruction.

24 But if you listen to me, says the LORD, and bring in no burden by the gates of this city on the sabbath day, but keep the sabbath day holy and do no work on it, [25]then there shall enter by the gates of this city kings[a] who sit on the throne of David, riding in chariots and on horses, they and their officials, the people of Judah and the inhabitants of Jerusalem; and this city shall be inhabited forever. [26]And people shall come from the towns of Judah and the places around Jerusalem, from the land of Benjamin, from the Shephelah, from the hill country, and from the Negeb, bringing burnt offerings and sacrifices, grain offerings and frankincense, and bringing thank offerings to the house of the LORD. [27]But if you do not listen to me, to keep the sabbath day holy, and to carry in no burden through the gates of Jerusalem on the sabbath day, then I will kindle a fire in its gates; it shall devour the palaces of Jerusalem and shall not be quenched.

The Potter and the Clay

18 The word that came to Jeremiah from the LORD: [2]"Come, go down to the potter's house, and there I will let you hear my words." [3]So I went down to the potter's house, and there he was working at his wheel. [4]The vessel he was making of clay was spoiled in the potter's hand, and he reworked it into another vessel, as seemed good to him.

5 Then the word of the LORD came to me: [6]Can I not do with you, O house of Israel, just as this potter has done? says the LORD. Just like the clay in the potter's hand, so are you in my hand, O house of Israel. [7]At one moment I may declare concerning a nation or a kingdom, that I will pluck up and break down and destroy it, [8]but if that nation, concerning which I have spoken, turns from its evil, I will change my mind about the disaster that I intended to bring on it. [9]And at another moment I may declare concerning a nation or a kingdom that I will build and plant it, [10]but if it does evil in my sight, not listening to my voice, then I will change my mind about the good that I had intended to do to it. [11]Now, therefore, say to the people of Judah and the inhabitants of Jerusalem: Thus says the LORD: Look, I am a potter shaping evil against you and devising a plan against you. Turn now, all of you from your evil way, and amend your ways and your doings.

Israel's Stubborn Idolatry

12 But they say, "It is no use! We will follow our own plans, and each of us will act according to the stubbornness of our evil will."

13　Therefore thus says the LORD:
　　Ask among the nations:
　　　Who has heard the like of this?
　　The virgin Israel has done
　　　a most horrible thing.
14　Does the snow of Lebanon leave
　　　the crags of Sirion?[b]
　　Do the mountain[c] waters run dry,[d]
　　　the cold flowing streams?
15　But my people have forgotten me,
　　　they burn offerings to a delusion;
　　they have stumbled[e] in their ways,
　　　in the ancient roads,
　　and have gone into bypaths,
　　　not the highway,
16　making their land a horror,
　　　a thing to be hissed at forever.
　　All who pass by it are horrified
　　　and shake their heads.
17　Like the wind from the east,
　　　I will scatter them before the
　　　　enemy.
　　I will show them my back, not my face,
　　　in the day of their calamity.

A Plot against Jeremiah

18 Then they said, "Come, let us make plots against Jeremiah—for instruction shall not perish from the priest, nor counsel from the wise, nor the word from the prophet. Come, let us bring charges against him,[f] and let us not heed any of his words."

---

a Cn: Heb *kings and officials*　b Cn: Heb *of the field*　c Cn: Heb *foreign*　d Cn: Heb *Are . . . plucked up?*　e Gk Syr Vg: Heb *they made them stumble*
f Heb *strike him with the tongue*

19 Give heed to me, O Lord,
     and listen to what my adversaries say!
20 Is evil a recompense for good?
     Yet they have dug a pit for my life.
   Remember how I stood before you
     to speak good for them,
     to turn away your wrath from them.
21 Therefore give their children over to famine;
     hurl them out to the power of the sword,
   let their wives become childless and widowed.
   May their men meet death by pestilence,
     their youths be slain by the sword in battle.
22 May a cry be heard from their houses,
     when you bring the marauder suddenly
          upon them!
   For they have dug a pit to catch me,
     and laid snares for my feet.
23 Yet you, O Lord, know
     all their plotting to kill me.
   Do not forgive their iniquity,
     do not blot out their sin from your sight.
   Let them be tripped up before you;
     deal with them while you are angry.

The Broken Earthenware Jug

19 Thus said the Lord: Go and buy a potter's earthenware jug. Take with you*a* some of the elders of the people and some of the senior priests, ²and go out to the valley of the son of Hinnom at the entry of the Potsherd Gate, and proclaim there the words that I tell you. ³You shall say: Hear the word of the Lord, O kings of Judah and inhabitants of Jerusalem. Thus says the Lord of hosts, the God of Israel: I am going to bring such disaster upon this place that the ears of everyone who hears of it will tingle. ⁴Because the people have forsaken me, and have profaned this place by making offerings in it to other gods whom neither they nor their ancestors nor the kings of Judah have known, and

because they have filled this place with the blood of the innocent, ⁵and gone on building the high places of Baal to burn their children in the fire as burnt offerings to Baal, which I did not command or decree, nor did it enter my mind; ⁶therefore the days are surely coming, says the Lord, when this place shall no more be called Topheth, or the valley of the son of Hinnom, but the valley of Slaughter. ⁷And in this place I will make void the plans of Judah and Jerusalem, and will make them fall by the sword before their enemies, and by the hand of those who seek their life. I will give their dead bodies for food to the birds of the air and to the wild animals of the earth. ⁸And I will make this city a horror, a thing to be hissed at; everyone who passes by it will be horrified and will hiss because of all its disasters. ⁹And I will make them eat the flesh of their sons and the flesh of their daughters, and all shall eat the flesh of their neighbors in the siege, and in the distress with which their enemies and those who seek their life afflict them.

10 Then you shall break the jug in the sight of those who go with you, ¹¹and shall say to them: Thus says the Lord of hosts: So will I break this people and this city, as one breaks a potter's vessel, so that it can never be mended. In Topheth they shall bury until there is no more room to bury. ¹²Thus will I do to this place, says the Lord, and to its inhabitants, making this city like Topheth. ¹³And the houses of Jerusalem and the houses of the kings of Judah shall be defiled like the place of Topheth— all the houses upon whose roofs offerings have been made to the whole host of heaven, and libations have been poured out to other gods.

14 When Jeremiah came from Topheth, where the Lord had sent him to prophesy, he stood in the court of the Lord's house and said to all the people: ¹⁵Thus says the Lord of hosts, the God of Israel: I am now bringing upon this city and upon all its towns all the disaster that I have pronounced against it, because they have stiffened their necks, refusing to hear my words.

Jeremiah Persecuted by Pashhur

20 Now the priest Pashhur son of Immer, who was chief officer in the house of the Lord, heard Jeremiah prophesying these things. ²Then Pashhur struck the prophet Jeremiah, and put him in the stocks that were in the upper Benjamin Gate of the house of the Lord. ³The next morning when

a Syr Tg Compare Gk: Heb lacks *take with you*

Pashhur released Jeremiah from the stocks, Jeremiah said to him, The LORD has named you not Pashhur but "Terror-all-around." ⁴For thus says the LORD: I am making you a terror to yourself and to all your friends; and they shall fall by the sword of their enemies while you look on. And I will give all Judah into the hand of the king of Babylon; he shall carry them captive to Babylon, and shall kill them with the sword. ⁵I will give all the wealth of this city, all its gains, all its prized belongings, and all the treasures of the kings of Judah into the hand of their enemies, who shall plunder them, and seize them, and carry them to Babylon. ⁶And you, Pashhur, and all who live in your house, shall go into captivity, and to Babylon you shall go; there you shall die, and there you shall be buried, you and all your friends, to whom you have prophesied falsely.

Jeremiah Denounces His Persecutors

⁷ O LORD, you have enticed me,
    and I was enticed;
  you have overpowered me,
    and you have prevailed.
  I have become a laughingstock all day
      long;
    everyone mocks me.

⁸ For whenever I speak, I must cry out,
    I must shout, "Violence and destruction!"
  For the word of the LORD has become for me
    a reproach and derision all day long.
⁹ If I say, "I will not mention him,
    or speak any more in his name,"
  then within me there is something like a
      burning fire
    shut up in my bones;
  I am weary with holding it in,
    and I cannot.
¹⁰ For I hear many whispering:
    "Terror is all around!
  Denounce him! Let us denounce him!"
    All my close friends
    are watching for me to stumble.
  "Perhaps he can be enticed,
    and we can prevail against him,
    and take our revenge on him."
¹¹ But the LORD is with me like a dread warrior;
    therefore my persecutors will stumble,
    and they will not prevail.
  They will be greatly shamed,
    for they will not succeed.
  Their eternal dishonor
    will never be forgotten.

STUDY IT!

Introducing . . . Jeremiah · Jeremiah 20:7

Have you ever felt ridiculed for defending your values or doing a good deed? If so, then you can probably relate to Jeremiah, who knew what it was like to be rejected for delivering God's message. He once told God: "O LORD, you have enticed me, and I was enticed; . . . I have become a laughingstock all day long; everyone mocks me" (Jeremiah 20:7). Jeremiah's message to the Israelites was often of coming judgment and destruction—not popular words, for sure! But he was faithful to the message God gave him.

Jeremiah was born in 645 B.C., into a priestly family belonging to a northern Israelite tribe. He was very young when he was called by God to be a prophet. Like Isaiah, Jeremiah was a prophet for all seasons. He was both optimistic (Jeremiah 31) and condemning (Jeremiah 22:18-23). He was courageous (Jeremiah 37), enduring beatings, imprisonment, and even being thrown into a well to die (Jeremiah 38:1-6) for the sake of delivering God's message. He loved his people so much that he was sometimes called the weeping prophet because of his bitter tears for them and their fast-approaching doom (Jeremiah 8:23; 13:7).

The book of Jeremiah gives us a fascinating inside look at the prophet's relationship with God. Several passages, called the confessions of Jeremiah, are personal accounts of his struggles with God (Jeremiah 12:1-6; 15:10-21; 17:14-18; 18:18-23; 20:7-18). Take the time to read these passages. You might just find that your own doubts and struggles aren't all that different.

12 O Lord of hosts, you test the righteous,
   you see the heart and the mind;
let me see your retribution upon them,
   for to you I have committed my cause.

13 Sing to the Lord;
   praise the Lord!
For he has delivered the life of the needy
   from the hands of evildoers.

14 Cursed be the day
   on which I was born!
The day when my mother bore me,
   let it not be blessed!
15 Cursed be the man
   who brought the news to my father, saying,
"A child is born to you, a son,"
   making him very glad.
16 Let that man be like the cities
   that the Lord overthrew without pity;
let him hear a cry in the morning
   and an alarm at noon,
17 because he did not kill me in the womb;
   so my mother would have been my grave,
   and her womb forever great.
18 Why did I come forth from the womb
   to see toil and sorrow,
   and spend my days in shame?

21 **Jerusalem Will Fall to Nebuchadrezzar**
This is the word that came to Jeremiah from the Lord, when King Zedekiah sent to him Pashhur son of Malchiah and the priest Zephaniah son of Maaseiah, saying, 2"Please inquire of the Lord on our behalf, for King Nebuchadrezzar of Babylon is making war against us; perhaps the Lord will perform a wonderful deed for us, as he has often done, and will make him withdraw from us."

3 Then Jeremiah said to them: 4Thus you shall say to Zedekiah: Thus says the Lord, the God of Israel: I am going to turn back the weapons of war that are in your hands and with which you are fighting against the king of Babylon and against the Chaldeans who are besieging you outside the walls; and I will bring them together into the center of this city. 5I myself will fight against you with outstretched hand and mighty arm, in anger, in fury, and in great wrath. 6And I will strike down the inhabitants of this city, both human beings and ani-

mals; they shall die of a great pestilence. 7Afterward, says the Lord, I will give King Zedekiah of Judah, and his servants, and the people in this city—those who survive the pestilence, sword, and famine—into the hands of King Nebuchadrezzar of Babylon, into the hands of their enemies, into the hands of those who seek their lives. He shall strike them down with the edge of the sword; he shall not pity them, or spare them, or have compassion.

8 And to this people you shall say: Thus says the Lord: See, I am setting before you the way of life and the way of death. 9Those who stay in this city shall die by the sword, by famine, and by pestilence; but those who go out and surrender to the Chaldeans who are besieging you shall live and shall have their lives as a prize of war. 10For I have set my face against this city for evil and not for good, says the Lord: it shall be given into the hands of the king of Babylon, and he shall burn it with fire.

Message to the House of David

11 To the house of the king of Judah say: Hear the word of the Lord, 12O house of David! Thus says the Lord:

Execute justice in the morning,
   and deliver from the hand of the oppressor
   anyone who has been robbed,
or else my wrath will go forth like fire,
   and burn, with no one to quench it,
   because of your evil doings.

13 See, I am against you, O inhabitant of the
   valley,
   O rock of the plain,
                    says the Lord;
you who say, "Who can come down
   against us,
   or who can enter our places of refuge?"
14 I will punish you according to the fruit of
   your doings,
                    says the Lord;
I will kindle a fire in its forest,
   and it shall devour all that is around it.

22 **Exhortation to Repent**
Thus says the Lord: Go down to the house of the king of Judah, and speak there this word, 2and say: Hear the word of the Lord, O King of Judah sitting on the throne of David— you, and your servants, and your people who enter

these gates. ³Thus says the LORD: Act with justice and righteousness, and deliver from the hand of the oppressor anyone who has been robbed. And do no wrong or violence to the alien, the orphan, and the widow, or shed innocent blood in this place. ⁴For if you will indeed obey this word, then through the gates of this house shall enter kings who sit on the throne of David, riding in chariots and on horses, they, and their servants, and their people. ⁵But if you will not heed these words, I swear by myself, says the LORD, that this house shall become a desolation. ⁶For thus says the LORD concerning the house of the king of Judah:

You are like Gilead to me,
    like the summit of Lebanon;
but I swear that I will make you a desert,
    an uninhabited city.ᵃ
⁷ I will prepare destroyers against you,
    all with their weapons;
they shall cut down your choicest cedars
    and cast them into the fire.

8 And many nations will pass by this city, and all of them will say one to another, "Why has the LORD dealt in this way with that great city?" ⁹And they will answer, "Because they abandoned the covenant of the LORD their God, and worshiped other gods and served them."

¹⁰ Do not weep for him who is dead,
    nor bemoan him;
weep rather for him who goes away,
    for he shall return no more
    to see his native land.

Message to the Sons of Josiah

11 For thus says the LORD concerning Shallum son of King Josiah of Judah, who succeeded his father Josiah, and who went away from this place: He shall return here no more, ¹²but in the place where they have carried him captive he shall die, and he shall never see this land again.

¹³ Woe to him who builds his house by
        unrighteousness,
    and his upper rooms by injustice;
who makes his neighbors work for nothing,
    and does not give them their wages;
¹⁴ who says, "I will build myself a spacious house
        with large upper rooms,"
    and who cuts out windows for it,

paneling it with cedar,
    and painting it with vermilion.
¹⁵ Are you a king
    because you compete in cedar?
Did not your father eat and drink
    and do justice and righteousness?
    Then it was well with him.
¹⁶ He judged the cause of the poor and
        needy;
    then it was well.
Is not this to know me?
    says the LORD.
¹⁷ But your eyes and heart
    are only on your dishonest gain,
for shedding innocent blood,
    and for practicing oppression and violence.

18 Therefore thus says the LORD concerning King Jehoiakim son of Josiah of Judah:

They shall not lament for him, saying,
    "Alas, my brother!" or "Alas, sister!"
They shall not lament for him, saying,
    "Alas, lord!" or "Alas, his majesty!"
¹⁹ With the burial of a donkey he shall be
        buried—
    dragged off and thrown out beyond the
        gates of Jerusalem.

²⁰ Go up to Lebanon, and cry out,
    and lift up your voice in Bashan;
cry out from Abarim,
    for all your lovers are crushed.
²¹ I spoke to you in your prosperity,
    but you said, "I will not listen."
This has been your way from your youth,
    for you have not obeyed my voice.
²² The wind shall shepherd all your shepherds,
    and your lovers shall go into captivity;
then you will be ashamed and dismayed
    because of all your wickedness.
²³ O inhabitant of Lebanon,
    nested among the cedars,
how you will groanᵇ when pangs come
        upon you,
    pain as of a woman in labor!

Judgment on Coniah (Jehoiachin)

24 As I live, says the LORD, even if King Coniah son of Jehoiakim of Judah were the signet ring on my right hand, even from there I would tear you off ²⁵and give you into the hands of those who seek your life,

ᵃ Cn: Heb *uninhabited cities* ᵇ Gk Vg Syr: Heb *will be pitied*

Admit It! · Jeremiah 22:18–23

Jeremiah's words against King Jehoiakim in **Jeremiah 22:21–23** are harsh. Jehoiakim is guilty of some serious sin and is leading the nation to destruction. But he doesn't want to hear about it. In fact, when Jehoiakim is presented with a scroll of Jeremiah's prophecies, he burns it (Jeremiah 36:23)! Sounds bold to burn the words of God, but how often do we have a similar response when faced with the harsh messages of our own lives? Pray this prayer and ask God to help you remember to follow God's ways:

Forgiving God,

Help me to hear the prophets in today's world who call me to own my sin,

the prophets who call me to end discrimination,

who call me to care for the needy,

who call me to care for the earth,

who call me to end violence,

who call me to healthy relationships,

who call me to be a person of integrity, avoiding sin in all its forms.

May I be humble enough to admit my faults

and courageous enough to do something about them.

into the hands of those of whom you are afraid, even into the hands of King Nebuchadrezzar of Babylon and into the hands of the Chaldeans. ²⁶I will hurl you and the mother who bore you into another country, where you were not born, and there you shall die. ²⁷But they shall not return to the land to which they long to return.

²⁸ Is this man Coniah a despised broken pot,
    a vessel no one wants?
Why are he and his offspring hurled out
    and cast away in a land that they do not
        know?
²⁹ O land, land, land,
    hear the word of the Lord!
³⁰ Thus says the Lord:
Record this man as childless,
    a man who shall not succeed in his
        days;
for none of his offspring shall succeed
    in sitting on the throne of David,
    and ruling again in Judah.

Restoration after Exile

23 Woe to the shepherds who destroy and scatter the sheep of my pasture! says the Lord. ²Therefore thus says the Lord, the God of Israel, concerning the shepherds who shepherd my people: It is you who have scattered my flock, and have driven them away, and you have not attended to them. So I will attend to you for your evil doings, says the Lord. ³Then I myself will gather the remnant of my flock out of all the lands where I have driven them, and I will bring them back to their fold, and they shall be fruitful and multiply. ⁴I will raise up shepherds over them who will shepherd them, and they shall not fear any longer, or be dismayed, nor shall any be missing, says the Lord.

The Righteous Branch of David

5 The days are surely coming, says the Lord, when I will raise up for David a righteous Branch, and he shall reign as king and deal wisely, and shall execute justice and righteousness in the land. ⁶In his days Judah will be saved and Israel will live in safety. And this is the name by which he will be called: "The Lord is our righteousness."

7 Therefore, the days are surely coming, says the Lord, when it shall no longer be said, "As the Lord lives who brought the people of Israel up out of the land of Egypt," ⁸but "As the Lord lives who brought out and led the offspring of the house of Israel out of the land of the north and out of all the lands where he*ᵃ* had driven them." Then they shall live in their own land.

ᵃ Gk: Heb *I*

False Prophets of Hope Denounced

9 Concerning the prophets:

My heart is crushed within me,
　　all my bones shake;
I have become like a drunkard,
　　like one overcome by wine,
because of the LORD
　　and because of his holy words.

10 For the land is full of adulterers;
　　because of the curse the land mourns,
　　and the pastures of the wilderness are
　　　　dried up.
Their course has been evil,
　　and their might is not right.

11 Both prophet and priest are ungodly;
　　even in my house I have found their
　　　　wickedness,
　　　　　　　　says the LORD.

12 Therefore their way shall be to them
　　like slippery paths in the darkness,
　　into which they shall be driven and fall;
for I will bring disaster upon them
　　in the year of their punishment,
　　　　　　　　says the LORD.

13 In the prophets of Samaria
　　I saw a disgusting thing:
they prophesied by Baal
　　and led my people Israel astray.

14 But in the prophets of Jerusalem
　　I have seen a more shocking thing:
they commit adultery and walk in lies;
　　they strengthen the hands of evildoers,
　　so that no one turns from wickedness;
all of them have become like Sodom
　　　　to me,
　　and its inhabitants like Gomorrah.

15 Therefore thus says the LORD of hosts
　　concerning the prophets:
"I am going to make them eat wormwood,
　　and give them poisoned water to drink;
for from the prophets of Jerusalem
　　ungodliness has spread throughout the
　　　　land."

16 Thus says the LORD of hosts: Do not listen to the words of the prophets who prophesy to you; they are deluding you. They speak visions of their own minds, not from the mouth of the LORD. [17] They keep saying to those who despise the word of the LORD, "It shall be well with you"; and to all who stubbornly follow their own stubborn hearts, they say, "No calamity shall come upon you."

18 For who has stood in the council of the LORD
　　so as to see and to hear his word?
Who has given heed to his word so as to
　　　　proclaim it?

19 Look, the storm of the LORD!
　　Wrath has gone forth,
a whirling tempest;
　　it will burst upon the head of the wicked.

20 The anger of the LORD will not turn back
　　until he has executed and accomplished
　　　　the intents of his mind.
In the latter days you will understand it clearly.

21 I did not send the prophets,
　　yet they ran;
I did not speak to them,
　　yet they prophesied.

22 But if they had stood in my council,
　　then they would have proclaimed my
　　　　words to my people,
and they would have turned them from their
　　　　evil way,
　　and from the evil of their doings.

23 Am I a God near by, says the LORD, and not a God far off? [24]Who can hide in secret places so that I cannot see them? says the LORD. Do I not fill heaven and earth? says the LORD. [25]I have heard what the prophets have said who prophesy lies in my name, saying, "I have dreamed, I have dreamed!" [26]How long? Will the hearts of the prophets ever turn back—those who prophesy lies, and who prophesy the deceit of their own heart? [27]They plan to make my people forget my name by their dreams that they tell one another, just as their ancestors forgot my name for Baal. [28]Let the prophet who has a dream tell the dream, but let the one who has my word speak my word faithfully. What has straw in common with wheat? says the LORD. [29]Is not my word like fire, says the LORD, and like a hammer that breaks a rock in pieces? [30]See, therefore, I am against the prophets, says the LORD, who steal my words from one another. [31]See, I am against the prophets, says the LORD, who use their own tongues and say, "Says the LORD." [32]See, I am against those who prophesy lying dreams, says the LORD, and who tell them, and who lead my people astray by their lies

and their recklessness, when I did not send them or appoint them; so they do not profit this people at all, says the LORD.

33 When this people, or a prophet, or a priest asks you, "What is the burden of the LORD?" you shall say to them, "You are the burden,[a] and I will cast you off, says the LORD." [34] And as for the prophet, priest, or the people who say, "The burden of the LORD," I will punish them and their households. [35] Thus shall you say to one another, among yourselves, "What has the LORD answered?" or "What has the LORD spoken?" [36] But "the burden of the LORD" you shall mention no more, for the burden is everyone's own word, and so you pervert the words of the living God, the LORD of hosts, our God. [37] Thus you shall ask the prophet, "What has the LORD answered you?" or "What has the LORD spoken?" [38] But if you say, "the burden of the LORD," thus says the LORD: Because you have said these words, "the burden of the LORD," when I sent to you, saying, You shall not say, "the burden of the LORD," [39] therefore, I will surely lift you up[b] and cast you away from my presence, you and the city that I gave to you and your ancestors. [40] And I will bring upon you everlasting disgrace and perpetual shame, which shall not be forgotten.

The Good and the Bad Figs

24 The LORD showed me two baskets of figs placed before the temple of the LORD. This was after King Nebuchadrezzar of Babylon had taken into exile from Jerusalem King Jeconiah son of Jehoiakim of Judah, together with the officials of Judah, the artisans, and the smiths, and had brought them to Babylon. [2] One basket had very good figs, like first-ripe figs, but the other basket had very bad figs, so bad that they could not be eaten. [3] And the LORD said to me, "What do you see, Jeremiah?" I said, "Figs, the good figs very good, and the bad figs very bad, so bad that they cannot be eaten."

4 Then the word of the LORD came to me: [5] Thus says the LORD, the God of Israel: Like these good figs, so I will regard as good the exiles from Judah, whom I have sent away from this place to the land of the Chaldeans. [6] I will set my eyes upon them for good, and I will bring them back to this land. I will build them up, and not tear them down; I will plant them, and not pluck them up. [7] I will give them a heart to know that I am the LORD; and they shall

STUDY IT!

Fig Trees
Jeremiah 24

Have you ever eaten a fig? Or maybe a Fig Newton? Figs were common in Jeremiah's day, and fig trees were widely cultivated in the ancient Near East. Its sweet fruit was a delight to taste, and its broad leaves offered welcome shade from the scorching summer sun. There are numerous places in the Bible where the fig tree is used as a symbol of Israel. In **Jeremiah 24:5–8**, ripe figs are presented as an image of the faithful exiles in Babylon, while the bad figs represent those who have turned away from God. In **1 Kings 4:25**, fig leaves symbolize protection and safety. Jesus also tells a parable about a fig tree in **Luke 13:6–9** to point out that God does not give up on anyone and is a God of grace.

be my people and I will be their God, for they shall return to me with their whole heart.

8 But thus says the LORD: Like the bad figs that are so bad they cannot be eaten, so will I treat King Zedekiah of Judah, his officials, the remnant of Jerusalem who remain in this land, and those who live in the land of Egypt. [9] I will make them a horror, an evil thing, to all the kingdoms of the earth—a disgrace, a byword, a taunt, and a curse in all the places where I shall drive them. [10] And I will send sword, famine, and pestilence upon them, until they are utterly destroyed from the land that I gave to them and their ancestors.

The Babylonian Captivity Foretold

25 The word that came to Jeremiah concerning all the people of Judah, in the fourth year of King Jehoiakim son of Josiah of Judah (that was the first year of King Nebuchadrezzar of Babylon), [2] which the prophet Jeremiah spoke to all the people of Judah and all the inhabitants of Jerusalem: [3] For twenty-three years, from the thirteenth year of King Josiah son of Amon of Judah, to this day, the word of the LORD has come to me, and I have spo-

---

a Gk Vg: Heb *What burden*   *b* Heb Mss Gk Vg: MT *forget you* ken persistently to you, but you have not listened. [4]And though the LORD persistently sent you all his servants the prophets, you have neither listened nor inclined your ears to hear [5]when they said, "Turn now, every one of you, from your evil way and wicked doings, and you will remain upon the land that the LORD has given to you and your ancestors from of old and forever; [6]do not go after other gods to serve and worship them, and do not provoke me to anger with the work of your hands. Then I will do you no harm." [7]Yet you did not listen to me, says the LORD, and so you have provoked me to anger with the work of your hands to your own harm.

8 Therefore thus says the LORD of hosts: Because you have not obeyed my words, [9]I am going to send for all the tribes of the north, says the LORD, even for King Nebuchadrezzar of Babylon, my servant, and I will bring them against this land and its inhabitants, and against all these nations around; I will utterly destroy them, and make them an object of horror and of hissing, and an everlasting disgrace.[a] [10]And I will banish from them the sound of mirth and the sound of gladness, the voice of the bridegroom and the voice of the bride, the sound of the millstones and the light of the lamp. [11]This whole land shall become a ruin and a waste, and these nations shall serve the king of Babylon seventy years. [12]Then after seventy years are completed, I will punish the king of Babylon and that nation, the land of the Chaldeans, for their iniquity, says the LORD, making the land an everlasting waste. [13]I will bring upon that land all the words that I have uttered against it, everything written in this book, which Jeremiah prophesied against all the nations. [14]For many nations and great kings shall make slaves of them also; and I will repay them according to their deeds and the work of their hands.

The Cup of God's Wrath

15 For thus the LORD, the God of Israel, said to me: Take from my hand this cup of the wine of wrath, and make all the nations to whom I send you drink it. [16]They shall drink and stagger and go out of their minds because of the sword that I am sending among them.

17 So I took the cup from the LORD's hand, and made all the nations to whom the LORD sent me drink it: [18]Jerusalem and the towns of Judah, its kings and officials, to make them a desolation and a waste, an object of hissing and of cursing, as they

are today; [19]Pharaoh king of Egypt, his servants, his officials, and all his people; [20]all the mixed people;[b] all the kings of the land of Uz; all the kings of the land of the Philistines—Ashkelon, Gaza, Ekron, and the remnant of Ashdod; [21]Edom, Moab, and the Ammonites; [22]all the kings of Tyre, all the kings of Sidon, and the kings of the coastland across the sea; [23]Dedan, Tema, Buz, and all who have shaven temples; [24]all the kings of Arabia and all the kings of the mixed peoples[b] that live in the desert; [25]all the kings of Zimri, all the kings of Elam, and all the kings of Media; [26]all the kings of the north, far and near, one after another, and all the kingdoms of the world that are on the face of the earth. And after them the king of Sheshach[c] shall drink.

27 Then you shall say to them, Thus says the LORD of hosts, the God of Israel: Drink, get drunk and vomit, fall and rise no more, because of the sword that I am sending among you.

28 And if they refuse to accept the cup from your hand to drink, then you shall say to them: Thus says the LORD of hosts: You must drink! [29]See, I am beginning to bring disaster on the city that is called by my name, and how can you possibly avoid punishment? You shall not go unpunished, for I am summoning a sword against all the inhabitants of the earth, says the LORD of hosts.

30 You, therefore, shall prophesy against them all these words, and say to them:

The LORD will roar from on high,
   and from his holy habitation utter his
      voice;
he will roar mightily against his fold,
   and shout, like those who tread grapes,
      against all the inhabitants of the earth.
[31] The clamor will resound to the ends of the
      earth,
   for the LORD has an indictment against the
      nations;
he is entering into judgment with all flesh,
   and the guilty he will put to the sword,
           says the LORD.

[32] Thus says the LORD of hosts:
   See, disaster is spreading
      from nation to nation,
   and a great tempest is stirring
      from the farthest parts of the earth!
33 Those slain by the LORD on that day shall extend from one end of the earth to the other. They

---

a Gk Compare Syr: Heb and everlasting desolations   b Meaning of Heb uncertain   c Sheshach is a cryptogram for Babel, Babylon shall not be lamented, or gathered, or buried; they shall become dung on the surface of the ground. ³⁴ Wail, you shepherds, and cry out;

 roll in ashes, you lords of the flock,

 for the days of your slaughter have come—and

  your dispersions,*a*

 and you shall fall like a choice vessel.

³⁵ Flight shall fail the shepherds,

 and there shall be no escape for the lords

  of the flock.

³⁶ Hark! the cry of the shepherds,

 and the wail of the lords of the flock!

For the LORD is despoiling their pasture,

³⁷ and the peaceful folds are devastated,

 because of the fierce anger of the LORD.

³⁸ Like a lion he has left his covert;

 for their land has become a waste

because of the cruel sword,

 and because of his fierce anger.

Jeremiah's Prophecies in the Temple

26 At the beginning of the reign of King Jehoiakim son of Josiah of Judah, this word came from the LORD: ²Thus says the LORD: Stand in the court of the LORD's house, and speak to all the cities of Judah that come to worship in the house of the LORD; speak to them all the words that I command you; do not hold back a word. ³It may be that they will listen, all of them, and will turn from their evil way, that I may change my mind about the disaster that I intend to bring on them because of their evil doings. ⁴You shall say to them: Thus says the LORD: If you will not listen to me, to walk in my law that I have set before you, ⁵and to heed the words of my servants the prophets whom I send to you urgently—though you have not heeded— ⁶then I will make this house like Shiloh, and I will make this city a curse for all the nations of the earth.

⁷ The priests and the prophets and all the people heard Jeremiah speaking these words in the house of the LORD. ⁸And when Jeremiah had finished speaking all that the LORD had commanded him to speak to all the people, then the priests and the prophets and all the people laid hold of him, saying, "You shall die! ⁹Why have you prophesied in the name of the LORD, saying, 'This house shall be like Shiloh, and this city shall be desolate, without inhabitant'?" And all the people gathered around Jeremiah in the house of the LORD.

¹⁰ When the officials of Judah heard these things, they came up from the king's house to the house of the LORD and took their seat in the entry of the New Gate of the house of the LORD. ¹¹Then the priests and the prophets said to the officials and to all the people, "This man deserves the sentence of death because he has prophesied against this city, as you have heard with your own ears."

¹² Then Jeremiah spoke to all the officials and all the people, saying, "It is the LORD who sent me to prophesy against this house and this city all the words you have heard. ¹³Now therefore amend your ways and your doings, and obey the voice of the LORD your God, and the LORD will change his mind about the disaster that he has pronounced against you. ¹⁴But as for me, here I am in your hands. Do with me as seems good and right to you. ¹⁵Only know for certain that if you put me to death, you will be bringing innocent blood upon yourselves and upon this city and its inhabitants, for in truth the LORD sent me to you to speak all these words in your ears."

¹⁶ Then the officials and all the people said to the priests and the prophets, "This man does not deserve the sentence of death, for he has spoken to us in the name of the LORD our God." ¹⁷And some of the elders of the land arose and said to all the assembled people, ¹⁸"Micah of Moresheth, who prophesied during the days of King Hezekiah of Judah, said to all the people of Judah: 'Thus says the LORD of hosts,

 Zion shall be plowed as a field;

  Jerusalem shall become a heap of ruins,

  and the mountain of the house a wooded

   height.'

¹⁹Did King Hezekiah of Judah and all Judah actually put him to death? Did he not fear the LORD and entreat the favor of the LORD, and did not the LORD change his mind about the disaster that he had pronounced against them? But we are about to bring great disaster on ourselves!"

²⁰ There was another man prophesying in the name of the LORD, Uriah son of Shemaiah from Kiriath-jearim. He prophesied against this city and against this land in words exactly like those of Jeremiah. ²¹And when King Jehoiakim, with all his warriors and all the officials, heard his words, the king sought to put him to death; but when Uriah heard of it, he was afraid and fled and escaped to Egypt. ²²Then King Jehoiakim sent*b* Elnathan son of Achbor and men with him to Egypt, ²³and they

---

a Meaning of Heb uncertain **b** Heb adds *men to Egypt*

took Uriah from Egypt and brought him to King Jehoiakim, who struck him down with the sword and threw his dead body into the burial place of the common people.

24 But the hand of Ahikam son of Shaphan was with Jeremiah so that he was not given over into the hands of the people to be put to death.

The Sign of the Yoke

27 In the beginning of the reign of King Zedekiah[a] son of Josiah of Judah, this word came to Jeremiah from the LORD. [2] Thus the LORD said to me: Make yourself a yoke of straps and bars, and put them on your neck. [3] Send word[b] to the king of Edom, the king of Moab, the king of the Ammonites, the king of Tyre, and the king of Sidon by the hand of the envoys who have come to Jerusalem to King Zedekiah of Judah. [4] Give them this charge for their masters: Thus says the LORD of hosts, the God of Israel: This is what you shall say to your masters: [5] It is I who by my great power and my outstretched arm have made the earth, with the people and animals that are on the earth, and I give it to whomever I please. [6] Now I have given all these lands into the hand of King Nebuchadnezzar of Babylon, my servant, and I have given him even the wild animals of the field to serve him. [7] All the nations shall serve him and his son and his grandson, until the time of his own land comes; then many nations and great kings shall make him their slave.

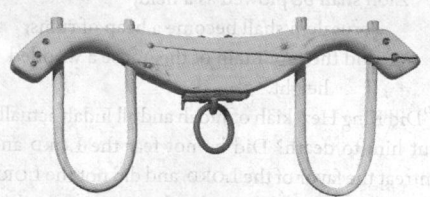

8 But if any nation or kingdom will not serve this king, Nebuchadnezzar of Babylon, and put its neck under the yoke of the king of Babylon, then I will punish that nation with the sword, with famine, and with pestilence, says the LORD, until I have completed its[c] destruction by his hand. [9] You, therefore, must not listen to your prophets, your diviners, your dreamers,[d] your soothsayers, or your sorcerers, who are saying to you, "You shall not serve the king of Babylon." [10] For they are prophesying a lie to you, with the result that you will be removed far from your land; I will drive you out, and you will perish.

[11] But any nation that will bring its neck under the yoke of the king of Babylon and serve him, I will leave on its own land, says the LORD, to till it and live there.

12 I spoke to King Zedekiah of Judah in the same way: Bring your necks under the yoke of the king of Babylon, and serve him and his people, and live. [13] Why should you and your people die by the sword, by famine, and by pestilence, as the LORD has spoken concerning any nation that will not serve the king of Babylon? [14] Do not listen to the words of the prophets who are telling you not to serve the king of Babylon, for they are prophesying a lie to you. [15] I have not sent them, says the LORD, but they are prophesying falsely in my name, with the result that I will drive you out and you will perish, you and the prophets who are prophesying to you.

16 Then I spoke to the priests and to all this people, saying, Thus says the LORD: Do not listen to the words of your prophets who are prophesying to you, saying, "The vessels of the LORD's house will soon be brought back from Babylon," for they are prophesying a lie to you. [17] Do not listen to them; serve the king of Babylon and live. Why should this city become a desolation? [18] If indeed they are prophets, and if the word of the LORD is with them, then let them intercede with the LORD of hosts, that the vessels left in the house of the LORD, in the house of the king of Judah, and in Jerusalem may not go to Babylon. [19] For thus says the LORD of hosts concerning the pillars, the sea, the stands, and the rest of the vessels that are left in this city, [20] which King Nebuchadnezzar of Babylon did not take away when he took into exile from Jerusalem to Babylon King Jeconiah son of Jehoiakim of Judah, and all the nobles of Judah and Jerusalem— [21] thus says the LORD of hosts, the God of Israel, concerning the vessels left in the house of the LORD, in the house of the king of Judah, and in Jerusalem: [22] They shall be carried to Babylon, and there they shall stay, until the day when I give attention to them, says the LORD. Then I will bring them up and restore them to this place.

Hananiah Opposes Jeremiah and Dies

28 In that same year, at the beginning of the reign of King Zedekiah of Judah, in the fifth month of the fourth year, the prophet Hananiah son of Azzur, from Gibeon, spoke to me in the house of the LORD,

---

a Another reading is *Jehoiakim*   b Cn: Heb *send them*   c Heb *their*   d Gk Syr Vg: Heb *dreams*

in the presence of the priests and all the people, saying, [2]"Thus says the LORD of hosts, the God of Israel: I have broken the yoke of the king of Babylon. [3]Within two years I will bring back to this place all the vessels of the LORD's house, which King Nebuchadnezzar of Babylon took away from this place and carried to Babylon. [4]I will also bring back to this place King Jeconiah son of Jehoiakim of Judah, and all the exiles from Judah who went to Babylon, says the LORD, for I will break the yoke of the king of Babylon."

[5] Then the prophet Jeremiah spoke to the prophet Hananiah in the presence of the priests and all the people who were standing in the house of the LORD; [6]and the prophet Jeremiah said, "Amen! May the LORD do so; may the LORD fulfill the words that you have prophesied, and bring back to this place from Babylon the vessels of the house of the LORD, and all the exiles. [7]But listen now to this word that I speak in your hearing and in the hearing of all the people. [8]The prophets who preceded you and me from ancient times prophesied war, famine, and pestilence against many countries and great kingdoms. [9]As for the prophet who prophesies peace, when the word of that prophet comes true, then it will be known that the LORD has truly sent the prophet."

[10] Then the prophet Hananiah took the yoke from the neck of the prophet Jeremiah, and broke it. [11]And Hananiah spoke in the presence of all the people, saying, "Thus says the LORD: This is how I will break the yoke of King Nebuchadnezzar of Babylon from the neck of all the nations within two years." At this, the prophet Jeremiah went his way.

[12] Sometime after the prophet Hananiah had broken the yoke from the neck of the prophet Jeremiah, the word of the LORD came to Jeremiah: [13]Go, tell Hananiah, Thus says the LORD: You have broken wooden bars only to forge iron bars in place of them! [14]For thus says the LORD of hosts, the God of Israel: I have put an iron yoke on the neck of all these nations so that they may serve King Nebuchadnezzar of Babylon, and they shall indeed serve him; I have even given him the wild animals. [15]And the prophet Jeremiah said to the prophet Hananiah, "Listen, Hananiah, the LORD has not sent you, and you made this people trust in a lie. [16]Therefore thus says the LORD: I am going to send you off the face of the earth. Within this year you will be dead, because you have spoken rebellion against the LORD."

[17] In that same year, in the seventh month, the prophet Hananiah died.

29 Jeremiah's Letter to the Exiles in Babylon

These are the words of the letter that the prophet Jeremiah sent from Jerusalem to the remaining elders among the exiles, and to the priests, the prophets, and all the people, whom Nebuchadnezzar had taken into exile from Jerusalem to Babylon. [2]This was after King Jeconiah, and the queen mother, the court officials, the leaders of Judah and Jerusalem, the artisans, and the smiths had departed from Jerusalem. [3]The letter was sent by the hand of Elasah son of Shaphan and Gemariah son of Hilkiah, whom King Zedekiah of Judah sent to Babylon to King Nebuchadnezzar of Babylon. It said: [4]Thus says the LORD of hosts, the God of Israel, to all the exiles whom I have sent into exile from Jerusalem to Babylon: [5]Build houses and live in them; plant gardens and eat what they produce. [6]Take wives and have sons and daughters; take wives for your sons, and give your daughters in marriage, that they may bear sons and daughters; multiply there, and do not decrease. [7]But seek the welfare of the city where I have sent you into exile, and pray to the LORD on its behalf, for in its welfare you will find your welfare. [8]For thus says the LORD of hosts, the God of Israel: Do not let the prophets and the diviners who are among you deceive you, and do not listen to the dreams that they dream,[a] [9]for it is a lie that they are prophesying to you in my name; I did not send them, says the LORD.

[10] For thus says the LORD: Only when Babylon's seventy years are completed will I visit you, and I will fulfill to you my promise and bring you back to this place. [11]For surely I know the plans I have for you, says the LORD, plans for your welfare and not for harm, to give you a future with hope. [12]Then when you call upon me and come and pray to me, I will hear you. [13]When you search for me, you will find me; if you seek me with all your heart, [14]I will let you find me, says the LORD, and I will restore your fortunes and gather you from all the nations and all the places where I have driven you, says the LORD, and I will bring you back to the place from which I sent you into exile.

[15] Because you have said, "The LORD has raised up prophets for us in Babylon,"— [16]Thus says the LORD concerning the king who sits on the throne

a Cn: Heb *your dreams that you cause to dream*

LIVE IT!

Good Plans · Jeremiah 29:11

This verse is a familiar one, quoted often when people want assurance that the plans they have will succeed and be blessed by God. And while **Jeremiah 29:11** and other verses in the Bible do show God's commitment to direct our plans and bring good into our lives, a deeper look at this verse gives us a different picture of the way this may play out. This promise was part of a letter sent by Jeremiah to the Israelites who had been taken into exile in Babylon. They longed to return to their own land. But God, through Jeremiah, tells them to settle where they are—to put down roots and to work for the good of the city of Babylon rather than fighting against it. And on top of that, they are told God is going to destroy those who remain in Jerusalem who have been disobedient to him. This was not what the people wanted to hear. This was not their idea of "good plans." It is with this as a backdrop that God assures them that, after a time, they will call on God's name and be restored.

- What are some of the plans you have made or things you want to see happen in your life?
- How does this verse remind you that God is working to give you a future with hope, even when God's plans look different from your own?

of David, and concerning all the people who live in this city, your kinsfolk who did not go out with you into exile: ¹⁷Thus says the LORD of hosts, I am going to let loose on them sword, famine, and pestilence, and I will make them like rotten figs that are so bad they cannot be eaten. ¹⁸I will pursue them with the sword, with famine, and with pestilence, and will make them a horror to all the kingdoms of the earth, to be an object of cursing, and horror, and hissing, and a derision among all the nations where I have driven them, ¹⁹because they did not heed my words, says the LORD, when I persistently sent to you my servants the prophets, but they*ᵃ* would not listen, says the LORD. ²⁰But now, all you exiles whom I sent away from Jerusalem to Babylon, hear the word of the LORD: ²¹Thus says the LORD of hosts, the God of Israel, concerning Ahab son of Kolaiah and Zedekiah son of Maaseiah, who are prophesying a lie to you in my name: I am going to deliver them into the hand of King Nebuchadrezzar of Babylon, and he shall kill them before your eyes. ²²And on account of them this curse shall be used by all the exiles from Judah in Babylon: "The LORD make you like Zedekiah and Ahab, whom the king of Babylon roasted in the fire," ²³because they have perpetrated outrage in Israel and have committed adultery with their neighbors' wives, and have spoken in my name lying words that I did not command them; I am the one who knows and bears witness, says the LORD.

The Letter of Shemaiah

24 To Shemaiah of Nehelam you shall say: ²⁵Thus says the LORD of hosts, the God of Israel: In your own name you sent a letter to all the people who are in Jerusalem, and to the priest Zephaniah son of Maaseiah, and to all the priests, saying, ²⁶The LORD himself has made you priest instead of the priest Jehoiada, so that there may be officers in the house of the LORD to control any madman who plays the prophet, to put him in the stocks and the collar. ²⁷So now why have you not rebuked Jeremiah of Anathoth who plays the prophet for you? ²⁸For he has actually sent to us in Babylon, saying, "It will be a long time; build houses and live in them, and plant gardens and eat what they produce."

29 The priest Zephaniah read this letter in the

> "For surely I know the plans I have for you, says the LORD, plans for your welfare and not for harm, to give you a future with hope."
> —Jeremiah 29:11

ᵃ Syr: Heb *you*

hearing of the prophet Jeremiah. [30]Then the word of the LORD came to Jeremiah: [31]Send to all the exiles, saying, Thus says the LORD concerning Shemaiah of Nehelam: Because Shemaiah has prophesied to you, though I did not send him, and has led you to trust in a lie, [32]therefore thus says the LORD: I am going to punish Shemaiah of Nehelam and his descendants; he shall not have anyone living among this people to see[a] the good that I am going to do to my people, says the LORD, for he has spoken rebellion against the LORD.

Restoration Promised for Israel and Judah

30 The word that came to Jeremiah from the LORD: [2]Thus says the LORD, the God of Israel: Write in a book all the words that I have spoken to you. [3]For the days are surely coming, says the LORD, when I will restore the fortunes of my people, Israel and Judah, says the LORD, and I will bring them back to the land that I gave to their ancestors and they shall take possession of it.

4 These are the words that the LORD spoke concerning Israel and Judah:

5   Thus says the LORD:
We have heard a cry of panic,
    of terror, and no peace.
6   Ask now, and see,
    can a man bear a child?
Why then do I see every man
    with his hands on his loins like a woman in
        labor?
Why has every face turned pale?
7   Alas! that day is so great
        there is none like it;
    it is a time of distress for Jacob;
        yet he shall be rescued from it.

8 On that day, says the LORD of hosts, I will break the yoke from off his[b] neck, and I will burst his[c] bonds, and strangers shall no more make a servant of him. [9]But they shall serve the LORD their God and David their king, whom I will raise up for them.

10   But as for you, have no fear, my servant Jacob,
        says the LORD,
    and do not be dismayed, O Israel;
    for I am going to save you from far away,
        and your offspring from the land of their
            captivity.
Jacob shall return and have quiet and ease,

and no one shall make him afraid.
11   For I am with you, says the LORD, to save you;
    I will make an end of all the nations
        among which I scattered you,
        but of you I will not make an end.
    I will chastise you in just measure,
        and I will by no means leave you
            unpunished.

12   For thus says the LORD:
Your hurt is incurable,
    your wound is grievous.
13   There is no one to uphold your cause,
    no medicine for your wound,
    no healing for you.
14   All your lovers have forgotten you;
        they care nothing for you;
    for I have dealt you the blow of an enemy,
        the punishment of a merciless foe,
    because your guilt is great,
        because your sins are so numerous.
15   Why do you cry out over your hurt?
    Your pain is incurable.
Because your guilt is great,
    because your sins are so numerous,
    I have done these things to you.
16   Therefore all who devour you shall be
            devoured,
    and all your foes, every one of them, shall
            go into captivity;
    those who plunder you shall be plundered,
    and all who prey on you I will make a prey.
17   For I will restore health to you,
        and your wounds I will heal,
                        says the LORD,
    because they have called you an outcast:
        "It is Zion; no one cares for her!"

18   Thus says the LORD:
I am going to restore the fortunes of the tents
        of Jacob,
    and have compassion on his dwellings;
    the city shall be rebuilt upon its mound,
        and the citadel set on its rightful site.
19   Out of them shall come thanksgiving,
        and the sound of merrymakers.
    I will make them many, and they shall not
        be few;
    I will make them honored, and they shall
        not be disdained.

a Gk: Heb *and he shall not see* b Cn: Heb *your*

20 Their children shall be as of old,
    their congregation shall be established
        before me;
    and I will punish all who oppress them.
21 Their prince shall be one of their own,
    their ruler shall come from their midst;
I will bring him near, and he shall
        approach me,
    for who would otherwise dare to
        approach me?
                says the LORD.
22 And you shall be my people,
    and I will be your God.

23 Look, the storm of the LORD!
    Wrath has gone forth,
a whirling*a* tempest;
    it will burst upon the head of the wicked.
24 The fierce anger of the LORD will not turn back
    until he has executed and accomplished
    the intents of his mind.
In the latter days you will understand this.

The Joyful Return of the Exiles

31 At that time, says the LORD, I will be the
God of all the families of Israel, and they
shall be my people.
2 Thus says the LORD:
The people who survived the sword
    found grace in the wilderness;
when Israel sought for rest,
3   the LORD appeared to him*b* from far away.*c*
I have loved you with an everlasting love;
    therefore I have continued my faithfulness
        to you.
4 Again I will build you, and you shall be built,
    O virgin Israel!
Again you shall take*d* your tambourines,
    and go forth in the dance of the
        merrymakers.
5 Again you shall plant vineyards
    on the mountains of Samaria;
the planters shall plant,
    and shall enjoy the fruit.
6 For there shall be a day when sentinels will call
    in the hill country of Ephraim:
"Come, let us go up to Zion,
    to the LORD our God."

7 For thus says the LORD:

Sing aloud with gladness for Jacob,
    and raise shouts for the chief of the nations;
proclaim, give praise, and say,
    "Save, O LORD, your people,
    the remnant of Israel."
8 See, I am going to bring them from the land of
    the north,
    and gather them from the farthest parts of
        the earth,
among them the blind and the lame,
    those with child and those in labor,
        together;
a great company, they shall return here.
9 With weeping they shall come,
    and with consolations*e* I will lead them
        back,
I will let them walk by brooks of water,
    in a straight path in which they shall not
        stumble;
for I have become a father to Israel,
    and Ephraim is my firstborn.

10 Hear the word of the LORD, O nations,
    and declare it in the coastlands far away;
say, "He who scattered Israel will gather him,
    and will keep him as a shepherd a flock."
11 For the LORD has ransomed Jacob,
    and has redeemed him from hands too
        strong for him.
12 They shall come and sing aloud on the height
    of Zion,
    and they shall be radiant over the goodness
        of the LORD,
over the grain, the wine, and the oil,
    and over the young of the flock and the
        herd;
their life shall become like a watered garden,
    and they shall never languish again.
13 Then shall the young women rejoice in the
    dance,
    and the young men and the old shall be
        merry.
I will turn their mourning into joy,
    I will comfort them, and give them gladness
        for sorrow.
14 I will give the priests their fill of
    fatness,
    and my people shall be satisfied with my
        bounty,
                says the LORD.

---

a One Ms: Meaning of MT uncertain *b* Gk: Heb *me* *c* Or *to him long ago* *d* Or *adorn yourself with* *e* Gk Compare Vg Tg: Heb *supplications*

15 Thus says the LORD:
A voice is heard in Ramah,
    lamentation and bitter weeping.
Rachel is weeping for her children;
    she refuses to be comforted for her
        children,
    because they are no more.
16 Thus says the LORD:
Keep your voice from weeping,
    and your eyes from tears;
for there is a reward for your work,
                        says the LORD:
    they shall come back from the land of the
        enemy;
17 there is hope for your future,
                        says the LORD:
    your children shall come back to their own
        country.
18 Indeed I heard Ephraim pleading:
"You disciplined me, and I took the discipline;
    I was like a calf untrained.
Bring me back, let me come back,
    for you are the LORD my God.
19 For after I had turned away I repented;
    and after I was discovered, I struck my
        thigh;
I was ashamed, and I was dismayed
    because I bore the disgrace of my youth."
20 Is Ephraim my dear son?
    Is he the child I delight in?
As often as I speak against him,
    I still remember him.
Therefore I am deeply moved for him;
    I will surely have mercy on him,
                        says the LORD.

21 Set up road markers for yourself,
    make yourself signposts;
consider well the highway,
    the road by which you went.
Return, O virgin Israel,
    return to these your cities.
22 How long will you waver,
    O faithless daughter?
For the LORD has created a new thing on the
    earth:
    a woman encompasses^a a man.

23 Thus says the LORD of hosts, the God of Israel:

Once more they shall use these words in the land of
Judah and in its towns when I restore their fortunes:
    "The LORD bless you, O abode of
        righteousness,
        O holy hill!"
24 And Judah and all its towns shall live there together, and the farmers and those who wander^b with
their flocks.
25 I will satisfy the weary,
    and all who are faint I will replenish.

26 Thereupon I awoke and looked, and my sleep
was pleasant to me.

Individual Retribution

27 The days are surely coming, says the LORD,
when I will sow the house of Israel and the house
of Judah with the seed of humans and the seed of
animals. 28 And just as I have watched over them to
pluck up and break down, to overthrow, destroy, and
bring evil, so I will watch over them to build and to
plant, says the LORD. 29 In those days they shall no
longer say:
    "The parents have eaten sour grapes,
        and the children's teeth are set on edge."
30 But all shall die for their own sins; the teeth of
everyone who eats sour grapes shall be set on edge.

A New Covenant

31 The days are surely coming, says the LORD,
when I will make a new covenant with the house of
Israel and the house of Judah. 32 It will not be like the
covenant that I made with their ancestors when I
took them by the hand to bring them out of the land
of Egypt—a covenant that they broke, though I was
their husband,^c says the LORD. 33 But this is the
covenant that I will make with the house of Israel
after those days, says the LORD: I will put my law
within them, and I will write it on their hearts; and
I will be their God, and they shall be my people. 34 No
longer shall they teach one another, or say to each
other, "Know the LORD," for they shall all know me,
from the least of them to the greatest, says the LORD;
for I will forgive their iniquity, and remember their
sin no more.

35 Thus says the LORD,
    who gives the sun for light by day
        and the fixed order of the moon and the
            stars for light by night,
    who stirs up the sea so that its waves roar—

---

a Meaning of Heb uncertain b Cn Compare Syr Vg Tg: Heb *and they shall wander* c Or *master*

The Heart of the Matter
Jeremiah 31:31–34

The Ten Commandments. The stone tablets on which they were written are the most famous stone tablets in the world, and yet no one knows where they are. The ark of the covenant, in which they were once kept, was taken during a raid on the temple (Jeremiah 52:17–23). What a find they would be today! Imagine all the people flocking to see the original Ten Commandments.

But perhaps their absence makes Jeremiah's beautiful words about the new covenant in **Jeremiah 31:31–34** even more fitting. What was etched in stone on those tablets needs to be etched in our hearts. We keep in our heart what is most valuable to us. If we keep God's law there, we have no need for it written in stone.

- When you look into your heart, what do you find written there?
- Jesus fulfills this description of the new covenant in which God's law is written on our hearts and our sins are remembered no more. How will that change the way you live today?

the LORD of hosts is his name:
36 If this fixed order were ever to cease
   from my presence, says the LORD,
then also the offspring of Israel would cease
   to be a nation before me forever.

37 Thus says the LORD:
If the heavens above can be measured,
   and the foundations of the earth below can
      be explored,
then I will reject all the offspring of Israel
   because of all they have done,
                              says the LORD.

Jerusalem to Be Enlarged

38 The days are surely coming, says the LORD, when the city shall be rebuilt for the LORD from the tower of Hananel to the Corner Gate. 39 And the measuring line shall go out farther, straight to the hill Gareb, and shall then turn to Goah. 40 The whole valley of the dead bodies and the ashes, and all the fields as far as the Wadi Kidron, to the corner of the Horse Gate toward the east, shall be sacred to the LORD. It shall never again be uprooted or overthrown.

32   Jeremiah Buys a Field During the Siege

The word that came to Jeremiah from the LORD in the tenth year of King Zedekiah of Judah, which was the eighteenth year of Nebuchadrezzar. 2 At that time the army of the king of Babylon was besieging Jerusalem, and the prophet Jeremiah was confined in the court of the guard that was in the palace of the king of Judah, 3 where King Zedekiah of Judah had confined him. Zedekiah had said, "Why do you prophesy and say: Thus says the LORD: I am going to give this city into the hand of the king of Babylon, and he shall take it; 4 King Zedekiah of Judah shall not escape out of the hands of the Chaldeans, but shall surely be given into the hands of the king of Babylon, and shall speak with him face to face and see him eye to eye; 5 and he shall take Zedekiah to Babylon, and there he shall remain until I attend to him, says the LORD; though you fight against the Chaldeans, you shall not succeed?"

6 Jeremiah said, The word of the LORD came to me: 7 Hanamel son of your uncle Shallum is going to come to you and say, "Buy my field that is at Anathoth, for the right of redemption by purchase is yours." 8 Then my cousin Hanamel came to me in the court of the guard, in accordance with the word of the LORD, and said to me, "Buy my field that is at Anathoth in the land of Benjamin, for the right of possession and redemption is yours; buy it for yourself." Then I knew that this was the word of the LORD.

9 And I bought the field at Anathoth from my cousin Hanamel, and weighed out the money to him, seventeen shekels of silver. 10 I signed the deed, sealed it, got witnesses, and weighed the money on scales. 11 Then I took the sealed deed of purchase, containing the terms and conditions, and the open copy; 12 and I gave the deed of purchase to Baruch son of Neriah son of Mahseiah, in the presence of my cousin Hanamel, in the presence of the witnesses

who signed the deed of purchase, and in the presence of all the Judeans who were sitting in the court of the guard. [13]In their presence I charged Baruch, saying, [14]Thus says the LORD of hosts, the God of Israel: Take these deeds, both this sealed deed of purchase and this open deed, and put them in an earthenware jar, in order that they may last for a long time. [15]For thus says the LORD of hosts, the God of Israel: Houses and fields and vineyards shall again be bought in this land.

Jeremiah Prays for Understanding

16 After I had given the deed of purchase to Baruch son of Neriah, I prayed to the LORD, saying: [17]Ah Lord GOD! It is you who made the heavens and the earth by your great power and by your outstretched arm! Nothing is too hard for you. [18]You show steadfast love to the thousandth generation,[a] but repay the guilt of parents into the laps of their children after them, O great and mighty God whose name is the LORD of hosts, [19]great in counsel and mighty in deed; whose eyes are open to all the ways of mortals, rewarding all according to their ways and according to the fruit of their doings. [20]You showed signs and wonders in the land of Egypt, and to this day in Israel and among all humankind, and have made yourself a name that continues to this very day. [21]You brought your people Israel out of the land of Egypt with signs and wonders, with a strong hand and outstretched arm, and with great terror; [22]and you gave them this land, which you swore to their ancestors to give them, a land flowing with milk and honey; [23]and they entered and took possession of it. But they did not obey your voice or follow your law; of all you commanded them to do, they did nothing. Therefore you have made all these disasters come upon them. [24]See, the siege ramps have been cast up against the city to take it, and the city, faced with sword, famine, and pestilence, has been given into the hands of the Chaldeans who are fighting against it. What you spoke has happened, as you yourself can see. [25]Yet you, O Lord GOD, have said to me, "Buy the field for money and get witnesses"—though the city has been given into the hands of the Chaldeans.

God's Assurance of the People's Return

26 The word of the LORD came to Jeremiah: [27]See, I am the LORD, the God of all flesh; is anything too hard for me? [28]Therefore, thus says the

LORD: I am going to give this city into the hands of the Chaldeans and into the hand of King Nebuchadrezzar of Babylon, and he shall take it. [29]The Chaldeans who are fighting against this city shall come, set it on fire, and burn it, with the houses on whose roofs offerings have been made to Baal and libations have been poured out to other gods, to provoke me to anger. [30]For the people of Israel and the people of Judah have done nothing but evil in my sight from their youth; the people of Israel have done nothing but provoke me to anger by the work of their hands, says the LORD. [31]This city has aroused my anger and wrath, from the day it was built until this day, so that I will remove it from my sight [32]because of all the evil of the people of Israel and the people of Judah that they did to provoke me to anger—they, their kings and their officials, their priests and their prophets, the citizens of Judah and the inhabitants of Jerusalem. [33]They have turned their backs to me, not their faces; though I have taught them persistently, they would not listen and accept correction. [34]They set up their abominations in the house that bears my name, and defiled it. [35]They built the high places of Baal in the valley of the son of Hinnom, to offer up their sons and daughters to Molech, though I did not command them, nor did it enter my mind that they should do this abomination, causing Judah to sin.

36 Now therefore thus says the LORD, the God of Israel, concerning this city of which you say, "It is being given into the hand of the king of Babylon by the sword, by famine, and by pestilence": [37]See, I am going to gather them from all the lands to which I drove them in my anger and my wrath and in great indignation; I will bring them back to this place, and I will settle them in safety. [38]They shall be my people, and I will be their God. [39]I will give them one heart and one way, that they may fear me for all time, for their own good and the good of their children after them. [40]I will make an everlasting covenant with them, never to draw back from doing good to them; and I will put the fear of me in their hearts, so that they may not turn from me. [41]I will rejoice in doing good to them, and I will plant them in this land in faithfulness, with all my heart and all my soul.

42 For thus says the LORD: Just as I have brought all this great disaster upon this people, so I will bring upon them all the good fortune that I now promise them. [43]Fields shall be bought in this land of which

---

a Or to thousands

you are saying, It is a desolation, without human beings or animals; it has been given into the hands of the Chaldeans. ⁴⁴Fields shall be bought for money, and deeds shall be signed and sealed and witnessed, in the land of Benjamin, in the places around Jerusalem, and in the cities of Judah, of the hill country, of the Shephelah, and of the Negeb; for I will restore their fortunes, says the LORD.

33 **Healing after Punishment**

The word of the LORD came to Jeremiah a second time, while he was still confined in the court of the guard: ²Thus says the LORD who made the earth,^a the LORD who formed it to establish it—the LORD is his name: ³Call to me and I will answer you, and will tell you great and hidden things that you have not known. ⁴For thus says the LORD, the God of Israel, concerning the houses of this city and the houses of the kings of Judah that were torn down to make a defense against the siege ramps and before the sword:^b ⁵The Chaldeans are coming in to fight^c and to fill them with the dead bodies of those whom I shall strike down in my anger and my wrath, for I have hidden my face from this city because of all their wickedness. ⁶I am going to bring it recovery and healing; I will heal them and reveal to them abundance^b of prosperity and security. ⁷I will restore the fortunes of Judah and the fortunes of Israel, and rebuild them as they were at first. ⁸I will cleanse them from all the guilt of their sin against me, and I will forgive all the guilt of their sin and rebellion against me. ⁹And this city^d shall be to me a name of joy, a praise and a glory before all the nations of the earth who shall hear of all the good that I do for them; they shall fear and tremble because of all the good and all the prosperity I provide for it.

10 Thus says the LORD: In this place of which you say, "It is a waste without human beings or animals," in the towns of Judah and the streets of Jerusalem that are desolate, without inhabitants, human or animal, there shall once more be heard ¹¹the voice of mirth and the voice of gladness, the voice of the bridegroom and the voice of the bride, the voices of those who sing, as they bring thank offerings to the house of the LORD:

"Give thanks to the LORD of hosts,
    for the LORD is good,
    for his steadfast love endures forever!"
For I will restore the fortunes of the land as at first, says the LORD.

12 Thus says the LORD of hosts: In this place that is waste, without human beings or animals, and in all its towns there shall again be pasture for shepherds resting their flocks. ¹³In the towns of the hill country, of the Shephelah, and of the Negeb, in the land of Benjamin, the places around Jerusalem, and in the towns of Judah, flocks shall again pass under the hands of the one who counts them, says the LORD.

The Righteous Branch and the Covenant with David

14 The days are surely coming, says the LORD, when I will fulfill the promise I made to the house of Israel and the house of Judah. ¹⁵In those days and at that time I will cause a righteous Branch to spring up for David; and he shall execute justice and righteousness in the land. ¹⁶In those days Judah will be saved and Jerusalem will live in safety. And this is the name by which it will be called: "The LORD is our righteousness."

17 For thus says the LORD: David shall never lack a man to sit on the throne of the house of Israel, ¹⁸and the levitical priests shall never lack a man in my presence to offer burnt offerings, to make grain offerings, and to make sacrifices for all time.

19 The word of the LORD came to Jeremiah: ²⁰Thus says the LORD: If any of you could break my covenant with the day and my covenant with the night, so that day and night would not come at their appointed time, ²¹only then could my covenant with my servant David be broken, so that he would not have a son to reign on his throne, and my covenant with my ministers the Levites. ²²Just as the host of heaven cannot be numbered and the sands of the sea cannot be measured, so I will increase the offspring of my servant David, and the Levites who minister to me.

23 The word of the LORD came to Jeremiah: ²⁴Have you not observed how these people say, "The two families that the LORD chose have been rejected by him," and how they hold my people in such contempt that they no longer regard them as a nation? ²⁵Thus says the LORD: Only if I had not established my covenant with day and night and the ordinances of heaven and earth, ²⁶would I reject the offspring of Jacob and of my servant David and not choose any of his descendants as rulers over the offspring of Abraham, Isaac, and Jacob. For I will restore their fortunes, and will have mercy upon them.

a Gk: Heb *it*   *b* Meaning of Heb uncertain   *c* Cn: Heb *They are coming in to fight against the Chaldeans*   *d* Heb *And it*

Death in Captivity Predicted for Zedekiah

34 The word that came to Jeremiah from the LORD, when King Nebuchadrezzar of Babylon and all his army and all the kingdoms of the earth and all the peoples under his dominion were fighting against Jerusalem and all its cities: ²Thus says the LORD, the God of Israel: Go and speak to King Zedekiah of Judah and say to him: Thus says the LORD: I am going to give this city into the hand of the king of Babylon, and he shall burn it with fire. ³And you yourself shall not escape from his hand, but shall surely be captured and handed over to him; you shall see the king of Babylon eye to eye and speak with him face to face; and you shall go to Babylon. ⁴Yet hear the word of the LORD, O King Zedekiah of Judah! Thus says the LORD concerning you: You shall not die by the sword; ⁵you shall die in peace. And as spices were burned^a for your ancestors, the earlier kings who preceded you, so they shall burn spices^b for you and lament for you, saying, "Alas, lord!" For I have spoken the word, says the LORD.

6 Then the prophet Jeremiah spoke all these words to Zedekiah king of Judah, in Jerusalem, ⁷when the army of the king of Babylon was fighting against Jerusalem and against all the cities of Judah that were left, Lachish and Azekah; for these were the only fortified cities of Judah that remained.

Treacherous Treatment of Slaves

8 The word that came to Jeremiah from the LORD, after King Zedekiah had made a covenant with all the people in Jerusalem to make a proclamation of liberty to them— ⁹that all should set free their Hebrew slaves, male and female, so that no one should hold another Judean in slavery. ¹⁰And they obeyed, all the officials and all the people who had entered into the covenant that all would set free their slaves, male or female, so that they would not be enslaved again; they obeyed and set them free. ¹¹But afterward they turned around and took back the male and female slaves they had set free, and brought them again into subjection as slaves. ¹²The word of the LORD came to Jeremiah from the LORD: ¹³Thus says the LORD, the God of Israel: I myself made a covenant with your ancestors when I brought them out of the land of Egypt, out of the house of slavery, saying, ¹⁴"Every seventh year each of you must set free any Hebrews who have been sold to you and have served you six years; you must set them free from your service." But your ancestors did not listen to me or incline their ears to me. ¹⁵You yourselves recently repented and did what was right in my sight by proclaiming liberty to one another, and you made a covenant before me in the house that is called by my name; ¹⁶but then you turned around and profaned my name when each of you took back your male and female slaves, whom you had set free according to their desire, and you brought them again into subjection to be your slaves. ¹⁷Therefore, thus says the LORD: You have not obeyed me by granting a release to your neighbors and friends; I am going to grant a release to you, says the LORD—a release to the sword, to pestilence, and to famine. I will make you a horror to all the kingdoms of the earth. ¹⁸And those who transgressed my covenant and did not keep the terms of the covenant that they made before me, I will make like^c the calf when they cut it in two and passed between its parts: ¹⁹the officials of Judah, the officials of Jerusalem, the eunuchs, the priests, and all the people of the land who passed between the parts of the calf ²⁰shall be handed over to their enemies and to those who seek their lives. Their corpses shall become food for the birds of the air and the wild animals of the earth. ²¹And as for King Zedekiah of Judah and his officials, I will hand them over to their enemies and to those who seek their lives, to the army of the king of Babylon, which has withdrawn from you. ²²I am going to command, says the LORD, and will bring them back to this city; and they will fight against it, and take it, and burn it with fire. The towns of Judah I will make a desolation without inhabitant.

The Rechabites Commended

35 The word that came to Jeremiah from the LORD in the days of King Jehoiakim son of Josiah of Judah: ²Go to the house of the Rechabites, and speak with them, and bring them to the house of the LORD, into one of the chambers; then offer them wine to drink. ³So I took Jaazaniah son of Jeremiah son of Habazziniah, and his brothers, and all his sons, and the whole house of the Rechabites. ⁴I brought them to the house of the LORD into the chamber of the sons of Hanan son of Igdaliah, the man of God, which was near the chamber of the officials, above the chamber of Maaseiah son of Shallum, keeper of the threshold. ⁵Then I set before the Rechabites pitchers full of wine, and

---

a Heb *as there was burning* b Heb *shall burn* c Cn: Heb lacks *like*

cups; and I said to them, "Have some wine." [6]But they answered, "We will drink no wine, for our ancestor Jonadab son of Rechab commanded us, 'You shall never drink wine, neither you nor your children; [7]nor shall you ever build a house, or sow seed; nor shall you plant a vineyard, or even own one; but you shall live in tents all your days, that you may live many days in the land where you reside.' [8]We have obeyed the charge of our ancestor Jonadab son of Rechab in all that he commanded us, to drink no wine all our days, ourselves, our wives, our sons, or our daughters, [9]and not to build houses to live in. We have no vineyard or field or seed; [10]but we have lived in tents, and have obeyed and done all that our ancestor Jonadab commanded us. [11]But when King Nebuchadrezzar of Babylon came up against the land, we said, 'Come, and let us go to Jerusalem for fear of the army of the Chaldeans and the army of the Arameans.' That is why we are living in Jerusalem."

12 Then the word of the LORD came to Jeremiah: [13]Thus says the LORD of hosts, the God of Israel: Go and say to the people of Judah and the inhabitants of Jerusalem, Can you not learn a lesson and obey my words? says the LORD. [14]The command has been carried out that Jonadab son of Rechab gave to his descendants to drink no wine; and they drink none to this day, for they have obeyed their ancestor's command. But I myself have spoken to you persistently, and you have not obeyed me. [15]I have sent to you all my servants the prophets, sending them persistently, saying, "Turn now every one of you from your evil way, and amend your doings, and do not go after other gods to serve them, and then you shall live in the land that I gave to you and your ancestors." But you did not incline your ear or obey me. [16]The descendants of Jonadab son of Rechab have carried out the command that their ancestor gave them, but this people has not obeyed me. [17]Therefore, thus says the LORD, the God of hosts, the God of Israel: I am going to bring on Judah and on all the inhabitants of Jerusalem every disaster that I have pronounced against them; because I have spoken to them and they have not listened, I have called to them and they have not answered.

18 But to the house of the Rechabites Jeremiah said: Thus says the LORD of hosts, the God of Israel: Because you have obeyed the command of your ancestor Jonadab, and kept all his precepts, and done all that he commanded you, [19]therefore thus says

the LORD of hosts, the God of Israel: Jonadab son of Rechab shall not lack a descendant to stand before me for all time.

The Scroll Read in the Temple

36 In the fourth year of King Jehoiakim son of Josiah of Judah, this word came to Jeremiah from the LORD: [2]Take a scroll and write on it all the words that I have spoken to you against Israel and Judah and all the nations, from the day I spoke to you, from the days of Josiah until today. [3]It may be that when the house of Judah hears of all the disasters that I intend to do to them, all of them may turn from their evil ways, so that I may forgive their iniquity and their sin.

4 Then Jeremiah called Baruch son of Neriah, and Baruch wrote on a scroll at Jeremiah's dictation all the words of the LORD that he had spoken to him. [5]And Jeremiah ordered Baruch, saying, "I am prevented from entering the house of the LORD; [6]so you go yourself, and on a fast day in the hearing of the people in the LORD's house you shall read the words of the LORD from the scroll that you have written at my dictation. You shall read them also in the hearing of all the people of Judah who come up from their towns. [7]It may be that their plea will come before the LORD, and that all of them will turn from their evil ways, for great is the anger and wrath that the LORD has pronounced against this people." [8]And Baruch son of Neriah did all that the prophet Jeremiah ordered him about reading from the scroll the words of the LORD in the LORD's house.

9 In the fifth year of King Jehoiakim son of Josiah of Judah, in the ninth month, all the people in Jerusalem and all the people who came from the towns of Judah to Jerusalem proclaimed a fast before the LORD. [10]Then, in the hearing of all the people, Baruch read the words of Jeremiah from the scroll, in the house of the LORD, in the chamber of Gemariah son of Shaphan the secretary, which was in the upper court, at the entry of the New Gate of the LORD's house.

The Scroll Read in the Palace

11 When Micaiah son of Gemariah son of Shaphan heard all the words of the LORD from the scroll, [12]he went down to the king's house, into the secretary's chamber; and all the officials were sitting there: Elishama the secretary, Delaiah son of Shemaiah, Elnathan son of Achbor, Gemariah son of

Shaphan, Zedekiah son of Hananiah, and all the officials. [13] And Micaiah told them all the words that he had heard, when Baruch read the scroll in the hearing of the people. [14] Then all the officials sent Jehudi son of Nethaniah son of Shelemiah son of Cushi to say to Baruch, "Bring the scroll that you read in the hearing of the people, and come." So Baruch son of Neriah took the scroll in his hand and came to them. [15] And they said to him, "Sit down and read it to us." So Baruch read it to them. [16] When they heard all the words, they turned to one another in alarm, and said to Baruch, "We certainly must report all these words to the king." [17] Then they questioned Baruch, "Tell us now, how did you write all these words? Was it at his dictation?" [18] Baruch answered them, "He dictated all these words to me, and I wrote them with ink on the scroll." [19] Then the officials said to Baruch, "Go and hide, you and Jeremiah, and let no one know where you are."

Jehoiakim Burns the Scroll

20 Leaving the scroll in the chamber of Elishama the secretary, they went to the court of the king; and they reported all the words to the king. [21] Then the king sent Jehudi to get the scroll, and he took it from the chamber of Elishama the secretary; and Jehudi read it to the king and all the officials who stood beside the king. [22] Now the king was sitting in his winter apartment (it was the ninth month), and there was a fire burning in the brazier before him. [23] As Jehudi read three or four columns, the king[a] would cut them off with a penknife and throw them into the fire in the brazier, until the entire scroll was consumed in the fire that was in the brazier. [24] Yet neither the king, nor any of his servants who heard all these words, was alarmed, nor did they tear their garments. [25] Even when Elnathan and Delaiah and Gemariah urged the king not to burn the scroll, he would not listen to them. [26] And the king commanded Jerahmeel the king's son and Seraiah son of Azriel and Shelemiah son of Abdeel to arrest the secretary Baruch and the prophet Jeremiah. But the LORD hid them.

Jeremiah Dictates Another

27 Now, after the king had burned the scroll with the words that Baruch wrote at Jeremiah's dictation, the word of the LORD came to Jeremiah: [28] Take another scroll and write on it all the former words that were in the first scroll, which King Jehoiakim

of Judah has burned. [29] And concerning King Jehoiakim of Judah you shall say: Thus says the LORD, You have dared to burn this scroll, saying, Why have you written in it that the king of Babylon will certainly come and destroy this land, and will cut off from it human beings and animals? [30] Therefore thus says the LORD concerning King Jehoiakim of Judah: He shall have no one to sit upon the throne of David, and his dead body shall be cast out to the heat by day and the frost by night. [31] And I will punish him and his offspring and his servants for their iniquity; I will bring on them, and on the inhabitants of Jerusalem, and on the people of Judah, all the disasters with which I have threatened them—but they would not listen.

32 Then Jeremiah took another scroll and gave it to the secretary Baruch son of Neriah, who wrote on it at Jeremiah's dictation all the words of the scroll that King Jehoiakim of Judah had burned in the fire; and many similar words were added to them.

Zedekiah's Vain Hope

37 Zedekiah son of Josiah, whom King Nebuchadrezzar of Babylon made king in the land of Judah, succeeded Coniah son of Jehoiakim. [2] But neither he nor his servants nor the people of the land listened to the words of the LORD that he spoke through the prophet Jeremiah.

3 King Zedekiah sent Jehucal son of Shelemiah and the priest Zephaniah son of Maaseiah to the prophet Jeremiah saying, "Please pray for us to the LORD our God." [4] Now Jeremiah was still going in and out among the people, for he had not yet been put in prison. [5] Meanwhile, the army of Pharaoh had come out of Egypt; and when the Chaldeans who were besieging Jerusalem heard news of them, they withdrew from Jerusalem.

6 Then the word of the LORD came to the prophet Jeremiah: [7] Thus says the LORD, God of Israel: This is what the two of you shall say to the king of Judah, who sent you to me to inquire of me: Pharaoh's army, which set out to help you, is going to return to its own land, to Egypt. [8] And the Chaldeans shall return and fight against this city; they shall take it and burn it with fire. [9] Thus says the LORD: Do not deceive yourselves, saying, "The Chaldeans will surely go away from us," for they will not go away. [10] Even if you defeated the whole army of Chaldeans who are fighting against you, and there remained of them only wounded men in their tents, they would rise up and burn this city with fire.

a Heb *he*

Jeremiah Is Imprisoned

11 Now when the Chaldean army had withdrawn from Jerusalem at the approach of Pharaoh's army, [12]Jeremiah set out from Jerusalem to go to the land of Benjamin to receive his share of property[a] among the people there. [13]When he reached the Benjamin Gate, a sentinel there named Irijah son of Shelemiah son of Hananiah arrested the prophet Jeremiah saying, "You are deserting to the Chaldeans." [14]And Jeremiah said, "That is a lie; I am not deserting to the Chaldeans." But Irijah would not listen to him, and arrested Jeremiah and brought him to the officials. [15]The officials were enraged at Jeremiah, and they beat him and imprisoned him in the house of the secretary Jonathan, for it had been made a prison. [16]Thus Jeremiah was put in the cistern house, in the cells, and remained there many days.

17 Then King Zedekiah sent for him, and received him. The king questioned him secretly in his house, and said, "Is there any word from the LORD?" Jeremiah said, "There is!" Then he said, "You shall be handed over to the king of Babylon." [18]Jeremiah also said to King Zedekiah, "What wrong have I done to you or your servants or this people, that you have put me in prison? [19]Where are your prophets who prophesied to you, saying, 'The king of Babylon will not come against you and against this land'? [20]Now please hear me, my lord king: be good enough to listen to my plea, and do not send me back to the house of the secretary Jonathan to die there." [21]So King Zedekiah gave orders, and they committed Jeremiah to the court of the guard; and a loaf of bread was given him daily from the bakers' street, until all the bread of the city was gone. So Jeremiah remained in the court of the guard.

Jeremiah in the Cistern

38 Now Shephatiah son of Mattan, Gedaliah son of Pashhur, Jucal son of Shelemiah, and Pashhur son of Malchiah heard the words that Jeremiah was saying to all the people, [2]Thus says the LORD, Those who stay in this city shall die by the sword, by famine, and by pestilence; but those who go out to the Chaldeans shall live; they shall have their lives as a prize of war, and live. [3]Thus says the LORD, This city shall surely be handed over to the army of the king of Babylon and be taken. [4]Then the officials said to the king, "This man ought to be put to death, because he is discouraging the soldiers who are left in this city, and all the people, by speaking such words to them. For this man is not seeking the welfare of this people, but their harm." [5]King Zedekiah said, "Here he is; he is in your hands; for the king is powerless against you." [6]So they took Jeremiah and threw him into the cistern of Malchiah, the king's son, which was in the court of the guard, letting Jeremiah down by ropes. Now there was no water in the cistern, but only mud, and Jeremiah sank in the mud.

Face the Fear · Jeremiah 37:11–21

The motto "No Fear" didn't apply to Jeremiah. With messages as unpopular as the ones he was delivering, Jeremiah felt intense fear. For example, Jeremiah has just been beaten and imprisoned (Jeremiah 37:15). Then King Zedekiah asks the prophet if he has had any word from God (Jeremiah 37:17). Jeremiah knows the message he has is going to make the king mad. But Jeremiah courageously tells the king that he, Zedekiah, will be handed over to the king of Babylon (Jeremiah 37:17).

If we live our lives trying to serve God, at some point we will face situations that cause us to fear for our safety and reputation. We may even fear that our closest friends will abandon us. This isn't the thrilling fear of watching a horror film or riding a roller coaster. It is an intense anxiety that can cause us to shut down and quit trying. We need to offer that fear to God and ask the Lord to calm our hearts.

Quiet your mind and pray:

Lord, give me the courage I need to be faithful to you. Let my love for you and for other people be so great that my fears will never be able to keep me from doing what is right. Amen.

a Meaning of Heb uncertain

Jeremiah Is Rescued by Ebed-melech

7 Ebed-melech the Ethiopian,[a] a eunuch in the king's house, heard that they had put Jeremiah into the cistern. The king happened to be sitting at the Benjamin Gate, [8]So Ebed-melech left the king's house and spoke to the king, [9]"My lord king, these men have acted wickedly in all they did to the prophet Jeremiah by throwing him into the cistern to die there of hunger, for there is no bread left in the city." [10]Then the king commanded Ebed-melech the Ethiopian,[a] "Take three men with you from here, and pull the prophet Jeremiah up from the cistern before he dies." [11]So Ebed-melech took the men with him and went to the house of the king, to a wardrobe of[b] the storehouse, and took from there old rags and worn-out clothes, which he let down to Jeremiah in the cistern by ropes. [12]Then Ebed-melech the Ethiopian[a] said to Jeremiah, "Just put the rags and clothes between your armpits and the ropes." Jeremiah did so. [13]Then they drew Jeremiah up by the ropes and pulled him out of the cistern. And Jeremiah remained in the court of the guard.

Zedekiah Consults Jeremiah Again

14 King Zedekiah sent for the prophet Jeremiah and received him at the third entrance of the temple of the LORD. The king said to Jeremiah, "I have something to ask you; do not hide anything from me." [15]Jeremiah said to Zedekiah, "If I tell you, you will put me to death, will you not? And if I give you advice, you will not listen to me." [16]So King Zed-ekiah swore an oath in secret to Jeremiah, "As the LORD lives, who gave us our lives, I will not put you to death or hand you over to these men who seek your life."

17 Then Jeremiah said to Zedekiah, "Thus says the LORD, the God of hosts, the God of Israel, If you will only surrender to the officials of the king of Babylon, then your life shall be spared, and this city shall not be burned with fire, and you and your house shall live. [18]But if you do not surrender to the officials of the king of Babylon, then this city shall be handed over to the Chaldeans, and they shall burn it with fire, and you yourself shall not escape from their hand." [19]King Zedekiah said to Jeremiah, "I am afraid of the Judeans who have deserted to the Chaldeans, for I might be handed over to them and they would abuse me." [20]Jeremiah said, "That will not happen. Just obey the voice of the LORD in what I say to you, and it shall go well with you, and your life shall be spared. [21]But if you are determined not to surrender, this is what the LORD has shown me— [22]a vision of all the women

PRAY IT!

Down in the Well
Jeremiah 38:1–13

Have you ever suffered like Jeremiah for doing what was right? Think of those times and say this prayer.

God, you know my ups and downs. You know that, like Jeremiah, I often find myself at the bottom. Sometimes I just fall there; other times I am thrown there. It's cold, dark, and lonely.

Bless me with friends, like Ebed-melech, who will care for me and lift me up when I am down or in trouble. And make me the kind of friend who is loyal enough to advocate for those in need and willing to do what is necessary to lift others up. Amen.

remaining in the house of the king of Judah being led out to the officials of the king of Babylon and saying,

'Your trusted friends have seduced you
     and have overcome you;
Now that your feet are stuck in the mud,
     they desert you.'

[23]All your wives and your children shall be led out to the Chaldeans, and you yourself shall not escape from their hand, but shall be seized by the king of Babylon; and this city shall be burned with fire."

24 Then Zedekiah said to Jeremiah, "Do not let anyone else know of this conversation, or you will die. [25]If the officials should hear that I have spoken with you, and they should come and say to you, 'Just tell us what you said to the king; do not conceal it from us, or we will put you to death. What did the king say to you?' [26]then you shall say to them, 'I was presenting my plea to the king not to send me back to the house of Jonathan to die there.' " [27]All the officials did come to Jeremiah and questioned him; and he answered them in the very words the king had commanded. So they stopped questioning him, for the conversation had not been overheard. [28]And Jeremiah remained in the court of the guard until the day that Jerusalem was taken.

a Or Nubian; Heb Cushite   b Cn: Heb to under

39 The Fall of Jerusalem

In the ninth year of King Zedekiah of Judah, in the tenth month, King Nebuchadrezzar of Babylon and all his army came against Jerusalem and besieged it; ²in the eleventh year of Zedekiah, in the fourth month, on the ninth day of the month, a breach was made in the city. ³When Jerusalem was taken,^a all the officials of the king of Babylon came and sat in the middle gate: Nergal-sharezer, Samgar-nebo, Sarsechim the Rabsaris, Nergal-sharezer the Rabmag, with all the rest of the officials of the king of Babylon. ⁴When King Zedekiah of Judah and all the soldiers saw them, they fled, going out of the city at night by way of the king's garden through the gate between the two walls; and they went toward the Arabah. ⁵But the army of the Chaldeans pursued them, and overtook Zedekiah in the plains of Jericho; and when they had taken him, they brought him up to King Nebuchadrezzar of Babylon, at Riblah, in the land of Hamath; and he passed sentence on him. ⁶The king of Babylon slaughtered the sons of Zedekiah at Riblah before his eyes; also the king of Babylon slaughtered all the nobles of Judah. ⁷He put out the eyes of Zedekiah, and bound him in fetters to take him to Babylon. ⁸The Chaldeans burned the king's house and the houses of the people, and broke down the walls of Jerusalem. ⁹Then Nebuzaradan the captain of the guard exiled to Babylon the rest of the people who were left in the city, those who had deserted to him, and the people who remained. ¹⁰Nebuzaradan the captain of the guard left in the land of Judah some of the poor people who owned nothing, and gave them vineyards and fields at the same time.

Jeremiah, Set Free, Remembers Ebed-melech

11 King Nebuchadrezzar of Babylon gave command concerning Jeremiah through Nebuzaradan, the captain of the guard, saying, ¹²"Take him, look after him well and do him no harm, but deal with him as he may ask you." ¹³So Nebuzaradan the captain of the guard, Nebushazban the Rabsaris, Nergal-sharezer the Rabmag, and all the chief officers of the king of Babylon sent ¹⁴and took Jeremiah from the court of the guard. They entrusted him to Gedaliah son of Ahikam son of Shaphan to be brought home. So he stayed with his own people.

15 The word of the LORD came to Jeremiah while he was confined in the court of the guard: ¹⁶Go and say to Ebed-melech the Ethiopian:^b Thus says the LORD of hosts, the God of Israel: I am going to fulfill my words against this city for evil and not for good, and they shall be accomplished in your presence on that day. ¹⁷But I will save you on that day, says the LORD, and you shall not be handed over to those whom you dread. ¹⁸For I will surely save you, and you shall not fall by the sword; but you shall have your life as a prize of war, because you have trusted in me, says the LORD.

40 Jeremiah with Gedaliah the Governor

The word that came to Jeremiah from the LORD after Nebuzaradan the captain of the guard had let him go from Ramah, when he took him bound in fetters along with all the captives of Jerusalem and Judah who were being exiled to Babylon. ²The captain of the guard took Jeremiah and said to him, "The LORD your God threatened this place with this disaster; ³and now the LORD has brought it about, and has done as he said, because

---

Risky Business · Jeremiah 39:15–18

Ebed-melech who? You've probably never heard of him, but this obscure character with a funny name played a significant role in Jeremiah's life, because he was available to God and willing to do risky business. When King Zedekiah's officials threw Jeremiah into the cistern and left him to die, Ebed-melech pulled him out. Although Ebed-melech had the king's permission to rescue Jeremiah, he would have lost his life if his plan had been discovered by the king's generals and counselors (Jeremiah 38:7-13). Ebed-melech's example shows us that being a servant of God is risky business. We cannot do God's will without taking risks. There is just no such thing as playing it safe and doing what God wants us to do.

When destruction finally came upon Jerusalem, God rewarded Ebed-melech by keeping him safe (Jeremiah 39:18), because he had trusted in God and helped Jeremiah.

---

a This clause has been transposed from 38.28   b Or *Nubian*; Heb *Cushite*

all of you sinned against the LORD and did not obey his voice. Therefore this thing has come upon you. [4]Now look, I have just released you today from the fetters on your hands. If you wish to come with me to Babylon, come, and I will take good care of you; but if you do not wish to come with me to Babylon, you need not come. See, the whole land is before you; go wherever you think it good and right to go. [5]If you remain,[a] then return to Gedaliah son of Ahikam son of Shaphan, whom the king of Babylon appointed governor of the towns of Judah, and stay with him among the people; or go wherever you think it right to go." So the captain of the guard gave him an allowance of food and a present, and let him go. [6]Then Jeremiah went to Gedaliah son of Ahikam at Mizpah, and stayed with him among the people who were left in the land.

7 When all the leaders of the forces in the open country and their troops heard that the king of Babylon had appointed Gedaliah son of Ahikam governor in the land, and had committed to him men, women, and children, those of the poorest of the land who had not been taken into exile to Babylon, [8]they went to Gedaliah at Mizpah—Ishmael son of Nethaniah, Johanan son of Kareah, Seraiah son of Tanhumeth, the sons of Ephai the Netophathite, Jezaniah son of the Maacathite, they and their troops. [9]Gedaliah son of Ahikam son of Shaphan swore to them and their troops, saying, "Do not be afraid to serve the Chaldeans. Stay in the land and serve the king of Babylon, and it shall go well with you. [10]As for me, I am staying at Mizpah to represent you before the Chaldeans who come to us; but as for you, gather wine and summer fruits and oil, and store them in your vessels, and live in the towns that you have taken over." [11]Likewise, when all the Judeans who were in Moab and among the Ammonites and in Edom and in other lands heard that the king of Babylon had left a remnant in Judah and had appointed Gedaliah son of Ahikam son of Shaphan as governor over them, [12]then all the Judeans returned from all the places to which they had been scattered and came to the land of Judah, to Gedaliah at Mizpah; and they gathered wine and summer fruits in great abundance.

13 Now Johanan son of Kareah and all the leaders of the forces in the open country came to Gedaliah at Mizpah [14]and said to him, "Are you at all aware that Baalis king of the Ammonites has sent Ishmael son of Nethaniah to take your life?" But Gedaliah

son of Ahikam would not believe them. [15]Then Johanan son of Kareah spoke secretly to Gedaliah at Mizpah, "Please let me go and kill Ishmael son of Nethaniah, and no one else will know. Why should he take your life, so that all the Judeans who are gathered around you would be scattered, and the remnant of Judah would perish?" [16]But Gedaliah son of Ahikam said to Johanan son of Kareah, "Do not do such a thing, for you are telling a lie about Ishmael."

Insurrection against Gedaliah

41 In the seventh month, Ishmael son of Nethaniah son of Elishama, of the royal family, one of the chief officers of the king, came with ten men to Gedaliah son of Ahikam, at Mizpah. As they ate bread together there at Mizpah, [2]Ishmael son of Nethaniah and the ten men with him got up and struck down Gedaliah son of Ahikam son of Shaphan with the sword and killed him, because the king of Babylon had appointed him governor in the land. [3]Ishmael also killed all the Judeans who were with Gedaliah at Mizpah, and the Chaldean soldiers who happened to be there.

4 On the day after the murder of Gedaliah, before anyone knew of it, [5]eighty men arrived from Shechem and Shiloh and Samaria, with their beards shaved and their clothes torn, and their bodies gashed, bringing grain offerings and incense to present at the temple of the LORD. [6]And Ishmael son of Nethaniah came out from Mizpah to meet them, weeping as he came. As he met them, he said to them, "Come to Gedaliah son of Ahikam." [7]When they reached the middle of the city, Ishmael son of Nethaniah and the men with him slaughtered them, and threw them[b] into a cistern. [8]But there were ten men among them who said to Ishmael, "Do not kill us, for we have stores of wheat, barley, oil, and honey hidden in the fields." So he refrained, and did not kill them along with their companions.

9 Now the cistern into which Ishmael had thrown all the bodies of the men whom he had struck down was the large cistern[c] that King Asa had made for defense against King Baasha of Israel; Ishmael son of Nethaniah filled that cistern with those whom he had killed. [10]Then Ishmael took captive all the rest of the people who were in Mizpah, the king's daughters and all the people who were left at Mizpah, whom Nebuzaradan, the captain of the guard, had committed to Gedaliah son of Ahikam. Ishmael son

---

a Syr: Meaning of Heb uncertain   b Syr: Heb lacks *and threw them*; compare verse 9   c Gk: Heb *whom he had killed by the hand of Gedaliah*

of Nethaniah took them captive and set out to cross over to the Ammonites.

11 But when Johanan son of Kareah and all the leaders of the forces with him heard of all the crimes that Ishmael son of Nethaniah had done, [12]they took all their men and went to fight against Ishmael son of Nethaniah. They came upon him at the great pool that is in Gibeon. [13]And when all the people who were with Ishmael saw Johanan son of Kareah and all the leaders of the forces with him, they were glad. [14]So all the people whom Ishmael had carried away captive from Mizpah turned around and came back, and went to Johanan son of Kareah. [15]But Ishmael son of Nethaniah escaped from Johanan with eight men, and went to the Ammonites. [16]Then Johanan son of Kareah and all the leaders of the forces with him took all the rest of the people whom Ishmael son of Nethaniah had carried away captive[a] from Mizpah after he had slain Gedaliah son of Ahikam— soldiers, women, children, and eunuchs, whom Johanan brought back from Gibeon.[b] [17]And they set out, and stopped at Geruth Chimham near Bethlehem, intending to go to Egypt [18]because of the Chaldeans; for they were afraid of them, because Ishmael son of Nethaniah had killed Gedaliah son of Ahikam, whom the king of Babylon had made governor over the land.

Jeremiah Advises Survivors Not to Migrate

42 Then all the commanders of the forces, and Johanan son of Kareah and Azariah[c] son of Hoshaiah, and all the people from the least to the greatest, approached [2]the prophet Jeremiah and said, "Be good enough to listen to our plea, and pray to the LORD your God for us—for all this remnant. For there are only a few of us left out of many, as your eyes can see. [3]Let the LORD your God show us where we should go and what we should do." [4]The prophet Jeremiah said to them, "Very well: I am going to pray to the LORD your God as you request, and whatever the LORD answers you I will tell you; I will keep nothing back from you." [5]They in their turn said to Jeremiah, "May the LORD be a true and faithful witness against us if we do not act according to everything that the LORD your God sends us through you. [6]Whether it is good or bad, we will obey the voice of the LORD our God to whom we are sending you, in order that it may go well with us when we obey the voice of the LORD our God."

7 At the end of ten days the word of the LORD came to Jeremiah. [8]Then he summoned Johanan son of Kareah and all the commanders of the forces who were with him, and all the people from the least to the greatest, [9]and said to them, "Thus says the LORD, the God of Israel, to whom you sent me to present your plea before him: [10]If you will only remain in this land, then I will build you up and not pull you down; I will plant you, and not pluck you up; for I am sorry for the disaster that I have brought upon you. [11]Do not be afraid of the king of Babylon, as you have been; do not be afraid of him, says the LORD, for I am with you, to save you and to rescue you from his hand. [12]I will grant you mercy, and he will have mercy on you and restore you to your native soil. [13]But if you continue to say, 'We will not stay in this land,' thus disobeying the voice of the LORD your God [14]and saying, 'No, we will go to the land of Egypt, where we shall not see war, or hear the sound of the trumpet, or be hungry for bread, and there we will stay,' [15]then hear the word of the LORD, O remnant of Judah. Thus says the LORD of hosts, the God of Israel: If you are determined to enter Egypt and go to settle there, [16]then the sword that you fear shall overtake you there, in the land of Egypt; and the famine that you dread shall follow close after you into Egypt; and there you shall die. [17]All the people who have determined to go to Egypt to settle there shall die by the sword, by famine, and by pestilence; they shall have no remnant or survivor from the disaster that I am bringing upon them.

18 "For thus says the LORD of hosts, the God of Israel: Just as my anger and my wrath were poured out on the inhabitants of Jerusalem, so my wrath will be poured out on you when you go to Egypt. You shall become an object of execration and horror, of cursing and ridicule. You shall see this place no more. [19]The LORD has said to you, O remnant of Judah, Do not go to Egypt. Be well aware that I have warned you today [20]that you have made a fatal mistake. For you yourselves sent me to the LORD your God, saying, 'Pray for us to the LORD our God, and whatever the LORD our God says, tell us and we will do it.' [21]So I have told you today, but you have not obeyed the voice of the LORD your God in anything that he sent me to tell you. [22]Be well aware, then, that you shall die by the sword, by famine, and by pestilence in the place where you desire to go and settle."

---

a Cn: Heb *whom he recovered from Ishmael son of Nethaniah*　b Meaning of Heb uncertain　c Gk: Heb *Jezaniah*

43 Taken to Egypt, Jeremiah Warns of Judgment

When Jeremiah finished speaking to all the people all these words of the LORD their God, with which the LORD their God had sent him to them, [2]Azariah son of Hoshaiah and Johanan son of Kareah and all the other insolent men said to Jeremiah, "You are telling a lie. The LORD our God did not send you to say, 'Do not go to Egypt to settle there'; [3]but Baruch son of Neriah is inciting you against us, to hand us over to the Chaldeans, in order that they may kill us or take us into exile in Babylon." [4]So Johanan son of Kareah and all the commanders of the forces and all the people did not obey the voice of the LORD, to stay in the land of Judah. [5]But Johanan son of Kareah and all the commanders of the forces took all the remnant of Judah who had returned to settle in the land of Judah from all the nations to which they had been driven— [6]the men, the women, the children, the princesses, and everyone whom Nebuzaradan the captain of the guard had left with Gedaliah son of Ahikam son of Shaphan; also the prophet Jeremiah and Baruch son of Neriah. [7]And they came into the land of Egypt, for they did not obey the voice of the LORD. And they arrived at Tahpanhes.

8 Then the word of the LORD came to Jeremiah in Tahpanhes: [9]Take some large stones in your hands, and bury them in the clay pavement[a] that is at the entrance to Pharaoh's palace in Tahpanhes. Let the Judeans see you do it, [10]and say to them, Thus says the LORD of hosts, the God of Israel: I am going to send and take my servant King Nebuchadrezzar of Babylon, and he[b] will set his throne above these stones that I have buried, and he will spread his royal canopy over them. [11]He shall come and ravage the land of Egypt, giving

> those who are destined for pestilence, to
>   pestilence,
>   and those who are destined for captivity, to
>   captivity,
>   and those who are destined for the sword,
>   to the sword.

[12]He[c] shall kindle a fire in the temples of the gods of Egypt; and he shall burn them and carry them away captive; and he shall pick clean the land of Egypt, as a shepherd picks his cloak clean of vermin; and he shall depart from there safely. [13]He shall break the obelisks of Heliopolis, which is in the land of Egypt; and the temples of the gods of Egypt he shall burn with fire.

44 Denunciation of Persistent Idolatry

The word that came to Jeremiah for all the Judeans living in the land of Egypt, at Migdol, at Tahpanhes, at Memphis, and in the land of Pathros, [2]Thus says the LORD of hosts, the God of Israel: You yourselves have seen all the disaster that I have brought on Jerusalem and on all the towns of Judah. Look at them; today they are a desolation, without an inhabitant in them, [3]because of the wickedness that they committed, provoking me to anger, in that they went to make offerings and serve other gods that they had not known, neither they, nor you, nor your ancestors. [4]Yet I persistently sent to you all my servants the prophets, saying, "I beg you not to do this abominable thing that I hate!" [5]But they did not listen or incline their ear, to turn from their wickedness and make no offerings to other gods. [6]So my wrath and my anger were poured out and kindled in the towns of Judah and in the streets of Jerusalem; and they became a waste and a desolation, as they still are today. [7]And now thus says the LORD God of hosts, the God of Israel: Why are you doing such great harm to yourselves, to cut off man and woman, child and infant, from the midst of Judah, leaving yourselves without a remnant? [8]Why do you provoke me to anger with the works of your hands, making offerings to other gods in the land of Egypt where you have come to settle? Will you be cut off and become an object of cursing and ridicule among all the nations of the earth? [9]Have you forgotten the crimes of your ancestors, of the kings of Judah, of their[d] wives, your own crimes and those of your wives, which they committed in the land of Judah and in the streets of Jerusalem? [10]They have shown no contrition or fear to this day, nor have they walked in my law and my statutes that I set before you and before your ancestors.

11 Therefore thus says the LORD of hosts, the God of Israel: I am determined to bring disaster on

---

a Meaning of Heb uncertain   b Gk Syr: Heb I   c Gk Syr Vg: Heb I   d Heb his you, to bring all Judah to an end. [12]I will take the remnant of Judah who are determined to come to the land of Egypt to settle, and they shall perish, everyone; in the land of Egypt they shall fall; by the sword and by famine they shall perish; from the least to the greatest, they shall die by the sword and by famine; and they shall become an object of execration and horror, of cursing and ridicule. [13]I will punish those who live in the land of Egypt, as I have punished Jerusalem, with the sword, with famine, and with pestilence, [14]so that none of the remnant of Judah who have come to settle in the land of Egypt shall escape or survive or return to the land of Judah. Although they long to go back to live there, they shall not go back, except some fugitives.

15 Then all the men who were aware that their wives had been making offerings to other gods, and all the women who stood by, a great assembly, all the people who lived in Pathros in the land of Egypt, answered Jeremiah: [16]"As for the word that you have spoken to us in the name of the LORD, we are not going to listen to you. [17]Instead, we will do everything that we have vowed, make offerings to the queen of heaven and pour out libations to her, just as we and our ancestors, our kings and our officials, used to do in the towns of Judah and in the streets of Jerusalem. We used to have plenty of food, and prospered, and saw no misfortune. [18]But from the time we stopped making offerings to the queen of heaven and pouring out libations to her, we have lacked everything and have perished by the sword and by famine." [19]And the women said,[a] "Indeed we will go on making offerings to the queen of heaven and pouring out libations to her; do you think that we made cakes for her, marked with her image, and poured out libations to her without our husbands' being involved?"

20 Then Jeremiah said to all the people, men and women, all the people who were giving him this answer: [21]"As for the offerings that you made in the towns of Judah and in the streets of Jerusalem, you and your ancestors, your kings and your officials, and the people of the land, did not the LORD remember them? Did it not come into his mind? [22]The LORD could no longer bear the sight of your evil doings, the abominations that you committed; therefore your land became a desolation and a waste and a curse, without inhabitant, as it is to this day. [23]It is because you burned offerings, and because

you sinned against the LORD and did not obey the voice of the LORD or walk in his law and in his statutes and in his decrees, that this disaster has befallen you, as is still evident today."

24 Jeremiah said to all the people and all the women, "Hear the word of the LORD, all you Judeans who are in the land of Egypt, [25]Thus says the LORD of hosts, the God of Israel: You and your wives have accomplished in deeds what you declared in words, saying, 'We are determined to perform the vows that we have made, to make offerings to the queen of heaven and to pour out libations to her.' By all means, keep your vows and make your libations! [26]Therefore hear the word of the LORD, all you Judeans who live in the land of Egypt: Lo, I swear by my great name, says the LORD, that my name shall no longer be pronounced on the lips of any of the people of Judah in all the land of Egypt, saying, 'As the Lord GOD lives.' [27]I am going to watch over them for harm and not for good; all the people of Judah who are in the land of Egypt shall perish by the sword and by famine, until not one is left. [28]And those who escape the sword shall return from the land of Egypt to the land of Judah, few in number; and all the remnant of Judah, who have come to the land of Egypt to settle, shall know whose words will stand, mine or theirs! [29]This shall be the sign to you, says the LORD, that I am going to punish you in this place, in order that you may know that my words against you will surely be carried out: [30]Thus says the LORD, I am going to give Pharaoh Hophra, king of Egypt, into the hands of his enemies, those who seek his life, just as I gave King Zedekiah of Judah into the hand of King Nebuchadrezzar of Babylon, his enemy who sought his life."

A Word of Comfort to Baruch

45 The word that the prophet Jeremiah spoke to Baruch son of Neriah, when he wrote these words in a scroll at the dictation of Jeremiah, in the fourth year of King Jehoiakim son of Josiah of Judah: [2]Thus says the LORD, the God of Israel, to you, O Baruch: [3]You said, "Woe is me! The LORD has added sorrow to my pain; I am weary with my groaning, and I find no rest." [4]Thus you shall say to him, "Thus says the LORD: I am going to break down what I have built, and pluck up what I have planted— that is, the whole land. [5]And you, do you seek great things for yourself? Do not seek them; for I am going to bring disaster upon all flesh, says the LORD;

---

a Compare Syr: Heb lacks *And the women said*

but I will give you your life as a prize of war in every place to which you may go."

46 Judgment on Egypt

The word of the LORD that came to the prophet Jeremiah concerning the nations.

2 Concerning Egypt, about the army of Pharaoh Neco, king of Egypt, which was by the river Euphrates at Carchemish and which King Nebuchadrezzar of Babylon defeated in the fourth year of King Jehoiakim son of Josiah of Judah:

3 Prepare buckler and shield,
    and advance for battle!
4 Harness the horses;
    mount the steeds!
Take your stations with your helmets,
    whet your lances,
    put on your coats of mail!
5 Why do I see them terrified?
    They have fallen back;
their warriors are beaten down,
    and have fled in haste.
They do not look back—
    terror is all around!
                    says the LORD.
6 The swift cannot flee away,
    nor can the warrior escape;
in the north by the river Euphrates
    they have stumbled and fallen.

7 Who is this, rising like the Nile,
    like rivers whose waters surge?
8 Egypt rises like the Nile,
    like rivers whose waters surge.
It said, Let me rise, let me cover the earth,
    let me destroy cities and their inhabitants.

9 Advance, O horses,
    and dash madly, O chariots!
Let the warriors go forth:
    Ethiopia[a] and Put who carry the
        shield,
    the Ludim, who draw[b] the bow.
10 That day is the day of the Lord GOD of hosts,
    a day of retribution,
    to gain vindication from his foes.
The sword shall devour and be sated,
    and drink its fill of their blood.
For the Lord GOD of hosts holds a sacrifice
    in the land of the north by the river
        Euphrates.
11 Go up to Gilead, and take balm,
    O virgin daughter Egypt!
In vain you have used many medicines;
    there is no healing for you.
12 The nations have heard of your shame,
    and the earth is full of your cry;
for warrior has stumbled against warrior;
    both have fallen together.

Babylonia Will Strike Egypt

13 The word that the LORD spoke to the prophet Jeremiah about the coming of King Nebuchadrezzar of Babylon to attack the land of Egypt:

14 Declare in Egypt, and proclaim in Migdol;
    proclaim in Memphis and Tahpanhes;
Say, "Take your stations and be ready,
    for the sword shall devour those around
        you."
15 Why has Apis fled?[c]
    Why did your bull not stand?
    —because the LORD thrust him down.
16 Your multitude stumbled[d] and fell,

Oracles Against the Nations · Jeremiah 46–51

The oracles against the nations in **Jeremiah 46–51** resemble the oracles in **Isaiah 13–23**. God makes it clear in both books that, although Israel has suffered greatly, the covenant still remains and God will not desert them. The enemies of Israel will have their due.

The nations named here were great, powerful nations, but they did not have the promise of the presence of God. The vengeful voice can be hard for us to hear and must be balanced with the words of Jesus about loving our enemies and living in peace. The amazing thing to recognize here is that God can use even pagan countries to accomplish God's purposes—no country or leader or movement is outside of God's ultimate sovereign plan to bring hope and salvation to God's people.

a Or Nubia; Heb Cush   b Cn: Heb who grasp, who draw   c Gk: Heb Why was it swept away   d Gk: Meaning of Heb uncertain

and one said to another,[a]
"Come, let us go back to our own people
and to the land of our birth,
because of the destroying sword."
17 Give Pharaoh, king of Egypt, the name
"Braggart who missed his chance."

18 As I live, says the King,
whose name is the LORD of hosts,
one is coming
like Tabor among the mountains,
and like Carmel by the sea.
19 Pack your bags for exile,
sheltered daughter Egypt!
For Memphis shall become a waste,
a ruin, without inhabitant.

20 A beautiful heifer is Egypt—
a gadfly from the north lights
upon her.
21 Even her mercenaries in her midst
are like fatted calves;
they too have turned and fled together,
they did not stand;
for the day of their calamity has come upon
them,
the time of their punishment.

22 She makes a sound like a snake gliding away;
for her enemies march in force,
and come against her with axes,
like those who fell trees.
23 They shall cut down her forest,
says the LORD,
though it is impenetrable,
because they are more numerous
than locusts;
they are without number.

24 Daughter Egypt shall be put to shame;
she shall be handed over to a people from
the north.

25 The LORD of hosts, the God of Israel, said:
See, I am bringing punishment upon Amon of
Thebes, and Pharaoh, and Egypt and her gods and
her kings, upon Pharaoh and those who trust in him.
26 I will hand them over to those who seek their life,
to King Nebuchadrezzar of Babylon and his officers.
Afterward Egypt shall be inhabited as in the days of
old, says the LORD.

God Will Save Israel

27 But as for you, have no fear, my servant Jacob,
and do not be dismayed, O Israel;
for I am going to save you from far away,
and your offspring from the land of their
captivity.
Jacob shall return and have quiet and ease,
and no one shall make him afraid.
28 As for you, have no fear, my servant Jacob,
says the LORD,
for I am with you.
I will make an end of all the nations
among which I have banished you,
but I will not make an end of you!
I will chastise you in just measure,
and I will by no means leave you
unpunished.

47 Judgment on the Philistines

The word of the LORD that came to the
prophet Jeremiah concerning the Philistines, before Pharaoh attacked Gaza:
2 Thus says the LORD:
See, waters are rising out of the north
and shall become an overflowing torrent;
they shall overflow the land and all that fills it,
the city and those who live in it.
People shall cry out,
and all the inhabitants of the land shall
wail.
3 At the noise of the stamping of the hoofs of his
stallions,
at the clatter of his chariots, at the
rumbling of their wheels,
parents do not turn back for children,
so feeble are their hands,
4 because of the day that is coming
to destroy all the Philistines,
to cut off from Tyre and Sidon
every helper that remains.
For the LORD is destroying the Philistines,
the remnant of the coastland of Caphtor.
5 Baldness has come upon Gaza,
Ashkelon is silenced.
O remnant of their power![b]
How long will you gash yourselves?
6 Ah, sword of the LORD!
How long until you are quiet?
Put yourself into your scabbard,
rest and be still!

---

a Gk: Heb *and fell one to another and they said*   b Gk: Heb *their valley*

7 How can it[a] be quiet,
  when the LORD has given it an order?
  Against Ashkelon and against the seashore—
  there he has appointed it.

48 Judgment on Moab
Concerning Moab.

Thus says the LORD of hosts, the God of Israel:
    Alas for Nebo, it is laid waste!
      Kiriathaim is put to shame, it is taken;
    the fortress is put to shame and broken
        down;
2   the renown of Moab is no more.
    In Heshbon they planned evil against her:
    "Come, let us cut her off from being a
        nation!"
    You also, O Madmen, shall be brought to
        silence;[b]
      the sword shall pursue you.

3 Hark! a cry from Horonaim,
    "Desolation and great destruction!"
4 "Moab is destroyed!"
    her little ones cry out.
5 For at the ascent of Luhith
    they go[c] up weeping bitterly;
  for at the descent of Horonaim
    they have heard the distressing cry of
        anguish.
6 Flee! Save yourselves!
    Be like a wild ass[d] in the desert!

7 Surely, because you trusted in your
        strongholds[e] and your treasures,
    you also shall be taken;
  Chemosh shall go out into exile,
    with his priests and his attendants.
8 The destroyer shall come upon every town,
    and no town shall escape;
  the valley shall perish,
    and the plain shall be destroyed,
  as the LORD has spoken.

9 Set aside salt for Moab,
    for she will surely fall;
  her towns shall become a desolation,
    with no inhabitant in them.

10 Accursed is the one who is slack in doing the
work of the LORD; and accursed is the one who
keeps back the sword from bloodshed.

11 Moab has been at ease from his youth,
    settled like wine[f] on its dregs;
  he has not been emptied from vessel to vessel,
    nor has he gone into exile;
  therefore his flavor has remained
    and his aroma is unspoiled.

12 Therefore, the time is surely coming, says the
LORD, when I shall send to him decanters to decant
him, and empty his vessels, and break his[g] jars in
pieces. 13Then Moab shall be ashamed of Chemosh,
as the house of Israel was ashamed of Bethel, their
confidence.

14 How can you say, "We are heroes
    and mighty warriors"?
15 The destroyer of Moab and his towns has
        come up,
    and the choicest of his young men have
        gone down to slaughter,
    says the King, whose name is the LORD of
        hosts.
16 The calamity of Moab is near at hand
    and his doom approaches swiftly.
17 Mourn over him, all you his neighbors,
    and all who know his name;
  say, "How the mighty scepter is broken,
    the glorious staff!"

18 Come down from glory,
    and sit on the parched ground,
    enthroned daughter Dibon!
  For the destroyer of Moab has come up
        against you;
    he has destroyed your strongholds.
19 Stand by the road and watch,
    you inhabitant of Aroer!
  Ask the man fleeing and the woman escaping;
    say, "What has happened?"
20 Moab is put to shame, for it is broken down;
    wail and cry!
  Tell it by the Arnon,
    that Moab is laid waste.

21 Judgment has come upon the tableland, upon
Holon, and Jahzah, and Mephaath, 22and Dibon,
and Nebo, and Beth-diblathaim, 23and Kiriathaim,
and Beth-gamul, and Beth-meon, 24and Kerioth,

---

a Gk Vg: Heb *you*   b The place-name *Madmen* sounds like the Hebrew verb *to be silent*   c Cn: Heb *he goes*   d Gk Aquila: Heb *like Aroer*   e Gk: Heb
works   f Heb lacks *like wine*   g Gk Aquila: Heb *their*

and Bozrah, and all the towns of the land of Moab, far and near. [25]The horn of Moab is cut off, and his arm is broken, says the LORD.

26 Make him drunk, because he magnified himself against the LORD; let Moab wallow in his vomit; he too shall become a laughingstock. [27]Israel was a laughingstock for you, though he was not caught among thieves; but whenever you spoke of him you shook your head!

[28] Leave the towns, and live on the rock,
      O inhabitants of Moab!
  Be like the dove that nests
      on the sides of the mouth of a gorge.
[29] We have heard of the pride of Moab—
      he is very proud—
  of his loftiness, his pride, and his arrogance,
      and the haughtiness of his heart.
[30] I myself know his insolence, says the LORD;
      his boasts are false,
      his deeds are false.
[31] Therefore I wail for Moab;
      I cry out for all Moab;
      for the people of Kir-heres I mourn.
[32] More than for Jazer I weep for you,
      O vine of Sibmah!
  Your branches crossed over the sea,
      reached as far as Jazer;[a]
  upon your summer fruits and your vintage
      the destroyer has fallen.
[33] Gladness and joy have been taken away
      from the fruitful land of Moab;
  I have stopped the wine from the wine presses;
      no one treads them with shouts of joy;
      the shouting is not the shout of joy.

34 Heshbon and Elealeh cry out;[b] as far as Jahaz they utter their voice, from Zoar to Horonaim and Eglath-shelishiyah. For even the waters of Nimrim have become desolate. [35]And I will bring to an end in Moab, says the LORD, those who offer sacrifice at a high place and make offerings to their gods. [36]Therefore my heart moans for Moab like a flute, and my heart moans like a flute for the people of Kir-heres; for the riches they gained have perished.

37 For every head is shaved and every beard cut off; on all the hands there are gashes, and on the loins sackcloth. [38]On all the housetops of Moab and in the squares there is nothing but lamentation; for I have broken Moab like a vessel that no one wants,

says the LORD. [39]How it is broken! How they wail! How Moab has turned his back in shame! So Moab has become a derision and a horror to all his neighbors.

[40] For thus says the LORD:
  Look, he shall swoop down like an eagle,
      and spread his wings against Moab;
[41] the towns[c] shall be taken
      and the strongholds seized.
  The hearts of the warriors of Moab, on
          that day,
      shall be like the heart of a woman in
          labor.
[42] Moab shall be destroyed as a people,
      because he magnified himself against the
          LORD.
[43] Terror, pit, and trap
      are before you, O inhabitants of Moab!
          says the LORD.
[44] Everyone who flees from the terror
      shall fall into the pit,
  and everyone who climbs out of the pit
      shall be caught in the trap.
  For I will bring these things[d] upon Moab
      in the year of their punishment,
          says the LORD.

[45] In the shadow of Heshbon
      fugitives stop exhausted;
  for a fire has gone out from Heshbon,
      a flame from the house of Sihon;
  it has destroyed the forehead of Moab,
      the scalp of the people of tumult.[e]
[46] Woe to you, O Moab!
      The people of Chemosh have perished,
  for your sons have been taken captive,
      and your daughters into captivity.
[47] Yet I will restore the fortunes of Moab
      in the latter days, says the LORD.
  Thus far is the judgment on Moab.

49 Judgment on the Ammonites

Concerning the Ammonites.

Thus says the LORD:
  Has Israel no sons?
      Has he no heir?
  Why then has Milcom dispossessed Gad,
      and his people settled in its towns?
[2] Therefore, the time is surely coming,

a Two Mss and Isa 16.8: MT *the sea of Jazer* b Cn: Heb *From the cry of Heshbon to Elealeh* c Or Kerioth d Gk Syr: Heb *bring upon it* e Or *of Shaon*

says the Lord,
when I will sound the battle alarm
    against Rabbah of the Ammonites;
it shall become a desolate mound,
    and its villages shall be burned with
        fire;
then Israel shall dispossess those who
    dispossessed him,
    says the Lord.

3 Wail, O Heshbon, for Ai is laid waste!
    Cry out, O daughters*a* of Rabbah!
Put on sackcloth,
    lament, and slash yourselves with whips!*b*
For Milcom shall go into exile,
    with his priests and his attendants.
4 Why do you boast in your strength?
    Your strength is ebbing,
O faithless daughter.
    You trusted in your treasures, saying,
    "Who will attack me?"
5 I am going to bring terror upon you,
    says the Lord God of hosts,
    from all your neighbors,
and you will be scattered, each headlong,
    with no one to gather the fugitives.

6 But afterward I will restore the fortunes of the Ammonites, says the Lord.

Judgment on Edom

7 Concerning Edom.

Thus says the Lord of hosts:
    Is there no longer wisdom in Teman?
        Has counsel perished from the prudent?
        Has their wisdom vanished?
8 Flee, turn back, get down low,
    inhabitants of Dedan!
For I will bring the calamity of Esau
        upon him,
    the time when I punish him.
9 If grape-gatherers came to you,
    would they not leave gleanings?
If thieves came by night,
    even they would pillage only what they
        wanted.
10 But as for me, I have stripped Esau bare,
    I have uncovered his hiding places,
    and he is not able to conceal himself.
His offspring are destroyed, his kinsfolk

and his neighbors; and he is no more.
11 Leave your orphans, I will keep them alive;
    and let your widows trust in me.

12 For thus says the Lord: If those who do not deserve to drink the cup still have to drink it, shall you be the one to go unpunished? You shall not go unpunished; you must drink it. 13 For by myself I have sworn, says the Lord, that Bozrah shall become an object of horror and ridicule, a waste, and an object of cursing; and all her towns shall be perpetual wastes.
14 I have heard tidings from the Lord,
    and a messenger has been sent among the
        nations:
    "Gather yourselves together and come
        against her,
    and rise up for battle!"
15 For I will make you least among the nations,
    despised by humankind.
16 The terror you inspire
    and the pride of your heart have
        deceived you,
you who live in the clefts of the rock,*c*
    who hold the height of the hill.
Although you make your nest as high as the
        eagle's,
    from there I will bring you down,
        says the Lord.

17 Edom shall become an object of horror; everyone who passes by it will be horrified and will hiss because of all its disasters. 18 As when Sodom and Gomorrah and their neighbors were overthrown, says the Lord, no one shall live there, nor shall anyone settle in it. 19 Like a lion coming up from the thickets of the Jordan against a perennial pasture, I will suddenly chase Edom*d* away from it; and I will appoint over it whomever I choose.*e* For who is like me? Who can summon me? Who is the shepherd who can stand before me? 20 Therefore hear the plan that the Lord has made against Edom and the purposes that he has formed against the inhabitants of Teman: Surely the little ones of the flock shall be dragged away; surely their fold shall be appalled at their fate. 21 At the sound of their fall the earth shall tremble; the sound of their cry shall be heard at the Red Sea.*f* 22 Look, he shall mount up and swoop down like an eagle, and spread his wings against Bozrah, and the heart of the warriors of Edom in that day shall be like the heart of a woman in labor.

a Or *villages* *b* Cn: Meaning of Heb uncertain *c* Or *of Sela* *d* Heb *him* *e* Or *and I will single out the choicest of his rams:* Meaning of Heb uncertain
f Or *Sea of Reeds*

Judgment on Damascus

23 Concerning Damascus.

Hamath and Arpad are confounded,
　for they have heard bad news;
they melt in fear, they are troubled like
　the sea[a]
　that cannot be quiet.
24 Damascus has become feeble, she turned to
　flee,
　and panic seized her;
anguish and sorrows have taken hold of her,
　as of a woman in labor.
25 How the famous city is forsaken,[b]
　the joyful town![c]
26 Therefore her young men shall fall in her
　　squares,
　and all her soldiers shall be destroyed in
　　that day,
　　　　　says the Lord of hosts.
27 And I will kindle a fire at the wall of
　　Damascus,
　and it shall devour the strongholds of
　　Ben-hadad.

Judgment on Kedar and Hazor

28 Concerning Kedar and the kingdoms of Hazor that King Nebuchadrezzar of Babylon defeated.

Thus says the Lord:
Rise up, advance against Kedar!
　Destroy the people of the east!
29 Take their tents and their flocks,
　their curtains and all their goods;
carry off their camels for yourselves,
　and a cry shall go up: "Terror is all
　　around!"
30 Flee, wander far away, hide in deep places,
　O inhabitants of Hazor!
　　　　　says the Lord.
For King Nebuchadrezzar of Babylon
　has made a plan against you
　and formed a purpose against you.

31 Rise up, advance against a nation at ease,
　that lives secure,
　　　　　says the Lord,
that has no gates or bars,
　that lives alone.
32 Their camels shall become booty,

　their herds of cattle a spoil.
I will scatter to every wind
　those who have shaven temples,
　and I will bring calamity
　against them from every side,
　　　　　says the Lord.
33 Hazor shall become a lair of jackals,
　an everlasting waste;
no one shall live there,
　nor shall anyone settle in it.

Judgment on Elam

34 The word of the Lord that came to the prophet Jeremiah concerning Elam, at the beginning of the reign of King Zedekiah of Judah.

35 Thus says the Lord of hosts: I am going to break the bow of Elam, the mainstay of their might; 36 and I will bring upon Elam the four winds from the four quarters of heaven; and I will scatter them to all these winds, and there shall be no nation to which the exiles from Elam shall not come. 37 I will terrify Elam before their enemies, and before those who seek their life; I will bring disaster upon them, my fierce anger, says the Lord. I will send the sword after them, until I have consumed them; 38 and I will set my throne in Elam, and destroy their king and officials, says the Lord.

39 But in the latter days I will restore the fortunes of Elam, says the Lord.

Judgment on Babylon

50 The word that the Lord spoke concerning Babylon, concerning the land of the Chaldeans, by the prophet Jeremiah:
2 Declare among the nations and proclaim,
　set up a banner and proclaim,
　do not conceal it, say:
Babylon is taken,
　Bel is put to shame,
　Merodach is dismayed.

---

a Cn: Heb *there is trouble in the sea*   b Vg: Heb *is not forsaken*   c Syr Vg Tg: Heb *the town of my joy*

Her images are put to shame,
  her idols are dismayed.
3 For out of the north a nation has come up against her; it shall make her land a desolation, and no one shall live in it; both human beings and animals shall flee away.

4 In those days and in that time, says the LORD, the people of Israel shall come, they and the people of Judah together; they shall come weeping as they seek the LORD their God. ⁵They shall ask the way to Zion, with faces turned toward it, and they shall come and join^a themselves to the LORD by an everlasting covenant that will never be forgotten.

6 My people have been lost sheep; their shepherds have led them astray, turning them away on the mountains; from mountain to hill they have gone, they have forgotten their fold. ⁷All who found them have devoured them, and their enemies have said, "We are not guilty, because they have sinned against the LORD, the true pasture, the LORD, the hope of their ancestors."

8 Flee from Babylon, and go out of the land of the Chaldeans, and be like male goats leading the flock. ⁹For I am going to stir up and bring against Babylon a company of great nations from the land of the north; and they shall array themselves against her; from there she shall be taken. Their arrows are like the arrows of a skilled warrior who does not return empty-handed. ¹⁰Chaldea shall be plundered; all who plunder her shall be sated, says the LORD.

11 Though you rejoice, though you exult,
  O plunderers of my heritage,
  though you frisk about like a heifer on the
      grass,
  and neigh like stallions,
12 your mother shall be utterly shamed,
  and she who bore you shall be disgraced.
  Lo, she shall be the last of the nations,
  a wilderness, dry land, and a desert.
13 Because of the wrath of the LORD she shall not
      be inhabited,
  but shall be an utter desolation;
  everyone who passes by Babylon shall be
      appalled
  and hiss because of all her wounds.
14 Take up your positions around Babylon,

all you that bend the bow;
shoot at her, spare no arrows,
  for she has sinned against the LORD.
15 Raise a shout against her from all sides,
  "She has surrendered;
her bulwarks have fallen,
  her walls are thrown down."
For this is the vengeance of the LORD:
  take vengeance on her,
  do to her as she has done.
16 Cut off from Babylon the sower,
  and the wielder of the sickle in time of
      harvest;
because of the destroying sword
  all of them shall return to their own
      people,
  and all of them shall flee to their own land.

17 Israel is a hunted sheep driven away by lions. First the king of Assyria devoured it, and now at the end King Nebuchadrezzar of Babylon has gnawed its bones. ¹⁸Therefore, thus says the LORD of hosts, the God of Israel: I am going to punish the king of Babylon and his land, as I punished the king of Assyria. ¹⁹I will restore Israel to its pasture, and it shall feed on Carmel and in Bashan, and on the hills of Ephraim and in Gilead its hunger shall be satisfied. ²⁰In those days and at that time, says the LORD, the iniquity of Israel shall be sought, and there shall be none; and the sins of Judah, and none shall be found; for I will pardon the remnant that I have spared.

21 Go up to the land of Merathaim;^b
  go up against her,
  and attack the inhabitants of Pekod^c
  and utterly destroy the last of them,^d
          says the LORD;
  do all that I have commanded you.
22 The noise of battle is in the land,
  and great destruction!
23 How the hammer of the whole earth
  is cut down and broken!
How Babylon has become
  a horror among the nations!
24 You set a snare for yourself and you were
          caught, O Babylon,
  but you did not know it;
you were discovered and seized,
  because you challenged the LORD.

a Gk: Heb *toward it. Come! They shall join*   b Or *of Double Rebellion*   c Or *of Punishment*   d Tg: Heb *destroy after them*

25 The LORD has opened his armory,
    and brought out the weapons of his wrath,
for the Lord GOD of hosts has a task
    to do
    in the land of the Chaldeans.
26 Come against her from every quarter;
    open her granaries;
pile her up like heaps of grain, and destroy
        her utterly;
    let nothing be left of her.
27 Kill all her bulls,
    let them go down to the slaughter.
Alas for them, their day has come,
    the time of their punishment!

28 Listen! Fugitives and refugees from the land of Babylon are coming to declare in Zion the vengeance of the LORD our God, vengeance for his temple.

29 Summon archers against Babylon, all who bend the bow. Encamp all around her; let no one escape. Repay her according to her deeds; just as she has done, do to her—for she has arrogantly defied the LORD, the Holy One of Israel. 30 Therefore her young men shall fall in her squares, and all her soldiers shall be destroyed on that day, says the LORD.

31 I am against you, O arrogant one,
    says the Lord GOD of hosts;
for your day has come,
    the time when I will punish you.
32 The arrogant one shall stumble and fall,
    with no one to raise him up,
and I will kindle a fire in his cities,
    and it will devour everything around him.

33 Thus says the LORD of hosts: The people of Israel are oppressed, and so too are the people of Judah; all their captors have held them fast and refuse to let them go. 34 Their Redeemer is strong; the LORD of hosts is his name. He will surely plead their cause, that he may give rest to the earth, but unrest to the inhabitants of Babylon.

35 A sword against the Chaldeans, says the LORD,
    and against the inhabitants of Babylon,
    and against her officials and her sages!
36 A sword against the diviners,
    so that they may become fools!
A sword against her warriors,
    so that they may be destroyed!
37 A sword against her[a] horses and against her[a]
        chariots,
    and against all the foreign troops in her
        midst,
    so that they may become women!
A sword against all her treasures,
    that they may be plundered!
38 A drought[b] against her waters,
    that they may be dried up!
For it is a land of images,
    and they go mad over idols.

39 Therefore wild animals shall live with hyenas in Babylon,[c] and ostriches shall inhabit her; she shall never again be peopled, or inhabited for all generations. 40 As when God overthrew Sodom and Gomorrah and their neighbors, says the LORD, so no one shall live there, nor shall anyone settle in her.

41 Look, a people is coming from the north;
    a mighty nation and many kings
    are stirring from the farthest parts of the
        earth.
42 They wield bow and spear,
    they are cruel and have no mercy.
The sound of them is like the roaring sea;
    they ride upon horses,
set in array as a warrior for battle,
    against you, O daughter Babylon!

43 The king of Babylon heard news of them,
    and his hands fell helpless;
anguish seized him,
    pain like that of a woman in labor.

44 Like a lion coming up from the thickets of the Jordan against a perennial pasture, I will suddenly chase them away from her; and I will appoint over her whomever I choose.[d] For who is like me? Who can summon me? Who is the shepherd who can stand before me? 45 Therefore hear the plan that the LORD has made against Babylon, and the purposes that he has formed against the land of the Chaldeans: Surely the little ones of the flock shall be dragged away; surely their[e] fold shall be appalled at their fate. 46 At the sound of the capture of Babylon the earth shall tremble, and her cry shall be heard among the nations.

a Cn: Heb *his*   b Another reading is *A sword*   c Heb lacks *in Babylon*   d Or *and I will single out the choicest of her rams*: Meaning of Heb uncertain
e Syr Gk Tg Compare 49.20: Heb lacks *their*

51 Thus says the Lord:
I am going to stir up a destructive wind[a]
    against Babylon
and against the inhabitants of
        Leb-qamai;[b]
2 and I will send winnowers to Babylon,
    and they shall winnow her.
They shall empty her land
    when they come against her from
        every side
    on the day of trouble.
3 Let not the archer bend his bow,
    and let him not array himself in his coat of
        mail.
Do not spare her young men;
    utterly destroy her entire army.
4 They shall fall down slain in the land of the
        Chaldeans,
    and wounded in her streets.
5 Israel and Judah have not been forsaken
    by their God, the Lord of hosts,
though their land is full of guilt
    before the Holy One of Israel.

6 Flee from the midst of Babylon,
    save your lives, each of you!
Do not perish because of her guilt,
    for this is the time of the Lord's
        vengeance;
he is repaying her what is due.
7 Babylon was a golden cup in the Lord's hand,
    making all the earth drunken;
the nations drank of her wine,
    and so the nations went mad.
8 Suddenly Babylon has fallen and is shattered;
    wail for her!
Bring balm for her wound;
    perhaps she may be healed.
9 We tried to heal Babylon,
    but she could not be healed.
Forsake her, and let each of us go
    to our own country;
for her judgment has reached up to heaven
    and has been lifted up even to the skies.
10 The Lord has brought forth our vindication;
    come, let us declare in Zion
    the work of the Lord our God.

11 Sharpen the arrows!
    Fill the quivers!

The Lord has stirred up the spirit of the kings of
the Medes, because his purpose concerning Babylon
is to destroy it, for that is the vengeance of the Lord,
vengeance for his temple.
12 Raise a standard against the walls of Babylon;
    make the watch strong;
post sentinels;
    prepare the ambushes;
for the Lord has both planned and done
    what he spoke concerning the inhabitants
        of Babylon.
13 You who live by mighty waters,
    rich in treasures,
your end has come,
    the thread of your life is cut.
14 The Lord of hosts has sworn by
        himself:
Surely I will fill you with troops like a swarm
        of locusts,

STUDY IT!

Whatever Happened to Babylon? Jeremiah 51

Jeremiah prophesied about the destruction of Babylon, the powerful empire with the most glamorous and glittering capital in the Middle East (see Jeremiah 50-51). But not long afterward, in 587 B.C., King Nebuchadrezzar (also called Nebuchadnezzar) of Babylon destroyed Jerusalem, blinded the king of Judah, and led the leaders of Judah off into exile. This seemed to be the end of Jerusalem and perhaps even the Israelites. So what about Jeremiah's prophecy? Eventually Babylon was defeated by Persia, and the captives were released. Today, Jerusalem is a thriving city, and Judaism—as it emerged after the exile—is one of the world's great religions. Babylon is long gone, and no one worships its chief god, Marduk. Jeremiah saw past the immediate destruction of Jerusalem to the eventual doom of Babylon.

a Or *stir up the spirit of a destroyer*   b *Leb-qamai* is a cryptogram for *Kasdim*, Chaldea

and they shall raise a shout of victory
over you.

15 It is he who made the earth by his power,
who established the world by his wisdom,
and by his understanding stretched out the
heavens.

16 When he utters his voice there is a tumult of
waters in the heavens,
and he makes the mist rise from the ends
of the earth.
He makes lightnings for the rain,
and he brings out the wind from his
storehouses.

17 Everyone is stupid and without knowledge;
goldsmiths are all put to shame by their
idols;
for their images are false,
and there is no breath in them.

18 They are worthless, a work of delusion;
at the time of their punishment they shall
perish.

19 Not like these is the LORD,[a] the portion of
Jacob,
for he is the one who formed all things,
and Israel is the tribe of his inheritance;
the LORD of hosts is his name.

Israel the Creator's Instrument

20 You are my war club, my weapon of battle:
with you I smash nations;
with you I destroy kingdoms;

21 with you I smash the horse and its rider;
with you I smash the chariot and the
charioteer;

22 with you I smash man and woman;
with you I smash the old man and the boy;
with you I smash the young man and the girl;

23 with you I smash shepherds and their
flocks;
with you I smash farmers and their teams;
with you I smash governors and deputies.

The Doom of Babylon

24 I will repay Babylon and all the inhabitants of
Chaldea before your very eyes for all the wrong that
they have done in Zion, says the LORD.

25 I am against you, O destroying mountain,
says the LORD,

that destroys the whole earth;
I will stretch out my hand against you,
and roll you down from the crags,
and make you a burned-out mountain.

26 No stone shall be taken from you for a corner
and no stone for a foundation,
but you shall be a perpetual waste,
says the LORD.

27 Raise a standard in the land,
blow the trumpet among the nations;
prepare the nations for war against her,
summon against her the kingdoms,
Ararat, Minni, and Ashkenaz;
appoint a marshal against her,
bring up horses like bristling locusts.

28 Prepare the nations for war against her,
the kings of the Medes, with their
governors and deputies,
and every land under their dominion.

29 The land trembles and writhes,
for the LORD's purposes against Babylon
stand,
to make the land of Babylon a desolation,
without inhabitant.

30 The warriors of Babylon have given up
fighting,
they remain in their strongholds;
their strength has failed,
they have become women;
her buildings are set on fire,
her bars are broken.

31 One runner runs to meet another,
and one messenger to meet another,
to tell the king of Babylon
that his city is taken from end to end:

32 the fords have been seized,
the marshes have been burned with fire,
and the soldiers are in panic.

33 For thus says the LORD of hosts, the God of
Israel:
Daughter Babylon is like a threshing floor
at the time when it is trodden;
yet a little while
and the time of her harvest will come.

34 "King Nebuchadrezzar of Babylon has
devoured me,
he has crushed me;
he has made me an empty vessel,

---

a Heb lacks the LORD

he has swallowed me like a monster;
he has filled his belly with my delicacies,
he has spewed me out.
35 May my torn flesh be avenged on Babylon,"
the inhabitants of Zion shall say.
"May my blood be avenged on the inhabitants
of Chaldea,"
Jerusalem shall say.
36 Therefore thus says the LORD:
I am going to defend your cause
and take vengeance for you.
I will dry up her sea
and make her fountain dry;
37 and Babylon shall become a heap of ruins,
a den of jackals,
an object of horror and of hissing,
without inhabitant.

38 Like lions they shall roar together;
they shall growl like lions' whelps.
39 When they are inflamed, I will set out their
drink
and make them drunk, until they become
merry
and then sleep a perpetual sleep
and never wake, says the LORD.
40 I will bring them down like lambs to the
slaughter,
like rams and goats.

41 How Sheshach[a] is taken,
the pride of the whole earth seized!
How Babylon has become
an object of horror among the nations!
42 The sea has risen over Babylon;
she has been covered by its tumultuous
waves.
43 Her cities have become an object of horror,
a land of drought and a desert,
a land in which no one lives,
and through which no mortal passes.
44 I will punish Bel in Babylon,
and make him disgorge what he has
swallowed.
The nations shall no longer stream to him;
the wall of Babylon has fallen.

45 Come out of her, my people!
Save your lives, each of you,
from the fierce anger of the LORD!

46 Do not be fainthearted or fearful
at the rumors heard in the land—
one year one rumor comes,
the next year another,
rumors of violence in the land
and of ruler against ruler.

47 Assuredly, the days are coming
when I will punish the images of Babylon;
her whole land shall be put to shame,
and all her slain shall fall in her midst.
48 Then the heavens and the earth,
and all that is in them,
shall shout for joy over Babylon;
for the destroyers shall come against them
out of the north,
       says the LORD.
49 Babylon must fall for the slain of Israel,
as the slain of all the earth have fallen
because of Babylon.

50 You survivors of the sword,
go, do not linger!
Remember the LORD in a distant land,
and let Jerusalem come into your mind:
51 We are put to shame, for we have heard
insults;
dishonor has covered our face,
for aliens have come
into the holy places of the LORD's house.

52 Therefore the time is surely coming, says the
LORD,
when I will punish her idols,
and through all her land
the wounded shall groan.
53 Though Babylon should mount up to heaven,
and though she should fortify her strong
height,
from me destroyers would come upon her,
says the LORD.

54 Listen!—a cry from Babylon!
A great crashing from the land of the
Chaldeans!
55 For the LORD is laying Babylon waste,
and stilling her loud clamor.
Their waves roar like mighty waters,
the sound of their clamor resounds;
56 for a destroyer has come against her,

a *Sheshach* is a cryptogram for *Babel*, Babylon

against Babylon;
　her warriors are taken,
　　their bows are broken;
　for the LORD is a God of recompense,
　　he will repay in full.
57 I will make her officials and her sages drunk,
　　also her governors, her deputies, and her
　　　warriors;
　they shall sleep a perpetual sleep and never
　　wake,
　says the King, whose name is the LORD of
　　hosts.

58 Thus says the LORD of hosts:
　The broad wall of Babylon
　　shall be leveled to the ground,
　and her high gates
　　shall be burned with fire.
　The peoples exhaust themselves for nothing,
　　and the nations weary themselves only for
　　　fire.^{a}

Jeremiah's Command to Seraiah

59 The word that the prophet Jeremiah commanded Seraiah son of Neriah son of Mahseiah, when he went with King Zedekiah of Judah to Babylon, in the fourth year of his reign. Seraiah was the quartermaster. ^{60}Jeremiah wrote in a^b scroll all the disasters that would come on Babylon, all these words that are written concerning Babylon. ^{61}And Jeremiah said to Seraiah: "When you come to Babylon, see that you read all these words, ^{62}and say, 'O LORD, you yourself threatened to destroy this place so that neither human beings nor animals shall live in it, and it shall be desolate forever.' ^{63}When you finish reading this scroll, tie a stone to it, and throw it into the middle of the Euphrates, ^{64}and say, 'Thus shall Babylon sink, to rise no more, because of the disasters that I am bringing on her.' "^{c} Thus far are the words of Jeremiah.

52 The Destruction of Jerusalem Reviewed

Zedekiah was twenty-one years old when he began to reign; he reigned eleven years in Jerusalem. His mother's name was Hamutal daughter of Jeremiah of Libnah. ^{2}He did what was evil in the sight of the LORD, just as Jehoiakim had done. ^{3}Indeed, Jerusalem and Judah so angered the LORD that he expelled them from his presence.

Zedekiah rebelled against the king of Babylon. ^{4}And in the ninth year of his reign, in the tenth month, on the tenth day of the month, King Nebuchadrezzar of Babylon came with all his army against Jerusalem, and they laid siege to it; they built siegeworks against it all around. ^{5}So the city was besieged until the eleventh year of King Zedekiah. ^{6}On the ninth day of the fourth month the famine became so severe in the city that there was no food for the people of the land. ^{7}Then a breach was made in the city wall;^{d} and all the soldiers fled and went out from the city by night by the way of the gate between the two walls, by the king's garden, though the Chaldeans were all around the city. They went in the direction of the Arabah. ^{8}But the army of the Chaldeans pursued the king, and overtook Zedekiah in the plains of Jericho; and all his army was scattered, deserting him. ^{9}Then they captured the king, and brought him up to the king of Babylon at Riblah in the land of Hamath, and he passed sentence on him. ^{10}The king of Babylon killed the sons of Zedekiah before his eyes, and also killed all the officers of Judah at Riblah. ^{11}He put out the eyes of Zedekiah, and bound him in fetters, and the king of Babylon took him to Babylon, and put him in prison until the day of his death.

12 In the fifth month, on the tenth day of the month—which was the nineteenth year of King Nebuchadrezzar, king of Babylon—Nebuzaradan the captain of the bodyguard who served the king of Babylon, entered Jerusalem. ^{13}He burned the house of the LORD, the king's house, and all the houses of Jerusalem; every great house he burned down. ^{14}All the army of the Chaldeans, who were with the captain of the guard, broke down all the walls around Jerusalem. ^{15}Nebuzaradan the captain of the guard carried into exile some of the poorest of the people and the rest of the people who were left in the city and the deserters who had defected to the king of Babylon, together with the rest of the artisans. ^{16}But Nebuzaradan the captain of the guard left some of the poorest people of the land to be vinedressers and tillers of the soil.

17 The pillars of bronze that were in the house of the LORD, and the stands and the bronze sea that were in the house of the LORD, the Chaldeans broke in pieces, and carried all the bronze to Babylon. ^{18}They took away the pots, the shovels, the snuffers, the basins, the ladles, and all the vessels of bronze used in the temple service. ^{19}The captain of the

---

^{a} Gk Syr Compare Hab 2.13: Heb *and the nations for fire, and they are weary*　^{b} Or *one*　^{c} Gk: Heb *on her. And they shall weary themselves*　^{d} Heb lacks *wall*

guard took away the small bowls also, the firepans, the basins, the pots, the lampstands, the ladles, and the bowls for libation, both those of gold and those of silver. [20]As for the two pillars, the one sea, the twelve bronze bulls that were under the sea, and the stands,[a] which King Solomon had made for the house of the LORD, the bronze of all these vessels was beyond weighing. [21]As for the pillars, the height of the one pillar was eighteen cubits, its circumference was twelve cubits; it was hollow and its thickness was four fingers. [22]Upon it was a capital of bronze; the height of the capital was five cubits; latticework and pomegranates, all of bronze, encircled the top of the capital. And the second pillar had the same, with pomegranates. [23]There were ninety-six pomegranates on the sides; all the pomegranates encircling the latticework numbered one hundred.

24 The captain of the guard took the chief priest Seraiah, the second priest Zephaniah, and the three guardians of the threshold; [25]and from the city he took an officer who had been in command of the soldiers, and seven men of the king's council who were found in the city; the secretary of the commander of the army who mustered the people of the land; and sixty men of the people of the land who were found inside the city. [26]Then Nebuzaradan the captain of the guard took them, and

brought them to the king of Babylon at Riblah. [27]And the king of Babylon struck them down, and put them to death at Riblah in the land of Hamath. So Judah went into exile out of its land.

28 This is the number of the people whom Nebuchadrezzar took into exile: in the seventh year, three thousand twenty-three Judeans; [29]in the eighteenth year of Nebuchadrezzar he took into exile from Jerusalem eight hundred thirty-two persons; [30]in the twenty-third year of Nebuchadrezzar, Nebuzaradan the captain of the guard took into exile of the Judeans seven hundred forty-five persons; all the persons were four thousand six hundred.

Jehoiachin Favored in Captivity

31 In the thirty-seventh year of the exile of King Jehoiachin of Judah, in the twelfth month, on the twenty-fifth day of the month, King Evil-merodach of Babylon, in the year he began to reign, showed favor to King Jehoiachin of Judah and brought him out of prison; [32]he spoke kindly to him, and gave him a seat above the seats of the other kings who were with him in Babylon. [33]So Jehoiachin put aside his prison clothes, and every day of his life he dined regularly at the king's table. [34]For his allowance, a regular daily allowance was given him by the king of Babylon, as long as he lived, up to the day of his death.

a Cn: Heb *that were under the stands*

Lamentations

▶▶▶▶▶▶▶▶▶▶▶▶▶▶▶▶▶▶

The grief and sadness of having someone close to you die can be almost too much for words. At such times of deep emotion, many people often resort to poetry or song to express their feelings. Written during the Babylonian exile, the book of Lamentations poetically expresses the overwhelming grief the Israelites felt over the loss of their homes, freedom, capital, and temple. The poetic images of Lamentations give us insight into how devastating and destructive those days actually were.

IN DEPTH

Lamentations is a collection of five poetic songs, each a separate chapter in the book. If you take a quick look, you will notice that each poem has twenty-two verses, except the third, which has sixty-six. This is not an accident. In the original Hebrew language, each verse of the first, second, and fourth poems begins with successive letters of the Hebrew alphabet, which has twenty-two letters. In the third poem, every set of three verses begins with a different letter of the alphabet. This poetic structure, called acrostic, cannot be successfully translated into English. It is found in several poetic sections of the Old Testament, including Psalm 119.

Scholars are not sure why the Lamentation poems were written in this fashion. It may be because the structure made them easier to memorize. Some scholars believe that it may have been a sign of order and completeness. Another possibility is that the poem's structure helped give form to the feeling of uncontrollable grief. Knowing that the poem had a definite end may have reminded them that their sorrow would also come to an end.

Through these beautiful poems, the Israelites were able to grieve and acknowledge the sin that led to their destruction. By recalling their experience of the goodness of God in the past, they were also able to hope for the day when God would lead them back to their land to rebuild their lives in faithfulness to the covenant.

QUICK FACTS

● **Date Written:** During the Babylonian exile (587-538 B.C.)

● **Author:** Unknown, but the book is sometimes attributed to Jeremiah

● **Themes:** Expressions of grief showing us how we can cry out to God in hard times

AT A GLANCE

● **Lamentations 1** The desolation of Mount Zion and Jerusalem

● **Lamentations 2** God's wrath upon Jerusalem fulfilled

● **Lamentations 3** An account of God's steadfast love

● **Lamentations 4** The punishment of Zion

● **Lamentations 5** A prayer for mercy

1 The Deserted City

How lonely sits the city
　　that once was full of people!
How like a widow she has become,
　　she that was great among the nations!
She that was a princess among the provinces
　　has become a vassal.

2 She weeps bitterly in the night,
　　with tears on her cheeks;
among all her lovers
　　she has no one to comfort her;
all her friends have dealt treacherously
　　　　with her,
　　they have become her enemies.

3 Judah has gone into exile with suffering
　　and hard servitude;
she lives now among the nations,
　　and finds no resting place;
her pursuers have all overtaken her
　　in the midst of her distress.

4 The roads to Zion mourn,
　　for no one comes to the festivals;
all her gates are desolate,
　　her priests groan;
her young girls grieve,[a]
　　and her lot is bitter.

5 Her foes have become the masters,
　　her enemies prosper,
because the LORD has made her suffer
　　for the multitude of her transgressions;
her children have gone away,
　　captives before the foe.

6 From daughter Zion has departed
　　all her majesty.
Her princes have become like stags
　　that find no pasture;
they fled without strength
　　before the pursuer.

7 Jerusalem remembers,
　　in the days of her affliction and wandering,
all the precious things
　　that were hers in days of old.
When her people fell into the hand of the foe,
　　and there was no one to help her,

the foe looked on mocking
　　over her downfall.

8 Jerusalem sinned grievously,
　　so she has become a mockery;
all who honored her despise her,
　　for they have seen her nakedness;
she herself groans,
　　and turns her face away.

9 Her uncleanness was in her skirts;
　　she took no thought of her future;
her downfall was appalling,
　　with none to comfort her.
"O LORD, look at my affliction,
　　for the enemy has triumphed!"

10 Enemies have stretched out their hands
　　over all her precious things;
she has even seen the nations
　　invade her sanctuary,
those whom you forbade
　　to enter your congregation.

11 All her people groan
　　as they search for bread;
they trade their treasures for food
　　to revive their strength.
Look, O LORD, and see
　　how worthless I have become.

12 Is it nothing to you,[a] all you who
　　　　pass by?
　　Look and see
if there is any sorrow like my sorrow,
　　which was brought upon me,
which the LORD inflicted
　　on the day of his fierce anger.

13 From on high he sent fire;
　　it went deep into my bones;
he spread a net for my feet;
　　he turned me back;
he has left me stunned,
　　faint all day long.

14 My transgressions were bound[a] into a yoke;
　　by his hand they were fastened together;
they weigh on my neck,
　　sapping my strength;

a Meaning of Heb uncertain

the Lord handed me over
  to those whom I cannot withstand.

15 The LORD has rejected
    all my warriors in the midst of me;
  he proclaimed a time against me
    to crush my young men;
  the Lord has trodden as in a wine press
    the virgin daughter Judah.

16 For these things I weep;
    my eyes flow with tears;
  for a comforter is far from me,
    one to revive my courage;
  my children are desolate,
    for the enemy has prevailed.

17 Zion stretches out her hands,
    but there is no one to comfort her;
  the LORD has commanded against Jacob
    that his neighbors should become his
      foes;
  Jerusalem has become
    a filthy thing among them.

18 The LORD is in the right,
    for I have rebelled against his word;
  but hear, all you peoples,
    and behold my suffering;
  my young women and young men
    have gone into captivity.

19 I called to my lovers
    but they deceived me;
  my priests and elders
    perished in the city
  while seeking food
    to revive their strength.

20 See, O LORD, how distressed I am;
    my stomach churns,
  my heart is wrung within me,
    because I have been very rebellious.
  In the street the sword bereaves;
    in the house it is like death.

21 They heard how I was groaning,
    with no one to comfort me.
  All my enemies heard of my trouble;
    they are glad that you have done it.

Bring on the day you have announced,
  and let them be as I am.

22 Let all their evil doing come before you;
    and deal with them
  as you have dealt with me
    because of all my transgressions;
  for my groans are many
    and my heart is faint.

God's Warnings Fulfilled

2 How the Lord in his anger
    has humiliated*a* daughter Zion!
  He has thrown down from heaven to earth
    the splendor of Israel;
  he has not remembered his footstool
    in the day of his anger.

2 The Lord has destroyed without mercy
    all the dwellings of Jacob;
  in his wrath he has broken down
    the strongholds of daughter Judah;
  he has brought down to the ground in
      dishonor
    the kingdom and its rulers.

3 He has cut down in fierce anger
    all the might of Israel;
  he has withdrawn his right hand from them
    in the face of the enemy;
  he has burned like a flaming fire in Jacob,
    consuming all around.

4 He has bent his bow like an enemy,
    with his right hand set like a foe;
  he has killed all in whom we took pride
    in the tent of daughter Zion;
  he has poured out his fury like fire.

5 The Lord has become like an enemy;
    he has destroyed Israel.
  He has destroyed all its palaces,
    laid in ruins its strongholds,
  and multiplied in daughter Judah
    mourning and lamentation.

6 He has broken down his booth like a garden,
    he has destroyed his tabernacle;
  the LORD has abolished in Zion
    festival and sabbath,

a Meaning of Heb uncertain

and in his fierce indignation has spurned
    king and priest.

7 The Lord has scorned his altar,
    disowned his sanctuary;
he has delivered into the hand of the enemy
    the walls of her palaces;
a clamor was raised in the house of the LORD
    as on a day of festival.

8 The LORD determined to lay in ruins
    the wall of daughter Zion;
he stretched the line;
    he did not withhold his hand from
        destroying;
he caused rampart and wall to lament;
    they languish together.

9 Her gates have sunk into the ground;
    he has ruined and broken her bars;
her king and princes are among the nations;
    guidance is no more,
and her prophets obtain
    no vision from the LORD.

10 The elders of daughter Zion
    sit on the ground in silence;
they have thrown dust on their heads
    and put on sackcloth;
the young girls of Jerusalem
    have bowed their heads to the ground.

11 My eyes are spent with weeping;
    my stomach churns;
my bile is poured out on the ground
    because of the destruction of my people,
because infants and babes faint
    in the streets of the city.

12 They cry to their mothers,
    "Where is bread and wine?"
as they faint like the wounded
    in the streets of the city,
as their life is poured out
    on their mothers' bosom.

13 What can I say for you, to what compare you,
    O daughter Jerusalem?
To what can I liken you, that I may
    comfort you,

O virgin daughter Zion?
For vast as the sea is your ruin;
    who can heal you?

14 Your prophets have seen for you
    false and deceptive visions;
they have not exposed your iniquity
    to restore your fortunes,
but have seen oracles for you
    that are false and misleading.

15 All who pass along the way
    clap their hands at you;
they hiss and wag their heads
    at daughter Jerusalem;
"Is this the city that was called

PRAY IT!

Poetry's Purpose
Lamentations 2

Poetry has a special way of expressing emotion that other forms of writing often miss. But it's not often intended to be taken literally. As you read it, be open to the spiritual and emotional truth this type of scripture contains.

The poetry of Lamentations helps us reflect on the feelings and thoughts of the Jewish people after the destruction of Jerusalem. They were suffering from the loss of their homes, freedom, security, and so much more. **Lamentations 2:12–19** paints a picture of hunger and violence in the streets. It is a tragic and heart-wrenching scene.

None of us has to look far to find hunger, violence, and hopelessness in our own cities and around the world. Let your prayers for the suffering echo those of Lamentations.

When will the violence stop, Lord? How many will die today from drug overdoses and domestic abuse? How many children will go hungry because nobody took the time to care for them? Have mercy on your people, Lord!

the perfection of beauty,
the joy of all the earth?"

16 All your enemies
open their mouths against you;
they hiss, they gnash their teeth,
they cry: "We have devoured her!
Ah, this is the day we longed for;
at last we have seen it!"

17 The LORD has done what he purposed,
he has carried out his threat;
as he ordained long ago,
he has demolished without pity;
he has made the enemy rejoice over you,
and exalted the might of your foes.

18 Cry aloud[a] to the Lord!
O wall of daughter Zion!
Let tears stream down like a torrent
day and night!
Give yourself no rest,
your eyes no respite!

19 Arise, cry out in the night,
at the beginning of the watches!
Pour out your heart like water
before the presence of the Lord!
Lift your hands to him
for the lives of your children,
who faint for hunger
at the head of every street.

20 Look, O LORD, and consider!
To whom have you done this?
Should women eat their offspring,
the children they have borne?
Should priest and prophet be killed
in the sanctuary of the Lord?

21 The young and the old are lying
on the ground in the streets;
my young women and my young men
have fallen by the sword;
in the day of your anger you have killed them,
slaughtering without mercy.

22 You invited my enemies from all around
as if for a day of festival;
and on the day of the anger of the LORD

no one escaped or survived;
those whom I bore and reared
my enemy has destroyed.

God's Steadfast Love Endures

3 I am one who has seen affliction
under the rod of God's[b] wrath;
2 he has driven and brought me
into darkness without any light;
3 against me alone he turns his hand,
again and again, all day long.

4 He has made my flesh and my skin waste away,
and broken my bones;
5 he has besieged and enveloped me
with bitterness and tribulation;
6 he has made me sit in darkness
like the dead of long ago.

7 He has walled me about so that I cannot
escape;
he has put heavy chains on me;
8 though I call and cry for help,
he shuts out my prayer;
9 he has blocked my ways with hewn stones,
he has made my paths crooked.

10 He is a bear lying in wait for me,
a lion in hiding;
11 he led me off my way and tore me to pieces;
he has made me desolate;
12 he bent his bow and set me
as a mark for his arrow.

13 He shot into my vitals
the arrows of his quiver;
14 I have become the laughingstock of all my
people,
the object of their taunt-songs all day long.
15 He has filled me with bitterness,
he has sated me with wormwood.

16 He has made my teeth grind on
gravel,
and made me cower in ashes;
17 my soul is bereft of peace;
I have forgotten what happiness is;
18 so I say, "Gone is my glory,
and all that I had hoped for from the
LORD."

---

a Cn: Heb *Their heart cried*   b Heb *his*

19 The thought of my affliction and my
         homelessness
     is wormwood and gall!
20 My soul continually thinks of it
     and is bowed down within me.
21 But this I call to mind,
     and therefore I have hope:

22 The steadfast love of the LORD never ceases,[a]
     his mercies never come to an end;
23 they are new every morning;
     great is your faithfulness.
24 "The LORD is my portion," says my soul,
     "therefore I will hope in him."

25 The LORD is good to those who wait for him,
     to the soul that seeks him.
26 It is good that one should wait quietly
     for the salvation of the LORD.
27 It is good for one to bear
     the yoke in youth,
28 to sit alone in silence
     when the Lord has imposed it,
29 to put one's mouth to the dust
     (there may yet be hope),
30 to give one's cheek to the smiter,
     and be filled with insults.

LIVE IT!

Each New Day
Lamentations
3:22–33

There is hope! Just
when the descriptions
of destruction and suffering seem hopeless,
Lamentations reminds the Israelites, and us,
that God's love, mercy, and goodness never
end (Lamentations 3:22–25). Even in the most
hopeless situation, we can put our trust in
God's faithfulness.

- When have you felt trapped in the
  darkness of suffering or hopelessness?
- Write down **Lamentations 3:22–24**
  and put it in a place where you can
  read it each morning as a reminder of
  God's faithfulness and hope.

> "The steadfast love
> of the LORD never
> ceases, his mercies
> never come to an end;
> they are new every
> morning; great is
> your faithfulness."
> —Lamentations
> 3:22–23

31 For the Lord will not
     reject forever.
32 Although he causes grief, he will have
         compassion
     according to the abundance of his steadfast
         love;
33 for he does not willingly afflict
     or grieve anyone.

34 When all the prisoners of the land
     are crushed under foot,
35 when human rights are perverted
     in the presence of the Most High,
36 when one's case is subverted
     —does the Lord not see it?

37 Who can command and have it done,
     if the Lord has not ordained it?
38 Is it not from the mouth of the Most High
     that good and bad come?
39 Why should any who draw breath complain
     about the punishment of their sins?

40 Let us test and examine our ways,
     and return to the LORD.
41 Let us lift up our hearts as well as our hands
     to God in heaven.
42 We have transgressed and rebelled,
     and you have not forgiven.

43 You have wrapped yourself with anger and
         pursued us,
     killing without pity;
44 you have wrapped yourself with a
         cloud
     so that no prayer can pass through.

a Syr Tg: Heb LORD, *we are not cut off*

45 You have made us filth and rubbish
   among the peoples.

46 All our enemies
   have opened their mouths against us;
47 panic and pitfall have come upon us,
   devastation and destruction.
48 My eyes flow with rivers of tears
   because of the destruction of my
   people.

49 My eyes will flow without ceasing,
   without respite,
50 until the LORD from heaven
   looks down and sees.
51 My eyes cause me grief
   at the fate of all the young women in my city.

52 Those who were my enemies without
   cause
   have hunted me like a bird;
53 they flung me alive into a pit
   and hurled stones on me;
54 water closed over my head;
   I said, "I am lost."

55 I called on your name, O LORD,
   from the depths of the pit;
56 you heard my plea, "Do not close your ear
   to my cry for help, but give me relief!"
57 You came near when I called on you;
   you said, "Do not fear!"

58 You have taken up my cause, O Lord,
   you have redeemed my life.
59 You have seen the wrong done to me,
   O LORD;
   judge my cause.
60 You have seen all their malice,
   all their plots against me.

61 You have heard their taunts, O LORD,
   all their plots against me.
62 The whispers and murmurs of my assailants
   are against me all day long.
63 Whether they sit or rise—see,
   I am the object of their taunt-songs.

64 Pay them back for their deeds, O LORD,
   according to the work of their hands!
65 Give them anguish of heart;
   your curse be on them!
66 Pursue them in anger and destroy them
   from under the LORD's heavens.

4 **The Punishment of Zion**
How the gold has grown dim,
   how the pure gold is changed!
The sacred stones lie scattered
   at the head of every street.

2 The precious children of Zion,
   worth their weight in fine gold—
how they are reckoned as earthen pots,
   the work of a potter's hands!

Growing Through Loss · Lamentations 3:48

One purpose of the poems in Lamentations was to help the ancient Israelites heal from the horrible tragedy of their loss. The poems accomplish this in three ways. First, in describing Israel's present loss and tragedy, they acknowledge that grief and mourning are needed. Second, they challenge Israel to look at its past, both to accept responsibility for its sin and to remember its great blessings from God. Third, they encourage Israel to have hope for the future. In image after image, Israel is assured that the door to God's mercy is still open, in spite of great pain and loss.

When have you felt the grief of loss in your life? These same principles of healing apply. First, it's okay to cry. **Lamentations 3:48** says, "My eyes flow with rivers of tears." Let yourself mourn, and surround yourself with friends and family who will comfort you. Second, remember the person you've lost, celebrating the good times and healing the hurtful memories. Finally, when the time is right, open yourself to the future. God's love is there for you, calling you to new life.

3 Even the jackals offer the breast
   and nurse their young,
 but my people has become cruel,
   like the ostriches in the wilderness.

4 The tongue of the infant sticks
   to the roof of its mouth for thirst;
 the children beg for food,
   but no one gives them anything.

5 Those who feasted on delicacies
   perish in the streets;
 those who were brought up in purple
   cling to ash heaps.

6 For the chastisement*a* of my people has been
     greater
   than the punishment*b* of Sodom,
 which was overthrown in a moment,
   though no hand was laid on it.*c*

7 Her princes were purer than snow,
   whiter than milk;
 their bodies were more ruddy than coral,
   their hair*c* like sapphire.*d*

8 Now their visage is blacker than soot;
   they are not recognized in the streets.
 Their skin has shriveled on their bones;
   it has become as dry as wood.

9 Happier were those pierced by the sword
   than those pierced by hunger,
 whose life drains away, deprived
   of the produce of the field.

10 The hands of compassionate women
    have boiled their own children;
  they became their food
    in the destruction of my people.

11 The LORD gave full vent to his wrath;
    he poured out his hot anger,
  and kindled a fire in Zion
    that consumed its foundations.

12 The kings of the earth did not believe,
    nor did any of the inhabitants of the world,
  that foe or enemy could enter
    the gates of Jerusalem.

13 It was for the sins of her prophets
    and the iniquities of her priests,
  who shed the blood of the righteous
    in the midst of her.

14 Blindly they wandered through the streets,
    so defiled with blood
  that no one was able
    to touch their garments.

15 "Away! Unclean!" people shouted at them;
    "Away! Away! Do not touch!"
  So they became fugitives and wanderers;
    it was said among the nations,
      "They shall stay here no longer."

16 The LORD himself has scattered them,
    he will regard them no more;
  no honor was shown to the priests,
    no favor to the elders.

17 Our eyes failed, ever watching
    vainly for help;
  we were watching eagerly
    for a nation that could not save.

18 They dogged our steps
    so that we could not walk in our streets;
  our end drew near; our days were numbered;
    for our end had come.

19 Our pursuers were swifter
    than the eagles in the heavens;
  they chased us on the mountains,
    they lay in wait for us in the wilderness.

20 The LORD's anointed, the breath of our life,
    was taken in their pits—
  the one of whom we said, "Under his shadow
    we shall live among the nations."

21 Rejoice and be glad, O daughter Edom,
    you that live in the land of Uz;
  but to you also the cup shall pass;
    you shall become drunk and strip yourself
      bare.

22 The punishment of your iniquity, O daughter
      Zion, is accomplished,
  he will keep you in exile no longer;

a Or *iniquity* *b* Or *sin* *c* Meaning of Heb uncertain *d* Or *lapis lazuli*

CONNECT IT!

Invisible Children: Healing the Wounds of War
Lamentations 5

Uganda is an African country torn by years of war. The description of the plight of the Israelites in **Lamentations 5** could easily be the words of those who have suffered at the hand of the Lord's Resistance Army (LRA) in Uganda. A complicated regional conflict with no easy solutions has left millions of victims in its wake—widows, orphans, child soldiers, and others who desperately need help in dealing with the impact of war in their lives. Three young filmmakers from Southern California visited Uganda in 2003 and recorded the stories they saw. As the film they created spread, Invisible Children was formed to bring healing to the victims of war in Uganda. Focusing on long-term development, education, and creative economic opportunities, Invisible Children (**invisiblechildren.com**) is partnering with Ugandans to create hope and a future for this war-torn region.

but your iniquity, O daughter Edom, he will
    punish,
he will uncover your sins.

A Plea for Mercy

5 Remember, O LORD, what has
    befallen us;
  look, and see our disgrace!
2 Our inheritance has been turned over to
    strangers,
  our homes to aliens.
3 We have become orphans, fatherless;
  our mothers are like widows.
4 We must pay for the water we drink;
  the wood we get must be bought.
5 With a yoke*a* on our necks we are hard driven;
  we are weary, we are given no rest.
6 We have made a pact with*b* Egypt and Assyria,
  to get enough bread.
7 Our ancestors sinned; they are no more,
  and we bear their iniquities.
8 Slaves rule over us;
  there is no one to deliver us from their
    hand.
9 We get our bread at the peril of our lives,
  because of the sword in the wilderness.
10 Our skin is black as an oven
  from the scorching heat of famine.

11 Women are raped in Zion,
  virgins in the towns of Judah.
12 Princes are hung up by their hands;
  no respect is shown to the elders.
13 Young men are compelled to grind,
  and boys stagger under loads of wood.
14 The old men have left the city gate,
  the young men their music.
15 The joy of our hearts has ceased;
  our dancing has been turned to mourning.
16 The crown has fallen from our head;
  woe to us, for we have sinned!
17 Because of this our hearts are sick,
  because of these things our eyes have
    grown dim:
18 because of Mount Zion, which lies desolate;
  jackals prowl over it.

19 But you, O LORD, reign forever;
  your throne endures to all generations.
20 Why have you forgotten us completely?
  Why have you forsaken us these many
    days?
21 Restore us to yourself, O LORD, that we may
    be restored;
  renew our days as of old—
22 unless you have utterly rejected us,
  and are angry with us beyond measure.

a Symmachus: Heb lacks *With a yoke* *b* Heb *have given the hand to*

Ezekiel

Four-headed creatures, a strange craft made up of wheels within wheels, a being of light that appears out of the sky—the first chapter of Ezekiel sounds like a preview for a science-fiction movie! Ezekiel, more than any other prophet, proclaims astonishing visions that are filled with bizarre images, symbols, and creatures.

IN DEPTH

Ezekiel lived during the last days of Judah, just before it was destroyed by the Babylonians. He was probably among an early group of captives sent into exile in Babylon before Judah and the city of Jerusalem were demolished in 587 B.C. (see the chart "Prophets and Kings (1050–571 B.C.)," p. 680). He began his prophetic ministry in 593 B.C., when he received a fantastic vision and call, described in Ezekiel 1–3. We also know that Ezekiel came from a priestly family (Ezekiel 1:3) and that he was married (Ezekiel 24:16–18).

Ezekiel preached many of the traditional themes of the other prophets, but in a unique way. Note these examples:

• **The Lord's presence in the temple.** Possibly because of Ezekiel's priestly heritage, he gave God's presence—or lack of presence—in the temple a more central role than did the other prophets. In his vision, the temple will be the center of the new Israel, and a great priest will rule instead of a king.

• **The awesomeness of God.** For Ezekiel, the Lord did not appear as a parent or someone to be argued with; rather, God was awesome and overpowering, beyond human explanations. Ezekiel often spoke of God's glory and holiness.

• **Personal responsibility.** Ezekiel did not condemn the previous generation for the destruction of Judah, but preached that every generation is responsible for its own acts. Individuals can direct their own lives according to God's will.

• **Apocalyptic prophecy.** Some of Ezekiel's prophecies take the form of symbolic images. The images are so mysterious they require special explanation by heavenly beings. The books of Daniel and Revelation continue this type of writing, which is called apocalyptic literature.

(see the chart "Prophets and Kings (1050–571 B.C.)," p. 680)

QUICK FACTS

• **Dates Covered:** Between 593 and 571 B.C.

• **Authors:** Ezekiel, and the scribes who recorded his words and actions

• **Themes:** God's glory, redemption, and restoration even during times of God's discipline

AT A GLANCE

• **Ezekiel 1–3** Ezekiel's call and vision of God's glory

• **Ezekiel 4–24** Visions and prophecies about Jerusalem

• **Ezekiel 25–32** Oracles against foreign nations

• **Ezekiel 33–39** Oracles of the restoration of Judah and Jerusalem

• **Ezekiel 40–48** Visions of a new temple and restored community

The Vision of the Chariot

1 In the thirtieth year, in the fourth month, on the fifth day of the month, as I was among the exiles by the river Chebar, the heavens were opened, and I saw visions of God. [2]On the fifth day of the month (it was the fifth year of the exile of King Jehoiachin), [3]the word of the LORD came to the priest Ezekiel son of Buzi, in the land of the Chaldeans by the river Chebar; and the hand of the LORD was on him there.

4 As I looked, a stormy wind came out of the north: a great cloud with brightness around it and fire flashing forth continually, and in the middle of the fire, something like gleaming amber. [5]In the middle of it was something like four living creatures. This was their appearance: they were of human form. [6]Each had four faces, and each of them had four wings. [7]Their legs were straight, and the soles of their feet were like the sole of a calf's foot; and they sparkled like burnished bronze. [8]Under their wings on their four sides they had human hands. And the four had their faces and their wings thus: [9]their wings touched one another; each of them moved straight ahead, without turning as they moved. [10]As for the appearance of their faces: the four had the face of a human being, the face of a lion on the right side, the face of an ox on the left side, and the face of an eagle; [11]such were their faces. Their wings were spread out above; each creature had two wings, each of which touched the wing of another, while two covered their bodies. [12]Each moved straight ahead; wherever the spirit would go, they went, without turning as they went. [13]In the middle of[a] the living creatures there was something that looked like burning coals of fire, like torches moving to and fro among the living creatures; the fire was bright, and lightning issued from the fire. [14]The living creatures darted to and fro, like a flash of lightning.

15 As I looked at the living creatures, I saw a wheel on the earth beside the living creatures, one for each of the four of them.[b] [16]As for the appearance of the wheels and their construction: their appearance was like the gleaming of beryl; and the four had the same form, their construction being something like a wheel within a wheel. [17]When they moved, they moved in any of the four directions without veering as they moved. [18]Their rims were tall and awesome, for the rims of all four were full of eyes all around. [19]When the living creatures moved, the wheels moved beside them; and when the living creatures rose from the earth, the wheels rose. [20]Wherever the spirit would go, they went, and the wheels rose along with them; for the spirit of the living creatures was in the wheels. [21]When they moved, the others moved; when they stopped, the others stopped; and when they rose from the earth, the wheels rose along with them; for the spirit of the living creatures was in the wheels.

22 Over the heads of the living creatures there was something like a dome, shining like crystal,[c] spread

Introducing . . . Ezekiel • Ezekiel 1–3

Ezekiel's Hebrew name means "God strengthens." He was a complex person. Priest and prophet, poet and teacher, he was tender one moment and angry the next. He experienced God in mysterious ways, often through visions that greatly influenced his life and prophetic ministry.

Ezekiel's vision of creatures from heaven (Ezekiel 1-3) was the basis for his call and ministry as a prophet. His vision of the defilement of the temple (Ezekiel 8-11) was a major turning point in his faith. He, along with most of the Israelites, believed that God's glory resided in the temple, and that nothing could ever change that. The vision revealed corruption in Jerusalem and that the glory of God had left the temple and had come to Babylon. His vision of dry bones coming to life (Ezekiel 37) helped him understand that God would breathe new life into Israel. His final visions of a new temple (Ezekiel 40; 43; 47) told him that God would restore Jerusalem and the temple.

Besides having symbolic visions, Ezekiel also performed many dramatic, symbolic actions (see "Live It: Street Theater," near Ezekiel 5). These were designed to catch people's attention and communicate God's message.

a Gk OL: Heb *And the appearance of* **b** Heb *of their faces* **c** Gk: Heb *like the awesome crystal*

out above their heads. ²³Under the dome their wings were stretched out straight, one toward another; and each of the creatures had two wings covering its body. ²⁴When they moved, I heard the sound of their wings like the sound of mighty waters, like the thunder of the Almighty,ᵃ a sound of tumult like the sound of an army; when they stopped, they let down their wings. ²⁵And there came a voice from above the dome over their heads; when they stopped, they let down their wings.

26 And above the dome over their heads there was something like a throne, in appearance like sapphire;ᵇ and seated above the likeness of a throne was something that seemed like a human form. ²⁷Upward from what appeared like the loins I saw something like gleaming amber, something that looked like fire enclosed all around; and downward from what looked like the loins I saw something that looked like fire, and there was a splendor all around. ²⁸Like the bow in a cloud on a rainy day, such was the appearance of the splendor all around. This was the appearance of the likeness of the glory of the Lord.

When I saw it, I fell on my face, and I heard the voice of someone speaking.

The Vision of the Scroll

2 He said to me: O mortal,ᶜ stand up on your feet, and I will speak with you. ²And when he spoke to me, a spirit entered into me and set me on my feet; and I heard him speaking to me. ³He said to me, Mortal, I am sending you to the people of Israel, to a nationᵈ of rebels who have rebelled against me; they and their ancestors have transgressed against me to this very day. ⁴The descendants are impudent and stubborn. I am sending you to them, and you shall say to them, "Thus says the Lord God." ⁵Whether they hear or refuse to hear (for they are a rebellious house), they shall know that there has been a prophet among them. ⁶And you, O mortal, do not be afraid of them, and do not be afraid of their words, though briers and thorns surround you and you live among scorpions; do not be afraid of their words, and do not be dismayed at their looks, for they are a rebellious house. ⁷You shall speak my words to them, whether they hear or refuse to hear; for they are a rebellious house.

8 But you, mortal, hear what I say to you; do not be rebellious like that rebellious house; open your mouth and eat what I give you. ⁹I looked, and a hand was stretched out to me, and a written scroll was in

LIVE IT!

Just Eat It!
Ezekiel 2:1–3:11

God gave Ezekiel words to eat. WHAT? The image of Ezekiel eating a scroll is an odd one (Ezekiel 3:1-3). But even Jesus compared the Word of God to food in **Matthew 4:4** when he said, "One does not live by bread alone, but by every word that comes from the mouth of God."

God nourished Ezekiel, so that Ezekiel could carry out his calling, and **Ezekiel 3:3** says the scroll was sweet. God gives us the Word as nourishment as well, to help us carry out our calling. The Word of God is good for you!

• How are you relying on God's Word to sustain you?

it. ¹⁰He spread it before me; it had writing on the front and on the back, and written on it were words of lamentation and mourning and woe.

3 He said to me, O mortal, eat what is offered to you; eat this scroll, and go, speak to the house of Israel. ²So I opened my mouth, and he gave me the scroll to eat. ³He said to me, Mortal, eat this scroll that I give you and fill your stomach with it. Then I ate it; and in my mouth it was as sweet as honey.

4 He said to me: Mortal, go to the house of Israel and speak my very words to them. ⁵For you are not sent to a people of obscure speech and difficult language, but to the house of Israel— ⁶not to many peoples of obscure speech and difficult language, whose words you cannot understand. Surely, if I sent you to them, they would listen to you. ⁷But the house of Israel will not listen to you, for they are not willing to listen to me; because all the house of Israel have a hard forehead and a stubborn heart. ⁸See, I have made your face hard against their faces, and your forehead hard against their foreheads. ⁹Like the hardest stone, harder than flint, I have made your forehead; do not fear them or be dismayed at their looks, for they are a rebellious house. ¹⁰He said to me: Mortal, all my words that I shall speak to you receive in your heart and hear with your ears; ¹¹then go to the exiles, to

ᵃ Traditional rendering of Heb *Shaddai* ᵇ Or *lapis lazuli* ᶜ Or *son of man*; Heb *ben adam* (and so throughout the book when Ezekiel is addressed)
ᵈ Syr: Heb *to nations*

your people, and speak to them. Say to them, "Thus says the Lord GOD"; whether they hear or refuse to hear.

Ezekiel at the River Chebar

12 Then the spirit lifted me up, and as the glory of the LORD rose[a] from its place, I heard behind me the sound of loud rumbling; [13]it was the sound of the wings of the living creatures brushing against one another, and the sound of the wheels beside them, that sounded like a loud rumbling. [14]The spirit lifted me up and bore me away; I went in bitterness in the heat of my spirit, the hand of the LORD being strong upon me. [15]I came to the exiles at Tel-abib, who lived by the river Chebar.[b] And I sat there among them, stunned, for seven days.

16 At the end of seven days, the word of the LORD came to me: [17]Mortal, I have made you a sentinel for the house of Israel; whenever you hear a word from my mouth, you shall give them warning from me. [18]If I say to the wicked, "You shall surely die," and you give them no warning, or speak to warn the wicked from their wicked way, in order to save their life, those wicked persons shall die for their iniquity; but their blood I will require at your hand. [19]But if you warn the wicked, and they do not turn from their wickedness, or from their wicked way, they shall die for their iniquity; but you will have saved your life. [20]Again, if the righteous turn from their righteousness and commit iniquity, and I lay a stumbling block before them, they shall die; because you have not warned them, they shall die for

their sin, and their righteous deeds that they have done shall not be remembered; but their blood I will require at your hand. [21]If, however, you warn the righteous not to sin, and they do not sin, they shall surely live, because they took warning; and you will have saved your life.

Ezekiel Isolated and Silenced

22 Then the hand of the LORD was upon me there; and he said to me, Rise up, go out into the valley, and there I will speak with you. [23]So I rose up and went out into the valley; and the glory of the LORD stood there, like the glory that I had seen by the river Chebar; and I fell on my face. [24]The spirit entered into me, and set me on my feet; and he spoke with me and said to me: Go, shut yourself inside your house. [25]As for you, mortal, cords shall be placed on you, and you shall be bound with them, so that you cannot go out among the people; [26]and I will make your tongue cling to the roof of your mouth, so that you shall be speechless and unable to reprove them; for they are a rebellious house. [27]But when I speak with you, I will open your mouth, and you shall say to them, "Thus says the Lord GOD"; let those who will hear, hear; and let those who refuse to hear, refuse; for they are a rebellious house.

The Siege of Jerusalem Portrayed

And you, O mortal, take a brick and set it before you. On it portray a city, Jerusalem; [2]and put siegeworks against it, and build a siege wall

---

Shack-a-thon: Homeless for a Night · Ezekiel 3:17

Ezekiel was called as a prophet to speak the words of God to the Israelites. Ezekiel 3:17 says when he heard a word from the mouth of God, he was to give it as a warning to the people. Our call is somewhat different, but God still asks us to take the message of God to our communities and the world.

Sometimes that is a message of love and forgiveness, sometimes one challenging others to take a stand for what is right. A shack-a-thon is an event used by young people across the country to get people's attention and challenge them to face the issues of homelessness. It can take different forms and may be associated with a larger organization such as Habitat for Humanity, but a shack-a-thon is basically a gathering of people who create a "home" out of cardboard, trash, or other materials and sleep in it for a night or set period of time. The purpose is to remind the community of the plight of the homeless and to raise money to meet the needs of people in this situation. You can learn more about a shack-a-thon at habitat.org/youthprograms.

---

a Cn: Heb and blessed be the glory of the LORD b Two Mss Syr: Heb Chebar, and to where they lived. Another reading is Chebar, and I sat where they sat

Street Theater
Ezekiel 3:22–5:4

Ezekiel used some dramatic tactics to get the attention of the Israelites and make a point everyone could understand. His "street theater" in these chapters was the result of God working through him to get people's attention before the fall of Jerusalem in 587 B.C.

His speechlessness (Ezekiel 3:22-27) was a sign that the people were rebellious and unwilling to hear God's word. He lay on his left side for days and then his right (Ezekiel 4:4-5), signifying the number of years that Israel (left) and then Judah (right) would be in exile. He ate small amounts of food cooked on dung (Ezekiel 4:10-15) as a sign of the shortage of food during the siege of the city.

We can learn from Ezekiel's creative ways of communicating. Sometimes it takes something out of the ordinary to draw people's attention to God's truth and move them to action in changing a society that violates human rights.

- What does your church do to create awareness and move people to change their ways?
- What creative things can you do to share God's truth?

the punishment of the house of Israel. [6]When you have completed these, you shall lie down a second time, but on your right side, and bear the punishment of the house of Judah; forty days I assign you, one day for each year. [7]You shall set your face toward the siege of Jerusalem, and with your arm bared you shall prophesy against it. [8]See, I am putting cords on you so that you cannot turn from one side to the other until you have completed the days of your siege.

9 And you, take wheat and barley, beans and lentils, millet and spelt; put them into one vessel, and make bread for yourself. During the number of days that you lie on your side, three hundred ninety days, you shall eat it. [10]The food that you eat shall be twenty shekels a day by weight; at fixed times you shall eat it. [11]And you shall drink water by measure, one-sixth of a hin; at fixed times you shall drink. [12]You shall eat it as a barley-cake, baking it in their sight on human dung. [13]The LORD said, "Thus shall the people of Israel eat their bread, unclean, among the nations to which I will drive them." [14]Then I said, "Ah Lord GOD! I have never defiled myself; from my youth up until now I have never eaten what died of itself or was torn by animals, nor has carrion flesh come into my mouth." [15]Then he said to me, "See, I will let you have cow's dung instead of human dung, on which you may prepare your bread."

16 Then he said to me, Mortal, I am going to break the staff of bread in Jerusalem; they shall eat bread by weight and with fearfulness; and they shall drink water by measure and in dismay. [17]Lacking bread and water, they will look at one another in dismay, and waste away under their punishment.

against it, and cast up a ramp against it; set camps also against it, and plant battering rams against it all around. [3]Then take an iron plate and place it as an iron wall between you and the city; set your face toward it, and let it be in a state of siege, and press the siege against it. This is a sign for the house of Israel.

4 Then lie on your left side, and place the punishment of the house of Israel upon it; you shall bear their punishment for the number of the days that you lie there. [5]For I assign to you a number of days, three hundred ninety days, equal to the number of the years of their punishment; and so you shall bear

A Sword against Jerusalem

5 And you, O mortal, take a sharp sword; use it as a barber's razor and run it over your head and your beard; then take balances for weighing, and divide the hair. [2]One third of the hair you shall burn in the fire inside the city, when the days of the siege are completed; one third you shall take and strike with the sword all around the city;[a] and one third you shall scatter to the wind, and I will unsheathe the sword after them. [3]Then you shall take from these a small number, and bind them in the skirts of your robe. [4]From these, again, you shall take some, throw them into the fire and burn them up; from there a fire will come out against all the house of Israel.

5 Thus says the Lord God: This is Jerusalem; I have set her in the center of the nations, with countries all around her. [6]But she has rebelled against my ordinances and my statutes, becoming more wicked than the nations and the countries all around her, rejecting my ordinances and not following my statutes. [7]Therefore thus says the Lord God: Because you are more turbulent than the nations that are all around you, and have not followed my statutes or kept my ordinances, but have acted according to the ordinances of the nations that are all around you; [8]therefore thus says the Lord God: I, I myself, am coming against you; I will execute judgments among you in the sight of the nations. [9]And because of all your abominations, I will do to you what I have never yet done, and the like of which I will never do again. [10]Surely, parents shall eat their children in your midst, and children shall eat their parents; I will execute judgments on you, and any of you who survive I will scatter to every wind. [11]Therefore, as I live, says the Lord God, surely, because you have defiled my sanctuary with all your detestable things and with all your abominations—therefore I will cut you down;[b] my eye will not spare, and I will have no pity. [12]One third of you shall die of pestilence or be consumed by famine among you; one third shall fall by the sword around you; and one third I will scatter to every wind and will unsheathe the sword after them.

13 My anger shall spend itself, and I will vent my fury on them and satisfy myself; and they shall know that I, the Lord, have spoken in my jealousy, when I spend my fury on them. [14]Moreover I will make you a desolation and an object of mocking among the nations around you, in the sight of all that pass by. [15]You shall be[c] a mockery and a taunt, a warning and a horror, to the nations around you, when I execute judgments on you in anger and fury, and with furious punishments—I, the Lord, have spo-

ken— [16]when I loose against you[d] my deadly arrows of famine, arrows for destruction, which I will let loose to destroy you, and when I bring more and more famine upon you, and break your staff of bread. [17]I will send famine and wild animals against you, and they will rob you of your children; pestilence and bloodshed shall pass through you; and I will bring the sword upon you. I, the Lord, have spoken.

Judgment on Idolatrous Israel

6 The word of the Lord came to me: [2]O mortal, set your face toward the mountains of Israel, and prophesy against them, [3]and say, You mountains of Israel, hear the word of the Lord God! Thus says the Lord God to the mountains and the hills, to the ravines and the valleys: I, I myself will bring a sword upon you, and I will destroy your high places. [4]Your altars shall become desolate, and your incense stands shall be broken; and I will throw down your slain in front of your idols. [5]I will lay the corpses of the people of Israel in front of their idols; and I will scatter your bones around your altars. [6]Wherever you live, your towns shall be waste and your high places ruined, so that your altars will be waste and ruined,[e] your idols broken and destroyed, your incense stands cut down, and your works wiped out. [7]The slain shall fall in your midst; then you shall know that I am the Lord.

8 But I will spare some. Some of you shall escape the sword among the nations and be scattered through the countries. [9]Those of you who escape shall remember me among the nations where they are carried captive, how I was crushed by their wanton heart that turned away from me, and their wanton eyes that turned after their idols. Then they will be loathsome in their own sight for the evils that they have committed, for all their abominations. [10]And they shall know that I am the Lord; I did not threaten in vain to bring this disaster upon them.

11 Thus says the Lord God: Clap your hands and stamp your foot, and say, Alas for all the vile abominations of the house of Israel! For they shall fall by the sword, by famine, and by pestilence. [12]Those far off shall die of pestilence; those nearby shall fall by the sword; and any who are left and are spared shall die of famine. Thus I will spend my fury upon them. [13]And you shall know that I am the Lord, when their slain lie among their idols around their

---

a Heb it   b Another reading is *I will withdraw*   c Gk Syr Vg Tg: Heb *It shall be*   d Heb *them*   e Syr Vg Tg: Heb *and be made guilty*

altars, on every high hill, on all the mountain tops, under every green tree, and under every leafy oak, wherever they offered pleasing odor to all their idols. ¹⁴I will stretch out my hand against them, and make the land desolate and waste, throughout all their settlements, from the wilderness to Riblah.^a Then they shall know that I am the LORD.

Impending Disaster

7 The word of the LORD came to me: ²You, O mortal, thus says the Lord GOD to the land of Israel:

An end! The end has come
  upon the four corners of the land.
³ Now the end is upon you,
  I will let loose my anger upon you;
  I will judge you according to your ways,
    I will punish you for all your abominations.
⁴ My eye will not spare you, I will have no pity.
  I will punish you for your ways,
    while your abominations are among you.
Then you shall know that I am the LORD.
  5 Thus says the Lord GOD:
Disaster after disaster! See, it comes.
⁶ An end has come, the end has come.
It has awakened against you; see, it comes!
⁷ Your doom^b has come to you,
  O inhabitant of the land.
The time has come, the day is near—
    of tumult, not of reveling on the
      mountains.
⁸ Soon now I will pour out my wrath upon you;
  I will spend my anger against you.
I will judge you according to your ways,
  and punish you for all your abominations.
⁹ My eye will not spare; I will have no pity.
  I will punish you according to your ways,
    while your abominations are among you.
Then you shall know that it is I the LORD who strike.
¹⁰ See, the day! See, it comes!
  Your doom^b has gone out.
The rod has blossomed, pride has budded.
¹¹ Violence has grown into a rod of
    wickedness.
None of them shall remain,
  not their abundance, not their wealth;
  no pre-eminence among them.^b
¹² The time has come, the day draws near;
  let not the buyer rejoice, nor the seller
    mourn,

for wrath is upon all their multitude.
¹³For the sellers shall not return to what has been sold as long as they remain alive. For the vision concerns all their multitude; it shall not be revoked. Because of their iniquity, they cannot maintain their lives.^b
¹⁴ They have blown the horn and made
    everything ready;
  but no one goes to battle,
  for my wrath is upon all their multitude.
¹⁵ The sword is outside, pestilence and famine
    are inside;
  those in the field die by the sword;
  those in the city—famine and pestilence
    devour them.
¹⁶ If any survivors escape,
  they shall be found on the mountains
  like doves of the valleys,
all of them moaning over their iniquity.
¹⁷ All hands shall grow feeble,
  all knees turn to water.
¹⁸ They shall put on sackcloth,
  horror shall cover them.
Shame shall be on all faces,
  baldness on all their heads.
¹⁹ They shall fling their silver into the streets,
  their gold shall be treated as unclean.
Their silver and gold cannot save them on the day of the wrath of the LORD. They shall not satisfy their hunger or fill their stomachs with it. For it was the stumbling block of their iniquity. ²⁰From their^c beautiful ornament, in which they took pride, they made their abominable images, their detestable things; therefore I will make of it an unclean thing to them.
²¹ I will hand it over to strangers as booty,
  to the wicked of the earth as plunder;
  they shall profane it.
²² I will avert my face from them,
  so that they may profane my treasured^d
    place;
the violent shall enter it,
  they shall profane it.
²³ Make a chain!^b
For the land is full of bloody crimes;
  the city is full of violence.
²⁴ I will bring the worst of the nations
  to take possession of their houses.
I will put an end to the arrogance of the
    strong,

---

a Another reading is *Diblah*   **b** Meaning of Heb uncertain   **c** Syr Symmachus: Heb *its*   **d** Or *secret*

and their holy places shall be profaned.
25 When anguish comes, they will seek peace,
but there shall be none. .
26 Disaster comes upon disaster,
rumor follows rumor;
they shall keep seeking a vision from the
prophet;
instruction shall perish from the priest,
and counsel from the elders.
27 The king shall mourn,
the prince shall be wrapped in despair,
and the hands of the people of the land
shall tremble.
According to their way I will deal with them;
according to their own judgments I will
judge them.
And they shall know that I am the LORD.

8 Abominations in the Temple

In the sixth year, in the sixth month, on
the fifth day of the month, as I sat in my
house, with the elders of Judah sitting before me,
the hand of the Lord GOD fell upon me there. [2]I
looked, and there was a figure that looked like a
human being;[a] below what appeared to be its loins
it was fire, and above the loins it was like the appearance of brightness, like gleaming amber. [3]It stretched
out the form of a hand, and took me by a lock of my
head; and the spirit lifted me up between earth and
heaven, and brought me in visions of God to Jerusalem, to the entrance of the gateway of the inner
court that faces north, to the seat of the image of
jealousy, which provokes to jealousy. [4]And the glory
of the God of Israel was there, like the vision that I
had seen in the valley.

5 Then God[b] said to me, "O mortal, lift up your
eyes now in the direction of the north." So I lifted
up my eyes toward the north, and there, north of
the altar gate, in the entrance, was this image of
jealousy. [6]He said to me, "Mortal, do you see what
they are doing, the great abominations that the
house of Israel are committing here, to drive me far
from my sanctuary? Yet you will see still greater
abominations."

7 And he brought me to the entrance of the court;
I looked, and there was a hole in the wall. [8]Then he
said to me, "Mortal, dig through the wall"; and when
I dug through the wall, there was an entrance. [9]He
said to me, "Go in, and see the vile abominations
that they are committing here." [10]So I went in and

looked; there, portrayed on the wall all around, were
all kinds of creeping things, and loathsome animals,
and all the idols of the house of Israel. [11]Before them
stood seventy of the elders of the house of Israel,
with Jaazaniah son of Shaphan standing among
them. Each had his censer in his hand, and the fragrant cloud of incense was ascending. [12]Then he
said to me, "Mortal, have you seen what the elders
of the house of Israel are doing in the dark, each in
his room of images? For they say, 'The LORD does
not see us, the LORD has forsaken the land.' " [13]He
said also to me, "You will see still greater abominations that they are committing."

14 Then he brought me to the entrance of the
north gate of the house of the LORD; women were
sitting there weeping for Tammuz. [15]Then he said
to me, "Have you seen this, O mortal? You will see
still greater abominations than these."

16 And he brought me into the inner court of
the house of the LORD; there, at the entrance
of the temple of the LORD, between the porch and
the altar, were about twenty-five men, with their
backs to the temple of the LORD, and their faces
toward the east, prostrating themselves to the sun
toward the east. [17]Then he said to me, "Have you
seen this, O mortal? Is it not bad enough that the
house of Judah commits the abominations done
here? Must they fill the land with violence, and
provoke my anger still further? See, they are putting the branch to their nose! [18]Therefore I will
act in wrath; my eye will not spare, nor will I have
pity; and though they cry in my hearing with a loud
voice, I will not listen to them."

9 The Slaughter of the Idolaters

Then he cried in my hearing with a loud
voice, saying, "Draw near, you execution-
ers of the city, each with his destroying weapon in
his hand." [2]And six men came from the direction of
the upper gate, which faces north, each with his
weapon for slaughter in his hand; among them was
a man clothed in linen, with a writing case at his
side. They went in and stood beside the bronze altar.

3 Now the glory of the God of Israel had gone up
from the cherub on which it rested to the threshold
of the house. The LORD called to the man clothed
in linen, who had the writing case at his side; [4]and
said to him, "Go through the city, through Jerusalem,
and put a mark on the foreheads of those who sigh
and groan over all the abominations that are com-

a Gk: Heb *like fire*   b Heb *he*

mitted in it." ⁵To the others he said in my hearing, "Pass through the city after him, and kill; your eye shall not spare, and you shall show no pity. ⁶Cut down old men, young men and young women, little children and women, but touch no one who has the mark. And begin at my sanctuary." So they began with the elders who were in front of the house. ⁷Then he said to them, "Defile the house, and fill the courts with the slain. Go!" So they went out and killed in the city. ⁸While they were killing, and I was left alone, I fell prostrate on my face and cried out, "Ah Lord GOD! will you destroy all who remain of Israel as you pour out your wrath upon Jerusalem?" ⁹He said to me, "The guilt of the house of Israel and Judah is exceedingly great; the land is full of bloodshed and the city full of perversity; for they say, 'The LORD has forsaken the land, and the LORD does not see.' ¹⁰As for me, my eye will not spare, nor will I have pity, but I will bring down their deeds upon their heads."

11 Then the man clothed in linen, with the writing case at his side, brought back word, saying, "I have done as you commanded me."

God's Glory Leaves Jerusalem

10 Then I looked, and above the dome that was over the heads of the cherubim there appeared above them something like a sapphire,ᵃ in form resembling a throne. ²He said to the man clothed in linen, "Go within the wheelwork underneath the cherubim; fill your hands with burning coals from among the cherubim, and scatter them over the city." He went in as I looked on. ³Now the cherubim were standing on the south side of the house when the man went in; and a cloud filled the inner court. ⁴Then the glory of the LORD rose up from the cherub to the threshold of the house; the house was filled with the cloud, and the court was full of the brightness of the glory of the LORD. ⁵The sound of the wings of the cherubim was heard as far as the outer court, like the voice of God Almightyᵇ when he speaks.

6 When he commanded the man clothed in linen, "Take fire from within the wheelwork, from among the cherubim," he went in and stood beside a wheel. ⁷And a cherub stretched out his hand from among the cherubim to the fire that was among the cherubim, took some of it and put it into the hands of the man clothed in linen, who took it and went out. ⁸The cherubim appeared to have the form of a human hand under their wings.

9 I looked, and there were four wheels beside the cherubim, one beside each cherub; and the appearance of the wheels was like gleaming beryl. ¹⁰And as for their appearance, the four looked alike, something like a wheel within a wheel. ¹¹When they moved, they moved in any of the four directions without veering as they moved; but in whatever direction the front wheel faced, the others followed without veering as they moved. ¹²Their entire body, their rims, their spokes, their wings, and the wheels—the wheels of the four of them—were full of eyes all around. ¹³As for the wheels, they were called in my hearing "the wheelwork." ¹⁴Each one had four faces: the first face was that of the cherub, the second face was that of a human being, the third that of a lion, and the fourth that of an eagle.

15 The cherubim rose up. These were the living creatures that I saw by the river Chebar. ¹⁶When the cherubim moved, the wheels moved beside them; and when the cherubim lifted up their wings to rise up from the earth, the wheels at their side did not veer. ¹⁷When they stopped, the others stopped, and when they rose up, the others rose up with them; for the spirit of the living creatures was in them.

18 Then the glory of the LORD went out from the threshold of the house and stopped above the cherubim. ¹⁹The cherubim lifted up their wings and rose up from the earth in my sight as they went out with the wheels beside them. They stopped at the entrance of the east gate of the house of the LORD; and the glory of the God of Israel was above them.

20 These were the living creatures that I saw underneath the God of Israel by the river Chebar; and I knew that they were cherubim. ²¹Each had four faces, each four wings, and underneath their wings something like human hands. ²²As for what their faces were like, they were the same faces whose appearance I had seen by the river Chebar. Each one moved straight ahead.

Judgment on Wicked Counselors

11 The spirit lifted me up and brought me to the east gate of the house of the LORD, which faces east. There, at the entrance of the gateway, were twenty-five men; among them I saw Jaazaniah son of Azzur, and Pelatiah son of Benaiah, officials of the people. ²He said to me, "Mortal, these are the men who devise iniquity and who give wicked counsel in this city; ³they say, 'The time is not near to build houses; this city is the pot, and we

---

ᵃ Or *lapis lazuli*   ᵇ Traditional rendering of Heb *El Shaddai* are the meat.' [4]Therefore prophesy against them; prophesy, O mortal."

5 Then the spirit of the LORD fell upon me, and he said to me, "Say, Thus says the LORD: This is what you think, O house of Israel; I know the things that come into your mind. [6]You have killed many in this city, and have filled its streets with the slain. [7]Therefore thus says the Lord GOD: The slain whom you have placed within it are the meat, and this city is the pot; but you shall be taken out of it. [8]You have feared the sword; and I will bring the sword upon you, says the Lord GOD. [9]I will take you out of it and give you over to the hands of foreigners, and execute judgments upon you. [10]You shall fall by the sword; I will judge you at the border of Israel. And you shall know that I am the LORD. [11]This city shall not be your pot, and you shall not be the meat inside it; I will judge you at the border of Israel. [12]Then you shall know that I am the LORD, whose statutes you have not followed, and whose ordinances you have not kept, but you have acted according to the ordinances of the nations that are around you."

13 Now, while I was prophesying, Pelatiah son of Benaiah died. Then I fell down on my face, cried with a loud voice, and said, "Ah Lord GOD! will you make a full end of the remnant of Israel?"

God Will Restore Israel

14 Then the word of the LORD came to me: [15]Mortal, your kinsfolk, your own kin, your fellow exiles,[a] the whole house of Israel, all of them, are those of whom the inhabitants of Jerusalem have said, "They have gone far from the LORD; to us this land is given for a possession." [16]Therefore say: Thus says the Lord GOD: Though I removed them far away among the nations, and though I scattered them among the countries, yet I have been a sanctuary to them for a little while[b] in the countries where they have gone. [17]Therefore say: Thus says the Lord GOD: I will gather you from the peoples, and assemble you out of the countries where you have been scattered, and I will give you the land of Israel. [18]When they come there, they will remove from it all its detestable things and all its abominations. [19]I will give them one[c] heart, and put a new spirit within them; I will remove the heart of stone from their flesh and give them a heart of flesh, [20]so that they may follow my statutes and keep my ordinances and obey them. Then they shall be my people, and I will be their God. [21]But as for those whose heart goes after their detestable things and their abominations,[d] I will bring their deeds upon their own heads, says the Lord GOD.

22 Then the cherubim lifted up their wings, with the wheels beside them; and the glory of the God of Israel was above them. [23]And the glory of the LORD ascended from the middle of the city, and stopped on the mountain east of the city. [24]The spirit lifted me up and brought me in a vision by the spirit of God into Chaldea, to the exiles. Then the vision that I had seen left me. [25]And I told the exiles all the things that the LORD had shown me.

Judah's Captivity Portrayed

12 The word of the LORD came to me: [2]Mortal, you are living in the midst of a rebellious house, who have eyes to see but do not see, who have ears to hear but do not hear; [3]for they are a rebellious house. Therefore, mortal, prepare for

PRAY IT!

Have a Heart! · Ezekiel 11:19–20

The Old Testament prophets spend a lot of time talking about people's hearts. That's probably because the ancient Israelites understood the heart as the center of intelligence, feelings, and human will. Jeremiah says the new covenant will be written on people's hearts (Jeremiah 31:33), and Ezekiel says God will take away their heart of stone and give them a heart of flesh (Ezekiel 11:19).

During your prayer time, reflect or journal on the following questions:

- What's the difference between having a heart of flesh and a cold heart of stone?
- Why would a natural heart, or heart of flesh, lead to obeying God (Ezekiel 11:20)?
- When does your heart feel natural and open to God's direction? When does it feel stony?
- Say a prayer asking God to give you a heart of flesh.

---

a Gk Syr: Heb *people of your kindred* b Or *to some extent* c Another reading is *a new* d Cn: Heb *And to the heart of their detestable things and their abominations their heart goes*

yourself an exile's baggage, and go into exile by day in their sight; you shall go like an exile from your place to another place in their sight. Perhaps they will understand, though they are a rebellious house. ⁴You shall bring out your baggage by day in their sight, as baggage for exile; and you shall go out yourself at evening in their sight, as those do who go into exile. ⁵Dig through the wall in their sight, and carry the baggage through it. ⁶In their sight you shall lift the baggage on your shoulder, and carry it out in the dark; you shall cover your face, so that you may not see the land; for I have made you a sign for the house of Israel.

7 I did just as I was commanded. I brought out my baggage by day, as baggage for exile, and in the evening I dug through the wall with my own hands; I brought it out in the dark, carrying it on my shoulder in their sight.

8 In the morning the word of the LORD came to me: ⁹Mortal, has not the house of Israel, the rebellious house, said to you, "What are you doing?" ¹⁰Say to them, "Thus says the Lord GOD: This oracle concerns the prince in Jerusalem and all the house of Israel in it." ¹¹Say, "I am a sign for you: as I have done, so shall it be done to them; they shall go into exile, into captivity." ¹²And the prince who is among them shall lift his baggage on his shoulder in the dark, and shall go out; he*ᵃ* shall dig through the wall and carry it through; he shall cover his face, so that he may not see the land with his eyes. ¹³I will spread my net over him, and he shall be caught in my snare; and I will bring him to Babylon, the land of the Chaldeans, yet he shall not see it; and he shall die there. ¹⁴I will scatter to every wind all who are around him, his helpers and all his troops; and I will unsheathe the sword behind them. ¹⁵And they shall know that I am the LORD, when I disperse them among the nations and scatter them through the countries. ¹⁶But I will let a few of them escape from the sword, from famine and pestilence, so that they may tell of all their abominations among the nations where they go; then they shall know that I am the LORD.

Judgment Not Postponed

17 The word of the LORD came to me: ¹⁸Mortal, eat your bread with quaking, and drink your water with trembling and with fearfulness; ¹⁹and say to the people of the land, Thus says the Lord GOD concerning the inhabitants of Jerusalem in the land

of Israel: They shall eat their bread with fearfulness, and drink their water in dismay, because their land shall be stripped of all it contains, on account of the violence of all those who live in it. ²⁰The inhabited cities shall be laid waste, and the land shall become a desolation; and you shall know that I am the LORD.

21 The word of the LORD came to me: ²²Mortal, what is this proverb of yours about the land of Israel, which says, "The days are prolonged, and every vision comes to nothing"? ²³Tell them therefore, "Thus says the Lord GOD: I will put an end to this proverb, and they shall use it no more as a proverb in Israel." But say to them, The days are near, and the fulfillment of every vision. ²⁴For there shall no longer be any false vision or flattering divination within the house of Israel. ²⁵But I the LORD will speak the word that I speak, and it will be fulfilled. It will no longer be delayed; but in your days, O rebellious house, I will speak the word and fulfill it, says the Lord GOD.

26 The word of the LORD came to me: ²⁷Mortal, the house of Israel is saying, "The vision that he sees is for many years ahead; he prophesies for distant times." ²⁸Therefore say to them, Thus says the Lord GOD: None of my words will be delayed any longer, but the word that I speak will be fulfilled, says the Lord GOD.

13 False Prophets Condemned

The word of the LORD came to me: ²Mortal, prophesy against the prophets of Israel who are prophesying; say to those who prophesy out of their own imagination: "Hear the word of the LORD!" ³Thus says the Lord GOD, Alas for the senseless prophets who follow their own spirit, and have seen nothing! ⁴Your prophets have been like jackals among ruins, O Israel. ⁵You have not gone up into the breaches, or repaired a wall for the house of Israel, so that it might stand in battle on the day of the LORD. ⁶They have envisioned falsehood and lying divination; they say, "Says the LORD," when the LORD has not sent them, and yet they wait for the fulfillment of their word! ⁷Have you not seen a false vision or uttered a lying divination, when you have said, "Says the LORD," even though I did not speak?

8 Therefore thus says the Lord GOD: Because you have uttered falsehood and envisioned lies, I am against you, says the Lord GOD. ⁹My hand will be against the prophets who see false visions and utter lying divinations; they shall not be in the council of

---

ᵃ Gk Syr: Heb *they*

my people, nor be enrolled in the register of the house of Israel, nor shall they enter the land of Israel; and you shall know that I am the Lord God. [10]Because, in truth, because they have misled my people, saying, "Peace," when there is no peace; and because, when the people build a wall, these prophets[a] smear whitewash on it. [11]Say to those who smear whitewash on it that it shall fall. There will be a deluge of rain,[b] great hailstones will fall, and a stormy wind will break out. [12]When the wall falls, will it not be said to you, "Where is the whitewash you smeared on it?" [13]Therefore thus says the Lord God: In my wrath I will make a stormy wind break out, and in my anger there shall be a deluge of rain, and hailstones in wrath to destroy it. [14]I will break down the wall that you have smeared with whitewash, and bring it to the ground, so that its foundation will be laid bare; when it falls, you shall perish within it; and you shall know that I am the Lord. [15]Thus I will spend my wrath upon the wall, and upon those who have smeared it with whitewash; and I will say to you, The wall is no more, nor those who smeared it— [16]the prophets of Israel who prophesied concerning Jerusalem and saw visions of peace for it, when there was no peace, says the Lord God.

17 As for you, mortal, set your face against the daughters of your people, who prophesy out of their own imagination; prophesy against them [18]and say, Thus says the Lord God: Woe to the women who sew bands on all wrists, and make veils for the heads of persons of every height, in the hunt for human lives! Will you hunt down lives among my people, and maintain your own lives? [19]You have profaned me among my people for handfuls of barley and for pieces of bread, putting to death persons who should not die and keeping alive persons who should not live, by your lies to my people, who listen to lies.

20 Therefore thus says the Lord God: I am against your bands with which you hunt lives;[c] I will tear them from your arms, and let the lives go free, the lives that you hunt down like birds. [21]I will tear off your veils, and save my people from your hands; they shall no longer be prey in your hands; and you shall know that I am the Lord. [22]Because you have disheartened the righteous falsely, although I have not disheartened them, and you have encouraged the wicked not to turn from their wicked way and save their lives; [23]therefore you

shall no longer see false visions or practice divination; I will save my people from your hand. Then you will know that I am the Lord.

14 God's Judgments Justified

Certain elders of Israel came to me and sat down before me. [2]And the word of the Lord came to me: [3]Mortal, these men have taken their idols into their hearts, and placed their iniquity as a stumbling block before them; shall I let myself be consulted by them? [4]Therefore speak to them, and say to them, Thus says the Lord God: Any of those of the house of Israel who take their idols into their hearts and place their iniquity as a stumbling block before them, and yet come to the prophet—I the Lord will answer those who come with the multitude of their idols, [5]in order that I may take hold of the hearts of the house of Israel, all of whom are estranged from me through their idols.

6 Therefore say to the house of Israel, Thus says the Lord God: Repent and turn away from your idols; and turn away your faces from all your abominations. [7]For any of those of the house of Israel, or of the aliens who reside in Israel, who separate themselves from me, taking their idols into their hearts and placing their iniquity as a stumbling block before them, and yet come to a prophet to inquire of me by him, I the Lord will answer them myself. [8]I will set my face against them; I will make them a sign and a byword and cut them off from the midst of my people; and you shall know that I am the Lord.

9 If a prophet is deceived and speaks a word, I, the Lord, have deceived that prophet, and I will stretch out my hand against him, and will destroy him from the midst of my people Israel. [10]And they shall bear their punishment—the punishment of the inquirer and the punishment of the prophet shall be the same— [11]so that the house of Israel may no longer go astray from me, nor defile themselves any more with all their transgressions. Then they shall be my people, and I will be their God, says the Lord God.

12 The word of the Lord came to me: [13]Mortal, when a land sins against me by acting faithlessly, and I stretch out my hand against it, and break its staff of bread and send famine upon it, and cut off from it human beings and animals, [14]even if Noah, Daniel,[d] and Job, these three, were in it, they would save only their own lives by their righteousness, says the

---

a Heb *they*   b Heb *rain and you*   c Gk Syr: Heb *lives for birds*   d Or, as otherwise read, *Danel*

Lord GOD. [15] If I send wild animals through the land to ravage it, so that it is made desolate, and no one may pass through because of the animals; [16] even if these three men were in it, as I live, says the Lord GOD, they would save neither sons nor daughters; they alone would be saved, but the land would be desolate. [17] Or if I bring a sword upon that land and say, "Let a sword pass through the land," and I cut off human beings and animals from it; [18] though these three men were in it, as I live, says the Lord GOD, they would save neither sons nor daughters, but they alone would be saved. [19] Or if I send a pestilence into that land, and pour out my wrath upon it with blood, to cut off humans and animals from it; [20] even if Noah, Daniel,[a] and Job were in it, as I live, says the Lord GOD, they would save neither son nor daughter; they would save only their own lives by their righteousness.

21 For thus says the Lord GOD: How much more when I send upon Jerusalem my four deadly acts of judgment, sword, famine, wild animals, and pestilence, to cut off humans and animals from it! [22] Yet, survivors shall be left in it, sons and daughters who will be brought out; they will come out to you. When you see their ways and their deeds, you will be consoled for the evil that I have brought upon Jerusalem, for all that I have brought upon it. [23] They shall console you, when you see their ways and their deeds; and you shall know that it was not without cause that I did all that I have done in it, says the Lord GOD.

The Useless Vine

15 The word of the LORD came to me: [2] O mortal, how does the wood of the vine surpass all other wood— the vine branch that is among the trees of the forest? [3] Is wood taken from it to make anything?

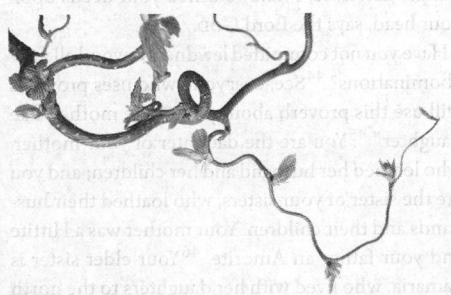

Does one take a peg from it on which to hang any object? [4] It is put in the fire for fuel; when the fire has consumed both ends of it and the middle of it is charred, is it useful for anything? [5] When it was whole it was used for nothing; how much less—when the fire has consumed it, and it is charred— can it ever be used for anything!

6 Therefore thus says the Lord GOD: Like the wood of the vine among the trees of the forest, which I have given to the fire for fuel, so I will give up the inhabitants of Jerusalem. [7] I will set my face against them; although they escape from the fire, the fire shall still consume them; and you shall know that I am the LORD, when I set my face against them. [8] And I will make the land desolate, because they have acted faithlessly, says the Lord GOD.

God's Faithless Bride

16 The word of the LORD came to me: [2] Mortal, make known to Jerusalem her abominations, [3] and say, Thus says the Lord GOD to Jerusalem: Your origin and your birth were in the land of the Canaanites; your father was an Amorite, and your mother a Hittite. [4] As for your birth, on the day you were born your navel cord was not cut, nor were you washed with water to cleanse you, nor rubbed with salt, nor wrapped in cloths. [5] No eye pitied you, to do any of these things for you out of compassion for you; but you were thrown out in the open field, for you were abhorred on the day you were born.

6 I passed by you, and saw you flailing about in your blood. As you lay in your blood, I said to you, "Live! [7] and grow up[b] like a plant of the field." You grew up and became tall and arrived at full womanhood;[c] your breasts were formed, and your hair had grown; yet you were naked and bare.

8 I passed by you again and looked on you; you were at the age for love. I spread the edge of my cloak over you, and covered your nakedness: I pledged myself to you and entered into a covenant with you, says the Lord GOD, and you became mine. [9] Then I bathed you with water and washed off the blood from you, and anointed you with oil. [10] I clothed you with embroidered cloth and with sandals of fine leather; I bound you in fine linen and covered you with rich fabric.[d] [11] I adorned you with ornaments: I put

---

a Or, as otherwise read, *Danel*   **b** Gk Syr: Heb *Live! I made you a myriad*   **c** Cn: Heb *ornament of ornaments*   **d** Meaning of Heb uncertain

bracelets on your arms, a chain on your neck, [12]a ring on your nose, earrings in your ears, and a beautiful crown upon your head. [13]You were adorned with gold and silver, while your clothing was of fine linen, rich fabric,[a] and embroidered cloth. You had choice flour and honey and oil for food. You grew exceedingly beautiful, fit to be a queen. [14]Your fame spread among the nations on account of your beauty, for it was perfect because of my splendor that I had bestowed on you, says the Lord GOD.

15 But you trusted in your beauty, and played the whore because of your fame, and lavished your whorings on any passer-by.[b] [16]You took some of your garments, and made for yourself colorful shrines, and on them played the whore; nothing like this has ever been or ever shall be.[a] [17]You also took your beautiful jewels of my gold and my silver that I had given you, and made for yourself male images, and with them played the whore; [18]and you took your embroidered garments to cover them, and set my oil and my incense before them. [19]Also my bread that I gave you—I fed you with choice flour and oil and honey—you set it before them as a pleasing odor; and so it was, says the Lord GOD. [20]You took your sons and your daughters, whom you had borne to me, and these you sacrificed to them to be devoured. As if your whorings were not enough! [21]You slaughtered my children and delivered them up as an offering to them. [22]And in all your abominations and your whorings you did not remember the days of your youth, when you were naked and bare, flailing about in your blood.

23 After all your wickedness (woe, woe to you! says the Lord GOD), [24]you built yourself a platform and made yourself a lofty place in every square; [25]at the head of every street you built your lofty place and prostituted your beauty, offering yourself to every passer-by, and multiplying your whoring. [26]You played the whore with the Egyptians, your lustful neighbors, multiplying your whoring, to provoke me to anger. [27]Therefore I stretched out my hand against you, reduced your rations, and gave you up to the will of your enemies, the daughters of the Philistines, who were ashamed of your lewd behavior. [28]You played the whore with the Assyrians, because you were insatiable; you played the whore with them, and still you were not satisfied. [29]You multiplied your whoring with Chaldea, the land of merchants; and even with this you were not satisfied.

30 How sick is your heart, says the Lord GOD, that you did all these things, the deeds of a brazen whore; [31]building your platform at the head of every street, and making your lofty place in every square! Yet you were not like a whore, because you scorned payment. [32]Adulterous wife, who receives strangers instead of her husband! [33]Gifts are given to all whores; but you gave your gifts to all your lovers, bribing them to come to you from all around for your whorings. [34]So you were different from other women in your whorings: no one solicited you to play the whore; and you gave payment, while no payment was given to you; you were different.

35 Therefore, O whore, hear the word of the LORD: [36]Thus says the Lord GOD, Because your lust was poured out and your nakedness uncovered in your whoring with your lovers, and because of all your abominable idols, and because of the blood of your children that you gave to them, [37]therefore, I will gather all your lovers, with whom you took pleasure, all those you loved and all those you hated; I will gather them against you from all around, and will uncover your nakedness to them, so that they may see all your nakedness. [38]I will judge you as women who commit adultery and shed blood are judged, and bring blood upon you in wrath and jealousy. [39]I will deliver you into their hands, and they shall throw down your platform and break down your lofty places; they shall strip you of your clothes and take your beautiful objects and leave you naked and bare. [40]They shall bring up a mob against you, and they shall stone you and cut you to pieces with their swords. [41]They shall burn your houses and execute judgments on you in the sight of many women; I will stop you from playing the whore, and you shall also make no more payments. [42]So I will satisfy my fury on you, and my jealousy shall turn away from you; I will be calm, and will be angry no longer. [43]Because you have not remembered the days of your youth, but have enraged me with all these things; therefore, I have returned your deeds upon your head, says the Lord GOD.

Have you not committed lewdness beyond all your abominations? [44]See, everyone who uses proverbs will use this proverb about you, "Like mother, like daughter." [45]You are the daughter of your mother, who loathed her husband and her children; and you are the sister of your sisters, who loathed their husbands and their children. Your mother was a Hittite and your father an Amorite. [46]Your elder sister is Samaria, who lived with her daughters to the north

---

a Meaning of Heb uncertain   b Heb adds *let it be his*

of you; and your younger sister, who lived to the south of you, is Sodom with her daughters. ⁴⁷You not only followed their ways, and acted according to their abominations; within a very little time you were more corrupt than they in all your ways. ⁴⁸As I live, says the Lord GOD, your sister Sodom and her daughters have not done as you and your daughters have done. ⁴⁹This was the guilt of your sister Sodom: she and her daughters had pride, excess of food, and prosperous ease, but did not aid the poor and needy. ⁵⁰They were haughty, and did abominable things before me; therefore I removed them when I saw it. ⁵¹Samaria has not committed half your sins; you have committed more abominations than they, and have made your sisters appear righteous by all the abominations that you have committed. ⁵²Bear your disgrace, you also, for you have brought about for your sisters a more favorable judgment; because of your sins in which you acted more abominably than they, they are more in the right than you. So be ashamed, you also, and bear your disgrace, for you have made your sisters appear righteous.

53 I will restore their fortunes, the fortunes of Sodom and her daughters and the fortunes of Samaria and her daughters, and I will restore your own fortunes along with theirs, ⁵⁴in order that you may bear your disgrace and be ashamed of all that you have done, becoming a consolation to them. ⁵⁵As for your sisters, Sodom and her daughters shall return to their former state, Samaria and her daughters shall return to their former state, and you and your daughters shall return to your former state. ⁵⁶Was not your sister Sodom a byword in your mouth in the day of your pride, ⁵⁷before your wickedness was uncovered? Now you are a mockery to the daughters of Aram*ᵃ* and all her neighbors, and to the daughters of the Philistines, those all around who despise you. ⁵⁸You must bear the penalty of your lewdness and your abominations, says the LORD.

An Everlasting Covenant

59 Yes, thus says the Lord GOD: I will deal with you as you have done, you who have despised the oath, breaking the covenant; ⁶⁰yet I will remember my covenant with you in the days of your youth, and I will establish with you an everlasting covenant. ⁶¹Then you will remember your ways, and be ashamed when I*ᵇ* take your sisters, both your elder and your younger, and give them to you as daughters, but not on account of my*ᶜ* covenant with you.

⁶²I will establish my covenant with you, and you shall know that I am the LORD, ⁶³in order that you may remember and be confounded, and never open your mouth again because of your shame, when I forgive you all that you have done, says the Lord GOD.

17

The Two Eagles and the Vine

The word of the LORD came to me: ²O mortal, propound a riddle, and speak an allegory to the house of Israel. ³Say: Thus says the Lord GOD:

A great eagle, with great wings and long
    pinions,
    rich in plumage of many colors,
    came to the Lebanon.
He took the top of the cedar,
⁴   broke off its topmost shoot;
he carried it to a land of trade,
    set it in a city of merchants.
⁵ Then he took a seed from the land,
    placed it in fertile soil;
a plant*ᵈ* by abundant waters,
    he set it like a willow twig.
⁶ It sprouted and became a vine
    spreading out, but low;
its branches turned toward him,
    its roots remained where it stood.
So it became a vine;
    it brought forth branches,
    put forth foliage.

⁷ There was another great eagle,
    with great wings and much plumage.
And see! This vine stretched out
    its roots toward him;
it shot out its branches toward him,
    so that he might water it.
From the bed where it was planted
⁸   it was transplanted
to good soil by abundant waters,
    so that it might produce branches
    and bear fruit
    and become a noble vine.
⁹Say: Thus says the Lord GOD:
Will it prosper?
Will he not pull up its roots,
    cause its fruit to rot*ᵈ* and wither,
    its fresh sprouting leaves to fade?
No strong arm or mighty army will be needed

ᵃ Another reading is *Edom*   *ᵇ* Syr: Heb *you*   *ᶜ* Heb lacks *my*   *ᵈ* Meaning of Heb uncertain

to pull it from its roots.
¹⁰ When it is transplanted, will it thrive?
When the east wind strikes it,
will it not utterly wither,
wither on the bed where it grew?

11 Then the word of the LORD came to me: ¹²Say now to the rebellious house: Do you not know what these things mean? Tell them: The king of Babylon came to Jerusalem, took its king and its officials, and brought them back with him to Babylon. ¹³He took one of the royal offspring and made a covenant with him, putting him under oath (he had taken away the chief men of the land), ¹⁴so that the kingdom might be humble and not lift itself up, and that by keeping his covenant it might stand. ¹⁵But he rebelled against him by sending ambassadors to Egypt, in order that they might give him horses and a large army. Will he succeed? Can one escape who does such things? Can he break the covenant and yet escape? ¹⁶As I live, says the Lord GOD, surely in the place where the king resides who made him king, whose oath he despised, and whose covenant with him he broke—in Babylon he shall die. ¹⁷Pharaoh with his mighty army and great company will not help him in war, when ramps are cast up and siege walls built to cut off many lives. ¹⁸Because he despised the oath and broke the covenant, because he gave his hand and yet did all these things, he shall not escape. ¹⁹Therefore thus says the Lord GOD: As I live, I will surely return upon his head my oath that he despised, and my covenant that he broke. ²⁰I will spread my net over him, and he shall be caught in my snare; I will bring him to Babylon and enter into judgment with him there for the treason he has committed against me. ²¹All the pick[a] of his troops shall fall by the sword, and the survivors shall be scattered to every wind; and you shall know that I, the LORD, have spoken.

Israel Exalted at Last

22 Thus says the Lord GOD:
I myself will take a sprig
from the lofty top of a cedar;
I will set it out.
I will break off a tender one
from the topmost of its young twigs;
I myself will plant it
on a high and lofty mountain.
²³ On the mountain height of Israel
I will plant it,

in order that it may produce boughs and bear fruit,
and become a noble cedar.
Under it every kind of bird will live;
in the shade of its branches will nest
winged creatures of every kind.
²⁴ All the trees of the field shall know
that I am the LORD.
I bring low the high tree,
I make high the low tree;
I dry up the green tree
and make the dry tree flourish.
I the LORD have spoken;
I will accomplish it.

18 Individual Retribution

The word of the LORD came to me: ²What do you mean by repeating this proverb concerning the land of Israel, "The parents have eaten sour grapes, and the children's teeth are set on edge"? ³As I live, says the Lord GOD, this proverb shall no more be used by you in Israel. ⁴Know that all lives are mine; the life of the parent as well as the life of the child is mine: it is only the person who sins that shall die.

5 If a man is righteous and does what is lawful and right— ⁶if he does not eat upon the mountains or lift up his eyes to the idols of the house of Israel, does not defile his neighbor's wife or approach a woman during her menstrual period, ⁷does not oppress anyone, but restores to the debtor his pledge, commits no robbery, gives his bread to the hungry and covers the naked with a garment, ⁸does not take advance or accrued interest, withholds his hand from iniquity, executes true justice between contending parties, ⁹follows my statutes, and is careful to observe my ordinances, acting faithfully—such a one is righteous; he shall surely live, says the Lord GOD.

10 If he has a son who is violent, a shedder of blood, ¹¹who does any of these things (though his father[b] does none of them), who eats upon the mountains, defiles his neighbor's wife, ¹²oppresses the poor and needy, commits robbery, does not restore the pledge, lifts up his eyes to the idols, commits abomination, ¹³takes advance or accrued interest; shall he then live? He shall not. He has done all these abominable things; he shall surely die; his blood shall be upon himself.

14 But if this man has a son who sees all the sins

---

a Another reading is *fugitives* b Heb *he*

that his father has done, considers, and does not do likewise, [15]who does not eat upon the mountains or lift up his eyes to the idols of the house of Israel, does not defile his neighbor's wife, [16]does not wrong anyone, exacts no pledge, commits no robbery, but gives his bread to the hungry and covers the naked with a garment, [17]withholds his hand from iniquity,[a] takes no advance or accrued interest, observes my ordinances, and follows my statutes; he shall not die for his father's iniquity; he shall surely live. [18]As for his father, because he practiced extortion, robbed his brother, and did what is not good among his people, he dies for his iniquity.

19 Yet you say, "Why should not the son suffer for the iniquity of the father?" When the son has done what is lawful and right, and has been careful to observe all my statutes, he shall surely live. [20]The person who sins shall die. A child shall not suffer for the iniquity of a parent, nor a parent suffer for the iniquity of a child; the righteousness of the righteous shall be his own, and the wickedness of the wicked shall be his own.

21 But if the wicked turn away from all their sins that they have committed and keep all my statutes and do what is lawful and right, they shall surely live; they shall not die. [22]None of the transgressions that they have committed shall be remembered against them; for the righteousness that they have done they shall live. [23]Have I any pleasure in the death of the wicked, says the Lord GOD, and not rather that they should turn from their ways and live? [24]But when the righteous turn away from their righteousness and commit iniquity and do the same abominable things that the wicked do, shall they live? None of the righteous deeds that they have done shall be remembered; for the treachery of which they are guilty and the sin they have committed, they shall die.

25 Yet you say, "The way of the Lord is unfair." Hear now, O house of Israel: Is my way unfair? Is it not your ways that are unfair? [26]When the righteous turn away from their righteousness and commit iniquity, they shall die for it; for the iniquity that they have committed they shall die. [27]Again, when the wicked turn away from the wickedness they have committed and do what is lawful and right, they shall save their life. [28]Because they considered and turned away from all the transgressions that they had committed, they shall surely live; they shall not die. [29]Yet the house of Israel says, "The way of the Lord is unfair." O house of Israel, are my ways unfair? Is it not your ways that are unfair?

30 Therefore I will judge you, O house of Israel, all of you according to your ways, says the Lord GOD. Repent and turn from all your transgressions; otherwise iniquity will be your ruin.[b] [31]Cast away from you all the transgressions that you have committed against me, and get yourselves a new heart and a new spirit! Why will you die, O house of Israel? [32]For I have no pleasure in the death of anyone, says the Lord GOD. Turn, then, and live.

Israel Degraded

19 As for you, raise up a lamentation for the princes of Israel, [2]and say:

What a lioness was your mother
 among lions!
She lay down among young lions,
 rearing her cubs.
[3] She raised up one of her cubs;
 he became a young lion,
and he learned to catch prey;
 he devoured humans.
[4] The nations sounded an alarm against him;
 he was caught in their pit;
and they brought him with hooks
 to the land of Egypt.
[5] When she saw that she was thwarted,
 that her hope was lost,
she took another of her cubs
 and made him a young lion.
[6] He prowled among the lions;
 he became a young lion,
and he learned to catch prey;
 he devoured people.
[7] And he ravaged their strongholds,[c]
 and laid waste their towns;
the land was appalled, and all in it,
 at the sound of his roaring.
[8] The nations set upon him
 from the provinces all around;
they spread their net over him;
 he was caught in their pit.
[9] With hooks they put him in a cage,
 and brought him to the king of Babylon;
 they brought him into custody,
so that his voice should be heard no more
 on the mountains of Israel.
[10] Your mother was like a vine in a vineyard[d]
 transplanted by the water,
fruitful and full of branches

a Gk: Heb *the poor*   b Or *so that they shall not be a stumbling block of iniquity to you*   c Heb *his widows*   d Cn: Heb *in your blood*

from abundant water.
11 Its strongest stem became
    a ruler's scepter;ᵃ
it towered aloft
    among the thick boughs;
it stood out in its height
    with its mass of branches.
12 But it was plucked up in fury,
    cast down to the ground;
the east wind dried it up;
    its fruit was stripped off,
its strong stem was withered;
    the fire consumed it.
13 Now it is transplanted into the wilderness,
    into a dry and thirsty land.
14 And fire has gone out from its stem,
    has consumed its branches and fruit,
so that there remains in it no strong stem,
    no scepter for ruling.

This is a lamentation, and it is used as a lamentation.

20   Israel's Continuing Rebellion

In the seventh year, in the fifth month, on the tenth day of the month, certain elders of Israel came to consult the LORD, and sat down before me. ²And the word of the LORD came to me: ³Mortal, speak to the elders of Israel, and say to them: Thus says the Lord GOD: Why are you coming? To consult me? As I live, says the Lord GOD, I will not be consulted by you. ⁴Will you judge them, mortal, will you judge them? Then let them know the abominations of their ancestors, ⁵and say to them: Thus says the Lord GOD: On the day when I chose Israel, I swore to the offspring of the house of Jacob—making myself known to them in the land of Egypt—I swore to them, saying, I am the LORD your God. ⁶On that day I swore to them that I would bring them out of the land of Egypt into a land that I had searched out for them, a land flowing with milk and honey, the most glorious of all lands. ⁷And I said to them, Cast away the detestable things your eyes feast on, every one of you, and do not defile yourselves with the idols of Egypt; I am the LORD your God. ⁸But they rebelled against me and would not listen to me; not one of them cast away the detestable things their eyes feasted on, nor did they forsake the idols of Egypt.

Then I thought I would pour out my wrath upon them and spend my anger against them in the midst of the land of Egypt. ⁹But I acted for the sake of my name, that it should not be profaned in the sight of the nations among whom they lived, in whose sight I made myself known to them in bringing them out of the land of Egypt. ¹⁰So I led them out of the land of Egypt and brought them into the wilderness. ¹¹I gave them my statutes and showed them my ordinances, by whose observance everyone shall live. ¹²Moreover I gave them my sabbaths, as a sign between me and them, so that they might know that I the LORD sanctify them. ¹³But the house of Israel rebelled against me in the wilderness; they did not observe my statutes but rejected my ordinances, by whose observance everyone shall live; and my sabbaths they greatly profaned.

Then I thought I would pour out my wrath upon them in the wilderness, to make an end of them. ¹⁴But I acted for the sake of my name, so that it should not be profaned in the sight of the nations, in whose sight I had brought them out. ¹⁵Moreover I swore to them in the wilderness that I would not bring them into the land that I had given them, a land flowing with milk and honey, the most glorious of all lands, ¹⁶because they rejected my ordinances and did not observe my statutes, and profaned my sabbaths; for their heart went after their idols. ¹⁷Nevertheless my eye spared them, and I did not destroy them or make an end of them in the wilderness.

18 I said to their children in the wilderness, Do not follow the statutes of your parents, nor observe their ordinances, nor defile yourselves with their idols. ¹⁹I the LORD am your God; follow my statutes, and be careful to observe my ordinances, ²⁰and hallow my sabbaths that they may be a sign between me and you, so that you may know that I the LORD am your God. ²¹But the children rebelled against me; they did not follow my statutes, and were not careful to observe my ordinances, by whose observance everyone shall live; they profaned my sabbaths.

Then I thought I would pour out my wrath upon them and spend my anger against them in the wilderness. ²²But I withheld my hand, and acted for the sake of my name, so that it should not be profaned in the sight of the nations, in whose sight I had brought them out. ²³Moreover I swore to them in the wilderness that I would scatter them among the nations and disperse them through the coun-

---

ᵃ Heb *Its strongest stems became rulers' scepters*

tries, [24]because they had not executed my ordinances, but had rejected my statutes and profaned my sabbaths, and their eyes were set on their ancestors' idols. [25]Moreover I gave them statutes that were not good and ordinances by which they could not live. [26]I defiled them through their very gifts, in their offering up all their firstborn, in order that I might horrify them, so that they might know that I am the LORD.

27 Therefore, mortal, speak to the house of Israel and say to them, Thus says the Lord GOD: In this again your ancestors blasphemed me, by dealing treacherously with me. [28]For when I had brought them into the land that I swore to give them, then wherever they saw any high hill or any leafy tree, there they offered their sacrifices and presented the provocation of their offering; there they sent up their pleasing odors, and there they poured out their drink offerings. [29](I said to them, What is the high place to which you go? So it is called Bamah[a] to this day.) [30]Therefore say to the house of Israel, Thus says the Lord GOD: Will you defile yourselves after the manner of your ancestors and go astray after their detestable things? [31]When you offer your gifts and make your children pass through the fire, you defile yourselves with all your idols to this day. And shall I be consulted by you, O house of Israel? As I live, says the Lord GOD, I will not be consulted by you.

32 What is in your mind shall never happen—the thought, "Let us be like the nations, like the tribes of the countries, and worship wood and stone."

God Will Restore Israel

33 As I live, says the Lord GOD, surely with a mighty hand and an outstretched arm, and with wrath poured out, I will be king over you. [34]I will bring you out from the peoples and gather you out of the countries where you are scattered, with a mighty hand and an outstretched arm, and with wrath poured out; [35]and I will bring you into the wilderness of the peoples, and there I will enter into judgment with you face to face. [36]As I entered into judgment with your ancestors in the wilderness of the land of Egypt, so I will enter into judgment with you, says the Lord GOD. [37]I will make you pass under the staff, and will bring you within the bond of the covenant. [38]I will purge out the rebels among you, and those who transgress against me; I will bring them out of the land where they reside as aliens, but they shall not enter the land of Israel. Then you shall know that I am the LORD.

39 As for you, O house of Israel, thus says the Lord GOD: Go serve your idols, every one of you now and hereafter, if you will not listen to me; but my holy name you shall no more profane with your gifts and your idols.

40 For on my holy mountain, the mountain height of Israel, says the Lord GOD, there all the house of Israel, all of them, shall serve me in the land; there I will accept them, and there I will require your contributions and the choicest of your gifts, with all your sacred things. [41]As a pleasing odor I will accept you, when I bring you out from the peoples, and gather you out of the countries where you have been scattered; and I will manifest my holiness among you in the sight of the nations. [42]You shall know that I am the LORD, when I bring you into the land of Israel, the country that I swore to give to your ancestors. [43]There you shall remember your ways and all the deeds by which you have polluted yourselves; and you shall loathe yourselves for all the evils that you have committed. [44]And you shall know that I am the LORD, when I deal with you for my name's sake, not according to your evil ways, or corrupt deeds, O house of Israel, says the Lord GOD.

A Prophecy against the Negeb

45[b] The word of the LORD came to me: [46]Mortal, set your face toward the south, preach against the south, and prophesy against the forest land in the Negeb; [47]say to the forest of the Negeb, Hear the word of the LORD: Thus says the Lord GOD, I will kindle a fire in you, and it shall devour every green tree in you and every dry tree; the blazing flame shall not be quenched, and all faces from south to north shall be scorched by it. [48]All flesh shall see that I the LORD have kindled it; it shall not be quenched. [49]Then I said, "Ah Lord GOD! they are saying of me, 'Is he not a maker of allegories?'"

The Drawn Sword of God

21 [c] The word of the LORD came to me: [2]Mortal, set your face toward Jerusalem and preach against the sanctuaries; prophesy against the land of Israel [3]and say to the land of Israel, Thus says the LORD: I am coming against you, and will draw my sword out of its sheath, and will cut off from you both righteous and wicked. [4]Because I will cut off from you both righteous and wicked, there-

---

a That is *High Place*   b Ch 21.1 in Heb   c Ch 21.6 in Heb fore my sword shall go out of its sheath against all flesh from south to north; [5]and all flesh shall know that I the LORD have drawn my sword out of its sheath; it shall not be sheathed again. [6]Moan therefore, mortal; moan with breaking heart and bitter grief before their eyes. [7]And when they say to you, "Why do you moan?" you shall say, "Because of the news that has come. Every heart will melt and all hands will be feeble, every spirit will faint and all knees will turn to water. See, it comes and it will be fulfilled," says the Lord GOD.

[8] And the word of the LORD came to me: [9]Mortal, prophesy and say: Thus says the Lord; Say:

A sword, a sword is sharpened,
　　it is also polished;
[10] it is sharpened for slaughter,
　　honed to flash like lightning!
How can we make merry?
　　You have despised the rod,
　　and all discipline.[a]
[11] The sword[b] is given to be polished,
　　to be grasped in the hand;
it is sharpened, the sword is polished,
　　to be placed in the slayer's hand.
[12] Cry and wail, O mortal,
　　for it is against my people;
it is against all Israel's princes;
　　they are thrown to the sword,
　　together with my people.
Ah! Strike the thigh!
[13]For consider: What! If you despise the rod, will it not happen?[a] says the Lord GOD.
[14] And you, mortal, prophesy;
　　strike hand to hand.
Let the sword fall twice, thrice;
　　it is a sword for killing.
A sword for great slaughter—
　　it surrounds them;
[15] therefore hearts melt
　　and many stumble.
At all their gates I have set
　　the point[a] of the sword.
Ah! It is made for flashing,
　　it is polished[c] for slaughter.

[16] Attack to the right!
　　Engage to the left!
　　—wherever your edge is directed.
[17] I too will strike hand to hand,
　　I will satisfy my fury;
　　I the LORD have spoken.

[18] The word of the LORD came to me: [19]Mortal, mark out two roads for the sword of the king of Babylon to come; both of them shall issue from the same land. And make a signpost, make it for a fork in the road leading to a city; [20]mark out the road for the sword to come to Rabbah of the Ammonites or to Judah and to[d] Jerusalem the fortified. [21]For the king of Babylon stands at the parting of the way, at the fork in the two roads, to use divination; he shakes the arrows, he consults the teraphim,[e] he inspects the liver. [22]Into his right hand comes the lot for Jerusalem, to set battering rams, to call out for slaughter, for raising the battle cry, to set battering rams against the gates, to cast up ramps, to build siege towers. [23]But to them it will seem like a false divination; they have sworn solemn oaths; but he brings their guilt to remembrance, bringing about their capture.

[24] Therefore thus says the Lord GOD: Because you have brought your guilt to remembrance, in that your transgressions are uncovered, so that in all your deeds your sins appear—because you have come to remembrance, you shall be taken in hand.[f]
[25] As for you, vile, wicked prince of Israel,
　　you whose day has come,
　　the time of final punishment,
[26] thus says the Lord GOD:
Remove the turban, take off the crown;
　　things shall not remain as they are.
Exalt that which is low,
　　abase that which is high.
[27] A ruin, a ruin, a ruin—
　　I will make it!
(Such has never occurred.)
Until he comes whose right it is;
　　to him I will give it.

[28] As for you, mortal, prophesy, and say, Thus says the Lord GOD concerning the Ammonites, and concerning their reproach; say:
A sword, a sword! Drawn for slaughter,
　　polished to consume,[g] to flash like lightning.
[29] Offering false visions for you,
　　divining lies for you,

---

a Meaning of Heb uncertain　b Heb It　c Tg: Heb wrapped up　d Gk Syr: Heb Judah in　e Or the household gods　f Or be taken captive　g Cn: Heb to contain

they place you over the necks
    of the vile, wicked ones—
those whose day has come,
    the time of final punishment.
30 Return it to its sheath!
In the place where you were created,
    in the land of your origin,
    I will judge you.
31 I will pour out my indignation upon you,
    with the fire of my wrath
    I will blow upon you.
I will deliver you into brutish hands,
    those skillful to destroy.
32 You shall be fuel for the fire,
    your blood shall enter the earth;
you shall be remembered no more,
    for I the LORD have spoken.

The Bloody City

22 The word of the LORD came to me: 2You, mortal, will you judge, will you judge the bloody city? Then declare to it all its abominable deeds. 3You shall say, Thus says the Lord GOD: A city! Shedding blood within itself; its time has come; making its idols, defiling itself. 4You have become guilty by the blood that you have shed, and defiled by the idols that you have made; you have brought your day near, the appointed time of your years has come. Therefore I have made you a disgrace before the nations, and a mockery to all the countries. 5Those who are near and those who are far from you will mock you, you infamous one, full of tumult.

6 The princes of Israel in you, everyone according to his power, have been bent on shedding blood. 7Father and mother are treated with contempt in you; the alien residing within you suffers extortion; the orphan and the widow are wronged in you. 8You have despised my holy things, and profaned my sabbaths. 9In you are those who slander to shed blood, those in you who eat upon the mountains, who commit lewdness in your midst. 10In you they uncover their fathers' nakedness; in you they violate women in their menstrual periods. 11One commits abomination with his neighbor's wife; another lewdly defiles his daughter-in-law; another in you defiles his sister, his father's daughter. 12In you, they take bribes to shed blood; you take both advance interest and accrued interest, and make gain of your neighbors by extortion; and you have forgotten me, says the Lord GOD.

13 See, I strike my hands together at the dishonest gain you have made, and at the blood that has been shed within you. 14Can your courage endure, or can your hands remain strong in the days when I shall deal with you? I the LORD have spoken, and I will do it. 15I will scatter you among the nations and disperse you through the countries, and I will purge your filthiness out of you. 16And I*a* shall be profaned through you in the sight of the nations; and you shall know that I am the LORD.

17 The word of the LORD came to me: 18Mortal, the house of Israel has become dross to me; all of them, silver,*b* bronze, tin, iron, and lead. In the smelter they have become dross. 19Therefore thus says the Lord GOD: Because you have all become dross, I will gather you into the midst of Jerusalem. 20As one gathers silver, bronze, iron, lead, and tin into a smelter, to blow the fire upon them in order to melt them; so I will gather you in my anger and in my wrath, and I will put you in and melt you. 21I will gather you and blow upon you with the fire of my wrath, and you shall be melted within it. 22As silver is melted in a smelter, so you shall be melted in it; and you shall know that I the LORD have poured out my wrath upon you.

23 The word of the LORD came to me: 24Mortal, say to it: You are a land that is not cleansed, not rained upon in the day of indignation. 25Its princes*c* within it are like a roaring lion tearing the prey; they have devoured human lives; they have taken treasure and precious things; they have made many widows within it. 26Its priests have done violence to my teaching and have profaned my holy things; they have made no distinction between the holy and the common, neither have they taught the difference between the unclean and the clean, and they have disregarded my sabbaths, so that I am profaned among them. 27Its officials within it are like wolves tearing the prey, shedding blood, destroying lives to get dishonest gain. 28Its prophets have smeared whitewash on their behalf, seeing false visions and divining lies for them, saying, "Thus says the Lord GOD," when the LORD has not spoken. 29The people of the land have practiced extortion and committed robbery; they have oppressed the poor and needy, and have extorted from the alien without redress. 30And I sought for anyone among them who would repair the wall and stand in the breach before me on behalf of the land, so that I would not destroy it; but I found no one. 31Therefore I have poured

a Gk Syr Vg: Heb *you*   b Transposed from the end of the verse; compare verse 20   c Gk: Heb *indignation.* 25*A conspiracy of its prophets*

Irresponsible Children
Ezekiel 23:1–21

"Bad choice. Now here is your consequence."

None of us like to hear those words, and we'll do anything to dodge the negative consequences of our actions. But Ezekiel says we've got to face them.

Ezekiel 13–24 contains prophecies, allegories, fables, and symbolic actions, all intended to encourage the people of Judah to take responsibility for their sinful actions. In a graphic allegory in **Ezekiel 23**, the northern and southern kingdoms are compared to promiscuous daughters who will sleep with almost anyone who comes their way. God is using just about every possible means to say, "Take responsibility for your actions, my children, and live with the consequences!"

- What consequences are you avoiding or trying to ignore?
- How might dodging those consequences lead to more trouble?
- What can you do today to face the consequences and learn from them?

out my indignation upon them; I have consumed them with the fire of my wrath; I have returned their conduct upon their heads, says the Lord GOD.

23   Oholah and Oholibah

The word of the LORD came to me: [2]Mortal, there were two women, the daughters of one mother; [3]they played the whore in Egypt; they played the whore in their youth; their breasts were caressed there, and their virgin bosoms were fondled. [4]Oholah was the name of the elder and Oholibah the name of her sister. They became mine, and they bore sons and daughters. As for their names, Oholah is Samaria, and Oholibah is Jerusalem.

[5]Oholah played the whore while she was mine; she lusted after her lovers the Assyrians, warriors[a] [6]clothed in blue, governors and commanders, all of them handsome young men, mounted horsemen. [7]She bestowed her favors upon them, the choicest men of Assyria all of them; and she defiled herself with all the idols of everyone for whom she lusted. [8]She did not give up her whorings that she had practiced since Egypt; for in her youth men had lain with her and fondled her virgin bosom and poured out their lust upon her. [9]Therefore I delivered her into the hands of her lovers, into the hands of the Assyrians, for whom she lusted. [10]These uncovered her nakedness; they seized her sons and her daughters; and they killed her with the sword. Judgment was executed upon her, and she became a byword among women.

[11]Her sister Oholibah saw this, yet she was more corrupt than she in her lusting and in her whorings, which were worse than those of her sister. [12]She lusted after the Assyrians, governors and commanders, warriors[a] clothed in full armor, mounted horsemen, all of them handsome young men. [13]And I saw that she was defiled; they both took the same way. [14]But she carried her whorings further; she saw male figures carved on the wall, images of the Chaldeans portrayed in vermilion, [15]with belts around their waists, with flowing turbans on their heads, all of them looking like officers—a picture of Babylonians whose native land was Chaldea. [16]When she saw them she lusted after them, and sent messengers to them in Chaldea. [17]And the Babylonians came to her into the bed of love, and they defiled her with their lust; and after she defiled herself with them, she turned from them in disgust. [18]When she carried on her whorings so openly and flaunted her nakedness, I turned in disgust from her, as I had turned from her sister. [19]Yet she increased her whorings, remembering the days of her youth, when she played the whore in the land of Egypt [20]and lusted after her paramours there, whose members were like those of donkeys, and whose emission was like that of stallions. [21]Thus you longed for the lewdness of your youth, when the Egyptians[b] fondled your bosom and caressed[c] your young breasts.

[22]Therefore, O Oholibah, thus says the Lord GOD: I will rouse against you your lovers from whom you turned in disgust, and I will bring them against you from every side: [23]the Babylonians and all the Chaldeans, Pekod and Shoa and Koa, and all the Assyrians with them, handsome young men, governors and commanders all of them, officers and warriors,[d] all of them riding on horses. [24]They shall

---

a Meaning of Heb uncertain   b Two Mss: MT *from Egypt*   c Cn: Heb *for the sake of*   d Compare verses 6 and 12: Heb *officers and called ones*

come against you from the north[a] with chariots and wagons and a host of peoples; they shall set themselves against you on every side with buckler, shield, and helmet, and I will commit the judgment to them, and they shall judge you according to their ordinances. [25]I will direct my indignation against you, in order that they may deal with you in fury. They shall cut off your nose and your ears, and your survivors shall fall by the sword. They shall seize your sons and your daughters, and your survivors shall be devoured by fire. [26]They shall also strip you of your clothes and take away your fine jewels. [27]So I will put an end to your lewdness and your whoring brought from the land of Egypt; you shall not long for them, or remember Egypt any more. [28]For thus says the Lord God: I will deliver you into the hands of those whom you hate, into the hands of those from whom you turned in disgust; [29]and they shall deal with you in hatred, and take away all the fruit of your labor, and leave you naked and bare, and the nakedness of your whorings shall be exposed. Your lewdness and your whorings [30]have brought this upon you, because you played the whore with the nations, and polluted yourself with their idols. [31]You have gone the way of your sister; therefore I will give her cup into your hand. [32]Thus says the Lord God:

You shall drink your sister's cup,
   deep and wide;
you shall be scorned and derided,
   it holds so much.
[33] You shall be filled with drunkenness and
   sorrow.
A cup of horror and desolation
   is the cup of your sister Samaria;
[34] you shall drink it and drain it out,
   and gnaw its sherds,
   and tear out your breasts;
for I have spoken, says the Lord God. [35]Therefore thus says the Lord God: Because you have forgotten me and cast me behind your back, therefore bear the consequences of your lewdness and whorings.

36 The Lord said to me: Mortal, will you judge Oholah and Oholibah? Then declare to them their abominable deeds. [37]For they have committed adultery, and blood is on their hands; with their idols they have committed adultery; and they have even offered up to them for food the children whom they had borne to me. [38]Moreover this they have done to me: they have defiled my sanctuary on the same day and profaned my sabbaths. [39]For when they had slaughtered their children for their idols, on the same day they came into my sanctuary to profane it. This is what they did in my house.

40 They even sent for men to come from far away, to whom a messenger was sent, and they came. For them you bathed yourself, painted your eyes, and decked yourself with ornaments; [41]you sat on a stately couch, with a table spread before it on which you had placed my incense and my oil. [42]The sound of a raucous multitude was around her, with many of the rabble brought in drunken from the wilderness; and they put bracelets on the arms[b] of the women, and beautiful crowns upon their heads.

43 Then I said, Ah, she is worn out with adulteries, but they carry on their sexual acts with her. [44]For they have gone in to her, as one goes in to a whore. Thus they went in to Oholah and to Oholibah, wanton women. [45]But righteous judges shall declare them guilty of adultery and of bloodshed; because they are adulteresses and blood is on their hands.

46 For thus says the Lord God: Bring up an assembly against them, and make them an object of terror and of plunder. [47]The assembly shall stone them and with their swords they shall cut them down; they shall kill their sons and their daughters, and burn up their houses. [48]Thus will I put an end to lewdness in the land, so that all women may take warning and not commit lewdness as you have done. [49]They shall repay you for your lewdness, and you shall bear the penalty for your sinful idolatry; and you shall know that I am the Lord God.

The Boiling Pot

24 In the ninth year, in the tenth month, on the tenth day of the month, the word of the Lord came to me: [2]Mortal, write down the name of this day, this very day. The king of Babylon has laid siege to Jerusalem this very day. [3]And utter an allegory to the rebellious house and say to them, Thus says the Lord God:

---

a Gk: Meaning of Heb uncertain   b Heb hands

Set on the pot, set it on,
pour in water also;
4 put in it the pieces,
all the good pieces, the thigh and the
shoulder;
fill it with choice bones.
5 Take the choicest one of the flock,
pile the logs*a* under it;
boil its pieces,*b*
seethe*c* also its bones in it.

6 Therefore thus says the Lord GOD:
Woe to the bloody city,
the pot whose rust is in it,
whose rust has not gone out of it!
Empty it piece by piece,
making no choice at all.*d*
7 For the blood she shed is inside it;
she placed it on a bare rock;
she did not pour it out on the ground,
to cover it with earth.
8 To rouse my wrath, to take vengeance,
I have placed the blood she shed
on a bare rock,
so that it may not be covered.
9 Therefore thus says the Lord GOD:
Woe to the bloody city!
I will even make the pile great.
10 Heap up the logs, kindle the fire;
boil the meat well, mix in the spices,
let the bones be burned.
11 Stand it empty upon the coals,
so that it may become hot, its copper
glow,
its filth melt in it, its rust be consumed.
12 In vain I have wearied myself;*e*
its thick rust does not depart.
To the fire with its rust!*f*
13 Yet, when I cleansed you in your filthy
lewdness,
you did not become clean from your filth;
you shall not again be cleansed
until I have satisfied my fury upon you.
14 I the LORD have spoken; the time is coming, I
will act. I will not refrain, I will not spare, I will not
relent. According to your ways and your doings I
will judge you, says the Lord GOD.

Ezekiel's Bereavement

15 The word of the LORD came to me: 16 Mortal,

with one blow I am about to take away from you the
delight of your eyes; yet you shall not mourn or weep,
nor shall your tears run down. 17 Sigh, but not aloud;
make no mourning for the dead. Bind on your turban,
and put your sandals on your feet; do not cover your
upper lip or eat the bread of mourners.*g* 18 So I spoke
to the people in the morning, and at evening my wife
died. And on the next morning I did as I was commanded.

19 Then the people said to me, "Will you not tell
us what these things mean for us, that you are acting
this way?" 20 Then I said to them: The word of the
LORD came to me: 21 Say to the house of Israel, Thus
says the Lord GOD: I will profane my sanctuary, the
pride of your power, the delight of your eyes, and your
heart's desire; and your sons and your daughters
whom you left behind shall fall by the sword. 22 And
you shall do as I have done; you shall not cover your
upper lip or eat the bread of mourners.*g* 23 Your turbans shall be on your heads and your sandals on your
feet; you shall not mourn or weep, but you shall pine
away in your iniquities and groan to one another.
24 Thus Ezekiel shall be a sign to you; you shall do
just as he has done. When this comes, then you shall
know that I am the Lord GOD.

25 And you, mortal, on the day when I take from
them their stronghold, their joy and glory, the delight
of their eyes and their heart's affection, and also*h* their
sons and their daughters, 26 on that day, one who has
escaped will come to you to report to you the news.
27 On that day your mouth shall be opened to the one
who has escaped, and you shall speak and no longer
be silent. So you shall be a sign to them; and they shall
know that I am the LORD.

Proclamation against Ammon

25 The word of the LORD came to me: 2 Mortal, set your face toward the Ammonites and
prophesy against them. 3 Say to the Ammonites, Hear
the word of the Lord GOD: Thus says the Lord GOD:
Because you said, "Aha!" over my sanctuary when it
was profaned, and over the land of Israel when it was
made desolate, and over the house of Judah when it
went into exile; 4 therefore I am handing you over to
the people of the east for a possession. They shall set
their encampments among you and pitch their tents
in your midst; they shall eat your fruit, and they shall
drink your milk. 5 I will make Rabbah a pasture for
camels and Ammon a fold for flocks. Then you shall
know that I am the LORD. 6 For thus says the Lord

---

a Compare verse 10: Heb *the bones*   *b* Two Mss: Heb *its boilings*   *c* Cn: Heb *its bones seethe*   *d* Heb *piece, no lot has fallen on it*   *e* Cn: Meaning of Heb
uncertain   *f* Meaning of Heb uncertain   *g* Vg Tg: Heb *of men*   *h* Heb lacks *and also*

GOD: Because you have clapped your hands and stamped your feet and rejoiced with all the malice within you against the land of Israel, [7] therefore I have stretched out my hand against you, and will hand you over as plunder to the nations. I will cut you off from the peoples and will make you perish out of the countries; I will destroy you. Then you shall know that I am the LORD.

Proclamation against Moab

8 Thus says the Lord GOD: Because Moab[a] said, The house of Judah is like all the other nations, [9] therefore I will lay open the flank of Moab from the towns[b] on its frontier, the glory of the country, Beth-jeshimoth, Baal-meon, and Kiriathaim. [10] I will give it along with Ammon to the people of the east as a possession. Thus Ammon shall be remembered no more among the nations, [11] and I will execute judgments upon Moab. Then they shall know that I am the LORD.

Proclamation against Edom

12 Thus says the Lord GOD: Because Edom acted revengefully against the house of Judah and has grievously offended in taking vengeance upon them, [13] therefore thus says the Lord GOD, I will stretch out my hand against Edom, and cut off from it humans and animals, and I will make it desolate; from Teman even to Dedan they shall fall by the sword. [14] I will lay my vengeance upon Edom by the hand of my people Israel; and they shall act in Edom according to my anger and according to my wrath; and they shall know my vengeance, says the Lord GOD.

Proclamation against Philistia

15 Thus says the Lord GOD: Because with unending hostilities the Philistines acted in vengeance, and with malice of heart took revenge in destruction; [16] therefore thus says the Lord GOD, I will stretch out my hand against the Philistines, cut off the Cherethites, and destroy the rest of the seacoast. [17] I will execute great vengeance on them with wrathful punishments. Then they shall know that I am the LORD, when I lay my vengeance on them.

Proclamation against Tyre

26 In the eleventh year, on the first day of the month, the word of the LORD came to me: [2] Mortal, because Tyre said concerning Jerusalem, "Aha, broken is the gateway of the peoples;

it has swung open to me;
I shall be replenished,
now that it is wasted,"
[3] therefore, thus says the Lord GOD:
See, I am against you, O Tyre!
I will hurl many nations against you,
as the sea hurls its waves.
[4] They shall destroy the walls of Tyre
and break down its towers.
I will scrape its soil from it
and make it a bare rock.
[5] It shall become, in the midst of the sea,
a place for spreading nets.
I have spoken, says the Lord GOD.
It shall become plunder for the nations,
[6]   and its daughter-towns in the country
shall be killed by the sword.
Then they shall know that I am the LORD.

7 For thus says the Lord GOD: I will bring against Tyre from the north King Nebuchadrezzar of Babylon, king of kings, together with horses, chariots, cavalry, and a great and powerful army.
[8] Your daughter-towns in the country
he shall put to the sword.
He shall set up a siege wall against you,
cast up a ramp against you,
and raise a roof of shields against you.
[9] He shall direct the shock of his battering rams
against your walls
and break down your towers with his axes.
[10] His horses shall be so many
that their dust shall cover you.
At the noise of cavalry, wheels, and chariots
your very walls shall shake,
when he enters your gates
like those entering a breached city.
[11] With the hoofs of his horses
he shall trample all your streets.
He shall put your people to the sword,
and your strong pillars shall fall to the
ground.
[12] They will plunder your riches
and loot your merchandise;
they shall break down your walls
and destroy your fine houses.
Your stones and timber and soil
they shall cast into the water.
[13] I will silence the music of your songs;
the sound of your lyres shall be heard no
more.

---

a Gk Old Latin: Heb *Moab and Seir*   **b** Heb *towns from its towns*

14 I will make you a bare rock;
    you shall be a place for spreading nets.
You shall never again be rebuilt,
    for I the LORD have spoken,
    says the Lord GOD.

15 Thus says the Lord GOD to Tyre: Shall not the coastlands shake at the sound of your fall, when the wounded groan, when slaughter goes on within you? 16 Then all the princes of the sea shall step down from their thrones; they shall remove their robes and strip off their embroidered garments. They shall clothe themselves with trembling, and shall sit on the ground; they shall tremble every moment, and be appalled at you. 17 And they shall raise a lamentation over you, and say to you:

How you have vanished[a] from the seas,
    O city renowned,
once mighty on the sea,
    you and your inhabitants,[b]
who imposed your[c] terror
    on all the mainland![d]
18 Now the coastlands tremble
    on the day of your fall;
the coastlands by the sea
    are dismayed at your passing.

19 For thus says the Lord GOD: When I make you a city laid waste, like cities that are not inhabited, when I bring up the deep over you, and the great waters cover you, 20 then I will thrust you down with those who descend into the Pit, to the people of long ago, and I will make you live in the world below, among primeval ruins, with those who go down to the Pit, so that you will not be inhabited or have a place[e] in the land of the living. 21 I will bring you to a dreadful end, and you shall be no more; though sought for, you will never be found again, says the Lord GOD.

Lamentation over Tyre

27 The word of the LORD came to me: 2 Now you, mortal, raise a lamentation over Tyre, 3 and say to Tyre, which sits at the entrance to the sea, merchant of the peoples on many coastlands, Thus says the Lord GOD:

O Tyre, you have said,
    "I am perfect in beauty."
4 Your borders are in the heart of the seas;
    your builders made perfect your beauty.
5 They made all your planks
    of fir trees from Senir;

they took a cedar from Lebanon
    to make a mast for you.
6 From oaks of Bashan
    they made your oars;
they made your deck of pines[f]
    from the coasts of Cyprus,
    inlaid with ivory.
7 Of fine embroidered linen from Egypt
    was your sail,
    serving as your ensign;
blue and purple from the coasts of Elishah
    was your awning.
8 The inhabitants of Sidon and Arvad
    were your rowers;
skilled men of Zemer[g] were within you,
    they were your pilots.
9 The elders of Gebal and its artisans were
        within you,
    caulking your seams;
all the ships of the sea with their mariners
        were within you,
    to barter for your wares.
10 Paras[h] and Lud and Put
    were in your army,
    your mighty warriors;
they hung shield and helmet in you;
    they gave you splendor.
11 Men of Arvad and Helech[i]
    were on your walls all around;
    men of Gamad were at your towers.
They hung their quivers all around your walls;
    they made perfect your beauty.

12 Tarshish did business with you out of the abundance of your great wealth; silver, iron, tin, and lead they exchanged for your wares. 13 Javan, Tubal, and Meshech traded with you; they exchanged human beings and vessels of bronze for your merchandise. 14 Beth-togarmah exchanged for your wares horses, war horses, and mules. 15 The Rhodians[j] traded with you; many coastlands were your own special markets; they brought you in payment ivory tusks and ebony. 16 Edom[k] did business with you because of your abundant goods; they exchanged for your wares turquoise, purple, embroidered work, fine linen, coral, and rubies. 17 Judah and the land of Israel traded with you; they exchanged for your merchandise wheat from Minnith, millet,[l] honey, oil, and balm. 18 Damascus traded with you for your abundant goods—because of your great wealth of every kind—wine of Helbon, and

---

a Gk OL Aquila: Heb *have vanished, O inhabited one,*   b Heb *it and its inhabitants*   c Heb *their*   d Cn: Heb *its inhabitants*   e Gk: Heb *I will give beauty*   f Or *boxwood*   g Cn Compare Gen 10.18: Heb *your skilled men, O Tyre*   h Or *Persia*   i Or *and your army*   j Gk: Heb *The Dedanites*   k Another reading is *Aram*   l Meaning of Heb uncertain

white wool. ¹⁹Vedan and Javan from Uzal*ᵃ* entered into trade for your wares; wrought iron, cassia, and sweet cane were bartered for your merchandise. ²⁰Dedan traded with you in saddlecloths for riding. ²¹Arabia and all the princes of Kedar were your favored dealers in lambs, rams, and goats; in these they did business with you. ²²The merchants of Sheba and Raamah traded with you; they exchanged for your wares the best of all kinds of spices, and all precious stones, and gold. ²³Haran, Canneh, Eden, the merchants of Sheba, Asshur, and Chilmad traded with you. ²⁴These traded with you in choice garments, in clothes of blue and embroidered work, and in carpets of colored material, bound with cords and made secure; in these they traded with you.*ᵇ* ²⁵The ships of Tarshish traveled for you in your trade.

So you were filled and heavily laden
　　in the heart of the seas.
²⁶ Your rowers have brought you
　　into the high seas.
The east wind has wrecked you
　　in the heart of the seas.
²⁷ Your riches, your wares, your merchandise,
　　your mariners and your pilots,
your caulkers, your dealers in merchandise,
　　and all your warriors within you,
with all the company
　　that is with you,
sink into the heart of the seas
　　on the day of your ruin.
²⁸ At the sound of the cry of your pilots
　　the countryside shakes,
²⁹ and down from their ships
　　come all that handle the oar.
The mariners and all the pilots of the sea
　　stand on the shore
³⁰ and wail aloud over you,
　　and cry bitterly.
They throw dust on their heads
　　and wallow in ashes;
³¹ they make themselves bald for you,
　　and put on sackcloth,
and they weep over you in bitterness of soul,
　　with bitter mourning.
³² In their wailing they raise a lamentation
　　for you,
　　and lament over you:
"Who was ever destroyed*ᶜ* like Tyre
　　in the midst of the sea?

³³ When your wares came from the seas,
　　you satisfied many peoples;
with your abundant wealth and merchandise
　　you enriched the kings of the earth.
³⁴ Now you are wrecked by the seas,
　　in the depths of the waters;
your merchandise and all your crew
　　have sunk with you.
³⁵ All the inhabitants of the coastlands
　　are appalled at you;
and their kings are horribly afraid,
　　their faces are convulsed.
³⁶ The merchants among the peoples hiss
　　at you;
you have come to a dreadful end
　　and shall be no more forever."

28 Proclamation against the King of Tyre

The word of the LORD came to me: ²Mortal, say to the prince of Tyre, Thus says the Lord GOD:

Because your heart is proud
　　and you have said, "I am a god;
I sit in the seat of the gods,
　　in the heart of the seas,"
yet you are but a mortal, and no god,
　　though you compare your mind
　　with the mind of a god.
³ You are indeed wiser than Daniel;*ᵈ*
　　no secret is hidden from you;
⁴ by your wisdom and your understanding
　　you have amassed wealth for yourself,
and have gathered gold and silver
　　into your treasuries.
⁵ By your great wisdom in trade
　　you have increased your wealth,
and your heart has become proud in your
　　wealth.
⁶ Therefore thus says the Lord GOD:
Because you compare your mind
　　with the mind of a god,
⁷ therefore, I will bring strangers against you,
　　the most terrible of the nations;
they shall draw their swords against the
　　beauty of your wisdom
　　and defile your splendor.
⁸ They shall thrust you down to the Pit,
　　and you shall die a violent death
　　in the heart of the seas.

ᵃ Meaning of Heb uncertain ᵇ Cn: Heb *in your market* ᶜ Tg Vg: Heb *like silence* ᵈ Or, as otherwise read, *Danel*

9 Will you still say, "I am a god,"
   in the presence of those who kill you,
though you are but a mortal, and no god,
   in the hands of those who wound you?
10 You shall die the death of the uncircumcised
   by the hand of foreigners;
   for I have spoken, says the Lord GOD.

Lamentation over the King of Tyre

11 Moreover the word of the LORD came to me:
12Mortal, raise a lamentation over the king of Tyre,
and say to him, Thus says the Lord GOD:
   You were the signet of perfection,[a]
      full of wisdom and perfect in beauty.
13 You were in Eden, the garden of God;
      every precious stone was your covering,
   carnelian, chrysolite, and moonstone,
      beryl, onyx, and jasper,
   sapphire,[b] turquoise, and emerald;
      and worked in gold were your settings
      and your engravings.[a]
   On the day that you were created
      they were prepared.
14 With an anointed cherub as guardian I
         placed you;[a]
      you were on the holy mountain of God;
      you walked among the stones of fire.
15 You were blameless in your ways
      from the day that you were created,
      until iniquity was found in you.
16 In the abundance of your trade
      you were filled with violence, and you
         sinned;
   so I cast you as a profane thing from the
         mountain of God,
      and the guardian cherub drove you out
      from among the stones of fire.
17 Your heart was proud because of your beauty;
      you corrupted your wisdom for the sake of
         your splendor.
   I cast you to the ground;
      I exposed you before kings,
      to feast their eyes on you.
18 By the multitude of your iniquities,
      in the unrighteousness of your trade,
      you profaned your sanctuaries.
   So I brought out fire from within you;
      it consumed you,
   and I turned you to ashes on the earth
      in the sight of all who saw you.

19 All who know you among the peoples
      are appalled at you;
   you have come to a dreadful end
      and shall be no more forever.

Proclamation against Sidon

20 The word of the LORD came to me: 21Mortal,
set your face toward Sidon, and prophesy against it,
22and say, Thus says the Lord GOD:
   I am against you, O Sidon,
      and I will gain glory in your midst.
   They shall know that I am the LORD
      when I execute judgments in it,
      and manifest my holiness in it;
23 for I will send pestilence into it,
      and bloodshed into its streets;
   and the dead shall fall in its midst,
      by the sword that is against it on every
         side.
   And they shall know that I am the LORD.

24 The house of Israel shall no longer find a prick-
ing brier or a piercing thorn among all their neighbors who have treated them with contempt. And
they shall know that I am the Lord GOD.

Future Blessing for Israel

25 Thus says the Lord GOD: When I gather the
house of Israel from the peoples among whom they
are scattered, and manifest my holiness in them in
the sight of the nations, then they shall settle on
their own soil that I gave to my servant Jacob.
26They shall live in safety in it, and shall build
houses and plant vineyards. They shall live in safety,
when I execute judgments upon all their neighbors
who have treated them with contempt. And they
shall know that I am the LORD their God.

Proclamation against Egypt

29 In the tenth year, in the tenth month, on
the twelfth day of the month, the word of
the LORD came to me: 2Mortal, set your face against
Pharaoh king of Egypt, and prophesy against him
and against all Egypt; 3speak, and say, Thus says the
Lord GOD:
   I am against you,
      Pharaoh king of Egypt,
   the great dragon sprawling
      in the midst of its channels,
   saying, "My Nile is my own;
      I made it for myself."

---

a Meaning of Heb uncertain b Or lapis lazuli

⁴ I will put hooks in your jaws,
　　and make the fish of your channels stick to
　　　　your scales.
　I will draw you up from your channels,
　　with all the fish of your channels
　　　sticking to your scales.
⁵ I will fling you into the wilderness,
　　you and all the fish of your channels;
　you shall fall in the open field,
　　and not be gathered and buried.
　To the animals of the earth and to the birds of
　　the air
　　I have given you as food.
⁶ Then all the inhabitants of Egypt shall know
　　that I am the LORD
　because you*a* were a staff of reed
　　to the house of Israel;
⁷ when they grasped you with the hand, you
　　broke,
　　and tore all their shoulders;
　and when they leaned on you, you broke,
　　and made all their legs unsteady.*b*

8 Therefore, thus says the Lord GOD: I will bring a sword upon you, and will cut off from you human being and animal; ⁹and the land of Egypt shall be a desolation and a waste. Then they shall know that I am the LORD.

Because you*c* said, "The Nile is mine, and I made it," ¹⁰therefore, I am against you, and against your channels, and I will make the land of Egypt an utter waste and desolation, from Migdol to Syene, as far as the border of Ethiopia.*d* ¹¹No human foot shall pass through it, and no animal foot shall pass through it; it shall be uninhabited forty years. ¹²I will make the land of Egypt a desolation among desolated countries; and her cities shall be a desolation forty years among cities that are laid waste. I will scatter the Egyptians among the nations, and disperse them among the countries.

13 Further, thus says the Lord GOD: At the end of forty years I will gather the Egyptians from the peoples among whom they were scattered; ¹⁴and I will restore the fortunes of Egypt, and bring them back to the land of Pathros, the land of their origin; and there they shall be a lowly kingdom. ¹⁵It shall be the most lowly of the kingdoms, and never again exalt itself above the nations; and I will make them so small that they will never again rule over the nations. ¹⁶The Egyptians*e* shall never again be the reliance of the house of Israel; they will recall their

iniquity, when they turned to them for aid. Then they shall know that I am the Lord GOD.

Babylonia Will Plunder Egypt

17 In the twenty-seventh year, in the first month, on the first day of the month, the word of the LORD came to me: ¹⁸Mortal, King Nebuchadrezzar of Babylon made his army labor hard against Tyre; every head was made bald and every shoulder was rubbed bare; yet neither he nor his army got anything from Tyre to pay for the labor that he had expended against it. ¹⁹Therefore thus says the Lord GOD: I will give the land of Egypt to King Nebuchadrezzar of Babylon; and he shall carry off its wealth and despoil it and plunder it; and it shall be the wages for his army. ²⁰I have given him the land of Egypt as his payment for which he labored, because they worked for me, says the Lord GOD.

21 On that day I will cause a horn to sprout up for the house of Israel, and I will open your lips among them. Then they shall know that I am the LORD.

Lamentation for Egypt

30 The word of the LORD came to me: ²Mortal, prophesy, and say, Thus says the Lord GOD:
　　Wail, "Alas for the day!"
³　　For a day is near,
　　　the day of the LORD is near;
　　it will be a day of clouds,
　　　a time of doom.*f* for the nations.
⁴　A sword shall come upon Egypt,
　　　and anguish shall be in Ethiopia,*d*
　　when the slain fall in Egypt,
　　　and its wealth is carried away,
　　　and its foundations are torn down.
⁵Ethiopia,*d* and Put, and Lud, and all Arabia, and Libya,*g* and the people of the allied land*h* shall fall with them by the sword.

⁶　Thus says the LORD:
　　Those who support Egypt shall fall,
　　　and its proud might shall come
　　　　down;
　　from Migdol to Syene
　　　they shall fall within it by the sword,
　　says the Lord GOD.
⁷　They shall be desolated among other
　　　desolated countries,

---

a Gk Syr Vg: Heb *they*　*b* Syr: Heb *stand*　*c* Gk Syr Vg: Heb *he*　*d* Or *Nubia*; Heb *Cush*　*e* Heb *It*　*f* Heb lacks *of doom*　*g* Compare Gk Syr Vg: Heb *Cub*　*h* Meaning of Heb uncertain

and their cities shall lie among cities laid
    waste.
8 Then they shall know that I am the LORD,
    when I have set fire to Egypt,
    and all who help it are broken.

9 On that day, messengers shall go out from me in ships to terrify the unsuspecting Ethiopians;[a] and anguish shall come upon them on the day of Egypt's doom;[b] for it is coming!

10 Thus says the Lord GOD:
    I will put an end to the hordes of Egypt,
      by the hand of King Nebuchadrezzar of
        Babylon.
11 He and his people with him, the most terrible
      of the nations,
      shall be brought in to destroy the land;
    and they shall draw their swords against Egypt,
    and fill the land with the slain.
12 I will dry up the channels,
    and will sell the land into the hand of
      evildoers;
    I will bring desolation upon the land and
      everything in it
    by the hand of foreigners;
    I the LORD have spoken.

13 Thus says the Lord GOD:
    I will destroy the idols
      and put an end to the images in Memphis;
    there shall no longer be a prince in the land of
      Egypt;
    so I will put fear in the land of Egypt.
14 I will make Pathros a desolation,
    and will set fire to Zoan,
    and will execute acts of judgment on
      Thebes.
15 I will pour my wrath upon Pelusium,
    the stronghold of Egypt,
    and cut off the hordes of Thebes.
16 I will set fire to Egypt;
    Pelusium shall be in great agony;
    Thebes shall be breached,
    and Memphis face adversaries by day.
17 The young men of On and of Pi-beseth shall
      fall by the sword;
    and the cities themselves[c] shall go into
      captivity.
18 At Tehaphnehes the day shall be dark,
    when I break there the dominion of Egypt,

and its proud might shall come to an end;
    the city[d] shall be covered by a cloud,
    and its daughter-towns shall go into
      captivity.
19 Thus I will execute acts of judgment on Egypt.
    Then they shall know that I am the LORD.

Proclamation against Pharaoh

20 In the eleventh year, in the first month, on the seventh day of the month, the word of the LORD came to me: [21] Mortal, I have broken the arm of Pharaoh king of Egypt; it has not been bound up for healing or wrapped with a bandage, so that it may become strong to wield the sword. [22] Therefore thus says the Lord GOD: I am against Pharaoh king of Egypt, and will break his arms, both the strong arm and the one that was broken; and I will make the sword fall from his hand. [23] I will scatter the Egyptians among the nations, and disperse them throughout the lands. [24] I will strengthen the arms of the king of Babylon, and put my sword in his hand; but I will break the arms of Pharaoh, and he will groan before him with the groans of one mortally wounded. [25] I will strengthen the arms of the king of Babylon, but the arms of Pharaoh shall fall. And they shall know that I am the LORD, when I put my sword into the hand of the king of Babylon. He shall stretch it out against the land of Egypt, [26] and I will scatter the Egyptians among the nations and disperse them throughout the countries. Then they shall know that I am the LORD.

The Lofty Cedar

31 In the eleventh year, in the third month, on the first day of the month, the word of the LORD came to me: [2] Mortal, say to Pharaoh king of Egypt and to his hordes:
    Whom are you like in your greatness?
3   Consider Assyria, a cedar of Lebanon,
    with fair branches and forest shade,
    and of great height,
      its top among the clouds.[e]
4 The waters nourished it,
    the deep made it grow tall,
    making its rivers flow[f]
    around the place it was planted,
    sending forth its streams
      to all the trees of the field.
5 So it towered high
    above all the trees of the field;

---

a Or *Nubians*; Heb *Cush* b Heb *the day of Egypt* c Heb *and they* d Heb *she* e Gk: Heb *thick boughs* f Gk: Heb *rivers going*

its boughs grew large
 and its branches long,
  from abundant water in its shoots.
6 All the birds of the air
 made their nests in its boughs;
  under its branches all the animals of the field
   gave birth to their young;
 and in its shade
  all great nations lived.

7 It was beautiful in its greatness,
 in the length of its branches;
  for its roots went down
   to abundant water.
8 The cedars in the garden of God could not
  rival it,
  nor the fir trees equal its boughs;
 the plane trees were as nothing
  compared with its branches;
 no tree in the garden of God
  was like it in beauty.
9 I made it beautiful
 with its mass of branches,
  the envy of all the trees of Eden
   that were in the garden of God.

10 Therefore thus says the Lord God: Because it[a] towered high and set its top among the clouds,[b] and its heart was proud of its height, [11]I gave it into the hand of the prince of the nations; he has dealt with it as its wickedness deserves. I have cast it out. [12]Foreigners from the most terrible of the nations have cut it down and left it. On the mountains and in all the valleys its branches have fallen, and its boughs lie broken in all the watercourses of the land; and all the peoples of the earth went away from its shade and left it.
13 On its fallen trunk settle
 all the birds of the air,
  and among its boughs lodge
   all the wild animals.
[14]All this is in order that no trees by the waters may grow to lofty height or set their tops among the clouds,[b] and that no trees that drink water may reach up to them in height.
 For all of them are handed over to death,
  to the world below;
 along with all mortals,
  with those who go down to the Pit.

15 Thus says the Lord God: On the day it went down to Sheol I closed the deep over it and covered it; I restrained its rivers, and its mighty waters were checked. I clothed Lebanon in gloom for it, and all the trees of the field fainted because of it. [16]I made the nations quake at the sound of its fall, when I cast it down to Sheol with those who go down to the Pit; and all the trees of Eden, the choice and best of Lebanon, all that were well watered, were consoled in the world below. [17]They also went down to Sheol with it, to those killed by the sword, along with its allies,[c] those who lived in its shade among the nations.

18 Which among the trees of Eden was like you in glory and in greatness? Now you shall be brought down with the trees of Eden to the world below; you shall lie among the uncircumcised, with those who are killed by the sword. This is Pharaoh and all his horde, says the Lord God.

Lamentation over Pharaoh and Egypt

32 In the twelfth year, in the twelfth month, on the first day of the month, the word of the Lord came to me: [2]Mortal, raise a lamentation over Pharaoh king of Egypt, and say to him:
 You consider yourself a lion among the
  nations,
 but you are like a dragon in the seas;
  you thrash about in your streams,
  trouble the water with your feet,
  and foul your[d] streams.
3 Thus says the Lord God:
 In an assembly of many peoples
  I will throw my net over you;
  and I[e] will haul you up in my dragnet.
4 I will throw you on the ground,
 on the open field I will fling you,
  and will cause all the birds of the air to settle
   on you,
 and I will let the wild animals of the whole
  earth gorge themselves with you.
5 I will strew your flesh on the mountains,
 and fill the valleys with your carcass.[f]
6 I will drench the land with your flowing blood

a Syr Vg: Heb *you* b Gk: Heb *thick boughs* c Heb *its arms* d Heb *their* e Gk Vg: Heb *they* f Symmachus Syr Vg: Heb *your height*

up to the mountains,
and the watercourses will be filled with you.
7 When I blot you out, I will cover the heavens,
and make their stars dark;
I will cover the sun with a cloud,
and the moon shall not give its light.
8 All the shining lights of the heavens
I will darken above you,
and put darkness on your land,
says the Lord GOD.
9 I will trouble the hearts of many peoples,
as I carry you captive[a] among the nations,
into countries you have not known.
10 I will make many peoples appalled at you;
their kings shall shudder because of you.
When I brandish my sword before them,
they shall tremble every moment
for their lives, each one of them,
on the day of your downfall.
11 For thus says the Lord GOD:
The sword of the king of Babylon shall come
against you.
12 I will cause your hordes to fall
by the swords of mighty ones,
all of them most terrible among the nations.
They shall bring to ruin the pride of Egypt,
and all its hordes shall perish.
13 I will destroy all its livestock
from beside abundant waters;
and no human foot shall trouble them any
more,
nor shall the hoofs of cattle trouble them.
14 Then I will make their waters clear,
and cause their streams to run like oil, says
the Lord GOD.
15 When I make the land of Egypt desolate
and when the land is stripped of all that
fills it,
when I strike down all who live in it,
then they shall know that I am the LORD.
16 This is a lamentation; it shall be chanted.
The women of the nations shall
chant it.
Over Egypt and all its hordes they shall chant it,
says the Lord GOD.

Dirge over Egypt

17 In the twelfth year, in the first month,[b] on the
fifteenth day of the month, the word of the LORD
came to me:

18 Mortal, wail over the hordes of Egypt,
and send them down,
with Egypt[c] and the daughters of majestic
nations,
to the world below,
with those who go down to the Pit.
19 "Whom do you surpass in beauty?
Go down! Be laid to rest with the
uncircumcised!"
20 They shall fall among those who are killed by the
sword. Egypt[c] has been handed over to the sword;
carry away both it and its hordes. 21 The mighty chiefs
shall speak of them, with their helpers, out of the
midst of Sheol: "They have come down, they lie still,
the uncircumcised, killed by the sword."

22 Assyria is there, and all its company, their
graves all around it, all of them killed, fallen by the
sword. 23 Their graves are set in the uttermost parts
of the Pit. Its company is all around its grave, all of
them killed, fallen by the sword, who spread terror
in the land of the living.

24 Elam is there, and all its hordes around its
grave; all of them killed, fallen by the sword, who
went down uncircumcised into the world below,
who spread terror in the land of the living. They
bear their shame with those who go down to the Pit.
25 They have made Elam[d] a bed among the slain
with all its hordes, their graves all around it, all of
them uncircumcised, killed by the sword; for terror
of them was spread in the land of the living, and they
bear their shame with those who go down to the
Pit; they are placed among the slain.

26 Meshech and Tubal are there, and all their
multitude, their graves all around them, all of them
uncircumcised, killed by the sword; for they spread
terror in the land of the living. 27 And they do not
lie with the fallen warriors of long ago[e] who went
down to Sheol with their weapons of war, whose
swords were laid under their heads, and whose
shields[f] are upon their bones; for the terror of the
warriors was in the land of the living. 28 So you shall
be broken and lie among the uncircumcised, with
those who are killed by the sword.

29 Edom is there, its kings and all its princes, who
for all their might are laid with those who are killed
by the sword; they lie with the uncircumcised, with
those who go down to the Pit.

30 The princes of the north are there, all of them,
and all the Sidonians, who have gone down in shame
with the slain, for all the terror that they caused by

---

a Gk: Heb *bring your destruction*   b Gk: Heb lacks *in the first month*   c Heb *it*   d Heb *It*   e Gk Old Latin: Heb *of the uncircumcised*   f Cn: Heb
iniquities

their might; they lie uncircumcised with those who are killed by the sword, and bear their shame with those who go down to the Pit.

31 When Pharaoh sees them, he will be consoled for all his hordes—Pharaoh and all his army, killed by the sword, says the Lord GOD. [32]For he[a] spread terror in the land of the living; therefore he shall be laid to rest among the uncircumcised, with those who are slain by the sword—Pharaoh and all his multitude, says the Lord GOD.

Ezekiel Israel's Sentry

33 The word of the LORD came to me: [2]O Mortal, speak to your people and say to them, If I bring the sword upon a land, and the people of the land take one of their number as their sentinel; [3]and if the sentinel sees the sword coming upon the land and blows the trumpet and warns the people; [4]then if any who hear the sound of the trumpet do not take warning, and the sword comes and takes them away, their blood shall be upon their own heads. [5]They heard the sound of the trumpet and did not take warning; their blood shall be upon themselves. But if they had taken warning, they would have saved their lives. [6]But if the sentinel sees the sword coming and does not blow the trumpet, so that the people are not warned, and the sword comes and takes any of them, they are taken away in their iniquity, but their blood I will require at the sentinel's hand.

7 So you, mortal, I have made a sentinel for the house of Israel; whenever you hear a word from my mouth, you shall give them warning from me. [8]If I say to the wicked, "O wicked ones, you shall surely die," and you do not speak to warn the wicked to turn from their ways, the wicked shall die in their iniquity, but their blood I will require at your hand. [9]But if you warn the wicked to turn from their ways, and they do not turn from their ways, the wicked shall die in their iniquity, but you will have saved your life.

God's Justice and Mercy

10 Now you, mortal, say to the house of Israel, Thus you have said: "Our transgressions and our sins weigh upon us, and we waste away because of them; how then can we live?" [11]Say to them, As I live, says the Lord GOD, I have no pleasure in the death of the wicked, but that the wicked turn from their ways and live; turn back, turn back from your evil ways; for why will you die, O house of Israel?

[12]And you, mortal, say to your people, The righteousness of the righteous shall not save them when they transgress; and as for the wickedness of the wicked, it shall not make them stumble when they turn from their wickedness; and the righteous shall not be able to live by their righteousness[b] when they sin. [13]Though I say to the righteous that they shall surely live, yet if they trust in their righteousness and commit iniquity, none of their righteous deeds shall be remembered; but in the iniquity that they have committed they shall die. [14]Again, though I say to the wicked, "You shall surely die," yet if they turn from their sin and do what is lawful and right— [15]if the wicked restore the pledge, give back what they have taken by robbery, and walk in the statutes of life, committing no iniquity—they shall surely live, they shall not die. [16]None of the sins that they have committed shall be remembered against them; they have done what is lawful and right, they shall surely live.

17 Yet your people say, "The way of the Lord is not just," when it is their own way that is not just. [18]When the righteous turn from their righteousness, and commit iniquity, they shall die for it.[c] [19]And when the wicked turn from their wickedness, and do what is lawful and right, they shall live by it.[c] [20]Yet you say, "The way of the Lord is not just." O house of Israel, I will judge all of you according to your ways!

The Fall of Jerusalem

21 In the twelfth year of our exile, in the tenth month, on the fifth day of the month, someone who had escaped from Jerusalem came to me and said, "The city has fallen." [22]Now the hand of the LORD had been upon me the evening before the fugitive came; but he had opened my mouth by the time the fugitive came to me in the morning; so my mouth was opened, and I was no longer unable to speak.

The Survivors in Judah

23 The word of the LORD came to me: [24]Mortal, the inhabitants of these waste places in the land of Israel keep saying, "Abraham was only one man, yet he got possession of the land; but we are many; the land is surely given us to possess." [25]Therefore say to them, Thus says the Lord GOD: You eat flesh with the blood, and lift up your eyes to your idols, and shed blood; shall you then possess the land? [26]You depend on your swords, you commit abominations,

a Cn: Heb *I*   b Heb *by it*   c Heb *them*

and each of you defiles his neighbor's wife; shall you then possess the land? ²⁷ Say this to them, Thus says the Lord GOD: As I live, surely those who are in the waste places shall fall by the sword; and those who are in the open field I will give to the wild animals to be devoured; and those who are in strongholds and in caves shall die by pestilence. ²⁸I will make the land a desolation and a waste, and its proud might shall come to an end; and the mountains of Israel shall be so desolate that no one will pass through. ²⁹Then they shall know that I am the LORD, when I have made the land a desolation and a waste because of all their abominations that they have committed.

30 As for you, mortal, your people who talk together about you by the walls, and at the doors of the houses, say to one another, each to a neighbor, "Come and hear what the word is that comes from the LORD." ³¹They come to you as people come, and they sit before you as my people, and they hear your words, but they will not obey them. For flattery is on their lips, but their heart is set on their gain. ³²To them you are like a singer of love songs,*a* one who has a beautiful voice and plays well on an instrument; they hear what you say, but they will not do it. ³³When this comes—and come it will!—then they shall know that a prophet has been among them.

34 **Israel's False Shepherds**

The word of the LORD came to me: ²Mortal, prophesy against the shepherds of Israel: prophesy, and say to them—to the shepherds: Thus says the Lord GOD: Ah, you shepherds of Israel who have been feeding yourselves! Should not shepherds feed the sheep? ³You eat the fat, you clothe yourselves with the wool, you slaughter the fatlings; but you do not feed the sheep. ⁴You have not strengthened the weak, you have not healed the sick, you have not bound up the injured, you have not brought back the strayed, you have not sought the lost, but with force and harshness you have ruled them. ⁵So they were scattered, because there was no shepherd; and scattered, they became food for all the wild animals. ⁶My sheep were scattered, they wandered over all the mountains and on every high hill; my sheep were scattered over all the face of the earth, with no one to search or seek for them.

7 Therefore, you shepherds, hear the word of the LORD: ⁸As I live, says the Lord GOD, because my sheep have become a prey, and my sheep have become food for all the wild animals, since there was no shepherd; and because my shepherds have not searched for my sheep, but the shepherds have fed themselves, and have not fed my sheep; ⁹therefore, you shepherds, hear the word of the LORD: ¹⁰Thus says the Lord GOD, I am against the shepherds; and I will demand my sheep at their hand, and put a stop to their feeding the sheep; no longer shall the shepherds feed themselves. I will rescue my sheep from their mouths, so that they may not be food for them.

God, the True Shepherd

11 For thus says the Lord GOD: I myself will search for my sheep, and will seek them out. ¹²As shepherds seek out their flocks when they are among their scattered sheep, so I will seek out my sheep. I will rescue them from all the places to which they have been scattered on a day of clouds and thick darkness. ¹³I will bring them out from the peoples and gather them from the countries, and will bring them into their own land; and I will feed them on

PRAY IT!

The Good Shepherd Ezekiel 34

The theme of the good shepherd is common in the Bible. **Psalm 23** compares God to a protective shepherd, and in **John 10:1–18** Jesus compares himself to a good shepherd.

Ezekiel 34 describes bad shepherds and contrasts them with God, the true shepherd, who feeds the flock with justice. Think about the ways the concept of God as our shepherd is both a comfort and a challenge as you pray today.

God, the true shepherd, thank you for your care and protection. Make me aware of the people in my life who are weak, injured, straying, or lost. Help me do what I can to strengthen them, comfort them, and bring them back to you. Guide me today. I want to be more like a shepherd than like a sheep that merely follows!

a Cn: Heb *like a love song*

the mountains of Israel, by the watercourses, and in all the inhabited parts of the land. [14] I will feed them with good pasture, and the mountain heights of Israel shall be their pasture; there they shall lie down in good grazing land, and they shall feed on rich pasture on the mountains of Israel. [15] I myself will be the shepherd of my sheep, and I will make them lie down, says the Lord God. [16] I will seek the lost, and I will bring back the strayed, and I will bind up the injured, and I will strengthen the weak, but the fat and the strong I will destroy. I will feed them with justice.

17 As for you, my flock, thus says the Lord God: I shall judge between sheep and sheep, between rams and goats: [18] Is it not enough for you to feed on the good pasture, but you must tread down with your feet the rest of your pasture? When you drink of clear water, must you foul the rest with your feet? [19] And must my sheep eat what you have trodden with your feet, and drink what you have fouled with your feet?

20 Therefore, thus says the Lord God to them: I myself will judge between the fat sheep and the lean sheep. [21] Because you pushed with flank and shoulder, and butted at all the weak animals with your horns until you scattered them far and wide, [22] I will save my flock, and they shall no longer be ravaged; and I will judge between sheep and sheep.

23 I will set up over them one shepherd, my servant David, and he shall feed them: he shall feed them and be their shepherd. [24] And I, the Lord, will be their God, and my servant David shall be prince among them; I, the Lord, have spoken.

25 I will make with them a covenant of peace and banish wild animals from the land, so that they may live in the wild and sleep in the woods securely. [26] I will make them and the region around my hill a blessing; and I will send down the showers in their season; they shall be showers of blessing. [27] The trees of the field shall yield their fruit, and the earth shall yield its increase. They shall be secure on their soil; and they shall know that I am the Lord, when I break the bars of their yoke, and save them from the hands of those who enslaved them. [28] They shall no more be plunder for the nations, nor shall the animals of the land devour them; they shall live in safety, and no one shall make them afraid. [29] I will provide for them a splendid vegetation so that they shall no more be consumed with hunger in the land, and no longer suffer the insults of the nations.

[30] They shall know that I, the Lord their God, am with them, and that they, the house of Israel, are my people, says the Lord God. [31] You are my sheep, the sheep of my pasture[a] and I am your God, says the Lord God.

Judgment on Mount Seir

35 The word of the Lord came to me: [2] Mortal, set your face against Mount Seir, and prophesy against it, [3] and say to it, Thus says the Lord God:

I am against you, Mount Seir;
   I stretch out my hand against you
   to make you a desolation and a waste.
4 I lay your towns in ruins;
   you shall become a desolation,
   and you shall know that I am the Lord.

[5] Because you cherished an ancient enmity, and gave over the people of Israel to the power of the sword at the time of their calamity, at the time of their final punishment; [6] therefore, as I live, says the Lord God, I will prepare you for blood, and blood shall pursue you; since you did not hate bloodshed, bloodshed shall pursue you. [7] I will make Mount Seir a waste and a desolation; and I will cut off from it all who come and go. [8] I will fill its mountains with the slain; on your hills and in your valleys and in all your watercourses those killed with the sword shall fall. [9] I will make you a perpetual desolation, and your cities shall never be inhabited. Then you shall know that I am the Lord.

10 Because you said, "These two nations and these two countries shall be mine, and we will take possession of them,"—although the Lord was there— [11] therefore, as I live, says the Lord God, I will deal with you according to the anger and envy that you showed because of your hatred against them; and I will make myself known among you,[b] when I judge you. [12] You shall know that I, the Lord, have heard all the abusive speech that you uttered against the mountains of Israel, saying, "They are laid desolate, they are given us to devour." [13] And you magnified yourselves against me with your mouth, and multiplied your words against me; I heard it. [14] Thus says the Lord God: As the whole earth rejoices, I will make you desolate. [15] As you rejoiced over the inheritance of the house of Israel, because it was desolate, so I will deal with you; you shall be desolate, Mount Seir, and all Edom, all of it. Then they shall know that I am the Lord.

a Gk OL: Heb pasture, you are people b Gk: Heb them

Blessing on Israel

36 And you, mortal, prophesy to the mountains of Israel, and say: O mountains of Israel, hear the word of the LORD. [2]Thus says the Lord GOD: Because the enemy said of you, "Aha!" and, "The ancient heights have become our possession," [3]therefore prophesy, and say: Thus says the Lord GOD: Because they made you desolate indeed, and crushed you from all sides, so that you became the possession of the rest of the nations, and you became an object of gossip and slander among the people; [4]therefore, O mountains of Israel, hear the word of the Lord GOD: Thus says the Lord GOD to the mountains and the hills, the watercourses and the valleys, the desolate wastes and the deserted towns, which have become a source of plunder and an object of derision to the rest of the nations all around; [5]therefore thus says the Lord GOD: I am speaking in my hot jealousy against the rest of the nations, and against all Edom, who, with wholehearted joy and utter contempt, took my land as their possession, because of its pasture, to plunder it. [6]Therefore prophesy concerning the land of Israel, and say to the mountains and hills, to the watercourses and valleys, Thus says the Lord GOD: I am speaking in my jealous wrath, because you have suffered the insults of the nations; [7]therefore thus says the Lord GOD: I swear that the nations that are all around you shall themselves suffer insults.

[8] But you, O mountains of Israel, shall shoot out your branches, and yield your fruit to my people Israel; for they shall soon come home. [9]See now, I am for you; I will turn to you, and you shall be tilled and sown; [10]and I will multiply your population, the whole house of Israel, all of it; the towns shall be inhabited and the waste places rebuilt; [11]and I will multiply human beings and animals upon you. They shall increase and be fruitful; and I will cause you to be inhabited as in your former times, and will do more good to you than ever before. Then you shall know that I am the LORD. [12]I will lead people upon you—my people Israel—and they shall possess you, and you shall be

their inheritance. No longer shall you bereave them of children.

[13] Thus says the Lord GOD: Because they say to you, "You devour people, and you bereave your nation of children," [14]therefore you shall no longer devour people and no longer bereave your nation of children, says the Lord GOD; [15]and no longer will I let you hear the insults of the nations, no longer shall you bear the disgrace of the peoples; and no longer shall you cause your nation to stumble, says the Lord GOD.

The Renewal of Israel

[16] The word of the LORD came to me: [17]Mortal, when the house of Israel lived on their own soil, they defiled it with their ways and their deeds; their conduct in my sight was like the uncleanness of a woman in her menstrual period. [18]So I poured out my wrath upon them for the blood that they had shed upon the land, and for the idols with which they had defiled it. [19]I scattered them among the nations, and they were dispersed through the countries; in accordance with their conduct and their deeds I judged them. [20]But when they came to the nations, wherever they came, they profaned my holy name, in that it was said of them, "These are the people of the LORD, and yet they had to go out of his land." [21]But I had concern for my holy name, which the house of Israel had profaned among the nations to which they came.

[22] Therefore say to the house of Israel, Thus says the Lord GOD: It is not for your sake, O house of Israel, that I am about to act, but for the sake of my holy name, which you have profaned among the nations to which you came. [23]I will sanctify my great name, which has been profaned among the nations, and which you have profaned among them; and the nations shall know that I am the LORD, says the Lord GOD, when through you I display my holiness before their eyes. [24]I will take you from the nations, and gather you from all the countries, and bring you into your own land. [25]I will sprinkle clean water upon you, and you shall be clean from all your unclean-

> "A new heart I will give you, and a new spirit I will put within you; and I will remove from your body the heart of stone and give you a heart of flesh."
> —Ezekiel 36:26

nesses, and from all your idols I will cleanse you. ²⁶A new heart I will give you, and a new spirit I will put within you; and I will remove from your body the heart of stone and give you a heart of flesh. ²⁷I will put my spirit within you, and make you follow my statutes and be careful to observe my ordinances. ²⁸Then you shall live in the land that I gave to your ancestors; and you shall be my people, and I will be your God. ²⁹I will save you from all your uncleannesses, and I will summon the grain and make it abundant and lay no famine upon you. ³⁰I will make the fruit of the tree and the produce of the field abundant, so that you may never again suffer the disgrace of famine among the nations. ³¹Then you shall remember your evil ways, and your dealings that were not good; and you shall loathe yourselves for your iniquities and your abominable deeds. ³²It is not for your sake that I will act, says the Lord GOD; let that be known to you. Be ashamed and dismayed for your ways, O house of Israel.

33 Thus says the Lord GOD: On the day that I cleanse you from all your iniquities, I will cause the towns to be inhabited, and the waste places shall be rebuilt. ³⁴The land that was desolate shall be tilled, instead of being the desolation that it was in the sight of all who passed by. ³⁵And they will say, "This land that was desolate has become like the garden of Eden; and the waste and desolate and ruined towns are now inhabited and fortified." ³⁶Then the nations that are left all around you shall know that I, the LORD, have rebuilt the ruined places, and replanted that which was desolate; I, the LORD, have spoken, and I will do it.

37 Thus says the Lord GOD: I will also let the house of Israel ask me to do this for them: to increase their population like a flock. ³⁸Like the flock for sacrifices,ᵃ like the flock at Jerusalem during her appointed festivals, so shall the ruined towns be filled with flocks of people. Then they shall know that I am the LORD.

37 The Valley of Dry Bones

The hand of the LORD came upon me, and he brought me out by the spirit of the LORD and set me down in the middle of a valley; it was full of bones. ²He led me all around them; there were very many lying in the valley, and they were very dry. ³He said to me, "Mortal, can these bones live?" I answered, "O Lord GOD, you know." ⁴Then he said to me, "Prophesy to these bones, and say to them: O dry bones, hear the word of the LORD. ⁵Thus says the Lord GOD to these bones: I will cause breathᵇ to enter you, and you shall live. ⁶I will lay sinews on you, and will cause flesh to come upon you, and cover you with skin, and put breathᵇ in you, and you shall live; and you shall know that I am the LORD."

7 So I prophesied as I had been commanded; and as I prophesied, suddenly there was a noise, a rattling, and the bones came together, bone to its bone. ⁸I looked, and there were sinews on them, and flesh had come upon them, and skin had covered them; but there was no breath in them. ⁹Then he said to me, "Prophesy to the breath, prophesy, mortal, and say to the breath:ᶜ Thus says the Lord GOD: Come from the four winds, O breath,ᶜ and breathe upon

STUDY IT!

Wind, Breath, and Spirit · Ezekiel 37:1–14

The English words "wind," "breath," and "spirit" have different meanings. Hebrew has only one word for all three: "ruah." The "wind from God (that) swept over the face of the waters" at creation is "ruah" (Genesis 1:2). The "breath of life" that God blows into the lifeless clay of the first human is "ruah" (Genesis 2:7). And the "spirit of the LORD (that) came mightily upon David" at his anointing (1 Samuel 16:13) is "ruah."

In **Ezekiel 37:1–14**, all three meanings of the word "ruah" come into play. Ezekiel cries out, "Thus says the Lord GOD: Come from the **four winds**, O **breath** (or "spirit"), and breathe upon these slain, that they may live" (Ezekiel 37:9, emphasis added). In the prophet's vision, the bones scattered across the battlefield are the exiled people of God, who have experienced the "death" of defeat and humiliation. God promises that the **spirit** of God (Ezekiel 37:14, emphasis added) will bring the people of Israel back from the exile and restore them to their land.

---

a Heb *flock of holy things*   **b** Or *spirit*   **c** Or *wind or spirit*

Bone Dry
Ezekiel 37:1–14

Have you ever broken a bone? If so, you probably gained a greater appreciation for the fact that bones are our body's physical support structure. But the bones Ezekiel sees in his vision (Ezekiel 37:1-2) represent a spiritual lack of life, not a physical one (Ezekiel 37:11-13). And it is God's spirit that restores life (Ezekiel 37:14).

- What are the dry bones in your life?
- How can calling out to God in prayer open you up to God's reviving Spirit?
- How can God use your help to energize and breathe life into others who seem dry and hopeless?

these slain, that they may live." [10]I prophesied as he commanded me, and the breath came into them, and they lived, and stood on their feet, a vast multitude.

11 Then he said to me, "Mortal, these bones are the whole house of Israel. They say, 'Our bones are dried up, and our hope is lost; we are cut off completely.' [12]Therefore prophesy, and say to them, Thus says the Lord GOD: I am going to open your graves, and bring you up from your graves, O my people; and I will bring you back to the land of Israel. [13]And you shall know that I am the LORD, when I open your graves, and bring you up from your graves, O my people. [14]I will put my spirit within you, and you shall live, and I will place you on your own soil; then you shall know that I, the LORD, have spoken and will act, says the LORD."

The Two Sticks

15 The word of the LORD came to me: [16]Mortal, take a stick and write on it, "For Judah, and the Israelites associated with it"; then take another stick and write on it, "For Joseph (the stick of Ephraim) and all the house of Israel associated with it"; [17]and join them together into one stick, so that they may become one in your hand. [18]And when your people say to you, "Will you not show us what you mean by these?" [19]say to them, Thus says the Lord GOD: I

am about to take the stick of Joseph (which is in the hand of Ephraim) and the tribes of Israel associated with it; and I will put the stick of Judah upon it,[a] and make them one stick, in order that they may be one in my hand. [20]When the sticks on which you write are in your hand before their eyes, [21]then say to them, Thus says the Lord GOD: I will take the people of Israel from the nations among which they have gone, and will gather them from every quarter, and bring them to their own land. [22]I will make them one nation in the land, on the mountains of Israel; and one king shall be king over them all. Never again shall they be two nations, and never again shall they be divided into two kingdoms. [23]They shall never again defile themselves with their idols and their detestable things, or with any of their transgressions. I will save them from all the apostasies into which they have fallen,[b] and will cleanse them. Then they shall be my people, and I will be their God.

24 My servant David shall be king over them; and they shall all have one shepherd. They shall follow my ordinances and be careful to observe my statutes. [25]They shall live in the land that I gave to my servant Jacob, in which your ancestors lived; they and their children and their children's children shall live there forever; and my servant David shall be their prince forever. [26]I will make a covenant of peace with them; it shall be an everlasting covenant with them; and I will bless[c] them and multiply them, and will set my sanctuary among them forevermore. [27]My dwelling place shall be with them; and I will be their God, and they shall be my people. [28]Then the nations shall know that I the LORD sanctify Israel, when my sanctuary is among them forevermore.

Invasion by Gog

38 The word of the LORD came to me: [2]Mortal, set your face toward Gog, of the land of Magog, the chief prince of Meshech and Tubal. Prophesy against him [3]and say: Thus says the Lord GOD: I am against you, O Gog, chief prince of Meshech and Tubal; [4]I will turn you around and put hooks into your jaws, and I will lead you out with all your army, horses and horsemen, all of them clothed in full armor, a great company, all of them with shield and buckler, wielding swords. [5]Persia, Ethiopia,[d] and Put are with them, all of them with buckler and helmet; [6]Gomer and all its troops;

---

a Heb *I will put them upon it*   b Another reading is *from all the settlements in which they have sinned*   c Tg: Heb *give*   d Or *Nubia*; Heb *Cush*

Beth-togarmah from the remotest parts of the north with all its troops—many peoples are with you.

7 Be ready and keep ready, you and all the companies that are assembled around you, and hold yourselves in reserve for them. [8]After many days you shall be mustered; in the latter years you shall go against a land restored from war, a land where people were gathered from many nations on the mountains of Israel, which had long lain waste; its people were brought out from the nations and now are living in safety, all of them. [9]You shall advance, coming on like a storm; you shall be like a cloud covering the land, you and all your troops, and many peoples with you.

10 Thus says the Lord GOD: On that day thoughts will come into your mind, and you will devise an evil scheme. [11]You will say, "I will go up against the land of unwalled villages; I will fall upon the quiet people who live in safety, all of them living without walls, and having no bars or gates"; [12]to seize spoil and carry off plunder; to assail the waste places that are now inhabited, and the people who were gathered from the nations, who are acquiring cattle and goods, who live at the center[a] of the earth. [13]Sheba and Dedan and the merchants of Tarshish and all its young warriors[b] will say to you, "Have you come to seize spoil? Have you assembled your horde to carry off plunder, to carry away silver and gold, to take away cattle and goods, to seize a great amount of booty?"

14 Therefore, mortal, prophesy, and say to Gog: Thus says the Lord GOD: On that day when my people Israel are living securely, you will rouse yourself[c] [15]and come from your place out of the remotest parts of the north, you and many peoples with you, all of them riding on horses, a great horde, a mighty army; [16]you will come up against my people Israel, like a cloud covering the earth. In the latter days I will bring you against my land, so that the nations may know me, when through you, O Gog, I display my holiness before their eyes.

Judgment on Gog

17 Thus says the Lord GOD: Are you he of whom I spoke in former days by my servants the prophets of Israel, who in those days prophesied for years that I would bring you against them? [18]On that day, when Gog comes against the land of Israel, says the Lord GOD, my wrath shall be aroused. [19]For in my jealousy and in my blazing wrath I declare: On that day there shall be a great shaking in the land of Israel; [20]the fish of the sea, and the birds of the air, and the animals of the field, and all creeping things that creep on the ground, and all human beings that are on the face of the earth, shall quake at my presence, and the mountains shall be thrown down, and the cliffs shall fall, and every wall shall tumble to the ground. [21]I will summon the sword against Gog[d] in[e] all my mountains, says the Lord GOD; the swords of all will be against their comrades. [22]With pestilence and bloodshed I will enter into judgment with him; and I will pour down torrential rains and hailstones, fire and sulfur, upon him and his troops and the many peoples that are with him. [23]So I will display my greatness and my holiness and make myself known in the eyes of many nations. Then they shall know that I am the LORD.

Gog's Armies Destroyed

39 And you, mortal, prophesy against Gog, and say: Thus says the Lord GOD: I am against you, O Gog, chief prince of Meshech and Tubal! [2]I will turn you around and drive you forward, and bring you up from the remotest parts of the north, and lead you against the mountains of Israel. [3]I will strike your bow from your left hand, and will make your arrows drop out of your right hand. [4]You shall fall on the mountains of Israel, you and all your troops and the peoples that are with you; I will give you to birds of prey of every kind and to the wild animals to be devoured. [5]You shall fall in the open field; for I have spoken, says the Lord GOD. [6]I will send fire on Magog and on those who live securely in the coastlands; and they shall know that I am the LORD.

7 My holy name I will make known among my people Israel; and I will not let my holy name be profaned any more; and the nations shall know that I am the LORD, the Holy One in Israel. [8]It has come! It has happened, says the Lord GOD. This is the day of which I have spoken.

9 Then those who live in the towns of Israel will go out and make fires of the weapons and burn them—bucklers and shields, bows and arrows, handpikes and spears—and they will make fires of them for seven years. [10]They will not need to take wood out of the field or cut down any trees in the forests, for they will make their fires of the weapons; they will despoil those who despoiled them, and plunder those who plundered them, says the Lord GOD.

a Heb *navel*   b Heb *young lions*   c Gk: Heb *will you not know?*   d Heb *him*   e Heb *to* or *for*

The Burial of Gog

11 On that day I will give to Gog a place for burial in Israel, the Valley of the Travelers^a east of the sea; it shall block the path of the travelers, for there Gog and all his horde will be buried; it shall be called the Valley of Hamon-gog.^{b} ^{12}Seven months the house of Israel shall spend burying them, in order to cleanse the land. ^{13}All the people of the land shall bury them; and it will bring them honor on the day that I show my glory, says the Lord GOD. ^{14}They will set apart men to pass through the land regularly and bury any invaders^c who remain on the face of the land, so as to cleanse it; for seven months they shall make their search. ^{15}As the searchers^c pass through the land, anyone who sees a human bone shall set up a sign by it, until the buriers have buried it in the Valley of Hamon-gog.^{b} ^{16}(A city Hamonah^d is there also.) Thus they shall cleanse the land.

17 As for you, mortal, thus says the Lord GOD: Speak to the birds of every kind and to all the wild animals: Assemble and come, gather from all around to the sacrificial feast that I am preparing for you, a great sacrificial feast on the mountains of Israel, and you shall eat flesh and drink blood. ^{18}You shall eat the flesh of the mighty, and drink the blood of the princes of the earth—of rams, of lambs, and of goats, of bulls, all of them fatlings of Bashan. ^{19}You shall eat fat until you are filled, and drink blood until you are drunk, at the sacrificial feast that I am preparing for you. ^{20}And you shall be filled at my table with horses and charioteers,^{e} with warriors and all kinds of soldiers, says the Lord GOD.

Israel Restored to the Land

21 I will display my glory among the nations; and all the nations shall see my judgment that I have executed, and my hand that I have laid on them. ^{22}The house of Israel shall know that I am the LORD their God, from that day forward. ^{23}And the nations shall know that the house of Israel went into captivity for their iniquity, because they dealt treacherously with me. So I hid my face from them and gave them into the hand of their adversaries, and they all fell by the sword. ^{24}I dealt with them according to their uncleanness and their transgressions, and hid my face from them.

25 Therefore thus says the Lord GOD: Now I will restore the fortunes of Jacob, and have mercy on the whole house of Israel; and I will be jealous for my holy name. ^{26}They shall forget^f their shame, and all the treachery they have practiced against me, when they live securely in their land with no one to make them afraid, ^{27}when I have brought them back from the peoples and gathered them from their enemies' lands, and through them have displayed my holiness in the sight of many nations. ^{28}Then they shall know that I am the LORD their God because I sent them into exile among the nations, and then gathered them into their own land. I will leave none of them behind; ^{29}and I will never again hide my face from them, when I pour out my spirit upon the house of Israel, says the Lord GOD.

The Vision of the New Temple

40 In the twenty-fifth year of our exile, at the beginning of the year, on the tenth day of the month, in the fourteenth year after the city was struck down, on that very day, the hand of the LORD was upon me, and he brought me there. ^{2}He brought me, in visions of God, to the land of Israel, and set me down upon a very high mountain, on which was a structure like a city to the south. ^{3}When he brought me there, a man was there, whose appearance shone like bronze, with a linen cord and a measuring reed in his hand; and he was standing in the gateway. ^{4}The man said to me, "Mortal, look closely and listen attentively, and set your mind upon all that I shall show you, for you were brought here in order that I might show it to you; declare all that you see to the house of Israel."

5 Now there was a wall all around the outside of the temple area. The length of the measuring reed in the man's hand was six long cubits, each being a cubit and a handbreadth in length; so he measured the thickness of the wall, one reed; and the height, one reed. ^{6}Then he went into the gateway facing east, going up its steps, and measured the threshold of the gate, one reed deep.^{g} There were ^{7}recesses, and each recess was one reed wide and one reed deep; and the space between the recesses, five cubits; and the threshold of the gate by the vestibule of the gate at the inner end was one reed deep. ^{8}Then he measured the inner vestibule of the gateway, one cubit. ^{9}Then he measured the vestibule of the gateway, eight cubits; and its pilasters, two cubits; and the vestibule of the gate was at the inner end. ^{10}There were three recesses on either side of the east gate; the three were of the same size; and the pilasters on either side were of the same size. ^{11}Then he measured the width of the opening of the gateway, ten

---

a Or *of the Abarim* b That is, *the Horde of Gog* c Heb *travelers* d That is *The Horde* e Heb *chariots* f Another reading is *They shall bear* g Heb *deep, and one threshold, one reed deep*

cubits; and the width of the gateway, thirteen cubits. [12]There was a barrier before the recesses, one cubit on either side; and the recesses were six cubits on either side. [13]Then he measured the gate from the back[a] of the one recess to the back[a] of the other, a width of twenty-five cubits, from wall to wall.[b] [14]He measured[c] also the vestibule, twenty cubits; and the gate next to the pilaster on every side of the court.[d] [15]From the front of the gate at the entrance to the end of the inner vestibule of the gate was fifty cubits. [16]The recesses and their pilasters had windows, with shutters[e] on the inside of the gateway all around, and the vestibules also had windows on the inside all around; and on the pilasters were palm trees.

17 Then he brought me into the outer court; there were chambers there, and a pavement, all around the court; thirty chambers fronted on the pavement. [18]The pavement ran along the side of the gates, corresponding to the length of the gates; this was the lower pavement. [19]Then he measured the distance from the inner front of[e] the lower gate to the outer front of the inner court, one hundred cubits.[f]

20 Then he measured the gate of the outer court that faced north—its depth and width. [21]Its recesses, three on either side, and its pilasters and its vestibule were of the same size as those of the first gate; its depth was fifty cubits, and its width twenty-five cubits. [22]Its windows, its vestibule, and its palm trees were of the same size as those of the gate that faced toward the east. Seven steps led up to it; and its vestibule was on the inside.[g] [23]Opposite the gate on the north, as on the east, was a gate to the inner court; he measured from gate to gate, one hundred cubits.

24 Then he led me toward the south, and there was a gate on the south; and he measured its pilasters and its vestibule; they had the same dimensions as the others. [25]There were windows all around in it and in its vestibule, like the windows of the others; its depth was fifty cubits, and its width twenty-five cubits. [26]There were seven steps leading up to it; its vestibule was on the inside.[g] It had palm trees on its pilasters, one on either side. [27]There was a gate on the south of the inner court; and he measured from gate to gate toward the south, one hundred cubits.

28 Then he brought me to the inner court by the south gate, and he measured the south gate; it was of the same dimensions as the others. [29]Its recesses, its pilasters, and its vestibule were of the same size as the others; and there were windows all around in

it and in its vestibule; its depth was fifty cubits, and its width twenty-five cubits. [30]There were vestibules all around, twenty-five cubits deep and five cubits wide. [31]Its vestibule faced the outer court, and palm trees were on its pilasters, and its stairway had eight steps.

32 Then he brought me to the inner court on the east side, and he measured the gate; it was of the same size as the others. [33]Its recesses, its pilasters, and its vestibule were of the same dimensions as the others; and there were windows all around in it and in its vestibule; its depth was fifty cubits, and its width twenty-five cubits. [34]Its vestibule faced the outer court, and it had palm trees on its pilasters, on either side; and its stairway had eight steps.

35 Then he brought me to the north gate, and he measured it; it had the same dimensions as the others. [36]Its recesses, its pilasters, and its vestibule were of the same size as the others;[h] and it had windows all around. Its depth was fifty cubits, and its width twenty-five cubits. [37]Its vestibule[i] faced the outer court, and it had palm trees on its pilasters, on either side; and its stairway had eight steps.

38 There was a chamber with its door in the vestibule of the gate,[j] where the burnt offering was to be washed. [39]And in the vestibule of the gate were two tables on either side, on which the burnt offering and the sin offering and the guilt offering were to be slaughtered. [40]On the outside of the vestibule[k] at the entrance of the north gate were two tables; and on the other side of the vestibule of the gate were two tables. [41]Four tables were on the inside, and four tables on the outside of the side of the gate, eight tables, on which the sacrifices were to be slaughtered. [42]There were also four tables of hewn stone for the burnt offering, a cubit and a half long, and one cubit and a half wide, and one cubit high, on which the instruments were to be laid with which the burnt offerings and the sacrifices were slaughtered. [43]There were pegs, one handbreadth long, fastened all around the inside. And on the tables the flesh of the offering was to be laid.

44 On the outside of the inner gateway there were chambers for the singers in the inner court, one[l] at the side of the north gate facing south, the other at the side of the east gate facing north. [45]He said to me, "This chamber that faces south is for the priests who have charge of the temple, [46]and the chamber that faces north is for the priests who have charge of the altar; these are the descendants of Zadok, who alone

a Gk: Heb roof   b Heb opening facing opening   c Heb made   d Meaning of Heb uncertain   e Compare Gk: Heb from before   f Heb adds the east and the north   g Gk: Heb before them   h One Ms: Compare verses 29 and 33: MT lacks were of the same size as the others   i Gk Vg Compare verses 26, 31, 34: Heb pilasters   j Cn: Heb at the pilasters of the gates   k Cn: Heb to him who goes up   l Heb lacks one

among the descendants of Levi may come near to the LORD to minister to him." [47]He measured the court, one hundred cubits deep, and one hundred cubits wide, a square; and the altar was in front of the temple.

The Temple

48 Then he brought me to the vestibule of the temple and measured the pilasters of the vestibule, five cubits on either side; and the width of the gate was fourteen cubits; and the sidewalls of the gate were three cubits[a] on either side. [49]The depth of the vestibule was twenty cubits, and the width twelve[b] cubits; ten steps led up[c] to it; and there were pillars beside the pilasters on either side.

41   Then he brought me to the nave, and measured the pilasters; on each side six cubits was the width of the pilasters.[d] 2The width of the entrance was ten cubits; and the sidewalls of the entrance were five cubits on either side. He measured the length of the nave, forty cubits, and its width, twenty cubits. [3]Then he went into the inner room and measured the pilasters of the entrance, two cubits; and the width of the entrance, six cubits; and the sidewalls[e] of the entrance, seven cubits. [4]He measured the depth of the room, twenty cubits, and its width, twenty cubits, beyond the nave. And he said to me, This is the most holy place.

5 Then he measured the wall of the temple, six cubits thick; and the width of the side chambers, four cubits, all around the temple. [6]The side chambers were in three stories, one over another, thirty in each story. There were offsets[f] all around the wall of the temple to serve as supports for the side chambers, so that they should not be supported by the wall of the temple. [7]The passageway[g] of the side chambers widened from story to story; for the structure was supplied with a stairway all around the temple. For this reason the structure became wider from story to story. One ascended from the bottom story to the uppermost story by way of the middle one. [8]I saw also that the temple had a raised platform all around; the foundations of the side chambers measured a full reed of six long cubits. [9]The thickness of the outer wall of the side chambers was five cubits; and the free space between the side chambers of the temple [10]and the chambers of the court was a width of twenty cubits all around the temple on every side. [11]The side chambers opened onto the area left free, one door toward the north, and an-

other door toward the south; and the width of the part that was left free was five cubits all around.

12 The building that was facing the temple yard on the west side was seventy cubits wide; and the wall of the building was five cubits thick all around, and its depth ninety cubits.

13 Then he measured the temple, one hundred cubits deep; and the yard and the building with its walls, one hundred cubits deep; [14]also the width of the east front of the temple and the yard, one hundred cubits.

15 Then he measured the depth of the building facing the yard at the west, together with its galleries[h] on either side, one hundred cubits.

The nave of the temple and the inner room and the outer[i] vestibule [16]were paneled,[j] and, all around, all three had windows with recessed[k] frames. Facing the threshold the temple was paneled with wood all around, from the floor up to the windows (now the windows were covered), [17]to the space above the door, even to the inner room, and on the outside. And on all the walls all around in the inner room and the nave there was a pattern.[l] [18]It was formed of cherubim and palm trees, a palm tree between cherub and cherub. Each cherub had two faces: [19]a human face turned toward the palm tree on the one side, and the face of a young lion turned toward the palm tree on the other side. They were carved on the whole temple all around; [20]from the floor to the area above the door, cherubim and palm trees were carved on the wall.[m]

21 The doorposts of the nave were square. In front of the holy place was something resembling [22]an altar of wood, three cubits high, two cubits long, and two cubits wide;[n] its corners, its base,[o] and its walls were of wood. He said to me, "This is the table that stands before the LORD." [23]The nave and the holy place had each a double door. [24]The doors had two leaves apiece, two swinging leaves for each door. [25]On the doors of the nave were carved cherubim and palm trees, such as were carved on the walls; and there was a canopy of wood in front of the vestibule outside. [26]And there were recessed windows and palm trees on either side, on the sidewalls of the vestibule.[p]

42   ### The Holy Chambers and the Outer Wall

Then he led me out into the outer court, toward the north, and he brought me to the cham-

---

a Gk: Heb *and the width of the gate was three cubits* b Gk: Heb *eleven* c Gk: Heb *and by steps that went up* d Compare Gk: Heb *tent* e Gk: Heb *width*
f Gk Compare 1 Kings 6.6: Heb *they entered* g Cn: Heb *it was surrounded* h Cn: Meaning of Heb uncertain i Gk: Heb *of the court* j Gk: Heb *the*
thresholds k Cn Compare Gk 1 Kings 6.4: Meaning of Heb uncertain l Heb *measures* m Cn Compare verse 25: Heb *and the wall* n Gk: Heb lacks *two*
cubits wide o Gk: Heb *length* p Cn: Heb *vestibule. And the side chambers of the temple and the canopies*

bers that were opposite the temple yard and opposite the building on the north. [2]The length of the building that was on the north side[a] was[b] one hundred cubits, and the width fifty cubits. [3]Across the twenty cubits that belonged to the inner court, and facing the pavement that belonged to the outer court, the chambers rose[c] gallery[d] by gallery[d] in three stories. [4]In front of the chambers was a passage on the inner side, ten cubits wide and one hundred cubits deep,[e] and its[f] entrances were on the north. [5]Now the upper chambers were narrower, for the galleries[d] took more away from them than from the lower and middle chambers in the building. [6]For they were in three stories, and they had no pillars like the pillars of the outer[g] court; for this reason the upper chambers were set back from the ground more than the lower and the middle ones. [7]There was a wall outside parallel to the chambers, toward the outer court, opposite the chambers, fifty cubits long. [8]For the chambers on the outer court were fifty cubits long, while those opposite the temple were one hundred cubits long. [9]At the foot of these chambers ran a passage that one entered from the east in order to enter them from the outer court. [10]The width of the passage[h] was fixed by the wall of the court.

On the south[i] also, opposite the vacant area and opposite the building, there were chambers [11]with a passage in front of them; they were similar to the chambers on the north, of the same length and width, with the same exits[j] and arrangements and doors. [12]So the entrances of the chambers to the south were entered through the entrance at the head of the corresponding passage, from the east, along the matching wall.[d]

13 Then he said to me, "The north chambers and the south chambers opposite the vacant area are the holy chambers, where the priests who approach the LORD shall eat the most holy offerings; there they shall deposit the most holy offerings—the grain offering, the sin offering, and the guilt offering—for the place is holy. [14]When the priests enter the holy place, they shall not go out of it into the outer court without laying there the vestments in which they minister, for these are holy; they shall put on other garments before they go near to the area open to the people."

15 When he had finished measuring the interior of the temple area, he led me out by the gate that faces east, and measured the temple area all around.

[16]He measured the east side with the measuring reed, five hundred cubits by the measuring reed. [17]Then he turned and measured[k] the north side, five hundred cubits by the measuring reed. [18]Then he turned and measured[k] the south side, five hundred cubits by the measuring reed. [19]Then he turned to the west side and measured, five hundred cubits by the measuring reed. [20]He measured it on the four sides. It had a wall around it, five hundred cubits long and five hundred cubits wide, to make a separation between the holy and the common.

43

The Divine Glory Returns to the Temple

Then he brought me to the gate, the gate facing east. [2]And there, the glory of the God of Israel was coming from the east; the sound was like the sound of mighty waters; and the earth shone with his glory. [3]The[l] vision I saw was like the vision that I had seen when he came to destroy the city, and[m] like the vision that I had seen by the river Chebar; and I fell upon my face. [4]As the glory of the LORD entered the temple by the gate facing east, [5]the spirit lifted me up, and brought me into the inner court; and the glory of the LORD filled the temple.

6 While the man was standing beside me, I heard someone speaking to me out of the temple. [7]He said to me: Mortal, this is the place of my throne and the place for the soles of my feet, where I will reside among the people of Israel forever. The house of Israel shall no more defile my holy name, neither they nor their kings, by their whoring, and by the corpses of their kings at their death.[n] [8]When they placed their threshold by my threshold and their doorposts beside my doorposts, with only a wall between me and them, they were defiling my holy name by their abominations that they committed; therefore I have consumed them in my anger. [9]Now let them put away their idolatry and the corpses of their kings far from me, and I will reside among them forever.

10 As for you, mortal, describe the temple to the house of Israel, and let them measure the pattern; and let them be ashamed of their iniquities. [11]When they are ashamed of all that they have done, make known to them the plan of the temple, its arrangement, its exits and its entrances, and its whole form—all its ordinances and its entire plan and all its laws; and write it down in their sight, so that they may observe and follow the entire plan and all its ordinances.

STUDY IT!

Dwell
Ezekiel 43:1–5

Ezekiel's vision of God returning to the temple in **Ezekiel 43:1–5** completes the circle of his prophecy. Earlier, he had a unique vision of God's glory leaving the temple and coming to rest in Babylon (Ezekiel 10). For Ezekiel, the temple represented the heart of Israel's relationship with God, so the vision of God's presence returning was important and full of hope. This probably explains why Ezekiel brings that reality home by carefully recording the specifics of the new temple in the remaining chapters of his book.

The early Christians of the New Testament learned from Jesus that God's presence isn't limited to the physical structure of the temple. In fact, 1 Corinthians says, "Do you not know that you are God's temple and that God's Spirit dwells in you?" (3:16). Talk about a message of hope! God's spirit lives in you!

[12]This is the law of the temple: the whole territory on the top of the mountain all around shall be most holy. This is the law of the temple.

The Altar

13 These are the dimensions of the altar by cubits (the cubit being one cubit and a handbreadth): its base shall be one cubit high,[a] and one cubit wide, with a rim of one span around its edge. This shall be the height of the altar: [14]From the base on the ground to the lower ledge, two cubits, with a width of one cubit; and from the smaller ledge to the larger ledge, four cubits, with a width of one cubit; [15]and the altar hearth, four cubits; and from the altar hearth projecting upward, four horns. [16]The altar hearth shall be square, twelve cubits long by twelve wide. [17]The ledge also shall be square, fourteen cubits long by fourteen wide, with a rim around it half a cubit wide, and its surrounding base, one cubit. Its steps shall face east.

a Gk: Heb lacks *high*

18 Then he said to me: Mortal, thus says the Lord GOD: These are the ordinances for the altar: On the day when it is erected for offering burnt offerings upon it and for dashing blood against it, [19]you shall give to the levitical priests of the family of Zadok, who draw near to me to minister to me, says the Lord GOD, a bull for a sin offering. [20]And you shall take some of its blood, and put it on the four horns of the altar, and on the four corners of the ledge, and upon the rim all around; thus you shall purify it and make atonement for it. [21]You shall also take the bull of the sin offering, and it shall be burnt in the appointed place belonging to the temple, outside the sacred area.

22 On the second day you shall offer a male goat without blemish for a sin offering; and the altar shall be purified, as it was purified with the bull. [23]When you have finished purifying it, you shall offer a bull without blemish and a ram from the flock without blemish. [24]You shall present them before the LORD, and the priests shall throw salt on them and offer them up as a burnt offering to the LORD. [25]For seven days you shall provide daily a goat for a sin offering; also a bull and a ram from the flock, without blemish, shall be provided. [26]Seven days shall they make atonement for the altar and cleanse it, and so consecrate it. [27]When these days are over, then from the eighth day onward the priests shall offer upon the altar your burnt offerings and your offerings of well-being; and I will accept you, says the Lord GOD.

44 The Closed Gate

Then he brought me back to the outer gate of the sanctuary, which faces east; and it was shut. [2]The LORD said to me: This gate shall remain shut; it shall not be opened, and no one shall enter by it; for the LORD, the God of Israel, has entered by it; therefore it shall remain shut. [3]Only the prince, because he is a prince, may sit in it to eat food before the LORD; he shall enter by way of the vestibule of the gate, and shall go out by the same way.

Admission to the Temple

4 Then he brought me by way of the north gate to the front of the temple; and I looked, and lo! the glory of the LORD filled the temple of the LORD; and I fell upon my face. 5 The LORD said to me: Mortal, mark well, look closely, and listen attentively to all that I shall tell you concerning all the ordinances of the temple of the LORD and all its laws; and mark well those who may be admitted to*a* the temple and all those who are to be excluded from the sanctuary. 6 Say to the rebellious house,*b* to the house of Israel, Thus says the Lord GOD: O house of Israel, let there be an end to all your abominations 7 in admitting foreigners, uncircumcised in heart and flesh, to be in my sanctuary, profaning my temple when you offer to me my food, the fat and the blood. You*c* have broken my covenant with all your abominations. 8 And you have not kept charge of my sacred offerings; but you have appointed foreigners*d* to act for you in keeping my charge in my sanctuary.

9 Thus says the Lord GOD: No foreigner, uncircumcised in heart and flesh, of all the foreigners who are among the people of Israel, shall enter my sanctuary. 10 But the Levites who went far from me, going astray from me after their idols when Israel went astray, shall bear their punishment. 11 They shall be ministers in my sanctuary, having oversight at the gates of the temple, and serving in the temple; they shall slaughter the burnt offering and the sacrifice for the people, and they shall attend on them and serve them. 12 Because they ministered to them before their idols and made the house of Israel stumble into iniquity, therefore I have sworn concerning them, says the Lord GOD, that they shall bear their punishment. 13 They shall not come near to me, to serve me as priest, nor come near any of my sacred offerings, the things that are most sacred; but they shall bear their shame, and the consequences of the abominations that they have committed. 14 Yet I will appoint them to keep charge of the temple, to do all its chores, all that is to be done in it.

The Levitical Priests

15 But the levitical priests, the descendants of Zadok, who kept the charge of my sanctuary when the people of Israel went astray from me, shall come near to me to minister to me; and they shall attend me to offer me the fat and the blood, says the Lord GOD. 16 It is they who shall enter my sanctuary, it is they who shall approach my table, to minister to me, and they shall keep my charge. 17 When they enter the gates of the inner court, they shall wear linen vestments; they shall have nothing of wool on them, while they minister at the gates of the inner court, and within. 18 They shall have linen turbans on their heads, and linen undergarments on their loins; they shall not bind themselves with anything that causes sweat. 19 When they go out into the outer court to the people, they shall remove the vestments in which they have been ministering, and lay them in the holy chambers; and they shall put on other garments, so that they may not communicate holiness to the people with their vestments. 20 They shall not shave their heads or let their locks grow long; they shall only trim the hair of their heads. 21 No priest shall drink wine when he enters the inner court. 22 They shall not marry a widow, or a divorced woman, but only a virgin of the stock of the house of Israel, or a widow who is the widow of a priest. 23 They shall teach my people the difference between the holy and the common, and show them how to distinguish between the unclean and the clean. 24 In a controversy they shall act as judges, and they shall decide it according to my judgments. They shall keep my laws and my statutes regarding all my appointed festivals, and they shall keep my sabbaths holy. 25 They shall not defile themselves by going near to a dead person; for father or mother, however, and for son or daughter, and for brother or unmarried sister they may defile themselves. 26 After he has become clean, they shall count seven days for him. 27 On the day that he goes into the holy place, into the inner court, to minister in the holy place, he shall offer his sin offering, says the Lord GOD.

28 This shall be their inheritance: I am their inheritance; and you shall give them no holding in Israel; I am their holding. 29 They shall eat the grain offering, the sin offering, and the guilt offering; and every devoted thing in Israel shall be theirs. 30 The first of all the first fruits of all kinds, and every offering of all kinds from all your offerings, shall belong to the priests; you shall also give to the priests the first of your dough, in order that a blessing may rest on your house. 31 The priests shall not eat of anything, whether bird or animal, that died of itself or was torn by animals.

a Cn: Heb *the entrance of*   b Gk: Heb lacks *house*   c Gk Syr Vg: Heb *They*   d Heb lacks *foreigners*

45 The Holy District

When you allot the land as an inheritance, you shall set aside for the LORD a portion of the land as a holy district, twenty-five thousand cubits long and twenty[a] thousand cubits wide; it shall be holy throughout its entire extent. [2]Of this, a square plot of five hundred by five hundred cubits shall be for the sanctuary, with fifty cubits for an open space around it. [3]In the holy district you shall measure off a section twenty-five thousand cubits long and ten thousand wide, in which shall be the sanctuary, the most holy place. [4]It shall be a holy portion of the land; it shall be for the priests, who minister in the sanctuary and approach the LORD to minister to him; and it shall be both a place for their houses and a holy place for the sanctuary. [5]Another section, twenty-five thousand cubits long and ten thousand cubits wide, shall be for the Levites who minister at the temple, as their holding for cities to live in.[b]

6 Alongside the portion set apart as the holy district you shall assign as a holding for the city an area five thousand cubits wide, and twenty-five thousand cubits long; it shall belong to the whole house of Israel.

7 And to the prince shall belong the land on both sides of the holy district and the holding of the city, alongside the holy district and the holding of the city, on the west and on the east, corresponding in length to one of the tribal portions, and extending from the western to the eastern boundary [8]of the land. It is to be his property in Israel. And my princes shall no longer oppress my people; but they shall let the house of Israel have the land according to their tribes.

9 Thus says the Lord GOD: Enough, O princes of Israel! Put away violence and oppression, and do what is just and right. Cease your evictions of my people, says the Lord GOD.

Weights and Measures

10 You shall have honest balances, an honest ephah, and an honest bath.[c] [11]The ephah and the bath shall be of the same measure, the bath containing one-tenth of a homer, and the ephah one-tenth of a homer; the homer shall be the standard measure. [12]The shekel shall be twenty gerahs. Twenty shekels, twenty-five shekels, and fifteen shekels shall make a mina for you.

Offerings

13 This is the offering that you shall make: one-sixth of an ephah from each homer of wheat, and one-sixth of an ephah from each homer of barley, [14]and as the fixed portion of oil,[d] one-tenth of a bath from each cor (the cor,[e] like the homer, contains ten baths); [15]and one sheep from every flock of two hundred, from the pastures of Israel. This is the offering for grain offerings, burnt offerings, and offerings of well-being, to make atonement for them, says the Lord GOD. [16]All the people of the land shall join with the prince in Israel in making this offering. [17]But this shall be the obligation of the prince regarding the burnt offerings, grain offerings, and drink offerings, at the festivals, the new moons, and the sabbaths, all the appointed festivals of the house of Israel: he shall provide the sin offerings, grain offerings, the burnt offerings, and the offerings of well-being, to make atonement for the house of Israel.

Festivals

18 Thus says the Lord GOD: In the first month, on the first day of the month, you shall take a young bull without blemish, and purify the sanctuary. [19]The priest shall take some of the blood of the sin offering and put it on the doorposts of the temple, the four corners of the ledge of the altar, and the posts of the gate of the inner court. [20]You shall do the same on the seventh day of the month for anyone who has sinned through error or ignorance; so you shall make atonement for the temple.

21 In the first month, on the fourteenth day of the month, you shall celebrate the festival of the passover, and for seven days unleavened bread shall be eaten. [22]On that day the prince shall provide for himself and all the people of the land a young bull for a sin offering. [23]And during the seven days of the festival he shall provide as a burnt offering to the LORD seven young bulls and seven rams without blemish, on each of the seven days; and a male goat daily for a sin offering. [24]He shall provide as a grain offering an ephah for each bull, an ephah for each ram, and a hin of oil to each ephah. [25]In the seventh month, on the fifteenth day of the month and for the seven days of the festival, he shall make the same provision for sin offerings, burnt offerings, and grain offerings, and for the oil.

46 Miscellaneous Regulations

Thus says the Lord GOD: The gate of the inner court that faces east shall remain closed on the six working days; but on the sabbath

---

a Gk: Heb *ten*   b Gk: Heb *as their holding, twenty chambers*   c A Heb measure of volume   d Cn: Heb *oil, the bath the oil*   e Vg: Heb *homer*

day it shall be opened and on the day of the new moon it shall be opened. [2]The prince shall enter by the vestibule of the gate from outside, and shall take his stand by the post of the gate. The priests shall offer his burnt offering and his offerings of well-being, and he shall bow down at the threshold of the gate. Then he shall go out, but the gate shall not be closed until evening. [3]The people of the land shall bow down at the entrance of that gate before the LORD on the sabbaths and on the new moons. [4]The burnt offering that the prince offers to the LORD on the sabbath day shall be six lambs without blemish and a ram without blemish; [5]and the grain offering with the ram shall be an ephah, and the grain offering with the lambs shall be as much as he wishes to give, together with a hin of oil to each ephah. [6]On the day of the new moon he shall offer a young bull without blemish, and six lambs and a ram, which shall be without blemish; [7]as a grain offering he shall provide an ephah with the bull and an ephah with the ram, and with the lambs as much as he wishes, together with a hin of oil to each ephah. [8]When the prince enters, he shall come in by the vestibule of the gate, and he shall go out by the same way.

9 When the people of the land come before the LORD at the appointed festivals, whoever enters by the north gate to worship shall go out by the south gate; and whoever enters by the south gate shall go out by the north gate: they shall not return by way of the gate by which they entered, but shall go out straight ahead. [10]When they come in, the prince shall come in with them; and when they go out, he shall go out.

11 At the festivals and the appointed seasons the grain offering with a young bull shall be an ephah, and with a ram an ephah, and with the lambs as much as one wishes to give, together with a hin of oil to an ephah. [12]When the prince provides a freewill offering, either a burnt offering or offerings of well-being as a freewill offering to the LORD, the gate facing east shall be opened for him; and he shall offer his burnt offering or his offerings of well-being as he does on the sabbath day. Then he shall go out, and after he has gone out the gate shall be closed.

13 He shall provide a lamb, a yearling, without blemish, for a burnt offering to the LORD daily; morning by morning he shall provide it. [14]And he shall provide a grain offering with it morning by morning regularly, one-sixth of an ephah, and one-third of a hin of oil to moisten the choice flour, as a grain offering to the LORD; this is the ordinance for all time. [15]Thus the lamb and the grain offering and the oil shall be provided, morning by morning, as a regular burnt offering.

16 Thus says the Lord GOD: If the prince makes a gift to any of his sons out of his inheritance,[a] it shall belong to his sons, it is their holding by inheritance. [17]But if he makes a gift out of his inheritance to one of his servants, it shall be his to the year of liberty; then it shall revert to the prince; only his sons may keep a gift from his inheritance. [18]The prince shall not take any of the inheritance of the people, thrusting them out of their holding; he shall give his sons their inheritance out of his own holding, so that none of my people shall be dispossessed of their holding.

19 Then he brought me through the entrance, which was at the side of the gate, to the north row of the holy chambers for the priests; and there I saw a place at the extreme western end of them. [20]He said to me, "This is the place where the priests shall boil the guilt offering and the sin offering, and where they shall bake the grain offering, in order not to bring them out into the outer court and so communicate holiness to the people."

21 Then he brought me out to the outer court, and led me past the four corners of the court; and in each corner of the court there was a court— [22]in the four corners of the court were small[b] courts, forty cubits long and thirty wide; the four were of the same size. [23]On the inside, around each of the four courts[c] was a row of masonry, with hearths made at the bottom of the rows all around. [24]Then he said to me, "These are the kitchens where those who serve at the temple shall boil the sacrifices of the people."

Water Flowing from the Temple

47 Then he brought me back to the entrance of the temple; there, water was flowing from below the threshold of the temple toward the east (for the temple faced east); and the water was flowing down from below the south end of the threshold of the temple, south of the altar. [2]Then he brought me out by way of the north gate, and led me around on the outside to the outer gate that faces toward the east;[d] and the water was coming out on the south side.

a Gk: Heb *it is his inheritance*   b Gk Syr Vg: Meaning of Heb uncertain   c Heb *the four of them*   d Meaning of Heb uncertain

3 Going on eastward with a cord in his hand, the man measured one thousand cubits, and then led me through the water; and it was ankle-deep. [4]Again he measured one thousand, and led me through the water; and it was knee-deep. Again he measured one thousand, and led me through the water; and it was up to the waist. [5]Again he measured one thousand, and it was a river that I could not cross, for the water had risen; it was deep enough to swim in, a river that could not be crossed. [6]He said to me, "Mortal, have you seen this?"

Then he led me back along the bank of the river. [7]As I came back, I saw on the bank of the river a great many trees on the one side and on the other. [8]He said to me, "This water flows toward the eastern region and goes down into the Arabah; and when it enters the sea, the sea of stagnant waters, the water will become fresh. [9]Wherever the river goes,[a] every living creature that swarms will live, and there will be very many fish, once these waters reach there. It will become fresh; and everything will live where the river goes. [10]People will stand fishing beside the sea[b] from En-gedi to En-eglaim; it will be a place for the spreading of nets; its fish will be of a great many kinds, like the fish of the Great Sea. [11]But its swamps and marshes will not become fresh; they are to be left for salt. [12]On the banks, on both sides of the river, there will grow all kinds of trees for food. Their leaves will not wither nor their fruit fail, but they will bear fresh fruit every month, because the water for them flows from the sanctuary. Their fruit will be for food, and their leaves for healing."

The New Boundaries of the Land

13 Thus says the Lord GOD: These are the boundaries by which you shall divide the land for inheritance among the twelve tribes of Israel. Joseph shall have two portions. [14]You shall divide it equally; I swore to give it to your ancestors, and this land shall fall to you as your inheritance.

15 This shall be the boundary of the land: On the north side, from the Great Sea by way of Hethlon to Lebo-hamath, and on to Zedad,[c] [16]Berothah, Sibraim (which lies between the border of Damascus and the border of Hamath), as far as Hazer-hatticon, which is on the border of Hauran. [17]So the boundary shall run from the sea to Hazar-enon, which is north of the border of Damascus, with the border of Hamath to the north.[d] This shall be the north side.

18 On the east side, between Hauran and Damascus; along the Jordan between Gilead and the land of Israel; to the eastern sea and as far as Tamar.[e] This shall be the east side.

19 On the south side, it shall run from Tamar as far as the waters of Meribath-kadesh, from there along the Wadi of Egypt[f] to the Great Sea. This shall be the south side.

20 On the west side, the Great Sea shall be the boundary to a point opposite Lebo-hamath. This shall be the west side.

21 So you shall divide this land among you according to the tribes of Israel. [22]You shall allot it as an inheritance for yourselves and for the aliens who reside among you and have begotten children among you. They shall be to you as citizens of Israel; with you they shall be allotted an inheritance among the tribes of Israel. [23]In whatever tribe aliens reside, there you shall assign them their inheritance, says the Lord GOD.

The Tribal Portions

48 These are the names of the tribes: Beginning at the northern border, on the Hethlon road,[g] from Lebo-hamath, as far as Hazar-enon (which is on the border of Damascus, with Hamath to the north), and[h] extending from the east side to the west,[i] Dan, one portion. [2]Adjoining the territory of Dan, from the east side to the west, Asher, one portion. [3]Adjoining the territory of Asher, from the east side to the west, Naphtali, one portion. [4]Adjoining the territory of Naphtali, from the east side to the west, Manasseh, one portion. [5]Adjoining the territory of Manasseh, from the east side to the west, Ephraim, one portion. [6]Adjoining the territory of Ephraim, from the east side to the west, Reuben, one portion. [7]Adjoining the territory of Reuben, from the east side to the west, Judah, one portion.

8 Adjoining the territory of Judah, from the east side to the west, shall be the portion that you shall set apart, twenty-five thousand cubits in width, and in length equal to one of the tribal portions, from the east side to the west, with the sanctuary in the middle of it. [9]The portion that you shall set apart for the LORD shall be twenty-five thousand cubits in length, and twenty[j] thousand in width. [10]These shall be the allotments of the holy portion: the priests shall have an allotment measuring twenty-five thousand cubits on the northern side, ten thousand cubits in width on the western side, ten thousand in

---

a Gk Syr Vg Tg: Heb *the two rivers go*   b Heb *it*   c Gk: Heb *Lebo-zedad,* [16]*Hamath*   d Meaning of Heb uncertain   e Compare Syr: Heb *you shall measure*
f Heb lacks *of Egypt*   g Compare 47.15: Heb *by the side of the way*   h Cn: Heb *and they shall be his*   i Gk Compare verses 2-8: Heb *the east side the west*
j Compare 45.1: Heb *ten*

width on the eastern side, and twenty-five thousand in length on the southern side, with the sanctuary of the LORD in the middle of it. [11]This shall be for the consecrated priests, the descendants[a] of Zadok, who kept my charge, who did not go astray when the people of Israel went astray, as the Levites did. [12]It shall belong to them as a special portion from the holy portion of the land, a most holy place, adjoining the territory of the Levites. [13]Alongside the territory of the priests, the Levites shall have an allotment twenty-five thousand cubits in length and ten thousand in width. The whole length shall be twenty-five thousand cubits and the width twenty[b] thousand. [14]They shall not sell or exchange any of it; they shall not transfer this choice portion of the land, for it is holy to the LORD.

15 The remainder, five thousand cubits in width and twenty-five thousand in length, shall be for ordinary use for the city, for dwellings and for open country. In the middle of it shall be the city; [16]and these shall be its dimensions: the north side four thousand five hundred cubits, the south side four thousand five hundred, the east side four thousand five hundred, and the west side four thousand five hundred. [17]The city shall have open land: on the north two hundred fifty cubits, on the south two hundred fifty, on the east two hundred fifty, on the west two hundred fifty. [18]The remainder of the length alongside the holy portion shall be ten thousand cubits to the east, and ten thousand to the west, and it shall be alongside the holy portion. Its produce shall be food for the workers of the city. [19]The workers of the city, from all the tribes of Israel, shall cultivate it. [20]The whole portion that you shall set apart shall be twenty-five thousand cubits square, that is, the holy portion together with the property of the city.

21 What remains on both sides of the holy portion and of the property of the city shall belong to the prince. Extending from the twenty-five thousand cubits of the holy portion to the east border, and westward from the twenty-five thousand cubits to the west border, parallel to the tribal portions, it shall belong to the prince. The holy portion with the sanctuary of the temple in the middle of it, [22]and the property of the Levites and of the city, shall be in the middle of that which belongs to the prince. The portion of the prince shall lie between the territory of Judah and the territory of Benjamin.

23 As for the rest of the tribes: from the east side to the west, Benjamin, one portion. [24]Adjoining the territory of Benjamin, from the east side to the west, Simeon, one portion. [25]Adjoining the territory of Simeon, from the east side to the west, Issachar, one portion. [26]Adjoining the territory of Issachar, from the east side to the west, Zebulun, one portion. [27]Adjoining the territory of Zebulun, from the east side to the west, Gad, one portion. [28]And adjoining the territory of Gad to the south, the boundary shall run from Tamar to the waters of Meribath-kadesh, from there along the Wadi of Egypt[c] to the Great Sea. [29]This is the land that you shall allot as an inheritance among the tribes of Israel, and these are their portions, says the Lord GOD.

30 These shall be the exits of the city: On the north side, which is to be four thousand five hundred cubits by measure, [31]three gates, the gate of Reuben, the gate of Judah, and the gate of Levi, the gates of the city being named after the tribes of Israel. [32]On the east side, which is to be four thousand five hundred cubits, three gates, the gate of Joseph, the gate of Benjamin, and the gate of Dan. [33]On the south side, which is to be four thousand five hundred cubits by measure, three gates, the gate of Simeon, the gate of Issachar, and the gate of Zebulun. [34]On the west side, which is to be four thousand five hundred cubits, three gates,[d] the gate of Gad, the gate of Asher, and the gate of Naphtali. [35]The circumference of the city shall be eighteen thousand cubits. And the name of the city from that time on shall be, The LORD is There.

a One Ms Gk: Heb *of the descendants* b Gk: Heb *ten* c Heb lacks *of Egypt* d One Ms Gk Syr: MT *their gates three*

Daniel

▶▶▶▶▶▶▶▶▶▶▶▶▶▶▶▶▶▶▶▶▶▶▶▶▶▶▶▶

Spider-Man has his web. Wonder Woman has her strength and bulletproof bracelets. Superman has his power of flight and X-ray vision. And all of these larger-than-life heroes are committed to upholding moral values and saving victims of injustice. Sounds a bit like the character in this book of the Old Testament! Though you won't find him in the local comic-book store, Daniel is a superhero of biblical proportions. His superpowers? Strong commitment, unwavering courage, and an ability to see and interpret visions. These powers enable him to lead his people on the right path in a foreign land filled with injustice, persecution, and idolatry.

IN DEPTH

Daniel represents the ideal leader with the spiritual and prophetic insight to lead people through troubled times. Scholars question whether he was an actual person. If he was, he lived in the sixth century B.C.—but the book of Daniel was written four hundred years later, during the reign of an evil Greek-Syrian king, Antiochus IV Epiphanes. King Antiochus desecrated the temple and attempted to prohibit many of Israel's religious practices. To many Israelites, this seemed like the end of the world.

The author of this book writes about the great hero Daniel to give the people hope during this persecution. Chapters 1–6 present six stories of Daniel and three friends living out their faith during the Babylonian exile. Chapters 7–12 tell of Daniel's four visions about the empires that dominated Israel: Babylon, Media, Persia, and Greece. The visions are full of strange symbols meant to be understood by the Israelites, but not by the Greek rulers of the author's time.

Daniel is shown as the ideal Jew—the embodiment of all the best of the people in exile. In the face of unjust persecution and oppression, he leads his people in faithfulness to God, even through death itself. Now that's a superhero!

QUICK FACTS

- **Setting:** Babylon, during the exile in the sixth century B.C.
- **Date Written:** Around 165 B.C., during the persecution of the Jews by Antiochus IV Epiphanes
- **Author:** Unknown
- **Themes:** Hope for those feeling oppressed or persecuted; the reassurance that God will one day make everything right in the world

AT A GLANCE

- **Daniel 1–6** Stories of Daniel and his friends
- **Daniel 7–12** Daniel's visions and dreams

1 Four Young Israelites at the Babylonian Court

In the third year of the reign of King Jehoiakim of Judah, King Nebuchadnezzar of Babylon came to Jerusalem and besieged it. [2]The Lord let King Jehoiakim of Judah fall into his power, as well as some of the vessels of the house of God. These he brought to the land of Shinar,[a] and placed the vessels in the treasury of his gods.

3 Then the king commanded his palace master Ashpenaz to bring some of the Israelites of the royal family and of the nobility, [4]young men without physical defect and handsome, versed in every branch of wisdom, endowed with knowledge and insight, and competent to serve in the king's palace; they were to be taught the literature and language of the Chaldeans. [5]The king assigned them a daily portion of the royal rations of food and wine. They were to be educated for three years, so that at the end of that time they could be stationed in the king's court. [6]Among them were Daniel, Hananiah, Mishael, and Azariah, from the tribe of Judah. [7]The palace master gave them other names: Daniel he called Belteshazzar, Hananiah he called Shadrach, Mishael he called Meshach, and Azariah he called Abednego.

8 But Daniel resolved that he would not defile himself with the royal rations of food and wine; so he asked the palace master to allow him not to defile himself. [9]Now God allowed Daniel to receive favor and compassion from the palace master. [10]The palace master said to Daniel, "I am afraid of my lord the king; he has appointed your food and your drink. If he should see you in poorer condition than the other young men of your own age, you would endanger my head with the king." [11]Then Daniel asked the guard whom the palace master had appointed over Daniel, Hananiah, Mishael, and Azariah: [12]"Please test your servants for ten days. Let us be given vegetables to eat and water to drink. [13]You can then compare our appearance with the appearance of the young men who eat the royal rations, and deal with your servants according to what you observe." [14]So he agreed to this proposal and tested them for ten days. [15]At the end of ten days it was observed that they appeared better and fatter than all the young men who had been eating the royal rations. [16]So the guard continued to withdraw their royal rations and the wine they were to drink, and gave them vegetables. [17]To these four young men

God gave knowledge and skill in every aspect of literature and wisdom; Daniel also had insight into all visions and dreams.

18 At the end of the time that the king had set for them to be brought in, the palace master brought them into the presence of Nebuchadnezzar, [19]and the king spoke with them. And among them all, no one was found to compare with Daniel, Hananiah, Mishael, and Azariah; therefore they were stationed in the king's court. [20]In every matter of wisdom and understanding concerning which the king inquired of them, he found them ten times better than all the magicians and enchanters in his whole kingdom. [21]And Daniel continued there until the first year of King Cyrus.

2 Nebuchadnezzar's Dream

In the second year of Nebuchadnezzar's reign, Nebuchadnezzar dreamed such dreams that his spirit was troubled and his sleep left him. [2]So the king commanded that the magicians, the enchanters, the sorcerers, and the Chaldeans be summoned to tell the king his dreams. When they came in and stood before the king, [3]he said to them, "I have had such a dream that my spirit is troubled by the desire to understand it." [4]The Chaldeans said to the king (in Aramaic),[b] "O king, live forever! Tell your servants the dream, and we will reveal the interpretation." [5]The king answered the Chaldeans, "This is a public decree: if you do not tell me both the dream and its interpretation, you shall be torn limb from limb, and your houses shall be laid in ruins. [6]But if you do tell me the dream and its interpretation, you shall receive from me gifts and rewards and great honor. Therefore tell me the dream and its interpretation." [7]They answered a second time, "Let the king first tell his servants the dream, then we can give its interpretation." [8]The king answered, "I know with certainty that you are trying to gain time, because you see I have firmly decreed: [9]if you do not tell me the dream, there is but one verdict for you. You have agreed to speak lying and misleading words to me until things take a turn. Therefore, tell me the dream, and I shall know that you can give me its interpretation." [10]The Chaldeans answered the king, "There is no one on earth who can reveal what the king demands! In fact no king, however great and powerful, has ever asked such a thing of any magician or enchanter or Chaldean. [11]The thing that the king is asking is too difficult,

a Gk Theodotion: Heb adds *to the house of his own gods*   b The text from this point to the end of chapter 7 is in Aramaic

and no one can reveal it to the king except the gods, whose dwelling is not with mortals."

12 Because of this the king flew into a violent rage and commanded that all the wise men of Babylon be destroyed. [13]The decree was issued, and the wise men were about to be executed; and they looked for Daniel and his companions, to execute them. [14]Then Daniel responded with prudence and discretion to Arioch, the king's chief executioner, who had gone out to execute the wise men of Babylon; [15]he asked Arioch, the royal official, "Why is the decree of the king so urgent?" Arioch then explained the matter to Daniel. [16]So Daniel went in and requested that the king give him time and he would tell the king the interpretation.

God Reveals Nebuchadnezzar's Dream

17 Then Daniel went to his home and informed his companions, Hananiah, Mishael, and Azariah, [18]and told them to seek mercy from the God of heaven concerning this mystery, so that Daniel and his companions with the rest of the wise men of Babylon might not perish. [19]Then the mystery was revealed to Daniel in a vision of the night, and Daniel blessed the God of heaven.

20 Daniel said:
"Blessed be the name of God from age to age,
    for wisdom and power are his.
21 He changes times and seasons,
    deposes kings and sets up kings;
he gives wisdom to the wise
    and knowledge to those who have
        understanding.
22 He reveals deep and hidden things;
    he knows what is in the darkness,
    and light dwells with him.
23 To you, O God of my ancestors,
    I give thanks and praise,
for you have given me wisdom and power,
    and have now revealed to me what we
        asked of you,
    for you have revealed to us what the king
        ordered."

Daniel Interprets the Dream

24 Therefore Daniel went to Arioch, whom the king had appointed to destroy the wise men of Babylon, and said to him, "Do not destroy the wise men of Babylon; bring me in before the king, and I will give the king the interpretation."

25 Then Arioch quickly brought Daniel before the king and said to him: "I have found among the exiles from Judah a man who can tell the king the interpretation." [26]The king said to Daniel, whose name was Belteshazzar, "Are you able to tell me the dream that I have seen and its interpretation?" [27]Daniel answered the king, "No wise men, enchanters, magicians, or diviners can show to the king the mystery that the king is asking, [28]but there is a God in heaven who reveals mysteries, and he has disclosed to King Nebuchadnezzar what will happen at the end of days. Your dream and the visions of your head as you lay in bed were these: [29]To you, O king, as you lay in bed, came thoughts of what would be hereafter, and the revealer of mysteries disclosed to you what is to be. [30]But as for me, this mystery has not been revealed to me because of any wisdom that I have more than any other living being, but in order that the interpretation may be known to the king and that you may understand the thoughts of your mind.

31 "You were looking, O king, and lo! there was a great statue. This statue was huge, its brilliance extraordinary; it was standing before you, and its appearance was frightening. [32]The head of that statue was of fine gold, its chest and arms of silver, its middle and thighs of bronze, [33]its legs of iron, its feet partly of iron and partly of clay. [34]As you looked on, a stone was cut out, not by human hands, and it struck the statue on its feet of iron and clay and broke them in pieces. [35]Then the iron, the clay, the bronze, the silver, and the gold, were all broken in pieces and became like the chaff of the summer threshing floors; and the wind carried them away, so that not a trace of them could be found. But the stone that struck the statue became a great mountain and filled the whole earth.

36 "This was the dream; now we will tell the king its interpretation. [37]You, O king, the king of kings—to whom the God of heaven has given the kingdom, the power, the might, and the glory, [38]into whose hand he has given human beings, wherever they live, the wild animals of the field, and the birds of the air, and whom he has established as ruler over them all—you are the head of gold. [39]After you shall arise another kingdom inferior to yours, and yet a third kingdom of bronze, which shall rule over the whole earth. [40]And there shall be a fourth kingdom, strong as iron; just as iron crushes and smashes everything,[a] it shall crush

---

[a] Gk Theodotion Syr Vg: Aram adds *and like iron that crushes*

and shatter all these. [41]As you saw the feet and toes partly of potter's clay and partly of iron, it shall be a divided kingdom; but some of the strength of iron shall be in it, as you saw the iron mixed with the clay. [42]As the toes of the feet were part iron and part clay, so the kingdom shall be partly strong and partly brittle. [43]As you saw the iron mixed with clay, so will they mix with one another in marriage,[a] but they will not hold together, just as iron does not mix with clay. [44]And in the days of those kings the God of heaven will set up a kingdom that shall never be destroyed, nor shall this kingdom be left to another people. It shall crush all these kingdoms and bring them to an end, and it shall stand forever; [45]just as you saw that a stone was cut from the mountain not by hands, and that it crushed the iron, the bronze, the clay, the silver, and the gold. The great God has informed the king what shall be hereafter. The dream is certain, and its interpretation trustworthy."

Daniel and His Friends Promoted

46 Then King Nebuchadnezzar fell on his face, worshiped Daniel, and commanded that a grain offering and incense be offered to him. [47]The king said to Daniel, "Truly, your God is God of gods and Lord of kings and a revealer of mysteries, for you have been able to reveal this mystery!" [48]Then the king promoted Daniel, gave him many great gifts, and made him ruler over the whole province of Babylon and chief prefect over all the wise men of Babylon. [49]Daniel made a request of the king, and he appointed Shadrach, Meshach, and Abednego over the affairs of the province of Babylon. But Daniel remained at the king's court.

The Golden Image

3 King Nebuchadnezzar made a golden statue whose height was sixty cubits and whose width was six cubits; he set it up on the plain of Dura in the province of Babylon. [2]Then King Nebuchadnezzar sent for the satraps, the prefects, and the governors, the counselors, the treasurers, the justices, the magistrates, and all the officials of the provinces, to assemble and come to the dedication of the statue that King Nebuchadnezzar had set up. [3]So the satraps, the prefects, and the governors, the counselors, the treasurers, the justices, the magistrates, and all the officials of the provinces, assembled for the dedication of the statue that King Nebuchadnezzar had set up. When they were standing before the statue that Nebuchadnezzar had set up, [4]the herald proclaimed aloud, "You are commanded, O peoples, nations, and languages, [5]that when you hear the sound of the horn, pipe, lyre, trigon, harp, drum, and entire musical ensemble, you are to fall down and worship the golden statue that King Nebuchadnezzar has set up. [6]Whoever does not fall down and worship shall immediately be thrown into a furnace of blazing fire." [7]Therefore, as soon as all the peoples heard the sound of the horn, pipe, lyre, trigon, harp, drum, and entire musical ensemble, all the peoples, nations, and languages fell down and worshiped the golden statue that King Nebuchadnezzar had set up.

8 Accordingly, at this time certain Chaldeans came forward and denounced the Jews. [9]They said to King Nebuchadnezzar, "O king, live forever! [10]You, O king, have made a decree, that everyone who hears the sound of the horn, pipe, lyre, trigon, harp, drum, and entire musical ensemble, shall fall

Stand Up · Daniel 3:1–24

Daniel 3 tells us of Shadrach, Meshach, and Abednego, three companions of Daniel who refuse to compromise their religious beliefs. Even in the face of death, they don't denounce the Lord and worship the god of Nebuchadnezzar.

The pressure to do what we know is wrong takes many forms. We face temptations every day—cheating on a test, lying to our parents, experimenting with drugs, pirating music, shoplifting, and many more—that can create an overwhelming amount of pressure. Although giving in to that pressure may offer some short-term satisfaction, denying what we know is right is ultimately denying God and the fullness of life God has planned for us.

Follow Shadrach, Meshach, and Abednego's example and stand up for what is right—stand up for God!

LIVE IT!

a Aram *by human seed*

down and worship the golden statue, [11]and whoever does not fall down and worship shall be thrown into a furnace of blazing fire. [12]There are certain Jews whom you have appointed over the affairs of the province of Babylon: Shadrach, Meshach, and Abednego. These pay no heed to you, O king. They do not serve your gods and they do not worship the golden statue that you have set up."

13 Then Nebuchadnezzar in furious rage commanded that Shadrach, Meshach, and Abednego be brought in; so they brought those men before the king. [14]Nebuchadnezzar said to them, "Is it true, O Shadrach, Meshach, and Abednego, that you do not serve my gods and you do not worship the golden statue that I have set up? [15]Now if you are ready when you hear the sound of the horn, pipe, lyre, trigon, harp, drum, and entire musical ensemble to fall down and worship the statue that I have made, well and good.[a] But if you do not worship, you shall immediately be thrown into a furnace of blazing fire, and who is the god that will deliver you out of my hands?"

16 Shadrach, Meshach, and Abednego answered the king, "O Nebuchadnezzar, we have no need to present a defense to you in this matter. [17]If our God whom we serve is able to deliver us from the furnace of blazing fire and out of your hand, O king, let him deliver us.[b] [18]But if not, be it known to you, O king, that we will not serve your gods and we will not worship the golden statue that you have set up."

The Fiery Furnace

19 Then Nebuchadnezzar was so filled with rage against Shadrach, Meshach, and Abednego that his face was distorted. He ordered the furnace heated up seven times more than was customary, [20]and ordered some of the strongest guards in his army to bind Shadrach, Meshach, and Abednego and to throw them into the furnace of blazing fire. [21]So the

> "If our God whom we serve is able to deliver us … let him … But if not, be it known to you, O king, that we will not serve your gods."
> —Daniel 3:17–18

men were bound, still wearing their tunics,[c] their trousers,[c] their hats, and their other garments, and they were thrown into the furnace of blazing fire. [22]Because the king's command was urgent and the furnace was so overheated, the raging flames killed the men who lifted Shadrach, Meshach, and Abednego. [23]But the three men, Shadrach, Meshach, and Abednego, fell down, bound, into the furnace of blazing fire.

24 Then King Nebuchadnezzar was astonished and rose up quickly. He said to his counselors, "Was it not three men that we threw bound into the fire?" They answered the king, "True, O king." [25]He replied, "But I see four men unbound, walking in the middle of the fire, and they are not hurt; and the fourth has the appearance of a god."[d] [26]Nebuchadnezzar then approached the door of the furnace of blazing fire and said, "Shadrach, Meshach, and Abednego, servants of the Most High God, come out! Come here!" So Shadrach, Meshach, and Abednego came out from the fire. [27]And the satraps, the prefects, the governors, and the king's counselors gathered together and saw that the fire had not had any power over the bodies of those men; the hair of their heads was not singed, their tunics[c] were not harmed, and not even the smell of fire came from them. [28]Nebuchadnezzar said, "Blessed be the God of Shadrach, Meshach, and Abednego, who has sent his angel and delivered his servants who trusted in him. They disobeyed the king's command and yielded up their bodies rather than serve and worship any god except their own God. [29]Therefore I make a decree: Any people, nation, or language that utters blasphemy against the God of Shadrach, Meshach, and Abednego shall be torn limb from limb, and their houses laid in ruins; for there is no other god who is able to deliver in this way." [30]Then the

a Aram lacks *well and good* b Or *If our God whom we serve is able to deliver us, he will deliver us from the furnace of blazing fire and out of your hand, O king.* c Meaning of Aram word uncertain d Aram *a son of the gods*

king promoted Shadrach, Meshach, and Abednego in the province of Babylon.

Nebuchadnezzar's Second Dream

4 [a] King Nebuchadnezzar to all peoples, nations, and languages that live throughout the earth: May you have abundant prosperity! [2]The signs and wonders that the Most High God has worked for me I am pleased to recount.

[3] How great are his signs,
   how mighty his wonders!
He kingdom is an everlasting kingdom,
   and his sovereignty is from generation to
      generation.

[4][b] I, Nebuchadnezzar, was living at ease in my home and prospering in my palace. [5]I saw a dream that frightened me; my fantasies in bed and the visions of my head terrified me. [6]So I made a decree that all the wise men of Babylon should be brought before me, in order that they might tell me the interpretation of the dream. [7]Then the magicians, the enchanters, the Chaldeans, and the diviners came in, and I told them the dream, but they could not tell me its interpretation. [8]At last Daniel came in before me—he who was named Belteshazzar after the name of my god, and who is endowed with a spirit of the holy gods[c]—and I told him the dream: [9]"O Belteshazzar, chief of the magicians, I know that you are endowed with a spirit of the holy gods[c] and that no mystery is too difficult for you. Hear[d] the dream that I saw; tell me its interpretation.

[10][e] Upon my bed this is what I saw;
   there was a tree at the center of the earth,
   and its height was great.
[11] The tree grew great and strong,
   its top reached to heaven,
   and it was visible to the ends of the whole
      earth.
[12] Its foliage was beautiful,
   its fruit abundant,
   and it provided food for all.
The animals of the field found shade
      under it,
   the birds of the air nested in its branches,
   and from it all living beings were fed.

[13] "I continued looking, in the visions of my head as I lay in bed, and there was a holy watcher, coming down from heaven. [14]He cried aloud and said:
'Cut down the tree and chop off its branches,

strip off its foliage and scatter its fruit.
Let the animals flee from beneath it
   and the birds from its branches.
[15] But leave its stump and roots in the ground,
   with a band of iron and bronze,
   in the tender grass of the field.
Let him be bathed with the dew of heaven,
   and let his lot be with the animals of the
      field
   in the grass of the earth.

a Ch 3.31 in Aram   **b** Ch 4.1 in Aram   **c** Or *a holy, divine spirit*   **d** Theodotion: Aram *The visions of*   **e** Theodotion Syr Compare Gk: Aram adds *The visions of my head*

PRAY IT!

The King's Change
Daniel 4

God will go to extremes to get our attention. In **Daniel 4** (written like a letter from the king to his subjects), King Nebuchadnezzar tells how he had to go through some pretty intense humiliation before God got his attention. Daniel tried to warn the king, rein in his ego, and bring him to his senses (see Daniel 4:26-27). But King Nebuchadnezzar wouldn't see God's way until after he was driven away from society and forced to live like a wild animal (Daniel 4:32-33). Finally Nebuchadnezzar realized the power of God and turned to praise and honor of God instead.

Many people go through a conversion—a turning toward God—after they have suffered the consequences of their sinful actions. For others, the catalyst might be an illness or the death of a close friend or family member. Why does it take a crisis for us to realize our need for God? Maybe because, during such a time, we realize that we cannot control life and that we need God's loving presence.

During your prayer time, reflect or journal on the following questions:

- Where do you recognize your need for God?
- Is a conversion toward God in a crisis only a temporary thing, or can it lead to a lifelong commitment? Why?

16 Let his mind be changed from that of a
        human,
        and let the mind of an animal be given
        to him.
        And let seven times pass over him.
17 The sentence is rendered by decree of the
        watchers,
        the decision is given by order of the holy
        ones,
    in order that all who live may know
        that the Most High is sovereign over the
        kingdom of mortals;
    he gives it to whom he will
        and sets over it the lowliest of human
        beings.'

18 "This is the dream that I, King Nebuchadnezzar, saw. Now you, Belteshazzar, declare the interpretation, since all the wise men of my kingdom are
unable to tell me the interpretation. You are able,
however, for you are endowed with a spirit of the
holy gods."*a*

Daniel Interprets the Second Dream

19 Then Daniel, who was called Belteshazzar, was
severely distressed for a while. His thoughts terrified
him. The king said, "Belteshazzar, do not let the
dream or the interpretation terrify you." Belteshazzar
answered, "My lord, may the dream be for those who
hate you, and its interpretation for your enemies!
20The tree that you saw, which grew great and strong,
so that its top reached to heaven and was visible to
the end of the whole earth, 21whose foliage was
beautiful and its fruit abundant, and which provided
food for all, under which animals of the field lived,
and in whose branches the birds of the air had nests—
22it is you, O king! You have grown great and strong.
Your greatness has increased and reaches to heaven,
and your sovereignty to the ends of the earth. 23And
whereas the king saw a holy watcher coming down
from heaven and saying, 'Cut down the tree and destroy it, but leave its stump and roots in the ground,
with a band of iron and bronze, in the grass of the
field; and let him be bathed with the dew of heaven,
and let his lot be with the animals of the field, until
seven times pass over him'— 24this is the interpretation, O king, and it is a decree of the Most High that
has come upon my lord the king: 25You shall be
driven away from human society, and your dwelling
shall be with the wild animals. You shall be made to

eat grass like oxen, you shall be bathed with the dew
of heaven, and seven times shall pass over you, until
you have learned that the Most High has sovereignty
over the kingdom of mortals, and gives it to whom
he will. 26As it was commanded to leave the stump
and roots of the tree, your kingdom shall be re-
established for you from the time that you learn that
Heaven is sovereign. 27Therefore, O king, may my
counsel be acceptable to you: atone for*b* your sins
with righteousness, and your iniquities with mercy
to the oppressed, so that your prosperity may be
prolonged."

Nebuchadnezzar's Humiliation

28 All this came upon King Nebuchadnezzar. 29At
the end of twelve months he was walking on the
roof of the royal palace of Babylon, 30and the king
said, "Is this not magnificent Babylon, which I have
built as a royal capital by my mighty power and for
my glorious majesty?" 31While the words were still
in the king's mouth, a voice came from heaven:
"O King Nebuchadnezzar, to you it is declared: The
kingdom has departed from you! 32You shall be
driven away from human society, and your dwelling
shall be with the animals of the field. You shall be
made to eat grass like oxen, and seven times shall
pass over you, until you have learned that the Most
High has sovereignty over the kingdom of mortals
and gives it to whom he will." 33Immediately the
sentence was fulfilled against Nebuchadnezzar. He
was driven away from human society, ate grass like
oxen, and his body was bathed with the dew of
heaven, until his hair grew as long as eagles' feathers
and his nails became like birds' claws.

Nebuchadnezzar Praises God

34 When that period was over, I, Nebuchadnezzar, lifted my eyes to heaven, and my reason returned
to me.
    I blessed the Most High,
        and praised and honored the one who lives
        forever.
    For his sovereignty is an everlasting
        sovereignty,
        and his kingdom endures from generation
        to generation.
35 All the inhabitants of the earth are accounted
        as nothing,
        and he does what he wills with the host of
        heaven

---

a Or *a holy, divine spirit*   *b* Aram *break off*

and the inhabitants of the earth.
There is no one who can stay his hand
    or say to him, "What are you doing?"
³⁶At that time my reason returned to me; and my majesty and splendor were restored to me for the glory of my kingdom. My counselors and my lords sought me out, I was re-established over my kingdom, and still more greatness was added to me. ³⁷Now I, Nebuchadnezzar, praise and extol and honor the King of heaven,
    for all his works are truth,
        and his ways are justice;
    and he is able to bring low
        those who walk in pride.

Belshazzar's Feast

5 King Belshazzar made a great festival for a thousand of his lords, and he was drinking wine in the presence of the thousand.

2 Under the influence of the wine, Belshazzar commanded that they bring in the vessels of gold and silver that his father Nebuchadnezzar had taken out of the temple in Jerusalem, so that the king and his lords, his wives, and his concubines might drink from them. ³So they brought in the vessels of gold and silver^a that had been taken out of the temple, the house of God in Jerusalem, and the king and his lords, his wives, and his concubines drank from them. ⁴They drank the wine and praised the gods of gold and silver, bronze, iron, wood, and stone.

The Writing on the Wall

5 Immediately the fingers of a human hand appeared and began writing on the plaster of the wall of the royal palace, next to the lampstand. The king was watching the hand as it wrote. ⁶Then the king's face turned pale, and his thoughts terrified him. His limbs gave way, and his knees knocked together.

⁷The king cried aloud to bring in the enchanters, the Chaldeans, and the diviners; and the king said to the wise men of Babylon, "Whoever can read this writing and tell me its interpretation shall be clothed in purple, have a chain of gold around his neck, and rank third in the kingdom." ⁸Then all the king's wise men came in, but they could not read the writing or tell the king the interpretation. ⁹Then King Belshazzar became greatly terrified and his face turned pale, and his lords were perplexed.

10 The queen, when she heard the discussion of the king and his lords, came into the banqueting hall. The queen said, "O king, live forever! Do not let your thoughts terrify you or your face grow pale. ¹¹There is a man in your kingdom who is endowed with a spirit of the holy gods.^b In the days of your father he was found to have enlightenment, understanding, and wisdom like the wisdom of the gods. Your father, King Nebuchadnezzar, made him chief of the magicians, enchanters, Chaldeans, and diviners,^c ¹²because an excellent spirit, knowledge, and understanding to interpret dreams, explain riddles, and solve problems were found in this Daniel, whom the king named Belteshazzar. Now let Daniel be called, and he will give the interpretation."

The Writing on the Wall Interpreted

13 Then Daniel was brought in before the king. The king said to Daniel, "So you are Daniel, one of the exiles of Judah, whom my father the king brought from Judah? ¹⁴I have heard of you that a spirit of the gods^d is in you, and that enlightenment, understanding, and excellent wisdom are found in you. ¹⁵Now the wise men, the enchanters, have been brought in before me to read this writing and tell me its interpretation, but they were not able to give the interpretation of the matter. ¹⁶But I have heard that you can give interpretations and solve problems. Now if you are able to read the writing and tell me its interpretation, you shall be clothed in purple, have a chain of gold around your neck, and rank third in the kingdom."

17 Then Daniel answered in the presence of the king, "Let your gifts be for yourself, or give your rewards to someone else! Nevertheless I will read the writing to the king and let him know the interpretation. ¹⁸O king, the Most High God gave your father Nebuchadnezzar kingship, greatness, glory, and majesty. ¹⁹And because of the greatness that he gave him, all peoples, nations, and languages trem-

---

a Theodotion Vg: Aram lacks *and silver*   **b** Or *a holy, divine spirit*   **c** Aram adds *the king your father*   **d** Or *a divine spirit*

bled and feared before him. He killed those he wanted to kill, kept alive those he wanted to keep alive, honored those he wanted to honor, and degraded those he wanted to degrade. [20]But when his heart was lifted up and his spirit was hardened so that he acted proudly, he was deposed from his kingly throne, and his glory was stripped from him. [21]He was driven from human society, and his mind was made like that of an animal. His dwelling was with the wild asses, he was fed grass like oxen, and his body was bathed with the dew of heaven, until he learned that the Most High God has sovereignty over the kingdom of mortals, and sets over it whomever he will. [22]And you, Belshazzar his son, have not humbled your heart, even though you knew all this! [23]You have exalted yourself against the Lord of heaven! The vessels of his temple have been brought in before you, and you and your lords, your wives and your concubines have been drinking wine from them. You have praised the gods of silver and gold, of bronze, iron, wood, and stone, which do not see or hear or know; but the God in whose power is your very breath, and to whom belong all your ways, you have not honored.

24 "So from his presence the hand was sent and this writing was inscribed. [25]And this is the writing that was inscribed: MENE, MENE, TEKEL, and PARSIN. [26]This is the interpretation of the matter: MENE, God has numbered the days of[a] your kingdom and brought it to an end; [27]TEKEL, you have been weighed on the scales and found wanting; [28]PERES,[b] your kingdom is divided and given to the Medes and Persians."

29 Then Belshazzar gave the command, and Daniel was clothed in purple, a chain of gold was put around his neck, and a proclamation was made concerning him that he should rank third in the kingdom.

30 That very night Belshazzar, the Chaldean king, was killed. [31][c] And Darius the Mede received the kingdom, being about sixty-two years old.

6 The Plot against Daniel

It pleased Darius to set over the kingdom one hundred twenty satraps, stationed throughout the whole kingdom, [2]and over them three presidents, including Daniel; to these the satraps gave account, so that the king might suffer no loss. [3]Soon Daniel distinguished himself above all the other presidents and satraps because an excellent spirit was in him, and the king planned to appoint him over the whole kingdom. [4]So the presidents and the satraps tried to find grounds for complaint against Daniel in connection with the kingdom. But they could find no grounds for complaint or any corruption, because he was faithful, and no negligence or corruption could be found in him. [5]The men said, "We shall not find any ground for complaint against this Daniel unless we find it in connection with the law of his God."

6 So the presidents and satraps conspired and came to the king and said to him, "O King Darius, live forever! [7]All the presidents of the kingdom, the prefects and the satraps, the counselors and the governors are agreed that the king should establish an ordinance and enforce an interdict, that whoever prays to anyone, divine or human, for thirty days, except to you, O king, shall be thrown into a den of lions. [8]Now, O king, establish the interdict and sign the document, so that it cannot be changed, according to the law of the Medes and the Persians, which cannot be revoked." [9]Therefore King Darius signed the document and interdict.

Daniel in the Lions' Den

10 Although Daniel knew that the document had been signed, he continued to go to his house, which had windows in its upper room open toward Jerusalem, and to get down on his knees three times a day to pray to his God and praise him, just as he had done previously. [11]The conspirators came and found Daniel praying and seeking mercy before his God. [12]Then they approached the king and said concerning the interdict, "O king! Did you not sign an interdict, that anyone who prays to anyone, divine or human, within thirty days except to you, O king, shall be thrown into a den of lions?" The king answered, "The thing stands fast, according to the law of the Medes and Persians, which cannot be revoked." [13]Then they responded to the king, "Daniel, one of the exiles from Judah, pays no attention to you, O king, or to the interdict you have signed, but he is saying his prayers three times a day."

14 When the king heard the charge, he was very much distressed. He was determined to save Daniel, and until the sun went down he made every effort to rescue him. [15]Then the conspirators came to the king and said to him, "Know, O king, that it is a law of the Medes and Persians that no interdict or ordinance that the king establishes can be changed."

a Aram lacks *the days of* *b* The singular of *Parsin* *c* Ch 6.1 in Aram

16 Then the king gave the command, and Daniel was brought and thrown into the den of lions. The king said to Daniel, "May your God, whom you faithfully serve, deliver you!" [17]A stone was brought and laid on the mouth of the den, and the king sealed it with his own signet and with the signet of his lords, so that nothing might be changed concerning Daniel. [18]Then the king went to his palace and spent the night fasting; no food was brought to him, and sleep fled from him.

Daniel Saved from the Lions

19 Then, at break of day, the king got up and hurried to the den of lions. [20]When he came near the den where Daniel was, he cried out anxiously to Daniel, "O Daniel, servant of the living God, has your God whom you faithfully serve been able to deliver you from the lions?" [21]Daniel then said to the king, "O king, live forever! [22]My God sent his angel and shut the lions' mouths so that they would not hurt me, because I was found blameless before him; and also before you, O king, I have done no wrong." [23]Then the king was exceedingly glad and commanded that Daniel be taken up out of the den. So Daniel was taken up out of the den, and no kind of harm was found on him, because he had trusted in his God. [24]The king gave a command, and those who had accused Daniel were brought and thrown into the den of lions—they, their children, and their wives. Before they reached the bottom of the den the lions overpowered them and broke all their bones in pieces.

25 Then King Darius wrote to all peoples and nations of every language throughout the whole world: "May you have abundant prosperity! [26]I make a decree, that in all my royal dominion people should tremble and fear before the God of Daniel:

For he is the living God,
enduring forever.
His kingdom shall never be
destroyed,
and his dominion has no end.
[27] He delivers and rescues,
he works signs and wonders in heaven
and on earth;
for he has saved Daniel
from the power of the lions."
[28]So this Daniel prospered during the reign of Darius and the reign of Cyrus the Persian.

Visions of the Four Beasts

7 In the first year of King Belshazzar of Babylon, Daniel had a dream and visions of his head as he lay in bed. Then he wrote down the dream:[a] [2]I,[b] Daniel, saw in my vision by night the four winds of heaven stirring up the great sea, [3]and four great beasts came up out of the sea, different from one another. [4]The first was like a lion and had eagles' wings. Then, as I watched, its wings were plucked off, and it was lifted up from the ground and made to stand on two feet like a human being; and a human mind was given to it. [5]Another beast appeared, a second one, that looked like a bear. It was raised up on one side, had three tusks[c] in its mouth among its teeth and was told, "Arise, devour many bodies!" [6]After this, as I watched, another appeared, like a leopard. The beast had four wings of a bird on its back and four heads; and dominion was given to it. [7]After this I saw in the visions by night a fourth beast, terrifying and dreadful and exceedingly strong. It had great iron teeth and was devouring, breaking in pieces, and stamping what was left with its feet. It was different from all the beasts that preceded it, and it had ten horns. [8]I was considering the horns, when another horn appeared, a little one coming up among them; to make room for it, three of the earlier horns were plucked up by the roots. There were eyes like human eyes in this horn, and a mouth speaking arrogantly.

Judgment before the Ancient One

9 As I watched,
thrones were set in place,
and an Ancient One[d] took his throne,
his clothing was white as snow,
and the hair of his head like pure wool;
his throne was fiery flames,
and its wheels were burning fire.
[10] A stream of fire issued
and flowed out from his presence.
A thousand thousands served him,
and ten thousand times ten thousand
stood attending him.
The court sat in judgment,
and the books were opened.
[11]I watched then because of the noise of the arrogant words that the horn was speaking. And as I watched, the beast was put to death, and its body destroyed and given over to be burned with fire. [12]As for the rest of the beasts, their dominion was taken away,

---

a Q Ms Theodotion: MT adds *the beginning of the words; he said*   b Theodotion: Aram *Daniel answered and said, I*   c Or *ribs*   d Aram *an Ancient of Days*

but their lives were prolonged for a season and a time. [13]As I watched in the night visions,

I saw one like a human being[a]
    coming with the clouds of heaven.
And he came to the Ancient One[b]
    and was presented before him.
[14] To him was given dominion
    and glory and kingship,
that all peoples, nations, and languages
    should serve him.
His dominion is an everlasting dominion
    that shall not pass away,
and his kingship is one
    that shall never be destroyed.

Daniel's Visions Interpreted

15 As for me, Daniel, my spirit was troubled within me,[c] and the visions of my head terrified me. [16]I approached one of the attendants to ask him the truth concerning all this. So he said that he would disclose to me the interpretation of the matter: [17]"As for these four great beasts, four kings shall arise out of the earth. [18]But the holy ones of the Most High shall receive the kingdom and possess the kingdom forever—forever and ever."

19 Then I desired to know the truth concerning the fourth beast, which was different from all the rest, exceedingly terrifying, with its teeth of iron and claws of bronze, and which devoured and broke in pieces, and stamped what was left with its feet; [20]and concerning the ten horns that were on its head, and concerning the other horn, which came up and to make room for which three of them fell out—the horn that had eyes and a mouth that spoke arrogantly, and that seemed greater than the others. [21]As I looked, this horn made war with the holy ones and was prevailing over them, [22]until the Ancient One[b] came; then judgment was given for the holy ones of the Most High, and the time arrived when the holy ones gained possession of the kingdom.

23 This is what he said: "As for the fourth beast,
    there shall be a fourth kingdom on earth
    that shall be different from all the other
        kingdoms;
    it shall devour the whole earth,

Apocalyptic Literature · Daniel 7–10

What's with the four beasts (Daniel 7), and the goat with the horn (Daniel 8), and the man with a face like lightning (Daniel 10)? These are all examples of apocalyptic literature. "Apocalypse" comes from a Greek word meaning "to uncover or reveal." Apocalyptic literature is written to sound like an attempt to foretell the future by using symbols and visions. But the symbols are often codes for people and events in the present. This type of literature is frequently produced during a time of persecution, when using real names could get a person into trouble or even killed. Apocalyptic literature developed in Israel around 200 B.C., when the country was enduring great persecution and suffering. The book of Revelation in the New Testament is another example of apocalyptic literature.

The book of Daniel contains some explanation of the visions it describes. But sometimes you will have to consult a good Bible commentary (a book that gives additional background on Bible passages) to completely understand the symbols. For instance, you might need help recognizing that the four beasts are symbols for Babylon, Media, Persia, and Greece—the four nations that ruled over Israel, but would pass away. Or that the arrogant eleventh horn on the fourth beast's head is a symbol for Antiochus IV Epiphanes, the king who persecuted the Jews during the time Daniel was written.

Apocalyptic literature assured the people of Israel that God would triumph and the present evil would eventually pass away. It was one more way to reinforce the belief that evil would be punished and good rewarded, even when it didn't look that way at the moment.

a Aram *one like a son of man* b Aram *the Ancient of Days* c Aram *troubled in its sheath*

and trample it down, and break it to pieces.

24 As for the ten horns,
   out of this kingdom ten kings shall arise,
   and another shall arise after them.
This one shall be different from the former ones,
   and shall put down three kings.
25 He shall speak words against the Most High,
   shall wear out the holy ones of the Most High,
   and shall attempt to change the sacred seasons and the law;
and they shall be given into his power
   for a time, two times,*a* and half a time.
26 Then the court shall sit in judgment,
   and his dominion shall be taken away,
   to be consumed and totally destroyed.
27 The kingship and dominion
   and the greatness of the kingdoms under the whole heaven
   shall be given to the people of the holy ones of the Most High;
their kingdom shall be an everlasting kingdom,
   and all dominions shall serve and obey them."

28 Here the account ends. As for me, Daniel, my thoughts greatly terrified me, and my face turned pale; but I kept the matter in my mind.

Vision of a Ram and a Goat

8 In the third year of the reign of King Belshazzar a vision appeared to me, Daniel, after the one that had appeared to me at first. [2]In the vision I was looking and saw myself in Susa the capital, in the province of Elam,*b* and I was by the river Ulai.*c* [3]I looked up and saw a ram standing beside the river.*d* It had two horns. Both horns were long, but one was longer than the other, and the longer one came up second. [4]I saw the ram charging westward and northward and southward. All beasts were powerless to withstand it, and no one could rescue from its power; it did as it pleased and became strong.

5 As I was watching, a male goat appeared from the west, coming across the face of the whole earth without touching the ground. The goat had a horn*e* between its eyes. [6]It came toward the ram with the two horns that I had seen standing beside the river,*d* and it ran at it with savage force. [7]I saw it approaching the ram. It was enraged against it and struck the ram, breaking its two horns. The ram did not have power to withstand it; it threw the ram down to the ground and trampled upon it, and there was no one who could rescue the ram from its power. [8]Then the male goat grew exceedingly great; but at the height of its power, the great horn was broken, and in its place there came up four prominent horns toward the four winds of heaven.

9 Out of one of them came another*f* horn, a little one, which grew exceedingly great toward the south, toward the east, and toward the beautiful land. [10]It grew as high as the host of heaven. It threw down to the earth some of the host and some of the stars, and trampled on them. [11]Even against the prince of the host it acted arrogantly; it took the regular burnt offering away from him and overthrew the place of his sanctuary. [12]Because of wickedness, the host was given over to it together with the regular burnt offering;*g* it cast truth to the ground, and kept prospering in what it did. [13]Then I heard a holy one speaking, and another holy one said to the one that spoke, "For how long is this vision concerning the regular burnt offering, the transgression that makes desolate, and the giving over of the sanctuary and host to be trampled?"*g* [14]And he answered him,*h* "For two thousand three hundred evenings and mornings; then the sanctuary shall be restored to its rightful state."

Gabriel Interprets the Vision

15 When I, Daniel, had seen the vision, I tried to understand it. Then someone appeared standing before me, having the appearance of a man, [16]and I heard a human voice by the Ulai, calling, "Gabriel, help this man understand the vision." [17]So he came near where I stood; and when he came, I became frightened and fell prostrate. But he said to me,

---

a Aram *a time, times*   b Gk Theodotion: MT Q Ms repeat *in the vision I was looking*   c Or *the Ulai Gate*   d Or *gate*   e Theodotion: Gk *one horn*; Heb *a horn of vision*   f Cn Compare 7.8: Heb *one*   g Meaning of Heb uncertain   h Gk Theodotion Syr Vg: Heb *me*

"Understand, O mortal,[a] that the vision is for the time of the end."

18 As he was speaking to me, I fell into a trance, face to the ground; then he touched me and set me on my feet. [19]He said, "Listen, and I will tell you what will take place later in the period of wrath; for it refers to the appointed time of the end. [20]As for the ram that you saw with the two horns, these are the kings of Media and Persia. [21]The male goat[b] is the king of Greece, and the great horn between its eyes is the first king. [22]As for the horn that was broken, in place of which four others arose, four kingdoms shall arise from his[c] nation, but not with his power.

23 At the end of their rule,
　　when the transgressions have reached their
　　　　full measure,
　　a king of bold countenance shall arise,
　　　　skilled in intrigue.
24 He shall grow strong in power,[d]
　　shall cause fearful destruction,
　　and shall succeed in what he does.
　　He shall destroy the powerful
　　and the people of the holy ones.
25 By his cunning
　　he shall make deceit prosper under his
　　　　hand,
　　and in his own mind he shall be great.
　　Without warning he shall destroy many
　　　　and shall even rise up against the Prince of
　　　　princes.
　　But he shall be broken, and not by human
　　　　hands.
26The vision of the evenings and the mornings that has been told is true. As for you, seal up the vision, for it refers to many days from now."

27 So I, Daniel, was overcome and lay sick for some days; then I arose and went about the king's business. But I was dismayed by the vision and did not understand it.

Daniel's Prayer for the People

9 In the first year of Darius son of Ahasuerus, by birth a Mede, who became king over the realm of the Chaldeans— [2]in the first year of his reign, I, Daniel, perceived in the books the number of years that, according to the word of the Lord to the prophet Jeremiah, must be fulfilled for the devastation of Jerusalem, namely, seventy years.

3 Then I turned to the Lord God, to seek an answer by prayer and supplication with fasting and sackcloth and ashes. [4]I prayed to the Lord my God and made confession, saying,

"Ah, Lord, great and awesome God, keeping covenant and steadfast love with those who love you and keep your commandments, [5]we have sinned and done wrong, acted wickedly and rebelled, turning aside from your commandments and ordinances. [6]We have not listened to your servants the prophets, who spoke in your name to our kings, our princes, and our ancestors, and to all the people of the land.

7 "Righteousness is on your side, O Lord, but open shame, as at this day, falls on us, the people of Judah, the inhabitants of Jerusalem, and all Israel, those who are near and those who are far away, in all the lands to which you have driven them, because of the treachery that they have committed against you. [8]Open shame, O Lord, falls on us, our kings, our officials, and our ancestors, because we have sinned against you. [9]To the Lord our God belong mercy and forgiveness, for we have rebelled against him, [10]and have not obeyed the voice of the Lord our God by following his laws, which he set before us by his servants the prophets.

PRAY IT!

A Closer Look · Daniel 9

Let's look closely at the prayer in **Daniel 9**. Here the prophet uses four types of prayer:

- **Intercession**, in which he prays on behalf of the people
- **Praise**, in which he proclaims God to be awesome and great
- **Lament**, in which he expresses sadness for past sinfulness and asks for forgiveness
- **Petition**, in which he asks God for help

Daniel gives us a great example of the various ways we can pray to God. When you have a moment, pray by yourself or with a friend, trying to incorporate all four of these types of prayer.

---

a Heb *son of man*　b Or *shaggy male goat*　c Gk Theodotion Vg: Heb *the*　d Theodotion and one Gk Ms: Heb repeats (from 8.22) *but not with his power*

11 "All Israel has transgressed your law and turned aside, refusing to obey your voice. So the curse and the oath written in the law of Moses, the servant of God, have been poured out upon us, because we have sinned against you. [12] He has confirmed his words, which he spoke against us and against our rulers, by bringing upon us a calamity so great that what has been done against Jerusalem has never before been done under the whole heaven. [13] Just as it is written in the law of Moses, all this calamity has come upon us. We did not entreat the favor of the Lord our God, turning from our iniquities and reflecting on his[a] fidelity. [14] So the Lord kept watch over this calamity until he brought it upon us. Indeed, the Lord our God is right in all that he has done; for we have disobeyed his voice.

15 "And now, O Lord our God, who brought your people out of the land of Egypt with a mighty hand and made your name renowned even to this day— we have sinned, we have done wickedly. [16] O Lord, in view of all your righteous acts, let your anger and wrath, we pray, turn away from your city Jerusalem, your holy mountain; because of our sins and the iniquities of our ancestors, Jerusalem and your people have become a disgrace among all our neighbors. [17] Now therefore, O our God, listen to the prayer of your servant and to his supplication, and for your own sake, Lord,[b] let your face shine upon your desolated sanctuary. [18] Incline your ear, O my God, and hear. Open your eyes and look at our desolation and the city that bears your name. We do not present our supplication before you on the ground of our righteousness, but on the ground of your great mercies. [19] O Lord, hear; O Lord, forgive; O Lord, listen and act and do not delay! For your own sake, O my God, because your city and your people bear your name!"

The Seventy Weeks

20 While I was speaking, and was praying and confessing my sin and the sin of my people Israel, and presenting my supplication before the Lord my God on behalf of the holy mountain of my God— [21] while I was speaking in prayer, the man Gabriel, whom I had seen before in a vision, came to me in swift flight at the time of the evening sacrifice. [22] He came[c] and said to me, "Daniel, I have now come out to give you wisdom and understanding. [23] At the beginning of your supplications a word went out, and I have come to declare it, for you are greatly beloved. So consider the word and understand the vision:

24 "Seventy weeks are decreed for your people and your holy city: to finish the transgression, to put an end to sin, and to atone for iniquity, to bring in everlasting righteousness, to seal both vision and prophet, and to anoint a most holy place.[d] [25] Know therefore and understand: from the time that the word went out to restore and rebuild Jerusalem until the time of an anointed prince, there shall be seven weeks; and for sixty-two weeks it shall be built again with streets and moat, but in a troubled time. [26] After the sixty-two weeks, an anointed one shall be cut off and shall have nothing, and the troops of the prince who is to come shall destroy the city and the sanctuary. Its[e] end shall come with a flood, and to the end there shall be war. Desolations are decreed. [27] He shall make a strong covenant with many for one week, and for half of the week he shall make sacrifice and offering cease; and in their place[f] shall be an abomination that desolates, until the decreed end is poured out upon the desolator."

10   Conflict of Nations and Heavenly Powers

In the third year of King Cyrus of Persia a word was revealed to Daniel, who was named Belteshazzar. The word was true, and it concerned a great conflict. He understood the word, having received understanding in the vision.

2 At that time I, Daniel, had been mourning for three weeks. [3] I had eaten no rich food, no meat or wine had entered my mouth, and I had not anointed myself at all, for the full three weeks. [4] On the twenty-fourth day of the first month, as I was standing on the bank of the great river (that is, the Tigris), [5] I looked up and saw a man clothed in linen, with a belt of gold from Uphaz around his waist. [6] His

> "O Lord, hear; O Lord, forgive; O Lord, listen and act and do not delay!"
> —Daniel 9:19

a Heb *your*   b Theodotion Vg Compare Syr: Heb *for the Lord's sake*   c Gk Syr: Heb *He made to understand*   d Or *thing* or *one*   e Or *His*
f Cn: Meaning of Heb uncertain

body was like beryl, his face like lightning, his eyes like flaming torches, his arms and legs like the gleam of burnished bronze, and the sound of his words like the roar of a multitude. [7]I, Daniel, alone saw the vision; the people who were with me did not see the vision, though a great trembling fell upon them, and they fled and hid themselves. [8]So I was left alone to see this great vision. My strength left me, and my complexion grew deathly pale, and I retained no strength. [9]Then I heard the sound of his words; and when I heard the sound of his words, I fell into a trance, face to the ground.

10 But then a hand touched me and roused me to my hands and knees. [11]He said to me, "Daniel, greatly beloved, pay attention to the words that I am going to speak to you. Stand on your feet, for I have now been sent to you." So while he was speaking this word to me, I stood up trembling. [12]He said to me, "Do not fear, Daniel, for from the first day that you set your mind to gain understanding and to humble yourself before your God, your words have been heard, and I have come because of your words. [13]But the prince of the kingdom of Persia opposed me twenty-one days. So Michael, one of the chief princes, came to help me, and I left him there with the prince of the kingdom of Persia,[a] [14]and have come to help you understand what is to happen to your people at the end of days. For there is a further vision for those days."

15 While he was speaking these words to me, I turned my face toward the ground and was speechless. [16]Then one in human form touched my lips, and I opened my mouth to speak, and said to the one who stood before me, "My lord, because of the vision such pains have come upon me that I retain no strength. [17]How can my lord's servant talk with my lord? For I am shaking,[b] no strength remains in me, and no breath is left in me."

18 Again one in human form touched me and strengthened me. [19]He said, "Do not fear, greatly beloved, you are safe. Be strong and courageous!" When he spoke to me, I was strengthened and said, "Let my lord speak, for you have strengthened me." [20]Then he said, "Do you know why I have come to you? Now I must return to fight against the prince of Persia, and when I am through with him, the prince of Greece will come. [21]But I am to tell you what is inscribed in the book of truth. There is no one with me who contends against these princes except Michael, your prince.

11 [1]As for me, in the first year of Darius the Mede, I stood up to support and strengthen him. 2 "Now I will announce the truth to you. Three more kings shall arise in Persia. The fourth shall be far richer than all of them, and when he has become strong through his riches, he shall stir up all against the kingdom of Greece. [3]Then a warrior king shall arise, who shall rule with great dominion and take action as he pleases. [4]And while still rising in power, his kingdom shall be broken and divided toward the four winds of heaven, but not to his posterity, nor according to the dominion with which he ruled; for his kingdom shall be uprooted and go to others besides these.

5 "Then the king of the south shall grow strong, but one of his officers shall grow stronger than he and shall rule a realm greater than his own realm. [6]After some years they shall make an alliance, and the daughter of the king of the south shall come to the king of the north to ratify the agreement. But she shall not retain her power, and his offspring shall not endure. She shall be given up, she and her attendants and her child and the one who supported her.

"In those times [7]a branch from her roots shall rise up in his place. He shall come against the army and enter the fortress of the king of the north, and he shall take action against them and prevail. [8]Even their gods, with their idols and with their precious vessels of silver and gold, he shall carry off to Egypt as spoils of war. For some years he shall refrain from attacking the king of the north; [9]then the latter shall invade the realm of the king of the south, but will return to his own land.

10 "His sons shall wage war and assemble a multitude of great forces, which shall advance like a flood and pass through, and again shall carry the war as far as his fortress. [11]Moved with rage, the king of the south shall go out and do battle against the king of the north, who shall muster a great multitude, which shall, however, be defeated by his enemy. [12]When the multitude has been carried off, his heart shall be exalted, and he shall overthrow tens of thousands, but he shall not prevail. [13]For the king of the north shall again raise a multitude, larger than the former, and after some years[c] he shall advance with a great army and abundant supplies.

14 "In those times many shall rise against the king of the south. The lawless among your own people shall lift themselves up in order to fulfill the vision,

---

a Gk Theodotion: Heb *I was left there with the kings of Persia*   b Gk: Heb *from now*   c Heb *and at the end of the times years*

but they shall fail. [15]Then the king of the north shall come and throw up siegeworks, and take a well-fortified city. And the forces of the south shall not stand, not even his picked troops, for there shall be no strength to resist. [16]But he who comes against him shall take the actions he pleases, and no one shall withstand him. He shall take a position in the beautiful land, and all of it shall be in his power. [17]He shall set his mind to come with the strength of his whole kingdom, and he shall bring terms of peace[a] and perform them. In order to destroy the kingdom,[b] he shall give him a woman in marriage; but it shall not succeed or be to his advantage. [18]Afterward he shall turn to the coastlands, and shall capture many. But a commander shall put an end to his insolence; indeed,[c] he shall turn his insolence back upon him. [19]Then he shall turn back toward the fortresses of his own land, but he shall stumble and fall, and shall not be found.

20 "Then shall arise in his place one who shall send an official for the glory of the kingdom; but within a few days he shall be broken, though not in anger or in battle. [21]In his place shall arise a contemptible person on whom royal majesty had not been conferred; he shall come in without warning and obtain the kingdom through intrigue. [22]Armies shall be utterly swept away and broken before him, and the prince of the covenant as well. [23]And after an alliance is made with him, he shall act deceitfully and become strong with a small party. [24]Without warning he shall come into the richest parts[d] of the province and do what none of his predecessors had ever done, lavishing plunder, spoil, and wealth on them. He shall devise plans against strongholds, but only for a time. [25]He shall stir up his power and determination against the king of the south with a great army, and the king of the south shall wage war with a much greater and stronger army. But he shall not succeed, for plots shall be devised against him [26]by those who eat of the royal rations. They shall break him, his army shall be swept away, and many shall fall slain. [27]The two kings, their minds bent on evil, shall sit at one table and exchange lies. But it shall not succeed, for there remains an end at the time appointed. [28]He shall return to his land with great wealth, but his heart shall be set against the holy covenant. He shall work his will, and return to his own land.

29 "At the time appointed he shall return and come into the south, but this time it shall not be as it was before. [30]For ships of Kittim shall come against him, and he shall lose heart and withdraw. He shall be enraged and take action against the holy covenant. He shall turn back and pay heed to those who forsake the holy covenant. [31]Forces sent by him shall occupy and profane the temple and fortress. They shall abolish the regular burnt offering and set up the abomination that makes desolate. [32]He shall seduce with intrigue those who violate the covenant; but the people who are loyal to their God shall stand firm and take action. [33]The wise among the people shall give understanding to many; for some days, however, they shall fall by sword and flame, and suffer captivity and plunder. [34]When they fall victim, they shall receive a little help, and many shall join them insincerely. [35]Some of the wise shall fall, so that they may be refined, purified, and cleansed,[e] until the time of the end, for there is still an interval until the time appointed.

36 "The king shall act as he pleases. He shall exalt himself and consider himself greater than any god, and shall speak horrendous things against the God of gods. He shall prosper until the period of wrath is completed, for what is determined shall be done. [37]He shall pay no respect to the gods of his ancestors, or to the one beloved by women; he shall pay no respect to any other god, for he shall consider himself greater than all. [38]He shall honor the god of fortresses instead of these; a god whom his ancestors did not know he shall honor with gold and silver, with precious stones and costly gifts. [39]He shall deal with the strongest fortresses by the help of a foreign god. Those who acknowledge him he shall make more wealthy, and shall appoint them as rulers over many, and shall distribute the land for a price.

The Time of the End

40 "At the time of the end the king of the south shall attack him. But the king of the north shall rush upon him like a whirlwind, with chariots and horsemen, and with many ships. He shall advance against countries and pass through like a flood. [41]He shall come into the beautiful land, and tens of thousands shall fall victim, but Edom and Moab and the main part of the Ammonites shall escape from his power. [42]He shall stretch out his hand against the countries, and the land of Egypt shall not escape. [43]He shall become ruler of the treasures of gold and of silver, and all the riches of Egypt; and the Libyans

---

a Gk: Heb *kingdom, and upright ones with him*   b Heb *it*   c Meaning of Heb uncertain   d Or *among the richest men*   e Heb *made them white*

and the Ethiopians*a* shall follow in his train. [44]But reports from the east and the north shall alarm him, and he shall go out with great fury to bring ruin and complete destruction to many. [45]He shall pitch his palatial tents between the sea and the beautiful holy mountain. Yet he shall come to his end, with no one to help him.

STUDY IT!

Resurrection
Daniel 12:1–3

Most of the Old Testament contains no indication of a belief in life after death. But Daniel speaks here of individual resurrection, or rising to life from death, and tells of God's ultimate victory over the final enemy of death, as in **1 Corinthians 15:26**. This understanding of personal resurrection developed quite late in Israel's existence. It is described as the complete transformation of the human being, body and spirit, after death.

12 The Resurrection of the Dead

"At that time Michael, the great prince, the protector of your people, shall arise. There shall be a time of anguish, such as has never occurred since nations first came into existence. But at that time your people shall be delivered, everyone who is found written in the book. [2]Many of those who sleep in the dust of the earth*b* shall awake, some to everlasting life, and some to shame and everlasting contempt. [3]Those who are wise shall shine like the brightness of the sky,*c* and those who lead many to righteousness, like the stars forever and ever. [4]But you, Daniel, keep the words secret and the book sealed until the time of the end. Many shall be running back and forth, and evil*d* shall increase."

5 Then I, Daniel, looked, and two others appeared, one standing on this bank of the stream and one on the other. [6]One of them said to the man clothed in linen, who was upstream, "How long shall it be until the end of these wonders?" [7]The man clothed in linen, who was upstream, raised his right hand and his left hand toward heaven. And I heard him swear by the one who lives forever that it would be for a time, two times, and half a time,*e* and that when the shattering of the power of the holy people comes to an end, all these things would be accom-

plished. [8]I heard but could not understand; so I said, "My lord, what shall be the outcome of these things?" [9]He said, "Go your way, Daniel, for the words are to remain secret and sealed until the time of the end. [10]Many shall be purified, cleansed, and refined, but the wicked shall continue to act wickedly. None of the wicked shall understand, but those who are wise shall understand. [11]From the time that the regular burnt offering is taken away and the abomination that desolates is set up, there shall be one thousand two hundred ninety days. [12]Happy are those who persevere and attain the thousand three hundred thirty-five days. [13]But you, go your way,*f* and rest; you shall rise for your reward at the end of the days."

a Or *Nubians*; Heb *Cushites* *b* Or *the land of dust* *c* Or *dome* *d* Cn Compare Gk: Heb *knowledge* *e* Heb *a time, times, and a half* *f* Gk Theodotion: Heb adds *to the end*

Hosea

"**G**o marry a prostitute." "Say what, God?" That's what God told Hosea to do—marry a prostitute. Why? Because a picture is worth a thousand words, and Hosea's family life was a living picture of Israel's infidelity and God's continuing faithfulness. The book of Hosea captures this faithful prophet's commitment to God and his loving faithfulness to his straying wife.

IN DEPTH

Hosea preached to the northern kingdom, Israel, before it was conquered by the Assyrians in 722 B.C. As we learn from Hosea's speeches, the situation in the northern kingdom was not good. For twenty-five years, Hosea saw seven kings come and go, most of them corrupt (see 2 Kings 14:23–17:23 as well as the chart "Prophets and Kings (1050–571 B.C.)," p. 680). The ruling classes pursued their own greedy ends, played power politics, overlooked the poor and needy in their midst, and led the people into idolatry. Through Hosea, God called the people to remember: "I have been the LORD your God, ever since the land of Egypt" (Hosea 13:4).

Even more powerful than Hosea's words was the living symbol of his marriage. Early in Hosea's preaching, God commanded him to marry a prostitute and have children by her. Hosea remained faithful to her, loving her even when she wandered to other men. Hosea used the image of his own marriage to preach his message to Israel. As Hosea's wife was unfaithful to him, so too Israel was unfaithful to God, wandering off to worship other gods. However, just as Hosea was faithful to his wife and awaited her return, so too God was faithful to Israel and awaited its return from the distractions of power, wealth, and other gods.

Hosea and Amos were prophets in the northern kingdom at about the same time. But Amos had come from the southern kingdom and was more distant and cynical in describing the sins of the ruling class (see his description of well-off women in Amos 4:1-3). Hosea was from the northern kingdom—these people were his people! He took their sins personally and passionately. Initially, he had hopes that the people would repent and return to God (Hosea 2:16-23). But after a succession of selfish and violent rulers, he prophesied against his people with all the passion of a scorned lover (Hosea 13:7-11). Still, at the end, he hoped for Israel's return to God (Hosea 14:1-2).

QUICK FACTS

- **Date Written:** Between 750 and 725 B.C.
- **Authors:** Hosea and later scribes
- **Theme:** God's faithful love, even when people walk away from God

AT A GLANCE

- **Hosea 1–3** Descriptions of Hosea's marriage and family
- **Hosea 4–13** Israel's unfaithfulness to God
- **Hosea 14** A call to repentance and promise of forgiveness

1

The word of the LORD that came to Hosea son of Beeri, in the days of Kings Uzziah, Jotham, Ahaz, and Hezekiah of Judah, and in the days of King Jeroboam son of Joash of Israel.

The Family of Hosea

2 When the LORD first spoke through Hosea, the LORD said to Hosea, "Go, take for yourself a wife of whoredom and have children of whoredom, for the land commits great whoredom by forsaking the LORD." ³So he went and took Gomer daughter of Diblaim, and she conceived and bore him a son.

4 And the LORD said to him, "Name him Jezreel;[a] for in a little while I will punish the house of Jehu for the blood of Jezreel, and I will put an end to the kingdom of the house of Israel. ⁵On that day I will break the bow of Israel in the valley of Jezreel."

6 She conceived again and bore a daughter. Then the LORD said to him, "Name her Lo-ruhamah,[b] for I will no longer have pity on the house of Israel or forgive them. ⁷But I will have pity on the house of Judah, and I will save them by the LORD their God; I will not save them by bow, or by sword, or by war, or by horses, or by horsemen."

8 When she had weaned Lo-ruhamah, she conceived and bore a son. ⁹Then the LORD said, "Name him Lo-ammi,[c] for you are not my people and I am not your God."[d]

The Restoration of Israel

10[e] Yet the number of the people of Israel shall be like the sand of the sea, which can be neither measured nor numbered; and in the place where it was said to them, "You are not my people," it shall be said to them, "Children of the living God." ¹¹The people of Judah and the people of Israel shall be gathered together, and they shall appoint for themselves one head; and they shall take possession of[f] the land, for great shall be the day of Jezreel.

2

[g] Say to your brother,[h] Ammi,[i] and to your sister,[j] Ruhamah.[k]

Israel's Infidelity, Punishment, and Redemption

2 Plead with your mother, plead—
for she is not my wife,
and I am not her husband—
that she put away her whoring from her face,
and her adultery from between her breasts,
3 or I will strip her naked

and expose her as in the day she was born,
and make her like a wilderness,
and turn her into a parched land,
and kill her with thirst.
4 Upon her children also I will have no pity,
because they are children of whoredom.
5 For their mother has played the whore;
she who conceived them has acted
shamefully.
For she said, "I will go after my lovers;
they give me my bread and my water,
my wool and my flax, my oil and my
drink."
6 Therefore I will hedge up her[l] way with
thorns;
and I will build a wall against her,
so that she cannot find her paths.
7 She shall pursue her lovers,
but not overtake them;
and she shall seek them,
but shall not find them.
Then she shall say, "I will go
and return to my first husband,
for it was better with me then than now."
8 She did not know
that it was I who gave her
the grain, the wine, and the oil,
and who lavished upon her silver
and gold that they used for Baal.
9 Therefore I will take back
my grain in its time,
and my wine in its season;
and I will take away my wool and my flax,
which were to cover her nakedness.
10 Now I will uncover her shame
in the sight of her lovers,
and no one shall rescue her out of my
hand.
11 I will put an end to all her mirth,
her festivals, her new moons, her sabbaths,
and all her appointed festivals.
12 I will lay waste her vines and her fig trees,
of which she said,
"These are my pay,
which my lovers have given me."
I will make them a forest,
and the wild animals shall devour them.
13 I will punish her for the festival days of the
Baals,
when she offered incense to them

---

a That is *God sows*   b That is *Not pitied*   c That is *Not my people*   d Heb *I am not yours*   e Ch 2.1 in Heb   f Heb *rise up from*   g Ch 2.3 in Heb
h Gk: Heb *brothers*   i That is *My people*   j Gk Vg: Heb *sisters*   k That is *Pitied*   l Gk Syr: Heb *your*

and decked herself with her ring and jewelry,
    and went after her lovers,
    and forgot me, says the LORD.

14 Therefore, I will now allure her,
    and bring her into the wilderness,
    and speak tenderly to her.
15 From there I will give her her vineyards,
    and make the Valley of Achor a door of
      hope.
There she shall respond as in the days of her
    youth,
    as at the time when she came out of the
      land of Egypt.

16 On that day, says the LORD, you will call me, "My husband," and no longer will you call me, "My Baal."*a* 17 For I will remove the names of the Baals from her mouth, and they shall be mentioned by name no more. 18 I will make for you*b* a covenant on that day with the wild animals, the birds of the air, and the creeping things of the ground; and I will abolish*c* the bow, the sword, and war from the land; and I will make you lie down in safety. 19 And I will take you for my wife forever; I will take you for my wife in righteousness and in justice, in steadfast love, and in mercy. 20 I will take you for my wife in faithfulness; and you shall know the LORD.

21 On that day I will answer, says the LORD,
    I will answer the heavens
    and they shall answer the earth;
22 and the earth shall answer the grain, the wine,
      and the oil,
    and they shall answer Jezreel;*d*
23 and I will sow him*e* for myself in the land.
And I will have pity on Lo-ruhamah,*f*
    and I will say to Lo-ammi,*g* "You are my
      people";
    and he shall say, "You are my God."

Unconditional Faithfulness
Hosea 3:1–3

We don't know all the details of Hosea's relationship with his wife, Gomer. But most people understand **Hosea 3:1–3** to mean that Hosea accepted her back after she was unfaithful to him. We can only hope that Gomer was so touched by Hosea's unconditional forgiveness that she turned her life around and was faithful to him in return.

Have you ever tried to be faithful to someone who has betrayed you? The other person doesn't have to be an adulterous spouse. She or he can be a friend who starts spending time with someone else instead of you, a classmate who betrays your trust by telling secrets, or a family member who keeps breaking promises to be with you. A natural reaction is to return the hurt in some way. The much harder (and Christlike) reaction is to keep being faithful and caring.

- When have you been hurt by someone's unfaithful behavior? How did you react?
- How can you address a friend's or family member's unfaithful behavior and still remain faithful and loving yourself?

3 Further Assurances of God's Redeeming Love

The LORD said to me again, "Go, love a woman who has a lover and is an adulteress, just as the LORD loves the people of Israel, though they turn to other gods and love raisin cakes." 2 So I bought her for fifteen shekels of silver and a homer of barley and a measure of wine.*h* 3 And I said to her, "You must remain as mine for many days; you shall not play the whore, you shall not have intercourse with a man, nor I with you." 4 For the Israelites shall remain many days without king or prince, without sacrifice or pillar, without ephod or teraphim. 5 Afterward the Israelites shall return and seek the LORD their God, and David their king; they shall come in awe to the LORD and to his goodness in the latter days.

---

a That is, *"My master"* *b* Heb *them* *c* Heb *break* *d* That is *God sows* *e* Cn: Heb *her* *f* That is *Not pitied* *g* That is *Not my people* *h* Gk: Heb *a homer of barley and a lethech of barley*

God Accuses Israel

4 Hear the word of the Lord, O people of
Israel;
for the Lord has an indictment against the
inhabitants of the land.
There is no faithfulness or loyalty,
and no knowledge of God in the land.
2 Swearing, lying, and murder,
and stealing and adultery break out;
bloodshed follows bloodshed.
3 Therefore the land mourns,
and all who live in it languish;
together with the wild animals
and the birds of the air,
even the fish of the sea are perishing.

4 Yet let no one contend,
and let none accuse,
for with you is my contention, O priest.*a*
5 You shall stumble by day;
the prophet also shall stumble with you by
night,
and I will destroy your mother.
6 My people are destroyed for lack of
knowledge;
because you have rejected knowledge,
I reject you from being a priest to me.
And since you have forgotten the law of
your God,
I also will forget your children.

7 The more they increased,
the more they sinned against me;
they changed*b* their glory into shame.
8 They feed on the sin of my people;
they are greedy for their iniquity.
9 And it shall be like people, like priest;
I will punish them for their ways,
and repay them for their deeds.
10 They shall eat, but not be satisfied;
they shall play the whore, but not multiply;
because they have forsaken the Lord
to devote themselves to 11whoredom.

The Idolatry of Israel

Wine and new wine
take away the understanding.
12 My people consult a piece of wood,
and their divining rod gives them oracles.
For a spirit of whoredom has led them astray,

and they have played the whore,
forsaking their God.
13 They sacrifice on the tops of the mountains,
and make offerings upon the hills,
under oak, poplar, and terebinth,
because their shade is good.

Therefore your daughters play the whore,
and your daughters-in-law commit
adultery.
14 I will not punish your daughters when they
play the whore,
nor your daughters-in-law when they
commit adultery;
for the men themselves go aside with
whores,
and sacrifice with temple prostitutes;
thus a people without understanding comes
to ruin.

15 Though you play the whore, O Israel,
do not let Judah become guilty.
Do not enter into Gilgal,
or go up to Beth-aven,
and do not swear, "As the Lord lives."
16 Like a stubborn heifer,
Israel is stubborn;
can the Lord now feed them
like a lamb in a broad pasture?

17 Ephraim is joined to idols—
let him alone.
18 When their drinking is ended, they indulge
in sexual orgies;
they love lewdness more than their
glory.*c*
19 A wind has wrapped them*d* in its wings,
and they shall be ashamed because of
their altars.*e*

Impending Judgment on Israel and Judah

5 Hear this, O priests!
Give heed, O house of Israel!
Listen, O house of the king!
For the judgment pertains to you;
for you have been a snare at Mizpah,
and a net spread upon Tabor,
2 and a pit dug deep in Shittim;*a*
but I will punish all of them.

a Cn: Meaning of Heb uncertain *b* Ancient Heb tradition: MT *I will change* *c* Cn Compare Gk: Meaning of Heb uncertain *d* Heb *her* *e* Gk Syr:
Heb *sacrifices*

3 I know Ephraim,
  and Israel is not hidden from me;
for now, O Ephraim, you have played the
    whore;
  Israel is defiled.
4 Their deeds do not permit them
  to return to their God.
For the spirit of whoredom is within them,
  and they do not know the Lord.

5 Israel's pride testifies against him;
  Ephraim[a] stumbles in his guilt;
  Judah also stumbles with them.
6 With their flocks and herds they shall go
  to seek the Lord,
but they will not find him;
  he has withdrawn from them.
7 They have dealt faithlessly with the Lord;
  for they have borne illegitimate children.
  Now the new moon shall devour them
    along with their fields.

8 Blow the horn in Gibeah,
  the trumpet in Ramah.
Sound the alarm at Beth-aven;
  look behind you, Benjamin!
9 Ephraim shall become a desolation
  in the day of punishment;
among the tribes of Israel
  I declare what is sure.
10 The princes of Judah have become
  like those who remove the landmark;
on them I will pour out
  my wrath like water.
11 Ephraim is oppressed, crushed in judgment,
  because he was determined to go after
    vanity.[b]
12 Therefore I am like maggots to Ephraim,
  and like rottenness to the house of Judah.
13 When Ephraim saw his sickness,
  and Judah his wound,
then Ephraim went to Assyria,
  and sent to the great king.[c]
But he is not able to cure you
  or heal your wound.
14 For I will be like a lion to Ephraim,
  and like a young lion to the house of Judah.
I myself will tear and go away;
  I will carry off, and no one shall rescue.
15 I will return again to my place

until they acknowledge their guilt and seek
    my face.
In their distress they will beg my favor:

A Call to Repentance

6 "Come, let us return to the Lord;
  for it is he who has torn, and he will
    heal us;
he has struck down, and he will bind us up.
2 After two days he will revive us;
  on the third day he will raise us up,
  that we may live before him.
3 Let us know, let us press on to know the
    Lord;
  his appearing is as sure as the
    dawn;
he will come to us like the showers,
  like the spring rains that water the earth."

Impenitence of Israel and Judah

4 What shall I do with you, O Ephraim?
  What shall I do with you, O Judah?
Your love is like a morning cloud,
  like the dew that goes away early.
5 Therefore I have hewn them by the prophets,
  I have killed them by the words of my
    mouth,
  and my[d] judgment goes forth as the light.
6 For I desire steadfast love and not sacrifice,
  the knowledge of God rather than burnt
    offerings.
7 But at[e] Adam they transgressed the covenant;
  there they dealt faithlessly with me.
8 Gilead is a city of evildoers,
  tracked with blood.
9 As robbers lie in wait[f] for someone,
  so the priests are banded
    together;[g]

> "I desire steadfast love and not sacrifice, the knowledge of God rather than burnt offerings."
> —Hosea 6:6

a Heb Israel and Ephraim b Gk: Meaning of Heb uncertain c Cn: Heb to a king who will contend d Gk Syr: Heb your e Cn: Heb like
f Cn: Meaning of Heb uncertain g Syr: Heb are a company

they murder on the road to Shechem,
  they commit a monstrous crime.
10 In the house of Israel I have seen a horrible
    thing;
  Ephraim's whoredom is there, Israel
    is defiled.

11 For you also, O Judah, a harvest is appointed.

When I would restore the fortunes of my
    people,

7
  ¹when I would heal Israel,
  the corruption of Ephraim is revealed,
  and the wicked deeds of Samaria;
for they deal falsely,
  the thief breaks in,
  and the bandits raid outside.
2 But they do not consider
  that I remember all their wickedness.
Now their deeds surround them,
  they are before my face.
3 By their wickedness they make the king glad,
  and the officials by their treachery.
4 They are all adulterers;
  they are like a heated oven,
whose baker does not need to stir the fire,
  from the kneading of the dough until it is
    leavened.
5 On the day of our king the officials
  became sick with the heat of wine;
  he stretched out his hand with mockers.
6 For they are kindled[a] like an oven, their heart
    burns within them;
  all night their anger smolders;
  in the morning it blazes like a flaming fire.
7 All of them are hot as an oven,
  and they devour their rulers.
All their kings have fallen;
  none of them calls upon me.

8 Ephraim mixes himself with the peoples;
  Ephraim is a cake not turned.
9 Foreigners devour his strength,
  but he does not know it;
gray hairs are sprinkled upon him,
  but he does not know it.
10 Israel's pride testifies against[b] him;
  yet they do not return to the LORD
    their God,
  or seek him, for all this.

Futile Reliance on the Nations

11 Ephraim has become like a dove,
  silly and without sense;
  they call upon Egypt, they go to Assyria.
12 As they go, I will cast my net over them;
  I will bring them down like birds of the air;
  I will discipline them according to the
    report made to their assembly.[c]
13 Woe to them, for they have strayed from me!
  Destruction to them, for they have rebelled
    against me!
I would redeem them,
  but they speak lies against me.
14 They do not cry to me from the heart,
  but they wail upon their beds;
they gash themselves for grain and wine;
  they rebel against me.
15 It was I who trained and strengthened their
    arms,
  yet they plot evil against me.
16 They turn to that which does not profit;[d]
  they have become like a defective bow;
their officials shall fall by the sword
  because of the rage of their tongue.
So much for their babbling in the land of
    Egypt.

Israel's Apostasy

8
Set the trumpet to your lips!
  One like a vulture[c] is over the house of
    the LORD,
because they have broken my covenant,
  and transgressed my law.
2 Israel cries to me,
  "My God, we—Israel—know you!"
3 Israel has spurned the good;
  the enemy shall pursue him.

4 They made kings, but not through me;
  they set up princes, but without my
    knowledge.
With their silver and gold they made idols
  for their own destruction.
5 Your calf is rejected, O Samaria.
  My anger burns against them.
How long will they be incapable of innocence?
6   For it is from Israel,
an artisan made it;
  it is not God.

---

a Gk Syr: Heb *brought near* b Or *humbles* c Meaning of Heb uncertain d Cn: Meaning of Heb uncertain

The calf of Samaria
    shall be broken to pieces.*a*

7 For they sow the wind,
    and they shall reap the whirlwind.
The standing grain has no heads,
    it shall yield no meal;
if it were to yield,
    foreigners would devour it.
8 Israel is swallowed up;
    now they are among the nations
    as a useless vessel.
9 For they have gone up to Assyria,
    a wild ass wandering alone;
    Ephraim has bargained for lovers.
10 Though they bargain with the nations,
    I will now gather them up.
They shall soon writhe
    under the burden of kings and princes.

11 When Ephraim multiplied altars to expiate sin,
    they became to him altars for sinning.

PRAY IT!

Reaping the Whirlwind
Hosea 8:7

What significant decisions have you made recently? Were your choices the ones that God wanted you to make? Or did your choices "reap a whirlwind"?

Hosea uses metaphors, or symbols, to describe Israel's relationship with God. **Hosea 8:7** gives one of those metaphors, saying the Israelites have sowed the wind and will reap the whirlwind. The wind is their political scheming, injustice, and idolatry; the whirlwind is violence and injustice that will destroy the whole country. Like Israel, we are free to reject or accept God, but will have to reap the consequences of our choices.

Pray today, asking God to show you the areas of your life where your choices are about to reap a whirlwind.

12 Though I write for him the multitude of my
    instructions,
    they are regarded as a strange thing.
13 Though they offer choice sacrifices,*b*
    though they eat flesh,
    the LORD does not accept them.
Now he will remember their iniquity,
    and punish their sins;
    they shall return to Egypt.
14 Israel has forgotten his Maker,
    and built palaces;
and Judah has multiplied fortified cities;
    but I will send a fire upon his cities,
    and it shall devour his strongholds.

9   Punishment for Israel's Sin

Do not rejoice, O Israel!
    Do not exult*c* as other nations do;
for you have played the whore, departing
        from your God.
    You have loved a prostitute's pay
    on all threshing floors.
2 Threshing floor and wine vat shall not feed
        them,
    and the new wine shall fail them.
3 They shall not remain in the land of the
        LORD;
    but Ephraim shall return to Egypt,
    and in Assyria they shall eat unclean
        food.

4 They shall not pour drink offerings of wine
        to the LORD,
    and their sacrifices shall not please him.
Such sacrifices shall be like mourners' bread;
    all who eat of it shall be defiled;
for their bread shall be for their hunger only;
    it shall not come to the house of the
        LORD.

5 What will you do on the day of appointed
        festival,
    and on the day of the festival of the
        LORD?
6 For even if they escape destruction,
    Egypt shall gather them,
    Memphis shall bury them.
Nettles shall possess their precious things of
        silver;*d*
    thorns shall be in their tents.

a Or *shall go up in flames* *b* Cn: Meaning of Heb uncertain *c* Gk: Heb *To exultation* *d* Meaning of Heb uncertain

7 The days of punishment have come,
   the days of recompense have come;
   Israel cries,[a]
"The prophet is a fool,
   the man of the spirit is mad!"
Because of your great iniquity,
   your hostility is great.
8 The prophet is a sentinel for my God over
      Ephraim,
   yet a fowler's snare is on all his ways,
   and hostility in the house of his God.
9 They have deeply corrupted themselves
      as in the days of Gibeah;
he will remember their iniquity,
   he will punish their sins.

10 Like grapes in the wilderness,
      I found Israel.
Like the first fruit on the fig tree,
   in its first season,
   I saw your ancestors.
But they came to Baal-peor,
   and consecrated themselves to a thing of
      shame,
   and became detestable like the thing they
      loved.
11 Ephraim's glory shall fly away like a bird—
   no birth, no pregnancy, no conception!
12 Even if they bring up children,
   I will bereave them until no one is left.
Woe to them indeed
   when I depart from them!
13 Once I saw Ephraim as a young palm planted
      in a lovely meadow,[b]
   but now Ephraim must lead out his
      children for slaughter.
14 Give them, O Lord—
   what will you give?
Give them a miscarrying womb
   and dry breasts.

15 Every evil of theirs began at Gilgal;
   there I came to hate them.
Because of the wickedness of their deeds
   I will drive them out of my house.
I will love them no more;
   all their officials are rebels.

16 Ephraim is stricken,
   their root is dried up,

   they shall bear no fruit.
Even though they give birth,
   I will kill the cherished offspring of their
      womb.

17 Because they have not listened to him,
   my God will reject them;
they shall become wanderers among the
   nations.

Israel's Sin and Captivity

10 Israel is a luxuriant vine
   that yields its fruit.
The more his fruit increased
   the more altars he built;
as his country improved,
   he improved his pillars.
2 Their heart is false;
   now they must bear their guilt.
The Lord[c] will break down their altars,
   and destroy their pillars.

3 For now they will say:
   "We have no king,
for we do not fear the Lord,
   and a king—what could he do
      for us?"
4 They utter mere words;
   with empty oaths they make covenants;
so litigation springs up like poisonous weeds
   in the furrows of the field.
5 The inhabitants of Samaria tremble
   for the calf[d] of Beth-aven.
Its people shall mourn for it,
   and its idolatrous priests shall wail[e] over it,
   over its glory that has departed
      from it.
6 The thing itself shall be carried to Assyria
   as tribute to the great king.[f]
Ephraim shall be put to shame,
   and Israel shall be ashamed of his idol.[g]

a Cn Compare Gk: Heb *shall know*   b Meaning of Heb uncertain   c Heb *he*   d Gk Syr: Heb *calves*   e Cn: Heb *exult*   f Cn: Heb *to a king who will contend*   g Cn: Heb *counsel*

7 Samaria's king shall perish
   like a chip on the face of the waters.
8 The high places of Aven, the sin of Israel,
   shall be destroyed.
Thorn and thistle shall grow up
   on their altars.
They shall say to the mountains,
   Cover us,
   and to the hills, Fall on us.

9 Since the days of Gibeah you have sinned,
   O Israel;
   there they have continued.
Shall not war overtake them in Gibeah?
10 I will come^a against the wayward people to
       punish them;
   and nations shall be gathered against
       them
   when they are punished^b for their double
       iniquity.

11 Ephraim was a trained heifer
   that loved to thresh,
   and I spared her fair neck;
but I will make Ephraim break the ground;
   Judah must plow;
   Jacob must harrow for himself.
12 Sow for yourselves righteousness;
   reap steadfast love;
   break up your fallow ground;
for it is time to seek the Lord,
   that he may come and rain righteousness
       upon you.

13 You have plowed wickedness,
   you have reaped injustice,
   you have eaten the fruit of lies.
Because you have trusted in your power
   and in the multitude of your warriors,
14 therefore the tumult of war shall rise against
       your people,
   and all your fortresses shall be destroyed,
as Shalman destroyed Beth-arbel on the day
       of battle
   when mothers were dashed in pieces with
       their children.
15 Thus it shall be done to you, O Bethel,
   because of your great wickedness.
At dawn the king of Israel
   shall be utterly cut off.

11 God's Compassion Despite Israel's Ingratitude

When Israel was a child, I loved him,
   and out of Egypt I called my son.
2 The more I^c called them,
   the more they went from me;^d
they kept sacrificing to the Baals,
   and offering incense to idols.

3 Yet it was I who taught Ephraim to walk,
   I took them up in my^e arms;
   but they did not know that I healed them.
4 I led them with cords of human kindness,
   with bands of love.
I was to them like those
   who lift infants to their cheeks.^f
   I bent down to them and fed them.

5 They shall return to the land of Egypt,
   and Assyria shall be their king,
   because they have refused to return to me.

PRAY IT!

A Parent's Love
Hosea 11:1–7

Hosea 11 describes God as a loving parent. Despite God's tenderness and care, Israel behaves like a rebellious child. God is heartbroken by Israel's rejection, but is compassionate in calling for its return. Like Israel, we often make choices that go against God's desires for us. Pray that God will help you return to God's love instead of repeating the mistakes of the Israelites.

God, thank you for your generous and unconditional love. Thank you for loving me with the tender love of a parent. And thank you that your love is perfect, even when the love of my earthly parents fails. Let me remember and return your love, even when I have done something wrong. And help me to live in a way that is pleasing to you. Amen.

Now read **Hosea 14:4–7** for God's faithful promise of forgiveness.

---

a Cn Compare Gk: Heb *In my desire*   b Gk: Heb *bound*   c Gk: Heb *they*   d Gk: Heb *them*   e Gk Syr Vg: Heb *his*   f Or *who ease the yoke on their jaws*

⁶ The sword rages in their cities,
    it consumes their oracle-priests,
    and devours because of their schemes.
⁷ My people are bent on turning away from me.
    To the Most High they call,
    but he does not raise them up at all.ᵃ

⁸ How can I give you up, Ephraim?
    How can I hand you over, O Israel?
How can I make you like Admah?
    How can I treat you like Zeboiim?
My heart recoils within me;
    my compassion grows warm and tender.
⁹ I will not execute my fierce anger;
    I will not again destroy Ephraim;
for I am God and no mortal,
    the Holy One in your midst,
    and I will not come in wrath.ᵃ

¹⁰ They shall go after the LORD,
    who roars like a lion;
when he roars,
    his children shall come trembling from the
       west.
¹¹ They shall come trembling like birds from
       Egypt,
    and like doves from the land of Assyria;
    and I will return them to their homes, says
       the LORD.

¹²ᵇ Ephraim has surrounded me with lies,
    and the house of Israel with deceit;
but Judah still walksᶜ with God,
    and is faithful to the Holy One.

12
    Ephraim herds the wind,
    and pursues the east wind all day long;
    they multiply falsehood and violence;
    they make a treaty with Assyria,
    and oil is carried to Egypt.

The Long History of Rebellion
² The LORD has an indictment against Judah,
    and will punish Jacob according to his
      ways,
    and repay him according to his deeds.
³ In the womb he tried to supplant his brother,
    and in his manhood he strove with God.
⁴ He strove with the angel and prevailed,
    he wept and sought his favor;
he met him at Bethel,

and there he spoke with him.ᵈ
⁵ The LORD the God of hosts,
    the LORD is his name!
⁶ But as for you, return to your God,
    hold fast to love and justice,
    and wait continually for your God.

⁷ A trader, in whose hands are false balances,
    he loves to oppress.
⁸ Ephraim has said, "Ah, I am rich,
    I have gained wealth for myself;
in all of my gain
    no offense has been found in me
    that would be sin."ᵃ
⁹ I am the LORD your God
    from the land of Egypt;
I will make you live in tents again,
    as in the days of the appointed festival.

¹⁰ I spoke to the prophets;
    it was I who multiplied visions,

LIVE IT!

Waiting
Hosea 12:6

We live in an instant world. Everything in our culture is fast—fast food, fast Internet, fast cars . . . the list goes on. But **Hosea 12:6** speaks of a slower spiritual pace. One in which we are required to stop running full speed ahead—and to return, to hold fast, and to wait. None of those are easy tasks, but they are what God asked of the Israelites in order to bring about healing and restoration. The Israelites had sinned and were living in rebellion. They first needed to return to God. Their faithfulness to God would require holding on to love and justice. And the process would take patience. We are also called to wait on God. The concept is found throughout the book of Psalms and the New Testament. When you find yourself impatient with God, read **Psalm 27:14**: "Wait for the LORD; be strong, and let your heart take courage; wait for the LORD!"

ᵃ Meaning of Heb uncertain ᵇ Ch 12.1 in Heb ᶜ Heb *roams* or *rules* ᵈ Gk Syr: Heb *us*

and through the prophets I will bring
   destruction.
11 In Gilead[a] there is iniquity,
   they shall surely come to nothing.
In Gilgal they sacrifice bulls,
   so their altars shall be like stone heaps
   on the furrows of the field.
12 Jacob fled to the land of Aram,
   there Israel served for a wife,
   and for a wife he guarded sheep.[b]
13 By a prophet the LORD brought Israel up from
   Egypt,
   and by a prophet he was guarded.
14 Ephraim has given bitter offense,
   so his Lord will bring his crimes down
     on him
   and pay him back for his insults.

Relentless Judgment on Israel

13 When Ephraim spoke, there was
   trembling;
   he was exalted in Israel;
but he incurred guilt through Baal and
   died.
2 And now they keep on sinning
   and make a cast image for themselves,
idols of silver made according to their
   understanding,
   all of them the work of artisans.
"Sacrifice to these," they say.[c]
   People are kissing calves!
3 Therefore they shall be like the
     morning mist
   or like the dew that goes away early,
like chaff that swirls from the threshing
     floor
   or like smoke from a window.

4 Yet I have been the LORD your God
   ever since the land of Egypt;
you know no God but me,
   and besides me there is no savior.
5 It was I who fed[d] you in the wilderness,
   in the land of drought.
6 When I fed[e] them, they were satisfied;
   they were satisfied, and their heart was
     proud;
   therefore they forgot me.
7 So I will become like a lion to them,
   like a leopard I will lurk beside the way.

8 I will fall upon them like a bear robbed of her
     cubs,
   and will tear open the covering of their
     heart;
there I will devour them like a lion,
   as a wild animal would mangle them.
9 I will destroy you, O Israel;
   who can help you?[f]
10 Where now is[g] your king, that he may
     save you?
   Where in all your cities are your rulers,
of whom you said,
   "Give me a king and rulers"?
11 I gave you a king in my anger,
   and I took him away in my wrath.

12 Ephraim's iniquity is bound up;
   his sin is kept in store.
13 The pangs of childbirth come for him,
   but he is an unwise son;
for at the proper time he does not present
     himself
   at the mouth of the womb.

14 Shall I ransom them from the power of
     Sheol?
   Shall I redeem them from Death?
O Death, where are[h] your plagues?
   O Sheol, where is[h] your destruction?
   Compassion is hidden from my eyes.

15 Although he may flourish among rushes,[i]
   the east wind shall come, a blast from the
     LORD,
   rising from the wilderness;
and his fountain shall dry up,
   his spring shall be parched.
It shall strip his treasury
   of every precious thing.
16[j] Samaria shall bear her guilt,
   because she has rebelled against her God;
they shall fall by the sword,
   their little ones shall be dashed in pieces,
   and their pregnant women ripped open.

A Plea for Repentance

14 Return, O Israel, to the LORD your God,
   for you have stumbled because of
   your iniquity.

---

a Compare Syr: Heb *Gilead* b Heb lacks *sheep* c Cn Compare Gk: Heb *To these they say sacrifices of people* d Gk Syr: Heb *knew* e Cn: Heb *according to their pasture* f Gk Syr: Heb *for in me is your help* g Gk Syr Vg: Heb *I will be* h Gk Syr: Heb *I will be* i Or *among brothers* j Ch 14.1 in Heb

2 Take words with you
  and return to the LORD;
say to him,
  "Take away all guilt;
accept that which is good,
  and we will offer
  the fruit*a* of our lips.
3 Assyria shall not save us;
  we will not ride upon horses;
we will say no more, 'Our God,'
  to the work of our hands.
In you the orphan finds mercy."

Assurance of Forgiveness

4 I will heal their disloyalty;
  I will love them freely,
  for my anger has turned from them.
5 I will be like the dew to Israel;
  he shall blossom like the lily,
  he shall strike root like the forests of
    Lebanon.*b*

6 His shoots shall spread out;
  his beauty shall be like the olive tree,
  and his fragrance like that of Lebanon.
7 They shall again live beneath my*c* shadow,
  they shall flourish as a garden;*d*
they shall blossom like the vine,
  their fragrance shall be like the wine of
    Lebanon.

8 O Ephraim, what have I*e* to do with idols?
  It is I who answer and look after you.*f*
I am like an evergreen cypress;
  your faithfulness*g* comes from me.
9 Those who are wise understand these
    things;
  those who are discerning know
    them.
For the ways of the LORD are right,
  and the upright walk in them,
  but transgressors stumble in them.

a Gk Syr: Heb *bulls*   *b* Cn: Heb *like Lebanon*   *c* Heb *his*   *d* Cn: Heb *they shall grow grain*   *e* Or *What more has Ephraim*   *f* Heb *him*   *g* Heb *your fruit*

Joel

You're cruisin' along, in the groove, and everything is going your way. Then it happens. You hit a major bump in the road, and everything starts falling apart. This appears to have been the situation in Joel's time, when a major plague of locusts was causing widespread destruction. But when Joel looked at the destruction, he saw something more—a call from God to turn from sin. Joel paints a vivid picture of the choice the Israelites face to remain in sin and face more pain or to turn to God and receive abundant mercy.

IN DEPTH

The book of Joel doesn't state clearly when it was written, but it gives several clues that lead biblical scholars to believe it was written after the end of the Babylonian exile (538 B.C.). Israel was ruled by the Greeks at this time and did not have a king. Jerusalem and the temple had been rebuilt, and Israel enjoyed relative peace. The people of Israel were waiting and watching for the coming of a messiah—a savior.

Then natural disaster struck—a plague of locusts destroyed the land, leaving hunger, confusion, and fear in its wake. Joel uses this tragedy to call the Israelites to turn their attention toward God and to renew their faith. He compares the plague of locusts to an invading army that brings devastation to a city. Eventually, prayer and penance end the plague and bring rain for new crops. More important, the gift of the Spirit renews the people of God (Joel 2:28-29).

A major element of this book is a warrior-type song in which Joel speaks of the coming of the "day of the Lord" (Joel 2:1-17). He describes this as the day when judgment will be delivered against the nations that have destroyed Israel. The "day of the Lord" is a theme that runs throughout the Bible. It is sometimes described as a joyful time of celebration (Isaiah 9:3), and other times as a day of punishment and destruction (Amos 5:18-24). Initially, writers of the scriptures applied the term only to Israel; Joel applied it to all nations. Gradually, it became connected to the final judgment (Matthew 25:31-46).

The book of Joel ends by affirming that the Lord dwells in Zion (Jerusalem) and the land will be fruitful once more. This is Joel's central message: Despite plagues and even war, God is present, and there is reason for hope.

QUICK FACTS

- **Date Written:** Between the rebuilding of the temple (515 B.C.) and the destruction of Sidon (343 B.C.), probably around 400 B.C.

- **Authors:** Joel and scribes

- **Theme:** The call to turn away from sin and wrongdoing and to turn to the Lord

AT A GLANCE

- **Joel 1:1–2:17** A discussion of a plague of locusts and the "day of the Lord"

- **Joel 2:18–3:21** Several prophecies promising God's salvation for Israel

1

The word of the LORD that came to Joel son of Pethuel:

Lament over the Ruin of the Country

2 Hear this, O elders,
     give ear, all inhabitants of the land!
Has such a thing happened in your days,
     or in the days of your ancestors?
3 Tell your children of it,
     and let your children tell their children,
     and their children another generation.

4 What the cutting locust left,
     the swarming locust has eaten.
What the swarming locust left,
     the hopping locust has eaten,
and what the hopping locust left,
     the destroying locust has eaten.

5 Wake up, you drunkards, and weep;
     and wail, all you wine-drinkers,
over the sweet wine,
     for it is cut off from your mouth.
6 For a nation has invaded my land,
     powerful and innumerable;
its teeth are lions' teeth,
     and it has the fangs of a lioness.
7 It has laid waste my vines,
     and splintered my fig trees;
it has stripped off their bark and thrown it
          down;
     their branches have turned white.

8 Lament like a virgin dressed in sackcloth
     for the husband of her youth.
9 The grain offering and the drink offering are
          cut off
     from the house of the LORD.
The priests mourn,
     the ministers of the LORD.
10 The fields are devastated,
     the ground mourns;
for the grain is destroyed,
     the wine dries up,
     the oil fails.

11 Be dismayed, you farmers,
     wail, you vinedressers,
over the wheat and the barley;
     for the crops of the field are ruined.

12 The vine withers,
     the fig tree droops.
Pomegranate, palm, and apple—
     all the trees of the field are dried up;
surely, joy withers away
     among the people.

A Call to Repentance and Prayer

13 Put on sackcloth and lament, you priests;
     wail, you ministers of the altar.
Come, pass the night in sackcloth,
     you ministers of my God!
Grain offering and drink offering
     are withheld from the house of your God.

14 Sanctify a fast,
     call a solemn assembly.
Gather the elders
     and all the inhabitants of the land
to the house of the LORD your God,
     and cry out to the LORD.

15 Alas for the day!
For the day of the LORD is near,
     and as destruction from the Almighty[a] it
          comes.
16 Is not the food cut off
     before our eyes,
joy and gladness
     from the house of our God?

17 The seed shrivels under the clods,[b]
     the storehouses are desolate;
     the granaries are ruined
because the grain has failed.
18 How the animals groan!
     The herds of cattle wander about
because there is no pasture for them;
     even the flocks of sheep are dazed.[c]

19 To you, O LORD, I cry.
For fire has devoured

a Traditional rendering of Heb *Shaddai*   b Meaning of Heb uncertain   c Compare Gk Syr Vg: Meaning of Heb uncertain

the pastures of the wilderness,
and flames have burned
all the trees of the field.
20 Even the wild animals cry to you
because the watercourses are
dried up,
and fire has devoured
the pastures of the wilderness.

2 Blow the trumpet in Zion;
sound the alarm on my holy mountain!
Let all the inhabitants of the land
tremble,
for the day of the LORD is coming, it is
near—
2 a day of darkness and gloom,
a day of clouds and thick darkness!
Like blackness spread upon the mountains
a great and powerful army comes;
their like has never been from of old,
nor will be again after them
in ages to come.

3 Fire devours in front of them,
and behind them a flame burns.
Before them the land is like the garden of
Eden,
but after them a desolate wilderness,
and nothing escapes them.

4 They have the appearance of horses,
and like war-horses they charge.
5 As with the rumbling of chariots,
they leap on the tops of the mountains,
like the crackling of a flame of fire
devouring the stubble,

like a powerful army
drawn up for battle.
6 Before them peoples are in anguish,
all faces grow pale.[a]
7 Like warriors they charge,
like soldiers they scale the wall.
Each keeps to its own course,
they do not swerve from[b] their paths.
8 They do not jostle one another,
each keeps to its own track;
they burst through the weapons
and are not halted.
9 They leap upon the city,
they run upon the walls;
they climb up into the houses,
they enter through the windows like a
thief.
10 The earth quakes before them,
the heavens tremble.
The sun and the moon are darkened,
and the stars withdraw their shining.
11 The LORD utters his voice
at the head of his army;
how vast is his host!
Numberless are those who obey his
command.
Truly the day of the LORD is great;
terrible indeed—who can endure it?

12 Yet even now, says the LORD,
return to me with all your heart,
with fasting, with weeping, and with
mourning;
13 rend your hearts and not your clothing.

STUDY IT!

Return to God · Joel 2:12–13

Joel's description of the plague and its destruction in the first part of this book is downright scary. But just when dark hopelessness is setting in, God steps up and offers life. In **Joel 2:12** God calls the people to repent—to return to God with heartfelt sorrow for their sin. The people are guilty and deserving of punishment, but God calls them because God is gracious, merciful, and loving (Joel 2:13). God offers us the same hope. When we turn from our sin, no matter how hopeless or overwhelming our situation may seem, God pours out love and mercy. This idea that God is slow to anger and full of love is woven throughout the Old and New Testaments. Check out **Psalms 86:15; 103:8; 145:8; and 1 John 1:9** to read more on what you'll find when you choose to return to God.

a Meaning of Heb uncertain   b Gk Syr Vg: Heb *they do not take a pledge along*

Return to the LORD, your God,
    for he is gracious and merciful,
slow to anger, and abounding in steadfast
      love,
    and relents from punishing.
14 Who knows whether he will not turn and
      relent,
    and leave a blessing behind him,
a grain offering and a drink offering
    for the LORD, your God?

15 Blow the trumpet in Zion;
    sanctify a fast;
call a solemn assembly;
16   gather the people.
Sanctify the congregation;
    assemble the aged;
gather the children,
    even infants at the breast.
Let the bridegroom leave his room,
    and the bride her canopy.

17 Between the vestibule and the altar
    let the priests, the ministers of the LORD,
      weep.
Let them say, "Spare your people, O LORD,
    and do not make your heritage a mockery,
    a byword among the nations.
Why should it be said among the peoples,
    'Where is their God?'"

God's Response and Promise

18 Then the LORD became jealous for his land,
    and had pity on his people.
19 In response to his people the LORD said:
I am sending you
    grain, wine, and oil,
    and you will be satisfied;
and I will no more make you
    a mockery among the nations.

20 I will remove the northern army far from you,
    and drive it into a parched and desolate
      land,
its front into the eastern sea,
    and its rear into the western sea;
its stench and foul smell will rise up.
    Surely he has done great things!

21 Do not fear, O soil;

be glad and rejoice,
    for the LORD has done great things!
22 Do not fear, you animals of the field,
    for the pastures of the wilderness are
      green;
the tree bears its fruit,
    the fig tree and vine give their full yield.

23 O children of Zion, be glad
    and rejoice in the LORD your God;
for he has given the early rain[a] for your
      vindication,
he has poured down for you abundant
      rain,
    the early and the later rain, as before.
24 The threshing floors shall be full of grain,
    the vats shall overflow with wine and oil.

25 I will repay you for the years
    that the swarming locust has eaten,
the hopper, the destroyer, and the cutter,
    my great army, which I sent against you.

26 You shall eat in plenty and be satisfied,
    and praise the name of the LORD
      your God,
who has dealt wondrously with you.
And my people shall never again be put to
      shame.
27 You shall know that I am in the midst of
      Israel,
    and that I, the LORD, am your God and
      there is no other.
And my people shall never again be put to
      shame.

God's Spirit Poured Out

28[b] Then afterward
    I will pour out my spirit on all flesh;
your sons and your daughters shall prophesy,
    your old men shall dream dreams,
    and your young men shall see visions.
29 Even on the male and female slaves,
    in those days, I will pour out my spirit.

30 I will show portents in the heavens and on the earth, blood and fire and columns of smoke. 31 The sun shall be turned to darkness, and the moon to blood, before the great and terrible day of the LORD comes. 32 Then everyone who calls on the name of

---

a Meaning of Heb uncertain   b Ch 3.1 in Heb

the Lord shall be saved; for in Mount Zion and in Jerusalem there shall be those who escape, as the Lord has said, and among the survivors shall be those whom the Lord calls.

3 *a* For then, in those days and at that time, when I restore the fortunes of Judah and Jerusalem, ²I will gather all the nations and bring them down to the valley of Jehoshaphat, and I will enter into judgment with them there, on account of my people and my heritage Israel, because they have scattered them among the nations. They have divided my land, ³and cast lots for my people, and traded boys for prostitutes, and sold girls for wine, and drunk it down.

4 What are you to me, O Tyre and Sidon, and all the regions of Philistia? Are you paying me back for something? If you are paying me back, I will turn your deeds back upon your own heads swiftly and speedily. ⁵For you have taken my silver and my gold, and have carried my rich treasures into your temples.*b* ⁶You have sold the people of Judah and Jerusalem to the Greeks, removing them far from their own border. ⁷But now I will rouse them to leave the places to which you have sold them, and I will turn your deeds back upon your own heads. ⁸I will sell your sons and your daughters into the hand of the people of Judah, and they will sell them to the Sabeans, to a nation far away; for the Lord has spoken.

Judgment in the Valley of Jehoshaphat

9 Proclaim this among the nations:
Prepare war,*c*
     stir up the warriors.
Let all the soldiers draw near,
     let them come up.
10 Beat your plowshares into swords,
     and your pruning hooks into spears;
     let the weakling say, "I am a warrior."

11 Come quickly,*d*
     all you nations all around,
     gather yourselves there.
Bring down your warriors, O Lord.
12 Let the nations rouse themselves,
     and come up to the valley of Jehoshaphat;
for there I will sit to judge
     all the neighboring nations.

13 Put in the sickle,
     for the harvest is ripe.
Go in, tread,
     for the wine press is full.
The vats overflow,
     for their wickedness is great.

14 Multitudes, multitudes,
     in the valley of decision!
For the day of the Lord is near
     in the valley of decision.
15 The sun and the moon are darkened,
     and the stars withdraw their shining.

16 The Lord roars from Zion,
     and utters his voice from Jerusalem,
     and the heavens and the earth shake.
But the Lord is a refuge for his people,
     a stronghold for the people of Israel.

The Glorious Future of Judah

17 So you shall know that I, the Lord your God,
     dwell in Zion, my holy mountain.
And Jerusalem shall be holy,
     and strangers shall never again pass
          through it.

18 In that day
the mountains shall drip sweet wine,
     the hills shall flow with milk,
and all the stream beds of Judah
     shall flow with water;
a fountain shall come forth from the house of
          the Lord
     and water the Wadi Shittim.
19 Egypt shall become a desolation
     and Edom a desolate wilderness,
because of the violence done to the people of
          Judah,
     in whose land they have shed innocent
          blood.
20 But Judah shall be inhabited forever,
     and Jerusalem to all generations.
21 I will avenge their blood, and I will not clear
          the guilty,*e*
     for the Lord dwells in Zion.

a Ch 4.1 in Heb   *b* Or *palaces*   *c* Heb *sanctify war*   *d* Meaning of Heb uncertain   *e* Gk Syr: Heb *I will hold innocent their blood that I have not held innocent*

Amos

▶▶▶▶▶▶▶▶▶▶▶▶▶▶▶▶▶▶▶▶▶▶▶▶▶▶▶▶▶▶▶▶▶▶▶▶▶

"Ijust tell it like it is." Ever heard that from someone? It seems like those who say that bluntly state what they see going on, without much concern for what other people think. That's a perfect description of the prophet Amos. He didn't pull any punches in describing the sin of the wealthy class or the destruction God had planned for Israel. He was a powerful voice calling for justice and compassion in God's plan of salvation.

IN DEPTH

Amos lived during a time when the Israelites were divided into two separate kingdoms: a northern kingdom named Israel and a southern kingdom named Judah. He was born in the southern kingdom and worked as a shepherd and tree trimmer (Amos 7:14). But God called him to preach to the northern kingdom. Amos was not an official prophet of the king's court, so he was free to speak against the king and the court and to be brutally honest in delivering God's message.

Among the Old Testament prophecies, Amos' are the least hopeful. Amos stresses that Israel's destruction, complete and total, is certain. He condemns Israel for its failure to be faithful to the covenant, but he is especially harsh on the leaders—the king, the priests, and the wealthy class. He accuses them of being hypocrites who lead the people of Israel astray while pretending to be faithful themselves.

What was Amos' evidence? First, the covenant demanded special care for the poor, the outcast, and the marginalized. The king, the wealthy, and some of the priests were ignoring this demand. Instead of caring for the poor and the lowly, the wealthy were cheating them and treating them unjustly (Amos 2:6-8).

Second, with the money they cheated out of the poor, the ruling class and the wealthy staged lavish ceremonies to God that were modeled on ceremonies honoring foreign gods. They went through the motions of worshiping God, but they ignored the demand to care for their neighbor (Amos 5:21-24). For Amos, this was the heart of Israel's hypocrisy—its sinful habit of separating its religious rituals from concern for its citizens. This phoniness was repulsive to God, and because of Israel's sin, God would bring it to destruction. Amos is rightly called the prophet of the Lord's justice.

QUICK FACTS

- **Dates Covered:** Between 760 and 740 B.C.
- **Authors:** Amos and later scribes
- **Themes:** A call against the injustice and hypocrisy of the wealthy and the ruling class in Israel; a reminder to us of our own responsibility to help the less fortunate

AT A GLANCE

- **Amos 1:1–2:3** A condemnation of Israel's neighbors
- **Amos 2:4–9:8** A proclamation of the destruction of the northern kingdom, Israel
- **Amos 9:9–15** A word of hope, probably added by a later editor

1 The words of Amos, who was among the shepherds of Tekoa, which he saw concerning Israel in the days of King Uzziah of Judah and in the days of King Jeroboam son of Joash of Israel, two years[a] before the earthquake.

Judgment on Israel's Neighbors

[2] And he said:

The LORD roars from Zion,
and utters his voice from Jerusalem;
the pastures of the shepherds wither,
and the top of Carmel dries up.

[3] Thus says the LORD:
For three transgressions of Damascus,
and for four, I will not revoke the
punishment;[b]
because they have threshed Gilead
with threshing sledges of iron.
[4] So I will send a fire on the house of Hazael,
and it shall devour the strongholds of Ben-
hadad.
[5] I will break the gate bars of Damascus,
and cut off the inhabitants from the Valley
of Aven,
and the one who holds the scepter from Beth-
eden;
and the people of Aram shall go into exile
to Kir,
says the LORD.

[6] Thus says the LORD:
For three transgressions of Gaza,
and for four, I will not revoke the
punishment;[b]
because they carried into exile entire
communities,
to hand them over to Edom.
[7] So I will send a fire on the wall of
Gaza,
fire that shall devour its strongholds.
[8] I will cut off the inhabitants from Ashdod,
and the one who holds the scepter from
Ashkelon;
I will turn my hand against Ekron,
and the remnant of the Philistines shall
perish,
says the Lord GOD.

[9] Thus says the LORD:

For three transgressions of Tyre,
and for four, I will not revoke the
punishment;[b]
because they delivered entire communities
over to Edom,
and did not remember the covenant of
kinship.
[10] So I will send a fire on the wall of Tyre,
fire that shall devour its
strongholds.

[11] Thus says the LORD:
For three transgressions of Edom,
and for four, I will not revoke the
punishment;[b]
because he pursued his brother with the
sword
and cast off all pity;
he maintained his anger perpetually,[c]
and kept his wrath[d] forever.
[12] So I will send a fire on Teman,
and it shall devour the strongholds
of Bozrah.

[13] Thus says the LORD:
For three transgressions of the Ammonites,
and for four, I will not revoke the
punishment;[b]
because they have ripped open pregnant
women in Gilead
in order to enlarge their territory.
[14] So I will kindle a fire against the wall of
Rabbah,
fire that shall devour its
strongholds,
with shouting on the day of battle,
with a storm on the day of the whirlwind;
[15] then their king shall go into exile,
he and his officials together,
says the LORD.

2 Thus says the LORD:
For three transgressions of Moab,
and for four, I will not revoke the
punishment;[b]
because he burned to lime
the bones of the king of Edom.
[2] So I will send a fire on Moab,
and it shall devour the strongholds
of Kerioth,

a Or *during two years* b Heb *cause it to return* c Syr Vg: Heb *and his anger tore perpetually* d Gk Syr Vg: Heb *and his wrath kept*

and Moab shall die amid uproar,
　　amid shouting and the sound of the
　　　trumpet;
3 I will cut off the ruler from its midst,
　　and will kill all its officials with him,
　　　　　　　　　　says the LORD.

Judgment on Judah

4 Thus says the LORD:
　For three transgressions of Judah,
　　and for four, I will not revoke the
　　　punishment;[a]
　because they have rejected the law of the
　　LORD,
　　and have not kept his statutes,
　but they have been led astray by the same lies
　　after which their ancestors walked.
5 So I will send a fire on Judah,
　　and it shall devour the strongholds of
　　　Jerusalem.

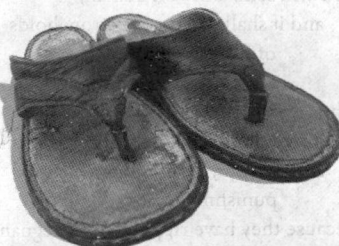

Judgment on Israel

6 Thus says the LORD:
　For three transgressions of Israel,
　　and for four, I will not revoke the
　　　punishment;[a]
　because they sell the righteous for silver,
　　and the needy for a pair of sandals—
7 they who trample the head of the poor into
　　the dust of the earth,
　　and push the afflicted out of the way;
　father and son go in to the same girl,
　　so that my holy name is profaned;
8 they lay themselves down beside every altar
　　on garments taken in pledge;
　and in the house of their God they drink
　　wine bought with fines they imposed.

9 Yet I destroyed the Amorite before them,
　　whose height was like the height of
　　　cedars,
　and who was as strong as oaks;
　I destroyed his fruit above,
　　and his roots beneath.
10 Also I brought you up out of the land of
　　Egypt,
　　and led you forty years in the wilderness,
　　to possess the land of the Amorite.
11 And I raised up some of your children to be
　　prophets
　　and some of your youths to be nazirites.[b]
　Is it not indeed so, O people of Israel?
　　　　　　　　　　says the LORD.

12 But you made the nazirites[b] drink wine,
　　and commanded the prophets,
　　saying, "You shall not prophesy."

13 So, I will press you down in your place,
　　just as a cart presses down
　　　when it is full of sheaves.[c]
14 Flight shall perish from the swift,
　　and the strong shall not retain their
　　　strength,
　　nor shall the mighty save their lives;
15 those who handle the bow shall not stand,
　　and those who are swift of foot shall not
　　　save themselves,
　　nor shall those who ride horses save their
　　　lives;
16 and those who are stout of heart among the
　　mighty
　　shall flee away naked in that day,
　　　　　　　　　　says the LORD.

Israel's Guilt and Punishment

3 Hear this word that the LORD has spoken
against you, O people of Israel, against
the whole family that I brought up out of the land
of Egypt:
2 You only have I known
　　of all the families of the earth;
　therefore I will punish you
　　for all your iniquities.

3 Do two walk together
　　unless they have made an appointment?
4 Does a lion roar in the forest,
　　when it has no prey?
　Does a young lion cry out from its den,
　　if it has caught nothing?

---

a Heb *cause it to return*　b That is, *those separated* or *those consecrated*　c Meaning of Heb uncertain

5 Does a bird fall into a snare on the earth,
    when there is no trap for it?
Does a snare spring up from the ground,
    when it has taken nothing?
6 Is a trumpet blown in a city,
    and the people are not afraid?
Does disaster befall a city,
    unless the LORD has done it?
7 Surely the Lord GOD does nothing,
    without revealing his secret
    to his servants the prophets.
8 The lion has roared;
    who will not fear?
The Lord GOD has spoken;
    who can but prophesy?

9 Proclaim to the strongholds in Ashdod,
    and to the strongholds in the land of
        Egypt,
    and say, "Assemble yourselves on Mount*a*
        Samaria,
        and see what great tumults are within it,
        and what oppressions are in its midst."
10 They do not know how to do right, says the
        LORD,
    those who store up violence and robbery
        in their strongholds.
11 Therefore thus says the Lord GOD:
    An adversary shall surround the land,
        and strip you of your defense;
        and your strongholds shall be plundered.

12 Thus says the LORD: As the shepherd rescues
from the mouth of the lion two legs, or a piece of
an ear, so shall the people of Israel who live in Samaria be rescued, with the corner of a couch and
part*b* of a bed.

13 Hear, and testify against the house of Jacob,
    says the Lord GOD, the God of hosts:
14 On the day I punish Israel for its
        transgressions,
    I will punish the altars of Bethel,
    and the horns of the altar shall be cut off
        and fall to the ground.
15 I will tear down the winter house as well as the
        summer house;
    and the houses of ivory shall perish,
    and the great houses*c* shall come to an end,
                        says the LORD.

 4 Hear this word, you cows of Bashan
    who are on Mount Samaria,
    who oppress the poor, who crush the
        needy,
    who say to their husbands, "Bring
        something to drink!"
2 The Lord GOD has sworn by his
        holiness:
    The time is surely coming upon you,
when they shall take you away with hooks,
    even the last of you with fishhooks.
3 Through breaches in the wall you shall leave,
    each one straight ahead;
    and you shall be flung out into Harmon,*b*
                        says the LORD.

4 Come to Bethel—and transgress;
    to Gilgal—and multiply transgression;
bring your sacrifices every morning,
    your tithes every three days;
5 bring a thank offering of leavened bread,
    and proclaim freewill offerings, publish
        them;
    for so you love to do, O people of Israel!
                        says the Lord GOD.

Israel Rejects Correction
6 I gave you cleanness of teeth in all your cities,
    and lack of bread in all your places,
yet you did not return to me,
                        says the LORD.

7 And I also withheld the rain from you
    when there were still three months to the
        harvest;
I would send rain on one city,
    and send no rain on another city;
one field would be rained upon,
    and the field on which it did not rain
        withered;
8 so two or three towns wandered to
        one town
    to drink water, and were not satisfied;
yet you did not return to me,
                        says the LORD.

9 I struck you with blight and mildew;
    I laid waste*d* your gardens and your
        vineyards;
    the locust devoured your fig trees and your
        olive trees;

a Gk Syr: Heb *the mountains of*   *b* Meaning of Heb uncertain   *c* Or *many houses*   *d* Cn: Heb *the multitude of*

yet you did not return to me,
     says the LORD.

10 I sent among you a pestilence after the manner
    of Egypt;
  I killed your young men with the sword;
  I carried away your horses;[a]
    and I made the stench of your camp go up
     into your nostrils;
yet you did not return to me,
     says the LORD.

11 I overthrew some of you,
  as when God overthrew Sodom and
   Gomorrah,
    and you were like a brand snatched from
     the fire;
yet you did not return to me,
     says the LORD.

12 Therefore thus I will do to you, O Israel;
  because I will do this to you,
  prepare to meet your God, O Israel!

13 For lo, the one who forms the mountains,
    creates the wind,
  reveals his thoughts to mortals,
makes the morning darkness,
    and treads on the heights of the earth—
    the LORD, the God of hosts, is his name!

A Lament for Israel's Sin

5 Hear this word that I take up over you in
lamentation, O house of Israel:
2 Fallen, no more to rise,
  is maiden Israel;
forsaken on her land,
  with no one to raise her up.

3 For thus says the Lord GOD:
The city that marched out a thousand
  shall have a hundred left,
and that which marched out a hundred
  shall have ten left.[b]

4 For thus says the LORD to the house of
    Israel:
Seek me and live;
5   but do not seek Bethel,
  and do not enter into Gilgal

or cross over to Beer-sheba;
for Gilgal shall surely go into exile,
  and Bethel shall come to nothing.

6 Seek the LORD and live,
  or he will break out against the house of
   Joseph like fire,
  and it will devour Bethel, with no one to
   quench it.
7 Ah, you that turn justice to wormwood,
  and bring righteousness to the ground!

8 The one who made the Pleiades and Orion,
  and turns deep darkness into the morning,
  and darkens the day into night,
who calls for the waters of the sea,
  and pours them out on the surface of the
   earth,
the LORD is his name,
9 who makes destruction flash out against the
   strong,
  so that destruction comes upon the
   fortress.

10 They hate the one who reproves in the gate,
  and they abhor the one who speaks the
   truth.
11 Therefore because you trample on the poor
  and take from them levies of grain,
you have built houses of hewn stone,
  but you shall not live in them;
you have planted pleasant vineyards,
  but you shall not drink their wine.
12 For I know how many are your transgressions,
  and how great are your sins—
you who afflict the righteous, who take a bribe,
  and push aside the needy in the gate.
13 Therefore the prudent will keep silent in such a
   time;
  for it is an evil time.

14 Seek good and not evil,
  that you may live;
and so the LORD, the God of hosts, will be
   with you,
  just as you have said.
15 Hate evil and love good,
  and establish justice in the gate;
it may be that the LORD, the God of hosts,
  will be gracious to the remnant of Joseph.

a Heb *with the captivity of your horses*   b Heb adds *to the house of Israel*

16 Therefore thus says the LORD, the God of
       hosts, the Lord:
In all the squares there shall be wailing;
       and in all the streets they shall say, "Alas!
       alas!"
They shall call the farmers to
       mourning,
       and those skilled in lamentation, to
       wailing;
17 in all the vineyards there shall be wailing,
       for I will pass through the midst of you,
                               says the LORD.

The Day of the LORD a Dark Day

18 Alas for you who desire the day of the LORD!
       Why do you want the day of the LORD?
It is darkness, not light;
19   as if someone fled from a lion,
       and was met by a bear;
or went into the house and rested a hand
              against the wall,
       and was bitten by a snake.
20 Is not the day of the LORD darkness, not
       light,
       and gloom with no brightness in it?

21 I hate, I despise your festivals,

> ## "Let justice roll down like waters, and righteousness like an ever-flowing stream."
> ## —Amos 5:24

       and I take no delight in your solemn
              assemblies.
22 Even though you offer me your burnt offerings
              and grain offerings,
       I will not accept them;
and the offerings of well-being of your fatted
              animals
       I will not look upon.
23 Take away from me the noise of your songs;
       I will not listen to the melody of your
              harps.
24 But let justice roll down like waters,
       and righteousness like an ever-flowing
              stream.

25 Did you bring to me sacrifices and offerings
the forty years in the wilderness, O house of Israel?
26 You shall take up Sakkuth your king, and Kaiwan

PRAY IT!

Let Justice Roll · Amos 5:21–24

In this passage, Amos shares some harsh words for the people who attend lavish religious ceremonies, but don't practice justice in their lives. To God and the prophets, justice is about living in right relationship with others and making sure that the dignity of all is protected and the basic needs of all are met.

Without a commitment to justice, the people's festivals, assemblies, and offerings will remain meaningless noise to God.

Amos' harsh words challenge us too.

- What does it mean to act justly as a young person in today's world?
- Think about how you treat other people, especially people who are in need. How are you responding to these needs?
- Have you ever been wasteful or consumed too much while others go in need of basic resources?
- Are you more committed to the fun activities of a youth group than to serving the poor?
- What changes can you make in your life in order to live more justly?

Pray today for all those who suffer from injustice in our world, and for the courage to personally respond by acting more justly in your own life. Pray the words of **Amos 5:24:** "Let justice roll down like waters, and righteousness like an ever-flowing stream."

your star-god, your images,^a which you made for yourselves; ²⁷ therefore I will take you into exile beyond Damascus, says the LORD, whose name is the God of hosts.

6 Complacent Self-Indulgence Will Be Punished

Alas for those who are at ease in
        Zion,
    and for those who feel secure on Mount
        Samaria,
the notables of the first of the nations,
    to whom the house of Israel resorts!
² Cross over to Calneh, and see;
    from there go to Hamath the great;
    then go down to Gath of the Philistines.
Are you better^b than these kingdoms?
    Or is your^c territory greater than their^d
        territory,
³ O you that put far away the evil day,
    and bring near a reign of violence?

⁴ Alas for those who lie on beds of ivory,
    and lounge on their couches,
and eat lambs from the flock,
    and calves from the stall;
⁵ who sing idle songs to the sound of the harp,
    and like David improvise on instruments
        of music;
⁶ who drink wine from bowls,
    and anoint themselves with the finest oils,
    but are not grieved over the ruin of
        Joseph!
⁷ Therefore they shall now be the first to go
        into exile,
    and the revelry of the loungers shall pass
        away.

⁸ The Lord GOD has sworn by himself
    (says the LORD, the God of hosts):
I abhor the pride of Jacob
    and hate his strongholds;
    and I will deliver up the city and all that
        is in it.

⁹ If ten people remain in one house, they shall die. ¹⁰ And if a relative, one who burns the dead,^e shall take up the body to bring it out of the house, and shall say to someone in the innermost parts of the house, "Is anyone else with you?" the answer

will come, "No." Then the relative^f shall say, "Hush! We must not mention the name of the LORD."

¹¹ See, the LORD commands,
    and the great house shall be shattered
        to bits,
    and the little house to pieces.
¹² Do horses run on rocks?
    Does one plow the sea with oxen?^g
But you have turned justice into poison
    and the fruit of righteousness into
        wormwood—
¹³ you who rejoice in Lo-debar,^h
    who say, "Have we not by our own
        strength
    taken Karnaimⁱ for ourselves?"
¹⁴ Indeed, I am raising up against you a nation,
    O house of Israel, says the LORD, the God
        of hosts,
and they shall oppress you from
        Lebo-hamath
    to the Wadi Arabah.

7 Locusts, Fire, and a Plumb Line

This is what the Lord GOD showed me: he was forming locusts at the time the latter growth began to sprout (it was the latter growth after the king's mowings). ² When they had finished eating the grass of the land, I said,
"O Lord GOD, forgive, I beg you!
    How can Jacob stand?
    He is so small!"
³ The LORD relented concerning this;
    "It shall not be," said the LORD.

⁴ This is what the Lord GOD showed me: the Lord GOD was calling for a shower of fire,^j and it devoured the great deep and was eating up the land. ⁵ Then I said,
"O Lord GOD, cease, I beg you!
    How can Jacob stand?
    He is so small!"
⁶ The LORD relented concerning this;
    "This also shall not be," said the Lord GOD.

⁷ This is what he showed me: the Lord was standing beside a wall built with a plumb line, with a plumb line in his hand. ⁸ And the LORD said to me, "Amos, what do you see?" And I said, "A plumb line." Then the Lord said,

---

a Heb *your images, your star-god* b Or *Are they better* c Heb *their* d Heb *your* e Or *who makes a burning for him* f Heb *he* g Or *Does one plow them with oxen* h Or *in a thing of nothingness* i Or *horns* j Or *for a judgment by fire*

"See, I am setting a plumb line
    in the midst of my people Israel;
    I will never again pass them by;
9 the high places of Isaac shall be made desolate,
    and the sanctuaries of Israel shall be laid
      waste,
    and I will rise against the house of Jeroboam
      with the sword."

Amaziah Complains to the King

10 Then Amaziah, the priest of Bethel, sent to King Jeroboam of Israel, saying, "Amos has conspired against you in the very center of the house of Israel; the land is not able to bear all his words. ¹¹For thus Amos has said,

'Jeroboam shall die by the sword,
    and Israel must go into exile
    away from his land.'"

¹²And Amaziah said to Amos, "O seer, go, flee away to the land of Judah, earn your bread there, and prophesy there; ¹³but never again prophesy at Bethel, for it is the king's sanctuary, and it is a temple of the kingdom."

14 Then Amos answered Amaziah, "I am*a* no prophet, nor a prophet's son; but I am*a* a herdsman, and a dresser of sycamore trees, ¹⁵and the LORD took me from following the flock, and the LORD said to me, 'Go, prophesy to my people Israel.'
16 "Now therefore hear the word of the LORD.
    You say, 'Do not prophesy against Israel,

    and do not preach against the house of
      Isaac.'
17 Therefore thus says the LORD:
    'Your wife shall become a prostitute in the city,
    and your sons and your daughters shall fall
      by the sword,
    and your land shall be parceled out by line;
    you yourself shall die in an unclean land,
    and Israel shall surely go into exile away
      from its land.' "

The Basket of Fruit

8 This is what the Lord GOD showed me—a basket of summer fruit.*b* ²He said, "Amos, what do you see?" And I said, "A basket of summer fruit."*b* Then the LORD said to me,

"The end*c* has come upon my people Israel;
    I will never again pass them by.
3 The songs of the temple*d* shall become wailings
    in that day,"
                 says the Lord GOD;
    "the dead bodies shall be many,
    cast out in every place. Be silent!"

4 Hear this, you that trample on the needy,
    and bring to ruin the poor of the land,
5 saying, "When will the new moon be over
    so that we may sell grain;
and the sabbath,
    so that we may offer wheat for sale?

Dave and Morgan Hansow: Light Gives Heat · Amos 8:4–6

When Dave and Morgan Hansow moved to Uganda to complete the adoption of their daughter, they had no visions of saving the world or transforming Africa. Once there, they saw a need and simply wanted to help Africans in any little ways they could. They went with open ears and hearts and what they found was everyday life—not the glorified picture of working for social justice in Africa that many of us hold on to, just life. But they also found beauty and love and hope in the women they met who had been widowed and displaced by war. They saw a need to provide these women with a way to earn a living. And so they started the organization Light Gives Heat (**lightgivesheat.org**) and specifically the Suubi ("hope") project, which buys and resells necklaces the women make from recycled paper. Unlike the people condemned for cheating the poor in this passage, Light Gives Heat buys the necklaces at a fair price that provides the women with a consistent income. They also provide literacy and English classes for the women. The Hansows have found that living justly is not glamorous, but it is filled with the beauty of relationships.

a Or *was*   b Heb *qayits*   c Heb *qets*   d Or *palace*

LIVE IT!

Fair Trade
Amos 8:4–10

Who made the clothes you are wearing? What about the shoes on your feet? Where was the food you ate for lunch grown? Chances are the answer to all those questions involves a country far from your home. We live in a society that is very removed from the majority of the original production, buying, and selling of goods. But if you take the time to read about the conditions and practices of some of the countries that produce what we consume, it's alarming. The harsh words in **Amos 8:4–10** condemn those who trample on the poor and treat them unfairly for their own gain.

Unfortunately, these words may indirectly apply to us more than we'd like to think. Amos challenges us, as he did the people of his day, to let our whole lives and the way we treat the poor be our worship to God. So how do we do that? By becoming educated about what we consume and choosing to support products and companies that treat people fairly. And by looking around our own schools and communities for people on the margins—the poor of the world who need us to be the hands and feet of Jesus.

We will make the ephah small and the shekel
    great,
  and practice deceit with false balances,
6 buying the poor for silver
    and the needy for a pair of sandals,
    and selling the sweepings of the wheat."

7 The LORD has sworn by the pride of Jacob:
  Surely I will never forget any of their deeds.
8 Shall not the land tremble on this account,
    and everyone mourn who lives in it,
  and all of it rise like the Nile,
    and be tossed about and sink again, like the
      Nile of Egypt?

9 On that day, says the Lord GOD,
  I will make the sun go down at noon,
    and darken the earth in broad daylight.
10 I will turn your feasts into mourning,
    and all your songs into lamentation;
  I will bring sackcloth on all loins,
    and baldness on every head;
  I will make it like the mourning for an
      only son,
    and the end of it like a bitter day.

11 The time is surely coming, says the Lord GOD,
    when I will send a famine on the land;
  not a famine of bread, or a thirst for water,
    but of hearing the words of the LORD.
12 They shall wander from sea to sea,
    and from north to east;
  they shall run to and fro, seeking the word of
      the LORD,
    but they shall not find it.

13 In that day the beautiful young women and the
      young men
    shall faint for thirst.
14 Those who swear by Ashimah of Samaria,
    and say, "As your god lives, O Dan,"
  and, "As the way of Beer-sheba lives"—
    they shall fall, and never rise again.

9

The Destruction of Israel

I saw the LORD standing beside*a* the altar,
    and he said:
Strike the capitals until the thresholds shake,
    and shatter them on the heads of all the
      people;*b*
and those who are left I will kill with the sword;
    not one of them shall flee away,
    not one of them shall escape.

2 Though they dig into Sheol,
    from there shall my hand take them;
  though they climb up to heaven,
    from there I will bring them down.
3 Though they hide themselves on the top of
      Carmel,
    from there I will search out and take them;
  and though they hide from my sight at the
      bottom of the sea,
    there I will command the sea-serpent, and it
      shall bite them.

a Or *on*   *b* Heb *all of them*

4 And though they go into captivity in front of
    their enemies,
    there I will command the sword, and it shall
      kill them;
and I will fix my eyes on them
    for harm and not for good.

5 The Lord, GOD of hosts,
he who touches the earth and it melts,
    and all who live in it mourn,
and all of it rises like the Nile,
    and sinks again, like the Nile of Egypt;
6 who builds his upper chambers in the heavens,
    and founds his vault upon the earth;
who calls for the waters of the sea,
    and pours them out upon the surface of the
      earth—
the LORD is his name.

7 Are you not like the Ethiopians[a] to me,
    O people of Israel? says the LORD.
Did I not bring Israel up from the land of
    Egypt,
    and the Philistines from Caphtor and the
      Arameans from Kir?
8 The eyes of the Lord GOD are upon the sinful
    kingdom,
    and I will destroy it from the face of the
      earth
—except that I will not utterly destroy the
    house of Jacob,
               says the LORD.

9 For lo, I will command,
    and shake the house of Israel among all the
      nations

as one shakes with a sieve,
    but no pebble shall fall to the ground.
10 All the sinners of my people shall die by the
    sword,
    who say, "Evil shall not overtake or
      meet us."

The Restoration of David's Kingdom

11 On that day I will raise up
    the booth of David that is fallen,
    and repair its[b] breaches,
    and raise up its[c] ruins,
    and rebuild it as in the days of old;
12 in order that they may possess the remnant
    of Edom
    and all the nations who are called by my
      name,
    says the LORD who does this.

13 The time is surely coming, says the LORD,
    when the one who plows shall overtake the
      one who reaps,
    and the treader of grapes the one who sows
      the seed;
the mountains shall drip sweet wine,
    and all the hills shall flow with it.
14 I will restore the fortunes of my people Israel,
    and they shall rebuild the ruined cities and
      inhabit them;
they shall plant vineyards and drink their wine,
    and they shall make gardens and eat their
      fruit.
15 I will plant them upon their land,
    and they shall never again be plucked up
    out of the land that I have given them,
      says the LORD your God.

a Or Nubians; Heb Cushites   b Gk: Heb their   c Gk: Heb his

Obadiah ▶▶▶▶▶▶▶▶▶▶▶▶▶▶▶▶

Betrayal. Violation by someone we trust is always difficult, and the pain only increases when the betrayal comes from someone in our own family. This is perhaps most true in abusive relationships, in which one person, through words and actions, mistreats and takes advantage of another. It can take a long time to heal these divisions and restore a sense of trust in the relationship. The Israelites knew the pain of betrayal.

Genesis records a conflict between Jacob (the father of the nation of Israel) and his brother, Esau (the father of the nation of Edom, later called Idumea). Hundreds of years later, the Israelites still fought with the Edomites (see Map 6: "Kingdoms of Israel and Judah.") In the book of Obadiah, the bitterness deepens.

In 587 B.C., Jerusalem was destroyed by the Babylonians. The Edomites, who were relatives of the Israelites, should have come to their rescue. But, instead, they betrayed them. Instead of offering aid to their "brother" (Obadiah 10), they took advantage of Israel's situation by gloating, boasting (Obadiah 12), looting (Obadiah 13), and capturing survivors (Obadiah 14). Because of the Edomites' cruelty, the prophet Obadiah prophesied the destruction of Edom by another country (Obadiah 15).

Obadiah has harsh words for Edom. And despite the suffering of Israel, Obadiah ultimately saw a hopeful future for God's people. There would come a day when all Israel's enemies would be wiped out, and the Jews would unite and return to Mount Zion (Obadiah 15-21). Mount Zion (the place where the temple stood in Jerusalem) would ultimately "rule Mount Esau; and the kingdoms shall be the LORD's" (Obadiah 21).

We are given no clues about the identity or life of the prophet Obadiah. We know only that he wrote the shortest book in the Old Testament—just one chapter long.

- **Date Written:** After the destruction of Jerusalem in 587 B.C.
- **Author:** Obadiah
- **Theme:** The message that God will restore hope and make everything right in the end
- **Noteworthy:** Obadiah means "servant/worshiper of the Lord."

- **Obadiah 1–9** Prophecies of Edom's destruction
- **Obadiah 10–14** A discussion of Edom's cruelty to the Israelites
- **Obadiah 15–21** A message about the "day of the LORD"

Proud Edom Will Be Brought Low

1 The vision of Obadiah.

Thus says the Lord GOD concerning Edom:
We have heard a report from the LORD,
     and a messenger has been sent among the
          nations:
"Rise up! Let us rise against it for battle!"
2 I will surely make you least among the
          nations;
     you shall be utterly despised.
3 Your proud heart has deceived you,
     you that live in the clefts of the rock,[a]
     whose dwelling is in the heights.
You say in your heart,
     "Who will bring me down to the
          ground?"
4 Though you soar aloft like the eagle,
     though your nest is set among the stars,
     from there I will bring you down,
                         says the LORD.

Pillage and Slaughter Will Repay Edom's Cruelty

5 If thieves came to you,
     if plunderers by night
     —how you have been destroyed!—
     would they not steal only what they
          wanted?
If grape-gatherers came to you,
     would they not leave gleanings?
6 How Esau has been pillaged,
     his treasures searched out!
7 All your allies have deceived you,
     they have driven you to the border;
your confederates have prevailed against you;
     those who ate[b] your bread have set a trap
          for you—
     there is no understanding of it.
8 On that day, says the LORD,
     I will destroy the wise out of Edom,
     and understanding out of Mount Esau.
9 Your warriors shall be shattered, O Teman,
     so that everyone from Mount Esau will be
          cut off.

Edom Mistreated His Brother

10 For the slaughter and violence done to your
          brother Jacob,
     shame shall cover you,

and you shall be cut off forever.
11 On the day that you stood aside,
     on the day that strangers carried off his
          wealth,
and foreigners entered his gates
     and cast lots for Jerusalem,
     you too were like one of them.
12 But you should not have gloated[c] over[d] your
          brother
     on the day of his misfortune;
you should not have rejoiced over the people
          of Judah
     on the day of their ruin;
you should not have boasted
     on the day of distress.
13 You should not have entered the gate of my
          people
     on the day of their calamity;
you should not have joined in the gloating
          over Judah's[e] disaster
     on the day of his calamity;
you should not have looted his goods
     on the day of his calamity.
14 You should not have stood at the crossings
     to cut off his fugitives;
you should not have handed over his
          survivors
     on the day of distress.

15 For the day of the LORD is near against all the
          nations.
As you have done, it shall be done to you;
     your deeds shall return on your own
          head.
16 For as you have drunk on my holy mountain,
     all the nations around you shall drink;
they shall drink and gulp down,[f]
     and shall be as though they had never
          been.

Israel's Final Triumph

17 But on Mount Zion there shall be those that
          escape,
     and it shall be holy;
and the house of Jacob shall take possession
          of those who dispossessed them.
18 The house of Jacob shall be a fire,
     the house of Joseph a flame,
     and the house of Esau stubble;
they shall burn them and consume them,

---

a Or *clefts of Sela* b Cn: Heb lacks *those who ate* c Heb *But do not gloat* (and similarly through verse 14) d Heb *on the day of* e Heb *his* f Meaning
of Heb uncertain

LIVE IT!

What Goes Around · Obadiah 15

"What goes around comes around." Isn't that exactly what Obadiah is saying in **Obadiah 15** when he states, "Your deeds shall return on your own head"?

Whatever you do eventually comes back to impact you. This is especially true when we consider our care for God's creation. We have a moral obligation to protect the earth on which we live. Care for the earth is a responsibility of our faith, not an option we can choose to ignore. God has entrusted us with the stewardship of all creation. To be good stewards, we must work to create a world where God's creation is always respected and protected. This means speaking out against individuals, governments, and corporations that pollute and destroy our environment. In a more personal way, it means we must be committed to things like recycling and reducing consumption in our everyday lives.

The impact we see on creation may seem minor, but it will only increase as it negatively affects the lives of future generations. In this way, the decisions we make today will come back around to impact both our own families and the larger human family.

- What individual changes can you make to be a better steward of the environment?
- In what ways are you being wasteful with the world's natural resources?
- How can you show more concern in your life for the gift of God's creation?

and there shall be no survivor of the house
of Esau;
for the LORD has spoken.
19 Those of the Negeb shall possess Mount
Esau,
and those of the Shephelah the land of the
Philistines;
they shall possess the land of Ephraim and the
land of Samaria,
and Benjamin shall possess Gilead.

20 The exiles of the Israelites who are in Halah[a]
shall possess[b] Phoenicia as far as
Zarephath;
and the exiles of Jerusalem who are in
Sepharad
shall possess the towns of the Negeb.
21 Those who have been saved[c] shall go up to
Mount Zion
to rule Mount Esau;
and the kingdom shall be the LORD's.

a Cn: Heb *in this army*   b Cn: Meaning of Heb uncertain   c Or *Saviors*

Jonah

Prophets. They're supposed to have overwhelming visions from God, speak truth to the people, and live righteously, right? Well, Jonah gets the first part—but then he runs away. Great prophet, huh? Even when he does obey, he is so full of hatred for the people God sends him to that he gets mad at God for saving them. Jonah is a satirical book, using humor to make the point that God's mercy is even greater than justice.

IN DEPTH

This story was written after the Jews returned from exile in Babylon. Their leaders encouraged the Jewish people to stay away from non-Jewish people (Ezra 9) in order to avoid falling into idolatry again. The result was religious bigotry against other nations—a belief that God was against every nation that opposed Israel. The book of Jonah was written to correct this narrow view resulting from Israel's religious self-righteousness.

Unlike other books in the Prophets, this one provides some humor. Right off the bat, Jonah is called by God and immediately takes off in the opposite direction (Jonah 1:1-3). What kind of prophet is this? When God tries to get his attention with a storm, it's the non-Jewish sailors who get the point (Jonah 1:14). Just as readers are probably wondering how God is going to get Jonah to Nineveh, along comes a taxi in the form of a large fish (Jonah 1:17).

There's more. Readers from the author's time would have expected Jonah to be ignored at best, more likely beaten or killed by the people of Nineveh. After all, these are Israel's mortal enemies. Instead, the Ninevites immediately respond to Jonah's short message and repent (Jonah 3:8). The point is clear—God's salvation is not limited to the nation of Israel.

So Jonah should be happy, right? By all standards he is an incredibly successful prophet—the people actually listened to his message. But Jonah is angry and upset. He didn't expect the Ninevites to convert—he wanted them punished. He goes outside the city to mope, and his favorite tree dies. The book ends with God chiding Jonah for his bigoted anger. If Jonah is so concerned for his little tree (Jonah 4:6-8), shouldn't God be concerned for the great city of Nineveh with its thousands of people (Jonah 4:11)? The point is driven home, and the humor has helped to make a challenging message easier to accept.

QUICK FACTS

- **Setting:** Nineveh, the capital of Assyria, during the seventh century B.C.
- **Date Written:** Probably during the fifth century B.C.
- **Author:** Unknown
- **Themes:** God's care for all people, even enemies; the greatness of God's mercy

AT A GLANCE

- **Jonah 1:1–16** Jonah sent by God to Nineveh
- **Jonah 1:17–2:10** Jonah in the belly of a large fish
- **Jonah 3** The Ninevites' conversion
- **Jonah 4** Jonah's anger outside of Nineveh

1   Jonah Tries to Run Away from God

Now the word of the LORD came to Jonah son of Amittai, saying, [2]"Go at once to Nineveh, that great city, and cry out against it; for their wickedness has come up before me." [3]But Jonah set out to flee to Tarshish from the presence of the LORD. He went down to Joppa and found a ship going to Tarshish; so he paid his fare and went on board, to go with them to Tarshish, away from the presence of the LORD.

4 But the LORD hurled a great wind upon the sea, and such a mighty storm came upon the sea that the ship threatened to break up. [5]Then the mariners were afraid, and each cried to his god. They threw the cargo that was in the ship into the sea, to lighten it for them. Jonah, meanwhile, had gone down into the hold of the ship and had lain down, and was fast asleep. [6]The captain came and said to him, "What are you doing sound asleep? Get up, call on your god! Perhaps the god will spare us a thought so that we do not perish."

7 The sailors[a] said to one another, "Come, let us cast lots, so that we may know on whose account this calamity has come upon us." So they cast lots, and the lot fell on Jonah. [8]Then they said to him, "Tell us why this calamity has come upon us. What is your occupation? Where do you come from? What is your country? And of what people are you?" [9]"I am a Hebrew," he replied. "I worship the LORD, the God of heaven, who made the sea and the dry land." [10]Then the men were even more afraid, and said to him, "What is this that you have done!" For the men knew that he was fleeing from the presence of the LORD, because he had told them so.

11 Then they said to him, "What shall we do to you, that the sea may quiet down for us?" For the sea was growing more and more tempestuous. [12]He said to them, "Pick me up and throw me into the sea; then the sea will quiet down for you; for I know it is because of me that this great storm has come upon you." [13]Nevertheless the men rowed hard to bring the ship back to land, but they could not, for the sea grew more and more stormy against them. [14]Then they cried out to the LORD, "Please, O LORD, we pray, do not let us perish on account of this man's life. Do not make us guilty of innocent blood; for you, O LORD, have done as it pleased you." [15]So they picked Jonah up and threw him into the sea; and the sea ceased from its raging. [16]Then the men feared the LORD even more, and they offered a sacrifice to the LORD and made vows.

[17][b] But the LORD provided a large fish to swallow up Jonah; and Jonah was in the belly of the fish three days and three nights.

2   A Psalm of Thanksgiving

Then Jonah prayed to the LORD his God from the belly of the fish, [2]saying,

"I called to the LORD out of my distress,
    and he answered me;
out of the belly of Sheol I cried,

PRAY IT!

Jesus and Jonah • **Jonah 2:2–10**

Do you see any similarities between Jonah and Jesus? Jonah is in the darkness of a fish's belly for three days before the Lord commands the fish to spit him out. Jesus experiences the darkness of death for three days before he bursts from the tomb in resurrected glory. In **Matthew 16:4** and **Luke 11:29**, Jesus even refers to the "sign of Jonah" in relation to his own ministry.

Jonah's prayer in **Jonah 2:2–10** could well have been Jesus' prayer. It reminds us that salvation comes from God when we are experiencing dark times. When you are going through a difficult time, use Jonah's prayer as a model for writing your own prayer of trust. Describe your difficulties and your situation, and end by expressing your ultimate trust in God.

a Heb *They* b Ch 2.1 in Heb

and you heard my voice.
3 You cast me into the deep,
    into the heart of the seas,
    and the flood surrounded me;
all your waves and your billows
    passed over me.
4 Then I said, 'I am driven away
    from your sight;
how*a* shall I look again
    upon your holy temple?'
5 The waters closed in over me;
    the deep surrounded me;
weeds were wrapped around my head
6   at the roots of the mountains.
I went down to the land
    whose bars closed upon me forever;
yet you brought up my life from the Pit,
    O Lord my God.
7 As my life was ebbing away,
    I remembered the Lord;
and my prayer came to you,
    into your holy temple.
8 Those who worship vain idols
    forsake their true loyalty.
9 But I with the voice of thanksgiving
    will sacrifice to you;
what I have vowed I will pay.
    Deliverance belongs to the Lord!"
10 Then the Lord spoke to the fish, and it spewed Jonah out upon the dry land.

Conversion of Nineveh

3 The word of the Lord came to Jonah a second time, saying, 2 "Get up, go to Nineveh, that great city, and proclaim to it the message that I tell you." 3 So Jonah set out and went to Nineveh, according to the word of the Lord. Now Nineveh was an exceedingly large city, a three days' walk across. 4 Jonah began to go into the city, going a day's walk. And he cried out, "Forty days more, and Nineveh shall be overthrown!" 5 And the people of Nineveh believed God; they proclaimed a fast, and everyone, great and small, put on sackcloth.

6 When the news reached the king of Nineveh, he rose from his throne, removed his robe, covered himself with sackcloth, and sat in ashes. 7 Then he had a proclamation made in Nineveh: "By the decree of the king and his nobles: No human being or animal, no herd or flock, shall taste anything. They shall not feed, nor shall they drink water. 8 Human beings

and animals shall be covered with sackcloth, and they shall cry mightily to God. All shall turn from their evil ways and from the violence that is in their hands. 9 Who knows? God may relent and change his mind; he may turn from his fierce anger, so that we do not perish."

10 When God saw what they did, how they turned from their evil ways, God changed his mind about the calamity that he had said he would bring upon them; and he did not do it.

Jonah's Anger

4 But this was very displeasing to Jonah, and he became angry. 2 He prayed to the Lord and said, "O Lord! Is not this what I said while I was still in my own country? That is why I fled to Tarshish at the beginning; for I knew that you are a gracious God and merciful, slow to anger, and abounding in steadfast love, and ready to relent from punishing. 3 And now, O Lord, please take my life from me, for it is better for me to die than to live." 4 And the Lord said, "Is it right for you to be angry?" 5 Then Jonah went out of the city and sat down east of the city, and made a booth for himself there. He sat under it in the shade, waiting to see what would become of the city.

6 The Lord God appointed a bush,*b* and made it come up over Jonah, to give shade over his head, to save him from his discomfort; so Jonah was very happy about the bush. 7 But when dawn came up the next day, God appointed a worm that attacked the bush, so that it withered. 8 When the sun rose, God prepared a sultry east wind, and the sun beat down on the head of Jonah so that he was faint and asked that he might die. He said, "It is better for me to die than to live."

Jonah Is Reproved

9 But God said to Jonah, "Is it right for you to be angry about the bush?" And he said, "Yes, angry

> "You are a gracious God and merciful, slow to anger, and abounding in steadfast love."
> —Jonah 4:2

---

a Theodotion: Heb *surely*   b Heb *qiqayon,* possibly *the castor bean plant*

That's Not Fair · Jonah 4:1–8

When God spares Nineveh, Jonah is furious! He is so angry he is willing to let his anger destroy him. Jonah thought he was loyal to God (which is funny, because at first he tried to run away from God), and he feels that God is being unfair to him by not destroying Nineveh. Jonah holds on to his own pride and doesn't want to look like a fool if what he predicted doesn't come true. He kept his end of the deal, and now he wants God to finish the job.

Do you see yourself in Jonah? Would you rather hold on to your judgment and anger toward someone than forgive? How do you feel when God forgives someone you consider wicked? **Ezekiel 18:23** says that God does not want the wicked to die, but to turn from their ways and live. We should have the same desire.

- Is there someone in your life you consider to be beyond God's grace?
- What would you do if God called you to talk to them about the love of God?
- What can you learn from Jonah about loyalty to God, who is much bigger than your own ideals?

enough to die." ¹⁰Then the LORD said, "You are concerned about the bush, for which you did not labor and which you did not grow; it came into being in a night and perished in a night. ¹¹And

should I not be concerned about Nineveh, that great city, in which there are more than a hundred and twenty thousand persons who do not know their right hand from their left, and also many animals?"

Micah

Justice. Compassion. Hope. These themes stand out in the words of the prophet Micah. The book of Micah echoes other prophets in laying out the devastation the Israelites will experience at the hand of their enemies, because they have turned away from God. But unlike other prophets, Micah's main message is not one of doom, but of hope. Micah's harsh words are balanced with a deep conviction that God's compassion and love will overcome.

IN DEPTH

The book of Micah is a collection of oracles (poemlike prophetic messages) taking different forms. Some of the oracles are harsh judgments (Micah 1:8-2:11), some are comforting promises that God will not desert the people (Micah 4), and some are the prophet's own confessions of faith (Micah 3:8; 7:7). The book of Micah shows us a God who is passionate for justice and fairness (Micah 3:9).

Micah prophesied in the city of Jerusalem, but was from a small town in the southern kingdom, Judah. His rural background provided him with a special connection to the land and the people who work it. Images of the countryside are woven throughout the book. Micah speaks against those who covet and seize fields and homes (Micah 2:2). He likens the destruction of Zion (Jerusalem) to plowing a field (Micah 3:12). He represents the ideal kingdom as a place where all the people have their own grapevines and fig trees (Micah 4:4).

His small-town background also gave him perspective on the impact the rulers had on the peasant class. Micah prophesied at about the same time as First Isaiah (see the chart "Prophets and Kings (1050-571 B.C.)," p. 680), during the days of Kings Jotham, Ahaz, and Hezekiah (2 Chronicles 27:1-31:21). But whereas Isaiah was a member of the upper class, defending the rights of the poor, Micah was a poor person, suffering with the poor. That is why he speaks so passionately about their mistreatment (Micah 3:1-3). When Micah condemns injustice, he is speaking as one who knows firsthand the suffering brought about by the gap between rich and poor. Even though his message went unheeded at the time, he models for us trust in the Lord's saving power (Micah 7:7).

QUICK FACTS

- **Date Written:** Late eighth century B.C.
- **Authors:** Micah and later editors
- **Themes:** Warnings against injustice and idolatry; and news of God's promises of hope and a brighter future

AT A GLANCE

- **Micah 1–2** A judgment against Israel and Judah
- **Micah 3:1–5:9** A judgment against rulers, prophets, and priests
- **Micah 5:10–6:8** A judgment against foreign religions, and a plea for justice
- **Micah 6:9–7:20** A judgment against the people, and a message of God's compassion

1 The word of the LORD that came to Micah of Moresheth in the days of Kings Jotham, Ahaz, and Hezekiah of Judah, which he saw concerning Samaria and Jerusalem.

Judgment Pronounced against Samaria

2 Hear, you peoples, all of you;
  listen, O earth, and all that is in it;
and let the Lord GOD be a witness against you,
  the Lord from his holy temple.
3 For lo, the LORD is coming out of his place,
  and will come down and tread upon the
    high places of the earth.
4 Then the mountains will melt under him
  and the valleys will burst open,
like wax near the fire,
  like waters poured down a steep place.
5 All this is for the transgression of Jacob
  and for the sins of the house of Israel.
What is the transgression of Jacob?
  Is it not Samaria?
And what is the high place*a* of Judah?
  Is it not Jerusalem?
6 Therefore I will make Samaria a heap in the
    open country,
  a place for planting vineyards.
I will pour down her stones into the valley,
  and uncover her foundations.
7 All her images shall be beaten to pieces,
  all her wages shall be burned with fire,
  and all her idols I will lay waste;
for as the wages of a prostitute she gathered
    them,
  and as the wages of a prostitute they shall
    again be used.

The Doom of the Cities of Judah

8 For this I will lament and wail;
  I will go barefoot and naked;
I will make lamentation like the jackals,
  and mourning like the ostriches.
9 For her wound*b* is incurable.
  It has come to Judah;
it has reached to the gate of my people,
  to Jerusalem.

10 Tell it not in Gath,
  weep not at all;
in Beth-leaphrah
  roll yourselves in the dust.

11 Pass on your way,
  inhabitants of Shaphir,
  in nakedness and shame;
the inhabitants of Zaanan
  do not come forth;
Beth-ezel is wailing
  and shall remove its support from you.
12 For the inhabitants of Maroth
  wait anxiously for good,
yet disaster has come down from the LORD
  to the gate of Jerusalem.
13 Harness the steeds to the chariots,
  inhabitants of Lachish;
it was the beginning of sin
  to daughter Zion,
for in you were found
  the transgressions of Israel.
14 Therefore you shall give parting gifts
  to Moresheth-gath;
the houses of Achzib shall be a deception
  to the kings of Israel.
15 I will again bring a conqueror upon you,
  inhabitants of Mareshah;
the glory of Israel
  shall come to Adullam.
16 Make yourselves bald and cut off your hair
  for your pampered children;
make yourselves as bald as the eagle,
  for they have gone from you into exile.

Social Evils Denounced

2 Alas for those who devise wickedness
  and evil deeds*c* on their beds!
When the morning dawns, they perform it,
  because it is in their power.
2 They covet fields, and seize them;
  houses, and take them away;
they oppress householder and house,
  people and their inheritance.
3 Therefore thus says the LORD:
Now, I am devising against this family an evil
  from which you cannot remove your necks;
and you shall not walk haughtily,
  for it will be an evil time.
4 On that day they shall take up a taunt song
    against you,
  and wail with bitter lamentation,
and say, "We are utterly ruined;
  the LORD*d* alters the inheritance of my
    people;

a Heb *what are the high places* *b* Gk Syr Vg: Heb *wounds* *c* Cn: Heb *work evil* *d* Heb *he*

Fight Injustice · Micah 2

In **Micah 2**, the prophet Micah challenges the people to take an honest look at their behavior. In harsh images and language, he articulates how greed and injustice have destroyed the well-being of the nation. In **Micah 2:3**, Micah implies that because of their injustice, the people will be like oxen whose necks are confined to yokes that hold their heads down in shame. Micah's message is that injustice forces all in the community and nation to carry a heavy burden.

This theme of examining injustices in the world has been repeated numerous times throughout scripture. The challenge is to keep looking with fresh perspective at what we can do in our communities and country to fight against modern instances of injustice such as racism, hunger, poverty, slavery, violence, and destruction of the environment.

- What injustices do you see in your school, your community, and your own life?
- What can you do to stop injustices from happening?

how he removes it from me!
  Among our captors[a] he parcels out our
      fields."

5 Therefore you will have no one to cast the line
      by lot
  in the assembly of the LORD.

6 "Do not preach"—thus they preach—
  "one should not preach of such things;
  disgrace will not overtake us."
7 Should this be said, O house of Jacob?
  Is the LORD's patience exhausted?
  Are these his doings?
  Do not my words do good
      to one who walks uprightly?
8 But you rise up against my people[b] as an
      enemy;
  you strip the robe from the peaceful,[c]
  from those who pass by trustingly
      with no thought of war.
9 The women of my people you drive out
      from their pleasant houses;
  from their young children you take away
      my glory forever.
10 Arise and go;
  for this is no place to rest,
  because of uncleanness that destroys
      with a grievous destruction.[d]
11 If someone were to go about uttering empty
      falsehoods,
  saying, "I will preach to you of wine and
      strong drink,"

such a one would be the preacher for this
      people!

A Promise for the Remnant of Israel

12 I will surely gather all of you, O Jacob,
  I will gather the survivors of Israel;
  I will set them together
      like sheep in a fold,
  like a flock in its pasture;
      it will resound with people.
13 The one who breaks out will go up before
      them;
  they will break through and pass the gate,
  going out by it.
  Their king will pass on before them,
      the LORD at their head.

Wicked Rulers and Prophets

3 And I said:
  Listen, you heads of Jacob
  and rulers of the house of Israel!
  Should you not know justice?—
2 you who hate the good and love the evil,
  who tear the skin off my people,[e]
      and the flesh off their bones;
3 who eat the flesh of my people,
      flay their skin off them,
  break their bones in pieces,
      and chop them up like meat[f] in a kettle,
      like flesh in a caldron.

4 Then they will cry to the LORD,

---

a Cn: Heb *the rebellious* **b** Cn: Heb *But yesterday my people rose* **c** Cn: Heb *from before a garment* **d** Meaning of Heb uncertain **e** Heb *from them*
f Gk: Heb *as*

but he will not answer them;
he will hide his face from them at that time,
because they have acted wickedly.

5 Thus says the LORD concerning the prophets
who lead my people astray,
who cry "Peace"
when they have something to eat,
but declare war against those
who put nothing into their mouths.

6 Therefore it shall be night to you, without
vision,
and darkness to you, without revelation.
The sun shall go down upon the prophets,
and the day shall be black over them;

7 the seers shall be disgraced,
and the diviners put to shame;
they shall all cover their lips,
for there is no answer from God.

8 But as for me, I am filled with power,
with the spirit of the LORD,
and with justice and might,
to declare to Jacob his transgression
and to Israel his sin.

9 Hear this, you rulers of the house of Jacob
and chiefs of the house of Israel,
who abhor justice
and pervert all equity,

10 who build Zion with blood
and Jerusalem with wrong!

11 Its rulers give judgment for a bribe,
its priests teach for a price,
its prophets give oracles for money;
yet they lean upon the LORD and say,
"Surely the LORD is with us!
No harm shall come upon us."

12 Therefore because of you
Zion shall be plowed as a field;
Jerusalem shall become a heap of ruins,
and the mountain of the house a wooded
height.

4

Peace and Security through Obedience

In days to come
the mountain of the LORD's house
shall be established as the highest of the
mountains,
and shall be raised up above the hills.

Peoples shall stream to it,
2 and many nations shall come and say:
"Come, let us go up to the mountain of the
LORD,
to the house of the God of Jacob;
that he may teach us his ways
and that we may walk in his paths."
For out of Zion shall go forth instruction,
and the word of the LORD from
Jerusalem.

3 He shall judge between many peoples,
and shall arbitrate between strong nations
far away;
they shall beat their swords into plowshares,
and their spears into pruning hooks;
nation shall not lift up sword against nation,
neither shall they learn war any more;

4 but they shall all sit under their own vines
and under their own fig trees,
and no one shall make them afraid;
for the mouth of the LORD of hosts has
spoken.

5 For all the peoples walk,
each in the name of its god,
but we will walk in the name of the LORD
our God
forever and ever.

Restoration Promised after Exile

6 In that day, says the LORD,
I will assemble the lame
and gather those who have been driven away,
and those whom I have afflicted.

7 The lame I will make the remnant,
and those who were cast off, a strong
nation;
and the LORD will reign over them in
Mount Zion
now and forevermore.

8 And you, O tower of the flock,
hill of daughter Zion,
to you it shall come,
the former dominion shall come,
the sovereignty of daughter Jerusalem.

9 Now why do you cry aloud?
Is there no king in you?
Has your counselor perished,

that pangs have seized you like a woman in
labor?
10 Writhe and groan,[a] O daughter Zion,
like a woman in labor;
for now you shall go forth from the city
and camp in the open country;
you shall go to Babylon.
There you shall be rescued,
there the LORD will redeem you
from the hands of your enemies.

11 Now many nations
are assembled against you,
saying, "Let her be profaned,
and let our eyes gaze upon Zion."
12 But they do not know
the thoughts of the LORD;
they do not understand his plan,
that he has gathered them as sheaves to the
threshing floor.
13 Arise and thresh,
O daughter Zion,
for I will make your horn iron
and your hoofs bronze;
you shall beat in pieces many peoples,
and shall[b] devote their gain to the LORD,
their wealth to the Lord of the whole earth.

5 [c] Now you are walled around with a
wall;[d]
siege is laid against us;
with a rod they strike the ruler of Israel
upon the cheek.

The Ruler from Bethlehem

2 [e] But you, O Bethlehem of Ephrathah,
who are one of the little clans of Judah,
from you shall come forth for me
one who is to rule in Israel,
whose origin is from of old,
from ancient days.
3 Therefore he shall give them up until the time
when she who is in labor has brought
forth;
then the rest of his kindred shall return
to the people of Israel.
4 And he shall stand and feed his flock in the
strength of the LORD,
in the majesty of the name of the LORD
his God.

PRAY IT!

From Humble Beginnings
Micah 5:2–5

As a country boy,
Micah has a different
vision than do some of the other prophets.
He doesn't see the ideal ruler, or savior,
coming out of a big city like Jerusalem.
Instead, he sees this great person coming
from Bethlehem—a tiny, insignificant city,
but also a place free from political
corruption. The gospel of Matthew shows
Micah's prophecy being fulfilled in the birth
of Jesus (Matthew 2:5-6).

The Bible is full of stories of God
accomplishing huge feats through small
and humble people, places, and situations.
During your prayer time, reflect or journal
on the following questions:

• Why does God often use small and
humble people to accomplish God's
purposes?

• What small or hidden gifts do you
have to offer God to work with?

And they shall live secure, for now he shall be
great
to the ends of the earth;
5 and he shall be the one of peace.

If the Assyrians come into our land
and tread upon our soil,[f]
we will raise against them seven shepherds
and eight installed as rulers.
6 They shall rule the land of Assyria with the
sword,
and the land of Nimrod with the drawn
sword;[g]
they[h] shall rescue us from the Assyrians
if they come into our land
or tread within our border.

The Future Role of the Remnant

7 Then the remnant of Jacob,
surrounded by many peoples,

---

a Meaning of Heb uncertain   b Gk Syr Tg: Heb and I will   c Ch 4.14 in Heb   d Cn Compare Gk: Meaning of Heb uncertain   e Ch 5.1 in Heb
f Gk: Heb in our palaces   g Cn: Heb in its entrances   h Heb he

shall be like dew from the Lord,
    like showers on the grass,
which do not depend upon people
    or wait for any mortal.

8 And among the nations the remnant of Jacob,
    surrounded by many peoples,
shall be like a lion among the animals of the
    forest,
    like a young lion among the flocks of
        sheep,
which, when it goes through, treads down
    and tears in pieces, with no one to deliver.

9 Your hand shall be lifted up over your
    adversaries,
    and all your enemies shall be cut off.

10 In that day, says the Lord,
    I will cut off your horses from among you
    and will destroy your chariots;

11 and I will cut off the cities of your land
    and throw down all your strongholds;

12 and I will cut off sorceries from your hand,
    and you shall have no more soothsayers;

13 and I will cut off your images
    and your pillars from among you,
and you shall bow down no more
    to the work of your hands;

14 and I will uproot your sacred poles[a] from
    among you
    and destroy your towns.

15 And in anger and wrath I will execute
    vengeance
    on the nations that did not obey.

6   God Challenges Israel

Hear what the Lord says:
    Rise, plead your case before the
        mountains,
    and let the hills hear your voice.

2 Hear, you mountains, the controversy of the
    Lord,
    and you enduring foundations of the
        earth;
for the Lord has a controversy with his
    people,
    and he will contend with Israel.

3 "O my people, what have I done to you?
    In what have I wearied you? Answer me!

4 For I brought you up from the land of Egypt,
    and redeemed you from the house of
        slavery;
and I sent before you Moses,
    Aaron, and Miriam.

5 O my people, remember now what King Balak
    of Moab devised,
    what Balaam son of Beor answered him,
and what happened from Shittim to Gilgal,
    that you may know the saving acts of the
        Lord."

LIVE IT!

What Do You Want from Me? · Micah 6:1–8

"God, what do you want from me?" How many times have you asked this question? It's a question Micah asks too for all the Israelites (Micah 6:6-7). The Israelites have just been reminded of the many times and ways God has saved them and are confronted with the question of what they should do in response. Sacrifice thousands of animals? Pour out rivers of oil? Sacrifice their firstborn children? The answer is a resounding no! God does not want sacrifice.

So what does God require?

Do justice. Love kindness. Walk humbly with God (Micah 6:8). It's a simple formula for doing God's will, but not so simple to put into practice. It covers all of life—physical, mental, and spiritual. We are to be active in working toward justice. We are to love and focus on kindness and mercy. And we are to do it all in a spirit of humility, walking with God and becoming more like God each day. God doesn't want a onetime sacrifice; God wants our entire lives.

- What are some simple steps you can take to show your thankfulness to God?
- How does your life show justice, kindness, and humility? How can you live out these traits?

a Heb *Asherim*

> "He has told you,
> O mortal, what is
> good; and what does
> the LORD require of you
> but to do justice, and
> to love kindness, and
> to walk humbly with
> your God?"
> —Micah 6:8

What God Requires

6 "With what shall I come before the LORD,
   and bow myself before God on
      high?
Shall I come before him with burnt offerings,
   with calves a year old?
7 Will the LORD be pleased with thousands of
      rams,
   with ten thousands of rivers of oil?
Shall I give my firstborn for my transgression,
   the fruit of my body for the sin of my soul?"
8 He has told you, O mortal, what is good;
   and what does the LORD require of you
but to do justice, and to love kindness,
   and to walk humbly with your God?

Cheating and Violence to Be Punished

9 The voice of the LORD cries to the city
   (it is sound wisdom to fear your name):
Hear, O tribe and assembly of the city!*a*
10   Can I forget*b* the treasures of wickedness in
         the house of the wicked,
      and the scant measure that is accursed?
11 Can I tolerate wicked scales
   and a bag of dishonest weights?
12 Your*c* wealthy are full of violence;
   your*d* inhabitants speak lies,
      with tongues of deceit in their mouths.
13 Therefore I have begun*e* to strike you down,
   making you desolate because of your sins.
14 You shall eat, but not be satisfied,
   and there shall be a gnawing hunger
      within you;
you shall put away, but not save,
   and what you save, I will hand over to the
      sword.

CONNECT IT!

Mother Teresa: Living Out God's Love
Micah 6:8

Mother Teresa arguably lived out the command of **Micah 6:8** to "do justice, and to love kindness, and to walk humbly with God" better than any other person in recent history. Her life as a nun working among the poorest of the poor in Calcutta, India, and around the world made her famous as a humanitarian and advocate for the poor, orphaned, sick, and dying. She served the poor in Calcutta for over forty-five years. She founded and ran the Missionaries of Charity, which included projects for everything from orphanages to soup kitchens to homes for HIV/AIDS victims around the world. She won the Nobel Peace Prize in 1979, along with many other honors and awards in her lifetime.

But although her own work was international in scope, over and over Mother Teresa encouraged and challenged people to live out compassion in their own lives, families, and communities. The commands of this verse are not only to be followed by leaving everything and serving the poor of another country. They are meant as guidelines for all of us, every day. And Mother Teresa challenged people not just to talk about it, but to do it, when she said, "Today it is fashionable to talk about the poor. Unfortunately, it is not fashionable to talk with them." Mother Teresa struggled with doubt and spiritual questions, but her actions revealed her unwavering commitment to living out the love of God in the world.

15 You shall sow, but not reap;
   you shall tread olives, but not anoint
      yourselves with oil;
   you shall tread grapes, but not drink wine.
16 For you have kept the statutes of Omri*f*

a Cn Compare Gk: Heb *tribe, and who has appointed it yet?*   **b** Cn: Meaning of Heb uncertain   **c** Heb *Whose*   **d** Heb *whose*   **e** Gk Syr Vg: Heb *have made sick*   **f** Gk Syr Vg Tg: Heb *the statutes of Omri are kept*

and all the works of the house of Ahab,
and you have followed their counsels.
Therefore I will make you a desolation, and
    your*a* inhabitants an object of
    hissing;
so you shall bear the scorn of my people.

The Total Corruption of the People

7 Woe is me! For I have become like
    one who,
after the summer fruit has been gathered,
after the vintage has been gleaned,
finds no cluster to eat;
    there is no first-ripe fig for which I hunger.
2 The faithful have disappeared from the land,
    and there is no one left who is upright;
they all lie in wait for blood,
    and they hunt each other with nets.
3 Their hands are skilled to do evil;
    the official and the judge ask for a bribe,
and the powerful dictate what they desire;
    thus they pervert justice.*b*
4 The best of them is like a brier,
    the most upright of them a thorn hedge.
The day of their*c* sentinels, of their*c*
    punishment, has come;
    now their confusion is at hand.

5 Put no trust in a friend,
    have no confidence in a loved one;
guard the doors of your mouth
    from her who lies in your embrace;
6 for the son treats the father with contempt,
    the daughter rises up against her mother,
the daughter-in-law against her mother-in-
    law;
    your enemies are members of your own
    household.
7 But as for me, I will look to the LORD,
    I will wait for the God of my salvation;
    my God will hear me.

Penitence and Trust in God

8 Do not rejoice over me, O my enemy;
    when I fall, I shall rise;
when I sit in darkness,
    the LORD will be a light to me.
9 I must bear the indignation of the LORD,
    because I have sinned against him,
until he takes my side
    and executes judgment for me.
He will bring me out to the light;
    I shall see his vindication.
10 Then my enemy will see,
    and shame will cover her who said
    to me,
    "Where is the LORD your God?"
My eyes will see her downfall;*d*
    now she will be trodden down
    like the mire of the streets.

A Prophecy of Restoration

11 A day for the building of your walls!
    In that day the boundary shall be far
    extended.
12 In that day they will come to you
    from Assyria to*e* Egypt,
and from Egypt to the River,
    from sea to sea and from mountain to
    mountain.
13 But the earth will be desolate
    because of its inhabitants,
    for the fruit of their doings.

14 Shepherd your people with your staff,
    the flock that belongs to you,
which lives alone in a forest
    in the midst of a garden land;
let them feed in Bashan and Gilead
    as in the days of old.
15 As in the days when you came out of the
    land of Egypt,
    show us*f* marvelous things.
16 The nations shall see and be ashamed
    of all their might;
they shall lay their hands on their
    mouths;
    their ears shall be deaf;
17 they shall lick dust like a snake,
    like the crawling things of the earth;
they shall come trembling out of their
    fortresses;

a Heb *its* *b* Cn: Heb *they weave it* *c* Heb *your* *d* Heb lacks *downfall* *e* One Ms: MT *Assyria and cities of* *f* Cn: Heb *I will show him*

they shall turn in dread to the LORD
    our God,
and they shall stand in fear of you.

God's Compassion and Steadfast Love

18 Who is a God like you, pardoning iniquity
    and passing over the transgression
    of the remnant of your[a] possession?
  He does not retain his anger forever,
    because he delights in showing clemency.

19 He will again have compassion
    upon us;
  he will tread our iniquities under foot.
  You will cast all our[b] sins
    into the depths of the sea.
20 You will show faithfulness to Jacob
    and unswerving loyalty to
       Abraham,
  as you have sworn to our ancestors
    from the days of old.

a Heb *his*   b Gk Syr Vg Tg: Heb *their*

Nahum ▶▶▶▶▶▶▶▶▶▶▶▶▶▶▶▶▶▶▶▶▶▶▶▶

Devastation, desolation, and destruction! If the book of Nahum were made into a movie, it would have to be rated R for graphic violence. You are about to read some angry words. They portray a vengeful God bringing destruction upon Israel's enemies. What could make the prophet Nahum so angry? What could make God so angry? Continue reading to find out.

IN DEPTH

At the time Nahum was written, the Assyrian Empire had been the terror of the Middle East for several centuries. In 722 B.C., it destroyed the northern kingdom, Israel. In 701 B.C., it invaded the southern kingdom, Judah, and laid siege to Jerusalem (see the chart "Prophets and Kings (1050-571 B.C.)," p. 680, and Map 8a: "Assyrian Empire"). The siege broke off, and Jerusalem did not fall, but the chosen people of God got a gruesome taste of Assyria's savage cruelty.

The sole concern of the prophet Nahum is the destruction of this evil world power. In the first chapter of his book, he declares the coming wrath of God, and in Nahum 2 and 3, he describes the destruction of Nineveh (the Assyrian capital). We shouldn't be too surprised that, when Assyria falls in 612 B.C., Nahum sees the justice of God being worked out: the Assyrians are finally getting a taste of their own medicine! Nahum seems almost to be gloating when he says in Nahum 3:19: "All who hear the news about you clap their hands over you. For who has ever escaped your endless cruelty?"

Hidden among the threats and violence against Assyria, we also find words of comfort for God's people: God will avenge their enemies (Nahum 1:2); good news and peace are coming for Judah (Nahum 2:1); the Lord will restore Israel to its original majesty (Nahum 2:3). We even find some wonderful reminders of God's love and protection, which balance the image of the God of vengeance and destruction: "The LORD is slow to anger but great in power" (Nahum 1:3); "The LORD is good, a stronghold in a day of trouble; he protects those who take refuge in him" (Nahum 1:7). The poetic images in Nahum remind us that God has many sides and is always more than we can imagine.

QUICK FACTS

- **Date Written:** Between 663 and 612 B.C.
- **Author:** Nahum
- **Themes:** The call for God's vengeance against Israel's cruel enemies, and a reminder of God's goodness

AT A GLANCE

- **Nahum 1:1–11** The coming of the Lord in judgment
- **Nahum 1:12–15** Good news for Judah
- **Nahum 2–3** The destruction of Nineveh

1

An oracle concerning Nineveh. The book of the vision of Nahum of Elkosh.

The Consuming Wrath of God

2 A jealous and avenging God is the LORD,
　　the LORD is avenging and wrathful;
the LORD takes vengeance on his adversaries
　　and rages against his enemies.
3 The LORD is slow to anger but great in power,
　　and the LORD will by no means clear the
　　　　guilty.

His way is in whirlwind and storm,
　　and the clouds are the dust of his feet.
4 He rebukes the sea and makes it dry,
　　and he dries up all the rivers;
Bashan and Carmel wither,
　　and the bloom of Lebanon fades.
5 The mountains quake before him,
　　and the hills melt;
the earth heaves before him,
　　the world and all who live in it.

6 Who can stand before his indignation?
　　Who can endure the heat of his anger?
His wrath is poured out like fire,
　　and by him the rocks are broken in pieces.
7 The LORD is good,
　　a stronghold in a day of trouble;
he protects those who take refuge in him,
8 　　even in a rushing flood.
He will make a full end of his adversaries,[a]
　　and will pursue his enemies into darkness.
9 Why do you plot against the LORD?
　　He will make an end;
　　no adversary will rise up twice.
10 Like thorns they are entangled,
　　like drunkards they are drunk;
　　they are consumed like dry straw.
11 From you one has gone out
　　who plots evil against the LORD,
　　one who counsels wickedness.

Good News for Judah

12 Thus says the LORD,
"Though they are at full strength and
　　　　many,[b]
　　they will be cut off and pass away.
Though I have afflicted you,
　　I will afflict you no more.

> "The LORD is good,
> a stronghold in
> a day of trouble;
> he protects those who
> take refuge in him."
> —Nahum 1:7

13 And now I will break off his yoke from you
　　and snap the bonds that bind you."

14 The LORD has commanded concerning you:
　　"Your name shall be perpetuated no
　　　　longer;
from the house of your gods I will cut off
　　the carved image and the cast image.
I will make your grave, for you are worthless."

15c Look! On the mountains the feet of one
　　who brings good tidings,
　　who proclaims peace!
Celebrate your festivals, O Judah,
　　fulfill your vows,
for never again shall the wicked invade you;
　　they are utterly cut off.

2

The Destruction of the Wicked City

A shatterer[d] has come up against you.
　　Guard the ramparts;
　　watch the road;
gird your loins;
　　collect all your strength.

2 (For the LORD is restoring the majesty of
　　　　Jacob,
　　as well as the majesty of Israel,
though ravagers have ravaged them
　　and ruined their branches.)

3 The shields of his warriors are red;
　　his soldiers are clothed in crimson.
The metal on the chariots flashes
　　on the day when he musters them;
　　the chargers[e] prance.
4 The chariots race madly through the streets,
　　they rush to and fro through the squares;
their appearance is like torches,
　　they dart like lightning.

a Gk: Heb *of her place*　b Meaning of Heb uncertain　c Ch 2.1 in Heb　d Cn: Heb *scatterer*　e Cn Compare Gk Syr: Heb *cypresses*

STUDY IT!

Images of God · Nahum 2:1–3:3

"Piles of dead, heaps of corpses, dead bodies without end . . ." (Nahum 3:3). The descriptions of God's vengeance on the Assyrians throughout these chapters are gruesome. They seem contradictory to Jesus' command to love one's enemies (Matthew 5:43-48). Was God different back in Old Testament times? Or was Nahum just mistaken? Are you comfortable imagining God in different—even opposite—ways? (See Nahum 1:6-7.) These are difficult but important questions! In understanding Nahum's message, it helps to keep in mind three things.

- Throughout the Bible, there is a strong theme of divine hatred for all sin. In the New Testament, though, a distinction emerges: although God hates the sin, God still loves the sinner. Nahum doesn't make that distinction.

- Christians today make a distinction between God directly causing something to happen and God allowing something to occur—usually as a result of human limitations, people's poor choices, or natural phenomena. Again, Nahum doesn't make this distinction—for Nahum, if something happens, God is the direct cause.

- We have to keep in mind that all our attempts to understand God will fall short. God is beyond human understanding. That is why the Bible's authors, including Nahum, describe God in many different—and often seemingly contradictory—ways.

5 He calls his officers;
    they stumble as they come forward;
they hasten to the wall,
    and the mantelet[a] is set up.
6 The river gates are opened,
    the palace trembles.
7 It is decreed[a] that the city[b] be exiled,
    its slave women led away,
moaning like doves
    and beating their breasts.
8 Nineveh is like a pool
    whose waters[c] run away.
"Halt! Halt!"—
    but no one turns back.
9 "Plunder the silver,
    plunder the gold!
There is no end of treasure!
    An abundance of every precious
        thing!"

10 Devastation, desolation, and destruction!
    Hearts faint and knees tremble,
all loins quake,
    all faces grow pale!
11 What became of the lions' den,
    the cave[d] of the young lions,
where the lion goes,

and the lion's cubs, with no one to disturb
    them?
12 The lion has torn enough for his whelps
    and strangled prey for his lionesses;
he has filled his caves with prey
    and his dens with torn flesh.

13 See, I am against you, says the LORD of hosts, and I will burn your[e] chariots in smoke, and the sword shall devour your young lions; I will cut off your prey from the earth, and the voice of your messengers shall be heard no more.

3   **Ruin Imminent and Inevitable**
Ah! City of bloodshed,
    utterly deceitful, full of booty—
no end to the plunder!
2 The crack of whip and rumble of wheel,
    galloping horse and bounding chariot!
3 Horsemen charging,
    flashing sword and glittering spear,
piles of dead,
    heaps of corpses,
dead bodies without end—
    they stumble over the bodies!
4 Because of the countless debaucheries of the
      prostitute,

a Meaning of Heb uncertain   b Heb *it*   c Cn Compare Gk: Heb *a pool, from the days that she has become, and they*   d Cn: Heb *pasture*   e Heb *her*

gracefully alluring, mistress of sorcery,
who enslaves[a] nations through her
        debaucheries,
    and peoples through her sorcery,
5 I am against you,
        says the LORD of hosts,
    and will lift up your skirts over your face;
    and I will let nations look on your nakedness
        and kingdoms on your shame.
6 I will throw filth at you
        and treat you with contempt,
        and make you a spectacle.
7 Then all who see you will shrink from you
            and say,
    "Nineveh is devastated; who will bemoan her?"
        Where shall I seek comforters for you?

8 Are you better than Thebes[b]
        that sat by the Nile,
    with water around her,
        her rampart a sea,
        water her wall?
9 Ethiopia[c] was her strength,
        Egypt too, and that without limit;
        Put and the Libyans were her[d] helpers.

10 Yet she became an exile,
        she went into captivity;
    even her infants were dashed in pieces
        at the head of every street;
    lots were cast for her nobles,
        all her dignitaries were bound in fetters.
11 You also will be drunken,
        you will go into hiding;[e]
    you will seek
        a refuge from the enemy.
12 All your fortresses are like fig trees
        with first-ripe figs—
    if shaken they fall

into the mouth of the eater.
13 Look at your troops:
        they are women in your midst.
    The gates of your land
        are wide open to your foes;
        fire has devoured the bars of your gates.

14 Draw water for the siege,
        strengthen your forts;
    trample the clay,
        tread the mortar,
        take hold of the brick mold!
15 There the fire will devour you,
        the sword will cut you off.
        It will devour you like the locust.

    Multiply yourselves like the locust,
        multiply like the grasshopper!
16 You increased your merchants
        more than the stars of the heavens.
        The locust sheds its skin and flies away.
17 Your guards are like grasshoppers,
        your scribes like swarms[e] of locusts
    settling on the fences
        on a cold day—
    when the sun rises, they fly away;
        no one knows where they have gone.

18 Your shepherds are asleep,
        O king of Assyria;
        your nobles slumber.
    Your people are scattered on the mountains
        with no one to gather them.
19 There is no assuaging your hurt,
        your wound is mortal.
    All who hear the news about you
        clap their hands over you.
    For who has ever escaped
        your endless cruelty?

a Heb sells b Heb No-amon c Or Nubia; Heb Cush d Gk: Heb your e Meaning of Heb uncertain

Habakkuk ▶▶▶▶▶▶▶▶▶▶

God, why aren't you answering my cry for help? How long must I endure this trial? If you are good and all-powerful, why let suffering or injustice go on? Have you ever asked these questions? Most people have asked them at some point in life. The prophet Habakkuk struggled with these same painful and disturbing questions. His hope in God's justice is a model of faith amid doubt.

IN DEPTH

Habakkuk was the first prophet who dared to ask God about God's behavior. He looked around at all the terrible things that were happening to his people and cried out: "God, where are you? Do you even care about us? Why do you allow evil people to oppress us?"

We know little about Habakkuk except that he was a prophet in Judah, the southern kingdom, in the late seventh century B.C. The Chaldeans (another name for the Babylonians) and the corrupt king of Judah, Jehoiakim (see 2 Kings 23:36–24:7), were causing so much trouble that Habakkuk was ready to despair. God answered him in a most surprising way, saying that the Chaldeans—as bad as they were—were chosen as God's instrument to punish the wicked all over the earth. Habakkuk was not satisfied. He asked why God was silent while the wicked destroyed the righteous. God then spoke to him in a vision (Habakkuk 2:2), saying that justice would come to the wicked in its own time, but the "righteous live by their faith" (Habakkuk 2:4). Later, Paul would use these same words to describe Christians (Romans 1:17; Galatians 3:11). For Habakkuk, faith in God and hope in God's justice were the same thing.

The short book of Habakkuk is unique among the prophetic books in the variety of its writings. Its reflections about the problem of evil in the world resemble the writings in wisdom literature (e.g., Job). Its dialogues with God (Habakkuk 1:2) are similar to Jeremiah's confessions (Jeremiah 12:6). Habakkuk 3 is written as a canticle (song) and is the prophet's final prayer of confidence in God's power to save the people. We too can pray in confidence, because God is just and will save us in our time of need.

QUICK FACTS

- **Date Written:** Probably between 609 and 598 B.C.
- **Author:** Habakkuk
- **Theme:** Faith in God's justice as the answer to evil

AT A GLANCE

- **Habakkuk 1:1–2:5** Habakkuk's complaints and God's responses
- **Habakkuk 2:6–20** Five warnings against wicked people
- **Habakkuk 3** Habakkuk's prayer of confidence

1

The oracle that the prophet Habakkuk saw.

The Prophet's Complaint

2 O Lord, how long shall I cry for help,
    and you will not listen?
Or cry to you "Violence!"
    and you will not save?
3 Why do you make me see wrongdoing
    and look at trouble?
Destruction and violence are before me;
    strife and contention arise.
4 So the law becomes slack
    and justice never prevails.
The wicked surround the righteous—
    therefore judgment comes forth perverted.

5 Look at the nations, and see!
    Be astonished! Be astounded!
For a work is being done in your days
    that you would not believe if you were
        told.
6 For I am rousing the Chaldeans,
    that fierce and impetuous nation,
who march through the breadth of the earth
    to seize dwellings not their own.
7 Dread and fearsome are they;
    their justice and dignity proceed from
        themselves.
8 Their horses are swifter than leopards,
    more menacing than wolves at dusk;
    their horses charge.
Their horsemen come from far away;
    they fly like an eagle swift to devour.
9 They all come for violence,
    with faces pressing[a] forward;
    they gather captives like sand.
10 At kings they scoff,
    and of rulers they make sport.
They laugh at every fortress,
    and heap up earth to take it.
11 Then they sweep by like the wind;
    they transgress and become guilty;
    their own might is their god!

12 Are you not from of old,
    O Lord my God, my Holy One?
You[b] shall not die.
O Lord, you have marked them for judgment;
    and you, O Rock, have established them
        for punishment.

13 Your eyes are too pure to behold evil,
    and you cannot look on wrongdoing;
why do you look on the treacherous,
    and are silent when the wicked swallow
        those more righteous than they?
14 You have made people like the fish of the sea,
    like crawling things that have no ruler.

15 The enemy[c] brings all of them up with a hook;
    he drags them out with his net,
he gathers them in his seine;
    so he rejoices and exults.
16 Therefore he sacrifices to his net
    and makes offerings to his seine;
for by them his portion is lavish,
    and his food is rich.
17 Is he then to keep on emptying his net,
    and destroying nations without mercy?

2

God's Reply to the Prophet's Complaint

I will stand at my watchpost,
    and station myself on the rampart;
I will keep watch to see what he will say to me,
    and what he[d] will answer concerning my
        complaint.
2 Then the Lord answered me and said:
Write the vision;
    make it plain on tablets,
    so that a runner may read it.
3 For there is still a vision for the appointed
        time;
    it speaks of the end, and does not lie.
If it seems to tarry, wait for it;
    it will surely come, it will not delay.
4 Look at the proud!
    Their spirit is not right in them,
    but the righteous live by their faith.[e]
5 Moreover, wealth[f] is treacherous;
    the arrogant do not endure.
They open their throats wide as Sheol;
    like Death they never have enough.
They gather all nations for themselves,
    and collect all peoples as their own.

The Woes of the Wicked

6 Shall not everyone taunt such people and, with
mocking riddles, say about them,
    "Alas for you who heap up what is not your
        own!"

---

a Meaning of Heb uncertain   b Ancient Heb tradition: MT We   c Heb He   d Syr: Heb I   e Or faithfulness   f Other Heb Mss read wine

LIVE IT!

Immediate Gratification · Habakkuk 2:3

"I want it all, and I want it now!" That statement could sum up the ambitions of a lot of people. It is how they define success. The key word in their goal is "now." They don't like to wait in lines; they want instant service and immediate gratification. Think about your own frustration if the Internet connection you're using is too slow or if you can't immediately reach a friend on your cell phone. We have grown used to getting things right away and become impatient when our expectations are not met.

There is a temptation to apply this goal to our spiritual lives, hoping for an immediate and fulfilling relationship with God. But the spiritual life does not work that way. Recall these words from **Ecclesiastes 3:1:** "For everything there is a season, and a time for every matter under heaven." We have to remind ourselves that many valuable things take time. Our growth in faith will take time. We need to be open, patient, and trusting. As God reminds Habakkuk in his vision in **Habakkuk 2:3,** "If it seems to tarry, wait for it; it will surely come, it will not delay."

- How patient are you with God in the midst of your own spiritual growth?
- How do you nurture your spiritual life day by day?
- What are your goals for your relationship with God?

How long will you load yourselves with
    goods taken in pledge?
7 Will not your own creditors suddenly rise,
    and those who make you tremble wake up?
    Then you will be booty for them.
8 Because you have plundered many nations,
    all that survive of the peoples shall
        plunder you—
    because of human bloodshed, and violence to
        the earth,
    to cities and all who live in them.

9 "Alas for you who get evil gain for your
        house,
    setting your nest on high
    to be safe from the reach of harm!"
10 You have devised shame for your
        house
    by cutting off many peoples;
    you have forfeited your life.
11 The very stones will cry out from the wall,
    and the plaster[a] will respond from the
        woodwork.

12 "Alas for you who build a town by bloodshed,
    and found a city on iniquity!"
13 Is it not from the LORD of hosts
    that peoples labor only to feed the flames,
    and nations weary themselves for nothing?

14 But the earth will be filled
    with the knowledge of the glory of the
        LORD,
    as the waters cover the sea.

15 "Alas for you who make your neighbors drink,
    pouring out your wrath[b] until they are
        drunk,
    in order to gaze on their nakedness!"
16 You will be sated with contempt instead of
        glory.
    Drink, you yourself, and stagger![c]
The cup in the LORD's right hand
    will come around to you,
    and shame will come upon your glory!
17 For the violence done to Lebanon will
        overwhelm you;
    the destruction of the animals will terrify
        you—[d]
because of human bloodshed and violence to
        the earth,
    to cities and all who live in them.

18 What use is an idol
    once its maker has shaped it—
    a cast image, a teacher of lies?
For its maker trusts in what has been made,
    though the product is only an idol that
        cannot speak!

---

a Or beam   b Or poison   c Q Ms Gk: MT be uncircumcised   d Gk Syr: Meaning of Heb uncertain

19 Alas for you who say to the wood,
       "Wake up!"
   to silent stone, "Rouse yourself!"
   Can it teach?
   See, it is gold and silver plated,
       and there is no breath in it at all.

20 But the LORD is in his holy temple;
       let all the earth keep silence before him!

> "O LORD, I have heard
> of your renown,
> and I stand in awe,
> O LORD, of your work."
> —Habakkuk 3:2

3 A prayer of the prophet Habakkuk according to Shigionoth.

The Prophet's Prayer

2 O LORD, I have heard of your renown,
       and I stand in awe, O LORD, of your work.
   In our own time revive it;
       in our own time make it known;
       in wrath may you remember mercy.
3 God came from Teman,
       the Holy One from Mount Paran.   *Selah*
   His glory covered the heavens,
       and the earth was full of his praise.
4 The brightness was like the sun;
       rays came forth from his hand,
       where his power lay hidden.
5 Before him went pestilence,
       and plague followed close behind.
6 He stopped and shook the earth;
       he looked and made the nations tremble.
   The eternal mountains were shattered;
       along his ancient pathways
       the everlasting hills sank low.
7 I saw the tents of Cushan under affliction;

   the tent-curtains of the land of Midian
       trembled.
8 Was your wrath against the rivers,*a* O LORD?
       Or your anger against the rivers,*a*
       or your rage against the sea,*b*
   when you drove your horses,
       your chariots to victory?
9 You brandished your naked bow,
       sated*c* were the arrows at your command.*d*
                                       Selah
   You split the earth with rivers.
10 The mountains saw you, and writhed;
       a torrent of water swept by;
   the deep gave forth its voice.
       The sun*e* raised high its hands;
11 the moon*f* stood still in its exalted place,
       at the light of your arrows speeding by,
       at the gleam of your flashing spear.
12 In fury you trod the earth,
       in anger you trampled nations.
13 You came forth to save your people,
       to save your anointed.
   You crushed the head of the wicked house,
       laying it bare from foundation to roof.*d*
                                       Selah

CONNECT IT!

Charles Spurgeon: A Prayer for Revival · Habakkuk 3:2

Charles Spurgeon (1834-1892) was a famous British preacher of his day. He was a powerful, captivating, and convincing speaker who often stirred up controversy within and outside of the Church. It's estimated that he spoke to more than 10 million people during his lifetime. One of his many famous sermons, titled "Spiritual Revival: The Want of the Church," called Christians to spiritual revival and renewal and was based on this verse. But his point was not that Christians should try really hard to be different. His point was that only God can cause our souls to be revived. It's the life of God in believers that the Church and the world need, because only God can truly fill us with love, kindness, self-control, and other traits like the fruit of the Spirit listed in **Galatians 5:22–23**. So our prayer should be that of Habakkuk for the revival of God's work.

a Or *against River* *b* Or *against Sea* *c* Cn: Heb *oaths* *d* Meaning of Heb uncertain *e* Heb *It* *f* Heb *sun, moon*

14 You pierced with their[a] own arrows the head[b]
   of his warriors,[c]
who came like a whirlwind to scatter us,[d]
   gloating as if ready to devour the poor who
     were in hiding.
15 You trampled the sea with your horses,
   churning the mighty waters.

16 I hear, and I tremble within;
   my lips quiver at the sound.
Rottenness enters into my bones,
   and my steps tremble[e] beneath me.
I wait quietly for the day of calamity
   to come upon the people who
     attack us.

Trust and Joy in the Midst of Trouble

17 Though the fig tree does not blossom,
   and no fruit is on the vines;
though the produce of the olive fails,
   and the fields yield no food;
though the flock is cut off from the fold,
   and there is no herd in the stalls,
18 yet I will rejoice in the LORD;
   I will exult in the God of my salvation.
19 GOD, the Lord, is my strength;
   he makes my feet like the feet of a deer,
   and makes me tread upon the heights.[f]

To the leader: with stringed[g]
   instruments.

---

a Heb *his* b Or *leader* c Vg Compare Gk Syr: Meaning of Heb uncertain d Heb *me* e Cn Compare Gk: Meaning of Heb uncertain f Heb *my heights* g Heb *my stringed*

Zephaniah

As kids we usually have to clean up messes, take time-outs, or lose privileges as consequences for poor choices we have made. As we get older, we learn that our wrongdoing has more personal and painful consequences: perhaps a parent's refusal to trust us, a friend's anger, or pain after hurting someone we love. The prophet Zephaniah warned the people of Judah of the severe consequences of their sin against the Lord.

IN DEPTH

The book of Zephaniah gives us few clues about the prophet Zephaniah's identity. We do know that he preached in the southern kingdom, Judah, during the reign of King Josiah (2 Chronicles 34-35), around 630 B.C. He followed First Isaiah and Micah and came a little before Habakkuk, during the time of Nahum.

Zephaniah follows the footsteps of the classical Old Testament prophets in denouncing the wrongdoing of society. His main contribution is considering pride (Zephaniah 1:6; 2:10; 3:11) as the source of problems such as smugness (Zephaniah 1:12), rebellion (Zephaniah 3:2), and treachery (Zephaniah 3:11). All these attitudes toward God lead to idolatry and social sin. Although all people sin, Zephaniah points out that all leaders have a greater responsibility, and their sins will provoke a harsh judgment during the coming "day of the LORD" (Zephaniah 1:14). Only those who worship God humbly and who seek justice will be spared. Zephaniah calls them the remnant (Zephaniah 3:12-13), meaning "a little piece that is left over." They are the ones who will stay faithful to God through both good times and bad.

The book ends with a song of joy reassuring the people of Jerusalem that God still loves them and will save them in the end. We are not sure whether the song is from Zephaniah himself or is the addition of a later editor. It is as if the writer knows that when people are experiencing the negative results of sinful actions, they need to be reassured they are still loved. The purpose of God's punishment is to teach us, not to destroy us. Therefore, God's people should not despair, but keep their trust in God.

QUICK FACTS

- **Date Written:** Around 630 B.C.
- **Author:** Zephaniah, and perhaps a later editor
- **Themes:** The consequences of sin, and a call to humility before God

AT A GLANCE

- **Zephaniah 1** A warning about Judah's idolatry
- **Zephaniah 2:1–3:7** A discussion of the destruction of the nations and the corrupt nature of Jerusalem
- **Zephaniah 3:8–20** A message about the conversion of the nations and salvation for Jerusalem

1

The word of the Lord that came to Zephaniah son of Cushi son of Gedaliah son of Amariah son of Hezekiah, in the days of King Josiah son of Amon of Judah.

The Coming Judgment on Judah

2 I will utterly sweep away everything
  from the face of the earth, says the Lord.
3 I will sweep away humans and animals;
  I will sweep away the birds of the air
  and the fish of the sea.
  I will make the wicked stumble.[a]
  I will cut off humanity
  from the face of the earth, says the Lord.
4 I will stretch out my hand against Judah,
  and against all the inhabitants of
    Jerusalem;
  and I will cut off from this place every
    remnant of Baal
  and the name of the idolatrous priests;[b]
5 those who bow down on the roofs
  to the host of the heavens;
  those who bow down and swear to the Lord,
  but also swear by Milcom;[c]
6 those who have turned back from following
    the Lord,
  who have not sought the Lord or inquired
    of him.

7 Be silent before the Lord God!
  For the day of the Lord is at hand;
  the Lord has prepared a sacrifice,
  he has consecrated his guests.
8 And on the day of the Lord's sacrifice
  I will punish the officials and the king's sons
  and all who dress themselves in foreign
    attire.
9 On that day I will punish
  all who leap over the threshold,
  who fill their master's house
  with violence and fraud.

10 On that day, says the Lord,
  a cry will be heard from the
    Fish Gate,
  a wail from the Second Quarter,
  a loud crash from the hills.
11 The inhabitants of the Mortar wail,
  for all the traders have perished;
  all who weigh out silver are cut off.

12 At that time I will search Jerusalem with
    lamps,
  and I will punish the people
  who rest complacently[d] on their dregs,
  those who say in their hearts,
  "The Lord will not do good,
  nor will he do harm."
13 Their wealth shall be plundered,
  and their houses laid waste.
  Though they build houses,
  they shall not inhabit them;
  though they plant vineyards,
  they shall not drink wine from them.

The Great Day of the Lord

14 The great day of the Lord is near,
  near and hastening fast;
  the sound of the day of the Lord is bitter,
  the warrior cries aloud there.
15 That day will be a day of wrath,
  a day of distress and anguish,
  a day of ruin and devastation,
  a day of darkness and gloom,
  a day of clouds and thick darkness,
16 a day of trumpet blast and battle cry
  against the fortified cities
  and against the lofty battlements.

17 I will bring such distress upon people
  that they shall walk like the blind;
  because they have sinned against the
    Lord,
  their blood shall be poured out like dust,
  and their flesh like dung.
18 Neither their silver nor their gold
  will be able to save them
  on the day of the Lord's wrath;
  in the fire of his passion
  the whole earth shall be consumed;
  for a full, a terrible end
  he will make of all the inhabitants of the
    earth.

2

Judgment on Israel's Enemies

Gather together, gather,
  O shameless nation,
2 before you are driven away
  like the drifting chaff,[e]
  before there comes upon you
  the fierce anger of the Lord,

---

a Cn: Heb *sea, and those who cause the wicked to stumble*   b Compare Gk: Heb *the idolatrous priests with the priests*   c Gk Mss Syr Vg: Heb *Malcam* (or, *their king*)   d Heb *who thicken*   e Cn Compare Gk Syr: Heb *before a decree is born; like chaff a day has passed away*

before there comes upon you
   the day of the LORD's wrath.
3 Seek the LORD, all you humble of the land,
   who do his commands;
seek righteousness, seek humility;
   perhaps you may be hidden
   on the day of the LORD's wrath.
4 For Gaza shall be deserted,
   and Ashkelon shall become a desolation;
Ashdod's people shall be driven out at noon,
   and Ekron shall be uprooted.

5 Ah, inhabitants of the seacoast,
   you nation of the Cherethites!
The word of the LORD is against you,
   O Canaan, land of the Philistines;
   and I will destroy you until no inhabitant
    is left.
6 And you, O seacoast, shall be pastures,
   meadows for shepherds
   and folds for flocks.
7 The seacoast shall become the possession
   of the remnant of the house of Judah,
   on which they shall pasture,
and in the houses of Ashkelon
   they shall lie down at evening.
For the LORD their God will be mindful
   of them
   and restore their fortunes.

8 I have heard the taunts of Moab
   and the revilings of the Ammonites,
how they have taunted my people
   and made boasts against their territory.
9 Therefore, as I live, says the LORD of hosts,
   the God of Israel,
Moab shall become like Sodom
   and the Ammonites like Gomorrah,
a land possessed by nettles and salt pits,
   and a waste forever.
The remnant of my people shall plunder
   them,
   and the survivors of my nation shall
    possess them.
10 This shall be their lot in return for their pride,
   because they scoffed and boasted
   against the people of the LORD of hosts.
11 The LORD will be terrible against them;
   he will shrivel all the gods of the earth,
   and to him shall bow down,

each in its place,
   all the coasts and islands of the nations.
12 You also, O Ethiopians,[a]
   shall be killed by my sword.

13 And he will stretch out his hand against the
    north,
   and destroy Assyria;
and he will make Nineveh a desolation,
   a dry waste like the desert.

14 Herds shall lie down in it,
   every wild animal;[b]
the desert owl[c] and the screech owl[c]
   shall lodge on its capitals;
the owl[d] shall hoot at the window,
   the raven[e] croak on the threshold;
   for its cedar work will be laid bare.
15 Is this the exultant city
   that lived secure,
that said to itself,
   "I am, and there is no one else"?
What a desolation it has become,
   a lair for wild animals!
Everyone who passes by it
   hisses and shakes the fist.

The Wickedness of Jerusalem

 3 Ah, soiled, defiled,
   oppressing city!
2 It has listened to no voice;
   it has accepted no correction.
It has not trusted in the LORD;
   it has not drawn near to its God.

3 The officials within it
   are roaring lions;
   its judges are evening wolves

a Or *Nubians*; Heb *Cushites* b Tg Compare Gk: Heb *nation* c Meaning of Heb uncertain d Cn: Heb *a voice* e Gk Vg: Heb *desolation* that leave nothing until the morning.

4 Its prophets are reckless,
faithless persons;
its priests have profaned what is sacred,
they have done violence to the law.

5 The LORD within it is righteous;
he does no wrong.
Every morning he renders his
judgment,
each dawn without fail;
but the unjust knows no shame.

6 I have cut off nations;
their battlements are in ruins;
I have laid waste their streets
so that no one walks in them;
their cities have been made desolate,
without people, without inhabitants.

7 I said, "Surely the city[a] will fear me,
it will accept correction;
it will not lose sight[b]
of all that I have brought upon it."
But they were the more eager
to make all their deeds corrupt.

Punishment and Conversion of the Nations

8 Therefore wait for me, says the LORD,
for the day when I arise as a witness.
For my decision is to gather nations,
to assemble kingdoms,
to pour out upon them my
indignation,
all the heat of my anger;
for in the fire of my passion
all the earth shall be consumed.

9 At that time I will change the speech of the
peoples to a pure speech,
that all of them may call on the name of the
LORD
and serve him with one accord.

10 From beyond the rivers of Ethiopia[c]
my suppliants, my scattered ones,
shall bring my offering.

11 On that day you shall not be put to shame
because of all the deeds by which you
have rebelled against me;
for then I will remove from your midst
your proudly exultant ones,
and you shall no longer be haughty
in my holy mountain.

12 For I will leave in the midst of you
a people humble and lowly.
They shall seek refuge in the name of the
LORD—

13 the remnant of Israel;
they shall do no wrong
and utter no lies,
nor shall a deceitful tongue
be found in their mouths.
Then they will pasture and lie down,
and no one shall make them afraid.

A Song of Joy

14 Sing aloud, O daughter Zion;
shout, O Israel!
Rejoice and exult with all your heart,
O daughter Jerusalem!

15 The LORD has taken away the judgments
against you,

The Promise · Zephaniah 3:11–13

Reading the prophets can be wearisome. It's like hearing the same song on repeat mode. The people reject God and choose their own ways. The prophets deliver bad news—all will be destroyed because of what they've done. Will God's people ever learn? At the end of his book Zephaniah offers hope for a time when this cycle will end and the repeat button will be switched off. Through Zephaniah, God promises that the people will be restored. And in his words we see not only a promise to the people of his time, but to all people. The promise is Jesus. The Lord will live among the people (Zephaniah 3:15, 17), save the lame, gather the outcast (Zephaniah 3:19), and renew the people with love. There are dark days ahead, but there is a promise of light that gives hope.

a Heb it   b Gk Syr: Heb its dwelling will not be cut off   c Or Nubia; Heb Cush

he has turned away your enemies.
The king of Israel, the LORD, is in your
    midst;
    you shall fear disaster no more.
16 On that day it shall be said to Jerusalem:
Do not fear, O Zion;
    do not let your hands grow weak.
17 The LORD, your God, is in your midst,
    a warrior who gives victory;
he will rejoice over you with gladness,
    he will renew you[a] in his love;
he will exult over you with loud singing
18   as on a day of festival.[b]
I will remove disaster from you,[c]
    so that you will not bear reproach
        for it.
19 I will deal with all your oppressors
    at that time.
And I will save the lame

> "The LORD, your God,
> is in your midst ... he
> will rejoice over you
> with gladness, he will
> renew you in his love."
> —Zephaniah 3:17

and gather the outcast,
and I will change their shame into praise
    and renown in all the earth.
20 At that time I will bring you home,
    at the time when I gather you;
for I will make you renowned and praised
    among all the peoples of the earth,
when I restore your fortunes
    before your eyes, says the LORD.

a Gk Syr: Heb *he will be silent*   b Gk Syr: Meaning of Heb uncertain   c Cn: Heb *I will remove from you; they were*

Haggai

▶▶▶▶▶▶▶▶▶▶▶▶▶▶▶▶▶▶▶▶▶▶▶▶▶

Imagine your entire city has been destroyed by a natural disaster—a fire, earthquake, or hurricane. Everyone is picking up the pieces and pulling together everything they have to rebuild. Now here is the question: Which would you put your money and effort toward rebuilding first—your home or your church? The Jews at the time of the prophet Haggai faced this very decision. Returning to Jerusalem after the Babylonian exile, which would they rebuild first—their homes or God's temple?

IN DEPTH

When the people of ancient Judah lost their temple in 587 B.C. and were deported to a strange land, they experienced a crisis in faith. Had God abandoned them? Were they no longer God's people? Was God punishing them for their sins? Some of them dreamed of a time when they could return to their land and rebuild God's temple. However, when they finally were able to return in 538 B.C., things weren't as easy as they had hoped. Suffering from poverty, droughts, and crop failures (Haggai 1:10-11), they put off completing the rebuilding of the temple. Into this scene came the prophet Haggai. He told the people that God was still with them, but life was so difficult because they didn't seem to care that God's house was in ruins (Haggai 1:9). They had to get their priorities in order!

The people heard God's word spoken through Haggai and immediately began working on the temple. In their minds, they knew the new temple would never be as beautiful as the original one (Haggai 2:3). Haggai used this opportunity to prophesy about a future temple that would be filled with God's glory (Haggai 2:7), a time when God would again bless these people and make their offerings holy. God would establish Judah as a powerful nation, and Zerubbabel (a descendant of David) would be its anointed king.

QUICK FACTS

- **Date Written:** Around 520 B.C.
- **Author:** Haggai
- **Theme:** The need to keep serving God as first priority

AT A GLANCE

- **Haggai 1** A command to rebuild the temple
- **Haggai 2:1–19** A description of the future glory of God's temple and the future prosperity of God's people
- **Haggai 2:20–23** A message about the future nation of Judah and its king

The Command to Rebuild the Temple

1 In the second year of King Darius, in the sixth month, on the first day of the month, the word of the LORD came by the prophet Haggai to Zerubbabel son of Shealtiel, governor of Judah, and to Joshua son of Jehozadak, the high priest: ²Thus says the LORD of hosts: These people say the time has not yet come to rebuild the LORD's house. ³Then the word of the LORD came by the prophet Haggai, saying: ⁴Is it a time for you yourselves to live in your paneled houses, while this house lies in ruins? ⁵Now therefore thus says the LORD of hosts: Consider how you have fared. ⁶You have sown much, and harvested little; you eat, but you never have enough; you drink, but you never have your fill; you clothe yourselves, but no one is warm; and you that earn wages earn wages to put them into a bag with holes.

7 Thus says the LORD of hosts: Consider how you have fared. ⁸Go up to the hills and bring wood and build the house, so that I may take pleasure in it and be honored, says the LORD. ⁹You have looked for much, and, lo, it came to little; and when you brought it home, I blew it away. Why? says the LORD of hosts. Because my house lies in ruins, while all of you hurry off to your own houses. ¹⁰Therefore the heavens above you have withheld the dew, and the earth has withheld its produce. ¹¹And I have called for a drought on the land and the hills, on the grain, the new wine, the oil, on what the soil produces, on human beings and animals, and on all their labors. 12 Then Zerubbabel son of Shealtiel, and Joshua

son of Jehozadak, the high priest, with all the remnant of the people, obeyed the voice of the LORD their God, and the words of the prophet Haggai, as the LORD their God had sent him; and the people feared the LORD. ¹³Then Haggai, the messenger of the LORD, spoke to the people with the LORD's message, saying, I am with you, says the LORD. ¹⁴And the LORD stirred up the spirit of Zerubbabel son of Shealtiel, governor of Judah, and the spirit of Joshua son of Jehozadak, the high priest, and the spirit of all the remnant of the people; and they came and worked on the house of the LORD of hosts, their God, ¹⁵on the twenty-fourth day of the month, in the sixth month.

The Future Glory of the Temple

2 In the second year of King Darius, ¹in the seventh month, on the twenty-first day of the month, the word of the LORD came by the prophet Haggai, saying: ²Speak now to Zerubbabel son of Shealtiel, governor of Judah, and to Joshua son of Jehozadak, the high priest, and to the remnant of the people, and say, ³Who is left among you that saw this house in its former glory? How does it look to you now? Is it not in your sight as nothing? ⁴Yet now take courage, O Zerubbabel, says the LORD; take courage, O Joshua, son of Jehozadak, the high priest; take courage, all you people of the land, says the LORD; work, for I am with you, says the LORD of hosts, ⁵according to the promise that I made you when you came out of Egypt. My spirit abides among you; do not fear.

PRAY IT!

God at the Center · Haggai 1

The people of Haggai's time needed to get their priorities straight! They thought they didn't have enough wealth to rebuild the temple (Haggai 1:2), but God told them they were poor and unsuccessful because they had not rebuilt it (Haggai 1:9). They needed to trust that God would provide. When you think about it, we are a lot like the people of Haggai's time. We put our energy into living a life we think will fulfill us—nice clothes, the best club or sports team, fun times, and people to share it all with. Not bad things to want, but when we make these things our focus, we lose sight of God as our first priority. Jesus makes this clear to his disciples when he tells them, "Strive first for the kingdom of God and his righteousness, and all these things will be given to you as well" (Matthew 6:33). If you want to get your priorities in line with God's priorities, pray this prayer today:

God, help me to put you first in my life. Help me to seek you, trusting you for everything I need. Amen.

[6] For thus says the LORD of hosts: Once again, in a little while, I will shake the heavens and the earth and the sea and the dry land; [7] and I will shake all the nations, so that the treasure of all nations shall come, and I will fill this house with splendor, says the LORD of hosts. [8] The silver is mine, and the gold is mine, says the LORD of hosts. [9] The latter splendor of this house shall be greater than the former, says the LORD of hosts; and in this place I will give prosperity, says the LORD of hosts.

A Rebuke and a Promise

10 On the twenty-fourth day of the ninth month, in the second year of Darius, the word of the LORD came by the prophet Haggai, saying: [11] Thus says the LORD of hosts: Ask the priests for a ruling: [12] If one carries consecrated meat in the fold of one's garment, and with the fold touches bread, or stew, or wine, or oil, or any kind of food, does it become holy? The priests answered, "No." [13] Then Haggai said, "If one who is unclean by contact with a dead body touches any of these, does it become unclean?" The priests answered, "Yes, it becomes unclean." [14] Haggai then said, So is it with this people, and with this nation before me, says the LORD; and so with every work of their hands; and what they offer there is unclean. [15] But now, consider what will come to pass from this day on. Before a stone was placed upon a stone in the LORD's temple, [16] how did you fare?[a] When one came to a heap of twenty measures, there were but ten; when one came to the wine vat to draw fifty measures, there were but twenty. [17] I struck you and all the products of your toil with blight and mildew and hail; yet you did not return to me, says the LORD. [18] Consider from this day on, from the twenty-fourth day of the ninth month. Since the day that the foundation of the LORD's temple was laid, consider: [19] Is there any seed left in the barn? Do the vine, the fig tree, the pomegranate, and the olive tree still yield nothing? From this day on I will bless you.

God's Promise to Zerubbabel

20 The word of the LORD came a second time to Haggai on the twenty-fourth day of the month: [21] Speak to Zerubbabel, governor of Judah, saying, I am about to shake the heavens and the earth, [22] and to overthrow the throne of kingdoms; I am about to destroy the strength of the kingdoms of the nations, and overthrow the chariots and their riders; and the horses and their riders shall fall, every one by the sword of a comrade. [23] On that day, says the LORD of hosts, I will take you, O Zerubbabel my servant, son of Shealtiel, says the LORD, and make you like a signet ring; for I have chosen you, says the LORD of hosts.

a Gk: Heb *since they were*

▷▷▷▷▷▷▷▷▷▷▷ Zechariah

What do you do when life is difficult and things seem to just be getting worse? Some people dream about the future; they imagine a time when all their troubles have ended and life is happy again. If their trouble is caused by certain people, they may imagine how these people will eventually pay for their wrongdoing. The book of Zechariah looks at Israel's future in both these ways.

IN DEPTH

Like the book of Isaiah, the book of Zechariah was written by at least two prophets. The original Zechariah—we'll call him First Zechariah—lived around the same time as Haggai, after the exiled Israelites returned to Jerusalem from Babylon. Second Zechariah, who may have been one or more prophets, wrote about two hundred years later.

The optimistic message of First Zechariah (chapters 1–8) is centered on two concerns: the rebuilding of the temple and the end of time. First Zechariah saw that a rebuilt temple was needed to restore the people's unity, identity, and relationship with God. Through a series of visions, he announced his message: under the guidance of the priest Joshua and the prince Zerubbabel (a descendant of King David) Israel would be restored. It would become a nation of justice, faith, love, mercy, and truth, where the Lord would dwell. Even the Gentiles (non-Jews) would come from faraway lands to worship God.

Second Zechariah (chapters 9–14) wrote later, when Israel was under Greek domination. He preached not through visions, but through oracles (prophetic speeches) of warning, violence, and also promise. He talked about a great battle that was about to take place between the forces of good and the forces of evil. This was the final war, which would bring an end to the present-day evil and corrupt world. But Second Zechariah also proclaimed the coming of a humble king who would bring peace to all nations. Jerusalem would be purified and become victorious as the city where God reigns as the highest power for good.

QUICK FACTS

- **Date Written:** First Zechariah, around 520 B.C.; Second Zechariah, sometime after 333 B.C.
- **Authors:** The original Zechariah, and an unknown prophet or prophets writing much later
- **Themes:** The call to stay faithful to God; the promise of God's ultimate, final victory
- **Noteworthy:** The prophecies of Zechariah are quoted in the New Testament, because they were understood by the early Church to have been fulfilled in Jesus Christ.

AT A GLANCE

- **Zechariah 1–6** Zechariah's visions
- **Zechariah 7–8** A discussion of fasting and God's promises
- **Zechariah 9–10** A description of the King of Peace and the evil shepherds of Judah
- **Zechariah 11–14** A message about the day of God's judgment and the final war

Israel Urged to Repent

1 In the eighth month, in the second year of Darius, the word of the Lord came to the prophet Zechariah son of Berechiah son of Iddo, saying: ²The Lord was very angry with your ancestors. ³Therefore say to them, Thus says the Lord of hosts: Return to me, says the Lord of hosts, and I will return to you, says the Lord of hosts. ⁴Do not be like your ancestors, to whom the former prophets proclaimed, "Thus says the Lord of hosts, Return from your evil ways and from your evil deeds." But they did not hear or heed me, says the Lord. ⁵Your ancestors, where are they? And the prophets, do they live forever? ⁶But my words and my statutes, which I commanded my servants the prophets, did they not overtake your ancestors? So they repented and said, "The Lord of hosts has dealt with us according to our ways and deeds, just as he planned to do."

> "Return to me, says the Lord of hosts, and I will return to you."
> —Zechariah 1:3

First Vision: The Horsemen

7 On the twenty-fourth day of the eleventh month, the month of Shebat, in the second year of Darius, the word of the Lord came to the prophet Zechariah son of Berechiah son of Iddo; and Zechariah[a] said, ⁸In the night I saw a man riding on a red horse! He was standing among the myrtle trees in the glen; and behind him were red, sorrel, and white horses. ⁹Then I said, "What are these, my lord?" The angel who talked with me said to me, "I will show you what they are." ¹⁰So the man who was standing among the myrtle trees answered, "They are those whom the Lord has sent to patrol the earth." ¹¹Then they spoke to the angel of the Lord who was standing among the myrtle trees, "We have patrolled the earth, and lo, the whole earth remains at peace." ¹²Then the angel of the Lord said, "O Lord of hosts, how long will you withhold mercy from Jerusalem and the cities of Judah, with which you have been angry these seventy years?" ¹³Then the Lord replied with gracious and comforting words to the angel who talked with me. ¹⁴So the angel who talked with me said to me, Proclaim this message: Thus says the Lord of hosts; I am very jealous for Jerusalem and for Zion. ¹⁵And I am extremely angry with the nations that are at ease; for while I was only a little angry, they made the disaster worse. ¹⁶Therefore, thus says the Lord, I have returned to Jerusalem with compassion; my house shall be built in it, says the Lord of hosts, and the measuring line shall be stretched out over Jerusalem. ¹⁷Proclaim further: Thus says the Lord of hosts: My cities shall again overflow with prosperity; the Lord will again comfort Zion and again choose Jerusalem.

Second Vision: The Horns and the Smiths

18[b] And I looked up and saw four horns. ¹⁹I asked the angel who talked with me, "What are these?" And he answered me, "These are the horns that have scattered Judah, Israel, and Jerusalem." ²⁰Then the Lord showed me four blacksmiths. ²¹And I asked, "What are they coming to do?" He answered, "These are the horns that scattered Judah, so that no head could be raised; but these have come to terrify them, to strike down the horns of the nations that lifted up their horns against the land of Judah to scatter its people."[c]

STUDY IT!

Night Visions
Zechariah 1:7–6:8

There are a lot of crazy images in the night visions of Zechariah. Even with their explanations, it is hard to interpret the meaning of the things Zechariah saw. The most important thing is to remember that the purpose of all the visions is to bring God's people back. God, through Zechariah, says, "Return to me, . . . and I will return to you, says the Lord" (Zechariah 1:3). The prophecies of old have come true, and now Zechariah points to a hopeful future when the people humbly repent and return to rebuild the temple and a peaceful kingdom.

a Heb *and he* b Ch 2.1 in Heb c Heb *it*

2

Third Vision: The Man with a Measuring Line

[a] I looked up and saw a man with a measuring line in his hand. [2]Then I asked, "Where are you going?" He answered me, "To measure Jerusalem, to see what is its width and what is its length." [3]Then the angel who talked with me came forward, and another angel came forward to meet him, [4]and said to him, "Run, say to that young man: Jerusalem shall be inhabited like villages without walls, because of the multitude of people and animals in it. [5]For I will be a wall of fire all around it, says the LORD, and I will be the glory within it."

Interlude: An Appeal to the Exiles

6 Up, up! Flee from the land of the north, says the LORD; for I have spread you abroad like the four winds of heaven, says the LORD. [7]Up! Escape to Zion, you that live with daughter Babylon. [8]For thus said the LORD of hosts (after his glory[b] sent me) regarding the nations that plundered you: Truly, one who touches you touches the apple of my eye.[c] [9]See now, I am going to raise[d] my hand against them, and they shall become plunder for their own slaves. Then you will know that the LORD of hosts has sent me. [10]Sing and rejoice, O daughter Zion! For lo, I will come and dwell in your midst, says the LORD. [11]Many nations shall join themselves to the LORD on that day, and shall be my people; and I will dwell in your midst. And you shall know that the LORD of hosts has sent me to you. [12]The LORD will inherit Judah as his portion in the holy land, and will again choose Jerusalem.

13 Be silent, all people, before the LORD; for he has roused himself from his holy dwelling.

3

Fourth Vision: Joshua and Satan

Then he showed me the high priest Joshua standing before the angel of the LORD, and Satan[e] standing at his right hand to accuse him. [2]And the LORD said to Satan,[e] "The LORD rebuke you, O Satan![e] The LORD who has chosen Jerusalem rebuke you! Is not this man a brand plucked from the fire?" [3]Now Joshua was dressed with filthy clothes as he stood before the angel. [4]The angel said to those who were standing before him, "Take off his filthy clothes." And to him he said, "See, I have taken your guilt away from you, and I will clothe you with festal apparel." [5]And I said, "Let them put a clean turban on his head." So they put a clean turban on

his head and clothed him with the apparel; and the angel of the LORD was standing by.

6 Then the angel of the LORD assured Joshua, saying [7]"Thus says the LORD of hosts: If you will walk in my ways and keep my requirements, then you shall rule my house and have charge of my courts, and I will give you the right of access among those who are standing here. [8]Now listen, Joshua, high priest, you and your colleagues who sit before you! For they are an omen of things to come: I am going to bring my servant the Branch. [9]For on the stone that I have set before Joshua, on a single stone with seven facets, I will engrave its inscription, says the LORD of hosts, and I will remove the guilt of this land in a single day. [10]On that day, says the LORD of hosts, you shall invite each other to come under your vine and fig tree."

4

Fifth Vision: The Lampstand and Olive Trees

The angel who talked with me came again, and wakened me, as one is wakened from sleep. [2]He said to me, "What do you see?" And I said, "I see a lampstand all of gold, with a bowl on the top of it; there are seven lamps on it, with seven lips on each of the lamps that are on the top of it. [3]And by it there are two olive trees, one on the right of the bowl and the other on its left." [4]I said to the angel who talked with me, "What are these, my lord?" [5]Then the angel who talked with me answered me, "Do you not know what these are?" I said, "No, my lord." [6]He said to me, "This is the word of the LORD to Zerubbabel: Not by might, nor by power, but by my spirit, says the LORD of hosts. [7]What are you, O great mountain? Before Zerubbabel you shall become a plain; and he shall bring out the top stone amid shouts of 'Grace, grace to it!' "

8 Moreover the word of the LORD came to me, saying, [9]"The hands of Zerubbabel have laid the foundation of this house; his hands shall also complete it. Then you will know that the LORD of hosts has sent me to you. [10]For whoever has despised the day of small things shall rejoice, and shall see the plummet in the hand of Zerubbabel.

"These seven are the eyes of the LORD, which range through the whole earth." [11]Then I said to him, "What are these two olive trees on the right and the left of the lampstand?" [12]And a second time I said to him, "What are these two branches of the olive trees, which pour out the oil[f] through the two golden

---

a Ch 2.5 in Heb **b** Cn: Heb *after glory he* **c** Heb *his eye* **d** Or *wave* **e** Or *the Accuser;* Heb *the Adversary* **f** Cn: Heb *gold*

pipes?" [13]He said to me, "Do you not know what these are?" I said, "No, my lord." [14]Then he said, "These are the two anointed ones who stand by the Lord of the whole earth."

Sixth Vision: The Flying Scroll

5 Again I looked up and saw a flying scroll. [2]And he said to me, "What do you see?" I answered, "I see a flying scroll; its length is twenty cubits, and its width ten cubits." [3]Then he said to me, "This is the curse that goes out over the face of the whole land; for everyone who steals shall be cut off according to the writing on one side, and everyone who swears falsely[a] shall be cut off according to the writing on the other side. [4]I have sent it out, says the LORD of hosts, and it shall enter the house of the thief, and the house of anyone who swears falsely by my name; and it shall abide in that house and consume it, both timber and stones."

Seventh Vision: The Woman in a Basket

5 Then the angel who talked with me came forward and said to me, "Look up and see what this is that is coming out." [6]I said, "What is it?" He said, "This is a basket[b] coming out." And he said, "This is their iniquity[c] in all the land." [7]Then a leaden cover was lifted, and there was a woman sitting in the basket! [b] [8]And he said, "This is Wickedness." So he thrust her back into the basket,[b] and pressed the leaden weight down on its mouth. [9]Then I looked up and saw two women coming forward. The wind was in their wings; they had wings like the wings of a stork, and they lifted up the basket[b] between earth and sky. [10]Then I said to the angel who talked with me, "Where are they taking the basket?"[b] [11]He said to me, "To the land of Shinar, to build a house for it; and when this is prepared, they will set the basket[b] down there on its base."

Eighth Vision: Four Chariots

6 And again I looked up and saw four chariots coming out from between two moun-

tains—mountains of bronze. [2]The first chariot had red horses, the second chariot black horses, [3]the third chariot white horses, and the fourth chariot dappled gray[d] horses. [4]Then I said to the angel who talked with me, "What are these, my lord?" [5]The angel answered me, "These are the four winds[e] of heaven going out, after presenting themselves before the Lord of all the earth. [6]The chariot with the black horses goes toward the north country, the white ones go toward the west country,[f] and the dappled ones go toward the south country." [7]When the steeds came out, they were impatient to get off and patrol the earth. And he said, "Go, patrol the earth." So they patrolled the earth. [8]Then he cried out to me, "Lo, those who go toward the north country have set my spirit at rest in the north country."

The Coronation of the Branch

9 The word of the LORD came to me: [10]Collect silver and gold[g] from the exiles—from Heldai, Tobijah, and Jedaiah—who have arrived from Babylon; and go the same day to the house of Josiah son of Zephaniah. [11]Take the silver and gold and make a crown,[h] and set it on the head of the high priest Joshua son of Jehozadak; [12]say to him: Thus says the LORD of hosts: Here is a man whose name is Branch: for he shall branch out in his place, and he shall build the temple of the LORD. [13]It is he that shall build the temple of the LORD; he shall bear royal honor, and shall sit upon his throne and rule. There shall be a priest by his throne, with peaceful understanding between the two of them. [14]And the crown[i] shall be in the care of Heldai,[j] Tobijah, Jedaiah, and Josiah[k] son of Zephaniah, as a memorial in the temple of the LORD.

15 Those who are far off shall come and help to build the temple of the LORD; and you shall know that the LORD of hosts has sent me to you. This will happen if you diligently obey the voice of the LORD your God.

Hypocritical Fasting Condemned

7 In the fourth year of King Darius, the word of the LORD came to Zechariah on the fourth day of the ninth month, which is Chislev. [2]Now the people of Bethel had sent Sharezer and Regem-melech and their men, to entreat the favor of the LORD, [3]and to ask the priests of the house of the LORD of hosts and the prophets, "Should I mourn and practice abstinence in the fifth month,

---

a The word *falsely* added from verse 4   b Heb *ephah*   c Gk Compare Syr: Heb *their eye*   d Compare Gk: Meaning of Heb uncertain   e Or *spirits*
f Cn: Heb *go after them*   g Cn Compare verse 11: Heb lacks *silver and gold*   h Gk Mss Syr Tg: Heb *crowns*   i Gk Syr: Heb *crowns*   j Syr Compare verse
10: Heb *Helem*   k Syr Compare verse 10: Heb *Hen*

as I have done for so many years?" ⁴Then the word of the LORD of hosts came to me: ⁵Say to all the people of the land and the priests: When you fasted and lamented in the fifth month and in the seventh, for these seventy years, was it for me that you fasted? ⁶And when you eat and when you drink, do you not eat and drink only for yourselves? ⁷Were not these the words that the LORD proclaimed by the former prophets, when Jerusalem was inhabited and in prosperity, along with the towns around it, and when the Negeb and the Shephelah were inhabited?

Punishment for Rejecting God's Demands

8 The word of the LORD came to Zechariah, saying: ⁹Thus says the LORD of hosts: Render true judgments, show kindness and mercy to one another; ¹⁰do not oppress the widow, the orphan, the alien, or the poor; and do not devise evil in your hearts against one another. ¹¹But they refused to listen, and turned a stubborn shoulder, and stopped their ears in order not to hear. ¹²They made their hearts adamant in order not to hear the law and the words that the LORD of hosts had sent by his spirit through the former prophets. Therefore great wrath came from the LORD of hosts. ¹³Just as, when I *ᵃ* called, they would not hear, so, when they called, I would not hear, says the LORD of hosts, ¹⁴and I scattered them with a whirlwind among all the nations that they had not known. Thus the land they left was desolate, so that no one went to and fro, and a pleasant land was made desolate.

God's Promises to Zion

8 The word of the LORD of hosts came to me, saying: ²Thus says the LORD of hosts: I am jealous for Zion with great jealousy, and I am jealous for her with great wrath. ³Thus says the LORD: I will return to Zion, and will dwell in the midst of Jerusalem; Jerusalem shall be called the faithful city, and the mountain of the LORD of hosts shall be called the holy mountain. ⁴Thus says the LORD of hosts: Old men and old women shall again sit in the streets of Jerusalem, each with staff in hand because of their great age. ⁵And the streets of the city shall be full of boys and girls playing in its streets. ⁶Thus says the LORD of hosts: Even though it seems impossible to the remnant of this people in these days, should it also seem impossible to me, says the LORD of hosts? ⁷Thus says the LORD of hosts: I will save my people from the east country and from the west country; ⁸and I will bring them to live in Jerusalem. They shall be my people and I will be their God, in faithfulness and in righteousness.

9 Thus says the LORD of hosts: Let your hands be strong—you that have recently been hearing these words from the mouths of the prophets who were present when the foundation was laid for the rebuilding of the temple, the house of the LORD of hosts. ¹⁰For before those days there were no wages for people or for animals, nor was there any safety from the foe for those who went out or came in, and I set them all against one another. ¹¹But now I will not deal with the remnant of this people as in the former days, says the LORD of hosts. ¹²For there shall be a sowing

The Same Message · Zechariah 7:1–10

In case you missed it in the other prophets, Zechariah once again spells out what God wants of the people. The Israelites wanted to know if they should continue performing the rituals they had done for many years (Zechariah 7:3). The response is the same one given to their ancestors—live out justice, mercy, and kindness; do not oppress widows, orphans, foreigners, and the poor (Zechariah 7:9-10).

The message is clear and simple, but obviously hard to live out. Because the people's ancestors didn't live according to this message, God was angry with them and scattered them (Zechariah 7:11-13). Both the repetition of this message and the punishment for not obeying should get our attention. Are we living out this message of justice today? Take time to journal your response and pray this prayer:

God, you have made your desires clear. Help me to know how to live out justice, kindness, and mercy every day. And give me the courage to love others, especially those in need.

ᵃ Heb *he*

Stay Strong
Zechariah 8:9–17

"Let your hands be strong." God, through Zechariah, gives this command to the people of Israel twice (Zechariah 8:9, 13). The Israelites had a job to do, but discouragement was getting in the way. Rebuilding the temple wasn't an easy job, but God tells the people to stay strong and keep working. And with the instruction comes a promise of peace, hope, and better times (Zechariah 8:11-13).

- What task do you need to finish? A school assignment? Helping your parents with a project at home? Volunteering at a local ministry?
- How has discouragement slowed you down?
- Commit to finishing well and following God's instruction to let your hands be strong.

of peace; the vine shall yield its fruit, the ground shall give its produce, and the skies shall give their dew; and I will cause the remnant of this people to possess all these things. ¹³ Just as you have been a cursing among the nations, O house of Judah and house of Israel, so I will save you and you shall be a blessing. Do not be afraid, but let your hands be strong.

14 For thus says the LORD of hosts: Just as I purposed to bring disaster upon you, when your ancestors provoked me to wrath, and I did not relent, says the LORD of hosts, ¹⁵ so again I have purposed in these days to do good to Jerusalem and to the house of Judah; do not be afraid. ¹⁶ These are the things that you shall do: Speak the truth to one another, render in your gates judgments that are true and make for peace, ¹⁷ do not devise evil in your hearts against one another, and love no false oath; for all these are things that I hate, says the LORD.

Joyful Fasting

18 The word of the LORD of hosts came to me, saying: ¹⁹ Thus says the LORD of hosts: The fast of the fourth month, and the fast of the fifth, and the fast of the seventh, and the fast of the tenth, shall be seasons of joy and gladness, and cheerful festivals for the house of Judah: therefore love truth and peace.

Many Peoples Drawn to Jerusalem

20 Thus says the LORD of hosts: Peoples shall yet come, the inhabitants of many cities; ²¹ the inhabitants of one city shall go to another, saying, "Come, let us go to entreat the favor of the LORD, and to seek the LORD of hosts; I myself am going." ²² Many peoples and strong nations shall come to seek the LORD of hosts in Jerusalem, and to entreat the favor of the LORD. ²³ Thus says the LORD of hosts: In those days ten men from nations of every language shall take hold of a Jew, grasping his garment and saying, "Let us go with you, for we have heard that God is with you."

Judgment on Israel's Enemies
An Oracle.

The word of the LORD is against the land of Hadrach
　　and will rest upon Damascus.
For to the LORD belongs the capital*ᵃ* of Aram,*ᵇ*
　　as do all the tribes of Israel;
2　Hamath also, which borders on it,
　　Tyre and Sidon, though they are very wise.
3　Tyre has built itself a rampart,
　　and heaped up silver like dust,
　　and gold like the dirt of the streets.
4　But now, the Lord will strip it of its possessions
　　and hurl its wealth into the sea,
　　and it shall be devoured by fire.

5　Ashkelon shall see it and be afraid;
　　Gaza too, and shall writhe in anguish;
　　Ekron also, because its hopes are withered.
　　The king shall perish from Gaza;
　　Ashkelon shall be uninhabited;
6　a mongrel people shall settle in Ashdod,
　　and I will make an end of the pride of
　　　Philistia.
7　I will take away its blood from its mouth,
　　and its abominations from between its
　　　teeth;
　　it too shall be a remnant for our God;
　　it shall be like a clan in Judah,
　　and Ekron shall be like the Jebusites.

ᵃ Heb *eye*　ᵇ Cn: Heb *of Adam* (or *of humankind*)

8 Then I will encamp at my house as a guard,
    so that no one shall march to and fro;
no oppressor shall again overrun them,
    for now I have seen with my own eyes.

The Coming Ruler of God's People

9 Rejoice greatly, O daughter Zion!
    Shout aloud, O daughter Jerusalem!
Lo, your king comes to you;
    triumphant and victorious is he,
humble and riding on a donkey,
    on a colt, the foal of a donkey.
10 He[a] will cut off the chariot from Ephraim
    and the war-horse from Jerusalem;
and the battle bow shall be cut off,
    and he shall command peace to the nations;
his dominion shall be from sea to sea,
    and from the River to the ends of the earth.

11 As for you also, because of the blood of my
      covenant with you,
    I will set your prisoners free from the
      waterless pit.
12 Return to your stronghold, O prisoners of
      hope;
    today I declare that I will restore to you
      double.
13 For I have bent Judah as my bow;
    I have made Ephraim its arrow.
I will arouse your sons, O Zion,
    against your sons, O Greece,
    and wield you like a warrior's sword.

14 Then the Lord will appear over them,
    and his arrow go forth like lightning;
the Lord God will sound the trumpet
    and march forth in the whirlwinds of the
      south.
15 The Lord of hosts will protect them,
    and they shall devour and tread down the
      slingers;[b]
they shall drink their blood[c] like wine,
    and be full like a bowl,
    drenched like the corners of the altar.

16 On that day the Lord their God will save them
    for they are the flock of his people;
for like the jewels of a crown
    they shall shine on his land.
17 For what goodness and beauty are his!

Grain shall make the young men flourish,
    and new wine the young women.

Restoration of Judah and Israel

10 Ask rain from the Lord
    in the season of the spring rain,
from the Lord who makes the storm clouds,
    who gives showers of rain to you,[d]
    the vegetation in the field to everyone.
2 For the teraphim[e] utter nonsense,
    and the diviners see lies;
the dreamers tell false dreams,
    and give empty consolation.
Therefore the people wander like sheep;
    they suffer for lack of a shepherd.

3 My anger is hot against the shepherds,
    and I will punish the leaders;[f]
for the Lord of hosts cares for his flock, the
      house of Judah,
    and will make them like his proud
      war-horse.
4 Out of them shall come the cornerstone,
    out of them the tent peg,
out of them the battle bow,
    out of them every commander.
5 Together they shall be like warriors in battle,
    trampling the foe in the mud of the
      streets;
they shall fight, for the Lord is with them,
    and they shall put to shame the riders on
      horses.

6 I will strengthen the house of Judah,
    and I will save the house of Joseph.
I will bring them back because I have
      compassion on them,
    and they shall be as though I had not
      rejected them;
for I am the Lord their God and I will
      answer them.
7 Then the people of Ephraim shall become like
      warriors,
    and their hearts shall be glad as with wine.
Their children shall see it and rejoice,
    their hearts shall exult in the Lord.

8 I will signal for them and gather
      them in,
    for I have redeemed them,

---

a Gk: Heb I   b Cn: Heb the slingstones   c Gk: Heb shall drink   d Heb them   e Or household gods   f Or male goats

and they shall be as numerous as they were
  before.
9 Though I scattered them among the nations,
  yet in far countries they shall
     remember me,
  and they shall rear their children and
     return.
10 I will bring them home from the land of Egypt,
  and gather them from Assyria;
  I will bring them to the land of Gilead and to
     Lebanon,
  until there is no room for them.
11 They[a] shall pass through the sea of distress,
  and the waves of the sea shall be struck
     down,
  and all the depths of the Nile dried up.
  The pride of Assyria shall be laid low,
  and the scepter of Egypt shall depart.
12 I will make them strong in the LORD,
  and they shall walk in his name,
                          says the LORD.

11 Open your doors, O Lebanon,
  so that fire may devour your cedars!
2 Wail, O cypress, for the cedar has fallen,
  for the glorious trees are ruined!
Wail, oaks of Bashan,
  for the thick forest has been felled!
3 Listen, the wail of the shepherds,
  for their glory is despoiled!
Listen, the roar of the lions,
  for the thickets of the Jordan are destroyed!

Two Kinds of Shepherds

4 Thus said the LORD my God: Be a shepherd of
the flock doomed to slaughter. 5 Those who buy them
kill them and go unpunished; and those who sell
them say, "Blessed be the LORD, for I have become
rich"; and their own shepherds have no pity on them.
6 For I will no longer have pity on the inhabitants of
the earth, says the LORD. I will cause them, every
one, to fall each into the hand of a neighbor, and each
into the hand of the king; and they shall devastate
the earth, and I will deliver no one from their hand.

7 So, on behalf of the sheep merchants, I became
the shepherd of the flock doomed to slaughter. I took
two staffs; one I named Favor, the other I named
Unity, and I tended the sheep. 8 In one month I
disposed of the three shepherds, for I had become
impatient with them, and they also detested me. 9 So

I said, "I will not be your shepherd. What is to die,
let it die; what is to be destroyed, let it be destroyed;
and let those that are left devour the flesh of one
another!" 10 I took my staff Favor and broke it, annulling the covenant that I had made with all the
peoples. 11 So it was annulled on that day, and the
sheep merchants, who were watching me, knew that
it was the word of the LORD. 12 I then said to them,
"If it seems right to you, give me my wages; but if
not, keep them." So they weighed out as my wages
thirty shekels of silver. 13 Then the LORD said to me,
"Throw it into the treasury"[b]—this lordly price at
which I was valued by them. So I took the thirty
shekels of silver and threw them into the treasury[b]
in the house of the LORD. 14 Then I broke my second
staff Unity, annulling the family ties between Judah
and Israel.

15 Then the LORD said to me: Take once more
the implements of a worthless shepherd. 16 For I am
now raising up in the land a shepherd who does not
care for the perishing, or seek the wandering,[c] or
heal the maimed, or nourish the healthy,[d] but devours the flesh of the fat ones, tearing off even their
hoofs.
17 Oh, my worthless shepherd,
  who deserts the flock!
May the sword strike his arm
  and his right eye!
Let his arm be completely withered,
  his right eye utterly blinded!

Jerusalem's Victory
An Oracle.

12 The word of the LORD concerning Israel: Thus says
the LORD, who stretched out the heavens and
founded the earth and formed the human spirit
within: 2 See, I am about to make Jerusalem a cup of
reeling for all the surrounding peoples; it will be
against Judah also in the siege against Jerusalem. 3 On
that day I will make Jerusalem a heavy stone for all
the peoples; all who lift it shall grievously hurt themselves. And all the nations of the earth shall come
together against it. 4 On that day, says the LORD, I
will strike every horse with panic, and its rider with
madness. But on the house of Judah I will keep a
watchful eye, when I strike every horse of the peoples
with blindness. 5 Then the clans of Judah shall say to
themselves, "The inhabitants of Jerusalem have
strength through the LORD of hosts, their God."

a Gk: Heb *He*   b Syr: Heb *it to the potter*   c Syr Compare Gk Vg: Heb *the youth*   d Meaning of Heb uncertain

STUDY IT!

The Jesus Connection Zechariah 12–14

Take a look at how the promise of Jesus permeates Zechariah. Chapters 12-14 in particular contain several prophecies on the final judgment, the restoration of Israel, and the reign of God. The first Christians saw Jesus as the fulfillment of many of these prophecies.

For example, Zechariah foretells a time of mourning for "one whom they have pierced" (Zechariah 12:10); the gospel of John applies this verse to Jesus' death on the cross (John 19:37). Zechariah says the sheep will be dispersed when the shepherd is struck (Zechariah 13:7); the gospel of Matthew uses this verse to describe the disciples' deserting Jesus (Matthew 26:31). And passages from Zechariah's description of the "day of the LORD" (Zechariah 14:6-9) show up in the book of Revelation's description of the new Jerusalem at Jesus' second coming (Revelation 11:15; 21:23).

These beautiful prophecies assured Israel's people of God's love and mercy. For Christians, they have additional meaning. They also describe Jesus Christ, whose death is our salvation and whose resurrection is the promise of the fullness of the kingdom of God.

6 On that day I will make the clans of Judah like a blazing pot on a pile of wood, like a flaming torch among sheaves; and they shall devour to the right and to the left all the surrounding peoples, while Jerusalem shall again be inhabited in its place, in Jerusalem.

7 And the LORD will give victory to the tents of Judah first, that the glory of the house of David and the glory of the inhabitants of Jerusalem may not be exalted over that of Judah. [8] On that day the LORD will shield the inhabitants of Jerusalem so that the feeblest among them on that day shall be like David, and the house of David shall be like God, like the angel of the LORD, at their head. [9] And on that day I will seek to destroy all the nations that come against Jerusalem.

Mourning for the Pierced One

10 And I will pour out a spirit of compassion and supplication on the house of David and the inhabitants of Jerusalem, so that, when they look on the one[a] whom they have pierced, they shall mourn for him, as one mourns for an only child, and weep bitterly over him, as one weeps over a firstborn. [11] On that day the mourning in Jerusalem will be as great as the mourning for Hadad-rimmon in the plain of Megiddo. [12] The land shall mourn, each family by itself; the family of the house of David by itself, and their wives by themselves; the family of the house of Nathan by itself, and their wives by themselves; [13] the family of the house of Levi by itself, and their wives by themselves; the family of the Shimeites by itself, and their wives by themselves; [14] and all the families that are left, each by itself, and their wives by themselves.

13 On that day a fountain shall be opened for the house of David and the inhabitants of Jerusalem, to cleanse them from sin and impurity.

Idolatry Cut Off

2 On that day, says the LORD of hosts, I will cut off the names of the idols from the land, so that they shall be remembered no more; and also I will remove from the land the prophets and the unclean spirit. [3] And if any prophets appear again, their fathers and mothers who bore them will say to them, "You shall not live, for you speak lies in the name of the LORD"; and their fathers and their mothers who bore them shall pierce them through when they prophesy. [4] On that day the prophets will be ashamed, every one, of their visions when they prophesy; they will not put on a hairy mantle in order to deceive, [5] but each of them will say, "I am no prophet, I am a tiller of the soil; for the land has been my possession[b] since my youth." [6] And if anyone asks them, "What are these wounds on your chest?"[c] the answer will be "The wounds I received in the house of my friends."

a Heb *on me* b Cn: Heb *for humankind has caused me to possess* c Heb *wounds between your hands*

The Shepherd Struck, the Flock Scattered

7 "Awake, O sword, against my shepherd,
　　against the man who is my associate,"
　　　　　　　　says the LORD of hosts.
　Strike the shepherd, that the sheep may be
　　scattered;
　I will turn my hand against the little ones.
8 In the whole land, says the LORD,
　　two-thirds shall be cut off and perish,
　　and one-third shall be left alive.
9 And I will put this third into the fire,
　　refine them as one refines silver,
　　and test them as gold is tested.
　They will call on my name,
　　and I will answer them.
　I will say, "They are my people";
　　and they will say, "The LORD is our God."

Future Warfare and Final Victory

14 See, a day is coming for the LORD, when the plunder taken from you will be divided in your midst. ²For I will gather all the nations against Jerusalem to battle, and the city shall be taken and the houses looted and the women raped; half the city shall go into exile, but the rest of the people shall not be cut off from the city. ³Then the LORD will go forth and fight against those nations as when he fights on a day of battle. ⁴On that day his feet shall stand on the Mount of Olives, which lies before Jerusalem on the east; and the Mount of Olives shall be split in two from east to west by a very wide valley; so that one half of the Mount shall withdraw northward, and the other half southward. ⁵And you shall flee by the valley of the LORD's mountain,ᵃ for the valley between the mountains shall reach to Azal;ᵇ and you shall flee as you fled from the earthquake in the days of King Uzziah of Judah. Then the LORD my God will come, and all the holy ones with him.

6 On that day there shall not beᶜ either cold or frost.ᵈ ⁷And there shall be continuous day (it is known to the LORD), not day and not night, for at evening time there shall be light.

8 On that day living waters shall flow out from Jerusalem, half of them to the eastern sea and half of them to the western sea; it shall continue in summer as in winter.

9 And the LORD will become king over all the earth; on that day the LORD will be one and his name one.

10 The whole land shall be turned into a plain from Geba to Rimmon south of Jerusalem. But Jerusalem shall remain aloft on its site from the Gate of Benjamin to the place of the former gate, to the Corner Gate, and from the Tower of Hananel to the king's wine presses. ¹¹And it shall be inhabited, for never again shall it be doomed to destruction; Jerusalem shall abide in security.

12 This shall be the plague with which the LORD will strike all the peoples that wage war against Jerusalem: their flesh shall rot while they are still on their feet; their eyes shall rot in their sockets, and their tongues shall rot in their mouths. ¹³On that day a great panic from the LORD shall fall on them, so that each will seize the hand of a neighbor, and the hand of the one will be raised against the hand of the other; ¹⁴even Judah will fight at Jerusalem. And the wealth of all the surrounding nations shall be collected—gold, silver, and garments in great abundance. ¹⁵And a plague like this plague shall fall on the horses, the mules, the camels, the donkeys, and whatever animals may be in those camps.

16 Then all who survive of the nations that have come against Jerusalem shall go up year after year to worship the King, the LORD of hosts, and to keep the festival of booths.ᵉ ¹⁷If any of the families of the earth do not go up to Jerusalem to worship the King, the LORD of hosts, there will be no rain upon them. ¹⁸And if the family of Egypt do not go up and present themselves, then on them shallᶠ come the plague that the LORD inflicts on the nations that do not go up to keep the festival of booths.ᵉ ¹⁹Such shall be the punishment of Egypt and the punishment of all the nations that do not go up to keep the festival of booths.ᵉ

20 On that day there shall be inscribed on the bells of the horses, "Holy to the LORD." And the cooking pots in the house of the LORD shall be as holy asᵍ the bowls in front of the altar; ²¹and every cooking pot in Jerusalem and Judah shall be sacred to the LORD of hosts, so that all who sacrifice may come and use them to boil the flesh of the sacrifice. And there shall no longer be tradersʰ in the house of the LORD of hosts on that day.

ᵃ Heb *my mountains*　ᵇ Meaning of Heb uncertain　ᶜ Cn: Heb *there shall not be light*　ᵈ Compare Gk Syr Vg Tg: Meaning of Heb uncertain
ᵉ Or *tabernacles*; Heb *succoth*　ᶠ Gk Syr: Heb *shall not*　ᵍ Heb *shall be like*　ʰ Or *Canaanites*

Malachi

▶▶▶▶▶▶▶▶▶▶▶▶▶▶▶▶▶▶▶▶▶

"You promised me!" These three words speak volumes. A promise is a sacred thing, and breaking promises hurts and destroys relationships. The last book of the Old Testament, Malachi, focuses on promises to God that have been broken. Like the other prophets, Malachi challenges the people to live with integrity, calling them to repentance and faithfulness. The book begins with a statement of God's love and ends with a promise of someone who will purify the people, punishing the wicked and rewarding the righteous.

IN DEPTH

The author of the book of Malachi wrote just before the reforms of Ezra and Nehemiah, starting around 458 B.C. The temple had been rebuilt, and temple worship had been restored, but people were still violating the law of the covenant.

The book of Malachi addresses two main problems. The first is the failure of Israel's priests to provide good leadership. Through a series of questions and answers, the prophet Malachi speaks harsh words against the priests of the temple for failing to live up to their calling to honor God. They offer inferior sacrifices on the altar of the temple, thinking that God won't notice. The prophet compares these priests with their ancestor Levi, who offered only the finest gifts to God. Levi was a good and honest man who kept God's covenant; these priests are not.

The second problem has to do with marriage and divorce. Evidently, many men are divorcing their Jewish wives and marrying non-Jewish women. The prophet challenges the people to be faithful to one another, because their marriages are a reminder of God's covenant with the people of Judah.

The book ends with a prophecy that forms a bridge to the New Testament and the coming of Jesus. It says that God will send a messenger (Malachi 3:1) before the day of judgment. His job will be to prepare the way for God. Those who repent will enjoy God's blessings; those who do not will be punished by God. New Testament writers saw this prophecy fulfilled by John the Baptist, who prepared the way for the coming of the Messiah, Jesus of Nazareth.

QUICK FACTS

- **Date Written:** Between 515 and 445 B.C.
- **Author:** Unknown
- **Themes:** The importance of good leaders and keeping our promises

AT A GLANCE

- **Malachi 1:1–2:9** A message about God's love for Israel and about the sins of the priests
- **Malachi 2:10–16** A call for faithfulness in marriage
- **Malachi 2:17–4:3** Prophecies about God's messenger and God's judgment
- **Malachi 4:4–6** God's promise to send the prophet Elijah

1 An oracle. The word of the Lord to Israel by Malachi.*a*

Israel Preferred to Edom

2 I have loved you, says the Lord. But you say, "How have you loved us?" Is not Esau Jacob's brother? says the Lord. Yet I have loved Jacob [3]but I have hated Esau; I have made his hill country a desolation and his heritage a desert for jackals. [4]If Edom says, "We are shattered but we will rebuild the ruins," the Lord of hosts says: They may build, but I will tear down, until they are called the wicked country, the people with whom the Lord is angry forever. [5]Your own eyes shall see this, and you shall say, "Great is the Lord beyond the borders of Israel!"

Corruption of the Priesthood

6 A son honors his father, and servants their master. If then I am a father, where is the honor due me? And if I am a master, where is the respect due me? says the Lord of hosts to you, O priests, who despise my name. You say, "How have we despised your name?" [7]By offering polluted food on my altar. And you say, "How have we polluted it?"*b* By thinking that the Lord's table may be despised. [8]When you offer blind animals in sacrifice, is that not wrong? And when you offer those that are lame or sick, is that not wrong? Try presenting that to your governor; will he be pleased with you or show you favor? says the Lord of hosts. [9]And now implore the favor of God, that he may be gracious to us. The fault is yours. Will he show favor to any of you? says the Lord of hosts. [10]Oh, that someone among you would shut the temple*c* doors, so that you would not kindle fire on my altar in vain! I have no pleasure in you, says the Lord of hosts, and I will not accept an offering from your hands. [11]For from the rising of the sun to its setting my name is great among the nations, and in every place incense is offered to my name, and a pure offering; for my name is great among the nations, says the Lord of hosts. [12]But you profane it when you say that the Lord's table is polluted, and the food for it*d* may be despised. [13]"What a weariness this is," you say, and you sniff at me,*e* says the Lord of hosts. You bring what has been taken by violence or is lame or sick, and this you bring as your offering! Shall I accept that from your hand? says the Lord. [14]Cursed be the cheat who has a male in the flock and vows to

give it, and yet sacrifices to the Lord what is blemished; for I am a great King, says the Lord of hosts, and my name is reverenced among the nations.

2 And now, O priests, this command is for you. [2]If you will not listen, if you will not lay it to heart to give glory to my name, says the Lord of hosts, then I will send the curse on you and I will curse your blessings; indeed I have already cursed them,*f* because you do not lay it to heart. [3]I will rebuke your offspring, and spread dung on your faces, the dung of your offerings, and I will put you out of my presence.*g*

4 Know, then, that I have sent this command to you, that my covenant with Levi may hold, says the Lord of hosts. [5]My covenant with him was a covenant of life and well-being, which I gave him; this called for reverence, and he revered me and stood in awe of my name. [6]True instruction was in his mouth, and no wrong was found on his lips. He walked with me in integrity and uprightness, and he turned many from iniquity. [7]For the lips of a priest should guard knowledge, and people should seek instruction from his mouth, for he is the messenger of the Lord of hosts. [8]But you have turned aside from the way; you have caused many to stumble by your instruction; you have corrupted the covenant of Levi, says the Lord of hosts, [9]and so I make you despised and abased before all the people, inasmuch as you have not kept my ways but have shown partiality in your instruction.

The Covenant Profaned by Judah

10 Have we not all one father? Has not one God created us? Why then are we faithless to one another, profaning the covenant of our ancestors? [11]Judah has been faithless, and abomination has been committed in Israel and in Jerusalem; for Judah has profaned the sanctuary of the Lord, which he loves, and has married the daughter of a foreign god. [12]May the Lord cut off from the tents of Jacob anyone who does this—any to witness*h* or answer, or to bring an offering to the Lord of hosts.

13 And this you do as well: You cover the Lord's altar with tears, with weeping and groaning because he no longer regards the offering or accepts it with favor at your hand. [14]You ask, "Why does he not?" Because the Lord was a witness between you and the wife of your youth, to whom you have been faithless, though she is your companion and your wife by covenant. [15]Did not one God make her?*i*

---

a Or *by my messenger* b Gk: Heb *you* c Heb lacks *temple* d Compare Syr Tg: Heb *its fruit, its food* e Another reading is *at it* f Heb *it* g Cn Compare Gk Syr: Heb *and he shall bear you to it* h Cn Compare Gk: Heb *arouse* i Or *Has he not made one?*

Both flesh and spirit are his.[a] And what does the one God[b] desire? Godly offspring. So look to yourselves, and do not let anyone be faithless to the wife of his youth. [16]For I hate[c] divorce, says the LORD, the God of Israel, and covering one's garment with violence, says the LORD of hosts. So take heed to yourselves and do not be faithless.

17 You have wearied the LORD with your words. Yet you say, "How have we wearied him?" By saying, "All who do evil are good in the sight of the LORD, and he delights in them." Or by asking, "Where is the God of justice?"

The Coming Messenger

3 See, I am sending my messenger to prepare the way before me, and the Lord whom you seek will suddenly come to his temple. The messenger of the covenant in whom you delight—indeed, he is coming, says the LORD of hosts. [2]But who can endure the day of his coming, and who can stand when he appears?

For he is like a refiner's fire and like fullers' soap; [3]he will sit as a refiner and purifier of silver, and he will purify the descendants of Levi and refine them like gold and silver, until they present offerings to the LORD in righteousness.[d] [4]Then the offering of Judah and Jerusalem will be pleasing to the LORD as in the days of old and as in former years.

5 Then I will draw near to you for judgment; I will be swift to bear witness against the sorcerers, against the adulterers, against those who swear falsely, against those who oppress the hired workers in their wages, the widow and the orphan, against those who thrust aside the alien, and do not fear me, says the LORD of hosts.

6 For I the LORD do not change; therefore you, O children of Jacob, have not perished. [7]Ever since the days of your ancestors you have turned aside from my statutes and have not kept them. Return to me, and I will return to you, says the LORD of hosts. But you say, "How shall we return?"

Do Not Rob God

8 Will anyone rob God? Yet you are robbing me! But you say, "How are we robbing you?" In your tithes and offerings! [9]You are cursed with a curse,

for you are robbing me—the whole nation of you! [10]Bring the full tithe into the storehouse, so that there may be food in my house, and thus put me to the test, says the LORD of hosts; see if I will not open the windows of heaven for you and pour down for you an overflowing blessing. [11]I will rebuke the locust[e] for you, so that it will not destroy the produce of your soil; and your vine in the field shall not be barren, says the LORD of hosts.

> "For I the LORD
> do not change."
> —Malachi 3:6

[12]Then all nations will count you happy, for you will be a land of delight, says the LORD of hosts.

13 You have spoken harsh words against me, says the LORD. Yet you say, "How have we spoken against you?" [14]You have said, "It is vain to serve God. What do we profit by keeping his command or by going about as mourners before the LORD of hosts? [15]Now we count the arrogant happy; evildoers not only prosper, but when they put God to the test they escape."

The Reward of the Faithful

16 Then those who revered the LORD spoke with one another. The LORD took note and listened, and a book of remembrance was written before him of those who revered the LORD and thought on his name. [17]They shall be mine, says the LORD of hosts, my special possession on the day when I act, and I will spare them as parents spare their children who serve them. [18]Then once more you shall see the difference between the righteous and the wicked, between one who serves God and one who does not serve him.

The Great Day of the LORD

4 [f] See, the day is coming, burning like an oven, when all the arrogant and all evildoers will be stubble; the day that comes shall burn them up, says the LORD of hosts, so that it will leave them neither root nor branch. [2]But for you who revere my name the sun of righteousness shall rise, with healing in its wings. You shall go out leaping like calves from the stall. [3]And you shall tread down the wicked, for they will be ashes under the soles of your feet, on the day when I act, says the LORD of hosts.

4 Remember the teaching of my servant Moses,

---

a Cn: Heb *and a remnant of spirit was his*   **b** Heb *he*   **c** Cn: Heb *he hates*   **d** Or *right offerings to the LORD*   **e** Heb *devourer*   **f** Ch 4.1-6 are Ch 3.19-24 in Heb

Coming Soon . . . • Malachi 4

Malachi is the last word of the Old Testament. And it kind of leaves us hanging.
Malachi 4 promises first the return of the prophet Elijah and then the coming of
a savior. But between Malachi and the first books of the New Testament, there
are four hundred years of silence. The Israelites had been promised a king on
the throne, but for now they wait.

And so it is with great expectation of a king that we look ahead to the New Testament and see
John the Baptist enter the story—the symbolic Elijah. In Matthew's gospel, Jesus states that it is John
the Baptist who fulfills Malachi's prophecy to prepare the way for Jesus (Matthew 11:10). The way is
prepared and, finally, a king has come.

- When have you had to wait for an answer to prayer or the fulfillment of a promise of God in
  your life?
- How does knowing that the savior and king promised in the Old Testament, who came in the
  birth of Jesus, help you to wait patiently for God's promises in your life?

the statutes and ordinances that I commanded him
at Horeb for all Israel.

5 Lo, I will send you the prophet Elijah before
the great and terrible day of the LORD comes. [6]He

will turn the hearts of parents to their children and
the hearts of children to their parents, so that I will
not come and strike the land with a curse.[a]

α *Or a ban of utter destruction*

THE NEW TESTAMENT

1

"I came that they may have life, and have it abundantly."

—John 10:10

Introduction to the
Gospels & Acts

If you have ever written a research paper for a class project, you know how important it is to have good sources. You want sources that have the most insight into your chosen topic, sources that provide inspiration. The books of the New Testament are those sources for the Christian faith. The gospels of Matthew, Mark, Luke, and John lay the foundation for understanding the message and the mission of Jesus, the center of Christianity. Acts continues with an inspiring account of how the earliest Christians continued Jesus' mission despite conflicts and persecution. The word "gospel" means "good news." And the good news in these books invites us to respond by accepting Jesus as the promised Messiah, the Son of God, the Savior of the world, and by giving our lives to following him.

IN DEPTH

The books of the New Testament continue the Old Testament's overarching story of God's saving work in the world. Their focus is on Jesus Christ—the hoped-for Messiah, the Savior. Jesus is revealed as God's Son, being both fully human and fully divine. In Jesus, God's promises to Abraham, Moses, and David were fulfilled. In Jesus, God's covenant is expanded beyond Judaism to include all peoples. In Jesus lie the forgiveness of sins and a new life of love and freedom for anyone who believes.

The New Testament tells of this good news through four types of books:

• **The Gospels,** four similar but unique views of Jesus' life and teaching;

• **Acts,** a book of stories about how the apostles spread the good news of Jesus;

• **Letters** from early Christian leaders to the first Christians and Christian communities; and

• **Apocalyptic writings** in the book of Revelation.

This introduction covers the four Gospels and Acts; another introduction will give more background on the letters and Revelation.

The gospels of Matthew, Mark, Luke, and John tell the story of Jesus from four different perspectives. They are not historical biographies or documents like those you might read today. They grew out of the teaching and preaching about Jesus in different early Christian communities. They reflect these early Christian communities' beliefs about Jesus, but they do not tell us everything Jesus said and did in his life on earth. The authors of the Gospels arranged the stories to bring out a particular understanding of Jesus' message, mission, and identity that had great importance in their Christian communities.

Matthew, Mark, and Luke are similar in their style and share much of the same content. They are called the "Synoptic" (from a Greek word that means "seeing the whole together") Gospels. It's likely that Mark was written first and the authors of Matthew and Luke used Mark as a source in creating their own gospels (Luke 1:1 mentions other accounts of Jesus). John is quite different from the Synoptic Gospels. It was written later and is more symbolic in its expression of who Jesus is.

Acts is a continuation of Luke's gospel (Acts 1:1). However, it is not itself a gospel. It picks up where Luke ends, telling the story of the origins of Christianity after the death and resurrection of Jesus, covering the period from about A.D. 30 to 64. Although Acts gives us a good deal of information about early Church leaders like Peter and Paul, its purpose is not to tell us their biographies. Instead, it gives us an interpretation of the beginnings of Christianity that emphasizes God's saving purpose. The book of Acts explains how Christianity, which began as an offshoot of the Jewish faith, gradually spread beyond Judaism into the Gentile, or non-Jewish, world.

The original Greek word for "gospel" is "evangelion," which means "big or important news" (sometimes translated "good news"). The authors of the Gospels wanted to share with others the important news of Jesus Christ. When you read these powerful stories of faith, let God use them to inspire and strengthen your faith in Jesus.

OTHER BACKGROUND

- Matthew emphasizes Jesus as the promised Messiah of the Jewish people. Jesus is portrayed as the greatest prophet, teaching the new law and calling people to be faithful to God.

- Mark was probably the first of the four Gospels to be written. It portrays Jesus as an active healer and miracle worker who accepts loneliness and suffering as the cost of obedience to God's will.

- Luke is a clear, orderly presentation of Jesus' mission to all people, Jews and Gentiles. This gospel emphasizes Jesus' mercy, compassion, and concern for the poor.

- John was the last gospel written and seeks to show Jesus as the unique Son of God. This gospel portrays Jesus as noble and powerful, fully in control of his own destiny.

- Acts was written by the author of Luke. It shows God at work in the growth of the early Christian communities, particularly through the efforts of Peter and Paul.

Titles of Jesus

Many names have been given to describe Jesus. Those who wrote the Gospels hoped to honor him with names, words, and titles that speak to faith in Jesus.

Name	Significance & Reference
Carpenter	Jesus was a craftsman who worked with his father, Joseph (Matt. 13:55; Mark 6:3).
Jesus	Yeshua (or Joshua) in Hebrew; it means "God saves" (Matt. 1:21; Luke 1:31).
King of the Jews	Jesus was born of David's royal line. Angels, shepherds, and the Magi adored the newborn king. Pilate mocked him with this title, which was nailed to the cross at his crucifixion (Matt. 2:2; Mark 15:2; Luke 23:38; John 19:19).
Lamb of God	Jesus is the worthy sacrifice who frees humanity from sin, who was slain, and who takes away grief (John 1:29, 36; Rev. 5:6; 17:14).
The Lord, "I Am"	Jesus Christ is Lord, the Glory of God, the manifestation of Yahweh among us. Jesus is the perfect image of true humanity and the one who calls us into eternal life (Matt. 1:23; Luke 1:66; John 11:25-27; 20:28-29; Acts 2:36; Phil. 2:11; Col. 2:9-10). Jesus is the "I am" of Yahweh; the bread of life; the light of the world; the door; the gate; the Good Shepherd; the resurrection and life; the way, the truth, and the life (John 6:35; 8:12; 10:7, 11; 11:25; 14:6).
Messiah ("Christ" in Greek)	Christ ("mashiah" in Hebrew) means "anointed one" and is a title used for kings, prophets, and war heroes. Jesus was the Messiah, who freed humanity from the bondage of slavery and from the pain and despair of sin. Over the centuries, this title honored Jesus' divinity (Matt. 1:1, 18; 16:16; Mark 1:1; 8:29; John 4:25-26; Acts 2:38).
Rabbi or Rabbouni	Jesus was a Jewish wisdom teacher, healer, and scholar of the Torah, the first five books of the Old Testament. His disciples honored and respected him by calling him "Rabbi" (Mark 9:5; 10:51; John 3:2; 20:16).
Savior	Jesus is Savior of the world, the one who releases humanity from bondage, sin, and death. The term is related to "Messiah" or "Christ" (Luke 2:11; John 4:42). Jesus is Israel's deliverer, the Redeemer; the God of history and of Israel is revealed in Christ (Acts 13:23). As Savior, Jesus grants forgiveness of sin (Acts 5:31).
Son of Abraham	Jesus is the descendant of Israel's great patriarch and shares in the election of Israel and the eternal covenant (Matt. 1:1; Luke 3:34; John 8:58).
Son of David	Jesus is a descendant of Israel's great King David and, as such, is the fulfillment of the prophecy of Nathan, who said the covenant would remain with the house of David (2 Sam. 7:11-16; Matt. 1:1; 12:23; Luke 18:38; Rev. 5:5).
Son of God	Jesus is the embodiment of the divine—Son of the Most High (Matt. 4:3; 14:33; 27:54; Mark 3:11; Luke 1:32; John 20:31).
Son of Man	The evangelists of the Gospels took this title, which Jesus called himself, and used it to identify Jesus as the expected Messiah (Matt. 12:8; 16:13-16; Luke 6:5). Jesus used this title when he spoke of his mission and of his suffering to come (Matt. 8:20; 17:9; 19:28; Luke 9:22, 58; 18:8). The Son of Man came as the "human one" from heaven with the authority to forgive sin (Matt. 9:6; 12:32; Mark 2:10; Luke 5:24; 12:10; John 3:13). The Son of Man will be betrayed and handed over (Matt. 17:12, 22-23; 26:24). The Son of Man will be condemned, die, be buried, and offer his life to redeem many (Matt. 20:18-19, 28; Mark 9:31). The Son of Man will rise from the dead (Mark 9:9). There will be signs of the coming of the Son of Man (Matt. 24:27, 37, 39, 44). The Son of Man will be glorified, honored before angels, and send angels to earth (Matt. 13:41; 16:27; 25:31; Luke 12:8; John 1:51; 12:23; 13:31). The Son of Man will judge the living and the dead and herald in a new age in glory (Matt. 19:28; 26:64; Luke 22:69; John 5:26-29).
Word of God	Jesus is the Word (Greek "logos") of God in the flesh. Jesus is the alpha and the omega; the beginning and end of all creation, the preexistent one (John 1:1-3; Rev. 19:13; 21:6).

Gospel Comparisons

	Mark	Matthew	Luke	John
Date Written	A.D. 65–70	A.D. 80–90	A.D. 80–95	A.D. 90–110
Writer	Mark: A second-generation Christian, traditionally thought to be a disciple of Peter named John Mark	Matthew: An unknown Jewish Christian, traditionally thought to be the apostle Matthew	Luke: A Gentile Christian, traditionally thought to be Luke the physician and Paul's traveling companion	John: A member of a Christian community possibly founded by John, the Beloved Disciple
Images of Christ	The suffering servant of God, Son of Man, Son of God, Messiah, and Lord	Teacher and prophet like Moses, Son of God, Son of Man, Messiah, and Lord	Great healer, merciful and compassionate toward the poor, Son of God, Son of Man, Messiah, and Lord	Logos, Word of God, Son of God, Son of Man, Lamb of God, Redeemer, Messiah, and Lord
The Author's Community	A Gentile Christian community undergoing persecution	A Jewish Christian community	A Greek community; the addressee, Theophilus (meaning "lover of God"), possibly represents any Christian	Community of Jews, Gentiles, and Samaritans
Theological Themes	Jesus shows that the suffering in our lives can be a source of grace when united to the sufferings of Christ.	Jesus teaches what it means to be a member of the kingdom of heaven. He prepares his followers to continue his teaching and ministry.	Jesus heals long-standing divisions between people. He calls his followers to have a special compassion for those excluded from wealth and power.	Jesus is the divine Son of God, the image of God in flesh. Salvation is available for those who believe in Jesus and commit their lives to him.
Historical Situation	The Romans subdued armed Jewish rebellions. Christians were experiencing persecution.	The Romans had destroyed all of Jerusalem, including the temple of Herod.	The persecution of Jews and Christians was intensifying	Emperor Domitian deified himself and mandated that all people worship him. Jewish leaders banned Christians from the synagogues.
Caesars	Nero (A.D. 54–68)	Vespasian and Titus (A.D. 70–81)	Domitian (A.D. 81–96)	Domitian (A.D. 81–96), Nerva (A.D. 96–98), Trajan (A.D. 98–117)

Matthew ▶▶▶▶▶▶▶▶▶▶▶▶▶▶

Holidays make for great celebrations, and every family has some kind of special or unique tradition. What's yours? How do you celebrate? Your family traditions might have been passed down for generations before you. Traditions give meaning to our special celebrations and help us know where we came from. The gospel of Matthew makes it clear to the early Jewish-Christian readers that believing in Jesus as the Son of God was not a break with their tradition, but the fulfillment of it.

IN DEPTH

Matthew is the first book in the New Testament, and it tells the story of Jesus in a way that both connects to the Old Testament and reaches beyond it into the New. The book begins with a list of Jesus' Jewish ancestors, connecting Jesus to Abraham, the father of Judaism, and David, Israel's greatest king. The author of Matthew was probably a Jewish Christian writing for a community of other Jewish Christians. It was important that he connect the dots for this group of new believers and show them how Jesus continued the story of their Jewish heritage. These people wanted to share the gospel message with their Jewish brothers and sisters (Matthew 10:6), but not everyone in their day liked the idea that these Jews had become followers of Christ. The book of Matthew helped the people defend their belief in Jesus by linking Jesus to important Jewish traditions, even though he gave them new meanings. The book also makes frequent references to Old Testament laws, prophecies, and events that Jesus fulfills or completes.

The author of Matthew also wanted to show how Jesus broke with certain Jewish beliefs—no doubt to help explain why his community of Jewish Christians was protesting against the Jewish religious establishment that it considered corrupt and wayward. The Sermon on the Mount (Matthew 5:1-7:29) shows Jesus giving a deeper interpretation to Jewish laws. And Jesus is frequently in conflict with the scribes and Pharisees over things like healing on the sabbath (Matthew 12:9-14).

Gradually, Matthew paints a picture of Jesus as the promised son of David who would reign as king forever and as a prophet-teacher like Moses, the true lawgiver. He is the Messiah, the fulfillment of all that the Jewish people had been waiting for, the one who would bring their liberation and salvation. This good news was to be proclaimed to Jews and non-Jews alike. And so the gospel ends with the risen Jesus telling his disciples, "Go therefore and make disciples of all nations" (Matthew 28:19).

QUICK FACTS

- **Author:** Unknown; traditionally thought to be the apostle Matthew, a tax collector
- **Date Written:** Around A.D. 80-90.
- **Audience:** Christian Jews
- **Image of Jesus:** The greatest prophet, the Messiah, who fulfills the old covenant and introduces the new covenant

AT A GLANCE

- **Matthew 1:1–4:17** The birth of Jesus and the beginning of Jesus' ministry
- **Matthew 4:18–9:38** The Sermon on the Mount and miracles in Galilee
- **Matthew 10–12** Teachings on mission and rejection
- **Matthew 13–18** Jesus, the kingdom, and the Church
- **Matthew 19–25** Jesus' ministry in Judea and Jerusalem
- **Matthew 26–28** Jesus' death and resurrection

The Genealogy of Jesus the Messiah

1 An account of the genealogy[a] of Jesus the Messiah,[b] the son of David, the son of Abraham.

2 Abraham was the father of Isaac, and Isaac the father of Jacob, and Jacob the father of Judah and his brothers, [3]and Judah the father of Perez and Zerah by Tamar, and Perez the father of Hezron, and Hezron the father of Aram, [4]and Aram the father of Aminadab, and Aminadab the father of Nahshon, and Nahshon the father of Salmon, [5]and Salmon the father of Boaz by Rahab, and Boaz the father of Obed by Ruth, and Obed the father of Jesse, [6]and Jesse the father of King David.

And David was the father of Solomon by the wife of Uriah, [7]and Solomon the father of Rehoboam, and Rehoboam the father of Abijah, and Abijah the father of Asaph,[c] [8]and Asaph[c] the father of Jehoshaphat, and Jehoshaphat the father of Joram, and Joram the father of Uzziah, [9]and Uzziah the father of Jotham, and Jotham the father of Ahaz, and Ahaz the father of Hezekiah, [10]and Hezekiah the father of Manasseh, and Manasseh the father of Amos,[d] and Amos[d] the father of Josiah, [11]and Josiah the father of Jechoniah and his brothers, at the time of the deportation to Babylon.

12 And after the deportation to Babylon: Jechoniah was the father of Salathiel, and Salathiel the father of Zerubbabel, [13]and Zerubbabel the father of Abiud, and Abiud the father of Eliakim, and Eliakim the father of Azor, [14]and Azor the father of Zadok, and Zadok the father of Achim, and Achim the father of Eliud, [15]and Eliud the father of Eleazar, and Eleazar the father of Matthan, and Matthan the father of Jacob, [16]and Jacob the father of Joseph the husband of Mary, of whom Jesus was born, who is called the Messiah.[e]

17 So all the generations from Abraham to David are fourteen generations; and from David to the deportation to Babylon, fourteen generations; and from the deportation to Babylon to the Messiah,[e] fourteen generations.

The Birth of Jesus the Messiah

18 Now the birth of Jesus the Messiah[b] took place in this way. When his mother Mary had been engaged to Joseph, but before they lived together, she was found to be with child from the Holy Spirit. [19]Her husband Joseph, being a righteous man and unwilling to expose her to public disgrace, planned to dismiss her quietly. [20]But just when he had resolved to do this, an angel of the Lord appeared to him in a dream and said, "Joseph, son of David, do not be afraid to take Mary as your wife, for the child conceived in her is from the Holy Spirit. [21]She will bear a son, and you are to name him Jesus, for he will save his people from their sins." [22]All this took place to fulfill what had been spoken by the Lord through the prophet:

STUDY IT!

Jesus' Family Tree · Matthew 1:1–17

Jesus is the fulfillment of all that was promised throughout Israel's history, and Matthew's gospel is uniquely focused on pointing that out to the Jews of that day. The author begins by tracing Jesus' family tree in the first two chapters.

Matthew lists Jesus' lineage in order to make his case that Jesus was the Messiah who would restore the covenant promised to Abraham, the father of the Jewish people. He also traces Jesus' ancestry back to David to show that Jesus is the fulfillment of the promises made to David (see 2 Samuel 7).

Things get even more interesting with a closer look at all the people mentioned in the list. There's a wide assortment of groups and social classes: patriarchs and slaves, kings and peasants, men and women, Jews and non-Jews. This genealogy is based on clan relations of which non-Jews are a part, because they have been incorporated into the clan that traces itself back to David and Abraham. Essentially, this genealogy demonstrates that God has been at work from the call of Abraham, the "father" of Judaism, through the high point of Israel's history (David), and even through their darkest times (the Babylonian exile) to bring a savior into the world. And Matthew promises the Jews that "God is with us" in Jesus (Matthew 1:23).

---

a Or *birth*　b Or *Jesus Christ*　c Other ancient authorities read *Asa*　d Other ancient authorities read *Amon*　e Or *the Christ*

STUDY IT!

Emmanuel . . . God with Us
Matthew 1:23

In announcing Jesus' birth, the gospel of Matthew quotes **Isaiah 7:14,** in which Isaiah tells King Ahaz that his young wife will conceive a son and they will name him Emmanuel, which means "God is with us" (Matthew 1:23). This is the perfect description for Jesus, the son of God, who fully shares our humanity. The gospel ends with the same promise, when the risen Jesus tells his disciples, "I am with you always" (Matthew 28:20).

23 "Look, the virgin shall conceive and bear
        a son,
    and they shall name him Emmanuel,"
which means, "God is with us." 24When Joseph awoke from sleep, he did as the angel of the Lord commanded him; he took her as his wife, 25but had no marital relations with her until she had borne a son;*a* and he named him Jesus.

The Visit of the Wise Men

2 In the time of King Herod, after Jesus was born in Bethlehem of Judea, wise men*b* from the East came to Jerusalem, 2asking, "Where is the child who has been born king of the Jews? For we observed his star at its rising,*c* and have come to pay him homage." 3When King Herod heard this, he was frightened, and all Jerusalem with him; 4and calling together all the chief priests and scribes of the people,

he inquired of them where the Messiah*d* was to be born. 5They told him, "In Bethlehem of Judea; for so it has been written by the prophet:

6 'And you, Bethlehem, in the land of Judah,
    are by no means least among the rulers of
        Judah;
    for from you shall come a ruler
        who is to shepherd*e* my people Israel.' "

7 Then Herod secretly called for the wise men*b* and learned from them the exact time when the star had appeared. 8Then he sent them to Bethlehem, saying, "Go and search diligently for the child; and when you have found him, bring me word so that I may also go and pay him homage." 9When they had heard the king, they set out; and there, ahead of them, went the star that they had seen at its rising,*c* until it stopped over the place where the child was. 10When they saw that the star had stopped,*f* they were overwhelmed with joy. 11On entering the house, they saw the child with Mary his mother; and they knelt down and paid him homage. Then, opening their treasure chests, they offered him gifts of gold, frankincense, and myrrh. 12And having been warned in a dream not to return to Herod, they left for their own country by another road.

The Escape to Egypt

13 Now after they had left, an angel of the Lord appeared to Joseph in a dream and said, "Get up, take the child and his mother, and flee to Egypt, and remain there until I tell you; for Herod is about to search for the child, to destroy him." 14Then Joseph*g* got up, took the child and his mother by night, and went to Egypt, 15and remained there until the death of Herod. This was to fulfill what had been spoken by the Lord through the prophet, "Out of Egypt I have called my son."

STUDY IT!

A Savior to All People · Matthew 2:1–12

Somehow the Christmas story has often gotten smashed into one snapshot image of the shepherds, wise men, and angels surrounding the baby Jesus one night in a stable. They're all there at the same time with the same outfits and often the same color skin. But the wise men were from another culture. They traveled a long way to see Jesus, and it's unlikely they were there with their gifts at the stable with everyone else. But they came to see the Messiah! And they are a symbol to us that Jesus came as the Savior not just to the Jews, but to all races and cultures.

a Other ancient authorities read *her firstborn son*   *b* Or *astrologers;* Gk *magi*   *c* Or *in the East*   *d* Or *the Christ*   *e* Or *rule*   *f* Gk *saw the star*   *g* Gk *he*

LIVE IT!

Compassion for Immigrants · Matthew 2:13

Joseph gets another visit from an angel. This time the message is to take Mary and Jesus to Egypt to protect them from Herod's massacre of all boys under age two. Why was Herod committing such an atrocity? To try to kill Jesus, whom he saw as a threat to his power. Jesus, Mary, and Joseph become refugees to avoid persecution.

Every year, millions of people in the world flee their countries because of hunger, poverty, or persecution. They often find themselves feeling like unwelcome strangers in their new land. Many can't communicate in the new language, and they're often persecuted by its inhabitants who think the immigrants have come simply to take advantage of government services. Christians, however, should have a special compassion for refugees and immigrants, because Jesus told us to love everyone, especially those who suffer.

- Imagine Jesus, Mary, and Joseph being in exile in our country. How would you treat them?
- What's your attitude toward refugees and immigrants in our country? How can you welcome them and show them love?

The Massacre of the Infants

16 When Herod saw that he had been tricked by the wise men,[a] he was infuriated, and he sent and killed all the children in and around Bethlehem who were two years old or under, according to the time that he had learned from the wise men.[a] 17 Then was fulfilled what had been spoken through the prophet Jeremiah:
18 "A voice was heard in Ramah,
    wailing and loud lamentation,
Rachel weeping for her children;
    she refused to be consoled, because they
      are no more."

The Return from Egypt

19 When Herod died, an angel of the Lord suddenly appeared in a dream to Joseph in Egypt and said, 20 "Get up, take the child and his mother, and go to the land of Israel, for those who were seeking the child's life are dead." 21 Then Joseph[b] got up, took the child and his mother, and went to the land of Israel. 22 But when he heard that Archelaus was ruling over Judea in place of his father Herod, he was afraid to go there. And after being warned in a dream, he went away to the district of Galilee. 23 There he made his home in a town called Nazareth, so that what had been spoken through the prophets might be fulfilled, "He will be called a Nazorean."

The Proclamation of John the Baptist

3 In those days John the Baptist appeared in the wilderness of Judea, proclaiming, 2 "Repent, for the kingdom of heaven has come near."[c] 3 This is the one of whom the prophet Isaiah spoke when he said,

"The voice of one crying out in the wilderness:
'Prepare the way of the Lord,
    make his paths straight.'"

4 Now John wore clothing of camel's hair with a leather belt around his waist, and his food was locusts and wild honey. 5 Then the people of Jerusalem and all Judea were going out to him, and all the region along the Jordan, 6 and they were baptized by him in the river Jordan, confessing their sins.

7 But when he saw many Pharisees and Sadducees coming for baptism, he said to them, "You brood of vipers! Who warned you to flee from the wrath to come? 8 Bear fruit worthy of repentance. 9 Do not presume to say to yourselves, 'We have Abraham

a Or *astrologers*; Gk *magi*   b Gk *he*   c Or *is at hand*

as our ancestor'; for I tell you, God is able from these stones to raise up children to Abraham. ¹⁰Even now the ax is lying at the root of the trees; every tree therefore that does not bear good fruit is cut down and thrown into the fire.

11 "I baptize you with*ᵃ* water for repentance, but one who is more powerful than I is coming after me; I am not worthy to carry his sandals. He will baptize you with*ᵃ* the Holy Spirit and fire. ¹²His winnowing fork is in his hand, and he will clear his

STUDY IT!

Pharisees and Sadducees · Matthew 3:7

So who are all these guys with strange names? They were upstanding citizens, religious experts, and community leaders. In Jesus' day, several groups of Jews held positions of status or leadership.

The Pharisees were scholars of the law of Moses. They used their expertise at interpreting the law to be sure that as many people as possible could obey it. People looked up to them for guidance about how they should live as good Jews.

The Sadducees were associated with the temple and the ruling class. They thought the well-being of the Jewish people was dependent on the proper operation and support of the temple.

The two groups were divided over certain beliefs, though. One example is that the Pharisees believed in resurrection of the body at the end-time, while the Sadducees did not. So why the harsh words from John the Baptist? Although the Pharisees and Sadducees were generally respected during this time, John saw their hypocrisy and their selfish ambitions. John called them to repent, because he knew that Jesus was coming—a savior who would look at their hearts rather than just their family associations and status in society.

STUDY IT!

Baptism · Matthew 3:13–17

Imagine the scene . . . John the Baptist dressed in camel hair, standing by the Jordan River, calling for people to turn from their sin and to be baptized in the water as a sign of their conversion. And who steps forward? Jesus, who is rumored to be the Messiah—the Son of God, who is without sin! Jesus convinces John to baptize him, and as Jesus comes out of the water, God reveals Jesus' true identity to the world: "This is my Son, the Beloved, with whom I am well pleased" (Matthew 3:17). This is considered the beginning of Jesus' public ministry, which ultimately leads to his death and resurrection.

Baptism is still an important practice for Christians today. It's an outward sign of the inward salvation that happens when we trust in Jesus. It's a symbol of our identity as adopted sons or daughters of God and members of the Christian community. Ritual washing like this was practiced before Jesus' death and resurrection, but it's now most often associated with Jesus. Going underwater signifies being buried with Christ, and coming out of the water signifies being raised again to new life with him.

Baptism traditions vary, depending on the church, with regard to the age of those baptized and the method. It may be done for infants, youths, or adults. People may be immersed (completely covered) in water or have water placed on or poured over their heads. The following words are often said as a person is baptized: "I baptize you in the name of the Father, and of the Son, and of the Holy Spirit." By being washed in water, the baptized person shows that they have died to sin and risen, freed from sin, as a new creation in Christ.

ᵃ Or *in*

threshing floor and will gather his wheat into the granary; but the chaff he will burn with unquenchable fire."

The Baptism of Jesus

13 Then Jesus came from Galilee to John at the Jordan, to be baptized by him. [14]John would have prevented him, saying, "I need to be baptized by you, and do you come to me?" [15]But Jesus answered him, "Let it be so now; for it is proper for us in this way to fulfill all righteousness." Then he consented. [16]And when Jesus had been baptized, just as he came up from the water, suddenly the heavens were opened to him and he saw the Spirit of God descending like a dove and alighting on him. [17]And a voice from heaven said, "This is my Son, the Beloved,[a] with whom I am well pleased."

Jesus Begins His Ministry in Galilee

12 Now when Jesus[b] heard that John had been arrested, he withdrew to Galilee. [13]He left Nazareth and made his home in Capernaum by the sea, in the territory of Zebulun and Naphtali, [14]so that what had been spoken through the prophet Isaiah might be fulfilled:

[15] "Land of Zebulun, land of Naphtali,
on the road by the sea, across the Jordan,
Galilee of the Gentiles—
[16] the people who sat in darkness
have seen a great light,
and for those who sat in the region and
shadow of death
light has dawned."

[17]From that time Jesus began to proclaim, "Repent, for the kingdom of heaven has come near."[c]

The Temptation of Jesus

4 Then Jesus was led up by the Spirit into the wilderness to be tempted by the devil. [2]He fasted forty days and forty nights, and afterwards he was famished. [3]The tempter came and said to him, "If you are the Son of God, command these stones to become loaves of bread." [4]But he answered, "It is written,

'One does not live by bread alone,
but by every word that comes from the
mouth of God.' "

5 Then the devil took him to the holy city and placed him on the pinnacle of the temple, [6]saying to him, "If you are the Son of God, throw yourself down; for it is written,

'He will command his angels concerning
you,'
and 'On their hands they will bear you up,
so that you will not dash your foot against a
stone.' "

[7]Jesus said to him, "Again it is written, 'Do not put the Lord your God to the test.' "

8 Again, the devil took him to a very high mountain and showed him all the kingdoms of the world and their splendor; [9]and he said to him, "All these I will give you, if you will fall down and worship me." [10]Jesus said to him, "Away with you, Satan! for it is written,

'Worship the Lord your God,
and serve only him.' "

[11]Then the devil left him, and suddenly angels came and waited on him.

PRAY IT!

Temptation
Matthew 4:1–11

Jesus faced temptation—real temptation—by the devil in the wilderness. So when you feel overwhelmed by temptation, follow Jesus' example and pray to the one who knows your struggle.

- "Command these stones to become loaves of bread" (Matthew 4:3). Jesus, you trusted God to provide your material needs—even when you must have been starving after not eating for forty days! Help me to avoid making material things my priority.

- "Throw yourself down; for it is written, . . . 'you will not dash your foot against a stone'" (Matthew 4:6). Jesus, you resisted using your power for vain and foolish reasons. Help me to resist doing foolish things only to impress others.

- "All these I will give you, if you will fall down and worship me" (Matthew 4:9). Jesus, you refused to cooperate with the devil to achieve status and power. Help me to follow you instead of getting trapped by evil compromises.

---

a Or *my beloved Son*   **b** Gk *he*   **c** Or *is at hand*

Jesus Calls the First Disciples

18 As he walked by the Sea of Galilee, he saw two brothers, Simon, who is called Peter, and Andrew his brother, casting a net into the sea—for they were fishermen. [19]And he said to them, "Follow me, and I will make you fish for people." [20]Immediately they left their nets and followed him. [21]As he went from there, he saw two other brothers, James son of Zebedee and his brother John, in the boat with their father Zebedee, mending their nets, and he called them. [22]Immediately they left the boat and their father, and followed him.

Jesus Ministers to Crowds of People

23 Jesus[a] went throughout Galilee, teaching in their synagogues and proclaiming the good news[b] of the kingdom and curing every disease and every sickness among the people. [24]So his fame spread throughout all Syria, and they brought to him all the sick, those who were afflicted with various diseases and pains, demoniacs, epileptics, and paralytics, and he cured them. [25]And great crowds followed him from Galilee, the Decapolis, Jerusalem, Judea, and from beyond the Jordan.

The Beatitudes

5 When Jesus[c] saw the crowds, he went up the mountain; and after he sat down, his disciples came to him. [2]Then he began to speak, and taught them, saying:

3 "Blessed are the poor in spirit, for theirs is the kingdom of heaven.

4 "Blessed are those who mourn, for they will be comforted.

5 "Blessed are the meek, for they will inherit the earth.

6 "Blessed are those who hunger and thirst for righteousness, for they will be filled.

7 "Blessed are the merciful, for they will receive mercy.

8 "Blessed are the pure in heart, for they will see God.

9 "Blessed are the peacemakers, for they will be called children of God.

10 "Blessed are those who are persecuted for righteousness' sake, for theirs is the kingdom of heaven.

11 "Blessed are you when people revile you and

LIVE IT!

Follow Me
Matthew 4:18–22

What did the first disciples leave behind when they chose to follow Jesus? Nets, boats, even families—the very things they depended on for life and security. But they gained so much more!

- Are you ready to follow Jesus?
- What are you willing to "leave behind" to follow him and continue his mission?

LIVE IT!

Mountaintop Wisdom · Matthew 5–7

Jesus speaks about life in ways that challenged the attitudes of his listeners in these chapters, known as the Sermon on the Mount. At that time, Jews were following the letter of the law by performing minimal acts of caring for the poor, burying the dead, and giving financial donations. But Jesus challenges their worldview—and ours—by giving new wisdom. He says people should do these things generously, compassionately, humbly, with a hunger for justice, with a pure heart, and in a desire for peace.

God has a special love for those who are poor and those who are oppressed. Living out an authentic faith means we must show a similar love for those who are most in need in our world.

- Think about your view of the topics in these chapters (obedience, anger, divorce, enemies, giving, worry). Which ones do you struggle with most?
- Is "good enough" your main priority? How can you begin to move from only focusing on the rules to adopting Jesus' perspective and attitude of love and generosity?

a Gk He b Gk gospel c Gk he

STUDY IT!

The Beatitudes · Matthew 5:1–12

Jesus repeatedly challenged the wisdom of his day, and the teachings in Matthew 5:1–12, known as the Beatitudes, are no exception. Their world was similar to ours—people valued intelligence, status, wealth, and a better quality of life. But Jesus turns that around and calls blessed the people who were not highly regarded. He makes the point that the poor, mournful, meek, and hungry are the ones who are blessed—not because of what they've done, but because of who God is. Their lowly place in life is a clear contrast to the love, power, and grace of God. It doesn't mean their lives will be great—their reward and rejoicing will be found in heaven (Matthew 5:12).

So what does that mean for us today? We can see others through the eyes of Jesus, no matter what status our culture gives them. We're called each and every day to love God and others generously, compassionately, humbly, with a hunger for justice, with a pure heart, and in a desire for peace. The Beatitudes also call us to turn from our desires for false or temporary happiness and to seek the eternal happiness only God can give. Our daily decisions and problems are seen in a new light—the light of Christ's life and resurrection. Based on the Beatitudes, we can:

- Realize that heaven is a gift we receive only through God's grace.
- Find comfort when we mourn the loss of a loved one.
- Be humble when tempted with pride.
- Desire righteousness (a right relationship with God and others) with every ounce of our being.
- Be merciful when others offend or hurt us.
- Purify our heart so that we only desire God.
- Seek peace when conflict arises.
- Stick to our convictions when it's a question of right and wrong.
- Endure being made fun of or threatened because of our faith in Jesus Christ.

persecute you and utter all kinds of evil against you falsely[a] on my account. [12]Rejoice and be glad, for your reward is great in heaven, for in the same way they persecuted the prophets who were before you.

Salt and Light

13 "You are the salt of the earth; but if salt has lost its taste, how can its saltiness be restored? It is no longer good for anything, but is thrown out and trampled under foot.

14 "You are the light of the world. A city built on a hill cannot be hid. [15]No one after lighting a lamp puts it under the bushel basket, but on the lampstand, and it gives light to all in the house. [16]In the same way, let your light shine before others, so that they may see your good works and give glory to your Father in heaven.

The Law and the Prophets

17 "Do not think that I have come to abolish the

law or the prophets; I have come not to abolish but to fulfill. [18]For truly I tell you, until heaven and earth pass away, not one letter,[b] not one stroke of a letter, will pass from the law until all is accomplished. [19]Therefore, whoever breaks[c] one of the least of these commandments, and teaches others to do the same, will be called least in the kingdom of heaven; but whoever does them and teaches them will be called great in the kingdom of heaven. [20]For I tell you, unless your righteousness exceeds that of the scribes and Pharisees, you will never enter the kingdom of heaven.

Concerning Anger

21 "You have heard that it was said to those of ancient times, 'You shall not murder'; and 'whoever murders shall be liable to judgment.' [22]But I say to you that if you are angry with a brother or sister,[d] you will be liable to judgment; and if you insult[e] a brother or sister,[f] you will be liable to the council;

a Other ancient authorities lack *falsely* b Gk *one iota* c Or *annuls* d Gk *a brother*; other ancient authorities add *without cause* e Gk *say Raca to* (an obscure term of abuse) f Gk *a brother*

and if you say, 'You fool,' you will be liable to the hell[a] of fire. [23]So when you are offering your gift at the altar, if you remember that your brother or sister[b] has something against you, [24]leave your gift there before the altar and go; first be reconciled to your brother or sister,[b] and then come and offer your gift. [25]Come to terms quickly with your accuser while you are on the way to court[c] with him, or your accuser may hand you over to the judge, and the judge to the guard, and you will be thrown into prison. [26]Truly I tell you, you will never get out until you have paid the last penny.

Concerning Adultery

27 "You have heard that it was said, 'You shall not commit adultery.' [28]But I say to you that everyone who looks at a woman with lust has already committed adultery with her in his heart. [29]If your right eye causes you to sin, tear it out and throw it away; it is better for you to lose one of your members than for your whole body to be thrown into hell.[a] [30]And if your right hand causes you to sin, cut it off and throw it away; it is better for you to lose one of your members than for your whole body to go into hell.[a]

Concerning Divorce

31 "It was also said, 'Whoever divorces his wife, let him give her a certificate of divorce.' [32]But I say to you that anyone who divorces his wife, except on the ground of unchastity, causes her to commit adultery; and whoever marries a divorced woman commits adultery.

Concerning Oaths

33 "Again, you have heard that it was said to those of ancient times, 'You shall not swear falsely, but carry out the vows you have made to the Lord.' [34]But I say to you, Do not swear at all, either by heaven, for it is the throne of God, [35]or by the earth, for it is his footstool, or by Jerusalem, for it is the city of the great King. [36]And do not swear by your head, for you cannot make one hair white or black. [37]Let your word be 'Yes, Yes' or 'No, No'; anything more than this comes from the evil one.[d]

Concerning Retaliation

38 "You have heard that it was said, 'An eye for an eye and a tooth for a tooth.' [39]But I say to you, Do not resist an evildoer. But if anyone strikes you on the right cheek, turn the other also; [40]and if anyone

PRAY IT!

An Eye, a Tooth, and the Other Cheek
Matthew 5:38–48

Jesus loves to turn our world upside down. And that's exactly what he was doing for the Jews of his time in **Matthew 5:38–48**. He takes laws that were accepted and followed by generations of Jews and expands them, providing a new way of looking at things. Jesus doesn't want us to live in abusive situations or endure harmful bullying, but he does make the point that our goal in all situations should be to respond in love rather than revenge—and that love is not reserved for people we like and who treat us well. So how can you actually follow Jesus' instructions?

During your prayer time, reflect or journal about the following questions:

- Who are your enemies?
- When someone hurts you, what is your usual reaction?
- How hard is it to forgive someone who has hurt you?
- What is the greatest challenge for you in living out these teachings from Jesus?

wants to sue you and take your coat, give your cloak as well; [41]and if anyone forces you to go one mile, go also the second mile. [42]Give to everyone who begs from you, and do not refuse anyone who wants to borrow from you.

Love for Enemies

43 "You have heard that it was said, 'You shall love your neighbor and hate your enemy.' [44]But I say to you, Love your enemies and pray for those who persecute you, [45]so that you may be children of your Father in heaven; for he makes his sun rise on the evil and on the good, and sends rain on the righteous and on the unrighteous. [46]For if you love those who love you, what reward do you have? Do not even the tax collectors do the same? [47]And if you greet only your brothers and sisters,[e] what more are you

a Gk *Gehenna*   b Gk *your brother*   c Gk lacks *to court*   d Or *evil*   e Gk *your brothers* doing than others? Do not even the Gentiles do the same? [48]Be perfect, therefore, as your heavenly Father is perfect.

6   Concerning Almsgiving

"Beware of practicing your piety before others in order to be seen by them; for then you have no reward from your Father in heaven.

2 "So whenever you give alms, do not sound a trumpet before you, as the hypocrites do in the synagogues and in the streets, so that they may be praised by others. Truly I tell you, they have received their reward. [3]But when you give alms, do not let your left hand know what your right hand is doing, [4]so that your alms may be done in secret; and your Father who sees in secret will reward you.[a]

Concerning Prayer

5 "And whenever you pray, do not be like the hypocrites; for they love to stand and pray in the synagogues and at the street corners, so that they may be seen by others. Truly I tell you, they have received their reward. [6]But whenever you pray, go into your room and shut the door and pray to your Father who is in secret; and your Father who sees in secret will reward you.[a]

7 "When you are praying, do not heap up empty phrases as the Gentiles do; for they think that they will be heard because of their many words. [8]Do not be like them, for your Father knows what you need before you ask him.

9 "Pray then in this way:

Our Father in heaven,
    hallowed be your name.
[10]   Your kingdom come.
    Your will be done,
        on earth as it is in heaven.
[11]   Give us this day our daily bread.[b]
[12]   And forgive us our debts,
        as we also have forgiven our debtors.
[13]   And do not bring us to the time of
        trial,[c]
    but rescue us from the evil one.[d]

[14]For if you forgive others their trespasses, your heavenly Father will also forgive you; [15]but if you do not forgive others, neither will your Father forgive your trespasses.

Concerning Fasting

16 "And whenever you fast, do not look dismal, like the hypocrites, for they disfigure their faces so as to show others that they are fasting. Truly I tell you, they have received their reward. [17]But when you fast, put oil on your head and wash your face,

---

PRAY IT!

A Lord's Prayer Reflection · Matthew 6:5–15

In the book of Matthew, Jesus teaches his followers the Lord's Prayer as an alternative to hypocritical and empty prayer. But even the Lord's Prayer can become empty words and phrases for us, if we don't pray them from the heart (Matthew 6:7). Use this reflection on Matthew 6:9-13 to help you to pray the Lord's Prayer thoughtfully:

"Our Father in heaven, hallowed be your name" (Matthew 6:9). How do I honor God as creator of all things? How do I honor God in my thoughts, my words, and my actions?

"Your kingdom come. Your will be done, on earth as it is in heaven" (Matthew 6:10). How does my life reflect God's reign of love, justice, and peace? Am I putting too much emphasis on material things?

"Give us this day our daily bread" (Matthew 6:11). Can I trust God to provide for my daily physical, emotional, and spiritual needs?

"And forgive us our debts, as we also have forgiven our debtors" (Matthew 6:12). When I have sinned, do I admit my wrong, ask God's forgiveness, and start again? When people have wronged me, do I hold a grudge? Am I able to forgive them as God forgives me?

"And do not bring us to the time of trial, but rescue us from the evil one" (Matthew 6:13). What are the temptations I face in life? How do I rely on God for the strength to resist them?

---

a Other ancient authorities add *openly* b Or *our bread for tomorrow* c Or *us into temptation* d Or *from evil*. Other ancient authorities add, in some form, *For the kingdom and the power and the glory are yours forever. Amen.*

[18]so that your fasting may be seen not by others but by your Father who is in secret; and your Father who sees in secret will reward you.[a]

Concerning Treasures

19 "Do not store up for yourselves treasures on earth, where moth and rust[b] consume and where thieves break in and steal; [20]but store up for yourselves treasures in heaven, where neither moth nor rust[b] consumes and where thieves do not break in and steal. [21]For where your treasure is, there your heart will be also.

Real Riches
Matthew 6:19–21

"You can't take it with you." You've probably heard that saying, and it's true. None of us—from the richest human in the world to the poorest of the poor—can take a single possession with us when we die. That's easy to forget in our materialistic world, where people are always flashing the coolest new gadget and the sleekest new stuff. Jesus reminds us to keep our heart focused on true wealth.

• What possessions could you absolutely not do without? Try giving them up for a day or a week.

• What steps can you take to keep your heart aimed in God's direction?

The Sound Eye

22 "The eye is the lamp of the body. So, if your eye is healthy, your whole body will be full of light; [23]but if your eye is unhealthy, your whole body will be full of darkness. If then the light in you is darkness, how great is the darkness!

Serving Two Masters

24 "No one can serve two masters; for a slave will either hate the one and love the other, or be devoted to the one and despise the other. You cannot serve God and wealth.[c]

Do Not Worry

25 "Therefore I tell you, do not worry about your life, what you will eat or what you will drink,[d] or about your body, what you will wear. Is not life more than food, and the body more than clothing? [26]Look at the birds of the air; they neither sow nor reap nor gather into barns, and yet your heavenly Father feeds them. Are you not of more value than they? [27]And can any of you by worrying add a single hour to your span of life?[e] [28]And why do you worry about clothing? Consider the lilies of the field, how they grow; they neither toil nor spin, [29]yet I tell you, even Solomon in all his glory was not clothed like one of these. [30]But if God so clothes the grass of the field, which is alive today and tomorrow is thrown into the oven, will he not much more clothe you—you of little faith? [31]Therefore do not worry, saying, 'What will we eat?' or 'What will we drink?' or 'What will we wear?' [32]For it is the Gentiles who strive for all these things; and indeed your heavenly Father knows that you need all these things. [33]But strive first for the kingdom of God[f] and his[g] righteousness, and all these things will be given to you as well.

Don't Worry · Matthew 6:25–34

Worrying comes with being human. That's because there's so much that's simply beyond our control. Jesus' teaching in this passage reminds us that no matter what our problem is, God is bigger and knows what we need. Using word pictures from his surroundings as he taught, Jesus reminds his listeners and us that God will provide for our most basic needs, including our food and clothing. He calls us to always focus on God rather than worrying.

• What do you worry about most?

• What Bible verses can you memorize to experience God's peace instead of anxiety? For ideas, look up the words "peace" and "worry" in the Concordance, located at the back of the Bible.

---

a Other ancient authorities add *openly* **b** Gk *eating* **c** Gk *mammon* **d** Other ancient authorities lack *or what you will drink* **e** Or *add one cubit to your height* **f** Other ancient authorities lack *of God* **g** Or *its*

> "Do not worry about tomorrow, for tomorrow will bring worries of its own. Today's trouble is enough for today."
> —Matthew 6:34

34 "So do not worry about tomorrow, for tomorrow will bring worries of its own. Today's trouble is enough for today.

Judging Others

7 "Do not judge, so that you may not be judged. [2]For with the judgment you make you will be judged, and the measure you give will be the measure you get. [3]Why do you see the speck in your neighbor's[a] eye, but do not notice the log in your own eye? [4]Or how can you say to your neighbor,[b] 'Let me take the speck out of your eye,' while the log is in your own eye? [5]You hypocrite, first take the log out of your own eye, and then you will see clearly to take the speck out of your neighbor's[a] eye.

Profaning the Holy

6 "Do not give what is holy to dogs; and do not throw your pearls before swine, or they will trample them under foot and turn and maul you.

Ask, Search, Knock

7 "Ask, and it will be given you; search, and you will find; knock, and the door will be opened for you. [8]For everyone who asks receives, and everyone who searches finds, and for everyone who knocks, the door will be opened. [9]Is there anyone among you who, if your child asks for bread, will give a stone? [10]Or if the child asks for a fish, will give a snake? [11]If you then, who are evil, know how to give good gifts to your children, how much more will your Father in heaven give good things to those who ask him!

The Golden Rule

12 "In everything do to others as you would have them do to you; for this is the law and the prophets.

The Narrow Gate

13 "Enter through the narrow gate; for the gate is wide and the road is easy[c] that leads to destruction, and there are many who take it. [14]For the gate is narrow and the road is hard that leads to life, and there are few who find it.

A Tree and Its Fruit

15 "Beware of false prophets, who come to you in sheep's clothing but inwardly are ravenous wolves. [16]You will know them by their fruits. Are grapes gathered from thorns, or figs from thistles? [17]In the same way, every good tree bears good fruit, but the bad tree bears bad fruit. [18]A good tree cannot bear bad fruit, nor can a bad tree bear good fruit. [19]Every tree that does not bear good fruit is cut down and thrown into the fire. [20]Thus you will know them by their fruits.

Concerning Self-Deception

21 "Not everyone who says to me, 'Lord, Lord,' will enter the kingdom of heaven, but only the one who does the will of my Father in heaven. [22]On that day many will say to me, 'Lord, Lord, did we not

LIVE IT!

Take Action
Matthew 7:21–27

In closing the Sermon on the Mount, Jesus calls people to action. It's not enough to talk the talk; you must also walk the walk. As part of our faith in Jesus, we need to follow his commands. Those who are rich need to share their wealth with those who are poor. Those who have power need to serve those who are powerless. Leaders need to serve without prejudice and govern with justice, taking into account the needs of the people, especially those who are poor and powerless.

• Do you feel more like the poor and powerless or the rich and powerful? Who are you comparing yourself to?

• In what areas of your life do you need to serve others in response to your faith?

a Gk brother's b Gk brother c Other ancient authorities read for the road is wide and easy

prophesy in your name, and cast out demons in your name, and do many deeds of power in your name?' [23]Then I will declare to them, 'I never knew you; go away from me, you evildoers.'

Hearers and Doers

24 "Everyone then who hears these words of mine and acts on them will be like a wise man who built his house on rock. [25]The rain fell, the floods came, and the winds blew and beat on that house, but it did not fall, because it had been founded on rock. [26]And everyone who hears these words of mine and does not act on them will be like a foolish man who built his house on sand. [27]The rain fell, and the floods came, and the winds blew and beat against that house, and it fell—and great was its fall!"

28 Now when Jesus had finished saying these things, the crowds were astounded at his teaching, [29]for he taught them as one having authority, and not as their scribes.

Jesus Cleanses a Leper

8 When Jesus[a] had come down from the mountain, great crowds followed him; [2]and there was a leper[b] who came to him and knelt before him, saying, "Lord, if you choose, you can make me clean." [3]He stretched out his hand and touched him, saying, "I do choose. Be made clean!" Immediately his leprosy[b] was cleansed. [4]Then Jesus said to him, "See that you say nothing to anyone; but go, show yourself to the priest, and offer the gift that Moses commanded, as a testimony to them."

Jesus Heals a Centurion's Servant

5 When he entered Capernaum, a centurion came to him, appealing to him [6]and saying, "Lord, my servant is lying at home paralyzed, in terrible distress." [7]And he said to him, "I will come and cure him." [8]The centurion answered, "Lord, I am not worthy to have you come under my roof; but only speak the word, and my servant will be healed. [9]For I also am a man under authority, with soldiers under me; and I say to one, 'Go,' and he goes, and to another, 'Come,' and he comes, and to my slave, 'Do this,' and the slave does it." [10]When Jesus heard him, he was amazed and said to those who followed him, "Truly I tell you, in no one[c] in Israel have I found such faith. [11]I tell you, many will come from east and west and will eat with Abraham and Isaac

It's a Miracle!
Matthew 8–9

Matthew 8–9 describes ten miracles that Jesus performed, intended as signs of the coming of the kingdom of God. Most of Jesus' miracles are healings, but some also show his power over demons and nature. The gospel of Mark records the most miracles (twenty-one). The gospel of John records the fewest (eight).

Most people today tend to view reports of miracles with suspicion. That's because our scientific minds want to believe that everything has a rational explanation. Because of this, we miss the point—and the miracle. People in Jesus' time were more concerned about what the miracle revealed than the miracle itself or even the miracle worker. Other people besides Jesus were known to perform miracles. In fact, Jesus' healing miracles were not taken as proof of his divinity (that he was God), only that he worked by the power of God.

In curing people of their illnesses and driving out demons, Jesus was revealing that the kingdom of God is a place where suffering and evil are banished. By curing sinners, women, and foreigners, he showed that the kingdom of God is also open to all, especially outcasts.

Miracles—then and now—point to God. Whether they are easily explained or beyond reasonable explanation doesn't matter. What matters is that they make us aware of God's loving presence in our lives. If we look at the events in our lives and ask what they tell us about God's presence in the world, we might find ourselves completely surrounded by miracles.

and Jacob in the kingdom of heaven, [12]while the heirs of the kingdom will be thrown into the outer darkness, where there will be weeping and gnashing

---

a Gk *he* b The terms *leper* and *leprosy* can refer to several diseases c Other ancient authorities read *Truly I tell you, not even*

of teeth." ¹³And to the centurion Jesus said, "Go; let it be done for you according to your faith." And the servant was healed in that hour.

Jesus Heals Many at Peter's House

14 When Jesus entered Peter's house, he saw his mother-in-law lying in bed with a fever; ¹⁵he touched her hand, and the fever left her, and she got up and began to serve him. ¹⁶That evening they brought to him many who were possessed with demons; and he cast out the spirits with a word, and cured all who were sick. ¹⁷This was to fulfill what had been spoken through the prophet Isaiah, "He took our infirmities and bore our diseases."

Would-Be Followers of Jesus

18 Now when Jesus saw great crowds around him, he gave orders to go over to the other side. ¹⁹A scribe then approached and said, "Teacher, I will follow you wherever you go." ²⁰And Jesus said to him, "Foxes have holes, and birds of the air have nests; but the Son of Man has nowhere to lay his head." ²¹Another of his disciples said to him, "Lord, first let me go and bury my father." ²²But Jesus said to him, "Follow me, and let the dead bury their own dead."

Jesus Stills the Storm

23 And when he got into the boat, his disciples followed him. ²⁴A windstorm arose on the sea, so great that the boat was being swamped by the waves; but he was asleep. ²⁵And they went and woke him up, saying, "Lord, save us! We are perishing!" ²⁶And he said to them, "Why are you afraid, you of little faith?" Then he got up and rebuked the winds and the sea; and there was a dead calm. ²⁷They were amazed, saying, "What sort of man is this, that even the winds and the sea obey him?"

Jesus Heals the Gadarene Demoniacs

28 When he came to the other side, to the country of the Gadarenes,ᵃ two demoniacs coming out of the tombs met him. They were so fierce that no one could pass that way. ²⁹Suddenly they shouted, "What have you to do with us, Son of God? Have you come here to torment us before the time?" ³⁰Now a large herd of swine was feeding at some distance from them. ³¹The demons begged him, "If you cast us out, send us into the herd of swine." ³²And he said to them, "Go!" So they came out and entered the swine; and suddenly, the whole herd rushed down the steep bank into the sea and perished in the water. ³³The swine-herds ran off, and on going into the town, they told the whole story about what had happened to the demoniacs. ³⁴Then the whole town came out to meet Jesus; and when they saw him, they begged him to leave their neighborhood. ¹And after getting into a boat he crossed the sea and came to his own town.

9

PRAY IT!

Spiritual Paralysis · Matthew 9:1–8

It's rare to encounter someone who is paralyzed. Our closest exposure might be the occasional story of a tragic accident, maybe in sports. The paralyzed man in **Matthew 9** had no hope of surgery or recovery. But even his hopeless physical state was not what Jesus addressed first. It was the man's spiritual situation. The first thing Jesus does is tell the man his sins are forgiven (Matthew 9:2). The physical healing comes only to help show Jesus' authority to those watching (Matthew 9:6). So although our modern world may have many tools for healing, it's still our spiritual paralysis that Jesus is most concerned with. Say this prayer, asking Jesus for spiritual healing:

Jesus, please be my healer. I get paralyzed too—not physically, but spiritually. I suffer spiritual paralysis that keeps me from walking with you. It happens at school and in my neighborhood, when I know the right thing to do, but am afraid to do it. I stand by frozen and do nothing while I see someone discriminating against or abusing another person. I'm afraid to risk ridicule and rejection, and my silence shows approval of wrong.

Forgive me of my sin of silence, Lord. Help me overcome my fears, so I can stand up for what's right. Heal my spiritual paralysis, so that I can walk with you. Amen.

a Other ancient authorities read *Gergesenes*; others, *Gerasenes*

Jesus Heals a Paralytic

2 And just then some people were carrying a paralyzed man lying on a bed. When Jesus saw their faith, he said to the paralytic, "Take heart, son; your sins are forgiven." [3]Then some of the scribes said to themselves, "This man is blaspheming." [4]But Jesus, perceiving their thoughts, said, "Why do you think evil in your hearts? [5]For which is easier, to say, 'Your sins are forgiven,' or to say, 'Stand up and walk'? [6]But so that you may know that the Son of Man has authority on earth to forgive sins"—he then said to the paralytic—"Stand up, take your bed and go to your home." [7]And he stood up and went to his home. [8]When the crowds saw it, they were filled with awe, and they glorified God, who had given such authority to human beings.

The Call of Matthew

9 As Jesus was walking along, he saw a man called Matthew sitting at the tax booth; and he said to him, "Follow me." And he got up and followed him.

10 And as he sat at dinner[a] in the house, many tax collectors and sinners came and were sitting[b] with him and his disciples. [11]When the Pharisees saw this, they said to his disciples, "Why does your teacher eat with tax collectors and sinners?" [12]But when he heard this, he said, "Those who are well have no need of a physician, but those who are sick. [13]Go and learn what this means, 'I desire mercy, not sacrifice.' For I have come to call not the righteous but sinners."

The Question about Fasting

14 Then the disciples of John came to him, saying, "Why do we and the Pharisees fast often,[c] but your disciples do not fast?" [15]And Jesus said to them, "The wedding guests cannot mourn as long as the bridegroom is with them, can they? The days will come when the bridegroom is taken away from them, and then they will fast. [16]No one sews a piece of unshrunk cloth on an old cloak, for the patch pulls away from the cloak, and a worse tear is made. [17]Neither is new wine put into old wineskins; otherwise, the skins burst, and the wine is spilled, and the skins are destroyed; but new wine is put into fresh wineskins, and so both are preserved."

A Girl Restored to Life and a Woman Healed

18 While he was saying these things to them, suddenly a leader of the synagogue[d] came in and knelt before him, saying, "My daughter has just died; but come and lay your hand on her, and she will live." [19]And Jesus got up and followed him, with his disciples. [20]Then suddenly a woman who had been suffering from hemorrhages for twelve years came up behind him and touched the fringe of his cloak, [21]for she said to herself, "If I only touch his cloak, I will be made well." [22]Jesus turned, and seeing her he said, "Take heart, daughter; your faith has made you well." And instantly the woman was made well. [23]When Jesus came to the leader's house and saw the flute players and the crowd making a commotion, [24]he said, "Go away; for the girl is not dead but sleeping." And they laughed at him. [25]But when the crowd had been put outside, he went in and took her by the hand, and the girl got up. [26]And the report of this spread throughout that district.

Jesus Heals Two Blind Men

27 As Jesus went on from there, two blind men followed him, crying loudly, "Have mercy on us, Son of David!" [28]When he entered the house, the blind men came to him; and Jesus said to them, "Do you believe that I am able to do this?" They said to him, "Yes, Lord." [29]Then he touched their eyes and said, "According to your faith let it be done to you." [30]And their eyes were opened. Then Jesus sternly ordered them, "See that no one knows of this." [31]But they went away and spread the news about him throughout that district.

Jesus Heals One Who Was Mute

32 After they had gone away, a demoniac who was mute was brought to him. [33]And when the demon had been cast out, the one who had been mute spoke; and the crowds were amazed and said, "Never has anything like this been seen in Israel." [34]But the Pharisees said, "By the ruler of the demons he casts out the demons."[e]

The Harvest Is Great, the Laborers Few

35 Then Jesus went about all the cities and villages, teaching in their synagogues, and proclaiming the good news of the kingdom, and curing every disease and every sickness. [36]When he saw the crowds, he had compassion for them, because they were harassed and helpless, like sheep without a shepherd. [37]Then he said to his disciples, "The harvest is plentiful, but the laborers are few; [38]therefore ask the Lord of the harvest to send out laborers into his harvest."

---

a Gk reclined b Gk were reclining c Other ancient authorities lack often d Gk lacks of the synagogue e Other ancient authorities lack this verse

The Twelve Apostles

10 Then Jesus[a] summoned his twelve disciples and gave them authority over unclean spirits, to cast them out, and to cure every disease and every sickness. [2]These are the names of the twelve apostles: first, Simon, also known as Peter, and his brother Andrew; James son of Zebedee, and his brother John; [3]Philip and Bartholomew; Thomas and Matthew the tax collector; James son of Alphaeus, and Thaddaeus;[b] [4]Simon the Cananaean, and Judas Iscariot, the one who betrayed him.

The Mission of the Twelve

[5] These twelve Jesus sent out with the following instructions: "Go nowhere among the Gentiles, and enter no town of the Samaritans, [6]but go rather to the lost sheep of the house of Israel. [7]As you go, proclaim the good news, 'The kingdom of heaven has come near.'[c] [8]Cure the sick, raise the dead, cleanse the lepers,[d] cast out demons. You received without payment; give without payment. [9]Take no gold, or silver, or copper in your belts, [10]no bag for your journey, or two tunics, or sandals, or a staff; for laborers deserve their food. [11]Whatever town or village you enter, find out who in it is worthy, and stay there until you leave. [12]As you enter the house, greet it. [13]If the house is worthy, let your peace come upon it; but if it is not worthy, let your peace return to you. [14]If anyone will not welcome you or listen to your words, shake off the dust from your feet as you leave that house or town. [15]Truly I tell you, it will be more tolerable for the land of Sodom and Gomorrah on the day of judgment than for that town.

Coming Persecutions

[16] "See, I am sending you out like sheep into the midst of wolves; so be wise as serpents and innocent as doves. [17]Beware of them, for they will hand you over to councils and flog you in their synagogues; [18]and you will be dragged before governors and kings because of me, as a testimony to them and the Gentiles. [19]When they hand you over, do not worry about how you are to speak or what you are to say; for what you are to say will be given to you at that time; [20]for it is not you who speak, but the Spirit of your Father speaking through you. [21]Brother will betray brother to death, and a father his child, and children will rise against parents and have them put to death; [22]and you will be hated by all because of

my name. But the one who endures to the end will be saved. [23]When they persecute you in one town, flee to the next; for truly I tell you, you will not have gone through all the towns of Israel before the Son of Man comes.

[24] "A disciple is not above the teacher, nor a slave above the master; [25]it is enough for the disciple to be like the teacher, and the slave like the master. If they have called the master of the house Beelzebul, how much more will they malign those of his household!

Whom to Fear

[26] "So have no fear of them; for nothing is covered up that will not be uncovered, and nothing secret that will not become known. [27]What I say to you in the dark, tell in the light; and what you hear whispered, proclaim from the housetops. [28]Do not fear those who kill the body but cannot kill the soul; rather fear him who can destroy both soul and body in hell.[e] [29]Are not two sparrows sold for a penny? Yet not one of them will fall to the ground apart from your Father. [30]And even the hairs of your head are all counted. [31]So do not be afraid; you are of more value than many sparrows.

[32] "Everyone therefore who acknowledges me before others, I also will acknowledge before my Father in heaven; [33]but whoever denies me before others, I also will deny before my Father in heaven.

Not Peace, but a Sword

[34] "Do not think that I have come to bring peace to the earth; I have not come to bring peace, but a sword.

[35] For I have come to set a man against his father,
and a daughter against her mother,
and a daughter-in-law against her
mother-in-law;
[36] and one's foes will be members of one's own
household.

[37]Whoever loves father or mother more than me is not worthy of me; and whoever loves son or daughter more than me is not worthy of me; [38]and whoever does not take up the cross and follow me is not worthy of me. [39]Those who find their life will lose it, and those who lose their life for my sake will find it.

Rewards

[40] "Whoever welcomes you welcomes me, and

a Gk *he* **b** Other ancient authorities read *Lebbaeus*, or *Lebbaeus called Thaddaeus* **c** Or *is at hand* **d** The terms *leper* and *leprosy* can refer to several diseases **e** Gk *Gehenna*

A Violent Jesus? · Matthew 10:34–39

Jesus says a curious thing as he prepares the twelve disciples for their mission: "I have not come to bring peace, but a sword" (Matthew 10:34). This is one of the many hard sayings attributed to Jesus in the Gospels. Jesus is speaking metaphorically to emphasize the extreme demands of discipleship. He is not advocating violence, but simply predicting how people will react to the new values and way of life of his followers. The author of Matthew lived in a community that knew living as Jesus' disciples wasn't always simple or easy. The people wished for peace, but living by Jesus' words brought them hatred and conflict with people in power. At the time Matthew was written, disciples and followers of Christ needed to be able to give up everything, including family attachments (Matthew 10:37), in order to follow Jesus.

- Is it any different today?
- What attachments would be difficult for you to leave behind?

whoever welcomes me welcomes the one who sent me. ⁴¹Whoever welcomes a prophet in the name of a prophet will receive a prophet's reward; and whoever welcomes a righteous person in the name of a righteous person will receive the reward of the righteous; ⁴²and whoever gives even a cup of cold water to one of these little ones in the name of a disciple—truly I tell you, none of these will lose their reward."

11 Now when Jesus had finished instructing his twelve disciples, he went on from there to teach and proclaim his message in their cities.

Messengers from John the Baptist

2 When John heard in prison what the Messiah*a* was doing, he sent word by his*b* disciples ³and said to him, "Are you the one who is to come, or are we to wait for another?" ⁴Jesus answered them, "Go and tell John what you hear and see: ⁵the blind receive their sight, the lame walk, the lepers*c* are cleansed, the deaf hear, the dead are raised, and the poor have good news brought to them. ⁶And blessed is anyone who takes no offense at me."

Jesus Praises John the Baptist

7 As they went away, Jesus began to speak to the crowds about John: "What did you go out into the wilderness to look at? A reed shaken by the wind? ⁸What then did you go out to see? Someone*d* dressed in soft robes? Look, those who wear soft

robes are in royal palaces. ⁹What then did you go out to see? A prophet?*e* Yes, I tell you, and more than a prophet. ¹⁰This is the one about whom it is written,

'See, I am sending my messenger ahead of you,
   who will prepare your way before you.'

¹¹Truly I tell you, among those born of women no one has arisen greater than John the Baptist; yet the least in the kingdom of heaven is greater than he. ¹²From the days of John the Baptist until now the kingdom of heaven has suffered violence,*f* and the violent take it by force. ¹³For all the prophets and the law prophesied until John came; ¹⁴and if you are willing to accept it, he is Elijah who is to come. ¹⁵Let anyone with ears*g* listen!

16 "But to what will I compare this generation? It is like children sitting in the marketplaces and calling to one another,

¹⁷ 'We played the flute for you, and you did not
   dance;
   we wailed, and you did not mourn.'

¹⁸For John came neither eating nor drinking, and they say, 'He has a demon'; ¹⁹the Son of Man came eating and drinking, and they say, 'Look, a glutton and a drunkard, a friend of tax collectors and sinners!' Yet wisdom is vindicated by her deeds."*h*

Woes to Unrepentant Cities

20 Then he began to reproach the cities in which most of his deeds of power had been done, because they did not repent. ²¹"Woe to you, Chorazin! Woe to you, Bethsaida! For if the deeds of power done

---

a Or *the Christ* **b** Other ancient authorities read *two of his* **c** The terms *leper* and *leprosy* can refer to several diseases **d** Or *Why then did you go out? To see someone* **e** Other ancient authorities read *Why then did you go out? To see a prophet?* **f** Or *has been coming violently* **g** Other ancient authorities add *to hear* **h** Other ancient authorities read *children*

in you had been done in Tyre and Sidon, they would have repented long ago in sackcloth and ashes. [22]But I tell you, on the day of judgment it will be more tolerable for Tyre and Sidon than for you. [23]And you, Capernaum,

will you be exalted to heaven?

No, you will be brought down to Hades. For if the deeds of power done in you had been done in Sodom, it would have remained until this day. [24]But I tell you that on the day of judgment it will be more tolerable for the land of Sodom than for you."

Jesus Thanks His Father

25 At that time Jesus said, "I thank[a] you, Father, Lord of heaven and earth, because you have hidden these things from the wise and the intelligent and have revealed them to infants; [26]yes, Father, for such was your gracious will.[b] [27]All things have been handed over to me by my Father; and no one knows the Son except the Father, and no one knows the Father except the Son and anyone to whom the Son chooses to reveal him.

28 "Come to me, all you that are weary and are carrying heavy burdens, and I will give you rest. [29]Take my yoke upon you, and learn from me; for I am gentle and humble in heart, and you will find rest for your souls. [30]For my yoke is easy, and my burden is light."

Plucking Grain on the Sabbath

12 At that time Jesus went through the grainfields on the sabbath; his disciples were hungry, and they began to pluck heads of grain and to eat. [2]When the Pharisees saw it, they said to him, "Look, your disciples are doing what is not lawful to do on the sabbath." [3]He said to them, "Have you not read what David did when he and his companions were hungry? [4]He entered the house of God and ate the bread of the Presence, which it was not lawful for him or his companions to eat, but only for the priests. [5]Or have you not read in the law that on the sabbath the priests in the temple break the sabbath and yet are guiltless? [6]I tell you, something greater than the temple is here. [7]But if you had known what this means, 'I desire mercy and not sacrifice,' you would not have condemned the guiltless. [8]For the Son of Man is lord of the sabbath."

The Man with a Withered Hand

9 He left that place and entered their synagogue; [10]a man was there with a withered hand, and they asked him, "Is it lawful to cure on the sabbath?" so that they might accuse him. [11]He said to them, "Suppose one of you has only one sheep and it falls into a pit on the sabbath; will you not lay hold of it and lift it out? [12]How much more valuable is a human being than a sheep! So it is lawful to do good on the sabbath." [13]Then he said to the man, "Stretch out your hand." He stretched it out, and it was restored, as sound as the other. [14]But the Pharisees went out and conspired against him, how to destroy him.

God's Chosen Servant

15 When Jesus became aware of this, he departed. Many crowds[c] followed him, and he cured all of them, [16]and he ordered them not to make him known. [17]This was to fulfill what had been spoken through the prophet Isaiah:
[18] "Here is my servant, whom I have chosen,
        my beloved, with whom my soul is well
            pleased.
    I will put my Spirit upon him,
        and he will proclaim justice to the
            Gentiles.
[19]   He will not wrangle or cry aloud,
        nor will anyone hear his voice in the
            streets.
[20]   He will not break a bruised reed
        or quench a smoldering wick
    until he brings justice to victory.
[21]   And in his name the Gentiles will hope."

Jesus and Beelzebul

22 Then they brought to him a demoniac who was blind and mute; and he cured him, so that the one who had been mute could speak and see. [23]All the crowds were amazed and said, "Can this be the Son of David?" [24]But when the Pharisees heard it, they said, "It is only by Beelzebul, the ruler of the demons, that this fellow casts out the demons." [25]He knew what they were thinking and said to them, "Every kingdom divided against itself is laid waste, and no city or house divided against itself will stand. [26]If Satan casts out Satan, he is divided against himself; how then will his kingdom stand? [27]If I cast out demons by Beelzebul, by whom do your own exorcists[d] cast them out? Therefore they will be your judges. [28]But if it is by the Spirit of God that I cast out demons, then the kingdom of God has come

---

a Or *praise*   b Or *for so it was well-pleasing in your sight*   c Other ancient authorities lack *crowds*   d Gk *sons* to you. [29]Or how can one enter a strong man's house and plunder his property, without first tying up the strong man? Then indeed the house can be plundered. [30]Whoever is not with me is against me, and whoever does not gather with me scatters. [31]Therefore I tell you, people will be forgiven for every sin and blasphemy, but blasphemy against the Spirit will not be forgiven. [32]Whoever speaks a word against the Son of Man will be forgiven, but whoever speaks against the Holy Spirit will not be forgiven, either in this age or in the age to come.

A Tree and Its Fruit

33 "Either make the tree good, and its fruit good; or make the tree bad, and its fruit bad; for the tree

LIVE IT!

Tripping over My Tongue
Matthew 12:33–37

We use words all day, every day. We speak, read, type, text, write, and listen. And the fact that words are so common sometimes makes us forget how powerful they are. **Matthew 12** reminds us of their power and importance. Jesus compares our words to the fruit of a tree. Good tree, good fruit. Bad tree, bad fruit. Sometimes we get that backwards, feeling guilty about our habit of swearing or our carelessness in saying bad things about others. We think that our bad words make us bad. But **Matthew 12:34** says, "Out of the abundance of the heart the mouth speaks." That means that our words don't make us sinful—it's our sin that causes us to use words for harm rather than good.

So how can you quit swearing, gossiping, or putting others down? Change your heart. Allow God to replace the sin in your heart with love, grace, and goodness. Then the abundant good in your heart will overflow, and your mouth will speak it. It won't happen completely or all at once, but more and more your words will reflect your good treasure (Matthew 12:35)—Jesus living in you.

is known by its fruit. [34]You brood of vipers! How can you speak good things, when you are evil? For out of the abundance of the heart the mouth speaks. [35]The good person brings good things out of a good treasure, and the evil person brings evil things out of an evil treasure. [36]I tell you, on the day of judgment you will have to give an account for every careless word you utter; [37]for by your words you will be justified, and by your words you will be condemned."

The Sign of Jonah

38 Then some of the scribes and Pharisees said to him, "Teacher, we wish to see a sign from you." [39]But he answered them, "An evil and adulterous generation asks for a sign, but no sign will be given to it except the sign of the prophet Jonah. [40]For just as Jonah was three days and three nights in the belly of the sea monster, so for three days and three nights the Son of Man will be in the heart of the earth. [41]The people of Nineveh will rise up at the judgment with this generation and condemn it, because they repented at the proclamation of Jonah, and see, something greater than Jonah is here! [42]The queen of the South will rise up at the judgment with this generation and condemn it, because she came from the ends of the earth to listen to the wisdom of Solomon, and see, something greater than Solomon is here!

The Return of the Unclean Spirit

43 "When the unclean spirit has gone out of a person, it wanders through waterless regions looking for a resting place, but it finds none. [44]Then it says, 'I will return to my house from which I came.' When it comes, it finds it empty, swept, and put in order. [45]Then it goes and brings along seven other spirits more evil than itself, and they enter and live there; and the last state of that person is worse than the first. So will it be also with this evil generation."

The True Kindred of Jesus

46 While he was still speaking to the crowds, his mother and his brothers were standing outside, wanting to speak to him. [47]Someone told him, "Look, your mother and your brothers are standing outside, wanting to speak to you."[a] [48]But to the one who had told him this, Jesus[b] replied, "Who is my mother, and who are my brothers?" [49]And pointing to his disciples, he said, "Here are my mother and

a Other ancient authorities lack verse 47   b Gk *he*

my brothers! [50]For whoever does the will of my Father in heaven is my brother and sister and mother."

The Parable of the Sower

13 That same day Jesus went out of the house and sat beside the sea. [2]Such great crowds gathered around him that he got into a boat and sat there, while the whole crowd stood on the beach. [3]And he told them many things in parables, saying: "Listen! A sower went out to sow. [4]And as he sowed, some seeds fell on the path, and the birds came and ate them up. [5]Other seeds fell on rocky ground, where they did not have much soil, and they sprang up quickly, since they had no depth of soil. [6]But when the sun rose, they were scorched; and since they had no root, they withered away. [7]Other seeds fell among thorns, and the thorns grew up and choked them. [8]Other seeds fell on good soil and brought forth grain, some a hundredfold, some sixty, some thirty. [9]Let anyone with ears[a] listen!"

The Purpose of the Parables

10 Then the disciples came and asked him, "Why do you speak to them in parables?" [11]He answered, "To you it has been given to know the secrets[b] of the kingdom of heaven, but to them it has not been given. [12]For to those who have, more will be given, and they will have an abundance; but from those who have nothing, even what they have will be taken away. [13]The reason I speak to them in parables is that 'seeing they do not perceive, and hearing they do not listen, nor do they understand.' [14]With them indeed is fulfilled the prophecy of Isaiah that says:

'You will indeed listen, but never understand,
    and you will indeed look, but never perceive.
[15] For this people's heart has grown dull,
    and their ears are hard of hearing,
    and they have shut their eyes;
    so that they might not look with their eyes,
    and listen with their ears,
and understand with their heart and turn—
    and I would heal them.'

[16]But blessed are your eyes, for they see, and your ears, for they hear. [17]Truly I tell you, many prophets and righteous people longed to see what you see, but did not see it, and to hear what you hear, but did not hear it.

The Parable of the Sower Explained

18 "Hear then the parable of the sower. [19]When anyone hears the word of the kingdom and does not understand it, the evil one comes and snatches away what is sown in the heart; this is what was sown on the path. [20]As for what was sown on rocky ground, this is the one who hears the word and immediately receives it with joy; [21]yet such a person has no root, but endures only for a while, and when trouble or persecution arises on account of the word, that person immediately falls away.[c] [22]As for what was sown among thorns, this is the one who hears the word, but the cares of the world and the lure of wealth choke the word, and it yields nothing. [23]But as for what was sown on good soil, this is the

STUDY IT!

The Riddle of Parables · Matthew 13:10–17

Jesus often taught in parables—fictional stories to make a point. Many of Jesus' parables are like riddles. They have surprising or shocking endings designed to tease the people of his time into examining certain beliefs they took for granted. The examples Jesus used (baking bread, planting crops, herding sheep, or fishing for supper) were familiar to the people of his day, because they were everyday activities. Because those examples aren't as familiar to us today, Jesus' parables can be hard to understand. But even with the cultural differences, the parables get our minds thinking—they get us to actively ask questions and seek the truths contained in them. Jesus says in **Matthew 13:15** that many people have hardened their hearts against the truth. The important thing for us is to seek understanding, so that it can be said of us, "Blessed are your eyes, for they see, and your ears, for they hear" (Matthew 13:16).

---

a Other ancient authorities add *to hear*   **b** Or *mysteries*   **c** Gk *stumbles*

one who hears the word and understands it, who indeed bears fruit and yields, in one case a hundredfold, in another sixty, and in another thirty."

The Parable of Weeds among the Wheat

24 He put before them another parable: "The kingdom of heaven may be compared to someone who sowed good seed in his field; 25but while everybody was asleep, an enemy came and sowed weeds among the wheat, and then went away. 26So when the plants came up and bore grain, then the weeds appeared as well. 27And the slaves of the householder came and said to him, 'Master, did you not sow good seed in your field? Where, then, did these weeds come from?' 28He answered, 'An enemy has done this.' The slaves said to him, 'Then do you want us to go and gather them?' 29But he replied, 'No; for in gathering the weeds you would uproot the wheat along with them. 30Let both of them grow together until the harvest; and at harvest time I will tell the reapers, Collect the weeds first and bind them in bundles to be burned, but gather the wheat into my barn.' "

The Parable of the Mustard Seed

31 He put before them another parable: "The kingdom of heaven is like a mustard seed that someone took and sowed in his field; 32it is the smallest of all the seeds, but when it has grown it is the greatest of shrubs and becomes a tree, so that the birds of the air come and make nests in its branches."

The Parable of the Yeast

33 He told them another parable: "The kingdom of heaven is like yeast that a woman took and mixed in with*a* three measures of flour until all of it was leavened."

The Use of Parables

34 Jesus told the crowds all these things in parables; without a parable he told them nothing. 35This was to fulfill what had been spoken through the prophet:*b*

"I will open my mouth to speak in parables;
    I will proclaim what has been hidden from
       the foundation of the world."*c*

Jesus Explains the Parable of the Weeds

36 Then he left the crowds and went into the house. And his disciples approached him, saying,

PRAY IT!

The Kingdom Is Like . . .
Matthew 13:10–53

In trying to get people to understand something as mysterious as the kingdom of heaven, Jesus used ordinary objects like seeds and light, salt and yeast. He chose everyday actions, such as farming, fishing, and baking, to illustrate truth. And in doing so he helped the people of his time to understand the new life that comes with the kingdom of heaven. These metaphors also make it clear that the kingdom of heaven is not some distant place we are trying to get to, but a reality we have to work toward creating here on earth. Heaven is living forever in perfect communion with Christ and all who believe in him.

What does the kingdom of heaven mean to you? Based on what you read in **Matthew 13:10–53**, meditate on the following questions:

- What would our world look like if it truly reflected Jesus' vision for the kingdom of heaven?
- What object, action, or image best describes your understanding of the kingdom of heaven?
- End your meditation with a prayer that your life will be a living sign to help others understand what the kingdom of heaven is all about.

"Explain to us the parable of the weeds of the field." 37He answered, "The one who sows the good seed is the Son of Man; 38the field is the world, and the good seed are the children of the kingdom; the weeds are the children of the evil one, 39and the enemy who sowed them is the devil; the harvest is the end of the age, and the reapers are angels. 40Just as the weeds are collected and burned up with fire, so will it be at the end of the age. 41The Son of Man will send his angels, and they will collect out of his kingdom all causes of sin and all evildoers, 42and they will throw

a Gk *hid in*   *b* Other ancient authorities read *the prophet Isaiah*   *c* Other ancient authorities lack *of the world*

them into the furnace of fire, where there will be weeping and gnashing of teeth. ⁴³Then the righteous will shine like the sun in the kingdom of their Father. Let anyone with ears*ᵃ* listen!

Three Parables

44 "The kingdom of heaven is like treasure hidden in a field, which someone found and hid; then in his joy he goes and sells all that he has and buys that field.

45 "Again, the kingdom of heaven is like a merchant in search of fine pearls; ⁴⁶on finding one pearl of great value, he went and sold all that he had and bought it.

47 "Again, the kingdom of heaven is like a net that was thrown into the sea and caught fish of every kind; ⁴⁸when it was full, they drew it ashore, sat down, and put the good into baskets but threw out the bad. ⁴⁹So it will be at the end of the age. The angels will come out and separate the evil from the righteous ⁵⁰and throw them into the furnace of fire, where there will be weeping and gnashing of teeth.

Treasures New and Old

51 "Have you understood all this?" They answered, "Yes." ⁵²And he said to them, "Therefore every scribe who has been trained for the kingdom of heaven is like the master of a household who brings out of his treasure what is new and what is old." ⁵³When Jesus had finished these parables, he left that place.

The Rejection of Jesus at Nazareth

54 He came to his hometown and began to teach the people*ᵇ* in their synagogue, so that they were astounded and said, "Where did this man get this wisdom and these deeds of power? ⁵⁵Is not this the carpenter's son? Is not his mother called Mary? And are not his brothers James and Joseph and Simon and Judas? ⁵⁶And are not all his sisters with us? Where then did this man get all this?" ⁵⁷And they took of-

fense at him. But Jesus said to them, "Prophets are not without honor except in their own country and in their own house." ⁵⁸And he did not do many deeds of power there, because of their unbelief.

The Death of John the Baptist

14 At that time Herod the ruler*ᶜ* heard reports about Jesus; ²and he said to his servants, "This is John the Baptist; he has been raised from the dead, and for this reason these powers are at work in him." ³For Herod had arrested John, bound him, and put him in prison on account of Herodias, his brother Philip's wife,*ᵈ* ⁴because John had been telling him, "It is not lawful for you to have her." ⁵Though Herod*ᵉ* wanted to put him to death, he feared the crowd, because they regarded him as a prophet. ⁶But when Herod's birthday came, the daughter of Herodias danced before the company, and she pleased Herod ⁷so much that he promised on oath to grant her whatever she might ask. ⁸Prompted by her mother, she said, "Give me the head of John the Baptist here on a platter." ⁹The king was grieved, yet out of regard for his oaths and for the guests, he commanded it to be given; ¹⁰he sent and had John beheaded in the prison. ¹¹The head was brought on a platter and given to the girl, who brought it to her mother. ¹²His disciples came and took the body and buried it; then they went and told Jesus.

Feeding the Five Thousand

13 Now when Jesus heard this, he withdrew from there in a boat to a deserted place by himself. But when the crowds heard it, they followed him on foot from the towns. ¹⁴When he went ashore, he saw a great crowd; and he had compassion for them and cured their sick. ¹⁵When it was evening, the disciples came to him and said, "This is a deserted place, and the hour is now late; send the crowds away so that they may go into the villages and buy food for themselves." ¹⁶Jesus said to them, "They need not go away; you give them something to eat." ¹⁷They replied, "We have nothing here but five loaves and two fish." ¹⁸And he said, "Bring them here to me." ¹⁹Then he ordered the crowds to sit down on the grass. Taking the five loaves and the two fish, he looked up to heaven, and blessed and broke the loaves, and gave them to the disciples, and the disciples gave them to the crowds. ²⁰And all ate and were filled; and they took up what was left over of

---

ᵃ Other ancient authorities add *to hear* *ᵇ* Gk *them* *ᶜ* Gk *tetrarch* *ᵈ* Other ancient authorities read *his brother's wife* *ᵉ* Gk *he*

the broken pieces, twelve baskets full. ²¹ And those who ate were about five thousand men, besides women and children.

Jesus Walks on the Water

22 Immediately he made the disciples get into the boat and go on ahead to the other side, while he dismissed the crowds. ²³ And after he had dismissed the crowds, he went up the mountain by himself to pray. When evening came, he was there alone, ²⁴ but by this time the boat, battered by the waves, was far from the land,ᵃ for the wind was against them. ²⁵ And early in the morning he came walking toward them on the sea. ²⁶ But when the disciples saw him walking on the sea, they were terrified, saying, "It is a ghost!" And they cried out in fear. ²⁷ But immediately Jesus spoke to them and said, "Take heart, it is I; do not be afraid."

28 Peter answered him, "Lord, if it is you, command me to come to you on the water." ²⁹ He said, "Come." So Peter got out of the boat, started walking on the water, and came toward Jesus. ³⁰ But when he noticed the strong wind,ᵇ he became frightened, and beginning to sink, he cried out, "Lord, save me!" ³¹ Jesus immediately reached out his hand and caught him, saying to him, "You of little faith, why did you doubt?" ³² When they got into the boat, the wind ceased. ³³ And those in the boat worshiped him, saying, "Truly you are the Son of God."

Jesus Heals the Sick in Gennesaret

34 When they had crossed over, they came to land at Gennesaret. ³⁵ After the people of that place recognized him, they sent word throughout the region and brought all who were sick to him, ³⁶ and begged him that they might touch even the fringe of his cloak; and all who touched it were healed.

The Tradition of the Elders

15 Then Pharisees and scribes came to Jesus from Jerusalem and said, ²"Why do your disciples break the tradition of the elders? For they do not wash their hands before they eat." ³ He answered them, "And why do you break the commandment of God for the sake of your tradition? ⁴ For God said,ᶜ 'Honor your father and your mother,' and, 'Whoever speaks evil of father or mother must surely die.' ⁵ But you say that whoever tells father or mother, 'Whatever support you might have had from me is given to God,'ᵈ then that person need not honor the father.ᵉ ⁶ So, for the sake of your tradition, you make void the wordᶠ of God. ⁷ You hypocrites! Isaiah prophesied rightly about you when he said:

8 'This people honors me with their
        lips,
    but their hearts are far from me;
9 in vain do they worship me,
        teaching human precepts as
                doctrines.' "

Do You Trust Jesus? · Matthew 14:22–33

At this point in Matthew, different groups are beginning to line up for or against Jesus. The Pharisees, Sadducees, and scribes don't trust him. The disciples still follow Jesus, but they don't yet understand who he really is. In **Matthew 14–17**, the true identity of Jesus is revealed to the disciples through several signs and wonders. Peter in particular is being prepared for his role as a leader.

Matthew is the only one of the four gospels that includes the story of Peter's walking on the water (Matthew 14:22-33). If you have gotten acquainted with Peter (see "Study It: Introducing . . . Peter," near Matthew 16:13-20), it won't surprise you that he was willing to take the risk. But why does Peter start to sink? When he's focused on Jesus, everything is fine. It's when he takes his eyes off Jesus, noticing the fierce storm, that he begins to sink.

Jesus invites you to risk a relationship with him. You have to step out in faith, maybe leaving some old ways of life behind. Learn from Peter's mistake: stay focused on Jesus. As the disciples learned, this is no ordinary man, but the Son of God! Following Jesus might get scary or difficult at times, but all great adventures involve some risk.

ᵃ Other ancient authorities read *was out on the sea* ᵇ Other ancient authorities read *the wind* ᶜ Other ancient authorities read *commanded, saying*
ᵈ Or *is an offering* ᵉ Other ancient authorities add *or the mother* ᶠ Other ancient authorities read *law* ; others, *commandment*

Things That Defile

10 Then he called the crowd to him and said to them, "Listen and understand: [11]it is not what goes into the mouth that defiles a person, but it is what comes out of the mouth that defiles." [12]Then the disciples approached and said to him, "Do you know that the Pharisees took offense when they heard what you said?" [13]He answered, "Every plant that my heavenly Father has not planted will be uprooted. [14]Let them alone; they are blind guides of the blind.[a] And if one blind person guides another, both will fall into a pit." [15]But Peter said to him, "Explain this parable to us." [16]Then he said, "Are you also still without understanding? [17]Do you not see that whatever goes into the mouth enters the stomach, and goes out into the sewer? [18]But what comes out of the mouth proceeds from the heart, and this is what defiles. [19]For out of the heart come evil intentions, murder, adultery, fornication, theft, false witness, slander. [20]These are what defile a person, but to eat with unwashed hands does not defile."

The Canaanite Woman's Faith

21 Jesus left that place and went away to the district of Tyre and Sidon. [22]Just then a Canaanite woman from that region came out and started shouting, "Have mercy on me, Lord, Son of David; my daughter is tormented by a demon." [23]But he did not answer her at all. And his disciples came and urged him, saying, "Send her away, for she keeps shouting after us." [24]He answered, "I was sent only to the lost sheep of the house of Israel." [25]But she came and knelt before him, saying, "Lord, help me." [26]He answered, "It is not fair to take the children's food and throw it to the dogs." [27]She said, "Yes, Lord, yet even the dogs eat the crumbs that fall from their masters' table." [28]Then Jesus answered her, "Woman, great is your faith! Let it be done for you as you wish." And her daughter was healed instantly.

Jesus Cures Many People

29 After Jesus had left that place, he passed along the Sea of Galilee, and he went up the mountain, where he sat down. [30]Great crowds came to him, bringing with them the lame, the maimed, the blind, the mute, and many others. They put them at his feet, and he cured them, [31]so that the crowd was amazed when they saw the mute speaking, the maimed whole, the lame walking, and the blind seeing. And they praised the God of Israel.

Feeding the Four Thousand

32 Then Jesus called his disciples to him and said, "I have compassion for the crowd, because they have been with me now for three days and have nothing to eat; and I do not want to send them away hungry, for they might faint on the way." [33]The disciples said to him, "Where are we to get enough bread in the desert to feed so great a crowd?" [34]Jesus asked them, "How many loaves have you?" They said, "Seven, and a few small fish." [35]Then ordering the crowd to sit down on the ground, [36]he took the seven loaves and the fish; and after giving thanks he broke them and gave them to the disciples, and the disciples gave them to the crowds. [37]And all of them ate and were filled; and they took up the broken pieces left over, seven baskets full. [38]Those who had eaten were four thousand men, besides women and children. [39]After sending away the crowds, he got into the boat and went to the region of Magadan.[b]

The Demand for a Sign

16 The Pharisees and Sadducees came, and to test Jesus[c] they asked him to show them a sign from heaven. [2]He answered them, "When it is evening, you say, 'It will be fair weather, for the sky is red.' [3]And in the morning, 'It will be stormy today, for the sky is red and threatening.' You know how to interpret the appearance of the sky, but you cannot interpret the signs of the times.[d] [4]An evil and adulterous generation asks for a sign, but no sign will be given to it except the sign of Jonah." Then he left them and went away.

The Yeast of the Pharisees and Sadducees

5 When the disciples reached the other side, they had forgotten to bring any bread. [6]Jesus said to them, "Watch out, and beware of the yeast of the Pharisees and Sadducees." [7]They said to one another, "It is because we have brought no bread." [8]And becoming aware of it, Jesus said, "You of little faith, why are you talking about having no bread? [9]Do you still not perceive? Do you not remember the five loaves for the five thousand, and how many baskets you gathered? [10]Or the seven loaves for the four thousand, and how many baskets you gathered? [11]How could you fail to perceive that I was not speaking about bread? Beware of the yeast of the Pharisees and Sadducees!" [12]Then they understood that he had not told them to beware of the yeast of bread, but of the teaching of the Pharisees and Sadducees.

---

a Other ancient authorities lack *of the blind*   b Other ancient authorities read *Magdala* or *Magdalan*   c Gk *him*   d Other ancient authorities lack *²When it is . . . of the times*

Peter's Declaration about Jesus

13 Now when Jesus came into the district of Caesarea Philippi, he asked his disciples, "Who do people say that the Son of Man is?" [14]And they said, "Some say John the Baptist, but others Elijah, and still others Jeremiah or one of the prophets." [15]He said to them, "But who do you say that I am?" [16]Simon Peter answered, "You are the Messiah,[a] the Son of the living God." [17]And Jesus answered him, "Blessed are you, Simon son of Jonah! For flesh and blood has not revealed this to you, but my Father in heaven. [18]And I tell you, you are Peter,[b] and on this rock[c] I will build my church, and the gates of Hades will not prevail against it. [19]I will give you the keys of the kingdom of heaven, and whatever you bind on earth will be bound in heaven, and whatever you loose on earth will be loosed in heaven." [20]Then he sternly ordered the disciples not to tell anyone that he was[d] the Messiah.[a]

Jesus Foretells His Death and Resurrection

21 From that time on, Jesus began to show his disciples that he must go to Jerusalem and undergo great suffering at the hands of the elders and chief priests and scribes, and be killed, and on the third day be raised. [22]And Peter took him aside and began to rebuke him, saying, "God forbid it, Lord! This must never happen to you." [23]But he turned and said to Peter, "Get behind me, Satan! You are a stumbling block to me; for you are setting your mind not on divine things but on human things."

The Cross and Self-Denial

24 Then Jesus told his disciples, "If any want to become my followers, let them deny themselves and take up their cross and follow me. [25]For those who want to save their life will lose it, and those who lose their life for my sake will find it. [26]For what will it profit them if they gain the whole world but forfeit their life? Or what will they give in return for their life?

27 "For the Son of Man is to come with his angels in the glory of his Father, and then he will repay everyone for what has been done. [28]Truly I tell you, there are some standing here who will not taste death before they see the Son of Man coming in his kingdom."

STUDY IT!

Introducing . . .
Peter
Matthew 16:13–20

The simple fisherman named Simon, called Peter, was among the first disciples called by Jesus (Matthew 4:18; Mark 1:16; Luke 5:10). The Bible paints a picture of a very human leader with sins and weaknesses along with many gifts and great faith. He was the hopeful believer who first recognized Jesus as the Messiah (Matthew 16:16; Mark 8:29; Luke 9:20). He was the fearful friend who denied Jesus three times (Matthew 26:69–74; Mark 14:66–72; Luke 22:54–61; John 18:15–27). And he was the leader of the early Church (John 21:15; Acts 2:14).

The author of Matthew uses a play on words to make a statement about Peter as the foundation of the Church. The new name Jesus gives him—Peter—means "rock." So Jesus is saying, "You are a rock, and on this rock I will build my church" (Matthew 16:18). Above all else, Peter is an example of how God uses people in all their human strengths and weaknesses for God's purposes and glory.

The Transfiguration

17 Six days later, Jesus took with him Peter and James and his brother John and led them up a high mountain, by themselves. [2]And he was transfigured before them, and his face shone like the sun, and his clothes became dazzling white. [3]Suddenly there appeared to them Moses and Elijah, talking with him. [4]Then Peter said to Jesus, "Lord, it is good for us to be here; if you wish, I[e] will make three dwellings[f] here, one for you, one for Moses, and one for Elijah." [5]While he was still speaking, suddenly a bright cloud overshadowed them, and from the cloud a voice said, "This is my Son, the Beloved;[g] with him I am well pleased; listen to him!" [6]When the disciples heard this, they fell to the ground and were overcome by fear. [7]But Jesus came and touched them, saying, "Get up and do not be afraid." [8]And when they looked up, they saw no one except Jesus himself alone.

a Or the Christ   b Gk Petros   c Gk petra   d Other ancient authorities add Jesus   e Other ancient authorities read we   f Or tents   g Or my beloved Son

The Old and New Testaments Working Together
Matthew 17:1–13

The word "old" can often be taken to mean outdated or no longer useful. Unfortunately, some people assume those meanings when they hear the words "Old Testament." But Matthew is clear that the Old Testament is indeed relevant and that Jesus is its fulfillment.

Look at the story of the transfiguration. It's packed with allusions and references to the Old Testament. According to Matthew, the event took place on a mountain, which immediately calls to mind Moses' meeting with God and establishing the covenant on Mount Sinai (see Exodus 24:12-18). The gospel of Matthew also says that Moses (who represents the law) and Elijah (who represents the prophets) appeared with Jesus on the mountain; their presence highlights how Jesus' work is in agreement with the Old Testament law and prophets. Another allusion can be found in the cloud that accompanies God's presence during the scene, a cloud much like the one that led the Israelites during their wanderings in the desert (see Exodus 40:34-37). A final reference to the Old Testament can be found in God's words commanding the disciples to listen to Jesus. This fulfills a prophecy in Deuteronomy that states that God would deliver a prophet who would speak God's words and all are called to listen to him (see Exodus 18:14-22).

From the beginning of creation to the sending of Jesus and the Holy Spirit, God gradually revealed himself and his plan for our salvation. Because God's one plan spans both the Old and New Testaments, the Church accepts and honors the natural unity of the two testaments. The Old Testament lays the foundation and prophesies the coming of Christ. The New Testament is the fulfillment of the prophecies and contains the story and teachings of Christ. We need to study both to fully understand God's plan for our salvation.

9 As they were coming down the mountain, Jesus ordered them, "Tell no one about the vision until after the Son of Man has been raised from the dead." [10]And the disciples asked him, "Why, then, do the scribes say that Elijah must come first?" [11]He replied, "Elijah is indeed coming and will restore all things; [12]but I tell you that Elijah has already come, and they did not recognize him, but they did to him whatever they pleased. So also the Son of Man is about to suffer at their hands." [13]Then the disciples understood that he was speaking to them about John the Baptist.

Jesus Cures a Boy with a Demon

14 When they came to the crowd, a man came to him, knelt before him, [15]and said, "Lord, have mercy on my son, for he is an epileptic and he suffers terribly; he often falls into the fire and often into the water. [16]And I brought him to your disciples, but they could not cure him." [17]Jesus answered, "You faithless and perverse generation, how much longer must I be with you? How much longer must I put up with you? Bring him here to me." [18]And Jesus rebuked the demon,[a] and it[b] came out of him, and the boy was cured instantly. [19]Then the disciples came to Jesus privately and said, "Why could we not cast it out?" [20]He said to them, "Because of your little faith. For truly I tell you, if you have faith the size of a[c] mustard seed, you will say to this mountain, 'Move from here to there,' and it will move; and nothing will be impossible for you."[d]

Jesus Again Foretells His Death and Resurrection

22 As they were gathering[e] in Galilee, Jesus said to them, "The Son of Man is going to be betrayed into human hands, [23]and they will kill him, and on the third day he will be raised." And they were greatly distressed.

Jesus and the Temple Tax

24 When they reached Capernaum, the collectors of the temple tax[f] came to Peter and said, "Does your teacher not pay the temple tax?"[f] [25]He said,

---

a Gk it or him b Gk the demon c Gk faith as a grain of d Other ancient authorities add verse 21, But this kind does not come out except by prayer and fasting e Other ancient authorities read living f Gk didrachma

"Yes, he does." And when he came home, Jesus spoke of it first, asking, "What do you think, Simon? From whom do kings of the earth take toll or tribute? From their children or from others?" [26]When Peter[a] said, "From others," Jesus said to him, "Then the children are free. [27]However, so that we do not give offense to them, go to the sea and cast a hook; take the first fish that comes up; and when you open its mouth, you will find a coin;[b] take that and give it to them for you and me."

18 | True Greatness

At that time the disciples came to Jesus and asked, "Who is the greatest in the kingdom of heaven?" [2]He called a child, whom he put among them, [3]and said, "Truly I tell you, unless you change and become like children, you will never enter the kingdom of heaven. [4]Whoever becomes humble like this child is the greatest in the kingdom of heaven. [5]Whoever welcomes one such child in my name welcomes me.

Temptations to Sin

6 "If any of you put a stumbling block before one of these little ones who believe in me, it would be better for you if a great millstone were fastened around your neck and you were drowned in the depth of the sea. [7]Woe to the world because of stumbling blocks! Occasions for stumbling are bound to come, but woe to the one by whom the stumbling block comes!

8 "If your hand or your foot causes you to stumble, cut it off and throw it away; it is better for you to enter life maimed or lame than to have two hands or two feet and to be thrown into the eternal fire. [9]And if your eye causes you to stumble, tear it out and throw it away; it is better for you to enter life with one eye than to have two eyes and to be thrown into the hell[c] of fire.

The Parable of the Lost Sheep

10 "Take care that you do not despise one of these little ones; for, I tell you, in heaven their angels continually see the face of my Father in heaven.[d] [12]What do you think? If a shepherd has a hundred sheep, and one of them has gone astray, does he not leave the ninety-nine on the mountains and go in search of the one that went astray? [13]And if he finds it, truly I tell you, he rejoices over it more than over the ninety-nine that never went astray. [14]So it is not

the will of your[e] Father in heaven that one of these little ones should be lost.

Reproving Another Who Sins

15 "If another member of the church[f] sins against you,[g] go and point out the fault when the two of you are alone. If the member listens to you, you have regained that one.[h] [16]But if you are not listened to, take one or two others along with you, so that every word may be confirmed by the evidence of two or three witnesses. [17]If the member refuses to listen to them, tell it to the church; and if the offender refuses to listen even to the church, let such a one be to you as a Gentile and a tax collector. [18]Truly I tell you, whatever you bind on earth will be bound in heaven, and whatever you loose on earth will be loosed in heaven. [19]Again, truly I tell you, if two of you agree on earth about anything you ask, it will be done for you by my Father in heaven. [20]For where two or three are gathered in my name, I am there among them."

Forgiveness

21 Then Peter came and said to him, "Lord, if another member of the church[i] sins against me, how often should I forgive? As many as seven times?" [22]Jesus said to him, "Not seven times, but, I tell you, seventy-seven[j] times.

The Parable of the Unforgiving Servant

23 "For this reason the kingdom of heaven may be compared to a king who wished to settle accounts with his slaves. [24]When he began the reckoning, one who owed him ten thousand talents[k] was brought to him; [25]and, as he could not pay, his lord ordered him to be sold, together with his wife and children and all his possessions, and payment to be made. [26]So the slave fell on his knees before him, saying, 'Have patience with me, and I will pay you everything.' [27]And out of pity for him, the lord of that slave released him and forgave him the debt. [28]But that same slave, as he went out, came upon one of his fellow slaves who owed him a hundred denarii;[l] and seizing him by the throat, he said, 'Pay what you owe.' [29]Then his fellow slave fell down and pleaded with him, 'Have patience with me, and I will pay you.' [30]But he refused; then he went and threw him into prison until he would pay the debt. [31]When his fellow slaves saw what had happened, they were greatly distressed, and they went and reported to

---

a Gk he   b Gk *stater*; the stater was worth two didrachmas   c Gk *Gehenna*   d Other ancient authorities add verse 11, *For the Son of Man came to save the lost*   e Other ancient authorities read *my*   f Gk *If your brother*   g Other ancient authorities lack *against you*   h Gk *the brother*   i Gk *if my brother*   j Or *seventy times seven*   k A talent was worth more than fifteen years' wages of a laborer   l The denarius was the usual day's wage for a laborer

Forgive Us
Our Debts
Matthew 18:23–35

The parable of the unforgiving servant is a clear challenge for us in view of the fact that we have been forgiven by God. It paints a perfect picture of how often we hold something against someone else, completely forgetting that we've been forgiven an even greater amount. Take some time to think of someone in your life you are struggling to forgive. Then pray this prayer:

God, your kindness and mercy overwhelm me. But I still struggle to turn that forgiveness around and show it to others. Please give me the strength to see how great a debt you have forgiven in me, and give me the courage to do the same for others in my life. Amen.

their lord all that had taken place. ³²Then his lord summoned him and said to him, 'You wicked slave! I forgave you all that debt because you pleaded with me. ³³Should you not have had mercy on your fellow slave, as I had mercy on you?' ³⁴And in anger his lord handed him over to be tortured until he would pay his entire debt. ³⁵So my heavenly Father will also do to every one of you, if you do not forgive your brother or sister[a] from your heart."

Teaching about Divorce

19 When Jesus had finished saying these things, he left Galilee and went to the region of Judea beyond the Jordan. ²Large crowds followed him, and he cured them there.

3 Some Pharisees came to him, and to test him they asked, "Is it lawful for a man to divorce his wife for any cause?" ⁴He answered, "Have you not read that the one who made them at the beginning 'made them male and female,' ⁵and said, 'For this reason a man shall leave his father and mother and be joined to his wife, and the two shall become one flesh'? ⁶So they are no longer two, but one flesh. Therefore what God has joined together, let no one separate."

⁷They said to him, "Why then did Moses command us to give a certificate of dismissal and to divorce her?" ⁸He said to them, "It was because you were so hard-hearted that Moses allowed you to divorce your wives, but from the beginning it was not so. ⁹And I say to you, whoever divorces his wife, except for unchastity, and marries another commits adultery."[b]

10 His disciples said to him, "If such is the case of a man with his wife, it is better not to marry." ¹¹But he said to them, "Not everyone can accept this teaching, but only those to whom it is given. ¹²For there are eunuchs who have been so from birth, and there are eunuchs who have been made eunuchs by others, and there are eunuchs who have made themselves eunuchs for the sake of the kingdom of heaven. Let anyone accept this who can."

Jesus Blesses Little Children

13 Then little children were being brought to him in order that he might lay his hands on them and pray. The disciples spoke sternly to those who brought them; ¹⁴but Jesus said, "Let the little children come to me, and do not stop them; for it is to such as these that the kingdom of heaven belongs." ¹⁵And he laid his hands on them and went on his way.

The Rich Young Man

16 Then someone came to him and said, "Teacher, what good deed must I do to have eternal life?" ¹⁷And he said to him, "Why do you ask me about what is good? There is only one who is good. If you wish to enter into life, keep the commandments." ¹⁸He said to him, "Which ones?" And Jesus said, "You shall not murder; You shall not commit adultery; You shall not steal; You shall not bear false witness; ¹⁹Honor your father and mother; also, You shall love your neighbor as yourself." ²⁰The young man said to him, "I have kept all these;[c] what do I still lack?" ²¹Jesus said to him, "If you wish to be perfect, go, sell your possessions, and give the money[d] to the poor, and you will have treasure in heaven; then come, follow me." ²²When the young man heard this word, he went away grieving, for he had many possessions.

23 Then Jesus said to his disciples, "Truly I tell you, it will be hard for a rich person to enter the kingdom of heaven. ²⁴Again I tell you, it is easier for a camel to go through the eye of a needle than for

a Gk *brother* b Other ancient authorities read *except on the ground of unchastity, causes her to commit adultery*; others add at the end of the verse *and he who marries a divorced woman commits adultery* c Other ancient authorities add *from my youth* d Gk lacks *the money*

someone who is rich to enter the kingdom of God." ²⁵When the disciples heard this, they were greatly astounded and said, "Then who can be saved?" ²⁶But Jesus looked at them and said, "For mortals it is impossible, but for God all things are possible."

27 Then Peter said in reply, "Look, we have left everything and followed you. What then will we have?" ²⁸Jesus said to them, "Truly I tell you, at the renewal of all things, when the Son of Man is seated on the throne of his glory, you who have followed me will also sit on twelve thrones, judging the twelve tribes of Israel. ²⁹And everyone who has left houses or brothers or sisters or father or mother or children or fields, for my name's sake, will receive a hundred-fold,ᵃ and will inherit eternal life. ³⁰But many who are first will be last, and the last will be first.

The Laborers in the Vineyard

20 "For the kingdom of heaven is like a land-owner who went out early in the morning to hire laborers for his vineyard. ²After agreeing with the laborers for the usual daily wage,ᵇ he sent them into his vineyard. ³When he went out about nine

o'clock, he saw others standing idle in the market-place; ⁴and he said to them, 'You also go into the vineyard, and I will pay you whatever is right.' So they went. ⁵When he went out again about noon and about three o'clock, he did the same. ⁶And about five o'clock he went out and found others standing around; and he said to them, 'Why are you standing here idle all day?' ⁷They said to him, 'Because no one has hired us.' He said to them, 'You also go into the vineyard.' ⁸When evening came, the owner of the vineyard said to his manager, 'Call the laborers and give them their pay, beginning with the last and then going to the first.' ⁹When those hired about five o'clock came, each of them received the usual daily wage.ᵇ ¹⁰Now when the first came, they thought they would receive more; but each of them also received the usual daily wage.ᵇ ¹¹And when they received it, they grumbled against the landowner, ¹²saying, 'These last worked only one hour, and you have made them equal to us who have borne the burden of the day and the scorching heat.' ¹³But he replied to one of them, 'Friend, I am doing you no wrong; did you not agree with me for the usual daily wage?ᵇ ¹⁴Take

LIVE IT!

Fairness vs. Justice · Matthew 20:1–16

In this parable, Jesus tells the story of a landowner who agrees on a daily wage with his workers and then pays them that established wage at the end of their workday, no matter whether they began early, in the middle of the day, or late in the afternoon. Because workers were paid the same amount for different lengths of work time, some of the workers thought the wage was unfair, even though they received the amount they had agreed to work for. There's the difference between fairness and justice. Fairness would mean paying more to the workers who worked longer. But justice means providing all people with what they need, as God, the landowner in this story, does. Such is the radical grace of God!

Throughout our world, many workers toil for long hours under brutal conditions for unjust wages. Even in the United States, a person working forty hours a week at minimum wage will rarely earn enough to cover all of life's basic needs—food, shelter, clothing, utilities, transportation, medical care—especially when caring for a family. Women and children often suffer the most from unjust wage practices.

Followers of Christ must advocate for a living wage and just conditions for all workers. A living wage is the minimum hourly wage necessary for a person to achieve a basic standard of living above the poverty line. Just conditions include safe and sanitary buildings, the ability to address problems, and freedom from inhumane treatment. (Read examples of Christians working toward this kind of justice in "Connect It: Dave and Morgan Hansow: Light Gives Heat," near Amos 8:4-6, and "Connect It: Krochet Kids: From Spokane to Uganda," near Numbers 13-14.)

ᵃ Other ancient authorities read *manifold*   ᵇ Gk *a denarius*

what belongs to you and go; I choose to give to this last the same as I give to you. ¹⁵Am I not allowed to do what I choose with what belongs to me? Or are you envious because I am generous?'ᵃ ¹⁶So the last will be first, and the first will be last."ᵇ

A Third Time Jesus Foretells His Death and Resurrection

17 While Jesus was going up to Jerusalem, he took the twelve disciples aside by themselves, and said to them on the way, ¹⁸"See, we are going up to Jerusalem, and the Son of Man will be handed over to the chief priests and scribes, and they will condemn him to death; ¹⁹then they will hand him over to the Gentiles to be mocked and flogged and crucified; and on the third day he will be raised."

The Request of the Mother of James and John

20 Then the mother of the sons of Zebedee came to him with her sons, and kneeling before him, she asked a favor of him. ²¹And he said to her, "What do you want?" She said to him, "Declare that these two sons of mine will sit, one at your right hand and one at your left, in your kingdom." ²²But Jesus answered, "You do not know what you are asking. Are you able to drink the cup that I am about to drink?"ᶜ They said to him, "We are able." ²³He said to them, "You

will indeed drink my cup, but to sit at my right hand and at my left, this is not mine to grant, but it is for those for whom it has been prepared by my Father."

24 When the ten heard it, they were angry with the two brothers. ²⁵But Jesus called them to him and said, "You know that the rulers of the Gentiles lord it over them, and their great ones are tyrants over them. ²⁶It will not be so among you; but whoever wishes to be great among you must be your servant, ²⁷and whoever wishes to be first among you must be your slave; ²⁸just as the Son of Man came not to be served but to serve, and to give his life a ransom for many."

Jesus Heals Two Blind Men

29 As they were leaving Jericho, a large crowd followed him. ³⁰There were two blind men sitting by the roadside. When they heard that Jesus was passing by, they shouted, "Lord,ᵈ have mercy on us, Son of David!" ³¹The crowd sternly ordered them to be quiet; but they shouted even more loudly, "Have mercy on us, Lord, Son of David!" ³²Jesus stood still and called them, saying, "What do you want me to do for you?" ³³They said to him, "Lord, let our eyes be opened." ³⁴Moved with compassion, Jesus touched their eyes. Immediately they regained their sight and followed him.

ᵃ Gk is your eye evil because I am good? ᵇ Other ancient authorities add for many are called but few are chosen ᶜ Other ancient authorities add or to be baptized with the baptism that I am baptized with? ᵈ Other ancient authorities lack Lord

True Greatness
Matthew 20:20–28

What good parents don't want their kids to find success in life? Like most people at the time of Jesus, the mother of James and John is confused about the kingdom Jesus had come to establish. She lobbies for her sons to be given places of honor and authority (Matthew 20:21).

The confusion and anger that results among the disciples allows Jesus the opportunity to remind them of how God defines true greatness. Jesus turns the tables on them in a veiled way by asking, "Are you able to drink the cup that I am about to drink?" (Matthew 20:22). He reminds them—and reminds us today—that true greatness is found by serving others (Matthew 20:26-27).

- When you're in a position of leadership, do you see it as a chance to control others in order to gain power or to impress your friends? Or do you see it as a chance to serve others and help them toward living full and healthy lives?
- Why is it that wanting power for ourselves so often gets in the way of wanting to serve the needs of others?
- What are some specific situations in your life where you can work on serving others better?

Jesus' Triumphal Entry into Jerusalem

21 When they had come near Jerusalem and had reached Bethphage, at the Mount of Olives, Jesus sent two disciples, ²saying to them, "Go into the village ahead of you, and immediately you will find a donkey tied, and a colt with her; untie them and bring them to me. ³If anyone says anything to you, just say this, 'The Lord needs them.' And he will send them immediately.ᵃ" ⁴This took place to fulfill what had been spoken through the prophet, saying,

⁵ "Tell the daughter of Zion,

Look, your king is coming to you,
humble, and mounted on a donkey,
and on a colt, the foal of a donkey."

⁶The disciples went and did as Jesus had directed them; ⁷they brought the donkey and the colt, and put their cloaks on them, and he sat on them. ⁸A very large crowdᵇ spread their cloaks on the road, and others cut branches from the trees and spread them on the road. ⁹The crowds that went ahead of him and that followed were shouting,

"Hosanna to the Son of David!
Blessed is the one who comes in the name of the Lord!
Hosanna in the highest heaven!"

¹⁰When he entered Jerusalem, the whole city was in turmoil, asking, "Who is this?" ¹¹The crowds were saying, "This is the prophet Jesus from Nazareth in Galilee."

Jesus Cleanses the Temple

12 Then Jesus entered the templeᶜ and drove out all who were selling and buying in the temple, and he overturned the tables of the money changers and the seats of those who sold doves. ¹³He said to them, "It is written,

'My house shall be called a house of prayer';
but you are making it a den of robbers."

14 The blind and the lame came to him in the temple, and he cured them. ¹⁵But when the chief priests and the scribes saw the amazing things that he did, and heardᵈ the children crying out in the temple, "Hosanna to the Son of David," they became angry ¹⁶and said to him, "Do you hear what these are saying?" Jesus said to them, "Yes; have you never read,

'Out of the mouths of infants and nursing babies
you have prepared praise for yourself'?"

STUDY IT!

Trouble in the Temple · Matthew 21:12–13

The cleansing of the temple is one of the few stories that occurs in all four gospels. To fully understand Jesus' anger in this situation, we need to remember that the Jews were required to offer sacrificial animals as part of their religious obligation. Money exchange was a necessary service for the operation of the temple. Pilgrims needed Jewish coinage to pay the temple tax. And buying animals for sacrifice at the temple ensured that only the best would be offered to God. Jesus was angry because the religious and civil leaders were too concerned about these things—they were forgetting that the temple was God's house, the place for encountering and worshiping God.

Jesus' clearing of the temple was an act of religious and civil disobedience, challenging the highest members of Jewish society. His actions would have been viewed as an attack on the temple. The gospels of Luke and Mark both say that immediately after this event, Jewish leaders began looking for a way to kill Jesus. They waited because Jesus was so popular with the people (Mark 11:18–19; Luke 19:47–48). Jesus knew that his actions and teachings made these corrupt leaders angry and would ultimately lead to his death (Matthew 20:17–19).

[17] He left them, went out of the city to Bethany, and spent the night there.

Jesus Curses the Fig Tree

18 In the morning, when he returned to the city, he was hungry. [19] And seeing a fig tree by the side of the road, he went to it and found nothing at all on it but leaves. Then he said to it, "May no fruit ever come from you again!" And the fig tree withered at once. [20] When the disciples saw it, they were amazed, saying, "How did the fig tree wither at once?" [21] Jesus answered them, "Truly I tell you, if you have faith and do not doubt, not only will you do what has been done to the fig tree, but even if you say to this mountain, 'Be lifted up and thrown into the sea,' it will be done. [22] Whatever you ask for in prayer with faith, you will receive."

The Authority of Jesus Questioned

23 When he entered the temple, the chief priests and the elders of the people came to him as he was teaching, and said, "By what authority are you doing these things, and who gave you this authority?" [24] Jesus said to them, "I will also ask you one question; if you tell me the answer, then I will also tell you by what authority I do these things. [25] Did the baptism of John come from heaven, or was it of human origin?" And they argued with one another, "If we say, 'From heaven,' he will say to us, 'Why then did you not believe him?' [26] But if we say, 'Of

human origin,' we are afraid of the crowd; for all regard John as a prophet." [27] So they answered Jesus, "We do not know." And he said to them, "Neither will I tell you by what authority I am doing these things.

The Parable of the Two Sons

28 "What do you think? A man had two sons; he went to the first and said, 'Son, go and work in the vineyard today.' [29] He answered, 'I will not'; but later he changed his mind and went. [30] The father[a] went to the second and said the same; and he answered, 'I go, sir'; but he did not go. [31] Which of the two did the will of his father?" They said, "The first." Jesus said to them, "Truly I tell you, the tax collectors and the prostitutes are going into the kingdom of God ahead of you. [32] For John came to you in the way of righteousness and you did not believe him, but the tax collectors and the prostitutes believed him; and even after you saw it, you did not change your minds and believe him.

The Parable of the Wicked Tenants

33 "Listen to another parable. There was a landowner who planted a vineyard, put a fence around it, dug a wine press in it, and built a watchtower. Then he leased it to tenants and went to another country. [34] When the harvest time had come, he sent his slaves to the tenants to collect his produce. [35] But the tenants seized his slaves and beat one, killed

a Gk *He*

another, and stoned another. [36]Again he sent other slaves, more than the first; and they treated them in the same way. [37]Finally he sent his son to them, saying, 'They will respect my son.' [38]But when the tenants saw the son, they said to themselves, 'This is the heir; come, let us kill him and get his inheritance.' [39]So they seized him, threw him out of the vineyard, and killed him. [40]Now when the owner of the vineyard comes, what will he do to those tenants?" [41]They said to him, "He will put those wretches to a miserable death, and lease the vineyard to other tenants who will give him the produce at the harvest time."

42 Jesus said to them, "Have you never read in the scriptures:

'The stone that the builders rejected
has become the cornerstone;[a]
this was the Lord's doing,
and it is amazing in our eyes'?

[43]Therefore I tell you, the kingdom of God will be taken away from you and given to a people that produces the fruits of the kingdom.[b] [44]The one who falls on this stone will be broken to pieces; and it will crush anyone on whom it falls."[c]

45 When the chief priests and the Pharisees heard his parables, they realized that he was speaking about them. [46]They wanted to arrest him, but they feared the crowds, because they regarded him as a prophet.

22 The Parable of the Wedding Banquet

Once more Jesus spoke to them in parables, saying: [2]"The kingdom of heaven may be compared to a king who gave a wedding banquet for his son. [3]He sent his slaves to call those who had been invited to the wedding banquet, but they would not come. [4]Again he sent other slaves, saying, 'Tell those who have been invited: Look, I have prepared my dinner, my oxen and my fat calves have been slaughtered, and everything is ready; come to the wedding banquet.' [5]But they made light of it and went away, one to his farm, another to his business, [6]while the rest seized his slaves, mistreated them, and killed them. [7]The king was enraged. He sent his troops, destroyed those murderers, and burned their city. [8]Then he said to his slaves, 'The wedding is ready, but those invited were not worthy. [9]Go therefore into the main streets, and invite everyone you find to the wedding banquet.' [10]Those slaves went out into the streets and gathered all whom they found, both good and bad; so the wed-

ding hall was filled with guests.

11 "But when the king came in to see the guests, he noticed a man there who was not wearing a wedding robe, [12]and he said to him, 'Friend, how did you get in here without a wedding robe?' And he was speechless. [13]Then the king said to the attendants, 'Bind him hand and foot, and throw him into the outer darkness, where there will be weeping and gnashing of teeth.' [14]For many are called, but few are chosen."

The Question about Paying Taxes

15 Then the Pharisees went and plotted to entrap him in what he said. [16]So they sent their disciples to him, along with the Herodians, saying, "Teacher, we know that you are sincere, and teach the way of God in accordance with truth, and show deference to no one; for you do not regard people with partiality. [17]Tell us, then, what you think. Is it lawful to pay taxes to the emperor, or not?" [18]But Jesus, aware of their malice, said, "Why are you putting me to the test, you hypocrites? [19]Show me the coin used for the tax." And they brought him a denarius. [20]Then he said to them, "Whose head is this, and whose title?" [21]They answered, "The emperor's." Then he said to them, "Give therefore to the emperor the things that are the emperor's, and to God the things that are God's." [22]When they heard this, they were amazed; and they left him and went away.

The Question about the Resurrection

23 The same day some Sadducees came to him, saying there is no resurrection;[d] and they asked him a question, saying, [24]"Teacher, Moses said, 'If a man dies childless, his brother shall marry the widow, and raise up children for his brother.' [25]Now there were seven brothers among us; the first married, and died childless, leaving the widow to his brother. [26]The second did the same, so also the third, down to the seventh. [27]Last of all, the woman herself died. [28]In the resurrection, then, whose wife of the seven will she be? For all of them had married her."

29 Jesus answered them, "You are wrong, because you know neither the scriptures nor the power of God. [30]For in the resurrection they neither marry nor are given in marriage, but are like angels[e] in heaven. [31]And as for the resurrection of the dead, have you not read what was said to you by God, [32]'I am the God of Abraham, the God of Isaac, and the

---

a Or *keystone*   b Gk *the fruits of it*   c Other ancient authorities lack verse 44   d Other ancient authorities read *who say that there is no resurrection*
e Other ancient authorities add *of God*

God of Jacob'? He is God not of the dead, but of the living." [33] And when the crowd heard it, they were astounded at his teaching.

The Greatest Commandment

34 When the Pharisees heard that he had silenced the Sadducees, they gathered together, [35] and one of them, a lawyer, asked him a question to test him. [36] "Teacher, which commandment in the law is the greatest?" [37] He said to him, " 'You shall love the Lord your God with all your heart, and with all your soul, and with all your mind.'

The Perfect Plan
Matthew 22:34–40

Can you imagine a world where every person lives according to the two commandments Jesus gives in **Matthew 22:34–40**? Where every word, thought, and action is motivated by a deep love for God and a desire for the well-being of others? Sounds a bit like the Garden of Eden! Libraries are filled with volumes describing philosophies for achieving the ideal human society, yet Jesus articulates the perfect plan in a few short sentences. In fact, these two commands summarize the Ten Commandments and were long considered a summary of the law of Moses.

The message of these two great commandments obviously remains real and relevant for us today. Following in the footsteps of the apostles who first heard Jesus' words, we now have the responsibility to live out these commandments in our world—becoming living, breathing examples of what it means to love God, our neighbors, and ourselves.

- List some practical steps you can take to better love God and others today.
- Who are the people around you who need some love?

[38] This is the greatest and first commandment. [39] And a second is like it: 'You shall love your neighbor as yourself.' [40] On these two commandments hang all the law and the prophets."

The Question about David's Son

41 Now while the Pharisees were gathered together, Jesus asked them this question: [42] "What do you think of the Messiah?[a] Whose son is he?" They said to him, "The son of David." [43] He said to them, "How is it then that David by the Spirit[b] calls him Lord, saying,

44 'The Lord said to my Lord,
   "Sit at my right hand,
      until I put your enemies under your
         feet" '?

[45] If David thus calls him Lord, how can he be his son?" [46] No one was able to give him an answer, nor from that day did anyone dare to ask him any more questions.

23 Jesus Denounces Scribes and Pharisees

Then Jesus said to the crowds and to his disciples, [2] "The scribes and the Pharisees sit on Moses' seat; [3] therefore, do whatever they teach you and follow it; but do not do as they do, for they do not practice what they teach. [4] They tie up heavy burdens, hard to bear,[c] and lay them on the shoulders of others; but they themselves are unwilling to lift a finger to move them. [5] They do all their deeds to be seen by others; for they make their phylacteries broad and their fringes long. [6] They love to have the place of honor at banquets and the best seats in the synagogues, [7] and to be greeted with respect in the marketplaces, and to have people call them rabbi. [8] But you are not to be called rabbi, for you have one teacher, and you are all students.[d] [9] And call no one your father on earth, for you have one Father—the one in heaven. [10] Nor are you to be called instructors, for you have one instructor, the Messiah.[e] [11] The greatest among you will be your servant. [12] All who exalt themselves will be humbled, and all who humble themselves will be exalted.

13 "But woe to you, scribes and Pharisees, hypocrites! For you lock people out of the kingdom of heaven. For you do not go in yourselves, and when others are going in, you stop them.[f] [15] Woe to you, scribes and Pharisees, hypocrites! For you

cross sea and land to make a single convert, and you make the new convert twice as much a child of hell[a] as yourselves.

16 "Woe to you, blind guides, who say, 'Whoever swears by the sanctuary is bound by nothing, but whoever swears by the gold of the sanctuary is bound by the oath.' [17]You blind fools! For which is greater, the gold or the sanctuary that has made the gold sacred? [18]And you say, 'Whoever swears by the altar is bound by nothing, but whoever swears by the gift that is on the altar is bound by the oath.' [19]How blind you are! For which is greater, the gift or the altar that makes the gift sacred? [20]So whoever swears by the altar, swears by it and by everything on it; [21]and whoever swears by the sanctuary, swears by it and by the one who dwells in it; [22]and whoever swears by heaven, swears by the throne of God and by the one who is seated upon it.

23 "Woe to you, scribes and Pharisees, hypocrites! For you tithe mint, dill, and cummin, and have neglected the weightier matters of the law: justice and mercy and faith. It is these you ought to have practiced without neglecting the others.

[24]You blind guides! You strain out a gnat but swallow a camel!

25 "Woe to you, scribes and Pharisees, hypocrites! For you clean the outside of the cup and of the plate, but inside they are full of greed and self-indulgence. [26]You blind Pharisee! First clean the inside of the cup,[b] so that the outside also may become clean.

27 "Woe to you, scribes and Pharisees, hypocrites! For you are like whitewashed tombs, which on the outside look beautiful, but inside they are full of the bones of the dead and of all kinds of filth. [28]So you also on the outside look righteous to others, but inside you are full of hypocrisy and lawlessness.

29 "Woe to you, scribes and Pharisees, hypocrites! For you build the tombs of the prophets and decorate the graves of the righteous, [30]and you say, 'If we had lived in the days of our ancestors, we would not have taken part with them in shedding the blood of the prophets.' [31]Thus you testify against yourselves that you are descendants of those who murdered the prophets. [32]Fill up, then, the measure of your ancestors. [33]You snakes, you brood of vipers!

PRAY IT!

No Respect · Matthew 23:1–36

The "woe" statements of Jesus in **Matthew 23:13–29** may be his harshest words in all the Gospels. Scholars think the community in which the author of Matthew lived may have had negative experiences with certain Jewish leaders such as the Pharisees, Sadducees, and scribes. Their hard feelings are reflected in Jesus' words. We should take **Matthew 23:3–4** not as a condemnation of Jewish people, but as a call to do the following:

• Practice what we preach (Matthew 23:3).

• Show compassion and not burden others (Matthew 23:4).

• Humbly respect the people who follow us (Matthew 23:8-15).

• Be guided by mercy and justice (Matthew 23:23-24).

Jesus' sharpest criticism here and in many other places in the Gospels is directed against hypocrisy—saying one thing and doing another, pretending to be holy and just while actually doing sinful things.

Spend some time praying, and ask God to help you answer these questions:

• How have you expressed your faith through words and actions?

• When has your life demonstrated what your faith is all about?

• When have you asked others to do something you weren't willing to do yourself?

• When have you used any power or influence you might have in a way that was humble and served the needs of others? How did you do that?

---

a Gk Gehenna   b Other ancient authorities add *and of the plate*

How can you escape being sentenced to hell?[a] 34Therefore I send you prophets, sages, and scribes, some of whom you will kill and crucify, and some you will flog in your synagogues and pursue from town to town, 35so that upon you may come all the righteous blood shed on earth, from the blood of righteous Abel to the blood of Zechariah son of Barachiah, whom you murdered between the sanctuary and the altar. 36Truly I tell you, all this will come upon this generation.

The Lament over Jerusalem

37 "Jerusalem, Jerusalem, the city that kills the prophets and stones those who are sent to it! How often have I desired to gather your children together as a hen gathers her brood under her wings, and you were not willing! 38See, your house is left to you, desolate.[b] 39For I tell you, you will not see me again until you say, 'Blessed is the one who comes in the name of the Lord.' "

24

The Destruction of the Temple Foretold

As Jesus came out of the temple and was going away, his disciples came to point out to him the buildings of the temple. 2Then he asked them, "You see all these, do you not? Truly I tell you, not one stone will be left here upon another; all will be thrown down."

Signs of the End of the Age

3 When he was sitting on the Mount of Olives, the disciples came to him privately, saying, "Tell us, when will this be, and what will be the sign of your coming and of the end of the age?" 4Jesus answered them, "Beware that no one leads you astray. 5For many will come in my name, saying, 'I am the Messiah!'[c] and they will lead many astray. 6And you will hear of wars and rumors of wars; see that you are not alarmed; for this must take place, but the end is not yet. 7For nation will rise against nation, and kingdom against kingdom, and there will be famines[d] and earthquakes in various places: 8all this is but the beginning of the birth pangs.

Persecutions Foretold

9 "Then they will hand you over to be tortured and will put you to death, and you will be hated by all nations because of my name. 10Then many will fall away,[e] and they will betray one another and hate

one another. 11And many false prophets will arise and lead many astray. 12And because of the increase of lawlessness, the love of many will grow cold. 13But the one who endures to the end will be saved. 14And this good news[f] of the kingdom will be proclaimed throughout the world, as a testimony to all the nations; and then the end will come.

The Desolating Sacrilege

15 "So when you see the desolating sacrilege standing in the holy place, as was spoken of by the prophet Daniel (let the reader understand), 16then those in Judea must flee to the mountains; 17the one on the housetop must not go down to take what is in the house; 18the one in the field must not turn back to get a coat. 19Woe to those who are pregnant and to those who are nursing infants in those days! 20Pray that your flight may not be in winter or on a sabbath. 21For at that time there will be great suffering, such as has not been from the beginning of the world until now, no, and never will be. 22And if those days had not been cut short, no one would be saved; but for the sake of the elect those days will be cut short. 23Then if anyone says to you, 'Look! Here is the Messiah!'[b] or 'There he is!'—do not believe it. 24For false messiahs[g] and false prophets will appear and produce great signs and omens, to lead astray, if possible, even the elect. 25Take note, I have told you beforehand. 26So, if they say to you, 'Look! He is in the wilderness,' do not go out. If they say, 'Look! He is in the inner rooms,' do not believe it. 27For as the lightning comes from the east and flashes as far as the west, so will be the coming of the Son of Man. 28Wherever the corpse is, there the vultures will gather.

The Coming of the Son of Man

29 "Immediately after the suffering of those days
　　the sun will be darkened,
　　　　and the moon will not give its light;
　　the stars will fall from heaven,
　　　　and the powers of heaven will be shaken.
30Then the sign of the Son of Man will appear in heaven, and then all the tribes of the earth will mourn, and they will see 'the Son of Man coming on the clouds of heaven' with power and great glory. 31And he will send out his angels with a loud trumpet call, and they will gather his elect from the four winds, from one end of heaven to the other.

---

a Gk *Gehenna* b Other ancient authorities lack *desolate* c Or *the Christ* d Other ancient authorities add *and pestilences* e Or *stumble* f Or *gospel*
g Or *christs*

The Lesson of the Fig Tree

32 "From the fig tree learn its lesson: as soon as its branch becomes tender and puts forth its leaves, you know that summer is near. [33] So also, when you see all these things, you know that he[a] is near, at the very gates. [34] Truly I tell you, this generation will not pass away until all these things have taken place. [35] Heaven and earth will pass away, but my words will not pass away.

The Necessity for Watchfulness

36 "But about that day and hour no one knows, neither the angels of heaven, nor the Son,[b] but only the Father. [37] For as the days of Noah were, so will be the coming of the Son of Man. [38] For as in those days before the flood they were eating and drinking, marrying and giving in marriage, until the day Noah entered the ark, [39] and they knew nothing until the flood came and swept them all away, so too will be the coming of the Son of Man. [40] Then two will be in the field; one will be taken and one will be left. [41] Two women will be grinding meal together; one will be taken and one will be left. [42] Keep awake therefore, for you do not know on what day[c] your Lord is coming. [43] But understand this: if the owner of the house had known in what part of the night the thief was coming, he would have stayed awake and would not have let his house be broken into. [44] Therefore you also must be ready, for the Son of Man is coming at an unexpected hour.

The Faithful or the Unfaithful Slave

45 "Who then is the faithful and wise slave, whom his master has put in charge of his household, to give the other slaves[d] their allowance of food at the proper time? [46] Blessed is that slave whom his master will find at work when he arrives. [47] Truly I tell you, he will put that one in charge of all his possessions. [48] But if that wicked slave says to himself, 'My master is delayed,' [49] and he begins to beat his fellow slaves, and eats and drinks with drunkards, [50] the master of that slave will come on a day when he does not expect him and at an hour that he does not know. [51] He will cut him in pieces[e] and put him with the hypocrites, where there will be weeping and gnashing of teeth.

25　### The Parable of the Ten Bridesmaids

"Then the kingdom of heaven will be like this. Ten bridesmaids[f] took their lamps and went to meet the bridegroom.[g] [2] Five of them were foolish, and five were wise. [3] When the foolish took their lamps, they took no oil with them; [4] but the wise took flasks of oil with their lamps. [5] As the bridegroom was delayed, all of them became drowsy and slept. [6] But at midnight there was a shout, 'Look! Here is the bridegroom! Come out to meet him.' [7] Then all those bridesmaids[f] got up and trimmed their lamps. [8] The foolish said to the wise, 'Give us some of your oil, for our lamps are going out.' [9] But the wise replied, 'No! there will not be enough for you and for us; you had better go to the dealers and buy some for yourselves.' [10] And while they went to buy it, the bridegroom came, and those who were ready went with him into the wedding banquet; and the door was shut. [11] Later the other bridesmaids[f] came also, saying, 'Lord, lord, open to us.' [12] But he replied, 'Truly I tell you, I do not know you.' [13] Keep awake therefore, for you know neither the day nor the hour.[h]

The Parable of the Talents

14 "For it is as if a man, going on a journey, summoned his slaves and entrusted his property to them; [15] to one he gave five talents,[i] to another two, to another one, to each according to his ability. Then he went away. [16] The one who had received the five

---

a Or it　b Other ancient authorities lack *nor the Son*　c Other ancient authorities read *at what hour*　d Gk *to give them*　e Or *cut him off*　f Gk *virgins*
g Other ancient authorities add *and the bride*　h Other ancient authorities add *in which the Son of Man is coming*　i A talent was worth more than fifteen years' wages of a laborer

Use It or Lose It · Matthew 25:14–30

What if your dad gave you his paycheck and said, "Take care of this for me while I'm gone on a long trip." What would you do? In the parable of the talents, the first two servants used the money they'd been entrusted with to make more. But the third servant hid his. Bad move. When the master came back, he took away the one timid servant's talent, because he'd kept it hidden. He hadn't even tried to use it. He just got scared or lazy and tried to pretend his gift wasn't even there.

A talent in this parable is actually a large sum of money, but we can gain important insight from reading the word "talent" as we use it today. We think of talents as abilities and skills, and, really, these are given to us by God. The lesson is the same too. Our gifts come from God, and we have a responsibility to use them wisely. We're called to use our abilities creatively and boldly in God's service. It may take some work, practice, and creative thinking to use what we've got, but we can honor God by being responsible with what we've been given.

- What are you good at? What skills and talents do you have? What can you do to use them to serve God and other people?
- What gifts or skills are you hiding? What steps can you take to share them with other people?
- How are you handling your money? Where can you invest it to earn more so you can give to those in need?

talents went off at once and traded with them, and made five more talents. [17]In the same way, the one who had the two talents made two more talents. [18]But the one who had received the one talent went off and dug a hole in the ground and hid his master's money. [19]After a long time the master of those slaves came and settled accounts with them. [20]Then the one who had received the five talents came forward, bringing five more talents, saying, 'Master, you handed over to me five talents; see, I have made five more talents.' [21]His master said to him, 'Well done, good and trustworthy slave; you have been trustworthy in a few things, I will put you in charge of many things; enter into the joy of your master.' [22]And the one with the two talents also came forward, saying, 'Master, you handed over to me two talents; see, I have made two more talents.' [23]His master said to him, 'Well done, good and trustworthy slave; you have been trustworthy in a few things, I will put you in charge of many things; enter into the joy of your master.' [24]Then the one who had received the one talent also came forward, saying, 'Master, I knew that you were a harsh man, reaping where you did not sow, and gathering where you did not scatter seed; [25]so I was afraid, and I went and hid your talent in the ground. Here you have what is yours.' [26]But his master replied, 'You wicked and lazy slave! You knew, did you, that I reap where I did not sow, and gather where I did not scatter? [27]Then you ought to have invested my money with the bankers, and on my return I would have received what was my own with interest. [28]So take the talent from him, and give it to the one with the ten talents. [29]For to all those who have, more will be given, and they will have an abundance; but from those who have nothing, even what they have will be taken away. [30]As for this worthless slave, throw him into the outer darkness, where there will be weeping and gnashing of teeth.'

The Judgment of the Nations

31 "When the Son of Man comes in his glory, and all the angels with him, then he will sit on the throne of his glory. [32]All the nations will be gathered before him, and he will separate people one from another as a shepherd separates the sheep from the goats, [33]and he will put the sheep at his right hand and the goats at the left. [34]Then the king will say to those at his right hand, 'Come, you that are blessed by my Father, inherit the kingdom prepared for you from the foundation of the world; [35]for I was hungry and you gave me food, I was thirsty and you gave me something to drink, I was a stranger and you welcomed me, [36]I was naked and you gave me clothing,

"You Did It to Me" · Matthew 25:31–46

"It's their own fault. If the poor would only get out and find work, they wouldn't be poor!" This attitude lets us off the hook too easily. Jesus says we shouldn't let people suffer; we must reach out to them. He doesn't just suggest or encourage us to respond—he demands it. He also states quite clearly that we will be judged by God based on how well we care for those who are disadvantaged. And **Matthew 25:40** makes it clear that we're not commanded to do this just because people need help, but because we encounter and minister to Christ by serving in this way.

Protecting the basic rights of humans isn't easy. The United Nations' "Universal Declaration of Human Rights" gives a good starting point in determining what these basic rights might be, listing thirty human rights that should always be guaranteed for all members of the human family. These rights include the right to work, education, fair legal treatment, and ownership of property.

There are also responsibilities that go along with these rights, and they're similar to what Jesus outlines for his disciples in this challenging passage—feeding the hungry, welcoming the stranger, clothing the naked, tending to the sick, supporting those who have been imprisoned. These are the demands of our faith as disciples of Jesus. Jesus makes it clear that there's no option, only an obligation.

- How does your local community respond to Jesus' call? Can hungry people get a free meal somewhere? Does your school or church have food or clothing drives? How are shut-ins and terminally ill people cared for? Who visits or writes to the prisoners in the county jail? How does your community, school, or church respond to refugees or immigrants?
- Who are the hungry, the thirsty, the strangers, the naked, the sick, or the imprisoned in your neighborhood or community? What can you do to help minister to them?

I was sick and you took care of me, I was in prison and you visited me.' ³⁷ Then the righteous will answer him, 'Lord, when was it that we saw you hungry and gave you food, or thirsty and gave you something to drink? ³⁸ And when was it that we saw you a stranger and welcomed you, or naked and gave you clothing? ³⁹ And when was it that we saw you sick or in prison and visited you?' ⁴⁰ And the king will answer them, 'Truly I tell you, just as you did it to one of the least of these who are members of my family,ᵃ you did it to me.' ⁴¹ Then he will say to those at his left hand, 'You that are accursed, depart from me into the eternal fire prepared for the devil and his angels; ⁴² for I was hungry and you gave me no food, I was thirsty and you gave me nothing to drink, ⁴³ I was a stranger and you did not welcome me, naked and you did not give me clothing, sick and in prison and you did not visit me.' ⁴⁴ Then they also will answer, 'Lord, when was it that we saw you hungry or thirsty or a stranger or naked or sick or in prison, and did not take care of you?' ⁴⁵ Then he will answer them, 'Truly I tell

you, just as you did not do it to one of the least of these, you did not do it to me.' ⁴⁶ And these will go away into eternal punishment, but the righteous into eternal life."

The Plot to Kill Jesus

26 When Jesus had finished saying all these things, he said to his disciples, ²"You know that after two days the Passover is coming, and the Son of Man will be handed over to be crucified."

3 Then the chief priests and the elders of the people gathered in the palace of the high priest, who was called Caiaphas, ⁴ and they conspired to arrest Jesus by stealth and kill him. ⁵ But they said, "Not during the festival, or there may be a riot among the people."

The Anointing at Bethany

6 Now while Jesus was at Bethany in the house of Simon the leper,ᵇ ⁷ a woman came to him with an alabaster jar of very costly ointment, and she poured it on his head as he sat at the table. ⁸ But when the

ᵃ Gk these my brothers　ᵇ The terms leper and leprosy can refer to several diseases

ment on my body she has prepared me for burial. [13]Truly I tell you, wherever this good news*a* is proclaimed in the whole world, what she has done will be told in remembrance of her."

Judas Agrees to Betray Jesus

14 Then one of the twelve, who was called Judas Iscariot, went to the chief priests [15]and said, "What will you give me if I betray him to you?" They paid him thirty pieces of silver. [16]And from that moment he began to look for an opportunity to betray him.

disciples saw it, they were angry and said, "Why this waste? [9]For this ointment could have been sold for a large sum, and the money given to the poor." [10]But Jesus, aware of this, said to them, "Why do you trouble the woman? She has performed a good service for me. [11]For you always have the poor with you, but you will not always have me. [12]By pouring this oint-

The Passover with the Disciples

17 On the first day of Unleavened Bread the disciples came to Jesus, saying, "Where do you want us to make the preparations for you to eat the

CONNECT IT!

Students Aiding Indigent Families: Bringing It Home
Matthew 25:34–40

"Wait a minute—there's poverty and homelessness all around my hometown too!" A thought like that struck Ashley Gunn after she returned home from a mission trip to Malawi, Africa. The twelve-year-old girl from the Jackson, Mississippi, area wanted to do something about it. "I couldn't believe I'd lived in a bubble my whole life. I wanted to do something about it," Ashley told WOMEN'S HEALTH magazine.*

After her younger brother, Brantley, had a similar experience in Kenya a few years later, the two knew it was time. "When my sister and I decided to start Students Aiding Indigent Families (SAIF) in 2003, it was because we knew we were blessed, and we knew we had to implement the golden rule of helping those less fortunate," Brantley told BREAKAWAY magazine.*

The brother and sister got their nonprofit organization rolling in 2005. Ashley was seventeen. Brantley was thirteen. The goal of SAIF is to renovate abandoned urban homes, then help poor or homeless families be able to afford them. The Gunns raise money from supportive friends, family, and investors to purchase the foreclosed properties. Then under the guidance of a contractor, they recruit students to help paint, demolish drywall, landscape, or hammer nails to help make the homes livable again. Once the construction is done, SAIF helps a family with the financing and continues to provide financial counseling—a big help, as most have terrible or nonexistent credit ratings. Families who were barely scraping together enough money to pay monthly rent are then able to own their own homes with a lower monthly mortgage payment. It's a big boost to their economic well-being and their sense of dignity and self-confidence.

"Jesus was concerned about both aspects of humanity—spiritual salvation and a person's physical needs," Brantley told BREAKAWAY. "Many Bible stories about Christ point out that He treated an individual's physical needs before He attended to their spiritual needs. After all, it's hard for a person to get serious about heaven if they are starving."* The Gunns and those who work alongside them are putting into practice their belief that when they serve others, they are serving God, just as Matthew says: "Just as you did it to one of the least of these who are members of my family, you did it to me" (Matthew 25:40).

a Or *gospel*

STUDY IT!

The Complete Covenant Story · Matthew 26:26–29

Covenant is such a key theme throughout scripture that the Bible itself is called the Old and New **Testaments,** which is the Latin word for "covenant." The word "covenant" is used to express the unique relationship between God and God's people. In the Old Testament, the laws and worship practices of the Israelites were a sign of this covenant relationship (see "Live It: The Power of Covenant," near Genesis 17).

But during the Last Supper, Jesus catapults humanity into a new and dynamic dimension of the covenant relationship with God. He shares the cup and says, "Drink from it, all of you; for this is my blood of the covenant" (Matthew 26:27-28). In Luke's gospel, Jesus calls it "the new covenant in my blood" (Luke 22:20). Jesus fully restores our relationship with God through his selfless love on the cross, and he creates a new, eternal covenant with God.

Jesus initiated the new covenant through the sacrifice of his life for all. He reinterpreted the life of a covenant people through his teaching and ministry. He taught that the covenant was truly about loving God totally and loving other people with the same unconditional love we get from God. Practicing kindness, justice, forgiveness, and righteousness are the qualities that lie at the heart of the covenant. Jesus' disciples entered into this new covenant when they took the body and blood of Christ at the Last Supper.

This communion in the body of Christ also reflects the communion of all believers to each other. No matter how different we may be in nationality, race, culture, or social status, our connection as the covenant people of God transcends all human divisions. When we participate in the Lord's Supper, we reaffirm the new covenant in Jesus. Our hearts are cleansed and renewed by Jesus' sacrifice on the cross, and we pledge to share our lives together as a Christian community and as an example for the world. The covenant, which began with Abraham and was fully revealed in Jesus, is God's way of bringing us back to the source of our lives in God and into unity with others.

Passover?" [18]He said, "Go into the city to a certain man, and say to him, 'The Teacher says, My time is near; I will keep the Passover at your house with my disciples.' " [19]So the disciples did as Jesus had directed them, and they prepared the Passover meal.

[20] When it was evening, he took his place with the twelve;[a] [21]and while they were eating, he said, "Truly I tell you, one of you will betray me." [22]And they became greatly distressed and began to say to him one after another, "Surely not I, Lord?" [23]He answered, "The one who has dipped his hand into the bowl with me will betray me. [24]The Son of Man goes as it is written of him, but woe to that one by whom the Son of Man is betrayed! It would have been better for that one not to have been born." [25]Judas, who betrayed him, said, "Surely not I, Rabbi?" He replied, "You have said so."

The Institution of the Lord's Supper

[26] While they were eating, Jesus took a loaf of bread, and after blessing it he broke it, gave it to the disciples, and said, "Take, eat; this is my body." [27]Then he took a cup, and after giving thanks he gave it to them, saying, "Drink from it, all of you; [28]for this is my blood of the[b] covenant, which is poured out for many for the forgiveness of sins. [29]I tell you, I will never again drink of this fruit of the vine until that day when I drink it new with you in my Father's kingdom."

[30] When they had sung the hymn, they went out to the Mount of Olives.

Peter's Denial Foretold

[31] Then Jesus said to them, "You will all become deserters because of me this night; for it is written,

'I will strike the shepherd,
    and the sheep of the flock will be scattered.'

a Other ancient authorities add *disciples*   b Other ancient authorities add *new*

³²But after I am raised up, I will go ahead of you to Galilee." ³³Peter said to him, "Though all become deserters because of you, I will never desert you." ³⁴Jesus said to him, "Truly I tell you, this very night, before the cock crows, you will deny me three times." ³⁵Peter said to him, "Even though I must die with you, I will not deny you." And so said all the disciples.

Jesus Prays in Gethsemane

36 Then Jesus went with them to a place called Gethsemane; and he said to his disciples, "Sit here while I go over there and pray." ³⁷He took with him Peter and the two sons of Zebedee, and began to be grieved and agitated. ³⁸Then he said to them, "I am deeply grieved, even to death; remain here,

LIVE IT!

Imperfect Friends
Matthew 26:36–45

When you're in the middle of a crisis, you probably want your best friends around to help you. Suppose you ask them to be there for you, they all promise they will, but then one friend after another fails to come through. You're left to face your problems alone.

That's what happened to Jesus. His friends, the disciples, had good intentions and meant to stay awake with him. But they got tired and let him down—not once, but three times (Matthew 26:40-45). It's easy to view the apostles as special, holy, and spiritually strong, but they were also human, with their own weaknesses. Even Peter, one of the greatest heroes of Christianity, got scared and wouldn't even admit he knew Jesus (Matthew 26:69-75). Yet Jesus loved his disciples despite their failings, even when they were disloyal.

- Is it easy for you to stay friends with those who let you down?
- How can you follow Jesus' example of understanding and forgiveness, even in the midst of frustration?

and stay awake with me." ³⁹And going a little farther, he threw himself on the ground and prayed, "My Father, if it is possible, let this cup pass from me; yet not what I want but what you want." ⁴⁰Then he came to the disciples and found them sleeping; and he said to Peter, "So, could you not stay awake with me one hour? ⁴¹Stay awake and pray that you may not come into the time of trial;ᵃ the spirit indeed is willing, but the flesh is weak." ⁴²Again he went away for the second time and prayed, "My Father, if this cannot pass unless I drink it, your will be done." ⁴³Again he came and found them sleeping, for their eyes were heavy. ⁴⁴So leaving them again, he went away and prayed for the third time, saying the same words. ⁴⁵Then he came to the disciples and said to them, "Are you still sleeping and taking your rest? See, the hour is at hand, and the Son of Man is betrayed into the hands of sinners. ⁴⁶Get up, let us be going. See, my betrayer is at hand."

The Betrayal and Arrest of Jesus

47 While he was still speaking, Judas, one of the twelve, arrived; with him was a large crowd with swords and clubs, from the chief priests and the elders of the people. ⁴⁸Now the betrayer had given them a sign, saying, "The one I will kiss is the man; arrest him." ⁴⁹At once he came up to Jesus and said, "Greetings, Rabbi!" and kissed him. ⁵⁰Jesus said to him, "Friend, do what you are here to do." Then they came and laid hands on Jesus and arrested him. ⁵¹Suddenly, one of those with Jesus put his hand on his sword, drew it, and struck the slave of the high priest, cutting off his ear. ⁵²Then Jesus said to him, "Put your sword back into its place; for all who take the sword will perish by the sword. ⁵³Do you think that I cannot appeal to my Father, and he will at once send me more than twelve legions of angels? ⁵⁴But how then would the scriptures be fulfilled, which say it must happen in this way?" ⁵⁵At that hour Jesus said to the crowds, "Have you come out with swords and clubs to arrest me as though I were a bandit? Day after day I sat in the temple teaching, and you did not arrest me. ⁵⁶But all this has taken place, so that the scriptures of the prophets may be fulfilled." Then all the disciples deserted him and fled.

Jesus before the High Priest

57 Those who had arrested Jesus took him to Caiaphas the high priest, in whose house the scribes

ᵃ Or *into temptation*

and the elders had gathered. [58] But Peter was following him at a distance, as far as the courtyard of the high priest; and going inside, he sat with the guards in order to see how this would end. [59] Now the chief priests and the whole council were looking for false testimony against Jesus so that they might put him to death, [60] but they found none, though many false witnesses came forward. At last two came forward [61] and said, "This fellow said, 'I am able to destroy the temple of God and to build it in three days.' " [62] The high priest stood up and said, "Have you no answer? What is it that they testify against you?" [63] But Jesus was silent. Then the high priest said to him, "I put you under oath before the living God, tell us if you are the Messiah,[a] the Son of God." [64] Jesus said to him, "You have said so. But I tell you,

From now on you will see the Son
    of Man
  seated at the right hand of Power
  and coming on the clouds of heaven."

[65] Then the high priest tore his clothes and said, "He has blasphemed! Why do we still need witnesses? You have now heard his blasphemy. [66] What is your verdict?" They answered, "He deserves death." [67] Then they spat in his face and struck him; and some slapped him, [68] saying, "Prophesy to us, you Messiah![a] Who is it that struck you?"

Peter's Denial of Jesus

69 Now Peter was sitting outside in the courtyard. A servant-girl came to him and said, "You also were with Jesus the Galilean." [70] But he denied it before all of them, saying, "I do not know what you are talking about." [71] When he went out to the porch, another servant-girl saw him, and she said to the bystanders, "This man was with Jesus of Nazareth."[b] [72] Again he denied it with an oath, "I do not know the man." [73] After a little while the bystanders came up and said to Peter, "Certainly you are also one of them, for your accent betrays you." [74] Then he began to curse, and he swore an oath, "I do not know the man!" At that moment the cock crowed. [75] Then Peter remembered what Jesus had said: "Before the cock crows, you will deny me three times." And he went out and wept bitterly.

Jesus Brought before Pilate

27 When morning came, all the chief priests and the elders of the people conferred together against Jesus in order to bring about his death. [2] They bound him, led him away, and handed him over to Pilate the governor.

The Suicide of Judas

3 When Judas, his betrayer, saw that Jesus[c] was condemned, he repented and brought back the thirty pieces of silver to the chief priests and the elders. [4] He said, "I have sinned by betraying innocent[d] blood." But they said, "What is that to us? See to it yourself." [5] Throwing down the pieces of silver

LIVE IT!

**Second Chances
Matthew 27:3–10**

We can only guess that Judas felt intense pain after his betrayal of Jesus and experienced a deep hopelessness that led him to commit suicide. Matthew presents Judas' suicide as the fulfillment of some Old Testament prophecies, but it doesn't tell us specifically why Judas killed himself. We don't know the historical circumstances around Judas' suicide or his thoughts or motivations in a culture very different from our own.

Sometimes when life looks hopeless, suicide can seem like the only way out of pain. Unfortunately, suicide ends everything—not just the current pain, but future possibilities for healing, growth, new relationships, and good times. Remember that both Judas and Peter betrayed Jesus. Judas ended his life, and it completed his story. But Peter trusted in God's love and forgiveness and got another chance to go on to become a great hero. Nothing you can do is so terrible that your only option is taking your life.

Do you ever have thoughts of suicide? If so, talk about them with someone you trust. Speak with a parent, a youth worker, a school counselor, a coach, or a trusted friend. Caring people will help you. Seeking their help is a better way out. (For more on suicide, see "Live It: Suicide Is Not the Answer," near 1 Samuel 31:1-6.)

---

a Or Christ b Gk the Nazorean c Gk he d Other ancient authorities read *righteous*

in the temple, he departed; and he went and hanged himself. [6]But the chief priests, taking the pieces of silver, said, "It is not lawful to put them into the treasury, since they are blood money." [7]After conferring together, they used them to buy the potter's field as a place to bury foreigners. [8]For this reason that field has been called the Field of Blood to this day. [9]Then was fulfilled what had been spoken through the prophet Jeremiah,[a] "And they took[b] the thirty pieces of silver, the price of the one on whom a price had been set,[c] on whom some of the people of Israel had set a price, [10]and they gave[d] them for the potter's field, as the Lord commanded me."

Pilate Questions Jesus

11 Now Jesus stood before the governor; and the governor asked him, "Are you the King of the Jews?" Jesus said, "You say so." [12]But when he was accused by the chief priests and elders, he did not answer. [13]Then Pilate said to him, "Do you not hear how many accusations they make against you?" [14]But he gave him no answer, not even to a single charge, so that the governor was greatly amazed.

Barabbas or Jesus?

15 Now at the festival the governor was accustomed to release a prisoner for the crowd, anyone whom they wanted. [16]At that time they had a notorious prisoner, called Jesus[e] Barabbas. [17]So after they had gathered, Pilate said to them, "Whom do you want me to release for you, Jesus[e] Barabbas or Jesus who is called the Messiah?"[f] [18]For he realized

that it was out of jealousy that they had handed him over. [19]While he was sitting on the judgment seat, his wife sent word to him, "Have nothing to do with that innocent man, for today I have suffered a great deal because of a dream about him." [20]Now the chief priests and the elders persuaded the crowds to ask for Barabbas and to have Jesus killed. [21]The governor again said to them, "Which of the two do you want me to release for you?" And they said, "Barabbas." [22]Pilate said to them, "Then what should I do with Jesus who is called the Messiah?"[f] All of them said, "Let him be crucified!" [23]Then he asked, "Why, what evil has he done?" But they shouted all the more, "Let him be crucified!"

Pilate Hands Jesus over to Be Crucified

24 So when Pilate saw that he could do nothing, but rather that a riot was beginning, he took some water and washed his hands before the crowd, saying, "I am innocent of this man's blood;[g] see to it yourselves." [25]Then the people as a whole answered, "His blood be on us and on our children!" [26]So he released Barabbas for them; and after flogging Jesus, he handed him over to be crucified.

The Soldiers Mock Jesus

27 Then the soldiers of the governor took Jesus into the governor's headquarters,[h] and they gathered the whole cohort around him. [28]They stripped him and put a scarlet robe on him, [29]and after twisting some thorns into a crown, they put

---

PRAY IT!

Prayer for the Suffering · Matthew 27:27–44

Matthew paints a graphic picture of the pain and humiliation Jesus experienced before he was hung on the cross. It was all part of the suffering he endured for us.

Everyone suffers at some time in life. Some suffer in silence. Some loudly complain, making it known to all. Some bitterly blame everyone around them. Jesus suffered ridicule, betrayal, persecution, crucifixion, and death. His burden was unimaginable, but he willingly endured it, sacrificing everything to give us the hope of eternal life. As you consider Jesus' sacrifice, reflect on this prayer:

Dear Jesus, give me strength to withstand the suffering I face in my life. When it feels like more than I can take, make me strong. Give me the patience to suffer injustices without lashing out at others. Fill me with mercy to forgive those who persecute me. Fill me with your loving presence, so I can be an example to others of God's glory and the promise of eternal life. Amen.

---

a Other ancient authorities read *Zechariah* or *Isaiah*   b Or *I took*   c Or *the price of the precious One*   d Other ancient authorities read *I gave*   e Other ancient authorities lack *Jesus*   f Or *the Christ*   g Other ancient authorities read *this righteous blood*, or *this righteous man's blood*   h Gk *the praetorium*

it on his head. They put a reed in his right hand and knelt before him and mocked him, saying, "Hail, King of the Jews!" [30] They spat on him, and took the reed and struck him on the head. [31] After mocking him, they stripped him of the robe and put his own clothes on him. Then they led him away to crucify him.

The Crucifixion of Jesus

32　As they went out, they came upon a man from Cyrene named Simon; they compelled this man to carry his cross. [33] And when they came to a place called Golgotha (which means Place of a Skull), [34] they offered him wine to drink, mixed with gall; but when he tasted it, he would not drink it. [35] And when they had crucified him, they divided his clothes among themselves by casting lots;[a] [36] then they sat down there and kept watch over him. [37] Over his head they put the charge against him, which read, "This is Jesus, the King of the Jews."

38　Then two bandits were crucified with him, one on his right and one on his left. [39] Those who passed by derided[b] him, shaking their heads [40] and saying, "You who would destroy the temple and build it in three days, save yourself! If you are the Son of God, come down from the cross." [41] In the same way the chief priests also, along with the scribes and elders, were mocking him, saying, [42] "He saved others; he cannot save himself.[c] He is the King of Israel; let him come down from the cross now, and we will believe in him. [43] He trusts in God; let God deliver him now, if he wants to; for he said, 'I am God's Son.' " [44] The bandits who were crucified with him also taunted him in the same way.

The Death of Jesus

45　From noon on, darkness came over the whole land[d] until three in the afternoon. [46] And about three o'clock Jesus cried with a loud voice, "Eli, Eli, lema sabachthani?" that is, "My God, my God, why have you forsaken me?" [47] When some of the bystanders heard it, they said, "This man is calling for Elijah." [48] At once one of them ran and got a sponge, filled it with sour wine, put it on a stick, and gave it to him to drink. [49] But the others said, "Wait, let us see whether Elijah will come to save him."[e] [50] Then Jesus cried again with a loud voice and breathed his last.[f] [51] At that moment the curtain of the temple was torn in two, from top to bottom. The earth shook, and

Jesus Prays
Psalm 22
Matthew 27:46

Matthew tells us that before Jesus gave up his spirit and breathed his last breath, he cried out, "My God, my God, why have you forsaken me?" Jesus was actually reciting and praying the opening lines of **Psalm 22**. This psalm begins in despair, but ends in triumph and confidence through God's saving help. With this prayer to God, Jesus invites all people gathered at the crucifixion to pray the entire psalm—not just the first words of despair, but also the hopeful conclusion (see Psalm 22:22-31).

The Dawn of a New Age · Matthew 27:45–54

According to the gospel of Matthew, some strange things happened when Jesus died. Each event tells us something about Jesus as the fulfillment of the long-awaited Savior. The darkness that covered the land (Matthew 27:45) and the earthquake (Matthew 27:51) show that all creation was aware that something significant had happened—a new age was dawning. The splitting of the sanctuary veil (Matthew 27:51), which was the barrier that separated the holiest part of the temple, where God was thought to dwell, from the rest of the temple area, symbolizes the direct access that people now had to God. And the dead saints who came out of their tombs to walk in the city symbolize God's triumph over death. These are all Old Testament signs of the end-times (see Joel 2:10; Isaiah 26:19; Nahum 12:2; Ezekiel 37:12).

---

a　Other ancient authorities add *in order that what had been spoken through the prophet might be fulfilled, "They divided my clothes among themselves, and for my clothing they cast lots."*　b　Or *blasphemed*　c　Or *is he unable to save himself?*　d　Or *earth*　e　Other ancient authorities add *And another took a spear and pierced his side, and out came water and blood*　f　Or *gave up his spirit*

the rocks were split. [52]The tombs also were opened, and many bodies of the saints who had fallen asleep were raised. [53]After his resurrection they came out of the tombs and entered the holy city and appeared to many. [54]Now when the centurion and those with him, who were keeping watch over Jesus, saw the earthquake and what took place, they were terrified and said, "Truly this man was God's Son!"[a]

55 Many women were also there, looking on from a distance; they had followed Jesus from Galilee and had provided for him. [56]Among them were Mary Magdalene, and Mary the mother of James and Joseph, and the mother of the sons of Zebedee.

The Burial of Jesus

57 When it was evening, there came a rich man from Arimathea, named Joseph, who was also a disciple of Jesus. [58]He went to Pilate and asked for the body of Jesus; then Pilate ordered it to be given to him. [59]So Joseph took the body and wrapped it in a clean linen cloth [60]and laid it in his own new tomb, which he had hewn in the rock. He then rolled a great stone to the door of the tomb and went away. [61]Mary Magdalene and the other Mary were there, sitting opposite the tomb.

The Guard at the Tomb

62 The next day, that is, after the day of Preparation, the chief priests and the Pharisees gathered before Pilate [63]and said, "Sir, we remember what that impostor said while he was still alive, 'After three days I will rise again.' [64]Therefore command the tomb to be made secure until the third day; otherwise his disciples may go and steal him away, and tell the people, 'He has been raised from the dead,' and the last deception would be worse than the first." [65]Pilate said to them, "You have a guard[b] of soldiers; go, make it as secure as you can."[c] [66]So they went with the guard and made the tomb secure by sealing the stone.

LIVE IT!

Go Out and Do It · Matthew 28:16–20

We often make a big deal about people's last words. Sometimes they leave profound statements or express an important final message before dying. The end of Matthew reveals Jesus' last important message before he returned to heaven. It was a command to his disciples that gave them their mission after Jesus was gone. They were to take his message to the whole world, so others could follow Jesus too.

It's important to note that discipleship in that day was a process of following and learning from a teacher (rabbi). It involved an active, daily relationship with the teacher—just like the one the Twelve had experienced with Jesus. They walked, traveled, worked, and ate with Jesus. Up to this point in the book of Matthew, Jesus is the only one doing the teaching. Now he tells his followers to teach others what they have learned—and to do it in a way that is rooted in relationships. Jesus didn't argue with people to convince them to believe in him. He took time to stop and pay attention to them. He showed them love and met their needs. He used words, and he used actions. And he calls us to do the same.

Sound like a big task? Jesus recognized that and promised that we have his help and his presence. We can find hope, encouragement, and help in the last words of the gospel of Matthew: Jesus is always with us. We are never alone, especially in the tasks he calls us to do.

- In what ways does your life reflect being a disciple of Jesus? How do you interact daily with him?
- Does making disciples sound intimidating? Journal about your fears or questions related to telling other people about Christ.
- Who around you needs God's love? List several ways you can show it to others in simple, practical ways.

a Or *a son of God* **b** Or *Take a guard* **c** Gk *you know how*

28

The Resurrection of Jesus

After the sabbath, as the first day of the week was dawning, Mary Magdalene and the other Mary went to see the tomb. [2]And suddenly there was a great earthquake; for an angel of the Lord, descending from heaven, came and rolled back the stone and sat on it. [3]His appearance was like lightning, and his clothing white as snow. [4]For fear of him the guards shook and became like dead men. [5]But the angel said to the women, "Do not be afraid; I know that you are looking for Jesus who was crucified. [6]He is not here; for he has been raised, as he said. Come, see the place where he[a] lay. [7]Then go quickly and tell his disciples, 'He has been raised from the dead,[b] and indeed he is going ahead of you to Galilee; there you will see him.' This is my message for you." [8]So they left the tomb quickly with fear and great joy, and ran to tell his disciples. [9]Suddenly Jesus met them and said, "Greetings!" And they came to him, took hold of his feet, and worshiped him. [10]Then Jesus said to them, "Do not be afraid; go and tell my brothers to go to Galilee; there they will see me."

The Report of the Guard

11 While they were going, some of the guard went into the city and told the chief priests everything that had happened. [12]After the priests[c] had assembled with the elders, they devised a plan to give a large sum of money to the soldiers, [13]telling them, "You must say, 'His disciples came by night and stole him away while we were asleep.' [14]If this comes to the governor's ears, we will satisfy him and keep you out of trouble." [15]So they took the money and did as they were directed. And this story is still told among the Jews to this day.

The Commissioning of the Disciples

16 Now the eleven disciples went to Galilee, to the mountain to which Jesus had directed them.

How to Be a Disciple
Matthew 28:19

How can we follow the path of a disciple today? What special principles and values must followers of Jesus take on in order to have God's love burn within them so brightly that others will actually see the light? The best answer is found in the Gospels, specifically through the words and actions of Jesus himself. This is where past generations began, and it's where all young disciples should also start. There are many admirable qualities, principles, and attributes that can be learned from the Gospels. But here are six that serve as a solid foundation for followers of Jesus to build their lives around:

- See God in everything.
- Trust in God always.
- Stand up for the poor and vulnerable.
- Be courageous.
- Serve humbly.
- Share the faith.

[17]When they saw him, they worshiped him; but some doubted. [18]And Jesus came and said to them, "All authority in heaven and on earth has been given to me. [19]Go therefore and make disciples of all nations, baptizing them in the name of the Father and of the Son and of the Holy Spirit, [20]and teaching them to obey everything that I have commanded you. And remember, I am with you always, to the end of the age."[d]

---

a Other ancient authorities read *the Lord*   b Other ancient authorities lack *from the dead*   c Gk *they*   d Other ancient authorities add *Amen*

Mark

▶▶▶▶▶▶▶▶▶▶▶▶▶▶▶▶▶▶▶▶▶▶▶▶▶▶▶▶▶▶▶▶

Have you ever been mocked or rejected by others—maybe even your friends—for trying to do something good? Jesus knows how you feel. In the gospel of Mark, Jesus is misunderstood and abandoned by those closest to him. This gospel was written for early Christians experiencing persecution or death for their faith. The author is reminding them to put their total trust in God as Jesus did, no matter what difficulties they encounter. That same message is for us today as well.

IN DEPTH

Mark is the shortest of the four gospels and can easily be read in one sitting. It portrays Jesus as a man of action—human in his feelings and always on the move fulfilling his mission. This gospel answers two fundamental questions: Who is this Jesus called the Christ? and What does it mean to be his disciple? Those questions were a matter of life and death to the people hearing this gospel, because they were being persecuted for believing in Jesus.

Who is this Jesus called the Christ? To answer, Mark tells stories about Jesus' power to heal and about his compassion for suffering people. Jesus tangles with demons and with religious and civil authorities, and he is misunderstood even by his own disciples. Through these stories, we learn that Jesus is the Son of God, the favored one who acts with God's authority, because he is obedient to God's will. Jesus did not come as the victorious king as many Jews expected. Instead, he accepted the suffering that comes with doing God's will. His painful, shameful death was needed before his glory could be revealed.

What does it mean to be his disciple? First, it means following courageously. When Jesus called them, the disciples left the life they knew and followed Jesus (Mark 1:16-19). It also means learning from his teaching. Mark 4:10-20 gives us an example of the extra teaching and understanding given to Jesus' disciples. It also means joining Jesus in his work (Mark 6:6-13). But it doesn't mean doing it all perfectly. The disciples Jesus called were eager to follow him at first, but they quickly became fearful. When Jesus was arrested, they were so afraid they ran away and left Jesus alone. But Jesus didn't abandon them. After he was raised from the dead, he sent them a message that he would meet them again in Galilee.

Jesus continually defied people's expectations. The disciples wanted power, importance, and approval from their peers. But Jesus called them to humble tasks. He even brought them into interactions with people who were shunned and looked down upon in their culture: a blind man, a leper, and Gentiles (non-Jews). These "lowly" people even became followers of Jesus, because they placed their total trust in him. Can we place our complete faith in Jesus, becoming his disciples and following his example in our daily lives?

QUICK FACTS

- **Author:** A Gentile Christian, traditionally thought to be a disciple of Peter named John Mark
- **Date Written:** Around A.D. 65-70; the first gospel written
- **Audience:** Non-Jewish Christians who were experiencing persecution because of their belief in Jesus
- **Image of Jesus:** Healer and miracle worker who accepts suffering as the cost for following God's will

AT A GLANCE

- **Mark 1:1–15** John the Baptist's announcement of Jesus' ministry
- **Mark 1:16–8:21** Jesus' preaching and miracles in Galilee
- **Mark 8:22–10:52** Jesus' teaching and healing on the way to Jerusalem
- **Mark 11–13** Jesus' teaching in Jerusalem
- **Mark 14–16** Jesus' death and resurrection

1

The Proclamation of John the Baptist

The beginning of the good news[a] of Jesus Christ, the Son of God.[b]

2 As it is written in the prophet Isaiah,[c]

"See, I am sending my messenger ahead
of you,[d]
who will prepare your way;
3 the voice of one crying out in the wilderness:
'Prepare the way of the Lord,
make his paths straight,' "

[4]John the baptizer appeared[e] in the wilderness, proclaiming a baptism of repentance for the forgiveness of sins. [5]And people from the whole Judean countryside and all the people of Jerusalem were going out to him, and were baptized by him in the river Jordan, confessing their sins. [6]Now John was clothed with camel's hair, with a leather belt around his waist, and he ate locusts and wild honey. [7]He proclaimed, "The one who is more powerful than I is coming after me; I am not worthy to stoop down and untie the thong of his sandals. [8]I have baptized you with[f] water; but he will baptize you with[f] the Holy Spirit."

The Baptism of Jesus

9 In those days Jesus came from Nazareth of Galilee and was baptized by John in the Jordan. [10]And just as he was coming up out of the water, he saw the heavens torn apart and the Spirit descending like a dove on him. [11]And a voice came from heaven, "You are my Son, the Beloved;[g] with you I am well pleased."

The Temptation of Jesus

12 And the Spirit immediately drove him out into the wilderness. [13]He was in the wilderness forty days, tempted by Satan; and he was with the wild beasts; and the angels waited on him.

The Beginning of the Galilean Ministry

14 Now after John was arrested, Jesus came to Galilee, proclaiming the good news[a] of God,[h] [15]and saying, "The time is fulfilled, and the kingdom of God has come near;[i] repent, and believe in the good news."[a]

Jesus Calls the First Disciples

16 As Jesus passed along the Sea of Galilee, he saw Simon and his brother Andrew casting a net into the sea—for they were fishermen. [17]And Jesus said to them, "Follow me and I will make you fish for people." [18]And immediately they left their nets and followed him. [19]As he went a little farther, he saw

LIVE IT!

Called to Follow Jesus · Mark 1:16–20

The response of Peter, Andrew, James, and John to Jesus is an example of obedience to God's call. Jesus calls them because he loves them and trusts them to share in his mission.

All Christians are called to be Jesus' disciples (followers) in whatever path their lives take. Some are called to serve through professional full-time ministry or missions, while most people are called to serve God in their everyday lives. So whether you end up a pastor or a plumber, married or single, poor or rich, faithfulness to God is the most important calling you can have. Consider these questions:

- Do you see school as a necessary evil to get a high-paying job? Or do you view it as preparation for a career that will allow you to serve others and contribute to society?
- If you work, do you approach your job halfheartedly, or are you enthusiastic, always giving your best effort? Do you treat co-workers and customers with warmth and respect?

It might be hard to imagine how school or a fast-food job is part of your call to follow Jesus. But Jesus is calling you to be his disciple wherever you are and in whatever you might be doing.

---

a Or *gospel* **b** Other ancient authorities lack *the Son of God* **c** Other ancient authorities read *in the prophets* **d** Gk *before your face* **e** Other ancient authorities read *John was baptizing* **f** Or *in* **g** Or *my beloved Son* **h** Other ancient authorities read *of the kingdom* **i** Or *is at hand*

James son of Zebedee and his brother John, who were in their boat mending the nets. [20]Immediately he called them; and they left their father Zebedee in the boat with the hired men, and followed him.

The Man with an Unclean Spirit

21 They went to Capernaum; and when the sabbath came, he entered the synagogue and taught. [22]They were astounded at his teaching, for he taught them as one having authority, and not as the scribes. [23]Just then there was in their synagogue a man with an unclean spirit, [24]and he cried out, "What have you to do with us, Jesus of Nazareth? Have you come to destroy us? I know who you are, the Holy One of God." [25]But Jesus rebuked him, saying, "Be silent, and come out of him!" [26]And the unclean spirit, convulsing him and crying with a loud voice, came out of him. [27]They were all amazed, and they kept on asking one another, "What is this? A new teaching—with authority! He[a] commands even the unclean spirits, and they obey him." [28]At once his fame began to spread throughout the surrounding region of Galilee.

Jesus Heals Many at Simon's House

29 As soon as they[b] left the synagogue, they entered the house of Simon and Andrew, with James and John. [30]Now Simon's mother-in-law was in bed with a fever, and they told him about her at once. [31]He came and took her by the hand and lifted her up. Then the fever left her, and she began to serve them.

32 That evening, at sunset, they brought to him all who were sick or possessed with demons. [33]And the whole city was gathered around the door. [34]And he cured many who were sick with various diseases, and cast out many demons; and he would not permit the demons to speak, because they knew him.

A Preaching Tour in Galilee

35 In the morning, while it was still very dark, he got up and went out to a deserted place, and there he prayed. [36]And Simon and his companions hunted for him. [37]When they found him, they said to him, "Everyone is searching for you." [38]He answered, "Let us go on to the neighboring towns, so that I may proclaim the message there also; for that is what I came out to do." [39]And he went throughout Galilee, proclaiming the message in their synagogues and casting out demons.

Jesus Cleanses a Leper

40 A leper[c] came to him begging him, and kneeling[d] he said to him, "If you choose, you can make me clean." [41]Moved with pity,[e] Jesus[f] stretched out his hand and touched him, and said to him, "I do choose. Be made clean!" [42]Immediately the leprosy[c] left him, and he was made clean. [43]After sternly warning him he sent him away at once, [44]saying to him, "See that you say nothing to anyone; but go, show yourself to the priest, and offer for your cleansing what Moses commanded, as a testimony to them." [45]But he went out and began to proclaim it freely, and to spread the word, so that Jesus[f] could no longer go into a town openly, but stayed out in the country; and people came to him from every quarter.

LIVE IT!

More to the Miracle
Mark 2:1–12

The physical healing Jesus provides for the paralytic in this story is considered miraculous, and rightly so. What we shouldn't lose sight of, however, is the first type of healing that Jesus offers to this man: the forgiveness of his sins (Mark 2:5). Imagine the sense of comfort this man must have felt as he walked away, his heart cleansed and his spirit lifted!

As followers of Jesus, we are meant to take part in his healing ministry. We experience it personally when we are honest about the sinfulness in our lives and accept God's forgiveness, or when we make things right with those who have wronged us. And we can share it with others by offering hope, strength, and spiritual comfort to those in need.

- When have you asked for forgiveness or reconciled with those who need forgiveness?
- In what ways can you bring comfort and hope to those who are in need of healing, either in body or spirit?

---

a Or *A new teaching! With authority he*   b Other ancient authorities read *he*   c The terms *leper* and *leprosy* can refer to several diseases   d Other ancient authorities lack *kneeling*   e Other ancient authorities read *anger*   f Gk *he*

2 Jesus Heals a Paralytic

When he returned to Capernaum after some days, it was reported that he was at home. [2]So many gathered around that there was no longer room for them, not even in front of the door; and he was speaking the word to them. [3]Then some people[a] came, bringing to him a paralyzed man, carried by four of them. [4]And when they could not bring him to Jesus because of the crowd, they removed the roof above him; and after having dug through it, they let down the mat on which the paralytic lay. [5]When Jesus saw their faith, he said to the paralytic, "Son, your sins are forgiven." [6]Now some of the scribes were sitting there, questioning in their hearts, [7]"Why does this fellow speak in this way? It is blasphemy! Who can forgive sins but God alone?" [8]At once Jesus perceived in his spirit that they were discussing these questions among themselves; and he said to them, "Why do you raise such questions in your hearts? [9]Which is easier, to say to the paralytic, 'Your sins are forgiven,' or to say, 'Stand up and take your mat and walk'? [10]But so that you may know that the Son of Man has authority on earth to forgive sins"—he said to the paralytic— [11]"I say to you, stand up, take your mat and go to your home." [12]And he stood up, and immediately took the mat and went out before all of them; so that they were all amazed and glorified God, saying, "We have never seen anything like this!"

Jesus Calls Levi

13 Jesus[b] went out again beside the sea; the whole crowd gathered around him, and he taught them. [14]As he was walking along, he saw Levi son of Alphaeus sitting at the tax booth, and he said to him, "Follow me." And he got up and followed him.

15 And as he sat at dinner[c] in Levi's[d] house, many tax collectors and sinners were also sitting[e] with Jesus and his disciples—for there were many who followed him. [16]When the scribes of[f] the Pharisees saw that he was eating with sinners and tax collectors, they said to his disciples, "Why does he eat[g] with tax collectors and sinners?" [17]When Jesus heard this, he said to them, "Those who are well have no need of a physician, but those who are sick; I have come to call not the righteous but sinners."

The Question about Fasting

18 Now John's disciples and the Pharisees were fasting; and people[a] came and said to him, "Why do John's disciples and the disciples of the Pharisees fast, but your disciples do not fast?" [19]Jesus said to them, "The wedding guests cannot fast while the bridegroom is with them, can they? As long as they have the bridegroom with them, they cannot fast. [20]The days will come when the bridegroom is taken away from them, and then they will fast on that day.

21 "No one sews a piece of unshrunk cloth on an old cloak; otherwise, the patch pulls away from it, the new from the old, and a worse tear is made. [22]And

PRAY IT!

Getting Personal
Mark 2:13–17

It's one thing to be seen with certain groups of people, but it is another to be seen hanging out and sharing meals in their homes. Jesus was often criticized for eating with the wrong kind of people, a charge he answers in **Mark 2:13–17**. He knew that the only way to help people grow was to get to know them personally. This is why he consistently invited people to sit down and share a meal with him, in the same way we share meals with our family and friends.

Jesus' "meal ministry" throughout the Gospels is a reminder to us that we too must live in community with all people in our world, especially those who are most in need. It didn't matter to Jesus whether a person was rich or poor, well known or unknown, a saint or a sinner. It didn't matter to him whether a person was black or white, male or female, young or old. What did matter to Jesus was whether the person he approached was interested in getting to know him—and his heavenly Father—personally.

Are you ready to get to know Jesus personally? If so, take a few minutes to close your eyes and think about what this passage says. Talk to Jesus about what is going on in your life and in your family's life. When you are done talking, spend some time quietly listening for what Jesus has to say to you.

---

a Gk *they*   b Gk *He*   c Gk *reclined*   d Gk *his*   e Gk *reclining*   f Other ancient authorities read *and*   g Other ancient authorities add *and drink*

no one puts new wine into old wineskins; otherwise, the wine will burst the skins, and the wine is lost, and so are the skins; but one puts new wine into fresh wineskins."[a]

Pronouncement about the Sabbath

23 One sabbath he was going through the grainfields; and as they made their way his disciples began to pluck heads of grain. [24]The Pharisees said to him, "Look, why are they doing what is not lawful on the sabbath?" [25]And he said to them, "Have you never read what David did when he and his companions were hungry and in need of food? [26]He entered the house of God, when Abiathar was high priest, and ate the bread of the Presence, which it is not lawful for any but the priests to eat, and he gave some to his companions." [27]Then he said to them, "The sabbath was made for humankind, and not humankind for the sabbath; [28]so the Son of Man is lord even of the sabbath."

The Man with a Withered Hand

3 Again he entered the synagogue, and a man was there who had a withered hand. [2]They watched him to see whether he would cure him on the sabbath, so that they might accuse him. [3]And he said to the man who had the withered hand, "Come forward." [4]Then he said to them, "Is it lawful to do good or to do harm on the sabbath, to save life or to kill?" But they were silent. [5]He looked around at them with anger; he was grieved at their hardness of heart and said to the man, "Stretch out your hand." He stretched it out, and his hand was restored. [6]The Pharisees went out and immediately conspired with the Herodians against him, how to destroy him.

A Multitude at the Seaside

7 Jesus departed with his disciples to the sea, and a great multitude from Galilee followed him; [8]hearing all that he was doing, they came to him in great numbers from Judea, Jerusalem, Idumea, beyond the Jordan, and the region around Tyre and Sidon. [9]He told his disciples to have a boat ready for him because of the crowd, so that they would not crush him; [10]for he had cured many, so that all who had diseases pressed upon him to touch him. [11]Whenever the unclean spirits saw him, they fell down before him and shouted, "You are the Son of God!" [12]But he sternly ordered them not to make him known.

Jesus Appoints the Twelve

13 He went up the mountain and called to him those whom he wanted, and they came to him. [14]And he appointed twelve, whom he also named apostles,[b] to be with him, and to be sent out to proclaim the message, [15]and to have authority to cast out demons. [16]So he appointed the twelve:[c] Simon (to whom he gave the name Peter); [17]James son of Zebedee and John the brother of James (to whom he gave the name Boanerges, that is, Sons of Thunder); [18]and

LIVE IT!

Trusting God · Mark 3:1–6

In **Mark 3:1–6**, among those gathered in the synagogue is a man with a withered hand. There is no indication that he is seeking out Jesus or that he commands any special attention. Jesus notices him and invites him to come forward. Jesus then asks the man to stretch out his disfigured hand for all to see.

It's safe to guess that the man did not feel proud of his hand, and it would have been understandable if, when invited by Jesus to show it off for all to see, the man had stormed out of the synagogue in anger and shame. Instead, he did what Jesus asked, and through his trust in Jesus his hand was restored to wholeness.

We are all disfigured in some way—whether physically, emotionally, or spiritually. We may feel a sense of shame or embarrassment at our imperfections and come to think of ourselves as less than what we were created to be. Jesus, however, invites us into relationship with him despite our limitations, offering us compassion, love, and mercy if we are willing to put our trust in him.

- What source of pain or shame in your own life might Jesus be inviting you to share with him?
- Will you risk becoming vulnerable and trusting him with it?

---

a Other ancient authorities lack *but one puts new wine into fresh wineskins*   b Other ancient authorities lack *whom he also named apostles*   c Other ancient authorities lack *So he appointed the twelve*

God's Plan · Mark 3:13–19

God has a plan for each of us, if we just have the courage to follow him. Look at the twelve disciples Jesus called to join him on the mountain. Each had the choice to go up the mountain or not, and each chose to go. Once on the mountain, Jesus appointed them apostles (which means "sent") to continue his mission. If the apostles had answered no to Jesus' call, they may have been spared the heartbreak of witnessing the crucifixion, but they also would have missed the joy of seeing Jesus after the resurrection!

Although some people may be called to a specific ministry, we are all invited to share in Jesus' mission—to follow God, surrender our lives to him, and spread God's message of love.

Andrew, and Philip, and Bartholomew, and Matthew, and Thomas, and James son of Alphaeus, and Thaddaeus, and Simon the Cananaean, [19]and Judas Iscariot, who betrayed him.

Jesus and Beelzebul

Then he went home; [20]and the crowd came together again, so that they could not even eat. [21]When his family heard it, they went out to restrain him, for people were saying, "He has gone out of his mind." [22]And the scribes who came down from Jerusalem said, "He has Beelzebul, and by the ruler of the demons he casts out demons." [23]And he called them to him, and spoke to them in parables, "How can Satan cast out Satan? [24]If a kingdom is divided against itself, that kingdom cannot stand. [25]And if a house is divided against itself, that house will not be able to stand. [26]And if Satan has risen up against himself and is divided, he cannot stand, but his end has come. [27]But no one can enter a strong man's house and plunder his property without first tying up the strong man; then indeed the house can be plundered.

28 "Truly I tell you, people will be forgiven for their sins and whatever blasphemies they utter; [29]but whoever blasphemes against the Holy Spirit can never have forgiveness, but is guilty of an eternal sin"— [30]for they had said, "He has an unclean spirit."

The True Kindred of Jesus

31 Then his mother and his brothers came; and standing outside, they sent to him and called him. [32]A crowd was sitting around him; and they said to him, "Your mother and your brothers and sisters[a] are outside, asking for you." [33]And he replied, "Who

are my mother and my brothers?" [34]And looking at those who sat around him, he said, "Here are my mother and my brothers! [35]Whoever does the will of God is my brother and sister and mother."

The Parable of the Sower

4 Again he began to teach beside the sea. Such a very large crowd gathered around him that he got into a boat on the sea and sat there, while the whole crowd was beside the sea on the land. [2]He began to teach them many things in parables, and in his teaching he said to them: [3]"Listen! A sower went out to sow. [4]And as he sowed, some seed fell on the path, and the birds came and ate it up. [5]Other seed fell on rocky ground, where it did not have much soil, and it sprang up quickly, since it had no depth of soil. [6]And when the sun rose, it was scorched; and since it had no root, it withered away. [7]Other seed fell among thorns, and the thorns grew up and choked it, and it yielded no grain. [8]Other seed fell into good soil and brought forth grain, growing up and increasing and yielding thirty and sixty and a hundredfold." [9]And he said, "Let anyone with ears to hear listen!"

The Purpose of the Parables

10 When he was alone, those who were around him along with the twelve asked him about the parables. [11]And he said to them, "To you has been given the secret[b] of the kingdom of God, but for those outside, everything comes in parables; [12]in order that

'they may indeed look, but not perceive,
     and may indeed listen, but not
          understand;

---

a Other ancient authorities lack *and sisters*   b Or *mystery* so that they may not turn again and be forgiven.' "

13 And he said to them, "Do you not understand this parable? Then how will you understand all the parables? ¹⁴The sower sows the word. ¹⁵These are the ones on the path where the word is sown: when they hear, Satan immediately comes and takes away the word that is sown in them. ¹⁶And these are the ones sown on rocky ground: when they hear the word, they immediately receive it with joy. ¹⁷But they have no root, and endure only for a while; then, when trouble or persecution arises on account of the word, immediately they fall away.ᵃ ¹⁸And others are those sown among the thorns: these are the ones who hear the word, ¹⁹but the cares of the world, and the lure of wealth, and the desire for other things come in and choke the word, and it yields nothing.

²⁰And these are the ones sown on the good soil: they hear the word and accept it and bear fruit, thirty and sixty and a hundredfold."

A Lamp under a Bushel Basket

21 He said to them, "Is a lamp brought in to be put under the bushel basket, or under the bed, and not on the lampstand? ²²For there is nothing hidden, except to be disclosed; nor is anything secret, except to come to light. ²³Let anyone with ears to hear listen!" ²⁴And he said to them, "Pay attention to what you hear; the measure you give will be the measure you get, and still more will be given you. ²⁵For to those who have, more will be given; and from those who have nothing, even what they have will be taken away."

The Parable of the Growing Seed

26 He also said, "The kingdom of God is as if someone would scatter seed on the ground, ²⁷and  would sleep and rise night and day, and the seed would sprout and grow, he does not know how. ²⁸The earth produces of itself, first the stalk, then the head, then the full grain in the head. ²⁹But when the grain is ripe, at once he goes in with his sickle, because the harvest has come."

The Parable of the Mustard Seed

30 He also said, "With what can we compare the kingdom of God, or what parable will we use for it? ³¹It is like a mustard seed, which, when sown upon the ground, is the smallest of all the seeds on earth; ³²yet when it is sown it grows up and becomes the greatest of all shrubs, and puts forth large branches, so that the birds of the air can make nests in its shade."

The Use of Parables

33 With many such parables he spoke the word to them, as they were able to hear it; ³⁴he did not speak to them except in parables, but he explained everything in private to his disciples.

Jesus Stills a Storm

35 On that day, when evening had come, he said

LIVE IT!

A Good Story Mark 4:1–34

How do you learn best? Some of us like to read, others like to listen. Still others learn best through experiencing or doing. But whatever form it takes, most of us respond well to stories. They draw us in, inviting us to explore meanings and answers as we go. They often have a lesson, but leave room for us to discover meaning from a different perspective. Jesus often used stories called parables to teach his followers. In this passage, Jesus teaches about God's kingdom through parables (see "Study It: The Riddle of Parables," near Matthew 13:10-17). Parables are often stories of comparison. Here Jesus uses comparisons between the kingdom of God and common, everyday objects or experiences to help explain a sometimes confusing aspect of faith.

- Do you find Jesus' parables easy or hard to understand?
- Choose one of Jesus' parables and rewrite it using a comparison to something that is common in your life today.

ᵃ Or *stumble*

Life's Storms
Mark 4:35–41

Storms on the Sea of Galilee are a common occurrence. They are a fisher's nightmare, and the one described in Mark 4:35–41 was really bad! It's no wonder the disciples felt fearful and powerless. As part of your prayer, try this meditation.

Begin by closing your eyes and relaxing. Then visualize yourself standing on the beach with Jesus and the disciples. Join them as they board the boat. When the storm comes, experience the rocking of the boat, the waves crashing on deck, and the winds blowing. Feel the disciples' anxiety and fear as the boat is tossed and water pours into the boat. Go with the disciples to wake Jesus, and watch as Jesus calms the storm. Now experience the peacefulness and tranquillity of the miracle you have witnessed.

All of us must face storms—that is, parts of our lives that are filled with anxiety or fear. Think about your life:

- What are the storms that batter and rock your world?
- Who in your family or in your community can calm your fears?
- When has Jesus replaced your fear with hope?
- How would you respond to Jesus' question, "Have you still no faith?" (Mark 4:40)?

to them, "Let us go across to the other side." ³⁶And leaving the crowd behind, they took him with them in the boat, just as he was. Other boats were with him. ³⁷A great windstorm arose, and the waves beat into the boat, so that the boat was already being swamped. ³⁸But he was in the stern, asleep on the cushion; and they woke him up and said to him, "Teacher, do you not care that we are perishing?" ³⁹He woke up and rebuked the wind, and said to the sea, "Peace! Be still!" Then the wind ceased, and there was a dead calm. ⁴⁰He said to them, "Why are you afraid? Have you still no faith?" ⁴¹And they were filled with great awe and said to one another, "Who then is this, that even the wind and the sea obey him?"

Jesus Heals the Gerasene Demoniac

5 They came to the other side of the sea, to the country of the Gerasenes.ᵃ ²And when he had stepped out of the boat, immediately a man out of the tombs with an unclean spirit met him. ³He lived among the tombs; and no one could restrain him any more, even with a chain; ⁴for he had often been restrained with shackles and chains, but the chains he wrenched apart, and the shackles he broke in pieces; and no one had the strength to subdue him. ⁵Night and day among the tombs and on the mountains he was always howling and bruising himself with stones. ⁶When he saw Jesus from a distance, he ran and bowed down before him; ⁷and he shouted at the top of his voice, "What have you to do with me, Jesus, Son of the Most High God? I adjure you by God, do not torment me." ⁸For he had said to him, "Come out of the man, you unclean spirit!" ⁹Then Jesusᵇ asked him, "What is your name?" He replied, "My name is Legion; for we are many." ¹⁰He begged him earnestly not to send them out of the country. ¹¹Now there on the hillside a great herd of swine was feeding; ¹²and the unclean spiritsᶜ begged him, "Send us into the swine; let us enter them." ¹³So he gave them permission. And the unclean spirits came out and entered the swine; and the herd, numbering about two thousand, rushed down the steep bank into the sea, and were drowned in the sea.

14 The swineherds ran off and told it in the city and in the country. Then people came to see what it was that had happened. ¹⁵They came to Jesus and saw the demoniac sitting there, clothed and in his right mind, the very man who had had the legion; and they were afraid. ¹⁶Those who had seen what had happened to the demoniac and to the swine reported it. ¹⁷Then they began to beg Jesusᵈ to leave their neighborhood. ¹⁸As he was getting into the boat, the man who had been possessed by demons begged him that he might be with him. ¹⁹But Jesusᵇ refused, and said to him, "Go home to your friends, and tell them how much the Lord has done for you, and what mercy he has shown you." ²⁰And he went away and began to

ᵃ Other ancient authorities read *Gergesenes*; others, *Gadarenes* ᵇ Gk *he* ᶜ Gk *they* ᵈ Gk *him*

proclaim in the Decapolis how much Jesus had done for him; and everyone was amazed.

A Girl Restored to Life and a Woman Healed

21 When Jesus had crossed again in the boat*a* to the other side, a great crowd gathered around him; and he was by the sea. ²²Then one of the leaders of the synagogue named Jairus came and, when he saw

him, fell at his feet ²³and begged him repeatedly, "My little daughter is at the point of death. Come and lay your hands on her, so that she may be made well, and live." ²⁴So he went with him.

And a large crowd followed him and pressed in on him. ²⁵Now there was a woman who had been suffering from hemorrhages for twelve years. ²⁶She had endured much under many physicians, and had spent all that she had; and she was no better, but rather grew worse. ²⁷She had heard about Jesus, and came up behind him in the crowd and touched his cloak, ²⁸for she said, "If I but touch his clothes, I will be made well." ²⁹Immediately her hemorrhage stopped; and she felt in her body that she was healed of her disease. ³⁰Immediately aware that power had gone forth from him, Jesus turned about in the crowd and said, "Who touched my clothes?" ³¹And his disciples said to him, "You see the crowd pressing in on you; how can you say, 'Who touched me?' " ³²He looked all around to see who had done it. ³³But the woman, knowing what had happened to her, came in fear and trembling, fell down before him, and told him the whole truth. ³⁴He said to her, "Daughter, your faith has made you well; go in peace, and be healed of your disease."

35 While he was still speaking, some people came from the leader's house to say, "Your daughter is dead. Why trouble the teacher any further?" ³⁶But overhearing*b* what they said, Jesus said to the leader of the synagogue, "Do not fear, only believe." ³⁷He allowed no one to follow him except Peter, James, and John, the brother of James. ³⁸When they came to the house of the leader of the synagogue, he saw a commotion, people weeping and wailing loudly. ³⁹When he had entered, he said to them, "Why do you make

a Other ancient authorities lack *in the boat*   ***b*** Or *ignoring* ; other ancient authorities read *hearing*

a commotion and weep? The child is not dead but sleeping." ⁴⁰And they laughed at him. Then he put them all outside, and took the child's father and mother and those who were with him, and went in where the child was. ⁴¹He took her by the hand and said to her, "Talitha cum," which means, "Little girl, get up!" ⁴²And immediately the girl got up and began to walk about (she was twelve years of age). At this they were overcome with amazement. ⁴³He strictly ordered them that no one should know this, and told them to give her something to eat.

6 The Rejection of Jesus at Nazareth

He left that place and came to his hometown, and his disciples followed him. ²On the sabbath he began to teach in the synagogue, and many who heard him were astounded. They said, "Where did this man get all this? What is this wisdom that has been given to him? What deeds of power are being done by his hands! ³Is not this the carpenter, the son of Mary*a* and brother of James and Joses and Judas and Simon, and are not his sisters here with us?" And they took offense*b* at him. ⁴Then Jesus said to them, "Prophets are not without honor, except in their hometown, and among their own kin, and in their own house." ⁵And he could do no deed of power there, except that he laid his hands on a few sick people and cured them. ⁶And he was amazed at their unbelief.

The Mission of the Twelve

Then he went about among the villages teaching. ⁷He called the twelve and began to send them out two by two, and gave them authority over the unclean spirits. ⁸He ordered them to take nothing for their journey except a staff; no bread, no bag, no money in their belts; ⁹but to wear sandals and not to put on two tunics. ¹⁰He said to them, "Wherever you enter a house, stay there until you leave the place. ¹¹If any place will not welcome you and they refuse to hear you, as you leave, shake off the dust that is on your feet as a testimony against them." ¹²So they went out and proclaimed that all should repent. ¹³They cast out many demons, and anointed with oil many who were sick and cured them.

The Death of John the Baptist

14 King Herod heard of it, for Jesus'*c* name had become known. Some were*d* saying, "John the baptizer has been raised from the dead; and for this

STUDY IT!

Jesus' Resume
Mark 6:1–6

"Is not this the carpenter?" (Mark 6:3).

The people of Nazareth were astounded by how a man who in their minds was merely a carpenter could speak and act with such wisdom and power. Perhaps they had low expectations of Jesus, given that his work was a humble trade, one that certainly was not associated with great wealth or prestige. Jesus shows us, however, that all workers, even those who engage in simple, unassuming work, are capable of great things.

This unique glimpse of Jesus as a worker is a reminder to us that Jesus was both a laborer and a minister to his people. We have a similar vocational call to be workers and ministers, no matter what kind of work we do. As Jesus did, we must ensure that the work we do is focused not on gaining wealth, power, or social status, but on preserving justice, fairness, and the dignity of all people. All those who work deserve to be treated with dignity. It doesn't matter whether someone is an underpaid factory worker, an overworked migrant farmer, or even a humble carpenter.

reason these powers are at work in him." ¹⁵But others said, "It is Elijah." And others said, "It is a prophet, like one of the prophets of old." ¹⁶But when Herod heard of it, he said, "John, whom I beheaded, has been raised."

17 For Herod himself had sent men who arrested John, bound him, and put him in prison on account of Herodias, his brother Philip's wife, because Herod*e* had married her. ¹⁸For John had been telling Herod, "It is not lawful for you to have your brother's wife." ¹⁹And Herodias had a grudge against him, and wanted to kill him. But she could not, ²⁰for Herod feared John, knowing that he was a righteous and holy man, and he protected him. When he heard him, he was greatly perplexed;*f* and yet he liked to listen to him. ²¹But an opportunity came when

---

a Other ancient authorities read *son of the carpenter and of Mary*   b Or *stumbled*   c Gk *his*   d Other ancient authorities read *He was*   e Gk *he*   f Other ancient authorities read *he did many things*

Herod on his birthday gave a banquet for his courtiers and officers and for the leaders of Galilee. [22]When his daughter Herodias[a] came in and danced, she pleased Herod and his guests; and the king said to the girl, "Ask me for whatever you wish, and I will give it." [23]And he solemnly swore to her, "Whatever you ask me, I will give you, even half of my kingdom." [24]She went out and said to her mother, "What should I ask for?" She replied, "The head of John the baptizer." [25]Immediately she rushed back to the king and requested, "I want you to give me at once the head of John the Baptist on a platter." [26]The king was deeply grieved; yet out of regard for his oaths and for the guests, he did not want to refuse her. [27]Immediately the king sent a soldier of the guard with orders to bring John's[b] head. He went and beheaded him in the prison, [28]brought his head on a platter, and gave it to the girl. Then the girl gave it to her mother. [29]When his disciples heard about it, they came and took his body, and laid it in a tomb.

Feeding the Five Thousand

30 The apostles gathered around Jesus, and told him all that they had done and taught. [31]He said to them, "Come away to a deserted place all by yourselves and rest a while." For many were coming and going, and they had no leisure even to eat. [32]And they went away in the boat to a deserted place by themselves. [33]Now many saw them going and recognized them, and they hurried there on foot from all the towns and arrived ahead of them. [34]As he went ashore, he saw a great crowd; and he had compassion for them, because they were like sheep without a shepherd; and he began to teach them many things. [35]When it grew late, his disciples came to him and

---

CONNECT IT!

Austin Gutwein: Hoops of Hope · Mark 6:35–44

Sometimes all it takes to make a big difference is using what you've got—no matter how small it is or how unimportant you may feel. Two boys separated by thousands of years would agree.

Austin Gutwein of Arizona was only nine years old when he heard about the millions of kids in Africa orphaned by AIDS and felt as though God was calling him to help. But how? Austin decided to use his favorite sport, basketball. He gathered sponsors and on World AIDS Day 2004 shot 2,057 free throws—one for each child whose parents would die that day. He raised nearly $3,000, and that was only the beginning.

Since then God has multiplied Austin's efforts exponentially. The boy's idea grew into Hoops of Hope (hoopsofhope.org), and thousands of people have joined in the basketball shoot-a-thons. Participants have raised almost $2 million, and the money has been used to build schools, medical clinics, and dormitories as well as to bring access to food, water, shelter, and education to children in Africa, India, and Haiti.

"People think that kids can't really make a difference and that they should wait until they're older," Austin told CBS Sports. "But that's totally wrong. You can do something as a kid."*

In this passage in Mark we see a similar story of a young Hebrew boy who lived a couple millennia ago. We don't know his name, but we know from John's gospel (John 6:9) that it was his five loaves of bread and two fishes that Jesus multiplied to feed the five thousand people told about here in Mark. What went through the boy's mind? Perhaps it was his idea to offer his food to Jesus. Maybe he believed Jesus could somehow make it enough for everyone, or maybe that thought never crossed his mind. What's important was that an average kid willingly gave what he had and trusted Jesus to work out the rest.

It's just the type of thing God likes to do—take what's offered from an "unimportant" source and multiply it into an overflow of provision for others in need. What is God calling you to make available to him?

---

a Other ancient authorities read *the daughter of Herodias herself*   b Gk *his*

said, "This is a deserted place, and the hour is now very late; ³⁶send them away so that they may go into the surrounding country and villages and buy something for themselves to eat." ³⁷But he answered them, "You give them something to eat." They said to him, "Are we to go and buy two hundred denarii*ᵃ* worth of bread, and give it to them to eat?" ³⁸And he said to them, "How many loaves have you? Go and see." When they had found out, they said, "Five, and two fish." ³⁹Then he ordered them to get all the people to sit down in groups on the green grass. ⁴⁰So they sat down in groups of hundreds and of fifties. ⁴¹Taking the five loaves and the two fish, he looked up to heaven, and blessed and broke the loaves, and gave them to his disciples to set before the people; and he divided the two fish among them all. ⁴²And all ate and were filled; ⁴³and they took up twelve baskets full of broken pieces and of the fish. ⁴⁴Those who had eaten the loaves numbered five thousand men.

Jesus Walks on the Water

45 Immediately he made his disciples get into the boat and go on ahead to the other side, to Bethsaida, while he dismissed the crowd. ⁴⁶After saying farewell to them, he went up on the mountain to pray.

47 When evening came, the boat was out on the sea, and he was alone on the land. ⁴⁸When he saw that they were straining at the oars against an adverse wind, he came towards them early in the morning, walking on the sea. He intended to pass them by. ⁴⁹But when they saw him walking on the sea, they thought it was a ghost and cried out; ⁵⁰for they all saw him and were terrified. But immediately he spoke to them and said, "Take heart, it is I; do not be afraid." ⁵¹Then he got into the boat with them and the wind ceased. And they were utterly astounded, ⁵²for they did not understand about the loaves, but their hearts were hardened.

Healing the Sick in Gennesaret

53 When they had crossed over, they came to land at Gennesaret and moored the boat. ⁵⁴When they got out of the boat, people at once recognized him, ⁵⁵and rushed about that whole region and began to bring the sick on mats to wherever they heard he was. ⁵⁶And wherever he went, into villages or cities or farms, they laid the sick in the marketplaces, and begged him that they might touch even the fringe of his cloak; and all who touched it were healed.

STUDY IT!

Those Thickheaded Disciples
Mark 6:30–52

The disciples seem unable to do anything right. During a storm at sea, they fail to put their trust in Jesus (Mark 4:35-41). Then they can't understand the miracle of the bread because their hearts are hardened (Mark 6:52). When Jesus gives them private tutoring sessions, they still fail to understand his teachings. Later, Peter proclaims that Jesus is the Messiah, but he ends up arguing with Jesus after Jesus tells him that he will be a suffering Messiah (Mark 8:27-33). Finally, when Jesus is arrested, the disciples all desert him (Mark 14:50).

The author of Mark intentionally emphasizes the lack of faith of the disciples in order to contrast it with the unexpected faith of people like the Syrophoenician woman in Mark 7:24–30. The gospel makes the point that Jesus' true disciples are the ones who hear Jesus and place their faith in him. But don't count out the original disciples. Their journey is like most of ours, a lifelong experience of growing in faith and understanding. The Acts of the Apostles tells how they fearlessly preached the news about the risen Christ. Despite their human weakness, God works through them. That goes for us too!

The Tradition of the Elders

7 Now when the Pharisees and some of the scribes who had come from Jerusalem gathered around him, ²they noticed that some of his disciples were eating with defiled hands, that is, without washing them. ³(For the Pharisees, and all the Jews, do not eat unless they thoroughly wash their hands,*ᵇ* thus observing the tradition of the elders; ⁴and they do not eat anything from the market unless they wash it;*ᶜ* and there are also many other

---

ᵃ The denarius was the usual day's wage for a laborer　**b** Meaning of Gk uncertain　**c** Other ancient authorities read *and when they come from the marketplace, they do not eat unless they purify themselves*

LIVE IT!

Sin's Source · Mark 7:14–23

Some people believe that spiritual depth is measured by how well certain rules or religious practices are followed. Jesus reminds us in **Mark 7:14–15** that our greater concern ought to be with what is in our hearts, because it is there that both our good and our bad actions originate. Ultimately, what is in our hearts should have a greater effect on our spiritual lives than things that influence us from the outside—no matter how powerful those forces may be.

• How can you guard your heart against envy, pride, and other sin that can form there?

traditions that they observe, the washing of cups, pots, and bronze kettles.*a*) *5*So the Pharisees and the scribes asked him, "Why do your disciples not live*b* according to the tradition of the elders, but eat with defiled hands?" *6*He said to them, "Isaiah prophesied rightly about you hypocrites, as it is written,

'This people honors me with their lips,
    but their hearts are far from me;
7 in vain do they worship me,
    teaching human precepts as doctrines.'

*8*You abandon the commandment of God and hold to human tradition."

9 Then he said to them, "You have a fine way of rejecting the commandment of God in order to keep your tradition! *10*For Moses said, 'Honor your father and your mother'; and, 'Whoever speaks evil of father or mother must surely die.' *11*But you say that if anyone tells father or mother, 'Whatever support you might have had from me is Corban' (that is, an offering to God*c*)— *12*then you no longer permit doing anything for a father or mother, *13*thus making void the word of God through your tradition that you have handed on. And you do many things like this."

14 Then he called the crowd again and said to them, "Listen to me, all of you, and understand: *15*there is nothing outside a person that by going in can defile, but the things that come out are what defile."*d*

17 When he had left the crowd and entered the house, his disciples asked him about the parable. *18*He said to them, "Then do you also fail to understand? Do you not see that whatever goes into a person from outside cannot defile, *19*since it enters, not the heart but the stomach, and goes out into the sewer?" (Thus he declared all foods clean.) *20*And he said, "It is what comes out of a person that defiles.

*21*For it is from within, from the human heart, that evil intentions come: fornication, theft, murder, *22*adultery, avarice, wickedness, deceit, licentiousness, envy, slander, pride, folly. *23*All these evil things come from within, and they defile a person."

The Syrophoenician Woman's Faith

24 From there he set out and went away to the region of Tyre.*e* He entered a house and did not want anyone to know he was there. Yet he could not escape notice, *25*but a woman whose little daughter had an unclean spirit immediately heard about him, and she came and bowed down at his feet. *26*Now the woman was a Gentile, of Syrophoenician origin. She begged him to cast the demon out of her daughter. *27*He said to her, "Let the children be fed first, for it is not fair to take the children's food and throw it to the dogs." *28*But she answered him, "Sir,*f* even the dogs under the table eat the children's crumbs." *29*Then he said to her, "For saying that, you may go—the demon has left your daughter." *30*So she went home, found the child lying on the bed, and the demon gone.

Jesus Cures a Deaf Man

31 Then he returned from the region of Tyre, and went by way of Sidon towards the Sea of Galilee, in the region of the Decapolis. *32*They brought to him a deaf man who had an impediment in his speech; and they begged him to lay his hand on him. *33*He took him aside in private, away from the crowd, and put his fingers into his ears, and he spat and touched his tongue. *34*Then looking up to heaven, he sighed and said to him, "Ephphatha," that is, "Be opened." *35*And immediately his ears were opened, his tongue was released, and he spoke plainly. *36*Then Jesus*g* ordered them to tell no one; but the more he ordered them, the more zealously they proclaimed it. *37*They

a Other ancient authorities add *and beds*   **b** Gk *walk*   **c** Gk lacks *to God*   **d** Other ancient authorities add verse 16, *"Let anyone with ears to hear listen"*
e Other ancient authorities add *and Sidon*   **f** Or *Lord*; other ancient authorities prefix *Yes*   **g** Gk *he*

were astounded beyond measure, saying, "He has done everything well; he even makes the deaf to hear and the mute to speak."

Feeding the Four Thousand

8 In those days when there was again a great crowd without anything to eat, he called his disciples and said to them, [2]"I have compassion for the crowd, because they have been with me now for three days and have nothing to eat. [3]If I send them away hungry to their homes, they will faint on the way—and some of them have come from a great distance." [4]His disciples replied, "How can one feed these people with bread here in the desert?" [5]He asked them, "How many loaves do you have?" They said, "Seven." [6]Then he ordered the crowd to sit down on the ground; and he took the seven loaves, and after giving thanks he broke them and gave them to his disciples to distribute; and they distributed them to the crowd. [7]They had also a few small fish; and after blessing them, he ordered that these too should be distributed. [8]They ate and were filled; and they took up the broken pieces left over, seven baskets full. [9]Now there were about four thousand people. And he sent them away. [10]And immediately he got into the boat with his disciples and went to the district of Dalmanutha.[a]

The Demand for a Sign

11 The Pharisees came and began to argue with him, asking him for a sign from heaven, to test him. [12]And he sighed deeply in his spirit and said, "Why does this generation ask for a sign? Truly I tell you, no sign will be given to this generation." [13]And he left them, and getting into the boat again, he went across to the other side.

The Yeast of the Pharisees and of Herod

14 Now the disciples[b] had forgotten to bring any bread; and they had only one loaf with them in the boat. [15]And he cautioned them, saying, "Watch out—beware of the yeast of the Pharisees and the yeast of Herod."[c] [16]They said to one another, "It is because we have no bread." [17]And becoming aware of it, Jesus said to them, "Why are you talking about having no bread? Do you still not perceive or understand? Are your hearts hardened? [18]Do you have eyes, and fail to see? Do you have ears, and fail to hear? And do you not remember? [19]When I broke the five loaves for the five thousand, how many baskets full of broken pieces did you collect?" They said to him, "Twelve." [20]"And the seven for the four thousand, how many baskets full of broken pieces did you collect?" And they said to him, "Seven." [21]Then he said to them, "Do you not yet understand?"

Jesus Cures a Blind Man at Bethsaida

22 They came to Bethsaida. Some people[d] brought a blind man to him and begged him to touch him. [23]He took the blind man by the hand and led him out of the village; and when he had put saliva on his eyes and laid his hands on him, he asked him, "Can you

Total Commitment · Mark 8:34–38

In **Mark 8:34–38**, Jesus calls for a total commitment requiring great sacrifice. He tells the disciples that to be truly alive, they must be willing to deny themselves, take up their own crosses, and follow him. The cross symbolizes denying the way of the world and embracing the way of Jesus. It means tough self-sacrifice and, at times, a willingness to suffer for what is right.

But what does it mean to deny ourselves and take up our own cross? When we deny ourselves, it means we cannot be fooled by what the world says about being truly alive. The world tells us to buy our happiness with wealth, power, prestige, or selfish pleasure. But those things can actually make us feel less alive and more anxious.

Taking up our own cross means being willing to cling to the right things—forgiveness, justice, service, and compassion for those who are poor and those who are unpopular—even if it brings us suffering, pain, and rejection from our peers. Being committed to Jesus and these virtues, or right things, will bring us real life, true freedom, joy, and inner peace.

---

a Other ancient authorities read *Mageda* or *Magdala*　b Gk *they*　c Other ancient authorities read *the Herodians*　d Gk *They*　e Gk *he*

> "If any want to become my followers, let them deny themselves and take up their cross and follow me."
> —Mark 8:34

¹And he said to them, "Truly I tell you, there are some standing here who will not taste death until they see that the kingdom of God has come with*^f* power."

The Transfiguration

2 Six days later, Jesus took with him Peter and James and John, and led them up a high mountain apart, by themselves. And he was transfigured before them, ³and his clothes became dazzling white, such

see anything?" ²⁴And the man*^a* looked up and said, "I can see people, but they look like trees, walking." ²⁵Then Jesus*^a* laid his hands on his eyes again; and he looked intently and his sight was restored, and he saw everything clearly. ²⁶Then he sent him away to his home, saying, "Do not even go into the village."*^b*

Peter's Declaration about Jesus

27 Jesus went on with his disciples to the villages of Caesarea Philippi; and on the way he asked his disciples, "Who do people say that I am?" ²⁸And they answered him, "John the Baptist; and others, Elijah; and still others, one of the prophets." ²⁹He asked them, "But who do you say that I am?" Peter answered him, "You are the Messiah."*^c* ³⁰And he sternly ordered them not to tell anyone about him.

Jesus Foretells His Death and Resurrection

31 Then he began to teach them that the Son of Man must undergo great suffering, and be rejected by the elders, the chief priests, and the scribes, and be killed, and after three days rise again. ³²He said all this quite openly. And Peter took him aside and began to rebuke him. ³³But turning and looking at his disciples, he rebuked Peter and said, "Get behind me, Satan! For you are setting your mind not on divine things but on human things."

34 He called the crowd with his disciples, and said to them, "If any want to become my followers, let them deny themselves and take up their cross and follow me. ³⁵For those who want to save their life will lose it, and those who lose their life for my sake, and for the sake of the gospel,*^d* will save it. ³⁶For what will it profit them to gain the whole world and forfeit their life? ³⁷Indeed, what can they give in return for their life? ³⁸Those who are ashamed of me and of my words*^e* in this adulterous and sinful generation, of them the Son of Man will also be ashame when he comes in the glory of his Father with the holy angels."

On Top of the World
Mark 9:2–8

The story of the transfiguration takes place after Jesus tells his disciples about his coming suffering, death, and resurrection (Mark 8:31). They need hope and a boost of faith. Jesus takes three disciples to a mountaintop to see the kingdom of God coming in power. The three disciples see Jesus in a glorious state talking with Moses and Elijah.

The two Old Testament figures are key symbols: Moses represents the law, and Elijah, the prophets. The message is clear: Jesus is the person who fulfills the law and God's promises to the prophets. It was a profound experience for the disciples as they glimpsed Jesus' glory, but they could not understand it. Understanding came only after Jesus' resurrection.

It is understandable to want to base our faith on mountaintop experiences (see "Pray It: Spiritual Highs," near Luke 9:28–36). But while profound religious experiences enliven our faith, listening and following Jesus' words daily are what really fortify our faith and give us new life.

- What mountaintop experiences have impacted your life?
- How can you apply those experiences to help you live closer to God every day?

a Gk *he* **b** Other ancient authorities add *or tell anyone in the village* **c** Or *the Christ* **d** Other ancient authorities read *lose their life for the sake of the gospel*
e Other ancient authorities read *and of mine* **f** Or *in*

as no one[a] on earth could bleach them. [4]And there appeared to them Elijah with Moses, who were talking with Jesus. [5]Then Peter said to Jesus, "Rabbi, it is good for us to be here; let us make three dwellings,[b] one for you, one for Moses, and one for Elijah." [6]He did not know what to say, for they were terrified. [7]Then a cloud overshadowed them, and from the cloud there came a voice, "This is my Son, the Beloved;[c] listen to him!" [8]Suddenly when they looked around, they saw no one with them any more, but only Jesus.

The Coming of Elijah

9 As they were coming down the mountain, he ordered them to tell no one about what they had seen, until after the Son of Man had risen from the dead. [10]So they kept the matter to themselves, questioning what this rising from the dead could mean. [11]Then they asked him, "Why do the scribes say that Elijah must come first?" [12]He said to them, "Elijah is indeed coming first to restore all things. How then is it written about the Son of Man, that he is to go through many sufferings and be treated with contempt? [13]But I tell you that Elijah has come, and they did to him whatever they pleased, as it is written about him."

The Healing of a Boy with a Spirit

14 When they came to the disciples, they saw a great crowd around them, and some scribes arguing with them. [15]When the whole crowd saw him, they were immediately overcome with awe, and they ran forward to greet him. [16]He asked them, "What are you arguing about with them?" [17]Someone from the crowd answered him, "Teacher, I brought you my son; he has a spirit that makes him unable to speak; [18]and whenever it seizes him, it dashes him down; and he foams and grinds his teeth and becomes rigid; and I asked your disciples to cast it out, but they could not do so." [19]He answered them, "You faithless generation, how much longer must I be among you? How much longer must I put up with you? Bring him to me." [20]And they brought the boy[d] to him. When the spirit saw him, immediately it convulsed the boy,[d] and he fell on the ground and rolled about, foaming at the mouth. [21]Jesus[e] asked the father, "How long has this been happening to him?" And he said, "From childhood. [22]It has often cast him into the fire and into the water, to destroy him; but if you are able to do anything, have pity on

PRAY IT!

"I Believe; Help My Unbelief!"
Mark 9:14–29

Saying that we believe in something may not be enough to prove that we truly believe. Faith in God means knowing that God is totally with us even when it doesn't seem that way!

When we have nagging doubts whether even God can help us in a particular situation—like the father here (Mark 9:24)—we can turn to God by praying for faith. We don't have to have our faith or our lives perfectly together before we ask God for help. The test of faith is trusting that God cares for us and provides what we need, even when our prayers are not answered in the way we desire.

us and help us." [23]Jesus said to him, "If you are able!—All things can be done for the one who believes." [24]Immediately the father of the child cried out,[f] "I believe; help my unbelief!" [25]When Jesus saw that a crowd came running together, he rebuked the unclean spirit, saying to it, "You spirit that keeps this boy from speaking and hearing, I command you, come out of him, and never enter him again!" [26]After crying out and convulsing him terribly, it came out, and the boy was like a corpse, so that most of them said, "He is dead." [27]But Jesus took him by the hand and lifted him up, and he was able to stand. [28]When he had entered the house, his disciples asked him privately, "Why could we not cast it out?" [29]He said to them, "This kind can come out only through prayer."[g]

Jesus Again Foretells His Death and Resurrection

30 They went on from there and passed through Galilee. He did not want anyone to know it; [31]for he was teaching his disciples, saying to them, "The Son of Man is to be betrayed into human hands, and they will kill him, and three days after being killed, he will rise again." [32]But they did not understand what he was saying and were afraid to ask him.

a Gk *no fuller* b Or *tents* c Or *my beloved Son* d Gk *him* e Gk *He* f Other ancient authorities add *with tears* g Other ancient authorities add *and fasting*

Who Is the Greatest?

33 Then they came to Capernaum; and when he was in the house he asked them, "What were you arguing about on the way?" 34But they were silent, for on the way they had argued with one another who was the greatest. 35He sat down, called the twelve, and said to them, "Whoever wants to be first must be last of all and servant of all." 36Then he took a little child and put it among them; and taking it in his arms, he said to them, 37"Whoever welcomes one such child in my name welcomes me, and whoever welcomes me welcomes not me but the one who sent me."

Another Exorcist

38 John said to him, "Teacher, we saw someone[a] casting out demons in your name, and we tried to stop him, because he was not following us." 39But Jesus said, "Do not stop him; for no one who does a deed of power in my name will be able soon afterward to speak evil of me. 40Whoever is not against us is for us. 41For truly I tell you, whoever gives you a cup of water to drink because you bear the name of Christ will by no means lose the reward.

Temptations to Sin

42 "If any of you put a stumbling block before one of these little ones who believe in me,[b] it would be better for you if a great millstone were hung around your neck and you were thrown into the sea. 43If your hand causes you to stumble, cut it off; it is better for you to enter life maimed than to have two hands and to go to hell,[c] to the unquenchable fire.[d] 45And if your foot causes you to stumble, cut it off; it is better for

you to enter life lame than to have two feet and to be thrown into hell.[c,d] 47And if your eye causes you to stumble, tear it out; it is better for you to enter the kingdom of God with one eye than to have two eyes and to be thrown into hell,[c] 48where their worm never dies, and the fire is never quenched.

49 "For everyone will be salted with fire.[e] 50Salt is good; but if salt has lost its saltiness, how can you season it?[f] Have salt in yourselves, and be at peace with one another."

Teaching about Divorce

10 He left that place and went to the region of Judea and[g] beyond the Jordan. And crowds again gathered around him; and, as was his custom, he again taught them.

2 Some Pharisees came, and to test him they asked, "Is it lawful for a man to divorce his wife?" 3He answered them, "What did Moses command you?" 4They said, "Moses allowed a man to write a certificate of dismissal and to divorce her." 5But Jesus said to them, "Because of your hardness of heart he wrote this commandment for you. 6But from the beginning of creation, 'God made them male and female.' 7'For this reason a man shall leave his father and mother and be joined to his wife,[h] 8and the two shall become one flesh.' So they are no longer two, but one flesh. 9Therefore what God has joined together, let no one separate."

10 Then in the house the disciples asked him again about this matter. 11He said to them, "Whoever divorces his wife and marries another commits adultery against her; 12and if she divorces her husband and marries another, she commits adultery."

Don't Get Burned · Mark 9:42–49

It's easy to give in to temptation. Every day, we face decisions that can hurt our relationship with God. Self-control is the strength to resist temptation, but sometimes we find ourselves in situations where our self-control isn't enough. So the best way to beat temptation is to avoid the situations completely. **Mark 9:42–49** seems a bit extreme if taken literally, but its point is the same. If something or some situation tempts you, get rid of it. No matter how painful or sad that feels, it is better than living in sin.

You've heard the old saying, "If you play with fire, you might get burned." It is often used by people recovering from addictions, but applies to any strong temptation. The best way to avoid getting burned is to stay far away.

- What desires tempt you most?
- How can you avoid getting burned?

---

a Other ancient authorities add *who does not follow us*   b Other ancient authorities lack *in me*   c Gk *Gehenna*   d Verses 44 and 46 (which are identical with verse 48) are lacking in the best ancient authorities   e Other ancient authorities either add or substitute *and every sacrifice will be salted with salt*   f Or *how can you restore its saltiness?*   g Other ancient authorities lack *and*   h Other ancient authorities lack *and be joined to his wife*

STUDY IT!

Positively Good
Mark 10:1–12

Jesus always had a great way of seeing the good in everything. For example, when the Pharisees try to test Jesus with a question about divorce, Jesus speaks about marriage. Rather than focus on the negative, Jesus turns everyone's attention to the positive—the beauty of two people who "are no longer two, but one flesh" (Mark 10:8). And just a few verses later Jesus challenges the rich man to give up all he owns in order to follow him (Mark 10:17–27). It's a tough challenge, and Jesus plainly tells his followers how hard it is for a rich man to enter the kingdom of God. But he doesn't leave it at that. Instead, Jesus brings out the positive by reminding his followers that there is still hope—what is impossible for people is possible with God.

Jesus Blesses Little Children

13 People were bringing little children to him in order that he might touch them; and the disciples spoke sternly to them. [14]But when Jesus saw this, he was indignant and said to them, "Let the little children come to me; do not stop them; for it is to such as these that the kingdom of God belongs. [15]Truly I tell you, whoever does not receive the kingdom of God as a little child will never enter it." [16]And he took them up in his arms, laid his hands on them, and blessed them.

The Rich Man

17 As he was setting out on a journey, a man ran up and knelt before him, and asked him, "Good Teacher, what must I do to inherit eternal life?" [18]Jesus said to him, "Why do you call me good? No one is good but God alone. [19]You know the commandments: 'You shall not murder; You shall not commit adultery; You shall not steal; You shall not bear false witness; You shall not defraud; Honor your father and mother.'" [20]He said to him, "Teacher, I have kept all these since my youth."

[21]Jesus, looking at him, loved him and said, "You lack one thing; go, sell what you own, and give the money[a] to the poor, and you will have treasure in heaven; then come, follow me." [22]When he heard this, he was shocked and went away grieving, for he had many possessions.

23 Then Jesus looked around and said to his disciples, "How hard it will be for those who have wealth to enter the kingdom of God!" [24]And the disciples were perplexed at these words. But Jesus said to them again, "Children, how hard it is[b] to enter the kingdom of God! [25]It is easier for a camel to go through the eye of a needle than for someone who is rich to enter the kingdom of God." [26]They were greatly astounded and said to one another,[c] "Then who can be saved?" [27]Jesus looked at them and said, "For mortals it is impossible, but not for God; for God all things are possible."

28 Peter began to say to him, "Look, we have left everything and followed you." [29]Jesus said, "Truly I tell you, there is no one who has left house or brothers or sisters or mother or father or children or fields, for my sake and for the sake of the good news,[d] [30]who will not receive a hundredfold now in this age—houses, brothers and sisters, mothers and children, and fields, with persecutions—and in the age to come eternal life. [31]But many who are first will be last, and the last will be first."

A Third Time Jesus Foretells His Death and Resurrection

32 They were on the road, going up to Jerusalem, and Jesus was walking ahead of them; they were amazed, and those who followed were afraid. He took the twelve aside again and began to tell them what was to happen to him, [33]saying, "See, we are going up to Jerusalem, and the Son of Man will be handed over to the chief priests and the scribes, and they will condemn him to death; then they

---

a Gk lacks *the money* **b** Other ancient authorities add *for those who trust in riches* **c** Other ancient authorities read *to him* **d** Or *gospel*

will hand him over to the Gentiles; [34] they will mock him, and spit upon him, and flog him, and kill him; and after three days he will rise again."

The Request of James and John

35 James and John, the sons of Zebedee, came forward to him and said to him, "Teacher, we want you to do for us whatever we ask of you." [36] And he said to them, "What is it you want me to do for you?" [37] And they said to him, "Grant us to sit, one at your right hand and one at your left, in your glory." [38] But Jesus said to them, "You do not know what you are asking. Are you able to drink the cup that I drink, or be baptized with the baptism that I am baptized with?" [39] They replied, "We are able." Then Jesus said to them, "The cup that I drink you will drink; and with the baptism with which I am baptized, you will be baptized; [40] but to sit at my right hand or at my left is not mine to grant, but it is for those for whom it has been prepared."

41 When the ten heard this, they began to be angry with James and John. [42] So Jesus called them and said to them, "You know that among the Gentiles those whom they recognize as their rulers lord it over them, and their great ones are tyrants over them. [43] But it is not so among you; but whoever wishes to become great among you must be your servant, [44] and whoever wishes to be first among you must be slave of all. [45] For the Son of Man came not to be served but to serve, and to give his life a ransom for many."

The Healing of Blind Bartimaeus

46 They came to Jericho. As he and his disciples and a large crowd were leaving Jericho, Bartimaeus son of Timaeus, a blind beggar, was sitting by the roadside. [47] When he heard that it was Jesus of Nazareth, he began to shout out and say, "Jesus, Son of David, have mercy on me!" [48] Many sternly ordered him to be quiet, but he cried out even more loudly, "Son of David, have mercy on me!" [49] Jesus stood still and said, "Call him here." And they called the blind man, saying to him, "Take heart; get up, he is calling you." [50] So throwing off his cloak, he sprang up and came to Jesus. [51] Then Jesus said to him, "What do you want me to do for you?" The blind man said to him, "My teacher,[a] let me see again." [52] Jesus said to him, "Go; your faith has made you well." Immediately he regained his sight and followed him on the way.

a Aramaic *Rabbouni*

Jesus' Triumphal Entry into Jerusalem

11 When they were approaching Jerusalem, at Bethphage and Bethany, near the Mount of Olives, he sent two of his disciples [2] and said to them, "Go into the village ahead of you, and immediately as you enter it, you will find tied there a colt that has never been ridden; untie it and bring it. [3] If anyone says to you, 'Why are you doing this?' just say this, 'The Lord needs it and will send it back here immediately.' " [4] They went away and found a colt tied near a door, outside in the street. As they were untying it, [5] some of the bystanders said to them, "What are you doing, untying the colt?" [6] They told them what Jesus had said; and they allowed them to take it. [7] Then they brought the colt to Jesus and threw their cloaks on it; and he sat on it. [8] Many people spread their cloaks on the road, and others spread leafy branches that they had cut in the fields. [9] Then those who went ahead and those who followed were shouting,

"Hosanna!

Blessed is the one who comes in the name
of the Lord!

10   Blessed is the coming kingdom of our
ancestor David!

Hosanna in the highest heaven!"

11 Then he entered Jerusalem and went into the temple; and when he had looked around at everything, as it was already late, he went out to Bethany with the twelve.

Jesus Curses the Fig Tree

12 On the following day, when they came from Bethany, he was hungry. [13] Seeing in the distance a fig tree in leaf, he went to see whether perhaps he would find anything on it. When he came to it, he found nothing but leaves, for it was not the season for figs. [14] He said to it, "May no one ever eat fruit from you again." And his disciples heard it.

Jesus Cleanses the Temple

15 Then they came to Jerusalem. And he entered the temple and began to drive out those who were selling and those who were buying in the temple, and he overturned the tables of the money changers and the seats of those who sold doves; [16] and he would not allow anyone to carry anything through the temple. [17] He was teaching and saying, "Is it not written,

Unanswered Prayer · Mark 11:24

Have you ever wanted something so badly that you prayed for it? Sometimes when things turn out the way we want, we say that God has answered our prayers. But when things don't turn out the way we want, we say that God didn't answer our prayers. But that's not always the case—God's perspective on answered prayer is much larger than ours. God sees beyond the immediate situation and into the depths of our hearts.

Mark 11:24 seems to say that we have the power to obtain what we want from God just by stating our wishes. And though stories throughout the Bible show us that God wants us to pray and hears our prayers, it's not a magic formula for getting anything we want. One of God's purposes in prayer is to shape our hearts to be more like his. As we pray and seek to know God better, we learn more of what God wants in this world and wants of us. So although our situation may not always change, our hearts and perspectives can be changed through prayer.

And what about the times when something horrible happens despite all our prayers? Tragedy happens because we live in a fallen, sinful world, but the good news is that God can and does use every situation for the good of those who love him (see Romans 8:28). We may not see it right away, but we can continue to trust in the God we know—a God who loves us intimately and hates to see us suffering and who ultimately is at work for our good.

'My house shall be called a house of prayer for all the nations'?

But you have made it a den of robbers."

[18]And when the chief priests and the scribes heard it, they kept looking for a way to kill him; for they were afraid of him, because the whole crowd was spellbound by his teaching. [19]And when evening came, Jesus and his disciples[a] went out of the city.

The Lesson from the Withered Fig Tree

20 In the morning as they passed by, they saw the fig tree withered away to its roots. [21]Then Peter remembered and said to him, "Rabbi, look! The fig tree that you cursed has withered." [22]Jesus answered them, "Have[b] faith in God. [23]Truly I tell you, if you say to this mountain, 'Be taken up and thrown into the sea,' and if you do not doubt in your heart, but believe that what you say will come to pass, it will be done for you. [24]So I tell you, whatever you ask for in prayer, believe that you have received[c] it, and it will be yours. 25 "Whenever you stand praying, forgive, if you have anything against anyone; so that your Father in heaven may also forgive you your trespasses."[d]

Jesus' Authority Is Questioned

27 Again they came to Jerusalem. As he was walking in the temple, the chief priests, the scribes, and the elders came to him [28]and said, "By what authority are you doing these things? Who gave you this authority to do them?" [29]Jesus said to them, "I will ask you one question; answer me, and I will tell you by what authority I do these things. [30]Did the baptism of John come from heaven, or was it of human origin? Answer me." [31]They argued with one another, "If we say, 'From heaven,' he will say, 'Why then did you not believe him?' [32]But shall we say, 'Of human origin'?"—they were afraid of the crowd, for all regarded John as truly a prophet. [33]So they answered Jesus, "We do not know." And Jesus said to them, "Neither will I tell you by what authority I am doing these things."

The Parable of the Wicked Tenants

12 Then he began to speak to them in parables. "A man planted a vineyard, put a fence around it, dug a pit for the wine press, and built a watchtower; then he leased it to tenants and went to another country. [2]When the season came, he sent a slave to the tenants to collect from them his share of the produce of the vineyard. [3]But they seized him, and beat him, and sent him away empty-handed. [4]And again he sent another slave to them; this one they beat over the head and insulted. [5]Then he sent another, and that one they killed. And so it was with

---

a Gk *they*: other ancient authorities read *he*　b Other ancient authorities read *"If you have*　c Other ancient authorities read *are receiving*　d Other ancient authorities add verse 26, *"But if you do not forgive, neither will your Father in heaven forgive your trespasses."*

many others; some they beat, and others they killed. ⁶He had still one other, a beloved son. Finally he sent him to them, saying, 'They will respect my son.' ⁷But those tenants said to one another, 'This is the heir; come, let us kill him, and the inheritance will be ours.' ⁸So they seized him, killed him, and threw him out of the vineyard. ⁹What then will the owner of the vineyard do? He will come and destroy the tenants and give the vineyard to others. ¹⁰Have you not read this scripture:

'The stone that the builders rejected
    has become the cornerstone;ᵃ
¹¹ this was the Lord's doing,
    and it is amazing in our eyes'?"

12 When they realized that he had told this parable against them, they wanted to arrest him, but they feared the crowd. So they left him and went away.

The Question about Paying Taxes

13 Then they sent to him some Pharisees and some Herodians to trap him in what he said. ¹⁴And they came and said to him, "Teacher, we know that you are sincere, and show deference to no one; for you do not regard people with partiality, but teach the way of God in accordance with truth. Is it lawful to pay taxes to the emperor, or not? ¹⁵Should we pay them, or should we not?" But knowing their hypocrisy, he said to them, "Why are you putting me to the test? Bring me a denarius and let me see it." ¹⁶And they brought one. Then he said to them, "Whose head is this, and whose title?" They answered, "The emperor's." ¹⁷Jesus said to them, "Give to the emperor the things that are the emperor's, and to God the things that are God's." And they were utterly amazed at him.

The Question about the Resurrection

18 Some Sadducees, who say there is no resurrection, came to him and asked him a question, saying, ¹⁹"Teacher, Moses wrote for us that if a man's brother dies, leaving a wife but no child, the manᵇ shall marry the widow and raise up children for his brother. ²⁰There were seven brothers; the first married and, when he died, left no children; ²¹and the second married the widowᶜ and died, leaving no children; and the third likewise; ²²none of the seven left children. Last of all the woman herself died. ²³In the resurrectionᵈ whose wife will she be? For the seven had married her."

24 Jesus said to them, "Is not this the reason you are wrong, that you know neither the scriptures nor the power of God? ²⁵For when they rise from the dead, they neither marry nor are given in marriage, but are like angels in heaven. ²⁶And as for the dead being raised, have you not read in the book of Moses, in the story about the bush, how God said to him, 'I am the God of Abraham, the God of Isaac, and the God of Jacob'? ²⁷He is God not of the dead, but of the living; you are quite wrong."

PRAY IT!

What Do You Want from Me?
Mark 12:13–17

When asked about whether Jews should pay taxes to the emperor, Jesus answers in a way that teaches a much more important lesson. In **Mark 12:17**, Jesus says to give to God the things that are God's. Think about that—what is God's? Everything! So how can you give back what God has given to you? Reflect on this passage in Mark and close with this prayer.

Dear God, Jesus tells us to give to you what is yours. What do you want from me, God? What can I give to you?

As a young person, I don't have much to offer financially. I can make a small contribution to the church or those in need. But what more can I give?

I can offer my time and talents to serve in my church. I can sing, play an instrument, draw posters, greet visitors, clean, decorate, organize, and help teach children. What more can I give?

I can reach out to serve and share your love with my family, my neighbors, my classmates, my community. What more can I give?

I want to serve you with my whole heart, Lord. Speak to me, and I will listen. Amen.

---

a Or *keystone* b Gk *his brother* c Gk *her* d Other ancient authorities add *when they rise*

The First Commandment

28 One of the scribes came near and heard them disputing with one another, and seeing that he answered them well, he asked him, "Which commandment is the first of all?" [29]Jesus answered, "The first is, 'Hear, O Israel: the Lord our God, the Lord is one; [30]you shall love the Lord your God with all your heart, and with all your soul, and with all your mind, and with all your strength.' [31]The second is this, 'You shall love your neighbor as yourself.' There is no other commandment greater than these." [32]Then the scribe said to him, "You are right, Teacher; you have truly said that 'he is one, and besides him there is no other'; [33]and 'to love him with all the heart, and with all the understanding, and with all the strength,' and 'to love one's neighbor as oneself,'—this is much more important than all whole burnt offerings and sacrifices." [34]When Jesus saw that he answered wisely, he said to him, "You are not far from the kingdom of God." After that no one dared to ask him any question.

The Question about David's Son

35 While Jesus was teaching in the temple, he said, "How can the scribes say that the Messiah[a] is the son of David? [36]David himself, by the Holy Spirit, declared,

'The Lord said to my Lord,
    "Sit at my right hand,
        until I put your enemies under your feet." '
[37]David himself calls him Lord; so how can he be his son?" And the large crowd was listening to him with delight.

Jesus Denounces the Scribes

38 As he taught, he said, "Beware of the scribes, who like to walk around in long robes, and to be greeted with respect in the marketplaces, [39]and to have the best seats in the synagogues and places of honor at banquets! [40]They devour widows' houses and for the sake of appearance say long prayers. They will receive the greater condemnation."

The Widow's Offering

41 He sat down opposite the treasury, and watched the crowd putting money into the treasury. Many rich people put in large sums. [42]A poor widow came and put in two small copper coins, which are worth a penny. [43]Then he called his disciples and said to them, "Truly I tell you, this poor widow has put in more than all those who are contributing to the treasury. [44]For all of them have contributed out of their abundance; but she out of her poverty has put in everything she had, all she had to live on."

13 The Destruction of the Temple Foretold

As he came out of the temple, one of his disciples said to him, "Look, Teacher, what large stones and what large buildings!" [2]Then Jesus asked him, "Do you see these great buildings? Not one stone will be left here upon another; all will be thrown down."

3 When he was sitting on the Mount of Olives opposite the temple, Peter, James, John, and Andrew asked him privately, [4]"Tell us, when will this be, and what will be the sign that all these things are about to be accomplished?" [5]Then Jesus began to say to them, "Beware that no one leads you astray. [6]Many will come in my name and say, 'I am he!'[b] and they will lead many astray. [7]When you hear of wars and rumors of wars, do not be alarmed; this must take place, but

STUDY IT!

Signs and Omens
Mark 13

The gospel of Mark was written for a community that saw its sufferings as part of the troubles that would come with the end-time. However, the author didn't intend that his readers take Jesus' signs and omens of wars and earthquakes to mean that the end of the world was literally at hand; rather, these descriptions were used symbolically (see "Study It: Apocalyptic Literature," near Daniel 7-10) to help the community make sense of its persecutions. The message of this gospel is that Christians who were getting beaten up and thrown in jail would be saved by God. And ultimately human history would climax in the return of Jesus and the complete coming of his kingdom. It was their job to hang on and endure to the end. All they had to worry about was spreading the good news of Jesus Christ, and God would take care of the rest.

a Or *the Christ*   *b* Gk *I am*

the end is still to come. [8]For nation will rise against nation, and kingdom against kingdom; there will be earthquakes in various places; there will be famines. This is but the beginning of the birth pangs.

Persecution Foretold

9 "As for yourselves, beware; for they will hand you over to councils; and you will be beaten in synagogues; and you will stand before governors and kings because of me, as a testimony to them. [10]And the good news[a] must first be proclaimed to all nations. [11]When they bring you to trial and hand you over, do not worry beforehand about what you are to say; but say whatever is given you at that time, for it is not you who speak, but the Holy Spirit. [12]Brother will betray brother to death, and a father his child, and children will rise against parents and have them put to death; [13]and you will be hated by all because of my name. But the one who endures to the end will be saved.

The Desolating Sacrilege

14 "But when you see the desolating sacrilege set up where it ought not to be (let the reader understand), then those in Judea must flee to the mountains; [15]the one on the housetop must not go down or enter the house to take anything away; [16]the one in the field must not turn back to get a coat. [17]Woe to those who are pregnant and to those who are nursing infants in those days! [18]Pray that it may not be in winter. [19]For in those days there will be suffering, such as has not been from the beginning of the creation that God created until now, no, and never will be. [20]And if the Lord had not cut short those days, no one would be saved; but for the sake of the elect, whom he chose, he has cut short those days. [21]And if anyone says to you at that time, 'Look! Here is the Messiah!'[b] or 'Look! There he is!'—do not believe it. [22]False messiahs[c] and false prophets will appear and produce signs and omens, to lead astray, if possible, the elect. [23]But be alert; I have already told you everything.

The Coming of the Son of Man

24 "But in those days, after that suffering,

the sun will be darkened,
    and the moon will not give its light,
[25]   and the stars will be falling from heaven,
        and the powers in the heavens will be
        shaken.

[26]Then they will see 'the Son of Man coming in clouds' with great power and glory. [27]Then he will send out the angels, and gather his elect from the four winds, from the ends of the earth to the ends of heaven.

The Lesson of the Fig Tree

28 "From the fig tree learn its lesson: as soon as its branch becomes tender and puts forth its leaves, you know that summer is near. [29]So also, when you see these things taking place, you know that he[d] is near, at the very gates. [30]Truly I tell you, this generation will not pass away until all these things have taken place. [31]Heaven and earth will pass away, but my words will not pass away.

The Necessity for Watchfulness

32 "But about that day or hour no one knows, neither the angels in heaven, nor the Son, but only the Father. [33]Beware, keep alert;[e] for you do not know when the time will come. [34]It is like a man going on a journey, when he leaves home and puts his slaves in charge, each with his work, and commands the doorkeeper to be on the watch. [35]Therefore, keep awake—for you do not know when the master of the house will come, in the evening, or at midnight, or at cockcrow, or at dawn, [36]or else he may find you asleep when he comes suddenly. [37]And what I say to you I say to all: Keep awake."

14 The Plot to Kill Jesus

It was two days before the Passover and the festival of Unleavened Bread. The chief priests and the scribes were looking for a way to arrest Jesus[f] by stealth and kill him; [2]for they said, "Not during the festival, or there may be a riot among the people."

The Anointing at Bethany

3 While he was at Bethany in the house of Simon the leper,[g] as he sat at the table, a woman came with an alabaster jar of very costly ointment of nard, and she broke open the jar and poured the ointment on his head. [4]But some were there who said to one another in anger, "Why was the ointment wasted in this way? [5]For this ointment could have been sold for more than three hundred denarii,[h] and the money given to the poor." And they scolded her. [6]But Jesus said, "Let her alone; why do you trouble her? She has performed a good service for me. [7]For

---

a Gk gospel   b Or the Christ   c Or christs   d Or it   e Other ancient authorities add and pray   f Gk him   g The terms leper and leprosy can refer to several diseases   h The denarius was the usual day's wage for a laborer

you always have the poor with you, and you can show kindness to them whenever you wish; but you will not always have me. [8]She has done what she could; she has anointed my body beforehand for its burial. [9]Truly I tell you, wherever the good news[a] is proclaimed in the whole world, what she has done will be told in remembrance of her."

Judas Agrees to Betray Jesus

10 Then Judas Iscariot, who was one of the twelve, went to the chief priests in order to betray him to them. [11]When they heard it, they were greatly pleased, and promised to give him money. So he began to look for an opportunity to betray him.

The Passover with the Disciples

12 On the first day of Unleavened Bread, when the Passover lamb is sacrificed, his disciples said to him, "Where do you want us to go and make the preparations for you to eat the Passover?" [13]So he sent two of his disciples, saying to them, "Go into the city, and a man carrying a jar of water will meet you; follow him, [14]and wherever he enters, say to the owner of the house, 'The Teacher asks, Where is my guest room where I may eat the Passover with my disciples?' [15]He will show you a large room upstairs, furnished and ready. Make preparations for us there." [16]So the disciples set out and went to the city, and found everything as he had told them; and they prepared the Passover meal.

17 When it was evening, he came with the twelve. [18]And when they had taken their places and were eating, Jesus said, "Truly I tell you, one of you will betray me, one who is eating with me." [19]They began to be distressed and to say to him one after another, "Surely, not I?" [20]He said to them, "It is one of the twelve, one who is dipping bread[b] into the bowl[c] with me. [21]For the Son of Man goes as it is written of him, but woe to that one by whom the Son of Man is betrayed! It would have been better for that one not to have been born."

The Institution of the Lord's Supper

22 While they were eating, he took a loaf of bread, and after blessing it he broke it, gave it to them, and said, "Take; this is my body." [23]Then he took a cup, and after giving thanks he gave it to them, and all of them drank from it. [24]He said to them, "This is my blood of the[d] covenant, which is poured out for many. [25]Truly I tell you, I will never again drink of

the fruit of the vine until that day when I drink it new in the kingdom of God."

Peter's Denial Foretold

26 When they had sung the hymn, they went out to the Mount of Olives. [27]And Jesus said to them, "You will all become deserters; for it is written,

'I will strike the shepherd,
 and the sheep will be scattered.'

[28]But after I am raised up, I will go before you to Galilee." [29]Peter said to him, "Even though all become deserters, I will not." [30]Jesus said to him, "Truly I tell you, this day, this very night, before the cock crows twice, you will deny me three times."

a Or gospel b Gk lacks bread c Other ancient authorities read same bowl d Other ancient authorities add new

³¹But he said vehemently, "Even though I must die with you, I will not deny you." And all of them said the same.

Jesus Prays in Gethsemane

32 They went to a place called Gethsemane; and he said to his disciples, "Sit here while I pray." ³³He took with him Peter and James and John, and began to be distressed and agitated. ³⁴And he said to them, "I am deeply grieved, even to death; remain here, and keep awake." ³⁵And going a little farther, he threw himself on the ground and prayed that, if it were possible, the hour might pass from him. ³⁶He said, "Abba,ᵃ Father, for you all things are possible; remove this cup from me; yet, not what I want, but what you want." ³⁷He came and found them sleeping; and he said to Peter, "Simon, are you asleep? Could you not keep awake one hour? ³⁸Keep awake and pray that you may not come into the time of trial;ᵇ the spirit indeed is willing, but the flesh is weak." ³⁹And again he went away and prayed, saying the same words. ⁴⁰And once more he came and found them sleeping, for their eyes were very heavy; and they did not know what to say to him. ⁴¹He came a third time and said to them, "Are you still sleeping and taking your rest? Enough! The hour has come; the Son of Man is betrayed into the hands of sinners. ⁴²Get up, let us be going. See, my betrayer is at hand."

The Betrayal and Arrest of Jesus

43 Immediately, while he was still speaking, Judas, one of the twelve, arrived; and with him there was a crowd with swords and clubs, from the chief priests, the scribes, and the elders. ⁴⁴Now the betrayer had given them a sign, saying, "The one I will kiss is the man; arrest him and lead him away under guard." ⁴⁵So when he came, he went up to him at once and said, "Rabbi!" and kissed him. ⁴⁶Then they laid hands on him and arrested him. ⁴⁷But one of those who stood near drew his sword and struck the slave of the high priest, cutting off his ear. ⁴⁸Then Jesus said to them, "Have you come out with swords and clubs to arrest me as though I were a bandit? ⁴⁹Day after day I was with you in the temple teaching, and you did not arrest me. But let the scriptures be fulfilled." ⁵⁰All of them deserted him and fled.

51 A certain young man was following him, wearing nothing but a linen cloth. They caught hold of him, ⁵²but he left the linen cloth and ran off naked.

Jesus before the Council

53 They took Jesus to the high priest; and all the chief priests, the elders, and the scribes were assembled. ⁵⁴Peter had followed him at a distance, right into the courtyard of the high priest; and he was sitting with the guards, warming himself at the fire. ⁵⁵Now the chief priests and the whole council were looking for testimony against Jesus to put him to death; but they found none. ⁵⁶For many gave false testimony against him, and their testimony did not agree. ⁵⁷Some stood up and gave false testimony against him, saying, ⁵⁸"We heard him say, 'I will destroy this temple that is made with hands, and in three days I will build another, not made with hands.' " ⁵⁹But even on this point their testimony did not agree. ⁶⁰Then the high priest stood up before them and asked Jesus, "Have you no answer? What is it that they testify against you?" ⁶¹But he was silent and did not answer. Again the high priest asked him, "Are you the Messiah,ᶜ the Son of the Blessed One?" ⁶²Jesus said, "I am; and

'you will see the Son of Man
   seated at the right hand of the Power,'
   and 'coming with the clouds of heaven.' "

⁶³Then the high priest tore his clothes and said, "Why do we still need witnesses? ⁶⁴You have heard his blasphemy! What is your decision?" All of them condemned him as deserving death. ⁶⁵Some began to spit on him, to blindfold him, and to strike him, saying to him, "Prophesy!" The guards also took him over and beat him.

Peter Denies Jesus

66 While Peter was below in the courtyard, one of the servant-girls of the high priest came by. ⁶⁷When she saw Peter warming himself, she stared at him and said, "You also were with Jesus, the man from Nazareth." ⁶⁸But he denied it, saying, "I do not know or understand what you are talking about." And he went out into the forecourt.ᵈ Then the cock crowed.ᵉ ⁶⁹And the servant-girl, on seeing him, began again to say to the bystanders, "This man is one of them." ⁷⁰But again he denied it. Then after a little while the bystanders again said to Peter, "Certainly you are one of them; for you are a Galilean." ⁷¹But he began to curse, and he swore an oath, "I do not know this man you are talking about." ⁷²At that moment the cock crowed for the second time. Then Peter remembered that Jesus had said to him, "Before the cock crows twice, you will deny me three times." And he broke down and wept.

---

a Aramaic for *Father* **b** Or *into temptation* **c** Or *the Christ* **d** Or *gateway* **e** Other ancient authorities lack *Then the cock crowed*

Facing the Hard Times · Mark 15:16–20

Read the events in **Mark 15:16–20** that led up to Jesus' crucifixion. Then say this prayer:

Lord, you really do know what it is like to be beaten, teased, pushed around, and rejected. If you could put up with this torment, then maybe there is hope for me when I feel the same way at times. Like when I'm made fun of or rejected because of the way I look or act or for what I believe in. Or when I feel all alone or that no one understands what I'm feeling.

But now I know that you understand, Lord. You took these difficult steps even before I did. You have been there. You show me the way through these tough times.

Teach me to pray as you did: "Abba, Father, for you all things are possible; remove this cup (suffering) from me; yet, not what I want, but what you want" (Mark 14:36). Give me the strength to overcome my despair. Give me faith to abandon myself in God's hands as you did. Give me hope to see a new life beyond these moments of pain and hopelessness. Amen.

15 Jesus before Pilate

As soon as it was morning, the chief priests held a consultation with the elders and scribes and the whole council. They bound Jesus, led him away, and handed him over to Pilate. ²Pilate asked him, "Are you the King of the Jews?" He answered him, "You say so." ³Then the chief priests accused him of many things. ⁴Pilate asked him again, "Have you no answer? See how many charges they bring against you." ⁵But Jesus made no further reply, so that Pilate was amazed.

Pilate Hands Jesus over to Be Crucified

6 Now at the festival he used to release a prisoner for them, anyone for whom they asked. ⁷Now a man called Barabbas was in prison with the rebels who had committed murder during the insurrection. ⁸So the crowd came and began to ask Pilate to do for them according to his custom. ⁹Then he answered them, "Do you want me to release for you the King of the Jews?" ¹⁰For he realized that it was out of jealousy that the chief priests had handed him over. ¹¹But the chief priests stirred up the crowd to have him release Barabbas for them instead. ¹²Pilate spoke to them again, "Then what do you wish me to do[a] with the man you call[b] the King of the Jews?" ¹³They shouted back, "Crucify him!" ¹⁴Pilate asked them, "Why, what evil has he done?" But they shouted all the more, "Crucify him!" ¹⁵So Pilate, wishing to satisfy the crowd, released Barabbas for them; and after flogging Jesus, he handed him over to be crucified.

The Soldiers Mock Jesus

16 Then the soldiers led him into the courtyard of the palace (that is, the governor's headquarters[c]); and they called together the whole cohort. ¹⁷And they clothed him in a purple cloak; and after twisting some thorns into a crown, they put it on him. ¹⁸And they began saluting him, "Hail, King of the Jews!" ¹⁹They struck his head with a reed, spat upon him, and knelt down in homage to him. ²⁰After mocking him, they stripped him of the purple cloak and put his own clothes on him. Then they led him out to crucify him.

The Crucifixion of Jesus

21 They compelled a passer-by, who was coming in from the country, to carry his cross; it was Simon of Cyrene, the father of Alexander and Rufus. ²²Then they brought Jesus[d] to the place called Golgotha (which means the place of a skull). ²³And they offered him wine mixed with myrrh; but he did not take it. ²⁴And they crucified him, and divided his clothes among them, casting lots to decide what each should take.

25 It was nine o'clock in the morning when they crucified him. ²⁶The inscription of the charge against him read, "The King of the Jews." ²⁷And with him they crucified two bandits, one on his right and one on his left.[e] ²⁹Those who passed by derided[f] him, shaking their heads and saying, "Aha! You who would destroy the temple and build it in three days, ³⁰save yourself, and come down from the cross!"

a Other ancient authorities read *what should I do*   b Other ancient authorities lack *the man you call*   c Gk *the praetorium*   d Gk *him*   e Other ancient authorities add verse 28, *And the scripture was fulfilled that says, "And he was counted among the lawless."*   f Or *blasphemed*

Never Alone
Mark 15:33–34

Have you ever felt lost, alone, or abandoned? Sometimes, we may actually be physically lost or abandoned, but more often these feelings are deeply emotional or spiritual as we struggle to find our way, feeling that there is no one in our lives who can fully help and support us.

Jesus may have had similar feelings. As he faced his death, he may have felt alone and completely abandoned by his friends and even by God (Mark 15:34). Can you imagine anything more lonely? His prayers did not change his circumstances, but gave him a way to lament, to cry out to God to express his distress.

What makes you the most lonely and afraid? When have you felt abandoned? In these situations of distress, it is always okay to lament. Crying out does not always change our circumstances, but it can help to remind us that we are not truly alone—God is with us.

³¹ In the same way the chief priests, along with the scribes, were also mocking him among themselves and saying, "He saved others; he cannot save himself. ³² Let the Messiah,ᵃ the King of Israel, come down from the cross now, so that we may see and believe." Those who were crucified with him also taunted him.

The Death of Jesus

33 When it was noon, darkness came over the whole landᵇ until three in the afternoon. ³⁴ At three o'clock Jesus cried out with a loud voice, "Eloi, Eloi, lema sabachthani?" which means, "My God, my God, why have you forsaken me?"ᶜ ³⁵ When some of the bystanders heard it, they said, "Listen, he is calling for Elijah." ³⁶ And someone ran, filled a sponge with sour wine, put it on a stick, and gave

We Were There · Mark 15:21

According to **Mark 15:21**, the Roman soldiers compelled a North African black man from Cyrene by the name of Simon, a passerby, to carry the cross of Jesus. We do not know anything more about Simon of Cyrene, except that Mark identifies him as the father of Alexander and Rufus. The reference to Simon's sons by name and the possibility that Rufus is the same person Paul greets in **Romans 16:13** indicate that they were known among the early Christians. This is significant for African Americans, because it is evidence of the prominence and influence of African people in the early Christian Church.

African people were there from the beginning of Christianity (see also Acts 8:26–40). They were not latecomers to the Christian faith. African Americans and other people who have experienced oppression are in danger of forgetting who they are and where they come from—not because they are forgetful people, but because the oppressors have tried to erase their culture and identity to cripple and control them. Yet despite all this, somebody always remembers.

We praise you, God, for having African people there to minister to Jesus in his time of need. We praise you in knowing that people of all races will be with you at the end. Hallelujah. Amen!

ᵃ Or the Christ   ᵇ Or earth   ᶜ Other ancient authorities read made me a reproach

it to him to drink, saying, "Wait, let us see whether Elijah will come to take him down." ³⁷Then Jesus gave a loud cry and breathed his last. ³⁸And the curtain of the temple was torn in two, from top to bottom. ³⁹Now when the centurion, who stood facing him, saw that in this way he*ᵃ* breathed his last, he said, "Truly this man was God's Son!"*ᵇ*

40 There were also women looking on from a distance; among them were Mary Magdalene, and Mary the mother of James the younger and of Joses, and Salome. ⁴¹These used to follow him and provided for him when he was in Galilee; and there were many other women who had come up with him to Jerusalem.

The Burial of Jesus

42 When evening had come, and since it was the day of Preparation, that is, the day before the sabbath, ⁴³Joseph of Arimathea, a respected member of the council, who was also himself waiting expectantly for the kingdom of God, went boldly to Pilate and asked for the body of Jesus. ⁴⁴Then Pilate wondered if he were already dead; and summoning the centurion, he asked him whether he had been dead for some time. ⁴⁵When he learned from the centurion that he was dead, he granted the body to Joseph. ⁴⁶Then Joseph*ᶜ* bought a linen cloth, and taking down the body,*ᵈ* wrapped it in the linen cloth, and laid it in a tomb that had been hewn out of the rock.

STUDY IT!

Faith and Reason · Mark 16:20

When we hear a person make some incredible claim on television, we often want to see proof that the claim is true. This was also the case for the disciples after Jesus rose from the dead. Some saw the risen Lord and believed, but others refused to believe, because they had not witnessed the risen Lord with their own eyes (Mark 16:9-13). Jesus scolds these disciples for their lack of faith (Mark 16:14). If the disciples who were with Jesus throughout his ministry were slow to believe, how difficult would it then be for the rest of the world to believe? Perhaps that is why Mark's gospel concludes by saying that Jesus himself confirms the message of the good news with signs like healings and miracles.

Although that is the end of Mark's gospel, the story has continued for more than two thousand years. Countless people have come to faith in Jesus Christ through the ongoing preaching of the good news and the signs that confirm Christ's message. Through this combination of the message and signs, we begin to see the natural relationship that exists between faith and reason.

To understand this relationship, we must begin by examining the Church's understanding of faith. First and foremost, faith is a gift from God. Through God's grace and the help of the Holy Spirit, our heart is turned toward God. Through this change, God then opens our mind so that we may accept and believe the truth. We too play an active role in receiving the gift of faith by welcoming God's grace and accepting the truth.

Our acceptance of the truth is not by blind faith; it involves our use of reason. And because God created everything, including both faith and reason, God did not create them to contradict one another, but to work together to arrive at the truth. Therefore, God provides external proofs like the signs and miracles mentioned in the gospel. But God also provides more ordinary proofs like the existence and growth of the Church or the presence of God working in the daily lives of other Christ followers.

An interesting thing can occur when our faith and reason work together. Our faith leads us to desire and to know God better, so we then use our reason to learn more about God. Once we learn more about God, our faith is deepened and we desire to know God even more! The use of faith and reason becomes a never-ending circle that continues to draw us closer and closer to God, whom we love and who loves us.

ᵃ Other ancient authorities add *cried out and*   ᵇ Or *a son of God*   ᶜ Gk *he*   ᵈ Gk *it*

He then rolled a stone against the door of the tomb. [47]Mary Magdalene and Mary the mother of Joses saw where the body[a] was laid.

The Resurrection of Jesus

16 When the sabbath was over, Mary Magdalene, and Mary the mother of James, and Salome bought spices, so that they might go and anoint him. [2]And very early on the first day of the week, when the sun had risen, they went to the tomb. [3]They had been saying to one another, "Who will roll away the stone for us from the entrance to the tomb?" [4]When they looked up, they saw that the stone, which was very large, had already been rolled back. [5]As they entered the tomb, they saw a young man, dressed in a white robe, sitting on the right side; and they were alarmed. [6]But he said to them, "Do not be alarmed; you are looking for Jesus of Nazareth, who was crucified. He has been raised; he is not here. Look, there is the place they laid him. [7]But go, tell his disciples and Peter that he is going ahead of you to Galilee; there you will see him, just as he told you." [8]So they went out and fled from the tomb, for terror and amazement had seized them; and they said nothing to anyone, for they were afraid.[b]

THE SHORTER ENDING OF MARK

[[And all that had been commanded them they told briefly to those around Peter. And afterward Jesus himself sent out through them, from east to west, the sacred and imperishable proclamation of eternal salvation.[c]]]

THE LONGER ENDING OF MARK

Jesus Appears to Mary Magdalene

9 [[Now after he rose early on the first day of the week, he appeared first to Mary Magdalene, from whom he had cast out seven demons. [10]She went out and told those who had been with him, while they were mourning and weeping. [11]But when they heard that he was alive and had been seen by her, they would not believe it.

Jesus Appears to Two Disciples

12 After this he appeared in another form to two of them, as they were walking into the country. [13]And they went back and told the rest, but they did not believe them.

Jesus Commissions the Disciples

14 Later he appeared to the eleven themselves as they were sitting at the table; and he upbraided them for their lack of faith and stubbornness, because they had not believed those who saw him after he had risen.[d] [15]And he said to them, "Go into all the world and proclaim the good news[e] to the whole creation. [16]The one who believes and is

LIVE IT!

Jesus Strengthens Our Faith
Mark 16

A group of faithful women watch from afar when Jesus dies on the cross, and they look to see where he is buried (Mark 15:40-47). They are witnesses to the terrible violence of Jesus' death. Two days later, after the sabbath, three of the women go to the tomb to anoint Jesus' body, giving him a proper burial. When they receive the news that Jesus is alive, they flee from the tomb terrified and amazed.

This is where the original gospel of Mark ends (Mark 16:8). Immediately we want to ask lots of questions. What happened to the disciples? Did they go to Galilee? How did the word get out that Jesus had risen from the dead? Apparently, early Christians found this abrupt ending troublesome, so they added other endings similar to those of the other Gospels.

These additions (starting at Mark 16:9) emphasize the surprise of the disciples. It seems as if they are paralyzed. Only a strong scolding by Jesus and being commissioned to proclaim the good news to the whole creation bring them around.

If doubts and confusion paralyze you in living your faith, pay attention to Jesus! Hear his voice! He is telling you to carry his message of love to other people. By doing so, you will strengthen your faith, and your life will be full of joy!

---

a Gk *it* **b** Some of the most ancient authorities bring the book to a close at the end of verse 8. One authority concludes the book with the shorter ending; others include the shorter ending and then continue with verses 9-20. In most authorities verses 9-20 follow immediately after verse 8, though in some of these authorities the passage is marked as being doubtful. **c** Other ancient authorities add *Amen* **d** Other ancient authorities add, in whole or in part, *And they excused themselves, saying, "This age of lawlessness and unbelief is under Satan, who does not allow the truth and power of God to prevail over the unclean things of the spirits. Therefore reveal your righteousness now"—thus they spoke to Christ. And Christ replied to them, "The term of years of Satan's power has been fulfilled, but other terrible things draw near. And for those who have sinned I was handed over to death, that they may return to the truth and sin no more, that they may inherit the spiritual and imperishable glory of righteousness that is in heaven."* **e** Or *gospel*

baptized will be saved; but the one who does not believe will be condemned. [17]And these signs will accompany those who believe: by using my name they will cast out demons; they will speak in new tongues; [18]they will pick up snakes in their hands,[a] and if they drink any deadly thing, it will not hurt them; they will lay their hands on the sick, and they will recover."

The Ascension of Jesus

[19] So then the Lord Jesus, after he had spoken to them, was taken up into heaven and sat down at the right hand of God. [20]And they went out and proclaimed the good news everywhere, while the Lord worked with them and confirmed the message by the signs that accompanied it.[b]]]

---

a Other ancient authorities lack *in their hands*   **b** Other ancient authorities add *Amen*

Luke

Black and white. Male and female. Rich and poor. Have you ever been put in a category and judged according to it? It often feels unfair whether it's accurate or not. But despite its unfairness, it's all too easy to divide ourselves into distinct categories instead of focusing on what unites us. These divisions can lead to discrimination, inequality, and injustice, as one group is considered "less than" another. In the gospel of Luke, Jesus asserts that such divisions have no place in the kingdom of God. Outcasts, sinners, women, the poor—all are compassionately welcomed to be followers of Christ.

IN DEPTH

The author of the gospel of Luke was a Gentile (non-Jewish) convert to Christianity. So one of Luke's important concerns is to show how Gentiles came to be included in God's plan of salvation, which first belonged to the Jews alone. In Luke's gospel, Jesus praises the faith of a centurion (Luke 7:1-10), who is a Gentile. Jesus also makes a Samaritan the hero of a parable (Samaritans were considered foreigners by other Jews; Luke 10:25-37).

Other "in-groups" for Jesus in Luke's gospel are women and poor people. Most women had little status in society at the time. But Luke includes many stories about women, including Mary's visit to her cousin Elizabeth before the births of their sons, Jesus and John the Baptist (Luke 1:39-66). This gospel also shows how Jesus loved the poor and scolded the rich for their lack of concern for the poor.

Finally, Luke's gospel shows Jesus' compassion for and forgiveness of outcasts and sinners. It includes stories about the tax collector Zacchaeus, who climbs a tree to see Jesus (Luke 19:1-10), the good Samaritan (Luke 10:25-37), and the penitent sinner who was crucified beside Jesus (Luke 23:39-43). In the gospel of Luke, Jesus is also the ultimate prophet and Savior who will be rejected by his own people (Luke 4:16-30). The gospel presents a vivid picture of how Jesus made the kingdom of God present, inspiring his disciples to take the gospel message to other lands and cultures.

QUICK FACTS

- **Author:** A Gentile Christian named Luke, traditionally thought to be a disciple of Paul (Colossians 4:14)

- **Date Written:** Around A.D. 80-95

- **Audience:** Gentile (Greek) Christians

- **Image of Jesus:** Merciful, compassionate, with a special concern for the poor, women, and non-Jews

- **Noteworthy:** Luke also wrote Acts

AT A GLANCE

- **Luke 1–2** Introduction; stories about Jesus' birth and early childhood

- **Luke 3:1–9:50** Jesus' ministry in Galilee

- **Luke 9:51–19:27** Parables and miracles on the way to Jerusalem

- **Luke 19:28–21:38** Jesus in Jerusalem; conflict with the religious authorities

- **Luke 22–24** Stories about Jesus' death, resurrection, and ascension

1 Dedication to Theophilus

Since many have undertaken to set down an orderly account of the events that have been fulfilled among us, [2]just as they were handed on to us by those who from the beginning were eyewitnesses and servants of the word, [3]I too decided, after investigating everything carefully from the very first,[a] to write an orderly account for you, most excellent Theophilus, [4]so that you may know the truth concerning the things about which you have been instructed.

The Birth of John the Baptist Foretold

5 In the days of King Herod of Judea, there was a priest named Zechariah, who belonged to the priestly order of Abijah. His wife was a descendant of Aaron, and her name was Elizabeth. [6]Both of them were righteous before God, living blamelessly according to all the commandments and regulations of the Lord. [7]But they had no children, because Elizabeth was barren, and both were getting on in years.

8 Once when he was serving as priest before God and his section was on duty, [9]he was chosen by lot, according to the custom of the priesthood, to enter the sanctuary of the Lord and offer incense. [10]Now at the time of the incense offering, the whole assembly of the people was praying outside. [11]Then there appeared to him an angel of the Lord, standing at the right side of the altar of incense. [12]When Zechariah saw him, he was terrified; and fear overwhelmed him. [13]But the angel said to him, "Do not be afraid, Zechariah, for your prayer has been heard. Your wife Elizabeth will bear you a son, and you will name him John. [14]You will have joy and gladness, and many will rejoice at his birth, [15]for he will be great in the sight of the Lord. He must never drink wine or strong drink; even before his birth he will be filled with the Holy Spirit. [16]He will turn many of the people of Israel to the Lord their God. [17]With the spirit and power of Elijah he will go before him, to turn the hearts of parents to their children, and the disobedient to the wisdom of the righteous, to make ready a people prepared for the Lord." [18]Zechariah said to the angel, "How will I know that this is so? For I am an old man, and my wife is getting on in years." [19]The angel replied, "I am Gabriel. I stand in the presence of God, and I have been sent to speak to you and to bring you this good news. [20]But now, because you did not believe my words, which will be fulfilled in their time, you will become mute, unable to speak, until the day these things occur."

21 Meanwhile the people were waiting for Zechariah, and wondered at his delay in the sanctuary. [22]When he did come out, he could not speak to them, and they realized that he had seen a vision in the sanctuary. He kept motioning to them and remained unable to speak. [23]When his time of service was ended, he went to his home.

24 After those days his wife Elizabeth conceived,

LIVE IT!

Waiting • Luke 1:5–25

The story of Elizabeth and her husband, Zechariah, is a story of waiting. They are both righteous and living blamelessly, but they have no children (Luke 1:6-7). They are also getting old and have been waiting a long time for the gift of a child. Then, when the angel Gabriel appears to Zechariah and tells him that they will have a son, Zechariah finds it hard to believe, so he is made unable to speak until his son is born. Talk about a long nine months of waiting! And when Elizabeth discovers she is pregnant, she goes into seclusion for five months. We don't know exactly why, but five months alone and pregnant is a long time to wait, no matter what the reasons.

Try to place yourself in Elizabeth's or Zechariah's shoes. How would you be at waiting and trusting God for the outcome in your life? Their waiting was long, but in the end they saw the glory of God in the birth of their son, John the Baptist, and in the one John came to proclaim—Jesus.

• What kind of a "waiter" are you? Impatient? Peaceful? Worried? Eager?

• Think of something you are waiting for now. How are you waiting patiently for God to work?

a Or for a long time

and for five months she remained in seclusion. She said, [25] "This is what the Lord has done for me when he looked favorably on me and took away the disgrace I have endured among my people."

The Birth of Jesus Foretold

26 In the sixth month the angel Gabriel was sent by God to a town in Galilee called Nazareth, [27] to a virgin engaged to a man whose name was Joseph, of the house of David. The virgin's name was Mary. [28] And he came to her and said, "Greetings, favored one! The Lord is with you." [a] [29] But she was much perplexed by his words and pondered what sort of greeting this might be. [30] The angel said to her, "Do not be afraid, Mary, for you have found favor with God. [31] And now, you will conceive in your womb and bear a son, and you will name him Jesus. [32] He will be great, and will be called the Son of the Most High, and the Lord God will give to him the throne

STUDY IT!

Introducing . . . Mary
Luke 1:26–56

Luke's gospel makes it clear that Mary has a special place in God's plan of salvation. Beginning with Mary's humble acceptance of God's will revealed by the angel Gabriel (Luke 1:26-38), Mary is presented as the true, first disciple who does the will of God. Her "yes" to God leads to Jesus' presence among us. She follows Jesus to the cross and is with the disciples in the upper room during the coming of the Holy Spirit (Acts 1:14). Mary reveals to us the meaning of true faith—a willingness to accept God's call and to gradually discover the full meaning of God's will.

In choosing Mary to be the mother of Jesus, God selects not a rich queen, but a poor young girl open to the action of the Holy Spirit in her life. In Mary, Luke emphasizes God's preference for children and the poor (see "Live It: The Prayer of the Poor," near Luke 1:39-56).

of his ancestor David. [33] He will reign over the house of Jacob forever, and of his kingdom there will be no end." [34] Mary said to the angel, "How can this be, since I am a virgin?" [b] [35] The angel said to her, "The Holy Spirit will come upon you, and the power of the Most High will overshadow you; therefore the child to be born [c] will be holy; he will be called Son of God. [36] And now, your relative Elizabeth in her old age has also conceived a son; and this is the sixth month for her who was said to be barren. [37] For nothing will be impossible with God." [38] Then Mary said, "Here am I, the servant of the Lord; let it be with me according to your word." Then the angel departed from her.

Mary Visits Elizabeth

39 In those days Mary set out and went with haste to a Judean town in the hill country, [40] where she entered the house of Zechariah and greeted Elizabeth. [41] When Elizabeth heard Mary's greeting, the child leaped in her womb. And Elizabeth was filled with the Holy Spirit [42] and exclaimed with a loud cry, "Blessed are you among women, and blessed is the fruit of your womb. [43] And why has this happened to me, that the mother of my Lord comes to me? [44] For as soon as I heard the sound of your greeting, the child in my womb leaped for joy. [45] And blessed is she who believed that there would be [d] a fulfillment of what was spoken to her by the Lord."

Mary's Song of Praise

46 And Mary [e] said,
  "My soul magnifies the Lord,
[47]   and my spirit rejoices in God my Savior,
[48] for he has looked with favor on the lowliness
        of his servant.
      Surely, from now on all generations will
        call me blessed;
[49] for the Mighty One has done great things
        for me,
      and holy is his name.
[50] His mercy is for those who fear him
        from generation to generation.
[51] He has shown strength with his arm;
      he has scattered the proud in the thoughts
        of their hearts.
[52] He has brought down the powerful from their
        thrones,
      and lifted up the lowly;
[53] he has filled the hungry with good things,

The Prayer of the Poor
Luke 1:39–56

Mary gives a testimony of her faith not long after she receives the news that she will be the mother of God. During her visit to her cousin Elizabeth, she sings a song of praise (also called the Magnificat, which means "(my soul) praises"). This prayer is mainly made up of verses taken from Psalms and the prophets. Mary first sings of her salvation; then she sings of God's salvation brought to the humble, the poor, and the hungry; and she finishes by singing of the salvation brought to all the people of God as promised to Abraham.

Mary's song is the song of the poor—those who expected salvation from God, not from people in power or through wars and conquests. The prayer is directed to God and talks about God's care for the poor. Jesus is the one who acts as God's agent, accomplishing these things on God's behalf; he raises up the lowly and brings down the powerful.

- In a world marked by huge gaps between rich and poor people, how do you think Christians are doing in caring for the poor?
- How are you helping the poor? How can you make choices now to continue to care for them throughout your life?

and sent the rich away empty.
54 He has helped his servant Israel,
in remembrance of his mercy,
55 according to the promise he made to our
ancestors,
to Abraham and to his descendants
forever."

56 And Mary remained with her about three months and then returned to her home.

a Gk a horn of salvation

The Birth of John the Baptist

57 Now the time came for Elizabeth to give birth, and she bore a son. 58 Her neighbors and relatives heard that the Lord had shown his great mercy to her, and they rejoiced with her.

59 On the eighth day they came to circumcise the child, and they were going to name him Zechariah after his father. 60 But his mother said, "No; he is to be called John." 61 They said to her, "None of your relatives has this name." 62 Then they began motioning to his father to find out what name he wanted to give him. 63 He asked for a writing tablet and wrote, "His name is John." And all of them were amazed. 64 Immediately his mouth was opened and his tongue freed, and he began to speak, praising God. 65 Fear came over all their neighbors, and all these things were talked about throughout the entire hill country of Judea. 66 All who heard them pondered them and said, "What then will this child become?" For, indeed, the hand of the Lord was with him.

Zechariah's Prophecy

67 Then his father Zechariah was filled with the Holy Spirit and spoke this prophecy:
68 "Blessed be the Lord God of Israel,
for he has looked favorably on his people
and redeemed them.
69 He has raised up a mighty savior*a* for us
in the house of his servant David,
70 as he spoke through the mouth of his holy
prophets from of old,
71 that we would be saved from our enemies
and from the hand of all who hate us.
72 Thus he has shown the mercy promised to our
ancestors,
and has remembered his holy covenant,
73 the oath that he swore to our ancestor
Abraham,
to grant us 74 that we, being rescued from
the hands of our enemies,
might serve him without fear, 75 in holiness
and righteousness
before him all our days.
76 And you, child, will be called the prophet of
the Most High;
for you will go before the Lord to prepare
his ways,
77 to give knowledge of salvation to his people
by the forgiveness of their sins.

78 By the tender mercy of our God,
    the dawn from on high will break
        upon[a] us,
79 to give light to those who sit in darkness and
      in the shadow of death,
    to guide our feet into the way of
      peace."

80 The child grew and became strong in spirit, and he was in the wilderness until the day he appeared publicly to Israel.

The Birth of Jesus

2 In those days a decree went out from Emperor Augustus that all the world should be registered. 2This was the first registration and was taken while Quirinius was governor of Syria. 3All went to their own towns to be registered. 4Joseph also went from the town of Nazareth in Galilee to Judea, to the city of David called Bethlehem, because he was descended from the house and family of David. 5He went to be registered with Mary, to whom he was engaged and who was expecting a child. 6While they were there, the time came for her to deliver her child. 7And she gave birth to her firstborn son and wrapped him in bands of cloth, and laid him in a manger, because there was no place for them in the inn.

The Shepherds and the Angels

8 In that region there were shepherds living in the fields, keeping watch over their flock by night. 9Then an angel of the Lord stood before them, and the glory of the Lord shone around them, and they were terrified. 10But the angel said to them, "Do not be afraid; for see—I am bringing you good news of great joy for all the people: 11to you is born this day in the city of David a Savior, who is the Messiah,[b] the Lord. 12This will be a sign for you: you will find a child wrapped in bands of cloth and lying in a manger." 13And suddenly there was with the angel a multitude of the heavenly host,[c] praising God and saying,

14 "Glory to God in the highest heaven,
    and on earth peace among those whom he
      favors!"[d]

15 When the angels had left them and gone into heaven, the shepherds said to one another, "Let us go now to Bethlehem and see this thing that has

a Other ancient authorities read *has broken upon* b Or *the Christ* c Gk *army* d Other ancient authorities read *peace, goodwill among people*

Jesus' Birth: Good News to the Poor · Luke 2:8–20

Jesus' birth was a defining moment in the history of salvation. Our Christmas celebrations include many traditions, but at the core of the holiday is the amazing fact that God entered the world as a human to save all people. But God's grand entrance doesn't look quite like we'd expect. As Luke records the moment of the birth of the Messiah, who are the stars of the show? Who hears the message of the angels telling of this remarkable event that is "good news of great joy for all the people" (Luke 2:10)? The high priest? The rich and important residents of Bethlehem? No. The announcement is made to shepherds—poor workers living in the fields nearby.

Like Mary, the shepherds are people of little power or social status. Luke makes the point that sometimes what the world sees as unimportant, God honors. This is the justice of God. It is the same today. The poorest in our world, the most hidden people who have no power, hold a special place in the heart of God. This truth is a challenge, but also good news for all of us, rich and poor alike.

- How do your attitudes and actions—even the way you celebrate Christmas—reflect God's special attention to those who are poor?
- How can reaching out to the poor help bring you closer to the heart of God?

taken place, which the Lord has made known to us." ¹⁶So they went with haste and found Mary and Joseph, and the child lying in the manger. ¹⁷When they saw this, they made known what had been told them about this child; ¹⁸and all who heard it were amazed at what the shepherds told them. ¹⁹But Mary treasured all these words and pondered them in her heart. ²⁰The shepherds returned, glorifying and praising God for all they had heard and seen, as it had been told them.

Jesus Is Named

21 After eight days had passed, it was time to circumcise the child; and he was called Jesus, the name given by the angel before he was conceived in the womb.

Jesus Is Presented in the Temple

22 When the time came for their purification according to the law of Moses, they brought him up to Jerusalem to present him to the Lord ²³(as it is written in the law of the Lord, "Every firstborn male shall be designated as holy to the Lord"), ²⁴and they offered a sacrifice according to what is stated in the law of the Lord, "a pair of turtledoves or two young pigeons."

25 Now there was a man in Jerusalem whose name was Simeon;^{a} this man was righteous and devout, looking forward to the consolation of Israel, and the

Holy Spirit rested on him. ²⁶It had been revealed to him by the Holy Spirit that he would not see death before he had seen the Lord's Messiah.^{b} ²⁷Guided by the Spirit, Simeon^c came into the temple; and when the parents brought in the child Jesus, to do for him what was customary under the law, ²⁸Simeon^d took him in his arms and praised God, saying,

29 "Master, now you are dismissing your servant^e
        in peace,
        according to your word;
30 for my eyes have seen your salvation,
31   which you have prepared in the presence of
        all peoples,
32 a light for revelation to the Gentiles
        and for glory to your people Israel."

33 And the child's father and mother were amazed at what was being said about him. ³⁴Then Simeon^a blessed them and said to his mother Mary, "This child is destined for the falling and the rising of many in Israel, and to be a sign that will be opposed ³⁵so that the inner thoughts of many will be revealed—and a sword will pierce your own soul too."

36 There was also a prophet, Anna^f the daughter of Phanuel, of the tribe of Asher. She was of a great age, having lived with her husband seven years after her marriage, ³⁷then as a widow to the age of eighty-four. She never left the temple but worshiped there with fasting and prayer night and day. ³⁸At that

a Gk *Symeon*   b Or *the Lord's Christ*   c Gk *In the Spirit, he*   d Gk *he*   e Gk *slave*   f Gk *Hanna*

LIVE IT!

The Wisdom of Age
Luke 2:25–38

When was the last time you listened to an older person—really listened? It's not something we do much in our society. Elderly relatives often live in nursing homes, away from family, where it is difficult for us to know and learn from them. But God clearly values the wisdom of the elderly. This passage tells of two old people who had greater wisdom and understanding about Jesus' coming than anyone. Simeon and Anna both saw the baby Jesus at the temple when he was presented for purification according to the law of Moses. Many people were at the temple that day, but it was these two who were shown by God that this baby was the Savior of the world.

- Is there an elderly person in your life whom you can spend time with?
- Make some time to spend with that person, just asking questions and listening. You might be surprised at the wisdom you gain.

moment she came, and began to praise God and to speak about the child*a* to all who were looking for the redemption of Jerusalem.

The Return to Nazareth

39 When they had finished everything required by the law of the Lord, they returned to Galilee, to their own town of Nazareth. 40 The child grew and became strong, filled with wisdom; and the favor of God was upon him.

The Boy Jesus in the Temple

41 Now every year his parents went to Jerusalem for the festival of the Passover. 42 And when he was twelve years old, they went up as usual for the festival. 43 When the festival was ended and they started to return, the boy Jesus stayed behind in Jerusalem, but his parents did not know it. 44 Assuming that he was in the group of travelers, they went a day's journey. Then they started to look for him among their relatives and friends. 45 When they did not find him, they returned to Jerusalem to search for him. 46 After three days they found him in the temple, sitting among the teachers, listening to them and asking them questions. 47 And all who heard him were amazed at his understanding and his answers. 48 When his parents*b* saw him they were astonished; and his mother said to him, "Child, why have you treated us like this? Look, your father and I have been searching for you in great anxiety." 49 He said to them, "Why were you searching for me? Did you

PRAY IT!

Jesus' Family · Luke 2:41–52

The Bible doesn't tell us a lot about Jesus' family. We know that Joseph was a kind and compassionate man, eager to do God's will. He raised Jesus as his own son, even though he was not Jesus' biological father. Jesus was raised in a home in which love and faith were the norm.

We can be sure that the family had their moments of conflict and crisis—all families do. Luke's story of Jesus' getting separated from his parents demonstrates their natural frustration (Luke 2:48). But we can also be sure that their love and faith helped them to survive such conflicts and grow stronger because of them.

Think about how the members of your family relate to each other as you say this prayer:

Lord, help me to learn from Jesus' family what it means to love and respect my family. Help us be real with the conflicts and hardships we face, but please help us learn to grow together rather than being driven apart. Help me to learn to be more patient, honest, generous, and compassionate with the people in my family. And help the love we share to flow to others. Amen.

a Gk *him* *b* Gk *they*

Growing Up God
Luke 2:41–52

Luke is the only gospel that includes any stories of Jesus' childhood.

When Jesus was twelve, he came to Jerusalem with his family to celebrate the pilgrimage festival of Passover. He was left behind, and when Mary and Joseph searched for him, they found him in the temple. At the temple, Jesus listened to the teachers and asked questions. His questions and his understanding amazed all who heard him.

Your teen years are an important time for exploring life's questions—including life's spiritual questions. But asking questions and seeking real answers can be hard work and may make some people uncomfortable. So seek out wise teachers and mentors who will welcome and encourage your questions. As you continue to dig in and learn more about what you believe, reflect on these questions:

- How well do you know your faith?
- What are your main questions about faith and life?
- Who are the wise teachers you can go to for help in searching out the answers?

not know that I must be in my Father's house?"[a] [50]But they did not understand what he said to them. [51]Then he went down with them and came to Nazareth, and was obedient to them. His mother treasured all these things in her heart.

52　And Jesus increased in wisdom and in years,[b] and in divine and human favor.

The Proclamation of John the Baptist

3 In the fifteenth year of the reign of Emperor Tiberius, when Pontius Pilate was governor of Judea, and Herod was ruler[c] of Galilee, and his brother Philip ruler[c] of the region of Ituraea and Trachonitis, and Lysanias ruler[c] of Abilene, [2]during the high priesthood of Annas and Caiaphas, the word of God came to John son of Zechariah in the wilderness. [3]He went into all the region around the Jordan, proclaiming a baptism of repentance for the forgiveness of sins, [4]as it is written in the book of the words of the prophet Isaiah,

"The voice of one crying out in the
　　　　wilderness:
'Prepare the way of the Lord,
　　make his paths straight.
[5]　Every valley shall be filled,
　　　and every mountain and hill shall be
　　　　　made low,
and the crooked shall be made straight,
　　and the rough ways made smooth;
[6]　and all flesh shall see the salvation of God.' "

7　John said to the crowds that came out to be baptized by him, "You brood of vipers! Who warned you to flee from the wrath to come? [8]Bear fruits worthy of repentance. Do not begin to say to yourselves, 'We have Abraham as our ancestor'; for I tell you, God is able from these stones to raise up children to Abraham. [9]Even now the ax is lying at the root of the trees; every tree therefore that does not bear good fruit is cut down and thrown into the fire."

10　And the crowds asked him, "What then should we do?" [11]In reply he said to them, "Whoever has two coats must share with anyone who has none; and whoever has food must do likewise." [12]Even tax collectors came to be baptized, and they asked him, "Teacher, what should we do?" [13]He said to them, "Collect no more than the amount prescribed for you." [14]Soldiers also asked him, "And we, what should we do?" He said to them, "Do not extort money from anyone by threats or false accusation, and be satisfied with your wages."

15　As the people were filled with expectation, and all were questioning in their hearts concerning John, whether he might be the Messiah,[d] [16]John answered all of them by saying, "I baptize you with water; but one who is more powerful than I is coming; I am not worthy to untie the thong of his sandals. He will baptize you with[e] the Holy Spirit and fire. [17]His winnowing fork is in his hand, to clear his threshing floor and to gather the wheat into his granary; but the chaff he will burn with unquenchable fire."

18　So, with many other exhortations, he proclaimed the good news to the people. [19]But Herod the ruler,[c] who had been rebuked by him because of Herodias, his brother's wife, and because of all the evil things that Herod had done, [20]added to them all by shutting up John in prison.

a Or be about my Father's interests?　b Or in stature　c Gk tetrarch　d Or the Christ　e Or in

STUDY
IT!

Introducing . . . John the Baptist · Luke 3:1–20

Picture a man living in the desert, eating locusts and wild honey, and wearing a camel's-hair coat. That's John the Baptist. Despite his unconventional image, John the Baptist plays an important role in all four gospels. John is a lot like an Old Testament prophet, calling people to repentance for their sins. And his ministry was so similar to Jesus' ministry that after Herod had John killed (Matthew 14:1-12), he thought that Jesus might have been John raised from the dead (Luke 9:7-9). The power of John's preaching is demonstrated by the fact that Jesus' disciples still encountered John's followers years after John's death (Acts 19:1-7).

John the Baptist was Jesus' cousin, and the gospel of Luke presents many parallels between the two men. John's preaching gives us a preview into Jesus' message. John was preparing the way for Jesus. He was a humble servant "not worthy to untie the thong of (Jesus') sandals" (Luke 3:16). He described his baptism as a baptism of water in contrast with Jesus' baptism with the Holy Spirit and fire.

John the Baptist is a model of the role we can play in pointing others toward Jesus with passion and humility.

The Baptism of Jesus

21 Now when all the people were baptized, and when Jesus also had been baptized and was praying, the heaven was opened, [22]and the Holy Spirit descended upon him in bodily form like a dove. And a voice came from heaven, "You are my Son, the Beloved;[a] with you I am well pleased."[b]

The Ancestors of Jesus

23 Jesus was about thirty years old when he began his work. He was the son (as was thought) of Joseph son of Heli, [24]son of Matthat, son of Levi, son of Melchi, son of Jannai, son of Joseph, [25]son of Mattathias, son of Amos, son of Nahum, son of Esli, son of Naggai, [26]son of Maath, son of Mattathias, son of Semein, son of Josech, son of Joda, [27]son of Joanan, son of Rhesa, son of Zerubbabel, son of Shealtiel,[c] son of Neri, [28]son of Melchi, son of Addi, son of Cosam, son of Elmadam, son of Er, [29]son of Joshua, son of Eliezer, son of Jorim, son of Matthat, son of Levi, [30]son of Simeon, son of Judah, son of Joseph, son of Jonam, son of Eliakim, [31]son of Melea, son of Menna, son of Mattatha, son of Nathan, son of David, [32]son of Jesse, son of Obed, son of Boaz, son of Sala,[d] son of Nahshon, [33]son of Amminadab, son of Admin, son of Arni,[e] son of Hezron, son of Perez, son of Judah, [34]son of Jacob, son of Isaac, son of Abraham, son of Terah, son of Nahor, [35]son of Serug, son of Reu, son of Peleg, son of Eber, son of Shelah, [36]son

of Cainan, son of Arphaxad, son of Shem, son of Noah, son of Lamech, [37]son of Methuselah, son of Enoch, son of Jared, son of Mahalaleel, son of Cainan, [38]son of Enos, son of Seth, son of Adam, son of God.

The Temptation of Jesus

4 Jesus, full of the Holy Spirit, returned from the Jordan and was led by the Spirit in the wilderness, [2]where for forty days he was tempted by the devil. He ate nothing at all during those days, and when they were over, he was famished. [3]The devil said to him, "If you are the Son of God, command this stone to become a loaf of bread." [4]Jesus answered him, "It is written, 'One does not live by bread alone.'"

5 Then the devil[f] led him up and showed him in an instant all the kingdoms of the world. [6]And the devil[f] said to him, "To you I will give their glory and all this authority; for it has been given over to me, and I give it to anyone I please. [7]If you, then, will worship me, it will all be yours." [8]Jesus answered him, "It is written,

'Worship the Lord your God,
    and serve only him.'"

9 Then the devil[f] took him to Jerusalem, and placed him on the pinnacle of the temple, saying to him, "If you are the Son of God, throw yourself down from here, [10]for it is written,

---

a Or my beloved Son b Other ancient authorities read You are my Son, today I have begotten you c Gk Salathiel d Other ancient authorities read Salmon e Other ancient authorities read Amminadab, son of Aram; others vary widely f Gk he

STUDY IT!

Tempted
Luke 4:1–13

After his baptism, Jesus went out into the wilderness to be alone, so he could discern what God wanted him to do. While he was out there, he faced temptation from the devil's prodding. Imagine how tempting it might have been for Jesus to use his power to prove to the world how great he was, instead of living in obedience, so the world might know God's amazing love. But he never gave in!

So what kept him strong? Scripture. Jesus quotes scripture several times as a means to refute the devil and his temptations. But the devil also quotes scripture in an effort to lead Jesus astray. The confrontation ends with the departure of the devil and Jesus' holding fast to God's truth and, ultimately, his role as the obedient son of God.

Knowing scripture and applying God's word and truth to our lives is essential for us as Jesus' followers. We can use scripture to withstand temptation just as Jesus did. But when we are studying and interpreting scripture, we must be mindful of what the human authors intended. This requires learning about the history, culture, literary expressions, and language of the time. By doing this we learn what God wanted to communicate through scripture and how to best apply it to our own situations.

'He will command his angels concerning you,
to protect you,'
[11]and
'On their hands they will bear you up,
so that you will not dash your foot against a stone.' "
[12]Jesus answered him, "It is said, 'Do not put the Lord your God to the test.' " [13]When the devil had finished every test, he departed from him until an opportune time.

> "The Spirit of the Lord is upon me, because he has anointed me to bring good news to the poor."
> —Luke 4:18

The Beginning of the Galilean Ministry

14 Then Jesus, filled with the power of the Spirit, returned to Galilee, and a report about him spread through all the surrounding country. [15]He began to teach in their synagogues and was praised by everyone.

The Rejection of Jesus at Nazareth

16 When he came to Nazareth, where he had been brought up, he went to the synagogue on the sabbath day, as was his custom. He stood up to read, [17]and the scroll of the prophet Isaiah was given to him. He unrolled the scroll and found the place where it was written:
18 "The Spirit of the Lord is upon me,
because he has anointed me
to bring good news to the poor.
He has sent me to proclaim release to the captives
and recovery of sight to the blind,
to let the oppressed go free,
19 to proclaim the year of the Lord's favor."
[20]And he rolled up the scroll, gave it back to the attendant, and sat down. The eyes of all in the synagogue were fixed on him. [21]Then he began to say to them, "Today this scripture has been fulfilled in your hearing." [22]All spoke well of him and were amazed at the gracious words that came from his mouth. They said, "Is not this Joseph's son?" [23]He said to them, "Doubtless you will quote to me this proverb, 'Doctor, cure yourself!' And you will say, 'Do here also in your hometown the things that we have heard you did at Capernaum.' " [24]And he said, "Truly I tell you, no prophet is accepted in the prophet's hometown. [25]But the truth is, there were many widows in Israel in the time of Elijah, when the heaven was shut up three years and six months, and there was a severe famine over all the land; [26]yet Elijah was sent to none of them except to a widow

at Zarephath in Sidon. ²⁷There were also many lepers[a] in Israel in the time of the prophet Elisha, and none of them was cleansed except Naaman the Syrian." ²⁸When they heard this, all in the synagogue were filled with rage. ²⁹They got up, drove him out of the town, and led him to the brow of the hill on which their town was built, so that they might hurl him off the cliff. ³⁰But he passed through the midst of them and went on his way.

The Man with an Unclean Spirit

31　He went down to Capernaum, a city in Galilee,

Jesus Delivers · Luke 4:14–30

Jesus begins his mission by referring to Isaiah's prophecy (see Isaiah 61:1). In the gospel of Luke, we see Jesus fulfilling this prophecy to bring good news to the oppressed, healing to the brokenhearted, and freedom to captives and prisoners by:

• Healing the sick, who have a variety of issues including demon possession

• Touching and curing lepers, who are separated from the rest of society

• Speaking to and spending time with Samaritans, who are looked down on and rejected by the Jews

• Accepting women, who are generally not viewed as social and religious equals, as disciples

• Forgiving and eating with sinners, who are put down and discriminated against by leaders of the temple.

Throughout his ministry, Jesus treats everyone he encounters with great respect. He recognizes that all people possess dignity and that their lives, even when afflicted by sin, sickness, or poverty, are a reflection of God's own self. As followers of Jesus, we can do the same by never discriminating against or marginalizing others because of their race, gender, health, or social status. Instead, our energy can be spent protecting and building the dignity and respect of others.

• How and where is human dignity being diminished in our world?

• Where is human dignity being uplifted and protected?

• Do you know of anyone who needs to be shown respect? How can you uphold their dignity?

Zach Hunter: Justice for Modern Slaves · Luke 4:16–20

Zach Hunter was twelve years old when he learned that slavery still exists today. And he felt as though God wanted him to do something about it. He started Loose Change to Loosen Chains, a campaign that initially raised almost $10,000, mostly from collecting spare coins, toward freeing slaves. And that was just the beginning. Through his teen years, Zach has spoken to hundreds of thousands of people across the country and written three books encouraging his peers to change the world by blending their passions with love for God.

There are 27 million slaves in the world today! And many of them are children forced into hard labor. Zach is committed to seeing this change in his lifetime, and he is driven by the belief that God's Word is serious when it calls believers to justice—or righting wrongs such as slavery (see Isaiah 1:17; James 1:27). Zach's way of following Jesus is to join him in the things Jesus cares about, such as "proclaim(ing) release to the captives" (Luke 4:18). Find out more about Zach and how you can get involved at **zachhunter.me**.

---

a　The terms *leper* and *leprosy* can refer to several diseases

and was teaching them on the sabbath. [32]They were astounded at his teaching, because he spoke with authority. [33]In the synagogue there was a man who had the spirit of an unclean demon, and he cried out with a loud voice, [34]"Let us alone! What have you to do with us, Jesus of Nazareth? Have you come to destroy us? I know who you are, the Holy One of God." [35]But Jesus rebuked him, saying, "Be silent, and come out of him!" When the demon had thrown him down before them, he came out of him without having done him any harm. [36]They were all amazed and kept saying to one another, "What kind of utterance is this? For with authority and power he commands the unclean spirits, and out they come!" [37]And a report about him began to reach every place in the region.

Healings at Simon's House

38 After leaving the synagogue he entered Simon's house. Now Simon's mother-in-law was suffering from a high fever, and they asked him about her. [39]Then he stood over her and rebuked the fever, and it left her. Immediately she got up and began to serve them.

40 As the sun was setting, all those who had any who were sick with various kinds of diseases brought them to him; and he laid his hands on each of them and cured them. [41]Demons also came out of many, shouting, "You are the Son of God!" But he rebuked them and would not allow them to speak, because they knew that he was the Messiah.[a]

Jesus Preaches in the Synagogues

42 At daybreak he departed and went into a deserted place. And the crowds were looking for him; and when they reached him, they wanted to prevent him from leaving them. [43]But he said to them, "I must proclaim the good news of the kingdom of God to the other cities also; for I was sent for this purpose." [44]So he continued proclaiming the message in the synagogues of Judea.[b]

Jesus Calls the First Disciples

5 Once while Jesus[c] was standing beside the lake of Gennesaret, and the crowd was pressing in on him to hear the word of God, [2]he saw two boats there at the shore of the lake; the fishermen had gone out of them and were washing their nets. [3]He got into one of the boats, the one belonging to Simon, and asked him to put out a little way

LIVE IT!

Do Not Be Afraid
Luke 5:1–11

How would you feel if someone walked into the room right now and announced that God wanted to see you in the next room in five minutes? Astonished? Excited? Frightened? Overwhelmed? Most of us would probably feel a little anxious and want a little more time to get some things in our lives straightened out first!

The gospel of Luke reveals something interesting when it describes a miraculous catch of fish and the call of the first disciples. Upon seeing the miraculous catch, Peter knows he is in the presence of God. Peter asks Jesus to leave, because he is overwhelmed by his own sinfulness and he knows that no one can see the face of God and live (Luke 5:8). If we found ourselves in a boat with God, we might respond the same way. Jesus reassures Peter, saying words so important that they are repeated six times in Luke: "Do not be afraid." God knows we are sinners too. Jesus came not to condemn us, but to save us and to make God's love known to us. Jesus is also saying to us: "Do not be afraid. Come, follow me!"

from the shore. Then he sat down and taught the crowds from the boat. [4]When he had finished speaking, he said to Simon, "Put out into the deep water and let down your nets for a catch." [5]Simon answered, "Master, we have worked all night long but have caught nothing. Yet if you say so, I will let down the nets." [6]When they had done this, they caught so many fish that their nets were beginning to break. [7]So they signaled their partners in the other boat to come and help them. And they came and filled both boats, so that they began to sink. [8]But when Simon Peter saw it, he fell down at Jesus' knees, saying, "Go away from me, Lord, for I am a sinful man!" [9]For he and all who were with him were amazed at the catch of fish that they had taken; [10]and so also were James and John, sons of Zebedee, who were partners with

a Or *the Christ* b Other ancient authorities read *Galilee* c Gk *he*

Simon. Then Jesus said to Simon, "Do not be afraid; from now on you will be catching people." [11]When they had brought their boats to shore, they left everything and followed him.

Jesus Cleanses a Leper

12 Once, when he was in one of the cities, there was a man covered with leprosy.[a] When he saw Jesus, he bowed with his face to the ground and begged him, "Lord, if you choose, you can make me clean." [13]Then Jesus[b] stretched out his hand, touched him, and said, "I do choose. Be made clean." Immediately the leprosy[a] left him. [14]And he ordered him to tell no one. "Go," he said, "and show yourself to the priest, and, as Moses commanded, make an offering for your cleansing, for a testimony to them." [15]But now more than ever the word about Jesus[c] spread abroad; many crowds would gather to hear him and to be cured of their diseases. [16]But he would withdraw to deserted places and pray.

Jesus Heals a Paralytic

17 One day, while he was teaching, Pharisees and teachers of the law were sitting near by (they had come from every village of Galilee and Judea and from Jerusalem); and the power of the Lord was with him to heal.[d] [18]Just then some men came, carrying a paralyzed man on a bed. They were trying to bring him in and lay him before Jesus;[b] [19]but finding no way to bring him in because of the crowd, they went up on the roof and let him down with his bed through the tiles into the middle of the crowd[e]

in front of Jesus. [20]When he saw their faith, he said, "Friend,[f] your sins are forgiven you." [21]Then the scribes and the Pharisees began to question, "Who is this who is speaking blasphemies? Who can forgive sins but God alone?" [22]When Jesus perceived their questionings, he answered them, "Why do you raise such questions in your hearts? [23]Which is easier, to say, 'Your sins are forgiven you,' or to say, 'Stand up and walk'? [24]But so that you may know that the Son of Man has authority on earth to forgive sins"—he said to the one who was paralyzed—"I say to you, stand up and take your bed and go to your home." [25]Immediately he stood up before them, took what he had been lying on, and went to his home, glorifying God. [26]Amazement seized all of them, and they glorified God and were filled with awe, saying, "We have seen strange things today."

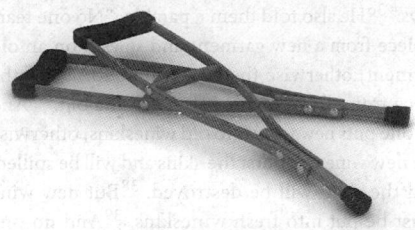

Jesus Calls Levi

27 After this he went out and saw a tax collector named Levi, sitting at the tax booth; and he said to him, "Follow me." [28]And he got up, left everything, and followed him.

LIVE IT!

Friends Like This · Luke 5:17–26

Need a picture of solid friendship? Check out the story of the paralyzed man in **Luke 5:17–26.** The man is so paralyzed he can't get out of bed to go see Jesus, so his friends pick up the bed and carry it to the house where Jesus is teaching. But it's so crowded there is no chance they'll get in. Do they say, "Sorry, man. We tried, but it's just not going to work"? NO! They don't say that. They don't give up. They stick by their friend and find a way to get him to Jesus. When they can't get in through the door, they take him to the roof, remove some tiles, and lower him down. And when Jesus sees the faith of these friends, he heals the man spiritually and physically (Luke 5:20). These are the kind of friends we all want, and the kind of friend we should be.

- Who do you know who needs a good friend?
- What can you do to not only help that friend yourself, but bring others along to help as well?
- How can you be persistent in bringing a hurting friend to Jesus?

---

a The Terms *leper* and *leprosy* can refer to several diseases   **b** Gk *he*   **c** Gk *him*   **d** Other ancient authorities read *was present to heal them*   **e** Gk *into the midst*   **f** Gk *Man*

29 Then Levi gave a great banquet for him in his house; and there was a large crowd of tax collectors and others sitting at the table *a* with them. 30 The Pharisees and their scribes were complaining to his disciples, saying, "Why do you eat and drink with tax collectors and sinners?" 31 Jesus answered, "Those who are well have no need of a physician, but those who are sick; 32 I have come to call not the righteous but sinners to repentance."

The Question about Fasting

33 Then they said to him, "John's disciples, like the disciples of the Pharisees, frequently fast and pray, but your disciples eat and drink." 34 Jesus said to them, "You cannot make wedding guests fast while the bridegroom is with them, can you? 35 The days will come when the bridegroom will be taken away from them, and then they will fast in those days." 36 He also told them a parable: "No one tears a piece from a new garment and sews it on an old garment; otherwise the new will be torn, and the piece from the new will not match the old. 37 And no one puts new wine into old wineskins; otherwise the new wine will burst the skins and will be spilled, and the skins will be destroyed. 38 But new wine must be put into fresh wineskins. 39 And no one after drinking old wine desires new wine, but says, 'The old is good.' " *b*

The Question about the Sabbath

6 One sabbath *c* while Jesus *d* was going through the grainfields, his disciples plucked some heads of grain, rubbed them in their hands, and ate them. 2 But some of the Pharisees said, "Why are you doing what is not lawful *e* on the sabbath?" 3 Jesus answered, "Have you not read what David did when he and his companions were hungry? 4 He entered the house of God and took and ate the bread of the Presence, which it is not lawful for any but the priests to eat, and gave some to his companions?" 5 Then he said to them, "The Son of Man is lord of the sabbath."

The Man with a Withered Hand

6 On another sabbath he entered the synagogue and taught, and there was a man there whose right hand was withered. 7 The scribes and the Pharisees watched him to see whether he would cure on the sabbath, so that they might find an accusation against him. 8 Even though he knew what they were thinking, he said to the man who had the withered hand, "Come and stand here." He got up and stood there. 9 Then Jesus said to them, "I ask you, is it lawful to do good or to do harm on the sabbath, to save life or to destroy it?" 10 After looking around at all of them, he said to him, "Stretch out your hand." He did so, and his hand was restored. 11 But they were filled with fury and discussed with one another what they might do to Jesus.

Jesus Chooses the Twelve Apostles

12 Now during those days he went out to the mountain to pray; and he spent the night in prayer to God. 13 And when day came, he called his disciples and chose twelve of them, whom he also named apostles: 14 Simon, whom he named Peter, and his brother Andrew, and James, and John, and Philip, and Bartholomew, 15 and Matthew, and Thomas, and James son of Alphaeus, and Simon, who was called the Zealot, 16 and Judas son of James, and Judas Iscariot, who became a traitor.

Jesus Teaches and Heals

17 He came down with them and stood on a level place, with a great crowd of his disciples and a great multitude of people from all Judea, Jerusalem, and the coast of Tyre and Sidon. 18 They had come to hear him and to be healed of their diseases; and those who were troubled with unclean spirits were cured. 19 And all in the crowd were trying to touch him, for power came out from him and healed all of them.

Blessings and Woes

20 Then he looked up at his disciples and said:
"Blessed are you who are poor,
    for yours is the kingdom
        of God.
21 "Blessed are you who are hungry now,
    for you will be filled.
"Blessed are you who weep now,
    for you will laugh.
22 "Blessed are you when people hate you, and when they exclude you, revile you, and defame you *f* on account of the Son of Man. 23 Rejoice in that day and leap for joy, for surely your reward is great in heaven; for that is what their ancestors did to the prophets.
24 "But woe to you who are rich,
    for you have received your consolation.

---

a Gk *reclining* b Other ancient authorities read *better*; others lack verse 39 c Other ancient authorities read *On the second first sabbath* d Gk *he*
e Other ancient authorities add *to do* f Gk *cast out your name as evil*

Jesus' Preference for the Poor
Luke 6:17–26

In Luke 6:17–26, Jesus teaches that God's justice has a preference for the poor and the little ones. So it's not surprising that the four Beatitudes (blessings) in Luke are balanced by four woes ("Woe!" is like saying, "Trouble ahead!"). For example, "Blessed are you who are poor" (Luke 6:20) is countered by "Woe to you who are rich" (Luke 6:24). Jesus shows his care for both the rich and the poor by calling the rich to practice justice and the poor to have hope.

Unlike the gospel of Matthew, Luke does not spiritualize the Beatitudes. Matthew says, "Blessed are the poor in spirit" (Matthew 5:3), but Luke simply says, "Blessed are you who are poor" (Luke 6:20), meaning materially poor. Matthew is concerned about people's salvation; Luke is concerned about their salvation AND their material needs.

25 "Woe to you who are full now,
    for you will be hungry.
"Woe to you who are laughing now,
    for you will mourn and weep.
26 "Woe to you when all speak well of you, for that is what their ancestors did to the false prophets.

Love for Enemies

27 "But I say to you that listen, Love your enemies, do good to those who hate you, 28 bless those who curse you, pray for those who abuse you. 29 If anyone strikes you on the cheek, offer the other also; and from anyone who takes away your coat do not withhold even your shirt. 30 Give to everyone who begs from you; and if anyone takes away your goods, do not ask for them again. 31 Do to others as you would have them do to you.

32 "If you love those who love you, what credit is that to you? For even sinners love those who love them. 33 If you do good to those who do good to you, what credit is that to you? For even sinners do the same. 34 If you lend to those from whom you hope to receive, what credit is that to you? Even sinners lend to sinners, to receive as much again. 35 But love your enemies, do good, and lend, expecting nothing in return.[a] Your reward will be great, and you will be children of the Most High; for he is kind to the ungrateful and the wicked. 36 Be merciful, just as your Father is merciful.

Hannah Turner: Warm Feet, Warm Heart · Luke 6:27–36

"Mommy, won't his feet be cold?" Hannah Turner was only four years old when she was helping serve Thanksgiving dinner to those in need. She saw a man without socks and, in her childlike stubbornness, was determined to do something about it. The next day, she and her mom collected and donated over a hundred pairs of socks to shelters around Toledo, Ohio. It was a practical application of the Golden Rule: "Do to others as you would have them do to you" (Luke 6:31).

In the process, Hannah and her family learned that socks and undergarments are one of the things needed most and donated least at shelters. So they started Hannah's Socks and have now donated over three hundred thousand pairs of socks to homeless and domestic violence shelters in Ohio, Kentucky, and Michigan. Their mission is that no one should lack the basic necessity of a clean, warm pair of socks. It took the simple eyes of a child to see the need and be willing to give without questioning. Some judge those in a position of need for making poor choices or spending their money on things other than life's necessities, but Hannah simply saw cold feet that needed to be warm. Luke 6:29 tells us that we are to give even to our enemies—if they take our coat, we are to give our shirt too. Or in this case, socks. Learn more at **hannahssocks.org**.

---

a Other ancient authorities read *despairing of no one*

Judging Others

37 "Do not judge, and you will not be judged; do not condemn, and you will not be condemned. Forgive, and you will be forgiven; [38] give, and it will be given to you. A good measure, pressed down, shaken together, running over, will be put into your lap; for the measure you give will be the measure you get back."

39 He also told them a parable: "Can a blind person guide a blind person? Will not both fall into a pit? [40] A disciple is not above the teacher, but everyone who is fully qualified will be like the teacher. [41] Why do you see the speck in your neighbor's[a] eye, but do not notice the log in your own eye? [42] Or how can you say to your neighbor,[b] 'Friend,[b] let me take out the speck in your eye,' when you yourself do not see the log in your own eye? You hypocrite, first take the log out of your own eye, and then you will see clearly to take the speck out of your neighbor's[a] eye.

A Tree and Its Fruit

43 "No good tree bears bad fruit, nor again does a bad tree bear good fruit; [44] for each tree is known by its own fruit. Figs are not gathered from thorns, nor are grapes picked from a bramble bush. [45] The good person out of the good treasure of the heart produces good, and the evil person out of evil treasure produces evil; for it is out of the abundance of the heart that the mouth speaks.

The Two Foundations

46 "Why do you call me 'Lord, Lord,' and do not do what I tell you? [47] I will show you what someone is like who comes to me, hears my words, and acts on them. [48] That one is like a man building a house, who dug deeply and laid the foundation on rock; when a flood arose, the river burst against that house but could not shake it, because it had been well built.[c] [49] But the one who hears and does not act is like a man who built a house on the ground without a foundation. When the river burst against it, immediately it fell, and great was the ruin of that house."

> "Do not judge, and you will not be judged; do not condemn, and you will not be condemned. Forgive, and you will be forgiven."
> —Luke 6:37

Jesus Heals a Centurion's Servant

7 After Jesus[d] had finished all his sayings in the hearing of the people, he entered Capernaum. [2] A centurion there had a slave whom he valued highly, and who was ill and close to death. [3] When he heard about Jesus, he sent some Jewish elders to him, asking him to come and heal his slave. [4] When they came to Jesus, they appealed to him earnestly, saying, "He is worthy of having you do this for him, [5] for he loves our people, and it is he who built our synagogue for us." [6] And Jesus went with them, but when he was not far from the house, the centurion sent friends to say to him, "Lord, do not trouble yourself, for I am not worthy to have you come under my roof; [7] therefore I did not presume to come to you. But only speak the word, and let my servant be healed. [8] For I also am a man set under authority, with soldiers under me; and I say to one, 'Go,' and he goes, and to another, 'Come,' and he comes, and to my slave, 'Do this,' and the slave does it." [9] When Jesus heard this he was amazed at him, and turning to the crowd that followed him, he said, "I tell you, not even in Israel have I found such faith." [10] When those who had been sent returned to the house, they found the slave in good health.

Jesus Raises the Widow's Son at Nain

11 Soon afterwards[e] he went to a town called Nain, and his disciples and a large crowd went with him. [12] As he approached the gate of the town, a man who had died was being carried out. He was his mother's only son, and she was a widow; and with her was a large crowd from the town. [13] When the Lord saw her, he had compassion for her and said to her, "Do not weep." [14] Then he came forward and touched the bier, and the bearers stood still. And he said, "Young man, I say to you, rise!" [15] The dead man sat up and began to speak, and Jesus[d] gave him to his mother. [16] Fear seized all of them; and they glorified God, saying, "A great prophet has risen among us!" and "God has looked favorably on his people!" [17] This word about him spread throughout Judea and all the surrounding country.

a Gk brother's   b Gk brother   c Other ancient authorities read founded upon the rock   d Gk he   e Other ancient authorities read Next day

Messengers from John the Baptist

18 The disciples of John reported all these things to him. So John summoned two of his disciples ¹⁹and sent them to the Lord to ask, "Are you the one who is to come, or are we to wait for another?" ²⁰When the men had come to him, they said, "John the Baptist has sent us to you to ask, 'Are you the one who is to come, or are we to wait for another?' " ²¹Jesus*a* had just then cured many people of diseases, plagues, and evil spirits, and had given sight to many who were blind. ²²And he answered them, "Go and tell John what you have seen and heard: the blind receive their sight, the lame walk, the lepers*b* are cleansed, the deaf hear, the dead are raised, the poor have good news brought to them. ²³And blessed is anyone who takes no offense at me."

24 When John's messengers had gone, Jesus*a* began to speak to the crowds about John:*c* "What did you go out into the wilderness to look at? A reed shaken by the wind? ²⁵What then did you go out to see? Someone *d* dressed in soft robes? Look, those who put on fine clothing and live in luxury are in royal palaces. ²⁶What then did you go out to see? A prophet? Yes, I tell you, and more than a prophet. ²⁷This is the one about whom it is written,

'See, I am sending my messenger ahead of you,
who will prepare your way before you.'

²⁸I tell you, among those born of women no one is greater than John; yet the least in the kingdom of God is greater than he." ²⁹(And all the people who heard this, including the tax collectors, acknowledged the justice of God,*e* because they had been baptized with John's baptism. ³⁰But by refusing to be baptized by him, the Pharisees and the lawyers rejected God's purpose for themselves.)

31 "To what then will I compare the people of this generation, and what are they like? ³²They are like children sitting in the marketplace and calling to one another,

'We played the flute for you, and you did not dance;
we wailed, and you did not weep.'

³³For John the Baptist has come eating no bread and drinking no wine, and you say, 'He has a demon'; ³⁴the Son of Man has come eating and drinking, and you say, 'Look, a glutton and a drunkard, a friend of tax collectors and sinners!' ³⁵Nevertheless, wisdom is vindicated by all her children."

A Sinful Woman Forgiven

36 One of the Pharisees asked Jesus*c* to eat with him, and he went into the Pharisee's house and took his place at the table. ³⁷And a woman in the city, who was a sinner, having learned that he was eating in the Pharisee's house, brought an alabaster jar of ointment. ³⁸She stood behind him at his feet, weeping, and began to bathe his feet with her tears and to dry them with her hair. Then she continued kissing his feet and anointing them with the ointment. ³⁹Now when the Pharisee who had invited him saw it, he said to himself, "If this man were a prophet, he would have known who and what kind of woman this is who is touching him—that she is a sinner." ⁴⁰Jesus spoke up and said to him, "Simon, I have something to say to you." "Teacher," he replied, "speak." ⁴¹"A certain creditor had two debt-

Great Love
Luke 7:36–50

Have you ever felt unworthy of God's love? Have you ever felt that the sin in your life was too great, that even if God could love you, you couldn't get past all those "good" or perfect people standing in the way? The story of the sinful woman in **Luke 7:36–50** is an amazing picture of the grace, forgiveness, and love of Jesus.

The woman who came to Jesus at a Pharisee's house to anoint his feet with oil was most likely a prostitute. She was looked down on by all and considered sinful and unclean (Luke 7:39). But she broke through the barriers and came to Jesus. And although the response of those around him was to judge her, Jesus did not! He forgave her. And not only that. He used a story to tell the religious people there that the woman had even greater love, because she had been forgiven of so much (Luke 7:41-43). Don't let your sin, no matter how bad it seems, keep you from God. Come to God, and let him forgive you and replace your sin with great love.

---

a Gk He *b* The terms *leper* and *leprosy* can refer to several diseases *c* Gk him *d* Or *Why then did you go out? To see someone* *e* Or *praised God*

ors; one owed five hundred denarii,^a and the other fifty. ⁴²When they could not pay, he canceled the debts for both of them. Now which of them will love him more?" ⁴³Simon answered, "I suppose the one for whom he canceled the greater debt." And Jesus^b said to him, "You have judged rightly." ⁴⁴Then turning toward the woman, he said to Simon, "Do you see this woman? I entered your house; you gave me no water for my feet, but she has bathed my feet with her tears and dried them with her hair. ⁴⁵You gave me no kiss, but from the time I came in she has not stopped kissing my feet. ⁴⁶You did not anoint my head with oil, but she has anointed my feet with ointment. ⁴⁷Therefore, I tell you, her sins, which were many, have been forgiven; hence she has shown great love. But the one to whom little is forgiven, loves little." ⁴⁸Then he said to her, "Your sins are forgiven." ⁴⁹But those who were at the table with him began to say among themselves, "Who is this who even forgives sins?" ⁵⁰And he said to the woman, "Your faith has saved you; go in peace."

Some Women Accompany Jesus

8 Soon afterwards he went on through cities and villages, proclaiming and bringing the good news of the kingdom of God. The twelve were with him, ²as well as some women who had been cured of evil spirits and infirmities: Mary, called Magdalene, from whom seven demons had gone out, ³and Joanna, the wife of Herod's steward Chuza, and Susanna, and many others, who provided for them^c out of their resources.

The Parable of the Sower

4 When a great crowd gathered and people from town after town came to him, he said in a parable: ⁵"A sower went out to sow his seed; and as he sowed, some fell on the path and was trampled on, and the birds of the air ate it up. ⁶Some fell on the

rock; and as it grew up, it withered for lack of moisture. ⁷Some fell among thorns, and the thorns grew with it and choked it. ⁸Some fell into good soil, and when it grew, it produced a hundredfold." As he said this, he called out, "Let anyone with ears to hear listen!"

The Purpose of the Parables

9 Then his disciples asked him what this parable meant. ¹⁰He said, "To you it has been given to know the secrets^d of the kingdom of God; but to others I speak^e in parables, so that

'looking they may not perceive,
    and listening they may not understand.'

The Parable of the Sower Explained

11 "Now the parable is this: The seed is the word of God. ¹²The ones on the path are those who have heard; then the devil comes and takes away the word from their hearts, so that they may not believe and be saved. ¹³The ones on the rock are those who, when they hear the word, receive it with joy. But these have no root; they believe only for a while and in a time of testing fall away. ¹⁴As for what fell among the thorns, these are the ones who hear; but as they go on their way, they are choked by the cares and riches and pleasures of life, and their fruit does not mature. ¹⁵But as for that in the good soil, these are the ones who, when they hear the word, hold it fast in an honest and good heart, and bear fruit with patient endurance.

A Lamp under a Jar

16 "No one after lighting a lamp hides it under a jar, or puts it under a bed, but puts it on a lampstand, so that those who enter may see the light. ¹⁷For nothing is hidden that will not be disclosed, nor is anything secret that will not become known and come to light. ¹⁸Then pay attention to how you listen; for to those who have, more will be given; and from those who do not have, even what they seem to have will be taken away."

The True Kindred of Jesus

19 Then his mother and his brothers came to him, but they could not reach him because of the crowd. ²⁰And he was told, "Your mother and your brothers are standing outside, wanting to see you." ²¹But he said to them, "My mother and my brothers are those who hear the word of God and do it."

a The denarius was the usual day's wage for a laborer   b Gk he   c Other ancient authorities read him   d Or mysteries   e Gk lacks I speak

Jesus Calms a Storm

22 One day he got into a boat with his disciples, and he said to them, "Let us go across to the other side of the lake." So they put out, 23 and while they were sailing he fell asleep. A windstorm swept down on the lake, and the boat was filling with water, and they were in danger. 24 They went to him and woke him up, shouting, "Master, Master, we are perishing!" And he woke up and rebuked the wind and the raging waves; they ceased, and there was a calm. 25 He said to them, "Where is your faith?" They were afraid and amazed, and said to one another, "Who then is this, that he commands even the winds and the water, and they obey him?"

Jesus Heals the Gerasene Demoniac

26 Then they arrived at the country of the Gerasenes,[a] which is opposite Galilee. 27 As he stepped out on land, a man of the city who had demons met him. For a long time he had worn[b] no clothes, and he did not live in a house but in the tombs. 28 When he saw Jesus, he fell down before him and shouted at the top of his voice, "What have you to do with me, Jesus, Son of the Most High God? I beg you, do not torment me"— 29 for Jesus[c] had commanded the unclean spirit to come out of the man. (For many times it had seized him; he was kept under guard and bound with chains and shackles, but he would break the bonds and be driven by the demon into the wilds.) 30 Jesus then asked him, "What is your name?" He said, "Legion"; for many demons had entered him. 31 They begged him not to order them to go back into the abyss.

32 Now there on the hillside a large herd of swine was feeding; and the demons[d] begged Jesus[e] to let them enter these. So he gave them permission. 33 Then the demons came out of the man and entered the swine, and the herd rushed down the steep bank into the lake and was drowned.

34 When the swineherds saw what had happened, they ran off and told it in the city and in the country. 35 Then people came out to see what had happened, and when they came to Jesus, they found the man from whom the demons had gone sitting at the feet of Jesus, clothed and in his right mind. And they were afraid. 36 Those who had seen it told them how the one who had been possessed by demons had been healed. 37 Then all the people of the surrounding country of the Gerasenes[a] asked Jesus[e] to leave them; for they were seized with great fear. So he got into the boat and returned. 38 The man from whom the demons had gone begged that he might be with him; but Jesus[c] sent him away, saying, 39 "Return to your home, and declare how much God has done for you." So he went away, proclaiming throughout the city how much Jesus had done for him.

A Girl Restored to Life and a Woman Healed

40 Now when Jesus returned, the crowd welcomed him, for they were all waiting for him. 41 Just then there came a man named Jairus, a leader of the synagogue. He fell at Jesus' feet and begged him to come to his house, 42 for he had an only daughter, about twelve years old, who was dying.

As he went, the crowds pressed in on him. 43 Now there was a woman who had been suffering from hemorrhages for twelve years; and though she had spent all she had on physicians,[f] no one could cure her. 44 She came up behind him and touched the fringe of his clothes, and immediately her hemorrhage stopped. 45 Then Jesus asked, "Who touched me?" When all denied it, Peter[g] said, "Master, the crowds surround you and press in on you." 46 But Jesus said, "Someone touched me; for I noticed that power had gone out from me." 47 When the woman saw that she could not remain hidden, she came trembling; and falling down before him, she declared in the presence of all the people why she had touched him, and how she had been immediately healed. 48 He said to her, "Daughter, your faith has made you well; go in peace."

49 While he was still speaking, someone came from the leader's house to say, "Your daughter is dead; do not trouble the teacher any longer." 50 When Jesus heard this, he replied, "Do not fear. Only believe, and she will be saved." 51 When he came to the house, he did not allow anyone to enter with him, except Peter, John, and James, and the child's father and mother. 52 They were all weeping and wailing for her; but he said, "Do not weep; for she is not dead but sleeping." 53 And they laughed at him, knowing that she was dead. 54 But he took her by the hand and called out, "Child, get up!" 55 Her spirit returned, and she got up at once. Then he directed them to give her something to eat. 56 Her parents were astounded; but he ordered them to tell no one what had happened.

---

a Other ancient authorities read *Gadarenes*; others, *Gergesenes* b Other ancient authorities read *a man of the city who had had demons for a long time met him. He wore* c Gk *he* d Gk *they* e Gk *him* f Other ancient authorities lack *and though she had spent all she had on physicians* g Other ancient authorities add *and those who were with him*

9

The Mission of the Twelve

Then Jesus[a] called the twelve together and gave them power and authority over all demons and to cure diseases, [2]and he sent them out to proclaim the kingdom of God and to heal. [3]He said to them, "Take nothing for your journey, no staff, nor bag, nor bread, nor money—not even an extra tunic. [4]Whatever house you enter, stay there, and leave from there. [5]Wherever they do not welcome you, as you are leaving that town shake the dust off your feet as a testimony against them." [6]They departed and went through the villages, bringing the good news and curing diseases everywhere.

Herod's Perplexity

7 Now Herod the ruler[b] heard about all that had taken place, and he was perplexed, because it was said by some that John had been raised from the dead, [8]by some that Elijah had appeared, and by others that one of the ancient prophets had arisen. [9]Herod said, "John I beheaded; but who is this about whom I hear such things?" And he tried to see him.

Feeding the Five Thousand

10 On their return the apostles told Jesus[c] all they had done. He took them with him and withdrew privately to a city called Bethsaida. [11]When the crowds found out about it, they followed him; and he welcomed them, and spoke to them about the kingdom of God, and healed those who needed to be cured.

12 The day was drawing to a close, and the twelve came to him and said, "Send the crowd away, so that they may go into the surrounding villages and countryside, to lodge and get provisions; for we are here in a deserted place." [13]But he said to them, "You give them something to eat." They said, "We have no more than five loaves and two fish—unless we are to go and buy food for all these people." [14]For there were about five thousand men. And he said to his disciples, "Make them sit down in groups of about fifty each." [15]They did so and made them all sit down. [16]And taking the five loaves and the two fish, he looked up to heaven, and blessed and broke them, and gave them to the disciples to set before the crowd. [17]And all ate and were filled. What was left over was gathered up, twelve baskets of broken pieces.

Peter's Declaration about Jesus

18 Once when Jesus[a] was praying alone, with only the disciples near him, he asked them, "Who do the crowds say that I am?" [19]They answered, "John the Baptist; but others, Elijah; and still others, that one of the ancient prophets has arisen." [20]He said to them, "But who do you say that I am?" Peter answered, "The Messiah[d] of God."

Jesus Foretells His Death and Resurrection

21 He sternly ordered and commanded them not to tell anyone, [22]saying, "The Son of Man must undergo great suffering, and be rejected by the elders, chief priests, and scribes, and be killed, and on the third day be raised."

23 Then he said to them all, "If any want to become my followers, let them deny themselves and take up their cross daily and follow me. [24]For those who want to save their life will lose it, and those who lose their life for my sake will save it. [25]What does it profit them if they gain the whole world, but lose or forfeit themselves? [26]Those who are ashamed of me and of my words, of them the Son of Man will be ashamed when he comes in his glory and the glory of the Father and of the holy angels. [27]But truly I tell you, there are some standing here who will not taste death before they see the kingdom of God."

LIVE IT!

Mission Possible
Luke 9:1–6

"Mission: Impossible" makes for a good action movie, but Jesus tells his disciples in **Luke 9:1–6** that, although their mission won't always be easy or popular, it is "mission: possible."

Followers of Jesus are asked to share in that mission, knowing that it's not easy. Most of us will not leave our homes with no food, clothing, or money as the disciples did. But taking the good news of Jesus to the world will often mean going against the norm.

- Are you ready to accept Jesus' mission?
- What does that look like in your life today?
- What is the hardest part for you?

---

a Gk he b Gk tetrarch c Gk him d Or The Christ

The Messiah · Luke 9:18-20

Have you ever noticed that when a dramatic event takes place, people want to gather and talk about it? When a natural disaster hits, a new president is elected, a teacher is fired, or a team wins a championship, we like to talk about the event and how it impacts our lives. The same was probably true when Jesus walked the earth teaching and performing miracles. It's not difficult to imagine people talking over dinner or in the public square about Jesus and the things he was doing. Jesus was probably aware of this talk, so he turned to the disciples and asked them what the crowds were saying about him. The disciples replied that the people thought Jesus was John the Baptist or some other great hero brought back to life (Luke 9:19). The crowds were on the right track thinking Jesus was someone special, but only the disciples realized his true identity as the Messiah.

Humankind had been anxiously awaiting the arrival of the Messiah ever since sin entered the world with Adam and Eve. God was laying the foundation throughout the Old Testament for the coming of the Messiah. The prophecies in Isaiah tell us a lot about the identity and role of the Messiah. The Messiah is described as fully possessing the gifts of the Holy Spirit (see "Pray It: The Character of the King," near Isaiah 11:1-2). The Messiah is the one who will usher in an era of peace that will be evident in all of God's creation, just as it was intended before Adam and Eve fell into sin. In Isaiah, the Messiah is described as God's servant who, even though he is without sin, willingly takes on the punishment for the sins of the world (52:13-53:12). His suffering and death would restore humankind's relationship with God.

Although Jesus is the Messiah hoped for in the Old Testament, many did not recognize him, because they mistakenly thought the Messiah was going to be a king who would establish his political rule over Israel like King David or King Solomon. They wanted a messiah who would do battle with earthly powers and save them from oppressive rulers. Jesus showed the world that the Messiah was a king, but one who would bring the kingdom of God through his suffering and death for the sins of all, just as Isaiah had prophesied. And when the time was right, Jesus willingly suffered crucifixion and offered his life on our behalf. He did battle with the powers of spiritual darkness and saved us from oppression of sin. As the Messiah, Jesus died and rose again, opening up for us the way to heaven, where the lamb and the wolf will lie together in peace.

The Transfiguration

28 Now about eight days after these sayings Jesus[a] took with him Peter and John and James, and went up on the mountain to pray. [29]And while he was praying, the appearance of his face changed, and his clothes became dazzling white. [30]Suddenly they saw two men, Moses and Elijah, talking to him. [31]They appeared in glory and were speaking of his departure, which he was about to accomplish at Jerusalem. [32]Now Peter and his companions were weighed down with sleep; but since they had stayed awake,[b] they saw his glory and the two men who stood with him. [33]Just as they were leaving him, Peter said to Jesus, "Master, it is good for us to be here; let us make three dwellings,[c] one for you, one for Moses,

and one for Elijah"—not knowing what he said. [34]While he was saying this, a cloud came and overshadowed them; and they were terrified as they entered the cloud. [35]Then from the cloud came a voice that said, "This is my Son, my Chosen;[d] listen to him!" [36]When the voice had spoken, Jesus was found alone. And they kept silent and in those days told no one any of the things they had seen.

Jesus Heals a Boy with a Demon

37 On the next day, when they had come down from the mountain, a great crowd met him. [38]Just then a man from the crowd shouted, "Teacher, I beg you to look at my son; he is my only child. [39]Suddenly a spirit seizes him, and all at once he[e] shrieks.

a Gk he b Or but when they were fully awake c Or tents d Other ancient authorities read my Beloved e Or it

PRAY IT!

Spiritual Highs · Luke 9:28–36

Have you ever been on a great retreat, camping trip, or service trip with your church? They can be amazing times that help you feel really close to God and to others who share the same spiritual high. You may even have wished the experience wouldn't end.

Peter, James, and John must have felt that way when they saw Jesus in his glory talking with Moses and Elijah on the mountaintop. Peter wanted to stay up on the mountain, but it quickly became clear that he couldn't.

Faith has its high moments as well as its low moments. And though the spiritual highs are encouraging and strengthening, it is unrealistic to think we can maintain some kind of spiritual high all the time. Faith that isn't grounded often fizzles out. The continuing challenge is to learn what it means to live as a Christian down in the realities of everyday life. Remember, our faith and God's love and mercy are all more than feelings.

Think of a special time in your life when you had a spiritual high and felt on top of the world. Relive the moment in your mind, this time looking for how God was present in that experience. Then say this prayer:

God, I love the feeling of being close to you—of being awed, inspired, and encouraged. Thank you for taking me to the mountaintop and showing me your greatness. Now please help me know how to live every day through what I experienced. Show me the direction you want me to go and give me the strength to move that way. Please teach me what it means to trust in you, not just the emotional highs of life. Amen.

It convulses him until he foams at the mouth; it mauls him and will scarcely leave him. ⁴⁰I begged your disciples to cast it out, but they could not." ⁴¹Jesus answered, "You faithless and perverse generation, how much longer must I be with you and bear with you? Bring your son here." ⁴²While he was coming, the demon dashed him to the ground in convulsions. But Jesus rebuked the unclean spirit, healed the boy, and gave him back to his father. ⁴³And all were astounded at the greatness of God.

Jesus Again Foretells His Death

While everyone was amazed at all that he was doing, he said to his disciples, ⁴⁴"Let these words sink into your ears: The Son of Man is going to be betrayed into human hands." ⁴⁵But they did not understand this saying; its meaning was concealed from them, so that they could not perceive it. And they were afraid to ask him about this saying.

True Greatness

46 An argument arose among them as to which one of them was the greatest. ⁴⁷But Jesus, aware of

> "Whoever welcomes this child in my name welcomes me, and whoever welcomes me welcomes the one who sent me; for the least among all of you is the greatest."
> —Luke 9:48

their inner thoughts, took a little child and put it by his side, ⁴⁸and said to them, "Whoever welcomes this child in my name welcomes me, and whoever welcomes me welcomes the one who sent me; for the least among all of you is the greatest."

Another Exorcist

49 John answered, "Master, we saw someone

casting out demons in your name, and we tried to stop him, because he does not follow with us." [50]But Jesus said to him, "Do not stop him; for whoever is not against you is for you."

A Samaritan Village Refuses to Receive Jesus

51 When the days drew near for him to be taken up, he set his face to go to Jerusalem. [52]And he sent messengers ahead of him. On their way they entered a village of the Samaritans to make ready for him; [53]but they did not receive him, because his face was set toward Jerusalem. [54]When his disciples James and John saw it, they said, "Lord, do you want us to command fire to come down from heaven and consume them?"[a] [55]But he turned and rebuked them. [56]Then[b] they went on to another village.

Would-Be Followers of Jesus

57 As they were going along the road, someone said to him, "I will follow you wherever you go." [58]And Jesus said to him, "Foxes have holes, and birds of the air have nests; but the Son of Man has nowhere to lay his head." [59]To another he said, "Follow me." But he said, "Lord, first let me go and bury my father." [60]But Jesus[c] said to him, "Let the dead bury their own dead; but as for you, go and proclaim the kingdom of God." [61]Another said, "I will follow you, Lord; but let me first say farewell to those at my home." [62]Jesus said to him, "No one who puts a hand to the plow and looks back is fit for the kingdom of God."

10

The Mission of the Seventy

After this the Lord appointed seventy[d] others and sent them on ahead of him in pairs to every town and place where he himself intended to go. [2]He said to them, "The harvest is plentiful, but the laborers are few; therefore ask the Lord of the harvest to send out laborers into his harvest. [3]Go on your way. See, I am sending you out like lambs into the midst of wolves. [4]Carry no purse, no bag, no sandals; and greet no one on the road. [5]Whatever house you enter, first say, 'Peace to this house!' [6]And if anyone is there who shares in peace, your peace will rest on that person; but if not, it will return to you. [7]Remain in the same house, eating and drinking whatever they provide, for the laborer deserves to be paid. Do not move about from house to house. [8]Whenever you enter a town and its people welcome you, eat what is set before you; [9]cure the sick who are there, and say to them, 'The kingdom of God has come near to you.'[e] [10]But whenever you enter a town and they do not welcome you, go out into its streets and say, [11]'Even the dust of your town that clings to our feet, we wipe off in protest against you. Yet know this: the kingdom of God has come near.'[f] [12]I tell you, on that day it will be more tolerable for Sodom than for that town.

Woes to Unrepentant Cities

13 "Woe to you, Chorazin! Woe to you, Bethsaida! For if the deeds of power done in you had been done in Tyre and Sidon, they would have repented long ago, sitting in sackcloth and ashes. [14]But at the judgment it will be more tolerable for Tyre and Sidon than for you. [15]And you, Capernaum,

will you be exalted to heaven?

No, you will be brought down to Hades.

16 "Whoever listens to you listens to me, and whoever rejects you rejects me, and whoever rejects me rejects the one who sent me."

The Return of the Seventy

17 The seventy[d] returned with joy, saying, "Lord, in your name even the demons submit to us!" [18]He said to them, "I watched Satan fall from heaven like a flash of lightning. [19]See, I have given you authority to tread on snakes and scorpions, and over all the power of the enemy; and nothing will hurt you. [20]Nevertheless, do not rejoice at this, that the spirits submit to you, but rejoice that your names are written in heaven."

Jesus Rejoices

21 At that same hour Jesus[c] rejoiced in the Holy Spirit[g] and said, "I thank[h] you, Father, Lord of heaven and earth, because you have hidden these things from the wise and the intelligent and have revealed them to infants; yes, Father, for such was your gracious will.[i] [22]All things have been handed over to me by my Father; and no one knows who the Son is except the Father, or who the Father is except the Son and anyone to whom the Son chooses to reveal him."

23 Then turning to the disciples, Jesus[c] said to them privately, "Blessed are the eyes that see what you see! [24]For I tell you that many prophets and kings desired to see what you see, but did not see it, and to hear what you hear, but did not hear it."

---

a Other ancient authorities add as Elijah did   b Other ancient authorities read rebuked them, and said, "You do not know what spirit you are of, [56]for the Son of Man has not come to destroy the lives of human beings but to save them." Then   c Gk he   d Other ancient authorities read seventy-two   e Or is at hand for you   f Or is at hand   g Other authorities read in the spirit   h Or praise   i Or for so it was well-pleasing in your sight

The Parable of the Good Samaritan

25 Just then a lawyer stood up to test Jesus.[a] "Teacher," he said, "what must I do to inherit eternal life?" [26]He said to him, "What is written in the law? What do you read there?" [27]He answered, "You shall love the Lord your God with all your heart, and with all your soul, and with all your strength, and with all your mind; and your neighbor as yourself." [28]And

he said to him, "You have given the right answer; do this, and you will live."

29 But wanting to justify himself, he asked Jesus, "And who is my neighbor?" [30]Jesus replied, "A man was going down from Jerusalem to Jericho, and fell into the hands of robbers, who stripped him, beat him, and went away, leaving him half dead. [31]Now by chance a priest was going down that road; and

The Good Samaritan · Luke 10:25–37

The good Samaritan is a popular Bible story with an obvious message: We must not only help others, but also love the ones who hate us. In Jesus' day, Jews despised the Samaritans and vice versa. Because the hero of the story was a Samaritan, it would have given the lawyer and other people listening to Jesus something to think about.

The parable itself is told as a response to the question posed of Jesus, "Who is my neighbor?" (Luke 10:29). The answer to this question? "Everyone!" Jesus reminds us through this parable that we are called to treat all people with great compassion regardless of their race, religion, ethnicity, gender, or social status. We are to love our neighbor as ourselves and welcome the stranger into our midst.

Imagine that this story takes place in your community:
• Who are the Samaritans in your community—that is, the culture or people that others judge and reject?
• How does Jesus' teaching through this story affect your understanding of discrimination and racism?
• What can you do to better accept and care for all people in your community?

Too Busy to Be Still · Luke 10:38–42

We live in a busy world. New inventions, progress, hard work, and success are all valued in our culture. So the story of Jesus' visit to Mary and Martha can be a tough one. Martha was a hard worker. She was being responsible and getting things done. Mary was just sitting. And in our culture, we typically value those who accomplish a lot rather than those who sit around. But Jesus says Mary has made the better choice by making spending time with Jesus her most important task. This story is not intended to make us feel guilty. It is an encouragement to slow down and enjoy the peace of simply spending time with Jesus. If you are struggling with finding times to be with God, pray this prayer:

Help me to slow down, Lord, right now, before I think of something else that I should be doing—as if it really is more important than you. Let me sit in the quiet peace of your presence and soak up all that you have to say to me. Give me the patience and perception to do nothing else for these next few moments except to be totally, completely, and wonderfully centered on you.

α Gk him

when he saw him, he passed by on the other side. ³²So likewise a Levite, when he came to the place and saw him, passed by on the other side. ³³But a Samaritan while traveling came near him; and when he saw him, he was moved with pity. ³⁴He went to him and bandaged his wounds, having poured oil and wine on them. Then he put him on his own animal, brought him to an inn, and took care of him. ³⁵The next day he took out two denarii,ᵃ gave them to the innkeeper, and said, 'Take care of him; and when I come back, I will repay you whatever more you spend.' ³⁶Which of these three, do you think, was a neighbor to the man who fell into the hands of the robbers?" ³⁷He said, "The one who showed him mercy." Jesus said to him, "Go and do likewise."

Jesus Visits Martha and Mary

38 Now as they went on their way, he entered a certain village, where a woman named Martha welcomed him into her home. ³⁹She had a sister named Mary, who sat at the Lord's feet and listened to what he was saying. ⁴⁰But Martha was distracted by her many tasks; so she came to him and asked, "Lord, do you not care that my sister has left me to do all the work by myself? Tell her then to help me." ⁴¹But the Lord answered her, "Martha, Martha, you are worried and distracted by many things; ⁴²there is need of only one thing.ᵇ Mary has chosen the better part, which will not be taken away from her."

The Lord's Prayer

11 He was praying in a certain place, and after he had finished, one of his disciples said to him, "Lord, teach us to pray, as John taught his disciples." ²He said to them, "When you pray, say:

Father,ᶜ hallowed be your name.
   Your kingdom come.ᵈ
3   Give us each day our daily bread.ᵉ
4   And forgive us our sins,
      for we ourselves forgive everyone
         indebted to us.
   And do not bring us to the time of
      trial."ᶠ

Perseverance in Prayer

5 And he said to them, "Suppose one of you has a friend, and you go to him at midnight and say to him, 'Friend, lend me three loaves of bread; ⁶for a friend of mine has arrived, and I have nothing to set before him.' ⁷And he answers from within, 'Do not

STUDY IT!

The Lord's Prayer
Luke 11:1–4

Sometimes the simplest question brings the most profound answer. The disciples had been traveling with Jesus for some time and saw how frequently Jesus prayed, especially before important events. So it is no wonder that the disciples ask Jesus to teach them to pray. Jesus responds by teaching them the Lord's Prayer, which is now the model for Christian prayer. It covers our relationship with God and our needs as God's children.

The first part of the prayer focuses on God (Luke 11:2). It begins by calling God "Father," which reflects our own identity as adopted daughters and sons of God. Then it acknowledges God's holiness, and expresses a desire for God's kingdom. By placing our attention on God, we draw closer to God and begin to leave behind all that would hold us back from loving him.

The second part (Luke 11:3-4 acknowledges our own weaknesses and calls on God's mercy. It addresses our basic human need for nourishment (both physical and spiritual) and for forgiveness (for both ourselves and others). These verses conclude with a request for deliverance. By acknowledging our weaknesses and asking for help, we place our hope in God. The Lord's Prayer teaches us how to love God and gives us the words to express and deepen that love.

bother me; the door has already been locked, and my children are with me in bed; I cannot get up and give you anything.' ⁸I tell you, even though he will not get up and give him anything because he is his friend, at least because of his persistence he will get up and give him whatever he needs.

9 "So I say to you, Ask, and it will be given you; search, and you will find; knock, and the door will be opened for you. ¹⁰For everyone who asks re-

---

ᵃ The denarius was the usual day's wage for a laborer   **b** Other ancient authorities read *few things are necessary, or only one*   **c** Other ancient authorities read *Our Father in heaven*   **d** A few ancient authorities read *Your Holy Spirit come upon us and cleanse us.* Other ancient authorities add *Your will be done, on earth as in heaven*   **e** Or *our bread for tomorrow*   **f** Or *us into temptation.* Other ancient authorities add *but rescue us from the evil one* (or *from evil*)

PRAY IT!

Ask and You Shall Receive
Luke 11:5–13

Have you ever asked your parents for something over and over again? They may have replied, "Will you stop asking me?!"

This is one response you will never hear from God. In fact, Jesus tells us to always be persistent in prayer. God wants to hear from us! Too often we hesitate to bring everything inside of us to God. We sort through what we think God wants to hear. Don't be selective! Bring it all to God—the big stuff as well as the little stuff. Be persistent and relentless in seeking God. He will respond (Luke 11:10). But don't be afraid of God's answers. God loves us deeply and will give us good gifts (Luke 11:11-13). Don't hold back out of fear—God has your best in mind.

ceives, and everyone who searches finds, and for everyone who knocks, the door will be opened. [11]Is there anyone among you who, if your child asks for[a] a fish, will give a snake instead of a fish? [12]Or if the child asks for an egg, will give a scorpion? [13]If you then, who are evil, know how to give good gifts to your children, how much more will the heavenly Father give the Holy Spirit[b] to those who ask him!"

Jesus and Beelzebul

14 Now he was casting out a demon that was mute; when the demon had gone out, the one who had been mute spoke, and the crowds were amazed. [15]But some of them said, "He casts out demons by Beelzebul, the ruler of the demons." [16]Others, to test him, kept demanding from him a sign from heaven. [17]But he knew what they were thinking and said to them, "Every kingdom divided against itself becomes a desert, and house falls on house. [18]If Satan also is divided against himself, how will his kingdom stand? —for you say that I cast out the demons by Beelzebul. [19]Now if I cast out the demons by Beelzebul, by whom do your exorcists[c] cast them out? Therefore they will be your judges. [20]But

if it is by the finger of God that I cast out the demons, then the kingdom of God has come to you. [21]When a strong man, fully armed, guards his castle, his property is safe. [22]But when one stronger than he attacks him and overpowers him, he takes away his armor in which he trusted and divides his plunder. [23]Whoever is not with me is against me, and whoever does not gather with me scatters.

The Return of the Unclean Spirit

24 "When the unclean spirit has gone out of a person, it wanders through waterless regions looking for a resting place, but not finding any, it says, 'I will return to my house from which I came.' [25]When it comes, it finds it swept and put in order. [26]Then it goes and brings seven other spirits more evil than itself, and they enter and live there; and the last state of that person is worse than the first."

True Blessedness

27 While he was saying this, a woman in the crowd raised her voice and said to him, "Blessed is the womb that bore you and the breasts that nursed you!" [28]But he said, "Blessed rather are those who hear the word of God and obey it!"

The Sign of Jonah

29 When the crowds were increasing, he began to say, "This generation is an evil generation; it asks for a sign, but no sign will be given to it except the sign of Jonah. [30]For just as Jonah became a sign to the people of Nineveh, so the Son of Man will be to this generation. [31]The queen of the South will rise at the judgment with the people of this generation and condemn them, because she came from the ends of the earth to listen to the wisdom of Solomon, and see, something greater than Solomon is here! [32]The people of Nineveh will rise up at the judgment with this generation and condemn it, because they repented at the proclamation of Jonah, and see, something greater than Jonah is here!

a Other ancient authorities add *bread, will give a stone; or if your child asks for*   b Other ancient authorities read *the Father give the Holy Spirit from heaven*
c Gk *sons*

The Light of the Body

33 "No one after lighting a lamp puts it in a cellar,[a] but on the lampstand so that those who enter may see the light. [34]Your eye is the lamp of your body. If your eye is healthy, your whole body is full of light; but if it is not healthy, your body is full of darkness. [35]Therefore consider whether the light in you is not darkness. [36]If then your whole body is full of light, with no part of it in darkness, it will be as full of light as when a lamp gives you light with its rays."

Jesus Denounces Pharisees and Lawyers

37 While he was speaking, a Pharisee invited him to dine with him; so he went in and took his place at the table. [38]The Pharisee was amazed to see that he did not first wash before dinner. [39]Then the Lord said to him, "Now you Pharisees clean the outside of the cup and of the dish, but inside you are full of greed and wickedness. [40]You fools! Did not the one who made the outside make the inside also? [41]So give for alms those things that are within; and see, everything will be clean for you.

42 "But woe to you Pharisees! For you tithe mint and rue and herbs of all kinds, and neglect justice and the love of God; it is these you ought to have practiced, without neglecting the others. [43]Woe to you Pharisees! For you love to have the seat of honor in the synagogues and to be greeted with respect in the marketplaces. [44]Woe to you! For you are like unmarked graves, and people walk over them without realizing it."

45 One of the lawyers answered him, "Teacher, when you say these things, you insult us too." [46]And he said, "Woe also to you lawyers! For you load people with burdens hard to bear, and you yourselves do not lift a finger to ease them. [47]Woe to you! For you build the tombs of the prophets whom your ancestors killed. [48]So you are witnesses and approve of the deeds of your ancestors; for they killed them, and you build their tombs. [49]Therefore also the Wisdom of God said, 'I will send them prophets and apostles, some of whom they will kill and persecute,' [50]so that this generation may be charged with the blood of all the prophets shed since the foundation of the world, [51]from the blood of Abel to the blood of Zechariah, who perished between the altar and the sanctuary. Yes, I tell you, it will be charged against this generation. [52]Woe to you lawyers! For you have taken away the key of knowledge; you did not enter yourselves, and you hindered those who were entering."

53 When he went outside, the scribes and the Pharisees began to be very hostile toward him and to cross-examine him about many things, [54]lying in wait for him, to catch him in something he might say.

A Warning against Hypocrisy

12 Meanwhile, when the crowd gathered by the thousands, so that they trampled on one another, he began to speak first to his disciples, "Beware of the yeast of the Pharisees, that is, their hypocrisy. [2]Nothing is covered up that will not be uncovered, and nothing secret that will not become known. [3]Therefore whatever you have said in the dark will be heard in the light, and what you have whispered behind closed doors will be proclaimed from the housetops.

Exhortation to Fearless Confession

4 "I tell you, my friends, do not fear those who kill the body, and after that can do nothing more. [5]But I will warn you whom to fear: fear him who, after he has killed, has authority[b] to cast into hell.[c] Yes, I tell you, fear him! [6]Are not five sparrows sold for two pennies? Yet not one of them is forgotten in God's sight. [7]But even the hairs of your head are all counted. Do not be afraid; you are of more value than many sparrows.

8 "And I tell you, everyone who acknowledges me before others, the Son of Man also will acknowledge before the angels of God; [9]but whoever denies me before others will be denied before the angels of God. [10]And everyone who speaks a word against the Son of Man will be forgiven; but whoever blasphemes against the Holy Spirit will not be forgiven. [11]When they bring you before the synagogues, the rulers, and the authorities, do not worry about how[d] you are to defend yourselves or what you are to say; [12]for the Holy Spirit will teach you at that very hour what you ought to say."

The Parable of the Rich Fool

13 Someone in the crowd said to him, "Teacher, tell my brother to divide the family inheritance with me." [14]But he said to him, "Friend, who set me to be a judge or arbitrator over you?" [15]And he said to them, "Take care! Be on your guard against all kinds of greed; for one's life does not consist in the abundance of possessions." [16]Then he told them a par-

---

a Other ancient authorities add *or under the bushel basket*   b Or *power*   c Gk *Gehenna*   d Other ancient authorities add *or what*

LIVE IT!

The Greed Trap · Luke 12:13–21

It's easy to let our possessions possess us—driving us to wanting more and more. This is the greed trap Jesus warns against in **Luke 12:13–21**.

So how do we get trapped in letting our stuff become our identity?

Advertisements play a role in convincing us we need to own everything that is new and improved (see "Study It: New and Improved!" near Ecclesiastes 1:1–11). Our own insecurities also play a role—the more we possess, the more important we tend to think we are. Greed is a sin that is addictive (Luke 12:18). Instead of feeling fulfilled by attaining the things we crave, we feel that what we have still isn't enough. It's a vicious cycle.

The solution to greed is simple. It's sharing—that value we learned when we were very small. Sharing our time and possessions makes us "rich toward God" (Luke 12:21).

- Where do you see the sin of greed at work in your world? In your own life?
- Where and when could you, your friends, and your family share more?

STUDY IT!

Trust God
Luke 12:22–34

It sounds good—trust God and you'll have everything you need.

Don't worry about the everyday things like clothing, food, and shelter, or even things like work, grades in school, or relationships. He's got it covered. But isn't that a bit naive? Trusting God for all that seems risky.

Indeed, putting our faith in God is a risk, but it's one that comes with the potential for great reward. Jesus tells us to not worry so much about everyday needs. Instead, we should look around for the simple signs that show God's care for us. If we do so, we won't fail to notice the many ways God is already working in our lives. In **Luke 12:33**, God's promise is not that every need or desire will be met, but that by trusting God we will be storing up treasure that cannot be destroyed by this world. You could spend your whole life worrying and working toward great wealth, which could all be stolen or destroyed in an instant. Instead, God wants us to give to the poor and build an eternal treasure that will last forever (Luke 12:34).

able: "The land of a rich man produced abundantly. [17] And he thought to himself, 'What should I do, for I have no place to store my crops?' [18] Then he said, 'I will do this: I will pull down my barns and build larger ones, and there I will store all my grain and my goods. [19] And I will say to my soul, Soul, you have ample goods laid up for many years; relax, eat, drink, be merry.' [20] But God said to him, 'You fool! This very night your life is being demanded of you. And the things you have prepared, whose will they be?' [21] So it is with those who store up treasures for themselves but are not rich toward God."

Do Not Worry

22 He said to his disciples, "Therefore I tell you, do not worry about your life, what you will eat, or about your body, what you will wear. [23] For life is more than food, and the body more than clothing. [24] Consider the ravens: they neither sow nor reap, they have neither storehouse nor barn, and yet God feeds them. Of how much more value are you than the birds! [25] And can any of you by worrying add a single hour to your span of life?[a] [26] If then you are not able to do so small a thing as that, why do you worry about the rest? [27] Consider the lilies, how they grow: they neither toil nor spin;[b] yet I tell you, even Solomon in all his glory was not clothed like one of these. [28] But if God so clothes the grass of the field, which is alive today and tomorrow is thrown into the oven, how much more will he clothe you—you of little faith! [29] And do not keep striving for what you are to eat and what you are to drink, and do not

a Or *add a cubit to your stature*   b Other ancient authorities read *Consider the lilies; they neither spin nor weave*

keep worrying. [30]For it is the nations of the world that strive after all these things, and your Father knows that you need them. [31]Instead, strive for his[a] kingdom, and these things will be given to you as well.

32 "Do not be afraid, little flock, for it is your Father's good pleasure to give you the kingdom. [33]Sell your possessions, and give alms. Make purses for yourselves that do not wear out, an unfailing treasure in heaven, where no thief comes near and no moth destroys. [34]For where your treasure is, there your heart will be also.

Watchful Slaves

35 "Be dressed for action and have your lamps lit; [36]be like those who are waiting for their master to return from the wedding banquet, so that they may open the door for him as soon as he comes and knocks. [37]Blessed are those slaves whom the master finds alert when he comes; truly I tell you, he will fasten his belt and have them sit down to eat, and he will come and serve them. [38]If he comes during the middle of the night, or near dawn, and finds them so, blessed are those slaves.

39 "But know this: if the owner of the house had known at what hour the thief was coming, he[b] would not have let his house be broken into. [40]You also must be ready, for the Son of Man is coming at an unexpected hour."

The Faithful or the Unfaithful Slave

41 Peter said, "Lord, are you telling this parable for us or for everyone?" [42]And the Lord said, "Who then is the faithful and prudent manager whom his master will put in charge of his slaves, to give them their allowance of food at the proper time? [43]Blessed is that slave whom his master will find at work when he arrives. [44]Truly I tell you, he will put that one in charge of all his possessions. [45]But if that slave says to himself, 'My master is delayed in coming,' and if he begins to beat the other slaves, men and women, and to eat and drink and get drunk, [46]the master of that slave will come on a day when he does not expect him and at an hour that he does not know, and will cut him in pieces,[c] and put him with the unfaithful. [47]That slave who knew what his master wanted, but did not prepare himself or do what was wanted, will receive a severe beating. [48]But the one who did not know and did what deserved a beating will receive a light beating. From everyone to whom much has been given, much will be required; and from the one to whom much has been entrusted, even more will be demanded.

Jesus the Cause of Division

49 "I came to bring fire to the earth, and how I wish it were already kindled! [50]I have a baptism with which to be baptized, and what stress I am under until it is completed! [51]Do you think that I have come to bring peace to the earth? No, I tell you, but rather division! [52]From now on five in one household will be divided, three against two and two against three; [53]they will be divided:

> father against son
>   and son against father,
> mother against daughter
>   and daughter against mother,
> mother-in-law against her
>   daughter-in-law
>   and daughter-in-law against
>   mother-in-law."

Interpreting the Time

54 He also said to the crowds, "When you see a cloud rising in the west, you immediately say, 'It is going to rain'; and so it happens. [55]And when you see the south wind blowing, you say, 'There will be scorching heat'; and it happens. [56]You hypocrites! You know how to interpret the appearance of earth and sky, but why do you not know how to interpret the present time?

Settling with Your Opponent

57 "And why do you not judge for yourselves what is right? [58]Thus, when you go with your accuser before a magistrate, on the way make an effort to settle the case,[d] or you may be dragged before the judge, and the judge hand you over to the officer, and the officer throw you in prison. [59]I tell you, you will never get out until you have paid the very last penny."

13 Repent or Perish

At that very time there were some present who told him about the Galileans whose blood Pilate had mingled with their sacrifices. [2]He asked them, "Do you think that because these Galileans suffered in this way they were worse sinners than all other Galileans? [3]No, I tell you; but unless you repent, you will all perish as they did. [4]Or those

---

[a] Other ancient authorities read *God's*   [b] Other ancient authorities add *would have watched and*   [c] Or *cut him off*   [d] Gk *settle with him*

eighteen who were killed when the tower of Siloam fell on them—do you think that they were worse offenders than all the others living in Jerusalem? [5]No, I tell you; but unless you repent, you will all perish just as they did."

The Parable of the Barren Fig Tree

6 Then he told this parable: "A man had a fig tree planted in his vineyard; and he came looking for fruit on it and found none. [7]So he said to the gardener, 'See here! For three years I have come looking for fruit on this fig tree, and still I find none. Cut it down! Why should it be wasting the soil?' [8]He replied, 'Sir, let it alone for one more year, until I dig around it and put manure on it. [9]If it bears fruit next year, well and good; but if not, you can cut it down.' "

Jesus Heals a Crippled Woman

10 Now he was teaching in one of the synagogues on the sabbath. [11]And just then there appeared a woman with a spirit that had crippled her for eighteen years. She was bent over and was quite unable to stand up straight. [12]When Jesus saw her, he called her over and said, "Woman, you are set free from your ailment." [13]When he laid his hands on her, immediately she stood up straight and began praising God. [14]But the leader of the synagogue, indignant because Jesus had cured on the sabbath, kept saying to the crowd, "There are six days on which work ought to be done; come on those days and be cured, and not on the sabbath day." [15]But the Lord answered him and said, "You hypocrites! Does not each of you on the sabbath untie his ox or his donkey from the manger, and lead it away to give it water? [16]And ought not this woman, a daughter of Abraham whom Satan bound for eighteen long years, be set free from this bondage on the sabbath day?" [17]When he said this, all his opponents were put to shame; and the entire crowd was rejoicing at all the wonderful things that he was doing.

The Parable of the Mustard Seed

18 He said therefore, "What is the kingdom of God like? And to what should I compare it? [19]It is like a mustard seed that someone took and sowed in the garden; it grew and became a tree, and the birds of the air made nests in its branches."

The Parable of the Yeast

20 And again he said, "To what should I compare the kingdom of God? [21]It is like yeast that a woman took and mixed in with[a] three measures of flour until all of it was leavened."

The Narrow Door

22 Jesus[b] went through one town and village after another, teaching as he made his way to Jerusalem. [23]Someone asked him, "Lord, will only a few be saved?" He said to them, [24]"Strive to enter through the narrow door; for many, I tell you, will try to enter and will not be able. [25]When once the owner of the house has got up and shut the door, and you begin to stand outside and to knock at the door, saying, 'Lord, open to us,' then in reply he will say to you, 'I do not know where you come from.' [26]Then you will begin to say, 'We ate and drank with you, and you taught in our streets.' [27]But he will say, 'I do not know where you come from; go away from me, all you evildoers!' [28]There will be weeping and gnashing of teeth when you see Abraham and Isaac and Jacob and all the prophets in the kingdom of God, and you yourselves thrown out. [29]Then people will come from east and west, from north and south, and will eat in the kingdom of God. [30]Indeed, some are last who will be first, and some are first who will be last."

The Lament over Jerusalem

31 At that very hour some Pharisees came and said to him, "Get away from here, for Herod wants to kill you." [32]He said to them, "Go and tell that fox for me,[c] 'Listen, I am casting out demons and performing cures today and tomorrow, and on the third day I finish my work. [33]Yet today, tomorrow, and the next day I must be on my way, because it is impossible for a prophet to be killed outside of Jerusalem.' [34]Jerusalem, Jerusalem, the city that kills the prophets and stones those who are sent to it! How often have I desired to gather your children together as a hen gathers her brood under her wings, and you were not willing! [35]See, your house is left to you. And I tell you, you will not see me until the time comes when[d] you say, 'Blessed is the one who comes in the name of the Lord.' "

Jesus Heals the Man with Dropsy

14 On one occasion when Jesus[e] was going to the house of a leader of the Pharisees to eat a meal on the sabbath, they were watching him closely. [2]Just then, in front of him, there was a man

---

a Gk *hid in*   b Gk *He*   c Gk lacks *for me*   d Other ancient authorities lack *the time comes when*   e Gk *he*

who had dropsy. ³And Jesus asked the lawyers and Pharisees, "Is it lawful to cure people on the sabbath, or not?" ⁴But they were silent. So Jesus*a* took him and healed him, and sent him away. ⁵Then he said to them, "If one of you has a child*b* or an ox that has fallen into a well, will you not immediately pull it out on a sabbath day?" ⁶And they could not reply to this.

Humility and Hospitality

7 When he noticed how the guests chose the places of honor, he told them a parable. ⁸"When you are invited by someone to a wedding banquet, do not sit down at the place of honor, in case someone more distinguished than you has been invited by your host; ⁹and the host who invited both of you may come and say to you, 'Give this person your place,' and then in disgrace you would start to take the lowest place. ¹⁰But when you are invited, go and sit down at the lowest place, so that when your host comes, he may say to you, 'Friend, move up higher'; then you will be honored in the presence of all who sit at the table with you. ¹¹For all who exalt themselves will be humbled, and those who humble themselves will be exalted."

12 He said also to the one who had invited him, "When you give a luncheon or a dinner, do not invite your friends or your brothers or your relatives or rich neighbors, in case they may invite you in return, and you would be repaid. ¹³But when you give a banquet, invite the poor, the crippled, the lame, and the blind. ¹⁴And you will be blessed, because they cannot repay you, for you will be repaid at the resurrection of the righteous."

The Parable of the Great Dinner

15 One of the dinner guests, on hearing this, said to him, "Blessed is anyone who will eat bread in the kingdom of God!" ¹⁶Then Jesus*a* said to him, "Someone gave a great dinner and invited many. ¹⁷At the time for the dinner he sent his slave to say to those who had been invited, 'Come; for everything is ready now.' ¹⁸But they all alike began to make excuses. The first said to him, 'I have bought a piece of land, and I must go out and see it; please accept my regrets.' ¹⁹Another said, 'I have bought five yoke of oxen, and I am going to try them out; please accept my regrets.' ²⁰Another said, 'I have just been married, and therefore I cannot come.' ²¹So the slave returned and reported this to his master. Then the owner of the house became angry and said to his slave, 'Go out at once into the streets and lanes of the town and bring in the poor, the crippled, the blind, and the lame.' ²²And the slave said, 'Sir, what you ordered has been done, and there is still room.' ²³Then the master said to the slave, 'Go out into the roads and lanes, and compel people to come in, so that my house may be filled. ²⁴For I tell you,*c* none of those who were invited will taste my dinner.' "

The Cost of Discipleship

25 Now large crowds were traveling with him; and he turned and said to them, ²⁶"Whoever comes to me and does not hate father and mother, wife and children, brothers and sisters, yes, and even life itself, cannot be my disciple. ²⁷Whoever does not carry the cross and follow me cannot be my disciple. ²⁸For which of you, intending to build a tower, does not first sit down and estimate the cost, to see whether he has enough to complete it? ²⁹Otherwise, when he has laid a foundation and is not able to finish, all who see it will begin to ridicule him, ³⁰saying, 'This fellow began to build and was not able to finish.' ³¹Or what king, going out to wage war against an-

God's Invitation List · Luke 14:7–24

Jesus uses the image of a banquet to describe the inclusive nature of God's grace. Jesus' point is not about what is on the menu, but who is on the invitation list: the weak, the poor, and the little ones. These are the people who will be in heaven as guests of honor at a feast. It's a beautiful picture of God's grace and love that includes everyone, not just those the world deems worthy.

- Who is on your "invitation list"?
- Who do you spend time with?
- Who are the people you reach out to and serve?

---

a Gk *he*   b Other ancient authorities read *a donkey*   c The Greek word for *you* here is plural

other king, will not sit down first and consider whether he is able with ten thousand to oppose the one who comes against him with twenty thousand? ³²If he cannot, then, while the other is still far away, he sends a delegation and asks for the terms of peace. ³³So therefore, none of you can become my disciple if you do not give up all your possessions.

Making a Difference
Luke 14:34–35

Have you ever made a recipe and forgot the salt? The result is often not just bland, but gross! Followers of Christ are to be the salt of the world, bringing God's flavor to everything. Think about your saltiness, and say this prayer:

Lord, I want to be where I can make a difference, where I can enrich and add flavor to the lives of others by bringing them the good news of your love and justice.

Help me to discover all the gifts you have given me, so that I can help turn this world around—starting with my own life! Show me how to keep my commitment fresh as I serve you each day. Amen.

About Salt

34 "Salt is good; but if salt has lost its taste, how can its saltiness be restored?[a] ³⁵It is fit neither for the soil nor for the manure pile; they throw it away. Let anyone with ears to hear listen!"

15 The Parable of the Lost Sheep

Now all the tax collectors and sinners were coming near to listen to him. ²And the Pharisees and the scribes were grumbling and saying, "This fellow welcomes sinners and eats with them."

3 So he told them this parable: ⁴"Which one of you, having a hundred sheep and losing one of them, does not leave the ninety-nine in the wilderness and go after the one that is lost until he finds it? ⁵When he has found it, he lays it on his shoulders and rejoices. ⁶And when he comes home, he calls together his friends and neighbors, saying to them, 'Rejoice with me, for I have found my sheep that was lost.' ⁷Just so, I tell you, there will be more joy in heaven over one sinner who repents than over ninety-nine righteous persons who need no repentance.

The Parable of the Lost Coin

8 "Or what woman having ten silver coins,[b] if she loses one of them, does not light a lamp, sweep the house, and search carefully until she finds it? ⁹When she has found it, she calls together her friends and neighbors, saying, 'Rejoice with me, for I have found the coin that I had lost.' ¹⁰Just so, I tell you, there is joy in the presence of the angels of God over one sinner who repents."

Lost and Found · Luke 15:1–7

Lost. It's a scary place to be, filled with frustration, fear, and loneliness. We can all identify with the feelings of being lost . . . which means everyone can also identify with being found! What a wonderful feeling it is to finally see the familiar landmark, or to make the right turn to the main road, or to have someone help you get your life back on track.

If you identify with that lone sheep who strayed from the flock (Luke 15:1-7), remember that God never stops looking for you. Stop and listen for God's call, so God can embrace you and celebrate your return.

• What recent experiences have led you astray and made you feel lost?

• Where do you need to repent and ask for forgiveness?

• Take some time to picture God holding you tight and lifting you high onto his shoulders as a shepherd who celebrates the return of his sheep.

---

a Or *how can it be used for seasoning?* b Gk *drachmas*, each worth about a day's wage for a laborer

The Parable of the Prodigal and His Brother

11 Then Jesus[a] said, "There was a man who had two sons. [12] The younger of them said to his father, 'Father, give me the share of the property that will belong to me.' So he divided his property between them. [13] A few days later the younger son gathered all he had and traveled to a distant country, and there he squandered his property in dissolute living. [14] When he had spent everything, a severe famine took place throughout that country, and he began to be in need. [15] So he went and hired himself out to one of the citizens of that country, who sent him to his fields to feed the pigs. [16] He would gladly have filled himself with[b] the pods that the pigs were eating; and no one gave him anything. [17] But when he came to himself he said, 'How many of my father's hired hands have bread enough and to spare, but here I am dying of hunger! [18] I will get up and go to my father, and I will say to him, "Father, I have sinned against heaven and before you; [19] I am no longer worthy to be called your son; treat me like one of your hired hands." ' [20] So he set off and went to his father. But while he was still far off, his father saw him and was filled with compassion; he ran and put his arms around him and kissed him. [21] Then the son said to him, 'Father, I have sinned against heaven and before you; I am no longer worthy to be called your son.'[c] [22] But the father said to his slaves, 'Quickly, bring out a robe—the best one—and put it on him; put a ring on his finger and sandals on his feet. [23] And get the fatted calf and kill it, and let us eat and celebrate; [24] for this son of mine was dead and is alive again; he was lost and is found!' And they began to celebrate.

25 "Now his elder son was in the field; and when he came and approached the house, he heard music and dancing. [26] He called one of the slaves and asked what was going on. [27] He replied, 'Your brother has come, and your father has killed the fatted calf, because he has got him back safe and sound.' [28] Then he became angry and refused to go in. His father came out and began to plead with him. [29] But he answered his father, 'Listen! For all these years I have been working like a slave for you, and I have never disobeyed your command; yet you have never given me even a young goat so that I might celebrate with

God's Limitless Love · Luke 15:11–32

Read the story of the prodigal son in **Luke 15:11–32**. Think about the story for a moment. What does it really say about God? Not only is the father not upset about his son wasting all his money, but the father is incredibly happy to see his son return home. He runs to meet him! Picture it—this man so eager to welcome his son that he runs down the road toward him and then hugs and kisses him. After all the pain the son has caused, doesn't the father's excitement seem a bit excessive?

But it doesn't end there. Despite the son's apology, which the father ignores, the father tells his servants to throw a huge party—to go all out for his son. This seems almost too much to believe, doesn't it? Music, dancing, expensive robes and rings, and a feast for everyone! What's going on here? If we're honest, many of us actually agree with the older brother in thinking that the prodigal doesn't deserve the welcome he receives. And we're right—he doesn't deserve it.

Luke is trying to show us, in the most visual way possible, that there is simply no limit to God's love for us. It is not a conditional love. It is an extravagant, outrageous love. God doesn't hold back. How can we refuse such boundless love? How can we hold back from such divine eagerness? The next time you think you have separated yourself from God's love, picture yourself walking down a road and God running toward you with open arms. What is your response?

---

a Gk *he*   **b** Other ancient authorities read *filled his stomach with*   **c** Other ancient authorities add *Treat me like one of your hired servants*

my friends. [30]But when this son of yours came back, who has devoured your property with prostitutes, you killed the fatted calf for him!' [31]Then the father[a] said to him, 'Son, you are always with me, and all that is mine is yours. [32]But we had to celebrate and rejoice, because this brother of yours was dead and has come to life; he was lost and has been found.' "

16 The Parable of the Dishonest Manager

Then Jesus[a] said to the disciples, "There was a rich man who had a manager, and charges were brought to him that this man was squandering his property. [2]So he summoned him and said to him, 'What is this that I hear about you? Give me an accounting of your management, because you cannot be my manager any longer.' [3]Then the manager said to himself, 'What will I do, now that my master is taking the position away from me? I am not strong enough to dig, and I am ashamed to beg. [4]I have decided what to do so that, when I am dismissed as manager, people may welcome me into their homes.' [5]So, summoning his master's debtors one by one, he asked the first, 'How much do you owe my master?' [6]He answered, 'A hundred jugs of olive oil.' He said to him, 'Take your bill, sit down quickly, and make it fifty.' [7]Then he asked another, 'And how much do you owe?' He replied, 'A hundred containers of wheat.' He said to him, 'Take your bill and make it eighty.' [8]And his master commended the dishonest manager because he had acted shrewdly; for the children of this age are more shrewd in dealing with their own generation than are the children of light. [9]And I tell you, make friends for yourselves by means of dishonest wealth[b] so that when it is gone, they may welcome you into the eternal homes.[c]

[10] "Whoever is faithful in a very little is faithful also in much; and whoever is dishonest in a very little is dishonest also in much. [11]If then you have not been faithful with the dishonest wealth,[c] who will entrust to you the true riches? [12]And if you have not been faithful with what belongs to another, who will give you what is your own? [13]No slave can serve two masters; for a slave will either hate the one and love the other, or be devoted to the one and despise the other. You cannot serve God and wealth."[b]

The Law and the Kingdom of God

14 The Pharisees, who were lovers of money, heard all this, and they ridiculed him. [15]So he said to them, "You are those who justify yourselves in the sight of others; but God knows your hearts; for what is prized by human beings is an abomination in the sight of God.

16 "The law and the prophets were in effect until John came; since then the good news of the kingdom of God is proclaimed, and everyone tries to enter it by force.[d] [17]But it is easier for heaven and earth to pass away, than for one stroke of a letter in the law to be dropped.

18 "Anyone who divorces his wife and marries another commits adultery, and whoever marries a woman divorced from her husband commits adultery.

The Rich Man and Lazarus

19 "There was a rich man who was dressed in purple and fine linen and who feasted sumptuously every day. [20]And at his gate lay a poor man named Lazarus, covered with sores, [21]who longed to satisfy

STUDY IT!

Understanding Parables
Luke 16:1–13

Jesus often used parables or stories in his teaching. In some of Jesus' parables, the characters represent someone else. For example, in the parable of the prodigal son (Luke 15:11-32), the forgiving father represents God. In other parables, the characters are examples for us to follow, as in the parable of the good Samaritan (Luke 10:29-37). However, in some parables, the characters neither represent God nor are role models for us.

For example, in the parable of the dishonest steward (Luke 16:1-13), the master doesn't represent God. And Jesus is not encouraging us to be dishonest like the manager. Jesus is simply saying that we need to be even more clever than dishonest people in using our money and talents for the sake of the gospel. In each parable there is a key lesson for us to learn and apply to our lives.

---

a Gk he   b Gk mammon   c Gk tents   d Or everyone is strongly urged to enter it

his hunger with what fell from the rich man's table; even the dogs would come and lick his sores. ²²The poor man died and was carried away by the angels to be with Abraham.^a The rich man also died and was buried. ²³In Hades, where he was being tormented, he looked up and saw Abraham far away with Lazarus by his side.^b ²⁴He called out, 'Father Abraham, have mercy on me, and send Lazarus to dip the tip of his finger in water and cool my tongue; for I am in agony in these flames.' ²⁵But Abraham said, 'Child, remember that during your lifetime you received your good things, and Lazarus in like manner evil things; but now he is comforted here, and you are in agony. ²⁶Besides all this, between you and us a great chasm has been fixed, so that those who might want to pass from here to you cannot do so, and no one can cross from there to us.' ²⁷He said, 'Then, father, I beg you to send him to my father's house— ²⁸for I have five brothers—that he may warn them, so that they will not also come into this place of torment.' ²⁹Abraham replied, 'They have Moses and the prophets; they should listen to them.' ³⁰He said, 'No, father Abraham; but if someone goes to them from the dead, they will repent.' ³¹He said to him, 'If they do not listen to Moses and the prophets, neither will they be convinced even if someone rises from the dead.' "

Some Sayings of Jesus

17 Jesus^c said to his disciples, "Occasions for stumbling are bound to come, but woe to anyone by whom they come! ²It would be better for you if a millstone were hung around your neck and you were thrown into the sea than for you to cause one of these little ones to stumble. ³Be on your

guard! If another disciple^d sins, you must rebuke the offender, and if there is repentance, you must forgive. ⁴And if the same person sins against you seven times a day, and turns back to you seven times and says, 'I repent,' you must forgive."

5 The apostles said to the Lord, "Increase our faith!" ⁶The Lord replied, "If you had faith the size of a^e mustard seed, you could say to this mulberry tree, 'Be uprooted and planted in the sea,' and it would obey you.

7 "Who among you would say to your slave who has just come in from plowing or tending sheep in the field, 'Come here at once and take your place at the table'? ⁸Would you not rather say to him, 'Prepare supper for me, put on your apron and serve me while I eat and drink; later you may eat and drink'? ⁹Do you thank the slave for doing what was commanded? ¹⁰So you also, when you have done all that you were ordered to do, say, 'We are worthless slaves; we have done only what we ought to have done!' "

Jesus Cleanses Ten Lepers

11 On the way to Jerusalem Jesus^f was going through the region between Samaria and Galilee. ¹²As he entered a village, ten lepers^g approached him. Keeping their distance, ¹³they called out, saying, "Jesus, Master, have mercy on us!" ¹⁴When he saw them, he said to them, "Go and show yourselves to the priests." And as they went, they were made clean. ¹⁵Then one of them, when he saw that he was healed, turned back, praising God with a loud voice. ¹⁶He prostrated himself at Jesus'^h feet and thanked him. And he was a Samaritan. ¹⁷Then Jesus asked, "Were not ten made clean? But the other nine, where are they? ¹⁸Was none of them found to return and

Humility and Thankfulness · Luke 17:1–19

Humility and thankfulness—two character traits that don't come easily. But Jesus makes a point of telling stories in Luke that illustrate the importance of both. First, he lets his disciples know that when they have done all he asks, they should not feel proud or self-righteous. Instead, they should remember that they have only done what they were instructed by Jesus to do. He then tells the story of ten lepers who are healed, but only one returns to say thank you.

- How are you doing in your own life with humility and thankfulness?
- Think of an area where you need to practice humility, and a way to remind yourself when tempted with pride.
- Think of something you need to say thank you for—either to God or someone else in your life.

^a Gk to Abraham's bosom ^b Gk in his bosom ^c Gk He ^d Gk your brother ^e Gk faith as a grain of ^f Gk he ^g The terms leper and leprosy can refer to several diseases ^h Gk his

give praise to God except this foreigner?" [19]Then he said to him, "Get up and go on your way; your faith has made you well."

The Coming of the Kingdom

20 Once Jesus[a] was asked by the Pharisees when the kingdom of God was coming, and he answered, "The kingdom of God is not coming with things that can be observed; [21]nor will they say, 'Look, here it is!' or 'There it is!' For, in fact, the kingdom of God is among[b] you."

22 Then he said to the disciples, "The days are coming when you will long to see one of the days of the Son of Man, and you will not see it. [23]They will say to you, 'Look there!' or 'Look here!' Do not go, do not set off in pursuit. [24]For as the lightning flashes and lights up the sky from one side to the other, so will the Son of Man be in his day.[c] [25]But first he must endure much suffering and be rejected by this generation. [26]Just as it was in the days of Noah, so too it will be in the days of the Son of Man. [27]They were eating and drinking, and marrying and being given in marriage, until the day Noah entered the ark, and the flood came and destroyed all of them. [28]Likewise, just as it was in the days of Lot: they were eating and drinking, buying and selling, planting and building, [29]but on the day that Lot left Sodom, it rained fire and sulfur from heaven and destroyed all of them [30]—it will be like that on the day that the Son of Man is revealed. [31]On that day, anyone on the housetop who has belongings in the house must not come down to take them away; and likewise anyone in the field must not turn back. [32]Remember Lot's wife. [33]Those who try to make their life secure will lose it, but those who lose their life will keep it. [34]I tell you, on that night there will be two in one bed; one will be taken and the other left. [35]There will be two women grinding meal together; one will be taken and the other left."[d] [37]Then they asked him, "Where, Lord?" He said to them, "Where the corpse is, there the vultures will gather."

18 The Parable of the Widow and the Unjust Judge

Then Jesus[a] told them a parable about their need to pray always and not to lose heart. [2]He said, "In a certain city there was a judge who neither feared God nor had respect for people. [3]In that city there was a widow who kept coming to him and saying, 'Grant me justice against my opponent.' [4]For a while he refused; but later he said to himself, 'Though I have no fear of God and no respect for anyone, [5]yet because this widow keeps bothering me, I will grant her justice, so that she may not wear me out by continually coming.' "[e] [6]And the Lord said, "Listen to what the unjust judge says. [7]And will not God grant justice to his chosen ones who cry to him day and night? Will he delay long in helping them? [8]I tell you, he will quickly grant justice to them. And yet, when the Son of Man comes, will he find faith on earth?"

The Parable of the Pharisee and the Tax Collector

9 He also told this parable to some who trusted

PRAY IT!

Hellooooo . . . Can You Hear Me?
Luke 18:1–8

A poor widow pleads for help. An unjust judge ignores her until he is so sick of her that he decides to act just to get rid of her. It's not a pretty picture of justice. But Jesus uses this story to give us a clear picture of our just and loving judge—God, who hears our cries and acts quickly. It may not always feel as though God is answering our prayers as quickly as we'd like, but Jesus reassures us that God is listening and acting.

Dear Jesus, you remind us to pray always and not to lose hope when faced with injustice. I need to hear that too. Sometimes it seems as if I pray and pray, but you are not answering. But you have promised to answer—help me to be patient.

I know I have to be willing to look and listen for your response. I know I have to pray always, not just in times of need. I know I need to share my daily life with you. Help me to do these things I know I need to do. Help me to trust your justice, timing, and amazing love. Amen.

---

a Gk he b Or within c Other ancient authorities lack in his day d Other ancient authorities add verse 36, "Two will be in the field; one will be taken and the other left." e Or so that she may not finally come and slap me in the face

in themselves that they were righteous and regarded others with contempt: [10]"Two men went up to the temple to pray, one a Pharisee and the other a tax collector. [11]The Pharisee, standing by himself, was praying thus, 'God, I thank you that I am not like other people: thieves, rogues, adulterers, or even like this tax collector. [12]I fast twice a week; I give a tenth of all my income.' [13]But the tax collector, standing far off, would not even look up to heaven, but was beating his breast and saying, 'God, be merciful to me, a sinner!' [14]I tell you, this man went down to his home justified rather than the other; for all who exalt themselves will be humbled, but all who humble themselves will be exalted."

Jesus Blesses Little Children

15 People were bringing even infants to him that he might touch them; and when the disciples saw it, they sternly ordered them not to do it. [16]But Jesus called for them and said, "Let the little children come to me, and do not stop them; for it is to such as these that the kingdom of God belongs. [17]Truly I tell you, whoever does not receive the kingdom of God as a little child will never enter it."

The Rich Ruler

18 A certain ruler asked him, "Good Teacher, what must I do to inherit eternal life?" [19]Jesus said to him, "Why do you call me good? No one is good but God alone. [20]You know the commandments: 'You shall not commit adultery; You shall not mur-der; You shall not steal; You shall not bear false witness; Honor your father and mother.' " [21]He replied, "I have kept all these since my youth." [22]When Jesus heard this, he said to him, "There is still one thing lacking. Sell all that you own and distribute the money[a] to the poor, and you will have treasure in heaven; then come, follow me." [23]But when he heard this, he became sad; for he was very rich. [24]Jesus looked at him and said, "How hard it is for those who have wealth to enter the kingdom of God! [25]Indeed, it is easier for a camel to go through the eye of a needle than for someone who is rich to enter the kingdom of God."

26 Those who heard it said, "Then who can be saved?" [27]He replied, "What is impossible for mortals is possible for God."

28 Then Peter said, "Look, we have left our homes and followed you." [29]And he said to them, "Truly I tell you, there is no one who has left house or wife or brothers or parents or children, for the sake of the kingdom of God, [30]who will not get back very much more in this age, and in the age to come eternal life."

A Third Time Jesus Foretells His Death and Resurrection

31 Then he took the twelve aside and said to them, "See, we are going up to Jerusalem, and everything that is written about the Son of Man by the prophets will be accomplished. [32]For he will be handed over to the Gentiles; and he will be mocked

The Loaded Question · Luke 18:18–30

If you ask a loaded question, you should expect a loaded answer, especially if you're talking to God! Picture the rich ruler in **Luke 18:18–30**, who devoutly followed the commandments all his life. After hearing Jesus talk about the kingdom of God, he eagerly asks Jesus, "What must I do to inherit eternal life?" (Luke 18:18).

Jesus answers, "Sell all that you own and distribute the money to the poor" (Luke 18:22). It must have felt like a blow. Jesus asked for a radical commitment from this rich ruler, just as Jesus asks for a radical commitment from us. As often happens in Luke's portrayal of Jesus, that radical commitment has something to do with wealth and those who are poor. If we dare to ask the loaded question, "What must I do?" we must be prepared to unload something too. Our human tendency is to hoard our money and our material goods. But with God's help (Luke 18:27), we can become generous to those in need. And Jesus promises that the treasure we give up will be restored, even multiplied, in heaven (Luke 18:22, 29–30).

a Gk lacks *the money*

and insulted and spat upon. [33]After they have flogged him, they will kill him, and on the third day he will rise again." [34]But they understood nothing about all these things; in fact, what he said was hidden from them, and they did not grasp what was said.

Jesus Heals a Blind Beggar Near Jericho

35 As he approached Jericho, a blind man was sitting by the roadside begging. [36]When he heard a crowd going by, he asked what was happening. [37]They told him, "Jesus of Nazareth[a] is passing by." [38]Then he shouted, "Jesus, Son of David, have mercy on me!" [39]Those who were in front sternly ordered him to be quiet; but he shouted even more loudly, "Son of David, have mercy on me!" [40]Jesus stood still and ordered the man to be brought to him; and when he came near, he asked him, [41]"What do you want me to do for you?" He said, "Lord, let me see again." [42]Jesus said to him, "Receive your sight; your faith has saved you." [43]Immediately he regained his sight and followed him, glorifying God; and all the people, when they saw it, praised God.

Jesus and Zacchaeus

19 He entered Jericho and was passing through it. [2]A man was there named Zacchaeus; he was a chief tax collector and was rich. [3]He was trying to see who Jesus was, but on account of the crowd he could not, because he was short in stature. [4]So he ran ahead and climbed a sycamore tree to see him, because he was going to pass that way. [5]When Jesus came to the place, he looked up and said to him, "Zacchaeus, hurry and come down; for I must stay at your house today." [6]So he hurried down and was happy to welcome him. [7]All who saw it began to grumble and said, "He has gone to be the guest of one who is a sinner." [8]Zacchaeus stood there and said to the Lord, "Look, half of my possessions, Lord, I will give to the poor; and if I have defrauded anyone of anything, I will pay back four times as much." [9]Then Jesus said to him, "Today salvation has come to this house, because he too is a son of Abraham. [10]For the Son of Man came to seek out and to save the lost."

The Parable of the Ten Pounds

11 As they were listening to this, he went on to tell a parable, because he was near Jerusalem, and because they supposed that the kingdom of God was to appear immediately. [12]So he said, "A nobleman went to a distant country to get royal power for himself and then return. [13]He summoned ten of his slaves, and gave them ten pounds,[b] and said to them, 'Do business with these until I come back.' [14]But the citizens of his country hated him and sent a delegation after him, saying, 'We do not want this man to rule over us.' [15]When he returned,

Look Up! · Luke 19:1–10

Jesus looked up. With this simple act, Jesus changed a man's life, inviting him down from the tree and into relationship with him. Why would Jesus choose Zacchaeus, who was hated and despised as a tax collector, to come follow him? Besides his reputation, he was pretty short and did not stand out in a crowd. Perhaps Luke is trying to tell us that our physical attributes, our past history, and other people's perceptions do not figure into God's equation.

After Jesus looks up and notices Zacchaeus, Zacchaeus ends up not only believing in Jesus, but also doing something surprising. He gives away half of his possessions to the poor and promises to pay back four times the amount to anyone he cheated. It's an amazing picture of conversion—a change of heart and behavior. Conversion calls us to act in ways we would not have acted before.

- Jesus has been with you from the start. How have you tried to know him better?
- How does it make you feel knowing that Jesus sees past externals and loves you for who you truly are?
- Who in your own life have you been failing to notice by not taking the time to look up?

---

a Gk *the Nazorean*   b The mina, rendered here by *pound*, was about three months' wages for a laborer

having received royal power, he ordered these slaves, to whom he had given the money, to be summoned so that he might find out what they had gained by trading. [16]The first came forward and said, 'Lord, your pound has made ten more pounds.' [17]He said to him, 'Well done, good slave! Because you have been trustworthy in a very small thing, take charge of ten cities.' [18]Then the second came, saying, 'Lord, your pound has made five pounds.' [19]He said to him, 'And you, rule over five cities.' [20]Then the other came, saying, 'Lord, here is your pound. I wrapped it up in a piece of cloth, [21]for I was afraid of you, because you are a harsh man; you take what you did not deposit, and reap what you did not sow.' [22]He said to him, 'I will judge you by your own words, you wicked slave! You knew, did you, that I was a harsh man, taking what I did not deposit and reaping what I did not sow? [23]Why then did you not put my money into the bank? Then when I returned, I could have collected it with interest.' [24]He said to the bystanders, 'Take the pound from him and give it to the one who has ten pounds.' [25](And they said to him, 'Lord, he has ten pounds!') [26]'I tell you, to all those who have, more will be given; but from those who have nothing, even what they have will be taken away. [27]But as for these enemies of mine who did not want me to be king over them—bring them here and slaughter them in my presence.' "

Jesus' Triumphal Entry into Jerusalem

28 After he had said this, he went on ahead, going up to Jerusalem.

29 When he had come near Bethphage and Bethany, at the place called the Mount of Olives, he sent two of the disciples, [30]saying, "Go into the village ahead of you, and as you enter it you will find tied there a colt that has never been ridden. Untie it and bring it here. [31]If anyone asks you, 'Why are you untying it?' just say this, 'The Lord needs it.' " [32]So those who were sent departed and found it as he had told them. [33]As they were untying the colt, its owners asked them, "Why are you untying the colt?" [34]They said, "The Lord needs it." [35]Then they brought it to Jesus; and after throwing their cloaks on the colt, they set Jesus on it. [36]As he rode along, people kept spreading their cloaks on the road. [37]As he was now approaching the path down from the Mount of Olives, the whole multitude of the disciples began to praise

God joyfully with a loud voice for all the deeds of power that they had seen, [38]saying,

"Blessed is the king
who comes in the name of the Lord!
Peace in heaven,
and glory in the highest heaven!"

[39]Some of the Pharisees in the crowd said to him, "Teacher, order your disciples to stop." [40]He answered, "I tell you, if these were silent, the stones would shout out."

Jesus Weeps over Jerusalem

41 As he came near and saw the city, he wept over it, [42]saying, "If you, even you, had only recognized on this day the things that make for peace! But now they are hidden from your eyes. [43]Indeed,

LIVE IT!

Shouting Stones
Luke 19:28–40

As Jesus enters Jerusalem to celebrate the Passover, the crowd joyfully hails him as the king and Messiah returning to the City of David. They celebrate the amazing things they have seen him do, and quote **Psalm 118:26** in praise. The whole scene fulfills words spoken in the Old Testament about the Messiah (1 Kings 1:33, 44; Zechariah 9:9; 1 Samuel 6:7). But the Pharisees don't like it. When they tell Jesus to command the people to stop, Jesus says the most remarkable thing: "I tell you, if these were silent, the stones would shout out" (Luke 19:40). This amazing statement makes it clear that Jesus' kingship is not based on what people think of him or do to him. Nature itself proclaims that he is God, and worthy of praise.

- Picture yourself in the crowd welcoming Jesus. Does Jesus' arrival fill you with joy and hope?

- How does it make you feel to know that nothing people can say or do can change Jesus' identity and mission to save the world?

Jesus' Tears
Luke 19:41–42

Have you ever been so disappointed in something that you just sat down and cried? Jesus has. In this passage we see Jesus' great disappointment and frustration that he cannot help Jerusalem and its people. The people of Jerusalem do not accept his message of justice and peace, so the temple and Jerusalem are to be destroyed again. Jesus is so upset that he weeps.

We often forget that although Jesus is fully God, he is also fully human and experienced all the things that normal people experience. He enjoyed excitement, laughter, and fun times with friends. He also experienced fear, sadness, and frustration. He was completely human in all things, but sin. We can take comfort in knowing that Jesus understands our human emotions and tears.

the days will come upon you, when your enemies will set up ramparts around you and surround you, and hem you in on every side. [44] They will crush you to the ground, you and your children within you, and they will not leave within you one stone upon another; because you did not recognize the time of your visitation from God."[a]

Jesus Cleanses the Temple

45 Then he entered the temple and began to drive out those who were selling things there; [46] and he said, "It is written,

'My house shall be a house of prayer';
　　but you have made it a den of robbers.'"

47 Every day he was teaching in the temple. The chief priests, the scribes, and the leaders of the people kept looking for a way to kill him; [48] but they did not find anything they could do, for all the people were spellbound by what they heard.

The Authority of Jesus Questioned

20 One day, as he was teaching the people in the temple and telling the good news, the chief priests and the scribes came with the elders [2] and said to him, "Tell us, by what authority are you doing these things? Who is it who gave you this authority?" [3] He answered them, "I will also ask you

Rosa Parks: Standing Against Injustice · Luke 19:45–48

Jesus not only claimed to be God's son, but also took an active stand against injustice, greed, and religious hypocrisy. When Jesus entered the temple in **Luke 19:45** and saw that people had made it a marketplace of greed, he threw them out. The selling of items for sacrifice was an accepted practice, and even considered holy, because it was part of religious law. But Jesus saw the greedy hearts of the people and revealed that it was not a just system of obedience to the law. Naturally, the religious leaders were not happy with Jesus' actions, and they looked for ways to kill him.

Despite the risks, other people have followed Jesus' example of working against injustice, even when it is an accepted part of society. On December 1, 1955, in Selma, Alabama, a black woman named Rosa Parks boarded a public bus and sat in one of the seats toward the front, where only white people were allowed to sit. For her bravery, she was arrested, jailed, and fined. This event triggered a bus boycott that lasted for months and finally put an end to that policy.

Another example of uncommon bravery in the face of injustice occurred on February 1, 1960, in Greensboro, North Carolina, when four first-year college students began a sit-in at a diner that did not allow black people. These students' actions against injustice sparked similar sit-ins across the country. Thousands of courageous people protested against unfair and cruel policies that gave white people privileges denied to black people.

---

a Gk lacks *from God*

a question, and you tell me: ⁴Did the baptism of John come from heaven, or was it of human origin?" ⁵They discussed it with one another, saying, "If we say, 'From heaven,' he will say, 'Why did you not believe him?' ⁶But if we say, 'Of human origin,' all the people will stone us; for they are convinced that John was a prophet." ⁷So they answered that they did not know where it came from. ⁸Then Jesus said to them, "Neither will I tell you by what authority I am doing these things."

The Parable of the Wicked Tenants

9 He began to tell the people this parable: "A man planted a vineyard, and leased it to tenants, and went to another country for a long time. ¹⁰When the season came, he sent a slave to the tenants in order that they might give him his share of the produce of the vineyard; but the tenants beat him and sent him away empty-handed. ¹¹Next he sent another slave; that one also they beat and insulted and sent away empty-handed. ¹²And he sent still a third; this one also they wounded and threw out. ¹³Then the owner of the vineyard said, 'What shall I do? I will send my beloved son; perhaps they will respect him.' ¹⁴But when the tenants saw him, they discussed it among themselves and said, 'This is the heir; let us kill him so that the inheritance may be ours.' ¹⁵So they threw him out of the vineyard and killed him. What then will the owner of the vineyard do to them? ¹⁶He will come and destroy those tenants and give the vineyard to others." When they heard this, they said, "Heaven forbid!" ¹⁷But he looked at them and said, "What then does this text mean:

'The stone that the builders rejected
    has become the cornerstone'?ᵃ

¹⁸Everyone who falls on that stone will be broken to pieces; and it will crush anyone on whom it falls." ¹⁹When the scribes and chief priests realized that he had told this parable against them, they wanted to lay hands on him at that very hour, but they feared the people.

The Question about Paying Taxes

20 So they watched him and sent spies who pretended to be honest, in order to trap him by what he said, so as to hand him over to the jurisdiction and authority of the governor. ²¹So they asked him, "Teacher, we know that you are right in what you say and teach, and you show deference to no one, but teach the way of God in accordance with truth.

²²Is it lawful for us to pay taxes to the emperor, or not?" ²³But he perceived their craftiness and said to them, ²⁴"Show me a denarius. Whose head and whose title does it bear?" They said, "The emperor's." ²⁵He said to them, "Then give to the emperor the things that are the emperor's, and to God the things that are God's." ²⁶And they were not able in the presence of the people to trap him by what he said; and being amazed by his answer, they became silent.

The Question about the Resurrection

27 Some Sadducees, those who say there is no resurrection, came to him ²⁸and asked him a question, "Teacher, Moses wrote for us that if a man's brother dies, leaving a wife but no children, the manᵇ shall marry the widow and raise up children for his brother. ²⁹Now there were seven brothers; the first married, and died childless; ³⁰then the second ³¹and the third married her, and so in the same way all seven died childless. ³²Finally the woman also died. ³³In the resurrection, therefore, whose wife will the woman be? For the seven had married her."

34 Jesus said to them, "Those who belong to this age marry and are given in marriage; ³⁵but those who are considered worthy of a place in that age and in the resurrection from the dead neither marry nor are given in marriage. ³⁶Indeed they cannot die anymore, because they are like angels and are children of God, being children of the resurrection. ³⁷And the fact that the dead are raised Moses himself showed, in the story about the bush, where he speaks of the Lord as the God of Abraham, the God of Isaac, and the God of Jacob. ³⁸Now he is God not of the dead, but of the living; for to him all of them are alive." ³⁹Then some of the scribes answered, "Teacher, you have spoken well." ⁴⁰For they no longer dared to ask him another question.

The Question about David's Son

41 Then he said to them, "How can they say that the Messiahᶜ is David's son? ⁴²For David himself says in the book of Psalms,

'The Lord said to my Lord,
    "Sit at my right hand,
⁴³   until I make your enemies your
                footstool." '

⁴⁴David thus calls him Lord; so how can he be his son?"

ᵃ Or keystone ᵇ Gk his brother ᶜ Or the Christ

Jesus Denounces the Scribes

45 In the hearing of all the people he said to the[a] disciples, [46]"Beware of the scribes, who like to walk around in long robes, and love to be greeted with respect in the marketplaces, and to have the best seats in the synagogues and places of honor at banquets. [47]They devour widows' houses and for the sake of appearance say long prayers. They will receive the greater condemnation."

21

The Widow's Offering

He looked up and saw rich people putting their gifts into the treasury; [2]he also saw a poor widow put in two small copper coins. [3]He said, "Truly I tell you, this poor widow has put in more

LIVE IT!

Less Is More
Luke 21:1–4

You've heard the stories—millionaires who give their wealth to charity, celebrities who use their influence to bring about change, or artists who use their talents to move the hearts of people to action. They are inspiring! But they can also leave us feeling as though our smaller contributions are pointless. What difference will our pocket change or spare time make in the world compared to what these people are doing? It can be depressing. But in **Luke 21:1–4**, Jesus points out that it is the disposition of our hearts, not the amount in our wallet, that matters. Jesus says that the widow who gave two small copper coins gave more than anyone, because it was all she had. She sacrificed, and trusted God to care for her. And that is more important to God than all the wealth in the world.

- What can you give of your time, talents, and treasure?
- Think about ways you can move from giving out of your abundance to sacrificing more and trusting God to provide.

than all of them; [4]for all of them have contributed out of their abundance, but she out of her poverty has put in all she had to live on."

The Destruction of the Temple Foretold

5 When some were speaking about the temple, how it was adorned with beautiful stones and gifts dedicated to God, he said, [6]"As for these things that you see, the days will come when not one stone will be left upon another; all will be thrown down."

Signs and Persecutions

7 They asked him, "Teacher, when will this be, and what will be the sign that this is about to take place?" [8]And he said, "Beware that you are not led astray; for many will come in my name and say, 'I am he!'[b] and, 'The time is near!'[c] Do not go after them.

9 "When you hear of wars and insurrections, do not be terrified; for these things must take place first, but the end will not follow immediately." [10]Then he said to them, "Nation will rise against nation, and kingdom against kingdom; [11]there will be great earthquakes, and in various places famines and plagues; and there will be dreadful portents and great signs from heaven.

12 "But before all this occurs, they will arrest you and persecute you; they will hand you over to synagogues and prisons, and you will be brought before kings and governors because of my name. [13]This will give you an opportunity to testify. [14]So make up your minds not to prepare your defense in advance; [15]for I will give you words[d] and a wisdom that none of your opponents will be able to withstand or contradict. [16]You will be betrayed even by parents and brothers, by relatives and friends; and they will put some of you to death. [17]You will be hated by all because of my name. [18]But not a hair of your head will perish. [19]By your endurance you will gain your souls.

The Destruction of Jerusalem Foretold

20 "When you see Jerusalem surrounded by armies, then know that its desolation has come near.[e] [21]Then those in Judea must flee to the mountains, and those inside the city must leave it, and those out in the country must not enter it; [22]for these are days of vengeance, as a fulfillment of all that is written. [23]Woe to those who are pregnant and to those who are nursing infants in those days! For there will be great distress on the earth and

a Other ancient authorities read his   b Gk I am   c Or at hand   d Gk a mouth   e Or is at hand

wrath against this people; [24]they will fall by the edge of the sword and be taken away as captives among all nations; and Jerusalem will be trampled on by the Gentiles, until the times of the Gentiles are fulfilled.

The Coming of the Son of Man

25 "There will be signs in the sun, the moon, and the stars, and on the earth distress among nations confused by the roaring of the sea and the waves. [26]People will faint from fear and foreboding of what is coming upon the world, for the powers of the heavens will be shaken. [27]Then they will see 'the Son of Man coming in a cloud' with power and great glory. [28]Now when these things begin to take place, stand up and raise your heads, because your redemption is drawing near."

The Lesson of the Fig Tree

29 Then he told them a parable: "Look at the fig tree and all the trees; [30]as soon as they sprout leaves you can see for yourselves and know that summer is already near. [31]So also, when you see these things taking place, you know that the kingdom of God is near. [32]Truly I tell you, this generation will not pass away until all things have taken place. [33]Heaven and earth will pass away, but my words will not pass away.

Exhortation to Watch

34 "Be on guard so that your hearts are not weighed down with dissipation and drunkenness and the worries of this life, and that day does not catch you unexpectedly, [35]like a trap. For it will come upon all who live on the face of the whole earth. [36]Be alert at all times, praying that you may have the strength to escape all these things that will take place, and to stand before the Son of Man."

37 Every day he was teaching in the temple, and at night he would go out and spend the night on the Mount of Olives, as it was called. [38]And all the people would get up early in the morning to listen to him in the temple.

22 The Plot to Kill Jesus

Now the festival of Unleavened Bread, which is called the Passover, was near. [2]The chief priests and the scribes were looking for a way to put Jesus[a] to death, for they were afraid of the people.

3 Then Satan entered into Judas called Iscariot, who was one of the twelve; [4]he went away and conferred with the chief priests and officers of the temple police about how he might betray him to them. [5]They were greatly pleased and agreed to give him money. [6]So he consented and began to look for an opportunity to betray him to them when no crowd was present.

The Preparation of the Passover

7 Then came the day of Unleavened Bread, on which the Passover lamb had to be sacrificed. [8]So Jesus[b] sent Peter and John, saying, "Go and prepare the Passover meal for us that we may eat it." [9]They asked him, "Where do you want us to make preparations for it?" [10]"Listen," he said to them, "when you have entered the city, a man carrying a jar of water will meet you; follow him into the house he enters [11]and say to the owner of the house, 'The teacher asks you, "Where is the guest room, where I may eat the Passover with my disciples?" ' [12]He will show you a large room upstairs, already furnished. Make preparations for us there." [13]So they went and found everything as he had told them; and they prepared the Passover meal.

The Institution of the Lord's Supper

14 When the hour came, he took his place at the table, and the apostles with him. [15]He said to them, "I have eagerly desired to eat this Passover with you before I suffer; [16]for I tell you, I will not eat it[c] until it is fulfilled in the kingdom of God." [17]Then he took a cup, and after giving thanks he said, "Take this and divide it among yourselves; [18]for I tell you that from now on I will not drink of the fruit of the vine until the kingdom of God comes." [19]Then he took a loaf of bread, and when he had given thanks, he broke it and gave it to them, saying, "This is my body, which is given for you. Do this in remembrance of

---

a Gk *him* b Gk *he* c Other ancient authorities read *never eat it again*

me." [20] And he did the same with the cup after supper, saying, "This cup that is poured out for you is the new covenant in my blood.[a] [21] But see, the one who betrays me is with me, and his hand is on the table. [22] For the Son of Man is going as it has been determined, but woe to that one by whom he is betrayed!" [23] Then they began to ask one another which one of them it could be who would do this.

The Dispute about Greatness

24 A dispute also arose among them as to which one of them was to be regarded as the greatest. [25] But he said to them, "The kings of the Gentiles lord it over them; and those in authority over them are called benefactors. [26] But not so with you; rather the greatest among you must become like the youngest, and the leader like one who serves. [27] For who is greater, the one who is at the table or the one who serves? Is it not the one at the table? But I am among you as one who serves.

28 "You are those who have stood by me in my trials; [29] and I confer on you, just as my Father has conferred on me, a kingdom, [30] so that you may eat and drink at my table in my kingdom, and you will sit on thrones judging the twelve tribes of Israel.

Jesus Predicts Peter's Denial

31 "Simon, Simon, listen! Satan has demanded[b] to sift all of you like wheat, [32] but I have prayed for you that your own faith may not fail; and you, when

PRAY IT!

Who Is Greatest?
Luke 22:24–27

"Me first, me first!"

"Quit cutting in line!"

"I'm the best!"

When we hear these comments we're more likely to picture schoolkids than Jesus' disciples, but in **Luke 22:24–27** we find them fighting over who is the greatest. And Jesus uses the opportunity to turn their ideas of greatness upside down. It was a new way of looking at things for the disciples, as it still is for us today. Reflect on and journal about times when you have given in to pride, then close with this prayer:

> Dear Jesus, you made it clear that those who are greatest are the ones who serve, not the ones who have fame, fortune, or authority. Help me to adjust my priorities to put others first. Give me a genuine desire to serve. Show me the daily opportunities I have to reach out to those in need in my family, school, and community. Guide me as I strive to follow your example to become a servant leader. Amen.

STUDY IT!

The Passover Lamb · Luke 22:14–20

Each of the gospels has an account of the Lord's Supper (Matthew 26:26–30; Mark 14:12–21; John 13:1–30). It is an essential piece of the story of Jesus' life, death, and resurrection. It is a simple account of Jesus eating a meal with his disciples, but it is packed with meaning. The meal they were eating together was the Passover—a Jewish celebration of how God had spared and freed the Israelites when they were slaves in Egypt. Each family had sacrificed a lamb and put the blood on their doorposts as a sign for the angel of death to pass over their house (see Exodus 12). Jesus is often called the Passover Lamb, because his sacrifice frees those who believe from the slavery of sin. Each time we eat the bread and drink the wine of the Lord's Supper, we are showing our belief in Jesus as the ultimate and final Passover Lamb—the sacrifice that brought us freedom from sin and death. We commit ourselves then to dying to our own selfish and sinful ways and living the new life given to us in Jesus. Celebrating Jesus as the Passover Lamb can give us a deeper understanding of how pain and death, lovingly embraced, can result in growth and new life. It's a reminder of our purpose in life—to love and serve God by loving and serving each other as Christ did.

---

a Other ancient authorities lack, in whole or in part, verses 19b-20 (*which is given . . . in my blood*)   **b** Or *has obtained permission*

once you have turned back, strengthen your brothers." ³³And he said to him, "Lord, I am ready to go with you to prison and to death!" ³⁴Jesus^a said, "I tell you, Peter, the cock will not crow this day, until you have denied three times that you know me."

Purse, Bag, and Sword

35 He said to them, "When I sent you out without a purse, bag, or sandals, did you lack anything?" They said, "No, not a thing." ³⁶He said to them, "But now, the one who has a purse must take it, and likewise a bag. And the one who has no sword must sell his cloak and buy one. ³⁷For I tell you, this scripture must be fulfilled in me, 'And he was counted among the lawless'; and indeed what is written about me is being fulfilled." ³⁸They said, "Lord, look, here are two swords." He replied, "It is enough."

Jesus Prays on the Mount of Olives

39 He came out and went, as was his custom, to the Mount of Olives; and the disciples followed him. ⁴⁰When he reached the place, he said to them, "Pray that you may not come into the time of trial."^b ⁴¹Then he withdrew from them about a stone's throw, knelt down, and prayed, ⁴²"Father, if you are willing, remove this cup from me; yet, not my will but yours be done." ⟦ ⁴³Then an angel from heaven

appeared to him and gave him strength. ⁴⁴In his anguish he prayed more earnestly, and his sweat became like great drops of blood falling down on the ground.⟧^c ⁴⁵When he got up from prayer, he came to the disciples and found them sleeping because of grief, ⁴⁶and he said to them, "Why are you sleeping? Get up and pray that you may not come into the time of trial."^b

The Betrayal and Arrest of Jesus

47 While he was still speaking, suddenly a crowd came, and the one called Judas, one of the twelve, was leading them. He approached Jesus to kiss him; ⁴⁸but Jesus said to him, "Judas, is it with a kiss that you are betraying the Son of Man?" ⁴⁹When those who were around him saw what was coming, they asked, "Lord, should we strike with the sword?" ⁵⁰Then one of them struck the slave of the high priest and cut off his right ear. ⁵¹But Jesus said, "No more of this!" And he touched his ear and healed him. ⁵²Then Jesus said to the chief priests, the officers of the temple police, and the elders who had come for him, "Have you come out with swords and clubs as if I were a bandit? ⁵³When I was with you day after day in the temple, you did not lay hands on me. But this is your hour, and the power of darkness!"

STUDY IT!

Same Story . . . Different Lessons · Luke 22:47–23:56

The stories of Jesus' Passion—the name Christians use to describe his suffering and death—differ in all four gospels. The differences don't create a contradiction, but give a deeper view of the events and the specific elements of the story and Jesus' character that each author wants to emphasize. Let's take a closer look at the perspective in the gospel of Luke.

First, Luke describes the openness of Gentiles to Jesus' message of salvation. The Roman centurion who praises God at the moment of Jesus' death (Luke 23:47) is an example.

Second, Luke emphasizes Jesus' compassion and forgiveness, even during his greatest suffering. While carrying the cross, Jesus shows his concern for the women who are following him (Luke 23:28-31). As he is nailed to the cross, he forgives those responsible (Luke 23:34). And when one of the criminals asks for Jesus to remember him, Jesus goes beyond that to promise that he will be with him in paradise (Luke 23:43).

Third, Mark portrays Jesus as abandoned in his suffering (Mark 15:34). But Luke surrounds Jesus with sympathetic people: a crowd, including the women of Jerusalem (Luke 23:27); the good thief (Luke 23:40-41); and the centurion (Luke 23:47). In Mark, Jesus feels God's absence (Mark 15:34). But Luke presents Jesus as obedient even at his death, handing his spirit over to God (Luke 23:46). Luke is emphasizing that Jesus is the loving, forgiving Savior of all humankind.

a Gk He   **b** Or *into temptation*   **c** Other ancient authorities lack verses 43 and 44

Peter Denies Jesus

54 Then they seized him and led him away, bringing him into the high priest's house. But Peter was following at a distance. [55]When they had kindled a fire in the middle of the courtyard and sat down together, Peter sat among them. [56]Then a servant-girl, seeing him in the firelight, stared at him and said, "This man also was with him." [57]But he denied it, saying, "Woman, I do not know him." [58]A little later someone else, on seeing him, said, "You also are one of them." But Peter said, "Man, I am not!" [59]Then about an hour later still another kept insisting, "Surely this man also was with him; for he is a Galilean." [60]But Peter said, "Man, I do not know what you are talking about!" At that moment, while he was still speaking, the cock crowed. [61]The Lord turned and looked at Peter. Then Peter remembered the word of the Lord, how he had said to him, "Before the cock crows today, you will deny me three times." [62]And he went out and wept bitterly.

The Mocking and Beating of Jesus

63 Now the men who were holding Jesus began to mock him and beat him; [64]they also blindfolded him and kept asking him, "Prophesy! Who is it that struck you?" [65]They kept heaping many other insults on him.

Jesus before the Council

66 When day came, the assembly of the elders of the people, both chief priests and scribes, gathered together, and they brought him to their council. [67]They said, "If you are the Messiah,[a] tell us." He replied, "If I tell you, you will not believe; [68]and if I question you, you will not answer. [69]But from now on the Son of Man will be seated at the right hand of the power of God." [70]All of them asked, "Are you, then, the Son of God?" He said to them, "You say that I am." [71]Then they said, "What further testimony do we need? We have heard it ourselves from his own lips!"

23 Jesus before Pilate

Then the assembly rose as a body and brought Jesus[b] before Pilate. [2]They began to accuse him, saying, "We found this man perverting our nation, forbidding us to pay taxes to the emperor, and saying that he himself is the Messiah, a king."[c] [3]Then Pilate asked him, "Are you the king of the Jews?" He answered, "You say so." [4]Then Pilate said to the chief priests and the crowds, "I find no basis for an accusation against this man." [5]But they were insistent and said, "He stirs up the people by teaching throughout all Judea, from Galilee where he began even to this place."

a Or the Christ   b Gk him   c Or is an anointed king

STUDY IT!

Stations of the Cross
Luke 23

Jesus' journey to the cross was not an easy one. Sometimes, in our excitement to celebrate his resurrection, we skip over the painful journey that took place in the days leading up to Jesus' death. As a way to remember, many Christians take part in some form of walking through what is known as the Stations of the Cross during the season of Lent or on Good Friday. These stations are based on the places and events that many Christians visit when they go to Jerusalem to retrace Jesus' steps. But if you can't make it to Jerusalem, you can still take part in this form of worship. The stations are set up differently by different churches and can take many forms including paintings, sculpture, and readings. The form is not as important as the fact that the stations take us on a journey of remembering the final hours of Jesus and making our own journey of confession and dependence on God.

Some churches include different numbers of stations, but the basic list includes the main events told in scripture:

- Station 1: Pilate condemns Jesus to die.
- Station 2: Jesus accepts his cross.
- Station 3: Simon helps carry the cross.
- Station 4: Jesus speaks to the women.
- Station 5: Jesus is stripped of his garments.
- Station 6: Jesus is nailed to the cross.
- Station 7: Jesus cares for his mother.
- Station 8: Jesus dies on the cross.

Jesus before Herod

6 When Pilate heard this, he asked whether the man was a Galilean. [7]And when he learned that he was under Herod's jurisdiction, he sent him off to Herod, who was himself in Jerusalem at that time. [8]When Herod saw Jesus, he was very glad, for he had been wanting to see him for a long time, because he had heard about him and was hoping to see him perform some sign. [9]He questioned him at some length, but Jesus[a] gave him no answer. [10]The chief priests and the scribes stood by, vehemently accusing him. [11]Even Herod with his soldiers treated him with contempt and mocked him; then he put an elegant robe on him, and sent him back to Pilate. [12]That same day Herod and Pilate became friends with each other; before this they had been enemies.

Jesus Sentenced to Death

13 Pilate then called together the chief priests, the leaders, and the people, [14]and said to them, "You brought me this man as one who was perverting the people; and here I have examined him in your presence and have not found this man guilty of any of your charges against him. [15]Neither has Herod, for he sent him back to us. Indeed, he has done nothing to deserve death. [16]I will therefore have him flogged and release him."[b]

18 Then they all shouted out together, "Away with this fellow! Release Barabbas for us!" [19](This was a man who had been put in prison for an insurrection that had taken place in the city, and for murder.) [20]Pilate, wanting to release Jesus, addressed them again; [21]but they kept shouting, "Crucify, crucify him!" [22]A third time he said to them, "Why, what evil has he done? I have found in him no ground for the sentence of death; I will therefore have him flogged and then release him." [23]But they kept urgently demanding with loud shouts that he should be crucified; and their voices prevailed. [24]So Pilate gave his verdict that their demand should be granted. [25]He released the man they asked for, the one who had been put in prison for insurrection and murder, and he handed Jesus over as they wished.

The Crucifixion of Jesus

26 As they led him away, they seized a man, Simon of Cyrene, who was coming from the country, and they laid the cross on him, and made him carry it behind Jesus. [27]A great number of the people followed him, and among them were women who were beating their breasts and wailing for him. [28]But Jesus turned to them and said, "Daughters of Jerusalem, do not weep for me, but weep for yourselves and for your children. [29]For the days are surely coming when they will say, 'Blessed are the barren, and the wombs that never bore, and the breasts that never nursed.' [30]Then they will begin to say to the mountains, 'Fall on us'; and to the hills, 'Cover us.' [31]For if they do this when the wood is green, what will happen when it is dry?"

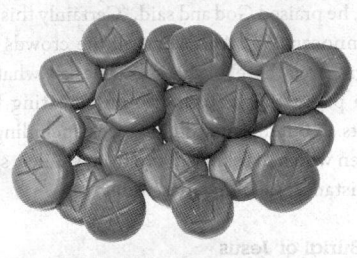

32 Two others also, who were criminals, were led away to be put to death with him. [33]When they came to the place that is called The Skull, they crucified Jesus[c] there with the criminals, one on his right and one on his left. [[[34]Then Jesus said, "Father, forgive them; for they do not know what they are doing."]][d]

And they cast lots to divide his clothing. [35]And the people stood by, watching; but the leaders scoffed at him, saying, "He saved others; let him save himself if he is the Messiah[e] of God, his chosen one!" [36]The soldiers also mocked him, coming up and offering him sour wine, [37]and saying, "If you are the King of the Jews, save yourself!" [38]There was also an inscription over him,[f] "This is the King of the Jews."

39 One of the criminals who were hanged there kept deriding[g] him and saying, "Are you not the Messiah?[e] Save yourself and us!" [40]But the other

> "Then Jesus said,
> 'Father, forgive them;
> for they do not know
> what they are doing.'"
> —Luke 23:34

---

a Gk *he* b Here, or after verse 19, other ancient authorities add verse 17, *Now he was obliged to release someone for them at the festival* c Gk *him* d Other ancient authorities lack the sentence *Then Jesus . . . what they are doing* e Or *the Christ* f Other ancient authorities add *written in Greek and Latin and Hebrew* (that is, *Aramaic*) g Or *blaspheming*

rebuked him, saying, "Do you not fear God, since you are under the same sentence of condemnation? [41] And we indeed have been condemned justly, for we are getting what we deserve for our deeds, but this man has done nothing wrong." [42] Then he said, "Jesus, remember me when you come into[a] your kingdom." [43] He replied, "Truly I tell you, today you will be with me in Paradise."

The Death of Jesus

44 It was now about noon, and darkness came over the whole land[b] until three in the afternoon, [45] while the sun's light failed;[c] and the curtain of the temple was torn in two. [46] Then Jesus, crying with a loud voice, said, "Father, into your hands I commend my spirit." Having said this, he breathed his last. [47] When the centurion saw what had taken place, he praised God and said, "Certainly this man was innocent."[d] [48] And when all the crowds who had gathered there for this spectacle saw what had taken place, they returned home, beating their breasts. [49] But all his acquaintances, including the women who had followed him from Galilee, stood at a distance, watching these things.

The Burial of Jesus

50 Now there was a good and righteous man named Joseph, who, though a member of the council, [51] had not agreed to their plan and action. He came from the Jewish town of Arimathea, and he was waiting expectantly for the kingdom of God. [52] This man went to Pilate and asked for the body of Jesus. [53] Then he took it down, wrapped it in a linen cloth, and laid it in a rock-hewn tomb where no one had ever been laid. [54] It was the day of Preparation, and the sabbath was beginning.[e] [55] The women who had come with him from Galilee followed, and they saw the tomb and how his body was laid. [56] Then they returned, and prepared spices and ointments.

On the sabbath they rested according to the commandment.

24 The Resurrection of Jesus

But on the first day of the week, at early dawn, they came to the tomb, taking the spices that they had prepared. [2] They found the stone rolled away from the tomb, [3] but when they went in, they did not find the body.[f] [4] While they were perplexed about this, suddenly two men in

LIVE IT!

He Is Alive!
Luke 24:1–12

Think about a time when you felt hopeless. Were you depressed? Lonely? Angry? Afraid? These were probably some of the feelings of the women who approached Jesus' tomb on the Sunday morning after his death. Their leader, their teacher, and their Lord had just been horribly executed before a huge crowd, and his wonderful vision of love, justice, and forgiveness had been shattered.

But what they encountered in that tomb changed everything. The tomb was empty. Two dazzling men appeared and spoke to them. The women were terrified, but the message they received was full of hope. Jesus was not there—he was alive!

When you think that a situation is hopeless, that no end is in sight, that evil is winning out, remember this story. Along with the resurrection stories in the other three gospels, this story is proof that despair and death do not win, that God is at work in the most hopeless situations! And he offers the hope of life to you.

dazzling clothes stood beside them. [5] The women[g] were terrified and bowed their faces to the ground, but the men[h] said to them, "Why do you look for the living among the dead? He is not here, but has risen.[i] [6] Remember how he told you, while he was still in Galilee, [7] that the Son of Man must be handed over to sinners, and be crucified, and on the third day rise again." [8] Then they remembered his words, [9] and returning from the tomb, they told all this to the eleven and to all the rest. [10] Now it was Mary Magdalene, Joanna, Mary the mother of James, and the other women with them who told this to the apostles. [11] But these words seemed to them an idle tale, and they did not believe them. [12] But Peter got up and ran to the tomb; stooping and looking in, he saw the linen cloths by themselves; then he went home, amazed at what had happened.[j]

a Other ancient authorities read in　b Or earth　c Or the sun was eclipsed. Other ancient authorities read the sun was darkened　d Or righteous　e Gk was dawning　f Other ancient authorities add of the Lord Jesus　g Gk They　h Gk but they　i Other ancient authorities lack He is not here, but has risen　j Other ancient authorities lack verse 12

Jesus Is with Us! · Luke 24:13–35

It's strange to think that the disciples on the road to Emmaus in **Luke 24:13–35** didn't recognize Jesus after being with him for years. We don't know if Jesus looked different after the resurrection, but we do know that the two disciples walking on the road were not expecting Jesus. After all, they had seen with their own eyes Jesus crucified and buried. The events of the previous days had brought their whole world crashing down, and they were unable to recognize Jesus even when he was right there with them, walking, talking, and teaching them. It wasn't until he broke and blessed the bread, as he had the last time they were together, that the disciples realized it was Jesus.

- How often do you miss the presence of Jesus in your life, because you don't expect him?
- Even when you feel disappointed, broken, and sad, what can you do to stay encouraged and keep your eyes open to the things Jesus wants to teach you?

The Walk to Emmaus

13 Now on that same day two of them were going to a village called Emmaus, about seven miles*a* from Jerusalem, 14and talking with each other about all these things that had happened. 15While they were talking and discussing, Jesus himself came near and went with them, 16but their eyes were kept from recognizing him. 17And he said to them, "What are you discussing with each other while you walk along?" They stood still, looking sad.*b* 18Then one of them, whose name was Cleopas, answered him, "Are you the only stranger in Jerusalem who does not know the things that have taken place there in these days?" 19He asked them, "What things?" They replied, "The things about Jesus of Nazareth,*c* who was a prophet mighty in deed and word before God and all the people, 20and how our chief priests and leaders handed him over to be condemned to death and crucified him. 21But we had hoped that he was the one to redeem Israel.*d* Yes, and besides all this, it is now the third day since these things took place. 22Moreover, some women of our group astounded us. They were at the tomb early this morning, 23and when they did not find his body there, they came back and told us that they had indeed seen a vision of angels who said that he was alive. 24Some of those who were with us went to the tomb and found it just as the women had said; but they did not see him." 25Then he said to them, "Oh, how foolish you are, and how slow of heart to believe all that the prophets have declared! 26Was it not necessary that the Messiah*e* should suffer these things and then enter into his glory?" 27Then beginning with Moses and all the prophets, he interpreted to them the things about himself in all the scriptures.

28 As they came near the village to which they were going, he walked ahead as if he were going on. 29But they urged him strongly, saying, "Stay with us, because it is almost evening and the day is now nearly over." So he went in to stay with them. 30When he was at the table with them, he took bread, blessed and broke it, and gave it to them. 31Then their eyes were opened, and they recognized him; and he vanished from their sight. 32They said to each other, "Were not our hearts burning within us*f* while he was talking to us on the road, while he was opening the scriptures to us?" 33That same hour they got up and returned to Jerusalem; and they found the eleven and their companions gathered together. 34They were saying, "The Lord has risen indeed, and he has appeared to Simon!" 35Then they told what had happened on the road, and how he had been made known to them in the breaking of the bread.

Jesus Appears to His Disciples

36 While they were talking about this, Jesus himself stood among them and said to them, "Peace be with you."*g* 37They were startled and terrified, and thought that they were seeing a ghost. 38He said to them, "Why are you frightened, and why do doubts arise in your hearts? 39Look at my hands and my feet; see that it is I myself. Touch me and see; for a ghost does not have flesh and bones as you see that I have." 40And when he had said this, he showed them his hands and his feet.*h* 41While in their joy

a Gk *sixty stadia*; other ancient authorities read *a hundred sixty stadia*   b Other ancient authorities read *walk along, looking sad?"*   c Other ancient authorities read *Jesus the Nazorean*   d Or *to set Israel free*   e Or *the Christ*   f Other ancient authorities lack *within us*   g Other ancient authorities lack *and said to them, "Peace be with you."*   h Other ancient authorities lack verse 40

they were disbelieving and still wondering, he said to them, "Have you anything here to eat?" [42]They gave him a piece of broiled fish, [43]and he took it and ate in their presence.

44 Then he said to them, "These are my words that I spoke to you while I was still with you—that everything written about me in the law of Moses, the prophets, and the psalms must be fulfilled." [45]Then he opened their minds to understand the scriptures, [46]and he said to them, "Thus it is written, that the Messiah[a] is to suffer and to rise from the dead on the third day, [47]and that repentance and forgiveness of sins is to be proclaimed in his name to all nations, beginning from Jerusalem. [48]You are witnesses[b] of these things. [49]And see, I am sending upon you what my Father promised; so stay here in the city until you have been clothed with power from on high."

The Ascension of Jesus

50 Then he led them out as far as Bethany, and, lifting up his hands, he blessed them. [51]While he was blessing them, he withdrew from them and was carried up into heaven.[c] [52]And they worshiped him, and[d] returned to Jerusalem with great joy; [53]and they were continually in the temple blessing God.[e]

a Or *the Christ*　b Or *nations. Beginning from Jerusalem* [48]*you are witnesses*　c Other ancient authorities lack *and was carried up into heaven*　d Other ancient authorities lack *worshiped him, and*　e Other ancient authorities add *Amen*

John

John

▶▶

"**W**e're like two peas in a pod." "Our friendship is as solid as a rock." We use analogies and symbolic images all the time to describe things, including our relationships. The author of the gospel of John does it too. He uses symbolic imagery throughout the gospel to describe a relationship with Jesus. John's gospel is different in style from the other gospels, but it also gives us the clearest picture of Jesus' unique relationship with God the Father.

IN DEPTH

The gospel of John begins with symbolic language describing Jesus as the Word, who was with God in the beginning of creation and who became flesh to live among us. The author goes on to describe Jesus as the light that overcomes darkness. Those who believe in Jesus walk in the light and their lives have meaning and direction. Those who do not believe stumble in the darkness of confusion and sin. John is clear that Jesus is the divine Son of God and that to belong to God, we must follow Jesus.

This symbolic language and emphasis on Jesus' unique relationship with God the Father separates John's gospel from other writings. The Synoptic Gospels—Matthew, Mark, and Luke—share many similarities including many of the same stories, in the same sequence, written in similar language. But John is different from the Synoptic Gospels in many ways:

• In the Synoptic Gospels, Jesus' teaching focuses on the kingdom (or reign) of God. In John's gospel, Jesus' teaching stresses relationships: Jesus' relationship with God the Father and our relationship with Jesus.

• In the Synoptic Gospels, Jesus teaches through parables and performs many healings and miracles. In the gospel of John, Jesus doesn't use parables. Instead, Jesus performs seven miraculous signs and teaches in long discourses.

• John's gospel has several passages about the role of the Holy Spirit. The Synoptic Gospels hardly mention the Holy Spirit.

Although the climax of John's story is Jesus' death, it is not tragic at all—it is his glorious return to the Father, whom he was with from the beginning. This gospel assures us that trusting in God will pay off in the end: "I will come again and will take you to myself, so that where I am, there you may be also" (John 14:3).

QUICK FACTS

● **Author:** A member of a Christian community possibly founded by John, the Beloved Disciple

◢ **Date Written:** Most likely between A.D. 90 and 110

◔ **Audience:** A Jewish-Christian community that was going through a difficult separation from its former Jewish society

● **Image of Jesus:** Noble and powerful; one with the Father; fully in control of his destiny

AT A GLANCE

● **John 1:1–18** Prologue: a poem about the Word of God

◢ **John 1:19–12:50** Jesus' miracles and teachings, disputes with "the Jews"

● **John 13–20** The Last Supper, and Jesus' suffering, death, and resurrection

◔ **John 21** Epilogue: another appearance of the risen Jesus

The Word Became Flesh

1 In the beginning was the Word, and the Word was with God, and the Word was God. [2] He was in the beginning with God. [3] All things came into being through him, and without him not one thing came into being. What has come into being [4] in him was life,[a] and the life was the light of all people. [5] The light shines in the darkness, and the darkness did not overcome it.

6 There was a man sent from God, whose name was John. [7] He came as a witness to testify to the light, so that all might believe through him. [8] He himself was not the light, but he came to testify to the light. [9] The true light, which enlightens everyone, was coming into the world.[b]

10 He was in the world, and the world came into being through him; yet the world did not know him. [11] He came to what was his own,[c] and his own people did not accept him. [12] But to all who received him, who believed in his name, he gave power to become children of God, [13] who were born, not of blood or of the will of the flesh or of the will of man, but of God.

14 And the Word became flesh and lived among us, and we have seen his glory, the glory as of a father's only son,[d] full of grace and truth. [15] (John testified to him and cried out, "This was he of whom I said, 'He who comes after me ranks ahead of me because he was before me.' ") [16] From his fullness we have all received, grace upon grace. [17] The law indeed was given through Moses; grace and truth came through Jesus Christ. [18] No one has ever seen God. It is God the only Son,[e] who is close to the Father's heart,[f] who has made him known.

The Testimony of John the Baptist

19 This is the testimony given by John when the Jews sent priests and Levites from Jerusalem to ask him, "Who are you?" [20] He confessed and did not deny it, but confessed, "I am not the Messiah."[g] [21] And they asked him, "What then? Are you Elijah?" He said, "I am not." "Are you the prophet?" He answered, "No." [22] Then they said to him, "Who are you? Let us have an answer for those who sent us. What do you say about yourself?" [23] He said,

"I am the voice of one crying out in the
  wilderness,
'Make straight the way of the Lord,' "

as the prophet Isaiah said.

LIVE IT!

Recognizing Jesus
John 1:1–18

Science fiction and fantasy movies and books often include important eternal beings or powers. STAR WARS has "the Force." The Chronicles of Narnia has Aslan, the noble lion who is the creator and savior of Narnia.

The poem that begins the gospel of John reads a little bit like something from a science fiction classic. But this story isn't fiction—it's God's revelation! The poem presents Jesus as the Word, who has existed from all time, the one through whom all things came into being. Scripture tells us a great mystery here: the man named Jesus, who lived in Nazareth some two thousand years ago, is the creative power of God, who "became flesh and lived among us" (John 1:14). No one has ever seen God. But Jesus, the revealer of God, "has made him known" (John 1:18) in flesh and blood.

Many people in John don't recognize or accept Jesus, and many people still don't today.

- What does it mean for you to accept Jesus?
- Who or what has helped you recognize or accept Jesus?

24 Now they had been sent from the Pharisees. [25] They asked him, "Why then are you baptizing if you are neither the Messiah,[g] nor Elijah, nor the prophet?" [26] John answered them, "I baptize with water. Among you stands one whom you do not know, [27] the one who is coming after me; I am not worthy to untie the thong of his sandal." [28] This took place in Bethany across the Jordan where John was baptizing.

The Lamb of God

29 The next day he saw Jesus coming toward him and declared, "Here is the Lamb of God who takes

---

a Or [3] through him. And without him not one thing came into being that has come into being. [4] In him was life **b** Or He was the true light that enlightens everyone coming into the world **c** Or to his own home **d** Or the Father's only Son **e** Other ancient authorities read It is an only Son, God, or It is the only Son **f** Gk bosom **g** Or the Christ

away the sin of the world! [30]This is he of whom I said, 'After me comes a man who ranks ahead of me because he was before me.' [31]I myself did not know him; but I came baptizing with water for this reason, that he might be revealed to Israel." [32]And John testified, "I saw the Spirit descending from heaven like a dove, and it remained on him. [33]I myself did not know him, but the one who sent me to baptize with water said to me, 'He on whom you see the Spirit descend and remain is the one who baptizes with the Holy Spirit.' [34]And I myself have seen and have testified that this is the Son of God."[a]

The First Disciples of Jesus

35 The next day John again was standing with two of his disciples, [36]and as he watched Jesus walk by, he exclaimed, "Look, here is the Lamb of God!" [37]The two disciples heard him say this, and they followed Jesus. [38]When Jesus turned and saw them following, he said to them, "What are you looking for?" They said to him, "Rabbi" (which translated means Teacher), "where are you staying?" [39]He said to them, "Come and see." They came and saw where he was staying, and they remained with him that day. It was about four o'clock in the afternoon. [40]One of the two who heard John speak and followed him was Andrew, Simon Peter's brother. [41]He first found his brother Simon and said to him, "We have found the Messiah" (which is translated Anointed[b]). [42]He brought Simon[c] to Jesus, who looked at him and said, "You are Simon son of John.

You are to be called Cephas" (which is translated Peter[d]).

Jesus Calls Philip and Nathanael

43 The next day Jesus decided to go to Galilee. He found Philip and said to him, "Follow me." [44]Now Philip was from Bethsaida, the city of Andrew and Peter. [45]Philip found Nathanael and said to him, "We have found him about whom Moses in the law and also the prophets wrote, Jesus son of Joseph from Nazareth." [46]Nathanael said to him, "Can anything good come out of Nazareth?" Philip said to him, "Come and see." [47]When Jesus saw Nathanael coming toward him, he said of him, "Here is truly an Israelite in whom there is no deceit!" [48]Nathanael asked him, "Where did you get to know me?" Jesus answered, "I saw you under the fig tree before Philip called you." [49]Nathanael replied, "Rabbi, you are the Son of God! You are the King of Israel!" [50]Jesus answered, "Do you believe because I told you that I saw you under the fig tree? You will see greater things than these." [51]And he said to him, "Very truly, I tell you,[e] you will see heaven opened and the angels of God ascending and descending upon the Son of Man."

The Wedding at Cana

2 On the third day there was a wedding in Cana of Galilee, and the mother of Jesus was there. [2]Jesus and his disciples had also been invited to the wedding. [3]When the wine gave out,

STUDY IT!

The First Sign · John 2:1–11

Your wedding day is the one day you want everything to go exactly as planned. Months of planning, and usually lots of money, go into ensuring the big day will go smoothly. Imagine if there wasn't enough food to feed everyone. How embarrassing! Imagine if the cake never arrived, or if there wasn't enough wine for all the guests.

That's exactly what happens at the wedding in Cana. Jesus is there, along with his followers and his mother, Mary. Mary mentions to Jesus that they are running out of wine. Take a minute to study Jesus' reaction to his mother's comment. Does it seem a bit strange? Why do you think Jesus hesitates? Why does Mary persist?

This is the first of seven miracles, or signs, as John calls them, that Jesus performs in the gospel of John. Why do you think this one is first? What happens because of this miracle? What might it be a sign of? As you read on in John's gospel, pay attention to what each of Jesus' seven miracles teaches us about Jesus and his mission.

a Other ancient authorities read *is God's chosen one* b Or *Christ* c Gk *him* d From the word for *rock* in Aramaic (*kepha*) and Greek (*petra*), respectively e Both instances of the Greek word for *you* in this verse are plural

"The Jews" in John · John 2:18–20

The writer of John often makes references to "the Jews." They are often portrayed challenging or questioning Jesus, as we see in **John 2:18**. Around the time John was written, Christian Jews were being forcibly removed from Jewish synagogues (John 16:1–4). With this rivalry in the background, the gospel writer sometimes lumps all Jews together, portraying them as the bad guys. We shouldn't take John's references to "the Jews" as a basis for prejudice or anger against Jewish people. Instead, we can learn from Jesus' emphasis on the motivations of our hearts rather than the Jewish leaders' often legalistic approach to religion.

the mother of Jesus said to him, "They have no wine." [4] And Jesus said to her, "Woman, what concern is that to you and to me? My hour has not yet come." [5] His mother said to the servants, "Do whatever he tells you." [6] Now standing there were six stone water jars for the Jewish rites of purification, each holding twenty or thirty gallons. [7] Jesus said to them, "Fill the jars with water." And they filled them up to the brim. [8] He said to them, "Now draw some out, and take it to the chief steward." So they took it. [9] When the steward tasted the water that had become wine, and did not know where it came from (though the servants who had drawn the water knew), the steward called the bridegroom [10] and said to him, "Everyone serves the good wine first, and then the inferior wine after the guests have become drunk. But you have kept the good wine until now." [11] Jesus did this, the first of his signs, in Cana of Galilee, and revealed his glory; and his disciples believed in him.

[12] After this he went down to Capernaum with his mother, his brothers, and his disciples; and they remained there a few days.

Jesus Cleanses the Temple

[13] The Passover of the Jews was near, and Jesus went up to Jerusalem. [14] In the temple he found people selling cattle, sheep, and doves, and the money changers seated at their tables. [15] Making a whip of cords, he drove all of them out of the temple, both the sheep and the cattle. He also poured out the coins of the money changers and overturned their tables. [16] He told those who were selling the doves, "Take these things out of here! Stop making my Father's house a marketplace!" [17] His disciples remembered that it was written, "Zeal for your house will consume me." [18] The Jews then said to him, "What sign can you show us for doing this?" [19] Jesus answered them, "Destroy this temple, and in three days I will raise it up." [20] The Jews then said, "This temple has been under construction for forty-six years, and will you raise it up in three days?" [21] But he was speaking of the temple of his body. [22] After he was raised from the dead, his disciples remembered that he had said this; and they believed the scripture and the word that Jesus had spoken.

[23] When he was in Jerusalem during the Passover festival, many believed in his name because they saw the signs that he was doing. [24] But Jesus on his part would not entrust himself to them, because he knew all people [25] and needed no one to testify about anyone; for he himself knew what was in everyone.

Nicodemus Visits Jesus

3 Now there was a Pharisee named Nicodemus, a leader of the Jews. [2] He came to Jesus[a] by night and said to him, "Rabbi, we know that you are a teacher who has come from God; for no one can do these signs that you do apart from the presence of God." [3] Jesus answered him, "Very

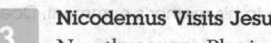

a Gk him

Introducing . . . Nicodemus
John 3:1–21

Nicodemus was a Jewish teacher with a high position of leadership who came to meet secretly with Jesus. Nicodemus has been waiting for a sign that God's promise of salvation through a savior will happen in his lifetime. He senses that maybe Jesus is this savior. But he doesn't yet believe in Jesus, as is emphasized by his coming to Jesus "by night" (John 3:2). Jesus symbolically outlines what it takes for salvation: to believe in Jesus as the one sent by God and to be born again through baptism and the Holy Spirit. The same is true for people today.

Nicodemus most likely knew that to accept Jesus publicly would put him in bad standing with the other Jewish leaders. Like Nicodemus, we also may need to make choices that might make us look foolish to others as we follow Jesus.

truly, I tell you, no one can see the kingdom of God without being born from above."*a* *4*Nicodemus said to him, "How can anyone be born after having grown old? Can one enter a second time into the mother's womb and be born?" *5*Jesus answered, "Very truly, I tell you, no one can enter the kingdom of God without being born of water and Spirit. *6*What is born of the flesh is flesh, and what is born of the Spirit is spirit.*b* *7*Do not be astonished that I said to you, 'You*c* must be born from above.'*d* *8*The wind*b* blows where it chooses, and you hear the sound of it, but you do not know where it comes from or where it goes. So it is with everyone who is born of the Spirit." *9*Nicodemus said to him, "How can these things be?" *10*Jesus answered him, "Are you a teacher of Israel, and yet you do not understand these things?

11 "Very truly, I tell you, we speak of what we know and testify to what we have seen; yet you*e* do not receive our testimony. *12*If I have told you about earthly things and you do not believe, how can you

believe if I tell you about heavenly things? *13*No one has ascended into heaven except the one who descended from heaven, the Son of Man.*f* *14*And just as Moses lifted up the serpent in the wilderness, so must the Son of Man be lifted up, *15*that whoever believes in him may have eternal life.*g*

16 "For God so loved the world that he gave his only Son, so that everyone who believes in him may not perish but may have eternal life.

17 "Indeed, God did not send the Son into the world to condemn the world, but in order that the world might be saved through him. *18*Those who believe in him are not condemned; but those who do not believe are condemned already, because they have not believed in the name of the only Son of God. *19*And this is the judgment, that the light has come into the world, and people loved darkness rather than light because their deeds were evil. *20*For all who do evil hate the light and do not come to the light, so that their deeds may not be exposed. *21*But those who do what is true come to the light, so that it may be clearly seen that their deeds have been done in God."*g*

Jesus and John the Baptist

22 After this Jesus and his disciples went into the Judean countryside, and he spent some time there with them and baptized. *23*John also was baptizing at Aenon near Salim because water was abundant there; and people kept coming and were being baptized *24*—John, of course, had not yet been thrown into prison.

25 Now a discussion about purification arose between John's disciples and a Jew.*h* *26*They came to John and said to him, "Rabbi, the one who was with you across the Jordan, to whom you testified, here he is baptizing, and all are going to him." *27*John answered, "No one can receive anything except what has been given from heaven. *28*You yourselves are my witnesses that I said, 'I am not the Messiah,*i* but I have been sent ahead of him.' *29*He who has the bride is the bridegroom. The friend of the bridegroom, who stands and hears him, rejoices greatly at the bridegroom's voice. For this reason my joy has been fulfilled. *30*He must increase, but I must decrease."*j*

The One Who Comes from Heaven

31 The one who comes from above is above all; the one who is of the earth belongs to the earth and speaks about earthly things. The one who comes

a Or *born anew* *b* The same Greek word means both *wind* and *spirit* *c* The Greek word for *you* here is plural *d* Or *anew* *e* The Greek word for *you* here and in verse 12 is plural *f* Other ancient authorities add *who is in heaven* *g* Some interpreters hold that the quotation concludes with verse 15 *h* Other ancient authorities read *the Jews* *i* Or *the Christ* *j* Some interpreters hold that the quotation continues through verse 36

from heaven is above all. [32]He testifies to what he has seen and heard, yet no one accepts his testimony. [33]Whoever has accepted his testimony has certified[a] this, that God is true. [34]He whom God has sent speaks the words of God, for he gives the Spirit without measure. [35]The Father loves the Son and has placed all things in his hands. [36]Whoever believes in the Son has eternal life; whoever disobeys the Son will not see life, but must endure God's wrath.

Jesus and the Woman of Samaria

4 Now when Jesus[b] learned that the Pharisees had heard, "Jesus is making and baptizing more disciples than John" [2]—although it was not Jesus himself but his disciples who baptized— [3]he left Judea and started back to Galilee. [4]But he had to go through Samaria. [5]So he came to a Samaritan city called Sychar, near the plot of ground that Jacob had given to his son Joseph.

[6]Jacob's well was there, and Jesus, tired out by his journey, was sitting by the well. It was about noon.

[7] A Samaritan woman came to draw water, and Jesus said to her, "Give me a drink." [8](His disciples had gone to the city to buy food.) [9]The Samaritan woman said to him, "How is it that you, a Jew, ask a drink of me, a woman of Samaria?" (Jews do not share things in common with Samaritans.)[c] [10]Jesus answered her, "If you knew the gift of God, and who it is that is saying to you, 'Give me a drink,' you would have asked him, and he would have given you living water." [11]The woman said to him, "Sir, you have no bucket, and the well is deep. Where do you get that living water? [12]Are you greater than our ancestor Jacob, who gave us the well, and with his sons and his flocks drank from it?" [13]Jesus said to her, "Everyone who drinks of this water will be thirsty again, [14]but those who drink of the water that I will give them will never

Dry Tears: Water Brings Life · John 4:13–14

People die every day simply because they don't have clean water—not just a few people, but about six thousand people every day, mostly children. More than a billion people around the world don't have clean water. They drink whatever they can get, including water with germs and bacteria that make them sick or kill them.

It's a big problem. Some might say too big. But not Conner Cress. As a sixteen-year-old, he decided to do something about it with the help of four of his high-school friends, Jared Ciervo, Kyle Blakely, Dan Mirolli, and Logan Weber. Together they started the Dry Tears campaign to raise money to build clean wells in Africa (see **drytearsmi.wordpress.com**). The name Dry Tears came from reading about some kids who were so dehydrated from lack of water that they couldn't even cry real tears.

The idea was simple. Create and sell bracelets and T-shirts to raise awareness about the problem and raise money that they could donate to Blood:Water Mission to build clean wells (see **bloodwatermission.com**). Within three years, their efforts produced enough to build twelve wells in four African countries. Each well represents a life-saving change for a village of people.

"What's cool is that when they build wells, they actually get people in the community to help," says Connor.* "So at the same time they provide jobs, giving back to the community."

"I like to think of what we're doing as just telling God that we love him," Jared says. "Through everything that he has given us, we are just giving back."

And what they are giving back is more than just a drink of cool water. The freshwater well gives the people an introduction to a well that will never run dry. In **John 4:13–14**, Jesus says that anyone who drinks of the water of life that he gives will never be thirsty again. He's not talking about physical thirst, but spiritual thirst. Jesus offers the living water of eternal life to everyone who believes in him.

be thirsty. The water that I will give will become in them a spring of water gushing up to eternal life." ¹⁵The woman said to him, "Sir, give me this water, so that I may never be thirsty or have to keep coming here to draw water."

16 Jesus said to her, "Go, call your husband, and come back." ¹⁷The woman answered him, "I have no husband." Jesus said to her, "You are right in saying, 'I have no husband'; ¹⁸for you have had five husbands, and the one you have now is not your husband. What you have said is true!" ¹⁹The woman said to him, "Sir, I see that you are a prophet. ²⁰Our ancestors worshiped on this mountain, but you[a] say that the place where people must worship is in Jerusalem." ²¹Jesus said to her, "Woman, believe me, the hour is coming when you will worship the Father neither on this mountain nor in Jerusalem. ²²You worship what you do not know; we worship what we know, for salvation is from the Jews. ²³But the hour is coming, and is now here, when the true worshipers will worship the Father in spirit and truth, for the Father seeks such as these to worship him. ²⁴God is spirit, and those who worship him must worship in spirit and truth." ²⁵The woman said to him, "I know that Messiah is coming" (who is called Christ). "When he comes, he will proclaim all things to us." ²⁶Jesus said to her, "I am he,[b] the one who is speaking to you."

27 Just then his disciples came. They were astonished that he was speaking with a woman, but no one said, "What do you want?" or, "Why are you

PRAY IT!

How Deep Is Your Well?
John 4:1–42

In John 4:1–42, Jesus initiates a conversation with a Samaritan woman while she is drawing water from a well during the heat of the day. She has no idea who Jesus is and what living water he is referring to, but she stands and listens. She is changed as a result. She believes in Jesus and goes to tell others about the Messiah. John uses her as a role model for those who believe.

Look inside the "well" of faith within you. How deep is that well? Do you thirst for a deeper relationship with Jesus? Are you ready to share the good news with others? Jesus invites each of us to join him in a personal relationship. All we have to do is ask. Begin your relationship with Jesus by praying:

Jesus, you are the Savior, the holy one. I am thirsty—please quench my thirst. I know I can never be satisfied without you, and I can never be clean without your cleansing of my sin. Please give me new life and a fresh start. Amen.

STUDY IT!

Why Are the Disciples Surprised? · John 4:1–42

The disciples "were astonished that he (Jesus) was speaking with a woman" (John 4:27). It was unusual for Jesus to be talking to this woman for several reasons. First, during that time in Israel men did not talk to women, especially strangers, in public places. Second, Jews didn't talk to Samaritans (see "Live It: Who Belongs and Who Doesn't?" near Ezra 9-10; and "Live It: The Good Samaritan," near Luke 10:25-37), because Samaritans were not considered real Jews (John 4:20). And finally, the woman with whom Jesus was speaking was accused of having had five husbands. Some scholars think that "five husbands" is symbolic of the five books of the Torah that the Samaritans revered. On the other hand, most first-century women didn't have the right to divorce; only their husbands did. So it may be that she was terribly unlucky, having been widowed or dismissed numerous times, and was now taken in as a servant in someone's household.

This episode is one more example in the gospel of John that shows Jesus is not bound by customs and stereotypes when the message of the gospel is at stake.

---

a The Greek word for *you* here and in verses 21 and 22 is plural   b Gk *I am*

speaking with her?" [28] Then the woman left her water jar and went back to the city. She said to the people, [29] "Come and see a man who told me everything I have ever done! He cannot be the Messiah,[a] can he?" [30] They left the city and were on their way to him.

31 Meanwhile the disciples were urging him, "Rabbi, eat something." [32] But he said to them, "I have food to eat that you do not know about." [33] So the disciples said to one another, "Surely no one has brought him something to eat?" [34] Jesus said to them, "My food is to do the will of him who sent me and to complete his work. [35] Do you not say, 'Four months more, then comes the harvest'? But I tell you, look around you, and see how the fields are ripe for harvesting. [36] The reaper is already receiving[b] wages and is gathering fruit for eternal life, so that sower and reaper may rejoice together. [37] For here the saying holds true, 'One sows and another reaps.' [38] I sent you to reap that for which you did not labor. Others have labored, and you have entered into their labor."

39 Many Samaritans from that city believed in him because of the woman's testimony, "He told me everything I have ever done." [40] So when the Samaritans came to him, they asked him to stay with them; and he stayed there two days. [41] And many more believed because of his word. [42] They said to the woman, "It is no longer because of what you said that we believe, for we have heard for ourselves, and we know that this is truly the Savior of the world."

Jesus Returns to Galilee

43 When the two days were over, he went from that place to Galilee [44] (for Jesus himself had testified that a prophet has no honor in the prophet's own country). [45] When he came to Galilee, the Galileans welcomed him, since they had seen all that he had done in Jerusalem at the festival; for they too had gone to the festival.

Jesus Heals an Official's Son

46 Then he came again to Cana in Galilee where he had changed the water into wine. Now there was a royal official whose son lay ill in Capernaum. [47] When he heard that Jesus had come from Judea to Galilee, he went and begged him to come down and heal his son, for he was at the point of death. [48] Then Jesus said to him, "Unless you[c] see signs and wonders you will not believe." [49] The official said to

him, "Sir, come down before my little boy dies." [50] Jesus said to him, "Go; your son will live." The man believed the word that Jesus spoke to him and started on his way. [51] As he was going down, his slaves met him and told him that his child was alive. [52] So he asked them the hour when he began to recover, and they said to him, "Yesterday at one in the afternoon the fever left him." [53] The father realized that this was the hour when Jesus had said to him, "Your son will live." So he himself believed, along with his whole household. [54] Now this was the second sign that Jesus did after coming from Judea to Galilee.

5 Jesus Heals on the Sabbath

After this there was a festival of the Jews, and Jesus went up to Jerusalem.

2 Now in Jerusalem by the Sheep Gate there is a pool, called in Hebrew[d] Beth-zatha,[e] which has five porticoes. [3] In these lay many invalids—blind, lame, and paralyzed.[f] [5] One man was there who had been ill for thirty-eight years. [6] When Jesus saw him lying there and knew that he had been there a long time, he said to him, "Do you want to be made well?" [7] The sick man answered him, "Sir, I have no one to put me into the pool when the water is stirred up; and while I am making my way, someone else steps down ahead of me." [8] Jesus said to him, "Stand up, take your mat and walk." [9] At once the man was made well, and he took up his mat and began to walk.

Now that day was a sabbath. [10] So the Jews said to the man who had been cured, "It is the sabbath; it is not lawful for you to carry your mat." [11] But he answered them, "The man who made me well said to me, 'Take up your mat and walk.'" [12] They asked him, "Who is the man who said to you, 'Take it up and walk'?" [13] Now the man who had been healed did not know who it was, for Jesus had disappeared[g] the crowd that was there. [14] Later Jesus found him in the temple and said to him, "See, you have been made well! Do not sin any more, so that nothing worse happens to you." [15] The man went away and told the Jews that it was Jesus who had made him well. [16] Therefore the Jews started persecuting Jesus, because he was doing such things on the sabbath. [17] But Jesus answered them, "My Father is still working, and I also am working." [18] For this reason the Jews were seeking all the more to kill him, because he was not only breaking the sabbath, but was

---

a Or the Christ b Or [35] . . . the fields are already ripe for harvesting. [36] The reaper is receiving c Both instances of the Greek word for you in this verse are plural d That is, Aramaic e Other ancient authorities read Bethesda, others Bethsaida f Other ancient authorities add, wholly or in part, waiting for the stirring of the water; [for an angel of the Lord went down at certain seasons into the pool, and stirred up the water; whoever stepped in first after the stirring of the water was made well from whatever disease that person had. g Or had left because of

The "I Am" Sayings of Jesus
John 5:16–18

In John 5:16–18, the Jews were upset that Jesus was equating himself with God. John contains a whole series of "I am" sayings from Jesus that explain his role as the Messiah. For example:

- "I am the bread of life." (John 6:35)
- "I am the light of the world." (John 8:12)
- "I am the gate for the sheep." (John 10:7)
- "I am the good shepherd." (John 10:11)
- "I am the resurrection and the life." (John 11:25)
- "I am the way, and the truth, and the life." (John 14:6)
- "I am the vine, you are the branches." (John 15:5)

The "I am" sayings are also a means of establishing the divine nature of Jesus. Jesus' use of "I am" is similar to when God revealed his name—"I am"—to Moses at the burning bush (Exodus 3:14). Ironically, the Jewish leaders in John are correct in thinking that Jesus is equating himself with God (John 5:18). But they are wrong in not recognizing that Jesus is right!

also calling God his own Father, thereby making himself equal to God.

The Authority of the Son

19 Jesus said to them, "Very truly, I tell you, the Son can do nothing on his own, but only what he sees the Father doing; for whatever the Father[a] does, the Son does likewise. 20 The Father loves the Son and shows him all that he himself is doing; and he will show him greater works than these, so that you will be astonished. 21 Indeed, just as the Father raises the dead and gives them life, so also the Son gives life to whomever he wishes. 22 The Father judges no one but has given all judgment to the Son, 23 so that all may honor the Son just as they honor the Father. Anyone who does not honor the Son does not honor the Father who sent him. 24 Very truly, I tell you, anyone who hears my word and believes him who sent me has eternal life, and does not come under judgment, but has passed from death to life.

25 "Very truly, I tell you, the hour is coming, and is now here, when the dead will hear the voice of the Son of God, and those who hear will live. 26 For just as the Father has life in himself, so he has granted the Son also to have life in himself; 27 and he has given him authority to execute judgment, because he is the Son of Man. 28 Do not be astonished at this; for the hour is coming when all who are in their graves will hear his voice 29 and will come out—those who have done good, to the resurrection of life, and those who have done evil, to the resurrection of condemnation.

Witnesses to Jesus

30 "I can do nothing on my own. As I hear, I judge; and my judgment is just, because I seek to do not my own will but the will of him who sent me.

31 "If I testify about myself, my testimony is not true. 32 There is another who testifies on my behalf, and I know that his testimony to me is true. 33 You sent messengers to John, and he testified to the truth. 34 Not that I accept such human testimony, but I say these things so that you may be saved. 35 He was a burning and shining lamp, and you were willing to rejoice for a while in his light. 36 But I have a testimony greater than John's. The works that the Father has given me to complete, the very works that I am doing, testify on my behalf that the Father has sent me. 37 And the Father who sent me has himself testified on my behalf. You have never heard his voice or seen his form, 38 and you do not have his word abiding in you, because you do not believe him whom he has sent.

39 "You search the scriptures because you think that in them you have eternal life; and it is they that testify on my behalf. 40 Yet you refuse to come to me to have life. 41 I do not accept glory from human beings. 42 But I know that you do not have the love of God in[b] you. 43 I have come in my Father's name, and you do not accept me; if another comes in his own name, you will accept him. 44 How can you believe when you accept glory from one another and do not seek the glory that comes from the one

a Gk *that one*   b Or *among*

who alone is God? ⁴⁵Do not think that I will accuse you before the Father; your accuser is Moses, on whom you have set your hope. ⁴⁶If you believed Moses, you would believe me, for he wrote about me. ⁴⁷But if you do not believe what he wrote, how will you believe what I say?"

Feeding the Five Thousand

6 After this Jesus went to the other side of the Sea of Galilee, also called the Sea of Tiberias.ᵃ ²A large crowd kept following him, because they saw the signs that he was doing for the sick. ³Jesus went up the mountain and sat down there with his disciples. ⁴Now the Passover, the festival of the Jews, was near. ⁵When he looked up and saw a large crowd coming toward him, Jesus said to Philip, "Where are we to buy bread for these people to eat?" ⁶He said this to test him, for he himself knew what he was going to do. ⁷Philip answered him, "Six months' wagesᵇ would not buy enough bread for each of them to get a little." ⁸One of his disciples, Andrew, Simon Peter's brother, said to him, ⁹"There is a boy here who has five barley loaves and two fish. But what are they among so many people?" ¹⁰Jesus said, "Make the people sit down." Now there was a great deal of grass in the place; so theyᶜ sat down, about five thousand in all. ¹¹Then Jesus took the loaves, and when he had given thanks, he distributed them to those who were seated; so also the fish, as much as they wanted.

PRAY IT!

A Little Gift Goes a Long Way
John 6:1-14

From all the people around Jesus, he chose a kid's small offering—five loaves and two fish—and turned it into a meal for thousands!

How do you think those people felt when that little bit of food was given by a boy? Did they laugh at his foolishness? Or did they feel guilty that they hadn't offered their own food? Either way, Jesus accepted the gift and did miraculous things with it.

Read this passage again and consider the role of the boy. Close with this prayer:

God, could you use me like the boy who helped feed the five thousand? Please help me have his courage and trust in you. Can you take my simple gifts and do wondrous things with them? Help me to take the risk and not worry what other people think. Please use my small gifts. Even if things don't work out as I plan, I'll trust that you are in charge and know better than I do. Amen.

CONNECT IT!

Loaves and Fishes: Feeding the Hungry · John 6:8-11

Nearly thirty years ago, a pot of soup was being prepared at St. John's Episcopal Church in Ithaca, New York. That one pot was intended to be shared by a few people selected to serve on a "hospitality and advocacy" committee. But their ministry began before they even got to discuss it. Three homeless people showed up at the door and were invited to share the group's first pot of soup. According to loaves.org, it was the beginning of much more soup for the hungry of their community.

After this first meal with the homeless, the church members began quietly serving community meals. Word spread fast, and they had twenty people sharing a meal within the first week. Today their Loaves & Fishes community kitchen provides all kinds of activities centered around sharing a nutritious meal each weekday. Many volunteers are students from local colleges, but others include families, professionals, retired people, and various community groups. The meals are open to any and all who come.

Like the boy who offered his lunch to Jesus in **John 6:9**, the people of Loaves & Fishes are offering daily what they have and watching God feed the hungry of their community.

ᵃ Gk *of Galilee of Tiberias*   ᵇ Gk *Two hundred denarii*; the denarius was the usual day's wage for a laborer   ᶜ Gk *the men*

¹²When they were satisfied, he told his disciples, "Gather up the fragments left over, so that nothing may be lost." ¹³So they gathered them up, and from the fragments of the five barley loaves, left by those who had eaten, they filled twelve baskets. ¹⁴When the people saw the sign that he had done, they began to say, "This is indeed the prophet who is to come into the world."

15 When Jesus realized that they were about to come and take him by force to make him king, he withdrew again to the mountain by himself.

Jesus Walks on the Water

16 When evening came, his disciples went down to the sea, ¹⁷got into a boat, and started across the sea to Capernaum. It was now dark, and Jesus had not yet come to them. ¹⁸The sea became rough because a strong wind was blowing. ¹⁹When they had rowed about three or four miles,ᵃ they saw Jesus walking on the sea and coming near the boat, and they were terrified. ²⁰But he said to them, "It is I;ᵇ do not be afraid." ²¹Then they wanted to take him into the boat, and immediately the boat reached the land toward which they were going.

The Bread from Heaven

22 The next day the crowd that had stayed on the other side of the sea saw that there had been only one boat there. They also saw that Jesus had not got into the boat with his disciples, but that his disciples had gone away alone. ²³Then some boats from Tiberias came near the place where they had eaten the bread after the Lord had given thanks.ᶜ ²⁴So when the crowd saw that neither Jesus nor his disciples were there, they themselves got into the boats and went to Capernaum looking for Jesus.

25 When they found him on the other side of the sea, they said to him, "Rabbi, when did you come here?" ²⁶Jesus answered them, "Very truly, I tell you, you are looking for me, not because you saw signs, but because you ate your fill of the loaves. ²⁷Do not work for the food that perishes, but for the food that endures for eternal life, which the Son of Man will give you. For it is on him that God the Father has set his seal." ²⁸Then they said to him, "What must we do to perform the works of God?" ²⁹Jesus answered them, "This is the work of God, that you believe in him whom he has sent." ³⁰So they said to him, "What sign are you going to give us then, so

PRAY IT!

Bread of Life · John 6:22–65

Jesus calls himself the "bread of life" (John 6:35). Some type of bread is part of the basic diet of almost every culture in the world. So Jesus is telling us in a symbolic way that he is part of the basic diet for spiritual life. And just as bread is shared and valued in every culture, Jesus shares himself with all people who are willing to believe.

Many of Jesus' early followers were troubled when he taught that they must eat his flesh and drink his blood in order to have true life (John 6:56-60). Their confusion and arguing is understandable; his words must have sounded strange. His words became more clear to the twelve disciples later when he served them bread and wine as his body and blood at the Last Supper. (See "Study It: The Complete Covenant Story," near Matthew 26:26-29; "Live It: The Lord's Supper," near Mark 14:22-25; and "Study It: The Passover Lamb," near Luke 22:14-20.) This teaching about the body and blood of Christ remains central to the Christian faith in the observance of Communion.

During your prayer time, reflect or journal on the following questions:

• How is Jesus a source of nourishment for you?

• How does celebrating Communion help you recognize more clearly Jesus' presence?

• How are you called to be the body and blood of Christ to the world around you?

Close with this prayer:

Lord, please be my nourishment and source of life. Thank you for your sacrifice, so that I can have true life. Amen.

ᵃ Gk *about twenty-five or thirty stadia*   ᵇ Gk *I am*   ᶜ Other ancient authorities lack *after the Lord had given thanks*

STUDY IT!

Jesus Fulfills Jewish Festivals · John 5–10

These chapters feature several references to four Old Testament festivals. During each festival, Jesus says or does something that cleverly indicates he is the fulfillment of the festival's intent.

After healing on the sabbath, Jesus says, "My Father is still working, and I also am working" (John 5:17). He is essentially declaring himself equal to God. Jesus feeds five thousand people and teaches that he is the bread of life near the Festival of Passover (see "Study It: The Passover," near Exodus 12:14-28). The implication is that, although Moses gave the Israelites manna during the exodus, God gives an even greater gift in Jesus, the bread of everlasting life.

The Festival of Booths, also called Tabernacles, is a weeklong harvest festival. Two of the main symbols of the Festival of Booths are water and light, and Jesus promises living water (John 7:38) and proclaims himself the light of the world (John 8:12).

Finally, the Festival of Dedication, also called Hanukkah, celebrates the dedication of the temple. During this festival, Jesus claims to be the one who is consecrated and sent into the world (John 10:36).

Jesus' saving mission is made clear in fulfilling these festivals, but his actions also lead to continued conflicts with the Jewish leaders.

---

that we may see it and believe you? What work are you performing? ³¹Our ancestors ate the manna in the wilderness; as it is written, 'He gave them bread from heaven to eat.'" ³²Then Jesus said to them, "Very truly, I tell you, it was not Moses who gave you the bread from heaven, but it is my Father who gives you the true bread from heaven. ³³For the bread of God is that which^a comes down from heaven and gives life to the world." ³⁴They said to him, "Sir, give us this bread always."

35 Jesus said to them, "I am the bread of life. Whoever comes to me will never be hungry, and whoever believes in me will never be thirsty. ³⁶But I said to you that you have seen me and yet do not believe. ³⁷Everything that the Father gives me will come to me, and anyone who comes to me I will never drive away; ³⁸for I have come down from heaven, not to do my own will, but the will of him who sent me. ³⁹And this is the will of him who sent me, that I should lose nothing of all that he has given me, but raise it up on the last day. ⁴⁰This is indeed the will of my Father, that all who see the Son and believe in him may have eternal life; and I will raise them up on the last day."

41 Then the Jews began to complain about him because he said, "I am the bread that came down from heaven." ⁴²They were saying, "Is not this Jesus, the son of Joseph, whose father and mother we know? How can he now say, 'I have come down from heaven'?" ⁴³Jesus answered them, "Do not complain among yourselves. ⁴⁴No one can come to me unless drawn by the Father who sent me; and I will raise that person up on the last day. ⁴⁵It is written in the prophets, 'And they shall all be taught by God.' Everyone who has heard and learned from the Father comes to me. ⁴⁶Not that anyone has seen the Father except the one who is from God; he has seen the Father. ⁴⁷Very truly, I tell you, whoever believes has eternal life. ⁴⁸I am the bread of life. ⁴⁹Your ancestors ate the manna in the wilderness, and they died. ⁵⁰This is the bread that comes down from heaven, so that one may eat of it and not die. ⁵¹I am the living bread that came down from heaven. Whoever eats of this bread will live forever; and the bread that I will give for the life of the world is my flesh."

52 The Jews then disputed among themselves, saying, "How can this man give us his flesh to eat?" ⁵³So Jesus said to them, "Very truly, I tell you, unless you eat the flesh of the Son of Man and drink his blood, you have no life in you. ⁵⁴Those who eat my flesh and drink my blood have eternal life, and I will raise them up on the last day; ⁵⁵for my flesh is true food and my blood is true drink. ⁵⁶Those who eat my flesh and drink my blood abide in me, and I in them. ⁵⁷Just as the living Father sent me, and I live because of the Father, so whoever eats me will live

a Or he who

because of me. [58]This is the bread that came down from heaven, not like that which your ancestors ate, and they died. But the one who eats this bread will live forever." [59]He said these things while he was teaching in the synagogue at Capernaum.

The Words of Eternal Life

60 When many of his disciples heard it, they said, "This teaching is difficult; who can accept it?" [61]But Jesus, being aware that his disciples were complaining about it, said to them, "Does this offend you? [62]Then what if you were to see the Son of Man ascending to where he was before? [63]It is the spirit that gives life; the flesh is useless. The words that I have spoken to you are spirit and life. [64]But among you there are some who do not believe." For Jesus knew from the first who were the ones that did not believe, and who was the one that would betray him. [65]And he said, "For this reason I have told you that no one can come to me unless it is granted by the Father."

66 Because of this many of his disciples turned back and no longer went about with him. [67]So Jesus asked the twelve, "Do you also wish to go away?" [68]Simon Peter answered him, "Lord, to whom can we go? You have the words of eternal life. [69]We have come to believe and know that you are the Holy One of God."[a] [70]Jesus answered them, "Did I not choose you, the twelve? Yet one of you is a devil." [71]He was speaking of Judas son of Simon Iscariot,[b] for he, though one of the twelve, was going to betray him.

7   The Unbelief of Jesus' Brothers

After this Jesus went about in Galilee. He did not wish[c] to go about in Judea because the Jews were looking for an opportunity to kill him. [2]Now the Jewish festival of Booths[d] was near. [3]So his brothers said to him, "Leave here and go to Judea so that your disciples also may see the works you are doing; [4]for no one who wants[e] to be widely known acts in secret. If you do these things, show yourself to the world." [5](For not even his brothers believed in him.) [6]Jesus said to them, "My time has not yet come, but your time is always here. [7]The world cannot hate you, but it hates me because I testify against it that its works are evil. [8]Go to the festival yourselves. I am not[f] going to this festival, for my time has not yet fully come." [9]After saying this, he remained in Galilee.

Jesus at the Festival of Booths

10 But after his brothers had gone to the festival, then he also went, not publicly but as it were[g] in secret. [11]The Jews were looking for him at the festival and saying, "Where is he?" [12]And there was considerable complaining about him among the crowds. While some were saying, "He is a good man," others were saying, "No, he is deceiving the crowd." [13]Yet no one would speak openly about him for fear of the Jews.

14 About the middle of the festival Jesus went up into the temple and began to teach. [15]The Jews were astonished at it, saying, "How does this man have such learning,[h] when he has never been taught?" [16]Then Jesus answered them, "My teaching is not mine but his who sent me. [17]Anyone who resolves to do the will of God will know whether the teaching is from God or whether I am speaking on my own. [18]Those who speak on their own seek their own glory; but the one who seeks the glory of him who sent him is true, and there is nothing false in him.

19 "Did not Moses give you the law? Yet none of you keeps the law. Why are you looking for an opportunity to kill me?" [20]The crowd answered, "You have a demon! Who is trying to kill you?" [21]Jesus answered them, "I performed one work, and all of you are astonished. [22]Moses gave you circumcision (it is, of course, not from Moses, but from the patriarchs), and you circumcise a man on the sabbath. [23]If a man receives circumcision on the sabbath in order that the law of Moses may not be broken, are you angry with me because I healed a man's whole body on the sabbath? [24]Do not judge by appearances, but judge with right judgment."

Is This the Christ?

25 Now some of the people of Jerusalem were saying, "Is not this the man whom they are trying to kill? [26]And here he is, speaking openly, but they say nothing to him! Can it be that the authorities really know that this is the Messiah?[i] [27]Yet we know where this man is from; but when the Messiah[i] comes, no one will know where he is from." [28]Then Jesus cried out as he was teaching in the temple, "You know me, and you know where I am from. I have not come on my own. But the one who sent me is true, and you do not know him. [29]I know him, because I am from him, and he sent me." [30]Then they tried to arrest him, but no one laid hands on

---

a Other ancient authorities read the Christ, the Son of the living God   b Other ancient authorities read Judas Iscariot son of Simon; others, Judas son of Simon from Karyot (Kerioth)   c Other ancient authorities read was not at liberty   d Or Tabernacles   e Other ancient authorities read wants it   f Other ancient authorities add yet   g Other ancient authorities lack as it were   h Or this man know his letters   i Or the Christ

him, because his hour had not yet come. [31]Yet many in the crowd believed in him and were saying, "When the Messiah[a] comes, will he do more signs than this man has done?"[b]

Officers Are Sent to Arrest Jesus

32 The Pharisees heard the crowd muttering such things about him, and the chief priests and Pharisees sent temple police to arrest him. [33]Jesus then said, "I will be with you a little while longer, and then I am going to him who sent me. [34]You will search for me, but you will not find me; and where I am, you cannot come." [35]The Jews said to one another, "Where does this man intend to go that we will not find him? Does he intend to go to the Dispersion among the Greeks and teach the Greeks? [36]What does he mean by saying, 'You will search for me and you will not find me' and 'Where I am, you cannot come'?"

Rivers of Living Water

37 On the last day of the festival, the great day, while Jesus was standing there, he cried out, "Let anyone who is thirsty come to me, [38]and let the one who believes in me drink. As[c] the scripture has said, 'Out of the believer's heart[d] shall flow rivers of living water.' " [39]Now he said this about the Spirit, which believers in him were to receive; for as yet there was no Spirit,[e] because Jesus was not yet glorified.

Division among the People

40 When they heard these words, some in the crowd said, "This is really the prophet." [41]Others said, "This is the Messiah."[a] But some asked, "Surely the Messiah[a] does not come from Galilee, does he? [42]Has not the scripture said that the Messiah[a] is descended from David and comes from Bethlehem, the village where David lived?" [43]So there was a division in the crowd because of him. [44]Some of

STUDY IT!

Jewish Sects · John 7:32

Several different ways of being Jewish emerged during the last two centuries before Christ. Various groups rose up and emphasized different ways of remaining faithful to their Jewish heritage. These groups, or factions, within a religion are sometimes called sects. Three primary sects emerged within Judaism. Their leaders disagreed with each other on points of Jewish law, but many were united in their dislike of Jesus.

The **Pharisees** were descendants of the Hasidim, Jews devoted to a strict observance of the law who opposed King Antiochus IV Epiphanes' attempts to destroy the Jewish religion. "Pharisee" means "separated" and probably reflects the Pharisees' rigorous observance of the law. They were often greatly respected. In the New Testament, Jesus argues with some Pharisees, but is also a guest of others. The apostle Paul was a Pharisee. Not surprisingly, some of the Pharisees' teachings were similar to those of the early Christians.

The **Sadducees** were a conservative Jewish sect that emerged in the first century B.C. and lasted only to around A.D. 70. The Sadducees were wealthy and politically influential landowners, and some of them had important roles in the temple. They emphasized the necessity of worshiping at the temple in Jerusalem. Unlike the Pharisees, they did not believe in the resurrection of the body.

The **Essenes**, like the Pharisees, seem to have descended from the Hasidim. They existed in the first century B.C. and disappeared after A.D. 70. "Essene" can mean "healer" or "pious." The Essenes did not believe in the necessity of temple sacrifice and often lived together in isolated communities where they practiced a simple lifestyle. Some of them were connected with the desert community at Qumran and were responsible for writing the Dead Sea Scrolls. John the Baptist's preaching and some of Jesus' teaching in the Gospels closely reflected the writings and teachings of the Essenes.

---

a Or *the Christ* b Other ancient authorities read *is doing* c Or *come to me and drink.* [38]*The one who believes in me, as* d Gk *out of his belly* e Other ancient authorities read *for as yet the Spirit* (others, *Holy Spirit*) *had not been given*

them wanted to arrest him, but no one laid hands on him.

The Unbelief of Those in Authority

45 Then the temple police went back to the chief priests and Pharisees, who asked them, "Why did you not arrest him?" [46]The police answered, "Never has anyone spoken like this!" [47]Then the Pharisees replied, "Surely you have not been deceived too, have you? [48]Has any one of the authorities or of the Pharisees believed in him? [49]But this crowd, which does not know the law—they are accursed." [50]Nicodemus, who had gone to Jesus[a] before, and who was one of them, asked, [51]"Our law does not judge people without first giving them a hearing to find out what they are doing, does it?" [52]They replied, "Surely you are not also from Galilee, are you? Search and you will see that no prophet is to arise from Galilee."

The Woman Caught in Adultery

⟦ [53]Then each of them went home, [1]while Jesus went to the Mount of Olives. [2]Early in the morning he came again to the temple. All the people came to him and he sat down and began to teach them. [3]The scribes and the Pharisees brought a woman who had been caught in adultery; and making her stand before all of them, [4]they said to him, "Teacher, this woman was caught in the very act of committing adultery. [5]Now in the law Moses commanded us to stone such women. Now what do you say?" [6]They said this to test him, so that they might have some charge to bring against him. Jesus bent down and wrote with his finger on the ground. [7]When they kept on questioning him, he straightened up and said to them, "Let anyone among you who is without sin be the first to throw a stone at her." [8]And once again he bent down and wrote on the ground.[b] [9]When they heard it, they went away, one by one, beginning with the elders; and Jesus was left alone with the woman standing before him. [10]Jesus straightened up and said to her, "Woman, where are they? Has no one condemned you?" [11]She said, "No one, sir."[c] And Jesus said, "Neither do I condemn you. Go your way, and from now on do not sin again."⟧[d]

Jesus the Light of the World

12 Again Jesus spoke to them, saying, "I am the light of the world. Whoever follows me will never

---

LIVE IT!

Divine Compassion · John 8:2–11

Jesus was great at turning the tables on those who considered themselves his enemies. In **John 8:2–11**, the scribes and Pharisees think they have come up with a perfect trap. They want Jesus to save the woman from being stoned by giving a "wrong" interpretation of the law. Making such a wrong judgment publicly would cause Jesus to lose his credibility quickly.

But Jesus redefines the game with one amazing sentence. The focus moves away from the woman and onto the accusers, who cannot deny that they too are guilty of sin. The trap fails miserably, and the humbled religious leaders leave in silence.

We are often quick to notice others' sin while minimizing our own. Jesus reminds us to be compassionate toward the sins of others. Notice how tenderly Christ dealt with the woman, whose dignity and reputation had been trampled on. When you recognize your own guilt and stand exposed and shamed before God and others, remember that God is just as tender and compassionate toward you.

- Are you quick to jump on the bandwagon of blame and accusation? Or are you willing to stand up for the persecuted or those who have publicly made mistakes?
- Who in your world is a constant scapegoat? How can you show the person compassion?

---

[a] Gk *him*   [b] Other ancient authorities add *the sins of each of them*   [c] Or *Lord*   [d] The most ancient authorities lack 7.53—8.11; other authorities add the passage here or after 7.36 or after 21.25 or after Luke 21.38, with variations of text; some mark the passage as doubtful.

The Light of Life
John 8:12

Once again, the author of the gospel of John creates a sharp distinction between light and darkness, belief and unbelief. Those who follow Jesus will never walk in darkness, but will have the light of life. Light is a symbol of belief that results in life, happiness, and the joy of salvation and liberation in Christ. Darkness is a symbol of unbelief that results in death, disgrace, and condemnation.

We need the light of Christ to live the life God has called us to and to illuminate what's important to help us keep our activities and material possessions in order. The light of Christ also directs us in our journey with God and shines through us to radiate God's love to those around us.

- Where in your life do you need the light of Christ?
- Give thanks to Jesus for inviting you to share in the life of God.

walk in darkness but will have the light of life." [13]Then the Pharisees said to him, "You are testifying on your own behalf; your testimony is not valid." [14]Jesus answered, "Even if I testify on my own behalf, my testimony is valid because I know where I have come from and where I am going, but you do not know where I come from or where I am going. [15]You judge by human standards;[a] I judge no one. [16]Yet even if I do judge, my judgment is valid; for it is not I alone who judge, but I and the Father[b] who sent me. [17]In your law it is written that the testimony of two witnesses is valid. [18]I testify on my own behalf, and the Father who sent me testifies on my behalf." [19]Then they said to him, "Where is your Father?" Jesus answered, "You know neither me nor my Father. If you knew me, you would know my Father also." [20]He spoke these words while he was teaching in the treasury of the temple, but no one arrested him, because his hour had not yet come.

Jesus Foretells His Death

21 Again he said to them, "I am going away, and you will search for me, but you will die in your sin. Where I am going, you cannot come." [22]Then the Jews said, "Is he going to kill himself? Is that what he means by saying, 'Where I am going, you cannot come'?" [23]He said to them, "You are from below, I am from above; you are of this world, I am not of this world. [24]I told you that you would die in your sins, for you will die in your sins unless you believe that I am he."[c] [25]They said to him, "Who are you?" Jesus said to them, "Why do I speak to you at all?[d] [26]I have much to say about you and much to condemn; but the one who sent me is true, and I declare to the world what I have heard from him." [27]They did not understand that he was speaking to them about the Father. [28]So Jesus said, "When you have lifted up the Son of Man, then you will realize that I am he,[c] and that I do nothing on my own, but I speak these things as the Father instructed me. [29]And the one who sent me is with me; he has not left me alone, for I always do what is pleasing to him." [30]As he was saying these things, many believed in him.

True Disciples

31 Then Jesus said to the Jews who had believed in him, "If you continue in my word, you are truly my disciples; [32]and you will know the truth, and the truth will make you free." [33]They answered him, "We are descendants of Abraham and have never been slaves to anyone. What do you mean by saying, 'You will be made free'?"

34 Jesus answered them, "Very truly, I tell you, everyone who commits sin is a slave to sin. [35]The slave does not have a permanent place in the household; the son has a place there forever. [36]So if the Son makes you free, you will be free indeed. [37]I know that you are descendants of Abraham; yet you look for an opportunity to kill me, because there is no place in you for my word. [38]I declare what I have seen in the Father's presence; as for you, you should do what you have heard from the Father."[e]

Jesus and Abraham

39 They answered him, "Abraham is our father." Jesus said to them, "If you were Abraham's children, you would be doing[f] what Abraham did, [40]but now you are trying to kill me, a man who has told you the truth that I heard from God. This is not what Abraham did. [41]You are indeed doing what your father

a Gk *according to the flesh* b Other ancient authorities read *he* c Gk *I am* d Or *What I have told you from the beginning* e Other ancient authorities read *you do what you have heard from your father* f Other ancient authorities read *If you are Abraham's children, then do*

Desmond Tutu: Standing for Truth, Calling for Freedom
John 8:31–32

Archbishop Desmond Tutu grew up in the deeply divided nation of South Africa and became an Anglican priest in 1960. From the 1950s to the 1990s, the country was ruled under apartheid, a political system of segregation that kept blacks and whites completely separated—and made sure that blacks had little or no rights or privileges, even though they greatly outnumbered the white minority. Blacks were not allowed citizenship and were outlawed from white areas, including schools and hospitals. The educational, medical, and few public services they received were far inferior and designed to deny them opportunity.

Mass uprising against apartheid began in the 1970s. And though some used violent means, Tutu called for freedom using nonviolence. He spoke out boldly against his nation's unjust government system for several decades, calling it evil and unchristian. Tutu called for freedom for blacks and whites, and he became well known internationally as the moral conscience of South Africa.

It took until the 1990s to repeal apartheid in South Africa, and in 1994 Nelson Mandela was elected as the country's first black president. Tutu continued to be a leading voice for equality and justice in the nation and urged the government to bring relief to its poor and oppressed citizens. He has continued to be involved in peacemaking efforts around the world. His opinions have not always been popular, but that has never kept Tutu from calling world leaders to moral truth and justice that reflects God's standards, especially on behalf of those who have no voice.

"This is God's world!" he wrote in the British newspaper THE GUARDIAN. "We live in a moral universe. The apartheid government was very powerful, but today it no longer exists. Injustice and oppression will never prevail. Those who are powerful have to remember the litmus test that God gives to the powerful: what is your treatment of the poor, the hungry, the voiceless?"* By living according to this standard of love and justice, we show that we are truly Jesus' disciples and know his truth. And, as John says, it is that truth that will make us free (John 8:32).

does." They said to him, "We are not illegitimate children; we have one father, God himself." [42]Jesus said to them, "If God were your Father, you would love me, for I came from God and now I am here. I did not come on my own, but he sent me. [43]Why do you not understand what I say? It is because you cannot accept my word. [44]You are from your father the devil, and you choose to do your father's desires. He was a murderer from the beginning and does not stand in the truth, because there is no truth in him. When he lies, he speaks according to his own nature, for he is a liar and the father of lies. [45]But because I tell the truth, you do not believe me. [46]Which of you convicts me of sin? If I tell the truth, why do you not believe me? [47]Whoever is from God hears the words of God. The reason you do not hear them is that you are not from God."

48 The Jews answered him, "Are we not right in saying that you are a Samaritan and have a demon?"

[49]Jesus answered, "I do not have a demon; but I honor my Father, and you dishonor me. [50]Yet I do not seek my own glory; there is one who seeks it and he is the judge. [51]Very truly, I tell you, whoever keeps my word will never see death." [52]The Jews said to him, "Now we know that you have a demon. Abraham died, and so did the prophets; yet you say, 'Whoever keeps my word will never taste death.' [53]Are you greater than our father Abraham, who died? The prophets also died. Who do you claim to be?" [54]Jesus answered, "If I glorify myself, my glory is nothing. It is my Father who glorifies me, he of whom you say, 'He is our God,' [55]though you do not know him. But I know him; if I would say that I do not know him, I would be a liar like you. But I do know him and I keep his word. [56]Your ancestor Abraham rejoiced that he would see my day; he saw it and was glad." [57]Then the Jews said to him, "You are not yet fifty years old, and have

you seen Abraham?"[a] [58]Jesus said to them, "Very truly, I tell you, before Abraham was, I am." [59]So they picked up stones to throw at him, but Jesus hid himself and went out of the temple.

9 A Man Born Blind Receives Sight

As he walked along, he saw a man blind from birth. [2]His disciples asked him, "Rabbi, who sinned, this man or his parents, that he was born blind?" [3]Jesus answered, "Neither this man nor his parents sinned; he was born blind so that God's works might be revealed in him. [4]We[b] must work the works of him who sent me[c] while it is day; night is coming when no one can work. [5]As long as I am in the world, I am the light of the world." [6]When he had said this, he spat on the ground and made mud with the saliva and spread the mud on the man's eyes, [7]saying to him, "Go, wash in the pool of Siloam" (which means Sent).

PRAY IT!

Seeing with God's Eyes
John 9

Lord, can you fix my eyesight, as you did for the blind man?

I want to see with your eyes those who are mocked for being different at school.

I want to see with your eyes the homeless person on a park bench.

I want to see with your eyes people from other races and cultures.

I want to see beyond people who think being thinner or stronger makes you more lovable.

I want to see beyond people who view wealth as the key to life.

Help me to see with your eyes, Lord! Blind me to the way the world sees, so that I won't give in to judging people on their looks, skin color, social status, or personality.

Help me to see and to love as you love, Lord—with eyes so wide open that they see past the outside and right into the hearts of others.

Then he went and washed and came back able to see. [8]The neighbors and those who had seen him before as a beggar began to ask, "Is this not the man who used to sit and beg?" [9]Some were saying, "It is he." Others were saying, "No, but it is someone like him." He kept saying, "I am the man." [10]But they kept asking him, "Then how were your eyes opened?" [11]He answered, "The man called Jesus made mud, spread it on my eyes, and said to me, 'Go to Siloam and wash.' Then I went and washed and received my sight." [12]They said to him, "Where is he?" He said, "I do not know."

The Pharisees Investigate the Healing

13 They brought to the Pharisees the man who had formerly been blind. [14]Now it was a sabbath day when Jesus made the mud and opened his eyes. [15]Then the Pharisees also began to ask him how he had received his sight. He said to them, "He put mud on my eyes. Then I washed, and now I see." [16]Some of the Pharisees said, "This man is not from God, for he does not observe the sabbath." But others said, "How can a man who is a sinner perform such signs?" And they were divided. [17]So they said again to the blind man, "What do you say about him? It was your eyes he opened." He said, "He is a prophet."

18 The Jews did not believe that he had been blind and had received his sight until they called the parents of the man who had received his sight [19]and asked them, "Is this your son, who you say was born blind? How then does he now see?" [20]His parents answered, "We know that this is our son, and that he was born blind; [21]but we do not know how it is that now he sees, nor do we know who opened his eyes. Ask him; he is of age. He will speak for himself." [22]His parents said this because they were afraid of the Jews; for the Jews had already agreed that anyone who confessed Jesus[d] to be the Messiah[e] would be put out of the synagogue. [23]Therefore his parents said, "He is of age; ask him."

24 So for the second time they called the man who had been blind, and they said to him, "Give glory to God! We know that this man is a sinner." [25]He answered, "I do not know whether he is a sinner. One thing I do know, that though I was blind, now I see." [26]They said to him, "What did he do to you? How did he open your eyes?" [27]He answered them, "I have told you already, and you

---

a Other ancient authorities read *has Abraham seen you?*   b Other ancient authorities read *I*   c Other ancient authorities read *us*   d Gk *him*   e Or *the Christ*

would not listen. Why do you want to hear it again? Do you also want to become his disciples?" ²⁸Then they reviled him, saying, "You are his disciple, but we are disciples of Moses. ²⁹We know that God has spoken to Moses, but as for this man, we do not know where he comes from." ³⁰The man answered, "Here is an astonishing thing! You do not know where he comes from, and yet he opened my eyes. ³¹We know that God does not listen to sinners, but he does listen to one who worships him and obeys his will. ³²Never since the world began has it been heard that anyone opened the eyes of a person born blind. ³³If this man were not from God, he could do nothing." ³⁴They answered him, "You were born entirely in sins, and are you trying to teach us?" And they drove him out.

Spiritual Blindness

35 Jesus heard that they had driven him out, and when he found him, he said, "Do you believe in the Son of Man?"[a] ³⁶He answered, "And who is he, sir?[b] Tell me, so that I may believe in him." ³⁷Jesus said to him, "You have seen him, and the one speaking with you is he." ³⁸He said, "Lord,[b] I believe." And he worshiped him. ³⁹Jesus said, "I came into this world for judgment so that those who do not see may see, and those who do see may become blind." ⁴⁰Some of the Pharisees near him heard this and said to him, "Surely we are not blind, are we?" ⁴¹Jesus said to them, "If you were blind, you would not have sin. But now that you say, 'We see,' your sin remains.

10 Jesus the Good Shepherd

"Very truly, I tell you, anyone who does not enter the sheepfold by the gate but climbs in by another way is a thief and a bandit. ²The one who enters by the gate is the shepherd of the sheep. ³The gatekeeper opens the gate for him, and the sheep hear his voice. He calls his own sheep by name and leads them out. ⁴When he has brought out all his own, he goes ahead of them, and the sheep follow him because they know his voice. ⁵They will not follow a stranger, but they will run from him because they do not know the voice of strangers." ⁶Jesus used this figure of speech with them, but they did not understand what he was saying to them.

7 So again Jesus said to them, "Very truly, I tell you, I am the gate for the sheep. ⁸All who came before me are thieves and bandits; but the sheep did not listen to them. ⁹I am the gate. Whoever enters by me will be saved, and will come in and go out and find

Jesus, the Good Shepherd · John 10:1–18

Shepherds and sheep are a recurring topic or theme in the Bible. God is sometimes portrayed as a shepherd in the Old Testament. For example, see **Psalm 23** and **Ezekiel 34**. David, the greatest king of Israel, is also portrayed as a shepherd in **Psalm 78:70–72**. In passages such as **Jeremiah 23:1–6**, God promises to raise up new shepherds who will follow in David's legacy. So it's natural that Jesus compares himself to a shepherd in this passage in John.

Being a shepherd is not an easy job. Sheep are defenseless creatures, and shepherds have to protect them from predators like lions and wolves. Sheep also have a tendency to stray from the flock, making them especially vulnerable. Shepherds endure the hardships of being away from their homes and putting up with simple food and harsh weather while pasturing sheep. Their lives can be endangered when confronted by desperate predators. Sheep learn to recognize their shepherd's voice, which makes it easier to separate different flocks when flocks are mixed together for grazing or protection.

- How do you relate to Jesus as the Good Shepherd?
- When is it reassuring to know that Jesus is watching out for you? How do you see yourself helping to "shepherd" other people as a follower of Jesus?
- In what areas do you keep wandering off like a lost sheep? Confess your sin and ask for help to stay close to Jesus, the Good Shepherd.

a Other ancient authorities read *the Son of God*   b *Sir* and *Lord* translate the same Greek word

"I came that they may have life, and have it abundantly."
—John 10:10

pasture. ¹⁰The thief comes only to steal and kill and destroy. I came that they may have life, and have it abundantly.

11 "I am the good shepherd. The good shepherd lays down his life for the sheep. ¹²The hired hand, who is not the shepherd and does not own the sheep, sees the wolf coming and leaves the sheep and runs away—and the wolf snatches them and scatters them. ¹³The hired hand runs away because a hired hand does not care for the sheep. ¹⁴I am the good shepherd. I know my own and my own know me, ¹⁵just as the Father knows me and I know the Father. And I lay down my life for the sheep. ¹⁶I have other sheep that do not belong to this fold. I must bring them also, and they will listen to my voice. So there will be one flock, one shepherd. ¹⁷For this reason the Father loves me, because I lay down my life in order to take it up again. ¹⁸No one takes[a] it from me, but I lay it down of my own accord. I have power to lay it down, and I have power to take it up again. I have received this command from my Father."

19 Again the Jews were divided because of these words. ²⁰Many of them were saying, "He has a demon and is out of his mind. Why listen to him?" ²¹Others were saying, "These are not the words of one who has a demon. Can a demon open the eyes of the blind?"

Jesus Is Rejected by the Jews

22 At that time the festival of the Dedication took place in Jerusalem. It was winter, ²³and Jesus was walking in the temple, in the portico of Solomon. ²⁴So the Jews gathered around him and said to him, "How long will you keep us in suspense? If you are the Messiah,[b] tell us plainly." ²⁵Jesus answered, "I have told you, and you do not believe. The works that I do in my Father's name testify to me; ²⁶but you do not believe, because you do not belong to my sheep. ²⁷My sheep hear my voice. I know them, and they follow me. ²⁸I give them eternal life, and they will never perish. No one will snatch them out of my hand. ²⁹What my Father has given me is

greater than all else, and no one can snatch it out of the Father's hand.[c] ³⁰The Father and I are one."

31 The Jews took up stones again to stone him. ³²Jesus replied, "I have shown you many good works from the Father. For which of these are you going to stone me?" ³³The Jews answered, "It is not for a good work that we are going to stone you, but for blasphemy, because you, though only a human being, are making yourself God." ³⁴Jesus answered, "Is it not written in your law,[d] 'I said, you are gods'? ³⁵If those to whom the word of God came were called 'gods'—and the scripture cannot be annulled— ³⁶can you say that the one whom the Father has sanctified and sent into the world is blaspheming because I said, 'I am God's Son'? ³⁷If I am not doing the works of my Father, then do not believe me. ³⁸But if I do them, even though you do not believe me, believe the works, so that you may know and understand[e] that the Father is in me and I am in the Father." ³⁹Then they tried to arrest him again, but he escaped from their hands.

40 He went away again across the Jordan to the place where John had been baptizing earlier, and he remained there. ⁴¹Many came to him, and they were saying, "John performed no sign, but everything that John said about this man was true." ⁴²And many believed in him there.

The Death of Lazarus

11 Now a certain man was ill, Lazarus of Bethany, the village of Mary and her sister Martha. ²Mary was the one who anointed the Lord with perfume and wiped his feet with her hair; her brother Lazarus was ill. ³So the sisters sent a message to Jesus,[f] "Lord, he whom you love is ill." ⁴But when Jesus heard it, he said, "This illness does not lead to death; rather it is for God's glory, so that the Son of God may be glorified through it." ⁵Accordingly, though Jesus loved Martha and her sister and Lazarus, ⁶after having heard that Lazarus[g] was ill, he stayed two days longer in the place where he was.

7 Then after this he said to the disciples, "Let us go to Judea again." ⁸The disciples said to him, "Rabbi, the Jews were just now trying to stone you, and are you going there again?" ⁹Jesus answered, "Are there not twelve hours of daylight? Those who walk during the day do not stumble, because they see the light of this world. ¹⁰But those who walk at night stumble, because the light is not in them."

---

a Other ancient authorities read has taken   b Or the Christ   c Other ancient authorities read My Father who has given them to me is greater than all, and no one can snatch them out of the Father's hand   d Other ancient authorities read in the law   e Other ancient authorities lack and understand; others read and believe   f Gk him   g Gk he

Alive Again! John 11:1–44

"Jesus began to weep" (John 11:35). Some believe Jesus wept because he couldn't help himself when he saw his dear friend Mary crying over the death of her brother, Lazarus. Jesus expressed both compassion for Mary and his own grief at the loss of his friend Lazarus. What a beautiful, powerful expression of Jesus' humanity!

What follows next is another powerful expression of Jesus' impending death and resurrection—his glorification. It's the seventh and final sign in John's gospel. What a dramatic moment, as Jesus steps into the tomb of a man who has been dead for four days. He calls to Lazarus to come out—and Lazarus, wrapped in burial cloth, indeed comes out! He is alive again. Can you imagine being there? It must have blown the minds of onlookers! Imagine how grateful Martha and Mary would have been to have their brother alive again.

You've got to wonder, though, what it would feel like to be alive again after being in the grave for four days. How would people react to this man knowing that he had been dead? Why do you think this is the last sign of Jesus' power in the gospel of John? Notice that this event occurs about a week before the last days of Jesus' life. Why is this sign such a threat to the ruling officials of Jerusalem?

¹¹ After saying this, he told them, "Our friend Lazarus has fallen asleep, but I am going there to awaken him." ¹² The disciples said to him, "Lord, if he has fallen asleep, he will be all right." ¹³ Jesus, however, had been speaking about his death, but they thought that he was referring merely to sleep. ¹⁴ Then Jesus told them plainly, "Lazarus is dead. ¹⁵ For your sake I am glad I was not there, so that you may believe. But let us go to him." ¹⁶ Thomas, who was called the Twin,ᵃ said to his fellow disciples, "Let us also go, that we may die with him."

Jesus the Resurrection and the Life

17 When Jesus arrived, he found that Lazarusᵇ had already been in the tomb four days. ¹⁸ Now Bethany was near Jerusalem, some two milesᶜ away, ¹⁹ and many of the Jews had come to Martha and Mary to console them about their brother. ²⁰ When Martha heard that Jesus was coming, she went and met him, while Mary stayed at home. ²¹ Martha said to Jesus, "Lord, if you had been here, my brother would not have died. ²² But even now I know that God will give you whatever you ask of him." ²³ Jesus said to her, "Your brother will rise again." ²⁴ Martha said to him, "I know that he will rise again in the resurrection on the last day." ²⁵ Jesus said to her, "I am the resurrection and the life.ᵈ Those who believe in me, even though they die, will live, ²⁶ and everyone who lives and believes in me will never die. Do you believe this?" ²⁷ She said to him, "Yes, Lord, I believe that you are the Messiah,ᵉ the Son of God, the one coming into the world."

Jesus Weeps

28 When she had said this, she went back and called her sister Mary, and told her privately, "The Teacher is here and is calling for you." ²⁹ And when she heard it, she got up quickly and went to him. ³⁰ Now Jesus had not yet come to the village, but was still at the place where Martha had met him. ³¹ The Jews who were with her in the house, consoling her, saw Mary get up quickly and go out. They followed her because they thought that she was going to the tomb to weep there. ³² When Mary came where Jesus was and saw him, she knelt at his feet and said to him, "Lord, if you had been here, my brother would not have died." ³³ When Jesus saw her weeping, and the Jews who came with her also weeping, he was greatly disturbed in spirit and deeply moved. ³⁴ He said, "Where have you laid him?" They said to him, "Lord, come and see." ³⁵ Jesus began to weep. ³⁶ So the Jews said, "See how he loved him!" ³⁷ But some of them said, "Could not he who opened the eyes of the blind man have kept this man from dying?"

ᵃ Gk Didymus   ᵇ Gk he   ᶜ Gk fifteen stadia   ᵈ Other ancient authorities lack and the life   ᵉ Or the Christ

Jesus Raises Lazarus to Life

38 Then Jesus, again greatly disturbed, came to the tomb. It was a cave, and a stone was lying against it. ³⁹Jesus said, "Take away the stone." Martha, the sister of the dead man, said to him, "Lord, already there is a stench because he has been dead four days." ⁴⁰Jesus said to her, "Did I not tell you that if you believed, you would see the glory of God?" ⁴¹So they took away the stone. And Jesus looked upward and said, "Father, I thank you for having heard me. ⁴²I knew that you always hear me, but I have said this for the sake of the crowd standing here, so that they may believe that you sent me." ⁴³When he had said this, he cried with a loud voice, "Lazarus, come out!" ⁴⁴The dead man came out, his hands and feet bound with strips of cloth, and his face wrapped in a cloth. Jesus said to them, "Unbind him, and let him go."

The Plot to Kill Jesus

45 Many of the Jews therefore, who had come with Mary and had seen what Jesus did, believed in him. ⁴⁶But some of them went to the Pharisees and told them what he had done. ⁴⁷So the chief priests and the Pharisees called a meeting of the council, and said, "What are we to do? This man is performing many signs. ⁴⁸If we let him go on like this, everyone will believe in him, and the Romans will come and destroy both our holy place[a] and our nation." ⁴⁹But one of them, Caiaphas, who was high priest that year, said to them, "You know nothing at all! ⁵⁰You do not understand that it is better for you to have one man die for the people than to have the whole nation destroyed." ⁵¹He did not say this on his own, but being high priest that year he prophesied that Jesus was about to die for the nation, ⁵²and not for the nation only, but to gather into one the dispersed children of God. ⁵³So from that day on they planned to put him to death.

54 Jesus therefore no longer walked about openly among the Jews, but went from there to a town called Ephraim in the region near the wilderness; and he remained there with the disciples.

55 Now the Passover of the Jews was near, and many went up from the country to Jerusalem before the Passover to purify themselves. ⁵⁶They were looking for Jesus and were asking one another as they stood in the temple, "What do you think? Surely he will not come to the festival, will he?" ⁵⁷Now the chief priests and the Pharisees had given orders that anyone who knew where Jesus[b] was should let them know, so that they might arrest him.

Mary Anoints Jesus

12 Six days before the Passover Jesus came to Bethany, the home of Lazarus, whom he had raised from the dead. ²There they gave a dinner for him. Martha served, and Lazarus was one of those at the table with him. ³Mary took a pound of costly perfume made of pure nard, anointed Jesus' feet, and wiped them[c] with her hair. The house was filled with the fragrance of the perfume. ⁴But Judas Iscariot, one of his disciples (the one who was about to betray him), said, ⁵"Why was this perfume not sold for three hundred denarii[d] and the money given to the poor?" ⁶(He said this not because he cared about the poor, but because he was a thief; he kept the common purse and used to steal what was put into it.) ⁷Jesus said, "Leave her alone. She bought it[e] so that she might keep it for the day of my burial. ⁸You always

---

a Or *our temple*; Greek *our place*   b Gk *he*   c Gk *his feet*   d Three hundred denarii would be nearly a year's wages for a laborer   e Gk lacks *She bought it*

have the poor with you, but you do not always have me."

The Plot to Kill Lazarus

9 When the great crowd of the Jews learned that he was there, they came not only because of Jesus but also to see Lazarus, whom he had raised from the dead. [10]So the chief priests planned to put Lazarus to death as well, [11]since it was on account of him that many of the Jews were deserting and were believing in Jesus.

Jesus' Triumphal Entry into Jerusalem

12 The next day the great crowd that had come to the festival heard that Jesus was coming to Jerusalem. [13]So they took branches of palm trees and went out to meet him, shouting,

"Hosanna!
Blessed is the one who comes in the name of
the Lord—
the King of Israel!"

[14]Jesus found a young donkey and sat on it; as it is written:

[15] "Do not be afraid, daughter of Zion.
Look, your king is coming,
sitting on a donkey's colt!"

[16]His disciples did not understand these things at first; but when Jesus was glorified, then they remembered that these things had been written of him and had been done to him. [17]So the crowd that had been with him when he called Lazarus out of the tomb and raised him from the dead continued to testify.[a] [18]It was also because they heard that he had performed this sign that the crowd went to meet him. [19]The Pharisees then said to one another, "You see, you can do nothing. Look, the world has gone after him!"

Some Greeks Wish to See Jesus

20 Now among those who went up to worship at the festival were some Greeks. [21]They came to Philip, who was from Bethsaida in Galilee, and said to him, "Sir, we wish to see Jesus." [22]Philip went and told Andrew; then Andrew and Philip went and told Jesus. [23]Jesus answered them, "The hour has come for the Son of Man to be glorified. [24]Very truly, I tell you, unless a grain of wheat falls into the earth and dies, it remains just a single grain; but if it dies, it bears much fruit. [25]Those who love their life lose it, and those who hate their life in this world will keep it for eternal life. [26]Whoever serves me must follow me, and where I am, there will my servant be also. Whoever serves me, the Father will honor.

Jesus Speaks about His Death

27 "Now my soul is troubled. And what should I say—'Father, save me from this hour'? No, it is for this reason that I have come to this hour. [28]Father, glorify your name." Then a voice came from heaven, "I have glorified it, and I will glorify it again." [29]The crowd standing there heard it and said that it was thunder. Others said, "An angel has spoken to him." [30]Jesus answered, "This voice has come for your sake, not for mine. [31]Now is the judgment of this world; now the ruler of this world will be driven out. [32]And I, when I am lifted up from the earth, will draw all people[b] to myself." [33]He said this to indicate the kind

LIVE IT!

Dying for New Life · John 12:24–26

In John 12:24–26, Jesus describes new life coming out of suffering and death. God used Christ's sacrifice to free us from the bonds of sin and Christ's resurrection to open the path to new life. This belief that new life can come out of sin and death is a continuously unfolding mystery that no one can fully explain, and yet it's perhaps the most essential foundation of our faith.

We bear the fruit of new life in death just like the grain of wheat in this passage. The path to new life is through sacrifice and death to ourselves. By dying to our selfishness and focusing on loving others, we experience the fullness of life in Christ.

• What kinds of attitudes, desires, or actions do you need to let go of?
• What keeps you from living completely for God? Ask for courage and strength to be free of those fears or sins.

---

a Other ancient authorities read *with him began to testify that he had called . . . from the dead*   b Other ancient authorities read *all things*

of death he was to die. [34]The crowd answered him, "We have heard from the law that the Messiah[a] remains forever. How can you say that the Son of Man must be lifted up? Who is this Son of Man?" [35]Jesus said to them, "The light is with you for a little longer. Walk while you have the light, so that the darkness may not overtake you. If you walk in the darkness, you do not know where you are going. [36]While you have the light, believe in the light, so that you may become children of light."

The Unbelief of the People

After Jesus had said this, he departed and hid from them. [37]Although he had performed so many signs in their presence, they did not believe in him. [38]This was to fulfill the word spoken by the prophet Isaiah:

"Lord, who has believed our message,
　　and to whom has the arm of the Lord been
　　　revealed?"

[39]And so they could not believe, because Isaiah also said,

[40]　"He has blinded their eyes
　　and hardened their heart,
　so that they might not look with their eyes,
　　and understand with their heart and
　　　turn—
　　and I would heal them."

[41]Isaiah said this because[b] he saw his glory and spoke about him. [42]Nevertheless many, even of the authorities, believed in him. But because of the Pharisees they did not confess it, for fear that they would be put out of the synagogue; [43]for they loved human glory more than the glory that comes from God.

Summary of Jesus' Teaching

[44] Then Jesus cried aloud: "Whoever believes in me believes not in me but in him who sent me. [45]And whoever sees me sees him who sent me. [46]I have come as light into the world, so that everyone who believes in me should not remain in the darkness. [47]I do not judge anyone who hears my words and does not keep them, for I came not to judge the world, but to save the world. [48]The one who rejects me and does not receive my word has a judge; on the last day the word that I have spoken will serve as judge, [49]for I have not spoken on my own, but the Father who sent me has himself given me a commandment about what to say and what to speak. [50]And I know that his commandment is eternal life. What I speak, therefore, I speak just as the Father has told me."

Jesus Washes the Disciples' Feet

13 Now before the festival of the Passover, Jesus knew that his hour had come to depart from this world and go to the Father. Having loved his own who were in the world, he loved them to the end. [2]The devil had already put it into the heart of Judas son of Simon Iscariot to betray him. And during supper [3]Jesus, knowing that the Father had given all things into his hands, and that he had

STUDY IT!

Passover · John 13:1–20

Chapter 13 is the beginning of the second part of the gospel of John, sometimes called the Book of Glory. Its main theme is how Jesus is glorified through his suffering, death, and resurrection. It begins with Jesus washing the disciples' feet at the Last Supper, before the Passover.

The Jewish festival of Passover, also called the Festival of Unleavened Bread, reminds us of how God "passed over" the homes of the Israelites in Egypt before the exodus. It was the blood of a lamb smeared on the doorposts of the Israelites' houses that signaled the angel of death to spare the firstborn of God's people.

The festival was traditionally celebrated with a meal of lamb, bitter herbs, and unleavened bread (see "Study It: The Passover," near Exodus 12:14-28). In the other gospels, the last meal Jesus shares with his disciples is the Passover meal. But in the gospel of John, Jesus is arrested before Passover. He is crucified on the preparation day of the Festival of Unleavened Bread, at the same time the lambs are being sacrificed in the temple. The symbolism would not be missed by Jewish readers of John: Jesus is the new and perfect Passover lamb.

a Or *the Christ*　**b** Other ancient witnesses read *when*

LIVE IT!

Serve Like Jesus · John 13:1–17

Think of the most faith-filled person you know. Chances are it's one of the most humble individuals you can name. Humility and faith go hand in hand. Humble people proclaim through their actions and words, "It's not about me!"

In Matthew, Mark, and Luke, the focus of the Last Supper is on Communion. But John's focus is on Jesus washing his disciples' feet, and John makes the point that serving others is at the heart of following Jesus.

Living our faith as disciples of Jesus requires us to place God first, so that our actions point to God and not to ourselves. Living out a humble faith doesn't mean we must be quiet about what we believe; it simply means we let the light of God's love and grace shine through us to others. It means we choose to be a window to God's presence, not a wall to ourselves.

• Who's the most humble person you know? What can you learn from him or her?

• How is Jesus calling you to serve others, humbly and compassionately?

come from God and was going to God, [4]got up from the table,[a] took off his outer robe, and tied a towel around himself. [5]Then he poured water into a basin and began to wash the disciples' feet and to wipe them with the towel that was tied around him. [6]He came to Simon Peter, who said to him, "Lord, are you going to wash my feet?" [7]Jesus answered, "You do not know now what I am doing, but later you will understand." [8]Peter said to him, "You will never wash my feet." Jesus answered, "Unless I wash you, you have no share with me." [9]Simon Peter said to him, "Lord, not my feet only but also my hands and my head!" [10]Jesus said to him, "One who has bathed does not need to wash, except for the feet,[b] but is entirely clean. And you[c] are clean, though not all of you." [11]For he knew who was to betray him; for this reason he said, "Not all of you are clean."

12 After he had washed their feet, had put on his robe, and had returned to the table, he said to them, "Do you know what I have done to you? [13]You call me Teacher and Lord—and you are right, for that is what I am. [14]So if I, your Lord and Teacher, have washed your feet, you also ought to wash one another's feet. [15]For I have set you an example, that you also should do as I have done to you. [16]Very truly, I tell you, servants[d] are not greater than their master, nor are messengers greater than the one who sent them. [17]If you know these things, you are blessed if you do them. [18]I am not speaking of all of you; I know whom I have chosen. But it is to fulfill the scripture, 'The one who ate my bread[e] has lifted his heel against me.' [19]I tell you this now, before it

occurs, so that when it does occur, you may believe that I am he.[f] [20]Very truly, I tell you, whoever receives one whom I send receives me; and whoever receives me receives him who sent me."

Jesus Foretells His Betrayal

21 After saying this Jesus was troubled in spirit, and declared, "Very truly, I tell you, one of you will betray me." [22]The disciples looked at one another, uncertain of whom he was speaking. [23]One of his disciples—the one whom Jesus loved—was reclining next to him; [24]Simon Peter therefore motioned to him to ask Jesus of whom he was speaking. [25]So while reclining next to Jesus, he asked him, "Lord, who is it?" [26]Jesus answered, "It is the one to whom I give this piece of bread when I have dipped it in the dish."[g] So when he had dipped the piece of bread, he gave it to Judas son of Simon Iscariot.[h] [27]After he received the piece of bread,[i] Satan entered into him. Jesus said to him, "Do quickly what you are going to do." [28]Now no one at the table knew why he said this to him. [29]Some thought that, because Judas had the common purse, Jesus was telling him, "Buy what we need for the festival"; or, that he should give something to the poor. [30]So, after receiving the piece of bread, he immediately went out. And it was night.

The New Commandment

31 When he had gone out, Jesus said, "Now the Son of Man has been glorified, and God has been glorified in him. [32]If God has been glorified in him,[j]

a Gk *from supper*   b Other ancient authorities lack *except for the feet*   c The Greek word for *you* here is plural   d Gk *slaves*   e Other ancient authorities read *ate bread with me*   f Gk *I am*   g Gk *dipped it*   h Other ancient authorities read *Judas Iscariot son of Simon*; others, *Judas son of Simon from Karyot* (Kerioth)   i Gk *After the piece of bread*   j Other ancient authorities lack *If God has been glorified in him*

The Mysterious Disciple
John 13:23–25

We are introduced to a mysterious character at the Last Supper. The disciple "whom Jesus loved" (John 13:23) is found only in the gospel of John. He is mentioned several more times: at the foot of the cross with Jesus' mother (John 19:25-27), on Easter morning when he enters the empty tomb with Peter (John 20:2-12), and after the resurrection when he identifies Jesus from the boat (John 21:7, 20). He is always with Peter or where Peter should be (at the cross).

So who is the mystery man? He has traditionally been identified as John the son of Zebedee, one of the twelve apostles, and as the writer of the gospel of John. But if that's true, why does he refer to himself so strangely? Many scholars today believe that the Beloved Disciple was a lesser known follower of Jesus who was the founder of the Christian community that ultimately produced the gospel of John. They think his eyewitness accounts (John 21:24) were passed on and are the basis for this book in the Bible we have today.

God will also glorify him in himself and will glorify him at once. [33]Little children, I am with you only a little longer. You will look for me; and as I said to the Jews so now I say to you, 'Where I am going, you cannot come.' [34]I give you a new commandment, that you love one another. Just as I have loved you, you also should love one another. [35]By this everyone will know that you are my disciples, if you have love for one another."

Jesus Foretells Peter's Denial

36 Simon Peter said to him, "Lord, where are you going?" Jesus answered, "Where I am going, you cannot follow me now; but you will follow afterward." [37]Peter said to him, "Lord, why can I not follow you now? I will lay down my life for you."

[38]Jesus answered, "Will you lay down your life for me? Very truly, I tell you, before the cock crows, you will have denied me three times.

Jesus the Way to the Father

14 "Do not let your hearts be troubled. Believe[a] in God, believe also in me. [2]In my Father's house there are many dwelling places. If it were not so, would I have told you that I go to prepare a place for you?[b] [3]And if I go and prepare a place for you, I will come again and will take you to myself, so that where I am, there you may be also. [4]And you know the way to the place where I am going."[c] [5]Thomas said to him, "Lord, we do not know where you are going. How can we know the way?" [6]Jesus said to him, "I am the way, and the truth, and the life. No one comes to the Father except through me. [7]If you know me, you will know[d] my Father also. From now on you do know him and have seen him."

8 Philip said to him, "Lord, show us the Father, and we will be satisfied." [9]Jesus said to him, "Have I been with you all this time, Philip, and you still do not know me? Whoever has seen me has seen the Father. How can you say, 'Show us the Father'? [10]Do you not believe that I am in the Father and the Father is in me? The words that I say to you I do not speak on my own; but the Father who dwells in me does his works. [11]Believe me that I am in the Father and the Father is in me; but if you do not, then believe me because of the works themselves. [12]Very truly, I tell you, the one who believes in me will also do the works that I do and, in fact, will do greater works than these, because I am going to the Father. [13]I will do whatever you ask in my name, so that the Father may be glorified in the Son. [14]If in my name you ask me[e] for anything, I will do it.

The Promise of the Holy Spirit

15 "If you love me, you will keep[f] my commandments. [16]And I will ask the Father, and he will give you another Advocate,[g] to be with you forever. [17]This is the Spirit of truth, whom the world cannot receive, because it neither sees him nor knows him. You know him, because he abides with you, and he will be in[h] you.

18 "I will not leave you orphaned; I am coming to you. [19]In a little while the world will no longer see me, but you will see me; because I live, you also will live. [20]On that day you will know that I am in my

---

a Or *You believe*   b Or *If it were not so, I would have told you; for I go to prepare a place for you*   c Other ancient authorities read *Where I am going you know, and the way you know*   d Other ancient authorities read *If you had known me, you would have known*   e Other ancient authorities lack *me*   f Other ancient authorities read *me, keep*   g Or *Helper*   h Or *among*

Father, and you in me, and I in you. ²¹They who have my commandments and keep them are those who love me; and those who love me will be loved by my Father, and I will love them and reveal myself to them." ²²Judas (not Iscariot) said to him, "Lord, how is it that you will reveal yourself to us, and not to the world?" ²³Jesus answered him, "Those who love me will keep my word, and my Father will love them, and we will come to them and make our home with them. ²⁴Whoever does not love me does not keep my words; and the word that you hear is not mine, but is from the Father who sent me.

25 "I have said these things to you while I am still with you. ²⁶But the Advocate,^a the Holy Spirit, whom the Father will send in my name, will teach you everything, and remind you of all that I have said to you. ²⁷Peace I leave with you; my peace I give to you. I do not give to you as the world gives. Do not let your hearts be troubled, and do not let them be afraid. ²⁸You heard me say to you, 'I am going away, and I am coming to you.' If you loved me, you would rejoice that I am going to the Father, because the Father is greater than I. ²⁹And now I have told you this before it occurs, so that when it does occur, you may believe. ³⁰I will no longer talk much with you, for the ruler of this world is coming. He has no power over me; ³¹but I do as the Father has commanded me, so that the world may know that I love the Father. Rise, let us be on our way.

Jesus the True Vine

15 "I am the true vine, and my Father is the vinegrower. ²He removes every branch in me that bears no fruit. Every branch that bears fruit

he prunes^b to make it bear more fruit. ³You have already been cleansed^b by the word that I have spoken to you. ⁴Abide in me as I abide in you. Just as the branch cannot bear fruit by itself unless it abides in the vine, neither can you unless you abide in me. ⁵I am the vine, you are the branches. Those who abide in me and I in them bear much fruit, because apart from me you can do nothing. ⁶Who-

a Or *Helper* **b** The same Greek root refers to pruning and cleansing

ever does not abide in me is thrown away like a branch and withers; such branches are gathered, thrown into the fire, and burned. [7]If you abide in me, and my words abide in you, ask for whatever you wish, and it will be done for you. [8]My Father is glorified by this, that you bear much fruit and become[a] my disciples. [9]As the Father has loved me, so I have loved you; abide in my love. [10]If you keep my commandments, you will abide in my love, just as I have kept my Father's commandments and abide in his love. [11]I have said these things to you so that my joy may be in you, and that your joy may be complete.

12 "This is my commandment, that you love one another as I have loved you. [13]No one has greater love than this, to lay down one's life for one's friends. [14]You are my friends if you do what I command you. [15]I do not call you servants[b] any longer, because the servant[c] does not know what the master is doing; but I have called you friends, because I have made known to you everything that I have heard from my Father. [16]You did not choose me but I chose you. And I appointed you to go and bear fruit, fruit that will last, so that the Father will give you whatever you ask him in my name. [17]I am giving you these commands so that you may love one another.

The World's Hatred

18 "If the world hates you, be aware that it hated me before it hated you. [19]If you belonged to the world,[d] the world would love you as its own. Because you do not belong to the world, but I have chosen you out of the world—therefore the world hates you. [20]Remember the word that I said to you, 'Servants[e] are not greater than their master.' If they persecuted me, they will persecute you; if they kept my word, they will keep yours also. [21]But they will do all these things to you on account of my name, because they do not know him who sent me. [22]If I had not come and spoken to them, they would not have sin; but now they have no excuse for their sin. [23]Whoever hates me hates my Father also. [24]If I had not done among them the works that no one else did, they would not have sin. But now they have seen and hated both me and my Father. [25]It was to fulfill the word that is written in their law, 'They hated me without a cause.'

26 "When the Advocate[f] comes, whom I will send to you from the Father, the Spirit of truth who comes from the Father, he will testify on my behalf. [27]You also are to testify because you have been with me from the beginning.

"I have said these things to you to keep you from stumbling. [2]They will put you out of the synagogues. Indeed, an hour is coming when those who kill you will think that by doing so they are offering worship to God. [3]And they will do this because they have not known the Father or me. [4]But I have said these things to you so that when their hour comes you may remember that I told you about them.

LIVE IT!

Not of This World · John 15:18–25

It's easy to get caught up in the pressures put on us by our classmates, friends, and society. We feel as though we have to dress a certain way, have certain possessions, and live in a certain kind of neighborhood just to be considered average. People who resist those pressures are often labeled weird or different. They often feel out of place—maybe not "of this world."

The community from which the gospel of John emerged didn't feel at home in this world either. Its message of the divine Jesus had been rejected by Jews, Gentiles, and perhaps even other early Christians. No wonder the author has Jesus emphasize, "Because you do not belong to the world, . . . therefore the world hates you" (John 15:19).

• How might Christians today be considered not of this world?

• What pressures do you need to resist?

• How does Jesus' warning to his disciples about the world's hatred (John 15:18-25) apply to you today? Ask for God's wisdom and strength to endure.

a Or be b Gk slaves c Gk slave d Gk were of the world e Gk Slaves f Or Helper

Our Guide: The Holy Spirit
John 14:15–31; 16:5–15

Jesus told his disciples that after his death, God would send the Spirit of truth to be with them forever. Jesus calls the Holy Spirit the Advocate, the one who defends us from sin. The Holy Spirit also guides us into all truth, helping us grasp the meaning of Jesus' words, actions, and miracles. As we live out our faith, it's the Spirit that guides us as disciples and empowers us to use our unique gifts to make a difference in our world.

- Jesus promises his followers that the Holy Spirit will abide in us (John 14:17). How are you aware of the Holy Spirit's presence in your life?
- Ask the Holy Spirit to protect you from all sin and evil and to bring you peace.

The Work of the Spirit

"I did not say these things to you from the beginning, because I was with you. ⁵But now I am going to him who sent me; yet none of you asks me, 'Where are you going?' ⁶But because I have said these things to you, sorrow has filled your hearts. ⁷Nevertheless I tell you the truth: it is to your advantage that I go away, for if I do not go away, the Advocate*ᵃ* will not come to you; but if I go, I will send him to you. ⁸And when he comes, he will prove the world wrong about*ᵇ* sin and righteousness and judgment: ⁹about sin, because they do not believe in me; ¹⁰about righteousness, because I am going to the Father and you will see me no longer; ¹¹about judgment, because the ruler of this world has been condemned.

12 "I still have many things to say to you, but you cannot bear them now. ¹³When the Spirit of truth comes, he will guide you into all the truth; for he will not speak on his own, but will speak whatever he hears, and he will declare to you the things that are to come. ¹⁴He will glorify me, because he will take what is mine and declare it to

you. ¹⁵All that the Father has is mine. For this reason I said that he will take what is mine and declare it to you.

Sorrow Will Turn into Joy

16 "A little while, and you will no longer see me, and again a little while, and you will see me." ¹⁷Then some of his disciples said to one another, "What does he mean by saying to us, 'A little while, and you will no longer see me, and again a little while, and you will see me'; and 'Because I am going to the Father'?" ¹⁸They said, "What does he mean by this 'a little while'? We do not know what he is talking about." ¹⁹Jesus knew that they wanted to ask him, so he said to them, "Are you discussing among yourselves what I meant when I said, 'A little while, and you will no longer see me, and again a little while, and you will see me'? ²⁰Very truly, I tell you, you will weep and mourn, but the world will rejoice; you will have pain, but your pain will turn into joy. ²¹When a woman is in labor, she has pain, because her hour has come. But when her child is born, she no longer remembers the anguish because of the joy of having brought a human being into the world. ²²So you have pain now; but I will see you again, and your hearts will rejoice, and no one will take your joy from you. ²³On that day you will ask nothing of me.*ᶜ* Very truly, I tell you, if you ask anything of the Father in my name, he will give it to you.*ᵈ* ²⁴Until now you have not asked for anything in my name. Ask and you will receive, so that your joy may be complete.

Peace for the Disciples

25 "I have said these things to you in figures of speech. The hour is coming when I will no longer speak to you in figures, but will tell you plainly of the Father. ²⁶On that day you will ask in my name. I do not say to you that I will ask the Father on your behalf; ²⁷for the Father himself loves you, because you have loved me and have believed that I came from God.*ᵉ* ²⁸I came from the Father and have come into the world; again, I am leaving the world and am going to the Father."

29 His disciples said, "Yes, now you are speaking plainly, not in any figure of speech! ³⁰Now we know that you know all things, and do not need to have anyone question you; by this we believe that you came from God." ³¹Jesus answered them, "Do you now believe? ³²The hour is coming, indeed it

has come, when you will be scattered, each one to his home, and you will leave me alone. Yet I am not alone because the Father is with me. [33]I have said this to you, so that in me you may have peace. In the world you face persecution. But take courage; I have conquered the world!"

17 Jesus Prays for His Disciples

After Jesus had spoken these words, he looked up to heaven and said, "Father, the hour has come; glorify your Son so that the Son may glorify you, [2]since you have given him authority over all people,[a] to give eternal life to all whom you have given him. [3]And this is eternal life, that they may know you, the only true God, and Jesus Christ whom you have sent. [4]I glorified you on earth by finishing the work that you gave me to do. [5]So now, Father, glorify me in your own presence with the glory that I had in your presence before the world existed.

PRAY IT!

A Prayer for Friends
John 17

Jesus prays for his friends, the disciples, in John 17. He also prays for us, his future disciples (John 17:20)! Here's a prayer you can say for your friends:

Dear Jesus, thank you for my true friends. They accept me for who I am. I don't have to pretend to be someone else with them. They support me when I feel as if the world is caving in around me. They're honest with me even if what they say isn't what I want to hear. They offer their sense of humor so that we can laugh together.

Please watch over these friends just as you watch over me. Show them your loving acceptance and support. Help them to honestly see themselves and the decisions they're making. Give them strength to lean on you in their pain, frustration, or failure. Fill them with laughter and love. Protect them and keep them safe. Amen.

6 "I have made your name known to those whom you gave me from the world. They were yours, and you gave them to me, and they have kept your word. [7]Now they know that everything you have given me is from you; [8]for the words that you gave to me I have given to them, and they have received them and know in truth that I came from you; and they have believed that you sent me. [9]I am asking on their behalf; I am not asking on behalf of the world, but on behalf of those whom you gave me, because they are yours. [10]All mine are yours, and yours are mine; and I have been glorified in them. [11]And now I am no longer in the world, but they are in the world, and I am coming to you. Holy Father, protect them in your name that you have given me, so that they may be one, as we are one. [12]While I was with them, I protected them in your name that[b] you have given me. I guarded them, and not one of them was lost except the one destined to be lost,[c] so that the scripture might be fulfilled. [13]But now I am coming to you, and I speak these things in the world so that they may have my joy made complete in themselves.[d] [14]I have given them your word, and the world has hated them because they do not belong to the world, just as I do not belong to the world. [15]I am not asking you to take them out of the world, but I ask you to protect them from the evil one.[e] [16]They do not belong to the world, just as I do not belong to the world. [17]Sanctify them in the truth; your word is truth. [18]As you have sent me into the world, so I have sent them into the world. [19]And for their sakes I sanctify myself, so that they also may be sanctified in truth.

20 "I ask not only on behalf of these, but also on behalf of those who will believe in me through their word, [21]that they may all be one. As you, Father, are in me and I am in you, may they also be in us,[f] so that the world may believe that you have sent me. [22]The glory that you have given me I have given them, so that they may be one, as we are one, [23]I in them and you in me, that they may become completely one, so that the world may know that you have sent me and have loved them even as you have loved me. [24]Father, I desire that those also, whom you have given me, may be with me where I am, to see my glory, which you have given me because you loved me before the foundation of the world.

25 "Righteous Father, the world does not know you, but I know you; and these know that you have sent me. [26]I made your name known to them, and I

---

a Gk flesh　**b** Other ancient authorities read protected in your name those whom　**c** Gk except the son of destruction　**d** Or among themselves　**e** Or from evil
f Other ancient authorities read be one in us

The Trinity · John 17:20–26

If you knew you were about to die, how would you spend your final moments with your friends? **John 13–17** gives us a window into Jesus' final moments with his disciples right before his arrest and crucifixion. During that time, Jesus washes their feet, tells them about the promise of the Holy Spirit, and shares his hopes for them. Jesus concludes with a prayer that reveals and reflects on the unity that exists between Jesus, God the Father, and his disciples. The unity between the Father and the Son, which Jesus refers to in his prayer, points to one of the greatest mysteries of the Christian faith: that there is one God in three persons—the Father, Son, and Holy Spirit. We call this mystery the Trinity.

This mystery is known only because God chose to reveal it to the world. In the Old Testament, God revealed himself as the Father of all creation. In the New Testament, God revealed himself as Father (in relationship to the Son), as Son (in the person of Jesus Christ), and as Holy Spirit (sent from the Father and the Son). The Father, Son, and Holy Spirit united as one God work together to bring about our salvation.

The Church teaches that the Father is God, Jesus is God, and the Holy Spirit is God, and together they are the one God. They are not just a way to name the different ways God acts in the world. Each is distinct, but because of their unity, each person of the Trinity is entirely in the other two, and all work together. For example, when we follow the Son, we're doing so because the Father invited us and the Holy Spirit moved us.

Jesus' prayer calls us to share in and reflect the unity that exists in the Trinity. When we are baptized in the name of the Father, Son, and Holy Spirit, we enter into the life and mystery of the Trinity. We are called to reflect God's unity in our relationships with each other by working together to help all people find salvation in God the Father, Son, and Holy Spirit.

---

will make it known, so that the love with which you have loved me may be in them, and I in them."

18
The Betrayal and Arrest of Jesus

After Jesus had spoken these words, he went out with his disciples across the Kidron valley to a place where there was a garden, which he and his disciples entered. ²Now Judas, who betrayed him, also knew the place, because Jesus often met there with his disciples. ³So Judas brought a detachment of soldiers together with police from the chief priests and the Pharisees, and they came there with lanterns and torches and weapons. ⁴Then Jesus, knowing all that was to happen to him, came forward and asked them, "Whom are you looking for?" ⁵They answered, "Jesus of Nazareth."ᵃ Jesus replied, "I am he."ᵇ Judas, who betrayed him, was standing with them. ⁶When Jesusᶜ said to them, "I am he,"ᵇ they stepped back and fell to the ground. ⁷Again he asked them, "Whom are you looking for?" And they said, "Jesus of Nazareth."ᵃ ⁸Jesus answered,

"I told you that I am he.ᵇ So if you are looking for me, let these men go." ⁹This was to fulfill the word that he had spoken, "I did not lose a single one of those whom you gave me." ¹⁰Then Simon Peter, who had a sword, drew it, struck the high priest's slave, and cut off his right ear. The slave's name was Malchus. ¹¹Jesus said to Peter, "Put your sword back into its sheath. Am I not to drink the cup that the Father has given me?"

Jesus before the High Priest

12 So the soldiers, their officer, and the Jewish police arrested Jesus and bound him. ¹³First they took him to Annas, who was the father-in-law of Caiaphas, the high priest that year. ¹⁴Caiaphas was the one who had advised the Jews that it was better to have one person die for the people.

Peter Denies Jesus

15 Simon Peter and another disciple followed Jesus. Since that disciple was known to the high priest, he

---

ᵃ Gk *the Nazorean*   ᵇ Gk *I am*   ᶜ Gk *he*

went with Jesus into the courtyard of the high priest, [16]but Peter was standing outside at the gate. So the other disciple, who was known to the high priest, went out, spoke to the woman who guarded the gate, and brought Peter in. [17]The woman said to Peter, "You are not also one of this man's disciples, are you?" He said, "I am not." [18]Now the slaves and the police had made a charcoal fire because it was cold, and they were standing around it and warming themselves. Peter also was standing with them and warming himself.

The High Priest Questions Jesus

19 Then the high priest questioned Jesus about his disciples and about his teaching. [20]Jesus answered, "I have spoken openly to the world; I have always taught in synagogues and in the temple, where all the Jews come together. I have said nothing in secret. [21]Why do you ask me? Ask those who heard what I said to them; they know what I said." [22]When he had said this, one of the police standing nearby struck Jesus on the face, saying, "Is that how you answer the high priest?" [23]Jesus answered, "If I have spoken wrongly, testify to the wrong. But if I have spoken rightly, why do you strike me?" [24]Then Annas sent him bound to Caiaphas the high priest.

Peter Denies Jesus Again

25 Now Simon Peter was standing and warming himself. They asked him, "You are not also one of his disciples, are you?" He denied it and said, "I am not." [26]One of the slaves of the high priest, a relative of the man whose ear Peter had cut off, asked, "Did I not see you in the garden with him?" [27]Again Peter denied it, and at that moment the cock crowed.

Jesus before Pilate

28 Then they took Jesus from Caiaphas to Pilate's headquarters.[a] It was early in the morning. They themselves did not enter the headquarters,[a] so as to avoid ritual defilement and to be able to eat the Passover. [29]So Pilate went out to them and said,

Jesus Triumphs · John 18–19

The gospel of John most resembles the other three gospels in its stories of Jesus' trial, death, and resurrection. But John's portrayal is still unique. The most obvious difference is that, in John, Jesus is clearly in charge and in his glory from the moment he is arrested. There is no agony in the garden. When the soldiers and police come to arrest Jesus, they fall to the ground as he speaks (John 18:6). He teaches Pilate about his identity and mission, in essence putting Pilate on trial (John 18:33-38). Jesus brings together his mother and the Beloved Disciple (John 19:26-27). Jesus isn't the victim. Instead, he decides the moment of his death when he gives up his spirit (John 19:30).

John is also careful to detail the ways Jesus' crucifixion fulfills Old Testament prophecies of the Messiah. He identifies Jesus with the just man who was persecuted in **Psalm 22** and **Psalm 69**. He does this by connecting the gambling for Jesus' seamless tunic (John 19:24) with **Psalm 22:18**, and the offering of sour wine (John 19:29) with **Psalm 69:21**. Jesus' unbroken legs (John 19:33) are a reference to the Passover lamb in **Exodus 12:46**, and his pierced side (John 19:34) is seen as the fulfillment of **Zechariah 12:10**.

John wants us to know that these events are the central "hour" in the world's history and the time of Jesus' triumph. Jesus is clearly the divine Son of God, and by Jesus' self-sacrifice God brings salvation to the entire world. The author of John wants us to focus not on the tragedy, but on God's power at work in Jesus.

a Gk the praetorium

"What accusation do you bring against this man?" [30]They answered, "If this man were not a criminal, we would not have handed him over to you." [31]Pilate said to them, "Take him yourselves and judge him according to your law." The Jews replied, "We are not permitted to put anyone to death." [32](This was to fulfill what Jesus had said when he indicated the kind of death he was to die.)

33 Then Pilate entered the headquarters[a] again, summoned Jesus, and asked him, "Are you the King of the Jews?" [34]Jesus answered, "Do you ask this on your own, or did others tell you about me?" [35]Pilate replied, "I am not a Jew, am I? Your own nation and the chief priests have handed you over to me. What have you done?" [36]Jesus answered, "My kingdom is not from this world. If my kingdom were from this world, my followers would be fighting to keep me from being handed over to the Jews. But as it is, my kingdom is not from here." [37]Pilate asked him, "So you are a king?" Jesus answered, "You say that I am a king. For this I was born, and for this I came into the world, to testify to the truth. Everyone who belongs to the truth listens to my voice." [38]Pilate asked him, "What is truth?"

Jesus Sentenced to Death

After he had said this, he went out to the Jews again and told them, "I find no case against him. [39]But you have a custom that I release someone for you at the Passover. Do you want me to release for you the King of the Jews?" [40]They shouted in reply, "Not this man, but Barabbas!" Now Barabbas was a bandit.

19 Then Pilate took Jesus and had him flogged. [2]And the soldiers wove a crown of thorns and put it on his head, and they dressed him in a purple robe. [3]They kept coming up to him, saying, "Hail, King of the Jews!" and striking him on the face. [4]Pilate went out again and said to them, "Look, I am bringing him out to you to let you know that I find no case against him." [5]So Jesus came out, wearing the crown of thorns and the purple robe. Pilate said to them, "Here is the man!" [6]When the chief priests and the police saw him, they shouted, "Crucify him! Crucify him!" Pilate said to them, "Take him yourselves and crucify him; I find no case against him." [7]The Jews answered him, "We have a law, and according to that law he ought to die because he has claimed to be the Son of God."

8 Now when Pilate heard this, he was more afraid

than ever. [9]He entered his headquarters[a] again and asked Jesus, "Where are you from?" But Jesus gave him no answer. [10]Pilate therefore said to him, "Do you refuse to speak to me? Do you not know that I have power to release you, and power to crucify you?" [11]Jesus answered him, "You would have no power over me unless it had been given you from above; therefore the one who handed me over to you is guilty of a greater sin." [12]From then on Pilate tried to release him, but the Jews cried out, "If you release this man, you are no friend of the emperor. Everyone who claims to be a king sets himself against the emperor."

13 When Pilate heard these words, he brought Jesus outside and sat[b] on the judge's bench at a place called The Stone Pavement, or in Hebrew[c] Gabbatha. [14]Now it was the day of Preparation for the Passover; and it was about noon. He said to the Jews, "Here is your King!" [15]They cried out, "Away with him! Away with him! Crucify him!" Pilate asked

STUDY IT!

King on the Cross
John 19:19–22

Pontius Pilate acts as a mediator between two worlds—the outside world of darkness and unbelief and the inner world of light and truth. During Jesus' trial, Pilate goes back and forth between the Jewish religious authorities, who are outside (in the dark), and Jesus, who is inside Pilate's headquarters (in the light).

Does Pilate know the truth about Jesus? When he writes out the charges to be placed on the cross, "the Jews" (see "Study It: 'The Jews' in John," near John 2:18–20) argue with him about the wording. He answers, "What I have written I have written" (John 19:22). The words are "Jesus of Nazareth, the King of the Jews" (John 19:19).

In another of the gospel's ironies, Pilate recognizes what the Jewish leaders rejected—Jesus Christ is a king. Christians believe a deeper truth—Christ is king of not only the Jews, but of all creation!

---

a Gk *the praetorium*   **b** Or *seated him*   **c** That is, *Aramaic*

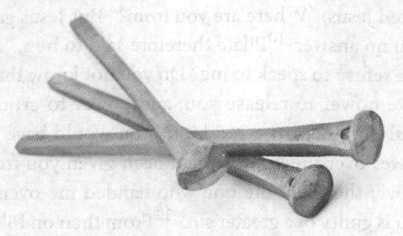

them, "Shall I crucify your King?" The chief priests answered, "We have no king but the emperor." [16]Then he handed him over to them to be crucified.

The Crucifixion of Jesus

So they took Jesus; [17]and carrying the cross by himself, he went out to what is called The Place of the Skull, which in Hebrew[a] is called Golgotha. [18]There they crucified him, and with him two others, one on either side, with Jesus between them. [19]Pilate also had an inscription written and put on the cross. It read, "Jesus of Nazareth,[b] the King of the Jews." [20]Many of the Jews read this inscription, because the place where Jesus was crucified was near the city; and it was written in Hebrew,[a] in Latin, and in Greek. [21]Then the chief priests of the Jews said to Pilate, "Do not write, 'The King of the Jews,' but, 'This man said, I am King of the Jews.' " [22]Pilate answered, "What I have written I have written." [23]When the soldiers had crucified Jesus, they took his clothes and divided them into four parts, one for each soldier. They also took his tunic; now the tunic was seamless, woven in one piece from the top. [24]So they said to one another, "Let us not tear it, but cast lots for it to see who will get it." This was to fulfill what the scripture says,

"They divided my clothes among themselves,
    and for my clothing they cast lots."

[25]And that is what the soldiers did.

Meanwhile, standing near the cross of Jesus were his mother, and his mother's sister, Mary the wife of Clopas, and Mary Magdalene. [26]When Jesus saw his mother and the disciple whom he loved standing beside her, he said to his mother, "Woman, here is your son." [27]Then he said to the disciple, "Here is your mother." And from that hour the disciple took her into his own home.

[28]After this, when Jesus knew that all was now finished, he said (in order to fulfill the scripture), "I am thirsty." [29]A jar full of sour wine was standing there. So they put a sponge full of the wine on a branch of hyssop and held it to his mouth. [30]When Jesus had received the wine, he said, "It is finished." Then he bowed his head and gave up his spirit.

Jesus' Side Is Pierced

31 Since it was the day of Preparation, the Jews did not want the bodies left on the cross during the sabbath, especially because that sabbath was a day of great solemnity. So they asked Pilate to have the legs of the crucified men broken and the bodies removed. [32]Then the soldiers came and broke the legs of the first and of the other who had been crucified with him. [33]But when they came to Jesus and saw that he was already dead, they did not break his legs. [34]Instead, one of the soldiers pierced his side with a spear, and at once blood and water came out. [35](He who saw this has testified so that you also may believe. His testimony is true, and he knows[c] that he tells the truth.) [36]These things occurred so that the scripture might be fulfilled, "None of his bones shall be broken." [37]And again another passage of scripture says, "They will look on the one whom they have pierced."

The Burial of Jesus

38 After these things, Joseph of Arimathea, who was a disciple of Jesus, though a secret one because of his fear of the Jews, asked Pilate to let him take away the body of Jesus. Pilate gave him permission; so he came and removed his body. [39]Nicodemus, who had at first come to Jesus by night, also came, bringing a mixture of myrrh and aloes, weighing about a hundred pounds. [40]They took the body of Jesus and wrapped it with the spices in linen cloths, according to the burial custom of the Jews. [41]Now there was a garden in the place where he was crucified, and in the garden there was a new tomb in which no one had ever been laid. [42]And so, because it was the Jewish day of Preparation, and the tomb was nearby, they laid Jesus there.

The Resurrection of Jesus

20 Early on the first day of the week, while it was still dark, Mary Magdalene came to the tomb and saw that the stone had been removed from the tomb. [2]So she ran and went to Simon Peter and the other disciple, the one whom Jesus loved, and said to them, "They have taken the Lord out of the tomb, and we do not know where they have laid him." [3]Then Peter and the other disciple set out and went

---

a That is, *Aramaic* *b* Gk *the Nazorean* *c* Or *there is one who knows*

toward the tomb. [4]The two were running together, but the other disciple outran Peter and reached the tomb first. [5]He bent down to look in and saw the linen wrappings lying there, but he did not go in. [6]Then Simon Peter came, following him, and went into the tomb. He saw the linen wrappings lying there, [7]and the cloth that had been on Jesus' head, not lying with the linen wrappings but rolled up in a place by itself. [8]Then the other disciple, who reached the tomb first, also went in, and he saw and believed; [9]for as yet they did not understand the scripture, that he must rise from the dead. [10]Then the disciples returned to their homes.

Jesus Appears to Mary Magdalene

11 But Mary stood weeping outside the tomb. As she wept, she bent over to look[a] into the tomb; [12]and she saw two angels in white, sitting where the body of Jesus had been lying, one at the head and the other at the feet. [13]They said to her, "Woman, why are you weeping?" She said to them, "They have taken away my Lord, and I do not know where they have laid him." [14]When she had said this, she turned around and saw Jesus standing there, but she did not know that it was Jesus. [15]Jesus said to her, "Woman, why are you weeping? Whom are you looking for?" Supposing him to be the gardener, she said to him, "Sir, if you have carried him away, tell me where you have laid him, and I will take him away." [16]Jesus said to her, "Mary!" She turned and said to him in Hebrew,[b] "Rabbouni!" (which means Teacher). [17]Jesus said to her, "Do not hold on to me, because I have not yet ascended to the Father. But go to my brothers and say to them, 'I am ascending to my Father and your Father, to my God and your God.' " [18]Mary Magdalene went and announced to the disciples, "I have seen the Lord"; and she told them that he had said these things to her.

Jesus Appears to the Disciples

19 When it was evening on that day, the first day of the week, and the doors of the house where the disciples had met were locked for fear of the Jews, Jesus came and stood among them and said, "Peace be with you." [20]After he said this, he showed them his hands and his side. Then the disciples rejoiced when they saw the Lord. [21]Jesus said to them again, "Peace be with you. As the Father has sent me, so I send you." [22]When he had said this, he breathed on them and said to them, "Receive the Holy Spirit.

STUDY IT!

Introducing . . . Mary Magdalene
John 20:1–18

A Samaritan woman is the first to spread the word that Jesus is the Messiah (John 4:1-42). Now another woman, Mary Magdalene, is the first to announce that Jesus has been raised from the dead. She comes to the tomb while it's still dark (symbolizing unbelief). She encounters the risen Jesus and begins to see with eyes of faith. Belief prompts her to action, and she goes to tell the disciples, "I have seen the Lord" (John 20:18).

Mary Magdalene is first in every list of Jesus' female disciples (see Matthew 27:55-56; Mark 15:40-41; Luke 8:2-3). She seems to have been a leader of a group of women who followed Jesus from the beginning of his ministry, through his death and beyond. **Luke 8:2** indicates that Jesus cured her of seven demons. All four gospels name her as one of the first eyewitnesses of Jesus' resurrection. All these facts indicate that she was a special friend and disciple of Jesus and an important leader among the first Christians.

[23]If you forgive the sins of any, they are forgiven them; if you retain the sins of any, they are retained."

Jesus and Thomas

24 But Thomas (who was called the Twin[c]), one of the twelve, was not with them when Jesus came. [25]So the other disciples told him, "We have seen the Lord." But he said to them, "Unless I see the mark of the nails in his hands, and put my finger in the mark of the nails and my hand in his side, I will not believe."

26 A week later his disciples were again in the house, and Thomas was with them. Although the doors were shut, Jesus came and stood among them

a Gk lacks to look   b That is, Aramaic   c Gk Didymus

and said, "Peace be with you." [27] Then he said to Thomas, "Put your finger here and see my hands. Reach out your hand and put it in my side. Do not doubt but believe." [28] Thomas answered him, "My Lord and my God!" [29] Jesus said to him, "Have you believed because you have seen me? Blessed are those who have not seen and yet have come to believe."

The Purpose of This Book

30 Now Jesus did many other signs in the presence of his disciples, which are not written in this book. [31] But these are written so that you may come to believe[a] that Jesus is the Messiah,[b] the Son of God, and that through believing you may have life in his name.

LIVE IT!

Free from Fear
John 20:19–23

Imagine the disciples, full of fear, huddled in their meeting room, which they had locked against outsiders. Their world had been turned upside down. Their Messiah had been killed; they could be next. They were grieving and reeling.

Then Jesus miraculously appears, showing them that neither fear nor human obstacles can keep out Christ and his peace. The disciples' fear is suddenly turned into rejoicing. Jesus hands on his mission to the disciples. He gives them purpose, and he gives them his Spirit to help them in all ways, including forgiving sins in God's name, just as Jesus had done.

- What are your greatest fears? What problem seems overwhelming?
- How can you look for Jesus? In what ways can you bring your fear, questions, and pain to him to exchange it all for peace and hope?

Jesus Appears to Seven Disciples

21 After these things Jesus showed himself again to the disciples by the Sea of Tiberias; and he showed himself in this way. [2] Gathered there together were Simon Peter, Thomas called the Twin,[c] Nathanael of Cana in Galilee, the sons of Zebedee, and two others of his disciples. [3] Simon Peter said to them, "I am going fishing." They said to him, "We will go with you." They went out and got into the boat, but that night they caught nothing.

4 Just after daybreak, Jesus stood on the beach; but the disciples did not know that it was Jesus. [5] Jesus said to them, "Children, you have no fish, have you?" They answered him, "No." [6] He said to them, "Cast the net to the right side of the boat, and you will find some." So they cast it, and now they were not able to haul it in because there were so many fish. [7] That disciple whom Jesus loved said to Peter, "It is the Lord!" When Simon Peter heard that it was the Lord, he put on some clothes, for he was naked, and jumped into the sea. [8] But the other

STUDY IT!

Resurrection Stories · John 21:1–14

There are fourteen stories about Jesus' resurrection in the four gospels. None of the stories describe the actual resurrection, but instead focus on the ways the followers of Jesus knew he was alive again. Matthew emphasizes God's power with dramatic symbols like earthquakes and lightning (Matthew 28:2-3). Mark focuses on the empty tomb (Mark 16:1-8). Luke emphasizes the living presence of Jesus in scripture and the Lord's Supper (Luke 24:13-35). John brings out the authority of the leaders of the early Church, especially Peter's role as its shepherd (John 20:19-23, 21:15-19).

All these stories together convey the faith of the disciples that Jesus is alive. Life has triumphed over death through God's power. The disciples' mission is to communicate this good news. And it's our mission too!

---

a Other ancient authorities read *may continue to believe* b Or *the Christ* c Gk *Didymus*

disciples came in the boat, dragging the net full of fish, for they were not far from the land, only about a hundred yards^a off.

9 When they had gone ashore, they saw a charcoal fire there, with fish on it, and bread. ^{10}Jesus said to them, "Bring some of the fish that you have just caught." ^{11}So Simon Peter went aboard and hauled the net ashore, full of large fish, a hundred fifty-three of them; and though there were so many, the net was not torn. ^{12}Jesus said to them, "Come and have breakfast." Now none of the disciples dared to ask him, "Who are you?" because they knew it was the Lord. ^{13}Jesus came and took the bread and gave it to them, and did the same with the fish. ^{14}This was now the third time that Jesus appeared to the disciples after he was raised from the dead.

Jesus and Peter

15 When they had finished breakfast, Jesus said to Simon Peter, "Simon son of John, do you love me more than these?" He said to him, "Yes, Lord; you know that I love you." Jesus said to him, "Feed my lambs." ^{16}A second time he said to him, "Simon son of John, do you love me?" He said to him, "Yes, Lord; you know that I love you." Jesus said to him, "Tend my sheep." ^{17}He said to him the third time, "Simon son of John, do you love me?" Peter felt hurt because he said to him the third time, "Do you love me?" And he said to him, "Lord, you know everything; you know that I love you." Jesus said to him, "Feed my sheep. ^{18}Very truly, I tell you, when you were younger, you used to fasten your own belt and to go wherever you wished. But when you grow old, you will stretch out your hands, and someone else will

PRAY IT!

Deep Forgiveness · John 21:15–19

Peter never did things halfheartedly. The Gospels give us plenty of examples of Peter's willingness to jump into action, even when it got him into trouble (Matthew 14:28-31; Mark 8:31-33). This leader among the disciples was the first to declare that he would give up his life for Jesus, which prompted Jesus to predict Peter's denial (John 13:36-38; Matthew 26:31-35). It's Peter's denial of Jesus that is most famous and most inglorious (John 18:15-18, 25-27). How quickly he went back on his word! Peter tried to stay strong when the going got tough; he even followed Jesus to the high priest's courtyard. But when the servants and slaves—not even the guards—asked if he knew Jesus, he flat out lied three times in a row, just as Jesus had said he would. Brash, bold Peter turned out to be a coward.

Can you imagine the guilt and disappointment Peter must have been carrying along with his grief through the events of Jesus' crucifixion? He must have been overjoyed to see Jesus alive again, but he must have also felt embarrassed about his earlier failure. He probably hoped that whole denial event would just quietly be forgotten.

Jesus had a better plan, and John's account of his interaction with Peter in **John 21:15–19** shows us God's priorities—healing and forgiveness. Jesus brought up Peter's pain—not to rub it in, but to heal it. "Do you love me?" Jesus asked three times. Peter was clearly hurting by the third question (John 21:17). But it seems clear that Jesus was symbolically cleaning out Peter's emotional wounds from each of his three denials. He was picking up Peter's broken pieces and replacing them with a mission: "Feed my sheep." He was renewing Peter's calling: "Follow me."

Peter had failed Jesus miserably, but Jesus was making it clear that he still loved and wanted Peter. It's a powerful lesson for us too. God knows we will fail him. But God still loves us and offers his forgiveness, no matter how great our sin. Don't let guilt drive you from God. Come to Jesus for healing and restoration.

• How have you let God down? What are you feeling guilty about?

• Pray or journal your confession and embarrassment and ask for God's healing. Open your heart to let God's Spirit draw you close to God again.

^{a} Gk *two hundred cubits*

LIVE IT!

The Gospel According to . . . • John 21:24–25

John ends by saying that if everything Jesus did were to be written down, the entire world couldn't contain it. It almost sounds like a challenge, doesn't it? Maybe the author was thinking of all the things the risen Christ continues to do in the lives of his followers.

- What marvelous stories would you write in your own gospel story, one based on the risen Jesus working in your life?
- What messages and teachings would you offer to people today?
- How does your life reveal and reflect the good news of Jesus?

fasten a belt around you and take you where you do not wish to go." ¹⁹(He said this to indicate the kind of death by which he would glorify God.) After this he said to him, "Follow me."

Jesus and the Beloved Disciple

20 Peter turned and saw the disciple whom Jesus loved following them; he was the one who had reclined next to Jesus at the supper and had said, "Lord, who is it that is going to betray you?" ²¹When Peter saw him, he said to Jesus, "Lord, what about him?" ²²Jesus said to him, "If it is my will that

he remain until I come, what is that to you? Follow me!" ²³So the rumor spread in the community[a] that this disciple would not die. Yet Jesus did not say to him that he would not die, but, "If it is my will that he remain until I come, what is that to you?"[b]

24 This is the disciple who is testifying to these things and has written them, and we know that his testimony is true. ²⁵But there are also many other things that Jesus did; if every one of them were written down, I suppose that the world itself could not contain the books that would be written.

a Gk *among the brothers*   b Other ancient authorities lack *what is that to you*

Acts

Think of Acts as the collection of DVD extras, bonus materials, the continuing story of the Gospels. The stories of the apostles take us behind the scenes and give us a real-life look at what happened when the followers of Christ started living out their new beliefs. Jesus was gone from the earth. He had sent the Holy Spirit to help his followers proclaim the gospel, but they still had to work out the everyday realities of living in community and obedience as they worked to share the good news of Jesus with the world. Acts is full of compromise, conflict, love, community, greed, generosity, powerful living, and violent death.

IN DEPTH

Acts was written by the author of the gospel of Luke. So, essentially, Acts is the second volume of a two-volume history. Like the Gospels, it is not a history in the sense of an eyewitness account of the beginnings of Christianity; rather, it is an interpretation of this history, explaining how Christianity spread outside of Judaism to the Gentile world under the direction of the Holy Spirit.

Acts is packed with action. We read about the descent of the Holy Spirit on the apostles (Acts 2:1-41), Paul's conversion to the Christian way (Acts 9:1-19), and some miraculous escapes from prisons and riots (Acts 12:6-11; 16:16-40). We learn about the first Church council in Jerusalem, where a decision was made to accept Gentiles (non-Jews) as Christians without requiring that they also become practicing Jews (Acts 15:1-35). Acts continuously emphasizes how faith in Christ is shared and supported through Christian community.

Acts also gives us instruction based on how Christians lived in the years after Jesus' resurrection and ascension. We learn how the believers celebrated the Lord's Supper together and shared everything they owned (Acts 2:42-47). We learn how the gospel message was preached, first to Jews in the synagogues and later to Gentiles. We learn how traveling missionaries like Paul went on long journeys and suffered many hardships to form new groups of believers across the Roman Empire. Under the guidance of the Holy Spirit, the Church miraculously went from a small group of disciples in Jerusalem to a movement spreading across the entire Roman Empire, even to Rome itself.

QUICK FACTS

- **Author:** A Gentile Christian named Luke, who also wrote the gospel of Luke
- **Date Written:** Around A.D. 80
- **Audience:** Gentile (Greek) Christians, represented by Theophilus
- **Themes:** God is sovereign over history and the future; Jesus is present in the world through the Holy Spirit and through the lives of his followers.

AT A GLANCE

- **Acts 1:1–6:7** The new Pentecost, the mission in Jerusalem
- **Acts 6:8–9:43** The martyrdom of Stephen, the spread of the mission outside Jerusalem, Paul's conversion
- **Acts 10:1–15:35** Continuing the spread of the mission to the Gentiles, the Council of Jerusalem
- **Acts 15:36–28:31** Paul's mission to the ends of the earth

The Promise of the Holy Spirit

1 In the first book, Theophilus, I wrote about all that Jesus did and taught from the beginning [2] until the day when he was taken up to heaven, after giving instructions through the Holy Spirit to the apostles whom he had chosen. [3] After his suffering he presented himself alive to them by many convincing proofs, appearing to them during forty days and speaking about the kingdom of God. [4] While staying[a] with them, he ordered them not to leave Jerusalem, but to wait there for the promise of the Father. "This," he said, "is what you have heard from me; [5] for John baptized with water, but you will be baptized with[b] the Holy Spirit not many days from now."

The Ascension of Jesus

6 So when they had come together, they asked him, "Lord, is this the time when you will restore the kingdom to Israel?" [7] He replied, "It is not for you to know the times or periods that the Father has set by his own authority. [8] But you will receive power when the Holy Spirit has come upon you; and you will be my witnesses in Jerusalem, in all Judea and Samaria, and to the ends of the earth." [9] When he had said this, as they were watching, he was lifted up, and a cloud took him out of their sight. [10] While he was going and they were gazing up toward heaven, suddenly two men in white robes stood by them. [11] They said, "Men of Galilee, why do you stand looking up toward heaven? This Jesus, who has been taken up from you into heaven, will come in the same way as you saw him go into heaven."

Matthias Chosen to Replace Judas

12 Then they returned to Jerusalem from the mount called Olivet, which is near Jerusalem, a sabbath day's journey away. [13] When they had entered the city, they went to the room upstairs where they were staying, Peter, and John, and James, and Andrew, Philip and Thomas, Bartholomew and Matthew, James son of Alphaeus, and Simon the Zealot, and Judas son of[c] James. [14] All these were constantly devoting themselves to prayer, together with certain women, including Mary the mother of Jesus, as well as his brothers.

15 In those days Peter stood up among the believers[d] (together the crowd numbered about one hundred twenty persons) and said, [16] "Friends,[e] the scripture had to be fulfilled, which the Holy Spirit

PRAY IT!

Send Us Your Spirit!
Acts 1:1–11

After Jesus was taken up to heaven, the apostles, Mary, and other women and men gathered to pray together. They knew they needed the Holy Spirit, promised by Jesus, to begin the difficult task of sharing the good news of Jesus with the world. Today, we continue to pray:

Jesus, send us your Spirit, and renew the face of the earth. You know our strengths and weaknesses. Transform us into messengers of your gospel for those who yearn for you.

Jesus, send us your Spirit, and renew the face of the earth. You know our history, with its beautiful and painful experiences. Help us to share your message of love, justice, and peace.

Jesus, send us your Spirit, and renew the face of the earth. You know our longing for love and community. Make us instruments of unity and service, especially for those who are weak and those who are lonely. Amen.

through David foretold concerning Judas, who became a guide for those who arrested Jesus— [17] for he was numbered among us and was allotted his share in this ministry." [18] (Now this man acquired a field with the reward of his wickedness; and falling headlong,[f] he burst open in the middle and all his bowels gushed out. [19] This became known to all the residents of Jerusalem, so that the field was called in their language Hakeldama, that is, Field of Blood.) [20] "For it is written in the book of Psalms,

'Let his homestead become desolate,
    and let there be no one to live in it';

and

'Let another take his position of overseer.'

[21] So one of the men who have accompanied us during all the time that the Lord Jesus went in and out among us, [22] beginning from the baptism of John until the day when he was taken up from us—one

a Or eating b Or by c Or the brother of d Gk brothers e Gk Men, brothers f Or swelling up

of these must become a witness with us to his resurrection." [23]So they proposed two, Joseph called Barsabbas, who was also known as Justus, and Matthias. [24]Then they prayed and said, "Lord, you know everyone's heart. Show us which one of these two you have chosen [25]to take the place[a] in this ministry and apostleship from which Judas turned aside to go to his own place." [26]And they cast lots for them, and the lot fell on Matthias; and he was added to the eleven apostles.

The Coming of the Holy Spirit

2 When the day of Pentecost had come, they were all together in one place. [2]And suddenly from heaven there came a sound like the rush of a violent wind, and it filled the entire house where they were sitting. [3]Divided tongues, as of fire, appeared among them, and a tongue rested on each of them. [4]All of them were filled with the Holy Spirit and began to speak in other languages, as the Spirit gave them ability.

5 Now there were devout Jews from every nation under heaven living in Jerusalem. [6]And at this sound the crowd gathered and was bewildered, because each one heard them speaking in the native language of each. [7]Amazed and astonished, they asked, "Are not all these who are speaking Galileans? [8]And how is it that we hear, each of us, in our own native language? [9]Parthians, Medes, Elamites, and residents of Mesopotamia, Judea and Cappadocia, Pontus and Asia, [10]Phrygia and Pamphylia, Egypt and the parts of Libya belonging to Cyrene, and visitors from Rome, both Jews and proselytes, [11]Cretans and Arabs—in our own languages we hear them speaking about God's deeds of power." [12]All were amazed and perplexed, saying to one another, "What does this mean?" [13]But others sneered and said, "They are filled with new wine."

Peter Addresses the Crowd

14 But Peter, standing with the eleven, raised his voice and addressed them, "Men of Judea and all who live in Jerusalem, let this be known to you, and listen to what I say. [15]Indeed, these are not drunk, as you suppose, for it is only nine o'clock in the morning. [16]No, this is what was spoken through the prophet Joel:

[17] 'In the last days it will be, God declares,
    that I will pour out my Spirit upon all flesh,
       and your sons and your daughters shall
          prophesy,
    and your young men shall see visions,

STUDY IT!

Pentecost · Acts 2:1–13

Jesus made his disciples a promise, and on Pentecost, fifty days after his resurrection, Jesus fulfilled his promise by sending the Holy Spirit, or the Advocate (John 14:26). Jesus told his followers that the Holy Spirit would guide them in truth and give them power from heaven. The dramatic descent of the Holy Spirit on Pentecost brought about more than the disciples could have ever imagined (Acts 2:3-4). The Spirit gave them the ability to speak in languages that everyone could understand. And they were given power that transformed their fears into courage and confidence to tell the world about Jesus. And that was just on day one!

The descent of the Holy Spirit on Pentecost also brought about several interesting events in the history of the world. First, Pentecost marks the day the Trinity was made fully known to believers as the Father, Son, and Holy Spirit. Second, it marks the day the kingdom of God was first made available to all who believed in Jesus Christ. And third, the world entered into what is called the time of the church, when God's kingdom is, in part, here on earth.

It's been over two thousand years since Pentecost, and the Holy Spirit is still guiding believers in carrying out their mission to lead people to salvation through Jesus Christ. The same Holy Spirit can also work wonders through each of us, giving us courage, confidence, and excitement about following God and telling others about Jesus. All we need to do is ask, knowing that Jesus always keeps his promises, often in ways we never could have dreamed!

a Other ancient authorities read *the share*

and your old men shall dream dreams.

18 Even upon my slaves, both men and women,
 in those days I will pour out my Spirit;
 and they shall prophesy.

19 And I will show portents in the heaven above
 and signs on the earth below,
 blood, and fire, and smoky mist.

20 The sun shall be turned to darkness
 and the moon to blood,
 before the coming of the Lord's great
 and glorious day.

21 Then everyone who calls on the name of the
 Lord shall be saved.'

22 "You that are Israelites,*a* listen to what I have to say: Jesus of Nazareth,*b* a man attested to you by God with deeds of power, wonders, and signs that God did through him among you, as you yourselves know— 23this man, handed over to you according to the definite plan and foreknowledge of God, you crucified and killed by the hands of those outside the law. 24But God raised him up, having freed him from death,*c* because it was impossible for him to be held in its power. 25For David says concerning him,

'I saw the Lord always before me,
 for he is at my right hand so that I will not
 be shaken;

26 therefore my heart was glad, and my tongue
 rejoiced;
 moreover my flesh will live in hope.

27 For you will not abandon my soul to Hades,
 or let your Holy One experience
 corruption.

28 You have made known to me the ways of life;
 you will make me full of gladness with your
 presence.'

29 "Fellow Israelites,*d* I may say to you confidently of our ancestor David that he both died and was buried, and his tomb is with us to this day. 30Since he was a prophet, he knew that God had sworn with an oath to him that he would put one of his descendants on his throne. 31Foreseeing this, David*e* spoke of the resurrection of the Messiah,*f* saying,

'He was not abandoned to Hades,
 nor did his flesh experience corruption.'

32This Jesus God raised up, and of that all of us are witnesses. 33Being therefore exalted at*g* the right hand of God, and having received from the Father the promise of the Holy Spirit, he has poured out this that you both see and hear. 34For David did not ascend into the heavens, but he himself says,

'The Lord said to my Lord,
 "Sit at my right hand,

35 until I make your enemies your
 footstool." '

36Therefore let the entire house of Israel know with certainty that God has made him both Lord and Messiah,*h* this Jesus whom you crucified."

The First Converts

37 Now when they heard this, they were cut to the heart and said to Peter and to the other apos-

LIVE IT!

Radical Living
Acts 2:42–47

Imagine living the way the believers did in this passage. It might be tough to share everything—time, space, food, possessions. We're so used to our own space and our own belongings. But think about the benefit of living in community—no one would lack anything! And you would never have to worry about having enough, knowing that the community would always care for you. Sound impossible in today's world?

The core of this kind of community is glad and generous hearts (Acts 2:46). And although today's community of believers is much larger, even global, we are called to be participants in helping to promote this reality in the world. It's not always easy, but we can find ways to incorporate these principles into our lives, starting with our own home community.

- What do you think society would be like today if everyone lived as the early Christian community tried to live?
- How can you work to create community among your family, friends, and believers in your city?
- With the use of technology and travel, how can your community reach out to the global Christian community?

---

a Gk *Men, Israelites* *b* Gk *the Nazorean* *c* Gk *the pains of death* *d* Gk *Men, brothers* *e* Gk *he* *f* Or *the Christ* *g* Or *by* *h* Or *Christ*

tles, "Brothers,*ª* what should we do?" [38] Peter said to them, "Repent, and be baptized every one of you in the name of Jesus Christ so that your sins may be forgiven; and you will receive the gift of the Holy Spirit. [39] For the promise is for you, for your children, and for all who are far away, everyone whom the Lord our God calls to him." [40] And he testified with many other arguments and exhorted them, saying, "Save yourselves from this corrupt generation." [41] So those who welcomed his message were baptized, and that day about three thousand persons were added. [42] They devoted themselves to the apostles' teaching and fellowship, to the breaking of bread and the prayers.

Life among the Believers

43 Awe came upon everyone, because many wonders and signs were being done by the apostles. [44] All who believed were together and had all things in common; [45] they would sell their possessions and goods and distribute the proceeds*ᵇ* to all, as any had need. [46] Day by day, as they spent much time together in the temple, they broke bread at home*ᶜ* and ate their food with glad and generous*ᵈ* hearts, [47] praising God and having the goodwill of all the people. And day by day the Lord added to their number those who were being saved.

Peter Heals a Crippled Beggar

3 One day Peter and John were going up to the temple at the hour of prayer, at three o'clock in the afternoon. [2] And a man lame from birth was being carried in. People would lay him daily at the gate of the temple called the Beautiful Gate so that he could ask for alms from those entering the temple. [3] When he saw Peter and John about to go into the temple, he asked them for alms. [4] Peter looked intently at him, as did John, and said, "Look at us." [5] And he fixed his attention on them, expecting to receive something from them. [6] But Peter said, "I have no silver or gold, but what I have I give you; in the name of Jesus Christ of Nazareth,*ᵉ* stand up and walk." [7] And he took him by the right hand and raised him up; and immediately his feet and ankles were made strong. [8] Jumping up, he stood and began to walk, and he entered the temple with them, walking and leaping and praising God. [9] All the people saw him walking and praising God, [10] and they recognized him as the one who used to sit and ask for alms at the Beautiful Gate of the temple; and they were filled with wonder and amazement at what had happened to him.

Peter Speaks in Solomon's Portico

11 While he clung to Peter and John, all the people

Shane Claiborne: Living in Simple Community
Acts 2:44–47

Think the idea of living in community was nice for the early Christians in Acts, but impossible in our world today? Shane Claiborne disagrees. He is one of the founding members of The Simple Way, an organization that brings together people who want to live out the radical commands of Christ. The Simple Way, with its houses on Potter Street in the Kensington neighborhood of Philadelphia, is all about community. Its website (thesimpleway.org) lists the principles on which the community is built—things like simplicity, nonviolence, spirituality, relationships, justice, and rest. But, like the early Christians, its members don't have a desire to live in isolation. In fact, just the opposite. They want their community to impact and help transform the larger community around them. They do this through building relationships and engaging in things like daily prayer, weekly community meals, and simply providing food and necessities for those in need around them. They've even built a community park where their former building burned down. Living in the poorest neighborhood in Philadelphia, the members of the community know the needs up close and personal and are able to help in many ways. On a larger scale, The Simple Way has also become a sort of connection point for similar communities who are part of the New Monastic movement. You can read more about Claiborne and the movement in his book, THE IRRESISTIBLE REVOLUTION: LIVING AS AN ORDINARY RADICAL.

a Gk *Men, brothers*   *b* Gk *them*   *c* Or *from house to house*   *d* Or *sincere*   *e* Gk *the Nazorean*

LIVE IT!

Share Christ · Acts 3:1–10

You're walking down the street. A homeless man approaches, asking for money. What do you do? What is your reaction? If you're like many people, you look away, avoiding eye contact. Maybe you mumble something about "not today" or perhaps quickly hand over some change.

Beggars were not uncommon on the streets in Jerusalem during the first century. And probably, like today, some people averted their eyes and walked by while others stopped to offer a few coins. When Peter and John encounter a beggar in **Acts 3:3**, they don't have a whole lot of money to share with him, but they stop just the same. Looking him in the eye, Peter offers the lame man the one thing of value he does have: the powerful gift of healing found in the name of Jesus Christ. You may not have the gift of healing or lots of extra money to give to those in need. But Peter and John remind us that knowing Jesus is the greatest treasure one can acquire in life. That treasure frees us to see those in need as real people with real needs beyond their request for some change. Whether it's with a smile, a moment of your time, an encouraging word, or a listening ear, don't forget to share Christ's love with others!

ran together to them in the portico called Solomon's Portico, utterly astonished. [12]When Peter saw it, he addressed the people, "You Israelites,[a] why do you wonder at this, or why do you stare at us, as though by our own power or piety we had made him walk? [13]The God of Abraham, the God of Isaac, and the God of Jacob, the God of our ancestors has glorified his servant[b] Jesus, whom you handed over and rejected in the presence of Pilate, though he had decided to release him. [14]But you rejected the Holy and Righteous One and asked to have a murderer given to you, [15]and you killed the Author of life, whom God raised from the dead. To this we are witnesses. [16]And by faith in his name, his name itself has made this man strong, whom you see and know; and the faith that is through Jesus[c] has given him this perfect health in the presence of all of you.

[17] "And now, friends,[d] I know that you acted in ignorance, as did also your rulers. [18]In this way God fulfilled what he had foretold through all the prophets, that his Messiah[e] would suffer. [19]Repent therefore, and turn to God so that your sins may be wiped out, [20]so that times of refreshing may come from the presence of the Lord, and that he may send the Messiah[f] appointed for you, that is, Jesus, [21]who must remain in heaven until the time of universal restoration that God announced long ago through his holy prophets. [22]Moses said, 'The Lord your God will raise up for you from your own people[d] a prophet like me. You must listen to whatever he tells you.

[23]And it will be that everyone who does not listen to that prophet will be utterly rooted out of the people.' [24]And all the prophets, as many as have spoken, from Samuel and those after him, also predicted these days. [25]You are the descendants of the prophets and of the covenant that God gave to your ancestors, saying to Abraham, 'And in your descendants all the families of the earth shall be blessed.' [26]When God raised up his servant,[b] he sent him first to you, to bless you by turning each of you from your wicked ways."

Peter and John before the Council

4 While Peter and John[g] were speaking to the people, the priests, the captain of the temple, and the Sadducees came to them, [2]much annoyed because they were teaching the people and proclaiming that in Jesus there is the resurrection of the dead. [3]So they arrested them and put them in custody until the next day, for it was already evening. [4]But many of those who heard the word believed; and they numbered about five thousand.

[5] The next day their rulers, elders, and scribes assembled in Jerusalem, [6]with Annas the high priest, Caiaphas, John,[h] and Alexander, and all who were of the high-priestly family. [7]When they had made the prisoners[i] stand in their midst, they inquired, "By what power or by what name did you do this?" [8]Then Peter, filled with the Holy Spirit, said to them, "Rulers of the people and elders, [9]if we are questioned

today because of a good deed done to someone who was sick and are asked how this man has been healed, [10]let it be known to all of you, and to all the people of Israel, that this man is standing before you in good health by the name of Jesus Christ of Nazareth,[a] whom you crucified, whom God raised from the dead. [11]This Jesus[b] is

> 'the stone that was rejected by you, the
>   builders;
>   it has become the cornerstone.'[c]

[12]There is salvation in no one else, for there is no other name under heaven given among mortals by which we must be saved."

13 Now when they saw the boldness of Peter and John and realized that they were uneducated and ordinary men, they were amazed and recognized them as companions of Jesus. [14]When they saw the man who had been cured standing beside them, they had nothing to say in opposition. [15]So they ordered them to leave the council while they discussed the

PRAY IT!

Can't Argue with That!
Acts 4:1–22

When Peter and John are arrested, the council hopes to find something it can punish them for. But it can find nothing questionable in the apostles' words or actions. Their words are clearly inspired by Jesus' teaching, and their power to perform miracles is unquestionable. Even as the council tries to convict Peter and John of something, the man they healed stands before them (Acts 4:13-14). How can you argue with that? After some debate, Peter and John are let go. Pray that your own words and actions will be like those of Peter and John:

God, make my words and actions so solid in you that nobody can argue with them. Give me the courage to speak of you, even when others don't like it. And help me act in ways that show my commitment to sharing your love and grace with the world. Amen.

matter with one another. [16]They said, "What will we do with them? For it is obvious to all who live in Jerusalem that a notable sign has been done through them; we cannot deny it. [17]But to keep it from spreading further among the people, let us warn them to speak no more to anyone in this name." [18]So they called them and ordered them not to speak or teach at all in the name of Jesus. [19]But Peter and John answered them, "Whether it is right in God's sight to listen to you rather than to God, you must judge; [20]for we cannot keep from speaking about what we have seen and heard." [21]After threatening them again, they let them go, finding no way to punish them because of the people, for all of them praised God for what had happened. [22]For the man on whom this sign of healing had been performed was more than forty years old.

The Believers Pray for Boldness

23 After they were released, they went to their friends[d] and reported what the chief priests and the elders had said to them. [24]When they heard it, they raised their voices together to God and said, "Sovereign Lord, who made the heaven and the earth, the sea, and everything in them, [25]it is you who said by the Holy Spirit through our ancestor David, your servant:[e]

> 'Why did the Gentiles rage,
>   and the peoples imagine vain things?
> [26] The kings of the earth took their stand,
>   and the rulers have gathered together
>   against the Lord and against his
>   Messiah.'[f]

[27]For in this city, in fact, both Herod and Pontius Pilate, with the Gentiles and the peoples of Israel, gathered together against your holy servant[e] Jesus, whom you anointed, [28]to do whatever your hand and your plan had predestined to take place. [29]And now, Lord, look at their threats, and grant to your servants[g] to speak your word with all boldness, [30]while you stretch out your hand to heal, and signs and wonders are performed through the name of your holy servant[e] Jesus." [31]When they had prayed, the place in which they were gathered together was shaken; and they were all filled with the Holy Spirit and spoke the word of God with boldness.

The Believers Share Their Possessions

32 Now the whole group of those who believed were of one heart and soul, and no one claimed

---

a Gk the Nazorean   b Gk This   c Or keystone   d Gk their own   e Or child   f Or his Christ   g Gk slaves

An Open Hand · Acts 4:32–37

Acts 4:32–37 describes the value of stewardship. Stewardship involves sharing the gifts of time, talents, and treasure that God has placed in your care (see "Live It: Less Is More," near Luke 21:1-4). It means living your life with an open hand, holding out everything God has given you to share with others. It is key to the life of any Christian community.

Sharing our treasure by giving money and possessions is the most obvious way of sharing. But consider Joseph (Acts 4:36-37). Yes, he sold a field and gave the money. But he also gave encouragement to others from his heart and through his life—so much so that he was given the name Barnabas, which means "son of encouragement."

- What are you good at that you could share with your church, school, or community? Don't discount even the simplest ability or character trait. For example, maybe you are persistent; this talent can help with the success of any project. Or perhaps you love children and can babysit for overwhelmed parents.
- When you are tempted to hold tight to your time, talents, and treasure, how can you remind yourself to release those gifts with an open hand?

private ownership of any possessions, but everything they owned was held in common. ³³With great power the apostles gave their testimony to the resurrection of the Lord Jesus, and great grace was upon them all. ³⁴There was not a needy person among them, for as many as owned lands or houses sold them and brought the proceeds of what was sold. ³⁵They laid it at the apostles' feet, and it was distributed to each as any had need. ³⁶There was a Levite, a native of Cyprus, Joseph, to whom the apostles gave the name Barnabas (which means "son of encouragement"). ³⁷He sold a field that belonged to him, then brought the money, and laid it at the apostles' feet.

Ananias and Sapphira

5 But a man named Ananias, with the consent of his wife Sapphira, sold a piece of property; ²with his wife's knowledge, he kept back some of the proceeds, and brought only a part and laid it at the apostles' feet. ³"Ananias," Peter asked, "why has Satan filled your heart to lie to the Holy Spirit and to keep back part of the proceeds of the land? ⁴While it remained unsold, did it not remain your own? And after it was sold, were not the proceeds at your disposal? How is it that you have contrived this deed in your heart? You did not lie to us[a] but to God!" ⁵Now when Ananias heard these words, he fell down and died. And great fear seized all who

heard of it. ⁶The young men came and wrapped up his body,[b] then carried him out and buried him.

7 After an interval of about three hours his wife came in, not knowing what had happened. ⁸Peter said to her, "Tell me whether you and your husband sold the land for such and such a price." And she said, "Yes, that was the price." ⁹Then Peter said to her, "How is it that you have agreed together to put the Spirit of the Lord to the test? Look, the feet of those who have buried your husband are at the door, and they will carry you out." ¹⁰Immediately she fell down at his feet and died. When the young men came in they found her dead, so they carried her out and buried her beside her husband. ¹¹And great fear seized the whole church and all who heard of these things.

The Apostles Heal Many

12 Now many signs and wonders were done among the people through the apostles. And they were all together in Solomon's Portico. ¹³None of the rest dared to join them, but the people held them in high esteem. ¹⁴Yet more than ever believers were added to the Lord, great numbers of both men and women, ¹⁵so that they even carried out the sick into the streets, and laid them on cots and mats, in order that Peter's shadow might fall on some of them as he came by. ¹⁶A great number of people would also gather from the towns around Jerusalem, bringing

a Gk *to men*　**b** Meaning of Gk uncertain

the sick and those tormented by unclean spirits, and they were all cured.

The Apostles Are Persecuted

17 Then the high priest took action; he and all who were with him (that is, the sect of the Sadducees), being filled with jealousy, [18]arrested the apostles and put them in the public prison. [19]But during the night an angel of the Lord opened the prison doors, brought them out, and said, [20]"Go, stand in the temple and tell the people the whole message about this life." [21]When they heard this, they entered the temple at daybreak and went on with their teaching.

When the high priest and those with him arrived, they called together the council and the whole body of the elders of Israel, and sent to the prison to have them brought. [22]But when the temple police went there, they did not find them in the prison; so they returned and reported, [23]"We found the prison securely locked and the guards standing at the doors, but when we opened them, we found no one inside." [24]Now when the captain of the temple and the chief priests heard these words, they were perplexed about them, wondering what might be going on. [25]Then someone arrived and announced, "Look, the men

STUDY IT!

Just a Little White Lie
Acts 5:1–11

Ananias and Sapphira were doing a great thing, right? Others were selling fields and bringing the money to the apostles, so they decided to do the same. They sold a piece of property and presented the money to the apostles as a gift to the community of believers. So what's with both of them keeling over dead? Their deaths were a result of their sin—dishonesty. The money was theirs to do with as they pleased, but they lied and pretended they were giving the full price of the land while keeping some back for themselves. But still, the severity of the punishment is jarring. If the punishment for lying was always death, none of us would be here. Thankfully, it's not. But God's message is clear to the early Christians and to us today: Sin is serious business. Lying to others is lying to God. Dishonesty as well as the underlying selfishness and desire for recognition are all unacceptable to God. In God's eyes there is no such thing as a little white lie.

LIVE IT!

Ultimate Success or Epic Failure?
Acts 5:17–39

When we catch up with the apostles in **Acts 5:17–39**, they have been thrown in prison for their teaching and then set free by an angel. When the council sends for the prisoners, it finds them in the temple courtyard teaching again! The council members are angry, and they want the men dead. But a wise man named Gamaliel talks them out of killing the apostles on the following argument: if the disciples' mission is from God, it will succeed despite anything the council does, but if it is not of God's design, it will fail and Jesus' followers will eventually disappear anyway.

When you look at your own mission, the purpose and goals of your life, how does it stand up to this test? We can take encouragement that if our plans are from God, ultimately nothing can stop our mission. That doesn't mean it will be easy or go according to plan! But in the bigger picture our mission, God's mission, cannot be stopped.

whom you put in prison are standing in the temple and teaching the people!" ²⁶Then the captain went with the temple police and brought them, but without violence, for they were afraid of being stoned by the people.

27 When they had brought them, they had them stand before the council. The high priest questioned them, ²⁸saying, "We gave you strict orders not to teach in this name,ᵃ yet here you have filled Jerusalem with your teaching and you are determined to bring this man's blood on us." ²⁹But Peter and the apostles answered, "We must obey God rather than any human authority.ᵇ ³⁰The God of our ancestors raised up Jesus, whom you had killed by hanging him on a tree. ³¹God exalted him at his right hand as Leader and Savior that he might give repentance to Israel and forgiveness of sins. ³²And we are witnesses to these things, and so is the Holy Spirit whom God has given to those who obey him."

33 When they heard this, they were enraged and wanted to kill them. ³⁴But a Pharisee in the council named Gamaliel, a teacher of the law, respected by all the people, stood up and ordered the men to be put outside for a short time. ³⁵Then he said to them, "Fellow Israelites,ᶜ consider carefully what you propose to do to these men. ³⁶For some time ago Theudas rose up, claiming to be somebody, and a number of men, about four hundred, joined him; but he was killed, and all who followed him were dispersed and disappeared. ³⁷After him Judas the Galilean rose up at the time of the census and got people to follow him; he also perished, and all who followed him were scattered. ³⁸So in the present case, I tell you, keep away from these men and let them alone; because if this plan or this undertaking is of human origin, it will fail; ³⁹but if it is of God, you will not be able to overthrow them—in that case you may even be found fighting against God!"

They were convinced by him, ⁴⁰and when they had called in the apostles, they had them flogged. Then they ordered them not to speak in the name of Jesus, and let them go. ⁴¹As they left the council, they rejoiced that they were considered worthy to suffer dishonor for the sake of the name. ⁴²And every day in the temple and at homeᵈ they did not cease to teach and proclaim Jesus as the Messiah.ᵉ

Seven Chosen to Serve

6 Now during those days, when the disciples were increasing in number, the Hellenists complained against the Hebrews because their widows were being neglected in the daily distribution of food. ²And the twelve called together the whole community of the disciples and said, "It is not right that we should neglect the word of God in order to wait on tables.ᶠ ³Therefore, friends,ᵍ select from among yourselves seven men of good standing, full of the Spirit and of wisdom, whom we may appoint to this task, ⁴while we, for our part, will devote ourselves to prayer and to serving the word." ⁵What they said pleased the whole community, and they chose Stephen, a man full of faith and the Holy Spirit, together with Philip, Prochorus, Nicanor, Timon, Parmenas, and Nicolaus, a proselyte of Antioch. ⁶They had these men stand before the apostles, who prayed and laid their hands on them.

7 The word of God continued to spread; the number of the disciples increased greatly in Jerusalem, and a great many of the priests became obedient to the faith.

PRAY IT!

A Secure Identity
Acts 6:8–7:60

The story of Stephen's brave defense of his faith is both heartbreaking and inspiring. Stephen is falsely accused and questioned by those who want to stop his work, but instead of fighting back he responds with an amazing account of the history of his ancestors. Stephen was secure in his identity, because he knew his spiritual history. Knowing the stories of those who had come before him gave Stephen divine courage, even in the face of death.

How many people today would be willing to make similar sacrifices in the struggle for freedom, equality, and truth? Would you? What is your spiritual history, and how does it shape your identity today?

Dear God, help me to learn about and treasure the bravery and sacrifice of those who have come before me. Help me to follow their example in working for justice with love and courage. Amen.

ᵃ Other ancient authorities read *Did we not give you strict orders not to teach in this name?* ᵇ Gk *than men* ᶜ Gk *Men, Israelites* ᵈ Or *from house to house* ᵉ Or *the Christ* ᶠ Or *keep accounts* ᵍ Gk *brothers*

The Arrest of Stephen

8 Stephen, full of grace and power, did great wonders and signs among the people. [9]Then some of those who belonged to the synagogue of the Freedmen (as it was called), Cyrenians, Alexandrians, and others of those from Cilicia and Asia, stood up and argued with Stephen. [10]But they could not withstand the wisdom and the Spirit[a] with which he spoke. [11]Then they secretly instigated some men to say, "We have heard him speak blasphemous words against Moses and God." [12]They stirred up the people as well as the elders and the scribes; then they suddenly confronted him, seized him, and brought him before the council. [13]They set up false witnesses who said, "This man never stops saying things against this holy place and the law; [14]for we have heard him say that this Jesus of Nazareth[b] will destroy this place and will change the customs that Moses handed on to us." [15]And all who sat in the council looked intently at him, and they saw that his face was like the face of an angel.

Stephen's Speech to the Council

7 Then the high priest asked him, "Are these things so?" [2]And Stephen replied:

"Brothers[c] and fathers, listen to me. The God of glory appeared to our ancestor Abraham when he was in Mesopotamia, before he lived in Haran, [3]and said to him, 'Leave your country and your relatives and go to the land that I will show you.' [4]Then he left the country of the Chaldeans and settled in Haran. After his father died, God had him move from there to this country in which you are now living. [5]He did not give him any of it as a heritage, not even a foot's length, but promised to give it to him as his possession and to his descendants after him, even though he had no child. [6]And God spoke in these terms, that his descendants would be resident aliens in a country belonging to others, who would enslave them and mistreat them during four hundred years. [7]'But I will judge the nation that they serve,' said God, 'and after that they shall come out and worship me in this place.' [8]Then he gave him the covenant of circumcision. And so Abraham[d] became the father of Isaac and circumcised him on the eighth day; and Isaac became the father of Jacob, and Jacob of the twelve patriarchs.

9 "The patriarchs, jealous of Joseph, sold him into Egypt; but God was with him, [10]and rescued him from all his afflictions, and enabled him to win favor and to show wisdom when he stood before Pharaoh, king of Egypt, who appointed him ruler over Egypt and over all his household. [11]Now there came a famine throughout Egypt and Canaan, and great suffering, and our ancestors could find no food. [12]But when Jacob heard that there was grain in Egypt, he sent our ancestors there on their first visit. [13]On the second visit Joseph made himself known to his brothers, and Joseph's family became known to Pharaoh. [14]Then Joseph sent and invited his father Jacob and all his relatives to come to him, seventy-five in all; [15]so Jacob went down to Egypt. He himself died there as well as our ancestors, [16]and their bodies[e] were brought back to Shechem and laid in the tomb that Abraham had bought for a sum of silver from the sons of Hamor in Shechem.

17 "But as the time drew near for the fulfillment of the promise that God had made to Abraham, our people in Egypt increased and multiplied [18]until another king who had not known Joseph ruled over Egypt. [19]He dealt craftily with our race and forced our ancestors to abandon their infants so that they would die. [20]At this time Moses was born, and he was beautiful before God. For three months he was brought up in his father's house; [21]and when he was abandoned, Pharaoh's daughter adopted him and brought him up as her own son. [22]So Moses was instructed in all the wisdom of the Egyptians and was powerful in his words and deeds.

23 "When he was forty years old, it came into his heart to visit his relatives, the Israelites.[f] [24]When he saw one of them being wronged, he defended the oppressed man and avenged him by striking down the Egyptian. [25]He supposed that his kinsfolk would understand that God through him was rescuing them, but they did not understand. [26]The next day he came to some of them as they were quarreling and tried to reconcile them, saying, 'Men, you are brothers; why do you wrong each other?' [27]But the man who was wronging his neighbor pushed Moses[g] aside, saying, 'Who made you a ruler and a judge over us? [28]Do you want to kill me as you killed the Egyptian yesterday?' [29]When he heard this, Moses fled and became a resident alien in the land of Midian. There he became the father of two sons.

30 "Now when forty years had passed, an angel appeared to him in the wilderness of Mount Sinai, in the flame of a burning bush. [31]When Moses saw it, he was amazed at the sight; and as he approached to look, there came the voice of the Lord: [32]'I am

---

a Or *spirit*   **b** Gk *the Nazorean*   **c** Gk *Men, brothers*   **d** Gk *he*   **e** Gk *they*   **f** Gk *his brothers, the sons of Israel*   **g** Gk *him*

Martyrs • Acts 6:8–8:1

The stoning of Stephen is a turning point in Luke's account of the first Christians. Up until this point, it has been power and strength and success even in the face of hardship. But Stephen is the first recorded martyr—one who dies for one's faith. Luke makes it clear that Stephen's death, rather than causing the Christian movement to fall apart now that the stakes were higher, actually strengthened the Church. His heroic sacrifice is even presented as a model for Christians. Notice all the similarities between his death and that of Jesus.

Stephen was convinced that following the teachings of Jesus was the most important way to live—even to the point of death. He died for his beliefs, and the Church became stronger because of his faith and heroism. What would you die for?

the God of your ancestors, the God of Abraham, Isaac, and Jacob.' Moses began to tremble and did not dare to look. [33] Then the Lord said to him, 'Take off the sandals from your feet, for the place where you are standing is holy ground. [34] I have surely seen the mistreatment of my people who are in Egypt and have heard their groaning, and I have come down to rescue them. Come now, I will send you to Egypt.'

35 "It was this Moses whom they rejected when they said, 'Who made you a ruler and a judge?' and whom God now sent as both ruler and liberator through the angel who appeared to him in the bush. [36] He led them out, having performed wonders and signs in Egypt, at the Red Sea, and in the wilderness for forty years. [37] This is the Moses who said to the Israelites, 'God will raise up a prophet for you from your own people[a] as he raised me up.' [38] He is the one who was in the congregation in the wilderness with the angel who spoke to him at Mount Sinai, and with our ancestors; and he received living oracles to give to us. [39] Our ancestors were unwilling to obey him; instead, they pushed him aside, and in their hearts they turned back to Egypt, [40] saying to Aaron, 'Make gods for us who will lead the way for us; as for this Moses who led us out from the land of Egypt, we do not know what has happened to him.' [41] At that time they made a calf, offered a sacrifice to the idol, and reveled in the works of their hands. [42] But God turned away from them and handed them over to worship the host of heaven, as it is written in the book of the prophets:

'Did you offer to me slain victims and sacrifices
    forty years in the wilderness, O house of
        Israel?

[43] No; you took along the tent of Moloch,
    and the star of your god Rephan,
        the images that you made to worship;
    so I will remove you beyond Babylon.'

44 "Our ancestors had the tent of testimony in the wilderness, as God[b] directed when he spoke to Moses, ordering him to make it according to the pattern he had seen. [45] Our ancestors in turn brought it in with Joshua when they dispossessed the nations that God drove out before our ancestors. And it was there until the time of David, [46] who found favor with God and asked that he might find a dwelling place for the house of Jacob.[c] [47] But it was Solomon who built a house for him. [48] Yet the Most High does not dwell in houses made with human hands;[d] as the prophet says,

49 'Heaven is my throne,
    and the earth is my footstool.
What kind of house will you build for me, says
        the Lord,
    or what is the place of my rest?
50 Did not my hand make all these things?'

51 "You stiff-necked people, uncircumcised in heart and ears, you are forever opposing the Holy Spirit, just as your ancestors used to do. [52] Which of the prophets did your ancestors not persecute? They killed those who foretold the coming of the Righteous One, and now you have become his betrayers and murderers. [53] You are the ones that received the law as ordained by angels, and yet you have not kept it."

The Stoning of Stephen

54 When they heard these things, they became

a Gk your brothers   b Gk he   c Other ancient authorities read for the God of Jacob   d Gk with hands enraged and ground their teeth at Stephen.[a] 55But filled with the Holy Spirit, he gazed into heaven and saw the glory of God and Jesus standing at the right hand of God. 56"Look," he said, "I see the heavens opened and the Son of Man standing at the right hand of God!" 57But they covered their ears, and with a loud shout all rushed together against him. 58Then they dragged him out of the city and began to stone him; and the witnesses laid their coats at the feet of a young man named Saul. 59While they were stoning Stephen, he prayed, "Lord Jesus, receive my spirit." 60Then he knelt down and cried out in a loud voice, "Lord, do not hold this sin against them." When he had said this, he died.[b] 1And Saul approved of their killing him.

8

Saul Persecutes the Church

That day a severe persecution began against the church in Jerusalem, and all except the apostles were scattered throughout the countryside of Judea and Samaria. 2Devout men buried Stephen and made loud lamentation over him. 3But Saul was ravaging the church by entering house after house; dragging off both men and women, he committed them to prison.

Philip Preaches in Samaria

4 Now those who were scattered went from place to place, proclaiming the word. 5Philip went down to the city[c] of Samaria and proclaimed the Messiah[d] to them. 6The crowds with one accord listened eagerly to what was said by Philip, hearing and seeing the signs that he did, 7for unclean spirits, crying with loud shrieks, came out of many who were possessed; and many others who were paralyzed or lame were cured. 8So there was great joy in that city.

9 Now a certain man named Simon had previously practiced magic in the city and amazed the people of Samaria, saying that he was someone great. 10All of them, from the least to the greatest, listened to him eagerly, saying, "This man is the power of God that is called Great." 11And they listened eagerly to him because for a long time he had amazed them with his magic. 12But when they believed Philip, who was proclaiming the good news about the kingdom of God and the name of Jesus Christ, they were baptized, both men and women. 13Even Simon himself believed. After being baptized, he stayed constantly with Philip and was amazed when he saw the signs and great miracles that took place.

CONNECT IT!

Voice of the Martyrs: Assisting the Persecuted Church
Acts 8:1

After Stephen was killed, **Acts 8:1** tells us that a severe persecution of the Church broke out and believers were scattered. It's easy to assume that religious persecution does not exist today. We don't normally hear stories of people being killed for their beliefs in Jesus or being Christians. But all around the world, including places close to home, people are mistreated and even killed because of their religious beliefs.

Voice of the Martyrs is an organization that assists the persecuted Church throughout the world. Its website (**persecution.com**) tells how this is done through:

- Help: Providing medical assistance, food, clothing, and other forms of aid to Christians who have been persecuted for their involvement in spreading the gospel of Christ
- Love: Supporting Christians who are willing to invite people, even their persecutors, to Jesus Christ through faithful deeds of love in a hostile environment
- Encouragement: Giving the testimony of persecuted Christians a voice, informing other Christians about how to help

As followers of Christ, we believe that the lives and the testimony of persecuted Christians are a vital part of the fellowship of all believers and will challenge and strengthen the faith of Christians everywhere.

14 Now when the apostles at Jerusalem heard that Samaria had accepted the word of God, they sent Peter and John to them. 15The two went down and prayed for them that they might receive the Holy Spirit 16(for as yet the Spirit had not come[e] upon any of them; they had only been baptized in the name

---

a Gk him   b Gk fell asleep   c Other ancient authorities read a city   d Or the Christ   e Gk fallen

Introducing . . . Paul · Acts 8:1–3

Saul of Tarsus is standing on the sidelines when Stephen is stoned, and he is about to enter as a major character in the story of the early Church. Saul begins as a persecutor of the early Christians. He is a member of the Pharisees, a group that holds to a rigid interpretation of Jewish law (Acts 26:4-5). He probably sees the Christians as a threat to the Jewish faith. But after a profound experience of the risen Christ, Saul is converted to the Christian faith and given the name Paul. Paul is initially distrusted by other Christians who remember his persecution of them. However, another early Christian leader, Barnabas, becomes Paul's companion and advocate (Acts 9:27).

Paul's major insight is that God has made salvation available to everyone, Jews and Gentiles alike. He also knows that God's offer of salvation is a free gift, that no one could do anything to actually earn it. But many of the early Christians, who are former Jews, disagree with him. This conflict comes to a head at the Council of Jerusalem (Acts 15), where Paul stands toe-to-toe with Peter and James (Galatians 2:1-10) and argues that the Gentiles can become Christians without following Jewish laws and customs, including circumcision.

Paul took it upon himself to spread the good news of God's salvation in Jesus to the Gentiles. During three different missionary journeys, he was instrumental in founding new Christian communities throughout the Mediterranean area. He stayed in touch with those communities through letters, some of which are included as books in the New Testament. Paul's impact in spreading the faith was so great that he is sometimes called the second founder of Christianity.

---

of the Lord Jesus). [17] Then Peter and John[a] laid their hands on them, and they received the Holy Spirit. [18] Now when Simon saw that the Spirit was given through the laying on of the apostles' hands, he offered them money, [19] saying, "Give me also this power so that anyone on whom I lay my hands may receive the Holy Spirit." [20] But Peter said to him, "May your silver perish with you, because you thought you could obtain God's gift with money! [21] You have no part or share in this, for your heart is not right before God. [22] Repent therefore of this wickedness of yours, and pray to the Lord that, if possible, the intent of your heart may be forgiven you. [23] For I see that you are in the gall of bitterness and the chains of wickedness." [24] Simon answered, "Pray for me to the Lord, that nothing of what you[b] have said may happen to me."

25　Now after Peter and John[c] had testified and spoken the word of the Lord, they returned to Jerusalem, proclaiming the good news to many villages of the Samaritans.

Philip and the Ethiopian Eunuch

26　Then an angel of the Lord said to Philip, "Get up and go toward the south[d] to the road that goes down from Jerusalem to Gaza." (This is a wilderness road.) [27] So he got up and went. Now there was an Ethiopian eunuch, a court official of the Candace, queen of the Ethiopians, in charge of her entire treasury. He had come to Jerusalem to worship [28] and was returning home; seated in his chariot, he was reading the prophet Isaiah. [29] Then the Spirit said to Philip, "Go over to this chariot and join it." [30] So Philip ran up to it and heard him reading the prophet Isaiah. He asked, "Do you understand what you are reading?" [31] He replied, "How can I, unless someone guides me?" And he invited Philip to get in and sit beside him. [32] Now the passage of the scripture that he was reading was this:

"Like a sheep he was led to the slaughter,
　　and like a lamb silent before its shearer,
　　　so he does not open his mouth.
[33]　In his humiliation justice was denied him.
　　Who can describe his generation?
　　　For his life is taken away from the
　　　　earth."

[34] The eunuch asked Philip, "About whom, may I ask you, does the prophet say this, about himself or about

---

a　Gk *they*　b　The Greek word for *you* and the verb *pray* are plural　c　Gk *after they*　d　Or *go at noon*

someone else?" [35]Then Philip began to speak, and starting with this scripture, he proclaimed to him the good news about Jesus. [36]As they were going along the road, they came to some water; and the eunuch said, "Look, here is water! What is to prevent me from being baptized?"[a] [38]He commanded the chariot to stop, and both of them, Philip and the eunuch, went down into the water, and Philip[b] baptized him. [39]When they came up out of the water, the Spirit of the Lord snatched Philip away; the eunuch saw him no more, and went on his way rejoicing. [40]But Philip found himself at Azotus, and as he was passing through the region, he proclaimed the good news to all the towns until he came to Caesarea.

The Conversion of Saul

9 Meanwhile Saul, still breathing threats and murder against the disciples of the Lord, went to the high priest [2]and asked him for letters to the synagogues at Damascus, so that if he found any who belonged to the Way, men or women, he might bring them bound to Jerusalem. [3]Now as he was going along and approaching Damascus, suddenly a light from heaven flashed around him. [4]He fell to the ground and heard a voice saying to him, "Saul, Saul, why do you persecute me?" [5]He asked, "Who are you, Lord?" The reply came, "I am Jesus, whom you are persecuting. [6]But get up and enter the city, and you will be told what you are to do." [7]The men who were traveling with him stood speechless because they heard the voice but saw no one. [8]Saul got up from the ground, and though his eyes were open, he could see nothing; so they led him by the hand and brought him into Damascus. [9]For three days he was without sight, and neither ate nor drank.

10 Now there was a disciple in Damascus named Ananias. The Lord said to him in a vision, "Ananias." He answered, "Here I am, Lord." [11]The Lord said to him, "Get up and go to the street called Straight, and at the house of Judas look for a man of Tarsus named Saul. At this moment he is praying, [12]and he has seen in a vision[c] a man named Ananias come in and lay his hands on him so that he might regain his sight." [13]But Ananias answered, "Lord, I have heard from many about this man, how much evil he has done to your saints in Jerusalem; [14]and here he has authority from the chief priests to bind all who invoke your name." [15]But the Lord said to him, "Go, for he is an instrument whom I have chosen to bring my name before Gentiles and kings and before the people of Israel; [16]I myself will show him how much he must suffer for the sake of my name." [17]So Ananias went and entered the house. He laid his hands on Saul[d] and said, "Brother Saul, the Lord Jesus, who appeared to you on your way here, has sent me so that you may regain your sight and be filled with the Holy Spirit." [18]And immediately something like scales fell from his eyes, and his sight was restored. Then he got up and was baptized, [19]and after taking some food, he regained his strength.

LIVE IT!

Bearing Good News
Acts 8:26–40

Acts 8:26–40 tells the story of an Ethiopian eunuch returning from a visit to Jerusalem. A eunuch is a man who has been castrated, either by accident or by design. Eunuchs often served as guards of the harems of kings. This eunuch was reading a text from Isaiah while traveling in his carriage. The Holy Spirit moved the missionary Philip to explain to him how Isaiah's prophecies pointed to Jesus, and the eunuch believed. Geographical, ethnic, and legal barriers were washed away as Philip baptized the eunuch. Praise God for the salvation brought by Jesus to all people!

The eunuch's faith was dependent on the interaction of the three in the story: the searching eunuch; Philip, bearing the good news; and the Holy Spirit, who brought them together.

Think about the following questions:
- How are you like the Ethiopian? What are you searching for in your faith?
- How are you like Philip? How do you share the good news with others?
- How can you share in the work of the Holy Spirit? How can you motivate other people to become bearers of the good news?

a Other ancient authorities add all or most of verse 37, And Philip said, "If you believe with all your heart, you may." And he replied, "I believe that Jesus Christ is the Son of God." b Gk he c Other ancient authorities lack in a vision d Gk him

A Life-Changing Experience · Acts 9:1-19

Saul (whose name was changed to Paul) experienced some dramatic events that converted him from a persecutor of Christians to a believer in Jesus Christ. He had a powerful experience of the risen Christ during which he was blinded. His physical blindness is symbolic of his previous spiritual blindness. For three days, Paul was practically lifeless—not seeing, not eating, not drinking. This period reminds us of Jesus' three days in the tomb. In many ways, going through a conversion is like dying—dying to old ways of thinking and acting. But after three days, Paul's blindness was lifted, and he was filled with the Holy Spirit.

Paul's life had been changed—he would never be the same again. Once a persecutor of Christians, he now felt compelled to learn more about Jesus and to share the good news with others. Paul's change told the early Christians that even the most unlikely person can be called by God and radically transformed.

Conversions can also happen in our own lives in more subtle, ordinary ways. Sometimes it's a new realization about how we should live as Jesus did, or how we might be kinder to others, or how we might sacrifice some of the things we think we need to help someone else—even when that may seem difficult.

During your prayer time, reflect or journal on the following questions:

• Have you ever been suddenly aware of God's presence and calling in your life?

• What plans do you think God might have for your life?

• How will you respond?

Then close with these words:

Dear Jesus, following you is a lifelong journey of learning about being changed by you. At times it is an easy journey; other times it is a struggle. Help me to be open to your light in scripture, in others, and within myself. Amen.

Saul Preaches in Damascus

For several days he was with the disciples in Damascus, [20] and immediately he began to proclaim Jesus in the synagogues, saying, "He is the Son of God." [21] All who heard him were amazed and said, "Is not this the man who made havoc in Jerusalem among those who invoked this name? And has he not come here for the purpose of bringing them bound before the chief priests?" [22] Saul became increasingly more powerful and confounded the Jews who lived in Damascus by proving that Jesus[a] was the Messiah.[b]

Saul Escapes from the Jews

23 After some time had passed, the Jews plotted to kill him, [24] but their plot became known to Saul. They were watching the gates day and night so that they might kill him; [25] but his disciples took him by night and let him down through an opening in the wall,[c] lowering him in a basket.

Saul in Jerusalem

26 When he had come to Jerusalem, he attempted to join the disciples; and they were all afraid of him, for they did not believe that he was a disciple. [27] But Barnabas took him, brought him to the apostles, and described for them how on the road he had seen the Lord, who had spoken to him, and how in Damascus he had spoken boldly in the name of Jesus. [28] So he went in and out among them in Jerusalem, speaking boldly in the name of the Lord. [29] He spoke and argued with the Hellenists; but they were attempting to kill him. [30] When the believers[d] learned of it, they brought him down to Caesarea and sent him off to Tarsus.

31 Meanwhile the church throughout Judea, Galilee, and Samaria had peace and was built up. Living in the fear of the Lord and in the comfort of the Holy Spirit, it increased in numbers.

a Gk *that this*   b Or *the Christ*   c Gk *through the wall*   d Gk *brothers*

The Healing of Aeneas

32 Now as Peter went here and there among all the believers,[a] he came down also to the saints living in Lydda. [33]There he found a man named Aeneas, who had been bedridden for eight years, for he was paralyzed. [34]Peter said to him, "Aeneas, Jesus Christ heals you; get up and make your bed!" And immediately he got up. [35]And all the residents of Lydda and Sharon saw him and turned to the Lord.

Peter in Lydda and Joppa

36 Now in Joppa there was a disciple whose name was Tabitha, which in Greek is Dorcas.[b] She was devoted to good works and acts of charity. [37]At that time she became ill and died. When they had washed her, they laid her in a room upstairs. [38]Since Lydda was near Joppa, the disciples, who heard that Peter was there, sent two men to him with the request, "Please come to us without delay." [39]So Peter got up and went with them; and when he arrived, they took him to the room upstairs. All the widows stood beside him, weeping and showing tunics and other clothing that Dorcas had made while she was with them. [40]Peter put all of them outside, and then he knelt down and prayed. He turned to the body and said, "Tabitha, get up." Then she opened her eyes, and seeing Peter, she sat up. [41]He gave her his hand and helped her up. Then calling the saints and widows, he showed her to be alive. [42]This became known throughout Joppa, and many believed in the Lord. [43]Meanwhile he stayed in Joppa for some time with a certain Simon, a tanner.

Peter and Cornelius

10 In Caesarea there was a man named Cornelius, a centurion of the Italian Cohort, as it was called. [2]He was a devout man who feared God with all his household; he gave alms generously to the people and prayed constantly to God. [3]One afternoon at about three o'clock he had a vision in which he clearly saw an angel of God coming in and saying to him, "Cornelius." [4]He stared at him in terror and said, "What is it, Lord?" He answered, "Your prayers and your alms have ascended as a memorial before God. [5]Now send men to Joppa for a certain Simon who is called Peter; [6]he is lodging with Simon, a tanner, whose house is by the seaside." [7]When the angel who spoke to him had left, he called two of his slaves and a devout soldier from the ranks of those who served him, [8]and after telling them everything, he sent them to Joppa.

9 About noon the next day, as they were on their journey and approaching the city, Peter went up on the roof to pray. [10]He became hungry and wanted something to eat; and while it was being prepared, he fell into a trance. [11]He saw the heaven opened and something like a large sheet coming down, being lowered to the ground by its four corners. [12]In it were all kinds of four-footed creatures and reptiles and birds of the air. [13]Then he heard a voice saying, "Get up, Peter; kill and eat." [14]But Peter said, "By no means, Lord; for I have never eaten anything that is profane or unclean." [15]The voice said to him again, a second time, "What God has made clean, you must not call profane." [16]This happened three times, and the thing was suddenly taken up to heaven.

17 Now while Peter was greatly puzzled about what to make of the vision that he had seen, suddenly the men sent by Cornelius appeared. They were asking for Simon's house and were standing by the gate. [18]They called out to ask whether Simon, who was called Peter, was staying there. [19]While Peter was still thinking about the vision, the Spirit said to him, "Look, three[c] men are searching for you. [20]Now get up, go down, and go with them without hesitation; for I have sent them." [21]So Peter went down to the men and said, "I am the one you are looking for; what is the reason for your coming?" [22]They answered, "Cornelius, a centurion, an upright and God-fearing man, who is well spoken of by the whole Jewish nation, was directed by a holy angel to send for you to come to his house and to hear what you have to say." [23]So Peter[d] invited them in and gave them lodging.

The next day he got up and went with them, and some of the believers[e] from Joppa accompanied him. [24]The following day they came to Caesarea. Cornelius was expecting them and had called together his relatives and close friends. [25]On Peter's arrival Cornelius met him, and falling at his feet, worshiped him. [26]But Peter made him get up, saying, "Stand up; I am only a mortal." [27]And as he talked with him, he

---

a Gk *all of them* b The name Tabitha in Aramaic and the name Dorcas in Greek mean *a gazelle* c One ancient authority reads *two*; others lack the word d Gk *he* e Gk *brothers*

went in and found that many had assembled; [28]and he said to them, "You yourselves know that it is unlawful for a Jew to associate with or to visit a Gentile; but God has shown me that I should not call anyone profane or unclean. [29]So when I was sent for, I came without objection. Now may I ask why you sent for me?"

30 Cornelius replied, "Four days ago at this very hour, at three o'clock, I was praying in my house when suddenly a man in dazzling clothes stood before me. [31]He said, 'Cornelius, your prayer has been heard and your alms have been remembered before God. [32]Send therefore to Joppa and ask for Simon, who is called Peter; he is staying in the home of Simon, a tanner, by the sea.' [33]Therefore I sent for you immediately, and you have been kind enough to come. So now all of us are here in the presence of God to listen to all that the Lord has commanded you to say."

Gentiles Hear the Good News

34 Then Peter began to speak to them: "I truly understand that God shows no partiality, [35]but in every nation anyone who fears him and does what is right is acceptable to him. [36]You know the message he sent to the people of Israel, preaching peace by Jesus Christ—he is Lord of all. [37]That message spread throughout Judea, beginning in Galilee after the baptism that John announced: [38]how God anointed Jesus of Nazareth with the Holy Spirit and with power; how he went about doing good and healing all who were oppressed by the devil, for God was with him. [39]We are witnesses to all that he did both in Judea and in Jerusalem. They put him to death by hanging him on a tree; [40]but God raised him on the third day and allowed him to appear, [41]not to all the people but to us who were chosen by God as witnesses, and who ate and drank with him after he rose from the dead. [42]He commanded us to preach to the people and to testify that he is the one ordained by God as judge of the living and the dead. [43]All the prophets testify about him that everyone who believes in him receives forgiveness of sins through his name."

Gentiles Receive the Holy Spirit

44 While Peter was still speaking, the Holy Spirit fell upon all who heard the word. [45]The circumcised believers who had come with Peter were astounded that the gift of the Holy Spirit had been poured out even on the Gentiles, [46]for they heard them speaking in tongues and extolling God. Then Peter said, [47]"Can anyone withhold the water for baptizing these people who have received the Holy Spirit just as we have?" [48]So he ordered them to be baptized in the name of Jesus Christ. Then they invited him to stay for several days.

11 Peter's Report to the Church at Jerusalem

Now the apostles and the believers[a] who were in Judea heard that the Gentiles had also accepted the word of God. [2]So when Peter went up to Jerusalem, the circumcised believers[b] criticized him, [3]saying, "Why did you go to uncircumcised men and eat with them?" [4]Then Peter began to explain it to them, step by step, saying, [5]"I was in the city of Joppa praying, and in a trance I saw a vision. There was something like a large sheet coming down from heaven, being lowered by its four corners; and it came close to me. [6]As I looked at it closely I saw four-footed animals, beasts of prey, reptiles, and birds of the air. [7]I also heard a voice saying to me, 'Get up, Peter; kill and eat.' [8]But I replied, 'By no means, Lord; for nothing profane or unclean has ever entered my mouth.' [9]But a second time the voice answered from heaven, 'What God has made clean, you must not call profane.' [10]This happened three times; then everything was pulled up again to heaven. [11]At that very moment three men, sent to me from Caesarea, arrived at the house where we were. [12]The Spirit told me to go with them and not to make a distinction between them and us.[c] These six brothers also accompanied me, and we entered the man's house. [13]He told us how he had seen the angel standing in his house and saying, 'Send to Joppa and bring Simon, who is called Peter; [14]he will give you a message by which you and your entire household will be saved.' [15]And as I began to speak, the Holy Spirit fell upon them just as it had upon us at the beginning. [16]And I remembered the word of the Lord, how he had said, 'John baptized with water, but you will be baptized with the Holy Spirit.' [17]If then God gave them the same gift that he gave us when we believed in the Lord Jesus Christ, who was I that I could hinder God?" [18]When they heard this, they were silenced. And they praised God, saying, "Then God has given even to the Gentiles the repentance that leads to life."

a Gk brothers   b Gk lacks believers   c Or not to hesitate

The Church in Antioch

19 Now those who were scattered because of the persecution that took place over Stephen traveled as far as Phoenicia, Cyprus, and Antioch, and they spoke the word to no one except Jews. [20]But among them were some men of Cyprus and Cyrene who, on coming to Antioch, spoke to the Hellenists[a] also, proclaiming the Lord Jesus. [21]The hand of the Lord was with them, and a great number became believers and turned to the Lord. [22]News of this came to the ears of the church in Jerusalem, and they sent Barnabas to Antioch. [23]When he came and saw the grace of God, he rejoiced, and he exhorted them all to remain faithful to the Lord with steadfast devotion; [24]for he was a good man, full of the Holy Spirit and of faith. And a great many people were brought to the Lord. [25]Then Barnabas went to Tarsus to look for Saul, [26]and when he had found him, he brought him to Antioch. So it was that for an entire year they met with[b] the church and taught a great many people, and it was in Antioch that the disciples were first called "Christians."

27 At that time prophets came down from Jerusalem to Antioch. [28]One of them named Agabus stood up and predicted by the Spirit that there would be a severe famine over all the world; and this took place during the reign of Claudius. [29]The disciples determined that according to their ability, each would send relief to the believers[c] living in Judea; [30]this they did, sending it to the elders by Barnabas and Saul.

James Killed and Peter Imprisoned

12 About that time King Herod laid violent hands upon some who belonged to the church. [2]He had James, the brother of John, killed with the sword. [3]After he saw that it pleased the Jews, he proceeded to arrest Peter also. (This was during the festival of Unleavened Bread.) [4]When he had seized him, he put him in prison and handed him over to four squads of soldiers to guard him, intending to bring him out to the people after the Passover. [5]While Peter was kept in prison, the church prayed fervently to God for him.

Peter Delivered from Prison

6 The very night before Herod was going to bring him out, Peter, bound with two chains, was sleeping between two soldiers, while guards in front of the door were keeping watch over the prison. [7]Suddenly an angel of the Lord appeared and a light shone in the cell. He tapped Peter on the side and woke him, saying, "Get up quickly." And the chains fell off his wrists. [8]The angel said to him, "Fasten your belt and put on your sandals." He did so. Then he said to him, "Wrap your cloak around you and follow me." [9]Peter[d] went out and followed him; he did not realize that what was happening with the angel's help was real; he thought he was seeing a vision. [10]After they had passed the first and the second guard, they came before the iron gate leading into the city. It opened for them of its own accord, and they went outside and walked along a lane, when suddenly the angel

STUDY IT!

Introducing . . . Barnabas · Acts 11:19–26

We first meet Barnabas when he sells a field and gives the money to support the early Christian community (Acts 4:36-37). He then shows up supporting and defending Paul after Paul's conversion (Acts 9:27). Here we are told that Barnabas "was a good man, full of the Holy Spirit and of faith" (Acts 11:24). Barnabas' name literally means "son of encouragement," and his gift was encouraging others.

There are numerous accounts of times when Barnabas encouraged and stood up for people. Barnabas recognized Paul's gifts and brought Paul to minister to the new Christians in Antioch when no one else trusted Paul. Later, Barnabas reached out to Mark, disagreeing with Paul on whether to give Mark a second chance to travel with them (Acts 15:36-39). Barnabas sounds like the friend we would all like to have—someone who would believe in us through good times and bad.

- Have you had a Barnabas in your life, someone who encouraged you and believed in you even after you made mistakes?
- Who do you know who needs you to be that kind of encouraging friend?

---

a Other ancient authorities read *Greeks*   b Or *were guests of*   c Gk *brothers*   d Gk *He*

PRAY IT!

What Imprisons You? · Acts 12:6–19

Peter is imprisoned—bound with two chains, sleeping between two soldiers, with guards watching over the door of the prison. There is no chance for escape. But then God shows up, and Peter is guided by an angel past all the security to freedom (Acts 12:11). Although most of us won't ever see the inside of a prison cell, we all have experienced the chains of suffering or trials. Even when it seems that you are imprisoned with no hope for escape, look for God to show up. Pray this prayer of freedom: Holy Spirit, come! Open my mind to seek the truth. Break down the barriers that imprison me. Empower me to overcome any guilt by asking for forgiveness. Enable me to forgive others and release my past hurt and anger. Open my eyes to desires, habits, and attitudes that are destructive to me and to others. Guide me to true freedom with your word. Amen.

left him. [11]Then Peter came to himself and said, "Now I am sure that the Lord has sent his angel and rescued me from the hands of Herod and from all that the Jewish people were expecting."

12 As soon as he realized this, he went to the house of Mary, the mother of John whose other name was Mark, where many had gathered and were praying. [13]When he knocked at the outer gate, a maid named Rhoda came to answer. [14]On recognizing Peter's voice, she was so overjoyed that, instead of opening the gate, she ran in and announced that Peter was standing at the gate. [15]They said to her, "You are out of your mind!" But she insisted that it was so. They said, "It is his angel." [16]Meanwhile Peter continued knocking; and when they opened the gate, they saw him and were amazed. [17]He motioned to them with his hand to be silent, and described for them how the Lord had brought him out of the prison. And he added, "Tell this to James and to the believers."[a] Then he left and went to another place.

18 When morning came, there was no small commotion among the soldiers over what had become of Peter. [19]When Herod had searched for him and could not find him, he examined the guards and ordered them to be put to death. Then he went down from Judea to Caesarea and stayed there.

The Death of Herod

20 Now Herod[b] was angry with the people of Tyre and Sidon. So they came to him in a body; and after winning over Blastus, the king's chamberlain, they asked for a reconciliation, because their country depended on the king's country for food. [21]On an appointed day Herod put on his royal robes, took his seat on the platform, and delivered a public address to them. [22]The people kept shouting, "The voice of a god, and not of a mortal!" [23]And immediately, because he had not given the glory to God, an angel of the Lord struck him down, and he was eaten by worms and died.

24 But the word of God continued to advance and gain adherents. [25]Then after completing their mission Barnabas and Saul returned to[c] Jerusalem and brought with them John, whose other name was Mark.

Barnabas and Saul Commissioned

13 Now in the church at Antioch there were prophets and teachers: Barnabas, Simeon who was called Niger, Lucius of Cyrene, Manaen a member of the court of Herod the ruler,[d] and Saul. [2]While they were worshiping the Lord and fasting, the Holy Spirit said, "Set apart for me Barnabas and Saul for the work to which I have called them." [3]Then after fasting and praying they laid their hands on them and sent them off.

The Apostles Preach in Cyprus

4 So, being sent out by the Holy Spirit, they went down to Seleucia; and from there they sailed to Cyprus. [5]When they arrived at Salamis, they proclaimed the word of God in the synagogues of the Jews. And they had John also to assist them. [6]When they had gone through the whole island as far as Paphos, they met a certain magician, a Jewish false prophet, named Bar-Jesus. [7]He was with the proconsul, Sergius Paulus, an intelligent man, who summoned Barnabas and Saul and wanted to hear the

a Gk *brothers* **b** Gk *he* **c** Other ancient authorities read *from* **d** Gk *tetrarch* word of God. [8]But the magician Elymas (for that is the translation of his name) opposed them and tried to turn the proconsul away from the faith. [9]But Saul, also known as Paul, filled with the Holy Spirit, looked intently at him [10]and said, "You son of the devil, you enemy of all righteousness, full of all deceit and villainy, will you not stop making crooked the straight paths of the Lord? [11]And now listen—the hand of the Lord is against you, and you will be blind for a while, unable to see the sun." Immediately mist and darkness came over him, and he went about groping for someone to lead him by the hand. [12]When the proconsul saw what had happened, he believed, for he was astonished at the teaching about the Lord.

Paul and Barnabas in Antioch of Pisidia

13 Then Paul and his companions set sail from Paphos and came to Perga in Pamphylia. John, however, left them and returned to Jerusalem; [14]but they went on from Perga and came to Antioch in Pisidia. And on the sabbath day they went into the synagogue and sat down. [15]After the reading of the law and the prophets, the officials of the synagogue sent them a message, saying, "Brothers, if you have any word of exhortation for the people, give it." [16]So Paul stood up and with a gesture began to speak:

"You Israelites,[a] and others who fear God, listen. [17]The God of this people Israel chose our ancestors and made the people great during their stay in the land of Egypt, and with uplifted arm he led them out of it. [18]For about forty years he put up with[b] them in the wilderness. [19]After he had destroyed seven nations in the land of Canaan, he gave them their land as an inheritance [20]for about four hundred fifty years. After that he gave them judges until the time of the prophet Samuel. [21]Then they asked for a king; and God gave them Saul son of Kish, a man of the tribe of Benjamin, who reigned for forty years. [22]When he had removed him, he made David their king. In his testimony about him he said, 'I have found David, son of Jesse, to be a man after my heart, who will carry out all my wishes.' [23]Of this man's posterity God has brought to Israel a Savior, Jesus, as he promised; [24]before his coming John had already proclaimed a baptism of repentance to all the people of Israel. [25]And as John was finishing his work, he said, 'What do you suppose that I am? I am not he. No, but one is coming after me; I am not worthy to untie the thong of the sandals[c] on his feet.'

26 "My brothers, you descendants of Abraham's family, and others who fear God, to us[d] the message of this salvation has been sent. [27]Because the residents of Jerusalem and their leaders did not recognize him or understand the words of the prophets that are read every sabbath, they fulfilled those words by condemning him. [28]Even though they found no cause for a sentence of death, they asked Pilate to have him killed. [29]When they had carried out everything that was written about him, they took him down from the tree and laid him in a tomb. [30]But God raised him from the dead; [31]and for many days he appeared to those who came up with him from Galilee to Jerusalem, and they are now his witnesses to the people. [32]And we bring you the good news that what God promised to our ancestors [33]he has fulfilled for us, their children, by raising Jesus; as also it is written in the second psalm,

'You are my Son;
    today I have begotten you.'

[34]As to his raising him from the dead, no more to return to corruption, he has spoken in this way,

'I will give you the holy promises made to
    David.'

[35]Therefore he has also said in another psalm,

'You will not let your Holy One experience
    corruption.'

[36]For David, after he had served the purpose of God in his own generation, died,[e] was laid beside his ancestors, and experienced corruption; [37]but he whom God raised up experienced no corruption. [38]Let it be known to you therefore, my brothers, that through this man forgiveness of sins is proclaimed to you; [39]by this Jesus[f] everyone who believes is set free from all those sins[g] from which you could not be freed by the law of Moses. [40]Beware, therefore, that what the prophets said does not happen to you:

[41] 'Look, you scoffers!
    Be amazed and perish,
for in your days I am doing a work,
    a work that you will never believe, even if
      someone tells you.' "

42 As Paul and Barnabas[h] were going out, the people urged them to speak about these things again the next sabbath. [43]When the meeting of the synagogue broke up, many Jews and devout converts to Judaism followed Paul and Barnabas, who spoke to them and urged them to continue in the grace of God.

44 The next sabbath almost the whole city gathered to hear the word of the Lord.[i] [45]But when the

---

a Gk *Men, Israelites*   b Other ancient authorities read *cared for*   c Gk *untie the sandals*   d Other ancient authorities read *you*   e Gk *fell asleep*   f Gk *this*
g Gk *all*   h Gk *they*   i Other ancient authorities read *God*

Jews saw the crowds, they were filled with jealousy; and blaspheming, they contradicted what was spoken by Paul. ⁴⁶Then both Paul and Barnabas spoke out boldly, saying, "It was necessary that the word of God should be spoken first to you. Since you reject it and judge yourselves to be unworthy of eternal life, we are now turning to the Gentiles. ⁴⁷For so the Lord has commanded us, saying,

'I have set you to be a light for the Gentiles,
　　so that you may bring salvation to the ends
　　　of the earth.'"

48 When the Gentiles heard this, they were glad and praised the word of the Lord; and as many as had been destined for eternal life became believers. ⁴⁹Thus the word of the Lord spread throughout the region. ⁵⁰But the Jews incited the devout women of high standing and the leading men of the city, and stirred up persecution against Paul and Barnabas, and drove them out of their region. ⁵¹So they shook the dust off their feet in protest against them, and went to Iconium. ⁵²And the disciples were filled with joy and with the Holy Spirit.

14 **Paul and Barnabas in Iconium**

The same thing occurred in Iconium, where Paul and Barnabas*ᵃ* went into the Jewish synagogue and spoke in such a way that a great number of both Jews and Greeks became believers. ²But the unbelieving Jews stirred up the Gentiles and poisoned their minds against the brothers. ³So they remained for a long time, speaking

boldly for the Lord, who testified to the word of his grace by granting signs and wonders to be done through them. ⁴But the residents of the city were divided; some sided with the Jews, and some with the apostles. ⁵And when an attempt was made by both Gentiles and Jews, with their rulers, to mistreat them and to stone them, ⁶the apostles*ᵃ* learned of it and fled to Lystra and Derbe, cities of Lycaonia, and to the surrounding country; ⁷and there they continued proclaiming the good news.

Paul and Barnabas in Lystra and Derbe

8 In Lystra there was a man sitting who could not use his feet and had never walked, for he had been crippled from birth. ⁹He listened to Paul as he was speaking. And Paul, looking at him intently and seeing that he had faith to be healed, ¹⁰said in a loud voice, "Stand upright on your feet." And the man*ᵇ* sprang up and began to walk. ¹¹When the crowds saw what Paul had done, they shouted in the Lycaonian language, "The gods have come down to us in human form!" ¹²Barnabas they called Zeus, and Paul they called Hermes, because he was the chief speaker. ¹³The priest of Zeus, whose temple was just outside the city,*ᶜ* brought oxen and garlands to the gates; he and the crowds wanted to offer sacrifice. ¹⁴When the apostles Barnabas and Paul heard of it, they tore their clothes and rushed out into the crowd, shouting, ¹⁵"Friends,*ᵈ* why are you doing this? We are mortals just like you, and we bring you good news, that you should turn from these worthless things to

The Journeys of Paul · Acts 13–14, 16–21

Luke tells us in Acts that Paul made three missionary journeys over a ten-year period to spread the gospel message. The details of his first journey are covered in **Acts 13–14**. The second journey is reported in **Acts 16–18**. The third journey is described in **Acts 19–21**.

Paul himself may have seen these not as three separate journeys, but as one continuous mission. On these journeys, Paul made converts and started Christian communities. On the second and third journeys, he also visited established communities to give them guidance and support. (See Map 3: "Paul's Missionary Journeys.")

Paul's third journey landed him back in Jerusalem, where some Jews had him arrested. On the basis of his Roman citizenship, Paul appealed to the emperor. So he was transported to Rome (this trip is often referred to as his fourth journey). He probably died there as a martyr around A.D. 65. Some traditions say that Paul wasn't martyred there, but went on to evangelize in Spain.

a Gk *they*　*b* Gk *he*　*c* Or *The priest of Zeus-Outside-the-City*　*d* Gk *Men*

Courage on the Run • Acts 14:1–7

One thing is clear about taking a stand and sharing your faith—it takes great courage. The story of Paul and Barnabas in Iconium is another example of how spreading the good news of Jesus was dangerous business. They taught in the synagogue, and many came to believe—but many others felt threatened. Paul and Barnabas first responded by taking a courageous stand to stay and speak boldly about the grace and power of the Lord (Acts 14:3). But they also knew when to run. When they learned of the plot to stone them, they fled (Acts 14:5–6). But they didn't give up! They continued telling the good news of Jesus everywhere they went.

• In what ways is God inviting you to speak and act boldly to share your faith in your school, neighborhood, and community?

• What keeps you from sharing?

the living God, who made the heaven and the earth and the sea and all that is in them. ¹⁶In past generations he allowed all the nations to follow their own ways; ¹⁷yet he has not left himself without a witness in doing good—giving you rains from heaven and fruitful seasons, and filling you with food and your hearts with joy." ¹⁸Even with these words, they scarcely restrained the crowds from offering sacrifice to them.

19 But Jews came there from Antioch and Iconium and won over the crowds. Then they stoned Paul and dragged him out of the city, supposing that he was dead. ²⁰But when the disciples surrounded him, he got up and went into the city. The next day he went on with Barnabas to Derbe.

The Return to Antioch in Syria

21 After they had proclaimed the good news to that city and had made many disciples, they returned to Lystra, then on to Iconium and Antioch. ²²There they strengthened the souls of the disciples and encouraged them to continue in the faith, saying, "It is through many persecutions that we must enter the kingdom of God." ²³And after they had appointed elders for them in each church, with prayer and fasting they entrusted them to the Lord in whom they had come to believe.

24 Then they passed through Pisidia and came to Pamphylia. ²⁵When they had spoken the word in Perga, they went down to Attalia. ²⁶From there they sailed back to Antioch, where they had been commended to the grace of God for the work*ᵃ* that they had completed. ²⁷When they arrived, they called the church together and related all that God had done with them, and how he had opened a door of faith for the Gentiles. ²⁸And they stayed there with the disciples for some time.

The Council at Jerusalem

15 Then certain individuals came down from Judea and were teaching the brothers, "Unless you are circumcised according to the custom of Moses, you cannot be saved." ²And after Paul and Barnabas had no small dissension and debate with them, Paul and Barnabas and some of the others were appointed to go up to Jerusalem to discuss this question with the apostles and the elders. ³So they were sent on their way by the church, and as they passed through both Phoenicia and Samaria, they reported the conversion of the Gentiles, and brought great joy to all the believers.*ᵇ* ⁴When they came to Jerusalem, they were welcomed by the church and the apostles and the elders, and they reported all that God had done with them. ⁵But some believers who belonged to the sect of the Pharisees stood up and said, "It is necessary for them to be circumcised and ordered to keep the law of Moses."

6 The apostles and the elders met together to consider this matter. ⁷After there had been much debate, Peter stood up and said to them, "My brothers,*ᶜ* you know that in the early days God made a choice among you, that I should be the one through whom the Gentiles would hear the message of the good news and become believers. ⁸And God, who knows the human heart, testified to them by giving them the Holy Spirit, just as he did to us; ⁹and in

a Or *committed in the grace of God to the work*   **b** Gk *brothers*   **c** Gk *Men, brothers*

cleansing their hearts by faith he has made no distinction between them and us. ¹⁰Now therefore why are you putting God to the test by placing on the neck of the disciples a yoke that neither our ancestors nor we have been able to bear? ¹¹On the contrary, we believe that we will be saved through the grace of the Lord Jesus, just as they will."

12 The whole assembly kept silence, and listened to Barnabas and Paul as they told of all the signs and wonders that God had done through them among the Gentiles. ¹³After they finished speaking, James replied, "My brothers,*a* listen to me. ¹⁴Simeon has related how God first looked favorably on the Gentiles, to take from among them a people for his name. ¹⁵This agrees with the words of the prophets, as it is written,

¹⁶ 'After this I will return,
and I will rebuild the dwelling of David, which
has fallen;
from its ruins I will rebuild it,
and I will set it up,
¹⁷ so that all other peoples may seek the Lord—
even all the Gentiles over whom my name
has been called.
Thus says the Lord, who has been
making these things ¹⁸known from
long ago.'*b*

¹⁹Therefore I have reached the decision that we should not trouble those Gentiles who are turning to God, ²⁰but we should write to them to abstain only from things polluted by idols and from fornication and from whatever has been strangled*c* and from blood. ²¹For in every city, for generations past, Moses has had those who proclaim him, for he has been read aloud every sabbath in the synagogues."

The Council's Letter to Gentile Believers

22 Then the apostles and the elders, with the consent of the whole church, decided to choose men from among their members*d* and to send them to Antioch with Paul and Barnabas. They sent Judas called Barsabbas, and Silas, leaders among the brothers, ²³with the following letter: "The brothers, both the apostles and the elders, to the believers*e* of Gentile origin in Antioch and Syria and Cilicia, greetings. ²⁴Since we have heard that certain persons who have gone out from us, though with no instructions from us, have said things to disturb you and have unsettled your minds,*f* ²⁵we have decided unanimously to choose representatives*g* and send them to you, along

Compromise
Acts 15:1–35

Disagreements among believers are nothing new. We see in **Acts 15:1–35** that the early Christians had to learn to disagree and reach compromise on many issues not spelled out in Jesus' teaching. The earliest Christians were Jews. They believed in Jesus and continued to follow the rules of the Jewish faith as a sign that they were a covenant people. But as Gentiles became Christians, questions came up over whether they needed to follow all the Jewish rules. A major source of disagreement was circumcision as a sign of the covenant. Jews said it had to be done. Gentile converts did not see the need for it.

Paul and Barnabas insisted that Christians were free from such Jewish laws; they went to Jerusalem to meet with the other apostles to defend their position. With Peter's support, the community decided that Paul and Barnabas were right. And so the apostles at the council agreed that the center of the Christian faith was believing in the risen Christ, not conforming to specific Jewish rituals. This meeting of the apostles is called the Council of Jerusalem and was a pivotal point in the history of the Church.

- How do you, your friends, family, or youth group handle conflict?
- How can this story in Acts be a reminder of the importance of compromise and unity in love despite differences?

with our beloved Barnabas and Paul, ²⁶who have risked their lives for the sake of our Lord Jesus Christ. ²⁷We have therefore sent Judas and Silas, who themselves will tell you the same things by word of mouth. ²⁸For it has seemed good to the Holy Spirit and to us to impose on you no further burden than these essentials: ²⁹that you abstain from what has been sacrificed to idols and from blood and from what is

---

a Gk *Men, brothers* *b* Other ancient authorities read *things.* *¹⁸Known to God from of old are all his works.'* *c* Other ancient authorities lack *and from whatever has been strangled* *d* Gk *from among them* *e* Gk *brothers* *f* Other ancient authorities add *saying, 'You must be circumcised and keep the law,'* *g* Gk *men*

strangled[a] and from fornication. If you keep yourselves from these, you will do well. Farewell."

30 So they were sent off and went down to Antioch. When they gathered the congregation together, they delivered the letter. [31]When its members[b] read it, they rejoiced at the exhortation. [32]Judas and Silas, who were themselves prophets, said much to encourage and strengthen the believers.[c] [33]After they had been there for some time, they were sent off in peace by the believers[c] to those who had sent them.[d] [35]But Paul and Barnabas remained in Antioch, and there, with many others, they taught and proclaimed the word of the Lord.

Paul and Barnabas Separate

36 After some days Paul said to Barnabas, "Come, let us return and visit the believers[c] in every city where we proclaimed the word of the Lord and see how they are doing." [37]Barnabas wanted to take with them John called Mark. [38]But Paul decided not to take with them one who had deserted them in Pamphylia and had not accompanied them in the work. [39]The disagreement became so sharp that they parted company; Barnabas took Mark with him and sailed away to Cyprus. [40]But Paul chose Silas and set out, the believers[c] commending him to the grace of the Lord. [41]He went through Syria and Cilicia, strengthening the churches.

16 Timothy Joins Paul and Silas

Paul[e] went on also to Derbe and to Lystra, where there was a disciple named Timothy, the son of a Jewish woman who was a believer; but his father was a Greek. [2]He was well spoken of by the believers[c] in Lystra and Iconium. [3]Paul wanted Timothy to accompany him; and he took him and had him circumcised because of the Jews who were in those places, for they all knew that his father was a Greek. [4]As they went from town to town, they delivered to them for observance the decisions that had been reached by the apostles and elders who were in Jerusalem. [5]So the churches were strengthened in the faith and increased in numbers daily.

Paul's Vision of the Man of Macedonia

6 They went through the region of Phrygia and Galatia, having been forbidden by the Holy Spirit to speak the word in Asia. [7]When they had come opposite Mysia, they attempted to go into Bithynia, but the Spirit of Jesus did not allow them; [8]so, passing

by Mysia, they went down to Troas. [9]During the night Paul had a vision: there stood a man of Macedonia pleading with him and saying, "Come over to Macedonia and help us." [10]When he had seen the vision, we immediately tried to cross over to Macedonia, being convinced that God had called us to proclaim the good news to them.

The Conversion of Lydia

11 We set sail from Troas and took a straight course to Samothrace, the following day to Neapolis, [12]and from there to Philippi, which is a leading city of the district[f] of Macedonia and a Roman colony. We remained in this city for some days. [13]On the sabbath day we went outside the gate by the river, where we supposed there was a place of prayer; and we sat down and spoke to the women who had gathered there. [14]A certain woman named Lydia, a worshiper of God, was listening to us; she was from the city of Thyatira and a dealer in purple cloth. The Lord opened her heart to listen eagerly to what was said by Paul. [15]When she and her household were baptized, she urged us, saying, "If you have judged me to be faithful to the Lord, come and stay at my home." And she prevailed upon us.

Paul and Silas in Prison

16 One day, as we were going to the place of prayer, we met a slave-girl who had a spirit of divination and brought her owners a great deal of money by fortune-telling. [17]While she followed Paul and us, she would cry out, "These men are slaves of the Most High God, who proclaim to you[g] a way of salvation." [18]She kept doing this for many days. But Paul, very much annoyed, turned and said to the spirit, "I order you in the name of Jesus Christ to come out of her." And it came out that very hour.

19 But when her owners saw that their hope of making money was gone, they seized Paul and Silas and dragged them into the marketplace before the authorities. [20]When they had brought them before the magistrates, they said, "These men are disturbing our city; they are Jews [21]and are advocating customs that are not lawful for us as Romans to adopt or observe." [22]The crowd joined in attacking them, and the magistrates had them stripped of their clothing and ordered them to be beaten with rods. [23]After they had given them a severe flogging, they threw them into prison and ordered the jailer to keep them securely. [24]Following these instructions, he put them

---

a Other ancient authorities lack *and from what is strangled* b Gk *When they* c Gk *brothers* d Other ancient authorities add verse 34, *But it seemed good to Silas to remain there* e Gk *He* f Other authorities read *a city of the first district* g Other ancient authorities read *to us*

STUDY IT!

Introducing . . . Lydia and Priscilla · Acts 16:14–15; 18

Acts names two women who were instrumental in Paul's missionary journeys: Lydia and Priscilla. Lydia was Paul's first convert in Philippi, which is in modern-day Greece. She was a textile merchant and was wealthy enough to support a household and open her home to Paul and Silas to stay for an extended time.

Priscilla and her husband, Aquila, hosted Paul in Corinth. Later, they accompanied him from Corinth to Antioch. While there they turned the teaching they had received into instruction for a man named Apollos (Acts 18:26). Luke's inclusion of these women indicates that women were active in the early Church and a crucial part of Christianity from its beginnings. They not only supported the missionary work of Paul, but also played an important role in leading and teaching.

in the innermost cell and fastened their feet in the stocks.

25 About midnight Paul and Silas were praying and singing hymns to God, and the prisoners were listening to them. ²⁶Suddenly there was an earthquake, so violent that the foundations of the prison were shaken; and immediately all the doors were opened and everyone's chains were unfastened. ²⁷When the jailer woke up and saw the prison doors wide open, he drew his sword and was about to kill himself, since he supposed that the prisoners had escaped. ²⁸But Paul shouted in a loud voice, "Do not harm yourself, for we are all here." ²⁹The jailer[a] called for lights, and rushing in, he fell down trembling before Paul and Silas. ³⁰Then he brought them outside and said, "Sirs, what must I do to be saved?" ³¹They answered, "Believe on the Lord Jesus, and you will be saved, you and your household." ³²They spoke the word of the Lord[b] to him and to all who were in his house. ³³At the same hour of the night he took them and washed their wounds; then he and his entire family were baptized without delay. ³⁴He brought them up into the house and set food before them; and he and his entire household rejoiced that he had become a believer in God.

35 When morning came, the magistrates sent the police, saying, "Let those men go." ³⁶And the jailer reported the message to Paul, saying, "The magistrates sent word to let you go; therefore come out now and go in peace." ³⁷But Paul replied, "They have beaten us in public, uncondemned, men who are Roman citizens, and have thrown us into prison; and now are they going to discharge us in secret? Certainly not! Let them come and take us out themselves." ³⁸The police reported these words to the

LIVE IT!

Praise Under Pressure
Acts 16:16–40

Paul and Silas are falsely accused, stripped of their clothes, beaten with rods, and thrown in jail. Their response? In the middle of the night they prayed and sang hymns to God (Acts 16:25). It's not just surprising—it's amazing. Faced with incredible pressure and pain, Paul and Silas don't change their tune one bit. Their faith in God is secure and no beating or chains can change that.

- How do you think you would respond if you found yourself in Paul and Silas' position?

- What does it take on a daily basis to change your attitude from complaining to praise?

- How can you work to remember to keep an eternal perspective even in the midst of pain and suffering?

a Gk He **b** Other ancient authorities read *word of God*

magistrates, and they were afraid when they heard that they were Roman citizens; [39]so they came and apologized to them. And they took them out and asked them to leave the city. [40]After leaving the prison they went to Lydia's home; and when they had seen and encouraged the brothers and sisters[a] there, they departed.

The Uproar in Thessalonica

17 After Paul and Silas[b] had passed through Amphipolis and Apollonia, they came to Thessalonica, where there was a synagogue of the Jews. [2]And Paul went in, as was his custom, and on three sabbath days argued with them from the scriptures, [3]explaining and proving that it was necessary for the Messiah[c] to suffer and to rise from the dead, and saying, "This is the Messiah,[c] Jesus whom I am proclaiming to you." [4]Some of them were persuaded and joined Paul and Silas, as did a great many of the devout Greeks and not a few of the leading women. [5]But the Jews became jealous, and with the help of some ruffians in the marketplaces they formed a mob and set the city in an uproar. While they were searching for Paul and Silas to bring them out to the assembly, they attacked Jason's house. [6]When they could not find them, they dragged Jason and some believers[a] before the city authorities,[d] shouting, "These people who have been turning the world upside down have come here also, [7]and Jason has entertained them as guests. They are all acting contrary to the decrees of the emperor, saying that there is another king named Jesus." [8]The people and the city officials were disturbed when they heard this, [9]and after they had taken bail from Jason and the others, they let them go.

Paul and Silas in Beroea

10 That very night the believers[a] sent Paul and Silas off to Beroea; and when they arrived, they went to the Jewish synagogue. [11]These Jews were more receptive than those in Thessalonica, for they welcomed the message very eagerly and examined the scriptures every day to see whether these things were so. [12]Many of them therefore believed, including not a few Greek women and men of high standing. [13]But when the Jews of Thessalonica learned that the word of God had been proclaimed by Paul in Beroea as well, they came there too, to stir up and incite the crowds. [14]Then the believers[a] immediately sent Paul away to the coast, but Silas and Timothy remained behind. [15]Those who conducted Paul brought him as far as Athens; and after receiving instructions to have Silas and Timothy join him as soon as possible, they left him.

Paul in Athens

16 While Paul was waiting for them in Athens, he was deeply distressed to see that the city was full of idols. [17]So he argued in the synagogue with the Jews and the devout persons, and also in the marketplace[e] every day with those who happened to be there. [18]Also some Epicurean and Stoic philosophers debated with him. Some said, "What does this babbler want to say?" Others said, "He seems to be a pro-

PRAY IT!

Speak Up! · Acts 17

Paul was wonderfully gifted for his work as an evangelist. He had the ability to communicate with both common people and intellectuals. He was familiar with three cultures—Jewish, Greek, and Roman—and proclaimed the gospel message in ways all three could understand. He was skilled at building Christian communities. And he was absolutely fearless in preaching about Jesus Christ. These are qualities we can all work toward and ask God to build in our own lives.

God, I would love to see your Holy Spirit work through me, as you did through Paul, to spread the good news of Jesus. Help me to reach out to classmates, no matter what clique or group they belong to. Help me to bring out the best in our culture and to challenge what is wrong or misleading. Give me wisdom to know the right time to listen and the right time to speak up about my faith. Build in me the courage to speak fearlessly. Let me be your instrument in building communities of faith, hope, and love. Amen.

a Gk brothers   b Gk they   c Or the Christ   d Gk politarchs   e Or civic center; Gk agora

claimer of foreign divinities." (This was because he was telling the good news about Jesus and the resurrection.) [19]So they took him and brought him to the Areopagus and asked him, "May we know what this new teaching is that you are presenting? [20]It sounds rather strange to us, so we would like to know what it means." [21]Now all the Athenians and the foreigners living there would spend their time in nothing but telling or hearing something new.

22 Then Paul stood in front of the Areopagus and said, "Athenians, I see how extremely religious you are in every way. [23]For as I went through the city and looked carefully at the objects of your worship, I found among them an altar with the inscription, 'To an unknown god.' What therefore you worship as unknown, this I proclaim to you. [24]The God who made the world and everything in it, he who is Lord of heaven and earth, does not live in shrines made by human hands, [25]nor is he served by human hands, as though he needed anything, since he himself gives to all mortals life and breath and all things. [26]From one ancestor[a] he made all nations to inhabit the whole earth, and he allotted the times of their existence and the boundaries of the places where they would live, [27]so that they would search for God[b] and perhaps grope for him and find him—though indeed he is not far from each one of us. [28]For 'In him we live and move and have our being'; as even some of your own poets have said,

'For we too are his offspring.'

[29]Since we are God's offspring, we ought not to think that the deity is like gold, or silver, or stone, an image formed by the art and imagination of mortals. [30]While God has overlooked the times of human ignorance, now he commands all people everywhere to repent, [31]because he has fixed a day on which he will have the world judged in righteousness by a man whom he has appointed, and of this he has given assurance to all by raising him from the dead."

32 When they heard of the resurrection of the dead, some scoffed; but others said, "We will hear you again about this." [33]At that point Paul left them. [34]But some of them joined him and became believers, including Dionysius the Areopagite and a woman named Damaris, and others with them.

Paul in Corinth

18 After this Paul[c] left Athens and went to Corinth. [2]There he found a Jew named Aquila, a native of Pontus, who had recently come from Italy with his wife Priscilla, because Claudius had ordered all Jews to leave Rome. Paul[d] went to see them, [3]and, because he was of the same trade, he stayed with them, and they worked together—by trade they were tentmakers. [4]Every sabbath he would argue in the synagogue and would try to convince Jews and Greeks.

5 When Silas and Timothy arrived from Macedonia, Paul was occupied with proclaiming the word,[e] testifying to the Jews that the Messiah[f] was Jesus. [6]When they opposed and reviled him, in protest he shook the dust from his clothes[g] and said to them, "Your blood be on your own heads! I am innocent. From now on I will go to the Gentiles." [7]Then he left the synagogue[h] and went to the house of a man named Titius[i] Justus, a worshiper of God; his house was next door to the synagogue. [8]Crispus, the official of the synagogue, became a believer in the Lord, together with all his household; and many of the Corinthians who heard Paul became believers and were baptized. [9]One night the Lord said to Paul in a vision, "Do not be afraid, but speak and do not be silent; [10]for I am with you, and no one will lay a hand on you to harm you, for there are many in this city who are my people." [11]He stayed there a year and six months, teaching the word of God among them.

12 But when Gallio was proconsul of Achaia, the Jews made a united attack on Paul and brought him before the tribunal. [13]They said, "This man is persuading people to worship God in ways that are contrary to the law." [14]Just as Paul was about to speak, Gallio said to the Jews, "If it were a matter of crime or serious villainy, I would be justified in accepting the complaint of you Jews; [15]but since it is a matter of questions about words and names and your own law, see to it yourselves; I do not wish to be a judge of these matters." [16]And he dismissed them from the tribunal. [17]Then all of them[j] seized Sosthenes, the official of the synagogue, and beat him in front of the tribunal. But Gallio paid no attention to any of these things.

Paul's Return to Antioch

18 After staying there for a considerable time, Paul said farewell to the believers[k] and sailed for Syria, accompanied by Priscilla and Aquila. At Cenchreae he had his hair cut, for he was under a vow. [19]When they reached Ephesus, he left them there, but first he himself went into the synagogue and had a discussion

with the Jews. [20]When they asked him to stay longer, he declined; [21]but on taking leave of them, he said, "I[a] will return to you, if God wills." Then he set sail from Ephesus.

22 When he had landed at Caesarea, he went up to Jerusalem[b] and greeted the church, and then went down to Antioch. [23]After spending some time there he departed and went from place to place through the region of Galatia[c] and Phrygia, strengthening all the disciples.

Ministry of Apollos

24 Now there came to Ephesus a Jew named Apollos, a native of Alexandria. He was an eloquent man, well-versed in the scriptures. [25]He had been instructed in the Way of the Lord; and he spoke with burning enthusiasm and taught accurately the things concerning Jesus, though he knew only the baptism of John. [26]He began to speak boldly in the synagogue; but when Priscilla and Aquila heard him, they took him aside and explained the Way of God to him more accurately. [27]And when he wished to cross over to Achaia, the believers[c] encouraged him and wrote to the disciples to welcome him. On his arrival he greatly helped those who through grace had become believers, [28]for he powerfully refuted the Jews in public, showing by the scriptures that the Messiah[e] is Jesus.

Paul in Ephesus

19 While Apollos was in Corinth, Paul passed through the interior regions and came to Ephesus, where he found some disciples. [2]He said to them, "Did you receive the Holy Spirit when you became believers?" They replied, "No, we have not even heard that there is a Holy Spirit." [3]Then he said, "Into what then were you baptized?" They answered, "Into John's baptism." [4]Paul said, "John baptized with the baptism of repentance, telling the people to believe in the one who was to come after him, that is, in Jesus." [5]On hearing this, they were baptized in the name of the Lord Jesus. [6]When Paul had laid his hands on them, the Holy Spirit came upon them, and they spoke in tongues and prophesied— [7]altogether there were about twelve of them.

8 He entered the synagogue and for three months spoke out boldly, and argued persuasively about the kingdom of God. [9]When some stubbornly refused to believe and spoke evil of the Way before the congregation, he left them, taking the disciples with

him, and argued daily in the lecture hall of Tyrannus.[f] [10]This continued for two years, so that all the residents of Asia, both Jews and Greeks, heard the word of the Lord.

The Sons of Sceva

11 God did extraordinary miracles through Paul, [12]so that when the handkerchiefs or aprons that had touched his skin were brought to the sick, their diseases left them, and the evil spirits came out of them. [13]Then some itinerant Jewish exorcists tried to use the name of the Lord Jesus over those who had evil spirits, saying, "I adjure you by the Jesus whom Paul proclaims." [14]Seven sons of a Jewish high priest named Sceva were doing this. [15]But the evil spirit said to them in reply, "Jesus I know, and Paul I know; but who are you?" [16]Then the man with the evil spirit leaped on them, mastered them all, and so overpowered them that they fled out of the house naked and wounded. [17]When this became known to all residents of Ephesus, both Jews and Greeks, everyone was awestruck; and the name of the Lord Jesus was praised. [18]Also many of those who became believers confessed and disclosed their practices. [19]A number of those who practiced magic collected their books and burned them publicly; when the value of these books[g] was calculated, it was found to come to fifty thousand silver coins. [20]So the word of the Lord grew mightily and prevailed.

The Riot in Ephesus

21 Now after these things had been accomplished, Paul resolved in the Spirit to go through Macedonia and Achaia, and then to go on to Jerusalem. He said, "After I have gone there, I must also see Rome." [22]So he sent two of his helpers, Timothy and Erastus, to Macedonia, while he himself stayed for some time longer in Asia.

23 About that time no little disturbance broke out concerning the Way. [24]A man named Demetrius, a silversmith who made silver shrines of Artemis, brought no little business to the artisans. [25]These he gathered together, with the workers of the same trade, and said, "Men, you know that we get our wealth from this business. [26]You also see and hear that not only in Ephesus but in almost the whole of Asia this Paul has persuaded and drawn away a considerable number of people by saying that gods made with hands are not gods. [27]And there is danger not only that this trade of ours may come into disrepute

---

a Other ancient authorities read *I must at all costs keep the approaching festival in Jerusalem, but I*   **b** Gk *went up*   **c** Gk *the Galatian region*   **d** Gk *brothers*
e Or *the Christ*   **f** Other ancient authorities read *of a certain Tyrannus, from eleven o'clock in the morning to four in the afternoon*   **g** Gk *them*

but also that the temple of the great goddess Artemis will be scorned, and she will be deprived of her majesty that brought all Asia and the world to worship her."

28 When they heard this, they were enraged and shouted, "Great is Artemis of the Ephesians!" [29] The city was filled with the confusion; and people[a] rushed together to the theater, dragging with them Gaius and Aristarchus, Macedonians who were Paul's travel companions. [30] Paul wished to go into the crowd, but the disciples would not let him; [31] even some officials of the province of Asia,[b] who were friendly to him, sent him a message urging him not to venture into the theater. [32] Meanwhile, some were shouting one thing, some another; for the assembly was in confusion, and most of them did not know why they had come together. [33] Some of the crowd gave instructions to Alexander, whom the Jews had pushed forward. And Alexander motioned for silence and tried to make a defense before the people. [34] But when they recognized that he was a Jew, for about two hours all of them shouted in unison, "Great is Artemis of the Ephesians!" [35] But when the town clerk had quieted the crowd, he said, "Citizens of Ephesus, who is there that does not know that the city of the Ephesians is the temple keeper of the great Artemis and of the statue that fell from heaven?[c] [36] Since these things cannot be denied, you ought to be quiet and do nothing rash. [37] You have brought these men here who are neither temple robbers nor blasphemers of our[d] goddess. [38] If therefore Demetrius and the artisans with him have a complaint against anyone, the courts are open, and there are proconsuls; let them bring charges there against one another. [39] If there is anything further[e] you want to know, it must be settled in the regular assembly. [40] For we are in danger of being charged with rioting today, since there is no cause that we can give to justify this commotion." [41] When he had said this, he dismissed the assembly.

20 Paul Goes to Macedonia and Greece

After the uproar had ceased, Paul sent for the disciples; and after encouraging them and saying farewell, he left for Macedonia. [2] When he had gone through those regions and had given the believers[f] much encouragement, he came to Greece, [3] where he stayed for three months. He was about to set sail for Syria when a plot was made against him by the Jews, and so he decided to return

through Macedonia. [4] He was accompanied by Sopater son of Pyrrhus from Beroea, by Aristarchus and Secundus from Thessalonica, by Gaius from Derbe, and by Timothy, as well as by Tychicus and Trophimus from Asia. [5] They went ahead and were waiting for us in Troas; [6] but we sailed from Philippi after the days of Unleavened Bread, and in five days we joined them in Troas, where we stayed for seven days.

Paul's Farewell Visit to Troas

7 On the first day of the week, when we met to break bread, Paul was holding a discussion with them; since he intended to leave the next day, he continued speaking until midnight. [8] There were many lamps in the room upstairs where we were meeting. [9] A young man named Eutychus, who was sitting in the window, began to sink off into a deep sleep while Paul talked still longer. Overcome by sleep, he fell to the ground three floors below and was picked up dead. [10] But Paul went down, and bending over him took him in his arms, and said, "Do not be alarmed, for his life is in him." [11] Then Paul went upstairs, and after he had broken bread and eaten, he continued to converse with them until dawn; then he left. [12] Meanwhile they had taken the boy away alive and were not a little comforted.

The Voyage from Troas to Miletus

13 We went ahead to the ship and set sail for Assos, intending to take Paul on board there; for he had made this arrangement, intending to go by land himself. [14] When he met us in Assos, we took him on board and went to Mitylene. [15] We sailed from there, and on the following day we arrived opposite Chios. The next day we touched at Samos, and[g] the day after that we came to Miletus. [16] For Paul had decided to sail past Ephesus, so that he might not have to spend time in Asia; he was eager to be in Jerusalem, if possible, on the day of Pentecost.

Paul Speaks to the Ephesian Elders

17 From Miletus he sent a message to Ephesus, asking the elders of the church to meet him. [18] When they came to him, he said to them:

"You yourselves know how I lived among you the entire time from the first day that I set foot in Asia, [19] serving the Lord with all humility and with tears, enduring the trials that came to me through the plots of the Jews. [20] I did not shrink from doing anything helpful, proclaiming the message to you and teaching

---

a Gk *they* b Gk *some of the Asiarchs* c Meaning of Gk uncertain d Other ancient authorities read *your* e Other ancient authorities read *about other matters* f Gk *given them* g Other ancient authorities add *after remaining at Trogyllium*

you publicly and from house to house, [21] as I testified to both Jews and Greeks about repentance toward God and faith toward our Lord Jesus. [22] And now, as a captive to the Spirit,[a] I am on my way to Jerusalem, not knowing what will happen to me there, [23] except that the Holy Spirit testifies to me in every city that imprisonment and persecutions are waiting for me. [24] But I do not count my life of any value to myself, if only I may finish my course and the ministry that I received from the Lord Jesus, to testify to the good news of God's grace.

[25] "And now I know that none of you, among whom I have gone about proclaiming the kingdom, will ever see my face again. [26] Therefore I declare to you this day that I am not responsible for the blood of any of you, [27] for I did not shrink from declaring to you the whole purpose of God. [28] Keep watch over yourselves and over all the flock, of which the Holy Spirit has made you overseers, to shepherd the church of God[b] that he obtained with the blood of his own Son.[c] [29] I know that after I have gone, savage wolves will come in among you, not sparing the flock. [30] Some even from your own group will come distorting the truth in order to entice the disciples to follow them. [31] Therefore be alert, remembering that for three years I did not cease night or day to warn everyone with tears. [32] And now I commend you to God and to the message of his grace, a message that is able to build you up and to give you the inheritance among all who are sanctified. [33] I coveted no one's silver or gold or clothing. [34] You know for yourselves that I worked with my own hands to support myself and my companions. [35] In all this I have given you an example that by such work we must support the weak, remembering the words of the Lord Jesus, for he himself said, 'It is more blessed to give than to receive.'"

[36] When he had finished speaking, he knelt down with them all and prayed. [37] There was much weeping among them all; they embraced Paul and kissed him, [38] grieving especially because of what he had said, that they would not see him again. Then they brought him to the ship.

Paul's Journey to Jerusalem

21 When we had parted from them and set sail, we came by a straight course to Cos,

> "But I do not count my life of any value to myself, if only I may finish my course and the ministry that I received from the Lord Jesus, to testify to the good news of God's grace."
> —Acts 20:24

PRAY IT!

Good-bye to a Friend · Acts 20:36–38

When Paul takes his leave from the people he taught in Ephesus, it is an emotional good-bye. He has been an important person in their lives, and they have come to depend on him. Their grief overwhelms them, and they all experience great pain over his departure.

When we have to say good-bye to someone we care for deeply, we go through a grieving process. We often feel sad and mad at the same time. Even after our friend has been gone for a long time, our heart has an empty space that our friend used to fill. If you've recently had to say good-bye to a friend, consider praying this prayer:

Lord, it's so difficult to say good-bye to my friend. We have shared so much together. I thank you for blessing me with this friendship. As we go our separate ways, be our constant guardian and companion. Guide each of us. And until our paths cross again, surround us with your loving and protective embrace. Amen.

---

a Or *And now, bound in the spirit*　b Other ancient authorities read *of the Lord*　c Or *with his own blood*; Gk *with the blood of his Own*

and the next day to Rhodes, and from there to Patara.[a] [2]When we found a ship bound for Phoenicia, we went on board and set sail. [3]We came in sight of Cyprus; and leaving it on our left, we sailed to Syria and landed at Tyre, because the ship was to unload its cargo there. [4]We looked up the disciples and stayed there for seven days. Through the Spirit they told Paul not to go on to Jerusalem. [5]When our days there were ended, we left and proceeded on our journey; and all of them, with wives and children, escorted us outside the city. There we knelt down on the beach and prayed [6]and said farewell to one another. Then we went on board the ship, and they returned home.

7 When we had finished[b] the voyage from Tyre, we arrived at Ptolemais; and we greeted the believers[c] and stayed with them for one day. [8]The next day we left and came to Caesarea; and we went into the house of Philip the evangelist, one of the seven, and stayed with him. [9]He had four unmarried daughters[d] who had the gift of prophecy. [10]While we were staying there for several days, a prophet named Agabus came down from Judea. [11]He came to us and took Paul's belt, bound his own feet and hands with it, and said, "Thus says the Holy Spirit, 'This is the way the Jews in Jerusalem will bind the man who owns this belt and will hand him over to the Gentiles.'" [12]When we heard this, we and the people there urged him not to go up to Jerusalem. [13]Then Paul answered, "What are you doing, weeping and breaking my heart? For I am ready not only to be bound but even to die in Jerusalem for the name of the Lord Jesus." [14]Since he would not be persuaded, we remained silent except to say, "The Lord's will be done."

15 After these days we got ready and started to go up to Jerusalem. [16]Some of the disciples from Caesarea also came along and brought us to the house of Mnason of Cyprus, an early disciple, with whom we were to stay.

Paul Visits James at Jerusalem

17 When we arrived in Jerusalem, the brothers welcomed us warmly. [18]The next day Paul went with us to visit James; and all the elders were present. [19]After greeting them, he related one by one the things that God had done among the Gentiles through his ministry. [20]When they heard it, they praised God. Then they said to him, "You see, brother, how many thousands of believers there are among the Jews, and they are all zealous for the law.

[21]They have been told about you that you teach all the Jews living among the Gentiles to forsake Moses, and that you tell them not to circumcise their children or observe the customs. [22]What then is to be done? They will certainly hear that you have come. [23]So do what we tell you. We have four men who are under a vow. [24]Join these men, go through the rite of purification with them, and pay for the shaving of their heads. Thus all will know that there is nothing in what they have been told about you, but that you yourself observe and guard the law. [25]But as for the Gentiles who have become believers, we have sent a letter with our judgment that they should abstain from what has been sacrificed to idols and from blood and from what is strangled[e] and from fornication." [26]Then Paul took the men, and the next day, having purified himself, he entered the temple with them, making public the completion of the days of purification when the sacrifice would be made for each of them.

Paul Arrested in the Temple

27 When the seven days were almost completed, the Jews from Asia, who had seen him in the temple, stirred up the whole crowd. They seized him, [28]shouting, "Fellow Israelites, help! This is the man who is teaching everyone everywhere against our people, our law, and this place; more than that, he has actually brought Greeks into the temple and has defiled this holy place." [29]For they had previously seen Trophimus the Ephesian with him in the city, and they supposed that Paul had brought him into the temple. [30]Then all the city was aroused, and the people rushed together. They seized Paul and dragged him out of the temple, and immediately the doors were shut. [31]While they were trying to kill him, word came to the tribune of the cohort that all Jerusalem was in an uproar. [32]Immediately he took soldiers and centurions and ran down to them. When they saw the tribune and the soldiers, they stopped beating Paul. [33]Then the tribune came, arrested him, and ordered him to be bound with two chains; he inquired who he was and what he had done. [34]Some in the crowd shouted one thing, some another; and as he could not learn the facts because of the uproar, he ordered him to be brought into the barracks. [35]When Paul[f] came to the steps, the violence of the mob was so great that he had to be carried by the soldiers. [36]The crowd that followed kept shouting, "Away with him!"

---

a Other ancient authorities add *and Myra* b Or *continued* c Gk *brothers* d Gk *four daughters, virgins,* e Other ancient authorities lack *and from what is strangled* f Gk *he*

STUDY IT!

Paul's Opponents? · Acts 21:17–26

Paul's return to Jerusalem in **Acts 21** can get confusing. The following information should help you keep track of the main characters.

- One group is the Jewish Christians, represented by James and the elders (Acts 21:17–26). Although the Jewish Christians might be suspicious of Paul's defense of the Gentile Christians, they support Paul and come up with a plan for him to try to prove his Jewish loyalty.
- Another group is the Jews who don't believe in Jesus. These Jews see the rise of the Jesus movement, with Paul as its most well-known representative, as a threat to Judaism. They attempt to arrest him and have him killed in a mob scene (Acts 21:27–36).
- The third group is the Roman rulers. The Romans probably have no interest in this conflict except to keep the peace. The Roman tribune (governor) thinks he can keep the Jews happy by having Paul flogged (Acts 22:22–29). But surprise! Paul is a Roman citizen and has civil rights that the tribune must honor.

So who are Paul's—and Christianity's—opponents? Luke tells us that at first they are the Jews who don't believe in Jesus. Still later—after this story occurs—they will be the Romans. Luke writes all this in Acts after the fact, so his hindsight allows him to bring all of Paul's opponents into play in describing Paul's arrest and imprisonment.

Paul Defends Himself

37 Just as Paul was about to be brought into the barracks, he said to the tribune, "May I say something to you?" The tribune[a] replied, "Do you know Greek? [38]Then you are not the Egyptian who recently stirred up a revolt and led the four thousand assassins out into the wilderness?" [39]Paul replied, "I am a Jew, from Tarsus in Cilicia, a citizen of an important city; I beg you, let me speak to the people." [40]When he had given him permission, Paul stood on the steps and motioned to the people for silence; and when there was a great hush, he addressed them in the Hebrew[b] language, saying:

"Brothers and fathers, listen to the defense that I now make before you."

22 2 When they heard him addressing them in Hebrew,[b] they became even more quiet. Then he said:

3 "I am a Jew, born in Tarsus in Cilicia, but brought up in this city at the feet of Gamaliel, educated strictly according to our ancestral law, being zealous for God, just as all of you are today. [4]I persecuted this Way up to the point of death by binding both men and women and putting them in prison, [5]as the high priest and the whole council of elders can testify about me. From them I also received letters to the brothers in Damascus, and I went there in order to bind those who were there and to bring them back to Jerusalem for punishment.

Paul Tells of His Conversion

6 "While I was on my way and approaching Damascus, about noon a great light from heaven suddenly shone about me. [7]I fell to the ground and heard a voice saying to me, 'Saul, Saul, why are you persecuting me?' [8]I answered, 'Who are you, Lord?' Then he said to me, 'I am Jesus of Nazareth[c] whom you are persecuting.' [9]Now those who were with me saw the light but did not hear the voice of the one who was speaking to me. [10]I asked, 'What am I to do, Lord?' The Lord said to me, 'Get up and go to Damascus; there you will be told everything that has been assigned to you to do.' [11]Since I could not see because of the brightness of that light, those who were with me took my hand and led me to Damascus.

12 "A certain Ananias, who was a devout man according to the law and well spoken of by all the Jews living there, [13]came to me; and standing beside me, he said, 'Brother Saul, regain your sight!' In that very hour I regained my sight and saw him. [14]Then he said, 'The God of our ancestors has chosen you to know his will, to see the Righteous One and to hear his own voice; [15]for you will be his witness to all the world of what you have seen and heard. [16]And now

a Gk He   b That is, *Aramaic*   c Gk *the Nazorean*

why do you delay? Get up, be baptized, and have your sins washed away, calling on his name.'

Paul Sent to the Gentiles

17 "After I had returned to Jerusalem and while I was praying in the temple, I fell into a trance [18] and saw Jesus[a] saying to me, 'Hurry and get out of Jerusalem quickly, because they will not accept your testimony about me.' [19]And I said, 'Lord, they themselves know that in every synagogue I imprisoned and beat those who believed in you. [20]And while the blood of your witness Stephen was shed, I myself was standing by, approving and keeping the coats of those who killed him.' [21]Then he said to me, 'Go, for I will send you far away to the Gentiles.' "

LIVE IT!

Sharing Your Story
Acts 22:6–16

Have you ever heard a dramatic conversion story? Retreats and large youth conferences are common places for individuals to share personal stories of how their belief in Jesus helped them overcome addictions, terrible problems, or great sin. Other stories may include how someone came to recognize and accept God as a result of a serious illness or the death of a close friend or family member. Listening to these dramatic stories can be inspiring. But it may also make you feel that your own story of following Christ doesn't quite measure up. Nothing could be farther from the truth in God's eyes.

We all have our own conversion stories—and the turning of a heart toward God is a miraculous event, regardless of the circumstances that surround it.

• Do you believe God can use your story to encourage others to put their faith in Christ?
• Are you willing to share your story of faith with others?
• Take some time to write down your story and share it with someone you know.

Paul and the Roman Tribune

22 Up to this point they listened to him, but then they shouted, "Away with such a fellow from the earth! For he should not be allowed to live." [23]And while they were shouting, throwing off their cloaks, and tossing dust into the air, [24]the tribune directed that he was to be brought into the barracks, and ordered him to be examined by flogging, to find out the reason for this outcry against him. [25]But when they had tied him up with thongs,[b] Paul said to the centurion who was standing by, "Is it legal for you to flog a Roman citizen who is uncondemned?" [26]When the centurion heard that, he went to the tribune and said to him, "What are you about to do? This man is a Roman citizen." [27]The tribune came and asked Paul,[c] "Tell me, are you a Roman citizen?" And he said, "Yes." [28]The tribune answered, "It cost me a large sum of money to get my citizenship." Paul said, "But I was born a citizen." [29]Immediately those who were about to examine him drew back from him; and the tribune also was afraid, for he realized that Paul was a Roman citizen and that he had bound him.

Paul before the Council

30 Since he wanted to find out what Paul[c] was being accused of by the Jews, the next day he released him and ordered the chief priests and the entire council to meet. He brought Paul down and had him stand before them.

23 While Paul was looking intently at the council he said, "Brothers,[d] up to this day I have lived my life with a clear conscience before God." [2]Then the high priest Ananias ordered those standing near him to strike him on the mouth. [3]At this Paul said to him, "God will strike you, you whitewashed wall! Are you sitting there to judge me according to the law, and yet in violation of the law you order me to be struck?" [4]Those standing nearby said, "Do you dare to insult God's high priest?" [5]And Paul said, "I did not realize, brothers, that he was high priest; for it is written, 'You shall not speak evil of a leader of your people.' "

6 When Paul noticed that some were Sadducees and others were Pharisees, he called out in the council, "Brothers, I am a Pharisee, a son of Pharisees. I am on trial concerning the hope of the resurrection[e] of the dead." [7]When he said this, a dissension began between the Pharisees and the Sadducees, and the assembly was divided. [8](The Sadducees say that

---

a Gk him   b Or up for the lashes   c Gk he   d Gk Men, brothers   e Gk concerning hope and resurrection

What About the Jews? · Acts 22:30–28:31

The earliest Christians were Jews. It was agonizing to them that so many of their Jewish friends wouldn't believe in Jesus. Indeed, not only did those friends not believe in Jesus, but some tried to stop the spread of Christianity, because they viewed Christian beliefs as blasphemy. **Acts 22–28** tell of Jewish attacks against Paul, which ultimately end with Paul's traveling to Rome to make his case before the emperor.

But the questions remain. If the Jews are God's people, why don't they believe that Jesus is the Jewish Messiah? Couldn't God make it easier for them to believe? Does God cause their lack of faith in Jesus? Who is ultimately responsible for anyone's faith? Read **Romans 9–11**, where Paul tries to answer those questions.

there is no resurrection, or angel, or spirit; but the Pharisees acknowledge all three.) [9] Then a great clamor arose, and certain scribes of the Pharisees' group stood up and contended, "We find nothing wrong with this man. What if a spirit or an angel has spoken to him?" [10] When the dissension became violent, the tribune, fearing that they would tear Paul to pieces, ordered the soldiers to go down, take him by force, and bring him into the barracks.

11 That night the Lord stood near him and said, "Keep up your courage! For just as you have testified for me in Jerusalem, so you must bear witness also in Rome."

The Plot to Kill Paul

12 In the morning the Jews joined in a conspiracy and bound themselves by an oath neither to eat nor drink until they had killed Paul. [13] There were more than forty who joined in this conspiracy. [14] They went to the chief priests and elders and said, "We have strictly bound ourselves by an oath to taste no food until we have killed Paul. [15] Now then, you and the council must notify the tribune to bring him down to you, on the pretext that you want to make a more thorough examination of his case. And we are ready to do away with him before he arrives."

16 Now the son of Paul's sister heard about the ambush; so he went and gained entrance to the barracks and told Paul. [17] Paul called one of the centurions and said, "Take this young man to the tribune, for he has something to report to him." [18] So he took him, brought him to the tribune, and said, "The prisoner Paul called me and asked me to bring this young man to you; he has something to tell you."

[19] The tribune took him by the hand, drew him aside privately, and asked, "What is it that you have to report to me?" [20] He answered, "The Jews have agreed to ask you to bring Paul down to the council tomorrow, as though they were going to inquire more thoroughly into his case. [21] But do not be persuaded by them, for more than forty of their men are lying in ambush for him. They have bound themselves by an oath neither to eat nor drink until they kill him. They are ready now and are waiting for your consent." [22] So the tribune dismissed the young man, ordering him, "Tell no one that you have informed me of this."

Paul Sent to Felix the Governor

23 Then he summoned two of the centurions and said, "Get ready to leave by nine o'clock tonight for Caesarea with two hundred soldiers, seventy horsemen, and two hundred spearmen. [24] Also provide mounts for Paul to ride, and take him safely to Felix the governor." [25] He wrote a letter to this effect:

26 "Claudius Lysias to his Excellency the governor Felix, greetings. [27] This man was seized by the Jews and was about to be killed by them, but when I had learned that he was a Roman citizen, I came with the guard and rescued him. [28] Since I wanted to know the charge for which they accused him, I had him brought to their council. [29] I found that he was accused concerning questions of their law, but was charged with nothing deserving death or imprisonment. [30] When I was informed that there would be a plot against the man, I sent him to you at once, ordering his accusers also to state before you what they have against him.*[a]*"

[a] Other ancient authorities add *Farewell*

31 So the soldiers, according to their instructions, took Paul and brought him during the night to Antipatris. ³²The next day they let the horsemen go on with him, while they returned to the barracks. ³³When they came to Caesarea and delivered the letter to the governor, they presented Paul also before him. ³⁴On reading the letter, he asked what province he belonged to, and when he learned that he was from Cilicia, ³⁵he said, "I will give you a hearing when your accusers arrive." Then he ordered that he be kept under guard in Herod's headquarters.*a*

24 Paul before Felix at Caesarea

Five days later the high priest Ananias came down with some elders and an attorney, a certain Tertullus, and they reported their case against Paul to the governor. ²When Paul*b* had been summoned, Tertullus began to accuse him, saying:

"Your Excellency,*c* because of you we have long enjoyed peace, and reforms have been made for this people because of your foresight. ³We welcome this in every way and everywhere with utmost gratitude. ⁴But, to detain you no further, I beg you to hear us briefly with your customary graciousness. ⁵We have, in fact, found this man a pestilent fellow, an agitator among all the Jews throughout the world, and a ringleader of the sect of the Nazarenes.*d* ⁶He even tried to profane the temple, and so we seized him.*e* ⁸By examining him yourself you will be able to learn from him concerning everything of which we accuse him."

9 The Jews also joined in the charge by asserting that all this was true.

Paul's Defense before Felix

10 When the governor motioned to him to speak, Paul replied:

"I cheerfully make my defense, knowing that for many years you have been a judge over this nation. ¹¹As you can find out, it is not more than twelve days since I went up to worship in Jerusalem. ¹²They did not find me disputing with anyone in the temple or stirring up a crowd either in the synagogues or throughout the city. ¹³Neither can they prove to you the charge that they now bring against me. ¹⁴But this I admit to you, that according to the Way, which they call a sect, I worship the God of our ancestors, believing everything laid down according to the law or written in the prophets. ¹⁵I have a hope in God—a hope that they themselves also accept—that there

will be a resurrection of both*f* the righteous and the unrighteous. ¹⁶Therefore I do my best always to have a clear conscience toward God and all people. ¹⁷Now after some years I came to bring alms to my nation and to offer sacrifices. ¹⁸While I was doing this, they found me in the temple, completing the rite of purification, without any crowd or disturbance. ¹⁹But there were some Jews from Asia—they ought to be here before you to make an accusation, if they have anything against me. ²⁰Or let these men here tell what crime they had found when I stood before the council, ²¹unless it was this one sentence that I called out while standing before them, 'It is about the resurrection of the dead that I am on trial before you today.'"

22 But Felix, who was rather well informed about the Way, adjourned the hearing with the comment, "When Lysias the tribune comes down, I will decide your case." ²³Then he ordered the centurion to keep him in custody, but to let him have some liberty and not to prevent any of his friends from taking care of his needs.

Paul Held in Custody

24 Some days later when Felix came with his wife Drusilla, who was Jewish, he sent for Paul and heard him speak concerning faith in Christ Jesus. ²⁵And as he discussed justice, self-control, and the coming judgment, Felix became frightened and said, "Go away for the present; when I have an opportunity, I will send for you." ²⁶At the same time he hoped that money would be given him by Paul, and for that reason he used to send for him very often and converse with him.

27 After two years had passed, Felix was succeeded by Porcius Festus; and since he wanted to grant the Jews a favor, Felix left Paul in prison.

25 Paul Appeals to the Emperor

Three days after Festus had arrived in the province, he went up from Caesarea to Jerusalem ²where the chief priests and the leaders of the Jews gave him a report against Paul. They appealed to him ³and requested, as a favor to them against Paul,*g* to have him transferred to Jerusalem. They were, in fact, planning an ambush to kill him along the way. ⁴Festus replied that Paul was being kept at Caesarea, and that he himself intended to go there shortly. ⁵"So," he said, "let those of you who have the authority come down with me, and

---

a Gk praetorium b Gk he c Gk lacks *Your Excellency* d Gk *Nazoreans* e Other ancient authorities add *and we would have judged him according to our law. ⁷But the chief captain Lysias came and with great violence took him out of our hands, ⁸commanding his accusers to come before you.* f Other ancient authorities read *of the dead, both of* g Gk *him*

if there is anything wrong about the man, let them accuse him."

6 After he had stayed among them not more than eight or ten days, he went down to Caesarea; the next day he took his seat on the tribunal and ordered Paul to be brought. [7]When he arrived, the Jews who had gone down from Jerusalem surrounded him, bringing many serious charges against him, which they could not prove. [8]Paul said in his defense, "I have in no way committed an offense against the law of the Jews, or against the temple, or against the emperor." [9]But Festus, wishing to do the Jews a favor, asked Paul, "Do you wish to go up to Jerusalem and be tried there before me on these charges?" [10]Paul said, "I am appealing to the emperor's tribunal; this is where I should be tried. I have done no wrong to the Jews, as you very well know. [11]Now if I am in the wrong and have committed something for which I deserve to die, I am not trying to escape death; but if there is nothing to their charges against me, no one can turn me over to them. I appeal to the emperor." [12]Then Festus, after he had conferred with his council, replied, "You have appealed to the emperor; to the emperor you will go."

Festus Consults King Agrippa

13 After several days had passed, King Agrippa and Bernice arrived at Caesarea to welcome Festus. [14]Since they were staying there several days, Festus laid Paul's case before the king, saying, "There is a man here who was left in prison by Felix. [15]When I was in Jerusalem, the chief priests and the elders of the Jews informed me about him and asked for a sentence against him. [16]I told them that it was not the custom of the Romans to hand over anyone before the accused had met the accusers face to face and had been given an opportunity to make a defense against the charge. [17]So when they met here, I lost no time, but on the next day took my seat on the tribunal and ordered the man to be brought. [18]When the accusers stood up, they did not charge him with any of the crimes[a] that I was expecting. [19]Instead they had certain points of disagreement with him about their own religion and about a certain Jesus, who had died, but whom Paul asserted to be alive. [20]Since I was at a loss how to investigate these questions, I asked whether he wished to go to Jerusalem and be tried there on these charges.[b] [21]But when Paul had appealed to be kept in custody for the decision of his Imperial Majesty, I ordered him to be held

until I could send him to the emperor." [22]Agrippa said to Festus, "I would like to hear the man myself." "Tomorrow," he said, "you will hear him."

Paul Brought before Agrippa

23 So on the next day Agrippa and Bernice came with great pomp, and they entered the audience hall with the military tribunes and the prominent men of the city. Then Festus gave the order and Paul was brought in. [24]And Festus said, "King Agrippa and all here present with us, you see this man about whom the whole Jewish community petitioned me, both in Jerusalem and here, shouting that he ought not to live any longer. [25]But I found that he had done nothing deserving death; and when he appealed to his Imperial Majesty, I decided to send him. [26]But I have nothing definite to write to our sovereign about him. Therefore I have brought him before all of you, and especially before you, King Agrippa, so that, after we have examined him, I may have something to write— [27]for it seems to me unreasonable to send a prisoner without indicating the charges against him."

26

Paul Defends Himself before Agrippa

Agrippa said to Paul, "You have permission to speak for yourself." Then Paul stretched out his hand and began to defend himself:

2 "I consider myself fortunate that it is before you, King Agrippa, I am to make my defense today against all the accusations of the Jews, [3]because you are especially familiar with all the customs and controversies of the Jews; therefore I beg of you to listen to me patiently.

4 "All the Jews know my way of life from my youth, a life spent from the beginning among my own people and in Jerusalem. [5]They have known for a long time, if they are willing to testify, that I have belonged to the strictest sect of our religion and lived as a Pharisee. [6]And now I stand here on trial on account of my hope in the promise made by God to our ancestors, [7]a promise that our twelve tribes hope to attain, as they earnestly worship day and night. It is for this hope, your Excellency,[c] that I am accused by Jews! [8]Why is it thought incredible by any of you that God raises the dead?

9 "Indeed, I myself was convinced that I ought to do many things against the name of Jesus of Nazareth.[d] [10]And that is what I did in Jerusalem; with authority received from the chief priests, I not only locked up many of the saints in prison, but I also cast

---

a Other ancient authorities read *with anything*   b Gk *on them*   c Gk *O king*   d Gk *the Nazorean*

my vote against them when they were being condemned to death. [11]By punishing them often in all the synagogues I tried to force them to blaspheme; and since I was so furiously enraged at them, I pursued them even to foreign cities.

Paul Tells of His Conversion

12 "With this in mind, I was traveling to Damascus with the authority and commission of the chief priests, [13]when at midday along the road, your Excellency,[a] I saw a light from heaven, brighter than the sun, shining around me and my companions. [14]When we had all fallen to the ground, I heard a voice saying to me in the Hebrew[b] language, 'Saul, Saul, why are you persecuting me? It hurts you to kick against the goads.' [15]I asked, 'Who are you, Lord?' The Lord answered, 'I am Jesus whom you are persecuting. [16]But get up and stand on your feet; for I have appeared to you for this purpose, to appoint you to serve and testify to the things in which you have seen me[c] and to those in which I will appear to you. [17]I will

rescue you from your people and from the Gentiles— to whom I am sending you [18]to open their eyes so that they may turn from darkness to light and from the power of Satan to God, so that they may receive forgiveness of sins and a place among those who are sanctified by faith in me.'

Paul Tells of His Preaching

19 "After that, King Agrippa, I was not disobedient to the heavenly vision, [20]but declared first to those in Damascus, then in Jerusalem and throughout the countryside of Judea, and also to the Gentiles, that they should repent and turn to God and do deeds consistent with repentance. [21]For this reason the Jews seized me in the temple and tried to kill me. [22]To this day I have had help from God, and so I stand here, testifying to both small and great, saying nothing but what the prophets and Moses said would take place: [23]that the Messiah[d] must suffer, and that, by being the first to rise from the dead, he would proclaim light both to our people and to the Gentiles."

STUDY IT!

Paul, Live from Caesarea! · Acts 26

Reporters MARISA and RICARDO (speaking into their microphones): We're here, live, in Caesarea, where Paul of Tarsus has just spoken with King Agrippa and Governor Festus. Here comes Paul now. Let's see what he has to say. Paul, why has your message caused so much controversy?

PAUL: It was never my intention to cause strife or conflict. But I must speak the truth, and the truth is that God has revealed his salvation for us in Jesus Christ. In Jesus, salvation is available to everyone— Jews and Gentiles, slaves and free people, men and women—and we are all equal as sons and daughters of God. Unfortunately, this truth is upsetting to some people, and they have gone to great lengths to try to get rid of me.

MARISA AND RICARDO: But hasn't your message been well received by many people—including many different types of people?

PAUL: Yes, it has. I think this is because Jesus taught us always to respect all persons as sons or daughters of God regardless of their culture or social class. Under the guidance of the Holy Spirit, Christian communities allow for diversity while keeping a common unity in Jesus Christ. I think people are hungry for this.

MARISA AND RICARDO: Soon you will be heading for Rome, where you will be on trial for alleged crimes against the empire. Are you worried?

PAUL (smiling): Why be worried? No one has ultimate power over me except my Lord Jesus Christ. I only need to be faithful to my calling, and I will receive my prize—eternal life with God. Plus I have the prayers and support of many close friends. But thank you for your concern. God's grace and peace be with you.

MARISA AND RICARDO: And thank you, Paul.

a Gk O king   b That is, Aramaic   c Other ancient authorities read the things that you have seen   d Or the Christ

Paul Appeals to Agrippa to Believe

24 While he was making this defense, Festus exclaimed, "You are out of your mind, Paul! Too much learning is driving you insane!" 25 But Paul said, "I am not out of my mind, most excellent Festus, but I am speaking the sober truth. 26 Indeed the king knows about these things, and to him I speak freely; for I am certain that none of these things has escaped his notice, for this was not done in a corner. 27 King Agrippa, do you believe the prophets? I know that you believe." 28 Agrippa said to Paul, "Are you so quickly persuading me to become a Christian?"*a* 29 Paul replied, "Whether quickly or not, I pray to God that not only you but also all who are listening to me today might become such as I am—except for these chains."

30 Then the king got up, and with him the governor and Bernice and those who had been seated with them; 31 and as they were leaving, they said to one another, "This man is doing nothing to deserve death or imprisonment." 32 Agrippa said to Festus, "This man could have been set free if he had not appealed to the emperor."

Paul Sails for Rome

27 When it was decided that we were to sail for Italy, they transferred Paul and some other prisoners to a centurion of the Augustan Cohort, named Julius. 2 Embarking on a ship of Adramyttium that was about to set sail to the ports along the coast of Asia, we put to sea, accompanied by Aristarchus, a Macedonian from Thessalonica. 3 The next day we put in at Sidon; and Julius treated Paul kindly, and allowed him to go to his friends to be cared for. 4 Putting out to sea from there, we sailed under the lee of Cyprus, because the winds were against us. 5 After we had sailed across the sea that is off Cilicia and Pamphylia, we came to Myra in Lycia. 6 There the centurion found an Alexandrian ship bound for Italy and put us on board. 7 We sailed slowly for a number of days and arrived with difficulty off Cnidus, and as the wind was against us, we sailed under the lee of Crete off Salmone. 8 Sailing past it with difficulty, we came to a place called Fair Havens, near the city of Lasea.

9 Since much time had been lost and sailing was now dangerous, because even the Fast had already gone by, Paul advised them, 10 saying, "Sirs, I can see that the voyage will be with danger and much heavy loss, not only of the cargo and the ship, but also of

our lives." 11 But the centurion paid more attention to the pilot and to the owner of the ship than to what Paul said. 12 Since the harbor was not suitable for spending the winter, the majority was in favor of putting to sea from there, on the chance that somehow they could reach Phoenix, where they could spend the winter. It was a harbor of Crete, facing southwest and northwest.

The Storm at Sea

13 When a moderate south wind began to blow, they thought they could achieve their purpose; so they weighed anchor and began to sail past Crete, close to the shore. 14 But soon a violent wind, called the northeaster, rushed down from Crete.*b* 15 Since the ship was caught and could not be turned head-on into the wind, we gave way to it and were driven. 16 By running under the lee of a small island called Cauda*c* we were scarcely able to get the ship's boat under control. 17 After hoisting it up they took measures*d* to undergird the ship; then, fearing that they would run on the Syrtis, they lowered the sea anchor and so were driven. 18 We were being pounded by the storm so violently that on the next day they began to throw the cargo overboard, 19 and on the third day with their own hands they threw the ship's tackle overboard. 20 When neither sun nor stars appeared for many days, and no small tempest raged, all hope of our being saved was at last abandoned.

21 Since they had been without food for a long time, Paul then stood up among them and said, "Men, you should have listened to me and not have set sail from Crete and thereby avoided this damage and loss. 22 I urge you now to keep up your courage, for there will be no loss of life among you, but only of the ship. 23 For last night there stood by me an angel of the God to whom I belong and whom I worship, 24 and he said, 'Do not be afraid, Paul; you must stand before the emperor; and indeed, God has granted safety to all those who are sailing with you.' 25 So keep up your courage, men, for I have faith in God that it will be exactly as I have been told. 26 But we will have to run aground on some island."

27 When the fourteenth night had come, as we were drifting across the sea of Adria, about midnight

a Or *Quickly you will persuade me to play the Christian*   *b* Gk *it*   *c* Other ancient authorities read *Clauda*   *d* Gk *helps*

the sailors suspected that they were nearing land. [28]So they took soundings and found twenty fathoms; a little farther on they took soundings again and found fifteen fathoms. [29]Fearing that we might run on the rocks, they let down four anchors from the stern and prayed for day to come. [30]But when the sailors tried to escape from the ship and had lowered the boat into the sea, on the pretext of putting out anchors from the bow, [31]Paul said to the centurion and the soldiers, "Unless these men stay in the ship, you cannot be saved." [32]Then the soldiers cut away the ropes of the boat and set it adrift.

33 Just before daybreak, Paul urged all of them to take some food, saying, "Today is the fourteenth day that you have been in suspense and remaining without food, having eaten nothing. [34]Therefore I urge you to take some food, for it will help you survive; for none of you will lose a hair from your heads." [35]After he had said this, he took bread; and giving thanks to God in the presence of all, he broke it and began to eat. [36]Then all of them were encouraged and took food for themselves. [37](We were in all two hundred seventy-six[a] persons in the ship.) [38]After they had satisfied their hunger, they lightened the ship by throwing the wheat into the sea.

The Shipwreck

39 In the morning they did not recognize the land, but they noticed a bay with a beach, on which they planned to run the ship ashore, if they could. [40]So they cast off the anchors and left them in the sea. At the same time they loosened the ropes that tied the steering-oars; then hoisting the foresail to the wind, they made for the beach. [41]But striking a reef,[b] they ran the ship aground; the bow stuck and remained immovable, but the stern was being broken up by the force of the waves. [42]The soldiers' plan was to kill the prisoners, so that none might swim away and escape; [43]but the centurion, wishing to save Paul, kept them from carrying out their plan. He ordered those who could swim to jump overboard first and make for the land, [44]and the rest to follow, some on planks and others on pieces of the ship. And so it was that all were brought safely to land.

28

Paul on the Island of Malta

After we had reached safety, we then learned that the island was called Malta. [2]The natives showed us unusual kindness. Since it had begun to rain and was cold, they kindled a fire and welcomed all of us around it. [3]Paul had gathered a bundle of brushwood and was putting it on the fire, when a viper, driven out by the heat, fastened itself on his hand. [4]When the natives saw the creature hanging from his hand, they said to one another, "This man must be a murderer; though he has escaped from the sea, justice has not allowed him to live." [5]He, however, shook off the creature into the fire and suffered no harm. [6]They were expecting him to swell up or drop dead, but after they had waited a long time and saw that nothing unusual had happened to him, they changed their minds

PRAY IT!

The Storms of Life · Acts 27:13–25

Facing danger requires courage. But it's not easy to feel brave when you find yourself in a situation completely out of your control. That's where Paul finds himself in **Acts 27:20**—caught in a storm at sea, with no hope for survival. But Paul's faith in God does not waiver. When the storms of life come and are crashing all around you, hold tight to faith. Say this prayer:

Help, Lord, I'm lost at sea! When I started this journey, I thought I knew where I was headed, but then a few waves started to rock the boat, and I became frightened.

Next, the wind picked up, and my fear turned into confusion. Then the night fell, and my confusion turned into despair. And now I am lost and need you to help calm the waves in my life and stand beside me until the night turns into day.

Help me to find my bearings again, Lord. And when this storm is over, give me wisdom to learn from this experience—to go back and make right what was wrong, not to lose hope at the first sign of trouble, and to hang on to you, my anchor, in the rough seas of life. Amen.

a Other ancient authorities read *seventy-six*; others, *about seventy-six*   b Gk *place of two seas*

and began to say that he was a god.

7 Now in the neighborhood of that place were lands belonging to the leading man of the island, named Publius, who received us and entertained us hospitably for three days. [8]It so happened that the father of Publius lay sick in bed with fever and dysentery. Paul visited him and cured him by praying and putting his hands on him. [9]After this happened, the rest of the people on the island who had diseases also came and were cured. [10]They bestowed many honors on us, and when we were about to sail, they put on board all the provisions we needed.

Paul Arrives at Rome

11 Three months later we set sail on a ship that had wintered at the island, an Alexandrian ship with the Twin Brothers as its figurehead. [12]We put in at Syracuse and stayed there for three days; [13]then we weighed anchor and came to Rhegium. After one day there a south wind sprang up, and on the second day we came to Puteoli. [14]There we found believers[a] and were invited to stay with them for seven days. And so we came to Rome. [15]The believers[a] from there, when they heard of us, came as far as the Forum of Appius and Three Taverns to meet us. On seeing them, Paul thanked God and took courage.

16 When we came into Rome, Paul was allowed to live by himself, with the soldier who was guarding him.

Paul and Jewish Leaders in Rome

17 Three days later he called together the local leaders of the Jews. When they had assembled, he said to them, "Brothers, though I had done nothing against our people or the customs of our ancestors, yet I was arrested in Jerusalem and handed over to the Romans. [18]When they had examined me, the Romans[b] wanted to release me, because there was no reason for the death penalty in my case. [19]But when the Jews objected, I was compelled to appeal to the emperor—even though I had no charge to bring against my nation. [20]For this reason therefore I have asked to see you and speak with you,[c] since it is for the sake of the hope of Israel that I am bound with this chain." [21]They replied, "We have received no letters from Judea about you, and none of the brothers coming here has reported or spoken anything evil about you. [22]But we would like to hear from you what you think, for with regard to this sect we know that everywhere it is spoken against."

Paul Preaches in Rome

23 After they had set a day to meet with him, they came to him at his lodgings in great numbers. From morning until evening he explained the matter to them, testifying to the kingdom of God and trying to convince them about Jesus both from the law of Moses and from the prophets. [24]Some were convinced by what he had said, while others refused to believe. [25]So they disagreed with each other; and as they were leaving, Paul made one further statement: "The Holy Spirit was right in saying to your ancestors through the prophet Isaiah,

26   'Go to this people and say,
       You will indeed listen, but never
              understand,
          and you will indeed look, but never
              perceive.
27   For this people's heart has grown
              dull,
       and their ears are hard of hearing,
          and they have shut their eyes;
              so that they might not look with their
                  eyes,
          and listen with their ears,
       and understand with their heart and turn—
          and I would heal them.'

[28]Let it be known to you then that this salvation of God has been sent to the Gentiles; they will listen."[d]

30 He lived there two whole years at his own expense[e] and welcomed all who came to him, [31]proclaiming the kingdom of God and teaching about the Lord Jesus Christ with all boldness and without hindrance.

---

a Gk brothers b Gk they c Or I have asked you to see me and speak with me d Other ancient authorities add verse 29, And when he had said these words, the Jews departed, arguing vigorously among themselves e Or in his own hired dwelling

Introduction to the Letters & Revelation

Before there was texting, e-mail, and social networking, there was letter writing. Yes, it still exists. People can often express themselves more clearly in writing than they can in person. Some people still turn to letters to say things that are difficult to say face-to-face or to mark a special occasion. Maybe you've received some special letters. Letters between parents and children, engaged couples, and even pen pals are often saved to be read again and again. They are treasured for their stories, advice, and expressions of love. The next twenty-one books of the New Testament are treasured letters. Their stories, advice, and confidence in God's loving guidance have inspired generations of Christians.

IN DEPTH

When you read someone else's mail, you see only one side of the conversation. So you have to do some reading between the lines to understand the issues being addressed. That's also true of the New Testament letters, but they give you a firsthand look at the earliest Christian communities and what they believed. In fact, the letters written by Paul are the oldest Christian documents we have, written even before the Gospels. Paul's earliest letter, 1 Thessalonians, was probably written around A.D. 50. That's only a little more than twenty years after the death and resurrection of Jesus!

These letters follow a common pattern. They usually begin with a greeting from the sender to the receiver or receivers. Next is a prayer, most often of thanksgiving. This is followed by the body of the letter, which addresses whatever issues the author wants to discuss. It often includes general advice about Christian living. The letters close with greetings and instructions to specific people and a final blessing.

There are exceptions to this pattern. The books of Hebrews and 1 John don't have all four of these features and are more like essays about faith. The book of James has more of the features, but reads like a good sermon rather than a letter.

Paul was the most prolific writer of the letters. At one time, it was thought that he wrote thirteen of the twenty-one. However, modern scholars believe that some of the letters traditionally attributed to Paul were actually written by his associates or later followers. Scholars have reached this conclusion because of differences in writing style, vocabulary, and thought. Those associates or followers of Paul applied his teaching to new situations faced by the early Christian communities. The letters of James, Peter, and John also were probably written by associates or later followers of those men.

That might seem like forgery to us today. But it wasn't uncommon in the ancient world for followers to write in an important person's name after the person's death. It was a way of honoring the person and keeping his or her traditions alive.

Although Revelation is grouped together with the letters in this introduction, it's not a letter at all. Revelation was written as a series of visions by a Christian prophet named John. The visions are filled with dramatic imagery and events. Some people interpret them as prophecies about the way the world will end, but many experts interpret them as coded messages about events happening in John's own time. Ultimately, the book of Revelation is a hopeful message to persecuted Christians that God is in control and that goodness and justice will triumph.

As you explore these letters and the book of Revelation, you'll see the church at its best: the miraculous growth, the Spirit-filled enthusiasm, and the deep love the early Christians had for each other and for Jesus. You'll also see how the early Church was threatened by intense disagreements, jealousy, and scandals. Through it all, the authors reveal a deep faith and missionary spirit. They focus again and again on the death and resurrection of Jesus and on the mystery of the Church as the living body of Christ acting in the world through the power of the Holy Spirit. These letters had a specific audience in the first century A.D., but their words are for you too!

OTHER BACKGROUND

- Nine letters by Paul or his followers are named for the cities where the recipient churches were located: Romans, 1 and 2 Corinthians, Galatians, Ephesians (called a captivity letter because it is attributed to Paul writing from jail), Philippians (also a captivity letter), Colossians (also a captivity letter), and 1 and 2 Thessalonians.

- Four letters by Paul or his followers are named for the individuals they were sent to: 1 and 2 Timothy and Titus (called the Pastoral Letters), and Philemon (a captivity letter).

- Hebrews is named for the Christian Jews for whom it was intended.

- Seven letters are named after their stated authors: James; 1 and 2 Peter; 1, 2, and 3 John; and Jude. They are general letters to all Christians.

- Revelation is not a letter. It's a collection of the prophecies and visions of John of Patmos, a Christian prophet.

Romans ▶▶▶▶▶▶▶▶▶▶▶▶▶▶▶▶▶▶

You can probably name a dozen love songs without even thinking. Chances are many of them are about unconditional love. It's what we all long for. And it was the message Paul was trying to get across to the people of Rome: God loves us unconditionally.

In his letter to the Romans, Paul addresses some big and important questions of life and faith. He wanted to share his understanding that, although we may not always do what's right, God still desires a relationship with us through Jesus. We are justified—made right with God—by faith in Jesus Christ.

IN DEPTH

Many people consider Romans to be the deepest expression of Paul's thinking. This was the only letter Paul wrote to a community he had not yet visited. He was planning to go to Rome at the time and was trying to prepare the way by explaining his teaching on justification and faith. Paul's message is that only God can forgive us of sin, so we can be restored to a right relationship with God. One verse from the first chapter sums up his ideas: "For I am not ashamed of the gospel; it is the power of God for salvation to everyone who has faith" (Romans 1:16).

Romans isn't always easy reading. Paul often makes his case by using arguments that might seem strange to us today. Here are some of his main points:

• Justification, or being made right with God, is available to both Jews and Gentiles (non-Jews).

• All people have sinned, so no one has earned justification.

• Justification and salvation come through faith in Jesus, not through following the Jewish religious law.

• Even though the gospel has come to the Gentiles, God has not abandoned the Jews.

Romans also includes many wonderfully comforting words. It tells us that when we don't know how to pray, God prays for us "with sighs too deep for words" (Romans 8:26). Romans 8:28 says, "All things work together for good for those who love God." And Romans 8:31 asks, "If God is for us, who is against us?"

So let go of your fears as you read this powerful letter. Even though we're not perfect, God will never leave us. As Paul says, "I am convinced that neither death, nor life, nor angels, nor rulers, nor things present, nor things to come, nor powers, nor height, nor depth, nor anything else in all creation, will be able to separate us from the love of God in Christ Jesus our Lord" (Romans 8:38-39).

QUICK FACTS

● **Author:** Paul

● **Date Written:** Between A.D. 56 and 58

● **Audience:** Jewish and Gentile (non-Jewish) Christians in Rome

● **Themes:** The righteousness and faithfulness of God, and how people are put right with God by faith and their relationship with God is restored

AT A GLANCE

● **Romans 1:1–15** A greeting and thanks

● **Romans 1:16–4:25** The lesson that humanity was once under the power of sin, but is now justified

● **Romans 5–8** A description of the life of the justified

● **Romans 9–11** A discussion of Judaism's place in God's plan of salvation

● **Romans 12–16** Moral advice, personal notes, and blessings

1

Salutation

Paul, a servant[a] of Jesus Christ, called to be an apostle, set apart for the gospel of God, [2]which he promised beforehand through his prophets in the holy scriptures, [3]the gospel concerning his Son, who was descended from David according to the flesh [4]and was declared to be Son of God with power according to the spirit[b] of holiness by resurrection from the dead, Jesus Christ our Lord, [5]through whom we have received grace and apostleship to bring about the obedience of faith among all the Gentiles for the sake of his name, [6]including yourselves who are called to belong to Jesus Christ,

7 To all God's beloved in Rome, who are called to be saints:

Grace to you and peace from God our Father and the Lord Jesus Christ.

Prayer of Thanksgiving

8 First, I thank my God through Jesus Christ for all of you, because your faith is proclaimed throughout the world. [9]For God, whom I serve with my spirit by announcing the gospel[c] of his Son, is my witness that without ceasing I remember you always in my prayers, [10]asking that by God's will I may somehow at last succeed in coming to you. [11]For I am longing to see you so that I may share with you some spiritual gift to strengthen you— [12]or rather so that we may be mutually encouraged by each other's faith, both yours and mine. [13]I want you to know, brothers and sisters,[d] that I have often intended to come to you (but thus far have been prevented), in order that I may reap some harvest among you as I have among the rest of the Gentiles. [14]I am a debtor both to Greeks and to barbarians, both to the wise and to the foolish [15]—hence my eagerness to proclaim the gospel to you also who are in Rome.

The Power of the Gospel

16 For I am not ashamed of the gospel; it is the power of God for salvation to everyone who has faith, to the Jew first and also to the Greek. [17]For in it the righteousness of God is revealed through faith for faith; as it is written, "The one who is righteous will live by faith."[e]

The Guilt of Humankind

18 For the wrath of God is revealed from heaven against all ungodliness and wickedness of those who by their wickedness suppress the truth. [19]For what can be known about God is plain to them, because God has shown it to them. [20]Ever since the creation of the world his eternal power and divine nature, invisible though they are, have been understood and seen through the things he has made. So they are without excuse; [21]for though they knew God, they did not honor him as God or give thanks to him,

---

STUDY IT!

The Many Meanings of "Gospel" · Romans 1:16

Paul says he's not ashamed of the gospel. So exactly what gospel is he referring to? The Greek word "euangelion," used in this passage, means "to evangelize" or "to share the good news." The word "gospel" is the best translation of the Greek word "euangelion" and comes from the Old English word "godspel," which means "good news." So Paul is saying he is not ashamed of the good news of Jesus.

The meaning of the word "gospel" goes through an evolution in the New Testament. For Paul, whose writings are the earliest in the New Testament, "gospel" referred to the good news of salvation for all who believe. Paul associated the gospel directly with Jesus himself, centering on his death and resurrection.

As Christian faith developed, the understanding of the word "gospel" expanded to include the kingdom of God that Jesus preached. The gospel wasn't just associated with Jesus' saving death and resurrection, but included all his teachings, miracles, promises, and demands. After the original apostles died or were killed, Christian communities wanted a record of their teachings about Jesus, and the gospel message was written down. So "gospel" came also to refer to the writings named for Matthew, Mark, Luke, and John.

---

a Gk *slave* b Or *Spirit* c Gk *my spirit in the gospel* d Gk *brothers* e Or *The one who is righteous through faith will live*

STUDY IT!

Lusts of the Heart
Romans 1:18–32

In making his case that all people are in need of salvation, Paul talks about the sinfulness of humankind in **Romans 1:18–32**. He talks about sexual debauchery in **Romans 1:26–27** as a specific example of what happens when people refuse to acknowledge God as Lord and creator and instead worship created things.

Some people interpret these verses to mean Paul is condemning homosexual persons. But a closer look at the context shows that right after this specific example, Paul lists all kinds of sinful behaviors in **Romans 1:28–32** including envy, deceit, gossiping, boastfulness, and rebelliousness. He is not commenting on homosexual behavior; instead, he is generally showing that people are guilty of sin when they abandon themselves to their desires and pleasures and ignore God.

but they became futile in their thinking, and their senseless minds were darkened. ²²Claiming to be wise, they became fools; ²³and they exchanged the glory of the immortal God for images resembling a mortal human being or birds or four-footed animals or reptiles.

24 Therefore God gave them up in the lusts of their hearts to impurity, to the degrading of their bodies among themselves, ²⁵because they exchanged the truth about God for a lie and worshiped and served the creature rather than the Creator, who is blessed forever! Amen.

26 For this reason God gave them up to degrading passions. Their women exchanged natural intercourse for unnatural, ²⁷and in the same way also the men, giving up natural intercourse with women, were consumed with passion for one another. Men committed shameless acts with men and received in their own persons the due penalty for their error.

28 And since they did not see fit to acknowledge God, God gave them up to a debased mind and to things that should not be done. ²⁹They were filled with every kind of wickedness, evil, covetousness, malice. Full of envy, murder, strife, deceit, craftiness, they are gossips, ³⁰slanderers, God-haters,ᵃ insolent, haughty, boastful, inventors of evil, rebel-

PRAY IT!

Judge and Be Judged · Romans 2:1–4, 9–11

It's so easy to see the sin of others and ignore our own. But Paul tells us that when we pass judgment on others, we condemn ourselves because we are doing the same thing. God's kindness is meant to show us our own sin and turn us to God for forgiveness. That forgiveness is offered to everyone. Ask yourself:

• Have you been patient with people around you?

• Have you offered forgiveness to those who have hurt you?

• Have you had the courage to admit when you are wrong?

• Have you treated your parents, brothers, and sisters with respect?

• Have you been sensitive to the feelings and needs of people around you?

• Have you tried to become more aware of how your actions contribute to larger social problems such as hunger, poverty, and damage to the environment?

Close with this prayer:

God, you're loving and forgiving. Help me to be aware of those times when I think I've earned the right to judge others. Paul reminds us that we're all guilty of sin and in need of your grace. Please forgive me, God, because I have sinned. Help me recognize the generosity of your forgiveness and love. Help me also to have strength and courage to follow the ways of your Son, Jesus. Amen.

ᵃ Or *God-hated*

lious toward parents, ³¹foolish, faithless, heartless, ruthless. ³²They know God's decree, that those who practice such things deserve to die—yet they not only do them but even applaud others who practice them.

2　The Righteous Judgment of God

Therefore you have no excuse, whoever you are, when you judge others; for in passing judgment on another you condemn yourself, because you, the judge, are doing the very same things. ²You say,^a "We know that God's judgment on those who do such things is in accordance with truth." ³Do you imagine, whoever you are, that when you judge those who do such things and yet do them yourself, you will escape the judgment of God? ⁴Or do you despise the riches of his kindness and forbearance and patience? Do you not realize that God's kindness is meant to lead you to repentance? ⁵But by your hard and impenitent heart you are storing up wrath for yourself on the day of wrath, when God's righteous judgment will be revealed. ⁶For he will repay according to each one's deeds: ⁷to those who by patiently doing good seek for glory and honor and immortality, he will give eternal life; ⁸while for those who are self-seeking and who obey not the truth but wickedness, there will be wrath and fury. ⁹There will be anguish and distress for everyone who does evil, the Jew first and also the Greek, ¹⁰but glory and honor and peace for everyone who does good, the Jew first and also the Greek. ¹¹For God shows no partiality.

12 All who have sinned apart from the law will also perish apart from the law, and all who have sinned under the law will be judged by the law. ¹³For it is not the hearers of the law who are righteous in God's sight, but the doers of the law who will be justified. ¹⁴When Gentiles, who do not possess the law, do instinctively what the law requires, these, though not having the law, are a law to themselves. ¹⁵They show that what the law requires is written on their hearts, to which their own conscience also bears witness; and their conflicting thoughts will accuse or perhaps excuse them ¹⁶on the day when, according to my gospel, God, through Jesus Christ, will judge the secret thoughts of all.

The Jews and the Law

17　But if you call yourself a Jew and rely on the law and boast of your relation to God ¹⁸and know his will and determine what is best because you are

STUDY IT!

Circumcision, Law, and Faith
Romans 2:25–29

For cultural and sometimes medical reasons, circumcision is practiced today in some parts of the world, including North America. But in biblical times, it was a spiritual practice. It was the sign of the covenant (agreement) between Israel and God (Genesis 17:2). As Gentiles became Christians, many Jewish Christians claimed that all new Christians had to live by Jewish religious laws, including circumcision.

Paul consistently insists that such rituals are not necessary for Gentile converts. He says "real circumcision is a matter of the heart" (Romans 2:29), which leads to "faith working through love" (Galatians 5:6). Later Paul sheds more light on this by using Abraham as an example. Abraham was considered the father of the Jewish faith. He was made righteous by God before he was circumcised (Romans 4:10). Why? Because of his strong and heroic faith in God. Christians are called to this kind of faith in God, whose plan of salvation is now fully revealed in Jesus.

instructed in the law, ¹⁹and if you are sure that you are a guide to the blind, a light to those who are in darkness, ²⁰a corrector of the foolish, a teacher of children, having in the law the embodiment of knowledge and truth, ²¹you, then, that teach others, will you not teach yourself? While you preach against stealing, do you steal? ²²You that forbid adultery, do you commit adultery? You that abhor idols, do you rob temples? ²³You that boast in the law, do you dishonor God by breaking the law? ²⁴For, as it is written, "The name of God is blasphemed among the Gentiles because of you."

25 Circumcision indeed is of value if you obey the law; but if you break the law, your circumcision has become uncircumcision. ²⁶So, if those who are uncircumcised keep the requirements of the law,

will not their uncircumcision be regarded as circumcision? ²⁷Then those who are physically uncircumcised but keep the law will condemn you that have the written code and circumcision but break the law. ²⁸For a person is not a Jew who is one outwardly, nor is true circumcision something external and physical. ²⁹Rather, a person is a Jew who is one inwardly, and real circumcision is a matter of the heart—it is spiritual and not literal. Such a person receives praise not from others but from God.

3 Then what advantage has the Jew? Or what is the value of circumcision? ²Much, in every way. For in the first place the Jews^a were entrusted with the oracles of God. ³What if some were unfaithful? Will their faithlessness nullify the faithfulness of God? ⁴By no means! Although everyone is a liar, let God be proved true, as it is written,

"So that you may be justified in your words,
and prevail in your judging."^b

⁵But if our injustice serves to confirm the justice of God, what should we say? That God is unjust to inflict wrath on us? (I speak in a human way.) ⁶By no means! For then how could God judge the world?

⁷But if through my falsehood God's truthfulness abounds to his glory, why am I still being condemned as a sinner? ⁸And why not say (as some people slander us by saying that we say), "Let us do evil so that good may come"? Their condemnation is deserved!

None Is Righteous

9 What then? Are we any better off?^c No, not at all; for we have already charged that all, both Jews and Greeks, are under the power of sin, ¹⁰as it is written:

"There is no one who is righteous, not
even one;

¹¹ there is no one who has understanding,
there is no one who seeks God.

¹² All have turned aside, together they have
become worthless;

there is no one who shows kindness,
there is not even one."

¹³ "Their throats are opened graves;
they use their tongues to deceive."

"The venom of vipers is under their lips."

¹⁴ "Their mouths are full of cursing and
bitterness."

STUDY IT!

The Law, Faith, and Justification · Romans 3

Paul spends a lot of time explaining the relationship between the law, faith, and justification (righteousness). He shows that the Jewish law of the Old Testament can't save us from the effect of sin (Romans 2:17-3:8). But he recognizes the value of the law (Romans 3:31). The law was the expression of the Jewish people's covenant relationship with God and each other.

We often think of sin as breaking God's law. But at its core, sin is really breaking our relationship with God and distancing ourselves from God. Remember what Adam and Eve did after their first sin? They hid from God, ashamed of their action. Paul is clear that we're all guilty of sin. Separated from God, the source of all life, we would eventually die without God's help. But God is always seeking us out. The ultimate act of love was God sending Jesus to reconnect the break in our relationship caused by sin. Jesus' life, death, resurrection, and ascension show us that God's great love is far more powerful than any sin we can commit.

Paul uses the word "justification" to explain the process that brings us back into a good relationship with God. It's a state of being right with God and being connected rather than separated from God.

How are we justified or considered righteous? Not by our ability to keep any laws—but by God's free gift to those who have faith in Christ. God's justification has the opposite effect of sin. Sin creates distance, but Christ draws us close. Sin kills, but Christ gives life. Sin produces hate and misery, but Christ brings love and peace.

a Gk *they* b Gk *when you are being judged* c Or *at any disadvantage?*

15 "Their feet are swift to shed blood;
16   ruin and misery are in their paths,
17 and the way of peace they have not known."
18   "There is no fear of God before their eyes."

19 Now we know that whatever the law says, it speaks to those who are under the law, so that every mouth may be silenced, and the whole world may be held accountable to God. 20For "no human being will be justified in his sight" by deeds prescribed by the law, for through the law comes the knowledge of sin.

Righteousness through Faith

21 But now, apart from law, the righteousness of God has been disclosed, and is attested by the law and the prophets, 22the righteousness of God through faith in Jesus Christ*a* for all who believe. For there is no distinction, 23since all have sinned and fall short of the glory of God; 24they are now justified by his grace as a gift, through the redemption that is in Christ Jesus, 25whom God put forward as a sacrifice of atonement*b* by his blood, effective through faith. He did this to show his righteousness, because in his divine forbearance he had passed over the sins previously committed; 26it was to prove at the present time that he himself is righteous and that he justifies the one who has faith in Jesus.*c*

27 Then what becomes of boasting? It is excluded. By what law? By that of works? No, but by the law of faith. 28For we hold that a person is justified by faith apart from works prescribed by the law. 29Or is God the God of Jews only? Is he not the God of Gentiles also? Yes, of Gentiles also, 30since God is one; and he will justify the circumcised on the ground of faith and the uncircumcised through that same faith. 31Do we then overthrow the law by this faith? By no means! On the contrary, we uphold the law.

The Example of Abraham

4 What then are we to say was gained by*d* Abraham, our ancestor according to the flesh? 2For if Abraham was justified by works, he has something to boast about, but not before God. 3For what does the scripture say? "Abraham believed God, and it was reckoned to him as righteousness." 4Now to one who works, wages are not reckoned as a gift but as something due. 5But to one who without works trusts him who justifies the ungodly, such faith is reckoned as righteousness. 6So also David speaks of the blessedness of those to whom God reckons righteousness apart from works:

7 "Blessed are those whose iniquities are
         forgiven,
      and whose sins are covered;
8 blessed is the one against whom the Lord will
         not reckon sin."

9 Is this blessedness, then, pronounced only on the circumcised, or also on the uncircumcised? We say, "Faith was reckoned to Abraham as righteousness." 10How then was it reckoned to him? Was it before or after he had been circumcised? It was not after, but before he was circumcised. 11He received the sign of circumcision as a seal of the righteousness that he had by faith while he was still uncircumcised. The purpose was to make him the ancestor of all who believe without being circumcised and who thus have righteousness reckoned to them, 12and likewise the ancestor of the circumcised who are not only circumcised but who also follow the example of the faith that our ancestor Abraham had before he was circumcised.

God's Promise Realized through Faith

13 For the promise that he would inherit the world did not come to Abraham or to his descendants through the law but through the righteousness of faith. 14If it is the adherents of the law who are to be the heirs, faith is null and the promise is void. 15For the law brings wrath; but where there is no law, neither is there violation.

16 For this reason it depends on faith, in order that the promise may rest on grace and be guaranteed to all his descendants, not only to the adherents of the law but also to those who share the faith of Abraham (for he is the father of all of us, 17as it is written, "I have made you the father of many nations")—in the presence of the God in whom he believed, who gives life to the dead and calls into

---

a Or *through the faith of Jesus Christ* b Or *a place of atonement* c Or *who has the faith of Jesus* d Other ancient authorities read *say about*

existence the things that do not exist. [18]Hoping against hope, he believed that he would become "the father of many nations," according to what was said, "So numerous shall your descendants be." [19]He did not weaken in faith when he considered his own body, which was already[a] as good as dead (for he was about a hundred years old), or when he considered the barrenness of Sarah's womb. [20]No distrust made him waver concerning the promise of God, but he grew strong in his faith as he gave glory to God, [21]being fully convinced that God was able to do what he had promised. [22]Therefore his faith[b] "was reckoned to him as righteousness." [23]Now the words, "it was reckoned to him," were written not for his sake alone, [24]but for ours also. It will be reckoned to us who believe in him who raised Jesus our Lord from the dead, [25]who was handed over to death for our trespasses and was raised for our justification.

Results of Justification

5 Therefore, since we are justified by faith, we[c] have peace with God through our Lord Jesus Christ, [2]through whom we have obtained access[d] to this grace in which we stand; and we[e] boast in our hope of sharing the glory of God. [3]And not only that, but we[e] also boast in our sufferings, knowing that suffering produces endurance, [4]and endurance produces character, and character produces hope, [5]and hope does not disappoint us, because God's love has been poured into our hearts through the Holy Spirit that has been given to us.

6 For while we were still weak, at the right time Christ died for the ungodly. [7]Indeed, rarely will anyone die for a righteous person—though perhaps for a good person someone might actually dare to die. [8]But God proves his love for us in that while we still were sinners Christ died for us. [9]Much more surely then, now that we have been justified by his blood, will we be saved through him from the wrath of God.[f] [10]For if while we were enemies, we were reconciled to God through the death of his Son, much more surely, having been reconciled, will we be saved by his life. [11]But more than that, we even boast in God through our Lord Jesus Christ, through whom we have now received reconciliation.

Adam and Christ

12 Therefore, just as sin came into the world through one man, and death came through sin, and so death spread to all because all have sinned— [13]sin was indeed in the world before the law, but sin is not reckoned when there is no law. [14]Yet death exercised dominion from Adam to Moses, even over those whose sins were not like the transgression of Adam, who is a type of the one who was to come.

> "We also boast in our sufferings, knowing that suffering produces endurance, and endurance produces character, and character produces hope, and hope does not disappoint us."
> —Romans 5:3–5

LIVE IT!

Trusting the Grace of God · Romans 5:1–11

A mother pushes her son out of the path of a speeding car, but she is hit and dies. A stranger jumps into a surging river to save a young girl, but he loses his own life. A firefighter is killed battling a blaze to rescue three trapped people. Their concern for others leads these real-life heroes to make the ultimate sacrifice.

Like the son, the young girl, and the three trapped people, we too have been saved from death at a great cost—Jesus' loving sacrifice in obedience to God's will. Paul reminds us that our reconciliation with God (our justification) isn't a reward we deserve for being good. It's God's free gift of love despite our weakness and sin. And that is grace. Don't put your faith in your own ability to please God, but put your faith in God's abundant grace.

---

a Other ancient authorities lack *already* **b** Gk *Therefore it* **c** Other ancient authorities read *let us* **d** Other ancient authorities add *by faith* **e** Or *let us* **f** Gk *the wrath*

15 But the free gift is not like the trespass. For if the many died through the one man's trespass, much more surely have the grace of God and the free gift in the grace of the one man, Jesus Christ, abounded for the many. [16]And the free gift is not like the effect of the one man's sin. For the judgment following one trespass brought condemnation, but the free gift following many trespasses brings justification. [17]If, because of the one man's trespass, death exercised dominion through that one, much more surely will those who receive the abundance of grace and the free gift of righteousness exercise dominion in life through the one man, Jesus Christ.

18 Therefore just as one man's trespass led to condemnation for all, so one man's act of righteousness leads to justification and life for all. [19]For just as by the one man's disobedience the many were made sinners, so by the one man's obedience the many will be made righteous. [20]But law came in, with the result that the trespass multiplied; but where sin increased, grace abounded all the more, [21]so that, just as sin exercised dominion in death, so grace might also exercise dominion through justification[a] leading to eternal life through Jesus Christ our Lord.

Dying and Rising with Christ

6 What then are we to say? Should we continue in sin in order that grace may abound? [2]By no means! How can we who died to sin go on living in it? [3]Do you not know that all of us who have been baptized into Christ Jesus were baptized into his death? [4]Therefore we have been buried with him by baptism into death, so that, just as Christ was raised from the dead by the glory of the Father, so we too might walk in newness of life.

5 For if we have been united with him in a death like his, we will certainly be united with him in a resurrection like his. [6]We know that our old self was crucified with him so that the body of sin might be destroyed, and we might no longer be enslaved to sin. [7]For whoever has died is freed from sin. [8]But if we have died with Christ, we believe that we will also live with him. [9]We know that Christ, being raised from the dead, will never die again; death no longer has dominion over him. [10]The death he died, he died to sin, once for all; but the life he lives, he lives to God. [11]So you also must consider yourselves dead to sin and alive to God in Christ Jesus.

12 Therefore, do not let sin exercise dominion in your mortal bodies, to make you obey their passions.

[13]No longer present your members to sin as instruments[b] of wickedness, but present yourselves to God as those who have been brought from death to life, and present your members to God as instruments[b] of righteousness. [14]For sin will have no dominion over you, since you are not under law but under grace.

Slaves of Righteousness

15 What then? Should we sin because we are not under law but under grace? By no means! [16]Do you not know that if you present yourselves to anyone as obedient slaves, you are slaves of the one whom you obey, either of sin, which leads to death, or of obedience, which leads to righteousness? [17]But thanks be to God that you, having once been slaves of sin, have become obedient from the heart to the form of teaching to which you were entrusted, [18]and that you, having been set free from sin, have become

PRAY IT!

New Life
Romans 6

In **Romans 6**, Paul tells us that we die to sin and receive new life in Jesus Christ—who died for the forgiveness of all sin and rose from the dead. We are no longer enslaved to sin when we trust in Jesus.

He shares, "The end is eternal life. For the wages of sin is death, but the free gift of God is eternal life in Christ Jesus our Lord" (Romans 6:22-23). Let the message of this passage fill you. Feel God's liberating grace inside you. Never forget that this isn't something you must strive for—God has already restored you to a right relationship with him. Reflect on this passage, closing with this prayer:

Loving God, I confess that I have sinned. My actions have hurt others and myself. Help me to do better, to learn from my mistakes, and to model my life on the ways of Jesus. Please help me to understand better the many gifts you have offered me. Amen.

---

a Or *righteousness*　*b* Or *weapons*

PRAY IT!

I'm Not Perfect · Romans 6:15–7:6

If God has already forgiven me, why should I worry about sinning? It's easy to think that way—today and during Paul's time (see Romans 6:15). But this passage reminds us that faith in Christ should be a matter of the heart, not simply a robotlike commitment. Our love for Christ should make us want to live in the light, free from sin, in the same way a married couple's love calls them to commit to each other (Romans 7:2). Why would we want to return to things that bring death to the soul (Romans 6:21)?

But sin is still a constant challenge even when we commit to follow Jesus. Paul encourages us to keep our focus on God and refrain from sin even in the face of temptation. When you are faced with temptation, pray and ask God to help you follow Jesus' example:

Jesus, you experienced temptation throughout your ministry. But you always made the decision to avoid sin and live in the light. I'm committed to following you. Give me the strength to overcome temptations and avoid sin. Please forgive me and help me find the right path again, if I let my sin and passions steer me in the wrong direction. Amen.

slaves of righteousness. [19]I am speaking in human terms because of your natural limitations.[a] For just as you once presented your members as slaves to impurity and to greater and greater iniquity, so now present your members as slaves to righteousness for sanctification.

20 When you were slaves of sin, you were free in regard to righteousness. [21]So what advantage did you then get from the things of which you now are ashamed? The end of those things is death. [22]But now that you have been freed from sin and enslaved to God, the advantage you get is sanctification. The end is eternal life. [23]For the wages of sin is death, but the free gift of God is eternal life in Christ Jesus our Lord.

An Analogy from Marriage

7 Do you not know, brothers and sisters[b]— for I am speaking to those who know the law—that the law is binding on a person only during that person's lifetime? [2]Thus a married woman is bound by the law to her husband as long as he lives; but if her husband dies, she is discharged from the law concerning the husband. [3]Accordingly, she will be called an adulteress if she lives with another man while her husband is alive. But if her husband dies, she is free from that law, and if she marries another man, she is not an adulteress.

4 In the same way, my friends,[b] you have died to the law through the body of Christ, so that you may belong to another, to him who has been raised from the dead in order that we may bear fruit for God. [5]While we were living in the flesh, our sinful passions, aroused by the law, were at work in our members to bear fruit for death. [6]But now we are discharged from the law, dead to that which held us captive, so that we are slaves not under the old written code but in the new life of the Spirit.

The Law and Sin

7 What then should we say? That the law is sin? By no means! Yet, if it had not been for the law, I would not have known sin. I would not have known what it is to covet if the law had not said, "You shall not covet." [8]But sin, seizing an opportunity in the commandment, produced in me all kinds of covetousness. Apart from the law sin lies dead. [9]I was once alive apart from the law, but when the commandment came, sin revived [10]and I died, and the very commandment that promised life proved to be death to me. [11]For sin, seizing an opportunity in the commandment, deceived me and through it killed me. [12]So the law is holy, and the commandment is holy and just and good.

13 Did what is good, then, bring death to me? By no means! It was sin, working death in me through what is good, in order that sin might be shown to be sin, and through the commandment might become sinful beyond measure.

The Inner Conflict

14 For we know that the law is spiritual; but I am

---

a Gk *the weakness of your flesh* **b** Gk *brothers*

LIVE IT!

Our Inner Struggle
Romans 7:13–25

In **Romans 7:15–16**, Paul reveals his own struggle to do what's right.

It seems there's a part of us that wants to do right, and another part that wants to do wrong. Even when we try to be good, "evil lies close at hand" (Romans 7:21), ready to have its way.

Paul uses the words "spirit" and "flesh" to describe this struggle. He says our flesh tempts us to do wrong, and our spirit wants us to do right. Paul doesn't mean that our physical bodies are evil and the source of sin; he means that we're all at war with ourselves.

Sin is hard to resist sometimes. Doing what's right requires us to stop and think clearly about our choices and to choose good over sin. The good news is that God, the understanding forgiver, is on our side in the struggle.

- What struggles feel like a tug-of-war inside you? What temptations keep dragging you down?
- For what sins do you need to accept God's freedom from shame and judgment?

of the flesh, sold into slavery under sin.*a* ¹⁵I do not understand my own actions. For I do not do what I want, but I do the very thing I hate. ¹⁶Now if I do what I do not want, I agree that the law is good. ¹⁷But in fact it is no longer I that do it, but sin that dwells within me. ¹⁸For I know that nothing good dwells within me, that is, in my flesh. I can will what is right, but I cannot do it. ¹⁹For I do not do the good I want, but the evil I do not want is what I do. ²⁰Now if I do what I do not want, it is no longer I that do it, but sin that dwells within me.

21 So I find it to be a law that when I want to do what is good, evil lies close at hand. ²²For I delight in the law of God in my inmost self, ²³but I see in my members another law at war with the law of my mind, making me captive to the law of sin that dwells in my members. ²⁴Wretched man that I am! Who will rescue me from this body of death? ²⁵Thanks be to God through Jesus Christ our Lord!

So then, with my mind I am a slave to the law of God, but with my flesh I am a slave to the law of sin.

8 Life in the Spirit

There is therefore now no condemnation for those who are in Christ Jesus. ²For the law of the Spirit*b* of life in Christ Jesus has set you*c* free from the law of sin and of death. ³For God has done what the law, weakened by the flesh, could not do: by sending his own Son in the likeness of sinful flesh, and to deal with sin,*d* he condemned sin in the flesh, ⁴so that the just requirement of the law might be fulfilled in us, who walk not according to the flesh but according to the Spirit.*b* ⁵For those who live according to the flesh set their minds on the things of the flesh, but those who live according to the Spirit*b* set their minds on the things of the Spirit.*b* ⁶To set the mind on the flesh is death, but to set the mind on the Spirit*b* is life and peace. ⁷For this reason the mind that is set on the flesh is hostile to God; it does not submit to God's law—indeed it cannot, ⁸and those who are in the flesh cannot please God.

9 But you are not in the flesh; you are in the Spirit,*b* since the Spirit of God dwells in you. Anyone who does not have the Spirit of Christ does not belong to him. ¹⁰But if Christ is in you, though the body is dead because of sin, the Spirit*b* is life because of righteousness. ¹¹If the Spirit of him who raised Jesus from the dead dwells in you, he who raised Christ*e* from the dead will give life to your mortal bodies also through*f* his Spirit that dwells in you.

12 So then, brothers and sisters,*g* we are debtors, not to the flesh, to live according to the flesh— ¹³for if you live according to the flesh, you will die; but if by the Spirit you put to death the deeds of the body, you will live. ¹⁴For all who are led by the Spirit of God are children of God. ¹⁵For you did not receive a spirit of slavery to fall back into fear, but you have received a spirit of adoption. When we cry, "Abba!*h* Father!" ¹⁶it is that very Spirit bearing witness*i* with our spirit that we are children of God, ¹⁷and if children, then heirs, heirs of God and joint heirs with Christ—if, in fact, we suffer with him so that we may also be glorified with him.

a Gk *sold under sin* **b** Or *spirit* **c** Here the Greek word *you* is singular number; other ancient authorities read *me* or *us* **d** Or *and as a sin offering* **e** Other ancient authorities read *the Christ* or *Christ Jesus* or *Jesus Christ* **f** Other ancient authorities read *on account of* **g** Gk *brothers* **h** Aramaic for *Father* **i** Or ¹⁵*a spirit of adoption, by which we cry, "Abba! Father!"* ¹⁶*The Spirit itself bears witness*

Future Glory

18 I consider that the sufferings of this present time are not worth comparing with the glory about to be revealed to us. ^{19}For the creation waits with eager longing for the revealing of the children of God; ^{20}for the creation was subjected to futility, not of its own will but by the will of the one who subjected it, in hope ^{21}that the creation itself will be set free from its bondage to decay and will obtain the freedom of the glory of the children of God. ^{22}We know that the whole creation has been groaning in labor pains until now; ^{23}and not only the creation, but we ourselves, who have the first fruits of the Spirit, groan inwardly while we wait for adop-tion, the redemption of our bodies. ^{24}For in^a hope we were saved. Now hope that is seen is not hope. For who hopes^b for what is seen? ^{25}But if we hope for what we do not see, we wait for it with patience.

26 Likewise the Spirit helps us in our weakness; for we do not know how to pray as we ought, but that very Spirit intercedes^c with sighs too deep for words. ^{27}And God,^{d} who searches the heart, knows what is the mind of the Spirit, because the Spirit^e intercedes for the saints according to the will of God.^{f}

28 We know that all things work together for good^g for those who love God, who are called according to his purpose. ^{29}For those whom he foreknew he also

> "We know that all things work together for good for those who love God, who are called according to his purpose."
> —Romans 8:28

STUDY IT!

The Holy Spirit · Romans 8:1–17

Do you allow the Holy Spirit to lead your life? What does that even look like? Romans reminds us that through the gift of the Holy Spirit we are all children of God, and as his children we are called to live a life of freedom (Romans 8:2). When we believe in Jesus as our Savior, we become temples, or homes, for God's Spirit (Romans 8:9). The same Spirit who makes us children of God is the one who helps us live out God's will in our lives (Romans 8:14). As we grow in faith, the Holy Spirit is there guiding us and interceding for us when we pray (Romans 8:26).

The Holy Spirit takes various forms throughout the Bible. Understanding these forms can help us understand how the Spirit can guide us in our daily lives. For example:

- The Holy Spirit in the form of a dove symbolizes the end of the flood during the time of Noah (see Genesis 8:8-12) and the descent of God's spirit after Jesus was baptized (see Matthew 3:16). It can serve as a reminder of our own baptism and that we're called to live as followers of Christ.
- The Holy Spirit is seen in the form of a cloud, leading the Israelites on their journey out of slavery toward the promised land (see Exodus 40:34-38), and overshadowing Mary when the angel told her she would be the mother of God's Son (see Luke 1:35). This reminds us that God's Spirit can give us clarity when we have tough decisions to make and can guide us on our journey through life.
- The Holy Spirit is seen in the form of fire, which descended on the disciples at Pentecost and transformed everyone who was present. This can serve as a reminder that God's Spirit is present and transforming our lives today (see Acts 2:3-12).

The same Spirit who is at work in our lives individually is also active in helping and guiding all believers. It's the Holy Spirit who unites us as the body of Christ and empowers us to bring God's message to the world.

---

a Or by b Other ancient authorities read *awaits* c Other ancient authorities add *for us* d Gk *the one* e Gk *he or it* f Gk *according to God* g Other ancient authorities read *God makes all things work together for good*, or *in all things God works for good*

predestined to be conformed to the image of his Son, in order that he might be the firstborn within a large family.*a* 30 And those whom he predestined he also called; and those whom he called he also justified; and those whom he justified he also glorified.

God's Love in Christ Jesus

31 What then are we to say about these things? If God is for us, who is against us? 32 He who did not withhold his own Son, but gave him up for all of us, will he not with him also give us everything else? 33 Who will bring any charge against God's elect? It

PRAY IT!
Absolutely Nothing!
Romans 8:31–39

Have you ever felt that God was out of reach? **Romans 8:31–39** is the encouragement we all need when we doubt God's love for us or feel distant from God. It reminds us that God, who loved us enough to give his own son, won't withhold other good things from us. It also reminds us that absolutely nothing can separate us from God's amazing love.

God, what could separate me from your love? Not a failed test or a broken promise or a hurtful insult.

What could tear you away from me? Not the lure of popularity or unnatural highs.

If you are on my side, who could be against me? Not a vengeful peer or an uncaring date or someone who has turned against me.

What situation could divide you and me, God? Not depression over a loss or anger over being laughed at or guilt from being caught red-handed.

No, in all these things, I know I'm never alone because you, God, conquered sin, despair, and even death itself through your endless love. I'm convinced, Lord, that nothing, absolutely nothing, will ever separate me from your love . . . ever! Amen.

is God who justifies. 34 Who is to condemn? It is Christ Jesus, who died, yes, who was raised, who is at the right hand of God, who indeed intercedes for us.*b* 35 Who will separate us from the love of Christ? Will hardship, or distress, or persecution, or famine, or nakedness, or peril, or sword? 36 As it is written,

> "For your sake we are being killed all day long;
> we are accounted as sheep to be
> slaughtered."

37 No, in all these things we are more than conquerors through him who loved us. 38 For I am convinced that neither death, nor life, nor angels, nor rulers, nor things present, nor things to come, nor powers, 39 nor height, nor depth, nor anything else in all creation, will be able to separate us from the love of God in Christ Jesus our Lord.

9

God's Election of Israel

I am speaking the truth in Christ—I am not lying; my conscience confirms it by the Holy Spirit— 2 I have great sorrow and unceasing anguish in my heart. 3 For I could wish that I myself were accursed and cut off from Christ for the sake of my own people,*c* my kindred according to the flesh. 4 They are Israelites, and to them belong the adoption, the glory, the covenants, the giving of the law, the worship, and the promises; 5 to them belong the patriarchs, and from them, according to the flesh, comes the Messiah,*d* who is over all, God blessed forever.*e* Amen.

6 It is not as though the word of God had failed. For not all Israelites truly belong to Israel, 7 and not all of Abraham's children are his true descendants; but "It is through Isaac that descendants shall be named for you." 8 This means that it is not the children of the flesh who are the children of God, but the children of the promise are counted as descendants. 9 For this is what the promise said, "About this time I will return and Sarah shall have a son." 10 Nor is that all; something similar happened to Rebecca when she had conceived children by one husband, our ancestor Isaac. 11 Even before they had been born or had done anything good or bad (so that God's purpose of election might continue, 12 not by works but by his call) she was told, "The elder shall serve the younger." 13 As it is written,

> "I have loved Jacob,
> but I have hated Esau."

14 What then are we to say? Is there injustice on God's part? By no means! 15 For he says to Moses,

---

a Gk *among many brothers*   *b* Or *Is it Christ Jesus . . . for us?*   *c* Gk *my brothers*   *d* Or *the Christ*   *e* Or *Messiah, who is God over all, blessed forever;* or *Messiah. May he who is God over all be blessed forever*

STUDY IT!

The Fate of Israel · Romans 9–11

Paul takes on a difficult question in **Romans 9–11**: What will happen to Israel (the Jews), God's chosen people, if they reject Jesus? This was an important question without easy answers for the early Jewish Christians, who probably had friends and family members who didn't believe in Jesus.

Paul answers by making several points. In the beginning, he affirms Israel's special place in God's plan of salvation (Romans 9). But the people's righteousness is based on faith, not on fulfilling the law (see "Study It: The Law, Faith, and Justification," near Romans 3). Paul also notes that justification is available for all, even Gentiles (Romans 10).

Paul uses the analogy of grafting branches onto a tree (Romans 11). The Gentiles were grafted, or grown, onto the original tree, which is Israel. Paul warns the Gentile Christians not to think they are better than the Jews. God can remove the Gentiles as easily as he added them. Paul says the Jews can also be grafted back onto that tree (Romans 11:23). In fact, he ends with the hopeful promise in **Romans 11:26** that, after the salvation of the Gentiles, all Israel will be saved!

Paul's teachings are not always easy to understand. But we do know that Jews have played an important role in the faith history of Christians. The ancestry and story of Jesus began with the Jews. Jewish people clearly have held a special place in history. Although we don't know exactly how Paul's promise for the Jews will come about, we can trust in the love and grace of God for the future of the Jews.

"I will have mercy on whom I have mercy,
    and I will have compassion on whom I
        have compassion."
[16]So it depends not on human will or exertion, but on God who shows mercy. [17]For the scripture says to Pharaoh, "I have raised you up for the very purpose of showing my power in you, so that my name may be proclaimed in all the earth." [18]So then he has mercy on whomever he chooses, and he hardens the heart of whomever he chooses.

God's Wrath and Mercy

19 You will say to me then, "Why then does he still find fault? For who can resist his will?" [20]But

who indeed are you, a human being, to argue with God? Will what is molded say to the one who molds it, "Why have you made me like this?"

[21]Has the potter no right over the clay, to make out of the same lump one object for special use and another for ordinary use? [22]What if God, desiring to show his wrath and to make known his power, has endured with much patience the objects of wrath that are made for destruction; [23]and what if he has done so in order to make known the riches of his glory for the objects of mercy, which he has prepared beforehand for glory— [24]including us whom he has called, not from the Jews only but also from the Gentiles? [25]As indeed he says in Hosea,

"Those who were not my people I will call 'my
        people,'
    and her who was not beloved I will call
        'beloved.' "
[26] "And in the very place where it was said to
        them, 'You are not my people,'
    there they shall be called children of the
        living God."

27 And Isaiah cries out concerning Israel, "Though the number of the children of Israel were like the sand of the sea, only a remnant of them will

be saved; [28]for the Lord will execute his sentence on the earth quickly and decisively."[a] [29]And as Isaiah predicted,

"If the Lord of hosts had not left survivors[b]
> to us,
> we would have fared like Sodom
> and been made like Gomorrah."

Israel's Unbelief

30 What then are we to say? Gentiles, who did not strive for righteousness, have attained it, that is, righteousness through faith; [31]but Israel, who did strive for the righteousness that is based on the law, did not succeed in fulfilling that law. [32]Why not? Because they did not strive for it on the basis of faith, but as if it were based on works. They have stumbled over the stumbling stone, [33]as it is written,

"See, I am laying in Zion a stone that will make
> people stumble, a rock that will make
> them fall,
> and whoever believes in him[c] will not be
> put to shame."

10 Brothers and sisters,[d] my heart's desire and prayer to God for them is that they may be saved. [2]I can testify that they have a zeal for God, but it is not enlightened. [3]For, being ignorant of the righteousness that comes from God, and seeking to establish their own, they have not submitted to God's righteousness. [4]For Christ is the end of the law so that there may be righteousness for everyone who believes.

Salvation Is for All

5 Moses writes concerning the righteousness that comes from the law, that "the person who does these things will live by them." [6]But the righteousness that comes from faith says, "Do not say in your heart, 'Who will ascend into heaven?'" (that is, to bring Christ down) [7]"or 'Who will descend into the abyss?'" (that is, to bring Christ up from the dead). [8]But what does it say?

"The word is near you,
> on your lips and in your heart"

(that is, the word of faith that we proclaim); [9]because[e] if you confess with your lips that Jesus is Lord and believe in your heart that God raised him from the dead, you will be saved. [10]For one believes with the heart and so is justified, and one confesses with the mouth and so is saved. [11]The scripture says, "No one who believes in him will be put to shame." [12]For

LIVE IT!

Are Your Feet Beautiful?
Romans 10:11–15

Marketing is big business. It's how companies survive—developing new, amazing ways of grabbing our attention. Think of the last thing you bought. That purchase may have been indirectly influenced by the company's efforts to create an appealing image of the product. Even a company with an amazing product would fail in its mission if no one knew about it.

The Church has what the world needs—the saving power that comes from faith in Jesus Christ. The promise in **Romans 10:11–15** is that all who know and call on the name of Jesus will be saved. God does the saving, but it's our job to get the message out to others. And it's okay to find appealing ways of doing this.

How do others hear about this good news? Paul says it's through us. And he adds, "How beautiful are the feet of those who bring good news!" (Romans 10:15). In other words, action, not just words, is needed to spread the gospel message.

- Who are some of the people who first helped you to know Jesus, and how did they do that?
- In what ways can you show others how important your faith is to you?
- Which of your friends need to hear this good news about Jesus? How can you share your faith with them, perhaps through a message of hope, forgiveness, or encouragement?

there is no distinction between Jew and Greek; the same Lord is Lord of all and is generous to all who call on him. [13]For, "Everyone who calls on the name of the Lord shall be saved."

14 But how are they to call on one in whom they have not believed? And how are they to believe in

---

a Other ancient authorities read *for he will finish his work and cut it short in righteousness, because the Lord will make the sentence shortened on the earth*
b Or *descendants*; Gk *seed*   c Or *trusts in it*   d Gk *Brothers*   e Or *namely, that*

one of whom they have never heard? And how are they to hear without someone to proclaim him? [15]And how are they to proclaim him unless they are sent? As it is written, "How beautiful are the feet of those who bring good news!" [16]But not all have obeyed the good news;[a] for Isaiah says, "Lord, who has believed our message?" [17]So faith comes from what is heard, and what is heard comes through the word of Christ.[b]

18 But I ask, have they not heard? Indeed they have; for

"Their voice has gone out to all the earth,
    and their words to the ends of the world."

[19]Again I ask, did Israel not understand? First Moses says,

"I will make you jealous of those who are not a
    nation;
  with a foolish nation I will make you angry."

[20]Then Isaiah is so bold as to say,

"I have been found by those who did not
    seek me;
I have shown myself to those who did not
    ask for me."

[21]But of Israel he says, "All day long I have held out my hands to a disobedient and contrary people."

11   Israel's Rejection Is Not Final

I ask, then, has God rejected his people? By no means! I myself am an Israelite, a descendant of Abraham, a member of the tribe of Benjamin. [2]God has not rejected his people whom he foreknew. Do you not know what the scripture says of Elijah, how he pleads with God against Israel? [3]"Lord, they have killed your prophets, they have demolished your altars; I alone am left, and they are seeking my life." [4]But what is the divine reply to him? "I have kept for myself seven thousand who have not bowed the knee to Baal." [5]So too at the present time there is a remnant, chosen by grace. [6]But if it is by grace, it is no longer on the basis of works, otherwise grace would no longer be grace.[c]

7 What then? Israel failed to obtain what it was seeking. The elect obtained it, but the rest were hardened, [8]as it is written,

"God gave them a sluggish spirit,
  eyes that would not see
  and ears that would not hear,
down to this very day."

[9]And David says,

"Let their table become a snare and a trap,

a stumbling block and a retribution for
  them;
10 let their eyes be darkened so that they
    cannot see,
  and keep their backs forever bent."

The Salvation of the Gentiles

11 So I ask, have they stumbled so as to fall? By no means! But through their stumbling[d] salvation has come to the Gentiles, so as to make Israel[e] jealous. [12]Now if their stumbling[d] means riches for the world, and if their defeat means riches for Gentiles, how much more will their full inclusion mean!

13 Now I am speaking to you Gentiles. Inasmuch then as I am an apostle to the Gentiles, I glorify my ministry [14]in order to make my own people[f] jealous, and thus save some of them. [15]For if their rejection is the reconciliation of the world, what will their acceptance be but life from the dead! [16]If the part of the dough offered as first fruits is holy, then the whole batch is holy; and if the root is holy, then the branches also are holy.

17 But if some of the branches were broken off, and you, a wild olive shoot, were grafted in their place to share the rich root[g] of the olive tree, [18]do not boast over the branches. If you do boast, remember that it is not you that support the root, but the root that supports you. [19]You will say, "Branches were broken off so that I might be grafted in." [20]That is true. They were broken off because of their unbelief, but you stand only through faith. So do not become proud, but stand in awe. [21]For if God did not spare the natural branches, perhaps he will not spare you.[h] [22]Note then the kindness and the severity of God: severity toward those who have fallen, but God's kindness toward you, provided you continue in his kindness; otherwise you also will be cut off. [23]And even those of Israel,[i] if they do not persist in unbelief, will be grafted in, for God has the power

---

a Or gospel   b Or about Christ; other ancient authorities read of God   c Other ancient authorities add But if it is by works, it is no longer on the basis of grace, otherwise work would no longer be work   d Gk transgression   e Gk them   f Gk my flesh   g Other ancient authorities read the richness   h Other ancient authorities read neither will he spare you   i Gk lacks of Israel

to graft them in again. ²⁴For if you have been cut from what is by nature a wild olive tree and grafted, contrary to nature, into a cultivated olive tree, how much more will these natural branches be grafted back into their own olive tree.

All Israel Will Be Saved

25 So that you may not claim to be wiser than you are, brothers and sisters,^a I want you to understand this mystery: a hardening has come upon part of Israel, until the full number of the Gentiles has come in. ²⁶And so all Israel will be saved; as it is written,

> "Out of Zion will come the Deliverer;
>   he will banish ungodliness from Jacob."

²⁷ "And this is my covenant with them,
     when I take away their sins."

²⁸As regards the gospel they are enemies of God^b for your sake; but as regards election they are beloved, for the sake of their ancestors; ²⁹for the gifts and the calling of God are irrevocable. ³⁰Just as you were once disobedient to God but have now received mercy because of their disobedience, ³¹so they have now been disobedient in order that, by the mercy shown to you, they too may now^c receive mercy. ³²For God has imprisoned all in disobedience so that he may be merciful to all.

33 O the depth of the riches and wisdom and knowledge of God! How unsearchable are his judgments and how inscrutable his ways!
³⁴ "For who has known the mind of the Lord?
     Or who has been his counselor?"
³⁵ "Or who has given a gift to him,
     to receive a gift in return?"
³⁶For from him and through him and to him are all things. To him be the glory forever. Amen.

The New Life in Christ

12 I appeal to you therefore, brothers and sisters,^a by the mercies of God, to present your bodies as a living sacrifice, holy and acceptable to God, which is your spiritual^d worship. ²Do not be conformed to this world,^e but be transformed by the renewing of your minds, so that you may discern what is the will of God—what is good and acceptable and perfect.^f

3 For by the grace given to me I say to everyone among you not to think of yourself more highly than you ought to think, but to think with sober judgment, each according to the measure of faith

We Are the Body of Christ
Romans 12:1–8

We are the body of Christ. That means each of us has a different but important role to play. Imagine the power if all Christians really acted like the living body of Christ in their homes, churches, neighborhoods, countries, and world. So how do we become the body of Christ?

In **Romans 12:1,** Paul calls us to present our bodies to God as living, holy, and acceptable sacrifices. The best thing we can offer to God is our whole life—all we are and all we do—in worship to God.

In **Romans 12:2,** Paul calls us not to be conformed to this world, but to be transformed. We are transformed by renewing our minds. That means we make choices about what we look at, read, and think about—choices that help us focus on what pleases God rather than the messages the world gives. Renewing our minds helps us discern God's good, true, and perfect will.

In **Romans 12:3–8,** Paul explains that each of us has a different role to play. We don't get to choose whether we're the lungs or the heart, but we are to fill a specific role, because the body cannot function without each part. Christians become one body in Christ by recognizing our gifts and working together.

that God has assigned. ⁴For as in one body we have many members, and not all the members have the same function, ⁵so we, who are many, are one body in Christ, and individually we are members one of another. ⁶We have gifts that differ according to the grace given to us: prophecy, in proportion to faith; ⁷ministry, in ministering; the teacher, in teaching; ⁸the exhorter, in exhortation; the giver, in generosity; the leader, in diligence; the compassionate, in cheerfulness.

---

a Gk brothers **b** Gk lacks of God **c** Other ancient authorities lack now **d** Or reasonable **e** Gk age **f** Or what is the good and acceptable and perfect will of God

LIVE IT!

Becoming a Peacemaker · Romans 12:17–19

What is your natural response when someone mistreats you? Revenge? In **Romans 12:17–19**, Paul tells us we should never try to avenge wrong against us—God will take care of it in God's own time. Paul goes on to remind us of Jesus' teaching to treat our enemies with kindness. Easier said than done! It's tough to respond with good when we are hurt.

So can it be done? Not perfectly, but there are people who have lived out the idea of living peaceably (for example, see "Connect It: Martin Luther King Jr.: Unseen Freedom," near Deuteronomy 34:4–5; "Connect It: Mother Teresa: Living Out God's Love," near Micah 6:8; and "Connect It: Desmond Tutu: Standing for Truth, Calling for Freedom," near John 8:31–32). But there are also countless unnamed people in our world who respond to hurt with love and respond to assault with peace. Maybe you know some people in your own community who have made similar commitments.

- Think of the people you know. Who are the peacemakers in your life?
- How can you follow the example of these people in your own family, school, or community?

Marks of the True Christian

9 Let love be genuine; hate what is evil, hold fast to what is good; [10]love one another with mutual affection; outdo one another in showing honor. [11]Do not lag in zeal, be ardent in spirit, serve the Lord.[a] [12]Rejoice in hope, be patient in suffering, persevere in prayer. [13]Contribute to the needs of the saints; extend hospitality to strangers.

14 Bless those who persecute you; bless and do not curse them. [15]Rejoice with those who rejoice, weep with those who weep. [16]Live in harmony with one another; do not be haughty, but associate with the lowly;[b] do not claim to be wiser than you are. [17]Do not repay anyone evil for evil, but take thought for what is noble in the sight of all. [18]If it is possible, so far as it depends on you, live peaceably with all. [19]Beloved, never avenge yourselves, but leave room for the wrath of God;[c] for it is written, "Vengeance is mine, I will repay, says the Lord." [20]No, "if your enemies are hungry, feed them; if they are thirsty, give them something to drink; for by doing this you will heap burning coals on their heads." [21]Do not be overcome by evil, but overcome evil with good.

Being Subject to Authorities

13 Let every person be subject to the governing authorities; for there is no authority except from God, and those authorities that exist have been instituted by God. [2]Therefore whoever resists authority resists what God has appointed, and those who resist will incur judgment. [3]For rulers are not a terror to good conduct, but to bad. Do you wish to have no fear of the authority? Then do what is good, and you will receive its approval; [4]for it is God's servant for your good. But if you do what is wrong, you should be afraid, for the authority[d] does not bear the sword in vain! It is the servant of God to execute wrath on the wrongdoer. [5]Therefore one must be subject, not only because of wrath but also because of conscience. [6]For the same reason you also pay taxes, for the authorities are God's servants, busy with this very thing. [7]Pay to all what is due them—taxes to whom taxes are due, revenue to whom revenue is due, respect to whom respect is due, honor to whom honor is due.

Love for One Another

8 Owe no one anything, except to love one another; for the one who loves another has fulfilled the law. [9]The commandments, "You shall not commit adultery; You shall not murder; You shall not steal; You shall not covet"; and any other commandment, are summed up in this word, "Love your neighbor as yourself." [10]Love does no wrong to a neighbor; therefore, love is the fulfilling of the law.

An Urgent Appeal

11 Besides this, you know what time it is, how it is now the moment for you to wake from sleep. For salvation is nearer to us now than when we became

a Other ancient authorities read *serve the opportune time* b Or *give yourselves to humble tasks* c Gk *the wrath* d Gk *it*

PRAY IT!

Real Love
Romans 13:8–10

Sometimes faith can feel like a list of things we can't do. But that's not the faith Jesus taught! Paul reminds us again that all of the commandments can be kept by following the one that says, "Love your neighbor as yourself" (Romans 13:9). It's a simple rule, but not always so simple to live by.

Lord, why is it so hard to love? Love is mentioned so much in the Bible that it makes me wonder why we don't get it. It seems that we're good at talking about love, but not so good at living love. We easily see where there is no love, but it sure is hard to bring love where it's needed. Jesus, fill me with your love to share with others—the kind of love that changes people forever, breaks down barriers, overcomes fears, and gives without counting the costs. Amen.

believers; [12] the night is far gone, the day is near. Let us then lay aside the works of darkness and put on the armor of light; [13] let us live honorably as in the day, not in reveling and drunkenness, not in debauchery and licentiousness, not in quarreling and jealousy. [14] Instead, put on the Lord Jesus Christ, and make no provision for the flesh, to gratify its desires.

14 Do Not Judge Another

Welcome those who are weak in faith,[a] but not for the purpose of quarreling over opinions. [2] Some believe in eating anything, while the weak eat only vegetables. [3] Those who eat must not despise those who abstain, and those who abstain must not pass judgment on those who eat; for God has welcomed them. [4] Who are you to pass judgment on servants of another? It is before their own lord that they stand or fall. And they will be upheld, for the Lord[b] is able to make them stand.

5 Some judge one day to be better than another, while others judge all days to be alike. Let all be fully convinced in their own minds. [6] Those who observe the day, observe it in honor of the Lord. Also those who eat, eat in honor of the Lord, since they give thanks to God; while those who abstain, abstain in honor of the Lord and give thanks to God.

7 We do not live to ourselves, and we do not die to ourselves. [8] If we live, we live to the Lord, and if we die, we die to the Lord; so then, whether we live or whether we die, we are the Lord's. [9] For to this end Christ died and lived again, so that he might be Lord of both the dead and the living.

10 Why do you pass judgment on your brother or sister?[c] Or you, why do you despise your brother or sister?[c] For we will all stand before the judgment seat of God.[d] [11] For it is written,

"As I live, says the Lord, every knee shall bow to me,
and every tongue shall give praise to[e] God."

[12] So then, each of us will be accountable to God.[f]

Do Not Make Another Stumble

13 Let us therefore no longer pass judgment on one another, but resolve instead never to put a stumbling block or hindrance in the way of another.[g] [14] I know and am persuaded in the Lord Jesus that nothing is unclean in itself; but it is unclean for anyone who thinks it unclean. [15] If your brother or sister[c] is being injured by what you eat, you are no longer walking in love. Do not let what you eat cause the ruin of one for whom Christ died. [16] So do not let your good be spoken of as evil. [17] For the kingdom of God is not food and drink but righteousness and peace and joy in the Holy Spirit. [18] The one who thus serves Christ is acceptable to God and has human approval. [19] Let us then pursue what makes for peace and for mutual upbuilding. [20] Do not, for the sake of food, destroy the work of God. Everything is indeed clean, but it is wrong for you to make others fall by what you eat; [21] it is good not to eat meat or drink wine or do anything that makes your brother or sister[c] stumble.[h] [22] The faith that you have, have as your own conviction before God. Blessed are those who have no reason to condemn themselves because of what they approve. [23] But those who have doubts are condemned if they eat, because they do not act from faith;[a] for whatever does not proceed from faith[a] is sin.[i]

---

a Or *conviction* b Other ancient authorities read *for God* c Gk *brother* d Other ancient authorities read *of Christ* e Or *confess* f Other ancient authorities lack *to God* g Gk *of a brother* h Other ancient authorities add *or be upset or be weakened* i Other authorities, some ancient, add here 16.25-27

Just a Little Respect · Romans 14

Worship band or choir? Formal dress or casual? Grape juice or wine? The smallest issues can become dividing points for Christians and whole churches. And this isn't a new problem. In **Romans 14:2, 5,** Paul has heard that the Christians in Rome disagree about what to eat and what days to set apart as holy. He tells them not to fight over these differences. Whatever they do, they should do it "in honor of the Lord" (Romans 14:6). Paul says that in these small issues, the most important thing is our motivation. We are to do what we believe is right and pleasing to God, and we are not to judge others when they act differently.

But Paul does give one restriction. He says that whatever we do should not "cause the ruin of one for whom Christ died" (Romans 14:15). That means we should respect others by avoiding actions that cause a problem for someone else—even if those actions aren't wrong. For example, if you feel that a certain movie is okay, but you know a friend who has issues with it, don't plan to play that movie at the next party you both attend. Or if you have a friend who has chosen not to listen to certain kinds of music, don't play that kind in the car when you're driving together. Instead, limit your own freedom, so that you don't cause a problem for someone else. By doing this, followers of Christ avoid wasting energy on arguing and instead spend their time helping others discover and know the love of Jesus.

- In what situations is it most difficult for you to give up your freedom in order to respect someone else?
- Think of the last time you disagreed with a friend over whether something was acceptable or not. How did you handle it? How could you have handled it better?

Please Others, Not Yourselves

15 We who are strong ought to put up with the failings of the weak, and not to please ourselves. ²Each of us must please our neighbor for the good purpose of building up the neighbor. ³For Christ did not please himself; but, as it is written, "The insults of those who insult you have fallen on me." ⁴For whatever was written in former days was written for our instruction, so that by steadfastness and by the encouragement of the scriptures we might have hope. ⁵May the God of steadfastness and encouragement grant you to live in harmony with one another, in accordance with Christ Jesus, ⁶so that together you may with one voice glorify the God and Father of our Lord Jesus Christ.

The Gospel for Jews and Gentiles Alike

7 Welcome one another, therefore, just as Christ has welcomed you, for the glory of God. ⁸For I tell you that Christ has become a servant of the circumcised on behalf of the truth of God in order that he might confirm the promises given to the patriarchs,

⁹and in order that the Gentiles might glorify God for his mercy. As it is written,

"Therefore I will confess*a* you among the
    Gentiles,
    and sing praises to your name";

¹⁰and again he says,

"Rejoice, O Gentiles, with his people";

¹¹and again,

"Praise the Lord, all you Gentiles,
    and let all the peoples praise him";

¹²and again Isaiah says,

"The root of Jesse shall come,
    the one who rises to rule the Gentiles;
    in him the Gentiles shall hope."

¹³May the God of hope fill you with all joy and peace in believing, so that you may abound in hope by the power of the Holy Spirit.

Paul's Reason for Writing So Boldly

14 I myself feel confident about you, my brothers and sisters,*b* that you yourselves are full of goodness, filled with all knowledge, and able to instruct

a Or *thank*   b Gk *brothers*

one another. [15]Nevertheless on some points I have written to you rather boldly by way of reminder, because of the grace given me by God [16]to be a minister of Christ Jesus to the Gentiles in the priestly service of the gospel of God, so that the offering of the Gentiles may be acceptable, sanctified by the Holy Spirit. [17]In Christ Jesus, then, I have reason to boast of my work for God. [18]For I will not venture to speak of anything except what Christ has accomplished[a] through me to win obedience from the Gentiles, by word and deed, [19]by the power of signs and wonders, by the power of the Spirit of God,[b] so that from Jerusalem and as far around as Illyricum I have fully proclaimed the good news[c] of Christ. [20]Thus I make it my ambition to proclaim the good news,[c] not where Christ has already been named, so that I do not build on someone else's foundation, [21]but as it is written,

"Those who have never been told of him
    shall see,
and those who have never heard of him
    shall understand."

Paul's Plan to Visit Rome

[22] This is the reason that I have so often been hindered from coming to you. [23]But now, with no further place for me in these regions, I desire, as I have for many years, to come to you [24]when I go to Spain. For I do hope to see you on my journey and to be sent on by you, once I have enjoyed your company for a little while. [25]At present, however, I am going to Jerusalem in a ministry to the saints; [26]for Macedonia and Achaia have been pleased to share their resources with the poor among the saints at Jerusalem. [27]They were pleased to do this, and indeed they owe it to them; for if the Gentiles have come to share in their spiritual blessings, they ought also to be of service to them in material things. [28]So, when I have completed this, and have delivered to them what has been collected,[d] I will set out by way of you to Spain; [29]and I know that when I come to you, I will come in the fullness of the blessing[e] of Christ.

[30] I appeal to you, brothers and sisters,[f] by our Lord Jesus Christ and by the love of the Spirit, to join me in earnest prayer to God on my behalf, [31]that I may be rescued from the unbelievers in Judea, and that my ministry[g] to Jerusalem may be acceptable to the saints, [32]so that by God's will I may come to you with joy and be refreshed in your company. [33]The God of peace be with all of you.[h] Amen.

16 Personal Greetings

I commend to you our sister Phoebe, a deacon[i] of the church at Cenchreae, [2]so that you may welcome her in the Lord as is fitting for the saints, and help her in whatever she may require from you, for she has been a benefactor of many and of myself as well.

[3] Greet Prisca and Aquila, who work with me in Christ Jesus, [4]and who risked their necks for my life, to whom not only I give thanks, but also all the churches of the Gentiles. [5]Greet also the church in their house. Greet my beloved Epaenetus, who was the first convert[j] in Asia for Christ. [6]Greet Mary, who has worked very hard among you. [7]Greet An-

STUDY IT!

Introducing . . . Phoebe and Junia
Romans 16:1-16

In Romans 16:1–16, Paul greets almost thirty people and their families in Rome—more people than he greets in any of his other letters. Some experts think maybe he was trying to establish a connection among the Christians in Rome by mentioning mutual acquaintanes. About a third of the people he greets are women, highlighting the important role women played in Paul's ministry and in the leadership of the early Church.

Especially interesting are Paul's comments about Phoebe, whom he calls a deacon, and Junia (also called Julia), whom he declares "prominent among the apostles" (Romans 16:7). In Paul's time, deacons were usually associated with a ministry of service, and apostles with a ministry of leadership. Even though women were not allowed to fill official positions in government or society, the early Church recognized them as being as important as men in service, leadership, and bringing the gospel to others.

---

a Gk *speak of those things that Christ has not accomplished* **b** Other ancient authorities read *of the Spirit* or *of the Holy Spirit* **c** Or *gospel* **d** Gk *have sealed to them this fruit* **e** Other ancient authorities add *of the gospel* **f** Gk *brothers* **g** Other ancient authorities read *my bringing of a gift* **h** One ancient authority adds 16.25-27 here **i** Or *minister* **j** Gk *first fruits*

dronicus and Junia,[a] my relatives[b] who were in prison with me; they are prominent among the apostles, and they were in Christ before I was. [8]Greet Ampliatus, my beloved in the Lord. [9]Greet Urbanus, our co-worker in Christ, and my beloved Stachys. [10]Greet Apelles, who is approved in Christ. Greet those who belong to the family of Aristobulus. [11]Greet my relative[c] Herodion. Greet those in the Lord who belong to the family of Narcissus. [12]Greet those workers in the Lord, Tryphaena and Tryphosa. Greet the beloved Persis, who has worked hard in the Lord. [13]Greet Rufus, chosen in the Lord; and greet his mother—a mother to me also. [14]Greet Asyncritus, Phlegon, Hermes, Patrobas, Hermas, and the brothers and sisters[d] who are with them. [15]Greet Philologus, Julia, Nereus and his sister, and Olympas, and all the saints who are with them. [16]Greet one another with a holy kiss. All the churches of Christ greet you.

Final Instructions

[17] I urge you, brothers and sisters,[d] to keep an eye on those who cause dissensions and offenses, in opposition to the teaching that you have learned; avoid them. [18]For such people do not serve our Lord Christ, but their own appetites,[e] and by smooth talk and flattery they deceive the hearts of the simple-minded. [19]For while your obedience is known to all, so that I rejoice over you, I want you to be wise in what is good and guileless in what is evil. [20]The God of peace will shortly crush Satan under your feet. The grace of our Lord Jesus Christ be with you.[f]

[21] Timothy, my co-worker, greets you; so do Lucius and Jason and Sosipater, my relatives.[b]

[22] I Tertius, the writer of this letter, greet you in the Lord.[g]

[23] Gaius, who is host to me and to the whole church, greets you. Erastus, the city treasurer, and our brother Quartus, greet you.[h]

Final Doxology

[25] Now to God[i] who is able to strengthen you according to my gospel and the proclamation of Jesus Christ, according to the revelation of the mystery that was kept secret for long ages [26]but is now disclosed, and through the prophetic writings is made known to all the Gentiles, according to the command of the eternal God, to bring about the obedience of faith— [27]to the only wise God, through Jesus Christ, to whom[j] be the glory forever! Amen.[k]

---

a Or *Junias*; other ancient authorities read *Julia* **b** Or *compatriots* **c** Or *compatriot* **d** Gk *brothers* **e** Gk *their own belly* **f** Other ancient authorities lack this sentence **g** Or *I Tertius, writing this letter in the Lord, greet you* **h** Other ancient authorities add verse 24, *The grace of our Lord Jesus Christ be with all of you. Amen.* **i** Gk *the one* **j** Other ancient authorities lack *to whom*. The verse then reads, *to the only wise God be the glory through Jesus Christ forever. Amen.* **k** Other ancient authorities lack 16.25-27 or include it after 14.23 or 15.33; others put verse 24 after verse 27

►►► 1 Corinthians

I t's no big secret: churches have problems. You've heard it on the news—power struggles, sex scandals, troubled marriages, bitter disagreements, and alcohol abuse. Maybe you've been part of a Christian community that's had some of these problems. Or maybe you know someone who has. The early Church in Corinth had them all. That's why Paul gave them guidance and encouragement in his first letter to the Corinthians. His words can also help churches today as we try to follow and honor Christ.

Corinth was an important seaport city in what is now southern Greece. It was a center of commerce for people from many cultures. It also had quite a reputation for sexual immorality. Paul established the Christian church in Corinth around A.D. 51 and spent about eighteen months with the new believers there. After Paul left, a man named Apollos came to help the young church grow.

Later, when Paul was in Ephesus, he got a letter from the Corinthian church (1 Corinthians 7:1) and a report from others about them (1 Corinthians 1:11). The church was having problems. The problems were natural in a young Christian community whose members included both Jewish Christians and Gentile (non-Jewish) converts. The community was divided into groups with different leaders. There were some disagreements on how to worship properly, and there were different opinions about eating meat that had been sacrificed to pagan idols. In addition, some of the wealthy Christians were ignoring those who were poorer. And those with certain spiritual gifts were claiming to be more important than others.

In response to all these divisions and questions, Paul gives the Corinthians good, practical advice. At the same time, he reminds them of what is truly important for Christian believers. The death and resurrection of Jesus is central to faith; human wisdom is foolish when measured against God's wisdom; others' needs and concerns must always be put before our own; and love should be the primary focus in everything we do and say.

Paul offers a picture of unity to this divided, confused community: we are all different parts of the same body of Christ (1 Corinthians 12:12–26). Paul celebrates our diversity and insists on our unity. The advice and teaching he gives in this letter are good for Christians of any time or place to take to heart.

- **Author:** Paul
- **Date Written:** A.D. 56
- **Audience:** The mainly Gentile (non-Jewish) church in Corinth (modern-day Greece)
- **Themes:** Belonging to Christ is to be a member of the body or community of believers in Christ; a life of faith should be lived out through relationships with others.

- **1 Corinthians 1:1–9** A greeting and thanks
- **1 Corinthians 1:10–4:21** A discussion of divisions in the Church and their implications for the gospel
- **1 Corinthians 5–11** Advice and answers to questions
- **1 Corinthians 12–14** An explanation of spiritual gifts and the priority of love
- **1 Corinthians 15** Paul's teaching about the resurrection of the body
- **1 Corinthians 16** Paul's plans and final blessing

1 **Salutation**

Paul, called to be an apostle of Christ Jesus by the will of God, and our brother Sosthenes,

2 To the church of God that is in Corinth, to those who are sanctified in Christ Jesus, called to be saints, together with all those who in every place call on the name of our Lord Jesus Christ, both their Lord[a] and ours:

3 Grace to you and peace from God our Father and the Lord Jesus Christ.

4 I give thanks to my[b] God always for you because of the grace of God that has been given you in Christ Jesus, [5]for in every way you have been enriched in him, in speech and knowledge of every kind— [6]just as the testimony of[c] Christ has been strengthened among you— [7]so that you are not lacking in any spiritual gift as you wait for the revealing of our Lord Jesus Christ. [8]He will also strengthen you to the end, so that you may be blameless on the day of our Lord Jesus Christ. [9]God is faithful; by him you were called into the fellowship of his Son, Jesus Christ our Lord.

Divisions in the Church

10 Now I appeal to you, brothers and sisters,[d] by the name of our Lord Jesus Christ, that all of you be in agreement and that there be no divisions among you, but that you be united in the same mind and the same purpose. [11]For it has been reported to me by Chloe's people that there are quarrels among you, my brothers and sisters.[e] [12]What I mean is that each of you says, "I belong to Paul," or "I belong to Apollos," or "I belong to Cephas," or "I belong to Christ." [13]Has Christ been divided? Was Paul crucified for you? Or were you baptized in the name of Paul? [14]I thank God[f] that I baptized none of you except Crispus and Gaius, [15]so that no one can say that you were baptized in my name. [16](I did baptize also the household of Stephanas; beyond that, I do not know whether I baptized anyone else.) [17]For Christ did not send me to baptize but to proclaim the gospel, and not with eloquent wisdom, so that the cross of Christ might not be emptied of its power.

Christ the Power and Wisdom of God

18 For the message about the cross is foolishness to those who are perishing, but to us who are being saved it is the power of God. [19]For it is written,

"I will destroy the wisdom of the wise,
  and the discernment of the discerning I
  will thwart."

[20]Where is the one who is wise? Where is the scribe? Where is the debater of this age? Has not God made foolish the wisdom of the world? [21]For since, in the wisdom of God, the world did not know God through wisdom, God decided, through the foolishness of our proclamation, to save those who believe. [22]For Jews demand signs and Greeks desire wisdom,

---

LIVE IT!

When a Fight Breaks Out · 1 Corinthians 1:10–17

Shawn brags at a party about his school's win over his cousin Nate's school in a recent football game. Nate argues that the referees missed a crucial penalty. Before long, the entire party is fighting over which team is the best. Everybody's mad, and no one is having fun anymore.

That's similar to what happened to the Christians in Corinth. They were divided over which missionary was the best and which leaders to follow. Paul challenges them to get over this foolish division and focus on the important thing they share—the love of God and their salvation through the cross of Christ.

Christians today still struggle with Paul's challenge to be united. There are significant differences between Christian churches and denominations. Too often we are divided over those differences instead of respecting them and working together to "be united in the same mind and the same purpose" (1 Corinthians 1:10).

- What disagreements cause problems in your church or youth group?
- How can you bring unity to those situations?

---

a Gk *theirs* b Other ancient authorities lack *my* c Or *to* d Gk *brothers* e Gk *my brothers* f Other ancient authorities read *I am thankful*

Foolish Wisdom
1 Corinthians
1:18–31

What's the difference between a smart person and a wise person? Many smart people excel in a school subject or a work skill. A person has to be very smart to run an illegal drug ring or to steal nuclear secrets. But being smart in these ways doesn't make a person wise in the ways of God.

Paul reminds the Corinthians that the central Christian message—that Christ was crucified for our salvation—seems foolish to many wise people of their time. The Greeks of this period prided themselves on their wisdom. And the Jews hoped for signs of a kingly messiah who would make the nation strong. Both the Jews and the Greeks thought the idea of a crucified messiah, or a god who could suffer and die, was foolish.

But there is a great mystery here. The foolishness of God is wiser than the greatest wisdom of the world (1 Corinthians 1:25). Our ways are not God's ways. Christ's hanging on a cross turns upside down the world's ideas of success and failure, victory and defeat, and power and weakness. And Paul says the reason for all of this is so God will get the glory—we can't boast in ourselves, but only in God (1 Corinthians 1:31).

- When in your life does the world's wisdom seem to make more sense than God's wisdom?
- What can you do to remind yourself of the truth Paul teaches?
- Has your idea of success, victory, and power been turned upside down by the cross?

---

foolishness is wiser than human wisdom, and God's weakness is stronger than human strength.

26 Consider your own call, brothers and sisters:[a] not many of you were wise by human standards,[b] not many were powerful, not many were of noble birth. [27] But God chose what is foolish in the world to shame the wise; God chose what is weak in the world to shame the strong; [28] God chose what is low and despised in the world, things that are not, to reduce to nothing things that are, [29] so that no one[c] might boast in the presence of God. [30] He is the source of your life in Christ Jesus, who became for us wisdom from God, and righteousness and sanctification and redemption, [31] in order that, as it is written, "Let the one who boasts, boast in[d] the Lord."

Proclaiming Christ Crucified

2 When I came to you, brothers and sisters,[a] I did not come proclaiming the mystery[e] of God to you in lofty words or wisdom. [2] For I decided to know nothing among you except Jesus Christ, and him crucified. [3] And I came to you in weakness and in fear and in much trembling. [4] My speech and my proclamation were not with plausible words of wisdom,[f] but with a demonstration of the Spirit and of power, [5] so that your faith might rest not on human wisdom but on the power of God.

The True Wisdom of God

6 Yet among the mature we do speak wisdom, though it is not a wisdom of this age or of the rulers of this age, who are doomed to perish. [7] But we speak God's wisdom, secret and hidden, which God decreed before the ages for our glory. [8] None of the rulers of this age understood this; for if they had, they would not have crucified the Lord of glory. [9] But, as it is written,

"What no eye has seen, nor ear heard,
    nor the human heart conceived,
what God has prepared for those who love
    him"—

[10] these things God has revealed to us through the Spirit; for the Spirit searches everything, even the depths of God. [11] For what human being knows what is truly human except the human spirit that is within? So also no one comprehends what is truly God's except the Spirit of God. [12] Now we have received not the spirit of the world, but the Spirit that is from God, so that we may understand the gifts bestowed on us by God. [13] And we speak of these things in words not

---

[23] but we proclaim Christ crucified, a stumbling block to Jews and foolishness to Gentiles, [24] but to those who are the called, both Jews and Greeks, Christ the power of God and the wisdom of God. [25] For God's

---

taught by human wisdom but taught by the Spirit, interpreting spiritual things to those who are spiritual.[a]

14 Those who are unspiritual[b] do not receive the gifts of God's Spirit, for they are foolishness to them, and they are unable to understand them because they are spiritually discerned. [15]Those who are spiritual discern all things, and they are themselves subject to no one else's scrutiny.
16 "For who has known the mind of the Lord
    so as to instruct him?"
But we have the mind of Christ.

On Divisions in the Corinthian Church

3 And so, brothers and sisters,[c] I could not speak to you as spiritual people, but rather as people of the flesh, as infants in Christ. [2]I fed you with milk, not solid food, for you were not ready for solid food. Even now you are still not ready, [3]for you are still of the flesh. For as long as there is jealousy and quarreling among you, are you not of the flesh, and behaving according to human inclinations? [4]For when one says, "I belong to Paul," and another, "I belong to Apollos," are you not merely human?

5 What then is Apollos? What is Paul? Servants through whom you came to believe, as the Lord assigned to each. [6]I planted, Apollos watered, but God gave the growth. [7]So neither the one who plants nor the one who waters is anything, but only God who gives the growth. [8]The one who plants and the one who waters have a common purpose, and each will receive wages according to the labor of each. [9]For we are God's servants, working together; you are God's field, God's building.

10 According to the grace of God given to me, like a skilled master builder I laid a foundation, and someone else is building on it. Each builder must choose with care how to build on it. [11]For no one can lay any foundation other than the one that has been laid; that foundation is Jesus Christ. [12]Now if anyone builds on the foundation with gold, silver, precious stones, wood, hay, straw— [13]the work of each builder will become visible, for the Day will disclose it, because it will be revealed with fire, and the fire will test what sort of work each has done. [14]If what has been built on the foundation survives, the builder will receive a reward. [15]If the work is burned up, the builder will suffer loss; the builder will be saved, but only as through fire.

16 Do you not know that you are God's temple

STUDY IT!

**Humble Servants
1 Corinthians
3:1–15**

Sometimes Christians are motivated by personal pride. Jealousy and fighting divide us. But Paul says clearly that all Christians are God's servants, who should work together toward a common purpose—God's purpose. Whatever we do for the gospel is part of Jesus' mission. It's not about gaining recognition for what we do or deciding which leader we like best to follow. Christians are all merely servants working to make Jesus known.

Paul uses two images to explain this. First, he uses the image of growing crops: "So neither the one who plants nor the one who waters is anything, but only God who gives the growth" (1 Corinthians 3:7). Second, Paul uses the image of building: "Like a skilled master builder I laid a foundation, and someone else is building on it. . . . For no one can lay any foundation other than the one that has been laid; that foundation is Jesus Christ" (1 Corinthians 3:10-11). Paul goes on to explain that this doesn't take away our responsibility, but it does mean that ultimately everything comes down to our foundation—Jesus.

and that God's Spirit dwells in you?[d] [17]If anyone destroys God's temple, God will destroy that person. For God's temple is holy, and you are that temple.

18 Do not deceive yourselves. If you think that you are wise in this age, you should become fools so that you may become wise. [19]For the wisdom of this world is foolishness with God. For it is written,
"He catches the wise in their craftiness,"
[20]and again,
"The Lord knows the thoughts of the
    wise,
    that they are futile."
[21]So let no one boast about human leaders. For all things are yours, [22]whether Paul or Apollos or Cephas or the world or life or death or the present or

---

a Or interpreting spiritual things in spiritual language, or comparing spiritual things with spiritual   b Or natural   c Gk brothers   d In verses 16 and 17 the Greek word for you is plural

Build Strong · 1 Corinthians 3:10–17

The most important part of a building is its foundation. Without a good foundation, even the best building materials will collapse. The same is true for people. Paul says that our foundation is Jesus, but each of us is responsible to build on that foundation. We choose our building materials by choosing our values, principles, and actions. Paul uses the imagery of gold, silver, precious stones, wood, hay, and straw to show that some building materials are better than others. We get to choose what to use, but the better the materials, the better our lives will be able to stand the tests that come.

Paul makes it clear that this is not a matter of whether or not we are saved. The foundation is Jesus, and **1 Corinthians 3:15** says even if the building is burned up, the builder will be saved. So it isn't about salvation, but about building a life that's worthy of Christ and can withstand the fires that come. Paul tells the people of Corinth that whatever they choose to use in building their foundation will show itself in the end.

- Is Christ the foundation you build your life on?
- What kind of person do you want to be remembered as when you are gone?
- What qualities, values, and virtues do you want to have and build your life around?

the future—all belong to you, [23] and you belong to Christ, and Christ belongs to God.

4 The Ministry of the Apostles

Think of us in this way, as servants of Christ and stewards of God's mysteries. [2] Moreover, it is required of stewards that they be found trustworthy. [3] But with me it is a very small thing that I should be judged by you or by any human court. I do not even judge myself. [4] I am not aware of anything against myself, but I am not thereby acquitted. It is the Lord who judges me. [5] Therefore do not pronounce judgment before the time, before the Lord comes, who will bring to light the things now hidden in darkness and will disclose the purposes of the heart. Then each one will receive commendation from God.

6 I have applied all this to Apollos and myself for your benefit, brothers and sisters,[a] so that you may learn through us the meaning of the saying, "Nothing beyond what is written," so that none of you will be puffed up in favor of one against another. [7] For who sees anything different in you?[b] What do you have that you did not receive? And if you received it, why do you boast as if it were not a gift?

8 Already you have all you want! Already you have become rich! Quite apart from us you have become kings! Indeed, I wish that you had become kings, so that we might be kings with you! [9] For I think that God

has exhibited us apostles as last of all, as though sentenced to death, because we have become a spectacle to the world, to angels and to mortals. [10] We are fools for the sake of Christ, but you are wise in Christ. We are weak, but you are strong. You are held in honor, but we are in disrepute. [11] To the present hour we are hungry and thirsty, we are poorly clothed and beaten and homeless, [12] and we grow weary from the work of our own hands. When reviled, we bless; when persecuted, we endure; [13] when slandered, we speak kindly. We have become like the rubbish of the world, the dregs of all things, to this very day.

Fatherly Admonition

14 I am not writing this to make you ashamed, but to admonish you as my beloved children. [15] For though you might have ten thousand guardians in Christ, you do not have many fathers. Indeed, in Christ Jesus I became your father through the gospel. [16] I appeal to you, then, be imitators of me. [17] For this reason I sent[c] you Timothy, who is my beloved and faithful child in the Lord, to remind you of my ways in Christ Jesus, as I teach them everywhere in every church. [18] But some of you, thinking that I am not coming to you, have become arrogant. [19] But I will come to you soon, if the Lord wills, and I will find out not the talk of these arrogant people but their power. [20] For the kingdom of God depends not on talk but on power. [21] What would you prefer? Am

a Gk brothers **b** Or Who makes you different from another? **c** Or am sending

I to come to you with a stick, or with love in a spirit of gentleness?

Sexual Immorality Defiles the Church

5 It is actually reported that there is sexual immorality among you, and of a kind that is not found even among pagans; for a man is living with his father's wife. ²And you are arrogant! Should you not rather have mourned, so that he who has done this would have been removed from among you?

3 For though absent in body, I am present in spirit; and as if present I have already pronounced judgment ⁴in the name of the Lord Jesus on the man who has done such a thing.^a When you are assembled, and my spirit is present with the power of our Lord Jesus, ⁵you are to hand this man over to Satan for the destruction of the flesh, so that his spirit may be saved in the day of the Lord.^b

6 Your boasting is not a good thing. Do you not know that a little yeast leavens the whole batch of dough? ⁷Clean out the old yeast so that you may be a new batch, as you really are unleavened. For our paschal lamb, Christ, has been sacrificed. ⁸Therefore, let us celebrate the festival, not with the old yeast, the yeast of malice and evil, but with the unleavened bread of sincerity and truth.

Sexual Immorality Must Be Judged

9 I wrote to you in my letter not to associate with sexually immoral persons— ¹⁰not at all meaning the immoral of this world, or the greedy and robbers, or idolaters, since you would then need to go out of the world. ¹¹But now I am writing to you not to associate with anyone who bears the name of brother or sister^c who is sexually immoral or greedy, or is an idolater, reviler, drunkard, or robber. Do not even eat with such a one. ¹²For what have I to do with judging those outside? Is it not those who are inside that you are to judge? ¹³God will judge those outside. "Drive out the wicked person from among you."

Lawsuits among Believers

6 When any of you has a grievance against another, do you dare to take it to court before the unrighteous, instead of taking it before the saints? ²Do you not know that the saints will judge the world? And if the world is to be judged by you, are you incompetent to try trivial cases? ³Do you not know that we are to judge angels—to say

Life to the Fullest · 1 Corinthians 6:12–20

"Don't act that way." "Don't do that." "Don't say that." Unfortunately, some people think of Christianity as a religion of "don'ts." They see the Bible as a book of rules, the Church as boring, and God as impersonal and judgmental.

But nothing could be farther from the truth! Paul helps us understand that God's desire for us is that we live well. All good gifts from God, including food and sexuality, are meant to be enjoyed to the fullest. But they also can be misused, and if they are, we miss out on the joy and purpose intended by God. So God gives us guidelines to allow us to experience these gifts to their fullest—not to take away our fun.

Take sex, for example. In **1 Corinthians 6:12–20**, Paul affirms that sex is meant to bond a man and woman for life. Fornication—sex between people who are not married—defeats its true purpose. Fornication takes away from the full joy and beauty of sexual intimacy as intended by God.

God created our sexuality. Our sexual desires are not sinful; they're a normal part of being human. As the author of our sexuality, God wants us to experience its fullness in marriage for the long run—not be hurt emotionally or physically—so commit your body, emotions, and desires to God.

- Have you thought of your sexuality as a gift from God? Picture sex as a wonderful present to be opened and enjoyed with God's blessing on your wedding day.
- What steps can you take to draw sexual boundaries that honor God? Have you set parameters for your physical and emotional interaction with the opposite sex?

---

a Or *on the man who has done such a thing in the name of the Lord Jesus*   **b** Other ancient authorities add *Jesus*   **c** Gk *brother*

nothing of ordinary matters? ⁴If you have ordinary cases, then, do you appoint as judges those who have no standing in the church? ⁵I say this to your shame. Can it be that there is no one among you wise enough to decide between one believer*a* and another, ⁶but a believer*a* goes to court against a believer*a*—and before unbelievers at that?

7 In fact, to have lawsuits at all with one another is already a defeat for you. Why not rather be wronged? Why not rather be defrauded? ⁸But you yourselves wrong and defraud—and believers*b* at that.

9 Do you not know that wrongdoers will not inherit the kingdom of God? Do not be deceived! Fornicators, idolaters, adulterers, male prostitutes, sodomites, ¹⁰thieves, the greedy, drunkards, revilers, robbers—none of these will inherit the kingdom of God. ¹¹And this is what some of you used to be. But you were washed, you were sanctified, you were justified in the name of the Lord Jesus Christ and in the Spirit of our God.

Glorify God in Body and Spirit

12 "All things are lawful for me," but not all things are beneficial. "All things are lawful for me," but I will not be dominated by anything. ¹³"Food is meant for the stomach and the stomach for food,"*c* and God will destroy both one and the other. The body is meant not for fornication but for the Lord, and the Lord for the body. ¹⁴And God raised the Lord and will also raise us by his power. ¹⁵Do you not know that your bodies are members of Christ? Should I therefore take the members of Christ and make them members of a prostitute? Never! ¹⁶Do you not know that whoever is united to a prostitute becomes one body with her? For it is said, "The two shall be one flesh." ¹⁷But anyone united to the Lord becomes one spirit with him. ¹⁸Shun fornication! Every sin that a person commits is outside the body; but the fornicator sins against the body itself. ¹⁹Or do you not know that your body is a temple*d* of the Holy Spirit within you, which you have from God, and that you are not your own? ²⁰For you were bought with a price; therefore glorify God in your body.

Directions concerning Marriage

7 Now concerning the matters about which you wrote: "It is well for a man not to touch a woman." ²But because of cases of sexual immorality, each man should have his own wife and each

STUDY IT!

You Want Me to Do What?! 1 Corinthians 7

In this chapter Paul says people shouldn't marry, uncircumcised people shouldn't get circumcised, and slaves should remain slaves. Why is Paul giving such strange advice? Because he thinks Jesus will be returning soon to establish God's kingdom for all time (1 Corinthians 7:31). So he advises the Corinthians to remain in whatever condition they were when they were called to Jesus in order to stay focused on preparing for Christ's return instead of being distracted with other cares.

But Jesus didn't come back during Paul's time. In fact, if you're reading this Bible, we're still waiting for his return. When will Jesus come again? Don't try to figure it out. Jesus told us we'll never know (Matthew 24:36-44). So what do we do with Paul's words? We look at the intent. Paul's purpose was not to condemn marriage and circumcision or justify slavery. The purpose of his advice was to keep people focused on God and ready for his return. Paul says that these instructions are not meant to restrain or limit people, but "to promote good order and unhindered devotion to the Lord" (1 Corinthians 7:35). That's advice we can follow.

woman her own husband. ³The husband should give to his wife her conjugal rights, and likewise the wife to her husband. ⁴For the wife does not have authority over her own body, but the husband does; likewise the husband does not have authority over his own body, but the wife does. ⁵Do not deprive one another except perhaps by agreement for a set time, to devote yourselves to prayer, and then come together again, so that Satan may not tempt you because of your lack of self-control. ⁶This I say by way of concession, not of command. ⁷I wish that all were as I myself am. But each has a particular gift from God, one having one kind and another a different kind.

---

a Gk *brother*   **b** Gk *brothers*   **c** The quotation may extend to the word *other*   **d** Or *sanctuary*

8 To the unmarried and the widows I say that it is well for them to remain unmarried as I am. ⁹But if they are not practicing self-control, they should marry. For it is better to marry than to be aflame with passion.

10 To the married I give this command—not I but the Lord—that the wife should not separate from her husband ¹¹(but if she does separate, let her remain unmarried or else be reconciled to her husband), and that the husband should not divorce his wife.

12 To the rest I say—I and not the Lord—that if any believer*ᵃ* has a wife who is an unbeliever, and she consents to live with him, he should not divorce her. ¹³And if any woman has a husband who is an unbeliever, and he consents to live with her, she should not divorce him. ¹⁴For the unbelieving husband is made holy through his wife, and the unbelieving wife is made holy through her husband. Otherwise, your children would be unclean, but as it is, they are holy. ¹⁵But if the unbelieving partner separates, let it be so; in such a case the brother or sister is not bound. It is to peace that God has called you.*ᵇ* ¹⁶Wife, for all you know, you might save your husband. Husband, for all you know, you might save your wife.

The Life that the Lord Has Assigned

17 However that may be, let each of you lead the life that the Lord has assigned, to which God called you. This is my rule in all the churches. ¹⁸Was anyone at the time of his call already circumcised? Let him not seek to remove the marks of circumcision. Was anyone at the time of his call uncircumcised? Let him not seek circumcision. ¹⁹Circumcision is nothing, and uncircumcision is nothing; but obeying the commandments of God is everything. ²⁰Let each of you remain in the condition in which you were called.

21 Were you a slave when called? Do not be concerned about it. Even if you can gain your freedom, make use of your present condition now more than ever.*ᶜ* ²²For whoever was called in the Lord as a slave is a freed person belonging to the Lord, just as whoever was free when called is a slave of Christ. ²³You were bought with a price; do not become slaves of human masters. ²⁴In whatever condition you were called, brothers and sisters,*ᵈ* there remain with God.

The Unmarried and the Widows

25 Now concerning virgins, I have no command of the Lord, but I give my opinion as one who by

the Lord's mercy is trustworthy. ²⁶I think that, in view of the impending*ᵉ* crisis, it is well for you to remain as you are. ²⁷Are you bound to a wife? Do not seek to be free. Are you free from a wife? Do not seek a wife. ²⁸But if you marry, you do not sin, and if a virgin marries, she does not sin. Yet those who marry will experience distress in this life,*ᶠ* and I would spare you that. ²⁹I mean, brothers and sisters,*ᵈ* the appointed time has grown short; from now on, let even those who have wives be as though they had none, ³⁰and those who mourn as though they were not mourning, and those who rejoice as though they were not rejoicing, and those who buy as though they had no possessions, ³¹and those who deal with the world as though they had no dealings with it. For the present form of this world is passing away.

32 I want you to be free from anxieties. The unmarried man is anxious about the affairs of the Lord, how to please the Lord; ³³but the married man is anxious about the affairs of the world, how to please his wife, ³⁴and his interests are divided. And the unmarried woman and the virgin are anxious about the affairs of the Lord, so that they may be holy in body and spirit; but the married woman is anxious about the affairs of the world, how to please her husband. ³⁵I say this for your own benefit, not to put any restraint upon you, but to promote good order and unhindered devotion to the Lord.

36 If anyone thinks that he is not behaving properly toward his fiancée,*ᵍ* if his passions are strong, and so it has to be, let him marry as he wishes; it is no sin. Let them marry. ³⁷But if someone stands firm in his resolve, being under no necessity but having his own desire under control, and has determined in his own mind to keep her as his fiancée,*ᵍ* he will do well. ³⁸So then, he who marries his fiancée*ᵍ* does well; and he who refrains from marriage will do better.

39 A wife is bound as long as her husband lives. But if the husband dies,*ʰ* she is free to marry anyone she wishes, only in the Lord. ⁴⁰But in my judgment she is more blessed if she remains as she is. And I think that I too have the Spirit of God.

Food Offered to Idols

8 Now concerning food sacrificed to idols: we know that "all of us possess knowledge." Knowledge puffs up, but love builds up. ²Anyone who claims to know something does not yet have

---

ᵃ Gk *brother* *ᵇ* Other ancient authorities read *us* *ᶜ* Or *avail yourself of the opportunity* *ᵈ* Gk *brothers* *ᵉ* Or *present* *ᶠ* Gk *in the flesh* *ᵍ* Gk *virgin*
ʰ Gk *falls asleep*

Freedom or Friends · 1 Corinthians 8:1–13

Katie quit going to parties—not that she was drinking alcohol there like many of her friends from school. She had always told her parents where she was going and talked about what went on there. But Katie just wasn't comfortable in that environment and was struggling because she wanted to be with her friends who didn't follow Jesus. The friends in Katie's youth group had two different opinions; some felt strongly that it was absolutely wrong for Christians to go to those parties, while others felt it was okay to go to parties to be with their friends, even though they steered clear of any activities that would displease God.

So who's right? Paul wrote about a similar debate in the Corinthian church. Paul recognizes that it's not necessarily wrong for some members of the community to eat meat sacrificed to idols, because they don't believe in those pagan gods. But he still recommends that they don't do it, because some members of the community find it upsetting. For Paul, paying attention to the welfare of everyone in the community is more important than always being right. He repeats this concept later when he tells the Corinthians not to seek their own interests, but to put others first and to do everything for God's glory (1 Corinthians 10:23-33).

- Do you ever do things just because you can, even if it upsets your friends or family members?
- When you catch yourself doing something like that, think about Paul's advice. Are you making your freedom more important than other people's feelings or convictions?

the necessary knowledge; [3]but anyone who loves God is known by him.

4 Hence, as to the eating of food offered to idols, we know that "no idol in the world really exists," and that "there is no God but one." [5]Indeed, even though there may be so-called gods in heaven or on earth— as in fact there are many gods and many lords— [6]yet for us there is one God, the Father, from whom are all things and for whom we exist, and one Lord, Jesus Christ, through whom are all things and through whom we exist.

7 It is not everyone, however, who has this knowledge. Since some have become so accustomed to idols until now, they still think of the food they eat as food offered to an idol; and their conscience, being weak, is defiled. [8]"Food will not bring us close to God."[a] We are no worse off if we do not eat, and no better off if we do. [9]But take care that this liberty of yours does not somehow become a stumbling block to the weak. [10]For if others see you, who possess knowledge, eating in the temple of an idol, might they not, since their conscience is weak, be encouraged to the point of eating food sacrificed to idols? [11]So by your knowledge those weak believers for whom Christ died are destroyed.[b] [12]But when you thus sin against members of your family,[c] and wound

their conscience when it is weak, you sin against Christ. [13]Therefore, if food is a cause of their falling,[d] I will never eat meat, so that I may not cause one of them[e] to fall.

The Rights of an Apostle

9 Am I not free? Am I not an apostle? Have I not seen Jesus our Lord? Are you not my work in the Lord? [2]If I am not an apostle to others, at least I am to you; for you are the seal of my apostleship in the Lord.

3 This is my defense to those who would examine me. [4]Do we not have the right to our food and drink? [5]Do we not have the right to be accompanied by a believing wife,[f] as do the other apostles and the brothers of the Lord and Cephas? [6]Or is it only Barnabas and I who have no right to refrain from working for a living? [7]Who at any time pays the expenses for doing military service? Who plants a vineyard and does not eat any of its fruit? Or who tends a flock and does not get any of its milk?

8 Do I say this on human authority? Does not the law also say the same? [9]For it is written in the law of Moses, "You shall not muzzle an ox while it is treading out the grain." Is it for oxen that God is concerned? [10]Or does he not speak entirely for our sake? It was

a The quotation may extend to the end of the verse   b Gk *the weak brother . . . is destroyed*   c Gk *against the brothers*   d Gk *my brother's falling*   e Gk *cause my brother*   f Gk *a sister as wife*

indeed written for our sake, for whoever plows should plow in hope and whoever threshes should thresh in hope of a share in the crop. [11] If we have sown spiritual good among you, is it too much if we reap your material benefits? [12] If others share this rightful claim on you, do not we still more?

Nevertheless, we have not made use of this right, but we endure anything rather than put an obstacle in the way of the gospel of Christ. [13] Do you not know that those who are employed in the temple service get their food from the temple, and those who serve at the altar share in what is sacrificed on the altar? [14] In the same way, the Lord commanded that those who proclaim the gospel should get their living by the gospel.

15 But I have made no use of any of these rights, nor am I writing this so that they may be applied in my case. Indeed, I would rather die than that—no one will deprive me of my ground for boasting! [16] If I proclaim the gospel, this gives me no ground for boasting, for an obligation is laid on me, and woe to me if I do not proclaim the gospel! [17] For if I do this of my own will, I have a reward; but if not of my own will, I am entrusted with a commission. [18] What then is my reward? Just this: that in my proclamation I may make the gospel free of charge, so as not to make full use of my rights in the gospel.

19 For though I am free with respect to all, I have made myself a slave to all, so that I might win more of them. [20] To the Jews I became as a Jew, in order to win Jews. To those under the law I became as one under the law (though I myself am not under the law) so that I might win those under the law. [21] To those outside the law I became as one outside the law (though I am not free from God's law but am under Christ's law) so that I might win those outside the law. [22] To the weak I became weak, so that I might win the weak. I have become all things to all people, that I might by all means save some. [23] I do it all for the sake of the gospel, so that I may share in its blessings.

24 Do you not know that in a race the runners all compete, but only one receives the prize? Run in such a way that you may win it. [25] Athletes exercise self-control in all things; they do it to receive a perishable wreath, but we an imperishable one. [26] So I do not run aimlessly, nor do I box as though beating the air; [27] but I punish my body and enslave it, so that after proclaiming to others I myself should not be disqualified.

LIVE IT!

Run for the Prize · 1 Corinthians 9:24–27

Did you know that the greatest pro basketball player in history had difficulty making his high-school varsity team? Michael Jordan could have quit trying, but he set a goal for himself and made it his priority to practice every day. Not only did he finally make the team; he broke state scoring records and was named all-state. And later he went on to lead the Chicago Bulls to six NBA championships.

Perseverance means setting priorities, sticking to them even when you get discouraged, and trying over and over to accomplish your goals. Although athletes do this to win a temporary prize, we practice the same kind of discipline in our spiritual lives for a prize that lasts forever.

• What are your desires for growing closer to God?

• What race do you feel God is calling you to run in your life?

• Decide on one goal and concentrate on it for the next month. What will you have to do to accomplish it? What priorities will you have to establish to focus on that goal?

Warnings from Israel's History

10 I do not want you to be unaware, brothers and sisters,[a] that our ancestors were all under the cloud, and all passed through the sea, [2]and all were baptized into Moses in the cloud and in the sea, [3]and all ate the same spiritual food, [4]and all drank the same spiritual drink. For they drank from the spiritual rock that followed them, and the rock was Christ. [5]Nevertheless, God was not pleased with most of them, and they were struck down in the wilderness.

6 Now these things occurred as examples for us, so that we might not desire evil as they did. [7]Do not become idolaters as some of them did; as it is written, "The people sat down to eat and drink, and they rose up to play." [8]We must not indulge in sexual immorality as some of them did, and twenty-three thousand fell in a single day. [9]We must not put Christ[b] to the test, as some of them did, and were destroyed by serpents. [10]And do not complain as some of them did, and were destroyed by the destroyer. [11]These things happened to them to serve as an example, and they were written down to instruct us, on whom the ends of the ages have come. [12]So if you think you are standing, watch out that you do not fall. [13]No testing has overtaken you that is not common to everyone. God is faithful, and he will not let you be tested beyond your strength, but with the testing he will also provide the way out so that you may be able to endure it.

> "God is faithful, and he will not let you be tested beyond your strength, but with the testing he will also provide the way out so that you may be able to endure it."
> —1 Corinthians 10:13

14 Therefore, my dear friends,[c] flee from the worship of idols. [15]I speak as to sensible people; judge for yourselves what I say. [16]The cup of blessing that we bless, is it not a sharing in the blood of Christ? The bread that we break, is it not a sharing in the body of Christ? [17]Because there is one bread, we who are many are one body, for we all partake of the one bread. [18]Consider the people of Israel;[d] are not those who eat the sacrifices partners in the altar? [19]What do I imply then? That food sacrificed to idols is anything, or that an idol is anything? [20]No, I imply that what pagans sacrifice, they sacrifice to demons and not to God. I do not want you to be partners with demons. [21]You cannot drink the cup of the Lord and the cup of demons. You cannot partake of the table of the Lord and the table of demons. [22]Or are we provoking the Lord to jealousy? Are we stronger than he?

Do All to the Glory of God

23 "All things are lawful," but not all things are

---

a Gk brothers   b Other ancient authorities read the Lord   c Gk my beloved   d Gk Israel according to the flesh beneficial. "All things are lawful," but not all things build up. [24]Do not seek your own advantage, but that of the other. [25]Eat whatever is sold in the meat market without raising any question on the ground of conscience, [26]for "the earth and its fullness are the Lord's." [27]If an unbeliever invites you to a meal and you are disposed to go, eat whatever is set before you without raising any question on the ground of conscience. [28]But if someone says to you, "This has been offered in sacrifice," then do not eat it, out of consideration for the one who informed you, and for the sake of conscience— [29]I mean the other's conscience, not your own. For why should my liberty be subject to the judgment of someone else's conscience? [30]If I partake with thankfulness, why should I be denounced because of that for which I give thanks?

31　So, whether you eat or drink, or whatever you do, do everything for the glory of God. [32]Give no offense to Jews or to Greeks or to the church of God, [33]just as I try to please everyone in everything I do, not seeking my own advantage, but that of many, so that they may be saved. **11** [1]Be imitators of me, as I am of Christ.

Head Coverings

2　I commend you because you remember me in everything and maintain the traditions just as I handed them on to you. [3]But I want you to understand that Christ is the head of every man, and the husband[a] is the head of his wife,[b] and God is the head of Christ. [4]Any man who prays or prophesies with something on his head disgraces his head, [5]but any woman who prays or prophesies with her head unveiled disgraces her head—it is one and the same thing as having her head shaved. [6]For if a woman will not veil herself, then she should cut off her hair; but if it is disgraceful for a woman to have her hair cut off or to be shaved, she should wear a veil. [7]For a man ought not to have his head veiled, since he is the image and reflection[c] of God; but woman is the reflection[c] of man. [8]Indeed, man was not made from woman, but woman from man. [9]Neither was man created for the sake of woman, but woman for the sake of man. [10]For this reason a woman ought to have a symbol of[d] authority on her head,[e] because of the angels. [11]Nevertheless, in the Lord woman is not independent of man or man independent of woman. [12]For just as woman came from man, so man comes through woman; but all things come

from God. [13]Judge for yourselves: is it proper for a woman to pray to God with her head unveiled? [14]Does not nature itself teach you that if a man wears long hair, it is degrading to him, [15]but if a woman has long hair, it is her glory? For her hair is given to her for a covering. [16]But if anyone is disposed to be contentious—we have no such custom, nor do the churches of God.

Abuses at the Lord's Supper

17　Now in the following instructions I do not commend you, because when you come together it is not for the better but for the worse. [18]For, to begin with, when you come together as a church, I hear that there are divisions among you; and to some extent I believe it. [19]Indeed, there have to be factions among you, for only so will it become clear who among you are genuine. [20]When you come

LIVE IT!

Called to Share
1 Corinthians 11:17–33

Those in the early Church in Corinth often met in one another's homes to talk about their faith, share a meal, and celebrate the Lord's Supper. But Paul tells the Corinthians the way they're doing it isn't in line with its purpose. Jesus spent his life creating community for the poor and outcast, bringing people together in unity. But the Corinthians are acting out of their own desires and eating their "own suppers," not the Lord's Supper. And they are not including the poor (1 Corinthians 11:21). Truly celebrating the Lord's Supper requires remembering Jesus' life and death and living out the values he taught.

- What would Paul say if he sat in on your church or youth group worship service or time of Communion?
- How do you share with people who have little or nothing?
- What can you do to make your youth group or worship service a sign of generosity, justice, and love?

---

a The same Greek word means *man* or *husband*　**b** Or *head of the woman*　**c** Or *glory*　**d** Gk lacks *a symbol of*　**e** Or *have freedom of choice regarding her head*

together, it is not really to eat the Lord's supper. [21]For when the time comes to eat, each of you goes ahead with your own supper, and one goes hungry and another becomes drunk. [22]What! Do you not have homes to eat and drink in? Or do you show contempt for the church of God and humiliate those who have nothing? What should I say to you? Should I commend you? In this matter I do not commend you!

The Institution of the Lord's Supper

23　For I received from the Lord what I also handed on to you, that the Lord Jesus on the night when he was betrayed took a loaf of bread, [24]and when he had given thanks, he broke it and said, "This is my body that is for[a] you. Do this in remembrance of me." [25]In the same way he took the cup also, after supper, saying, "This cup is the new covenant in my blood. Do this, as often as you drink it, in remembrance of me." [26]For as often as you eat this bread and drink the cup, you proclaim the Lord's death until he comes.

Partaking of the Supper Unworthily

27　Whoever, therefore, eats the bread or drinks the cup of the Lord in an unworthy manner will be answerable for the body and blood of the Lord. [28]Examine yourselves, and only then eat of the bread and drink of the cup. [29]For all who eat and drink[b] without discerning the body,[c] eat and drink judgment against themselves. [30]For this reason many of you are weak and ill, and some have died.[d] [31]But if we judged ourselves, we would not be judged. [32]But when we are judged by the Lord, we are disciplined[e] so that we may not be condemned along with the world.

33　So then, my brothers and sisters,[f] when you come together to eat, wait for one another. [34]If you are hungry, eat at home, so that when you come together, it will not be for your condemnation. About the other things I will give instructions when I come.

12

Spiritual Gifts

Now concerning spiritual gifts,[g] brothers and sisters,[f] I do not want you to be uninformed. [2]You know that when you were pagans, you were enticed and led astray to idols that could not speak. [3]Therefore I want you to understand that no one speaking by the Spirit of God ever says "Let Jesus be cursed!" and no one can say "Jesus is Lord" except by the Holy Spirit.

4　Now there are varieties of gifts, but the same Spirit; [5]and there are varieties of services, but the same Lord; [6]and there are varieties of activities, but it is the same God who activates all of them in everyone. [7]To each is given the manifestation of the Spirit for the common good. [8]To one is given through the Spirit the utterance of wisdom, and to another the utterance of knowledge according to the same Spirit, [9]to another faith by the same Spirit, to another gifts of healing by the one Spirit, [10]to another the working of miracles, to another prophecy, to another the discernment of spirits, to another various kinds of tongues, to another the interpretation of tongues. [11]All these are activated by one and the same Spirit, who allots to each one individually just as the Spirit chooses.

STUDY IT!

Parts of the Whole · 1 Corinthians 12:12–31

Remember playing with Mr. Potato Head? Each part of his body was separate, and you got to choose how to put the pieces together to make a whole. It didn't matter if you put the arms on the head or left them off altogether—it was a plastic potato. But our bodies and the body of Christ are not like that.

Our bodies depend on each and every part to function correctly. Paul says that God has given us different gifts, designed to work together in the body of Christ. That's true for each person—all are needed for the Church to function properly. Many look at pastors, priests, famous speakers, or worship leaders—the most visible people—and conclude that they are more important than others. But God sees things differently (1 Corinthians 12:24-25). God values the gifts and roles of every single individual and often chooses the "unknown" people to do the most important work of God.

a Other ancient authorities read *is broken for*　b Other ancient authorities add *in an unworthy manner,*　c Other ancient authorities read *the Lord's body*　d Gk *fallen asleep*　e Or *When we are judged, we are being disciplined by the Lord*　f Gk *brothers*　g Or *spiritual persons*

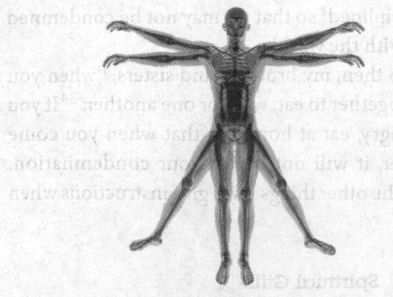

One Body with Many Members

12 For just as the body is one and has many members, and all the members of the body, though many, are one body, so it is with Christ. [13]For in the one Spirit we were all baptized into one body—Jews or Greeks, slaves or free—and we were all made to drink of one Spirit. 14 Indeed, the body does not consist of one member but of many. [15]If the foot would say, "Because I am not a hand, I do not belong to the body," that would not make it any less a part of the body. [16]And if the ear would say, "Because I am not an eye, I do not belong to the body," that would not make it any less a part of the body. [17]If the whole body were an eye, where would the hearing be? If the whole body were hearing, where would the sense of smell be? [18]But as it is, God arranged the members in the body, each one of them, as he chose. [19]If all were a single member, where would the body be? [20]As it is, there are many members, yet one body. [21]The eye cannot say to the hand, "I have no need of you," nor again the head to the feet, "I have no need of you." [22]On the contrary, the members of the body that seem to be weaker are indispensable, [23]and those members of the body that we think less honorable we clothe with greater honor, and our less respectable members are treated with greater respect; [24]whereas our more respectable members do not need this. But God has so arranged the body, giving the greater honor to the inferior member, [25]that there may be no dissension within the body, but the members may have the same care for one another. [26]If one member suffers, all suffer together with it; if one member is honored, all rejoice together with it.

27 Now you are the body of Christ and individually members of it. [28]And God has appointed in the church first apostles, second prophets, third teachers; then deeds of power, then gifts of healing, forms of assistance, forms of leadership, various kinds of tongues. [29]Are all apost...

teachers? Do all work ...

gifts of healing? Do al...

interpret? [31]But strive ...

will show you a still mo...

The Gift of L...

13 If I speak in th...

angels, but do ...

gong or a clanging cym...

powers, and understan...

edge, and if I have all f...

tains, but do not have ...

PRAY IT!

all followers of Christ ...

passage is often rea...

for the new couple. ...

love should strive to ...

romance. We are all ...

capacity to love, an...

complicated and ex...

love we most often ...

Ask yourself these ...

the prayer below to ...

to fill you with the gi...

• What is your vi...

been shaped?

• When have you ...

patient and kin...

or resentful?

• Who shares lov...

you grow in yo...

and learn to lov...

Dear Lord, help ...

in my life who s...

call us to do. Ple...

understanding ot...

can express this ...

friends, and even ...

me to love. Am...

Jamie Tworkowski: To Write Love on Her Arms
1 Corinthians 13

Jamie Tworkowski believes that hope is real and that love is the answer to all of life's hardest questions. Sounds nice. But the reality he has lived out shows that his belief is far more than nice words.

It all started when he and some friends spent a week saving the life of their friend Renee. Renee's life was scarred by more darkness and evil than most of us can imagine, and her arms showed the physical razor-inflicted scars of her pain and depression. When she was denied entry into a drug treatment center, a group of friends, including Jamie, became the body of Christ to her. They met her needs and wrote love on her arms to heal the wounds—not a temporary love that satisfies for a moment, but the true love spoken of in 1 Corinthians 13.

The movement To Write Love on Her Arms began as an attempt to tell a story and help a friend. Jamie designed the original T-shirts and began selling them to raise money for Renee's treatment, once she was accepted into rehab. But Jamie soon discovered the issue was so much greater than his friend. This conversation about pain, addiction, depression, and hopelessness needed to be started around the world. Today TWLOHA is a nonprofit organization dedicated to presenting hope and finding help for people struggling with depression, addiction, self-injury, and suicide. You can read Jamie's powerful story of helping Renee and more about this movement at **twloha.org**.

away all my possessions, and if I hand over my body so that I may boast,[a] but do not have love, I gain nothing.

4 Love is patient; love is kind; love is not envious or boastful or arrogant [5]or rude. It does not insist on its own way; it is not irritable or resentful; [6]it does not rejoice in wrongdoing, but rejoices in the truth. [7]It bears all things, believes all things, hopes all things, endures all things.

8 Love never ends. But as for prophecies, they will come to an end; as for tongues, they will cease; as for knowledge, it will come to an end. [9]For we know only in part, and we prophesy only in part; [10]but when the complete comes, the partial will come to an end. [11]When I was a child, I spoke like a child, I thought like a child, I reasoned like a child; when I became an adult, I put an end to childish ways. [12]For now we see in a mirror, dimly,[b] but then we will see face to face. Now I know only in part; then I will know fully, even as I have been fully known. [13]And now faith, hope, and love abide, these three; and the greatest of these is love.

Gifts of Prophecy and Tongues

14 Pursue love and strive for the spiritual gifts, and especially that you may prophesy.

[2]For those who speak in a tongue do not speak to other people but to God; for nobody understands them, since they are speaking mysteries in the Spirit. [3]On the other hand, those who prophesy speak to other people for their upbuilding and encouragement and consolation. [4]Those who speak in a tongue build up themselves, but those who prophesy build up the church. [5]Now I would like all of you to speak in tongues, but even more to prophesy. One who prophesies is greater than one who speaks in tongues, unless someone interprets, so that the church may be built up.

6 Now, brothers and sisters,[c] if I come to you speaking in tongues, how will I benefit you unless I speak to you in some revelation or knowledge or prophecy or teaching? [7]It is the same way with lifeless instruments that produce sound, such as the flute or the harp. If they do not give distinct notes, how will anyone know what is being played? [8]And if the bugle gives an indistinct sound, who will get ready for battle? [9]So with yourselves; if in a tongue you utter speech that is not intelligible, how will anyone know what is being said? For you will be speaking into the air. [10]There are doubtless many different kinds of sounds in the world, and nothing is without sound. [11]If then I do not know the mean-

a Other ancient authorities read *body to be burned*   b Gk *in a riddle*   c Gk *brothers*

STUDY IT!

Faith, Hope, and Love · 1 Corinthians 13:13

Have you ever seen one group of students at school putting down another group? That's the kind of problem Paul was addressing in his letter to the Corinthians. Some people in their church were claiming that their particular spiritual gift made them better than others in the church. Paul challenged the Corinthians to be unified as one community and to respect their diversity of gifts. And he called them all to seek something even greater: faith, hope, and love.

These three attitudes or habits direct our hearts and minds toward God and strengthen our relationship with God. They serve as a basis for all our actions and help open our hearts to living according to God's will. Ultimately, they help us live as God's children.

Faith: Faith helps us believe in God and all that God has revealed. Through faith we give our lives to God and actively seek to do God's will. To be truly alive, our faith must be evident in the love we show others and in good works we do. Along with having and living faith, we're also called to share our faith in God with others.

Hope: Hope is the virtue that helps keep our hearts and minds focused on the goal—eternal life with God. Through hope our actions take on new direction and purpose, namely, working to build the kingdom of God here on earth. Our daily struggles and sufferings take on new meaning when we place our hope in God's plan for our lives. Hope gives us the strength to endure what seemed impossible before. Jesus' teachings on the Beatitudes (see Matthew 5:1-12) and the Lord's Prayer (see Luke 11:1-4) express the fullness of what is hoped for, and **Hebrews 11:4–38** gives examples of the faith of God's people through ancient history.

Love: Paul leaves no doubt that love is the most important of the three. Love helps us fulfill the two greatest commandments: to love God with our whole heart and to love others as we love ourselves. Jesus showed us how much God loves us by his words and life and even more by dying for us and our sinfulness. Jesus calls us to love God and each other with the same limitless love.

Faith, hope, and love are all essential to our lives in Christ, but, as Paul points out, without love everything else is worth nothing.

ing of a sound, I will be a foreigner to the speaker and the speaker a foreigner to me. ¹²So with yourselves; since you are eager for spiritual gifts, strive to excel in them for building up the church.

13 Therefore, one who speaks in a tongue should pray for the power to interpret. ¹⁴For if I pray in a tongue, my spirit prays but my mind is unproductive. ¹⁵What should I do then? I will pray with the spirit, but I will pray with the mind also; I will sing praise with the spirit, but I will sing praise with the mind also. ¹⁶Otherwise, if you say a blessing with the spirit, how can anyone in the position of an outsider say the "Amen" to your thanksgiving, since the outsider does not know what you are saying? ¹⁷For you may give thanks well enough, but the other person is not built up. ¹⁸I thank God that I speak in tongues more than all of you; ¹⁹neverthe-

less, in church I would rather speak five words with my mind, in order to instruct others also, than ten thousand words in a tongue.

20 Brothers and sisters,ᵃ do not be children in your thinking; rather, be infants in evil, but in thinking be adults. ²¹In the law it is written,

"By people of strange tongues
　　and by the lips of foreigners
I will speak to this people;
　　yet even then they will not listen
　　　　to me,"

says the Lord. ²²Tongues, then, are a sign not for believers but for unbelievers, while prophecy is not for unbelievers but for believers. ²³If, therefore, the whole church comes together and all speak in tongues, and outsiders or unbelievers enter, will they not say that you are out of your mind? ²⁴But if all

α Gk brothers

prophesy, an unbeliever or outsider who enters is reproved by all and called to account by all. [25] After the secrets of the unbeliever's heart are disclosed, that person will bow down before God and worship him, declaring, "God is really among you."

Orderly Worship

26 What should be done then, my friends?[a] When you come together, each one has a hymn, a lesson, a revelation, a tongue, or an interpretation. Let all things be done for building up. [27] If anyone speaks in a tongue, let there be only two or at most three, and each in turn; and let one interpret. [28] But if there is no one to interpret, let them be silent in church and speak to themselves and to God. [29] Let two or three prophets speak, and let the others weigh what is said. [30] If a revelation is made to someone else sitting nearby, let the first person be silent. [31] For you can all prophesy one by one, so that all may learn and all be encouraged. [32] And the spirits of prophets are subject to the prophets, [33] for God is a God not of disorder but of peace.

(As in all the churches of the saints, [34] women should be silent in the churches. For they are not permitted to speak, but should be subordinate, as the law also says. [35] If there is anything they desire to know, let them ask their husbands at home. For it is shameful for a woman to speak in church.[b] [36] Or did the word of God originate with you? Or are you the only ones it has reached?)

37 Anyone who claims to be a prophet, or to have spiritual powers, must acknowledge that what I am writing to you is a command of the Lord. [38] Anyone who does not recognize this is not to be recognized. [39] So, my friends,[c] be eager to prophesy, and do not forbid speaking in tongues; [40] but all things should be done decently and in order.

15 The Resurrection of Christ

Now I would remind you, brothers and sisters,[a] of the good news[d] that I proclaimed to you, which you in turn received, in which also you stand, [2] through which also you are being saved, if you hold firmly to the message that I proclaimed to you—unless you have come to believe in vain.

3 For I handed on to you as of first importance what I in turn had received: that Christ died for our sins in accordance with the scriptures, [4] and that he was buried, and that he was raised on the third day in

Women: Speaking or Silent?
1 Corinthians 14:34–36

Here Paul says women should be silent in church. Yet earlier he implies that women can pray and prophesy in church (1 Corinthians 11:5). Paul supported and worked closely with many different women throughout his ministry (see "Study It: Introducing . . . Lydia and Priscilla," near Acts 16:14-15; 18; and "Study It: Introducing . . . Phoebe and Junia," near Romans 16:1-16).

What explains Paul's seemingly different attitudes? It appears that these three verses (1 Corinthians 14:34-36) may have been added to Paul's original letter by a later writer. Perhaps someone copying Paul's letters needed to show that Christianity was not a movement that would disrupt the social order by allowing women to speak in public. It's important to note that this cultural expectation in the ancient world is not directly transferable to our contemporary setting, where women's knowledge and leadership are highly valued.

accordance with the scriptures, [5] and that he appeared to Cephas, then to the twelve. [6] Then he appeared to more than five hundred brothers and sisters[a] at one time, most of whom are still alive, though some have died.[e] [7] Then he appeared to James, then to all the apostles. [8] Last of all, as to one untimely born, he appeared also to me. [9] For I am the least of the apostles, unfit to be called an apostle, because I persecuted the church of God. [10] But by the grace of God I am what I am, and his grace toward me has not been in vain. On the contrary, I worked harder than any of them—though it was not I, but the grace of God that is with me. [11] Whether then it was I or they, so we proclaim and so you have come to believe.

The Resurrection of the Dead

12 Now if Christ is proclaimed as raised from the dead, how can some of you say there is no resurrec-

---

a Gk brothers   b Other ancient authorities put verses 34-35 after verse 40   c Gk my brothers   d Or gospel   e Gk fallen asleep

tion of the dead? [13]If there is no resurrection of the dead, then Christ has not been raised; [14]and if Christ has not been raised, then our proclamation has been in vain and your faith has been in vain. [15]We are even found to be misrepresenting God, because we testified of God that he raised Christ—whom he did not raise if it is true that the dead are not raised. [16]For if the dead are not raised, then Christ has not been raised. [17]If Christ has not been raised, your faith is futile and you are still in your sins. [18]Then those also who have died[a] in Christ have perished. [19]If for this life only we have hoped in Christ, we are of all people most to be pitied.

20 But in fact Christ has been raised from the dead, the first fruits of those who have died.[a] [21]For since death came through a human being, the resurrection of the dead has also come through a human being; [22]for as all die in Adam, so all will be made alive in Christ. [23]But each in his own order: Christ the first fruits, then at his coming those who belong to Christ. [24]Then comes the end,[b] when he hands over the kingdom to God the Father, after he has destroyed every ruler and every authority and power. [25]For he must reign until he has put all his enemies under his feet. [26]The last enemy to be destroyed is death. [27]For "God[c] has put all things in subjection under his feet." But when it says, "All things are put in subjection," it is plain that this does not include the one who put all things in subjection under him. [28]When all things are subjected to him, then the Son himself will also be subjected to the one who put all things in subjection under him, so that God may be all in all.

29 Otherwise, what will those people do who receive baptism on behalf of the dead? If the dead are not raised at all, why are people baptized on their behalf?

30 And why are we putting ourselves in danger every hour? [31]I die every day! That is as certain, brothers and sisters,[d] as my boasting of you—a boast that I make in Christ Jesus our Lord. [32]If with merely human hopes I fought with wild animals at Ephesus, what would I have gained by it? If the dead are not raised,

"Let us eat and drink,
    for tomorrow we die."

[33]Do not be deceived:

"Bad company ruins good morals."

[34]Come to a sober and right mind, and sin no more; for some people have no knowledge of God. I say this to your shame.

The Resurrection Body

35 But someone will ask, "How are the dead raised? With what kind of body do they come?" [36]Fool! What you sow does not come to life unless it dies. [37]And as for what you sow, you do not sow the body that is to be, but a bare seed, perhaps of wheat or of some other grain. [38]But God gives it a body as he has chosen, and to each kind of seed its own body. [39]Not all flesh is alike, but there is one flesh for human beings, another for animals, another for birds, and another for fish. [40]There are both heavenly bodies and earthly bodies, but the glory of the heavenly is one thing, and that of the earthly is another. [41]There is one glory of the sun, and another glory of the moon, and another glory of the stars; indeed, star differs from star in glory.

42 So it is with the resurrection of the dead. What is sown is perishable, what is raised is imperishable. [43]It is sown in dishonor, it is raised in glory. It is sown in weakness, it is raised in power. [44]It is sown a physical body, it is raised a spiritual body. If there is a physical body, there is also a spiritual body. [45]Thus it is written, "The first man, Adam, became a living being"; the last Adam became a life-giving spirit. [46]But it is not the spiritual that is first, but the physical, and then the spiritual. [47]The first man was from the earth, a man of dust; the second man is[e] from heaven. [48]As was the man of dust, so are those who are of the dust; and as is the man of heaven, so are those who are of heaven. [49]Just as we have borne the image of the man of dust, we will[f] also bear the image of the man of heaven.

50 What I am saying, brothers and sisters,[d] is this: flesh and blood cannot inherit the kingdom of God, nor does the perishable inherit the imperishable. [51]Listen, I will tell you a mystery! We will not all die,[g] but we will all be changed, [52]in a moment, in the twinkling of an eye, at the last trumpet. For the trumpet will sound, and the dead will be raised imperishable, and we will be changed. [53]For this perishable body must put on imperishability, and this mortal body must put on immortality. [54]When this perishable body puts on imperishability, and this mortal body puts on immortality, then the saying that is written will be fulfilled:

"Death has been swallowed up in victory."
55 "Where, O death, is your victory?
      Where, O death, is your sting?"
[56]The sting of death is sin, and the power of sin is the law. [57]But thanks be to God, who gives us the

---

a Gk *fallen asleep*   b Or *Then come the rest*   c Gk *he*   d Gk *brothers*   e Other ancient authorities add *the Lord*   f Other ancient authorities read *let us*
g Gk *fall asleep*

STUDY
IT!

Life After Death · 1 Corinthians 15:35–58

Reality and fantasy are often confusing for kids. When we're young we might believe in Santa Claus, the Easter Bunny, the Tooth Fairy, and even a monster living under our beds. We may picture heaven as having pearly gates with chubby angels flying around clouds with harps. As we grow older, some exchange this fantasy image for a more mature belief in the mystery of the resurrection. But it is confusing and hard to know exactly what to believe about life after death.

Christians from Corinth had problems with this concept too. Common ideas influenced by Greek philosophy made it difficult for them to think that a body could return to life after it had died. They believed body and soul were separate. Their view was that the immortal soul continued living after the body died.

In contrast, the Hebrews saw a unity between the spiritual and physical aspects of the human person. When the prophets, such as Daniel, had visions of a blessed life after death, they didn't think in terms of a soul freed from the body. They thought in terms of a body filled once more with life (see "Study It: Resurrection," near Daniel 12:1–3).

Believing in the resurrection of the body is a core part of the Christian faith. The gospel writers describe the risen Jesus as different from the Jesus who died on the cross. The disciples didn't recognize him at first sight. They knew him only through their faith.

Paul gets right to the point. Jesus' followers need to believe in the resurrection of the body; otherwise the belief that Christ was raised from death is in vain. Paul explains that in the resurrection, our earthly bodies will be transformed—becoming glorious, imperishable, and immortal bodies (1 Corinthians 15:44–46). We will not be spirits or souls without bodies when we have eternal life in communion with God (1 Corinthians 15:53–57). And we will be made alive in Christ, whether our mind can comprehend that idea or not. Our end is not death, but eternal life with Christ!

---

victory through our Lord Jesus Christ.

58 Therefore, my beloved,*a* be steadfast, immovable, always excelling in the work of the Lord, because you know that in the Lord your labor is not in vain.

The Collection for the Saints

16 Now concerning the collection for the saints: you should follow the directions I gave to the churches of Galatia. ²On the first day of every week, each of you is to put aside and save whatever extra you earn, so that collections need not be taken when I come. ³And when I arrive, I will send any whom you approve with letters to take your gift to Jerusalem. ⁴If it seems advisable that I should go also, they will accompany me.

Plans for Travel

5 I will visit you after passing through Macedonia—for I intend to pass through Macedonia—

⁶and perhaps I will stay with you or even spend the winter, so that you may send me on my way, wherever I go. ⁷I do not want to see you now just in passing, for I hope to spend some time with you, if the Lord permits. ⁸But I will stay in Ephesus until Pentecost, ⁹for a wide door for effective work has opened to me, and there are many adversaries.

10 If Timothy comes, see that he has nothing to fear among you, for he is doing the work of the Lord just as I am; ¹¹therefore let no one despise him. Send him on his way in peace, so that he may come to me; for I am expecting him with the brothers.

12 Now concerning our brother Apollos, I strongly urged him to visit you with the other brothers, but he was not at all willing*b* to come now. He will come when he has the opportunity.

Final Messages and Greetings

13 Keep alert, stand firm in your faith, be courageous, be strong. ¹⁴Let all that you do be done in love.

---

a Gk beloved brothers *b* Or it was not at all God's will for him

Be Courageous · 1 Corinthians 16:13–14

Young people are often excellent risk takers, and taking risks requires courage. Though some of these risky actions are seen in a negative light, there are other risks that often serve to bring light to others. Befriending an isolated student, speaking out against unjust practices, confronting discrimination, or standing up to those who abuse the environment are not always the easiest things to do. Yet young people are often found leading the way. So we celebrate risk takers who have given up their comfort, their lifestyle, and sometimes their very lives to proclaim their faith with courage. The lives of these people challenge and inspire others to live out that same courageous faith.

- What risks are you willing to take in making God's message known to the world?
- Who can you follow as examples? Check out the "Connect It!" sections throughout this Bible for the stories of people who are going against the grain and courageously taking risks for Christ.

15 Now, brothers and sisters,[a] you know that members of the household of Stephanas were the first converts in Achaia, and they have devoted themselves to the service of the saints; [16]I urge you to put yourselves at the service of such people, and of everyone who works and toils with them. [17]I rejoice at the coming of Stephanas and Fortunatus and Achaicus, because they have made up for your absence; [18]for they refreshed my spirit as well as yours. So give recognition to such persons.

19 The churches of Asia send greetings. Aquila and Prisca, together with the church in their house, greet you warmly in the Lord. [20]All the brothers and sisters[a] send greetings. Greet one another with a holy kiss.

21 I, Paul, write this greeting with my own hand. [22]Let anyone be accursed who has no love for the Lord. Our Lord, come![b] [23]The grace of the Lord Jesus be with you. [24]My love be with all of you in Christ Jesus.[c]

a Gk brothers b Gk Marana tha. These Aramaic words can also be read Maran atha, meaning Our Lord has come c Other ancient authorities add Amen

2 Corinthians

▶▶▶▶▶▶▶▶▶▶▶▶▶▶▶▶▶

We've all felt the pain of conflict and criticism. It's no fun to be picked on or attacked. Our instinct is to get defensive and strike back. But in his second letter to the Corinthians, Paul shows us how God helps us rise above our instincts. Paul responds to personal attacks with directness and honesty. He demonstrates how to witness about Jesus—even when we're in the middle of conflict.

IN DEPTH

The relationship between Paul and the Corinthians went downhill after Paul wrote 1 Corinthians. Apparently, some other traveling missionaries came to Corinth and undermined Paul's credibility. They attacked him as a person (2 Corinthians 10:10), implied that he was mentally imbalanced (2 Corinthians 5:13), and criticized him as a speaker (2 Corinthians 10:10). They even suggested that Paul wasn't trustworthy with money (2 Corinthians 8:20-21).

As part of these attacks, some people claimed that Paul couldn't make up his mind about returning to visit Corinth. They said he kept changing between yes and no. Paul defends himself skillfully by changing the focus and saying that in Jesus we always find a yes. In Jesus, every one of God's promises is a yes (2 Corinthians 1:19-20). And although Paul's opponents make boastful claims for themselves, Paul realizes that God's grace is all he needs. In fact, he says, "I will boast all the more gladly of my weaknesses, so that the power of Christ may dwell in me" (2 Corinthians 12:9). Paul's decision not to return to Corinth is also an attempt to avoid causing the community any more pain as a result of another conflict that happened within the Corinthian community (2 Corinthians 2:1-11).

Paul loves the people he is writing to. Before he addresses the issues between them, he makes this clear by telling them that he wrote to let them know the abundant love he has for them (2 Corinthians 2:4). What an amazing example of where God starts with us, and where we should start with others—love. It sets the tone for dealing with differences and tears down the walls of defensiveness. Then Paul is free to speak truth and put things into perspective. Then he and the Corinthians can work through their differences and look for unity in Christ.

QUICK FACTS

- **Author:** Paul
- **Date Written:** Around 57 A.D.
- **Audience:** The mainly Gentile (non-Jewish) church in Corinth (in modern-day Greece)
- **Theme:** God's power is made perfect in our weakness.

AT A GLANCE

- **2 Corinthians 1:1–11**
  Greetings
- **2 Corinthians 1:12–7:16**
  A description of how Paul and the Corinthians resolve their conflict; teaching on the nature of Paul's ministry
- **2 Corinthians 8–9**
  A discussion of a collection for the church at Jerusalem
- **2 Corinthians 10:1–13:10**
  A defense of Paul's ministry as an apostle
- **2 Corinthians 13:11–13**
  Final greeting and a blessing

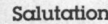
1 Salutation

Paul, an apostle of Christ Jesus by the will of God, and Timothy our brother,

To the church of God that is in Corinth, including all the saints throughout Achaia:

2 Grace to you and peace from God our Father and the Lord Jesus Christ.

Paul's Thanksgiving after Affliction

3 Blessed be the God and Father of our Lord Jesus Christ, the Father of mercies and the God of all consolation, [4]who consoles us in all our affliction, so that we may be able to console those who are in any affliction with the consolation with which we ourselves are consoled by God. [5]For just as the sufferings of Christ are abundant for us, so also our consolation is abundant through Christ. [6]If we are being afflicted, it is for your consolation and salvation; if we are being consoled, it is for your consolation, which you experience when you patiently endure the same sufferings that we are also suffering. [7]Our hope for you is unshaken; for we know that as you share in our sufferings, so also you share in our consolation.

8 We do not want you to be unaware, brothers and sisters,[a] of the affliction we experienced in Asia; for we were so utterly, unbearably crushed that we despaired of life itself. [9]Indeed, we felt that we had received the sentence of death so that we would rely not on ourselves but on God who raises the dead. [10]He who rescued us from so deadly a peril will continue to rescue us; on him we have set our hope that he will rescue us again, [11]as you also join in helping us by your prayers, so that many will give thanks on our[b] behalf for the blessing granted us through the prayers of many.

The Postponement of Paul's Visit

12 Indeed, this is our boast, the testimony of our conscience: we have behaved in the world with frankness[c] and godly sincerity, not by earthly wis-

dom but by the grace of God—and all the more toward you. [13]For we write you nothing other than what you can read and also understand; I hope you will understand until the end— [14]as you have already understood us in part—that on the day of the Lord Jesus we are your boast even as you are our boast.

15 Since I was sure of this, I wanted to come to you first, so that you might have a double favor;[d] [16]I wanted to visit you on my way to Macedonia, and to come back to you from Macedonia and have you send me on to Judea. [17]Was I vacillating when I wanted to do this? Do I make my plans according to ordinary human standards,[e] ready to say "Yes, yes" and "No, no" at the same time? [18]As surely as God is faithful, our word to you has not been "Yes and No." [19]For the Son of God, Jesus Christ, whom we proclaimed among you, Silvanus and Timothy and I, was not "Yes and No"; but in him it is always "Yes." [20]For in him every one of God's promises is a "Yes." For this reason it is through him that we say the "Amen," to the glory of God. [21]But it is God who establishes us with you in Christ and has anointed us, [22]by putting his seal on us and giving us his Spirit in our hearts as a first installment.

23 But I call on God as witness against me: it was to spare you that I did not come again to Corinth. [24]I do not mean to imply that we lord it over your faith; rather, we are workers with you for your joy, because you stand firm in the faith. ## 2 [1]So I made up my mind not to make you another painful visit. [2]For if I cause you pain, who is there to make me glad but the one whom I have pained? [3]And I wrote as I did, so that when I came, I might not suffer pain from those who should have made me rejoice; for I am confident about all of you, that my joy would be the joy of all of you. [4]For I wrote you out of much distress and anguish of heart and with many tears, not to cause you pain, but to let you know the abundant love that I have for you.

> "Blessed be the God and Father of our Lord Jesus Christ ... who consoles us in all our affliction, so that we may be able to console those who are in any affliction with the consolation with which we ourselves are consoled by God."
> —2 Corinthians 1:3–4

---

a Gk brothers b Other ancient authorities read your c Other ancient authorities read holiness d Other ancient authorities read pleasure
e Gk according to the flesh

to Christ, so also wives ought to be, in everything, to their husbands.

25 Husbands, love your wives, just as Christ loved the church and gave himself up for her, ²⁶in order to make her holy by cleansing her with the washing of water by the word, ²⁷so as to present the church to himself in splendor, without a spot or wrinkle or anything of the kind—yes, so that she may be holy and without blemish. ²⁸In the same way, husbands should love their wives as they do their own bodies. He who loves his wife loves himself. ²⁹For no one ever hates his own body, but he nourishes and tenderly cares for it, just as Christ does for the church, ³⁰because we are members of his body.[a] ³¹"For this reason a man will leave his father and mother and be joined to his wife, and the two will become one flesh." ³²This is a great mystery, and I am applying it to Christ and the church. ³³Each of you, however, should love his wife as himself, and a wife should respect her husband.

Children and Parents

6 Children, obey your parents in the Lord,[b] for this is right. ²"Honor your father and mother"—this is the first commandment with a promise: ³"so that it may be well with you and you may live long on the earth."

4 And, fathers, do not provoke your children to anger, but bring them up in the discipline and instruction of the Lord.

Slaves and Masters

5 Slaves, obey your earthly masters with fear and trembling, in singleness of heart, as you obey Christ; ⁶not only while being watched, and in order to please them, but as slaves of Christ, doing the will of God from the heart. ⁷Render service with enthusiasm, as to the Lord and not to men and women, ⁸knowing that whatever good we do, we will receive the same again from the Lord, whether we are slaves or free.

9 And, masters, do the same to them. Stop threatening them, for you know that both of you have the same Master in heaven, and with him there is no partiality.

The Whole Armor of God

10 Finally, be strong in the Lord and in the strength of his power. ¹¹Put on the whole armor of God, so that you may be able to stand against the wiles of the devil. ¹²For our[c] struggle is not against enemies of blood and flesh, but against the rulers, against the authorities, against the cosmic powers of this present darkness, against the spiritual forces of evil in the heavenly places. ¹³Therefore take up the whole armor of God, so that you may be able to withstand on that evil day, and having done everything, to stand firm. ¹⁴Stand therefore, and fasten the belt of truth around your waist, and put on the breastplate of righteousness. ¹⁵As shoes for your feet put on whatever will

---

PRAY IT!

The Armor of God · Ephesians 6:10–17

The military imagery of this passage is a strong signal that we face a battle as followers of Jesus. Look closely at this armor. Most of it is intended as defense against an evil enemy (Ephesians 6:11). Our main offensive weapon, the sword of the Spirit, isn't a tool that we create (Ephesians 6:17). It's the Word of God, and it shows us that we must rely on God's truth and words in every aspect of our battle against evil. Our enemy is not a natural one, but a spiritual one (Ephesians 6:12). Although we may face struggles in our life, the real struggle is between spiritual forces of good and evil. The good news is that God's truth, righteousness, peace, salvation, and Word will ultimately be victorious.

Dear God, thank you that your power and strength are greater than any of the forces of darkness. Give me your protection and help me to always stand firm in you. Amen.

---

a Other ancient authorities add *of his flesh and of his bones*   b Other ancient authorities lack *in the Lord*   c Other ancient authorities read *your*   d Or *In all circumstances*

make you ready to proclaim the gospel of peace. [16]With all of these,[d] take the shield of faith, with which you will be able to quench all the flaming arrows of the evil one. [17]Take the helmet of salvation, and the sword of the Spirit, which is the word of God. 18 Pray in the Spirit at all times in every prayer and supplication. To that end keep alert and always persevere in supplication for all the saints. [19]Pray also for me, so that when I speak, a message may be given to me to make known with boldness the mystery of the gospel,[a] [20]for which I am an ambassador in chains. Pray that I may declare it boldly, as I must speak.

Personal Matters and Benediction

21 So that you also may know how I am and what I am doing, Tychicus will tell you everything. He is a dear brother and a faithful minister in the Lord. [22]I am sending him to you for this very purpose, to let you know how we are, and to encourage your hearts.

23 Peace be to the whole community,[b] and love with faith, from God the Father and the Lord Jesus Christ. [24]Grace be with all who have an undying love for our Lord Jesus Christ.[c]

a Other ancient authorities lack *of the gospel*   b Gk *to the brothers*   c Other ancient authorities add *Amen*

Philippians

▶▶▶▶▶▶▶

"To be, or not to be: that is the question." In this line from Shakespeare's "Hamlet," Hamlet wonders which is better for him—to live or to die. He doesn't want to live and suffer, but he's afraid the "sleep of death" may be worse. Either way, he loses. In the letter to the Philippians, Paul struggles with a similar question. Paul looks forward to dying to be with God. But he also wants to stay alive in order to continue serving and helping other believers grow in their joy in faith.

IN DEPTH

Paul wrote this letter when he was imprisoned, facing a charge that might end in his death. He wrote it either near the end of his life when he was under house arrest in Rome or, more likely, during an earlier imprisonment in Ephesus (1 Corinthians 15:32; 2 Corinthians 1:8).

Paul is torn: "I am hard pressed between the two," life and **death (Philippians 1:23).** But Paul feels he'll win either way: "For to me, living is Christ and dying is gain" (Philippians 1:21). In addition, Paul believes this imprisonment will not end with his death, because he is still needed to support the new churches he helped start.

Incredibly, even in prison Paul exhibits a spirit of hope and encouragement. He uses the words "rejoice" and "joy" fifteen times in this short letter! Living in Christ doesn't mean everything will always go wonderfully. But it does mean that God can get you through the good times and the difficult times with joy.

In this letter, Paul asks the Philippians—and us—to imitate Christ. Imitating Christ is to think and act as Christ did, even when things aren't going our way. Paul quotes an early Christian song (Philippians 2:6-11) to the Philippians to show what imitating Christ means. The song praises Jesus, who chose to humble himself, become a servant, and remain "obedient to the point of death" (Philippians 2:8). God exalted him above all things.

It's clear from this letter that Paul had a close relationship with the Philippians. No doubt, they were worried about him. Paul wants them to rejoice in Christ and in their suffering, and to stop worrying (Philippians 4:4-6). He encourages them to present their concerns—all of them—to God in prayer. And he promises that if they do so, "the peace of God, which surpasses all understanding, will guard [their] hearts and [their] minds in Christ Jesus" (Philippians 4:7). His words offer great advice and comfort for all people.

QUICK FACTS

- **Author:** Paul
- **Date Written:** A.D. 55, if from Ephesus; 59-63, if from Rome
- **Audience:** The Christian community in Philippi (in modern-day Greece)
- **Theme:** Nothing is more important than knowing Christ.

AT A GLANCE

- **Philippians 1:1–26** Greeting, thanks, and discussion of Paul's imprisonment
- **Philippians 1:27–2:18** Advice to imitate Christ
- **Philippians 2:19–3:1** Plans for Timothy and Epaphroditus
- **Philippians 3:2–4:9** Warning against false teachers and advice for Christian living
- **Philippians 4:10–23** Thanks, final greeting, and a blessing

1

Salutation

Paul and Timothy, servants*a* of Christ Jesus,
To all the saints in Christ Jesus who are in
Philippi, with the bishops*b* and deacons:*c*

2 Grace to you and peace from God our Father
and the Lord Jesus Christ.

Paul's Prayer for the Philippians

3 I thank my God every time I remember you, *4*constantly praying with joy in every one of my prayers for all of you, *5*because of your sharing in the gospel from the first day until now. *6*I am confident of this, that the one who began a good work among you will bring it to completion by the day of Jesus Christ. *7*It is right for me to think this way about all of you, because you hold me in your heart,*d* for all of you share in God's grace*e* with me, both in my imprisonment and in the defense and confirmation of the gospel. *8*For God is my witness, how I long for all of you with the compassion of Christ Jesus. *9*And this is my prayer, that your love may overflow more and more with knowledge and full insight *10*to help you to determine what is best, so that in the day of Christ you may be pure and blameless, *11*having produced the harvest of righteousness that comes through Jesus Christ for the glory and praise of God.

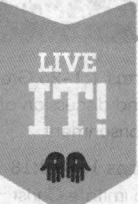

LIVE IT!

True BFF
Philippians 1:3–11

Here Paul writes beautifully of his love for and friendship with the people living in Philippi. Remember that Paul—like all the others who wrote the words of scripture—was a real person with problems and needs. He had some dear friends in Philippi. His words to them provide a great model of true friendship: sharing the ups and downs, being committed, being thankful for each other, and wanting the best for one another. Friendship in Christ is like that!

- Who are your true friends?
- Who considers you a true friend?
- How can you keep Christ at the center of your friendships?

Paul's Present Circumstances

12 I want you to know, beloved,*f* that what has happened to me has actually helped to spread the gospel, *13*so that it has become known throughout the whole imperial guard*g* and to everyone else that my imprisonment is for Christ; *14*and most of the brothers and sisters,*f* having been made confident in the Lord by my imprisonment, dare to speak the word*h* with greater boldness and without fear.

15 Some proclaim Christ from envy and rivalry, but others from goodwill. *16*These proclaim Christ out of love, knowing that I have been put here for the defense of the gospel; *17*the others proclaim Christ out of selfish ambition, not sincerely but intending to increase my suffering in my imprisonment. *18*What does it matter? Just this, that Christ is proclaimed in every way, whether out of false motives or true; and in that I rejoice.

Yes, and I will continue to rejoice, *19*for I know that through your prayers and the help of the Spirit of Jesus Christ this will turn out for my deliverance. *20*It is my eager expectation and hope that I will not be put to shame in any way, but that by my speaking with all boldness, Christ will be exalted now as always in my body, whether by life or by death. *21*For to me, living is Christ and dying is gain. *22*If I am to live in the flesh, that means fruitful labor for me; and I do not know which I prefer. *23*I am hard pressed between the two: my desire is to depart and be with Christ, for that is far better; *24*but to remain in the flesh is more necessary for you. *25*Since I am convinced of this, I know that I will remain and continue with all of you for your progress and joy in faith, *26*so that I may share abundantly in your boasting in Christ Jesus when I come to you again.

27 Only, live your life in a manner worthy of the gospel of Christ, so that, whether I come and see you or am absent and hear about you, I will know that you are standing firm in one spirit, striving side by side with one mind for the faith of the gospel, *28*and are in no way intimidated by your opponents. For them this is evidence of their destruction, but of your salvation. And this is God's doing. *29*For he has graciously granted you the privilege not only of believing in Christ, but of suffering for him as well— *30*since you are having the same struggle that you saw I had and now hear that I still have.

---

a Gk *slaves* *b* Or *overseers* *c* Or *overseers and helpers* *d* Or *because I hold you in my heart* *e* Gk *in grace* *f* Gk *brothers* *g* Gk *whole praetorium*
h Other ancient authorities read *word of God*

Super Humility · Philippians 2:1–11

Paul tells his friends that nothing would make him happier than knowing that they are unified in love (Philippians 2:2). This requires humility—thinking of others as better than yourself and putting their interests first. And who is a better example of this than Jesus?

In **Philippians 2:6–11**, Paul borrows a hymn sung in the earliest days of the Church to explain how the community should have the same mind-set as Jesus. Jesus gave up his right to equality with God (Philippians 2:6) and entered our world as a human being. He lived in utter humility, from his simple birth to his crucifixion. Because of his humility and obedience, Jesus' name is exalted by God, so that Christ is now Lord of all and worshiped by all creation.

To be the loving people God calls us to be, we must imitate Christ's humility in our love for and service to each other. It's more common for us to see those who are powerful in our world being served by others. But Paul reminds us it's Jesus' nature to serve. Christians are called to be powerful in a radically different way—by humbly serving with the "same mind . . . that was in Christ Jesus" (Philippians 2:5).

Imitating Christ's Humility

2 If then there is any encouragement in Christ, any consolation from love, any sharing in the Spirit, any compassion and sympathy, ²make my joy complete: be of the same mind, having the same love, being in full accord and of one mind. ³Do nothing from selfish ambition or conceit, but in humility regard others as better than yourselves. ⁴Let each of you look not to your own interests, but to the interests of others. ⁵Let the same mind be in you that was*ᵃ* in Christ Jesus,

6 who, though he was in the form of God,
    did not regard equality with God
    as something to be exploited,
7 but emptied himself,
    taking the form of a slave,
    being born in human likeness.
    And being found in human form,
8   he humbled himself
    and became obedient to the point of
        death—
    even death on a cross.

9 Therefore God also highly exalted him
    and gave him the name
    that is above every name,
10   so that at the name of Jesus
    every knee should bend,
    in heaven and on earth and under the
        earth,

11   and every tongue should confess
    that Jesus Christ is Lord,
    to the glory of God the Father.

Shining as Lights in the World

12 Therefore, my beloved, just as you have always obeyed me, not only in my presence, but much more now in my absence, work out your own salvation with fear and trembling; ¹³for it is God who is at work in you, enabling you both to will and to work for his good pleasure.

14 Do all things without murmuring and arguing, ¹⁵so that you may be blameless and innocent, children of God without blemish in the midst of a crooked and perverse generation, in which you shine like stars in the world. ¹⁶It is by your holding fast to the word of life that I can boast on the day of Christ that I did not run in vain or labor in vain. ¹⁷But even if I am being poured out as a libation over the sacrifice and the offering of your faith, I am glad and

a Or *that you have*

rejoice with all of you— [18] and in the same way you also must be glad and rejoice with me.

Timothy and Epaphroditus

19 I hope in the Lord Jesus to send Timothy to you soon, so that I may be cheered by news of you. [20] I have no one like him who will be genuinely concerned for your welfare. [21] All of them are seeking their own interests, not those of Jesus Christ. [22] But Timothy's[a] worth you know, how like a son with a father he has served with me in the work of the gospel. [23] I hope therefore to send him as soon as I see how things go with me; [24] and I trust in the Lord that I will also come soon.

25 Still, I think it necessary to send to you Epaphroditus—my brother and co-worker and fellow soldier, your messenger[b] and minister to my need; [26] for he has been longing for[c] all of you, and has been distressed because you heard that he was ill. [27] He was indeed so ill that he nearly died. But God had mercy on him, and not only on him but on me also, so that I would not have one sorrow after another. [28] I am the more eager to send him, therefore, in order that you may rejoice at seeing him again, and that I may be less anxious. [29] Welcome him then in the Lord with all joy, and honor such people, [30] because he came close to death for the work of Christ,[d] risking his life to make up for those services that you could not give me.

3   Finally, my brothers and sisters,[e] rejoice[f] in the Lord.

Breaking with the Past

To write the same things to you is not troublesome to me, and for you it is a safeguard.

2 Beware of the dogs, beware of the evil workers, beware of those who mutilate the flesh![g] [3] For it is we who are the circumcision, who worship in the Spirit of God[h] and boast in Christ Jesus and have no confidence in the flesh— [4] even though I, too, have reason for confidence in the flesh.

If anyone else has reason to be confident in the flesh, I have more: [5] circumcised on the eighth day, a member of the people of Israel, of the tribe of Benjamin, a Hebrew born of Hebrews; as to the law, a Pharisee; [6] as to zeal, a persecutor of the church; as to righteousness under the law, blameless.

7 Yet whatever gains I had, these I have come to regard as loss because of Christ. [8] More than that, I regard everything as loss because of the surpassing value of knowing Christ Jesus my Lord. For his sake I have suffered the loss of all things, and I regard them as rubbish, in order that I may gain Christ [9] and be found in him, not having a righteousness of my own that comes from the law, but one that comes through faith in Christ,[i] the righteousness from God based on faith. [10] I want to know Christ[j] and the power of his resurrection and the sharing of his sufferings by becoming like him in his death, [11] if somehow I may attain the resurrection from the dead.

Pressing toward the Goal

12 Not that I have already obtained this or have already reached the goal;[k] but I press on to make it my own, because Christ Jesus has made me his own. [13] Beloved,[l] I do not consider that I have made it my own;[m] but this one thing I do: forgetting what lies behind and straining forward to what lies ahead, [14] I press on toward the goal for the prize of the heavenly[n] call of God in Christ Jesus. [15] Let those of us then who are mature be of the same mind; and if you think differently about anything, this too God will reveal to you. [16] Only let us hold fast to what we have attained.

17 Brothers and sisters,[l] join in imitating me, and observe those who live according to the example

LIVE IT!

**The Ultimate Goal
Philippians 3:12–16**

Paul measures maturity by how well people are able to stick to the goal and commitment of following Christ all the way. Mature people—whether age sixteen or sixty—are always looking ahead and striving to move forward in pursuit of their goals. Paul says the goal that guides his life is "to know Christ and the power of his resurrection" (Philippians 3:10).

- Is knowing Christ and the power of his resurrection the goal that guides your life?
- How are you moving forward in pursuit of your goals?
- If you are a follower of Jesus, how does your life show your commitment to him?

---

a Gk *his* b Gk *apostle* c Other ancient authorities read *longing to see* d Other ancient authorities read *of the Lord* e Gk *my brothers* f Or *farewell* g Gk *the mutilation* h Other ancient authorities read *worship God in spirit* i Or *through the faith of Christ* j Gk *him* k Or *have already been made perfect* l Gk *Brothers* m Other ancient authorities read *my own yet* n Gk *upward*

you have in us. [18]For many live as enemies of the cross of Christ; I have often told you of them, and now I tell you even with tears. [19]Their end is destruction; their god is the belly; and their glory is in their shame; their minds are set on earthly things. [20]But our citizenship[a] is in heaven, and it is from there that we are expecting a Savior, the Lord Jesus Christ. [21]He will transform the body of our humiliation[b] that it may be conformed to the body of his glory,[c] by the power that also enables him to make all things subject to himself.

> "I can do all things through him who strengthens me."
> —Philippians 4:13

4 [1]Therefore, my brothers and sisters,[d] whom I love and long for, my joy and crown, stand firm in the Lord in this way, my beloved.

Exhortations

2 I urge Euodia and I urge Syntyche to be of the same mind in the Lord. [3]Yes, and I ask you also, my loyal companion,[e] help these women, for they have struggled beside me in the work of the gospel, together with Clement and the rest of my co-workers, whose names are in the book of life.

4 Rejoice[f] in the Lord always; again I will say, Rejoice.[f] [5]Let your gentleness be known to everyone. The Lord is near. [6]Do not worry about anything, but in everything by prayer and supplication with thanksgiving let your requests be made known to God. [7]And the peace of God, which surpasses all understanding, will guard your hearts and your minds in Christ Jesus.

8 Finally, beloved,[g] whatever is true, whatever is honorable, whatever is just, whatever is pure, whatever is pleasing, whatever is commendable, if there is any excellence and if there is anything worthy of praise, think about[h] these things. [9]Keep on doing the things that you have learned and received and heard and seen in me, and the God of peace will be with you.

Acknowledgment of the Philippians' Gift

10 I rejoice[i] in the Lord greatly that now at last you have revived your concern for me; indeed, you were concerned for me, but had no opportunity to show it.[j] [11]Not that I am referring to being in need; for I have learned to be content with whatever I have. [12]I know what it is to have little, and I know what it is to have plenty. In any and all circumstances I have learned the secret of being well-fed and of going hungry, of having plenty and of being in need. [13]I can do all things through him who strengthens me. [14]In any case, it was kind of you to share my distress.

15 You Philippians indeed know that in the early days of the gospel, when I left Macedonia, no church shared with me in the matter of giving and

Praise, Prayer, and Peace · Philippians 4:4–7

Paul provides the Philippians with instructions to rejoice in the Lord always (Philippians 4:4) and to pray instead of worrying (Philippians 4:6). The promise he gives them is a promise for us as well, that "the peace of God, which surpasses all understanding, will guard (our) hearts and (our) minds in Christ Jesus" (Philippians 4:7). That's a peace that sustains us even when earthly logic says our circumstances and problems are so bad that we will never have any peace at all! If you are consumed with worry, consider praying this prayer today:

God, I praise you for who you are. I know you love me, but I get caught up in my problems and start to worry. I want to trust you, but I try to figure it all out myself. Help me to turn to you. Thank you that you never turn away or lose interest in me. Please give me your peace, even beyond what I can understand, and help me to rest in you. Amen.

---

a Or *commonwealth* **b** Or *our humble bodies* **c** Or *his glorious body* **d** Gk *my brothers* **e** Or *loyal Syzygus* **f** Or *Farewell* **g** Gk *brothers* **h** Gk *take account of* **i** Gk *I rejoiced* **j** Gk lacks *to show it*

receiving, except you alone. [16]For even when I was in Thessalonica, you sent me help for my needs more than once. [17]Not that I seek the gift, but I seek the profit that accumulates to your account. [18]I have been paid in full and have more than enough; I am fully satisfied, now that I have received from Epaphroditus the gifts you sent, a fragrant offering, a sacrifice acceptable and pleasing to God. [19]And my God will fully satisfy every need of yours according to his riches in glory in Christ Jesus. [20]To our God and Father be glory forever and ever. Amen.

Final Greetings and Benediction

21 Greet every saint in Christ Jesus. The friends[a] who are with me greet you. [22]All the saints greet you, especially those of the emperor's household.

23 The grace of the Lord Jesus Christ be with your spirit.[b]

a Gk *brothers*   b Other ancient authorities add *Amen*

Colossians

The health-and-wealth message that claims that Christians will be rewarded with prosperity is a nice thought. It's easy to start looking at biblical teaching in a way that reflects the comfort and ease of a wealthy lifestyle. But although this message may be attractive, it's not the message of Christ. This isn't a new phenomenon. Even in first-century Colossae there were some who were applying pagan religious practices and beliefs from Greek philosophy to the Christian community. The author's advice in the letter to the Colossians is pretty direct: stay focused on Christ!

IN DEPTH

This letter attacks a group that was teaching a weird mixture of ideas. It insisted on Jewish rituals and regulations (Colossians 2:16, 22), severe treatment of one's own body (Colossians 2:23), and a philosophy that mixed "the elemental spirits of the universe" (Colossians 2:8) and pagan religious practices. These teachers probably had Jewish roots, because they observed the sabbath and other Jewish festivals (Colossians 2:16).

Against the backdrop of all this thinking, the author—who may have been a disciple of Paul, rather than Paul himself—declares the supreme mystery of Christ. He quotes a Christian hymn to say Christ is honored as the firstborn of creation and as the one who created everything (Colossians 1:15-20). Christ is above everything that is and holds all creation together.

Christians believe Jesus is more than just a great teacher. They believe Jesus is God who chose to become human and live on earth. This letter gives us an early statement of that belief: "In (Christ) the whole fullness of deity dwells bodily" (Colossians 2:9).

Colossians also offers comforting words about God. God has given us life and forgiveness. God erased the record of our sins and set it aside, "nailing it to the cross" (Colossians 2:14). Unlike those teachers who burden their followers with guilt and impossible rules, our God frees us from guilt and gives us life! As you read this letter, you'll find these and many other words to live by: "God's chosen ones, . . . forgive each other, . . . clothe yourselves with love, . . . and let the peace of Christ rule in your hearts" (Colossians 3:12-15).

QUICK FACTS

- **Author:** Paul, or more likely a follower of Paul
- **Date Written:** Around A.D. 61, if by Paul; around 80, if by a follower
- **Audience:** The Christian community in Colossae (in modern-day Turkey)
- **Themes:** Jesus is Lord of all and reconciles all things in heaven and on earth.

AT A GLANCE

- **Colossians 1:1–2** Greeting
- **Colossians 1:3–23** Thanksgiving and hymn of praise to Christ as the first of creation and Lord of all
- **Colossians 1:24–2:23** Relations with the community and warnings against false teachers
- **Colossians 3:1–4:6** Advice for Christian living
- **Colossians 4:7–18** Final greetings and a blessing

1

Salutation

Paul, an apostle of Christ Jesus by the will of God, and Timothy our brother,

2 To the saints and faithful brothers and sisters[a] in Christ in Colossae:

Grace to you and peace from God our Father.

Paul Thanks God for the Colossians

3 In our prayers for you we always thank God, the Father of our Lord Jesus Christ, [4]for we have heard of your faith in Christ Jesus and of the love that you have for all the saints, [5]because of the hope laid up for you in heaven. You have heard of this hope before in the word of the truth, the gospel [6]that has come to you. Just as it is bearing fruit and growing in the whole world, so it has been bearing fruit among yourselves from the day you heard it and truly comprehended the grace of God. [7]This you learned from Epaphras, our beloved fellow servant.[b] He is a faithful minister of Christ on your[c] behalf, [8]and he has made known to us your love in the Spirit.

9 For this reason, since the day we heard it, we have not ceased praying for you and asking that you may be filled with the knowledge of God's[d] will in all spiritual wisdom and understanding, [10]so that you may lead lives worthy of the Lord, fully pleasing to him, as you bear fruit in every good work and as you grow in the knowledge of God. [11]May you be made strong with all the strength that comes from his glorious power, and may you be prepared to endure everything with patience, while joyfully [12]giving thanks to the Father, who has enabled[e] you[f] to share in the inheritance of the saints in the light. [13]He has rescued us from the power of darkness and transferred us into the kingdom of his beloved Son, [14]in whom we have redemption, the forgiveness of sins.[g]

The Supremacy of Christ

15 He is the image of the invisible God, the firstborn of all creation; [16]for in[h] him all things in heaven and on earth were created, things visible and invisible, whether thrones or dominions or rulers or powers—all things have been created through him and for him. [17]He himself is before all things, and in[h] him all things hold together. [18]He is the head of the body, the church; he is the beginning, the firstborn from the dead, so that he might come to have first place in everything. [19]For in him all the fullness of God was pleased to dwell, [20]and through him God was pleased to reconcile to himself all things, whether on earth or in heaven, by making peace through the blood of his cross.

> "Lead lives worthy of the Lord, fully pleasing to him, as you bear fruit in every good work and as you grow in the knowledge of God."
> —Colossians 1:10

STUDY IT!

The Image of God · Colossians 1:15–20

It's possible to describe God by naming certain characteristics. We can say God is all-powerful, all-knowing, and eternal. But knowing about God is not the same as knowing God. So how can we really understand the mysterious, invisible, eternal God?

The author of Colossians gives us a clue. He calls Jesus "the image of the invisible God" (Colossians 1:15). If we want to know God, who is hidden from us in mystery, we look at Jesus. Christ has existed for all eternity, and through him all things were created and all things continue to hold together. God chose to use Christ as the way to reconcile all creation to God (Colossians 1:20).

Is there still the unknown? Yes. We cannot comprehend God completely. But we can understand more about God by getting to know Jesus Christ.

---

a Gk brothers b Gk slave c Other ancient authorities read our d Gk his e Other ancient authorities read called f Other ancient authorities read us
g Other ancient authorities add through his blood h Or by

21 And you who were once estranged and hostile in mind, doing evil deeds, [22]he has now reconciled[a] in his fleshly body[b] through death, so as to present you holy and blameless and irreproachable before him— [23]provided that you continue securely established and steadfast in the faith, without shifting from the hope promised by the gospel that you heard, which has been proclaimed to every creature under heaven. I, Paul, became a servant of this gospel.

Paul's Interest in the Colossians

24 I am now rejoicing in my sufferings for your sake, and in my flesh I am completing what is lacking in Christ's afflictions for the sake of his body, that is, the church. [25]I became its servant according to God's commission that was given to me for you, to make the word of God fully known, [26]the mystery that has been hidden throughout the ages and generations but has now been revealed to his saints. [27]To them God chose to make known how great among the Gentiles are the riches of the glory of this mystery, which is Christ in you, the hope of glory. [28]It is he whom we proclaim, warning everyone and teaching everyone in all wisdom, so that we may present everyone mature in Christ. [29]For this I toil and struggle with all the energy that he powerfully inspires within me.

2 For I want you to know how much I am struggling for you, and for those in Laodicea, and for all who have not seen me face to face. [2]I want their hearts to be encouraged and united in love, so that they may have all the riches of assured understanding and have the knowledge of God's mystery, that is, Christ himself,[c] [3]in whom are hidden all the treasures of wisdom and knowledge. [4]I am saying this so that no one may deceive you with plausible arguments. [5]For though I am absent in body, yet I am with you in spirit, and I rejoice to see your morale and the firmness of your faith in Christ.

Fullness of Life in Christ

6 As you therefore have received Christ Jesus the Lord, continue to live your lives[d] in him, [7]rooted and built up in him and established in the faith, just as you were taught, abounding in thanksgiving.

8 See to it that no one takes you captive through philosophy and empty deceit, according to human

LIVE IT!

What Are Your Priorities? Colossians 2:6–7

What's one thing that motivates you? What keeps you going? Is it a special friendship? The drive to succeed or be the best at something? Maybe it's a goal of owning a car or holding down a job.

The author of Colossians says we should be "rooted and built up in [Christ]" (Colossians 2:7). Wherever you put down your roots, that's where your motivation will come from. Think again about what motivates you. There's nothing wrong with working toward earthly goals and accomplishments, but are your roots or priorities drawing from something deeper that is enough to nourish a full, rich life?

- What things are most important in your life right now?
- Where is God in each of those things?
- What do you need to reorder so that Christ "might come to have first place" (Colossians 1:18) in your life?

tradition, according to the elemental spirits of the universe,[e] and not according to Christ. [9]For in him the whole fullness of deity dwells bodily, [10]and you have come to fullness in him, who is the head of every ruler and authority. [11]In him also you were circumcised with a spiritual circumcision,[f] by putting off the body of the flesh in the circumcision of Christ; [12]when you were buried with him in baptism, you were also raised with him through faith in the power of God, who raised him from the dead. [13]And when you were dead in trespasses and the uncircumcision of your flesh, God[g] made you[h] alive together with him, when he forgave us all our trespasses, [14]erasing the record that stood against us with its legal demands. He set this aside, nailing it to the cross. [15]He disarmed[i] the rulers and authorities and made a public example of them, triumphing over them in it.

16 Therefore do not let anyone condemn you in

---

a Other ancient authorities read *you have now been reconciled*   b Gk *in the body of his flesh*   c Other ancient authorities read *of the mystery of God, both of the Father and of Christ*   d Gk *to walk*   e Or *the rudiments of the world*   f Gk *a circumcision made without hands*   g Gk *he*   h Other ancient authorities read *made us*; others, *made*   i Or *divested himself of*

matters of food and drink or of observing festivals, new moons, or sabbaths. [17] These are only a shadow of what is to come, but the substance belongs to Christ. [18] Do not let anyone disqualify you, insisting on self-abasement and worship of angels, dwelling[a] on visions,[b] puffed up without cause by a human way of thinking,[c] [19] and not holding fast to the head, from whom the whole body, nourished and held together by its ligaments and sinews, grows with a growth that is from God.

Warnings against False Teachers

20 If with Christ you died to the elemental spirits of the universe,[d] why do you live as if you still belonged to the world? Why do you submit to regulations, [21] "Do not handle, Do not taste, Do not touch"? [22] All these regulations refer to things that perish with use; they are simply human commands and teachings. [23] These have indeed an appearance of wisdom in promoting self-imposed piety, humility, and severe treatment of the body, but they are of no value in checking self-indulgence.[e]

The New Life in Christ

3 So if you have been raised with Christ, seek the things that are above, where Christ is, seated at the right hand of God. [2] Set your minds on things that are above, not on things that are on earth, [3] for you have died, and your life is hidden with Christ in God. [4] When Christ who is your[f] life is revealed, then you also will be revealed with him in glory.

5 Put to death, therefore, whatever in you is earthly: fornication, impurity, passion, evil desire, and greed (which is idolatry). [6] On account of these the wrath of God is coming on those who are disobedient.[g] [7] These are the ways you also once followed, when you were living that life.[h] [8] But now you must get rid of all such things—anger, wrath, malice, slander, and abusive[i] language from your mouth. [9] Do not lie to one another, seeing that you have stripped off the old self with its practices [10] and have clothed yourselves with the new self, which is being renewed in knowledge according to the image of its creator. [11] In that renewal[j] there is no longer Greek and Jew, circumcised and uncircumcised, barbarian, Scythian, slave and free; but Christ is all and in all!

12 As God's chosen ones, holy and beloved, clothe yourselves with compassion, kindness, humility, meekness, and patience. [13] Bear with one another and, if anyone has a complaint against another, forgive each other; just as the Lord[k] has forgiven you, so you also must forgive. [14] Above all, clothe yourselves with love, which binds everything together in perfect harmony. [15] And let the peace of Christ rule in your hearts, to which indeed you were called in the one body. And be thankful. [16] Let the word of Christ[l] dwell in you richly; teach and admonish one another in all wisdom; and with gratitude in your hearts sing psalms, hymns, and spiritual songs to God.[m] [17] And whatever you do, in word or deed, do everything in the name of the Lord Jesus, giving thanks to God the Father through him.

STUDY IT!

You Are What You Wear · Colossians 3:1–17

We're surrounded by sights, smells, and sounds—the physical stuff we see every day. But at the same time, there is a spiritual reality that we can't see with our eyes. The author uses the imagery of clothing to talk about this spiritual reality and to illustrate what our new lives in Christ should look like. We should take off "anger, wrath, malice, slander, and abusive language" (Colossians 3:8). Instead, we need to put on new clothes—compassion, kindness, humility, meekness, and patience (Colossians 3:12). Most important, we are to dress up in love. It's like the final accessory that ties the whole outfit together (Colossians 3:14). This clothing is more than just an outward appearance; it's a reflection of our style—who we are on the inside. It reflects the peace of Christ that rules in our hearts (Colossians 3:15) and the word of Christ that dwells in us richly (Colossians 3:16). According to Colossians, we truly are what we wear.

---

a Other ancient authorities read *not dwelling* b Meaning of Gk uncertain c Gk *by the mind of his flesh* d Or *the rudiments of the world* e Or *are of no value, serving only to indulge the flesh* f Other authorities read *our* g Other ancient authorities lack *on those who are disobedient* (Gk *the children of disobedience*) h Or *living among such people* i Or *filthy* j Gk *its creator, ¹¹where* k Other ancient authorities read *just as Christ* l Other ancient authorities read *of God*, or *of the Lord* m Other ancient authorities read *to the Lord*

Rules for Christian Households

18 Wives, be subject to your husbands, as is fitting in the Lord. [19]Husbands, love your wives and never treat them harshly.

20 Children, obey your parents in everything, for this is your acceptable duty in the Lord. [21]Fathers, do not provoke your children, or they may lose heart. [22]Slaves, obey your earthly masters[a] in everything, not only while being watched and in order to please them, but wholeheartedly, fearing the Lord.[b] [23]Whatever your task, put yourselves into it, as done for the Lord and not for your masters,[a] [24]since you know that from the Lord you will receive the inheritance as your reward; you serve[c] the Lord Christ. [25]For the wrongdoer will be paid back for whatever wrong has been done, and there is no partiality. [1]Masters, treat your slaves justly and fairly, for you know that you also have a Master in heaven.

4

Further Instructions

2 Devote yourselves to prayer, keeping alert in it with thanksgiving. [3]At the same time pray for us as well that God will open to us a door for the word, that we may declare the mystery of Christ, for which I am in prison, [4]so that I may reveal it clearly, as I should.

5 Conduct yourselves wisely toward outsiders, making the most of the time.[d] [6]Let your speech always be gracious, seasoned with salt, so that you may know how you ought to answer everyone.

Final Greetings and Benediction

7 Tychicus will tell you all the news about me; he is a beloved brother, a faithful minister, and a fellow servant[e] in the Lord. [8]I have sent him to you for this very purpose, so that you may know how we are[f] and that he may encourage your hearts; [9]he is coming with Onesimus, the faithful and beloved brother, who is one of you. They will tell you about everything here.

10 Aristarchus my fellow prisoner greets you, as does Mark the cousin of Barnabas, concerning whom you have received instructions—if he comes to you, welcome him. [11]And Jesus who is called Justus greets you. These are the only ones of the circumcision among my co-workers for the kingdom of God, and they have been a comfort to me. [12]Epaphras, who is one of you, a servant[e] of Christ Jesus, greets you. He is always wrestling in his prayers on

All in the Family
Colossians 3:18–4:1

The rules for Christian families in this passage might seem a little strange in our culture. It's easy to get caught in the cultural differences between the time Colossians was written and today. But looking past the cultural trappings and into the core ethical standards makes these teachings relevant to us today. Colossians simply calls all people, especially families, to be rooted in loving relationships (see also "Study It: Family Relationships," near Ephesians 5:21–6:4).

A family is a gift from God. It's intended to be a community where mutual love and respect exist between its members, both young and old. It's a community we can turn to for comfort and support. But those things don't just happen. Every family member has to make an effort. That means taking time to listen, to help each other out, and to respect each individual. Sometimes selfishness gets in the way of making God's love real. At those times, family members must try even harder. Praying together as well as reading and talking about the Bible together can help a family focus on God's presence in their lives. Family relationships take patience and commitment, but they are worth it.

- How would you describe your family life? Is love the guiding rule? Does everyone take time to pray together? Do you support and participate in family activities and chores willingly?

- If your family doesn't look like the description in Colossians, what can you do to improve your relationships? Do you know a family you can learn from?

- If your family fits these descriptions, how can you reach out to include others to encourage the growth of healthy, close relationships?

---

a In Greek the same word is used for *master* and *Lord*   **b** Gk *not for men*   **c** Or *you are slaves of*, or *be slaves of*   **d** Or *opportunity*   **e** Gk *slave*   **f** Other authorities read *that I may know how you are*

your behalf, so that you may stand mature and fully assured in everything that God wills. [13] For I testify for him that he has worked hard for you and for those in Laodicea and in Hierapolis. [14] Luke, the beloved physician, and Demas greet you. [15] Give my greetings to the brothers and sisters[a] in Laodicea, and to Nympha and the church in her house. [16] And when this letter has been read among you,

have it read also in the church of the Laodiceans; and see that you read also the letter from Laodicea. [17] And say to Archippus, "See that you complete the task that you have received in the Lord."

18 I, Paul, write this greeting with my own hand. Remember my chains. Grace be with you.[b]

a Gk *brothers*   b Other ancient authorities add *Amen*

1 Thessalonians

▸▸▸▸▸▸▸▸▸▸▸▸▸▸▸▸▸

You're about to read what is probably the oldest book in the New Testament. It was written a little over twenty years after Jesus' death and resurrection. It's the very first Christian letter we still have! Paul, the author, answers some questions that were on people's minds at the time. You might be surprised to find these ancient questions are the same ones you have today.

IN DEPTH

Thessalonica was the capital of a Roman province called Macedonia. Today that area is in northern Greece (see Map 13, "Paul's Missionary Journeys.") Acts 17 tells us that Paul spent three weeks in Thessalonica preaching about Jesus Christ. Many people, mainly Gentiles (non-Jews), became Christians after hearing his teaching. Paul worried about the new Christian community after he left the city, so he sent his co-worker Timothy back to check things out. When Timothy rejoined Paul, he had some great news. The Thessalonians were staying strong in their faith and love, even though they were being persecuted (1 Thessalonians 3:6–7).

It's clear from his writing that **Paul is thankful the Church is thriving!** Four different times he expresses his gratitude. But he also apparently feels the need to defend himself against some critics. So he reminds everyone that he has been genuine and has cared for them "like a nurse tenderly caring for her own children" (1 Thessalonians 2:7).

After reassuring the Thessalonians that the persecution they are suffering is to be expected (1 Thessalonians 3:3–4), Paul takes the time to answer some questions about the coming of the Lord at the end of time. Some of the Thessalonians are concerned about their friends who have already died. Will they join the living when Christ returns again?

Paul tells them they don't have to worry about those who die before Jesus returns; **the dead will be raised first and join the living to "be with the Lord forever" (1 Thessalonians 4:17).** When will that happen? No one knows, Paul says, but Christians don't have to be afraid of that day. Their job is to watch for that day and clothe themselves with "faith and love . . . and . . . hope" (1 Thessalonians 5:8).

QUICK FACTS

- **Author:** Paul
- **Date Written:** A.D. 51
- **Audience:** The mainly Gentile (non-Jewish) church in Thessalonica (in modern-day Greece)
- **Themes:** Jesus has conquered evil and death and will return soon; how we are to live until his return

AT A GLANCE

- **1 Thessalonians 1** Greeting and thanksgiving
- **1 Thessalonians 2–3** Discussion of Paul's ministry in Thessalonica and Timothy's report
- **1 Thessalonians 4:1–12** Advice about the Christian life
- **1 Thessalonians 4:13–5:11** Teaching about the end-times
- **1 Thessalonians 5:12–28** Final advice and a blessing

1

Salutation

Paul, Silvanus, and Timothy,

To the church of the Thessalonians in God the Father and the Lord Jesus Christ:

Grace to you and peace.

The Thessalonians' Faith and Example

2 We always give thanks to God for all of you and mention you in our prayers, constantly [3]remembering before our God and Father your work of faith and labor of love and steadfastness of hope in our Lord Jesus Christ. [4]For we know, brothers and sisters[a] beloved by God, that he has chosen you, [5]because our message of the gospel came to you not in word only, but also in power and in the Holy Spirit and with full conviction; just as you know what kind of persons we proved to be among you for your sake. [6]And you became imitators of us and of the Lord, for in spite of persecution you received the word with joy inspired by the Holy Spirit, [7]so that you became an example to all the believers in Macedonia and in Achaia. [8]For the word of the Lord has sounded forth from you not only in Macedonia and Achaia, but in every place your faith in God has become known, so that we have no need to speak about it. [9]For the people of those regions[b] report about us what kind of welcome we had among you, and how you turned to God from idols, to serve a living and true God, [10]and to wait for his Son from heaven, whom he raised from the dead—Jesus, who rescues us from the wrath that is coming.

CONNECT IT!

Leslie and Lauren Reavely: Hope 2 Others (H2O)
1 Thessalonians 1:6–7

Teenage sisters Leslie and Lauren Reavely had their eyes opened to the struggles of the poor at World Venture's kids' missions camp held at Camp Jonah in Trout Lake, Washington. When they returned home, they wanted to put into action their new passion for the poor. So like the believers commended in 1 Thessalonians, the Reavely sisters became imitators of Christ and an example for all believers (1 Thessalonians 1:6-7).

Leslie and Lauren started Hope 2 Others, or H2O, which aims to bring spiritual and physical hope to homeless people by providing them with food and basic necessities like socks, hand wipes, and a rescue mission meal voucher. People can hand out bags of these supplies to people they see on the streets. The bags are designed to meet needs and start conversations with the recipients. H2O is reaching the poor across the United States and in the Philippines by working with partners who want to start a ministry in their own community. Find out more about how H2O is giving hope to the poor, one bag at a time, at **H2Obags.com**.

Paul's Ministry in Thessalonica

2

You yourselves know, brothers and sisters,[a] that our coming to you was not in vain, [2]but though we had already suffered and been shamefully mistreated at Philippi, as you know, we had courage in our God to declare to you the gospel of God in spite of great opposition. [3]For our appeal does not spring from deceit or impure motives or trickery, [4]but just as we have been approved by God to be entrusted with the message of the gospel, even so we speak, not to please mortals, but to please God who tests our hearts. [5]As you know and as God is our witness, we never came with words of flattery or with a pretext for greed; [6]nor did we seek praise from mortals, whether from you or from others, [7]though we might have made demands as apostles of Christ. But we were gentle[c] among you, like a nurse tenderly caring for her own children. [8]So deeply do we care for you that we are determined to share with you not only the gospel of God but also our own selves, because you have become very dear to us.

9 You remember our labor and toil, brothers and sisters;[a] we worked night and day, so that we might not burden any of you while we proclaimed to you the gospel of God. [10]You are witnesses, and God also, how pure, upright, and blameless our conduct was toward you believers. [11]As you know, we dealt with each one of you like a father with his children, [12]urging and encouraging you and pleading that you

---

a Gk brothers **b** Gk For they **c** Other ancient authorities read infants

lead a life worthy of God, who calls you into his own kingdom and glory.

13 We also constantly give thanks to God for this, that when you received the word of God that you heard from us, you accepted it not as a human word but as what it really is, God's word, which is also at work in you believers. [14]For you, brothers and sisters,[a] became imitators of the churches of God in Christ Jesus that are in Judea, for you suffered the same things from your own compatriots as they did from the Jews, [15]who killed both the Lord Jesus and the prophets,[b] and drove us out; they displease God and oppose everyone [16]by hindering us from speaking to the Gentiles so that they may be saved. Thus they have constantly been filling up the measure of their sins; but God's wrath has overtaken them at last.[c]

Paul's Desire to Visit the Thessalonians Again

17 As for us, brothers and sisters,[a] when, for a short time, we were made orphans by being separated from you—in person, not in heart—we longed with great eagerness to see you face to face. [18]For we wanted to come to you—certainly I, Paul, wanted to again and again—but Satan blocked our way. [19]For what is our hope or joy or crown of boasting before our Lord Jesus at his coming? Is it not you? [20]Yes, you are our glory and joy!

3 Therefore when we could bear it no longer, we decided to be left alone in Athens; [2]and we sent Timothy, our brother and co-worker for God in proclaiming[d] the gospel of Christ, to strengthen and encourage you for the sake of your faith, [3]so that no one would be shaken by these persecutions. Indeed, you yourselves know that this is what we are destined for. [4]In fact, when we were with you, we told you beforehand that we were to suffer persecution; so it turned out, as you know. [5]For this reason, when I could bear it no longer, I sent to find out about your faith; I was afraid that somehow the tempter had tempted you and that our labor had been in vain.

Timothy's Encouraging Report

6 But Timothy has just now come to us from you, and has brought us the good news of your faith and love. He has told us also that you always remember us kindly and long to see us—just as we long to see you. [7]For this reason, brothers and sisters,[a] during all our distress and persecution we have been encouraged about you through your faith. [8]For we now live, if you continue to stand firm in the Lord. [9]How can we thank God enough for you in return for all the joy that we feel before our God because of you? [10]Night and day we pray most earnestly that we may see you face to face and restore whatever is lacking in your faith.

11 Now may our God and Father himself and our Lord Jesus direct our way to you. [12]And may the Lord make you increase and abound in love for one another and for all, just as we abound in love for you. [13]And may he so strengthen your hearts in holiness that you may be blameless before our God and Father at the coming of our Lord Jesus with all his saints.

A Life Pleasing to God

4 Finally, brothers and sisters,[a] we ask and urge you in the Lord Jesus that, as you

Encouragement · 1 Thessalonians 3:6–13

Do you ever feel alone in your faith? It's easy to wonder if anyone feels, thinks, or prays the way we do. As one of the first missionaries of the faith, Paul must have experienced his share of dark days when he wondered if the people would really accept the good news. He must have been so encouraged when Timothy returned to tell him of the faith and love of the Thessalonians (1 Thessalonians 3:6).

The Christian faith is never meant to be held privately. We don't grow in our faith, hope, and love by being isolated from others. Like Paul, we need the encouragement and challenge of other people: our family, friends, and the entire Christian community.

- How do you encourage others to grow in Christ?
- How do others encourage or challenge you to grow in faith, hope, and love?
- How can you avoid isolation and stay connected to other believers?

---

a Gk brothers   b Other ancient authorities read their own prophets   c Or completely or forever   d Gk lacks proclaiming

learned from us how you ought to live and to please God (as, in fact, you are doing), you should do so more and more. [2]For you know what instructions we gave you through the Lord Jesus. [3]For this is the will of God, your sanctification: that you abstain from fornication; [4]that each one of you know how to control your own body[a] in holiness and honor, [5]not with lustful passion, like the Gentiles who do not know God; [6]that no one wrong or exploit a brother or sister[b] in this matter, because the Lord is an avenger in all these things, just as we have already told you beforehand and solemnly warned you. [7]For God did not call us to impurity but in holiness. [8]Therefore whoever rejects this rejects not human authority but God, who also gives his Holy Spirit to you.

9 Now concerning love of the brothers and sisters,[c] you do not need to have anyone write to you, for you yourselves have been taught by God to love one another; [10]and indeed you do love all the brothers and sisters[c] throughout Macedonia. But we urge you, beloved,[c] to do so more and more, [11]to aspire to live quietly, to mind your own affairs, and to work with your hands, as we directed you, [12]so that you may behave properly toward outsiders and be dependent on no one.

The Coming of the Lord

13 But we do not want you to be uninformed, brothers and sisters,[c] about those who have died,[d] so that you may not grieve as others do who have no hope. [14]For since we believe that Jesus died and rose again, even so, through Jesus, God will bring with him those who have died.[d] [15]For this we declare to you by the word of the Lord, that we who are alive, who are left until the coming of the Lord, will by no means precede those who have died.[d]

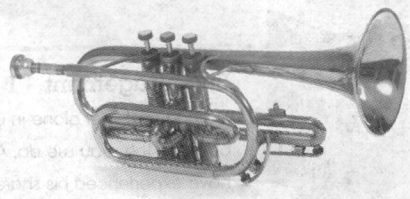

[16]For the Lord himself, with a cry of command, with the archangel's call and with the sound of God's trumpet, will descend from heaven, and the dead in Christ will rise first. [17]Then we who are alive, who are left, will be caught up in the clouds together with them to meet the Lord in the air; and so we will be with the Lord forever. [18]Therefore encourage one another with these words.

STUDY IT!

Sex Is a Gift
1 Thessalonians 4:1–8

Paul's teaching clearly explains that fornication (sex outside of marriage), including premarital sex, is wrong. Paul reminds the Thessalonians to live in ways pleasing to God. When they don't, they are saying no to the gift of the Holy Spirit and to the holiness God wants for all believers.

If we get involved in a sexual relationship outside of marriage, we risk exploiting another person (1 Thessalonians 4:6)—even if that person is a willing partner. God designed sex to be part of a long-term bond between two people, and God wants us to enjoy sex in the right context. It's the special gift God gave to couples for pleasure, connectedness, and to create new life. But sex outside of this context can undermine those beautiful purposes. Each sex act bonds us to that partner in a way that never goes away, and those physical and emotional bonds can interfere in intimacy with our partner in the future.

Much of our culture views and portrays sex as a recreational activity, but treating sex casually violates the gift of sexuality God created in us. God's message calls us to sexual restraint until marriage. Taking that stand can be unpopular with some people, and it's not always easy to value our gift of sexuality enough to express it only as God intended. But ultimately it's the most rewarding, because we live according to God's purpose and pave the road to freely enjoying sex in marriage.

a Or how to take a wife for himself b Gk brother c Gk brothers d Gk fallen asleep

5 Now concerning the times and the seasons, brothers and sisters,[a] you do not need to have anything written to you. [2]For you yourselves know very well that the day of the Lord will come like a thief in the night. [3]When they say, "There is peace and security," then sudden destruction will come upon them, as labor pains come upon a pregnant woman, and there will be no escape! [4]But you, beloved,[a] are not in darkness, for that day to surprise you like a thief; [5]for you are all children of light and children of the day; we are not of the night or of darkness. [6]So then let us not fall asleep as others do, but let us keep awake and be sober; [7]for those who sleep sleep at night, and those who are drunk get drunk at night. [8]But since we belong to the day, let us be sober, and put on the breastplate of faith and love, and for a helmet the hope of salvation. [9]For God has destined us not for wrath but for obtaining salvation through our Lord Jesus Christ, [10]who died for us, so that whether we are awake or asleep we may live with him. [11]Therefore encourage one another and build up each other, as indeed you are doing.

Final Exhortations, Greetings, and Benediction

12 But we appeal to you, brothers and sisters,[a] to respect those who labor among you, and have charge of you in the Lord and admonish you; [13]esteem them very highly in love because of their work. Be at peace among yourselves. [14]And we urge you, beloved,[a] to admonish the idlers, encourage the fainthearted, help

> "Rejoice always, pray without ceasing, give thanks in all circumstances: for this is the will of God in Christ Jesus for you."
> —1 Thessalonians 5:16–18

the weak, be patient with all of them. [15]See that none of you repays evil for evil, but always seek to do good to one another and to all. [16]Rejoice always, [17]pray without ceasing, [18]give thanks in all circumstances; for this is the will of God in Christ Jesus for you. [19]Do not quench the Spirit. [20]Do not despise the words of prophets,[b] [21]but test everything; hold fast to what is good; [22]abstain from every form of evil.

23 May the God of peace himself sanctify you entirely; and may your spirit and soul and body be kept sound[c] and blameless at the coming of our Lord Jesus Christ. [24]The one who calls you is faithful, and he will do this.

25 Beloved,[d] pray for us.

26 Greet all the brothers and sisters[a] with a holy kiss. [27]I solemnly command you by the Lord that this letter be read to all of them.[e]

28 The grace of our Lord Jesus Christ be with you.[f]

PRAY IT!

God's Will for You · 1 Thessalonians 5:16–22

How many times have you prayed, "God what should I do? What is your will for my life?" Although God may have specific direction for you in certain choices, much of following God's will involves doing what Paul describes in this passage. We are to rejoice always, pray without ceasing, and give thanks in all circumstances. Living this way every day is living out the will of God—which usually makes it easier to make good choices in specific situations as well. Paul's words in the next few verses can also help when making choices. He says to test everything and hold on to the good while staying away from evil (1 Thessalonians 5:21-22). So the next time you face a tough choice, start here with these guidelines for living in God's will and see where they lead you. And don't forget to seek God in prayer:

God, I face so many tough choices in my life. Help me to live according to your will every day and choose what is good. Thank you that through it all you love me more than I'll ever know. Amen.

---

a Gk *brothers*   b Gk *despise prophecies*   c Or *complete*   d Gk *Brothers*   e Gk *to all the brothers*   f Other ancient authorities add *Amen*

2 Thessalonians

"You know, when I was your age . . ." Cue the parent or other adult launching into some story about how hard it was in the good old days, right? It seems all past generations, including those who lived in biblical times, had their struggles and challenges. When the Thessalonians were going through some really tough times, Paul's second letter to them promised that if they continued to trust God and endure, they would receive salvation and be able to give glory to God.

IN DEPTH

The book of 2 Thessalonians is short and basically covers two problems the Thessalonians were experiencing. First, they were being persecuted by non-Christians. Second, some of them were becoming confused over "the coming of our Lord Jesus Christ" (2 Thessalonians 2:1), sometimes called the second coming. Word was being spread that Jesus had already come again (2 Thessalonians 2:2), and the Thessalonians were afraid that they hadn't seen the signs of the end-times or properly interpreted them.

This letter speaks to the Thessalonians using apocalyptic language (see "Study It: Apocalyptic Literature," near Daniel 7–10; and the introduction to Revelation). This language is rich in cosmic symbolism. The Thessalonians are to have peace and not let themselves be deceived, because "all who have not believed the truth but took pleasure in unrighteousness will be condemned" (2 Thessalonians 2:12). They are to have hope, because at the end-time Christ will overcome all evil and destroy the lawless one (2 Thessalonians 2:8).

This letter isn't as warm and personal as 1 Thessalonians. Perhaps that's because it's filled with the sobering awareness that more suffering is to come before the end-time. In such an environment, the letter advises the Thessalonians—and us—to "stand firm and hold fast to the traditions that were taught" (2 Thessalonians 2:15).

QUICK FACTS

- **Author:** Possibly Paul, but more likely a disciple of Paul
- **Date Written:** After A.D. 51, if by Paul; 90-100, if by a disciple
- **Audience:** The mainly Gentile (non-Jewish) church in Thessalonica (in modern-day Greece)
- **Themes:** Do not be idle as you wait for Jesus to return.

AT A GLANCE

- **2 Thessalonians 1:1–4**
  Greeting and thanksgiving
- **2 Thessalonians 1:5–2:17**
  Information about the day of judgment
- **2 Thessalonians 3:1–15**
  Prayer request, and warning against idleness
- **2 Thessalonians 3:16–18**
  Final greetings and a blessing

1

Salutation

Paul, Silvanus, and Timothy,

To the church of the Thessalonians in God our Father and the Lord Jesus Christ:

2 Grace to you and peace from God our[a] Father and the Lord Jesus Christ.

Thanksgiving

3 We must always give thanks to God for you, brothers and sisters,[b] as is right, because your faith is growing abundantly, and the love of every one of you for one another is increasing. [4]Therefore we ourselves boast of you among the churches of God for your steadfastness and faith during all your persecutions and the afflictions that you are enduring.

The Judgment at Christ's Coming

5 This is evidence of the righteous judgment of God, and is intended to make you worthy of the kingdom of God, for which you are also suffering. [6]For it is indeed just of God to repay with affliction those who afflict you, [7]and to give relief to the afflicted as well as to us, when the Lord Jesus is revealed from heaven with his mighty angels [8]in flaming fire, inflicting vengeance on those who do not know God and on those who do not obey the gospel of our Lord Jesus. [9]These will suffer the punishment of eternal destruction, separated from the presence of the Lord and from the glory of his might, [10]when he comes to be glorified by his saints and to be marveled at on that day among all who have believed, because our testimony to you was believed.

[11]To this end we always pray for you, asking that our God will make you worthy of his call and will fulfill by his power every good resolve and work of faith, [12]so that the name of our Lord Jesus may be glorified in you, and you in him, according to the grace of our God and the Lord Jesus Christ.

2

The Man of Lawlessness

As to the coming of our Lord Jesus Christ and our being gathered together to him, we beg you, brothers and sisters,[b] [2]not to be quickly shaken in mind or alarmed, either by spirit or by word or by letter, as though from us, to the effect that the day of the Lord is already here. [3]Let no one deceive you in any way; for that day will not come unless the rebellion comes first and the lawless one[c] is revealed, the one destined for destruction.[d] [4]He opposes and exalts himself above every so-called god or object of worship, so that he takes his seat in the temple of God, declaring himself to be God. [5]Do you not remember that I told you these things when I was still with you? [6]And you know what is now restraining him, so that he may be revealed when his time comes. [7]For the mystery of lawlessness is already at work, but only until the one who now restrains it is removed. [8]And then the lawless one will be revealed, whom the Lord Jesus[e] will destroy[f] with the breath of his mouth, annihilating him by the manifestation of his coming. [9]The coming of the lawless one is apparent in the working of Satan, who uses all power, signs, lying wonders, [10]and every kind of wicked deception for those who are

STUDY IT!

The Second Coming · 2 Thessalonians 1:5–2:17

The early Christians started to wait for Jesus' second coming after his death and resurrection. During the time 2 Thessalonians was written, the early Church thought Jesus would return soon in glory to judge the living and the dead and to completely fulfill the kingdom of God. They even saw some signs of his coming and issued an urgent call to be prepared. Paul seems to expect Christ's return in the near future, but insists that nobody can predict the time. He emphasizes the importance of living the gospel and always being prepared for "our being gathered together to him" (2 Thessalonians 2:1).

The important message for us today is that our history has meaning and purpose and that Christ will ultimately triumph over sin and death. We can trust that God has always been and always will be faithful. The various descriptions of the signs preceding the end-time are intended not to predict the future, but rather to encourage us to live the gospel as we wait in hope for Christ's glorious return. We don't need to put our hope in a prediction of the future, because our hope is in the One who knows and determines the future.

STUDY IT!

Family Traditions of Faith
2 Thessalonians 2:13–17

What are some of your favorite family traditions? The traditions you celebrate when you gather with your relatives say something about who you are as a family. The same is true for Christianity. This letter emphasizes the importance of the traditions that had been handed on to the church in Thessalonica through the apostles' preaching and written letters about Jesus (2 Thessalonians 2:15).

Before 2 Thessalonians was written, God had been slowly revealing himself through words and deeds even before Christ came. God spoke to Moses out of the burning bush (Exodus 3:1–22) and led the Israelites across the Red Sea (Exodus 14:1–31). These words and deeds guided people in the ways and traditions of obeying and worshiping God. The same words and deeds also laid the foundation for the ultimate and final revelation of God in the Word made flesh, Jesus Christ.

In the early days of the Church, the apostles led Christians in new ways to worship and serve God. The new ways were based on the fact that, through Jesus, believers could have a relationship with the Father. The apostles built new traditions to remember and follow Jesus' teachings, such as Communion, gathering together for worship, and sending messengers around the world to share the message about Jesus. Our culture is extremely different from the early Christians', but we are able to draw close to God through some of the same actions and traditions established centuries ago. We can learn from our spiritual ancestors, benefit from their knowledge of God's Son, and live like members of God's family.

perishing, because they refused to love the truth and so be saved. [11] For this reason God sends them a powerful delusion, leading them to believe what is false, [12] so that all who have not believed the truth but took pleasure in unrighteousness will be condemned.

Chosen for Salvation

13 But we must always give thanks to God for you, brothers and sisters[a] beloved by the Lord, because God chose you as the first fruits[b] for salvation through sanctification by the Spirit and through belief in the truth. [14] For this purpose he called you through our proclamation of the good news,[c] so that you may obtain the glory of our Lord Jesus Christ. [15] So then, brothers and sisters,[a] stand firm and hold fast to the traditions that you were taught by us, either by word of mouth or by our letter.

16 Now may our Lord Jesus Christ himself and God our Father, who loved us and through grace gave us eternal comfort and good hope, [17] comfort your hearts and strengthen them in every good work and word.

Request for Prayer

3 Finally, brothers and sisters,[a] pray for us, so that the word of the Lord may spread rapidly and be glorified everywhere, just as it is among you, [2] and that we may be rescued from wicked and evil people; for not all have faith. [3] But the Lord is faithful; he will strengthen you and guard you from the evil one.[d] [4] And we have confidence in the Lord concerning you, that you are doing and will go on doing the things that we command. [5] May the Lord direct your hearts to the love of God and to the steadfastness of Christ.

Warning against Idleness

6 Now we command you, beloved,[a] in the name of our Lord Jesus Christ, to keep away from believers who are[e] living in idleness and not according to the tradition that they[f] received from us. [7] For you yourselves know how you ought to imitate us; we were not idle when we were with you, [8] and we did not eat anyone's bread without paying for it; but with toil and labor we worked night and day, so that we might not burden any of you. [9] This was not because we do not have that right, but in order to give you an example to imitate. [10] For even when we were with you, we gave you this command: Anyone

---

a Gk *brothers* b Other ancient authorities read *from the beginning* c Or *through our gospel* d Or *from evil* e Gk *from every brother who is* f Other ancient authorities read *you*

LIVE IT!

Lazy Bones · 2 Thessalonians 3:6–13

Where are you on the lazy scale? Do you tend to get things done on your own or let others take care of things while you hang out? How does it make you feel when others expect you to work while they do nothing?

The author of 2 Thessalonians sees the idleness of certain people in the early Church as destructive to relationships and the Christian community. He challenges those who are being lazy to follow the example he set and to work and earn a living (2 Thessalonians 3:12). He tells those who are already working hard to avoid those who are lazy and to warn them that their actions are hurtful (2 Thessalonians 3:14).

But before you set out to tell the lazy people in your life to get their act together, don't miss these final words: "Do not regard them as enemies, but warn them as believers" (2 Thessalonians 3:15).

- Is there someone in your life whose laziness has become hurtful to your relationship? Is there someone who might feel that way about you?
- What can you do to make the relationship right either by confronting the person in love or by working harder to do your share?
- In what areas of your life do you need encouragement to "not be weary in doing what is right" (2 Thessalonians 3:13)?

unwilling to work should not eat. [11]For we hear that some of you are living in idleness, mere busybodies, not doing any work. [12]Now such persons we command and exhort in the Lord Jesus Christ to do their work quietly and to earn their own living. [13]Brothers and sisters,[a] do not be weary in doing what is right.

14 Take note of those who do not obey what we say in this letter; have nothing to do with them, so that they may be ashamed. [15]Do not regard them as enemies, but warn them as believers.[b]

Final Greetings and Benediction

16 Now may the Lord of peace himself give you peace at all times in all ways. The Lord be with all of you.

17 I, Paul, write this greeting with my own hand. This is the mark in every letter of mine; it is the way I write. [18]The grace of our Lord Jesus Christ be with all of you.[c]

> "Do not be weary in doing what is right."
> —2 Thessalonians 3:13

a Gk Brothers b Gk a brother c Other ancient authorities add Amen

1 Timothy

Imagine you're a pastor writing to good friends who are also leaders in ministry. How do you encourage them? What do you warn them about? The two letters to Timothy and the letter to Titus are written to give good, practical advice to the leaders of the early Church. They don't deal so much with the big spiritual questions, but rather with the nitty-gritty of living in community with other believers.

IN DEPTH

The letters to Timothy and Titus are called the Pastoral Letters, because they were written to Church leaders, or pastors. These letters sound as if they were written by Paul. But a great deal of evidence suggests they may have been written by later disciples of Paul, adapting Paul's teaching and advice to the situation of the churches a generation later.

1 Timothy addresses practical issues the churches needed to deal with in order to achieve stability and respond to new challenges as Christianity became more visible in society: How should the churches deal with people teaching false beliefs? What qualities should Church leaders have? Who deserves financial help from the community? How should Christians view success?

In 2 Timothy it appears that Paul's impending execution is near. As you read this letter, you will experience his sadness at death, hear his reflections on his life and ministry, and see a man who feels deserted by many. This letter tells Timothy—who stands for all faithful Christians—that he needs to endure suffering with hope. Doing the right thing often means more pain than popularity. But even when other people desert us, God "remains faithful—for he cannot deny himself" (2 Timothy 2:13).

Titus gives advice for elders, older men, older women, slaves, younger men, and younger women. It also offers repeated warnings to guard against temptations and false teachings and encouragement to be self-controlled.

The Pastoral Letters give us a picture of the Church that looks much like the Church today. The early Christians struggled to be faithful in applying the gospel of Jesus Christ to their culture and time. Today's churches struggle in the same way to be relevant to the world, while maintaining character and identity apart from the many other organizations out there. Living out faith in community isn't easy, but our hope comes in the words that end each letter, "Grace be with you."

QUICK FACTS

- **Author:** Attributed to Paul, but most likely followers of Paul
- **Date Written:** Around A.D. 100
- **Audience:** Leaders of the early churches
- **Themes:** Church leadership, false teaching, and strength in the face of suffering for those who follow Jesus

AT A GLANCE

- **1 Timothy 1–2** Advice on prayer and worship
- **1 Timothy 3:1–13** Qualifications for Church leaders
- **1 Timothy 3:14–6:21** A guide for Christian living
- **2 Timothy 1** Thanksgiving and words of encouragement
- **2 Timothy 2:1–3:9** True teaching vs. false teaching
- **2 Timothy 3:10–4:22** Last words of advice and blessing
- **Titus 1** Appointing Church leaders; dealing with false teachers
- **Titus 2–3** Teachings about the Christian life

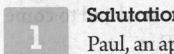

Salutation

1 Paul, an apostle of Christ Jesus by the command of God our Savior and of Christ Jesus our hope,

2 To Timothy, my loyal child in the faith:

Grace, mercy, and peace from God the Father and Christ Jesus our Lord.

Warning against False Teachers

3 I urge you, as I did when I was on my way to Macedonia, to remain in Ephesus so that you may instruct certain people not to teach any different doctrine, [4]and not to occupy themselves with myths and endless genealogies that promote speculations rather than the divine training[a] that is known by faith. [5]But the aim of such instruction is love that comes from a pure heart, a good conscience, and sincere faith. [6]Some people have deviated from these and turned to meaningless talk, [7]desiring to be teachers of the law, without understanding either what they are saying or the things about which they make assertions.

8 Now we know that the law is good, if one uses it legitimately. [9]This means understanding that the law is laid down not for the innocent but for the lawless and disobedient, for the godless and sinful, for the unholy and profane, for those who kill their father or mother, for murderers, [10]fornicators, sodomites, slave traders, liars, perjurers, and whatever else is contrary to the sound teaching [11]that conforms to the glorious gospel of the blessed God, which he entrusted to me.

Gratitude for Mercy

12 I am grateful to Christ Jesus our Lord, who has strengthened me, because he judged me faithful and appointed me to his service, [13]even though I was formerly a blasphemer, a persecutor, and a man of violence. But I received mercy because I had acted ignorantly in unbelief, [14]and the grace of our Lord overflowed for me with the faith and love that are in Christ Jesus. [15]The saying is sure and worthy of full acceptance, that Christ Jesus came into the world to save sinners—of whom I am the foremost. [16]But for that very reason I received mercy, so that in me, as the foremost, Jesus Christ might display the utmost patience, making me an example to those who would come to believe in him for eternal life. [17]To the King of the ages, immortal, invisible, the only God, be honor and glory forever and ever.[b] Amen.

18 I am giving you these instructions, Timothy, my child, in accordance with the prophecies made earlier about you, so that by following them you may fight the good fight, [19]having faith and a good conscience. By rejecting conscience, certain persons have suffered shipwreck in the faith; [20]among them are Hymenaeus and Alexander, whom I have turned over to Satan, so that they may learn not to blaspheme.

PRAY IT!

Conscience: God in the Gut
1 Timothy 1:18–19

Do you ever wonder where God is during those really difficult moments of making a decision? Like when you feel pressured by the group to do something you know is wrong. Or when you have to decide whether to spend your money on what you want or give it to a homeless person you pass on the street.

One of the best places to look for God's direction in the middle of life's dilemmas is that feeling in the center of your stomach—your gut. That feeling may be a sign of your conscience and the Holy Spirit prompting you to act.

Timothy is told to have "faith and a good conscience" (1 Timothy 1:19). A good conscience is based on making good moral decisions and acting in a way that's true to your faith. Take time to develop your conscience by studying moral issues, which include things like cheating, honesty, gossiping, drinking alcohol, sexual purity, pornography, slavery, and fair trade. Then ask God to help you to act according to that conscience.

God, it's not easy to live by faith and good conscience. Help me to learn more about what pleases you, so that what I feel in my gut will reflect you. Give me wisdom to recognize what is right and courage to act with integrity. Please help me, like Timothy, to fight the good fight in living for you. Amen.

2 Instructions concerning Prayer

First of all, then, I urge that supplications, prayers, intercessions, and thanksgivings be made for everyone, [2]for kings and all who are in high positions, so that we may lead a quiet and peaceable life in all godliness and dignity. [3]This is right and is acceptable in the sight of God our Sav-ior, [4]who desires everyone to be saved and to come to the knowledge of the truth. [5]For

there is one God;

there is also one mediator between God
and humankind,
Christ Jesus, himself human,
[6]   who gave himself a ransom for all

—this was attested at the right time. [7]For this I was appointed a herald and an apostle (I am telling the truth,[a] I am not lying), a teacher of the Gentiles in faith and truth.

8 I desire, then, that in every place the men should pray, lifting up holy hands without anger or argument; [9]also that the women should dress themselves modestly and decently in suitable clothing, not with their hair braided, or with gold, pearls, or expensive clothes, [10]but with good works, as is proper for women who profess reverence for God. [11]Let a woman[b] learn in silence with full submission. [12]I permit no woman[b] to teach or to have authority over a man;[c] she is to keep silent. [13]For Adam was formed first, then Eve; [14]and Adam was not deceived, but the woman was deceived and became a transgressor. [15]Yet she will be saved through childbearing, provided they continue in faith and love and holiness, with modesty.

STUDY IT!

Women's Roles
1 Timothy 2:8–15

What's your response to this passage? Scripture like this can easily be misunderstood and even misused against women. It's important to realize that this is a reflection of women's roles in the ancient world. Whatever her religious background, a woman's place at that time was in the home. Women generally married young, had no education, and were not allowed to hold a position of public authority.

The earliest Christian communities gathered in members' homes. In this less public arena, women taught and performed other ministries. As Christianity became more widely accepted, concern for how the Church appeared to outsiders grew—including concern about drunken leaders, immodest dress, and women teaching in public. That's probably why the author of 1 Timothy says, "I permit no woman to teach" (1 Timothy 2:12).

Are things different for women in the Church today? Yes! Society has changed. Today, people in North America are not scandalized if a woman manages a business, runs for public office, or leads a private foundation. Today, if you ask people to name influential church leaders, Mother Teresa often comes up. Think of women you know who are involved in church life. In your own church or community, for example, there are probably women who are religious education directors, coordinators of youth ministry, or even pastors and ministers.

3 Qualifications of Bishops

The saying is sure:[d] whoever aspires to the office of bishop[e] desires a noble task. [2]Now a bishop[f] must be above reproach, married only once,[g] temperate, sensible, respectable, hospitable, an apt teacher, [3]not a drunkard, not violent but gentle, not quarrelsome, and not a lover of money. [4]He must manage his own household well, keeping his children submissive and respectful in every way— [5]for if someone does not know how to manage his own household, how can he take care of God's church? [6]He must not be a recent convert, or he may be puffed up with conceit and fall into the condemnation of the devil. [7]Moreover, he must be well thought of by outsiders, so that he may not fall into disgrace and the snare of the devil.

Qualifications of Deacons

8 Deacons likewise must be serious, not double-tongued, not indulging in much wine, not greedy for money; [9]they must hold fast to the mystery of the faith with a clear conscience. [10]And let them first be tested; then, if they prove themselves blame-

---

a Other ancient authorities add *in Christ*   b Or *wife*   c Or *her husband*   d Some interpreters place these words at the end of the previous paragraph. Other ancient authorities read *The saying is commonly accepted*   e Or *overseer*   f Or *an overseer*   g Gk *the husband of one wife*

Jesus Is Really God · 1 Timothy 3:14–16

Being new at something can be difficult, and it helps to have someone experienced show you the way. This is what Paul was doing for Timothy in his first letter. Timothy was new at leading his local church and was apparently facing some difficulties with people promoting false beliefs about Jesus. Paul helps by providing Timothy with a brief summary of beliefs and acknowledges that faith in Christ involves mystery, or things that go beyond understanding. In this brief summary, Paul mentions that Jesus "was revealed in flesh" (1 Timothy 3:16). This verse points to the mystery that Jesus is both fully divine and fully human.

Similar to the challenges that Timothy faced, the Church has also had to address those who preached competing beliefs. During its first five hundred years, some said Jesus was created by God and therefore only semidivine. Others said the two natures remained totally separate in Jesus. And still others claimed Jesus' human nature ceased to exist once it was assumed by Christ when God came in the flesh.

Scripture provides evidence of the presence and role of both a divine and human nature united in one Jesus. This mysterious relationship is known as the incarnation. We see that Jesus is truly human, for he had to learn and grow (see Luke 2:52), he experienced emotions (see John 11:28-37), and he faced temptations just as we do (see Matthew 4:1-11). We also see that Jesus is truly divine, for he could read the hearts of those he encountered (see John 4:5-42) and performed many miracles (see Matthew 9:18-26).

With the exception of sinning, Jesus is just like each one of us in every way. By becoming human, Jesus showed us how God would live and act. He gave us an example of how to live totally obedient to the Father's will. Through his love and service to others, he showed us how much God loves us and how much we should love others. By becoming human, Jesus revealed to us our true nature as sons and daughters of God.

---

less, let them serve as deacons. [11]Women[a] likewise must be serious, not slanderers, but temperate, faithful in all things. [12]Let deacons be married only once,[b] and let them manage their children and their households well; [13]for those who serve well as deacons gain a good standing for themselves and great boldness in the faith that is in Christ Jesus.

The Mystery of Our Religion

14 I hope to come to you soon, but I am writing these instructions to you so that, [15]if I am delayed, you may know how one ought to behave in the household of God, which is the church of the living God, the pillar and bulwark of the truth. [16]Without any doubt, the mystery of our religion is great:

He[c] was revealed in flesh,
    vindicated[d] in spirit,[e]
    seen by angels,
proclaimed among Gentiles,
    believed in throughout the world,
    taken up in glory.

False Asceticism

4 Now the Spirit expressly says that in later[f] times some will renounce the faith by paying attention to deceitful spirits and teachings of demons, [2]through the hypocrisy of liars whose consciences are seared with a hot iron. [3]They forbid marriage and demand abstinence from foods, which God created to be received with thanksgiving by those who believe and know the truth. [4]For everything created by God is good, and nothing is to be rejected, provided it is received with thanksgiving; [5]for it is sanctified by God's word and by prayer.

A Good Minister of Jesus Christ

6 If you put these instructions before the brothers and sisters,[g] you will be a good servant[h] of Christ

---

a Or *Their wives,* or *Women deacons* **b** Gk *be husbands of one wife* **c** Gk *Who;* other ancient authorities read *God;* others, *Which* **d** Or *justified*
e Or *by the Spirit* **f** Or *the last* **g** Gk *brothers* **h** Or *deacon*

Jesus, nourished on the words of the faith and of the sound teaching that you have followed. ⁷Have nothing to do with profane myths and old wives' tales. Train yourself in godliness, ⁸for, while physical training is of some value, godliness is valuable in every way, holding promise for both the present life and the life to come. ⁹The saying is sure and worthy of full acceptance. ¹⁰For to this end we toil and struggle,ᵃ because we have our hope set on the living God, who is the Savior of all people, especially of those who believe.

11 These are the things you must insist on and teach. ¹²Let no one despise your youth, but set the believers an example in speech and conduct, in love, in faith, in purity. ¹³Until I arrive, give attention to the public reading of scripture,ᵇ to exhorting, to teaching. ¹⁴Do not neglect the gift that is in you, which was given to you through prophecy with the laying on of hands by the council of elders.ᶜ ¹⁵Put these things into practice, devote yourself to them, so that all may see your progress. ¹⁶Pay close attention to yourself and to your teaching; continue in these things, for in doing this you will save both yourself and your hearers.

> "Let no one despise your youth, but set the believers an example in speech and conduct."
> —1 Timothy 4:12

Duties toward Believers

5 Do not speak harshly to an older man,ᵈ but speak to him as to a father, to younger men as brothers, ²to older women as mothers, to younger women as sisters—with absolute purity.

3 Honor widows who are really widows. ⁴If a widow has children or grandchildren, they should first learn their religious duty to their own family and make some repayment to their parents; for this is pleasing in God's sight. ⁵The real widow, left alone, has set her hope on God and continues in supplications and prayers night and day; ⁶but the widowᵉ who lives for pleasure is dead even while

PRAY IT!

The Power of Youth
1 Timothy 4:12

Timothy was young.

But he was challenged to never let that stand in the way of setting an example for the other believers. Although some in the world may look down on youth, it's clear that God does not. When you feel discouraged by the limitations of your age, say this prayer based on this verse:

God, help me to be like Timothy. Give me courage to set an example for my friends in the way I talk and the way I act. Help them to see you in my life. Amen.

LIVE IT!

Pump It Up · 1 Timothy 4:6–10

We spend countless hours training to become better athletes, musicians, scientists, teachers, electricians, and more. You name it, we train for it, if we want to be good at it. Paul says the soul needs that same kind of training.

In your journal or on a piece of paper, make two columns—one to list the ways you train for your sporting event or other activity and the other to list ways you might train your soul to become a more loving person in the image of Jesus.

- How do your two training columns compare?
- What are some ways you can increase your spiritual training efforts?
- Put your lists where you can see them and continue adding to your list as training starts to pay off.

ᵃ Other ancient authorities read *suffer reproach*   ᵇ Gk *to the reading*   ᶜ Gk *by the presbytery*   ᵈ Or *an elder, or a presbyter*   ᵉ Gk *she*

CONNECT IT!

Alex and Brett Harris: Starting a Rebelution · 1 Timothy 4:12

Alex and Brett Harris are twin brothers who started a rebelution. Think that should be spelled "revolution"? Nope, it's a combination of "rebellion" and "revolution," and it's a movement to encourage teens to rise above low expectations and be used by God in big ways. The brothers began TheRebelution.com when they were sixteen, and the blog became the most popular Christian teen blog on the Web in two years. They built on their ideas and wrote the bestselling book Do Hard Things when they were nineteen. They followed that up with national conferences and another book called Start Here.

So what's it all about? Basically about pursuing God into big ideas. Not trivial ideas for fleeting fame, but ones that defy stereotypes of teen laziness, apathy, and inability. Alex and Brett inspire teens to set goals, sharpen their skills, and pursue their passions to change the world around them for God. Their actions have started a movement and a community of young people living out this verse, setting examples "in speech and conduct, in love, in faith, in purity." And there's no looking down on their youth!

she lives. [7] Give these commands as well, so that they may be above reproach. [8] And whoever does not provide for relatives, and especially for family members, has denied the faith and is worse than an unbeliever.

9 Let a widow be put on the list if she is not less than sixty years old and has been married only once;[a] [10] she must be well attested for her good works, as one who has brought up children, shown hospitality, washed the saints' feet, helped the afflicted, and devoted herself to doing good in every way. [11] But refuse to put younger widows on the list; for when their sensual desires alienate them from Christ, they want to marry, [12] and so they incur condemnation for having violated their first pledge. [13] Besides that, they learn to be idle, gadding about from house to house; and they are not merely idle, but also gossips and busybodies, saying what they should not say. [14] So I would have younger widows marry, bear children, and manage their households, so as to give the adversary no occasion to revile us. [15] For some have already turned away to follow Satan. [16] If any believing woman[b] has relatives who are really widows, let her assist them; let the church not be burdened, so that it can assist those who are real widows.

17 Let the elders who rule well be considered worthy of double honor,[c] especially those who labor in preaching and teaching; [18] for the scripture says, "You shall not muzzle an ox while it is treading out the grain," and, "The laborer deserves to be paid." [19] Never accept any accusation against an elder except on the evidence of two or three witnesses. [20] As for those who persist in sin, rebuke them in the presence of all, so that the rest also may stand in fear. [21] In the presence of God and of Christ Jesus and of the elect angels, I warn you to keep these instructions without prejudice, doing nothing on the basis of partiality. [22] Do not ordain[d] anyone hastily, and do not participate in the sins of others; keep yourself pure.

23 No longer drink only water, but take a little wine for the sake of your stomach and your frequent ailments.

24 The sins of some people are conspicuous and precede them to judgment, while the sins of others follow them there. [25] So also good works are conspicuous; and even when they are not, they cannot remain hidden.

6 Let all who are under the yoke of slavery regard their masters as worthy of all honor, so that the name of God and the teaching may not be blasphemed. [2] Those who have believing masters must not be disrespectful to them on the ground that they are members of the church;[e] rather they must serve them all the more, since those who benefit by their service are believers and beloved.[f]

---

a Gk *the wife of one husband* b Other ancient authorities read *believing man or woman*; others, *believing man* c Or *compensation* d Gk *Do not lay hands on* e Gk *are brothers* f Or *since they are believers and beloved, who devote themselves to good deeds*

LIVE IT!

The Dangers of Money
1 Timothy 6:6–10

We live in a culture that glorifies material things, money, and consumption. Even when individuals or families have the essential things to live comfortably, many are driven to get more and more.

An important truth, found in many places in scripture (e.g., Luke 12:20), is repeated here: You can't take it with you. Another truth about money is: "The love of money is a root of all kinds of evil" (1 Timothy 6:10). In our eagerness to become financially rich, we can lose sight of God.

Sure, all of us need the basic stuff of life: food, clothing, and shelter. God wants us to have these things. But ultimately, real riches or success won't be measured by bank accounts or material things. It will be measured by the love and generosity with which we have lived.

- How do you measure success or wealth?
- How rich are you becoming in eternal things?

False Teaching and True Riches

Teach and urge these duties. [3]Whoever teaches otherwise and does not agree with the sound words of our Lord Jesus Christ and the teaching that is in accordance with godliness, [4]is conceited, understanding nothing, and has a morbid craving for controversy and for disputes about words. From these come envy, dissension, slander, base suspicions, [5]and wrangling among those who are depraved in mind and bereft of the truth, imagining that godliness is a means of gain.[a] [6]Of course, there is great gain in godliness combined with contentment; [7]for we brought nothing into the world, so that[b] we can take nothing out of it; [8]but if we have food and clothing, we will be content with these. [9]But those who want to be rich fall into temptation and are trapped by many senseless and harmful desires that plunge people into ruin and destruction. [10]For the love of money is a root of all kinds of evil, and in their eagerness to be rich some have wandered away from the faith and pierced themselves with many pains.

The Good Fight of Faith

11 But as for you, man of God, shun all this; pursue righteousness, godliness, faith, love, endurance, gentleness. [12]Fight the good fight of the faith; take hold of the eternal life, to which you were called and for which you made[c] the good confession in the presence of many witnesses. [13]In the presence of God, who gives life to all things, and of Christ Jesus, who in his testimony before Pontius Pilate made the good confession, I charge you [14]to keep the commandment without spot or blame until the manifestation of our Lord Jesus Christ, [15]which he will bring about at the right time—he who is the blessed and only Sovereign, the King of kings and Lord of lords. [16]It is he alone who has immortality and dwells in unapproachable light, whom no one has ever seen or can see; to him be honor and eternal dominion. Amen.

17 As for those who in the present age are rich, command them not to be haughty, or to set their hopes on the uncertainty of riches, but rather on God who richly provides us with everything for our enjoyment. [18]They are to do good, to be rich in good works, generous, and ready to share, [19]thus storing up for themselves the treasure of a good foundation for the future, so that they may take hold of the life that really is life.

Personal Instructions and Benediction

20 Timothy, guard what has been entrusted to you. Avoid the profane chatter and contradictions of what is falsely called knowledge; [21]by professing it some have missed the mark as regards the faith. Grace be with you.[d]

---

a Other ancient authorities add *Withdraw yourself from such people*   **b** Other ancient authorities read *world—it is certain that*   **c** Gk *confessed*
d The Greek word for *you* here is plural; in other ancient authorities it is singular. Other ancient authorities add *Amen*

2 Timothy

For background on this letter, see the introduction to 1 Timothy, 2 Timothy, and Titus at the beginning of 1 Timothy.

1 Salutation

Paul, an apostle of Christ Jesus by the will of God, for the sake of the promise of life that is in Christ Jesus,

2 To Timothy, my beloved child:

Grace, mercy, and peace from God the Father and Christ Jesus our Lord.

Thanksgiving and Encouragement

3 I am grateful to God—whom I worship with a clear conscience, as my ancestors did—when I remember you constantly in my prayers night and day. [4]Recalling your tears, I long to see you so that I may be filled with joy. [5]I am reminded of your sincere faith, a faith that lived first in your grandmother Lois and your mother Eunice and now, I am sure, lives in you. [6]For this reason I remind you to rekindle the gift of God that is within you through the laying on of my hands; [7]for God did not give us a spirit of cowardice, but rather a spirit of power and of love and of self-discipline.

8 Do not be ashamed, then, of the testimony about our Lord or of me his prisoner, but join with me in suffering for the gospel, relying on the power of God, [9]who saved us and called us with a holy calling, not according to our works but according to his own purpose and grace. This grace was given to us in Christ Jesus before the ages began, [10]but it has now been revealed through the appearing of our Savior Christ Jesus, who abolished death and brought life and immortality to light through the gospel. [11]For this gospel I was appointed a herald and an apostle and a teacher,[a] [12]and for this reason I suffer as I do. But I am not ashamed, for I know the one in whom I have put my trust, and I am sure that he is able to guard until that day what I have entrusted to him.[b] [13]Hold to the standard of sound teaching that you have heard from me, in the faith

and love that are in Christ Jesus. [14]Guard the good treasure entrusted to you, with the help of the Holy Spirit living in us.

15 You are aware that all who are in Asia have turned away from me, including Phygelus and Hermogenes. [16]May the Lord grant mercy to the household of Onesiphorus, because he often refreshed me and was not ashamed of my chain; [17]when he arrived in Rome, he eagerly[c] searched for me and found me [18]—may the Lord grant that he will find mercy from the Lord on that day! And you know very well how much service he rendered in Ephesus.

PRAY IT!

Power, Love, and Self-Discipline
2 Timothy 1:7

What are you afraid of? What are you afraid to do? We all face fear in our lives, even when it comes to spiritual things. We fear standing up for what is right. We fear what others will think of us. We even face fear when doubt challenges our deepest beliefs. Like Timothy, we need to be reminded that God's spirit in us is not one of cowardice, but of power, love, and self-discipline. When you face fear, pray:

God, I am afraid. Please remind me that your spirit lives inside of me—and that spirit is not one of fear. Please give me your power and love, and teach me to be self-disciplined, so that I can live for you and share your love with the world. Amen.

---

a Other ancient authorities add *of the Gentiles* b Or *what has been entrusted to me* c Or *promptly*

2

A Good Soldier of Christ Jesus

You then, my child, be strong in the grace that is in Christ Jesus; [2]and what you have heard from me through many witnesses entrust to faithful people who will be able to teach others as well. [3]Share in suffering like a good soldier of Christ Jesus. [4]No one serving in the army gets entangled in everyday affairs; the soldier's aim is to please the enlisting officer. [5]And in the case of an athlete, no one is crowned without competing according to the rules. [6]It is the farmer who does the work who ought to have the first share of the crops. [7]Think over what I say, for the Lord will give you understanding in all things.

8 Remember Jesus Christ, raised from the dead, a descendant of David—that is my gospel, [9]for which I suffer hardship, even to the point of being chained like a criminal. But the word of God is not chained. [10]Therefore I endure everything for the sake of the elect, so that they may also obtain the salvation that is in Christ Jesus, with eternal glory. [11]The saying is sure:

If we have died with him, we will also live
　　with him;
[12] if we endure, we will also reign
　　with him;
if we deny him, he will also deny us;
[13] if we are faithless, he remains faithful—
　　for he cannot deny himself.

A Worker Approved by God

14 Remind them of this, and warn them before God[a] that they are to avoid wrangling over words, which does no good but only ruins those who are listening. [15]Do your best to present yourself to God as one approved by him, a worker who has no need to be ashamed, rightly explaining the word of truth. [16]Avoid profane chatter, for it will lead people into more and more impiety, [17]and their talk will spread like gangrene. Among them are Hymenaeus and Philetus, [18]who have swerved from the truth by claiming that the resurrection has already taken place. They are upsetting the faith of some. [19]But God's firm foundation stands, bearing this inscription: "The Lord knows those who are his," and, "Let everyone who calls on the name of the Lord turn away from wickedness."

20 In a large house there are utensils not only of gold and silver but also of wood and clay, some for special use, some for ordinary. [21]All who cleanse themselves of the things I have mentioned[b] will become special utensils, dedicated and useful to the owner of the house, ready for every good work. [22]Shun youthful passions and pursue righteousness, faith, love, and peace, along with those who call on the Lord from a pure heart. [23]Have nothing to do with stupid and senseless controversies; you know that they breed quarrels. [24]And the Lord's servant[c] must not be quarrelsome but kindly to everyone, an apt teacher, patient, [25]correcting opponents with gentleness. God may perhaps grant that they will repent and come to know the truth, [26]and that they may escape from the snare of the devil, having been held captive by him to do his will.[d]

3

Godlessness in the Last Days

You must understand this, that in the last days distressing times will come. [2]For people will be lovers of themselves, lovers of money, boasters, arrogant, abusive, disobedient to their parents, ungrateful, unholy, [3]inhuman, implacable, slanderers, profligates, brutes, haters of good, [4]treacherous, reckless, swollen with conceit, lovers of pleasure rather than lovers of God, [5]holding to the outward form of godliness but denying its power. Avoid them! [6]For among them are those who make their way into households and captivate silly women, overwhelmed by their sins and swayed by all kinds of desires, [7]who are always being instructed and can never arrive at a knowledge of the truth. [8]As Jannes and Jambres opposed Moses, so these people, of corrupt mind and counterfeit faith, also oppose the truth. [9]But they will not make much progress, because, as in the case of those two men,[e] their folly will become plain to everyone.

Paul's Charge to Timothy

10 Now you have observed my teaching, my conduct, my aim in life, my faith, my patience, my love, my steadfastness, [11]my persecutions, and my suffering the things that happened to me in Antioch, Iconium, and Lystra. What persecutions I endured! Yet the Lord rescued me from all of them. [12]Indeed, all who want to live a godly life in Christ Jesus will be persecuted. [13]But wicked people and impostors will go from bad to worse, deceiving others and being deceived. [14]But as for you, continue in what you have learned and firmly believed, knowing from whom you learned it, [15]and how from childhood you have known the sacred writings that are able to

---

a Other ancient authorities read *the Lord* 　**b** Gk *of these things*　**c** Gk *slave*　**d** Or *by him, to do his* (that is, God's) *will*　**e** Gk lacks *two men*

> "All scripture is inspired by God and is useful for teaching, for reproof, for correction, and for training in righteousness."
> —2 Timothy 3:16

instruct you for salvation through faith in Christ Jesus. [16]All scripture is inspired by God and is[a] useful for teaching, for reproof, for correction, and for training in righteousness, [17]so that everyone who belongs to God may be proficient, equipped for every good work.

4 In the presence of God and of Christ Jesus, who is to judge the living and the dead, and in view of his appearing and his kingdom, I solemnly urge you: [2]proclaim the message; be persistent whether the time is favorable or unfavorable; convince, rebuke, and encourage, with the utmost patience in teaching. [3]For the time is coming when people will not put up with sound doctrine, but having itching ears, they will accumulate for themselves teachers to suit their own desires, [4]and will turn away from listening to the truth and wander away to myths. [5]As for you, always be sober, endure suffering, do the work of an evangelist, carry out your ministry fully.

[6] As for me, I am already being poured out as a libation, and the time of my departure has come. [7]I have fought the good fight, I have finished the race, I have kept the faith. [8]From now on there is reserved for me the crown of righteousness, which the Lord, the righteous judge, will give me on that day, and not only to me but also to all who have longed for his appearing.

Personal Instructions

[9] Do your best to come to me soon, [10]for Demas, in love with this present world, has deserted me and gone to Thessalonica; Crescens has gone to Galatia,[b] Titus to Dalmatia. [11]Only Luke is with me. Get Mark and bring him with you, for he is useful in my ministry. [12]I have sent Tychicus to Ephesus. [13]When you come, bring the cloak that I left with Carpus at Troas, also the books, and above all the parchments. [14]Alexander the coppersmith did me great harm; the Lord will pay him back for his deeds. [15]You also must beware of him, for he strongly opposed our message.

[16] At my first defense no one came to my support, but all deserted me. May it not be counted against them! [17]But the Lord stood by me and gave me strength, so that through me the message might be fully proclaimed and all the Gentiles might hear it. So I was rescued from the lion's mouth. [18]The Lord will rescue me from every evil attack and save me for his heavenly kingdom. To him be the glory forever and ever. Amen.

LIVE IT!

Share the Faith · 2 Timothy 4:2–5

It's one thing to know the faith, another to live the faith, and yet another to share the faith. Disciples of Christ are called to do all three. A faith that is alive, that echoes the reason for its being, is one that's meant to be passed along, so others may be transformed by the God at the center of it all (2 Timothy 4:2). But a challenging faith that demands much isn't always a faith that's easily shared. People want a nice, convenient faith that allows them to live their lives undisturbed and unencumbered. So to share this total, radical, and world-changing faith that Jesus lived, died, and rose for is not the easiest of assignments. It's an assignment that requires a lot of courage, integrity, and commitment (2 Timothy 4:5).

- What's your biggest challenge in sharing your faith? How can you work to overcome it? Who can you ask for help?
- How can you use the tips in 2 Timothy 2:22-26 (live a good moral life, do good works, have a pure heart, be kind, patient, gentle, and prepared) to help you share your faith with others?

---

a Or *Every scripture inspired by God is also*   b Other ancient authorities read *Gaul*

PRAY IT!

Misleading Messages · 2 Timothy 4:3–4

Sticking with something can be difficult. When things get tough, many people are tempted to quit or walk away. If swim practice is boring, quit the team. If homework is too complicated, just don't finish it. If a friend starts to get annoying, stop hanging around with her or him. We're surrounded by messages like, "If it feels good, do it" and "You deserve whatever your heart desires."

But this passage warns us against being taken in by deceptive messages that suit our own desires—like the belief that life should always be easy and pleasurable. Such messages water down the real challenge of living as a follower of Jesus!

God, it's so much easier to follow the messages that tell me what I want to hear and give me instant gratification. But I know in my head they're shallow and short-lived. Please help me to believe and trust in you and to listen to your truth instead of the messages of this world. Amen.

Final Greetings and Benediction

19 Greet Prisca and Aquila, and the household of Onesiphorus. [20]Erastus remained in Corinth; Trophimus I left ill in Miletus. [21]Do your best to come before winter. Eubulus sends greetings to you, as do Pudens and Linus and Claudia and all the brothers and sisters.[a]

22 The Lord be with your spirit. Grace be with you.[b]

---

a Gk all the brothers   b The Greek word for you here is plural. Other ancient authorities add Amen

Titus

For background on this letter, see the introduction to 1 Timothy, 2 Timothy, and Titus at the beginning of 1 Timothy.

1

Salutation

Paul, a servant[a] of God and an apostle of Jesus Christ, for the sake of the faith of God's elect and the knowledge of the truth that is in accordance with godliness, [2]in the hope of eternal life that God, who never lies, promised before the ages began— [3]in due time he revealed his word through the proclamation with which I have been entrusted by the command of God our Savior,

4 To Titus, my loyal child in the faith we share: Grace[b] and peace from God the Father and Christ Jesus our Savior.

Titus in Crete

5 I left you behind in Crete for this reason, so that you should put in order what remained to be done, and should appoint elders in every town, as I directed you: [6]someone who is blameless, married only once,[c] whose children are believers, not accused of debauchery and not rebellious. [7]For a bishop,[d] as God's steward, must be blameless; he must not be arrogant or quick-tempered or addicted to wine or violent or greedy for gain; [8]but he must be hospitable, a lover of goodness, prudent, upright, devout, and self-controlled. [9]He must have a firm grasp of the word that is trustworthy in accordance with the teaching, so that he may be able both to preach with sound doctrine and to refute those who contradict it.

10 There are also many rebellious people, idle talkers and deceivers, especially those of the circumcision; [11]they must be silenced, since they are upsetting whole families by teaching for sordid gain what it is not right to teach. [12]It was one of them, their very own prophet, who said,

"Cretans are always liars, vicious brutes, lazy
    gluttons."

LIVE IT!

Follow the Leader · Titus 1:5–9

Who do you follow? Why? Even if you consider yourself a leader, you still follow other people in certain areas of life. Making good choices about who to follow is important. It's easy to follow people who have great vision and can inspire us to action. But even people with those skills can be bad leaders, if they lead in a wrong direction. Good leaders live with integrity in their lifestyle and their commitment and service to the values of Christ. Good leaders serve others and know how to motivate people to grow and serve.

Make a list of the values you think a leader should have. Now compare your list to the qualities in this passage. How closely does your list match the characteristics listed here? The qualities listed in Titus are a great guide both as you choose who to follow and as you take on leadership roles of your own.

- Which leaders in your school, community, or church do you admire most? What qualities make them good leaders?
- How do these leaders stack up against the good-leader characteristics you listed and against the ones given in Titus?
- What leadership qualities do you need to work on in your own life? Make a list of ways you can begin to build those characteristics.

---

a Gk *slave*   b Other ancient authorities read *Grace, mercy,*   c Gk *husband of one wife*   d Or *an overseer*

¹³That testimony is true. For this reason rebuke them sharply, so that they may become sound in the faith, ¹⁴not paying attention to Jewish myths or to commandments of those who reject the truth. ¹⁵To the pure all things are pure, but to the corrupt and unbelieving nothing is pure. Their very minds and consciences are corrupted. ¹⁶They profess to know God, but they deny him by their actions. They are detestable, disobedient, unfit for any good work.

Teach Sound Doctrine

2 But as for you, teach what is consistent with sound doctrine. ²Tell the older men to be temperate, serious, prudent, and sound in faith, in love, and in endurance.

3 Likewise, tell the older women to be reverent in behavior, not to be slanderers or slaves to drink; they are to teach what is good, ⁴so that they may encourage the young women to love their husbands, to love their children, ⁵to be self-controlled, chaste, good managers of the household, kind, being submissive to their husbands, so that the word of God may not be discredited.

6 Likewise, urge the younger men to be self-controlled. ⁷Show yourself in all respects a model of good works, and in your teaching show integrity, gravity, ⁸and sound speech that cannot be censured; then any opponent will be put to shame, having nothing evil to say of us.

9 Tell slaves to be submissive to their masters and to give satisfaction in every respect; they are not to talk back, ¹⁰not to pilfer, but to show complete and perfect fidelity, so that in everything they may be an ornament to the doctrine of God our Savior.

11 For the grace of God has appeared, bringing salvation to all,ᵃ ¹²training us to renounce impiety and worldly passions, and in the present age to live lives that are self-controlled, upright, and godly, ¹³while we wait for the blessed hope and the manifestation of the glory of our great God and Savior,ᵇ Jesus Christ. ¹⁴He it is who gave himself for us that he might redeem us from all iniquity and purify for himself a people of his own who are zealous for good deeds.

15 Declare these things; exhort and reprove with all authority.ᶜ Let no one look down on you.

Maintain Good Deeds

3 Remind them to be subject to rulers and authorities, to be obedient, to be ready for every good work, ²to speak evil of no one, to avoid quarreling, to be gentle, and to show every courtesy to everyone. ³For we ourselves were once foolish, disobedient, led astray, slaves to various passions and pleasures, passing our days in malice and envy, despicable, hating one another. ⁴But when the goodness and loving kindness of God our Savior appeared, ⁵he saved us, not because of any works of righteousness that we had done, but according to his mercy, through the waterᵈ of rebirth and renewal by the Holy Spirit. ⁶This Spirit he poured out on us richly through Jesus Christ our Savior, ⁷so that, having been justified by his grace, we might become heirs according to the hope of eternal life. ⁸The saying is sure.

I desire that you insist on these things, so that those who have come to believe in God may be careful to devote themselves to good works; these things are excellent and profitable to everyone. ⁹But avoid stupid controversies, genealogies, dissensions, and quarrels about the law, for they are unprofitable and worthless. ¹⁰After a first and second admonition, have nothing more to do with anyone who causes divisions, ¹¹since you know that such a person is perverted and sinful, being self-condemned.

By Grace · Titus 3:3–8

The letter to Titus is full of challenges to live a moral life, make good choices, and do good works. But just when we think it's up to us to do good things, we are reminded by these verses that it's not our actions that save us. Instead, it's God's loving-kindness and mercy. God poured out grace on us before we did any good thing. So why should we follow the instructions of Titus in doing good works? Not so we can gain salvation, but because we have been given the gift of salvation. It's a great reminder that God loved us first—and that we can live our lives as a gift of thanks for God's mercy and grace.

ᵃ Or *has appeared to all, bringing salvation* ᵇ Or *of the great God and our Savior* ᶜ Gk *commandment* ᵈ Gk *washing*

Final Messages and Benediction

12 When I send Artemas to you, or Tychicus, do your best to come to me at Nicopolis, for I have decided to spend the winter there. [13]Make every effort to send Zenas the lawyer and Apollos on their way, and see that they lack nothing. [14]And let people learn to devote themselves to good works in order to meet urgent needs, so that they may not be unproductive.

15 All who are with me send greetings to you. Greet those who love us in the faith.

Grace be with all of you.[a]

Philemon ▶▶▶▶▶▶▶▶▶▶▶▶▶

On the surface, the brief letter to Philemon is the story of a slave who escaped and is now being returned to his master. But on a much deeper level, this book is about love and fellowship among believers in Christ. Although it doesn't condemn slavery outright, this letter challenges the early believers not only to look at slavery differently, but to act on their beliefs.

IN DEPTH

The letter is addressed to a slave owner named Philemon, a woman named Apphia, and a soldier named Archippus, who all live in Colossae. Philemon's slave, Onesimus, ran away, wound up in prison with Paul, and became a Christian. Now Paul is sending him back to Philemon as the law requires. That same law gives Philemon the right to punish Onesimus for escaping. But Paul asks not only for Onesimus' freedom, but for something far more challenging—that Philemon, Apphia, and Archippus accept Onesimus as "a beloved brother" in Christ (v. 16).

So why doesn't Paul come right out and say slavery is wrong? It's great that he is pleading the case of this one slave, but why does he seem to tolerate an institution we think of as unjust? To answer that we have to look at the culture in which the letter was written. Slavery was accepted at this time and practiced by many. But we see in this letter the beginning of a new attitude toward slavery. Recall Paul's basic statement on Christian freedom in Galatians: "There is no longer Jew or Greek, there is no longer slave or free, there is no longer male and female; for all of you are one in Christ Jesus" (Galatians 3:28). In this letter he is challenging Philemon and other believers to put this into practice.

Paul may not have been a social revolutionary by our standards, but he did believe the Christian community ought to live by a higher standard than the surrounding culture. This letter is a masterpiece of persuasion, as it urges Philemon and the church community in Colossae to accept Onesimus as a beloved brother in Christ. It uses compliments (vv. 4-7), a veiled reference to Paul's authority (vv. 8-9), Paul's personal relationship with everyone involved (vv. 12-17), and Paul's backing up his words with actions in his offer to pay for anything Onesimus stole (vv. 18-19). Paul's message to the household of Philemon and to us is this: we must get beyond whatever cultural boundaries prevent us from treating one another as brothers and sisters in Christ.

QUICK FACTS

- **Author:** Paul
- **Date Written:** A.D. 54-56, if from Ephesus; 61-63, if from Rome while Paul was in prison
- **Audience:** Philemon and his household, who lived in Colossae (in modern-day Turkey)
- **Themes:** Love for Jesus and for others is central to Christian faith.

AT A GLANCE

- **Philemon 1-7** Greeting and gratitude for Philemon
- **Philemon 8-22** Paul's request
- **Philemon 23-25** Final greetings and a blessing

Salutation

1 Paul, a prisoner of Christ Jesus, and Timothy our brother,[a]

To Philemon our dear friend and co-worker, [2]to Apphia our sister,[b] to Archippus our fellow soldier, and to the church in your house:

3 Grace to you and peace from God our Father and the Lord Jesus Christ.

Philemon's Love and Faith

4 When I remember you[c] in my prayers, I always thank my God [5]because I hear of your love for all the saints and your faith toward the Lord Jesus. [6]I pray that the sharing of your faith may become effective when you perceive all the good that we[d] may do for Christ. [7]I have indeed received much joy and encouragement from your love, because the hearts of the saints have been refreshed through you, my brother.

Paul's Plea for Onesimus

8 For this reason, though I am bold enough in Christ to command you to do your duty, [9]yet I would rather appeal to you on the basis of love—and I, Paul, do this as an old man, and now also as a prisoner of Christ Jesus.[e] [10]I am appealing to you for my child, Onesimus, whose father I have become during my imprisonment. [11]Formerly he was useless to you, but now he is indeed useful[f] both to you and to me. [12]I am sending him, that is, my own heart, back to you. [13]I wanted to keep him with me, so that he might be of service to me in your place during my imprisonment for the gospel; [14]but I preferred to do nothing without your consent, in order that your good deed might be voluntary and not some-

thing forced. [15]Perhaps this is the reason he was separated from you for a while, so that you might have him back forever, [16]no longer as a slave but more than a slave, a beloved brother—especially to me but how much more to you, both in the flesh and in the Lord.

17 So if you consider me your partner, welcome him as you would welcome me. [18]If he has wronged you in any way, or owes you anything, charge that to my account. [19]I, Paul, am writing this with my own hand: I will repay it. I say nothing about your owing me even your own self. [20]Yes, brother, let me have this benefit from you in the Lord! Refresh my heart in Christ. [21]Confident of your obedience, I am writing to you, knowing that you will do even more than I say.

22 One thing more—prepare a guest room for me, for I am hoping through your prayers to be restored to you.

Final Greetings and Benediction

23 Epaphras, my fellow prisoner in Christ Jesus, sends greetings to you,[g] [24]and so do Mark, Aristarchus, Demas, and Luke, my fellow workers.

25 The grace of the Lord Jesus Christ be with your spirit.[h]

LIVE IT!

Rethinking Social Structures · Philemon 8–21

In sending the slave Onesimus back to his wealthy owner, Philemon, Paul asks Philemon not only to forgive his runaway slave, but to rethink his relationship with him. Paul's plea to Philemon and the church in Colossae to look on Onesimus as a brother in Christ was radical for the time. People expected runaway slaves to be punished severely. Accepting Onesimus as a Christian would be a sign that Paul's intended notion of the Church as one body in Christ was being lived out in concrete ways!

- What commonly accepted social structures in our day need a fresh look?
- What privileges do we take for granted that may actually prevent true equality in Christ?
- Who do you look down on? How can you change your attitude and treat them equally?

---

a Gk *the brother* b Gk *the sister* c From verse 4 through verse 21, *you* is singular d Other ancient authorities read *you* (plural) e Or *as an ambassador of Christ Jesus, and now also his prisoner* f The name Onesimus means *useful* or (compare verse 20) *beneficial* g Here *you* is singular h Other ancient authorities add *Amen*

Hebrews ▶▶▶▶▶▶▶▶▶▶▶▶▶▶▶▶▶▶▶

Have you ever wondered why it makes sense to believe that Jesus is the Savior of all humanity? It's an honest question. Evidently, some early Christians asked it. The letter to the Hebrews is a sermon—to them and to us—to strengthen faith and belief in Jesus, the Son of God.

IN DEPTH

Hebrews gives almost no information about its author and the community it's addressed to. But it appears that some members of the community are in danger of giving up their faith—and this is happening after the group has already survived a period of persecution. The letter encourages them to be strong in their faith. It also seeks to give a sound foundation for believing in Jesus. It's a statement on the saving power of Christ's sacrificial death and his unique role as high priest of the new covenant.

The letter says that Christ is the divine Son of God through whom the world was created, superior to any angel, and the culmination of all the promises and expectations of the Old Testament. In explaining Christ's importance, the letter uses a type of argument called "from the lesser to the greater." This type of argument is based on the idea that if you accept something as true in a lesser situation, then it is certainly true in a greater situation. The author uses it to show that Christ's sacrifice is far greater than the sacrifices offered by the Jewish priests in the temple for the forgiveness of sins. As the perfect high priest, Christ offers the perfect sacrifice—his death on the cross. And through it God saves us once and for all from sin.

This letter reads like one complete message made up of interconnecting parts. Try reading the whole thing out loud first to truly appreciate its power and wording. Then look up some of its references to people and events in the Old Testament to better appreciate its explanation of Christ's mission.

QUICK FACTS

- **Author:** Unknown
- **Date Written:** Between A.D. 60 and 95
- **Audience:** Hellenistic (Greek-speaking) Christians and possibly Jewish Christians
- **Themes:** Salvation and faith in Christ is superior over other faith traditions.

AT A GLANCE

- **Hebrews 1–2** Introduction, and a message that Christ is greater than the angels
- **Hebrews 3–7** Christ, greater than Moses, Melchizedek, and the priests of the temple
- **Hebrews 8:1–10:18** Christ as the perfect sacrifice of the new covenant
- **Hebrews 10:19–12:29** Call to perseverance, list of heroes of the faith, the example of Christ, warnings based on Old Testament stories
- **Hebrews 13:1–19** Exhortations to right behavior
- **Hebrews 13:20–25** Blessing and final greeting

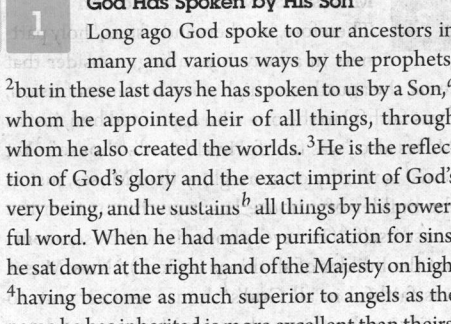

God Has Spoken by His Son

1 Long ago God spoke to our ancestors in many and various ways by the prophets, [2]but in these last days he has spoken to us by a Son,[a] whom he appointed heir of all things, through whom he also created the worlds. [3]He is the reflection of God's glory and the exact imprint of God's very being, and he sustains[b] all things by his powerful word. When he had made purification for sins, he sat down at the right hand of the Majesty on high, [4]having become as much superior to angels as the name he has inherited is more excellent than theirs.

The Son Is Superior to Angels

[5] For to which of the angels did God ever say,

"You are my Son;
today I have begotten you"?

Or again,

"I will be his Father,
and he will be my Son"?

[6]And again, when he brings the firstborn into the world, he says,

"Let all God's angels worship him."

[7]Of the angels he says,

"He makes his angels winds,
and his servants flames of fire."

[8]But of the Son he says,

"Your throne, O God, is[c] forever and ever,
and the righteous scepter is the scepter of
your[d] kingdom.
[9] You have loved righteousness and hated
wickedness;
therefore God, your God, has anointed you

with the oil of gladness beyond your
companions."

[10]And,

"In the beginning, Lord, you founded the
earth,
and the heavens are the work of your
hands;
[11] they will perish, but you remain;
they will all wear out like clothing;
[12] like a cloak you will roll them up,
and like clothing[e] they will be changed.
But you are the same,
and your years will never end."

[13]But to which of the angels has he ever said,

"Sit at my right hand
until I make your enemies a footstool for
your feet"?

[14]Are not all angels[f] spirits in the divine service, sent to serve for the sake of those who are to inherit salvation?

Warning to Pay Attention

2 Therefore we must pay greater attention to what we have heard, so that we do not drift away from it. [2]For if the message declared through angels was valid, and every transgression or disobedience received a just penalty, [3]how can we escape if we neglect so great a salvation? It was declared at first through the Lord, and it was attested to us by those who heard him, [4]while God added his testimony by signs and wonders and various miracles, and by gifts of the Holy Spirit, distributed according to his will.

STUDY IT!

The Exact Imprint · Hebrews 1

There have been many opinions throughout history about who Jesus of Nazareth was. Some have called him a great teacher, some a prophet, some a charismatic preacher, and others a miracle worker. Christians believe Jesus was all of these and more—much more.

The letter to the Hebrews makes a bold claim about Jesus. It says the historical human being from Nazareth named Jesus is the perfect human image of God. Jesus reflects God's glory and is "the exact imprint of God's very being" (Hebrews 1:3). In other words, Jesus is a human being like us, and Jesus is God.

This astonishing claim is central to the Christian faith. If you accept it as true, it will change your life. And if you believe it, you need to know the whole story behind it and all the evidence that supports it. The best place to start is with the book in your hands. Read on!

---

a Or *the Son* b Or *bears along* c Or *God is your throne* d Other ancient authorities read *his* e Other ancient authorities lack *like clothing* f Gk all of them

Exaltation through Abasement

5 Now God[a] did not subject the coming world, about which we are speaking, to angels. [6]But someone has testified somewhere,

> "What are human beings that you are mindful
>　　of them,[b]
>　or mortals, that you care for them?[c]
> 7 You have made them for a little while lower[d]
>　　than the angels;
>　you have crowned them with glory and
>　　honor,[e]
> 8 subjecting all things under
>　　their feet."

Now in subjecting all things to them, God[a] left nothing outside their control. As it is, we do not yet see everything in subjection to them, [9]but we do see Jesus, who for a little while was made lower[f] than the angels, now crowned with glory and honor because of the suffering of death, so that by the grace of God[g] he might taste death for everyone.

10 It was fitting that God,[a] for whom and through whom all things exist, in bringing many children to glory, should make the pioneer of their salvation perfect through sufferings. [11]For the one who sanctifies and those who are sanctified all have one Father.[h] For this reason Jesus[a] is not ashamed to call them brothers and sisters,[i] [12]saying,

> "I will proclaim your name to my brothers and
>　　sisters,[i]
>　in the midst of the congregation I will
>　　praise you."

[13]And again,

> "I will put my trust in him."

And again,

> "Here am I and the children whom God has
>　　given me."

14 Since, therefore, the children share flesh and blood, he himself likewise shared the same things, so that through death he might destroy the one who has the power of death, that is, the devil, [15]and free those who all their lives were held in slavery by the fear of death. [16]For it is clear that he did not come to help angels, but the descendants of Abraham. [17]Therefore he had to become like his brothers and sisters[i] in every respect, so that he might be a merciful and faithful high priest in the service of God, to make a sacrifice of atonement for the sins of the people. [18]Because he himself was tested by what he suffered, he is able to help those who are being tested.

Moses a Servant, Christ a Son

3 Therefore, brothers and sisters,[i] holy partners in a heavenly calling, consider that Jesus, the apostle and high priest of our confession, [2]was faithful to the one who appointed him, just as Moses also "was faithful in all[j] God's[k] house." [3]Yet Jesus[l] is worthy of more glory than Moses, just as the builder of a house has more honor than the house itself. [4](For every house is built by someone, but the builder of all things is God.) [5]Now Moses was faithful in all God's[k] house as a servant, to testify to the things that would be spoken later. [6]Christ, however, was faithful over God's[k] house as a son, and we are his house if we hold firm[m] the confidence and the pride that belong to hope.

Warning against Unbelief

7 Therefore, as the Holy Spirit says,

> "Today, if you hear his voice,
> 8 do not harden your hearts as in the
>　　rebellion,
>　　as on the day of testing in the wilderness,
> 9 where your ancestors put me to the test,
>　　though they had seen my works [10]for forty
>　　years.
> Therefore I was angry with that generation,
> and I said, 'They always go astray in their
>　　hearts,
>　and they have not known my ways.'
> 11 As in my anger I swore,
>　'They will not enter my rest.' "

[12]Take care, brothers and sisters,[i] that none of you may have an evil, unbelieving heart that turns away from the living God. [13]But exhort one another every day, as long as it is called "today," so that none of you may be hardened by the deceitfulness of sin. [14]For we have become partners of Christ, if only we hold our first confidence firm to the end. [15]As it is said,

> "Today, if you hear his voice,
>　do not harden your hearts as in the rebellion."

[16]Now who were they who heard and yet were rebellious? Was it not all those who left Egypt under the leadership of Moses? [17]But with whom was he angry forty years? Was it not those who sinned, whose bodies fell in the wilderness? [18]And to whom did he swear that they would not enter his rest, if not to those who were disobedient? [19]So we see that they were unable to enter because of unbelief.

---

a Gk he　b Gk *What is man that you are mindful of him?*　c Gk *or the son of man that you care for him?* In the Hebrew of Psalm 8.4-6 both *man* and *son of man* refer to all humankind　d Or *them only a little lower*　e Other ancient authorities add *and set them over the works of your hands*　f Or *who was made a little lower*　g Other ancient authorities read *apart from God*　h Gk *are all of one*　i Gk *brothers*　j Other ancient authorities lack *all*　k Gk *his*　l Gk *this one*　m Other ancient authorities add *to the end*

4 The Rest That God Promised

Therefore, while the promise of entering his rest is still open, let us take care that none of you should seem to have failed to reach it. [2] For indeed the good news came to us just as to them; but the message they heard did not benefit them, because they were not united by faith with those who listened.[a] [3] For we who have believed enter that rest, just as God[b] has said,

"As in my anger I swore,
'They shall not enter my rest,' "

though his works were finished at the foundation of the world. [4] For in one place it speaks about the seventh day as follows, "And God rested on the seventh day from all his works." [5] And again in this place it says, "They shall not enter my rest." [6] Since therefore it remains open for some to enter it, and those who formerly received the good news failed to enter because of disobedience, [7] again he sets a certain day—"today"—saying through David much later, in the words already quoted,

"Today, if you hear his voice,
do not harden your hearts."

[8] For if Joshua had given them rest, God[b] would not speak later about another day. [9] So then, a sabbath rest still remains for the people of God; [10] for those who enter God's rest also cease from their labors as God did from his. [11] Let us therefore make every effort to enter that rest, so that no one may fall through such disobedience as theirs.

[12] Indeed, the word of God is living and active, sharper than any two-edged sword, piercing until it divides soul from spirit, joints from marrow; it is able to judge the thoughts and intentions of the heart. [13] And before him no creature is hidden, but all are naked and laid bare to the eyes of the one to whom we must render an account.

Jesus the Great High Priest

[14] Since, then, we have a great high priest who has passed through the heavens, Jesus, the Son of God, let us hold fast to our confession. [15] For we do not have a high priest who is unable to sympathize with our weaknesses, but we have one who in every respect has been tested[c] as we are, yet without sin. [16] Let us therefore approach the throne of grace with boldness, so that we may receive mercy and find grace to help in time of need.

> "For we do not have a high priest who is unable to sympathize with our weaknesses, but we have one who in every respect has been tested as we are, yet without sin."
> —Hebrews 4:15

LIVE IT!

Come Boldly · Hebrews 4:14–16

Have you ever done something you felt God could never forgive? Or do you ever have thoughts that make you feel so ashamed you don't dare talk with God about them?

Here we are reminded of a remarkable truth: Jesus was fully human even though he was fully divine. He never sinned, but this scripture passage tells us that he was tempted in every way, just as we are today. Think about that! Jesus grew up with pressure from friends. He experienced the hormonal changes of adolescence. He was once fourteen, seventeen, and twenty-two years old. There is no temptation you face that Jesus can't understand. That's why you can come to him boldly in any circumstance—even your deepest trouble—and find compassion and grace.

- In what area of your life do you face the greatest temptation?
- How can taking that to Jesus help you face it and experience freedom in the understanding and grace he provides?

a Other ancient authorities read *it did not meet with faith in those who listened*   b Gk *he*   c Or *tempted*

STUDY IT!

The Highest Priest · Hebrews 4:14–5:10

The role of the priesthood in the Old Testament evolved after Israel became a nation, and it underwent a long process of development. The priesthood was considered hereditary within the tribe of Levi. After the exile, three classes of clergy emerged: high priests, priests, and Levites. Priestly functions included maintaining religion as the center of Israel's life, taking care of the temple of Jerusalem, and interpreting and teaching scripture (see Numbers 18; and "Study It: The Covenant Laws," near Leviticus 3). The priests of Israel represented the people in a special way before God by offering prayer and sacrifices for the forgiveness of sin.

Here Jesus is described as the high priest who doesn't come from the tribe of Levi, but from the heavens. He sympathizes with us, understands our weaknesses, was tested like us, yet was without sin. Israel's priestly sacrifices foreshadowed the sacrifice of Jesus, the Son of God, the only sacrifice truly capable of reconciling a broken relationship with God caused by sin.

5 Every high priest chosen from among mortals is put in charge of things pertaining to God on their behalf, to offer gifts and sacrifices for sins. ²He is able to deal gently with the ignorant and wayward, since he himself is subject to weakness; ³and because of this he must offer sacrifice for his own sins as well as for those of the people. ⁴And one does not presume to take this honor, but takes it only when called by God, just as Aaron was.

5 So also Christ did not glorify himself in becoming a high priest, but was appointed by the one who said to him,

"You are my Son,
today I have begotten you";

⁶as he says also in another place,

"You are a priest forever,
according to the order of
Melchizedek."

7 In the days of his flesh, Jesus[a] offered up prayers and supplications, with loud cries and tears, to the one who was able to save him from death, and he was heard because of his reverent submission. ⁸Although he was a Son, he learned obedience through what he suffered; ⁹and having been made perfect, he became the source of eternal salvation for all who obey him, ¹⁰having been designated by God a high priest according to the order of Melchizedek.

Warning against Falling Away

11 About this[b] we have much to say that is hard to explain, since you have become dull in understanding. ¹²For though by this time you ought to be teachers, you need someone to teach you again the basic elements of the oracles of God. You need milk, not solid food; ¹³for everyone who lives on milk, being still an infant, is unskilled in the word of righteousness. ¹⁴But solid food is for the mature, for those whose faculties have been trained by practice to distinguish good from evil.

The Peril of Falling Away

6 Therefore let us go on toward perfection,[c] leaving behind the basic teaching about Christ, and not laying again the foundation: repentance from dead works and faith toward God, ²instruction about baptisms, laying on of hands, resurrection of the dead, and eternal judgment. ³And we will do[d] this, if God permits. ⁴For it is impossible to restore again to repentance those who have once been enlightened, and have tasted the heavenly gift, and have shared in the Holy Spirit, ⁵and have tasted the goodness of the word of God and the powers of the age to come, ⁶and then have fallen away, since on their own they are crucifying again the Son of God and are holding him up to contempt. ⁷Ground that drinks up the rain falling on it repeatedly, and that produces a crop useful to those for whom it is cultivated, receives a blessing from God. ⁸But if it produces thorns and thistles, it is worthless and on the verge of being cursed; its end is to be burned over.

9 Even though we speak in this way, beloved, we are confident of better things in your case, things

---

a Gk *he* b Or *him* c Or *toward maturity* d Other ancient authorities read *let us do* that belong to salvation. [10]For God is not unjust; he will not overlook your work and the love that you showed for his sake[a] in serving the saints, as you still do. [11]And we want each one of you to show the same diligence so as to realize the full assurance of hope to the very end, [12]so that you may not become sluggish, but imitators of those who through faith and patience inherit the promises.

The Certainty of God's Promise

[13] When God made a promise to Abraham, because he had no one greater by whom to swear, he swore by himself, [14]saying, "I will surely bless you and multiply you." [15]And thus Abraham,[b] having patiently endured, obtained the promise. [16]Human beings, of course, swear by someone greater than themselves, and an oath given as confirmation puts an end to all dispute. [17]In the same way, when God desired to show even more clearly to the heirs of the promise the unchangeable character of his purpose, he guaranteed it by an oath, [18]so that through two unchangeable things, in which it is impossible that God would prove false, we who have taken refuge might be strongly encouraged to seize the hope set before us. [19]We have this hope, a sure and steadfast anchor of the soul, a hope that enters the inner shrine behind the curtain, [20]where Jesus, a forerunner on our behalf, has entered, having become a high priest forever according to the order of Melchizedek.

The Priestly Order of Melchizedek

7 This "King Melchizedek of Salem, priest of the Most High God, met Abraham as he was returning from defeating the kings and blessed him"; [2]and to him Abraham apportioned "one-tenth of everything." His name, in the first place, means "king of righteousness"; next he is also king of Salem, that is, "king of peace." [3]Without father, without mother, without genealogy, having neither beginning of days nor end of life, but resembling the Son of God, he remains a priest forever.

[4] See how great he is! Even[c] Abraham the patriarch gave him a tenth of the spoils. [5]And those descendants of Levi who receive the priestly office have a commandment in the law to collect tithes[d] from the people, that is, from their kindred,[e] though these also are descended from Abraham. [6]But this man, who does not belong to their ancestry, collected tithes[d] from Abraham and blessed him who had received the promises. [7]It is beyond dispute that the inferior is blessed by the superior. [8]In the one case, tithes are received by those who are mortal; in the other, by one of whom it is testified that he lives. [9]One might even say that Levi himself, who receives tithes, paid tithes through Abraham, [10]for he was still in the loins of his ancestor when Melchizedek met him.

Another Priest, Like Melchizedek

[11] Now if perfection had been attainable through the levitical priesthood—for the people received the law under this priesthood—what further need would there have been to speak of another priest arising according to the order of Melchizedek, rather than one according to the order of Aaron? [12]For when there is a change in the priesthood, there is necessarily a change in the law as well. [13]Now the one of whom these things are spoken belonged to another tribe, from which no one has ever served at the altar. [14]For it is evident that our Lord was descended from Judah, and in connection with that tribe Moses said nothing about priests.

[15] It is even more obvious when another priest arises, resembling Melchizedek, [16]one who has become a priest, not through a legal requirement concerning physical descent, but through the power of an indestructible life. [17]For it is attested of him,

"You are a priest forever,
　　according to the order of Melchizedek."

[18]There is, on the one hand, the abrogation of an earlier commandment because it was weak and ineffectual [19](for the law made nothing perfect); there is, on the other hand, the introduction of a better hope, through which we approach God.

[20] This was confirmed with an oath; for others who became priests took their office without an oath, [21]but this one became a priest with an oath, because of the one who said to him,

"The Lord has sworn
　　and will not change his mind,
'You are a priest forever' "—

[22]accordingly Jesus has also become the guarantee of a better covenant.

[23] Furthermore, the former priests were many in number, because they were prevented by death from continuing in office; [24]but he holds his priesthood permanently, because he continues forever. [25]Consequently he is able for all time to save[f] those who approach God through him, since he always lives to make intercession for them.

---

a Gk *for his name*　b Gk *he*　c Other ancient authorities lack *Even*　d Or *a tenth*　e Gk *brothers*　f Or *able to save completely*

26 For it was fitting that we should have such a high priest, holy, blameless, undefiled, separated from sinners, and exalted above the heavens. 27 Unlike the other[a] high priests, he has no need to offer sacrifices day after day, first for his own sins, and then for those of the people; this he did once for all when he offered himself. 28 For the law appoints as high priests those who are subject to weakness, but the word of the oath, which came later than the law, appoints a Son who has been made perfect forever.

Mediator of a Better Covenant

8 Now the main point in what we are saying is this: we have such a high priest, one who is seated at the right hand of the throne of the Majesty in the heavens, 2 a minister in the sanctuary and the true tent[b] that the Lord, and not any mortal, has set up. 3 For every high priest is appointed to offer gifts and sacrifices; hence it is necessary for this priest also to have something to offer. 4 Now if he were on earth, he would not be a priest at all, since there are priests who offer gifts according to the law. 5 They offer worship in a sanctuary that is a sketch and shadow of the heavenly one; for Moses, when he was about to erect the tent,[b] was warned, "See that you make everything according to the pattern that was shown you on the mountain." 6 But Jesus[c] has now obtained a more excellent ministry, and to that degree he is the mediator of a better covenant, which has been enacted through better promises. 7 For if that first covenant had been faultless, there would have been no need to look for a second one. 8 God[d] finds fault with them when he says:

"The days are surely coming, says the Lord,
    when I will establish a new covenant with
        the house of Israel
    and with the house of Judah;
9 not like the covenant that I made with their
        ancestors,
    on the day when I took them by the hand
        to lead them out of the land of Egypt;
    for they did not continue in my covenant,
    and so I had no concern for them, says the
        Lord.
10 This is the covenant that I will make with the
        house of Israel
    after those days, says the Lord:
    I will put my laws in their minds,
        and write them on their hearts,
    and I will be their God,

and they shall be my people.
11 And they shall not teach one another
    or say to each other, 'Know the Lord,'
    for they shall all know me,
        from the least of them to the greatest.
12 For I will be merciful toward their iniquities,
    and I will remember their sins no more."
13 In speaking of "a new covenant," he has made the first one obsolete. And what is obsolete and growing old will soon disappear.

The Earthly and the Heavenly Sanctuaries

9 Now even the first covenant had regulations for worship and an earthly sanctuary. 2 For a tent[b] was constructed, the first one, in which were the lampstand, the table, and the bread of the Presence;[e] this is called the Holy Place. 3 Behind the second curtain was a tent[b] called the Holy of Holies. 4 In it stood the golden altar of incense and the ark of the covenant overlaid on all sides with gold, in which there were a golden urn holding the manna, and Aaron's rod that budded, and the tablets of the covenant; 5 above it were the cherubim of glory overshadowing the mercy seat.[f] Of these things we cannot speak now in detail.

6 Such preparations having been made, the priests go continually into the first tent[b] to carry out their ritual duties; 7 but only the high priest goes into the second, and he but once a year, and not without taking the blood that he offers for himself and for the sins committed unintentionally by the people. 8 By this the Holy Spirit indicates that the way into the sanctuary has not yet been disclosed as long as the first tent[b] is still standing. 9 This is a symbol[g] of the present time, during which gifts and sacrifices are offered that cannot perfect the conscience of the worshiper, 10 but deal only with food and drink and various baptisms, regulations for the body imposed until the time comes to set things right.

a Gk lacks other b Or tabernacle c Gk he d Gk He e Gk the presentation of the loaves f Or the place of atonement g Gk parable

11 But when Christ came as a high priest of the good things that have come,[a] then through the greater and perfect[b] tent[c] (not made with hands, that is, not of this creation), [12]he entered once for all into the Holy Place, not with the blood of goats and calves, but with his own blood, thus obtaining eternal redemption. [13]For if the blood of goats and bulls, with the sprinkling of the ashes of a heifer, sanctifies those who have been defiled so that their flesh is purified, [14]how much more will the blood of Christ, who through the eternal Spirit[d] offered himself without blemish to God, purify our[e] conscience from dead works to worship the living God!

15 For this reason he is the mediator of a new covenant, so that those who are called may receive the promised eternal inheritance, because a death has occurred that redeems them from the transgressions under the first covenant.[f] [16]Where a will[f] is involved, the death of the one who made it must be established. [17]For a will[f] takes effect only at death, since it is not in force as long as the one who made it is alive. [18]Hence not even the first covenant was inaugurated without blood. [19]For when every commandment had been told to all the people by Moses in accordance with the law, he took the blood of calves and goats,[g] with water and scarlet wool and hyssop, and sprinkled both the scroll itself and all the people, [20]saying, "This is the blood of the covenant that God has ordained for you." [21]And in the same way he sprinkled with the blood both the tent[c]

and all the vessels used in worship. [22]Indeed, under the law almost everything is purified with blood, and without the shedding of blood there is no forgiveness of sins.

Christ's Sacrifice Takes Away Sin

23 Thus it was necessary for the sketches of the heavenly things to be purified with these rites, but the heavenly things themselves need better sacrifices than these. [24]For Christ did not enter a sanctuary made by human hands, a mere copy of the true one, but he entered into heaven itself, now to appear in the presence of God on our behalf. [25]Nor was it to offer himself again and again, as the high priest enters the Holy Place year after year with blood that is not his own; [26]for then he would have had to suffer again and again since the foundation of the world. But as it is, he has appeared once for all at the end of the age to remove sin by the sacrifice of himself. [27]And just as it is appointed for mortals to die once, and after that the judgment, [28]so Christ, having been offered once to bear the sins of many, will appear a second time, not to deal with sin, but to save those who are eagerly waiting for him.

Christ's Sacrifice Once for All

10 Since the law has only a shadow of the good things to come and not the true form of these realities, it[h] can never, by the same sacrifices that are continually offered year after year, make

PRAY IT!

The Perfect Sacrifice · Hebrews 10:1-18

The priests of the Old Testament had great job security! People never stopped sinning, so they never stopped working to offer sacrifices for the forgiveness of sin. But Jesus put an end to all that. Jesus was "holy, blameless . . . and exalted above the heavens" (Hebrews 7:26), so when he offered himself as a sacrifice for sin on the cross, it ended the need for sacrifices.

The author of Hebrews uses the "from the lesser to the greater" argument again to explain that Christ's sacrifice on the cross is greater than any sacrifice that could ever be offered in the temple. Even though perfect animals were offered over and over, they never could take away sins (Hebrews 10:1-4). Christ's sacrifice was perfect, offered only once for the sins of all (Hebrews 10:12-14). After Christ's death, there is no longer any need for anyone else to offer a sacrifice for the forgiveness of sins. Say a prayer of thanks to Jesus:

Jesus, thank you for your willingness to give up your life to save me. Thank you for sacrificing yourself to fulfill God's requirements once and for all. Help me to never forget what my forgiveness cost you, and to live my life in the freedom your sacrifice brings. Amen.

---

a Other ancient authorities read *good things to come*   b Gk *more perfect*   c Other ancient authorities read *Holy Spirit*   d Other ancient authorities read *your*   e The Greek word used here means both *covenant* and *will*   f Other ancient authorities lack *and goats*   g Or *tabernacle*   h Other ancient authorities read *they*

perfect those who approach. [2]Otherwise, would they not have ceased being offered, since the worshipers, cleansed once for all, would no longer have any consciousness of sin? [3]But in these sacrifices there is a reminder of sin year after year. [4]For it is impossible for the blood of bulls and goats to take away sins. [5]Consequently, when Christ[a] came into the world, he said,

> "Sacrifices and offerings you have not desired,
>> but a body you have prepared for me;
> [6] in burnt offerings and sin offerings
>> you have taken no pleasure.
> [7] Then I said, 'See, God, I have come to do your
>> will, O God'
>> (in the scroll of the book[b] it is written of
>> me)."

[8]When he said above, "You have neither desired nor taken pleasure in sacrifices and offerings and burnt offerings and sin offerings" (these are offered according to the law), [9]then he added, "See, I have come to do your will." He abolishes the first in order to establish the second. [10]And it is by God's will[c] that we have been sanctified through the offering of the body of Jesus Christ once for all.

11 And every priest stands day after day at his service, offering again and again the same sacrifices that can never take away sins. [12]But when Christ[d] had offered for all time a single sacrifice for sins, "he sat down at the right hand of God," [13]and since then has been waiting "until his enemies would be made a footstool for his feet." [14]For by a single offering he has perfected for all time those who are sanctified. [15]And the Holy Spirit also testifies to us, for after saying,

> [16] "This is the covenant that I will make
>> with them
>> after those days, says the Lord:
> I will put my laws in their hearts,
>> and I will write them on their minds,"

[17]he also adds,

> "I will remember[e] their sins and their lawless
>> deeds no more."

[18]Where there is forgiveness of these, there is no longer any offering for sin.

A Call to Persevere

19 Therefore, my friends,[f] since we have confidence to enter the sanctuary by the blood of Jesus, [20]by the new and living way that he opened for us through the curtain (that is, through his flesh), [21]and since we have a great priest over the house of God, [22]let us approach with a true heart in full assurance of faith, with our hearts sprinkled clean from an evil conscience and our bodies washed with pure water. [23]Let us hold fast to the confession of our hope without wavering, for he who has promised is faithful. [24]And let us consider how to provoke one another to love and good deeds, [25]not neglecting to meet together, as is the habit of some, but encouraging one another, and all the more as you see the Day approaching.

26 For if we willfully persist in sin after having received the knowledge of the truth, there no longer remains a sacrifice for sins, [27]but a fearful prospect of judgment, and a fury of fire that will consume the adversaries. [28]Anyone who has violated the law of Moses dies without mercy "on the testimony of two or three witnesses." [29]How much worse punishment do you think will be deserved by those who have spurned the Son of God, profaned the blood of the covenant by which they were sanctified, and outraged the Spirit of grace? [30]For we know the one who said, "Vengeance is mine, I will repay." And again, "The Lord will judge his people." [31]It is a fearful thing to fall into the hands of the living God.

32 But recall those earlier days when, after you had been enlightened, you endured a hard struggle with sufferings, [33]sometimes being publicly exposed to abuse and persecution, and sometimes being partners with those so treated. [34]For you had compassion for those who were in prison, and you cheerfully accepted the plundering of your possessions, knowing that you yourselves possessed something better and more lasting. [35]Do not, therefore, abandon that confidence of yours; it brings a great reward. [36]For you need endurance, so that when you have done the will of God, you may receive what was promised. [37]For yet

> "in a very little while,
>> the one who is coming will come and will
>> not delay;
> [38] but my righteous one will live by faith.
>> My soul takes no pleasure in anyone who
>> shrinks back."

[39]But we are not among those who shrink back and so are lost, but among those who have faith and so are saved.

The Meaning of Faith

11 Now faith is the assurance of things hoped for, the conviction of things not seen. [2]In-

---

a Gk he   **b** Meaning of Gk uncertain   **c** Gk by that will   **d** Gk this one   **e** Gk on their minds and I will remember   **f** Gk Therefore, brothers

Run the Race
Hebrews 11

Have you ever made a family tree, read through old family letters, looked at old family photos, or listened to a grandparent's family stories? The perspective we gain from looking back can often help us understand our own identity. This chapter is a type of family history, recounting the stories of heroes of the faith, who lived by faith. It begins, "Now faith is the assurance of things hoped for, the conviction of things not seen" (Hebrews 11:1). And the heroes listed here all lived their lives with the hope of something they never saw revealed. Through Jesus, we now see the fulfillment of all their hopes. Hebrews challenges all readers to let the history of the faithful encourage us to get rid of the things that hold us back and to "run with perseverance the race that is set before us" (Hebrews 12:1).

- What holds you back from running the race of life that God has given you? How can you let go of it?
- What do you hope for? How can the examples of these heroes help you live by faith even when your hopes have not been fulfilled?

deed, by faith[a] our ancestors received approval. [3]By faith we understand that the worlds were prepared by the word of God, so that what is seen was made from things that are not visible.[b]

The Examples of Abel, Enoch, and Noah

4 By faith Abel offered to God a more acceptable[c] sacrifice than Cain's. Through this he received approval as righteous, God himself giving approval to his gifts; he died, but through his faith[d] he still speaks. [5]By faith Enoch was taken so that he did not experience death; and "he was not found, because God had taken him." For it was attested before he was taken away that "he had pleased God." [6]And

without faith it is impossible to please God, for whoever would approach him must believe that he exists and that he rewards those who seek him. [7]By faith Noah, warned by God about events as yet unseen, respected the warning and built an ark to save his household; by this he condemned the world and became an heir to the righteousness that is in accordance with faith.

The Faith of Abraham

8 By faith Abraham obeyed when he was called to set out for a place that he was to receive as an inheritance; and he set out, not knowing where he was going. [9]By faith he stayed for a time in the land he had been promised, as in a foreign land, living in tents, as did Isaac and Jacob, who were heirs with him of the same promise. [10]For he looked forward to the city that has foundations, whose architect and builder is God. [11]By faith he received power of procreation, even though he was too old—and Sarah herself was barren—because he considered him faithful who had promised.[e] [12]Therefore from one person, and this one as good as dead, descendants were born, "as many as the stars of heaven and as the innumerable grains of sand by the seashore."

13 All of these died in faith without having received the promises, but from a distance they saw and greeted them. They confessed that they were strangers and foreigners on the earth, [14]for people who speak in this way make it clear that they are seeking a homeland. [15]If they had been thinking of the land that they had left behind, they would have had opportunity to return. [16]But as it is, they desire a better country, that is, a heavenly one. Therefore God is not ashamed to be called their God; indeed, he has prepared a city for them.

17 By faith Abraham, when put to the test, offered up Isaac. He who had received the promises was ready to offer up his only son, [18]of whom he had been told, "It is through Isaac that descendants shall be named for you." [19]He considered the fact that God is able even to raise someone from the dead—and figuratively speaking, he did receive him back. [20]By faith Isaac invoked blessings for the future on Jacob and Esau. [21]By faith Jacob, when dying, blessed each of the sons of Joseph, "bowing in worship over the top of his staff." [22]By faith Joseph, at the end of his life, made mention of the exodus of the Israelites and gave instructions about his burial.[f]

a Gk by this   b Or was not made out of visible things   c Gk greater   d Gk through it   e Or By faith Sarah herself, though barren, received power to conceive, even when she was too old, because she considered him faithful who had promised.   f Gk his bones

The Faith of Moses

23 By faith Moses was hidden by his parents for three months after his birth, because they saw that the child was beautiful; and they were not afraid of the king's edict.[a] 24By faith Moses, when he was grown up, refused to be called a son of Pharaoh's daughter, 25choosing rather to share ill-treatment with the people of God than to enjoy the fleeting pleasures of sin. 26He considered abuse suffered for the Christ[b] to be greater wealth than the treasures of Egypt, for he was looking ahead to the reward. 27By faith he left Egypt, unafraid of the king's anger; for he persevered as though[c] he saw him who is invisible. 28By faith he kept the Passover and the sprinkling of blood, so that the destroyer of the firstborn would not touch the firstborn of Israel.[d]

The Faith of Other Israelite Heroes

29 By faith the people passed through the Red Sea as if it were dry land, but when the Egyptians attempted to do so they were drowned. 30By faith the walls of Jericho fell after they had been encircled for seven days. 31By faith Rahab the prostitute did not perish with those who were disobedient,[e] because she had received the spies in peace.

32 And what more should I say? For time would fail me to tell of Gideon, Barak, Samson, Jephthah, of David and Samuel and the prophets— 33who through faith conquered kingdoms, administered justice, obtained promises, shut the mouths of lions, 34quenched raging fire, escaped the edge of the sword, won strength out of weakness, became mighty in war, put foreign armies to flight. 35Women

> "Therefore, since we are surrounded by so great a cloud of witnesses, let us also lay aside every weight and the sin that clings so closely, and let us run with perseverance the race that is set before us."
> —Hebrews 12:1

received their dead by resurrection. Others were tortured, refusing to accept release, in order to obtain a better resurrection. 36Others suffered mocking and flogging, and even chains and imprisonment. 37They were stoned to death, they were sawn in two,[f] they were killed by the sword; they went about in skins of sheep and goats, destitute, persecuted, tormented— 38of whom the world was not worthy. They wandered in deserts and mountains, and in caves and holes in the ground.

39 Yet all these, though they were commended for their faith, did not receive what was promised, 40since God had provided something better so that they would not, apart from us, be made perfect.

The Example of Jesus

12 Therefore, since we are surrounded by so great a cloud of witnesses, let us also lay aside every weight and the sin that clings so closely,[g] and let us run with perseverance the race that is set before us, 2looking to Jesus the pioneer and perfecter of our faith, who for the sake of[h] the joy that was set before him endured the cross, disregarding its shame, and has taken his seat at the right hand of the throne of God.

3 Consider him who endured such hostility against himself from sinners,[i] so that you may not grow weary or lose heart. 4In your struggle against sin you have not yet resisted to the point of shedding your blood. 5And you have forgotten the exhortation that addresses you as children—

"My child, do not regard lightly the discipline
　　of the Lord,
　　or lose heart when you are punished
　　　　by him;
6 for the Lord disciplines those whom he loves,
　　and chastises every child whom he
　　　　accepts."

7Endure trials for the sake of discipline. God is treating you as children; for what child is there whom a parent does not discipline? 8If you do not have that discipline in which all children share, then you are illegitimate and not his children. 9Moreover, we had human parents to discipline us, and we respected them. Should we not be even more willing to be subject to the Father of spirits and live? 10For they disciplined us for a short time as seemed best to them, but he disciplines us for our good, in order that we may share his holiness. 11Now, discipline always seems painful rather than pleasant at the time, but

---

a Other ancient authorities add *By faith Moses, when he was grown up, killed the Egyptian, because he observed the humiliation of his people* (Gk *brothers*) b Or *the Messiah* c Or *because* d Gk *would not touch them* e Or *unbelieving* f Other ancient authorities add *they were tempted* g Other ancient authorities read *sin that easily distracts* h Or *who instead of* i Other ancient authorities read *such hostility from sinners against themselves*

Eric Liddell: Running to Win · Hebrews 12:1

Eric Liddell was the "Flying Scotsman," who won gold in the 400 meters at the 1924 Paris Olympics. It was a surprising performance. Liddell's best event was the 100 meters, but his convictions about keeping the sabbath kept him from running the 100, because it fell on a Sunday. No one expected him to win the 400.

Liddell's story was made even more famous decades later by the classic movie CHARIOTS OF FIRE, and he's still an excellent example of running the race of life with perseverance (Hebrews 12:1). Neither his running nor his fame defined Liddell. His greatest race was living for Christ. He left Scotland in 1924, at the top of his running career, and spent the rest of his life sharing the love of Jesus as a missionary in China. Why? Because he knew the truth of this verse, and also the one that says, "Athletes . . . do it to receive a perishable wreath, but we an imperishable one" (1 Corinthians 9:25). Liddell loved to run, and his running gave him a platform to speak of his beliefs. But he knew the glory and the reward were temporary. Instead, he chose to run the race he felt God calling him to—a race of eternal glory.

later it yields the peaceful fruit of righteousness to those who have been trained by it.

12 Therefore lift your drooping hands and strengthen your weak knees, [13] and make straight paths for your feet, so that what is lame may not be put out of joint, but rather be healed.

Warnings against Rejecting God's Grace

14 Pursue peace with everyone, and the holiness without which no one will see the Lord. [15] See to it that no one fails to obtain the grace of God; that no root of bitterness springs up and causes trouble, and through it many become defiled. [16] See to it that no one becomes like Esau, an immoral and godless person, who sold his birthright for a single meal. [17] You know that later, when he wanted to inherit the blessing, he was rejected, for he found no chance to repent,[a] even though he sought the blessing[b] with tears.

18 You have not come to something[c] that can be touched, a blazing fire, and darkness, and gloom, and a tempest, [19] and the sound of a trumpet, and a voice whose words made the hearers beg that not another word be spoken to them. [20] (For they could not endure the order that was given, "If even an animal touches the mountain, it shall be stoned to death." [21] Indeed, so terrifying was the sight that Moses said, "I tremble with fear.") [22] But you have come to Mount Zion and to the city of the living God, the heavenly Jerusalem, and to innumerable angels in festal gathering, [23] and to the assembly[d] of the firstborn who are enrolled in heaven, and to God the judge of all, and to the spirits of the righteous made perfect, [24] and to Jesus, the mediator of a new covenant, and to the sprinkled blood that speaks a better word than the blood of Abel.

25 See that you do not refuse the one who is speaking; for if they did not escape when they refused the one who warned them on earth, how much less will we escape if we reject the one who warns from heaven! [26] At that time his voice shook the earth; but now he has promised, "Yet once more I will shake not only the earth but also the heaven." [27] This phrase, "Yet once more," indicates the removal of what is shaken—that is, created things—so that what cannot be shaken may remain. [28] Therefore, since we are receiving a kingdom that cannot be shaken, let us give thanks, by which we offer to God an acceptable worship with reverence and awe; [29] for indeed our God is a consuming fire.

Service Well-Pleasing to God

13 Let mutual love continue. [2] Do not neglect to show hospitality to strangers, for by doing that some have entertained angels without knowing it. [3] Remember those who are in prison, as though you were in prison with them; those who are being tortured, as though you yourselves were being tortured.[e] [4] Let marriage be held in honor by all, and let the marriage bed be kept undefiled; for God will judge fornicators and adulterers. [5] Keep your lives free from the love of money, and be con-

a Or *no chance to change his father's mind*   b Gk *it*   c Other ancient authorities read *a mountain*   d Or *angels, and to the festal gathering* [23] *and assembly*
e Gk *were in the body*

STUDY IT!

Entertaining Angels
Hebrews 13:1–5

Angels fascinate us. But the media portrayal isn't always biblical. Although we don't know much about these beings, we do know that God created angelic beings and that they are portrayed in the Bible as God's messengers. Some people have even entertained angels without knowing it (Hebrews 13:2). So should we live our lives looking for angels around every corner? No. We should follow the instructions of mutual love that surround this angelic reference in Hebrews: show hospitality to strangers, remember those who are in prison or being tortured, honor marriage, be content, and trust God for our security (Hebrews 13:2-5).

have no right to eat. [11]For the bodies of those animals whose blood is brought into the sanctuary by the high priest as a sacrifice for sin are burned outside the camp. [12]Therefore Jesus also suffered outside the city gate in order to sanctify the people by his own blood. [13]Let us then go to him outside the camp and bear the abuse he endured. [14]For here we have no lasting city, but we are looking for the city that is to come. [15]Through him, then, let us continually offer a sacrifice of praise to God, that is, the fruit of lips that confess his name. [16]Do not neglect to do good and to share what you have, for such sacrifices are pleasing to God.

17 Obey your leaders and submit to them, for they are keeping watch over your souls and will give an account. Let them do this with joy and not with sighing—for that would be harmful to you.

18 Pray for us; we are sure that we have a clear conscience, desiring to act honorably in all things. [19]I urge you all the more to do this, so that I may be restored to you very soon.

Benediction

20 Now may the God of peace, who brought back from the dead our Lord Jesus, the great shepherd of the sheep, by the blood of the eternal covenant, [21]make you complete in everything good so that you may do his will, working among us[c] that which is pleasing in his sight, through Jesus Christ, to whom be the glory forever and ever. Amen.

Final Exhortation and Greetings

22 I appeal to you, brothers and sisters,[d] bear with my word of exhortation, for I have written to you briefly. [23]I want you to know that our brother Timothy has been set free; and if he comes in time, he will be with me when I see you. [24]Greet all your leaders and all the saints. Those from Italy send you greetings. [25]Grace be with all of you.[e]

tent with what you have; for he has said, "I will never leave you or forsake you." [6]So we can say with confidence,

"The Lord is my helper;
    I will not be afraid.
What can anyone do to me?"

7 Remember your leaders, those who spoke the word of God to you; consider the outcome of their way of life, and imitate their faith. [8]Jesus Christ is the same yesterday and today and forever. [9]Do not be carried away by all kinds of strange teachings; for it is well for the heart to be strengthened by grace, not by regulations about food,[a] which have not benefited those who observe them. [10]We have an altar from which those who officiate in the tent[b]

a Gk *not by foods* b Or *tabernacle* c Other ancient authorities read *you* d Gk *brothers* e Other ancient authorities add *Amen*

James

Have you ever noticed how a kite strains at the string as it soars in the sky? It seems to want to be free of the string that ties it down, free to fly on its own. But if that string does break, the kite may soar for a short time, but then founders and crashes. The kite has the freedom to fly only as long as it's tied to something. That's the way we are under the new covenant in Christ. We may think we're free to do whatever we want, but if we break from a faithful response to God's love for us, we founder and crash. James provides guidance for living "the perfect law, the law of liberty" (James 1:25), which leads to real freedom.

IN DEPTH

Defining the literary form of James is a little difficult. It opens like the other letters, but lacks the typical closing. In ways, it is similar to the wisdom literature of the Old Testament. It provides practical advice for how wise people ought to live. It is also similar to Greek moral teaching, which used famous people as models for how we ought to live. This has led scholars to think the book might have been written by an educated Jewish Christian and admirer of James, the first leader of the early Church in Jerusalem.

The letter addresses several issues in Christian living. It warns that rich people should not discriminate against poor people. It insists that Christians' actions must reflect their beliefs. It cautions against careless speech and a poorly controlled tongue. It encourages believers to patiently endure suffering.

James also addresses a misunderstanding of Paul's teaching that "a person is justified by faith apart from works prescribed by the law" (Romans 3:28). Using Abraham and Rahab as examples, the author of James declares, "A person is justified by works and not by faith alone" (James 2:24). After all, "faith by itself, if it has no works, is dead" (James 2:17). James is making the point that to say you love Jesus and then do unloving things makes no sense; it's just plain hypocritical.

But if we act on God's word and live our faith intensely from the heart, as the letter of James instructs, we will keep from foundering and be able to soar in the freedom of God's love!

QUICK FACTS

- **Author:** Possibly James the relative of Jesus, but most likely a later admirer of James
- **Date Written:** A.D. 57–62, if by James; 70–110, if by a later writer
- **Audience:** Christians in Palestine, Syria, or Rome
- **Theme:** Faith without works is dead.

AT A GLANCE

- **James 1** Greetings, and proverbs for Christian living
- **James 2:1–13** Discussion of discrimination within the Christian community
- **James 2:14–26** Message that faith without works is dead
- **James 3:1–12** Warnings about controlling the tongue
- **James 3:13–5:20** More advice for Christian living

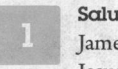

1 Salutation

James, a servant[a] of God and of the Lord Jesus Christ,

To the twelve tribes in the Dispersion:
Greetings.

Faith and Wisdom

2 My brothers and sisters,[b] whenever you face trials of any kind, consider it nothing but joy, [3]because you know that the testing of your faith produces endurance; [4]and let endurance have its full effect, so that you may be mature and complete, lacking in nothing.

5 If any of you is lacking in wisdom, ask God, who gives to all generously and ungrudgingly, and it will be given you. [6]But ask in faith, never doubting, for the one who doubts is like a wave of the sea, driven and tossed by the wind; [7, 8]for the doubter, being double-minded and unstable in every way, must not expect to receive anything from the Lord.

Poverty and Riches

9 Let the believer[c] who is lowly boast in being raised up, [10]and the rich in being brought low, because the rich will disappear like a flower in the field. [11]For the sun rises with its scorching heat and withers the field; its flower falls, and its beauty perishes. It is the same way with the rich; in the midst of a busy life, they will wither away.

> "Whenever you face trials of any kind, consider it nothing but joy, because you know that the testing of your faith produces endurance."
> —James 1:2–3

Trial and Temptation

12 Blessed is anyone who endures temptation. Such a one has stood the test and will receive the crown of life that the Lord[d] has promised to those who love him. [13]No one, when tempted, should say, "I am being tempted by God"; for God cannot be tempted by evil and he himself tempts no one. [14]But one is tempted by one's own desire, being lured and enticed by it; [15]then, when that desire has conceived, it gives birth to sin, and that sin, when it is fully grown, gives birth to death. [16]Do not be deceived, my beloved.[e]

17 Every generous act of giving, with every perfect gift, is from above, coming down from the Father of lights, with whom there is no variation or shadow due to change.[f] [18]In fulfillment of his own purpose he gave us birth by the word of truth, so that we would become a kind of first fruits of his creatures.

Hearing and Doing the Word

19 You must understand this, my beloved:[e] let everyone be quick to listen, slow to speak, slow to anger; [20]for your anger does not produce God's righteousness. [21]Therefore rid yourselves of all sordidness and rank growth of wickedness, and welcome with meekness the implanted word that has the power to save your souls.

22 But be doers of the word, and not merely hearers who deceive themselves. [23]For if any are hearers of

PRAY IT!

The Equation for Joy · James 1:2–4

Most of us are joyful when things are going well, but not so much when times are hard. But James starts out by challenging the idea that joy comes from circumstances. Instead, we are to consider our troubles nothing but joy. Why? Because the testing of our faith leads to endurance, which leads to our maturity. And since that is our goal in Christ, we should be glad for the hard things that produce that in us.

God, I confess that I don't always find joy in my troubles. I'm more likely to complain and feel down than to look for the end result. Help me to recognize the ways you are at work in my life, even in the hard times. And please give me your joy, no matter what comes my way. Amen.

---

a Gk slave b Gk brothers c Gk brother d Gk he; other ancient authorities read God e Gk my beloved brothers f Other ancient authorities read variation due to a shadow of turning

the word and not doers, they are like those who look at themselves[a] in a mirror; [24]for they look at themselves and, on going away, immediately forget what they were like. [25]But those who look into the perfect law, the law of liberty, and persevere, being not hearers who forget but doers who act—they will be blessed in their doing.

26 If any think they are religious, and do not bridle their tongues but deceive their hearts, their religion is worthless. [27]Religion that is pure and undefiled before God, the Father, is this: to care for orphans and widows in their distress, and to keep oneself unstained by the world.

2 Warning against Partiality

My brothers and sisters,[b] do you with your acts of favoritism really believe in our glorious Lord Jesus Christ?[c] [2]For if a person with gold rings and in fine clothes comes into your assembly, and if a poor person in dirty clothes also comes in, [3]and if you take notice of the one wearing the fine clothes and say, "Have a seat here, please," while to the one who is poor you say, "Stand there," or, "Sit at my feet,"[d] [4]have you not made distinctions among

LIVE IT!

Playing Favorites
James 2:1–13

When was the last time you watched someone receive special treatment? It doesn't seem fair when a person gets singled out because of his or her good looks, money, or athletic ability. Too often it makes others feel hurt and diminished. Here the author clearly spells out where God stands on the issue of favoritism and partiality. God's response is to turn things upside down by raising up the poor and the lowly (James 2:5). We too should live by God's standard and give priority to the needs of those who are poor and vulnerable.

In our world, there is a big difference between rich and poor. God needs us to respond to this injustice by recognizing that we have a special responsibility to care for those who are struggling the most just to live.

- How can you, your family, or your church provide opportunities to the poor?
- Think of someone you know personally who is vulnerable in some way and needs you to reach out in love. How will you do that this week?

CONNECT IT!

Ashley Clements: Diving into Disasters · James 1:27

Ashley Clements doesn't hold back. As a member of World Vision's Global Rapid Response Team, Ashley gets himself into disaster zones often before other aid groups or the press. He takes pictures and video, helps victims, and advises World Vision on where aid is needed most. The job has taken Ashley into Haiti following its catastrophic earthquake, Myanmar after its devastating cyclone, Iraqi refugee camps in Jordan and Lebanon, and Georgia after the Russian invasion. Sound dangerous? It is. Ashley is committed to giving his all to fight for justice and help people in their direst needs. His life is a picture of what James calls pure religion as he enters places of crisis and works to care for "orphans and widows in their distress" (James 1:27). You can see some of Clements' amazing photographs of the places he has worked at **worldvision.org**.

---

a Gk *at the face of his birth* **b** Gk *My brothers* **c** Or *hold the faith of our glorious Lord Jesus Christ without acts of favoritism* **d** Gk *Sit under my footstool*

yourselves, and become judges with evil thoughts? [5]Listen, my beloved brothers and sisters.[a] Has not God chosen the poor in the world to be rich in faith and to be heirs of the kingdom that he has promised to those who love him? [6]But you have dishonored the poor. Is it not the rich who oppress you? Is it not they who drag you into court? [7]Is it not they who blaspheme the excellent name that was invoked over you?

8 You do well if you really fulfill the royal law according to the scripture, "You shall love your neighbor as yourself." [9]But if you show partiality, you commit sin and are convicted by the law as transgressors. [10]For whoever keeps the whole law but fails in one point has become accountable for all of it. [11]For the one who said, "You shall not commit adultery," also said, "You shall not murder." Now if you do not commit adultery but if you murder, you have become a transgressor of the law. [12]So speak and so act as those who are to be judged by the law of liberty. [13]For judgment will be without mercy to anyone who has shown no mercy; mercy triumphs over judgment.

Faith without Works Is Dead

14 What good is it, my brothers and sisters,[a] if you say you have faith but do not have works? Can faith save you? [15]If a brother or sister is naked and lacks daily food, [16]and one of you says to them, "Go in peace; keep warm and eat your fill," and yet you do not supply their bodily needs, what is the good of that? [17]So faith by itself, if it has no works, is dead.

CONNECT IT!

Dr. Bob Pierce: A Vision for the World
James 2:15–17

Bob Pierce was traveling through Asia preaching at large evangelistic meetings in 1948. Just before he returned home, he spoke to a group of children at a missionary school in China and asked them to give their lives to Jesus. One little girl did, but was disowned and kicked out of her home when she told her parents. Pierce found her in the arms of the school's director, who had no more resources to take care of another child. Pierce realized that if he didn't do something to help, this child would live a life much worse than the one she had before. He realized that he couldn't just tell the good news and leave without meeting her needs. He couldn't just say to her "Go in peace; keep warm and eat your fill" (James 2:16) without supplying the most basic physical needs. He pledged to send the money it would take to care for this child, and the core of World Vision was begun. Today World Vision is changing the lives of hundreds of millions of men, women, and children in one hundred countries. Find out more at **worldvision.org**.

STUDY IT!

Faith and Works · James 2:14–26

A person who insists that faith alone is necessary for our salvation might think: "I don't have to demonstrate my faith with action at all. I just have to believe in Jesus, and then I can do anything I want." Such an attitude isn't very helpful.

Yet a person who insists that particular actions alone are necessary for our salvation might think: "I don't have to really believe in what I'm doing. I'll just go through the motions of faith, and that way I'll play it safe." This attitude is not very helpful either.

James is nearly saying the same thing—show me a person who has real faith, and I will show you a person doing good works. Which makes it seem as though he is disagreeing with Paul, who takes the faith side (Romans 3:21-31; Galatians 2:15-3:14). So how are we to understand these two? A look at **James 1:26** sheds some light. Although James is arguing that works are part of our justification, he concludes by saying "faith without works is also dead" (James 2:26), acknowledging that it is not one or the other, but works as a central expression of faith.

---

a Gk *brothers*

18 But someone will say, "You have faith and I have works." Show me your faith apart from your works, and I by my works will show you my faith. [19]You believe that God is one; you do well. Even the demons believe—and shudder. [20]Do you want to be shown, you senseless person, that faith apart from works is barren? [21]Was not our ancestor Abraham justified by works when he offered his son Isaac on the altar? [22]You see that faith was active along with his works, and faith was brought to completion by the works. [23]Thus the scripture was fulfilled that says, "Abraham believed God, and it was reckoned to him as righteousness," and he was called the friend of God. [24]You see that a person is justified by works and not by faith alone. [25]Likewise, was not Rahab the prostitute also justified by works when she welcomed the messengers and sent them out by another road? [26]For just as the body without the spirit is dead, so faith without works is also dead.

Taming the Tongue

3 Not many of you should become teachers, my brothers and sisters,[a] for you know that we who teach will be judged with greater strictness. [2]For all of us make many mistakes. Anyone who makes no mistakes in speaking is perfect, able to keep the whole body in check with a bridle. [3]If we put bits into the mouths of horses to make them obey us, we guide their whole bodies. [4]Or look at ships: though they are so large that it takes strong winds to drive them, yet they are guided by a very small rudder wherever the will of the pilot directs. [5]So also the tongue is a small member, yet it boasts of great exploits.

How great a forest is set ablaze by a small fire! [6]And the tongue is a fire. The tongue is placed among our members as a world of iniquity; it stains the whole body, sets on fire the cycle of nature,[b] and is itself

set on fire by hell.[c] [7]For every species of beast and bird, of reptile and sea creature, can be tamed and has been tamed by the human species, [8]but no one can tame the tongue—a restless evil, full of deadly poison. [9]With it we bless the Lord and Father, and with it we curse those who are made in the likeness of God. [10]From the same mouth come blessing and cursing. My brothers and sisters,[d] this ought not to be so. [11]Does a spring pour forth from the same opening both fresh and brackish water? [12]Can a fig tree, my brothers and sisters,[e] yield olives, or a grapevine figs? No more can salt water yield fresh.

Two Kinds of Wisdom

13 Who is wise and understanding among you? Show by your good life that your works are done with gentleness born of wisdom. [14]But if you have bitter envy and selfish ambition in your hearts, do not be

LIVE IT!

Taming the Tongue
James 3:1–12

Sometimes we are advised to hold it. Other times we are ordered to bite it. Try as we might to keep this counsel, our tongue often proves to be much stronger than our will to control it. But it's not a new problem. James addresses it as an issue in the early Church. And he says that although all kinds of wild animals have been tamed, we have not succeeded in taming the tongue (James 3:7-8).

All of us have said things that hurt or offend others and God. But James says it shouldn't be that way. We should speak out of the life that is in us (James 3:10-11).

• When have you spoken words that were hurtful to another person, directly or behind the person's back?

• How might you use your tongue to begin to heal someone's hurt through an apology, compliment, or words of forgiveness?

---

a Gk *brothers*   **b** Or *wheel of birth*   **c** Gk *Gehenna*   **d** Gk *My brothers*   **e** Gk *my brothers*

boastful and false to the truth. [15]Such wisdom does not come down from above, but is earthly, unspiritual, devilish. [16]For where there is envy and selfish ambition, there will also be disorder and wickedness of every kind. [17]But the wisdom from above is first pure, then peaceable, gentle, willing to yield, full of mercy and good fruits, without a trace of partiality or hypocrisy. [18]And a harvest of righteousness is sown in peace for[a] those who make peace.

4 Friendship with the World

Those conflicts and disputes among you, where do they come from? Do they not come from your cravings that are at war within you? [2]You want something and do not have it; so you commit murder. And you covet[b] something and cannot obtain it; so you engage in disputes and conflicts. You do not have, because you do not ask. [3]You ask and do not receive, because you ask wrongly, in order to spend what you get on your pleasures. [4]Adulterers! Do you not know that friendship with the world is enmity with God? Therefore whoever wishes to be a friend of the world becomes an enemy of God. [5]Or do you suppose that it is for nothing that the scripture says, "God[c] yearns jealously for the spirit that he has made to dwell in us"?

[6]But he gives all the more grace; therefore it says,
"God opposes the proud,
     but gives grace to the humble."
[7]Submit yourselves therefore to God. Resist the devil, and he will flee from you. [8]Draw near to God, and he will draw near to you. Cleanse your hands, you sinners, and purify your hearts, you double-minded. [9]Lament and mourn and weep. Let your laughter be turned into mourning and your joy into dejection. [10]Humble yourselves before the Lord, and he will exalt you.

Warning against Judging Another

11 Do not speak evil against one another, brothers and sisters.[d] Whoever speaks evil against another or judges another, speaks evil against the law and judges the law; but if you judge the law, you are not a doer of the law but a judge. [12]There is one lawgiver and judge who is able to save and to destroy. So who, then, are you to judge your neighbor?

Boasting about Tomorrow

13 Come now, you who say, "Today or tomorrow we will go to such and such a town and spend a year there, doing business and making money." [14]Yet you do not even know what tomorrow will bring. What

STUDY IT!

Justice for the Poor · James 5:1–6

Warnings to the rich are common in the Bible, and they can be of special concern to Christians living in a wealthy nation like the United States. Based on this passage, here are two tough questions to ask yourself:

• Where is your trust? In the comfort and pleasure of wealth and material possessions, or in God?

• How does your lifestyle—including the way you spend money, the choices you make about your future work, and the way you use your time—affect the poor people of this world?

God's justice requires that we care about the abuse of poor people. God does not want us to become paralyzed with guilt because we are wealthy compared with most of the people in the world. But scripture reminds us that the life choices we make matter and that those choices may either contribute to a more just world or support an unequal system that keeps rich people comfortable and poor people suffering. To make good life choices, we must educate ourselves about the situations that cause poverty, examine how our own lifestyle or beliefs might unintentionally contribute to the misery of those who are poor, and actively work to alleviate the suffering of others. That is hard work—perhaps work we would rather avoid. But ignoring the plight of the poor is exactly what scripture warns against! Money in itself is not evil; it's what we do (or don't do) with it that matters.

---

a Or by b Or you murder and you covet c Gk He d Gk brothers

is your life? For you are a mist that appears for a little while and then vanishes. [15]Instead you ought to say, "If the Lord wishes, we will live and do this or that." [16]As it is, you boast in your arrogance; all such boasting is evil. [17]Anyone, then, who knows the right thing to do and fails to do it, commits sin.

5 Warning to Rich Oppressors

Come now, you rich people, weep and wail for the miseries that are coming to you. [2]Your riches have rotted, and your clothes are moth-eaten. [3]Your gold and silver have rusted, and their rust will be evidence against you, and it will eat your flesh like fire. You have laid up treasure[a] for the last days. [4]Listen! The wages of the laborers who mowed your fields, which you kept back by fraud, cry out, and the cries of the harvesters have reached the ears of the Lord of hosts. [5]You have lived on the earth in luxury and in pleasure; you have fattened your hearts in a day of slaughter. [6]You have condemned and murdered the righteous one, who does not resist you.

Patience in Suffering

7 Be patient, therefore, beloved,[b] until the coming of the Lord. The farmer waits for the precious crop from the earth, being patient with it until it receives the early and the late rains. [8]You also must be patient. Strengthen your hearts, for the coming of the Lord is near.[c] [9]Beloved,[d] do not grumble against one another, so that you may not be judged. See, the Judge is standing at the doors! [10]As an example of suffering and patience, beloved,[b] take the prophets who spoke in the name of the Lord. [11]Indeed we call blessed those who showed endurance. You have heard of the endurance of Job, and you have seen the purpose of the Lord, how the Lord is compassionate and merciful.

12 Above all, my beloved,[b] do not swear, either by heaven or by earth or by any other oath, but let your "Yes" be yes and your "No" be no, so that you may not fall under condemnation.

The Prayer of Faith

13 Are any among you suffering? They should pray. Are any cheerful? They should sing songs of praise. [14]Are any among you sick? They should call for the elders of the church and have them pray over them, anointing them with oil in the name of the Lord. [15]The prayer of faith will save the sick, and

PRAY IT!

The Making of a Prayer
James 5:13–18

Do you ever feel as though your prayers are just words without much meaning? It happens when you get stuck on saying the same prayer every time, no matter what the situation. It becomes a habit and, like all habits, after a while you may stop thinking about why you are even doing it.

James offers some advice that can help you. This passage says that no matter what situation we are in, we should pray. We can think about the needs and feelings we have at any given moment of the day and turn them into a prayer. Feeling down? Tell God about it. Just had the best day of your life? Share it with God. Want to get even with a person who hurt you? Let God know about it. In fact, there is nothing you can't tell God—even if you are mad and God is the one you are mad at.

Get in touch with what is occupying your mind the most right now—good, bad, or ordinary—and turn it into a prayer by sharing it with God, who is always ready to hear what you have to say.

the Lord will raise them up; and anyone who has committed sins will be forgiven. [16]Therefore confess your sins to one another, and pray for one another, so that you may be healed. The prayer of the righteous is powerful and effective. [17]Elijah was a human being like us, and he prayed fervently that it might not rain, and for three years and six months it did not rain on the earth. [18]Then he prayed again, and the heaven gave rain and the earth yielded its harvest.

19 My brothers and sisters,[e] if anyone among you wanders from the truth and is brought back by another, [20]you should know that whoever brings back a sinner from wandering will save the sinner's[f] soul from death and will cover a multitude of sins.

---

a Or will eat your flesh, since you have stored up fire   b Gk brothers   c Or is at hand   d Gk Brothers   e Gk My brothers   f Gk his

1 Peter

You confront a friend about shoplifting, and he won't speak to you. You and some classmates start a prayer group before school and become the target of ridicule. You say no to having sex with your boyfriend and become the object of gossip and insults. The tension between living for Christ and living in the world is real in your life and in the world. On the news you hear that Christian leaders who have spoken out publicly against racism are the target of vandalism. Or that the government has intercepted a plot to bomb a prominent church. It's enough to make some Christians ask, "Is living our faith worth this risk and persecution?" This is a major concern addressed by 1 Peter.

IN DEPTH

The first letter of Peter was written to a group of Christians that was alienated and persecuted because of its Christian lifestyle. Its members faced the challenge of living as part of the Roman Empire while also living as followers of Christ. They were ridiculed, treated as evildoers, and insulted by unbelieving neighbors who didn't understand their faith or moral code of behavior. The author—who may have been Peter, but was more likely a later disciple of his—wants to console them and help them make sense of what they're going through.

The author of 1 Peter says that Christ suffered, and so we should expect to suffer too. He also says that suffering purifies our faith and makes it more genuine (1 Peter 1:7). When we suffer, we are united with all the world's people who are suffering (1 Peter 5:9). And no matter how great our suffering, we should be hopeful and willing to give a reason for our hope. Then our persecutors will be ashamed and repent of their wrongdoing (1 Peter 3:14-16).

Despite all this attention to suffering, 1 Peter is a hope-filled letter. It offers constant reminders of the wonderful things God has done—and will do—for us. When you are going through a hard time, turn to this letter for hope and encouragement. "And after you have suffered for a little while, the God of all grace, who has called you to his eternal glory in Christ, will himself restore, support, strengthen, and establish you" (1 Peter 5:10).

QUICK FACTS

- **Author:** Possibly Peter, but most likely a later disciple of Peter
- **Date Written:** A.D. 60-63, if by Peter; 70-90, if by a later disciple
- **Audience:** A Gentile (non-Jewish) Christian community living in Asia Minor (modern-day Turkey)
- **Theme:** Endurance in the midst of suffering and the comfort and hope God provides

AT A GLANCE

- **1 Peter 1:1-2** Greeting and thanksgiving
- **1 Peter 1:3-2:10** Message that Christians are called to be a chosen race and a royal priesthood
- **1 Peter 2:11-3:12** Description of the Christian way of life
- **1 Peter 3:13-5:11** Discussion of Christian suffering
- **1 Peter 5:12-14** Closing

Salutation

1 Peter, an apostle of Jesus Christ,

To the exiles of the Dispersion in Pontus, Galatia, Cappadocia, Asia, and Bithynia, [2] who have been chosen and destined by God the Father and sanctified by the Spirit to be obedient to Jesus Christ and to be sprinkled with his blood:

May grace and peace be yours in abundance.

A Living Hope

3 Blessed be the God and Father of our Lord Jesus Christ! By his great mercy he has given us a new birth into a living hope through the resurrection of Jesus Christ from the dead, [4] and into an inheritance that is imperishable, undefiled, and unfading, kept in heaven for you, [5] who are being protected by the power of God through faith for a salvation ready to be revealed in the last time. [6] In this you rejoice,[a] even if now for a little while you have had to suffer various trials, [7] so that the genuineness of your faith—being more precious than gold that, though perishable, is tested by fire—may be found to result in praise and glory and honor when Jesus Christ is revealed. [8] Although you have not seen[b] him, you love him; and even though you do not see him now, you believe in him and rejoice with an indescribable and glorious joy, [9] for you are receiving the outcome of your faith, the salvation of your souls.

10 Concerning this salvation, the prophets who prophesied of the grace that was to be yours made careful search and inquiry, [11] inquiring about the person or time that the Spirit of Christ within them indicated when it testified in advance to the sufferings destined for Christ and the subsequent glory. [12] It was revealed to them that they were serving not themselves but you, in regard to the things that have now been announced to you through those who brought you good news by the Holy Spirit sent from heaven—things into which angels long to look!

A Call to Holy Living

13 Therefore prepare your minds for action;[c] discipline yourselves; set all your hope on the grace that Jesus Christ will bring you when he is revealed. [14] Like obedient children, do not be conformed to the desires that you formerly had in ignorance. [15] Instead, as he who called you is holy, be holy yourselves in all your conduct; [16] for it is written, "You shall be holy, for I am holy."

17 If you invoke as Father the one who judges all people impartially according to their deeds, live in reverent fear during the time of your exile. [18] You know that you were ransomed from the futile ways inherited from your ancestors, not with perishable things like silver or gold, [19] but with the precious blood of Christ, like that of a lamb without defect or blemish. [20] He was destined before the foundation of the world, but was revealed at the end of the ages for your sake. [21] Through him you have come to trust in God, who raised him from the dead and gave him

PRAY IT!

Live the Belief · 1 Peter 1:13–25

Believing in Jesus is active. It definitely involves our hearts and minds, but it also involves our hands and feet. When we believe in Jesus, we serve him by helping people who also need to know God's love. Believing in Jesus is seen in the ways we spend our time and the choices we make about how to act in ways that please God. This passage says that we are not to live by the desires we used to have, but to be holy in everything we do. Those who believe in Jesus have been made new and are to be holy as Jesus is holy (1 Peter 1:13-15). Spend some time writing in your journal about the ways your belief in God is impacting both your thoughts and your actions. Then talk to God about it.

Holy God, you invite me to live the gospel message, not just hear and accept it. It's not enough to say I believe. I am called to live that belief. I want to lovingly serve you, God, and all my brothers and sisters. I want to seek your word and follow it faithfully. I want to exercise self-control and avoid temptations. I want to build endurance to stand firm against life's trials. I want to value truth and goodness. Provide me with the fruit of your Spirit to sustain me for my journey, as I work to imitate your Son, Jesus Christ. Amen.

---

a Or *Rejoice in this*   *b* Other ancient authorities read *known*   *c* Gk *gird up the loins of your mind*

glory, so that your faith and hope are set on God.

22 Now that you have purified your souls by your obedience to the truth[a] so that you have genuine mutual love, love one another deeply[b] from the heart.[c] 23 You have been born anew, not of perishable but of imperishable seed, through the living and enduring word of God.[d] 24 For

"All flesh is like grass
       and all its glory like the flower of grass.
The grass withers,
       and the flower falls,
25 but the word of the Lord endures forever."
That word is the good news that was announced to you.

2 The Living Stone and a Chosen People

Rid yourselves, therefore, of all malice, and all guile, insincerity, envy, and all slander. 2 Like newborn infants, long for the pure, spiritual milk, so that by it you may grow into salvation— 3 if indeed you have tasted that the Lord is good.

4 Come to him, a living stone, though rejected by mortals yet chosen and precious in God's sight, and 5 like living stones, let yourselves be built[e] into a spiritual house, to be a holy priesthood, to offer spiritual sacrifices acceptable to God through Jesus Christ. 6 For it stands in scripture:

"See, I am laying in Zion a stone,
       a cornerstone chosen and precious;
and whoever believes in him[f] will not be put
              to shame."

7 To you then who believe, he is precious; but for those who do not believe,

> "But you are a chosen race, a royal priesthood, a holy nation, God's own people, in order that you may proclaim the mighty acts of him who called you out of darkness into his marvelous light."
> —1 Peter 2:9

"The stone that the builders rejected
       has become the very head of the corner,"
8 and

"A stone that makes them stumble,
       and a rock that makes them fall."
They stumble because they disobey the word, as they were destined to do.

9 But you are a chosen race, a royal priesthood, a holy nation, God's own people,[g] in order that you may proclaim the mighty acts of him who called you out of darkness into his marvelous light.
10 Once you were not a people,
       but now you are God's people;
once you had not received mercy,
       but now you have received mercy.

Live as Servants of God

11 Beloved, I urge you as aliens and exiles to ab-

STUDY IT!

A Royal Priesthood · 1 Peter 2:1–17

Other than the Jewish priests, the only person who is actually called a priest in the New Testament is Jesus. A new priesthood has been born in Christ, one that surpasses the priesthood of the Old Testament (see "Study It: The Highest Priest," near Hebrews 4:14–5:10).

But did you know that every Christian shares in Christ's priesthood as well (1 Peter 2:9)? In ancient Israel, only the priests had direct access to God in the temple; now we are able to go directly to God through Jesus. And we are considered priests to our friends, family, and the world in order that we may "proclaim the mighty acts of him who called you out of darkness into his marvelous light" (1 Peter 2:9). Being a part of the priesthood of all believers means that you become an instrument in the hand of God and a light to the world.

a Other ancient authorities add *through the Spirit* b Or *constantly* c Other ancient authorities read *a pure heart* d Or *through the word of the living and enduring God* e Or *you yourselves are being built* f Or *it* g Gk *a people for his possession*

Part of the Family · 1 Peter 2:9-17

All of us come from and belong to a family. Some families are large and some small; some have two parents and others one; and some include aunts, uncles, or grandparents. Every family is unique.

As Christians, we belong to a family that extends well beyond the relationships of blood or adoption. As followers of Christ, we make up a "royal priesthood" and a "holy nation," and are called "God's own people" (1 Peter 2:9). What exactly does that mean?

First, it means that our faith is not just between us and God, but is shared with others. Yes, our relationship with the Lord is personal, but we are also called by God into a community of disciples who share a common faith. Second, God has chosen us to live together in such a way that others who see our example will see something so good that they will want to be a part of it.

• How connected do you feel to the Christian family?
• What kind of support would you like to receive from other believers? What kind of support can you give?

stain from the desires of the flesh that wage war against the soul. ¹²Conduct yourselves honorably among the Gentiles, so that, though they malign you as evildoers, they may see your honorable deeds and glorify God when he comes to judge.ᵃ

13 For the Lord's sake accept the authority of every human institution,ᵇ whether of the emperor as supreme, ¹⁴or of governors, as sent by him to punish those who do wrong and to praise those who do right. ¹⁵For it is God's will that by doing right you should silence the ignorance of the foolish. ¹⁶As servantsᶜ of God, live as free people, yet do not use your freedom as a pretext for evil. ¹⁷Honor everyone. Love the family of believers.ᵈ Fear God. Honor the emperor.

The Example of Christ's Suffering

18 Slaves, accept the authority of your masters with all deference, not only those who are kind and gentle but also those who are harsh. ¹⁹For it is a credit to you if, being aware of God, you endure pain while suffering unjustly. ²⁰If you endure when you are beaten for doing wrong, what credit is that? But if you endure when you do right and suffer for it, you have God's approval. ²¹For to this you have been called, because Christ also suffered for you, leaving you an example, so that you should follow in his steps.

²² "He committed no sin,
    and no deceit was found in his mouth."
²³When he was abused, he did not return abuse; when he suffered, he did not threaten; but he entrusted himself to the one who judges justly. ²⁴He

himself bore our sins in his body on the cross,ᵉ so that, free from sins, we might live for righteousness; by his woundsᶠ you have been healed. ²⁵For you were going astray like sheep, but now you have returned to the shepherd and guardian of your souls.

Wives and Husbands

3 Wives, in the same way, accept the authority of your husbands, so that, even if some of them do not obey the word, they may be won over without a word by their wives' conduct, ²when they see the purity and reverence of your lives. ³Do not adorn yourselves outwardly by braiding your hair, and by wearing gold ornaments or fine clothing; ⁴rather, let your adornment be the inner self with the lasting beauty of a gentle and quiet spirit, which is very precious in God's sight. ⁵It was in this way long ago that the holy women who hoped in

a Gk *God on the day of visitation*   b Or *every institution ordained for human beings*   c Gk *slaves*   d Gk *Love the brotherhood*   e Or *carried up our sins in his body to the tree*   f Gk *bruise*

LIVE IT!

Good Suffering?
1 Peter 3:13–22

Taking a stand for what is right sounds good, but it's easy to back down when doing good causes us suffering. It seems unfair. But it's proof that those who belong to God are not at home in this world. There's a tension between the good God calls us to and the values of our mainstream culture. It's tempting to just blend in with the rest of the world around us. But the author of 1 Peter says, "It is better to suffer for doing good . . . than to suffer for doing evil" (1 Peter 3:17). It is reassuring to know that the suffering we experience now is temporary and that it makes us stronger as we await Jesus' return (1 Peter 1:6–7).

• When do you feel caught in the middle between your faith and mainstream culture?

• Ask some friends to join you in encouraging each other to do good even when it's hard.

God used to adorn themselves by accepting the authority of their husbands. [6]Thus Sarah obeyed Abraham and called him lord. You have become her daughters as long as you do what is good and never let fears alarm you.

7 Husbands, in the same way, show consideration for your wives in your life together, paying honor to the woman as the weaker sex,[a] since they too are also heirs of the gracious gift of life—so that nothing may hinder your prayers.

Suffering for Doing Right

8 Finally, all of you, have unity of spirit, sympathy, love for one another, a tender heart, and a humble mind. [9]Do not repay evil for evil or abuse for abuse; but, on the contrary, repay with a blessing. It is for this that you were called—that you might inherit a blessing. [10]For

"Those who desire life
    and desire to see good days,

let them keep their tongues from evil
    and their lips from speaking deceit;
[11] let them turn away from evil and do good;
    let them seek peace and pursue it.
[12] For the eyes of the Lord are on the righteous,
    and his ears are open to their prayer.
But the face of the Lord is against those who
    do evil."

13 Now who will harm you if you are eager to do what is good? [14]But even if you do suffer for doing what is right, you are blessed. Do not fear what they fear,[b] and do not be intimidated, [15]but in your hearts sanctify Christ as Lord. Always be ready to make your defense to anyone who demands from you an accounting for the hope that is in you; [16]yet do it with gentleness and reverence.[c] Keep your conscience clear, so that, when you are maligned, those who abuse you for your good conduct in Christ may be put to shame. [17]For it is better to suffer for doing good, if suffering should be God's will, than to suffer for doing evil. [18]For Christ also suffered[d] for sins once for all, the righteous for the unrighteous, in order to bring you[e] to God. He was put to death in the flesh, but made alive in the spirit, [19]in which also he went and made a proclamation to the spirits in prison, [20]who in former times did not obey, when God waited patiently in the days of Noah, during the building of the ark, in which a few, that is, eight persons, were saved through water. [21]And baptism, which this prefigured, now saves you—not as a removal of dirt from the body, but as an appeal to God for[f] a good conscience, through the resurrection of Jesus Christ, [22]who has gone into heaven and is at the right hand of God, with angels, authorities, and powers made subject to him.

4 [18]Slaves, accept the authority of your masters with all defer

Good Stewards of God's Grace

Since therefore Christ suffered in the flesh,[g] arm yourselves also with the same intention (for whoever has suffered in the flesh has finished with sin), [2]so as to live for the rest of your earthly life[h] no longer by human desires but by the will of God. [3]You have already spent enough time in doing what the Gentiles like to do, living in licentiousness, passions, drunkenness, revels, carousing, and lawless idolatry. [4]They are surprised that you no longer join them in the same excesses of dissipation, and so they blaspheme.[i] [5]But they will have to give an accounting to him who stands ready to judge the living and the dead. [6]For this is the reason the

a Gk vessel b Gk their fear c Or respect d Other ancient authorities read died e Other ancient authorities read us f Or a pledge to God from
g Other ancient authorities add for us; others, for you h Gk rest of the time in the flesh i Or they malign you

gospel was proclaimed even to the dead, so that, though they had been judged in the flesh as everyone is judged, they might live in the spirit as God does.

7 The end of all things is near;[a] therefore be serious and discipline yourselves for the sake of your prayers. [8]Above all, maintain constant love for one another, for love covers a multitude of sins. [9]Be hospitable to one another without complaining. [10]Like good stewards of the manifold grace of God, serve one another with whatever gift each of you has received. [11]Whoever speaks must do so as one speaking the very words of God; whoever serves must do so with the strength that God supplies, so that God may be glorified in all things through Jesus Christ. To him belong the glory and the power forever and ever. Amen.

Suffering as a Christian

12 Beloved, do not be surprised at the fiery ordeal that is taking place among you to test you, as though something strange were happening to you. [13]But rejoice insofar as you are sharing Christ's sufferings, so that you may also be glad and shout for joy when his glory is revealed. [14]If you are reviled for the name of Christ, you are blessed, because the spirit of glory,[b] which is the Spirit of God, is resting on you.[c] [15]But let none of you suffer as a murderer, a thief, a criminal, or even as a mischief maker. [16]Yet if any of you suffers as a Christian, do not consider it a disgrace, but glorify God because you bear this name. [17]For the time has come for judgment to begin with the household of God; if it begins with us, what will be the end for those who do not obey the gospel of God? [18]And

"If it is hard for the righteous to be saved,
    what will become of the ungodly and the
        sinners?"

[19]Therefore, let those suffering in accordance with God's will entrust themselves to a faithful Creator, while continuing to do good.

Tending the Flock of God

5 Now as an elder myself and a witness of the sufferings of Christ, as well as one who shares in the glory to be revealed, I exhort the elders among you [2]to tend the flock of God that is in your charge, exercising the oversight,[d] not under compulsion but willingly, as God would have you do it[e]—not for sordid gain but eagerly. [3]Do not lord it over those in your charge, but be examples to the flock. [4]And when the chief shepherd appears, you will win the crown of glory that never fades away. [5]In the same way, you who are younger must accept the authority of the elders.[f] And all of you must clothe yourselves with humility in your dealings with one another, for

"God opposes the proud,
    but gives grace to the humble."

6 Humble yourselves therefore under the mighty hand of God, so that he may exalt you in due time. [7]Cast all your anxiety on him, because he cares for you. [8]Discipline yourselves, keep alert.[g] Like a roaring lion your adversary the devil prowls around, looking for someone to devour. [9]Resist him, steadfast in your faith, for you know that your brothers and sisters[h] in all the world are undergoing the same

---

Shout for Joy • 1 Peter 4:12–19

No healthy person likes to suffer. But when we suffer for resisting evil and doing good—like being identified as a follower of Christ or defending someone who is under attack by others—we are called blessed (1 Peter 4:14). God notices when we are mocked or ridiculed for our faith. We are challenged to rejoice when we experience such treatment, instead of taking it as a sign of failure. Didn't Christ suffer for doing good? Won't he be with us when we suffer for his name? The gospel has a strange way of turning things upside down—it says that we can find joy even in suffering.

God, I don't want to suffer. And even though it doesn't make sense by worldly logic, I trust that you see suffering from a much bigger perspective. Please help me to see it through your eyes and to find joy in the midst of it. Keep me faithful in doing good, until I can shout for joy when the world sees Christ's glory. Amen.

---

a Or *is at hand* **b** Other ancient authorities add *and of power* **c** Other ancient authorities add *On their part he is blasphemed, but on your part he is glorified* **d** Other ancient authorities lack *exercising the oversight* **e** Other ancient authorities lack *as God would have you do it* **f** Or *of those who are older* **g** Or *be vigilant* **h** Gk *your brotherhood*

kinds of suffering. [10]And after you have suffered for a little while, the God of all grace, who has called you to his eternal glory in Christ, will himself restore, support, strengthen, and establish you. [11]To him be the power forever and ever. Amen.

Final Greetings and Benediction

12 Through Silvanus, whom I consider a faithful brother, I have written this short letter to encourage you and to testify that this is the true grace of God. Stand fast in it. [13]Your sister church[a] in Babylon, chosen together with you, sends you greetings; and so does my son Mark. [14]Greet one another with a kiss of love.

Peace to all of you who are in Christ.[b]

a Gk *She who is*   b Other ancient authorities add *Amen*

2 Peter

What happens to us when we die? What is heaven like? Does God care what happens to us? These are common questions everyone asks, yet people have responded through the ages with all kinds of different answers. Some believe there is no heaven, no hell, and no God. Some say that when we die, our bodies simply decay and we no longer exist in any form. Some say there is no life after death, no punishment, and no reward. But the Bible tells us differently. Second Peter was written to reassure believers that God does indeed care, that there is eternal life, and that those who believe in Jesus will be rewarded for leading faithful lives.

IN DEPTH

Biblical scholars have convincing evidence that 2 Peter is one of the latest books in the New Testament. The letter appears to have been written by someone who is appealing to the authority of the dead apostle Peter. At the time of its writing—perhaps as much as one hundred years after Jesus' death and resurrection— some Christians were starting to wonder if what they believed was true. People were even teaching that there would be no reward or punishment after death. So why not live any way you wanted?

The author of 2 Peter is arguing against these false teachers. This writer uses famous examples from the Old Testament to remind readers how God has acted through history. And the author promises that those who have chosen to separate themselves from God in their lifetime will experience the fullness of separation from God in death—a separation that Christians call hell. Those who have stayed faithful to God's calling will enjoy eternal life in union with God—a life that Christians call heaven.

Tied to this argument is another concern. Many of the earliest Christians believed Christ would return soon after his resurrection, probably within their lifetime, to establish God's kingdom once and for all. When generations had passed and Christ had not yet returned, false teachers claimed he would never return. The author of 2 Peter reminds readers that God does not operate within our system of time—Christ is simply waiting so more people have a chance to repent of their sins before he comes for judgment (2 Peter 3:9).

QUICK FACTS

- **Author:** An unknown person writing in Peter's name
- **Date Written:** Between A.D. 100 and 125
- **Audience:** A community of both Jewish and Gentile (non-Jewish) Christians
- **Themes:** Be on the lookout for false teachers and stand firm in God's promises.

AT A GLANCE

- **2 Peter 1** Greeting, and encouragement to lead a holy life
- **2 Peter 2** Warning to beware of false teachers
- **2 Peter 3** Message that the day of God's judgment is coming

1

Salutation

Simeon[a] Peter, a servant[b] and apostle of Jesus Christ,

To those who have received a faith as precious as ours through the righteousness of our God and Savior Jesus Christ:[c]

2 May grace and peace be yours in abundance in the knowledge of God and of Jesus our Lord.

The Christian's Call and Election

3 His divine power has given us everything needed for life and godliness, through the knowledge of him who called us by[d] his own glory and goodness. [4]Thus he has given us, through these things, his precious and very great promises, so that through them you may escape from the corruption that is in the world because of lust, and may become participants of the divine nature. [5]For this very reason, you must make every effort to support your faith with goodness, and goodness with knowledge, [6]and knowledge with self-control, and self-control with endurance, and endurance with godliness, [7]and godliness with mutual[e] affection, and mutual[e] affection with love. [8]For if these things are yours and are increasing among you, they keep you from being ineffective and unfruitful in the knowledge of our Lord Jesus Christ. [9]For anyone who lacks these things is short-sighted and blind, and is forgetful of the cleansing of past sins. [10]Therefore, brothers and sisters,[f] be all the more eager to confirm your call and election, for if you do this, you will never stumble. [11]For in this way, entry into the eternal kingdom of our Lord and Savior Jesus Christ will be richly provided for you.

12 Therefore I intend to keep on reminding you of these things, though you know them already and are established in the truth that has come to you. [13]I think it right, as long as I am in this body,[g] to refresh your memory, [14]since I know that my death[h] will come soon, as indeed our Lord Jesus Christ has made clear to me. [15]And I will make every effort so that after my departure you may be able at any time to recall these things.

> "Make every effort to support your faith with goodness, and goodness with knowledge, and knowledge with self-control, and self-control with endurance."
> —2 Peter 1:5–6

Eyewitnesses of Christ's Glory

16 For we did not follow cleverly devised myths when we made known to you the power and coming of our Lord Jesus Christ, but we had been eyewitnesses of his majesty. [17]For he received honor and glory from God the Father when that voice was conveyed to him by the Majestic Glory, saying, "This is my Son, my Beloved,[i] with whom I am well pleased." [18]We ourselves heard this voice come from heaven, while we were with him on the holy mountain.

19 So we have the prophetic message more fully confirmed. You will do well to be attentive to this as to a lamp shining in a dark place, until the day dawns and the morning star rises in your hearts. [20]First of all you must understand this, that no prophecy of scripture is a matter of one's own interpretation, [21]because no prophecy ever came by human will, but men and women moved by the Holy Spirit spoke from God.[j]

2

False Prophets and Their Punishment

But false prophets also arose among the people, just as there will be false teachers among you, who will secretly bring in destructive opinions. They will even deny the Master who bought them—bringing swift destruction on themselves. [2]Even so, many will follow their licentious ways, and because of these teachers[k] the way of truth will be maligned. [3]And in their greed they will exploit you with deceptive words. Their condemnation, pronounced against them long ago, has not been idle, and their destruction is not asleep.

4 For if God did not spare the angels when they sinned, but cast them into hell[l] and committed them to chains[m] of deepest darkness to be kept until the judgment; [5]and if he did not spare the ancient world, even though he saved Noah, a herald of righteousness, with seven others, when he brought a flood on a world of the ungodly; [6]and if by turning the cities of Sodom and Gomorrah to ashes he condemned them to extinction[n] and made them an example of

---

a Other ancient authorities read *Simon*   b Gk *slave*   c Or *of our God and the Savior Jesus Christ*   d Other ancient authorities read *through*
e Gk *brotherly*   f Gk *brothers*   g Gk *tent*   h Gk *the putting off of my tent*   i Other ancient authorities read *my beloved Son*   j Other ancient authorities
read *but moved by the Holy Spirit saints of God spoke*   k Gk *because of them*   l Gk *Tartaros*   m Other ancient authorities read *pits*   n Other ancient
authorities lack *to extinction*

what is coming to the ungodly;*a* *7*and if he rescued Lot, a righteous man greatly distressed by the licentiousness of the lawless *8*(for that righteous man, living among them day after day, was tormented in his righteous soul by their lawless deeds that he saw and heard), *9*then the Lord knows how to rescue the godly from trial, and to keep the unrighteous under punishment until the day of judgment *10*—especially those who indulge their flesh in depraved lust, and who despise authority.

Bold and willful, they are not afraid to slander the glorious ones,*b* *11*whereas angels, though greater in might and power, do not bring against them a slanderous judgment from the Lord.*c* *12*These people, however, are like irrational animals, mere creatures of instinct, born to be caught and killed. They slander what they do not understand, and when those creatures are destroyed,*d* they also will be destroyed, *13*suffering*e* the penalty for doing wrong. They count it a pleasure to revel in the daytime. They are blots and blemishes, reveling in their dissipation*f* while they feast with you. *14*They have eyes full of adultery, insatiable for sin. They entice unsteady souls. They have hearts trained in greed. Accursed children! *15*They have left the straight road and have gone astray, following the road of Balaam son of Bosor,*g* who loved the wages of doing wrong, *16*but was rebuked for his own transgression; a speechless donkey spoke with a human voice and restrained the prophet's madness.

17 These are waterless springs and mists driven by a storm; for them the deepest darkness has been reserved. *18*For they speak bombastic nonsense, and with licentious desires of the flesh they entice people who have just*h* escaped from those who live in error. *19*They promise them freedom, but they themselves are slaves of corruption; for people are slaves to whatever masters them. *20*For if, after they have escaped the defilements of the world through the knowledge of our Lord and Savior Jesus Christ, they are again entangled in them and overpowered, the last state has become worse for them than the first. *21*For it would have been better for them never to have known the way of righteousness than, after knowing it, to turn back from the holy commandment that was passed on to them. *22*It has happened to them according to the true proverb,

"The dog turns back to its own vomit,"

and,

"The sow is washed only to wallow in the mud."

The Promise of the Lord's Coming

3 This is now, beloved, the second letter I am writing to you; in them I am trying to arouse your sincere intention by reminding you *2*that you should remember the words spoken in the past by the holy prophets, and the commandment of the Lord and Savior spoken through your apostles. *3*First of all you must understand this, that in the last days scoffers will come, scoffing and indulging their own lusts *4*and saying, "Where is the promise of his coming? For ever since our ancestors died,*i* all things continue as they were from the beginning of creation!" *5*They deliberately ignore this fact, that by the word of God heavens existed long ago and an earth was formed out of water and by means of water, *6*through which the world of that time was deluged with water and perished. *7*But by the same word the present heavens and earth have been reserved for fire, being kept until the day of judgment and destruction of the godless.

STUDY IT!

Identifying False Prophets · 2 Peter 2:1–3

Many people throughout history have misled others in the name of God. The Nazi dictator Adolf Hitler is probably the best-known such leader in the twentieth century. Some of these leaders have even convinced their followers to commit mass suicide as part of their beliefs. These extreme examples show how people can be misguided by false prophets.

Here the author gives guidelines for identifying false prophets, explaining that false prophets use secrets, propose destructive opinions, deny God's teachings, twist the truth to their needs, and exploit their followers. Beware of any leaders, religious or nonreligious, who use these techniques—even if they make them look attractive. They exploit the truth (2 Peter 2:2).

---

a Other ancient authorities read *an example to those who were to be ungodly*   **b** Or *angels*; Gk *glories*   **c** Other ancient authorities read *before the Lord*; others lack the phrase   **d** Gk *in their destruction*   **e** Other ancient authorities read *receiving*   **f** Other ancient authorities read *love-feasts*   **g** Other ancient authorities read *Beor*   **h** Other ancient authorities read *actually*   **i** Gk *our fathers fell asleep*

8 But do not ignore this one fact, beloved, that with the Lord one day is like a thousand years, and a thousand years are like one day. [9] The Lord is not slow about his promise, as some think of slowness, but is patient with you,[a] not wanting any to perish, but all to come to repentance. [10] But the day of the Lord will come like a thief, and then the heavens will pass away with a loud noise, and the elements will be dissolved with fire, and the earth and everything that is done on it will be disclosed.[b]

11 Since all these things are to be dissolved in this way, what sort of persons ought you to be in leading lives of holiness and godliness, [12] waiting for and hastening[c] the coming of the day of God, because of which the heavens will be set ablaze and dissolved, and the elements will melt with fire? [13] But, in accordance with his promise, we wait for new heavens and a new earth, where righteousness is at home.

Final Exhortation and Doxology

14 Therefore, beloved, while you are waiting for these things, strive to be found by him at peace, without spot or blemish; [15] and regard the patience of our Lord as salvation. So also our beloved brother Paul wrote to you according to the wisdom given him, [16] speaking of this as he does in all his letters. There are some things in them hard to understand, which the ignorant and unstable twist to their own destruction, as they do the other scriptures. [17] You therefore, beloved, since you are forewarned, beware that you are not carried away with the error of the lawless and lose your own stability. [18] But grow in the grace and knowledge of our Lord and Savior Jesus Christ. To him be the glory both now and to the day of eternity. Amen.[d]

LIVE IT!

Waiting for God
2 Peter 3:8–9

Have you ever trusted God for something and waited . . . and waited . . . and waited? During times of waiting, sometimes we begin to doubt even the things we felt were clear from the Lord. The early readers of 2 Peter were in that same place—confused that Jesus had not yet returned (see "Study It: The Second Coming," near 2 Thessalonians 1:5-2:17). The author reminds them, and us, not to apply human limits to God's response.

God is outside of time, so what feels like an eternity to us is nothing to God: "With the Lord one day is like a thousand years, and a thousand years are like one day" (2 Peter 3:8). We live in an instant culture. But God isn't slow or behind schedule. It's just that God's timetable doesn't look like our own.

- What have you prayed for or felt God promising you that you are still waiting for?
- How does looking at God's response through your own perspective of time limit the ways you can see God working?
- What can you do to remain patient and trust God's ultimate timing in your life?

---

a Other ancient authorities read *on your account* b Other ancient authorities read *will be burned up* c Or *earnestly desiring* d Other ancient authorities lack *Amen*

1 John

Betrayal is painful. It often begins with a misunderstanding. Sometimes harsh words are exchanged, and people part ways feeling sad and bitter. The letters of John were addressed to a group that had experienced sharp division and conflict. It's impossible to miss the author's feeling of betrayal as you read these letters.

IN DEPTH

All three letters of John were probably written by the same person, the elder referred to in the second and third letters. This writer probably belonged to the same community that the gospel of John was written to. He saw himself and his community as being faithful to the true meaning of John's gospel. But others who had once belonged to this community had abandoned it in a time of need. They read the gospel of John too, but interpreted it very differently. The disagreement between these two groups resulted in a bitter conflict.

It's difficult to determine exactly what the disagreement was about even after carefully studying the first letter. One issue seems to have been the proper understanding of Jesus' humanity. Apparently, the people didn't fully believe in Jesus' humanity and its connection to salvation through Jesus' death and resurrection. The author emphasizes Jesus' humanity by mentioning that Jesus came in the flesh, and he comments on the saving power of the blood of Jesus.

The author also challenges the people's claims that they were free to do anything they wanted and still love God. If they truly loved God, they would also love their brothers and sisters and would not have abandoned the community.

The second letter of John is brief and seems to be a follow-up to the first letter addressed to the same community. The third letter of John is also brief. It's addressed to a man named Gaius, and in it the elder is complaining about a church leader named Diotrephes, who refused to provide hospitality to some missionaries sent by the elder.

Through these letters, God reminds us today that Christ's followers will inevitably have profoundly different understandings about what they believe. Conflict and disagreement will occur even within the Christian community. But the challenge for Christians is to learn to handle such conflict with love and respect.

QUICK FACTS

- **Author:** Unknown, but possibly someone associated with the same community that the gospel of John was written to
- **Date Written:** Around A.D. 100
- **Audience:** Christians who were suffering from a split in their church
- **Theme:** Love one another.

AT A GLANCE

- **1 John 1:1–3:10** A message that God is light, and we must walk in the light
- **1 John 3:11–5:21** A message that those who are God's children show it by their love
- **2 John** A warning about false messages
- **3 John** A letter to Gaius, a man who provides hospitality to missionaries

1

The Word of Life

We declare to you what was from the beginning, what we have heard, what we have seen with our eyes, what we have looked at and touched with our hands, concerning the word of life— ²this life was revealed, and we have seen it and testify to it, and declare to you the eternal life that was with the Father and was revealed to us— ³we declare to you what we have seen and heard so that you also may have fellowship with us; and truly our fellowship is with the Father and with his Son Jesus Christ. ⁴We are writing these things so that our*ᵃ* joy may be complete.

God Is Light

5 This is the message we have heard from him and proclaim to you, that God is light and in him there is no darkness at all. ⁶If we say that we have fellowship with him while we are walking in darkness, we lie and do not do what is true; ⁷but if we walk in the light as he himself is in the light, we have fellowship with one another, and the blood of Jesus his Son cleanses us from all sin. ⁸If we say that we have no sin, we deceive ourselves, and the truth is not in us. ⁹If we confess our sins, he who is faithful and just will forgive us our sins and cleanse us from all unrighteousness. ¹⁰If we say that we have not sinned, we make him a liar, and his word is not in us.

2

Christ Our Advocate

My little children, I am writing these things to you so that you may not sin. But if anyone does sin, we have an advocate with the Father, Jesus Christ the righteous; ²and he is the atoning sacrifice for our sins, and not for ours only but also for the sins of the whole world.

3 Now by this we may be sure that we know him, if we obey his commandments. ⁴Whoever says, "I have come to know him," but does not obey his commandments, is a liar, and in such a person the truth does not exist; ⁵but whoever obeys his word,

Live in the Light
1 John 1:5–10

Darkness hides things. Light reveals them. This can be good, unless you are trying to hide something. But 1 John tells us that our forgiveness and righteousness depend on living in the light and allowing it to reveal what's in us—even sin. Sin is there either way (1 John 1:8), but when we confess it, God is faithful to forgive us and cleanse us (1 John 1:9). A much better option than trying to hide sin in the darkness!

- Is there any area of your life where you are allowing sin to hide in the darkness? How is it impacting your relationship with others and with God?
- Take some time to confess your sin and experience the forgiveness God offers to those who live in the light.

truly in this person the love of God has reached perfection. By this we may be sure that we are in him: ⁶whoever says, "I abide in him," ought to walk just as he walked.

A New Commandment

7 Beloved, I am writing you no new commandment, but an old commandment that you have had from the beginning; the old commandment is the word that you have heard. ⁸Yet I am writing you a new commandment that is true in him and in you, because*ᵇ* the darkness is passing away and the true light is already shining. ⁹Whoever says, "I am in the light," while hating a brother or sister,*ᶜ* is still in the darkness. ¹⁰Whoever loves a brother or sister*ᵈ* lives in the light, and in such a person*ᵉ* there is no cause for stumbling. ¹¹But whoever hates another believer*ᶠ* is in the darkness, walks in the darkness, and does not know the way to go, because the darkness has brought on blindness.

¹² I am writing to you, little children,
because your sins are forgiven on account of his name.
¹³ I am writing to you, fathers,

ᵃ Other ancient authorities read *your* *ᵇ* Or *that* *ᶜ* Gk *hating a brother* *ᵈ* Gk *loves a brother* *ᵉ* Or *in it* *ᶠ* Gk *hates a brother*

because you know him who is from the
beginning.
I am writing to you, young people,
because you have conquered the evil one.

14 I write to you, children,
because you know the Father.
I write to you, fathers,
because you know him who is from the
beginning.
I write to you, young people,
because you are strong
and the word of God abides
in you,
and you have overcome the evil one.

15 Do not love the world or the things in the
world. The love of the Father is not in those who
love the world; 16for all that is in the world—the
desire of the flesh, the desire of the eyes, the pride
in riches—comes not from the Father but from the
world. 17And the world and its desire*a* are passing
away, but those who do the will of God live forever.

Warning against Antichrists

18 Children, it is the last hour! As you have heard
that antichrist is coming, so now many antichrists
have come. From this we know that it is the last hour.
19They went out from us, but they did not belong
to us; for if they had belonged to us, they would have
remained with us. But by going out they made it
plain that none of them belongs to us. 20But you
have been anointed by the Holy One, and all of
you have knowledge.*b* 21I write to you, not because
you do not know the truth, but because you know
it, and you know that no lie comes from the truth.

22Who is the liar but the one who denies that Jesus
is the Christ?*c* This is the antichrist, the one who
denies the Father and the Son. 23No one who denies
the Son has the Father; everyone who confesses the
Son has the Father also. 24Let what you heard from
the beginning abide in you. If what you heard
from the beginning abides in you, then you will
abide in the Son and in the Father. 25And this is
what he has promised us,*d* eternal life.

26 I write these things to you concerning those
who would deceive you. 27As for you, the anointing
that you received from him abides in you, and so
you do not need anyone to teach you. But as his
anointing teaches you about all things, and is true
and is not a lie, and just as it has taught you, abide
in him.*e*

28 And now, little children, abide in him, so that
when he is revealed we may have confidence and
not be put to shame before him at his coming.

Children of God

29 If you know that he is righteous, you may be
sure that everyone who does right has been

3 born of him. 1See what love the Father has
given us, that we should be called children
of God; and that is what we are. The reason
the world does not know us is that it did not know
him. 2Beloved, we are God's children now; what we
will be has not yet been revealed. What we do know
is this: when he*e* is revealed, we will be like him, for
we will see him as he is. 3And all who have this hope
in him purify themselves, just as he is pure.

4 Everyone who commits sin is guilty of lawlessness; sin is lawlessness. 5You know that he was re-

---

PRAY IT!

A World of Desires · 1 John 2:15–17

We live in the world, but we are told not to love the world or the things in it
(1 John 2:15). That's not easy. The things of the world look good, and it can be
easier to desire the things that are right in front of us than things we have to
wait for. So why should we not love the world? It's because the world is passing
away—the things of the world are temporary and empty (1 John 2:17). But in Christ our hope is in
eternal life with Jesus.

Lord, I confess that many times I want the things of the world more than I desire you. But I know
they are only a shadow of the amazing things you have in store for me in eternity. Please help
me to love you more than the world. Help me to remember what's temporary and what's eternal.
Teach me to live well in this world, knowing that true life is found with you forever. Amen.

---

a Or *the desire for it*   *b* Other ancient authorities read *you know all things*   *c* Or *the Messiah*   *d* Other ancient authorities read *you*   *e* Or *it*

vealed to take away sins, and in him there is no sin. [6]No one who abides in him sins; no one who sins has either seen him or known him. [7]Little children, let no one deceive you. Everyone who does what is right is righteous, just as he is righteous. [8]Everyone who commits sin is a child of the devil; for the devil has been sinning from the beginning. The Son of God was revealed for this purpose, to destroy the works of the devil. [9]Those who have been born of God do not sin, because God's seed abides in them;[a] they cannot sin, because they have been born of God. [10]The children of God and the children of the devil are revealed in this way: all who do not do what is right are not from God, nor are those who do not love their brothers and sisters.[b]

Love One Another

11 For this is the message you have heard from the beginning, that we should love one another. [12]We must not be like Cain who was from the evil one and murdered his brother. And why did he murder him? Because his own deeds were evil and his brother's righteous. [13]Do not be astonished, brothers and sisters,[c] that the world hates you. [14]We know that we have passed from death to life because we love one another. Whoever does not love abides in death. [15]All who hate a brother or sister[b] are murderers, and you know that murderers do not have eternal life abiding in them. [16]We know love by this, that he laid down his life for us—and we ought to lay down our lives for one another. [17]How does God's love abide in anyone who has the world's

Love in Action
1 John 3:16–18

Love is not just a feeling; it is an action. And we know what that action looks like, because Jesus showed us. He lived out love in both his life and his death. Jesus laid down his life for others, and our challenge as his followers is to do the same (1 John 3:16). Does that mean we are supposed to die for someone else? Probably not. But loving does mean sacrifice. We are commanded to show love by helping those who don't have food, clothing, shelter, and other necessities (1 John 3:17). It's not enough to say we love the poor, if we aren't willing to give of what we have to help them. We must love in truth and action (1 John 3:18).

- Think about how you have lived and acted during the past week. Have you shown love in truth and action?

- Ask God to forgive you for any situations in which you failed to act lovingly or to help someone in need.

- Who needs you to put your love into action? How can you do that this week?

Compassion = Helping Others in Need · 1 John 3:16–18

There are 925 million undernourished people in the world according to the 2010 report by the United Nations Food and Agriculture Organization.* That's enough to fill New York City about 114 times! And it doesn't even count those in need of clean water, medical services, shelter, or education. Most of those people live in developing nations, but some are in your own city. So the question posed in 1 John 3:17 is not a hypothetical question: "How does God's love abide in anyone who has the world's goods and sees a brother or sister in need and yet refuses help?"

Need a way to move your faith and love for God from words to action? Compassion International describes itself as a child advocacy ministry that releases children from spiritual, economic, social, and physical poverty and enables them to become responsible, fulfilled Christian adults. That means they do the hard work to provide you with an easy and personal way to change the life of a child through sponsorship. Check it out at **compassion.com**.

---

a *Or because the children of God abide in him*   b *Gk his brother*   c *Gk brothers*

goods and sees a brother or sister*a* in need and yet refuses help?

18 Little children, let us love, not in word or speech, but in truth and action. [19] And by this we will know that we are from the truth and will reassure our hearts before him [20] whenever our hearts condemn us; for God is greater than our hearts, and he knows everything. [21] Beloved, if our hearts do not condemn us, we have boldness before God; [22] and we receive from him whatever we ask, because we obey his commandments and do what pleases him.

23 And this is his commandment, that we should believe in the name of his Son Jesus Christ and love one another, just as he has commanded us. [24] All who obey his commandments abide in him, and he abides in them. And by this we know that he abides in us, by the Spirit that he has given us.

> "This is love, not that we loved God but that he loved us and sent his Son to be the atoning sacrifice for our sins."
> —1 John 4:10

Testing the Spirits

4 Beloved, do not believe every spirit, but test the spirits to see whether they are from God; for many false prophets have gone out into the world. [2] By this you know the Spirit of God: every spirit that confesses that Jesus Christ has come in the flesh is from God, [3] and every spirit that does not confess Jesus*b* is not from God. And this is the spirit of the antichrist, of which you have heard that it is coming; and now it is already in the world. [4] Little children, you are from God, and have conquered them; for the one who is in you is greater than the one who is in the world. [5] They are from the world; therefore what they say is from the world, and the world listens to them. [6] We are from God. Whoever knows God listens to us, and whoever is not from God does not listen to us. From this we know the spirit of truth and the spirit of error.

STUDY IT!

Testing Spirits · 1 John 4:1–6

Ancient peoples believed in different kinds of spirits that could affect the way things happened in the world. This passage talks about two kinds of spirits: the spirit that comes from God and the spirit that does not come from God. This letter gives us two ways for testing whether we are filled with God's Spirit. The first is whether God's love flows from our lives as we love others (1 John 3:18). The second is that we will confess our belief that Jesus Christ is the Word made flesh, who revealed God to us.

These two tests came as a result of recent events in this group of believers. Some people had left the community, because they didn't believe Jesus was the Christ (1 John 2:22). Some additional clarification is provided in **2 John 7**; it says that these people didn't believe that Jesus came as a human. They believed Jesus came to live among us, but they didn't believe he actually became one of us and suffered and died as we do. But this is what the author of 1 John believed and what Christians today believe. This is what we mean when we talk about the incarnation—God takes on flesh and becomes like us.

So what does all this mean for us today? These two tests are still meaningful. You can apply them to just about any spiritual idea or practice you come across. To see if it's of God, ask yourself: "Does this help me to love God and other people? Does this support the Christian belief that Jesus Christ is fully God and fully human and that faith in him is necessary for salvation?" If you can't answer yes to both of these questions, then you can be confident that the idea or practice is not of God.

---

a Gk *brother*   *b* Other ancient authorities read *does away with Jesus* (Gk *dissolves Jesus*)

LIVE IT!

All About the Love · 1 John 4:7–21

The Bible contains some of the most beautiful prose and poetry about love. This is an especially eloquent passage that captures the heart of the good news. God has loved us in Christ Jesus, who came as the Savior of the world. Now we have been given the Holy Spirit, and we are commanded to love others as we have been loved by God. There's a lot here about love, but at the core these verses tell us that God's story is and has always been all about love.

It's easy to say we love God. But **1 John 4:21** tells us we show it by loving other people. Loving one another is much harder than simply saying, "I love God" or even "I love you." What does this love for God look like? It's not the romantic, gushy love the world usually presents to us. Read **Matthew 25:31–36** or **1 Corinthians 13** for some ideas.

- What aspect about love from **1 John 4:7–21** speaks most powerfully to you?
- How does knowing God's love for you motivate you to love others?

God Is Love

7 Beloved, let us love one another, because love is from God; everyone who loves is born of God and knows God. [8]Whoever does not love does not know God, for God is love. [9]God's love was revealed among us in this way: God sent his only Son into the world so that we might live through him. [10]In this is love, not that we loved God but that he loved us and sent his Son to be the atoning sacrifice for our sins. [11]Beloved, since God loved us so much, we also ought to love one another. [12]No one has ever seen God; if we love one another, God lives in us, and his love is perfected in us.

13 By this we know that we abide in him and he in us, because he has given us of his Spirit. [14]And we have seen and do testify that the Father has sent his Son as the Savior of the world. [15]God abides in those who confess that Jesus is the Son of God, and they abide in God. [16]So we have known and believe the love that God has for us.

God is love, and those who abide in love abide in God, and God abides in them. [17]Love has been perfected among us in this: that we may have boldness on the day of judgment, because as he is, so are we in this world. [18]There is no fear in love, but perfect love casts out fear; for fear has to do with punishment, and whoever fears has not reached perfection in love. [19]We love[a] because he first loved us. [20]Those who say, "I love God," and hate their brothers or sisters,[b] are liars; for those who do not love a brother or sister[c] whom they have seen, cannot love God whom they have not seen. [21]The

STUDY IT!

Perfect Love
1 John 4:16

Greek, the language of the New Testament, has several words for "love." There are words for parental love, romantic love, and love between friends or relatives. The Greek word Paul uses in this verse is the same one used in **1 Corinthians 13**, the love chapter. It is "agape," and it is reserved for a special kind of love.

Agape is love without conditions or motivations. It's there no matter who you are or what you do. It willingly chooses to serve without expecting service in return. God is agape. The source of agape is the unconditional love of God. God's agape is revealed to us in Jesus Christ. And through the Holy Spirit, we become a channel for communicating this wonderful love to others.

We are created in God's image. God wants us to love each other with agape, knowing that we'll experience the fullness of agape only when we meet Jesus face-to-face.

---

a Other ancient authorities add *him*; others add *God*   *b* Gk *brothers*   *c* Gk *brother*

commandment we have from him is this: those who love God must love their brothers and sisters[a] also.

5

Faith Conquers the World

Everyone who believes that Jesus is the Christ[b] has been born of God, and everyone who loves the parent loves the child. [2]By this we know that we love the children of God, when we love God and obey his commandments. [3]For the love of God is this, that we obey his commandments. And his commandments are not burdensome, [4]for whatever is born of God conquers the world. And this is the victory that conquers the world, our faith. [5]Who is it that conquers the world but the one who believes that Jesus is the Son of God?

Testimony concerning the Son of God

6 This is the one who came by water and blood, Jesus Christ, not with the water only but with the water and the blood. And the Spirit is the one that testifies, for the Spirit is the truth. [7]There are three that testify:[c] [8]the Spirit and the water and the blood, and these three agree. [9]If we receive human testimony, the testimony of God is greater; for this is the testimony of God that he has testified to his Son. [10]Those who believe in the Son of God have the testimony in their hearts. Those who do not believe in God[d] have made him a liar by not believing in the testimony that God has given concerning his Son. [11]And this is the testimony: God gave us eter-nal life, and this life is in his Son. [12]Whoever has the Son has life; whoever does not have the Son of God does not have life.

Epilogue

13 I write these things to you who believe in the name of the Son of God, so that you may know that you have eternal life.

14 And this is the boldness we have in him, that if we ask anything according to his will, he hears us. [15]And if we know that he hears us in whatever we ask, we know that we have obtained the requests made of him. [16]If you see your brother or sister[e] committing what is not a mortal sin, you will ask, and God[f] will give life to such a one—to those whose sin is not mortal. There is sin that is mortal; I do not say that you should pray about that. [17]All wrongdoing is sin, but there is sin that is not mor-tal.

18 We know that those who are born of God do not sin, but the one who was born of God protects them, and the evil one does not touch them. [19]We know that we are God's children, and that the whole world lies under the power of the evil one. [20]And we know that the Son of God has come and has given us understanding so that we may know him who is true;[g] and we are in him who is true, in his Son Jesus Christ. He is the true God and eternal life.

21 Little children, keep yourselves from idols.[h]

---

a Gk *brother*   b Or *the Messiah*   c A few other authorities read (with variations) [7]*There are three that testify in heaven, the Father, the Word, and the Holy Spirit, and these three are one.* [8]*And there are three that testify on earth:*   d Other ancient authorities read *in the Son*   e Gk *your brother*   f Gk *he*   g Other ancient authorities read *know the true God*   h Other ancient authorities add *Amen*

2 John

▶▶▶▶▶▶▶▶▶▶▶▶▶▶▶▶▶▶▶▶▶▶▶▶▶▶▶▶▶▶

For background on this letter, see the introduction at the beginning of 1 John.

Salutation

1 The elder to the elect lady and her children, whom I love in the truth, and not only I but also all who know the truth, ²because of the truth that abides in us and will be with us forever:

3 Grace, mercy, and peace will be with us from God the Father and from*ª* Jesus Christ, the Father's Son, in truth and love.

Truth and Love

4 I was overjoyed to find some of your children walking in the truth, just as we have been commanded by the Father. ⁵But now, dear lady, I ask you, not as though I were writing you a new commandment, but one we have had from the beginning, let us love one another. ⁶And this is love, that we walk according to his commandments; this is the commandment just as you have heard it from the beginning—you must walk in it.

7 Many deceivers have gone out into the world, those who do not confess that Jesus Christ has come in the flesh; any such person is the deceiver and the antichrist! ⁸Be on your guard, so that you do not lose what we*ᵇ* have worked for, but may receive a full reward. ⁹Everyone who does not abide in the teaching of Christ, but goes beyond it, does not have God; whoever abides in the teaching has both the Father and the Son. ¹⁰Do not receive into the house or welcome anyone who comes to you and does not bring this teaching; ¹¹for to welcome is to participate in the evil deeds of such a person.

Final Greetings

12 Although I have much to write to you, I would rather not use paper and ink; instead I hope to come to you and talk with you face to face, so that our joy may be complete.

13 The children of your elect sister send you their greetings.*ᶜ*

LIVE IT!

Unwelcome Guests
2 John 10–11

The author of 2 John is warning a Christian group—called the elect lady and her children—about false messages from those who would lead them astray. The author cautions the community to have nothing to do with such people, not even to let them into their homes (2 John 10–11). The words sound harsh, but the reasoning is sound.

We are faced every day with the chance to let false messages into our homes and lives through television, books, magazines, music, and the Internet. There's a lot of truth to be found in many of these forms of media, but the messages, values, and behaviors they promote are often contrary to a healthy and holy way of life. It may seem like no big deal, but these "guests" can affect our attitudes and choices, especially if we welcome them blindly without thinking about the impact of their messages.

- Think about the media you most frequently look at or listen to. Make a list of the positive and negative messages they contain. How do the lists compare?
- How can you manage your media exposure wisely in order to grow in truth and love and resist negative influences?

---

a Other ancient authorities add *the Lord*   b Other ancient authorities read *you*   c Other ancient authorities add *Amen*

3 John

For background on this letter, see the introduction at the beginning of 1 John.

Salutation

1 The elder to the beloved Gaius, whom I love in truth.

Gaius Commended for His Hospitality

2 Beloved, I pray that all may go well with you and that you may be in good health, just as it is well with your soul. [3]I was overjoyed when some of the friends[a] arrived and testified to your faithfulness to the truth, namely how you walk in the truth. [4]I have no greater joy than this, to hear that my children are walking in the truth.

5 Beloved, you do faithfully whatever you do for the friends,[a] even though they are strangers to you; [6]they have testified to your love before the church. You will do well to send them on in a manner worthy of God; [7]for they began their journey for the sake of Christ,[b] accepting no support from non-believers.[c]

[8]Therefore we ought to support such people, so that we may become co-workers with the truth.

Diotrephes and Demetrius

9 I have written something to the church; but Diotrephes, who likes to put himself first, does not acknowledge our authority. [10]So if I come, I will call attention to what he is doing in spreading false charges against us. And not content with those charges, he refuses to welcome the friends,[a] and even prevents those who want to do so and expels them from the church.

11 Beloved, do not imitate what is evil but imitate what is good. Whoever does good is from God; whoever does evil has not seen God. [12]Everyone has testified favorably about Demetrius, and so has the truth itself. We also testify for him,[d] and you know that our testimony is true.

LIVE IT!

Supporting the Ministry of Others • 3 John 5–8

Gaius was a man of faith who opened his home to missionaries passing through his city. Gaius didn't personally know these missionaries, but he provided hospitality for them, because he knew they were helping to spread the good news. In 3 John, the writer appeals to Gaius to welcome his messenger, Demetrius, even when others refuse to do so.

Do you ever feel overwhelmed by the issues of the world? Do you feel as though there's only so much—or so little—you can do because of your age or life circumstances? The story of Gaius shows how you can partner with Christians who are ministering in some way you can't. You can offer your hospitality, time, or money, and you can promote their work in your church, school, or community.

- Think of a person or a ministry you would like to partner with. (There are lots of great ones in the "Connect It!" study notes throughout this Bible.)
- Find out what they need and how it matches with what you have to offer. You may even want to talk to your family about how you can all work together in partnership with someone.

---

a Gk brothers b Gk for the sake of the name c Gk the Gentiles d Gk lacks for him

> "Do not imitate what
> is evil but imitate
> what is good."
> —3 John 11

Final Greetings

13 I have much to write to you, but I would rather not write with pen and ink; [14]instead I hope to see you soon, and we will talk together face to face.

15 Peace to you. The friends send you their greetings. Greet the friends there, each by name.

Jude

They pretend to be part of your group, but all they really do is cause trouble. They claim to have all the right answers, but they won't listen to other people's opinions. They flatter people to get what they want, but then they grumble and complain behind people's backs. They cause division wherever they go. Do you know people like this? Maybe you even find yourself acting like them sometimes. The letter of Jude has some things to say about these people.

IN DEPTH

The purpose of Jude is to warn churches about false teachers who come into the Christian community with lies and tricks, making trouble wherever they go. The author recalls stories from the past in which God punished such people: stories about the Egyptians, who opposed God's plan to bring the Hebrew people to the promised land; the immoral people of Sodom and Gomorrah; the angels who revolted against God; and Cain, who killed his brother. Not really people you want to be associated with! The author also encourages believers to build themselves up in the faith. Finally, the author cautions Christians to ignore ungodly people—unless those people truly want to change, in which case Christians should be examples of the mercy of Christ.

Notice that this letter includes some terms that are unfamiliar to modern Christians or that have different meanings today. For instance, the term "holy ones" refers to the members of the Christian community, and a "love feast" is a celebration of the Lord's Supper. Not knowing for sure who wrote this book or who it was written to can also limit our understanding. But the overall lesson is still true for us today. There will always be people and teachings that threaten to invade the Christian church and tear it apart. We are not to be surprised by their twisted thinking or living. Instead, we should be prepared and keep our focus on God's love and mercy (Jude 21).

QUICK FACTS

- **Author:** Unknown, traditionally thought to be Jude, the brother of James (see Mark 3)
- **Date Written:** Possibly A.D. 80–90
- **Audience:** Unknown
- **Themes:** Warning against false teaching in the Church; ground yourself in God's love through prayer

AT A GLANCE

- **Jude 1–2** Opening
- **Jude 3–23** Warnings about judgment
- **Jude 24–25** Closing

Salutation

1 Jude,[a] a servant[b] of Jesus Christ and brother of James,

To those who are called, who are beloved[c] in[d] God the Father and kept safe for[d] Jesus Christ:

2 May mercy, peace, and love be yours in abundance.

Occasion of the Letter

3 Beloved, while eagerly preparing to write to you about the salvation we share, I find it necessary to write and appeal to you to contend for the faith that was once for all entrusted to the saints. [4]For certain intruders have stolen in among you, people who long ago were designated for this condemnation as ungodly, who pervert the grace of our God into licentiousness and deny our only Master and Lord, Jesus Christ.[e]

Judgment on False Teachers

5 Now I desire to remind you, though you are fully informed, that the Lord, who once for all saved[f] a people out of the land of Egypt, afterward destroyed those who did not believe. [6]And the angels who did not keep their own position, but left their proper dwelling, he has kept in eternal chains in deepest darkness for the judgment of the great day. [7]Likewise, Sodom and Gomorrah and the surrounding cities, which, in the same manner as they, indulged in sexual

immorality and pursued unnatural lust,[g] serve as an example by undergoing a punishment of eternal fire.

8 Yet in the same way these dreamers also defile the flesh, reject authority, and slander the glorious ones.[h] [9]But when the archangel Michael contended with the devil and disputed about the body of Moses, he did not dare to bring a condemnation of slander[i] against him, but said, "The Lord rebuke you!" [10]But these people slander whatever they do not understand, and they are destroyed by those things that, like irrational animals, they know by instinct. [11]Woe to them! For they go the way of Cain, and abandon themselves to Balaam's error for the sake of gain, and perish in Korah's rebellion. [12]These are blemishes[j] on your love-feasts, while they feast with you without fear, feeding themselves.[k] They are waterless clouds carried along by the winds; autumn trees without fruit, twice dead, uprooted; [13]wild waves of the sea,

LIVE IT!

Pay Attention · Jude 3–4

Things aren't always what they seem—or sound like. There have always been people who are good at twisting God's Word for their own means. These verses warn the people of the Church to watch out for teachers or "intruders" who "pervert the grace of our God into licentiousness and deny our only Master and Lord, Jesus Christ" (v. 4). "Licentiousness" is an old-fashioned word that means rebelliousness and often suggests sexual impurity. It seems that some people in the early Church were saying that, because Jesus forgave them, they could do whatever they wanted.

Sound familiar? Have you heard teachers or other Christians claiming that they know God, so they can do whatever they want? Have you been tempted to think and act like that? It is true that God promises to forgive us whatever we do when we confess it (1 John 1:9), but God cares very much what we do and how we live (John 14:21). The Bible gives us guidance about the kinds of actions and traits God wants to build into our lives, and Jude reminds us of the importance of staying focused on God, so we won't be led away from God's truth. We are instructed to keep praying and growing toward Jesus (vv. 20-23). As we learn more and more to hear and follow his voice, we'll be able to recognize and avoid lies and false voices that can hurt us and pull us away from God.

a Gk Judas b Gk slave c Other ancient authorities read sanctified d Or by e Or the only Master and our Lord Jesus Christ f Other ancient authorities read though you were once for all fully informed, that Jesus (or Joshua) who saved g Gk went after other flesh h Or angels; Gk glories i Or condemnation for blasphemy j Or reefs k Or without fear. They are shepherds who care only for themselves casting up the foam of their own shame; wandering stars, for whom the deepest darkness has been reserved forever.

14 It was also about these that Enoch, in the seventh generation from Adam, prophesied, saying, "See, the Lord is coming[a] with ten thousands of his holy ones, [15]to execute judgment on all, and to convict everyone of all the deeds of ungodliness that they have committed in such an ungodly way, and of all the harsh things that ungodly sinners have spoken against him." [16]These are grumblers and malcontents; they indulge their own lusts; they are bombastic in speech, flattering people to their own advantage.

Warnings and Exhortations

17 But you, beloved, must remember the predictions of the apostles of our Lord Jesus Christ; [18]for they said to you, "In the last time there will be scoffers, indulging their own ungodly lusts." [19]It is these worldly people, devoid of the Spirit, who are causing divisions. [20]But you, beloved, build yourselves up on your most holy faith; pray in the Holy Spirit; [21]keep yourselves in the love of God; look forward to the mercy of our Lord Jesus Christ that leads to[b] eternal life. [22]And have mercy on some who are wavering; [23]save others by snatching them out of the fire; and have mercy on still others with fear, hating even the tunic defiled by their bodies.[c]

Benediction

24 Now to him who is able to keep you from falling, and to make you stand without blemish in the presence of his glory with rejoicing, [25]to the only God our Savior, through Jesus Christ our Lord, be glory, majesty, power, and authority, before all time and now and forever. Amen.

---

a Gk *came* b Gk *Christ to* c Gk *by the flesh*. The Greek text of verses 22-23 is uncertain at several points

Revelation ▶▶▶▶▶▶▶▶▶▶

Have you ever shown someone a text message from a friend and he or she just couldn't understand it? It makes perfect sense to you, but others don't get it, because they weren't part of the whole conversation. In a similar way, it's hard to understand the message in Revelation. The symbols and visions that appear in this book aren't always clear. Many people think Revelation is a frightening book about the end of the world, but much of its symbolism represents events that were taking place when the book was written. For early Christians and the Church today, the book of Revelation is a message of hope that proclaims God's ultimate triumph over evil both in history and in the future.

IN DEPTH

This book is unique in that the author, who calls himself John, received a series of visions from God that form most of the content. The recorded visions take the form of apocalyptic literature (see "Study It: Apocalyptic Literature," near Daniel 7-10) and are full of symbols. These symbols are like the language of a secret club. You use it when you want to keep people who don't belong to your club from understanding what you are saying.

Why did the writer want to hide the meaning from people outside the early Christian churches? Most likely because the Christians still remembered their persecution under the Roman emperor Nero Caesar (A.D. 54-68) and were suffering a new persecution under the Roman emperor Domitian (A.D. 81-96). This coded language allowed John to write about the persecution taking place, cry for justice in the face of it, and even criticize the Roman Empire without necessarily putting his readers at risk of more persecution or death. John himself was exiled to an island off Asia Minor for preaching the gospel (Revelation 1:9).

Understanding the symbolism of Revelation and setting aside a linear concept of time that we're used to help us understand the book as a message of hope to a church under persecution. It expresses belief in God's justice and victory over evil—an evil that at John's time was embodied in the Roman Empire. But it also expresses the great Christian belief that God will ultimately be victorious at the end of time, when Christ will come again in his full glory and power. It's a mistake for Christians to try to decipher Revelation as a prediction as to exactly when and how that final coming will occur. But we can take great joy and hope in the promise of a new world in which God will wipe away every tear and suffering and death will be no more (Revelation 21:4).

QUICK FACTS

- **Author:** A Jewish-Christian prophet named John
- **Date Written:** Probably A.D. 92-96
- **Audience:** Christian churches in Asia Minor (modern-day Turkey) during a time of Roman persecution
- **Themes:** There is hope because God is in control of the future and will be victorious.

AT A GLANCE

- **Revelation 1–3** Introduction, and letters to the seven churches
- **Revelation 4–11** Visions of God's throne, the Lamb, the seven seals, and the seven trumpets
- **Revelation 12–14** Visions of the dragon and the two beasts
- **Revelation 15–18** Visions of the seven plagues and the fall of Babylon (Rome)
- **Revelation 19–22** Visions of the victory of Christ and the end of history

Introduction and Salutation

1 The revelation of Jesus Christ, which God gave him to show his servants[a] what must soon take place; he made[b] it known by sending his angel to his servant[c] John, [2]who testified to the word of God and to the testimony of Jesus Christ, even to all that he saw.

3 Blessed is the one who reads aloud the words of the prophecy, and blessed are those who hear and who keep what is written in it; for the time is near.

4 John to the seven churches that are in Asia:

Grace to you and peace from him who is and who was and who is to come, and from the seven spirits who are before his throne, [5]and from Jesus Christ, the faithful witness, the firstborn of the dead, and the ruler of the kings of the earth.

To him who loves us and freed[d] us from our sins by his blood, [6]and made[b] us to be a kingdom, priests serving[e] his God and Father, to him be glory and dominion forever and ever. Amen.

7 Look! He is coming with the clouds;
  every eye will see him,
even those who pierced him;
  and on his account all the tribes of the
    earth will wail.
So it is to be. Amen.

8 "I am the Alpha and the Omega," says the Lord God, who is and who was and who is to come, the Almighty.

A Vision of Christ

9 I, John, your brother who share with you in Jesus the persecution and the kingdom and the patient endurance, was on the island called Patmos because of the word of God and the testimony of Jesus.[f] [10]I was in the spirit[g] on the Lord's day, and I heard behind me a loud voice like a trumpet [11]saying, "Write in a book what you see and send it to the seven churches, to Ephesus, to Smyrna, to Pergamum, to Thyatira, to Sardis, to Philadelphia, and to Laodicea."

12 Then I turned to see whose voice it was that spoke to me, and on turning I saw seven golden lampstands, [13]and in the midst of the lampstands I saw one like the Son of Man, clothed with a long robe and with a golden sash across his chest. [14]His head and his hair were white as white wool, white as snow; his eyes were like a flame of fire, [15]his feet were like burnished bronze, refined as in a furnace, and his voice was like the sound of many waters. [16]In his right hand he held seven stars, and from his mouth came a sharp, two-edged sword, and his face was like the sun shining with full force.

17 When I saw him, I fell at his feet as though dead. But he placed his right hand on me, saying,

PRAY IT!

The Alpha and the Omega · Revelation 1:7–20

In the first chapter of Revelation, John introduces God's message to the seven churches. After explaining that he received the message through a vision and that an angel instructed him to communicate it to them, John describes a vision of Christ.

A vision is like a dream. Instead of interpreting it literally, we must look for its deep meaning and be open to its message. For example, in the vision of **Revelation 1:12–16,** a magnificently robed Christ stands amid seven lampstands. **Revelation 1:20** reveals that the lampstands are actually the seven churches. The deeper meaning is that the resurrected Jesus in all his glory and power is watching over the seven churches. Here's another example: **Revelation 1:8** has God saying, "I am the Alpha and the Omega." In the Greek alphabet, "alpha" is the first letter, and "omega" is the last letter. This passage is telling us that God is the beginning and the end, in control of all time, past and future.

If there are some current events that frighten you, take hope from John's image of the risen Christ and pray:

Lord Jesus, all of history and all of the future is in your hands—everything that happens in the world and in my life. Please remind me that you are always with me. Fill me with hope in your love and promise of justice to make everything right again someday. Amen.

---

a Gk *slaves* **b** Gk *and he made* **c** Gk *slave* **d** Other ancient authorities read *washed* **e** Gk *priests to* **f** Or *testimony to Jesus* **g** Or *in the Spirit*

"Do not be afraid; I am the first and the last, [18] and the living one. I was dead, and see, I am alive forever and ever; and I have the keys of Death and of Hades. [19] Now write what you have seen, what is, and what is to take place after this. [20] As for the mystery of the seven stars that you saw in my right hand, and the seven golden lampstands: the seven stars are the angels of the seven churches, and the seven lampstands are the seven churches.

The Message to Ephesus

2 "To the angel of the church in Ephesus write: These are the words of him who holds the seven stars in his right hand, who walks among the seven golden lampstands:

2 "I know your works, your toil and your patient endurance. I know that you cannot tolerate evildoers; you have tested those who claim to be apostles but are not, and have found them to be false. [3] I also know that you are enduring patiently and bearing up for the sake of my name, and that you have not grown weary. [4] But I have this against you, that you have abandoned the love you had at first. [5] Remember then from what you have fallen; repent, and do the works you did at first. If not, I will come to you and remove your lampstand from its place, unless you repent. [6] Yet this is to your credit: you hate the works of the Nicolaitans, which I also hate. [7] Let anyone who has an ear listen to what the Spirit is saying to the churches. To everyone who conquers, I will give permission to eat from the tree of life that is in the paradise of God.

The Message to Smyrna

8 "And to the angel of the church in Smyrna write: These are the words of the first and the last, who was dead and came to life:

9 "I know your affliction and your poverty, even though you are rich. I know the slander on the part of those who say that they are Jews and are not, but are a synagogue of Satan. [10] Do not fear what you are about to suffer. Beware, the devil is about to throw some of you into prison so that you may be tested, and for ten days you will have affliction. Be faithful until death, and I will give you the crown of life. [11] Let anyone who has an ear listen to what the Spirit is saying to the churches. Whoever conquers will not be harmed by the second death.

The Message to Pergamum

12 "And to the angel of the church in Pergamum write: These are the words of him who has the sharp two-edged sword:

13 "I know where you are living, where Satan's throne is. Yet you are holding fast to my name, and you did not deny your faith in me[a] even in the days of Antipas my witness, my faithful one, who was killed among you, where Satan lives. [14] But I have a few things against you: you have some there who hold to the teaching of Balaam, who taught Balak to

LIVE IT!

Lukewarm Faith · Revelation 2–3

The messages addressed to the seven churches in Asia Minor (modern-day Turkey) are not predictions of the future. John calls these actual communities to deeper faith in the same way the prophets of the Old Testament called Israel to return to God's covenant. Two churches are praised (Smyrna and Philadelphia), two are scolded (Sardis and Laodicea), and the remaining three receive both praise and criticism. The churches are corrected, because they have tolerated leaders whose teaching contradicts the true gospel message and because their faith has become "lukewarm," lacking the devotion it had when they first became Christians.

• If John wrote a prophecy to your church or youth group, what would he praise and what would he criticize?

• Is your community on fire in living the gospel, or is it lukewarm in its commitment? What can you do to encourage it toward deeper faith?

• How does your own faith measure up? What steps can you take to deepen your love and devotion for Jesus?

a Or *deny my faith*

put a stumbling block before the people of Israel, so that they would eat food sacrificed to idols and practice fornication. ¹⁵So you also have some who hold to the teaching of the Nicolaitans. ¹⁶Repent then. If not, I will come to you soon and make war against them with the sword of my mouth. ¹⁷Let anyone who has an ear listen to what the Spirit is saying to the churches. To everyone who conquers I will give some of the hidden manna, and I will give a white stone, and on the white stone is written a new name that no one knows except the one who receives it.

The Message to Thyatira

18 "And to the angel of the church in Thyatira write: These are the words of the Son of God, who has eyes like a flame of fire, and whose feet are like burnished bronze:

19 "I know your works—your love, faith, service, and patient endurance. I know that your last works are greater than the first. ²⁰But I have this against you: you tolerate that woman Jezebel, who calls herself a prophet and is teaching and beguiling my servants*a* to practice fornication and to eat food sacrificed to idols. ²¹I gave her time to repent, but she refuses to repent of her fornication. ²²Beware, I am throwing her on a bed, and those who commit adultery with her I am throwing into great distress, unless they repent of her doings; ²³and I will strike her children dead. And all the churches will know that I am the one who searches minds and hearts, and I will give to each of you as your works deserve. ²⁴But to the rest of you in Thyatira, who do not hold this teaching, who have not learned what some call 'the deep things of Satan,' to you I say, I do not lay on you any other burden; ²⁵only hold fast to what you have until I come. ²⁶To everyone who conquers and continues to do my works to the end,

I will give authority over the nations;
²⁷ to rule*b* them with an iron rod,

as when clay pots are shattered—
²⁸even as I also received authority from my Father. To the one who conquers I will also give the morning star. ²⁹Let anyone who has an ear listen to what the Spirit is saying to the churches.

The Message to Sardis

3 "And to the angel of the church in Sardis write: These are the words of him who has the seven spirits of God and the seven stars:

"I know your works; you have a name of being

Opening the Door
Revelation 3:20

Imagine a door in a garden, overgrown with vines. The vines show that it obviously hasn't been opened in a long time. And as you look closer, you realize it has no outside latch or knob—it can be opened only from the inside. And Jesus is standing in front of the door, knocking patiently.

The door is the door to our hearts, and Jesus is standing on the other side, knocking, not pounding. Jesus will not force his way into our lives. He seeks a close friendship with us, and a real friendship. Real love always involves a free choice. No one can choose to open the door but you.

- What's your relationship with Christ like right now? Is the door of your life open to let Jesus in, or has it been closed for a while?
- What steps can you take to open your heart and life to Jesus?

alive, but you are dead. ²Wake up, and strengthen what remains and is on the point of death, for I have not found your works perfect in the sight of my God. ³Remember then what you received and heard; obey it, and repent. If you do not wake up, I will come like a thief, and you will not know at what hour I will come to you. ⁴Yet you have still a few persons in Sardis who have not soiled their clothes; they will walk with me, dressed in white, for they are worthy. ⁵If you conquer, you will be clothed like them in white robes, and I will not blot your name out of the book of life; I will confess your name before my Father and before his angels. ⁶Let anyone who has an ear listen to what the Spirit is saying to the churches.

The Message to Philadelphia

7 "And to the angel of the church in Philadelphia write:

These are the words of the holy one, the
true one,

a Gk slaves *b* Or to shepherd

who has the key of David,
who opens and no one will
shut,
who shuts and no one opens:

8 "I know your works. Look, I have set before you an open door, which no one is able to shut. I know that you have but little power, and yet you have kept my word and have not denied my name. [9] I will make those of the synagogue of Satan who say that they are Jews and are not, but are lying— I will make them come and bow down before your feet, and they will learn that I have loved you. [10] Because you have kept my word of patient endurance, I will keep you from the hour of trial that is coming on the whole world to test the inhabitants of the earth. [11] I am coming soon; hold fast to what you have, so that no one may seize your crown. [12] If you conquer, I will make you a pillar in the temple of my God; you will never go out of it. I will write on you the name of my God, and the name of the city of my God, the new Jerusalem that comes down from my God out of heaven, and my own new name. [13] Let anyone who has an ear listen to what the Spirit is saying to the churches.

The Message to Laodicea

14 "And to the angel of the church in Laodicea write: The words of the Amen, the faithful and true witness, the origin[a] of God's creation:

15 "I know your works; you are neither cold nor hot. I wish that you were either cold or hot. [16] So, because you are lukewarm, and neither cold nor hot, I am about to spit you out of my mouth. [17] For you say, 'I am rich, I have prospered, and I need nothing.' You do not realize that you are wretched, pitiable, poor, blind, and naked. [18] Therefore I counsel you to buy from me gold refined by fire so that you may be rich; and white robes to clothe you and to keep the shame of your nakedness from being seen; and salve to anoint your eyes so that you may see. [19] I reprove and discipline those whom I love. Be earnest, therefore, and repent. [20] Listen! I am standing at the door, knocking; if you hear my voice and open the door, I will come in to you and eat with you, and you with me. [21] To the one who conquers I will give a place with me on my throne, just as I myself conquered and sat down with my Father on his throne. [22] Let anyone who has an ear listen to what the Spirit is saying to the churches."

a Or beginning b Or in the Spirit

The Heavenly Worship

4 After this I looked, and there in heaven a door stood open! And the first voice, which I had heard speaking to me like a trumpet, said, "Come up here, and I will show you what must take place after this." [2] At once I was in the spirit,[b] and there in heaven stood a throne, with one seated on the throne! [3] And the one seated there looks like jasper and carnelian, and around the throne is a rainbow that looks like an emerald. [4] Around the throne are twenty-four thrones, and seated on the thrones are twenty-four elders, dressed in white robes, with golden crowns on their heads. [5] Coming from the throne are flashes of lightning, and rumblings and peals of thunder, and in front of the

STUDY IT!

Jesus, Lord of All Time
Revelation 4–5

After the messages to the churches in Asia, John presents several visions that reveal God's actions through time in chapter 4. The vision of God's throne is the background of the whole book of Revelation. It symbolizes God's authority over all time. The vision is enhanced by heavenly worship in which God is proclaimed and praised: "Holy, holy, holy, the Lord God the Almighty, who was and is and is to come" (Revelation 4:8).

The vision continues with two standout symbols in chapter 5: a sealed scroll and a lamb. God holds a scroll, but its meaning is hidden—until a bloody lamb appears. It's the risen Jesus, carrying in his body the signs of his death as a reminder that his sacrifice was a victorious event. Because of it, he is the only one who can open the scroll and reveal the mystery of death and life.

Read both visions again and experience the honor, glory, and power of Christ. Let these visions reinforce your faith and renew your hope every time you wonder about the meaning of an event you can't make sense of.

throne burn seven flaming torches, which are the seven spirits of God; [6]and in front of the throne there is something like a sea of glass, like crystal.

Around the throne, and on each side of the throne, are four living creatures, full of eyes in front and behind: [7]the first living creature like a lion, the second living creature like an ox, the third living creature with a face like a human face, and the fourth living creature like a flying eagle. [8]And the four living creatures, each of them with six wings, are full of eyes all around and inside. Day and night without ceasing they sing,

"Holy, holy, holy,
the Lord God the Almighty,
who was and is and is to come."

[9]And whenever the living creatures give glory and honor and thanks to the one who is seated on the throne, who lives forever and ever, [10]the twenty-four elders fall before the one who is seated on the throne and worship the one who lives forever and ever; they cast their crowns before the throne, singing,

[11] "You are worthy, our Lord and God,
to receive glory and honor and power,
for you created all things,
and by your will they existed and were created."

The Scroll and the Lamb

5 Then I saw in the right hand of the one seated on the throne a scroll written on the inside and on the back, sealed[a] with seven seals; [2]and I saw a mighty angel proclaiming with a loud

voice, "Who is worthy to open the scroll and break its seals?" [3]And no one in heaven or on earth or under the earth was able to open the scroll or to look into it. [4]And I began to weep bitterly because no one was found worthy to open the scroll or to look into it. [5]Then one of the elders said to me, "Do not weep. See, the Lion of the tribe of Judah, the Root of David, has conquered, so that he can open the scroll and its seven seals."

6 Then I saw between the throne and the four living creatures and among the elders a Lamb standing as if it had been slaughtered, having seven horns and seven eyes, which are the seven spirits of God sent out into all the earth. [7]He went and took the scroll from the right hand of the one who was seated on the throne. [8]When he had taken the scroll, the four living creatures and the twenty-four elders fell before the Lamb, each holding a harp and golden bowls full of incense, which are the prayers of the saints. [9]They sing a new song:

"You are worthy to take the scroll
and to open its seals,

LIVE IT!

Pure Praise · Revelation 4–5

Over and over in John's vision of heaven, we find enthusiastic praise being offered to God or to the Lamb of God, who is Jesus. There are angels, incense, fantastic creatures, jewels, gold, elders, white-robed martyrs, and a crowd too great to number. The scenes of this vision inspire us to add our voice to theirs, to praise the majesty of God and the saving sacrifice of Christ.

Some Christians and churches praise God with loud, spontaneous praise. But many others express their praise through softer songs and more solemn prayers. Whatever our preference, we should be enthusiastic and authentic with our praise. It's not a matter of style, but of the sincerity of our hearts.

- How does the vision of the "thousands, singing with full voice" (Revelation 5:11-12) encourage you to be more bold in your praise of God?
- How can you sing and pray more from your heart in church and when you're alone?
- Practice praising God without asking for anything.

---

a Or *written on the inside, and sealed on the back*

STUDY IT!

Numbers and Colors · Revelation 4–7

There's deeper meaning to the numbers and colors of Revelation, and learning about them adds understanding to these verses. The numbers seven and twelve symbolize fullness or perfection. The number four symbolizes universality (as in the four directions on a compass). One thousand symbolizes a multitude or a quantity too big to count. So the twenty-four elders (Revelation 4:4) represent the perfection of the twelve tribes of Israel and the twelve disciples. The Lamb with horns and eyes (Revelation 5:6) represents the risen Christ, who has the fullness of power (seven horns) and perfect knowledge (seven eyes). The 144,000 who will be saved (Revelation 7:4) represent a chosen multitude too big to count, because 144,000 equals twelve times twelve times a thousand.

The color white symbolizes victory or worthiness, and red symbolizes bloodshed. The people who are slaughtered and given white robes are the martyrs who gave up their lives for their faith (Revelation 6:9-11). They are victorious, because God raised them to eternal life.

for you were slaughtered and by your blood
    you ransomed for God
    saints from[a] every tribe and language and
      people and nation;
10 you have made them to be a kingdom and
    priests serving[b] our God,
    and they will reign on earth."

11 Then I looked, and I heard the voice of many angels surrounding the throne and the living creatures and the elders; they numbered myriads of myriads and thousands of thousands, 12 singing with full voice,

"Worthy is the Lamb that was slaughtered
to receive power and wealth and wisdom and
    might
and honor and glory and blessing!"

13 Then I heard every creature in heaven and on earth and under the earth and in the sea, and all that is in them, singing,

"To the one seated on the throne and to the
    Lamb
be blessing and honor and glory and might
forever and ever!"

14 And the four living creatures said, "Amen!" And the elders fell down and worshiped.

The Seven Seals

6 Then I saw the Lamb open one of the seven seals, and I heard one of the four living creatures call out, as with a voice of thunder, "Come!"[c] 2 I looked, and there was a white horse! Its rider had a bow; a crown was given to him, and

he came out conquering and to conquer.

3 When he opened the second seal, I heard the second living creature call out, "Come!"[c] 4 And out came[d] another horse, bright red; its rider was permitted to take peace from the earth, so that people would slaughter one another; and he was given a great sword.

5 When he opened the third seal, I heard the third living creature call out, "Come!"[c] I looked, and there was a black horse! Its rider held a pair of scales in his hand, 6 and I heard what seemed to be a voice in the midst of the four living creatures saying, "A quart of wheat for a day's pay,[e] and three quarts of barley for a day's pay,[e] but do not damage the olive oil and the wine!"

7 When he opened the fourth seal, I heard the voice of the fourth living creature call out, "Come!"[c] 8 I looked and there was a pale green horse! Its rider's name was Death, and Hades followed with him; they were given authority over a fourth of the earth, to kill with sword, famine, and pestilence, and by the wild animals of the earth.

9 When he opened the fifth seal, I saw under the altar the souls of those who had been slaughtered for the word of God and for the testimony they had given; 10 they cried out with a loud voice, "Sovereign Lord, holy and true, how long will it be before you judge and avenge our blood on the inhabitants of the earth?" 11 They were each given a white robe and told to rest a little longer, until the number would be complete both of their fellow servants[f] and of their brothers and sisters,[g] who were soon to be

a Gk ransomed for God from   b Gk priests to   c Or "Go!"   d Or went   e Gk a denarius   f Gk slaves   g Gk brothers

STUDY IT!

The Seven Seals and Seven Trumpets
Revelation 6–9

As the vision continues, the Lamb opens the seven seals on the scroll and reveals the great forces in salvation history. The opening of the first four seals reveals the four horses of the apocalypse, which bring conquest, strife, famine, and plagues. These are the things that throughout history have made people yearn for God's salvation.

The opening of the fifth seal reveals the souls of the martyrs, who demand justice. Their white robes indicate that they are already with the risen Christ. They are waiting for other martyrs, but this stage will end soon.

The opening of the sixth seal reveals how God will get justice for the martyrs. History will change, and all people, even the powerful, will suffer. The visions of the census and of the great crowd (Revelation 7) reveal the destiny of Christians. The vision contains many reminders of the Exodus story (Exodus 12–14). After this, a countless multitude from all nations, tribes, peoples, and languages will experience God's salvation and sing of God's glory.

Finally, the Lamb opens the last seal. Seven more trumpets are revealed. When they are blown by angels, a new series of plagues is released (Revelation 8:6–9:21). One-third of the people are destroyed by these plagues, so that those remaining might repent. But many people do not change in spite of these warnings.

This vision tells us that no matter what evil besets us in the past, present, or future, God has saved, is saving, and will save the faithful. One day God's justice will be complete and God's kingdom will be restored perfectly.

---

killed as they themselves had been killed.

12 When he opened the sixth seal, I looked, and there came a great earthquake; the sun became black as sackcloth, the full moon became like blood, [13] and the stars of the sky fell to the earth as the fig tree drops its winter fruit when shaken by a gale. [14] The sky vanished like a scroll rolling itself up, and every mountain and island was removed from its place. [15] Then the kings of the earth and the magnates and the generals and the rich and the powerful, and everyone, slave and free, hid in the caves and among the rocks of the mountains, [16] calling to the mountains and rocks, "Fall on us and hide us from the face of the one seated on the throne and from the wrath of the Lamb; [17] for the great day of their wrath has come, and who is able to stand?"

7   The 144,000 of Israel Sealed

After this I saw four angels standing at the four corners of the earth, holding back the four winds of the earth so that no wind could blow on earth or sea or against any tree. [2] I saw another angel ascending from the rising of the sun, having the seal of the living God, and he called with a loud voice to the four angels who had been given power to damage earth and sea, [3] saying, "Do not damage the earth or the sea or the trees, until we have marked the servants[a] of our God with a seal on their foreheads."

4 And I heard the number of those who were sealed, one hundred forty-four thousand, sealed out of every tribe of the people of Israel:

5 From the tribe of Judah twelve thousand sealed,
   from the tribe of Reuben twelve thousand,
   from the tribe of Gad twelve thousand,
6 from the tribe of Asher twelve thousand,
   from the tribe of Naphtali twelve thousand,
   from the tribe of Manasseh twelve thousand,
7 from the tribe of Simeon twelve thousand,
   from the tribe of Levi twelve thousand,
   from the tribe of Issachar twelve thousand,
8 from the tribe of Zebulun twelve thousand,
   from the tribe of Joseph twelve thousand,
   from the tribe of Benjamin twelve thousand sealed.

The Multitude from Every Nation

9 After this I looked, and there was a great multitude that no one could count, from every nation, from all tribes and peoples and languages, standing

---

a Gk *slaves*

STUDY IT!

Life After Suffering · Revelation 7:2–14

What do you do when things get really difficult? John was answering that question for his readers. John describes a looming ordeal and how the faithful will be marked on the forehead as a sign of God's protection. This sign does not free them from the suffering and death that happen to all humanity, but provides God's protection and a reminder to trust God during it. John then describes a multitude in heaven that have already survived the ordeal and remained faithful to God.

The important message for John's audience is how those in heaven survived. The angel says that they were made pure through the blood of the Lamb. That is, they united their lives with the suffering, death, and resurrection of Jesus Christ and remained faithful throughout. And God remained faithful to them in fulfilling the covenant and providing the promised eternal spiritual life.

We too are called to resist sin and offer our lives to God, just like the faithful in John's vision, even if it means facing a time of suffering. We are called to be the new generation of witnesses—to be an example to others to strengthen them on their journey.

---

before the throne and before the Lamb, robed in white, with palm branches in their hands. ¹⁰They cried out in a loud voice, saying,

"Salvation belongs to our God who is seated
on the throne, and to the Lamb!"
¹¹And all the angels stood around the throne and around the elders and the four living creatures, and they fell on their faces before the throne and worshiped God, ¹²singing,

"Amen! Blessing and glory and wisdom
and thanksgiving and honor
and power and might
be to our God forever and ever! Amen."
13 Then one of the elders addressed me, saying, "Who are these, robed in white, and where have they come from?" ¹⁴I said to him, "Sir, you are the one that knows." Then he said to me, "These are they

who have come out of the great ordeal; they have washed their robes and made them white in the blood of the Lamb.

¹⁵ For this reason they are before the throne
of God,
and worship him day and night within his
temple,
and the one who is seated on the throne
will shelter them.
¹⁶ They will hunger no more, and thirst no more;
the sun will not strike them,
nor any scorching heat;
¹⁷ for the Lamb at the center of the throne will
be their shepherd,
and he will guide them to springs of the
water of life,
and God will wipe away every tear from their
eyes."

> "They will hunger no more, and thirst no more ... for the Lamb at the center of the throne will be their shepherd ... and God will wipe away every tear from their eyes."
> —Revelation 7:16–17

8 The Seventh Seal and the Golden Censer

When the Lamb opened the seventh seal, there was silence in heaven for about half an hour. ²And I saw the seven angels who stand before God, and seven trumpets were given to them.

3 Another angel with a golden censer came and stood at the altar; he was given a great quantity of incense to offer with the prayers of all the saints on the golden altar that is before the throne. ⁴And the smoke of the incense, with the prayers of the saints, rose before God from the hand of the angel. ⁵Then

the angel took the censer and filled it with fire from the altar and threw it on the earth; and there were peals of thunder, rumblings, flashes of lightning, and an earthquake.

The Seven Trumpets

6 Now the seven angels who had the seven trumpets made ready to blow them.

7 The first angel blew his trumpet, and there came hail and fire, mixed with blood, and they were hurled to the earth; and a third of the earth was burned up, and a third of the trees were burned up, and all green grass was burned up.

8 The second angel blew his trumpet, and something like a great mountain, burning with fire, was thrown into the sea. 9A third of the sea became blood, a third of the living creatures in the sea died, and a third of the ships were destroyed.

10 The third angel blew his trumpet, and a great star fell from heaven, blazing like a torch, and it fell on a third of the rivers and on the springs of water. 11The name of the star is Wormwood. A third of the waters became wormwood, and many died from the water, because it was made bitter.

12 The fourth angel blew his trumpet, and a third of the sun was struck, and a third of the moon, and a third of the stars, so that a third of their light was darkened; a third of the day was kept from shining, and likewise the night.

13 Then I looked, and I heard an eagle crying with a loud voice as it flew in midheaven, "Woe, woe, woe to the inhabitants of the earth, at the blasts of the other trumpets that the three angels are about to blow!"

9 And the fifth angel blew his trumpet, and I saw a star that had fallen from heaven to earth, and he was given the key to the shaft of the bottomless pit; 2he opened the shaft of the bottomless pit, and from the shaft rose smoke like the smoke of a great furnace, and the sun and the air were darkened with the smoke from the shaft. 3Then from the smoke came locusts on the earth, and they were given authority like the authority of scorpions of the earth. 4They were told not to damage the grass of the earth or any green growth or any tree, but only those people who do not have the seal of God on their foreheads. 5They were allowed to torture them for five months, but not to kill them, and their torture was like the torture of a scorpion when it stings someone. 6And in those days people will seek death but will not find it; they will long to die, but death will flee from them.

7 In appearance the locusts were like horses equipped for battle. On their heads were what looked like crowns of gold; their faces were like human faces, 8their hair like women's hair, and their teeth like lions' teeth; 9they had scales like iron

breastplates, and the noise of their wings was like the noise of many chariots with horses rushing into battle. [10]They have tails like scorpions, with stingers, and in their tails is their power to harm people for five months. [11]They have as king over them the angel of the bottomless pit; his name in Hebrew is Abaddon,[a] and in Greek he is called Apollyon.[b]

12 The first woe has passed. There are still two woes to come.

13 Then the sixth angel blew his trumpet, and I heard a voice from the four[c] horns of the golden altar before God, [14]saying to the sixth angel who had the trumpet, "Release the four angels who are bound at the great river Euphrates." [15]So the four angels were released, who had been held ready for the hour, the day, the month, and the year, to kill a third of humankind. [16]The number of the troops of cavalry was two hundred million; I heard their number. [17]And this was how I saw the horses in my vision: the riders wore breastplates the color of fire and of sapphire[d] and of sulfur; the heads of the horses were like lions' heads, and fire and smoke and sulfur came out of their mouths. [18]By these three plagues a third of humankind was killed, by the fire and smoke and sulfur coming out of their mouths. [19]For the power of the horses is in their mouths and in their tails; their tails are like serpents, having heads; and with them they inflict harm.

20 The rest of humankind, who were not killed by these plagues, did not repent of the works of their hands or give up worshiping demons and idols of gold and silver and bronze and stone and wood, which cannot see or hear or walk. [21]And they did not repent of their murders or their sorceries or their fornication or their thefts.

The Angel with the Little Scroll

10 And I saw another mighty angel coming down from heaven, wrapped in a cloud, with a rainbow over his head; his face was like the sun, and his legs like pillars of fire. [2]He held a little scroll open in his hand. Setting his right foot on the sea and his left foot on the land, [3]he gave a great shout, like a lion roaring. And when he shouted, the seven thunders sounded. [4]And when the seven thunders had sounded, I was about to write, but I heard a voice from heaven saying, "Seal up what the seven thunders have said, and do not write it down." [5]Then the angel whom I saw standing on the sea

and the land
    raised his right hand to heaven
6   and swore by him who lives forever and ever,

who created heaven and what is in it, the earth and what is in it, and the sea and what is in it: "There will be no more delay, [7]but in the days when the seventh angel is to blow his trumpet, the mystery of God will be fulfilled, as he announced to his servants[e] the prophets."

8 Then the voice that I had heard from heaven spoke to me again, saying, "Go, take the scroll that is open in the hand of the angel who is standing on the sea and on the land." [9]So I went to the angel and told him to give me the little scroll; and he said to me, "Take it, and eat; it will be bitter to your stomach, but sweet as honey in your mouth." [10]So I took the little scroll from the hand of the angel and ate it; it was sweet as honey in my mouth, but when I had eaten it, my stomach was made bitter.

11 Then they said to me, "You must prophesy again about many peoples and nations and languages and kings."

The Two Witnesses

11 Then I was given a measuring rod like a staff, and I was told, "Come and measure the temple of God and the altar and those who worship there, [2]but do not measure the court outside the temple; leave that out, for it is given over to the nations, and they will trample over the holy city for forty-two months. [3]And I will grant my two witnesses authority to prophesy for one thousand two hundred sixty days, wearing sackcloth."

4 These are the two olive trees and the two lampstands that stand before the Lord of the earth. [5]And if anyone wants to harm them, fire pours from their mouth and consumes their foes; anyone who wants to harm them must be killed in this manner. [6]They have authority to shut the sky, so that no rain may fall during the days of their prophesying, and they have authority over the waters to turn them into blood, and to strike the earth with every kind of plague, as often as they desire.

7 When they have finished their testimony, the beast that comes up from the bottomless pit will make war on them and conquer them and kill them, [8]and their dead bodies will lie in the street of the great city that is prophetically[f] called Sodom and Egypt, where also their Lord was crucified. [9]For

---

a That is, *Destruction* b That is, *Destroyer* c Other ancient authorities lack *four* d Gk *hyacinth* e Gk *slaves* f Or *allegorically*; Gk *spiritually*

God Is in Control
Revelation 11:15–18

The world is a wonderful place, full of life and hope. At the same time, it's full of pain, suffering, sickness, and death. It can seem frightening and out of control. Wars break out. Drought threatens the lives of millions. A friend dies in a senseless car accident. Terrorists attack and kill innocent people. Climate change threatens life as we know it. It's easy to wonder why God allows such things.

The book of Revelation was written to encourage the people of John's time that, despite the evil that happens, God is in control. It can do the same for us too. The song in **Revelation 11:15–18** reminds us that there will come a time when the just will be rewarded and the wicked punished. And although God's reign isn't yet fully realized, we are called to be people of justice, peace, and hope to a world desperately seeking these things.

three and a half days members of the peoples and tribes and languages and nations will gaze at their dead bodies and refuse to let them be placed in a tomb; [10] and the inhabitants of the earth will gloat over them and celebrate and exchange presents, because these two prophets had been a torment to the inhabitants of the earth.

[11] But after the three and a half days, the breath[a] of life from God entered them, and they stood on their feet, and those who saw them were terrified. [12] Then they[b] heard a loud voice from heaven saying to them, "Come up here!" And they went up to heaven in a cloud while their enemies watched them. [13] At that moment there was a great earthquake, and a tenth of the city fell; seven thousand people were killed in the earthquake, and the rest were terrified and gave glory to the God of heaven.

[14] The second woe has passed. The third woe is coming very soon.

The Seventh Trumpet

[15] Then the seventh angel blew his trumpet, and there were loud voices in heaven, saying,

"The kingdom of the world has become the
kingdom of our Lord
and of his Messiah,[c]
and he will reign forever and ever."

[16] Then the twenty-four elders who sit on their thrones before God fell on their faces and worshiped God, [17] singing,

"We give you thanks, Lord God Almighty,
who are and who were,
for you have taken your great power
and begun to reign.
[18] The nations raged,
but your wrath has come,
and the time for judging the dead,
for rewarding your servants,[d] the prophets
and saints and all who fear your name,
both small and great,
and for destroying those who destroy the
earth."

[19] Then God's temple in heaven was opened, and the ark of his covenant was seen within his temple; and there were flashes of lightning, rumblings, peals of thunder, an earthquake, and heavy hail.

The Woman and the Dragon

12 A great portent appeared in heaven: a woman clothed with the sun, with the moon under her feet, and on her head a crown of twelve stars. [2] She was pregnant and was crying out in birth pangs, in the agony of giving birth. [3] Then another portent appeared in heaven: a great red dragon, with seven heads and ten horns, and seven diadems on his heads. [4] His tail swept down a third of the stars of heaven and threw them to the earth. Then the dragon stood before the woman who was about to bear a child, so that he might devour her child as soon as it was born. [5] And she gave birth to a son, a male child, who is to rule[e] all the nations with a rod of iron. But her child was snatched away and taken to God and to his throne; [6] and the woman fled into the wilderness, where she has a place prepared by God, so that there she can be nourished for one thousand two hundred sixty days.

Michael Defeats the Dragon

[7] And war broke out in heaven; Michael and his angels fought against the dragon. The dragon and

a Or *the spirit* b Other ancient authorities read *I* c Gk *Christ* d Gk *slaves* e Or *to shepherd*

The Woman and the Dragon · Revelation 12

The vision in this chapter symbolizes the great battle between Christ and Satan. The pregnant woman in the opening scene represents Israel, from which the Messiah will come. The dragon waiting to devour her child is a symbol for Satan (Revelation 12:9). This child is the Messiah, Jesus Christ, who will rule all the nations. So some Christians have equated the woman with Mary, the mother of Jesus.

The conflict moves from heaven to earth when Satan fails to devour the child and is thrown down from his place in heaven. The dragon continues his pursuit of the woman on earth. The woman now represents the Church. The "rest of her children" represent its members, whom the dragon angrily persecutes, because he didn't succeed in devouring her child.

The images in this vision can be hard to follow, but through them John is telling the persecuted Christians of his time to have hope because, in the end, Christ will totally and completely destroy Satan (Revelation 20:1-10).

his angels fought back, [8]but they were defeated, and there was no longer any place for them in heaven. [9]The great dragon was thrown down, that ancient serpent, who is called the Devil and Satan, the deceiver of the whole world—he was thrown down to the earth, and his angels were thrown down with him.

10 Then I heard a loud voice in heaven, proclaiming,

"Now have come the salvation and the power
and the kingdom of our God
and the authority of his Messiah,[a]
for the accuser of our comrades[b] has been
thrown down,
who accuses them day and night before
our God.
[11] But they have conquered him by the blood of
the Lamb
and by the word of their testimony,
for they did not cling to life even in the face of
death.
[12] Rejoice then, you heavens
and those who dwell in them!
But woe to the earth and the sea,
for the devil has come down to you
with great wrath,
because he knows that his time is short!"

The Dragon Fights Again on Earth

13 So when the dragon saw that he had been thrown down to the earth, he pursued[c] the woman who had given birth to the male child. [14]But the woman was given the two wings of the great eagle, so that she could fly from the serpent into the wilderness, to her place where she is nourished for a time, and times, and half a time. [15]Then from his mouth the serpent poured water like a river after the woman, to sweep her away with the flood. [16]But the earth came to the help of the woman; it opened its mouth and swallowed the river that the dragon had poured from his mouth. [17]Then the dragon was angry with the woman, and went off to make war on the rest of her children, those who keep the commandments of God and hold the testimony of Jesus.

The First Beast

18 Then the dragon[d] took his stand on the sand of the seashore. [1]And I saw a beast rising out of the sea, having ten horns and seven heads; and on its horns were ten diadems, and on its heads were blasphemous names. [2]And the beast that I saw was like a leopard, its feet were like a bear's, and its mouth was like a lion's mouth. And the dragon gave it his power and his throne and great authority. [3]One of its heads seemed to have received a death-blow, but its mortal wound[e] had been healed. In amazement the whole earth followed the beast. [4]They worshiped the dragon, for he had given his authority to the beast, and they worshiped the beast, saying, "Who is like the beast, and who can fight against it?"

5 The beast was given a mouth uttering haughty and blasphemous words, and it was allowed to exercise authority for forty-two months. [6]It opened

13

---

a Gk *Christ*   b Gk *brothers*   c Or *persecuted*   d Gk *Then he*; other ancient authorities read *Then I stood*   e Gk *the plague of its death*

its mouth to utter blasphemies against God, blaspheming his name and his dwelling, that is, those who dwell in heaven. ⁷Also it was allowed to make war on the saints and to conquer them.ᵃ It was given authority over every tribe and people and language and nation, ⁸and all the inhabitants of the earth will worship it, everyone whose name has not been written from the foundation of the world in the book of life of the Lamb that was slaughtered.ᵇ

9 Let anyone who has an ear listen:

¹⁰ If you are to be taken captive,
　　into captivity you go;
　if you kill with the sword,
　　with the sword you must be
　　　killed.

Here is a call for the endurance and faith of the saints.

The Second Beast

11 Then I saw another beast that rose out of the earth; it had two horns like a lamb and it spoke like a dragon. ¹²It exercises all the authority of the first beast on its behalf, and it makes the earth and its inhabitants worship the first beast, whose mortal woundᶜ had been healed. ¹³It performs great signs, even making fire come down from heaven to earth in the sight of all; ¹⁴and by the signs that it is allowed to perform on behalf of the beast, it deceives the inhabitants of earth, telling them to make an image for the beast that had been wounded by the swordᵈ

and yet lived; ¹⁵and it was allowed to give breathᵉ to the image of the beast so that the image of the beast could even speak and cause those who would not worship the image of the beast to be killed. ¹⁶Also it causes all, both small and great, both rich and poor, both free and slave, to be marked on the right hand or the forehead, ¹⁷so that no one can buy or sell who does not have the mark, that is, the name of the beast or the number of its name. ¹⁸This calls for wisdom: let anyone with understanding calculate the number of the beast, for it is the number of a person. Its number is six hundred sixty-six.ᶠ

The Lamb and the 144,000

14 Then I looked, and there was the Lamb, standing on Mount Zion! And with him were one hundred forty-four thousand who had his name and his Father's name written on their foreheads. ²And I heard a voice from heaven like the sound of many waters and like the sound of loud thunder; the voice I heard was like the sound of harpists playing on their harps, ³and they sing a new song before the throne and before the four living creatures and before the elders. No one could learn that song except the one hundred forty-four thousand who have been redeemed from the earth. ⁴It is these who have not defiled themselves with women, for they are virgins; these follow the Lamb wherever he goes. They have been redeemed from humankind as first fruits for God and the Lamb,

STUDY IT!

The Number of the Beast · Revelation 13

The vision of the two beasts in chapter 13 is a continuation of the vision about the woman and the dragon. The beasts represent the Roman Empire and its emperor, which at the time threatened the true practice of Christianity. Roman leaders expected all citizens, including Christians, to offer sacrifices to the Roman gods and to worship the emperor as though he were a god. This may have been especially true in the cities in Asia Minor, which were trying to prove their loyalty to the Roman emperor.

The number of the second beast is 666 (Revelation 13:18). Most scholars believe that this stands for Nero Caesar, who was the emperor of Rome from A.D. 54 to 68. Their reasoning is that when the Greek letters for Nero's name and title are converted into Hebrew letters, which also have numerical equivalents, they add up to the number 666. Six is one less than seven, the perfect number, so 666 represents something less than perfect—or evil itself. Nero was responsible for some vicious attacks on Christians in Rome. The book of Revelation was written after Nero committed suicide, but there were widespread rumors that he hadn't died and had come out of hiding in the east to lead this new wave of persecution against Christians (Revelation 13:3).

ᵃ Other ancient authorities lack this sentence ᵇ Or *written in the book of life of the Lamb that was slaughtered from the foundation of the world* ᶜ Gk *whose plague of its death* ᵈ Or *that had received the plague of the sword* ᵉ Or *spirit* ᶠ Other ancient authorities read *six hundred sixteen*

[5] and in their mouth no lie was found; they are blameless.

The Messages of the Three Angels

6 Then I saw another angel flying in midheaven, with an eternal gospel to proclaim to those who live[a] on the earth—to every nation and tribe and language and people. [7] He said in a loud voice, "Fear God and give him glory, for the hour of his judgment has come; and worship him who made heaven and earth, the sea and the springs of water."

8 Then another angel, a second, followed, saying, "Fallen, fallen is Babylon the great! She has made all nations drink of the wine of the wrath of her fornication."

9 Then another angel, a third, followed them, crying with a loud voice, "Those who worship the beast and its image, and receive a mark on their foreheads or on their hands, [10] they will also drink the wine of God's wrath, poured unmixed into the cup of his anger, and they will be tormented with fire and sulfur in the presence of the holy angels and in the presence of the Lamb. [11] And the smoke of their torment goes up forever and ever. There is no rest day or night for those who worship the beast and its image and for anyone who receives the mark of its name."

12 Here is a call for the endurance of the saints, those who keep the commandments of God and hold fast to the faith of[b] Jesus.

13 And I heard a voice from heaven saying, "Write this: Blessed are the dead who from now on die in the Lord." "Yes," says the Spirit, "they will rest from their labors, for their deeds follow them."

Reaping the Earth's Harvest

14 Then I looked, and there was a white cloud, and seated on the cloud was one like the Son of Man, with a golden crown on his head, and a sharp sickle in his hand! [15] Another angel came out of the temple, calling with a loud voice to the one who sat on the cloud, "Use your sickle and reap, for the hour to reap has come, because the harvest of the earth is fully ripe." [16] So the one who sat on the cloud swung his sickle over the earth, and the earth was reaped.

17 Then another angel came out of the temple in heaven, and he too had a sharp sickle. [18] Then another angel came out from the altar, the angel who has authority over fire, and he called with a loud voice to him who had the sharp sickle, "Use your

sharp sickle and gather the clusters of the vine of the earth, for its grapes are ripe." [19] So the angel swung his sickle over the earth and gathered the vintage of the earth, and he threw it into the great wine press of the wrath of God. [20] And the wine press was trodden outside the city, and blood flowed from the wine press, as high as a horse's bridle, for a distance of about two hundred miles.[c]

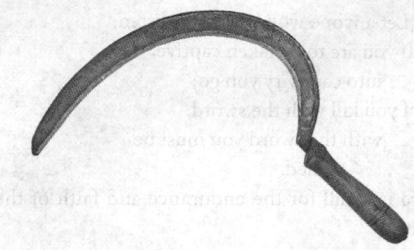

15 The Angels with the Seven Last Plagues

Then I saw another portent in heaven, great and amazing: seven angels with seven plagues, which are the last, for with them the wrath of God is ended.

2 And I saw what appeared to be a sea of glass mixed with fire, and those who had conquered the beast and its image and the number of its name, standing beside the sea of glass with harps of God in their hands. [3] And they sing the song of Moses, the servant[d] of God, and the song of the Lamb:

"Great and amazing are your deeds,
    Lord God the Almighty!
Just and true are your ways,
    King of the nations![e]
4 Lord, who will not fear
    and glorify your name?
For you alone are holy.
    All nations will come
    and worship before you,
for your judgments have been revealed."

5 After this I looked, and the temple of the tent[f] of witness in heaven was opened, [6] and out of the temple came the seven angels with the seven plagues, robed in pure bright linen,[g] with golden sashes across their chests. [7] Then one of the four living creatures gave the seven angels seven golden bowls full of the wrath of God, who lives forever and ever; [8] and the temple was filled with smoke from the glory of God and from his power, and no one

---

a Gk *sit* b Or *to their faith in* c Gk *one thousand six hundred stadia* d Gk *slave* e Other ancient authorities read *the ages* f Or *tabernacle* g Other ancient authorities read *stone*

could enter the temple until the seven plagues of the seven angels were ended.

The Bowls of God's Wrath

16 Then I heard a loud voice from the temple telling the seven angels, "Go and pour out on the earth the seven bowls of the wrath of God." 2 So the first angel went and poured his bowl on the earth, and a foul and painful sore came on those who had the mark of the beast and who worshiped its image.

3 The second angel poured his bowl into the sea, and it became like the blood of a corpse, and every living thing in the sea died.

4 The third angel poured his bowl into the rivers and the springs of water, and they became blood. 5And I heard the angel of the waters say,

"You are just, O Holy One, who are and were,
     for you have judged these things;
6   because they shed the blood of saints and prophets,
     you have given them blood to drink.
It is what they deserve!"
7And I heard the altar respond,

"Yes, O Lord God, the Almighty,
     your judgments are true and just!"

8 The fourth angel poured his bowl on the sun, and it was allowed to scorch people with fire; 9they were scorched by the fierce heat, but they cursed the name of God, who had authority over these plagues, and they did not repent and give him glory.

10 The fifth angel poured his bowl on the throne of the beast, and its kingdom was plunged into darkness; people gnawed their tongues in agony, 11and cursed the God of heaven because of their pains and sores, and they did not repent of their deeds.

12 The sixth angel poured his bowl on the great river Euphrates, and its water was dried up in order to prepare the way for the kings from the east. 13And I saw three foul spirits like frogs coming from the mouth of the dragon, from the mouth of the beast, and from the mouth of the false prophet. 14These are demonic spirits, performing signs, who go abroad to the kings of the whole world, to assemble them for battle on the great day of God the Almighty. 15("See, I am coming like a thief! Blessed is the one who stays awake and is clothed,[a] not going about naked and exposed to shame.") 16And they assembled them at the place that in Hebrew is called Harmagedon.

17 The seventh angel poured his bowl into the air, and a loud voice came out of the temple, from the throne, saying, "It is done!" 18And there came flashes of lightning, rumblings, peals of thunder, and a violent earthquake, such as had not occurred since people were upon the earth, so violent was that earthquake. 19The great city was split into three parts, and the cities of the nations fell. God remembered great Babylon and gave her the wine-cup of the fury of his wrath. 20And every island fled away, and no mountains were to be found; 21and huge hailstones, each weighing about a hundred pounds,[b] dropped from heaven on people, until they cursed God for the plague of the hail, so fearful was that plague.

The Great Whore and the Beast

17 Then one of the seven angels who had the seven bowls came and said to me, "Come, I will show you the judgment of the great whore who is seated on many waters, 2with whom the kings of the earth have committed fornication, and with the wine of whose fornication the inhabitants of the earth have become drunk." 3So he carried me away in the spirit[c] into a wilderness, and I saw a woman sitting on a scarlet beast that was full of blasphemous names, and it had seven heads and ten horns. 4The woman was clothed in purple and scarlet, and adorned with gold and jewels and pearls, holding in her hand a golden cup full of abominations and the impurities of her fornication; 5and on her forehead was written a name, a mystery: "Babylon the great, mother of whores and of earth's abominations." 6And I saw that the woman was drunk with the blood of the saints and the blood of the witnesses to Jesus.

When I saw her, I was greatly amazed. 7But the angel said to me, "Why are you so amazed? I will tell you the mystery of the woman, and of the beast with seven heads and ten horns that carries her. 8The beast that you saw was, and is not, and is about to ascend from the bottomless pit and go to destruction. And the inhabitants of the earth, whose names have not been written in the book of life from the foundation of the world, will be amazed when they see the beast, because it was and is not and is to come.

9 "This calls for a mind that has wisdom: the seven heads are seven mountains on which the woman is seated; also, they are seven kings,

---

a Gk *and keeps his robes*   b Gk *weighing about a talent*   c Or *in the Spirit*

Out of the Lap of Luxury
Revelation 17–18

In John's coded language, the whore called Babylon is Rome, a city built on seven hills. She is dressed in colors that symbolize her royalty (purple) and her obscene and immoral behavior (scarlet). Her gold and pearls are signs of her wealth and excessive luxury. The blasphemous names on her forehead are the titles that should be given to God, such as Lord, Savior, and Son of God, but that Roman emperors claimed instead. By calling her Babylon, John is creating a tie with the capital of another evil empire from the Old Testament (see "Study It: The Fall of Jerusalem," near 2 Kings 25:1–21).

The whore is drunk on the blood of the saints she killed because of their faith. John indicates that her evil is caused by her unrestrained desire for wealth and luxury and her abuse of power (Revelation 18:3–19). He tells his Christian readers that they can be hopeful, even in the midst of so much suffering, because the Lamb (Christ) will conquer the beast in the end (Revelation 17:14).

Since Revelation was written, many other countries have abused their power. The United States is no exception. Consider, for example, its treatment of Native Americans, the practice of slavery, and destruction of the natural environment.

- Where do you think the desire for wealth and luxury has gone too far?
- In what ways can your church or community walk away from pursuing wealth and take more responsibility to ensure justice for all people?
- Have you gotten caught up in the obsession for more stuff?
- What steps can you take to use your resources to help others?

[10]of whom five have fallen, one is living, and the other has not yet come; and when he comes, he must remain only a little while. [11]As for the beast that was and is not, it is an eighth but it belongs to the seven, and it goes to destruction. [12]And the ten horns that you saw are ten kings who have not yet received a kingdom, but they are to receive authority as kings for one hour, together with the beast. [13]These are united in yielding their power and authority to the beast; [14]they will make war on the Lamb, and the Lamb will conquer them, for he is Lord of lords and King of kings, and those with him are called and chosen and faithful."

15 And he said to me, "The waters that you saw, where the whore is seated, are peoples and multitudes and nations and languages. [16]And the ten horns that you saw, they and the beast will hate the whore; they will make her desolate and naked; they will devour her flesh and burn her up with fire. [17]For God has put it into their hearts to carry out his purpose by agreeing to give their kingdom to the beast, until the words of God will be fulfilled. [18]The woman you saw is the great city that rules over the kings of the earth."

The Fall of Babylon

18 After this I saw another angel coming down from heaven, having great authority; and the earth was made bright with his splendor. [2]He called out with a mighty voice,

"Fallen, fallen is Babylon the great!
It has become a dwelling place of demons,
a haunt of every foul spirit,
a haunt of every foul bird,
a haunt of every foul and hateful beast.[a]
3 For all the nations have drunk[b]
of the wine of the wrath of her fornication,
and the kings of the earth have committed fornication with her,
and the merchants of the earth have grown rich from the power[c] of her luxury."
4 Then I heard another voice from heaven saying,
"Come out of her, my people,
so that you do not take part in her sins,
and so that you do not share in her plagues;
5 for her sins are heaped high as heaven,
and God has remembered her iniquities.

---

a Other ancient authorities lack the words *a haunt of every foul beast* and attach the words *and hateful* to the previous line so as to read *a haunt of every foul and hateful bird*   b Other ancient authorities read *She has made all nations drink*   c Or *resources*

6 Render to her as she herself has rendered,
     and repay her double for her deeds;
     mix a double draught for her in the cup
          she mixed.
7 As she glorified herself and lived luxuriously,
     so give her a like measure of torment and
          grief.
   Since in her heart she says,
     'I rule as a queen;
   I am no widow,
     and I will never see grief,'
8 therefore her plagues will come in a single
          day—
     pestilence and mourning and famine—
   and she will be burned with fire;
     for mighty is the Lord God who judges
          her."

9 And the kings of the earth, who committed
fornication and lived in luxury with her, will weep
and wail over her when they see the smoke of her
burning; 10they will stand far off, in fear of her
torment, and say,

   "Alas, alas, the great city,
     Babylon, the mighty city!
   For in one hour your judgment has
          come."

11 And the merchants of the earth weep and
mourn for her, since no one buys their cargo anymore, 12cargo of gold, silver, jewels and pearls, fine
linen, purple, silk and scarlet, all kinds of scented
wood, all articles of ivory, all articles of costly
wood, bronze, iron, and marble, 13cinnamon, spice,
incense, myrrh, frankincense, wine, olive oil,
choice flour and wheat, cattle and sheep, horses
and chariots, slaves—and human lives.ª
14 "The fruit for which your soul longed
     has gone from you,
   and all your dainties and your splendor
     are lost to you,
     never to be found again!"
15The merchants of these wares, who gained
wealth from her, will stand far off, in fear of her
torment, weeping and mourning aloud,
16 "Alas, alas, the great city,
     clothed in fine linen,
          in purple and scarlet,
     adorned with gold,
          with jewels, and with pearls!
17 For in one hour all this wealth has been laid
          waste!"

And all shipmasters and seafarers, sailors and all
whose trade is on the sea, stood far off 18and cried
out as they saw the smoke of her burning,
     "What city was like the great city?"
19And they threw dust on their heads, as they wept
and mourned, crying out,
   "Alas, alas, the great city,
     where all who had ships at sea
          grew rich by her wealth!
   For in one hour she has been laid waste."

20 Rejoice over her, O heaven, you saints and
apostles and prophets! For God has given judgment for you against her.

21 Then a mighty angel took up a stone like a
great millstone and threw it into the sea, saying,
   "With such violence Babylon the great city
     will be thrown down,
     and will be found no more;
22 and the sound of harpists and minstrels and
          of flutists and trumpeters
     will be heard in you no more;
   and an artisan of any trade
     will be found in you no more;
   and the sound of the millstone
     will be heard in you no more;
23 and the light of a lamp
     will shine in you no more;
   and the voice of bridegroom and bride
     will be heard in you no more;
   for your merchants were the magnates of the
          earth,
   and all nations were deceived by your
          sorcery.
24 And in youᵇ was found the blood of prophets
          and of saints,
   and of all who have been slaughtered on
          earth."

The Rejoicing in Heaven

19 After this I heard what seemed to be the
loud voice of a great multitude in heaven,
saying,
   "Hallelujah!
   Salvation and glory and power to our God,
2   for his judgments are true and just;
   he has judged the great whore
     who corrupted the earth with her
          fornication,
   and he has avenged on her the blood of his
          servants."ᶜ

ª Or chariots, and human bodies and souls   ᵇ Gk her   ᶜ Gk slaves

³Once more they said,

"Hallelujah!

The smoke goes up from her forever and ever."

⁴And the twenty-four elders and the four living creatures fell down and worshiped God who is seated on the throne, saying,

"Amen. Hallelujah!"

5 And from the throne came a voice saying,

"Praise our God,

all you his servants,ᵃ

and all who fear him,

small and great."

⁶Then I heard what seemed to be the voice of a great multitude, like the sound of many waters and like the sound of mighty thunderpeals, crying out,

"Hallelujah!

For the Lord our God

the Almighty reigns.

7 Let us rejoice and exult

and give him the glory,

for the marriage of the Lamb has come,

and his bride has made herself ready;

8 to her it has been granted to be clothed

with fine linen, bright and pure"—

for the fine linen is the righteous deeds of the saints.

9 And the angel saidᵇ to me, "Write this: Blessed are those who are invited to the marriage supper of the Lamb." And he said to me, "These are true words of God." ¹⁰Then I fell down at his feet to worship him, but he said to me, "You must not do that! I am a fellow servantᶜ with you and your comradesᵈ who hold the testimony of Jesus.ᵉ Worship God! For the testimony of Jesusᵉ is the spirit of prophecy."

The Rider on the White Horse

11 Then I saw heaven opened, and there was a white horse! Its rider is called Faithful and True, and in righteousness he judges and makes war. ¹²His eyes are like a flame of fire, and on his head are many diadems; and he has a name inscribed that no one knows but himself. ¹³He is clothed in a robe dipped inᶠ blood, and his name is called The Word of God. ¹⁴And the armies of heaven, wearing fine linen, white and pure, were following him on white horses. ¹⁵From his mouth comes a sharp sword with which to strike down the nations, and he will ruleᵍ them with a rod of iron; he will tread the wine press of the fury of the wrath of God the Almighty. ¹⁶On his robe and on his thigh he has a name inscribed, "King of kings and Lord of lords."

The Beast and Its Armies Defeated

17 Then I saw an angel standing in the sun, and with a loud voice he called to all the birds that fly in midheaven, "Come, gather for the great supper of God, ¹⁸to eat the flesh of kings, the flesh of captains, the flesh of the mighty, the flesh of horses and their riders—flesh of all, both free and slave, both small and great." ¹⁹Then I saw the beast and the kings of the earth with their armies gathered to make war against the rider on the horse and against his army. ²⁰And the beast was captured, and with it the false prophet who had performed in its presence the signs by which he deceived those who had received the mark of the beast and those who worshiped its image. These two were thrown alive into the lake of fire that burns with sulfur. ²¹And the rest were killed by the sword of the rider on the horse, the sword that came from his mouth; and all the birds were gorged with their flesh.

The Thousand Years

20 Then I saw an angel coming down from heaven, holding in his hand the key to the bottomless pit and a great chain. ²He seized the dragon, that ancient serpent, who is the Devil and Satan, and bound him for a thousand years, ³and threw him into the pit, and locked and sealed it over him, so that he would deceive the nations no more, until the thousand years were ended. After that he must be let out for a little while.

4 Then I saw thrones, and those seated on them were given authority to judge. I also saw the souls of those who had been beheaded for their testimony to Jesusʰ and for the word of God. They had not worshiped the beast or its image and had not received its mark on their foreheads or their hands. They came to life and reigned with Christ a thousand years. ⁵(The rest of the dead did not come to life until the thousand years were ended.) This is the first resurrection. ⁶Blessed and holy are those who share in the first resurrection. Over these the second death has no power, but they will be priests of God and of Christ, and they will reign with him a thousand years.

Satan's Doom

7 When the thousand years are ended, Satan will be released from his prison ⁸and will come out to deceive the nations at the four corners of the earth, Gog and Magog, in order to gather them for battle;

ᵃ Gk *slaves* ᵇ Gk *he said* ᶜ Gk *slave* ᵈ Gk *brothers* ᵉ Or *to Jesus* ᶠ Other ancient authorities read *sprinkled with* ᵍ Or *will shepherd* ʰ Or *for the testimony of Jesus*

The New Jerusalem · Revelation 20:1–22:5

The last three chapters of Revelation contain John's visions of God's reign, the end of history, and eternal life. Satan is alive, but has limited power. This is symbolized by the dragon's thousand-year imprisonment and the time when the martyrs reign with Christ (Revelation 20:2-5). The thousand-year reign has been interpreted in many different ways through the centuries, but no one knows its true significance. At the end of the thousand years, Satan is defeated, and Christ sits in final judgment over all the dead.

In chapter 21, John describes a new heaven and a new earth. The Bible begins in Genesis with the story of the creation of a world in which everything is good. It ends in Revelation with a new creation in which God's goodness again overflows. A holy city, the New Jerusalem, comes down out of heaven. The New Jerusalem is described as a beautiful bride who is preparing to marry Jesus. John tells his Christian readers that they should look forward to the time of this new city with joy because, when it comes, God and Christ will live in their midst. The whole city will be God's temple. The sun will always shine. A river of living water will flow from God's throne, and the trees will produce fruit year-round, recalling the Garden of Eden, where Adam and Eve lived before their sin. The New Jerusalem is a symbol for the new world that God will establish when evil is destroyed and suffering is banished.

These visions helped Christians at the end of the first century maintain their hope by focusing on the glorious victory of God. They can also help us renew our commitment to Christ and keep our hope alive, especially when we face times of trials or are misunderstood because of our faith. No matter where we are in life or where our lives fall in the eternal scope of the cosmic battle between good and evil, we can hope for the day when God completes the ultimate victory that Christ has already won.

they are as numerous as the sands of the sea. [9]They marched up over the breadth of the earth and surrounded the camp of the saints and the beloved city. And fire came down from heaven[a] and consumed them. [10]And the devil who had deceived them was thrown into the lake of fire and sulfur, where the beast and the false prophet were, and they will be tormented day and night forever and ever.

The Dead Are Judged

11 Then I saw a great white throne and the one who sat on it; the earth and the heaven fled from his presence, and no place was found for them. [12]And I saw the dead, great and small, standing before the throne, and books were opened. Also another book was opened, the book of life. And the dead were judged according to their works, as recorded in the books. [13]And the sea gave up the dead that were in it, Death and Hades gave up the dead that were in them, and all were judged according to

what they had done. [14]Then Death and Hades were thrown into the lake of fire. This is the second death, the lake of fire; [15]and anyone whose name was not found written in the book of life was thrown into the lake of fire.

The New Heaven and the New Earth

21 Then I saw a new heaven and a new earth; for the first heaven and the first earth had passed away, and the sea was no more. [2]And I saw the holy city, the new Jerusalem, coming down out of heaven from God, prepared as a bride adorned for her husband. [3]And I heard a loud voice from the throne saying,

"See, the home[b] of God is among mortals.
He will dwell[c] with them;
they will be his peoples,[d]
and God himself will be with them;[e]
4   he will wipe every tear from their eyes.
Death will be no more;

a Other ancient authorities read *from God, out of heaven*, or *out of heaven from God* b Gk *the tabernacle* c Gk *will tabernacle* d Other ancient authorities read *people* e Other ancient authorities add *and be their God*

> "Death will be no more;
> mourning and crying
> and pain will be no
> more, for the first things
> have passed away."
> —Revelation 21:4

> mourning and crying and pain will be no
> more,
> for the first things have passed away."

5 And the one who was seated on the throne said, "See, I am making all things new." Also he said, "Write this, for these words are trustworthy and true." [6]Then he said to me, "It is done! I am the Alpha and the Omega, the beginning and the end. To the thirsty I will give water as a gift from the spring of the water of life. [7]Those who conquer will inherit these things, and I will be their God and they will be my children. [8]But as for the cowardly, the faithless,[a] the polluted, the murderers, the fornicators, the sorcerers, the idolaters, and all liars, their place will be in the lake that burns with fire and sulfur, which is the second death."

Vision of the New Jerusalem

9 Then one of the seven angels who had the seven bowls full of the seven last plagues came and said to me, "Come, I will show you the bride, the wife of the Lamb." [10]And in the spirit[b] he carried me away to a great, high mountain and showed me the holy city Jerusalem coming down out of heaven from God. [11]It has the glory of God and a radiance like a very rare jewel, like jasper, clear as crystal. [12]It has a great, high wall with twelve gates, and at the gates twelve angels, and on the gates are inscribed the names of the twelve tribes of the Israelites; [13]on the east three gates, on the north three gates, on the south three gates, and on the west three gates. [14]And the wall of the city has twelve foundations, and on them are the twelve names of the twelve apostles of the Lamb.

15 The angel[c] who talked to me had a measuring rod of gold to measure the city and its gates and walls. [16]The city lies foursquare, its length the same as its width; and he measured the city with his rod, fifteen hundred miles;[d] its length and width and height are equal. [17]He also measured its wall, one hundred forty-four cubits[e] by human measurement, which the angel was using. [18]The wall is built of jasper, while the city is pure gold,

LIVE IT!

The Return of the King · Revelation 22:7–21

Kids want immediate gratification. Waiting for Christmas or a birthday is nearly impossible. Saving a piece of candy for after dinner is downright torture. And a long trip in the car produces the infamous persistent question, "Are we there yet?"

The Bible tells us that Jesus will return. But when? Like impatient children, some people have tried to predict the Lord's second coming. Some still try to predict a specific day that Jesus will return. But Jesus said, "About that day and hour no one knows, . . . only the Father" (Matthew 24:36).

Can we say with John, "Amen. Come, Lord Jesus!" (Revelation 22:20), and really hope that Jesus will come today? We may hesitate, wanting to hang on to the life we know here and now along with the hopes and dreams we want to accomplish. But the coming of Christ will be the most glorious event imaginable for those who have put their trust in God. So keep preparing and praying for the return of Christ!

- How does picturing Christ's return make you feel?
- What hopes and dreams do you have for the future? How can you surrender them to God whether you have a chance to pursue them on earth or not?
- Talk to Jesus about your mixed feelings about his return. Ask for his attitude and perspective for life on earth and in eternity.

---

a Or *the unbelieving* b Or *in the Spirit* c Gk *He* d Gk *twelve thousand stadia* e That is, almost seventy-five yards

clear as glass. ¹⁹The foundations of the wall of the city are adorned with every jewel; the first was jasper, the second sapphire, the third agate, the fourth emerald, ²⁰the fifth onyx, the sixth carnelian, the seventh chrysolite, the eighth beryl, the ninth topaz, the tenth chrysoprase, the eleventh jacinth, the twelfth amethyst. ²¹And the twelve gates are twelve pearls, each of the gates is a single pearl, and the street of the city is pure gold, transparent as glass.

22 I saw no temple in the city, for its temple is the Lord God the Almighty and the Lamb. ²³And the city has no need of sun or moon to shine on it, for the glory of God is its light, and its lamp is the Lamb. ²⁴The nations will walk by its light, and the kings of the earth will bring their glory into it. ²⁵Its gates will never be shut by day—and there will be no night there. ²⁶People will bring into it the glory and the honor of the nations. ²⁷But nothing unclean will enter it, nor anyone who practices abomination or falsehood, but only those who are written in the Lamb's book of life.

The River of Life

22 Then the angel ᵃ showed me the river of the water of life, bright as crystal, flowing from the throne of God and of the Lamb ²through the middle of the street of the city. On either side of the river is the tree of life ᵇ with its twelve kinds of fruit, producing its fruit each month; and the leaves of the tree are for the healing of the nations. ³Nothing accursed will be found there any more. But the throne of God and of the Lamb will be in it, and his servants ᶜ will worship him; ⁴they will see his face, and his name will be on their foreheads. ⁵And there will be no more night; they need no light of lamp or sun, for the Lord God will be their light, and they will reign forever and ever.

6 And he said to me, "These words are trustworthy and true, for the Lord, the God of the spirits of the prophets, has sent his angel to show his servants ᶜ what must soon take place."

7 "See, I am coming soon! Blessed is the one who keeps the words of the prophecy of this book."

Epilogue and Benediction

8 I, John, am the one who heard and saw these things. And when I heard and saw them, I fell down to worship at the feet of the angel who showed them to me; ⁹but he said to me, "You must not do that! I am a fellow servant ᵈ with you and your comrades ᵉ

LIVE IT!

Amen
Revelation 22:20

In Hebrew, "amen" means "So be it" or "Yes, it's true." So saying amen in your prayers is the same as saying, "Yes, I believe it!" It's an appropriate way to conclude the last book of the Bible, and it shouldn't be said lightly. Each of us is invited to join the great amen, to say: "Yes, I believe in a loving God who is father to us all! Yes, I believe in God's Son, Jesus Christ, who is my Lord and Savior! Yes, I believe in the Holy Spirit, who will help me continue Jesus' mission of justice, reconciliation, and love!" But these words remain just words until people with courage and conviction take the risk to live them out in their own corner of the world. Take the risk. Join God's story. Amen!

- Are you able to say amen to all you have read, prayed, and reflected on in the Bible?
- Have the stories and poems, teachings and parables, songs and sayings led you to believe in a God who is with you every step of your journey, every minute of the day and night?
- How can you live your daily life to reflect Christ's kingdom?

the prophets, and with those who keep the words of this book. Worship God!"

10 And he said to me, "Do not seal up the words of the prophecy of this book, for the time is near. ¹¹Let the evildoer still do evil, and the filthy still be filthy, and the righteous still do right, and the holy still be holy."

12 "See, I am coming soon; my reward is with me, to repay according to everyone's work. ¹³I am the Alpha and the Omega, the first and the last, the beginning and the end."

14 Blessed are those who wash their robes, ᶠ so that they will have the right to the tree of life and

ᵃ Gk he ᵇ Or the Lamb. ²In the middle of the street of the city, and on either side of the river, is the tree of life ᶜ Gk slaves ᵈ Gk slave ᵉ Gk brothers
ᶠ Other ancient authorities read do his commandments

may enter the city by the gates. [15]Outside are the dogs and sorcerers and fornicators and murderers and idolaters, and everyone who loves and practices falsehood.

16 "It is I, Jesus, who sent my angel to you with this testimony for the churches. I am the root and the descendant of David, the bright morning star."

17 The Spirit and the bride say, "Come."
And let everyone who hears say, "Come."
And let everyone who is thirsty come.
Let anyone who wishes take the water
        of life as a gift.

a Other ancient authorities lack *all*; others lack *the saints*; others lack *Amen*

18 I warn everyone who hears the words of the prophecy of this book: if anyone adds to them, God will add to that person the plagues described in this book; [19]if anyone takes away from the words of the book of this prophecy, God will take away that person's share in the tree of life and in the holy city, which are described in this book.

20 The one who testifies to these things says, "Surely I am coming soon."
Amen. Come, Lord Jesus!

21 The grace of the Lord Jesus be with all the saints. Amen.[a]

Where Do I Find it?

Abbreviations

The following abbreviations are used for the books of the Bible:

Old Testament

Gen.	Genesis
Exod.	Exodus
Lev.	Leviticus
Num.	Numbers
Deut.	Deuteronomy
Josh.	Joshua
Judg.	Judges
Ruth	Ruth
1 Sam.	1 Samuel
2 Sam.	2 Samuel
1 Kings	1 Kings
2 Kings	2 Kings
1 Chron.	1 Chronicles
2 Chron.	2 Chronicles
Ezra	Ezra
Neh.	Nehemiah
Esther	Esther
Job	Job
Ps(s).	Psalms
Prov.	Proverbs
Eccl.	Ecclesiastes
Song of Sol.	Song of Solomon
Isa.	Isaiah
Jer.	Jeremiah
Lam.	Lamentations
Ezek.	Ezekiel
Dan.	Daniel
Hos.	Hosea
Joel	Joel
Amos	Amos
Obad.	Obadiah
Jon.	Jonah
Mic.	Micah
Nah.	Nahum
Hab.	Habakkuk
Zeph.	Zephaniah
Hag.	Haggai
Zech.	Zechariah
Mal.	Malachi

New Testament

Matt.	Matthew
Mark	Mark
Luke	Luke
John	John
Acts	Acts of the Apostles
Rom.	Romans
1 Cor.	1 Corinthians
2 Cor.	2 Corinthians
Gal.	Galatians
Eph.	Ephesians
Phil.	Philippians
Col.	Colossians
1 Thess.	1 Thessalonians
2 Thess.	2 Thessalonians
1 Tim.	1 Timothy
2 Tim.	2 Timothy
Titus	Titus
Philem.	Philemon
Heb.	Hebrews
James	James
1 Pet.	1 Peter
2 Pet.	2 Peter
1 John	1 John
2 John	2 John
3 John	3 John
Jude	Jude
Rev.	Revelation

In the NRSV notes to the books of the Old Testament the following abbreviations are used:

Ant.	Josephus, *Antiquities of the Jews*
Aram	Aramaic
Ch(s)	Chapter(s)
Cn	Correction; made where the text has suffered in transmission and the versions provide no satisfactory restoration, but where the Standard Bible Committee agrees with the judgment of competent scholars as to the most probable reconstruction of the original text.
Gk	Septuagint, Greek version of the OT
Heb	Hebrew of the consonantal Masoretic Text of the OT
Josephus	Flavius Josephus (Jewish historian, ca. A.D. 37–95)

Macc.	The book(s) of the Maccabees
Ms(s)	Manuscript(s)
MT	The Hebrew of the pointed Masoretic Text of the OT
OL	Old Latin
Q Ms(s)	Manuscript(s) found at Qumran by the Dead Sea
Sam	Samaritan Hebrew text of the OT
Syr	Syriac Version of the OT
Syr H	Syriac Version of Origen's Hexapla
Tg	Targum
Vg	Vulgate, Latin Version of the OT

Events and Teachings Index

All entries are listed in the order in which they appear in the Bible.

Old Testament Stories

- Creation, Gen. 1–2
- original sin and its punishment, Gen. 3
- Cain and Abel, Gen. 4:1–16
- Noah and the flood, Gen. 6–9
- God's covenant with Abraham, Gen. 17:1–18:15
- God's command to sacrifice Isaac, Gen. 22:1–19
- Isaac's blessing of Jacob, Gen. 27:1–29
- Jacob's dream, Gen. 28:10–22
- Joseph and his brothers, Gen. 37–46
- birth and youth of Moses, Exod. 2:1–10
- Moses at the burning bush, Exod. 3:1–12
- plagues on Egypt, Exod. 7–12
- Passover and the exodus, Exod. 12–14
- Ten Commandments, Exod. 20:1–17
- destruction of Jericho, Josh. 5:13–6:27
- Gideon and the sign of the fleece, Judg. 6:36–40
- Samson, Judg. 13–16
- Samuel's birth and calling, 1 Sam. 1–3
- David and Goliath, 1 Sam. 17
- David and Bathsheba, 2 Sam. 11
- Solomon's wisdom, 1 Kings 3
- Elijah's triumph over the priests of Baal, 1 Kings 18:20–40
- miracles of Elisha, 2 Kings 4:1–6:23
- end of the Babylonian exile, Ezra 1
- Ezekiel and the valley of dry bones, Ezek. 37:1–14
- Daniel, Dan. 1–6
- Jonah and the Ninevites, Jon. 1–3

New Testament Stories

- birth of Jesus, Matt. 1:18–2:12; Luke 1–2
- baptism of Jesus, Matt. 3:13–17; Mark 1:9–11; Luke 3:21–22
- temptation of Jesus, Matt. 4:1–11; Mark 1:12–13; Luke 4:1–13
- Peter's declaration about Jesus, Matt. 16:13–20; Mark 8:27–30; Luke 9:18–20
- transfiguration of Jesus, Matt. 17:1–13; Mark 9:2–13; Luke 9:28–36
- Jesus' triumphal entry into Jerusalem, Matt. 21:1–11; Mark 11:1–11; Luke 19:28–40; John 12:12–19

- Jesus in the temple, Matt. 21:12–17; Mark 11:15–19; Luke 19:45–48; John 2:13–16
- Judas' betrayal of Jesus, Matt. 26:14–16, 47–56; Mark 14:10–11, 43–52; Luke 22:1–53; John 13:21–30; 18:1–5
- Last Supper, Matt. 26:17–30; Mark 14:12–25; Luke 22:7–38; 1 Cor. 11:23–26
- Jesus at Gethsemane, Matt. 26:36–56; Mark 14:32–51; Luke 22:39–53
- Peter's denial of Christ, Matt. 26:69–75; Mark 14:66–72; Luke 22:54–62; John 18:15–18, 25–27
- crucifixion, Matt. 27:32–56; Mark 15:21–41; Luke 23:26–49; John 19:16–30
- resurrection and appearances, Matt. 28; Mark 16; Luke 24; John 20–21; Acts 1:1–11
- Jesus washing his disciples' feet, John 13:1–17
- Holy Spirit at Pentecost, Acts 2:1–42
- stoning of Stephen, Acts 6–7
- conversion of Saul, Acts 9:1–31
- Peter's escape from prison, Acts 12:1–19
- Paul and Silas' escape from prison, Acts 16:16–40
- Paul's journey to Rome for his trial, Acts 27–28

Miracles of Jesus

Healing Individuals

- leper, Matt. 8:1–4; Mark 1:40–45; Luke 5:12–16
- centurion's servant, Matt. 8:5–13; Luke 7:1–10
- many at Peter's house, Matt. 8:14–17; Mark 1:29–34; Luke 4:38–41
- Gadarene (Gerasene) demoniacs, Matt. 8:28–34; Mark 5:1–20; Luke 8:26–39
- paralytic, Matt. 9:2–8; Mark 2:1–12; Luke 5:17–26
- woman with bleeding, Matt. 9:20–22; Mark 5:25–34; Luke 8:43–48
- two blind men, Matt. 9:27–31
- mute man, Matt. 9:32–34
- man with a withered hand, Matt. 12:9–13; Mark 3:1–5; Luke 6:6–11
- blind, mute, and possessed man, Matt. 12:22
- Canaanite woman's daughter, Matt. 15:21–28; Mark 7:24–30
- boy with a demon, Matt. 17:14–21; Mark 9:14–29; Luke 9:37–43
- blind Bartimaeus, Matt. 20:29–34; Mark 10:46–52; Luke 18:35–43

Life and Faith Issues Index

Here are some passages that can give you comfort or direction for life and issues you might be facing today. There are many other passages in the Bible that also address these and other topics, but this will give you a starting place. For a more complete index, see the concordance on p. 1386.

anger
Matt. 5:21–24
John 2:13–17
Eph. 4:25–27, 31–32
James 1:19–21

calling
Gen. 12:1–9
1 Sam. 1–3
Isa. 6:1–8
Jer. 1:4–10
Matt. 4:18–22;
    28:16–20
Mark 1:16–20
Luke 5:1–11

commitment
Num. 30:2–4
Deut. 6:1–9; 11:8–9
Josh. 24:14–15
Mark 8:34–38

courage
Josh. 1:9
1 Sam. 17
Ps. 31

discipleship
Mark 8:34–38
Luke 9:1–6
John 4:1–42

family
Gen. 4:9; 12:10–20
Eph. 5:21–6:4

fear
Pss. 27; 91
Zeph. 3:14–20
Matt. 14:22–33
Mark 4:35–41
Luke 22:54–62

forgiveness
Gen. 33:1–17
Ps. 51
Matt. 18:21–35
Luke 6:27–36; 23:34
John 8:2–11

friendship
Ruth 1:1–19
1 Sam. 20
John 15:12–17

friendship with God
Gen. 28:10–22
Mic. 6:8
John 15:12–17

giving
2 Chron. 31:2–10
Ezra 1:6–11
Mark 12:41–44
Luke 21:1–4

happiness
Luke 12:22–34
Phil. 4:4–9

honesty with God
Gen. 18:22–33
Jer. 12:1–16
Mark 14:32–42

hope
Eccl. 3:1–8
Lam. 3:22–26
Rom. 8:18–30

hypocrisy
Matt. 6:1–6; 23:1–36
Luke 18:9–14
James 1:22–2:4

images of God
Gen. 1:26–27;
    32:22–32
Ps. 23
Jer. 18:1–11

judgment of others
Matt. 7:1–5
Rom. 14:1–12
Gal. 3:26–28

**loneliness and
abandonment**
Ps. 22:1–12
Mark 15:33–34
2 Tim. 4:9–18

love
Song of Sol. 8:6–7
Matt. 5:43–48
Mark 12:28–34
1 Cor. 13

peace
Isa. 11:1–9
Mic. 4:1–5
John 14:25–31

persistence
Luke 11:5–8; 18:1–8

popularity
Mark 9:33–37
1 Cor. 3:1–9
Phil. 2:1–11

presence of God
Gen. 15:7
Exod. 3:1–6; 33:17–23
Matt. 18:20

promises of God
Exod. 6:1–9
Jer. 29:11
Luke 4:14–30

repentance
1 Chron. 21:1–17
Joel 2:12–18
Luke 15:11–32

responsibility
Ezek. 18

service
Isa. 42:1–6
Matt. 20:20–28;
    25:31–46
Mark 10:35–45
John 13:1–17

sexuality
Gen. 1:26–31
Song of Sol.
Eph. 5:1–14
1 Thess. 4:3–8

suffering
Job 1:13–21
Ps. 22
Matt. 5:1–12
1 Pet. 3:13–18

temptation
Gen. 3
Matt. 4:1–11
Mark 1:12–13;
    7:14–23
Luke 4:1–13

trust in God
Ps. 62
Isa. 43:1–5
Matt. 11:28–30
Mark 10:46–52

wisdom
2 Chron. 1:7–13
Prov. 8:1–21

Connect It! Profile Index

These are the names of the people and organizations profiled in the Connect It! study notes throughout this Bible. They are listed, with corresponding scripture reference and page number, in the order in which they appear throughout the Bible.

Study Note Index

This subject index is not an index to the Bible itself, but to the subjects covered in the various study note articles throughout **The Guidebook**. Each article is based on a passage of scripture, so you can also find verses related to these subjects by looking up the study note.

A

Abraham
15, 20, 21, 22, 24, 26, 27, 34, 1183

abuse
22, 29, 44, 321

addiction
1215, 1246

Advocate
See Holy Spirit.

African Americans
219, 484, 1045, 1240

AIDS
14, 581

angels
1298

anger
592, 643, 1003

anointing
301

anxiety
See worry.

apocalyptic literature
886

apocryphal books
481

apostles
See disciples.

appearance
1226, 1258

ark of the covenant
106

armor
1247

attitude
83

attributes of God
523, 541

B

Babel, tower of
18

baptism
976, 1190

Barnabas
1155, 1159, 1160

Beatitudes
979

belief
1034, 1046, 1100, 1103, 1307, 1321

Beloved Disciple
1124

betrayal
265, 562

blessings
150

body of Christ
1195, 1213

busy
1072

C

Caleb
158, 180

carpenter
1028

character
695

Christmas
1053, 1054

church
1202, 1212, 1213, 1217, 1332

circumcision
25, 1183

comfort
1223

commitment
1032, 1252, 1349

Communication
831

Communion
See Lord's Supper.

community
1140, 1141, 1212, 1259, 1263, 1269, 1309

compassion
581, 1113, 1220, 1262, 1301, 1302, 1320

compromise
1160

contradictions
938

conscience
1271

conversion
433, 881, 907, 1152, 1170

Study Aids

Cro-Magnon people appear. (35,000)

Humans live in permanent settlements. (10,000)

35,000 | 10,000 | 9000

B.C.

Timeline of Human History

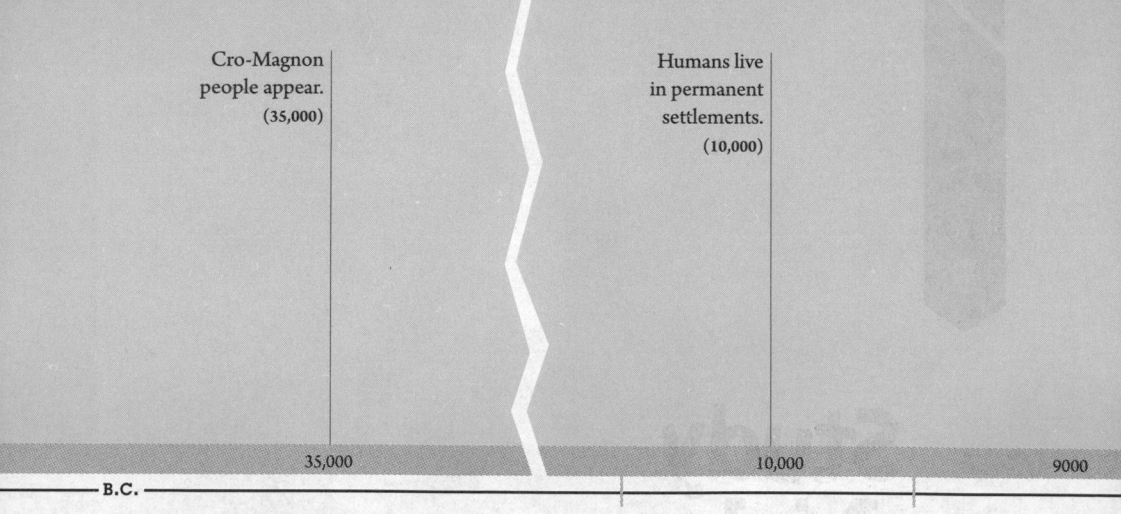

Expanded Timeline of Biblical History

B.C.

PREHISTORY | 2000 | 1900 | 1800 | 1700

Note: All dates are approximate.

Also, the black and dark green sections of the *Timeline of Human History* on pages 1372 and 1373 correspond to the entire *Expanded Timeline of Biblical History* on all four pages.

Jacob's descendants settle in Egypt. (1750)

Abraham and Sarah arrive in Canaan. (1850)

BIBLICAL PREHISTORY

Important Biblical Figures

Adam and Eve

Cain and Abel

Noah

TIME OF THE PATRIARCHS AND MATRIARCHS

Important Biblical Figures

Abraham and Sarah

Isaac and Rebekah

Jacob, Leah, and Rachel

Joseph and Asenath

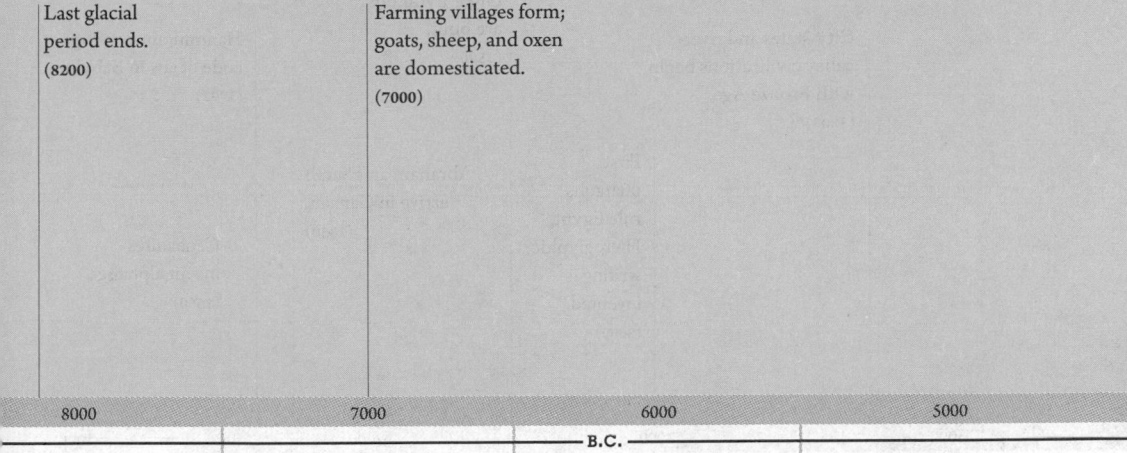

Last glacial
period ends.
(8200)

Farming villages form;
goats, sheep, and oxen
are domesticated.
(7000)

| 8000 | 7000 | 6000 | 5000 |

B.C.

Timeline of Human History

Expanded Timeline of Biblical History

B.C.

| 1600 | 1500 | 1400 | 1300 | 1200 | 1100 |

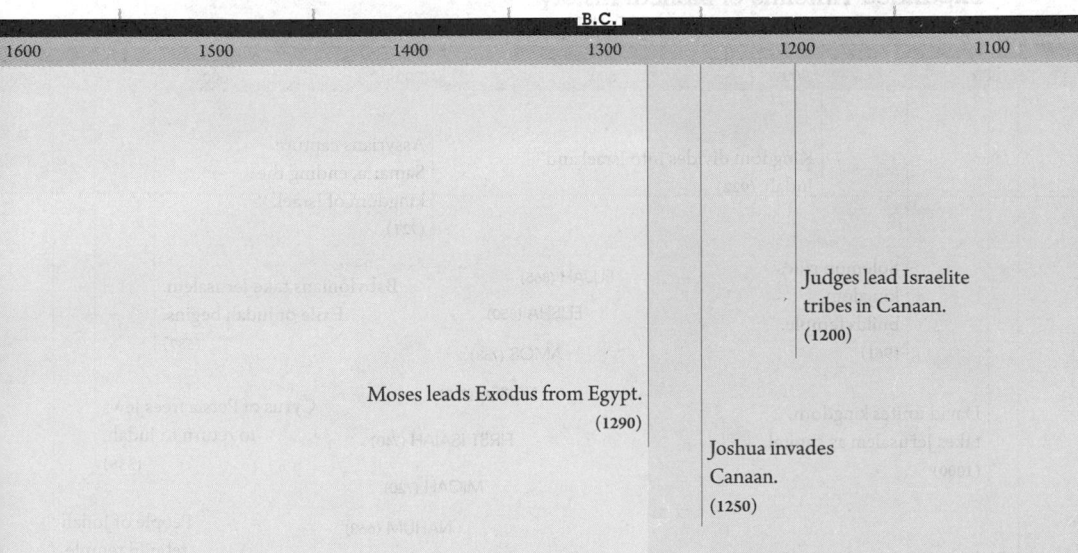

Judges lead Israelite
tribes in Canaan.
(1200)

Moses leads Exodus from Egypt.
(1290)

Joshua invades
Canaan.
(1250)

TIME IN EGYPT AND THE EXODUS

Important Biblical Figures
Moses
Aaron
Miriam

TIME OF THE JUDGES

Important Biblical Figures
Deborah
Gideon
Samson
Samuel

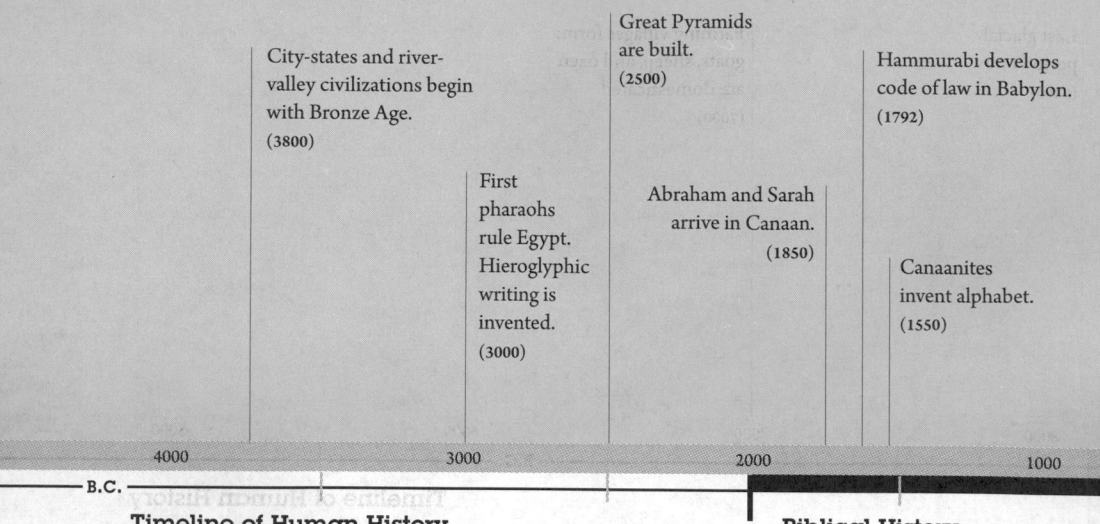

City-states and river-valley civilizations begin with Bronze Age. (3800)

Great Pyramids are built. (2500)

Hammurabi develops code of law in Babylon. (1792)

First pharaohs rule Egypt. Hieroglyphic writing is invented. (3000)

Abraham and Sarah arrive in Canaan. (1850)

Canaanites invent alphabet. (1550)

4000   3000   2000   1000

B.C.

Timeline of Human History

Biblical History

Expanded Timeline of Biblical History

PROPHETS   Prominent Kings of Israel   Prominent Kings of Judah

B.C.

1000   900   800   700   600   500

Kingdom divides into Israel and Judah. (922)

Assyrians capture Samaria, ending the kingdom of Israel. (721)

Solomon rules kingdom, builds temple. (961)

ELIJAH (865)

ELISHA (850)

AMOS (783)

Babylonians take Jerusalem. Exile of Judah begins. (587)

HOSEA (760)

David unites kingdom, takes Jerusalem as capital. (1000)

FIRST ISAIAH (740)

Cyrus of Persia frees Jews to return to Judah. (538)

MICAH (720)

NAHUM (663)

People of Judah rebuild temple. (515)

ZEPHANIAH (630)

Saul is named first king of Israel. (1020)

JEREMIAH (626)   SECOND ISAIAH (540)

HABAKKUK (609)   ZECHARIAH (520)

EZEKIEL (593)   HAGGAI (520)

OBADIAH (586)

TIME OF THE KINGS AND PROPHETS

UNITED KINGDOM

DIVIDED KINGDOM

PERSIAN DOMINATION

			Jeroboam I (922)	Ahab (869)	Ahaziah (850)	Jeroboam II (786)	Hoshea (732)			
Saul	David	Solomon	Rehoboam (922)	Ahaziah (842)	Jehoash (837)	Uzziah (783)	Hezekiah (715)	Josiah (640)	Jehoiachin (598)	Zedekiah (597)

1370

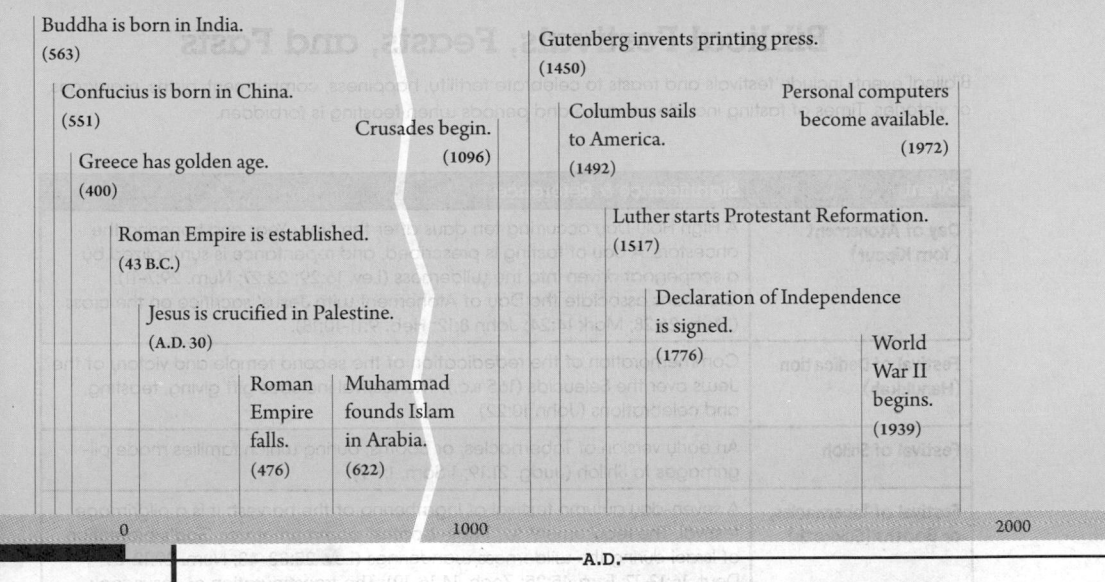

Buddha is born in India.
(563)

Confucius is born in China.
(551)

Greece has golden age.
(400)

Roman Empire is established.
(43 B.C.)

Jesus is crucified in Palestine.
(A.D. 30)

Roman Empire falls. (476)

Muhammad founds Islam in Arabia. (622)

Gutenberg invents printing press.
(1450)

Columbus sails to America.
(1492)

Crusades begin.
(1096)

Personal computers become available.
(1972)

Luther starts Protestant Reformation.
(1517)

Declaration of Independence is signed.
(1776)

World War II begins.
(1939)

0   1000   2000

A.D.

iblical History

Timeline of Human History

Expanded Timeline of Biblical History

New Testament Books

B.C.   A.D.

400   300   200   100   0   100

Revolt against Greeks by Maccabees begins.
(166)

Romans conquer Holy Land.
(63)

Greeks conquer Holy Land.
(332)

Temple is rededicated.
(165)

Jesus is born.
(5 BC)

Ezra brings Torah to Jerusalem. (398)

Simon, Jonathan's brother, establishes Hasmonean dynasty.
(142)

Jesus is crucified.
(AD 30)

Saul is converted.
(31)

Nehemiah becomes governor of Judah, starts renewal. (445)

James is martyred.
(61)

Nero persecutes Christians. Peter and Paul are martyred.
(64-68)

MALACHI (458)

JOEL (400)

Romans destroy Jerusalem temple.
(70)

TIME OF FOREIGN DOMINATION

TIME OF NEW TESTAMENT

GREEK DOMINATION

HASMONEAN DYNASTY
(FREE FROM FOREIGN DOMINATION)

ROMAN DOMINATION

Nehemiah   Ezra   The Maccabees

Domitian persecutes Christians.
(95)

1 Thess. (51), Paul's major letters (mid- to late 50s)

Colossians, Philemon (early 60s)

Gospel of Mark (mid-60s)

Gospels of Matthew and Luke, Acts, Hebrews (70s to 80s)

Gospel of John; 1, 2, and 3 John; and Revelation (90s); 2 Peter (after 100)

Biblical Festivals, Feasts, and Fasts

Biblical events include festivals and feasts to celebrate fertility, happiness, commitment, births, marriages, or victories. Times of fasting include penance and periods when feasting is forbidden.

Event	Significance & Reference
Day of Atonement (Yom Kippur)	A High Holy Day occurring ten days after the New Year and honoring the ancestors. A day of fasting is prescribed, and repentance is symbolized by a scapegoat driven into the wilderness (Lev. 16:29; 23:27; Num. 29:7-11). Christians associate the Day of Atonement with Jesus' sacrifice on the cross (Matt. 26:28; Mark 14:24; John 8:12; Heb. 9:11-10:18).
Festival of Dedication (Hanukkah)	Commemoration of the rededication of the second temple and victory of the Jews over the Seleucids (165 B.C.). The festival includes gift giving, feasting, and celebrations (John 10:22).
Festival of Shiloh	An early version of Tabernacles, or Booths, during which families made pilgrimages to Shiloh (Judg. 21:19; 1 Sam. 1:1-7).
Festival of Tabernacles, or Booths (Sukkoth)	A seven-day autumn festival of ingathering of the harvest; it is a pilgrimage festival. The requirement to "live in booths" commemorates God's protection of Israel during the wilderness wanderings (Lev. 23:33-43; Num. 29:12-39; Deut. 16:13-17; Ezra 45:25; Zech. 14:16-19). The transfiguration of Jesus took place during this festival (Luke 9:33; John 7:2, 37).
Festival of Trumpets, or New Year Festival (Rosh Hashanah)	The new-moon festival celebrated on the seventh day of the seventh month, a day of prayers, rest, and "trumpet blasts" (Lev. 23:23-25; Num. 29:1-6).
Festival of Weeks (Shavuot)	Celebration of the beginning of the wheat harvest, seven weeks after the presentation of the barley omer; it is a pilgrimage festival. It came to be associated with the giving of the Torah at Mount Sinai (Exod. 23:16; 34:22-23; Lev. 23:15; Num. 28:26-31; Deut. 16:9-10).
Jubilee Year	The fiftieth year (occurring after seven sabbatical cycles of seven years each), in which property was returned to its original owner, Israelite slaves were freed, debts were cancelled, and the land rested (Lev. 25:8-22; 2 Chron. 36:21; Isa. 61:1-2).
Passover, and Festival of Unleavened Bread	A weeklong spring memorial of the exodus from Egypt, beginning with the "seder" meal, at which prayers and blessings are offered for Jews across the world; it is a pilgrimage festival (Exod. 12:1-28; 23:14-17; 34:18, 25; Lev. 23:4-14; Num. 9:1-14; 28:16-25; Deut. 16:1-8; Ezra 45:18-24). Jesus memorialized Passover, as he offered himself as the bread of life at the Last Supper (Matt. 26:17-19, 26-29; 1 Cor. 10:1; 11:23-26; Eph. 2:19-20).
Pentecost	The Greek name for the Festival of Weeks, which occurred fifty days after Passover. Pentecost, for Christians, marks the descent of the Holy Spirit and reveals Christ's church (Acts 2:1-11; 20:16; 1 Cor. 16:8).
Purim	A holy day that marks the deliverance of the Jewish people from the Persians by Esther and honors Mordecai's faith. It is a day of feasting, rejoicing, and wearing costumes, as the story of Esther is retold and often dramatized (Esther 9:20-32).
Sabbath	The seventh day, a day of rest to honor God and family. No work is permitted (Exod. 20:8-11; Lev. 23:1-3; Deut. 5:12-15). Christians celebrate the Sabbath on Sunday to honor Christ's life, death, and resurrection (Matt. 28:1-10; Mark 16:1-8; Luke 24:1-12; John 21:1-14).
Sabbatical Year	Every seventh year, when the land rested, slaves were freed, and all debts were suspended or erased (Exod. 21:2; 23:10-11; Lev. 25:1-7; Deut. 15:1-6).

Glossary

A

abba An Aramaic word—a language spoken in Palestine at the time of Jesus—meaning "father," used by children in addressing their fathers. Jesus used the word to express his relationship with God (see Mark 14:36) and taught his disciples to pray to God as a loving and lovable parent.

Adam A name signifying "one formed from the earth," related to the Hebrew word *adamah,* meaning "ground." According to Genesis, Adam was the first man to be formed; he was the husband of Eve and the father of Cain and Abel. Christ is sometimes called the "new Adam" or the "second Adam," as Christ initiated the new or second creation by restoring the divine friendship that had been lost as a result of the first couple's disobedience.

allegory An extended metaphor using symbolic figures and actions, often to communicate a hidden meaning commonly understood by the people to whom it is addressed. The Bible often uses allegories to explain spiritual reality. For example, Jesus is called the Lamb of God in Revelation, an allegory in which Jesus is seen as the sacrifice for our sins.

alleluia An exclamation, from the Hebrew meaning "praise to Yahweh" or "praise to God," used in the Christian liturgy as a way of praising God, especially during the Easter season.

amen A Hebrew word meaning "So be it" or "Yes, it is true." As a conclusion to prayer, it represents the agreement by the person praying to what has been said in the prayer.

angel Based on a word meaning "messenger," a personal and immortal creature, with intelligence and free will, who constantly glorifies God and serves as a messenger from God to humans.

anointing The act of applying oil in a religious ceremony or as part of a blessing (from the Latin *inungere,* "to smear" or "to rub on" oil or ointment for medicinal purposes). In the Old Testament, kings, priests, and prophets were anointed as a sign of their divine mission.

Antichrist An adversary of Christ, from the Greek literally meaning "against Christ." In the New Testament, the antichrist is a deceitful figure associated with the mystery of the iniquity that is to precede the second coming of Christ. In modern usage, the term describes both one who falsely claims to speak in the name of Christ and an enemy of Christ.

apocalypse In a general sense, the end of the world when God will destroy the forces of evil (from the Greek meaning "revelation," "unveiling," or "uncovering"). In scripture, the Apocalypse, or book of Revelation, which is the last book of the New Testament, describes the conflict between good and evil, the end of the world, and heaven.

apocalyptic literature A genre of literature, with roots in both Jewish and Christian tradition, that appears in the books of Ezekiel, Daniel, and Revelation. It is associated with the end-times or the last things and anticipates the time of last judgment when Jesus returns and the world as we know it disappears. Frequently referred to as "crisis literature," it generally appears in the context of historical, political, or religious turmoil and is characterized by symbols and images used to communicate a message to the intended audience, while preventing the enemies of faith from understanding its true meaning.

Apocrypha. *See* canon of scripture; deuterocanonical books.

apostle A general term meaning "one who is sent" that can be used in reference to any missionary of the Church during the New Testament period. In reference to the twelve companions chosen by Jesus, also known as "the Twelve," the term refers to those special witnesses of Jesus on whose ministry the early Church was built.

ark of the covenant In the Old Testament, the sacred chest that housed the holy presence of God. Exodus contains the details of its construction (Exod. 25:10–22; 37:1–9; 39:16–21). In the time of Moses, the ark was carried during the desert wanderings (1250 B.C.) and kept in the tent of meeting. In the period of the kings (about 1000 B.C.), it was placed in the Holy of Holies in the temple (see 1 Kings 8:6–8). It held the tablets of the law of Moses, manna from heaven, and the rod of Aaron. It was also called the ark of God (see 1 Sam. 3:3).

ascension The "going up" into heaven of the risen Christ forty days after his resurrection (Mark 16:19; Luke 24:50–53).

B

Baal A generic Semitic word meaning "master," "owner," "husband," or "lord." However, in scripture, the word is most often associated with the practices of idolatry or the worship of gods other than Yahweh. Baal was both the name of a specific god and a generic title that could refer to any number of gods, such as Baal of Peor or Baal of Hermon. Often, the religion included the use of temple prostitutes and even demanded human sacrifice, especially of infants. The worshipers of Baal were generally seen as the enemies of the Israelites (1 Kings 18:20–40).

Babylonian exile The period during which the Israelites were in exile in Babylon after the destruction of Judah, Jerusalem, and the temple by the Babylonian king Nebuchadnezzar in 587 B.C. The conquest resulted in the deaths of multitudes, the destruction of the land, the deportation of the population, and despair and loss of national identity. The exile lasted an entire generation (586–539 B.C.), until the Persian emperor Cyrus conquered the Babylonians and let the Israelites return home to Jerusalem (see Ezra 1). *See also* Diaspora; exile.

Beatitudes The blessings enunciated by Jesus as part of the Sermon on the Mount (Matt. 5:3–12) and the Sermon on the Plain (Luke 6:20–26). The Beatitudes are often considered to represent the heart of the preaching of Jesus.

Bible The collection of Jewish and Christian writings considered inspired for belief (from the Greek *biblia,* "books"). The Hebrew Bible contains many of the works of what Christians call the Old Testament; the Christian Bible also includes writings known as the New Testament. *See also* New Testament; Old Testament.

biblical criticism A term referring to two different approaches to studying the Bible: (1) "lower criticism" attempts to reconstruct the original biblical text (because none of the original manuscripts have survived); and (2) "higher criticism" compares this reconstructed text with other documents of the time.

biblical interpretation Scripture study that looks not only at what the human authors intended to say, but also at what God reveals to humans through their words. Criteria for interpreting scripture include consideration of (1) the kind of writing—that is, the literary form—in which a particular passage appears, (2) the context of each author's historical time and the presumptions the author and the audience shared, and (3) the context of the process of revelation that occurred over time. Early insights often represent one step in understanding a mystery, not the fullness of revelation.

C

canon of scripture The official list of the books of the Bible regarded as sacred. The canons of scripture vary among different churches. The list of books accepted by Protestant churches does not include some books and parts of books that are accepted by Catholic and Orthodox churches. *See also* deuterocanonical books.

chosen people According to the Old Testament, descendants of Abraham, the Jewish people, who were chosen by God to be the recipients of divine revelation and to play a unique role in salvation history (Gen. 12:2–3).

Christian A follower of Christ. According to Acts 11:26, the disciples of Jesus were first called Christians in Antioch. "Christ" comes from the Greek *christos,* the "anointed one" or Messiah.

church Used in three related ways: (1) The entire people of God throughout the world. (2) The local church. (3) Any assembly of believers gathered for celebration, especially of the Lord's Supper. In the Nicene Creed, the church is recognized as one—holy, catholic (universal), and apostolic.

circumcision The act of surgically removing the foreskin of the penis. According to Jewish law, males are to be circumcised eight days after birth (Gen. 17:12–14; Lev. 12:3). Circumcision was the mark of the covenant for Jews and a point of conflict for the early Church. Today circumcision is a personal and sometimes medical choice, more commonly practiced in some cultures than others.

cities of refuge Cities designated in the Old Testament as safe places where an individual who had accidentally caused the death of another could seek protection from the victim's family members who were seeking revenge (Josh. 20). Initially the accused would seek safety by clinging to the horns of the altar in the sanctuary. Later on, various cities in strategic locations were set aside as safe havens. Offering sanctuary was a humanitarian effort to protect people who were falsely accused and to prevent blood feuds between families that would continue until one family was completely annihilated. Still practiced today, sanctuary is often in the form of aid to the homeless and persecuted.

contextualist A person who interprets biblical passages by considering the literary and historical context and the whole process of revelation in order to correctly understand what the Bible is teaching.

covenant A solemn agreement between human beings or between God and human beings in which mutual commitments are recognized. A covenant can also be called a testament. In the Bible, two covenants are central: (1) the covenant between God and the people of ancient Israel established at Mount Sinai through Moses, also called the Old Testament or old covenant; and (2) the new covenant established by Jesus through his sacrificial death and resurrection, also called the New Testament. The term *testament* has come to be associated primarily with the sacred scriptures that record the history and meaning of the two biblical covenants.

Creation accounts The two accounts of God's creation of all things presented in Gen. 1:1–2:4a; 2:4b–3:24. Although different in their details, both accounts present Creation as a divine action that affirms the goodness of all creatures; in particular, humans were created in the image of God (Gen. 1:27) and called to live in mutual and life-giving friendships (Gen. 2:18–22).

D

day of judgment The biblical name for the time when God's justice will prevail, also known as the "day of the LORD" or the "day of wrath." In the Old Testament, the prophets proclaimed a "day of the LORD," in which all of humanity will share the bounty of the earth, "beat their swords into plowshares," and make war no more (Isa. 2:2–4). The prophets also declared that the "day of the LORD" was a time when God's wrath would be brought against those who practiced idolatry and injustice (Zeph. 2:1–3). In the New Testament, the day of judgment came to mean the last judgment, when Jesus Christ will judge each person (Matt. 10:15; 12:36).

Dead Sea Scrolls Scrolls found in 1947 in clay jars in a cave on the northwest shore of the Dead Sea containing portions of the Hebrew scriptures and other writings (in Hebrew, Aramaic, and Greek) that date to as early as 250 B.C. Scholars believe a group called the Essenes hid them there, perhaps in connection with the Roman destruction of Jerusalem in A.D. 70. The scrolls are older by a thousand years than any other copies of Old Testament books in existence. *See also* Essenes.

deuterocanonical books Also called the Apocrypha, seven books that are part of the Catholic Old Testament, but are not included in many Protestant Bibles. The deuterocanonical books were part of a Greek-language collection of the Jewish scriptures called the Septuagint. They are Tobit, Judith, 1 Maccabees, 2 Maccabees, Sirach, Baruch, and Wisdom of Solomon, along with additions to Esther and Daniel.

Deuteronomist A term for the person or group responsible for writing the history contained in the Old Testament books of Deuteronomy through 2 Kings. The Deuteronomist emphasized that God's just punishment occurred whenever the people sinned and broke their covenant with God. The Deuteronomist also emphasized that if the people repented and returned to obedience to the law of Moses, God's favor would return.

devil, demon A fallen angel—one who was created naturally good, but who sinned against God by refusing to accept God's authority. *Devil* refers to Satan, Lucifer, or the Evil One, the chief of the fallen angels; a *demon* is an agent of the Evil One.

Diaspora A community of people who live in exile from their native land (from the Greek *diaspeirein,* "to scatter"). In the Old Testament, the Diaspora of the Jewish people began in 587 B.C., when the temple in Jerusalem was destroyed and many Jews were taken into exile in Babylon.

disciple A follower of Christ. Based on a word for "pupil" or "student," the term is used to designate both those who learned from and followed Jesus in New Testament times (the disciples) and those who commit to follow him today.

dispersion. *See* Diaspora.

E

Elohim One of the names for God in the Old Testament. Some scholars translate the word in the plural to mean "divinities" or "host of heaven"; other scholars consider Elohim a "majestic plural."

Elohist (E) tradition The materials in the Pentateuch that come from the group of writers (seventh to sixth centuries B.C.) who use Elohim for the name of God. The materials portray God as a humanlike figure who appears in person at different events and who is capable of regret.

Emmanuel A name for Jesus (Matt. 1:23), from the Hebrew meaning "God with us."

Essenes A group of pious, ultraconservative Jews who left the temple in Jerusalem and began a community beside the Dead Sea at Qumran. Originating in 100 B.C., the Essenes thrived until A.D. 70, when the Romans violently put down a Jewish rebellion. The Essene community copied, wrote, and preserved the library of texts known today as the Dead Sea Scrolls.

E tradition. *See* Elohist (E) tradition.

evangelist Based on a word for "good news," a term that describes anyone who actively works to spread the gospel of Jesus; more commonly and specifically, one of the persons traditionally recognized as an author of one of the four gospels: Matthew, Mark, Luke, and John.

Eve The name (related to the Hebrew *hawwah,* "a living being") given to the first woman, who was the partner of Adam and the mother of Cain and Abel.

exegesis An explanation or critical interpretation of scripture, from the Greek *exegesis,* which means "to draw out" or "to explain." The writers and editors of the Bible lived in various countries and cultures, wrote in several different languages, and wrote about events that spanned thousands of years. Faithful scholars have dedicated their lives to understanding the languages, symbols, culture, history, and meanings intended by those who wrote the Bible. The work of scholars assists church leaders and believers in their interpretation. Modern scholars use a number of methods to deepen understanding of the Bible. These methods are often called criticisms, not in the sense of being critically negative, but in the sense of taking a disciplined approach to the Bible as literature. *See also* form criticism; historical-critical method; literary criticism; redaction criticism; source criticism; textual criticism.

exile The forced or voluntary relocation from one's native land to another land, from the Latin *exilium,* meaning "banishment." *See also* Babylonian exile; Diaspora.

exodus The departure of the Israelites from Egypt under the leadership of Moses, described in the book of Exodus (a word meaning "going out"). The exodus is celebrated at Passover as the liberation of the chosen people.

F

fall, the The biblical revelation about the origins of sin and evil in the world, expressed figuratively in the story of Adam and Eve in Genesis; also called the "fall from grace." *See also* original sin.

Father A way of speaking about and relating to God. Jesus called God *abba* ("father") and taught his disciples to pray to God as "Our Father."

form criticism A method of studying the literary forms of a document in order to ascertain the background of a particular passage. For example, biblical form criticism studies such forms as parables, proverbs, and poems in order to discover the origin and history of a particular scriptural text.

fundamentalism A way of interpreting the Bible and Christian doctrine based on the literal meaning of the words and without regard to the historical setting in which the writings or teachings were first developed. A person who holds such a perspective is called a fundamentalist.

G

Gehenna The name (from the Hebrew *ge hinnom,* the "Valley of Hinnom") of the place where children were once sacrificed to Molech (Baal; Jer. 19:5). Jesus spoke of Gehenna as a place of punishment for those who refused to repent and be converted.

genre A category of literature, art, or music. Genres in scripture include prose, poetry, myths, law codes, historical narratives, didactic (teaching) narratives, parables, and miracle stories. The first step in correctly interpreting a scripture passage is to know its genre.

Gentile A term (from the Latin *gens,* meaning "race" or "clan") usually used in the New Testament to designate a person who is not Jewish; in other contexts it can be used to refer to a person who is not Christian.

gospel The "good news" of the revelation of God in and through Jesus Christ, proclaimed initially by him, then by the apostles, and now by the Church. The term also refers to the four gospels of the New Testament (Matthew, Mark, Luke, and John), which focus on the person, life, teachings, death, and resurrection of Jesus.

H

heaven A term from the Old English meaning "home of God": has various meanings: (1) in the ancient world, the sky or firmament, considered the dwelling place of the divine; (2) in Judaism, because of the reluctance to pronounce the name

of God, a term sometimes used as a substitute for God's name; or (3) the final goal of all Christians, where they are definitively united with God and reunited with their fellow Christians.

Hebrew A member of the Israelite people; also their language. The term derives from Hebrew words meaning either "one from the other side" or possibly "immigrant."

Hebrew scriptures. *See* Old Testament.

hermeneutics The study of the interpretation of texts, especially the study of the theory and method of biblical interpretation, from the Greek *hermeneus,* "interpreter."

high place An elevated location used for religious rites. Both the Hebrews and the Canaanites established places of worship on high ground (Gen. 12:7–8; 1 Kings 13:32). The Canaanite high places were used for fertility rites and human sacrifices offered to Baal, Molech, and Asherah. Over the centuries, the Hebrews destroyed the high places of the Canaanites (Deut. 12:2–3).

historical books Books making up a continuous narrative of Israel's history from the conquest of the land of Canaan to the rebuilding of Jerusalem after the Babylonian exile: Joshua, Judges, Ruth, 1 and 2 Samuel, 1 and 2 Kings, 1 and 2 Chronicles, Ezra, Nehemiah, and Esther.

historical-critical method A method of studying texts, especially the Bible, that considers the historical context, the philosophical presuppositions, and the theological perspective (from the Greek *historia,* "record" or "account," and *kritikos,* "able to judge"). *See also* biblical criticism.

Holy of Holies The innermost part of the temple in Jerusalem and the repository for the ark of the covenant. Only the high priest was permitted to enter the Holy of Holies and then only once a year, on the Day of Atonement.

Holy Spirit The third person of the Trinity (from the Latin *spiritus,* "breath" or "soul"), the Paraclete divinely sent to teach and guide the Church to the end of times. *See also* Paraclete.

I

I AM The name (also "I AM WHO I AM") God called himself when talking to Moses from the burning bush (Exod. 3:14). It expresses that God simply is, God has no beginning and no end, and everything else exists because of God. Yahweh, the most common name for God in the Old Testament, was probably based on that phrase. The New Testament contains suggestions of this title in connection with Jesus. Jesus asks Peter, "Who do you say that I am?" And Peter says, "You are the Messiah, the Son of the living God" (Matt. 16:16).

idolatry Worship of other beings, creatures, or material goods in a way that is fitting for God alone. It is a violation of the first commandment (Exod. 20:3; Deut. 5:7).

incarnation, the Based on words meaning "in flesh," a term that refers to the mystery and belief that the Son of God assumed human nature and "became flesh" in the person of Jesus of Nazareth (John 1:14). The incarnation means that Jesus, the Son of God and second person of the Trinity, is both fully God and fully human.

Israel A name that comes from Jacob's experience of "wrestling with God" (Gen. 32:28): (1) the twelve tribes of Israel as descendants of the twelve sons of Jacob; (2) the chosen people or Jewish people as a whole; (3) the northern kingdom (Israel) in contrast to the southern kingdom (Judah); or (4) the modern nation of Israel.

Israelites Members of the twelve tribes of Israel descended from Jacob, who inhabited the land of Israel during biblical times.

J

Jesus Christ The central figure in the New Testament, the Savior and Son of God. In Hebrew Jesus means "God saves" and was the name given to the historical Jesus at the annunciation. Christ comes from the Greek *christos*, meaning the "anointed one," and translates the Hebrew word meaning "messiah." In the Old Testament, kings, priests, and prophets were anointed; in giving Jesus the title Christ, the New Testament indicates that Jesus fulfilled the messianic hope of Israel through his threefold office of king, prophet, and priest.

J tradition. *See* Yahwist (J) tradition.

jubilee The fiftieth year occurring at the end of seven sabbatical cycles of seven years each, in which all landed property was returned to its original owners, slaves were set free, all debts were erased, and the land was let rest (Lev. 25:8–55). The intent of the jubilee was to create a just society, in which the bounty and the land were shared, to prevent abject poverty, and to restore God's intended equality to human relationships.

Judah, Judea Terms stemming from the Hebrew word *yehudah*, meaning "praise the Lord." Judah was a son of Jacob and Leah and founder of one of the twelve tribes of Israel. The tribe of Judah became the most powerful of the twelve and occupied the territory around Jerusalem. During the monarchy, Jerusalem was the headquarters for the administration of the nation of Israel, the location of the temple, and the dwelling place of the royal family of David. After the civil war at the end of Solomon's reign, the northern tribes separated and became known as the kingdom of Israel, and the southern tribes became known as the kingdom of Judah. In the time of Roman rule, the area was called Judea.

Judaism The monotheistic religion of the Jewish people, who trace their origin to Abraham and whose religious observance is based on the Torah. The term traces back to Judah, the fourth son of Jacob, and the tribe descended from him.

judges Men and women who served the Hebrew people as tribal leaders and military commanders, as recounted in the book of Judges. They were not like today's judges, presiding over legal cases. Instead, they were charismatic leaders raised up by God to lead the Israelites when they were a loosely knit federation of tribes (1200–1000 B.C.). The judges were clan heroes who empowered the faith of the people in times of crisis and focused their attention on the promises of the covenant.

K

kingdom of God The rule of God over the hearts of people and, as a consequence of that, the development of a new social order based on unconditional love; also referred to as the "reign of God."

kingdom of heaven Phrase used in the gospel of Matthew for "kingdom of God," which may reflect the Jewish custom of not speaking directly about God.

L

Last Supper The last meal Jesus shared with his disciples, during the Jewish celebration of Passover, before being handed over for crucifixion. It is commemorated by believers on the Thursday before Easter.

law (law of Moses) The Torah, or the law of Moses, which consists of the first five books of the Bible (Genesis through Deuteronomy), which are followed by the Prophets in the Hebrew Bible. In the New Testament, Jesus often refers to "the law and the prophets." *See also* Tanakh.

law, new The law of the gospel of Jesus Christ, a law of love, grace, and freedom. It is distinguished from the old law, or the law of Moses.

lectio divina A form of meditative prayer, usually focused on a passage from scripture, that involves repetitive readings and periods of reflection. It can serve as either private or communal prayer.

Levites Descendants of Levi, one of Jacob and Leah's sons (Gen. 29:34), and one of the twelve tribes of Israel. Moses and Aaron were descendants of Levi (Exod. 2:1). According to God's command, only Aaron and his sons could serve as priests (Exod. 28:1). Thus, the Levites became the tribe entrusted with sacred ministries, the caretakers of the tabernacle and the temple (Num. 1:48–54). *See also* priest; sacrifice.

literal sense A form of biblical interpretation that translates a biblical text word for word and emphasizes the explicit meaning of the text. *See also* senses of scripture.

literary criticism A method of studying scripture that seeks to understand a text as a work of literature. Literary criticism considers what literary form (poetry, letter, story, and so on) or device (pun, parable, exaggeration, and so on) is used and how the particular literary forms or devices functioned in an ancient society. *See also* exegesis.

literary forms Categories of smaller units of text that can be used within a particular genre. For example, the newspaper genre contains many literary forms, including national news stories, editorials, obituaries, sports stories, and classified ads.

LORD The English rendering of the Hebrew word for God YHWH (Yahweh). Because this divine name was considered too sacred to be spoken, readers would automatically substitute the Hebrew word for "Lord," *Adonai*, for it.

Lord In the New Testament, a term used both for God the Father and, on occasion, for Jesus, to reflect awareness of Jesus' identity as the Son of God.

Lord's Supper A sacramental rite, also called Communion, established by Jesus at the Last Supper, in which his sacrificial death and resurrection are both remembered ("Do this in remembrance of me") and renewed ("This is my body, given for you"). The celebration of the Lord's Supper is a very important and meaningful aspect of worship for many believers.

M

messiah An anointed agent of God, from the Hebrew *mashiah*, meaning "to anoint" (which in Greek is *christos*, English "Christ"). Many Jews of Jesus' time were awaiting the arrival of a messiah to deliver them from oppression. Jesus was hailed as the Messiah, but he was not the expected military messiah. Instead, as Savior, he preached the kingdom of God and gave his life for the forgiveness of sins.

monotheism The belief in and worship of one true God. The Israelites were unique in their monotheism; other peoples in biblical times were polytheistic, believing in many gods and goddesses.

Mosaic law. *See* law (law of Moses).

N

natural law Our God-given instinct to be in right relationship with God, other people, the world, and ourselves. The basis for natural law is our participation in God's wisdom and goodness, because we are created in the divine likeness. The fundamental expressions of natural law remain fixed and unchanging, which is why natural law is the foundation for both personal morality and civil norms.

new covenant The covenant or law established by God and fulfilled in Jesus Christ. Jesus speaks of the new covenant at the Last Supper. The new covenant does not replace the old covenant, Mosaic law, much less oppose it; rather it fulfills it and brings the old covenant to completion. *See also* law, new; old covenant.

New Testament The name of the twenty-seven books of the Bible written during the early years of the Church in response to the life, mission, death, and resurrection of Jesus. It is also another name for the new covenant established between God and humanity by Jesus.

northern kingdom. *See* Israel.

O

old covenant The covenant or law that was given by God to Moses on Mount Sinai for the Israelites. Although Christians consider the old law a preparation for the new covenant or new law given by Christ, the old covenant has never been revoked. *See also* law, new; new covenant.

Old Testament The name of the thirty-nine books of the Bible that record the history of salvation from creation, through the story of ancient Israel, and up to the time of Jesus. It also refers to the old covenant established between God and the people of Israel in God's encounter with Moses on Mount Sinai. *See also* Septuagint; Tanakh.

oral tradition In the ancient world, the sacred wisdom, parables, stories, and rules of life revealed to the ancestors and passed down by storytellers. By telling these stories around campfires and at religious festivals, the sacred wisdom was passed from one generation to the next, until later scribes wrote it down. Many of the stories and teachings in both the Old and New Testaments were passed on by oral tradition for generations before they were written down.

original sin The sin of the first human beings, Adam and Eve, who disobeyed God's command, lost their original holiness, and thereby became subject to death. Original sin affects every person born into the world.

P

parable A story with a double meaning intended to convey a religious truth or particular teaching through the use of metaphors. Parables are a central feature of Jesus' teaching ministry.

Paraclete A name for the Holy Spirit based on a word for "helper" or "advocate." *See also* Holy Spirit.

paradise A word referring to both the Garden of Eden in Genesis and the New Jerusalem in Revelation; it has also come to be identified with heaven.

Parousia The second coming of Christ, when his kingdom will be fully established and his triumph over evil will be complete.

Passion The sufferings of Jesus during the final days of his life: his agony in the garden at Gethsemane, his trial, and his crucifixion. Contemporary theologians often relate the Passion of Christ to the present-day suffering of people, especially those who are needy and marginalized.

Passover The Jewish festival that memorializes the exodus, God's deliverance of the Israelites from slavery in Egypt. Before the tenth plague, the killing of the firstborn, the Israelites were to sacrifice a lamb and smear its blood on their doorposts; seeing the blood, the Lord would "pass over" those houses, sparing the Hebrew firstborn (Exod. 12:13). The Israelites escaped from Egypt, crossed the Red Sea when it opened for them (it closed over Pharaoh's army), and became a free people. The Passover festival, with its seder meal and Paschal lamb, honors

God, who heard the cries of his people and responded with miraculous power to free them. Jesus gathered his disciples together at a Passover meal and offered them the bread of life (Matt. 26:17–30; Mark 14:12–26; Luke 22:7–23; 1 Cor. 10:1, 11:23–26). *See also* exodus; Last Supper; Lord's Supper.

patriarch A traditional term for Abraham, Isaac, and Jacob, the progenitors of the Israelites. Today the term *ancestors* is preferred, so as to include the wives of these fathers of the Israelite people: Sarah, Rebekah, Leah, and Rachel.

Pentateuch The English term (from the Greek *pente,* meaning "five," and *teuchos,* meaning "vessels" or "containers for scrolls") for the Torah, the first five books of the Hebrew scriptures: Genesis, Exodus, Leviticus, Numbers, and Deuteronomy. *See also* Old Testament; Torah.

Pentecost The biblical event that followed the resurrection and ascension of Jesus at which the Holy Spirit was poured out on his disciples. The first Pentecost is often identified as the birth of the Church (Acts 2:1–13). In the Christian liturgical year, Pentecost recalls the biblical event and is celebrated fifty days after Easter.

people of God The biblical image for the Church, referring to those who share in Christ's mission as priest, prophet, and king.

Pharisees A Jewish sect during the time of Jesus known for its study of and strict adherence to the law.

priest One who offers sacrifices to God on behalf of the people. The first priest in the Hebrew tradition was Melchizedek of Salem. With Abraham he offered bread and wine and was a "priest of God Most High" (Gen. 14:18). As part of the Sinai covenant, God instituted that the tribe of Levi, the Levites, would receive no allotment of land, but were to be the priests for Israel (Josh. 18:7). As the Israelites settled Canaan, they worshiped at local sanctuaries, where the priests offered the required animal sacrifices. Once the temple was built in Jerusalem, religious observances became centered there. All local sanctuaries

were destroyed, and the priests were all moved to Jerusalem, where they assisted with worship and sacrifice in the temple. The high priest was the chief priest and led all the major religious rituals in the temple. The priesthood of Christ fulfills the expectations of the Old Testament priesthood through Christ's perfect sacrifice on the cross (Heb. 7:1–28). *See also* Levites.

Priestly (P) tradition A theological tradition present in the Pentateuch that is the work of priestly scribes who hoped to restore the memory of the divided kingdom, Israel and Judah, and restore focus on the Sinai covenant. In this tradition the scribes blended the sacred names from northern Israel and southern Judah into a unified title, which in English translates as "Lord God." God is portrayed as transcendent and distant, thus the need for priestly intercession.

promised land The land that God promised to the descendants of Abraham (Gen. 12), the land of Canaan, or Palestine.

prophet A person chosen by God to communicate a divine message to the people (from the Greek *prophetes,* "interpreter" or "spokesperson"). A prophet was not necessarily a person who predicted the future. Prophecy refers to the messages communicated by prophets on behalf of God. Sixteen books in the Bible are named for prophets: Isaiah, Jeremiah, Ezekiel, Daniel, Hosea, Joel, Amos, Obadiah, Jonah, Micah, Nahum, Habakkuk, Zephaniah, Haggai, Zechariah, and Malachi. The prophecies of other prophets, such as Moses, Deborah, Nathan, Elijah, Elisha, and Anna, are recorded in other books. Isaiah, Jeremiah, and Ezekiel are called the major prophets, because so many of their prophecies were written down.

proverb Any short wisdom saying that has been orally passed down as advice from generation to generation. The book of Proverbs in the Old Testament contains many examples of such wisdom sayings, which provide an understanding of human experience from a religious perspective.

psalm A hymn or song that expresses praise, thanksgiving, petition, lamentation, or a historical memory of God's actions on behalf of the people. The Psalter, or the book of Psalms, in the Old Testament contains 150 psalms.

P tradition. *See* Priestly (P) tradition.

R

redaction criticism The technical effort to determine the editorial history of a particular text, especially in biblical studies.

redemption The process by which we are "bought back" (the meaning of *redeem*) from slavery to sin into a right relationship with God. We are redeemed by the grace of God and through the life, death, and resurrection of Jesus Christ. As the agent of redemption, Jesus is called the Redeemer.

reign of God. *See* kingdom of God.

resurrection of Christ The passage of Jesus from death to life "on the third day" after his crucifixion. This is the heart of the paschal mystery and the basis of our hope in the resurrection of the dead.

resurrection of the dead The Christian doctrine that all those deemed righteous by God will be raised and will live forever with God in heaven. It is the conviction that not only our souls, but also our transformed bodies will live on after death (Apostles' Creed: "I believe in the resurrection of the body").

revelation God's self-communication and disclosure of the divine plan for humankind through creation, events, persons, and, most fully, Jesus Christ.

S

sabbath In the Old Testament, the "seventh day" on which God rested after the work of creation was completed. In Jewish law, this is the weekly day of rest to remember God's work through private prayer, communal worship, and spiritual disciplines such as fasting. For most Christians, this is Sunday, the day on which Jesus was raised from the dead.

sacrifice An offering made to God by a priest on behalf of the people as a sign of adoration,

thanksgiving, petition, or communion (from the Latin *sacer*, "sacred," and *facere*, "to make"; Lev. 1–7). In the Old Testament, a sacrifice was needed as atonement—that is, a healing rite that restored holiness by cleansing the people from infractions of the law. Sacrifices also reconciled their covenant relationship with God (Ps. 51:1–17). The only perfect sacrifice is that offered by Christ on the cross (Heb. 7:22–28).

salvation Liberation from sin and eternal union with God in heaven. Salvation is accomplished by God alone through the dying and rising of Jesus Christ.

salvation history The pattern of events in human history that exemplify God's presence and saving actions.

Samaritans The inhabitants of Samaria. The Samaritans rejected the Jerusalem temple and worshiped on Mount Gerizim. The New Testament describes the Jewish rejection of Samaritans in both the parable of the good Samaritan (Luke 10:29–37) and the account of Jesus' speaking with the Samaritan woman at the well (John 4:1–42).

Satan The name, from a Hebrew word meaning "adversary," of the fallen angel or spirit of evil who is the enemy of God and a continuing instigator of temptation and sin in the world.

Savior A title (from the Latin *salvator*, meaning "saver" or "preserver") appropriately given to Jesus, whose Hebrew name means "God saves."

scribes In biblical times, government officials and scholars of the law of Moses.

scripture A sacred writing; for Christians, the Old and New Testaments, which make up the Bible and are recognized as the Word of God.

Semites A group of peoples of the ancient Near East, including Arabs, Arameans, Assyrians, Babylonians, Canaanites, Hebrews, and Phoenicians, who share similarities in ethnicity, language, and culture. The term derives from Shem, one of Noah's three sons (Gen. 10:1).

senses of scripture Ways of interpreting

scripture. Every text is open to a variety of interpretations, or senses. In the history of Christian biblical interpretation, the following meanings or senses of scripture have been proposed: (1) the literal sense seeks the word-for-word meaning of a text; (2) the allegorical sense seeks the symbolic meaning behind the text; (3) the anagogical sense seeks the spiritual meaning of a text; (4) the tropological sense searches for the ethical implications of a text; and (5) the typological sense shows how the Old Testament prefigured the New Testament.

Septuagint The name (from the Latin *septuaginta,* meaning "seventy") given to the Greek translation of the Hebrew Bible that was widely used among hellenized Jews at the time of Jesus. According to a popular legend, a group of seventy (or seventy-two) Jewish scholars, working independently, produced the identically same translation in seventy (or seventy-two) days; hence the name Septuagint ("seventy"; abbreviated LXX). *See also* Old Testament; Torah.

Shema The prayer said by observant Jews three times a day for thousands of years to honor the unity of God. In essence, it calls the faithful across the centuries: "Hear, O Israel: the LORD [Yahweh] is our God [Elohim], the LORD alone. You shall love the LORD your God with all your heart, and with all your soul, and with all your might" (Deut. 6:4–5). Jesus uses the Shema to summarize the law and the faith of Moses as the first of the two great commandments (see Matt. 22:36–40).

source criticism A method of studying scripture that identifies writings from other ancient cultures that influenced the writers of a specific passage. It considers whether the writers build on an existing story, myth, or other literature as a basis for their work and whether the theology or justice ethic of the biblical version varies from that of the cultural source. *See also* exegesis.

southern kingdom. *See* Judah, Judea.

suffering servant An image used by the prophet Isaiah for the people of Israel, who endured the pain of alienation and grief across history. Yet the prophet also proclaimed that one to come, the promised one of God, would suffer as a result of his compassion for humanity. He was to be Immanuel—"God with us." The suffering servant of the Lord would be one with the people and would be one who knew suffering. He would bear our sufferings and bring us redemption (Isa. 52:13–53:12).

synagogue A Greek word, meaning "meeting" or "assembly," that refers to the worship assemblies of Jews who, living outside of Jerusalem, gathered, prayed, read scripture, and heard teaching. Jesus is depicted in Luke 4:14–30 as beginning his Galilean ministry in the synagogue at Nazareth.

Synoptic Gospels A term (from a Greek word meaning "seeing together") for the gospels of Matthew, Mark, and Luke, because they follow a similar pattern in both their overall structure and their individual narratives.

T

tabernacle The portable dwelling carried by the Israelites during their wilderness wandering that housed the presence of God (Exod. 25:8–9).

Talmud A Hebrew word meaning "instruction" that refers to the collection of rabbinic writings that constitute the basic religious authority in Judaism.

Tanakh A name for the Hebrew Bible that is an acronym referring to the three major divisions; TaNaKh: Torah ("Law"), Nebi'im ("Prophets"), and Ketubim ("Writings").

temple A term that almost always, in the Old Testament, refers to the temple in Jerusalem. The so-called First Temple period (1006–586 B.C.) began with David's occupation of Jerusalem and included Solomon's building the first temple. This period ended with the Babylonian exile. The Second Temple period (538 B.C.–A.D. 70) began with the return of the Jewish exiles, who rebuilt the temple, which was dedicated in 515 B.C. Shortly before the birth of Jesus, Herod the Great renovated the temple, enlarging and decorating it magnificently. This temple was destroyed by the Romans in A.D. 70.

Ten Commandments The ten laws given by God to Moses on Mount Sinai (Exod. 20:2–17; Deut. 5:6–21) as the fundamental rules of conduct for the Israelites. The first three of the Ten Commandments concern the relationship with God; the other seven commandments concern relationships with others.

testament A word (from the Latin *testamentum,* meaning "will" or "covenant") used for the two parts of the Bible, the Old Testament and the New Testament, both of which are covenants offered by God. *See also* covenant.

textual criticism A method of studying scripture that compares and contrasts various translations of scripture to more clearly understand the meaning of a given passage. It considers whether the modern translations are in agreement with the oldest versions of scripture available. *See also* exegesis.

Torah A Hebrew word meaning "law" or "instruction" used for Mosaic law or the Pentateuch, the first five books of the Hebrew scriptures: Genesis, Exodus, Leviticus, Numbers, and Deuteronomy. *See also* Old Testament; Tanakh.

twelve tribes A confederation of twelve Hebrew tribes that traced their origin to the twelve sons of Jacob by his wives, Leah and Rachel, and their maidservants Zilpah and Bilhah: Reuben, Simeon, Levi, Judah, Issachar, Zebulun, Gad, Asher, Dan, Naphtali, Joseph, and Benjamin. The stories in the Pentateuch tell how God renewed with Jacob the promises of the covenant he had originally made with Abraham, including the giving of the land (Gen. 28:10–17). The twelve tribes settled in the promised land, each in its own area, except for the Levites, who were to be the priests (Josh. 13–19).

W

wisdom depicted in the Hebrew scriptures as the action of God in the world; in Christian theology it is one of the seven gifts of the Holy Spirit that enables a person to know God's divine plan of salvation.

wisdom literature A genre of ancient literature that extolled the virtue of wisdom and gave practical advice on what it meant to be wise. In the Old Testament, the books of Proverbs, Job, Ecclesiastes, and Song of Solomon are wisdom literature. Typical themes are the value of wisdom, self-control, patience, honesty, diligence, and respect for elders. Wisdom is sometimes personified as Woman Wisdom (Prov. 1:1–36). In wisdom literature there is little mention of Israelite history, the law of Moses, or the covenant; the emphasis is on what can be learned by experience and applied in daily life.

Word of God (1) God's word, or the power through which God created all that is (Ps. 33:6). (2) The Bible, which has the power to create new life within the soul, to renew spirits, to teach, and to give hope (2 Tim. 3:14–16). (3) Jesus—the Logos in Greek (John 1:1; Rev. 19:13), a title that describes the divine nature of Christ: "The Word was with God, and the Word was God" (John 1:1). *See also* Bible.

Y

Yahweh A word reconstructed by modern biblical scholars from the four consonants, YHWH, used in the Hebrew scriptures for the name of God. Scholars believe YHWH is connected to the Hebrew verb "to be." At the burning bush God tells his name to Moses as "I AM WHO I AM" (Exod. 3:14).

Yahwist (J) tradition A particular school of writing woven throughout the Pentateuch attributed to authors or a school that used Yahweh for the name of God. (The first scholars to discover this source were German, and in German *Yahweh* is spelled "Jahweh," hence the J tradition.) This is the oldest literary source in the Pentateuch. It was probably written by unknown scribes from Judah around 950 B.C. To the Yahwists, God had human, or anthropomorphic, qualities. This God walked in the garden (Gen. 3:8), sculpted humanity with divine hands (Gen. 2:7), and planted groves of trees (Gen. 2:8).

Yom Kippur The Day of Atonement, a Jewish holy day that is observed with prayer and fasting in accord with Leviticus 16.

Z

Zealots A Jewish group at the beginning of the first century A.D. who sought religious and political independence from the Romans and rose up in open rebellion. After their defeat, they carried on guerrilla warfare against the Romans.

Zion, Mount The hill on which the citadel of David and the city of Jerusalem stood. On Zion, David built his palace, and Solomon later built the temple of Jerusalem. The city of Jerusalem came to represent the people and faith of Israel (Pss. 87:2; 149:2). In scripture, the use of the phrase "virgin Zion" represents the ideal, pure relationship between the people of Israel and God (2 Kings 19:21; Lam. 2:13–22). During the Babylonian exile (587–539 B.C.), the prophets promised a time when God would make his home again in Zion (Zech. 2:10–11). In the book of Revelation, Jesus Christ, the Lamb of God, appears on Mount Zion (14:1).

Concordance

Abbreviations

The following abbreviations are used for the books of the Bible:

1Ch	1 Chronicles	Hos	Hosea
1Co	1 Corinthians	Isa	Isaiah
1Jn	1 John	Jas	James
1Ki	1 Kings	Jdg	Judges
1Pe	1 Peter	Jer	Jeremiah
1Sa	1 Samuel	Jn	John
1Th	1 Thessalonians	Jnh	Jonah
1Ti	1 Timothy	Job	Job
2Ch	2 Chronicles	Joel	Joel
2Co	2 Corinthians	Jos	Joshua
2Jn	2 John	Jude	Jude
2Ki	2 Kings	La	Lamentations
2Pe	2 Peter	Lev	Leviticus
2Sa	2 Samuel	Lk	Luke
2Th	2 Thessalonians	Mal	Malachi
2Ti	2 Timothy	Mic	Micah
3Jn	3 John	Mk	Mark
Ac	Acts	Mt	Matthew
Am	Amos	Na	Nahum
Col	Colossians	Ne	Nehemiah
Da	Daniel	Nu	Numbers
Dt	Deuteronomy	Ob	Obadiah
Ecc	Ecclesiastes	Phm	Philemon
Eph	Ephesians	Php	Philippians
Est	Esther	Pr	Proverbs
Ex	Exodus	Ps	Psalms
Eze	Ezekiel	Rev	Revelation
Ezr	Ezra	Ro	Romans
Gal	Galatians	Ru	Ruth
Ge	Genesis	SS	Song of Solomon
Hab	Habakkuk	Tit	Titus
Hag	Haggai	Zec	Zechariah
Heb	Hebrews	Zep	Zephaniah

Other abbreviations and special symbols used:

S . . . . Shorter ending of Mark

T . . . . Psalm titles

† . . . . A dagger distinguishes "LORD" and "GOD" from "Lord" and "God" in Hebrew Bible references

→ . . . . An arrow following an entry heading points to related words for additional study

[[ ]] . . . . Contexts in double brackets are from passages that are similarly bracketed in the NRSV (e.g., John 7:53–8:11)

For further study consult *The Concise Concordance to the New Revised Standard Version* (Oxford University Press, 1993) and *The NRSV Concordance Unabridged* (Zondervan, 1991).

—John R. Kohlenberger III

A

ABANDON → ABANDONED
Dt 4.31 will neither a you nor destroy you;
2Ch 15. 2 but if you a him, he will a you.
Ac 2.27 For you will not a my soul to Hades

ABANDONED → ABANDON
Dt 29.25 they a the covenant of the LORD,
Isa 54. 7 For a brief moment I a you,

ABBA
Mk 14.36 "A, Father, for you all things are possible;
Ro 8.15 When we cry, "A! Father!"
Gal 4. 6 into our hearts, crying, "A! Father!"

ABIDE
Ge 6. 3 My spirit shall not a in mortals forever,
Ps 91. 1 a in the shadow of the Almighty,
Jn 15. 4 A in me as I a in you.
1Co 13.13 faith, hope, and love a, these three;
1Jn 2.28 And now, little children, a in him,

ABILITY → ABLE
Mt 25.15 to each according to his a.
Ac 2. 4 as the Spirit gave them a.

ABLE → ABILITY
Da 3.17 God whom we serve is a to deliver
Mk 10.38 you a to drink the cup that I drink,
Ro 14. 4 the Lord is a to make them stand.
2Co 9. 8 God is a to provide you with every
Eph 6.11 a to stand against the wiles of the devil.
Heb 2.18 a to help those who are being tested.
7.25 he is a for all time to save

ABOLISH → ABOLISHED
Da 11.31 shall a the regular burnt offering
Mt 5.17 I have come not to a but to fulfill.

ABOLISHED → ABOLISH
Eph 2.15 a the law with its commandments
2Ti 1.10 who a death and brought life

ABOMINABLE → ABOMINATION
2Ch 28. 3 the a practices of the nations
Eze 7.20 they made their a images,

ABOMINATION → ABOMINABLE
Pr 6.16 seven that are an a to him:
Da 9.27 shall be an a that desolates,

ABOUND → ABOUNDED, ABOUNDING
Dt 28.11 LORD will make you a in prosperity,
Ro 6. 1 in sin in order that grace may a?

ABOUNDED → ABOUND
Ro 5.20 sin increased, grace a all the more,

ABOUNDING → ABOUND
Ex 34. 6 a in steadfast love and faithfulness,
Ps 86. 5 a in steadfast love to all who call
Joel 2.13 to anger, and a in steadfast love,
Jnh 4. 2 to anger, and a in steadfast love,

ABUNDANCE → ABUNDANTLY
Lk 12.15 one's life does not consist in the a
2Co 9. 8 provide you with every blessing in a

ABUNDANTLY → ABUNDANCE
Jn 10.10 that they may have life, and have it a.

ACCEPT → ACCEPTABLE
Jn 1.11 his own people did not a him.

ACCEPTABLE → ACCEPT
Ps 19.14 meditation of my heart be a to you,
51.17 sacrifice a to God is a broken spirit;
Ro 12. 1 a living sacrifice, holy and a to God,

ACCOUNT → ACCOUNTABLE
Mt 12.36 judgment you will have to give an a
Heb 4.13 to whom we must render an a.

ACCOUNTABLE → ACCOUNT
Ro 14.12 each of us will be a to God.

ACCURSED → CURSE
Ro 9. 3 I could wish that I myself were a
Rev 22. 3 Nothing a will be found there

ACCUSATION → ACCUSE
Lk 23. 4 no basis for an a against this man."

ACCUSE → ACCUSATION, ACCUSER
Ps 103. 9 He will not always a,
Zec 3. 1 Satan standing at his right hand to a
Mt 12.10 so that they might a him.

ACCUSER → ACCUSE
Rev 12.10 the a of our comrades has been thrown

ACKNOWLEDGE
Dt 4.35 would a that the LORD is God;
Pr 3. 6 In all your ways a him,
Mt 10.32 I also will a before my Father in

ACTIVE
Heb 4.12 the word of God is living and a,

ADD → ADDED
Dt 4. 2 You must neither a anything
Pr 30. 6 Do not a to his words, or else
Lk 12.25 by worrying a a single hour to your

ADDED → ADD
Ecc 3.14 nothing can be a to it, nor anything

ADOPTION
Ro 8.23 groan inwardly while we wait for a,
Gal 4. 5 that we might receive a as children.

ADORNMENT
Pr 3.22 for your soul and a for your neck.
1Pe 3. 4 let your a be the inner self with the

ADULTERERS → ADULTERY
Jer 23.10 For the land is full of a;
1Co 6. 9 idolaters, a, male prostitutes,

ADULTERESS → ADULTERY
Lev 20.10 the a shall be put to death.
Pr 2.16 from the a with her smooth words,

ADULTERY → ADULTERERS, ADULTERESS
Ex 20.14 You shall not commit a.
Jer 3. 9 committing a with stone and tree.
Mt 5.28 committed a with her in his heart.
Lk 16.18 and marries another commits a,
Jn 8. 3 [[a woman who had been caught in a;]]

ADVANTAGE
Ecc 7.12 a of knowledge is that wisdom gives
1Co 10.24 Do not seek your own a, but that of

ADVERSARY
1Pe 5. 8 roaring lion your a the devil prowls

ADVICE
Ps 1. 1 do not follow the a of the wicked,
Pr 8.14 I have good a and sound wisdom;

ADVOCATE
Jn 14.26 But the A, the Holy Spirit,
15.26 the A comes, whom I will send
1Jn 2. 1 we have an a with the Father,

AFFLICT → AFFLICTED, AFFLICTION, AFFLICTIONS
2Sa 7.10 evildoers shall a them no more,
La 3.33 for he does not willingly a
2Th 1. 6 repay with affliction those who a

AFFLICTED → AFFLICT
Na 1.12 Though I have a you, I will afflict
2Co 4. 8 are a in every way, but not crushed;

AFFLICTION → AFFLICT
Ps 25.18 Consider my a and my trouble,
La 1. 9 "O LORD, look at my a,
2Co 4.17 this slight momentary a is preparing

AFFLICTIONS → AFFLICT
Ps 34.19 Many are the a of the righteous,

AFRAID → FEAR
Ex 3. 6 for he was a to look at God.
Lev 26. 6 and no one shall make you a;
Dt 20. 3 Do not lose heart, or be a,
Ps 3. 6 I am not a of ten thousands
27. 1 of whom shall I be a?
Isa 12. 2 I will trust, and will not be a,
Mt 28.10 Jesus said to them, "Do not be a;
Lk 12.32 "Do not be a, little flock,
Heb 13. 6 Lord is my helper; I will not be a.

AGE → AGES
Mt 28.20 with you always, to the end of the a."
Gal 1. 4 to set us free from the present evil a,

AGES → AGE
Col 1.26 has been hidden throughout the a
1Ti 1.17 To the King of the a, immortal,

AGREE
Mt 18.19 if two of you a on earth about
Mk 14.56 and their testimony did not a.

AIR
Eph 2. 2 the ruler of the power of the a,
1Th 4.17 to meet the Lord in the a;

ALERT
Lk 12.37 slaves whom the master finds a
1Co 16.13 Keep a, stand firm in your faith,
Eph 6.18 keep a and always persevere
1Pe 5. 8 Discipline yourselves, keep a.

ALIEN → ALIENS
Ex 2.22 an a residing in a foreign land."
Lev 19.34 you shall love the a as yourself,
Dt 24.17 You shall not deprive a resident a

ALIENS → ALIEN
Eph 2.19 you are no longer strangers and a,
1Pe 2.11 I urge you as a and exiles to abstain

ALIVE → LIVE
Ac 1. 3 suffering he presented himself a
Ro 6.11 dead to sin and a to God
Eph 2. 5 made us a together with Christ—
1Th 4.17 Then we who are a, who are left,
Rev 1.18 I am a forever and ever;
19.20 were thrown a into the lake of fire

ALMIGHTY → MIGHT
Ge 17. 1 "I am God A; walk before me,
Ps 91. 1 who abide in the shadow of the A,
Rev 1. 8 who was and who is to come, the A.
21.22 its temple is the Lord God the A

ALMS
Mt 6. 2 "So whenever you give a,

ALONE
Ge 2.18 not good that the man should be a;
Dt 6. 4 The LORD is our God, the LORD a.
Mk 2. 7 Who can forgive sins but God a?"
10.18 No one is good but God a.

ALPHA
Rev 1. 8 "I am the A and the Omega,"
22.13 I am the A and the Omega,

ALTAR
Ex 27. 1 shall make the a of acacia wood,
30. 1 an a on which to offer incense;
Heb 13.10 We have an a from which those
Rev 6. 9 I saw under the a the souls of those

ALWAYS
Mt 28.20 And remember, I am with you a,
Php 4. 4 Rejoice in the Lord a; again I will

AMAZED → AMAZING
Mt 8.27 a, saying, "What sort of man is this,
Mk 6. 6 And he was a at their unbelief.
Ac 2. 7 A and astonished, they asked,

AMAZING → AMAZED
Mk 12.11 and it is a in our eyes'?"
Rev 15. 3 "Great and a are your deeds,

AMBASSADORS
2Co 5.20 So we are a for Christ,

AMBITION
Php 2. 3 Do nothing from selfish a or conceit

Jas   3.14   envy and selfish **a** in your hearts,

AMEN

Dt   27.15   people shall respond, saying, "**A**!"
2Co   1.20   through him that we say the "**A**,"
Rev   3.14   The words of the **A**, the faithful and

ANCESTORS

Ex   3.13   'The God of your **a** has sent me to
Dt   4.31   not forget the covenant with your **a**
La   5. 7   Our **a** sinned; they are no more,
Ac   5.30   The God of our **a** raised up Jesus,
Heb   1. 1   Long ago God spoke to our **a** in

ANCHOR

Heb   6.19   a sure and steadfast **a** of the soul,

ANCIENT

Da   7. 9   and an **A** One took his throne,
Mic   5. 2   origin is from of old, from **a** days.
Rev   20. 2   He seized the dragon, that **a** serpent,

ANGEL → ANGELS, ARCHANGEL, ARCHANGEL'S

Ex   3. 2   the **a** of the LORD appeared to him
    23.20   going to send an **a** in front of you,
Ps   34. 7   The **a** of the LORD encamps
Isa   37.36   the **a** of the LORD set out and
Da   3.28   who has sent his **a** and delivered
    6.22   God sent his **a** and shut the lions'
Mt   1.20   an **a** of the Lord appeared to him in
Lk   1.26   In the sixth month the **a** Gabriel
Ac   5.19   during the night an **a** of the Lord
    23. 8   say that there is no resurrection, or **a**,
2Co   11.14   Satan disguises himself as an **a** of light.

ANGELS → ANGEL

Ge   28.12   **a** of God were ascending and
Ps   103.20   Bless the LORD, O you his **a**,
Mk   12.25   but are like **a** in heaven.
Jn   1.51   and the **a** of God ascending and
Ro   8.38   that neither death, nor life, nor **a**,
1Co   6. 3   not know that we are to judge **a**—
Heb   2. 7   for a little while lower than the **a**;
2Pe   2. 4   not spare the **a** when they sinned,
Rev   1.20   stars are the **a** of the seven churches,
    21.12   and at the gates twelve **a**,

ANGER → ANGRY

Ex   34. 6   merciful and gracious, slow to **a**,
Jdg   2.12   they provoked the LORD to **a**.
1Ki   16.13   God of Israel to **a** with their idols.
Ps   30. 5   For his **a** is but for a moment;
Pr   12.16   Fools show their **a** at once,
Joel   2.13   slow to **a**, and abounding in
Jnh   4. 2   slow to **a**, and abounding in
Mk   3. 5   He looked around at them with **a**;
Eph   4.26   not let the sun go down on your **a**,
Jas   1.19   slow to speak, slow to **a**;

ANGRY → ANGER

Jer   3.12   I will not be **a** forever.
Mt   5.22   that if you are **a** with a brother

ANGUISH

Isa   53.11   Out of his **a** he shall see light;
Da   12. 1   There shall be a time of **a**,
Zep   1.15   a day of distress and **a**,

ANIMAL → ANIMALS

Ge   2.19   God formed every **a** of the field

ANIMALS → ANIMAL

Ge   3.14   cursed are you among all **a**
Ps   36. 6   save humans and **a** alike, O LORD.

ANOINT → ANOINTED, ANOINTING

Ex   30.30   You shall **a** Aaron and his sons,
1Sa   15. 1   "The LORD sent me to **a** you king
Ps   23. 5   you **a** my head with oil; my cup
Da   9.24   and to **a** a most holy place.

ANOINTED → ANOINT

1Ch   16.22   "Do not touch my **a** ones;
Ps   2. 2   against the LORD and his **a**,
Isa   61. 1   because the LORD has **a** me;
Da   9.26   an **a** one shall be cut off and

Lk   4.18   he has **a** me to bring good news to
Jn   1.41   Messiah" (which is translated **A**).

ANOINTING → ANOINT

Ex   30.25   it shall be a holy **a** oil.
Jas   5.14   **a** them with oil in the name of the Lord
1Jn   2.27   as his **a** teaches you about all things,

ANOTHER

Isa   48.11   My glory I will not give to **a**.
Jn   14.16   and he will give you **a** Advocate,
Gal   1. 7   not that there is **a** gospel,

ANSWER

Pr   15. 1   A soft **a** turns away wrath,
Isa   65.24   Before they call I will **a**,
Lk   23. 9   but Jesus gave him no **a**.

ANT

Pr   6. 6   Go to the **a**, you lazybones;

ANTICHRIST

1Jn   2.18   As you have heard that **a** is coming,
    2.22   the **a**, the one who denies the Father
    4. 3   And this is the spirit of the **a**,
2Jn   1. 7   person is the deceiver and the **a**!

ANXIETIES → ANXIETY

1Co   7.32   I want you to be free from **a**.

ANXIETY → ANXIETIES

Ecc   11.10   Banish **a** from your mind,
1Pe   5. 7   Cast all your **a** on him, because he

ANYTHING

Ge   18.14   Is **a** too wonderful for the LORD?
Jer   32.27   is **a** too hard for me?
Mt   18.19   if two of you agree on earth about **a**
Jn   16.23   if you ask **a** of the Father in my name,

APART

Jn   15. 5   **a** from me you can do nothing.
Jas   2.20   that faith **a** from works is barren?

APOSTASIES

Jer   2.19   and your **a** will convict you.
Eze   37.23   I will save them from all the **a**

APOSTLE → APOSTLES

Ro   11.13   as I am an **a** to the Gentiles,
1Co   9. 1   Am I not an **a**?
2Co   12.12   signs of a true **a** were performed
Heb   3. 1   **a** and high priest of our confession,

APOSTLES → APOSTLE

Mt   10. 2   the names of the twelve **a**:
Ac   2.43   and signs were being done by the **a**.
1Co   12.28   has appointed in the church first **a**,
Eph   2.20   foundation of the **a** and prophets,
    4.11   he gave were that some would be **a**,
Rev   21.14   are the twelve names of the twelve **a**

APPEAR → APPEARANCE, APPEARANCES, APPEARED, APPEARING

Mt   24.30   the sign of the Son of Man will **a** in
Mk   13.22   messiahs and false prophets will **a**

APPEARANCE → APPEAR

1Sa   16. 7   not look on his **a** or on the height
2Co   5.12   those who boast in outward **a**

APPEARANCES → APPEAR

Jn   7.24   not judge by **a**, but judge with right

APPEARED → APPEAR

Jn   21.14   that Jesus **a** to the disciples after he
1Co   15. 5   he **a** to Cephas, then to the twelve.
Heb   9.26   **a** once for all at the end of the age

APPEARING → APPEAR

Ac   1. 3   **a** to them during forty days and
2Ti   4. 8   to all who have longed for his **a**.

APPETITES

Ro   16.18   our Lord Christ, but their own **a**,

APPOINTED → APPOINT

Mk   3.16   So he **a** the twelve: Simon (to whom
Ac   3.20   that he may send the Messiah **a** for
Heb   1. 2   whom he **a** heir of all things,

Heb   9.27   as it is **a** for mortals to die once,

APPROACH

Heb   4.16   **a** the throne of grace with boldness,
    11. 6   whoever would **a** him must believe

APPROVAL → APPROVED

Gal   1.10   I now seeking human **a**, or God's **a**?
Heb   11. 2   by faith our ancestors received **a**.

APPROVED → APPROVAL

1Th   2. 4   but just as we have been **a** by God
2Ti   2.15   to present yourself to God as one **a**

ARARAT

Ge   8. 4   ark came to rest on the mountains of **A**.

ARCHANGEL → ANGEL

Jude   1. 9   **a** Michael contended with the devil

ARCHANGEL'S → ANGEL

1Th   4.16   a call and with the sound of God's

ARCHITECT

Heb   11.10   whose **a** and builder is God.

AREOPAGUS

Ac   17.22   Then Paul stood in front of the **A**

ARGUE → ARGUMENTS

Isa   1.18   let us **a** it out, says the LORD:
Ac   18. 4   Every sabbath he would **a** in the
Ro   9.20   a human being, to **a** with God?

ARGUMENTS → ARGUE

2Co   10. 4   destroy strongholds. We destroy **a**
Col   2. 4   may deceive you with plausible **a**.

ARISE → RISE

Isa   60. 1   **A**, shine; for your light has come,
Mt   24.11   false prophets will **a** and lead many

ARK

Ge   6.14   Make yourself an **a** of cypress wood
Ex   25.10   shall make an **a** of acacia wood;
1Sa   4.11   The **a** of God was captured;
Rev   11.19   the **a** of his covenant was seen

ARM → ARMOR, ARMS, ARMY

Ex   6. 6   redeem you with an outstretched **a**
Dt   7.19   mighty hand and the outstretched **a**
2Ch   32. 8   With him is an **a** of flesh;
Ps   98. 1   his holy **a** have gotten him victory.
Isa   53. 1   the **a** of the LORD been revealed?
Jn   12.38   the **a** of the Lord been revealed?"

ARMOR → ARM

Ro   13.12   and put on the **a** of light;
Eph   6.11   Put on the whole **a** of God,

ARMS → ARM

Hos   11. 3   I took them up in my **a**;
Mk   10.16   And he took them up in his **a**,

ARMY → ARM

Jos   5.14   as commander of the **a** of the LORD
Ps   27. 3   Though an **a** encamp against me,
    33.16   A king is not saved by his great **a**;
Rev   19.19   rider on the horse and against his **a**.

AROMA

2Co   2.15   For we are the **a** of Christ to God

ARRESTED

Mt   26.50   and laid hands on Jesus and **a** him.
Ac   5.18   **a** the apostles and put them in the

ARROGANCE → ARROGANT

Pr   8.13   Pride and **a** and the way of evil
Eze   7.24   put an end to the **a** of the strong,

ARROGANT → ARROGANCE

Ps   73. 3   For I was envious of the **a**;
1Co   13. 4   love is not envious or boastful or **a**

ARROW

Ps   64. 7   But God will shoot his **a** at them;
Isa   49. 2   he made me a polished **a**,

ASCEND → ASCENDED

Ps   139. 8   If I **a** to heaven, you are there;

Isa 14. 13 in your heart, "I will a to heaven;
Ro 10. 6 'Who will a into heaven?' "

ASCENDED → ASCEND
2Ki 2. 11 Elijah a in a whirlwind into heaven.
Jn   3. 13 No one has a into heaven except

ASHAMED → SHAME
Ge   2. 25 were both naked, and were not a.
Mk   8. 38 who are a of me and of my words
Ro   1. 16 For I am not a of the gospel;
2Ti 2. 15 a worker who has no need to be a,
Heb 2. 11 Jesus is not a to call them brothers
     11. 16 God is not a to be called their God;

ASHES
Ge 18. 27 I who am but dust and a.
Est 4. 1 and put on sackcloth and a,
Job 42. 6 and repent in dust and a."
Jnh 3. 6 himself with sackcloth, and sat in a.
Mt 11. 21 long ago in sackcloth and a.

ASK
Isa 65. 1 sought out by those who did not a,
Mt   6. 8 knows what you need before you a
     7. 7 "A, and it will be given you;
Jn 16. 24 A and you will receive,
Jas 4. 3 You a and do not receive, because
1Jn 5. 14 we a anything according to his will,

ASLEEP → SLEEP
Jnh 1. 5 had lain down, and was fast a.
Mt   8. 24 by the waves; but he was a.
1Th 5. 6 So then let us not fall a as others do,

ASSIGNED
Ro 12. 3 the measure of faith that God has a.
1Co 3. 5 as the Lord a to each.
     7. 17 lead the life that the Lord has a,

ASSURANCE
Dt 28. 66 in dread, with no a of your life.
Heb 6. 11 so as to realize the full a of hope
     11. 1 faith is the a of things hoped for,

ASTONISHED
Isa 52. 14 there were many who were a at him
Lk   2. 48 his parents saw him they were a;

ASTRAY → STRAY
Dt 30. 17 are led a to bow down to other gods
Isa 53. 6 All we like sheep have gone a;
Jer 50. 6 their shepherds have led them a,
Mt 18. 12 go in search of the one that went a?
1Pe 2. 25 For you were going a like sheep,

ATE → EAT
Ge   3. 6 she took of its fruit and a;
Ex 16. 35 The Israelites a manna forty years,
Ps 78. 25 Mortals a of the bread of angels;
Mt 14. 20 And all a and were filled;
     15. 37 And all of them a and were filled;

ATHLETE → ATHLETES
2Ti 2. 5 And in the case of an a,

ATHLETES → ATHLETE
1Co 9. 25 A exercise self-control in all

ATONE → ATONEMENT
Da   9. 24 an end to sin, and to a for iniquity,

ATONED → ATONEMENT
Pr 16. 6 and faithfulness iniquity is a for,

ATONEMENT → ATONE, ATONED, ATONING
Ex 29. 36 a bull as a sin offering for a.
    30. 10 Aaron shall perform the rite of a
    32. 30 perhaps I can make a for your sin."
Lev 23. 28 for it is a day of a,
Ro   3. 25 God put forward as a sacrifice of a
Heb 2. 17 to make a sacrifice of a for the sins

ATONING → ATONEMENT
1Jn 2. 2 and he is the a sacrifice for our sins,
     4. 10 sent his Son to be the a sacrifice for

ATTENTION
Heb 2. 1 greater a to what we have heard,

AUTHOR
Ac   3. 15 and you killed the A of life,

AUTHORITIES → AUTHORITY
Ro 13. 1 be subject to the governing a;
Col 2. 15 He disarmed the rulers and a and

AUTHORITY → AUTHORITIES
Pr 29. 2 When the righteous are in a,
Mk   1. 27 A new teaching—with a!
Lk   5. 24 Son of Man has a on earth to forgive
Ac   5. 29 obey God rather than any human a.
Ro 13. 1 for there is no a except from God,
1Co 11. 10 woman ought to have a symbol of a
Col 2. 10 who is the head of every ruler and a.
1Ti 2. 12 no woman to teach or to have a over a
           man
Rev 12. 10 and the a of his Messiah,
    20. 4 on them were given a to judge.

AVENGE → VENGEANCE
Dt 32. 43 he will a the blood of his children,
Ro 12. 19 Beloved, never a yourselves,
Rev 6. 10 and a our blood on the inhabitants

AVENGER → VENGEANCE
Nu 35. 12 shall be for you a refuge from the a,
Ps   8. 2 to silence the enemy and the a.
1Th 4. 6 the Lord is an a in all these things,

AVENGING → VENGEANCE
Na   1. 2 A jealous and a God is the LORD,

AWAKE
Da 12. 2 in the dust of the earth shall a,
Mk 14. 37 Could you not keep a one hour?
Eph 5. 14 "Sleeper, a! Rise from the dead,
1Th 5. 6 but let us keep a and be sober;
Rev 16. 15 Blessed is the one who stays a and

AWE → AWESOME
Ps 119.161 my heart stands in a of your words.
Isa 29. 23 will stand in a of the God of Israel.
Mt   9. 8 saw it, they were filled with a,
Ac   2. 43 A came upon everyone, because
Ro 11. 20 do not become proud, but stand in a.

AWESOME → AWE
Ex 15. 11 majestic in holiness, a in splendor,
Dt 10. 17 the great God, mighty and a,
Ne   1. 5 and a God who keeps covenant
Ps 47. 2 For the LORD, the Most High, is a,
Da   9. 4 saying, "Ah, Lord, great and a God,

B

BAAL
Jdg 2. 13 and worshiped B and the Astartes.
1Ki 18. 25 Elijah said to the prophets of B,
Jer 2. 8 the prophets prophesied by B,
Ro 11. 4 not bowed the knee to B."

BABEL → BABYLON
Ge 11. 9 Therefore it was called B,

BABES
Ps   8. 2 Out of the mouths of b and infants
Isa 3. 4 and b shall rule over them.

BABYLON → BABEL
2Ki 24. 15 into captivity from Jerusalem to B.
Ps 137. 1 By the rivers of B—there we sat
Isa 14. 4 this taunt against the king of B:
     21. 9 he responded, "Fallen, fallen is B;
Jer 25. 11 serve the king of B seventy years.
1Pe 5. 13 Your sister church in B, chosen
Rev 14. 8 "Fallen, fallen is B the great!

BACKSLIDING
Jer 8. 5 people turned away in perpetual b?

BAD
Mt   7. 17 but the b tree bears b fruit.
1Co 15. 33 "B company ruins good morals."

BALM
Jer 8. 22 Is there no b in Gilead?

BANISH
Ecc 11. 10 B anxiety from your mind,
Ro 11. 26 he will b ungodliness from Jacob."

BANNER
Ex 17. 15 and called it, The LORD is my b.

BAPTISM → BAPTIZE
Mk   1. 4 proclaiming a b of repentance for
    10. 38 be baptized with the b that I am
Lk 20. 4 the b of John come from heaven,
Ac 18. 25 though he knew only the b of John.
    19. 3 They answered, "Into John's b."
Ro   6. 4 buried with him by b into death,
1Co 15. 29 receive b on behalf of the dead?
Eph 4. 5 one Lord, one faith, one b,
Col 2. 12 when you were buried with him in b,
1Pe 3. 21 b, which this prefigured, now saves

BAPTISMS → BAPTIZE
Heb 6. 2 about b, laying on of hands,

BAPTIST → BAPTIZE
Mt   3. 1 In those days John the B appeared
    11. 11 has arisen greater than John the B;
Mt 14. 8 the head of John the B here on a

BAPTIZE → BAPTISM, BAPTISMS, BAPTIST, BAPTIZED, BAPTIZING
Mt   3. 11 "I b you with water for repentance,
Lk   3. 16 He will b you with the Holy Spirit
1Co 1. 17 For Christ did not send me to b but

BAPTIZED → BAPTIZE
Mt   3. 13 to John at the Jordan, to be b
Ac   1. 5 John b with water, but you will be b
           with the Holy
     2. 38 "Repent, and be b every one of you
Ro   6. 3 b into Christ Jesus were b into his
1Co 10. 2 all were b into Moses in the cloud
    12. 13 one Spirit we were all b into one

BAPTIZING → BAPTIZE
Mt 28. 19 b them in the name of the Father
Jn   4. 1 "Jesus is making and b more

BARN → BARNS
Lk 12. 24 they have neither storehouse nor b,

BARNS → BARN
Dt 28. 8 the blessing upon you in your b,
Ps 144. 13 May our b be filled, with produce
Lk 12. 18 pull down my b and build larger

BARREN
Ge 11. 30 Now Sarai was b; she had no child.
Ex 23. 26 No one shall miscarry or be b in
1Sa 2. 5 The b has borne seven, but she who
Ps 113. 9 He gives the b woman a home,
Isa 54. 1 Sing, O b one who did not bear;
Lk   1. 7 because Elizabeth was b,
Heb 11. 11 too old—and Sarah herself was b—

BASIN
Ex 30. 18 You shall make a bronze b with a
1Ki 7. 30 four corners were supports for a b.
Jn 13. 5 b and began to wash the disciples'

BASKET
Mt   5. 15 a lamp puts it under the bushel b,
Ac   9. 25 in the wall, lowering him in a b.

BATTLE
Ps 24. 8 and mighty, the LORD, mighty in b.
Ecc 9. 11 nor the b to the strong, nor bread to
Rev 16. 14 them for b on the great day of God
    20. 8 Magog, in order to gather them for b;

BEAR → BEARS, BIRTH, BIRTHRIGHT, BORE, BORN, CHILDBEARING, FIRSTBORN
Ge   4. 13 punishment is greater than I can b!

Isa   7.14   is with child and shall **b** a son,
Mt   1.23   virgin shall conceive and **b** a son,
    7.18   A good tree cannot **b** bad fruit,
Lk   11.46   load people with burdens hard to **b**,
Jn   15. 2   he prunes to make it **b** more fruit.
Gal   6. 2   **B** one another's burdens,
Col   3.13   **B** with one another and,
Heb   9.28   offered once to **b** the sins of many,
Rev   12. 4   woman who was about to **b** a child,

BEARS → BEAR
Ps   68.19   Blessed be the Lord, who daily **b** us
1Co   13. 7   It **b** all things, believes all things,

BEAST → BEASTS
Rev   11. 7   **b** that comes up from the bottomless pit
    13.18   calculate the number of the **b**,
    16. 2   who had the mark of the **b**
    19.20   who had received the mark of the **b**

BEASTS → BEAST
Da   7. 3   four great **b** came up out of the sea,

BEAT → BEATEN
Isa   2. 4   shall **b** their swords into plowshares,
Joel   3.10   **B** your plowshares into swords,
Lk   22.63   began to mock him and **b** him;

BEATEN → BEAT
2Co   11.25   Three times I was **b** with rods.
1Pe   2.20   If you endure when you are **b** for

BEAUTIFUL → BEAUTY
Ge   12.11   you are a woman **b** in appearance;
1Sa   25. 3   The woman was clever and **b**,
Est   2. 7   the girl was fair and **b**,
Job   42.15   no women so **b** as Job's daughters;
SS   1. 5   I am black and **b**, O daughters of
Isa   4. 2   the branch of the Lord shall be **b**
    52. 7   How **b** upon the mountains are the
Ac   3. 2   the temple called the **B** Gate so that
Ro   10.15   **b** are the feet of those who bring

BEAUTY → BEAUTIFUL
Ps   27. 4   to behold the **b** of the Lord,
Pr   31.30   Charm is deceitful, and **b** is vain,
1Pe   3. 4   with the lasting **b** of a gentle

BEGGAR → BEGS
Mk   10.46   son of Timaeus, a blind **b**,
Jn   9. 8   who had seen him before as a **b**

BEGINNING
Ge   1. 1   In the **b** when God created the
Ps   111.10   fear of the Lord is the **b** of wisdom;
Pr   1. 7   The fear of the Lord is the **b** of
    8.22   The Lord created me at the **b** of his
Isa   40.21   Has it not been told you from the **b**?
Mt   24. 8   this is but the **b** of the birth pangs.
Jn   1. 1   In the **b** was the Word,
1Jn   1. 1   declare to you what was from the **b**,
2Jn   1. 6   as you have heard it from the **b**—
Rev   21. 6   and the Omega, the **b** and the end.

BEGOTTEN
Ps   2. 7   You are my son; today I have **b** you.
Ac   13.33   are my Son; today I have **b** you.'
Heb   1. 5   are my Son; today I have **b** you"?

BEGS → BEG
Lk   6.30   Give to everyone who **b** from you;

BEHEADED → HEAD
Lk   9. 9   Herod said, "John I **b**,"
Rev   20. 4   the souls of those who had been **b**

BEHEMOTH
Job   40.15   "Look at **B**, which I made just as I

BELIEF → BELIEVE
2Th   2.13   the Spirit and through **b** in the truth.

BELIEVE → BELIEF, BELIEVED, BELIEVER, BELIEVERS, BELIEVES
Nu   14.11   long will they refuse to **b** in me,
2Ki   17.14   not **b** in the Lord their God.
Ps   119.66   for I **b** in your commandments.
Mt   18. 6   one of these little ones who **b** in me,
    24.23   or 'There he is!'—do not **b** it.

Mk   1.15   repent, and **b** in the good news."
    9.24   "I **b**; help my unbelief!"
Lk   24.25   how slow of heart to **b** all that the
Jn   1. 7   so that all might **b** through him.
    3.18   who **b** in him are not condemned;
    5.46   believed Moses, you would **b** me,
    6.29   you **b** in him whom he has sent."
    14. 1   **B** in God, **b** also in me.
    17.20   will **b** in me through their word,
    20.29   not seen and yet have come to **b**."
Ac   16.31   answered, "**B** on the Lord Jesus,
    28.24   while others refused to **b**.
Ro   3.22   faith in Jesus Christ for all who **b**.
    10. 9   **b** in your heart that God raised him
Gal   3. 9   this reason, those who **b** are blessed
1Th   4.14   For since we **b** that Jesus died and
Heb   11. 6   would approach him must **b**
Jas   2.19   Even the demons **b**—and shudder.
1Pe   1. 8   you do not see him now, you **b**
1Jn   4. 1   Beloved, do not **b** every spirit,
Jude   1. 5   destroyed those who did not **b**.

BELIEVED → BELIEVE
Ge   15. 6   And he **b** the Lord;
Ex   14.31   **b** in the Lord and in his
Isa   53. 1   Who has **b** what we have heard?
Jn   1.12   received him, who **b** in his name,
    12.38   "Lord, who has **b** our message,
Ac   2.44   All who **b** were together and had
Ro   4. 3   "Abraham **b** God, and it was
2Co   4.13   "I **b**, and so I spoke"—
Gal   3. 6   Just as Abraham "**b** God,
1Ti   3.16   **b** in throughout the world, taken up
Heb   4. 3   For we who have **b** enter that rest,
Jas   2.23   that says, "Abraham **b** God,

BELIEVER → BELIEVE
1Co   7.12   **b** has a wife who is an unbeliever,
2Co   6.15   Or what does a **b** share with an

BELIEVERS → BELIEVE
Gal   2. 4   because of false **b** secretly brought
2Th   3. 6   keep away from **b** who are living in
1Pe   2.17   Love the family of **b**.

BELIEVES → BELIEVE
Jn   3.15   whoever **b** in him may have eternal
    11.26   everyone who lives and **b** in me
Ro   10.10   **b** with the heart and so is justified,
1Co   13. 7   It bears all things, **b** all things,

BELLY
Ge   3.14   upon your **b** you shall go,
Jnh   1.17   and Jonah was in the **b** of the fish
Mt   12.40   three days and three nights in the **b**

BELOVED → LOVE
SS   2.16   My **b** is mine and I am his;
Mt   3.17   heaven said, "This is my Son, the **B**,
    12.18   my **b**, with whom my soul is well
    17. 5   "This is my Son, the **B**;
Col   3.12   As God's chosen ones, holy and **b**,
Rev   20. 9   camp of the saints and the **b** city.

BEND → BENT
Php   2.10   name of Jesus every knee should **b**,

BENEFICIAL → BENEFIT
1Co   6.12   but not all things are **b**.
    10.23   lawful," but not all things are **b**.

BENEFIT → BENEFICIAL, BENEFITS
Gal   5. 2   Christ will be of no **b** to you.
Phm   1.20   have this **b** from you in the Lord!
Heb   4. 2   message they heard did not **b** them,

BENEFITS → BENEFIT
Ps   103. 2   and do not forget all his **b**—
1Co   9.11   if we reap your material **b**?

BENT → BEND
Hos   11. 4   I **b** down to them and fed them.
Jn   8. 6   [[Jesus **b** down and wrote with his]]

BEST → GOOD
Dt   33.21   He chose the **b** for himself,
Mk   12.39   the **b** seats in the synagogues and

2Ti   2.15   your **b** to present yourself to God

BETHANY
Mt   26. 6   Jesus was at **B** in the house of
Jn   11. 1   a certain man was ill, Lazarus of **B**,

BETHLEHEM
1Sa   17.12   David was the son of an Ephrathite of **B**
Mic   5. 2   But you, O **B** of Ephrathah,
Mt   2. 1   after Jesus was born in **B** of Judea,
Lk   2.15   "Let us go now to **B** and see this

BETRAY → BETRAYED
Mt   10.21   Brother will **b** brother to death,
Mk   14.11   to look for an opportunity to **b** him.
Jn   13.11   For he knew who was to **b** him;

BETRAYED → BETRAY
Lk   21.16   You will be **b** even by parents and
1Co   11.23   Jesus on the night when he was **b**

BETTER → GOOD
1Sa   15.22   Surely, to obey is **b** than sacrifice,
Ps   63. 3   your steadfast love is **b** than life,
Pr   15.16   **B** is a little with the fear of
Ecc   2.24   There is nothing **b** for mortals than
SS   1. 2   For your love is **b** than wine,
Mt   5.29   it is **b** for you to lose one of your
Mk   14.21   It would have been **b** for that one
Jn   11.50   **b** for you to have one man die for
Php   1.23   be with Christ, for that is far **b**;
    2. 3   in humility regard others as **b** than
Heb   7.22   the guarantee of a **b** covenant.
    9.23   need **b** sacrifices than these.

BIND → BINDS
Dt   6. 8   **B** them as a sign on your hand,
Pr   6.21   **B** them upon your heart always;
Isa   61. 1   to **b** up the brokenhearted,
Mt   16.19   whatever you **b** on earth will be

BINDS → BIND
Job   5.18   For he wounds, but he **b** up;
Col   3.14   **b** everything together in perfect

BIRD → BIRDS
Ge   1.21   and every winged **b** of every kind.
Lev   20.25   the unclean **b** and the clean;

BIRDS → BIRD
Ge   7. 3   and seven pairs of the **b** of the air
Ps   50.11   I know all the **b** of the air,
Mt   6.26   Look at the **b** of the air;

BIRTH → BEAR
Dt   32.18   you forgot the God who gave you **b**.
Ps   22.10   On you I was cast from my **b**,
Mt   24. 8   is but the beginning of the **b** pangs.
Jas   1.18   he gave us **b** by the word of truth,
1Pe   1. 3   given us a new **b** into a living hope

BIRTHRIGHT → BEAR, RIGHT
Ge   25.34   Thus Esau despised his **b**.
Heb   12.16   who sold his **b** for a single meal.

BISHOP
1Ti   3. 1   whoever aspires to the office of **b**
Tit   1. 7   For a **b**, as God's steward, must be

BITE
Gal   5.15   If, however, you **b** and devour one

BITTER → BITTERNESS
Ex   1.14   made their lives **b** with hard service
    12. 8   with unleavened bread and **b** herbs.
Rev   8.11   the water, because it was made **b**.

BITTERNESS → BITTER
Pr   14.10   The heart knows its own **b**,
Ro   3.14   mouths are full of cursing and **b**."
Eph   4.31   Put away from you all **b** and wrath

BLACK
SS   1. 5   I am **b** and beautiful, O daughters
Zec   6. 2   the second chariot **b** horses,
Mt   5.36   cannot make one hair white or **b**.
Rev   6. 5   I looked, and there was a **b** horse!

BLAMELESS
2Sa   22.26   with the **b** you show yourself **b**;

Ps 37.18 The Lord knows the days of the **b,**
Pr 11.20 but those of **b** ways are his delight.
Eph 1. 4 holy and **b** before him in love.
Php 2.15 so that you may be **b** and innocent,
1Th 5.23 and **b** at the coming of our Lord
Tit 1. 7 bishop, as God's steward, must be **b**
Heb 7.26 **b,** undefiled, separated from sinners,
Rev 14. 5 mouth no lie was found; they are **b.**

BLASPHEME → BLASPHEMED,
BLASPHEMER, BLASPHEMES,
BLASPHEMIES, BLASPHEMOUS
Ac 26.11 I tried to force them to **b;**
1Ti 1.20 so that they may learn not to **b.**

BLASPHEMED → BLASPHEME
Eze 20.27 In this again your ancestors **b** me,
Mt 26.65 tore his clothes and said, "He has **b!**

BLASPHEMER → BLASPHEME
1Ti 1.13 even though I was formerly a **b,**

BLASPHEMES → BLASPHEME
Lev 24.16 One who **b** the name of the Lord
Lk 12.10 whoever **b** against the Holy Spirit

BLASPHEMIES → BLASPHEME
Mk 3.28 their sins and whatever **b** they utter;
Rev 13. 6 its mouth to utter **b** against God,

BLASPHEMOUS → BLASPHEME
Ac 6.11 "We have heard him speak **b** words
Rev 13. 1 and on its heads were **b** names.

BLEMISH
Ex 12. 5 Your lamb shall be without **b,**
Lev 22.20 not offer anything that has a **b,**
Eph 5.27 that she may be holy and without **b.**
Heb 9.14 offered himself without **b** to God,
1Pe 1.19 that of a lamb without defect or **b.**
Jude 1.24 to make you stand without **b** in the

BLESS → BLESSED, BLESSING, BLESSINGS
Ge 12. 2 I will **b** you, and make your name
    22.17 I will indeed **b** you, and I will make
    26. 3 I will be with you, and will **b** you;
    20.24 I will come to you and **b** you.
Ex 23.25 **b** you and keep you;
Nu 6.24 The Lord **b** you and keep you;
    23.20 See, I received a command to **b;**
Dt 7.13 he will love you, **b** you,
    30.16 the Lord your God will **b** you
1Ch 29.20 "**B** the Lord your God."
Ps 5.12 For you **b** the righteous, O Lord;
    34. 1 I will **b** the Lord at all times;
  103. 1 **B** the Lord, O my soul,
Hag 2.19 From this day on I will **b** you.
Lk 6.28 **b** those who curse you, pray
Ro 12.14 **B** those who persecute you;
1Co 4.12 When reviled, we **b;**
Jas 3. 9 With it we **b** the Lord and Father,

BLESSED → BLESS
Ge 1.22 God **b** them, saying, "Be fruitful
    2. 3 So God **b** the seventh day and
    14.19 He **b** him and said, "**B** be Abram
Nu 24. 9 **B** is everyone who blesses you,
Job 1.21 **b** be the name of the Lord."
Ps 118.26 **B** is the one who comes in the name
Isa 30.18 **b** are all those who wait for him.
Jer 17. 7 **B** are those who trust in the Lord,
Mt 5. 3 "**B** are the poor in spirit,
Mk 10.16 laid his hands on them, and **b** them.
Lk 1.42 "**B** are you among women,
    6.20 "**B** are you who are poor,
Jn 12.13 **B** is the one who comes in the name
    20.29 **B** are those who have not seen and
Ac 20.35 It is more **b** to give than to receive.
Gal 3. 8 "All the Gentiles shall be **b** in you."
Eph 1. 3 who has **b** us in Christ
1Pe 3.14 for doing what is right, you are **b.**
Rev 22. 7 **B** is the one who keeps the words of

BLESSING → BLESS
Ge 12. 2 so that you will be a **b.**
    22.18 the nations of the earth gain by for
Dt 11.26 before you today a **b** and a curse:

Dt 23. 5 your God turned the curse into a **b**
Ne 13. 2 our God turned the curse into a **b.**
Eze 34.26 they shall be showers of **b.**
Mk 14.22 bread, and after **b** it he broke it,
Lk 24.51 While he was **b** them, he withdrew
1Co 10.16 The cup of **b** that we bless,
Gal 3.14 in Christ Jesus the **b** of Abraham
Eph 1. 3 every spiritual **b** in the heavenly
Rev 5.12 might and honor and glory and **b!**
    7.12 **B** and glory and wisdom and

BLESSINGS → BLESS
Dt 28. 2 all these **b** shall come upon you
Jos 8.34 the words of the law, **b** and curses,
Mal 2. 2 and I will curse your **b;**
Ro 15.27 come to share in their spiritual **b,**

BLIND → BLINDED, BLINDNESS
Ex 4.11 mute or deaf, seeing or **b?**
Ps 146. 8 the Lord opens the eyes of the **b.**
Isa 35. 5 the eyes of the **b** shall be opened,
Mt 11. 5 **b** receive their sight, the lame walk,
Lk 6.39 "Can a **b** person guide a **b** person?
Jn 9.25 though I was **b,** now I see."
Ro 2.19 sure that you are a guide to the **b,**

BLINDED → BLIND
Jn 12.40 "He has **b** their eyes and hardened
2Co 4. 4 has **b** the minds of the unbelievers,

BLINDNESS → BLIND
Dt 28.28 will afflict you with madness, **b,**
1Jn 2.11 the darkness has brought on **b.**

BLOCK → BLOCKS
Eze 14. 7 their iniquity as a stumbling **b**
Mt 16.23 You are a stumbling **b** to me;
Ro 11. 9 a stumbling **b** and a retribution for
1Co 1.23 stumbling **b** to Jews and foolishness

BLOCKS → BLOCK
Jer 6.21 before this people stumbling **b**
Mt 18. 7 the world because of stumbling **b!**

BLOOD → BLOODSHED
Ge 9. 6 sheds the **b** of a human, by a human shall
          that person's **b** be shed;
Ex 7.17 and it shall be turned to **b.**
    12.13 when I see the **b,** I will pass over
    24. 8 the **b** of the covenant that the Lord
Lev 17.11 it is the **b** that makes atonement.
Nu 35.33 for **b** pollutes the land,
Ps 72.14 and precious is their **b** in his sight.
Isa 1.11 I do not delight in the **b** of bulls,
Eze 33. 4 **b** shall be upon their own heads.
Joel 2.30 **b** and fire and columns of smoke.
Mt 27. 8 field has been called the Field of **B**
Mk 14.24 "This is my **b** of the covenant,
Lk 22.44 [[sweat became like great drops of **b**]]
Jn 1.13 who were born, not of **b**
    6.53 of the Son of Man and drink his **b,**
    19.34 and at once **b** and water came out.
Ac 2.20 to darkness and the moon to **b,**
Ro 5. 9 that we have been justified by his **b,**
1Co 11.25 cup is the new covenant in my **b.**
Eph 1. 7 we have redemption through his **b,**
Heb 9.12 the **b** of goats and calves, but with his
          own **b,**
    9.22 without the shedding of **b** there is no
1Jn 5. 6 the one who came by water and **b,**
Rev 6.12 the full moon became like **b,**
    8. 9 A third of the sea became **b,**
    12.11 conquered him by the **b** of the Lamb

BLOODSHED → BLOOD, SHED
Isa 5. 7 he expected justice, but saw **b;**
Eze 35. 6 you did not hate **b,** **b** shall pursue
Hab 2. 8 because of human **b,** and violence

BLOT
Ge 6. 7 "I will **b** out from the earth
Ex 32.32 **b** me out of the book that you have
Ps 51. 1 mercy **b** out my transgressions.
Rev 3. 5 not **b** your name out of the book of

BOAST → BOASTERS, BOASTING
Ps 34. 2 My soul makes its **b** in the Lord;
Pr 27. 1 Do not **b** about tomorrow,
Jer 9.24 but let those who **b** **b** in this,
Ro 2.23 You that **b** in the law,
1Co 1.31 the one who boasts, **b** in the Lord."
2Co 11.30 If I must **b,** I will **b** of the things that
Gal 6.14 never **b** of anything except the cross
Eph 2. 9 of works, so that no one may **b.**

BOASTERS → BOAST
2Co 11.13 For such **b** are false apostles,
2Ti 3. 2 **b,** arrogant, abusive, disobedient to

BOASTING → BOAST
1Co 5. 6 Your **b** is not a good thing.
1Th 2.19 or crown of **b** before our Lord Jesus

BODIES → BODY
Ro 12. 1 present your **b** as a living sacrifice,
1Co 6.15 that your **b** are members of Christ?
Heb 10.22 and our **b** washed with pure water.

BODILY → BODY
Lk 3.22 upon him in **b** form like a dove.
Col 2. 9 the whole fullness of deity dwells **b,**

BODY → BODIES, BODILY
Mic 6. 7 fruit of my **b** for the sin of my soul?
Mt 6.22 "The eye is the lamp of the **b.**
Mk 14.22 and said, "Take; this is my **b.**"
Lk 12. 4 do not fear those who kill the **b,**
Jn 2.21 speaking of the temple of his **b.**
1Co 15.44 It is sown a physical **b,** it is raised a
          spiritual **b.**
2Co 5. 8 from the **b** and at home with the Lord.
Eph 4. 4 There is one **b** and one Spirit,

BOLD → BOLDNESS
Dt 31. 6 Be strong and **b;** have no fear
Pr 28. 1 the righteous are as **b** as a lion.

BOLDNESS → BOLD
Eph 3.12 whom we have access to God in **b**
Heb 4.16 approach the throne of grace with **b,**
1Jn 4.17 may have **b** on the day of judgment,

BONE → BONES
Ge 2.23 "This at last is **b** of my bones and
Eze 37. 7 came together, **b** to its **b.**

BONES → BONE
Ex 12.46 you shall not break any of its **b.**
Ps 34.20 He keeps all their **b;** not one of
Jn 19.36 "None of his **b** shall be broken."

BOOK → BOOKS
Ex 17.14 "Write this as a reminder in a **b** and
Dt 31.24 writing down in a **b** the words of
Jos 1. 8 This **b** of the law shall not depart
Ps 69.28 be blotted out of the **b** of the living;
Rev 1.11 "Write in a **b** what you see and
    21.27 who are written in the Lamb's **b**

BOOKS → BOOK
Ecc 12.12 Of making many **b** there is no end,
Da 7.10 in judgment, and the **b** were opened.
Jn 21.25 world itself could not contain the **b**

BOOTHS
Lev 23.34 the festival of **b** to the Lord.
Ezr 3. 4 kept the festival of **b,** as prescribed,
Zec 14.16 and to keep the festival of **b.**

BORE → BEAR
Isa 53.12 yet he **b** the sin of many,
Mt 8.17 our infirmities and **b** our diseases."
1Pe 2.24 He himself **b** our sins in his body

BORN → BEAR
Ecc 3. 2 a time to be **b,** and a time to die;
Isa 9. 6 For a child has been **b** for us,
    66. 8 Shall a land be **b** in one day?
Lk 2.11 is **b** this day in the city of David
Jn 3. 7 'You must be **b** from above.'
1Pe 1.23 You have been **b** anew,
1Jn 4. 7 everyone who loves is **b** of God

BORROW → BORROWER
Dt   28.12   to many nations, but you will not **b.**
Ps   37.21   The wicked **b,** and do not pay back,
Mt   5.42   anyone who wants to **b** from you.

BORROWER → BORROW
Pr   22. 7   the **b** is the slave of the lender.

BOUGHT → BUY
1Co   6.20   For you were **b** with a price;
2Pe   2. 1   even deny the Master who **b** them—

BOW → RAINBOW
Ge   9.13   I have set my **b** in the clouds,
Ex   20. 5   You shall not **b** down to them or
Ps   95. 6   O come, let us worship and **b** down,
Isa   45.23   "To me every knee shall **b,**
Ro   14.11   every knee shall **b** to me,

BOWLS
Rev   16. 1   the seven **b** of the wrath of God."

BRANCH → BRANCHES
Isa   4. 2   On that day the **b** of the LORD shall
      11. 1   and a **b** shall grow out of his roots.
Jer   23. 5   raise up for David a righteous **B,**
Zec   3. 8   going to bring my servant the **B.**
Jn   15. 2   every **b** in me that bears no fruit.

BRANCHES → BRANCH
Ro   11.21   if God did not spare the natural **b,**

BREAD
Ge   3.19   sweat of your face you shall eat **b**
Ex   12. 8   with unleavened **b** and bitter herbs.
      25.30   set the **b** of the Presence on the table
Dt   8. 3   that one does not live by **b** alone,
Ecc   11. 1   Send out your **b** upon the waters,
Mt   6.11   Give us this day our daily **b.**
Lk   4. 4   'One does not live by **b** alone.'"
Jn   6.35   said to them, "I am the **b** of life.
1Co   11.26   For as often as you eat this **b** and

BREAK → BREAKING, BROKEN, BROKENHEARTED
Mt   6.19   where thieves **b** in and steal;
Jn   19.33   they did not **b** his legs.

BREASTPIECE → BREASTPLATE
Ex   28.15   You shall make a **b** of judgment,

BREASTPLATE → BREASTPIECE
Isa   59.17   He put on righteousness like a **b,**
Eph   6.14   and put on the **b** of righteousness.

BREATH
Ge   2. 7   into his nostrils the **b** of life;
      6.17   all flesh in which is the **b** of life;
Job   7. 7   "Remember that my life is a **b;**
Ecc   12. 7   the **b** returns to God who gave it.
2Th   2. 8   will destroy with the **b** of his mouth,

BRIBE
Dt   16.19   for a **b** blinds the eyes of the wise
Pr   6.35   and refuses a **b** no matter how great.

BRIDE → BRIDEGROOM
Isa   62. 5   the bridegroom rejoices over the **b,**
Rev   21. 9   the **b,** the wife of the Lamb."

BRIDEGROOM → BRIDE
Mt   9.15   as long as the **b** is with them,
Jn   3.29   He who has the bride is the **b.**

BRIGHT
Mt   17. 5   suddenly a **b** cloud overshadowed
Rev   15. 6   robed in pure **b** linen,
      22.16   of David, the **b** morning star."

BROKE → BREAK
Ex   32.19   tablets from his hands and **b** them
2Ch   36.19   **b** down the wall of Jerusalem,
Jer   31.32   a covenant that they **b,**
Mt   14.19   and blessed and **b** the loaves,
1Co   11.24   he **b** it and said, "This is my body

BROKEN → BREAK
Ne   1. 3   the wall of Jerusalem is **b** down,
Ps   51.17   acceptable to God is a **b** spirit;

Mt   15.37   they took up the **b** pieces left over,
Lk   20.18   who falls on that stone will be **b**
Ro   11.20   were **b** off because of their unbelief,

BROKENHEARTED → BREAK, HEART
Ps   147. 3   He heals the **b,** and binds up their
Isa   61. 1   the oppressed, to bind up the **b,**

BRONZE
Nu   21. 9   look at the serpent of **b** and live.
Dt   28.23   The sky over your head shall be **b,**
Da   10. 6   legs like the gleam of burnished **b,**
Rev   1.15   his feet were like burnished **b,**

BROTHER → BROTHER'S, BROTHERS
Ge   4. 8   Cain rose up against his **b** Abel,
Mt   5.24   first be reconciled to your **b** or
      10.21   **B** will betray **b** to death,

BROTHER'S → BROTHER
Dt   25. 7   has no desire to marry his **b** widow,
Mk   6.18   lawful for you to have your **b** wife."

BROTHERS → BROTHER
Ge   9.25   lowest of slaves shall he be to his **b.**
      37.11   So his **b** were jealous of him,
Mk   3.33   "Who are my mother and my **b?**"
Lk   22.32   turned back, strengthen your **b.**"
Heb   2.11   not ashamed to call them **b** and

BUILD → BUILDER, BUILDERS, BUILDING, BUILDS, BUILT, REBUILD
Ge   11. 4   "Come, let us **b** ourselves a city,
Ps   127. 1   those who **b** it labor in vain.
Mt   16.18   and on this rock I will **b** my church,
      27.40   destroy the temple and **b** it in three
1Co   10. 9   must choose with care how to **b**
      10.23   are lawful," but not all things **b** up.

BUILDER → BUILD
Heb   3. 4   but the **b** of all things is God.)
      11.10   whose architect and **b** is God.

BUILDERS → BUILD
Ps   118.22   The stone that the **b** rejected has
Mk   12.10   'The stone that the **b** rejected has
1Pe   2. 7   "The stone that the **b** rejected has

BUILDING → BUILD
1Co   3. 9   you are God's field, God's **b.**
2Co   5. 1   we have a **b** from God,
Eph   4.12   for **b** up the body of Christ,

BUILDS → BUILD
Ps   127. 1   Unless the LORD **b** the house,
Pr   14. 1   The wise woman **b** her house,
1Co   8. 1   Knowledge puffs up, but love **b** up.

BUILT → BUILD
1Ki   6.14   Solomon **b** the house, and finished
Ne   7. 1   the wall had been **b** and I had set up
Pr   9. 1   Wisdom has **b** her house,
Da   9.25   sixty-two weeks it shall be **b** again
Eph   2.20   **b** upon the foundation of the

BULL → BULLS
Ps   50. 9   will not accept a **b** from your house,

BULLS → BULL
Ps   22.12   encircle me, strong **b** of Bashan
Isa   1.11   I do not delight in the blood of **b,**
Heb   10. 4   it is impossible for the blood of **b**

BURDEN → BURDENS, BURDENSOME
Ps   55.22   Cast your **b** on the LORD,
Mt   11.30   my yoke is easy, and my **b** is light."

BURDENS → BURDEN
Ex   6. 6   free you from the **b** of the Egyptians
Lk   11.46   you load people with **b** hard to bear,
Gal   6. 2   Bear one another's **b,** and

BURDENSOME → BURDEN
1Jn   5. 3   And his commandments are not **b,**

BURIED → BURY
Ro   6. 4   have been **b** with him by baptism
1Co   15. 4   he was **b,** and that he was raised on

BURN → BURNED, BURNT
Ex   21.25   **b** for **b,** wound for wound,
Mal   4. 1   the day that comes shall **b** them up,
Lk   3.17   but the chaff he will **b** with

BURNED → BURN
Ex   3. 3   and see why the bush is not **b** up."
Jn   15. 6   thrown into the fire, and **b.**
1Co   3.15   If the work is **b** up, the builder

BURNT → BURN
Ex   40. 6   You shall set the altar of **b** offering
Lev   1. 3   If the offering is a **b** offering from
1Sa   15.22   LORD as great delight in **b** offerings
Ps   51.16   if I were to give a **b** offering,
Da   8.11   it took the regular **b** offering away
Hos   6. 6   the knowledge of God rather than **b**
Mic   6. 6   Shall I come before him with **b**
Mk   12.33   more important than all whole **b**

BURY → BURIED
Lk   9.60   "Let the dead **b** their own dead;

BUSH
Ex   3. 2   he looked, and the **b** was blazing,
Jnh   4. 6   The LORD God appointed a **b,**

C

CALAMITIES → CALAMITY
1Sa   10.19   who saves you from all your **c** and
2Co   6. 4   in afflictions, hardships, **c,**
      12.10   and **c** for the sake of Christ;

CALAMITY → CALAMITIES
Da   9.13   all this **c** has come upon us.
Hab   3.16   wait quietly for the day of **c** to come

CALF
Ex   32. 4   and cast an image of a **c;**
Lk   15.23   And get the fatted **c** and kill it,

CALL → CALLED, CALLING
1Ch   16. 8   to the LORD, **c** on his name,
Ps   61. 2   From the end of the earth I **c** to you,
Pr   8. 1   Does not wisdom **c,** and does
Isa   65.24   Before they I will answer,
Mt   9.13   to **c** not the righteous but sinners."
Lk   6.46   "Why do you **c** me 'Lord, Lord,'
Jn   15.15   I do not **c** you servants any longer,
Php   3.14   goal for the prize of the heavenly **c**

CALLED → CALL
2Sa   22. 7   In my distress I **c** upon the LORD;
Isa   43. 1   I have **c** you by name, you are mine.
1Co   7.15   It is to peace that God has **c** you.
Eph   1.18   the hope to which he has **c** you,
1Jn   3. 1   that we should be **c** children of God;

CALLING → CALL
Ro   11.29   and the **c** of God are irrevocable.
Eph   4. 1   lead a life worthy of the **c** to which

CAMEL
Mt   23.24   strain out a gnat but swallow a **c!**
Mk   10.25   **c** to go through the eye of a needle

CANAAN
Ge   9.25   "Cursed be **C;** lowest of slaves
Nu   13. 2   "Send men to spy out the land of **C,**
1Ch   16.18   "To you I will give the land of **C**

CAPTIVE → CAPTIVITY
2Ki   15.29   he carried the people **c** to Assyria.
      24.16   king of Babylon brought **c** to
Ro   7.23   making me **c** to the law of sin
Eph   4. 8   he made captivity itself a **c;**

CAPTIVITY → CAPTIVE
Dt   28.41   for they shall go into **c.**
Ezr   8.35   those who had come from **c,**

CARE → CAREFUL, CARES, CARING
Ps   8. 4   mortals that you **c** for them?
Heb   2. 6   or mortals, that you **c** for them?

Jas 1.27 to c for orphans and widows in

CAREFUL → CARE

Dt 4.23 So be c not to forget the covenant
Jos 1. 8 you may be c to act in accordance
Eph 5.15 Be c then how you live,

CARES → CARE

1Pe 5. 7 on him, because he c for you.

CARPENTER'S

Mt 13.55 Is not this the c son?

CASE

Isa 41.21 Set forth your c, says the LORD;
Lk 12.58 make an effort to settle the c,
Jn 18.38 "I find no c against him.

CAST

Ex 34.17 You shall not make c idols.
Ps 22.18 and for my clothing they c lots.
     55.22 C your burden on the LORD,
Mk 3.23 "How can Satan c out Satan?
Jn 19.24 and for my clothing they c lots."
1Pe 5. 7 C all your anxiety on him,

CATTLE

Ge 1.25 and the c of every kind,
Ps 50.10 the c on a thousand hills.

CELEBRATE

Lev 23.37 shall c as times of holy convocation,
1Co 5. 8 Therefore, let us c the festival,

CENSER

Lev 10. 1 Nadab and Abihu, each took his c,
Eze 8.11 Each had his c in his hand,
Rev 8. 3 Another angel with a golden c came

CENTURION

Mt 8. 5 he entered Capernaum, a c came to
Lk 23.47 the c saw what had taken place,
Ac 10. 1 a man named Cornelius, a c

CERTIFICATE

Dt 24. 1 so he writes her a c of divorce,
Mt 5.31 let him give her a c of divorce.'
Mk 10. 4 a man to write a c of dismissal

CHAFF

Ps 1. 4 like c that the wind drives away.
Lk 3.17 c he will burn with unquenchable

CHAINS

Eph 6.20 for which I am an ambassador in c.
Heb 11.36 and even c and imprisonment.
2Pe 2. 4 them to c of deepest darkness

CHANGE → CHANGERS

Ex 32.12 c your mind and do not bring
Nu 23.19 a mortal, that he should c his mind.
1Sa 15.29 will not recant or c his mind;
Jer 18. 8 I will c my mind about the disaster
Jas 1.17 is no variation or shadow due to c.

CHANGERS → CHANGE

Mk 11.15 overturned the tables of the money c
Jn 2.15 poured out the coins of the money c

CHARGE

Mt 25.21 I will put you in c of many things;
Mk 15.26 The inscription of the c against him
Ro 8.33 will bring any c against God's elect?
1Co 9.18 I may make the gospel free of c,

CHARM

Pr 31.30 C is deceitful, and beauty is vain,

CHASTISEMENT → CHASTISES

La 4. 6 the c of my people has been greater

CHASTISES → CHASTISEMENT

Heb 12. 6 and c every child whom he accepts.

CHEEK

Ps 3. 7 you strike all my enemies on the c;
Mt 5.39 if anyone strikes you on the right c,

CHEERFUL

Pr 15.13 A glad heart makes a c countenance,

Pr 17.22 A c heart is a good medicine,
2Co 9. 7 for God loves a c giver.
Jas 5.13 Are any c? They should sing songs

CHERUB → CHERUBIM

2Ch 3.11 touched the wing of the other c;
Ps 18.10 He rode on a c, and flew;
Eze 10.14 the first face was that of the c,
     28.14 an anointed c as guardian I placed

CHERUBIM → CHERUB

Ge 3.24 the garden of Eden he placed the c,
Ex 25.18 You shall make two c of gold;
Ps 80. 1 You who are enthroned upon the c,
Heb 9. 5 the c of glory overshadowing the

CHIEF

Ps 118.22 has become the c cornerstone.
Mk 15. 3 the c priests accused him of many
1Pe 5. 4 And when the c shepherd appears,

CHILD → CHILDBEARING, CHILDREN

Isa 11. 6 and a little c shall lead them.
     49.15 Can a woman forget her nursing c,
Hos 11. 1 When Israel was a c, I loved him,
Mt 1.18 with c from the Holy Spirit.
Mk 10.15 the kingdom of God as a little c
Lk 2.12 you will find a c wrapped in bands
1Co 13.11 When I was a c, I spoke like a
Rev 12. 4 that he might devour her c as soon

CHILDBEARING → CHILD, BEAR

Ge 3.16 greatly increase your pangs in c;
1Ti 2.15 Yet she will be saved through c,

CHILDREN → CHILD

Pr 22. 6 Train c in the right way, and when
Mt 3. 9 stones to raise up c to Abraham.
Lk 18.16 "Let the little c come to me,
Jn 1.12 he gave power to become c of God,
Ro 8.14 by the Spirit of God are c of God.
Eph 6. 4 do not provoke your c to anger,
Heb 12. 7 God is treating you as c;
1Jn 3.10 The c of God and the c of the devil

CHOOSE → CHOOSES, CHOSE, CHOSEN

Dt 30.19 C life so that you and your
Jos 24.15 c this day whom you will serve,
Jn 15.16 You did not c me but I chose you.

CHOOSES → CHOOSE

Ro 9.18 he has mercy on whomever he c,

CHOSE → CHOOSE

Mk 13.20 for the sake of the elect, whom he c,
1Co 1.27 God c what is foolish in the world

CHOSEN → CHOOSE

Isa 42. 1 my servant, whom I uphold, my c,
Mt 22.14 For many are called, but few are c."
Ro 11. 5 there is a remnant, c by grace.
1Pe 2. 6 a cornerstone and precious;
     2. 9 are a c race, a royal priesthood,

CHRIST → CHRISTIAN, CHRISTIANS, JESUS, MESSIAH

Jn 4.25 Messiah is coming" (who is called C).
Ro 5. 6 right time C died for the ungodly.
     8.35 will separate us from the love of C?
1Co 1.23 but we proclaim C crucified,
     3.11 that foundation is Jesus C.
     11. 1 Be imitators of me, as I am of C.
Gal 5. 1 For freedom C has set us free.
Eph 4.15 into him who is the head, into C,
Php 1.21 to me, living is C and dying is gain.
     2.11 should confess that Jesus C is Lord,
Col 1.27 C in you, the hope of glory.
Rev 20. 4 reigned with C a thousand years.

CHRISTIAN → CHRIST

Ac 26.28 persuading me to become a C?"
1Pe 4.16 Yet if any of you suffers as a C,

CHRISTIANS → CHRIST

Ac 11.26 the disciples were first called "C."

CHURCH

Mt 16.18 on this rock I will build my c,

Ac 8. 1 persecution began against the c
1Co 12.28 appointed in the c first apostles,
     14. 4 those who prophesy build up the c.
Col 1.18 He is the head of the body, the c;

CIRCUMCISE → CIRCUMCISED, CIRCUMCISION

Ge 17.11 shall c the flesh of your foreskins,
Dt 10.16 C, then, the foreskin of your heart,
Lk 1.59 the eighth day they came to c the
Jn 7.22 and you c a man on the sabbath.

CIRCUMCISED → CIRCUMCISE

Ge 17.10 Every male among you shall be c.
Gal 6.13 c do not themselves obey the law,
Col 2.11 also you were c with a spiritual

CIRCUMCISION → CIRCUMCISE

Ro 2.29 real c is a matter of the heart—
Gal 5. 6 For in Christ Jesus neither c

CITIES → CITY

Jos 20. 2 'Appoint the c of refuge,
Rev 16.19 and the c of the nations fell.

CITIZENSHIP

Php 3.20 But our c is in heaven,

CITY → CITIES

1Ch 11. 7 it was called the c of David.
Ps 127. 1 Unless the LORD guards the c,
Mt 5.14 A c built on a hill cannot be hid.
Heb 12.22 Zion and to the c of the living God,
Rev 21. 2 I saw the holy c, the new Jerusalem,

CLAY

Isa 45. 9 Does the c say to the one who
Jer 18. 6 Just like the c in the potter's hand,
Ro 9.21 Has the potter no right over the c,
2Co 4. 7 But we have this treasure in c jars,

CLEAN → CLEANSE, CLEANSING

Ge 7. 2 seven pairs of all c animals,
Lev 10.10 and between the unclean and the c;
Ps 51. 7 with hyssop, and I shall be c;
Mk 7.19 (Thus he declared all foods c.)
Heb 10.22 and our hearts sprinkled c from

CLEANSE → CLEAN

Ps 51. 2 and c me from my sin.
1Jn 1. 9 c us from all unrighteousness.

CLEANSING → CLEAN

Eph 5.26 by c her with the washing of water
2Pe 1. 9 is forgetful of the c of past sins.

CLOTH

Isa 64. 6 righteous deeds are like a filthy c.
Lk 2. 7 and wrapped him in bands of c,

CLOTHE → CLOTHED, CLOTHING

Col 3.14 Above all, c yourselves with love,
1Pe 5. 5 you must c yourselves with humility

CLOTHED → CLOTHE

2Co 5. 2 longing to be c with our heavenly
Gal 3.27 have c yourselves with Christ.
Rev 12. 1 a woman c with the sun,

CLOTHING → CLOTHE

Ps 22.18 and for my c they cast lots.
Mt 25.36 I was naked and you gave me c,
Jn 19.24 and for my c they cast lots."

CLOUD → CLOUDS

Ex 13.21 went in front of them in a pillar of c
Mk 9. 7 Then a c overshadowed them,
Lk 21.27 'the Son of Man coming in a c'
Heb 12. 1 by so great a c of witnesses,
Rev 14.14 on the c was one like the Son of Man,

CLOUDS → CLOUD

Ge 9.13 I have set my bow in the c,
Da 7.13 being coming with the c of heaven.
Mt 24.30 'the Son of Man coming on the c of
1Th 4.17 be caught up in the c together with
Rev 1. 7 He is coming with the c;

COIN
Mt   17.27   open its mouth, you will find a **c**;
      22.19   Show me the **c** used for the tax."
Lk   15. 9   I have found the **c** that I had lost.'

COLLECTOR → COLLECTORS
Mt   10. 3   Thomas and Matthew the tax **c**;
Lk   18.10   one a Pharisee and the other a tax **c**.
      19. 2   he was a chief tax **c** and was rich.

COLLECTORS → COLLECTOR
Mt   5.46   Do not even the tax **c** do the same?
    11.19   a friend of tax **c** and sinners!'

COLT
Ge   49.11   his donkey's **c** to the choice vine,
Zec   9. 9   and riding on a donkey, on a **c**,
Jn   12.15   coming, sitting on a donkey's **c!**"

COME → COMES, COMING
Mt   6.10   Your kingdom **c**. Your will be done,
Lk   7.20   'Are you the one who is to **c**,
1Co   16.22   Our Lord, **c**!
Rev   1. 4   who is and who was and who is to **c**,
    22.20   Amen. **C**, Lord Jesus!

COMES → COME
Ps   118.26   who **c** in the name of the LORD.
Lk   19.38   "Blessed is the king who **c** in the
Jn   14. 6   No one **c** to the Father except through

COMFORT → COMFORTED, COMFORTS
Ps   23. 4   your rod and your staff—they **c** me.
Isa   40. 1   **C**, O **c** my people, says your God.

COMFORTED → COMFORT
Ps   86.17   LORD, have helped me and **c** me.
Isa   49.13   For the LORD has **c** his people,
Mt   5. 4   those who mourn, for they will be **c**.

COMFORTS → COMFORT
Isa   66.13   As a mother **c** her child, so I will

COMING → COME
Mal   3. 2   But who can endure the day of his **c**,
Heb   10.37   is **c** will come and will not delay;
2Pe   3. 4   "Where is the promise of his **c**?
Rev   22.20   "Surely I am **c** soon."

COMMAND → COMMANDED,
COMMANDING, COMMANDMENT,
COMMANDMENTS
Ex   34.11   Observe what I **c** you today.
Jdg   2. 2   But you have not obeyed my **c**.

COMMANDED → COMMAND
Mt   28.20   to obey everything that I have **c** you.
Jn   14.31   but I do as the Father has **c** me,

COMMANDING → COMMAND
Dt   4.40   **c** you today for your own well-being
    30.11   **c** you today is not too hard for you,

COMMANDMENT → COMMAND
Dt   6. 1   Now this is the **c**—the statutes
Ps   19. 8   **c** of the LORD is clear,
Mt   22.38   This is the greatest and first **c**.
Ro   7.12   and the **c** is holy and just and good.
Gal   5.14   law is summed up in a single **c**,
1Jn   3.23   this is his **c**, that we should believe

COMMANDMENTS → COMMAND
Ex   20. 6   those who love me and keep my **c**,
Dt   4.13   to observe, that is, the ten **c**;
Ps   119.66   for I believe in your **c**.
Pr   10. 8   The wise of heart will heed **c**,
Ecc   12.13   Fear God, and keep his **c**;
Mt   22.40   On these two **c** hang all the law and
Jn   14.15   If you love me, you will keep my **c**.
1Co   7.19   obeying the **c** of God is everything.
1Jn   5. 3   And his **c** are not burdensome,
Rev   14.12   those who keep the **c** of God and

COMMON
Lev   10.10   between the holy and the **c**,
Eze   22.26   between the holy and the **c**,
Ac   2.44   and had all things in **c**;

COMMUNION
2Co   13.13   the **c** of the Holy Spirit be with

COMPANY
1Co   15.33   "Bad **c** ruins good morals."

COMPASSION → COMPASSIONATE
Dt   32.36   will vindicate his people, have **c**
Ps   103.13   As a father has **c** for his children,
Hos   11. 8   my **c** grows warm and tender.
Mt   14.14   had **c** for them and cured their sick.
Ro   9.15   I will have **c** on whom I have **c**."
Col   3.12   clothe yourselves with **c**, kindness,

COMPASSIONATE → COMPASSION
Ex   22.27   I will listen, for I am **c**.
Jas   5.11   how the Lord is **c** and merciful.

COMPLAIN → COMPLAINING,
COMPLAINT
Nu   14.27   shall this wicked congregation **c**
Jer   2.29   Why do you **c** against me?
1Co   10.10   And do not **c** as some of them did,

COMPLAINING → COMPLAIN
Ex   16. 7   heard your **c** against the LORD.
1Pe   4. 9   hospitable to one another without **c**.

COMPLAINT → COMPLAIN
Ps   142. 2   I pour out my **c** before him;
Hab   2. 1   he will answer concerning my **c**.
Col   3.13   if anyone has a **c** against another,

COMPLETE → COMPLETED
Jn   4.34   him who sent me and to **c** his work.
Rev   6.11   until the number would be **c**

COMPLETED → COMPLETE
Jer   25.12   Then after seventy years are **c**,
Da   11.36   until the period of wrath is **c**,

CONCEIT → CONCEITED
Php   2. 3   nothing from selfish ambition or **c**,
1Ti   3. 6   he may be puffed up with **c** and fall

CONCEITED → CONCEIT
Gal   5.26   Let us not become **c**, competing
1Ti   6. 4   is **c**, understanding nothing,

CONCEIVE
Mt   1.23   the virgin shall **c** and bear a son,
Lk   1.31   you will **c** in your womb and bear

CONDEMN → CONDEMNATION,
CONDEMNED
Lk   11.31   of this generation and **c** them,
Jn   3.17   not send the Son into the world to **c**
Ro   8.34   Who is to **c**?
1Jn   3.21   Beloved, if our hearts do not **c** us,

CONDEMNATION → CONDEMN
Mk   12.40   They will receive the greater **c**."
Ro   5.18   one man's trespass led to **c** for all,
1Ti   3. 6   fall into the **c** of the devil.
Jas   5.12   so that you may not fall under **c**.

CONDEMNED → CONDEMN
Mt   12.37   and by your words you will be **c**."
Lk   24.20   handed him over to be **c** to death
Jn   3.18   Those who believe in him are not **c**;
    16.11   the ruler of this world has been **c**.
1Co   11.32   disciplined so that we may not be **c**

CONDUCT
1Pe   1.15   be holy yourselves in all your **c**;

CONFESS → CONFESSES, CONFESSION
Lev   5. 5   you shall **c** the sin that you have
Ps   38.18   my iniquity; I am sorry for my sin.
Php   2.11   should **c** that Jesus Christ is Lord,
1Jn   1. 9   If we **c** our sins, he who is faithful
Rev   3. 5   will **c** your name before my Father

CONFESSES → CONFESS
Ro   10.10   **c** with the mouth and so is saved.
1Jn   2.23   who **c** the Son has the Father also.

CONFESSION → CONFESS
Da   9. 4   to the LORD my God and made **c**,

CONFIDENCE
Ps   118. 8   LORD than to put **c** in mortals.
Php   3. 3   and have no **c** in the flesh—
Heb   10.19   we have **c** to enter the sanctuary

CONFORMED
Ro   8.29   predestined to be **c** to the image of
    12. 2   Do not be **c** to this world,
Php   3.21   may be **c** to the body of his glory,
1Pe   1.14   do not be **c** to the desires that you

CONFUSE
Ge   11. 7   go down, and **c** their language there,

CONGREGATION
Ps   1. 5   nor sinners in the **c** of the righteous;
Heb   2.12   the midst of the **c** I will praise you."

CONQUER → CONQUERED,
CONQUERORS, CONQUERS
Rev   17.14   and the Lamb will **c** them,
    21. 7   who **c** will inherit these things,

CONQUERED → CONQUER
Jn   16.33   take courage; I have **c** the world!"
Heb   11.33   who through faith **c** kingdoms,
1Jn   2.13   because you have **c** the evil one.
Rev   15. 2   who had **c** the beast and its image

CONQUERORS → CONQUER
Ro   8.37   all these things we are more than **c**

CONQUERS → CONQUER
1Jn   5. 4   victory that **c** the world, our faith.
Rev   2. 7   To everyone who **c**, I will give

CONSCIENCE
Ro   2.15   their own **c** also bears witness;
1Co   8. 7   and their **c**, being weak, is defiled.
1Ti   1. 5   a good **c**, and sincere faith.
Heb   9.14   purify our **c** from dead works to
1Pe   3.21   as an appeal to God for a good **c**,

CONSIDER
1Sa   12.24   for **c** what great things he has done
Ps   107.43   and **c** the steadfast love of the LORD.
Lk   12.27   **C** the lilies, how they grow:

CONSOLATION
Lk   2.25   looking forward to the **c** of Israel,
2Co   1. 3   of mercies and the God of all **c**,

CONSPIRED
Da   6. 6   So the presidents and satraps **c**
Mt   26. 4   they **c** to arrest Jesus by stealth

CONSUME → CONSUMED, CONSUMING
Ex   32.12   **c** them from the face of the earth'?
Nu   16.21   so that I may **c** them in a moment.
Mt   6.19   where moth and rust **c** and where
Jn   2.17   "Zeal for your house will **c** me."

CONSUMED → CONSUME
Ex   3. 2   bush was blazing, yet it was not **c**.
Ps   69. 9   zeal for your house that has **c** me;
Zep   3. 8   all the earth shall be **c**.
Gal   5.15   that you are not **c** by one another.

CONSUMING → CONSUME
Heb   12.29   for indeed our God is a **c** fire.

CONTEMPT
Da   12. 2   some to shame and everlasting **c**.
Mk   9.12   sufferings and be treated with **c**?
Heb   6. 6   and are holding him up to **c**.

CONTENT → CONTENTMENT
2Co   12.10   Therefore I am **c** with weaknesses,
Php   4.11   learned to be **c** with whatever I have
Heb   13. 5   and be **c** with what you have;

CONTENTMENT → CONTENT
1Ti   6. 6   gain in godliness combined with **c**;

CONTRITE
Ps   51.17   broken and **c** heart, O God, you
Isa   57.15   who are **c** and humble in spirit,

CONVERT
Mt 23. 15 sea and land to make a single **c**,
1Ti 3. 6 He must not be a recent **c**,

CONVICT → CONVICTION
Dt 19. 15 to **c** a person of any crime
Jude 1. 15 to **c** everyone of all the deeds of

CONVICTION → CONVICT
Heb 11. 1 the **c** of things not seen.

CONVINCE → CONVINCED, CONVINCING
Ac 28. 23 and trying to **c** them about Jesus
2Ti 4. 2 **c**, rebuke, and encourage,

CONVINCED → CONVINCE
Lk 16. 31 neither will they be **c** even if
Ro 8. 38 For I am **c** that neither death, nor
2Co 5. 14 we are **c** that one has died for all;

CONVINCING → CONVINCE
Ac 1. 3 to them by many **c** proofs,

COPPER
Mk 12. 42 and put in two small **c** coins,

CORNERSTONE → STONE
Ps 118. 22 rejected has become the chief **c**.
Isa 28. 16 a tested stone, a precious **c**, a sure
Zec 10. 4 Out of them shall come the **c**,
Lk 20. 17 builders rejected has become the **c**'?
Eph 2. 20 with Christ Jesus himself as the **c**.
1Pe 2. 6 laying in Zion a stone, a **c** chosen

CORRECT → CORRECTING, CORRECTION
Ps 141. 5 let the faithful **c** me.

CORRECTING → CORRECT
2Ti 2. 25 **c** opponents with gentleness.

CORRECTION → CORRECT
Jer 5. 3 but they refused to take **c**.
2Ti 3. 16 **c**, and for training in righteousness,

CORRUPT → CORRUPTION
Ge 6. 11 Now the earth was **c** in God's sight,
Ac 2. 40 yourselves from this **c** generation."
Eph 4. 22 your old self, **c** and deluded

CORRUPTION → CORRUPT
Ac 2. 31 nor did his flesh experience **c**.'
2Pe 1. 4 you may escape from the **c**

COST
1Ch 21. 24 burnt offerings that **c** me nothing."
Lk 14. 28 not first sit down and estimate the **c**,

COUNCIL → COUNCILS
Jer 23. 18 who has stood in the **c** of the LORD
Mt 26. 59 the whole **c** were looking for false

COUNCILS → COUNCIL
Mk 13. 9 for they will hand you over to **c**;

COUNSEL → COUNSELOR, COUNSELORS
Ps 2. 2 and the rulers take **c** together,
33. 11 The **c** of the LORD stands forever,
Isa 28. 29 he is wonderful in **c**, and excellent

COUNSELOR → COUNSEL
Isa 9. 6 and he is named Wonderful **C**,
Ro 11. 34 Or who has been his **c**?"

COUNSELORS → COUNSEL
Pr 11. 14 in an abundance of **c** there is safety.
24. 6 in abundance of **c** there is victory.

COUNTENANCE
Nu 6. 26 the LORD lift up his **c** upon you,
Ps 89. 15 O LORD, in the light of your **c**;
Pr 15. 13 A glad heart makes a cheerful **c**,

COURAGE → COURAGEOUS
1Ch 22. 13 Be strong and of good **c**.
Jn 16. 33 But take **c**; I have conquered

COURAGEOUS → COURAGE
Jos 1. 6 Be strong and **c**; for you shall put
Da 10. 19 Be strong and **c**!"

1Co 16. 13 stand firm in your faith, be **c**,

COURT → COURTS
Ex 27. 9 shall make the **c** of the tabernacle.
Pr 25. 8 do not hastily bring into **c**;
Mt 5. 25 while you are on the way to **c**
1Co 6. 6 believer goes to **c** against a believer

COURTS → COURT
Ps 84. 10 in your **c** is better than a thousand
96. 8 an offering, and come into his **c**.

COVENANT → COVENANTS
Ge 6. 18 But I will establish my **c** with you;
9. 9 I am establishing my **c** with you
15. 18 the LORD made a **c** with Abram,
Ex 19. 5 you obey my voice and keep my **c**,
24. 7 Then he took the book of the **c**,
40. 3 put in it the ark of the **c**,
Jdg 2. 1 'I will never break my **c** with you.
1Ki 8. 23 keeping **c** and steadfast love
Ps 105. 8 He is mindful of his **c** forever,
Isa 61. 8 I will make an everlasting **c** with
Jer 31. 31 when I will make a new **c** with
Eze 16. 60 establish with you an everlasting **c**.
Mal 3. 1 The messenger of the **c** in whom
Lk 22. 20 is the new **c** in my blood.
1Co 11. 25 "This cup is the new **c** in my blood.
2Co 3. 6 be ministers of a new **c**, not of letter
Heb 7. 22 become the guarantee of a better **c**.
12. 24 the mediator of a new **c**,
Rev 11. 19 the ark of his **c** was seen within his

COVENANTS → COVENANT
Ro 9. 4 the adoption, the glory, the **c**,
Gal 4. 24 an allegory: these women are two **c**.

COVET
Ex 20. 17 shall not **c** your neighbor's house;
Ro 7. 7 had not said, "You shall not **c**."
Jas 4. 2 you **c** something and cannot obtain

CRAFTINESS → CRAFTY
Ro 1. 29 of envy, murder, strife, deceit, **c**,
1Co 3. 19 "He catches the wise in their **c**,"

CRAFTY → CRAFTINESS
Ge 3. 1 serpent was more **c** than any other

CRAVING
Nu 11. 4 rabble among them had a strong **c**;
Ps 78. 30 But before they had satisfied their **c**,

CREATE → CREATED, CREATION, CREATOR
Ps 51. 10 **C** in me a clean heart, O God,
Isa 65. 17 to **c** new heavens and a new earth;
Eph 2. 15 **c** in himself one new humanity

CREATED → CREATE
Ge 1. 1 In the beginning when God **c** the
1. 27 So God **c** humankind in his image,
Dt 32. 6 Is not he your father, who **c** you,
Pr 8. 22 The LORD **c** me at the beginning
Mal 2. 10 Has not one God **c** us?
1Co 11. 9 Neither was man **c** for the sake of
Eph 2. 10 **c** in Christ Jesus for good works,
Col 1. 16 all things have been **c** through him
1Ti 4. 4 For everything **c** by God is good,
Rev 4. 11 you **c** all things, and by your will

CREATION → CREATE
Ge 2. 3 all the work that he had done in **c**.
Mk 10. 6 But from the beginning of **c**,
Ro 8. 19 the **c** waits with eager longing for
2Co 5. 17 anyone is in Christ, there is a new **c**:
Col 1. 15 invisible God, the firstborn of all **c**;

CREATOR → CREATE
Ecc 12. 1 Remember your **c** in the days of
Ro 1. 25 served the creature rather than the **C**
1Pe 4. 19 to a faithful **C**,

CREATURE → CREATURES
Ge 2. 19 the man called every living **c**,

CREATURES → CREATURE
Lev 11. 2 these are the **c** that you may eat.

Ps 104. 24 the earth is full of your **c**.

CRIED → CRY
Ps 22. 5 To you they **c**, and were saved;
Mt 27. 46 Jesus **c** with a loud voice,

CRIMINAL → CRIMINALS
Jn 18. 30 "If this man were not a **c**,
2Ti 2. 9 the point of being chained like a **c**.
1Pe 4. 15 suffer as a murderer, a thief, a **c**,

CRIMINALS → CRIMINAL
Lk 23. 32 Two others also, who were **c**,

CROOKED
Dt 32. 5 a perverse and **c** generation.
Ps 18. 26 the **c** you show yourself perverse.
Ecc 1. 15 What is **c** cannot be made straight,
Lk 3. 5 and the **c** shall be made straight,

CROSS
Dt 31. 3 your God himself will **c** over before
Mk 15. 30 and come down from the **c**!"
Lk 14. 27 the **c** and follow me cannot be my
1Co 1. 18 the **c** is foolishness to those who are
Gal 6. 14 never boast of anything except the **c**
Php 2. 8 of death—even death on a **c**.
Col 1. 20 peace through the blood of his **c**.
Heb 12. 2 was set before him endured the **c**,

CROW
Lk 22. 34 the cock will not **c** this day,

CROWD → CROWDS
Mk 8. 2 "I have compassion for the **c**,
14. 43 a **c** with swords and clubs,

CROWDS → CROWD
Mt 7. 28 **c** were astounded at his teaching,

CROWN → CROWNED, CROWNS
Lev 8. 9 the golden ornament, the holy **c**,
Jn 19. 2 soldiers wove a **c** of thorns and put
Php 4. 1 my joy and **c**, stand firm in the Lord
2Ti 4. 8 there is reserved for me the **c**
1Pe 5. 4 the **c** of glory that never fades away.
Rev 6. 2 Its rider had a bow; a **c** was given
14. 14 with a golden **c** on his head,

CROWNED → CROWN
Ps 8. 5 and **c** them with glory and honor.
2Ti 2. 5 no one is **c** without competing
Heb 2. 9 now **c** with glory and honor

CROWNS → CROWN
Rev 4. 10 they cast their **c** before the throne,

CRUCIFIED → CRUCIFY
Mt 27. 22 All of them said, "Let him be **c**!"
Lk 24. 7 and on the third day rise again."
Ac 4. 10 whom you **c**, whom God raised
Ro 6. 6 We know that our old self was **c**
1Co 1. 23 but we proclaim Christ **c**,
Gal 2. 19 I have been **c** with Christ;

CRUCIFY → CRUCIFIED, CRUCIFYING
Lk 23. 21 they kept shouting, "**C**, **c** him!"
Jn 19. 15 asked them, "Shall I **c** your King?"

CRUCIFYING → CRUCIFY
Heb 6. 6 they are **c** again the Son of God

CRUSH
Mt 21. 44 it will **c** anyone on whom it falls."
Ro 16. 20 will shortly **c** Satan under your feet.

CRY → CRIED, CRYING
Pr 130. 1 Out of the depths I **c** to you,
Hab 1. 2 how long shall I **c** for help,
Mk 15. 37 Then Jesus gave a loud **c**

CRYING → CRY
Mk 1. 3 the voice of one **c** out in the
Rev 21. 4 and pain will be no more,

CUP
Ps 23. 5 my head with oil; my **c** overflows.
Mt 26. 39 if it is possible, let this **c** pass
Mk 10. 38 you able to drink the **c** that I drink,

Lk   22. 17 he took a **c**, and after giving thanks
1Co 11. 25 **c** is the new covenant in my blood.
Rev 14. 10 unmixed into the **c** of his anger,

CURED
Mt   8. 16 and **c** all who were sick.
Ac   5. 16 and they were all **c**.

CURSE → ACCURSED, CURSED, CURSES
Ge   8. 21 "I will never again **c** the ground
     12. 3 the one who curses you I will **c;**
Job   2. 9 **C** God, and die."
Ps 109. 28 Let them **c**, but you will bless.
Mal   4. 6 come and strike the land with a **c**.
Mk 14. 71 he began to **c**, and he swore an oath,
Lk   6. 28 bless those who **c** you, pray
Ro   12. 14 bless and do not **c** them.
Gal   3. 13 redeemed us from the **c** of the law by
               becoming a **c** for us—

CURSED → CURSE
Ge   3. 17 **c** is the ground because of you;
     27. 29 **C** be everyone who curses you,
Nu   23. 8 can I curse whom God has not **c**?
Mk 11. 21 fig tree that you **c** has withered."
Gal   3. 10 "**C** is everyone who does not
Rev   16. 9 but they **c** the name of God,

CURSES → CURSE
Lev 24. 15 who **c** God shall bear the sin.

CURTAIN
Ex   26. 31 You shall make a **c** of blue, purple,
2Ch   3. 14 And Solomon made the **c** of blue
Lk   23. 45 the **c** of the temple was torn in two.
Heb 10. 20 that he opened for us through the **c**

CUT
Ge   9. 11 never again shall all flesh be **c** off
Ps   37. 9 For the wicked shall be **c** off,
Isa   53. 8 **c** off from the land of the living,
Mt   3. 10 does not bear good fruit is **c** down
Mk   9. 43 hand causes you to stumble, **c** it off;
Ro   11. 22 otherwise you also will be **c** off.

D

DAILY → DAY
Mt   6. 11 Give us this day our **d** bread.
Lk   9. 23 take up their cross **d** and follow me.

DANCE → DANCED
Ps 150. 4 Praise him with tambourine and **d**;
Ecc   3. 4 a time to mourn, and a time to **d**;
Lk   7. 32 the flute for you, and you did not **d**;

DANCED → DANCE
2Sa   6. 14 David **d** before the LORD with all
Mt   14. 6 the daughter of Herodias **d** before

DARK → DARKEST, DARKNESS
Ps 139. 12 even the darkness is not **d** to you;
Lk   12. 3 whatever you have said in the **d** will
2Pe   1. 19 as to a lamp shining in a **d** place,

DARKEST → DARK
Ps   23. 4 though I walk through the **d** valley,

DARKNESS → DARK
Ge   1. 2 the earth was a formless void and **d**
Ex   10. 22 was dense **d** in all the land of Egypt
Isa   9. 2 walked in **d** have seen a great light;
Joel   2. 31 The sun shall be turned to **d**,
Mt   4. 16 who sat in **d** have seen a great light,
Jn   1. 5 light shines in the **d**, and the **d** did not
Col   1. 13 from the power of **d** and transferred
1Jn   1. 5 God is light and in him there is no **d**

DAUGHTER → DAUGHTERS
Mic   7. 6 the **d** rises up against her mother,
Lk   12. 53 against **d** and **d** against mother,

DAUGHTERS → DAUGHTER
Ge   6. 4 of God went in to the **d** of humans,
Joel   2. 28 sons and your **d** shall prophesy,
Ac   2. 17 sons and your **d** shall prophesy,

2Co   6. 18 and you shall be my sons and **d**,

DAWN → DAWNS
Isa   14. 12 from heaven, O Day Star, son of **D**!
Hos   6. 3 his appearing is as sure as the **d**;

DAWNS → DAWN
Ps   97. 11 Light **d** for the righteous,
2Pe   1. 19 until the day **d** and the morning star

DAY → DAILY, DAYS
Ge   1. 5 God called the light **D**, and
Ex   13. 21 of them in a pillar of cloud by **d**,
     20. 8 Remember the sabbath **d**, and keep
Ps   1. 2 his law they meditate **d** and night.
     118. 24 is the **d** that the LORD has made;
Joel   1. 15 For the **d** of the LORD is near,
Zec   1. 16 a **d** is coming for the LORD,
Mal   3. 2 who can endure the **d** of his coming,
Mt   25. 13 you know neither the **d** nor the hour.
Lk   11. 3 Give us each **d** our daily bread.
     24. 46 to rise from the dead on the third **d**,
Jn   6. 40 I will raise them up on the last **d**."
Ro   14. 5 Some judge one **d** to be better than
1Th   5. 2 very well that the **d** of the Lord
2Pe   3. 8 one **d** is like a thousand years,
     3. 10 of the Lord will come like a thief,
1Jn   4. 17 have boldness on the **d** of judgment,
Rev   16. 14 for battle on the great **d** of God

DAYS → DAY
Ge   1. 14 and for seasons and for **d** and years,
Ex   24. 18 on the mountain for forty **d** and
1Ki   19. 8 that food forty **d** and forty nights
Ps   90. 10 The **d** of our life are seventy years,
Eph   5. 16 of the time, because the **d** are evil.
2Ti   3. 1 in the last **d** distressing times will

DEACON → DEACONS
Ro   16. 1 a **d** of the church at Cenchreae,

DEACONS → DEACON
1Ti   3. 8 **D** likewise must be serious, not

DEAD → DEATH, DIE, DIED, DYING
Mt   8. 22 and let the **d** bury their own **d**."
Mk   12. 27 God not of the **d**, but of the living;
Lk   24. 5 look for the living among the **d**?
Ro   6. 11 must consider yourselves **d** to sin
Eph   2. 1 You were **d** through the trespasses
Rev   1. 5 witness, the firstborn of the **d**,
     20. 12 And the **d** were judged according to

DEAF
Ex   4. 11 Who makes them mute or **d**,
Isa   29. 18 On that day the **d** shall hear the
Lk   7. 22 the lepers are cleansed, the **d** hear,

DEATH → DEAD
Dt   30. 19 that I have set before you life and **d**,
Isa   25. 7 he will swallow up **d** forever.
Hos   13. 14 O **D**, where are your plagues?
Lk   1. 79 in darkness and in the shadow of **d**,
Jn   5. 24 but has passed from **d** to life.
Ro   6. 23 For the wages of sin is **d**,
1Co   15. 55 "Where, O **d**, is your victory?
Heb   2. 14 through **d** he might destroy the one who
               has the power of **d**,
1Jn   3. 14 that we have passed from **d** to life
Rev   1. 18 I have the keys of **D** and of Hades.
     20. 14 **D** and Hades were thrown into the lake
     21. 4 **D** will be no more;

DEBTS
Mt   6. 12 And forgive us our **d**, as we

DECEIT → DECEITFUL, DECEIVE
Dt   32. 4 A faithful God, without **d**,
Isa   53. 9 and there was no **d** in his mouth.
Ro   1. 29 Full of envy, murder, strife, **d**,
1Pe   2. 22 and no **d** was found in his mouth."

DECEITFUL → DECEIT
1Ti   4. 1 by paying attention to **d** spirits

DECEIVE → DECEIT
Eph   5. 6 Let no one **d** you with empty words,
1Jn   1. 8 that we have no sin, we **d** ourselves,

Rev   20. 8 to **d** the nations at the four corners

DECREES
Dt   6. 2 and keep all his **d** and his
Ps   19. 7 the **d** of the LORD are sure,
     119. 2 Happy are those who keep his **d**,

DEDICATION
2Ch   7. 9 the **d** of the altar seven days and
Ezr   6. 16 the **d** of this house of God with joy.

DEED → DEEDS
Ecc   12. 14 will bring every **d** into judgment,
Mt   19. 16 good **d** must I do to have eternal life
Col   3. 17 And whatever you do, in word or **d**,

DEEDS → DEED
Jer   50. 29 Repay her according to her **d**;
Lk   23. 41 getting what we deserve for our **d**,
Ro   2. 6 repay according to each one's **d**:
Rev   15. 3 "Great and amazing are your **d**,
     19. 8 the righteous **d** of the saints.

DEEP → DEPTH, DEPTHS
Ge   1. 2 darkness covered the face of the **d**,
     7. 11 the fountains of the great **d** burst
Ro   8. 26 with sighs too **d** for words.

DEFEND
Ps   72. 4 May he **d** the cause of the poor of
Pr   31. 9 **d** the rights of the poor and needy.

DEFILE
Lev   11. 43 you shall not **d** yourselves
Nu   35. 34 You shall not **d** the land
Mk   7. 15 things that come out are what **d**."

DEITY
Col   2. 9 whole fullness of **d** dwells bodily,

DELAY
Dt   7. 10 He does not **d** but repays
Ps   70. 5 my deliverer; O LORD, do not **d**!
Heb   10. 37 will come and will not **d**;

DELIGHT
1Sa   15. 22 "Has the LORD as great **d** in burnt
Ps   1. 2 their **d** is in the law of the LORD,
     40. 8 I **d** to do your will, O my God;
Pr   8. 30 I was daily his **d**, rejoicing before
Ro   7. 22 For I **d** in the law of God in my

DELIVER → DELIVERANCE, DELIVERER, DELIVERS
Ex   3. 8 to **d** them from the Egyptians,
Da   3. 17 able to **d** us from the furnace
     6. 20 able to **d** you from the lions?"
Mt   27. 43 let God **d** him now,

DELIVERANCE → DELIVER
Ex   14. 13 and see the **d** that the LORD will
Ps   3. 8 **D** belongs to the LORD;
Php   1. 19 this will turn out for my **d**.

DELIVERER → DELIVER
Ps   140. 7 O LORD, my Lord, my strong **d**,
Ro   11. 26 "Out of Zion will come the **D**;

DEMON → DEMONIACS, DEMONIC, DEMONS
Mt   11. 18 and they say, 'He has a **d**';
     17. 18 Jesus rebuked the **d**, and it came out
Jn   8. 48 you are a Samaritan and have a **d**?"
     10. 21 not the words of one who has a **d**.

DEMONIACS → DEMON
Mt   4. 24 **d**, epileptics, and paralytics, and he
     8. 28 two **d** coming out of the tombs met

DEMONIC → DEMON
Rev   16. 14 These are **d** spirits, performing signs

DEMONS → DEMON
Dt   32. 17 They sacrificed to **d**, not God,
Lk   11. 18 that I cast out the **d** by Beelzebul.
1Co   10. 20 not want you to be partners with **d**.
1Ti   4. 1 deceitful spirits and teachings of **d**,
Jas   2. 19 Even the **d** believe—and shudder.

Rev 9.20 their hands or give up worshiping **d**

DEN

Jer 7.11 a **d** of robbers in your sight?
Da 6. 7 shall be thrown into a **d** of lions.
Mk 11.17 you have made it a **d** of robbers."

DENARIUS

Mk 12.15 Bring me a **d** and let me see it."

DENIED → DENY

Mt 26.70 But he **d** it before all of them,
1Ti 5. 8 has **d** the faith and is worse than
Rev 3. 8 my word and have not **d** my name.

DENIES → DENY

Lk 12. 9 but whoever **d** me before others
1Jn 2.22 liar but the one who **d** that Jesus

DENY → DENIED, DENIES

Mt 16.24 let them **d** themselves and take up
2Ti 2.12 if we **d** him, he will also **d** us;
2Pe 2. 1 **d** the Master who bought them—

DEPRAVED → DEPRAVITY

1Ti 6. 5 among those who are **d** in mind
2Pe 2.10 who indulge their flesh in **d** lust,

DEPRAVITY → DEPRAVED

Lev 20.14 that there may be no **d** among you.

DEPTH → DEEP

Mt 13. 5 since they had no **d** of soil.
Ro 11.33 O the **d** of the riches and wisdom
Eph 3.18 and length and height and **d**,

DEPTHS → DEEP

Ps 130. 1 Out of the **d** I cry to you,
1Co 2.10 even the **d** of God.

DESCENDANTS

Ge 15.18 saying, "To your **d** I give this land,
Dt 4.37 he chose their **d** after them.
Isa 44. 3 I will pour my spirit upon your **d**,
Ro 9. 7 Abraham's children are his true **d**;
Gal 3. 7 who believe are the **d** of Abraham.

DESERT

Ps 106.14 and put God to the test in the **d**;
Isa 40. 3 make straight in the **d** a highway
Mk 8. 4 with bread here in the **d**?"

DESERVE

Pr 14.14 and the good, what their deeds **d**.
Lk 23.15 he has done nothing to **d** death.
Ac 26.31 man is doing nothing to **d** death
Rev 2.23 give to each of you as your works **d**.

DESIRE → DESIRES

Ge 3.16 your **d** shall be for your husband,
Ps 20. 4 May he grant you your heart's **d**,
Hos 6. 6 I **d** steadfast love and not sacrifice,
Mt 9.13 learn what this means, 'I **d** mercy,
1Jn 2.16 the **d** of the flesh, the **d** of the eyes,

DESIRES → DESIRE

1Ti 2. 4 who **d** everyone to be saved
2Ti 4. 3 teachers to suit their own **d**,

DESOLATE → DESOLATES

Da 11.31 the abomination that makes **d**.

DESOLATES → DESOLATE

Da 9.27 shall be an abomination that **d**,

DESPISE → DESPISED

Job 5.17 not **d** the discipline of the Almighty.
Pr 1. 7 fools **d** wisdom and instruction.
Lk 16.13 devoted to the one and **d** the other.

DESPISED → DESPISE

Isa 53. 3 He was **d** and rejected by others;
1Co 1.28 God chose what is low and **d** in the

DESTINED

Eph 1. 5 He **d** us for adoption as his children
1Th 5. 9 For God has **d** us not for wrath but
1Pe 1.11 to the sufferings **d** for Christ

DESTROY → DESTROYED, DESTRUCTION

Ge 6.13 to **d** them along with the earth.
Mt 10.28 rather fear him who can **d** both soul
Jn 10.10 comes only to steal and kill and **d**.
Jas 4.12 who is able to save and to **d**.
1Jn 3. 8 to **d** the works of the devil.

DESTROYED → DESTROY

Da 6.26 His kingdom shall never be **d**,
1Co 15.26 The last enemy to be **d** is death.

DESTRUCTION → DESTROY

Pr 16.18 Pride goes before **d**, and a haughty
Mt 7.13 and the road is easy that leads to **d**,

DEVIL

Mt 4. 1 wilderness to be tempted by the **d**.
Lk 8.12 **d** comes and takes away the word
Jn 8.44 You are from your father the **d**,
Eph 4.27 and do not make room for the **d**.
6.11 to stand against the wiles of the **d**,
1Ti 3. 6 fall into the condemnation of the **d**;
Heb 2.14 the power of death, that is, the **d**,
Jas 4. 7 Resist the **d**, and he will flee from
1Pe 5. 8 lion your adversary the **d** prowls
1Jn 3. 8 to destroy the works of the **d**.
Jude 1. 9 Michael contended with the **d**
Rev 12. 9 who is called the **D** and Satan,
20. 2 that ancient serpent, who is the **D**

DIE → DEAD

Ge 2.17 eat of it you shall **d**."
3. 4 to the woman, "You will not **d**;
Ru 1.17 Where you **d**, I will **d**—
Ecc 3. 2 a time to be born, and a time to **d**;
Isa 22.13 eat and drink, for tomorrow we **d**."
Jer 31.30 But all shall **d** for their own sins;
Mt 26.35 "Even though I must **d** with you,
Jn 11.26 and believes in me will never **d**.
Ro 14. 8 if we **d**, we **d** to the Lord;
1Co 15.32 eat and drink, for tomorrow we **d**."
Heb 9.27 appointed for mortals to **d** once,

DIED → DEAD

Ro 5. 6 right time Christ **d** for the ungodly.
1Co 15. 3 Christ **d** for our sins in accordance
Gal 2.19 the law I **d** to the law,

DIFFERENT

2Co 11. 4 or a **d** gospel from the one you
Gal 1. 6 and are turning to a **d** gospel—

DISAPPOINT

Ro 5. 5 and hope does not **d** us,

DISCIPLE → DISCIPLES

Mt 10.24 "A **d** is not above the teacher,
Lk 14.26 even life itself, cannot be my **d**.

DISCIPLES → DISCIPLE

Mt 26.56 all the **d** deserted him and fled.
28.19 therefore and make **d** of all nations,
Lk 6.13 he called his **d** and chose twelve of
Jn 8.31 in my word, you are truly my **d**;
Ac 11.26 the **d** were first called "Christians."

DISCIPLINE → DISCIPLINED

Job 5.17 not despise the **d** of the Almighty.
Ps 94.12 Happy are those whom you **d**,
Eph 6. 4 in the **d** and instruction of the Lord.
Heb 12. 5 not regard lightly the **d** of the Lord,

DISCIPLINED → DISCIPLINE

1Co 11.32 **d** so that we may not be condemned

DISEASE → DISEASES

Mt 4.23 of the kingdom and curing every **d**
9.35 curing every **d** and every sickness.

DISEASES → DISEASE

Ex 15.26 **d** that I brought upon the Egyptians;
Ps 103. 3 your iniquity, who heals all your **d**,
Isa 53. 4 our infirmities and carried our **d**;
Mt 8.17 took our infirmities and bore our **d**."

DISMAYED

Dt 1.21 do not fear or be **d**."
Jos 1. 9 do not be frightened or **d**,

DISOBEDIENT → DISOBEY

Ne 9.26 they were **d** and rebelled
Ro 10.21 I have held out my hands to a **d**
Tit 3. 3 ourselves were once foolish, **d**,

DISOBEY → DISOBEDIENT

Lev 26.27 But if, despite this, you **d** me,
1Pe 2. 8 stumble because they **d** the word,

DISTINCTION → DISTINCTIONS

Ex 8.23 I will make a **d** between my people
Lev 11.47 make a **d** between the unclean and
Eze 22.26 have made no **d** between the holy

DISTINCTIONS → DISTINCTION

Jas 2. 4 you not made **d** among yourselves,

DISTRESS → DISTRESSED

2Sa 22. 7 In my **d** I called upon the LORD;
Ps 81. 7 In **d** you called, and I rescued you;
Lk 21.23 For there will be great **d** on the earth
Ro 8.35 Will hardship, or **d**, or persecution,

DISTRESSED → DISTRESS

La 1.20 See, O LORD, how **d** I am;

DISTRIBUTED

Ac 4.35 it was **d** to each as any had need.
Heb 2. 4 gifts of the Holy Spirit, **d** according

DIVIDED

Lev 11. 3 Any animal that has **d** hoofs
Ps 136.13 who **d** the Red Sea in two,
Lk 11.18 If Satan also is **d** against himself,

DIVINE

Ro 1.20 his eternal power and **d** nature,
2Pe 1. 4 become participants of the **d** nature.

DIVORCE → DIVORCED

Dt 24. 1 so he writes her a certificate of **d**,
Isa 50. 1 Where is your mother's bill of **d**
Jer 3. 8 sent her away with a decree of **d**;
Mal 2.16 For I hate **d**, says the LORD,
Mt 5.31 let him give her a certificate of **d**.'
19. 3 a man to **d** his wife for any cause?"
1Co 7.11 the husband should not **d** his wife.

DIVORCED → DIVORCE

Lev 21. 7 neither shall they marry a woman **d**
Mt 5.32 whoever marries a **d** woman

DOCTOR

Lk 4.23 this proverb, '**D**, cure yourself!'

DOCTRINE → DOCTRINES

Eph 4.14 blown about by every wind of **d**,
1Ti 1. 3 not to teach any different **d**,
2Ti 4. 3 people will not put up with sound **d**,
Tit 1. 9 able both to preach with sound **d**

DOCTRINES → DOCTRINE

Mk 7. 7 teaching human precepts as **d**.'

DOERS

Jas 1.22 But be **d** of the word,

DOGS

Mt 7. 6 "Do not give what is holy to **d**;

DOMINION

Ge 1.26 let them have **d** over
Ps 22.28 For **d** belongs to the LORD,
Da 7.14 His **d** is an everlasting **d**
Rev 1. 6 to him be glory and **d** forever

DONKEY

Zec 9. 9 humble and riding on a **d**,
Mt 21. 5 humble, and mounted on a **d**,

DOOR → DOORPOSTS

Mt 7. 7 knock, and the **d** will be opened
Lk 13.24 Strive to enter through the narrow **d**
Rev 3.20 I am standing at the **d**, knocking;

DOORPOSTS → DOOR

Ex 12. 7 the blood and put it on the two **d**

DOUBT → DOUBTED, DOUBTING

Mt 14.31 of little faith, why did you **d**?"

Jn 20.27 Do not **d** but believe."

DOUBTED → DOUBT
Mt 28.17 they worshiped him; but some **d.**

DOUBTING → DOUBT
Jas 1.6 But ask in faith, never **d,**

DOVE
Ge 8.8 Then he sent out the **d** from him,
Mk 1.10 Spirit descending like a **d** on him.

DRAGON
Isa 27.1 and he will kill the **d** that
Rev 12.3 a great red **d,** with seven heads and
20.2 seized the **d,** that ancient serpent,

DRANK → DRINK
Ex 24.11 beheld God, and they ate and **d.**
Mk 14.23 and all of them **d** from it.
1Co 10.4 all **d** the same spiritual drink.

DRAW
Jas 4.8 **D** near to God, and he will **d** near

DREAM → DREAMS
Joel 2.28 your old men shall **d** dreams,
Ac 2.17 and your old men shall **d** dreams.

DREAMS → DREAM
Nu 12.6 I speak to them in **d.**

DRIED → DRY
Ge 8.13 the waters were **d** up from the earth;
Jos 5.1 had **d** up the waters of the Jordan
Isa 51.10 Was it not you who **d** up the sea,

DRINK → DRANK, DRUNK, DRUNKARD, DRUNKENNESS
Ex 32.6 the people sat down to eat and **d,**
Ecc 9.7 and **d** your wine with a merry heart;
Isa 22.13 eat and **d,** for tomorrow we die."
Mt 20.22 to **d** the cup that I am about to **d?**"
Jn 18.11 not to **d** the cup that the Father has
Ro 14.17 kingdom of God is not food and **d,**
1Co 12.13 we were all made to **d** of one Spirit.
Rev 14.10 also **d** the wine of God's wrath,

DRUNK → DRINK
Jn 2.10 after the guests have become **d.**
Ac 2.15 these are not **d,** as you suppose,
Eph 5.18 Do not get **d** with wine,

DRUNKARD → DRINK
Mt 11.19 they say, 'Look, a glutton and a **d,**
1Co 5.11 is an idolater, reviler, **d,** or robber.
1Ti 3.3 not a **d,** not violent but gentle,

DRUNKENNESS → DRINK
Gal 5.21 **d,** carousing, and things like these.

DRY → DRIED
Ge 1.9 and let the **d** land appear."
Ex 14.16 may go into the sea on **d** ground.
Eze 37.4 **d** bones, hear the word of the LORD.

DUST
Ge 2.7 LORD God formed man from the **d**
1Sa 2.8 He raises up the poor from the **d;**
Ps 103.14 he remembers that we are **d.**
Ecc 3.20 from the **d,** and all turn to **d** again.
Mt 10.14 shake off the **d** from your feet
1Co 15.47 man was from the earth, a man of **d;**

DWELL → DWELLING, DWELLS
Ex 25.8 so that I may **d** among them.
1Ki 8.27 But will God indeed **d** on the earth?
Ps 23.6 and I shall **d** in the house of
Eph 3.17 that Christ may **d** in your hearts
Col 1.19 fullness of God was pleased to **d,**
Rev 21.3 He will **d** with them as their God;

DWELLING → DWELL
Ps 90.1 our **d** place in all generations.
Jn 14.2 my Father's house there are many **d**
2Co 5.2 to be clothed with our heavenly **d**—
Eph 2.22 spiritually into a **d** place for God.

DWELLS → DWELL
Jn 14.10 but the Father who **d** in me

Ro 7.17 but sin that **d** within me.
1Co 3.16 and that God's Spirit **d** in you?
Col 2.9 whole fullness of deity **d** bodily,

E

EAGLES
Isa 40.31 shall mount up with wings like **e,**

EAR
Isa 64.4 has heard, no **e** has perceived,
Lk 22.51 he touched his **e** and healed him.
1Co 2.9 "What no eye has seen, nor **e** heard,

EARTH
Ge 1.1 God created the heavens and the **e,**
6.11 the **e** was corrupt in God's sight,
Isa 6.3 the whole **e** is full of his glory."
65.17 to create new heavens and a new **e;**
Mt 5.5 meek, for they will inherit the **e.**
24.35 Heaven and **e** will pass away,
2Pe 3.13 wait for new heavens and a new **e,**
Rev 21.1 I saw a new heaven and a new **e;**

EAST
Ge 2.8 planted a garden in Eden, in the **e;**
Ps 103.12 as far as the **e** is from the west,
Mt 2.1 wise men from the **E** came to

EASY
Mt 11.30 For my yoke is **e,** and my burden is

EAT → ATE, EATS
Ge 2.16 freely **e** of every tree of the garden;
Lev 11.4 you shall not **e** the following:
Mt 26.26 to the disciples, and said, "Take, **e;**
Ac 10.13 "Get up, Peter; kill and **e.**"
1Co 10.31 whether you **e** or drink, or whatever
Rev 3.20 I will come in to you and **e** with you

EATS → EAT
Jn 6.51 **e** of this bread will live forever;
1Co 11.27 **e** the bread or drinks the cup of the

EDEN
Ge 2.8 a garden in **E,** in the east;

EGYPT
Ge 47.27 Israel settled in the land of **E,**
Hos 11.1 and out of **E** I called my son.
Mt 2.15 "Out of **E** I have called my son."
Rev 11.8 prophetically called Sodom and **E,**

ELDER → ELDERS
1Ti 5.19 any accusation against an **e** except
1Pe 5.1 as an **e** myself and a witness of the

ELDERS → ELDER
Ex 24.1 and seventy of the **e** of Israel,
Mt 27.12 accused by the chief priests and **e,**
Mk 7.3 thus observing the tradition of the **e;**
1Ti 5.17 the **e** who rule well be considered
Jas 5.14 **e** of the church and have them pray
1Pe 5.5 must accept the authority of the **e.**
Rev 4.4 on the thrones are twenty-four **e,**

ELECT → ELECTION
Mt 24.22 sake of the **e** those days will be cut
Mk 13.22 to lead astray, if possible, the **e.**

ELECTION → ELECT
Ro 9.11 God's purpose of **e** might continue,
2Pe 1.10 eager to confirm your call and **e,**

ELEVEN
Mt 28.16 Now the **e** disciples went to Galilee,
Ac 1.26 and he was added to the **e** apostles.

EMMANUEL → IMMANUEL
Mt 1.23 and they shall name him **E,**"

ENCOURAGE → ENCOURAGEMENT
1Th 4.18 **e** one another with these words.
1Pe 5.12 written this short letter to **e** you

ENCOURAGEMENT → ENCOURAGE
Ro 15.5 God of steadfastness and **e** grant

Php 2.1 If then there is any **e** in Christ,

END
Ge 6.13 determined to make an **e** of all flesh,
Pr 14.12 but its **e** is the way to death.
Ecc 12.12 making many books there is no **e,**
Mt 24.13 But the one who endures to the **e**
28.20 always, to the **e** of the age."
Ro 10.4 For Christ is the **e** of the law so
Rev 22.13 the beginning and the **e.**"

ENDURANCE → ENDURE
Ro 5.3 knowing that suffering produces **e,**
1Ti 6.11 godliness, faith, love, **e,**
Heb 10.36 For you need **e,** so that when you
Jas 1.3 the testing of your faith produces **e;**
2Pe 1.6 and self-control with **e,**

ENDURE → ENDURANCE, ENDURED, ENDURES
Mal 3.2 who can **e** the day of his coming,
1Co 10.13 so that you may be able to **e** it.
2Ti 2.12 if we **e,** we will also reign with him;

ENDURED → ENDURE
Heb 12.2 that was set before him **e** the cross,

ENDURES → ENDURE
1Co 13.7 hopes all things, **e** all things.
1Pe 1.25 but the word of the Lord **e** forever."

ENEMIES → ENEMY
Mt 5.44 But I say to you, Love your **e** and
Ro 5.10 For if while we were **e,**

ENEMY → ENEMIES, ENMITY
Mt 13.39 the **e** who sowed them is the devil;
1Co 15.26 The last **e** to be destroyed is death.

ENGAGED
Mt 1.18 mother Mary had been **e** to Joseph,

ENJOYMENT
Ecc 8.15 So I commend **e,** for there is nothing
1Ti 6.17 with everything for our **e.**

ENLIGHTENED → LIGHT
Ro 10.2 a zeal for God, but it is not **e.**
Eph 1.18 with the eyes of your heart **e,**
Heb 6.4 those who have once been **e,**

ENLIGHTENS → LIGHT
Jn 1.9 The true light, which **e** everyone,

ENMITY → ENEMY
Ge 3.15 put **e** between you and the woman,
Jas 4.4 with the world is **e** with God?

ENTER → ENTRY
Mt 7.13 "**E** through the narrow gate;
Mk 10.15 as a little child will never **e** it."
Jn 3.5 no one can **e** the kingdom of God
Rev 21.27 But nothing unclean will **e** it,

ENTRUSTED → TRUST
Lk 12.48 the one to whom much has been **e,**
2Ti 1.12 guard until that day what I have **e**
Jude 1.3 the faith that was once for all **e**

ENVY
Pr 23.17 Do not let your heart **e** sinners,
Mk 7.22 deceit, licentiousness, **e,** slander,
Ro 1.29 Full of **e,** murder, strife, deceit,

EPHOD
Ex 28.6 They shall make the **e** of gold,

EQUAL → EQUALITY
Isa 40.25 you compare me, or who is my **e?**
46.5 will you liken me and make me **e,**
Jn 5.18 thereby making himself **e** to God.

EQUALITY → EQUAL
Php 2.6 not regard **e** with God as something

ERROR
Lev 5.18 for the **e** that you committed
Ro 1.27 the due penalty for their **e.**
1Jn 4.6 of truth and the spirit of **e.**

ESTABLISH → ESTABLISHED
Eze 16. 60 e with you an everlasting covenant.
Heb 8. 8 when I will e a new covenant with

ESTABLISHED → ESTABLISH
2Sa 7. 16 your throne shall be e forever.
Ps 89. 2 your steadfast love is e forever;
103. 19 The LORD has e his throne in the

ETERNAL → ETERNITY
Mt 25. 46 but the righteous into e life."
Mk 10. 17 what must I do to inherit e life?"
Jn 3. 16 may not perish but may have e life.
Ro 5. 21 e life through Jesus Christ our Lord.
2Co 4. 17 an e weight of glory beyond all
Heb 5. 9 the source of e salvation for all who
1Jn 5. 13 may know that you have e life.

ETERNITY → ETERNAL
Isa 57. 15 high and lofty one who inhabits e,
2Pe 3. 18 glory both now and to the day of e.

EUNUCH
Ac 8. 27 Now there was an Ethiopian e,

EVANGELIST → EVANGELISTS
2Ti 4. 5 do the work of an e, carry out your

EVANGELISTS → EVANGELIST
Eph 4. 11 some e, some pastors and teachers,

EVERLASTING → LAST
Ge 9. 16 remember the e covenant between
Ps 90. 2 from e to e you are God.
Isa 9. 6 E Father, Prince of Peace.
Jer 31. 3 I have loved you with an e love;
Da 4. 3 His kingdom is an e kingdom,

EVIL
Ge 2. 9 tree of the knowledge of good and e.
Jdg 2. 11 Then the Israelites did what was e
Ps 23. 4 the darkest valley, I fear no e;
Pr 8. 13 fear of the LORD is hatred of e.
Mt 6. 13 but rescue us from the e one.
12. 35 e person brings e things out of an e
Lk 11. 13 who are e, know how to give good
Jn 17. 15 to protect them from the e one.
Ro 12. 17 Do not repay anyone e for e,
Eph 5. 16 of the time, because the days are e.
1Ti 6. 10 of money is a root of all kinds of e,
1Jn 5. 18 and the e one does not touch them.
2Jn 1. 11 to welcome is to participate in the e
3Jn 1. 11 do not imitate what is e but imitate

EXALT → EXALTED
Lk 14. 11 who e themselves will be humbled,
Jas 4. 10 before the Lord, and he will e you.

EXALTED → EXALT
Ps 57. 5 Be e, O God, above the heavens.
Php 2. 9 highly e him and gave him the name

EXAMPLES
1Co 10. 6 these things occurred as e for us,
1Pe 5. 3 but be e to the flock.

EXCELLENCE → EXCELLENT
Php 4. 8 if there is any e and if there is

EXCELLENT → EXCELLENCE
Isa 28. 29 in counsel, and e in wisdom.
1Co 12. 31 I will show you a still more e way.
Heb 1. 4 the name he has inherited is more e

EXCUSE
Jn 15. 22 they have no e for their sin.
Ro 1. 20 So they are without e;

EXHORT
Tit 2. 15 e and reprove with all authority.
Heb 3. 13 But e one another every day,

EXILE
2Ki 25. 11 carried into e the rest of the people
Ezr 6. 21 of Israel who had returned from e,

EYE → EYES, EYEWITNESSES
Ex 21. 24 e for e, tooth for tooth,
Ps 17. 8 Guard me as the apple of the e;

Mt 5. 29 If your right e causes you to sin,
5. 38 An e for an e and a tooth for
7. 3 see the speck in your neighbor's e,
Mk 10. 25 to go through the e of a needle
1Co 15. 52 in the twinkling of an e, at the last
Rev 1. 7 the clouds; every e will see him,

EYES → EYE
Ge 3. 7 Then the e of both were opened,
Ps 121. 1 I lift up my e to the hills—
Pr 3. 7 Do not be wise in your own e;
Mt 9. 30 And their e were opened.
Eph 1. 18 with the e of your heart enlightened,
1Pe 3. 12 e of the Lord are on the righteous,
1Jn 2. 16 of the flesh, the desire of the e,
Rev 21. 4 he will wipe every tear from their e.

EYEWITNESSES → EYE, WITNESS
Lk 1. 2 who from the beginning were e
2Pe 1. 16 but we had been e of his majesty.

F

FACE
Ge 32. 30 "For I have seen God f to f,
Nu 6. 25 LORD make his f to shine upon
12. 8 With him I speak f to f—
Ps 4. 6 Let the light of your f shine on us,
Isa 54. 8 wrath for a moment I hid my f
Eze 39. 29 I will never again hide my f from
Lk 9. 29 the appearance of his f changed,

FADE → FADES
Ps 37. 2 for they will soon f like the grass,
Isa 64. 6 We all f like a leaf,

FADES → FADE
Isa 40. 7 The grass withers, the flower f,
1Pe 5. 4 crown of glory that never f away.

FAINT
Ps 142. 3 When my spirit is f, you know
Isa 40. 31 they shall walk and not f.

FAITH → FAITHFUL, FAITHFULNESS
Isa 7. 9 If you do not stand firm in f,
Hab 2. 4 but the righteous live by their f.
Mt 17. 20 have f the size of a mustard seed,
Ac 3. 16 and the f that is through Jesus
Ro 3. 28 that a person is justified by f apart
1Co 13. 13 And now f, hope, and love abide,
Eph 4. 5 one Lord, one f, one baptism,
Heb 11. 1 f is the assurance of things hoped
Jas 2. 17 f by itself, if it has no works,
1Jn 5. 4 that conquers the world, our f.
Rev 2. 13 and you did not deny your f in me

FAITHFUL → FAITH
Dt 32. 4 A f God, without deceit, just and
Ps 4. 3 LORD has set apart the f for
Mt 24. 45 "Who then is the f and wise slave,
1Th 5. 24 The one who calls you is f,
Heb 10. 23 for he who has promised is f.
1Jn 1. 9 f and just will forgive us our sins
Rev 19. 11 Its rider is called F and True,

FAITHFULNESS → FAITH
Ex 34. 6 abounding in steadfast love and f,
Jos 24. 14 and serve him in sincerity and in f;
Isa 11. 5 and f the belt around his loins.
La 3. 23 new every morning; great is your f.
Gal 5. 22 patience, kindness, generosity, f,

FALL → FELL
Pr 16. 18 and a haughty spirit before a f.
Ro 9. 33 a rock that will make them f,
1Co 10. 12 watch out that you do not f.

FALSE
Dt 5. 20 Neither shall you bear f witness
Mk 13. 22 F messiahs and f prophets will
Heb 6. 18 impossible that God would prove f,
2Pe 2. 1 there will be f teachers among you,
Rev 20. 10 where the beast and the f prophet

FAMILY
Pr 6. 19 and one who sows discord in a f.
Gal 6. 10 especially for those of the f of faith.
Eph 3. 15 from whom every f in heaven and
1Pe 2. 17 Love the f of believers.

FAST
Isa 58. 5 Is such the f that I choose,
Mt 6. 16 "And whenever you f,

FATHER → FATHER'S
Ge 2. 24 a man leaves his f and his mother
Ex 20. 12 Honor your f and your mother,
Ps 89. 26 cry to me, 'You are my F, my God,
Isa 9. 6 Mighty God, Everlasting, F, Prince
Mt 6. 9 Our F in heaven, hallowed be your
28. 19 the name of the F and of the Son and
Jn 5. 18 but was also calling God his own F,
14. 6 comes to the F except through me.
Gal 4. 6 into our hearts, crying, "Abba! F!"
Rev 3. 5 confess your name before my F

FATHER'S → FATHER
Lk 2. 49 that I must be in my F house?"
Jn 1. 14 the glory as of a f only son,
14. 2 F house there are many dwelling

FAVOR
Ps 30. 5 his f is for a lifetime.
Isa 49. 8 In a time of f I have answered you,
Lk 4. 19 proclaim the year of the Lord's f."

FEAR → AFRAID
Dt 6. 13 The LORD your God you shall f;
Ps 19. 9 the f of the LORD is pure,
23. 4 the darkest valley, I f no evil;
Pr 1. 7 f of the LORD is the beginning
Ecc 12. 13 F God, and keep his commandments
Mt 10. 28 rather f him who can destroy both
Mk 5. 36 "Do not f, only believe."
1Pe 3. 14 Do not f what they f,
1Jn 4. 18 but perfect love casts out f;
Rev 14. 7 "F God and give him glory,

FEET
Ps 119. 105 Your word is a lamp to my f
Lk 24. 39 Look at my hands and my f;
Jn 13. 5 and began to wash the disciples' f
1Co 15. 25 put all his enemies under his f.

FELLOWSHIP
Ac 2. 42 to the apostles' teaching and f,
2Co 6. 14 Or what f is there between light and
1Jn 1. 3 and truly our f is with the Father

FEMALE
Ge 1. 27 male and f he created them.
Mk 10. 6 'God made them male and f.'
Gal 3. 28 there is no longer male and f;

FESTIVAL → FESTIVALS
Ex 23. 14 in the year you shall hold a f for me.
1Co 5. 8 Therefore, let us celebrate the f,

FESTIVALS → FESTIVAL
Lev 23. 2 the appointed f of the LORD
Ne 10. 33 the new moons, the appointed f,
Col 2. 16 of food and drink or of observing f,

FEW
Mt 22. 14 many are called, but f are chosen."
Lk 13. 23 "Lord, will only a f be saved?"

FIG
Ge 3. 7 and they sewed f leaves together
Hab 3. 17 Though the f tree does not blossom,
Mt 24. 32 "From the f tree learn its lesson:

FILL → FILLED, FULL, FULLNESS
Ge 1. 28 and f the earth and subdue it;
Jer 23. 24 Do I not f heaven and earth?
Eph 4. 10 so that he might f all things.)

FILLED → FILL
Lk 1. 15 will be f with the Holy Spirit.
Ac 2. 4 were f with the Holy Spirit and
Eph 5. 18 but be f with the Spirit,

FIND

Dt   4. 29   you will f him if you search after
Jer 29. 13   you search for me, you will f me;
Mt 16. 25   lose their life for my sake will f it.

FINISHED

Ge   2. 2   on the seventh day God f the work
Jn 19. 30   the wine, he said, "It is f."

FIRE → FIERY

Ex 13. 21   and in a pillar of f by night,
Da   3. 25   walking in the middle of the f,
Mal   3. 2   For he is like a refiner's f and like
Mt   3. 11   baptize you with the Holy Spirit and f.
Mk   9. 43   to go to hell, to the unquenchable f.
Ac   2. 3   Divided tongues, as of f, appeared
Heb 12. 29   indeed our God is a consuming f.
Rev 20. 14   the second death, the lake of f;

FIRST → FIRSTBORN

Ge   1. 5   and there was morning, the f day.
Pr   8. 22   the f of his acts of long ago.
Isa 41. 4   I, the LORD, am f,
Mt   6. 33   But strive f for the kingdom of God
Mk 10. 31   But many who are f will be last, and the last will be f."
1Th   4. 16   the dead in Christ will rise f.
1Jn   4. 19   We love because he f loved us.
Rev   1. 17   I am the f and the last,
     20. 5   This is the f resurrection.
     21. 1   the f heaven and the f earth

FIRSTBORN → BEAR, FIRST

Ex   4. 22   'Thus says the LORD: Israel is my f
Ps 78. 51   He struck all the f in Egypt,
Zec 12. 10   as one weeps over a f.
Lk   2. 7   And she gave birth to her f son and
Col   1. 15   invisible God, the f of all creation;
Rev   1. 5   faithful witness, the f of the dead,

FISH

Jnh   2. 1   his God from the belly of the f,
Jn   6. 9   has five barley loaves and two f.

FLESH

Ge   2. 23   of my bones and f of my f;
     2. 24   and they become one f.
Eze 36. 26   of stone and give you a heart of f.
Mt 16. 17   For f and blood has not revealed this
     26. 41   but the f is weak."
Jn   1. 14   the Word became f and lived among
     3. 6   What is born of the f is f,
Ro   8. 4   to the f but according to the Spirit.
2Co 12. 7   a thorn was given me in the f,
Gal   5. 19   Now the works of the f are obvious:
1Pe   1. 24   "All f is like grass and all its glory
1Jn   4. 2   that Jesus Christ has come in the f

FLOOD

Ge   7. 7   the ark to escape the waters of the f.
2Pe   2. 5   a f on a world of the ungodly;

FLOWING

Ex   3. 8   a land f with milk and honey,
Jos   5. 6   a land f with milk and honey.

FOLLOW → FOLLOWED

1Ki 18. 21   If the LORD is God, f him;
Lk   9. 23   take up their cross daily and f me.

FOLLOWED → FOLLOW

Mk   1. 18   they left their nets and f him.
Rev 13. 3   the whole earth f the beast.

FOOD

Ge   1. 30   I have given every green plant for f.
Ps 136. 25   who gives f to all flesh,
Jn   6. 55   for my flesh is true f and my blood
1Co   8. 8   "F will not bring us close to God."

FOOL → FOOLISH, FOOLISHNESS, FOOLS

Pr 15. 5   A f despises a parent's instruction,

FOOLISH → FOOL

Mt   7. 26   like a f man who built his house
1Co   1. 20   Has not God made f the wisdom of
Tit   3. 3   For we ourselves were once f,

FOOLISHNESS → FOOL

1Co   1. 18   cross is f to those who are perishing,
     3. 19   wisdom of this world is f with God.

FOOLS → FOOL

Ps 14. 1   F say in their hearts, "There is no God."
Pr   1. 7   f despise wisdom and instruction.
Ro   1. 22   Claiming to be wise, they became f;
1Co   4. 10   We are f for the sake of Christ,

FOREHEADS

Eze   9. 4   and put a mark on the f of those
Rev   7. 3   of our God with a seal on their f."
     20. 4   not received its mark on their f

FOREKNEW → KNOW

Ro   8. 29   whom he f he also predestined to
     11. 2   not rejected his people whom he f.

FOREVER

Ge   3. 22   the tree of life, and eat, and live f"
     6. 3   spirit shall not abide in mortals f,
Ex   3. 15   This is my name f, and this my title
Ps 110. 4   "You are a priest f according to the
Ecc   3. 14   that whatever God does endures f;
Isa 40. 8   the word of our God will stand f.
Jn   6. 51   eats of this bread will live f;
     14. 16   another Advocate, to be with you f.
Heb 13. 8   the same yesterday and today and f.
Rev 11. 15   and he will reign f and ever."

FORGET

Dt   4. 23   So be careful not to f the covenant
Isa 49. 15   these may f, yet I will not f you.

FORGIVE → FORGAVE, FORGIVEN, FORGIVENESS, FORGIVING

Ne   9. 17   But you are a God ready to f,
Mt   6. 12   And f us our debts, as we
Lk   5. 24   has authority on earth to f sins"—
1Jn   1. 9   is faithful and just will f us our sins

FORGIVEN → FORGIVE

Ps 32. 1   are those whose transgression is f,
Mt   6. 12   as we also have f our debtors.
     12. 31   against the Spirit will not be f.
Ro   4. 7   are those whose iniquities are f,
Eph   4. 32   as God in Christ has f you.

FORGIVENESS → FORGIVE

Mk   1. 4   a baptism of repentance for the f
Col   1. 14   we have redemption, the f of sins.

FORGIVING → FORGIVE

Ex 34. 7   f iniquity and transgression and sin,
Eph   4. 32   f one another, as God in Christ has

FORMED → FORMLESS

Ge   2. 7   LORD God f man from the dust
Ps 139. 13   you who f my inward parts;

FORMLESS → FORMED

Ge   1. 2   the earth was a f void and darkness

FORSAKE → FORSAKEN

Dt 31. 6   he will not fail you or f you."
Jos   1. 5   I will not fail you or f you.
Heb 13. 5   "I will never leave you or f you."

FORSAKEN → FORSAKE

Ps 22. 1   my God, why have you f me?
Mt 27. 46   my God, why have you f me?"
2Co   4. 9   persecuted, but not f;

FORTRESS

2Sa 22. 2   The LORD is my rock, my f,
Ps 71. 3   for you are my rock and my f.

FORTY

Ge   7. 4   rain on the earth for f days and f
Nu 14. 34   f days, for every day a year,
1Ki 19. 8   f days and f nights to Horeb
Jnh   3. 4   And he cried out, "F days more,
Mt   4. 2   He fasted f days and f nights,
Heb   3. 17   with whom was he angry f years?

FOUNDATION → FOUNDATIONS

Isa 28. 16   See, I am laying in Zion a f stone,

FOUNDATIONS → FOUNDATION

Heb 11. 10   looked forward to the city that has f,
Rev 21. 14   the wall of the city has twelve f,

FRANKINCENSE → INCENSE

Isa 60. 6   They shall bring gold and f,
Mt   2. 11   gifts of gold, f, and myrrh.

FREE

Jn   8. 32   and the truth will make you f."
Ro   6. 23   the f gift of God is eternal life
Gal   3. 28   there is no longer slave or f,

FRIEND → FRIENDS

Pr 18. 24   but a true f sticks closer than
Mt 11. 19   a f of tax collectors and sinners!'
Jas   2. 23   and he was called the f of God.

FRIENDS → FRIEND

Jn 15. 13   to lay down one's life for one's f.

FRUIT → FRUITFUL, FRUITLESS, FRUITS

Ge   3. 6   she took of its f and ate;
Lk   6. 44   each tree is known by its own f.
Jn 15. 2   branch that bears f he prunes to make it bear more f.
Rev 22. 2   tree of life with its twelve kinds of f,

FRUITFUL → FRUIT

Ge   9. 1   said to them, "Be f and multiply,

FRUITS → FRUIT

Ro   8. 23   who have the first f of the Spirit,
1Co 15. 23   in his own order: Christ the first f,
Rev 14. 4   as first f for God and the Lamb,

FULFILL → FULFILLED, FULFILLING

Mt   5. 17   I have come not to abolish but to f.

FULFILLED → FULFILL

Mk   1. 15   "The time is f, and the kingdom
Lk 24. 44   prophets, and the psalms must be f."
Ro   8. 4   requirement of the law might be f

FULFILLING → FULFILL

Ro 13. 10   love is the f of the law.

FULL → FILL

Isa   6. 3   the whole earth is f of his glory."
Jn   1. 14   f of grace and truth.

FULLNESS → FILL

Jn   1. 16   From his f we have all received,
1Co 10. 26   "the earth and its f are the Lord's."
Gal   4. 4   But when the f of time had come,
Eph   3. 19   may be filled with all the f of God
Col   1. 19   in him all the f of God was pleased

FURNACE

Da   3. 6   be thrown into a f of blazing fire."

FUTURE

Pr 24. 20   for the evil have no f;
Jer 31. 17   hope for your f, says the LORD:
1Co   3. 22   or death or the present or the f—

G

GAIN

Lk   9. 25   if they g the whole world,
Php   1. 21   living is Christ and dying is g.

GALILEE

Isa   9. 1   beyond the Jordan, G of the nations.
Mt   4. 15   across the Jordan, G of the Gentiles
Jn   7. 41   the Messiah does not come from G,

GARDEN

Ge   2. 8   LORD God planted a g in Eden,
Jn 19. 41   and in the g there was a new tomb

GATE → GATES

Mt   7. 13   "Enter through the narrow g;
Jn 10. 7   I am the g for the sheep.

GATES → GATE
Mt 16. 18 and the g of Hades will not prevail
Rev 21. 21 And the twelve g are twelve pearls,

GATHERED
Mt 18. 20 two or three are g in my name,

GENERATION
Ex 20. 6 steadfast love to the thousandth g
Da 4. 34 his kingdom endures from g to g.
Mt 12. 39 evil and adulterous g asks for a sign,
Lk 21. 32 this g will not pass away

GENEROSITY
Gal 5. 22 joy, peace, patience, kindness, g,

GENTILE → GENTILES
Mt 18. 17 as a G and a tax collector.
Gal 2. 14 live like a G and not like a Jew,

GENTILES → GENTILE
Ro 3. 29 Is he not the God of G also?

GENTLENESS
Gal 5. 23 g, and self-control.
Php 4. 5 Let your g be known to everyone.
1Ti 6. 11 godliness, faith, love, endurance, g.

GETHSEMANE
Mk 14. 32 They went to a place called G;

GHOST
Mt 14. 26 were terrified, saying, "It is a g!"
Lk 24. 39 for a g does not have flesh and

GIFT → GIFTS
Ecc 5. 19 this is the g of God.
Jn 4. 10 "If you knew the g of God,
Ac 2. 38 will receive the g of the Holy Spirit.
Ro 6. 23 but the free g of God is eternal life
1Co 7. 7 each has a particular g from God,
Jas 1. 17 with every perfect g, is from above,
Rev 21. 6 the thirsty I will give water as a g

GIFTS → GIFT
Mt 2. 11 offered him g of gold, frankincense,
1Co 12. 1 Now concerning spiritual g,

GIVE → GIVEN, GIVER
Mt 6. 11 G us this day our daily bread.
Mk 10. 45 to g his life a ransom for many."
Jn 10. 28 I g them eternal life, and they will
Ac 20. 35 more blessed to g than to receive.' "

GIVEN → GIVE
Mt 7. 7 "Ask, and it will be g you;
Lk 22. 19 "This is my body, which is g for
Ro 5. 5 Holy Spirit that has been g to us.

GIVER → GIVE
2Co 9. 7 for God loves a cheerful g.

GLADNESS
Ps 100. 2 Worship the LORD with g;
Pr 10. 28 The hope of the righteous ends in g,
Isa 16. 10 Joy and g are taken away from the
Zep 3. 17 he will rejoice over you with g,
Heb 1. 9 has anointed you with the oil of g

GLORIFIED → GLORY
Jn 13. 31 "Now the Son of Man has been g,
Ac 3. 13 has g his servant Jesus,
Ro 8. 30 those whom he justified he also g.

GLORIFY → GLORY
Ps 86. 12 and I will g your name forever.
Jn 17. 1 g your Son so that the Son may g you,
1Co 6. 20 therefore g God in your body.

GLORY → GLORIFIED, GLORIFY
Ex 33. 18 Moses said, "Show me your g,
1Sa 4. 21 "The g has departed from Israel,"
Ps 8. 5 crowned them with g and honor.
Isa 6. 3 the whole earth is full of his g."
Mt 25. 31 the Son of Man comes in his g,
Lk 2. 14 "G to God in the highest heaven,
Jn 1. 14 and we have seen his g,
Ro 3. 23 sinned and fall short of the g of God;
1Co 10. 31 do everything for the g of God.

2Co 4. 17 for an eternal weight of g beyond
Heb 1. 3 reflection of God's g and the exact
Rev 4. 11 to receive g and honor and power,
     21. 23 for the g of God is its light,

GNASHING
Mt 8. 12 will be weeping and g of teeth."
     25. 30 will be weeping and g of teeth.'

GOAT → GOATS
Lev 16. 9 Aaron shall present the g on which

GOATS → GOAT
Mt 25. 32 separates the sheep from the g,

GOD → GOD'S, GODLINESS, GODLY, GODS
Ge 1. 1 In the beginning when G created
     1. 27 So G created humankind in his image,
     6. 2 sons of G saw that they were fair;
Ex 34. 6 a G merciful and gracious, slow to
Nu 23. 19 G is not a human being,
Dt 6. 5 love the LORD your G with all
1Ki 8. 27 will G indeed dwell on the earth?
2Ch 2. 5 for our G is greater than other gods.
Ps 19. 1 heavens are telling the glory of G;
     22. 1 My G, my G, why have you forsaken
     46. 10 "Be still, and know that I am G!
     53. 1 Fools say in their hearts, "There is no G."
Ecc 12. 13 Fear G, and keep his
Isa 9. 6 Wonderful Counselor, Mighty G,
     44. 6 besides me there is no g.
Jer 10. 10 But the LORD is the true G;
Mt 1. 23 which means, "G is with us."
     6. 24 You cannot serve G and wealth.
Mk 1. 1 news of Jesus Christ, the Son of G.
     2. 7 Who can forgive sins but G alone?"
Lk 2. 14 "Glory to G in the highest heaven,
     18. 19 No one is good but G alone.
     22. 70 "Are you, then, the Son of G?"
Jn 1. 1 was with G, and the Word was G.
     1. 18 It is G the only Son,
     3. 16 so loved the world that he gave his
     5. 18 calling G his own Father, thereby making
         himself equal to G.
Ac 5. 29 "We must obey G rather than any
Ro 6. 23 gift of G is eternal life in Christ
2Co 4. 4 Christ, who is the image of G.
Eph 4. 6 one G and Father of all,
Php 2. 6 though he was in the form of G,
Col 1. 19 fullness of G was pleased to dwell,
1Jn 4. 16 G is love, and those who abide
Rev 4. 8 "Holy, holy, holy, the Lord G

GOD'S → GOD
Mt 27. 43 for he said, 'I am G Son.' "
     27. 54 "Truly this man was G Son!"

GODLINESS → GOD
1Ti 4. 7 Train yourself in g,
2Pe 1. 3 everything needed for life and g,

GODLY → GOD
2Co 7. 10 For g grief produces a repentance
2Pe 2. 9 how to rescue the g from trial,

GODS → GOD
Ex 20. 3 you shall have no other g before me.
1Co 8. 5 so-called g in heaven or on earth—

GOLD
Ps 119. 127 love your commandments more than g,
1Pe 1. 7 being more precious than g that,
Rev 21. 21 and the street of the city is pure g,

GOLGOTHA
Mt 27. 33 G (which means Place of a Skull),

GOMORRAH
Ge 19. 24 LORD rained on Sodom and G sulfur
Jude 1. 7 Sodom and G and the surrounding

GOOD → BEST, BETTER, GOODNESS
Ge 1. 31 and indeed, it was very g.
     2. 9 tree of the knowledge of g and evil.
2Ch 7. 3 "For he is g, for his steadfast love
Ps 34. 8 taste and see that the LORD is g;
Isa 52. 7 who brings g news, who announces

Mt 5. 45 his sun rise on the evil and on the g,
Mk 10. 18 No one is g but God alone.
Jn 10. 11 "I am the g shepherd.
Ro 12. 21 but overcome evil with g.
Eph 2. 10 created in Christ Jesus for g works,

GOODNESS → GOOD
Ps 23. 6 Surely g and mercy shall follow me
Heb 6. 5 tasted the g of the word of God and
2Pe 1. 5 support your faith with g,

GOSPEL
Mk 8. 35 and for the sake of the g,
Ro 1. 16 For I am not ashamed of the g;
Gal 1. 6 and are turning to a different g—
Php 1. 27 life in a manner worthy of the g
Rev 14. 6 an eternal g to proclaim to those

GRACE → GRACIOUS
Jn 1. 14 father's only son, full of g and truth.
     1. 16 we have all received, g upon g.
Ac 15. 11 that we will be saved through the g
Ro 3. 24 are now justified by his g as a gift,
     11. 6 otherwise g would no longer be g.
2Co 12. 9 "My g is sufficient for you,
Eph 2. 5 by g you have been saved—
Heb 4. 16 approach the throne of g with
Jas 4. 6 But he gives all the more g;

GRACIOUS → GRACE
Ex 34. 6 the LORD, a God merciful and g,
Nu 6. 25 to shine upon you, and be g to you;
Ps 116. 5 G is the LORD, and righteous;

GREAT → GREATER, GREATEST
Ge 1. 16 God made the two g lights—
     12. 2 I will make of you a g nation,
Dt 10. 17 the g God, mighty and awesome,
La 3. 23 g is your faithfulness.
Mt 4. 16 sat in darkness have seen a g light,
     20. 26 whoever wishes to be g among you
Heb 2. 3 if we neglect so g a salvation?
     13. 20 the g shepherd of the sheep,
Rev 12. 9 The g dragon was thrown down,
     20. 11 I saw a g white throne and the one

GREATER → GREAT
Ex 18. 11 that the LORD is g than all gods,
Mk 12. 31 no other commandment g than these
Jn 14. 12 in fact, will do g works than these,
     15. 13 No one has g love than this,

GREATEST → GREAT
Mt 22. 38 the g and first commandment.
Lk 9. 48 the least among all of you is the g."
1Co 13. 13 and the g of these is love.

GREEK
Jn 19. 20 in Hebrew, in Latin, and in G.
Ro 1. 16 to the Jew first and also to the G.
Gal 3. 28 There is no longer Jew or G,

GRIEF → GRIEVE, GRIEVED
2Co 7. 9 your g led to repentance;

GRIEVE → GRIEF
Eph 4. 30 do not g the Holy Spirit of God,
1Th 4. 13 not g as others do who have no hope

GRIEVED → GRIEF
Isa 63. 10 they rebelled and g his holy spirit;

GROUND
Ge 2. 7 formed man from the dust of the g,
Isa 53. 2 and like a root out of dry g;
Mt 13. 5 Other seeds fell on rocky g,

GROW
Col 1. 10 as you g in the knowledge of God.
2Pe 3. 18 But g in the grace and knowledge of

GUARANTEE → GUARANTEED
2Co 5. 5 who has given us the Spirit as a g.
Heb 7. 22 Jesus has also become the g of a

GUARANTEED → GUARANTEE
Ro 4. 16 promise may rest on grace and be g
Heb 6. 17 he g it by an oath,

GUIDE

Ps   48. 14 He will be our **g** forever.
Isa   58. 11 The Lord will **g** you continually,
Lk   6. 39 Can a blind person **g** a blind person?
Jn   16. 13 he will **g** you into all the truth;

GUILT → GUILTY

Ps   32. 5 and you forgave the **g** of my sin.
Hos 14. 2 say to him, "Take away all **g**;
Zec   3. 9 I will remove the **g** of this land

GUILTY → GUILT

Ex   23. 7 for I will not acquit the **g.**
Nu   14. 18 but by no means clearing the **g,**
Mk   3. 29 but is **g** of an eternal sin"—

H

HADES

Mt   16. 18 and the gates of **H** will not prevail
Ac   2. 27 not abandon my soul to **H,**
Rev   1. 18 I have the keys of Death and of **H.**
     20. 14 **H** were thrown into the lake of fire.

HALLOWED

Ge   2. 3 blessed the seventh day and **h** it,
Mt   6. 9 Father in heaven, **h** be your name.

HAND → HANDS

Ex   15. 6 Your right **h,** O Lord, glorious
Dt   19. 21 tooth for tooth, **h** for **h,**
Ps 110. 1 says to my lord, "Sit at my right **h**
Mk   9. 43 If your **h** causes you to stumble, cut
Lk   20. 42 said to my Lord, "Sit at my right **h,**
Heb 10. 12 "he sat down at the right **h** of God,"
Rev   5. 1 saw in the right **h** of the one seated

HANDS → HAND

Ps   24. 4 who have clean **h** and pure hearts,
Lk   23. 46 into your **h** I commend my spirit."
     24. 40 he showed them his **h** and his feet.
Jn   3. 35 has placed all things in his **h.**
Ac   8. 18 the laying on of the apostles' **h,**
Heb   6. 2 laying on of **h,** resurrection of the

HARD → HARDENED

Jer 32. 17 Nothing is too **h** for you.
Mt   7. 14 the road is **h** that leads to life,
     19. 23 **h** for a rich person to enter the

HARDENED → HARD

Ex   10. 20 But the Lord **h** Pharaoh's heart,
Mk   8. 17 Are your hearts **h?**
2Co   3. 14 But their minds were **h.**

HARVEST → HARVESTING

Ge   8. 22 the earth endures, seedtime and **h,**
Mt   13. 39 **h** is the end of the age, and the
Rev 14. 15 the **h** of the earth is fully ripe."

HARVESTING → HARVEST

Jn   4. 35 see how the fields are ripe for **h.**

HATE → HATES, HATING

Ps   97. 10 the Lord loves those who **h** evil;
Ecc   3. 8 a time to love, and a time to **h;**
Am   5. 15 **H** evil and love good, and establish
Mt   5. 43 your neighbor and **h** your enemy.'
Lk   6. 27 do good to those who **h** you,

HATES → HATE

Pr   6. 16 six things that the Lord **h,**

HEAD

Mt   8. 20 of Man has nowhere to lay his **h."**
Mk   6. 28 brought his **h** on a platter,
Eph   1. 22 has made him the **h** over all things

HEAL → HEALED, HEALING, HEALS, HEALTH

Dt   32. 39 and I make alive; I wound and I **h;**
Ecc   3. 3 a time to kill, and a time to **h;**
Jn   12. 40 and turn—and I would **h** them."

HEALED → HEAL

Isa 53. 5 and by his bruises we are **h.**

Jas   5. 16 one another, so that you may be **h.**
1Pe   2. 24 by his wounds you have been **h.**

HEALING → HEAL

Eze 47. 12 for food, and their leaves for **h."**
Mal   4. 2 shall rise, with **h** in its wings.
1Co 12. 9 another gifts of **h** by the one Spirit,
Rev 22. 2 leaves of the tree are for the **h** of

HEALS → HEAL

Ex   15. 26 for I am the Lord who **h** you."
Ps 103. 3 iniquity, who **h** all your diseases,

HEALTH → HEAL

3Jn   1. 2 and that you may be in good **h,**

HEAR → HEARERS, HEARS

Dt   6. 4 **H,** O Israel: The Lord is our God,
Mk   12. 29 answered, "The first is, 'H, O Israel:
Lk   7. 22 the lepers are cleansed, the deaf **h,**
Heb   3. 7 says, "Today, if you **h** his voice,

HEARERS → HEAR

Ro   2. 13 For it is not the **h** of the law who
Jas   1. 22 merely **h** who deceive themselves.

HEARS → HEAR

Ps   69. 33 For the Lord **h** the needy,
Pr   15. 29 but he **h** the prayer of the righteous.
Mt   7. 24 then who **h** these words of mine
1Jn   5. 14 according to his will, he **h** us.

HEART → BROKENHEARTED, HEARTS

Dt   6. 5 the Lord your God with all your **h,**
     30. 14 in your mouth and in your **h** for you
Jos 22. 5 all your **h** and with all your soul."
1Sa 16. 7 but the Lord looks on the **h."**
Ps   51. 10 Create in me a clean **h,** O God,
Pr   3. 5 Trust in the Lord with all your **h,**
Jer   9. 26 of Israel is uncircumcised in **h.**
Eze 36. 26 A new **h** I will give you,
Mt   5. 8 "Blessed are the pure in **h,** for they
Mk   12. 30 the Lord your God with all your **h,**
Ro   2. 29 circumcision is a matter of the **h**—

HEARTS → HEART

Jer 31. 33 and I will write it on their **h;**
Jn   14. 1 "Do not let your **h** be troubled.
Ro   2. 15 law requires is written on their **h,**
Eph   3. 17 Christ may dwell in your **h** through
Col   3. 15 the peace of Christ rule in your **h,**
Heb 10. 16 I will put my laws in their **h,**
1Jn   3. 20 for God is greater than our **h,**
Rev   2. 23 the one who searches minds and **h,**

HEAVEN → HEAVENLY, HEAVENS

Dt   30. 12 "Who will go up to **h** for us,
Ecc   3. 1 and a time for every matter under **h:**
Mt   6. 9 Father in **h,** hallowed be your name.
     24. 35 **H** and earth will pass away,
     26. 64 and coming on the clouds of **h."**
Mk   10. 21 and you will have treasure in **h;**
Lk   24. 51 and was carried up into **h.**
Ro   10. 6 'Who will ascend into **h?'** "
Php   3. 20 But our citizenship is in **h,**
1Th   1. 10 to wait for his Son from **h,**
Heb   9. 24 but he entered into **h** itself,
Rev 21. 1 I saw a new **h** and a new earth;

HEAVENLY → HEAVEN

Mt   5. 48 as your **h** Father is perfect.
Eph   1. 3 spiritual blessing in the **h** places,
Heb   3. 1 holy partners in a **h** calling,

HEAVENS → HEAVEN

Ge   1. 1 when God created the **h** and
Isa 65. 17 to create new **h** and a new earth;
Heb   4. 14 priest who has passed through the **h,**
2Pe   3. 10 the **h** will pass away with a loud

HEIR → HEIRS

Gal   4. 7 then also an **h,** through God.
Heb   1. 2 whom he appointed **h** of all things,

HEIRS → HEIR

Ro   8. 17 **h** of God and joint **h** with Christ—
Eph   3. 6 the Gentiles have become fellow **h,**
1Pe   3. 7 also **h** of the gracious gift of life—

HELL

Mt   10. 28 both soul and body in **h.**
Mk   9. 43 to have two hands and to go to **h,**
2Pe   2. 4 cast them into **h** and committed

HELP → HELPER, HELPS

Ps   46. 1 a very present **h** in trouble.
Mk   9. 24 "I believe; **h** my unbelief!"
Heb   2. 18 able to **h** those who are being tested.

HELPER → HELP

Ge   2. 18 will make him a **h** as his partner."
Ps   30. 10 O Lord, be my **h!"**
Heb 13. 6 Lord is my **h;** I will not be afraid.

HELPS → HELP

Ps   37. 40 The Lord **h** them and rescues
Ro   8. 26 the Spirit **h** us in our weakness;

HIDDEN → HIDE

Mt   13. 44 is like treasure **h** in a field,
Mk   4. 22 nothing **h,** except to be disclosed;
Col   3. 3 your life is **h** with Christ in God.
Rev   2. 17 the **h** manna, and I will give a white

HIDE → HIDDEN

Dt   31. 17 I will forsake them and **h** my face
Ps   13. 1 How long will you **h** your face
     17. 8 **h** me in the shadow of your wings,

HIGH → HIGHEST

Ps   91. 1 live in the shelter of the Most **H,**
Mk   5. 7 Jesus, Son of the Most **H** God?
Eph   4. 8 "When he ascended on **h** he made
Heb   2. 17 a merciful and faithful **h** priest
     7. 26 that we should have such a **h** priest,

HIGHEST → HIGH

1Ki   8. 27 the **h** heaven cannot contain you,
Mt   21. 9 Hosanna in the **h** heaven!"
Lk   2. 14 "Glory to God in the **h** heaven,

HOLINESS → HOLY

Ro   1. 4 according to the spirit of **h** by
2Co   6. 6 **h** of spirit, genuine love,
1Ti   2. 15 continue in faith and love and **h,**
Heb 12. 14 **h** without which no one will see

HOLY → HOLINESS

Ex   20. 8 the sabbath day, and keep it **h.**
     26. 33 the **h** place from the most **h.**
Lev 11. 44 and be **h,** for I am **h.**
1Sa   2. 2 "There is no **H** One like the Lord,
Isa   6. 3 "H, **h, h** is the Lord of hosts;
Mt   1. 18 to be with child from the **H** Spirit.
     3. 11 baptize you with the **H** Spirit and
Mk   1. 24 who you are, the **H** One of God."
     3. 29 against the **H** Spirit can never have
Lk   3. 22 the **H** Spirit descended upon him in
Jn   14. 26 But the Advocate, the **H** Spirit,
Ac   2. 4 were filled with the **H** Spirit and
Ro   12. 1 living sacrifice, **h** and acceptable
Eph   4. 30 do not grieve the **H** Spirit of God,
Heb   6. 4 and have shared in the **H** Spirit,
1Pe   1. 16 "You shall be **h,** for I am **h."**
1Jn   2. 20 have been anointed by the **H** One,
Jude 1. 14 with ten thousands of his **h** ones,
Rev   4. 8 **H, h, h,** the Lord God the Almighty
     21. 2 I saw the **h** city, the new Jerusalem,

HOMETOWN

Mk   6. 4 not without honor, except in their **h,**

HONEY

Ex   3. 8 a land flowing with milk and **h,**
Mt   3. 4 and his food was locusts and wild **h.**

HONOR

Dt   5. 16 **H** your father and your mother,
Ps   8. 5 and crowned them with glory and **h.**
Mt   15. 4 For God said, 'H your father and
Ro   13. 7 **h** to whom **h** is due.
Eph   6. 2 "H your father and mother"—
Rev   4. 11 to receive glory and **h** and power,

HOPE → HOPES

La   3. 21 and therefore I have **h:**

1Co 13.13 And now faith, **h**, and love abide,
Col 1.27 Christ in you, the **h** of glory.
1Jn 3. 3 all who have this **h** in him purify

HOPES → HOPE
1Co 13. 7 believes all things, **h** all things,

HOSANNA
Mk 11.10 **H** in the highest heaven!"
Jn 12.13 went out to meet him, shouting, "**H!**

HOSPITABLE → HOSPITALITY
1Ti 3. 2 temperate, sensible, respectable, **h**,
Tit 1. 8 but he must be **h**, a lover
1Pe 4. 9 Be **h** to one another without

HOSPITALITY → HOSPITABLE
Ro 12.13 of the saints; extend **h** to strangers.
1Ti 5.10 has brought up children, shown **h**,
Heb 13. 2 not neglect to show **h** to strangers,

HOSTS
Ps 46. 7 The LORD of **h** is with us;
Isa 48. 2 the LORD of **h** is his name.

HOUR
Mt 24.36 about that day and **h** no one knows,
Jn 2. 4 My **h** has not yet come."
17. 1 "Father, the **h** has come;
Rev 3.10 I will keep you from the **h** of trial
14. 7 for the **h** of his judgment has come;

HOUSE → HOUSEHOLD, STOREHOUSE
Ex 20.17 shall not covet your neighbor's **h**;
1Ch 22. 1 "Here shall be the **h** of the LORD
Ezr 1. 5 rebuild the **h** of the LORD in
Ps 69. 9 zeal for your **h** that has consumed
Mt 7.24 like a wise man who built his **h**
Jn 2.17 "Zeal for your **h** will consume me."
14. 2 In my Father's **h** there are many
1Pe 2. 5 be built into a spiritual **h**,

HOUSEHOLD → HOUSE
Jos 24.15 my **h**, we will serve the LORD."

HUMAN → HUMANKIND
Ps 8. 4 are **h** beings that you are mindful
Mt 15. 9 teaching **h** precepts as doctrines.' "
Ac 5.29 obey God rather than any **h**
Php 2. 7 being born in **h** likeness.

HUMANKIND → HUMAN
Ge 1.26 "Let us make **h** in our image,
1Ti 2. 5 one mediator between God and **h**,

HUMBLE → HUMBLED, HUMBLY, HUMILITY
Ps 25. 9 He leads the **h** in what is right,
Isa 57.15 to revive the spirit of the **h**,
Mt 11.29 for I am gentle and **h** in heart,
Jas 4.10 **H** yourselves before the Lord,

HUMBLED → HUMBLE
Lk 14.11 all who exalt themselves will be **h**,
Php 2. 8 he **h** himself and became obedient

HUMBLY → HUMBLE
Mic 6. 8 and to walk **h** with your God?

HUMILITY → HUMBLE
Pr 15.33 and **h** goes before honor.
Zep 2. 3 seek righteousness, seek **h**;
Php 2. 3 in **h** regard others as better than

HUNGER → HUNGRY
Mt 5. 6 "Blessed are those who **h** and thirst
Rev 7.16 will **h** no more, and thirst no more;

HUNGRY → HUNGER
Ps 146. 7 who gives food to the **h**.
Jn 6.35 comes to me will never be **h**,
Ro 12.20 "if your enemies are **h**, feed them;

HUSBAND → HUSBANDS
Isa 54. 5 For your Maker is your **h**,
Eph 5.23 **h** is the head of the wife just as
Rev 21. 2 as a bride adorned for her **h**.

HUSBANDS → HUSBAND
Eph 5.25 **H**, love your wives, just as Christ

Col 3.18 Wives, be subject to your **h**,
1Pe 3. 7 **H**, in the same way, show

I

IDOL → IDOLS
Ex 20. 4 shall not make for yourself an **i**,
Isa 40.19 An **i**?—A workman casts it,
1Co 10.19 or that an **i** is anything?

IDOLS → IDOL
Ex 34.17 You shall not make cast **i**.
1Co 8. 1 concerning food sacrificed to **i**:

IMAGE
Ge 1.26 "Let us make humankind in our **i**,
1Co 15.49 the **i** of the man of heaven.
Col 1.15 He is the **i** of the invisible God,
Rev 20. 4 not worshiped the beast or its **i**

IMMANUEL → EMMANUEL
Isa 7.14 bear a son, and shall name him **I**.

IMMORAL → IMMORALITY
1Co 5. 9 not to associate with sexually **i**
Heb 12.16 an **i** and godless person,

IMMORALITY → IMMORAL
2Co 12.21 sexual **i**, and licentiousness
Jude 1. 7 indulged in sexual **i** and pursued

IMMORTAL → IMMORTALITY
Ro 1.23 the glory of the **i** God for images
1Ti 1.17 the King of the ages, **i**, invisible,

IMMORTALITY → IMMORTAL
1Co 15.53 and this mortal body must put on **i**.
1Ti 6.16 It is he alone who has **i** and dwells

IMPOSSIBLE
Mt 17.20 and nothing will be **i** for you."
Mk 10.27 "For mortals it is **i**, but not for God;
Heb 11. 6 without faith it is **i** to please God,

INCENSE → FRANKINCENSE
Ex 25. 6 anointing oil and for the fragrant **i**,

INFANTS
Ps 8. 2 Out of the mouths of babes and **i**
Mt 21.16 'Out of the mouths of **i** and nursing
1Co 14.20 **i** in evil, but in thinking be adults.

INHERIT → INHERITANCE
Ps 37.11 But the meek shall **i** the land,
Lk 10.25 "what must I do to **i** eternal life?"
1Co 6. 9 wrongdoers will not **i** the kingdom
Heb 1.14 sake of those who are to **i** salvation?

INHERITANCE → INHERIT
Eph 1.11 In Christ we have also obtained an **i**,
Heb 9.15 the promised eternal **i**,

INIQUITY
Ex 34. 7 forgiving **i** and transgression and
Ps 103. 3 who forgives all your **i**,
Isa 53. 6 has laid on him the **i** of us all.
Tit 2.14 that he might redeem us from all **i**

INN
Lk 2. 7 no place for them in the **i**.

INNOCENT
Pr 6.17 and hands that shed **i** blood,
Mt 27.24 "I am **i** of this man's blood;

INSPIRED
Ex 35.34 And he has **i** him to teach,
2Ti 3.16 All scripture is **i** by God and is

INSTRUCT → INSTRUCTED, INSTRUCTION, INSTRUCTOR
Dt 17.10 observing everything they **i** you.
Ne 9.20 You gave your good spirit to **i** them,

INSTRUCTED → INSTRUCT
Isa 40.13 or as his counselor has **i** him?
Jn 8.28 these things as the Father **i** me.

INSTRUCTION → INSTRUCT
Pr 8.10 Take my **i** instead of silver,
Ro 15. 4 in former days was written for our **i**,
1Ti 1. 5 But the aim of such **i** is love

INSTRUCTOR → INSTRUCT
Mt 23.10 for you have one **i**, the Messiah.

INTERCEDES → INTERCESSION
Ro 8.26 Spirit **i** with sighs too deep for

INTERCESSION → INTERCEDES
1Sa 2.25 against the LORD, who can make **i**?"
Isa 53.12 and made **i** for the transgressors.
Heb 7.25 he always lives to make **i** for them.

INTERPRET → INTERPRETATION, INTERPRETATIONS
Mt 16. 3 cannot **i** the signs of the times.
1Co 12.30 Do all speak in tongues? Do all **i**?

INTERPRETATION → INTERPRET
1Co 12.10 to another the **i** of tongues.

INTERPRETATIONS → INTERPRET
Ge 40. 8 to them, "Do not **i** belong to God?

INVISIBLE
Col 1.15 He is the image of the **i** God,
1Ti 1.17 To the King of the ages, immortal, **i**,

ISRAEL → JACOB
Ge 49.28 All these are the twelve tribes of **I**,
Ex 28.11 with the names of the sons of **I**;
Nu 24.17 and a scepter shall rise out of **I**;
Dt 6. 4 Hear, O **I**: The LORD is our God,
Jer 31.31 a new covenant with the house of **I**
Mt 2. 6 who is to shepherd my people **I**.' "
Mk 12.29 answered, "The first is, 'Hear, O **I**:
Ac 1. 6 you will restore the kingdom to **I**?"
Heb 8. 8 a new covenant with the house of **I**
Rev 7. 4 out of every tribe of the people of **I**:

J

JACOB → ISRAEL
Ps 135. 4 the LORD has chosen **J** for himself,
Mic 7.20 You will show faithfulness to **J**
Ro 9.13 "I have loved **J**,

JARS
2Co 4. 7 But we have this treasure in clay **j**,

JEALOUS
Ex 34.14 whose name is **J**, is a **j** God).
Dt 4.24 God is a devouring fire, a **j** God.
Ro 10.19 "I will make you **j** of those

JERUSALEM
2Sa 5. 5 and at **J** he reigned over all Israel
2Ki 25.10 broke down the walls around **J**.
Ezr 2. 1 they returned to **J** and Judah,
Ne 2.17 Come, let us rebuild the wall of **J**,
Isa 40. 2 Speak tenderly to **J**,
La 1. 8 **J** sinned grievously, so she has
Da 9.25 went out to restore and rebuild **J**
Mt 23.37 "**J, J**, the city that kills the prophets
Gal 4.25 corresponds to the present **J**,
Heb 12.22 of the living God, the heavenly **J**,
Rev 21. 2 And I saw the holy city, the new **J**,

JESUS → CHRIST
LIFE: Genealogy (Mt 1.1–17; Lk 3.21–37). Birth announced (Mt 1.18–25; Lk 1.26–45). Birth (Mt 2.1–12; Lk 2.1–40). Escape to Egypt (Mt 2.13–23). As a boy in the temple (Lk 2.41–52). Baptism (Mt 3.13–17; Mk 1.9–11; Lk 3.21–22; Jn 1.32–34). Temptation (Mt 4.1–11; Mk 1.12–13; Lk 4.1–13). Ministry in Galilee (Mt 4.12–18.35; Mk 1.14–9.50; Lk 4.14–13.9; Jn 1.35–2.11; 4; 6), Transfiguration (Mt 17.1–8; Mk 9.2–8; Lk 9.28–36), on the way to Jerusalem (Mt 19–20; Mk 10; Lk 13.10–19.27), in Jerusalem (Mt 21–25; Mk 11–13; Lk 19.28–21.38; Jn 2.12–3.36; 5; 7–12). Last supper (Mt 26.17–35; Mk 14.12–31; Lk 22.1–38; Jn 13–17). Arrest and trial (Mt 26.36–27.31; Mk 14.43–

15.20; Lk 22.39–23.25; Jn 18.1–19.16). Crucifixion (Mt 27.32–66; Mk 15.21–47; Lk 23.26–55; Jn 19.28–42). Resurrection and appearances (Mt 28; Mk 16; Lk 24; Jn 20–21; Ac 1.1–11; 7.56; 9.3–6; 1Co 15.1–8; Rev 1.1–20).

MIRACLES. *Healings:* official's son (Jn 4.43–54), demoniac in Capernaum (Mk 1.23–26; Lk 4.33–35), Peter's mother-in-law (Mt 8.14–17; Mk 1.29–31; Lk 4.38–39), leper (Mt 8.2–4; Mk 1.40–45; Lk 5.12–16), paralytic (Mt 9.1–8; Mk 2.1–12; Lk 5.17–26), cripple (Jn 5.1–9), shriveled hand (Mt 12.10–13; Mk 3.1–5; Lk 6.6–11), centurion's servant (Mt 8.5–13; Lk 7.1–10), widow's son raised (Lk 7.11–17), demoniac (Mt 12.22–23; Lk 11.14), Gadarene demoniacs (Mt 8.28–34; Mk 5.1–20; Lk 8.26–39), woman's bleeding and Jairus' daughter (Mt 9.18–26; Mk 5.21–43; Lk 8.40–56), blind man (Mt 9.27–31), mute man (Mt 9.32–33), Canaanite woman's daughter (Mt 15.21–28; Mk 7.24–30), deaf man (Mk 7.31–37), blind man (Mk 8.22–26), demoniac boy (Mt 17.14–18; Mk 9.14–29; Lk 9.37–43), ten lepers (Lk 17.11–19), man born blind (Jn 9.1–7), Lazarus raised (Jn 11), crippled woman (Lk 13.11–17), man with dropsy (Lk 14.1–6), two blind men (Mt 20.29–34; Mk 10.46–52; Lk 18.35–43), Malchus' ear (Lk 22.50–51). *Other Miracles:* water to wine (Jn 2.1–11), storm stilled (Mt 8.23–27; Mk 4.37–41; Lk 8.22–25), 5,000 fed (Mt 14.15–21; Mk 6.35–44; Lk 9.10–17; Jn 6.1–14), walking on water (Mt 14.25–33; Mk 6.48–52; Jn 6.15–21), 4,000 fed (Mt 15.32–39; Mk 8.1–9), money from fish (Mt 17.24–27), fig tree cursed (Mt 21.18–22; Mk 11.12–14), catch of fish (Jn 21.1–14).

MAJOR TEACHING: Sermon on the Mount (Mt 5–7; Lk 6.17–49), to Nicodemus (Jn 3), to Samaritan woman (Jn 4), Bread of Life (Jn 6.22–59), at Feast of Tabernacles (Jn 7–8), woes to Pharisees (Mt 23; Lk 11.37–54), Good Shepherd (Jn 10.1–18), Olivet Discourse (Mt 24–25; Mk 13; Lk 21.5–36), Upper Room Discourse (Jn 13–16).

PARABLES: Sower (Mt 13.3–23; Mk 4.3–25; Lk 8.5–18), seed's growth (Mk 4.26–29), wheat and weeds (Mt 13.24–30, 36–43), mustard seed (Mt 13.31–32; Mk 4.30–32), yeast (Mt 13.33; Lk 13.20–21), hidden treasure (Mt 13.44), valuable pearl (Mt 13.45–46), net (Mt 13.47–51), house owner (Mt 13.52), good Samaritan (Lk 10.25–37), unmerciful servant (Mt 18.15–35), lost sheep (Mt 18.10–14; Lk 15.4–7), lost coin (Lk 15.8–10), prodigal son (Lk 15.11–32), dishonest manager (Lk 16.1–13), rich man and Lazarus (Lk 16.19–31), persistent widow (Lk 18.1–8), Pharisee and tax collector (Lk 18.9–14), payment of workers (Mt 20.1–16), tenants and the vineyard (Mt 21.28–46; Mt 12.1–12; Lk 20.9–19), wedding banquet (Mt 22.1–14), faithful servant (Mt 24.45–51), ten virgins (Mt 25.1–13), talents (Mt 25.1–30; Lk 19.12–27).

DISCIPLES see APOSTLES. Call (Jn 1.35–51; Mt 4.18–22; 9.9; Mk 1.16–20; 2.13–14; Lk 5.1–11, 27–28). Named Apostles (Mk 3.13–19; Lk 6.12–16). Twelve sent out (Mt 10; Mk 6.7–11; Lk 9.1–5). Seventy sent out (Lk 10.1–24). Defection of (Jn 6.60–71; Mt 26.56; Mk 14.50–52). Final commission (Mt 28.16–20; Jn 21.15–23; Ac 1.3–8).

Ac   9. 5 "I am J, whom you are persecuting.
1Co   8. 6 and one Lord, J Christ,
Php   2.10 name of J every knee should bend,
2Th   2. 1 the coming of our Lord J Christ
1Ti   1.15 J came into the world to save
Heb   12. 2 to J the pioneer and perfecter of our
        13. 8 J Christ is the same yesterday and
1Jn   1. 7 the blood of J his Son cleanses us
Rev   1. 1 The revelation of J Christ,
       22.20 Amen. Come, Lord J!

JEW → JEWS
Ro   1.16 to the J first and also to the Greek.
        2.29 a person is a J who is one inwardly,
Col   3.11 there is no longer Greek and J,

JEWEL → JEWELS
Rev   21.19 of the city are adorned with every j;

JEWELS → JEWEL
Pr   3.15 She is more precious than j,
Isa   54.12 your gates of j, and all your wall

Rev   17. 4 adorned with gold and j and pearls,

JEWS → JEW
Est   3.13 to kill, and to annihilate all J,
Mt   2. 2 who has been born king of the J?
       27.11 "Are you the King of the J?"
Ro   3.29 Or is God the God of J only?

JOINED
Mt   19. 6 what God has j together, let no one
Eph   2.21 the whole structure is j together

JORDAN
Ge   13.10 the plain of the J was well watered
Nu   34.12 the boundary shall go down to the J,
Mt   3. 6 were baptized by him in the river J,

JOY
Ne   8.10 the j of the LORD is your strength."
Job   20. 5 j of the godless is but for a moment?
Ps   51.12 Restore to me the j of your salvation
Pr   21.15 When justice is done, it is a j to the
Isa   35.10 everlasting j shall be upon their
La   2.15 of beauty, the j of all the earth?"
Lk   1.44 the child in my womb leaped for j.
        2.10 bringing you good news of great j
Ro   5. 2 but righteousness and peace and j in
Gal   5.22 the fruit of the Spirit is love, j,
Heb   12. 2 j that was set before him endured
Jas   1. 2 consider it nothing but j,

JUBILEE
Lev   25.10 It shall be a j for you:
Nu   36. 4 when the j of the Israelites comes,

JUDEA
Mt   2. 1 Jesus was born in Bethlehem of J,
Lk   3. 1 Pontius Pilate was governor of J,
Ac   1. 8 my witnesses in Jerusalem, in all J

JUDGE → JUDGED, JUDGES, JUDGMENT, JUDGMENTS
1Sa   2.10 LORD will j the ends of the earth;
Ps   96.13 for he is coming to j the earth.
Eze   34.17 I shall j between sheep and sheep,
Lk   6.37 not j, and you will not be judged;
Jn   7.24 Do not j by appearances,
Ro   3. 6 then how could God j the world?
1Co   6. 2 that the saints will j the world?
2Ti   4. 1 who is to j the living and the dead,
Rev   20. 4 on them were given authority to j.

JUDGED → JUDGE
1Co   11.31 if we j ourselves, we would not be j
Rev   20.12 dead were j according to their works

JUDGES → JUDGE
Jdg   2.16 Then the LORD raised up j,
Lk   11.19 Therefore they will be your j.

JUDGMENT → JUDGE
Ex   6. 6 arm and with mighty acts of j.
Ps   1. 5 wicked will not stand in the j,
Ecc   12.14 God will bring every deed into j,
Jer   25.31 he is entering into j with all flesh,
Ro   14.10 we will all stand before the j seat of
2Co   5.10 all of us must appear before the j
Heb   9.27 to die once, and after that the j,
Jas   2.13 mercy triumphs over j.
1Jn   4.17 may have boldness on the day of j,
Rev   18.10 For in one hour your j has come."

JUDGMENTS → JUDGE
Ps   119.75 LORD, that your j are right,
Ro   11.33 How unsearchable are his j and
Rev   19. 2 for his j are true and just;

JUST → JUSTICE, JUSTIFICATION, JUSTIFIED, JUSTIFY
Ge   18.25 Judge of all the earth do what is j?"
1Jn   1. 9 he who is faithful and j will forgive
Rev   15. 3 J and true are your ways, King of

JUSTICE → JUST
Ex   23. 6 not pervert the j due to your poor
Ps   33. 5 He loves righteousness and j;

Isa   30.18 For the LORD is a God of j;
Jer   9.24 I act with steadfast love, j,
Hos   12. 6 to your God, hold fast to love and j,
Am   5.24 But let j roll down like waters,
Lk   11.42 and neglect j and the love of God;

JUSTIFICATION → JUST
Ro   4.25 trespasses and was raised for our j.
2Co   3. 9 more does the ministry of j abound
Gal   2.21 for if j comes through the law,

JUSTIFIED → JUST
Mt   12.37 for by your words you will be j,
Ro   5. 1 Therefore, since we are j by faith,
       10.10 believes with the heart and so is j,
Gal   2.16 that we might be j by faith in Christ,
Jas   2.24 is j by works and not by faith alone.

K

KEEP → KEEPER
Ge   17. 9 for you, you shall k my covenant,
Ex   19. 5 obey my voice and k my covenant,
Nu   6.24 The LORD bless you and k you;
Dt   5.10 love me and k my commandments.
Ne   1. 5 love him and k his commandments;
Pr   7. 2 k my commandments and live,
Ecc   3. 6 time to k, and a time to throw away;
       12.13 Fear God, and k his commandments
Lk   17.33 those who lose their life will k it.

KEEPER → KEEP
Ge   4. 9 am I my brother's k?"
Ps   121. 5 The LORD is your k;

KEY → KEYS
Rev   3. 7 true one, who has the k of David,

KEYS → KEY
Mt   16.19 you the k of the kingdom of heaven,
Rev   1.18 I have the k of Death and of Hades,

KILL → KILLED, KILLS
Ecc   3. 3 a time to k, and a time to heal;
Mt   10.28 not fear those who k the body but cannot k the soul;
Mk   14. 1 to arrest Jesus by stealth and k him;

KILLED → KILL
Mk   9.31 after being k, he will rise again."
Ac   3.15 and you k the Author of life,

KILLS → KILL
2Co   3. 6 the letter k, but the Spirit gives life.

KIND → KINDNESS
1Co   13. 4 Love is patient; love is k;
Eph   4.32 and be k to one another,

KINDNESS → KIND
Pr   31.26 teaching of k is on her tongue.
Ro   2. 4 k is meant to lead you to repentance
Gal   5.22 joy, peace, patience, k, generosity,

KING → KINGDOM, KINGS
2Sa   2. 4 there they anointed David k over
Ps   2. 6 set my k on Zion, my holy hill."
       10.16 The LORD is k forever and ever;
Isa   6. 5 have seen the K, the LORD of hosts!
Mt   2. 2 who has been born k of the Jews?
       27.37 "This is Jesus, the K of the Jews."
1Ti   1.17 To the K of the ages, immortal,
Rev   19.16 "K of kings and Lord of lords."

KINGDOM → KING
Ex   19. 6 you shall be for me a priestly k and
2Sa   7.12 and I will establish his k.
Ps   145.13 Your k is an everlasting k,
Mt   4.17 "Repent, for the k of heaven has
        5. 3 for theirs is the k of heaven.
        6.10 Your k come. Your will be done,
Mk   10.24 how hard it is to enter the k of God!
Lk   17.21 in fact, the k of God is among us."
Jn   18.36 "My k is not from this world.
Ro   14.17 the k of God is not food and drink

1Co   6. 9 wrongdoers will not inherit the **k**
1Th   2.12 calls you into his own **k** and glory.
Heb 12.28 receiving a **k** that cannot be shaken,
Rev 11.15 world has become the **k** of our Lord

KINGS → KING
Ps   2. 2 The **k** of the earth set themselves,
Isa 52.15 **k** shall shut their mouths because of
Ac   4.26 The **k** of the earth took their stand,
1Ti   6.15 the King of **k** and Lord of lords.
Rev 19.16 "King of **k** and Lord of lords."

KISS
Ps   2.12 **k** his feet, or he will be angry,
SS   1. 2 Let him **k** me with the kisses of his
Mt   26.48 "The one I will **k** is the man; arrest
2Co 13.12 Greet one another with a holy **k**.

KNEE → KNEES
Isa 45.23 "To me every **k** shall bow,
Ro   14.11 says the Lord, every **k** shall bow to
Php   2.10 at the name of Jesus every **k** should

KNEES → KNEE
1Ki 19.18 the **k** that have not bowed to Baal,
Eph   3.14 I bow my **k** before the Father,

KNOCK → KNOCKING
Lk   11. 9 **k**, and the door will be opened for

KNOCKING → KNOCK
Rev 3.20 I am standing at the door, **k**;

KNOW → FOREKNEW, KNOWLEDGE,
KNOWN, KNOWS
Job 19.25 For I **k** that my Redeemer lives,
Ps   46.10 "Be still, and **k** that I am God!
Jer 31.34 "**K** the Lord," for they shall all **k**
Mt   6. 3 left hand **k** what your right hand is
      22.34 denied three times that you **k** me."
Jn   10.14 I **k** my own and my own **k** me,
1Co 13.12 I **k** only in part; then I will **k** fully,
Heb 8.11 '**K** the Lord,' for they shall all **k** me,
1Jn   2. 4 Whoever says, "I have come to **k**
Rev   3. 3 not **k** at what hour I will come to

KNOWLEDGE → KNOW
Ge   2. 9 the tree of the **k** of good and evil.
Pr   1. 7 of the Lord is the beginning of **k**;
1Co   8. 1 **K** puffs up, but love builds up.
Eph   3.19 the love of Christ that surpasses **k**,
Col   2. 3 the treasures of wisdom and **k**.
1Jn   2.20 and all of you have **k**.

KNOWN → KNOW
Ps 139. 1 you have searched me and **k** me.
Lk   6.44 for each tree is **k** by its own fruit.

KNOWS → KNOW
Ps   94.11 The Lord **k** our thoughts,
Mt   6. 8 your Father **k** what you need before
     24.36 about that day and hour no one **k**,

L

LABOR
Ex   20. 9 Six days you shall **l** and do all your

LADDER
Ge   28.12 there was a **l** set up on the earth,

LAID → LAY
Isa 53. 6 the Lord has **l** on him the iniquity
Mk   16. 6 Look, there is the place they **l** him.
1Jn   3.16 that he **l** down his life for us—

LAKE
Rev 19.20 were thrown alive into the **l** of fire
     20.14 This is the second death, the **l** of fire

LAMB
Ge   22. 8 "God himself will provide the **l** for
Ex   12.21 and slaughter the passover **l**.
Isa 53. 7 like a **l** that is led to the slaughter,
Mk   14.12 when the Passover **l** is sacrificed,

Jn   1.29 **L** of God who takes away the sin of
1Co   5. 7 For our paschal **l**, Christ, has been
1Pe   1.19 like that of a **l** without defect or
Rev   5.12 the **L** that was slaughtered to
     21.23 and its lamp is the **L**.

LAME
Isa 35. 6 then the **l** shall leap like a deer,
Zep   3.19 And I will save the **l** and gather the
Mt   11. 5 the **l** walk, the lepers are cleansed,

LAMP → LAMPS, LAMPSTAND,
LAMPSTANDS
Ps 119.105 Your word is a **l** to my feet and a
Mt   5.15 lighting a **l** puts it under the bushel

LAMPS → LAMP
Ex   25.37 You shall make the seven **l** for it;

LAMPSTAND → LAMP
Ex   25.31 You shall make a **l** of pure gold.

LAMPSTANDS → LAMP
Rev   1.20 the seven **l** are the seven churches.

LAND
Ge   1.10 God called the dry **l** Earth,
Ex   3. 8 a **l** flowing with milk and honey,
Nu   13. 2 to spy out the **l** of Canaan,
Jos 11.23 So Joshua took the whole **l**,
2Ki 17. 5 the king of Assyria invaded all the **l**
     25.21 So Judah went into exile out of its **l**.
2Ch   7.14 will forgive their sin and heal their **l**.
Ps   37.11 But the meek shall inherit the **l**,

LANGUAGE
Ge   11. 9 Lord confused the **l** of all the earth;

LAST → EVERLASTING
Isa 44. 6 I am the first and I am the **l**;
Mt   19.30 first will be **l**, and the **l** will be first.
Heb   1. 2 **l** days he has spoken to us by a Son,
Rev   1.17 I am the first and the **l**,

LAUGH
Ecc   3. 4 a time to weep, and a time to **l**;
Lk   6.21 you who weep now, for you will **l**.

LAW → LAWFUL
Dt   1. 5 Moses undertook to expound this **l**
      31. 9 Then Moses wrote down this **l**,
Jos   1. 8 book of the **l** shall not depart out of
Ps   1. 2 their delight is in the **l** of the Lord,
    119.97 Oh, how I love your **l**!
Jer 31.33 I will put my **l** within them,
Mt   5.17 come to abolish the **l** or the prophets
Lk   24.44 written about me in the **l** of Moses,
     10. 4 For Christ is the end of the **l** so that
Heb 10. 1 Since the **l** has only a shadow of the
Jas   2.10 For whoever keeps the whole **l** but

LAWFUL → LAW
1Co   6.12 "All things are **l** for me,"
     10.23 "All things are **l**," but

LAY → LAID
Mt   28. 6 Come, see the place where he **l**.
Jn   10.15 I **l** down my life for the sheep.

LEAD → LEADS
Isa 11. 6 and a little child shall **l** them.

LEADS → LEAD
Ps   23. 2 he **l** me beside still waters;

LEAST
Mt   2. 6 are by no means **l** among the rulers
      5.19 called **l** in the kingdom of heaven;
Lk   9.48 **l** among all of you is the greatest."

LEAVE → LEFT
Mk   10. 7 this reason a man shall **l** his father
Heb 13. 5 said, "I will never **l** you or forsake

LEAVEN
Ex   12.15 on the first day you shall remove **l**

LEAVES
Ge   3. 7 and they sewed fig **l** together

Eze 47.12 and their **l** for healing."
Rev 22. 2 **l** of the tree are for the healing of

LEFT → LEAVE
Mt   6. 3 your **l** hand know what your right
Lk   17.34 one will be taken and the other **l**.

LEGS
Jn   19.33 they did not break his **l**.

LEPER → LEPROUS
Mt   8. 2 and there was a **l** who came to him
      26. 6 in the house of Simon the **l**,

LEPERS → LEPROUS
Lk   7.22 the lame walk, the **l** are cleansed,

LEPROUS → LEPER, LEPERS
Ex   4. 6 he took it out, his hand was **l**,
Nu   12.10 Miriam had become **l**,

LETTER
Mt   5.18 not one **l**, not one stroke of a **l**,
2Co   3. 6 the **l** kills, but the Spirit gives life.

LEVIATHAN
Job 41. 1 you draw out **L** with a fishhook,
Ps   74.14 You crushed the heads of **L**;

LEVITES → LEVITICAL
Nu   1.53 **L** shall camp around the tabernacle
Jos 14. 4 no portion was given to the **L** in the
Ne   8. 9 **L** who taught the people said to all

LEVITICAL → LEVITES
Heb   7.11 attainable through the **l** priesthood

LIAR → LIE
Pr   19.22 and it is better to be poor than a **l**.
Jn   8.44 for he is a **l** and the father of lies.

LIE → LIAR, LYING
Nu   23.19 that he should **l**, or a mortal,
Ps   23. 2 makes me **l** down in green pastures;
1Jn   2.21 know that no **l** comes from the truth.

LIFE → LIVE
Ge   2. 7 into his nostrils the breath of **l**;
      2. 9 the tree of **l** also in the midst of the
      9. 5 require a reckoning for human **l**.
Ex   21.23 then you shall give **l** for **l**,
Dt   30.19 Choose **l** so that you and your
Isa 53.10 you make his **l** an offering for sin,
Da   12. 2 shall awake, some to everlasting **l**,
Mt   7.14 and the road is hard that leads to **l**,
     10.39 Those who find their **l** will lose it,
     20.28 to give his **l** a ransom for many."
Jn   1. 4 in him was **l**, and the **l** was the light
      3.15 believes in him may have eternal **l**.
      6.35 said to them, "I am the bread of **l**.
Jn   11.25 "I am the resurrection and the **l**.
     14. 6 "I am the way, and the truth, and the **l**.
Ac   3.15 and you killed the Author of **l**,
Ro   5.21 eternal **l** through Jesus Christ our
2Co   3. 6 the letter kills, but the Spirit gives **l**.
Php   4. 3 whose names are in the book of **l**.
1Jn   5.20 He is the true God and eternal **l**.
Rev   2. 8 who was dead and came to **l**:
     20. 4 came to **l** and reigned with Christ
     20.12 book was opened, the book of **l**.
     22. 2 the tree of **l** with its twelve kinds

LIGHT → ENLIGHTENED, ENLIGHTENS,
LIGHTS
Ge   1. 3 "Let there be **l**"; and there was **l**.
Isa   9. 2 in darkness have seen a great **l**;
     60. 1 Arise, shine; for your **l** has come,
Mt   4.16 in darkness have seen a great **l**,
      5.14 "You are the **l** of the world.
Jn   1. 9 true **l**, which enlightens everyone,
      8.12 saying, "I am the **l** of the world.
Ro   13.12 and put on the armor of **l**;
2Co 11.14 Satan disguises himself as an angel of **l**.
Rev 22. 5 for the Lord God will be their **l**,

LIGHTS → LIGHT
Ge   1.16 God made the two great **l**—
Jas   1.17 coming down from the Father of **l**,

LIKENESS
Ge   1.26 in our image, according to our **l**;
Ro   8. 3 his own Son in the **l** of sinful flesh,
Php   2. 7 of a slave, being born in human **l.**

LION → LIONS
Isa   11. 7 the **l** shall eat straw like the ox.
Rev   5. 5 See, the **L** of the tribe of Judah,

LIONS → LION
Da   6.20 able to deliver you from the **l**?"

LISTEN
Ex   23.22 But if you **l** attentively to his voice
2Ki   17.40 They would not **l**, however,
Mk   9. 7 my Son, the Beloved; **l** to him!"
Lk   16.31 'If they do not **l** to Moses and the
Jas   1.19 be quick to **l**, slow to speak,

LIVE → ALIVE, LIFE, LIVES, LIVING
Ge   3.22 and eat, and **l** forever'—
Ex   33.20 for no one shall see me and **l.**"
Lev   18. 5 by doing so one shall **l**:
Dt   8. 3 one does not **l** by bread alone,
Hab   2. 4 but the righteous **l** by their faith.
Mt   4. 4 'One does not **l** by bread alone,
Jn   11.25 even though they die, will **l**,
Ro   14. 8 If we **l**, we **l** to the Lord,
2Co   5.15 those who **l** might **l** no longer for

LIVES → LIVE
Job   19.25 For I know that my Redeemer **l**,
Ro   6.10 but the life he **l**, he **l** to God.
Rev   15. 7 of God, who **l** forever and ever;

LIVING → LIVE
Ge   2. 7 and the man became a **l** being.
Dt   5.26 the voice of the **l** God speaking out
Jer   2.13 forsaken me, the fountain of **l** water,
Zec   14. 8 that day **l** waters shall flow out from
Mt   16.16 the Messiah, the Son of the **l** God."
Jn   4.10 he would have given you **l** water."
    6.51 I am the **l** bread that came down
Ro   12. 1 present your bodies as a **l** sacrifice,
Heb   4.12 the word of God is **l** and active,

LOAVES
Mk   6.41 Taking the five **l** and the two fish,
    8. 6 and he took the seven **l**,

LOCUSTS
Ex   10. 4 I will bring **l** into your country.
Mt   3. 4 and his food was **l** and wild honey.
Rev   9. 3 from the smoke came **l** on the earth,

LONG
Ex   20.12 that your days may be **l** in the land
Ps   13. 1 How **l**, O Lord?
Rev   6.10 how **l** will it be before you judge

LORD → LORD'S, LORDS
Dt   10.17 God is God of gods and **L** of lords,
Ps   110. 1 The Lord says to my **l**,
Mt   7.22 many will say to me, '**L**, **L**,
Mk   1. 3 'Prepare the way of the **L**,
    12.29 the **L** our God, the **L** is one;
Lk   2.11 who is the Messiah, the **L.**
Jn   13.13 You call me Teacher and **L**—
    20.28 "My **L** and my God!"
Ac   2.34 'The **L** said to my **L**, "Sit at my
Ro   4.24 in him who raised Jesus our **L**
    10.12 the same **L** is **L** of all and
1Co   8. 6 and one **L**, Jesus Christ,
2Co   3.17 Now the **L** is the Spirit,
Eph   4. 5 one **L**, one faith, one baptism,
Php   2.11 that Jesus Christ is **L**, to the glory
1Pe   3.15 in your hearts sanctify Christ as **L.**
Rev   4. 8 "Holy, holy, holy, the **L** God
    19.16 "King of kings and **L** of lords."
    22.20 Amen. Come, **L** Jesus!

†LORD → †LORD'S
Ge   2. 7 **L** God formed man from the dust of
    13. 4 Abram called on the name of the **L.**
    18.14 Is anything too wonderful for the **L?**
Ex   15. 3 The **L** is a warrior; the **L** is his name.
    34. 6 and proclaimed, "The **L**, the **L**,

Lev   19. 2 for I the **L** your God am holy.
Nu   6.24 The **L** bless you and keep you;
Dt   6. 4 The **L** is our God, the **L** alone.
Jos   24.15 my household, we will serve the **L.**"
1Sa   2. 2 "There is no Holy One like the **L**,
Ne   8.10 the joy of the **L** is your strength."
Job   1.21 the **L** gave, and the **L** has taken
Ps   1. 2 their delight is in the law of the **L**,
    10.16 The **L** is king forever and ever;
    23. 1 The **L** is my shepherd, I shall not
    33.12 Happy is the nation whose God is the **L**
    110. 1 The **L** says to my lord,
    150. 6 that breathes praise the **L!**
Pr   1. 7 fear of the **L** is the beginning of
    3. 5 Trust in the **L** with all your heart,
Isa   6. 3 "Holy, holy, holy is the **L** of hosts;
    53. 6 the **L** has laid on him the iniquity
Jer   31.34 "Know the **L**," for they shall all
La   3.25 The **L** is good to those who wait for
Eze   37. 4 O dry bones, hear the word of the **L.**
    48.35 time on shall be, The **L** is There.
Hos   14. 1 Return, O Israel, to the **L** your God,
Joel   1.15 For the day of the **L** is near,
Am   5. 6 Seek the **L** and live,
Ob   1.15 the day of the **L** is near against all
Na   1. 3 The **L** is slow to anger but great in
Zep   1.14 The great day of the **L** is near,
Zec   14. 9 the **L** will be one and his name one.
Mal   4. 5 and terrible day of the **L** comes.

LORD'S → LORD
Mk   12.11 was the **L** doing, and it is amazing
Lk   4.19 to proclaim the year of the **L** favor."
Ro   14. 8 or whether we die, we are the **L.**
1Co   10.26 the earth and its fullness are the **L.**"

†LORD'S → †LORD
Dt   32. 9 the **L** own portion was his people,
Isa   59. 1 the **L** hand is not too short to save,
Ob   1.21 and the kingdom shall be the **L.**

LORDS → LORD
Dt   10.17 God is God of gods and Lord of **l**,
Rev   19.16 "King of kings and Lord of **l.**"

LOSS → LOST
Php   3. 8 I regard everything as **l** because of

LOST → LOSS
Ps   119.176 I have gone astray like a **l** sheep;
Lk   15. 6 I have found my sheep that was **l.**"
    19.10 came to seek out and to save the **l.**"

LOTS
Ps   22.18 and for my clothing they cast **l.**
Mt   27.35 among themselves by casting **l**;

LOVE → BELOVED, LOVED, LOVES
Ex   20. 6 but showing steadfast **l** to the
    34. 6 and abounding in steadfast **l** and
Lev   19.18 shall **l** your neighbor as yourself:
Dt   6. 5 You shall **l** the Lord your God
2Ch   6.42 Remember your steadfast **l**
Ne   1. 5 steadfast **l** with those who **l** him
Ps   18. 1 I **l** you, O Lord, my strength.
    86. 5 abounding in steadfast **l** to all who
    119.97 Oh, how I **l** your law!
Ps   136. 1 for his steadfast **l** endures forever.
Pr   8.17 I **l** those who **l** me,
Ecc   3. 8 a time to **l**, and a time to hate;
SS   1. 2 For your **l** is better than wine,
Isa   54. 8 but with everlasting **l** I will have
La   3.22 steadfast **l** of the Lord never ceases,
Hos   11. 4 of human kindness, with bands of **l.**
Joel   2.13 and abounding in steadfast **l**,
Jnh   4. 2 and abounding in steadfast **l**,
Mt   5.44 **L** your enemies and pray
    6.24 either hate the one and **l** the other,
Mk   12.31 shall **l** your neighbor as yourself.
Lk   6.32 For even sinners **l** those who **l** them.
    10.27 "You shall **l** the Lord your God
Jn   12.25 Those who **l** their life lose it,
    13.34 new commandment, that you **l** one
    14.15 "If you **l** me, you will keep my
    15.13 No one has greater **l** than this,

Ro   5. 8 But God proves his **l** for us in that
    12. 9 Let **l** be genuine; hate what is evil,
1Co   8. 1 Knowledge puffs up, but **l** builds up.
    13. 4 **L** is patient; **l** is kind;
    13.13 and the greatest of these is **l.**
Gal   5.22 the fruit of the Spirit is **l**, joy,
Eph   3.19 **l** of Christ that surpasses knowledge
    5.25 Husbands, **l** your wives,
1Ti   6.10 For the **l** of money is a root of all
Heb   10.24 provoke one another to **l** and good
    13. 5 your lives free from the **l** of money,
2Pe   1. 7 and mutual affection with **l.**
1Jn   2.15 not **l** the world or the things in the
    3. 1 See what **l** the Father has given us,
    5. 3 For the **l** of God is this,
2Jn   1. 6 And this is **l**, that we walk according
Jude   1.21 keep yourselves in the **l** of God;
Rev   2. 4 abandoned the **l** you had at first.

LOVED → LOVE
Jer   31. 3 have **l** you with an everlasting love;
Jn   3.16 God so **l** the world that he gave his
    15. 9 the Father has **l** me, so I have **l** you;
    15.12 love one another as I have **l** you.
1Jn   4.19 We love because he first **l** us.

LOVES → LOVE
Pr   3.12 the Lord reproves the one he **l**,
    17.17 A friend **l** at all times,
Lk   7.47 to whom little is forgiven, **l** little."
Ro   13. 8 who **l** another has fulfilled the law.
Eph   5.28 He who **l** his wife **l** himself.
Heb   12. 6 Lord disciplines those whom he **l**,
Rev   1. 5 who **l** us and freed us from our sins

LOWER → LOWLY
Ps   8. 5 have made them a little **l** than God,
Heb   2. 7 made them for a little while **l** than

LOWLY → LOWER
Pr   16.19 It is better to be of a **l** spirit
Ro   12.16 but associate with the **l**;

LOYALTY
Dt   7. 9 God who maintains covenant **l**
Ru   3.10 this last instance of your **l**
Ps   101. 1 I will sing of **l** and of justice;
Hos   4. 1 There is no faithfulness or **l**,

LUKEWARM
Rev   3.16 because you are **l**, and neither cold

LUST → LUSTS
Mt   5.28 looks at a woman with **l** has already
2Pe   1. 4 that is in the world because of **l**,

LUSTS → LUST
Ro   1.24 gave them up in the **l** of their hearts

LYING → LIE
Pr   6.17 a **l** tongue, and hands that shed

M

MADE → MAKE
Ge   1.31 God saw everything that he had **m**,
Ge   2.22 he **m** into a woman and brought her
    6. 6 was sorry that he had **m** humankind
    15.18 the Lord **m** a covenant with Abram,
Ex   20.11 For in six days the Lord **m** heaven
Ps   8. 5 have **m** them a little lower than God
    118.24 This is the day that the Lord has **m**;
    139.14 I am fearfully and wonderfully **m.**
Ac   2.36 that God has **m** him both Lord and
Eph   2. 5 **m** us alive together with Christ—

MAGDALENE
Mt   27.56 Among them were Mary **M**,

MAJESTIC → MAJESTY
Ex   15.11 Who is like you, **m** in holiness,
Ps   8. 1 how **m** is your name in all the earth!

MAJESTY → MAJESTIC
1Ch   29.11 the glory, the victory, and the **m**;

Ps   93. 1 The LORD is king, he is robed in **m**;
2Pe   1. 16 we had been eyewitnesses of his **m**.

MAKE → MADE, MAKER
Ge   1. 26 "Let us **m** humankind in our image,
      2. 18 will **m** him a helper as his partner."
Ex   20. 4 You shall not **m** for yourself an idol,
Nu   6. 25 LORD **m** his face to shine upon you,
Mt   28. 19 and **m** disciples of all nations,

MAKER → MAKE
Ge   14. 19 God Most High, **m** of heaven and
Ps   95. 6 kneel before the LORD, our **M**!
Isa   54. 5 For your **M** is your husband,

MALE
Ge   1. 27 **m** and female he created them.
Lev   20. 13 If a man lies with a **m** as with a
Rev   12. 5 she gave birth to a son, a **m** child,

MAN
Ge   2. 7 LORD God formed **m** from the dust
      2. 18 not good that the **m** should be alone;
Mt   9. 6 Son of **M** has authority on earth to
Lk   6. 5 The Son of **M** is lord of the sabbath.
Jn   9. 35 "Do you believe in the Son of **M**?"
1Co   11. 3 that Christ is the head of every **m**,
Rev   1. 13 I saw one like the Son of **M**,

MANGER
Lk   2. 12 in bands of cloth and lying in a **m**."

MANNA
Ex   16. 31 The house of Israel called it **m**;
Jn   6. 49 ate the **m** in the wilderness,
Rev   2. 17 I will give some of the hidden **m**,

MANY
Mt   22. 14 **m** are called, but few are chosen."
Mk   10. 45 and to give his life a ransom for **m**."
Ro   12. 5 who are **m**, are one body in Christ,

MARK
Ge   4. 15 And the LORD put a **m** on Cain,
Eze   9. 6 but touch no one who has the **m**.
Rev   19. 20 who had received the **m** of the beast

MARRIAGE → MARRIED, MARRIES
Mt   22. 30 are given in **m**, but are like angels
Heb   13. 4 Let **m** be held in honor by all,
Rev   19. 7 for the **m** of the Lamb has come,

MARRIED → MARRIAGE
1Ti   3. 2 be above reproach, **m** only once,
Tit   1. 6 m only once, whose children are

MARRIES → MARRIAGE
Mk   10. 11 and **m** another commits adultery
Ro   7. 3 if she **m** another man, she is not an
1Co   7. 28 and if a virgin **m**, she does not sin.

MASTER → MASTERS, TASKMASTERS
Mal   1. 6 if I am a **m**, where is the respect due
Jn   15. 20 Servants are not greater than their **m**
2Pe   2. 1 deny the **M** who bought them—

MASTERS → MASTER
Mt   6. 24 "No one can serve two **m**;

MEDIATOR
Gal   3. 19 ordained through angels by a **m**.
1Ti   2. 5 **m** between God and humankind,
Heb   8. 6 he is the **m** of a better covenant,

MEDITATE → MEDITATION
Jos   1. 8 you shall **m** on it day and night,
Ps   1. 2 on his law they **m** day and night.

MEDITATION → MEDITATE
Ps   19. 14 of my mouth and the **m** of my heart
      119. 97 It is my **m** all day long.

MEEK → MEEKNESS
Ps   37. 11 But the **m** shall inherit the land,
Mt   5. 5 "Blessed are the **m**, for they will

MEEKNESS → MEEK
Col   3. 12 kindness, humility, **m**, and patience.
Jas   1. 21 with **m** the implanted word

MEETING
Ex   27. 21 In the tent of **m**, outside the curtain
      40. 34 the cloud covered the tent of **m**,

MELCHIZEDEK
Ge   14. 18 King **M** of Salem brought out bread
Ps   110. 4 forever according to the order of **M**."
Heb   7. 1 This "King **M** of Salem, priest of

MEMBERS
Ro   7. 23 I see in my **m** another law at war
1Co   6. 15 that your bodies are **m** of Christ?
      12. 18 God arranged the **m** in the body,

MERCIES → MERCY
La   3. 22 his **m** never come to an end;
2Co   1. 3 the Father of **m** and the God of all

MERCIFUL → MERCY
Dt   4. 31 the LORD your God is a **m** God,
Ps   111. 4 the LORD is gracious and **m**.
Jer   3. 12 not look on you in anger, for I am **m**
Mt   5. 7 "Blessed are the **m**, for they will
Lk   6. 36 Be **m**, just as your Father is **m**.

MERCY → MERCIES, MERCIFUL
Ex   25. 17 make a **m** seat of pure gold;
1Ch   21. 13 of the LORD, for his **m** is very great;
Hab   3. 2 in wrath may you remember **m**.
Mt   9. 13 learn what this means, 'I desire **m**,
      23. 23 of the law: justice and **m** and faith.
Ro   9. 15 "I will have **m** on whom I have **m**,
Eph   2. 4 But God, who is rich in **m**,
Jas   2. 13 **m** triumphs over judgment.

MESSENGER → MESSAGE
Mt   11. 10 I am sending my **m** ahead of you,
2Co   12. 7 a **m** of Satan to torment me,

MESSIAH → CHRIST, MESSIAHS
Mt   16. 16 Peter answered, "You are the **M**,
Lk   2. 11 a Savior, who is the **M**, the Lord.
Ac   2. 36 God has made him both Lord and **M**
Ro   9. 5 according to the flesh, comes the **M**,
Rev   11. 15 kingdom of our Lord and of his **M**,

MESSIAHS → MESSIAH
Mk   13. 22 False **m** and false prophets will

MIDWIVES
Ex   1. 17 But the **m** feared God; they did not

MIGHT → ALMIGHTY, MIGHTY
2Ch   20. 6 In your hand are power and **m**,
Zec   4. 6 **m**, nor by power, but by my spirit,

MIGHTY → MIGHT
Ge   49. 24 by the hands of the **M** One of Jacob,
Ex   6. 1 by a **m** hand he will let them go;
Ps   99. 4 **M** King, lover of justice, you have
Isa   9. 6 Wonderful Counselor, **M** God,
Rev   18. 8 for **m** is the Lord God who judges

MILE
Mt   5. 41 one **m**, go also the second **m**.

MILK
Ex   3. 8 a land flowing with **m** and honey,
Heb   5. 12 You need **m**, not solid food;

MILLSTONE → STONE
Lk   17. 2 better for you if a **m** were hung

MIND → MINDFUL
Nu   23. 19 mortal, that he should change his **m**.
Jnh   3. 9 God may relent and change his **m**;
Mt   22. 37 all your soul, and with all your **m**.'
1Co   2. 16 who has known the **m** of the Lord
Php   2. 5 same **m** be in you that was in Christ
Heb   7. 21 sworn and will not change his **m**,

MINDFUL → MIND
Ps   8. 4 beings that you are **m** of them,
Heb   2. 6 beings that you are **m** of them,

MINISTERS → MINISTRY
2Co   3. 6 to be **m** of a new covenant,
      11. 15 if his **m** also disguise themselves as **m**

MINISTRY → MINISTERS
2Co   5. 18 has given us the **m** of reconciliation;
Eph   4. 12 equip the saints for the work of **m**,
Heb   8. 6 now obtained a more excellent **m**,

MIRACLES → See also JESUS: MIRACLES
Ps   78. 11 and the **m** that he had shown them.
Ac   19. 11 did extraordinary **m** through Paul,
1Co   12. 29 Are all teachers? Do all work **m**?
Heb   2. 4 signs and wonders and various **m**,

MOCKED → MOCK
Gal   6. 7 God is not **m**, for you reap

MOMENT → MOMENTARY
Ps   30. 5 For his anger is but for a **m**;
Isa   54. 7 For a brief **m** I abandoned you,
1Co   15. 52 in a **m**, in the twinkling of an eye,

MOMENTARY → MOMENT
2Co   4. 17 this slight **m** affliction is preparing

MONEY
Mk   11. 15 the tables of the **m** changers
1Ti   6. 10 love of **m** is a root of all kinds
Heb   13. 5 your lives free from the love of **m**,

MOON → MOONS
Joel 2. 31 to darkness, and the **m** to blood,
Ac   2. 20 to darkness and the **m** to blood,
Rev   6. 12 the full **m** became like blood,
      21. 23 no need of sun or **m** to shine on it,

MOONS → MOON
2Ch   8. 13 the new **m**, and the three annual
Col   2. 16 or of observing festivals, new **m**,

MORALS
1Co   15. 33 "Bad company ruins good **m**."

MORNING
Ge   1. 5 and there was **m**, the first day.
Ps   30. 5 but joy comes with the **m**.
La   3. 23 every **m**; great is your faithfulness.
Lk   24. 22 They were at the tomb early this **m**,
2Pe   1. 19 the day dawns and the **m** star rises
Rev   22. 16 of David, the bright **m** star."

MOST
Ge   14. 18 he was priest of God **M** High.
Ex   26. 33 the holy place from the **m** holy.
Ps   91. 1 live in the shelter of the **M** High,
Mk   5. 7 Jesus, Son of the **M** High God?

MOTH
Ps   39. 11 consuming like a **m** what is dear to
Mt   6. 19 where **m** and rust consume and

MOTHER
Ge   2. 24 a man leaves his father and his **m**
      3. 20 because she was the **m** of all living.
Ex   20. 12 Honor your father and your **m**,
Isa   66. 13 As a **m** comforts her child, so I will
Mt   10. 37 loves father or **m** more than me is
Jn   19. 27 to the disciple, "Here is your **m**."
Eph   5. 31 a man will leave his father and **m**
Rev   17. 5 **m** of whores and of earth's

MOUNT → MOUNTAIN, MOUNTAINS
Ex   19. 20 the LORD descended upon **M** Sinai,
Ps   78. 68 **M** Zion, which he loves.
Mk   13. 3 he was sitting on the **M** of Olives
Rev   14. 1 the Lamb, standing on **M** Zion!

MOUNTAIN → MOUNT
Isa   2. 2 the **m** of the LORD's house shall
Mt   4. 8 a very high **m** and showed him all
      17. 20 you will say to this **m**,

MOUNTAINS → MOUNT
1Co   13. 2 have all faith, so as to remove **m**,

MOURN → MOURNFUL, MOURNING
Ecc   3. 4 a time to **m**, and a time to dance;
Mt   5. 4 "Blessed are those who **m**,

MOURNING → MOURN
Rev   21. 4 **m** and crying and pain will be no

MOUTH

Dt 8. 3 that comes from the **m** of the LORD.
Ps 19. 14 Let the words of my **m** and
Mt 4. 4 every word that comes from the **m**
Rev 19. 15 From his **m** comes a sharp sword

MULTIPLY

Ge 1. 28 to them, "Be fruitful and **m**,
9. 7 And you, be fruitful and **m**,
Dt 6. 3 that you may **m** greatly in a land

MULTITUDE

Jas 5. 20 and will cover a **m** of sins.
1Pe 4. 8 for love covers a **m** of sins.

MURDER → MURDERER

Ex 20. 13 You shall not **m**.
Hos 4. 2 lying, and **m**, and stealing and
Mt 5. 21 of ancient times, 'You shall not **m**';

MURDERER → MURDER

Nu 35. 16 the **m** shall be put to death.
Jn 8. 44 He was a **m** from the beginning

MUSTARD

Mt 17. 20 have faith the size of a **m** seed,
Mk 4. 31 It is like a **m** seed, which,

MYRRH

Mt 2. 11 gifts of gold, frankincense, and **m**.
Mk 15. 23 offered him wine mixed with **m**;

MYSTERY

Da 2. 19 **m** was revealed to Daniel in a vision
Ro 11. 25 I want you to understand this **m:**
1Co 15. 51 Listen, I will tell you a **m!**
Eph 3. 4 my understanding of the **m** of Christ
1Ti 3. 9 must hold fast to the **m** of the faith
Rev 17. 5 a name, a **m:** "Babylon the great,

N

NAILING → NAILS

Col 2. 14 He set this aside, **n** it to the cross.

NAILS → NAILING

Jn 20. 25 put my finger in the mark of the **n**

NAKED

Ge 2. 25 the man and his wife were both **n**,
Job 1. 21 "**N** I came from my mother's womb,
and **n** shall

NAME → NAMES

Ge 2. 19 every living creature, that was its **n**.
4. 26 people began to invoke the **n** of
Ex 3. 15 my **n** forever, and this my title
20. 7 wrongful use of the **n** of the LORD
Ps 9. 10 know your **n** put their trust in you,
Pr 18. 10 The **n** of the LORD is a strong tower;
Isa 42. 8 I am the LORD, that is my **n**;
Eze 20. 9 But I acted for the sake of my **n**,
Joel 2. 32 on the **n** of the LORD shall be saved;
Mt 1. 21 a son, and you are to **n** him Jesus,
6. 9 Father in heaven, hallowed be your **n**.
28. 19 baptizing them in the **n** of the Father
Jn 1. 12 received him, who believed in his **n**,
20. 31 believing you may have life in his **n**.
Ac 4. 12 for there is no other **n** under heaven
Php 2. 9 gave him the **n** that is above every **n**
Rev 13. 17 **n** of the beast or the number of its **n**.
19. 13 his **n** is called The Word of God.

NAMES → NAME

Mt 10. 2 are the **n** of the twelve apostles:
Rev 21. 14 the twelve **n** of the twelve apostles

NARROW

Lk 13. 24 "Strive to enter through the **n** door;

NATION → NATIONS

Ge 12. 2 I will make of you a great **n**, and
Ex 32. 10 and of you I will make a great **n**."
Isa 66. 8 a **n** be delivered in one moment?
1Pe 2. 9 a holy **n**, God's own people,

NATIONS → NATION

Ge 18. 18 the **n** of the earth shall be blessed in
Am 9. 12 and all the **n** who are called
Mt 28. 19 and make disciples of all **n**,
Mk 11. 17 a house of prayer for all the **n**'?
Ro 4. 18 become "the father of many **n**,"
Rev 22. 2 the tree are for the healing of the **n**.

NAZARETH

Mt 2. 23 made his home in a town called **N**,
Jn 1. 46 Can anything good come out of **N**?
19. 19 "Jesus of **N**, the King of the Jews."

NAZIRITE

Nu 6. 2 make a special vow, the vow of a **n**,
Jdg 13. 5 boy shall be a **n** to God from birth.

NEAR

Dt 30. 14 No, the word is very **n** to you;
Isa 55. 6 call upon him while he is **n**;
Lk 10. 9 'The kingdom of God has come **n**
Jas 4. 8 Draw **n** to God, and he will draw **n** to

NEED → NEEDY

Mt 6. 8 for your Father knows what you **n**
Heb 4. 16 and find grace to help in time of **n**.

NEEDLE

Lk 18. 25 a camel to go through the eye of a **n**

NEEDY → NEED

1Sa 2. 8 he lifts the **n** from the ash heap,
Ps 113. 7 and lifts the **n** from the ash heap,

NEIGHBOR

Lev 19. 18 shall love your **n** as yourself:
Dt 5. 20 bear false witness against your **n**.
Mt 19. 19 You shall love your **n** as yourself."

NEVER

La 3. 22 steadfast love of the LORD **n** ceases,
1Co 13. 8 Love **n** ends. But as for prophecies,
Heb 13. 5 he has said, "I will **n** leave you or

NEW

Ecc 1. 9 there is nothing **n** under the sun.
Isa 65. 17 create **n** heavens and a **n** earth;
Jer 31. 31 I will make a **n** covenant with the
La 3. 23 they are **n** every morning;
Eze 36. 26 A **n** heart I will give you,
Mt 9. 17 is **n** wine put into old wineskins;
Lk 22. 20 is the **n** covenant in my blood.
Jn 13. 34 I give you a **n** commandment,
2Co 3. 6 to be ministers of a **n** covenant,
Heb 8. 8 when I will establish a **n** covenant
2Pe 3. 13 we wait for **n** heavens and a **n** earth,
Rev 21. 1 I saw a **n** heaven and a **n** earth;
21. 5 "See, I am making all things **n**."

NEWS

Isa 52. 7 who brings good **n**, who announces
Mt 11. 5 the poor have good **n** brought to
Mk 1. 15 repent, and believe in the good **n**."

NIGHT → NIGHTS

Ge 1. 5 and the darkness he called **N**.
1Th 5. 2 Lord will come like a thief in the **n**.
Rev 22. 5 And there will be no more **n**;

NIGHTS → NIGHT

Ge 7. 12 on the earth forty days and forty **n**.
Jnh 1. 17 of the fish three days and three **n**.
Mt 4. 2 He fasted forty days and forty **n**,
12. 40 for three days and three **n** the Son

NOISE

Ps 66. 1 Make a joyful **n** to God, all the earth
2Pe 3. 10 will pass away with a loud **n**,

NOTHING

Ecc 1. 9 there is **n** new under the sun.
Jer 32. 17 **N** is too hard for you.
Mt 17. 20 and **n** will be impossible for you."
Jn 15. 5 apart from me you can do **n**.

NUMBER

Rev 13. 18 Its **n** is six hundred sixty-six.

O

OATH

Dt 7. 8 and kept the **o** that he swore to your
Heb 7. 20 This was confirmed with an **o**;

OBEDIENCE → OBEY

Ro 5. 19 so by the one man's **o** the many will
Heb 5. 8 learned **o** through what he suffered;

OBEDIENT → OBEY

Php 2. 8 and became **o** to the point of death

OBEY → OBEDIENCE, OBEDIENT

Ex 19. 5 if you **o** my voice and keep my
Dt 12. 28 Be careful to **o** all these words that
Mt 28. 20 **o** everything that I have commanded
Ac 5. 29 "We must **o** God rather than any
Eph 6. 1 Children, **o** your parents in the Lord,
1Jn 5. 3 love of God is this, that we **o** his

OFFENSE

Mk 6. 3 And they took **o** at him.
Gal 5. 11 **o** of the cross has been removed.

OFFERING → OFFERINGS

Ge 4. 4 LORD had regard for Abel and his **o**,
Ps 40. 6 Sacrifice and **o** you do not desire,
Da 11. 31 shall abolish the regular burnt **o**
Eph 5. 2 a fragrant **o** and sacrifice to God.
Heb 10. 14 For by a single **o** he has perfected

OFFERINGS → OFFERING

Hos 6. 6 of God rather than burnt **o**.
Mk 12. 33 important than all whole burnt **o**

OIL

Ex 25. 6 **o** for the lamps, spices for the anointing **o**
Ps 23. 5 you anoint my head with **o**;
Jas 5. 14 anointing them with **o** in the name

OLD

Mk 2. 22 puts new wine into **o** wineskins;
Eph 4. 22 your **o** self, corrupt and deluded by

OLIVE → OLIVES

Zec 4. 3 And by it there are two **o** trees,
Ro 11. 17 and you, a wild **o** shoot,
Rev 11. 4 two **o** trees and the two lampstands

OLIVES → OLIVE

Zec 14. 4 Mount of **O** shall be split in two
Mt 24. 3 he was sitting on the Mount of **O**,

OMEGA

Rev 1. 8 "I am the Alpha and the **O**,"

ONCE → ONE

Ro 6. 10 he died, he died to sin, **o** for all;
Heb 7. 27 this he did **o** for all when he offered
9. 27 it is appointed for mortals to die **o**,

ONE → FIRST, ONCE

Ge 2. 24 and they become **o** flesh.
Zec 14. 9 the LORD will be **o** and his name **o**.
Mk 12. 29 the Lord our God, the Lord is **o**;
Jn 10. 30 The Father and I are **o**."
1Co 12. 13 For in the **o** Spirit we were all baptized
Eph 4. 5 **o** Lord, **o** faith, **o** baptism,

ONLY

Jn 1. 14 the glory as of a father's **o** son,
3. 16 that he gave his **o** Son,
1Ti 1. 17 the **o** God, be honor and glory
1Jn 4. 9 God sent his **o** Son into the world so

OPPRESSED

Ps 146. 7 who executes justice for the **o**;
Isa 53. 7 He was **o**, and he was afflicted,

ORACLES

Ro 3. 2 entrusted with the **o** of God.

ORDAIN

Ex 29. 9 shall then **o** Aaron and his sons.
1Ti 5. 22 Do not **o** anyone hastily,

ORPHAN → ORPHANED, ORPHANS

Ex 22. 22 You shall not abuse any widow or **o**.

Hos 14. 3 In you the **o** finds mercy."

ORPHANED → ORPHAN
Jn 14. 18 will not leave you **o**; I am coming

ORPHAN → ORPHAN
Jas 1. 27 to care for **o** and widows in their

OUTSTRETCHED
Ex 6. 6 I will redeem you with an **o** arm
Ps 136. 12 an **o** arm, for his steadfast love
Jer 27. 5 by my great power and my **o** arm

OVERCOME
Jn 1. 5 and the darkness did not **o** it.
Ro 12. 21 Do not be **o** by evil, but **o** evil with
1Jn 2. 14 and you have **o** the evil one.

OVERSHADOW → OVERSHADOWED
Lk 1. 35 power of the Most High will **o** you;

OVERSHADOWED → OVERSHADOW
Lk 9. 34 a cloud came and **o** them;

OWE
Mt 18. 28 he said, 'Pay what you **o**.'
Ro 13. 8 **O** no one anything, except to love

P

PAIN
Ge 3. 16 in **p** you shall bring forth children,
Rev 21. 4 and crying and **p** will be no more,

PALM
Jn 12. 13 So they took branches of **p** trees
Rev 7. 9 robed in white, with **p** branches in

PARABLE → PARABLES
Ps 78. 2 I will open my mouth in a **p**;

PARABLES → PARABLE; See also JESUS: PARABLES
Mt 13. 35 I will open my mouth to speak in **p**;

PARADISE
Lk 23. 43 today you will be with me in **P**."
2Co 12. 4 was caught up into **P** and heard
Rev 2. 7 tree of life that is in the **p** of God.

PARALYTIC → PARALYZED
Mt 9. 2 saw their faith, he said to the **p**,

PARALYZED → PARALYTIC
Jn 5. 3 many invalids—blind, lame, and **p**.
Ac 8. 7 who were **p** or lame were cured.

PARCHMENTS
2Ti 4. 13 also the books, and above all the **p**.

PARDON
Ex 34. 9 **p** our iniquity and our sin,
Isa 55. 7 our God, for he will abundantly **p**.

PARENTS
Eph 6. 1 Children, obey your **p** in the Lord,

PARTIALITY
Dt 16. 19 distort justice; you must not show **p**;
Pr 24. 23 **P** in judging is not good.
Ro 2. 11 For God shows no **p**.
Jas 3. 17 without a trace of **p** or hypocrisy.

PARTNERS
1Co 10. 20 not want you to be **p** with demons.
Heb 3. 1 holy **p** in a heavenly calling,

PASS → PASSED, PASSING
Ex 12. 13 when I see the blood, I will **p** over
   33. 19 make all my goodness **p** before you,
Am 5. 17 I will **p** through the midst of you,
Mt 24. 35 Heaven and earth will **p** away, but my
       words will not **p**
2Pe 3. 10 then the heavens will **p** away

PASSED → PASS
Ex 12. 27 he **p** over the houses of the Israelites
2Co 5. 17 everything old has **p** away;

Rev 21. 4 for the first things have **p** away."

PASSING → PASS
1Co 7. 31 present form of this world is **p** away
1Jn 2. 17 the world and its desire are **p** away,

PASSIONS
Gal 5. 24 have crucified the flesh with its **p**
2Ti 2. 22 Shun youthful **p** and pursue

PASSOVER
Ex 12. 11 It is the **p** of the LORD.
Dt 16. 1 the month of Abib by keeping the **p**
Mk 14. 12 when the **P** lamb is sacrificed,

PASTORS
Eph 4. 11 evangelists, some **p** and teachers,

PASTURES
Ps 23. 2 He makes me lie down in green **p**;

PATH → PATHS
Ps 119. 105 lamp to my feet and a light to my **p**.

PATHS → PATH
Mt 3. 3 of the Lord, make his **p** straight.'"
Heb 12. 13 and make straight **p** for your feet,

PATIENCE → PATIENT
Mic 2. 7 Is the LORD's **p** exhausted?
Ro 2. 4 his kindness and forbearance and **p**?
Gal 5. 22 fruit of the Spirit is love, joy, peace, **p**,
2Pe 3. 15 regard the **p** of our Lord as salvation

PATIENT → PATIENCE
1Co 13. 4 Love is **p**; love is kind;

PEACE → PEACEMAKERS
Ps 122. 6 Pray for the **p** of Jerusalem:
Isa 57. 19 **P, p**, to the far and the near,
Jer 6. 14 saying, "**P, p**," when there is no **p**.
Mic 5. 5 and he shall be the one of **p**.
Lk 2. 14 on earth **p** among those whom he
Jn 14. 27 **P** I leave with you; my **p** I give
1Co 14. 33 is a God not of disorder but of **p**.
Gal 5. 22 the fruit of the Spirit is love, joy, **p**,
Php 4. 7 the **p** of God, which surpasses all

PEACEMAKERS → PEACE
Mt 5. 9 "Blessed are the **p**, for they will be

PEARLS
Mt 7. 6 do not throw your **p** before swine,

PENTECOST
Ac 2. 1 When the day of **P** had come,

PEOPLE
Ex 5. 1 the God of Israel, 'Let my **p** go,
Dt 4. 20 a **p** of his very own possession,
Ru 1. 16 your **p** shall be my **p**,
Ps 29. 11 the LORD bless his **p** with peace!
Isa 40. 1 Comfort, O comfort my **p**, says
Mt 1. 21 he will save his **p** from their sins."
Heb 8. 10 their God, and they shall be my **p**,
1Pe 2. 9 a holy nation, God's own **p**,

PERFECT → PERFECTER, PERFECTION
2Sa 22. 31 This God—his way is **p**;
Ps 19. 7 The law of the LORD is **p**, reviving
Mt 5. 48 Be **p**, therefore, as your heavenly Father
       is **p**.
Ro 12. 2 what is good and acceptable and **p**.
Heb 7. 19 (for the law made nothing **p**);
1Jn 4. 18 in love, but **p** love casts out fear;

PERFECTER → PERFECT
Heb 12. 2 Jesus the pioneer and **p** of our faith,

PERFECTION → PERFECT
Heb 6. 1 Therefore let us go on toward **p**,
1Jn 2. 5 the love of God has reached **p**.

PERISH → PERISHABLE
Est 4. 16 and if I **p**, I **p**."
Ps 1. 6 but the way of the wicked will **p**.
Jn 3. 16 who believes in him may not **p**
2Pe 3. 9 with you, not wanting any to **p**,

PERISHABLE → PERISH
1Co 9. 25 they do it to receive a **p** wreath,
   15. 42 What is sown is **p**, what is raised is
1Pe 1. 23 not of **p** but of imperishable seed,

PERSECUTE → PERSECUTED, PERSECUTION
Mt 5. 44 and pray for those who **p** you,
Ac 9. 4 "Saul, Saul, why do you **p** me?"
Ro 12. 14 Bless those who **p** you; bless

PERSECUTED → PERSECUTE
2Co 4. 9 **p**, but not forsaken; struck down,
2Ti 3. 12 godly life in Christ Jesus will be **p**.

PERSECUTION → PERSECUTE
Mt 13. 21 or **p** arises on account of the word,
Ro 8. 35 Will hardship, or distress, or **p**, or
Heb 10. 33 publicly exposed to abuse and **p**,

PERSEVERANCE → PERSEVERE
Heb 12. 1 let us run with **p** the race that is set

PERSEVERE → PERSEVERANCE
Da 12. 12 Happy are those who **p**
Ro 12. 12 be patient in suffering, **p** in prayer.

PHARAOH → PHARAOH'S
Ex 14. 17 I will gain glory for myself over **P**

PHARAOH'S → PHARAOH
Ex 7. 3 But I will harden **P** heart,
Heb 11. 24 refused to be called a son of **P**

PHARISEE → PHARISEES
Lk 11. 37 a **P** invited him to dine with him;
Jn 3. 1 a **P** named Nicodemus,
Ac 5. 34 a **P** in the council named Gamaliel,
Php 3. 5 as to the law, a **P**;

PHARISEES → PHARISEE
Mt 5. 20 that of the scribes and **P**,
   16. 6 beware of the yeast of the **P** and
   23. 13 "But woe to you, scribes and **P**,

PHILISTINE → PHILISTINES
1Sa 17. 37 save me from the hand of this **P**."

PHILISTINES → PHILISTINE
1Sa 5. 1 the **P** captured the ark of God,
Am 1. 8 the remnant of the **P** shall perish,

PIERCED
Zec 12. 10 look on the one whom they have **p**,
Jn 19. 37 look on the one whom they have **p**."
Rev 1. 7 even those who **p** him;

PIG
Dt 14. 8 the **p**, because it divides the hoof

PILLAR
Ge 19. 26 and she became a **p** of salt.
Ex 13. 21 and in a **p** of fire by night,

PIONEER
Heb 2. 10 make the **p** of their salvation perfect
   12. 2 Jesus the **p** and perfecter of our faith

PIT
Rev 20. 3 into the **p**, and locked and sealed it

PLACE
Jn 14. 3 And if I go and prepare a **p** for you,

PLAGUE → PLAGUES
Zec 14. 12 the **p** with which the LORD will
Rev 11. 6 strike the earth with every kind of **p**,

PLAGUES → PLAGUE
Hos 13. 14 O Death, where are your **p**?
Rev 15. 1 seven angels with seven **p**, which

PLANT
Ge 1. 29 I have given you every **p** yielding
Ecc 3. 2 time to **p**, and a time to pluck up

PLEASE → PLEASED, PLEASES, PLEASING
Ro 8. 8 who are in the flesh cannot **p** God.
   15. 3 For Christ did not **p** himself;
Heb 11. 6 without faith it is impossible to **p** God,

PLEASED → PLEASE
Mic   6. 7   Will the LORD be **p** with thousands
Mt   3. 17   Beloved, with whom I am well **p.**"
Col   1. 19   the fullness of God was **p** to dwell,

PLEASES → PLEASE
1Jn   3. 22   commandments and do what **p** him.

PLEASING → PLEASE
Ps 104. 34   May my meditation be **p** to him,
Eph   5. 10   to find out what is **p** to the Lord.
Php   4. 18   a sacrifice acceptable and **p** to God.

PLOT
Ps   2. 1   and the peoples **p** in vain?
Na   1. 9   Why do you **p** against the LORD?

PLOWSHARES
Isa   2. 4   they shall beat their swords into **p,**
Joel 3. 10   Beat your **p** into swords, and your

POLLUTED → POLLUTES
Ac   15. 20   from things **p** by idols and from
Rev 21. 8   the cowardly, the faithless, the **p,**

POLLUTES → POLLUTED
Nu   35. 33   blood **p** the land, and no expiation

POOR → POVERTY
Ex   23. 6   not pervert the justice due to your **p**
1Sa   2. 8   He raises up the **p** from the dust;
Ps 113. 7   He raises the **p** from the dust,
Mt   5. 3   "Blessed are the **p** in spirit,
Mk   10. 21   own, and give the money to the **p,**
     12. 42   **p** widow came and put in two small
2Co   6. 10   as **p,** yet making many rich;
      8. 9   yet for your sakes he became **p,**
Jas   2. 5   Has not God chosen the **p** in the

PORTION
Dt   32. 9   the LORD's own **p** was his people,
La   3. 24   "The LORD is my **p,**" says my soul,

POSSESSED → POSSESSION
Mt   8. 16   many who were **p** with demons;

POSSESSION → POSSESSED, POSSESSIONS
Ex   19. 5   treasured **p** out of all the peoples.
Ps   2. 8   and the ends of the earth your **p.**

POSSESSIONS → POSSESSION
Lk   12. 15   not consist in the abundance of **p.**"
1Co 13. 3   If I give away all my **p,**

POSSIBLE
Mt   19. 26   but for God all things are **p.**"
     26. 39   if it is **p,** let this cup pass from me;

POTTER
Isa 64. 8   we are the clay, and you are our **p;**
Ro   9. 21   Has the **p** no right over the clay,

POUR → POURED
Isa 44. 3   I will **p** my spirit upon your
Eze 39. 29   I **p** out my spirit upon the house of
Joel 2. 28   I will **p** out my spirit on all flesh;
Ac   2. 17   I will **p** out my Spirit upon all flesh,

POURED → POUR
Mt   26. 28   is **p** out for many for the forgiveness
Ac   2. 33   he has **p** out this that you both see
Tit   3. 6   This Spirit he **p** out on us richly

POVERTY → POOR
Mk   12. 44   out of her **p** has put in everything
2Co   8. 9   by his **p** you might become rich.

POWER → POWERFUL, POWERS
1Ch 29. 11   O LORD, are the greatness, the **p,**
Isa 40. 29   He gives **p** to the faint,
Zec   4. 6   by might, nor by **p,** but by my spirit,
Mt   22. 29   the scriptures nor the **p** of God.
Mk   13. 26   coming in clouds' with great **p** and
1Co   1. 17   might not be emptied of its **p.**
Eph   1. 19   the immeasurable greatness of his **p**
Php   3. 10   Christ and the **p** of his resurrection
2Pe   1. 3   divine **p** has given us everything
Rev 19. 1   and glory and **p** to our God,
     20. 6   these the second death has no **p,**

POWERFUL → POWER
Mk   1. 7   one who is more **p** than I is coming

POWERS → POWER
Ro   8. 38   present, nor things to come, nor **p,**
Eph   6. 12   against the cosmic **p** of this present

PRACTICE → PRACTICES
Mt   23. 3   for they do not **p** what they teach.

PRACTICES → PRACTICE
Ex   23. 24   or worship them, or follow their **p,**
Col   3. 9   stripped off the old self with its **p**

PRAISE
Ex   15. 2   this is my God, and I will **p** him,
Dt   10. 21   He is your **p;** he is your God,
Ps 150. 6   that breathes the **p** the LORD!
Pr   27. 2   Let another **p** you, and not your own
     31. 31   let her works **p** her in the city gates.
Mt   21. 16   nursing babies you have prepared **p**
Rev 19. 5   "**P** our God, all you his servants,

PRAY → PRAYED, PRAYER, PRAYERS
2Ch   7. 14   humble themselves, **p,** seek my face
Ps 122. 6   **P** for the peace of Jerusalem!
Mt   5. 44   and **p** for those who persecute you,
      6. 5   you **p,** do not be like the hypocrites;
Lk   11. 1   teach us to **p,** as John taught his
Ro   8. 26   do not know how to **p** as we ought,
1Th   5. 17   **p** without ceasing,

PRAYED → PRAY
Mk   1. 35   to a deserted place, and there he **p.**
     14. 35   threw himself on the ground and **p**

PRAYER → PRAY
Pr   15. 29   but he hears the **p** of the righteous.
Isa 56. 7   house shall be called a house of **p**
Mt   21. 13   house shall be called a house of **p';**
Mk   11. 24   I tell you, whatever you ask for in **p,**
Ro   12. 12   patient in suffering, persevere in **p.**
Jas   5. 16   The **p** of the righteous is powerful

PRAYERS → PRAY
Heb   5. 7   Jesus offered up **p** and supplications
Rev   5. 8   which are the **p** of the saints.

PREACH → PREACHING
Tit   1. 9   able both to **p** with sound doctrine

PREACHING → PREACH
1Ti   5. 17   those who labor in **p** and teaching;

PRECEPTS → PRECEPT
Ps   19. 8   the **p** of the LORD are right,
Mt   15. 9   teaching human **p** as doctrines.' "

PRECIOUS
Ps   72. 14   and **p** is their blood in his sight.
Pr   3. 15   She is more **p** than jewels,
Isa 28. 16   a tested stone, a **p** cornerstone,
1Pe   1. 19   but with the **p** blood of Christ,
      2. 6   a cornerstone chosen and **p;**
2Pe   1. 1   received a faith as **p** as ours

PREDESTINED
Ro   8. 30   those whom he **p** he also called;

PREDICTION → PREDICTIONS
Isa 44. 26   and fulfills the **p** of his messengers;

PREDICTIONS → PREDICT
Jude 1. 17   the **p** of the apostles of our Lord

PREPARE
Ps   23. 5   You **p** a table before me in the
Mt   3. 3   '**P** the way of the Lord, make his
Jn   14. 2   I have told you that I go to **p** a place

PRESENCE → PRESENT
Ex   25. 30   the bread of the **P** on the table
Ps   51. 11   Do not cast me away from your **p,**
    139. 7   Or where can I flee from your **p?**
Jn   17. 5   with the glory that I had in your **p**

PRESENT → PRESENCE
Ro   6. 13   but **p** yourselves to God as
1Co   3. 22   or death or the **p** or the future—

Eph   5. 27   **p** the church to himself in splendor,
2Ti   2. 15   **p** yourself to God as one approved

PRICE
Mt   27. 9   the one on whom a **p** had been set,
1Co   6. 20   For you were bought with a **p;**

PRIDE → PROUD
Ps   20. 7   our **p** is in the name of the LORD
Pr   16. 18   **P** goes before destruction,
Mk   7. 22   licentiousness, envy, slander, **p,**
1Jn   2. 16   the desire of the eyes, the **p** in riches

PRIEST → PRIESTHOOD, PRIESTS
Ge   14. 18   he was **p** of God Most High.
Ps 110. 4   "You are a **p** forever according to
Mk   14. 63   Then the high **p** tore his clothes and
Heb   3. 1   apostle and high **p** of our confession
      7. 3   the Son of God, he remains a **p**

PRIESTHOOD → PRIEST
Ex   29. 9   the **p** shall be theirs by a perpetual
Heb   7. 24   but he holds his **p** permanently,
1Pe   2. 5   a holy **p,** to offer spiritual sacrifices

PRIESTS → PRIEST
Ex   28. 1   the Israelites, to serve me as **p**—
Mk   15. 3   the chief **p** accused him of many
Heb   7. 27   Unlike the other high **p,** he has no
Rev 20. 6   they will be **p** of God and of Christ,

PRINCE → PRINCES
Isa   9. 6   Everlasting Father, **P** of Peace.
Eze 37. 25   David shall be their **p** forever.

PRINCES → PRINCE
1Sa   2. 8   to make them sit with **p** and inherit
Da   8. 25   even rise up against the Prince of **p.**

PRISONER → PRISONERS
Mk   15. 6   at the festival he used to release a **p**
Eph   3. 1   that I Paul am a **p** for Christ Jesus

PRISONERS → PRISONER
Ps 146. 7   The LORD sets the **p** free;
Isa 61. 1   to the captives, and release to the **p;**

PRIZE
1Co   9. 24   but only one receives the **p?**
Php   3. 14   the **p** of the heavenly call of God in

PROMISE → PROMISED, PROMISES
Ps 105. 42   For he remembered his holy **p,**
Eph   2. 12   and strangers to the covenants of **p,**
2Pe   3. 9   The Lord is not slow about his **p,**

PROMISED → PROMISE
Dt   1. 11   and bless you, as he has **p** you!
Ac   13. 23   to Israel a Savior, Jesus, as he **p;**
Eph   1. 13   with the seal of the **p** Holy Spirit;
Heb 10. 23   for he who has **p** is faithful.

PROMISES → PROMISE
Jos 21. 45   the good **p** that the LORD had made
2Co   1. 20   every one of God's **p** is a "Yes."

PROOFS → PROVE
Ac   1. 3   to them by many convincing **p,**

PROPHECIES → PROPHESY
1Co 13. 8   as for **p,** they will come to an end;

PROPHECY → PROPHESY
Ac   21. 9   daughters who had the gift of **p.**
1Co 12. 10   to another **p,** to another
2Pe   1. 20   that no **p** of scripture is a matter

PROPHESY → PROPHECIES, PROPHECY, PROPHET, PROPHETS
Joel 2. 28   sons and your daughters shall **p,**
Mt   7. 22   Lord, did we not **p** in your name,
1Co 13. 9   only in part, and we **p** only in part;
Rev 11. 3   my two witnesses authority to **p**

PROPHET → PROPHESY
Dt   18. 18   a **p** like you from among their own
Mal   4. 5   the **p** Elijah before the great and
Lk   4. 24   no **p** is accepted in the prophet's
Rev 16. 13   and from the mouth of the false **p.**

PROPHETS → PROPHESY
Nu 11.29 that all the LORD's people were p,
Mt 5.17 come to abolish the law or the p;
22.40 hang all the law and the p."
1Co 12.28 the church first apostles, second p,
Eph 2.20 the foundation of the apostles and p,
4.11 some p, some evangelists,
Rev 11.10 these two p had been a torment to
18.20 you saints and apostles and p!

PROSPER → PROSPERITY
Ps 1.3 In all that they do, they p.
Isa 53.10 the will of the LORD shall p.

PROSPERITY → PROSPER
Dt 30.15 have set before you today life and p,

PROSTITUTE → PROSTITUTES
Jos 2.1 a p whose name was Rahab,
1Co 6.15 and make them members of a p?
Heb 11.31 By faith Rahab the p did not perish

PROSTITUTES → PROSTITUTE
Mt 21.31 the p are going into the kingdom of

PROUD → PRIDE
Ps 94.2 give to the p what they deserve!
Pr 21.4 Haughty eyes and a p heart—
Jas 4.6 God opposes the p, but gives grace

PROVERBS
Pr 1.1 The p of Solomon son of David,
Ecc 12.9 and studying and arranging many p.

PROVOKE → PROVOKED
Jer 25.6 not p me to anger with the work of
Heb 10.24 how to p one another to love

PROVOKED → PROVOKE
Ps 78.41 and p the Holy One of Israel.

PRUNES
Jn 15.2 he p to make it bear more fruit.

PSALMS
Lk 24.44 and the p must be fulfilled."
Eph 5.19 you sing p and hymns and spiritual

PUFFS
1Co 8.1 Knowledge p up, but love builds up.

PUNISH → PUNISHING, PUNISHMENT
Ex 32.34 I will p them for their sin."
1Pe 2.14 by him to p those who do wrong

PUNISHING → PUNISH
Dt 5.9 p children for the iniquity of parents
Joel 2.13 in steadfast love, and relents from p.

PUNISHMENT → PUNISH
Isa 53.5 was the p that made us whole,
Mt 25.46 these will go away into eternal p,
1Jn 4.18 for fear has to do with p,

PURE → PURIFICATION, PURIFIED
2Sa 22.27 with the p you show yourself p,
Ps 19.9 the fear of the LORD is p, enduring
Hab 1.13 Your eyes are too p to behold evil,
Mt 5.8 "Blessed are the p in heart, for they
Php 4.8 whatever is p, whatever is pleasing,
Tit 1.15 To the p all things are p,
1Jn 3.3 purify themselves, just as he is p.

PURIFICATION → PURE
Heb 1.3 When he had made p for sins,

PURIFIED → PURE
1Pe 1.22 p your souls by your obedience to

PURPLE
Ex 25.4 p, and crimson yarns and fine linen,
Mk 15.17 And they clothed him in a p cloak;

PURPOSE
Isa 46.10 saying, "My p shall stand,
Ro 8.28 who are called according to his p.
2Ti 1.9 works but according to his own p

Q

QUAILS
Ex 16.13 In the evening q came up
Nu 11.31 and it brought q from the sea and

QUARRELED
Ex 17.7 the Israelites q and tested the LORD,
Nu 20.3 The people q with Moses and said,

QUEEN
1Ki 10.1 the q of Sheba heard of the fame of
Rev 18.7 in her heart she says, 'I rule as a q;

QUIET
1Ti 2.2 q and peaceable life in all godliness
1Pe 3.4 beauty of a gentle and q spirit,

R

RABBI
Jn 1.38 "R" (which translated means Teacher),

RACE
Ecc 9.11 the sun the r is not to the swift,
1Co 9.24 that in a r the runners all compete,
Heb 12.1 let us run with perseverance the r
1Pe 2.9 But you are a chosen r, a royal

RAIN → RAINBOW
Ge 7.4 For in seven days I will send r on
Isa 45.8 let the skies r down righteousness;
Mt 5.45 sends r on the righteous and on the
Rev 11.6 so that no r may fall during the days

RAINBOW → BOW
Rev 4.3 the throne is a r that looks like an

RAISE → RISE
Jn 2.19 and in three days I will r it up."
2Co 4.14 who raised the Lord Jesus will r us

RAISED → RISE
Mt 17.23 and on the third day he will be r."
Ac 2.24 God r him up, having freed him
Ro 4.25 and was r for our justification.
1Co 15.4 r on the third day in accordance

RANSOM
Ps 49.8 For the r of life is costly, and can
Mt 20.28 and to give his life a r for many."
1Ti 2.6 who gave himself a r for all

REAP
Gal 6.7 for you r whatever you sow.
Rev 14.15 for the hour to r has come,

REBUILD → BUILD
Ezr 1.3 and r the house of the LORD,
Ne 2.17 let us r the wall of Jerusalem,
Da 9.25 went out to restore and r Jerusalem
Ac 15.16 and I will r the dwelling of David,

REBUKE
Pr 27.5 Better is open r than hidden love.
Zec 3.2 said to Satan, "The LORD r you,
Mk 8.32 Peter took him aside and began to r
2Ti 4.2 convince, r, and encourage,

RECEIVE
Jn 16.24 Ask and you will r, so that your joy
Ac 2.38 you will r the gift of the Holy Spirit.
20.35 'It is more blessed to give than to r.'
Rev 4.11 to r glory and honor and power,

RECKONED
Ge 15.6 LORD r it to him as righteousness.
Ro 4.3 it was r to him as righteousness."

RECONCILIATION
Ro 5.11 whom we have now received r.
2Co 5.18 and has given us the ministry of r;

REDEEM → REDEEMER, REDEMPTION
Ex 6.6 I will r you with an outstretched
Gal 4.5 to r those who were under the law,

REDEEMER → REDEEM
Job 19.25 For I know that my R lives,
Ps 19.14 O LORD, my rock and my r.

REDEMPTION → REDEEM
Lk 21.28 because your r is drawing near."
Eph 1.7 In him we have r through his blood,
Heb 9.12 own blood, thus obtaining eternal r.

REFINE
Jer 9.7 I will now r and test them,
Zec 13.9 r them as one refines silver,

REFLECTED → REFLECTION
2Co 3.18 though r in a mirror,

REFLECTION → REFLECTED
1Co 11.7 since he is the image and r of God;
Heb 1.3 He is the r of God's glory

REFUGE
Nu 35.11 select cities to be cities of r for you,
Ps 2.12 Happy are all who take r in him.

REGULATIONS
Col 2.20 Why do you submit to r,
Heb 9.10 r for the body imposed until the

REIGN
Ex 15.18 The LORD will r forever and ever."
Ps 146.10 The LORD will r forever,
1Co 15.25 r until he has put all his enemies
2Ti 2.12 we will also r with him;
Rev 11.15 and he will r forever and ever."
22.5 and they will r forever and ever.

REJECTED
Ps 118.22 The stone that the builders r
Isa 53.3 He was despised and r by others;
Mt 21.42 The stone that the builders r

REJOICE
Ps 118.24 let us r and be glad in it.
Zep 3.17 he will r over you with gladness,
Php 4.4 R in the Lord always; again I will say, R.

RELENT → RELENTED
Eze 24.14 I will not spare, I will not r.
Joel 2.14 whether he will not turn and r,
Jnh 3.9 God may r and change his mind;

RELENTED → RELENT
1Ch 21.15 LORD took note and r concerning
Jer 4.28 I have not r nor will I turn back.

REMEMBER → REMEMBRANCE
Ge 9.15 I will r my covenant that is between
Ex 20.8 R the sabbath day, and keep it holy.
Dt 8.18 But r the LORD your God,
2Ti 2.8 R Jesus Christ, raised from the dead
Heb 8.12 and I will r their sins no more."

REMEMBRANCE → REMEMBER
Lk 22.19 Do this in r of me."

REMNANT
Isa 10.21 A r will return, the r of Jacob,
Jer 50.20 will pardon the r that I have spared.
Ro 9.27 only a r of them will be saved;

RENEW → RENEWAL, RENEWED, RENEWING
Isa 40.31 the LORD shall r their strength,
La 5.21 r our days as of old—

RENEWAL → RENEW
Mt 19.28 I tell you, at the r of all things,

RENEWED → RENEW
2Co 4.16 inner nature is being r day by day.
Eph 4.23 to be r in the spirit of your minds,

RENEWING → RENEW
Ro 12.2 transformed by the r of your minds,

REPENT → REPENTANCE
Mt 3.2 "R, for the kingdom of heaven has
Ac 2.38 "R, and be baptized every one of

REPENTANCE → REPENT

Mk   1.   4   a baptism of **r** for the forgiveness
Lk   3.   8   Bear fruits worthy of **r**.
Ro   2.   4   kindness is meant to lead you to **r**?
2Co   7.10   **r** that leads to salvation and brings
2Pe   3.   9   any to perish, but all to come to **r**.

REPROVE

Pr   19.25   **r** the intelligent, and they will gain
Tit   2.15   exhort and **r** with all authority.
Rev   3.19   **r** and discipline those whom I love.

REQUIRE

Dt   10.12   does the LORD your God **r** of you?
Mic   6.   8   the LORD **r** of you but to do justice,

RESCUE → RESCUED

Mt   6.13   but **r** us from the evil one.
2Pe   2.   9   the Lord knows how to **r** the godly

RESCUED → RESCUE

Col   1.13   has **r** us from the power of darkness

RESIST

Mt   5.39   I say to you, Do not **r** an evildoer.
Ro   9.19   For who can **r** his will?"
Jas   4.   7   **R** the devil, and he will flee from

REST → RESTED

Ex   31.15   seventh day is a sabbath of solemn **r**
Ps   95.11   swore, "They shall not enter my **r**."
Mt   11.28   and I will give you **r**.
Heb   4.10   those who enter God's **r** also cease

RESTED → REST

Ge   2.   2   he **r** on the seventh day from all the
Ex   20.11   all that is in them, but **r** the seventh

RESURRECTION

Mt   22.30   For in the **r** they neither marry nor
Mk   12.18   Sadducees, who say there is no **r**,
Jn   11.25   said to her, "I am the **r** and the life.
1Co   15.12   you say there is no **r** of the dead?
Php   3.10   know Christ and the power of his **r**
Rev   20.   5   This is the first **r**.

RETURN

Ge   3.19   you are dust, and to dust you shall **r**.
Mal   3.   7   **R** to me, and I will **r** to you,

REVEAL → REVEALED, REVELATION

Mt   11.27   to whom the Son chooses to **r** him.

REVEALED → REVEAL

Isa   40.   5   the glory of the LORD shall be **r**,
Mt   16.17   flesh and blood has not **r** this to you
Lk   17.30   on the day that the Son of Man is **r**.
Ro   1.17   in it the righteousness of God is **r**

REVELATION → REVEAL

1Co   14.   6   some **r** or knowledge or prophecy
Eph   3.   3   was made known to me by **r**,

REVERE → REVERENCE

Jos   24.14   "Now therefore **r** the LORD,
Mal   4.   2   But for you who **r** my name the sun

REVERENCE → REVERE

Eph   5.21   subject to one another out of **r** for

REVILE → REVILED

Ex   22.28   You shall not **r** God, or curse
Mt   5.11   people **r** you and persecute you

REVILED → REVILE

1Co   4.12   When **r**, we bless;
1Pe   4.14   If you are **r** for the name of Christ,

REWARD

Ps   19.11   in keeping them there is great **r**.
Isa   40.10   **r** is with him, and his recompense
Mt   6.   5   I tell you, they have received their **r**.
Lk   6.23   for surely your **r** is great in heaven;
Rev   22.12   I am coming soon; my **r** is with me,

RIB

Ge   2.22   **r** that the LORD God had taken from

RICH → RICHES

Mt   19.23   hard for a **r** person to enter the
2Co   8.   9   by his poverty you might become **r**.
Eph   2.   4   But God, who is **r** in mercy,

RICHES → RICH

Lk   8.14   they are choked by the cares and **r**
Ro   11.33   O the depth of the **r** and wisdom
1Jn   2.16   the desire of the eyes, the pride in **r**

RIGHT → BIRTHRIGHT

Ex   15.   6   Your **r** hand, O LORD, glorious in
Dt   6.18   Do what is **r** and good in the sight
Ps   110. 1   says to my lord, "Sit at my **r** hand
Pr   14.12   a way that seems **r** to a person,
Ac   2.34   said to my Lord, "Sit at my **r** hand,
Heb   1.13   "Sit at my **r** hand until I make your

RIGHTEOUS → RIGHTEOUSNESS

Ps   11.   7   For the LORD is **r**; he loves **r** deeds;
Jer   23.   5   I will raise up for David a **r** Branch,
Eze   3.20   if the **r** turn from their righteousness
Hab   2.   4   but the **r** live by their faith.
Mt   5.45   rain on the **r** and on the unrighteous.
Mk   2.17   come to call not the **r** but sinners."
Ro   1.17   one who is **r** will live by faith."
Heb   10.38   but my **r** one will live by faith.
1Jn   2.   1   with the Father, Jesus Christ the **r**;
Rev   19.   8   the fine linen is the **r** deeds of the

RIGHTEOUSNESS → RIGHTEOUS

Ge   15.   6   the LORD reckoned it to him as **r**.
Isa   11.   5   **R** shall be the belt around his waist,
Jer   23.   6   be called: "The LORD is our **r**."
Da   9.24   to bring in everlasting **r**,
Hos   10.12   Sow for yourselves **r**; reap steadfast
Mt   5.   6   those who hunger and thirst for **r**,
Jn   16.   8   about sin and **r** and judgment:
Ro   5.18   act of **r** leads to justification
Gal   3.   6   and it was reckoned to him as **r**,"
Eph   6.14   and put on the breastplate of **r**.
2Pe   3.13   heavens and a new earth, where **r**

RIPE

Jn   4.35   how the fields are **r** for harvesting.
Rev   14.15   the harvest of the earth is fully **r**."

RISE → ARISE, RAISE, RAISED, ROSE

Da   12.13   shall **r** for your reward at the end of
Mal   4.   2   the sun of righteousness shall **r**,
Mt   27.63   'After three days I will **r** again.'
1Th   4.16   and the dead in Christ will **r** first.

ROAD

Mt   7.13   and the **r** is easy that leads to

ROBBERS

Jer   7.11   become a den of **r** in your sight?
Mt   21.13   but you are making it a den of **r**."

ROBE

Ex   28.   4   a breastpiece, an ephod, a **r**,
Jn   19.   5   crown of thorns and the purple **r**.
Rev   6.11   They were each given a white **r** and
  19.13   He is clothed in a **r** dipped in blood,

ROCK

Ex   17.   6   Strike the **r**, and water will come
Nu   20.   8   you shall bring water out of the **r**
1Sa   2.   2   there is no **R** like our God.
Mt   16.18   and on this **r** I will build my church,
Mk   15.46   that had been hewn out of the **r**.
1Pe   2.   8   and a **r** that makes them fall."

ROD

Ps   2.   9   shall break them with a **r** of iron,
  23.   4   your **r** and your staff—they comfort
Pr   13.24   who spare the **r** hate their children,
Rev   2.27   to rule them with an iron **r**,

ROLL

Mk   16.   3   "Who will **r** away the stone for us

ROOT

Isa   11.10   On that day the **r** of Jesse
  53.   2   and like a **r** out of dry ground;
Ro   15.12   "The **r** of Jesse shall come,

1Ti   6.10   For the love of money is a **r** of all
Rev   5.   5   the tribe of Judah, the **R** of David,

ROSE → RISE

SS   2.   1   I am a **r** of Sharon, a lily
1Th   4.14   believe that Jesus died and **r** again,

RULE

Eph   1.21   far above all **r** and authority and
Col   3.15   the peace of Christ **r** in your hearts,

RUMORS

Mt   24.   6   you will hear of wars and **r** of wars;

RUN

Isa   40.31   they shall **r** and not be weary,
Heb   12.   1   let us **r** with perseverance the race

RUST

Mt   6.19   where moth and **r** consume

S

SABBATH

Ex   20.   8   Remember the **s** day, and keep it holy.
Mk   2.28   Son of Man is lord even of the **s**."

SACRIFICE → SACRIFICED

Ex   12.27   'It is the passover **s** to the LORD,
1Sa   15.22   Surely, to obey is better than **s**,
Ps   40.   6   **S** and offering you do not desire,
Da   9.27   he shall make **s** and offering cease;
Hos   6.   6   For I desire steadfast love and not **s**,
Mt   9.13   this means, 'I desire mercy, not **s**.'
Ro   3.25   put forward as a **s** of atonement
Heb   13.15   let us continually offer a **s** of praise
1Jn   2.   2   and he is the atoning **s** for our sins,

SACRIFICED → SACRIFICE

1Co   5.   7   our paschal lamb, Christ, has been **s**.
  8.   1   Now concerning food **s** to idols:

SADDUCEES

Mt   16.   6   the yeast of the Pharisees and **S**."
Mk   12.18   **S**, who say there is no resurrection,

SAFE → SAFETY

Ps   37.28   righteous shall be kept **s** forever,
Pr   18.10   the righteous run into it and are **s**.

SAFETY → SAFE

Dt   12.10   around so that you live in **s**,
Eze   34.28   they shall live in **s**,

SAINTS

Ps   31.23   Love the LORD, all you his **s**.
Ro   8.27   the Spirit intercedes for the **s**
1Co   6.   2   that the **s** will judge the world?
Eph   4.12   equip the **s** for the work of ministry,
Rev   5.   9   by your blood you ransomed for God **s**

SALT

Ge   19.26   back, and she became a pillar of **s**.
Mt   5.13   "You are the **s** of the earth;

SALVATION → SAVE

Ex   15.   2   and he has become my **s**;
Ps   27.   1   The LORD is my light and my **s**;
Isa   52.   7   brings good news, who announces **s**,
Lk   3.   6   all flesh shall see the **s** of God.'"
Ac   4.12   There is **s** in no one else,
Php   2.12   work out your own **s** with fear
Heb   2.   3   escape if we neglect so great a **s**?
2Pe   3.15   regard the patience of our Lord as **s**.

SAMARITAN

Lk   10.33   But a **S** while traveling came near
Jn   4.   7   A **S** woman came to draw water,

SANCTIFICATION → SANCTIFY

Ro   6.19   as slaves to righteousness for **s**.
1Th   4.   3   For this is the will of God, your **s**:

SANCTIFIED → SANCTIFY

Jn   17.19   so that they also may be **s** in truth.
1Co   6.11   But you were washed, you were **s**,

SANCTIFY → SANCTIFICATION, SANCTIFIED
Lev 11.44 s yourselves therefore, and be holy,
Heb 13.12 to s the people by his own blood.

SANCTUARY
Ex 25. 8 And have them make me a s,
1Ch 22.19 build the s of the LORD God
Heb 9.24 Christ did not enter a s made by

SAND
Mt 7.26 foolish man who built his house on s.

SAT → SIT
Heb 10.12 "he s down at the right hand of God,
Rev 3.21 and s down with my Father

SATAN
1Ch 21. 1 S stood up against Israel,
Job 1. 6 and S also came among them.
Zec 3. 2 "The LORD rebuke you, O S!
Mt 4.10 Jesus said to him, "Away with you, S!
  16.23 said to Peter, "Get behind me, S!
2Co 11.14 S disguises himself as an angel of light.
Rev 12. 9 who is called the Devil and S,
  20. 7 S will be released from his prison

SAVE → SALVATION, SAVED, SAVIOR
Isa 59. 1 LORD's hand is not too short to s,
Jer 15.20 for I am with you to s you
Mt 1.21 he will s his people from their sins."
  16.25 who want to s their life will lose it,
Lk 19.10 came to seek out and to s the lost."

SAVED → SAVE
Isa 45.22 Turn to me and be s,
Joel 2.32 on the name of the LORD shall be s;
Mt 10.22 who endures to the end will be s.
Mk 15.31 He s others; he cannot save himself.
Ro 10.13 on the name of the Lord shall be s."
Eph 2. 8 For by grace you have been s

SAVIOR → SAVE
Isa 49.26 know that I am the LORD your S,
Hos 13. 4 and besides me there is no s.
1Ti 4.10 who is the S of all people,
Tit 2.13 of the glory of our great God and S,
2Pe 3.18 knowledge of our Lord and S Jesus

SCARLET
Isa 1.18 your sins are like s, they shall be
Mt 27.28 stripped him and put a s robe on him

SCEPTER
Ge 49.10 The s shall not depart from Judah,
Nu 24.17 and a s shall rise out of Israel;

SCRIBES
Mt 7.29 having authority, and not as their s.
  23.13 "But woe to you, s and Pharisees,

SCRIPTURE → SCRIPTURES
Lk 4.21 "Today this s has been fulfilled in
Jn 10.35 and the s cannot be annulled—
1Ti 4.13 attention to the public reading of s,
2Ti 3.16 All s is inspired by God and is useful

SCRIPTURES → SCRIPTURE
Mt 22.29 know neither the s nor the power
Lk 24.45 their minds to understand the s,
Jn 5.39 "You search the s because you think

SEA
Ps 95. 5 The s is his, for he made it,
Mic 7.19 all our sins into the depths of the s.
Rev 4. 6 there is something like a s of glass,
  21. 1 and the s was no more.

SEAL
2Co 1.22 by putting his s on us and giving us
Eph 1.13 the s of the promised Holy Spirit;
Rev 7. 3 our God with a s on their foreheads.

SEASON → SEASONS
Ps 1. 3 which yield their fruit in its s,
Ecc 3. 1 For everything there is a s,

SEASONS → SEASON
1Th 5. 1 Now concerning the times and the s,

SEAT
Ex 25.17 make a mercy s of pure gold;
Ro 14.10 stand before the judgment s of God.
2Co 5.10 must appear before the judgment s

SECRET
Dt 29.29 The s things belong to the LORD
Ro 2.16 will judge the s thoughts of all.

SEE → SEEN, SEES, SIGHT
Ex 33.20 for no one shall s me and live."
Jn 9.25 that though I was blind, now I s."
Rev 1. 7 the clouds; every eye will s him,

SEED → SEEDS, SEEDTIME
Mt 17.20 have faith the size of a mustard s,

SEEDS → SEED
Mt 13. 8 Other s fell on good soil
Mk 4.31 the smallest of all the s on earth;

SEEK
1Ch 28. 9 If you s him, he will be found by
Ps 34.10 those who s the LORD lack no good
Isa 55. 6 S the LORD while he may be found,
Lk 19.10 came to s out and to save
Heb 11. 6 that he rewards those who s him.

SEEN → SEE
Jn 1.18 No one has ever s God.
  14. 9 Whoever has s me has s the Father.

SELF-CONTROL
2Pe 1. 6 with s, and s with endurance,

SEPARATE
Mt 19. 6 joined together, let no one s."
Ro 8.35 will s us from the love of Christ?

SERPENT
Ge 3. 1 the s was more crafty than any other
2Co 11. 3 the s deceived Eve by its cunning,
Rev 20. 2 He seized the dragon, that ancient s,

SERVANT
Isa 42. 1 Here is my s, whom I uphold,
  53.11 my s, shall make many righteous,
Zec 3. 8 going to bring my s the Branch.
Lk 1.38 "Here am I, the s of the Lord;
Ac 3.13 has glorified his s Jesus,
Heb 3. 5 faithful in all God's house as a s,

SERVE
Jos 24.15 my household, we will s the LORD."
1Sa 12.20 but s the LORD with all your heart;
Mt 6.24 You cannot s God and wealth.
Mk 10.45 Son of Man came not to be served but to s,
1Pe 4.10 s one another with whatever gift

SEVEN → SEVENTH
Ge 7. 2 with you s pairs of all clean animals,
Ex 25.37 You shall make the s lamps for it;
Jos 6. 4 march around the city s times,
Da 9.25 prince, there shall be s weeks;
Mt 18.22 "Not s times, but, I tell you, seventy-seven
Rev 1.12 turning I saw s golden lampstands,
  5. 1 and on the back, sealed with s seals;
  8. 2 I saw the s angels who stand before
  12. 3 a great red dragon, with s heads and
  15. 1 s angels with s plagues,

SEVENTH → SEVEN
Ge 2. 2 on the s day God finished the work
Ex 20.10 the s day is a sabbath to the LORD
Heb 4. 4 God rested on the s day from all his

SEVENTY → SEVENTY-SEVEN
Da 9.24 S weeks are decreed for your people

SEVENTY-SEVEN → SEVENTY
Mt 18.22 "Not seven times, but, I tell you, s

SHADOW
Ps 17. 8 hide me in the s of your wings,
  91. 1 who abide in the s of the Almighty,

SHAME → ASHAMED
Da 12. 2 some to s and everlasting contempt.

SHARE
1Co 1.27 foolish in the world to s the wise;
Heb 12. 2 endured the cross, disregarding its s,
1Jn 2.28 be put to s before him at his coming.

SHARE
Col 1.12 to s in the inheritance of the saints
Heb 12.10 in order that we may s his holiness.
Jude 1. 3 to you about the salvation we s,

SHARPENS → SHARPER
Pr 27.17 Iron s iron, and one person s

SHARPER → SHARPENS
Heb 4.12 s than any two-edged sword,

SHED
Ge 9. 6 shall that person's blood be s;
Rev 16. 6 s the blood of saints and prophets,

SHEEP
Isa 53. 6 All we like s have gone astray;
Mt 9.36 like s without a shepherd.
Jn 10. 7 I am the gate for the s.
  10.15 And I lay down my life for the s.
Heb 13.20 the great shepherd of the s,
1Pe 2.25 For you were going astray like s,

SHEOL
Ps 139. 8 if I make my bed in S, you are there.
Hos 13.14 O S, where is your destruction?

SHEPHERD → SHEPHERDS
Ps 23. 1 The LORD is my s, I shall not want.
Isa 40.11 He will feed his flock like a s;
Mt 2. 6 ruler who is to s my people Israel.' "
Jn 10.11 "I am the good s.
Heb 13.20 the great s of the sheep,
1Pe 5. 4 And when the chief s appears,

SHEPHERDS → SHEPHERD
Lk 2. 8 there were s living in the fields,

SHIELD
Eph 6.16 With all of these, take the s of faith,

SHINE → SHINES
Nu 6.25 LORD make his face to s upon you,
Ps 4. 6 light of your face s on us, O LORD!"
Da 12. 3 Those who are wise shall s like the
Mt 5.16 let your light s before others,

SHINES → SHINE
Jn 1. 5 The light s in the darkness,

SHORT
Ro 3.23 sinned and fall s of the glory of God;

SHOW → SHOWED
Ex 33.18 Moses said, "S me your glory,
Ps 85. 7 S us your steadfast love, O LORD,
Jn 14. 8 said to him, "Lord, s us the Father,
1Co 12.31 will s you a still more excellent way

SHOWED → SHOW
Jn 20.20 he s them his hands and his side.

SICK → SICKNESS
Mt 8.16 and cured all who were s.
Jas 5.14 Are any among you s?

SICKNESS → SICK
Ex 23.25 I will take s away from among you.
Mt 4.23 and curing every disease and every s

SIDE
Jn 19.34 soldiers pierced his s with a spear,

SIGHT → SEE
Mt 11. 5 blind receive their s, the lame walk,
2Co 5. 7 for we walk by faith, not by s.

SIGN → SIGNS
Mt 24. 3 the s of your coming and of the end
Mk 8.12 does this generation ask for a s?

SIGNS → SIGN
Ge 1.14 be for s and for seasons and for days
Mt 16. 3 cannot interpret the s of the times.
Jn 20.30 Jesus did many other s in the
1Co 1.22 Jews demand s and Greeks desire
Rev 16.14 demonic spirits, performing s,

SILENT
Isa 53. 7 a sheep that before its shearers is **s**,
Mk 14.61 But he was **s** and did not answer.

SILVER
Mt 26.15 They paid him thirty pieces of **s**.
Ac 3. 6 But Peter said, "I have no **s** or gold,

SIN → SINNED, SINNER, SINNERS, SINS
Nu 32.23 and be sure your **s** will find you out.
2Ch 7.14 forgive their **s** and heal their land.
Ps 119.11 so that I may not **s** against you.
Isa 53.12 yet he bore the **s** of many,
Mt 5.29 If your right eye causes you to **s**,
Jn 1.29 who takes away the **s** of the world!
Ro 6.23 For the wages of **s** is death,
Heb 4.15 tested as we are, yet without **s**.
1Jn 1. 7 Jesus his Son cleanses us from all **s**.

SINAI
Ex 19.20 the LORD descended upon Mount **S**,

SING → SONG, SONGS, SUNG
Ps 47. 6 **S** praises to God, **s** praises;
1Co 14.15 I will **s** praise with the spirit,
Col 3.16 gratitude in your hearts **s** psalms,
Rev 5. 9 They **s** a new song:

SINNED → SIN
Ps 51. 4 Against you, you alone, have I **s**,
La 5. 7 Our ancestors **s**; they are no more,
Ro 3.23 all have **s** and fall short of the glory
1Jn 1.10 If we say that we have not **s**,

SINNER → SIN
Lk 15. 7 over one **s** who repents than
Jas 5.20 that whoever brings back a **s**

SINNERS → SIN
Pr 23.17 Do not let your heart envy **s**,
Ro 5. 8 we still were **s** Christ died for us.
1Ti 1.15 Jesus came into the world to save **s**

SINS → SIN
1Sa 2.25 if someone **s** against the LORD,
Eze 18. 4 only the person who **s** that shall die.
Mt 9. 6 has authority on earth to forgive **s**"—
Lk 11. 4 forgive us our **s**, for we ourselves
Ac 3.19 to God so that your **s** may be wiped
1Co 15. 3 Christ died for our **s** in accordance
Heb 9.28 offered once to bear the **s** of many,
1Jn 1. 9 If we confess our **s**, he who is faithful
Rev 1. 5 loves us and freed us from our **s**

SISTER
Pr 7. 4 Say to wisdom, "You are my **s**,"
Mk 3.35 the will of God is my brother and **s**

SIT → SAT
Ps 110. 1 says to my lord, "**S** at my right hand
Mt 20.23 to **s** at my right hand and at my left,
Heb 1.13 "**S** at my right hand until I make

SIX
Ex 20. 9 **S** days you shall labor and do all
Pr 6.16 are **s** things that the LORD hates,

SKULL
Mt 27.33 Golgotha (which means Place of a **S**)

SLANDER → SLANDERED
Ps 15. 3 who do not **s** with their tongue,
Pr 10.18 and whoever utters **s** is a fool.
Mt 15.19 fornication, theft, false witness, **s**.
1Pe 2. 1 all guile, insincerity, envy, and all **s**.

SLANDERED → SLANDER
1Co 4.13 when **s**, we speak kindly.

SLAUGHTER
Isa 53. 7 like a lamb that is led to the **s**,
Ac 8.32 "Like a sheep he was led to the **s**,

SLAVE → SLAVERY
Mk 10.44 first among you must be **s** of all.
Jn 8.34 who commits sin is a **s** to sin.
Gal 3.28 there is no longer **s** or free,

SLAVERY → SLAVE
Gal 5. 1 do not submit again to a yoke of **s**.

SLEEP → ASLEEP, SLEEPER, SLEEPING
Ps 121. 4 keeps Israel who neither slumber nor **s**.
Da 12. 2 Many of those who **s** in the dust of

SLEEPER → SLEEP
Eph 5.14 "**S**, awake! Rise from the dead,

SLEEPING → SLEEP
Mt 9.24 for the girl is not dead but **s**."
26.40 to the disciples and found them **s**;

SLING
1Sa 17.50 over the Philistine with a **s** and a stone,

SLOW → SLOWNESS
Ex 34. 6 merciful and gracious, **s** to anger,
2Pe 3. 9 The Lord is not **s** about his promise,

SLOWNESS → SLOW
2Pe 3. 9 think of **s**, but is patient with you,

SNOW
Ps 51. 7 and I shall be whiter than **s**.
Isa 1.18 sins are like scarlet, they shall be like **s**;
Da 7. 9 his clothing was white as **s**,
Rev 1.14 as white wool, white as **s**;

SOBER
1Th 5. 6 but let us keep awake and be **s**;
2Ti 4. 5 always be **s**, endure suffering,

SODOM
Ge 19.24 rained on **S** and Gomorrah sulfur
Lk 10.12 it will be more tolerable for **S** than
Rev 11. 8 city that is prophetically called **S**

SOLDIERS
Mt 28.12 give a large sum of money to the **s**,
Jn 19.23 When the **s** had crucified Jesus,

SON → SONS
Ex 4.23 now I will kill your firstborn **s**.' "
2Sa 7.14 and he shall be a **s** to me.
Ps 2. 7 He said to me, "You are my **s**;
Isa 7.14 is with child and shall bear a **s**,
Mt 1.23 virgin shall conceive and bear a **s**,
3.17 from heaven said, "This is my **S**,
16.16 the Messiah, the **S** of the living God."
Mk 10.45 **S** of Man came not to be served but to
Lk 1.35 he will be called **S** of God.
Jn 3.16 loved the world that he gave his only **S**,
1Th 1.10 to wait for his **S** from heaven,
Heb 1. 2 last days he has spoken to us by a **S**,
1Jn 4. 9 God sent his only **S** into the world
Rev 12. 5 she gave birth to a **s**, a male child,
14.14 the cloud was one like the **S** of Man,

SONG → SING
Ps 40. 3 He put a new **s** in my mouth,
Rev 5. 9 They sing a new **s**: "You are worthy
15. 3 and the **s** of the Lamb:

SONGS → SING
Col 3.16 hymns, and spiritual **s** to God.

SONS → SON
Ac 2.17 **s** and your daughters shall prophesy,
2Co 6.18 you shall be my **s** and daughters,

SOON
Rev 22.20 says, "Surely I am coming **s**."

SOUL → SOULS
Dt 6. 5 all your **s**, and with all your might.
Jos 22. 5 all your heart and with all your **s**."
Mt 10.28 fear him who can destroy both **s** and
Heb 4.12 piercing until it divides **s** from spirit
Jas 5.20 will save the sinner's **s** from death
3Jn 1. 2 just as it is well with your **s**.

SOULS → SOUL
Jer 6.16 walk in it, and find rest for your **s**.
Mt 11.29 and you will find rest for your **s**.

SOWS
Jn 4.37 'One **s** and another reaps.'

2Co 9. 6 who **s** sparingly will also reap

SPARROWS
Lk 12. 7 you are of more value than many **s**.

SPEAK → SPEAKING
Ecc 3. 7 time to keep silence, and a time to **s**;
Mt 13.13 The reason I **s** to them in parables is
Ac 2. 4 began to **s** in other languages,
1Co 12.30 Do all **s** in tongues?

SPEAKING → SPEAK
1Co 14.39 and do not forbid **s** in tongues;
Eph 4.15 But **s** the truth in love,

SPEAR → SPEARS
Jn 19.34 the soldiers pierced his side with a **s**,

SPIES → SPY
Nu 13.32 we have gone through as **s**
Jos 2. 1 two men secretly from Shittim as **s**,

SPIRIT → SPIRITS, SPIRITUAL
Ge 6. 3 My **s** shall not abide in mortals forever,
Nu 11.25 rested upon them, they prophesied.
Ps 31. 5 Into your hand I commit my **s**;
51.17 acceptable to God is a broken **s**;
Isa 42. 1 I have put my **s** upon him;
Eze 36.26 and a new **s** I will put within you;
Joel 2.28 I will pour out my **s** on all flesh;
Mt 1.18 to be with child from the Holy **S**.
5. 3 "Blessed are the poor in **s**,
26.41 the **s** indeed is willing, but the flesh
Mk 1. 8 will baptize you with the Holy **S**."
Jn 3. 5 without being born of water and **S**.
4.24 God is **s**, and those who worship him
must worship in **s** and truth."
14.26 But the Advocate, the Holy **S**,
Ac 2. 4 of them were filled with the Holy **S**
Ro 8.26 the **S** helps us in our weakness;
1Co 12. 4 are varieties of gifts, but the same **S**;
2Co 3. 6 the letter kills, but the **S** gives life.
Gal 5.22 the fruit of the **S** is love, joy, peace,
Eph 1.13 the seal of the promised Holy **S**;
5.18 but be filled with the **S**,
1Th 5.19 Do not quench the **S**.
Heb 4.12 piercing until it divides soul from **s**,
1Jn 4. 1 Beloved, do not believe every **s**,

SPIRITS → SPIRIT
Lk 4.36 power he commands the unclean **s**,
Rev 1. 4 seven **s** who are before his throne,

SPIRITUAL → SPIRIT
1Co 2.13 interpreting **s** things to those who are **s**.
12. 1 Now concerning **s** gifts,
14. 1 Pursue love and strive for the **s** gifts,
Eph 1. 3 every **s** blessing in the heavenly
1Pe 2. 5 yourselves be built into a **s** house,

SPIT
Mk 14.65 began to **s** on him, to blindfold him,
Rev 3.16 am about to **s** you out of my mouth.

SPY → SPIES
Nu 13. 2 men to **s** out the land of Canaan,
Jos 6.25 whom Joshua sent to **s** out Jericho.

STAFF
Ex 4. 4 and it became a **s** in his hand—
Nu 17. 6 the **s** of Aaron was among theirs.
Ps 23. 4 your rod and your **s**—they comfort me.

STAND → STANDING
Ex 14.13 "Do not be afraid, **s** firm,
Job 19.25 at the last he will **s** upon the earth;
Ps 1. 5 wicked will not **s** in the judgment,
Mt 12.25 house divided against itself will **s**.
Ro 14.10 all **s** before the judgment seat of God.

STANDING → STAND
1Co 10.12 So if you think you are **s**,
Rev 3.20 I am **s** at the door, knocking;

STAR → STARS
Nu 24.17 a **s** shall come out of Jacob,
Isa 14.12 are fallen from heaven, O Day **S**,
Mt 2. 2 For we observed his **s** at its rising,

2Pe   1. 19   day dawns and the morning **s** rises
Rev   9. 1   saw a **s** that had fallen from heaven
    22. 16   of David, the bright morning **s."**

STARS → STAR
Ge   1. 16   to rule the night—and the **s.**
Job   38. 7   when the morning **s** sang together
Rev   1. 16   In his right hand he held seven **s,**

STATUE
Da   2. 31   there was a great **s.**

STATUTE → STATUTES
Lev   16. 29   This shall be a **s** to you forever:
Nu   19. 21   It shall be a perpetual **s** for them.

STATUTES → STATUTE
Ge   26. 5   commandments, my **s,** and my laws.
Dt   4. 1   give heed to the **s** and ordinances
Ne   9. 13   good **s** and commandments,
Ps   119. 8   I will observe your **s;**

STEADFAST
Heb   6. 19   a sure and **s** anchor of the soul,
1Pe   5. 9   Resist him, **s** in your faith,

STEAL
Ex   20. 15   You shall not **s.**
Mt   6. 19   and where thieves break in and **s;**

STILL
Ps   46. 10   "Be **s,** and know that I am God!
Mk   4. 39   said to the sea, "Peace! Be **s!"**

STING
1Co   15. 55   Where, O death, is your **s?"**

STONE → CORNERSTONE, MILLSTONE, STONED, STONES
Ex   31. 18   tablets of **s,** written with the finger of
1Sa   17. 50   the Philistine with a sling and a **s,**
Ps   118. 22   The **s** that the builders rejected has
Isa   28. 16   in Zion a foundation **s,** a tested **s,**
Eze   36. 26   from your body the heart of **s**
Mt   4. 6   will not dash your foot against a **s.' "**
Mk   12. 10   'The **s** that the builders rejected has
    16. 3   "Who will roll away the **s** for us
Ro   9. 32   have stumbled over the stumbling **s,**
2Co   3. 3   not on tablets of **s** but on tablets

STONED → STONE
Ac   14. 19   Then they **s** Paul and dragged him
Heb   11. 37   **s** to death, they were sawn in two,

STONES → STONE
Mt   3. 9   God is able from these **s** to raise
Lk   19. 40   were silent, the **s** would shout out."
1Co   3. 12   precious **s,** wood, hay, straw—
1Pe   2. 5   like living **s,** let yourselves be built

STRAIGHT
Pr   3. 6   and he will make your paths.
Isa   40. 3   **s** in the desert a highway for our God.
Mt   3. 3   way of the Lord, make his paths **s.' "**
Ac   9. 11   Get up and go to the street called **S,**

STRANGER → STRANGERS
Dt   10. 19   You shall also love the **s.**
Mt   25. 35   I was a **s** and you welcomed me,

STRANGERS → STRANGER
Ro   12. 13   extend hospitality to **s.**
Heb   11. 13   They confessed that they were **s**

STREAMS
Ps   1. 3   like trees planted by **s** of water,
    42. 1   As a deer longs for flowing **s,**

STRENGTH → STRONG
Ex   15. 2   The Lord is my **s** and my might,
1Ch   16. 11   Seek the Lord and his **s,**
Ne   8. 10   for the joy of the Lord is your **s."**
Ps   46. 1   God is our refuge and **s,**
Isa   40. 31   The Lord shall renew their **s,**
Mk   12. 30   all your mind, and with all your **s.'**

STRENGTHEN → STRONG
Ps   119. 28   **s** me according to your word.
Heb   12. 12   hands and **s** your weak knees,

STRENGTHENS → STRONG
Php   4. 13   do all things through him who **s** me.

STRIFE
Pr   23. 29   Who has sorrow? Who has **s?**
Ro   1. 29   Full of envy, murder, **s,** deceit,
Gal   5. 20   enmities, **s,** jealousy, anger,

STRIKE
Ge   3. 15   he will **s** your head, and you will **s**
Ex   17. 6   **S** the rock, and water will come out
Mk   14. 27   'I will **s** the shepherd, and the sheep

STRONG → STRENGTH, STRENGTHEN, STRENGTHENS, STRONGHOLD
Dt   31. 6   Be **s** and bold; have no fear
Jos   1. 6   Be **s** and courageous; for you shall
Ecc   9. 11   nor the battle to the **s,** nor bread to
Ro   15. 1   We who are **s** ought to put up with
1Co   1. 27   in the world to shame the **s;**
2Co   12. 10   whenever I am weak, then I am **s.**
Eph   6. 10   be in the Lord and in the strength

STRONGHOLD → STRONG
Ps   9. 9   The Lord is a **s** for the oppressed,
Na   1. 7   a **s** in a day of trouble;

STUDY
Ezr   7. 10   Ezra had set his heart to **s** the law
Ecc   12. 12   much **s** is a weariness of the flesh.

STUMBLE → STUMBLING
Mt   18. 9   And if your eye causes you to **s,**
Ro   9. 33   a stone that will make people **s,**

STUMBLING → STUMBLE
Mt   16. 23   You are a **s** block to me;
Ro   11. 9   a **s** block and a retribution for them;
1Co   8. 9   not somehow become a **s** block

SUBDUE
Ge   1. 28   and fill the earth and **s** it;

SUBJECT
Ro   13. 1   be **s** to the governing authorities;
Eph   5. 21   **s** to one another out of reverence

SUBMISSION → SUBMIT
1Ti   2. 11   a woman learn in silence with full **s.**
Heb   5. 7   was heard because of his reverent **s.**

SUBMISSIVE → SUBMIT
1Ti   3. 4   keeping his children **s** and respectful
Tit   2. 5   kind, being **s** to their husbands,

SUBMIT → SUBMISSION, SUBMISSIVE
Heb   13. 17   Obey your leaders and **s** to them,

SUCCEED → SUCCESSFUL
Pr   15. 22   but with many advisers they **s.**
Ecc   10. 10   but wisdom helps one to **s.**

SUCCESSFUL → SUCCEED
Jos   1. 7   that you may be **s** wherever you go.

SUDDENLY
Mal   3. 1   Lord whom you seek will **s** come to
Mk   13. 36   find you asleep when he comes **s.**

SUFFER → SUFFERED, SUFFERING, SUFFERINGS
Lk   22. 15   this Passover with you before I **s;**
    24. 46   the Messiah is to **s** and to rise from
Heb   9. 26   then he would have had to **s** again

SUFFERED → SUFFER
1Pe   2. 21   because Christ also **s** for you,

SUFFERING → SUFFER
Isa   53. 3   a man of **s** and acquainted with
Mk   8. 31   Son of Man must undergo great **s,**

SUFFERINGS → SUFFER
Ro   8. 18   the **s** of this present time are not

SUFFICIENT
2Co   12. 9   "My grace is **s** for you,

SULFUR
Ge   19. 24   rained on Sodom and Gomorrah **s**

Ps   11. 6   he will rain coals of fire and **s;**
Rev   21. 8   in the lake that burns with fire and **s,**

SUN
Jos   10. 13   And the **s** stood still,
Ecc   1. 9   there is nothing new under the **s.**
Mt   5. 45   he makes his **s** rise on the evil and
Rev   22. 5   they need no light of lamp or **s,**

SUPPER
Lk   22. 20   he did the same with the cup after **s,**
Rev   19. 9   to the marriage **s** of the Lamb."

SUPPLICATION → SUPPLICATIONS
Eph   6. 18   at all times in every prayer and **s.**

SUPPLICATIONS → SUPPLICATION
1Ti   2. 1   then, I urge that **s,** prayers,
Heb   5. 7   Jesus offered up prayers and **s,**

SURPASSES
Eph   3. 19   the love of Christ that **s** knowledge,
Php   4. 7   the peace of God, which **s** all

SUSTAINS
Ps   3. 5   for the Lord **s** me.
Heb   1. 3   he **s** all things by his powerful word.

SWALLOW → SWALLOWED
Jnh   1. 17   provided a large fish to **s** up Jonah;
Mt   23. 24   You strain out a gnat but **s** a camel!

SWALLOWED → SWALLOW
1Co   15. 54   "Death has been **s** up in victory."

SWEAR
Dt   10. 20   and by his name you shall **s.**
Ps   24. 4   and do not **s** deceitfully.
Mt   5. 34   Do not **s** at all, either by heaven,

SWEAT
Ge   3. 19   By the **s** of your face you shall eat
Lk   22. 44   [[**s** became like great drops of blood]]

SWINE
Mt   7. 6   do not throw your pearls before **s,**

SWORD → SWORDS
Ge   3. 24   and a **s** flaming and turning to guard
Mt   10. 34   not come to bring peace, but a **s.**
Eph   6. 17   the **s** of the Spirit, which is the word
Heb   4. 12   sharper than any two-edged **s,**
Rev   1. 16   mouth came a sharp, two-edged **s,**

SWORDS → SWORD
Isa   2. 4   shall beat their **s** into plowshares,
Joel   3. 10   Beat your plowshares into **s,**

SYMPATHIZE → SYMPATHY
Heb   4. 15   unable to **s** with our weaknesses,

SYMPATHY → SYMPATHIZE
Php   2. 1   any compassion and **s,**
1Pe   3. 8   all of you, have unity of spirit, **s,**

SYNAGOGUE → SYNAGOGUES
Lk   4. 16   he went to the **s** on the sabbath day,
Ac   18. 26   He began to speak boldly in the **s;**

SYNAGOGUES → SYNAGOGUE
Mt   4. 23   teaching in their **s** and proclaiming
Jn   18. 20   always taught in **s** and in the temple,

T

TABERNACLE
Ex   25. 9   concerning the pattern of the **t**
    40. 34   the glory of the Lord filled the **t.**
1Ch   6. 48   for all the service of the **t** of the house

TABLE → TABLES
Ex   25. 23   You shall make a **t** of acacia wood,
Ps   23. 5   a **t** before me in the presence of my

TABLES → TABLE
Mk   11. 15   overturned the **t** of the money changers

TABLETS
Ex   31. 18   gave him the two **t** of the covenant,

2Co 3. 3 not on t of stone but on t of human
          hearts.

TALENT
Mt 25.25 and hid your t in the ground.

TAX → TAXES
Mt 11.19 a friend of t collectors and sinners!'
Lk 18.10 Pharisee and the other a t collector.

TAXES → TAX
Mt 22.17 Is it lawful to pay t to the emperor,
Ro 13. 7 t to whom t are due,

TEACH → TEACHER, TEACHERS,
TEACHING
Dt   6. 1 to you to observe in the land that
Jer 31.34 No longer shall they t one another,
Col 3.16 t and admonish one another in all
1Jn 2.27 so you do not need anyone to t you.

TEACHER → TEACH
Ecc 1. 1 words of the T, the son of David,
Jn   1.38 "Rabbi" (which translated means T)

TEACHERS → TEACH
Ps 119.99 more understanding than all my t,
1Co 12.28 second prophets, third t;
Eph 4.11 evangelists, some pastors and t,
Jas 3. 1 Not many of you should become t,

TEACHING → TEACH
Mk 1.27 A new t—with authority!

TEAR
Rev 7.17 God will wipe away every t from

TEETH → TOOTH
Mt 8.12 will be weeping and gnashing of t."

TEMPLE
2Ch 2.12 who will build a t for the LORD,
Mt   4. 5 placed him on the pinnacle of the t,
     12. 6 something greater than the t is here.
1Co 3.16 you are God's t and that God's Spirit
Eph 2.21 and grows into a holy t in the Lord;
Rev 21.22 its t is the Lord God the Almighty and

TEMPTATION → TEMPTED
1Ti 6. 9 who want to be rich into t and
Jas 1.12 Blessed is anyone who endures t.

TEMPTED → TEMPTATION
Mk 1.13 wilderness forty days, t by Satan;
Gal 6. 1 care that you yourselves are not t.

TEN
Ex 34.28 the covenant, the t commandments.

TENT
Ex 27.21 the t of meeting, outside the curtain
2Co 5. 1 the earthly we live in is destroyed,

TEST → TESTED, TESTING
Dt   6.16 put the LORD your God to the t,
Lk   4.12 not put the Lord your God to the t.'
     10.25 then a lawyer stood up to t Jesus.
2Co 13. 5 indeed, you fail to meet the t!
1Jn 4. 1 t the spirits to see whether they are

TESTED → TEST
Ge 22. 1 After these things God t Abraham.
Ps 78.41 They t God again and again,
Heb 4.15 been t as we are, yet without sin.

TESTIMONY
Mk 14.59 on this point their t did not agree.
Rev 1. 9 the word of God and the t of Jesus.

TESTING → TEST
1Co 10.13 No t has overtaken you that is not
Jas 1. 3 t of your faith produces endurance;

THANK → THANKS, THANKSGIVING
2Ch 29.31 bring sacrifices and t offerings to
Ps 52. 9 I will t you forever,

THANKS → THANK
1Co 11.24 and when he had given t,

THANKSGIVING → THANK
Ps 50.14 Offer to God a sacrifice of t,
Php 4. 6 with t let your requests be made known
Rev 7.12 glory and wisdom and t and honor

THIEF → THIEVES
Ex 22. 1 The t shall make restitution.
Jn 10.10 The t comes only to steal and kill
1Th 5. 2 day of the Lord will come like a t in
Rev 16.15 ("See, I am coming like a t!

THIEVES → THIEF
Mt 6.19 and where t break in and steal;

THINK → THOUGHTS
Ro 12. 3 not to t of yourself more highly than
1Co 10.12 So if you t you are standing,

THIRD → THREE
Mt 26.44 and prayed for the t time,
Lk 18.33 and on the t day he will rise again."

THIRST → THIRSTY
Mt   5. 6 who hunger and t for righteousness,
Rev 7.16 will hunger no more, and t no more;

THIRSTY → THIRST
Mt 25.35 I was t and you gave me something
Jn   6.35 believes in me will never be t.
Rev 22.17 And let everyone who is t come.

THORN → THORNS
2Co 12. 7 a t was given me in the flesh,

THORNS → THORN
Jn 19. 2 the soldiers wove a crown of t and

THOUGHTS → THINK
Isa 55. 8 For my t are not your t,
1Co 3.20 "The Lord knows the t of the wise,
Heb 4.12 judge the t and intentions of the heart.

THOUSAND
Ps 90. 4 t years in your sight are like yesterday
2Pe 3. 8 one day is like a t years, and a t years
Rev 20. 4 and reigned with Christ a t years.

THREE → THIRD
Mt 18.20 two or t are gathered in my name,
    26.34 you will deny me t times."
Mk   8.31 be killed, and after t days rise again.
2Co 12. 8 T times I appealed to the Lord
1Jn 5. 7 There are t that testify:

THRONE
Ps 45. 6 Your t, O God, endures forever
Isa 6. 1 I saw the Lord sitting on a t, high
Mt 19.28 the Son of Man is seated on the t
Heb 4.16 approach the t of grace with boldness,
Rev 4.10 they cast their crowns before the t,
    20.11 I saw a great white t and the one

THUMMIM
Ex 28.30 you shall put the Urim and the T,

THUNDER
Ex   9.23 and the LORD sent t and hail,
Rev 4. 5 and rumblings and peals of t,

TIME → TIMES
nEst 4.14 dignity for just such a t as this."
Ecc 3. 1 a t for every matter under heaven:
Da   7.25 for a t, two times, and half a
Ro   5. 6 the right t Christ died for the ungodly.
2Co 6. 2 See, now is the acceptable t;
Gal 4. 4 when the fullness of t had come,
Rev 12.14 for a t, and times, and half a t.

TIMES → TIME
Mt 16. 3 cannot interpret the signs of the t.
    18.22 seven t, but, I tell you, seventy-seven t.
Mk 14.30 you will deny me three t."

TITHE
Dt 12.17 the t of your grain, your wine, and
Mal 3.10 Bring the full t into the storehouse,

TODAY
Ps   2. 7 my son; t I have begotten you.

Heb 1. 5 my Son; t I have begotten you"?
    13. 8 Christ is the same yesterday and t

TOMB
Mk 15.46 laid it in a t that had been hewn out
Lk 24. 2 the stone rolled away from the t,

TOMORROW
Mt   6.34 "So do not worry about t,
Jas 4.14 do not even know what t will bring.

TONGUE → TONGUES
Isa 45.23 shall bow, every t shall swear."
Php 2.11 every t should confess that Jesus Christ

TONGUES → TONGUE
Ac   2. 3 Divided t, as of fire, appeared
1Co 12.10 t, to another the interpretation of t.

TOOTH → TEETH
Ex 21.24 t for t, hand for hand, foot for foot,
Mt   5.38 'An eye for an eye and a t for a t.'

TOWER
Ge 11. 4 and a t with its top in the heavens,
Pr 18.10 The name of the LORD is a strong t;

TRADITION
Mt 15. 2 disciples break the t of the elders?
Col 2. 8 empty deceit, according to human t,

TRAIN → TRAINING
Pr 22. 6 T children in the right way, and
1Ti 4. 7 T yourself in godliness,

TRAINING → TRAIN
1Ti 4. 8 while physical t is of some value,
2Ti 3.16 and for t in righteousness,

TRAITOR
Lk 6.16 and Judas Iscariot, who became a t.

TRANSFIGURED
Mt 17. 2 And he was t before them,

TRANSFORM → TRANSFORMED
Php 3.21 will t the body of our humiliation

TRANSFORMED → TRANSFORM
Ro   12. 2 be t by the renewing of your minds,
2Co 3.18 are being t into the same image

TRANSGRESSION → TRANSGRESSIONS
Ex 23.21 for he will not pardon your t;
Da   9.24 to finish the t, to put an end to sin,

TRANSGRESSIONS → TRANSGRESSION
Ps 103.12 so far he removes our t from us.
Isa 53. 5 But he was wounded for our t,

TREASURE → TREASURES
Mt   6.21 where your t is, there your heart
2Co 4. 7 But we have this t in clay jars,
2Ti 1.14 Guard the good t entrusted to you,

TREASURES → TREASURE
Col 2. 3 are hidden all the t of wisdom

TREE
Ge   3.24 to guard the way to the t of life.
Mt 12.33 for the t is known by its fruit.
Rev 22. 2 the t of life with its twelve kinds

TREMBLING
Ps   2.11 Serve the LORD with fear, with t
Php 2.12 your own salvation with fear and t;

TRESPASS → TRESPASSES
Ro   5.15 But the free gift is not like the t.

TRESPASSES → TRESPASS
Mt   6.14 For if you forgive others their t,
2Co 5.19 not counting their t against them,

TRIAL → TRIALS
Lk 11. 4 do not bring us to the time of t."
2Pe 2. 9 knows how to rescue the godly from t,
Rev 3.10 I will keep you from the hour of t

TRIALS → TRIAL
Jas 1. 2 whenever you face t of any kind,

1Pe 1. 6 you have had to suffer various **t,**

TRIBES
Ge 49. 28 All these are the twelve **t** of Israel,
Ex 24. 4 to the twelve **t** of Israel.
Mt 19. 28 judging the twelve **t** of Israel.
Rev 21. 12 inscribed the names of the twelve **t**

TRIUMPHAL → TRIUMPHS
2Co 2. 14 Christ always leads us in **t** procession,

TRIUMPHS → TRIUMPHAL
Jas 2. 13 mercy **t** over judgment.

TROUBLE → TROUBLED
Ps 9. 9 a stronghold in times of **t.**
Pr 11. 8 The righteous are delivered from **t,**
Isa 33. 2 our salvation in the time of **t.**
Mt 6. 34 Today's **t** is enough for today.

TROUBLED → TROUBLE
Jn 14. 1 "Do not let your hearts be **t.**

TRUE → TRUTH
Ps 119.151 and all your commandments are **t.**
Jn 1. 9 The **t** light, which enlightens
1Jn 5. 20 He is the **t** God and eternal life.
Rev 3. 14 the Amen, the faithful and **t** witness,
19. 11 Its rider is called Faithful and **T,**

TRUMPET
1Co 15. 52 twinkling of an eye, at the last **t.**
1Th 4. 16 and with the sound of God's **t,**

TRUST → ENTRUSTED, TRUSTED, TRUSTWORTHY
Ps 37. 3 **T** in the LORD, and do good;
Pr 3. 5 **T** in the LORD with all your heart,

TRUSTED → TRUST
Da 3. 28 delivered his servants who **t** in him.
6. 23 because he had **t** in his God.

TRUSTWORTHY → TRUST
Ps 111. 7 and just; all his precepts are **t.**
Rev 22. 6 "These words are **t** and true,

TRUTH → TRUE
Pr 23. 23 Buy **t,** and do not sell it;
Jn 1. 17 grace and **t** came through Jesus Christ.
4. 23 worship the Father in spirit and **t,**
Jn 8. 32 and the **t** will make you free."
14. 6 "I am the way, and the **t,** and the life.
14. 17 This is the Spirit of **t,**
Eph 4. 15 But speaking the **t** in love,
2Ti 2. 15 rightly explaining the word of **t.**

TURNED → TURN
Isa 53. 6 we have all **t** to our own way,
Ro 3. 12 All have **t** aside, together they have

TWELVE
Ge 49. 28 All these are the twelve **t** tribes of Israel,
Mt 10. 1 Jesus summoned his **t** disciples
Lk 9. 17 **t** baskets of broken pieces.
Rev 21. 12 inscribed the names of the **t** tribes
22. 2 tree of life with its **t** kinds of fruit,

TWINKLING
1Co 15. 52 in the **t** of an eye, at the last trumpet

TWO → TWICE, TWO-EDGED
Ge 1. 16 God made the **t** great lights—
6. 19 bring **t** of every kind into the ark,
Ex 31. 18 the **t** tablets of the covenant,
Dt 17. 6 of **t** or three witnesses the death
Mt 6. 24 "No one can serve **t** masters;
19. 5 and the **t** shall become one flesh'?

TWO-EDGED → TWO
Heb 4. 12 sharper than any **t** sword,
Rev 1. 16 his mouth came a sharp, **t** sword,

U

UNBELIEF → UNBELIEVER, UNBELIEVERS
Mk 6. 6 And he was amazed at their **u.**
9. 24 cried out, "I believe; help my **u!**"

UNBELIEVER → UNBELIEF
1Co 10. 27 If an **u** invites you to a meal and
2Co 6. 15 does a believer share with an **u?**

UNBELIEVERS → UNBELIEF
2Co 6. 14 Do not be mismatched with **u.**

UNCIRCUMCISED → UNCIRCUMCISION
Ac 7. 51 people, **u** in heart and ears,
Ro 4. 11 he had by faith while he was still **u.**
Col 3. 11 circumcised and **u,** barbarian,

UNCIRCUMCISION → UNCIRCUMCISED
1Co 7. 19 Circumcision is nothing, and **u** is
Gal 5. 6 neither circumcision nor **u** counts

UNCLEAN → UNCLEANNESS
Lev 5. 2 when any of you touch any **u** thing
Isa 52. 11 Touch no **u** thing;
Mk 3. 11 Whenever the **u** spirits saw him,
Rev 21. 27 But nothing **u** will enter it,

UNDERSTAND → UNDERSTANDING
Lk 24. 45 opened their minds to **u** the scriptures,
Eph 5. 17 but **u** what the will of the Lord is.

UNDERSTANDING → UNDERSTAND
Ex 36. 1 has given skill and **u** to know how
Pr 2. 6 from his mouth come knowledge and **u**
Lk 2. 47 heard him were amazed at his **u**
Php 4. 7 peace of God, which surpasses all **u,**

UNGODLY
Ro 5. 6 the right time Christ died for the **u.**
2Pe 2. 6 example of what is coming to the **u;**

UNITY
Ps 133. 1 when kindred live together in **u!**
Eph 4. 3 to maintain the **u** of the Spirit

UNJUST
Ro 3. 5 That God is **u** to inflict wrath on us?
Heb 6. 10 For God is not **u;** he will

UNLEAVENED
Ex 12. 17 shall observe the festival of **u** bread,
Mt 26. 17 first day of **U** Bread the disciples

UNRIGHTEOUS → UNRIGHTEOUSNESS
Mt 5. 45 rain on the righteous and on the **u.**
2Pe 2. 9 **u** under punishment until the day

UNRIGHTEOUSNESS → UNRIGHTEOUS
Ps 92. 15 and there is no **u** in him.
1Jn 1. 9 and cleanse us from all **u.**

URIM
Ex 28. 30 of judgment you shall put the **U**

USEFUL
2Ti 3. 16 scripture is inspired by God and is **u**

V

VAIN → VANITY
Ps 2. 1 and the peoples plot in **v?**
Mt 15. 9 in **v** do they worship me,
Php 2. 16 that I did not run in **v** or labor in **v.**

VALLEY
Ps 23. 4 through the darkest **v,** I fear no evil;

VANITY → VAIN
Ecc 1. 2 **v** of vanities! All is **v.**

VEIL
Ex 34. 33 he put a **v** on his face;
2Co 3. 15 a **v** lies over their minds;

VENGEANCE → AVENGE, AVENGER, AVENGING
Ps 94. 1 O LORD, you God of **v,**
Isa 34. 8 For the LORD has a day of **v,**
Na 1. 2 the LORD takes **v** on his adversaries

VICTORY
Pr 21. 31 but the **v** belongs to the LORD.

1Co 15. 54 Death has been swallowed up in **v."**

VINE → VINEYARD
Jn 15. 1 "I am the true **v,** and my Father is

VINEYARD → VINE
Isa 5. 1 had a **v** on a very fertile hill.
Mt 21. 33 a landowner who planted a **v,**

VIOLENCE
Ge 6. 11 and the earth was filled with **v.**
Isa 53. 9 although he had done no **v,**
Hab 2. 17 because of human bloodshed and **v**

VIRGIN
Mt 1. 23 the **v** shall conceive and bear a son,
Lk 1. 34 "How can this be, since I am a **v?**"

VISION → VISIONS
Isa 22. 1 oracle concerning the valley of **v.**
Da 8. 26 As for you, seal up the **v,**

VISIONS → VISION
Nu 12. 6 make myself known to them in **v;**
Eze 1. 1 were opened, and I saw **v** of God.
Da 1. 17 Daniel also had insight into all **v**
Joel 2. 28 and your young men shall see **v.**
Ac 2. 17 and your young men shall see **v,**

VOICE
Heb 3. 7 says, "Today, if you hear his **v,**
Rev 3. 20 if you hear my **v** and open the door,

VOID
Ge 1. 2 the earth was a formless **v**

VOW
Ecc 5. 4 Fulfill what you **v.**

W

WAGES
Ro 6. 23 For the **w** of sin is death,

WAIT
Ps 27. 14 **W** for the LORD; be strong,
1Th 1. 10 to **w** for his Son from heaven,

WALK
Dt 10. 12 to **w** in all his ways, to love him,
Ps 23. 4 I **w** through the darkest valley,
Isa 40. 31 they shall **w** and not faint.
2Co 5. 7 for we **w** by faith, not by sight.

WALL
Jos 6. 20 shout, and the **w** fell down flat;
Ne 2. 17 let us rebuild the **w** of Jerusalem,
Eph 2. 14 has broken down the dividing **w,**

WANT
Ps 23. 1 LORD is my shepherd, I shall not **w.**

WAR → WARRIOR, WARS
Ecc 3. 8 a time for **w,** and a time for peace.

WARRIOR → WAR
Ex 15. 3 LORD is a **w;**

WARS → WAR
Mt 24. 6 you will hear of **w** and rumors of **w;**

WASH
Ps 51. 7 **w** me, and I shall be whiter than snow.
Jn 13. 5 and began to **w** the disciples' feet

WATER → WATERS
Jer 2. 13 the fountain of living **w,**
Eze 36. 25 I will sprinkle clean **w** upon you,
Mk 1. 8 I have baptized you with **w;**
Jn 2. 9 tasted the **w** that had become wine,
3. 5 without being born of **w** and Spirit.
4. 10 he would have given you living **w."**
1Jn 5. 6 the one who came by **w** and blood,
Rev 22. 1 showed me the river of the **w** of life,

WATERS → WATER
Ge 7. 7 the ark to escape the **w** of the flood.

Isa 55. 1 who thirsts, come to the **w**;

WAY → WAYS

Ps 1. 6 watches over the **w** of the righteous,
Pr 22. 6 Train children in the right **w**,
Mt 3. 3 'Prepare the **w** of the Lord,
Jn 14. 6 "I am the **w**, and the truth, and the life.
1Co 12.31 show you a still more excellent **w**.
Heb 10.20 the new and living **w** that he opened

WAYS → WAY

Dt 10.12 to walk in all his **w**, to love him,

WEAK → WEAKNESS, WEAKNESSES

Mt 26.41 indeed is willing, but the flesh is **w**."
1Co 1.27 God chose what is **w** in the world
2Co 12.10 whenever I am **w**, then I am strong.

WEAKNESS → WEAK

Ro 8.26 the Spirit helps us in our **w**;

WEAKNESSES → WEAK

Heb 4.15 to sympathize with our **w**,

WEALTH

Rev 5.12 receive power and **w** and wisdom

WEARY

Isa 40.31 they shall run and not be **w**,
Heb 12. 3 you may not grow **w** or lose heart.

WEDDING

Jn 2. 1 there was a **w** in Cana of Galilee;

WEEKS

Ex 34.22 You shall observe the festival of **w**,
Lev 23.15 you shall count off seven **w**;

WEEP → WEEPING

Ecc 3. 4 a time to **w**, and a time to laugh;
Ro 12.15 **w** with those who **w**.

WEEPING → WEEP

Ps 30. 5 **W** may linger for the night,
Mt 8.12 will be **w** and gnashing of teeth."

WELL

Dt 6. 3 so that it may go **w** with you,
Mt 3.17 with whom I am **w** pleased."
    17. 5 I am **w** pleased; listen to him!"
2Pe 1.17 with whom I am **w** pleased."

WICKED → WICKEDNESS

Ps 1. 5 the **w** will not stand in the judgment,
Isa 48.22 no peace," says the LORD, "for the **w**."
Eze 18.23 any pleasure in the death of the **w**,

WICKEDNESS → WICKED

Ps 45. 7 you love righteousness and hate **w**.
Lk 11.39 inside you are full of greed and **w**.

WIDOW → WIDOWS

Ex 22.22 shall not abuse any **w** or orphan.
Ps 146. 9 he upholds the orphan and the **w**,
1Ti 5. 4 If a **w** has children or grandchildren,

WIDOWS → WIDOW

1Ti 5. 3 Honor **w** who are really **w**.
Jas 1.27 to care for orphans and **w**

WIFE → WIVES

Ge 2.24 and his mother and clings to his **w**,
Ex 20.17 shall not covet your neighbor's **w**,
Pr 18.22 who finds a **w** finds a good thing,
Mt 5.32 that anyone who divorces his **w**,
Eph 5.28 He who loves his **w** loves himself.
Rev 21. 9 the bride, the **w** of the Lamb."

WILDERNESS

Isa 40. 3 the **w** prepare the way of the LORD,
Mt 3. 3 voice of one crying out in the **w**:

WILL → WILLING

Ps 40. 8 I delight to do your **w**, O my God;
Mt 6.10 Your **w** be done, on earth as it is in
Lk 22.42 yet, not my **w** but yours be done."
Jn 4.34 "My food is to do the **w** of him who
Eph 6. 6 doing the **w** of God from the heart.
1Jn 5.14 if we ask anything according to his **w**,

WILLING → WILL

Mt 26.41 spirit indeed is **w**, but the flesh is weak.
Lk 22.42 if you are **w**, remove this cup from

WIND

Ecc 1.14 all is vanity and a chasing after **w**.
Jn 3. 8 The **w** blows where it chooses,
Ac 2. 2 a sound like the rush of a violent **w**,

WINE

Mt 9.17 is new **w** put into old wineskins;
Jn 2. 9 tasted the water that had become **w**,
Eph 5.18 Do not get drunk with **w**, for that is

WINGS

Ex 19. 4 and how I bore you on eagles' **w**
Ps 17. 8 hide me in the shadow of your **w**,
Mal 4. 2 shall rise, with healing in its **w**.
Lk 13.34 hen gathers her brood under her **w**,

WIPE

Isa 25. 8 GOD will **w** away the tears from all
Rev 21. 4 he will **w** every tear from their eyes.

WISDOM → WISE

1Ki 4.29 God gave Solomon very great **w**,
Pr 1.20 **W** cries out in the street;
    9.10 fear of the LORD is the beginning of **w**,
Jer 9.23 Do not let the wise boast in their **w**,
Mt 13.54 this man get this **w** and these deeds
Lk 2.52 Jesus increased in **w** and in years,
Ro 11.33 the depth of the riches and **w** and
1Co 1.19 "I will destroy the **w** of the wise,
Col 2. 3 whom are hidden all the treasures of **w**
Jas 3.17 But the **w** from above is first pure,
Rev 5.12 wealth and **w** and might and honor

WISE → WISDOM

Ps 19. 7 are sure, making **w** the simple;
Pr 3. 7 Do not be **w** in your own eyes;
Da 12. 3 are **w** shall shine like the brightness
1Co 1.26 not many of you were **w** by human
Eph 5.15 not as unwise people but as **w**,

WITHER → WITHERS

Ps 1. 3 and their leaves do not **w**.
Eze 47.12 Their leaves will not **w** nor their

WITHERS → WITHER

Jn 15. 6 is thrown away like a branch and **w**;
1Pe 1.24 The grass **w**, and the flower falls,

WITNESS → EYEWITNESSES, WITNESSES

Dt 19.15 single **w** shall not suffice to convict
Rev 1. 5 faithful **w**, the firstborn of the dead,

WITNESSES → WITNESS

Mt 26.60 though many false **w** came forward.
Heb 12. 1 surrounded by so great a cloud of **w**,
Rev 11. 3 my two **w** authority to prophesy

WIVES → WIFE

Eph 5.22 **W**, be subject to your husbands as
1Pe 3. 1 **W**, in the same way, accept the

WOMAN → WOMEN

Ge 2.22 he made into a **w** and brought her to
    3.15 enmity between you and the **w**,
Ps 113. 9 He gives the barren **w** a home,
Pr 11.16 A gracious **w** gets honor,
    31.30 **w** who fears the LORD is to be praised.
Rev 12. 1 a **w** clothed with the sun,

WOMEN → WOMAN

Lk 1.42 "Blessed are you among **w**,
    23.55 **w** who had come with him from
1Pe 3. 5 that the holy **w** who hoped in God

WONDERFUL → WONDERS

Ge 18.14 Is anything too **w** for the LORD?
Isa 9. 6 named **W** Counselor, Mighty God,

WONDERS → WONDERFUL

Ex 3.20 and strike Egypt with all my **w** that
Ps 136. 4 who alone does great **w**,
Jn 4.48 signs and **w** you will not believe."
2Th 2. 9 who uses all power, signs, lying **w**,

WORD → BYWORD, WORDS

Dt 30.14 No, the **w** is very near to you;
Ps 119.105 Your **w** is a lamp to my feet and
Pr 30. 5 Every **w** of God proves true;
Isa 40. 8 the **w** of our God will stand forever.
Jn 1. 1 In the beginning was the **W**, and the **W**
        was with God, and the **W** was God.
    1.14 the **W** became flesh and lived among
2Ti 2.15 rightly explaining the **w** of truth.
Jas 1.22 But be doers of the **w**,
Rev 19.13 his name is called The **W** of God.

WORDS → WORD

Ex 20. 1 Then God spoke all these **w**:
Dt 11.18 put these **w** of mine in your heart
Mt 24.35 but my **w** will not pass away.

WORK → WORKS

Ge 2. 2 the seventh day God finished the **w**
Ex 20.10 you shall not do any **w**—
Php 2.12 **w** out your own salvation with fear
2Ti 3.17 equipped for every good **w**.

WORKS → WORK

Gal 2.16 and not by doing the **w** of the law,
    5.19 the **w** of the flesh are obvious:
Eph 2. 9 not the result of **w**, so that no one may
1Ti 6.18 to do good, to be rich in good **w**,

WORLD

Mt 5.14 "You are the light of the **w**.
    16.26 gain the whole **w** but forfeit their life?
Jn 1.10 yet he **w** did not know him.
    3.16 loved the **w** that he gave his only Son,
    8.12 saying, "I am the light of the **w**.
1Jn 2.15 not love the **w** or the things in the **w**.
Rev 11.15 kingdom of the **w** has become the

WORRY

Mt 6.25 do not **w** about your life,
    10.19 not **w** about how you are to speak

WORSHIP

Ex 20. 5 not bow down to them or **w** them;
Ps 100. 2 **W** the LORD with gladness;
Mt 4. 9 if you will fall down and **w** me."
Jn 4.24 who **w** him must **w** in spirit and truth."
Ro 12. 1 which is your spiritual **w**.

WORTHY

2Sa 22. 4 LORD, who is **w** to be praised,
Eph 4. 1 to lead a life **w** of the calling
Rev 4.11 "You are **w**, our Lord and God,
    5.12 **W** is the Lamb that was slaughtered

WOUNDS

1Pe 2.24 by his **w** you have been healed.

WRAPPED

Mk 15.46 the body, **w** it in the linen cloth,
Lk 2. 7 **w** him in bands of cloth,

WRATH

Nu 16.46 For **w** has gone out from the LORD;
Ps 2. 5 Then he will speak to them in his **w**,
Pr 15. 1 A soft answer turns away **w**,
Zep 1.15 That day will be a day of **w**,
Mt 3. 7 you to flee from the **w** to come?
Ro 1.18 **w** of God is revealed from heaven
1Th 1.10 rescues us from the **w** that is coming
Rev 6.17 the great day of their **w** has come,

WRITE → WRITING, WRITTEN, WROTE

Ex 34.27 LORD said to Moses: **W** these words;
Dt 6. 9 **w** them on the doorposts of your house
Pr 7. 3 **w** them on the tablet of your heart.
Jer 31.33 and I will **w** it on their hearts;
Heb 8.10 and **w** them on their hearts,

WRITING → WRITE

Ex 32.16 and the **w** was the **w** of God,

WRITTEN → WRITE

Lk 24.44 everything **w** about me in the law
Jn 21.25 if every one of them were **w** down,
Rev 21.27 are **w** in the Lamb's book of life.

WRONG → WRONGED
Lk 23. 41 but this man has done nothing **w**."
Ac 23. 9 "We find nothing **w** with this man.

WRONGED → WRONG
1Co 6. 7 Why not rather be **w**?

WROTE → WRITE
Ex 24. 4 And Moses **w** down all the words

Y

YEAR → YEARS
Ex 23. 14 Three times in the **y** you shall hold a
Heb 10. 1 continually offered **y** after **y**,

YEARS → YEAR
Ps 90. 4 For a thousand **y** in your sight are like
Jer 25. 12 Then after seventy **y** are completed,
Da 9. 2 of Jerusalem, namely, seventy **y**.
2Pe 3. 8 the Lord one day is like a thousand **y**,
Rev 20. 2 and bound him for a thousand **y**,

YEAST
Mt 16. 6 beware of the **y** of the Pharisees and
Gal 5. 9 A little **y** leavens the whole batch of

YESTERDAY
Heb 13. 8 Jesus Christ is the same **y** and today

YOKE
Mt 11. 30 my **y** is easy, and my burden is light."

YOUTH → YOUNG
Ecc 12. 1 Remember your creator in the days of
your **y**,

Z

ZEAL
Ps 69. 9 **z** for your house that has consumed me
Jn 2. 17 "**Z** for your house will consume me.
Ro 10. 2 testify that they have a **z** for God,

ZION
2Sa 5. 7 David took the stronghold of **Z**,
Ps 2. 6 I have set my king on **Z**, my holy hill.
Isa 28. 16 I am laying in **Z** a foundation stone,
Mic 4. 2 For out of **Z** shall go forth instruction,
Zec 9. 9 Rejoice greatly, O daughter **Z**!
Mt 21. 5 "Tell the daughter of **Z**,
Ro 11. 26 "Out of **Z** will come the Deliverer;
1Pe 2. 6 "See, I am laying in **Z** a stone,
Rev 14. 1 the Lamb, standing on Mount **Z**!

Works Cited

The information in the Getting Started section on pp. xiii–xvi is adapted from three *Saint Mary's Press* *Essential Quick Charts: Bible Basics* © 2007, *Salvation History* © 2007, and *Interpreting the Bible* © 2009, by Saint Mary's Press, Winona, Minnesota. All rights reserved.

The information about prayer on pp. xvi–xvii is adapted in part from the *Personal Journey Bible: The Catholic Youth Bible New Testament and Psalms* (Winona, MN: Saint Mary's Press, 2009), pp. c1–c8. Copyright © 2009 by Saint Mary's Press. All rights reserved.

Pray It!, Exodus 5:22–23: Thomas Merton, *He Is Risen* (Allen, TX: RCL Enterprises, 1975), p. 22. Copyright © 1975 by RCL Enterprises. Used with permission of the Merton Legacy Trust.

Connect It!, Exodus 22:21–27: "Teen Immigrants, Five American Stories," PBS *In the Mix*, www.pbs .org/inthemix/shows/show_teen_immigrants5.html#neema.

Connect It!, Leviticus, 12:1–8: Suzanne Slesin and Emily Gwathmey, comp., *Amen: Prayers and Blessings from Around the World* (New York: Viking Penguin, 1995).

Live It!, Deuteronomy 5:1–21: Ron Zeilinger, *Sacred Ground* (Chamberlain, SD: Tipi Press, 1986), pp. 74–75.

Connect It!, 1 Chronicles 16:1–37: Matt Conner, "Living on a Prayer," *Relevant,* January/February 2009.

Connect It!, 2 Chronicles 35:22: Kelly Rippin, "High School Students Wash Cars for Uganda Awareness," 12 News WBOY, West Virginia, September 18, 2010.

Connect It!, Esther 4:9–16: Sojourner Truth, "Ain't I a Woman?," Women's Convention, Akron, Ohio, 1851, www.fordham.edu/halsall/mod/sojtruth-woman.html.

Connect It!, Job 1:20–22: Rachel Scott, "My Ethics, My Codes of Life," www.rachelschallenge.org/ LearnMore/RachelsEssay.php.

Connect It!, Psalm 84:10: Matt Redman, "We Shall Not Be Shaken," www.mattredman.com/chordcharts .php.

Connect It!, Proverbs 31:8–9: "Injustice Today," www.ijm.org/ourwork/injusticetoday.

Connect It!, Ecclesiastes 3:1–8: Dr. Robi Sonderegger, untitled video, www.thefrontline.org.au/index .cfm.

Connect It!, Matthew 25:34–40: "How Action Figure Ashley Gunn Helps the Homeless," *Women's Health,* December 22, 2009, www.womenshealthmag.com/life/fighting-to-end-homelessness; Sarah Corrigan, "Brantley Gunn: World-Changer," *Breakaway,* July 2007.

Connect It!, Mark 6:35–44: "Hoops of Hope" on "The Final Four Show," CBS Sports, April 5, 2010.

Connect It!, John 4:13–14: Jeremy V. Jones, "One Tear at a Time," *Breakaway,* December 2007.

Connect It!, John 8:31–32: Desmond Tutu, "Apartheid in the Holy Land," *The Guardian,* April 29, 2002.

Connect It!, 1 John 3:16–18: "The State of Food Insecurity in the World," reported by the United Nations Food and Agriculture Organization, www.fao.org, 2010.

Notes

Notes

Notes

Notes

Notes

Notes

Notes

Notes

Notes

Index to Maps

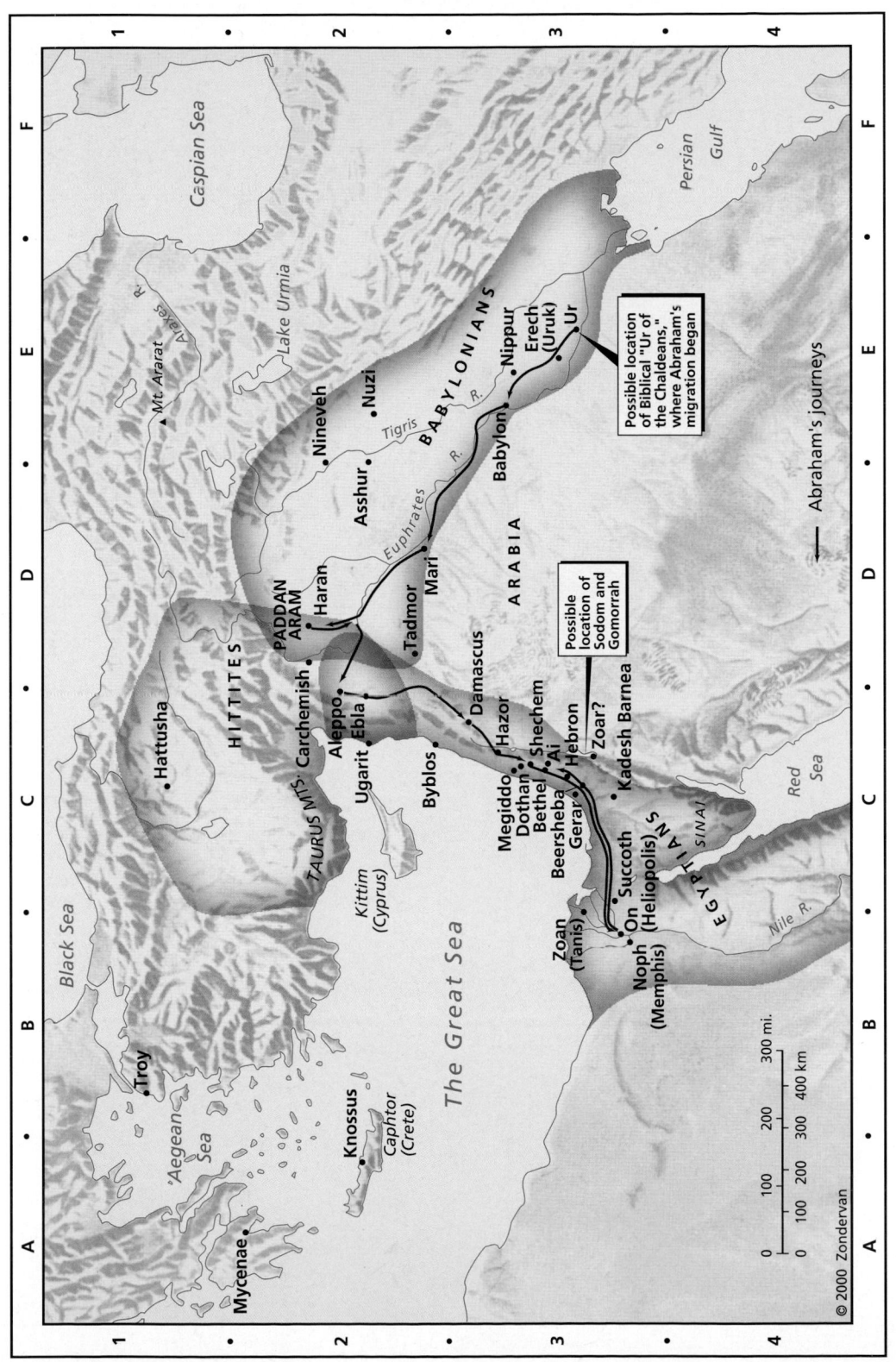

Map 1: WORLD OF THE PATRIARCHS

Caspian Sea

Black Sea

Aegean Sea

Mycenae

Troy

Knossus

Caphtor (Crete)

Kittim (Cyprus)

The Great Sea

Mt Ararat

Araxes R.

Lake Urmia

Nineveh

Nuzi

Asshur

Tigris R.

Zab R.

BABYLONIANS

Babylon

Nippur

Erech (Uruk)

Ur

Euphrates R.

HITTITES

Hattusha

TAURUS MTS.

Carchemish

Aleppo

Ugarit

Ebla

Byblos

Haran

PADDAN ARAM

Tadmor

Mari

Damascus

Hazor

Shechem

Megiddo

Dothan

Bethel

Ai

Beersheba

Hebron

Gerar

Zoar?

Kadesh Barnea

ARABIA

EGYPTIANS

SINAI

Succoth

On (Heliopolis)

Zoan (Tanis)

Noph (Memphis)

Nile R.

Red Sea

Persian Gulf

Possible location of Biblical "Ur of the Chaldeans," where Abraham's migration began

Possible location of Sodom and Gomorrah

→ Abraham's journeys

300 mi.

400 km

0   100   200   300

0   100   200   300

© 2000 Zondervan

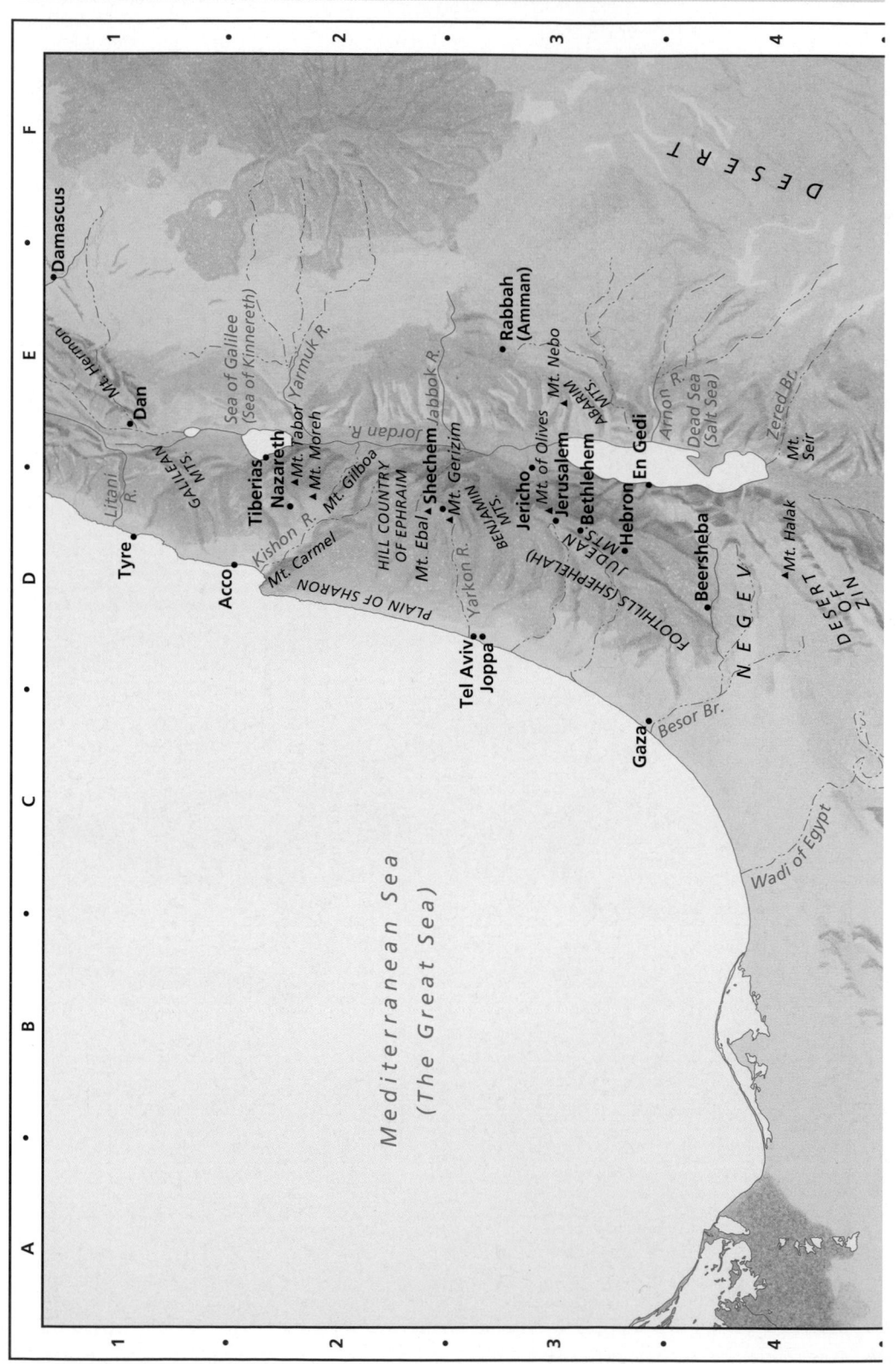

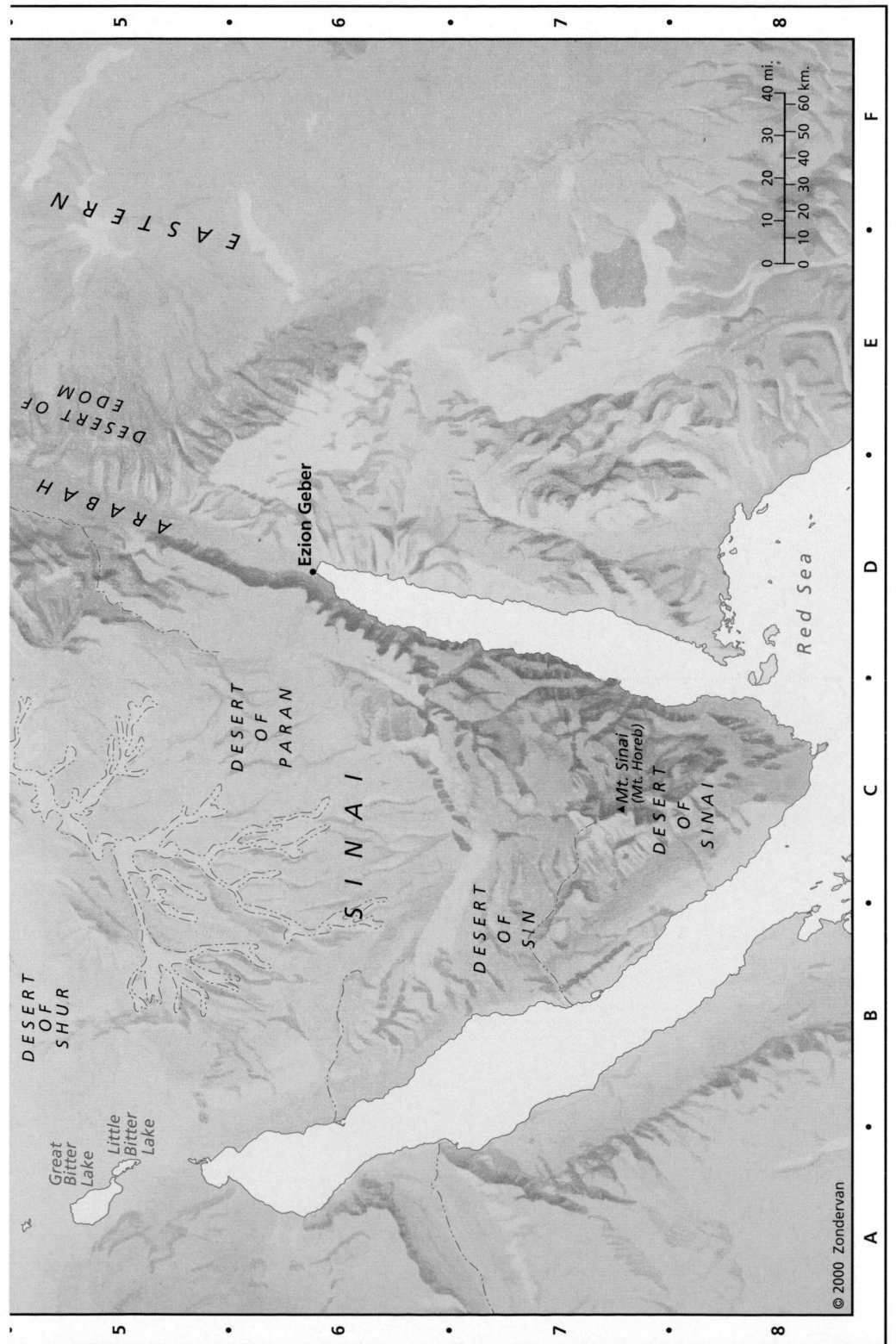

© 2000 Zondervan

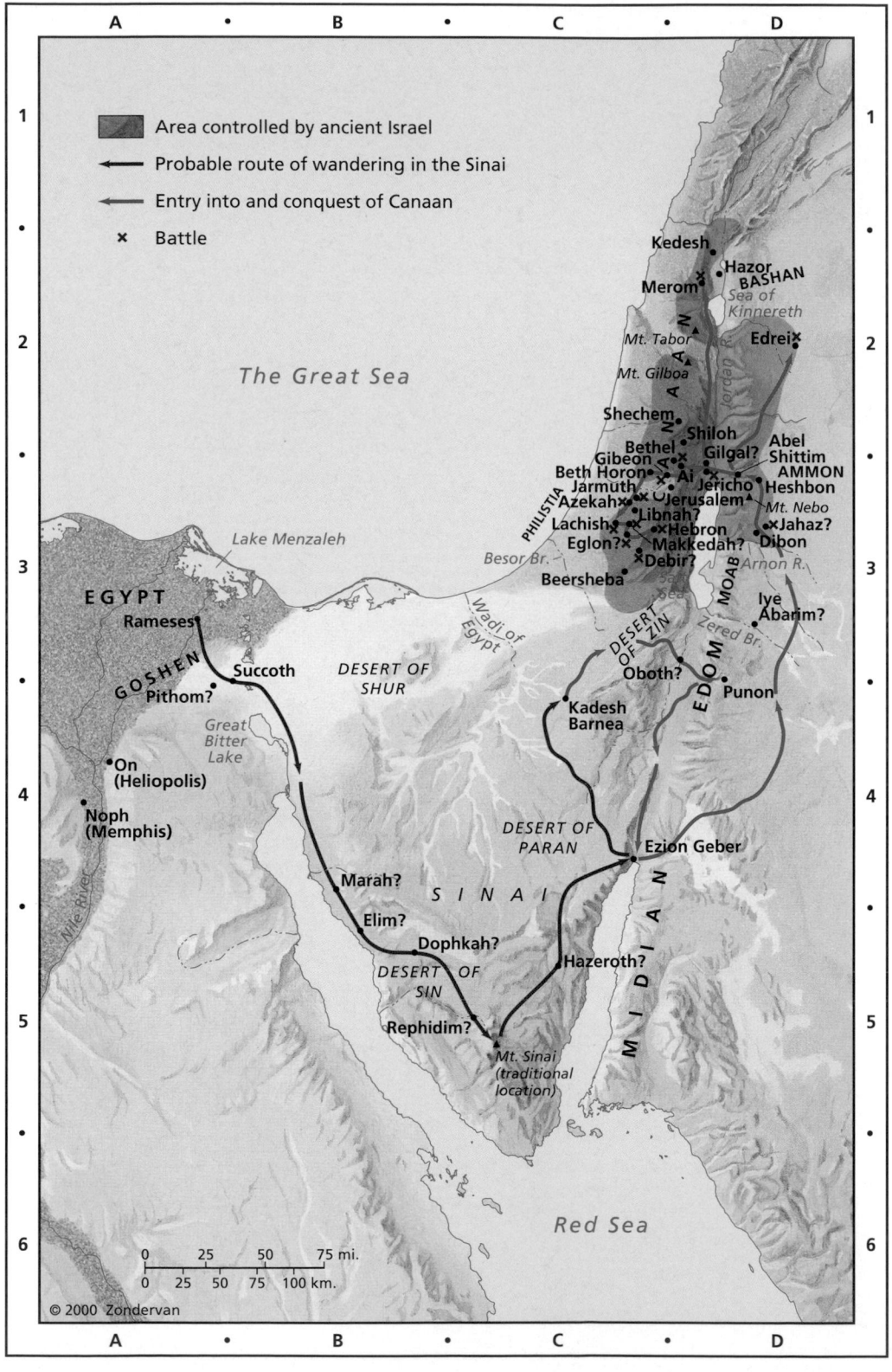

Area controlled by ancient Israel

Probable route of wandering in the Sinai

Entry into and conquest of Canaan

× Battle

The Great Sea

Kedesh
Merom ×
Hazor
BASHAN
Sea of Kinnereth
Mt. Tabor
Edrei ×
Mt. Gilboa
Shechem
Shiloh
Bethel ×
Gibeon ×
Gilgal?
Abel Shittim
Beth Horon ×
Ai ×
AMMON
Jarmuth ×
Jericho
Heshbon
Azekah ×
Jerusalem
Mt. Nebo
Lachish ×
Libnah?
Eglon? ×
Hebron ×
Jahaz? ×
Debir? ×
Makkedah?
Dibon
Beersheba
Iye Abarim?
Arnon R.
Besor Br.
DESERT OF ZIN
Zered Br.
EGYPT
Rameses
Oboth?
MOAB
EDOM
Punon
GOSHEN
Succoth
DESERT OF SHUR
Wadi of Egypt
Pithom?
Kadesh Barnea
On (Heliopolis)
Great Bitter Lake
Noph (Memphis)
Nile River
DESERT OF PARAN
Ezion Geber
Marah?
S I N A I
Elim?
Dophkah?
Hazeroth?
MIDIAN
DESERT OF SIN
Rephidim?
Mt. Sinai (traditional location)

Red Sea

0   25   50   75 mi.
0 25 50 75 100 km.

© 2000 Zondervan

Map 4: LAND OF THE TWELVE TRIBES

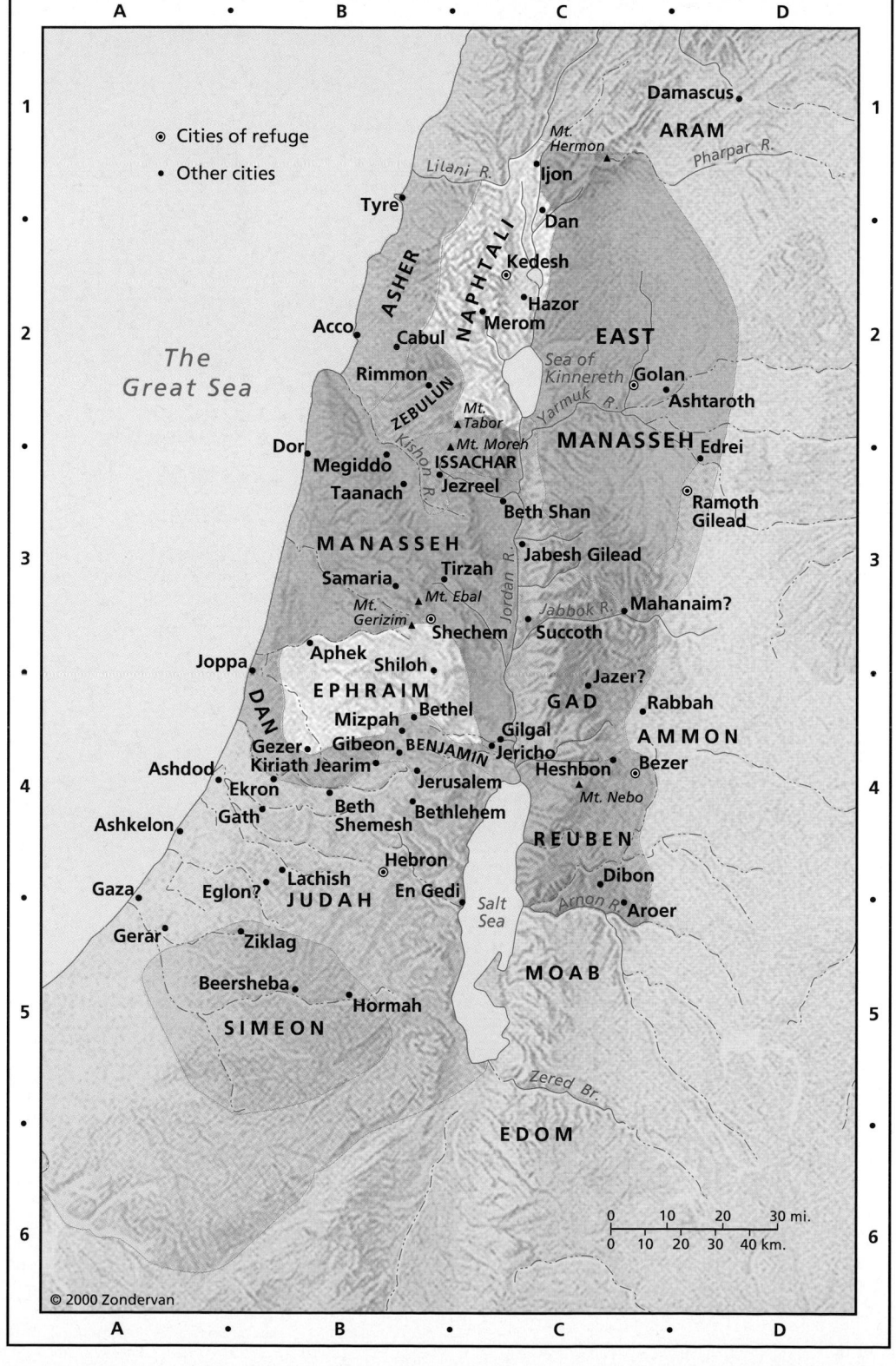

⊙ Cities of refuge
• Other cities

Damascus
ARAM
Mt. Hermon
Ijon
Tyre
Dan
Kedesh
Hazor
Acco
Cabul
Merom
EAST
The Great Sea
Rimmon
Sea of Kinnereth
Golan
Ashtaroth
Dor
Mt. Tabor
Mt. Moreh
MANASSEH
Edrei
Megiddo
ISSACHAR
Jezreel
Ramoth Gilead
Taanach
Beth Shan
MANASSEH
Jabesh Gilead
Tirzah
Samaria
Mt. Ebal
Mahanaim?
Mt. Gerizim
Shechem
Succoth
Aphek
Shiloh
Jazer?
EPHRAIM
GAD
Rabbah
Joppa
Mizpah
Bethel
Gilgal
AMMON
Gezer
Gibeon
BENJAMIN
Jericho
Ashdod
Kiriath Jearim
Jerusalem
Heshbon
Bezer
Ekron
Gath
Beth Shemesh
Bethlehem
Mt. Nebo
Ashkelon
REUBEN
Gaza
Eglon?
Lachish
Hebron
En Gedi
Dibon
Gerar
JUDAH
Salt Sea
Aroer
Ziklag
Arnon R.
Beersheba
MOAB
Hormah
SIMEON
Zered Br.
EDOM

ASHER
NAPHTALI
ZEBULUN
DAN

Litani R.
Pharpar R.
Yarmuk R.
Kishon R.
Jordan R.
Jabbok R.

0   10   20   30 mi.
0 10 20 30 40 km.

© 2000 Zondervan

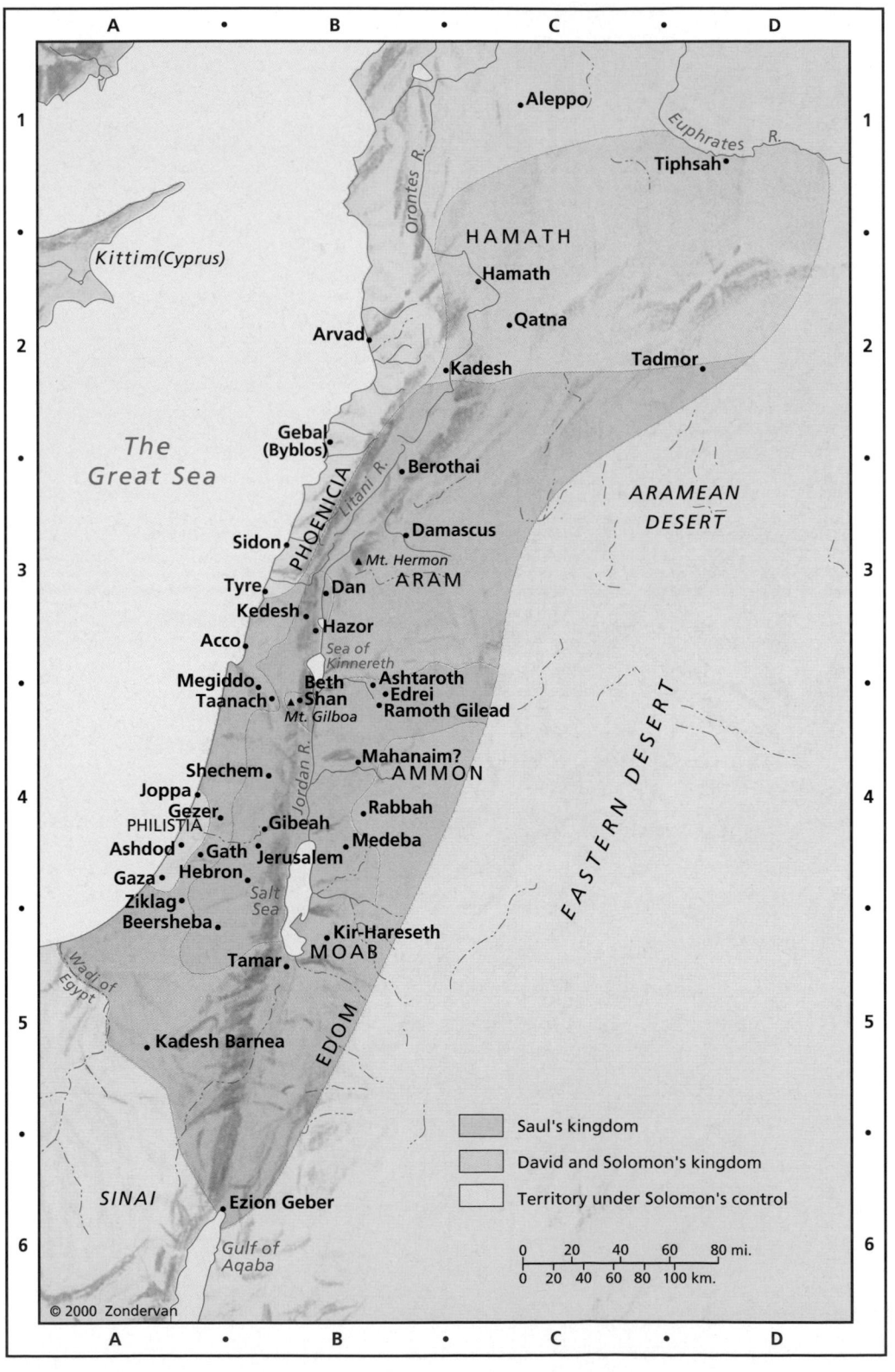

Map 5: **KINGDOM OF DAVID AND SOLOMON**

Aleppo

Euphrates R.

Tiphsah

Orontes R.

HAMATH

Kittim (Cyprus)

Hamath

Qatna

Arvad

Kadesh

Tadmor

The Great Sea

Gebal (Byblos)

Berothai

ARAMEAN DESERT

Sidon

PHOENICIA

Litani R.

Damascus

▲ Mt. Hermon

Tyre

Dan

ARAM

Kedesh

Hazor

Acco

Sea of Kinnereth

Megiddo

Beth

Ashtaroth

Taanach

▲ Shan

Edrei

Mt. Gilboa

Ramoth Gilead

Jordan R.

Shechem

Mahanaim?

AMMON

Joppa

Gezer

PHILISTIA

Gibeah

Rabbah

Ashdod

Gath

Medeba

Gaza

Hebron

Jerusalem

Ziklag

Salt Sea

Beersheba

Kir-Hareseth

Tamar

MOAB

Wadi of Egypt

EASTERN DESERT

EDOM

Kadesh Barnea

SINAI

Ezion Geber

Gulf of Aqaba

Saul's kingdom

David and Solomon's kingdom

Territory under Solomon's control

| 0 | 20 | 40 | 60 | 80 mi. |
| 0 | 20 | 40 | 60 | 80 | 100 km. |

© 2000 Zondervan

Map 6: KINGDOMS OF ISRAEL AND JUDAH

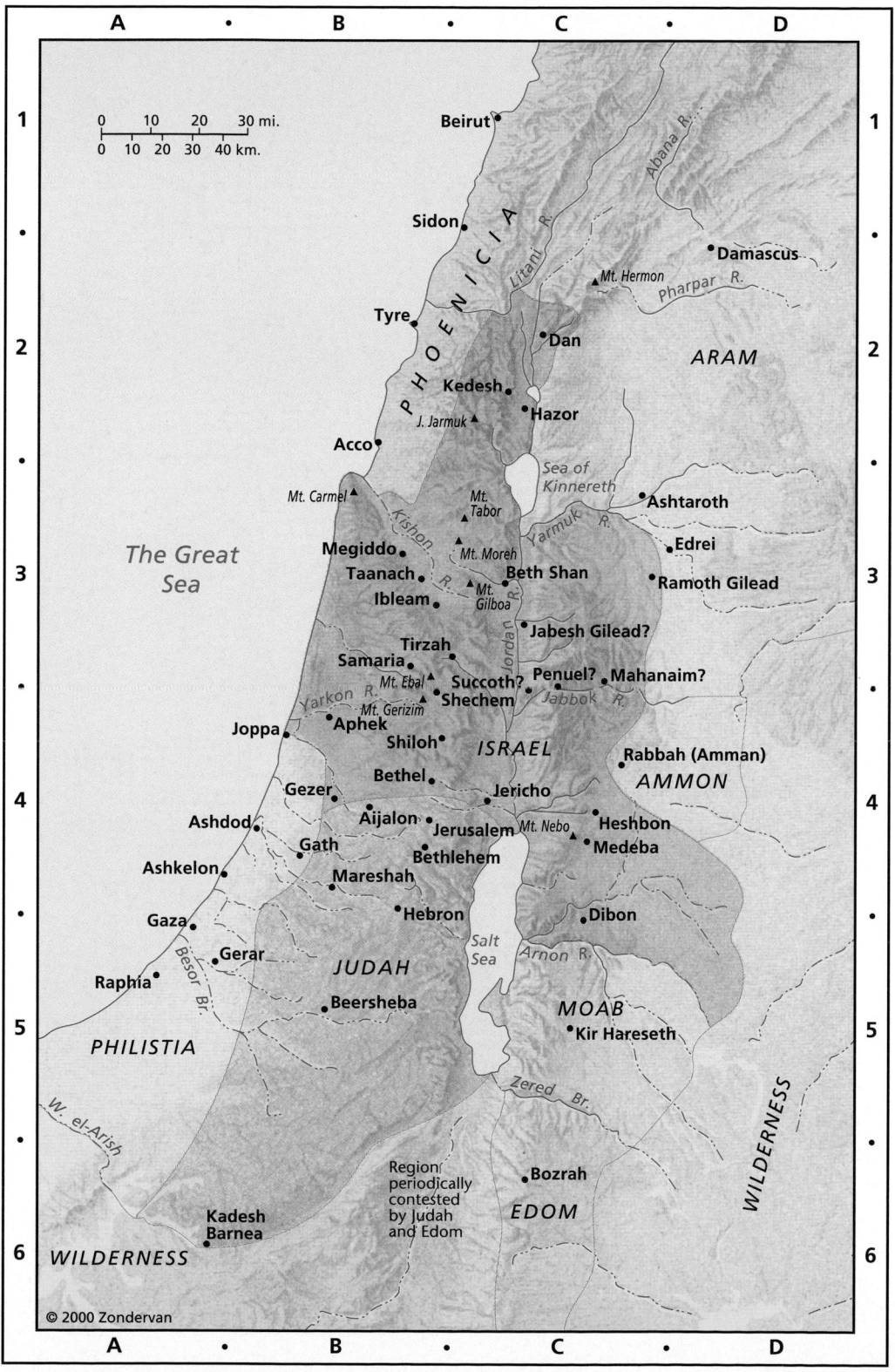

Beirut

Sidon

Damascus

PHOENICIA

Mt. Hermon

Pharpar R.

Abana R.

Litani R.

Tyre

Dan

ARAM

Kedesh

Hazor

J. Jarmuk

Acco

Sea of Kinnereth

Ashtaroth

Mt. Carmel

Mt. Tabor

Edrei

The Great Sea

Kishon R.

Yarmuk R.

Megiddo

Mt. Moreh

Beth Shan

Ramoth Gilead

Taanach

Mt. Gilboa

Ibleam

Jabesh Gilead?

Jordan R.

Tirzah

Samaria

Mt. Ebal

Succoth?

Penuel?

Mahanaim?

Mt. Gerizim

Shechem

Jabbok R.

Yarkon R.

Joppa

Aphek

Shiloh

ISRAEL

Rabbah (Amman)

Bethel

AMMON

Gezer

Jericho

Ashdod

Aijalon

Jerusalem

Mt. Nebo

Heshbon

Gath

Bethlehem

Medeba

Ashkelon

Mareshah

Gaza

Hebron

Dibon

Gerar

Salt Sea

Arnon R.

Raphia

JUDAH

Besor Br.

Beersheba

MOAB

Kir Haseth

W. el-Arish

Zered Br.

WILDERNESS

PHILISTIA

Region periodically contested by Judah and Edom

Bozrah

EDOM

Kadesh Barnea

WILDERNESS

0 10 20 30 mi.
0 10 20 30 40 km.

© 2000 Zondervan

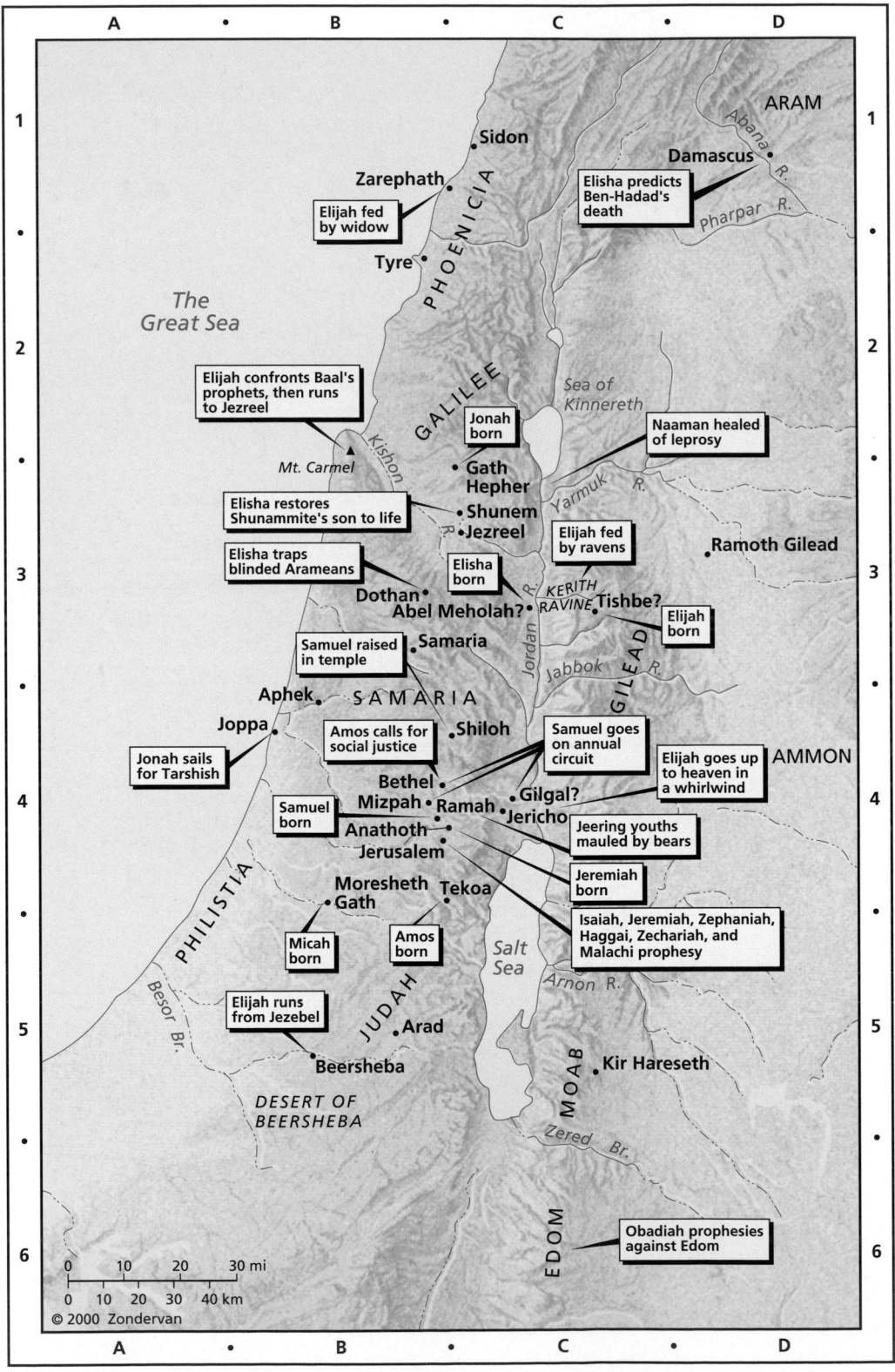

A • B • C • D

ARAM

Abana R.

• Sidon

Damascus •

Elisha predicts
Ben-Hadad's
death

Zarephath •

PHOENICIA

Pharpar R.

Elijah fed
by widow

Tyre •

The Great Sea

Sea of
Kinnereth

Elijah confronts Baal's
prophets, then runs
to Jezreel

GALILEE

Jonah
born

Naaman healed
of leprosy

Kishon

▲
Mt. Carmel

• Gath
Hepher

Elisha restores
Shunammite's son to life

• Shunem

• Jezreel

Yarmuk R.

Elijah fed
by ravens

Ramoth Gilead •

Elisha traps
blinded Arameans

Elisha
born

KERITH
RAVINE Tishbe? •

Dothan •

Abel Meholah? •

Jordan R.

Elijah
born

Samuel raised
in temple

• Samaria

Jabbok R.

GILEAD

Aphek •

S A M A R I A

Joppa •

Amos calls for
social justice

• Shiloh

Samuel goes
on annual
circuit

Elijah goes up
to heaven in
a whirlwind

AMMON

Jonah sails
for Tarshish

Bethel •

Samuel
born

Mizpah •

Ramah •

Gilgal? •

Jericho •

Jeering youths
mauled by bears

Anathoth •

Jerusalem •

Jeremiah
born

Moresheth
Gath •

• Tekoa

Isaiah, Jeremiah, Zephaniah,
Haggai, Zechariah, and
Malachi prophesy

Micah
born

Amos
born

*Salt
Sea*

PHILISTIA

Arnon R.

Elijah runs
from Jezebel

JUDAH

• Arad

MOAB

Kir Hareseth •

Besor Br.

• Beersheba

*DESERT OF
BEERSHEBA*

Zered Br.

EDOM

Obadiah prophesies
against Edom

0   10   20   30 mi
0 10 20 30 40 km

© 2000 Zondervan

A • B • C • D

Map 8: ASSYRIAN AND BABYLONIAN EMPIRES

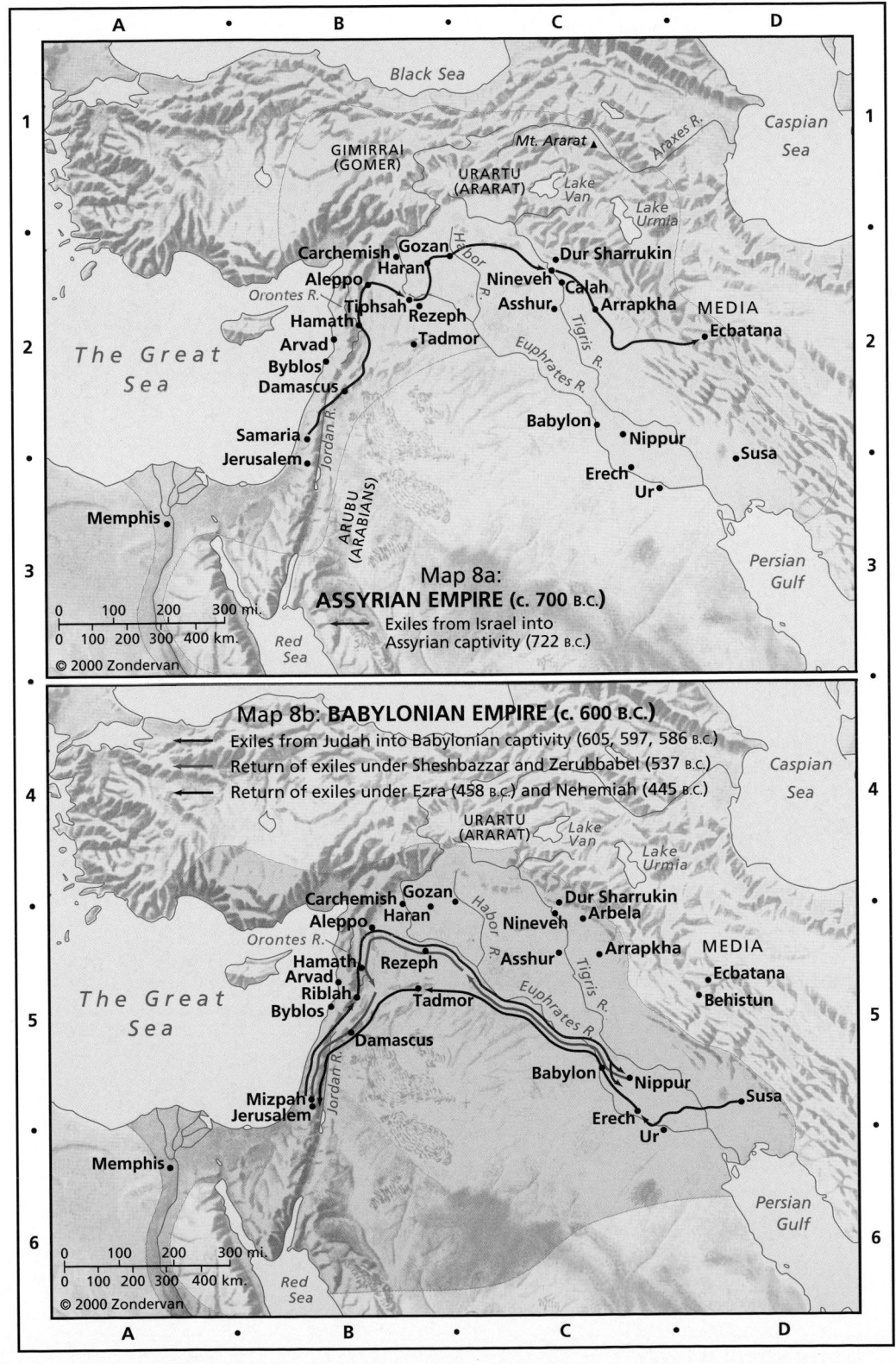

Black Sea

GIMIRRAI
(GOMER)

URARTU
(ARARAT)

Mt. Ararat

Araxes R.

Caspian
Sea

Lake
Van

Lake
Urmia

Carchemish
Gozan
Haran
Aleppo
Tiphsah
Rezeph
Hamath
Tadmor
Arvad
Byblos
Damascus

Orontes R.

Habor R.

Dur Sharrukin
Nineveh
Asshur
Calah
Arrapkha

Euphrates R.

Tigris R.

MEDIA
Ecbatana

The Great
Sea

Samaria
Jerusalem

Jordan R.

ARUBU
(ARABIANS)

Babylon
Nippur
Erech
Ur

Susa

Memphis

Persian
Gulf

Map 8a:
ASSYRIAN EMPIRE (c. 700 B.C.)

→ Exiles from Israel into
Assyrian captivity (722 B.C.)

0 100 200 300 mi.
0 100 200 300 400 km.

© 2000 Zondervan

Red
Sea

Map 8b: BABYLONIAN EMPIRE (c. 600 B.C.)

→ Exiles from Judah into Babylonian captivity (605, 597, 586 B.C.)
→ Return of exiles under Sheshbazzar and Zerubbabel (537 B.C.)
→ Return of exiles under Ezra (458 B.C.) and Nehemiah (445 B.C.)

URARTU
(ARARAT)

Lake
Van

Lake
Urmia

Caspian
Sea

Carchemish
Gozan
Aleppo
Haran
Hamath
Rezeph
Arvad
Riblah
Byblos
Tadmor
Damascus

Orontes R.

Habor R.

Dur Sharrukin
Arbela
Nineveh
Asshur
Arrapkha

Euphrates R.

Tigris R.

MEDIA
Ecbatana
Behistun

The Great
Sea

Mizpah
Jerusalem

Jordan R.

Babylon
Nippur
Erech
Ur

Susa

Memphis

Persian
Gulf

0 100 200 300 mi.
0 100 200 300 400 km.

© 2000 Zondervan

Red
Sea

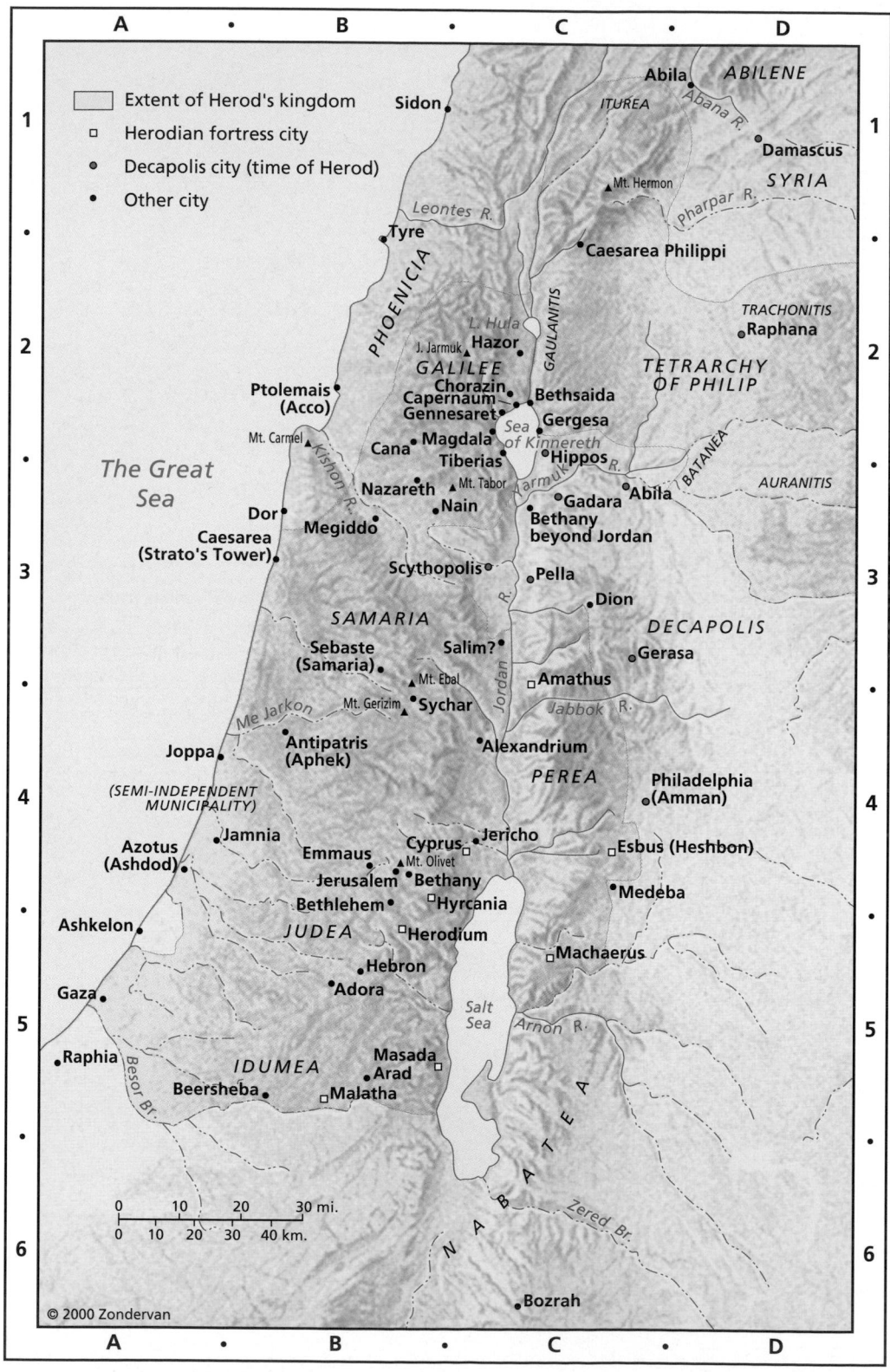

Map 9: HOLY LAND IN THE TIME OF JESUS

Extent of Herod's kingdom
Herodian fortress city
Decapolis city (time of Herod)
Other city

Abila
ABILENE
ITUREA
Abana R.
Sidon
Damascus
SYRIA
Mt. Hermon
Pharpar R.
Tyre
Leontes R.
Caesarea Philippi
PHOENICIA
TRACHONITIS
Raphana
L. Hula
GAULANITIS
J. Jarmuk
Hazor
GALILEE
Ptolemais
(Acco)
Chorazin
Capernaum
Bethsaida
Gennesaret
Gergesa
TETRARCHY
OF PHILIP
Mt. Carmel
Cana
Magdala
Sea
of Kinnereth
BATANEA
Tiberias
Hippos
AURANITIS
Nazareth
Mt. Tabor
Gadara
Abila
The Great
Sea
Nain
Bethany
beyond Jordan
Dor
Megiddo
Caesarea
(Strato's Tower)
Scythopolis
Pella
Dion
SAMARIA
DECAPOLIS
Sebaste
(Samaria)
Salim?
Gerasa
Mt. Ebal
Amathus
Me Jarkon
Mt. Gerizim
Sychar
Jabbok R.
Joppa
Antipatris
(Aphek)
Alexandrium
PEREA
Philadelphia
(Amman)
(SEMI-INDEPENDENT
MUNICIPALITY)
Jamnia
Cyprus
Jericho
Esbus (Heshbon)
Azotus
(Ashdod)
Emmaus
Mt. Olivet
Jerusalem
Bethany
Medeba
Ashkelon
Bethlehem
Hyrcania
JUDEA
Herodium
Machaerus
Hebron
Adora
Gaza
Salt
Sea
Arnon R.
Raphia
Besor Br.
IDUMEA
Masada
Arad
Beersheba
Malatha
NABATEA
Zered Br.
Bozrah

0 10 20 30 mi.
0 10 20 30 40 km.

© 2000 Zondervan

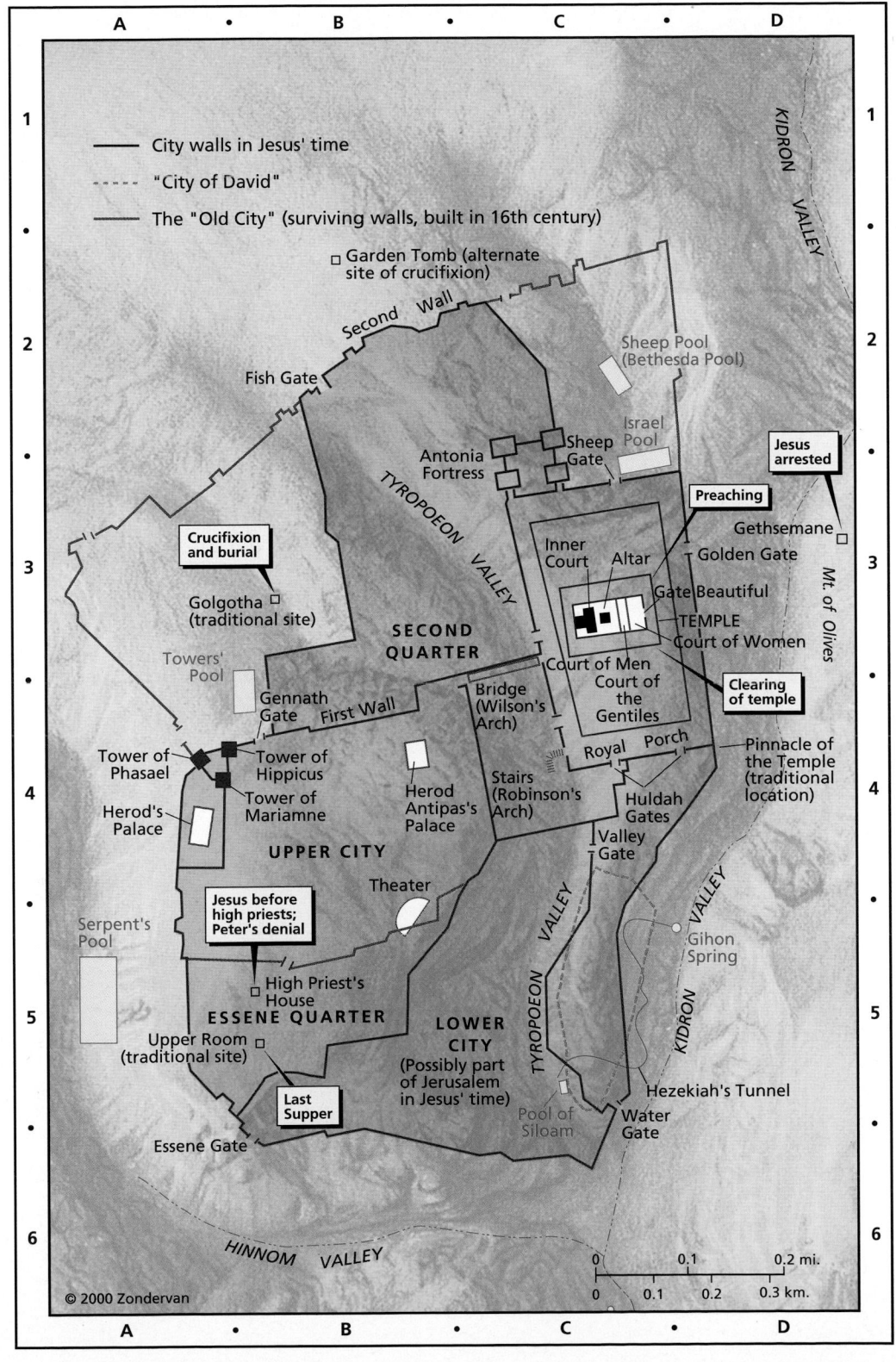

Map 10: **JERUSALEM IN THE TIME OF JESUS**

— City walls in Jesus' time
---- "City of David"
— The "Old City" (surviving walls, built in 16th century)

Garden Tomb (alternate site of crucifixion)

KIDRON VALLEY

Second Wall

Sheep Pool (Bethesda Pool)

Fish Gate

Israel Pool

Jesus arrested

Antonia Fortress

Sheep Gate

Preaching

TYROPOEON VALLEY

Inner Court

Altar

Gethsemane

Golden Gate

Crucifixion and burial

Gate Beautiful

TEMPLE
Court of Women

Mt. of Olives

Golgotha (traditional site)

SECOND QUARTER

Court of Men
Court of the Gentiles

Towers' Pool

Gennath Gate

First Wall

Bridge (Wilson's Arch)

Clearing of temple

Royal Porch

Pinnacle of the Temple (traditional location)

Tower of Phasael

Tower of Hippicus

Stairs (Robinson's Arch)

Huldah Gates

Tower of Mariamne

Herod's Palace

Herod Antipas's Palace

Valley Gate

UPPER CITY

Theater

KIDRON VALLEY

Serpent's Pool

Jesus before high priests; Peter's denial

Gihon Spring

High Priest's House

ESSENE QUARTER

Upper Room (traditional site)

TYROPOEON VALLEY

LOWER CITY
(Possibly part of Jerusalem in Jesus' time)

Hezekiah's Tunnel

Last Supper

Pool of Siloam

Water Gate

KIDRON

Essene Gate

HINNOM VALLEY

0   0.1   0.2 mi.
0   0.1   0.2   0.3 km.

© 2000 Zondervan

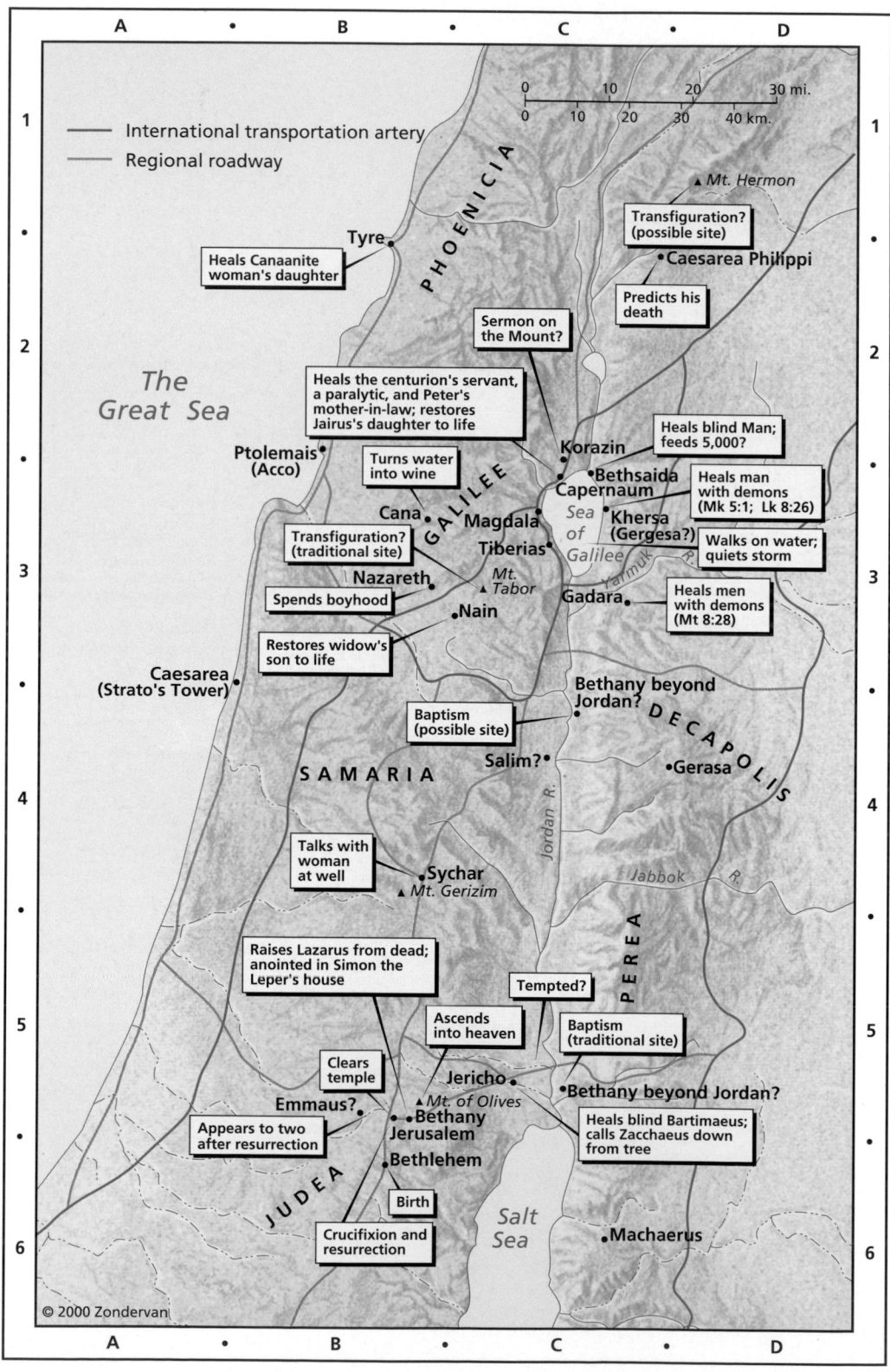

International transportation artery
Regional roadway

0   10   20   30 mi.
0   10   20   30   40 km.

PHOENICIA

Mt. Hermon

Transfiguration?
(possible site)

●Caesarea Philippi

Predicts his
death

Sermon on
the Mount?

*The
Great Sea*

Heals Canaanite
woman's daughter

Tyre●

Heals the centurion's servant,
a paralytic, and Peter's
mother-in-law; restores
Jairus's daughter to life

Korazin●

Heals blind Man;
feeds 5,000?

Ptolemais●
(Acco)

Turns water
into wine

●Bethsaida
Capernaum●

GALILEE

Heals man
with demons
(Mk 5:1; Lk 8:26)

Cana●

Magdala●

*Sea
of
Galilee*

Khersa
(Gergesa?)

Walks on water;
quiets storm

Transfiguration?
(traditional site)

Tiberias●

Yarmuk R.

Nazareth●

*Mt.
Tabor*

Gadara●

Heals men
with demons
(Mt 8:28)

Spends boyhood

●Nain

Restores widow's
son to life

Caesarea
(Strato's Tower)●

Bethany beyond
Jordan?●

DECAPOLIS

Baptism
(possible site)

SAMARIA

Salim?●

Jordan R.

●Gerasa

Jabbok R.

Talks with
woman
at well

●Sychar
Mt. Gerizim

PEREA

Raises Lazarus from dead;
anointed in Simon the
Leper's house

Tempted?

Ascends
into heaven

Baptism
(traditional site)

Clears
temple

Jericho●

Emmaus?●

Mt. of Olives

●Bethany beyond Jordan?

Appears to two
after resurrection

●Bethany
Jerusalem●

Heals blind Bartimaeus;
calls Zacchaeus down
from tree

●Bethlehem

JUDEA

Birth

*Salt
Sea*

Crucifixion and
resurrection

●Machaerus

© 2000 Zondervan

A   B   C   D
1   1
2   2
3   3
4   4
5   5
6   6

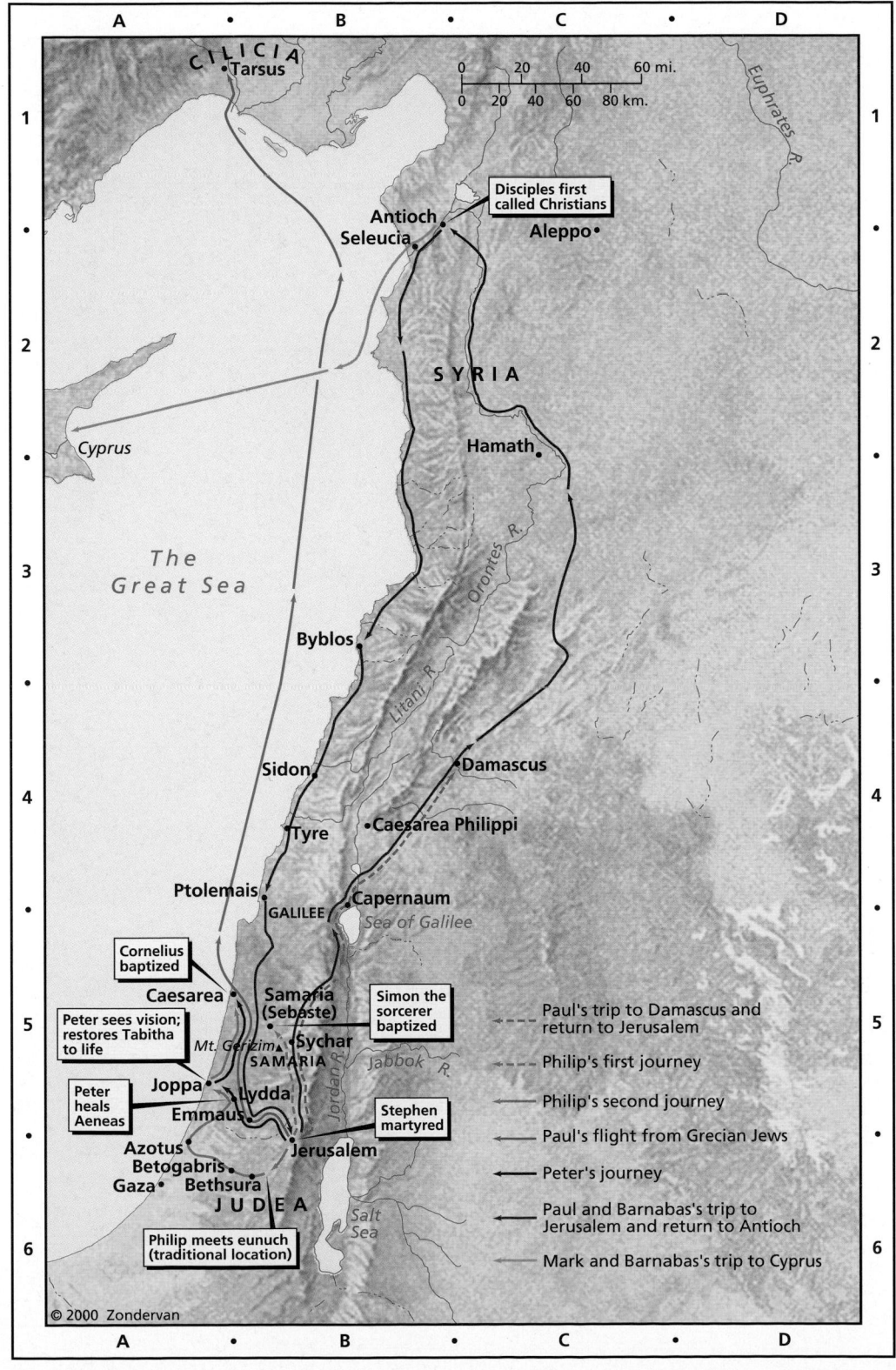

Map 12: **APOSTLES' EARLY TRAVELS**

C I L I C I A
Tarsus

0   20   40   60 mi.
0   20   40   60   80 km.

Euphrates R.

Disciples first
called Christians

Antioch
Seleucia

Aleppo

S Y R I A

Cyprus

Hamath

*The
Great Sea*

Orontes R.

Byblos

Litani R.

Sidon

Damascus

Tyre

Caesarea Philippi

Ptolemais

GALILEE

Capernaum
Sea of Galilee

Cornelius
baptized

Caesarea

Samaria
(Sebaste)

Simon the
sorcerer
baptized

Peter sees vision;
restores Tabitha
to life

Mt. Gerizim

Sychar
SAMARIA

Jabbok R.

Peter
heals
Aeneas

Joppa

Lydda

Emmaus

Jordan R.

Stephen
martyred

Azotus
Betogabris

Gaza

Bethsura

Jerusalem

J U D E A

Salt
Sea

Philip meets eunuch
(traditional location)

- - - Paul's trip to Damascus and
return to Jerusalem

- - - Philip's first journey

—— Philip's second journey

—— Paul's flight from Grecian Jews

—— Peter's journey

—— Paul and Barnabas's trip to
Jerusalem and return to Antioch

—— Mark and Barnabas's trip to Cyprus

© 2000 Zondervan

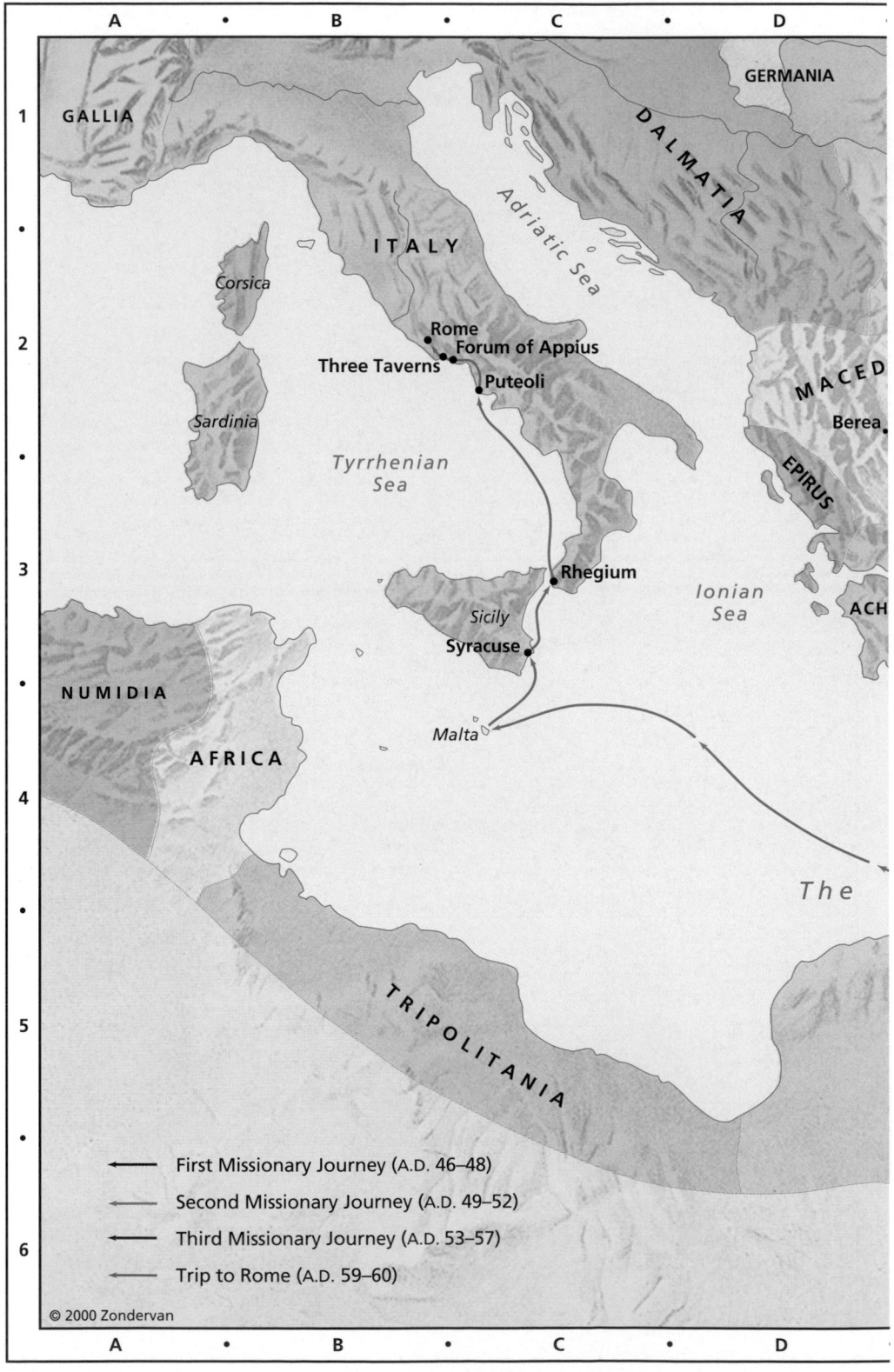

GALLIA

GERMANIA

DALMATIA

Adriatic Sea

ITALY

Corsica

Rome
Forum of Appius
Three Taverns
Puteoli

MACED

Berea

EPIRUS

Sardinia

Tyrrhenian Sea

Rhegium

Ionian Sea

ACH

Sicily

Syracuse

Malta

NUMIDIA

AFRICA

The

TRIPOLITANIA

First Missionary Journey (A.D. 46–48)

Second Missionary Journey (A.D. 49–52)

Third Missionary Journey (A.D. 53–57)

Trip to Rome (A.D. 59–60)

© 2000 Zondervan

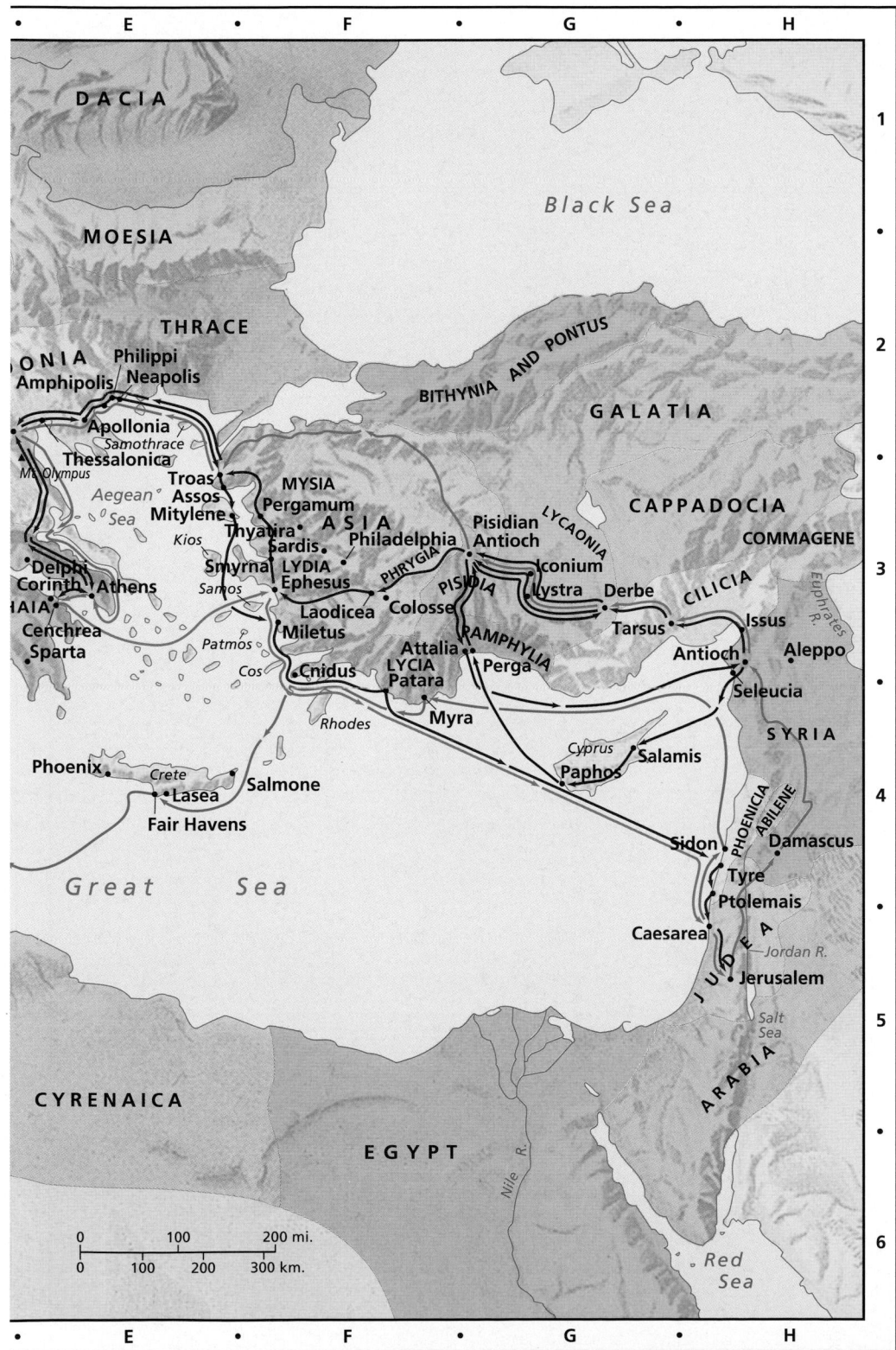

Map 14: ROMAN EMPIRE

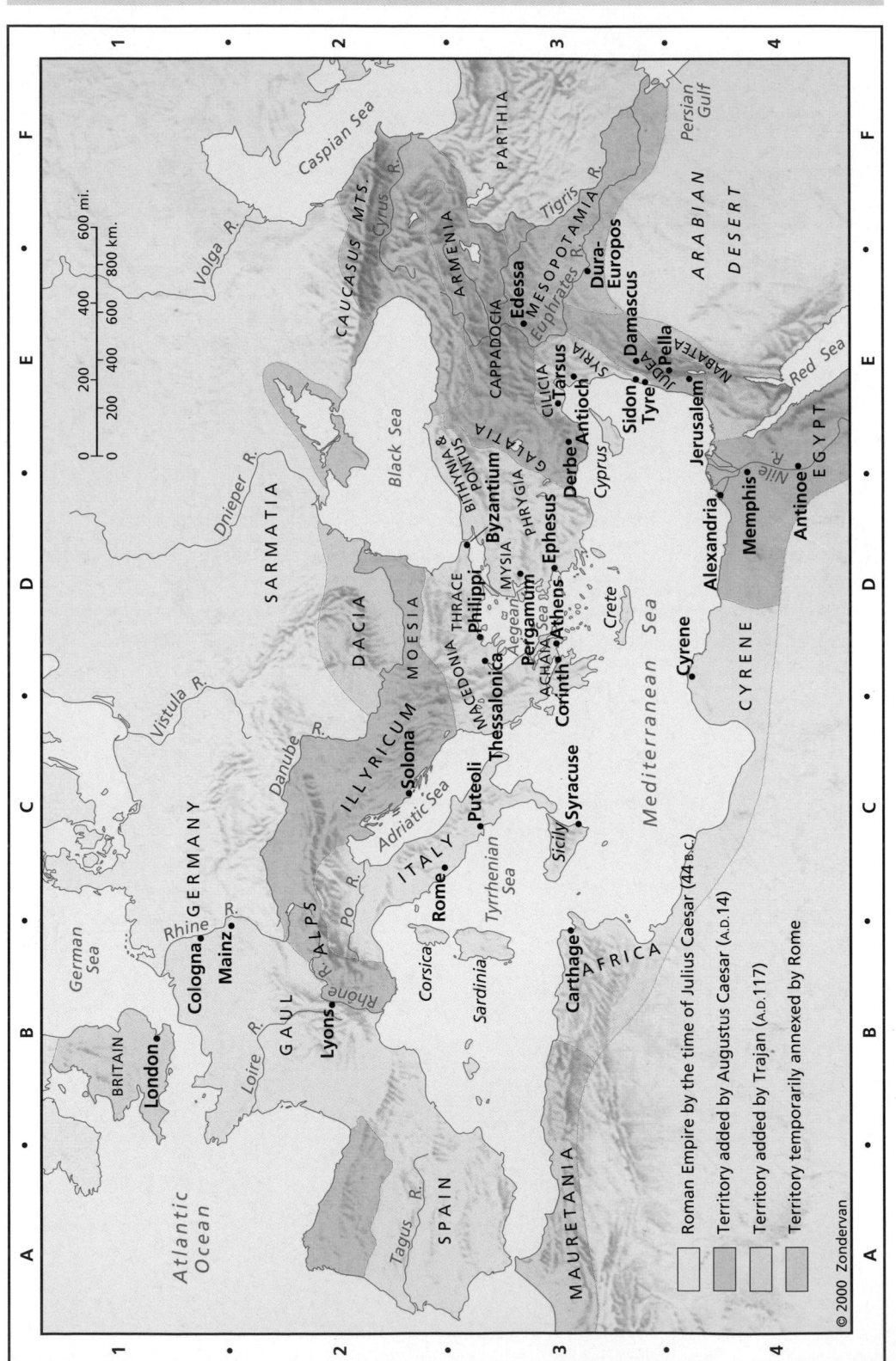

Roman Empire by the time of Julius Caesar (44 B.C.)

Territory added by Augustus Caesar (A.D.14)

Territory added by Trajan (A.D.117)

Territory temporarily annexed by Rome

© 2000 Zondervan